THE ENCYCLOPEDIA
OF THE THIRD REICH

Edited by

Christian Zentner and Friedemann Bedürftig

English translation edited by Amy Hackett

DA CAPO PRESS • NEW YORK

Library of Congress Cataloging-in-Publication Data

Grosse Lexikon des Dritten Reiches. English.
    The encyclopedia of the Third Reich / edited by Christian Zentner and
Friedemann Bedürftig; English translation edited by Amy Hackett.—1st Da
Capo Press ed.
        p.   cm.
    Includes bibliographical references and index.
    ISBN 0-306-80793-9 (alk. paper)
    1. Germany—History—1933–1945—Encyclopedias. 2. National socialism—
Germany—Encyclopedias. I. Zentner, Christian. II. Bedürftig, Friedemann,
1949– . III. Title.
DD256.5.G76313 1997
943.086′03—dc21   97-12744
                                                                                CIP

First Da Capo Press edition 1997

This Da Capo Press paperback edition of *The Encyclopedia of the Third Reich*
is an unabridged republication of the edition originally published in New York
in 1991 in two volumes, here reprinted in one. It is published by arrangement
with Macmillan Reference, a division of Simon & Schuster, Inc.

Published by Da Capo Press, Inc.
A Subsidiary of Plenum Publishing Corporation
233 Spring Street, New York, N.Y. 10013

Manufactured in the United States of America

Editorial and Production Staff

Project Editor
Sylvia Juran

Translators
Paul Bernabeo   Margaret Dalton   Paul A. Duggan   Christine Ann Evans

Copy Editors
Candice L. Gianetti   Eric L. Haralson   David Olivenbaum

Production Manager
Morton I. Rosenberg

Contents

Preliminary Remarks

The Third Reich and its related phenomena are the subjects of intense controversy. This is due in part to the subject's complexity, but also to the epoch's usefulness for current political and journalistic controversies, to issues of guilt and allegations of guilt—and to the great deficits of information about this omnipresent past. The overcoming of the past that is universally called for usually founders in the maze of legends and in the ruins of a historical consciousness that is characterized not least by repression or demonization, glorification or trivialization.

This is certainly not the fault of the scholars. Quite the contrary: the thicket of works covering every conceivable aspect of this period becomes daily more impenetrable and demands multiple specializations, because even historians find their way only with difficulty. The amateur gives up, and falls back on whatever the media supply on the occasion of anniversaries or to explain current events. Answers to concrete questions are seldom available. Only a comprehensive reference work, such as *The Encyclopedia of the Third Reich* represents for the first time, can provide such answers.

Dimensions

A reference work on the National Socialist period derives its key words from the events of the years 1933 to 1945, presents the ideological jargon and biographies of the actors, portrays significant organizations and treaties, and describes the crucial settings. Without reference to the prior history, however, it would be as much a mere torso as if there were no consideration of the immediate sequels. Thus, significant articles discuss Versailles, the Weimar Republic, the early history of the National Socialist party, and Hitler's origins, as well as denazification, the Nuremberg Trials, and neo-Nazism. The biographies are complete, although emphasis is on their subjects' connections with the Third Reich.

[With regard to the Second World War], extensive individual articles describe all the campaigns, detail the lives of the important military leaders, and discuss such key terms as "partisans" and "prisoners of war"; no attempt was made to account for all weapons, aircraft models, or individual operations. Important places such as Dunkerque, Stalingrad, and Dresden appear as short entries, and a large article, "Second World War," provides the necessary overview.

Presentation

Our primary task was to create the greatest possible number of points of information while maintaining the connections between them. The former aim is served by the more than 3,000 entries, and the latter by longer articles (see page xi for a listing) distinct in format, which in focused essays link together themes that can easily become lost in the alphabetical dispersion of individual entries. These signed contributions, which intentionally break with the encyclopedia's general format, have helped to create a usable reference work. More than a data bank, it does not disappoint the layperson in search of an overview, yet it expeditiously provides the expert with needed details.

The straightforward arrangement of articles contributes to this end. All entries begin with the boldface key word (alphabetized according to international standards), followed by a short definition within the thematic boundaries. For persons, biographical details appear at the head of the article, followed by a generally chronological text. Cross-references to other articles are set off [in small capitals in the English edition] only where they add necessary depth or lead further; not every key name or term in an article is stressed in this way, and certainly not the obvious ones. Thus, references to Hitler and his most important colleagues are generally not set off, nor are countries or concentration camps;

these of course are given their own articles. Quotations that are not attributed are from contemporary reference works.

A listing of works for further reading on the most important topics is provided in a separate bibliography, with subject headings arranged alphabetically.

Format

Without illustrations, the presentation of lexicographic information would be deficient: more than 1,200 photographs, graphics, and other depictions help the user to visualize the persons portrayed, the atmosphere of the period, and the drama of the events, along with the sense of the words. In particular, thematic full-page illustrations communicate messages necessary for understanding the period as no text could.

Outlook

The philologist Moritz Haupt (1808–1874) once noted: "The author of an encyclopedia builds, as the old saying goes, in the middle of the path, and exposes his work to criticism." We accept this, especially since everyone engaged in such work discovers how susceptible to error texts crammed with facts are, and how long the choice of entries and data can be disputed. Suggestions for future editions are therefore welcome, for "it is in the nature of an encyclopedia," according to the Germanist Matthias Lexer (1830–1892), "that it can approach its goal only gradually and after long effort."

THE EDITORS
Munich, October 1985

Preface to the English Translation

The Encyclopedia of the Third Reich is the most extensive reference work now available in English on the National Socialist phenomenon. As the editors of the original German *Das Grosse Lexikon des Dritten Reiches* note in their introductory remarks, their intent was to make available to the nonspecialist the wealth of research available on this subject. (The quantity of this research continues to grow, and the bibliography in the English edition has been updated, especially with English-language sources. The German editors have also added a few articles not found in the 1985 *Lexikon*.) The reader will find articles on the expected National Socialist leaders, but also discussions of more obscure party members. Relatively minor party groupings are allotted articles as well. In keeping with the totalitarian impulses of the Third Reich, the encyclopedia includes articles on such disparate areas as sports, culture, religion, and economics. Figures who were not themselves National Socialists but who had a significant relationship to the period are covered; indeed, considerable attention is paid to individuals and organizations opposed to National Socialism. The focus is necessarily on Germany, but the encyclopedia includes articles on other nations and their citizens who were touched by the Third Reich, whether through occupation, alliance, resistance, or collaboration.

The translator of a work such as this—indeed, anyone attempting to explain the Third Reich in a language other than German—confronts a daunting challenge. The National Socialists themselves, of course, believed that they were engaged in a specifically German enterprise; this led, for example, to an attempt to expunge "foreign" borrowings from the German language. Perhaps ironically, scholars of the Third Reich, more than those of other periods in German history or those of other nations, tend to adhere to this idea of an untranslatable "Germanness" and to retain National Socialist terminology in their writings. This is surely not because of any sympathy with National Socialist ideology. Rather, it most likely stems from an understandable difficulty in assimilating into the normal language of history and human behavior events that were so heinous. The effect of this linguistic untouchability is, however, a kind of mystification that may well interfere with comprehension, particularly for anyone not fluent in German—and perhaps even for those who are.

In the course of working with this English translation, German terminology was treated with a minimally "protective" approach. In fact, the large number of German-English cognates facilitates the finding of satisfactory English equivalents. Certain terms continued to elude this effort. Some have gained sufficient standing in English that it seemed potentially confusing to translate them. (An example is *Schutzstaffeln*, or SS.) Other German words or terms had such multiple connotations and associations that it seemed unwise to contrive a replacement. For example, the German word *Einsatz* and its derivative *Einsatzgruppen* could plausibly be translated as "task" and "task group" or "task force," respectively. But the complex connotations of the root noun, the frequency with which the second term is found in discussions of these murder squads, and the very particularity of the "task" assigned to these particular "groups" made it seem right to leave the name in German. (Individual articles may, of course, refer to "task groups" as a synonym, for stylistic reasons.) *Leistung*, on the other hand, although it might connote "performance" or "achievement," or both concepts simultaneously, is found under the key word "performance," the more often intended usage; the article "Performance," however, makes note of the other potential translations of *Leistung*, which are used when appropriate.

Two frequently used concepts deserve special discussion. The German word *Volk* has been retained when in a National Socialist context, though elsewhere it has been translated as "folk" or "people." National Socialists implicitly used the term most often to refer exclusively to those of German ethnicity; thus it seemed reasonable to retain the original. Conversely, "folk" or "people" was used when the meaning was more inclusive or universal, notably in the rhetoric of anthropology or of leftist or populist politics. The related term *völkisch* also seemed too peculiarly rooted in German tradition to Anglicize. (See the articles "Volk" and "völkisch.") By the same logic, *Führer* has usually not been translated. (Hitler, moreover, made the term universally notorious.) While the meaning is, roughly, "leader," it seemed advisable to make a distinction between this more powerful and charismatic personification of

leadership and the somewhat more pedestrian and managerial *Leiter* (as in *Gauleiter*), which is, of course, the cognate for the English "leader."

The encyclopedia's blind entries and/or index include the German terminology, so that a reader knowing only the German name of a given organization or concept will be directed to the desired article. The acronyms of organizations are also included, since many of the Nationalist Socialist organizations were widely known by their initials. Following the *Lexikon's* practice, the encyclopedia routinely uses "National Socialism" or "National Socialist," rather than the more familiar "Nazism" or "Nazi." A brief article on the latter term notes that it originated as an epithet, parallel to the similarly derogatory "Sozi" (for the Social Democrats), and that it was not used by the National Socialists themselves. This usage was retained both out of faithfulness to the original and in the belief that, although there is no wish to protect those so addressed, "Nazi" obscures a name that in its countervailing appeal does much to explain the movement's success.

The translations of the articles seek to be accurate vis-à-vis the originals, but they have been updated as individuals have died, or to reflect changes such as the Soviet acknowledgment of accountability for the Katyn massacre. The German editors have supplied a few corrections and, as noted above, have added a few new articles. Our translation was made at a time of great change in Germany, and it was impossible to reflect all these changes. In a few articles, interpolations explicate a matter for the English-language reader; such changes are in brackets.

The cliché that something is always lost in translation is balanced, to an extent, by the fact that a translation may also shed light on the uses or abuses of language. The necessity of finding equivalent terms forces one to scrutinize what is being said in a way that does not necessarily occur when the language is taken as a given. Thus, the encyclopedia clarifies the most important sources of National Socialist language and jargon. These were:

1. An imagined "pure" German vocabulary that the National Socialists wanted to substitute for "alien" incursions and contaminations, as discussed above. An example was *Allbuch*—"all-book" or "book of everything"—substituting for *Lexikon*. This retrieval enterprise led them to forage about for arcane words: hence the frequent awkwardness of some of the English translations, which attempt to render a German that was itself somewhat tortured.

2. A quasi-bureaucratic language usage known as "language regulation" (*Sprachregelung*), which was insisted upon in correspondence among functionaries, in particular. Such lingo proliferated in reference to what—precisely in this style—became known as the "Final Solution." As Hannah Arendt (among others) has noted, the effect of this practice was "not to keep these people ignorant of what they were doing, but to prevent them from equating it with their old, 'normal' knowledge." As with any bureaucratic practice, this "regulation" also served to dilute responsibility.

3. A pseudo-religious language of exaltation, which flourished in the National Socialist world of "blood sacrifice" even as the movement tried to strike an ultimately uneasy arrangement with established Christianity.

4. A linguistic complex fashioned from the vocabularies of medicine, eugenics, "racial hygiene," Social Darwinism, and animal husbandry. National Socialist jargon abounded with metaphors of infection and with injunctions to counter threats to the German *Volk* body. There was a Social Darwinist urgency to the various "struggles" that characterized the Third Reich. It was the former agricultural student Heinrich Himmler who no doubt promoted the notions of "culling out" and "species upgrading."

5. A further related set of metaphors from technology, most notably "synchronization" (*Gleichschaltung*), borrowed from electrotechnology. These last two categories look simulta-neously forward—to some vision of science and modernity—and backward, a fact altogether characteristic of National Socialism and its paradoxical and internally contradictory appeal.

As editor of the English translation, I have several people to thank. From the long term, I want to mention my parents for their constant support and encouragement; Dell Lewis, with whom I began the study of German in high school; Rudolph Binion, Peter Gay, and Fritz Stern, who fostered my interest in German history; and Robert Jay Lifton, who encouraged me to move into a period of German history that I had frankly avoided. More immediately, I want to thank for their cooperation those who did the bulk of the translating: Margaret Dalton, Paul A. Duggan, and Christine Ann Evans. Sylvia Juran, the editor at Macmillan with primary responsibility for the encyclopedia, deserves particular acknowledgment. Without her mastery of the details of editing, her patience as I learned some of these skills, and her high standards of scholarship and craft, this book would have been far less than the handsome work of publishing that it is. The New York German Women's History Study Group provided scholarly comradeship. Finally, I want to thank Stoney, Eugene, and Louisa for their support and cooperation, and Louisa for her expert alphabetizing.

AMY HACKETT
Brooklyn, N.Y., October 1990

Contributors

Volker Albers *Hamburg*	V. A.	Prof. Dr. Herbert Obenaus *Hannover*	H. O.
Ulrich Bachmann *Hannover*	U. B.	Dr. Sibylle Obenaus *Hannover*	S. O.
Dr. Reinhard Barth *Hamburg*	Ba.	Dr. Wolfgang Petter *Freiburg*	W. P.
Prof. Dr. Reinhart Beck *Esslingen*	R. B.	Wilhelm M. Rissmann *Hannover*	W. R.
Volker Brennecke *Hannover*	V. B.	Prof. Dr. Adelheid von Saldern *Göttingen*	A. v. S.
Claudia Brinner *Hannover*	C. B.	Alisa Schapira *Hannover*	Sch.
Dr. Alexander von Brünneck *Hannover*	A. v. B.	Christoph Schmidt *Hannover*	C. S.
Christa Dopatka *Hannover*	C. D.	Prof. Dr. Harald Scholtz *Berlin*	H. S.
Willy Dressen *Ludwigsburg*	W. D.	Prof. Dr. Jürgen Seifert *Hannover*	J. S.
Mathias Forster *Hamburg*	M. F.	Rainer Sontowski *Hannover*	R. S.
Ivo Frenzel *Düsseldorf*	I. F.	Dr. Harald Steffahn *Hamburg*	H. St.
Sebastian Haffner *Berlin*	S. H.	Alfred Streim *Ludwigsburg*	A. St.
Dr. Gode Hartmann *Hannover*	Ha.	Prof. Dr. Klaus Vondung *Siegen*	K. V.
Reinhold Hartmann *Kirchhain*	R. H.	Dr. Bernd Wegner *Freiburg*	We.
Dr. Horst Heidtmann *Hamburg*	H. H.	Prof. Dr. Bernd-Jürgen Wendt *Hamburg*	B.-J. W.
Dr. Gerhard Hümmelchen *Stuttgart*	G. H.	Prof. Dr. Dr. Rolf Winau *Berlin*	R. W.
Dr. Dorothee Klinksiek *Würzburg*	D. K.	Birgit Wulff *Hamburg*	B. W.
Prof. Dr. Dieter Langewiesche *Tübingen*	D. L.	Dr. Christian Zentner *Munich*	C. Z.

Major Articles and Overviews

The issue is not one of overcoming the past. For that is impossible. It cannot be changed retroactively or be undone. He who closes his eyes to the past, however, will be blind to the present.

Richard von Weizsäcker, President of the Federal
   Republic of Germany, in an address on May 8, 1985

Volume 1
A - L

AB-Aktion. *See* Extraordinary Pacification Operation.

Abetz, Otto, b. Schwetzingen, March 26, 1903; d. Langenfeld bei Düsseldorf, May 5, 1958, German diplomat with a paradoxical National Socialist career. Trained as an art teacher, Abetz came from the German-French youth movement into the NSDAP in 1931, with ideas of reconciling peoples. As an expert on France, he worked in the Paris RIBBENTROP OFFICE as of January 1935. He was expelled in July 1939, and after the French defeat of August 1940 became German ambassador to the VICHY regime. It was he who arranged the Hitler-Pétain meeting in MONTOIRE. Made an SS-*Brigadeführer* in 1941, Abetz was arrested by the Allies in 1945. He was found guilty of the deportation of Jews, among other crimes, and was condemned to 20 years' forced labor in 1949. Released in 1954, he died in an automobile accident.

abkindern (verb), ironically intended colloquial designation for the cancellation of a marriage loan (*see* MARRIAGE LOANS) through the production of offspring (*ab* means "off" and *Kind* means "child").

Abmeierung. *See* Farmers, dispossession of.

Abortion, criminal offense whose penalty (Criminal Code ¶218) was made harsher during the Third Reich because abortion was said to offend the "German *Volk*'s will to life and a future." Exceptional permission for an abortion was granted only through the Law to Prevent HEREDITARILY ILL OFFSPRING (*Gesetz zur Verhütung erbkranken Nachwuchses*). Propaganda was directed above all against individualistic motives for abortion; the "duty to the *Volk*" had precedence over the "right to one's own body." The awakening of the "will for a child" was to be the primary goal of all POPULATION POLICY.

Abs, Hermann Josef, b. Bonn, October 15, 1901, German banker. A lawyer, Abs became a partner in the Berlin banking house Delbrück, Schickler and Co. in 1935, and director of the Deutsche Bank in 1938. He accumulated directorships and by 1942 had a vote on 40 boards. His great

Otto Abetz.

Hermann Josef Abs.

1

economic influence during the National Socialist period, partly through firms operating in German-occupied territory during the war, attracted much hostility after 1945; he was condemned in absentia as a war criminal in Yugoslavia. Abs became a financial adviser to Konrad ADENAUER, headed the German delegation at the London Debt Conference of 1951–1953, and in 1957 assumed leadership of the Deutsche Bank. He has a reputation as a patron of the arts.

Abschnitt, subdivision of the STURMABTEILUNG and SS.

Abstammungsnachweis. *See* Certificate of Descent.

Abwehr, military counterintelligence and counterespionage service; its official designation after February 4, 1938, was Bureau Abwehr (Amtsgruppe A.), and after 1939, Abwehr Foreign Office (Amt Ausland/A.) in the WEHRMACHT HIGH COMMAND (OKW). The Abwehr was created in 1920; its name (*abwehren,* to ward off) was intended to stress the defensive character of this department of the Reichswehr (Armed Forces) Ministry after the First World War. This changed as Germany rearmed following the Seizure of Power.

From 1933 to 1934 the Abwehr was directed by Naval Capt. Conrad Patzig, who came into conflict with the NSDAP and was followed, after January 1, 1935, by Rear Adm. (after January 1, 1940, Adm.) Wilhelm CANARIS. The effective secret service that then developed consisted of a Foreign Office (Capt., then Vice Adm., Leopold Bürkner), a Central Division for Administration and Records (Col. Hans OSTER), and Divisions I (intelligence; Col. Hans Piekenbrock), II (sabotage, subversion, minorities; Colonel von Lahousen), and III (defense against espionage, counterespionage; Colonel von Bentivegni). The Canaris offices shared intelligence duties with Division IV of the Quartermaster General's Office and the "Foreign Army" division of the ARMY HIGH COMMAND (OKH). Rivalry for military intelligence came from the SS SECURITY SERVICE (Sicherheitsdienst; SD) under Reinhard HEYDRICH until 1942, then Walter SCHELLENBERG.

After the FRITSCH CRISIS, Oster made the Abwehr Foreign Office a center of military opposition. For some time he was able to conceal the conspirators, cover their plans, and provide opponents of the war with intelligence. By April 1943, the arrest of Hans von DOHNÁNYI, and Oster's dismissal as a result of careless currency

transactions in the V7 rescue operation, had diminished the potential for opposition. It was finally extinguished when Canaris was removed in February 1944 and the SD took over the Abwehr as a military office (Amt MIL).

Abyssinia, empire in East Africa (the residents' own term, Ethiopia [Äthiopien], first prevailed in German usage after 1945). In 1933 Abyssinia covered 1.2 million sq km (.5 million sq miles) and had a population of approximately 12 million. Italy's first attempt to establish itself as a colonial power in Abyssinia failed in 1896 at the Battle of Adwa. This only temporarily dampened Rome's claims, which were actually recognized by Great Britain and France in 1906.

From the early 1930s, MUSSOLINI's imperialistic plans received renewed impetus from the world economic crisis. In the belief that the Western powers were preoccupied with National Socialist Germany's threats to foreign and security policy, the Duce used a border incident to attack Abyssinia.

On October 2, 1935, some 360,000 Italian troops marched against the Abyssinian capital of Addis Ababa, one attack column coming northward from Eritrea, the other southeast from Italian Somaliland. On May 5, 1936, it was conquered, and four days later King VICTOR EMMANUEL III assumed the title Emperor of Abyssinia. The Italian victory was less surprising

Abyssinia. Soldiers of Negus (Emperor) Haile Selassie.

than the great effort required by Mussolini's well-equipped troops to defeat the barely organized 300,000 soldiers of Negus (Emperor) Haile Selassie (1892–1975; r. 1930–1936 and 1941–1974).

Mussolini had also made a diplomatic error: the great colonial powers, France and Great Britain, reacted more sharply than anticipated and pushed economic sanctions against Italy through the LEAGUE OF NATIONS (October 18, 1935). That they failed with their policy of half measures was to the credit of Hitler and was also due to the reluctance of Paris, in particular, to jeopardize the cooperation with Rome just achieved at STRESA. Hitler used the Abyssinian conflict to lessen German-Italian tensions that had built up since the Viennese putsch attempt against Chancellor Engelbert DOLLFUSS (July 25, 1934). German coal and steel deliveries put Mussolini in Hitler's debt and marked the first step toward the Berlin-Rome AXIS. To what extent Hitler was involved in dealing with the Negus for German weapons, and was carrying out a double cross to lengthen the war for diplomatic gains, is not clear.

The new Italian colony of Abyssinia was lost in the Second World War as early as 1941.

Academic (*Akademiker*), often characterized by the National Socialists as a "brainworker" (*Arbeiter der Stirn*), a member of those professions whose exercise required university study as a prerequisite. The term "academic" was avoided because it fostered caste mentality and contradicted the ideal of the VOLK COMMUNITY. The proportion of academics from a working-class background increased during the Third Reich, but remained minuscule in actual numbers.

Academies of the NSD University Teachers' League (Akademien des NSD-Dozentenbundes), institutions created to permeate the entire university realm with National Socialist principles and to supervise all scholarly work in terms of ideology. The first academies were established in Kiel, Tübingen, Heidelberg, and Göttingen.

Academy for German Law (Akademie für deutsches Recht), institute founded in 1933 on the initiative of Hans FRANK; after July 11, 1934, a public corporation of the Reich (*Reich Law Gazette* I, p. 608). It was financed largely by business donations. The academy's members were prominent representatives of politics, business, and academia, including Hermann GÖRING, Joseph GOEBBELS, Carl Bosch, Friedrich

FLICK, Carl SCHMITT, and Hans Carl NIPPERDEY; its presidents were Frank (1933–1943) and Otto THIERACK (1942–1945). Frank's original goal for the academy—influence on National Socialist legislation—did not prevail because the ministerial bureaucracies successfully defended their prerogatives. The academy developed extensive representative and publishing activities. By holding attractive international congresses, it contributed to the reputation of the Third Reich. Its committees attempted to develop the foundations for a new NS law (*see* VOLK LAW CODE). Publications: *Jahrbuch der Akademie f. d. R.* (Yearbook of the Academy for German Law), *Zeitschrift der Akademie f. d. R.* (Journal of the Academy for German Law; monthly), and *Schriftenreihe der Akademie f. d. R.* (Publications of the Academy for German Law).

Sch.

Academy for Youth Leadership (Akademie für Jugendführung), Hitler Youth (HJ) leadership school in Braunschweig. Any "Hitler Youth who is above reproach in terms of descent, health, performance, and behavior" was eligible for the one-year academy course if he had completed his labor and military service and had already taken some leadership courses. Successful completion of the academy course obligated the graduate to 12 years of HJ service. The academy had little effect because the war began soon after its founding.

Action Française, French right-radical movement founded in 1898. Action Française and its intellectual leader, Charles MAURRAS, attacked the Third Republic, demanded revenge for the Franco-Prussian War (1870–1871), and planned the establishment of a hereditary monarchy based on a society divided by rank ("integral nationalism"). Not a parliamentary party, Action Française remained without political influence after the First World War I, but it did affect the intellectual youth of the interwar period. Its glorification of violence, its antisemitic slogans, and its doctrine of the absolute primacy of politics resulted in conflict with the church (it was condemned by the pope in 1926) and made it a precursor of French FASCISM. Despite continuing hostility to Germany, the adherents of Action Française vehemently opposed the war in 1939, and after the French defeat of 1940 supported the PÉTAIN government. Thus discredited by COLLABORATION, Action Française disappeared after 1944. Its ideology surfaced again with some changes in the programs of the New Right in France (*see* NEOFASCISM).

Activism (*Aktivismus*), political maxim of National Socialism as a "fighting movement," as opposed to "bourgeois passivity." It was claimed that only through an activist stance had it been possible to "defeat terrorist Marxism." However, that which propaganda ennobled as activism was, especially at the grass-roots level, often only blind action for action's sake.

Adam, Karl, b. Pursruck (Upper Palatinate), October 22, 1876; d. Tübingen, April 1, 1966, German Catholic theologian. Ordained in 1900, Adam was a professor of Catholic theology in Tübingen from 1919. His main work was *Wesen des Katholizismus* (The Essence of Catholicism; 1924). In 1933 Adam greeted Hitler's seizure of power lyrically; he sought a theological reconciliation of the German *Volk* and Catholic Christendom as "nature and super-nature." Despite its "clear, firm affirmation . . . of the moral forces" of National Socialism as an ideology of "determined brotherliness," National Socialists saw Adam's *völkisch* theology as an attempt to embrace Catholicism. They also criticized his attacks on the GERMAN FAITH MOVEMENT and his stress on the Jewish origins of Christianity. After becoming a professor emeritus in 1948, Adam lived a reclusive life in Tübingen.

Adenauer, Konrad, b. Cologne, January 5, 1876; d. Rhöndorf, April 19, 1967, German politician. Adenauer entered the CENTER party in 1906 and became deputy mayor in the Cologne City Council. From 1917 to 1933 he was lord mayor of his home city; as a member of the Prussian State Council (president, 1920–1933) during the WEIMAR REPUBLIC, he gained great political influence, but in 1926 he refused the Reich chancellorship as Hans LUTHER's successor. As a Catholic, Adenauer opposed National Socialism, and on March 12, 1933, he was removed from office as a result of SYNCHRONIZATION. He was accused of malfeasance as well as separatism because he had proposed a Rhenish Free State separated from Prussia (but not the Republic) during the RUHR CONFLICT. Imprisoned for a time in 1934, Adenauer retreated into private life. Imprisoned again in connection with the assassination attempt of the TWENTIETH OF JULY, 1944, he was soon released.

After the German collapse Adenauer helped build the Christian Democratic Union, for a short time serving again as lord mayor of Cologne. As president of the Parliamentary Coun-

Konrad Adenauer.

cil, he was one of the creators of the Basic Law (*Grundgesetz*) of the Federal Republic of Germany. As first federal chancellor (September 15, 1949–October 16, 1963), he took a stance against the burdensome inheritance of the National Socialist period, with an agreement on RESTITUTION with Israel, negotiations in Moscow for release of prisoners of war, and reconciliation with France. However, he also drew criticism for too great leniency toward such politically compromised individuals as Hans GLOBKE and Theodor OBERLÄNDER. Adenauer led the Federal Republic into the Western alliance. Not least because of growing prosperity, his era established a stable, free political culture in the western part of Germany.

ADGB. *See* General German Trade Union Federation.

Adler, Friedrich, b. Vienna, July 9, 1879; d. Zurich, January 2, 1960, Austrian politician. Originally a physicist, Adler turned down a Zurich professorship that then went to Albert EINSTEIN. Adler joined the Social Democrats; on October 21, 1916, he shot to death Austrian prime minister Stürgkh, in protest against his party's war policies. His death sentence commuted to imprisonment, Adler was amnestied in 1918; in 1923 he became general secretary of the Socialist Workers International. In 1940 he emigrated to the United States, but he returned in 1946. The National Socialists persecuted Adler as a "Jewish rabble-rouser and Marxist" despite his anti-Communist efforts.

Adlerhorst (Eagle's Nest), Führer headquarters built in 1940 at Ziegenhain, near Bad Nauheim; at first unused. Hitler directed the ARDENNES OFFENSIVE from the Adlerhorst, beginning on December 10, 1944. After it failed, he returned to Berlin on January 16, 1945.

Adlerorden (Eagle Order; Service Order of the German Eagle [Verdienstorden vom Deutschen Adler]), commendation for foreigners established by Hitler on May 1, 1937. There were five levels of this military medal with swords; after April 20, 1939, there was also a Grand Cross in gold.

Adlerschild des Deutschen Reiches (Eagle Shield of the German Reich), "honorary award" (*Ehrengabe*) granted by the German president beginning in 1922 for scholarly or artistic achievements. It was a metal disc with a German imperial eagle (after 1933, a swastika) on a pedestal, a high and infrequently awarded honor.

Adler und Falke (Eagle and Falcon), NSDAP youth organization during the early TIME OF STRUGGLE (*Kampfzeit*).

Administration (*Verwaltung*), an instrument important to National Socialism for carrying out the political goals of the regime. The National Socialists centralized the administrative structure taken over from the Weimar Republic by SYNCHRONIZATION. In particular, the state (*Land*) administrations, which had been independent until that time, became part of a unified REICH AUTHORITY. Besides the governmental administrative organs, the NSDAP offices had administrative authority in many spheres, although the competence of these agencies was not always clearly defined. Traditional administration greatly expanded in two areas: (1) organization of the economy in the National Socialist spirit, especially to facilitate the preparation for and conduct of war; and (2) combating political enemies of the system, notably by instituting the Gestapo, the SD, and the REICH SECURITY MAIN OFFICE. Between 1933 and 1945 the administration was not subject to any control by an independent judiciary. Administrative jurisdiction continued to exist in principle, but its competence had been strongly curtailed, and in all political questions it conformed to the regime's expectations.

A. v. B.

Adolf Hitler Canal, canal built between 1933 and 1939 as a WORK CREATION measure to connect the Upper Silesian industrial district near Gleiwitz with the Oder River; its mouth was at Cosel. It is now known as the Gliwice Canal (Poland).

Adolf-Hitler-Dank. *See* Hitler-Dank.

Adolf Hitler Donation (*Adolf-Hitler-Spende*), "voluntary" contribution from German business to the NSDAP, agreed to in the spring of 1933 by the main business and economic associations as an "expression of thanks to the Führer," equaling about .5 percent of wages. Martin BORMANN initiated the donation and administered it as Hitler's financial representative. It was considered a substitute for many earlier uncoordinated efforts to raise party funds from business.

Adolf-Hitler-Koog, new land (1,330 hectares, or 3,285 acres) created by dikes as a WORK CREATION measure in Süderdithmarschen; now called Dieksanderkoog.

Adolf Hitler March of German Youth, yearly pilgrimage of some 2,000 HITLER YOUTH (HJ) from all parts of the Reich to the REICH PARTY CONGRESSES in Nuremberg, where they marched with flags past Hitler in a huge parade. Some groups covered as many as 800 km (490 miles). The HJ goal of "combat readiness" (*Wehrhaftmachung*) underlay the watchword given the youth by Reich Youth Führer Baldur von SCHIRACH: "We are marching to the Führer —if he wishes, we will also march for him." After 1937, the march was extended beyond Nuremberg to LANDSBERG AM LECH, where the viewing of Hitler's prison cell crowned the program.

Adolf Hitler Pass, connection between Ostrachtal and Vilstal in Allgäu, 1,180 m (3,870 feet) high; now called Gaichpass.

Adolf Hitler Schools (AHS), association of 10, ultimately 12, "National Socialist Schools," which Hitler allowed, on January 15, 1937, to bear his name (as he earlier had other schools). Their founding was based on Robert LEY's plan to erect a "Gauburg" (citadel) in every GAU, thereby creating an NSDAP school system. This would also have transformed the state-supported NATIONAL-POLITICAL EDUCATIONAL INSTITUTES. Education minister Bernhard RUST, however, agreed only to boarding-school "Aufbauschulen" (advanced grade schools with some college preparation), supported by the party, to educate future party leaders. Neither plan was realized. Until 1941, the AHS was supported by the financial office of the GERMAN LABOR

Adolf Hitler Streets and Squares

The zeal with which German municipal authorities attempted, immediately after the Seizure of Power, to play their part in the NATIONAL RISING (*Erhebung*) is shown by the practice of conferring honorary municipal citizenship on Hitler, and even more by naming a street (*Strasse*), a square or place (*Platz*), a promenade (*Anlage*), an avenue (*Damm, Allee*), a stadium (*Kampfbahn*), or a bridge (*Brücke*) after the new chancellor. As early as March and April of 1933, a wave of renamings swept through Germany's cities. Most of the examples in Table 1 come from this period.

TABLE 1. *Adolf Hitler Streets and Squares*

City	1933–1945 Name	Pre-1933/Post-1945 Name
Berlin	A.-H.-Platz (Charlottenburg; further renamings were planned for after the "Final Victory")	Reichskanzlerplatz/Theodor-Heuss-Platz
Bremen	A.-H.-Brücke (Lüderitzbrücke after 1939)	Grosse Weserbrücke (torn down, 1961)
	A.-H.-Brücke (new in 1939)	Westbrücke/Stephaniebrücke
	A.-H.-Platz (Hemelingen)	Rathausplatz
	A.-H.-Platz (Lesum)	An der Lesumer Kirche
	A.-H.-Strasse (Aumund)	Hammersbecker Strasse
	A.-H.-Strasse (Lesum)	Kellerstrasse
Cologne	A.-H.-Platz	Platz der Republik/Deutscher Platz (Ebertplatz after 1950)
Dortmund	A.-H.-Allee	Hainallee
Düsseldorf	A.-H.-Platz	Graf-Adolf-Platz
	A.-H.-Strasse	Haroldstrasse
Essen	A.-H.-Platz	Burgplatz
	A.-H.-Strasse	Kettwiger Strasse; Viehofer Strasse
Frankfurt am Main	A.-H.-Anlage	Gallus-Anlage
Hamburg	A.-H.-Platz	Rathausmarkt
	A.-H.-Strasse (Winterhude)	Bebelallee
	A.-H.-Platz (Altona)	Platz der Republik
	A.-H.-Damm (Wandsbek)	Friedrich-Ebert-Damm
	A.-H.-Strasse (Wilhelmsburg)	Wilhelmsburger Reichsstrasse
Hannover	A.-H.-Platz (Hermann-Göring-Platz after September 15, 1933)	Corvinusplatz
	A.-H.-Platz	Theaterplatz
	A.-H.-Strasse	Bahnhofstrasse
Kiel	A.-H.-Platz	Neumarkt/Rathausplatz
Munich	A.-H.-Platz (Pasing)	Avenariusplatz
	A.-H.-Allee (Solln)	Diefenbachstrasse
	A.-H.-Strasse (Obermenzing)	Verdistrasse
	A.-H.-Strasse (Untermenzing)	Eversbuschstrasse
	A.-H.-Strasse (Allach)	Vesaliusstrasse
	A.-H.-Strasse (Aubing)	Limesstrasse
	A.-H.-Strasse (Lochhausen)	Schussenrieder Strasse

(cont.)

TABLE 1 (cont.)

CITY	1933–1945 NAME	PRE-1933/POST-1945 NAME
Nuremberg	A.-H.-Platz	Hauptmarkt
Saarbrücken	A.-H.-Strasse (1935–1945)	Bahnhofstrasse
Stuttgart	A.-H.-Strasse	Planie
	A.-H.-Platz (Birkach)	Bei der Linde
	A.-H.-Platz (Stammheim)	—
	A.-H.-Strasse (Feuerbach)	Stuttgarter Strasse
	A.-H.-Strasse (Plieningen)	Paracelsusstrasse
	A.-H.-Strasse (Möhringen)	Laustrasse
	A.-H.-Strasse (Vaihingen)	Böblinger Strasse/Hauptstrasse
	A.-H.-Kampfbahn (Bad Cannstatt)	Neckarstadion
Vienna	A.-H.-Platz (1938–1945)	Rathausplatz

FRONT. Built up class by class, the schools were housed with the similarly financed ORDER FORTRESSES until 1941. Responsibility for the schools' structure was assumed not by the NSDAP but by the REICH YOUTH LEADERSHIP.

The AHS were to set an example for the "revolution in education": "The responsibility of youth for itself is also possible in school" (Baldur von SCHIRACH). Thus the HITLER YOUTH (HJ) announced its intent to transform schooling. Yet in practice the AHS achieved hardly more than the Education Institutes' model of a duplicate leadership structure for the boarding schools. HJ leaders and Order Fortress teachers were employed as "school leaders" (Schulführer); all had HJ ranks and were addressed familiarly with "Du." A GAULEITER did not supervise schools in his territory; this was done by a "commander" (Kommandeur) from the Youth Leadership. Thus with varied ambitions and usually little expertise, the "educators" worked on "educational and curricular plans." Only the plans for art and vocational education were published (1944). Unity was as meager in the effort to combine basic subjects in a Volkskunde (folklore) as it was in the content and introduction of such new subjects as "schooling in worldview" (sometimes called "NSDAP") or "religion

Dedication of the Adolf Hitler School for Lower Silesia in Wartha. From left: Gauleiter Karl Hanke, Reich Organization Leader Robert Ley, and Reich Youth Führer Baldur von Schirach.

Adolphe Légalité. "How Herr Hitler puts the word 'legal' in his mouth." Caricature in the Social Democratic humor magazine *Der Wahre Jakob* (The Right Way), Berlin, 1932.

lore." Denominational religious instruction was not offered. Latin ranked first as a foreign language. As in the Education Institutes, a broad range of athletic and musical offerings was guaranteed. *Einsätze* (action groups; *see* EINSATZ) were part of the educational theory in both kinds of schools, countering the isolation of boarding schools and allowing pupils to "prove" themselves, usually in HJ leadership functions. The AHS gathered together for "performance weeks" (*Leistungswochen*).

Beginning in 1941, the AHS became "Reich Schools of the NSDAP." (Only the Feldafing school, which since 1936 had been patronized and financed by the party leadership, was so designated.) After 1941 several AHS were housed in emptied sanatoriums and cloister schools. Assignment of pupils from an area to a particular school stopped at this point, and some German-speaking pupils from occupied territories were accepted. The disparate criteria according to which the HJ, under control of the local *Gau* leaders, had selected pupils thereby became more evident. The educational concept was based primarily on the individual's proving himself one of "the best." In 1941 the Education Ministry certified that the "final review"

(*Abschlussbeurteilung*, conferred after five school years) qualified students for university study. Most pupils also received a "diploma." A solid instructional program, for which there were no commonly accepted goals, was sacrificed to the idea of "proving oneself" (*Bewährung*). Within the five years, this was ultimately extended to the assumption of leadership positions in the CHILDREN'S COUNTRY EVACUATION, and, after 1943, to assignment as FLAK HELPERS. Graduates could choose their profession.

H. S.

Adolphe Légalité, derisory nickname for Hitler in social-revolutionary SA circles (*see* STURMABTEILUNG) following the REICHSWEHR TRIAL held before the Leipzig Supreme Court in late September 1930. In the eyes of radical National Socialists, Hitler's LEGALITY OATH had conceded too much to his political enemies, in the same way as had the Duke of Orleans, who adopted the name Philippe Egalité during the French Revolution.

Adult education (*Erwachsenenbildung*), institutional continuing education for persons who have completed their schooling. After the synchronization of university extension programs (Volkshochschulen) and their municipal or private sponsors, the GERMAN LABOR FRONT (DAF) made its influence felt in two ways. Within its National Socialist STRENGTH THROUGH JOY organization, it founded the GERMAN PUBLIC INSTRUCTION AGENCY (Deutsche Volksbildungswerk; DVW) in 1935. Moreover, after 1933 it used the Office for Vocational Education and Business Management to influence commercial education. The GERMAN INSTITUTE FOR NATIONAL SOCIALIST TECHNICAL VOCATIONAL TRAINING (Dinta) gave rise to the German Vocational Education Agency (Deutsches Berufserziehungswerk), which organized "practice groups" (*Übungsgemeinschaften*) that by 1938 had 2 million participants; its workplace programs involved another 1.3 million. These operations should be distinguished from the "community schooling" (*Gemeinschaftsschulung*) of employers, foremen, and workers through courses in the DAF's Reich schools.

Above all, adult education had functions not provided by the mass organizations of National Socialism, with their "ideological orientation and selection" and their military training. The adult education offerings had more to do with the economic predicament and the demand for continuing education and ideological orientation than with political schooling (*see* SCHOOLING, POLITICAL). During the war, new areas of activity arose through the combining of work with vocational or general-educational correspondence courses, as well as through continuing education for persons with war-related disabilities. In 1943, the DVW established a night school (*Abendoberschule*) in Munich. It supported social and cultural courses given by so-called guardians of public instruction (*Volksbildungswarte*) in the workplaces.

The 300 offices for public instruction also attempted to mobilize the rural population for culture. Their program of instruction was largely based on a model curriculum created in 1939 by Reich and *Gau* work groups for adult education. Instead of consolidation of adult education taking place through Reich legislation, a goal aimed at in 1933, the DVW gained dominance through the financial resources made available from DAF dues; in 1943 it was upgraded to a leadership office (Führungsamt) in the DAF. Adult education should not be underestimated as an integrating element, even if its educational offerings primarily served the collective increase of power.

H. S.

Adventists, Christian religious sect, founded by American farmer William Miller (1782–1849), that expects the Last Judgment to be immediately at hand (originally expected in 1843–1844). In Germany, the offshoot Seventh-day Adventists grew to some 30,000 members by 1930; its ritual, strongly influenced by Judaism, was banned in 1936 during the National Socialist persecution of sects (*see* SECTS, PERSECUTION OF).

Advertising Council of German Industry (Werberat der deutschen Wirtschaft), panel established by the Law on Commercial Advertising of September 12, 1933. Comprised of knowledgeable representatives of business, it had a mandate to oversee all publicity, posters, exhibits, fairs, and advertising. The council members were appointed by the Propaganda Ministry, which thereby secured control over the content and format of all advertising campaigns. These had to be submitted to and approved by the council.

Aesthetics, general theory of the beautiful, especially in art. For the National Socialists, aesthetics was important only where politically expedient. The arts were seen to have no purpose of their own, and did not serve as a means to knowledge; rather they were seen as an instru-

Aesthetics. *Monument to the Road,* by Josef Thorak.

ment of rule: "Questions of destiny with the importance of a *Volk*'s struggle for existence obviate any obligation to beauty" (*Mein Kampf*). The arts were expected to provide models for the "new people," especially the idealization of the heroic ("heroic realism").

National Socialist aesthetic theories were based on the ideal of classical antiquity, of the "Nordic Occident" (including Greece); Plotinus's *Enneads* were cited for theoretical authority. "Symmetry and harmony of content and form" were stressed. The aesthetic values of German classicism, especially as represented by Immanuel Kant, in whose works the thinking, self-determining subject assumes a central position, were largely rejected. Hitler legitimized normative, imitative aesthetics through the determination that it was better "to copy the good than to produce something new but bad." "Heroic ages," he concluded, always sought "bridges to the heroic past." Formal severity, the setting of artistic norms, corresponded to conceptions of state order: "This state is the most supreme work of art" (Alfred BAEUMLER). Through the creation of cultural values (*see* FÜHRER CULT) and through "concrete images of friend and enemy," the National Socialists strove for an "aestheticizing of political life" (Walther Benjamin), which disguised the absence of any rational justification. Thus Hitler elevated his role as politician to that of an artist working with "human material," who arranges the human masses according to aesthetic criteria; mass deployments were considered "human architecture."

Citing Friedrich Nietzsche and Charles Darwin as authorities, aesthetics was supported with racial biology: "A particular ideal of beauty is unique to a people or race, and no historical art form, so far as it is genuine, can survive independent of this group-specific ideal" (Baeumler). Man was seen as a work of art determined through evolution; a "racially related maximum value of a spiritual kind" should correspond to a "racial ideal of physical beauty" (Alfred ROSENBERG).

H. H.

Afabund, abbreviation of Allgemeiner Freier Angestelltenbund (General Free Federation of Employees), chief association of private-sector employees in the Weimar Republic. Member organizations encompassed groups as diverse as artists, theater workers, bank clerks, foremen, and technical employees and managers. It was

dissolved in early May 1933, following the destruction of the TRADE UNIONS.

Africa Corps, German (Afrika-Korps). *See* African Campaign.

African Campaign, term for the German-Italian military operations against British and American troops in North Africa between 1940 and May 13, 1943. When Italy entered the war on Germany's side on June 10, 1940, Marshal Pietro BADOGLIO commanded a military force of two armies with 14 divisions in the Italian colony of Libya. An attack on the weak British forces (approximately 36,000 troops) seemed promising to Mussolini. The Italian offensive began on September 13, 1940; by September 16 it reached Sidi Barrani, but stalled on September 18 because of alleged supply problems. Mussolini rejected German offers of help; he later told Badoglio that he feared becoming dependent. On December 12, 1940, the British Thirteenth Army Corps, with only 31,000 troops, 275 tanks, and 120 artillery pieces, began a counteroffensive, which quickly became a catastrophe for the Italians. Sidi Barrani fell on December 10, and Sollum (Salūm) on December 16. On January 5, 1941, the British were in Bardia (Bardïyah), on January 22 in Tobruk, and on February 6 in Benghazi. With only 558 dead and 1,373 wounded, they had destroyed 10 Italian divisions and had captured 130,000 prisoners, 408 tanks, and 1,290 artillery pieces. Logistic problems forced them to stop at Al-Agheila on February 8, 1941.

On January 9, 1941, Hitler ordered a German "barrage unit" (*Sperrverband*) to Libya in answer to an Italian request for help of December 19, 1940. The newly formed Fifth Light Division began to move on February 8, followed soon by the Fifteenth Tank Division. Gen. Erwin ROMMEL took command of the German Africa Corps on February 2, 1941, and, contrary to Hitler's delaying tactics, ordered a reconnaissance thrust toward Al-Agheila on March 22.

The British then drove eastward. Rommel followed, took Benghazi on April 4, and after marching through the desert, took Derna on April 8. The attack on Tobruk collapsed; Rommel reached Bardia on April 11, and conquered the Halfaya Pass on April 14. A British counteroffensive in June 1941 failed; a second one, begun on November 18, to relieve Tobruk (which had been blockaded since April 11), was carried out with superior forces and was more successful. On December 7, Rommel was forced to give up the battle for the fortress and make an

African Campaign. A German tank crew tries to cool off in the Mediterranean.

orderly retreat. He evacuated Benghazi on December 23; in early January 1942, after heavy losses on both sides, he stood approximately where he had begun.

Protected by heavy sandstorms, Rommel renewed the attack on his totally surprised opponent on January 23, 1942; he entered Benghazi on January 29, and reached Derna on February 3. He could not continue the offensive until May 26, 1942. The British suspected that Rommel wanted to push on to Egypt, but on June 18, he broke off his march to the east, turned west, and conquered Tobruk on June 21, taking 33,000 prisoners and enormous booty. Rommel was made general field marshal. On June 23 the German-Italian African tank corps again crossed the Egyptian border, and on June 30 reached El-Alamein, 100 km (62 miles) west of Alexandria. An attempted breakthrough failed; Rommel had to go on the defensive. The facts that the supply problem had not been addressed more energetically and that the British had not been dislodged from the Mediterranean island of Malta now took their toll. Rommel's last attempt to break through the Alamein position failed between August 31 and September 2. A British offensive against Tobruk failed on September 14.

Yet the next attack, by the British Eighth Army under Gen. Bernard MONTGOMERY, could not be held off. On October 23, 10 divisions and four brigades, with 1,114 tanks and 880 aircraft, attacked 5 German and 7 Italian divisions, with only 530 tanks and 372 airplanes. Gen. Georg

Stumme, in charge during Rommel's absence, was killed. On November 2, Montgomery broke through the German lines and took 30,000 prisoners. Concurrently, the Allies landed in Morocco and Algeria on November 7–8, 1942 (Operation "Torch"). The German leadership responded by occupying VICHY France. Rapid deployment of troops to Tunisia prevented loss of this part of French North Africa. Because of the threat from his rear, Rommel retreated with the African Tank Corps, abandoning Tobruk on November 13, 1942, and Al-Agheila a month later. Italy's Libyan colony was lost with the surrender of Tripoli on January 23, 1943. On March 9, illness led Rommel to turn over command of the Africa Corps to Col. Gen. Jürgen von Arnim, who on May 13, 1943, was forced to capitulate with the remainder of the Eleventh German and the Sixth Italian division; 130,000 German and 120,000 Italian soldiers were captured. Hitler had rejected a plausible attempt to save a great many troops.

German losses in Africa were 18,594 dead and 3,400 missing; Italian, 13,748 dead and 8,821 missing; British, 35,476 dead; United States, 16,500 dead.

G. H.

After-work organization (*Feierabendgestaltung*), the "planned" structuring of daily leisure time attempted by the National Socialists through individual state agencies, including the Office for After-Work Activity (Amt für Feierabend), within the STRENGTH THROUGH JOY program. In

National Socialist usage the term "after-work organization" was increasingly applied to the entire area of organized leisure activity (including vacations and weekends).

Agrarian Movement (*Agrarbewegung*), farmers' movement during the economic crisis that protested difficulties of a structural nature (as indebtedness and forced liquidations) and an economic nature (as the decline in prices). In Schleswig-Holstein a mass farmers' movement arose as early as 1928; it became increasingly radical, and ultimately benefited the NSDAP in particular. On the national level, various agricultural associations united in a common front ("GREEN FRONT") in 1929, despite continuing internal tensions. Leadership was assumed by the REICH COUNTRY LEAGUE, which represented primarily major agricultural interests. Despite considerable subsidies (*see* EASTERN AID) and high protective tariffs, farmers—especially large landowners—were not satisfied. Both actively and passively, they contributed to the decline of the Weimar Republic.

A. v. S.

Agricultural policy, all measures related to agriculture in the National Socialist state. The most important were creation of the REICH FOOD ESTATE (Reichsnährstand) and the introduction of market regulations with fixed prices for all important farm products. Markets were also regulated and rationalized (for example, a new organization of the consumer milk market). In 1936–1937 there followed legislative intervention in the production of milk (regulation of quantities delivered) and grain (regulation of the variety mix). The continued depression of some grower prices, despite increases, reflected the overall economic strategy of austerity in favor of rearmament. This, however, contradicted the other prime goal of agricultural policy, the "battle for agricultural production," to achieve greater self-sufficiency in agricultural products.

The contradiction between relatively low prices to farmers and the expectation of increased production was dealt with through compulsory measures and the encouragement of mechanization, rationalization, and the use of fertilizers. (During the war, resort was made to financial incentives.) A further problem was the scarcity of labor. The number of agricultural workers sank by 440,000 between 1933 and 1939. State-sponsored compensatory efforts (Country Service, Labor Service, Service Year) could not create a qualitative substitute for the "flight from the countryside." Despite these problems and contradictions, the degree of self-sufficiency was "successfully" increased from 68 percent in 1927–1928 to 83 percent in 1938–1939. The "FAT GAP" could not, however, be closed.

The second important area of agricultural policy consisted of efforts to restructure agriculture. Examples here are debt-forgiveness policies, which continued at a higher level what was begun with EASTERN AID, and the HEREDITARY FARM LAW, which was meant to take some agricultural property off the free market in order to prevent fragmentation of holdings and indebtedness. The constraints on those affected, particularly the diminished creditworthiness of entailed farms, made this law a prototype of unsuccessful structural policy in the agricultural sector.

A. v. S.

Agricultural Policy Apparatus of the NSDAP (Agrarpolitischer Apparat), party organization created by Walther DARRÉ on June 1, 1930, to coordinate measures and statements dealing with agricultural policy. It was later renamed the REICH OFFICE FOR AGRICULTURAL POLICY (*see also* REICH FOOD ESTATE).

Agricultural Program ("Official Party Proclamation regarding the Position of the NSDAP toward the Countryfolk and Agriculture" of March 6, 1930), NSDAP statement, formulated by Walther DARRÉ, on agricultural policy. It arose mainly from consideration of election tactics and the attempt to profit from growing dissatisfaction among the rural population after the beginning of the world economic crisis. Along with suggestions for a general improvement of agriculture, the central demand was for a "German Soil Policy" (*Deutsche Bodenpolitik*); this included such measures as a ban on mortgaging land to private creditors, and a general inheritance law to prevent fragmentation of farms and burdening with debt. Contrary to Point 17 of the PARTY PROGRAM OF THE NSDAP of February 24, 1920, the confiscation of land was not mentioned. Specifically National Socialist elements of the program were antisemitism ("only members of the German *Volk* may be owners of German soil") and expansionism (creation of room for farming and colonizing). In sum, the vague formulations of the Agricultural Program were oriented toward the expectations and needs, the emotions and latent resentments of the rural population. The success registered by

Agricultural policy. Propaganda demonstration on the Bückeberg for the Reich Food Estate.

the NSDAP in the Reichstag elections of September 14, 1930, particularly among this group, justified the program.

Ahasuerus. *See* Wandering Jew.

Ahlwardt, Hermann, b. Krien bei Anklam, December 21, 1846; d. Leipzig, April 16, 1914; German antisemitic journalist. Ahlwardt was originally an elementary school (*Volksschule*) teacher, but was dismissed in 1893 because of his anti-Jewish pamphlets (such as "Jew Rifles" [*Judenflinten*], which attacked the Loewe Weapons Factory) and sentenced to prison. He was a co-founder of the Antisemitic People's Party (Antisemitische Volkspartei); his three-volume work *Verzweiflungskampf der arischen Völker mit dem Judentum* (The Desperate Struggle of the Aryan Peoples with Judaism; 1890–1892) later influenced National Socialist ANTISEMITISM.

Ahnenerbe. *See* Ancestral Inheritance.

Aid Service (Hilfsdienst), division of the GERMAN WOMEN'S AGENCY (Frauenwerk) that coordinated and organized the deployment of women from the agency and from the National Socialist WOMEN'S UNION (Frauenschaft) into the various social welfare agencies (the Red Cross, the NS Volk Welfare, the Committee for the Nursing Profession, and the Reich Air Defense League).

The women's work was done under the supervision of the individual organizations, and the Women's Union was responsible for the ideological schooling of all women so deployed.

Air Battle for England (*Luftschlacht um England*; Anglo-Amer., Battle of Britain), in the narrower sense, the conflict between the German Luftwaffe and the Royal Air Force (RAF) in 1940–1941 for mastery in the air over the English Channel and southern England. In general, it refers to all attacks from 1940 to 1945 on targets in Great Britain, which because it was an island could be carried out only from the air. Since England did not give up after the defeat of France, the Wehrmacht had to develop a military plan that called for an invasion of Great Britain. Yet this would be possible, in the opinion of the army, only after the RAF had been removed as a factor. On July 2, 1940, the Wehrmacht High Command (OKW) notified the three Wehrmacht divisions of Hitler's decision —under particular preconditions, which in view of the navy's weakness included air domination—to invade southern England (Operation "Seelöwe" [Sea Lion]). According to an advisory of June 30, 1940, the battle for England would be fought first against the British air force and its ground operations, as well as against the aircraft and related armaments industry. On

August 1, 1940, Hitler commanded that the Luftwaffe should then, "ready-for-battle, put itself at the disposal" of Operation "Sea Lion" (Advisory No. 17).

On August 13 ("Day of the Eagle" [*Adlertag*]), the Luftwaffe had available in the Second, Third, and Fifth Air Forces in France, Belgium, and Norway, over 875 battle-ready bombers, 316 dive bombers, 45 long-range reconnaissance planes, 702 fighters (*Jäger*), and 227 escort fighters (*Zerstörer*). On this first day of the air battle they flew 1,485 missions, with 34 planes lost. On August 24, the first bombs fell on London—unintentionally, in keeping with Hitler's orders up to that point. By August 31, the Luftwaffe had flown 4,779 missions, dropped 4,638 tons of bombs, and lost 215 bombers and 252 fighters. The RAF lost 359 fighters. Although the primary goal of removing the RAF from action was not attained, on September 7 and throughout that night, massive attacks on London took place, carried out by 625 bombers, which by day were covered by 648 fighters. Further attacks followed for the following 65 nights. In September 1940, the Luftwaffe flew 7,260 missions against Great Britain. The mounting losses proved that the British fighters could not be defeated, and that new production could maintain the force at equivalent strength. Daytime attacks, which provided sufficient precision of targets, had to be given up by the fall because of losses and deteriorating weather conditions. The range of the German fighters was insufficient to offer the bombers adequate protection. Total radar cover prevented surprise attacks. The Me 110 escort fighter proved to be inadequate as a long-distance fighter, and the

dive bomber had to be withdrawn after heavy losses.

Germany greatly overestimated the effect of the nighttime attacks on British industry that followed. Even the devastation in London or in COVENTRY (November 14–15, 1940) could not break the will to resist of the British people, as was the case with the far more terrible attacks on the German population carried out later by Allied bombers. The use of the Luftwaffe for the RUSSIAN CAMPAIGN forced the abandonment of the Air Battle for England. The Luftwaffe had inflicted heavy damage, killing 41,294 British civilians and injuring 52,128 more (July 1, 1940–May 31, 1941). But it did not achieve its goal of making England ready for peace, or even create the preconditions for an invasion. Operation "Sea Lion" had to be abandoned. Germany's Luftwaffe suffered total losses between August 1, 1940, and March 31, 1941, of 1,142 bombers, 802 fighters, 330 escort fighters, and 128 dive bombers.

On April 14, 1942, Hitler commanded that the air war against England was "to be carried on aggressively to a fuller extent." Targets were to be chosen "whose attack would have the greatest possible repercussions for public life." From March 23 to October 31, 1942, the German Luftwaffe, though weakened in force, bombed 22 British cities containing valuable old buildings, such as Exeter, Canterbury, Norwich, and York (the so-called Baedecker Attacks), as "vengeance" for RAF attacks on the medieval centers of such cities as Lübeck and Rostock. In 1943 some 1,975 nighttime raids (with 105 planes lost) were carried out against British harbors and industrial cities, while during the daytime hours, 434 fighter-bomber attacks (with 25 shot down) were directed against 15 cities. Although aircraft were lacking on all fronts, in 1944 Hitler ordered further "vengeance attacks." In the night of January 21–22, 1944, the Ninth Air Corps bombed London with 447 planes. These nighttime attacks (the "Baby Blitz") lasted until May 29, 1944 (4,269 missions, with 329 losses).

The final great test for the British population was bombardment with the so-called V-Weapon (V for *Vergeltung*, or vengeance): between June 12, 1944, and March 29, 1945, 10,492 V1 flying bombs ("buzz bombs") were fired. Three thousand exploded on firing, and 3,957 were destroyed by British defenses. They killed 6,184 civilians and wounded 17,981. From September 8, 1944, to March 27, 1945, in addition, 1,045 long-distance rockets of the A4 type (V2),

Air Battle for England. A German ME 109 fighter pursues a British Spitfire.

against which there was no defense, were fired at southern England, killing 2,754 civilians and wounding 6,523. The "miracle" that German propaganda had promised from their use—a turning point in the war—did not take place.

G. H.

Aircraft-damaged. *See* Fliegergeschädigt.

Air defense (Lufschutz), the totality of measures for defense against bombing attacks. The creation of a civilian air defense was the defensive complement to REARMAMENT and had a relatively high priority after the Seizure of Power. The Reich Air Defense League (Reichsluftschutzbund; RLB) was founded as early as April 29, 1933; responsible to the Reich Ministry for Air Travel and the supreme commander of the Luftwaffe, it was taken over by the NSDAP in 1944. It was responsible for training the volunteer "air defense watchers" (*Luftschutzwarte*), who led the so-called air defense communities in individual apartment buildings or on residential blocks. The Air Defense Law of May 26, 1935, introduced an air defense duty (*Luftschutzpflicht*), which foresaw for all Germans a service requirement (as for the AIR RAID ALARM, blackout, firefighting, first aid, or clearing rubble), as well as a requirement concerning material provisions (such as constructing air defense spaces or supplying equipment).

When the war began, the RLB had over 13.5 million members, 820,000 officers, and 28,000 air defense teachers in 3,800 air defense schools, whose courses could be made obligatory for everyone. Particular tasks were given to workplace air defense (*Werk-Luftschutz*). The Allied AIR WAR after 1942 demonstrated the narrow limits of air defense in a modern war. Many air defense helpers were killed in service.

Air-emergency region (*Luftnotgebiet*), euphemistic National Socialist propaganda term for regions destroyed and endangered by bombing, especially major and industrial cities in western Germany. The term was required for press and radio reporting.

Air Force, German. *See* Air Battle for England.

Air Huns (*Lufthunnen*; also "air barbarians"), curse coined by Joseph Goebbels in 1944 for the Allied bomber crews. The expression was meant to go beyond the expression "terror flyers" (*Terrorflieger*), and alluded to the British catchword of the First World War that demonized the German soldiers as "beastly Huns."

Air defense. Poster from 1943: "The enemy sees your light! Black out!"

Air raid alarm (*Fliegeralarm; Luftalarm*), siren warning against bombing attacks during the AIR WAR. Three equally long and loud signals meant "public air raid warning," or a preliminary alarm. The infirm and families with small children were to go to air raid shelters, at first in their own homes, and later, as attacks intensified, to the nearest bunker—if one was available. A full alarm—signals fluctuating in volume—was sounded when bomber squadrons approached at a distance of approximately 100 km (62 miles). Alarms often lasted many hours and cost an already overstressed population its sleep, especially when many had to leave the cellars to fight fires and clear away debris even before the sounding of the all-clear signal, an extended, non-fluctuating siren.

Air war (*Luftkrieg*), in general, all military engagements that involve aircraft; in the narrower sense for the Second World War, the Allied bombing campaign against Germany. On the same day that Britain declared war (September 3, 1939), several airplanes from the Royal Air Force (RAF) dropped leaflets over Hamburg, Bremen, and the Ruhr area. German air operations in the West were limited to surveillance

"Air raid alarm. Instructions for the workers of the AUER German Incandescent Light Factory in Oranienburg.

Keep calm. Obey the warden. Keep gas mask ready.

When the air raid alarm (fire alarm) sounds: Put on gas mask, go immediately to the shelter by the prescribed route. Keep gas mask on until in the shelter.

When the all-clear signal (factory alarm) sounds: Put on gas mask; wait until warden orders a return to the workplace. Follow the orders of the workplace decontamination unit. Don't remove mask until you are at your workplace."

flights as long as most of the Luftwaffe was involved over Poland. Both sides avoided dropping bombs on land targets in order to prevent reprisals.

This tentative initial strategy changed with the beginning of the French Campaign when the British cabinet—now under Winston CHUR-CHILL—on May 11, 1940, allowed the Bomber Command (BC) to attack Germany's hinterland. The strategic air war against Germany began on May 16–17, 1940, with the deployment of 99 bombers over the Ruhr region. A French naval long-distance reconnaissance plane dropped the first bombs (2 tons) on Berlin on the night of June 8. Because all the German planes were involved in the western campaign, there was initially no reaction. A strong German counterattack came on July 10, 1940; this attack, over southern England, began the AIR BATTLE FOR ENGLAND.

After the first German nighttime attacks against London, Churchill ordered an attack on Berlin, which was carried out by 81 two-engine bombers on August 25, 1940. Only a few of them found Berlin on this night mission, and they inflicted little damage. The first significant attack was carried out by 189 bombers against Hannover (February 10–11, 1941) and by 359 against Hamburg and Bremen on the night of May 9, 1941. Other targets, most of which were attacked by fewer than 100 bombers, were Berlin, Kiel, Hannover, Cologne, Frankfurt, Stettin, and Mannheim. Up to this point, damages were less than those inflicted on England by the Luftwaffe, which included 3,623 deaths. A considerable intensification of the British attacks followed when Air Marshal Arthur T. HARRIS took over the BC, on February 23, 1942. Shortly before this (February 14), the British War Cabinet had decided, despite the failure of similar German strategies, that the target of future attacks should be the "morale of the civilian population and particularly of the industrial worker."

The threat from the air set in motion considerable defense efforts on the German side. At the outset of the war, the Luftwaffe did not have a single night fighter (*Nachtjäger*). By late 1939/early 1940 an initial group of single-engine fighters had been produced, and by April 21, 1940, they had achieved their first kill. On July 17, 1940, the creation of the First Night Fighter Division was ordered. By September 20, 1944, the number of planes in the Reich Air Fleet (Luftflotte Reich) had increased to 1,181 daytime and 772 nighttime fighters. The number of antiaircraft batteries increased from 423 heavy batteries in July 1940 to 1,432 heavy and 498 medium and light batteries in September 1944 (*see* HOME FLAK; FLAK HELPERS). Nonetheless, the "roof" of "Fortress Europa" remained full of holes. The loss rate of the BC sank from 3.9 percent in 1942 to 1.7 percent in 1944, in part because of the sometimes successful disturbance of German radar gear through the dropping of chaff.

In March 1942 the BC began a new phase of the air war with four nighttime attacks against Essen; on March 28–29, 1942, 234 bombers destroyed Lübeck's Inner City (1,425 buildings destroyed, 320 dead, 785 injured). A month later Rostock was hit (204 dead; 60 percent of the Old City destroyed). The first "1,000-bomber strike" of the Second World War took place on May 30–31, 1942: 1,046 planes were sent by the BC against Cologne. At the cost of 48 planes lost, they dropped 1,459 tons of bombs, killed 469 people, injured 5,027, and left 45,132 homeless. Further large attacks followed, with the Ruhr region and Bremen as targets, until June 26, 1942. Thereafter the number of almost-nightly raids decreased again. The BC was joined on January 27, 1943, by the United States Eighth Air Force, which had been assembling in England since mid-1942. The Americans avoided night attacks because of the difficulty of precision bombing. The CASABLANCA Conference in January 1943 established American precision attacks by day and RAF carpet bombing by night.

The bombing of Hamburg between July 24 and 30, 1943, marked a terrible intensification of the air war: 2,205 British planes (with 57 losses) dropped 6,889 tons of bombs, killed 30,482 people, and destroyed 277,330 residences, 3,212 businesses, 24 hospitals, 227 schools, and 58 churches. From this point on, the Allies attacked nearly every large German city, and after the INVASION laid waste to many smaller cities as well, such as Darmstadt (August 11–12, 1944; 12,300 dead), Heilbronn (December 4–5, 1944; 7,147 dead), and Pforzheim (February 23–24, 1945; 17,600 dead). The Allied attacks on DRESDEN on February 13–14, 1945, caused the largest losses of human life, with over 35,000 victims.

For a long time the attacks on German industry caused negligible damage to the production of armaments. The American bombardment of the Fuel Hydrogenation Works was successful, causing a decline in production of 6 percent from May to September 1944. The psychological goal of the air war was never attained. If anything, it produced a greater will to resist and supported the credibility of National Socialist propaganda. This failure was admitted by the Allied side after the war.

The air war over Germany destroyed 3.37 million residences, killed 609,000 people, and injured 917,000. The BC lost 8,325 planes and 58,309 air force personnel; the United States Eighth Air Force lost 11,687 planes and 43,742 men.

G. H.

a. Kr., abbreviation of Auf Kriegsdauer ("for the duration of the war"); it was added to a title to indicate the limited promotion prospects for bureaucrats.

Aktion 14f13, camouflage designation chosen from the file code of the Inspectorate of Concentration Camps to identify the killing of camp prisoners as part of the so-called INVALID OPERATION.

Aktion Reinhard. *See* Reinhard Operation.

Aktion T4, camouflage designation for the killing activities in the EUTHANASIA program; it was taken from the address of the relevant Reich Chancellery office at Tiergartenstrasse 4.

Ala. *See* Allgemeine Anzeigen GmbH.

Albania, Balkan kingdom; area, 27,000 sq km (10,400 sq miles); population, 1.1 million (1939). After centuries of Turkish rule, Albania declared its independence in 1913; during the First World War, it was occupied in the south by Italy and in the north by the Central Powers. Albania was established as an independent state in 1919 and was recognized by Italy on August 8 of that year. In 1925 Ahmed Zogu profited from domestic unrest to stage a coup; in 1928 he assumed the royal title Zog I. After a period of great Albanian dependence on Italy, Rome responded to tentative attempts to break the tie by occupying the country in April 1939; the king went into exile. Italy used Albania to stage an attack on Greece on October 28, 1940; a Greek counteroffensive pushed far into Albanian territory and provoked the German BALKAN CAMPAIGN. Albania remained nominally Italian until November 1944; after September of that year it was occupied by Germany, but was the scene of

Air war. Survivors of a bombing raid in Mannheim.

active partisan activity supported by Josip TITO. After the war, Albania became a Communist People's Republic (January 11, 1946).

Albers, Hans, b. Hamburg, September 22, 1892; d. Berg bei Starnberg, July 24, 1960, German actor. Albers came to film from the Deutsches Theater in Berlin and became one of the most beloved film stars of the Third Reich. He liked to play noble and strong characters and was himself not meek, even with important National Socialists. Joseph GOEBBELS made use of Albers's popularity in the anti-British film CARL PETERS (1941), about the German colonial explorer. Other films included *Peer Gynt* (1934), *Wasser für Canitoga* (Water for Canitoga; 1939), MÜNCHHAUSEN (1943), and *Grosse Freiheit Nr. 7* (Great Freedom No. 7; 1944). After the war Albers continued as a successful actor.

Albiker, Karl, b. Ühlingen bei Waldshut, September 16, 1878; d. Ettlingen, February 26, 1961, German sculptor. Albiker studied with Rodin in Paris; from 1919 to 1945 he was a professor at the Dresden Academy. His monumental statues, like those of Georg KOLBE, reflected National Socialist heroic realism. Albiker created the relay racers for Berlin's REICH SPORTS FIELD and various war monuments, including those in Karlsruhe, Freiburg im Breisgau, and Greiz.

Albion, Celtic name for England. During the French revolutionary wars, and especially in the First World War, the name was transformed into the curse "perfidious Albion"; it was revived in National Socialist propaganda during the Second World War.

Alfarth, Felix, b. Leipzig, July 5, 1901; d. Munich, November 9, 1923, National Socialist martyr; a salesman for Siemanns. A fanatical Hitler admirer, Alfarth fell during the MARCH ON THE FELDHERRNHALLE, allegedly with the GERMAN NATIONAL ANTHEM on his lips. His name led the list of "blood witnesses" (*see* BLOOD WITNESS) that was read yearly by torchlight at the anniversary of the HITLER PUTSCH in Munich.

Alfieri, Dino, b. Bologna, July 8, 1886; d. Milan, January 2, 1966, Italian politician and one of MUSSOLINI's first followers in the Fascist struggle for power. In 1924 he was a deputy; in 1929, state secretary; in 1936–1939, minister of education; in 1939–1940, ambassador to the Holy See; in 1940–1942, ambassador in Berlin at Hitler's request; after May 1942, member of the Fascist Grand Council. A close friend of Galeazzo CIANO, Alfieri voted for Mussolini's removal on July 25, 1943, and fled to Switzerland after the latter's liberation. Alfieri escaped extradition because he was condemned to death in absentia before a special court in Verona. He returned to Italy after the war and was pensioned as a diplomat.

Hans Albers in *Unter heissem Himmel* (Under a Hot Sky).

Alien-blooded (*fremdblütig*), in National Socialist usage, a term for persons of "non-Aryan" heritage, who accordingly were not GERMAN-BLOODED.

Alien morality (*Fremdmoral*), in National Socialist usage, a term for moral principles that do not originate with one's own "species" (*Artung*), and thus undermine "species-specific" (*art-eigene*) ETHICS. For the "Nordic" person, for example, Christian morality was a typical alien morality.

Alien workers (*Fremdarbeiter*), civilian workers from German-occupied territories in the Second World War, at first recruited voluntarily, but after 1942 increasingly coerced. Alien workers were placed on farms and in factories within the German Reich or else in satellite plants in their homelands. Most of them came from Poland, Russia, France, Belgium, and the Netherlands. As the war continued, the mask of volunteering gradually fell away—from the outset, "volunteering" had been reinforced by threats such as the withholding of ration cards.

On March 21, 1942, Hitler named Fritz SAUCKEL General Deputy for LABOR DEPLOYMENT. A decree of August 22, 1942, authorized forcible employment of alien workers in all the occupied territories and in prison camps. In his first annual report, on April 15, 1943, Sauckel reported that 3,638,056 "new alien laborers" (*neue fremdvölkische Arbeitskräfte*) and 1,622,829 prisoners of war had been "procured" for the German war economy. At the Nuremberg Trials, the presupposition was of a total of 12 million alien workers, of whom the overwhelming majority had been pressed into service in Germany, often through brutal coercion, by commandos from the labor bureaus, supported by the SS and SD (at times using outright kidnapping).

Alien workers were monitored by the Security Police and the Gestapo's "Alien Worker" desk. While alien workers from the Western countries were more or less equal to their German coworkers (especially coveted skilled workers), the "eastern workers" (*Ostarbeiter*) from the Soviet Union and those from Poland and southeastern Europe who were "unsuited for RE-GERMANIZATION" were subjected to numerous restraints. They had to wear badges on their clothing ("OST" [East] for Russians, "P" for Poles), were not allowed to attend cultural or church functions, and were forbidden access to radio and newspapers; relations with German women were punishable by death as RACIAL INFAMY. More-

Alien workers. A Russian "eastern worker" in an armament factory.

over, alien workers from the east received substantially lower pay, from which they furthermore had 15 percent withheld (the "Eastern Worker Tax"), on the ground that they would have had an even lower standard of living in their homeland.

Allbuch (Book of Everything), National Socialist Germanization of *Lexikon*.

Alldeutscher Verband. *See* All-German Association.

Allgemeine Anzeigen GmbH (General Advertisements, Ltd.; Ala), central advertising agency of the NSDAP, created in 1926 from "Ausland GmbH" (Foreign Lands, Ltd.). It was part of the Alfred HUGENBERG concern, taken over by the EHER PRESS in 1934 in order to improve the advertising position of the National Socialist *Gau* presses.

S. O.

Allgemeiner Deutscher Gewerkschaftsbund. *See* General German Trade Union Federation.

Allgemeiner freier Angestelltenbund. *See* Afabund.

Allgemeiner Verband der deutschen Bankangestellten. *See* Afabund.

Allgemeine SS (General SS), common term for the SS, as contrasted to the militarized WAFFEN-SS.

All-German Association (Alldeutscher Verband), nationalist organization founded on April 9,

1891, as the "General German Association" (Allgemeiner Deutscher Verband); it changed its name on July 1, 1894. The organization was engendered by the protest movement against the putative sell-out of German interests in the Anglo-German treaty of 1890, in which Germany exchanged her African territory of Zanzibar for the North Sea island of Helgoland. The All-German Association promoted the "union of all German elements on earth" for the purpose of an active pro-German policy throughout the world. Its chauvinistic and imperialistic program was expressed during the First World War in the promotion of exaggerated war aims. In the Weimar Republic the struggle against democracy and for a national dictatorship moved to the fore.

Although the association never had a very large membership—its high point came in 1922, with 40,000 members—it achieved considerable influence with its *Alldeutsche Blätter* (1894–1939) because it was supported by such influential politicians as Alfred HUGENBERG. The National Socialists disparaged its "reactionary tendencies," but nonetheless took much from the All-German terminology, for example, "master people" (*Herrenvolk*) and "LIVING SPACE." The strongly antisemitic and anti-Catholic Austrian offshoot of the All-Germans, under Georg von SCHÖNERER, had a significant influence on Hitler. In the Third Reich, the association (led by Heinrich CLASS) was tolerated until 1939 and then dissolved, ostensibly because it had fulfilled its mission.

Alliance of German Organizations Abroad (Verband deutscher Vereine im Ausland; VdV), National Socialist umbrella organization founded in 1934 to unite all FOREIGN GERMANS outside the Reich; its headquarters was in Berlin. The VdV was supposed to organize these Germans and to influence and win them over with NS propaganda, insofar as they were not yet part of the FOREIGN ORGANIZATION of the NSDAP. Its journal was the *Heimatbrief* (Letter from Home).

Allied Control Council (Alliierter Kontrollrat), Allied organization that exercised supreme government authority in Germany following the collapse; its legal basis was the JUNE DECLARATION of June 5, 1945. Members were the supreme commanders of the occupying armies. The council first met on July 30, 1945, then every 10 days, with a monthly rotation of chairmen in the court of appeals building (Berliner Kammergericht) in the American Sector of Ber-

lin. Its responsibilities included the settlement of all issues relating to Germany as a whole and the ensuring of uniform policies among the occupying powers. Because of incompatibility between British-American and Soviet, and sometimes also French, occupation policies, the council could not achieve its intended unity on most questions. The council collapsed after the USSR withdrew on March 20, 1948.

Alljuda, antisemitic Germanization of the term "international Jewry" that borrowed from the word *alldeutsch* (all- or pan-German), as in the antisemitic slogan "All-Germany against All-Jewry!" The National Socialists used the word *Alljuda* to suggest the *Allgegenwart* (omnipresence) of the Jewish danger and the "world conspiracy of Judaism."

Alpine fortress (*Alpenfestung*), final defensive position discussed by Hitler during a meeting in the Führerbunker on April 18, 1945; he would wait there until, after the meeting of Anglo-American and Soviet forces, differences broke apart the "unnatural" wartime coalition. On April 24, German outfits fighting in northern Italy were to withdraw to the Alpine fortress, which was to be commanded by the Tyrolean Gauleiter Franz HOFER as Reich deputy. The plan failed because of Hitler's decision to stay in Berlin.

The notion of a fully defended Alpine fortress also figured in Allied plans. Supreme Comdr. Dwight D. EISENHOWER telegraphed Stalin on March 28, 1945, that he would proceed along the line between Erfurt and Leipzig and wait there for the Red Army, but that he would use most of his forces to capture Germany's Alpine fortress. This considerably slowed the American march eastward.

Alquen, Gunter d', b. Essen, October 24, 1910, German journalist. Alquen entered the Hitler Youth in 1925, the SA in 1927, the NSDAP in 1928, and the SS in 1931. After beginning his career with Bremen's National Socialist newspaper and in the home office of the VÖLKISCHER BEOBACHTER, in early 1935 the talented Alquen was named by Himmler as editor in chief of the new SS journal, *Das* SCHWARZE KORPS (The Black Corps). Alquen fashioned the journal into the voice of an aggressive, revolutionary, but thoroughly self-critical National Socialism. His invective and intellectual arrogance were feared; his radical antisemitism was more effective than the primitive Jew-baiting of *Der* STÜRMER. During the war, Alquen went to the front as chief war correspondent for the SS and worked in psychological warfare against the Red Army. He published an official history of the SS in 1939. In 1955 and 1958, Alquen was fined for inflaming racial hatred and inciting to murder.

Alsace-Lorraine (Elsass-Lothringen), territory on the left bank of the Rhine between Luxembourg and Switzerland; in its boundaries as German Reichsland (1871–1918), its area was approximately 14,500 sq km (about 5,800 sq miles). In the VERSAILLES TREATY, Alsace-Lorraine was ceded to France without a plebiscite. During the 1920s and 1930s, France had to combat a strong Alsatian separatist movement, as Germany had earlier. Despite Germany's renunciation of the territory in the LOCARNO PACT in 1925, and despite Hitler's repeated assurances after 1933 that he would no longer contest the "centuries-old bone of contention," after Germany's victory in the West in 1940 the area was *de facto* annexed to the German Reich over the protests of the VICHY regime. (Administratively, Alsace was joined to Baden, and Lorraine to the Westmark *Gau.*) In 1945, Alsace-Lorraine was split among the French Bas-Rhin, Haut-Rhin, and Moselle departments.

Alte Kämpfer. *See* Old Combatants.

Altmann, Klaus, alias used by Klaus BARBIE in Bolivia after the war.

Altmark Incident ("*Altmark*"-*Zwischenfall*), capture of the German auxiliary ship *Altmark* by the British destroyer *Cossack* in Norwegian waters on February 12, 1940, in order to free captured English merchant sailors. Four German sailors lost their lives. Norway's mild protests against the incident encouraged German suspicions of a planned British landing in NORWAY and hastened German invasion plans.

Altona Bloody Sunday (*Altonaer Blutsonntag*), name for the bloody confrontation among the SA and SS, the police, and Communist party (KPD) supporters in Altona, near Hamburg, on July 17, 1932. In a policy of making concessions to the NSDAP, the Papen government on June 28, 1932, lifted a ban that had been placed on the SA and SS in April. This action rekindled political street fighting, which had reached a peak in April, and which Papen had used as an excuse for his PRUSSIAN COUP. The SA and the SS had announced a propaganda march through the workers' quarter of Prussian Altona that had been approved by the Social Democratic police

president, Otto EGGERSTEDT, despite warnings by the KPD. Eggerstedt himself was on an election trip, and his deputy was on vacation. Predictably, it came to blows between the near-military invasion of some 7,000 National Socialists and Altona's Communist residents, leading to massive police intervention. Eighteen people, including two SA men, were killed, most by stray police bullets. After the Seizure of Power in May 1933, 15 arrested Communists were tried for murder; in addition to jail sentences, four death sentences were levied, which were carried out on August 1, 1933.

Ba.

Altreich. *See* Old Reich.

Alverdes, Paul, b. Strasbourg, May 6, 1897; d. Munich, February 28, 1979, German writer. As a volunteer in World War I, Alverdes suffered a serious throat wound. After 1922 he was a freelance author in Munich, and from 1934 to 1944, co-editor of the journal *Das innere Reich* (The Inner Reich). Alverdes's work was influenced by the youth movement and by the "FRONT EXPERIENCE," whose purifying and "transforming" power he praised, as in the autobiographical story *Die Pfeiferstube* (The Whistler's Room; 1929). Nonetheless, he was only moderately popular with National Socialists because he lacked an "activist-dynamic attitude." Further works include the poems *Die Nördlichen* (The Northerners; 1922), the radio play *Die Freiwilligen* (The Volunteers; 1934), the fairy-tale *Das Männlein Mittenzwei* (The Little In-Between Man; 1937), and *Grimbarts Haus* (Grimbart's House; 1949).

Amann, Max, b. Munich, November 24, 1891; d. Munich, March 30, 1957, German politician and journalist. Amann, a salesclerk, served as a sergeant in the same company as Corporal Hitler during the First World War; he joined the NSDAP immediately upon its founding (membership no. 3) and became its secretary-general in 1922. In the midst of building the NSDAP's central publishing house (EHER PRESS), Amann's rise was interrupted by the HITLER PUTSCH. With Hitler, he served six months' imprisonment in Landsberg. Once again director of the Eher Press in 1925, Amann became a member of the party's national executive committee and coordinator of the entire National Socialist press. After the Seizure of Power the NS press became increasingly identical with the German press itself, thanks to Amann's unscrupulous methods of SYNCHRONIZATION. (By 1942 some

Max Amann.

80 percent of all newspapers belonged to Amann's empire.) This assured him an enormous income. As chairman of the Association of Newspaper Publishers (May to November 1933) and president of the REICH PRESS CHAMBER (after November 15, 1933), Amann was responsible for silencing all opposition. He was aided in this by his consistently good relationship with Hitler, whose royalties from *Mein Kampf* and other publications he administered. Amann, who in 1941 became an SS-*Obergruppenführer*, was condemned after the war (September 8, 1948) to 10 years' hard labor as a major perpetrator.

Amateur theater. *See* Lay theater.

Ambassadors' Conference (*Botschafterkonferenz*), commission of Allied ambassadors, formed in Paris on January 10, 1920, to supervise the carrying out of the PARIS SUBURBAN TREATIES, especially the one signed at Versailles (*see* VERSAILLES TREATY). After Germany joined the League of Nations in 1926, the conference lost importance; it was dissolved in 1931.

Amber Room (*Bernstein-Zimmer*), amber wainscoting of an entire banquet hall, commissioned by Frederick I of Prussia in 1701, presented by Frederick William I to Tsar Peter the Great in 1717, and shipped to Saint Petersburg. The Amber Room—today worth some $50 million —was installed in the Pushkin imperial palace at Tsarskoe Selo. During the Russian Campaign, in late September and early October 1941, it

was dismantled by the Third Company of Supply Battalion 553 and shipped to Königsberg on October 14. There it was temporarily reassembled and displayed to the public. In January 1945, this most prominent example of National Socialist ART PLUNDER was presumably evacuated, along with the coffins of Gen. Paul von Hindenburg and his wife. Torn apart in transit, it was stored in damaged condition in an unknown location. Most clues point to a tunnel of the former Wittekind potash mine in Volpriehausen, near Göttingen; the mine was buried in the explosion of a munitions factory in the autumn of 1945.

Amnesty, general pardon of particular crimes or misdemeanors; it is meant to reflect changing legal consciousness or is granted as a political demonstration of mercy. In the Third Reich, a first amnesty was granted on March 21, 1933, on the occasion of the POTSDAM CELEBRATION of the Reichstag opening, for all acts committed "in the struggle for NATIONAL RISING [*Erhebung*]." The amnesty of August 7, 1934, on the occasion of the unification of the offices of chancellor and Reich president, benefited SA members who had been arrested during the RÖHM AFFAIR. At the outbreak of war on September 1, 1939, there was an amnesty for Wehrmacht members who had been subjected to punishment, followed by an amnesty for civilians on September 9. Victory in the Polish Campaign was "crowned" by the amnesty of October 4, 1939, according to which members of the shooting commandos of the SS (*see* EINSATZGRUPPEN) were relieved of sentences imposed by Wehrmacht courts for the massacre of Polish civilians.

Amt Ausland/Abwehr. *See* Abwehr.

Amt "K." *See* Office "K."

Amtsblatt (gazette), periodical that published official notices and that consequently was compulsory reading for many. Soon after the Seizure of Power, only organs of the National Socialist press were allowed to call themselves such, thus cementing their monopoly.

Amtsgruppe Allgemeine Wehrmachtsangelegenheiten (Office Group for General Wehrmacht Affairs), division of the Wehrmacht High Command (OKW). In 1938–1939 it was designated the Wehrwirtschaftsstab (Military Economy Staff).

Amtsgruppe Auslandsnachrichten und Abwehr (Foreign Intelligence and Counterintelligence

Bureau), 1938–1939 name for the ABWEHR Foreign Office.

Amtsleiter (Office Leader [Director]), NSDAP rank, as of a *Gau-* or *Reichsamtsleiter.*

Amtswalter (office steward), Old German–sounding National Socialist synonym for "official" or "civil servant" (*Beamter*) and therefore the preferred term for professional functionaries of the party and its branches. Those persons working in the state apparatus continued to be called *Beamten.*

Anacker, Heinrich, b. Aarau (Switzerland), January 29, 1901, German author. Anacker entered National Socialist circles in Vienna in 1922, joined the SA, and after 1933 lived in Berlin as a freelance writer. He wrote a spate of SA and Hitler youth songs and was considered the "lyricist of the Brown Front"; he won the 1934 Dietrich Eckart Prize and the 1936 NSDAP Prize for Art. Nonetheless, after the war he was classified as only minimally incriminated. His poetry collections include *Die Trommel* (The Drum; 1931), *Der Aufbau* (Uplift; 1936), and *Glück auf, es geht gen Morgen* (Hurrah, It Will Soon Be Morning; 1943).

Anbauschlacht. *See* Battle for Cultivation.

Ancestral Inheritance (Ahnenerbe), SS "Teaching and Research Group," founded on July 1, 1935, as a "Society to Study the Intellectual History of the German Ancestral Inheritance"; its founders were Heinrich HIMMLER (president after 1937), Walther DARRÉ, and "researcher in intellectual prehistory" (*Geistesurgeschichtsforscher*) H. Wirth. The Reich secretary-general, located in Waischenfeld, was Wolfram Sievers (hanged in Nuremberg in 1948). By 1944 the group had some 40 academic divisions, which, however, worked side by side more often than in an interdisciplinary way. Ancestral Inheritance, which employed famous scientists as well as *völkisch* opportunists, aimed to research Germanic prehistory using racial criteria; to promote the study of German folklore; and to accumulate scientific evidence for the National Socialist worldview. Even before the war, this led to excursions into the natural sciences, and, after 1939, into research projects directly related to the war, such as the human experiments in military medicine of Sigmund Rascher (DACHAU) and August Hirt (NATZWEILER). Ancestral Inheritance also propagandized in German-occupied territories for the SS Great-German concept of the "Germanic scientific task" (*Wissenschaftseinsatz*); this had little effect, however, because of Hitler's lack of interest. Even the gaining of a monopoly on scientific work within the SS miscarried. On the other hand, Ancestral Inheritance inadvertently provided protection for many scientists who were criticized or even persecuted by the party.

Ancestral Passport (*Ahnenpass*), booklet with the form for the CERTIFICATE OF DESCENT, published by the Reich Federation of Civil Registrars; it cost .60 RM. A complete passport, certified by government office or church, replaced the previously required birth, baptismal, and marriage certificates. Opposition clergy helped many racially persecuted individuals by providing them with fake passports as a personal document necessary for survival.

Heinrich Anacker.

Brothers, what will remain from our
  time?
Runes will forever glow!
Our bodies will disappear,
As dust in the winds they will blow.
. . . .
It was we who built the streets,
That our grandchildren first saw
  complete;
Along them, cars will boldly whiz,
For a hundred and a thousand years.
What we wrote in inflexible deeds
Unshaken will ever remain,
Forever, beginning and amen,
The most vivid rune: The Führer's
  name!
(Heinrich Anacker, "Brothers, What
Will Remain?," in *Das Schwarze
Korps,* August 14, 1935.)

Anders, Władysław, b. Błonie, near Warsaw, August 11, 1892; d. London, May 12, 1970, Polish general (from 1936). Anders was captured by the Soviet army in 1939, but escaped the fate of his comrades in the KATYN Forest. He was released in 1941 and formed a Polish volunteer army, which joined the Allied Eastern Army and fought in Africa and Italy (notably at Monte Cassino). In February 1945, Anders became commander in chief of all Polish troops in the West, nearly 200,000 men, of whom nearly 80 percent refused repatriation after the Communist revolution in Poland. Anders remained in English exile.

Andienungspflicht. *See* Purveyance duty.

Anglo-German Naval Agreement. *See* German-British Naval Agreement.

Angriff, Der (The Attack; "The German Monthly Paper in Berlin"), newspaper of the National Socialist *Kampfpresse* (fighting press), published from July 4, 1927, by the Angriff Press. The official organ of Gauleiter Goebbels, its motto was "For the oppressed, against the exploiters." After October 1, 1929, *Der Angriff* appeared twice weekly; after November 1, 1930, as a daily paper with the subtitle "The German Evening Paper in Berlin"; after October 1, 1932, twice daily, as "The Attack at Noon" and "Night Attack." First founded to rally NSDAP members

Der Angriff. Title page of the November 9, 1931, edition. The headline reads: "Our Dead Exhort. The Service of Mourning in the Sports Palace."

during the nearly two-year ban on the party in Berlin, *Der Angriff* was also conceived as a mass circulation paper that fought the hated "System" with rude and aggressive language. Antiparliamentarianism and antisemitism were its self-defining themes. The most regular contributors were party functionaries; lead articles were usually written by the publisher, Goebbels, until 1933, and signed "Dr. G." A further attraction were the political caricatures by Hans SCHWEITZER ("Mjölnir"). The editor in chief was Julius LIPPERT; circulation in 1927 was 2,000.

After February 1, 1933, *Der Angriff* appeared as the "Daily Newspaper of the German Labor Front" from the EHER PRESS. Goebbels remained the publisher; editors in chief were Karoly Kampmann (1933) and Hans Schwarz van Berk (1934–1937). After February 19, 1945, *Der Angriff* was merged with the *Berliner Illustrierte Nachtausgabe* (Berlin Illustrated Night Edition). Its circulation in 1939 was 146,694; in 1944, 306,000; the last edition was published on April 24, 1945.

S. O.

Angstbrosche (badge of fear), derogatory name for the National Socialist badge; it ridiculed the mass party entries resulting from cowardice and opportunism after the Seizure of Power.

Anhaltelager. *See* Detention camps.

Animal-feed coupon (*Futtermittelschein*), official permission to purchase food for domestic animals and livestock in line with the rationing of foodstuffs during the Second World War through RATION CARDS; at times there was even a separate coupon for dogs.

Annunzio, Gabriele d'. *See* D'Annunzio, Gabriele.

Ansatz ([roughly] attack), First World War military term, used in the National Socialist vocabulary in the same ways as the word EINSATZ, though less frequently; one referred to bringing a piece of equipment, troops, or a weapon "zum Ansatz" (into attack, or play).

Anschluss (union), in particular, the shorthand designation for the union of Austria with Germany; after 1918 it served as a political slogan. The idea of an Anschluss went back to the wars of liberation from Napoleon (1813–1815) and referred to the unification of German-speaking parts of Austria with Germany. Particularist interests, Bismarck's "small-German" politics, and the multiethnic character of the Habsburg monarchy long stood in its way. Only with their collapse in the First World War did an Anschluss seem feasible; indeed, it was promoted by concern for the economic survival of the German-Austrian rump state after the defeat.

On November 12, 1918, Austria's Provisional National Assembly passed a constitutional law which declared that German-Austria, including the Sudeten territories, was part of the German Republic; it was unanimously ratified on March 12, 1919. However, the peace treaty of SAINT-GERMAIN-EN-LAYE forbade even the designation "German-Austria," and made any change in Austrian independence dependent upon agreement by the League of Nations and therefore illusory for the moment. Hence Austria's Federal Constitution of October 10, 1920, lacked any mention of Anschluss, and on September 22, 1919, Allied pressure forced the striking of Article 61 of the Weimar Constitution, which gave Austria an advisory voice in the REICHSRAT until an Anschluss. This significant disregard for the right of SELF-DETERMINATION OF PEOPLES was a not insignificant reason for the discrediting of the peace treaties; it also ensured attention to the agitation for an Anschluss far beyond nationalist circles. Its effectiveness was demonstrated by ever-renewed demands, especially by France, to stipulate Austria's independence: in 1922 Vienna had to forswear an Anschluss for 20 years in order to receive a loan from the League of Nations, in 1931 a German-Austrian tariff union was torpedoed by the Great Powers, and in 1932 the Lausanne Protocol again made a loan dependent on the renunciation of an Anschluss. This led to considerable domestic political difficulties, because nearly all Austrian party programs supported an Anschluss. Only after Hitler seized power did Christian Socials and Social Democrats drop their demands; the Catholic church also abandoned the idea of Anschluss and demanded Austria's independent statehood. Anschluss politics became the preserve of the Great-German People's Party and Austria's National Socialists.

This was true in a second way: for tactical reasons Hitler himself at first downplayed an Anschluss as a foreign-policy demand, since the sincerity of his concern for peace would be measured not least by his political relationship to his homeland; the National Socialist (NS) press was instructed to avoid the term "German-Austrian Anschluss." To be sure, this did not change the goal announced at the beginning of *Mein Kampf:* "German-Austria must return again to the great German motherland," a basic demand in terms of both REVISIONIST POLICY and ideology: "The same blood belongs in a common Reich."

Although not undesired, the NS putsch against the government of Engelbert DOLLFUSS on July 25, 1934, definitely came too early for Hitler (*see* AUSTRIA). Mussolini stationed Italian troops at the Brenner Pass, and forced Hitler to quickly distance himself from the Viennese putsch attempt. However, the Duce also showed him that the key to an Anschluss lay in Rome. Italy was the only Great Power that had a common border with Austria; it would also have to fear a demand for the return of the South Tyrol from a Great-Germany. Every Anschluss policy was therefore an Italian policy, which Hitler could not yet bring into play at his first meeting with Mussolini in February 1934. The opportunity soon offered itself through the imperialist policies of Fascist Italy: in the conflict with ABYSSINIA, he allied himself with Mussolini; in the SPANISH CIVIL WAR he broadened the friendly relationship to a partnership in combat.

While France was increasingly preoccupied with domestic problems, and England engaged in appeasement, the AXIS connection allowed Hitler to shift again to an active foreign policy. This consisted at first in improving the situation of Austria's National Socialists, who on June 19, 1933, had been banned, and who now filled DETENTION CAMPS. Here was a lever Hitler could use to intervene in the domestic affairs of the neighboring country: on July 11, 1936, German pressure produced the JULY AGREEMENT with the SCHUSCHNIGG government, which, however, dragged out implementation of agreed-upon improvements for the National Socialists. After several threats, Hitler invited Schuschnigg to the Obersalzberg on February 12, 1938, and issued an ultimatum: to include Hitler's man in Vienna, Arthur SEYSS-INQUART, as interior minister in the Austrian government, to adjust foreign policy to that of the Reich, to legalize the Austrian NSDAP, and to issue a general amnesty. In the so-called BERCHTESGADEN DIKTAT, Schuschnigg accepted these terms, as well as other economic and military conditions. Three days later, Austrian president Wilhelm MIKLAS appointed Seyss-Inquart, and thereby delivered his nation's security agencies to the National Socialists.

In a last desperate attempt to prevent the Anschluss, on March 9, 1938, Schuschnigg issued a surprise announcement of a popular referendum for the 13th: for or against a "free

Anschluss. Scene at the Heldenplatz in Vienna on March 15, 1938, as Hitler announces "the entry of my homeland into the German Reich."

and German, independent and social, Christian and united Austria." Irregularities during preparations for the vote (increase of the voting age to 24 years; missing voter lists), and the limited time, only hastened German intervention. On March 11, Hitler demanded cancellation of the referendum and Schuschnigg's resignation in favor of Seyss-Inquart; he also declared his intention, "if other means do not succeed, to invade Austria with armed forces." Hitler's intended goal was clearly the Anschluss, and he never really considered "other means" than invasion, even after the fulfillment of his ultimatum: at midnight on March 12, 1938, Miklas surmounted considerable resistance and named Seyss-Inquart chancellor. That morning, after Göring and Seyss-Inquart had agreed by telephone to a request for help by the Austrian government, Wehrmacht units crossed the borders. On March 15, Hitler, amid thunderous jubilation on Vienna's Heldenplatz, announced "the entry of my homeland into the German Reich." Concurrently, the Law concerning the Reunification of Austria with the German Reich went into force. Austria, divided into Reichs-

gaue, was now called Ostmark (East March). The Western powers made only perfunctory protests.

There can be no doubt that even with every reservation regarding NS election data, the results of the Anschluss referendum of April 10, 1938, reflected overwhelming agreement in both nations (officially, Austria: 99.7 percent; German Reich: 99 percent). Even Austrian Socialist leader Karl RENNER greeted Hitler's action in clear appreciation of the referendum and publicly voted in favor of it, although he could calculate precisely the consequences for Austrian Social Democracy. The Austrian episcopacy under Theodor Cardinal INNITZER allowed the churches to be decorated with swastikas and "joyfully" acknowledged that the National Socialists had "accomplished outstanding things . . . in the area of *völkisch* and economic uplift," ignoring the persecution of political opponents and Jews, which had begun [in Austria] immediately after the Anschluss. The MAUTHAUSEN camp was erected in early August of 1938.

Ansiedlung. *See* Colonization.

Anthropology, biological and philosophical dis-

Election poster for the April 10, 1938, plebiscite on the Austrian Anschluss: "Great-Germany YES! on April 10."

cipline that includes such subdisciplines as human biology, psychology, and ethnology. During the Third Reich, anthropology was under great ideological pressure: thus techniques for human biology were applied using racist criteria. The National Socialists attempted to obscure the historical dimension of human existence with the demand that anthropology should conceive of man primarily as a "branch of the whole *Volk*," as an "ethnic-political" (*volkhaft-politisch*) being."

Anthropometry, methods of physical anthropology used to measure the human body, data from which allow inferences regarding physiological evolution. In the Third Reich, anthropometry also served the purposes of race lore (*see* RACE), particularly cranioscopy (study of skull measurements), for the purpose of selecting "racially valuable" children in the conquered territories (*see* GENERAL PLAN FOR THE EAST) and giving them to German foster parents for "NORDIC UPGRADING."

Anthroposophy (Gr.; "wisdom about humankind"), ideological doctrine, founded by Rudolf Steiner (1861–1925), in which Christian, Indian, gnostic, and cabalistic elements are interwoven. Anthroposophy aims to help humankind gain "higher" spiritual capabilities and thus "supernatural" knowledge. The adherents of anthroposophy were organized in the Anthroposophical Society, with its center in the "Goe-

theanum" in Dornach bei Basel. The National Socialists fought anthroposophy as internationalist, pacifist, and an "enemy of racial principles"; its Waldorf Schools, whose pedagogy mocked the idea of a natural FÜHRER PRINCIPLE, were "breeding grounds for Talmudism." The Anthroposophical Society was banned in the German Reich on November 1, 1935.

Antiaircraft. *See* Air defense.

Anti-Comintern Pact, treaty with five years' validity against "Communist sedition" by the Communist INTERNATIONAL, that is, against the Soviet Union. Proposed by Japan's military attaché in Berlin, Oshima, it was negotiated with Joachim von RIBBENTROP, thus bypassing the foreign minister. The Anti-Comintern Pact was signed by Japan and the German Reich on November 25, 1936; a supplementary secret protocol provided for mutual benevolent neutrality in case of an unprovoked Soviet attack, and forbade treaties with the Soviet Union directed against the spirit of the pact "without mutual agreement." Other nations entered into the Anti-Comintern Pact without knowing of the secret addition: Italy (November 6, 1937), Hun-

Joachim von Ribbentrop signing the Anti-Comintern Pact. On the left is Japan's Extraordinary Ambassador, Mushakoji.

gary and Manchukuo (February 1939), Spain (March 1939), and Finland, Denmark, Slovakia, Romania, Croatia, Bulgaria, and the Nanking government on November 11, 1941, when the pact was extended for five years. The pact was the preliminary step to the THREE-POWER AGREEMENT (1940) but less effective, since even the secret protocol hindered neither Hitler's signing of the GERMAN-SOVIET NONAGGRESSION PACT (August 23, 1939) nor Japan's Neutrality Agreement with Moscow (April 13, 1941). The Anti-Comintern Pact became irrelevant with Germany's capitulation (May 5, 1945).

Antifa. (abbreviation of *Antifascismus*). *See* Antifascist committees.

Antifascism, general opposition to all forms of FASCISM, whether ideological, political, or organizational; in a narrower sense, a slogan, influenced by Communist doctrine, that makes a term for the struggle against fascist parties and regimes in the past into a label for the general Communist-revolutionary struggle, something like a reverse definition of communism.

As a term, "antifascism" was first generally applied to the Italian situation after Mussolini's assumption of power in 1922, and meant opposition from the Left or the Right to the buildup of Fascist domination. It was extended to the political struggle against fascist movements in other states, and was applied to opposition to the Hitler movement in disregard of the much more extensive goals of National Socialism. Here were demonstrated the first results of the Communist theory that viewed fascism—and National Socialism as one of its varieties—as only a symptom of the final crisis of capitalism. Social democracy was seen in this light as the opposite (Left) side of the same coin, or as "social fascism," while antifascism became the struggle against all forms of bourgeois rule, a struggle that was to be carried out by a "united front from below" that included all workers, and that would complete the inevitable victory of the working class.

This illusory position exceeded all other forms of antifascism in conciseness and unwillingness to compromise; more differentiated analyses paled in comparison. Thus antifascism retained its shortsighted equation of fascism and National Socialism even after Hitler's victory had revealed its ideological miscalculation, and it remained Communist-oriented. The KPD (Communist Party of Germany) did promote a new antifascist tactic, the POPULAR FRONT, at the so-called Brussels Conference in Moscow in October 1935. The front would include all Hitler opponents, but the KPD continued to claim political leadership. In the long run this impeded cooperation with bourgeois forms of antifascism, as well as with Jewish organizations, because insight into the racist character of National Socialism was still rudimentary or even blocked by traditional antisemitism. This "birth defect" of antifascism permanently weakened the German OPPOSITION.

Internationally as well, the popular-front concept found little favor after the failure of the International Brigade in the SPANISH CIVIL WAR, particularly given the confusion caused by the German-Soviet Nonaggression Pact of August 23, 1939. Support for antifascism and its resistance movements in German-occupied areas during the Second World War came from bourgeois groups in western and northern Europe, which, however, promptly made tactical alliances with Communist groups. Exceptions were the Comitato di Liberazione Nazionale (CLN), formed in Italy in 1943 as a common liberation effort in the motherland of fascism, and TITO's partisan movement in Yugoslavia, which could not base its unity on nationalism. Because the diverse forms of struggle against fascism and National Socialism are not easily combined under one subsuming concept, the historical meaning of the word is conflated with the modern polemical use of the term "antifascism" in propaganda waged by the socialist states against allegedly or actually fascist or "fascistoid" regimes.

Antifascist committees, committees ("Antifas") formed spontaneously, shortly before or after the entry of Allied troops in 1945, in nearly all cities and many other communities in Germany. Composed of SPD (Social Democratic Party of Germany), KPD (Communist Party of Germany), and sometimes Center party members, they temporarily took over the administration in these communities until Allied organizations could replace them.

Antifascist-Democratic Order (Antifascistisch-demokratische Ordnung), in official Communist terminology, the political order of the SOVIET OCCUPATION ZONE until the founding of the German Democratic Republic (October 1949). Characterized by the alliance of all "democratic" parties in an "Antifascist-Democratic Bloc" ("Antifablock") under the leadership of the Socialist Unity Party (SED), it was to lay the foundation for the "building up of socialism."

Antisemitism

The National Socialist (NS) PERSECUTION OF JEWS expanded on the preexisting antisemitism in the national histories of Germany and Austria. The basis for antisemitism was the minority status of Jews in many European national societies. Like other minorities, the Jewish minority became an object of aggression for the majority. The Jews took over the role of scapegoat on whom guilt or at least partial guilt for national disaster was heaped.

The historical moment for the birth of modern antisemitism in Germany was the economic and social crisis of 1873, the "speculation crisis" (*Gründerkrise*), which was part of a worldwide economic crisis and led into a cyclical depression. A spreading mood of deep pessimism expressed itself as criticism of the "spirit of capitalism." A further negative factor was the weakness of political liberalism in Germany, which had never succeeded in profoundly influencing society. Antiliberal forces seized on the crisis as an opportunity for a countermovement, in which social and cultural politics would assume a central position. Since the mid-1870s, an antisemitic press had developed, including the originally liberal *Gartenlaube* (Arbor), the conservative *Kreuzzeitung* (Cross News), and Catholic publications. An initial high point was the racist journalism of Wilhelm MARR and the mass meetings held by Court Preacher Adolf STOECK-ER in 1879, when the term "antisemitism" became common. In November 1880 an "Antisemite Petition" provoked a debate in the Prussian House of Deputies, in which members of the Conservative and Center factions condemned the Jews.

During the economic crisis of 1873, which represented a systemic crisis of capitalism, a diversion of social aggression against the socialist workers' movement would theoretically have been imaginable. That the Jews above all were attacked may be explained by the particular circumstances of Jewish life in Germany. In the 18th century, the Jews formed a marginal group alongside bourgeoisie, clergy, and nobility in a society of estates. The process of overcoming this ordered society ran parallel for Jews and bourgeoisie, but in Germany it involved great difficulties, reversals, and constant compromises. Just as the German bourgeoisie had to be satisfied with partial modernization throughout the 19th century, in that it was unable fully to realize its claim to power, so Jews too were relegated to an intermediate stage in the process of emancipation. The "Jewish question" remained a theme for public debate for many generations; constant discussion breathed renewed life into anti-Jewish stereotypes, whose roots reached into the Middle Ages. Thus it is not surprising that a few years after the conclusion of emancipation through the Reich Constitution in 1871, the "Jewish question" in the sense of antisemitism could again be raised. Moreover, as a social group the Jews exhibited particular characteristics that connected them with the economic crisis: they were overrepresented in banking, commerce, and the press; they profited from the chances for advancement in the capitalist system; and they were frequently "spokesmen for the criticism of tradition and for a secularized culture and society" (Reinhold Rürup).

Although antisemitism expanded on the Jew-hatred of the medieval and early modern periods, there were great differences. Antisemitism was a movement directed not, as the hatred during the medieval period, against the religion of the Jews; rather, it was ignited in the situation that followed the attainment of emancipation. The Antisemite League (Antisemiten-Liga), founded with help from Marr in September and October 1879, had as its goal "to push the Jews we find so obnoxious back behind the barriers that incautious legislation abolished, to our detriment." All antisemites were agreed that Jews must be removed from the positions of power they had attained in society. Beyond this point, the antisemitic movement divided into radicals and moderates, into those who thought in terms of racist biology and those who wanted primarily to remove Jews from public positions and to oppose the "Jewish spirit."

Antisemitism was not, however, identical with the renewed discussion of the "Jewish question." As ideology it was a movement against the agenda of the French Revolution and liberalism. Antisemitism was closely connected with the crisis of the bourgeois mentality that erupted during the recession of the 1870s and 1880s. This crisis expressed itself in a new and more vehement nationalism, in xenophobia, and in antisocialism. The antisemitic movement and its related parties found followers particularly among the petite bourgeoisie. In 1878 Stoecker sought followers within the working class for the antisemitic party he had founded. When this tactic failed, he changed the party's name from Christian-Social Worker's Party to Christian-Social Party. Rather than workers, he attracted artisans, shopkeepers, and, to a lesser degree, peasants, as well as members of the academic elite. The working class largely resisted antisemitism, as did Social Democracy, which sharply rejected it at the 1893 party congress.

In terms of the development of a party, there were two tendencies among the antisemites: one viewed antisemitism as a worldview to be expressed within all parties if possible; the other wanted to make it the central program point of one party. The founding of antisemitic parties did not bring great successes. They reached a high point in the 1893 Reichstag elections with 2.9 percent of the vote and 16 deputies, declined thereafter, and developed into sect-like groups. On the other hand, antisemitism played a role in several associations of great importance during the imperial period of the late 19th and early 20th centuries, including the LEAGUE OF AGRICULTURALISTS, the GERMAN NATIONAL SHOP ASSISTANTS' ASSOCIATION, the ALL-GERMAN ASSOCIATION, the Organization of German Students, and some BURSCHENSCHAFTEN. These

"Teut[on] against Juda: The Showdown." Antisemitic pamphlet from the early 1920s.

organizations supported the spread of antisemitism at the turn of the century, and indeed supported an "antisemitic social tone" altogether (Friedrich Naumann). At the same time, antisemitism and racial ideology, as formulated by Houston Stewart CHAMBERLAIN, established a close relationship. A people was no longer to be molded by history and culture, but rather primarily in accordance with RACE. The possibility of assimilation, which the old-style antisemitism had permitted for the integration of Jews, was thus discounted.

Hitler presupposed a connection between antisemitism and racial ideology in his programmatic remarks and his book MEIN KAMPF. Influenced by such Austrian antisemites as Georg Ritter von SCHÖNERER and Karl LUEGER, Hitler announced his intention to practice antisemitism with utmost consistency and harshness, particularly through the social restriction and exclusion of Jews. His political perspective was to give the German *Volk*, through antisemitism, "the great, unifying thought for combat." Finally, Hitler wanted to exploit the new importance antisemitism had won after the defeat of the First World War. The belief that the Jews were responsible for the collapse of the German Empire and for the "stab in the back" of the undefeated frontline troops strengthened the role of the Jews as scapegoats, even after the economic upturn in the last prewar years had resulted in rather a decline in antisemitic tendencies. Antisemites also blamed the Jews for the Communist movement that had achieved power during and after the war. They saw communism as led and manipulated by Jews. Typical of postwar antisemitism was an increasing "unscrupulousness, and a growing acceptance of physical violence" (Peter G. J. Pulzer). Jewish organizations tried to argue energetically against the accusations of guilt for the world war and the defeat: the REICH LEAGUE OF JEWISH FRONTLINE SOLDIERS, for example, in a 1924 pamphlet pointed to the 12,000 Jewish war deaths and urged "German women" not to tolerate "the mocking of German mothers in their grief." Such actions remained totally without success. Antisemitism, as a subconsciously anchored prejudice, could not be "refuted" by pointing out the incorrect or illogical nature of its ideas.

Hitler's NSDAP was one of the antisemitic parties of the Weimar Republic, among which the German Völkisch Freedom Party of Gen. Erich LUDENDORFF should also be mentioned. Initially the antisemitic slogans of the German

The coarse slogan "Juda perish" became a terrible reality in Hitler's extermination camps.

National People's Party or the All-Germans had a larger audience. The NSDAP program of 1920 mentioned the Jews especially in Point 4, according to which a "*Volk* comrade" (*Volksgenosse*) and citizen had to have "German blood"; "No Jew can therefore be a *Volk* comrade." Realization of this demand would have to mean revoking the citizenship of all Jews and dismissing them from all public posts. Other program points, such as "breaking interest servitude," the communalization of department stores, and agricultural reform were spelled out so as to be understood as directed exclusively against Jews. The NSDAP attempted to create its own accent after 1927 by carrying out boycotts against department stores and one-price shops in conformity with its pro-MITTELSTAND policies. It described these businesses as "Jewish inventions," and claimed that department stores were all run by Jews. The *Völkischer Beobachter* commented on January 28, 1927: "One may carry out the struggle against department stores as one will: as long as one is silent about the true reason for the danger (insatiable Jewish lust for power), as long as one does not dare to speak of Jews . . . so long will the struggle against the department store be only a half-hearted one.

Therefore the middle class can be saved only by National Socialists."

The WORLD ECONOMIC CRISIS of 1930, like that of 1873, again provoked strong antisemitic emotions. "An antisemitic frenzy" favored the growth of National Socialism (E. G. Reichmann). That the NSDAP intended to follow its antisemitic propaganda with real deeds was demonstrated soon after the Seizure of Power with the BOYCOTT AGAINST JEWS of April 1, 1933, and the CIVIL SERVICE LAW of April 7, 1933. From the antisemitic program grew—as many in bourgeois circles or even among German Jews had not thought possible—the persecution of the Jews and, ultimately, the FINAL SOLUTION. After establishing themselves in power, the National Socialists wanted nothing more to do with the term "antisemitism": in 1935 the Propaganda Ministry advised the German press "to avoid the words 'antisemitic' or 'antisemitism' in discussing the Jewish question, because the German policy is opposed only to Jews, not Semites as such. The word 'anti-Jewish' should be used instead." Foreign-policy considerations, particularly regarding the Arab world, caused the National Socialists to ban the central term from the campaign against the

1
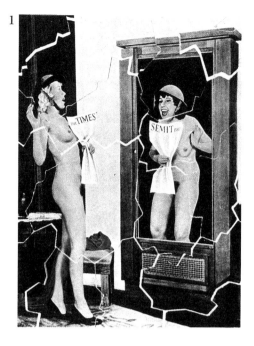

2

1
In the mirror, the "true" face of the London *Times* is revealed as "Times" becomes "Semit[e]." War leaflet in puzzle form.

2
"Behind the enemy powers: the Jew." Propaganda poster.

3
(See facing page.)

3

Jude verdufte!

In unserm weiten Vaterland
Manch Fleckchen Erde ist bekannt
Durch Schönheit und durch seine Kraft,
Wodurch Gesundheit es verschafft.
Drum wird besucht es gar so gern
Von vielen Menschen nah und fern.
Wie Ihr auf diesem Bilde seht,
Auch eine Tafel dabei steht,
Die allen Menschen groß verkündt',
Daß Juden unerwünschet sind!
Den Deutschen nur gehört die Luft,
Drum Freundchen Jude, hier verduft!

Facing page:
3
From the children's book *Don't Trust a Fox on a Green Heath or a Jew by His Oath*, Stürmer Press, 1936. The sign reads: "!Jews! Are Not Wanted Here." The poem, "Jew, Get Lost!," reads:
In our broad fatherland
Many a spot is known
For its beauty and efficacy
Whereby health is restored.
Thus it is fondly visited
By people coming from far and wide.
As you see in this picture,
A sign has been put up
Announcing to all people
That Jews are not wanted!
The air belongs only to Germans,
And therefore, little Jewish friend, get lost!

Jews. In 1944 another official statement sought to replace the term "antisemitism" with the neologism "anti-Judaism" (*Antijudaismus*). The replacement of this central polemical term was more than a political regulation of speech. It demonstrated that antisemitism as a "'world-view' . . . had become an integrating component of the National Socialist 'worldview,'" while "antisemitism as a political movement . . . had been subsumed in the National Socialist 'movement'" (Thomas Nipperdey and Reinhold Rürup).

After all political counterpositions, save for remnants in the churches, were extinguished in 1933, a "dynamic" and aggressive antisemitism based on broad latent antisemitism could develop unhindered (Ian Kershaw). It was dominant in the NSDAP, and constituted an important source of cohesion for the party, and especially for the SS. Among the population, the party found only limited resonance for a dynamic antisemitism. This became clear on the occasion of KRISTALLNACHT, when the population was actively involved only here and there, and often only in marginal groups. The role of spectator

Marked with the Jewish Star: an elderly woman on the way [to the gas chamber] in a German extermination camp.

was dominant; indeed, critical views grew in significance, as can be seen from the increase of such cases before the Special Court in Munich. The NSDAP did ultimately succeed in rooting more firmly the antisemitic views held by the population. The result was that the deportations of German Jews after 1941, and the recurrent rumors about their murder, called forth only very weak reactions. Latent antisemitism, as well as general intimidation and the weight of personal worries regarding daily life in wartime, encouraged an indifference to the fate of Jews that made it possible for the NSDAP to carry out unhindered its annihilation policies.

Herbert Obenaus

Antonescu, Ion, b. Piteşti, Romania, June 15, 1882; d. Jilava (now part of Bucharest), June 1, 1946 (executed), Romanian politician. In 1933 Antonescu became chief of the General Staff; in 1937–1938, he was minister of war. As an extreme nationalist, Antonescu enjoyed great popularity, to the extent that King Carol II was forced to accept him as head of the government on September 4, 1940. Two days later the new Conducător (leader) overthrew the king and created a fascist-style personal dictatorship. He was able to defend himself against a putsch attempt by the IRON GUARD. Antonescu came increasingly under German influence because of the Wehrmacht's dependence on Romanian oil. Romania was forced to join the THREE-POWER AGREEMENT (November 23, 1940), and in June 1941 it participated in the attack on the Soviet Union. As the Red Army moved toward Romania in 1944, Antonescu was overthrown (August 23, 1944) and tried before a people's tribunal, which sentenced him to death.

AO. *See* Foreign Organization.

Ion Antonescu.

APA. *See* Foreign Policy Office of the NSDAP.

Appeals Boards (Spruchkammern), court-like organs to implement DENAZIFICATION. They were created through the Law for the Liberation from National Socialism and Militarism, enacted on March 5, 1946, by the state (*Land*) governments in the American occupation zone. Through a directive of the Allied Control Council on December 10, 1946, the law was also applied to the other occupation zones. The boards consisted of lay judges and public prosecutors and were subordinate to the supervision of the "Liberation Ministries" (Befreiungsministerien) of the individual states.

Appeasement, term for the British policy during the interwar period that was meant to assure peace and "peaceful change" at the negotiating table. At least by the time of the MUNICH AGREEMENT, "appeasement" had become a political catchword signifying an impotent capitulation to dictators. Beyond its immediate identification with British prime minister Neville CHAMBERLAIN and his controversial attempts to negotiate with Hitler over the SUDETEN CRISIS, appeasement resulted from the crises of British domestic politics, as well as from dangerous developments in the international balance of power, especially following the WORLD ECONOMIC CRISIS, notably the simultaneous challenge to Britain's position of world power by totalitarian and aggressive world powers (Japan in East Asia, Italy in the Mediterranean, Germany in Europe). Combining both aspects, appeasement was the attempt of a satiated and already declining world power to survive on the basis of sharply reduced political, economic, and military strength. The domestic social-economic crisis that began in the late 19th century was dramatically worsened by the world depression. Survival required avoiding the renewed burdens of an international arms race and a new world war. At the same time, advancing the needed modernization process required the absence of an external threat.

Appeals Boards. Swearing-in of the chairman.

Appeasement. Returning from the Munich conference, Prime Minister Neville Chamberlain, at the London airport, believes that he can promise "peace in our time."

Behind the concept of appeasement lay fear of the significant burdens and dangers of an arms race and military entanglements: renewed growth of foreign and domestic indebtedness (especially to the United States), which had still not been settled from the First World War; the weakness of the British pound; the danger of inflation; the flight of capital; unhealthy distortions in the system of production; the loss of export markets; changes in England's social profile to the detriment of the conservative establishment; and the vulnerability of the British sea-lanes. Appeasement was the tactical effort to delay armed conflict in Europe until it was perceived as a common threat throughout the Empire. It arose from fears of a Communist threat, especially in conservative circles, which saw National Socialist Germany as a dependable "bulwark" against communism, as well as from a "bad conscience" because of the long-recognized problems created at Versailles in 1919. British peace policies could count on widespread pacifist sentiments. In an illusory misreading of the NS regime and its expansionist intentions, appeasement was based on the hope that timely revisionist economic concessions and a degree of recognition of German hegemony in central and southeastern Europe would strengthen the "moderates" in Berlin (Göring, Schacht, and the like; sometimes even Hitler himself) against the "extremists" (Himmler, Goebbels, and Ribbentrop), with the moderates'

support ultimately implementing a peace policy in Germany. In British eyes, the Munich conference was the last attempt to deal with European matters through the region's "Big Four," in conscious distance from the Soviet Union and the United States, and thereby to delay the post-1918 decline of Europe as a world power.

Appeasement was further developed under continuing German threats, in the winter of 1938–1939, into a double strategy of "peace and rearmament." Its limits were clearly marked by the English and French guarantees to Poland (March 31, 1939) and to Romania and Greece (April 13, 1939) as a response to the German march on Prague (March 15, 1939). Even though hopes for a continuation of appeasement in the form of peace contacts persisted in British government circles beyond March 9, 1939, indeed, until Chamberlain's resignation (May 10, 1940), Germany's unleashing of war finally removed the basis for it in three respects: domestically, as a policy of acquiescence without German counterconcessions; in foreign policy, as a significant disturbance of the European "balance of power" that underlay Britain's existence; and all this the result of a unilateral German ultimatum, rather than an internationally negotiated compromise.

B.-J. W.

Arbeiter. *See* Worker.

Arbeiterbanken. *See* Bank of German Labor, Ltd.

Arbeiterheime. *See* Homestead.

Arbeiter-Illustrierte-Zeitung (Workers' Illustrated News; AIZ), Berlin newspaper published after November 30, 1924, by the New German Press, associated with the International Workers Aid (IAH) of Willi MÜNZENBERG. The AIZ developed out of the IAH journal *Sowjetrussland im Bild* (Soviet Russia in Pictures), founded in the summer of 1921, which in 1923–1924 became *Hammer und Sichel* (Hammer and Sickle) and appeared twice monthly (weekly after November 1, 1926). The editors in chief were Franz Höllering and, after 1927, Lily Corpus and Hans Lange. Conceived as an alternative to bourgeois tabloids, the AIZ, with its political and ideological loyalties to the KPD (Communist Party of Germany), intended to use photomontages and collages to capture and analyze areas of proletarian existence. John HEARTFIELD published his photomontages in the AIZ after 1929. Its circulation in 1925 was 200,000; in 1931, 500,000; the last issue appeared on March 5, 1933 (no. 10).

The paper continued in exile in Prague with numbers 11/12/13 (March 25); the AIZ was sometimes distributed illegally in Germany. Its editor in chief was F. C. Weiskopf; circulation was 6,000–7,000. After numbers 41/35, the AIZ bore the subtitle *Illustriertes Volksblatt* (Illustrated People's News); after numbers 34/36, the title *Volks-Illustrierte* (People's Illustrated). The last edition was published October 12, 1938; the 1936 circulation was 12,000. The attempt at a further continuation failed. Only seven issues were published in Strasbourg between January 15 and February 26, 1939, under the dual title *Die Volks-Illustrierte/Illustré Populaire* (People's Illustrated).

S. O.

Arbeitsausschüsse. *See* Labor Committees.

Arbeitsbuch. *See* Employment book.

Arbeitsdank, office of the GERMAN LABOR FRONT.

Arbeitsdienst. *See* Reich Labor Service.

Arbeitseinsatz. *See* Labor deployment.

Arbeitsfront. *See* Labor Front.

Arbeitskammer. *See* Labor Chamber.

Arbeitsmaid. *See* Workmaid.

Arbeitsmann. *See* Workman.

Arbeitsordnungsgesetz. *See* Labor Regulation Law.

Arbeitsschlacht. *See* Battle for Work.

Arbeitsspende. *See* Work Fund.

Arbeitswechsel. *See* Work Bill.

Architecture (*Architektur* or *Baukunst*), an art favored by National Socialism, and especially by Hitler; through monumental structures, architecture was supposed to convey the "greatness of intentions" of the National Socialist (NS) movement. NS aestheticians considered the functionalism and cosmopolitanism of modern architecture to be *Ausländerei* (foreign); flat roofs to be "oriental," and concrete, glass, and artificial materials to be "racially degenerate" (Paul SCHULTZE-NAUMBURG). The influence of national or regional traditions in architecture nonetheless remained secondary after 1933, limited to residences and community buildings, for example, the use of timber frames (*Fachwerk*). The model for Hitler and his architects (until 1934, especially Paul Ludwig TROOST, then Albert SPEER) was the "ideal of beauty of the peoples and states of antiquity," the super-dimensional massiveness of antique temples. A classically oriented AESTHETICS was considered "timeless." Expanded through stylistic borrowings from medieval fortresses, it was designated "Germanic tectonics." In the monumental architecture of the Third Reich, heavy, strongly geometric forms and horizontal or vertical symmetry dominate. In conscious contrast to everyday, functional architecture, political sacral buildings were to express a "community spirit" such as was thought to be incorporated in early German cathedrals.

Because Hitler saw architecture as a means of domination, the years 1934 to 1940 produced a building boom of "historical uniqueness." The new structures were supposed to function as "sites of national consecration," particularly for the masses, creating stages for assemblies and marches. They were fitted out with columns, towers, and tribunes, decorated with state insignia, flags, and banners, and during public events were artfully illuminated and lighted. The emphasis was at first on the "buildings of the [NS] movement"; the first huge structures arose on Munich's Königsplatz, followed by the completion of the Nuremberg Reich Party Congress Grounds, conceived as a "style-setting document" on 30 sq km (18.6 sq miles). The epitome was reached with planning for the Reich capital,

Berlin, which was to become a representative center, because "only the existence of such [a city] with the magical charm of a Mecca or Rome can give a movement strength in the long run" (Hitler). Drafts from 1937 depicted for the planned metropolis of 10 million residents a magnificent boulevard ("the longest shopping street in the world") and a "Great *Volk*-Hall," with a brick dome 300 m (984 feet) high. In 1944 the plans were still being worked on, with the intent of rebuilding war-torn Berlin as "Germania," capital of a Europe ruled by Germany.

Into the 1940s, numerous large buildings without economic or social uses were built; through size and mass they were meant to make state authority be felt as an "experience" and to intimidate critics: "Nothing is better suited to silence the petty complainer than the eternal language of art" (Hitler). Classical architecture, like natural building materials (especially granite and limestone), symbolized the permanence and steadfastness of the system. Long-range plans foresaw a "unification" of city structures through centers with political temples and parade grounds. Distributed throughout the country and the occupied territories, SS barracks and "castles" (*see* ORDER FORTRESSES) were to be—and in part were—erected on mountains and hills like medieval watchtowers. During the Second World War, the planning of mausoleums and monuments to the dead signaled the beginnings of a gigantic cemetery architecture.

In the private sector (influenced by the BEAUTY OF WORK Office of the German Labor Front), the principles of NS architecture affected the construction of industrial facilities: factories were built of natural stone and brick, office buildings contained columned halls. Private residential construction, on the other hand, lost much of its importance after 1933. Public funds fell far below the level of the Weimar period, and standards fell with use of the cheapest construction methods, mass production, and economizing on comfort and furnishings. Moreover, state-supported settlements for housing and work were supposed to tie the

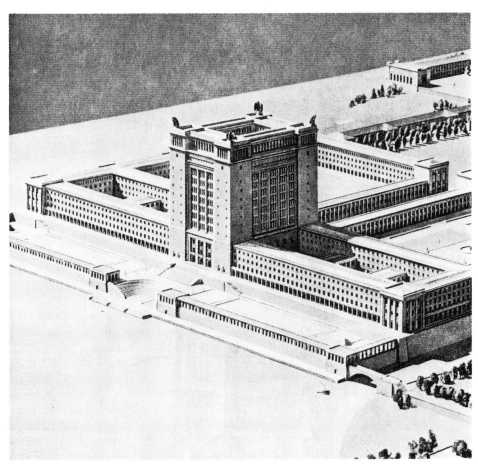

Architecture. Model of the projected party academy (*see* HOHE SCHULE DER NSDAP) at Chiemsee. Architect: Hermann Giesler.

worker more closely to the "production community" and were therefore kept decidedly simple.

H. H.

Ardeatine Caves (Fosse Ardeatine), volcanic rock (trass) caves on the southern boundary of Rome near the catacombs of Saint Calixt. On March 24, 1944, the German chief of police for Rome, SS-Obersturmbannführer Herbert Kappler, had 335 Italians shot in the caves. The massacre was a reprisal for an attack by Communist resistance forces the previous day on Rome's Via Rasella, in which 32 German soldiers were killed and 60 more severely wounded. Hitler had first ordered the shooting of 50 hostages for every German victim, a "quota" that Field Marshal Gen. Albert KESSELRING reduced to 10; he ordered that prisoners sentenced to death or awaiting a death sentence be selected. Because Kappler did not find enough such victims, he ordered further arrests, so that those executed in the Ardeatine Caves ultimately included women and two 14-year-old boys.

In July 1948, a Roman court sentenced Kappler to death. His sentence was reduced to life imprisonment, and in 1977 he was able, with the help of his wife, to escape from a hospital and flee to Germany, where he died a few weeks later. The escape led to a disruption in German-Italian relations.

Ardennes Offensive, final major German offensive operation in the Second World War (*see* INVASION). It began on December 16, 1944;

Benno von Arent.

after initial successes, by January 16, 1945, all territorial gains had again been lost. Hitler had intended that the offensive would lead the Wehrmacht out of its "eternally defensive" stance and would break the Allies' confidence in their victory. Instead, it only weakened the eastern front and hastened the COLLAPSE.

Arent, Benno von, b. Görlitz, June 19, 1898, German set designer. Self-taught, after various apprentice positions Arent obtained his first theater job in Berlin in 1923. In 1931 he joined the SS, and in 1932 the NSDAP. He was the founder of the Federation of National Socialist Stage and Film Artists (after 1933 the Comradeship [Kameradschaft] of German Artists). In 1935 Arent received Hitler's personal commission to stage celebrations; after 1936 he oversaw the German stage as "Reich Set Designer." Arent was also the architect for the German Labor Front House in Berlin. In 1939 he became Reich Commissioner for FASHION. He was commissioned an SS-*Oberführer* in 1944.

Arier. *See* Aryan.

Arisierung. *See* Aryanization.

Army, German. *See* Reichswehr; Wehrmacht.

Army High Command (Oberkommando des Heeres; OKH), the highest administrative and command level of the army under its supreme commander. The post was held from November 1, 1936, to February 4, 1938, by Werner Baron von FRITSCH, then by Walter von BRAUCHITSCH until December 19, 1941, and finally by Hitler. After Hitler's suicide (April 30, 1945) the OKH was dissolved.

Arndt, Walter, b. Landshut (Silesia), January 8, 1891; d. Brandenburg, June 26, 1944 (executed), German zoologist and victim of National Socialism. After graduating from the University of Breslau in 1920, Arndt joined the Zoological Museum in Berlin, where he became curator in 1925 and professor in 1931. He gained an international reputation through numerous publications. The search for and dissemination of truth not only distinguished him as a researcher, but made him a critic of political abuses. In 1944 he was denounced by acquaintances when, after a bombing attack, he predicted the end of the Third Reich. He admitted this before the VOLK COURT, so that even requests for mercy by leading scientists could not save him. Arndt was sentenced to death on May 11, 1944.

Benno von Arent's *Grecian Group*, in the festive parade "Two Thousand Years of German Culture."

Arnheim, Dutch city where an Allied paratroop operation (September 17–26, 1944) failed to gain the Rhine bridges (*see* INVASION).

Arrow Cross. Symbol of the Hungarian national guards.

Arrow Cross (Pfeilkreuzler), Hungarian fascist party (also called the "National Socialist Party" of Hungary), named after the party emblem. The Arrow Cross was founded in October 1937 by Ferenc SZÁLASI through the merger of three smaller fascist parties with the "Party of National Will" (sometimes called the "Hungarian Movement"), which he had founded and led since 1935. The Arrow Cross party was financially supported by Germany. As a radical nationalist and Great-Hungarian revisionist movement, the party addressed particularly the so-called *Lumpenproletariat* and petite bourgeoisie with its social-revolutionary and antisemitic program; otherwise, it had no audience in Hungary.

After the arrest of the regent, Adm. Miklós HORTHY, on October 16, 1944, the German occupation authorities named Szálasi premier ("state Führer") of a fascist government. As a German puppet, he was made a tool of the policies of Jewish extermination and bloody suppression in those areas not yet occupied by Soviet troops. Szálasi and the other Arrow Cross leaders were turned over to Hungary's postwar government after their capture by the Americans in Austria; nearly all were hanged after a trial in 1946.

B.-J. W.

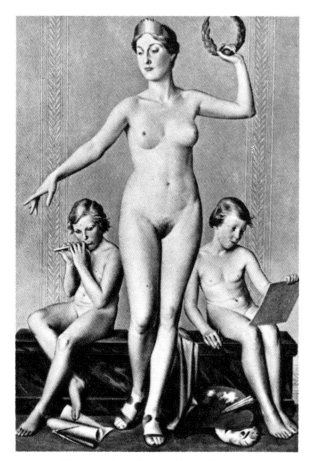

Art. *Goddesses of Art,* by Adolf Ziegler.

Arson (*Brandstiftung*), crime punishable with a long term of imprisonment. The REICHSTAG FIRE DECREE stipulated the death penalty for arson in public buildings; this was confirmed by the LEX VAN DER LUBBE and the Law to Prevent Political Violence of April 4, 1933. Marinus van der LUBBE was condemned according to these laws in the REICHSTAG FIRE TRIAL.

Art (*Kunst*), the totality of aesthetically formative creation (*see* LITERATURE; ARCHITECTURE; SCULPTURE; MUSIC; FILM), which National Socialist theorists explained not only by a "particular imagination" or a "realization of metaphysical energies," but also by its "identity as to race, blood, and *Volk.*" NS art policy was, after 1933, influenced more by the struggle to define itself against republican, leftist, modern art (*see* DEGENERATE ART; ART BOLSHEVISM) than by its own aesthetic alternative (*see* AESTHETICS). The "sensual-instinctual" quality of bourgeois modern art was rejected, but the "super-sensual" ideal of NS art remained a vague concept: "The most superior artistic

work of the West is . . . not something 'beautiful,' but rather the work whose exterior is permeated with spiritual impetus, [which] lifts it above itself from within" (Alfred ROSENBERG). In the culture politics of the Third Reich, art was less important than propaganda and was subordinated to political aims. This produced a tendency toward universally accessible art, as well as a hierarchy of political and material support based on popular impact: architecture and film had priority, while artistic forms that had an individual audience received little or no support (*see, for example,* RADIO PLAY).

H. H.

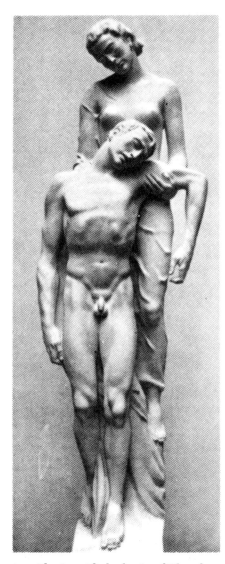

Art. *The Last Flight,* by Josef Thorak.

1

2

3

1
"Königsplatz. Temple of Honor for the Fallen [Heroes] of November 9, 1923. Führer's and Administrative Building." Postcard from the series Munich—Capital of the [National Socialist] Movement.
2
The Führer's Building in Munich. Living Room, Fireplace Group. Architects: Leonhard Gall and Gerdy Troost.
3
Sculpture by Georg Kolbe.

1

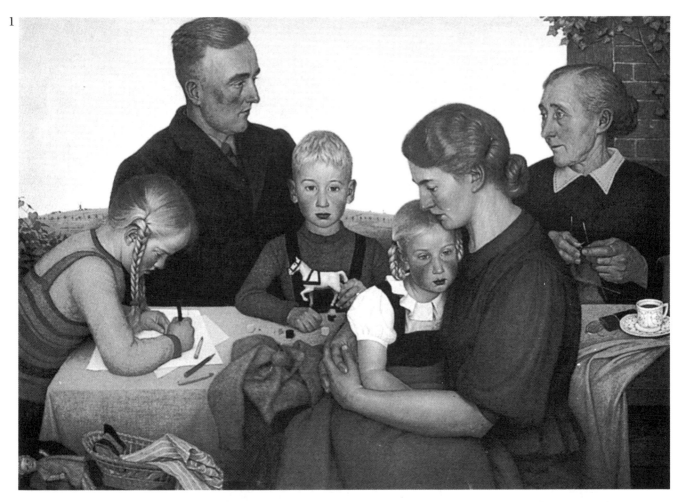

2

3

4

5

1
Adolf Wissel,
*Kahlberg Peasant
Family*, 1939.
2
Adolf Reich, *Collect-
ing Woolen Clothing
at a Munich Local
Party Group*, 1942.
3
Robert Schwarz,
Bathing Girls, 1943.
4
Will Tschech, *Com-
rades*, 1943.
5
Hubert Lanzinger,
The Standard-Bearer,
1938.

Artamanen (neologism coined from the Middle High German *art* [farming] and *manen* [men]), members of the Artam League, a nationalist-*völkisch* group founded in 1924, whose program included increased German settlement in the east, a stemming of the flight from the country-side, and a close relationship between BLOOD AND SOIL. Artam, which developed out of the *völkisch* wing of the YOUTH MOVEMENT, early on promoted rural labor service (*see* REICH LABOR SERVICE), demanded the resettlement of Polish agricultural workers from the eastern Reich provinces, and developed a model for later SS racism. It was no accident that the approximately 2,000 Artamanen (1924) included Heinrich HIMMLER, the later Reich Peasant Führer Walther DARRÉ, and Auschwitz commandant Rudolf HÖSS. The Artam League was absorbed by the NSDAP in 1933.

Art Bolshevism (*Kunstbolschewismus*), derogatory catchword of National Socialist propaganda, like CULTURE BOLSHEVISM directed against modern and socially critical art. The term was applied by Hitler himself to painting, in particular: "The Bolshevism of art is the only possible cultural life form and spiritual expression of Bolshevism"; thus, the "officially recognized art" in Bolshevist states was represented by the "sickly outgrowths of insane and debilitated people that we have come to know since the turn of the century as Cubism and Dadaism" (*Mein Kampf*).

Art cultivation (*Kunstpflege*), general term for all measures that serve to promote artists and the arts, as well as to preserve and care for works of art; it was motivated primarily by ideological and propagandistic viewpoints in the Third Reich. Exemplary accomplishments of cultivation of public art were considered to be commissions to artists for monuments and public spaces, the "lavish development of Berlin and Munich according to artistic criteria," the organizational inclusion of German artists in the REICH CULTURE CHAMBER, and the creation of an artists' social agency, the "German Fine Arts Relief agency" (Hilfswerk für deutsche bildende Kunst), in the NATIONAL SOCIALIST VOLK WELFARE agency. Art cultivation in the broader sense included art instruction, the promotion of contemporary National Socialist art in such journals as *Die Kunst im Dritten Reich* (Art in the Third Reich), support for art associations (some 100 in 1937), and the organization of workplace exhibits through the German Labor Front and of study groups, lectures, and museum

trips within the GERMAN PUBLIC INSTRUCTION AGENCY.

Art education (*Kunsterziehung*), general term used in the Third Reich for "the education of the *Volk* to understand the various expressions of art." This was achieved primarily by art criticism in newspapers and magazines (*see* ART VIEWING) that positively emphasized National Socialist content. In a narrower sense, art education was the official term used since the second half of the 19th century to denote a public school curricular field consisting primarily of drawing instruction. NS pedagogues wanted to reassess the subject by making ideological "art viewing" a subject of instruction and by creating a separate curriculum for art teachers.

Article 48 of the WEIMAR CONSTITUTION, provision according to which the Reich president could temporarily nullify important basic rights, for example, freedom of assembly and speech. Emergency measures based on this article, which was also called the "dictatorship paragraph," had to be lifted by a majority vote of the Reichstag. This did not appreciably weaken Article 48, since the Reich president could dissolve the Reichstag according to Article 25, and then rule again through EMERGENCY DECREES. After 1930 the Reichstag was unable to produce a majority capable of coalition. Article 48 then became the basis for the PRESIDIAL CABINETS that undermined the rights of the Reichstag and led to the fall of the Republic. It also underlay the REICHSTAG FIRE DECREE of February 28, 1933, the first step toward Hitler's dictatorship.

Article 231 of the VERSAILLES TREATY, provision attributing sole guilt for the First World War to Germany: "The Allied and Associated Governments affirm and Germany accepts the responsibility of Germany and her allies for causing all the loss and damage to which the Allied and Associated Governments and their nationals have been subjected as a consequence of the war imposed upon them by the aggression of Germany and her allies." The majority of Germans viewed this article as a WAR GUILT LIE; it stood in the way of assimilating defeat and became the most pointed weapon of rightist parties against the provisions of the peace treaty.

Art plunder (*Kunstraub*), organized looting of art treasures from German-occupied countries in the Second World War; it was carried out by state or party offices, especially the ROSENBERG

OPERATION STAFF of Reichsleiter Alfred ROSEN-BERG. Because Hitler planned to create the "greatest museum in the world" in Linz after the "final victory," the theft was intended to supply a basic collection. The real motive force was supplied by Göring, who obtained valuable pieces from the booty to decorate his villa KARINHALL, including 52 pictures from the Cranach School. The stolen art objects were stored in the Neuschwanstein and Herrenchiemsee castles and in mine tunnels, cloisters, and caverns, or were requisitioned by important party members for their offices. At the outset primarily Jewish collections were "secured," but later (especially in Poland, by Generalgouverneur Hans FRANK), the treasures of real or ostensible "enemies of the Reich" were stolen; finally, even public museums were plundered. According to an incomplete accounting of July 15, 1944, some 22,000 art objects had fallen victim, among them 5,281 paintings by artists from Goya to Watteau. The most prominent theft involved the AMBER ROOM of the Russian tsars.

Art viewing (*Kunstbetrachtung*), official Third Reich term for art criticism. Because art with a national or *völkisch* orientation was usually judged negatively by professional critics before 1933 (National Socialists considered this "criticism for the sake of criticism"), the term "art criticism" was suspect. For a few years after the Seizure of Power, even the narrow latitude available in the "synchronized" press was exploited to the extent that on November 27, 1936, Goebbels was forced to note: "Because the year 1936 has still produced no satisfactory improvement in art criticism, from today on I am forbidding any continuation of art criticism in the previous form." It was to be replaced immediately by an "art viewing" that described but did not judge, for "only the state or the party can give an absolute valuation" (*Völkischer Beobachter*).

Aryan (*Arier*), originally a purely linguistic term for the Indo-Germanic settlers in Persia and India, in contrast to the indigenous population. In the 19th century it was used by Count Arthur de GOBINEAU as a designation of racial value, whereby the greatest worth within the already superior white race was attributed to the Aryan, next to whom came the German. Taken over in this sense by National Socialist usage, the term gradually became purely a way to isolate Jews as the embodiment of the non-Aryan, and came to be equated with "member of the Nordic race." Because of this narrowing, the

adjective "Aryan" was increasingly replaced by such usages as "of German or related blood" and GERMAN-BLOODED.

Aryan Certificate. *See* Certificate of Descent.

Aryanization (*Arisierung*), National Socialist term for the transfer of Jewish property into "ARYAN" hands in order to "de-Jew the economy" (*see* DE-JEWING). Through the ARYAN PARAGRAPH and the NUREMBERG LAWS, Jews were early on largely excluded from public life. Reserved areas in the economy had been left to them, which Aryanization was to remove. On April 26, 1938, Jews were ordered to report all wealth over 5,000 marks, and their access to bank accounts was restricted; on June 14 of that year, the Interior Ministry ordered the registration of all Jewish businesses. The state set the sales value of Jewish firms at a fraction of their market worth, and used various pressure tactics to ensure sales only to desired persons. Among the largest "Aryanization profiteers" were the I.G. FARBEN Combine, the FLICK Group, and large banks. The proceeds from "Aryanized" firms had to be deposited in savings accounts, and were made available to their Jewish depositors only in limited amounts, so that in the final analysis Aryanization amounted to almost compensation-free confiscation.

After KRISTALLNACHT (November 9–11, 1938), the pressure of Aryanization was drastically increased. On November 12, Jews were forbidden to function as business managers, forcing Jewish owners to install "Aryan" surrogates. These people, who were often promoted by the party, first took over the office, and soon thereafter usually the whole business. "Compliant Aryans" (*Gefälligkeitsarier*) were threatened with punishment according to the Regulation against Complicity with the Camouflage of Jewish Firms (April 22, 1938). Because the Jews were burdened with heavy payments as "atonement" for the damage done by the SA and antisemitic mobs during Kristallnacht, the selling off of Jewish property was only a question of time. On December 3, 1938, the value of Jewish landed property was frozen at the lowest level, and valuables and jewels were permitted to be sold only through state offices. The impoverishment of the Jewish population caused by Aryanization often stood in the way of its goal—of promoting emigration through persecution—because those affected lacked the means to emigrate. They became victims of the FINAL SOLUTION. Aryanization combined the racial motives of National Socialism with traditional antisemitic resentments within the middle classes (*see* MITTELSTAND) and the expansionist tendencies of big business. The fear of being too late to share in the booty produced a fateful coalition of greed, so that little opposition to Aryanization arose. After the war, the Federal Republic of Germany paid RESTITUTION for the material losses.

Aryanization of Jesus (*Arisierung Jesu*), the attempt by GERMAN CHRISTIANS to use genealogical constructions to remove the taint of Judaism from Jesus. Galilee, from which Jesus' mother came, was accordingly conquered by Jews only later; moreover, Mary belonged to the lower class, and was therefore not of Jewish birth. Theodor FRITSCH even derived the word "Galilee" from "Gaul," and postulated Germanic origins. Paternally there was no problem, in that even racial fanatics stopped at the Holy Ghost. In their enthusiasm to Aryanize, genealogists even discovered an Aryan family name for Jesus: he and his cousin Skopas were occasionally called "sons of panthers," and therefore "their grandfather probably bore the Greek name Panther." Hitler never expressed an opinion on these speculations, but he liked to cite Jesus as an enemy of the Jews, seeing therein a close connection with National Socialist ANTISEMITISM.

Aryan Paragraph (*Arierparagraph*), regulation to exclude Jews from organizations, federations,

parties, and, ultimately, all public life. Based on the bylaws and programs of antisemitic organizations and parties of the late 19th century (as the German-Social Party in 1889), the Aryan Paragraph first appeared in the Third Reich in the formulation of the CIVIL SERVICE LAW. It stipulated that only those of Aryan descent, without Jewish parents or grandparents, could be employed in public service, especially in an official capacity (*see* CERTIFICATE OF DESCENT). The Aryan Paragraph was extended to education on April 25, 1933, in the Law against the Overcrowding of German Schools and Universities; on June 30 of that year, it was broadened so that even marriage to a "non-Aryan" sufficed for exclusion from a civil service career. In keeping with SYNCHRONIZATION, NSDAP pressure led many federations and organizations to adopt the Aryan Paragraph. Thus, Jews were barred from the public-health system, lost their honorary public offices, were driven from editorial offices (*see* EDITOR LAW) and theaters (*see* REICH CULTURE CHAMBER), and were excluded from agriculture (*see* HEREDITARY FARM LAW), a progression culminating in the NUREMBERG LAWS "for the final separation of Jewry from the German *Volk*." At the outset there were exceptions to this discrimination (combat veterans, service in the NATIONAL RISING [*Erhebung*], honorary Aryans, and so on), but now Jews and "Jewish MIXED-BREEDS" (*Mischlinge*) were confronted with a ban on nearly all professions. The

"Only for Aryans." Effect of the Aryan Paragraph in public parks.

Aryan Paragraph was accepted largely without protest, except that within the Evangelical Church it provoked the splitting off of the CON-FESSING CHURCH.

Ärzte-Prozess. *See* Doctors' Trial.

Aschendorfermoor, one of the Emsland penal camps, founded in 1936. Prisoners were used to cultivate the moors for the State Moor Administration; a sub-commando worked for the Höveler and Dieckhaus Clothing and Shoe Repair Workshop in Papenburg.

Asmussen, Hans Christian, b. Flensburg, August 21, 1898; d. Speyer, December 30, 1968, German Evangelical theologian. Asmussen was a pastor in Altona (now Hamburg-Altona); he was removed from office by the National Socialists because of his activity in the REICH FRATERNAL COUNCIL of the Confessing Church; he was jailed several times before 1945. He was co-author of the protest "Word and Affirmation of Altona Pastors amid the Misery and Confusion of Public Life" (January 11, 1933), which rejected a pact with National Socialism and thus became a preliminary step toward the theological declaration of the BARMEN CONFESSIONAL SYNOD. From 1945 to 1948, Asmussen presided over the Evangelical Church Chancellery, and from 1949 to 1955, he was dean (*Propst*) in Kiel; he was a promoter of ecumenical dialogue. His writings include *Seelsorge* (Pastoral Care; 1934) and *Der Römerbrief* (Letter to the Romans; 1952).

Asocials (*Asoziale*), in National Socialist usage, persons who "do not want to conform to the order of the VOLK COMMUNITY." According to this broad definition, the Reich Criminal Office in July 1938 ordered the arrest of such asocials as "vagabonds, beggars, GYPSIES, and persons who travel about like Gypsies." The operation also served to capture the WORK-SHY, an indication of the scarcity of labor. Asocials were sent without a trial to concentration camps, where they were identified as a separate prisoner category by means of a black cloth triangle.

Asphalt (*Asphalt*), in National Socialist (NS) usage, the negative antithesis of SOD (*Scholle*) as a concept; asphalt allegedly separated the city dweller from the land, so that he or she remained rootless. Typical asphalt-people were the Jews, who were those primarily blamed for the perversions that NS propaganda associated with asphalt: "asphalt news" and "asphalt press" as synonyms for the tabloid press and yellow journalism, the "asphalt democracy" of urbanized Western civilization, the "asphalt culture" of morally decayed big-city life, and the "asphalt literature" of "deracinated" (*artlos*) pacifist and socialist journalists. The word "asphalt" became the key term in NS hostility to civilization as against the BLOOD AND SOIL ideology, according to which "Germanic values" were "crippled by the red-hot, sterile asphalt of a bestialized monstrosity" (Alfred ROSENBERG).

Assassination Attempts on Hitler's Life

Until the end of the Third Reich, National Socialist propaganda successfully conveyed the picture of a Führer loved by all, who—in contrast to today's rulers—could safely move about among his Germans. The nearly suicidal carelessness with which Hitler ignored the security concerns of those around him contributed to this. The image of the Führer without enemies was strengthened by a series of incredible circumstances that repeatedly caused attacks to fail, so that it was easy to suppress reports—with the exception of the BÜRGERBRÄU ASSASSINATION ATTEMPT and the TWENTIETH OF JULY. The following list documents how often attempts were made to do away with Hitler; only attempts that reached the stage of realization are included.

Before 1933. Before the Seizure of Power, four attempts, including one with poison in the Hotel Kaiserhof (1930)

1933. Ten attacks, including one by an unknown SA man in Obersalzberg and another by the Lutter group in Königsberg

1934. Four attacks, among them one by Beppo RÖMER in Berlin and another by Helmut Mylius in Berlin

1935. The Marwitz group and Paul Josef Stuermer, both in Berlin

1936. Helmut Hirsch in Nuremberg

1937. Josef Thomas in Berlin; unknown SS man at the Berlin Sports Palace

1938–1939. Noel Mason-Macfarlane in Berlin

1939. Johann Georg ELSER in Munich; Erich Kordt in Berlin

Mussolini, who arrived at the "Wolfsschanze" Führer's headquarters shortly after the failed assassination attempt of July 20, 1944, surveys the damage from the bomb explosion.

1940. Erwin von WITZLEBEN in Paris
1941–1943. Nikolaus von Halem; several attempts by Beppo Römer in Berlin
1943. Hubert Lanz, Hans SPEIDEL, Hyazinth Count von Strachwitz in Walki (USSR); Friedrich König and Baron von Boeselager in Smolensk; Henning von TRESCKOW, Fabian von SCHLABRENDORFF, and Rudolph von Gersdorff; unknown Pole in the Führer's Wolfsschanze headquarters; Rudolph von Gersdorff in Berlin; Axel von dem Bussche-Streithorst at Wolfsschanze
1944. Ewald von KLEIST at Wolfsschanze; Eberhard von Breitenbuch in Obersalzberg; Claus Baron Schenk von STAUFFENBERG, several times in Berlin and at Wolfsschanze

Atlantic Charter, declaration of intent regarding the shape of a world at peace after the defeat of the Axis powers; it was announced by British prime minister Churchill and United States president Roosevelt aboard the British battleship *Prince of Wales* off the American coast on August 14, 1941. It proclaimed (1) no annexations; (2) territorial changes only after plebiscites; (3) peoples' right to self-determination; (4) universal access to raw materials and world trade; (5) economic progress through cooperation; (6) freedom from fear and misery through peace; (7) freedom of the seas; (8) renunciation of force, demilitarization of the aggressors, and general disarmament. The Atlantic Charter was recognized by 47 states (the Soviet Union accepted it with reservations) and it influenced the Charter of the UNITED NATIONS.

Atlantic Wall (*Atlantikwall*), propaganda term for the German defenses on the Atlantic designed to prevent the INVASION.

Atomic bomb, a weapon that uses energy released from the splitting of the atom, thus producing a force far in excess of traditional explosives. An atomic bomb became possible after the discovery of the fission of the uranium atom by the German chemist Otto Hahn (1879–1968) and his team in December 1938. Germany, however, lacked the industrial capacity necessary to build an atomic bomb. Prejudices against "Jewish atomic physics" also stood in the way, so that development of the bomb remained at a preliminary stage. The fear of such a weapon nonetheless prompted Albert EINSTEIN to send a letter of warning on August 2, 1939, to United States president Franklin D. Roosevelt, who turned the development of an atomic bomb over to the so-called Manhattan Project. The effort was made more urgent by German announcements of WONDER WEAPONS. The atomic bomb was not ready for deployment until after the war ended in Europe, so that Japan was its first victim (Hiroshima on August 6, 1945, and Nagasaki on August 9 of that year).

Atonement (*Sühneleistung*), the "penance" of 1 billion RM imposed on the German Jews upon Göring's initiative after KRISTALLNACHT (November 9–10, 1938) for the murder of Ernst vom RATH and the subsequent damages, which were said to have been caused by the "spontaneous *Volk* fury" unleashed by the bloody deed.

Atrocity stories (*Greuelpropaganda, -hetze, -märchen*), term for consciously fabricated reports of enemy crimes in wartime. In principle always a means of psychological warfare, atrocity stories were so widely used in the First World War, especially by the Allies, that their credibility suffered, and therefore the intended effect failed or the reverse was produced, when obvious lies were revealed. The most famous examples were the assertion that German soldiers—on the express and detailed order of Kaiser Wilhelm II—had chopped off the hands of Belgian children and had raped and tortured them, or, as in a London *Daily Telegraph* report of March 1916, that Austrians had gassed 700,000 Serbs. During the Second World War, these atrocity stories proved to be the SS's most effective camouflage for the genocide of the FINAL SOLUTION. In the summer of 1944, the highest Allied officials (for example, John Pehle, director of the American War Refugee Board) refused to believe reports of the gas chambers in AUSCHWITZ, citing these earlier atrocity stories. Despairing witnesses such as Kurt GERSTEIN confronted a wall of disbelief, which only became firmer because of the monstrous nature of the reports; German denials were considerably more successful. The fateful effects of the atrocity stories are still detectable in neo-Nazism (*see* AUSCHWITZ LIE).

Attlee, Clement, b. London, January 3, 1883; d. London, October 8, 1967, British politician and lawyer. In 1907 Attlee joined the Labour party; from 1922 to 1925, he was a member of Parliament; in 1924, he was under state secretary. Attlee became a party leader in 1935 and strongly opposed Chamberlain's APPEASEMENT policy. This recommended him for Churchill's War Cabinet, in which he served as Churchill's deputy from 1942 until the war's end. On July 28, 1945, Attlee replaced Churchill as prime minister in the difficult negotiations of the POTSDAM AGREEMENT. Many concessions to the Soviet Union were later attributed to him. Attlee granted India independence (1947), gave up

Atrocity stories. Belgian document from the First World War.

Clement Attlee.

Britain's Mandate over Palestine, and participated in the Korean War. From 1951 to 1955 he led the opposition against Churchill; thereafter he sat in the House of Lords.

Aufartung. *See* Species upgrading.

"Aufbau Ost" (Buildup in the East), code name for the first preparations to attack the USSR (*see* RUSSIAN CAMPAIGN).

Aufbruch der Nation ("a new start for the nation"), nationalist interpretation of the beginning of the First World War; it was adopted by the "National Socialist Revolution" to emphasize the overcoming of the party state and of pluralism. This was a parallel concept to the NATIONAL RISING (*Erhebung*).

Aufhäuser, Siegfried, b. Augsburg, January 1, 1884; d. Berlin, December 6, 1969, German politician and union leader; from 1921 to 1933, chairman of the largely white-collar AFABUND. Aufhäuser joined the SPD (Social Democratic Party) in 1912; after a brief period in the USPD (Independent Socialist Party), he served as an SPD Reichstag deputy from 1921 to 1933. Arrested several times in 1933, he emigrated the same year. Until 1935 he belonged to the executive committee of the SPD-in-exile, then strongly rejected the party's reformist course, viewing resistance to Hitler from a standpoint of class struggle. After 1939, Aufhäuser lived in New York as a journalist. In 1951 he returned to Germany, where he was chairman of the German Employees' Union (Deutsche Angestelltengewerkschaft; DAG).

Aufnordung. *See* Nordic upgrading.

August Wilhelm ("Auwi"), b. Potsdam, January 29, 1887; d. Stuttgart, March 25, 1949, prince of Prussia, fourth of six sons of Kaiser WILHELM II. Reared at court, August Wilhelm served in the First World War as a colonel, then entered the Prussian civil service. In 1927 he joined the STEEL HELMET, which he left two years later for the NSDAP and SA. Hitler first cultivated him as a monarchical fig leaf for the "movement," even honoring him with membership number 24. After the Seizure of Power, Hitler lost interest in August Wilhelm, who, however, paid him homage till the end; perhaps he also flirted with a monarchical restoration after Hitler. Named an SA-*Obergruppenführer* in 1939, August Wilhelm was categorized after the war as incriminated, and was sentenced to 30 months' hard labor; 40 percent of his wealth was confiscated.

Ausbürgerung. *See* Citizenship, revocation of.

Auschwitz, the largest National Socialist concentration and extermination camp. Auschwitz had a double function: its prisoners were used as forced labor; and it served as an extermination camp within the framework of the FINAL SOLUTION of the "Jewish question." Auschwitz was divided into three large camp areas: Auschwitz I (the main camp), Auschwitz II (Birkenau), and Auschwitz III (Monowitz). It was located in the Upper Silesian industrial region, near the city of Auschwitz (Pol., Oświęcim), on the Ostrau-Kraków (Kattowitz) railway line.

Auschwitz I, the main camp, was built between May and July 1940 in a former Austrian artillery barracks. It was first filled mostly with Polish prisoners (members of the resistance movement and the intelligentsia). By 1943 the prisoner population of the main camp had risen to some 30,000. This camp consisted of the protective-custody camp (*Schutzhaftlager*), where the prisoners were housed, and buildings outside the camp, which were under the commandant's jurisdiction. The protective-custody camp was surrounded with a barbed-wire fence 4 m (about 13 feet) high, which at night was electrified; watchtowers stood along the fence. Over the entrance gate to the camp was the motto "Work liberates" ("Arbeit macht frei").

Auschwitz II, the Birkenau camp, was built from late 1941 to early 1942, some 3 km (about 1.9 miles) from the main camp; it was constantly expanded until the war's end. The entire camp ultimately extended over an area of some 175 hectares (about 330 acres) and contained over

Prince August Wilhelm.

250 stone buildings and wooden barracks, divided into several subcamps separated by barbed wire. Men and women were housed separately. Newcomers capable of work were first quarantined, then divided among other camp sections. In September 1943, when Czech Jews were transferred in family groups from THERESIENSTADT, the so-called Czech family camp, or Theresienstadt camp, was formed in Auschwitz. Jews from this camp who were capable of work were ultimately sent to other camps; the remainder were gassed in March and July 1944. The Gypsy camp was another sub-unit. On the western side of the grounds was the "personal-effects camp," called "Canada" in local jargon, where the luggage, clothing, jewelry, watches, and the like belonging to the incoming Jews were stored and sorted. Birkenau was surrounded by a high double barbed-wire fence, electrically charged at night, as were the barbed-wire fences surrounding the separate subcamps. Some 150,000 prisoners were housed in Auschwitz II.

Auschwitz III, Monowitz, was built in 1941 for I.G. FARBEN Industries, which operated a plant for producing synthetic rubber (see BUNA) there. The camp was first called "Camp Buna." Monowitz was the largest of the external camps (Aussenlager) built in Upper Silesia; ultimately some 40 subsidiary camps (Nebenlager) arose. The Birkenau and Monowitz camps were made organizationally independent, with their own commandants, in 1943. The Political Division, the chief physician, and the telegraph office remained in the main camp. Otherwise, the camp's administration was like that at DACHAU.

Living conditions for the Auschwitz prisoners were the worst imaginable. Prisoners slept in unheated stone buildings or barracks on three-tiered plank beds covered only with straw or excelsior, with three and sometimes four prisoners in one bunk, usually without sheets, and with a single cover. The excelsior and straw were full of vermin. Sanitary and hygienic conditions were totally inadequate. In particular, given the frequent cases of diarrhea, there were far too few latrines, and all the wells in Birkenau were infected with coliform bacteria. At night prisoners could not leave the barracks, and used emergency buckets. Only prisoners charged with special functions and privileged prisoners had soap. The usual prisoner clothing consisted of a striped suit, underwear, a cap, and wooden shoes (clogs). The food was insufficient; within a short time prisoners became totally emaciated (see MUSELMANN). In many work squads, prisoners did receive better treatment (as in the SS's own agricultural operation and experimental institute). Besides the I.G. Farben facility, prisoners worked in the SS's own plants (GERMAN ARMAMENT WORKS, German Earth and Stone Works, and so on), and for other industrial firms in Upper Silesia. Malnourishment, exhaustion, disease, and epidemics (typhus, dysentery, cholera) led to mass deaths of prisoners. Mistreatment and arbitrary killings contributed further to increase the mortality rate.

Discipline of the SS men in Auschwitz was poor. Despite threats of severe punishment, there were hardly any who did not profit from the property confiscated from Jewish prisoners. Out of the "Canada" camp, SS men and certain trusted prisoners conducted an active business with such property. Corruption and bribery were the order of the day. Proceedings in SS courts against numerous SS men, some with high ranks, made no significant change in this regard.

In early September 1941, the first killings of prisoners with ZYKLON B began in the camp. Commandant Rudolf HÖSS preferred it to the carbon monoxide (CO) used in other places, because he thought it killed more quickly and reliably. The gassings took place in the Block 11 arrest cells (the "Bunker") of the main camp. However, because it was too difficult to conduct the gassings in these narrow cells, a gas chamber was soon built in the "old" or "small" crematorium of the main camp. A transport of 900 Russian prisoners was gassed there first. From October 1941 on, small groups of Jews were killed in this gas chamber. The victims were told to undress before a supposed delousing. The gas chamber in the old crematorium remained in operation until October 1942.

In January 1942 it was decided to rebuild a farmhouse ("Bunker I") in Auschwitz II as a gas chamber. Jews from Upper Silesia were killed here first, after being brought to the camp in so-called RSHA (REICH SECURITY MAIN OFFICE) transports. They were followed by transport trains from the GENERALGOUVERNEMENT, the Reich, the Protectorate of Bohemia and Moravia, and, finally, from all the European countries occupied and influenced by Germany. People in the first RSHA transports were killed without exception in Auschwitz, on Himmler's orders. Another order soon followed, however, according to which Jews were to be "selected" upon arrival; that is, those capable of work (on an average, 10 percent to 15 percent of a transport) were separated out for forced labor. Occasionally, entire transports were still killed immediately and without any SELEKTION.

Because of the constantly growing number of transports, a second Birkenau farmhouse ("Bunker II") was made into a gas chamber in June 1942. To further increase the killing capacity in Auschwitz II, two additional large crematoria and two somewhat smaller ones with attached gas chambers were built. The larger crematoria (I and II) began operating in spring 1943, and the two smaller ones (Crematoria III and IV) the same year. Bunker I was torn down, and Bunker II (then known as Bunker V) was used for supplementary killing. Aside from the men, women, and children in the arriving transports who were unfit for work, from time to time prisoners who were sick and unfit for work were separated out in all the camp divisions. They were gassed or were killed in the infirmary with phenol injections.

On Himmler's orders, destruction of the camp's gassing facilities was undertaken in late October and early November 1944. (The job was completed in January 1945, shortly before the arrival of Soviet troops.) The total number of Jews killed in Auschwitz is not known with precision, particularly since arriving prisoners chosen for immediate death were given no registration numbers. According to expert estimates, the number lies between 1 million and 1.5 million persons. Commandant Höss first gave the number of prisoners gassed as 2.5 million, with another half million dead of illness; he later estimated a total of 1.3 million.

As in other large concentration camps, there were numerous medical experiments on prisoners in Auschwitz. The most notorious are those performed by SS doctors Josef MENGELE, using Gypsies and twins, and Carl CLAUBERG, involving sterilization of women prisoners.

The commandants of the Auschwitz camp were Rudolf Höss (executed in Auschwitz, 1947), Arthur LIEBEHENSCHEL (executed in Kraków, 1948), Josef KRAMER (executed in Hameln, 1947), Heinrich Schwarz (executed in Sandweier, 1947), Fritz Hartjenstein (condemned to death; d. in a French prison, 1954), and Richard Baer (d. in prison pending trial, 1963).

W. D.

Auschwitz lie (*Auschwitzlüge*), term for denial of the mass murder of European Jewry in the so-called FINAL SOLUTION. An Auschwitz lie is punishable in the Federal Republic of Germany as a misdemeanor upon the complaint of survivors and the families of victims; it is politically controversial whether it should be an official misdemeanor. In a cynical reversal, neo-Nazi extremists refer to the results of historical re-

Selektion in Auschwitz.

Blown-up gas chamber in Auschwitz.

search on the Final Solution as the "Auschwitz lie."

Auschwitz trials, trials against former commanders and guards at AUSCHWITZ for crimes committed against camp prisoners. The majority of the trials took place in Poland; they involved at least 600 persons, most of whom were remanded to Poland by the western Allies in accordance with an agreement to try National Socialist criminals in courts of the countries where they had committed their crimes.

The most important trial was that against former Auschwitz commandant Rudolf HÖSS and his successor, Arthur LIEBEHENSCHEL, along with 39 others. On April 2, 1947, the Polish Supreme Court in Warsaw condemned Höss to death. The sentence was carried out in Auschwitz on April 16. In Kraków the same court, on December 22, 1947, condemned Liebehenschel and 22 other defendants to death, six to life imprisonment, seven to 15 years' imprisonment, and three to 10, 5, and 3 years' imprisonment, respectively; one defendant was acquitted. Of the 23 defendants condemned to death, 21 (including Liebehenschel) were executed; the sentences of the other two were commuted to life imprisonment.

Besides the Polish courts, Allied military tribunals in the four zones of occupation concerned themselves with crimes in Auschwitz. At issue were not only crimes committed in that camp, but also crimes committed by the accused during other assignments. Particularly significant among these proceedings was the trial, before a British military court in Lüneburg, of the former commandant of Auschwitz II (Birkenau) and later of BERGEN-BELSEN, Josef KRAMER, and 44 others, including several SS female guards, which took place as early as 1945. On November 17 of that year, Kramer and 10 other defendants were condemned to death, 1 to life imprisonment, and 18 to terms ranging from 1 to 15 years. The court acquitted 14 of the accused. During the trial, the proceedings against one defendant were cut short because of illness.

In the Federal Republic of Germany (FRG), few trials against former Auschwitz staff members were held before 1958. The turning point came in March 1958, with the testimony of a former prisoner that seriously incriminated Friedrich Wilhelm BOGER, a former SS-*Oberscharführer* in the political section at Auschwitz. Investigations in this case led to numerous Auschwitz trials, among them one of the largest trials dealing with National Socialist crimes in the FRG. Beginning on December 20, 1963, 20 defendants faced a jury in the State Court at Frankfurt am Main. In a judgment of August

19–20, 1965, 6 defendants were sentenced to life imprisonment and 10 to prison terms ranging from 3½ years to 14 years; one defendant was given a juvenile sentence of 10 years. The court acquitted 3 of the accused. After a review, a second defendant was acquitted on October 8, 1970. Reviews requested by the remaining defendants, the remaining plaintiffs, and the state prosecutor's office were quashed. The proceedings now known as the "first Auschwitz trial" were followed by others; investigations of crimes committed in Auschwitz continue to the present time.

Besides the trials of former commanders and guards, a number of proceedings against others are considered to be Auschwitz trials. These include the trial before a British military tribunal in Hamburg (1946) against the owners of the Tesch and Stabenow firm and others for supplying ZYKLON B gas to kill prisoners; the Nuremberg trial held by the United States (1948) against Carl Krauch and 22 others for "exploiting" Auschwitz prisoners (see I.G. FARBEN TRIAL); and the jury trial held before the State Court in Frankfurt am Main (1971) against Bruno Beger and a co-defendant for taking part in the killing of over 80 Auschwitz prisoners for the purpose of establishing a collection of skulls and skeletons. Finally, trials of Auschwitz criminals took place in the German Democratic Republic (for example, against the camp doctor Horst Fischer) and in Austria.

A. St.

Auslandsdeutsche. *See* Foreign Germans.

Auslandsorganisation. *See* Foreign Organization.

Auslese. *See* Selection.

Ausmerze. *See* Culling out.

Ausrichtung (alignment), favorite National Socialist word, borrowed from military usage, for external and internal "normalization" of the movement's followers (see VOLK COMRADE). External uniformity of dress corresponded to inner ideological alignment regarding NS goals.

Aussenpolitisches Amt der NSDAP. *See* Foreign Policy Office of the NSDAP.

Ausserordentliche Befriedungsaktion. *See* Extraordinary Pacification Operation.

Austria, federal state southeast of the German Reich's border; area, approximately 84,000 sq km (32,432 sq miles); population, 6.7 million (1930). The "German remnant" of the Habs-

burg Empire was denied the uniformly desired ANSCHLUSS with Germany by the peace treaty of SAINT-GERMAIN-EN-LAYE (September 10, 1919). After the collapse of the Great Coalition between Social Democrats and Christian Socials under Karl RENNER (June 10, 1920), Austria was faced with four fundamental contradictions, which prevented domestic peace and hindered the development of a national identity: (1) the glorified historical memory of an Old Austria; (2) ideological and partisan polarization between the anti-Marxist bourgeois bloc (consisting of Christian Socials under Ignaz Seipel [chancellor, 1922–1924 and 1926–1929], the Great-German People's Party, and the Land League) and the Austro-Marxist camp, which was intensified by paramilitary conflicts between the Home Guards and the Republican Defense League (*see* AUSTROFASCISM); (3) the social conflict between the industrialized "red" metropolis and bureaucratic hydrocephalus, Vienna (with 25 percent of Austria's population), and the overwhelmingly agrarian and conservative federal states, which after the dissolution of the Danube monarchy were incapable of feeding the capital sufficiently (causing hunger riots, 1918–1922); and, finally, (4) disagreement over the meaning of the Anschluss between Christian Socials who wanted the state's independence and Social Democrats who hoped for an "Anschluss with socialism" from a merger with the German state.

Austria. September 11, 1933: Chancellor Engelbert Dollfuss proclaims a corporatist constitution.

Austria. Propaganda to stay the course: "Capitulation—never! Vienna is declared a defense area. Women and children are advised to leave the city."

With the catastrophic results of the world economic crisis (the collapse of Austria's Creditanstalt bank on March 11, 1931), and with increasing pressure and agitation from Berlin, attempts by Engelbert DOLLFUSS (1932–1934) and Kurt von SCHUSCHNIGG (1934–1938) to preserve Austria's internal peace and external independence failed, despite such measures as a *coup d'état* (in March 1933, suspension of parliament and dissolution of the Republican Defense League); the banning of the NSDAP (June 19, 1933); the founding of the FATHERLAND FRONT; and the creation of an authoritarian CORPORATIST STATE, which was oriented toward Catholic social teachings and Italian Fascism. One price of these attempts was a bloody civil war in February 1934 over the banning of the Social Democratic party. Austria was isolated in its foreign policy and defenseless because of the failure of "collective security," the APPEASEMENT policy of the Western powers, and the Berlin-Rome AXIS ("the spit on which Austria will be roasted brown"). Thus it had to take the "German path," by way of the JULY AGREEMENT of 1936 and the Anschluss in 1938, on to the dissolution of its statehood as the "Eastern March" (OSTMARK).

B.-J. W.

Austrofascism, Austrian variety of fascism, represented especially by the armed self-defense leagues of the Home Guards (Heimwehren) in the 1920s and 1930s. The ideology of Austrofascism was first fed from nationalist sources and *völkisch* ideas after the collapse of the multi-ethnic Habsburg state. The Home Guards attracted a heterogeneous group with the potential to protest against the new democratic Austria and against Marxist elements in its constitution and government. Encouraged by Christian Socials and Great-Germans, and supported by industry, they developed into fighting leagues of the bourgeois camp for opposing the worker organizations of the Social Democrats and the Republican Defense League. Fascist tendencies peaked after the July unrest in 1927, under the influence of Othmar SPANN. Massive

Austrofascism. Veterans of the First World War as members of the Austrian Home Guards.

financial help began to arrive from Fascist Italy, whose programmatic influence was noticeable in the so-called Korneuburg Oath of May 18, 1930: rejection of parliamentarianism; demands for a state seizure of power and for overcoming the liberal-capitalist economic system and class struggle; and the FÜHRER PRINCIPLE.

Similarities between Austrofascism and early National Socialism are undeniable, but the further development of the Austrofascist concept into an Austrian CORPORATIST STATE made the differences clear. After Austria adopted a corporatist constitution on May 1, 1934, Catholic and bourgeois support for Austrofascism under Chancellor Engelbert DOLLFUSS led to unbridgeable opposition to National Socialism. The Home Guards, which some National Socialists had joined as early as 1933, participated actively in the defeat of the National Socialist putsch of July 25, 1934. Thereafter, followers of the NSDAP filled DETENTION CAMPS. On the other hand, after the ANSCHLUSS in 1938, Spann, the ideological foster father of Austrofascism, was arrested and was thereafter banned from teaching. Home Guard leader Ernst Rüdiger Prince STARHEMBERG went into exile.

Autarky, general self-sufficiency in food and raw materials; under National Socialist rule, both an ideological goal and an economic strategy for rearmament. At the center of the NS LIVING SPACE concept was the striving for national independence. In rejecting industrial society, the life of "free peasants on their own soil" became almost a substitute religion. The effects of the WORLD ECONOMIC CRISIS gave support to ideas of an autarkic ECONOMY UNDER NATIONAL SOCIALISM that would be untouched by such crises. However, since Germany could not support itself, the NS Living Space theory gained credibility. "Autarky in a large-scale economic space" promised to satisfy the political motives of power and race, as well as to open new export markets. After 1933, FOREIGN TRADE was relatively soon subordinated to these goals. But concerns regarding the economics and strategy of weapons procurement also played an important role during the period of rearmament and the war. The experience of the First World War demonstrated the importance of the economy's ability to function (*see* WAR ECONOMY). In the short and the intermediate run, the striving for autarky would protect rearmament against a blockade; in the long run, it would serve the

creation of a closed European economy under German leadership.

V. B.

Authoritarian regime (*autoritäre Regime*), form of rule in which all power is derived from one person, group, or party, without the mediation of other political groups, and without control over the executive. The PRESIDIAL CABINETS functioning at the end of the Weimar Republic were authoritarian in their approach. The National Socialists rejected the classification of the "Führer State" as an authoritarian regime because its authority was rooted in "the close tie between leadership and *Volk*." But with its absolute claims, the personal dictatorship of Hitler was a perfect authoritarian regime, which the precise term "total state" described (*see* TOTALITARIANISM).

Autobahn, limited-access highway intended exclusively for automobile traffic, originally also called *Nurautostrasse* ("only-autos street") and *Kraftfahrtbahn* (motorway); among the most important public-works projects of the Third Reich, in terms of transportation technology and symbolism: "The mission of the Reich Autobahn is to become Adolf Hitler's road. . . . To honor him, not only today, but for generations to come." The first Autobahn-like road was the "Avus," near Berlin, 8.9 km (about 5.5 miles) long, completed in 1921. It was planned in 1912 by the Automobil-Verkehrs- und Uebungs-Strasse GmbH (Automobile, Transport, and Maneuver Road, Ltd). In 1922, a *Kraftwagenstrasse* (motorcar road) 20 km (about 12.4 miles) long between Cologne and Bonn was opened.

The growth of automobile traffic during the 1920s created the need for long-distance roads that would make possible "great speeds with increased safety," a goal that was not feasible at the time for reasons of transportation technology and economics. Preliminary work for the Autobahn was done first by such semiprivate associations as the Research Group for Automobile Road Construction (Studiengesellschaft für Automobilstrassenbau; STUFA), founded in 1924, and the Association to Prepare for the Hamburg-Frankfurt-Basel Auto Road (Verein zur Vorbereitung der Autostrasse Hamburg-Frankfurt-Basel; HAFRABA), founded in 1926, which planned the Frankfurt-Mannheim-Heidelberg stretch as the first section.

The NSDAP, on the other hand, began with a statewide concept: as early as June 27, 1933, Hitler promulgated the Law to Create a "Reich

Autobahn" Agency (RAB) under Julius DORP-
MÜLLER, and appointed engineer Fritz TODT as
"General Inspector of the German Road Sys-
tem." The HAFRABA became the GEZUVOR,
or Gesellschaft zur Vorbereitung der Reichs-
Autobahn (Society to Prepare for the Reich
Autobahn). The law first proposed the following
stretches, a total of 6,900 km (4,278 miles):

1. Lübeck-Hamburg-Hannover-Kassel-Frankfurt
2. Stettin-Berlin-Leipzig-Hof-Nuremberg-
   Munich
3. Aachen-Cologne-Magdeburg-Berlin
4. Saarbrücken-Kaiserslautern-Mainz-Frankfurt-
   Fulda-Erfurt-Leipzig-Dresden-Breslau-
   Beuthen
5. Saarbrücken-Landau-Bruchsal-
   Ludwigshafen-Stuttgart-Ulm-Munich-
   Berchtesgaden
6. Hamburg-Wittenberg-Spandau-Berlin-
   Glogau-Breslau

On September 23, 1933, Hitler broke ground
for the Autobahn in Frankfurt. The first RAB
section, the Frankfurt-Darmstadt stretch, was
opened on May 19, 1935; by December 15,
1938, 3,000 km (1,860 miles) were finished.

In terms of construction technology, most of
the Autobahn had a breadth of 24 m (78.7 feet)
at the crown, divided into two lanes, each 7.5 m
(24.6 feet) wide. They were separated by a
middle strip 5 m (16.4 feet) wide; each side had
an edge strip of 2 m (6.6 feet). The roadway
consisted mostly of tamped concrete 20 cm (7.8
inches) thick. Autobahn routes were to blend
into the landscape, harmoniously "swerving" or
with "bold curves," and were conceived as
gigantic total artworks: "Fulfillment of the simple transportation function is not the ultimate
meaning of German road construction. The
German road must be an expression of its landscape and an expression of the German essence"
(Todt, 1934). Bridges, in particular, whose architecture was oriented on models of the 19th
century, were meant to be massive works of art
and "symbols of eternity"; thus, most were
constructed with hewn natural stone.

Such costly construction, intended "to last
many hundreds of years," was possible only in a
totalitarian state, which had no controls to observe, which could simply confiscate or transform land, and which had an army of laborers to
use at will. WORK CREATION had been the
central justification for Autobahn construction
even among private planners: "Nowhere can so
many unskilled workers find employment as in
road building" (HAFRABA, 1931). After 1933

Autobahn. Hitler inspects the work on the Mangfall
Bridge in the summer of 1935.

employment offices sent hundreds of thousands
of jobless men to the Autobahn construction sites
(refusal to go resulted in loss of unemployment
support). Although the industrial branches associated with construction flourished, wages remained low, even after unemployment declined;
moreover, concentration camp prisoners and foreign workers were employed (especially to break
stones). Most of the workers lived apart from
their families in paramilitary-like barracks (see
TODT ORGANIZATION).

Autobahn planning included military perspectives from early on. Transportation policymakers intoned: "Adolf Hitler's roads are roads
to peace. But, needless to say, the motorized
units of the new and strong German Wehrmacht
also roll along on them when there is a need to
secure the existence and right to live of the
German Volk" (the magazine Strasse [Street],
1938). Short-term troop movements could be
achieved more quickly on the Autobahn than by
rail; thus Gen. Heinz Guderian could declare in
1940: "We have enjoyed the blessings of the
Reich Autobahn on the march to liberate Vienna, and then on the march to the Sudetenland,

on the march against Czechoslovakia, against Poland, and against the Western powers. What a joy to march within Reich territory." During the war, parts of the Autobahn were destroyed; nonetheless, it is one of the few National Socialist monuments that could be used largely unchanged in postwar Germany. Its reputation has also proved to be lasting: in apologetic portrayals of the National Socialists, "Hitler's" Autobahn offers an important set piece.

H. H.

Automobile industry. *See* Motorization.

"Auwi," casual nickname within the SA for Prince AUGUST WILHELM of Prussia.

Auxiliary Caravan (*Hilfszug*), motorized supply column for mass meetings of the NSDAP and its organizations. The "Bavaria" unit was especially famous, and was glorified by propaganda as the "only mass supply caravan in the world": formed in 1933, it included 265 vehicles and could deliver provisions for 250,000 persons daily.

Auxiliary Fellowship for Reciprocity (Hilfsgemeinschaft auf Gegenseitigkeit; HIAG), association in the Federal Republic of Germany of former WAFFEN-SS soldiers; its first chairman was Paul HAUSSER. The purpose of the HIAG is to overcome the consequences of the war for veterans of the Waffen-SS (numbering about 300,000 to 400,000). Their situation was made particularly difficult by their collective classification as members of a "criminal organization" in the NUREMBERG TRIALS, since qualifications of this judgment did not sink into the general consciousness. Foreign-policy considerations also prevented these soldiers from being treated as the equivalent of Wehrmacht veterans until 1961.

After rather moderate beginnings, the embitterment of this "army of the despised" (*Armee der Geächteten*) produced an urge for justification that led to a growing disdain for historical truth and occasionally verged on neo-Nazism. Although the HIAG is officially nonpartisan, connections between it and right-radical circles are evident. Thus, the organization was cited in

Axis. Visit of Il Duce to Berlin in 1937. From left: War Minister Werner von Blomberg, Mussolini, Hitler, and Army Supreme Commander Werner von Fritsch.

the Interior Ministry's report on the protection of the constitution from 1979 to 1982. Its assemblies are regularly accompanied by protest demonstrations. The association's organ (since 1956) is *Der Freiwillige* (The Volunteer).

Axis (*Achse*), Berlin-Rome (also the Axis; Axis powers), term for the close foreign-policy relationship between Germany and Italy after Hitler's support for the Italian annexation of ABYSSINIA. Hans FRANK claimed credit for coining the term: at a meeting with Galeazzo CIANO in September 1936, he used the metaphor of a European political wagon, which must be driven forward on the "axis of Fascism and National Socialism." The terminology was popularized through a speech by MUSSOLINI on November 1, 1936, in Milan, a few weeks after Berlin's formal recognition of Italy's Abyssinian Empire (October 24, 1936); in it he referred to the common German-Italian support for FRANCO in the SPANISH CIVIL WAR. The Axis was expanded ideologically through Italy's entrance into the ANTI-COMINTERN PACT (November 6, 1937), and militarily and economically through the PACT OF STEEL (May 22, 1939). The term was later applied to the partners of the THREE-POWER AGREEMENT (September 27, 1940), Germany, Italy, and Japan, so that a Berlin-Rome-Tokyo Axis was spoken of. The term "Axis powers" became accepted for the states allied with Germany in the Second World War. The Axis ended with the Italian armistice in September 1943.

Axmann, Arthur, b. Hagen, February 18, 1913, Hitler Youth functionary. Axmann entered the HITLER YOUTH (HJ) as a 15-year-old gymnast, distinguished himself in the organization of National Socialist (NS) youth cells (*see* NATIONAL SOCIALIST WORKPLACE CELL ORGANIZATION), and entered the Reich HJ leadership in 1932. After the Seizure of Power he assumed leader-

Arthur Axmann.

ship of the social office of the REICH YOUTH LEADERSHIP, built up the state vocational training agency, and founded the REICH VOCATIONAL COMPETITION FOR GERMAN YOUTH, in which over a million young workers participated every year. As a soldier on the western front in 1939–1940, Axmann was appointed by Hitler as the successor to Baldur von SCHIRACH as Reich Youth Führer on August 8, 1940. Axmann mandated a strict program to militarize youth for the HJ, himself serving as a bad example: although he had lost an arm on the eastern front in 1941, this did not prevent him from allowing HJ groups to be used increasingly as combat reserves. In late April 1945 he spent some time in the Führer bunker, but left Berlin at the last moment. Arrested in December 1945, he was sentenced to three years and three months' imprisonment in May 1949, which was considered as time already served. In 1958 a West Berlin court levied on Axmann, then working as a salesman, a large monetary fine for inciting youth. His participation in further NS crimes was denied.

Babi Yar, ravine near Kiev where on September 29–30, 1941, 33,771 Jewish men, women, and children were murdered by Sonderkommando (SK) 4a (*see* SPECIAL COMMANDOS) of Einsatzgruppe C (*see* EINSATZGRUPPEN), assisted by two commando detachments of the "Russia-South" police regiment. Shortly after the conquest of Kiev, placards were posted calling upon the city's Jews to report to a specific place on September 29, 1941, for the purpose of resettlement. In an enormous column they were led to the ravine, where they were shot in groups. After the executions were completed, engineers blasted the rims of the ravine, burying the corpses under the soil. The commando report concluded: "Although at first the participation of only about 5,000 to 6,000 Jews was expected, over 30,000 reported. Because of very skillful organizing they believed in their resettlement until immediately before the execution" (Situation Report 128, November 3, 1941). The commanding officer of SK 4a, Paul BLOBEL, was sentenced to death at the OHLENDORF TRIAL and executed. The state court (*Landgericht*) in Darmstadt sentenced numerous members of the commandos to long prison terms in 1968. The Babi Yar massacre is the theme of a poem by the Russian writer Yevgeny Yevtushenko that is directed against antisemitism.

Baby Division, ironic but respectful Anglo-American nickname for the Twelfth SS Tank Division "HITLER YOUTH."

Bach-Zelewski, Erich von dem, b. Lauenberg (Pomerania), March 3, 1899; d. Munich, March 8, 1972, SS-*Obergruppenführer* (November 1941). Germany's youngest army volunteer in November 1914, Bach-Zelewski was a company commander by the end of the war. He then served in the Silesian border patrol and the Reichswehr. He joined the NSDAP in 1930 and the SS a year later, becoming, successively, Führer of the SS districts (*Oberabschnitte*)

Erich von dem Bach-Zelewski.

Northeast (Königsberg) and Southeast (Breslau). He served in the Reichstag from 1932 to 1944. As early as the RÖHM AFFAIR, he demonstrated particular brutality. Promoted to *Gruppenführer* when the Russian Campaign began (June 22, 1941), he was Higher SS and Police Leader (*Höherer SS- und Polizeiführer*) for the area of the Central Army Group (Heeresgruppe Mitte).

In July 1943 Himmler entrusted Bach-Zelewski with "combating gangs" (*Bandenbekämpfung*) on the entire eastern front. This entailed not only the persecution of partisans, but above all the persecution and liquidation of Jews. Bach-Zelewski was awarded the Knight's Cross for crushing the WARSAW UPRISING. After the end of the war, he made himself available as a prosecution witness at Nuremberg, and thus escaped extradition to the Soviet Union. It was not until 1949 that a German appeals court sentenced him to 10 years at hard labor (which he never served). In 1961 Bach-Zelewski was sentenced to 58 months' imprisonment for his participation in murders during the Röhm Affair, and in 1962 to life imprisonment for the murder of political enemies in 1933. His involvement in the shooting of Jews in the east—"There are no more Jews in Estonia," he wrote on October 31, 1941—remained unpunished.

Backe, Herbert, b. Batum (Caucasus), May 1, 1896; d. Nuremberg, April 7, 1947, National Socialist politician and SS-*Obergruppenführer.* Educated in Tiflis (Georgia), during the First World War Backe was subject to Russian internment. He emigrated to Germany, studied agriculture in Göttingen, and worked as an estate manager. An SA member from 1922 (in 1923 he joined the NSDAP), Backe first appeared in politics as a speaker for the NSDAP against the YOUNG PLAN. In 1933 he was appointed by Walther DARRÉ first to the post of Reich commissioner, then in October of that year as state secretary in the Reich Ministry for Nutrition and Agriculture. In 1936 Backe became head of the nutrition task force (*Geschäftsgruppe*) within the framework of the FOUR-YEAR PLAN. A capable organizer who preferred efficiency to ideology, and a supporter of strong state control of the economy, Backe crowded out the dreamy peasant-enthusiast (*Bauerntümler*) Darré. In May 1942 Backe took over Darré's functions as minister and leader of German peasants (*Reichsbauernführer*). On April 1, 1944, he was promoted to ministerial rank, which he retained in the DÖNITZ government. Backe committed suicide while in Allied custody.

Herbert Backe.

Badenweiler March, musical piece written by the military composer Georg Fürst (d. 1936) to commemorate the capture of the town of Badonviller in the Vosges mountain range (Meurthe-et-Moselle department). It was Hitler's favorite march. According to a police ordinance of May 17, 1939, the march was to be publicly performed only in Hitler's presence. Therefore it has been largely in disrepute since 1945.

Badge of Honor for Caring for the German Volk (Ehrenzeichen für deutsche Volkspflege), order-like award created by Hitler on May 1, 1939, for services in the social sector: the WINTER RELIEF AGENCY, NATIONAL SOCIALIST VOLK WELFARE, medical and rescue work, care of foreign and ethnic Germans, and so on. A replacement for Red Cross awards, it was conferred in four classes and consisted of a white-enameled gold Balkenkreuz with Reich eagle and swastika.

Badges of Honor of the NSDAP (Ehrenzeichen der NSDAP), several medallions or crosses awarded as medals that could also be worn on a military uniform: the BLOOD ORDER (the highest badge of honor), the Golden Badge of Honor (GOLDEN PARTY BADGE), the Nuremberg Party Badge of 1929, the Badge of the 1931 Braunschweig SA Rally, the Traditional *Gau* Badge, and the Golden Hitler Youth Badge.

Badoglio, Pietro, b. Grazzano Monteferrato (now Grazzano Badoglio), September 28, 1871; d. there, November 1, 1956, Italian marshal and politician. From 1919 to 1921, Badoglio was chief of the General Staff. He manifested a wavering attitude toward Mussolini until 1924, when he sought an approach to the latter. In 1925 Badoglio again became chief of the General Staff, and in 1926 he was made marshal. From 1929 to 1933 he was governor of Libya, and in 1935 he was supreme commander in ABYSSINIA (in 1936–1937, viceroy). Badoglio viewed Italy's dependence upon Germany with concern and in 1939–1940 supported a neutral course, while at the same time offering no opposition in serving Mussolini's imperialistic policy. He was forced to retire after the collapse of the attack on Greece (*see* BALKAN CAMPAIGN). Badoglio then established contact with Allied representatives. After Mussolini's overthrow he was charged by the king with forming a government; Badoglio negotiated an armistice with the Anglo-American forces, and declared war on Germany on October 13, 1943. In 1944 he had to defer to Ivanoe Bonomi as head of government.

Pietro Badoglio.

Badoglio lost his senate seat because of his cooperation with the Fascists, but he was rehabilitated in 1947.

Baeck, Leo, b. Lissa (Posen), May 23, 1873; d. London, November 2, 1956, Jewish theologian. Baeck was rabbi in Oppeln (1897), in Düsseldorf (1907), and in Berlin (1912–1943). He was a lecturer at the Institute for Judaic Studies (Hochschule für die Wissenschaft des Judentums) in Berlin. Not an outspoken opponent of ZIONISM, Baeck made a plea for improved mutual understanding of religions through better information; this was the aim of his main work,

Leo Baeck.

Das Wesen des Judentums (The Nature of Judaism; 1905). After 1933 he had to recognize the failure of this idea. As president of the REICH REPRESENTATION OF GERMAN JEWS from 1933, he refused to leave Germany, and in 1943 was transported to Theresienstadt after much persecution and interrogation by the Gestapo. As head of the Theresienstadt camp council he tried to console his fellow believers, most of whom were doomed to die. He himself witnessed the liberation and found a new home in London, where he tried to pick up again the torn thread of German-Jewish dialogue. The Leo Baeck Institute, founded in 1954, with branches in London and New York City, serves this purpose.

Baedecker attacks (*Baedecker-Angriffe*), bombing attacks carried out by the German Luftwaffe (March 23–October 31, 1942) on British cities with valuable cultural monuments, such as Canterbury, Exeter, Norwich, and York (*see* AIR BATTLE FOR ENGLAND). Named for the famous German guidebooks, the Baedecker attacks were described as "vengeance" for British bombings of Lübeck, Rostock, and other cities of value to cultural history.

Baeumler, Alfred, b. Neustadt an der Tafelfichte (Bohemia), November 19, 1887; d. Eningen bei Reutlingen, March 3, 1968, German philosopher and educator. In 1929, Baeumler became a professor at the Technical Institute in Dresden; in 1933, a professor of "political pedagogy" in Berlin; soon thereafter he became head of the "Academic Office" (Amt Wissenschaft) under Alfred ROSENBERG. Baeumler welcomed the BOOK BURNING in May 1933 as an elimination of "toxins," and called for "replacement of the educated man [*Gebildeter*] by the soldier-type" even in intellectual life. According to Baeumler, a direct path led from Nietzsche's "will to power" to the National Socialist Seizure of Power, which introduced a "masculine age."

Baeumler made a name for himself especially as an ideologist of sports; he developed "political physical education," which rejected both "individualistic striving for records" and games, which should be left to women and children. He advocated instead the "politically oriented team," as it had already been proposed by the "father of gymnastics," Friedrich JAHN, which would serve the "development of *völkisch* strength." Sports thus became an auxiliary military discipline in accordance with the NS concept of MILITARY SPORTS; it also could help demonstrate "racial superiority." Along with numerous separate publications, Baeumler published *Weltanschauung und Schule* (Worldview and School), a journal of radical culture politics.

Balbo, Italo, b. Quartesana (Ferrara), June 5, 1896; d. Tobruk, June 28, 1940, Italian Fascist politician. Balbo was one of Mussolini's first followers; the organizer of the March on Rome (October 28, 1922); in 1923, commanding general of the Fascist militia; in 1925, deputy state secretary; from 1929 to 1933, minister for aviation; in 1934, governor of Libya. As advocate of a social-revolutionary course, Balbo came into constant conflict with Mussolini, with whom, however, he later came to terms. New strains arose after the adoption in 1938 of Fascist legislation on Jews patterned on the National Socialist example, especially since Balbo advocated pro-Western neutrality. An ardent aviator, Balbo was mistakenly shot down by his own antiaircraft guns.

Balfour Declaration, pronouncement by British foreign minister Arthur Balfour (1848–1930) in a letter of November 2, 1917, addressed to the Zionist World Congress. Balfour promised to facilitate, as best as he could, the "establishment of a national homeland for the Jewish people in Palestine." The Balfour Declaration was interpreted by Zionists as a binding promise to create a Jewish state on the soil of the territory under British mandate; its opponents regarded it only as an assurance of a right to life and residence. By referring to the Balfour Declaration, the

Arthur James Balfour.

German Jews who were being persecuted in the Third Reich in particular tried to extract permission to immigrate. Out of regard for the Arab population, however, the British interpreted the declaration very narrowly; the White Paper of May 1939 expressly rejected the formation of a Jewish state.

Balkan Campaign, summary term for the operations of the German Wehrmacht against Greece and Yugoslavia from April 6, 1941, to June 1 of that year. After the Italians attacked Greece from their Albanian base on October 28, 1940, the Balkan Peninsula became a war zone. Following initial Italian success, the Greeks had gone over to a counterattack and penetrated deep into Italian Albania. To prevent a defeat of his ally, Hitler ordered a plan for German assistance (Order No. 18 of November 12, 1940) and an attack on Greece (Order No. 20 of December 13 for Operation "Marita"). As a reaction to the requisite deployment of German troops in Bulgaria, Great Britain landed about 58,000 men in Greece before April 24, 1941.

Nearly simultaneously, a *coup d'état* in YUGO-SLAVIA brought down the government of Prince Paul, which was friendly to Germany. This made Hitler decide to "smash Yugoslavia militarily and as a state" (Order No. 25). For the Balkan Campaign, 8 German divisions lined up on April 6, 1941, against Greece, and 15 divisions against Yugoslavia, supported by 780 aircraft. After breaking through the Greek Metaxas Line, German tanks reached Salonika on April 9. The threat from the north forced the Greeks to abandon Albania. In the meantime, the 32 Yugoslav divisions were beaten or fell apart, so that General Kalafatovich had to sign the Yugoslav capitulation on April 17. The same day, the British Supreme Command ordered the evacuation of Greece; three days later, the Greek Epirus Army capitulated. On April 27, German tanks rolled into Athens, and on April 30, German occupation of the Greek mainland (including the Peloponnesus) was completed. The Germans took 344,000 Yugoslav, 218,000 Greek, and 10,682 British soldiers prisoner. German losses amounted to 2,559 dead, 3,169 missing in action, and 5,820 wounded. The Luftwaffe lost 158 aircraft and the Royal Air Force 209.

Crete remained the last British bastion, defended by 31,000 British and 10,258 Greek soldiers. For its conquest the Wehrmacht put in readiness the Eleventh Air Corps (General Student), together with a paratrooper division and a

Balkan Campaign. German paratroopers with captured English soldiers.

mountain division, which landed on May 20, 1941. They were assisted by sea transport groups, which suffered heavy losses at the hands of the British navy. After seven days the defenders of Crete gave up, and evacuated the island by June 1. The British lost a total of 15,743 soldiers and 2,011 sailors; 10,700 British and 5,000 Greek troops were taken captive. Heavy German losses (6,580 men, including 3,250 dead and missing) led to an abandonment of future airborne operations. The Balkan Campaign had, moreover, delayed the long-planned RUSSIAN CAMPAIGN by several weeks, and thus possibly fatefully determined its outcome.

G. H.

Balkanization (*Balkanisierung*), National Socialist catchword to denote the results of the PARIS SUBURBAN TREATIES for central and southeastern Europe. Here the victorious powers had created—as previously existed only on the Balkan Peninsula—confused political conditions by setting up numerous rival states in the territory of the former Central Powers. The accusation of Balkanization was picked up by the National Socialists in their struggle against the Versailles treaty.

Baltendeutsche. *See* Baltic Germans.

Baltic Germans (*Baltendeutsche*), Germans (about 8 percent of the population) who had emigrated to the Baltic territory as a result of German colonization of the east since 1200. As large landed proprietors, they formed the upper social crust, and long preserved their independence, even under the increasing pressure of

Russification. After the First World War, the Baltic Germans received the right to self-government in the BALTIC STATES, while losing their landed property. Their position became untenable only after the surrender of these states in the secret supplementary protocol to the GERMAN-SOVIET NONAGGRESSION PACT of August 23, 1939. On the basis of individual treaties, about 70,000 Baltic Germans were resettled, primarily in the Warthegau and DANZIG–WEST PRUSSIA, in October 1939.

Baltic states, collective term for the states of ESTONIA, LATVIA, and LITHUANIA, which came into being after the First World War. They all lost their independence after the demarcation of German and Soviet spheres of influence in the secret supplementary protocol to the GERMAN-SOVIET NONAGGRESSION PACT of August 23, 1939. The Baltic states remained Soviet republics after the Second World War. The main body of the German population (the BALTIC GERMANS) was resettled in the Reich in 1939.

Baltikum, coastal strip on the Baltic Sea from East Prussia to Lake Peipus (on the Russian-Estonian border); *see* BALTIC STATES.

Bamberg Führer Conference (*Bamberger Führertagung*) of the NSDAP, meeting of *Gau* leaders of the newly founded party, scheduled by Hitler for February 14, 1926. During Hitler's imprisonment after the failed putsch of November 9, 1923, struggles had broken out in various wings of the party. The choice of locale clearly indicated Hitler's desire to play off the weight of his south German following against the social revolution–oriented "alliance" (*Arbeitsgemeinschaft*) of the north and west German *Gau* leaders. Ostensibly at issue was the party's attitude on the question of the EXPROPRIATION OF PRINCES. Hitler's programmatic speech on the topic, however, also ended the ideological dissension: antisocialism and the nationalist-populist notions of Gottfried FEDER prevailed against Gregor STRASSER. The Bamberg meeting prevented the drifting apart of the party's wings and marked the beginning of the career of the young Goebbels, who switched from the Strasser camp to Hitler and soon became *Gauleiter* of Berlin.

Bank for International Settlement (Bank für Internationalen Zahlungsausgleich; BIZ), international bank with headquarters in Basel; it was established after a conference at The Hague on January 20, 1930. The bank's purpose was settlement of the German REPARATIONS payments, which the YOUNG PLAN, signed at the same time, had renegotiated.

R. B.

Bank of German Labor, Inc. (Bank der Deutschen Arbeit A.G.), financial institution of the GERMAN LABOR FRONT (DAF). Founded in 1924 as the Bank of Workers, Employees, and Civil Servants by organizations representing these groups, it was taken over by the DAF and renamed after the destruction of the TRADE UNIONS on May 2, 1933.

Bann (ban), Old German word meaning area of command authority (thus, ban-mile). It was revived by the HITLER YOUTH (HJ) to designate a division of four to six *Stämme* (stems), or subbans, led by an HJ *Bannführer*. The *Bann* corresponded to the *Untergau* in the League of German Girls, and to the *Jungbann* in the JUNGVOLK.

Banse, Ewald, b. Braunschweig, May 23, 1883; d. there, October 31, 1953, German geographer. Banse was a professor at the technical college in his native city. Allied propaganda cited Banse's main work, *Raum und Volk im Weltkriege* (Space and *Volk* in the World War; 1925), as proof of Germany's war lust. Banse advocated the union of all areas settled by Germans in a Great-German Reich extending far beyond the 1914 frontiers. To achieve this he expressly demanded military action, for the warrior was to be the carrier of the coming rule of "Nordic nobility."

Barbaric (*barbarisch*), term often given a positive interpretation in National Socialist usage (comparable terms: brutal, merciless), which aimed to convey decisiveness and HARDNESS as against "simpering about humanity" (*Humanitätsduselei*).

Barbarossa Jurisdictional Decree (*Barbarossa-Gerichtsbarkeiterlass*), "Order concerning the Exercise of Military Jurisdiction in the 'Barbarossa' Region [Soviet Union], regarding Special Troop Measures." The decree was issued by the Wehrmacht High Command (OKW) at Hitler's orders on May 13, 1941. The Barbarossa decree, named after the code designation for the RUSSIAN CAMPAIGN, proclaimed that "any wrongful acts committed by enemy civilians" no longer fell under MILITARY JURISDICTION but were to be punished according to the decision of individual troop commanders. Against localities guilty of "insidious or treacherous" attacks, "collective violent measures" (*kollektive Gewaltmassnahmen*) were stipulated. Offenses by German soldiers against enemy civilians were not liable for prosecution. Like the COMMISSAR ORDER, the Barbarossa decree evoked strong criticism within the officer corps; it was transmitted by Army Commander in Chief Walther von BRAUCHITSCH, together with an order to strictly preserve traditional "manly discipline" (*Manneszucht*).

"Barbarossa" Operation, military code name for Germany's attack on the USSR on June 22, 1941 (*see* RUSSIAN CAMPAIGN).

Barbie, Klaus (alias Altmann, Willms, Müller), b. Bad Godesberg, October 25, 1913, SS-*Hauptsturmführer*. In 1935 Barbie joined the staff of the Western Division (Oberabschnitt West) of the SECURITY SERVICE (SD), later moving to the Dortmund office. In May 1940 he joined the foreign task force for Holland, Belgium, and France. He belonged to the Hitler Youth (April 1, 1933, to September 1, 1935), the SS (after September 26, 1935), and the NSDAP (after May 1, 1937).

German and French authorities sought Barbie after the war in connection with both war-related and National Socialist crimes that he was alleged to have committed between 1942 and 1944 as head of Section IV (Gestapo) of the headquarters of the commander of the Security Police and the SD in Lyons. On November 25, 1954, a military court in Lyons sentenced him to death in absentia. In the late 1960s Barbie was discovered in La Paz under the name of Klaus

Altmann, a Bolivian citizen. [United States counterintelligence, for which he had worked after the war, had assisted his escape.] Bolivia rejected French extradition demands. Similar demands by the German Federal Republic also remained unanswered. In early 1983 Barbie was expelled from Bolivia, captured during a stopover in Cayenne (French Guiana), and transported to France. [On July 4, 1987, the Rhône Court of Assizes sentenced him to life imprisonment for numerous crimes against humanity.]

Barkhorn, Gerhard, b. Königsberg, March 20, 1919; d. Frechen (near Cologne), January 12, 1983 (auto accident), German fighter pilot; the second in the record-list of "aces," with 301 planes shot down. In 1945 Barkhorn was a major in the Forty-fourth Fighter Squadron (jet fighter Me 262). He received the Iron Cross with Oak Leaves and Sword. He became a major general in the Bundeswehr in 1973, and retired in 1975.

Barlach, Ernst, b. Wedel (Holstein), January 2, 1870; d. Rostock, October 24, 1938, sculptor, dramatist, and graphic artist. In 1906 Barlach visited Russia; in 1909 he went to Florence on a scholarship from the German Artists' League. A friend of the author Thomas Däubler, from 1910 on Barlach resided in Güstrow (Mecklenburg). Active in literature after 1912, in 1919 he became a member of the Prussian Academy of the Arts; in 1923 he was awarded the Kleist Prize, and in 1925 he was elected to the Munich Academy of Fine Arts. During the National Socialist period, Barlach's works were considered "degenerate"; he himself was persecuted by the Gestapo. In 1937, 381 of his sculptures

Gerhard Barkhorn.

The Berserker, sculpture by Ernst Barlach.

were seized, and he was prohibited from exhibiting his works. Barlach's dramas, such as *Der blaue Boll* (The Blue Boll), were banned from the stage, and his books were burned. Suffering from persistent depression, Barlach died of a heart attack in 1938.

Barmat Scandal (*Barmat-Skandal*), corruption case in 1924–1925 involving the business of the Barmat brothers, Jews who had immigrated from Russia. The Reichstag appointed a committee to investigate rumors that the firm, which employed 14,000 people, had received official support through bribery. Although clear evidence was lacking, Postmaster General Höfle (CENTER party) had to resign, and former chancellor Gustav BAUER (Social Democratic Party of Germany; SPD) was expelled from his party in connection with the scandal. Both Communists and National Socialists (who charged "Judaization") made political capital of the case with propaganda hostile to the Weimar Republic.

Barmen Confessional Synod (*Barmer Bekenntnissynode*), conference of "representatives of Lutheran, Reformed, and United [Protestant] churches, free synods, church congresses [*Kirchentage*], and congregations" that took place in Barmen (now Wuppertal) from May 29 to 31, 1934. The delegates from a total of 19 among the 28 Evangelical state churches (*Landeskirchen*) were united in their opposition to the "synchronization" measures of the Reich Church regime under Ludwig MÜLLER. They also opposed the falsification of Christian doctrine through the National Socialist (NS) racist ideas being imposed by most church leaders with German-Christian leanings (*see* GERMAN CHRISTIANS; ARYAN PARAGRAPH).

The synod concluded with a "theological declaration" that formulated the basis of the Evangelical faith in six theses and six condemnations, and that rejected the totalitarian claims of the NS state, as well as state functions for the church. This document became the basic law for the CONFESSING CHURCH, which began to organize at this point: only the word of God as revealed through Christ was to be accepted as a basis for Christian behavior and pronouncement. The fact that the divergent Protestant tendencies came together in a common confession for the first time since the 16th century under the pressure of the NS revolution made the Barmen synod effective far beyond the CHURCH STRUGGLE. Organizationally, it legitimized the bodies of the Confessing Church as counterparts to the German-Christian church regime.

Bartels, Adolf, b. Wesselburen (Dithmarschen), November 15, 1862; d. Weimar, March 7, 1945, German writer. An artisan's son, Bartels studied literature. After 1895 a free-lance journalist in Weimar, he gained a reputation as a Hebbel scholar. In 1897 he wrote a history of German literature that was marked by racist evaluations and rabid antisemitism; it became a pioneering work for National Socialist literary reviews. According to Bartels, even authors whose names sounded Jewish, who wrote for the "Jewish press," or who were friendly with Jews were "contaminated with Jewishness." The noblest task of *völkisch* cultural policy would therefore be a radical DE-JEWING of the arts, and thus the "salvation of National Socialist Germany" (*National-sozialistisches Deutschlands Rettung*; 1924). Bartels's further literary productions, including *Die Dithmarscher* (1898), based on his native region, and *Martin Luther* (1903), are largely forgotten today.

Barth, Karl, b. Basel, May 10, 1886; d. there, December 10, 1968, Swiss Evangelical theologian. Barth was an assistant pastor in Geneva (1909) and a professor in Göttingen (1921), Münster (1925), and Bonn (1930). He belonged quite early to the religious socialists, and later joined the SPD (Social Democratic Party of Germany). He became known to a wider public through his commentary on *Romans* (1919), which clearly rejected political theology and saw human salvation only through the "predestined grace" (*Gnadenwahl*) of Jesus Christ. Barth argued that whatever theology might know of God it could grasp only in radically opposed statements. This so-called dialectical

Karl Barth.

theology, with its uncompromising return to divine revelation through the "Word," ignited church opposition to National Socialist efforts at subversion through the GERMAN CHRISTIANS. Barth's essay "Theologische Existenz heute" (Theological Existence Today) in the summer of 1933 became the basis for the theological declaration of the BARMEN CONFESSIONAL SYNOD, and thereby the foundation of the CONFESSING CHURCH. When Barth agreed to take the "oath of allegiance" only conditionally in late 1934, NS authorities used this for his dismissal. Barth accepted an invitation to Basel, where he taught until 1961 and worked on his uncompleted principal work, *Kirchliche Dogmatik* (Church Dogmatics; 14 vols.).

Barthel, Ludwig Friedrich, b. Marktbreit bei Kitzingen, June 12, 1898; d. Munich, February 14, 1962, German writer. Barthel served in the First World War and was a student in Munich; he was later an archivist (*Archivrat*) there. His poems, for example "Tannenburg: Ruf und Requiem" (Tannenburg: A Call and a Requiem; 1934), and such stories as "Das Leben ruft" (Life Calls; 1935), are influenced by the experience of war, which he made into a cult. Because of such tendencies, he venerated National Socialism, which he celebrated in such extravagant hymns as "Dom aller Deutschen" (The Cathedral of All Germans; 1938). Barthels also edited the letters of his friend Rudolf BINDING (1957).

Barthel, Max, b. Loschwitz (now part of Dresden), November 17, 1893; d. Waldbröl, June 17, 1975, German writer. A factory worker, Barthel was a member of the socialist youth movement; he was a frontline soldier from 1914 to 1918. He was co-founder of the Youth International in the Soviet Union in 1920, and was acquainted there with Lenin. In 1923 Barthel moved from the KPD (Communist Party of Germany) to the SPD (Social Democratic Party of Germany). He drew closer to National Socialism after the Seizure of Power; he was a reporter on Kraft durch Freude (*see* STRENGTH THROUGH JOY) trips, and a press correspondent during the war. In 1922 he had worked Communist ideas into the poem "Arbeiterseele" (The Worker's Soul), but in 1934 his novel *Das unsterbliche Volk* (The Immortal *Volk*) described "the transformation of a German worker [himself] from a Communist to a follower of the Führer." In a tone of resignation, Barthel titled his postwar autobiography *Kein Bedarf an Weltgeschichte* (No Need for World History; 1950).

Basic rights (*Grundrechte*), fundamental rights of a citizen vis-à-vis the state, guaranteed in the WEIMAR CONSTITUTION. Through the REICHSTAG FIRE DECREE of February 28, 1933 (*Reich Law Gazette* I, p. 83), the following basic civil rights were suspended: freedom of the person (Article 114); inviolability of the home (Article 115); secrecy in communication by letter, mail, telegraph, and telephone (Article 117); freedom to express opinions, including freedom of the press (Article 118); freedom of assembly (Article 123); freedom of association (Article 124); and the right to private property (Article 153). Between 1933 and 1945 there were no guaranteed basic rights, since the assurance of the individual's rights to freedom in the traditional constitutional sense was incompatible with National Socialist political theory and practice, which treated the individual "*Volk* comrade" (*Volksgenosse*) not as vested with his own rights vis-à-vis the state, but only as a member of a VOLK COMMUNITY.

A. v. B.

Battle for Cultivation (*Anbauschlacht*), agricultural counterpart to the BATTLE FOR WORK as related to WORK CREATION and AUTARKY efforts.

Battle for Production (*Erzeugungsschlacht*), propaganda motto related to AUTARKY efforts.

Battle for Work (*Arbeitsschlacht*), propaganda term for the totality of measures involved in WORK CREATION. Because of its military and activist sound, Battle for Work was one of Hitler's favorite terms until 1937 (the *de facto* end of unemployment). It was patterned after the Fascist Italian *battaglia del grano* (battle for grain).

Battle of Britain. *See* Air Battle for England.

Battle of the Atlantic (*Atlantikschlacht*), Second World War struggle over the western supply routes to England, and later to Allied troops in Europe (*see* NAVAL WAR).

Bauer, Gustav, b. Darkehmen (East Prussia), January 6, 1870; d. Berlin, September 16, 1944, German politician. Bauer worked as an office assistant; in 1903 he worked in the central secretariat of the Free Trade Unions; in 1912 he became an SPD (Social Democratic Party of Germany) Reichstag member; in 1918, labor minister. As chancellor, in June 1919 Bauer formed the cabinet that signed the Versailles treaty. He thereby became the quintessential representative of FULFILLMENT POLICY for the political Right, and a target of its anti-Republican propaganda. Resigning as chancellor after the KAPP PUTSCH, Bauer had responsibility for various ministries until 1922. In 1925 he was drawn into the BARMAT SCANDAL; he was expelled from the SPD, and resigned his Reichstag seat in 1928. Despite rapid rehabilitation, Bauer stayed away from politics.

Gustav Bauer.

Bauer, Josef Martin, b. Taufkirchen (Vils), March 11, 1901; d. Dorfen, March 15, 1970, German writer. Bauer's work had its origins in Bavarian vernacular poetry. He was a war correspondent in Russia; his reporting exuded a spirit of carefree soldiery and incorporated National Socialist propaganda about "subhumans." According to Bauer, the Red Army soldier was characterized by "soulless, animal-like behavior" (as in *Unterm Edelweiss in der Ukraine* [Under the Edelweiss in the Ukraine; 1943]). The same attitude glimmers through his extremely successful postwar novel, *So weit die Füsse tragen* (As Far as Feet Will Carry; 1955).

Bauer, Otto, b. Vienna, September 5, 1881; d. Paris, July 4, 1938, Austrian politician and lawyer. From a wealthy Jewish family of manufacturers, Bauer joined the radical wing of Austria's Social Democratic Party. After Russian captivity in 1918–1919, he became state secretary for foreign affairs. On March 2, 1919, Bauer concluded a secret agreement with the German foreign minister for an ANSCHLUSS of German Austria with Germany; this, however, was thwarted by the Allies' peace conditions. Considerably involved in drawing up the Austrian constitution, Bauer turned resolutely against authoritarian tendencies, and participated actively in the workers' uprising in Vienna in 1934. After its failure, he went into exile. Following Hitler's Seizure of Power, Bauer regarded the Anschluss he had earlier advocated as a threat to Austria's existence.

Bauern-. *See* Peasant.

Bauhaus, "Academy for Design" (Hochschule für Gestaltung), founded by Walter Gropius in 1919. As of 1925 it was located in Dessau; it dissolved in 1933. Teachers at the Bauhaus, such as Lionel Feininger and Wassily Kandinsky (denounced as "degenerate" after 1933), strove for a connection between art and functionality (as in furniture and wall coverings). The Bauhaus style in architecture—lack of ornamentation and limitation to basic elements—was considered by the National Socialists to be "Structural Bolshevism" (*Baubolschewismus*) and an expression of "emotional coldness that is contrary to the German nature."

Baukunst (building art), usual National Socialist Germanization of ARCHITECTURE.

Baum, Vicki, b. Vienna, January 24, 1888; d. Los Angeles, August 29, 1960, Austrian writer. Baum was an editor at the Ullstein publishing house from 1926 to 1931. Her principal literary work was *Menschen im Hotel* (People in a Hotel; 1929). In 1931 she went to Hollywood to work on its film version, *Grand Hotel* (1932). Because of her Jewish background, Baum did not return to Germany after the Seizure of Power. Her literary works were banned in the Third Reich. She became an American citizen in 1938.

Baumann, Hans, b. Amberg (Upper Palatinate), April 22, 1914, German writer and composer. Baumann was trained as a teacher. In 1934 he was invited by Baldur von Schirach to join the Reich Youth Leadership. As one of the most popular HITLER YOUTH poets, Baumann celebrated in song the "eternally German character," nature, the tiller of the soil, motherhood, and the "spirit of front-comradery," as in "Es zittern die morschen Knochen" (The brittle bones rattle . . .). His Nibelungen drama *Rüdiger von Bechelaren* (1939) was considered by contemporary critics the "song of songs" of "German military preparedness" and an "ideal open-air play." Baumann's nature and hiking songs, composed in folk-song style, are still sung, for example, "Gute Nacht, Kameraden" (Good Night, Comrades) and "Von allen blauen Hügeln" (From All the Blue Hills). Returned from Soviet captivity, Baumann became one of the most important writers of the new West German literature for children and youth. His adventure and true-life stories, some of which have won prizes, grappled with the past and stood for humanistic ideals; examples are *Der Sohn des Columbus* (The Son of Columbus; 1951) and *Ich zog mit Hannibal* (I Marched with Hannibal; 1960). Baumann also translated nu-

Bauhaus. Walter Gropius with models of his most important creations.

merous Russian poets, partly as a gesture of reparation.

H. H.

Baumbach, Werner, b. Cloppenburg, December 27, 1916; d. near Buenos Aires, October 20, 1953 (air crash), German Luftwaffe officer; a most successful bomber pilot. As a colonel with an appointment as a general of bomber pilots, Baumbach wrote a letter of protest to Göring in early 1945 against the senseless continuation of the war, offering to resign his post and relinquish his decorations. He was nonetheless left undisturbed, and was able to contribute to the peaceful surrender of Hamburg. After Allied captivity, Baumbach became an air force adviser in Argentina.

Werner Baumbach.

Bavarian People's Party (Bayerische Volkspartei; BVP), bourgeois party created on November 12, 1918, through a split in the CENTER party. (The party's paper was the *Bayrischer Kurier* [Bavarian Courier].) It absorbed the Center party in Bavaria, and became its rival on the national level on January 9, 1920, withdrawing from their Reichstag coalition. With its separatist origins, the BVP was a strong proponent of federalism. In 1922–1923 and from 1925 to 1932 the BVP belonged to governing coalitions in the Weimar Republic; from 1920 to 1933 it was the strongest party in Bavaria (*see* Heinrich HELD), a state that the party characterized as a "cell of national order" (*nationale Ordnungszelle*). Thus, despite its distance from the *völkisch* movement, it lent support to the HITLER PUTSCH. After the Reichstag elections of March 3, 1933, the BVP lost its parliamentary majority in Bavaria, voted for the ENABLING LAW, and dissolved itself on July 4, 1933.

Bavaud, Maurice, b. Neuenburg (Switzerland), January 15, 1916; d. Berlin-Plötzensee, May 14, 1941 (executed), Swiss would-be assassin. Bavaud began as a technical draftsman, but in 1934 he entered the seminary for priests in Saint Ilan (Brittany). At the seminary Bavaud met Marcel Gerbohay, who passed himself off as the tsar's son, and who intigated Bavaud to make an attempt on Hitler's life. In October 1938 Bavaud traveled to Germany, armed with a useless lady's pistol, but was unable to fire either during the memorial march to the Munich FELDHERRNHALLE (November 9) or at the Obersalzberg. Picked up for fare beating, Bavaud was unmasked, and was sentenced to death by the *Volk* Court on December 18, 1939. Gerbohay too was arrested, after the occupation of France, and was executed on April 9, 1943. The Bavaud case was partly responsible for the ban on the staging of Schiller's drama *Wilhelm Tell* (June 3, 1941).

Bayerische Volkspartei. *See* Bavarian People's Party.

Bayreuth Festivals (Bayreuther Festspiele), productions of Richard WAGNER's operas in his own Festival Hall in Bayreuth, first in 1876, and yearly from 1883. Since Wagner never saw his musical dramas achieve their full effect on the existing theatrical stages, he wanted to communicate "real emotional understanding" to an ideal public through "exemplary artistic performances" accessible to everyone. In the late 19th century a group of nationalist and *völkisch* artists, critics, and patrons banded together around Wagner. They saw in the festivals "the essence of Teutonism" (Prince Hohenlohe) and a "center of opposition" against "modern cultural degeneration." Wagner's reworking of Germanic mythology and his emphasis on the irrational and mythological coincided with the taste of his contemporaries, as did his orientation toward classicism and the cult-like nature of his productions.

Under the management of Winifred WAGNER (after 1930), the festivals took on a "decidedly *völkisch*-nationalist" character. A member of the NSDAP since 1926, Winifred was on friendly terms with Hitler, whom she saw as "an avid and mighty promoter of the festivals." Hitler

Bayreuth Festivals. In the garden of "Haus Wahnfried" in Bayreuth (1938), Hitler, flanked by Frau Winifred Wagner and Wieland Wagner.

considered the combination of "German musical art and German poetic art" in Wagner's operas to be a classic art form. The National Socialists also exploited Wagner's racist and antisemitic convictions, interpreted his cult of the hero in chauvinistic terms, and celebrated the festivals as "plays of national consecration" (*nationale Weihespiele*).

H. H.

BdA. *See* League of Foreign Germans.

BDM. *See* League of German Girls.

BDO. *See* League of German Officers.

Beamtenbund. *See* Reich League of German Civil Servants.

Beauftragter der NSDAP. *See* Delegate of the NSDAP.

Beauftragter für den Vierjahresplan. *See* Delegate for the Four-Year Plan.

Beauty of Work (Schönheit der Arbeit), office of the German Labor Front (DAF) agency STRENGTH THROUGH JOY. The main purpose of this office was, in today's terminology, workplace design. Its concern was less humanization than improvements relating to beautification and increased productivity. With great propagandistic éclat (mottoes included "Clean people in a clean workplace"), the office promoted revivification of the workplace through repainting, workplace libraries, floral displays for cafeterias and offices, and better lighting of offices and warehouses. The firms bore the cost of such improvements; any labor required was expected as a voluntary contribution of employees. Particularly successful beautifications were rewarded and publicly acknowledged as part of the PERFORMANCE COMPETITION FOR GERMAN WORKPLACES. Thus Beauty of Work was one of the propaganda instruments of National Socialist SOCIAL POLICY.

Becher, Johannes R(obert), b. Munich, May 22, 1891; d. Berlin, German Democratic Republic (GDR), October 11, 1958, German writer and politician. In 1912 Becher became associated with the Expressionist journal *Aktion.* He joined the USPD (Independent Socialists) in 1917, and the KPD (Communist Party of Germany) in 1919. In 1928 Becher was co-founder of the League of Proletarian Revolutionary Writers (Bund Proletarischer Revolutionärer Schriftsteller), and was its chairman until 1933. Because of his political speeches and writings, he had to emigrate in 1933, going to France via Switzerland and Czechoslovakia. In 1935 he went to the USSR, where he was editor in chief of the journal *Internationale Literatur, Deutsche*

Blätter (International Literature/German News) until 1945. Becher was president of the Academy of Arts in the GDR from 1953 to 1956, and served as minister of culture after 1954.

Becher, Kurt, b. Hamburg, September 12, 1909, *Standartenführer* in the Waffen-SS (reserves); businessman. Becher joined the equestrian unit of the SS on August 29, 1934, and on May 1, 1937, the NSDAP. After 1938 he served with the Second SS Death's-Head Unit "Brandenburg" at the ORANIENBURG concentration camp. In September 1939 he joined the SS Death's-Head Equestrian Unit 1 in Poland, which was deployed at the start of the RUSSIAN CAMPAIGN as an SS cavalry regiment. This unit later belonged to the notorious SS Calvalry Brigade, which participated in extermination operations against Jews. In March 1942 Becher was ordered to the Office of Equestrian and Transportation Affairs of the SS Leadership Main Office (SS-Führungshauptamt; SSFHA). After Germany invaded Hungary in March 1944, he was sent on a special mission to Budapest.

An ordinary SS man when the war began, by early 1945 Becher had been promoted to colonel in the Waffen-SS, probably in part for his "meritorious service" in Hungary: against the wishes of the Hungarian government, and without regard for diplomatic complications, he had taken under SS control the country's largest armaments firm, the Manfred Weiss Combine, which was partly owned by Jews. Becher also participated in Adolf EICHMANN's negotiations with representatives of Hungarian Jewry (*see* Joel BRAND) regarding the buying off of Jews from deportation to death camps (10,000 trucks for 1 million Jews). When the truck deal fell through, Becher continued negotiations, accepting jewelry and other valuables as "ransom" for 1,700 Jews, and arranging for the transfer of deportation victims to Switzerland. After the war Becher contended that his actions had saved thousands of Hungarian Jews. However, his actual role at the time remains unclarified.

A. St.

Beck, Józef, b. Warsaw, October 4, 1894; d. Stăneşti (Romania), June 5, 1944, Polish politician. Beck was a member of Józef PIŁSUDSKI's Polish Legion during the First World War and thenceforth his close friend; from 1932 to 1939 he was foreign minister. After Piłsudski's death in 1935, Beck became the real strongman of Poland. He was co-architect of the GERMAN-POLISH NONAGGRESSION PACT of January 26, 1934, and tried to create a bloc of east-central European nations, a so-called Third Europe under Polish leadership. His illusions about Hitler's expansionist policies received new nourishment after the MUNICH AGREEMENT (1938) owing to Poland's territorial gains (the region of Teschen). When Beck became aware of the real thrust of National Socialist foreign policy, his change of orientation through mutual assistance pacts with Great Britain (April 6) and France (May 19) came too late. After the POLISH CAMPAIGN Beck was interned in Romania, where he had fled.

Beauty of Work. Model workplace using natural lighting.

Józef Beck.

Beck, Ludwig, b. Biebrich (now part of Wiesbaden), June 29, 1880; d. Berlin, July 20, 1944 (executed), German officer and opposition fighter. Beck began army service in 1898; in 1911, General Staff service. In the First World War he was a General Staff officer (in 1918, a major) on the western front; he then served in the Reichswehr (major general, February 1, 1931) in the Weimar Republic. Beck hoped that Hitler's rearmament plans would restore German military parity, and he therefore welcomed the "revolutionary new beginning" of 1933. On October 1, 1933, he became chief of the Troop Office (Truppenamt)—a title changed to "Chief of the Army General Staff" on July 1, 1935—and on October 1, 1935, was promoted to the rank of artillery general.

When Beck realized that Hitler's rearmament plans aimed directly at a forcible solution of the "space question" (*Raumfrage*), he forcefully opposed them. After receiving directives (code name: "Case 'Green'" [Fall "Grün"]) for the "smashing" of Czechoslovakia on May 30, 1938, Beck tried to build opposition in the officer corps and to dissuade Hitler from military action through memoranda on the inadequacy of German armaments. Beck's course found little resonance, especially with the army commander in chief, Walther von BRAUCHITSCH. On August 18, 1938, Beck submitted his resignation, which was accepted with the rank of colonel general on October 1 of that year. (His successor was Franz HALDER.) Beck then became the central figure of the military opposition, and next to Carl

GOERDELER, the soul of the German opposition to Hitler. As a member of the "WEDNESDAY CLUB" he had close contact with leading representatives from the economy, politics, and academia. Through his ability to unite people he was able to unify non-Communist, bourgeois, and military resistance activities until the TWENTIETH OF JULY, 1944. It was presumed that Beck would become head of state if Hitler were assassinated. After the plot's failure and an unsuccessful suicide attempt, he was shot on order of Friedrich FROMM.

Ludwig Beck.

Beckmann, Max, b. Leipzig, February 2, 1884; d. New York, December 27, 1950, German painter and graphic artist. Beckmann's exaggerated pictures, created with Expressionistic techniques, were marked after 1914 by his experience in the First World War. In a disillusioned and anti-heroic mode, they expose violence, destruction, and cruelty. After 1929 Beckmann was attacked as a leading representative of "artistic Bolshevism" by the COMBAT LEAGUE FOR GERMAN CULTURE; his work was considered "seditious," and after 1933 was shown only at exhibitions meant to defame modern, socially critical painting, as The Spirit of November in the Service of Sedition (Stuttgart) and DEGENERATE ART (Munich). Beckmann emigrated to Paris in 1937, and later found recognition as an artist and university lecturer in the United States.

Bedarfsdeckungsscheine. *See* Scrip.

Beer-Bottle Gustav (Flaschenbier-Gustav), nick-

Max Beckmann.

name popularized by right-wing enemies of the Republic to deride Weimar foreign minister Gustav STRESEMANN, who had written a thesis on a gastronomic topic.

Beer-Hofmann, Richard, b. Rodann, near Vienna, July 11, 1866; d. New York City, September 26, 1945, Austrian writer and dramatist; friend of Hugo von Hofmannsthal and Arthur Schnitzler. Between 1924 and 1930 Beer-Hofmann wrote several plays on commission from Max REINHARDT for Vienna and Berlin stages. A Jew, he consciously emphasized the Jewish spirit in his writing, as in *Der Graf von Charolais* (The Count of Charolais; 1904). He emigrated to the United States in 1938 and became an American citizen in 1943.

Befreiungsgesetz. *See* Liberation Law; Denazification.

Beheim-Schwarzbach, Martin, b. London, April 27, 1900; d. Hamburg, May 7, 1985, German journalist and author. Beheim-Schwarzbach wrote novellas and poems with a religious angle, such as "Die Runen Gottes" (The Runes of God; 1927) and "Die Krypta" (The Crypt; 1935). In 1939 he went into exile in London, where he did factory and radio work. In 1946 he returned to Germany, where he received the Alexander Zinn Prize in 1964.

Behemoth, Old Testament monster (*Job* 40: 15–24); used by Thomas Hobbes (1588–1679) as a term to characterize the condition of total lawlessness and anarchy without political authority. The emigré lawyer Franz Neumann (1900–

1954) adopted the term for the National Socialist system of rule in 1942 in *Behemoth: The Structure and Practice of National Socialism,* because "National Socialism is a non-state, or is developing into one, a chaos, a rule of lawlessness and anarchy, which has 'devoured' the rights and dignity of man." According to Neumann, its sociological basis was a coalition of elite interests: party, bureaucracy, business, and military, all cooperating in shifting patterns for the sake of reciprocal benefits. Neumann's extensive analysis of the NS system of rule was especially applicable to the period after 1938 (*see also* DUAL STATE).

A. v. B.

Beimler, Hans, b. Munich, July 2, 1895; d. Madrid, December 1, 1936, German revolutionary and politician. Beimler worked as a locksmith; at the war's end in 1918, he was a member of the workers' and soldiers' council in Cuxhaven; he was imprisoned for sabotage until 1923; in 1930 he became a Communist member of the Bavarian legislature; in 1932 he became a Reichstag deputy. After the Reichstag fire, Beimler was arrested and taken to the Dachau concentration camp (brochure, "Im Mörderlager Dachau" [In the Dachau Murder Camp]; 1933). He escaped and crossed the border. In 1935 he took over the Zurich office of the Red Aid. Beimler soon clashed with the agency's central office; the conflict continued to smolder during the Spanish Civil War, in which he participated as "Political Commissar of All German Battalions in the International Brigade." Since he often denounced Stalinist persecution of fighters in Spain who deviated from the party line, the popular commissar was shot in the back by Soviet agents.

Bekennende Kirche. *See* Confessing Church.

Belange, Germanization of the word "interests" (*Interessen*), created as early as the 18th century from the verb *belangen* (to affect or concern); first used only with a preposition: *von Belang* (of interest). *Belange* became a fashionable National Socialist term, as in *politische und völkische Belange* (political and *völkisch* interests or consequences).

Belgium, kingdom on Germany's western border; area, 30,440 sq km (18,872 sq miles); population, 8.3 million (1939). By virtue of the Versailles treaty, Belgium obtained EUPEN-MALMÉDY, abandoned its traditional neutrality, and sought ties with France (in 1920, a military

Belgium. "The New Order . . . of servitude." Belgian resistance document, elaborating on the *Neue Ordnung* propagated by Germany.

"The pig as the symbol of the master race according to Walter [*sic*] Darré." Belgian resistance caricature of Darré's book *Das Schwein als Kriterium für nordische Völker und Semiten* (The Pig as Criterion for Nordic Peoples and Semites).

alliance), whose side it took in the RUHR CONFLICT. In internal affairs, the opposition between the two almost equally strong population groups (the Walloons and the Flemish) dominated the scene. The introduction of universal male suffrage in 1919 resulted in the loss of the Roman Catholic majority (from 1884), as well as a rapid change among coalition governments, which inhibited steady political and economic development. This increased the influence of the king—from 1934 Leopold III—as the connecting link between the Walloon nationalists (*see* REXISTS) and their Flemish counterparts.

After the LOCARNO PACT there was a relaxation in German-Belgian relations, which became endangered after Hitler's assumption of power because of Belgium's French ties. For this reason, as well as because of the weakness of the Western powers (*see* APPEASEMENT), Leopold III announced a return to neutrality on October 14, 1936. This did not save Belgium from German occupation during the FRENCH CAMPAIGN. The king remained in Belgium, while a government-in-exile was formed in London. During the occupation (until September–October 1944), 18,000 Belgians were deported to German concentration camps for political resistance; 24,387 Belgian Jews fell victim to the FINAL SOLUTION; and 140,000 forced laborers were recruited for the German armaments industry. COLLABORATION with the enemy tainted Belgium's postwar history, notably the volunteer detachments of the Waffen-SS: the Flemish Legion and the "Wallonie" Armored Division (*see* Léon DEGRELLE), each with some 20,000 men.

Bello, Heinz, b. Breslau, September 5, 1920; d. Berlin-Tegel, June 29, 1944 (executed), German victim of National Socialism. A medical student, in 1940 Bello was drafted into the medical corps, but in 1942 he was transferred back to his home region with a student company to continue his studies. A senseless order incited Bello to utter sharp words against militarism, National Socialism, and corrupt party bigwigs on July 20, 1943. Denounced by two fellow soldiers, he was sentenced to death for "undermining the military" by a field court-martial of the Central Army Court on March 18, 1944.

Belsen, Hannover locality (now in Lower Saxony) with the nearby BERGEN-BELSEN concentration camp.

Bełżec, National Socialist extermination camp on the southeastern border of the Lublin district in the GENERALGOUVERNEMENT of Poland. Construction began in late autumn 1941. By early March 1942 Bełżec was completed, and by mid-March extermination measures as part of the FINAL SOLUTION had begun. Gassing was at first carried out in a wooden barrack lined with tin that held 100 to 150 persons. The SS later erected a stone building with six gas chambers that could hold about 1,500 persons. After initial attempts at using bottled gas, for economic reasons the exhaust gas from a tank or a truck motor was finally used as the means of killing. The first commanding officer was SS-*Haupt-*

sturmführer and police captain Christian **WIRTH**, who had already collaborated on the **EUTHANASIA** program. He was replaced by another policeman and *Hauptsturmführer*, Gottlieb **HERING**. The camp personnel consisted of former participants in euthanasia projects, as well as specially detailed SS and police. The guard contingent consisted of Ukrainian **VOLUNTEER HELPERS** and ethnic Germans.

When "resettlement trains" (*Umsiedlerzügen*) arrived in Bełżec, the Jewish men (for security reasons) were driven into the gas chambers first, and then the women and children. As camouflage, the chambers were fitted out like showers. The gassing process took about 10 minutes. After the chambers were aired, they were cleared by "work Jews" (*Arbeitsjuden*). The corpses were first searched by special prisoner details for such valuables as gold teeth and rings, then thrown into nearby pits that had been prepared in advance. In early December 1942, the SS stopped the exterminations. By March 1943 the corpses were exhumed and burned (*see* **EXHUMATION OPERATION**), and the camp was then dissolved.

At least 400,000 Jews were murdered in Bełżec. The actual number of victims is probably more than 600,000. The first report on Bełżec was drawn up shortly before the war's end by SS-Obersturmführer of the Waffen-SS Kurt **GERSTEIN**, who had to make an official visit to the camp as a member of the Hygiene Division of SS Headquarters. The report was much disputed for a time, especially because it contained several inaccuracies. In the meantime it has been confirmed in all essential points through investigations of the **LUDWIGSBURG CENTRAL OFFICE**.

A. St.

Bendlerstrasse, street in Berlin where the Reich War Ministry and Wehrmacht High Command (OKW) were located; the name was often used to designate the ministry itself. The street was a main site of the failed putsch of the **TWENTIETH OF JULY**, 1944.

Beneš, Edvard, b. Kožlány (Bohemia), May 28, 1884; d. Sezimovo Ústí (Bohemia), September 3, 1948, Czechoslovak politician; a lawyer and political economist. During the First World War Beneš advocated the creation of a Czechoslovak state that would include regions with alien majorities for the sake of economic and political viability. He was able to carry his point at the Paris peace negotiations. Beneš served as minis-

Edvard Beneš.

ter of foreign affairs (1918–1935), prime minister (1921–1922), and president of the young Czechoslovak republic (1935–1938). He tried to secure this state through treaties with Yugoslavia and Romania (the Little Entente), as well as with France (1924) and the Soviet Union (1935). Beneš's hard line on the minority question, however, intensified the **SUDETEN CRISIS** and contributed to the loss of the Sudetenland in the **MUNICH AGREEMENT**. Beneš resigned, went to the United States, and in 1940 to England, where he headed a government-in-exile. He again became president of the republic in 1945, but was unable to ward off the Communist takeover. He resigned his post on July 7, 1948.

Benn, Gottfried, b. Mansfeld (Westprignitz), May 2, 1886; d. Berlin, July 7, 1956, German writer. Benn studied medicine, was a military doctor during the First World War, and settled in Berlin in 1917 as a specialist for skin and venereal diseases. His first volume of verse, *Morgue*, appeared in 1912, followed by essays, dramatic experiments, and further collections of lyric poetry in an Expressionist style. In 1932 Benn was accepted into the Prussian Academy of Arts. In his inaugural address ("After Nihilism"), he expressed his hopes for overcoming the cultural and political crisis of those years, which coincided with his personal crisis-laden development.

Benn welcomed Hitler's Seizure of Power in 1933 as an attempt at heroic self-affirmation of the German people and the white race, and he polemicized against emigrés. But after the **RÖHM AFFAIR** in 1934, he turned away in horror from National Socialism and its cultural institutions, which he scorned as "popular organs of excretion" (*völkische Ausscheidungsorgane*). Benn

Gottfried Benn.

came under party fire, was expelled from the Reich Writing Chamber, and was forbidden to publish. He fled into a kind of "aristocratic emigration," a "Two-Realm Theory" (*Zwei-Reiche-Theorie*), according to which his aesthetic realm was not of this world, and therefore was incompatible with the political realm. Benn's rejection of National Socialism thus seems born of bitter disappointment, rather than of critical insight. After the war, which he survived as a military doctor (from 1935), Benn again won poetic fame with works such as *Statische Ge-dichte* (Static Poems; 1949). However, he could never quite silence critics of his National Socialist entanglement, who accused him of "intellectual abdication before tyranny." This criticism has overshadowed Benn's great poetic significance.

A stanza from the poem "Einsamer nie . . ." (Lonely—never . . .), which Benn wrote during his "aristocratic emigration," reads: "When everything manifests itself through happiness / and exchanges glances / and exchanges rings / in the fragrance of wine, in the / intoxication of things—: / you serve the other happiness, / the spirit."

Benz, Richard, b. Reichenbach (Saxon Vogtland), June 12, 1884; d. Heidelberg, November 9, 1966, German literary and cultural historian. Benz strove for a complete portrayal of culture and the arts, especially of German Romanticism, as in "the renewal of a German nature out of the spirit of *Volk*dom." As an editor, he merited credit for rediscovering early forms of vernacular literature, in *Die deutsche Volksbücher* (German Folk Books; 6 vols., 1911–1926).

Berchtesgaden Diktat, German-Austrian agreement, concluded February 12, 1938, at the Berghof, near Berchtesgaden, after an ultimatum delivered by Hitler to Austrian chancellor Kurt SCHUSCHNIGG. Hitler's policies, which aimed at an ANSCHLUSS with Austria, could not be satisfied by the JULY AGREEMENT of 1936, especially since Austria carried out its provisions slowly and the international situation seemed conducive to further Austrian concessions. In the *Diktat*, Hitler demanded the inclusion of Arthur SEYSS-INQUART as interior minister, as well as the placement of further National Socialists in the Schuschnigg government, a general amnesty for Austrian National Socialists, preparations for German-Austrian economic unity, peace with the press, and so on. Intimidated by the high German military officers whom Hitler had brought into the talks, and by reports of German troop movements near the frontier, Schuschnigg accepted the *Diktat* after the term allowed, on February 15, 1938. In the end, he could not avert annexation.

Berend, Alice, b. Berlin, June 30, 1878; d. Florence, April 2, 1938, German journalist and author. Berend spent many years in Italy. She remained in Berlin until 1933, when her Jewish origins forced her to seek exile in Italy via Switzerland. Her writings consisted mainly of humorous novels about Berlin's petite bourgeoisie, as *Spiessbürger* (Philistines; 1938).

Berens-Totenohl, Josefa (real surname, Berens), b. Grevenstein (Sauerland), March 30, 1891; d. Meschede, September 6, 1969, German writer and painter. Berens-Totenohl composed prose and lyric poetry linked to Westphalia, where she made a home in Totenohl. She wrote about "woman as creator and preserver of the *Volk*" (*Die Frau als Schöpferin und Erhalterin des Volkstums*; 1938), and had her greatest success with two peasant novels set in the 14th century, *Der Femhof* (The Vehmnic Court; 1934) and *Frau Magdlene* (1935). They were "comparable to the great Norse family epics" (F. Lennartz, 1941).

Bergen-Belsen, National Socialist concentration camp in the Celle district, built between March and mid-July 1943. It was intended for about 10,000 female and male Jewish prisoners of various European nationalities, for whom emigration was promised in exchange for German returnees. At first the inmates were not to be drafted for work; only after 1944 was compulsory labor required of some inmates (unloading railroad cars, excavation work, and so on). Bergen-Belsen was divided into individual sections, the largest of which was the "star camp" (*Sternlager,* named after the "Jewish star"). Second came the so-called camp for neutrals (*Neutralenlager*), which housed Jews from neutral states who could not be exchanged. Food, housing, and hygienic conditions corresponded to the usual inadequate standards common to concentration camps. The inmates were bullied and mistreated by block and detachment leaders, despite the fact that Bergen-Belsen passed for a camp with preferential treatment.

In 1944 there were exchange operations with Palestine (222 persons), for German citizens interned there; with Switzerland (1,685 Hungarian Jews), for a per capita rate of about $1,000; and with the United States and North Africa (about 800 persons), in exchange for German citizens interned in the United States. In the course of 1943, sick inmates from other concentration camps were brought to a separate section (the convalescent camp), which eventually housed about 2,000 inmates. The lack of medicines and the miserable hygienic conditions led to many deaths. In June and July 1944, in particular, many seriously ill inmates were killed with injections of phenol. Besides the "convalescent camp," an "induction camp" (tent camp) was set up in mid-August for Polish women. It was totally overcrowded by late 1944 and early 1945 with thousands of sick female inmates from Auschwitz (among them Anne FRANK). Toward the end of the war Bergen-Belsen served as a collection camp for many thousands of inmates evacuated from other concentration camps. Catastrophe resulted, and after February 1945 new arrivals were not even registered. Losses through hunger, infectious disease, and exhaustion were terrible. From early January to mid-April 1945, some 35,000 people died in Bergen-Belsen. When the commandant, Josef Kramer, handed over the camp to the British on April 15, 1945, Bergen-Belsen still held about 60,000 survivors, of whom 13,000 died of exhaustion and disease after being liberated. Kramer was sentenced to death by the British and executed; his predecessor, Rudolf Haas, was declared dead in 1950.

W. D.

Bergengruen, Werner, b. Riga (Latvia), September 16, 1892; d. Baden-Baden, September 4, 1964, German author and journalist. In 1914 Bergengruen was an army volunteer; in 1919, a cornet in the "Baltic Militia"; after 1920, a journalist. He worked in Tilsit and Memel; in 1925 he became editor in chief of the *Baltische*

Bergen-Belsen. Captured SS guards.

Werner Bergengruen.

Blätter (Baltic News). In 1936 he openly converted to Roman Catholicism, which resulted in his exclusion from the Reich Writing Chamber in 1937. Many of his books were banned. Bergengruen moved to the Tyrol in 1942, and later to Rome. After the war ended, he lived in Zurich until 1958, then in Baden-Baden. For his literary works, such as *Der Grosstyrann und das Gericht* (The Great Tyrant and the Court, 1935; translated as *A Matter of Conscience*), he was awarded the Wilhelm Raabe Prize in 1951 and the Schiller Prize in 1962.

Berger, Gottlob, b. Gorstetten, July 16, 1896; d. Stuttgart, January 5, 1975, SS-*Obergruppenführer* (1940). Berger was a lieutenant in the First World War, and later a gymnastics teacher. He joined the NSDAP and the SA. After an internal dispute, Berger left the SA in the spring of 1933, and turned to the SS after the Röhm scandal. He became head of the recruitment office at SS Headquarters in 1938, and as such became the real founder of the WAFFEN-SS. Since the SS could not at first rely for its troops upon those liable for military duty, Berger recruited substitutes among the ETHNIC GERMANS and later developed the idea of VOLUNTEER UNITS from occupied western and northern European countries. His vision of a "Germanic army" ultimately suffered defeat because of Hitler's essentially nationalistic concept. A loyal collaborator with Himmler, Berger became chief of SS Headquarters (*Leiter des SS-Hauptamtes*) on August 15, 1940. As a state secretary, after July 1942 he directed Alfred Rosenberg's

Ministry for the Occupied Eastern Territories. He won prominence as a commanding officer by employing overly severe measures to suppress an uprising in Slovakia in September 1944. On October 1 of that year Berger was also put in charge of the prisoner-of-war department. He could not reduce the disastrous abuse rampant there because of the rapidly worsening overall situation. For this involvement, in particular, he was sentenced at Nuremberg to 25 years' imprisonment in 1949. After reduction of the sentence to 10 years on January 31, 1951, Berger was released from prison the same year.

Gottlob Berger.

Berghof, Hitler's country place, located on the 900–1,000-m-high (2,952–3,280 feet) Obersalzberg, northeast of Berchtesgaden. In a narrower sense it referred only to Haus Wachenfeld, acquired by Hitler in 1927, which was enlarged and built up (to about 30 rooms) especially after the Seizure of Power. In a broader sense the entire "Führer area" belonged to the Berghof, encompassing about 10 sq km (3.86 sq miles) with 800 hectares (1,976 acres) of woods in 1940. Goebbels, Göring, and BORMANN, the architect of the Obersalzberg, also built for themselves splendid country homes there. To this were added numerous supply institutions, SS guard barracks, and guesthouses, as well as Hitler's famous teahouse on the 1,800-m-high (5,904 feet) Kehlstein ("Cliff Nest"), which was reached by a 120-m-high (394 feet) elevator blasted through the rock. Hitler spent a great deal of time at the Berghof, and used it to

Hitler's Berghof on the Obersalzberg: Haus Wachenfeld.

receive high state visitors such as Austrian chancellor Kurt Schuschnigg (February 12, 1938) and British prime minister Neville Chamberlain (September 15, 1938). The Berghof area, which was continually under construction (with extensive bunkers and antiaircraft gun sites), was laid waste on April 25, 1945, by 318 British bombers. Nearly all the buildings except for the teahouse fell victim to 1,181 tons of bombs. On May 4 of that year, United States troops occupied the Berghof.

Berlin, Battle for (*Schlacht um Berlin*), term for the fighting around the Reich capital in late April and early May 1945. Berlin had been surrounded by Red Army detachments since April 25. The battle had special significance since Hitler had remained in the bunker under the Reich Chancellery. Although the city was strategically insignificant, its capture by the Soviets on May 2 was a clear gain in prestige, and provided Stalin with a pawn (*see* COLLAPSE).

Berlin Allied Headquarters (Berliner Alliierte Kommandantur), instrument for exercising supreme control in Greater Berlin; it was created on July 7, 1945, on the basis of the Berlin

Four-Power Statute. Subordinated to the ALLIED CONTROL COUNCIL, it consisted of the city commanders. Its tasks were to coordinate the policy of the Four Powers regarding Berlin and to supervise German officials there. Disagreement between the Western and Soviet commanders increasingly obstructed the activities of the headquarters. It ended with the withdrawal of the Soviet Union on June 16, 1948.

Berlin Declaration "in view of the defeat of Germany" (June 5, 1945). *See* June Declaration.

Berliner Illustri(e)rte Zeitung (Berlin Illustrated News; BI), the largest illustrated weekly in the Weimar Republic, founded in 1892. It was published by the Ullstein publishing house until its liquidation in 1938, and thereafter by the German Press (Deutscher Verlag). Kurt Korff was editor in chief until March 31, 1933, then Carl Schnebel. Circulation in 1933 was 1.9 million, and in 1944, 2.6 million, under editor in chief Ewald Wüsten. After October 1944, the BI was the only illustrated paper other than the ILLUSTRIERTER BEOBACHTER because of wartime concentration of the press. Large German cities received its content in ready-made matrixes and provided only the headlines. The last issue was published on April 22, 1945.

Berlin Four-Power Statute, statute concerning the joint administration of Greater Berlin by

Title page of the *Berliner Illustrirte Zeitung,* which fell victim to National Socialist press censorship for portraying Hermann Göring in a happy-go-lucky pose.

Great Britain, France, the United States, and the USSR, contained in the JUNE DECLARATION of June 5, 1945. It stipulated the city's occupation by troops of the Four Powers, its division into American, British, French, and Soviet sectors, and its joint government through the Berlin Allied Command. The statute was undermined by the East-West conflict.

Berlin press conference (*Berliner Pressekonferenz*), informational meeting of German journalists from the daily press, begun in 1919. Government representatives were "guests of the press"; government statements could be published freely. On June 20, 1933, the Propaganda Ministry abolished the press conference and substituted a forum that released official PRESS ADVISORIES.

Berlin Transit Workers' Strike, strike by workers of the Berlin Transit Authority that took place from November 3 to 7, 1932, over the planned reduction of hourly wages by 2 pfennigs. Although the original strike vote did not have the necessary three-quarters majority, the Communist trade union saw a possibility for adopting militant tactics, especially when it was able to bring the NATIONAL SOCIALIST WORKPLACE CELL ORGANIZATION over to its side. Since Gauleiter Goebbels did not want to be outdone in social-revolutionary spirit in "red" Berlin, he found himself in a joint strike leadership with such Communists as Walter ULBRICHT. This peculiar tactical alliance did not pay off for the National Socialists: they lost a considerable number of votes, especially in middle-class precincts, in the Reichstag elections of November 6, 1932. When the Papen government remained firm, the unsuccessful strike had to be broken off, on November 7.

Berlin Treaty (Berliner Vertrag), German-Soviet security and neutrality treaty concluded April 24, 1926, to provide an Eastern flank for the LOCARNO PACT. The Berlin Treaty was intended to counteract Soviet fears of a one-sided German connection with the West. It had an anti-Polish orientation and promoted secret cooperation between the Reichswehr and the Red Army. For the first five years, the partners committed themselves to remain neutral in case of conflict involving the other party, and to abstain from any boycotts. The treaty was extended in 1931 and confirmed for another five years on June 24, 1933, by Hitler, who wanted to avoid turbulence while the Third Reich consolidated its foreign policy.

Bernadotte, Folke, Count of Wisborg, b. Stockholm, January 2, 1895; d. Jerusalem, September 17, 1948, Swedish politician. Originally an officer, in 1943 Bernadotte became vice president, and in 1946 president, of the Swedish Red Cross. In February 1945 he made contact with Himmler, and achieved the rescue of Danish and Norwegian concentration camp inmates. In three further meetings with the SS-*Reichsführer*, Bernadotte discussed humanitarian problems of the war's end and Himmler's proposals for a separate peace with the Western powers. He was unable to establish the desired contact with General Eisenhower, since the Allies rejected talks with Himmler and insisted on UNCONDITIONAL SURRENDER. Bernadotte was murdered in Palestine by Jewish extremists while attempting to mediate on behalf of the United Nations.

Count Folke Bernadotte.

Bernburg an der Saale, one of six "killing facilities" in the EUTHANASIA program and INVALID OPERATION. Bernburg replaced the "hospital and nursing home" in Brandenburg an der Havel, which was closed in November 1940. It bore the code name "Anstalt Be" (Facility Be). According to existing records, 8,601 people were killed there in 1941 alone.

Bernhard, Georg, b. Berlin, October 20, 1875; d. New York, February 10, 1944, German politician and journalist. Bernhard was editor in chief of the *Vossische Zeitung* from 1909 to 1930, and a Reichstag deputy (German Democratic Party) from 1928 to 1930. He was persecuted as a Jew by the National Socialists, and deprived of German citizenship for "anti-German agitation." In 1933 he emigrated via Copenhagen to Paris, where he was active as founder and editor in chief of the PARISER TAGEBLATT (Paris Daily News) until 1937. In 1940 he was confined in the Bassens camp (Bordeaux). He succeeded in fleeing to the United States in 1941.

"Bernhard" Operation, code name for the counterfeiting of British pound notes, begun in early 1940 by Office VI (Sabotage) of the Reich Security Main Office (RSHA). Through massive production (as of mid-1941) of the highest quality of counterfeit bank notes, the attempt was made to create difficulties for Britain's wartime economy, and simultaneously to finance a widespread net of agents. The counterfeit bank notes, whose total sum could never be established, circulated throughout the world. An SS detachment buried some at the end of the war in Lake Toplitz.

Bernstein-Zimmer. *See* Amber Room.

Bertram, Adolf, b. Hildesheim, March 14, 1859; d. Johannesberg Castle (Bohemia), July 6, 1945, German Roman Catholic theologian and churchman. In 1881 Bertram was ordained as a priest; he became head of the cathedral chapter in 1894 and bishop of Hildesheim in 1906; in 1914, prince bishop of Breslau; in 1916, cardinal; from 1919 to 1945 he was chairman of the Fulda Conference of Bishops. Bertram led German Catholicism throughout the period of the Third Reich. He first rejected National Socialism, but accepted Rome's concordat policy; he again intensified his criticism as the CHURCH STRUGGLE continued. Publicity-shy because of a

"Bernhard" Operation. Counterfeit English bank note.

speech defect and concerned with the ultimate rights of the church, Bertram avoided open conflict. He confined himself to a policy of petitioning in his fight against NS encroachments and antisemitic excesses, incurring criticism for weakness even in Catholic circles.

Bertram, Ernst, b. Elberfeld (now Wuppertal-Elberfeld), July 27, 1884; d. Cologne, May 2, 1957, German writer. In 1922 Bertram became professor of German philology in Cologne. He made a name for himself in *völkisch*-German nationalist circles as a lyric poet and essayist by conjuring up German-Nordic myths as the primary basis of German history. Despite his friendship with Thomas MANN, whom he unsuccessfully tried to win over for the Third Reich, Bertram welcomed the BOOK BURNING on principle, and celebrated the national awakening in *Deutscher Aufbruch* (German New Start; 1933). For his literary work, which included *Wartburg* (aphoristic poems; 1933) and *Die Fenster von Chartres* (The Windows of Chartres; poems, 1944), he was awarded the Görres Prize in 1942 and the Rhenish Prize for Literature in 1944. After the war Bertram was temporarily prohibited from publishing; he was made a professor emeritus in 1950.

Berufsbeamtengesetz. *See* Civil Service Law.

Berufsschulung, zusätzliche. *See* Vocational training, continuing.

Berufswettkampf. *See* Vocational competition.

Besatzungspolitik. *See* Occupation policy.

Bessarabia, from 1918 to 1940, Romanian territory between the Prut and Dniester rivers; area, about 44,000 sq km (16,988 sq miles); population, 3 million (56 percent Romanians, 31 percent Russian nationalities). In the secret supplementary protocol of the GERMAN-SOVIET

Cardinal Adolf Bertram.

NONAGGRESSION PACT of August 23, 1939, Bessarabia was added to the Soviet sphere of interest, while the German side declared its "complete political disinterestedness." Nevertheless, the Bessarabian question became a burden for German-Soviet relations in the summer of 1940, since Moscow demanded the surrender of the area in an ultimatum, and extended the demand to BUKOVINA. On June 28, 1940, German pressure forced Romania to yield Bessarabia to the Soviet Union. Hitler's bitterness over this contributed to the acceleration of his attack plans against Russia.

Best, Werner, b. Darmstadt, July 10, 1903, German politician and SS-*Obergruppenführer* (1944). A lawyer, Best was twice arrested by the French during the RUHR CONFLICT. In 1929 he became a law clerk (*Gerichtsassessor*); he was dismissed in 1931 for co-authoring the so-called BOXHEIM DOCUMENTS, regarding National Socialist plans to seize power. A member of the NSDAP from 1930, Best was appointed state commissioner of all Hessian police forces in March 1933, and in July 1933 he became governor of Hesse. In 1935 he transferred to the Gestapo in Berlin, becoming its chief legal adviser; as an SS-*Standartenführer* he headed the Office of Administration and Law in the main office for security police in the Interior Ministry.

Best was Reinhard Heydrich's most important co-worker in creating the SS Security Service (SD). As chief of Office II of the REICH SECURITY MAIN OFFICE between September 1939 and June 1940, Best is assumed to have shared

Werner Best.

responsibility for the massacres in Poland. As part of the military government in France between 1940 and 1942, he combated the RÉSISTANCE. From November 1942 to the end of the war, Best governed DENMARK as Reich plenipotentiary. The unscrupulous manipulator of power seems here to have pulled back somewhat from the methods of police terror he had helped develop, and to have contributed to the rescue of Danish Jews. Nonetheless, in 1949 he was sentenced to death in Copenhagen. The sentence was reduced to 12 years' imprisonment, and Best was released in 1951; he returned to Germany, where he became a legal adviser to the Stinnes concern. In February 1972 he was accused of murders in Poland, but he remained unprosecuted for health reasons, although the accusation was never formally withdrawn.

Bestallung (appointment), National Socialist bureaucratic Germanization of the foreign word *Approbation* (certification) in reference to documents and orders; the term is occasionally still used.

Bestgestaltung der Arbeit ("best configuration of work"), social-political cliché in the campaign for optimal workplace organization and safe work procedures "for productive people."

Bestleistung ("best performance"), Germanization, from around 1930, of the foreign word *Rekord*, which it almost completely replaced in National Socialist usage. It is still used in sports, as to designate such accomplishments annually or worldwide (*Jahresbestleistung*; *Weltbestleistung*).

Bethge, Friedrich, b. Berlin, May 24, 1891; d. Bad Homburg, September 17, 1963, German writer. Bethge joined the NSDAP early on, and was state head (*Landesleiter*) of the REICH WRITING CHAMBER and also *Gau* culture steward (*Gaukulturwart*). In writings dealing with guilt and atonement, he represented the ethical slogan "strength through suffering" ("Kraft durch Leid"); in his First World War drama *Reims* (1930), a soldier "atones" for his desertion during the storming of that city.

Betreuung (care), fashionable National Socialist word; previously little used, but today still customary because it replaces such encumbered synonyms as *Fürsorge* and the awkward verb form *sich kümmern um* (to take care of; to concern oneself with). In NS figurative speech, *Betreuung* could also be negatively reinterpret-

Friedrich Bethge.

ed: the Gestapo "took care of" (*betreute*) the Jews; the commander of a protective-custody camp was responsible for the "care" (*Betreuung*) of the prisoners. Inflated positive usage also gave the word a somewhat forced quality, as in TROOP RECREATION (*Truppen-Betreuung*).

Betriebs-. *See* Workplace.

Betrothal order (*Verlobungsbefehl*), obligatory duty of SS members to report their engagement; a complement to the MARRIAGE ORDER.

Beumelburg, Werner, b. Traben-Trarbach, February 19, 1899; d. Würzburg, March 9, 1963, German writer. Beumelburg's first success came with a "chronicle of the World War," the novel *Sperrfeuer um Deutschland* (Barrage around Germany; 1930). He glorified the "spirit of the frontline soldier" in his works, which were awarded National Socialist prizes; he became especially popular with historical novels "on the *völkisch* Reich idea," about Bismarck, Frederick II, and the like. In his postwar works Beumelburg continued to maintain his German nationalist viewpoint, as in *Jahren ohne Gnade* (Years without Mercy; 1952), which was conceived as a "chronicle of the Second World War."

Bevin, Ernest, b. Winsfort (Somerset), March 9, 1881; d. London, April 14, 1951, English politician. Bevin worked as a farmhand and truck driver; in 1911 he became general secretary of the dockworkers' union. He was significantly involved with the unification of the British trade union movement. After 1935 he advocated British rearmament, and warned against APPEASEMENT of Hitler; he joined Churchill's wartime cabinet in 1940 as minister of labor and national service. As foreign secretary in the ATTLEE government, he participated in the POTSDAM AGREEMENT in 1945. Bevin was an architect of the North Atlantic Treaty Organization (NATO).

Bevölkerungspolitik. *See* Population policy.

Bewegung. *See* Movement.

Bezugsschein. *See* Purchase permit; War economy.

Bianchi, Michele, b. Belmonte Calabro, July 22, 1883; d. Rome, February 3, 1930, Italian politician. Bianchi, like Mussolini, was originally a socialist; the two men were also among the first Fascists. In 1922 it was largely Bianchi who organized the March on Rome that led to the Fascist takeover. In 1929, after holding high administrative posts, he was named minister for public works.

Bibelforscher. (Christian sect). *See* Jehovah's Witnesses.

Bie, Oskar, b. Breslau, February 9, 1864; d. Berlin, April 21, 1938, German writer and music critic. From 1894 to 1922 Bie was literary editor and publisher of the *Neue Rundschau* (New Review). He worked as a critic for the *Berliner Börsen-Courier* (Berlin Stock Exchange Courier). His works included *Das deutsche Lied* (The German Song) and *Die Oper* (Opera). After

Werner Beumelburg.

1921 Bie taught at the Berlin Academy of Music. His essays and literary works were branded as "testimonies to cultural decadence," and were banned from publication after 1933. Although Jewish, Bie remained in Berlin until his death.

Bierut, Bolesław, b. near Lublin, April 18, 1892; d. Moscow, March 12, 1956, Polish politician. Bierut became a Communist in 1918, and belonged to the Comintern until 1932. During the Second World War he built up, on the request of the Soviet Communist party, a Communist underground movement in German-occupied Poland. The so-called Lublin Committee that he headed became the nucleus for the Communist-dominated National Council. It succeeded in excluding Poland's "bourgeois" government-in-exile in London, and thereby became the agent of the postwar Communist takeover. Bierut served as Poland's president (1947–1952) and prime minister (1952–1954). After 1954 the chairman of the Polish Communist party, Bierut was an uncompromising hard-line Stalinist.

Big Three (*Grosse Drei*), designation for the United States, USSR, and Great Britain or their political leaders, ROOSEVELT, STALIN, and CHURCHILL. At conferences in TEHERAN (1943), YALTA (1945), and Potsdam (1945; *see* POTSDAM AGREEMENT), where TRUMAN replaced Roosevelt, they decided the fate of postwar Germany and Europe.

Bildberichter. *See* Picture reporter.

Bildung, wealth of knowledge and learning, as well as the process of its acquisition. In this traditional sense, it was an educational goal rejected by the National Socialists, because it neglected the "schooling of the will [*Willensschulung*] and character formation." Therefore National Socialist politicians preferred to speak about *Erziehung* (*see* EDUCATION), and defined *Bildung* as "fashioning of the racially impeccably born German person . . . into a fully developed, strong-willed, and solid personality within the framework of the *Volk* Community."

Binding, Rudolf Georg, b. Basel, August 13, 1867; d. Starnberg, August 4, 1938, German writer. Binding was successful from the 1920s with austerely stylized neoclassical prose and lyric poetry. He preferred such themes as chivalry, self-sacrifice, and chastity; he glorified war as a "heroic trial," for example, in the Richthofen story "Unsterblichkeit" (Immortality; 1922). From a wealthy bourgeois background, Binding had reservations about the fascist "plebeians,"

Rudolf Georg Binding.

but he espoused the cause of the "new Germany" in a kind of aesthetic glorification, as in his "Answer of a German to the World" (written in 1933 in response to attacks by the French writer Romain Rolland), which won praise as a "genuine German confession."

H. H.

Biologism (*Biologismus*), an essential feature of National Socialism, which acquired its ideological base largely by transferring biological principles to human social life. This is true both of the biological doctrine of race, with its inadmissible equation of SPECIES and RACE, and of the concept of "LIVING SPACE," which according to the ideas of SOCIAL DARWINISM was justified by the "eternal struggle for existence" and the "right of the stronger." The theory of heredity had a particular impact, influencing National Socialist marriage law and providing a logic for the EUTHANASIA program. The ideology of the "VOLK COMMUNITY" was also derived from NS biologism, which from the alleged primacy of species preservation over self-preservation inferred a natural law of the subordination of the individual to the community.

Birkenau (Pol., Brzezinka), name of the National Socialist extermination camp AUSCHWITZ II.

Birth control (*Geburtenregelung*; *Geburtenkontrolle*), general term for measures intended to regulate the frequency of births, especially by preventing conception. National Socialist population policymakers considered it, except where medically indicated, "indecent, immoral, and unnatural"; intentional childlessness was "treason against the *Volk*." The desire for birth control was said to arise from a "diminution of the biological will to live," and was an expression of "crises within the *Volk*" induced by Marxism and liberalism, with their overvaluation of individual freedoms. Even the extremely critical position of the Catholic church (birth control was allowed only by the "rhythm method" of nonfertile days) was rejected by NS POPU-LATION POLICY.

Birthrate decline. *See* Population policy.

Birth war (*Geburtenkrieg*), slogan coined in 1936 for National Socialist POPULATION POLI-CY. To defend against the threatening "*Volk* death," the birth war—"a momentous struggle of the community"—was declared. The martial expression "birth war" fit the NS militarization of language, as did the slogans "BATTLE FOR CULTIVATION" in agricultural policy and "BAT-TLE FOR WORK" in social policy. [Before the First World War, the Social Democratic Party of Germany had debated a "birth strike."]

BIZ. *See* Bank for International Settlement.

Bizone, unified economic region, consisting of American and British occupation zones, created by agreement between the foreign ministers of Great Britain and the United States on December 2, 1946; it was established on January 1, 1947. Bizonal organs were the two-zone office in Berlin, under the command of the American and British military governors; and bizonal German administrative offices (two-zone authorities) for the economy, nutrition, agriculture, transport, post, and law. When France joined the Bizone, it became a TRIZONE (by the treaty of April 8, 1949), which formed the basis for creation of the Federal Republic of Germany.

Black Friday (*Schwarzer Freitag*), name given to the stock market crash in New York on October 25, 1929. Black Friday is regarded as the beginning of the great WORLD ECONOMIC CRISIS of 1929 to 1932; it ended a boom in securities in the United States that had lasted for years, based on the economic upswing of 1925 and heated up by hectic speculation. An unfettered optimism, as well as favorable interest rates in the American money market, facilitated the purchase of stocks on credit. In October 1929 small index reversals led to panic selling, the proceeds of which had become necessary to pay off credit debts. The rapid loss of value in stocks had devastating effects not only in the United States but also in Europe and especially in Germany.

V. B.

Black Front (Schwarze Front), self-designation of an alliance of the "Combat Community [Kampf-gemeinschaft] of Revolutionary National Socialists," which Otto STRASSER founded after his withdrawal from the NSDAP (July 4, 1930), with similarly oriented groups (National Bolsheviks, disillusioned Communists, and so on). In its periodical of the same name, the Black Front

Black Friday. Hectic activity outside the New York Stock Exchange.

argued for nationalist and revolutionary "solidarity," as was also propagated by the spokesmen of the SECOND REVOLUTION. The front was active especially between 1931 and 1933. After Strasser emigrated in 1933, the disintegrating group still agitated so tenaciously against the Third Reich from outside the country that as late as in 1939 Himmler blamed them for the BÜRGERBRÄU ASSASSINATION ATTEMPT.

"Black List" (*Schwarze Liste*), designation for an official catalog of books that were to be "expurgated" from public libraries. Published on May 16, 1933, in the trade newspaper of German booksellers, the "Black List" was aimed against "asphalt literature," which was divided into three groups: (1) works slated for destruction, such as those of Erich Maria REMARQUE (*see* BOOK BURNING); (2) works that, like Lenin's writings, were to be locked away in the "poison cabinet," to be saved for later confrontations; and (3) uncertain cases, for example, the American novelist B. Traven [pseud. of Berwick Traven Torsvan].

Black market (*Schwarzmarkt*; *Schwarzer Markt*), the illegal sale or exchange of rationed goods or of goods whose price is fixed by the state. The black market price is therefore always substantially higher, which for the black marketeer means a high profit that also evades taxation. A black market always crops up when the available supply of goods does not meet the demand and becomes rationed. Under these conditions the beginnings of a black market developed in Germany and in the occupied territories in the last phase of the war. It then flourished after the war and was ended only by the currency reform of 1948. Thus the years from 1945 to 1948 were often referred to as the Black Market Period.

Blackout (*Verdunklung*), nighttime AIR DEFENSE measure, regulated by the ordinances of May 23, 1939, and October 22, 1940. The duty to comply with the ordinances was especially urgent during an AIR RAID ALARM; it required dimming the source of light or "openings through which light escapes," so that even in clear visibility not the faintest light could be seen at 500 m (about 1,700 feet). Motor vehicle and bicycle lights were also regulated; after October 1, 1940, they had to be equipped with camouflage devices (narrow light slits). Crimes committed during blackouts were punished in accordance with the ordinance against VOLK VERMIN.

Black market. Poster of the Bavarian Trade Union Federation (1948): "The black market is the DEATH of the new currency. Eradicate the black market! Black marketeers are parasites on the productive people!"

Black Reichswehr (*Schwarze Reichswehr*), term for the augmentation of the army between 1919 and 1924 through evasion of the conditions of the VERSAILLES TREATY. A system of so-called temporary volunteers (*Zeitfreiwilliger*) was set up by September 11, 1919; it was intended to allow the calling up of reinforcements in times of crisis. In 1920, under Allied pressure, it was at first relinquished, then replaced in 1921

Blackout. National Socialist poster: "Oh, if I had only blacked out properly and gone to the air raid shelter!"

Black Reichswehr. *White Book* published by the German League for Human Rights.

by so-called work squads (*Arbeitskommandos*) made up of former free corps combatants. To be sure, they were not officially acknowledged, nor did they have military status, yet they were provided with weapons, ammunition, and trainers from the Reichswehr, which also extensively financed them. The Black Reichswehr was put to use in defense of the Upper Silesia border area, in the suppression of uprisings, and in guard duty at illegal arsenals. Its members (some 20,000 in 1923), most of them hostile to the Weimar Republic, developed into a threat to the very state they were supposed to serve. They menaced internal peace with VEHM MURDERS and, under their organizer, Maj. Bruno Ernst Buchrucker, moved out from their main post at Küstrin on October 1, 1923, to make a *coup d'état*, an action blocked by the Reichswehr. This led to the disbanding of this form of Black Reichswehr. Because of the RUHR CONFLICT, recourse was had once again to the system of temporary volunteers; it was disbanded once again in August 1924, yet was never completely abandoned.

Black Troop (Schwarze Schar), self-designation of the SS. It was derived from the nickname of the Lützow free corps in the Wars of Liberation from Napoleon (1813–1814).

Black-White-Red Combat Front (Kampffront Schwarz-Weiss-Rot; the colors were those of Imperial Germany), self-designation chosen by the GERMAN NATIONAL PEOPLE'S PARTY (DNVP) and the STEEL HELMET for the Reichstag election of March 5, 1933, in order to fit in with the nationalistic political trend. The Front won 52 mandates, as the DNVP had in the elections of November 6, 1932; as coalition partner of the NSDAP (288 of 647 seats), it helped that party gain an absolute majority.

Blaskowitz, Johannes, b. Peterswalde (East Prussia), July 10, 1883; d. Nuremberg, February 5, 1948, German colonel general (October 1, 1939). In 1901 Blaskowitz joined the army; in 1916, General Staff service; he was taken into the Reichswehr in 1919; in 1932 he became a major general; in 1933, lieutenant general and inspector of military academies; in 1936, infantry general. During the Polish Campaign, Blaskowitz commanded the Eighth Army, and became Supreme Commander for the East in October 1939. In this capacity he wrote two memorandums about atrocities committed by the SS and the party in Poland. He fell into disfavor and was not promoted, despite his continued assignment (October 1940–May 1944 with the First Army in France). Repeatedly made supreme commander of army units, on April 7, 1945, Blaskowitz was given supreme command of "Fortress Holland," where he made agreements with the Allies to secure food sup-

Johannes Blaskowitz.

plies for the civilian population. After the capitulation he was interned in various camps, and was then accused of alleged war crimes. Blaskowitz avoided trial through suicide.

Blass, Ernst, b. Berlin, October 17, 1890; d. there, January 31, 1939, German lyric poet and journalist. Blass was associated with the Expressionist journal *Aktion*; in 1914–1915 he was publisher of the magazine *Die Argonauten*; he was a friend of the Expressionist and revolutionary Kurt Hiller. After 1924 Blass was a reader for the Cassirer publishing house. As a Jewish writer he was forbidden to publish after 1933, and was kept under surveillance. His early death saved him from deportation to a concentration camp.

Blei, Franz, b. Vienna, January 18, 1871; d. Long Island, N.Y., July 10, 1942, Austrian writer and literary critic. From 1906 to 1919 Blei was editor of various literary journals (with Carl Sternheim and Max Scheler, among others). In 1919 he joined the Roman Catholic church and professed his allegiance to communism. From 1923 to 1933 he worked as a film critic in Berlin. He left Germany after the Seizure of Power, and lived in exile on Majorca until 1936. Following the outbreak of the Spanish Civil War, Blei fled from the Gestapo to Vienna, and in 1938 to France (via Italy). After 1941 he resided in the United States, where he was a friend of the emigré authors Hermann Broch and Albert Ehrenstein.

"Blitz," English term adopted from National Socialist propaganda jargon for the German bomber offensive against British cities in the second phase of the AIR BATTLE FOR ENGLAND. The weak German nighttime attacks in the winter of 1943–1944 were, by ironic analogy, termed the "Baby Blitz."

Blitzkrieg (lightning war), term for the tactics of the German Wehrmacht in the early phase of the Second World War, which sought quick, peremptory battles. Since that time, the word has become a generic term for quickly decided campaigns. It was probably coined by Eugen HADAMOVSKY, in *Blitzmarsch nach Warschau* (Lightning March to Warsaw; 1940). Blitzkrieg strategy entailed the surprise deployment of massive tank units with strong air cover, breakthrough at the front, and rapid advance into enemy territory in order to cripple enemy forces. In 1939 a Blitzkrieg in the POLISH CAMPAIGN was the Wehrmacht's only chance to avoid a war of attrition and to utilize fully

Germany's short-term armaments advantage, which could not be maintained long in view of the insufficiency of German raw materials and of the economy. Thus, Hitler ordered an attack, despite quite incomplete preparations. The Blitzkrieg plans developed by the Allies, as by Charles de GAULLE or Sir Basil Liddell Hart, were hardly listened to, so that Germany again used these tactics in the FRENCH CAMPAIGN and the BALKAN CAMPAIGN.

G. H.

Blitzmädel (Blitz girl), term adopted from soldiers' jargon for women in the communications corps (*see* WEHRMACHT, WOMEN IN THE), whose uniform was marked with the lightning symbol of the corps.

Blobel, Paul, b. Potsdam, August 13, 1894; d. Landsberg (Lech), June 7, 1951 (executed), SS-*Standartenführer*. Initially an independent architect, Blobel joined the Security Service (SD) after professional setbacks. (On December 1, 1931, he had already joined the SA, SS, and NSDAP.) In the SD he was active primarily in the Western Division (Oberabschnitt West). Early in the Russian Campaign he became head of Special Commando (SK) 4a of Einsatzgruppe C. With SK 4a he carried out mass executions within the Sixth Army's theater of operation; the 60,000, primarily Jewish, victims included the Jews of Kiev (*see* BABI YAR). In January 1942 Blobel was relieved of this duty and charged with the EXHUMATION OPERATION. After the war the Americans tried him before a military court in Nuremberg (*see* OHLENDORF TRIAL). On April 10, 1948, he was sentenced to death by hanging for crimes against humanity, war crimes, and membership in a criminal organization.

Block, lowest organizational unit ("territory") of the NSDAP, averaging 40 to 60 families, or some 160 to 240 persons, led by a BLOCK LEADER.

Block leader (*Blockleiter*), the lowest "bearer of jurisdiction" (*Hoheitsträger*) in the NSDAP, responsible for the "overall political situation" on his block. This included the duty to report "harmful rumors," the collection of membership dues, and the keeping of card indexes on all residents. As "preacher and champion of the National Socialist worldview," the block leader was charged with such propaganda tasks as getting block residents to join the Hitler Youth, the SA, or other party organizations, and recruiting them for NS events. He was appointed by the district leader (*Kreisleiter*), and was responsible only to him. Many block leaders became petty tyrants, feared for possible denunciation.

Block warden (*Blockwart; Blockwalter*), lowest-level leader in the Reich Air Defense League; also the designation for the leader of a "block" in the German Labor Front or the National Socialist Volk Welfare organization (NSV); he was subordinate to a BLOCK LEADER (*Blockleiter*). Through the frequent union of these offices, a "warden" was often equivalent to a "leader."

Bloem, Walter, b. Elberfeld (now Wuppertal-Elberfeld), June 20, 1868; d. Lübeck, August 18, 1951, German writer. With his militant, Prussian-nationalist recreational and war novels, Bloem was one of the most widely read authors of his time. An early champion of National Socialist fiction, he had his greatest success with a trilogy (1911–1913) on the Franco-Prussian War of 1870–1871, *Das eiserne Jahr* (The Iron Year), *Volk wider Volk* (People against People), and *Die Schmiede der Zukunft* (The Forgers of the Future). Bloem's son, Walter Julius (b. Barmen, October 22, 1898; missing in action near Berlin, 1945), also wrote nationalistic escape literature, under the pseudonym Kilian Koll.

Blomberg, Werner von, b. Stargard (Pomerania), September 2, 1878; d. Nuremberg, March 14, 1946, German field marshal (April 20, 1936) and politician. In 1897 Blomberg joined the army; in 1910 he took a General Staff post; in

Werner von Blomberg.

1919–1920 he was in the Reichswehr Ministry. After occupying diverse high posts, in 1929 he became commander of Military District I (Königsberg). On January 30, 1933, on Hindenburg's recommendation, Hitler appointed Blomberg to his government as Reichswehr minister, and found in him an energetic advocate of rearmament. Blomberg also supported Hitler in eliminating the SA in the RÖHM AFFAIR, and made the Reichswehr take the oath of allegiance to Hitler after Hindenburg's death. Blomberg became Reich war minister on May 21, 1935, and supreme commander of the renamed Wehrmacht. He collaborated on the plan to occupy the RHINELAND (*see* RHINELAND OCCUPATION), and received the marshal's staff after the occupation.

Blomberg's compliance toward Hitler evoked displeasure among the officer corps. He attempted weak protests against Hitler's war policy in 1937, but remained unconditionally loyal. This did not help him when his "unsuitable" marriage (on January 1, 1938)—to a prostitute, as was ascertained afterward—gave his enemies Göring and Himmler a pretext for his downfall. In a countermove, Blomberg recommended to Hitler before being dismissed (February 4, 1938) that he himself should assume supreme command over the Wehrmacht, as indeed happened. Together with the FRITSCH CRISIS, which was taking place simultaneously, this brought the armed forces definitively under party control. After the war Blomberg was imprisoned by United States troops as a witness; he died in prison.

Blomberg-Fritsch Crisis, general term for the situation involving Reich War Minister Werner von Blomberg and the army's supreme commander, Werner von Fritsch; the more common designation is FRITSCH CRISIS.

Blondi, Hitler's German shepherd dog; it was kept especially at the BERGHOF, but also at Führer headquarters. Toward the end of the war, Hitler brought the dog into the bunker under the Reich Chancellery. There, on Hitler's order, Blondi was poisoned on April 30, 1945.

Blood (*Blut*), a central, mythically glorified concept in National Socialist thought, standing for the unity of soul and body, and for life in general. Symbolically, blood represented the "bearer of life," while in (scientifically untenable) "race lore" (*Rassenkunde*) it was regarded as the "bearer of inheritance" (*Träger des Erbgutes*) and of alleged racial qualities. In numer-

Hitler with his German shepherd Blondi.

ous word combinations, "blood" implied racial qualities in a broader sense, for example, "bound by blood" (*blutgebunden*), describing a character molded by racial origin; "blood circle" (*Blutkreis*), members of one race; "blood barrier" (*Blutschranke*), the alleged natural and ethical division between races; "blood soul" (*Blutseele*), the essential characteristics of a people, which are embodied in such outstanding figures as "poets and heroes" (Alfred Rosenberg, 1933); "of alien blood" (*blutsfremd*), belonging to another race; "blood feeling" (*Blutgefühl*), avowal of racial kinship; "blood pride" (*Blutstolz*), a feeling of superiority owing to racial kinship; "responsible to blood" (*blutsverantwortlich*), synonymous with "racially conscious"; "blood bearer" (*Blutträger*), representative of a race; "blood poisoning" (*Blutvergiftung*), symptoms of degeneration in races, nations, or cultures; "blood worth" (*Blutwert*), evaluation of a person according to his or her racial group.

H. H.

Blood, Law to Protect (*Blutschutzgesetz*), official term for the Law for the Protection of German Blood and German Honor, enacted in 1935 as part of the NUREMBERG LAWS. It prohibited marriage and "extramarital relations" between "Jews and citizens of German or kindred blood"; infractions were punishable by a jail or prison term. The law also forbade Jews to employ non-Jewish workers in their households or to hoist the German flag. In the Regulations for Implementation, the provisions of the law were extended to include Gypsies and Negroes, and special regulations dealt with Jewish MIXED-BREEDS (*Mischlinge*).

Blood and Soil (*Blut und Boden*), frequently used propaganda formula (abbreviated as "Blubo" in popular disparaging parlance) for the "basic idea of National Socialist ideology." According to it, "a healthy state" can rest only upon the unity of its "own *Volk*," therefore on BLOOD (that is, a uniform race) and its "own soil." The term was first introduced by Oswald SPENGLER (*The Decline of the West*) as a conceptual association, and was then popularized and culturally glorified as designating "eternal values," especially by Walther DARRÉ, later head of the SS Race and Settlement Main Office (RuSHA), in his book *Neuadel aus Blut und Boden* (The New Nobility of Blood and Soil; 1930).

Since the peasantry was regarded as the "blood source" of the German people, the Blood and Soil theory especially influenced agricultural policy; in which, for example, landed property was permanently fixed through the Reich HEREDITARY FARM LAW. The umbrella organization of the German food production industry, the REICH FOOD ESTATE, even adopted the words "Blood and Soil" for its official coat of arms. The Blood and Soil theory also served the National Socialists as a political justification for their so-called RE-GERMANIZATION (*Eindeutschung*) efforts in eastern Europe, which included expulsion of the native rural population. The idea of land seizure justified by "racial superiority" (not only) in the east was increasingly reflected from the 1920s on in German fiction, in so-called Blood-and-Soil novels. Sometimes clothed in historical garb, these novels continued a tradition of already conservative "homeland literature" (*Heimatliteratur*), or used the theme of German claims to African colonies (notably in the works of Hans GRIMM).

H. H.

Blood Banner (*Blutfahne*), official term for the swastika flag that was carried in Munich during the march to the Feldherrnhalle (*see* HITLER PUTSCH) on November 9, 1923, and that was allegedly stained with the blood of National Socialists who had been killed. After 1926, flags of the NSDAP and its member organizations

Hitler consecrates flags with the Blood Banner.

were consecrated by contact with the Blood Banner. This was a link to medieval tradition, according to which jurisdiction through drawing blood (*Blutgerichtsbarkeit*) was symbolized by a red flag at the ceremony conferring feudal grants.

Blood Order (Blutorden), the highest NSDAP decoration, a silver medal on a red band with white trim; it was instituted in 1934, and awarded by Hitler to roughly 1,500 participants in the HITLER PUTSCH of November 8–9, 1923. Later, it was a decoration for National Socialists who were seriously wounded or given long jail terms, thus making a BLOOD SACRIFICE.

Blood-relatedness (*Blutsverwandtschaft*), in general, membership in the same family; in National Socialist usage, it was also applied to the racial relatedness of different peoples or nations. For narrower racial and cultural ties, especially between German-speaking countries, the term "blood community" (*Blutsgemeinschaft*) was also used.

Blood sacrifice (*Blutopfer*), general term for those who died in national wars or movements;

more narrowly, and with some religio-mystical glorification, it referred to National Socialists who died in political battles.

Blood shame (*Blutschande; Blutsünde*), originally, a synonym for incest; in National Socialist usage, the meaning shifted to RACIAL INFAMY: sexual intercourse between members of different races and, more narrowly, between Jews and Aryans.

Blood witness (*Blutzeuge*), German term for "martyr" (from Gr.; witness), generally applied to one who suffers or dies for a belief; it was used more narrowly for the dead of the world wars and of the National Socialist "movement," who sacrificed their lives "for the sake of their racial and *völkisch* convictions."

Bloody Sunday (*Blutsonntag*), emotional designation for Sundays on which political confrontations or fights between hostile groups resulted in deaths; it was a favorite term of propagandists because of the contrast between the injunction for a peaceful Sunday, and ugly brutality, and therefore was most often used accusingly (*see* ALTONA BLOODY SUNDAY; BROMBERG BLOODY SUNDAY).

Blubo, popular belittling of the National Socialist mythology of *Blut und Boden* (BLOOD AND SOIL).

Blue Division (Blaue Division; Span., División Azul), Spanish volunteer corps in the RUSSIAN CAMPAIGN; its members were allowed to wear the blue Falange shirt with their Wehrmacht uniforms, hence the name.

Blüher, Hans, b. Freiburg (Silesia), February 17, 1888; d. Berlin, February 4, 1955, German author and culture critic. Blüher was an ideologist of the youth movement and the WANDERVOGEL; he supported nationalist elitism, but was rejected by the National Socialists "because of his emphasis on male HOMOSEXUALITY."

Blum, Léon, b. Paris, April 9, 1872; d. Jouy-en-Josas (Yvelines), March 3, 1950, French politician and literary critic. In 1902 Blum was a founder of the French Socialist Party; in 1918–1919, he decisively influenced its postwar program and its political strategy, which led to the so-called Popular Front with Communists and radical socialists in 1936. Although Blum, then premier, prohibited the formation of fascist military units, he could not make up his mind to intervene in the SPANISH CIVIL WAR, and thus alienated the Communists. After his final downfall in 1938 he fought the APPEASEMENT policy and called for increased armaments. Handed over to Germany in 1942, Blum remained incarcerated in a concentration camp until the end of the war. In 1946–1947 he was again premier, briefly.

Blumenkriege. *See* Flower Wars.

Blunck, Hans Friedrich, b. Altona (now Hamburg-Altona), September 3, 1888; d. Hamburg, April 25, 1961, German writer. Blunck worked as a judiciary civil servant. In the 1920s he began writing historical-mythological novel cycles whose action took place in the "unresearched depths of Germanic prehistory." From 1933 to 1935 he was president (afterward, president ex officio) of the REICH WRITING CHAMBER. In collections of North German fairy tales and sagas, in lyric poetry and prose, he interpreted the past in a nationalist sense and glorified leader figures as saviors, as in the novel *Der einsame König* (The Lonely King; 1936), which described the wanderings of the Vandals under Geiserich. (National Socialist literary criticism extolled this novel as an "epic of a new race and of Germanic Christianity.") Blunck's memoirs, *Unwegsame Zeiten* (Impassable Times; 1952), portray his totally uncritical relationship to the NS state.

Hans Friedrich Blunck.

Blutendes Deutschland (*Bleeding Germany*), the first National Socialist propaganda montage film, made by Johannes Häussler immediately after the Seizure of Power. First shown in Berlin on March 30, 1933, it was to convey to the masses a conviction of the victory of the "National Revolution." Material for the film came from old newsreels, documents, and photographs. After a portrayal of the rise and fall of the old German Empire (the prewar period, the outbreak of war, the upheaval in 1918), the film presented a section entitled "Germany Awakens!": a sketch of the history of the NSDAP up to March 5, 1933, the day of the Reichstag elections.

Blütenlese, literal Germanization of the word *Anthologie* (Gr.; flower collection); a collection of selected writings, especially poetry.

BNSDJ. *See* National Socialist League of Law Guardians.

Bock, Fedor von, b. Küstrin, December 3, 1880; d. Lensahn (Schleswig-Holstein), May 5, 1945, German field marshal (July 19, 1940). Bock was a First World War battalion commander and General Staff officer; he transferred into the Reichswehr and in 1929 became a major general. Promoted to colonel general (March 15, 1938), Bock led the German march into Austria, and commanded Army Group North in the Polish Campaign. During the French Campaign he led Army Group B, first against the Netherlands and Belgium (accepting their capitulation), and then during the advance to the Loire River. During the Russian Campaign, Bock's Central Army Group bore the main burden of attack. Replaced on December 18, 1941, during the winter crisis near Moscow, Bock took over Army Group South on January 16, 1942. He was

Fedor von Bock.

dismissed and removed from further service after protesting against Hitler's plan for a simultaneous attack on Stalingrad and the Caucasus. Bock lost his life during an attack by low-flying aircraft, after he had put himself at the disposal of the DÖNITZ government.

Böckel, Otto, b. Frankfurt am Main, July 2, 1859; d. Michendorf (Brandenburg), September 17, 1923, German politician. Böckel was the founder of the Central-German Peasants Organization (1889), and a Reichstag deputy (1887–1903). The National Socialists considered him to be the "pioneer of antisemitism," because his hostility to Jews had a racial basis. In the Reichstag he proposed putting the Jews under special legislation as foreigners. Böckel was also known as a folklorist.

Bodelschwingh, Friedrich von, b. Bethel, August 14, 1877; d. there, January 4, 1946, German Evangelical theologian. In 1904 Bodelschwingh joined the Bethel Institute for the Handicapped, founded by his father; in 1910 he was chosen its director. Bodelschwingh saw his primary task in acts of charity, but he became involved in the machinery of church politics in 1933. Recommended by the YOUNG REFORMERS, he was appointed Reich Bishop by an overwhelming majority of Evangelical regional churches on May 27, 1933, in order to forestall the election of Hitler's protégé, Ludwig MÜLLER. Because the Reich Church lacked a constitution, the political leadership refused to recognize Bodelschwingh and installed a state commissioner

Friedrich Wilhelm Boger.

(*Staatskommissar*) for the regulation of church affairs on June 24, 1933. Bodelschwingh capitulated to political pressure and resigned. In Bethel he fought against the encroachments of the National Socialist authorities; he managed to save his patients from EUTHANASIA, and was finally able to play a significant role in ending the killing program.

Boger, Friedrich Wilhelm, b. Stuttgart, December 19, 1906; d. Bietingheim-Bissingen, April 3, 1977, SS-*Hauptscharführer*. Boger joined the National Socialist Youth (a precursor of the Hitler Youth) in 1922 and the ARTAMANEN in 1925. In 1933 he joined the SS, and in 1937 began work in its criminal bureau. From December 1942 until the camp's dissolution in 1945, Boger was in the political section at AUSCHWITZ. He was notorious for inventing the "Boger swing" (*Boger-Schaukel*), an instrument of torture used to extort statements during interrogations: prisoners were tied to it and, in numerous instances, were tortured to death. Boger was arrested by the Americans after the war. During extradition from the American occupation zone to Poland, he managed to escape; he disappeared from sight, and worked as a farmhand and industrial laborer. Arrested again in 1958, he was sentenced to life imprisonment in August 1965 for the murder of Auschwitz inmates.

Bohemia and Moravia (Böhmen und Mähren), regions in Czechoslovakia; designation for the

Friedrich von Bodelschwingh.

German PROTECTORATE OF BOHEMIA AND MO-
RAVIA after that country's destruction in March
1939.

Bohle, Ernst Wilhelm, b. Bradford (England),
July 28, 1903; d. Düsseldorf, November 9,
1960, German politician. Bohle grew up in
Cape Town, South Africa, then studied economics in Cologne and Berlin. With a business
degree (1923), he engaged in wholesale trade.
In 1931 he was employed by the Foreign Division of the NSDAP. He joined the party on
March 1, 1932, and became head of its FOREIGN
ORGANIZATION on May 8, 1933, thereby becoming a *Gau* leader as well. On November 12,
1933, he was elected to the Reichstag. In charge
of foreign national organizations (*Landes-
verbände*), Bohle was able to increase their
memberships. He became a state secretary in
the Foreign Office on January 30, 1937. His
Foreign Organization served its functions of
propaganda and intelligence, but lost ground
because it was prohibited in many countries,
causing Bohle to lose influence. In the WILHELM-
STRASSE TRIAL, the Allies sentenced him on
April 14, 1949, to five years in prison, a term he
had nearly served in pretrial internment. He was
released on December 21, 1949, and became a
businessman.

Ernst Wilhelm Bohle.

Böhme, Herbert, b. Frankfurt an der Oder, October 17, 1907; d. Lochham, near Munich,
October 23, 1971, German writer. Primarily a
poet (for example, *Des Blutes Gesänge* [Songs of
the Blood]; 1934), he also wrote dramas (such as

Volk bricht auf [*Volk* Sets Out]; 1934) and novels
(including *Andreas Jemand* [Andreas Some-
body]; 1939). National Socialist literary criticism extolled Böhme as "a passionate harbinger
of the ideals of the Third Reich." He joined the
NSDAP and the SA in 1933, became head
(*Fachschaftsleiter*) of the lyric poetry guild in
the REICH WRITING CHAMBER, and edited the
Hitler Youth literature series Young *Volk* after
1935. He became a professor of German at the
University of Posen (now Poznań) in 1944. After
the war he was active on the extreme Right as a
publisher and author.

The last stanza of Böhme's poem "Der Führer" (1937) reads: "The Führer goes toward /
the light / With tense power; / With the rolling
of his / drums, you, / *Volk*, become passion."

Bolshevism (*Bolschewismus*; from Russ. *bolshe-
viki*, members of the majority faction), term for a
political group in the Russian Social Democratic
party, introduced by Lenin in 1903 after winning a vote over the "Mensheviks" (minority
faction). In the Soviet vocabulary, until Stalin's
death (1953) it was the general term for the
theory and practice of Soviet communism. In
HITLER'S WORLDVIEW, Bolshevism was one of
the masks worn by world Jewry, whose "nega-
tion of all order and culture" recurred in Bolshevism, and who wished to achieve world domination via the Bolshevik world revolution.

Bolshevism. Poster for the Great Anti-
Bolshevik Exhibition at the 1937
Reich Party Congress in Nuremberg.

German fears of Bolshevism after the Soviet October Revolution were fanned by the Spartacist Uprising, the Munich Republic of Councils, and Communist disturbances in Saxony, Hamburg, and elsewhere. This anxiety—vented in the murder of Walther RATHENAU for his "pact with Bolshevism" at RAPALLO—dominated foreign-policy debate. National Socialist (NS) propaganda used it in domestic politics as a weapon against Germany's Marxist Communist and Social Democratic parties. NS policy later utilized these fears against the Western powers, when Hitler presented himself as a bulwark against Bolshevism. The exploitation of the enemy image (for the National Socialists, an effective extension of antisemitism) paid off in two directions. The bourgeois forces accepted it at the time of the SEIZURE OF POWER; the Western nations, especially the Vatican (*see* CONCORDAT) and Great Britain, accommodated Hitler in return for his anticipated anti-Bolshevik services.

NS foreign policy also used the dreaded enemy to keep the fascist camp united in the ANTI-COMINTERN PACT. Anti-Bolshevism was one of the few continuities of foreign policy on which Hitler's partners thought they could rely. The fact that he was willing to change such a fundamental position (temporarily, and for tactical considerations) was manifested by the GERMAN-SOVIET NONAGGRESSION PACT of August 23, 1939. The RUSSIAN CAMPAIGN was subsequently conducted as a "crusade against Bolshevism," again with an eye on Germany's allies and western Europe. The struggle of ideologies and the "racial struggle" coincided thereby with the constant desire to gain LIVING SPACE.

Bolz, Eugen, b. Rottenburg, December 15, 1881; d. Berlin-Plötzensee, January 23, 1945 (executed), German politician. A pious Catholic and a member of the Center party from 1912, Bolz became justice minister in Württemberg in 1919, and in 1923 interior minister. He was president of Württemberg from 1928 to 1933. He strongly supported the policies of Chancellor BRÜNING and tried by every means to stem National Socialist machinations. Following the Seizure of Power, Bolz was imprisoned for a few weeks. Afterward, he attempted to take up contact with the opposition. The "continuous misuse of state power by the National Socialists" required "the people's right to self-defense." His connection with Carl GOERDELER led to his imprisonment and a death sentence after the failed attempt on Hitler's life on July 20, 1944. Therein Bolz was true to his motto: "My life means nothing when it is a question of Germany."

Bombed out. Soldier searching for his relatives.

Bombed out (*ausgebombt*), popular term for the official "aircraft-damaged" (*fliegergeschädigt*), that is, being without a roof over one's head as a result of bombing. Because the AIR WAR from 1939 to 1945 was carried out against the rules of international law, first by the Luftwaffe and then by the Allied bombers as well, in the German Reich alone 13.7 million persons lost their homes and were thus considered totally bombed out. Partial damage is not included in this figure. In legal proceedings against persons accused of criticizing the state leadership or making comments "subversive of military strength," a defendant's having been bombed out immediately before committing the crime was considered a mitigating circumstance.

Bombing war (*Bombenkrieg*), designation for the stragetic AIR WAR of the Allies against Germany.

Bonhoeffer, Dietrich, b. Breslau, February 4, 1906; d. Flossenbürg concentration camp, April 9, 1945 (executed), German Evangelical theologian and opposition fighter. After his studies, Bonhoeffer was a curate in Barcelona (1927–1929), an auditor at Union Theological Seminary in New York (1930), a student chaplain in Berlin (1931), a pastor of German congregations in London (1933), and an advisory member of the Ecumenical Council (1934). Although he knew the risk of professing Christianity in National Socialist Germany, he accepted a call to lead the illegal seminary for preachers of the CONFESSING CHURCH in Finkenwalde. In 1936

he was forbidden to teach, in 1940 to preach, and in 1941 to publish. Convinced of the worldly mission of Christianity, he criticized the purely churchly opposition in Christian circles and sought contact with the political opposition movement. Calling Hitler "Antichrist," Bonhoeffer wanted "to get rid of" (*auszumerzen*) him.

Through his brother-in-law Hans von DOHNÁNYI, Bonhoeffer found his way to the Abwehr circle around Adm. Wilhelm CANARIS, which gave him cover through official missions abroad. In May 1942 Bonhoeffer met in Sweden with Bishop Bell of Chichester and probed fruitlessly for possible peace negotiations after Hitler's elimination. On April 5, 1943, the Gestapo arrested him on the pretext that he had misused his office for church politics. Only after the failed attempt on Hitler's life of July 20, 1944, was proof of his conspiratorial activities found. After imprisonment by the Gestapo and at Buchenwald, he was transferred from the Tegel military prison to Flossenbürg. Following an SS summary court-martial, he was hanged, together with Hans OSTER and Canaris, shortly before the arrival of United States troops. After the war Bonhoeffer's literary testament appeared, titled *Auf dem Wege zur Freiheit* (*The Way to Freedom*). His prison notes were published in 1951 under the title *Widerstand und Ergebung* (Opposition and Resignation; translated as *Prisoner for God* and as *Letters and Papers from Prison*).

Bonhoeffer, Klaus, b. Breslau, January 5, 1901; d. Berlin, April 23, 1945 (executed), German

Dietrich Bonhoeffer.

Klaus Bonhoeffer.

opposition fighter and jurist. Bonhoeffer became an attorney (1930), then corporate counsel (*Syndikus*) for German Lufthansa (1936). A much-traveled man of the world, he was in contact with the church opposition through his brother Dietrich, with the military opposition through his brother-in-law Hans von DOHNÁNYI, and with the Social Democratic opposition through his wife's cousin Ernst von HARNACK. Arrested after the attempt on Hitler's life of July 20, 1944, Bonhoeffer was sentenced to death on February 2, 1945. He was killed with a shot in the back of the neck by SS guards in besieged Berlin.

Bono, Emilio de, b. Cassano d'Adda, March 19, 1866; d. Verona, January 11, 1944 (executed), Italian marshal (November 16, 1935). One of the first high-ranking officers to support Mussolini, Bono participated in the March on Rome in October 1922. He became governor of Libya in 1925, served as minister for the colonies from 1929 to 1935, and was commander in chief of Italy's East African Army in the war against ABYSSINIA from April to November 1935. On July 25, 1945, Bono voted in the Fascist Grand Council to depose Mussolini. After Il Duce's reinstatement by the Germans, Bono was sentenced to death and executed.

Bonze ("big shot"), National Socialist epithet, applied especially to Social Democratic Party functionaries, whose leadership was denounced as a "Bonzocracy." The word, which derived from the Japanese for "Buddhist priest," was widely whispered to describe NS functionaries.

Book Burning (*Bücherverbrennung*), ritual destruction of books written by "degenerate and Jewish litterateurs" in nearly all German university cities on the evening of May 10, 1933. The Book Burning culminated a series of actions "against the non-German spirit" carried out largely by the German Students' Corporation (Deutsche Studentenschaft). It organized the local conflagrations, for which students and professors, sub-units of the NSDAP, and nationalist leagues gathered.

In Berlin, 40,000 people gathered on the Opernplatz to hear Goebbels speak; his speech was transmitted further by radio. Trucks or oxcarts brought books; the "elders" of the student group, along with professors of German language and literature in their academic robes, made speeches. Then the works of philosophers

Emilio de Bono.

(Marx, Ernst Bloch), scientists (Freud, Magnus HIRSCHFELD), classical humanist poets (Heinrich Heine), and contemporary authors were thrown into the fire: "No to decadence and moral corruption! Yes to decency and morality in family and state! I consign to the flames the writings of Heinrich MANN, Ernst Glaeser, Erich KÄSTNER." Besides socialists such as Bertolt BRECHT and pacifists such as Erich Maria REMARQUE, critical bourgeois writers (Alfred KERR, Arthur Schnitzler) and foreign "corrupters" (Henri Barbusse, Ernest Hemingway, Jack London) predominated. The charges ranged from "membership in an intellectual underclass and political treason" to "journalism alien to the *Volk*."

As early as the Weimar Republic period, nationalist groups had conducted an increasingly bitter struggle against democratic and left-wing literature, and had used the FILTH-AND-TRASH LAW to censor and ban politically disagreeable books. After the Seizure of Power, measures against critical writers were immediately intensified; they were removed from academies, professional associations, and public service. In Berlin alone, the Political Police confiscated 500 tons of "Marxist" literature by May 30, 1933. The fight against political "trash literature" was most zealously carried on at universities, which considered themselves the "bulwark of German *Volk*dom." Anti-Republican students and professors composed blacklists; after the takeover of power, nearly all sections of the NSDAP, from

Book Burning on May 10, 1933, on the Opernplatz in Berlin.

the Hitler Youth to the Teachers' League, put up their own "cleansing lists" for publishers and libraries. Following appeals in the press, many citizens delivered "un-German" literature from their own libraries to the pyres of May 10.

Its organizers saw the Book Burning as a symbolic act. As in olden times, fire was considered to have a purifying and healing effect; thus the "spiritual foundation of the hated November Republic" was to sink through flames "to the ground." The Book Burning was to signify that the "German nation had cleansed itself internally and externally" (Goebbels). The "cleansing process" for German literature continued after May 1933 through regional book burnings. Thousands of "unreliable" and "non-Aryan" authors were prohibited from exercising their profession or publishing, were sent to concentration camps, or went into exile. Although the Book Burning was not directly initiated by state authorities or the NSDAP, it was a decisive break: the provincial nature of literature in the Third Reich was thereby assured; a further development of German literature could occur only in exile.

No opposition to the book burnings worth mention roused itself in Germany. Bookstores and publishers reacted opportunistically; authors whose books were not burned rarely showed real solidarity with those whose were, as

did Oskar Maria GRAF: "Burn me!" (letter of May 12, 1933). The educated German bourgeoisie regarded the Book Burning as a "beer-inspired student prank" (*Bierulk*). Abroad, the reaction was frequently "amusement" at this "expression of excessive student zeal." Only rarely was the Book Burning interpreted in light of Heine's warning: "Where books are burned, in the end people will be burned."

H. H.

Booty operations (*Beuteaktionen*), confiscations of private and public money and goods (in particular, such items as artworks) by Soviet occupation authorities in 1945, and their shipment (through the so-called TROPHY COMMISSION) to the USSR.

Borchardt, Georg Hermann, given name of the author Georg HERMANN.

Borchardt, Rudolf, b. Königsberg, June 9, 1877; d. Trins (Tyrol), January 10, 1945, German playwright and translator; a friend of Hugo von Hofmannsthal. After 1922 Borchardt lived in Italy, where until 1927 he edited the magazine *Neue deutsche Beiträge* (New German Contributions). He translated Dante's *Divine Comedy* into German in 1930. As a Jew he was prohibited from occasional sojourns into Germany after

1933. In 1944 Borchardt was arrested by the Gestapo during his Italian exile and taken to Innsbruck. He succeeded in fleeing to Trins, where he died of a heart attack.

Börgermoor, penal camp in the Surwald district, part of the EMSLAND CAMPS; its prisoners were used by the state peat-bog authority for labor on the peat bogs. The prisoners' song "Wir sind die Moorsoldaten" (We Are the Peat-Bog Soldiers) originated in Börgermoor.

Boris III, b. Sofia, January 30, 1894; d. there, August 28, 1943, king (tsar) of BULGARIA. After the abdication of his father, Boris ascended the throne on October 3, 1918. After 1934 he established a moderate royal dictatorship, looked for support from the Axis powers, and joined the THREE-POWER AGREEMENT in 1941. He let himself be induced to declare war on England, but did not take part in the war against the Soviet Union. After the German BALKAN CAMPAIGN, Boris annexed large parts of northern Greece. Following a visit with Hitler (on August 15, 1943), he died under circumstances that have never been clarified.

Bormann, Martin, b. Halberstadt, June 17, 1900; d. Berlin, May 2, 1945, German politician. The son of a postal official, Bormann attended the *Realgymnasium* in Weimar, leaving after six years with a *mittlere Reife* (ordinary level) certificate. Still training with a field artillery regiment in Parchim at the end of the First World War, he did not reach the front. In 1919 he began an apprenticeship in agriculture at the Herzberg estate near Parchim (the von Treuenfels manor), becoming an estate inspector within a few years. Bormann's early rise was already aided by qualities that considerably favored his advance to the power center of National Socialism and the Third Reich. These qualities, all of which can be (and were) turned to negative use, were: unflagging diligence, prudence, dependability, memory, and talent for organizing. In the *völkisch*–National Socialist (NS) climate of opposition to the Weimar Republic, rural Mecklenburg was a place where secret societies found shelter and an audience for their agitation, and where VEHM MURDERS against disloyal members and "traitors" took place. Bormann participated in one: a teacher, Walter Kadow, a former member of the Rossbach free corps, was killed under suspicion of being a Communist spy. Bormann was sentenced to a year in prison for aiding and abetting the crime.

He returned to Weimar, where he had grown up, and became a contributor to the weekly magazine *Der Nationalsozialist.* Bormann did not write, but he made himself indispensable by providing various services. In 1927 he became member no. 60508 in the NSDAP, and also joined the SA. He organized campaign appearances for *Gau* leader Fritz SAUCKEL, and prepared for Hitler's appearance in Weimar. The single-minded effort to further his own progress was already evident. Bormann combined tireless backstage activity with constant stage presence. Whenever Hitler appeared, Bormann was visible at his side. But he was a born servant and assistant, an organization man (*Apparatmensch*), incapable himself of appearing, speaking, or representing. No matter how often photographs documented Bormann—squat, thickset, broadnecked, robust—he remained unknown. He was Hitler's silent shadow, but most assiduous in the second rank.

Bormann proposed the formation of a motorized SA to the group's highest leader, Franz PFEFFER VON SALOMON, an idea that piqued Hitler's technical interests. Pfeffer von Salomon invited Bormann to the party headquarters in Munich in 1928, marking the beginning of his real career. Agile, and as well versed in money matters as he was dependable, Bormann took over and expanded the party's aid fund, which was used primarily as compensation for SA men who had been wounded or killed (or their families). In 1929 he married Gerda Buch, daughter of the highest party judge; Hitler attended the ceremony. Ten children were born of this typical NS marriage. With his wife's approval (indeed encouragement), Bormann had several affairs. She quite seriously proposed a marriage à trois, to ensure more valuable offspring for the state.

When Hitler seized power, the party fund lost its function. Bormann applied to deputy Führer Rudolf HESS for a new party post. In July 1933 Hess appointed him his staff leader. However, Robert LEY, Reich organization leader of the NSDAP, had the same rank. In the ensuing dispute over spheres of authority, Bormann easily crowded his rival out of his imprecisely defined responsibilities, since Ley was overburdened with other offices (such as the Labor Front), and could not keep up with Bormann in matters of discipline and conduct. Basically, Bormann was already head of the party bureau. He did not make disloyal use of his power against his dreamy and unrealistic superior, Hess. But he tirelessly wove tighter the network of his powerful influence: everything passed

Martin Bormann.

through his hands, and nothing escaped him. Using delegated power, he kept the various party organizations under constant control, "ruling by means of orders, forms, lists, and circulars" (von Lang).

At the same time, Bormann systematically consolidated his position at Hitler's side: he was his living file cabinet, recalling on command all utterances for their potential use; he managed the Führer's private purse and invested the ADOLF HITLER DONATION from German business, partly in extravagant construction projects on and around the Obersalzberg (see BERG-HOF). Moreover, a whole series of private domiciles were built, with questionable financial sources, for the Bormann clan, which finally reached 12 members: in Pullach (Sonnenstrasse), on the Obersalzberg, in Mecklenburg, and in the Black Forest.

Once the war began, Bormann became indispensable to Hitler. The dictator—goal-oriented, but disinclined to steady work—found in Bormann an absolutely reliable systemizer. Since Hitler was not very interested in internal policies, he delegated to Bormann all communication with the internal power structure, the NSDAP. (Hess, who was theoretically responsible for this, receded increasingly into the background.) All measures involving ideological battles over domestic policies from then on bore (at least partly, if not predominantly) the stamp of Bormann's involvement (see EUTHANASIA; CHURCH STRUGGLE; PERSECUTION OF JEWS). He was a fanatical executor of NS racial programs

and of the "master race" mentality, within the sphere of his competence and often beyond it. To this was added a dangerous ambition for power that was feared by all, with few exceptions: notably Himmler, with whom he was on friendly terms; Goebbels, whose circle he left alone; and above all Hitler, to whom alone Bormann remained absolutely and unconditionally devoted. Otherwise, Albert Speer's utterance is apt: "Only a few critical remarks by Hitler, and all of Bormann's enemies would have been at his throat." But such remarks were never made, for Hitler well knew what he had in Bormann's person: "I know that Bormann is brutal. But whatever he tackles is solid, and I can rely completely on the execution of my orders, immediately and despite any obstacles."

Thus Bormann ruled in Hitler's name in the Reich (only military matters remained unaffected) and was mocked as "General Teletype" (*General der Fernschreiber*). Since Hitler's orders often conflicted with one another, Bormann chose the harshest versions from his complete files and transformed them into the Führer's commands. His power in Hitler's shadow grew even stronger after Hess's flight to England in May 1941. Bormann became chief of the Party Chancellery and soon thereafter the official "secretary to the Führer" (April 1943). From Hess he also took over the rank of a Reich minister. The further the war progressed, the closer became the collaboration between Bormann and Hitler. Bormann's constant presence alone made him Hitler's closest confidant. Neither vacations nor illness existed for him. He worked up to 20 hours a day, and according to Goebbels, transformed "the Party Chancellery into a paper chancellery." Cynically altering the words of Jesus, Bormann himself coined the motto "No one can come to the Führer but through me!" Hitler's war policy and the related crimes were decisions for which he himself was ultimately responsible; but from various clues it can be ascertained that Bormann collaborated on them, and more than once made them harsher and more fanatical.

Bormann held out in the bunker under the Reich Chancellery until his master's suicide. Hitler in his political testament had elevated him to the rank of party minister, and privately had called him "my most faithful party comrade" (*meinen treuesten Parteigenossen*). On May 1, 1945, Bormann attempted to break out of surrounded and embattled Berlin. He doubted that he would succeed: "there is no longer any point." For decades he remained missing. During the NUREMBERG TRIALS of the major war criminals he was sentenced to death in absentia. Only in the early 1970s was it proved that Bormann had not survived his attempt to flee in 1945. His skeleton, showing clear evidence of suicide by cyanide poisoning, was found near the Invaliden Brücke in Berlin. He was officially declared dead in 1973.

                                        H. St.

Borowski, Tadeusz, b. Zhitomir, November 12, 1922; d. Warsaw, July 3, 1951, Polish writer. During the German occupation of Poland, Borowski studied at the underground university. In February 1943 he was arrested and taken to the Auschwitz concentration camp. After liberation he wrote bluntly realistic stories about everyday life in the death camp: *A World of Stone* (1948), *Farewell to Maria* (1948), and the report "We Were in Auschwitz" (1946). But he was unable to exorcise the horror, and chose suicide.

Bothmann, Hans, b. Lohe (Holstein), November 11, 1911; d. in British custody, April 4, 1946 (suicide), SS-*Hauptsturmführer* and commissioner in the criminal division. Bothmann joined the NSDAP and the SS in 1933, before graduating with an academic high school diploma (*Abitur*) in 1934. After a period with the Labor Service, he joined the LEIBSTANDARTE-SS "ADOLF HITLER" on August 1 of that year. In November 1935 he was called up to the Secret State Police (Gestapo), and on August 1, 1937, was transferred to State Police (Stapo) headquarters in Berlin as a criminal commissioner trainee (*Kriminalkommissaranwärter*). His apprenticeship completed, Bothmann served first with the Leipzig Stapo, then in Posen, and finally was ordered to KULMHOF (Chełmno). From about April or May 1942, he headed the "Special Commando [Sonderkommando; SK] Kulmhof," also called "SK Bothmann," which carried out mass murders of Jews in the extermination camp there.

Botschafterkonferenz. *See* Ambassadors' Conference.

Bottai, Giuseppe, b. Rome, September 3, 1895; d. there, January 9, 1959, Italian politician. Bottai was one of the original Fascists; he took part in the March on Rome (October 1922), and after the Fascist takeover became under secretary of state in 1926. From 1929 to 1932 he was minister for corporations, and from 1936 to 1943, minister for education. He had a reputa-

tion as a moderate spokesman for a Fascist CORPORATIST STATE. This was expressed in the CHARTER OF LABOR he worked out. An opponent of the war policy, he increasingly distanced himself from Mussolini, and on July 25, 1943, voted to remove him from power. In 1944 Bottai fled to Algeria, where he served in the Foreign Legion until 1948. Back in Italy, he unsuccessfully worked on behalf of the monarchists.

Bouhler, Philipp, b. Munich, September 11, 1899; d. near Dachau, May 19, 1945, German politician and SS-*Obergruppenführer* (January 30, 1936). Bouhler served a business apprenticeship; from November 1921 he was with the *Völkischer Beobachter*; he was among the first members of the NSDAP, and became its second business manager (1922). He was a participant in the HITLER PUTSCH; after the party's reinstitution, he served as Reich business manager from 1925 to 1934. Bouhler, who in June 1933 had become a "Reich leader" and Reichstag deputy, took control of the newly created (November 17, 1934) Chancellery of the Führer of the NSDAP. This body had a narrower sphere of competence than the later Party Chancellery under Martin BORMANN. Still, Bouhler was responsible for the "protection of National Socialist writing" and for clemency petitions. He temporarily held a key position when Hitler assigned him, together with Karl BRANDT, to implement the EUTHANASIA program on September 1, 1939. When the program was discontinued in August 1941, Bouhler placed his

Philipp Bouhler.

killing specialists at the disposal of the EXTERMINATION CAMPS. His influence declined rapidly, and he sought an alliance with Göring, in whose retinue he was taken prisoner by United States troops in May 1945. Before transfer to the internment camp at Dachau, Bouhler took poison. He wrote a history of the NS movement, *Kampf für Deutschland* (Struggle for Germany; 1938), and a biography of Napoleon, *Kometenbahn eines Genies* (The Comet Path of a Genius; 1941), which was one of Hitler's favorite books.

Bourgeoisie (*Bürgertum*), stratum of society dominated by the middle grouping or class (*see* MITTELSTAND); it gained in importance after the monarchy's collapse in 1918, since the working class could not achieve a dictatorship of the proletariat during the revolution, and its majority probably did not even want it. Because the traditional bourgeois elite, such as upper-level civil servants, still clung to the authoritarian prewar state, its new responsibility was accepted only halfheartedly. The Weimar Republic was considered an emergency solution, especially since wide circles of the bourgeoisie were proletarianized through the INFLATION and the WORLD ECONOMIC CRISIS, and they tended to drift into the camp of radical enemies of the Republic, notably the National Socialists. There, everything bourgeois was considered antithetical to the "new man" (*neuer Mensch*), who was envisioned as a classless VOLK COMRADE. The bourgeoisie, which had refused the chance at democracy, was nonetheless seen by the National Socialists as a "breeding ground of democratism" (*Brutstätte des Demokratismus*), and was made responsible for Germany's defeat in the First World War, as well as for the "manifestations of capitalist and Marxist degeneracy" of the so-called SYSTEM ERA of the Weimar Republic.

Boxheim Documents, notes of discussions by leading Hessian National Socialists in the "Boxheimer Hof" inn near Bürstadt (Bergstrasse); they were signed by Werner BEST. The documents were leaked to the police on November 25, 1931, and became widely known. Their plain language with regard to National Socialist action in case of a Communist uprising embarrassed Hitler, who had just taken his LEGALITY OATH. In case of the "abolition of the present highest state authority," a takeover of power by the NSDAP, with the help of the SA and the SS, was envisaged, as well as the elimination of political opponents and general conscription for labor service. The NS leadership managed to distance itself from the Boxheim notes. The Weimar courts stopped proceedings against Best in 1932, since the documents were regarded as only a utopian scenario.

Boycott, ban on the importation and purchase of German goods. Called for by American organizations in 1938 to protest National Socialist persecution of Jews, it had little effect. The boycott was also a reaction to the NS BOYCOTT AGAINST JEWS of April 1, 1933.

Boycott against Jews (*Judenboykott*), the first centrally directed action by the National Socialists against Jews after the Seizure of Power. On March 28, 1933, the party leadership ordered that it was to begin on April 1, at 10 a.m. The boycott was to be directed against Jewish businesses and department stores, lawyers and physicians. It was legitimized by the claim that it was necessary to counter the "atrocity mongering" (*Greuelhetze*) and the incitement to boycott German goods that "international Jewry" had initiated against National Socialist (NS) Germany. The boycott thus represented a challenge to the "Jewish world conspiracy" in keeping with NS ANTISEMITISM.

The action was led by a "Central Committee for Deflecting Jewish Atrocity and Boycott Mongering" under the leadership of Julius STREICHER in Munich. Its political function was to restrict Jews socially, while simultaneously stabilizing NS rule. "The Führer told me that even the Reich banner, the national emblem, was being insulted, and now we must tell World Jewry: this far, and no further" (Streicher, 1946). Everywhere in Germany, the NSDAP established local action committees, which were to disseminate and organize the boycott. In order to put force behind the call to boycott, SA and SS sentries were posted at 10 a.m. According to the official line, they were to "warn the population against entering Jewish businesses," which were often marked by posters and graffiti. Persons who nevertheless made purchases in Jewish stores were often subjected to bullying. Attacks against Jews were not infrequent, and led to a feeling of insecurity among Jewish citizens. The stabilization of NS rule was to be achieved, according to the program of the Munich Central Committee, by inducing the press to support the boycott, and by holding meetings in factories during which workers were to be convinced of its necessity.

The boycott, which took place on a Saturday, was not continued in the following weeks, since

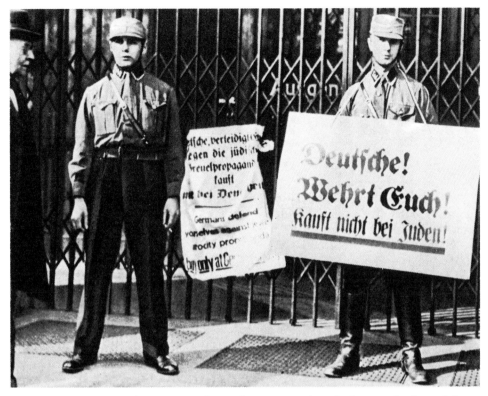

Boycott against Jews. The sign at right reads: "Germans! Defend yourselves! *Don't buy from Jews!*"

the domestic and foreign political consequences of the action caused anxiety to the NSDAP. Subsequently, actions were directed against individual Jewish businesses. In addition, NSDAP propaganda created a permanent boycott sentiment against the Jews.

H. O.

Bracht, Franz, b. Berlin, November 23, 1877; d. there, September 26, 1933, German politician. In 1923–1924 Bracht was state secretary in the Reich Chancellery; from 1924 to 1932, lord mayor of Essen. A member of the right wing of the Center party, he was nominated by Chancellor Franz von PAPEN to be deputy Reich commissioner on July 20, 1932. Following the PRUSSIAN COUP, this meant that Bracht had *de facto* become Prussian interior minister. Before being appointed to the Reich Interior Ministry by Chancellor Kurt von SCHLEICHER in December 1932, Bracht attained comic fame with the so-called GUSSET DECREE (*Zwickelerlass*), which made bathing apparel a police matter. Bracht resigned on January 28, 1933, despite inducements to continue governing for a time under the state of emergency and suspension of parliament.

Brack, Viktor, b. Haaren, November 11, 1904; d. Landsberg (Lech), June 2, 1948 (executed), SS-*Oberführer*. Brack pursued studies in economics. Originally Himmler's chauffeur, in 1936 he became SS liaison with the Chancellery of the Führer under Philipp BOUHLER; later he

Viktor Brack.

was the latter's deputy as senior officer manager (*Oberdienstleiter*). Coming from a medical family, Brack organized the EUTHANASIA program in Office T4 of the Reich Chancellery, and selected the medical personnel for it. He and his assistants then worked on the setting up of the EXTERMINATION CAMPS in occupied Poland. Brack was sentenced to death in the DOCTORS' TRIAL on August 20, 1947.

Bradfisch, Otto, b. Zweibrücken, May 10, 1903, SS-*Obersturmbannführer*. A lawyer, Bradfisch joined the NSDAP on January 1, 1931; after early 1936 he worked in the Upper Bavarian government and the Bavarian Interior Ministry. He joined the Gestapo in the spring of 1937, then became chief of the State Police (Sipo) office in Neustadt an der Weinstrasse in July 1938. On September 26 of that year, he joined the SS. At the outset of the Russian Campaign, Bradfisch assumed command of Einsatzkommando 8 of Einsatzgruppe B, which participated in the annihilation of Jews within the area of the Central Army Group. He was relieved of this task and given command of the State Police office in Litzmannstadt (Łódź) in April 1942. There, on the order of the Reich Security Main Office (RSHA), he directed the "resettlement" (*Umsiedlung*) of Jews from the ghetto, most of them to the KULMHOF extermination camp. In the summer of 1944 Bradfisch became commander of the Security Police and Security Service (SD) in Litzmannstadt. From early July 1943 to the end of 1944 he was also provisional lord mayor of that city.

After the war Bradfisch lived under an assumed name for a few years. A jury trial in the Munich I State Court sentenced him on July 21, 1961, to 10 years' imprisonment for his activities in Russia. Another jury trial, in Hannover's state court, sentenced him on November 18, 1963, to 13 years' imprisonment for his activities in Litzmannstadt, incorporating the sentence by the Munich court.

A. St.

Brand, Joel, b. Siebenbürgen (Hungary), 1906; d. Bad Kissingen, July 13, 1964, Jewish functionary in Hungary. Brand spent his youth in Germany, but in 1933 returned to Hungary, where he became a textile merchant. In 1941 he began saving Slovak and Hungarian Jews from deportation through payments and bribery. In 1943 he founded a "Jewish Rescue Committee." On May 8, 1944, Brand met with Adolf EICHMANN, who proposed a "goods for blood"

Joel Brand.

(*Ware für Blut*) deal: for 10,000 brand-new trucks, the SS would spare 1 million Jews. Brand traveled to Palestine to raise the money, but was imprisoned by the British. The deal fell through, and 400,000 Hungarian Jews were killed. In 1961 Brand was a main prosecution witness in the Eichmann Trial in Jerusalem. His tragedy is the subject of a play by Heinar Kipphardt, *Joel Brand, Geschichte eines Geschäfts* (Joel Brand: Story of a Business Deal; 1965).

Brandenburg an der Havel, one of the six "killing facilities" in the EUTHANASIA program. Brandenburg was established in late 1939 in an old prison, and had the code name "Facility B." It was decommissioned in November 1940, and its personnel were moved to the more efficient "hospital and nursing home" at BERNBURG AN DER SAALE. According to surviving records, 9,772 people were killed at Brandenburg.

A. St.

Brandt, Karl, b. Mühlhausen (Alsace), January 8, 1904; d. Landsberg (Lech), June 2, 1948 (executed), German physician and SS-*Gruppenführer* (April 20, 1944). Brandt received a medical license in 1928, and thereafter worked at a clinic in Bochum; he joined the NSDAP in January 1932 and the SA in 1933. In the summer of 1933 Brandt treated Hitler's adjutant Wilhelm BRÜCKNER and other members of the entourage, who had been badly injured in a car accident. On Brückner's recommendation, in 1934 Hitler named Brandt his "attending physician" (*Begleitarzt*). Brandt went to Berlin and in

July 1934 was admitted into the SS as an *Unter-sturmführer*. He advanced quickly (in 1939 he was already an *Obersturmbannführer*). In 1940 he joined the Waffen-SS and was assigned to Führer headquarters. Hitler in 1942 appointed him general commissioner (Reich commissioner after August 1944) for sanitation and health (with special assignments). This gave him control over all military and civilian medical institutions. As of 1942 Brandt belonged to the Presidial Council of the Reich Research Council. He fell into disfavor in late 1944 because of an intrigue against Hitler's personal physician, Theo MORELL.

On August 20, 1947, a United States military court sentenced Brandt to death for crimes against humanity, war crimes, and membership in a criminal organization (*see* DOCTORS' TRIAL). His crimes included responsibility for carrying out "cruel medical experiments with often fatal results" (*see* HUMAN EXPERIMENTS) on concentration camp inmates, prisoners of war, and other persons without their consent, as well as for the "aid-in-dying" (*Sterbehilfe*) program (*see* EUTHANASIA).

A. St.

Brandt, Walter, b. Hamburg, September 26, 1912; d. Munich, October 1937, German trade unionist. Brandt worked as a shipping agent; in 1929 he joined the Central Association of Employees (Zentralverband der Angestellten), and in 1931, the International Socialist Combat League (Internationaler sozialistischer Kampfbund), an association of young unionists. After the Seizure of Power, Brandt organized opposition worker groups in Hamburg. He escaped the Gestapo in 1935 by fleeing to Switzerland, where he made connections with emigré circles. On returning to Germany in 1937, Brandt was arrested because comrades who believed him safely abroad had incriminated him during interrogation. He committed suicide while in prison, in order not to betray comrades while under torture.

Brauchitsch, Walther von, b. Berlin, October 4, 1881; d. Hamburg, October 18, 1948, German field marshal (July 19, 1940). Brauchitsch was personal page to the empress while in cadet training. He was commissioned in 1900; during the First World War he was assigned to the General Staff at the western front; in 1921 he was taken into the Reichswehr; in 1930 he became a major general. As head of the Army Training Division, Brauchitsch visited the Red Army in 1931. He was made inspector of the artillery in 1932, and after further commands was appointed by Hitler to be the successor to Werner von FRITSCH as Army commander in chief on February 4, 1938. Simultaneously, he advanced to colonel general.

Brauchitsch was under obligation to Hitler for financial help during a divorce and remarriage. Therefore, and because he was an unpolitical and cautious soldier, Brauchitsch never dared to oppose Hitler's war policies, which he certainly regarded critically. Thus Brauchitsch was not

Karl Brandt as a defendant at Nuremberg.

Walther von Brauchitsch.

much respected in the officer corps, despite the "Blitz" victories in Poland, France, and the Balkans. Hitler increasingly interfered in military operations, bypassing Brauchitsch, who had repeatedly offered to resign, while making him the scapegoat for the winter crisis outside Moscow. On December 19, 1941, Hitler dismissed the general and himself assumed command of the army. On August 20, 1944, Brauchitsch published an article (allegedly to protect endangered friends) directed against the men of the TWENTIETH OF JULY. He called their attempted coup "an act of madness by a small number of men who have forgotten honor." He died in British captivity before the beginning of a planned military proceeding.

Brauchtum und Sitte ("usage and custom"), much-used propaganda formula (mockingly abbreviated as "Brausi" [cf. *Brause*, shower or douche] in popular parlance); a term for "forms of expression of a *völkisch* communal life." Such forms might be manifested by a whole people or race, or by individual groups, professions, landscapes, or epochs. Emphasis on *Brauchtum und Sitte* served to legitimize National Socialist rule. Institutions and hierarchies were portrayed as continuations of organic national traditions. The revival of such old Germanic customs as solstice celebrations, and the cultural glorification of official rituals and celebrations, was meant to create new usages and customs that would express the *völkisch* communal character of the system.

H. H.

Brauer, Max, b. Altona (now Hamburg-Altona), September 3, 1887; d. there, February 2, 1973, German municipal politician. Brauer worked as a glassblower's apprentice and a salesclerk. He joined the SPD (Social Democratic Party of Germany) in 1903, became deputy mayor of Altona in 1919, and was its lord mayor from 1924 to 1933. The National Socialists took Brauer, a committed opponent, into protective custody, but he managed to escape. For a short time he worked for the League of Nations; he then went to the United States as a lecturer in political science. Brauer returned to Germany in 1946 and served two terms as lord mayor of Hamburg (1946 to 1953 and 1957 to 1961), doing much to rebuild the heavily destroyed seaport. He also served in the Bundestag from 1961 to 1965.

Braun, Eva, b. Munich, February 6, 1912; d. Berlin, April 30, 1945, Hitler's mistress, and his

wife for one day. After the suicide of "Geli" RAUBAL in September 1931, the relationship between Hitler and Braun, whom he had met in the studio of his photographer Heinrich HOFFMANN, became intimate. The liaison was carefully hidden from the public, in order not to spoil the image of a Führer far removed from all earthly concerns. To compensate for Braun's loneliness, which brought her close to suicide, Hitler bought her a villa on Wasserburgerstrasse (now Delpstrasse) in Munich, and somewhat later let her move to the BERGHOF. Yet here too she had to remain in the background, and could appear as Hitler's "housewife" only in the most intimate circles. The Führer's headquarters was closed to her during the war. She had to correspond to Hitler's ideal woman—an unemanci-

Eva Braun and Hitler (1943).

pated, unpolitical "companion" (*Kameradin*)—although for reasons of state she was denied the children otherwise touted as blessings. On April 15, 1945, Braun followed Hitler into the bunker under the Chancellery, against his express desire. She was married to him on April 29. On the next day they both committed suicide; according to Hitler's wish, the corpses were burned in the garden.

Braun, Otto, b. Königsberg, January 28, 1872; d. Ascona (Switzerland), December 15, 1955, German politician. Braun joined the SPD (Social Democratic Party of Germany) as a printer's apprentice. From 1911 he was on the party executive committee; in 1919 he became a deputy in the Weimar National Assembly. After the Kapp Putsch (March 13, 1920), Braun became Prussian minister president, a position he held (with short intermissions) for 12 years. The "Red Tsar" (his nickname because of his strongly Social Democratic outlook) in the Republic's largest state (*Land*) was a stabilizing factor in a time of constantly changing state governments. Braun resolutely defended the Republic against radical parties. After the loss of his majority, he headed a minority cabinet, but defended himself only by legal means against Papen's PRUSSIAN COUP (July 20, 1932). Braun's ultimate vindication did not help him. By the Reich president's order of February 6, 1933, Braun was removed from office. To escape the National Socialists he settled in Switzerland. He published his memoirs, *Von Weimar zu Hitler* (From Weimar to Hitler), in 1940.

Braun, Wernher von, b. Wirsitz (Posen), February 23, 1912; d. Alexandria, Va., June 16, 1977, German engineer. Braun joined the Army Weapons Office in 1932. At age 25, he became head of the army's Rocket Research Facility at Peenemünde. In 1938 production of the first prototype of the later long-range ballistic rocket, the A4, was achieved. It was first successfully tested on October 3, 1942, under the propaganda name V2 (V for *Vergeltung*, or vengeance). The V2's first wartime use was on September 8, 1944, against London, which was hit by a total of 1,054 V2s; 2,100 hit Brussels and Antwerp. The SS mistrusted Braun, who was more interested in space travel than in arms technology: he was arrested on March 14, 1944, but was released through the intercession of Albert SPEER. In March 1945 Braun evacuated Peenemünde, and went into American captivity with his team of some 100 technicians. He continued his work after the war in the United

Wernher von Braun.

States, where he became a citizen in 1955. Braun joined NASA in 1959 and helped to develop manned rockets, notably for the "Apollo" moon flight program. In 1970 he became chief planner for NASA.

Braunau, Austrian town on the Inn River, with 5,011 inhabitants in 1934. On Saturday of Holy Week, April 20, 1889, at 7:30 p.m., Adolf Hitler was born on the second floor of the Gasthaus zum Pommer (Pommer Hotel). During the Third Reich, Braunau became a place of pilgrimage for enthusiastic adherents of National Socialism. Units of the "Black Cat" Thirteenth United States Armored Division occupied the town on May 2, 1945. The building where Hitler was born is now used by an organization for the physically handicapped, and attracts numerous, primarily American, tourists. After heated political debate the building was supplied with a memorial plaque bearing the words "Never again fascism."

Braunbuch. *See* Brown Book.

Brauns, Heinrich, b. Cologne, January 3, 1868; d. Lindenberg (Allgäu), October 19, 1939, German politician. Brauns was ordained as a priest (1890); he was prominent in the People's Union for Catholic Germany (1900–1920). From the Center party he tried unsuccessfully to found an ecumenical Christian people's party after the First World War. He served in the National Assembly in 1919 and then in the Reichstag (1920–1923). In 1920 he became labor minister, a post he retained under 13 governments, until 1928. In January 1931 Brauns assumed leadership of a "Committee to Fight Unemployment," which, however, found no recipe for success. The National Socialists held him responsible for the reduction of social welfare measures and accused him of economic and political impotence.

Braunschweig, one of the federal states (*Länder*) of the Weimar Republic, as well as a historical German territorial unit; it was part of the South Hannover–Braunschweig *Gau* of the NSDAP. Braunschweig was important for party history because of the appointment of the "author" Adolf Hitler as government councillor (*Regierungsrat*) on February 25, 1932. The Braunschweig government, which was partly under National Socialist rule from September 1930, thereby made the Austrian a German citizen, a prerequisite for the office of Reich president.

Brausi, derisive popular term for the propaganda slogan BRAUCHTUM UND SITTE ("usage and custom"; a *Brause* is a douche or shower).

Bread, freedom of (*Brotfreiheit;* similarly, *Nahrungsfreiheit,* freedom of nourishment), part of the ideology of National Socialist AUTARKY, the effort to make the German Reich self-sufficient in foodstuffs. The program of the so-called BATTLE FOR CULTIVATION, which was intended to defeat a "hunger blockade" such as that of the First World War and to counteract a dangerous involvement in foreign trade, was designed to serve this struggle.

"Breaking interest servitude" (*Brechung der Zinsknechtschaft*), demand formulated by Gottfried FEDER that was accepted under Article 11 into the NSDAP Program of February 24, 1920. The basically socialist idea of "abolishing income gained without work or effort" was later softened by the comment that the article in question was directed against "Jewish usury," not against interest as such.

Brecht, Bertolt, b. Augsburg, February 10, 1898; d. Berlin, August 14, 1956, German writer. Brecht was a medical orderly in the First World War; he was a haphazard student (natural sciences, medicine, literature). He became a theater critic and playwright (for example, for Max REINHARDT, 1924–1926). Brecht achieved fame with his *Dreigroschenoper* (Threepenny Opera; 1928). As a Marxist, he was considered by the National Socialists to be the embodiment of the kind of trashy scribbler (*Asphaltliterat*)

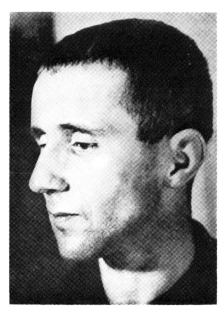

Bertolt Brecht.

whose works fell victim to the BOOK BURNING of May 10, 1933.

Brecht left Germany immediately after the Reichstag fire on February 28, 1933. During his exile (in Switzerland, France, Denmark, the USSR, Finland, Sweden, and the United States), he constantly concerned himself in his dramas with National Socialism, which he saw too one-sidedly as a "handmaiden of capital" and too simplistically as fascism; he did not recognize its racist components. His realistic sequence of scenes *Furcht und Elend des Dritten Reiches* (Fear and Misery of the Third Reich [also translated as *The Private Life of the Master Race*]; 1935–1938), which was based on press and eyewitness reports, can be termed the most successful literary portrait of everyday life under National Socialism. His plays *Die Rundköpfe und die Spitzköpfe* (Roundheads and Peakheads; 1932–1938) and *Die Horatier und die Kuratier* (The Horatii and the Curiatii; 1934) are both directed against National Socialism, as is *Die aufhaltsame Aufstieg des Arturo Ui* (The Resistible Rise of Arturo Ui; 1941), which presents Hitler's Seizure of Power as a gangster's career. The play *Die Gewehre der Frau Carrar* (Señora Carrar's Rifles; 1937) uses the Spanish Civil War to prove that there can be no neutrality in the struggle against fascism. Brecht's script for the Hollywood film *Hangmen Also Die* (1943) deals with the assassination attempt on Reinhard Heydrich. Further disagreements with National Socialism and its war were reflected in the *Svendborger Gedichte* (Svendborg Poems; 1939), *Flüchtlingsgespräche* (Refugee

Conversations; 1940–1941), and *Schweyk im zweiten Weltkrieg* (*Schweyk in the Second World War;* 1941–1944). Persecuted in the United States for "un-American activities," Brecht returned to Germany in 1947, and founded the "Berliner Ensemble" in East Berlin. His worldwide fame assured him some artistic tolerance in the state of German Socialist Unity.

Brechung der Zinsknechtschaft. *See* "Breaking interest servitude."

Bredel, Willi, b. Hamburg, May 2, 1907; d. East Berlin, October 27, 1964, German writer and journalist. Originally a dockworker in Hamburg, Bredel joined the KPD (Communist Party of Germany) in 1923, and was active as a journalist for such workers' newspapers as the *Hamburger Volkszeitung.* In 1930 he was sentenced to two years' imprisonment for literary "high treason." In 1933–1934 he was incarcerated in the Fuhlsbüttel concentration camp. He fled to Czechoslovakia in 1934 and was deprived of German citizenship in 1935. Bredel edited the exile journal *Das Wort* (The Word) in Moscow (with Bertolt **BRECHT** and Lion **FEUCHTWANGER**). From 1937 to 1939 he fought in the Spanish Civil War. Returning in 1945, he was president of the German Academy of Arts in the German Democratic Republic (GDR) after 1962.

Breeding (*Züchtung*), term that originally referred only to the systematic increase and eventual improvement of animals and plants, but that Charles Darwin applied to humans: "With the exception of the human case, no breeder is so ignorant as to allow his worst animals to reproduce." In this sense the term "breeding" was taken up by Houston Stewart **CHAMBERLAIN** and *völkisch* theorists such as Josef **LANZ** for their program of racial biology: "Racial breeding and pure breeding will be and must be the sole religion and church of the future." After the Seizure of Power, the National Socialists strove for the "rebirth" of the nation "through the conscious breeding of a new human" (Hitler). According to Walther **DARRÉ**, in animal breeding "only a few noble sires [were] often necessary in order to raise the whole level of breeding and transmit noble traits to the offspring." Because mankind was also "naturally subject to the same laws of breeding," National Socialist leaders wanted, alongside the "exclusion of the worst," the artificial **SELECTION** of the "best Germans by dint of blood." Himmler in particular attempted after 1932 to fill the SS with a "racial selection of men."

H. H.

Breeding Guardian (*Zuchtwart*), occupation discussed but never introduced in the Third Reich (it was to have had "a Reich main office, state offices, and local branch offices"). Trained in the biology of heredity, medicine, and marriage counseling, the guardian was to have responsibility for "all questions affecting the biological heritage [*Erbgut*] of our *Volk*" (Walther Darré).

Brehm, Bruno, b. Laibach (now Ljubljana, Yugoslavia), July 23, 1892; d. Altaussee (Styria), June 5, 1974, Austrian writer. Brehm was an officer in the First World War, and was gravely wounded; he was acquainted with the author Edwin **DWINGER**. He studied art history, and worked as a publisher's salesman; in 1928 he became a free-lance writer. Brehm's fictional trilogy *Apis und Este* (1931–1933; two volumes were translated as *They Call It Patriotism* and *That Was the End*), which made him famous and which was awarded the National Book Prize in 1939, deals with the collapse of the Habsburg Empire. After the Anschluss, which Brehm greeted as the realization of the "Greater-German *Volk* idea," he was a councilman in Vienna, then an ordinance officer. His postwar trilogy, *Das zwölfjährige Reich* (The Twelve-Year Reich; 1960–1964), was a not very successful attempt at a critical evaluation of National Socialism and Hitler.

Breitscheid, Rudolf, b. Cologne, November 2, 1874; d. Buchenwald concentration camp, August 24, 1944, German politician. Breitscheid was a political economist and journalist who

Bruno Brehm.

Rudolf Breitscheid.

moved from progressive politics to the SPD (Social Democratic Party of Germany) in 1912; he belonged to the USPD (Independent Socialists) from 1917 to 1922. After the revolution, Breitscheid was Prussia's first socialist interior minister (1918–1919); from 1920 he served as a Reichstag deputy, and from 1922, on the executive committee of the newly reunited SPD's Reichstag delegation. He was also the party spokesman on foreign affairs. As a committed supporter of the conciliatory course advocated by Gustav STRESEMANN, he was appointed to the German delegation at the League of Nations. Parties on the political Right, especially the National Socialists, attacked Breitscheid for seeking compliance with the terms of the Versailles treaty, as an *Erfüllungspolitiker* (fulfillment-politician). In late March 1933, Breitscheid moved to Switzerland to avoid seizure by the National Socialists. He was deprived of German citizenship in August of that year and went to Paris, where he unsuccessfully tried to establish a popular front with the Communists to fight Hitler. In 1940 Breitscheid fled before the German troops to Marseilles. The Vichy government extradited him to Germany on December 11, 1941. There he died during an air raid while interned in a concentration camp.

Breker, Arno, b. Elberfeld (now Wuppertal-Elberfeld), July 19, 1900, German sculptor. Breker studied in Düsseldorf (1928–1932), and after a stay in Paris, settled in Berlin in 1933. His statues for the Olympic Stadium (Silver Medal in 1936) so pleased Hitler and his master builder, Albert SPEER, that Breker was showered with public commissions. Cultural ideologue Alfred ROSENBERG saw in Breker's monumental figures a representation of the "force and willpower" (*Wucht und Willenhaftigkeit*) of the age. Among other creations, Breker sculpted the heroic statues "Party" and "Army" for the NEW REICH CHANCELLERY, where they flanked the main entrance. He became a professor at the Academy of Fine Arts in Berlin in 1938. In 1942 the VICHY government arranged a large exhibi-

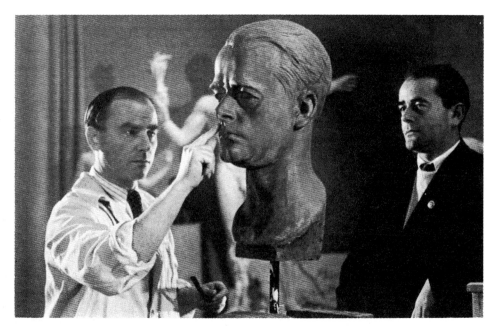

Arno Breker sculpts Albert Speer.

tion of Breker's works in Paris, on the occasion of which the elderly sculptor Aristide Maillol praised him as "the German Michelangelo." Postwar critics not only criticized Breker for his services to a criminal regime, but also found fault with the "empty pathos" of his "savage" giant figures. Labeled as a fellow traveler, Breker worked as an architect and sculptor for the Gerling company; his memoirs, *Im Strahlungsfeld der Ereignisse* (In the Focus of Events; 1972), deplored the alleged witch-hunt against him and his art.

Brennessel, Die (The Stinging [Burning] Nettle), National Socialist satirical journal, published from 1931 by the EHER PRESS; it appeared monthly from January to March of that year, bimonthly from April to September, and weekly after October. Its first editors were Karl Prühäussler and, after September 1931, Wilhelm WEISS, who also served as editor in chief from 1933 to 1938; the managing editors were Dietrich Loder and, after July 1937, C. M. Köhn. Circulation was approximately 29,000 in 1937. The journal was folio-size, and published expensive color pages. An introductory poem in the first issue proclaimed sentimentally and programmatically that the journal would "burn tirelessly, and by burning, extinguish German dishonor"; further, it would "know no mercy for those who disgraced Germany's honor." It con-

"For the health—Prague ham." *Brennessel* caricature of the Czech president, Edvard Beneš, during the 1938 Sudeten Crisis.

tained caricatures and satirical articles by Karl Prühäussler, Paul Schondorff, Hans SCHWEIT-ZER, and Jo-Hans Rösler, among others. The magazine was strongly antisemitic and anti-Weimar, but it also published sentimental NS self-portraits in print and pictures. After 1933 it also attacked emigrés and foreign opponents. The last issue was published on December 27, 1938.

S. O.

Brest-Litovsk, Polish city and fortress on the Bug River; population, 50,700 (1939). Brest-Litovsk was ceded to the Soviet Union after the Polish Campaign (*see* GERMAN-SOVIET NONAGGRESSION PACT). On March 3, 1918, a treaty dictated by the Central Powers to the young Soviet state, weakened by revolution, had been concluded in Brest-Litovsk. This treaty deprived Russia of 1.4 million sq km (540,540 sq miles) and some 60 million inhabitants (of Finland, Latvia, Estonia, Courland, Poland, Lithuania, the Ukraine, Georgia, and Armenia). The Reichstag approved the treaty, with the SPD (Social Democratic Party of Germany) abstaining from the vote, on March 22, 1918, thereby damaging for a long time the credibility of Germany's "eastern policy." The Treaty of Brest-Litovsk, which was the first occasion for promoting the right of peoples to self-determination, was declared void on November 11, 1918, at the armistice treaty of Compiègne, and on November 13, 1918, by the Soviet government.

Briand, Aristide, b. Nantes, March 28, 1862; d. Paris, March 7, 1932, French politician. Briand

Aristide Briand.

worked as a journalist and lawyer; originally a socialist, after 1910 he was a moderate social republican. From 1906 to 1932 he served 10 times as premier or foreign minister; he also headed the Foreign Ministry for 10 years, the uninterrupted tenure from 1925 to 1932 being especially significant. Together with Gustav STRESEMANN he guided a policy of German-French rapprochement by means of the LOCARNO PACT, and together with Stresemann (as well as Neville Chamberlain and Charles Dawes) was awarded the Nobel Peace Prize for 1926. In his own country, however, Briand was increasingly attacked as a "German lackey," and was unable to carry through his disarmament policy. His May 1930 memorandum on European union was referred to again after 1945 during the process of European unification.

Briansk and Viazma, Soviet cities in the path of the German offensive against Moscow (begun on October 2, 1941) in the RUSSIAN CAMPAIGN.

Bridal schools (*Bräuteschulen*), courses on an American model to prepare young women for marriage and motherhood; they were first offered in 1929 by the so-called domestic happiness movement (*Heimglückbewegung*). In 1936 the National Socialist Women's Agency adopted them under the name MARRIAGE SCHOOLS, and developed them in the MOTHERS' SERVICE bureau.

Brigade (*Brigade*), large military unit, between a division and a regiment; also a sub-unit in the SA, SS, and NSKK (National Socialist Motor Corps), under a *Brigadeführer* (major general). Such a brigade consisted of several "standards" (*see* STANDARTE).

Broad-gauge railroad (*Breitspurbahn*), proposal for new broad-gauge (3 m, or 9.84 feet) transcontinental stretches of the Reich Railroad (Reichsbahn) made by Fritz TODT in 1941. Taken up by Hitler, it was transmitted to the Transportation Ministry for planning. The broad-gauge cars would be twice as long and wide as normal cars, and would have an upper level, giving them eight times the normal capacity. A train consisting of seven passenger cars and a baggage car would transport 1,728 persons from Kazan via Moscow to Berlin, or from Istanbul via Vienna and Munich to Paris, at a speed of 250 km (about 155 miles) per hour. Passengers in the better classes could expect "the luxury of an ocean steamship." The broad-gauge railroad

of the "Great-Germanic Reich" belongs to the "gigantomaniac" construction plans (*see* ARCHITECTURE) that Hitler envisaged after the "final victory."

Broch, Hermann, b. Vienna, November 1, 1886; d. New Haven, Conn., May 31, 1951, Austrian writer and psychologist. Broch came from a Jewish industrialist family; he ran his father's factories from 1916 to 1927. He then lived as a free-lance writer in Styria (*Die Schlafwandler* [The Sleepwalkers]; 1931, and *Der Tod des Vergil* [The Death of Vergil]; 1937–1945). When Austria was occupied in 1938, Broch was arrested. After his release, he fled to the United States via Vienna and England in 1938. Between 1941 and 1948 he studied mass psychology at Princeton University. In 1949 he was appointed a professor of German literature at Yale University.

Brod, Max, b. Prague, May 27, 1884; d. Tel Aviv, December 20, 1960, Austrian-Israeli writer and essayist. Brod was a pacifist and active Zionist from 1913; he was a friend of Kafka, against whose will he was administrator of the Kafka estate. From 1929 to 1939 Brod was cultural affairs editor of the *Prager Tagblatt* (Prague Daily News). In 1933 his name appeared on the first National Socialist index of proscribed literature, and on May 10 of that year his books (including *Tycho Brahe;* 1912) were publicly burned. After 1939 Brod lived in Israel as a free-lance writer. In 1940 he became a dramatic adviser (*Dramaturg*) at the Hebrew National Theater (Habimah) in Tel Aviv.

Max Brod.

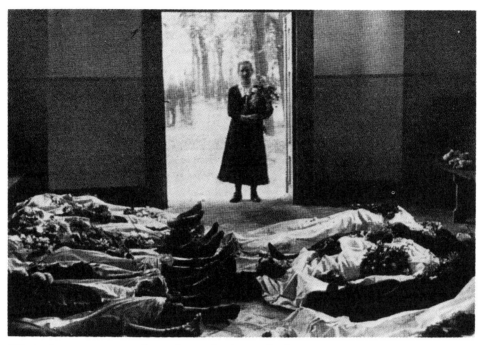

Ethnic German victims of Bromberg Bloody Sunday lying in state.

Bröger, Karl, b. Nuremberg, March 10, 1886; d. Erlangen, May 4, 1944, German writer. Bröger was a part-time construction worker, then a Social Democratic journalist. He belonged to those working-class poets (such as Max BARTHEL) who became nationalists after achieving literary success. Bröger extolled the First World War in various poems as "the greatest communal experience," thus becoming himself a "herald of German comradeship and national unity" (Lennartz). His best-known poem was "Bekenntnisse eines Arbeiters" (Confessions of a Worker; 1914). Bröger also made a name for himself as a Frankish vernacular poet. After the Seizure of Power he "freely avowed his loyalty" to National Socialism, which he hoped would eliminate class antagonisms.

Bromberg Bloody Sunday (*Bromberg Blutsonntag*), term for September 3, 1939, in the Polish city of Bromberg, whose total population of some 120,000 inhabitants included 15,000 ethnic Germans. Polish troops (especially the Fifteenth Infantry Division), retreating after the German attack of September 1 (*see* POLISH CAMPAIGN), together with incited civilians, caused a bloodbath among the German population. At least 1,100 people fell victim, according to findings by the WEHRMACHT INVESTIGATION OFFICE, before German troops captured the city on September 4. National Socialist propaganda used the Bromberg massacre to justify the German "defensive campaign" and "vengeance." Special courts were formed to try the acts committed in Bromberg, and many death sentences were meted out.

Bronnen, Arnolt (real name, Arne Bronner), b. Vienna, August 19, 1895; d. East Berlin, October 12, 1959, Austrian writer. Bronnen moved to Berlin in 1920, became friendly with the young Bertolt BRECHT, and made himself notorious through such scandalous plays as *Vatermord* (Parricide; 1920). Although of Jewish background, Bronnen moved from left-leaning anarchism to an admiration for Hitler. His novel *O. S.* (1929) so glorified the struggles of the FREE

Arnolt Bronnen.

CORPS that Goebbels noticed the author and rewarded him with the post of producer at Radio Berlin. After the Seizure of Power, this "salon fascist" (Kurt TUCHOLSKY) procured for himself an Aryan certificate (*see* CERTIFICATE OF DESCENT), but he still came under National Socialist attack as an "opportunist." In 1936 Bronnen was entrusted with programming for German television. In 1937, however, he was expelled from the REICH WRITING CHAMBER and retired to his Austrian homeland. After 1945 he again became a Communist, justified himself by writing *a.b. gibt zu protokoll* (a.b. gives his deposition; 1954), and moved to East Berlin, where he became a theater critic.

Brown, official color of the NSDAP. Since stronger, emotionally more evocative colors were already in use elsewhere (red by the Communists, black by the Italian Fascists), the National Socialists chose brown rather accidentally, inspired by FREE CORPS uniforms, when a standardized attire was needed for the SA: the BROWNSHIRT. In 1925, when the SA and NSDAP were reinstituted, "earthy" brown was declared the color of the movement. Later interpretations defined it as an expression of special ties with the "native soil" and the *Volk.* Brown soon became the symbol for the National Socialists, especially because of their mass processions in brown shirts.

Brown Book (*Braunbuch*), a publication, in August 1933, of the World Auxiliary Committee for Victims of German Fascism (Welthilfskomitee für die Opfer des deutschen Faschismus) that aimed to prove National Socialist guilt for the REICHSTAG FIRE. The initiator of the Brown Book and of the committee was the Communist publisher Willi MÜNZENBERG. With the help of documents, some of them forgeries, and alluding to the fire's usefulness for the National Socialists, the Brown Book has had considerable propaganda effect that has continued into scholarly postwar controversies. A second, lesser-known Brown Book dealt with the REICHSTAG FIRE TRIAL in April 1934.

Brown cult (*Brauner Kult*), postwar designation of the festivals and CELEBRATIONS established by the National Socialists.

Brown House (*Braunes Haus*), term for the former Barlow mansion in Munich (Briennerstrasse 45), built in 1829–1830 in a classical style; it was acquired by the NSDAP on June 5, 1930, with money from industry and from a special party appeal. The name derived from the color of the uniforms worn by the new owners, and was first used only popularly; the party later adopted it officially. By the time the Reich NSDAP leadership moved into the Brown House on January 1, 1931 (after extensive remodeling by Paul TROOST), it was too small because of large increases in membership after the successful elections of September 14, 1930. Adjacent buildings were rented, and the name Brown House was soon extended to the whole complex. Party buildings in other cities were also popularly called "brown houses."

Brownshirt (*Braunhemd*), part of the uniform worn beginning in 1926 by the SA and other party branches; it superseded the gray windbreakers worn until then. In plural form, the term (Brownshirts) was used to denote the National Socialists. The brown shirt was chosen as an inexpensive item of standardized clothing; its earthy color was later glorified as a symbol of the "movement's connections with sod and soil."

Bruckner, Ferdinand (real name, Theodor Tagger), b. Vienna, August 26, 1891; d. Berlin, December 5, 1958, Austrian playwright. From 1923 to 1927 Bruckner directed the Berlin Renaissance Theater. As a Jew he made a literary protest against antisemitism with *Die Rassen* (The Races; 1933), and was forced first into Austrian exile (1933) and then American exile (1936). He was co-founder of the Aurora publishing house. Bruckner returned to Germany in 1951 and became a dramatic adviser (*Dramaturg*) at the Schiller and Schlosspark theaters in West Berlin.

Brückner, Wilhelm, b. Baden-Baden, December 11, 1884; d. Herbstdorf (Chiemgau), August 1954, SA-*Obergruppenführer* (November 9, 1934). Brückner was an officer in the First World War and then fought with the EPP Free Corps; he studied political economy. He joined the NSDAP in 1922, and led the SA "Munich" regiment during the HITLER PUTSCH. After serving four months of his one-and-a-half-year term, he worked for a time as representative of the VOLK LEAGUE FOR GERMANDOM ABROAD. In 1930 he joined the SA; he became Hitler's SA adjutant and was thereafter part of Hitler's personal entourage. Through Brückner, Hitler made the acquaintance of his attending physician, Karl BRANDT. Because of internal disagreements, in 1940 Brückner transferred to the Wehrmacht, where he became a colonel by the end of the war.

Bruderräte. *See* Fraternal councils.

Brüning, Heinrich, b. Münster, November 26, 1885; d. Norwich, Conn., March 30, 1970, German politician. Brüning studied philosophy, history, and political economy; he was deeply affected by his experience as an officer at the front in the First World War. From 1919 he took part in the Catholic Christian Trade Union movement, from 1920 to 1930 as its general secretary. He was a Center party Reichstag deputy from 1924 to 1933, and was the party delegation chairman in 1929. As his party's financial expert, Brüning was appointed Reich chancellor on March 30, 1930, after the collapse of the Great Coalition (*see* Hermann MÜLLER) and in light of the intensifying WORLD ECONOMIC CRISIS. With a cabinet of bourgeois centrist politicians having no ties to their party delegations, he initiated a program of drastic overhaul that was intended to consolidate the budget and end the payment of REPARATIONS.

Both goals were reached at the price of a dramatic heightening of the crisis, which brought landslide victories in the next elections to the radical parties, and especially to the National Socialists, thus rendering illusory Brüning's parliamentary majority. He continued to lead the government (also serving as foreign minister after October 1931) with a presidial cabinet (*see* PRESIDIAL CABINETS), and was barely tolerated by the SPD (Social Democratic Party of Germany). His support for Hindenburg's re-election as Reich president contributed in particular to the diminution of his influence, since the president resented the fact that his victory over Hitler (April 1932) was won "with the help of *Sozis* and *Katholen*" (SPD and

Heinrich Brüning.

Center). Moreover, presidential advisers maligned Brüning's EASTERN AID program as "agrarian Bolshevism" in discussions with the large-estate owner Hindenburg. Thus Brüning lost his last political support, and he resigned on May 30, 1932.

By usurping parliamentary power, Brüning's government marks the transition from a democratic to an authoritarian system. Its austerity policies, moreover, contributed to the mood of fatigue with the Weimar Republic, while also creating the financial basis for Hitler's use of deficit financing to consolidate his power (*see* WORK CREATION). In vain Brüning opposed the ENABLING LAW in 1933; as new chairman of the Center party (May 1933) his options were limited to the decision to dissolve the party on July 5, 1933. In June 1934 Brüning went into exile. He was a professor at Harvard University from 1939 to 1950, and in Cologne, from 1951 to 1954. He never regained any political influence. His *Memoiren 1918–1934* were published in 1970.

Brutal (*brutal*), word often given a positive meaning in National Socialist usage, in the sense of "courageous" or "decisive," comparable to the transformed meaning of such words as "fantastic" or "ruthless."

Brzezinka, Polish name of the AUSCHWITZ-Birkenau extermination camp.

Buch, Eva-Maria, b. Berlin, January 31, 1921; d. there, August 5, 1943 (executed), German opposition fighter. Buch received a Catholic education and engaged in linguistic studies. In 1941 she came in contact with the group around Harro SCHULZE-BOYSEN (*see* RED ORCHESTRA); in light of the misery created by the war, she was attracted to Communist goals. Arrested on October 10, 1942, for inciting French slave laborers to resist, Buch was characterized by the Reich military court as combining "the slyness of a Catholic woman and the hostility to the [National Socialist] state of a Communist," and as such, deserving death. She was sentenced accordingly.

Buch, Walter, b. Bruchsal, October 24, 1883; d. Ammersee, November 12, 1949 (suicide), German politician. A major during the First World War, Buch joined the NSDAP in 1922; in August 1923 he became SA-Führer of Munich. After the party's reconstitution (February 1925), Buch belonged to it from the beginning. In 1927 he became chairman of the "Uschla" (*see* INQUIRY AND ARBITRATION COMMITTEE), and in 1928 a Reichstag deputy. After the Seizure of Power,

Walter Buch.

Buch's Uschla post was elevated to that of "supreme party arbitrator" (*Oberster Parteirichter*), and he was awarded the rank of SA-*Obergruppenführer*. Both during and after the RÖHM AF-

FAIR Buch was considerably involved in party purges. He had in the beginning promoted the career of Martin BORMANN, who was also his son-in-law. When the relationship broke down in 1942, Buch lost his influence. A radical antisemite, Buch was classified as a "major offender" by an appeals court in July 1949; he was sentenced to hard labor and loss of property.

Buchenwald, National Socialist concentration camp, constructed in the wooded area of Etter Mountain near Weimar in the summer of 1937. In November 1939 the camp contained some 12,600 inmates, of whom approximately 2,400 were Jews. Shortly before the war ended, Buchenwald temporarily housed up to 47,000 people, most in transit to other camp's. At the liberation, Americans found 21,000 survivors.

The inmates worked for the GERMAN ARMAMENT WORKS, in workshops (for example, locksmith and carpentry), in the camp's spacious plant nursery, in various equestrian facilities (stables, indoor and outdoor riding areas), and in a nearby quarry. The camp had about 130 satellite and auxiliary camps, some far removed from the main facility.

Barrack in Buchenwald.

Housing, food supplies, and sanitary conditions in Buchenwald were poor. Numerous inmates fell victim to hunger, illness (especially dysentery epidemics), exhaustion, maltreatment, hanging, torture (such as being bound to poles or trees), shootings (sometimes during alleged escape attempts), and medical experiments (such as spotted fever research). In an area designated for shooting inmates in the back of the neck (the "horse stables"), beginning in 1941 several thousand Russian prisoners of war were treacherously murdered under the pretext of medical experimentation by order of the Reich Security Main Office (RSHA). Executions by shooting also took place in the crematorium (the victims included Ernst THÄLMANN). In Operation 14f13 (see INVALID OPERATION), sick inmates were sent to the killing facilities of the EUTHANASIA program. In the camp's detention hall, many inmates were killed with injections of Evipan or phenol administered by camp doctor Erwin DING-SCHULER on orders of the commandant, Karl Koch. Tattooed human skin was used in Buchenwald to produce exhibition specimens or useful articles for SS family members (lampshades, briefcases, and so on).

Because of the widespread corruption in the camp (such as the theft of inmate property), combined with the killing of inmates, Commandant Koch was sentenced to death by an SS and police court and executed by shooting in the camp. His co-defendant and wife, Ilse KOCH (the "Witch of Buchenwald"), was accused of receiving stolen goods but acquitted owing to insufficient evidence. Koch's successor, Hermann Pister, was sentenced to death by a French military court and died in captivity.

W. D.

Bückeberg, mountain near Hameln; location of the main festivities of HARVEST THANKS DAY from 1933 to 1937 (canceled in 1938 because of the SUDETEN CRISIS and after 1939 because of the war). Hundreds of thousands of farmers were brought to the Bückeberg each year from all parts of the Reich, up to 1.2 million in 1937. The mountain slope formed a huge grandstand for the masses. In its middle a path 800 m (2,624 feet) long led to the summit, up which Hitler strode, and which was called, upon his wish, "the path through the *Volk.*" Before the "harvest altar" at the mountaintop, Hitler accepted the "harvest crown" as a sign that the peasantry was transmitting to the nation the harvest it had gathered. After the reintroduction of compulsory military service in 1935, a public exercise by the Wehrmacht took place that was meant to express the unity of peasants (*Nährstand*) and soldiers (*Wehrstand*).

K. V.

Bukovina, Romanian area (from 1918) on the outer edge of the Carpathian Mountains; area, about 10,000 sq km (approximately 3861 sq miles); population, 1 million. In the summer of 1940, Moscow demanded the cession of Bukovina in accordance with the secret supplementary protocol of the GERMAN-SOVIET NONAGGRESSION PACT, although the treaty had specified only BESSARABIA. Berlin succeeded only in reducing the Soviet demands to northern Bukovina. This fact, together with the Bessarabian issue, led to bitter resentment in the relations between Germany and the Soviet Union.

Bulgaria, kingdom in southeastern Europe; area, 103,000 sq km (39,768 sq miles); population, 6.1 million (1934). During the First World War, Bulgaria, which sided with the Central Powers after 1915, temporarily achieved its territorial goals in Romania and Serbia. However, in the Treaty of Neuilly (the Bulgarian "Versailles") in 1919, Bulgaria was pushed back to the borders of 1913 and was burdened with heavy reparations. The result was economic and political instability, which led to unrest in the 1920s, such as the Communist rebellion under Georgi DIMITROV in 1923. In 1934–1935 Tsar BORIS III established a "royal dictatorship" supported by the military, and aligned himself with the Axis powers out of national considerations. With Germany's help Bulgaria regained the southern Dobruja area from Romania, and joined the THREE-POWER AGREEMENT in March 1941.

German troops received permission for deployment in Bulgaria for the BALKAN CAMPAIGN (April–May 1941). Victory over Yugoslavia and Greece brought Bulgaria, in addition to its territory lost in 1918, all of Yugoslav Macedonia and, with the annexation of the Greek portion of Thrace, access to the Aegean Sea. Boris III entered the war on Germany's side against England and the United States at the end of 1941, but refused to participate in the RUSSIAN CAMPAIGN: "My people feel Russian and think German." The German wish to have about 50,000 Bulgarian Jews deported to extermination camps was countered by unanimous opposition of the Bulgarian parliament on March 17, 1943.

Bulgarian neutrality vis-à-vis the Soviet Union did not prevent occupation by the Red Army in the fall of 1944. The Communists soon won the upper hand in a putsch by the "Patriotic Front," and under Soviet pressure Bulgaria entered the war against Germany on October 28. In the postwar era Bulgaria was considered Moscow's closest ally in the Balkans. However, except for the Dobruja region, in 1945 it had to renounce its territorial gains of 1940–1941.

M. F.

Bullet Decree (*Kugelerlass*), order of the Wehrmacht High Command (OKW), presumably from early 1944, stating that escaped PRISONERS OF WAR who were recaptured—with the exception of British and American soldiers—were to be turned over to the Chief of the Security Police and the SD (CSSD) under the code name "Stage III" (*Stufe* III); it was stressed that the transfers should under no circumstances be made public. With a decree of March 2, 1944, and a telex of March 4, the CSSD informed its subordinate offices of the Bullet Decree and ordered that the transferred prisoners of war be moved to the MAUTHAUSEN concentration camp under the code name "Operation Bullet" (Aktion Kugel). The captives were killed in Mauthausen. The Bullet Decree itself has never been found. Its existence and content are inferred from, among other sources, the CSSD telex of March 4, 1944, which gives it verbatim.

A. St.

Bumke, Erwin, b. Stolp (Pomerania), July 7, 1874; d. Leipzig, April 20, 1945 (suicide), German jurist. Bumke studied in Freiburg, Leipzig, Munich, Berlin, and Greifswald, receiving a degree (*Promotion*) in 1896. In 1902 he became a law clerk in Stettin; in 1905, district judge (*Landrichter*) in Essen. In February 1907 Bumke joined the imperial Justice Ministry; he was named councillor (*Regierungsrat*) in April 1909, and privy councillor (*Geheimer Regierungsrat*) in May 1912. He worked primarily on the reform of criminal law and criminal proceedings. As of January 1, 1920, he became ministerial director, taking over the division of criminal law, criminal proceedings, and sentencing. On February 15, 1929, Bumke was named president of the SUPREME COURT (Reichsgericht) in Leipzig; he remained in office until 1945. Concurrently he was chairman of the State Law Court for the German Reich (Staatsgerichtshof für das Deutsche Reich), and, after December 1932, deputy to the Reich president.

Bumke had a reputation as an apolitical lawyer of the old school. Nevertheless, in 1919 he joined the GERMAN NATIONAL PEOPLE'S PARTY, and in May 1937 the NSDAP. He became a compliant servant of the National Socialist regime, which rewarded him by twice extending his term in office, despite his age. Under his presidency the Supreme Court increasingly yielded to the demands of the rulers and became an instrument of state power and terror. In addition, Bumke chaired a "Special Disciplinary Senate" (Besonderer Strafsenat), also called the "Führer's Court of Justice" (Gerichtshof des Führers). This body was created expressly to serve the manipulation of the law: it "corrected" valid but unsuitable sentences in keeping with Hitler's intent. Bumke took his own life shortly before the war's end.

U. B.

Buna, synthetic rubber, produced from butadiene, using sodium (Na) as a catalyst. In 1936 industrial mass production of Buna began at I.G. FARBEN, which was to supply this vital raw material. By 1939, however, only 22 percent of the need for synthetic rubber had been met (22,000 tons). In Zschoppau, Leverkusen, Hüls (after May 1940), and Ludwigshafen (after March 1943), about 117,000 tons were produced in 1943. Production then fell because of air raids.

Bund der Auslandsdeutschen. *See* League of Foreign Germans.

Bund der Landwirte. *See* League of Agriculturists.

Bund Deutscher Mädel. *See* League of German Girls.

Bund Deutscher Offiziere. *See* League of German Officers.

Bund Deutscher Osten. *See* League for the German East.

Bund für Deutsche Kirche. *See* League for a German Church.

Bund Nationalsozialistischer Deutscher Juristen. *See* National Socialist League of Law Guardians.

Bund Oberland. *See* Oberland League.

Bundschuh, shoe fastened with an ankle strap, worn by National Socialist youth organization members (Hitler Youth and League of German Girls), and created with intentional reference to the symbol of the 16th-century peasant wars. The historical allusion conformed to NS self-consciousness as a class-transcending ideology of VOLK COMMUNITY.

Bürckel, Josef, b. Lingenfeld (Palatinate), March 30, 1895; d. Neustadt (Haardt), September 28, 1944, German politician. Bürckel was a teacher; he fought as a frontline soldier in the First World War. He joined the NSDAP in 1921, and fought separatist tendencies in the Palatinate as *Gau* leader there after March 1926. He became a Reichstag deputy in 1930. As a skillful negotiator, Bürckel was made Reich commissioner in charge of reincorporating the Saarland in 1935, and for the unification of Austria with Germany in 1938. In 1938–1939 he was Reich governor (*Reichsstatthalter*) of Austria and *Gau* leader of Vienna. Bürckel returned to the West as head of the civilian administration in occupied Lorraine on August 2, 1940. He ruled here and in his "Westmark" *Gau* (Saar region and Saar-Palatinate) as a provincial dictator. On October 22, 1940, he had all the Jews in his "Westmark" territories deported to unoccupied France, where many died in the camp at GURS. This action only temporarily quelled the displeasure within the National Socialist hierarchy over his extravagant life-style and his autocratic rule. When the front neared his area and he only hesitantly took up the defense measures that had been ordered, Martin BORMANN suggested suicide to him. This was then announced as an accident and disguised with a state funeral.

Burckhardt, Carl Jacob, b. Basel, September 10, 1891; d. Vinzel, March 3, 1974, Swiss writer and diplomat. From 1918 to 1921 Burckhardt was an attaché in Vienna; in 1923 he became

Josef Bürckel.

Carl Jacob Burckhardt.

Red Cross representative in charge of prison conditions in Turkey; in 1929, a professor of history in Zurich (in 1932, in Geneva as well). In 1937 Burckhardt was appointed League of Nations high commissioner in Danzig, where he found himself in a hopeless position trying to resolve Polish and German conflicting interests, the latter becoming increasingly identical with National Socialist demands (*see* DANZIG QUESTION). After the outbreak of war, Burckhardt was active with the Red Cross (president, 1944–1948), concerning himself with prisoners of war and civilian internees. Besides his scholarly histories (such as *Richelieu*, 1935; 1965–1967), Burckhardt's memoirs of his political service are important eyewitness reports from a major crisis area before the Second World War (*Meine Danziger Mission 1937–1939* [My Mission in Danzig]; 1960).

Bürgerbräu assassination attempt (*Bürgerbräu-Attentat*), bomb attack on Hitler in Munich's Bürgerbräu Cellar on November 8, 1939, on the occasion of his yearly speech to longtime followers (*see* OLD COMBATANTS). In months of secret work at night, the carpenter Johann ELSER had built a powerful time bomb into a column of the hall behind the speaker's platform. It exploded at 9:30 p.m., causing the ceiling to collapse and killing seven people; an eighth person died later of injuries. Hitler was to have been eliminated as a perpetrator of the war, but he had left early, at 9:15. Speculations about those behind the attack, in public as well as within the National Socialist hierarchy, extended from the "British Secret Service" to "aid from above." But the

Bürgerbräu assassination attempt. Damage in the Bürgerbräu Cellar after the bomb explosion.

propaganda theory could not be proved valid, nor could the Gestapo deliver to Hitler the sought-for "foreign wire-pullers." There remained the individual act of Elser, who was liquidated in the Dachau concentration camp toward the end of the war, when the holding of the expected show trial became unrealistic.

Bürgermeister (mayor), according to the GERMAN COMMUNAL ORDINANCE of January 30, 1935, the manager of communal affairs and representative of a municipality. In localities with fewer than 10,000 inhabitants it was an honorary position; in larger ones it was full-time. In urban districts (*Stadtkreisen*), the post was called *Ober-Bürgermeister* (lord mayor). The mayor was appointed by the government inspectorate (*staatliche Aufsichtsbehörde*) on the recommendation of the DELEGATE OF THE NSDAP, as were the deputy mayors (*Beigeordneten*). The mayor's term of office was limited to 6 years if honorary and 12 if full-time.

Bürgersteuer. *See* Poll tax.

Bürgertum. *See* Bourgeoisie.

Burschell, Friedrich, b. Ludwigshafen, August 9, 1889; d. Munich, April 19, 1970, German writer and translator. Burschell worked for the journal *Die Neue Weltbühne* (The New World Stage) and the *Prager Tagblatt* (Prague Daily), went into French exile in 1933, and lived in Spain and Czechoslovakia from 1933 to 1938. After the outbreak of the Second World War he moved to England. Burschell resided in the Federal Republic after 1954.

Burschenschaften (student fraternities; from *Bursch*, youth; lad), movement—arising at the time of the Wars of Liberation from Napoleonic rule (1813–1815) in Germany—that sought reforms in all aspects of student life as well as the unification of Germany. After phases of political radicalization and of being banned as "demagogic alliances," the Burschenschaften split into various fraternities (Verbindungen), with an overwhelmingly conservative orientation. In the 1920s they cooperated with *völkisch* and nationalistic groups, adopted anti-Republican and *völkisch* positions, and fought alongside nationalistic professors against CULTURE BOLSHEVISM and leftist organizations. This did not shield the fraternities from SYNCHRONIZATION after the Seizure of Power, though it did delay it: although their dissolution was officially ordered in 1935, several years passed before they, like other student groups, were transformed into "Kameradschaften" (comradeships) of the NATIONAL SOCIALIST GERMAN STUDENTS' LEAGUE. Only in Austria and Czechoslovakia were the fraternities able to retain organizational independence, since they were intended to function there as "representatives of the *völkisch* Great-

German idea" in the German-language institutions of higher education.

H. H.

Burte, Hermann (pseud. of Hermann Strübe), b. Maulburg (Baden), February 15, 1879; d. Lörrach, March 22, 1960, German writer. Beginning as a lyric poet ("Patricia"; 1910), Burte achieved a breakthrough with his ideological novel *Wiltfeber, der ewige Deutsche* (Wiltfeber, the Eternal German; 1912). His *völkisch*-racist ideas and the doctrine of a "Pure Christ" (*Reiner Krist*), an antisemitic Germanization of Christianity that was expounded in this work, recommended Burte to the National Socialists, who honored him more than once (with the 1935 Hebel Prize and the 1938 Goethe Prize, among other awards). His drama *Katte* (1914), about the death of Frederick the Great's friend, was said by literary critics to have had a "deep influence" on the "National Socialist Rising." Burte underwent hardly any change after the war, as can be seen in his book of poems *Psalter um Krist* (Psalter for a Germanic Christ; 1953).

Busch, Ernst, b. Essen-Steele, July 6, 1885; d. Aldershot (England) prisoner-of-war camp, July 17, 1945, German field marshal. In 1904 Busch joined the army; he was a commanding general of the Eighth Army Corps at the outset of the Second World War, and was made a colonel general on June 19, 1940. In October 1943 Busch became commander in chief of the Central Army Group in the Russian Campaign. This unit was almost completely annihilated by the Red Army in the summer of 1944. Relieved of his duties on June 28, 1944, and made a scapegoat, this totally unpolitical soldier was later made commander in chief for the northwest; he was captured by the British.

Butenandt, Adolf, b. Lehe (now Bremerhaven-Lehe), March 24, 1903, German biochemist. In 1933 Butenandt became a professor in Danzig; in 1935 he rejected an appointment to Harvard; in 1936 he became president of the Kaiser Wilhelm Society. Butenandt had to refuse the Nobel prize, which he was awarded in 1939 for pathbreaking work in hormone research; in 1949 he was able to accept the prize. Meanwhile, he became a professor in Tübingen. In 1956 he went to Munich, where he was president of the Max Planck Society from 1960 to 1971.

Bver, term for those in the *Berufsverbrecher* (professional criminal) category in the CONCENTRATION CAMPS.

BVP. *See* Bavarian People's Party.

Ernst Busch.

Adolf Butenandt.

C

Cadaver obedience (*Kadavergehorsam*), blind, self-sacrificial obedience. The term is drawn from the rules of the JESUITS, who require from their members unconditional obedience toward God, the pope, and the order's superiors, by bypassing one's own will as if one were a cadaver. This form of total submission to the will of others was branded as "lack of character" by the National Socialists (Security Service training manual of August 1937), yet was demanded within their own ranks as proof of "high racial merit."

Calais, British broadcasting station for propaganda. Despite its title as "Soldiers' Station Calais," it transmitted a program from England especially for German soldiers, on medium wave (360, 420, and 492 m). From October 24, 1943, until April 14, 1945, a team of German emigrants and British journalists under the direction of D. Sefton Delmer broadcast skillfully selected news and excellent entertainment shows over this strongest transmitter in Europe. The Soldiers' Station Calais became one of the most feared weapons the Allies employed in psychological warfare. Despite draconian punishments for listening to "enemy transmitters," its effect could not be curbed.

Camp practices (*Lagerbrauchtum*), all-inclusive term for the fixed, recurring rituals and practices that were part of the camp life of the Hitler Youth, League of German Girls, Reich Labor Service, and Sturmabteilung (Storm Troopers; SA), and also of life in schools or institutions for political education (ORDER FORTRESSES; ADOLF HITLER SCHOOLS). They included raising of the flag, reveille, early-morning ceremonies, and campfire vigils. Camp practices were intended to integrate children and adolescents, in particular, into the "spirit" and "community life" of their respective groups and to contribute to an understanding of hierarchical subordination. (*See* BRAUCHTUM UND SITTE.)

Canaris, Wilhelm, b. Aplerbeck (Westphalia), January 1, 1887; d. Flossenbürg concentration camp, April 9, 1945, German admiral and Secret Service officer. Canaris entered the navy in 1905; after the Battle of the Falkland Islands in 1914, he was imprisoned in Chile but carried out an adventurous escape; he conducted a secret mission for the Admiralty in Spain (1916), then became a U-boat commander in the Mediterranean. In the early postwar turmoil, Canaris set up home guard units and sympathized with the free corps and the Kapp Putsch (March 13, 1920). Suspected of aiding the escape of the murderers of Rosa Luxemburg and Karl Liebknecht, he was jailed but later rehabilitated and kept in the adjutant's office of the SPD (Social Democratic Party of Germany) armed forces minister, Gustav NOSKE. Canaris held navy posts from 1924 to 1928, and thereafter various commands; in 1932 he was made a sea captain, and in 1934 he took a "retirement post" as a fortress commander in Swinemünde.

Canaris benefited from glowing appraisals ("energetic and circumspect") and from his earlier critical attitude toward the Weimar Republic to become a prospect for higher office in the National Socialist (NS) state. On January 1, 1935, as a rear admiral, he became head of the intelligence and espionage section (Abwehrabteilung) of the War Ministry (after 1938, Abwehr Foreign Office of the Wehrmacht High Command; *see* ABWEHR) because the assignment's political side intrigued him. He had the opportunity for a clear view of Hitler's war preparations and of the brutal wielding of NS power, circumstances that rapidly cooled his initial esteem for the "brown revolution." After the FRITSCH CRISIS in early 1938, Canaris purposely sought out ties with the military opposition around Generals Ludwig BECK and Franz HALDER; he extended covert support to them, in part through Hans OSTER, the head of the Abwehr's central section. At the same time,

Wilhelm Canaris.

Canaris filed unvarnished reports in order to steer the regime away from war, which he feared would be "the end of Germany."

That this double game—for the Reich, against Hitler—at first did not attract attention was due to Canaris's undoubted successes in counterespionage and reconnaissance. These accomplishments protected Canaris (an admiral after January 1, 1940) for a long time from the grasp of the Security Service (SD), under his friend and rival Reinhard HEYDRICH. They also enabled him to protest the excesses of the SS in Poland and Russia. Canaris sided personally with some persecuted individuals, protected Jews through paper assignments to the Abwehr, hindered Hitler's attempts to draw Franco into the war, and finally wore out himself and his reputation in this war of nerves.

When Abwehr agents deserted to the British, Canaris was removed from office, in February 1944. The Abwehr was then absorbed by the REICH SECURITY MAIN OFFICE (RSHA). Although he opposed any assassination plot, Canaris was arrested on July 23, 1944, following the attempt on Hitler's life by Claus von STAUFFENBERG. After a lengthy detention, Canaris was condemned to death and hanged by an SS summary court in the Flossenbürg camp shortly before the entry of the American army. According to Ernst von WEIZSÄCKER, Canaris was "one of the most interesting figures of the period." He played out his conspiratorial role so skillfully in the background that as late as the fall of 1944 the RSHA was still puzzling over the

question of on which side the Abwehr chief had really stood. Even today the question has never been totally clarified.

Cap Arcona, with 27,000 gross registered tons, the fourth largest passenger ship in the German merchant marine. In the last months of the war, the *Cap Arcona* was put into rescue service at the behest of the navy for refugees from areas in the east threatened by the Red Army. In late April 1945 Karl KAUFMANN, the *Gauleiter* of Hamburg and the Reich commissioner for merchant shipping, withdrew the *Cap Arcona* from naval command and had it anchored in the Bay of Lübeck. There some 5,000 prisoners of the evacuated NEUENGAMME concentration camp were brought on board on April 25–26, along with 400 SS guards, a protective detail of 500 naval gunnery crewmen, and a crew of 76. Many prisoners starved owing to insufficient provisions or to mistreatment in the completely overfilled holds. On May 3 the British air force attacked "concentrations of enemy shipping" in the Baltic Sea. The *Cap Arcona* and the THIELBEK were bombarded and fired upon in several waves by three squadrons. The hoisting of white flags proved useless. Only 500 people were rescued from the burning *Cap Arcona*. Most of those who were able to jump ship drowned in the cold sea.

Capitalism, term employed, especially since the time of Karl Marx, for an economic and social order characterized by private ownership of the means of production and by labor as a commodity, with consequent "alienation." Consistent with its self-definition, National Socialism as nationalism opposed MARXISM, and concomitantly as ostensible socialism, opposed capitalism. Nonetheless, it viewed both as being on the same collision course. Capitalism led to class hatred through the enslavement of LABOR, and its internationalist "lust for profits" undermined *Volk* communities. Marxism, through its "sham struggle" (*Scheinkampf*) against capitalism, also incited class struggle, with the same result. Both capitalism and Marxism were on the payroll of WORLD JEWRY, which held the controlling positions in both camps. Only National Socialism had overcome capitalism and had put it, like labor, in the service "of the life interests of the entire *Volk*." This assured "appropriate earnings" to capital, and the right to work to productive *Volk* comrades (*Volksgenossen*).

The reality of the ECONOMY UNDER NATIONAL SOCIALISM revealed this self-representation to be rhetorical propaganda. Nothing was changed regarding either capitalist means of production or property arrangements, aside from ARYANIZA-TION as part of the persecution of Jews. The National Socialist state practiced unrestrained capitalism, including state capitalism, in order to meet the ambitious goals for armaments and warfare. The ever-expanding regulations (*see* FOUR-YEAR PLAN) and the intensified political supervision nonetheless indicated that, in a victorious NS state, capitalism too would be forced into strict conformity; thus, Lenin's classification of fascism as "the highest level of capitalism" does not accurately reflect National Socialism and its racist program.

Capitulation, the end of fighting by the German Wehrmacht on May 7–8, 1945 (*see* UNCONDITIONAL SURRENDER).

CARE, acronym of Cooperative for American Remittances to Europe, a private relief organization founded in 1946 in the United States that contributed to the mitigation of postwar want in Europe, especially in Germany. The epitome of such aid was the CARE package for needy Europeans, which relatives, friends, and strangers could order with different contents (baby clothing, children's food, lard, and so on) from CARE headquarters in New York. CARE shipments to the Federal Republic of Germany were discontinued in 1960. The estimated total of CARE aid to Germany was over 300 million DM.

Care (concern). *See* Betreuung.

Carl Peters, German motion picture directed by Herbert Selpin (who also wrote the screenplay, with Ernst von SALOMON), with Hans ALBERS in the title role; it premiered on March 21, 1941. The film was officially rated "politically and artistically worthwhile, educational for the *Volk*,

beneficial to youth." It portrays the life of the German Africa explorer and colonial pioneer Carl Peters (1856–1918) in a heroic light. Thus, for him the establishment of German East Africa in 1885 was not—in contrast with English colonies—a matter of "lust for domination," but of "the respect and cooperation shown by Germans in the outside world" (*Film-Illustrierte*, 1941). Besides attacking the British, *Carl Peters* also served as antiparliament propaganda: the blond hero is called to account before the Reichstag for the execution of two "Negroes." Under cross-examination by "Jewish liberals and Social Democrats," he states: "In the Reichstag they hack and tear each other apart. Poor Germany, you are your own greatest enemy." Despite the official promotion and popular performers, the film was tiresome owing to its overly long scenes of parliamentary debate, and it failed to earn its production costs.

H. H.

Carossa, Hans, b. (Bad) Tölz, December 15, 1878; d. Rittsteig bei Passau, September 12, 1956, German author and physician. Carossa became one of the most popular writers of the middle class during the Weimar period with his semi-autobiographical poetry and prose. His work, influenced by Catholic humanism, manifests formal elegance as well as a commitment to traditional modes of storytelling. Because of his rejection of the literary avant-garde and his popularity, the National Socialists attempted to integrate him into official cultural life (Goethe

Distribution of CARE packages.

Hans Carossa.

Prize, 1938). Carossa declined election to the Prussian Academy of Letters in 1933, but in 1941 he reluctantly allowed himself to be named president of a fascist European writers' union. His books after 1933 reflect a retreat into the "inner emigration," and powerlessness in confrontation with the National Socialist "antispirit." After 1945 his works were highly regarded among foreigners as an expression of the "other" Germany. Carossa developed his experiences and problems with the Third Reich in the stories in *Ungleiche Welten* (Dissimilar Worlds; 1951).

Carpathian German Party (Karpatendeutsche Partei), subdivision of the SUDETEN GERMAN PARTY; it supported National Socialist goals in Slovakia after the MUNICH AGREEMENT (September 30, 1938).

Carpet biter (*Teppichbeisser*), rumor, arising from Hitler's feared attacks of rage, that the Reich chancellor occasionally so lost control of himself that he bit into a carpet. The rumor led to the following example of UNDERGROUND HUMOR: Hitler bought a bedside rug, whereupon the salesman inquired: "Should I wrap it, or do you want to eat it here?"

Casablanca, port city in Morocco where the heads of government of the United States (Franklin D. ROOSEVELT) and England (Winston CHURCHILL) conferred from January 14 to 25, 1943. Because of the Soviet winter offensive near Stalingrad, Stalin was unavailable; also present were the Allied chiefs of staff. Against the Soviet wish for a second front in France to take pressure off the Red Army, Churchill pushed through the priority for a landing in Sicily, with a vague plan for an invasion of France sometime in the fall of 1943. The conference's importance was confirmed by Churchill when, after the meetings with Roosevelt, he made the first call for UNCONDITIONAL SURRENDER by the Axis powers. A side event of the conference was the temporary reconciliation of the rival French generals Henri-Honoré GIRAUD and Charles de GAULLE.

Cassirer, Ernst, b. Breslau, July 28, 1874; d. New York, April 13, 1945, German philosopher. An important representative of Neo-Kantianism, Cassirer extended Kant's critique of reason over all areas of human culture. The National Socialists argued that his interpretation of the classic German philosopher proved "the incapacity of the Jewish mind to do justice to concrete reali-

Ernst Cassirer.

ty." Cassirer lost his professorship in Hamburg in 1933 and, being Jewish, was forced to flee into exile.

Catholic Action (Katholische Aktion), Catholic lay movement that began in Italy in 1886, at first with a mostly political agenda. Later, as a consequence of democratization after the First World War, Catholic parties took up political activity, and Pope Pius XI in 1922 redefined Catholic Action as a consciously religious and social movement (in the encyclical *Ubi arcano*). After the renunciation of partisan political activity in the LATERAN TREATIES, Catholic Action became the church's second-line organization for influencing secular affairs.

Since the Vatican increasingly backed the authoritarian approach, from 1928 onward the papal nuncio in Berlin, Eugenio Pacelli (later PIUS XII), called upon German laity as well to join together in Catholic Action. When political Catholicism had to be sacrificed in the CONCORDAT with Hitler, Rome hoped that Catholic Action would serve the same buffer function as in Italy. However, Hitler had intentionally left Article 31 of the Concordat (protection of Catholic organizations) to be negotiated, since he interpreted the term "political" much more narrowly than the Curia suspected. National Socialist totalitarianism could not tolerate alongside itself an ideological mass movement such as Catholic Action, which sought to "Christianize all of German life." Catholic Action was persecuted through administrative measures and selective acts of terrorism, which reached a peak on June 30, 1934, in the murder of its Berlin leader Erich KLAUSENER, who had protested NS harassment at mass meetings.

Catholic church (Roman Catholic church), one of two large Christian denominations in Germany (*see* CHURCH STRUGGLE).

Catholic Workers' Associations (Katholische Arbeitervereine), the Catholic church's answer to the rise of social democracy and trade unions: alliances of Catholic workers that grew in numbers toward the end of the 19th century. The associations joined together in 1911 in the Cartel Alliance (in 1927, the Reich Alliance) of Catholic Workers' Associations and, after long internal conflicts, they promoted the Christian trade union movement. After initial opposition to National Socialism, the associations attempted to avoid the threat of persecution in April 1933 through a declaration of loyalty to the "new state." Despite Article 31 of the CONCORDAT (protection of Catholic organizations), they became victims, in various ways, of the SYNCHRONIZATION measures, since the government arbitrarily classified them as "political" and thus unqualified for protection. In 1939 the last periodicals of the associations had to halt publication; their assets were seized and handed over to the GERMAN LABOR FRONT.

Caucasus Campaign, failed German offensive of the summer and fall of 1942; its high point was the surmounting of Mount Elbrus (August 21); *see* RUSSIAN CAMPAIGN.

Celebrations (*Feiern*), National Socialist (NS) rituals for cultic exaltation of ideology and institutions. The numerous celebrations were divided by their organizers into three main types: CELEBRATIONS IN THE NATIONAL SOCIALIST CALENDAR, LIFE CELEBRATIONS, and MORNING CELEBRATIONS. This classification put the NS celebrations in a parallel and competitive position with Christian worship: with the feasts of the church year; with baptism, marriage, and burial; and with the Sunday worship services. The content and forms of NS celebrations also had a cultic character, which resulted not least from the numerous borrowings from Christian worship. Nonetheless, in 1936 Goebbels forbade the use of the term "public worship" (*Kult*); Hitler himself, at the 1938 Reich Party Congress, again differentiated NS celebrations from "public worship." This semantic regulation, however, was only intended to obscure the fact that the celebrations did indeed constitute an attempt to compete with and replace Christian worship.

Their cultic character was clearly revealed by language, musical expressions, ritual, sites for celebration, and liturgical form. The texts used in NS celebrations—poems, song lyrics, CHORAL POETRY, words of the Führer—often employed a sacral vocabulary, in which the meaning was prefigured by the Christian religion: Hitler was referred to as a "redeemer," whom we "need like bread and wine," blood was "holy," the Third Reich was "of a holy spirit," the FELDHERRNHALLE was "an altar," the flag "a sacrament" and "a light of revelation." One of the musical expressions was the SONG, which imitated the liturgical plainchant and ranked first in importance. Instrumental music befitted the "solemn" surroundings or served as a background for ritual actions; deemed as especially suitable instruments were trumpets and trombones, field drums and kettledrums, as well as the organ. In the ritual, "striding" (*Schreiten*) played a special role: the parade was analogous to a procession, and the Führer's solemn pace to the Feldherrnhalle or to the "harvest altar" on the BÜCKEBERG was analogous to a priest's steps to the altar. The celebratory sites supported the ritual and provided a solemn atmosphere through their arrangement and monumentality (for example, the grounds for Reich Party Congresses); enclosed celebration halls bore a great resemblance to church structures. In the sequence of celebration there were obvious parallels to church liturgies: "the Führer's word" compared to the scriptural reading; the "address" to the sermon, "common song," "proclamation," "profession," and "vow."

Hitler himself set the principles for the NS style of celebration; Goebbels perfected it and developed it into new forms. He held the greatest control over the resources needed for conducting celebrations. Offices established by him in the Propaganda Ministry and in the Reich Propaganda Directorate planned, organized, and supervised—like ritual congregations—the NS celebrations; a special party periodical issued monthly after 1935 aided in the standardization and central control of celebrations at lower levels. For the "life" and "morning" celebrations, Albert ROSENBERG was able to secure control over resources in a jurisdictional dispute with Goebbels; these celebrations were more fully developed during the war.

The NS celebrations had multiple functions. At first they served as self-presentations of the party and its Führer, and as political advertisements. The cultic character of the celebrations revealed, however, even more pretentious func-

Celebrations. Annual march to Munich's Feldherrnhalle on November 9 to commemorate the Hitler Putsch of 1923.

tions: in the celebrations the contents of NS ideology and its symbols, BLOOD AND SOIL, *Volk* and Reich, the flag, even Hitler himself, were dedicated as "objects of belief"; they manifested themselves in cultic fullness as a "political religion" that sought to give meaning and security to life, one to which a person should make "confession." With this function the celebrations fully met the psychological needs of many participants, especially since the celebratory style adroitly aimed at an emotional effect. The establishment of a believing "community" had the final goal of making people into unconditional followers of National Socialism.

The long-range goal of the NS leadership was to suppress Christian religion and worship and to establish their own celebrations as the sole "cult." It is, then, not surprising that activity related to celebrations became more intense during the final war years, even though no great "Reich celebrations" took place after 1939. Because of their elaborate and sophisticated style they had impressed even skeptical observers, something wartime celebrations were less able to do.

K. V.

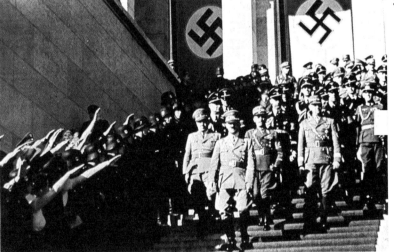

1
Harvest Thanks Day on the Bücke-berg.
2
Parade in Berlin for Hitler's 50th birthday, on April 20, 1939.
3
Entry of Hitler and his entourage at the Reich Party Congress in Nurem-berg.
4
Memorial celebration of the "Old Combatants" on November 9.

Celebrations in the National Socialist Calendar

("Celebrations of the Reich and of the Course of the Year")

As part of the spectrum of National Socialist CELEBRATIONS during the Third Reich, state holidays, the party's memorial days, and "customary" holidays were collected into a canonical National Socialist celebration year in a manner that paralleled and competed with the church year. Given a fixed order early on, its function was to lend expression to the might and unity of state and party, and to draw in the state's *Volk*. The Propaganda Ministry and the Reich Propaganda Directorate were responsible for organizing and carrying out events on the various occasions, except for Reich Party Congresses and celebrations within organizations. Holidays that did not have their origin in the history or ideology of the NSDAP were reinterpreted and "synchronized."

January 30: Day of the SEIZURE OF POWER
February 24: Party holiday in remembrance of the proclamation of the PARTY PROGRAM OF THE NSDAP in 1920
March: (1) *Reminiscere* (Remembrance) Sunday, the HEROES' MEMORIAL DAY, a recasting of the National Day of Mourning; after 1939, it was held on March 16 to commemorate the reintroduction of universal COMPULSORY MILITARY SERVICE in 1935; (2) on the last Sunday of the month, the "Commitment of Youth" (*Verpflichtung der Jugend*): ac-

Day of the Seizure of Power, January 30, 1933: SA units march through the Brandenburg Gate.

ceptance of 14-year-old children into the HITLER YOUTH and LEAGUE OF GERMAN GIRLS

April 20: Führer's Birthday

May 1: MAY HOLIDAY

May: MOTHER'S DAY, after 1933 on the second and after 1938 on the third Sunday of the month

June 21: Summer SOLSTICE

September: Reich Party Congress (*see* REICH PARTY CONGRESSES) in Nuremberg during the first half of the month

October: HARVEST THANKS DAY at the beginning of the month

November 9: Memorial day for the 16 "blood witnesses [*see* BLOOD WITNESS] of the Movement" in the HITLER PUTSCH of 1923; the highest National Socialist holiday

December 21: Winter Solstice, the unsuccessful attempt to replace Christmas with a yule feast

K. V.

Center (Zentrum), German party founded on December 13, 1870. The "German Center Party" (its official name) was a denominational (Catholic) party and at the same time a people's party, with members and adherents in all groups of the Catholic population. Both under the empire and in the Weimar Republic it formed the middle of the German party spectrum (hence its name).

Monarchist under the empire, after 1917 the Center converted itself into a republican party under the leadership of Matthias ERZBERGER; its 1923 program committed it to the democratic constitutional state, and it became the most important government party in the Weimar Republic. Between 1919 and 1932 the Center was involved in all 19 German governments, mostly in coalition with the SPD (Social Democratic Party of Germany) and the DDP (German Democratic Party; *see* WEIMAR COALITION). It provided more Reich chancellors than any other party.

The Center enjoyed a very stable constituency. In the 1919 elections to the National Assembly it received 19.7 percent of the votes, and in subsequent Reichstag elections, between 13.6 percent (1920) and 11.9 percent (November 1932). In contrast with the other bourgeois parties, during the end phase of the Republic the Center lost hardly any votes to the NSDAP; even in the Reichstag elections of March 1933, it received 11.2 percent, despite considerable obstructing of the electoral campaign by the National Socialists. Yet even the Center leadership misjudged the NSDAP and its political goals. This was shown by conversations of the prelate Ludwig KAAS (party chairman from December 1928) with the NSDAP as late as autumn 1932 concerning a share in a Hitler government, but especially by the consent of the party's Reichs-

Center. Election poster, 1931: "Brüning, the last bulwark of freedom and order. Truth, freedom, law. Elect the Center, List 4."

tag delegation to the ENABLING LAW on March 23, 1933. On July 5 of that year, the Center dissolved itself under National Socialist pressure.

After the Second World War the Center party was refounded, but it failed to gain any importance. Most of its former members and voters found their new political home in the Christian Democratic Union/Christian Social Union.

R. B.

Central Association of German Citizens of the Jewish Faith (Centralverein Deutscher Staatsbürger jüdischen Glaubens), organization to represent German Jews, founded in 1893. It promoted assimilation and opposed antisemitism with legal and journalistic means. It had 300,000 members when it was incorporated into the REICH REPRESENTATION OF GERMAN JEWS in 1933.

Certificate of Descent (*Abstammungsnachweis;* also called Aryan Certificate, or *Ariernachweis*), proof demanded by the NUREMBERG LAWS (September 15, 1935) of every German citizen in the Third Reich that he or she was of "Aryan descent." Birth, baptism, and marriage documents were used to prove that no parent or grandparent had "fully species-alien, especially Jewish, blood." A Certificate of Descent without gaps was a precondition for full citizenship rights (*see also* VOLK COMRADE). For acceptance into the NSDAP and its organizations a "long Certificate of Descent" was prescribed, which required proof of "German or related descent" back to the year 1800. The Reich Agency for Genealogy (Reichsstelle für Sippenforschung) in the Interior Ministry decided on questionable cases. Professional genealogists could be called upon to help document the certificate.

Chamberlain, Houston Stewart, b. Southsea by Portsmouth (England), September 9, 1855; d. Bayreuth, January 9, 1927, British-German publicist. Chamberlain's childhood was spent at Versailles, followed by schooling in England and higher studies in Switzerland. At the age of 20, he heard for the first time the music of Richard WAGNER and was drawn by its magic. Beginning in 1882 he attended every one of the BAYREUTH FESTIVALS. His second marriage was to Wagner's daughter Eva, and after 1909 he resided only in Bayreuth, becoming a German citizen in 1916.

Wagner's views on racial theories, stemming from Count Arthur de GOBINEAU, had an influence on Chamberlain. In his major work, *Die Grundlagen des 19. Jahrhunderts* (The Foundations of the 19th Century, 2 vols., 1899), he elaborated them into an "asemitic" culture theory: the Germanic peoples were culturally creative above others, and their "fundamental racial strength" was preserved with least depletion in the German *Volk*. The Jews, on the contrary, embodied the destructive principle. Chamberlain therefore appealed to the "racial conscience" of Germans and spoke out for "cleansing" Christendom of Jewish elements. He thereby became a forerunner both of National Socialist racist antisemitism and of the *Volk*-oriented theology of the GERMAN CHRISTIANS. Chamberlain's admirers included Kaiser WILHELM II and Hitler, whom Chamberlain personally met in 1924 and held in esteem. Nonetheless, Chamberlain's direct influence on Hitler is judged to be a good bit less, because of their very different attitudes on the religious question, than it was on Alfred ROSENBERG's racist constructions.

Chamberlain, Joseph Austen, b. Birmingham (England), October 16, 1863; d. London, March 16, 1937, British politician. A half brother of Neville Chamberlain, Austen Chamberlain served several terms as Conservative chancellor of the Exchequer, minister, and state secretary. His term as foreign minister was almost simultaneous with that of Gustav STRESEMANN (1924–1929). Like his German counterpart, he was significantly involved with German-French rec-

Houston Stewart Chamberlain.

Joseph Austen Chamberlain.

onciliation through the LOCARNO PACT. For this work he received the Nobel Peace Prize in 1925 (along with Charles Dawes; *see* DAWES PLAN).

Chamberlain, Neville, b. near Birmingham (England), March 18, 1869; d. Heckfield, near Reading, November 9, 1940, British politician. Chamberlain's first occupation was as a farmer in the Bahamas (1890–1897), then as a manufacturer. In 1918 he was elected a Conservative member of Parliament, then served as minister of health (1923 and 1924–1929) and chancellor of the Exchequer (1931–1937). In a period of severe economic problems and of signs of deterioration of the British Empire, on May 28, 1937, Chamberlain undertook, as prime minister, the direction of British politics, which he attempted to steer into calmer waters. By acknowledging Hitler's justifiable demands without considering the actual character of the National Socialist regime, Chamberlain sought to appease the German Reich and to transform it from a source of turmoil into a stabilizing force on the Continent. This APPEASEMENT policy led to the ANSCHLUSS of Austria and the MUNICH AGREEMENT. It failed, however, with regard to Hitler's broader goals. Despite several personal meetings with Hitler, Chamberlain never assessed him correctly or in any way succeeded in influencing his opinion. The switch of British policy after the German assault on Czechoslovakia in March 1939 came too late; subsequent British guarantees for Poland, Greece, Romania, and Turkey could not block the war. Chamberlain finally lost power owing to his unsuccessful conduct of the war (*see* NORWEGIAN CAMPAIGN). On May 10, 1940, he had to yield his post to Winston CHURCHILL.

Channel breakthrough (*Kanaldurchbruch*), successful German naval operation (February 11–12, 1942) to move three battleships from the French harbor at Brest through the English Channel into the North Sea (*see* NAVAL WAR).

Chaplin, Charlie (originally, Charles Spencer Chaplin), b. London, April 16, 1889; d. Vevey (Switzerland), December 25, 1977, English-American actor, screenwriter, and producer. Chaplin was famous worldwide as a movie comedian from 1914. Because of the political dimension of his comedy, and of his support for the "little man" and the oppressed under National Socialism, Chaplin was rejected early on by the NSDAP. Hitler referred to him contemptuously as a "jumping-Jew" (*Zappeljude*). The showing of his movies was forbidden in 1933. The facial resemblance between Hitler and Chaplin could not be overlooked; it inspired Chaplin in 1939 to work on a political film that he considered a protest against the oppression of the individual in Hitler's Germany. *The Great Dictator* premiered in New York on October 15, 1940, as a

Neville Chamberlain.

Charlie Chaplin in *The Great Dictator*.

sarcastic comedy of mistaken identity. Chaplin played the double role of a Jewish barber and the dictator Hynkel. Through overt intimidation and anonymous death threats, the National Socialists unsuccessfully sought to halt the production. Once released, the film was officially ignored in Germany; its showing was prohibited, although the Reich Film Archive had a copy that was allowed to be shown to leading politicians (for example, Foreign Minister Joachim von Ribbentrop) "under special circumstances."

Character (*Charakter;* literally, something imprinted), the totality of moral and mental qualities. National Socialist ideology described character as the entirety of a person's mind, conduct, and attitude, which "necessarily" results from belonging "to a certain race" and is "received through inheritance." For this reason, character education was more important than traditional EDUCATION. As a catchword for the NS image of man, the term "character" is found in a series of derivations and compounds: character qualities (*Charaktereigenschaften*), "feelings and tendencies of the will"; character lore (*Charakterkunde*), the doctrine of the racist conditionality of character, which is alterable "only in part" through education and "self-forming will"; character worth (*Charakterwerte*), the "final measure" (Albert Rosenberg) in judging a person's suitability for the "*Volk* Community."

Charter of Labor (*Carta del Lavoro*), the constitution for work that was developed in Fascist Italy on the principle of the CORPORATIST STATE; it was adopted on April 21, 1927, by the Fascist Grand Council. Under state supervision 22 corporations (in line with economic categories) were formed, in which both employers and employees were proportionately represented; they agreed upon collective "work contracts" (on price-setting, working conditions, and so on). Overall supervision was through the National Council of Corporations. The charter, through this combination of employers' associations and labor unions, was expected to contribute to the elimination of class struggle, while aiding state direction of the economy. The charter served as a model for the establishment of the GERMAN LABOR FRONT, which, as an association affiliated with the NSDAP, was conceived as a more far-reaching state organ.

Chef der Sicherheitspolizei und des SD (Chief of the Security Police and the SD; CSSD), office held by Reinhard HEYDRICH (to 1942) and Ernst KALTENBRUNNER.

Chełmno, Polish name of the KULMHOF extermination camp.

Children's and young people's literature in the Third Reich was the area in which National Socialist (NS) policies on literature were most active. Strict guidelines from the Interior Ministry soon after the SEIZURE OF POWER aimed at a "New Order" for children's literature with little delay. Along with the general agencies and committees in charge of cultural and literary policy, special directive and censorship authorities for children's literature were established: the Main Office for Writing for Youth (Hauptlektorat Jugendschrifttum) in Alfred Rosenberg's Office for the Cultivation of Writing (Amt für Schrifttumspflege); the Youth Publications Office (Jugendschriftenlektorat) in the Reich Youth Leadership; and the Reich Bureau for Writing for Youth (Reichsstelle für das Jugendschrifttum) of the NS Teachers' League, which produced obligatory "basic lists" for student libraries and published a yearly index of recommended titles, *Das Buch der Jugend* (The Book of Youth), for educators, parents, and librarians.

The SYNCHRONIZATION of children's literature was easily achieved in 1933: the publishers with the greatest market share (Ensslin & Laiblin, Franckh, Thienemann, Schneider, and so on) already had nationalistically oriented programs; the few progressive authors went into exile, and most of the others voluntarily acknowledged the NS state and cooperated in a "cleaning up of children's and young people's libraries" (this resulted in the removal of even such classics as those by Johann Peter Hebel for being too "favorable to Jews"). Mass-circulation periodicals for children and school-age youth, such as *Deutsche Jugendburg* (German Youth Fortress) and *Hilf mit* (Give Help), served for everyday political agitation. High honors and prizes (as the HANS SCHEMM PRIZE) were meant to influence authors to mold youth in line with Hitler's thought: "I want a youth that is violent, domineering, intrepid, and fierce."

NS children's literature captivated young readers through adventure and exotic elements (for example, the Tecumseh series by Erhard WITTEK); it also exploited the fascination with modern technology and presented heroic role models, as in Rolf Italiaander's *Manfred Freiherr von Richthofen* (1938). Colonial tales, Prussian war history, stories from the life of the Führer, and material from the history of National Socialism (such as Karl A. Schenzinger's HITLERJUNGE QUEX; 1932) were main subjects

Children's and young people's literature. Illustration from the antisemitic indoctrination book *Der Giftpilz* (The Poison Mushroom).

of this literature. In addition, there were illustrated books with patriotic content such as *Deine deutsche Heimat* (Your German Homeland) and books for antisemitic indoctrination such as *Der Giftpilz* (The Poison Mushroom; 1938) and *Trau keinem Fuchs auf grüner Heid und keinem Jud bei seinem Eid* (Don't Trust a Fox on a Green Heath or a Jew by His Oath; 1936).

The most important theme of NS children's literature was training for combat. From the mid-1930s, the demand increased for inspiring, "combat-related" books for youth, and once the war began, the ideal of HARDNESS predominated, as in *Jagdfliegergruppe G: Jäger an Polens*

Himmel (Fighter Group G: Fighters over Poland's Skies; 1940). Children's-book publishers engaged correspondents of the PROPAGANDA COMPANIES to write about "staying at the machine gun down to the last round" (*see* WARTIME LIBRARY FOR GERMAN YOUTH); cheap illustrated booklets prepared children for air war: "The bombs fall with harmful power / To earth helter-skelter, / And so they don't get you, / Run to the defense shelter!"

Along with ideologically arousing texts, up until the early war years a wide selection of idyllic children's literature dealing with safe worlds of fairy creatures was also available. Formerly critical authors wrote apolitical entertainments, and only rarely did children's books show merit, such as Hans FALLADA's *Geschichte aus der Murkelei* (Stories from Childhood; 1938).

H. H.

Children's Country Evacuation (*Kinderlandverschickung*; KLV), the organization of vacations for city children in rural care centers. After 1933, it was broadened by the NATIONAL SOCIALIST VOLK WELFARE (NSV) agency and the HITLER YOUTH (HJ). This phase was distinct from the "expanded" evacuation begun on September 27, 1940, which is more commonly understood by the term. Hitler gave Baldur von SCHIRACH—no longer responsible for the HJ, but still "Reich leader of youth education of the

Children's Country Evacuation.

NSDAP''—the mandate to coordinate state agencies, the NSV, the National Socialist Teachers' League, and the HJ in evacuating children and young people from cities menaced by bombing. Funded by the NSDAP, the evacuation was at first voluntary and planned for only six months. Divided by sex, children aged 10 to 14 years, along with their schoolteachers, were lodged in camps, often beyond the borders of the Reich.

As the air war intensified in 1943, many schools halted classes, and more than 5,000 such camps were established. Most were directed by older teachers; the "service" (*Dienst*) was rendered according to "guidance bulletins" ("Our Camp") by "camp team leaders" from the ranks of the National Socialist girls' and boys' organizations. Girls were more intensively prepared for their leadership tasks in courses for "health service" and practical instruction. The camps were concerned not only with health and nutrition, but above all with NS camp training, which also influenced classroom instruction. In the occupied territories they also demonstrated the political presence of the Reich. The KLV accustomed young people to a desired mobility and relieved of child care adults who were hard hit by the war. Approximately every third schoolchild of HJ age spent time in one of the 9,000 camps; almost as many younger children were evacuated by the KLV.

H. S.

Child-rich (*Kinderreiche*), term for families with four or more children ("full families") that was propagated by National Socialist POPULATION POLICY to maintain the position of the German *Volk*. The term had earlier connoted "thoughtlessness" or even "intentional hostility to the people" for its focus on solely the number of children; it was more often applied to "asocial and hereditarily diseased families" who "without any control put undesired children into the world." A "title of respect" for the National Socialists, it was henceforth to be used only for "German-blooded families, fit for life [*lebenstüchtig*] and hereditarily healthy." Large families were promoted through prohibitions (*see* BIRTH CONTROL) and such incentives as MARRIAGE LOANS or child subsidies (*see* SOCIAL POLICY). Their "well-being" was handled by the NSDAP Office for Racial Policy, which supervised the Reich League of the Child-Rich. To raise the propaganda value of large families, in 1938 the CROSS OF HONOR of the German Mother was created to reward meritorious service in the "birth war" (*Geburtenkrieg*), a slogan from 1936.

Choltitz, Dietrich von, b. near Neustadt (Upper Silesia), November 9, 1894; d. Baden-Baden, November 4, 1966, German infantry general (August 1, 1944). Choltitz was a career soldier after 1914, a colonel in 1941, and a lieutenant general as of February 1, 1943. Hitler named him the Wehrmacht commander for Paris on

Child-rich peasant family.

Dietrich von Choltitz.

August 7, 1944, ordering him, as the Allies approached, to have all bridges and supply facilities blown up, with no consideration for the populace or for buildings. Choltitz refused to obey, and handed Paris over to the Allies intact (August 25, 1944). Imprisoned by the French, he was freed in 1947.

Choral poetry (*Chorische Dichtung*), a literary pairing of poetry and drama. The range of forms extends from simple choral recitations to poems with one or more solo speakers and choirs, up to the choral play (*chorischer Spiel*) that has one— usually simple—performance. In the early years of the Third Reich, choral poetry was especially promoted and cultivated, since it provided suitable "liturgical texts" for National Socialist CELEBRATIONS. The alternating recitation between "callers" and chorus imitated the Responsorium of church liturgy and served to "proclaim" the content of NS ideology, with the chorus representing the *Volk* Community in making "confession." Choral poetry was preferred for the THING PLAYS. The authors were mainly younger writers: Hans BAUMANN, Herbert BÖHME, Kurt EGGERS, Herybert MENZEL, and Gerhard SCHUMANN.

K. V.

Christiansen, Friedrich, b. Wyk auf Föhr, December 12, 1879; d. Aukrug-Innien (Schleswig-Holstein), December 3, 1972, German general. Christiansen was a sailor, then a flyer in the First World War (decorated with the Pour le mérite); in 1929 he was a pilot for the Dornier flying boat Do X. In 1933 he was assigned to the ministerial council in the Reich Air Ministry; he supervised flight schools and later the NATIONAL SOCIALIST

FLYERS' CORPS. In 1939 he became an air marshal (*General der Flieger*), and the following year, Wehrmacht commander for occupied Holland. As such, he was held responsible after the war for the destruction of the village of Putten and the murder of its male inhabitants. In August 1948 he was sentenced to 12 years' imprisonment, but was pardoned in 1951. In the 1960s the municipal council of his hometown of Wyk, under pressure from the state government and public opinion, withdrew from him its award of distinguished citizenship (Ehrenbürgerrechte).

Christian-Social People's Service (Christlich-Sozialer Volksdienst; CSVD), party of national-minded Evangelical Christians ("Evangelical Center") who came from Pietistic and Free Church circles, mostly in Württemberg and eastern Westphalia, and who had moved away from the increasingly radical right-wing German National People's Party. The CSVD advocated the authoritarian political direction of the PRESIDIAL CABINETS; its 14 deputies (1930–1932) cooperated with the Brüning government. Its influence ebbed in the wake of National Socialism (in March 1933 it still had four seats), and it was forced to dissolve itself on June 30, 1933.

Churchill, Winston, b. Blenheim Palace (Oxfordshire), November 30, 1874; d. London, January 24, 1965, British politician. As the scion of the family of the Dukes of Marlborough, Churchill was educated at elite schools such as Harrow and the military academy at Sandhurst; he served as an officer in several campaigns. In 1899–1900 he was a war correspondent in the Boer War. By making a daring escape from a Boer prison he gained great popularity, and in 1900 won a seat in the House of Commons as a Conservative member of Parliament. In 1906 he switched over to the Liberals and held several cabinet posts, among them that of First Lord of the Admiralty (1911–1915). Having interrupted his parliamentary career as a frontline officer in France, after 1917 Churchill took on another series of ministerial duties (for example, chancellor of the Exchequer, 1924–1929), and returned to the Conservative party.

An energetic advocate of a British policy of strength against the rearming National Socialist Germany, Churchill fell increasingly into conflict with the Conservative APPEASEMENT policy; from 1929 to 1939 he was out of the government. His warnings against NS racism and imperialism found few listeners, and Berlin viewed them as the attacks of "an outsider not to be taken very seriously." When Britain's appeasement policy failed to curb Hitler's unrestrained expansionism, public opinion pressed for Churchill's inclusion in Neville CHAMBERLAIN's War Cabinet as First Lord of the Admiralty. Churchill's demands for the occupation of Norway's chief port of Narvik were taken to heart too late, and Hitler stole the march on Great Britain. On the day of Germany's attack in the west (May 10, 1940), Churchill replaced Chamberlain as head of government.

Churchill formed a "cabinet of national unity" that included the Labour party and declared unyielding resistance to the German conquerors ("blood, toil, tears, and sweat"). When Churchill rejected Hitler's peace offer in the summer of 1940, he already had hopes for American help, which came in the form of the LEND-LEASE ACT. After the German assault on the Soviet Union in June 1941, Churchill concluded a covenant with Stalin on July 12 of that year; he was the primary initiator of the "Big Three" alliance (the United States, the USSR, and Great

Britain). In CASABLANCA (January 1943), he could still push through his strategy to overthrow Germany with a southern offensive (against the "soft underbelly of Europe"), but his influence waned at the conferences in TEHERAN (late 1943) and YALTA (February 1945). Churchill's plan to detain the Red Army far from central Europe fell through with Roosevelt, who wanted to involve Stalin in the war against Japan.

Churchill shared only in the beginnings of the postwar ordering of Europe: his election defeat in July 1945 removed him from further collaboration in the POTSDAM AGREEMENT. A new term as prime minister (1951–1955) did not change the fact that Great Britain had lost its place as a superpower to the United States and the USSR. Churchill acknowledged as much in his memoirs (*The Second World War;* 1948–1954), which, with his other works, brought him the Nobel prize for literature in 1953. His successful advocacy of a Western alliance resulted in NATO.

Winston Churchill.

Church Struggle (*Kirchenkampf*), the designation, in church history in particular, for the history of the two major denominations in Germany during the Third Reich. In late 1933 this term, or the comparable terms "church dispute" (*Kirchenstreit*) and "church troubles" (*Kirchenwirren*), initially referred only to the contention within the Evangelical Church as to the authentic confession of faith and the defense against the errors of the GERMAN CHRISTIANS. Its meaning was then expanded to include the ideological conflict with National Socialism, and thus came to encompass the Catholic church's struggle for autonomy and freedom of preaching. Conversely, "church struggle" described the whole range of National Socialist measures and plans for disciplining, SYNCHRONIZATION, suppression, and, finally, extermination of the churches and of Christianity. (*See the longer article on the* Church Struggle, *following.*)

Church Struggle

"We must declare ourselves to be the true Christians. 'Christianity' is the watchword for the extermination of the clerics [*Pfaffen*], just as 'socialism' once served to exterminate the Marxist big shots" (*see* BONZE). Goebbels's statement describes in exaggerated form the National Socialist (NS) strategy in the Church Strug-

gle (*Kirchenkampf*), as well as Hitler's policy toward the churches in the period preceding the Seizure of Power. Although nearly all the details of Hitler's foreign policy and racist goals can be found in MEIN KAMPF, statements of his intentions regarding ecclesiastical policy are almost totally lacking or else serve to dissemble, as did

Point 24 of the NSDAP Program of February 24, 1920 (*see* PARTY PROGRAM OF THE NSDAP), which took the position of a "positive Christianity." What was meant by the phrase "the ethical and moral sense of the Germanic race"—and how seriously it was to be taken—became clear only much later. Officially, Hitler avoided to the very end any declaration of conflict with the churches. But to infer from this (as Eberhard Jäckel does) that the church question had a lesser ideological importance for him is to ignore the significance Hitler accorded it in the TABLE TALKS, for example, and would be a latter-day success for the smokescreen that concealed the deadly contradiction between National Socialism and Christianity.

Hitler achieved his first successes with the Protestants, who since the downfall of the monarchy and with it the tie between throne and altar, were without political direction; unlike the Catholics, they lacked their own political party and support from Rome. Fragmented into three denominations (Lutheran, Reformed, and United) and 28 regional churches (*Landeskirchen*), they sought different answers to contemporary questions, but they did agree on one: in the national distress after the defeat in 1918, the Evangelical Church discovered the *Volk* as a theological mission, and sought to be a "people's church" (*Volkskirche*) in the sense of Christian solidarity and moral appeal. This led not a few theologians, church leaders, and laity into dialogue with the VÖLKISCH MOVEMENT and into acceptance of many of its positions in a sort of political theology that later, in the new distress of the world economic crisis, made them vulnerable to the nationalistic and seemingly Christian rhetoric of National Socialism, especially of Hitler. Nonetheless, there was no dearth of warnings in the Evangelical Church against the totalitarian nature of the NS movement: the adherents of Karl BARTH's "dialectical theology" pointed out the growing menace of the perversion of the confession of faith. Yet Hitler's following among Protestants grew; organized in 1932 as the GERMAN CHRISTIANS, they won a third of the seats in the Prussian church elections (November 12–14, 1932). NS ANTISEMITISM proved to be no obstacle here, and indeed matched to some extent the latent hostility toward Jews in church circles.

This antisemitism—whose racist dimensions no one suspected—stood in the way of a rapprochement between National Socialism and the Catholic church less than did the NSDAP's official self-characterization as a "socialist" party; yet even this was not an insuperable hurdle. Until the Seizure of Power the German bishops' rejection of Hitler on principle was due more to the tie between the church and the CENTER party, to cultural, political, and theological reservations, and certainly to the bishops' firm anchoring in Rome. This last factor, although attacked by NS propaganda as INTERNATIONALISM and "anti-*Volk*," was to become the lever by which Hitler pried open Catholic defenses. The LATERAN TREATIES between the Curia and Mussolini in 1929 signaled the Vatican's readiness for arrangements with authoritarian but anti-Bolshevik regimes, and for the abandonment of political Catholicism, which might clear the way for Hitler's march to power. Moreover, when Eugenio Pacelli (*see* PIUS XII) became cardinal secretary of state in 1930, prospects for the church's toleration of National Socialism increased; as nuncio in Berlin he had worked long although unsuccessfully for a concordat with Germany.

The Center party's campaign for the March 3, 1933, elections was clearly directed against the NSDAP. But rifts between Rome's position and the attitude among the laity on the one hand and the German episcopacy on the other could no longer be overlooked. It is still debated whether the Center party's consent to the ENABLING LAW on March 23, 1933, and the withdrawal five days later of warnings by the Bishops' Conference against NS "religious and moral errors" were

The Center party as Hitler's coalition partner? Caricature from the Social Democratic humor magazine *Der Wahre Jakob* (The Right Way), September 1932.

consequences only of pressure by Rome and of trust in Hitler's agreement to a concordat. It is beyond dispute that the new chancellor's willingness to talk promoted the change and aroused remarkable illusions as to the regime's true character. It resulted in the CONCORDAT of July 20, 1933, ratified on September 10. Yet this official assent to the suppression of Catholic political and trade union organizations that had in fact already occurred was already overshadowed by the onset of the struggle against the Catholic church in Germany.

Just as the Concordat served as bait, so also did the catchword "Reichskirche" on the Evangelical side, expressing an ancient longing for unity and state protection. Moreover, in the spring of 1933 the Reich Church stood for the Evangelical counterpart of the treaty arrangements between the Reich and Rome. Reared as a Catholic, Hitler found Protestant pluralism incomprehensible, as well as a serious obstacle to SYNCHRONIZATION. He thus adopted the German Christian program for a Reich Church; on the advice of Ludwig MÜLLER he also pressed for passage of a Reich Church constitution and election of a REICH BISHOP. The church would then follow the FÜHRER PRINCIPLE, state control would be assured, and ideological access to it would be established. The first two aims provoked hardly any opposition, but farsighted theologians and laity, notably the YOUNG REFORM-

ERS, sought to oppose the third with their own initiative. They achieved only a respite with the appointment of Friedrich von BODELSCHWINGH as Reich Bishop, since the German Christians' victory in the church elections of July 23, 1933, and Müller's election as Reich Bishop on September 27 seemed to seal the long-desired NS embrace.

Only now did many recognize the danger for the confession, since the church's adoption of the ARYAN PARAGRAPH threatened, and the inclusion of Evangelical youngsters in the HITLER YOUTH (December 20, 1933) seriously imperiled Christian education. The first opposition took shape in Martin NIEMÖLLER's PASTORS' EMERGENCY LEAGUE. It was stiffened in the spring of 1934 by Reich Church regimentation, as Müller attempted to silence the opposition with suspensions and gag orders. The conflict reached a peak with the establishment of the CONFESSING CHURCH, which more sharply repudiated the heresies of the German Christians and withdrew adherence to the Reich Bishop. On the Catholic side, too, the first open opposition erupted with respect to a confession of faith; in his Advent homilies of 1933, Cardinal Michael FAULHABER of Munich denounced antisemitic attacks on the Old Testament.

Hitler himself deliberately remained aloof from the raging Church Struggle. Many regarded him as the last court of appeal where people could find some understanding for complaints about the excesses of party and state authorities. He knew how to use small concessions to cultivate an image as a statesmanlike mediator, as he did through pointed silence in the controversy over Alfred ROSENBERG's MYTHUS DES 20. JAHRHUNDERTS while theologians published attacks against NS ideologues. During the consolidation of power in 1933 and 1934, he allowed church attendance by entire SA units to be encouraged. Hitler also allowed his deputy Rudolf HESS to promulgate the so-called Tolerance Decree of December 17, 1933, forbidding discrimination because of denomination.

Concurrently, the state began to target opposition clergy with widespread intimidation measures. Whereas the party first left discipline in the Evangelical Church to the German Christian church authorities and to the Reich Bishop, the Catholic church was subjected to direct pressure. It was attacked in religious education, through monitoring of sermons, in associational activities (for example, the suppression of the GERMAN YOUTH FORCE athletic association), in Catholic journalism, in charitable works, in

The most important points of the Concordat on an election poster for November 12, 1933: "Why must a Catholic vote for the electoral list of Adolf Hitler?"

The cross is to yield to the swastika. Caricature from *Les Dernières Nouvelles*, October 1934.

Catholic schools, and in financial transactions (*see* FOREIGN CURRENCY MANAGEMENT); the pressure reached a peak in the PRIEST TRIALS.

The state ultimately also intervened in the Evangelical Church, since the Reich Bishop failed to gain control over the stubborn Confessing Church. On July 16, 1935, Hanns KERRL became Reich minister for church affairs; the Law for the Protection of the GERMAN EVANGELICAL CHURCH of September 24, 1935, was passed to restore a unified leadership, and in particular to assure control over theological training. After some initial success, however, this effort also failed, and led to vehement ideological controversy over a statement addressed by the Confessing Church to Hitler and published abroad (July 23, 1936). Similar to the papal encyclical MIT BRENNENDER SORGE that appeared soon afterward, this statement excoriated NS "de-Christianization," antisemitism, the Führer cult, and the destruction of justice. The state's response to both churches became manifest through tightening of controls, reduction in the church tax rate (beginning in March 1935), and restriction of all activities (assemblies, processions, and so on) not held in church facilities. In 1938, prosecution began against 2,256 clergymen for violations against the PULPIT PARAGRAPH, the MALICIOUS-GOSSIP LAW, and other statutes. Sixty-nine were found guilty, 72 (including Niemöller) were placed under PROTECTIVE CUSTODY, 37 were forbidden public speech, 100 were forced from their congregations, and 439 were issued warnings.

Still, most clergy and practicing laity strove for loyalty to the NS state, approved or even applauded most political measures, and made allowance for or ignored the NUREMBERG LAWS or KRISTALLNACHT. It is also true that a confrontational stance emerged only when direct church interests were involved. Efforts of high-ranking church leaders to search out some arrangement with the National Socialists did not cease. What the party—and that meant Hitler—understood by church struggle was something that church leaders understood least. The radical wartime attacks on the churches probably went back at least in part to the initial phase of the struggle, when Hitler came to realize on a practical level that coexistence with National Socialism was unthinkable and that winning the churches over to his racist and imperialist goals was not even desirable: from the outset, conflicting worldviews made it necessary that National Socialism aim to destroy the churches' firm base among the people, and to wean the people from the constricting shackles of Christian morality.

The way had already been prepared: especially in Hitler Youth education, anti-Christian propaganda was strongly emphasized (the "purging" of song lyrics, and so on), making it difficult for Evangelical organizations to recruit new members. The National Socialists attempted to achieve the same effect by hampering theological education (for example, through closing seminaries), despite the Catholic church's greater capacity for opposition. Members of NS associations and branches were encouraged to leave their churches and declare themselves as GOD-BELIEVING. CELEBRATIONS IN THE NATIONAL SOCIALIST CALENDAR were in-

"Germans, recognize the Jesuit." Anticlerical NSDAP sticker.

tended to gradually replace church festivals, but they made scarcely any inroads.

The war slowed but in no way ended the single-minded continuation of this program, despite the catchword of "truce" (*Burgfriede*). Hitler did prohibit direct reprisals out of concern for combat troops (as in the orders of September 8, 1939, and July 24, 1940). Still, he mostly gave a free hand to Bormann and others in their policy of petty harassment, and risked open conflict over the EUTHANASIA program. He quickly saw himself forced to alter this policy, partly through the protests of such religious leaders as Clemens von GALEN and Theophil WURM. This nourished the illusion among church circles that they had spoken "to [the state's] conscience," and furthered the churches' willingness to go along with the war (thanksgiving services for victories, prayers of petition, chaplaincies at the front, church bells donated to the METAL DONATION OF THE GERMAN VOLK, and so on).

That there was no possibility of addressing a NS "conscience" on religious matters should have been a lesson drawn from the ANSCHLUSS of Catholic Austria. The Reich government refused to apply the Concordat to the "Ostmark," and after further territorial expansion limited its application to the "Old Reich." Despite the emphatic welcome by the Austrian episcopacy, antichurch actions began in 1938, directed against Cardinal Theodor INNITZER, among others. A sample of what was planned for the churches was the Reichsgau WARTHELAND, where measures touched not only the local Polish Catholic church, but also German Lutherans who had believed that their role in the "*Volk* struggle" had earned them a place of merit in the Reich. Both churches underwent demotion to the status of private associations, a nearly total cessation of state support, prohibition against contact with sister churches in Germany, mass arrests of clergy, and the accompanying extensive crippling of congregational life under the guise of "wartime exigencies."

Neither church withstood the hardest test of the Church Struggle, which followed; very few —as the Breslau curate (*Vikarin*) Katharina Staritz, Pastor Heinrich GRÜBER, or Bishop Wurm—raised their voices against the FINAL SOLUTION, insofar as its reality penetrated at all. The Catholic church remained almost entirely silent. Many people helped quietly, but the institutional churches officially suppressed the problem of the "non-Aryans." They had their hands full in struggling for self-preservation: their press was hindered by paper rationing (as early as June 6, 1940), hospital chaplaincies were banned (June 1, 1940), candidates for religious orders were restricted in number "by reason of labor requirements" (October 30, 1940), distribution of religious literature among soldiers was banned (June 1, 1940), JESUITS were discharged from the Wehrmacht (May 31, 1941), church personnel were conscripted with priority into military service (September 14, 1943), and the commandeering of monasteries, convents, and congregational facilities for wartime purposes took on the dimensions of total expropriation.

The situation of the churches was hard, yet they were spared a true Church Struggle by the collapse of the Third Reich. Whether in the event of a "final victory" they would have rotted away "like a gangrenous limb" (Hitler's *Table Talks*, December 13, 1941) is open to doubt. Although the forces of church opposition, or more accurately of Christian recalcitrance, were timid, they still showed that a major onslaught by the state would have awakened the ancient powers of martyrdom. Examples such as Father Maximilian KOLBE, Dietrich BONHOEFFER, Paul SCHNEIDER, and many others gave proof that the rock on which the churches are built is firmer than their NS persecutors believed, and provided in 1945 a sound foundation for their rebuilding.

Friedemann Bedürftig

Ciano, Galeazzo, Count of Cortellazzo, b. Livorno, March 18, 1903; d. Verona, January 11, 1944, Italian politician. After completing his law degree in 1925, Ciano entered the diplomatic service. He married Edda Mussolini (b. 1913) in 1930 and was grandly promoted by his father-in-law: in 1930 he was press secretary; in 1934–1935, undersecretary of state; in 1935,

propaganda minister and member of the Fascist Grand Council. After combat service as an air force officer in ABYSSINIA, Ciano was named foreign minister on June 9, 1936. He promptly put into effect Mussolini's imperialist policy: the formation of the AXIS with Berlin, intervention in the SPANISH CIVIL WAR, occupation of Albania (1939), and an assault on Greece (October

Galeazzo Ciano.

1940). His first reservations over involvement in Germany's war policies became evident in August and September of 1939 and led to his alienation from Mussolini. In February 1943 he was relieved of his office and sent off as ambassador to the Holy See. He established contact with internal Fascist opposition, and on July 25, 1943, supported the Grand Council's decision to remove Il Duce from power. Detained by the Germans and then handed over to the Republic of SALÒ, Ciano was sentenced to death by a special tribunal and shot. His diaries are an important historical source for the Fascist era.

Citadels of the Dead (*Totenburgen*), gigantic monuments to the dead of the Second World War; they never got beyond the planning stage. In 1943 the architect Wilhelm KREIS, among others, drafted plans of such citadels for occupied Russia: rounded pyramids up to 165 m (550 feet) high, built atop hills, were intended to recall the "mighty victories and the greatest heroic struggle in history."

Citizenship, revocation of (*Ausbürgerung*), deprivation of nationality. Whereas before 1933 revocation of citizenship was possible only in exceptional situations (as flight from taxation), the Law Regulating the Revocation of Naturalized Citizenship and the Deprivation of Citizenship of July 14, 1933 (*Reich Law Gazette* [*Reichsgesetzblatt*; RGB] I, p. 480), contained blanket authority to revoke the citizenship of political emigrés and of Jews who had been naturalized after 1918. Although this law was

still designed for application to individual cases, the 11th ordinance to the Reich Citizenship Law of November 25, 1941 (RGBl I, p. 722), collectively affected all Jews outside the Reich —including those deported to concentration camps and extermination camps in the Generalgouvernement. Their property reverted to the Reich. Such revocation of citizenship is disallowed in the Federal Republic of Germany (Article 16I of the Basic Law). Those deprived of citizenship between 1933 and 1945 can regain German citizenship (Article 116II).

Sch.

Civil servants (*Beamte*), officials in public service who occupy positions of particular trust. In the Third Reich, the bases for the establishment of a civil service that was obligated to National Socialism and sworn personally to Hitler (*see* OATH) were the CIVIL SERVICE LAW of April 7, 1933 (*Reich Law Gazette* [*Reichsgesetzblatt*; RGBl] I, p. 175), and the German Civil Service Law of January 27, 1937 (RGBl I, p. 41). The status of the nonpartisan civil servant with lifelong tenure, as intended under the Weimar Constitution, was abolished. Politically unreliable and Jewish civil servants were terminated or forced into retirement. Most key positions were then filled with trustworthy National Socialists, many of whom had entered the party before 1933. Civil servants were organized into National Socialist cells in their workplaces, where they were politically instructed and controlled. In 1939 they constituted 28.2 percent of all NSDAP members. The Basic Law of the Federal Republic resumed the civil service laws of the Weimar Constitution, yet allowed for extensive

Citadels of the Dead. Sketch of a memorial for the bank of the Dnieper River in Russia.

continuity of civil service personnel through the regulations in Article 131.

Sch.

Civil Service Emergency Relief Tax (*Beamtennotopfer;* officially, *Reichshilfe der Personen des öffentlichen Dienstes* [Reich Assistance from Persons in Public Service]), reduction of the salaries of public servants by 2.5 percent. The measure was by emergency decree on July 26, 1930, as a result of Chancellor Heinrich Brüning's policy of DEFLATION during the economic crisis.

Civil Service Law (*Berufsbeamtengesetz*), shortened name for the Law to Restore the Civil Service of April 7, 1933. As early as 14 days after the ENABLING LAW, the National Socialist leadership utilized this legislative carte blanche to enact the Civil Service Law, which made it possible to remove Jewish (*see* ARYAN PARAGRAPH) and politically unpopular civil servants, employees, and workers from state service, "even if the necessary preconditions, according to valid law, are not present." At first only Communists and Jews were specified; shortly thereafter, Socialists and other real or alleged opponents of the regime were affected, a total of some 30,000 persons. Besides dismissal, the law allowed reduction of civil service rank and salary.

Claims Conference. *See* Conference on Jewish Material Claims against Germany.

Clan (also "kindred"), the approximate equivalent of *Sippe*, an Old High German word for "blood relationship"; among the Germanic tribes a term for the "community of peace, law, settlement, and arms" of a population group descended from common (in part mythical) ancestors. Originally it denoted a socially static formation, which, however, as early as the Germanic period made a transition to looser forms of kindred organization. In the Middle Ages the *Sippe* was replaced by the "family" (Lat., *familia*, household community), while by the late 19th century the term itself was used almost exclusively in the sense of consanguinity or even riffraff (*Sippschaft, Gelichter*). The *völkisch* and nationalist Germanic cult idealized the "sanctity of blood ties" in the *Sippe*, understood as a primeval Nordic existential community. The National Socialists attempted to substitute *Sippe* for "family" (*Familie*) in daily and official usage.

Clan Book (*Sippenbuch*), SS register of family and descent, introduced by SS order A-No. 65 (December 31, 1931), "in which the families of SS

members [are] to be entered after the granting of permission to marry or being approved for [SS] enrollment," in order to preserve and increase "this valuable blood inheritance [*Blutserbe*] for future generations of the German *Volk*" (*see* MARRIAGE ORDER).

Clan infamy (*Sippenschande*), in National Socialist propaganda and official jargon a term occasionally used in the sense of RACIAL INFAMY: the "destruction" of a "hereditarily healthy and gifted clan" through "species-alien blood" or "sick blood."

Clan liability (*Sippenhaft[ung]*), legal liability, usually in criminal law but also in property law, of the relatives of a person for that person's infractions. In the Third Reich it was used as a terrorist measure against relatives of political opponents, serving to exert pressure or to intimidate. After the failed coup (the attempt on Hitler's life) of July 20, 1944, wives and children of the alleged perpetrators, as well as some grandchildren, parents, and siblings, were incarcerated with their families in prisons or camps. Clan liability was also imposed on the families of officers who were punished as "traitors to their country" for ordering a retreat, or on the families of persons who expressed doubts as to the "final victory." On February 5, 1945, the Wehrmacht High Command (OKW) ordered: "The clan of a Wehrmacht member who commits treason while a prisoner of war and who is therefore sentenced to death, is liable to relinquish property, freedom, or life." It was hoped that this measure would check the cooperation of German prisoners with the authorities.

U. B.

Clan lore (*Sippenkunde [-forschung]*), National Socialist term for genealogy, the study of kinship and lineage, which in connection with NS racial theories experienced a peak of popularity in the Third Reich. Clan lore—the drawing up of ancestral charts and family trees and the issuance of genealogical documents (*see* CERTIFICATE OF DESCENT)—was the particular concern of the Reich Clan Office (Reichssippenamt) in Berlin, the Central Office for the History of German Persons and Families (Zentralstelle für Deutsche Personen- und Familiengeschichte) in Leipzig, the Main Office for Foreign-German Clan Lore (Hauptstelle für auslandsdeutsche Sippenkunde) in the German Foreign Institute in Stuttgart, the German Ancestral Catalog (Deutsche Ahnenstammkartei) in Dresden, the member organizations of the Volk League of

German Clan Lore Associations (Volksbund der deutschen sippenkundlichen Vereine), and of numerous freelance "researchers," whose professional organization was the Reich Association of Clan Researchers and Heraldists, Registered Association (Reichsverband der Sippenforscher und Heraldiker e.V.).

Clan Office (*Sippenamt*), **1.** SS office responsible for "investigating men already in the SS, both subaltern and major leaders, as well as recent inductees, in terms of race, descent, and hereditary health" (organization book of the NSDAP). Himmler intended the Clan Office particularly to ensure the racially elite character of the SS, which was to become a "clan of German Nordic traits, valuable for its hereditary health."

2. The Reich Office for Clan Research (Reichsstelle für Sippenforschung) in the Interior Ministry (renamed the Reich Clan Office on November 13, 1940), responsible for making and certifying a legally binding decision as to genealogy in all "difficult and ambiguous cases."

3. A renaming of the civil registry office (Standesamt), promoted by National Socialist racial policymakers but never carried through.

Clan passport (*Sippenpass*), additional personal document proposed for the Third Reich (but not officially introduced); it was meant to identify relatives of perpetrators (especially traitors) who eventually could be held "criminally responsible" (*see* CLAN LIABILITY).

Class, Heinrich, b. Alzey, February 29, 1868; d. Jena, April 16, 1953, German politician. Trained as a lawyer, Class joined the ALL-GERMAN ASSOCIATION in 1897, and was its chairman from 1908 until 1939. He supported an imperialist policy for Germany and promoted a vulgar biologism and antisemitism. In the First World War he produced aggressive anti-French and anti-British propaganda. After the war he bitterly resisted the Weimar Republic and democracy: in 1929 he took part in the resistance against the YOUNG PLAN, and in 1931 in the HARZBURG FRONT. In March 1933, Class entered the Reichstag with the NSDAP, but he wielded no influence and could not prevent the dissolution of his association in 1939.

Clauberg, Carl, b. Wupperhof, September 28, 1898; d. Kiel, August 9, 1957, German physician. After receiving his degree, Clauberg served at the university women's clinic in Kiel (November 1, 1925–June 30, 1932), as assistant physician and then physician. Beginning in 1932 he worked at the women's clinic in Königsberg,

Carl Clauberg.

where in 1934—after joining the NSDAP in 1933—he became chief physician (*Oberarzt*). On August 30, 1937, he became a lecturer (*ausserordentlicher Professor*), and on September 20, 1939, a non-budgeted (*ausserplanmässig*) professor; concurrently he was chief physician at the women's clinic in Königshütte (Upper Silesia). He was the author of numerous scientific publications.

In 1942 Himmler authorized Clauberg to conduct sterilization experiments on female prisoners in Research Block 10 of the AUSCHWITZ I extermination camp. Using Jewish and Gypsy women as subjects, Clauberg tested uterine injections, until 1944. Many of the weakened women died. In 1945 he was also in charge of sterilization experiments at the women's camp at RAVENSBRÜCK. The Soviets sentenced him to 25 years' imprisonment, from which he was freed in 1955 after 10 years. However, the Central Council of Jews in Germany strove to have him retried for his experiments, and he was jailed again on November 22, 1955. He died shortly before his trial in 1957. (*See* HUMAN EXPERIMENTS; STERILIZATION.)

Claudius, Hermann, b. Langenfelde bei Hamburg, October 19, 1898; d. September 8, 1980, German writer. Claudius was an elementary school teacher until 1934. The great-grandson of the poet Matthias Claudius, the "Herald of Wandsbek," he began as a "workers' poet," then developed a folk-song-like tone in his poems, as in "Heimkehr" (Homecoming; 1925). He also wrote regional stories such as "Stummel" (The Stump; 1925), and novels. Thoroughly unpolitical and deeply pious, he expressed thanks for

National Socialist recognition of his homely poetry in a naive ode to Hitler ("Lord, be close to the Führer anew, that his work might be for you"; 1941), which gave him an undeserved reputation as a National Socialist. His Low German poems and amateur plays (*see* LAY THEATER) remain popular.

Clauss, Ludwig Ferdinand (pseud. of Götz Brandeck), b. Offenburg/Baden, February 8, 1892; d. Huppert/Taunus, January 13, 1974, German psychologist. In publications such as *Von Seele und Antlitz der Rassen und Völker* (Soul and Countenance in Races and Peoples; 1929), Clauss strove to establish and justify a relationship between "race and soul." He was also co-publisher of the journal *Rasse* (Race). The National Socialists honored him as a spokesman for race psychology, but in 1943 the University of Berlin suspended him for resisting the political misuse of his theories.

Clemenceau, Georges, b. Mouilleron-en-Pareds (Vendée), September 28, 1841; d. Paris, November 24, 1929, French politician. Clemenceau was an opponent of the Franco-German peace treaty of 1871 and a radical socialist. He published the journal *L'Aurore,* a voice against antisemitism in the Dreyfus affair. As prime minister from 1906 to 1909, he carried out the law definitively separating church and state in France. During the First World War he agitated for the maximum effort against Germany. Again premier in 1917, he gained dictatorial powers; he presided over the Paris Peace Conference in 1919, and gained the nickname "the Tiger" for

Georges Clemenceau.

his fierce severity. The excessively harsh and fateful conditions of the peace treaty (*see* VERSAILLES TREATY) bear his stamp. Clemenceau retired from politics in 1920.

Clothing card (*Kleiderkarte*), ration card to buy textile goods (*see* REICH CLOTHING CARD).

Coal thief (*Kohlenklau*), fictitious figure created by National Socialist propaganda as the personification of an antisocial parasite: an ugly monster, half man, half beast, with a sack on his back. In one of the most massive propaganda operations of the Third Reich, the coal thief served as a negative symbol of an energy squanderer, beginning in the winter of 1942–1943: he was to campaign for the sparing use of fuel and bring attention to needlessly burning lamps and open windows. The figure was used on countless posters in railroad stations and stores, on matchboxes, and in radio sketches and announcements.

Coca-Cola, trademark of an American caffeine-containing soft drink that is internationally bottled by concession. The German company was established in Essen in 1929; by 1939, 50 bottling franchises had joined together. Although the product's image (openness to the world; the American way of life) was in clear contrast to *völkisch* and nationalistic ideals, Coca-Cola became the best-known German soft

Coal thief. National Socialist poster: "Watch out! The coal thief is after your bride."

drink, owing to expensive advertising campaigns in the late 1930s and also because National Socialist anti-Americanism was restrained until 1939. Coca-Cola was the official soft drink at the 1936 Olympic Games. Production was cut back in 1940 owing to a shortage of ingredients, and in 1942 the concessionaires had to replace the cola with the newly developed Fanta lemonade drink, which is still made in the Federal Republic of Germany.

H. H.

Codreanu, Corneliu Zelea, b. Jassy, September 13, 1899; d. Bucharest, November 30, 1938, Romanian politician. As an antisemite and anti-Marxist, in 1923 Codreanu founded the "Legion of the Archangel Michael," out of which the fascist IRON GUARD grew. Codreanu tended ideologically toward the Italian exemplar of Mussolini. Following the banning of the Iron Guard in 1933, he won 16 percent of the vote in the elections of 1937 with his new party, "All for the Fatherland," the so-called Green Shirts. However, in April 1938 Codreanu was sentenced to 10 years' imprisonment on the charge of high treason. Shortly thereafter he and 13 of his imprisoned followers were murdered by policemen.

Corneliu Zelea Codreanu.

Collaboration (*Kollaboration*), in general, cooperation with an occupying enemy; in the narrower sense, support for and supporters of German authorities in areas conquered by the Wehrmacht in the Second World War, especially France. The term was originated by the French, and was employed by Henri PÉTAIN on October 11, 1940, as a name for his government's program that sought to assure France a fitting place in a German-dominated Europe. That this involved no active complicity in National Socialist (NS) expansionism was demonstrated at MON-

TOIRE, where Pétain was able to keep his distance by putting Hitler off with vague promises. Motives for collaboration, besides the wish for survival, on the Left involved hopes derived from the "socialist" part of the NS program; the Right admired the strong fascist and antisemitic state, for which ACTION FRANÇAISE had already appealed. Newspapers supportive of collaboration bore appropriate titles such as *Les Nouveaux Temps* (The New Times) and *Le Cri du Peuple* (The Cry of the People). Various explicitly collaborationist parties were formed, like the RASSEMBLEMENT NATIONAL POPULAIRE (Popular National Assembly; RNP) and the PARTI POPULAIRE FRANÇAIS (French Popular Party; PPF).

The character of collaboration was altered by the German assault on the Soviet Union (June 22, 1941). First, it ended the crippling of French Communists through the Hitler-Stalin pact of August 23, 1939, and produced a sharp increase in activities of the RÉSISTANCE against the German occupation. On the other hand, it mobilized anti-Bolshevik resentment among the French citizenry, and thus split French society. An "Anti-Bolshevik Volunteer Legion" was formed, which later became the source for French units of the Waffen-SS, some of which defended Berlin to the very end. French militia in the occupied part of the country conducted an authentic civil war against the *maquisards* (partisans of the Résistance). The designation "collaboration" became politically discredited early on through the actions of such persistently ambitious politicians as Pierre LAVAL, and it became the embodiment of aiding and abetting the enemy, of secret police control, and of fratricide. It also soon came to mean assistance for NS antisemitism (*see* PERSECUTION OF JEWS) and support for a EUROPEAN NEW ORDER, in which France was accorded only a supernumerary's role.

After the turning point of the war, bitterness between Résistance and collaboration intensified. Prominent collaborators were transported to Germany ahead of the advancing Allies; after the German collapse they were imprisoned and most were condemned to death. The "hard core" of collaborationists found themselves exposed to a ruthless campaign of revenge, with victims numbering in the hundreds of thousands. Women who had given their favors to the enemy were especially mistreated in a fit of collective zeal, sometimes pilloried or even put to death. The wounds healed slowly, and even today the collaboration file is not yet closed in France.

Collaboration. French patriots settle accounts.

As in France, German occupation forces found support nearly everywhere: in Belgium from the Vlaamsch National Verbond (Flemish National Union; VNV) and from the REXISTS of Léon DEGRELLE. Belgian units fought in the Waffen-SS on the eastern front. In the Netherlands, in 1931 Anton MUSSERT had already founded the Nationaal Socialistisch Beweging (National Socialist Movement; NSB). It became the vehicle for Dutch collaboration and was recognized by Reich Commissioner Arthur SEYSS-INQUART as the only legal political party. On December 13, 1942, Mussert became the Dutch "Führer." The Waffen-SS found some recruits in the Netherlands as well.

The very synonym for collaborators ("quislings") was the name of the Norwegian fascist Führer Vidkun QUISLING, with his Nasjonal Samling (National Coalition). He had an even narrower base among his people than did Mussert, and played only the role of national fig leaf for the German authorities, alongside Reich Commissioner Josef TERBOVEN, during the occupation. Danish National Socialism under Frits Clausen had virtually no significance; even when the Wehrmacht seized government control over Denmark in 1943, he was given no say in the regime.

In Yugoslavia collaboration took the form of an "independent" Croatia under the Ustaša regime established by Ante PAVELIĆ after the Balkan Campaign. In Hungary, the instruments of collaboration were ARROW CROSS party members under Ferenc SZÁLASI, after Adm. Miklós HORTHY's fall from power. In the occupied eastern lands there was no organized collaboration, though the occupiers found support among those Balts and Ukrainians who were hoping for

Collaboration. In Italy a woman is subjected to scorn for having had relations with German soldiers.

national autonomy, but whose hopes soon lay dashed in the wake of oppression and exploitation. Even among Soviet peoples categorized as "subhumans," such as the Kirghiz, the Tatars, and the Circassians, VOLUNTEER HELPERS were available. The symbolic figure of this collaboration was Andrei VLASOV.

As in France, scores with the collaborators were settled bloodily in all countries vacated by the Germans. In the Soviet Union at times the mere fact of having been a prisoner of war of the Germans was grounds for conviction. A particularly sad chapter in this context was the remanding by the British of Cossacks who had fought on the German side over to the Soviet Union and to certain death. The revenge sought by Tito's partisans also claimed innumerable victims among the Ustaša and Croats. Even in Germany's former ally Italy, where state-directed collaboration had prevailed, vengeance raged.

Collapse (*Zusammenbruch*), a now common term for the political and moral end of National Socialist rule in 1944–1945, and thus for the destruction of the unified German state; in a more restricted sense, a term for the military defeat of the German Wehrmacht. On the eastern front, the Red Army had stopped at the Oder River at the end of January 1945 and armed itself for the last offensive; in the southeast, the Hungarian capital, Budapest, had to capitulate on February 13, after failed attempts to relieve it. Breslau was cut off from February 15 on, and had to be supplied by air. Weak German counterattacks in Pomerania in February and in Lower Silesia in March failed, as did Soviet attempts to wipe out the Kurland bridgehead, which was cut off from all land connections after October 10, 1944. Königsberg capitulated on April 9, Vienna fell on April 13, and two days later the Red Army suspended its advance in the southeast near Sankt Pölten.

After taking Pomerania and cutting off the Bay of Danzig, on April 16 the Soviets launched a final offensive on the Neisse and from the Oder bridgeheads; on April 20, they also proceeded on the lower Oder to capture Mecklenburg. On the same day they began bombing central Berlin. Five days later Soviet panzer units joined up west of Berlin, and completed the encirclement of the Reich capital. A relief attempt by the Twelfth Army (Wenck) from the west had failed by April 28. Hitler remained in the bunker under the Reich Chancellery, where he committed suicide on April 30, after naming First Admiral DÖNITZ to be his successor. Berlin

capitulated on May 2, as Soviet panzer units entered Rostock. Breslau held out until May 6. Army Group Kurland was the last large unit of the Wehrmacht to capitulate (with 208,000 men), on May 10, 1945.

To the south, the Allies reached Bologna on April 21, 1945. This opened the way into the Po Valley, which the English and Americans passed through three days later on a broad front. On April 29, German Army Group C with two armies (250,000 men) capitulated. The Italian Campaign had cost 47,000 dead and 170,000 wounded.

In the west, the Allied counteroffensive only slowly got under way, in January and February of 1945, after the shock of the Ardennes Campaign (*see* INVASION). On March 7 Cologne fell, and the United States First Army crossed the Rhine over a still intact bridge near REMAGEN, to be followed on March 24 by a British crossing near Wesel. By March 25, the Allies had taken possession of the entire left bank of the Rhine. Moving into the Ruhr region on April 1, they cut off Army Group B (General Model), which capitulated by April 18. Four days later the United States Third Army crossed the Czech border; on April 30, the United States Seventh Army entered Munich; and on April 19, Leipzig was reached. On April 25, American units had met troops of the Red Army near TORGAU on the

Collapse. Slogans, to the bitter end: "Our Walls Break, but Not Our Hearts."

Collapse. Soviet troops raise the red flag on the Reichstag building in Berlin.

Elbe River. In the north the British occupied Bremen on April 26, Lübeck and Schwerin on May 2, and Hamburg on May 3. On May 4, German forces in northwest Germany and the Netherlands capitulated. The UNCONDITIONAL SURRENDER of the Wehrmacht was signed three days later in Eisenhower's headquarters in Reims, and on May 8 in Soviet headquarters in Berlin-Karlshorst. The Second World War had ended in Europe; the German Reich was destroyed after the arrest of the Dönitz government (May 23) and the Allied JUNE DECLARATION (June 5). Germany's future fate was reserved for a peace treaty, but in fact was regulated for the time being by the POTSDAM AGREEMENT.

G. H.

Collective (*Kollektiv*), general work group; in socialist theory (and in socialist states) the designation for a group that works toward a common economic and political goal, and in which individual members have the same rights and duties. National Socialist ideology resolutely condemned the collective as a "communistic forced community" (the forced collectivization of Soviet agriculture in the 1920s serving as a perennial cautionary propaganda example), and made it the negative counterpart to the VOLK COMMUNITY based on insight and common experience.

Collective guilt (*Kollektivschuld*), the legal guilt of a community (such as a nation) for the crimes of some of its members. The term contradicts modern jurisprudence, which recognizes only the legal guilt of the individual perpetrator and rejects as a distortion of law such collective punishments as the National Socialist CLAN LIABILITY. After 1945, the allegation of a collective guilt of the German nation for NS crimes was abandoned on these very grounds. Theodor HEUSS spoke instead of a "collective shame" (*Kollektivscham*) that the German people must feel in the face of the outrages committed in its name; out of this attitude grew the commitment to RESTITUTION. Karl JASPERS expressed himself in a similar vein in 1946 by speaking of a "shared implication" (*Mitbetroffenheit*) "even if we have no moral or juridical liability." This is what the STUTTGART CONFESSION OF GUILT of the Evangelical Church intended to communicate. In a talk at the memorial monument in Auschwitz on November 23, 1977, West German chancellor Helmut Schmidt maintained that "today's Germans" were not personally guilty, but he affirmed a "shared responsibility" (*Mitverantwortung*) for German history even on the part of future generations.

Colonial lie (*Koloniallüge*), nationalist-conservative slogan to describe the justifications for the seizure of German colonies through the Versailles treaty; a term parallel to WAR GUILT LIE. The charge that Germany's treatment of her colonies had served "to eliminate the natives more than to develop them" was considered especially mendacious.

Colonial Policy Office (Kolonialpolitisches Amt),

office in the NSDAP Reich Headquarters, founded by Franz Xaver von EPP in 1934 to coordinate related policy matters, especially their treatment in the press.

Colonization (*Ansiedlung*), creation of new peasant farms through the division of large estates, reclamation of land, and—the goal of National Socialist LIVING SPACE policies—conquest. NS ideologues were less concerned with economic issues in this regard than with promoting their POPULATION POLICY, tying broader circles to the "soil," and securing conquered territories, as foreseen in the GENERAL PLAN FOR THE EAST. Thus, colonization was also known as "new creation of the German peasantry" (*Neubildung deutsches Bauerntums*). (*See also* PEASANT MILITIA.)

Combatants for the National Rising (*Kämpfer für die Nationale Erhebung*), term for members of the NSDAP, SA, SS, and other nationalist groups (STEEL HELMET, League of Frontline Soldiers) who had fought for the "National Socialist revolution" before January 30, 1933. Through the Law concerning Provisions for Combatants for the National Awakening, such groups were to be rewarded and honored; the injured and survivors were to be eligible for the same benefits as casualties of war.

Combat League for German Culture (Kampfbund für deutsche Kultur), organization founded by Alfred ROSENBERG in 1929 after an initial suggestion made at the third Reich Party Congress of the NSDAP on August 27. It opposed "degenerative phenomena" in modern art, and Jewish influence on German cultural life. On June 6, 1934, it merged with the Reich Association of the German Stage to form the NATIONAL SOCIALIST CULTURE COMMUNITY.

Combat Spoilage! (*Kampf dem Verderb*), National Socialist propaganda slogan; part of the AUTARKY efforts to attain self-sufficiency in the agricultural sector. The slogan appeared on placards in food stores and in advertisements, especially in wartime as supplies became increasingly scarce.

Comic War (*Komischer Krieg*), German rendering of the French *drôle de guerre* (Eng., "phony war"), denoting the phase of the Second World War between the declaration of war (September 3, 1939) and Germany's attack on France (May 10, 1940); *see* SITTING WAR.

Comintern, shortened form of Communist INTERNATIONAL.

Commando Order (*Kommandobefehl*), order issued by Hitler on October 18, 1942, for the extermination of terror and sabotage groups. From mid-1940, commando units were set up in England to harass German occupation troops through operations in the occupied western territories, as well as to destroy military and economic facilities. At the high point of commando warfare Hitler ordered, in a Wehrmacht bulletin of October 7, 1942, that "in the future all terror and sabotage troops of the British and their accomplices . . . shall be crushed ruthlessly in battle . . . by German troops." The Wehrmacht High Command staff was given the task of putting the statement into an appropriate order that would help subordinate levels as a basis and guideline for proper decisions in future cases. It was thereby made known that members of such commandos who fell into the hands of the Wehrmacht were to be handed over to the SECURITY SERVICE (SD); keeping them in custody under military supervision—even temporarily—was strictly forbidden. In an accompanying statement Hitler explained the reason for promulgating the Commando Order: since substantial personnel and material damages had been caused by the activity of enemy sabotage troops, it was necessary to make clear to the foe that every troop of saboteurs would be crushed to

"Combat Spoilage now above all!" National Socialist poster (1941).

the last man, without exception. Commando members who fell into captivity were handed over to the SD and then shot.

A. St.

Commercial policy (*Handelspolitik*). *See* Foreign trade; Organization of the Industrial Economy; Reich Food Estate; Wage-price policy.

Commissar Order (*Kommissarbefehl;* officially, Guidelines for the Handling of Political Commissars), Hitler's directive for the extermination of captive Soviet commissars. As early as March 30, 1941, Hitler declared in a meeting with his generals that in the impending Russian Campaign, commissars were to be killed. Shortly before the invasion of the USSR, a corresponding Commissar Order was drafted—under Hitler's influence—by the Wehrmacht High Command (OKW) staff (Section L). In areas of military operations, political commissars "of every type and rank" who had operated against the troops or were suspected of having done so were to be segregated from other prisoners of war right on the battlefield and then "finished off" (*erledigt*). Commissars caught in suspicious activities in rear military areas were to be handed over to EINSATZGRUPPEN of the Security Police and SECURITY SERVICE (SD).

On June 6, 1941, the guidelines were transmitted to commanding officers of the three Wehrmacht sections with the instruction that they be distributed only to army supreme commanders and air fleet chiefs; transmission to lower commanders was to be oral. The order, a violation of international law, remained in force for nearly a year. In the late summer of 1941, protests from the field accumulated in the Army High Command (OKH), which finally, on September 23, urged the OKW "to examine the need for carrying out the Commissar Order in its current form in light of the developing situation." Alfred JODL, head of the Wehrmacht command staff, on Hitler's instructions rebuffed any change on September 26, 1941. At the beginning of May 1942 Hitler finally ordered the tentative suspension of the order "to strengthen the inclination of surrounded Soviet troops to desert and surrender."

A. St.

Communal annexation (*Eingemeindung;* also translated as "incorporation"), means of territorial reform that was often used in the Third Reich, in accordance with the GERMAN COMMUNAL ORDINANCE of January 30, 1935. Its purpose was to create larger market areas, for example by uniting Hamburg and formerly Prussian Altona (January 1937). Communal annexation also served to dissolve established local structures so as to facilitate centralization and SYNCHRONIZATION by eliminating particularist opposition.

Communism (*Kommunismus*), in general, any form of society characterized by total community of property and a communal way of life; in the narrower sense, the schemes for society that in the 19th century strove for freedom from the ruling authorities and for classlessness. In the Marxist sense the term was used to denote the highest stage of socialism, and, by derivation, the world of socialist states ("the Communist camp"). National Socialist propaganda was directed against communism in its concrete manifestation, namely BOLSHEVISM, labeling it a "dogmatically formulated collectivist social doctrine of Jewry." Insofar as communism promoted the abolition of private property, Jewry was said to be attempting to "create shock troops out of the mass of socially desperate and subhuman people with whom it . . . seeks to achieve world domination." The NS notion of pincers saw CAPITALISM as the right arm and communism as the left arm exerting a stranglehold that turned the world over to the Jews.

Communist Party of Germany (Kommunistische Partei Deutschlands; KPD), extreme-left political party founded in Berlin on December 30, 1918, through a merger of the Spartacus

Communist Party of Germany. The party central office, Karl Liebknecht House, in Berlin.

Communist Party of Germany poster:
"Join the KPD! (Spartacus League)."

League, which split off from the SPD (Social
Democratic Party of Germany) in 1916, and the
"International Communists of Germany"; it was
augmented in December 1920 through union
with the left wing of the Independent Socialists
(USPD). Through numerous internal conflicts
the "left" wing prevailed in 1928–1929 under
the leadership of Ernst THÄLMANN (chairman
from 1925); in March 1929 the "right" wing
established the COMMUNIST PARTY OPPOSITION
(KPO). From then on the KPD oriented its
organization and politics toward the Soviet (Stalinist) Communist party. It effectively became
the German section of the Comintern, viewing
the "social fascist" SPD as its main opponent
and totally underestimating the NSDAP. It thus
impeded a united opposition on the part of the
German labor movement against National Socialism. On another level, the KPD and its
RED FRONTLINE FIGHTERS' LEAGUE, through
meeting-hall brawls and street battles such as
ALTONA BLOODY SUNDAY, contributed heavily
to the brutalization of political disagreements in
the final phase of the Weimar Republic. The
KPD's main publication was *Die* ROTE FAHNE
(The Red Flag).

In Reichstag elections the KPD succeeded in
almost continually augmenting its percentage of
the votes: from 2.1 percent in 1920 to 16.9
percent in November 1932. After the Reichstag
fire of February 27, 1933, which National Socialist propaganda blamed on the KPD, many of
its members and the majority of its 100 Reichstag deputies were arrested (some 3,000 persons). Nearly all its election propaganda was
seized. Yet it still received 12.3 percent of the
votes in the elections of March 5. Immediately
after the elections, all 81 Communist mandates
were annulled, and no Communist took part in
the Reichstag session of March 24, 1933, at
which the ENABLING LAW was passed.

The KPD was *de facto* the first German party
to be banned. Outside the country, it persisted
through the establishment, on January 30, 1933,
of a "foreign directorate" (in Paris and Prague,
and after 1941 in Moscow, under the direction
of Wilhelm PIECK and Walter ULBRICHT). Within Germany, the illegal party maintained a "domestic directorate" in Berlin. With the exception of the RED ORCHESTRA, the small and
splintered Communist opposition groups, weakened by widespread arrests (in 1936–1937
alone, about 20,000 persons), remained mainly
ineffective. Tardy attempts to bring together a
popular front based on ANTIFASCISM found no
echo among Social Democratic or bourgeois
opposition groups.

On June 11, 1945, the KPD was reestablished.
In the Soviet Zone it merged with the SPD to
form the Socialist Unity Party of Germany (So-
zialistische Einheitspartei Deutschlands; SED).
The Federal Republic of Germany banned the
KPD on August 17, 1956, as unconstitutional.

R. B.

Communist Party Opposition (Kommunistische
Partei Opposition; KPO), Communist organization founded in March 1929 by "right-wing"
Communists who had been expelled from the
KPD (Communist Party of Germany) in late
1928 and early 1929. Under such leaders as
August Thalheimer and Paul Fröhlich, the KPO
set itself against the Stalinist course of the KPD,
resisting particularly its insistence that the "social fascist" SPD (Social Democratic Party of
Germany) was communism's chief political adversary. The KPO was most influential in Saxony, Thuringia, Hesse, and Württemberg, but it
never rose to the level of a mass party. A number
of its leaders and members joined the Socialist
Workers' Party (Sozialistische Arbeiterpartei) in
1932.

R. B.

Community (*Gemeinschaft*), central concept in
the National Socialist (NS) worldview; beginning from the classical view of the human as
zoon politikon (political being), it meant to stress
the "obligatory mutuality" of human behavior.
The give-and-take in a community suggested by
this concept was, to be sure, arranged according

to clear priorities in National Socialism: individual rights were unconditionally subordinate to the interests of the community; what these interests might be was determined "from above," according to the FÜHRER PRINCIPLE. The NS concept of community was developed in contradistinction to traditional notions of community as well as to Marxist theories of class: while society (*Gesellschaft*) was said to be only subsequently a purposive combination of groups, "community" implied an "original life association" (*ursprünglicher Lebenszusammenhang*), a "primeval existence" (*Urdasein*). In contrast to "rootless, internationalist" class ideology, the community was rooted in "blood"; it obliged one to be concerned with the "material of heredity" (*Erbmasse*), the "constant factor" of the community. Thus it could be the basis for an inclusive VOLK COMMUNITY, even as the FRONT EXPERIENCE of the First World War had produced a genuine community of combatants. Similarly, "the experience of a common fate in the same space [*des gemeinsamen Schicksals auf gleichem Raum*]" must lead to a "community of sacrifice and fate."

NS ideologues defended themselves against the criticism of collectivism by referring to the "articulated" community structure they foresaw: the nucleus was the FAMILY, in its turn bound to "colleagueship" (*Berufskamerad-*

schaft) and a community (*Gemeinde*), which ultimately broadened out into the *Volk*. The practice of NS EDUCATION proves, however, that the totalitarian goals themselves stood in the way of this glorified family concept. The goal was an "organized" community, whose "supreme law" had to be "disciplined" according to the principle of "Führer and followers" (Robert Ley, December 11, 1934). Here there could be no talk of a community in which the individual "could first develop into a personality," as the official propaganda claimed.

Community settlement (*Gemeinschaftssiedlung*), form of settlement structured according to the National Socialist notion of COMMUNITY; it had a nucleus (*Ortskern*) with a school and community house (*Gemeinschaftshaus*). Care was to be taken that all possible occupational and age groups were represented, so that division into classes and social strata would be avoided.

Compiègne, French city northeast of Paris; its population was 18,000 in 1940. In the Pullman car of French marshal Ferdinand Foch in the forest of Compiègne, a German delegation under Matthias ERZBERGER, on November 9, 1918, accepted the harsh Allied conditions for a ceasefire that would lead to a peace treaty (*see* VERSAILLES TREATY). The delegation signed the

Community. Soldiers listen to the *Volk*'s receiver.

Compiègne (1940). Hitler with his entourage in front of the historic parlor car.

cease-fire on November 11, at the insistent recommendation of the army supreme commanders.

In the same car, at the same place, during the FRENCH CAMPAIGN, Hitler received a French delegation on June 21, 1940, and announced the German conditions for the cease-fire that was signed on the following day by Gen. Wilhelm KEITEL and French army general Huntziger. Its stipulations included demobilization of the French army, the occupation of France to the Loire River and along the entire coastline, and extradition of German emigrés. The historic rail car was brought to Berlin, and the Compiègne monument to the French victory of 1918 was destroyed.

Complete family (*Vollfamilie*), term used by National Socialist population theorists to denote the "hereditarily healthy family with four or more children, living an orderly life." These were the families that would be necessary to maintain and eventually increase Germany's "*Volk* energy and strength."

Compulsory military service (*Wehrpflicht*), universal obligatory military service reintroduced in Germany by the Law "for the Creation of the Wehrmacht," on March 16, 1935, violating the disarmament terms of the Versailles treaty (Article 173); it was supplemented by the Reich Defense Law of May 21, 1935. The preliminary peacetime strength of the Wehrmacht was stipulated at 36 divisions and 550,000 men. The introduction of compulsory military service was preceded on March 9 by an official declaration regarding the rebuilding of the Luftwaffe. The law was only the official statement of a rearmament that had secretly been going on for years. Hitler took as pretext the British defense "White Book" of March 4, 1935, which justified British armaments by reference to secret German remilitarization, as well as to the introduction of two years of military service in France (March 6, 1935) and the extension of the French-Belgian military agreement of 1921 (March 7, 1935).

In reality, compulsory military service was an important preparatory step in the transition from a REVISIONIST POLICY to a policy of expansion. At the same time, it was a tool of domestic policy, aiming to secure the consent of the people by dramatic foreign-policy actions. The British government protested in Berlin on March 18, 1935. The same diplomatic note inquired whether a state visit of Foreign Secretary Sir John Simon and Lord Privy Seal Anthony Eden, which had been postponed on March 7 because of Hitler's "cold," was still welcome. On June

> **Gesetz für den Aufbau der Wehrmacht vom 16. März 1935**
>
> Die Reichsregierung hat folgendes Gesetz beschlossen, das hiermit verkündet wird:
>
> **§ 1.**
> Der Dienst in der Wehrmacht erfolgt auf der Grundlage der allgemeinen Wehrpflicht.
>
> **§ 2.**
> Das deutsche Friedensheer einschließlich der überführten Truppenpolizeien gliedert sich in 12 Korpskommandos und 36 Divisionen.
>
> **§ 3.**
> Die ergänzenden Gesetze über die Regelung der allgemeinen Wehrpflicht sind durch den Reichswehrminister dem Reichsministerium vorzulegen.
>
> Berlin, den 16. März 1935
>
> Unterschriften des Führers und sämtlicher Mitglieder des Reichskabinetts

Compulsory military service. Law for the Creation of the Wehrmacht. Berlin, March 16, 1935, signed by the Führer and all members of the Reich Cabinet:

"The Reich government has adopted the following law, which is herewith announced:

1. Service in the Wehrmacht is based on universal compulsory military service.

2. The German peacetime army, including the transferred police units, is organized into 12 corps commandos and 36 divisions.

3. The supplementary laws regulating universal compulsory military service will be submitted to the Reich ministry by the armed forces minister."

18, the British sanctioned German rearmament in line with their APPEASEMENT policy by concluding the GERMAN-BRITISH NAVAL AGREEMENT. France, Italy, and the League of Nations Council, which had been invoked by Paris and the "antirevisionist front" of STRESA, protested only on paper. The Western powers let themselves be deceived by Hitler's "Peace Address" of May 21, 1935, which offered bilateral nonaggression pacts and the intentionally nurtured illusion that compulsory military service only "legalized" a secret process which had been known about for a long time and which had been regarded with great concern. Thus it allegedly was the necessary prerequisite for moving from German equality and the parity in armaments that Berlin desired to general disarmament or arms limitation through treaties.

B.-J. W.

Comrade (*Genosse*, from Celt. *neah* [Ger., *Vieh*, beast; livestock]), term originally referring to a person or companion who had the same animal, and used in the context of a cooperative trade association. The term *Genosse* was introduced in 1879 as the salutation for fellow members of the Socialist Workers' Party of Germany, a predecessor of the SPD (Social Democratic Party of Germany), which continued the practice. The National Socialists took over the term "party comrade" (*Parteigenosse*), as well as "comrade in struggle" (*Kampfgenosse*), and coined the term VOLK COMRADE, which in keeping with National Socialism's self-definition dropped the word's "character of class struggle" and reaffirmed its "Old German meaning of community and following."

Comradely marriage (*Kameradschaftsehe*), term coined in Weimar Germany [after the American "companionate marriage"] to refer to marriage-like cohabitations without marriage license and, above all, without the intent to produce children. Such cohabitations were sharply criticized by the National Socialists for endangering the "continued existence of the *Volk*" and for crippling the "will for a child."

Comrades' grave (*Kameradengrab*), National Socialist euphemism adopted to avoid using the term "mass grave" for burials of their own dead.

Comradeship (*Kameradschaft*), a high-ranking virtue in National Socialist ETHICS; like National Socialism itself, born "in the trenches of the World War" (*see* FRONT EXPERIENCE). A properly understood comradeship should overcome "all differences among classes" and was thus a precondition for the VOLK COMMUNITY. The emphasis on comradeship also went with the NS cult of manhood and the valued "soldierly attitude."

The term was further used as a designation for organizations, especially student groups ("new communities of education and life"). A *Kameradschaft* was the smallest unit in the HITLER YOUTH; artists' groups bore the same name, and in general NSDAP units were given the lofty title "Comradeships of the Third Reich." [The German *Genosse*, also translated as "COMRADE," has definite leftist-labor connotations, despite its appropriation in *Volksgenosse* (VOLK COMRADE). *Kamerad*, on the other hand, was favored for its military evocations. *Kameradschaft* should similarly be contrasted with *Genossenschaft; see* COOPERATIVES.]

Concentration Camps

The first concentration camps (*Konzentrationslager*) were set up by the British during the Boer War (1901) to intern civilian captives. In National Socialist Germany they served to confine and re-educate such "hostile elements" as Communists, Socialists, Centrists, and clerics, as well as to provide forced labor. The camps arose as a result of the wave of arrests following the SEIZURE OF POWER in 1933: overflow conditions in the jails soon necessitated expanded confinement facilities. The principal legal basis for arrests was the REICHSTAG FIRE DECREE. Confinement was characterized as a preventive police measure or protective detention of elements hostile to the state. Judicial recourse against these actions was not permitted.

The first concentration camps were organized partly by state agencies such as the police and partly by autonomous SA and SS groups, using such sites as factories and camp buildings. These "wild" camps (*see* PROTECTIVE CUSTODY) were gradually phased out, while administration and guarding of the other camps remained under the authority of SA and SS personnel appointed by the state as auxiliary police (Hilfspolizei); after the RÖHM AFFAIR (June 30, 1934) the SS alone was in charge.

The model for all concentration camps was DACHAU; its commandant, Theodor EICKE, named "Inspector of Concentration Camps" on July 4, 1934, issued a set of camp regulations on October 1, 1933, that provided the pattern for organizing other camps. A camp had five sections: the commandant's office (I), a political section (II), a protective-custody camp (III), an administrative office (IV), and a medical section (V). The political section (II) was in fact a field office of the existing local Gestapo, with a Gestapo official as chief. It conducted interrogations and maintained prisoner records and files. The commander of the protective-custody section (in large camps there was a first and a second commander) was also the commandant's deputy. Under him came one or more reporting officers (*Rapportführer*), beneath whom were the block leaders (*Blockführer*). Also under him were the work detail leader (*Arbeitseinsatzführer*) and the commando chief (*Kommandoführer*). Prisoners were billeted in the protective-custody section (III).

Discipline among SS members in the camps

was mostly poor. Even severe punishments (including the death penalty) imposed by SS courts failed to make any basic change. Parallel to the SS organization, a prisoners' administrative scheme was later arranged; at its head was the camp elder or elders (*Lagerältester*), followed by an elder from the individual barracks and the barracks detail. Prisoners with special work assignments (clerical workers, prisoner physicians, corpse bearers, and so on) were charged with the most varied work in the camp. They were placed in the work details as KAPOS and foremen. Most were criminals or political prisoners; between the two groups there was a constant overt or covert struggle for the best positions in the camp. Besides the SS personnel within the camp, SS guard troops maintained external security. These SS Guard Units (SS-Wachverbände) were later called the SS DEATH'S-HEAD UNITS.

At first only political prisoners were kept in protective custody in the camps, but later, as a result of a Reich Justice Ministry decree of December 14, 1937, "career and habitual criminals, and asocial persons," and the like, who were labeled as preventive police detainees, were placed in the camps, in part to discriminate against political prisoners. Joined by Jews, Gypsies, homosexuals, JEHOVAH'S WITNESSES, the so-called WORK-SHY (by Himmler's decree of January 26, 1938), and individuals who had already served out their sentences or who allegedly had been unjustly acquitted, various inmate categories were early on confined in camps. After the outbreak of war, foreign prisoners from German-occupied territories—such as "NN prisoners" (*see* "NIGHT AND FOG" DECREE)—were increasingly put into the camps. They came to constitute the majority of the prisoners.

The various types of prisoners were identified by an upside-down triangle (called "angle" [*Winkel*]) made of colored fabric attached to the clothing: criminals had green, politicals red, asocials black, homosexuals pink, and Jehovah's Witnesses violet triangles. Jewish prisoners were marked as such by a yellow triangle sewn on top of the first one to form a Star of David. Foreign prisoners were identified by the initial of their native land sewn onto their badge. Prisoners who had attempted to flee or were suspected thereof were identified by a large "escape mark"

(*Fluchtpunkt*) in red or black on their chest and back.

Since a gigantic reserve of forced laborers was available in the camps, the SS began to establish its own economic enterprises, and in February 1942 instituted the ECONOMIC-ADMINISTRATIVE MAIN OFFICE (WVHA), under the direction of the later SS-*Obergruppenführer* Oswald POHL, to which the Office of the Inspector of Concentration Camps was attached under the rubric "Office Group [Amtsgruppe] D." As the war dragged on, continual bombardment made it necessary to move most armament production underground, which increased the demand for prisoners and forced laborers. The small group of camps established by 1939—Dachau, Flossenbürg, Sachsenhausen, Buchenwald, Mauthausen, and the women's camp at Ravensbrück, with a total of 21,400 inmates—grew into an extensive system that included the occupied countries as well. Wherever industry needed labor, satellite camps (auxiliary camps) were set up. The prisoner count in all camps grew in this way to nearly 525,000 in August 1944, and rose to over 600,000 at the beginning of 1945.

The interests of the WVHA in utilizing labor resources was to some extent in conflict with the interests of the REICH SECURITY MAIN OFFICE (RSHA) in eliminating or re-educating political opponents. However, governance of the camps by the WVHA was hardly advantageous to the prisoners. According to an order from Pohl in April 1942, the exploitation of labor was expected to be "exhaustive, in the truest sense of the word": mealtimes, roll calls, and the like would be kept to the absolute minimum. After September 1942 certain prisoners processed by the judicial system (protective-custody detainees and Germans, Jews, Gypsies, Russians, and Poles, among others) were also to be placed in camps, "for extermination through work," in accordance with an agreement between justice minister Otto THIERACK and Himmler. Moreover, in the camps all prisoners no longer capable of work (*see* MUSELMANN) were segregated and transported to the killing facilities of the EUTHANASIA operation or to EXTERMINATION CAMPS, where they were killed. In many cases they were murdered by toxic injection in the concentration camps themselves.

Camp prisoners were subjected to the unconditional authority of the SS and Gestapo. In keeping with Eicke's camp regulations, the imposition of punishments—whippings, being

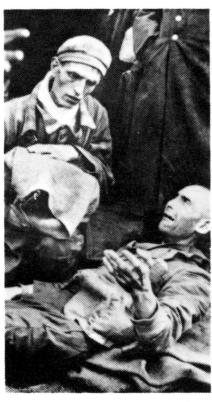

Concentration camps. Prisoners after the liberation (1945).

Victims of the Bergen-Belsen concentration camp being pushed into mass graves by a bulldozer.

hung on a stake, anything up to and including the death penalty—was up to the local commandant, although capital punishment for such offenses as escape attempts was normally ordered by the RSHA. The unauthorized killing or mistreatment of a prisoner was expressly forbidden. SS members were even prohibited from touching prisoners. Nevertheless, mistreatment and killing of prisoners (through beatings, hangings, drownings, lethal torture, and so on) were daily realities. Prison orderlies (the Kapos) took part in these actions along with SS personnel. The perpetrators were normally left unpunished, since the Office of the Inspector tolerated the practices.

Living conditions—hygiene, clothing, food supplies, and medical care—were altogether inadequate and inhuman. Most inmates were quartered in drafty wooden barracks, furnished with primitive three-tier bunk beds. Up to three prisoners slept in each bed, often under one blanket, on straw sacks for mattresses or even on the bare wood frame. Normal garments consisted—even in winter—of the thin, striped prisoner's uniform, which was seldom washed. Food was usually a small bread ration, most often with turnip soup or gruel. This, along with bad sanitary conditions that brought on repeat-ed epidemics, and inhuman working conditions, led to an extraordinarily high mortality rate. Even with the demand of the WVHA (Pohl's memorandum of January 20, 1943) to maintain through all means the prisoners' working strength, these mortality rates could not be stanched. Further, prisoners were used for numerous medical HUMAN EXPERIMENTS, which were sometimes planned to be terminal (that is, it was clear from the outset that the subjects would thereby die). In the framework of the FINAL SOLUTION, some camps were used for killing with poison gas and for SPECIAL HANDLING, namely, the execution of "elements hostile to the state" and of Russian prisoners of war (after the COMMISSAR ORDER of June 6, 1941).

Most concentration camps in the inner Reich were evacuated shortly before the war's end. In the chaos of the collapse, innumerable exhausted prisoners, some in open freight trains, died. If they could not keep up with the tempo of the forced marches, they were shot on the roadside by guards. Many died in the totally overcrowded collecting camps—an estimate of some one-third of all registered prisoners as of January 1945.

Willy Dressen

Concentration camps, "wild." *See* Protective custody.

Concordat (Reich Concordat), treaty of July 20, 1933, between the German Reich government and the Holy See. The Concordat came into being through continual negotiations conducted by Franz von PAPEN, Monsignor Ludwig KAAS, and Cardinal Secretary of State Eugenio Pacelli (*see* PIUS XII), starting in April 1933, after several failed attempts during the Weimar Republic. The treaty took effect on September 10, 1933, and guaranteed the continuance of existing state concordats (Bavaria, 1924; Prussia, 1929; Baden, 1932). Among other matters, its provisions included protection of "the freedom to confess and openly practice the Catholic religion" (Article 1); guarantees of the church's free right of patronage over all ecclesiastical offices and benefices (Article 14), of religious orders and communities (Article 15), of church property (Article 17), and of the maintenance of Catholic theological faculties at state institutions of higher education (Article 19); the establishment of new philosophical and theological schools for the clergy (Article 20); the recognition of Catholic religious education in public schools (Article 23); the maintenance and expansion of Catholic schools (Article 23); protection for Catholic organizations and associations "that serve exclusively religious, purely cultural, and charitable purposes" (Article 31, the specific details of which were reserved for negotiations with the German episcopate); and the prohibition against membership by clergy and religious in political parties (Article 32). A secret supplementary protocol governed the appointment of chaplains in the event of the reintroduction of universal military service.

By the sacrifice of German Catholicism's trade unions and political organizations (July 4–5, 1933, self-dissolution of the CENTER party and the BAVARIAN PEOPLE'S PARTY), the Vatican hoped, with an eye to the regime's continuing efforts toward totalitarian SYNCHRONIZATION, to bring a halt to the threat of a CHURCH STRUGGLE. It also hoped to establish a legally secure defensive position for the Catholic church's self-assertion, for its independence, and for the protection of important elements among the

Concordat. Franz von Papen (second from left) and State Secretary Cardinal Pacelli (center).

laity. The suspicion cannot be unequivocally proved that the Vatican—aware of the imminent agreement on a concordat, and planning to allow the Center party to expire immediately thereafter—through some sort of "stab in the back" forced the Center on March 23, 1933, to consent to the ENABLING LAW. For Hitler the Concordat meant foreign recognition and prestige, especially with regard to Catholic countries, a confirmation in international law of his worthiness for treaties, and a breakout from Germany's isolation. For his domestic policies, it meant a substantial gain of legitimacy and loyalty among Catholics, recognition of his regime by the Vatican, and also the breakup of political Catholicism and the depoliticization of the clergy.

The Concordat was unable to forestall its immediate and unilateral violation, especially of Articles 15, 17, 19, 23, and 31: notably, persecution of Catholic youth groups and professional organizations, offensives against Catholic schools, prosecution of priests and religious (*see* PRIEST TRIALS), and discrimination against Caritas, the Catholic social welfare organization. Continuing in spite of repeated protests by the Vatican, these violations aggravated the Church Struggle and led to issuance of the papal encyclical MIT BRENNENDER SORGE on March 14, 1937.

There are two sides to an appraisal of the Concordat. It clearly played an important role in the internal and external stabilization of the regime and in the removal of its opponents. On the other hand, it preserved for the Catholic church a certain amount of space for its self-defense and for non-accommodation of the regime's interventions and claims, as well as a legal foundation in the Church Struggle. It also set certain limits to the total synchronization of societal and religious life.

According to a judgment handed down by the Federal Constitutional Court (Bundesverfassungsgericht) on March 26, 1957, the Concordat remains valid for the Federal Republic of Germany.

B.-J. W.

Condor Legion (Legion Condor), volunteer Wehrmacht units that fought on Franco's side in the SPANISH CIVIL WAR. As early as the end of July 1936, an airlift of 15,000 Spanish Nationalist troops was organized with the aid of German airplanes. The legion was continually expanded and came to include air, communications, and transport units, which were augmented by tank troops to a total strength of about 6,000 men, who were regularly rotated. Their efforts were decisive in many ways to Franco's victory. Alongside the ideological goal of "confronting the spread of communism in this place" (Göring), the legion found in Spain a proving ground for new weapons and "thereby had the opportunity to test with live ammunition whether the matériel was satisfactorily developed for its purposes" (Göring). The venture was kept secret; however, it became known to world public opinion no later than the bombing of GUERNICA (April 1937). The homecoming of the legion —on cruise ships of the government's KdF (STRENGTH THROUGH JOY) program—turned into a pompous state celebration. On June 6, 1939, the legion paraded in Berlin, bearing

12, 1936). The Confessing Church was from then on only secondarily an organizational factor; above all, it was involved wherever Evangelical Christians refused the nationalist, racist, and antisemitic claims of National Socialism.

The church commission too foundered. Hitler lost any interest in pacifying the Evangelical Church and gave his ideologues (Albert Rosenberg) and his power holders (Martin Bormann) a free hand in combating and harassing the Confessing Church. Their cooperation in ecumenism was thwarted, their training of candidates was hindered, and pastors were banished from their congregations or prohibited from preaching (*see* PULPIT PARAGRAPH). In mid-1937 Niemöller was arrested. He was acquitted on March 2, 1938, only to be sent to a concentration camp as "the Führer's personal prisoner." He was followed by many clergymen, who were publicly remembered in lists of petitionary prayers kept by pastors in the Confessing Church. Political opposition to such policies as EUTHANASIA not uncommonly proceeded from theological conflict, even though active conspirators like Dietrich BONHOEFFER remained the exception.

With the beginning of the war a kind of civil peace developed between the Confessing Church and the NS authorities. Still, open confession of Jesus Christ, the "sole Word of God" (Barmen Theological Declaration), thereafter carried serious risks (18 pastors of the Confessing Church were confined in camps between 1937 and 1945) and personal disadvantages. Many did not shy away from these burdens, thereby providing a foundation for rebuilding the Evangelical Church after the COLLAPSE. Yet in the STUTTGART CONFESSION OF GUILT (October 19, 1945) it accused itself of "not having loved more ardently," because the Confessing Church had remained mostly silent with regard to the NS genocide against the Jews.

Confession of Guilt of the Evangelical Church (October 19, 1945). *See* Stuttgart Confession of Guilt.

Conscience (*Gewissen*), the human mental faculty for the ethical and moral control of judgment and behavior, for decisions regarding good and evil. National Socialism gave the Christian term "conscience" a racist reinterpretation: it was "tied to inheritance," so that one could speak of a specifically "German conscience" that would point out the way of "*Volk* responsibility." Thus, Hitler's creation of National Socialism could be traced back to a voice of conscience, while the

"call of the Führer" conversely had "stirred" all Germans "in their consciences."

Conscience, freedom of. *See* Freedom of conscience.

Conscription (*Dienstverpflichtung*), mobilization of workers and employees for jobs of particular importance to the state, with at the same time (at first for a set period) a severing of existing labor obligations; it was introduced through a decree of June 22, 1938. The immediate context for the decree, apotheosized as an "economic induction notice," was the erection of military defense facilities on the western border of Germany (*see* WESTWALL), for which some 400,000 persons were recruited. In the following period, the National Socialist state used conscription as a permanent instrument of maintaining a high employment level in the armaments industry and of controlling LABOR DEPLOYMENT. On February 13, 1939, the time limitation on conscription was lifted; in January 1943, on grounds of national defense, conscription was extended to women between 17 and 45 years of age.

Conservativism (*Konservativismus*), intellectual and political movement begun in the 18th century whose objective was to justify and retain existing conditions in society and state; it was supported by politically and economically privileged groups. During the Weimar Republic, Catholic and clerical conservative forces were organized especially in the CENTER party, liberal conservatives in the GERMAN PEOPLE'S PARTY (DVP), and the more Prussian-Evangelical conservative groups, landowners, representatives of heavy industry, and military officers in the GERMAN NATIONAL PEOPLE'S PARTY (DNVP). The conservativism cultivated in the DNVP, linked to one-sided advocacy of the interests of large landowners in particular, prepared the soil for National Socialism through its antirepublican and nationalist posture and increased its stature through alliances (*see* HARZBURG FRONT). The NSDAP criticized the conservatives' "rigid adherence to obsolete notions," yet was itself "perhaps best . . . described by the term 'conservative-revolutionary party'" (Hitler). Because of the partial identity of goals between conservativism and National Socialism (revision of the Versailles treaty, rearmament, abolition of democracy, and so on), Germany's traditional elite tolerated the revolutionary excesses so long that they themselves ended up as prisoners of the system.

"Conserves" (*Konserven*), SECURITY SERVICE (SD) code name for bodies of concentration camp prisoners, dressed in Polish uniforms, that were left behind as "evidence" after the fake attack on the GLEIWITZ radio station, the Hochlinden tollhouse, and the Pitschen forester's lodge.

Constitution (*Verfassung*), the totality of regulations regarding the form and direction of the state, the tasks of state institutions, and the BASIC RIGHTS of citizens. The German Reich had no written constitution between 1933 and 1945; there was, however, a constitutional practice (*Verfassungspraxis*) based on particular laws and unwritten principles. Although the WEIMAR CONSTITUTION had not been formally abolished, it was regarded as no longer valid for National Socialism. The point of departure for National Socialist constitutional development was the REICHSTAG FIRE DECREE of February 28, 1933 (*Reich Law Gazette* [*Reichsgesetzblatt;* RGBl] I, p. 83), which repealed the most important civil rights. This formed the basis for the abolition of traditional constitutional guarantees of individual freedoms against the state. The Reichstag Fire Decree was thus, according to Ernst Fraenkel, something like the "Basic Constitutional Document" (*Verfassungsurkunde*) of the Third Reich.

The ENABLING LAW of March 24, 1933 (RGBl I, p. 141), abolished the previous rights of the Reichstag, as well as the separation of legislative and executive power. Its application led to cancellation of the democratic elements in the Weimar Constitution, and especially to the prohibition of all parties except the NSDAP, through the Law against the New Formation of Parties of July 14, 1933 (RGBl I, p. 479). In 1933 and 1934 the federal structure of state bodies that was characteristic of German constitutional tradition was abolished through SYNCHRONIZATION. The states (*Länder*) lost their sovereign rights to the Reich, becoming only its lower administrative bodies.

The FÜHRER PRINCIPLE came to be the crucial principle of NS constitutional practice. Accordingly, the activity of all state institutions derived solely from the FÜHRER'S WILL. Since the democratic mechanisms for control were dismantled along with constitutional guarantees, all measures of the state up to and including such crimes as the FINAL SOLUTION could be justified.

A. v. B.

Consul Organization, radical right-wing successor organization that arose after the disbandment of the EHRHARDT Naval Brigade free corps following the failure of the KAPP PUTSCH of 1920. The organization had a distinctly secret-society character, gave itself a radically antirepublican charter, and demanded unconditional obedience from its 5,000 members, most of them former officers: "Traitors will be tried by the Vehm!" (*see* VEHM MURDERS). Under the code name "Consul Eichmann," Hermann Ehrhardt and his adjutant, Ernst von SALOMON, directed the group from Munich; together with other members they arranged the murder of the foreign minister, Walther RATHENAU. The Center party leader, Matthias ERZBERGER, also fell victim to the group. It was disbanded by legislation in 1922 (*see* REPUBLIC PROTECTION LAW), but it continued to exist until 1928 in the "Viking League." The Consul group's political attacks against Jews, Social Democrats, and others were viewed positively by the nationalist Right and by some members of the middle class, and the perpetrators of such acts could count on a lenient, biased justice.

Conti, Leonardo, b. Lugano (Switzerland), August 24, 1900; d. Nuremberg, October 6, 1945, German physician. From an Italian-Swiss family, Conti grew up in Germany, where he joined the Völkisch Movement. He took part in the KAPP PUTSCH as a FREE CORPS member and entered the SA in 1923. After graduating from medical school in 1924, he organized the SA medical service in Berlin. In 1927 he joined the NSDAP, and the SS in 1930. His patients included Horst WESSEL. In 1929 Conti was a co-founder of the NATIONAL SOCIALIST GERMAN PHYSICIANS'

Leonardo Conti.

LEAGUE. He was named to the Prussian State Council in January 1934. Among other activities, he directed medical services at the 1936 Olympics, and took a decisive part in the banning of Jewish physicians from medical practice. On April 20, 1939, he became director of the Main Office for Volk Health and thus Reich Physicians' Führer (*Reichsärzteführer*), succeeding Gerhard WAGNER. Good relations with Martin BORMANN assured Conti's further advancement: in 1941 he became a Reichstag deputy, and in 1944, an SS-*Obergruppenführer*. After the war's end, Conti took his life in an Allied prison.

Control Council. *See* Allied Control Council.

Cooper, Duff, b. London, February 22, 1890; d. near Vigo (Spain), January 1, 1954, British politician and historian. Cooper was a Conservative member of Parliament from 1923, war minister from 1935 to May 1937, and then First Lord of the Admiralty. To protest Prime Minister Neville Chamberlain's APPEASEMENT policy, Cooper resigned his post on September 30, 1938, after the MUNICH AGREEMENT, thereby gaining the National Socialist propaganda label of "leading warmonger." He joined Churchill's War Cabinet in 1940–1941 as information minister, and gave sharp anti-NS speeches. Cooper became ambassador to the French Liberation Committee in Algiers in 1943, and represented Great Britain in Paris from 1944 to 1948. His historical works were well received, particularly the significant biography *Talleyrand* (1932).

Cooperatives (*Genossenschaften*), commercial or economic arrangements for the purpose of overcoming major problems and offsetting the competitive advantages of big business. With its principles of self-help and trusteeship, the cooperative system suited the notions of a National Socialist organization of the economy (*see* ECONOMY UNDER NATIONAL SOCIALISM, THE). However, consumer unions, as workers' groups that were difficult to monitor, were attacked on the pretext of "Marxist" influence. A law on consumer cooperatives of May 21, 1935, ordered the dissolution of their savings programs, and their leadership and expansion were made subject to the Reich Economics Ministry. While the farming cooperatives were incorporated into the REICH FOOD ESTATE with retention of their legal autonomy, the industrial cooperatives—in the framework of the ORGANIZATION OF THE INDUSTRIAL ECONOMY—were organized into Reich groups of banks, trade, and crafts, which in turn

were subdivided into specialized groups (such as the Interest Group for Industrial Credit Cooperatives), according to a directive of the Reich and Prussian Economic Ministry (October 23, 1936).

Coordination (*Gleichschaltung*). *See* Synchronization.

Corporatist state (*Ständestaat*), form of societal organization in which the supporting pillars are the (occupational) estates (*Stände*). Originating in the Christian Middle Ages, the concept received new stimulus through Catholic social teaching in the 19th and early 20th centuries as a model for overcoming the class struggle. In secularized form it can be found in the universalist state theory of Othmar SPANN, and in combination with anti-Marxist and anti-democratic theories it influenced AUSTROFASCISM and its Home Guards. They introduced the basic idea into the discussion of Austrian constitutional reform, which Engelbert DOLLFUSS finally realized with the "May Constitution" (May 1, 1934): exclusion of parliament, abolition of basic rights, end of a separation of powers, and a one-party state (*see* FATHERLAND FRONT). In a narrower sense the term applies to the Austrian state form from 1934 to 1938, although there was never a functioning corporatist organization. Only two *Vollstände* (complete estates or corporations)—agriculture and forestry, and public service—were constituted; after the ANSCHLUSS (March 13, 1938) they were liquidated, as was the Dollfuss constitution. The National Socialists rejected the corporatist state idea as a "conservative symptom of decline" that contravened the principle of the VOLK COMMUNITY.

Corradini, Enrico, b. San Miniatello (now part of Montelupo Fiorentino), July 20, 1865; d. Rome, December 9, 1931, Italian writer and politician. Influenced by Gabriele D'ANNUNZIO, Corradini glorified in his writings the ancient heritage of Italy (as in the novel *Julius Caesar*; 1902) and military virtues. He developed into an extreme nationalist, in 1910 founding the Nationalist Association, and imposed a class-struggle model onto international politics: "proletarian" nations (such as Italy) against the rich (colonial) states. The language of a "national socialism" was evident early in Corradini, who became a pathbreaker for Fascism and one of the first followers of Mussolini. A senator in 1923, Corradini became a minister of state in 1928.

Corridor (*Korridor;* Polish Corridor), strip of territory in West Prussia between the Vistula

River (near Danzig) and Pomerania, delineated in line with the FOURTEEN POINTS at the Paris Peace Conference (*see* VERSAILLES TREATY), that the German state was forced to cede to the newly formed Poland without a plebiscite. The corridor comprised 15,865 sq km (approximately 6,125 sq miles), with 330,600 inhabitants, more than 50 percent of whom were German-speaking. It was meant to link Poland to the sea at the port of Gdynia. Cutting East Prussia off from the rest of Germany, it became a permanent crisis point despite free transit for German goods (in sealed trains with no customs inspection). A peaceful revision did not come about, and the expulsion of numerous German inhabitants (still 10 percent in 1939) added fuel to the fire, which Hitler used on March 21, 1939, in an ultimatum demanding extraterritorial traffic arteries through the Corridor, a plebiscite, and a 25-year nonaggression pact. Poland rejected all the demands on March 26. The Corridor and the DANZIG QUESTION thus became pretexts for unleashing the POLISH CAMPAIGN and thereby the Second World War. From 1939 to 1945 the Corridor territories belonged to the Reichsgau DANZIG–WEST PRUSSIA.

Corrosion (*Zersetzung;* also erosion, undermining, eating away), National Socialist propaganda catchword, used in particular to defame the critical intellect. The word was originally common only in the technical vocabulary of miners and chemistry, but in the 19th century it was adopted in the intellectual sphere. From that time it was applied to critical thinking, which was seen as especially embodied in Jewish intellectuals: "Jews and the accomplices of Jews . . . work untiringly, and always at the most extreme and radical Left, on the undermining and dissolution [*Auflösung*] of that which we Germans had seen until now as incorporating everything human and holy to us" (Ernst Moritz Arndt, 1848).

The National Socialists popularized the term in this sense, frequently in the combination "corrosive criticism" (*zersetzende Kritik*), which was often applied to Marxists as well as to Jews. Even before the outbreak of war, the Ordinance concerning Special Criminal Law in Wartime and in Particular Actions (*Verordnung über das Sonderstrafrecht im Kriege und bei besonderem Einsatz*) of August 26, 1939 (*Reich Law Gazette* I, p. 1455), made any kind of criticism of the regime's political and military measures subject to prosecution as UNDERMINING OF MILITARY STRENGTH.

Cosmetics (*Kosmetik*), beauty care, promoted for German women by the National Socialists primarily in the sense of hygiene: the body's natural beauty was to be maintained and encouraged; therefore products to "remove unpleasant odors" or "excessive perspiration" were permitted. But cosmetics to heighten a modern sense of the "chic" (*see* FASHION) or for erotic attraction were not reconcilable with the ideals of woman as "child-bearer" and *Kameradin*, and were thus rejected as "species-alien" to the German nature.

Cosmopolitanism (*Kosmopolitismus*), world citizenship; community with people of different nations and races. The National Socialists viewed cosmopolitanism, like INTERNATIONALISM, as diametrically opposed to their own worldview, which emphasized racial-*völkisch* ties and the obligations of an individual. In National Socialist propaganda usage, "cosmopolite" acquired the character of an epithet; it was used in particular to defame "rootless" pacifist intellectuals.

Coulondre, Robert, b. Nîmes, September 11, 1885; d. Paris, March 6, 1959, French diplomat. Coulondre was the French ambassador to Moscow from 1936 to 1938, and to Berlin in 1938 and 1939. He early anticipated German-Soviet rapprochement, and in vain gave warning to Premier Édouard DALADIER. Coulondre's memoirs from these years in the forefront of events and personalities (*De Staline à Hitler;* 1950) are fascinating in their clarity and exact detail.

Council of Foreign Ministers, standing body of the foreign ministers (or representatives named by them) of China, France, England, the United States, and the USSR, provided for in the POTSDAM AGREEMENT of August 2, 1945, to work out the peace treaty provisions for Germany, Italy, Romania, Bulgaria, Hungary, and Finland. The council's first session took place on September 11, 1945. The task of the council was accomplished where the onetime allies of the German Reich were concerned; the German question, on the other hand, was only hotly discussed and not settled, partly because the "unified German government" foreseen in the statute of the council to accept the eventual decisions had not materialized. With the sixth session, from May 23 to June 20, 1949, the council ended its deliberations.

Counseling Offices for Heredity and Race Cultivation (Beratungsstellen für Erb- und Rassenpflege), divisions established in all Health Of-

Council of Foreign Ministers in Moscow (1946). From the left: Ernest Bevin (Great Britain), Viacheslav Molotov (USSR), and James Byrnes (United States).

fices in 1933 to instruct prospective marriage partners on legal regulations related to the danger of HEREDITARILY ILL OFFSPRING and to clarify the race-related preconditions for marriage (*see* MARITAL FITNESS). The offices also aided in the process of applying for MARRIAGE LOANS and in providing the prescribed CERTIFICATES OF DESCENT.

Counter-race (*Gegenrasse;* also counter-nation, *Gegennation*), term in the National Socialist vocabulary for the putative Jewish race; it was meant to emphasize the irreconcilable opposition to their own "Nordic-Germanic" race. The counter-race did, to be sure, evolve through SELECTION, but not to a higher stage, as had the "culture-creating Aryan"; rather, it developed only in the refinement of its "parasitic life activity" (Alfred Rosenberg).

Countersignature (*Gegenzeichnung*), in accordance with the Weimar Constitution, the required co-signing, by the Reich chancellor or by the particular minister, of all orders and enactments of the Reich president. The chancellor or minister thus assumed parliamentary responsibility before the Reichstag. Since the FÜHRER'S WILL was the basis for all state activity in the Third Reich, the countersignature lost this function. Yet it was still generally carried out, although now as a sign of the responsibility of the minister to the chief of state ("Führer") for accuracy and appropriateness. The validity of the Führer's orders and decrees was no longer bound to a countersignature.

Countryfolk movement (*Landvolkbewegung*), the militant wing of the AGRARIAN MOVEMENT, which protested against its rapidly deteriorating

economic situation with tax strikes, mass demonstrations, and also acts of sabotage (especially in Schleswig-Holstein from 1928 to 1932). Leaders of the movement were found guilty in the "bomb-planters' trial" of 1930, but they were soon released. The NSDAP, which sided with the movement, became its political heir in the end, since it possessed the necessary mass support for a successful struggle.

Country Service (*Landdienst*), legally regulated labor service by elementary school (*Volksschule*) graduates (*see* COUNTRY YEAR).

Countrywomen's Schools (*Landfrauenschulen*), like the PEASANT SCHOOLS, educational institutions supported by the REICH FOOD ESTATE; they prepared young women to be farm wives. The one- or two-year schools offered vocational training in home economics. They stressed in particular the "duties of a mother" and were intended to transmit, above all, the ideology of racial hygiene. Thus, they largely lost the purely practical orientation of the "peasant vocational schools" and "economic schools for women" from which they developed.

Country Year (*Landjahr*), Prussian "national-political" institution established on a legal basis after the model of other countries as an eight-month-long "camp" for elementary school (*Volkschule*) graduates. The Country Year served to re-educate various target groups (working-class children, rural children, returning settlers). In contrast to the HITLER YOUTH'S (HJ) Country Service (*Landdienst*), for young people 14 to 25 years old, and the Country Aid (*Landhilfe*) and Harvest Aid (*Erntehilfe*) programs, paid labor was not the prime aspect of

Labor deployment in the Country Year.

the Country Year. Rather, participating 14- and 15-year-olds performed practical tasks without pay and only half-time—except at harvesttime. Of central importance were camp training and schooling, for which the country environment was intended to provide the experiential foundation. Teachers, many of whom came from the youth leagues (so-called *bündische Jugend; see* YOUTH MOVEMENT), could thus carry out more effectively the schooling task of the HJ.

The political function of the Country Year changed. In 1934 it was instituted as a substitute for a ninth school year for two-thirds of the young men and one-third of the young women from "economic and political risk groups." Its aim was to alleviate unemployment among young people who were to be won over to the HJ. The Catholic church in particular opposed this measure. Between 1937 and 1940 the Country Year maintained the appearance of a program for a "select group": predominantly young people from farming districts, whose tendency to leave the countryside was successfully countered by their service. During the war, the number of these camps was drastically reduced. Girls could serve out their DUTY YEAR in country service. Most camps (in 1938, there were 450; in 1944, 259) were set up near or over the Reich borders as a "weapon of ethnic policy" (*volkstumpolitische Waffe*) and to integrate ethnic German "return settlers" from eastern Europe. In 10 years some 264,000 participants passed through these camps.

H. S.

Coventry, British industrial city in the Midlands southeast of Birmingham; its population was 213,000 in 1938. During the AIR BATTLE FOR ENGLAND, on the night of November 14–15, 1940, a total of 449 German bombers launched a devastating attack on Coventry. Against only light air defenses, they dropped 500 tons of explosive bombs and 30 tons of firebombs. The old city with its Gothic cathedral went up in flames; 554 people were killed and 865 wounded, but industrial production in the armament factories dipped only temporarily. German propaganda announced that the Luftwaffe would "Coventrize" (*coventrieren*) other British cities. Coventry became the symbol of carpet bombing without regard for a civilian population, and the pattern for Allied bombardment of German cities, which to be sure was of a much different magnitude. By cracking German radio codes, the British were aware of general plans for a coming attack, but they had insufficient knowledge of the code names of operations to determine precise attack sites.

Cracow. *See* Kraków-Płaszów.

Cramer, Walter, b. Leipzig, May 1, 1886; d. Berlin-Plötzensee, November 11, 1944 (executed), German businessman. In 1928 Cramer became chairman of the board of Stöhr-Konzern, Germany's largest worsted yarn manufacturer. In 1933 he established ties with Carl GOERDELER, with whom he increasingly reject-

Coventry. Destroyed cathedral.

Gottfried von Cramm.

ed the National Socialist dictatorship. Within the spreading opposition movement, the conservative Cramer was especially involved in contacts with the military, without whom no overthrow attempt would have had a chance. At the same time, the sociopolitically engaged businessman worked in industry for the struggle against Hitler. This subjected him to Gestapo observation after a denunciation in February 1944. Following the assassination attempt of July 20, 1944, Cramer was arrested and sentenced to death.

Cramm, Gottfried von, b. Nettlingen bei Hannover, July 7, 1909; d. near Cairo, November 9, 1976 (automobile accident), German tennis player. The "tennis baron" Cramm ranked as a world-class player in the 1930s; in 1933 he won in the mixed competition at Wimbledon, and between 1935 and 1937 he reached the singles finals three times. He won 82 out of a total of 102 Davis Cup games. At first promoted by the National Socialists as a symbol of German sports, Cramm remained aloof from the regime, and after 1938 was harassed, jailed for a while, and several times interrogated. After the war he resumed his career.

Crete, Mediterranean island belonging to Greece, strategically located between Europe and North Africa. It was conquered in late May 1941 by German airborne troops, concluding the BALKAN CAMPAIGN.

Crimea, Soviet Black Sea peninsula; it was conquered in 1941–1942 by the German Eleventh Army (*see* RUSSIAN CAMPAIGN) and was evacuated in 1944.

Crimea Conference, less customary designation for the meeting of the Big Three in YALTA from February 4 to 11, 1945.

Crimes against humanity (*Verbrechen gegen die Menschlichkeit*), one of the four main charges at the NUREMBERG TRIALS before the International Military Tribunal (IMT) and at subsequent trials in accord with Control Council Law (CCL) No. 10 of December 20, 1945. All actions that caused the indiscriminate and systematic destruction of life and liberty (Second United States Court, verdict of April 10, 1948) were categorized as crimes against humanity. According to the outline of the LONDON AGREEMENT of August 8, 1945, which became the statute for

Crimes against humanity. German shooting squad in Poland.

the IMT, the following acts fell under this rubric: "murder, extermination, enslavement, deportation or other inhuman actions, which were perpetrated against any civilian population before or during the war, persecution for political, racial, or religious reasons carried out while committing a crime or in connection with a crime, for which a court of law has jurisdiction, regardless of whether the action was an infringement of the law of the land in which it was carried out." CCL 10, under Article II, contains a corresponding enumeration, while stressing that this should not be regarded as exhaustive.

A. St.

Crimes against peace (*Verbrechen gegen den Frieden*), one of the main charges at the NUREMBERG TRIALS before the International Military Tribunal (IMT) and in other law courts, according to Control Council Law (CCL) No. 10 of December 20, 1945. (The other main charges were WAR CRIMES, CRIMES AGAINST HUMANITY, and membership in a criminal organization; *see* CRIMINAL ORGANIZATIONS.) According to the outline of the LONDON AGREEMENT of August 8, 1945, which was the statute for the IMT, the following actions were specified as crimes against peace: "The planning, preparation, inception, or carrying through of an offensive war, or of a war that violates international agreements, treaties, or assurances, or participation in a common plan or a conspiracy for carrying out one of the aforementioned actions." In essence, this definition coincided with the corresponding definition in CCL 10, which, however, stressed that the enumeration should not be regarded "as exhaustive examples." The defense objected that the charge created retroactively a punishable offense, thus violating the principle of NULLA POENA SINE LEGE (no punishment without a law). The IMT, however, upheld its point with reference to the "progress of international common law" and to the proscription of war in the KELLOGG-BRIAND PACT of 1928.

A. St.

Criminal law (*Strafrecht*), the aggregate of legal norms for the protection of life within the political community, as well as the sanctions provided for violation of the norms. The National Socialist (NS) concept of a new criminal law was initially to have been realized through a comprehensive reform of criminal law. This never came to pass, since a basic element of NS policy on criminal law was that rules for punishment could be quickly adapted to the needs of

the situation; for this purpose, a codified body of law would have been too rigid. Thus, NS criminal law was largely a law of decrees (*Verordnungsrecht*).

The desire for such a large-scale adaptation of punishment norms to the particular needs of a state authority required a radical departure from previously dominant principles. The concept of NULLA POENA SINE LEGE (no punishment without a law; now Article 103, ¶2, of the Basic Law of the Federal Republic of Germany) was abandoned. Instead, the judge was to determine whether an act "deserved punishment according to the fundamental idea of a criminal law and according to sound *Volk* feeling," even if the act were not punishable by the letter of the law (Law to Amend the Criminal Code of June 28, 1935, *Reich Law Gazette* I, p. 839). "Healthy *Volk* sentiment" (*gesunde Volksempfinden*) was a circumlocution for the opinion of the party or state authority. Moreover, general clauses were introduced and evidence of criminal actions was intentionally broadly conceived, permitting a boundless range of interpretations. No one could with certainty foresee the consequence of an action. This incalculability was part and parcel of an obviously intentional insecurity under law.

Finally, the deed itself was no longer the determinant factor, but rather the intention of the perpetrator, his "criminal will." Thus, according to NS criminal law, failure to submit oneself unconditionally to the will and the ideas of the state authority as though it were the law itself would make one liable for punishment. The central concept here was the VOLK COMMUNITY, which served to exclude dissidents, malcontents, and ETHNIC ALIENS. Special regulations for Jews, Poles, and Gypsies breached the principle of equality. "Punishment," according to Alfred ROSENBERG, "is the sorting out of alien types and species-alien beings." Expiation for a criminal offense was no longer the main concern, but rather the elimination of the culprit, deterrence, and intimidation. Accordingly, the range of punishments was greatly expanded, and the death penalty was prescribed for a multitude of crimes, until by the late war years it became to some extent the standard punishment. Criminal procedural law was characterized by the total removal of constitutional procedural guarantees. Thus, criminal justice became an instrument of the arbitrariness of party and state.

Criminal organizations (*Verbrecherische Organisationen*), associations or organizations of the Third Reich whose criminal nature was established by the International Military Tribunal (IMT) at the NUREMBERG TRIALS in a verdict of October 1, 1946. According to the LONDON AGREEMENT of August 8, 1945, the IMT could classify a group or organization as criminal, given certain prerequisites (Article 9). The signatory powers had the right (Article 10) to institute legal proceedings before national military courts or occupation courts against persons belonging to such associations.

Charges were raised before the IMT against six groups or organizations: the SS, the SA, the GENERAL STAFF and Wehrmacht High Command (OKW), the Reich Cabinet, the Führer Corps of the NSDAP, and the GESTAPO and SECURITY SERVICE (SD). The court declared the SS, the Gestapo, the SD, and the Führer Corps to be criminal. It determined, however, that no one should be convicted for membership alone. A conviction required either knowledge of the criminal purposes or actions of the organization, or personal involvement in criminal acts. The signatory powers made use of the authority they had to try members of the condemned organizations. The actual judicial basis for these proceedings was created by Article II (1d) of Control Council Law No. 10.

A. St.

Croatia, part of YUGOSLAVIA; in the BALKAN CAMPAIGN it was proclaimed the "Independent State of Croatia" (April 10, 1941), under USTAŠA leader Ante PAVELIĆ.

Crooked cross (*Kruckenkreuz*), swastika-like emblem of the Austrian CORPORATIST STATE from 1934 to 1938. Despite the anti–National Socialist program of the FATHERLAND FRONT, its propagandists were clearly fascinated by the SWASTIKA, thereby substantiating the thesis of Ernst Nolte that "the opposition to fascism itself often bore fascist traits."

Crössinsee, one of the three NSDAP ORDER FORTRESSES, located near Falkenburg (East Pomerania). Founded in 1936, it began classes on April 24 of that year.

Cross of Honor (Ehrenkreuz), order established in 1934 "in memory of the imperishable achievements of the German *Volk* in the World War." A bronze-tinted iron cross with the dates 1914–1918 on the center shield, it came with varying details: for frontline soldiers it had crossed swords, for other military personnel it had an oak cluster rather than a laurel wreath, and for parents and widows of the fallen, it was made of matte-lacquered iron.

Cross of Honor of the German Mother.

Since mothers of many children (*see* CHILD-RICH) were thought to have shown the same "dedication of body and life" as "frontline soldiers in the thunder of battle" (quotation from the *Völkischer Beobachter*), a "Cross of Honor of the German Mother" (Mother's Cross) was instituted in 1938. In the middle it had a swastika encircled by the words "The child ennobles the mother." Mothers of four or five children received a bronze cross; mothers of six or seven children, one of silver; and mothers of eight or more children, one of gold. This cross was first awarded in 1939 to some 3 million mothers as a propaganda measure for National Socialist POPULATION POLICY.

CSSD, acronym of *Chef der Sicherheitspolizei und des SD* (Chief of the Security Police and the SD), post held by Reinhard HEYDRICH (until 1942) and Ernst KALTENBRUNNER.

CSVD, acronym of Christlich-Sozialer Volksdienst (CHRISTIAN-SOCIAL PEOPLE'S SERVICE).

Culling out (*Ausmerze*), conceptual opposite of SELECTION (*Auslese*); the natural or artificial "hindering or prevention of the further reproduction of the hereditarily ill or hereditarily unfit." The National Socialist population policy of culling out made inroads in marriage law and racial legislation, and culminated in EUTHANASIA and the FINAL SOLUTION.

Culture (*Kultur*; from Lat. *cultura*, working and tending the soil), broad term encompassing the development of a person, his or her capabilities and environment, and the resulting material products (such as tools) and intellectual products (such as science, art, and religion). National Socialist ideology employed the term exclusively as an expression of "ethnic-racial substance." Accordingly, only certain races were capable of establishing a culture and bringing it to full bloom, namely, as "Aryan states of work and culture," against which were juxtaposed unproductive "culture bearers" (*Kulturträger*) and "culture destroyers" (*Kulturzerstörer*) in "Jewish parasite colonies" (Hitler). In *Mein Kampf,* Hitler based the Aryans' predestination to rule on the idea that they were "the original bearers of human culture and thus the true founders of everything included in the word 'humankind' [*Menschheit*]." Harking back to the philosopher Fichte ("True culture is a culture of conviction"), the term "culture" also became a political catchword, aimed against "degenerate phenomena" and intellectual rootlessness.

Culture Bolshevism (*Kulturbolschewismus*), a catchword utilized both by National Socialists and by middle-class conservatives to defame the entirety of modern art and culture in the Weimar Republic: Expressionist and abstract art, socially critical theater, atonal music, Bauhaus architecture, scientific sex research, and so on. The term "Culture Bolshevism" originally derived from Soviet attempts, after the October Revolution, to establish a Proletkult, a proletarian and revolutionary art and culture. In German discourse, the term was intended to be derogatory and to tie in with anti-Communist reservations and sentiments. It was aimed against everything that in the view of nationalist circles represented a "conscious devaluation of morality, honor, family, and fatherland."

Culture creators (*Kulturschaffende*), National Socialist term introduced into general usage to describe persons active in cultural pursuits who came under the organizational aegis of the REICH CULTURE CHAMBER as the "professional organization and articulation of all culture creators." The term was intended to counteract the elite character of artistic work, since "creator" (*Schaffender*) referred to those who worked either with their hands (*Arbeiter der Faust*) or with their intellects (*Arbeiter der Stirn*).

Culture fertilizer (*Kulturdünger*), term coined in the 19th century to denote the enrichment of foreign cultures by German emigrants. In National Socialist usage, the "culture-fertilizing" functions of more highly developed peoples were seen as a threat to themselves. Accordingly, the German *Volk* should be protected from serving as a culture fertilizer for others to the point that "the last drop of our Aryan-Nordic blood is spoiled or extinguished" (*Mein Kampf*).

Culture management (*Kulturlenkung*), official term for the SYNCHRONIZATION and political institutionalization of art and culture in the Third Reich. In order to guarantee "*völkisch* symbols of the standard of accomplishment" and to overcome "hindrances and obstructions" in the way of a unified National Socialist culture, "one must . . . intervene. . . . That is the particular task of political leadership and the management of culture" (Goebbels).

Cuno, Wilhelm, b. Suhl (Thuringia), July 2, 1876; d. Aumühle bei Hamburg, January 3, 1933, German politician and lawyer. Cuno began as a civil servant; as of November 1, 1917, he was employed by the Hapag shipping line; on December 20, 1918, he became its director general. Cuno took part in the peace negotiations of 1918–1919 as a German economic expert. Because of the hope raised by his technical expertise, the nonpartisan Cuno was asked, in November 1922—the first sign of German weariness with political parties—to head a "government of the economy" (*Regierung der Wirtschaft*), which was to find a way out of INFLATION and reparations debts. Cuno could not master the problems; his proposals for REPARATIONS reform were rejected by France, and his policy of passive resistance in the RUHR CONFLICT hastened hyperinflation and lost him the support of the SPD (Social Democratic Party of Germany). Forced to resign on August 12, 1923, Cuno returned to his position at Hapag.

Curtius, Julius, b. Duisburg, February 7, 1877; d. Heidelberg, November 10, 1948, German politician and lawyer. From 1920 to 1932, Cur-

Wilhelm Cuno.

tius was a Reichstag deputy for the DVP (German People's Party). As Reich economics minister (1926–1929) and foreign minister (1929–October 3, 1931), Curtius advocated measures for WORK CREATION and fought for acceptance of the YOUNG PLAN to ease the reparations burden. He considered himself the "executor" of Gustav STRESEMANN's legacy in efforts at reconciliation with the Western powers and for economic cooperation with the Soviet Union. This elicited the hatred of the Right, especially that of the National Socialists. After the failure of his plan for a German-Austrian customs union, Curtius had to resign.

Curzon Line, boundary named after British foreign secretary George N. Curzon (1859–1925), who on July 11, 1920, suggested as the demarcation line between Poland and the Soviet Union a line going from Dünaburg (Daugavpils) to Vilna (Vilnius) to Grodno to Brest, then along the Bug River, cutting through Galicia to Przemyśl. After its defeat of the Red Army near Warsaw (August 1920), Poland rejected the Curzon Line and pushed the border 250 km (155 miles) farther to the east. In 1939 the Curzon Line served as a reference for dividing the spheres of influence in the GERMAN-SOVIET NONAGGRESSION PACT and, in 1945, for establishing the Polish-Soviet border.

"Czechia, remnant." *See* Residual Czech state.

Czechoslovakia, state to the east of Germany; area, 140,485 sq km (about 56,000 sq miles); population, 14.7 million (1930). The Czechoslovak Republic (ČSR) was founded on October 28, 1918, as a successor state of Austria-Hungary. It was made up of the "historic territories" of Bohemia, Moravia, and Silesia, as well as of Slovakia and the Carpathian Ukraine. Czechoslovakia had to overcome considerable nationality problems (only 50 percent of its people were Czechs, while 24 percent were Germans and 15.6 percent were Slovaks), strong national, cultural, and historical differences, and a clear socioeconomic difference between an industrialized west and the rural east.

The Czech program of a centralized unitary state (based on legal, geographic-strategic, and economic considerations) was continually contested by demands for autonomy of the Slovaks and national minorities. So pressed, the Czechs as the governing people failed to realize the model of a "middle-European Switzerland" that had originally been held out, and broke the promises made in particular to the Slovaks in 1918: on February 29, 1920, a centralist constitution was passed by an appointed provisional "Revolutionary National Assembly" without participation by minorities; and a "Czechification" policy for civil servants, as well as laws favoring the Czech language, were introduced.

Nevertheless, Czechoslovakia under Tomás MASARYK (president from 1918 to 1935) and Edvard BENEŠ had, in comparison to other states in east-central Europe, great parliamentary and democratic stability. This was the result of healthy economic development, the internal strength of the Czech parties and their ability to form coalitions, the loyalty of the minorities, and the readiness of the "activist" German parties to assume government responsibility. In foreign-policy matters Czechoslovakia relied on the LITTLE ENTENTE and on alliances with France (January 25, 1924) and the Soviet Union (May 19, 1925) to ward off territorial demands by Hungary (for southern Slovakia and the Carpathian Ukraine) and by Poland (for Teschen), as well as monarchist attempts at restoration from Austria. Relations with the Weimar Republic were correct, because Berlin had little interest in the Sudeten issue. It was only the devastating consequences of the world economic crisis that led to growing internal tension. The crisis affected, in particular, export-dependent small and middle-sized industry in the Sudetenland. After 1933, National Socialist propaganda (notably that of the SUDETEN GERMAN PARTY) encouraged separatism among the German and Hungarian minorities. These internal tensions were constantly exploited by Berlin after May 1938 in an effort to "smash" Czechoslovakia. Prague did not respond with timely concessions, and consequent-

Julius Curtius.

Czechoslovakia. Removal of the German-Czech border marker.

ly matters escalated into the SUDETEN CRISIS, which found temporary solution in the MUNICH AGREEMENT.

The so-called Second Republic of what was now Czecho-Slovakia (October 1938–March 14, 1939) ceded considerable territory (about 42,000 sq km, or some 16,000 sq miles) and population (about 5 million people), and gave autonomy to SLOVAKIA and the Carpathian Ukraine. Although the republic submitted completely to Berlin's will on such matters as proceedings against Jews, party restructuring, and special legislation against German emigrés, President Emil HÁCHA had to yield to Hitler's blackmail on March 14, 1939. Under the pretext that the state had dissolved itself (a declaration of independence by Slovakia and the Carpathian Ukraine was dictated in Berlin on March 14, 1939), the Wehrmacht occupied the "residual Czech state" (Resttschechei) on March 15. On March 16, Hitler signed at Prague's Hradčany Castle the Decree concerning the PROTECTORATE OF BOHEMIA AND MORAVIA.

In terms of international law, Czechoslovakia continued to exist in London in its government-in-exile (under Beneš), which was recognized by Great Britain, the United States, the USSR, and Charles de Gaulle. In close cooperation with Moscow (a treaty of friendship and assistance was concluded on December 12, 1943), the government-in-exile successfully pursued the nullification of the Munich Agreement, preparations for EXPULSION of the 2.3 million Sudeten Germans in 1945–1946, and plans for a new political and social order after the war. Following an uprising in Prague shortly before the German collapse (May 5–7, 1945), Beneš returned to the renascent Czechoslovakia. He was unable to ward off the subsequent Communist seizure of power, which meant the end of the Czechoslovak "middle course."

B.-J. W.

Czechoslovakia. Recruitment poster for Czech partisans.

D

D'Abernon, Edgar Vincent, Viscount, b. Slinfold, August 19, 1857; d. Hove, November 1, 1941, British diplomat. From 1899 to 1906 D'Abernon was a member of Parliament (Conservative party); from 1920 to 1926, ambassador to Berlin, where he influenced the conciliatory policies of Chancellor Joseph WIRTH and Foreign Minister Gustav STRESEMANN. D'Abernon supported adjudication of the reparations issue (*see* DAWES PLAN), and, as a father of the LOCARNO PACT, supported tying Germany to the Western powers.

Dachau, the first National Socialist concentration camp, opened on March 22, 1933, on the outskirts of the Upper Bavarian city of Dachau (8,240 inhabitants in 1933), in a former ammunitions factory; its original capacity was 5,000 prisoners (about 17,000 in 1943). At first thought of as a center for the "protective custody" of political offenders, the camp soon included all of the regime's unwanted groups: "politi-

Edgar Vincent D'Abernon.

cals," oppositional clergy, Jews, Gypsies, the handicapped, homosexuals, and criminals. The desired side effects were the fostering of mutual discrimination and spying, and the impeding of group solidarity.

During the war years the nationality of the "new arrivals" reflected German military successes. The Dachau camp grew into a complex organization, with 125 branches that supplied a labor force to the armaments industry in southern Germany. Surrounded by SS settlements and secluded, Dachau nonetheless could depend upon the infrastructure of nearby Munich.

On October 1, 1938, the camp commandant, Theodor EICKE, issued regulations for duty and punishment that, like Dachau's physical layout, were adopted by other concentration camps. The "model installation" at Dachau also served as a training center. Prospective camp commandants were required to complete a special course at Dachau by order of Reinhard Heydrich. The SS DEATH'S-HEAD UNITS began here. Adolf EICHMANN also attended Dachau's "school of violence."

Dachau was not planned as an extermination camp; its prisoners were shot "trying to escape," or died of hunger, disease, and exhaustion ("extermination through labor"), under torture, or as victims of pseudoscientific experiments, such as Dr. Sigmund Rascher's atmospheric-pressure and hypothermia experiments. (The findings were meant to benefit the poorly clad soldiers at the eastern front and pilots downed at sea.)

After the decision for the FINAL SOLUTION, a crematorium, including a gas chamber—whose use, however, cannot be proved—was built in 1942. By November 1944, 3,225 physically and mentally handicapped prisoners had been transferred to the euthanasia facility at HARTHEIM Castle (near Linz) and gassed. On the day that Dachau was liberated, April 29, 1945, the

177

The Dachau concentration camp.

Americans found 30,000 survivors in the barracks. By that date, 206,000 registered prisoners had passed through the camp; 31,951 deaths were recorded. The Dachau memorials (Catholic Chapel of the Agony of Christ, Protestant Reconciliation Chapel, and Israeli Memorial) were opened on May 9, 1965.

Commandants of the Dachau camp were Hilmar Wäckerle (until July 15, 1933; d. in action near Lemberg, July 2, 1941) and Theodor Eicke.

M. F.

DAF. *See* German Labor Front.

Dagger (*Dolch*), short stabbing weapon, considered a national emblem as early as Roman times. In Fascist Italy and National Socialist Germany, the dagger was worn by officers and SA and SS leaders as a symbol of their privileged position; in the SA (inscription: "Everything for Germany") and SS (inscription: "Our Honor Is Loyalty"), it was also part of the regular uniform. (*See* STAB-IN-THE-BACK LEGEND [*Dolchstosslegende*].)

Dagover, Lil (real name, Marie Seubert), b. Madiun (Java), September 30, 1897; d. Grünwald, near Munich, January 23, 1980, German actress. Dagover first appeared in silent films; after 1931, she also worked in the theater (with Max

REINHARDT, among others). She was a popular film star during the Third Reich, performing in such movies as *Die Kreutzersonate* (director, Veit HARLAN; 1936) and *Bismarck* (director, Wolfgang LIEBENEINER; 1940). For her efforts among the troops she received a War Service Cross in 1944. After the war Dagover's film career continued unabated with two films based

Lil Dagover.

on Thomas Mann, *Königliche Hoheit* (Royal Highness; 1953) and *Die Buddenbrooks* (1959), and *Der Richter und sein Henker* (The Judge and His Hangman; 1977), among others.

Dahlem, Franz, b. Rohrbach (Lorraine), January 13, 1892; d. East Berlin, December 17, 1981, German Communist politician. Dahlem joined the KPD (Communist Party of Germany) in 1920; he entered the Central Committee in 1927, and a year later the Politburo. He represented the KPD in the Reichstag from 1928 to 1933, when he emigrated to Prague (later continuing to Paris). Dahlem fought in the Spanish Civil War as a political commissar in the International Brigade (1937–1938). Interned in France from 1939 to 1941, he was released to the Germans, who put him in the Mauthausen concentration camp for the duration. After the war (again as a Central Committee and Politburo member) he worked toward building the Socialist Unity Party in the Soviet sector. In 1953 he was relieved of all offices for "blindness toward the activities of imperialist agents," but was eventually rehabilitated in 1956.

Dahlerus, Birger, b. Stockholm, February 6, 1891; d. there, March 8, 1957, Swedish industrialist and friend of Hermann Göring. During the height of the Polish crisis in the summer of 1939, Dahlerus tried repeatedly but in vain to mediate between Berlin and London. Germany demanded that England rescind its guarantee of support for Poland and allow Germany a free hand in the east, while London pressed for a negotiated settlement of German-Polish differences. Dahlerus's unofficial mission failed finally when Great Britain upgraded its guarantee to a formal pact with Poland on August 25, 1939. Dahlerus appeared in 1946 as a witness at the Nuremberg Trials. He wrote *Der letzte Versuch* (*The Last Attempt;* 1948).

Daladier, Édouard, b. Carpentras, June 18, 1884; d. Paris, October 10, 1970, French politician. A history teacher by profession, Daladier represented the Radical Socialists in the National Assembly after 1919, and frequently held the positions of minister and premier. In April 1938, when he was forming his third cabinet, the political landscape was overshadowed by the Sudeten crisis. At the MUNICH AGREEMENT in September 1938, Daladier and British prime minister Neville CHAMBERLAIN voted to cede the Sudetenland to Germany, thereby exchanging the viability of the Czechoslovak Republic for the vague hope of easing tensions in central Europe. Eleven months later, on September 3, 1939, Germany's invasion of Poland was answered with Britain's declaration of war, followed hours later by France's. After the French surrender (June 1940), Daladier was imprisoned by order of the VICHY government, deported to Germany in 1943, and freed by the Allies in 1945. He attempted a postwar political comeback, but never escaped the "shadow of Munich."

d'Alquen, Gunter. *See* Alquen, Gunter d'.

Birger Dahlerus.

Édouard Daladier.

Daluege, Kurt, b. Kreuzburg (Silesia), September 15, 1897; d. Prague, October 23, 1946 (executed), licensed engineer and SS-*Oberstgruppenführer* (April 20, 1944). Daluege joined the NSDAP in 1922. After its reconstitution in 1925, he recruited 500 men from the Berlin sanitation department into the ranks of the local SA through his contacts in the underworld (where he was known as "Dumm-Dummi"). He joined the SS in 1928. In 1933 he was named Prussian state councillor and lieutenant general of the Prussian state police during the National Socialist infiltration of the Prussian bureaucracy. As such, he was significantly involved in the "cleansing" of the SA in the RÖHM AFFAIR.

Daluege became chief of police in the Interior Ministry, where he came into rivalry with Reinhard HEYDRICH, Himmler's protégé. When Himmler gained control of all German police forces as *Reichsführer*-SS, Daluege was promoted (to SS-*Obergruppenführer*), but in fact he was bought off with the leadership of the ORDER-KEEPING POLICE (Orpo) and downgraded to Himmler's powerless representative. As a police expert, Daluege wrote *National-sozialistischer Kampf gegen das Verbrechertum* (NS Struggle against Criminality; 1936). On May 31, 1942, after the assassination attempt against Heydrich, Daluege became deputy Reich Protector of Bohemia and Moravia in Prague. As one of those held accountable after the war for the LIDICE massacre, he was sentenced to death and executed.

Kurt Daluege.

Damaging and undesirable writing (*Schädliches und unerwünschtes Schrifttum*), from the National Socialist viewpoint, all literature that might endanger the "NS cultural will." Within the party bureaucracy, the OFFICIAL PARTY REVIEW COMMISSION FOR SAFEGUARDING NATIONAL SOCIALIST WRITING concerned itself with the suppression of such material; within the state bureaucracy, the PROPAGANDA MINISTRY censored all publications and, if necessary, included them in this category to be confiscated or closed down.

Damica, National Socialist concentration camp in northern Croatia, established in May 1941 after the German occupation of Yugoslavia as the first of six camps. Some 2,000 Jewish prisoners lost their lives in Damica from shootings, mistreatment, hunger, and disease.

Dannecker, Theodor, b. Tübingen, March 27, 1913; d. Bad Tölz, December 10, 1945, SS officer. In 1937 the young lawyer became a SECURITY SERVICE (SD) operative in Adolf EICHMANN's Office IV B 4. As an SD specialist on Jewish affairs, beginning in 1940 Dannecker worked in France on the deportation of Jews (*see* DRANCY). Because of official misconduct, Eichmann transferred him in January 1943 to Bulgaria, where he organized transports of Jews to EXTERMINATION CAMPS. This service earned him promotion to the post of commissioner for Jewish affairs in Italy. Eyewitnesses identified Dannecker as a fanatical Nazi and brutal antisemite. He took his own life while in American imprisonment.

D'Annunzio, Gabriele, b. Francavilla, near Pescara, March 12, 1863; d. Gardone, March 1, 1938, Italian writer and politician. While still a high school student, D'Annunzio was recognized as a precocious poet (*Primo vere;* 1879). By the turn of the century, he was Italy's most celebrated lyric poet (*Laudi;* 1903–1904) and storyteller. Like his later idol Benito MUSSOLINI, he shifted politically from the Left to the Right. From 1897 to 1900 he was a Conservative party deputy, and he became a radical nationalist and imperialist. As a poet he glorified authority ("Paradise lies in the shadow of the sword") and worshiped the "SUPERMAN."

As a politician, D'Annunzio fought passionately for Italy's entrance into the First World War on the side of the Entente. He distinguished himself as an air force volunteer officer in daring actions. Disappointed by the disdainful treatment of Italy after the war, with a troop

Gabriele D'Annunzio (drawing by
E. M. Lilien).

of volunteers he conquered Fiume (now Rijeka,
Yugoslavia) in a surprise attack on September
12, 1918. After 16 months, he finally withdrew
his forces in order to avoid a civil war. Subsequently, his political influence waned as his
poetic fame grew to cultic dimensions. As the
bard of heroism, with the rise of Fascism he
became Italy's national poet and the intimate
friend of Mussolini, who ennobled him as
prince of Monte Nevoso and gave him a grand

villa on Lake Garda, where he enjoyed a comfortable old age, albeit under close watch by
the police.

Danzig Question (*Danzigfrage*), a growing conflict between Germany and Poland as of 1919.
On November 15, 1920, without the benefit of a
plebiscite among the city's 380,000 inhabitants
(of whom 12,000 were Poles), Danzig was proclaimed a Free City under the authority of the
League of Nations. The Swiss historian Carl J.
BURCKHARDT functioned as League high commissioner. Tariff authority and diplomatic representation of the territory were assumed by
Poland; the harbor was under joint administration.

In 1933, the National Socialists took power in
Danzig as in Germany, but the conflict over the
city's future was temporarily downplayed in
order not to jeopardize the consolidation of
power in the Third Reich (*see* GERMAN-POLISH
NONAGGRESSION PACT of January 26, 1934).
But in 1939, the Danzig Question played a key
role as the pretext for unleashing the war
against Poland. In April 1939, Hitler proposed
a comprehensive German-Polish settlement,
aimed against the USSR, including the return of
Danzig to Germany, construction of an extraterritorial highway through the Polish CORRIDOR,
and Poland's entrance into the ANTI-COMINTERN
PACT. Hitler also released his Führer Directive

Danzig.

"Case 'White'" (Fall "Weiss"; *see* POLISH CAM-
PAIGN). Warsaw brusquely rejected the offer,
not only for chauvinistic reasons but also because it considered a policy of strict neutrality
vis-à-vis its two neighbors to be a "matter of
survival."

Hitler now sought Poland's isolation (*see*
GERMAN-SOVIET NONAGGRESSION PACT). On
August 10, Danzig's *Gauleiter*, Albert FORSTER,
gave his "Back Home to the Reich" ("Heim-ins-
Reich") speech. The war with Poland began on
September 1, with bombardment from the battleship *Schleswig-Holstein*. Danzig was immediately declared part of the Third Reich. After the
defeat of Poland, National Socialist propaganda
sought, not without some success, to convince
the French public of the pointlessness of their
nation's declaration of war on September 3,
1939, with the slogan "Die for Danzig?"
("Mourir pour Danzig?"). The POTSDAM AGREE-
MENT placed Danzig under Polish control as the
city of Gdansk.

Danzig–West Prussia, Reichsgau formed in the
fall of 1939 after the Polish Campaign from the
annexed, formerly German province of West
Prussia together with Danzig and Bromberg, as
well as the formerly East Prussian government
district of Marienwerder; it was not attached to
the state of Prussia. The Reich governor was
Albert FORSTER; the capital was Danzig. In
1945 the territory was placed under Polish
administration, or returned to Poland.

DAP. *See* German Workers' Party.

Darlan, François, b. Nérac, August 7, 1881; d.
Algiers, December 23, 1942, French admiral;
commander in chief of the navy at the outbreak
of the war. Darlan's refusal to send the fleet into
Allied waters following the French defeat of
June 1940 led to the British attack on Oran that
July. Darlan served as minister in the VICHY
government. After the Allied landing in North
Africa (November 1942), Darlan—meanwhile
advanced to supreme commander of the armed
forces—sought a truce. He was apparently
killed by a follower of Charles de GAULLE.

Darré, Richard Walther (baptized Ricardo), b.
Belgrano, near Buenos Aires, July 14, 1895; d.
Munich, September 5, 1953, National Socialist
agricultural politician. The son of an emigrant
German-Argentine businessman, Darré fought
as a volunteer on the western front in the First
World War. He graduated with a degree in
colonial economics (as a "colonial manager")

and then studied agriculture at Halle/Salle, specializing in animal breeding and genetics. His
books, *Das Bauerntum als Lebensquell der
nordischen Rasse* (The Peasantry as the Life
Source of the Nordic Race; 1928), *Neuadel aus
Blut und Boden* (The New Nobility of Blood
and Soil; 1930), and *Das Zuchtziel des deutsch-
en Volkes* (The Breeding Goal of the German
Volk; 1931), promoted a "noble peasantry"
(*Adelsbauerntum*) as the biological germ of future history. He viewed urbanization as a major
contemporary evil.

Darré joined the NSDAP in 1930 and, as
Hitler's deputy for agricultural matters, formu-
lated the party's first agricultural program,
which broadened a policy that until then ap-
pealed to the petite bourgeoisie with the slogan
"BLOOD AND SOIL," aimed at the peasantry. In
1931 Darré was promoted to head of the RACE
AND SETTLEMENT MAIN OFFICE (RuSHA) of the
SS and to Reich Leader of the Office for Agricul-
tural Policy. He also published the newspapers
NS-Landpost (NS Country Post) and *Deutsche
Agrarpolitik* (German Agricultural Policy; called
Odal after 1939).

After the Seizure of Power, Darré carried out
the SYNCHRONIZATION of all agricultural associations under the authority of the REICH FOOD
ESTATE, which he directed from 1934 to 1942 as
"Reich Peasant Führer." He replaced Alfred
HUGENBERG as Reich minister for nutrition and
agriculture in June 1933 and issued the HEREDI-
TARY FARM LAW (September 1933), which secured in perpetuity the possession of debt-free
farms in peasant families and was meant to stem

François Darlan.

Richard Walther Darré.

the flight from the countryside; he also set fixed market prices.

Although Darré received the Golden Party Badge in 1936, that year also marked his downfall. His policy of concern for the fate of individual peasants did not suit Göring, whose Four-Year Plan aimed at maximizing production, and his Blood-and-Soil romanticism was criticized in RuSHA as "too theoretical." (He lost his RuSHA post in 1938.) Darré, who had helped prepare the spiritual soil for the NS policy of "Living Space," voiced opposition to Himmler's planned methods for carrying out settlement in the east, as well as to Hitler's command of the war. This led to his removal from office (he was replaced as Reich minister by Herbert BACKE) and banishment to his hunting lodge in the Schorfheide, outside Berlin. Here he wrote *Im Kampf um die Seele des deutschen Bauern* (In Struggle for the Soul of the German Peasant; 1943). After the war Darré was arrested and sentenced to seven years' imprisonment in the WILHELMSTRASSE TRIAL, but was released early in 1950.

Darwinism, doctrine of the British biologist Charles Darwin (1809–1882) that the multiplicity of species derives from a common root (descent or origin of species), and the process of evolution through natural selection. The more than questionable application of this model to human society led to SOCIAL DARWINISM, which greatly influenced National Socialist racial ideology and its theory of the "right of the stronger."

David, Star of. *See* Jewish Star.

DAW. *See* German Armament Works.

Dawes Plan, series of measures of the REPARATIONS Commission after the First World War to adjust the obligations placed on Germany by the Versailles treaty (set at 226 billion gold marks on March 19, 1923) to the nation's actual productive capacity. The plan was based on the testimony of the American banker Charles G. Dawes (1865–1951; co-winner of the Nobel Peace Prize in 1925). On April 9, 1924, he urged the stabilization of the German economy and, with allusions to French policy, the suspension of the "pawn politics" (*see* RUHR CONFLICT) as prerequisites to further German payments. The Dawes Plan called for yearly payments of 1 to 1.75 billion gold marks for a transition period of four years, followed by payments of 2.5 billion gold marks yearly. Germany received a subvention credit of 800 million gold marks and in return pledged its income from customs and excise duties. France agreed to withdraw from the Ruhr region within 12 months.

The agreement was signed in London on August 16, 1924, passed by the Reichstag on August 29, and took effect two days later. The result was an easing of political and psychological tensions in Germany and Europe, the growing involvement of American capital in the German economy, and a steadily rising foreign debt. The plan was superseded in 1930 by the YOUNG PLAN (vigorously opposed by the

Charles G. Dawes.

NSDAP), which cut Germany's total reparations obligation to 34.5 billion marks (payable by 1988).

D Day (Decision Day), Allied shorthand for the date of a large-scale military operation (the term is still used today by NATO). In the original sense, it refers to the day of the Allied INVASION of Normandy (June 6, 1944).

Death penalty (*Todesstrafe*), the most severe punishment, the use of which the National Socialists extended significantly. Whereas before 1933 the death penalty could be prescribed for only three crimes, by 1943–1944 it could be applied in over 40 crimes and misdemeanors. (For the number of death sentences imposed and carried out, *see* JUSTICE.)

Death's-Head Units (officially, SS-Totenkopfverbände), an armed SS troop under SS-Gruppenführer Theodor EICKE. Initially the SS Guard Unit (Wachverband), after March 29, 1936, it was officially also called by the Death's-Head name; it guarded the concentration camps, and recruited its members partly from the very young unemployed and peasants. Even in their external appearance, Eicke sought to distinguish his troops as a special unit: they wore a dark earth-colored uniform with a skull on the right collar patch, rather than the black outfit of the SS. They were literally "incited against" the prisoners (Eicke), and were to be relentlessly obedient and pitiless executors of the Führer's will. Eicke's own guard unit at the DACHAU

Death's-Head Units of the SS.

concentration camp had the opportunity to demonstrate these qualities during the RÖHM AFFAIR on June 30, 1934. Eicke himself shot Ernst RÖHM, and was rewarded by being named "Inspector of Concentration Camps and Führer of SS Guard Units" on July 4, 1934.

Eicke's brutalized Death's-Head Units grew to four *Standarten* with about 9,000 men by the end of 1938. They attracted the eye of Gottlob Berger, leader of the Recruitment Office in the SS Main Office, when he had to fill the SS STAND-BY TROOPS. Part of the Death's-Head Units were released from concentration camp service; police reinforcements from the General SS replaced them. Death's-Head Units, Standby Troops, and JUNKER SCHOOLS were then combined in the Armed SS (WAFFEN-SS), and on November 1, 1939, Eicke combined the Death's-Head Units and some of the police reinforcements as the SS "Death's-Head" (Totenkopf) Division. Within the by no means squeamish Waffen-SS they distinguished themselves by their extraordinarily inhumane conduct of war, including quite a number of war crimes. The indisputably impressive soldierly achievements of the Death's-Head Units, such as breaking out of the encirclement of Demiansk, in the USSR, in early 1942, fade in comparison.

Decartelization (*Entflechtung*), dissolution of trusts, concerns, and cartels on the basis of the POTSDAM AGREEMENT of August 2, 1945; it was carried out by the occupation powers in the Western occupation zones. A total of 80 such dismemberments were implemented, including those of I.G. FARBEN, the United Steel Works, and the Krupp concern.

Decker, Will, b. Rostock, December 13, 1899; d. May 1, 1945, National Socialist social policymaker and publicist. Elected to the Reichstag for the NSDAP in 1930, Decker became head of the Office for Education and Training in the headquarters of the REICH LABOR SERVICE in 1932. He was named general labor leader (*Generalarbeitsführer*) in 1935. Decker's writings included *Der deutsche Weg* (The German Path; 1933), *Die politische Aufgabe des Arbeitsdienstes* (The Political Task of the Labor Service; 1935), and *Mit dem Spaten durch Polen* (Through Poland with a Spade; 1939). He also edited the series Volk an der Arbeit (The *Volk* at Work; 1934ff.).

Deeg, Peter, b. Kissingen, May 15, 1908, German jurist and politician. After his studies, Deeg became a researcher for Julius STREICHER, publisher of *Der Stürmer*, whom he supplied with "scientific" ammunition for antisemitic campaigns: *Hofjuden* (Court Jews; 1938) and *Judengesetze Grossdeutschlands* (Jewish Legislation for Great-Germany; 1939). Deeg came into conflict with Streicher over charges of disloyalty, which led to rejection of his application for NSDAP membership. After the war he practiced law in Kissingen, joined the Christian Social Union (CSU), and played a role in the "*Spiegel* affair" of 1962, involving attacks on that journal for criticizing West German military preparedness.

Defamation (*Beschimpfung*), a criminal act according to Paragraph 134a–b of the Criminal Code; it applied especially to cases of intentional insults to the Reich, its constitution, the military services, the NSDAP, or its member organizations, flags, banners, symbols, or decorations. Defamation was punishable with a prison term.

Defense planning (*Abwehrplanung*), strategy for the limitation of damage from military attacks on Reich territory. It included AIR DEFENSE, relocation of industries, reconstruction, and fortifications.

Deflation (literally, removal of air), decrease in the circulation of money, with the effect that prices fall and the value of money rises; it is preceded by a market crisis. An intentional deflationary policy can be facilitated by a policy of rigorous austerity; its most immediate effect is a reduction in production ("shrinking for health"). The deflationary policy of Chancellor Heinrich BRÜNING had as its goal the reform of state finances as a precondition for stanching mass unemployment (in March 1930, 3.3 million were out of work). Moreover, the government's difficulties in meeting payments—in this sense, welcome—were meant to move the Western powers to give in on the reparations question. This strategy, aimed at gaining time, failed; the economic crisis intensified (in January 1933, 6 million were unemployed), while the Reichstag failed to gain control of the financial crisis. All this favored the propaganda successes and avalanche victories of the NSDAP.

De Gaulle, Charles. *See* Gaulle, Charles de.

Degenerate Art (*Entartete Kunst*), defamatory National Socialist catchphrase, later an official designation for modern, non-naturalistic art, in particular for art that was formally innovative or

Poster for the Degenerate Art exhibition.

that had a socially critical content (such as Expressionist, Dadaist, or abstract art). Originating from the biological and medical term denoting deterioration, it was introduced into art criticism by Max Nordau in his book *Entartung* (Degeneration; 1893) and was later picked up by the COMBAT LEAGUE FOR GERMAN CULTURE. At the culture conference of the NSDAP in 1933, the "Bolshevists of art" were declared the prime enemy in the "ruthless war for purification"; pictures by Max BECKMANN, Otto DIX, Paul KLEE, and the like were banned "because they have had a spiritually destructive impact in their unbridled individualistic tyranny . . . and have propagated a subhuman culture" (*Deutsche Kultur-Wacht* [German Culture Guardian], 1933).

The works of "artists of the era of decay" were systematically removed from public collections; a Führer decree of June 30, 1937, commanded the president of the Reich Chamber of Fine Arts, Adolf ZIEGLER, to put together a selection for an exhibition. Under the title "Degenerate Art," in the summer of 1937 in Munich Ziegler presented paintings, graphics, and sculpture, with provocative descriptions, as "the monstrous products of madness and arrogance." For Hitler, after the exhibition "patience . . . was henceforth at an end for all those who had not fallen into line in the area of fine arts"; the institutional synchronization of the official art world had thus been concluded.

1
Paul Klee, *The Revolution of the Viaduct,* 1937.
2
Otto Dix, *War,* 1914.
3
Emil Nolde, *The Great Gardener,* 1940.
4
Max Beckmann, *Liberation from Mortal Danger,* 1941.
5
Oskar Kokoschka, *Self-Portrait,* 1913.

Goebbels visits the Degenerate Art exhibition.

In the struggle against Degenerate Art, the National Socialists found widespread public support (over 20,000 visitors daily came to the Munich exhibition); inadequate understanding of modern art was intensified, through propaganda, to impassioned rejection. Even the younger generation, yearning for firm points of orientation, was unsettled by the appearance of formal dissolution in modern art. The Law regarding the Confiscation of Works of Degenerate Art of May 1938 allowed even private holdings to be confiscated without compensation. Numerous artworks were sold abroad to profit the Reich, and over 4,000 pictures were publicly burned in Berlin in 1939. "Degenerate" artists had to emigrate or were at the least forbidden to work. The term "degenerate art" has retained its currency in conservative art criticism of the artistic avant-garde after 1945, despite its historical baggage.

H. H.

Degeneration (*Entartung*), in the National Socialist vocabulary, a frequently used term for putative phenomena of decay in a people because of "racial mixing and the decline of physical and mental capacity based on heredity and race." In the first case, the decline of the people affected was ineluctable; but such cases as the Weimar Republic allegedly represented could "be overcome through a new idea that encompassed the entire *Volk*," as National Socialism indeed proved. According to the false NS notion of SPECIES, the "mixing of very different races" regularly produced degeneration, which was therefore preventable through measures of HEREDITY CULTIVATION and "blood protection" (*see* NUREMBERG LAWS).

DEGESCH. *See* German Society for Vermin Control.

Degrelle, Léon, b. Bouillon, June 15, 1906, Belgian politician. A trained jurist, Degrelle created the Catholic "Rexist movement" ("Christ-Is-King movement") in 1930. The REXISTS stood for an authoritarian and fascist corporative state based on "natural communities" (family, occupation, people [*Volk*]); at the high point of their popularity, in 1936, they elected 21 deputies to the Belgian parliament. In 1940 Degrelle was arrested when German troops occupied Belgium, and was transported to France. Freed by the Germans, he became their leading collaborator in Belgium.

Degrelle founded and commanded the "Walloon Legion" in the Waffen-SS (SS-Division blindée Wallonie); he returned from Russia as the most highly decorated foreigner in the Wehrmacht (Knight's Cross with Oak Leaves). At the end of the war, he escaped to Spain. Condemned to death by a Belgian court-martial on December 14, 1945, he lived in Spanish exile with a few interruptions, becoming head of a chain of laundries. Belgian efforts to have him extradited were without success. In 1964 Belgium's parliament discussed the extension of the statute of limitations for high treason, dubbed the "Lex Degrelle" in the press. In his *Memoirs of a Fascist*, published in 1969, Degrelle was still praising Hitler as "the greatest genius of all time."

Degrelle receives from Hitler the Oak-Leaf Cluster for the Knight's Cross, and the Golden Clasp for Hand-to-Hand Combat.

De-Jewing (*Entjudung*), term used as early as 1881 by Eugen DÜHRING to denote the exclusion of Jews, which he considered a *"völkisch task."* It was incorporated in the NSDAP Program under Point 4 ("No Jew can be a *Volk* comrade" [*see* VOLK COMRADE]), and meant at first the exclusion of Jews and citizens "with Jewish kin" from government service and public life (*see* ARYAN PARAGRAPH). Later it meant their expulsion from economic life (ARYANIZATION), and finally from life itself (*see* FINAL SOLUTION). In the biologistic jargon of National Socialism, this genocidal term signified a metabolic process aimed at "eliminating the Jewry that had deeply penetrated the German *Volk* body."

Delegate for the Four-Year Plan (*Beauftragter für den Vierjahresplan*), function delegated from Hitler to Göring (October 19, 1936) for the directing of the FOUR-YEAR PLAN.

Delegate of the NSDAP (*Beauftragter der NSDAP*), in accordance with the GERMAN COMMUNAL ORDINANCE of January 30, 1935, the representative of the party whose task was "to assure the conformity of communal administration and party." The delegate had a decisive role in the naming of mayors, municipal councils, and deputy mayors; statutes, municipal charters, and the bestowal of honorary citizenships required his approval. The deputy to the Führer ordinarily named the *Kreisleiter*

(district leader) to the post. The office of the delegate was intended to carry through the National Socialist principle of the "unity of party and state" and the FÜHRER PRINCIPLE on the communal level.

Delitzsch, Friedrich, b. Erlangen, September 3, 1850; d. Langenschwalbach, December 19, 1922, German scholar of the ancient Near East. Delitzsch's lectures on the Mesopotamian roots of the biblical view of the world set off a protracted controversy over Babel; *Die grosse Täuschung* (The Great Deception; 1920) provided arguments for the openly anti-Jewish and covertly anti-Christian cultural history of the National Socialist period.

Delp, Alfred, b. Mannheim, September 15, 1907; d. Berlin-Plötzensee, February 2, 1945 (executed), German Catholic theologian and opposition fighter. A Jesuit since 1926, Delp was ordained in 1937. In 1939 he became the editor of *Stimmen der Zeit* (Voices of the Day) in Munich; after his journal was banned in 1941, Delp conducted public and private services and discussions with friends in Munich-Bogenhausen. In a dialogue with Heidegger's existentialist philosophy he developed his own system of "theonomic humanism" (*Der Mensch und die Geschichte* [The Human and History]; 1943), which stood in sharp contrast to National Socialism and which Delp intended to serve as a basis for German postwar society. In 1942 he estab-

Alfred Delp.

lished contact with Helmut Count MOLTKE, in whose KREISAU CIRCLE he stated his ideas based on a Christian social order. Although not himself involved in the assassination attempt of July 20, 1944, Delp was arrested, condemned to death by the *Volk* Court, and executed. Delp's last writings were published in 1956 under the title *Im Angesicht des Todes* (In the Face of Death).

Demilitarization of Germany, declared Allied war aim in the Second World War, confirmed in the POTSDAM AGREEMENT (decree of August 2, 1945); it led to total German disarmament and the DISMANTLING of the arms industry.

Demilitarized Zone, area evacuated by German troops in accord with the Versailles treaty (*see* OCCUPIED TERRITORIES; RHINELAND OCCUPATION).

Democracy (*Demokratie;* from Gr., rule of the people), type of government rejected by National Socialism from the outset. Direct democracy by the whole people was said to be impossible in a mass society, whereas parliamentary or representative democracy led to individual lack of responsibility, bred "scared rabbits or artful dodgers," and crippled any accomplishment (Hitler speech of August 17, 1934). National Socialism, on the other hand, developed true, "Germanic" or "Führer democracy": the Führer was supported by the love and trust of the *Volk,* to whom alone he felt responsibility. Thus to juxtapose the authoritarian state and democracy was a "liberal falsification." Despite this

reclamation of "true democracy," National Socialist propaganda used the word almost exclusively in a pejorative sense; the Western powers were identified as "effeminate" or "Judaized democracies," and party ideologist Alfred Rosenberg spoke of chaotic, deracinating "humane" democracy.

Demoplutocratic (*demoplutokratisch*), neologism presumably coined by Joseph GOEBBELS from "democratic" and "plutocratic," and meant to denigrate the Anglo-American enemy during the war: "It is Mr. Winston Churchill, known as W. C., . . . first violin in the demonic concert that at the moment the whole demoplutocratic world has struck up against the Axis powers" (*Das Reich,* February 2, 1941).

Denazification (*Entnazifizierung*), removal of National Socialists from public offices and leading positions in the economy after 1945 in Germany (and Austria); in the broader sense, also the "cleansing" of political, economic, and cultural life of a National Socialist (NS) mentality. Conceived by the United States, denazification aimed at the total abolition of the personnel and ideological foundations of NATIONAL SOCIALISM and its system of rule, thereby creating the preconditions for a democratization of Germany. At the YALTA Conference (February 1945), the Allies had declared denazification to be a primary goal of their policy toward a defeated Germany.

In the POTSDAM AGREEMENT of August 2, 1945, the Allies decreed the following denazification measures:

1. Dissolution of the NSDAP, its "branches and subsidiary organizations"
2. The banning of "all Nazi and militaristic activity and propaganda"
3. Abolition of NS laws
4. Arrest and internment of NS party leaders, "influential" supporters of National Socialism, the heads of NS offices and organizations, "and all other persons who jeopardize the occupation [of Germany by the Allies] and its goals"
5. Removal of all more than simply nominal members of the NSDAP and "all persons hostile to the Allied goals" from public and semi-public offices, as well as from leading positions in the private economy
6. Complete removal of "Nazi and militarist doctrines" from educational and instructional institutions, and their supervision (*see* REEDUCATION)

Denazification. An appeals board stages a proceeding against "Hitler, Adolf; profession: painter and decorator." An empty chair symbolizes the absent defendant.

Denazification was carried out first on the basis of laws passed by the ALLIED CONTROL COUNCIL, notably Law No. 1 (of September 20, 1945) and No. 2 (of October 10, 1945), most intensively in the American zone, where every holder of a public office or other high position and every candidate for such had to fill out an extensive QUESTIONNAIRE. On the basis of his responses, the petitioner was classified in one of six categories: "automatically arrest," "dismissal required," "dismissal recommended," "dismissal not recommended," "no proof of National Socialist activities," or "anti–National Socialist activities proved." The Control Council law of December 25, 1945, extended this procedure to the other occupation zones, although it was only partially carried out there. In late 1945 it was revised, no doubt because it had produced an acute labor shortage, especially in public administration. The Law for the Liberation from Na-

tional Socialism and Militarism of March 5, 1946, divided (former) National Socialists into five categories (without accusing them of war crimes): (1) major offenders; (2) offenders; (3) lesser offenders; (4) fellow travelers; and (5) those exonerated. Local German APPEALS BOARDS were charged with denazification; they were supervised by "liberation ministries" in the states (*Länder*). A Control Council directive of October 12, 1946, applied this procedure to the other zones.

Denazification, with its PERSIL CERTIFICATE corruption, was criticized in particular by the churches and the conservative German parties. In late 1947 it was modified: the United States military government granted an amnesty to the young and socially disadvantaged (some 2.8 million cases); the French military governor amnestied all merely nominal National Socialists (decrees of November 17, 1947, and July 13, 1948); in the Soviet zone, an order of the military government of August 16, 1947, had already made merely nominal National Socialists equal to other citizens, and the decree of February 26, 1948, ended denazification there.

After the founding of the Federal Republic of Germany (FRG) in September 1949, responsibility for denazification in West Germany passed completely to the federal states; however, only persons in categories 1 and 2 were further prosecuted, and even they were in large part amnestied. "Termination laws" (*Abschlussgesetze*) passed in all states between 1949 and 1954 further limited denazification and its results: on the basis of the so-called 131 Law of May 11, 1951 (implementation law to Article 131 of the Basic Law), nearly all officials touched by denazification were restored to office. In the German Democratic Republic (GDR), the law of October 2, 1952, made former National Socialists (other than "war criminals") equal to all other citizens. According to an investigation by the Federal Interior Ministry of February 1950, some 6.08 million persons were affected by denazification in the Western zones and the Federal Republic. Of these, nearly 1,700 fell into category 1, some 23,000 in category 2, some 150,400 in category 3, and approximately 1,006,000 in category 4. Proceedings were dropped in 3,939,000 inquiries. Thus, nearly 98 percent of those affected by the denazification procedure were categorized as "exonerated" or only "fellow travelers."

R. B.

Denker (thinker), Germanization of "philosopher" that was used in National Socialist reference works.

Denmark, kingdom on the border with Schleswig-Holstein; area, 43,069 sq km (16,629 sq miles); population, 3.65 million (1933). Despite its strong economic connections with Germany, Denmark opposed National Socialist policies; because of Hitler's REVISIONIST POLICY it had to be prepared for conflict with Germany over North Schleswig. Alone among northern European nations, Denmark concluded a nonaggression pact with the German Reich (May 1939). The Great Belt between the main Danish islands was mined in November 1939 in order to keep the Royal Navy from the Baltic Sea. Even after the surprise occupation of the country (April 9, 1940) by German troops (*see* NORWEGIAN CAMPAIGN), Copenhagen remained cooperative. On the same day, the government accepted—under protest—Germany's demands (principally to refrain from resistance), which in an obliging tone asked for understanding regarding the operation, which was directed against England. As a result, the royal family, the government, the parliament, and the army remained untouched; Danish Jews were unmolested for the time, and there was no move to annex North Schleswig.

In 1943, after isolated strikes and acts of sabotage, the situation worsened. On August 29, Reich Commissioner Werner BEST placed Denmark under martial law, the government resigned, and a large part of the Danish fleet scuttled itself. SS plans to deport Danish Jews were largely frustrated through an unusual rescue effort. Warned in time, 7,906 Jews, half Jews, and Christians married to Jews were brought to safety in Sweden aboard fishing boats. The SS was able to deport only 492 Jews to Theresienstadt; 423 survived. The Danish resistance against the German occupation claimed 3,213 lives (113 executions). On May 9, 1945, British warships entered Copenhagen's harbor.

De-Nordicization (*Entnordung*), term invented by Hans GÜNTHER to denote the decrease of the "Nordic blood component" in a people through miscegenation, through wars in which primarily "aggressive Nordic men" perished, or through an inadequate birthrate within the Nordic elite groups; the conceptual opposite of NORDIC UPGRADING. According to Günther, de-Nordicization could be recognized by the increase in a people's garrulousness (*Geschwätzigkeit*). The general term "deracination" (*Entrassung*) was used as a synonym.

Deportation, forced removal of persons, especially in large numbers, to regions outside their traditional area of settlement, either by their

King Christian of Denmark during a ride in Copenhagen.

own government or by an occupying power; in international law, it is permissible only as "legalized criminal punishment" and under humane conditions. Neither criterion was met by the National Socialist deportation of some 4.5 million Jewish people, in particular (*see* FINAL SOLUTION), from areas under German control to the EXTERMINATION CAMPS. The further deportation of some 5 million people during the war from areas occupied by the Wehrmacht to FORCED LABOR in German armaments factories also ran counter to international law; "General Plenipotentiary for Labor Deployment" Fritz SAUCKEL, who was responsible, was condemned to death at the Nuremberg Trials. (On the deportation of Germans from the Eastern Territories, *see* EXPULSION.)

Deputy to the Führer (*Stellvertreter des Führers*), office created for Rudolf HESS by Hitler's appointment on April 21, 1933; Hess had previously been the leader of the NSDAP's political Central Commission. The deputy was intended to have the power to decide in Hitler's name "all questions of party [as against government] leadership." In order to realize the party's influence on policies, after June 29, 1933, he had the right to take part in all cabinet sessions; he became a Reich Minister without Portfolio through the Law for Securing the Unity of Party and State of December 1, 1933 (*Reich Law Gazette* I, p. 1016). As a result of the Führer's decree of July 27, 1934, he collaborated in all legislative projects, and in line with the

Deputy to the Führer. Rudolf Hess (right) with Martin Bormann.

decree of September 24, 1935, he also had a voice in the appointment and discharge of officials.

The deputy worked from the BROWN HOUSE in Munich; his tasks included "politically aligning in a uniform manner the branches and affiliated associations of the NSDAP, and communicating political guidelines to them." Toward this end he was served by an ample staff, which the managing staff director, Martin BORMANN, skillfully ran after July 1933. The true possessor of the powers of the deputy, Bormann finally inherited them after Hess had flown to England. The position was renamed, however, in the PARTY CHANCELLERY on May 12, 1941, and in April 1943, with expanded jurisdiction, Bormann was named Secretary to the Führer.

Descent, Theory of (*Abstammungslehre*). In contrast to the doctrine of the conservation of species, the Theory of Descent explains the present variety of species as the result of a process of natural selection. The struggle for existence allows only the best-adapted individuals to survive and reproduce, while the others are "culled out." In the biologistic worldview of National Socialism, the Theory of Descent became the model for human society, peoples, and races as well. Fantasies of master races and theories of racial value have their origins here (*see also* SOCIAL DARWINISM).

Detention camps (*Anhaltelager*), Austrian collection centers for interning political opponents, first of the DOLLFUSS, then the SCHUSCHNIGG regime; they were established by a decree of the federal chancellor of September 23, 1933 (after July 30, 1934, it was part of the constitution). At one time 20 detention camps were in operation, in which, after the worker unrest of February 1934, primarily Socialists were held. After the National Socialist putsch attempt of July 25, 1934, they held mainly National Socialists (on September 23, 1934, there were some 13,388 internees). In contrast to prisoners in the German CONCENTRATION CAMPS, detention camp prisoners were separated by political group, and were not forced to work. After 1935, only the largest detention camp, Wöllersdorf, continued to operate; following the German-Austrian JULY AGREEMENT (July 11, 1936), it was emptied and shut down. After the ANSCHLUSS, NS concentration camps replaced detention camps (*see* MAUTHAUSEN).

Detten, Georg von, b. Hagen, September 9, 1887; d. Berlin, July 2, 1934, SA Führer. Detten joined the NSDAP in 1924; in 1932 he was made a Reichstag deputy. As an SA *Gruppen-führer* in 1934, he headed the Political Office at SA headquarters. Considered a propagandist for the SECOND REVOLUTION, he was shot in connection with the RÖHM AFFAIR.

De-urbanization (*Entstädterung*), a goal of National Socialist settlement policies that was served by such measures as the grant of HOMESTEADS. Through the breaking up of large cities and metropolitan concentrations there was an ideological hope for a connection with the "native soil" that was deemed vital to the GERMAN MAN, but that had been lost through URBANIZATION. In terms of border policies, it implied more settlement of the east so as to push back Slavic influences.

Deutsch-. *See* Index.

Deutsch, Ernst, b. Prague, September 16, 1890; d. Berlin, March 22, 1969, German actor. Considered a pioneer of Expressionism on the stage, Deutsch worked with Max REINHARDT in Berlin after 1917. His Jewish heritage forced him to emigrate to Austria (where he was engaged by Vienna's Burgtheater) in April 1937, then to Prague, Paris, London, and finally Hollywood. In 1947, he returned to Europe and Vienna's

Ernst Deutsch.

"Burg"; he returned to Germany only in 1954. Deutsch's portrayals of Shylock and Nathan the Wise made theater history.

Deutsche Allgemeine Zeitung (German General News; DAZ), successor in 1918 to the *Norddeutsche Allgemeine Zeitung* (North German General News). Conservative in tone, until 1933 the newspaper was the voice of the GERMAN PEOPLE'S PARTY, and representative of the interests of large industry. In 1938, the DAZ was taken over by the NSDAP; the last issue was that of April 24, 1945.

Deutsche Erd- und Steinwerke (German Earth and Stone Works), one of the SS ECONOMIC ENTERPRISES, founded in 1938.

Deutsche Reichsbahn (German Reich Railroad; DR), transportation enterprise descended from the Deutsche Reichsbahn-Gesellschaft (German Reich Railroad Company), founded in 1924. A law of February 10, 1937, transferred ownership of the nationalized but largely independent company to direct national administration; its offices became government agencies. Supervision and direction came under the Reich transportation minister, who after 1937 was Julius Heinrich DORPMÜLLER. With invested capital of over 27 billion RM, the DR was the largest enterprise in the German economy.

The Reichsbahn played a central role in the FINAL SOLUTION, in support of which it transported over 3 million people to EXTERMINATION CAMPS, beginning in the fall of 1941. Under orders of the Reich Security Main Office (RSHA), and to keep up appearances, passenger cars—however painfully jammed—were made available to transport Jews from Germany and western Europe; eastern European victims, however, were hauled in often barely usable freight and livestock cars.

Legal punishment did not follow when the war ended: Dorpmüller died in 1945, and the probable chief perpetrator, Albert Ganzenmüller, state secretary in the Transportation Ministry, fled to Argentina in 1947. He returned in 1954, and judicial investigations began in 1957. In 1973 Ganzenmüller was tried for aiding and abetting murder and for using his office for deprivation of freedom resulting in death. In 1977 the proceeding was stayed because of the accused's inability to stand trial. The entanglement of the Reichsbahn in the National Socialist crimes was acknowledged for the first time in 1985, in the Nuremberg commemorative exhibition "150 Years of Railroad."

Deutscher Verlag (German Publishing House), successor enterprise to the Ullstein firm, which was acquired in 1938 by Max WINKLER for the NSDAP. The largest subsidiary of the EHER PRESS, its publications included *Das Reich, Signal,* and the *Deutsche Allgemeine Zeitung.*

Deutsches Jungvolk (German Young *Volk*), subdivision of the HITLER YOUTH for boys 10 to 14 years old.

Deutsches Reich, official name of the German state from 1871 to 1945. The name originated with the proclamation in Versailles on January 18, 1871, of the Prussian king, Wilhelm, as Deutscher Kaiser (German emperor), and with the announcement on April 16, 1871, of a Reich Constitution for a constitutional and monarchical federal state. The term "Deutsches Reich" was retained in the WEIMAR CONSTITUTION of August 11, 1919, although the monarchy denoted by the name (*Reich* means "monarchy" or "empire") was abolished. The federal organization was, however, retained in the now democratic German Reich and, like the constitution, never formally abrogated until 1945.

De facto, however, the National Socialist SEIZURE OF POWER (1933–1934) suspended all constitutional guarantees through SYNCHRONIZATION in a centralized, one-party state. "German Reich" became synonymous with Hitler's totalitarian, one-party state and was territorially extended to a GREAT-GERMAN REICH. It succumbed to the enemy coalition that formed against it during the Second World War, and ended with the UNCONDITIONAL SURRENDER on May 7–8, 1945. The formal end of the German Reich came after the arrest of the government of Karl DÖNITZ (May 23, 1945) with the JUNE DECLARATION of June 5, 1945. While the Federal Republic of Germany considers itself the legitimate successor to the German Reich, the German Democratic Republic views the concept as totally extinguished through creation of the two German states.

Deutschland (Germany), geographical term that until 1945 was generally synonymous with DEUTSCHES REICH (German empire or state); as a cultural and historical phenomenon it was the basis of national identity for the German people, especially through their common language. During the burgeoning of German nationalism that was provoked by the Napoleonic wars, it was increasingly glorified in a conservative myth of the Fatherland. The term acquired

almost religious significance in its National Socialist manifestation when it was elevated as the "blood source" (*Blutquelle*) and "racial primeval ground [*Urgrund*]" of the German *Volk.* Even though the NS racial programs pointed beyond solutions within a nation-state, the cult of Germany was tended in order to raise the collective consciousness as a prerequisite to expansionism. Anti-NS agitation also used the term's emotional weight by speaking of emigrants and opposition fighters as the "other," "upright," or "decent" Germany.

De Vecchi, Cesare Maria, b. Casale Monferrato, November 14, 1884; d. Rome, June 23, 1959, Italian politician. De Vecchi participated in the March on Rome (October 1922) and was governor of Italian Somaliland from 1923 to 1928, ambassador to the Vatican from 1929 to 1935, and later education minister. One of the principal representatives of the monarchist wing of the Fascist party, he voted in the Fascist Grand Council in July 1943 for Mussolini's ouster and supported the latter's arrest by King VICTOR EMMANUEL III. In return, he was condemned to death in absentia from SALÒ in 1944.

DFW. *See* German Women's Agency.

DGB. *See* German Trade Union Federation.

Dibelius, Otto, b. Berlin, May 15, 1880; d. there, January 31, 1967, German Evangelical theologian. In 1907 Dibelius became a pastor; in 1925, general superintendent of Kurmark. At first inclined toward nationalist ideas, he gave utterance to antisemitic prejudices, which brought him in conflict with the "dialectical theology" of Karl BARTH. Even at the National Socialist Seizure of Power he remained well-disposed and hopeful. At the POTSDAM CELEBRATION he blessed the course of the new regime in his sermon for the opening of the Reichstag.

Shocked by Hitler's antichurch tack, behind which he quickly saw anti-Christian objectives, Dibelius committed himself to the CONFESSING CHURCH and lost his post. He struggled tirelessly, even though at times incarcerated or forbidden to speak publicly, for freedom of religious practice; yet he did not carry his protests beyond church affairs, even though Kurt GERSTEIN had informed him during the war about the NS program for a Final Solution. The STUTTGART CONFESSION OF GUILT of October 19, 1945, which Dibelius helped to compose, can thus be understood as his personal avowal of failure. From 1949 to 1961, Dibelius served

Otto Dibelius.

as chairman of the Council of the Evangelical Church of Germany, and from 1954 to 1961 as the first German in the presidium of the World Council of Churches. He led the Evangelical Church of Berlin-Brandenburg as bishop from 1945 to 1966. His best-known book is *Das Jahrhundert der Kirche* (The Century of the Church; 1927).

Dichtung (also *Dichtkunst*), collective term for works of fiction or literary art. According to National Socialist artistic theory, German *Dichtung* was possible only for those who "by blood and temperament brought the inner preconditions for it," and who created on the basis of a "race idea." The National Socialists condemned much contemporary literature as "Jewish *Dichtung* in the German language." (*For approved writing, see* LITERATURE.)

Dictatorship (*Diktatur*), in contrast to DEMOCRACY, rule by one person or group independent of the will of the people. With the merger of the offices of head of government and REICH PRESIDENT in the person of Hitler as "leader and chancellor" (FÜHRER UND REICHSKANZLER) on August 1, 1934, the Third Reich became a personal dictatorship with despotic tendencies. The National Socialists denied this view on the ground that Hitler was the "delegate [*Beauftragter*] of the *Volk*," "supported by its trust and love." The formation of political will in the German Reich was therefore "the formation of a true and direct *Volk* will." The Führer state might be described as a "dictatorship of the *Volk*," but it did not represent a temporary makeshift such as the classic dictatorship of

ancient Rome or the PRESIDIAL CABINETS based on Article 48 (the DICTATORSHIP PARAGRAPH) of the Weimar Constitution. Thus, for the National Socialists it was "the exact opposite of every dictatorship: a political form intended to last."

Dictatorship Paragraph (*Diktaturparagraph*), polemical name for Article 48 of the Weimar Constitution, which enabled the Reich president to bestow the force of law on government decisions by EMERGENCY DECREES. It was the basis for the PRESIDIAL CABINETS and the REICHSTAG FIRE DECREE of February 28, 1933, and thus a crucial building block in Hitler's dictatorship.

Dieckhoff, Hans Heinrich, b. Strasbourg, December 23, 1884; d. Lenzkirch, March 21, 1952, German diplomat. In 1912 Dieckhoff entered the foreign service, becoming ministerial counselor in the Foreign Office in 1930 and head of the political division in 1935. He became ambassador to Washington in 1937, and for a time promoted the careful treatment of the United States in National Socialist foreign policy; in the end, however, he could not prevent the path to war and the misperception of American policy. In 1943–1944, he represented Germany in Madrid.

"Die Fahne hoch!" (Raise the banner!), beginning line and title of the "HORST-WESSEL-LIED."

Diels, Rudolf, b. Berghausen (Taunus), December 16, 1900; d. Katzenelnbogen (Hesse), November 18, 1957, German jurist. Diels was an army volunteer in 1918, studied in Marburg, and was a member of a student free corps. He then became a councillor (*Regierungsrat*) in the Prussian Interior Ministry under Carl SEVERING (1930), with the special assignment of combating communism. This background made Diels useful to Hermann GÖRING after the 1933 Reichstag fire. On April 26, Diels was made chief of the Gestapo office in Berlin, where he developed the first police regulations for PROTECTIVE CUSTODY and persecution of Jews, while seeking to control the SA's "wild" concentration camps.

In the power struggle with Heinrich Himmler and Reinhard Heydrich, Göring finally sacrificed his Gestapo chief by appointing Diels governor (*Regierungspräsident*) and sending him to Cologne in 1934 and to Hannover in 1936. Diels was imprisoned briefly in 1944 after the July 20 assassination attempt, but Göring protected him from further prosecution. Imprisoned by the Allies until 1948, Diels appeared as a prosecution witness at Nuremberg. His memoirs, *Lucifer ante portas* (Lucifer at the Door; 1953), although apologetic, give rich insight into the terrorist methods of the National Socialists' early consolidation of power.

Diem, Carl, b. Würzburg, June 24, 1882; d. Cologne, December 17, 1962, German sports academician and functionary. From 1913 to 1933 Diem was general secretary of the GERMAN REICH COMMITTEE FOR PHYSICAL EXERCISES. In 1920 he co-founded the German Academy for Physical Exercises. Diem despised the haste with which sports association leaders supported the Synchronization of German SPORTS; he even coined the slogan "as lacking in character as a sports leader." Nonetheless, he made himself available as organizer of the 1936 OLYMPIC GAMES, although otherwise remaining in the background. After the war he founded the German Sports Academy in Cologne (1947). His most famous book is *Weltgeschichte des Sports und der Leibesübungen* (World History of Sports and Physical Exercises, 2 vols., 1960).

Dienstgrade (service level), RANKS in the military, the bureaucracy, and in various National Socialist organizations.

Dienststelle Ribbentrop. *See* Ribbentrop Office.

Dieppe, French port city on the Channel coast. On August 19, 1942, a British reconnaissance and beachhead operation ("Jubilee"), intended as a dress rehearsal for the INVASION of the German-occupied mainland, collapsed near Dieppe, with many casualties.

Carl Diem.

Dietl, Eduard, b. Bad Aibling, July 21, 1890; d. (in a plane crash) near Harberg (Styria), June 23, 1944, German colonel general (June 1, 1942). In 1909 Dietl joined the army; he became a major general on April 1, 1938, and two years later to the day, advanced to lieutenant general. He was popular as the "hero of Narvik," which he defended (April–May 1940) with mountain troops and sailors against a force several times as large in the NORWEGIAN CAMPAIGN. An early National Socialist supporter—his first encounter with Hitler was in 1921—Dietl was nonetheless opposed to political fanaticism and was beloved as a good-humored and humane troop leader. From January 15, 1942, he led the German Twentieth Lappland Army in the Russian Campaign.

Eduard Dietl.

Dietrich, Hermann, b. Oberprechtal (Baden), December 14, 1879; d. Stuttgart, March 6, 1954, German politician. Dietrich studied law, and was active in local and state politics in Baden. He was elected to the National Assembly in 1919 for the German Democratic Party (DDP), of which he was a co-founder and which he represented in the Reichstag until 1933. The apex of his political career came with his appointment as minister for agriculture and nutrition in the Great Coalition cabinet of Hermann MÜLLER in 1928, and then in the economics and finance posts under Heinrich BRÜNING in 1930. With Brüning's fall on May 30, 1932, Dietrich's ministerial service ended. He had played a decisive role in the chancellor's deflationary policy (*see* DEFLATION). Forbidden political activity in 1933, he again took up the law. In

1945, he was among the founders of the Free Democratic Party (FDP) in the Federal Republic of Germany.

Dietrich, Joseph ("Sepp"), b. Hawangen (Upper Bavaria), May 28, 1892; d. Ludwigsburg, April 21, 1966, SS-*Oberstgruppenführer* (August 1, 1944). A butcher's apprentice, in 1911 Dietrich joined the Bavarian Army, serving as a sergeant in the First World War. Later a policeman, in 1923 he joined the SA. Discharged after the Hitler Putsch later that year, he held odd jobs, then joined the NSDAP in 1928. After the party's surprising electoral success of September 14, 1930, he represented Lower Bavaria in the Reichstag.

Dietrich became an SS-*Brigadeführer* in 1931, and on March 17, 1933, set up the Berlin SS Guard Staff, the basis for Hitler's bodyguard unit (LEIBSTANDARTE-SS "ADOLF HITLER"; LAH), established in September 1933; Dietrich remained its commander until July 1943. To reward his services in leading the execution of high SA officers in Munich during the "cleansing" of the RÖHM AFFAIR, he was promoted to SS-*Obergruppenführer*. Hitler spoke approvingly of Dietrich's "mixture of cunning, ruthlessness, and HARDNESS." Dietrich entered the war with the LAH as part of the Waffen-SS, but his great popularity could not compensate for his deficits as a military leader. As commanding general of the First SS Panzer Corps (July 27, 1943–October 24, 1944), he was awarded the Diamond Knight's Cross with Oak Leaves and Swords. As commander in chief of the Sixth SS Panzer Army (from October 1944 until the end of the war), he shared responsibility for the

Joseph Dietrich.

massacre of United States prisoners of war during the Ardennes Offensive, for which he was sentenced to life imprisonment in the MALMÉDY TRIAL. Because of procedural shortcomings, the term was reduced to 25 years and eventually to a pardon, on October 22, 1955. On May 14, 1957, Dietrich was sentenced again, to 18 months' imprisonment for manslaughter during the Röhm Affair; he was finally released in February 1959.

Dietrich, Marlene (originally, Maria Magdalena von Losch), b. Berlin, December 27, 1901, German film actress and singer. Dietrich went to the United States after her role in the Joseph von Sternberg film *Der Blaue Engel* (*The Blue Angel*, 1930), which made her an international star overnight. In 1934 she rejected an offer from Joseph Goebbels to return to Germany; the German film public was offered Swedish actress Zarah LEANDER as a Dietrich substitute. Branded a traitor in the Third Reich, in the United States Dietrich was celebrated (along with Thomas MANN) as a symbol of the "other Germany," and made frequent public appearances opposing National Socialism. She acquired American citizenship in 1937, and served during the war as a troop entertainer. Dietrich entered liberated Paris with Charles de Gaulle in 1944. National Socialist propaganda, which discredited her political engagement as "anti-German rabble-rousing," had influence even after the war; the relationship between Germany and Dietrich, defined by Jean Améry as "mutually disappointed love," remains warped even today.

M. F.

Dietrich, Otto, b. Essen, August 31, 1897; d. Düsseldorf, November 22, 1952, German journalist and politician. After First World War service and study, Dietrich worked in politics and economics, then with the *Essener Allgemeine Zeitung* (Essen General News). In 1928 he was chief of the business section of the German-nationalist *München-Augsburger Abendzeitung* (Munich-Augsburg Evening News), through which he grew close to Munich's National Socialist circles. On August 1, 1931, Hitler named Dietrich Reich Press Chief of the NSDAP. Dietrich entered the SS in 1932, and rose to *Obergruppenführer* (1941). He worked intensively on the great propaganda campaigns of 1932, and as NSDAP campaign manager he used his connections with the Rhineland's heavy industry to benefit Hitler.

Marlene Dietrich in *The Blue Angel*.

Dietrich played a major part in the SYNCHRO-NIZATION of the German PRESS after the Seizure of Power; as chairman of the Reich Association of the German Press he made the "formerly purely liberal-Marxist-led association an instrument of the New Reich." After the establishment of the Reich Culture Chamber, Dietrich became vice president of the REICH PRESS CHAMBER; from 1937 to 1945 he was a state secretary in the Propaganda Ministry and press chief for the Reich government, which made him responsible for PRESS ADVISORIES. In addition, he was

Otto Dietrich.

responsible for the publication of works in which National Socialism was glorified: *Mit Hitler an die Macht* (With Hitler on to Power; 1933), *Zwölf Jahre mit Hitler* (Twelve Years with Hitler; 1935), and *Auf den Strassen des Sieges* (On the Streets of Victory; 1939). At the end of the war he was taken prisoner and condemned to seven years' imprisonment in the WILHELM-STRASSE TRIAL, but was freed for good behavior in August 1950.

Dietwart (from Middle High Ger. *diet* [*Volk*] and *wart* [guardian]), leader of political instruction in gymnastics and sports clubs. First employed in the GERMAN GYMNASTS' UNION for "mental and moral hardening," after the synchronization of sports in the GERMAN REICH LEAGUE FOR PHYSICAL EXERCISES, the *Dietwart* became the "ideological goalie" for National Socialism in the clubs. Through "Diet exams," he routinely tested the "*völkisch* dependability" of athletes, and attended to the "cultivation of values of the German *Volk*" in sports.

Dimitrov, Georgi, b. Radomir, June 18, 1882; d. Moscow, July 2, 1949, Bulgarian politician. Dimitrov joined the Social Democratic party in 1902, and after 1918, the Communist party. He participated in a popular uprising in 1923, after which he sought exile in Moscow, Vienna, and finally Berlin. In 1933, he was arrested in Berlin in the wake of the Reichstag fire but was acquitted, along with his countrymen Popov and

Georgi Dimitrov.

Tanev, and the German Communist Reichstag leader Torgler. During the trial, Dimitrov cleverly succeeded in casting suspicion on the National Socialists as the arsonists, causing Göring as witness totally to lose his composure. Deported to the Soviet Union, Dimitrov served from 1935 to 1943 as general secretary of the Comintern. He returned to Bulgaria with the Red Army in 1944; on September 15, 1946, he proclaimed the Bulgarian People's Republic, and served as its premier until his death.

Ding-Schuler, Erwin Oskar [Ding was a pseudonym for Erwin Schuler], b. Bitterfeld/Saale, September 19, 1912; d. Freising (Upper Bavaria), August 11, 1945 (suicide), German physician. Ding-Schuler joined the NSDAP in 1932 and the SS in 1936. In 1937 he received his degree and passed his second state exam in medicine. An author of scientific publications, in 1939 he became camp physician at BUCHENWALD and head of the division for spotted fever and viral research of the Waffen-SS Hygiene Institute in Weimar-Buchenwald. Until 1945 he conducted extensive medical experiments (on some 1,000 inmates, many of whom lost their lives) in Experimental Station Block 46, using various poisons as well as infective agents for spotted fever, yellow fever, smallpox, typhus, and cholera.

W. D.

Dinta. *See* German Institute for National Socialist Technical Vocational Training.

Dinter, Artur, b. Mülhausen (Alsace), June 27, 1876; d. Offenburg, May 21, 1948, German

völkisch ideologue; student of natural sciences and philosophy, teacher, and theater director. Dinter gained fame as author of the antisemitic novel *Die Sünde wider das Blut* (The Sin against Blood; 1917), which by 1934 had 260,000 copies in print. After becoming acquainted with Hitler in 1923, Dinter organized the Great-German *Volk* Community in Thuringia as a successor to the NSDAP during Hitler's incarceration. He became party member no. 5 at the refounding of the party in February 1925, then Thuringian *Gauleiter.* Although Hitler had originally almost worshiped Dinter, the two fell into disagreement when Dinter promoted a debate over Christianity, notably the idea that Jesus, "the greatest antisemite of all time," had as a mission the purification of the Christian church from Judaism and the restoration of the "Aryan Savior image."

On September 30, 1927, Dinter was forced out as *Gauleiter.* He was thrown out of the party on October 11, 1928, after personal attacks on Hitler; on April 29, 1933, his application for readmission to membership was rejected, as was his appeal for pardon on June 15, 1937. After the banning that year of his "German *Volk* Church" (founded in 1927), he was removed in 1939 from the REICH WRITING CHAMBER.

Dirksen, Herbert von, b. Berlin, April 2, 1882; d. Munich, December 19, 1955, German diplomat. Dirksen was a law student, then a Prussian civil servant. In 1918 he entered the foreign service and in 1928 was appointed ambassador

Herbert von Dirksen.

to Moscow, where he continued the policy of German-Russian cooperation aimed at breaking the chains of the Versailles settlement. After the Seizure of Power, he was sent to Tokyo, where he participated in drafting the ANTI-COMINTERN PACT. In 1938 Dirksen replaced Joachim von Ribbentrop, whom he detested, as ambassador to London, where he tried in vain to use his influence to moderate Hitler's policies. His service in England ended on September 3, 1939, with the British declaration of war. In 1940 he retired at his own request. A denazification court exonerated him in 1947. Dirksen's memoirs, *Moskau-Tokio-London* (*Moscow, Tokyo, London*), were published in 1949.

Dirlewanger, Oskar, b. Würzburg, September 26, 1895; d. Altshausen (Upper Swabia), June 19, 1945, SS-*Oberführer* (1943). Dirlewanger served as a lieutenant in the First World War, completed a degree in political science in 1922, and joined the NSDAP in 1923. He became leader of the Esslingen SA-Sturmbann in 1932, was sentenced to two years' imprisonment in 1934 for seducing a dependent, joined the CONDOR LEGION in 1937, and became an *Obersturmführer* in the Waffen-SS in 1939.

In 1940 Dirlewanger developed the idea of forming a rifle unit of convicted criminals, whose "sharpshooting talents shouldn't lie fallow." On September 1 of that year, the first SS Special Battalion "Dirlewanger" came into being. Filled and refilled with professional criminals and desperadoes, the later SS Storm Brigade "Dirlewanger" developed into a unique band of incendiaries and murderers. Soviet marshal Georgi ZHUKOV placed a bounty on Dirlewanger. Even in the SS he provoked revulsion, especially for the excesses of his units in putting down the WARSAW UPRISING. His men were taken into Soviet captivity on May 5, 1945; Dirlewanger himself had decamped for the West, where he presumably died of mistreatment in a French prison. Rumors that he was still alive came to rest with the exhumation of his body in November 1960.

Disappearance (*Verschollenheit*), unclarified whereabouts of a person. The legal consequences of a person's disappearance were regulated by the law of July 4, 1939 (*Reich Law Gazette* I, p. 1168): in order to clarify the uncertainty of legal matters in such instances a declaration of death was generally possible after 10 years (¶2). The time limit was reduced to a minimum of one year in the case of persons missing during the war or through other emergency—in

other words, for missing soldiers and deported civilians (¶¶4–8). An application (for example, by family members or the public prosecutor's office) and public notice were required for a death certificate to be issued by the Civil Court in the missing person's place of residence (¶¶13–18). A death certificate could be reversed in a special procedure for which application had to be made, in case the missing person reappeared (¶¶30–33). In contrast to all other cases, proceedings for those missing in the war were free of charge.

Disarmament (*Abrüstung*), efforts to limit, reduce, and ultimately abolish the arsenals of weapons and military forces of nations. After several failed attempts, disarmament seemed to be a political goal toward which at least a few steps were possible after the First World War. In the Paris Suburban Treaties, the defeated Central Powers, Germany above all, had drastic arms limitations imposed on them (*see* VERSAILLES TREATY), which were proclaimed to be the first step toward general disarmament. Article 8 of the League of Nations Covenant, included in the peace treaties, contained an obligation to disarm, which to be sure was not to contravene national-security needs and thus from the outset remained subject to interpretation. Efforts at disarmament did not go beyond a limitation on naval forces negotiated between the sea powers (Washington Naval Conference, November 11, 1921–February 6, 1922). French security demands stood in the way of agreement on ground forces.

Only when the LOCARNO PACT created international guarantees for France's eastern boundaries was the League of Nations Council able to call a Preliminary Commission for the Disarmament Conference on December 12, 1925. After five, often month-long, sessions, on December 9, 1930, it presented the proposal for a disarmament convention, which was then rejected by the German government because it prescribed disarmament for the defeated nations without demanding a comparably low level of arms for the victors. The demand for German equality was added to the two previous topics of contention: "security through disarmament" and "disarmament after security." The Geneva conference, involving 51 states, met on February 2, 1932; the first round nearly failed over the German demand. Only after an adjournment and Germany's threat to halt participation did France go along with the other Great Powers and declare, on December 11, 1932, Germany's

Disarmament. German heavy artillery is scrapped.

basic military equality in the context of a "system offering security to all nations."

In terms of domestic politics, this agreement, as well as the earlier concessions on the REPARATIONS issue, came too late. Hitler, whose climb to power had been promoted by the hard-line stance of the Western powers, harvested the successes. Moreover, he used the moral lever of Germany's lack of weapons to increase pressure on the Great Powers. He conditionally accepted the plan of British prime minister Ramsay MacDonald (March 16, 1933) to grant Germany parity in armaments on the basis of a 200,000-man army, thus forcing France, in particular, into line. When the French delegation made agreement to MacDonald's plan conditional on a four-year time limit, the German government rejected this as unacceptable. On October 14, 1933, Germany left both the Geneva Disarmament Conference and the League of Nations. To the international public, France appeared as the stumbling block to disarmament.

The reintroduction of COMPULSORY MILITARY SERVICE in Germany on March 16, 1935, although long since planned, could be advertised as a morally justifiable response. This was particularly true after the GERMAN-BRITISH NAVAL AGREEMENT of June 18, 1935, seemed to confirm Germany's good faith regarding arms limitation. Disarmament in the sense of the League of Nations Covenant was nonetheless a lost cause. The Geneva Disarmament Conference met for the last time on June 11, 1934.

Discovery Aid (*Ermittlungshilfe*), auxiliary institution of the State Prosecutor's Office created by order of the Reich Justice Ministry on October 7, 1937. The new office replaced the Legal Aid (Gerichtshilfe) office, abolished in 1933, which the National Socialists saw as a misplaced protection for criminals, because it could inspire leniency in JUSTICE through exposure of the defendant's personal circumstances. The Discovery Aid office was totally at the service of the prosecution.

Dismantling (*Demontage*), taking apart production facilities to satisfy reparations demands of the victor powers. Plans for dismantling German industry were first discussed between Roosevelt and Churchill at the second Quebec Conference (September 1944). A compromise was finally reached between the soft line taken by American secretary of state Cordell Hull and the hard line of the MORGENTHAU PLAN. At YALTA (February 1945), the Allies agreed on the abolition of the armaments industry, international control over the Ruhr and Saar regions, and an extensive restitution program ($20 billion). In the POTSDAM AGREEMENT of August 2, 1945, they agreed to carry out their demands in the current occupation zones; because of the Allies' disparate industrial levels, the USSR was promised an additional 10 percent of dismantled facilities from the Western zones.

The goal of the Western powers was to reduce German industrial capacity to the level of 1932;

Dismantling. An American officer and his Soviet counterpart supervise the dismantling of a power station.

to accomplish this, the Level-of-Industry Plan of March 26, 1946, foresaw the dismantling of 1,636 factories. But in 1947, with the open outbreak of the East-West conflict, the Western zones became potential allies: a "Revised Industrial Plan" now sought a reduction to the 1936 industrial capacity, which still required the dismantling of 682 factories and inspired labor protests and demonstrations. The USSR attempted to prevent the establishment of a West German state and in 1948 halted its dismantling activities, which until then it had rigorously carried out. Instead, it sought an all-German solution, although its diversion of production from its zone ended only in 1952. On September 1, 1948, dismantling officially ended in the United States zone, and Washington pressed its allies to do the same in theirs. With the Petersberg Agreement of November 22, 1949, the Federal Republic of Germany's government effectively attained the end of dismantling, although it officially ended only with the Germany Treaty of May 26, 1952. In the West, approximately 8 percent of the economic potential of 1936 was lost.

Displaced Persons (DPs), in the parlance of the Allies, deportees—that is, people from German-occupied territories (especially in eastern Europe) who were forcibly removed to Germany for use as slave labor during the Second World War, as well as non-German refugees (totaling about 8.5 million) who fled westward before the Red Army. Most DPs were repatriated or resettled; a small number remained as stateless foreigners in the Federal Republic of Germany.

Dittmar, Kurt, b. Magdeburg, January 5, 1891; d. April 20, 1959, German lieutenant general (1941). An officer in the First World War, Dittmar became commander of the Berlin-Karlshorst Pioneer School in 1937. In 1941, because of illness from service at the front, he was transferred to Lappland, where he worked as a military and political expert for Radio Berlin under orders of the Army High Command. His relatively candid reporting on the situation made even euphemistic emendations of it seem credible, and was therefore permitted on tactical grounds.

Ditzen, Rudolf. *See* Fallada, Hans.

División Azul (Blue Division), Spanish volunteer corps in the RUSSIAN CAMPAIGN; it was named after the volunteers' blue FALANGE shirts.

Divisions (*Gliederungen*), subgroups of the NSDAP, as defined in Paragraph 4 of the Regulation of March 29, 1935, to Implement the Law to Secure the Unity of Party and State of December 1, 1933 (*Reich Law Gazette* I, p. 502). As against "affiliated associations" (*angeschlossene Verbände*), the divisions, as organizations of the NSDAP, had no legal personality of their own; rather, they were identical with the party in terms of civil and property law. The divisions included the SA, SS, National Socialist Motor Corps, Hitler Youth, National Socialist German Students' League, National Socialist German University Teachers' League, and National Socialist Women's Union.

Dix, Otto, b. Untermhaus bei Gera, December 2, 1891; d. Singen, July 25, 1969, German painter and graphic artist. An Expressionist, Dix was among the most important representatives of the "New Realism" (*Neue Sachlichkeit*). His aggressive, often grotesque depictions of the "nausea and horror" of war (as represented in his 1923–1924 series of etchings, "The War") unmasked the Berlin of the "Golden Twenties" as a nightmare of war cripples, prostitutes, and decadents. His bitter social criticism ("seditious, rabble-rousing, and inciting"), his realism ("merciless"), and his emphasis on what was ugly earned him the reputation among National Socialists as a particularly repulsive exponent of

Otto Dix.

DEGENERATE ART, for which he was relieved of his post as professor at the Dresden Academy of Art in 1933. By 1937, 260 of his paintings and etchings had been confiscated; some were burned and others sold abroad. After his years of prohibition from working, his late works reveal resignation in their emphasis on religious themes and landscapes.

Djakovo, National Socialist concentration camp in Croatia. It was built in May 1941, after the collapse of Yugoslavia, initially for Jews. Some 2,000 of them were murdered or died of starvation or disease there.

DNB. *See* German News Bureau.

DNSAP. *See* German National Socialist Workers' Party.

DNVP. *See* German National People's Party.

Döblin, Alfred, b. Stettin, August 10, 1878; d. Emmendingen (Breisgau), June 26, 1957, German author. Döblin came from a Jewish retailing family; he practiced medicine in Berlin until 1933. A member of the SPD (Social Democratic Party of Germany), together with other socialist authors and friends such as Bertolt Brecht, Döblin opposed nationalism and "Reaction" through his politics and writing. His major work, *Berlin Alexanderplatz* (1929), tells of the downfall of a part-time worker in a tire factory in the capitalist metropolis, using a technique of shifting perspective and narration unfamiliar at the time in the German novel. The National Socialists defamed it as "one of the worst products of Jewish ASPHALT literature." Döblin's books were banned and burned in 1933; he fled into exile. As an emigrant, he supported the Zionist "free land movement"; in his late work, psychoanalytic and religious themes predominate.

Doctors' Trial (*Ärzte-Prozess*), proceeding in Military Tribunal I of the United States in Nuremberg against former Reich Commissioner for Medicine and Health Karl BRANDT and others for crimes against humanity and membership in criminal organizations (Case 1). The defendants were 20 physicians from military and civilian agencies of the Third Reich, one private physician, and two nonmedical personnel. They were accused principally of responsibility for carrying out cruel and frequently fatal medical experiments on concentration camp prisoners and prisoners of war, as well as of participation in the EUTHANASIA program, to which tens of thousands of the mentally ill, persons with incurable illnesses, children with deformities, and others fell victim. The accusation against the private physician was limited to the charge that he had suggested methods of mass sterilization to Himmler.

A judgment of August 19, 1947, sentenced seven of the accused to death by hanging, five to life imprisonment, and four to prison terms of 10 to 20 years. Seven defendants were acquitted. The death sentences were ratified by the military governor and carried out. All other sentences were reduced through a pardon by United States High Commissioner John McCloy on January 31, 1951.

A. St.

Document Center (DC), archive in Berlin with surviving personnel records from the National Socialist period, under the authority of the United States Mission in Berlin. Shortly after the war, members of the United States Seventh Army discovered in a paper mill (and elsewhere) the nearly complete membership files of the NSDAP, which had been slated for destruction. The United States Third Army captured a large collection of records of the Race and Settlement Main Office (SS membership records and CERTIFICATES OF DESCENT of married and engaged SS members, as well as of their wives and fiancées); files from the party supreme court; 65,000 personnel files of SS leaders and Waffen-SS officers; about 80,500 Gestapo and police files; and 100,000 membership cards for the SA and other National Socialist organizations (such as the NSKK, NSFK, and Teachers' League). Over a

period of years, the records were reviewed, alphabetized, geographically arranged, and housed in Wasserkäfersteig, a former bunker in Berlin-Zehlendorf. These records have been central to denazification proceedings and the prosecution of NS crimes. For years, German and American authorities have negotiated regarding the transfer of these records to the Federal Republic of Germany.

A. St.

Dodd, William Edward, b. Wake County, near Clayton, N.C., October 21, 1869; d. Round Hill, Va., February 9, 1940, American historian and diplomat. From 1908 to 1933 Dodd was a professor at the University of Chicago. An opponent of isolationism, he was named ambassador to Berlin shortly after Franklin D. Roosevelt's inauguration in 1933. Despite Dodd's indignation over the harsh methods of the National Socialist police state, he had little influence in Berlin and was recalled in late 1937. Appearing in 1941, Dodd's notebooks reveal his mistaken appraisal of the Third Reich as a triumvirate, on the antique model, of Hitler, Göring, and Goebbels.

Dohnányi, Hans von, b. Vienna, January 1, 1902; d. Sachsenhausen concentration camp, April 8 or 9, 1945 (executed), German jurist and opposition fighter. Dohnányi joined the Reich Justice Ministry in 1929 and became personal counsel to Justice Minister Franz GÜRTNER in May 1933. After an unsuccessful legal struggle against the onset of concentration camp terror and National Socialist dismantling of the legal system, he

Hans von Dohnányi.

decided on active opposition. He built up a file of NS crimes, and made contact with the GOERDELER circle after the Röhm Affair (1934) and with the military opposition after the FRITSCH CRISIS (1938).

As a result of pressure from the NS justice official Roland FREISLER, Dohnányi was transferred to the Reich Court in Leipzig. Gen. Ludwig BECK then maneuvered him into the ABWEHR, where he directed the political desk under Hans Oster and set up a rich information collection. On April 5, 1943, he was arrested, along with Henning von TRESCKOW and Fabian von SCHLABRENDORFF, with whom he had organized an unsuccessful assassination attempt against Hitler. Dohnányi's Abwehr information, as well as material hinting at co-conspirators, fell into the hands of the Gestapo. (The currency manipulations of a Swiss contact had initially put investigators onto his trail.) Although the evidence was insufficient to try him, Dohnányi, like his brother-in-law Dietrich BONHOEFFER, died on the gallows after an improvised court-martial in the concentration camp.

Dohna-Schlobitten, Heinrich Count zu, b. Waldburg bei Königsberg (Prussia), October 15, 1882; d. Berlin, September 14, 1944 (executed), German officer. In the First World War, Dohna-Schlobitten was in the Operations Office of the General Staff; he was discharged in 1919 and returned to his family estates. An opponent of National Socialism, he was involved with the East Prussian Fraternal Council of the CONFESSING CHURCH, and was close to Carl Friedrich GOERDELER, whom he knew as onetime mayor of Königsberg. Dohna-Schlobitten was reactivated in the Second World War. He eventually held the rank of major general and was chief of the local army command in Danzig. His struggle against SS atrocities began as early as the Polish Campaign. After his discharge in 1943, he found his way into the inner circle of the assassination conspiracy of July 20, 1944, for which he paid with his life when the attempt failed.

Dolchstosslegende. *See* Stab-in-the-Back Legend.

Dollfuss, Engelbert, b. Texing (Lower Austria), October 4, 1892; d. Vienna, July 25, 1934, Austrian politician. Dollfuss was a reserve officer in the First World War. A jurist and national economist, in 1927 he became director of the Austrian Agricultural Chamber, and in 1931, minister of agriculture. Ambitious and short in stature (his nickname was "Millimetternich"),

Engelbert Dollfuss.

he became chancellor on May 20, 1932, with a hair-thin parliamentary majority. He led a coalition of Christian Socials, Home Block, and Country League members. Dollfuss instituted a program of economic reform with the help of the Lausanne loan of August 30, 1932, in return for which he again repudiated an ANSCHLUSS with Germany. To resist the Great-German movement for annexation, he also used autocratic methods (dissolving the National Council, March 4, 1933), cooperation with Fascist Italy (Riccione Treaty, August 20, 1933), and the Austrofascist program of the FATHERLAND FRONT, which he founded on September 11, 1933. After the banning of the Communist party (May 1933) and the National Socialists (June 1933)—following the bloody suppression of Social Democracy in the so-called February Putsch of 1934 and the declaration of the "Christian-German Federal State of Austria on a Corporatist Foundation" (*see* CORPORATIST STATE) in the May Constitution (May 1, 1934)—the Front supplanted parties and became the sole legal facilitator for forming the political will. The assault against workers' organizations, above all, cost Dollfuss possible allies in his struggle with the National Socialists, whose terror the reinstitution of the death penalty and the establishment of DETENTION CAMPS could not stop, and to which Dollfuss himself eventually succumbed. He was murdered by National Socialist putschists during the occupation of the Federal Chancellery.

Dominik, Hans, b. Zwickau, November 15, 1872; d. Berlin, December 9, 1945, German engineer and writer (initially) of technical books, then of reports from the colonies and nationalistic war novels. After 1922, Dominik's FUTURISTIC NOVELS made him one of the most popular contemporary authors. He anticipated the beginning of space travel (*Treibstoff SR* [Fuel Source SR]; 1940), atomic power, and laser weapons. His early novels dealt with global conflicts, as when German technicians save the world from the "yellow peril." After 1933, his chauvinism adapted well to the spirit of a new age, and his heroes used more realistic inventions for the good of the Fatherland. His celebration of the Führer Principle and his *völkisch* ideals prepared the way for fascism in mass literature. Although the National Socialists did not directly support Dominik, between 1940 and 1945 his books achieved their greatest circulation in FIELD POST editions. Through regular reprintings since 1945, his writings remain synonymous with futuristic fiction for the postwar generation.

Dönitz, Karl, b. Grünau bei Berlin, September 16, 1891; d. Aumühle bei Hamburg, December 24, 1980, German First Lord of the Admiralty (*Grossadmiral*; January 31, 1943). Dönitz joined the navy in 1910; during the First World War, in 1916, he joined the submarine corps. Following a period in an English prisoner-of-war camp for officers, he joined the Republican Navy (Reichsmarine). After numerous command and staff posts, he became "submarine leader" (*Führer der U-Boote*) on January 1, 1936, expanding the fleet in accordance with the terms of the GERMAN-BRITISH NAVAL AGREEMENT. Dönitz

Karl Dönitz.

was made commander of the U-boat fleet (*Befehlshaber der U-Boote*) on September 12, 1939. During the Second World War, he made up for the inadequate pace of the submarine-building program by his tactical skills. His pack assaults on Allied convoys broke for a time the British overseas supply routes (2,882 cargo ships equaling 14.5 million gross registered tons were sunk). In 1943, he succeeded Erich RAEDER as supreme naval commander (*Oberbefehlshaber der Kriegsmarine*), then shortly afterward broke off the Battle of the Atlantic (*see* NAVAL WAR) because of rising casualties.

Dönitz nonetheless supported the military oath of fealty to Hitler, and severely condemned the "dishonorable" officers who had planned the assassination attempt of July 20, 1944. Hitler thanked him in his political last will and testament by naming him his successor as Reich president, assuming that Dönitz would unflinchingly pursue the war. Dönitz's sole aim, however, was to use a partial capitulation in the West to save as many soldiers and refugees as possible from the Red Army. His "Executive Government" (Geschäftsführende Reichsregierung) in Flensburg (May 2–23, 1945), under Johann Ludwig SCHWERING VON KROSIGK, had only begun this attempt before it had to accept an UNCONDITIONAL SURRENDER. At the NUREMBERG TRIALS, Dönitz was sentenced to 10 years' imprisonment, which he spent at Spandau, for "crimes against peace."

Dopolavoro (from Ital. *dopo lavoro,* "after work"), shortened term for Opera Nazionale Dopolavoro (National Free Time Bureau; OND), a leisure organization in Fascist Italy, founded on May 1, 1925, the model for the German Labor Front bureau STRENGTH THROUGH JOY. Dopolavoro offered cultural, sports, and tourist programs, had at its disposal theaters (stage and screen), libraries, and vacation resorts, and thereby served the second part of the basic principle of mass appeal: bread and circuses. In 1939, over 5 million members were organized in 24,500 professional, workplace, and regional groups.

Dornier, Claude, b. Kempten (Allgäu), May 14, 1884; d. Zug (Switzerland), January 5, 1969, German airplane builder. In 1910 Dornier was employed in the Zeppelin factory in Friedrichshafen, where in 1914 he founded Dornier Metallbau GmbH (Dornier Metalworks, Ltd.), an aircraft factory. Dornier constructed all-metal machines, in particular, and in the 1920s was known for his flying boats, such as the

Do 18, Do "Whale," and Do X (1929), an enormous 12-engine airplane. A member of the NSDAP from 1940, during the Third Reich he was promoted to military-industrial leader (*Wehrwirtschaftsführer*). His factories supplied the Luftwaffe with such planes as the Do 17 bomber ("Flying Pencil") and the one-seat fighter plane Do 335 ("Anteater"), which with its tandem propulsion was the fastest propeller plane of the Second World War. Categorized as "exonerated" after the war, Dornier took up the aircraft business again in 1955, making rapid-acceleration machines.

Dorpmüller, Julius Heinrich, b. Elberfeld (now Wuppertal-Elberfeld), July 24, 1869; d. Malente, July 5, 1945, German transportation policymaker. Dorpmüller served with the railroad in Prussia from 1893 to 1908, then in China until 1917. In an adventurous journey, he fled China after it declared war on Germany, and returned home via Russia. In 1922 he became president of the national railroad office in Oppeln; he later served as longtime general director of the DEUTSCHE REICHSBAHN (1926–1937). Until the end of the war, Dorpmüller was transportation minister in Hitler's government, a position for which his activity since 1933 as

Claude Dornier.

head of the Reich AUTOBAHN project recommended him. Directly after the war, the western Allies proposed Dorpmüller as supervisor of the reconstruction of the German railroad system, a responsibility prevented by his death. Today it is considered certain that he must have been aware of the railroad's role in furthering the FINAL SOLUTION, since the RACE AND SETTLEMENT MAIN OFFICE demanded regular information on transport capacity from the Transportation Ministry.

Drancy, police internment camp established near Paris in 1941, used also as a prison and transit camp for Jews. The living conditions in Drancy were poor, provoking a hunger strike in October 1941. The majority of the French Jews deported to AUSCHWITZ were funneled through Drancy. In 1941 and 1942 a French commandant directed the camp, although under Theodor DANNECKER's supervision.

The first deportation from Drancy—about 1,000 Jews—took place in March 1942, although extensive deportations began only in July of that year. In conjunction with major police raids in the summer of 1942, between July 19 and September 30 some 22,000 Jews were deported to Auschwitz in trainloads of about 1,000 people each, three times a week. At the end of August 1942, the original age limit of 60 years for deportation was lifted, and henceforth sick Jews as well were deported. The last deportation of 1,000 adults and over 200 children took place on July 31, 1944.

Monumental sculpture from the first national exhibition of Dopolavoro.

W. D.

Drechsel, Max Ulrich Count von, b. Castle Karlstein, near Regensburg, October 3, 1911; d. Berlin-Plötzensee, September 4, 1944 (executed), German officer and jurist. After the Röhm Affair (June 30, 1934), Drechsel went into the Wehrmacht because he thought that "as a soldier [he could] better . . . distance [himself] from political events." Severely wounded in Africa in 1942, he then served in the Munich recruiting office, handling officers' applications. Inwardly, he had already long since abandoned his military oath when that year he again encountered Count Claus von STAUFFENBERG, his old friend from student days at Erlangen. Drechsel joined the effort to overthrow the government, and after the July 20, 1944, assassination attempt, was condemned to death as an "accomplice."

Drees, Willem, b. Amsterdam, July 5, 1886; d. The Hague, May 14, 1988, Dutch politician. In 1919 Drees joined the Social Democratic Party, serving as a deputy from 1933 to 1940. After the German occupation of the Netherlands, he was deported, but was freed in 1941. Thereafter he played a significant role in the resistance movement (he was chairman of the Central Committee) and in postwar reconstruction: from 1945 to 1948 he was social minister, and from 1948 to 1958 (with interruptions), prime minister and a fervent supporter of Western integration.

Dresden, German metropolis on the Elbe River; its population was 630,000 in 1940. Dresden had been spared in the war, but on February 13–14, 1945, British and American air forces attacked in three bombing waves. The city of arts, known as "Venice on the Elbe," was undefended, and at the time was jammed with Silesian refugees. According to official estimates, 35,000 people lost their lives. The actual losses were probably much higher, although there is no basis for the six-figure fatalities that were soon being reported. Even if the death rate did not reach those of Hiroshima and COVENTRY, Dresden has become a symbol of senseless terror from the sky, criticized harshly even from the Allied side.

Drexler, Anton, b. Munich, June 13, 1884; d. there, February 24, 1942, German politician; originally a locksmith. Discharged from the military during the First World War on health grounds, Drexler joined the Fatherland party and agitated among laborers. In March 1918 he founded the "Free Working Committee for a Good Peace," which was opposed to both capitalism and Marxism. This orientation again manifested itself in the "Political Working Circle" (Politischer Arbeitszirkel), which Drexler, along with the journalist Karl Harrer, founded in October 1918, and in the GERMAN WORKERS' PARTY, which they founded on January 5, 1919. Drexler presided over this group of about 40 members, more a group of beer-hall regulars than a political party, which however was invigorated by the appearance of Adolf Hitler in September 1919. Drexler had heard the former Reichswehr spokesman in a discussion meeting and, attracted by his oratorical powers, sent him a membership card.

Drexler became Hitler's political foster father; his 1919 tract *Mein politisches Erwachen* (My Political Awakening), with its Great-German ideas and plans for overcoming the class struggle, influenced MEIN KAMPF. The apprentice quickly outpaced Drexler tactically. Although Drexler played a significant role in the formulation of the program of what became the NATIONAL SOCIALIST GERMAN WORKERS' PARTY in February 1920, he was forced out of the party leadership in the summer of 1921. Elevated to honorary chairmanship of the NSDAP, Drexler had to sit by while his party became more and more an instrument of Hitler's will. Although he was implicated in the HITLER PUTSCH of November 1923, Drexler remained distant from the

Dresden after the British-American bombing raids.

Anton Drexler.

February 1925 refounding of the NSDAP. With the dissolution of his "National Socialist People's League" (Volksbund), founded in 1928, Drexler's political career came to an end.

DRK. *See* German Red Cross.

Drôle de guerre (Fr.; comic war), term used by French soldiers for the SITTING WAR (Eng., phony war).

Drückeberger (shirker), ironic 19th-century term, modeled on terminology for a city resident (such as *Heidelberger* for a resident of Heidelberg), for someone who avoids (*sich drücken*) work, responsibility, or military service. National Socialist propaganda used it to brand "those who refuse to produce" (*Leistungsverweigerer*), who were to be considered WORK-SHY.

Dualism (*Dualismus*; also *Zweiheitslehre*), philosophical model suggesting that reality is the tension between two opposing principles (such as good and evil, spirit and matter, sensuality and intellect). It was condemned by National Socialist ideology as causing "confusion" by its "overemphasis on opposition." National Socialism strove for total harmony (as in the abolition of social differences through the VOLK COMMUNITY) and adopted the notion of "dynamism," which suggested the active overcoming of all opposites, and which can be considered as the homely opposite to the despised "dialectic" of Hegel and Marx. NS ideology itself, meanwhile, presented a classic dualistic system: the "Aryan creator of culture" as a figure of light, in opposition to the "eternally culture-destroying Jew"; the "master" as opposed to the "subhuman."

Dual State (*Doppelstaat*), term coined by emigré jurist Ernst Fraenkel (1898–1975) to describe the two forms of political authority that characterized the National Socialist system. First, in order to ensure the proper functioning of the economic system, the "normative state" (*Normenstaat*) in most economic matters preserved a certain predictability of state behavior through the circumscribed application of norms, especially regarding civil, business, trade, and tax law. However, in areas regarding the state's authority and the combating of its political enemies, National Socialism recognized no normative restraint; rather, it conducted itself purely according to expediency. Fraenkel called this aspect of state behavior the "prerogative state" (*Massnahmenstaat*). The "Dual State," characterized by the coexistence of both types, applied particularly to the early phase of National Socialism, approximately up to 1938 (*see* BEHEMOTH).

A. v. B.

Duce (Ital., "leader"), Benito Mussolini's official title after 1922 as leader of the Fascist party. In 1938, his title was expanded to *Capo del governo e Duce del fascismo* (Head of the Government and Leader of Fascism), analogous to Hitler's title "FÜHRER UND REICHSKANZLER."

Duesterberg, Theodor, b. Darmstadt, October 19, 1875; d. Hameln, November 4, 1950, German officer. In 1900–1901 Duesterberg served in the East Asian Expeditionary Corps; he was a major at the front in the First World

Theodor Duesterberg.

War, held a post in the War Ministry, and was discharged as a lieutenant colonel. Deeply shocked by Germany's defeat, Duesterberg was a fervent opponent of the Weimar Republic, which he combated after 1924 as the second chairman of the STEEL HELMET league. This led to a tactical alliance with the NSDAP during the protest against the YOUNG PLAN in 1929 and in the HARZBURG FRONT (October 11, 1931), although Duesterberg rejected the party's revolutionary élan. His alienation grew as a result of National Socialist attacks on his "non-Aryan" origins on the occasion of the 1932 presidential election, which he entered without hope of victory as a candidate of the German Nationals (DNVP) and the Steel Helmet (the "Black-White-Red Combat Front"). His co-chairman Franz SELDTE cooperated with Hitler, and Alfred HUGENBERG ignored warnings about National Socialism. Imprisoned in Dachau after the Röhm Affair (June 30, 1934), Duesterberg later joined the opposition circle around Carl Friedrich GOERDELER, but he survived the persecutions after the failed assassination attempt of July 1944. He wrote *Der Stahlhelm und Hitler* (The Steel Helmet and Hitler; 1949).

Dühring, Eugen, b. Berlin, January 12, 1833; d. Nowawes bei Potsdam, September 21, 1921, German academic theorist. Dühring, who lost his sight while still young, was removed from his teaching position as a philosopher in 1877 because of his attacks on university policies. He was a man who made many enemies: his writings on political economy brought him into conflict most notably with Friedrich Engels, whose "Anti-Dühring" polemic attacked Dühring's "socializing" (*sozialitär*) harmony model of capital and labor. This anti-Marxist theory recommended Dühring to the National Socialists as an authority, as did his anticlericalism and his ANTISEMITISM, whose "founder" he considered to be himself (*Die Judenfrage* [The Jewish Question]; 1881). They also honored him as the herald of a "heroic view of life," as expressed in his book *Wert des Lebens* (Value of Life, 7th ed., 1916).

Dulles, Allen, b. Watertown, N.Y., April 7, 1893; d. Washington, D.C., January 29, 1969, American politician. In 1916 Dulles entered the diplomatic service; from 1922 to 1926 he was chief of the State Department's Near Eastern Division. Dulles served in various diplomatic posts. He played a central role as head of the Office of Strategic Services (OSS) bureau in Bern from

Allen Dulles.

1942 to 1945. One of the first Western politicians to learn details of the National Socialist FINAL SOLUTION, Dulles had contact with German opposition circles through Hans Bernd GISEVIUS, among others; he arranged the early capitulation of German forces in Italy (April 29, 1945) with SS-Obergruppenführer Karl WOLFF. After the war, Dulles became CIA chief in 1953, a post he had to leave in 1961 after the fiasco of the Bay of Pigs invasion of Cuba.

Dunkirk, French port city on the Channel coast. In the FRENCH CAMPAIGN, most of the British Expeditionary Force and remnants of France's Northern Army escaped to Great Britain from Dunkirk in late May and early June 1940.

Durchführung (carrying through; implementation), fashionable National Socialist word, referring both to the goal-oriented progression and to the successful completion of an enterprise. Thus, it was especially appropriate to describe perfect obedience to orders or the realization of a historic mission (carrying through an attack; carrying through the "German Revolution").

Duty Year (*Pflichtjahr*), compulsory-service plan for all young women under the age of 25, introduced on February 15, 1938, with the Regulation to Implement the FOUR-YEAR PLAN by the Increased Deployment of the Female Labor Force in the Rural and Household Economy. Exempt from the Duty Year were women who were already employed in a rural or domestic job or who were seeking such work. An

Duty Year. Labor deployment in agriculture.

attestation of the Duty Year in the EMPLOYMENT BOOK was a precondition for a later job. Service as part of the COUNTRY YEAR or with the REICH LABOR SERVICE counted for six months, and the HOME ECONOMICS YEAR gave a full exemption. Two years of the so-called Women's Aid Service (*Frauenhilfsdienst*) with the social service bureau of the GERMAN WOMEN'S AGENCY also counted as a Duty Year. In 1940, some 200,000 young women over the age of 18 participated in the program. The obligation could be met in the parental household or in that of a relative only if it contained at least four children under the age of 14. Approval was given through the Labor Offices. The Duty Year was an instrument for regulating the labor market (*see* LABOR DEPLOYMENT).

DVP. *See* German People's Party.

Dwinger, Edwin Erich, b. Kiel, April 23, 1898; d. Gmund am Tegernsee, December 17, 1981, German writer. A volunteer in 1915, Dwinger was held as a Russian prisoner of war and fought with the Whites against Bolshevism. He developed his war experiences into resentment-laden propaganda novels: *Armee hinter Stacheldraht* (*The Army behind Barbed Wire*; also translated as *Prisoner of War*; 1929) and *Wir rufen Deutschland* (We Call on Germany; 1932). In his often reprinted anti-Communist books, Dwinger presented the political leadership of the Weimar Republic as corrupt, the homeland as "usurers' booty," and the "front community"

as the model for a national community above class conflict. Praised by the National Socialists as "our . . . chronicler of the German Age," Dwinger advanced to Reich Culture Senator and SS-*Obersturmführer*, and was sent with the SS as a war correspondent to the USSR, as described in *Wiedersehen mit Sowjetrussland: Tagebuch vom Ostfeldzug* (translated as *Soviet Russia Revisited: Diary of the Eastern Campaign;* 1942). Even after 1945, Dwinger's chauvinistic and militaristic works—some of which, such as *General Wlassow: Eine Tragödie unserer Zeit* (Gen-

Edwin Erich Dwinger.

eral Vlasov: A Tragedy of Our Time; 1951), had a documentary basis—won a wide audience for their message of Soviet atrocities.

Dynamic (*Dynamik; Schwung*), in National Socialist usage, an ideological cliché for creative or idealistic energy or action (thus it was that National Socialism understood itself as a MOVE-MENT). To construct an irreconcilable ideological conflict, Alfred Rosenberg characterized the "feeling for life of the Nordic peoples" as "dynamic-Western," while denigrating the essence of the "Judeo-Christian sense of life" as "static."

E

Eagle. *See* Adler-.

Eastern Aid (Osthilfe), support program for eastern German agriculture (especially a debt conversion plan) enacted through the Eastern Aid Law of March 31, 1931. The program encompassed 33,619 farms with a total of 2.2 million hectares (about 5.5 million acres), but mainly benefited large estates. Funding came primarily (80 percent) from a newly founded industrial bank, whose capital was refinanced by an assessment on industry, but also from the Reich budget (8 percent) and from agriculture itself (12 percent), through land sales from farms undergoing debt conversion. The various measures brought an aggregate of 600 million RM, which improved the situation somewhat but did not eliminate the structural causes of agricultural indebtedness. The proposed resettlement of properties that could not be paid off became a hotly contested political issue and contributed to the fall of the BRÜNING and PAPEN governments. The National Socialists continued and expanded the debt reduction policies in the

Fund-raising event for Eastern Aid in Silesia (1931); Chancellor Brüning is second from right.

Law to Regulate Agricultural Debt Conditions of June 1, 1933.

R. S.

Eastern March. *See* Ostmark.

Eastern Territories (*Ostgebiete*), designation after 1945 for the territories of the German Reich as of December 31, 1937 (thus, without the Sudetenland), that lay east of the ODER-NEISSE LINE, 114,296 sq km (about 45,600 sq miles), with 9.62 million inhabitants in 1939. On the basis of the Potsdam Agreement of August 2, 1945, the Eastern Territories were temporarily (that is, until a definitive settlement of Germany's eastern border through a peace treaty) placed under Polish and Soviet administration. EXPULSION replaced the intended "humane" population transfer of Germans in the Eastern Territories. Violations of the agreement also took place as the areas under Soviet administration (on October 17, 1945) and those under Polish administration (on January 12, 1949) were incorporated into these states.

Eastern workers (*Ostarbeiter*), the worst-treated category of ALIEN WORKERS.

Ebensee, satellite camp of the MAUTHAUSEN concentration camp; in March and April 1945 it was a collection camp for evacuation transports from the camps in the east. Numerous inmates perished on these marches; in Ebensee, 182 of 2,000 Jews from Gross-Rosen died on March 3, 1945, alone.

Eberl, Irmfried, b. Bregenz (Austria), September 8, 1910; d. Ulm, February 6, 1948, SS-*Untersturmführer* (1942). Eberl joined the NSDAP on December 8, 1931, as a medical student, and was an assistant physician after February 1935. At the age of 29, on February 1, 1940, he became director of the BRANDENBURG "killing facility." In the fall of 1941 he took over the BERNBURG "euthanasia facility." Shortly thereafter he became commandant of the TREBLINKA extermination camp, part of the REINHARD OPERATION. In August or September 1942 Eberl was replaced for "incompetence," for causing indescribable conditions in the camp. The SS leadership, which valued the perfect deception of the victims, criticized him for ordering gassings before the corpses of the prior group had been removed. After the war, Eberl committed suicide while in investigative detention.

A. St.

Ebert, Friedrich, b. Heidelberg, February 4, 1871; d. Berlin, February 28, 1925, German politician. A trained saddler, Ebert became editor of the *Bremer Bürger-Zeitung* (Bremen Citizens' News) in 1893, and a member of the city council in 1900. In 1905 he became secretary of the SPD (Social Democratic Party of Germany) executive committee in Berlin. After 1912 Ebert was a Reichstag deputy. At the Jena SPD convention in 1913, he was chosen party chairman, succeeding August Bebel. Ebert was a pragmatic politician, averse to ideological disputes. In January 1918 he unsuccessfully tried to ward off a strike of munitions workers; he then led the strike, in order to turn it in a lawful direction.

As an opponent of revolutionary upheavals and chairman of the strongest German party, Ebert seemed to be the only suitable head of government for liquidating the empire and starting postwar reconstruction. Therefore Chancellor Max von Baden handed over the affairs of state to him on November 9, 1918. Elected chairman of the Council of People's Deputies on November 10, Ebert attempted to move beyond the revolu-

tionary postwar phase, and did not shun alliances with the former elites, especially the military. The Weimar National Assembly elected him the Republic's president on February 11, 1919. Ebert became the target of sharp attacks by the nationalist Right. Because of his participation in the January 1918 strike, an editor initiated a lawsuit against him; a Magdeburg court found him guilty in the legal sense of high treason on December 23, 1924. Nevertheless, his natural authority and personal integrity made Ebert an important mainstay of the young Republic.

Eckart, Dietrich, b. Neumarkt, March 23, 1868; d. Berchtesgaden, December 26, 1923, German writer. After interrupted medical studies, Eckart worked as a journalist and as an (unsuccessful) playwright and writer. From 1918 to 1920, he edited the nationalist weekly *Auf gut deutsch* (In Plain German), which combined anti-Republican pamphlets with primitive anti-Bolshevik and antisemitic propaganda. He used his connections with antisemitic and pan-German circles (*see* ALL-GERMAN ASSOCIATION) in Munich to establish Hitler, whom he came to know during this time, as the national "Messiah." Hitler valued Eckart's services on behalf of National Socialism so highly that he later dedicated MEIN KAMPF to him.

Eckart was not only Hitler's personal teacher and promoter, but also the intellectual inspirer of the building phase of the NSDAP. He procured the money to acquire the VÖLKISCHER BEOBACHTER, and became its first chief editor in 1921. The fighting slogan of National Socialism, "Germany Awaken" ("Deutschland erwache"),

Friedrich Ebert.

Dietrich Eckart.

was derived from one of Eckart's poems. Arrested in connection with the HITLER PUTSCH in November 1923, Eckart died shortly after his release.

Economic-Administrative Main Office (Wirtschafts-Verwaltungshauptamt; WVHA), department in the SS command. The administrative affairs of the SS were originally handled by an administrative office subordinate to the SS Main Office, which in its core dated back to the year 1929. Chief of this office after February 1, 1934, was Oswald POHL. The extension of administrative responsibility over the armed SS units as well led to Pohl's appointment on June 1, 1935, as Administrative Chief of the SS on the personal staff of the REICHSFÜHRER-SS (RFSS), while retaining his previous offices. He thus reported immediately to Himmler and was also chief of the administrative offices of the RACE AND SETTLEMENT MAIN OFFICE (RuSHA) and of the Security Service (SD) Main Office. At the same time, as Reich Treasurer of the SS, he handled budgetary affairs with the NSDAP's Reich treasurer.

On April 20, 1939, the Office of Administrative Chief was upgraded to the Main Office for Administration and Economy, which now broadly assumed the tasks of the Administrative Office in the SS Main Office as well. Since the new Main Office administered not only budget expenditures of the party but also government financial resources of the Reich Interior Ministry (for the armed SS units), with regard to the latter it signed off as the Main Office for Budget and [Public] Works. On February 1, 1942, both Main Offices were merged with the still-existing Administrative Office into the Economic-Administrative Main Office, with Pohl again as its chief.

The mammoth new office, which at times had as many as 1,500 personnel, was divided into five Office Groups (Amtsgruppen). The Troop Administrative Office (Amtsgruppe A) was responsible for the treasury, payroll, finance, and auditing systems, as well as for drawing up the SS budget; Amtsgruppe B (Troop Economy) managed the food, clothing, lodging, and procurement systems. In these groups the growing demands of the Waffen-SS predominated. The other three offices, however, reflected the wide-ranging economic ambitions of the SS. Amtsgruppe C (Construction) not only was responsible for the construction of work sites and living quarters, barracks and camps, but was also involved in special programs, such as the manufacture of the "V" weapons and the installation of underground plants for munitions industries.

The incorporation of the Inspectorate of the CONCENTRATION CAMPS into the WVHA (as Amtsgruppe D) on March 3, 1942, was a response to the constantly increasing importance of the camps as an economic factor. It also enabled the SS to organize the labor resources of its prisoners under its own direction, for example, avoiding the "General Plenipotentiary for Labor Deployment," newly named by Hitler. In close connection with the growing labor pool in the concentration camps came the rise of the SS ECONOMIC ENTERPRISES, whose administration was subordinate to Amtsgruppe W (Economic Enterprises) of the WVHA. This singular coupling of private economic and official functions clearly justified the special status of this Amtsgruppe within the WVHA: it had neither its own budget nor its own permanent office. Its command personnel were normally recruited from among the boards of directors of SS-owned businesses, from whence its revenue also came.

We.

The Economy under National Socialism

The economy—along with party, bureaucracy, and military—ranked among the pillars of National Socialist (NS) rule. Its history can be divided into three phases:

1. 1933–1935/1936: At the beginning of this phase the economy was under the influencé of the WORLD ECONOMIC CRISIS. From the outset, rearmament played a substantial role in its overcoming. The specific switchover occurred in 1933–1934, and on two levels: first, munitions expenditures rose in 1934 to 4.2 billion RM (*see* REARMAMENT); moreover, structural changes were undertaken in production, in order to accommodate the expected increase in demand for armaments. From 1933 to 1934, armaments production occupied the public's attention less than WORK CREATION measures. Particularly effective in terms of public relations were the

Election poster from the "Time of Struggle" of the NSDAP: "Workers. Elect the frontline soldier Hitler!"

construction of the Reich AUTOBAHN and MAR-RIAGE LOANS. Financing for arms as well as for jobs was accomplished mainly through creating money and credit by means of MEFO BILLS.

In FOREIGN TRADE as well, noticeable changes were effected on the basis of the NEW PLAN of September 1934 under Hjalmar SCHACHT, Reich Bank president and Reich economics minister. Although the beginnings of a new orientation in this sector dated back to the PRESIDIAL CABINETS, only the complete regulation of foreign trade (including currency management) and the bilateralization of foreign-trade relations achieved a shift of foreign trade from the Atlantic to the (southeastern) European area, which was intended to favor German plans for territorial expansion.

The economy was reorganized. In all sectors (industry, handicrafts, trade, agriculture), businesses became hierarchically (in line with the FÜHRER PRINCIPLE) structured organizations on both horizontal and vertical levels. In the new "Reich Estate of German Industry" (Reichsstand der deutschen Industrie) the large concerns set the tone. In addition, they profited from the advancing process of concentration in the economy, driven in part by forced combination into cartels and obligatory associations.

Repeated attempts have been made to gain an understanding of the relationship between industry and the NS leadership. The range of

attempted explanations is large—even within the set of theories on fascism. They extend from the hypothesis of certain functional and structural (operational) connections between politics and economics (with a concomitant expansion of governmental activity) to the hypothesis of an identity of interests between "monopoly capital" and fascist leadership. In contrast with theories of fascism, in theories of totalitarianism the coercive character of SYNCHRONIZATION and the political powerlessness of the economy are emphasized more.

The NS leadership did not possess a unified concept of the economy. It did, however, adhere to some guidelines: preservation of private ownership of means of production (with an exception, ARYANIZATION), with concomitant exclusion of free worker representation in businesses on the one hand, and orientation of the economy toward armaments and AUTARKY in view of the expansionist foreign (trade) policy on the other. Leading businessmen in general agreed with these basic elements of NS economic policy, which did not rule out conflicts in particular cases.

2. 1935/1936–1938/1939: This phase falls completely under the rubric of the FOUR-YEAR PLAN of 1936 and the related sharp increase (compared with the previous phase) in efforts toward armaments and autarky. Ever greater sections of the national economy became directly and indirectly involved in the armaments-and-autarky merry-go-round; in this connection note should be made of the "battle for agricultural production," the development of substitute raw materials, and the economically irrational exploitation and smelting of German iron ore reserves. The advantage of plan quotas and objectives, as well as the elaboration of "cost standards," provided the framework within which the munitions industry (in part, highly subsidized) did extremely profitable business, so that the greater part of investments could be financed by private capital. This system led in various sectors to considerable performance increases, though quotas could not be achieved (sometimes by a wide margin).

Although dependence upon foreign suppliers was lessened (relative autarky), the raw materials problem—leaving aside raw materials management—was still the regime's economic Achilles heel. Even the Military-Economic New Production Plan of 1938, which concentrated on somewhat fewer products, remained an unfinished work in this perspective. Moreover, the relative gains of the Four-Year Plan were

Aryanization. Advertisement from a North German daily newspaper: "Business takeover. The major linens firm Nebel & Sander, Wagnerstrasse 2, has been purchased by me. Thus this business, under my personal management, is now in Aryan hands. I request your confidence. Joachim Hagenow, formerly Nebel & Sander."

bought dearly, and economic problems came to light on several levels. For example, the first major currency crisis flared up in 1935–1936. A currency shortage resulted from the increased demand, caused by rearmament, for currencies to cover certain imports of raw materials, which demand could not be offset either by lowering imports of foodstuffs or by raising export profits.

Toward the end of this phase, problems also became manifest in the labor market. UNEMPLOYMENT was converted into a labor shortage by the domestic rearmament boom. Despite various attempts by the German Labor Front (DAF) to regulate the expansion of the labor pool, agriculture and the (consumer and) export goods industries were the first to suffer from lack of labor resources, while the munitions industry could attract an abundant labor supply by means of material incentives (despite a wage freeze). (*See* WAGE-PRICE POLICY).

The shift of laborers over to the munitions industries was a sign of the increasing disparity among the economic sectors. From 1936 on, as a result of government management of investments (as in the prohibition of investing in the consumer-goods industries), about half of all industrial plant investment was made just in the area of those munitions-related branches of the economy that were controlled by the Four-Year Plan. The curtailments in the consumer-goods industries had the result that, despite massive influence over consumers and control over demand, the slowly growing buying power of the people could be satisfied ever less with an adequate supply of merchandise. Taken as a whole, this phase was characterized by a covert austerity policy. The economy, finally, produced less "butter and guns"—as Göring once supposed—than it did "guns and artificial honey";

it built in the first place not homes, but bunkers and fortifications (such as the WESTWALL).

The problems of controlling the economy also grew visibly: offices sprouted like mushrooms out of the ground (agencies of the Four-Year Plan), and in turn were confronted with the system of special commissioners. On the one hand, a partial flexibility was achieved through the fulfillment of specific economic tasks; on the other, quarrels over jurisdiction often made for an unwieldy economic organization. In the literature, the term "polycracy" (*Polykratie*) has come to be used for this jurisdictional "undergrowth," and in particular for a phenomenon, typical of the system, of interests growing wild simultaneously with a straying from the principles of rational (in the Max Weber sense) rule in

"Will they be able to steer a steady course without me?" Caricature from the Swiss *Nebelspalter* on the removal of Finance Minister Schacht from power (March 1939).

the hands of a functioning bureaucracy. A further crisis area was that of state finances. In 1938–1939, gold and currency reserves were largely exhausted. The state's debt had tripled in the few years since 1933. The Mefo Bills, most recently issued with the backing of raw materials and markets still to be conquered, were pressing for "redemption."

It is debatable whether the above-named phenomena of economic crisis can be characterized as "only" limited crises, or whether the assertion is justified that in 1938–1939 the individual crises had condensed into a potent crisis syndrome, which helps explain the timing (not the reasons) for the outbreak of war as a "flight forward." If one grants the latter hypothesis, one must still reconsider the widespread opinion that the National Socialists had overcome the economic crisis in 1933–1934: in that case, the rearmament would have "overcome" the "old" economic crisis, but simultaneously would have planted the seed for a new one, which because of its different character (no unemployment) and because of the general lack of information re-

sources did not enter public awareness, or did so at most only to a small extent. An economics expert such as Schacht, who in the early years had himself communicated the new policy to responsible parties, did indeed clearly foresee the crisis danger since 1935–1936; to no avail, he and others suggested a slower rate of rearmament as well as strengthened efforts for a greater integration of the German economy in the world market. His replacement (by Walther FUNK) as Reich economics minister and Reich Bank president must be seen in this context.

3. **1938/1939–1945:** The economic problems that had increased before the outbreak of the war were at first lessened by the victorious "Blitzkriegs" and the ensuing economic exploitation of the vanquished countries. This was carried out in varying intensity and in varying forms, from state-managed plundering (eastern Europe) to the superficially "voluntary" mergers and acquisitions of companies (northern and western Europe). The task of carrying it all out lay with the large German concerns. Even the instituted trustee system (as in Poland) was put

Hitler addressing the workers at a Berlin armaments factory in 1940.

under the direction of these firms. Moreover, the economic organizations and large businesses developed their own New Order programs for the conquered and yet-to-be-conquered major economic areas, all of which fell into the category of unilateral exploitation.

The victorious campaigns had the further result that the structure of production went through little change in the early war years. A turnaround did not occur until the defeats in Russia. In the SPEER era the course was set for a total WAR ECONOMY, although it was not always consistently implemented. Changes in economic administration had already been undertaken under Fritz TODT to aid in the development of central economic planning. Under Speer a vigorous switch was made to standardized mass production of war materials; until then the production of crucial material had been more commonly done in smaller series with multipurpose machine tools. The introduction of assembly-line production provided the technical production requirements for expanded use of foreign and forced laborers, as well as of concentration camp inmates.

The increased bombardment of German cities indeed slowed productive output (for example, industrial relocations became necessary), but the actual destruction never reached the level that was conjectured immediately after the war's end. However, from 1943–1944, difficulties grew in supplying the population with economic goods, particularly after the country could no longer live at the expense of subjugated nations. In addition, by the end of the war the reichsmark currency was totally ruined. To be sure, the enduring long-term control of inflation had been able to conceal well this consequence of NS economic and financial policy until the very end.

Having itself grown out of a great economic crisis, the NS economy necessarily collapsed like a house of cards after its sole "long-term trump card," the exploitation of foreign countries and peoples, could no longer be played. Precisely the history of the NS economy can show how closely the dates January 30, 1933, September 1, 1939, and May 8, 1945, belong together.

Adelheid von Saldern

Edelweiss Pirates (*Edelweisspiraten*), opposition groups of young workers, apprentices, and pupils who came together, particularly in the Rhineland, without firm organizational structure or unitary ideology; their common mark of recognition was an edelweiss on or under their left lapel, or a pin the color of the flower. The National Socialists persecuted these youth groups as "juvenile cliques." After 1933 oppositional young people gathered, especially in cities, in "wild juvenile groups." They continued to foster illegally the structures and ideas of Christian, socialist, and federative branches of the YOUTH MOVEMENT, or they stressed only superficial nonconformity (long hair, listening to "un-German" swing music), and sometimes consciously distanced themselves from the military drill and intolerance of the Hitler Youth (HJ). Thus in-groups such as the Dresden "Mobs," the Hamburg "Death's-Head Gang" (*Totenkopfbande*), or the "Edelweiss Pirates" were formed.

Such groups initially wanted only to hike and camp without supervision; then spontaneously they began articulating political resistance, scuffled with the HJ, and distributed leaflets. Some

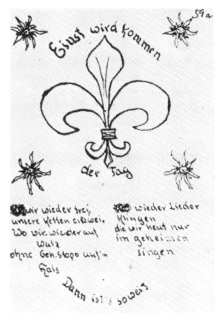

Pamphlet of an Edelweiss group in Wuppertal, "The Day Will Come": "We'll again be free, / Our chains will break. / We'll again walk about / without the Gestapo on our neck. / Songs will sound again / That we now sing only / in secret; / Then we'll be there."

Edelweiss Pirates are publicly hanged in Cologne.

Pirates committed illegal acts, such as sabotage in the armaments industry or assassination attempts against SA leaders. The number of young people who evaded HJ conscription was finally so large that "Regulations to Fight Juvenile Cliques" were issued in 1944. Acts that mainly expressed juvenile protest and generational conflict were criminalized by the Gestapo, who arrested 13 of the Pirates in late 1944 and had them hanged without judicial proceedings. After the war their families fought for a long time to have them recognized as opposition fighters. But as late as 1978, the president of the Cologne administrative district (*Regierungspräsident*) called them "state criminals" and refused to honor them. Meanwhile, a bronze memorial tablet on the corner of Schönsteinstrasse and Venloer Strasse in Cologne commemorates the gallows where, among others, 16-year-old Edelweiss Pirate Bartholomäus Schink died. A street has been named for him.

H. H.

Eden, Robert Anthony, Earl of Avon (after 1961), b. Windlestone Hall, June 12, 1897; d. near Salisbury (Wiltshire), January 14, 1977, British politician. In 1923 Eden became a Conservative Member of Parliament. He held various posts in the Foreign Office and in 1935 became secretary for League of Nations affairs. As foreign secretary in Neville CHAMBERLAIN's government (1935–1938), Eden decisively influenced Britain's APPEASEMENT policy. In Churchill's cabinet he served first as secretary of war (1940), then as foreign secretary (1940–1945). In 1942 Eden negotiated a 20-year Mutual Assistance Pact with the USSR. He participated in the conference establishing the United Nations in 1945. After the war, Eden, who was foreign secretary from 1951 to 1955 and prime minister from 1955 to 1957, advocated close cooperation among European countries. The fiasco of British and French intervention in the Suez crisis in 1956 ended his political career.

Robert Anthony Eden.

Edinita, National Socialist concentration camp in Bessarabia, established immediately after the German invasion of the Soviet Union. Primarily Romanian Jews were deported to Edinita, many of whom died en route. Of the 12,000 persons admitted, 70 to 100 died daily in the camp itself, from exhaustion or mistreatment. In September 1941 the Edinita camp was dissolved, and the few survivors were put in ghettos in Transnistria.

Editor, in National Socialist parlance, *Schriftleiter* (literally, leader or director of writing), a Germanization of the "foreign" *Redakteur*; thus, *Hauptschriftleiter* for *Chefredakteur* (editor in chief). To be employed as a *Schriftleiter* one had to fulfill the conditions of the EDITOR LAW. The word *Schriftleiter* first appeared in the late 19th century and seems to have Austrian origins; it appeared in the 1920 NSDAP Program.

Editor Law (*Schriftleitergesetz*), law of October 4, 1933, to achieve Synchronization of the German PRESS; it declared "collaboration in shaping the thought content of newspapers and political periodicals published within Reich territory by word, news, and pictures" to be a "public function regulated by law." To be a *Schriftleiter* (EDITOR), one had to be of "Aryan" ancestry and "not married to a person of non-Aryan ancestry"; one also had to possess "Reich citizenship" and "the capacity to assume public office," as well as all the "qualities . . . that the function of influencing public opinion requires." The law as applied made the journalist in the Third Reich "primarily a servant of the *Volk* Community and only secondarily an employee of a private publisher." The Editor Law also brought editors together in the Reich Association of the German Press (with over 20,000 members), which as a public and legal corporation belonged to the REICH PRESS CHAMBER.

Education

Under National Socialism the education (*Erziehung*) of youth was largely superseded by re-education (*Umerziehung*). In 1934 Hitler assigned his party the task of educating the German *Volk* "in the spirit of the National Socialist idea." For this purpose a new ritualization of public life was organized beyond existing educationally effective measures: the Hitler greeting, marching columns, the cult of banners, festivities, and mass meetings. Camps with a military structure emphasized training to discipline the body, to become accustomed to subordination, to revere symbols of political authority. This effort to influence conduct and value systems was not widely perceived as re-education because the consciousness of youth was directed (by propaganda) toward antidemocratic national and political values that were felt to be modern, and toward the myth of "BLOOD."

National resentment over the results of the First World War was intended to extinguish socioeconomic and sociocultural interest in political issues. Thereby educationally relevant needs could at times be set aside—for example, self-determination regarding one's body, the establishment of an interrelationship between personal development and society's demands, and, moreover, the decision as to what would give meaning to one's own life. Priority was given to the supreme significance of the development of political hegemony over other nations. Yet this was not justified by any plans to transform domestic power relationships. Thus re-education was effective only as compensation for the irrationality of a society that could not yet master its *de facto* modernization.

Because re-education took place in "camps," during free time, and outside the regular school world of curriculum and subject matter, it could more easily pass for an education that developed personal values (in the form of secondary virtues) without having any immediate goal. These camps offered an opportunity to "prove one's worth" through "youth leading itself"—to be sure, all prestructured. For this reason distinctions were made between service and work, schooling and instruction, leading (*Führung*) and pedagogic guidance or "steering" (*Lenkung*). Thus, despite the rigid organization of what Alfred BAEUMLER called "formation education" (*Formationserziehung*), one could have the sense of developing one's own initiative as a "Führer," in a kind of free space where one was absolved of the need to secure one's existence. This "formation education" (a significantly more precise expression than "community education" [*Gemeinschaftserziehung*]) depended, on the one hand, on the education by habituation that produced military obedience, and that does not concern itself with personal motivation or opinions. Yet it also utilized the susceptibility of youth to emotional thinking, moral rigor, joy in physical activity, and a life amid nature in the company of peers, as had earlier been cultivated by the middle-class youth movement in Germany.

Thus the illusion was sustained that for modern society, rationality and self-control, theoretical rigorousness and professional authority, the division of labor and industrial production, were of lesser significance. This "revaluation of all values" (Baeumler) had to lead to the loss of authority on the part of traditional educational institutions. Yet to allow only re-education to dominate in the education of youth would have endangered the existence of the complex society. The history of education under National Socialist (NS) rule should thus be described as the suspenseful struggle of a totalitarian movement that advocated re-education (exemplified by the Hitler Youth [HJ] and the German Labor Front; at times also by the NS Teachers' League and the school bureaucracy) with the at least equally strong tendencies to secure the continu-

ation of a complex society and, from a political perspective, to secure the loyalty of adults threatened by the loss of authority.

In a first phase (1933–1936), new institutions (HJ as an autonomous organization of youth for the state, camps, competitive games) were established alongside the traditional educational institutions. In the second phase (1936–1940), they became rivals. After 1940 the exceptional situation of the war in general undermined the old institutions; for example, the period of instruction was curtailed, parental influence was excluded as education moved to boarding schools and camps, and church influence was obstructed. It also led to the draining of personal motivation from political engagement, as through introduction of the Youth Service Duty and the limitation of personal perspectives to the attainment of the "Final Victory." Re-education led either to a fanaticism that was blind to reality or to a selfish will to survive.

What National Socialism meant by education can be seen in the changing functions of re-education. (Only a few spokesmen, such as Baeumler, referred to this in a consciously pragmatic way by deriving the concept of "fate"

"Hail to our Führer." School celebration for Hitler's birthday.

from the situation.) The influence of politics on education can be understood as a succession of phases: the contrasting of educational influences, the attempt at a synthesis, and the use of education as an instrument of imperialistic war. The first phase set up contrasts between "leadership" on command (*"Führen" auf Kommando*) and pedagogic influence, between "schools" and "instruction." Youths who responded to discipline, HARDNESS, and personal bonds with exemplary leaders could feel they belonged to the avant-garde. For a time, schools could also be involved in the political incorporation of students who did not belong to the HJ (State Youth Congress [*Staatsjugendtag*] of 1934 to 1936). Young people who were already employed were solicited through the REICH VOCATIONAL COMPETITION, begun in 1934, which gave them hope of greater social mobility.

In the second phase, the attempt was made to integrate political criteria into the process of educating youth through emphasizing "SELECTION" (*Auslese*), a concept involving the whole person in his or her social situation. The great need for functionaries, and the willingness of young people to contribute to the enhancement of the regime's power by working at unpaid or poorly paid posts, heightened the importance of selection in re-education. The new institutions could now compete with traditional institutions in gaining influence over youth. Apart from political socialization, they were able to awaken the need to develop skills that complemented the precepts of school education, for example, through "special units" in the HJ and "work communities" in the League of German Girls' (BDM) FAITH AND BEAUTY unit. The utilization of the educational sector for war and the total control of leisure activity for youth were tested.

The war released the system from the need to fulfill the expectations of social advancement raised through its idea of selection. The privilege of expanded training was offered to broader social strata (TEACHER TRAINING INSTITUTES, German Home Schools, Preparatory Schools for Noncommissioned Officers), but the period for "youth" was soon shortened. Middle school and high school students aged 15 and 16 served as FLAK HELPERS after 1943. The new boarding schools, the CHILDREN'S COUNTRY EVACUATION camps, the DUTY YEAR for girls, as well as the REICH LABOR SERVICE and the COUNTRY YEAR, were utilized to stress the Reich's presence in the occupied territories. Political demands on education were gradually reduced to an assurance of the demanded readiness to serve.

On the level of interaction, education was increasingly uncoupled from traditional institutions by legitimizing personal authority. "Self-leadership" (*Selbstführung*) in the HJ was based on the utilization and testing of leadership functions. Constant "transfers" of lower-level leaders made a continuous bond between a leader and his following possible only for the highest representatives of the regime. Fixation of consciousness on symbols (slogans as well as the visual representation of power in a ritualized public life) amounted to personal identification with the "Will of the Führer" in order to justify personal behavior. Only in this manner could an individual escape the experience of conflicting authorities.

If a sense of personal worth ("honor") was supposed to be developed only within a politically defined collectivity, it had to rely on these symbols of solidarity. "Community education" was to serve the ritualization of conforming behavior in order to achieve easily supervised virtues: cleanliness, discipline, comradeship, faithfulness, severity toward oneself, readiness to serve, but in no way the cultivation of relations with one's fellow humans.

In itself the system of re-education could not motivate anyone to accomplish the higher-level achievements essential to a complex society. Thus it had to fall back on the idea of self-realization, despite its inherent tendencies to eliminate personal motives and decisions. "Selection" could not be oriented only toward an attained conformism. It had to try to exploit aggressive impulses born out of frustrations, just as the prior development of potential for accomplishment in the education process was furthered in home and school. Yet a secure social position would have to be held out as an ostensible aim of selection, and would have necessitated the limitation of the regime's jurisdiction over the individual. Therefore educational institutions for the top positions (*see* ORDER FORTRESSES; UPPER SCHOOL OF THE NSDAP) remained more propaganda than reality.

The exercise of power over youth by the REICH YOUTH LEADERSHIP through programmed instruction and numerous rules was neither theoretically supervised nor based on a common conception of educational policy (as can be seen from the many "agreements" on individual problems). This made it possible to utilize the striving for prestige among young people interested in social mobility for the development of hectic activity. (This was less possible among those from the wealthy and proletarian strata.) At the same time, "leisure" as a precondition for the development of higher achievements was endangered. Consciousness of one's mission and readiness to serve were essential for an aggressive conduct of war. A rational attitude toward eventual failure had not been programmed.

SOCIAL DARWINISM turned out to be an unsuitable prescription for surviving defeat. Retreat into an unpolitical "inwardness" had been partly prepared by politically submissive teachers. Baeumler, the pragmatist of power, encouraged this tendency by assigning to the schools the task of concentrating on "formal education" (*formale Bildung*). But the school tried to ward off its loss of authority by producing politically conformist ideology. The latter, however, was subject to rapid wear and tear—as in a whispered joke that a "Rust" (Bernhard RUST was the Reich minister in charge of schools from 1934 to 1945) was the unit of time between a decree and its cancellation. This joke was indicative of the ministry's fruitless efforts to counteract the use of the schools as an instrument of pragmatic political power. Still, it was possible to secure the limited political loyalty of a public that was primarily concerned with school structure, despite the introduction of nondenominational community schools, the elimination of private schools, and the questionable viability of the middle school (*Mittelschule*) when threatened by the establishment of a "main school" (HAUPT-SCHULE) alongside the elementary school (*Volksschule*), and despite the drastic curtailment of religious instruction.

The possibility of downplaying problems of school structure that earlier had been hotly debated was fully exploited now that political interest could be deflected to foreign policy. Since re-education influenced primarily young teachers, and since until the war the teaching profession was largely in the hands of men, during the war education in the schools could mostly return again to its orientation toward proficiency: in Children's Country Evacuation camps, under the guidance of older teachers, reformist pedagogical goals were revived. NS re-education primarily depended on shifts of emphasis in the field of education. It thus had no tradition-building power for educating young people after the collapse of the system.

Harald Scholtz

Egalitarian bungling (*Gleichmacherei*), polemical National Socialist slogan against the demand for equality of all people as raised by the French Revolution. According to NS notions, such leveling subverted all "*völkisch* and racial order," as BOLSHEVISM recently had clearly demonstrated. Such egalitarianism contradicted the "aristocratic principle of selection in nature," and the "internationalism" derived from it undermined the "blood-bound" COMMUNITY. The reasonable hierarchy of a community could only succeed when the diverse values of individuals were recognized and thus the right place could be found for everyone. National Socialism was thought to have overcome egalitarianism with the FÜHRER PRINCIPLE.

Eggers, Kurt, b. Berlin, November 10, 1905; d. Bielograd, August 12, 1943, German writer and cultural policymaker. A free corps fighter, Eggers participated in the Kapp Putsch in 1920. The "passionate" nationalism of his early writings aroused National Socialist attention. In 1933 he became production director of Radio Leipzig, and in 1936 head of the department in charge of organizing celebrations in the SS Race and Settlement Main Office. Eggers interpreted German history in a *völkisch*-racist spirit on the stage, in Old German plays (*see* THING PLAYS) and musical dramas. Besides writing songs for hikers and soldiers, he produced spoken choruses as settings for cultural festivals.

Eggerstedt, Otto, b. Kiel, August 27, 1886; d. Papenburg concentration camp, October 12, 1933, German politician. Eggerstedt became a Social Democratic member of the Kiel Workers' and Soldiers' Council in 1918 and a Reichstag deputy in 1921. He was appointed to the Prussian Interior Ministry in 1928. Made police president of Altona-Wandsbek in 1929, Eggerstedt was in office on ALTONA BLOODY SUNDAY (July 19, 1932). Although he was not in town at the time, the event earned him the implacable hatred of the National Socialists. Thus he was arrested immediately upon the Seizure of Power. After a failed escape attempt he was taken to the Papenburg concentration camp, where he was shot in the back—officially "while attempting to escape" on a wood-clearing detail.

Ehe; Ehe-. *See* Marital; Marriage; Marriageability.

Eher Press (Eher-Verlag; Central Press of the NSDAP), shortened form of Franz Eher Nachfolger GmbH, Munich, later with branch offices in Berlin and Vienna. The enterprise was founded in 1923, and after 1933 became the publisher of all official National Socialist (NS) party literature, as well as the NS press trust. The general manager was Max MANN; managing directors were Rolf RIENHARDT (spring 1933–November 1943) and Wilhelm Baur (1943–1945). Amann put together his concern from Max Winkler's Cura enterprise (Cura-Gesellschaft), encompassing state-owned presses and others in which the Weimar government held shares, and large sections of the HUGENBERG concern.

All *Gau* newspapers were published by Standard, Ltd. (Standarte GmbH). Vera Publishers, Ltd. (Vera-Verlagsanstalt GmbH), taken over from Hugenberg, was the collective publisher for big-city middle-class newspapers. For middle-size cities and former Center party papers there was Phönix GmbH. Vera and Phönix were finally incorporated in the Herold Publishing Co., Ltd. (Herold-Verlagsgesellschaft GmbH). The Europe Publishing Co., Ltd. (Europa-Verlagsgesellschaft GmbH) was

added in 1940 for the press of the occupied European countries. Publishers under Eher's direct control included the Deutscher Verlag, which grew out of the Ullstein Verlag, and after 1944 Hugenberg's Scherl-Verlag. The legal successor of the Eher Press is the Free State of Bavaria.

S. O.

Ehre; Ehren-. *See* Honor.

Ehrenzeichen. *See* Badge of Honor for Caring for the German Volk; Badges of Honor of the NSDAP.

Ehrhardt, Hermann, b. Diersburg (Baden), November 29, 1881; d. Brunn am Walde (Lower Austria), September 27, 1971, German naval officer. In 1919 Ehrhardt founded the free corps "Ehrhardt Brigade," which was employed against Communist uprisings, and which participated in the KAPP PUTSCH under the anti-Republican slogan "Black-Red-Gold, incredible." After arrest and flight, he founded the right-radical secret CONSUL ORGANIZATION, which spawned the murderers of Matthias ERZBERGER and Walther RATHENAU. Ehrhardt conspired with other groups—including the NSDAP—that were hostile to the Republic, especially in southern Germany. He considered Hitler a dreamer, however, and at first spoke of him disparagingly as "the idiot." After another arrest and flight in 1923, he retreated from politics; the SS took over his brigade in 1933. After the RÖHM AFFAIR he went abroad, and after 1936 he lived in Austria as a farmer.

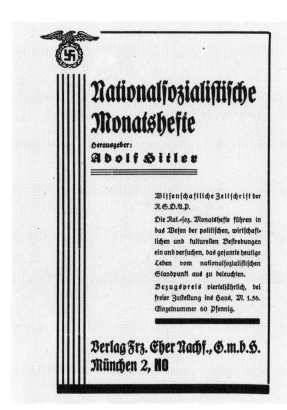

Advertisement for the Eher Press's *National Socialist Monthly*; editor, Adolf Hitler. ("The Scholarly Periodical of the NSDAP.")

Hermann Ehrhardt.

"Eiche" (Oak), military code name for the operation to free Benito MUSSOLINI from Gran Sasso on September 12, 1943.

Eichmann, Adolf, b. Solingen, March 19, 1906; d. Ramle, near Tel Aviv, June 1, 1962 (executed), SS-*Obersturmbannführer* (November 9, 1941). Eichmann grew up in Linz (Upper Austria). After dropping his mechanical engineering studies, he became a laborer, traveling salesman, and member of the WANDERVOGEL youth group and the Young Front Combatants' League. His acquaintance with Ernst KALTENBRUNNER brought Eichmann into the Austrian NSDAP and the SS on April 1, 1932. In Bavaria he went through military training with the SS STANDBY TROOPS. With the rank of SS-*Scharführer*, on October 1, 1934, he joined the Security Service (SD) Main Office, where he administered emigration matters in the "Jewish Office" (Judenreferat). Eichmann negotiated with Zionist functionaries, even learned a little Hebrew, and went on an inspection tour of Palestine in 1937— experience useful to him when he was charged with organizing a "Central Office for Jewish Emigration" in Vienna in August 1938. In less than a year and a half, the office drove 150,000 Austrian Jews into emigration.

Eichmann's next post brought less "success": the "Reich Central Office for Jewish Emigration" in Berlin, which he took over in October 1939, lost its importance during the war as deportation replaced emigration, although Eichmann retained a prominent role. After December 1939 he worked in the REICH SECURITY MAIN OFFICE (RSHA), Office IV, Bureau IV D 4,

Adolf Eichmann.

in charge of "Emigration and Evacuation," then in Bureau IV B 4, "Jewish Affairs and Evacuation." Here Eichmann became a central figure in the deportation of over 3 million Jews from the total area under German authority to death camps, as part of the so-called FINAL SOLUTION of the Jewish question. He visited AUSCHWITZ, urged Allied governments to extradite their Jewish citizens, negotiated with Joel BRAND in a failed attempt to buy freedom for Hungarian Jews in 1944, and also organized local transports to the death factories.

The obscure "desk criminal" was able to escape American captivity in 1946, then to escape with church assistance to Argentina, where he disappeared from sight under various aliases (including that of "Richard Klement"). He even managed later on to bring over his family. Israeli secret agents finally tracked him down and abducted him to Israel. In a sensational proceeding (April 2–December 11, 1961), Eichmann was tried and sentenced to death.

Eicke, Theodor, b. Hampont (Alsace-Lorraine), October 17, 1892; d. Orelka (USSR), February 26, 1943, SS-*Obergruppenführer* (1943). Eicke was a paymaster in the First World War; later, he worked as a policeman and businessman, serving as head of security for I.G. FARBEN from 1923 to 1932. In 1928 he joined the NSDAP and the SA; he entered the SS in 1930. Good relations with Himmler aided his rapid advancement and protected the notoriously aggressive Eicke from revenge at the hands of party comrades.

In the summer of 1933, Eicke was named commandant of the DACHAU concentration camp, which he developed into a kind of model under the slogan "Tolerance is a sign of weakness." His security measures (including corporal and capital punishment, the KAPO system, and the degradation of inmates) became obligatory when he was made inspector of CONCENTRATION CAMPS and head of the SS DEATH'S-HEAD UNITS in July 1934. This promotion reflected gratitude for his active involvement in the party leadership's murderous operations against the SA; the Death's-Head groups deployed in the RÖHM AFFAIR became the kernel of the "Death's-Head" Division of the Waffen-SS, established in 1939. Eicke assumed its command. Its brutality in combat and commission of war crimes contributed to the Waffen-SS's later condemnation as a "criminal organization." Eicke died in an airplane crash at the eastern front.

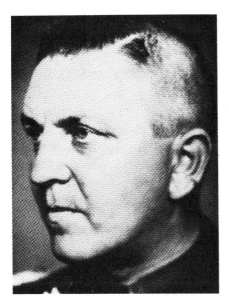

Theodor Eicke.

Eickstedt, Egon Freiherr von, b. Jersitz (near Posen), April 10, 1892; d. Mainz, December 20, 1965, German anthropologist. In 1933 Eickstedt became a professor and director of the Anthropological Institute of Breslau University; in 1946 he became a professor in Mainz. Eickstedt developed a "racial formula" to determine membership in a race. His works, which also utilized quotations from Hitler and Rosenberg, provided arguments for the alleged connections between race and character. His writings included *Rassische Grundlagen des deutschen Volkstums* (Racial Foundations of the German *Volk* Character; 1934) and *Grundlagen der Rassenpsychologie* (Fundamentals of Racial Psychology; 1936).

Eigengesetzlichkeit, Germanization of *Autonomie* (autonomy) that entered into general use through being frequently employed in National Socialist language (especially by Alfred Rosenberg.)

Einheitsfront. *See* Unity Front.

Einsatz (action; engagement; task; deployment), one of the most frequently used words in the Third Reich, especially through battlefield reports. Its originally passive meaning was expanded with active, strategic-planning, and technical-mechanical components: the *Einsatz* of troops referred to the "human matériel" with which one operated; the *Einsatz* of individuals made people "parts of a huge work mechanism" (*see* LABOR DEPLOYMENT).

Einsatzgruppen (attack or task groups), mobile units under the chief of the Security Police (Sipo) and the Security Service (SD). Free of control by and responsibility to the military forces, they carried out the tasks of security police in the course of army operations before (in Austria and the Sudetenland) and during the war. Their use is best known in the RUSSIAN CAMPAIGN, for which four groups (designated with the letters A, B, C, and D) were formed and assigned to the North, Central, and South Army Groups and to the Eleventh Army. Four to five SPECIAL COMMANDOS (SK) or EINSATZKOMMANDOS (EK) of company strength were subordinated to each Einsatzgruppe. They were filled from the Sipo (officials from the state [Stapo] and criminal police) and the SD.

Later on, members of police reserve battalions 9 or 3, and of the Waffen-SS special-assignment battalion, were added, to be distributed in platoons among the commandos. The units were reinforced with VOLUNTEER HELPERS and local militia. Their tasks as security police included operations against "individuals hostile to the Reich," notably the annihilation of Jews as carriers of the Bolshevik system, in accordance with the "Führer's order." On the order of Reinhard HEYDRICH, the Einsatzgruppen unleashed only POGROMS in the first days of the campaign. These were followed by executions of able-bodied men of the Jewish faith for such alleged causes as arson and support of partisans. After approximately August 1941, all Jews, including women and children, were shot.

The annihilation operations generally followed a standard course. Before each *Aktion,* the Einsatzgruppe chief or the commander of a subordinate commando group usually made contact with the Wehrmacht unit or office responsible for the locality or area involved, and informed it of the project. As far as was necessary, the counterparts agreed on such ancillary measures as blocking off the execution ground and the availability of trucks to transport victims to their execution. With the help of interpreters, and frequently with information from the native population, Jews were located and taken to collection points. From there they were driven on foot or in trucks to the execution sites, where prisoners of war had dug trenches for the corpses or where the victims themselves were forced to dig pits. The Jews were then forced to hand over their valuables and to undress. Initially executions were carried out in a "military style," but the increased number of executions led to the abandonment of that practice. Victims

```
Gruppe Arlt                    Minsk, den 3.August 1942

              T ä t i g k e i t s b e r i c h t .
          -.-.-.-.-.-.-.-.-.-.-.-.-.-.-.-.-.-.-.-.-.

Am 26.6. traf der erwartete Judentransport aus dem Reich ein.
Am 27.6. starteten wir samt ziemlich den ganzen Kdo. zu einer
Aktion nach Baranewitsche. Der Erfolg war wie immer negativ. Im
Zuge dieser Aktion räumten wir das Judenghetto in S l o n i m .
Etwa 4000 Juden wurden an diesem Tage der Erde übergeben.
Am 30.6. kehrten wir wieder nach Minsk zurück. Die nächstfolgenden
Tage waren mit Sacheninstandsetzen, Waffenreinigen, Waffendurchsicht
ausgefüllt.
Am 2.7. wurden bereits wieder die Vorkehrungen zum Empfang eines
Judentransportes, Aushebung der Gruben, getroffen.
Am 10.7. wurden wir und das lett. Kdo. gegen Partisanen im Walde
von Koydanow eingesetzt. Wir konnten dabei ein Munitionslager
ausheben. Plötzlich wurden wir dabei aus dem Hinterhalt mit einem
M.G. beschossen. Ein lettischer Kamerad wurde dabei getötet. Bei
der Verfolgung der Bande konnten vier Mann erschossen werden.
Am 12.7. wurde der lett. Kamerad im neuen Friedhof beigesetzt.
Am 17.7. traf ein Transport mit Juden ein und wurde zum Gut gebracht.
Am 21. 22. und 23.7. werden neue Gruben ausgehoben.
Am 24.7. trifft bereits wieder ein Transport mit 1000 Juden aus
dem Reich hier ein.
Vom 25.7. bis 27.7. werden neue Gruben ausgehoben.
Am 28.7. Großaktion im Minsker russ. Ghetto. 6000 Juden werden
zur Grube gebracht.
Am 29.7. 3000 deutsche Juden werden zur Grube gebracht.
Die nächstfolgenden Tage waren mit Waffenreinigen und
Sacheninstandsetzen ausgefüllt.

Das Betragen der Männer ist In- und -außer Dienst gut und
gibt zu keiner Beanstandung Anlass.


                          gez. Arlt
                       ⚡⚡-Unterscharführer.
```

Einsatzgruppen. Activity report of the Arlt Group. [A translation of the report is at the end of the Einsatzgruppen article.]

were made to lie down in the pit next to each other, face down, or, if one row was full, to put their head between the feet of those already shot. Sometimes a trench was filled in although all the victims were not yet dead. From the end of 1941, S[pezial]-*Wagen* (*see* GAS VANS) were used to kill Jews, in order to accelerate the pace of mass annihilation.

The extent of these operations emerges from so-called SITUATION REPORTS that were preserved, as well as from later documents from the occupied Eastern Territories summarizing Einsatzgruppen reports to the Reich Security Main Office. One such report, for example, told how SK 4a of Einsatzgruppe C, under the leadership of SS-Standartenführer Paul BLOBEL, had shot 33,771 Jewish men, women, and children in the BABI YAR ravine near Kiev on September 29 and 30, 1941, and at least 10,000 Jews in Kharkov in early 1942. Einsatzgruppen victims totaled at least 900,000 persons. Numerous judicial proceedings were conducted against former members of these detachments after the war, notably the OHLENDORF TRIAL.

[The text of the report in the illustration is as follows: "Arlt Group. Minsk, August 3, 1942.

Activity report.

On 6/26 the anticipated Jewish transport from the Reich arrived.

On 6/27 the entire commando set out toward Baranovichi on an operation. The outcome was negative as always. In the course of this operation we cleared out the Jewish ghetto in *Slonim*. On this day about 4,000 Jews were put in the earth.

On 6/30 we returned to Minsk. The following days were occupied with putting things in order and cleaning and inspecting weapons.

On 7/2 arrangements were again made for receiving a Jewish transport, with digging the pits.

On 7/10 we and the Latvian commando were deployed against partisans in the Kaidanov forest. While doing so we were able to raid a munitions depot. Suddenly we were fired at from behind by a machine gun. A Latvian comrade was killed. In pursuit of the band, we killed four men.

On 7/12 the Latvian comrade was buried in the new cemetery.

On 7/17 a transport with Jews arrived and was taken to the farm.

On 7/21, 22, and 23, new pits were dug.

On 7/24 another transport arrived here with 1,000 Jews from the Reich.

From 7/25 to 7/27, new pits were dug.

On 7/28 there was a major operation in the Minsk Russian ghetto. Six thousand Jews were taken to the pit.

On 7/29, 3,000 German Jews were taken to the pit.

The following days were occupied with cleaning weapons and putting things in order.

The conduct of the men in and out of service is good and gives no occasion for complaint."]

A. St.

Einsatzkommandos (Operational Commandos; EK), along with the SPECIAL COMMANDOS (Sonderkommandos; SK), units of the EINSATZGRUPPEN. By agreement between the Army High Command (OKH) and the chief of the Security Police on April 28, 1941 (Regulation of the Deployment of the Security Police and Security Service [SD] in Army Units), the EKs were to operate behind the combat lines, and the SKs were to follow immediately after the combat troops to which they were attached. Commandos from the headquarters and units of the Chief of the Security Police and SD were also designated as EKs. According to his deployment orders 8, 9, and 14, they were responsible for eliminating "politically intolerable" Soviet prisoners of war.

A. St.

Einstein, Albert, b. Ulm, March 14, 1879; d. Princeton, N.J., April 18, 1955, German physicist. In 1901 Einstein was a science expert at the "Office for Intellectual Property" (Patent Office) in Bern. He later became a professor in Zurich (1909), Prague (1911), and again Zurich (1912). From 1914 to 1933 he served as director of the Kaiser Wilhelm Institute for Physics in Berlin. Einstein's supreme position as a theoretical physicist was undisputed from early on: in 1905 he developed the Special Theory of Relativity, and in 1907 the Law of Equivalence of Energy and Mass; in 1921 he received a Nobel price in Physics for his work on the quantum theory. As a Jew, however, he was subjected to antisemitism, which grew stronger when he became a pacifist during the First World War. Einstein's membership in the German League for Human Rights was criticized in National Socialist circles as "salon Bolshevism."

After the Seizure of Power, Einstein's property was seized, and in March 1934 his German citizenship was revoked. Since 1933 he had been in the United States at the Institute for Advanced Study in Princeton. (In 1940 he became an American citizen.) The envy of experimental physicists (*see* Philipp LENARD) allied itself with political antisemitic persecution, and led to attempts to belittle Einstein's scientific achievements as of no practical significance because of their "purely conceptual and formal character." This was frighteningly contradicted—for Einstein himself, as well—by the construction of the ATOMIC BOMB, which Einstein had proposed to President Franklin D. Roosevelt in a letter of August 2, 1939, in fear of a German bomb. After the war, Einstein unsuccessfully fought against the further development of nuclear arsenals, and increasingly withdrew from public life. In 1952 he refused election as president of the young Israeli state.

"Ein Volk, ein Reich, ein Führer!" (One People, one Empire, one Leader!), National Socialist propaganda slogan expressing the demand for a "Great-Germany" (Grossdeutschland) that included all Germans in an ethnically uniform state. After the ANSCHLUSS with Austria, it was widely distributed on official placards with Hitler's picture to celebrate this interim success.

Eisenhower, Dwight D(avid), b. Denison, Tex., October 14, 1890; d. Washington, D.C., March 28, 1969, American general and politician. In 1911 Eisenhower entered the military academy at West Point. He fought in the First World War, eventually with tank units. From 1935 to 1940 he was chief of staff with Gen. Douglas MacArthur in the Philippines. In 1941 Eisenhower was made a general; from February 16, 1941, to June 26, 1942, as chief of operations in the War Department, he was significantly involved in planning the United States' entry into the European theater of war. After June 25, 1942, Eisenhower was supreme commander of United States troops in Europe; he directed the landings in

Albert Einstein.

Dwight D. Eisenhower.

North Africa (November 8, 1942), on Sicily (July 9, 1943), and on the Italian mainland (September 3, 1943). He later directed the combined Allied operation for the INVASION at Normandy (June 6, 1944), serving as supreme commander of the Allied Expeditionary Force after December 24, 1943.

Eisenhower rejected the daredevil tactics of his British deputy, Bernard Law MONTGOMERY, and to preserve American troops, depended entirely on superiority of matériel. Rejecting the idea of a partial German capitulation to the Western powers, he held strictly to the demand of President Franklin D. Roosevelt for UNCONDITIONAL SURRENDER, which Eisenhower received at his Reims headquarters on May 7, 1945. Until November of that year he served as supreme commander of American occupational forces in Germany; he was responsible for the "fraternization ban." Eisenhower later became army chief of staff (1945–1948) and supreme commander of Allied forces in Europe (1950–1952), participating in the organization of NATO. From 1953 to 1961 he was the 34th president of the United States.

Eisern-. *See* Iron.

Eisler, Elfriede. *See* Fischer, Ruth.

Eisler, Gerhart, b. Leipzig, February 20, 1897; d. Azerbaijan (USSR), March 21, 1968, German politician and journalist; brother of Ruth FISCHER. Eisler was an Austrian officer in the First World War. In 1918 he joined the Austrian Communist party; in 1921 he joined Berlin's Communist party. He worked as editor for the party paper ROTE FAHNE (The Red Flag) and held various party posts. Active for the KPD (Communist Party of Germany) in Prague and Paris after 1935, he was interned in France in 1940, but was able to escape to the United States. Suspected of espionage, Eisler moved to the German Democratic Republic in 1949. After various positions in the field of information, he became a member of the Socialist Unity Party's Central Committee in 1967.

El Alamein, village on the Mediterranean coast of northwest Egypt before which the German-Italian "Afrika" tank corps was halted on June 21, 1942; it was forced to retreat on November 2 of that year. The battle at El Alamein was the turning point of the AFRICAN CAMPAIGN.

Elite (Fr., *élite,* choice, select part), term commonly used in France since the 17th century; it was adapted by 19th-century social philosophy to designate the dominant stratum of a society. Membership in the elite depends on birth and/or power, or on a person's worth. Even such plans for egalitarian societies as Marxism-Leninism recognize the concept of an elite in their doctrines of the working class as the avant-garde of the revolution and the cadre as organizational core of the revolutionary party. Fascism, on the other hand, tries to build a consciously hierarchical, antidemocratic elite in order to ensure domination by dividing society vertically along the lines of estates or corporations (*see* CORPORATIST STATE). The corresponding National Socialist FÜHRER PRINCIPLE found a Social Darwinist legitimation in the alleged "aristocratic principle in nature." But unlike Fascism in Italy, National Socialism did not intend a partitioning into estates; rather, it intended to form a political, military, and economic functional elite through SELECTION and schooling (*see* SCHOOLING, POLITICAL), as exemplified by the SS or its military elite troops, the Waffen-SS.

Elsas, Fritz, b. Cannstatt (now Stuttgart–Bad Cannstatt), July 11, 1890; d. Sachsenhausen concentration camp, January 4, 1945, German municipal politician and lawyer. In 1926 Elsas was vice president of the German Municipal Congress (Städtetag); in 1931, first mayor of Berlin. The National Socialists dismissed him because of his Jewish origins in 1933; he then practiced law and advised emigrants. Although he was not in the most immediate circle of conspirators on July 20, 1944, Elsas was on friendly terms with many of them, and gave shelter to Carl GOERDELER more than once after the attempt failed. This led to his arrest. There was no trial; SS guards shot Elsas in the so-called industrial courtyard (*Industriehof*) of the Sachsenhausen concentration camp.

Elser, Johann Georg, b. Hermaringen (Württemberg), January 4, 1903; d. Dachau concentration camp, April 9, 1945, German opposition fighter. Elser, a skilled furniture maker, belonged for a time to the RED FRONTLINE FIGHTERS' LEAGUE but abandoned it because he found it lacking in determined opposition to National Socialist domination. A secretive loner, Elser began planning an assassination attempt on Hitler and the NS leaders after the MUNICH AGREEMENT, in order to prevent a war.

The locale that seemed to him most suitable for this was Munich's Bürgerbräu Celler, where Hitler spoke annually on the eve of November 9 to "Old Combatants" in memory of the MARCH ON THE FELDHERRNHALLE. Some 30 to 35 times

Johann Georg Elser.

Paul Baron von Eltz-Rübenach.

between August and November 1939, Elser let himself be locked up there at night so he could build a self-made time bomb into the column behind the speaker's lectern. The bomb was set for 9:20 p.m., since Hitler usually spoke until 10. But bad weather forced Hitler to return to Berlin by train rather than airplane, and therefore he left the hall at 9:13, after a short greeting. Minutes later, Elser's bomb devastated the hall: eight were killed, 63 injured, and (a whispered joke added) "60 million burned [*Verkohlte*, hoaxed]," since an NS propaganda ploy was suspected. But no evidence was found for this rumor, nor for Gestapo conjectures about instigators from Otto Strasser's BLACK FRONT or the British Secret Service.

Elser was arrested near the Swiss border that same night. He confessed on November 14, and was taken to the Sachsenhausen camp as a "special prisoner of the Führer." In late 1944 or early 1945, he was transferred to Dachau, and shot on order of the Reich Security Main Office on April 9, 1945 (*see* BÜRGERBRÄU ASSASSINATION ATTEMPT).

Eltz-Rübenach, Paul Baron von, b. Wahn, near Cologne, February 9, 1875; d. Linz am Rhein, August 25, 1943, German politician. After studying engineering in Aachen and Berlin, Eltz-Rübenach worked for the state railroad. He spent several years in the United States, and from 1911 to 1914 worked as a technical expert for the German consulate in New York. When the war began in 1914, he returned to Germany and worked in military rail transport. After the war, he served in several ministries, and in 1924 became president of the State Railroad [Reichsbahn] Board in Karlsruhe; in June 1932, he joined Franz von PAPEN's cabinet as minister for post and transportation. Eltz-Rübenach entered Hitler's cabinet on January 30, 1933, and fought unsuccessfully for the development of the state railroad against the National Socialist orientation toward highways (*see* AUTOBAHN). Influenced by his Catholic background, he refused to accept the Golden Party Badge in 1937 because of the party's anti-Christian attitude. He was thereupon removed from office. When his wife then refused the Mother's Cross, the family suffered further victimization, including Gestapo surveillance and temporary denial of pension.

Emergency Abitur (*Notabitur*), popular term for the academic high school diploma granted to pupils before completion of the regular school term because of induction into military service. Already used during the last stages of the First World War, the Emergency Abitur was made possible at the outset of the Second World War after the secondary school period for boys was shortened to eight years "for important reasons of population [read: military] policy" in January 1938 (extended to girls in 1940). This meant that 12 years of schooling led to the degree. The Emergency Abitur was introduced with the Ordinance on Diplomas (*Anordnung über Reifezeugnisse*) of September 8, 1939, which stipulated that pupils who left the eighth secondary school grade prematurely because of conscription would receive their diploma after an oral examination; they were excused from the written examinations. In 1941, examinations were dropped altogether. After February 1942 the ordinance was extended to 17-year-old pupils in the seventh secondary school class; toward the end of the war it was interpreted even more loosely. After the war, all emergency diplomas granted after January 1, 1943, were annulled.

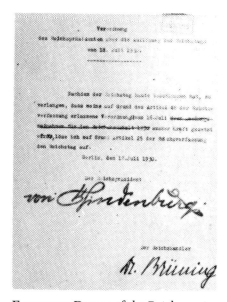

Emergency Decree of the Reich president upon the dissolution of the Reichstag (July 18, 1930).

Emergency Decrees (*Notverordnungen*), according to Paragraph 48 (the "Dictatorship Paragraph") of the Weimar Constitution, legally binding decrees issued by the Reich president, which could be revoked on demand of a Reichstag majority. Through Emergency Decrees, the Reich president, with Reichswehr assistance, could proceed against state (*Land*) governments that acted in violation of the Constitution (Article 1) and could invalidate BASIC RIGHTS (Article 2). The Emergency Decrees were, to be sure, intended to be limited to "necessary measures" (*nötige Massnahmen*), but this term was never legally defined. Thus, during the post-1930 crisis of the Weimar Republic, Emergency Decrees could develop into a substitute for legislation by the obstructed Reichstag, which could not use its right to revoke because it lacked the necessary majority, and because the Reich president could threaten it with the countermeasure of parliamentary dissolution according to Paragraph 25. The PRESIDIAL CABINETS governed primarily under the Emergency Decrees after they had lost significant parliamentary support. In 1932 only five laws were issued, as against 66 Emergency Decrees. They also smoothed the way for the dictatorship of Hitler, who initiated the liquidation of the Republic with the "Emergency Decree of the Reich President for the Protection of *Volk* and State" (*see* REICHSTAG FIRE DECREE) of February 28, 1933.

Emigration

The German emigration of 1933 to 1945 was not a collective movement; it never succeeded in creating an organization, and it accomplished nothing politically. The contrast with the Austrian and Czech emigrations of 1938–1939 — not to mention Charles de GAULLE's "Free France" in London — is striking. Each of these had from the outset a central political leadership around which to coalesce and which allowed dealing with the host country. During the war they were able — with more or less success — to form governments-in-exile, and Edvard BENEŠ and de Gaulle finally returned to their countries as heads of government.

The German emigrés included some formerly prominent politicians — Heinrich BRÜNING, Otto BRAUN, Hermann RAUSCHNING — but they

no longer played a role abroad. Occasional attempts to create something like a German National Committee in England or the United States never got off the ground. They failed not only because of the less than encouraging attitudes of the English and American governments. The German emigration itself — which comprised some 10,000 people at the beginning and several hundred thousand by the end — was too diffuse, politically too divided, and on the whole too unpolitical. Exaggerating somewhat, one could say there was no German emigration as such, there were only German emigrés. Yet not only in their numbers, but also frequently in their quality, these German emigrés were a factor that cannot be eliminated from the history of the 1930s and 1940s. It was impossible to overlook them; they made themselves conspicuous, in a negative as well as a positive way, at home and abroad.

How much of a thorn in the flesh they were to the National Socialists could be seen in such acts of revenge as the BOOK BURNING and revocation of citizenship. Talk of them in Germany never ceased: the fact that such men as Albert EINSTEIN and Thomas MANN had turned their backs on the Third Reich continued to have an impact—whether alarming or comforting depended on one's viewpoint. And besides such imponderable matters, the emigration had some very concrete consequences. It is quite possible that the competition for the ATOMIC BOMB was decided by the German emigration: it meant a growth in scientific capacity for America and England and a loss for Germany. This could not, of course, have been foreseen at the time they left Germany, even by the 10 or 20 scientists of the highest class upon whom this world-historic effort depended. One must distinguish between effects and motives. Moreover, prominent scientists were numerically less represented in the emigration than their literary counterparts. German science experienced a loss of blood through the emigration; German literature suffered a fatal hemorrhage. The losses were also enormous in such related areas as journalism, theater, and film. In the field of academic humanism, schools of thought were transplanted from Germany to America during the 1930s—for example, the Frankfurt School in sociology, and PSYCHOANALYSIS. All this made history; but it was intellectual, not political, history.

Emigration was in each case a lone, individual decision; and this decision nearly always had a double aspect: it meant flight and protest. The admixture of motives was different in each case, but the motives were never single-minded—not even in the case of the unpolitical Jews, who so vastly increased the number of emigrants in 1938–1939, when real persecution began. They fled persecution, but at the same time they protested against persecution by their flight, and carried the indictment against it into the world. As far as the Jewish emigrés of the "first hour" were concerned, the act of protest certainly was paramount. Many of them were members of the then-existing German-Jewish cultural aristocracy, and they left Germany primarily as cultural aristocrats, not as Jews. In this early period, flight was more often the motive behind emigration for politicians. In many cases they had good reasons to flee. Brüning and Gottfried TREVIRA-

NUS, for example, were on the death list of June 30, 1934 (see RÖHM AFFAIR), and would doubtless have been murdered had they not reached safety at the final hour. Should they have stayed?

This question has often been posed in a reproachful tone since 1945, especially in regard to politicians, but also in reference to outstanding personalities in literary and academic life, who made up a large percentage of early emigrés. If the best people left, what could be expected of the average person, it was asked? Was emigration desertion?

A counterquestion addresses such reproaches: What then could they have done in Germany? At least they made a point by emigrating. In Germany they could have made no further points. There was no possibility of political opposition, there was no longer even public, free speech. The alternatives after March 1933 were no longer to withdraw or to participate. Even those who tried to withdraw, who went into INNER EMIGRATION, who fell silent and hid in harmless, breadwinning jobs, could not fail to realize in the long run that they were collaborating, however reluctantly and indirectly. Everything, even the most harmless thing, ultimately served the regime that had taken possession of all of Germany, to its farthest corner.

There was only one other alternative: martyrdom. But it was a martyrdom behind closed doors. Martyrs such as Carl von OSSIETZKY or Hans and Sophie SCHOLL had little impact in Germany at the time. The emigrés at least could not be silenced—at least not the prominent among them.

In any case, emigration too brought suffering and deprivation, often for even the prominent. For fame in Germany was not the same as fame beyond its borders, and many emigrés who had been famous in Germany left their fame behind them. The writers, journalists, and actors who were so numerous in the emigration left behind them their tool: their language. And all left behind their property: in 1933, people were permitted to take out 200 RM; by 1938 only 10 RM. Everything else was lost. For most, emigration meant starting from scratch, and this under extremely difficult conditions. For German immigrants were welcome nowhere. Economic crisis and unemployment prevailed everywhere in the 1930s. A residence permit was a privilege; a work permit was unobtainable for most until the war. How they managed to get through, many could not themselves have explained later on.

A bitter emigré joke circulated about a man

The most important
figures of the intel-
lectual emigration in
a triptych by Arthur
Kaufmann.

(1) director Berthold Viertel; (2) director Fritz Lang; (3) writer Günther Anders; (4) composer Ernst Toch; (5) philosopher Ernst Bloch; (6) the painter of the triptych, Arthur Kaufmann; (7) his wife, Elisabeth Musset-Kaufmann; (8) psychologist Max Wertheimer; (9) violinist Emanuel Feuermann; (10) composer Arnold Schönberg; (11) painter George Grosz; (12) painter Joseph Floch; (13) writer Heinrich Mann; (14) lecturer Paul Zucker; (15) actress Luise Rainer; (16) chief physician Ulrich Friedemann; (17) conductor Otto Klemperer; (18) theologian Paul Tillich; (19) writer Arnold Zweig; (20) psychologist William Stern; (21) dramatist Ferdinand Bruckner; (22) physicist Albert Einstein; (23) writer Klaus Mann; (24) writer Thomas Mann; (25) writer Erika Mann; (26) writer Ludwig Renn; (27) art dealer Curt Valentin; (28) composer Hanns Jelinek; (29) writer Bruno Frank; (30) director Erwin Piscator; (31) journalist Lotte Goslar; (32) writer Oskar Maria Graf; (33) graphic artist B. F. Dolbin; (34) philosopher Kurt Goldstein; (35) composer Kurt Weill; (36) director Max Reinhardt; (37) actress Helene Thimig; (38) writer Ernst Toller.

searching the globe for a place of refuge. Finally he asks: "Would you perhaps have another globe?" Of the German-speaking countries where most would naturally have preferred to go, Austria was soon endangered, and SWITZER-LAND unfriendly; only those were admitted who brought with them great wealth, which ever fewer Germans were able to do because of the harsh regulations and tight control. The Soviet Union was considered only by Communists, and proved inhospitable even to them: many German Communists in exile fell victim to Stalin's purges. France, though liberal enough initially, proved difficult in the long run; during the war—even before the occupation—it became a trap. The best option was still to go to England or America; admission was difficult, but once there, one could stay without being threatened, and perhaps even work someday, if one assimilated. Some German emigrés in England and America gradually ceased being German emigrés, and became grateful voluntary Englishmen or Americans.

It is impossible to draw a uniform picture of the German emigration, or a heroic one, despite personal courage and readiness to sacrifice. The idea that a better Germany had been preserved or developed further abroad in order to return in triumph someday came to nothing. The reality of the emigration was a harsh individual struggle for existence; often enough, misery and embitterment; at best, a hard personal beginning in a new homeland, which sometimes derived a little or even a great deal of profit from the grateful and eager endeavors of its new citizens. Some may have been consoled during the hard years of their impotent exile by Goethe's words: "Germany is nothing," he said to Chancellor von Müller on December 14, 1808, "but each individual German is much; and yet the latter imagines the opposite. The Germans would have to be transplanted and dispersed throughout the world like the Jews, in order to develop fully the abundance of good that lies in them for the good of all nations."

Sebastian Haffner

Employment Book (*Arbeitsbuch*), document introduced by a law of February 26, 1935; every employee had to submit it to his or her employer when hired. Dates and type of employment were recorded in it. An implementation ordinance of May 16, 1935, specified that persons without an Employment Book could no longer be employed. Officially introduced to "direct the deployment of the labor force," the book served to control the labor market and to seek out the WORK-SHY. The Employment Offices had records of all entries.

Emsland camps, seven penal camps in the Emsland moors near Holland, under the authority of the Justice Ministry (not incorporated into the concentration camp organization). They were established as such in 1934 (although some had existed since 1923 as institutions of Prussia's justice department), and housed criminals as well as political prisoners. The Emsland camps came under the authority of the "commander of the penal camps in Emsland" in Papenburg, who in turn was directly under the Prussian Justice Ministry. Individual camp commandants were primarily old SA leaders, hired by the justice administration, who had not been trained as officials for penal institutions. Direct inmate supervision was carried out by the

"Guard Troop of Prisoners in Emsland": SA members in blue uniform (the "Blues") who were paid by the Justice Ministry.

After the dissolution in September 1936 of the Esterwegen camp, which until then had been under the authority of the Prussian Interior Ministry, it and the following camps were responsible to the Justice Ministry: Camp I, Börgermoor; Camp II, Aschendorfermoor; Camp III, Brual-Rhede; Camp IV, Walchum; Camp V, Neusustrum; Camp VI, Oberlangen; Camp VII, Esterwegen. In 1939, the Reich Justice Ministry established a bureau in Papenburg with the designation "Delegate of the Reich Justice Ministry for the Penal Camps in Emsland." The seven SA camp commandants were replaced by penal officials, and trained prison guards were installed alongside the SA guard troops for internal camp operations.

Until the war began, the Emsland camps held only non-Jewish German inmates. Thereafter Jews, French "NN" prisoners (*see* "NIGHT AND FOG" DECREE), Poles, Belgians, Dutch, ethnic German deserters, and prisoners of the Wehrmacht were sent there. The inmates were employed cultivating the moors. Work commandos were also used for the TODT ORGANIZATION in France, the Channel Islands, and in northern Norway. The Emsland camps used the same methods as the concentration camps. A person who was not up to the harsh labor demands was beaten with a rubber truncheon and subjected to punitive drill until completely exhausted. Prisoners were also beaten to death by guards, or killed in other ways. Allied troops liberated the Emsland camps in late March and early April 1945.

W. D.

Enabling Law (*Ermächtigungsgesetz*), Reich law with the title Law to Relieve the Distress of Volk and Reich (*Gesetz zur Behebung der Not von Volk und Reich*), which passed the Reichstag by a vote of 441–94 on March 23, 1933, and took effect the next day. Only the SPD (Social Democratic Party of Germany) voted against this law, which gave the Reich government the right to conclude laws, including budgetary laws (Article 1). These laws could deviate from the WEIMAR CONSTITUTION (Article 2) and could be drawn up by the Reich chancellor rather than the Reich president (Article 3). Reich treaties with other states did not require parliamentary ratification (Article 4). The law's validity initially expired on April 1, 1937, but the Reichstag extended it in 1937 (until April 4, 1941) and 1939 (until May 10, 1943). By order of the Führer it was finally extended indefinitely in 1943.

The Enabling Law abolished basic principles of democracy and of a constitutional state (legislative powers for parliament and the precept of the constitutionality of laws) and restricted the power of the Reich president. Together with the REICHSTAG FIRE DECREE of February 28, 1933, it formed the legislative base for the establishment of the National Socialist dictatorship, and even legalized it. Although the prescribed two-thirds majority of Reichstag members present passed the law, in reality its content and the background of its passage were unconstitutional. Elections to the Reichstag (March 5) had been only conditionally free; arrests and other chicanery kept all 81 Communist party members and 26 of the 120 Social Democrats away from the March 23 session; and armed SA and SS guards were posted in the chamber to intimidate potential opposition to the law.

Thus only the SPD rejected the Enabling Law. The Center party (73 seats) agreed to it after long hesitation when Hitler promised (orally) to limit the law's use, saying, for example, that he would safeguard the rights of the Reichstag, the Reichsrat, the Reich president, and the churches. He never kept these promises.

R. B.

Enabling Law. While Hitler speaks, Göring observes individual deputies through binoculars.

Encirclement (*Einkreisung*), catchword for international isolation. Imperial Chancellor Bernhard von Bülow first spoke of "encirclement" on November 14, 1906, in condemning the British policy of forming anti-German blocs, which were primarily an answer to Germany's immoderate "world policy." Owing to the multi-front war from 1914 to 1918, encirclement became a German nightmare and was therefore suitable as a propaganda argument for rearmament and an offensive National Socialist FOREIGN POLICY. The Franco-Soviet mutual assistance pact of May 2, 1935, was especially perceived as a sign of a new encirclement, despite the dominant British APPEASEMENT position and France's stationary "fortress" policy.

Endlösung. *See* Final Solution.

Enemy listener (*Feindhörer*), in National Socialist criminal law, VOLK VERMIN who listened to "enemy transmitters" or even to transmitters of neutral states. They could expect draconian punishment, even death sentences as the war continued. They were pursued with various tactics, including the use of children to spy on parents.

Enemy powers (*Feindmächte*), generic National Socialist propaganda term to circumvent the term "Allies," as the victors of the First World War were called, in describing Germany's current military enemies; a parallel term was "enemy side" (*Feindseite*).

Enemy-State Clauses (*Feindstaatenklauseln*), term for Article 53, Paragraph 1, Section 3, and Article 107 of the Statute of the UNITED NATIONS. The Enemy-State Clauses contain special provisions for the former wartime enemies of the world organization's founding members. Article 107 exempts the measures undertaken by the Allies toward the "Enemy States" as a consequence of war from the statutory restrictions. Article 53 revoked the Security Council's control power over measures undertaken by member nations in accord with treaties directed against the "renewal of aggressive policies by a former enemy state." The clauses became superfluous with the admission of the German Democratic Republic and the Federal Republic of Germany into the United Nations.

England. *See* Air Battle for England; Great Britain.

Enterdungsaktion. *See* Exhumation Operation.

Entjudung. *See* De-Jewing.

Epp, Franz Xaver Ritter von, b. Munich, October 16, 1868; d. there, December 31, 1946, German general and politician. After attending military school and military academy, Epp was a volunteer in the German Expeditionary Corps in China (1900–1901), served as company commander in colonial warfare against the Herero and Hottentot tribes in southwest Africa (1904–1906), and was commander of the Bavarian Royal Infantry Regiment in the First World War. After the war he received financial support from

Encirclement: France's "Little Entente" against Hitler (1934). From the left: Jevtić (Yugoslavia), Beneš (Czechoslovakia), Barthou (France), Titulescu (Romania).

Franz Xaver Ritter von Epp.

the Armed Forces Ministry to found the "Epp Free Corps" in Thuringia. It played a significant role in smashing the Republic of Councils in Munich and the Communist uprising in the Ruhr area. After 1920, Epp, who had come into contact with Hitler through his staff officer Ernst RÖHM, supported the National Socialist newspaper *Völkischer Beobachter*. He joined the Bavarian People's Party and in 1928 the NSDAP. From 1928 to 1945 a Reichstag deputy, he became Reich commissioner in Bavaria after the Seizure of Power (from April 10, 1933, Reich governor). As of May 1934 he headed the NSDAP Office for Colonial Policy. Epp's influence as a conservative monarchist shrank considerably when he protested the shooting of three Munich SA leaders during the RÖHM AFFAIR. In the final phase of the Third Reich, he belonged to Hitler's internal party critics. He died in American internment.

Equalization of burdens (*Lastenausgleich*), equalization of wealth between those demographic groups in the Federal Republic of Germany that were severely affected by the Second World War and those that were not at all or little hurt. Its legal basis was first the Law to Provide Immediate Help (*Soforthilfegesetz*) of August 8, 1949, and then the Law to Equalize Burdens (*Lasten-ausgleichsgesetz;* LAG) of August 14, 1952. According to the LAG, "equalization taxes" (*Aus-gleichsabgaben*)—until 1979 applied to property and interest on mortgages, until 1974 to interest on credit—were levied against individuals, corporations, and organizations. Together with subsidies from the Bonn government and

the states, these monies fed into an "Equalization Fund" (*Ausgleichsfond*). From it "Equalization Payments" (*Ausgleichsleistungen*) were distributed, according to the amount of loss and the level of need, to persons who had suffered property losses from acts of war, expulsion, or flight (from East Germany, Eastern Europe, and, after 1969, the Soviet zone or the GDR), or from the currency reform of 1948. Payments were direct or were made in the form of pensions, loans, and subsidies for education or training. By the end of 1974, the Equalization Fund had accrued 94.2 billion DM; payments came to 94 billion DM.

R. B.

Equestrian SS (Reiter-SS). *See* SS.

Erb-. *See* Hereditarily; Hereditary.

Erdmann, Lothar, b. Breslau, October 12, 1888; d. Sachsenhausen concentration camp, September 18, 1939, German trade unionist and Socialist. From 1924 to 1933 Erdmann was secretary of the General German Trade Union Federation and editor in chief of the journal *Die Arbeit* (Labor). After the unions were smashed (May 2, 1933), Erdmann refused to work for the GERMAN LABOR FRONT, and acquired a reputation for political unreliability from then on. He was thus taken into "protective custody" at the beginning of the war on September 1, 1939, and transported to the Sachsenhausen concentration camp. He rebelled against the arbitrary rule of the SS, and after a few weeks died from such punishments as "intensified drill" and "stake-hanging" (*Pfahlhängen*).

Erkelenz, Anton, b. Neuss, October 10, 1878; d. Berlin, April 25, 1945, German trade unionist and locksmith. In 1902 Erkelenz became secretary of the liberal Hirsch-Duncker trade union; in 1919 a deputy in the National Assembly (German Democratic Party). He was also editor in chief of the liberal journal *Die Hilfe* (Help) and the metalworkers' paper *Regulator*. Erkelenz opposed communism and materialism but advocated an active social policy and economic democratization. Despite ideological reservations he joined the SPD (Social Democratic Party of Germany) in 1932 in order to check the "National Socialist plague." His last attempt to achieve a trade union alliance across party lines, after Hitler's seizure of power, failed. He withdrew from political life, although he had contacts with the opposition circle around Julius

LEBER. Erkelenz was found stabbed to death in his garden in Zehlendorf the day after Soviet troops marched in.

Ernst, Karl, b. Berlin, June 24, 1904; d. there, June 30, 1934, hotel page; SA-*Gruppenführer* (March 1, 1933). Ernst joined the NSDAP and SA in 1923. The good-looking young man attracted the attention of Ernst RÖHM, who entered into homosexual relations with him and aided his rise in the SA. In 1931 he became a *Stabsführer*, and in 1932 a Reichstag deputy and SA-*Oberführer*. En route to his wedding trip, Ernst was arrested by an SS commando during the RÖHM AFFAIR, taken to Berlin, and shot.

Ernst, Paul, b. Elbingerode (Harz), March 7, 1866; d. Sankt Georgen (Styria), May 13, 1933, German author. Ernst studied theology, literature, and political economy. At first a Social Democrat and an adherent of literary Naturalism (his drama *Lumpenbagasch* [Riffraff] appeared in 1898), Ernst became a neoclassicist searching for a connection between "Germanic depth and Romantic formal severity." The National Socialists thought they saw in this an attempt to "renew German life with a historic consciousness," notably in *Das Kaiserbuch* (The Emperor's Book), a three-volume verse epic (1922–1928). They repeatedly honored Ernst, who professed his loyalty to the Third Reich shortly before his death. Veneration of the author was officially checked later, and his highly abstract and formal works were criticized as "bloodless."

Ernste Bibelforscher. *See* Jehovah's Witnesses.

Paul Ernst.

Ernte-. *See* Harvest.

Erzberger, Matthias, b. Buttenhausen (Württemberg), September 20, 1875; d. near Bad Griesbach (Baden), August 26, 1921, German politician. In 1896 Erzberger became editor of the Catholic *Deutsches Volksblatt* (German People's Paper); in 1903, a Reichstag deputy (Center party). During the First World War, he changed from a proponent of a "victorious peace" to an advocate of a policy of mutual understanding. In his capacity as state secretary (after October 1918), and upon the urgent request of the Army High Command, he signed the armistice at Compiègne on November 11, 1918, thus be-

Karl Ernst.

Matthias Erzberger.

coming the embodiment of a November Criminal (*see* NOVEMBER CRIMINALS) for the nationalist Right. His subsequent service as finance minister (June 1919–March 1920) was overshadowed by a corruption scandal. Erzberger fell victim to assassination by two former officers.

Espionage. *See* Abwehr.

Esser, Hermann, b. Röhrmoos, July 29, 1900; d. Munich, February 7, 1981, German politician. A First World War volunteer, Esser was initially a Social Democratic journalist. He joined the German Workers' Party in 1919, with membership book no. 2; the same year, he became managing editor of the VÖLKISCHER BEOBACHTER under Dietrich ECKART. Esser appeared as a speaker at party meetings and became the NSDAP's press agent in 1923. A notorious antisemitic agitator, he appealed to the basest instincts with dubious "revelations" and primitive slander. His fellow party member Otto STRASSER called him a "demagogue of the worst type."

Elected to the Bavarian legislature in 1932, Esser also became a Reichstag deputy, that body's second vice president, and Bavarian commerce minister, all in 1933. Burdened by his involvement in political intrigues and a scandal-ridden private life, he increasingly slipped into political oblivion. In 1935 he was shuffled off into the Propaganda Ministry as head of the Tourist Office. After publishing an inflammatory piece entitled *Die jüdische Weltpest* (The Jewish World Plague) in 1939, he made almost no further public appearances. For this reason he

Hermann Esser.

was released in 1947 after only two years of American imprisonment. In 1949 a German denazification tribunal categorized him as a major offender and sentenced him to five years in a labor camp. However, he was released in 1952.

Esterwegen, a so-called protective-custody camp, established in Emsland in March 1933; it was originally under the Prussian interior minister (Göring), rather than the Justice Ministry. Most prisoners were in PROTECTIVE CUSTODY; they included political prisoners such as Communists or socialists and high officials of the previous regime, such as provincial governors or police chiefs. There were also criminals and Jewish citizens at Esterwegen. Inmates were often mistreated by the SS guards, without cause or over trifles; they were kicked and beaten with fists, bars, truncheons, and rifle butts. Individual prominent and Jewish inmates were shot. The SS guards were paid as auxiliary policemen (50 RM a month with free board and lodging). Inmates were used to cultivate the moors.

The camp was dissolved in September 1936; the prisoners were transferred to the SACHSENHAUSEN concentration camp, which Esterwegen inmates helped construct. That same month, Esterwegen came under the authority of the Justice Ministry; it was filled with convicts, as were the other EMSLAND CAMPS. Esterwegen provided prisoners for work units in northern Norway in 1942, and in 1943 in France.

W. D.

Estonia (Estland), republic on the Baltic Sea, one of the Baltic states; area, 47,500 sq km (about 18,800 sq miles); population, 1.1 million (1934), with the capital at Reval (now Tallinn). At its founding on February 24, 1918, Estonia (until then under Russian rule) was still occupied by German troops. At first under a democratic government, it became an authoritarian state under President Konstantin Päts in 1934, after a fascist coup followed a severe economic crisis. The minority of BALTIC GERMANS constituted 1.5 percent of the population.

The GERMAN-SOVIET NONAGGRESSION PACT of August 23, 1939, brought Estonia into the Soviet sphere of influence. A German-Estonian pact in October 1939 regulated the resettlement of persons of German extraction in the German Reich. After a Soviet ultimatum, the Red Army occupied Estonia on June 16, 1940, but had to evacuate it in the fall of 1941 during Germany's Russian Campaign. The Estonians hoped for a re-establishment of their state; many of them served as volunteers in the Waffen-SS (for example, in the Twentieth Waffen-Grenadier Division). During the German occupation, Estonia was a Generalkommissariat belonging to Reichskommissariat OSTLAND. Soviet troops re-entered Estonia in August 1944, taking Reval on September 22.

Eternal (*ewig*), term frequently used by the National Socialists; though secularized, it retained religious associations. It was intended to imply the predestined and permanent nature of their system: the party made a "claim of eternal leadership" (Goebbels); party congress locations would have "eternal fame."

Eternal Jew. *See* Wandering Jew.

Ethics, branch of philosophy concerned with morality (the norms of human behavior) and its foundation. National Socialism promulgated a radical *völkisch*-collectivist ethics, according to which the individual meant nothing, while all acts were to be gauged according to their utility for the "*Volk* Community of fate and blood" (*Schicksals- und Blutgemeinschaft des Volkes*). Since moral perception was determined by "race and blood," the German's "natural Nordic-Germanic feeling" would instruct him on what was advantageous for this community. Besides traditional community virtues, National Socialist ethics emphasized, in particular, responsibility toward one's race: this included the "will to [produce] a child," as well as an impeccable attitude on racial hygiene; its supreme commandment was to respect the "race barrier" (*Rassenschranke*). In this demented racial ethics, only that which served victory in the "race war" could be ethical; this included finally both EUTHANASIA and the FINAL SOLUTION. Thus in Himmler's eyes (speech of May 5, 1944), genocide was the "claim to fame" of the SS and left its perpetrators "decent" (*anständig*).

Ethiopia, self-designation of the East African empire of ABYSSINIA before and after the Italian annexation of 1936–1941.

Ethnic aliens (*Fremdvölkische*), according to National Socialist (NS) categories, in general all persons who did not belong to the German *Volk*; in a narrower sense, all "elements incapable of RE-GERMANIZATION" in the occupied countries, especially in the east, during the Second World War. In Himmler's opinion as "Reich Commissioner for the Fortification of the German Volk-Nation," ethnic aliens constituted "a danger for the German *Volk* Community" and thus were placed under special penal law in December 1941. Within NS master-race ideology they were considered to be work slaves ("itinerant workers") who had to learn "to be obedient to Germans as a divine command" (Himmler in *Einige Gedanken über die Behandlung der Fremdvölkischen im Osten* [Some Thoughts on the Treatment of the Ethnic Aliens in the East]; 1940). NS occupation policies affected these aliens most harshly, since as "human beasts" (*Menschentiere*, in Himmler's speech of October 4, 1943) they were fair game.

Ethnic German Central Office (Volksdeutsche Mittelstelle; Vomi), NSDAP office under SS-Gruppenführer Werner LORENZ. Established in 1936 by Rudolf Hess to coordinate the concern for ETHNIC GERMANS by the state and the party, in 1938 it was placed directly under Hitler. The Vomi tried to win ethnic Germans over to National Socialism and to utilize them for Hitler's political goals, as in the SUDETEN CRISIS. Beginning in 1939 it organized the resettlement of German ethnic groups from foreign countries into the Reich, checked the racial and political credentials of new settlers, and sorted out foreigners according to their suitability for RE-GERMANIZATION. On October 7 of that year the Vomi was finally merged into the Reich Office for the Integration of the German Volk-Nation (Reichsamt für den Zusammenschluss des deutschen Volkstums) under the *Reichsführer-SS* (Heinrich Himmler) in his capacity as Reich Commissioner for the Fortification of the German Volk-Nation.

Ethnic Germans (*Volksdeutsche*; literally, *Volk*-Germans), National Socialist term for persons of German origin who lived beyond the borders of the Reich. In contrast to the FOREIGN GERMANS (*Auslandsdeutsche*), they did not have German citizenship. The *Volksdeutsche* had to be of "German or species-related blood" and to "speak the German language and to identify voluntarily with the German *Volk* Community and cultural community." The most diverse groups were included under this rubric, from Germans resident in southeastern and eastern Europe, some since the Middle Ages, to those who had emigrated overseas in the 19th century and those who had forcibly been given foreign citizenship through the territorial cessions of the VERSAILLES TREATY. These latter groups of former citizens of the German Reich sometimes formed minorities with considerable political weight in their host countries. The connection between the Reich and the ethnic Germans was maintained by organizations such as the VOLK LEAGUE FOR GERMANDOM ABROAD and, as of 1936, above all by the ETHNIC GERMAN CENTRAL OFFICE.

The often difficult situation of the ethnic Germans became favored grist for the NS propaganda mill at such times as the SUDETEN CRISIS and the POLISH CAMPAIGN, when it provided a justification for the aggressive policies of the Third Reich. On the other hand, it played no role when problems were unrelated to the political situation, as with the South Tyrol or in the case of the Baltic states after the GERMAN-SOVIET NONAGGRESSION PACT. The Baltic Germans were resettled as the first ethnic German group, and later some 900,000 other *Volksdeutsche* were resettled. The "Heim-ins-Reich" (Back home to the Reich) slogan was proclaimed, which *de facto* usually meant settlement in areas occupied by Germany (such as the Wartheland) and, after the war, EXPULSION. Expulsion was also the fate of most ethnic Germans who were not resettled, a total of some 7 million, of whom 1 million lost their lives in the upheaval. [The term *Volksdeutsche* continued to be used in the Federal Republic of Germany for those of German heritage, most of them in countries to the east, who sought entrance; the Basic Law of the Federal Republic granted automatic citizenship to ethnic Germans.]

Ethnic mush (*Völkerbrei*), term introduced in *völkisch* circles at the turn of the century. It was appropriated by National Socialist propaganda to defame multi-ethnic states that were not "racially pure" (the Roman empire, for example), but also to denote states that, as "host peoples" (*Wirtsvölker*), assimilated racial minorities.

Ettighofer, Paul Coelestin, b. Colmar, April 14, 1896; d. Zülpich, October 15, 1975, German writer. Ettighofer began with war literature, written in journalistic style; his novel *Feldgrau schafft Dividende* (Field-Gray Brings Dividends; 1934) describes the "awful exploitation" of German prisoners of war in French mines. In numerous penny novels Ettighofer described war as a thrilling adventure, which assured him of a wide audience even after 1945. Postwar critics justified the chauvinist spirit of his "factual novels" by pointing out that he pleaded for "chivalry during acts of war."

Eugenics (*Eugenik*), doctrine of hereditary health. The term "eugenics" was replaced by HEREDITY CULTIVATION.

Eupen-Malmédy, Belgian frontier area near Aachen; area, 1,036 sq km (about 380 sq miles); population, 62,000 (1933), of whom 52,000 were German-speaking. Eupen-Malmédy belonged to Prussia after 1815, and was assigned to the so-called PLEBISCITE REGIONS by the VERSAILLES TREATY as compensation for war damage. Belgium conducted only a public "consultation" (June 24, 1920), threatening advocates of continued union with Germany with massive penalties (such as deprivation of food supplies). Only 271 of the 33,726 eligible voters put their names down on the voting lists. The League of Nations ignored German protests. On Gustav Stresemann's suggestion, and with Belgian consent, negotiations on the return of the area began in 1926, but they failed because of French objections. On May 18, 1940, Hitler ordered the reincorporation of Eupen-Malmédy into the German Reich. After the war it again went to Belgium, with small border changes.

Euringer, Richard, b. Augsburg, April 4, 1891; d. Essen, August 29, 1953, German writer. Euringer was a pilot in the First World War, then a laborer and a bank employee. He became known as the author of the "best combat pilot novel," as critics termed his *Fliegerschule 4* (Flying School 4; 1929). He also wrote for the *Völkischer Beobachter* after 1931, and along with Hanns JOHST, Erwin Guido KOLBENHEYER, and other writers was among the best-known National Socialist authors. His *Deutsche Passion*

Richard Euringer.

(1933), a sort of modern miracle play, received the first State Prize of the Third Reich. Euringer also wrote and produced THING PLAYS, which he valued as "theater of nature" and which suited his cultural and literary predilections. His further works included *Die Fürsten fallen* (The Princes Fall; 1935) and *Chronik einer deutschen Wandlung* (Chronicle of a German Transformation; 1936).

European Advisory Commission (EAC), commission of representatives of the United States, the USSR, Great Britain, and (after November 27, 1944) France; it met first on December 5, 1943, and for the last time on July 26, 1945. It was founded by a resolution of the Moscow Foreign Ministers' Conference in October 1943. The task of the commission was to submit proposals to the Allied governments for the postwar treatment of Germany and Austria. The results of their deliberations were the division of both countries into OCCUPATION ZONES, the division of their capitals into four sectors, and the organization of Allied administration and control.

European New Order (*Europäische Neuordnung*), propagandistic euphemism for plans to transform Europe under German leadership and "from the center" (*aus der Mitte heraus*) (*see* WEST, THE) after the "final victory." It camouflaged the project of a "Great-German Reich of the German Nation" from the Atlantic to the Urals, which was to realize National Socialist racial and territorial goals in that area. This entailed the single-minded application of the FINAL SOLUTION of the Jewish question and the subjugation of the "Eastern peoples" in particular, the removal of great population masses eastward in order to "Germanize" the Russian area (*see* GENERAL PLAN FOR THE EAST), the repression of even the Western nations to the position of dependent helot-peoples, and the creation of an autarchic European "Greater Economic Area" (with Africa as a colonial "supplementary area"), which could then prevail in the coming final struggle with the United States for world domination. This brutal and utopian European New Order had no place for partners of the German master race. Hitler's treatment of even collaborationist fascist movements in other countries was marked with barely disguised contempt even during the war, giving the lie to the fraternization themes of the official EUROPE IDEOLOGY. Not even with the alleged "Germanic fraternal peoples" in the Netherlands, Norway, or Denmark were there arrangements compatible with peace.

Europe Ideology (*Europa-Ideologie*), embellishment of the National Socialist policy of expansion as a "Crusade against BOLSHEVISM" for the sake of Europe. According to the theses of this ideology, military assistance was to be recruited during the Russian Campaign from small and conquered countries as being in their own interest. The Europe Ideology, as circulated, for example, in the illustrated propaganda magazine SIGNAL, abandoned the usual emphasis on German claims to leadership and was restrained. It was used to recruit volunteers for the WAFFEN-SS and in exhibitions, films, and brochures, but its efforts to obscure the real goals of the NS EUROPEAN NEW ORDER during and after the war had only limited success.

Euthanasia (*Euthanasie*; Gr., "easy death"), assistance in death; aid that eases the death of someone certain to die. By law euthanasia is permissible only when no shortening of life is involved. The National Socialist (NS) authorities designated their extermination of so-called "LIFE UNWORTHY OF LIFE" in the years from 1939 to 1945 as "euthanasia."

The Euthanasia program during the Third Reich was the outgrowth of the NS worldview:

Europe Ideology. National Socialist propaganda poster: "Europe. Protect its 3,000-year-old culture against Bolshevism."

"The weak must be eliminated." The NS ideology was taken to the public with all available propaganda media. Film was especially favored as a means of suggestively raising the question of why the individual and the state should be burdened with the incurably mentally ill, who were classified as "useless eaters" (*unnütze Esser*), when a sensible physician could release them from their suffering (for example, *Das Erbe* [The Inheritance], 1935; *Opfer der Vergangenheit* [Victim of the Past], 1937). The issue was later expanded beyond the mentally ill to incurably ill persons (*see* ICH KLAGE AN).

Child-Euthanasia came first. The impulse behind this extermination operation came from without; in late 1938 relatives of a deformed child turned to Hitler with the plea to release the child from "his suffering." He gave the approval, delegating his attending physician Karl BRANDT to handle the situation as necessary. Simultaneously he gave Brandt and Reichsleiter Philipp BOUHLER, chief of the Chancellery of the Führer, the oral authorization to proceed similarly in other such cases, while ensuring that the Chancellery was not implicated. Under the name "Reich Committee for the Scientific Registration of Serious Hereditary and Congenital Diseases" (Reichsausschuss zur wissenschaftlichen Erfassung von erb- und anlagebedingten schweren Leiden), an organization was created that first dealt with mentally ill and deformed children to the age of three, and later on with older children as well. The children were evaluated by selected physicians on the basis of a report and a brief medical history. Children selected as "unworthy of life" were sent to so-called pediatric specialty divisions (*Kinderfachabteilungen*) of particular hospitals and sanatoriums, where they were killed.

The Euthanasia program for mentally ill adults ran parallel to the children's program. In October 1939, Hitler signed an authorization, backdated to September 1, 1939—the outbreak of the war—to kill such persons. "Operation T4," the mass killing by gas of mentally ill adults, was carried out on the basis of this authorization. Here too, the ill were registered through a questionnaire operation; the forms were evaluated by selected medical experts—the *Kreuzleschreiber* (writers of little *x*'s). Persons chosen for killing were taken to transit facilities for camouflage purposes, then to one of the six killing centers.

To avoid implicating Hitler's Chancellery, "Operation T4" used fake organizations for contact with the outside world. Because the killings became public knowledge despite the camouflage measures, the propaganda efforts had no success. Protests—especially from church circles—led Hitler to order the operation stopped in August 1941. This did not, however, end the murder of the mentally ill. The halt did not affect the children's program, nor did it stop "Operation 14f13," an extension of "Operation T4" to concentration camp prisoners who were mentally ill or incapable of work (*see* INVALID OPERATION). Finally, adult patients of hospitals and sanatoriums continued to be killed, although no longer by gas in the killing facilities. Rather, the killing was done by administering tablets or injections, or by withholding nourishment in the custodial institutions. According to available data, at least 100,000 people fell victim to the Euthanasia measures.

A. St.

Evangelical Church. *See* German Evangelical Church.

Evolution (*Evolution*). **1.** In the sense of uninterrupted development in the sociopolitical realm, evolution is the opposite of revolution. After the Seizure of Power, Hitler widely promoted the transition to an evolutionary phase in order to oppose demands for a SECOND REVOLUTION: "Revolutions only do away with the circumstances of power. Evolution alone transforms actual circumstances" (speech of September 5, 1934). **2.** In terms of the philosophy of history, evolution is the assumption of a systematic development of humankind, which according to National Socialist ideas could be positively

Euthanasia. Still photograph from the film *Ich klage an* (I Accuse).

influenced through the setting of "species-appropriate goals." **3.** In the biological sense, evolution refers to the process of species development as described by the Theory of DESCENT.

Ewers, Hanns Heinz, b. Düsseldorf, November 3, 1871; d. Berlin, June 12, 1943, German author. After writing cabaret lyrics, Ewers had his first success with *Deutsche Kriegslieder* (German War Songs; 1915). He became the most important representative of "Black Romanticism" in Germany, with cruel and fantastic horror stories. His main works included the best-seller *Alraune* (The Mandrakes; 1911). Made into a movie several times, it is the story of a "child artificially conceived from the sperm of a murderer and the womb of a whore." Contemporary critics called his prose a "compendium of decadent motifs." Ewers joined the NSDAP at an early date, and wrote two propaganda novels before the Seizure of Power: *Reiter in deutscher Nacht* (1932; translated as *Rider of the Night*) and *Horst Wessel: Ein deutsches Schicksal* (Horst Wessel: A German Fate; 1933). Despite his ideological adaptability, Ewers did not achieve the success he desired, since the National Socialists labeled his books "revolting," and banned them as "decadent" in 1934.

Ewiger Jude. *See* Wandering Jew.

Exhumation Operation (Enterdungsaktion), the clearance of mass graves by Special Commando (SK) 1005 (*see* SPECIAL COMMANDOS). In early 1942 the commander of SK 4a, Paul BLOBEL, relieved of his earlier command by Reinhard Heydrich, was charged with the removal of the corpses of murdered Jews. After experiments with flamethrowers and explosives, the burning of corpses on grates finally proved to be the most suitable method. While Blobel's activity was first limited to burning corpses in the EXTERMINATION CAMPS, as of late 1942 he also arranged for the removal of corpses from mass graves in the occupied Eastern Territories. The operation was named "1005" after a bureaucratic code in the Reich Security Main Office. The commandos were called "SK 1005," and functioned with or without additional personnel. They generally consisted of a leader from the Security Police or Security Service (SD), junior officers, and squads from the Security Police and SD, as well as Jewish or local work commandos.

The size of the SK fluctuated according to the size and difficulty of the operation. Members of the regular police were added to the units for concealment of the operation and to guard the work commandos. After completing their work, members of the work commandos were killed, although they had often been promised their freedom. Because of the rapid retreat of the German troops, the Exhumation Operation could be carried out only incompletely. Numerous mass graves remained, especially in the former eastern operational areas of EINSATZGRUPPEN B, C, and D.

A. St.

Exile (*Friedlosigkeit*), in the German legal tradition, a means of punishing criminals by expelling them from the community and declaring them outlaws or "fair game" (*Freiwild*). The National Socialist administration of justice prided itself on restoring this community-based punishment —which a liberalistic justice system had abandoned—in the Law Regulating the Revocation of Naturalized Citizenship and the Deprivation of Citizenship of July 14, 1933 (*see* CITIZENSHIP, REVOCATION OF).

Exile literature (*Exilliteratur*), or emigré literature, general term for works produced during a writer's period of residence, usually forced, outside his native land. The phenomenon is as old as literature itself and is remarkable because of the particularly frequent exile of writers, who have always been suspect by rulers. After the National Socialist Seizure of Power in 1933, many German authors left their homeland because of persecution for reasons of racial policy. Their works constitute "exile literature" in the narrow sense. The situation of these writers was initially marked by incisive changes: separation from the previous environment, total change in living conditions, economic problems, loss of a readership in the mother tongue, new orientation in a foreign language, and political homelessness. This contributed to an increased politicization of their literary production; yet, given the multiplicity of personalities and orientations, it is impossible to speak with uniformity and precision of an exile literature, especially since socially, the experience encompassed both the comfortable exile of a Nobel laureate such as Thomas MANN and the real starvation that befell other writers.

Various German emigrant presses and journals were founded, such as the PARISER TAGEBLATT (1933–1940) and New York's *Aufbau* (Rebuilding), which is still published. Besides political essays, literary works appeared that dealt with the exile experience or the hated regime back home, by authors such as Bertolt BRECHT,

Johannes BECHER, Franz WERFEL, Else Lasker-
Schüler, Walter MEHRING, Nelly Sachs, Anna
Seghers, Carl ZUCKMAYR, and others. But important works without any concrete connection
to the contemporary situation also arose in exile.
Their high status also owes something to the
largely provincial production of those writers
remaining in Germany. Thus exile literature
formed a bridge spanning the Third Reich's
hostility toward the intellect and assured continuity and a connection with international artistic movements.

Experience (*Erlebnis*), central cliché of National
Socialist propaganda: such experiences as the
world war and the TIME OF STRUGGLE were
mythically transfigured through emphasis on
communal fortitude. National Socialism itself
was characterized as an "experience" of "emotion and faith" (*Fühlen und Glauben*).

Expressionism (literally, the art of expression),
movement in art and literature arising after
1900 that is characterized by the dissolution of
fixed forms and an emphasis on exaggeration of
feeling. It was Expressionist authors, in particular, who voiced their moral indignation after
1914 through apocalyptic descriptions of war
and pacifist poems and plays. The texts and
pictures of the Expressionists "estrange" reality
in a grotesque, caricature-like manner; they
portray ugliness, they transmit a feeling of discomfort; they concern themselves with subjective feelings and (under the influence of Freud)
with the libido; they choose outsiders, cripples,
the insane, and prostitutes as their "heroes."

By its conscious contrast with the traditional,
petit-bourgeois concept of art, Expressionism
embodied for the National Socialists everything
that they rejected in modern art. It was seen as
"the worst aberration in the area of artistic
creation," "uninhibited daubing of paint," or
"incomprehensible stammering." In the "representation of the pathological, . . . the inferior
and ugly," the National Socialists saw the use of
a "conscious weapon" of Jewish as well as of
Marxist circles for the purpose of fostering moral
"CORROSION" (*Zersetzung*). After the Seizure of
Power, Expressionist art and literature were
prohibited; books by Johannes R. BECHER,
Leonhard Frank, and René Schickele were
burned; and paintings by Max BECKMANN and
Erich HECKEL were seized as "degenerate."
Expressionist artists were, at the least, forbidden to work; some were forced into exile or
died in concentration camps.

In its beginnings Expressionism manifested
elements common also to *völkisch* art: political
criticism and aesthetic hostility toward the
bourgeoisie. In early works influenced by Expressionism, some of the authors held in esteem
by the National Socialists (including Arnold
BRONNEN and Hanns JOHST) translated *völkisch*
ideas in emotionally exaggerated ways.

H. H.

Expropriation (*Enteignung*), procedure for transferring private property, especially landed property, to state ownership with compensation. The
possibilities for expropriation in the Third Reich
were widely expanded, since the need for state-
owned land rose by leaps and bounds: for the
Wehrmacht (law of March 29, 1935), civil aviation (law of June 27, 1933), highways (*see* AUTO-
BAHN; law of December 18, 1933), and the
power industry (law of December 13, 1935).
The acquisition of land for HOMESTEADS
also demanded regulations for expropriation,
which, however, had been created before 1933.

Expropriation of princes (*Fürstenenteignung*;
also *Fürstenabfindung*, indemnification), retention of the confiscated wealth of German prince-
ly houses after the end of the monarchy (November 11, 1918). After several states had made
indemnification agreements with their former
princes, the LUTHER government proposed a
law to create uniform compensation regulations

Demonstration for the expropriation of princes. The
signs read: "Not a penny to the princes" and "The
victims of capitalist greed."

on February 2, 1926. The Left, especially the KPD (Communist Party of Germany), was opposed, and itself proposed total expropriation, backed up with a popular initiative and 12.5 million signatures. After the Reichstag rejected expropriation (with the votes of the NSDAP) on May 6, 1926, a referendum became necessary. The proposal won 15.5 million votes on June 20, which, however, fell short of the required majority of 20 million. Despite the great popularity of expropriation, Hitler pledged his party's opposition at the BAMBERG FÜHRER CONFERENCE, because he feared being tarred with Bolshevism and he rejected common action with the Marxist parties.

Expulsion (*Vertreibung*), eviction of large population groups from their home territory, primarily during and after a war. As early as the conferences at TEHERAN (December 1943) and YALTA (February 1945), the Allies had discussed the expulsion of the German population from the German EASTERN TERRITORIES and from eastern and east-central Europe into a Germany west of the ODER-NEISSE LINE. The POTSDAM AGREEMENT of August 2, 1945 (Section XIII), determined "that the German population or parts of it who have remained in Poland, Czechoslovakia, and Hungary must be transported to Germany" in "an orderly and humane manner." The ALLIED CONTROL COUNCIL was to regulate the details of the plan.

The systematic expulsion of the German population began, however, as early as July and August 1945, that is, before the Control Council plan had been signed on October 17, 1945. It by no means happened in an "orderly and humane manner"; indeed, it flouted international law and human rights. It included the

Expulsion. Murdered Silesian peasant.

German population in the German Eastern Territories that were under Polish administration, as well as in northern East Prussia, which had been handed over to the Soviet Union. Moreover, millions of Germans had fled westward before the advancing Red Army since the end of 1944. The expelled and those who had fled lost not only their homeland but usually all their possessions as well.

In 1944–1945, a total of 19.17 million German citizens or ETHNIC GERMANS lived in eastern Germany and eastern Europe. Of them, 10.39 million were in Germany's Eastern Territories (including Danzig), 1.26 million were in Poland, 2.07 million in the USSR, 633,000 in Hungary, 3.62 million in Czechoslovakia (including the Sudetenland), 550,000 in Yugoslavia, 689,000 in Romania, and 6,000 in the other Balkan states. By 1950, 11.96 million people (expelled and fleeing) had come to what remained of Germany. Of them, 7.29 million came from the German Eastern Territories, 618,000 from Poland, 421,000 from the Soviet Union, 2.99 million from Czechoslovakia, 213,000 from Hungary, 297,000 from Yugoslavia, 137,000 from Romania, and 3,000 from the other Balkan states. Over 2 million lost their lives while fleeing or being expelled. The majority of the total of 4.4 million refugees who were initially received in what later became the German Democratic Republic or in East Berlin migrated later as "refugees from the Soviet zone" (*Sowjetzoneflüchtlinge*) to the Federal Republic of Germany or to West Berlin (from 1949 to July 1961, about 2.1 million).

Since 1950 the resettlement in Germany of Germans and ethnic Germans from Eastern Europe and east-central Europe has continued to a lesser extent, mostly on the basis of contractual agreements between the Federal Republic and the individual states. Between 1950 and 1982, about 1.14 million resettlers arrived. In 1982, an estimated 3.3 million Germans still lived in Eastern Europe, most of them (some 2 million) in the Soviet Union.

The judicial status of the expellees has been regulated in the Federal Republic by the Federal Law for the Expelled (*Bundesvertriebenengesetz*) of May 19, 1953. Their social and economic integration has been largely achieved with the aid of extensive legislation (*see* EQUALIZATION OF BURDENS). In the Charter of Those Expelled from Their Homeland (*Charta der Heimatvertriebenen*) of 1950, the expelled have expressly renounced vengeance for the injustice and violence done to them. But their organizations continue to demand the restoration of the German boundaries of 1937.

R. B.

Extermination camps (*Vernichtungslager*), camps or parts of camps that were established in accordance with the FINAL SOLUTION of the Jewish question, and that were basically designated for the killing of Jews. The term "extermination camp" refers to its purpose, not to the conditions within. Pure extermination camps were KULMHOF, BEŁŻEC, SOBIBÓR, and TREBLIN-

Extermination camps. Clothing of gassed prisoners.

KA. AUSCHWITZ (Birkenau) and MAIDANEK (at times) had a double function: they were both extermination camps and concentration camps. In the pure extermination camps Jews were killed immediately after their arrival, except for the few who were set aside for certain work squads (including removal of corpses and cleaning up). In the camps with a double function, a *Selektion* generally took place after the arrival of a transport. Those unable to work were driven into the gas chambers; those who could work were used in private or SS-owned businesses, and were killed only after their ability to work had been exhausted. Some killing of non-Jewish prisoners took place in the extermination camps, for example, of GYPSIES and "politically intolerable" Soviet PRISONERS OF WAR.

A. St.

Extraordinary Pacification Operation (Ausserordentliche Befriedungsaktion; AB-Aktion), code name for the liquidation of Polish political opponents and professional criminals in the Generalgouvernement (the occupied part of Poland) from mid-May to mid-June 1940. The operation was based on Hitler's order to Governor-General Hans FRANK, and was intended as a "preemptive *völkisch* counterattack." A total of some 3,500 men and women who were considered resistance fighters, along with about 3,000 criminals, fell victim to the operation. The so-called INTELLIGENTSIA OPERATION is to be distinguished from the AB-Aktion.

A. St.

Fachamt (specialized office or bureau), subdivision of the GERMAN REICH LEAGUE FOR PHYSICAL EXERCISES. It was also the designation for the trade subdivisions of the GERMAN LABOR FRONT, which initially were called Reichsbetriebsgemeinschaften (Reich Workplace Communities).

Fachgruppe (trade or occupational group), amalgamation of trade bureaus (*see* FACHAMT) in the GERMAN LABOR FRONT and of subdivisions in the NATIONAL SOCIALIST LEAGUE OF LAW GUARDIANS, the ORGANIZATION OF THE INDUSTRIAL ECONOMY, and the NATIONAL SOCIALIST LEAGUE FOR GERMAN TECHNOLOGY.

Fachschaft (occupational union; guild), compulsory union of all members of a profession or trade belonging to an organization based on a professional category or status. An example was the publishing guild (Fachschaft Verlag) in the "Book Trade" occupational group in the REICH WRITING CHAMBER.

Fähnlein (Little Flag), term for a subdivision of the German Jungvolk (*see* HITLER YOUTH [HJ]), chosen for its conscious reference to the 15th- and 16th-century divisions of peasant soldiers (*Landsknechte*) who fought together under a flag. One Fähnlein was made up of four Jungzüge (Young Platoons) and included about 160 boys under a single *Fähnleinführer*; it was comparable to a FOLLOWERSHIP (Gefolgschaft) in the HJ.

Faith (*Glaube*), belief in—and trust in—transcendental realities that are not "provable" either logically or physically, especially God. This religious concept of faith was utilized by National Socialism to enshrine its ideological positions as truths for salvation to which one could just as

trustingly submit oneself as to their herald (*see* FÜHRER CULT). In this context the propaganda readily spoke of "blind faith" and unquestioning obedience, legitimizing the demand for such through further sacral borrowings such as "faith in the gospel of his [HITLER's] doctrine" (Goebbels) or the "trinity of blood, faith, and the state" (Gottfried Feder). The Seizure of Power in 1933 was consequently celebrated at a Reich Party Congress (*see* REICH PARTY CONGRESSES) under the title "The Victory of Faith." Making a tool out of the concept of faith also served to mask antichurch and anti-Christian goals and was intended to show that National Socialism was a religiously based movement.

Faith and Beauty (Glaube und Schönheit), special unit (*Werk*, or "program") of the LEAGUE OF GERMAN GIRLS (BDM) for young women 17 to 21 years old. It was established at the Hitler Youth Leadership Assembly in Berlin on January 19, 1938. Very much in the forefront of this program was preparation for the role of housewife and mother, realized through personal hygiene, housekeeping, education, and home decorating. These areas were augmented by intensive physical activity, especially dance and gymnastics, as well as by issues of fashion, since one could not entirely ignore the natural interest in style and adornments despite National Socialist reservations regarding a "passion for self-beautifying" (*Putzsucht*). The intent to totally capture young people in this age category was only partially attained. As the war went on, Faith and Beauty with its ideal of "grace and charm" (*Anmut*), far removed from reality, lost its attraction in the deadly seriousness of daily life. Service obligations further curtailed the Faith and Beauty operations.

Faith and Beauty. Gymnastics with balls.

Falange (Span.; phalanx, in the sense of "shock troop"), the Spanish state party; a national movement in terms of its own image of itself. Its emblem was a bundle of radiating arrows joined by a yoke. The Falange began in 1934 through an agreement between the Spanish Falange (founded in 1933 by José Antonio PRIMO DE RIVERA) and the nationalist and syndicalist J.O.N.S. attack groups, which arose in 1931. An amalgam of fascism, National Socialism, and Spanish tradition, until 1936 it attained little political significance; it was not even directly involved with the military revolt of July 17, 1936, that set off the SPANISH CIVIL WAR. After the execution of Primo de Rivera, Gen. Francisco FRANCO assumed leadership of the Falange and in 1937 united it with other nationalist groups, notably the traditionalist Carlists, thus creating a "reservoir of all patriotic forces." The original Falange, a militant party of fascist stripe, gradually lost influence after the end of the civil war, since its role as bearer of state authority was alien to its nature. It declined into a mere label for the Franco dictatorship, which rested on the pillars of the military, the clergy, the large landowners, and industrial capital. The Falange was finally and officially dissolved in 1976–1977.

M. F.

Falkenhausen, Alexander von, b. Blumenthal bei Neisse, October 29, 1878; d. Nassau, July 31, 1966, German general. In 1900–1901, Falkenhausen participated in the German China Expedition; from 1910 to 1914 he was military attaché in Tokyo; he served on the western front during the First World War, as well as in Russia and Turkey. He retired in 1930, but was called back to active service by Hitler in 1939, promoted to infantry general on September 1, 1940, and in the same year was made military commander of Belgium and northern France. In this post, as an urbane and correct officer who was nevertheless sworn to unconditional obedience, Falkenhausen manifested some contrary atti-

Falange members march through the streets of the Spanish city of Valladolid on their way to the front.

Alexander von Falkenhausen.

253 Family

tudes. He initially opposed introduction of the wearing of the Star of David in Belgium and did not generally carry out the deportation of local Jews, but he did give orders for the shooting of hostages. Suspected by the Gestapo of ties with German military resistance circles, Falkenhausen was dismissed in July 1944 and remained imprisoned in the Dachau concentration camp until the end of the war. A Belgian war tribunal sentenced him in 1951 to 12 years' hard labor, but pardoned him after 16 days in view of the fact that he had shielded individual Belgian citizens from the grasp of the SS.

Falkenhorst, Nikolaus von, b. Breslau, January 17, 1885; d. Holzminden, June 18, 1968, German colonel general (July 19, 1940). Falkenhorst's First World War posts included that of General Staff officer; from 1925 to 1927 he was with the operations section of the Armed Forces Ministry; from 1933 to 1935 he was military attaché in Prague, Belgrade, and Bucharest. Promoted to major general (July 1, 1937), Falkenhorst became commanding general of the Twenty-first Army Corps in the Polish Campaign. He directed the NORWEGIAN CAMPAIGN (April 9–June 10, 1940) and then led the Wehrmacht attack on the Soviet Union at the Murmansk front in the summer of 1941. He was Wehrmacht commander from January 1, 1942, until December 18, 1944, when he was removed owing to differences with Reich Commissioner Josef TERBOVEN. Responsible for the execution of members of a British commando mission, Falkenhorst was sentenced to death on August 2,

1946, by a British-Norwegian military tribunal; he was later pardoned and released from imprisonment on July 23, 1953.

Fallada, Hans (originally, Rudolf Ditzen), b. Greifswald, July 21, 1893; d. Berlin, February 6, 1947, German writer. Fallada ran afoul of the law early in life: while still an adolescent, he shot a *Gymnasium* schoolmate in a duel and was committed to an asylum for two years. In 1920 he began his literary career with Expressionist writings, but in 1925 he had to begin a two-year prison term for alcohol and drug addiction. He achieved his first great success in 1931, with a novel on the COUNTRY FOLK MOVEMENT, *Bauern, Bonzen und Bomben* (Peasants, Bosses, and Bombs). This was surpassed in 1932 by his novel *Kleiner Mann—was nun?* (*Little Man, What Now?*), which dealt with the consequences of the worldwide economic crisis. Fallada was not bothered by the National Socialists, and published further successful novels, including *Wer einmal aus dem Blechnapf frisst* (*Who Once Eats Out of the Tin Bowl;* 1934) and *Wolf unter Wölfen* (*Wolf among Wolves;* 1937); yet he was considered suspect, since he lacked the "strong inner attitude." After the war's end Fallada lived in East Berlin.

Hans Fallada.

Nikolaus von Falkenhorst.

Family (*Familie*), in the narrower sense, a married couple with children (nuclear family); in the broader sense, also the designation for relatives or household (extended family). As the "germ cell of the *Volk*," the family played a crucial role in National Socialist POPULATION POLICY. Through measures to promote HEREDITY

CULTIVATION, the family was to be kept "racially pure" and genetically healthy. Through financial support (*see* MARRIAGE LOANS) and exaggerated propaganda (*see* WOMEN IN THE THIRD REICH), the "will for a child" was to be awakened and encouraged, so that the objective of a "full family" with at least four children would become the rule, and the continuation of the German *Volk* would be assured. The idea of "family" was also highly prized for its usefulness in binding FOREIGN GERMANS to the homeland. Where women and children "unnaturally" dominated the family, as in the United States, or where German families formed extended families with "ethnically alien" servants, as in southeastern Europe, UMVOLKUNG (de-ethnicization) was said to threaten—the transformation of ethnic character that jeopardized the cohesiveness of "all-Germandom" (*Gesamtdeutschtum*).

Family support (*Familienunterstützung*), financial compensation for dependents of men conscripted for military service or summoned to army or air defense exercises, in accordance with the Family Support Law of March 30, 1936. Family support payments exceeded those for social welfare and were provided by welfare agencies out of Reich funds. In wartime, this aid was received by relatives of men summoned to active duty who were entitled to support. Besides making direct payments, family support subsidized rent, insurance payments, educational and medical expenses, debt amortization, and the like. It could not exceed 85 percent of the breadwinner's last net income.

Fanal (beacon), word borrowed from French during the Napoleonic era; it became a fashionable National Socialist term for referring to a symbol or signpost. It was often used tautologically in the formulation "flaming beacon" to heighten emotion.

Fanaticism (*Fanatismus*; from Lat. *fanum*, sacred place, temple), the mentality of prejudiced personalities who cling with zealous passion to an idea, a religion, or some ideal, and who cannot be influenced by rational discussion. The term first came into use in the field of religion in order to impugn sectarianism. Its negative meaning was then extended to cover political intolerance. In the National Socialist vocabulary, however, it experienced a positive transformation. Beginning with *Mein Kampf*, one spoke of "holy fanaticism," of "fervid" or "defiant" fanaticism. The adjective "fanatic" became fashionable in NS propaganda, employed in the sense of "unconditional" or "ready for any sacrifice" for the Führer, Germany, or National Socialism. Today the negative meaning once again prevails.

Farmers, dispossession of (*Abmeierung*; *Meier* means "farmer," especially a tenant farmer), withdrawal of the management or ownership of a hereditary farm owing to loss of the so-called *Bauernfähigkeit* (capacity to be considered a peasant), according to the HEREDITARY FARM LAW.

Fasces (lictor's bundle), a number of sticks or rods, bound together with a cord, from the midst of which emerges the cutting edge of an ax. Originally a symbol of office or authority in ancient Rome, it was made by the Italian Fascists into a symbol of their movement in 1919. From *fascio* (band) the term FASCISM developed.

Fascism

Fascism was originally only the movement founded by Mussolini in Italy in 1919, which attained power through the 1922 "March on Rome," and the system of government control that depended on this movement until 1945. The term "fascism," however, soon came to stand for similar movements in other countries, insofar as they were nationalistic, anti-Communist, authoritarian, and antiparliamentarian. In the Communist camp as well as in many segments of the European New Left, "fascism" became a term useful for public agitation because it identified *the* enemy. From a psycholog- ical standpoint, the term seeks to comprehend dispositions, possibly acquired in early childhood, toward behavior that is both obedient to authority and obsessed with power. In the political controversies of the 20th century, hardly any other word has been so overused and given so many interpretations as that of fascism. It is necessary to distinguish among the historical phenomena of fascism, theories of fascism advanced by its adherents, and theories of fascism proposed by historians and political opponents.

The word derives from the Latin *fasces*, the old Roman bundle of rods, symbol of the lictors' authority. In Italian, *fascio* has the political meaning of "alliance" or "league." Mussolini's *fascio di combattimento* (combat league), established in 1919, was initially a leftist splinter group that in the early 1920s first gained a middle-class following after turning against socialism and communism, thereby becoming a mass movement (*movimento*).

The Fascist state was centralist as well as strictly hierarchical and authoritarian, with the "Duce" (Führer) at the apex as the sole representative of the nation: "This pseudodemocratic claim of the Führer principle to be the realization of the total identity between the rulers and the ruled was the basic fiction of the Fascist as well as of the National Socialist [NS] system. Moreover, social life was 'seized' in semimilitary fashion as extensively as possible through numerous state and party organizations; the highest right of the citizen was supposed to be, in direct opposition to a middle-class, liberal notion of state, service to the uniformed nation. More than the debated origins in middle-class society, this affinity to the total organizational forms of the socialist-Communist systems clearly stands out" (Karl Dietrich Bracher, 1984).

The ideology of Fascism was always a mixture of eclectic elements. Mussolini, originally a Marxist, adopted from Marx the idea of class struggle, from Georges Sorel the political principle of "direct action," from Vilfredo Pareto the conviction that a hierarchical and authoritarian structure of society was necessary, and from

Italian children's primer: "Benito Mussolini loves children very much. The Italian children love Il Duce very much."

Friedrich Nietzsche the concept of the "will to power" as the fundamental motive force in the process of history. Nationalism and its related ethic manifest traces of Hegel's political theory. *Völkisch* racism as the basis of a militant ANTISEMITISM, a fundamental component of NS ideology, was at first alien to Italian Fascism. It gained entry into Fascist theory only during the Second World War under NS pressure, but without ever gaining greater influence in Italy. In general, Italian Fascism, measured against the claims of its theory, was much less efficient politically than NATIONAL SOCIALISM, its German variation.

The phenomenon of nationalist, authoritarian, and, in each case, anti-Communist movements and systems of rule was not limited to Italy after the First World War. Hitler entered the scene with his NSDAP as a "socialist workers' party," which attracted a following from broader strata of the middle class only because of the fear of communism, thus becoming a mass movement. However, similar regimes also came to power in the 1930s and 1940s, in Spain (Francisco FRANCO), Portugal (Antonio SALAZAR), Hungary (Miklós HORTHY), Poland (Józef PIŁSUDSKI),

Election poster from the early period of Fascism.

Austria (Engelbert DOLLFUSS and Kurt SCHUSCH-
NIGG), Romania (Ion ANTONESCU), and Argentina (Juan Perón). Their leaders were all authoritarian, anti-Communist, and antidemocratic.
Therefore it has become usual to label all these
systems "fascist." It must be recognized, however, that the expression of fascism in these countries was quite varied and depended heavily on
the specific national and economic conditions.
Even the imperialist programs that were supposed to lead to a strengthening of the national
state differed. Along with Hitler and Mussolini,
Franco remains the outstanding example of a
fascist dictator. He was able to establish his
power, which endured for decades, through a
victorious civil war against Communists. It is
nonetheless striking that, in all states in which
fascism had a political chance, a Catholic tradition predominated, whose own mentality favored the establishment of a centralist and
strictly hierarchical state authority. In Germany
the "Führer" Hitler, coming from the Austrian-
Catholic tradition, also made use of the obedience of citizens brought up in the tradition of
the authoritarian Prussian state. In this way
National Socialism attained the greatest and
most fateful efficiency of all fascist movements.
(In contrast, fascism never had a realistic chance
in countries with old democratic traditions and
an early separation of spiritual and temporal
power, such as Switzerland, France, England,
and the United States. Even the fascist or outright NS parties that were helped into existence
in the occupied lands through German pressure
during the Second World War were until 1945
mere vassals of the military regimes, and they
disappeared with the downfall of the Third
Reich.)

The question of which political and social
conditions can give rise to fascism remains controversial. The following factors are repeatedly
mentioned as important: discontent with a difficult parliamentary system; disappointment as a
nation-state as a result of the First World War;
the world economic crisis; fear of international
communism; anxiety regarding cultural decadence; the irrational wish for "order" and for a
strong man at the top. These reasons are to the
point, but they explain the total phenomenon of
fascism as little as would the study of the biographies of fascist dictators.

The Marxist definitions of fascism have proved
to be mainly untenable. The thesis that fascism
is a symptom of the decline of capitalism was
refuted by historical reality, as was the Stalinist
theory of agents, according to which leaders and

functionaries of fascist movements are mere
lackeys or agents of international capital. To be
sure, Karl Radek—the Soviet journalist active in
Germany—in 1923 had warned against fascism
as "socialism for the little man" and as a new
mass movement. Yet the Comintern theoreticians succeeded in their dismissal of fascism as
trivial, which led to a disastrous underestimation of Hitler by the European Left before the
Second World War. In 1933 Ernst Bloch had
more correctly perceived that, contrary to leftist
hopes, the NS movement would not so easily be
pushed aside in light of social reality. Faced
with the irrationality of psychological forces at
work here, the traditional Marxist methods of
thought failed. In his book *Massenpsychologie
des Faschismus (The Mass Psychology of Fascism; 1933)*, Wilhelm Reich pointed out that in
the economic crisis the masses for the most part
turned not to the left, as Marxist theory had
predicted, but to the right. As a follower of
Sigmund FREUD, Reich believed that the psychological disposition toward fascism was acquired in earliest childhood, not under capitalist
conditions but rather through the long-
embedded authoritarian structures of the patriarchal society. The causes of fascism were thus
displaced into nearly prehistoric time. In the
empirical analysis *Studies in Prejudice* (5 vols.,
1949–1950), Max Horkheimer, Theodor
Adorno, and others from the Frankfurt School
published studies of the authoritarian character
in which they departed from the view of fascism
as a petit-bourgeois movement.

The Stalinist theory of fascism reached its
grotesque high point with the condemnation of
social democrats as "twin brothers of fascism"
and with the thesis of the "social fascism" of the
SPD (Social Democratic Party of Germany) as
the "archenemy": "In reality it was a matter of
drawing the line at democratic socialism and of a
justification for its own failures in 1922 as in
1933" (K. D. Bracher, 1984).

In richly documented studies, Ernst Nolte
(1963, 1968) sought to give a comprehensive
phenomenology of historical fascism. Beyond its
multiform variants in individual countries, he
posits the component of anti-Communism as a
unifying element, which makes fascism in its
totality a phenomenon characteristic of the period between the world wars. However, in saying
this he provides new justifications for the sim-
plistic Marxist theory that fascist equals anti-
Communist. Karl Dietrich Bracher (1984) takes
a stand against the inflationary use of the concept of fascism, against a purely ideological or

socioeconomic classification "which follows the fashionable notion of a supposed societal alternative of fascism or socialism" and thereby misconstrues the decisive criterion of the modern state, namely, political freedom. Hence Bracher emphasizes the relationship between right-wing and left-wing dictatorships.

Each new theory of fascism has to take it seriously as a mass movement that transcends classes. In Germany, as in Italy, workers, middle-and upper-class citizens, the military, artists, and scientists belonged to it. As a mass movement of this kind, fascism led to the catastrophe of the Second World War and then disappeared in the military and political defeat of 1945. Neofascist currents and groups in individual European countries have since then no longer been able to develop into mass movements.

Ivo Frenzel

Fascist Grand Council. *See* Grand Council of Fascism.

Fashion (*Mode*), the prevailing taste in (primarily feminine) clothing, hairstyles, accessories, and cosmetics. Beginning in the late 1920s a conservative trend made itself felt. The masculinization of women through the "Garçonne-Mode" of short hair and short skirts was followed by fashions geared to the traditional female role (*see* WOMEN IN THE THIRD REICH). Skirts, dresses, and hair grew increasingly longer until the mid-1930s. After 1933 the National Socialists attempted to neutralize the influence of international trends on German fashion by founding the GERMAN FASHION INSTITUTE. Simple and unerotic sports clothing was considered the "style for our times." Dresses of a uniform cut, with a well-defined waist and reaching to the calf, worn with thick-soled wedge-heeled shoes, were supposed to undercut class distinctions. Anything frivolous and exclusive was frowned upon. Fashion shows and women's magazines sponsored by the FAITH AND BEAUTY unit of the LEAGUE OF GERMAN GIRLS (BDM) advocated "BDM gowns" and pleated skirts. Economic consolidation in the second half of the 1930s and a growing demand for less uniformity brought modest changes in fashion: padding broadened women's shoulders and lace adorned petticoats, without overemphasizing individuality.

The war led to fashion stagnation. The introduction of the REICH CLOTHING CARD permitted only a few acquisitions. Women's magazines added patterns, among other reasons to allow "replacement of defective gussets"; fashion brochures were issued for home sewing ("New from old for small and tall—saves coupon points for you and all") and to increase variety. Skirts were shortened to save fabric, while pants made a breakthrough despite ideological reservations (they were "unfeminine") because they were warmer, more practical, and better suited to factory work or air raid shelters than skirts and stockings. Nets or turbans wound from kerchiefs and fabric remnants replaced ladies' hats, which were unobtainable.

Men's fashions underwent little change after 1933: the tuxedo, cutaway, and dinner jacket remained for festive occasions. Sports clothing, sometimes with knickerbocker pants, was for daytime wear. The 1936 Olympic Games generated some fashion impulses, such as the parkas worn by winter-sports athletes, which became general leisure wear. Full-cut, multicolored "bush shirts" (similar to the later Hawaiian shirts) became expressions of fashion extravagance. Once the war began, uniforms made fashionable civilian clothing for men practically superfluous.

When the war ended, women (especially the younger ones) immediately picked up the international fashion trends: a "New Look" with

Fashion show (1939).

lavishly tailored styles. Swinging skirts emphasized feminine forms and contours and bid adieu to the homely knot and braid as hairstyles.

H. H.

Fat gap (*Fettlücke*), shortage of foodstuffs that supplied fats (in 1936, 45 percent). To achieve AUTARKY in the supply of fats, a plan was implemented in 1933 that, beyond its propaganda content (a "battle for production"), provided measures to increase supply through (1) the expanded cultivation of plants from which fats and protein could be derived; (2) greater efficiency in the fattening of livestock; and (3) an increase in the fat content of milk. In addition, measures by the "Reich Office for Oils and Fats" (established April 4, 1933) to control consumption, including taxation of fats and rationing, were expected to help eliminate this deficit as well as a PROTEIN GAP. Customer lists were used to test the rationing that would be necessary in a war—the first such test.

Fatherland (*Vaterland*), patriotic-poetic term for the native country (*Heimatstaat*). It was largely avoided in National Socialist language usage, since it was regarded as tainted by bourgeois-conservative or monarchist sentiments ("With God for King and Fatherland"), and since it had also been much used by Jewish circles in the past. The press was instructed "no longer to use" the term "even in a positive sense" (March 16, 1942).

Fatherland Front (*Vaterländische Front*), Austrian movement for political unity founded on May 21, 1933, by Engelbert DOLLFUSS; it opposed the parliamentary system, class struggle, and the ANSCHLUSS. At the first "General Roll Call" on September 11, 1933, the Fatherland Front acquired an Austrofascist program and the CROOKED CROSS as a symbol. After the banning of political parties (May Constitution of May 1, 1934), it became the sole representative of political opinion in the Austrian CORPORATIST STATE. It was divided into a Civilian Front and a Military Front (which in 1937 became a Front Militia and a Storm Corps) and patterned itself on the German and Italian models. In 1936 an "Austrian Young *Volk*" (*Jungvolk*) came into existence and the cultural organization "New Life" was founded as an agency of the Fatherland Front; public political lectures [*Volkspolitische Referate*] were intended to win the cooperation of opposition groups, especially that of the National Socialists. Neither Prince STARHEMBERG, who succeeded Dollfuss at the end of

Fatherland Front. Rally on Vienna's Heldenplatz. In the foreground, Chancellor Dollfuss; to his left, Vice-Chancellor Fey; in back, to the right, Stepan, national leader of the front.

July 1934, nor Kurt SCHUSCHNIGG (after May 14, 1936) achieved this goal. Despite massive pressure (*see* DETENTION CAMPS), the working class could not be integrated. The Fatherland Front ended with the Anschluss (March 13, 1938).

Faulhaber, Michael, b. Heidenfeld bei Schweinfurt, March 5, 1869; d. Munich, June 12, 1952, German Catholic theologian. Ordained a priest in 1892, Faulhaber completed his postdoctoral *Habilitation* in Old Testament studies in 1899. He was a professor in Strasbourg (1903–1910), bishop of Speyer (1911–1917), and also a military bishop during the First World War. In 1917 he became archbishop of Munich-Freising, and in 1921 a cardinal. Faulhaber owed the high regard in which he was held by the Roman Curia not least to his bluntly conservative attitude, from which viewpoint he condemned the Weimar Republic as being built upon the "high treason and perjury" of the November Revolution.

While no friend of National Socialism, after a visit to Rome in March 1933 Faulhaber switched

Michael Faulhaber.

his position to favor the Vatican's policy objective of a CONCORDAT and contributed significantly to diminishing reservations among the German bishops. For all that, his attitude toward the National Socialist regime remained ambivalent. In his Advent homilies of 1933, as a "trained" Old Testament scholar he vehemently defended the Jewish origins of Christianity against antisemitism, and criticized violations of the Concordat as well. But he also thought he could procure leniency and respect from the state for church interests through good conduct (for example, his visit to Hitler at the Obersalzberg on November 4, 1936). On the one hand, he rendered assistance in formulating the encyclical MIT BRENNENDER SORGE (With Burning Concern; issued on July 14, 1937); on the other hand, in November 1939 he led a thanksgiving service for the "wondrous rescue of the Führer" during the BÜRGERBRÄU ASSASSINATION ATTEMPT. He protested against the EUTHANASIA program, yet willingly sacrificed church bells to be used for war matériel. He uttered no public word concerning the persecution and extermination of Jews.

Feder, Gottfried, b. Würzburg, January 27, 1883; d. Murnau (Upper Bavaria), September 24, 1941, German politician. A civil engineer, Feder became active in economic and political affairs. With his demand for "breaking the servitude to interest rates," he exerted strong influence over the program of the GERMAN WORKERS' PARTY (Point 11), which he had joined even before Hitler. As an economics expert, he repre-

sented the NSDAP in the Reichstag from 1924 to 1936; he was also a state secretary in the Reich Economics Ministry (1933–1934) and Reich Commissioner for Housing (1934–1935). His influence declined with the downfall of the social-revolutionary group around Gregor STRASSER (1932) and fell further when his rigorously anticapitalist theories proved to be a hindrance to Hitler in soliciting the support of businessmen. Feder's political career was stopped cold when he became a professor at Berlin's Technical College in 1936. His work *Das Programm der national-sozialistischen Arbeiterpartei und ihre weltanschaulichen Grundlagen* (The Program of the NSDAP and Its Ideological Foundations; 1927) is an important document for the history of National Socialism.

Gottfried Feder.

Federzoni, Luigi, b. Bologna, September 27, 1878; d. Rome, January 24, 1967, Italian politician. Federzoni was the publisher of the newspaper *Idea Nazionale* and an adviser to VICTOR EMMANUEL III. He took part in Mussolini's seizure of power in October 1922, and subsequently served as colonial minister (1922–1924, 1926–1928), interior minister (1924–1926), Senate president (1929–1939), and president of the Accademia d'Italia. An exponent of the moderate wing of the Fascist party, on July 25, 1943, Federzoni voted against Mussolini in the GRAND COUNCIL OF FASCISM. For this reason he was sentenced to death in absentia in 1944 by the regime in SALÒ.

Feeling (*Gefühl*), the sense of oneself (*Zumutesein*), which served as a basis for one's mood and instinctive sense of place in the world; according to the National Socialist view, it was contingent upon "racial constitution." Because feeling preceded will and action and had a decisive effect on them, the "Nordic-Germanic person" had the invaluable advantage of a predominating "pure, genuine, deep, open-to-the-world feeling."

Fegelein, Hermann, b. Ansbach, October 30, 1906; d. Berlin, April 28, 1945, SS-*Gruppenführer.* A former stableboy and jockey, Fegelein made a career with the Equestrian-SS. He served as inspector of cavalry and transport facilities in the Reich Security Main Office (RSHA) from May to October 1942 and was named an SS-*Obergruppenführer* on December 2, 1942. Wounded in late October 1943, he became Himmler's liaison with the Führer's headquarters; there, after his wedding to Gretel Braun, the sister of Eva BRAUN, Fegelein gained access to Hitler's innermost circle. In the final days of the Third Reich, he lived in the Führer's bunker, but he aroused Hitler's wrath by leaving without permission and was arrested. When news of Himmler's discussions with Count Folke BERNADOTTE arrived, Hitler had Fegelein shot as an accomplice despite his protestations of innocence. Eva Braun made no attempt to rescue her brother-in-law.

Fehrenbach, Konstantin, b. Wellendingen (Baden), January 11, 1852; d. Freiburg im Breisgau, March 26, 1926, German politician. Fehrenbach studied Catholic theology and jurisprudence and in 1882 began work as a lawyer in Freiburg; he was a Center party deputy in the Baden diet (1885–1887, 1901–1913; president, 1907–1909). Fehrenbach was elected to the Reichstag in 1903, becoming chairman of that body's Central Committee in 1917, and Reichstag president in 1918. He was president of the National Assembly in 1919. In 1920 he became Reich chancellor at the head of a middle-class cabinet. Fehrenbach took part in the reparations conferences at Spa in 1919 and London in 1920. His willingness to make an arrangement with the

Konstantin Fehrenbach.

victorious powers gave him a reputation as an apologist for a FULFILLMENT POLICY; this cost him the support of the GERMAN NATIONAL PEOPLE'S PARTY and consequently the chancellorship in May 1921. In March 1924 he became chairman of the Center party's Reichstag delegation.

Feldherrnhalle (cenotaph [empty tomb or monument] for generals), hall of fame built in Munich's Odeonsplatz between 1841 and 1844 by Bavarian king Ludwig I. A march to the hall was planned to crown the HITLER PUTSCH of November 9, 1923, but the putsch collapsed in

The Feldherrnhalle. Memorial tablet inscribed with the names of those who died in the Hitler Putsch of 1923.

Hermann Fegelein with Gretel Braun and Hitler.

front of the monument under fire from the Bavarian state police. During the Third Reich, an honor roll adorned the eastern side of the hall, bearing the names of the 16 National Socialist victims. Every year on November 9, Hitler led a memorial march from the Bürgerbräukeller to the Feldherrnhalle. The so-called Guard Standard of the SA bore the name "Feldherrnhalle," and in 1944 a tank-grenadier division (formerly the Sixtieth Motorized Infantry Division) received the same designation.

Fellgiebel, Fritz Erich, b. Pöpelwitz (Silesia), October 4, 1886; d. Berlin, September 4, 1944 (executed), German general. From 1939 Fellgiebel was chief of the Intelligence Communications Office of the Wehrmacht High Command. He rejected National Socialism, and at the outbreak of the war put himself at the disposal of the opposition movement. During the assassination attempt of July 20, 1944, he undertook to block the communications system at the Führer's headquarters, but achieved only temporary success. Designated as future postal minister by the conspirators, Fellgiebel was arrested that same evening, and sentenced to death by the *Volk* Court on August 10, 1944.

Female Wehrmacht Retinue (Weibliches Wehrmachtgefolge), official collective term for the *Wehrmachthelferinnen* (women in the Wehrmacht; *see* WEHRMACHT, WOMEN IN THE) who were deployed with the troops as part of the WAR AID SERVICE program.

Fememorde. *See* Vehm murders.

Feuchtwanger, Lion, b. Munich, July 7, 1884; d. Los Angeles, December 21, 1958, German writer. From an Orthodox Jewish family, Feuchtwanger repeatedly explored subjects from early Jewish history to portray "Jewish existence in a non-Jewish world." His novel *Jud Süss* (*Jew Süss;* 1925) depicted, among other things, the arousal of antisemitic mass psychosis in the 18th century. Given his pacifist and socialist worldview, Feuchtwanger was an early opponent of the NSDAP. In *Erfolg* (*Success;* 1930), he wrote a satirical chronicle of the HITLER PUTSCH and described the provincial petit-bourgeois character of National Socialism. During the Third Reich he was deprived of his citizenship because of "low-minded insults to the National Socialist movement" and "glorification of Jewry." Feuchtwanger went into exile in southern France. In 1940 he was interned in the Le Vernet camp, but was able to escape through

Lion Feuchtwanger.

Spain to the United States. After the war his works found more attention in the German Democratic Republic than in the Federal Republic of Germany.

Feuerstein, Heinrich, b. Freiburg im Breisgau, April 11, 1877; d. Dachau concentration camp, August 2, 1942, German Catholic theologian and pastor of Donaueschingen from 1908. Even before 1933, Feuerstein opposed National Socialism; after that date, he protested repeatedly against the government's arbitrary actions. Finally he denounced the crimes against the mentally ill (*see* EUTHANASIA). In 1941 he publicly saluted the "martyrs of Dachau." Soon afterward he joined them: arrested in January 1942, Feuerstein was brought to Dachau in June of that year, by then totally debilitated. He bore his imprisonment, in Christian humility, as a "school of holiness."

Field Post (Feldpost), the organization of letter and parcel mail between the war front and the homeland during the Second World War; the term also referred to the items forwarded by the Field Post. Tried out during maneuvers in 1936, it was designed with a system of field postal numbers that were intended to make it difficult for enemy intelligence to determine the location of the addressees or their units. The Field Post employed 12,000 field postmen, who handled some 25 million postage-free pieces a day (for a total of 40 billion). Of the deliveries, 75 percent went to the front through as many as 400 Field Post offices at the division level in all of German-occupied Europe. Field Post Inspection Stations

(Feldpostprüfstellen; F.P.P.) randomly censored the mail for counterintelligence purposes, and also to combat the UNDERMINING OF MILITARY STRENGTH. Regular sampling reports informed commanders about troop morale.

The Field Post had great propaganda value for the Wehrmacht, and was called the "heart of mental warfare" (*Herzstück der geistigen Kriegsführung*). In 1941 the anthology *Feldpostbriefe aus dem Osten—Deutsche Soldaten sehen die Sowjetunion* (Field Post Letters from the East—German Soldiers View the Soviet Union) was published. As the fortunes of war withered, however, the "Field Post weapon" backfired, since it was forwarding an increasing amount of bad news and could no longer fulfill its assigned role as the "blood donor of relatives' faith and will." The Allies used the propaganda potential of the Field Post by dropping captured or forged letters behind the front lines and over Germany. The best-known Field Post forgery was the so-called MÖLDERS LETTER.

Field Sports Teams (Geländesport-Arbeitsgemeinschaften), camouflage organizations of the SA during the later years of the Weimar Republic. Under this designation entire SA formations gained access to courses in Reichswehr-subsidized Gymnastic and Sports Schools (later the REICH CURATORIUM FOR YOUTH FITNESS TRAINING). In this way the SA accomplished some of the premilitary training of its followers.

Film, artistic medium that had priority in material support and that was politically exploited by the NSDAP: "We are convinced that film is one of the most modern and far-reaching means for influencing the masses" (Goebbels). German cinema in its beginnings gained worldwide esteem for its artistically distinguished productions, and despite the economic crisis, in 1933 it was still counted as among Hollywood's most important competitors. The German market, dominated by a small number of large companies (Tobis; Ufa), was nationalistically oriented and at an early stage offered the NSDAP the chance for collaboration with producers and theater owners. As early as 1927 the party produced its own propaganda films, and popularized what had until then been a city entertainment through the use of "movie-mobiles" (*Kinomobile*) in the rural areas. After the Seizure of Power, it organized "*Gau* film centers" to promote village movie evenings, school performances, and open-air theater viewings (at times with as many as 20,000 in attendance).

In 1933, then, conditions were favorable for the SYNCHRONIZATION of the film industry and its transformation into a single unified company, which was carried out by force because of the special interest of the Propaganda Ministry in motion pictures. First there were prohibitions and the cancellation of contracts with Jewish and left-wing directors. Then, an "entertainment tax" (June 7, 1933), combined with new regulations of the state film-rating service, gave substantial tax advantages to any film that exemplified the National Socialist (NS) spirit and that was "politically valuable." In 1934 the Reich Motion-Picture Law and the establishment of the position of "Reich Film Adviser" (*Reichsfilmdramaturg*) created a legal basis for advance censorship or prohibition. Even before the establishment of the REICH CULTURE CHAMBER, the "corporatist transformation of the film industry" took place, in which membership in a Film Chamber was a prerequisite for employment in motion pictures. Since Jewish and socially critical directors and actors were excluded, and Goebbels, as a generous financier, succeeded in gaining control over new productions through a film credit bank, synchronization proceeded very smoothly. Beginning in 1934 the Reich systematically bought up shares of the large film companies; a "Reich Agent for the German Film Industry" (Max WINKLER) was able in 1937–1938 to transform German film companies into a unified concern having the acronym Ufa (*see* UNIVERSE FILMS, INC.), with a Reich film manager (*Reichsfilmintendant*), one Fritz Hippler, at its head.

Film production flourished in NS Germany. With the start of the war, new production facilities and market outlets opened up in the occupied countries. Between 1933 and 1945 a total of some 1,100 motion pictures were released, of which 15 percent were primarily for propaganda purposes. In the early phase especially, films glorifying the party were made, such as SA-MANN BRAND, HANS WESTMAR, and HITLERJUNGE QUEX (all in 1933). These were followed by the artistically more accomplished works of Leni RIEFENSTAHL (TRIUMPH OF THE WILL, 1934; *Olympia*, 1936). As an aspect of the PERSECUTION OF JEWS, antisemitic agitation films came to the theaters in 1940: JUD SÜSS (Jew Süss) and *Der Ewige Jude* (*see* WANDERING JEW). After the war began, a growing number of WAR FILMS were meant to spread optimism.

Goebbels relied more, however, on indirect propaganda: he encouraged "good entertainment films," since "the war effort also requires

Goebbels congratulates Otto Gebühr on his appointment as State Actor. In the background, the director Veit Harlan and the actress Kristina Söderbaum.

that we keep our people in a good mood." He considered films to be "not merely entertainment," but rather "an educational medium"; he maintained, however, that it was "very advisable to cloak this pedagogical purpose." This was achieved with films that on the surface were mainly apolitical: HEROIC FILMS that told stories glorifying great Germans (*Bismarck;* 1940); high-budget operettas and REVUE FILMS such as *Stern von Rio* (Star of Rio; 1939–1940); comedies (MÜNCHHAUSEN; 1943) and comic society films; adventure films with Hans ALBERS or Harry Piel, such as *Ein Unsichtbarer geht durch die Stadt* (An Invisible Man Stalks the City; 1933). While movie propaganda of the Third Reich was mainly oriented toward the realism and social pathos of the proletarian film (Sergei Eisenstein, Slatan Dudow), feature films followed the popular-entertainment model. Movie heroes who invited imitation manifested obedience, submission to destiny, adaptation to authority structures, and the priority of the community over individual interests, as well as "moral purity." Along with providing desirable character models, films also fulfilled their aim of

diversion: the "little man" was expected, as Goebbels intended, "to forget the war for a few hours" in the movie theater.

Because of the political and propaganda significance of the medium, the National Socialists were more willing to make ideological and material compromises in the cinematic area than elsewhere. Thus, new Hollywood films (even MICKEY MOUSE) were shown in German theaters until 1940. Popular actors of half- or quarter-Jewish ancestry or with Jewish partners received special work permits (for example, Paul Henkels, Theo Lingen, and Heinz RÜHMANN). Movie actors were the best-paid artists of the Third Reich (top earners like Hans Albers, Heinrich GEORGE, and Hans Moser had yearly incomes of over 200,000 RM). Because of their skillful cinematic handling of the NS worldview, the directors Karl RITTER, Veit HARLAN, Hans STEINHOFF, and Wolfgang LIEBENEINER were given most of the projects.

As the war dragged on, the production volume of the film industry also receded; "staff workers" were summoned to military service, materials became scarce, and censorship mea-

1
Hans Albers in the color film *Münchhausen.*
2
Kristina Söderbaum.
3
Program for the *German Weekly Newsreel.*
4
Dutch advertisement for the film *The Wandering Jew.*

sures increased. Although movies continued to be made in the studios up to the last days of the Third Reich, beginning in 1944 many productions were either suspended or postponed. "War theme" films such as KOLBERG were given preference. Yet even in the closing phase some unconventional works, like Helmut KÄUTNER's *Unter den Brücken* (Under the Bridges; 1945), were produced, despite obstacles. As a whole, cinema was the only artistic medium during the Third Reich that, by exploiting its freedom of scope in content and form, produced more nuanced and aesthetically more complex works, which obtained and secured esteem for German films abroad despite any ideological doubts. After 1945, the German motion-picture industry was unable to follow up on its wartime and prewar successes. In the Soviet zone/German Democratic Republic the vestiges of Ufa were assimilated into the DEFA (*Deutsche Film-AG*); in the Western zones some 40 production companies started up between 1946 and 1948, since the western Allies through liquidation measures impeded the foundation of a new large company.

H. H.

Filth-and-Trash Law (*Schmutz- und Schundgesetz*), term for the Law to Protect Youth from Filthy and Trashy Writings, passed on December 18, 1926, to protect children and adolescents from a type of literature that was not more precisely defined. Conservative middle-class organizations with similar goals already existed, and had condemned the likes of "penny dreadfuls" about Indians, as well as erotic literature, while promoting patriotic literature that was formally little different. Review boards set up pursuant to the law were particularly concerned that books containing sexual depictions be put on a "List of Filthy and Trashy Writings" and thus be made subject to strict distribution regulations. Nationalist circles led the campaign, which had as a theme that such writings compromised "military fitness." Politically unpopular, socially critical, and socialist literature frequently became a target as well. After 1933, the synchronization of the book trade and the installation of authorities mandated to censor and control made special procedures and organizations to protect young people superfluous, and the law was set aside on April 10, 1935.

H. H.

Final Solution

The term "Final Solution" (*Endlösung*) of the Jewish question did not at the outset have the meaning in National Socialist (NS) usage of the "physical extermination" of the Jews. The term's earliest documented uses are in a bulletin from Adolf EICHMANN dated March 12, 1941, and an order from the REICH SECURITY MAIN OFFICE (RSHA) of May 29, 1941. As early as the antisemitic discussions at the turn of the century, the call was heard for a "solution" of the Jewish question, in the sense of creating a special legal category (legislation treating them as aliens) or, at most, expelling Jews. NS radicalization in the direction of a Final Solution at first did not go considerably farther, but it did take more concrete and brutal forms along the lines of population transfer (including the MADAGASCAR PLAN and the establishment of Jewish reservations in the east). Exactly when Hitler decided on the extermination of the Jews, as he had rhetorically threatened in his Reichstag speech of January 30, 1939, and when he gave the first orders for it, cannot now be precisely deter-

mined. In the course of preparations for the Russian Campaign, deciding factors accumulated with growing frequency in the gradual progression toward a Final Solution in the lethal sense. The ultimate general order for extermination was never fixed in writing.

The first extensive operations against the lives of Jews came about at the beginning of the attack on the Soviet Union (June 22, 1941). Reinhard HEYDRICH, the head of the Security Service (SD), ordered the EINSATZGRUPPEN under his command to surreptitiously unleash pogroms in the territories soon to be occupied, to intensify them, and to guide them in the "correct" paths. He further ordered that Jews in party and governmental positions were to be executed. A great number of pogroms resulted, especially in the Wehrmacht-occupied Baltic states and in the Ukraine, leading to the deaths of multitudes of Jews. Further, as "security measures" or as "vengeance" for incidents charged to Jews, Jewish men in particular were shot en masse. From approximately August

Roundup of Dutch Jews in Amsterdam.

1941 onward, all Jews were swept into the extermination measures "in order to leave no avengers at large," as the Einsatzgruppen commanders explained to their men. Along with the Einsatzgruppen, police units too carried out extermination actions. They generally acted on orders from the HIGHER SS AND POLICE LEADERS (*Höhere SS- und Polizeiführer*). Einsatzgruppen and police squadrons variously obtained support from Wehrmacht units or headquarters, which above all provided trucks for the removal of Jews to places of execution.

The scale of extermination operations is evident from SITUATION REPORTS and surviving individual reports of the EINSATZKOMMANDOS (EK) or Sonderkommandos (SPECIAL COMMANDOS; SK) under the Einsatzgruppen. Thus, for example, EK 3 of Einsatzgruppe A, according to a report of December 1, 1941, shot 133,346 Jews in "liberated" Lithuania as well as in the area of Minsk between early July of that year and the reporting day. Another 4,000 were killed when EK 3 took over "security police" tasks in the course of pogroms by the local militia. The reporter, SS-Standartenführer Karl JÄGER, in conclusion confirmed that "the goal of solving the Jewish problem for Lithuania . . . has been achieved. In Lithuania there are now no more Jews left, except for the work Jews. . . . These . . . too I wanted to do away with, which got me

into heated controversy with the civil administration and the Wehrmacht." The largest single operations were carried out by SK 4a of Einsatzgruppe C under SS-Standartenführer Paul BLOBEL (*see* BABI YAR). In the late autumn of 1941, the RSHA made available to the Einsatzgruppen GAS VANS for the killing of Jews and other "potential adversaries." These mobile gas chambers were generally utilized for "smaller" extermination operations, such as during the "cleanup" of smaller ghettos and of prisons.

While the extermination operations of the Einsatzgruppen were already proceeding, on July 31, 1941, Hermann Göring ordered Heydrich to draw up plans "for the attainment of the sought-after Final Solution to the Jewish question," and to initiate all preparations for it within the German sphere of influence in Europe. After completion of the plan, Heydrich invited representatives from the ministries and governing bodies needed for collaboration to Berlin on January 20, 1942 (*see* WANNSEE CONFERENCE), in order to ensure its execution. The plan intended essentially to put eastern Jews into labor squads and to decimate them through exploitation of the labor force. The "remainder" were to be "appropriately handled." It was planned to transport them first to "transit ghettos" and from there to deport them further into the east.

The deportation of German Jews had already begun in October 1941. They were brought mainly to the ghettos of Riga, Minsk, and Łódź (Litzmannstadt), which at the start of the resettlement of Jews from the Reich had been partially "cleared"—that is, the indigenous ghetto residents had been liquidated by members of the Einsatzgruppen, not infrequently with the cooperation of local militia units. If the destination did not yet have lodging available, the transported German Jews were immediately shot. Sometimes, after arrival, Jews who were incapable of working were sorted out from the rest and immediately murdered. As an example, from the 19th Berlin eastern transport to Riga, with approximately 1,500 men, women, and children, only 60 able-bodied men were exempted from immediate annihilation. Despite the tense war situation and the urgent need for transport space, such trains rolled continually out of the Reich and out of the Protectorate of Bohemia and Moravia into the occupied Eastern Territories. From Berlin alone, between October 18, 1941, until the end of October 1942, at least 22 transport trains took a minimum of 13,000 Jews to Łódź, Minsk, Kowno, Riga, Trawniki, and Reval (*see* DEUTSCHE REICHSBAHN).

As part of the preparations for the Final Solution, suitable locations for the extermination of Jews were chosen; Himmler himself decided on AUSCHWITZ for a concentration camp. In August 1941 (presumably), he ordered the (first) commandant, SS-Obersturmbannführer Rudolf HÖSS, to set up the necessary facilities for mass killings. After conferring with SS-Obersturmbannführer Adolf Eichmann, the head of Sec-

tion IV B 4 (later IV A 4), on "Jewish Affairs," in the RSHA, the decision was made to use gas as the means for killing. Höss ordered that a farmhouse situated in the area of the later Auschwitz II (Birkenau) camp be rebuilt for gassings; he began with trial gassings in the arrest cells of Block 11 and in the "mortuary" (*Leichenhalle*) of the (old) camp crematorium. Facilities for mass gassings were meanwhile constructed in another camp. At KULMHOF, beginning in December 1941, an SK under SS-Hauptsturmführer Herbert LANGE and his successor, SS-Hauptsturmführer Hans BOTHMANN, murdered Jews who had been transported mainly from the Warthegau and from the Łódź ghetto. The killings (by March 1943 a total of 143,000 Jews, and again in 1944 presumably at least 25,000) followed a method that had been used in the EUTHANASIA program: gassing with carbon monoxide, in gas vans rather than in chambers. At Auschwitz, ZYKLON B, a compound based on hydrocyanic acid, was used; Höss thought it brought on death more quickly and seemed more reliable.

Around the end of 1941 the gassing facility at Auschwitz-Birkenau (the so-called Bunker 1) was completed. From early 1942, ever-larger transport trains arrived carrying Jews, at first from eastern Upper Silesia, neighboring parts of the Generalgouvernement (GG) of Poland, the Reich, and the Protectorate of Bohemia and Moravia. Later transports also came from territories occupied by the Wehrmacht and European countries under German influence, from France to Romania. On their arrival in Auschwitz the Jews were sorted (*see* SELEKTION): the able-bodied—10 to 15 percent of a transport—

Entrance to the Auschwitz-Birkenau extermination camp.

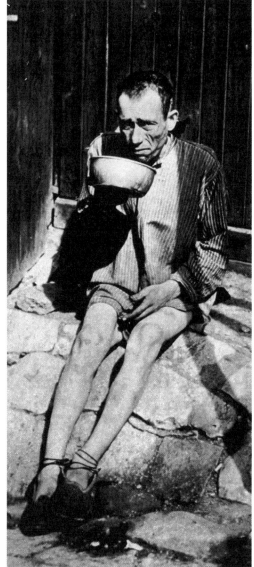

1
Last Walk of the Jews.
Watercolor by the concentration camp prisoner Waldemar Nawakowski, Auschwitz (1943).
2
Surviving concentration camp prisoner after the liberation by the Allies.
3
Execution. Scene from the American television series ''Holocaust.''

went into the labor pool for SS-owned factories and other enterprises in the general vicinity of the camp; those unfit for work were gassed. At times entire transports were killed immediately, without a *Selektion.*

The increasing number of deportation trains required additional gas chambers. In Birkenau (Auschwitz II) a total of five gassing facilities were constructed. During an uprising on October 7, 1944, prisoners blew up one installation; the remaining installations (with one exception) were dismantled by the SS beginning at the end of November 1944; the last one was destroyed in January 1945, shortly before the abandonment of the camp. The number of Jews killed in Auschwitz cannot be determined even approximately, since firm data are lacking. It is certain, however, that from May to October 1944 alone, when a great number of Hungarian Jews were deported to Auschwitz, more than 500,000 Jewish persons met their death.

Since from the beginning it was clear that Kulmhof and Auschwitz were not sufficient to exterminate all the European Jews, three more camps were set up for the SPECIAL HANDLING of the well over 2 million Jews living in the GG: BEŁŻEC (at the southeastern border of the Lublin district), SOBIBÓR (at the eastern border of the Lublin district), and TREBLINKA (northeast of Warsaw). The "resettlement" of Jews in these camps proceeded under the code name REINHARD OPERATION (named for Reinhard Heydrich, assassinated at the end of May 1942). It was directed by SS-Brigadeführer Odilo GLOBOCNIK, SS and Police Leader in the Lublin district. In all the camps, the killing of people was carried out primarily through the use of exhaust gases from truck or tank motors.

By the beginning of March 1942, Bełżec was ready for operation. On March 17, the first shipment of Jews arrived from Lublin. In Sobibór the first transports arrived in May 1942. Treblinka was the last camp to be put into operation, on July 23, 1942. The camps had been planned solely as places of extermination. After their arrival the Jews were immediately driven into the gas chambers and killed there. Selections for the gas chambers were made only when skilled workers were needed for specific projects or when the "cleaning and corpse-removal squads" were replaced; those replaced were themselves then killed.

The "resettlement" of Jews from individual districts of the GG into the extermination camps was hampered by wartime transport difficulties. In the summer of 1942 there were lulls that the

SS took advantage of to expand the capacity of the gas chambers. After the rebuilding, the gas chambers at Bełżec could hold 1,500 people (up from 150); at Treblinka, 4,000 (previously, 600); and at Sobibór, 1,200 to 1,300 (earlier, 200). From the beginning of August 1942 the extermination machinery once again ran in high gear. Continual transports arrived from the Reich and other countries at all the camps.

By the end of 1942 most of the Jewish population of the GG had been murdered, so the decision was made to shut the camps down. First, however, all traces of the exterminations had to be removed (*see* EXHUMATION OPERATION). The victims lying in mass graves (a minimum of 700,000 in Treblinka alone) were exhumed by "worker Jews" and cremated with around-the-clock toil. This activity was completed in Bełżec by March 1943; more time was required in Sobibór and Treblinka, where the gassing installations were kept in operation because of delays in closing down the ghettos (as when German firms refused to hand over Jewish workers, and because of the WARSAW GHETTO UPRISING). Revolts by prisoners in Treblinka (August 2, 1943) and Sobibór (October 14, 1943) finally hastened the shutdown of those camps. They were razed to the earth and the "worker Jews" were killed. In a letter dated November 4, 1943, Globocnik informed Himmler: "As of 10/19/43 I have concluded Operation Reinhard, which I conducted in the Generalgouvernement, and have broken up all the camps." According to conservative estimates, at least 1.75 million Jews fell victim to the operation.

Those Jews who worked in industries critical to the war effort were not drawn into the Reinhard Operation. After the liquidation of the ghettos—with the exception of Łódź—they lived in work camps operated by SS enterprises or by private businesses. Toward the end of the Reinhard Operation it was determined that in the Lublin district more Jews had been kept back from extermination than were necessary for the labor force. To hasten completion of the Final Solution and for "security" reasons (*see* "HARVEST FESTIVAL"), the decision was made to "decimate" these Jews. In early November 1943, Jews from Lublin and the camps around it were brought to Maidanek, in use at that time as an extermination camp, and, along with the Jews already there, were shot. The number of victims came to at least 17,000. Shootings on a large scale were also carried out in the camps at Poniatowa and Trawniki.

When the Red Army moved into Poland, the

commander of the Security Police and the SS in the GG, SS-Oberführer Eberhard Schöngarth, on July 20, 1944, gave the order to evacuate the camps. For the Jews that generally meant "Auschwitz," unless they had already been brought to a camp within Reich territory. The breakup of the Łódź ghetto followed, from the end of August to early September 1944. On August 21 there were still at least 62,000 Jews there. A short time later nearly all were on the way to Auschwitz, to camps in the Reich, or to Kulmhof, where for some months the extermination machinery was again in motion.

Numerous Jews still lived in the occupied parts of the USSR and in the Baltic area, despite the initial "cleanup operations" of the Einsatzgruppen. Many Jews who had fled from the murder commandos of the SS had returned to the cities after the massacres, in the belief that the persecution measures were past. Moreover, the Einsatzgruppen had not been able to conduct such operations everywhere. Because of the rapid advance of the troops, they had continually changed their positions in order to follow the army units. Once the civil administration was in place in the occupied Eastern Territories, ghettoization was implemented. By August 1941 there were ghettos in Libau (Liepāja), Dünaburg (Daugavpils), Vilna, Kowno, and Minsk. Shortly thereafter, killing operations resumed, and were often conducted with the help of police units under Higher SS and Police Leaders, in some areas aided by the local militia. In October 1942 Himmler personally ordered the liquidation of the last large ghetto in the Reichskommissariat Ukraine, in Pinsk. At the end of 1942 the Ukraine was essentially "Jewfree."

In the Reichskommissariat Ostland, ghettoization could not be effected so rapidly. By the autumn of 1941, mass shootings of ghetto residents were taking place; however, the ghettos were always refilled with Jews from the Reich and from other countries. It also happened that in some regions the German civil administration and the Wehrmacht—generally for economic reasons—obstructed the extermination measures. From the end of October 1942, after extensive selections, the ghettos were transformed into camps, or able-bodied selected individuals were transferred to existing camps. When the Red Army pressed closer, the SS deported some of the survivors to camps in the Reich and to Auschwitz; the remainder were shot on the spot. As with the breakup of the extermination camps, care was taken to eliminate the mass graves before the surrender of those areas.

The exact number of Jews who perished because they were caught up in the Final Solution cannot be established. From surviving reports about the killing operations of the Einsatzgruppen and other units, from transport lists of those heading toward the extermination camps, and from statistics about the Jewish population in the territories at the beginning of the operations, combined with tracing reports after the war, it can be estimated that some 5 million Jews were murdered or died as a result of conditions in the camps. The question of how many of them could have been saved if the Allies had shifted to systematic bombardment of the access routes, especially to Auschwitz, has recently been much discussed, sometimes for inappropriate [untauglichen] reasons of allocating guilt. No answer is possible. The Allies proceeded according to Roosevelt's motto that all the persecuted would best be helped by concentrating all resources on hastening the victory over Hitler.

Alfred Streim

Final victory (*Endsieg*), catchword in National Socialist propaganda that became increasingly used as the war situation grew worse. It was intended to suggest that all the setbacks could, after all, do nothing to hinder the final victory, for Germany would triumph "because triumph it must" (Goebbels). The word had already been utilized in the First World War, as well as in *Mein Kampf;* like the term WONDER WEAPONS, it was part of Goebbels's strategy of (vain) consolations aimed at upholding the will to stand fast as the enemy fronts drew nearer.

Finckh, Ludwig, b. Reutlingen, March 21, 1876; d. Gaienhofen (Bodensee), March 8, 1964, German writer and physician. Finckh wrote numerous popular stories and novels after 1906 whose subjects were rooted in the countryside and history of his Swabian homeland; among his best known is *Der Rosendoktor* (The Rose Doctor; 1906). He also published works on genealogy, such as *Heilige Ahnenschaft* (Holy Ancestry; 1926) and *Der Ahnenring* (The Ancestral Ring; 1934). Finckh considered his work to be a "struggle for the German soul, blood and earth, language and writing."

Finland, republic in northern Europe; area, 388,279 sq km (about 155,000 sq miles); population about 3.6 million (1928). After the November Revolution in 1917, Finland separated itself from Russia, became independent by a proclamation of the Finnish National Assembly on June 21, 1919, and assumed a republican constitution with a powerful position for the state president. After a terrible civil war from 1918 to 1920, between a "white" defense corps under Baron MANNERHEIM with occasional German support (under Colmar von der Goltz), and Soviet troops joined with Finnish "Red Guards," the Peace of Dorpat (October 14, 1920) brought recognition by the Soviet Union. Finland also gained a corridor to the Arctic Ocean with the port of Petsamo, in return for which Russia retained eastern Karelia. Deep distrust of Moscow, tensions with Sweden (language conflicts; dispute over the Finnish Åland Islands), cool distance from Germany, and the failed attempt to establish an entente with the Baltic states led to Finland's international isolation between the wars, with far-reaching repercussions in domestic politics (prohibition of the Communist party, and so on).

The GERMAN-SOVIET NONAGGRESSION PACT of August 23, 1939, which contained a secret supplemental protocol that expressly attached Finland to the Soviet sphere of interest, aroused grievous apprehensions in Helsinki concerning the country's own security and its freedom of action in foreign affairs; these fears proved to be justified by the WINTER WAR, provoked by Stalin. Without help from the Western powers, Sweden, or Germany, Finland was compelled to settle a devastating cease-fire with Moscow on March 12, 1940. Finland's total cutoff from Western help after the NORWEGIAN CAMPAIGN, Sweden's strict neutrality, the Sovietization of the Baltic states, increasing pressure from Moscow, and the desire for revision of the cease-fire on the one hand and Germany's strategic and military economic (nickel) interests on the other —all these factors brought Helsinki and Berlin together in 1940–1941: on June 26, 1941, Finland began participation in the RUSSIAN CAMPAIGN, with insistence on its autonomous conduct of war. On November 25, 1941, it joined the ANTI-COMINTERN PACT, and on December 6 of that year it entered into a state of war with Great Britain. The heavy German losses of 1943–1944 and the collapse of the Karelian front forced Finland into a cease-fire with Moscow on September 19, 1944. The terms, confirmed by the Treaty of Paris in 1947, were: war reparations of $300 million, withdrawal from the area around Petsamo, leasing of Porkkala, and cooperation in expelling the German Lapland Army, which led to heavy destruction. The skillful neutrality policy of President Juho Kusti Paasikivi (1946–1955), which maintained friendly relations with Moscow, ensured Finland's political independence.

B.-J. W.

Finnish-Soviet War (1939–1940). *See* Winter War.

Fischer, Eugen, b. Karlsruhe, June 5, 1874; d. Freiburg im Breisgau, July 9, 1967, German anthropologist. Fischer was a professor in Würzburg (1912), Freiburg (1918), and Berlin (1927–1942); he was director of the Kaiser Wilhelm Institute for Anthropology, Human Heredity, and Eugenics in Berlin. Through his collaboration on the standard work for RACIAL HYGIENE, *Menschliche Erblichkeitslehre und Rassenhygiene* (Theory of Human Heredity and Racial Hygiene; 1921), Fischer gained the respect of the National Socialists, and in 1937 he became a member of the Prussian Academy of Sciences. Despite his articles in the *Archiv für Rassen- und Gesellschaftsbiologie* (Archives of Racial and Social Biology) of the GERMAN SOCIETY FOR RACIAL HYGIENE, after the war Fischer was made an honorary member of the German Anthropological Society.

Fischer, Ruth (née Elfriede Eisler; married name, Golke), b. Leipzig, December 11, 1895; d. Paris, March 13, 1961, German politician and journalist; the sister of Gerhart EISLER. Fischer studied philosophy and political economy in Vienna. A Social Democrat during the First World War, in November 1918 she helped found the Austrian Communist party. Living in Berlin after 1919, she became the chairman of Berlin's Communist party. From 1924 to 1928 she was elected to the Reichstag for the German Communist Party (KPD). She served as its chairman after April 1924, leading the party along an ultra-left course. Replaced by Ernst THÄLMANN in September 1925, Fischer was expelled from the party in August 1926. After a failed attempt to found a left-wing Communist party, she abandoned political activity. In 1933 she emigrated to Paris, and in 1940, to the United States. After 1945 she published several works on the history of communism.

Flag oath (*Fahneneid;* also *Diensteid,* service oath), soldier's oath of allegiance, sworn before a flag, gun, or officer's saber. After August 1934, Wehrmacht members were obliged to take the flag oath in the name of "the Führer and Reich chancellor" (*see* OATH).

Flags (*Fahnen;* from Old High German *Gundfano,* battle cloth). Flags were used in classical antiquity, and also among the Germanic tribes, as battle, field, and victory emblems. Flags, especially the SWASTIKA flag as a symbol of nation and community, were given cultic veneration in the Third Reich. The raising of the national flag on holidays served as a "confirmation of the German *Volk* Community and . . . assent to the state" (Hanns KERRL), and was to be an honor as well as a duty for citizens (*see* HOUSE FLAG). NSDAP flags were "consecrated" by contact with the BLOOD BANNER at Reich Party Congresses. On March 18, 1936, the Wehrmacht

Flak Helpers in training.

first received a flag "bestowed" by Hitler, that it might be accorded military honors (presentation of colors); the soldiers' oath of allegiance was sworn on it (*see* FLAG OATH).

Flak, acronym of *Flugabwehrkanonen* (aircraft-defense artillery). *See* Air defense.

Flak Helpers (*Flakhelfer*), universally used designation for the official title Air Force and Navy Helpers (*Luftwaffen- und Marinehelfer*). It referred to pupils aged from 15 to 17 who after February 1943 were deployed to defend the Reich in the AIR WAR (*see* HOME FLAK). After the January 26, 1943, passage of the Regulation to Mobilize Pupils in an Auxiliary War Unit of German Youth in the Luftwaffe, a first group of 11,503 Flak Helpers were inducted according to school class. Some were housed in barracks. They received regular instruction, which, however, ultimately went by the boards. The helpers replaced antiaircraft soldiers, who were needed at the front: 100 helpers for 70 soldiers was the initial formula. It was soon established, however, that the fanatically engaged youths often exceeded, in their readiness to fight, the already jaded soldiers. The helpers soon assumed all functions from first gunner to gun captain, even using the heavy antiaircraft weapons. By June 1944, some 56,000 helpers were manning the antiaircraft batteries for a 50-pfennig daily wage. They belonged officially to the HITLER YOUTH (HJ) and wore the standard outdoor uniform of the HJ air force and navy units. Helpers had no combat status, and consequently could be treated as partisans if captured. This danger increased in the last phase of the war, when the Flak Helpers were also used in ground fighting. Their losses are unknown, although reports of numerous direct hits of antiaircraft positions document high casualties.

Flak militia (*Flakwehrmann*), designation for civilians with service obligations in antiaircraft and HOME FLAK.

Flex, Walter, b. Eisenach, July 6, 1887; d. Peudehof (Ösel island), October 16, 1917, German writer. A volunteer in 1914, Flex achieved wide success with patriotic war poems. His work combines the spirit of the youth movement, Protestantism, and the nationalism characteristic of student fraternities. In his best-known book, *Wanderer zwischen beiden Welten* (A Wanderer between Both Worlds; 1917), Flex idealized the spirit of frontline comradeship and readiness for sacrifice ("to die first" as the

Walter Flex.

Friedrich Flick.

highest duty of an officer) in the person of a fallen friend. Flex's poems exerted a strong influence over postwar youth, but attained their greatest circulation only after 1933, since the National Socialists saw in Flex a "blood witness of wartime experience" and valued highly his readiness to serve as a model for German youth. Even today some of his lyrics are popular, as "Wildgänse rauschen durch die Nacht..." (Wild geese rustle through the night).

Flick, Friedrich, b. Ernsdorf, July 10, 1883; d. Konstanz (Switzerland), July 20, 1972, German industrialist. Flick began his career as a merchant in the iron industry; by 1915 he had joined the board of directors of the Charlottenhütte foundry, and in 1919 he became its general director. In the 1920s Flick gained a central position in German heavy industry, profiting from inflation, speculation, and artfully packaged stock deals (in this way he held, through the Gelsenkirchen mine concern, great influence over the Vereinigte Stahlwerke AG, Germany's largest steel company).

In 1932 Flick donated 50,000 RM to the NSDAP, merely a fraction of his contributions to middle-class parties. Only in 1933 did he increase his gifts to the NSDAP, which by 1945 totaled about 7.65 million RM. In addition, as a member of the HIMMLER FRIENDS' CIRCLE, he subsidized the SS in the amount of 100,000 RM a year. In 1937 Flick joined the NSDAP, and a year later he was named MILITARY ECONOMY FÜHRER. The Flick-Konzern (after 1934, Friedrich Flick KG [limited partnership]) was among

the largest beneficiaries of the ARYANIZATION of the economy that began in 1938.

The visibly close cooperation between Flick and the National Socialist leadership continued into the Second World War, when the enterprises of the Flick combine used a great number of forced laborers and concentration camp prisoners. After his arrest on June 13, 1945, he was sentenced on December 22, 1947, to seven years' imprisonment (*see* FLICK TRIAL). Released early (August 25, 1950) because of an amnesty, Flick quickly rebuilt his concern, despite some lost assets (enterprises in central Germany) and despite Allied divestiture requirements. For decades the Flick concern refused to give material indemnification to its former forced laborers. Finally, in 1985, on the occasion of the concern's sale to the Deutsche Bank, the public debate was again ignited. Since few survivors were still alive, "for humanitarian reasons" (any claim as a matter of right was still rejected) a payment of 5 million DM was made.

R. S.

Flick Trial, proceedings of United States Military Court V in Nuremberg against steel magnate Friedrich FLICK and five of his fellow executives for crimes against humanity, war crimes, and membership in a criminal organization. The substance of the accusation of crimes against humanity and/or war crimes consisted mainly of the forced employment of foreign workers, concentration camp prisoners, and prisoners of war under inhuman conditions; the plundering of factories in France and the USSR; and the persecution of Jews from 1936 to 1939 by confiscating their industrial plants (*see* ARYANIZATION).

The Flick Trial began on April 19, 1947. On December 22 of that year Flick was sentenced to seven years' imprisonment, and two other accused were sentenced to 30 months and five years, respectively. The court acquitted two other defendants. It denied its competence over crimes against humanity alleged to have taken place before the war; its reasoning was that crimes committed before the war and which had no connection to the war did not fall under Control Council Law No. 10. Flick was released early for good behavior.

A. St.

Fliegergeschädigt (aircraft-damaged), German bureaucratic jargon for the more colloquial *ausgebombt* (BOMBED OUT).

Florian, Friedrich Karl, b. Essen, February 4, 1894, German politician. Florian was a First World War volunteer; he participated actively in the RUHR CONFLICT and was a mine worker. In August 1925 Florian founded the Buer (Gelsenkirchen) local of the NSDAP; he became a city councilman in 1927. Florian became the *Gauleiter* of Düsseldorf in 1929, a Reichstag deputy in 1930, a Prussian state councillor in 1933, an SA-*Obergruppenführer* in 1937, and Reich defense commissioner in 1942. Charged with having arranged the shooting of a police officer, he was acquitted in 1949.

Flossenbürg, National Socialist concentration camp, built in May 1938 near Weiden (Upper Palatinate), in the immediate area of a hillside quarry. The camp was occupied by an average of 5,000 to 6,000 prisoners, the number increasing to 15,000 to 18,000 in the closing months of the war. In March 1945 some 900 female prisoners arrived at Flossenbürg from the GROSS-ROSEN concentration camp, but in the same month they were transported to BERGEN-BELSEN. As time went on, more and more satellite and annex camps were established near the main Flossenbürg camp, their number growing to 90 and more. The prisoners in these satellite camps worked in such areas as armaments production, the aircraft industry, and mineral-oil extraction.

Flossenbürg's prisoners came from various European nations, the majority from the Eastern Territories (Poland, Russia, and so on). In the early years German political prisoners (in protective custody) and, later, criminals too (in preventive custody) were brought in. The prisoners worked in the quarry, 200 m (656 feet) from the camp, and in a variety of construction projects. Sick and disabled prisoners were sorted out by the camp physician and killed with an injection of phenol or other toxin, or were killed as part of Aktion 14f13 (*see* INVALID OPERATION). Housing conditions were bad: three or four prisoners slept in a single bunk, sparsely covered with one blanket. Food supplies, hygiene, clothing, and medical care were completely inadequate as well. Mistreatment of prisoners resulting in death was not uncommon.

Flossenbürg. Prisoners working in the quarry.

In particular, prisoners laden with heavy stones had to do "punishment drills" for hours in a "drainhole" (*Sumpfloch*) in a lower part of the quarry, the base of which was knee-high in mud. Aside from executions (including those of Dietrich BONHOEFFER and Adm. Wilhelm CANARIS), the prisoners' exhaustion and sickness were responsible for the very high mortality rate.

On April 20, 1945, Flossenbürg was evacuated. The prisoners were taken to Dachau on an eight-day forced march. Anyone who could not keep up with the pace was shot alongside the road. American troops liberated the camp's remaining prisoners on April 23.

Camp commandants in Flossenbürg were Jakob Weiseborn (committed suicide in 1939 after his embezzling was discovered); Egon Zill (sentenced to life imprisonment in 1955, later reduced to 15 years; d. 1974); Max Koenig (suicide, 1946); and Karl Künster (killed near Nuremberg, 1945).

W. D.

Flower Wars (*Blumenkriege*), term coined by Joseph Goebbels for the ANSCHLUSS of Austria and for Germany's march into the Sudetenland: "flowers, not bullets, greeted our soldiers."

Flyer (*Flugblatt*), one- to two-sided leaflet used since the invention of printing especially for political statements and propaganda; it was used by the National Socialists during the "Time of Struggle" (until 1933) as a central, cheap, and quickly produced medium for influencing the masses. During the Second World War both Germany and the Allies found flyers important for enemy propaganda, especially when dropped from aircraft. For antifascist opposition groups after 1933, flyers were the only instrument—because they could easily be duplicated with the simplest equipment—for enlightenment and counterpropaganda.

Folk song (*Volkslied*), type of SONG that was particularly cultivated by National Socialist culture policy. New soldiers' or combat songs deliberately borrowed from the genre.

Followership (following; *Gefolgschaft*), authority relationship between leader and led (*Führer* and *Geführten*), derived from the FÜHRER PRINCIPLE with conscious reference to Germanic feudalism; also, term for the collectivity of the led. The "Followership Principle" applied to the entire

Allied flyer (1944): "Where is the Luftwaffe? . . . Now, in broad daylight, masses of American bombers fly over Berlin. . . . Naturally, you . . . are asking, 'Where is the Luftwaffe?' Ask Göring! Ask Hitler!'"

Volk in relation to Hitler, as well as to the respective subgroups of the party or its mass organizations in relation to the most immediate leader. Followers were believed to be products of the "natural inequality of people"; the concept also arose from the conviction that "every true rule of a Führer [*Führertum*] was sent by fate." The Führer's duty with regard to the welfare of his followers had a counterpart in their duty to be loyal.

In the narrower sense, *Gefolgschaft* was used in National Socialist terminology to designate the employees of an enterprise in the terms of the LABOR REGULATION LAW of January 20, 1934. At their head was a WORKPLACE FÜHRER; workers were called *Gefolgschaftsmitglieder* (members of the following) and formed a WORKPLACE COMMUNITY. A sub-unit of the Hitler Youth was also a *Gefolgschaft*; it usually encompassed three troops with up to 250 boys, led by a *Gefolgschaftsführer*; three to five such groups formed an Unterbann.

Forced labor (*Zwangsarbeit*), according to the 1930 definition of the International Labor Organization (ILO), "any kind of labor or service that is demanded of a person under the threat of any kind of punishment and for which he has not freely made himself available." In the Second World War the German armaments industry was able to accomplish its astounding achievements only through a high level of participation of forced labor, which was performed chiefly by ALIEN WORKERS and PRISONERS OF WAR. Forced labor of German prisoners of war was demanded during and after the war in the Soviet Union and to a lesser degree also in France and Belgium, among other countries, as a reparations payment and restitution. In the Declaration of the Rights of Man of the United Nations of 1948, forced labor is outlawed; the Basic Law of the Federal Republic of Germany disallows it in Article 12.

Forced sterilization (*Zwangssterilisation*), the act of rendering a person incapable of reproduction without his or her consent. The first National Socialist program carried out in the course of the NS policy of SPECIES UPGRADING was the forced sterilization of the so-called hereditarily ill, which was made possible through the Law to Prevent HEREDITARILY ILL OFFSPRING. The law defined as "hereditarily ill" anyone suffering from congenital feeblemindedness, schizophrenia, manic-depressive insanity, hereditary epilepsy, Huntington's chorea, hereditary blindness or deafness, or severe physical malformations. Severe alcoholism could also be classified as a hereditary illness. Hereditary Health Courts decided on the recommendations for forced sterilization, which physicians in public service and heads of institutions were obliged to make. If sterilization was decided upon, it was to be carried out within 14 days. If the order was circumvented, forcible measures were resorted to, including police delivery of the person to a clinic. The release of such persons from hospitals and nursing homes without prior sterilization was forbidden.

In 1939 the Ordinance for Heredity Cultivation (*Erbpflegeverordnung*) limited forced sterilizations to "urgent cases." During the Third Reich between 250,000 and 300,000 people were forcibly sterilized. At first the measure provoked no notable resistance since the National Socialists skillfully adopted discussions from the Weimar period regarding eugenics (*see* HEREDITY CULTIVATION) and RACIAL HYGIENE. Methods for the forcible sterilization of entire groups and peoples were tried out in HUMAN EXPERIMENTS in the concentration camps at Auschwitz and Ravensbrück. *R. W.*

Foreign-currency management (*Devisenbewirtschaftung*), regulation of foreign financial transactions through governmental measures. By 1931, toward the end of the Weimar Republic, limited control over foreign currency was introduced for the purpose of stabilizing the overburdened balance of payments. The National Socialists strongly advocated such management as a way of controlling FOREIGN TRADE in the face of a chronic foreign-currency deficit. The primary underlying rationale was to support the basic goal of REARMAMENT through securing foreign-trade relations. At the start, foreign-exchange quotas determined the allocation of payments; after 1934 (*see* NEW PLAN) quotas on imported goods allowed direct political influence over the aggregate composition of goods traded.

Foreign Germans (*Auslandsdeutsche*), German citizens resident in foreign countries, as opposed to ETHNIC GERMANS (*Volksdeutsche*), who held citizenship in foreign countries. Sailors at sea were also numbered among foreign Germans. The number of such Germans increased sharply with German territorial concessions pursuant to the VERSAILLES TREATY (in 1934 the total was 1 million people). They were organized into the LEAGUE OF FOREIGN GERMANS, based in Berlin, which also attended to Germans returning to the Reich. After the Seizure of Power the league was absorbed by the FOREIGN ORGANIZATION of the NSDAP. Foreign Germans were consciously exploited by National Socialist propaganda as a fifth column, and were especially susceptible to the nationalistic rhetoric of the Third Reich.

Foreign Organization (Auslandsorganisation; AO) of the NSDAP, umbrella association of all NSDAP groups abroad, divided into country groups (*Landesgruppen*), districts (*Kreise*), local groups (*Ortsgruppen*), and bases (*Stützpunkte*). Its director as of May 8, 1933, was Ernst Wilhelm BOHLE. The AO was administered like a *Gau* (district). It provided party members abroad, "the emissaries of Germandom," with political and ideological instructional and propaganda material; it also organized travel in the Reich and set up sister-city arrangements. Although the AO proclaimed its strict nonintervention in the affairs of host countries, it used its connections for espionage and political pressure. These activities frequently provoked bans on the organization and, in the case of Wilhelm GUSTLOFF, even political murder.

Foreign Policy

The interpretation of National Socialist (NS) foreign policy leads to the controversy regarding the character of the NS system of rule and Hitler's role within it. Was this policy specifically National Socialist or fascist, or, rather, traditional Prussian-German, or was it Hitler's foreign policy? The issue of the place of the Third Reich and its foreign policy in the history of the Prussian-German great-power state after 1871, and the debate as to whether 1933 signified a break or continuity, is connected with the further controversy surrounding the programmatic coherence and long-range goals of this foreign policy, its political and social function, its supporters and institutions, and possible alternatives to it.

At this point two interpretations starkly confront each other. The first revolves mainly around Hitler and his "omnipotent key position" (Karl Dietrich Bracher), his intentions, and the dogmatic and uncompromisingly rigid "program" that guided his actions, from its first written appearance in *Mein Kampf* (1925–1927) and in the "SECOND BOOK" (1928), until 1945. This view alleges that Hitler's program, in its concrete historical realization, was evidently a "plan by stages." Its first phase was continental in scope and was realized by 1942; the second phase, transoceanic in scope, was planned for the following years. The policy was traditionally imperialistic and characterized by power politics. It sought to consolidate a blockade-proof and autarkic territorial base under German hegemony from the Atlantic to the Urals; utilizing this platform, it then sought world power through the establishment of a central African colonial empire and further Atlantic and overseas strongholds. The third phase, a struggle for world supremacy with the United States, became lost in visions of worldwide utopias. This politics of world power on the model of Kaiser Wilhelm II was, however, from the outset interspersed with explicitly novel and revolutionary traits, which had no prior model, through the connection with territorial ideology, racial dogmas, and a FINAL SOLUTION as core elements of National Socialism. It became a foreign policy based on racial biology and Social Darwinism. Predicating an "eternal and relentless struggle for existence," it intended to secure "LIVING SPACE" for the "racially more valuable Nordic *Volk*" and to subject a large part of the earth to a "Pax Germanica" based on this greater value and, moreover, "Jew-free."

The alternate position acknowledges the revolutionary ideological triad of living space, racial utopia, and anti-Bolshevism as the real essence and driving force of NS foreign policy. It does not, however, derive this foreign policy primarily from Hitler's intentions or from a "program" to which he constantly adhered. Rather, it sees foreign policy as "domestic policy projected outward" (Hans Mommsen) with the goals of stabilizing internal political control and the regime's monopoly of political power, of retaining the loyalty of the masses, and of integrating and diverting the "antagonistic forces of the unfettered society of the Third Reich" (Martin Broszat). The "program" here becomes an "aimless expansion"; with an anarchic chaos of conflicting bureaucratic responsibilities in the background, Hitler appears as the "indecisive, often insecure, and in many respects weak dictator, who was exclusively concerned with preserving his prestige and personal authority and most strongly influenced by his immediate surroundings" (H. Mommsen). His "program" writings and programmatic pronouncements even in the realm of foreign policy are essentially reduced to the functions of maintaining personal power and mobilizing the masses through propaganda for the regime.

A reconciliation of these positions seems possible and sensible if we, along with Karl Dietrich Bracher, refer to the ambivalence of the NS system of rule in general and of its foreign policy in particular: analogous to the DUAL STATE in internal affairs, a "twofold character trait of National Socialist foreign policy" (Hans-Adolf Jacobsen) emerged in external affairs through the co-existence of traditional and revolutionary objectives and means. NS foreign policy derived its "particular dynamism and aggressiveness" precisely from "its often contradictory mixture of dogmatic rigidity in principles and most extreme flexibility in applications" (W. Schieder). In a typical fusion of power politics, economics, and ideology, the orientation toward territory and its racist justification represent a thoroughly axiomatic and binding long-range program for foreign-policy actions, which with some consistency led to a Russian Campaign that had been

American caricature of Hitler's "peaceful" foreign policy.

planned from the outset as a war of racial extermination and "Holocaust" (*see* COMMISSAR ORDER). Nevertheless, the notion of a "plan by stages" should not make us retroactively force foreign-policy events into a precisely drawn-out "road map of world conquest" in Hitler's head. Mediated by propaganda and the self-styled youthful dynamism of the regime, foreign policy was always an integrative device (*Integrationsklammer*), an indispensable tool of domestic policy. Especially after the outbreak of war and under the impression of a radicalization and brutalization of the conduct of war, it served to bind anew the often disenchanted and despondent populace to the regime, to create among the masses an appearance of popular legitimacy, and to erase memories of terror and the deprivation of rights.

Agreement prevails among proponents of both positions on the point that foreign policy bore Hitler's personal stamp even more than domestic policy, and that he considered foreign affairs his special domain. Even from the impersonal perspective of the "functionalists," there still remains a considerable "Hitler residue" to explain. Indeed, the acceptance not of a minutely programmed "plan by stages," but rather of a strongly ideological and constant basic direction of foreign-policy planning and action rules out any talk of a peaceful and revisionist policy until 1938, followed by a subsequent totally altered, militarist, and expansionist foreign policy. On the contrary, under this common perspective of goals the individual steps in foreign policy before and after 1938 form a unity. In this category belong, above all, rearmament and the mobilization of the popular will for military preparedness, while shielding these internal events from the outside world (withdrawal from the League of Nations, reintroduction of a universal COMPULSORY MILITARY SERVICE); the overcoming of foreign-policy isolation (*see* CONCORDAT, the nonaggression pact with POLAND, the GERMAN-BRITISH NAVAL AGREEMENT, the JULY AGREEMENT with Austria, the Berlin-Rome AXIS, the ANTI-COMINTERN PACT, the PACT OF STEEL, the GERMAN-SOVIET NONAGGRESSION PACT); the gradual formation of a "southeast European economic zone" (*see* NEW PLAN); the transition to a military economy and to forced preparations

Negotiations over the German-British Naval Agreement (1935). At the left: Lord Privy Seal Anthony Eden and Foreign Secretary John Simon.

Demonstration. The banner reads: "We want to come back home to the Reich."

for a war economy in the name of AUTARKY; the consolidation of a Great-German hegemony and the broadening of the economic base in central Europe (*see*, for example, RHINELAND OCCUPATION; ANSCHLUSS; MUNICH AGREEMENT), while sheltered from three international political crises (Italy's invasion of ABYSSINIA, the SPANISH CIVIL WAR, Japan's attack on China in 1937); and, finally, the NS synchronization of responsible positions of leadership (Hjalmar SCHACHT's resignation as Reich economics minister in November 1937, the replacement of Konstantin von NEURATH as foreign minister by Joachim von RIBBENTROP, the FRITSCH CRISIS in February 1938).

Even the apparently almighty "Führer" could not cast into oblivion the fact that every nation's foreign policy is subject not only to internal forces and power blocs, but above all is also shaped by the structures and combinations of the international system of powers. The new regime's aggressive manifestations since 1933 had unmistakably aroused counterforces and the formation of fronts that markedly limited Germany's room to act unilaterally and to impose its aims of domination and territory. These forces also created objective pressures on the international scene to which Hitler had to adjust by temporary departures from his original "program." By doing so, as well as by setting for himself ever-tighter time pressures for the realization of his foreign-policy goals, he further restricted his room for action. A similar consequence ensued from the increasingly evi-

dent strains on German economic reserves—shortages in raw materials, foreign currency, and labor resources—which were at the disposition of rearmament before the war and which dramatically widened the gap between greatly overextended goals of territorial hegemony and the economic means to achieve them, even through war. As a "forward escape" and as a way out at the end of 1939, only "lightning-like" raids to broaden the economic base offered themselves, so long as there was no desire to make a 180-degree turn in foreign policy. This would have caused the NS regime to abandon its militarist and expansionist character. It thereby became necessary in 1939 to exploit the relatively narrow "strategic window" between advanced German armaments and still-inadequate Western military preparedness, as well as to force into place an international arrangement that would prevent the two-front war of attrition that had been feared since 1914.

In the history leading up to both world wars, which as German struggles for hegemony were undoubtedly connected "to one another as two acts of the same drama" (Ludwig Dehio), both pre-1914 "Wilhelmian imperialists". and pre-1939 National Socialists—in a singular "continuity of error"—firmly believed in their ability to secure English neutrality or even benevolent indulgence as Germany achieved continental hegemony. Both times the British, with consequences that were finally decisive for war, rejected German claims for "a free hand in Europe and in the east." Thus, even before the first shot,

1
Final rally during Mussolini's state visit, on the May Field in Berlin (September 29, 1937).
2
"Step by step, Hitler tears up the diktat of Versailles." Election poster for the April 10, 1938, plebiscite on the Anschluss of Austria.
3
Hitler's entry into Vienna on March 15, 1938.

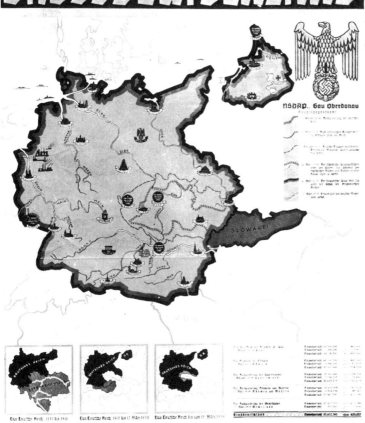

GROSSDEUTSCHLAND

Haltet das Reich nie für gesichert, wenn es nicht auf Jahrhunderte hinaus jedem Sprossen unseres Volkes sein eigenes Stück Grund und Boden zu geben vermag!

Adolf Hitler („Mein Kampf")

DANZIG IST DEUTSCH

1
"Great-Germany." NSDAP wall poster. "Never consider the Reich to be secure if it cannot for centuries into the future give every offspring of our *Volk* his own piece of land and soil!"

2
"Danzig is German." Propaganda poster (1939).

3
June 22, 1941. At a press conference, Foreign Minister Ribbentrop announces the beginning of the war with Russia.

decisive pieces of the projected "plan by stages" of NS foreign policy were broken off; inopportunely and against his will, Hitler himself was entangled in the dreaded two-front war with "reversed" fronts. The German-Soviet Nonaggression Pact of August 23, 1939, was obviously a merely temporary expedient, and in no way an expression of a fundamental departure from the long-envisaged military solution of the "living space" issue in the east.

To what extent was NS foreign policy, apart from short-range tactical shifts, at all open to other alternatives within its outlines as "dogmatically deranged power politics" (Klaus Hildebrand)? If it was, in what direction, and through what institutions and representative groups, did such programmatic alternatives perhaps present themselves? The controlled bureaucratic chaos explicated by David Schoenbaum as an essential trait of the NS system of rule, the "institutional Darwinism," did not stop at foreign policy. While Hitler reserved to himself personally the determination of the basic lines of foreign policy from the outset, "a series of new nongovernmental offices of the party and of the economy" (H.-A. Jacobsen) were established, often as instruments of a "revolutionary" and ideologized foreign policy. Located alongside and above the traditional Foreign Ministry as well as the other state agencies concerned with foreign relations, they competed with these bodies in the absence of clear jurisdictional demarcations: there were the Foreign Policy Office of the NSDAP under Alfred ROSENBERG, the FOREIGN ORGANIZATION of the NSDAP under Ernst Wilhelm BOHLE, the ETHNIC GERMAN AGENCY under Himmler's confidant Werner LORENZ (after 1938), and the RIBBENTROP OFFICE, which steadily lost influence after 1938. Foreign policy carried a double meaning: on the one hand, the pursuit of Germany's national interests on the level of power politics among other states, and on the other, above all the realization of the revolutionary NS goals, notably in the conquered territories. Especially during the war, other agencies were also involved, such as the Propaganda Ministry, various SS departments, the heads of the Generalgouvernement and the Reich commissioners, Rosenberg's Reich Ministry for the Occupied Eastern Territories (although powerless), and Göring's Office for the Four-Year Plan. In keeping with the trend toward an increasing "fragmentation" and breakdown of governmental institutions and competences, Hitler also assigned leading representatives of the state and party to special missions abroad.

As a reflex of this multiplicity of competing nstitutions, power centers, and party "satrapies," something of a "conceptual pluralism" repeatedly asserted itself. As a point of reference for the question of the basic openness of foreign-policy decision making to alternative goals, the period between the surrender of France (June 22, 1940) and the definitive command for "Barbarossa" (December 6, 1940) is often more closely analyzed. By the end of July 1940 at the latest, Hitler consciously and essentially without alternatives conducted "his own war" (Messerschmidt), that is, the campaign of conquest, plundering, and racial extermination against the Soviet Union—in temporal and causal connection with the FINAL SOLUTION. Nonetheless, in his circle, alternative options on a power-politics level were ventilated for one last time. As in the 1930s, the proponents recalled Wilhelmian imperialism and war aims from before and during the First World War. These advocates were found among the "traditionalists" in diplomacy, the bureaucracy, the economy, the naval command, and the old colonial lobby, and included Ribbentrop. Common to these very heterogeneous concepts was hostility toward England; the rejection of war in the east; a readiness for cooperation with the Soviet Union in the framework of a Euro-Asiatic continental bloc "from Madrid to Yokohama," with an anti-British edge; as well as the traditional interest in the development of a central African colonial empire and a transoceanic system of bases against Great Britain and the United States.

That none of these other foreign-policy models was ever able to prevail over Hitler's "program" was due to a very broad and relatively long-lasting consensus between Hitler and the "conservative elite." This was based on the "partial identity of goals" (Messerschmidt): namely, revision of the Versailles treaty, restoration of German great-power status in Europe, world-power politics, and anti-Bolshevism. Consensus was due also to the aura of undisputed success and to a certain charismatic radiance that surrounded the "Führer" after the rapid victory over France and the initial successes in Russia until 1942. Later, from 1943 to 1945, the mutually antagonistic forces were shackled together and to "their Führer" as though with ever-tighter clamps—by their common entanglement in the crimes of an NS state based on injustice, by the increasing siege mentality in "Fortress Europe," by the "Führer myth" that remained unshaken to the very end, by the

Allied demand for "unconditional surrender," by anti-Bolshevism, but also by terror and intimidation.

Marxist attempts to explain Hitler simply as an "agent" and a "stooge of finance capital" completely ignore his high degree of autonomy precisely in foreign-policy decisions. They also disregard the lack of documented testimony that could prove that any fundamental step in foreign policy was taken under pressure of "monopoly capitalism" (which in no way is to deny the broad confluence between economic goals and NS expansionism!). Even less can the cooperation between foreign policy and racist utopia, between imperialism and "Holocaust," the truly revolutionary components of National Socialism, be convincingly explained as inevitable or functional in the sense of capitalist rationality and maximization of profits.

With the attack on the Soviet Union, NS foreign policy may have finally wandered into a dead end of "self-inflicted constraints" (Wolfgang J. Mommsen), which had long since lain in wait, and into the dynamic tow of an equally long-evident national self-destruction. The irrational dogma of racist politics triumphed over calculations of power politics in occupied and plundered Russia and finally in Auschwitz. A foreign policy of the traditional type will always, consistent with its basic goals as "the art of the possible" (Bismarck), keep open several options and, as far as possible, avoid the path of irreversibility. NS foreign policy was different: Hitler's maxim, written down in *Mein Kampf*, that "Germany will either become a world power or will not exist at all," was neither an "ideological metaphor" (Broszat) nor a nonbinding propaganda flourish; rather, it expresses that unmistakable and—even in comparison with Italian Fascism—singular style of NS foreign policy that increasingly ran to extreme alternatives of "all or nothing" and thus excluded compromises, separate peace settlements, and divergent options. In this way foreign policy finally reduced itself *ad absurdum* and, had it followed Hitler's intentions, led toward total destruction and the collective suicide of the German *Volk* (*see* NERO COMMAND). Germany was rescued from complete self-annihilation in large part by compliant technocrats of the regime who, very late but not too late, came to their senses regarding the basis for a reasonable policy that would ensure the chance for survival of a people even in military defeat.

Bernd-Jürgen Wendt

Foreign Policy Office of the NSDAP (Aussenpolitisches Amt der NSDAP; APA), party office under Alfred ROSENBERG, created on April 1, 1933, as an intentional competitor of the Foreign Office. The APA was intended to bring into play against the traditionalists in the diplomatic corps the "dynamic line" of National Socialist foreign policy. However, it was never really able to implement this against the FOREIGN ORGANIZATION under Ernst BOHLE, the RIBBENTROP OFFICE, and the Foreign Office heads Konstantin von NEURATH and Joachim von RIBBENTROP. Hitler did not make use of the proposals of the party office, which in 1938 had 80 employees, and he mistrusted Rosenberg's diplomatic talents after the failure of a mission to England in May 1933. As a result, the APA was limited largely to contacts with fascist "fraternal parties." Its attempts to exploit the antisemitic potential in other nations for German foreign-policy goals remained insignificant. Only when Rosenberg became minister for the occupied Eastern Territories (July 17, 1941) did policy impulses from the office have even a modest impact.

Foreign trade, because of Germany's heavy dependence on foreign economies, an important part of National Socialist economic policy. Owing to the effects of the WORLD ECONOMIC CRISIS on Germany, there was a desire to increasingly retreat from world trade and, in national independence, to implement a policy of AUTARKY oriented toward the domestic economy. However, to obtain the raw materials needed for REARMAMENT and also to secure foodstuffs, a Germany poor in raw materials "necessarily" had to carry on foreign trade. Moreover, the terms of trade had developed in a way detrimental to Germany. Because of the international depression the prices for industrial goods fell, while those for raw materials stabilized.

In order to obtain German priorities in politics and armaments, the previously multilateral trade was subjected to comprehensive government planning and regulation. Strict FOREIGN-CURRENCY MANAGEMENT was able completely to control foreign trade. Foreign trade thus had the task of guaranteeing the necessary supplies of raw materials and foodstuffs, and, with a view toward foreign expansion, of creating the foundation for a large-scale European economic area. A permanent shortage of foreign currencies, together with later possibilities for attaining military security, led to a reorientation of foreign trade from overseas to Europe, especially to southeastern Europe. These industrially underdeveloped agrarian states would form the basis for providing raw materials and foodstuffs, and in the long run would provide an expanded living space for the German "Master Race." With the aid of bilateral trade agreements these nations would become economically and politically dependent on Germany.

Despite extensive political intervention (*see* NEW PLAN; FOUR-YEAR PLAN), foreign trade was unable to solve the problems of an increasing foreign-currency crisis and of insufficient raw materials for armaments.

V. B.

Foreign words (*Fremdwörter*), words that manifest themselves as coming from a foreign language by their sound and spelling. National Socialist linguists divided the German vocabulary into original "inherited" words (*Erbwörter*), which historically were handed down through the *Volk*; "borrowed words" (*Lehnwörter*), whose adoption from other languages was no longer obvious; and "foreign words," whose use was rejected as a "foreign affectation" (*Ausländerei*) and an expression of "poverty of thought," on the ground that the adoption of another people's words amounted to cultural subordination.

Even before 1933, a "movement for purification of language" was being promoted by such groups as the General German Language Association, founded in 1885, which advocated the avoidance and replacement of foreign words. The BOOK BURNING consumed many books by reason of their "extreme foreignness"(*Überfremdung*) and their "arrogant degradation of the German language." This linguistic purism was gradually imposed in public and governmental sectors, and in new designations for titles or offices, as the Office for Cultivation of Writing (*see* WRITING, CULTIVATION OF). Nonetheless, foreign words did not disappear from everyday speech after 1933, nor even from National Socialist journalism. Exaggerated attempts at Germanization—such as *Tagleuchter* ("daylighter," for window), *Fernzieh* ("long-distance puller," for electric locomotive), and *Steigrundling* ("climbing roundlet," for balloon)— generally aroused only amusement.

Forst, Willi, b. Vienna, April 7, 1903; d. there, August 12, 1980, Austrian actor and director. Forst performed mainly in light comedies and operetta films, such as *Atlantik* (1929) and *Peter Voss, der Millionendieb* (Peter Voss, Thief of Millions; 1932), before he took up directing in 1933 with *Leise flehen meine Lieder* (Softly My Songs Plead), without totally forsaking his acting. He specialized in stirring romantic entertainment films set in Vienna at the turn of the century. In contrast to the average entertainment fare of the National Socialist period, these manifested wit and elegance; examples were *Maskerade* (1934), *Bel Ami* (1939), *Operette* (1940), and *Wiener Blut* (Viennese Blood; 1942). They fulfilled especially well the desired purpose of diversion from everyday problems, particularly during wartime.

Willi Forst.

Forster, Albert, b. Fürth, 1902; d. in Poland, April 28, 1948 (executed), German politician and banker. Forster joined the NSDAP in 1923. As a speaker and active SA leader in his Franconian homeland, he attracted the attention of Julius STREICHER, became his protégé, and thus was elected to the Reichstag in 1930. Also named *Gauleiter* of the Free City of Danzig, supervised (from 1920) by the League of Nations, Forster had to reorganize the local NSDAP, which had been disbanded. Although he took on additional duties in Germany itself after the Seizure of Power (including those of head of the General Association of German Employees in the GERMAN LABOR FRONT), Forster was mainly active in carrying out the

Albert Forster.

"creeping National Socialist seizure of power" in Danzig, with the goal of reintegrating the city into the German Reich.

By winning an absolute majority for the NSDAP in Danzig (May 28, 1933), Forster could more or less infiltrate "from above" the government and administration of the free city. On August 23, 1939, one week before the outbreak of war with Poland, instigated under the pretext of the DANZIG QUESTION, Forster had himself elected head of state by the city senate, in order to be able officially to petition the Reich for protection. After the victory in Poland, Forster was named Reich governor (*Reichsstatthalter*) of Danzig and leader of the Danzig–West Prussia *Gau;* in 1940 he also became Reich war commissioner. A Polish court sentenced him to death in 1947 for war crimes attributed to him during the occupation.

Forster, Friedrich (pseud. of Waldfried Burggraf), b. Bremen, August 11, 1895; d. there, March 1, 1958, German writer. Forster began as an actor; from 1933 to 1938 he was a theater director in Munich, and subsequently a freelance author. The National Socialists appreciated his entertaining and stageworthy pieces, with their material drawn from the German past; these included his Widukind drama *Der Sieger* (The Victor; 1934). Even his school tragedy *Der Graue* (The Gray One; 1931), on teacher despotism and youth protest, was well received. Some plays by Forster, such as *Robinson soll nicht sterben* (Robinson Must Not Die; 1933), still enjoy success.

Forsthoff, Ernst, b. Laar (now Duisburg-Laar), September 13, 1902; d. Heidelberg, August 13, 1974, German scholar of constitutional and administrative law. In 1933, Forsthoff became a professor in Frankfurt am Main. In his work *Der totale Staat* (The Total State; 1933), he identified the FÜHRER PRINCIPLE as something that could be achieved only metaphysically—a process, bound up with the world of political experience, that was difficult to elucidate to foreigners. Forsthoff presented Jews as enemies to be rendered harmless, who by their otherness infringed on the territorial or spiritual LIVING SPACE of a *Volk.* The purely constitutional state (*Rechtsstaat*) was "the prototype of a community without honor and dignity." In further influential writings on basic political and legal questions, he took stands in line with National Socialist doctrine.

In 1935 Forsthoff accepted a teaching post in Hamburg, and then proceeded to Königsberg (1936), Vienna (1941), and Heidelberg (1943). In 1945 he was dismissed by order of the American Military Government. After working in the state administration of Schleswig-Holstein, Forsthoff again became a professor in Heidelberg (1949–1967). From 1960 to 1963 he was also president of the Supreme Constitutional Court of the Republic of Cyprus. Forsthoff's post-1945 writings on administrative and constitutional law and legal theory had great significance for the theory and practice of law in the Federal Republic of Germany.

Fortress (*Festung*), popular catchword in National Socialist propaganda; it was used after the turnaround in the Second World War to urge perseverance in line with Hitler's strategy: "Hold out at all cost!" Europe was declared a "fortress" before the INVASION; after the retreat behind Reich borders, Germany became one, as did cutoff areas (such as Fortress Holland) and, eventually, encircled German cities (such as Fortress Breslau). The fortress mentality, which in 1940 turned into a liability for France behind the MAGINOT LINE, also crippled Germany's conduct of war and proved to be pointless, since ultimately none of the "fortresses" defended by the German Wehrmacht possessed any "roof" against the Allies' heavy air superiority.

Fourteen Points, United States president Woodrow Wilson's program to end the First World War and create a peaceful order for the future. It was proclaimed in Congress on January 8, 1918, and consisted of 14 points: (1) open negotiations for peace and abolition of secret diplomacy; (2)

Fourteen Points. Demonstrators in Berlin. The sign in the middle reads: "We want only what was promised: Justice."

freedom of the seas; (3) freedom of international trade; (4) restrictions on national armaments and their guarantee; (5) "impartial" settlement of colonial claims; (6) the evacuation from Russia of the Central Powers; (7) restoration of Belgian sovereignty; (8) the return of Alsace-Lorraine to France; (9) the adjustment of Italian borders according to the nationality principle; (10) autonomy for the nations of the Danubian monarchy; (11) evacuation of Romania, Serbia, and Montenegro by the Central Powers; (12) independence of the Turkish state, autonomy for its non-Turkish nationalities, and the opening up of the Dardenelles; (13) creation of an independent Polish state; and (14) creation of a LEAGUE OF NATIONS. However, Wilson was unable to carry his points with his allies during the peace negotiations; the VERSAILLES TREATY and the other PARIS SUBURBAN TREATIES contradicted the Fourteen Points in important parts and in spirit.

R. B.

Four-Year Plan (*Vierjahresplan*), comprehensive National Socialist economic program aimed at giving an armaments-oriented direction to the ECONOMY UNDER NATIONAL SOCIALISM. In propaganda, the phase beginning with the Seizure of Power and running until 1936 was

retroactively declared to have been the first such plan, after which, at the Reich Party Congress of 1936, Hitler announced the real Four-Year Plan, which commenced with a decree of October 18, 1936. Under the standard of a drive for rearmament, the German economy was to achieve a "war economy in peacetime." The impetus for economic planning—which went beyond the control of FOREIGN TRADE—was a severe supply crisis in the summer of 1936. The shortage of raw materials and foodstuffs, as well as bottlenecks in the supply of fuels critical to munitions production, made obligatory a decision as to the future tempo of rearmament necessary. In order to keep the standard of living from falling, the intention was to exercise strict control over production and concentrate on products important to armaments (*see* RAW-MATERIALS ECONOMY).

Four-Year Plan. Newspaper ads urge that materials be saved. Top: "As you know, the Four-Year Plan demands the greatest economy. This also applies to *keys for opening tins,* since iron and steel are rationed. Our tins of fish will no longer come with key openers; instead, the shopkeeper will give a key for every two tins. Every opener can be used several times. . . . The savings will be even greater if you use a *can opener* to cut open the tin." Bottom: "Attention! Please don't throw away the empty tube . . . it is made of metal, which we urgently need and in part must import from abroad. Save empty tubes . . . you will help save *foreign currency!*"

Hitler had set down the most important goals of the Four-Year Plan in a secret memorandum of August 1936. The activation of all economic resources, he maintained, could bring only "temporary relief"; a "permanent solution" along the lines of AUTARKY could be attained "only through the expansion of living space or of the base of raw materials and foodstuffs." Hitler demanded: "I. The German army must be ready for action in four years. II. The German economy must be ready for war in four years." Fulfillment of these aggressive and expansionist goals demanded a relentless mobilization of the economy.

The Four-Year Plan concentrated on allocating important raw materials, on planning and channeling LABOR DEPLOYMENT, on WAGE-PRICE POLICY, and on investment and consumption. Göring, although no expert, was entrusted with the execution of the whole plan. As "Deputy for the Four-Year Plan" he had extensive authority, but because of jurisdictional confusion he ran into frequent conflicts, particularly with Hjalmar SCHACHT. The uncoordinated system of special deputies allowed the plan to become an aggregate of many separate measures and partial planning, so that until the war the plan's investments lagged by 40 percent of its goals. Despite failures in fulfilling these goals, the plan did achieve a substantial alteration of the economic structure in favor of the production goods industries, for which the investment volume in 1939 was 250 percent higher than in the boom year of 1928. Although the Four-Year Plan was claimed to be comprehensive in scope, it never created a planned economy in the strict sense. In the plan's final phase, until the transition to the total WAR ECONOMY, the I.G. FARBEN concern gained ever more influence over its organization. The failure of the BLITZKRIEG program by late 1941 revealed the weaknesses of the Four-Year Plan. Planning thereafter was fully centralized anew under Albert SPEER.

V. B.

Fragebogen. *See* Questionnaire.

France (officially, République Française), republic on Germany's western border; area, 551,000 sq km (about 220,400 sq miles); population, 40.7 million (1930). France presented a paradox: in the 1920s it was an antirevisionist power, defending the status quo and its own hegemony in Europe, yet in the 1930s it acquiesced to National Socialist demands without resistance, and abandoned its independent foreign policy

after 1936 as a "junior partner" in the tow of British APPEASEMENT. The explanation of this paradox lies in the deep internal and external political and moral crisis of the Third Republic (1870–1940), and in its inability either (1) to preserve its capacity to make foreign policy by reforming and stabilizing its political and social system, or (2) to control the catastrophic effects of the WORLD ECONOMIC CRISIS and the collapse of the Versailles security system. Largely formed in the liberal *belle époque* prior to 1914, state and society in France had not kept pace with the enormous burdens associated with the emerging modern industrial age and a democratic mass society. Accordingly, it was not able to confront the threat to national existence with a strong foreign and security policy or with a claim to European leadership.

The lasting economic crisis of the 1930s was deepened by past neglect (the modernization deficit) and an orthodox currency and finance policy (overvaluation of the franc) that limited growth and fed deflation. The social consequences were significant: high unemployment, heightened class tension, meager social security, impoverishment of broad sectors of the middle class, proletarianization of workers and of some sectors of the intelligentsia, and demographic stagnation. These conditions in turn produced political crises: crumbling of the liberal democratic-republican "ruling synthesis of the center"; declining ability of bourgeois democratic parties to unite and compromise; radicalization and proletaranization on both the Left and the Right, with antiparliamentary and right-wing extremist movements; instability of government coalitions; and the increasing dysfunction of bourgeois parliamentary democracy, while the executive, the army, and interest groups gained greater autonomy.

The RHINELAND OCCUPATION of 1936 took place amid rapidly changing configurations of government (*see* POPULAR FRONT), during the term of the weak and indecisive interim cabinet under Albert Sarraut. The general moral crisis of bourgeois society (marked by cultural pessimism, *décadence*, and defeatism) produced sympathies for authoritarian or even outright fascist solutions, such as the storming of the Palais Bourbon by radical leagues of the Right on February 6, 1934. The army meanwhile manifested a strong preference for a purely defensive strategy (*see* MAGINOT LINE). The gap grew ever wider between France's traditional claim to great-power status and its dwindling material resources and diminished desire for self-

France. French rightists ("Blue Shirts") at a Paris demonstration (1935).

assertion. The cease-fire of June 22, 1940, sealed both a military defeat (*see* FRENCH CAMPAIGN) and the fate of a political and social order that proved itself obsolete in many respects. It created room for two developments: for the short term, COLLABORATION and the bureaucratic and authoritarian VICHY regime under Henri Pétain (1940–1944). Pétain's proclaimed "National Revolution" temporarily attracted hopes for renewal of even many disappointed Third Republic democrats. For the long term, the RÉSISTANCE and the "Free France" (*La France libre*) of Gen. Charles de GAULLE led to the Fourth Republic (1946–1958), in which France was to make the decisive step into "modernization."

B.-J. W.

Franco, Francisco, b. El Ferrol (Spain), December 4, 1892; d. Madrid, November 20, 1975, Spanish politician and general. Franco entered the colonial service in 1912, and by 1922 was commander of the Spanish Foreign Legion in Morocco. He played a key role in the suppression of an anarchist revolt in Asturias in 1934, and became general chief of staff in 1935. The Popular Front government, regarding Franco as politically dangerous, sent him to the Canary Islands in 1936. Nevertheless, he established contact with the military in revolt in Morocco, becoming their head in July 1936; that September, they called on him to lead a Spanish Nationalist government. With German (*see* CONDOR LEGION) and Italian help, he was able to defeat the Popular Front, which was supported by

international brigades and by the Soviet Union, and to establish a clerical-fascist regime. Franco entered into the ANTI-COMINTERN PACT, yet he succeeded in keeping his country out of the Second World War, despite Hitler's personal intervention during their meeting in HENDAYE. Until his death Franco ruled Spain as chief of state (*Caudillo*) with full dictatorial powers through his fascist FALANGE party, though he arranged for the reinstatement of the monarchy.

François-Poncet, André, b. Provins (France), June 13, 1887; d. Paris, January 8, 1978, French politician; noted scholar of the German lan-

Francisco Franco.

André François-Poncet.

guage and historian (elected to the Académie Française in 1952). After several diplomatic assignments (including one during the RUHR CONFLICT), François-Poncet became French ambassador to Berlin in 1931. In the ensuing years he dedicated himself resolutely to Franco-German understanding, earning even Hitler's appreciation. In 1938 he was transferred to Rome as ambassador, and in 1940 became a member of the French National Assembly. He was deported to Germany in 1943 and interned until 1945. Even after the war François-Poncet remained politically and intellectually involved with Germany, as a foreign-policy adviser (an expert on Germany) to the French government, high commissioner (1949–1953), and ambassador to Bonn (1953–1955). His works included *Goethes Wahlverwandschaften* (Goethe's "Elective Affinities"), *The Fateful Years: Memoirs of a French Ambassador in Berlin* (1946), and *The Road from Versailles to Potsdam* (1948).

Frank, Anne, b. Frankfurt am Main, June 12, 1929; d. Bergen-Belsen concentration camp, March 1945, a Jewish girl. In reaction to the National Socialist persecution of Jews, the Frank family migrated in 1933 to the Netherlands, where Anne was able to attend school, even after the start of the German occupation in 1940. The situation became so threatening by 1942 that the Frank family, together with Jewish friends, on July 9 went underground in the rear house at Prinsengracht 263 in Amsterdam. There, until August 1, 1944, Anne held conversations with her diary ("Dear Kitty"), which with childlike

openness expresses movingly the fear and misery of the hunted as well as their hopes and prayers. On August 4, 1944, the Gestapo discovered the hidden people and deported them to concentration and extermination camps; only Anne's father, Otto Frank, survived. Anne succumbed to an epidemic in BERGEN-BELSEN. Her *Diary of Anne Frank* was published directly after the war. Its millions of copies carried worldwide the accusation against NS terror and a warning against racism everywhere. The house on Prinsengracht is now a memorial.

Anne Frank.

Frank, Hans, b. Karlsruhe, May 23, 1900; d. Nuremberg, October 16, 1946 (executed), German jurist and politician. As early as 1919, while a law student in Munich, Frank came into contact with the GERMAN WORKERS' PARTY, but he did not join the NSDAP until October 1923. Frank took part in the HITLER PUTSCH, then withdrew to Austria. In 1926 he opened a law office in Munich. By his own count, he handled some 150 trials merely against "slanderers" of Hitler. During the REICHSWEHR TRIAL in 1930 he provided the party leader with a forum for the sensation-causing LEGALITY OATH. In 1928, Frank founded what later became the National Socialist lawyers' organization (*see* NATIONAL SOCIALIST LEAGUE OF LAW GUARDIANS). He established the Reich Legal Office (Reichsrechtamt) of the NSDAP in 1930, and in 1933 the ACADEMY FOR GERMAN LAW. In 1930 he was elected to the Reichstag, from 1933 to 1934 served as Bavarian justice minister, and in 1934 became Reich Minister without Portfolio. Frank

Hans Frank.

was concerned with the "renewal of German law in line with the National Socialist worldview"; yet, blind to Hitler's deep contempt for all legalities, he never gained influence over legislation in the Führer state. Also in vain, he protested against the police state's evisceration of the law and against executions without trial during the RÖHM AFFAIR.

Frank's protests risked the goodwill of the fanatically revered Führer, so that in his appointment as governor-general (*Generalgouverneur*) in German-occupied Poland in October 1939 there was an element of his being kicked upstairs with praise. Frank, however, considered it an obligation to provide "representation in the name of the Führer and the Reich on the grandest scale." Exacerbated by his NS master-race conceit and his ruthless antisemitism, this devotion led to an indescribably brutal program of oppression. Frank, who held court lavishly in Kraków's Gothic Citadel —even the ostentatious Göring styled him "King Stanislaus"—took actions responsible for the liquidation of Poland's ruling echelon, for the total plundering of the country, and for the deportation of about a million Polish workers to German armaments factories. Even for the SS, which within Frank's jurisdiction perpetrated the genocide of the FINAL SOLUTION, it went too far. But when one of the closest collaborators of the "butcher of Poland" was arrested and shot as a warning, Frank drew an unexpected conclusion. In frenetically cheered speeches at German universities in 1942, he called for the return to a constitutional state. As a conse-

quence, Hitler removed him from all party offices, yet left him in the post of governorgeneral. Perhaps inside knowledge shielded Frank: in 1931, Hitler had entrusted to him the research into his own family tree.

Toward the end of the war and then during the NUREMBERG TRIALS, Frank converted, becoming a repentant sinner and a Catholic. This did not avert his death sentence: the ledger he had painstakingly maintained from 1939 to 1945 and had handed over intact to his judges (38 daybooks) was too full. Shortly before his execution, he wrote his questionable "interpretation of Hitler and his time" under the title *Im Angesicht des Galgens* (Facing the Gallows).

Frank, Karl Hermann, b. Karlsbad, January 24, 1898; d. Prague, May 22, 1946 (executed), Sudeten German politician. In 1933 Frank became chief of propaganda for Konrad HENLEIN; in 1935 he was elected deputy for the Sudeten German party in the Czechoslovak parliament, and after Germany's annexation of the Sudetenland in October 1938 he became deputy *Gauleiter*. After the German occupation of "rump Czechoslovakia" (March 1939), Frank became secretary of state under Reich Protector Konstantin von NEURATH; after the latter's removal as Reich minister in August 1943, Frank became the true power holder in the PROTECTORATE OF BOHEMIA AND MORAVIA, even though subordinate to Wilhelm FRICK. Frank displayed his unsparing hardness immediately after the assault on Reinhard HEYDRICH (May 27, 1942) through the "act of revenge" at LIDICE. He

Karl Hermann Frank.

carried out a terrorist policy, especially against the Jewish population, until the end of the war. Frank finally fled to the West, but was remanded by the Americans to Czechoslovakia. A court in Prague condemned him to death, and had him hanged in the courtyard of Pankraz prison before several thousand spectators.

Frank, Walter, b. Fürth, February 12, 1905; d. Gross-Brunsrode bei Braunschweig, May 9, 1945, German historian. As a young man, Frank was an assistant at the party newspaper, the *Völkischer Beobachter,* and was already a fanatical antisemite. He made Hitler's acquaintance in 1923, and upon completing his doctorate in 1934 became a consultant for the NSDAP "on questions concerning historical literature" on Rudolf HESS's staff. Although not a party member, Frank acquired great influence in the Third Reich. On July 1, 1935, he became director of the Reich Institute for the History of the New Germany in Berlin. He regarded himself as the "responsible leader of the German historical scholarship" that was intended to "form the soul of the nation in its understanding and struggle." In 1936 a research department for the "Jewish question" was established within his institute, which ran into competition with the Institute of the NSDAP for Research into the Jewish Question. The resulting ideological and scholarly quarrels that Frank noisily staged caused his influence to ebb, especially since he lost his powerful patron when Hess flew to England. Bormann finally removed Frank on December 11, 1941, and prohibited his further services as a speaker. His subsequent publications, notably on the colonial question, attracted little attention. When the war ended he committed suicide.

Frankfurter, David, b. Daruvar (Croatia), 1909; d. Tel Aviv, July 19, 1982, Jewish assassin. A rabbi's son, Frankfurter began medical studies in Germany, then transferred to Bern because of National Socialist persecution of Jews. On February 4, 1936, in Davos, Frankfurter shot Wilhelm GUSTLOFF, the group leader in Switzerland of the NSDAP's Foreign Organization. He later explained his motive: "The death of Gustloff could not have changed the Nazis, but I hoped that my deed would change the Jews." Also a factor was his personal situation, which included failed examinations and suicide fantasies. The deed badly damaged German-Swiss relations; despite German pressure, Frankfurter was given a relatively fair trial. He was sentenced on December 14, 1936, to 18 years'

David Frankfurter.

imprisonment, and in 1945 was released to go to Palestine. With the exception of one brother, his entire family perished in German extermination camps.

Frankfurter Zeitung (FZ), liberal daily newspaper in Frankfurt am Main, founded in 1866 by Leopold Sonnemann. It was managed by his grandsons Heinrich and K. Simon from 1910 to 1934, with the financial involvement of the I.G. Farben and Bosch firms after 1930. During the Weimar Republic the FZ was esteemed even abroad as a great source of industrial and business news. Its negative attitude toward the NSDAP, as well as Hitler's known personal antipathy toward it, made it seem a candidate for banning in 1933, yet at first only the Simons, as Jews and principal shareholders, were required to transfer their shares to I.G. Farben and Bosch, and Jewish journalists were forced from their jobs. Management of the newspaper was assumed by Wendelin Hecht, and Rudolf Kircher became editor in chief. Its circulation in 1934 was 100,000.

For the time being, I.G. Farben and Bosch retained ownership of the FZ. Evidently, however, it no longer seemed necessary or possible to exert journalistic influence over National Socialist policies. On April 21, 1939, the FZ was sold to the Herold-Verlagsgesellschaft, associated with the EHER PRESS. The core of the editorial staff—Benno Reifenberg, Dolf Sternberger, and Paul Sethe—was allowed to remain. The 1943 circulation was 30,000.

Within the context of the "pluralism of opinions" arranged by Goebbels, the FZ was able to express criticism of the regime during the Third Reich. As a distinguished newspaper with an international reputation, it enjoyed special privileges; its publication was not forbidden until August 10, 1943. FZ journalists were absorbed in part by the VÖLKISCHER BEOBACHTER, where Sethe became a military commentator. The last issue of the FZ was published on August 31, 1943.

Franz, Kurt Hubert, b. Düsseldorf, January 17, 1904, SS officer. By training, Franz was a cook and a butcher. In October 1937, he joined the Third SS Death's-Head Division—later called "Thüringen." Franz was initially a guard in the BUCHENWALD concentration camp, where he later became a cook for the SS. In late 1939, by then a corporal in the SS, he was assigned to the Public Welfare Foundation for Institutional Administration (Gemeinnützige Stiftung für Anstaltspflege), which functioned within the EUTHANASIA program. As a cook, he was posted to the "killing facilities" at Grafeneck, Hartheim, and Sonnenstein, and then to the Chancellery of the Führer. In early 1942 Franz was attached to the headquarters of the SS and Police Leader in the Lublin district (Odilo GLOBOCNIK) and detailed to the BEŁŻEC extermination camp with other veterans of the Euthanasia program (*see* REINHARD OPERATION). Transferred to TREBLINKA, in August 1943 he finally became a camp commandant with the rank of SS-*Untersturmführer.* In the late autumn of 1943 Franz was ordered to Trieste, where he remained until the war's end. On September 3, 1965, a Düsseldorf district court jury sentenced him to life imprisonment for the collective murder of at least 300,000 people, for 35 counts of murder involving at least 139 people, and for attempted murder.

A. St.

Fraternal Councils (Bruderräte), Evangelical regional church consistories (governing bodies) in the PASTORS' EMERGENCY LEAGUE that in March 1934 united in the REICH FRATERNAL COUNCIL. They conducted the main burden of the CHURCH STRUGGLE on a local basis.

Fraternities. *See* Burschenschaften.

Frau, Die (The Woman), subtitled *Monatsschrift für das gesamte Frauenleben unserer Zeit* (Monthly for the Complete Life of Women in our Time), journal founded in 1893; the original publisher was W. Moeser-Buchhandlung, followed in 1921 by F. A. Herbig. Its editors were

Helene Lange (1893–1931), Gertrud Bäumer (1916–1917 to 1944), and Frances Magnus von Hausen (1933–1944). After April/June 1943, *Die Frau* appeared as a quarterly.

First conceived as a "magazine for the struggle of the women's movement," after April 1921 *Die Frau* was also the official journal of the Federation of German Women's Organizations (Bund Deutscher Frauenvereine), which dissolved itself in May 1933. It increasingly avoided taking political stances during the Third Reich, while promoting a sort of Christian mysticism or, as Bäumer formulated it: "Aside from the practical issues of women's lives and women's activities," *Die Frau* should "attempt to keep alive spiritual values, from which in the final analysis all energy flows." For the Propaganda Ministry, the journal seemed to be useful as an example of the officially supported "plurality of opinions." After the war began, it received 80 percent of its prior paper allotment, and it survived both the large media suppression operations of 1941 and 1943. The 1929 circulation was 6,500; in 1941 it was 3,000. *Die Frau* ceased publication on September 30, 1944.

S. O.

Frauenfeld, Alfred Eduard, b. Vienna, May 18, 1898; d. Hamburg, May 10, 1977, Austrian-German politician. By occupation Frauenfeld was a mason, then a bank official. Active as a writer (with the play *Dämmerung* [Twilight]; 1925), he joined the Austrian NSDAP in 1928. Arrested after its banning on December 4, 1933, he escaped from the WÖLLERSDORF detention camp to Munich. In 1935 Frauenfeld became

Alfred Eduard Frauenfeld.

managing director of the REICH THEATER CHAMBER. After 1942 he was active in the German civilian administration in the Reich Commissariat of the Ukraine. For crimes committed there during the German occupation, Frauenfeld was sentenced in absentia by a Viennese court to 15 years' imprisonment in January 1947. In the meantime he was denazified in Lower Saxony as a "minor offender." In 1949, he moved to Hamburg, where he managed a branch of a construction business.

Free corps (*Freikorps*), in general, military volunteer units without firm attachment to a larger body of troops. After the disbandment of the Imperial Army in 1918, numerous volunteer bands coalesced, established mainly by nationalistic officers and named for them; members came from such groups as the unemployed, East Elbian junkers, and career soldiers, all of whom were disoriented in the everyday civilian world after their return from the war. Once-respected officers could not accept the breakdown of social divisions and rejected the Weimar Republic.

The free corps, numbering as many as 200, with over 400,000 members (the best known was the Ehrhardt Naval Brigade; *see* EHRHARDT, HERMANN), were used by the state, especially against the workers' movement, notably during the January 1919 strike in Berlin and during the suppression of Munich's republic of councils. They attacked the political Left through assaults and murders (such as those of Rosa Luxemburg, Karl Liebknecht, and Walther RATHENAU) or functioned as "border defense"

Kameraden!

Die spartakistische Gefahr ist noch nicht beseitigt. Der Pole dringt noch immer tiefer in Deutsches Gebiet hinein.

Könnt Ihr das ruhig mitansehen?

Nein!

Bedenkt, was Ihr Euren gefallenen Kameraden schuldig seid!

Freiwillige heraus!

Soldaten, kommt und zeigt, daß Deutschland nicht zum Gespött der Welt wird. Tretet sofort ein in das

Freikorps Hülsen!

Frontsoldaten! Keiner darf fehlen!

Mobile Löhnung; M.5. Tageszulage, freie Verpflegung, Unterbringung und Ausrüstung. Disziplinierte Truppe.

Besonders gebraucht werden Offiziere, Zahlmeister, Mannschaften aller Waffen, Gedientes Eisenbahnpersonal, Holz- und Eisenarbeiter, Schneider, Schuhmacher und Sattler.

Werbezentrale: Charlottenburg, Luisen-Café am Luisenplatz, Untergrundbahnstation Wilhelmplatz, Luisenplatz 5 b.

Werbebüros (dort auch Auskunft): Café Bauer, Unter den Linden; Tauentzien-Palast, Tauentzienstraße, Berlin N, Chausseestraße 1, Alchinger, C, Alexanderplatz 2, Alchinger, NW, Belle-Alliance-Platz 22, Potsdamer Bierhallen, Werder a. d. W., Thorstraße 177; Hannover, Georgspalast, Georgstraße.

Freikorps Hülsen!

Recruiting poster for the Hülsen Free Corps: "Comrades! The Spartacist danger is not yet over. . . . Think about what you owe your fallen comrades. Volunteers, come out! Soldiers, come and help so that Germany does not become the laughingstock of the world."

in the east. The decree dissolving the free corps in 1920 contributed to the uprising of the KAPP PUTSCH. Many free corps members attached themselves to the SA or the SS. After the Seizure of Power they were decorated with "certificates of honor" as an expression of "thanks" to confer the "recognition that has been withheld up until now."

Free corps. Members of the Ehrhardt Naval Brigade in Munich (1919).

Freedom (*Freiheit*), the highest moral value next to HONOR from the National Socialist perspective, said to arise in "Nordic people" from "Germanic force of will." Alfred ROSENBERG, in particular, opposed democratic freedom, which through anarchy would turn all freedom into despotism. Against this he juxtaposed the "creative freedom" of the Germanic man (*Germanen*), arising from the latter's return "to what is most truly his own." Along with this went the awareness that the individual could be only as free as his own "blood community." The community in turn would find that which was "deepest, most characteristic" in "the Führer," with the consequence that "true freedom" was realized only in "relationship with the Führer and his followers." As an example, while liberal thinkers saw military service as the epitome of the destruction of freedom, for the "Germanic man" it represented, on the contrary, the highest development of freedom, since it above all assured the freedom and honor of his *Volk*. Whereas Christian freedom was actually only the "freedom of a bad conscience" (to sin or not to sin), the "German" (*deutscher Mensch*) embraced a freedom that rested upon loyalty to the "Führer" and the "*Volk* Community."

Freedom of belief (*Glaubensfreiheit*), religious tolerance, the "basic characteristic of the Nordic-Germanic race"; like FREEDOM OF CONSCIENCE, a demand of Point 24 of the NSDAP program of February 24, 1920. This "freedom" was a tactical concession by Hitler to the Christian denominations, which he still courted after the Seizure of Power. A related measure was the so-called Toleration Decree (*Duldungserlass*) issued by his deputy Rudolf Hess on October 13, 1933, which expressly prohibited discrimination based on denomination. The CHURCH STRUGGLE soon demonstrated the tactical nature of such proclamations.

Freedom of conscience (*Gewissensfreiheit*), according to Point 24 of the NSDAP program of February 24, 1920, the freedom of religious affiliation, which was, however, conditioned by the "ethical and moral sentiment of the German race." Since conscience had a "racial" basis, it was misused by anyone who "surrendered his conscience to any alien political, ideological, or religious power." With this flexible restriction the GERMAN CHRISTIANS, to name an example, conducted their campaign against the Old Testament and its "Jewish payment morality" [*Lohnmoral*].

Freedom of opinion (*Meinungsfreiheit*), a basic right, protected by Article 118 of the Weimar Constitution, which was annulled by the REICHSTAG FIRE DECREE. Meanwhile, the National Socialists redefined the term: because the presumably free individual of the "SYSTEM ERA" had been superseded by the "*Volk* comrade bound to the community," freedom of opinion could apply only where it did not harm the common welfare. Because the party alone defined this common welfare, freedom of opinion, especially in the form of FREEDOM OF THE PRESS, was effectively revoked.

Freedom of the press (*Pressefreiheit*), the right of the media to free expression of opinion; in the Third Reich it was denigrated as a "liberal" notion based on the rejected pluralism of interests in the political journalism of the Weimar Republic, which had consigned journalists to "shackles of money." The National Socialists redefined it as the freedom of journalists "to serve only the welfare of the whole nation, uninfluenced by economic interests or by the involvements of their publishers."

S. O.

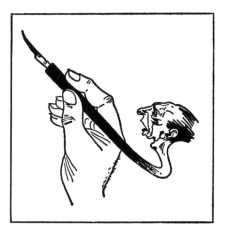

Freedom of the press. "The Penholder," caricature in the Swiss *Nebelspalter*.

Freemasonry (*Freimauerei*), international movement with humanitarian objectives based on tolerance and active brotherhood. Freemasonry developed in late medieval England from the cottage-based alliances of free stonemasons, which later were organized into temples, lodges, and grand lodges. When the future Frederick II of Prussia joined in 1738, Freemasonry achieved substantial gains in Germany. In the 18th and 19th centuries, many important figures from the worlds of culture, commerce, and politics joined the Freemasons, including Goethe, Napoleon's antagonist Gen. Gebhard von Blücher, and William I. Despite these associations, German Freemasonry was not immune from National Socialist persecution, which began in the so-called Time of Struggle and was incited especially by Alfred ROSENBERG, as in his *Das Verbrechen der Freimauerei* (The Crime of Freemasonry; 1922).

As did *völkisch* critics, the National Socialists blamed Freemasonry—one of Erich LUDENDORFF's array of hostile "cosmopolitan powers" —for having been swayed by "sentimental humanitarianism" to promote Jewish emancipation in the 19th century, thereby importing "alien" influences into German culture. The Catholic struggle against Freemasonry contributed the slogan about the complicity of "Jews and Masons," and the lodges were attacked as "hotbeds of Talmudery." The hermetic practices of Freemasonry and its character as a secret society made it especially suited to NS conspiracy theories, while its relative weakness (some 76,000 members in 1933) made it vulnerable to scapegoat strategies. The selection of members by social rank was construed as "separation by caste," and thus as irreconcilable with the goal of a "*Volk* Community." Freemasonry's international network was considered a security risk and a betrayal of *völkisch* and "racial thinking."

Immediately after the Seizure of Power, terrorism against Freemasonry intensified. The movement was hit particularly hard because it would willingly have been involved in the "task of national reconstruction." Flight to a forward position, however, as through Masonic petitions to Reich President Hindenburg, renaming the lodges the "German Christian Order," or adopting an ARYAN PARAGRAPH, proved useless. By the middle of 1935 most of the lodges had been harassed into self-dissolution, and on September 6 of that year, in line with the REICHSTAG FIRE DECREE, the remaining Masonic organizations were closed and lodge properties confiscated, on the ground that they served "activities hostile to the *Volk* and the state." Officials who had withdrawn from lodges only after January 30, 1933, were excluded from permanent employment and promotion or were terminated; the others were retained only on probation. At Security Service headquarters (later the Reich Security Main Office), Freemasonry Desk II/111 (later VII B 1) was established. "Stubborn" adherents of Freemasonry paid for their attitude in concentration camps or in combat ("frontline testing"). In the German-occupied lands as well, measures were taken against Freemasonry.

Freethinkers (*Freidenker*), term that originated in the Enlightenment (17th–18th centuries) to refer to people who submit even religious questions to the primacy of reason. The freethinker movement developed along deistic and atheistic lines, out of which grew a bourgeois antimaterialistic freethinking school (Monists); dialectical materialism produced its own social-revolutionary form of freethinking, which aroused National Socialist criticism. Itself profoundly atheistic, although committed to tactical religiosity, National Socialism attacked all freethinkers as "unprincipled" and "internationalistic," and accused proletarian freethinkers of "the systematic corruption of the morals of youth." The National Socialists also ordered a wholesale ban of all freethinker organizations after the Seizure of Power, something the NSDAP had already demanded without success in May 1932.

Free time (*Freizeit*), in general, the work-free time of employed people. For the National Socialists, free time was to be "at least as important as, if not more important than, everyday activity" (Robert LEY). In order not to leave too much individual latitude for recreational leisure and to guarantee the optimal generation of labor power, the state saw as one of its "most important tasks" the provision of "recreation in the most varied forms" (Ley). Organizing the free time of "working people" (*schaffende Menschen*) was the responsibility of the STRENGTH THROUGH JOY program, with its Office for Travel, Hiking, and Vacations, "After-Work" Office, Sports Office, and Office for "Beauty of Work," as well as its GERMAN PUBLIC INSTRUCTION AGENCY. The spectrum of the official organization of free time ranged from evening entertainment and continuing education to theater trips, the revival of "old folk customs," travel, and instructional camps.

Free trade, in general, economic activity that is free of all limitations; in the narrower sense, a type of FOREIGN TRADE without tariffs, import and export restrictions, quotas, and the like, which was rejected by the National Socialists as liberal and materialistic.

Freiburg Circle (Freiburger Kreis), loose nationalist and conservative group within the German OPPOSITION, centered on the historian Gerhard RITTER at the University of Freiburg.

Freikorps. *See* Free corps.

Freisler, Roland, b. Celle, October 30, 1893; d. Berlin, February 3, 1945, German jurist. A

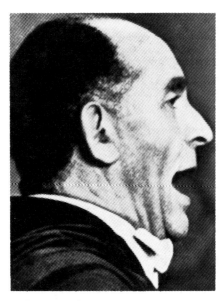

Roland Freisler.

prisoner of war in Russia during the First World War, Freisler had a career there as a Bolshevik commissar. After 1920 he was a prominent criminal defense attorney in Kassel. Politically, Freisler was first involved in the Völkisch-Social Bloc, and after 1925 in the NSDAP. Prior to 1933 he was a city councilman and a member of the provincial assembly, the Prussian parliament, and the Reichstag. During this period he was entangled in a finance scandal and in libel suits.

After 1933 Freisler became ministerial director in the Prussian Justice Ministry, then state secretary in the Reich Justice Ministry, where his responsibilities included the organization of the justice system. He curbed conflicts between the party and the justice system by quashing trials against National Socialist (NS) criminals, as well as by replacing or retiring unfavorable judges. As state secretary, Freisler represented the Justice Ministry at the WANNSEE CONFERENCE. He was editor of the journal of the ACADEMY FOR GERMAN LAW and the director of its research department. Freisler made key contributions to the implementation of NS perspectives in the justice system. His many articles on NS law and his numerous edicts and memorandums on issues of legal interpretation gained widespread attention.

In 1942 Freisler replaced Otto THIERACK as president of the VOLK COURT. He declared to Hitler that he wanted to judge each case as he believed the Führer himself might judge it. Freisler presided over many trials, 90 percent of which ended with the death penalty or with life

imprisonment. He sentenced, among others, Hans and Sophie SCHOLL and those accused in connection with the assassination attempt of the TWENTIETH OF JULY, 1944, whose trials were filmed. He was prone to insult the defendants, to attack them, to shout at them, and to make long speeches about National Socialism and loyalty to the Führer. His conduct of trials was criticized as unworthy even within the NS leadership. In early 1945 Freisler was still pronouncing death sentences, on defendants who challenged him with the threat that he himself would be hanged after the war's end. However, he died in a bombardment. The NS press reported Freisler's death only as an item without comment.

Sch.

Fremd-. *See* Alien; Ethnic; Foreign.

French Campaign, designation for the military operations in the west from the German attack on May 10, 1940, until the collapses of Holland (May 14), Belgium (May 28), and France (June 22). After the British and French declarations of war on September 3, 1939, which continued in force even after the German victory in the POLISH CAMPAIGN, the next stage was the SITTING WAR, during which German preparations advanced for a French campaign (Case "Yellow"); the first tentative plan was dated October 19, 1939. The definitive version of the operations plan originated with Gen. Erich von MANSTEIN, with the assent of the tank-warfare expert Gen. Heinz GUDERIAN; it was issued by the Army High Command (OKH) on February 24, 1940, as the new marching orders ("Sicklecut"). Manstein planned a two-phase French campaign: a thrust against the Somme and the English Channel coast with its focal point south of Namur, thereby destroying the Allied armies in Belgium; then, after regrouping, an advance of all forces toward the south, wiping out the remaining Allied units. Disregard of the neutrality of the Benelux states was part of the plan.

A revolutionary element of the plan, which was regarded with the greatest skepticism by the German generals, was the strike by the panzer corps through the Ardennes: heavily wooded and with few roads, this, it was supposed, would be the pivotal point of the Allied defeat. Manstein was expecting an enemy push through Belgium, as was intended in the so-called Dyle Plan. Despite Belgian and Dutch declarations of neutrality, the Allied Supreme Command under

Gen. Maurice-Gustave GAMELIN decided upon this thrust with an extension of the right flank into southern Holland in the event of a German invasion.

The German deployment at the beginning of the attack took this form: in the north, Army Group B (Col. Gen. Fedor von BOCK) faced the Dutch army (Gen. H. Winkelman), the Belgian army (King LEOPOLD III), and the French Army Group One (Gen. Gaston Billotte) with the British Expeditionary Force (General Lord Gort)—that is, 29 German against about 60 Allied divisions. The focal point of the attack lay with the tank units of Army Group A (Col. Gen. Gerd von RUNDSTEDT) in the middle zone against the Ninth and Second French armies, that is, 45 German against 18 French divisions. In the south, Army Group C (Col. Gen. Wil-

helm Ritter von LEEB) advanced to the WESTWALL and along the upper Rhine front against French Army Group Two (General Prételat) and Group Three (General Besson): 19 German against 27 French divisions. German Air Fleets Two and Three secured the operations with 2,288 aircraft against 1,604 French and 581 British airplanes.

Despite the Allies' superiority in tanks (3,373 against 2,445), the French Campaign followed its planned course. After airborne landings in "Fortress Holland" and a devastating air attack on Rotterdam (900 victims), the Dutch resistance collapsed on May 14 (2,890 dead, 29 missing, 6,899 wounded). On May 16, Army Group B broke through the Dyle Line; Brussels fell on the 17th, and on the 19th Abbeville was reached, as was the mouth of the Somme River

French Campaign. German cavalry before the Arc de Triomphe.

on the 20th. Allied Supreme Commander Gamelin was replaced on May 19 by Gen. Maxime WEYGAND. After only 10 days, all Allied combat divisions north of the "Sicklecut" were cut off, and the Belgian army surrendered on May 28 with 500,000 men (7,500 dead, 15,850 wounded). That 338,226 British and French soldiers were able to escape from the pocket around Dunkirk was due to the halt that Hitler ordered for the tanks on May 24, among other factors.

On June 5 the real French Campaign began with the second operations phase ("Red"). Army Group B reached the lower Seine on June 9, Paris fell without a battle on the 14th, and on the 16th, Army Group C broke through the MAGINOT LINE. When the German tanks reached the Swiss border on June 17, the bulk of the French army was surrounded. The Italian attack on the Alpine front after war was declared on France (June 6) ended unsuccessfully. On June 16, Winston CHURCHILL (British prime minister since May 10, 1940) proposed to the French government, which had withdrawn to Bordeaux, the union of both states, in order to continue conducting the war from the colonies and to secure France's strong battle fleet for Great Britain. The French cabinet refused and then resigned. Henri PÉTAIN became the new head of government; on June 17 he petitioned Germany for a cease-fire, which was signed on June 22 in the COMPIÈGNE forest (the one with Italy was signed on June 24 in Rome).

France mourned a total of 92,000 dead and 200,000 wounded; the Wehrmacht's toll was 27,074 dead, 18,383 missing, and 111,034 wounded. The British army lost 68,111 men, and 1.9 million Allied soldiers were captured. France remained occupied by German troops down to a line west and north of Geneva, Dôle, Tours, Mont de Marsan, and the Spanish border. The Pétain regime proceeded to function out of VICHY. In London, Charles de GAULLE appealed for the continuation of the struggle (*see* RÉSISTANCE) and formed a government-in-exile. However, it appeared that Hitler had finally attained hegemony over continental Europe.

G. H.

Frenssen, Gustav, b. Barlt (Dithmarschen), October 19, 1863; d. there, April 11, 1945, German writer. Frenssen studied Evangelical theology, then served as a pastor from 1890 to 1902. After a great success with the rural novel *Jörn Uhl* (1901; 500,000 copies sold by 1949), he withdrew from the ministry. As a freelance writer he

lived in, among other places, Blankenese, near Hamburg, where there is still a street named after him. For his German-*völkisch* stories, rooted in the homeland, Frenssen received various prizes during the Third Reich. Although honored in 1933 with an honorary doctorate of theology by the University of Heidelberg, Frenssen distanced himself ever more from the church and proclaimed a "Germanic belief in God" in his *Der Glaube der Nordmark* (The Faith of the Northern March; 1936), which during the war was published even in a field edition. According to this work, Christianity was "a form of the rule of the master race," which should allow itself to be led by its "Germanic conscience" as the "true voice of God."

Freud, Sigmund, b. Freiberg (Moravia), May 6, 1856; d. London, September 23, 1939, Austrian physician and psychologist; discoverer of the unconscious and founder of both theoretical and clinical PSYCHOANALYSIS. Freud regarded the sexual instinct as the central human instinct, and interpreted repressed sexuality as the cause of mental illnesses and failed development (Oedipus complex). He was the first to try to make emotional energies the "object of empirical science." Through his theories he wielded lasting influence not only over the fields of medicine and the social sciences, but beyond them over the contemporary arts; he influenced authors (such as Thomas MANN and Hanns Heinz EWERS) in their description of the "night sides of nature and mind." The National Socialists rejected Freud's materialistic concept of mind and

Sigmund Freud.

the determination of human activity by instinct as a "denial of all moral values." They consigned his writings to the flames in 1933 with the words "Down with the soul-devouring exaggeration of instinctive life, up with the nobility of the human soul!" (*see* BOOK BURNING). Although infirm, Freud had to flee Vienna and seek English exile in 1938, since for the National Socialists he and his teaching embodied "the high level of moral dissolution peculiar to Jewry."

H. H.

Freyer, Hans, b. Leipzig, July 31, 1887; d. Wiesbaden, January 18, 1969, German philosopher and sociologist. Freyer was a professor in Kiel (1922–1925), Leipzig (1925–1948), Münster (1953–1954), and Ankara, Turkey (1954–1955). With his major work, *Revolution von rechts* (Revolution on the Right; 1931), Freyer took his place among the intellectual forerunners of National Socialism. He indirectly but clearly referred to the movement in this half-poetic interpretation of the present, which called for "the *Volk* to become a state" that should then be freed from the clutches of interest groups (such as labor unions). Since class struggle had given way to class compromise in the modern industrial state, a "change of subject for revolution" had come about. With his work *Das politische Semester* (1933), Freyer propounded a reform of higher education along National Socialist lines, but he failed to recognize the much cruder educational plans of the new government. He achieved little response, despite his emphasis on "soldierly schooling" and on a "will for the Reich" that should "enliven" (*durchseelen*) everything. After the war, Freyer returned to liberal-conservative concepts, as in his *Theorie des gegenwärtigen Zeitalters* (Theory of the Present Age; 1955).

Frick, Wilhelm, b. Alsenz (Palatinate), March 12, 1877; d. Nuremberg, October 16, 1946 (executed), German politician. After studies in law, Frick entered the Bavarian state administration in 1904; as a senior magistrate (*Oberamtmann*), he became director of the political police in 1919. An early National Socialist sympathizer, Frick concealed the crimes of right-wing extremists, took part in the HITLER PUTSCH on November 9, 1923, and was sentenced to 15 months' imprisonment. The NS Freedom Movement (the substitute organization for the banned NSDAP) extricated him from prison by giving him a Reichstag mandate (May 4, 1924). As a deputy, Frick was leader of the NSDAP delega-

Wilhelm Frick.

tion after 1928, and on January 23, 1930, became the first National Socialist in a state government, as interior and education minister in Thuringia. There he campaigned against "Negro and jazz culture," prescribed prayer guidelines for the schools, and named the race ideologue Hans F. K. GÜNTHER to a professorship.

Hitler summoned Frick, at the time the only NS departmental head, into the Interior Ministry of his government of "National Rising" (January 30, 1933). Using his Reich governors, in accord with SYNCHRONIZATION Frick assumed government authority in the states. He significantly shaped everyday legal practices through his decisive contributions to many laws, including the GERMAN COMMUNAL ORDINANCE, the CIVIL SERVICE LAW, and, especially, the antisemitic NUREMBERG LAWS. Supervision of the police, however, was kept from him, first by Göring in Prussia, then later more generally by Himmler. Nonetheless, by transferring police jurisdiction from the states to the Reich, Frick provided the basis for the later total authority of the SS.

Frick's influence steadily ebbed during the war. On August 24, 1943, he lost his ministerial post to Himmler, but he remained Reich Minister without Portfolio and functioned as Reich Protector in Bohemia and Moravia, alongside his deputy Karl Hermann FRANK, the true power.

As architect of the police state and co-developer of the terror system of the CONCENTRATION CAMPS, Frick was charged with crimes against humanity, war crimes, and membership in the NS leadership responsible for planning a war of aggression. The Nuremberg Military Tribunals sentenced him to death by hanging on October 1, 1946.

Fried, Ferdinand (pseud. of Ferdinand Friedrich Zimmerman), b. Freienwalde, August 14, 1898; d. Cuxhaven, July 9, 1967, German journalist. From 1923 to 1932 Fried was economics editor for the *Vossische Zeitung* and the *Berliner Morgenpost*. As a contributor to the conservative cultural periodical *Die Tat* (The Deed; 1931–1933) and economics theoretician of the TAT CIRCLE, Fried advocated a policy of reagrarianization of Germany with the objective of assuring self-sufficiency in foodstuffs (as in his *Autarkie*; 1932). An SS member (*Obersturmbannführer*) from 1934, Fried worked from 1934 to 1938 on the staff of the Reich Peasant Führer; he subsequently wrote free-lance works on economic and political topics, including *Der Aufstieg der Juden* (The Rise of the Jews; 1937). After the war he was an economics editor for the newspapers *Sonntagsblatt* and *Die Welt*.

Friedeburg, Hans Georg von, b. Strasbourg, July 15, 1895; d. Flensburg, May 23, 1945, German fleet admiral (May 1, 1945). At the outbreak of war in 1939, Friedeburg was chief of the Organizational Section for U-boat commander Karl DÖNITZ. In February 1943, Friedeburg became commanding admiral of U-boats; after Dönitz was named Hitler's successor on May 1, 1945, Friedeburg was made the last supreme commander of the German navy. In this capacity he

Hans Georg von Friedeburg signs the German partial capitulation in Field Marshal Montgomery's headquarters.

signed the German partial surrender in the northwestern area in Field Marshal Bernard Montgomery's presence, and then the declarations of UNCONDITIONAL SURRENDER in Reims on May 7 and in Berlin-Karlshorst on May 8. Friedeburg committed suicide when the Dönitz government was placed under arrest.

Friedensdiktate (peace dictates), *völkisch* and nationalist propaganda term for the PARIS SUBURBAN TREATIES of 1919–1920, especially the VERSAILLES TREATY.

Fries, Jakob Friedrich, b. Barby (Elbe), August 23, 1773; d. Jena, August 10, 1843, German philosopher. In 1805 Fries became a professor in Heidelberg, and in 1816 in Jena. Discharged for participating in the nationalist Wartburg Celebration of 1817, he resumed teaching in Jena in 1824. Fries attempted to overcome the apparently growing discrepancy in Kantian theory between thought and being by means of the postulate of the "self-confidence of reason." As a natural scientist, Fries described knowledge as the consequence of "revenge" against the irrational, of mathematical thinking, and of observation of the sensory world. The emotional component of this teaching attracted National Socialist theoreticians, who saw in it a kind of "German positivism" that supposedly led Fries to be among the first to attain fundamental antisemitic insights. In this perspective his scholarly contributions receded, since his importance was derived above all from one obscure piece: *Über die Gefährdung des Wohlstands und des Charakters der Deutschen durch die Juden* (On the Threat to the Welfare and Character of the Germans by the Jews; 1816).

Fritsch, Theodor, b. Wiesenena bei Delitzsch, October 28, 1852; d. Gautzsch bei Leipzig, September 8, 1933, German publicist. Fritsch was originally a miller. In 1924 he served briefly as an NSDAP Reichstag deputy. His antisemitic "career" arose from a social motive: the struggle to preserve middle-class trades against the tide of industrialization. Thus an antisemitism based on envy of "Jewish capital" developed into his racial antisemitism. Fritsch expounded on this, along with arguments against the churches and against FREEMASONRY, in a periodical, *Hammer*, which he began in 1902. In this way he became a Nestor—the wise Greek elder during the Trojan War—for the *völkisch* movement, and he achieved cult status among the National Socialists with his *Antisemitischer Catechismus* (1887), which later appeared under the name *Hand-*

Theodor Fritsch.

buch der Judenfrage (Manual on the Jewish Question). Dietrich ECKART termed it "our complete spiritual arsenal."

Fritsch, Werner Baron von, b. Benrath (now Düsseldorf-Benrath), August 4, 1880; d. Praga, near Warsaw, September 22, 1939, German colonel general (April 1, 1936). From 1907 to 1910, Fritsch studied at the War Academy; in the First World War he held General Staff positions. As a confidant of General Hans von SEECKT, he held several posts connected with the buildup of the REICHSWEHR, and was made a lieutenant general on October 1, 1932. On February 1, 1934, he became Chief of Army Command (*Chef der Heeresleitung*), a title changed to Supreme Army Commander (*Oberbefehlshaber des Heeres*) on May 2, 1935. Fritsch approved Hitler's actions against the SA in the so-called RÖHM AFFAIR (June 30, 1934), which temporarily made the Reichswehr the sole arms bearer in the nation. A believer in the need for another war and a promoter of rearmament, Fritsch nonetheless resisted Hitler's hurried rate of buildup and opposed his plans for the use of force on November 5, 1937 (*see* HOSSBACH MEMORANDUM). As a result, he was accused of homosexuality and deposed in the FRITSCH CRISIS on February 4, 1938. His rehabilitation through a Reich court-martial in March 1938 fell through amid the euphoria of the Anschluss with Austria. Given the honorary post of Chief of Artillery Regiment 12, Fritsch fell in the Polish Campaign.

Fritsch Crisis (Blomberg-Fritsch Crisis), double intrigue engineered by Hermann Göring and Reinhard Heydrich against the military heads of the Wehrmacht in January and February 1938. Reich War Minister Werner von BLOMBERG and Supreme Army Comdr. Werner von FRITSCH, by warning against a course of war on November 5, 1937 (*see* HOSSBACH MEMORANDUM), only confirmed Hitler's low opinion of the vacillating generals. Hitler quickly found a pretext for Blomberg's dismissal: the divorced general field marshal had become engaged to a woman of inappropriate social standing. Göring encouraged Blomberg to go through with the wedding, arguing that outdated social prejudices had to be pushed aside. He and Hitler then served as Blomberg's witnesses at his wedding on January 12, 1938. A few days later it became known that not only was Mrs. Blomberg of inappropriate social station, she was unacceptable owing to

Fritsch Crisis. Blomberg (left) and Fritsch in conversation with Hitler.

her past as a prostitute; moreover, Hitler as chief of state had been disgraced. Blomberg had to submit his resignation on January 27.

Fritsch was assumed to be Blomberg's successor in the ministry post, but Göring also had his eyes on it. Göring now leaked Gestapo information that Fritsch had had homosexual relations with a male streetwalker, and was therefore a security risk. Fritsch's word of honor was not accepted by Hitler, and in the Reich Chancellery he was confronted with the "subject," one Schmid. The "witness" stood by his claim of intimate relations with Fritsch, who was then dismissed on February 4 and replaced by Walther von BRAUCHITSCH. Hitler himself assumed command of the Wehrmacht through the newly formed WEHRMACHT HIGH COMMAND (OKW), under Wilhelm KEITEL. Fritsch's complete rehabilitation through an honor court proceeding presided over by Göring on March 18, 1938, was spoiled by the vortex of events around the ANSCHLUSS with Austria. Through the Blomberg scandal, Hitler had gained a lockhold on the military forces; now, through the Fritsch Crisis, the moral backbone of the officer corps was broken. The latter surrendered honor and self-respect by offering no resistance as the highest-ranking soldier of the Reich became a victim of a criminal National Socialist plot.

Fritzsche, Hans, b. Bochum, April 21, 1900; d. Cologne, September 27, 1953, German journalist. After studying history and philosophy, in 1923 Fritzsche joined the German National People's Party and became an editor at a newspaper information service. In 1932 he was appointed director of the Wireless Service of the central news bureau of German Radio. When the Wireless Service was subordinated to the Propaganda Ministry on May 1, 1933, Fritzsche became director of the news service, now placed under the Propaganda Ministry press office; on the same day he joined the NSDAP. From then on, all news items had to be approved by Fritzsche's office—he controlled the news published in the German press as well as the flow of information to foreign outlets. After 1938, Fritzsche was director of the German Press Division; later he was given the post of ministerial director, and in November 1942 he took control of the Radio Division of the Propaganda Ministry.

Fritzsche became widely known after 1937 for his radio commentaries, entitled "Hans Fritzsche Speaking," which adhered to the party line but had a cloak of objectivity. Toward the end of the war the program was completely at the

Hans Fritzsche.

service of Goebbels's propaganda, urging the nation to stand fast. In early May 1945, Fritzsche was one of the highest-ranking government officials left after the flight or suicide of members of the political leadership; as such, he was involved in the surrender negotiations in Berlin. He also identified the bodies of Goebbels and his family for the Soviets, who then dispatched him to Moscow for confinement. In the NUREMBERG TRIALS, Fritzsche was acquitted; in 1947 a denazification court sentenced him to a work camp for nine years, but he was released on September 29, 1950.

Froelich, Carl August, b. Berlin, September 5, 1875; d. there, February 12, 1953, German film director and producer. From 1903, Froelich was a cameraman for the Messterfilm GmbH studio; in 1911 and 1912 he directed his own first important works. With Henny PORTEN, Froelich founded the Porten-Froelich Production Company in 1921; in 1929 they produced the first German sound film, *Die Nacht gehört uns* (The Night Belongs to Us), which also enjoyed foreign success. Froelich made the 1931 film *Mädchen in Uniform* (Girls in Uniform), using only actresses. For *Traumulus* (with Emil JANNINGS), he received the State Prize in 1936; he was officially commended for other movies, such as *Wenn wir alle Engel wären* (If We Were All Angels) and *Es war eine rauschende Ballnacht* (An Intoxicating Night at the Ball). Hitler named him a professor on January 20, 1937, and Goebbels appointed him president of the REICH FILM CHAMBER on July 1, 1939. Froelich succeeded in keeping German cinema at an international level despite its entanglement with propaganda.

Fromm, Friedrich, b. Berlin, October 8, 1888; d. Brandenburg, March 12, 1945 (executed), German colonel general (July 19, 1940). Fromm was chief of army weaponry and, after 1939, commander of the Reserve Army. Because of the strategic importance of his post in plans for the assassination attempt of the TWENTIETH OF JULY, 1944, he was let in on the secret; he opposed the plot, but without betraying the conspirators. As the attempt progressed, however, he finally came down on the side of the regime: when he learned that Hitler had survived, he had six principal conspirators, who were staying with him at the Army High Command, arrested, sentenced to death by summary courts-martial, and shot. Those executed included even his friend Erich HOEPNER. Fromm's attempt to conceal his complicity failed: on the next day he was arrested on Himmler's order, and in March 1945 he was sentenced to death "for cowardice" and executed.

Front (*Front*), military term for the flank of troops facing the enemy, or the line across which enemy troops confront one another. In the First and Second World Wars, it was generally used to designate a combat site or battlefield (often in such compounds as "front service"). Since service at the front in the First World War was held in higher propagandistic and patriotic esteem in Germany than staff or base duty, as a result of the militarization of National Socialist vocabulary, "front" was borrowed for designations of

Friedrich Fromm.

tasks and places that required especially active involvement. Thus, labor became a "labor front"; labor with political or military significance, such as the building of the WESTWALL, was performed by "front workers"; farmers with labor service obligations became "front farmers." Once the war began, the term "front" was used ever more frequently and ever more inclusively, generally in the sense of something advanced, current, or important: "new light beers . . . are now at the front" (*Das Reich*, 1940). The term HOME FRONT emerged at the time of the bombing war.

"Frontbann" (frontline unit), replacement organization for the SA (STURMABTEILUNG) during the period when the NSDAP was illegal (1924–1925).

Front bookstores (*Frontbuchhandlungen*), compact and portable bookstores for combat troops during the Second World War. The mobile stores each carried some 1,500 titles approved by the Propaganda Ministry, Labor Front (DAF), and REICH WRITING CHAMBER in specially armed omnibuses (12 vehicles for the French Campaign), with a trailer to increase the assortment.

Front experience (*Fronterlebnis*), the key event in the lives of the generation that took part in the First World War. The front experience was repeatedly portrayed in the literature of the 1920s and 1930s, mostly in a glorifying light (as in the work of Ernst JÜNGER). It was often viewed as a contrast to the political divisiveness of the Weimar Republic years and was at the

Carl August Froelich.

National Socialist poster invokes the front experience: "National Socialist, or the sacrifices will have been in vain."

core of the nostalgia for clear-cut hierarchical decision making, which groups such as the National Socialists offered. Hitler, who himself was decisively affected by his front experience, most convincingly succeeded in articulating these feelings: he oriented his choice of words and his statements toward the heroic, and invoked the solidarity derived from the threat of combat (*see* FRONT SOCIALISM) to overcome current problems. After the Seizure of Power, glorification of the front experience also served to deepen the inward assent of the population to a new armed conflict, which had been planned from the outset.

Front libraries (*Frontbüchereien*), lending libraries for soldiers at the front, stocked during the Second World War by the German Army Library (Berlin) from the holdings of troop and officers' libraries. The front libraries also received most of the books donated through public collections (in 1939–1940, over 8 million copies were collected). The books were transported in crates with the troops.

Front realignment (*Frontbegradigung*), National Socialist wartime propaganda euphemism for retreats and defeats.

Front socialism (*Frontsozialismus*), exaltation of the common experience and perseverance in the battles of the First World War into a "front community" or "social community of destiny" by nationalist and patriotic circles. The National Socialists saw in "front socialism" the model for the VOLK COMMUNITY to which they aspired; they therefore wanted it understood as the "genuine new birth of a German socialism" and as "a process that is lethal to Marxism. . . . The front of 1914 is now the whole *Volk*. From front socialism, therefore, National Socialism has now emerged" (Alfred Rosenberg).

Führer-Begleit-Bataillon (Führer Escort Battalion), military unit originally created to protect Hitler, his staff, and the current headquarters. Formed on October 1, 1939, from the Führer-begleitkommando (Führer Escort Commando), it was later broadened to a regiment. In November 1944, the Führer-Begleit-Brigade, under Col. Otto-Ernst REMER, was created from the Begleit-Bataillon; on January 26, 1945, it was broadened as the Führer-Grenadier-Division. First deployed during the ARDENNES OFFENSIVE, the division was destroyed in late April 1945 in the pocket at Spremberg.

Führerbunker, generally bombproof housing for Hitler in the FÜHRER'S HEADQUARTERS, especially the bunker under the Reich Chancellery, which was created in wartime, and the garden that belonged to it. The *Führerbunker* was located 16 m (about 50 feet) below ground on two levels, and could be reached by a stairway from the chancellery and the garden. Hitler spent the last months of the war here, during which time Albert SPEER considered eliminating the dictator with poison gas introduced through the ventilating machinery. On April 30, 1945, Hitler took his life, along with that of Eva BRAUN, in the *Führerbunker.*

"Führer commands, we follow" ("Führer befiehl, wir folgen"), National Socialist loyalty oath to Hitler, often used to close speeches at party gatherings. During the war a bitter parody was circulated in UNDERGROUND HUMOR, in light of the bombed-out cities: "The Führer commands, we bear the consequences" ("Führer befiehl, wir tragen die Folgen").

Führer cult (*Führerkult*), a kind of religious glorification and veneration of Hitler, staged through propaganda and self-styling, and encouraged by the circumstances of the period and by his own person. For large segments of the German people, the parliamentary Weimar Republic, with its conflicting interests and its pressure toward political compromise, was a questionable system. They were more accustomed to the clear

authoritarian order of the imperial state, as well
as to the military decision-making hierarchies
they had experienced during the war. Democratic traditions were lacking. Anxiety over the
future was generated by immense technological
and scientific progress and by economic crises;
the VERSAILLES TREATY was regarded as a "national degradation." People were looking for
guides and hoped for change through a "strong
man" at the head of the Reich. Many poems
promised predestined leaders: Stefan GEORGE
was one who sang of the leader who "breaks the
chains. . . . He leads through cruel signals . . .
and plants the New Reich."

In this situation, during the 1920s Hitler
became a "point of convergence for many long-
ings, anxieties, and resentments" (Joachim Fest).
He conjured up distinct images of an enemy,
directed hate toward the weaker and the foreign, invoked the fear of BOLSHEVISM, appealed
to emotions, and impressed hearers through his
ability to declaim about insignificant matters
with the greatest passion. In the early phase of
the National Socialist movement, Hitler sought
to surround himself with an aura of the extraordinary and an atmosphere of mystery. He promoted the growth of the legend and with tactical skill used all available means, including
terror and riots, in order to become known.
Within the NSDAP he imposed his claim to

Führer cult. Weekly maxim of the
NSDAP: "The Führer is always right."

leadership with scrupulousness and self-as-
surance. At the members' meeting on July 29,
1921, he secured the granting of "dictatorial
powers" and was celebrated for the first time as
"our Führer." In August 1921 the *Völkischer
Beobachter*, the party newspaper, fashioned
Hitler for the larger public as the predestined
"national rescuer" and "Führer."

Dietrich ECKART, the article's author, began,
along with Hermann ESSER and Rudolf HESS, to
elaborate a Führer myth around Hitler in the
ensuing period. Hitler's public appearances addressed the emotions of his hearers, in great part
through the crowd-pleasing arrangements of
flags, colors, symbols, uniforms, and military-
like marches. Hitler offered himself as a Führer
who stood above classes and material interests,
and called for willingness to submit and to
sacrifice. Through the ceremonial character of
public rallies and the consciously cultivated
mien of a bearer of salvation, a new Führer
emerged with ever stronger religious accents.
Hitler was exalted as the "fatherly redeemer"
(Haug) and as the "messiah of the *Volk*"
(Loewy); he himself emphasized his predestination by his continual references to "the Lord
God" and to "Providence." The elevation into a
Christlike hero was strengthened in the years
after the Seizure of Power by a series of publicly
effective performances of CHORAL POETRY, in
which a leader conducted the chosen German
people to redemption, using the pattern of the
Christian passion plays (one such play was *Deutsche Passion 1933* by Richard EURINGER).

"Führer commands, we follow." Banner on the Brandenburg Gate.

NS propaganda was also consciously oriented toward religious utterances: "On this earth we believe in Adolf Hitler alone"; the "Lord God has sent us Adolf Hitler, that he might be for all eternity a foundation for Germany" (NSDAP training letter, 1937). In the GERMAN GREETING, "Heil Hitler" took the place of "Grüss Gott" (literally, "greetings to God"). The "Führer's birthday" was turned into a kind of high religious feast day. With the motto "The Führer is always right!" Goebbels claimed divine infallibility for "our Hitler," as he declared in liturgical fashion toward the end of each of his birthday addresses right up until 1945.

Führer cult. Gymnastics festival in Breslau (1938). Ecstatic greeting by the masses. On the platform, from the left: Robert Ley, Martin Bormann, Heinrich Himmler, Hans von Tschammer und Osten, Hitler, Bernhard Rust, Hanns Kerrl, and Joseph Goebbels.

Hitler himself demanded the Führer cult around his person, and regarded as self-evident homages such as that from Gen. Wilhelm Keitel, who celebrated him as "the greatest military commander of all time." The early wartime successes confirmed Hitler as a victorious conqueror who swept away the "European debris of petty states." The contradictions and the terror of the system were blamed not on the Führer, but on the "little Adolfs": Hitler took on the nimbus of a statesman bestriding everyday affairs. "If only the Führer knew that!" became the slogan for disappointed hopes. While the manifest defeats in war aroused doubts about Hitler's infallibility, his position within the NS movement remained unquestioned until the war's end.

The Führer cult was among the main subjects of the literature and arts of the Third Reich, although with subtle differences. In lyric poetry, hymns and odes dedicated to the Führer developed into a distinct genre, in which he was lauded as "the heart of the *Volk*" (Ina SEIDEL). In novels and cinema, the Führer cult found expression more in a comparison with the personalities of such historical leaders as Otto von Bismarck. In order to conserve his image of being exceptional and inviolable, Hitler opposed the representation of his person in feature films. He considered his own ideal image to have been perfectly and incomparably realized in the film *Triumph des Willens* (TRIUMPH OF THE WILL). In sculpture and architecture, the Führer cult was reflected especially in the oversized dimensions of statues and of public buildings, which were meant to express the importance and might of the Führer working inside them.

After 1945, the Führer cult manifested aftereffects in Germany. The critical scholarly analysis of National Socialism suffered in part from it, since the explicit personalization of politics in the Führer cult moved to the foreground, and the Third Reich became investigated exclusively as "the personal work of Adolf Hitler" (F. Glum). The monstrous nature of his deeds and the Führer cult stand in the way even today of a sober consideration of Hitler, who becomes dehumanized as a nonbeing, as a "gutter demon" (George W. F. Hallgarten), a "fascist beast" (Ilya Ehrenburg), and a "disgusting object" (Golo Mann) who ought to be pulled down from the pedestal of the Führer cult. This negative emotionalization has shown itself to be useless against those who are unwilling to abandon the Führer cult: it is not only in nationalist-conservative circles that Hitler is still glorified in

such guises as the builder of highways and the eliminator of unemployment. Neo-Nazi groups still celebrate the anniversaries of Hitler's birth and death with solemn ceremonies.

H. H.

Führergrundsatz, later customary Germanization of the original term *Führerprinzip* (FÜHRER PRINCIPLE).

Führer Principle (*Führerprinzip*; also *Führergrundsatz* [Führer fundament], a later Germanization), a radically antidemocratic system of political leadership, which Hitler demanded for the entire state structure as early as in *Mein Kampf*, and which is typical of fascist dictatorships. According to this principle, only the highest leader is to be "confirmed" by the people (legitimation by plebiscite); in the case of National Socialism, this was Hitler. All other leaders were to be appointed by the leader immediately above, so that political decisions could be made in ostensible independence from all "entanglements of interests." In the National Socialist view, the Führer Principle was the basis of "Germanic DEMOCRACY" and rested upon the "unconditional bond between absolute responsibility and absolute authority" (*Mein Kampf*). It should penetrate all areas of society, since it was a "law of nature" that was rooted "deeply in Germanic-German thinking."

After the Seizure of Power, the principle that had prevailed since 1921 in the NSDAP and its divisions was applied to all organizations, such as the German Labor Front, the Reich Food Estate, the Reich League for Physical Exercises, and the member chambers of the Reich Culture Chamber. It was then extended into the economy through the LABOR REGULATION LAW, and into the communal bodies through the GERMAN COMMUNAL ORDINANCE. The motto was "Consultation instead of votes!" ("Beratung statt Abstimmung!").

Führer Schools (*Führerschulen*), instructional institutions for future party members (*see* SCHOOLING, POLITICAL).

Führer's headquarters (*Führerhauptquartiere*), Hitler's fortified command centers, with bunkers, living quarters, and other features, both inside and beyond Germany's borders. From them, Hitler and his staff (the Wehrmacht command staff) conducted operations in the Second World War. During the Polish Campaign, Hitler still had no fixed headquarters but rode in his "Adler" (Eagle) command railway car into the war zone on September 3, 1939; after several visits to the front, he left on September 26. Over the remaining course of the war, he used the following headquarters:

He occupied "Felsennest" (Cliff Nest), near Münstereifel, from May 10 to June 5, 1940; "Wolfsschlucht" (Wolf's Ravine; previously "Waldwiese" [Forest Meadow]), near Bruly de Peche in Belgium, from June 6 to 17 and June 19 to 28, 1940; and "Tannenberg" (Mount Fir), on the Kniebis in the Black Forest, from June 28 to July 5, 1940. During the Balkan Campaign, Hitler again rode in his command railway car.

For the Russian Campaign, the best-known of the Führer's headquarters, "Wolfsschanze" (Wolf's Stronghold), was built near Rastenburg in East Prussia. Hitler worked here from June 24, 1941, to June 17, 1942. From July 16 to October 31, 1942, he occupied the "Werwolf" headquarters near Vinnitsa in the Ukraine. After that he was at "Wolfsschanze" again, from October 31 to November 7, 1942, and from November 22 to February 17, 1943. He was again at "Werwolf" from February 19 to March 13, 1943, only to return once more to "Wolfsschanze."

After the D Day invasion, Hitler went on June 17, 1944, to "Wolfsschlucht II," near Soissons, his only stay in that headquarters. On July 14 he returned again to "Wolfsschanze," where he was the object of the assassination attempt of the TWENTIETH OF JULY. The approach of the Soviet front forced him to abandon that headquarters on November 20, 1944. Hitler then conducted the ARDENNES OFFENSIVE (from December 10, 1944, to January 16, 1945) from "Adlerhorst" (Eagle's Nest), near Bad Nauheim. After the offensive's failure, he withdrew to the command bunker under the Reich Chancellery.

G. H.

Führer's will (*Führerwille*; also *Führererlass* [Führer's edict/decree] or *Führerbefehl* [Führer's order]), in the National Socialist view, the basis for all governmental activity in legislation (see LAWS), ADMINISTRATION, and JUSTICE. As justification it was asserted that the Führer expressed the true will of the *Volk*, without any requirement that the Führer's will agree with any actual popular will. The expression of the Führer's will was not tied to any substantive criteria or to any formal prescriptions. The Führer's will, as expressed in speeches, for example, was binding for all state organs. By the Führer's order, individual—often vague—decisions were rendered for military and civilian spheres.

Through the Führer's decrees, both generally binding regulations and specific decisions were issued. These pronouncements often depended upon circumstances. Such crimes as the FINAL SOLUTION and the EUTHANASIA program, in particular, may be traced back to the Führer's will.

Führer Talks (*Führergespräche*), term for Martin Bormann's collection of notes on Hitler's TABLE TALKS.

Führer und Reichskanzler (Leader and Reich Chancellor), as of August 2, 1934, Hitler's official title in conformity with the Law on the Head of State of the German Reich, issued the day before (*Reich Law Gazette* I, p. 747). The designation "Führer" for Hitler as party chief, apparently in imitation of the Fascist example of "Duce," appeared in 1921–1922, but became firm practice only after the re-establishment of the NSDAP (February 27, 1925). The assumption of the responsibilities of the Reich president after Hindenburg's death completed Hitler's personal dictatorship; he thereby also became supreme commander of the military forces, and obligated soldiers and civil servants to himself personally by means of an OATH, sworn as a vow of loyalty to the *Führer und Reichskanzler*. In a plebiscite on August 19, 1934, according to official reports 89.9 percent of the voters approved the law that delineated the office. The designation "Führer" was thus given constitutional status and gradually supplanted the term "Reich chancellor." On January 14, 1939, the press was informed that from then on Hitler was to be spoken of only as the "Führer"; this was extended on January 22, 1942, to Hitler as supreme commander of the Wehrmacht as well. The Party Chancellery declared in April 1944 that the term "Führer" covered all of Hitler's functions as party chief, chief of state, Reich chancellor, and commander in chief.

Fulfillment policy (*Erfüllungspolitik*), foreign-policy strategy for demonstrating the impossibility of fulfilling terms of the VERSAILLES TREATY, especially its reparations demands. After 1921, Reich Chancellor Joseph WIRTH and his foreign minister, Walther RATHENAU, advocated a consistent policy of fulfillment, but because of the rigid French attitude they achieved no results except for the aggravation of the economic (*see* INFLATION) and political (*see* RUHR CONFLICT) situations. When passive resistance under Wilhelm CUNO also failed, Foreign Minister Gustav

STRESEMANN transformed the fulfillment policy into a policy of accommodation, with countermeasures from the Allies (such as the DAWES PLAN, LOCARNO PACT, and YOUNG PLAN). Their continuation under Heinrich BRÜNING during the world economic crisis, along with an austere economic policy, led Germany to the brink of economic collapse and thereby to political radicalization; success in ending the reparations in 1932 thus came too late. The always massive polemics of the nationalist Right had contributed to this outcome; in particular, the National Socialists had denounced fulfillment as "suicidal" and "disgraceful." Although essentially without alternatives, because of internal as well as external resistance this fulfillment policy became a crucial factor in weakening and finally bringing down the Weimar Republic.

Funder, Friedrich, b. Graz, November 1, 1872; d. Vienna, May 19, 1959, Austrian journalist. In 1896 Funder became an editor of the Christian-Social *Reichspost* and in 1902 its editor in chief. He played a key role in building up the newspaper into the most significant organ of Austrian Catholicism; from that base he opposed National Socialism and the ANSCHLUSS. Following the merger of Austria with the German Reich in 1938, Funder was arrested, and confined during 1938–1939 in the concentration camps at Dachau and Flossenbürg; in 1944 he was once again temporarily detained. After 1945 he resumed his earlier journalistic success with the cultural and political newspaper *Die Furche* (The Furrow).

Funger, Hans, b. Krefeld, December 10, 1891; d. spring 1945, German trade unionist. Originally a railroad worker, Funger was a radio operator in the First World War. After the RUHR CONFLICT, he joined the Railway Workers' Union of the GENERAL GERMAN TRADE UNION FEDERATION, serving as its deputy chairman in 1928; in 1926 he had joined the SPD (Social Democratic Party of Germany). After the Seizure of Power, Funger was concerned with maintaining the cohesiveness of the old trade union cadres. On December 3, 1937, he was sentenced by the *Volk* Court in Düsseldorf to a term of 15 years in the penitentiary for illegal union activity and for conspiracy with international labor organizations. During the war he was detailed to bomb-search squads in the area of Hannover, and died, probably from exhaustion, during an evacuation transport to the concentration camp at Bergen-Belsen.

Funk, Walther, b. Trakehnen, August 18, 1890; d. Düsseldorf, May 31, 1960, politican and economics expert. Funk studied law, economics, and philosophy; as of 1912 he was an editor, and from 1922 to 1930 editor in chief, of the conservative financial paper *Berliner Börsenzeitung.* A convinced anti-Marxist and nationalist, Funk joined the NSDAP in 1931 and advanced rapidly to become Hitler's personal economics adviser. In this position, he proved to be a valuable mediator between Hitler and powerful industrial circles that channeled a great part of their donations to the NSDAP through Funk, who was regarded as a moderate National Socialist. In this manner the donors intended to strengthen the economically liberal wing within the party.

On January 30, 1933, Funk became press secretary for the Reich government, and on March 11 of that year, state undersecretary in the Propaganda Ministry. At the same time, he co-opted several functions relating to control of National Socialist cultural agencies (for example, the posts of vice president of the REICH CULTURE CHAMBER and chairman of the Board of German Broadcasters). He also took an early part in planning the removal of the economic rights of Jews (*see* ARYANIZATION). As the successor to Hjalmar SCHACHT in the offices of Reich economics minister, general plenipotentiary for the war economy (1938), and Reichsbank president (1939), Funk shared responsibility for the looting of the occupied territories: for example, he had the gold reserves of the Czechoslovak National Bank confiscated, and was president of the Kontinentale Öl-Gesellschaft, which had the task of exploiting oil

Walther Funk.

deposits in the occupied Eastern Territories. Moreover, in 1942 Funk had made a secret accord with Himmler that enabled the Reichsbank to store for the SS the cash, gold, jewelry, and other valuables from the property of deported and murdered Jews. In 1943 Funk became a member of the Central Planning Board, which, among other things, organized the deployment in German industry of forced laborers who had been deported from occupied territories.

On October 1, 1946, Funk was sentenced to life imprisonment on charges of war crimes and crimes against humanity, in the Nuremberg proceedings against the major war criminals. Consideration was given to the fact that, although he had held high positions, he had never been a dominant figure in NS policy. In 1957 he was released from the Spandau prison on grounds of illness.

R. S.

Furtwängler, Wilhelm, b. Berlin, January 25, 1886; d. Ebersteinburg (Baden-Baden), November 30, 1954, German orchestra conductor. Furtwängler served as conductor (*Kapellmeister*) in Strasbourg, Lübeck, Mannheim, and Vienna. From 1922 to 1945, and again after 1947, he was primary conductor (*Dirigent*) of the Berlin Philharmonic; concurrently, he was conductor of the Leipzig Gewandhaus (Drapers' Hall) Orchestra (1922–1928), musical director of the Bayreuth Festival (1931), and director of the Berlin State Opera (1933). He gave international "Furtwängler Concerts" and produced many recordings. His first postwar concert was a Mendelssohn memorial concert in Vienna in 1947. (The National Socialists had forbidden the music of the "Jewish"—although a convert —composer.) Furtwängler's favorite composers were Bach, Mozart, Haydn, and especially Beethoven and the Romantics, as well as Richard STRAUSS and Paul HINDEMITH.

In 1933, Göring named Furtwängler to the Prussian State Council; with his international fame as a musician, he was a useful advertisement for National Socialist cultural propaganda. He became vice president of the REICH MUSIC CHAMBER. His insistence on artistic independence led to open conflict with Goebbels in November 1934, since Furtwängler stood by Hindemith when the latter's music had been outlawed as "degenerate." In protest, on December 4, 1934, Furtwängler resigned all his offices for the moment, but then reached an arrangement with the party that allowed him

Wilhelm Furtwängler.

considerable artistic freedom, such that he was able to protect Jewish members of his orchestra. Furtwängler was cleared by a denazification proceeding in 1945.

R. H.

Futuristic novels (*Zukunftsromane*), literary descriptions of the future; one of the most important forms of entertainment and escapist literature in Germany after the lost First World War. A flood of chauvinistic futuristic novels described, under the motto "Revenge for Versailles," how Germany uses technological miracle weapons to reconquer its hegemony and master other peoples. Many of these works reintroduced the monarchy, such as *1934— Deutschlands Auferstehung* (1934—Germany's Resurrection; 1921), by Ferdinand Eugen Solf. Literary descriptions and quasi-scientific and political myth building were blended together. Futuristic novels and political pamphleteering mythologized Atlantis and Thule as lost Aryan high cultures about to return.

German futuristic novels, like almost no other genre, laid the ideological ground for National Socialism. Numerous authors anticipated the Third Reich in the 1920s. Directly after the takeover of power, glorifying prognoses appeared, such as *Im Jahre 2000 im Dritten Reich* (In the Year 2000 in the Third Reich; 1933) by Edmund Schmid, who among other scenes described how Hitler's successor, "Herr König" (Mr. King), on the occasion of his 100th birthday has battalions of "wheat-blond," naked mothers with milk-filled breasts parade by. Popular series of futuristic novels promoted Führer figures, for example, *Sun Koh, der Erbe von Atlantis (Sun Koh, the Heir of Atlantis;* 1933–1935) and *Jan Mayen* (1936–1938). In antisemitic parables Jews were made alien as antlike "parasites" that plunder other planets (F. Freska, *Druso,* 1931). In *Deutschland ohne Deutsche* (Germany without Germans), H. Heyck depicted in 1929 how the last "Nordic men" leave the "nigger- and Jew-ridden" Weimar Republic in order to procreate the blond master race in Lappland, for which in later novels the "Race Office of Asgard" was responsible (in the Atlantis cycle by E. Kiss, 1930–1939).

Futuristic novels were not specifically promoted by the National Socialists (certain titles were even prohibited because of exaggerated theses on racial breeding), since the detailed planning of the future was to succeed only through the Führer himself; nonetheless, technological-chauvinistic futuristic novels reached their highest sales figures around 1940 (*see* Hans DOMINIK). Not only were they the favorite reading material of young readers, but as special editions and "Christmas gifts" they went to the front in millions of copies.

H. H.

Gaiser, Gerd, b. Oberriexingen/Enz, September 15, 1908; d. Reutlingen, June 9, 1976, German writer. An officer and fighter pilot in the Second World War, Gaiser began his literary career with poems inspired by youthful emotion (*Reiter am Himmel* [Riders to the Heavens]; 1941). On account of his support for National Socialism before 1945, his early postwar works were often criticized as a continuation of his *völkisch* poetics. Parts of his often noted novel of a flying squadron, *Die sterbende Jagd* (The Mortal Chase; 1953), appeared earlier during the war in the magazine *Das innere Reich.* Yet Gaiser's primary concern was with human isolation in wartime and in the postwar period. From a romantic viewpoint and using complex language, he criticized materialism and the satiety of postwar society, as in *Schlussball* (Final Ball; 1958).

Galen, Clemens August Count von, b. Dinklage, March 16, 1878; d. Münster, March 22, 1946, German Catholic theologian. Galen was educated by the Jesuits. Ordained a priest in 1904, he served as assistant pastor, then as pastor, in Berlin-Schöneberg (Saint Matthias) from 1906 to 1929. He transferred to Münster (Saint Lamberti), and was named local bishop there in September 1933. Galen was one of the first to take a "loyalty oath" before agents of the National Socialist state. This was not difficult for him to do, since he hoped for a moderating influence from the CONCORDAT, and at any rate was a conservative of nationalistic bent. However, Galen was also one of the first prelates, in early 1934, to warn against Nazi racism: that year he answered Alfred Rosenberg's new paganism, as expressed in *Der* MYTHUS DES 20. JAHRHUNDERTS (*The Myth of the 20th Century*), with *Studien zum Mythus des 20. Jahrhunderts* (Studies on the Myth of the 20th Century).

Consistent with his motto, "Nec laudibus nec timore" ("Neither to be enticed nor to be intimidated"), Galen turned against "an obedience that enslaves the soul" (September 6, 1936) and took action to distribute the encyclical MIT BRENNENDER SORGE (With Burning Concern; March 14, 1937). However, he earned his fame as "the Lion of Münster" through his intrepid and successful protest against EUTHANASIA in three homilies delivered during the summer of 1941 (July 13, July 20, and August 3); the Security Service (SD) characterized them as "the strongest attack to date against the state leadership." Galen eluded imprisonment and a death sentence only because of Hitler's worry over the combat morale of Catholic soldiers. Named a cardinal after the war (Christmas 1945), Galen showed himself to be equally intrepid toward the British occupation authorities, whom he admonished to show clemency and fairness.

Clemens August Count von Galen.

Galland, Adolf, b. Westerholt, March 19, 1912, German lieutenant general (November 1, 1944). Trained as a commercial pilot, Galland joined the Reichswehr; as of 1935 he was attached to the "Richthofen" Fighter Squadron. He was with the Condor Legion in the Spanish Civil War, and from 1940 was squadron commander for France and Great Britain, himself making 104 hits. From 1941 to January 1945, Galland was commander of fighter planes (*General der Jagdflieger*). After the war he lived in Argentina as a military adviser until 1954, when he returned to the Federal Republic as a businessman.

Gamelin, Maurice-Gustave, b. Paris, September 20, 1872; d. there, April 18, 1958, French general. During the First World War Gamelin was Marshal Joffre's chief of staff. In 1931 he became chief of the French General Staff, and in 1935, general inspector of the army and vice president of the Supreme War Council. As of September 1939 he was supreme commander of Allied military forces in France; on May 19, 1940, he was replaced by Gen. Maxime WEYGAND. Arrested in September 1940 and tried in Riom in 1942, Gamelin was charged with responsibility for France's military defeat. Incarcerated in France until April 1943, he was then remanded to Germany, where he was a prisoner of war until 1945.

Adolf Galland.

Maurice-Gustave Gamelin.

Garda de Fier. *See* Iron Guard.

Gas chambers (*Gaskammern*), rooms or buildings built or refitted to kill people by gassing. They were utilized in several National Socialist pro-

grams: EUTHANASIA, the "FINAL SOLUTION of the Jewish question," and the SPECIAL HANDLING of potential enemies in certain hospitals and nursing facilities, as well as in the EXTERMINATION CAMPS and numerous CONCENTRATION CAMPS. The chambers were often built to resemble bathing facilities in order to deceive the victims: on the ceiling were shower heads, some fake, but others connected to pipes for the introduction of gas. The walls were of tile. Airtight doors closed the chambers. In most cases the proceedings could be observed through a peephole in the door or a small window in the wall. For killing with carbon monoxide from steel tanks, the gas was introduced through a ("water") pipe system and the shower heads; when motor-exhaust gases were used, the gas came into the extermination rooms through pipes or tubes. The hydrocyanic compound ZYKLON B, in crystalline (pellet) form, was thrown through an opening into the chamber, where the toxic gas became released on contact with the air.

There were gas chambers in the extermination and concentration camps in the occupied Eastern Territories (Auschwitz, Bełżec, Sobibór, Treblinka, and Maidanek), in the euthanasia facilities (Bernburg, Brandenburg, Grafeneck, Hadamar, Hartheim, and Sonnenstein), and in several concentration camps in Reich territory (Neuengamme, Natzweiler, Mauthausen, Ravensbrück, Sachsenhausen, and Stutthof). In the Kulmhof extermination camp GAS VANS were used.

A. St.

Gassing (*Vergasen*), killing of the handicapped, Jews, and "potential enemies" of the Third Reich by means of poison gas. EUTHANASIA victims in killing facilities and victims of the FINAL SOLUTION in extermination camps were killed by gassing. This was done in GAS CHAMBERS and GAS VANS, in which carbon monoxide (CO) and prussic acid (hydrocyanic acid; HCN) were used. At first, CO in steel cylinders was used, but for reasons of economy a switch was made to CO-containing fumes from deliberately re-adjusted truck motors. Especially in AUSCHWITZ and the concentration camps, killing was carried out by means of the prussic acid compound ZYKLON B. It was thrown in stable crystalline form into the gas chambers, where it became released in contact with the air, and thus unleashed its deadly effect.

A. St.

Gas vans (*Gaswagen*; also S[*pezial*]-*Wagen*), mobile gas chambers used to kill Jews and other "potential enemies" by means of exhaust gases; they were used primarily in the occupied Eastern Territories. From approximately the late summer of 1941, officials in the Reich Security Main Office (RSHA), under the direction of SS-Obersturmführer (later Standartenführer) Walther RAUFF, worked on development of a gas van. The chassis was built by the Saurer and Diamond truck factory, the body by the Gaubschat firm in Berlin, and the gassing apparatus by the motor vehicle workshop of the RSHA. After a gas van was built, the SS ran test gassings, some using Soviet prisoners of war in the Sachsenhausen camp.

The first gas vans were deployed in the late fall of 1941; their technical performance proved satisfactory. Thus, a report of June 5, 1942, to Rauff noted that with three vans, since December 1941 "97,000 [had been] processed [*verarbeitet*]" without any problems showing up with the vans. Still, some improvements were considered expedient—such as quicker and easier unloading of the corpses and easier cleaning of the vans (memorandum, RSHA/II D 3 a (9) Nr. 214/42 g. RS. of June 5, 1942, in the LUDWIGSBURG CENTRAL OFFICE). The gas vans looked like furniture delivery trucks. To monitor the gassings, there was a small window in the cab that later was omitted. A removable hose led from the exhaust to a pipe going through the van's floor into its interior. At least 30 vans were ultimately deployed in the liquidation of ghettos and camps, as well as to "empty out" prisons.

A. St.

Gau, Old German term for particular (tribal) regions, retained in regional names (such as Hennegau). It was taken up again by the gymnastic and YOUTH MOVEMENTs for designating regional subdivisions. Although customary even before 1933, after that date the NSDAP officially used the term *Gau* to designate its highest "sovereign territory" (*Hoheitsgebiet*) below the Reich level. A *Gauleiter* directed a *Gau*; its subdivisions were the *Kreis* (district), *Ortsgruppe* (local group), *Zelle* (cell), and *Block*.

As of November 1941, the *Gaue* and their *Gau* leaders were:

Baden	Norbert Wagner
Bayerische Ostmark (Bavarian East March)	Fritz Wächtler
Berlin	Joseph GOEBBELS
Danzig-Westpreussen (Danzig–West Prussia)	Albert FORSTER
Düsseldorf	Friedrich Karl FLORIAN
Essen	Josef TERBOVEN
Franken (Franconia)	Karl Holz
Halle-Merseburg	Joachim Albrecht Eggeling
Hamburg	Karl KAUFMANN
Hessen-Nassau (Hesse-Nassau)	Jakob Sprenger
Kärnten (Carinthia)	Friedrich Rainer
Köln-Aachen (Cologne-Aachen)	Josef GROHÉ
Kurhessen (Electoral Hesse)	Karl Weinrich
Magdeburg-Anhalt	Rudolf JORDAN
Mainfranken	Otto Hellmuth

Gau. Joseph Goebbels with *"Gau* propaganda leaders" of the NSDAP.

Mark Brandenburg	Emil Stürtz
Mecklenburg	Friedrich HILDEBRAND
Moselland	Gustav SIMON
München-Oberbayern	Adolf WAGNER
(Munich–Upper Bavaria)	
Niederdonau (Lower Danube)	Hugo Jury
Niederschlesien (Lower Silesia)	Karl HANKE
Oberdonau (Upper Danube)	August Eigruber
Oberschlesien (Upper Silesia)	Fritz BRACHT
Osthannover	Otto Telschow
Ostpreussen (East Prussia)	Erich KOCH
Pommern (Pomerania)	Franz Schwede-Coburg
Sachsen (Saxony)	Martin MUTSCHMANN
Salzburg	Gustav Adolf SCHEEL
Schleswig-Holstein	Hinrich LOHSE
Schwaben (Swabia)	Karl Wahl
Steiermark (Styria)	Siegfried Uiberreither
Sudetenland	Konrad HENLEIN
Südhannover-Braunschweig	Hartmann Lauterbacher
Thüringen (Thuringia)	Fritz SAUCKEL
Tirol-Vorarlberg	Franz HOFER
Wartheland	Arthur GREISER
Weser-Ems	Carl RÖVER
Westfalen-Nord (North Westphalia)	Alfred MEYER
Westfalen-Süd (South Westphalia)	Josef WAGNER
Westmark	Josef BÜRCKEL
Wien (Vienna)	Baldur von SCHIRACH
Württemberg-Hohenzollern	Wilhelm MURR
Auslandsorganisation	Ernst Wilhelm BOHLE
(Foreign Organization)	

Gauger, Martin, b. Wuppertal, September 4, 1905; d. Buchenwald concentration camp, July 14, 1941, German opposition fighter. Gauger was a jurist and a political economist; in 1934 he refused the civil service oath and became an attorney for the CONFESSING CHURCH. He worked with all possible judicial means for persecuted and jailed pastors, for threatened congregation members, and for the rights of the church. He declined appointments to foreign institutes. His writings, including *Bekenntnis und Kirchenregiment* (Denomination and

Church Government; 1936), were seized by the Gestapo. When the war broke out and he refused to take the military oath and to serve with a weapon, he finally had no choice but to flee to the Netherlands in May 1940. There the war and the Gestapo caught up with him. After more than a year of confinement in the Düsseldorf police jail, Gauger was murdered in the Buchenwald concentration camp.

Gauleiter (*Gau* leaders), the "sovereignty-bearers" of the NSDAP in the different *Gaue* (regions), who were directly responsible to Hitler. The *Gau* leaders were often appointed as Reich governors (*Statthalter*) or provincial presidents (*Oberpräsidenten*) at the same time, in order to promote the fusion of state and party and also a kind of provincial dictatorship. Out of concern for their regional positions of power, the *Gau* leaders often opposed the decisions of Reich ministries. Many of them had ties to Hitler from the "Time of Struggle," and they used their direct lines to him to exert tyrannical rule, as in the cases of Josef BÜRCKEL and Adolf WAGNER. At the start of the Second World War, many *Gau* leaders were named Reich defense commissioners (*Reichsverteidigungskommissaren*); all *Gau* leaders were given this function on November 16, 1942, and on September 25, 1944, they received a mandate to assemble the VOLK STORM.

Gaulle, Charles de, b. Lille, November 22, 1890; d. Colombey-les-deux-Églises, November 9, 1970, French general and politician. After training at the Saint-Cyr military academy, de Gaulle was an officer in the First World War. In 1920–1921, he was an adviser on the Polish side of the Polish-Russian war. From 1922 to 1924 he was educated for General Staff service, and from 1932 to 1937 he was general secretary of the National Defense Council. In 1940 he was promoted to brigadier general. In contrast with the victorious field commanders of the First World War who clung to their obsolete notions of victory, de Gaulle had realized early on what tank and air forces meant for a future war, and he stubbornly but unsuccessfully demanded the restructuring of the French armed forces in this direction. Finally in 1938 he was sent away to garrison service in Metz. His book on the approaching motorized war, *Vers l'armée de métier* (Toward a Professional Army; 1934), attracted more attention in Germany under the title *Frankreichs Stossarmee* (France's Assault Army; 1935) than it did among French defense politicians.

At the start of the German attack in the west (*see* FRENCH CAMPAIGN), de Gaulle was commander of the Fourth Tank Division. Only when his predictions about the German tank attack proved to be a terrible reality was he allowed—on May 17, 1940, when it was far too late—to lead a concentrated strike against Gen. Heinz GUDERIAN's widely stretched flank. The only partial success for the French, it was indeed quickly lost again for lack of support; however, it led to de Gaulle's appointment on June 6 as state undersecretary in the War Ministry of the REYNAUD government, which had fled to Bordeaux. As the voices there grew louder for a cease-fire petition, de Gaulle brought his family to safety in England and followed them, contrary to orders, on June 17. On the following day his historic radio appeal to all the French was broadcast, calling for the continuation of resistance even after the defeat. The Vichy government had him sentenced to death in July 1940.

From exile, de Gaulle became the soul of the RÉSISTANCE. He was able to outmaneuver such rivals as François DARLAN and Henri-Honoré GIRAUD; he became chief of the French Committee for National Liberation, and in June 1943, chief of the government-in-exile in London, from which the provisional government of the French Republic emerged in May 1944. On August 25, 1944, he marched into liberated Paris, where he was confirmed as minister president and elected provisional chief of state. As new party conflicts threatened his work of unification, de Gaulle retired from politics in 1947.

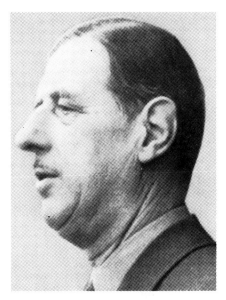

Charles de Gaulle.

In 1958, after the military revolt of May 13 in Algeria, he was summoned back and overcame the crisis through constitutional changes (the presidential system). As the first president of "his" Fifth Republic, he ended the Algerian conflict, led France out of NATO, and together with Konrad ADENAUER laid the foundation for lasting German-French reconciliation (the friendship treaty of January 20, 1963). After losing in a referendum on planned territorial and governmental reforms, he resigned on April 28, 1969.

Gayl, Wilhelm Baron von, b. Königsberg, February 4, 1879; d. Potsdam, November 7, 1945, German politician. A jurist, from 1909 to 1933 Gayl was in the management of the East Prussian Settlement Society. During the First World War he was a captain in the military administration. In 1920 Gayl received the thankless post of Reich commissioner for the plebiscite in East Prussia (*see* PLEBISCITE REGIONS). He was then active in the German National People's Party (DNVP). In 1932 Franz von Papen appointed Gayl to his "Cabinet of Barons" as Reich Interior Minister, and gained his support for the PRUSSIAN COUP. Attacked thenceforth by both the Left and the National Socialists as "helpless in the face of Marxist terror," Gayl was not brought into the Schleicher cabinet. In 1933 he disappeared from the political arena.

Gebühr, Otto, b. Kettwig (now Essen-Kettwig), May 29, 1877; d. Wiesbaden, March 13, 1954, German actor. Gebühr had already achieved fame by the 1920s performing the role of Frederick the Great (as in *Fridericus Rex;* 1922). As the demand for HEROIC FILMS grew in the Third Reich, he was kept busy. Best known was his portrayal of endurance in Veit HARLAN's Frederick the Great film *Der Grosse König* (The Great King; 1942). After the war Gebühr formed his own traveling theater company; he also acted in entertainment films such as *Rosen-Resli* (1954).

Geheime Staatspolizei. *See* Gestapo; Secret State Police.

Gehlen, Arnold, b. Leipzig, January 29, 1904; d. Hamburg, January 30, 1976, German philosopher and sociologist. Gehlen studied in Leipzig, where he was an assistant to Hans FREYER, and in Cologne. He was a professor in Leipzig from 1934 to 1938, in Königsberg until 1940, and from 1940 to 1944 in Vienna. Early on, Gehlen turned to philosophical anthropology and interpreted modern man as a "deficient being"

(*Mängelwesen*) in whom action-directed instincts had been lost, along with "protective organic obtuseness [*Borniertheit*]." Only the restoration of such institutions as family, state, and fatherland, in line with NIETZSCHE's thought, would again provide a footing, he believed.

This authoritarian philosophy matched National Socialist demands for a strong state and reached its height in Gehlen's *Rede über Fichte* (Discourse on Fichte; 1938), which affirmed the Führer myth. His major work, *Der Mensch—seine Natur und seine Stellung in der Welt* (Man—His Nature and His Place in the World; 1940), elaborated Gehlen's teachings on institutions. It also demanded systems of leadership that would provide "models for rearing" (*Zuchtbilder*)—in the sense of "educating"—for the "creature of rearing" (*Zuchtwesen*), which was man, for purposes of orientation and motivation. He even referred to Alfred Rosenberg's "Germanic character values" (*see* ETHICS). Temporarily without a professional post after the war, Gehlen took a position with the Administrative Academy in Speyer in 1947, then in 1962 obtained a post at the Technical College in Aachen. After 1945 Gehlen's formulations changed, but not his basic positions.

Gehlen, Reinhard, b. Erfurt, April 3, 1902; d. Berg bei Starnberg, June 8, 1979, German general. Gehlen entered the Reichswehr in 1920; from 1935 on, he was with the Army General Staff, and from 1942 to 1945 he was director of the division for "Foreign Armies: East." After the war he established an intelligence service

Otto Gebühr as Frederick II (the Great) in *Der Grosse König.*

Reinhard Gehlen.

(the "Gehlen Organization") under the mandate of the American occupation authority. From this came the Federal Intelligence Service (Bundesnachrichtendienst) in 1956, with Gehlen as its president until 1968. In 1971 he published his memoirs, *Der Dienst* (*The Service*); their justification of Germany's Russian Campaign as an anti-Bolshevik act of liberation aroused considerable attention and criticism.

Gekrat, shortened form of **Ge**meinnützige **Kran**kentransport GmbH (PUBLIC WELFARE AMBULANCE SERVICE, LTD.), utilized in the EUTHANASIA program.

"Gelb" (*Fall "Gelb,"* Case "Yellow"), military code name for the German attack in the west on May 10, 1940 (*see* FRENCH CAMPAIGN).

Gemeinde (commune; municipality), communal administrative unit; its governance was fundamentally transformed by the GERMAN COMMUNAL ORDINANCE of January 30, 1935.

Gemeinschaft. *See* Community.

Gempp, Walter, b. Rodach bei Coburg, September 13, 1878; d. Berlin, May 2, 1939, German firefighting expert. After studies in mechanical engineering, Gempp joined the Berlin Fire Department in 1908. He was given the project of developing a motorized fire extinguishing service, and in 1908 he produced the first engine-powered hose truck. In 1923 he became chief fire commissioner in the Reich capital. Immediately after the REICHSTAG FIRE of February 27, 1933, Gempp contradicted the National Socialist claim of arson by Communists, thereby incurring considerable harassment according to the terms of the CIVIL SERVICE LAW. Nonetheless, in the Reichstag Fire Trial he stood by his statements (for example, that Hermann Göring had prohibited sounding the most urgent alarm) and thereby fed the rumors of NS involvement in the deed. The authorities' revenge took the form of dismissal, and in 1937 Gempp was arrested and indicted for alleged wrongdoing in office. He appealed his sentence, but remained in investigatory confinement; shortly afterward he was found strangled in his cell.

General Council for the German Economy (Generalrat der deutschen Wirtschaft), executive coordination committee for the various departments involved in the FOUR-YEAR PLAN. Its members were the department heads of the plan, as well as the state secretaries of economic departments. From an overall standpoint the council remained a relatively uninfluential body, since it had no decision-making power. The important decisions were made in Hermann Göring's central office or within the particular divisions of the plan.

A. v. S.

General German Trade Union Federation (Allgemeiner Deutscher Gewerkschaftsbund; ADGB), umbrella organization of the "Free [Social Democratic] Trade Unions." It was founded in 1919 as the successor organization to the General Commission of German Trade Unions (Generalkommission der Gewerkschaften Deutschlands), which was founded in 1890. Its chairmen were Carl Legien (1919–1920) and Theodor LEIPART (1920–1933). The ADGB combined various trade organizations and industrial unions. In 1920–1921, the AFABUND and the General German Civil Servants' Federation joined together. As of 1923 the ADGB had a membership of approximately 8 million, which in 1928 had dropped to 4.5 million; its goal was a "democratization of the economy on the path to socialism."

Several public-service operations belonged to the ADGB: Public Welfare (Volksfürsorge), Bank for Workers and Employees, and German Housing Assistance. The socialist goals of the ADGB made it a target of sharp attacks by the National Socialists. Thus it was all the more amazing that after the Seizure of Power the ADGB's leaders attempted to strike an agreement, an illusion destroyed by the National Socialist attack on the trade unions on May 2, 1933.

General German Trade Union Federation. Occupation of a Berlin trade union headquarters by SA men on May 2, 1933.

Generalgouvernement (officially, after October 26, 1939, "for the occupied Polish Territories"; after July 1940 simply "Generalgouvernement"), a German "collateral country" (*Nebenland*) established after the POLISH CAMPAIGN in conquered Poland; it had no independent statehood and was under a *Generalgouverneur* (Hans FRANK), with limited Polish self-administration on the lowest level. It was divided into four districts (Kraków, Warsaw, Radom, and Lublin) under district governors. In addition, on August 1, 1941, Eastern Galicia with Lvov (Ger., Lemberg) was annexed as the "Galicia District"; this gave the Generalgouvernement 142,000 sq km (about 56,800 sq miles) and some 12 million inhabitants.

The Generalgouvernement was the labor reservoir for abducted Polish forced laborers; the reception area for Poles displaced from territories annexed to Germany (some 1.2 million); an object of industrial and agricultural exploitation; and, after 1942 and the ghettoization of Jews (*see* WARSAW GHETTO UPRISING), the scene of the implementation of the FINAL SOLUTION. After the closing of upper-level schools and universities and the extermination of parts of the Polish intelligentsia (*see* INTELLIGENTSIA OPERATION), the school system was reduced to simple and purely technical training centers.

In the broader perspective, the GENERAL PLAN FOR THE EAST provided for the banishment of 80 to 85 percent of the Poles from the Generalgouvernement to Siberia, and the settlement of German peasants in their place. Whereas Frank and his civil government occasionally sought, although unsuccessfully, to mitigate somewhat the occupation regime (for purely practical reasons), the completely autonomous reign of terror of the HIGHER SS AND POLICE LEADERS, who reported directly to Himmler and who held the jurisdiction and increasingly carried out the tasks of the executive, led from 1943 on to an aggravation of conditions in the Generalgouvernement. A relatively porous German control net in the Generalgouvernement permitted the organization of the Polish resistance into an underground government with an underground army. On August 1, 1944, in the WARSAW UPRISING, this army rose up against the German occupation, but after a two-month battle it went down in defeat for lack of Allied support.

B.-J. W.

General Inspectorate (*Generalinspektor*) for German Highways, position created on June 30, 1933, and assumed by Fritz TODT on July 5. On November 30 the office was upgraded to a Supreme Reich Authority (*oberste Reichsbehörde*), reporting directly to Hitler. The general inspectorate's responsibilities included construction of the AUTOBAHN; after 1934 its publication was *Die Strasse* (The Street). After 1941 Todt was also general inspector for water and energy.

General Plan for the East (*Generalplan Ost*), title of a memorandum of the Main Section on Planning (by Professor Konrad Meyer-Hetling) under the REICH COMMISSIONER FOR THE FORTIFICATION OF THE GERMAN VOLK-NATION. It concerned "legal, economic, and territorial principles of the buildup in the east"; mandated by Himmler, it was signed by him on June 12,

Generalgouvernement. Polish goods being loaded for shipment to Germany.

1942. Alfred Rosenberg's Ministry for the Occupied Eastern Territories and the NSDAP Office for Racial Policies also collaborated on it, so that the plan can be considered the official program of National Socialist conquest and OCCUPATION POLICY.

The plan stipulated that in the first 25 years after the end of the war, 31 million inhabitants of Poland, the Baltic region, and the Soviet western territories were to be forcibly moved to Siberia and decimated, while the remaining 14 million, especially "re-Germanizable" Balts and Ukrainians "belonging to the Nordic or Dinaric races," would cooperate in extending the German "*Volk*-nation border" a thousand kilometers to the east. They were intended to be labor slaves for the settlers who were to move from the Reich, from ethnic German areas in South Tirol, Romania, or Hungary, and from Scandinavia, Holland, and England to the east to accomplish the genuine "Germanization." As a net for enclosing and controlling the new frontiers, 36 settlement hubs, each with 20,000 inhabitants and surrounded by a ring of villages, were planned; among them were "Ingermanland," around Leningrad; "Gotengau," including the Crimea; the Memel-Narev territory; and the Generalgouvernement.

Based on former Germanic settlement of the designated territories, the plan was intended to shift the "geopolitical wind direction" toward the east and fulfill Hitler's demands in *Mein Kampf* for living space. A right to life for the

"Slavic subhumans" was not provided for in this racist conception. Even though its implementation did not progress beyond meager beginnings because of the changing war situation, the plan left its stamp on German occupation practices in the Reich Commissariats OSTLAND and UKRAINE, and caused initial enthusiasm among the populace for the Wehrmacht to turn quickly into implacable hatred toward the occupiers.

General Staff (*Generalstab*), officer corps consisting of select and specially trained officers for the preparation and execution of military operations and for the support of troop leaders. A German general staff was forbidden in 1919 by Article 160 of the Versailles treaty, yet it continued a covert existence; after the restoration of general COMPULSORY MILITARY SERVICE in 1935, it regained its name. The General Staff and the WEHRMACHT HIGH COMMAND (OKW) were indicted among the major war criminals in the NUREMBERG TRIALS but were not condemned as CRIMINAL ORGANIZATIONS. Indeed, the court characterized the members of the General Staff and the OKW as "blemishes on the honorable bearing of arms" and formally certified that they had "taken active part" in National Socialist crimes, but denied that they had the character of a group or organization and recommended that the members be judged individually.

Geneva Conventions (*Genfer Abkommen*; *Genfer Konventionen*), designation for a series of international treaties concluded in Geneva for the protection of wounded and sick soldiers, prisoners of war, and civilians in wartime. The first Geneva Convention was concluded on August 22, 1864, at the initiative of Henri Dunant (1828–1910) and signed by 16 states (including Prussia and other members of the German Confederation); it applied to soldiers in a land war (and was extended to naval war in 1899). In addition, it established the protective symbol of the RED CROSS. A second Geneva Convention of July 6, 1906, substantially expanded on the first and was ratified by 40 states.

On July 27, 1929, 15 states agreed on a broader, third Geneva Convention, which especially regulated the treatment of PRISONERS OF WAR. On August 12, 1949, 59 governments reached accord on the fourth Geneva Convention "for the protection of victims of war," which has since been ratified by nearly all countries. The first three conventions—valid at the outbreak of the Second World War and intended to shield persons affected by war particularly from killing, mutilation, torture, hostage taking, and violation of human dignity—were violated by nearly all the belligerents. On the German side, the conduct in the western war theaters generally adhered at least in the beginning to the conventions, whereas the "war of worldviews" in the east was conducted virtually without regard for the spirit or even the letter of the Geneva Conventions (*see, for example*, EINSATZGRUPPEN).

Geneva Disarmament Conference. *See* Disarmament.

Genocide (*Völkermord*), the physical (and cultural) extermination of national, ethnic, religious, social, or racial groups. The factual reality of genocide is as old as human history; its concept was developed in the 20th century and embodied in international law. The first attempts at a formulation resulted from the persecution of minorities in the Soviet Union after 1917, but the notion was codified after the experiences with National Socialism's policy to annihilate Poles, Slavs, and Jews (*see* FINAL SOLUTION). In Article 6c of the International Military Tribunal statute of August 8, 1945, for the NUREMBERG TRIALS, genocide was classified among the CRIMES AGAINST HUMANITY; on December 9, 1948, it was the object of the Agreement for the Prevention and Punishment of Genocide, which was unanimously accepted by the United Nations General Assembly. The agreement classifies as genocide physical and mental injury to a group, as well as killing of its

members, with the intent to destroy it. This can be done through the intentional creation of unbearable living conditions or through expulsion, restrictions on births, and so on. In 1954 the Federal Republic of Germany signed the United Nations agreement, and through Paragraph 220a of the State Law Code made genocide a punishable offense.

Genosse. *See* Comrade.

Geopolitics (*Geopolitik*), term coined by Swedish political scientist Rudolf Kjéllen in 1905 for the scientific inquiry into geographical constraints on political events. In its German form as expressed by Karl HAUSHOFER, who from 1923 to 1944 edited the journal *Zeitschrift für Geopolitik*, geopolitics never attained the status of a science. After the First World War it was used as the underpinning for REVISIONIST POLICY. Moreover, on the basis of a mythical conception of soil (*see* BLOOD AND SOIL), German geopolitics elaborated an imperialist theory that was antisemitic and hostile to civilization, and that demanded—if necessary, through military action—the formation of a middle-European continental bloc under German leadership. The foundation for this was anti-British ("sea pirates") notions of AUTARKY, as well as a sort of collective claustrophobia that demanded "breathing space" and outlets for "population pressure." Here geopolitics came close to the LIVING SPACE ideology of National Socialism, which eagerly exploited this "scientific" support for its expansionist policies even while criticizing the "un-*völkisch*" foundation of geopolitics.

George VI, b. Sandringham, December 14, 1895; d. there, February 6, 1952, king of England (r. 1936–1952). George VI was a naval officer; he pursued studies in history and political economy. He ascended to the British throne through the abdication of his brother Edward VIII, an event that made headlines for months. Politically, George remained in the background. During the AIR BATTLE FOR ENGLAND, his continued presence in London contributed substantially to the stiffening of the British will to hold out. His renunciation of the title "Emperor of India" (1948) made plain the rapidity of decolonialization and England's departure from the role of a world power as a consequence of the Second World War.

George, Heinrich (originally, Heinrich Georg Schulz), b. Stettin, October 9, 1893; d. Sachsenhausen internment camp, September 25,

Heinrich George as the Postmaster, with Hilde Krahl.

1946, German actor. George began his theatrical career in Kolberg. After military service during the war he acted at Vienna's Burgtheater and then at the State Theater (Schauspielhaus) in Berlin. George enjoyed innumerable successes as the embodiment of rough and somewhat primitive strength, both on the stage and in such films as Fritz Lang's *Metropolis.* He was scarcely interested in who allowed him to practice his acting craft. Thus, although initially opposed to the National Socialists, after 1933 he cooperated, thereby helping the German cinema to gain an international reputation despite the political restrictions imposed on it. He acted in ideological films (HITLERJUNGE QUEX; 1933), in HEROIC

George VI.

FILMS (*Friedrich Schiller;* 1940), in melodramas (*Heimat* [Home]; 1938), and in the inflammatory antisemitic film JUD SÜSS (1940).

Nonetheless, George's signature roles were in Goethe's *Götz* on the stage (after 1938 he was general manager of Berlin's Schiller Theater) and in the film version of Pushkin's *The Postmaster* (1940). Toward the end of the war his career returned to its origins: he played the main role in the morale-building KOLBERG (1945). Captured by the Red Army, George was interned in the former concentration camp at Sachsenhausen. There he again put together a theater company, but he finally perished from the harsh conditions.

George, Stefan, b. Büdesheim bei Bingen, July 12, 1868; d. Minusio, near Locarno (Switzerland), December 14, 1933, German writer. George was the author of symbolist, esoteric, and formalist lyrics. His early works were indebted to the principle of "art for art's sake," while his later books heralded a "new heroic era" (*Das Neue Reich* [The New Reich]; 1928). He supported a thoroughgoing purge of capitalized nouns in German.

After 1893 George surrounded himself with a circle of friends and students, which also included contemporary literary figures and influential academics. The discussions of issues of aesthetics and cultural policy increasingly developed *völkisch* and antisemitic dimensions. Extrapolating from his antirepublican circle, George hoped for a renewal of "spiritual Germany" (*geistiges Deutschland*) as the foundation for an "empire of the spirit" (*Reich des Geistes*). The National Socialists valued George more as a "language creator" (*Sprachschöpfer*) than as the "priestly-visionary creator of the 'New Reich,'" which they nevertheless—supported by disciples from the George Circle—equated with the Third Reich.

George's works, as well as his hangers-on, did have a lasting influence on the dissemination of a "Führer and Reich" ideology among the German middle class. But in 1933 he refused the presidency of the Prussian Academy of Letters that was offered him, on the ground of insufficient agreement with the "vulgar" (*ordinär*) dictatorship. He then went into exile. Although the Propaganda Ministry created a Stefan George Prize (awarded only in 1934), the poet's heroic and mythological notions ultimately aroused only limited interest among the National Socialists. George's followers saw with increasing clarity the contradiction between

Stefan George.

their elitist, aristocratic ideas of a New Reich and the political reality. As conservative critics of the Third Reich, some of them had to flee into exile; others ended in concentration camps. Still others, such as the Stauffenberg counts, joined the opposition to Hitler.

H. H.

Gereke, Günther, b. Gruna, October 6, 1893; d. Neuenhagen bei Berlin, May 1, 1970, German politician and social policymaker. In 1915 Gereke was appointed a district president (*Landrat*), and in this capacity served as president of the German Congress of Rural Communes (Deutscher Landgemeindetag). From 1924 to 1928 he was a member of the Reichstag for the German National People's Party (DNVP), but in 1930 he became a co-founder and deputy of the Christian National Peasants' and Country People's Party. In 1932 Gereke collaborated in drafting an employment program for rural communities. That same year, Reich Chancellor Kurt von Schleicher appointed him Reich Commissioner for Work Creation, leading to the drafting of the Urgent, or Gereke, Program.

In March 1933 Gereke was arrested; in a show trial he was sentenced to prison for embezzling money from the Hindenburg election fund. He was released in 1935. In connection with the assassination attempt of July 20, 1944, he was again jailed, and was later freed by the Allies. In 1946 Gereke joined the Christian Democratic Union (CDU). He was also Interior Minister of Lower Saxony, but resigned in 1947. In 1948 he became Deputy Minister President and Minister

for Food in that state. The CDU expelled him in 1950 for dealing with the German Democratic Republic (GDR). Gereke founded the German Social Party, and in 1952 emigrated to the GDR.

B. W.

Gerlach, Helmut Georg von, b. Mönchmotschelmitz (Silesia), February 2, 1866; d. Paris, August 1, 1935, German political journalist. After studies in law, Gerlach was from 1893 to 1896 the editor of the Christian Social daily newspaper *Das Volk*. In 1896, together with Friedrich Naumann, he founded the National Social Union (Nationalsozialer Verein); from 1898 to 1930 he served as editor in chief of the Berlin *Welt am Montag* (World on Monday). A convinced pacifist, until 1929 he was chairman of the German Peace Society. After the arrest of Carl von OSSIETZKY, Gerlach became editor in chief of the WELTBÜHNE (World Stage). In 1933 he managed to flee through Austria and Switzerland to exile in Paris. There he wrote his important autobiography, *Von rechts nach links* (From Right to Left; published posthumously in 1937).

Gerlich, Fritz, b. Stettin, February 15, 1883; d. Dachau concentration camp, June 30, 1934, German journalist. After studies in natural sciences and history, Gerlich worked as an archivist. Unfit for military service during the First World War, he vehemently advocated pan-German war goals in his political writings, and after 1918 struck a sharply anti-Communist tone. From 1920 to 1928 he was the editor in chief of the *Münchner Neueste Nachrichten* (Mu-

Helmut Georg von Gerlach.

Fritz Gerlich.

nich Latest News), which he made into the most important south German daily newspaper. A convert to Catholicism in 1931, Gerlich conducted an uncompromisingly radical fight against National Socialism as manager of the magazine *Der gerade Weg* (The Straight Path). On March 9, 1933, he was arrested. After severe mistreatment he was brought to the Dachau concentration camp, where he was murdered during the RÖHM AFFAIR.

German Academic Exchange Service (Deutscher Akademischer Austauschdienst; DAAD), central German authority founded in 1931 to foster international exchange among academics and students. It awards grants and arranges lecture tours, and has numerous branch offices abroad and at nearly all German institutions of higher education. As of 1933 its president was SS-Brigadeführer Ewald von Massow, who cultivated particularly intensive contacts with southeastern and western Europe and the United States. He viewed the DAAD as an instrument of National Socialist propaganda. Thus, German students were sent abroad as "conscious representatives of their *Volk*." In 1950, the DAAD was re-established as a politically neutral and self-governing organization of German institutions of higher education.

German Africa Corps (Deutsches Afrika-Korps; DAK), German troops sent to North Africa (February 8–11, 1941) as an armored defense force to support Italian troops; after February 18 the corps was called the DAK (*see* AFRICAN CAMPAIGN).

German Armament Works (Deutsche Ausrüstungswerke; DAW), SS enterprise founded in 1939 with numerous factories that produced primarily military armaments; it achieved large profits through massive exploitation of concentration camp prisoners. Its sales in 1941 amounted to 5.3 million RM; in 1942, 9.5 million RM; and in 1943, 23.2 million RM.

German Arts and Crafts League (Deutscher Werkbund; DWB), union of artists, architects, designers, industry, and crafts, founded in Munich in 1907. The Werkbund was originally influenced by the ideas of the English utopian socialist William Morris (1835–1896), who wanted to renew the applied arts through aesthetic form as against alienated labor; it became especially concerned with the standardization of industrially produced consumer goods. The National Socialists dissolved the Werkbund in 1933, then re-established it in 1935 to organize German handicrafts exhibits at home and abroad, and to propagandize for the GERMAN STYLE.

German-believing (*deutschgläubig*), term used for both the Christian *völkisch* doctrine of the GERMAN CHRISTIANS and the non-Christian dogmas of the GERMAN FAITH MOVEMENT.

German-blooded (*deutschblütig*), synonym for ARYAN. An Interior Ministry memorandum of November 26, 1935, made it the obligatory designation for persons "of German or species-related blood." It had cropped up even earlier, however, as in the *Völkischer Beobachter* of April 4, 1933: "Only German-blooded civil servants may embody the authority of the state." The term was rooted in the mythical concept of blood as the carrier of ethnic and racial traits.

German-British Naval Agreement (*Deutsch-Britisches Flottenabkommen*), treaty between Great Britain and Germany regarding naval armaments, signed on June 18, 1935; the idea

German Africa Corps armband.

behind it was first introduced to diplomacy by Hitler in late 1934 with the formula "35:100" (the ratio of German to British naval tonnage). Hitler had three goals: (1) to provide international sanctions for German naval rearmament; (2) to break up the collective-security system created at Versailles by means of a bilateral treaty with England; and (3) to take a first step in the direction of the vision in *Mein Kampf,* which granted England the oceans and Germany a free hand in the east. Hitler viewed Wilhelmian naval policy as an unnecessary provocation of England: he wanted to establish his colonial empire close at hand. To France's dismay, sounds of negotiation came from London: there were no eternal enemies, only eternal interests; and if there must be a burial (of the Versailles diktat), then if possible it should be while Hitler seemed inclined "to honor the duty of the gravedigger."

On March 24, 1935, Hitler received Lord Privy Seal Anthony EDEN and British foreign secretary John Simon, who already wanted an agreement with Germany because of the Japanese threat. The negotiations began in London on June 4, led by Hitler's ambassador-at-large, Joachim von RIBBENTROP, and Simon. They agreed to the 35:100 ratio on the seas as well as on basic parity in submarines, while renouncing unrestricted submarine warfare. Precisely on the anniversary of Waterloo (June 18), the treaty was signed; Paris was thus given additionally brusque treatment. Four years later (April 28, 1939), after Britain had offered guarantees to Poland, Hitler renounced the treaty.

M. F.

German Christians (Deutsche Christen), originally a general label for groups in the German Evangelical Church that supported nationalistic ideas and promoted the NSDAP. It was later a specific designation for members of the "Faith Movement of German Christians" (Glaubensbewegung Deutscher Christen), which came into being through the initiative of the *Gauleiter* of the Ostmark, Wilhelm KUBE. Pastor Joachim Hossenfelder became its "Reich leader" (*Reichsleiter*). The goal of the German Christians was an Evangelical Reich Church, organized according to the Führer principle on the basis of race and *Volk.*

Political theology had built the bridge between church and National Socialism, proceeding from the historical theology of the prewar

German-British Naval Agreement. The German delegation in London. From left to right: Ambassador-at-Large Ribbentrop, Rear Admiral Schuster, Captain Wassner, and Ambassador Bismarck.

Publication of the German Christians:
The De-Jewing of Religious Life.

period, which claimed a special place for Germans and their Reich in the divine plan of salvation. Unsettled by socialist revolution and the brutal persecution of churches in Bolshevik Russia, conservative forces in the Evangelical Church sought ties with the nationalist movement. The Gospel was seen as "the highest eternal good," and German nationality as "the highest temporal good." A landmark in this development was the Patriotic Church Congress (*Vaterländischer Kirchentag*) held in Königsberg in 1927, at which the theologian Paul Althaus made the shift toward a "German proclamation of the Gospel." The nebulous Point 24 ("positive Christianity") of the NSDAP party program made it seem that this notion was well received by the Hitler movement.

The church elections of 1932 in Prussia did not yield a victory for the newly established German Christians, although they won nearly a third of the seats in decision-making committees. Hitler's Seizure of Power gave them new vigor, particularly when in April 1933 the chancellor made Ludwig MÜLLER, the chaplain of the Königsberg army corps district, who favored the German Christians, his adviser for Evangelical Church affairs. The most attractive program point of the German Christians, the establishment of an Evangelical Reich Church, paradoxically produced an initial setback: by a vote of 91 to 8, the representatives of the 28 regional churches (*Landeskirchen*) on May 27, 1933, elected as the first Reich Bishop the head of

the Bethel Institutes, Friedrich von BODELSCHWINGH, instead of Hitler's protégé Müller.

It was obvious to Hitler that neither the Führer principle nor the ARYAN PARAGRAPH would gain acceptance in the church under someone like Bodelschwingh. Through procedural tricks (in the absence of a constitution for the Reich Church) and the appointment of state commissioners for church activities, Bodelschwingh was maneuvered into resigning. New and hastily arranged church elections on July 23, 1933, with Hitler's massive intervention, resulted in a landslide victory in the synods for the German Christians. On September 27, the National Synod in Wittenberg unanimously elected Ludwig Müller as Reich Bishop.

The regional churches, however, did not allow themselves to be so easily "synchronized." The first theological resistance against the intrusion above all of National Socialist racial ideology in the church manifested itself in the form of the PASTORS' EMERGENCY LEAGUE, founded by Martin NIEMÖLLER. The German Christians then overplayed their cards: at a rally in the Berlin Sports Palace on November 13, 1933, their radical wing sought to secure the acceptance of the Aryan Paragraph in church matters by a show of hands. By a vote of 20,000 to 1 (!), those assembled resolved, among other things, that the German "*Volk* church" had to free itself from "the Old Testament and its Jewish money morality," that it should present a "heroic image of Jesus," and that it should exclude non-Aryans from its ranks.

Out of the storm of indignation against this resolution, which turned the Jew Jesus into the chief witness for antisemitism, the CONFESSING CHURCH developed. Moreover, massive membership losses weakened the German Christians and "Reibi" (Reich Bishop) Müller, so that Hitler lost interest in his fifth column in the Evangelical Church. From then on he relied on administration and confrontation. Despite all efforts at ingratiating themselves, the German Christians never again gained decisive influence. After the resignation of the first *Reichsleiter*, Hossenfelder, at the end of 1933, Christian Kinder took over the leadership, and, using the name "Reich Movement of German Christians," steered a reform course of mission to the people. More splinter groups arose, however, such as the one in Thuringia under Siegfried Leffler and Julius Leutheuser, who had already founded a German Christian movement in 1927.

On the Reich level, after 1938 the German Christians, now under the leadership of Werner

Mass rally of the German Christians in Berlin's Sports Palace on November 13, 1933. The banner states: "The German Christian reads *The Gospel in the Third Reich.*"

Petersmann, called themselves "Luther Germans." Alongside them existed all kinds of working groups and regional church groups in shifting alliances, which in 1939 established an "Institute to Research [read: eliminate] Jewish Influence over German Church Life." Despite brusque handling by leading National Socialists, such as Heinrich Himmler, Alfred Rosenberg, and Martin Bormann, who mistrusted entanglement with the church, the German Christians never freed themselves from their antisemitic and nationalist beginnings; for many of them, Hitler had apocalyptic significance. Their magazines, *Evangelium im Dritten Reich* (The Gospel in the Third Reich; 1932–1936) and *Die Nationalkirche* (The National Church; 1932–1941), celebrated the rediscovery of the divinely created rules of *Volk*, state, race, and family.

After the collapse of the Reich, the Allies banned the German Christians. The regional churches instituted against some of their leaders "proceedings to restore a pastorate obligated to ministry and confession."

German Christians' League (Deutscher Christenbund), *völkisch* Evangelical group founded in 1925 by the Leipzig pastor Heinrich Vogel. That same year it merged with the LEAGUE FOR A GERMAN CHURCH. It was a forerunner of the GERMAN CHRISTIANS.

German Colonization Society (Deutsche Ansiedlungsgesellschaft; DAG), organization created by the SS to promote and administer German colonization in the conquered territory in Poland and the Soviet Union, as outlined in the GENERAL PLAN FOR THE EAST.

German Combat League (Deutscher Kampfbund), alliance of Hitler's NSDAP, the OBERLAND League (Friedrich Weber), and the Association of Reich Battle Flags (Adolf Heiss), formed on September 2, 1923, at a "German congress" of patriotic "fatherland leagues" in Nuremberg. Hitler was made leader of the league, which perpetrated the HITLER PUTSCH of November 8–9, 1923.

German Communal Ordinance (*Deutsche Gemeindeordnung;* DGO), Reich law of January 30, 1935, concerning the constitution and administration of municipalities or communes (*Kommunen*). The preamble announced the realization of the idea of communal self-administration (*Selbstverwaltung*) as conceived by Baron vom Stein (1757–1831); but because the DGO established the FÜHRER PRINCIPLE and strict party supervision, it meant the precise opposite. A DELEGATE OF THE NSDAP actually became the key figure in all community affairs by virtue of his authority to appoint and dismiss the mayor and communal council. The rights of communal council members shrank to those of a merely advisory role, with laws and ordinances under the control of the party and the state (the Reich interior minister). The DGO was an example of the National Socialist principle of the "unity of party and state" and thus spelled the end of the commune as a self-governing body.

German Competitive Games (*Deutsche Kampfspiele*), national festival called into being by the GERMAN REICH COMMITTEE FOR PHYSICAL EXERCISES in 1922; its high point was the athletic competition. The festival's creator, Carl DIEM, intended that the games should evoke "German art, German song, and the German *Volk* Community." After the last festival in 1934 in Nuremberg, the games were replaced by the GERMAN GYMNASTIC AND SPORTS FESTIVAL.

German Congress of Jurists (Deutscher Juristentag), organization of law school professors, judges, solicitors, and attorneys, founded in 1860; it held periodic congresses on legal issues. The last free assembly took place in Lübeck in 1931. The congress was "synchronized" into the League of National Socialist Jurists (Bund National-sozialistischer Juristen), which was renamed the NATIONAL SOCIALIST LEAGUE OF LAW GUARDIANS (National-sozialistischer Rechtswahrerbund) at the second congress held during the Third Reich, in Leipzig in 1936. Thereafter the congresses served only the purposes of political instruction and the ideological "alignment" of WORKERS IN THE LAW.

German Cross (Deutsches Kreuz), decoration established by Hitler in 1941. In gold for outstanding bravery and in silver for special achievements in troop leadership, it was an eight-pointed silver star with gold or silver laurel wreath. In soldiers' jargon, the gold version was ironically called a "fried egg" (*Spiegelei*) or a "party rear reflector" (*Parteirückstrahler*).

German Defense Wall Badge of Honor (Deutsches Schutzwall-Ehrenzeichen), bronze decoration established by Hitler on August 2, 1939, for services in building the WESTWALL. It bore

the inscription "For Work to Defend Germany." The badge was to be worn on the left side of the chest.

German Democratic Party (Deutsche Demokratische Partei; DDP), collective successor party to the left-liberal and National Liberal parties, founded on November 16, 1918. The National Liberal right wing by and large remained distant (*see* GERMAN PEOPLE'S PARTY; DVP), and the 1925 attempt at a merger failed. With 74 seats the third-largest faction in the Weimar National Assembly, the DDP participated in the governing WEIMAR COALITION, but it constantly lost votes to the Left and especially to the DVP; by 1928, it had only 25 seats. Moreover, the DDP lost its leading representatives through untimely deaths: co-founder Friedrich Naumann (1919), sociologist Max Weber (1920), Walther RATHENAU (1922), and Hugo Preuss (1925), the "father" of the Weimar Constitution. A merger with the YOUNG GERMAN ORDER in 1930 to create the German State Party (Deutsche Staatspartei) brought no upward turn for a party now supported only by the liberal press

German Democratic Party. Election poster, 1920: "For all honest labor in the city and in the country. Against dictatorship of the Left and the Right."

German Cross.

(such as the *Vossische Zeitung* and *Frankfurter Zeitung*). Its last five delegates voted for the ENABLING LAW, and it dissolved itself under National Socialist pressure on June 28, 1933.

German Eastern League (Deutscher Ostbund; DO), pressure organization, founded on September 27, 1920, to promote reparations demands from Germans in the ceded Eastern Territories (*see* VERSAILLES TREATY) who had suffered confiscation or other damages. In 1933 it became the LEAGUE FOR THE GERMAN EAST.

German Evangelical Church (Deutsche Evangelische Kirche), amalgamation of the 28 Evangelical regional churches (*Landeskirchen*) in accordance with the Reich Church Constitution of July 11, 1933, which was ratified by Reich law on July 14 and approved by parishioners in church elections on July 23. The church resulted from Hitler's efforts to create a unified Evangelical Reich Church and to subject it to his concept of SYNCHRONIZATION through a negotiated agreement analogous to the CONCORDAT. Despite a great majority of GERMAN CHRISTIANS in the church balloting and the election of Ludwig MÜLLER as Reich Bishop (September 27, 1933), unification by means of the church foundered against opposition. The CONFESSING CHURCH fought back against the intrusion of National Socialist thought and opposed the German Evangelical Church with its own "Provisional Church Leadership" (Vorläufige Kirchenleitung; VKL). The appointment of Hanns KERRL as Reich Church Minister with extensive authority on July 16, 1935, brought no progress. For that reason Hitler, on February 15, 1937, ordered the selection of a general synod for the purpose of reorganizing the church. It never assembled: a true German Evangelical Church could never be successfully established while the CHURCH STRUGGLE continued.

German Faith Movement (Deutsche Glaubensbewegung), federation of *völkisch* sects established on July 7, 1933, through the initiative of Jakob HAUER. The sects all strove for "a species-true faith" in estrangement from Christianity. They merged into the movement in May 1934, and confirmed Hauer as chairman and Ernst Count von REVENTLOW as deputy. The ideological basis of the movement was the conviction that every people "through its blood" developed its own religious knowledge, which was overlaid by Christianity. The movement sought to find in Germanic antiquity the sources of a "German knowledge of God," even

as it reinvigorated old rites. It was organized on town, district, and state levels; its activity was protected by the so-called Tolerance Edict (*Duldungserlass*) of October 13, 1933, but it conflicted with the totalitarian claims of National Socialism. The movement's rapid decline and dissolution were precipitated by harassment, for example the 1937 suppression of its magazine, *Durchbruch* (Breakthrough), and a prohibition against party members' even appearing at Faith Movement functions (as of November 11, 1937; for SS members, such a prohibition had been in force since September 20, 1935). A change in the movement's name in 1938 to "Combat Circle for German Faith" (Kampfring Deutscher Glaube) and its increasing anti-Christian radicalization did nothing to alter its situation.

German Fashion Institute (Deutsches Mode-Institut), Berlin institution founded in 1933 on the initiative of the Propaganda Ministry; its official functions were "fashion creation, fashion reporting, fashion propaganda, fashion shows." Given the backward-looking National Socialist view of women, however, the institute also had a mission to control and ward off "species-alien" (*artfremd*) influences.

German Front (Deutsche Front), working alliance formed in July 1933 by all German middle-class and right-wing parties (including the NSDAP) in the SAAR TERRITORY. In 1934 the groups established a united party in view of the plebiscite scheduled for January 1935, in order to promote the return of the Saar Territory to Germany. The party's key positions were occupied by National Socialists, its election expenses were subsidized by the German Propaganda Ministry, and the powerful German radio transmitters broadcast supportive messages. After the overwhelming plebiscite victory (90.36 percent of the votes), the German Front was absorbed into the NSDAP.

German Greeting (*Deutscher Gruss*; also *Hitlergruss*), raising of the outstretched right arm to eye level, with the palm out, accompanied by the words "Heil [Hail] Hitler!" This greeting was already common among National Socialists during the so-called Time of Struggle; it was established as the only form of greeting for the general German public in 1937. It was also used as the required closing in correspondence: "With German Greeting Heil Hitler!" Propaganda traced the greeting from the Germanic acclamation, the open hand being the sign of unarmed trust among "free men"; the German

Greeting was said to have cast off "everything subservient."

Like few other National Socialist prescriptions, the greeting met resistance, since in many regions, especially Catholic ones, it replaced religious greetings and was thus considered blasphemous. Despite numerous convictions for refusal to use it, failure to do so or deliberate misuse, such as bowdlerizing it as "Drei Liter!" (Three liters!), remained a common means of ventilating otherwise impossible criticism of the regime. A related form of the German Greeting increasingly replaced such special greeting forms as "Glückauf!" (Here's to luck!) and "Waidmanns Heil!" (Good hunting!—a drinking toast); in their place a uniform "Sieg Heil!" (Hail to victory!) was used. In the military, the German Greeting was prescribed instead of a salute when no headgear was worn. After the assassination attempt of July 20, 1944, it was made obligatory under all circumstances.

German Gymnastic and Sports Festival (*Deutsches Turn- und Sportsfest*), festival originally planned as a regular assemblage of the best

German Greeting.

Posters of the German Front for the 1935 plebiscite in the Saar Territory: "We died for you! And you want to betray us?" "To Germany. German Mothers, back home to you!"

German athletes, but held only once, between July 24 and 31, 1938. For political reasons it was held near the Polish border, in Breslau. The revanchist intent was clear from the confidential press directive of July 19, 1937, "that the festival's goals to a large extent will support German border policies." The Propaganda Ministry financed preparations for the festival with 1.3 million marks, making it the largest national sports event in the Third Reich. Among the 250,000 participants, 30,000 Sudeten German athletes competed for glory, a propaganda gesture preparing for the SUDETEN CRISIS.

German Gymnastics (*Deutsche Gymnastik*), physical exercises primarily developed for girls' education and used especially by the League of German Girls' (BDM) "FAITH AND BEAUTY" program. What the MILITARY SPORTS program meant for young men, German Gymnastics was to be for young women who wanted to be "faithful [to National Socialism], beautiful, and proud," and who above all were to be prepared for motherhood. Accordingly, a cyclical motif (circles and swinging) dominated in this program, "because the thorough functioning of primordial movements is the precondition for motherhood" and because rhythmic movement "can maintain that inner cheerfulness that a mother necessarily needs." Thus German Gymnastics was enlisted in the service of the Hitler Youth principle for health: "Your body belongs to your nation."

German Gymnastics. Girls with balls and hoops.

German Gymnasts' Union (Deutsche Turner-schaft; DT), the largest German sports association, with 13,000 clubs and 1.6 million members in 1933. It was founded in 1860 to revive the ideals of the "father of gymnastics," Friedrich Ludwig JAHN (1778–1852), "to raise whole and fit men for the Fatherland." This conflicted from the outset with its declared intent to shun "any and all political partisanship," and made it susceptible to German nationalist (and, ultimately, National Socialist) propaganda. Immediately after the Seizure of Power, the gymnasts' leadership embraced the "National Rising," submitted to the ARYAN PARAGRAPH, and joined the "onward march into the Third Reich." Yet even this flight forward—acceptance of the Führer principle and priority for "military gymnastics"—did not stave off SYN-CHRONIZATION. On April 18, 1936, the DT dissolved itself and became a bureau (*Fachamt*) in the GERMAN REICH LEAGUE FOR PHYSICAL EXERCISES.

Germanic cult (*Germanenkult*), overstated glorification of the history and the culture of the *Germanen* (Teutons or Germanic tribes). After the Teutons became a subject of German literature in the 19th century, they first were a subject of idyllicizing and romanticizing exaltation, and later came to symbolize German greatness and superiority as well as a national community free from social contradictions. After the defeat in the First World War, many nationalist authors, dissatisfied with the political reality, developed a Germanic cult with "forefather sagas"; with "novels from Germanic prehistory" and about "Germanic folk kings," as those by Hans Friedrich BLUNCK; or with Nordic mythical ballads, as those by Börries von MÜNCHHAU-SEN. In the early 20th century the literary Germanic cult was displaced by a positivist, nationalist academic history; with a newly interpreted "Germanic archaeology," it juxtaposed as equals a Germanic "classical" antiquity, with its own "intrinsic spiritual culture," and Greco-Roman antiquity (*Germanische Altertumskunde* [Germanic Archaeology], edited by Hermann Schneider, 1938). The National Socialists promoted the Germanic cult insofar as it conformed with their racist theory of life, and they expanded it through cultivation of folklore, through the restoration or new construction of Germanic cultural and memorial sites, through THING PLAYS, and so on. Since the Third Reich, in the minds of its leaders, carried on the Germanic heritage, the system's historical roots, permanence, and popular character were to be expressed in the Germanic cult.

H. H.

Germanic Democracy (*Germanische Demokratie*), National Socialist counterpart to parliamentary DEMOCRACY. In this sense, it referred to the acclamation of the "Führer," who made further democratic actions superfluous and replaced them with consultation (*see* FÜHRER PRINCIPLE).

German Institute for National Socialist Technical Vocational Training (Deutsches Institut für nationalsozialistische technische Arbeitsschulung; Dinta), GERMAN LABOR FRONT institute in Düsseldorf, with roots in a training school run by employer organizations. Established in 1925, the institute trained National Socialist leadership cadres for industry and promoted "education in community spirit" in the workplace.

Germanization (*Germanisierung*), as a term parallel to RE-GERMANIZATION (*Eindeutschung*), a designation applied to the appropriation of Slavic areas in eastern Europe by "Germanic" or German colonists, as the indigenous Slavic inhabitants were simultaneously expelled, suppressed, or themselves Germanized. The term was commonly used in pan-German propaganda; it returned initially in the territorial sense, as in Hitler's speech to the Reichswehr generals on February 3, 1933: "Conquest of new LIVING SPACE in the east and its ruthless Germanization." In the context of propaganda promoting

Germanic cult. "Old Germanic Group" from the "Two Thousand Years of German Culture" parade (1937), in front of the House of German Art.

the concept of a *Volk*-Nation (*Volkstum*), Germanization acquired traits of racial colonialism, and during the Second World War it became reality in the manner announced previously by Himmler on November 8, 1938: "I truly intend to obtain, plunder, and steal Germanic blood from anywhere in the world."

As Reich Commissioner for the Fortification of the German Volk-Nation, after October 7, 1939, Himmler had "persons qualified for re-Germanization" in the occupied areas searched out; their Germanization would at the same time effect a "qualitative decline in the leading stratum of the alien nation." In particular, "racially valuable" children, uncovered through racial-biological examinations carried out by the Race and Settlement Main Office of the SS, meant a "racially valuable population increase" for Himmler. They were taken from their parents and given over to German families or to "rearing" (*Aufzucht*) in a home of the LEBENSBORN organization. Finally, this racial Germanization arose from the shortage of settlers for territorial Germanization.

German Labor Front (Deutsche Arbeitsfront; DAF), organization created by a constitutive congress called for May 10, 1933, after the elimination of the trade unions. The Labor Front's stated aim was to represent workers rather than trade unions, through "the establishment of a community that is truly based on the *Volk* and productive work [*wirkliche Volks- und Leistungsgemeinschaft*] and that has abjured all thoughts of class conflict." The first, provisional organization plan was built on the trade union structure and was based on a four-pillar structure (worker, employee, entrepreneur, and commercial and artisan middle strata).

In November 1933 the relative independence of these corporate groups was abolished and a unified membership of all "working Germans" (*schaffende Deutsche*) was promulgated. In early 1934 a new, vertically linked and centralized organization gave the DAF a structure analogous to that of the NSDAP. There were *Gau*, district (*Kreis*), and local groups and, at the lowest level, workplace and street groups. Decisions came from the central office of Reichsleiter Robert LEY and its bureaus, such as those in charge of organization, personnel, and press and propaganda. In March 1935, the DAF acquired the status of a party-affiliated association, thereby reducing its independence.

The new organization could have become a powerful representative of the interests of workers, especially since, at the outset, representatives of the NATIONAL SOCIALIST WORKPLACE

German Labor Front. Recruiting poster: "Then as now. We remain comrades."

CELL ORGANIZATION (NSBO), with ideas of social revolution, held leading positions. But the NSBO lost influence with every reorganization of the DAF. The law of April 19, 1933, commissioning the appointment of government TRUSTEES OF LABOR diminished the DAF's sphere of activity even further, preparing the way for the abolition of employer and employee autonomy in setting wages and supplanting it with government regulations. The work of the DAF was limited to purely propagandistic activity, a development confirmed by the LABOR REGULATION LAW of January 20, 1934. The DAF had only an advisory role in wage and labor matters. It retained a right to make nominations to the MUTUAL TRUST COUNCIL, which was to be elected yearly by workers, but if they were rejected, places would be filled by the trustee. In general, the Labor Regulation Law gave the DAF an insignificant role in the social constitution of the Third Reich. The law detailed and confirmed the activity of the labor trustee. It also promoted the dismantling of employee rights and of any social partnership in favor of a leader-and-follower relationship. The DAF became a huge organization that supported the goals of the regime through social and cultural concerns, vocational training, and social appeasement (*Befriedung*) of the employee. It also functioned as an additional agency of control for the regime.

The activities of the Labor Front supported the concept of the VOLK COMMUNITY: the REICH VOCATIONAL COMPETITION awakened youth's will to perform; the "'Gehag' Homestead Office" (Gemeinnützige Heimstätten-Spar- und Bau AG [Public Welfare Homestead, Savings, and Building Corporation]) built model housing for workers. Every improvement in working conditions (the responsible office was "BEAUTY OF WORK"), from accident protection at the blast furnace to a flower vase on a bureaucrat's desk, was duly stressed; concerts during work breaks gave workers the feeling that in terms of culture they did not live in the shadows. The accomplishments of the leisure-time organization STRENGTH THROUGH JOY (KdF), which had the job of "breaking all prerogatives of property related to the nation's cultural wealth and the beauties of the world," made travel, which had been a luxury, a commodity that nearly anyone could afford. The "KdF Car" project, financed through loans, promised to place even car ownership in the realm of the possible (*see* VOLKSWAGEN). At the mass demonstrations on May 1, the "Day of National Labor" (*see* MAY HOLIDAY), the regime—with the help of the DAF—presented itself as a "*Volk* Community and Workers' State" (*volksgemeinschaftlicher Arbeiterstaat*). These suggestive mass demonstrations, with their pomp and pathos, had an important function in integrating the labor force into the National Socialist state.

The resources of the destroyed trade unions were not adequate to accomplish the whole DAF program. The organization supported itself by withholding compulsory dues of 1.5 percent of wages. In addition, increasing profits were generated by the Labor Front's own businesses and investments: the Bank of German Labor, the Insurance Combine of German Labor, the KdF-Car Works, publishing houses, and so on. Officially, membership was voluntary, but "desired" (*erwünscht*); in 1942, 25 million belonged. The largest labor organization in the world (40,000 full-time employees), the DAF was an essential participant in converting the economy to war production. On October 10, 1945, it was dissolved by Allied Control Council Law No. 2.

B. W.

German Law Front (Deutsche Rechtsfront), designation for the union of all professional groups involved with the legal system in the NATIONAL SOCIALIST LEAGUE OF LAW GUARDIANS; it was analogous to the concept behind the GERMAN LABOR FRONT.

German lore (*Deutschkunde*), broad designation for all academic subjects related to German culture: German language, history, geography, religion, art, and music. In conjunction with the school reforms of the 1920s, the Germanists' Association promoted an "inclusive German lore" in order to place German intellectual life "on a *völkisch* foundation." After 1933 the German lore subjects, along with physical exercises, were put at the center of National Socialist education. The aim was to "lead [pupils to] the sources of German *Volk*-nationhood [*Volkstum*]" and to contribute to "strengthening" those values that "slumber deep in the Germanic nature and must be painstakingly cultivated" (Alfred ROSENBERG).

German man (*Deutscher Mensch*; literally, person), racial and cultural propaganda formula for the ideal representative of the National Socialist worldview. The term distinguished the actual German, the product of biological and cultural history, from the German of an NS future, who was to be educated and bred. The German was especially suited to such ennobling, despite some racial mixing, because a preserved "Nordic racial nucleus" made him capable of both "heroic actions for the highest ideals and creative cultural achievement." The German man was said to exemplify "a capacity for enthusiasm, a need for genuineness, and a will to act." According to a well-known phrase of the composer Richard WAGNER, to be German meant to do "a thing for its own sake." This active side corresponded to a temperamental nature, which assured that German action and thought remained under the "discipline of a good heart." Such propaganda regarding the militant and fervent German was meant to intensify a feeling of national self-worth until it became a feeling of NS superiority.

German National Anthem ("Deutschlandlied"; literally, Song of Germany), from 1922 to 1945 the official national hymn of the German Reich (after 1933, together with the "HORST-WESSEL-LIED"). Written in 1841 on the North Sea island of Helgoland by Hoffmann von Fallersleben, who used a 1797 hymn to the Austrian emperor composed by Joseph Haydn, the anthem was

originally meant to be a call to unite Germany. Outside Germany, however, it was immediately perceived as an expression of German chauvinism, especially because of its opening line ("Deutschland, Deutschland über alles" [Germany, Germany above all]) and because of the reference in the first verse to the reclaimed territories ("von der Maas bis an die Memel . . ." [from the Meuse to the Niemen River]). In the First World War it was sung as a "hymn of allegiance" (*Bekenntnislied*), and as of 1922 it was the official anthem of the Weimar Republic. The Allies banned the text in 1945, but in the Federal Republic a "Hymn to Germany" (by Rudolf Alexander Schröder) did not gain acceptance. Consequently, since 1952 the third verse ("Einigkeit und Recht und Freiheit . . ." [Unity and law and freedom]) has officially been sung as the national anthem.

German National People's Party (Deutschnationale Volkspartei; DNVP), a consolidation of all right-wing groups from the fallen monarchy; it formed after the appeal to found such a party on November 22, 1918. The DNVP defined itself as a monarchist interest group of large landowners and the bourgeoisie. It rejected the Weimar Constitution and the Versailles treaty, cultivated the STAB-IN-THE-BACK LEGEND, and demanded an authoritarian and antisemitic state. It cooperated with branches of the Christian trade unions and patriotic leagues (such as the STEEL HELMET), sympathized with the KAPP PUTSCH, and enjoyed the support of influential media, such as those of the Hugenberg concern. When the Weimar Republic did not promptly collapse, as anticipated, the party began a phase of limited cooperation with the WEIMAR COALITION. DNVP abstention on the DAWES PLAN contributed to the plan's passage; the DNVP participated in the Luther government in 1925, partially supported Gustav Stresemann's foreign policy, and even sanctioned some pro-Republic legislation (*see* REPUBLIC PROTECTION LAW).

From 1924 to 1928 the DNVP was the strongest bourgeois faction in the Reichstag, with 106 to 103 seats. It was a significant factor in Paul von Hindenburg's election as Reich president in 1925. By changing the party leadership and engaging in nationalist radicalization under Alfred HUGENBERG, the DNVP sought to overcome an electoral reversal in 1928 (a decline to 78 seats), but in the process it lost moderate support and fell into the embrace of the National Socialists, as in the HARZBURG FRONT (1930, down to 41 seats; 1932, only 37). The flight

German National People's Party. Election poster (1924): "Free from Versailles! Free from Jewish-Socialist serfdom! For freedom and fatherland. Your watchword: German-National!"

forward into Hitler's "Cabinet of National Concentration" on January 30, 1933, only furthered the new chancellor's plan for the SEIZURE OF POWER, by procuring an absolute majority in the election of March 5, 1933, and supporting the ENABLING LAW, to which the DNVP itself fell victim through its decision to disband on June 27, 1933.

German National Shop Assistants' Association (Deutschnationaler Handlungsgehilfenverband; DHV), until 1933 the largest professional organization of retail employees and the most influential individual union in the bourgeois German Trade Union League (Deutscher Gewerkschaftsbund). The DHV was founded in 1893 as more than an economic interest group; its program combined social demands and nationalistic slogans. Even after the First World War, DHV members considered the organization a "like-minded community" (*Gesinnungsgemeinschaft*);

it did not accept Jews, only "salespeople of German blood." It rejected women in the workplace, opposed the Social Democratic and Communist parties, as well as parliamentary democracy, and sought a "*Volk* community based on occupational [*berufsständisch*] group." Initially oriented toward the German National People's Party (DNVP) and the German People's Party (DVP), the majority of DHV members were early sympathizers with the NSDAP, and won support for it in middle-class circles. In the period before 1933, the DHV contributed significantly to the spread of antisemitic, racist, and *völkisch* ideas. Despite its active support for the National Socialist movement it was "synchronized" in 1933, then attached to the GERMAN LABOR FRONT, and finally dissolved in February 1934.

H. H.

German National Socialist Workers' Party (Deutsche Nationalsozialistische Arbeiterpartei; DNSAP), after May 5, 1918, the name of the German Workers' Party of Austria (Deutsche Arbeiterpartei Österreichs), founded in 1904, which split into Austrian and Sudeten German organizations after the dissolution of the Austro-Hungarian monarchy. Although the Austrian members soon united with the NSDAP, the Czech group remained independent; it was nonetheless close to the NSDAP's Great-German line, ideologically and above all in terms of foreign policy. The DNSAP won five seats in the Prague parliament in 1925 and nine in 1929, and it ever more radically championed the merger of the Sudetenland with Germany. The party's SA-like combat group (Volkssport) was banned in 1932. The DNSAP averted a ban for its subversive relationship with the "enemy-of-the-state NSDAP" only by self-dissolution on October 4, 1933. Most of its members later ended up in the SUDETEN GERMAN PARTY.

German News Bureau (Deutsches Nachrichtenbüro; DNB), central state-owned news agency with numerous offices inside Germany and abroad. The DNB came into being in December 1933 through a merger carried out by Max WINKLER, on order of the Propaganda Ministry. The entities joined were the Wolff Telegraph Bureau (WTB; the official government agency of the Weimar Republic) and the Telegraph Union (TU) of the Hugenberg concern. The DNB offered the "General DNB Service," plus various economic, cultural, sports, and picture services. During the war, "DNB White" provided secret information to ministers and to Reich and *Gau* leaders. "DNB Red" and "DNB Blue" directed some of this information to a select group of persons, such as important editors and party functionaries.

S. O.

German Peasants' Party (Deutsche Bauernpartei), party founded in 1927 to represent agricultural interests in the Reichstag. It won five mandates in 1930, and formed a factional alliance with the Christian and nationalist Peasants' and Countryfolks' Party. It dissolved itself in the spring of 1933.

German People's Party (Deutsche Volkspartei; DVP), right-liberal party founded on December 15, 1918, as the successor to the right wing of the National Liberal party by the latter's last chairman, Gustav STRESEMANN. The DVP consciously distinguished itself from the left-liberal GERMAN DEMOCRATIC PARTY, and even after modification of both parties' positions, it resisted merger efforts in 1925. The party gained in significance as the majority party in the WEIMAR COALITION after changing its initially monarchist course and placing Stresemann, probably the most renowned politician in the Weimar Republic, in the government (as chancellor, August to November 1923, and as foreign minister, 1923 to 1929). Stresemann reinforced the traditional primacy of foreign policy in the DVP and reversed the party's harsh REVISIONIST POLICY. In the nationalistic climate that followed his death, the party's policy of reconciliation became a liability that led to the loss of support from industry and a rapid decline in votes. This development accelerated after an opening to the right in 1932–1933: from 45 mandates in 1928, the party dropped to 2 in March 1933. On July 4, 1933, the DVP was forced to disband.

German physics (*Deutsche Physik*), national (National Socialist) catchword for a "species-true" natural science. It was taken from the title of a book by the Nobel laureate Philipp LENARD, and was directed especially against Einstein's "Jewish" Theory of Relativity.

German-Polish Nonaggression Pact (*Deutsch-Polnischer Nichtangriffspakt*), agreement signed in Berlin on January 26, 1934, by the German foreign minister, Konstantin von NEURATH, and the Polish ambassador, Józef Lipski. It promised

German People's Party. Election poster with Stresemann (1930): "Vote for my party."

peaceful settlement of all German-Polish differences for a minimum of 10 years. The pact came into being on Hitler's personal initiative, as against his rejection of collective settlement of security issues. With this pact Hitler achieved the first loosening of Germany's international isolation, a breach in the French system of alliances with eastern European states, and a successful camouflage of his true ambitions in eastern Europe.

The pact's explicit renunciation of the use of unilateral force to alter Poland's western border contravened all previous German claims, especially Hitler's own stated policies, and supported the credibility of Germany's assurances of peace following its withdrawal from the LEAGUE OF NATIONS. Hitler abrogated the agreement, which had led to a closer alliance between France and Russia, on April 28, 1939, after Britain's Polish guarantee of March 31, 1939, and in preparation for the GERMAN-SOVIET NONAGGRESSION PACT and the POLISH CAMPAIGN.

German-Polish Nonaggression Pact. From the left: Germany's envoy, von Moltke; Piłsudski; Goebbels; and Poland's foreign minister, Beck.

German Public Instruction Agency (Deutsches Volksbildungswerk), institution under the authority of the Office for Schooling of the NSDAP and attached to the leisure-time organization STRENGTH THROUGH JOY; after 1933 the latter had responsibility for all public and adult instructional facilities. The agency's goal was the transmission of National Socialist culture and ideology, as well as professional and cultural education and physical training. Agency activities included courses and work groups, organized lectures, and solstice celebrations.

German Railroad. *See* Deutsche Reichsbahn.

German Red Cross (Deutsches Rotes Kreuz; DRK), German branch of the International Red Cross, founded in 1869. The Reich law of December 9, 1939, centralized the organization under Hitler's patronage. Membership in 1940 was about 2.5 million. The DRK and its facilities were used by party, state, and military welfare organizations as a relief society; they were promoted by the War Relief Agency (Kriegshilfswerk) after 1939. A large portion of the DRK's expenses were covered by national and international contributions. Humanitarian duties with regard to prisoners of war as defined by the GENEVA CONVENTIONS could be carried out only with great difficulty, especially in the east, where the Red Cross had only minimal influence on the treatment of PRISONERS OF WAR.

German Reich Committee for Physical Exercises (Deutscher Reichsausschuss für Leibesübungen; DRA), post–First World War overall organization of all bourgeois gymnastic and sports groups (about 40). Theodor LEWALD served as president and Carl DIEM as secretary general. The DRA organized Reich Youth Competitions, awarded the German Gymnastic and Sports Badge, and mounted the GERMAN COMPETITIVE GAMES. At Diem's urging, the DRA created the German Academy for Physical Exercises (1920) and the Berlin Sports Forum (1925), and organized the participation of German athletes in the 1928 and 1932 Olympic Games. The general assembly of the DRA met for the last time on April 12, 1933. It elected a negotiating committee, which on May 10, in an act of self-"synchronization," dissolved the DRA. The organization was supplanted by the National Socialist–controlled GERMAN REICH LEAGUE FOR PHYSICAL EXERCISES.

German Reich League for Physical Exercises (Deutscher Reichsbund für Leibesübungen; DRL), umbrella association of all gymnastics and sports clubs in the German Reich. After the dissolution of the GERMAN REICH COMMITTEE FOR PHYSICAL EXERCISES on May 10, 1933, Reich Sports Commissioner Hans von TSCHAMMER UND OSTEN (*Reichssportführer* after July 1933) announced: "The age of individualistic sports activity is over." Fifteen sports departments were created (*see* Table 1), with offices in Berlin. The chairmen of sports associations formed a leadership council (*Reichsführerring*) under the Reich Sports Führer. Sports clubs (*Vereine*), organized regionally by *Gau*, *Bezirk* (region), and *Kreis* (district), were supplanted by the associations (*Verbände*) and placed directly under the DRL, whose existence von Tschammer proclaimed on January 30, 1934, and whose bylaws went into effect on January 1, 1936. The ideological schooling of the athlete—known as

Dietarbeit (*Volk* work; *see* DIETWART)—ranked immediately below the association's athletic aims. Jews were excluded from the DRL, and members of the disbanded workers' gymnastics and sports clubs could join only conditionally. To protect the DRL from encroachments by the Hitler Youth, German Labor Front, and SA, in late 1938 von Tschammer founded the NATIONAL SOCIALIST REICH LEAGUE FOR PHYSICAL EXERCISES, which finally bound German sports to the party.

TABLE 1. *German Reich League for Physical Exercises*

DEPARTMENTS (*Fachämter*)	AFFILIATED ASSOCIATIONS (*Anschlussverbände*)
Gymnastics with apparatus; gymnastics; summer games	German Yachting Association
Soccer; rugby; cricket	Hiking Association
Handball	Alpine Association
Swimming	Bowlers' League
Light athletics (track and field)	Sharpshooters' League
Heavy athletics (wrestling; shot put)	Golfing Association
Boxing	Bobsled and Toboggan Sports Association
Fencing	Table Tennis League
Hockey	Amateur Billiards Association
Tennis	
Rowing	
Canoe sports	
Ice sports; roller skating	
Skiing	
Bicycling	

German Revolution (*Deutsche Revolution*), National Socialist slogan for the events of the SEIZURE OF POWER, which despite its legal course was said to be an "upheaval of the whole legal system and the whole life of the *Volk*" in order to secure the "unitary worldview on which to base the development of the German *Volk*" (Hans FRANK). The "German Revolution" concept consciously alluded to the so-designated upheaval created by the war with Austria in 1866 and the founding of a German Empire in 1871. Then, a "German Revolution" had won national unity, whereas the NS "German Revolution" had attained the "protection of the racial life source."

German Settlement Program (Deutsches Siedlungswerk), totality of measures meant to stem the flight from the countryside, according to a brochure of this name issued by settlement officials attached to the deputy to the Führer

(Rudolf HESS) in 1934. Perceiving increasing urbanization to be a "dangerous symptom of sickness in the body of the *Volk*," the National Socialists propagandized for a "tie with the home sod" and supported the acquisition of HOMESTEADS, though as early as 1934 these were implicitly viewed as an emergency solution. Because of the "space needs of the German *Volk*," the settlement program ultimately promoted a colonial solution, thus becoming an expression of National Socialist demands for LIVING SPACE.

German Settlers' League (Deutscher Siedlerbund; DSB), organization of private and homestead settlers, founded in March 1935. On behalf of the NSDAP Reich Homestead Office and the German Labor Front, the league was to advise proprietors of HOMESTEADS and look after their (ideological) schooling. Some 130,000 members in 32 *Gau* groups belonged in 1936; the league's publication was *Der deutscher Heimstättensiedler* (The German Homesteader; 1923–1943).

German Society for Economic Studies (Deutsche Wirtschaftswissenschaftliche Gesellschaft), academic organization, founded in Berlin on July 6, 1936, to restore "German economic studies" through the synthesis of political economy and business management, and through the encouragement of practice-oriented research.

German Society for Military Policy and Military Studies (Deutsche Gesellschaft für Wehrpolitik und Wehrwissenschaften), organization formed in June 1933 by the Seminar for Military Studies (Wehrwissenschaftliche Arbeitsgemeinschaft), founded in 1929. The society aimed to combine all "creative efforts in military policy." Its honorary president was Franz Xaver Ritter von EPP. The society was an instrument for military propaganda, urging the forthcoming militarization as a "concern for the whole nation." Its official journal was *Wehr und Wissen* (Weapon and Knowledge).

German Society for Public Works (Deutsche Gesellschaft für öffentliche Arbeiten AG; Öffa), joint-stock company founded on August 1, 1930; an instrument of the German government to promote and finance projects related to WORK CREATION without the need to consider the rigid provisions of budgetary law. The share capital of 150 million RM was supplemented by interest and amortizations of previous government loans. This operation on its own account must be distinguished from the society's trust branch, which began in 1932. The former financed itself from returns and interest as well as from its own resources; by 1936 it had granted some 200 million RM in loans, especially to states and municipalities. The trust operation primarily granted loans related to the government's employment program: some 1.257 billion RM by 1939. After the outbreak of the war, Öffa granted credits to employers to gear production to the demands of the war economy.

B. W.

German Society for Racial Hygiene (Deutsche Gesellschaft für Rassenhygiene), association founded in 1905 by Alfred PLOETZ; its office was in Berlin. The society's goal was to propagate the doctrine of racial purity as the sole means to stem the decline of the German *Volk*.

It applied principles of animal and plant husbandry to human society ("social biology"), thus foreshadowing National Socialist racism (*see* SOCIAL DARWINISM). It dissolved at the war's end in 1945.

German Society for Vermin Control (Deutsche Gesellschaft für Schädlingsbekämpfung; DEGESCH), subsidiary of I.G. FARBEN, located in Frankfurt am Main. It produced the poison gas compound ZYKLON B used in EXTERMINATION CAMPS, especially Auschwitz.

German-Soviet Nonaggression Pact (*Deutsch-Sowjetischer Nichtangriffsvertrag*), pact between Germany and the Soviet Union, signed in Moscow on August 23, 1939. Valid for 10 years, it contained a 1-year notification requirement for withdrawal and a provision for consultation. Hitler no doubt saw the pact as both a temporary arrangement with Stalin and an emergency response to the necessity of beginning with a "reversed front" the European war that had conclusively been planned since April 1939, at the latest. England and France had denied Germany's demand for a "free hand" on the Continent and in the east, while Poland had rejected the role Germany intended it to play as a satellite in the "war for living space." Japan and, at the last moment, Italy refused to help. The pact was a temporary deviation from the ideological and racist underpinnings of National Socialist FOREIGN POLICY in favor of strategic and military calculations. Its intended purposes were several: military neutralization of the Soviet Union during the attack on Poland, strategic ensnarement and isolation of Polish territory from the east and the west, intimidation of the Western powers, and, in the event of armed conflict in the west, security in the east from an attack from the rear.

The German-Soviet Economic Treaty of August 19, 1939, in the following years channeled Soviet shipments of raw materials and foodstuffs (both bilateral and transit trade from the Far East) to German armaments production and warfare, in return for German credits, weapons, and industrial goods, thus largely nullifying the British blockade. Moreover, the secret supplemental protocol of August 23, 1939 (expanded and modified through the Boundary and Friendship Treaty of September 28), created the preconditions for the "Fourth Polish Partition" between Berlin and Moscow, and for further mutual demarcations of spheres of influence, through which Finland, Estonia, Latvia,

Lithuania, and Bessarabia fell to the Soviet sphere.

Hitler underscored the purely expedient and tactical character of his actions to the League of Nations commissioner in Danzig, Carl Jacob BURCKHARDT. But the real pioneer and protagonist behind the alliance, German foreign minister Joachim von RIBBENTROP, apparently viewed it as a chance to achieve a long-term settlement by picking up the threads of the old RAPALLO TREATY line. The absence of a provision releasing either party from its obligations in case the other attacked a third party, unusual for a nonaggression pact, clearly indicates that both partners concluded the treaty in full awareness of a future German aggression and of the need to maintain their respective military-strategic and political security.

For Stalin, the treaty promised several advantages: a means of overcoming the international isolation imposed on the Soviet Union since the MUNICH AGREEMENT; shipments of German industrial goods urgently needed for Stalin's ambitious industrialization program; and a broad security buffer in east-central Europe, from which Moscow as the "laughing third party" could more or less coolly view a "self-laceration" of the capitalist states. The existence of the secret protocol to the German-Soviet treaty was officially denied by the Soviet Union until 1989. [In December 1989, the Soviet Congress of People's Deputies condemned the protocol on the ground that Stalin and Hitler had illegally conspired to divide eastern Europe into spheres of influence, in violation of the "sovereignty and independence" of other nations.]

B.-J. W.

German Sports Aid (Deutsche Sportshilfe), organization of the GERMAN REICH LEAGUE FOR PHYSICAL EXERCISES; it was created in 1936 from the Aid Fund for German Sports (founded in 1934). Its duties included financing the OLYMPIC GAMES, promoting gifted athletes, and supporting those disabled by sports injuries. Sports Aid financed itself with contributions, as well as the "sport groschen" (*Sportgroschen*), a levy on entrance tickets to sporting events.

German State Party (Deutsche Staatspartei), new name of the GERMAN DEMOCRATIC PARTY after its merger with the YOUNG GERMAN ORDER in July 1930.

German Style (*Deutscher Stil*), inclusive term for the artworks produced during the Third Reich —from painting to architecture and industrial design—that could be considered as the "artistic form of expression of the new Germany." Similar to the political New Beginnings, a new artistic epoch was also to have begun, which "later generations will perhaps one day proudly call the 'German Style'" (*Das Schwarze Korps*, 1935).

German Trade Union Federation (Deutscher Gewerkschaftsbund; DGB), umbrella association founded in 1919 for the Christian nationalist TRADE UNIONS: the General Association of Christian Trade Unions, the General Association of German Employees' Trade Unions, and the General Association of German Civil Servants in Transportation and Government. Its headquarters was in Berlin, and in 1930 it had some 1.4 million members. Because of the conflicting interests of its individual member groupings, the DGB was denied any great successes. Like the other trade unions, it was abolished on May 2, 1933.

German völkisch movement (*Deutschvölkische Bewegung*), general designation for various political and ideological tendencies and organiza-

German foreign minister Ribbentrop signing the German-Soviet Nonaggression Pact. Behind him, Molotov and Stalin.

tions that from the early 20th century promoted a distinctly nationalistic and antisemitic orientation for German politics. In 1914 it spawned the German Völkisch Party (Deutschvölkische Partei), which during the First World War belonged to the group advocating annexation and "peace through victory." In 1918 the party was absorbed into the GERMAN NATIONAL PEOPLE'S PARTY (DNVP). Similarly, the German Völkisch League for Defense and Offense (Deutschvölkischer Schutz- und Trutzbund), founded in 1919 by the ALL-GERMAN ASSOCIATION, opposed every effort at reconciliation with the former wartime enemy and was banned following Walther RATHENAU's murder in 1922.

A successor organization, the German Völkisch Freedom Party (Deutschvölkische Freiheitspartei), was founded at the end of 1922 as a splinter group from the DNVP. After the NSDAP was banned because of the Hitler Putsch (November 9, 1923), the two groups re-formed as the National Socialist Freedom Party, and in May 1924 temporarily won 32 seats in the Reichstag, 9 of them going to National Socialists. After its re-establishment in February 1925, the NSDAP absorbed practically all of the movement's organizations. Groups remaining outside had no significance.

German Volk List (*Deutsche Volksliste;* DVL), catalog for classifying persons of German descent in German-occupied territories during the Second World War. Intended to determine suitability for "RE-GERMANIZATION," it was instituted by order of the REICH COMMISSIONER FOR THE FORTIFICATION OF THE GERMAN VOLK-NATION on March 4, 1941.

German Weekly Newsreel (*Deutsche Wochenschau*), collection (15 to 20 minutes long) of short news clips on politics, culture, and sports, usually prepared twice a week and shown in nearly all movie houses before the feature film began. Regular weekly newsreels had existed in Germany since 1910. Some, such as the Ufa's (since 1927), had a nationalistic orientation; thus, in 1933, Goebbels found an already functioning "propaganda machine."

During the war, in 1940, the four newsreel presentations from the private film companies (Deulig, German, Tobis, and Ufa) were merged as the *German Weekly Newsreel* in order to increase political effectiveness. "The weekly newsreel is the especially appropriate vehicle for a propaganda impact that brings the world of the Führer close to the people and makes clear his nature as the embodiment of the whole-German being" (Ludwig Heyde). As a medium for war reporting, the newsreel was so important to the National Socialists that Goebbels himself controlled new programs and released them for showing.

German Women's Agency (Deutsches Frauenwerk; DFW), umbrella association of "synchronized" women's organizations, founded in 1933, which also accepted Aryans as individual members. It was independent in organization and finances, but nevertheless was closely tied to the National Socialist WOMEN'S UNION (Frauenschaft; NSF). Because of overlapping personnel and the DFW's close cooperation with the NSF, it is difficult to determine who was responsible for carrying out the program.

German Workers' Party (Deutsche Arbeiterpartei; DAP), party founded on January 5, 1919, in Munich, the center of counterrevolutionary organizations during the postwar upheaval. Its founders were the locksmith Anton DREXLER, who became its second chairman, and the sports journalist Karl Harrer, its first head. The party's political theme was the overcoming of the alienation between the radical Right and the masses. The THULE SOCIETY, a *völkisch* and antisemitic secret society with some 1,500 influential members, was the DAP's foster mother, remaining in the background but viewing the party as a platform for its own political propaganda. The society's symbol was the swastika; its publication was the *Münchner Beobachter* (Munich Observer), precursor of the VÖLKISCHER BEOBACHTER.

The DAP became a reservoir for nationalistic, anti-Bolshevik, and racist ideas (especially those of Dietrich ECKART), as well as for social-revolutionary currents (represented by Gottfried FEDER and later Ernst RÖHM), but it never lost the atmosphere of a beer-hall debating society. Rather than a platform, Drexler promulgated guidelines: alongside such concrete recommendations as the limitation of yearly salaries to 10,000 marks, parity in employment of state (*Land*) residents in the Foreign Office, and inclusion of skilled workers in the middle class (MITTELSTAND) were ideological platitudes (a classless leadership-state, reconciliation between nation and socialism) and nonbinding promises ("good work," "a full pot," "advancement for children"). The national socialism (*nationaler Sozialismus*) of the DAP was the expression of a longing for complete security. In place of class conflict, it offered the reconciliation of all social strata in a VOLK

Meeting room of the German Workers' Party in the Sterneckerbräu (Sternecker Beer Hall) in Munich.

COMMUNITY, whereas Jewry served as an enemy image of global dimensions, constituting a link between international Bolshevism ("abasement of the nation") and capitalism ("abasement of the person"). The DAP's claim to represent no single social rank or class, but rather the *Volk*, found its way into the NSDAP (NATIONAL SO-CIALIST GERMAN WORKERS' PARTY) through such tactical slogans as "BREAKING INTEREST SERVITUDE."

The DAP is historically significant as the precursor of the NSDAP and as the springboard for Hitler's career. On September 12, 1919, as Reichswehr representative under orders of his army superior, Capt. Karl Mayr, Hitler attend-ed a DAP meeting at Munich's Sterneckerbräu. The nature of his first spontaneous appearance as a speaker was corroborated in Drexler's Ba-varian dialect: "Mensch, der hat a Gosch'n, den könnt ma braucha!" (Man, could I use his jaw!). Hitler was then accepted into the party, given membership no. 555 (in fact, he was 55th: the additional digit was for prestige), and accepted as the 7th member of its 7-member executive committee. Made responsible for party propa-ganda, Hitler built up the party bureaucracy in the back room of the Sterneckerbräu. He won over Ernst Röhm, the Bavarian press officer for the Reichswehr, and went on to make the DAP a popular and effective fighting organization whose propaganda focused on combating the Versailles treaty and growing Jewish influence.

The party's first public meeting was held on October 16, 1919; before 111 people, Hitler experienced the revelation that he was a born orator: "I could speak!" (*Mein Kampf*). Follow-ing Hitler's strategy, the DAP replaced Harrer with Drexler as chairman. At its first large meeting, in the hall of the Hofbräuhaus on February 24, 1920, Hitler presented a thorough program. Besides the familiar anticapitalist, anti-Marxist, and antisemitic theses, it included some new points that emphasized the party's socialist character: the taxing away of all income not earned by labor, confiscation of war profits, a ban on land speculation, profit sharing with workers in large enterprises. Party legend was to compare Hitler's speech with Luther's Ninety-five Theses. In the event, one cannot gauge accurately Hitler's personal influence on the formulation of particular program points. One week later, the DAP became the NSDAP, and on June 29, 1921, Hitler became its chairman.

M. F.

Germany. *See* Deutsches Reich.

German Youth Force (Deutsche Jugendkraft; DJK), national alliance founded in 1920 to promote physical exercise in Catholic organizations; it had approximately 220,000 active members in 1933. Despite protection under the papal CONCORDAT, the DJK was "synchronized," and in 1934 it was forced to integrate its competitive activities with those of the GERMAN REICH LEAGUE FOR PHYSICAL EXERCISES. After the murder of DJK Reich Leader Adalbert Probst during the RÖHM AFFAIR (June 30, 1934), the political police, on July 23, 1935, banned religious groups from all sports activities.

Gerstein, Kurt, b. Münster, August 11, 1905; d. Paris, July 23, 1945, SS-*Obersturmführer.* An engineer, Gerstein joined the NSDAP in May 1933. Despite his party membership, he remained in the CONFESSING CHURCH; as a result he was dismissed from state service in 1936, and in 1938 was also expelled from the party after confinement in a concentration camp. He then studied medicine, but after the murder of a sister-in-law in the course of the EUTHANASIA program, he determined to "take a look into Hitler's kitchen." To that end he voluntarily enrolled in the Waffen-SS, was accepted, and in November 1941 was assigned to the Hygiene Institute as a disinfection expert for the SS Command Main Office. There he worked with the hydrocyanic acid compound ZYKLON B, of which, in August 1942, he had to bring 100 kg (220 lbs.) to Poland, where he witnessed mass killings in the extermination camps of Treblinka, Sobibór, and especially BEŁŻEC.

Gerstein then communicated with German friends (including Otto DIBELIUS) as well as with Swedish and Dutch contacts. They themselves were scarcely able to believe his reports, and found even less belief among Allied officials when they passed them along. A copy of the Dutch notes survived and confirmed the original Gerstein report, which he put into writing in May 1945 while in French custody. Accused of being an SS member, Gerstein was found a short while later hanging in his cell. Whether this was a suicide (as officially determined), out of despair over his failed attempt to hinder the genocide, or whether it was a form of secret assassination (*see* VEHM MURDERS) by other SS men confined in the same jail, can no longer be determined. Gerstein's report, often attacked for some inaccuracies, is now judged as fully truthful in every essential point.

Gerstenmaier, Eugen, b. Kirchheim (Teck), August 25, 1906; d. Oberwinter, near Bonn, March 13, 1986, German politician. Gerstenmaier studied German philology and Evangelical theology. Although he was numbered among the first adherents of the CONFESSING CHURCH, he worked from 1936 to 1944 in the foreign office of the GERMAN EVANGELICAL CHURCH, where, according to Karl BARTH, "the principle was the direct opposite of any ecclesiastical statement or action." While completing obligatory service in the cultural policy section of the Foreign Ministry during 1939–1940, Gerstenmaier came into contact with the KREISAU CIRCLE, although he was sentenced only to seven years' imprisonment following the failed assassination attempt of July 20, 1944. After the war he helped develop the Evangelical Aid Program, and was

Kurt Gerstein.

Eugen Gerstenmaier before the *Volk* Court.

its director until 1951. He joined the Christian Democratic Union, was elected to the Bundestag, and served as its president from 1954 to 1969. Gerstenmaier's career ended when his exaggerated claims for RESTITUTION became known. His self-presentation as an opposition fighter was publicly criticized by Barth as early as 1945.

Gessler, Otto, b. Ludwigsburg, February 6, 1875; d. Lindenburg (Allgäu), March 24, 1955, German politician. Gessler's studies were in law. In 1910 he became mayor of Regensburg, and in 1914 mayor of Nuremberg. In 1918 Gessler was a co-founder of the GERMAN DEMOCRATIC PARTY (DDP) in Franconia. After the KAPP PUTSCH and the resignation of Gustav NOSKE, in March 1920 Gessler was made armed forces minister. He held this post in 13 cabinets until 1928; from 1931 to 1933 he served as chairman of the Organization for German Nationals Abroad (Verein für das Deutschtum im Ausland). As an opponent of National Socialism, Gessler withdrew from political life in 1933. However, he maintained contact with opposition circles and after the assassination attempt of July 20, 1944, was confined to the Ravensbrück concentration camp for seven months. From 1950 to 1952 he was president of the German Red Cross.

Gestapo, short form of Geheime Staatspolizei (secret state police). It was originally officially shortened as Gestapa (for Geheimes Staatspolizeiamt [Secret State Police Office]), but was generally changed to conform to Sipo (Sicherheitspolizei [Security Police]), Kripo (Kriminal-

Otto Gessler.

polizei), and Schupo (Schutzpolizei [Protective Police]). When the bureau was named, the shorter Geheimes Polizeiamt (Secret Police Office) was consciously rejected because its acronym, GPA, was thought to be too reminiscent of the Soviet secret police, the GPU. [*See also the major article* Secret State Police.]

Gigantic (*gigantisch*), fashionable National Socialist term designating something as monumental, unheard of, unsurpassable; both the "upheaval of the age" effected by National Socialism and the community of "workers with brain and brawn" united in one front (Hitler, January 30, 1935) were termed "gigantic." "Gigantic" also were Germany's armaments, and—in an inflationary formula—so was the "contest" that would be carried out by means of them in the Second World War.

"Giovinezza" (Ital.; youth), name of the Fascist anthem, taken from the beginning of its refrain; after Mussolini's seizure of power it became the Italian national anthem alongside the "Royal March." Composed in 1909 by Giuseppe Blanc to accompany a patriotic text, in 1921 "Giovinezza" was matched with the words of Salvatore Gotta: "Su, compagni, in forti schieri" (Rise up, comrades, in strong array).

Giraud, Henri-Honoré, b. Paris, January 18, 1879; d. Dijon, March 13, 1949, French general. Giraud participated in the First World War and in the French colonial wars in North Africa; in 1939 he became a member of the Supreme War Council and supreme commander of the French Seventh Army. In 1940 he fell into German captivity, but in 1942 he was able to escape from the Königstein Fortress. From May to November 1943 he was, together with Charles de GAULLE, president of the National Liberation Committee; by 1944 he had supreme command of the Free French forces within the country. After the war he was vice president of the Supreme War Council until 1948.

Gisevius, Hans Bernd, b. Arnsberg, June 14, 1904; d. Müllheim (Baden), February 23, 1974, German Abwehr agent. A jurist by training, in 1933 Gisevius went from the German National People's Party (DNVP) to the NSDAP; he held posts in administration and the police (Gestapo). During the war he was conscripted into the ABWEHR and became a German agent under cover of being a vice-consul in Zurich. Soon coming into close contact with the opposition circle around Hans OSTER, he passed on messages from Ludwig BECK and Carl Friedrich GOER-

Hans Bernd Gisevius.

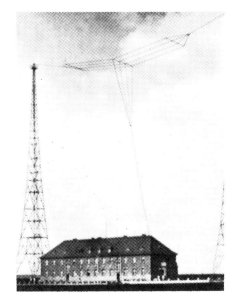

The Gleiwitz radio station.

DELER to Allen DULLES, the American intelligence agent in Bern, and collaborated in planning for the assassination attempt of July 20, 1944. After its failure, Gisevius was able to find refuge in Switzerland, and then spent several years in the United States. His fact-filled memoirs, *Bis zum bitteren Ende* (*To the Bitter End;* 1946), aroused disputes. Gisevius, who testified in the Nuremberg Trials, found himself subject to many suspicions because of the concealment required for a system-bound opposition movement. He was able to refute accusations of having grown rich from the fortunes of refugees in connection with Operation "v7."

Gleichschaltung. *See* Synchronization.

Gleiwitz (Pol., Gliwice), German city in the industrial region of Upper Silesia. A faked attack on the radio station at Gleiwitz was carried out by a specially assigned commando under SS-Sturmbannführer Alfred NAUJOCKS on the night of August 31, 1939, on the order of Security Service (SD) chief Reinhard HEYDRICH. This was intended to give international public opinion the proof that Polish border incursions had reached such a point that military countermeasures (*see* POLISH CAMPAIGN) would appear as a necessary defense.

In line with Hitler's statement to high military personnel at the Obersalzberg on August 22, 1939, that he would "provide a propaganda event for starting the war, regardless of whether or not it was believable," three operations were planned by Heydrich, of which the most spectacular was to be the one against the Glei-

witz radio station. At the signal code from Berlin, "Grandmother dead" (*Grossmutter gestorben*), at around 8:00 p.m. Naujocks occupied the broadcast studio with his group disguised as Polish "insurgents," interrupted the program, and had a Polish appeal read that called for battle against the Germans. However, it could be heard only locally: Gleiwitz could broadcast regionally only through the station at Breslau, which was not switched into it. Throughout, battle noises were simulated, and a drugged prisoner (in SS jargon, "canned goods") was put down at the door and shot. He was left after the 20-minute operation as proof of the alleged Polish perpetration.

The propaganda exploitation of the feigned attacks—there were simultaneous actions against the customs station at Hochlinden and the forestry station at Pitschen, where murdered concentration camp inmates in Polish uniforms were left behind—ran into difficulties because of the foul-up regarding the broadcast range and because of the greater impact of the subsequent war events. Also, from the time of the rumors surrounding the REICHSTAG FIRE, deep skepticism had prevailed at home and especially abroad concerning National Socialist provocation campaigns.

Globke, Hans, b. Düsseldorf, September 10, 1889; d. Bad Godesberg, February 13, 1973, German jurist and administrative official. Prior to 1933 Globke belonged to the Center party, was deputy police chief in Aachen, and, after 1929, was ministerial counselor in both the

Hans Globke.

Prussian and the Reich interior ministries. He became known through having written, with his superior Wilhelm STUCKART, a commentary on the NUREMBERG LAWS. While Globke limited the prohibition of extramarital sexual intercourse between Jews and Germans to sexual acts in the narrower sense, and termed "kisses, embraces, and lewd touches" as being outside the prohibition, he interpreted the Blood Protection Law (*Blutschutzgesetz*) more narrowly than did the judiciary and other commentators. At the same time in his commentary he discriminated against not only legally forbidden relations, but also those undesirable from a police standpoint between persons "tainted with Jewish blood and German-blooded persons."

To the end, Globke had a part in creating the legal principles for the PERSECUTION OF JEWS. In 1944 he personally signed a decree that regulated the transfer of the assets of dead (and murdered) Jews to the Reich. After 1945 he was at first jailed as a member of the National Socialist leadership echelon; later he was classified as a "fellow traveler" and was able—then as a member of the Christian Democratic Union —to continue his civil service career. His last post was that of state secretary (1953–1963) under Konrad Adenauer in the Federal Chancellor's Office.

Sch.

Globocnik, Odilo, b. Trieste, April 21, 1904; d. near Weisensee (Carinthia), May 21, 1945, SS-*Gruppenführer* and lieutenant general of the police (January 9, 1942). A construction engi-

neer, Globocnik was active in his homeland as a leader in the NSDAP years before the Anschluss of Austria (the date of his party enrollment was March 1, 1931). He was sentenced four times by Austrian courts for illegal activity on behalf of the party, receiving prison terms ranging from four weeks to six months; during 1936–1937 a warrant was issued for his arrest on a charge of high treason. After the Anschluss he was at first a state secretary and, for a while, *Gauleiter* of Vienna.

Globocnik took part in the Polish Campaign as an SS-*Unterscharführer* of the standby troops; in the General SS, which he joined on September 1, 1934, he was already a *Standartenführer*. Thereafter he was named SS and Police Leader in the Lublin district and promoted to SS-*Brigadeführer* and major general. On July 17, 1941, Himmler gave Globocnik the assignment of planning and building SS and police strongholds in eastern Europe. For labor resources Globocnik used mainly Jews. In May 1942 he was given responsibility for carrying out the REINHARD OPERATION. After Globocnik had had quarrels with party and SS leaders, Himmler, who called him "Globus," appointed him in August 1943 as *Höherer SS- und Polizeiführer* (Higher SS and Police Leader) in the "Adriatic Coast Operation Zone" in Trieste. Globocnik committed suicide when captured by Allied troops at the war's end.

A. St.

Gloeden, Elisabeth Charlotte ("Lilo"), b. Cologne, December 19, 1903; d. Berlin-Plötzensee, November 30, 1944 (executed), Ger-

Odilo Globocnik.

man resistance fighter and jurist. She married the architect Erich Gloeden in 1938. Politically and racially persecuted people regularly found refuge in the Gloeden home, among them Carl Friedrich GOERDELER. After the failed assassination attempt of July 20, 1944, Gen. Fritz Lindemann—for whose capture a reward of half a million marks was offered—also stayed there. When the Gestapo tracked him down on September 3, 1944, it arrested the whole family, the Gloedens as well as Lilo's 66-year-old mother. All three were sentenced to death on November 27, 1944, and were beheaded three days later.

Glücks, Richard, b. Düsseldorf, April 22, 1889; d. presumably Flensburg, May 10, 1945, SS-*Gruppenführer* (November 1943). Glücks was an officer in the First World War, and then became a businessman; he joined the NSDAP only after the Seizure of Power. He became a colleague of Theodor EICKE, the Inspector of CONCENTRATION CAMPS, and succeeded him in this post at the end of 1939. In March 1942 Glücks became the director of Office Group D in the SS Economic-Administrative Main Office; soon afterward he took charge of the EXTERMINATION CAMPS in German-occupied Poland, and relayed to them Himmler's orders for killing. He was also responsible for medical "care" at the concentration camps, including the HUMAN EXPERIMENTS there, and for the selection of labor slaves and of liquidation victims for the gas chambers. He is thought to have met his end through suicide in a naval hospital.

Gobineau, Count Arthur de, b. Ville d'Avray, July 14, 1816; d. Turin, October 13, 1882, French diplomat and writer. Beginning in 1849, Gobineau was assigned to a series of remote diplomatic posts (Teheran, Athens, Rio de Janeiro, Stockholm), allowing him time to produce poetry, most of which is now forgotten. He achieved success, however, with his four-volume *Essay on the Inequality of Human Races* (1853–1855; German edition, 1898–1901), which was essentially an attempt at a "scientific" legitimization of imperialism and colonialism after the loss of the missionary Christian justification. According to Gobineau, distinctions had to be made between "lower" races—notably blacks and Semites—and "higher" races such as the "Aryans," and especially the "Teutons." In his appeal to preserve the "high race" through the protection of "pure blood," he had especially the English and the Flemish in mind. It remained for his followers, such as Richard WAG-

Count Arthur de Gobineau.

NER and Houston Stewart CHAMBERLAIN, to reclaim the Germanic mythology for the Germans, thereby establishing the connection between Gobineau's key ideas and the National Socialist worldview.

God-believing (*gottgläubig*), official term (by a decree of November 26, 1936) for persons who had left a recognized religious community. The formal designation was meant to document the fact that distance from a church did not mean unbelief but, rather, was proper to the "species-appropriate piety of the German nature." Jews who had left their community thus could not so designate themselves. The term continued to be used for a time after the war.

Godesberg Conference (*Godesberger Konferenz*), meeting between British prime minister Neville Chamberlain and Hitler on September 22–23, 1938, at the Rheinhotel Dreesen in Bad Godesberg. They met in order to settle the SUDETEN CRISIS, which, however, was first accomplished through the MUNICH AGREEMENT.

Goebbels, Joseph, b. Rheydt, October 29, 1897; d. Berlin, May 1, 1945, German politician. The son of the bookkeeper of a small lamp-wick factory and the product of a strict Catholic household, Goebbels was to have become a priest. Instead, he decided to pursue studies in philosophy and literature, believing that his future lay in the literary field. In 1921 the young Goebbels attained his doctorate with a thesis on Romantic drama. Handicapped with a crippled foot, he had not taken part in the First World War.

In a frail body with a disproportionately large head lurked the will and ambition of a man visibly slighted by life—a diminishment of existence that sought out substitutes in a great number of love affairs. The small, limping man was unusually successful with women, endowed as he was with the charm of dark eyes, wit, and liveliness. Yet despite these victories there were defeats of another kind that gave his life its ultimate direction: his literary ambitions were never satisfied. Newspapers sent his articles back, and publishing houses returned his novels and dramas. In particular, his insistent submissions to the liberal *Berliner Tageblatt* under its editor in chief, Theodor Wolff, were rejected. Goebbels's development into a fanatic antisemite and a despiser of everything bourgeois is, one suspects, traceable in large part to these insults to his ego. The deficient belletristic qualities of the aesthete Goebbels make the refusals understandable. He wrote in a bombastic and high-flown style; his journals from the 1920s reveal the mental state of an adolescent, continually swinging between extremes, undergoing "emotional hot, then cold baths" (Helmut Heiber).

It is noteworthy that Goebbels's sentimental outpourings were compatible with his cutting trenchancy and precision as a political orator and editor. In this capacity he joined the *völkisch* camp in 1924—and met with success from the very beginning. Here he found the substitute for the recognition and praise that had been denied him as a belletrist. Helmut Heiber writes of Goebbels's "high intellectual varnish covering the emotional world of an adolescent." Politically, Goebbels stood close to the "leftist" National Socialist Gregor STRASSER; he became the managing director of the Rhineland-North *Gau* (whose seat was in Elberfeld) and edited the *National-Sozialistische Briefe* (National Socialist Letters). During the rivalry between Hitler and the Strasser group, Goebbels sided with the latter, until Hitler rhetorically abolished it at the BAMBERG FÜHRER CONFERENCE in 1926. Hitler recognized Goebbels's talent and shrewdly attracted him to himself. Soon Goebbels bowed to "the greater, the political genius," as he confided to his diary, adding, "Hitler, I love you, because you are great and simple at the same time." This bond ceased only with their nearly simultaneous deaths. Goebbels was as proficient an orator as Hitler, with better projection but with no charisma; he knew instinctively that he could only be the servant, the herald, the propagandist of someone who

was first, but never first himself. With this awareness he demagogically supported and reinforced Hitler's rise and rule until the very last.

A critical decision for both sides was taken in the autumn of 1926, when Hitler sent his best agitator into "red" Berlin in order to establish the NSDAP on the toughest turf in Germany. In point of fact, Goebbels conquered Berlin for National Socialism. The Reich capital remained his preeminent field of operation for 18 years. The hatred of the Communists for the *Gauleiter* was not without respect, for Goebbels was fearless: he would deliver his tirades in the middle of workers' neighborhoods, and would stand on a podium unscathed during a meeting-hall brawl. His brutally hard-hitting SA men would almost always emerge on top. If any "comrades in struggle" were killed, Goebbels would arrange a spectacular rite of mourning for the "blood witnesses" after the style of state funerals (as the one he arranged for Horst WESSEL). He kept Berlin in political suspense and attracted followers.

At the same time, Goebbels edited the newspaper *Der* ANGRIFF (The Attack); after 1930 he held the post of Reich Propaganda Director for the NSDAP as well. The overworked demagogue was also a member of the Reichstag for his party. He was always thinking up new devices for steering the masses. When such artifices are employed nowadays, Goebbels often stands behind them as the invisible instructor. He also put to consistent use as propaganda tools the new media of radio and motion pic-

Joseph Goebbels.

tures—which was possible, of course, only after the Seizure of Power. They were placed under the REICH CULTURE CHAMBER (founded in 1933), as were the press, literature, music, and art. Very few sectors of artistic expression evaded Goebbels's grasp in his position as Reich Minister for "Volk Enlightenment and Propaganda" (March 13, 1933). Göring allowed relative freedom in the Prussian State Theater, and ARCHITECTURE was retained by Hitler, an architectural enthusiast, under his own direction. It was primarily Goebbels who banished the fertile and, in some cases, dominant influence of Jewish writers, journalists, and artists from German cultural life, since professional practice in these fields required "Aryan" ancestry.

On the other hand, Goebbels was clever enough to tolerate islands of cheerfulness within the imposed worldview. Countless entertainment films, even in the regime's final days, were free from any political resonance. As press lord (*see* PRESS ADVISORIES), Goebbels saw to it that the NS state spoke with a single voice both at home and abroad. The decisive domestic and foreign political steps were always prepared, accompanied, and justified by campaigns. In the inflamed nationalist climate, Goebbels exploited isolated foreign attacks for his own press campaigns of unrestrained agitation. He could suddenly mobilize "healthy *Volk* sentiment" and was the chief organizer of the KRISTALLNACHT pogrom (November 9–10, 1938). As the ranking orchestrator of opinion he contributed substantially toward creating the at-

mosphere that made possible, during the war, the mass crimes against Jews. Similarly, along with Rudolf Hess and Baldur von Schirach, he consolidated the FÜHRER CULT.

Despite all of Goebbels's loyalty to Hitler, the Führer's trust in his paladin underwent a setback in the late 1930s because of Goebbels's love affairs. Married since 1931 to the divorcée Magda Quandt, the propaganda chief caused a stir by his passion for the Czech actress Lida Baarova. Hitler, intolerant of a second marital scandal among the higher ranks after the BLOMBERG affair, called Goebbels into line.

The propaganda energy of the "little doctor," already at a high pitch, released fresh reserves in wartime, invigorating himself and those around him. He produced an endless flow of speeches and articles (many published in *Das* REICH) aimed at improving war morale—all the more needed, given the crushing bomb attacks on German cities. With his calls to stay the course, Goebbels clearly was an important factor in the people's ability to patiently endure wartime distress well beyond physical and psychological limits. His developed strategy of (false) assurances, aided by fantasies of final victory or promises of WONDER WEAPONS, worked until the collapse. Goebbels's hate-filled nature shaped the public understanding of reality with effective formulas, as in his rhetorically ingenious SPORTS PALACE SPEECH promoting "total war" (February 18, 1943). He was always at his strongest while cutting and thrusting, when feelings and rage could be inflamed. He needed enemies, although his enemy images

Magda Goebbels with her children Helga, Helmuth, Hedda, Hilde, and Holde.

were less ideologically rooted than those of Hitler and Himmler.

Even in the rubble heaps of Berlin and other cities, Goebbels did not hesitate to go out among the people, although his Führer had long since stopped seeking out the masses. As General Plenipotentiary for Total War Measures (*Generalbevollmächtigter für den totalen Kriegseinsatz;* July 1944), he worked to squeeze from the *Volk* every bit of their strength to withstand to the end. Yet he had no illusions concerning the personal consequences of a defeat: "We are already so enmeshed above all in the Jewish question that there is no escape for us," he had written in his diary in March 1943. However, right up until the downfall, which he clearly recognized, Goebbels spared neither time nor energy. Named Reich chancellor by Hitler in the latter's political testament (April 29, 1945), Goebbels staged his departure in the style of a tragedy: a day after the suicide of his master, he poisoned his six children and then, along with his wife, took his own life in the bunker under the Reich Chancellery.

H. St.

Goebbels Home for German Composers (Goebbelsheim für deutsche Komponisten), convalescent home for musicians, named after the Minister for Volk Enlightenment and Propaganda and president of the REICH CULTURE CHAMBER. It belonged to the REICH MUSIC CHAMBER and was located in Bad Harzburg.

Goebbels snout (*Goebbelsschnauze*), folksy and ironic term for the VOLK'S RECEIVER.

Goerdeler, Carl Friedrich, b. Schneidemühl, July 31, 1884; d. Berlin-Plötzensee, February 2, 1945 (executed), German politician. Goerdeler studied law and specialized in public administration; after the First World War he joined the German National People's Party. From 1920 to 1930, he was deputy mayor of Königsberg. Goerdeler had a skeptical attitude toward the Weimar Republic; because of his experiences in the wartime economy, he was a convinced advocate of economic liberalism. In this connection he was successful as lord mayor of Leipzig (as of 1930) in combating unemployment, and was named Reich Commissioner for Price Supervision by Heinrich Brüning in December 1931. Goerdeler's hopes for becoming chancellor as Brüning's successor were not fulfilled.

Even after the Seizure of Power, Goerdeler remained in his post as mayor, and from November 5, 1934, he again served as price commis-

sioner. Despite his nationalist-conservative principles and his collaboration on the GERMAN COMMUNAL ORDINANCE of January 30, 1935, which was reshaped in line with National Socialist viewpoints, Goerdeler soon came into conflict with the party over the liquidation of the state based on law, and especially over Hitler's racial and church policies. On July 1, 1935, he resigned in protest as price commissioner; shortly after his re-election, he vacated his Leipzig mayoral post when the party forced the removal of a monument to the Jewish composer Felix Mendelssohn-Bartholdy. Goerdeler was a consultant to the Bosch firm, which enabled him to take extensive trips abroad.

After 1935, Goerdeler was in correspondence with General Staff chief Ludwig BECK; their development into opposition fighters ran parallel. After the outbreak of war, Goerdeler more and more became the political head of the civilian OPPOSITION; in many memorandums he developed models for a post-Hitler Germany. This being the case, it is astounding how long Goerdeler believed in the recovery of a Great-Germany (with the Sudetenland, Posen, Austria, and even the South Tyrol), and how even in domestic policies he sought to turn back the clock. He had in mind a strong, partly corporatist half-democratic state, led by the old elites, with possible monarchical features. He hoped to win over the Western powers in common cause against Bolshevism after removing Hitler, perhaps through a *coup d'état* by the Wehrmacht (he rejected the idea of murder). In this regard he was deeply disconcerted by the demand for UNCONDITIONAL SURRENDER. Intended as

Carl Friedrich Goerdeler.

Reich chancellor for the period after a successful putsch, by holding to his own plans he came into conflict with the KREISAU CIRCLE as well as with the Social Democrats around Julius LEBER. Even the young militants around Claus von Stauffenberg ultimately considered Goerdeler as only a transition figure.

Even before the attempted assassination of July 20, 1944, whose failure Goerdeler regarded as a "divine judgment," the Gestapo was on his trail. They were able to arrest him, however, only on August 12, after he was denounced (his female accuser received 1 million RM from Hitler). On September 8, the *Volk* Court sentenced Goerdeler to death. The execution was stalled in the hope that he would yield further information; five months later it was carried out by beheading, at Hitler's order, with a hand ax.

Goga, Octavian, b. near Hermannstadt, April 1, 1881; d. Ciucea, near Klausenburg, May 7, 1938, Romanian writer and politician. In the First World War, Goga favored struggle against the Central Powers and called for the incorporation of Transylvania into Romania. He was the founder and chairman of the Christian National Party, served as minister several times, and became prime minister on December 29, 1937, with a pronouncedly antisemitic and nationalist program. Unable to carry out his program, he resigned his office on February 10, 1938. His patriotic songs (including "The Earth Calls Us," 1909) became popular.

Gogarten, Friedrich, b. Dortmund, January 13, 1887; d. Göttingen, October 16, 1967, German Evangelical theologian. Gogarten became a pro-

Octavian Goga.

fessor in Breslau in 1931, and from 1935 to 1955 he taught in Göttingen. In 1920 he became known as a critic of the historical theology of the 19th century through his essay "Zwischen den Zeiten" (Between the Times). He then became involved with the dialectical theology of Karl BARTH, with whom he struggled against Christian liberalism and socialism, as well as against *völkisch* political theology, considering all of them false temporal approaches. His turnaround was marked by a 1930 polemic, "Wider die Ächtung der Autorität" (Against the Contempt for Authority), which called for a strong state. This led Gogarten to a break with Barth and finally to join the GERMAN CHRISTIANS. He announced his membership on August 4, 1933, after he had justified the harsh measures of the National Socialist regime on grounds that a people that had "lapsed so much from form" as had the Germans must "first be put into uniform." By the end of 1933 he already recognized his mistake and left the German Christians, but he did not join the church opposition. In 1955 Barth retrospectively called Gogarten one of the "intellectual founders of National Socialism."

Golden Flag of the German Labor Front (*Goldene Fahne der DAF*), swastika flag, its white circle bordered by a golden cogwheel. After 1937 it was awarded every May 1 by the GERMAN LABOR FRONT in the PERFORMANCE COMPETITION OF GERMAN WORKPLACES, along with the title "National Socialist Model Workplace."

Golden Party Badge (Goldenes Parteiabzeichen; also Goldenes Ehrenzeichen des NSDAP [Golden Honor Badge of the NSDAP]), highest National Socialist party award after the BLOOD ORDER. It was granted by Hitler to "party comrades" with membership numbers under 100,000 and to "those who have particularly distinguished themselves in the National Socialist movement and the attainment of its goals." The badge was a round pin with a gold oak-leaf wreath and the legend "National-sozialistische D. A. P." around a large swastika.

Golden pheasant (*Goldfasan*), mocking colloquial term (especially in soldiers' jargon) for party functionaries decked out with (gala) uniforms and medals. Especially during the war and in the occupied territories, such "birds" were responsible for bad blood among the population.

Golden Sunday (*Goldener Sonntag*), old-fashioned name for the last Sunday before Christmas. By reviving the term, National Socialist propaganda vainly attempted to supplant the Christian designation of the fourth Advent Sunday. Still less successful were the extensions to the third Advent Sunday ("Silver Sunday") and the second ("Copper Sunday").

Gold Oak-Leaf Cluster (Goldenes Eichenlaub), highest addition to the KNIGHT'S CROSS, awarded only once (to Flight Col. Hans-Ulrich RUDEL).

Gömbös von Jákfa, Gyula, b. Murga county (Hungary), December 26, 1886; d. Munich, October 6, 1936, Hungarian politician. In 1919 Gömbös was involved in the counterrevolution against Béla KUN; in 1921 he participated in the successful resistance against a Habsburg restoration. A close colleague of Miklós HORTHY, he was minister of war from 1929 to 1936, and after 1932 prime minister as well. He sought support from both Fascist Italy and National Socialist Germany. On June 17, 1933, Gömbös was the first foreign head of state to visit Reich Chancellor Hitler in Berlin.

Good Work! (*Gute Arbeit!*), propagandistic demand of the GERMAN WORKERS' PARTY, with its petit-bourgeois socialist program.

Goote, Thor (pseud. of Schultze von Langsdorff; second pseud., Johannes M. Berg), b. Forbach, May 27, 1899; d. off the Scottish coast (airplane crash), July 3, 1940, German writer and engineer. In the First World War, Goote was a frontline officer; later he was a free corps soldier, an SA leader, and a professor at the Karls-

Gyula Gömbös von Jákfa.

ruhe Technical College. Goote based his "factual" and war novels, imbued with "passionate" nationalist sentiment, on his own experience ("I do not want to live . . . or advance myself at any cost. Everything must be for Germany"— Goote's life motto). He had notable success, numbering among his readers the leading personages of the Third Reich, with his aviator books, whose heroes he styled "men who had proved themselves."

Göring, Emmy (née Sonnemann; first married name, Köstlin [divorced]), b. Hamburg, March 24, 1893; d. Munich, June 8, 1973, second wife

Emmy Göring with her husband and daughter Edda.

of Hermann GÖRING; an actress. She met the second man of the Third Reich a few months after the death of Karin Göring. They married with the greatest pomp on April 10, 1935; the nominally still functioning Reich Bishop, Ludwig MÜLLER, officiated for them in the Berlin Cathedral. Hitler acted as best man and made the couple a present of a painting by Franz von Lembach, *Bismarck.*

Since Hitler was unmarried, Emmy immediately undertook the role of a First Lady in National Socialist Germany; however, she stayed completely out of political activity. On June 2, 1938, she gave birth to a daughter, who was named after Mussolini's daughter Edda; the child's father idolized her. After the war's end, Emmy Göring was arrested and was confined with her daughter for several months in the Straubing Prison before she could visit her husband in the Nuremberg Military Prison. When he committed suicide, Emmy was suspected of having smuggled the poison to him, but this was never proved. Classified as an active National Socialist, she was forbidden to make public appearances for five years. In 1966 her memoirs, *Mein Leben mit Hermann Göring* (My Life with Hermann Göring), were published.

Göring, Hermann, b. Rosenheim, January 12, 1893; d. Nuremberg, October 15, 1946, German politician. Göring was the son of the first imperial Reich commissioner in German Southwest Africa. His childhood and youth, already under strong upper-class influence, took on an expressly feudal style when, around the turn of the century, his parents moved to the estates of his uncle and godfather, Hermann Ritter von Epenstein. In two castles in the Salzburg area and in Franconia, the youth lived in grandiose circumstances, which very overtly provided a foundation for his later famous (indeed notorious) penchant for pomp and splendor. His life's military direction grew out of attendance at the cadet institutes at Karlsruhe and Lichterfelde, near Berlin. His intellectual talent showed great promise.

In 1912, Göring joined the infantry in Alsace; a lieutenant, he promptly transferred into the newly formed aviator unit, in which he became one of the most successful fighter pilots (he was awarded the Pour le mérite medal in 1917). After the death of Baron von Richthofen, Göring was the last commander of that squadron. He escaped Germany's dreary postwar conditions by moving to Denmark and Sweden, where he was active as a stunt flyer and met Karin von

Kantzow. Their mutual love destroyed the Swedish woman's marriage; after her divorce, she married the 30-year-old air captain (inactive) in Munich. Göring had already returned to his home province in 1921, since he foresaw no career advancement in the north.

Göring's career was decisively altered in 1922 when he met Hitler, who entrusted the war hero, brimming with energy and willpower, with the further buildup of the SA. A year later, during the HITLER PUTSCH, Göring suffered serious wounds at the Feldherrnhalle. He evaded the warrant for his arrest by fleeing to Austria. He became addicted to morphine from injections used to control his pain; only years later was he able to break his dependency, through several withdrawal treatments in Sweden. The mid-1920s were the luckless phase of Göring's life: he was disabled, without a profession, in debt, and a fugitive from his country. An amnesty in 1927 enabled him to return, and a wartime friendship gave him a link to Lufthansa and thus to economic recovery.

Göring led an active and politically beneficial social life in Berlin. He resumed his contacts with Hitler, and in 1928 became a member of the Reichstag for the NSDAP. His house on Badensche Strasse served in cultivating his relations with the political and industrial powers he was courting. While Joseph GOEBBELS sought to win over Berlin on the street and in oratorical combat, Göring achieved successes in high-society salons. His worldly-wise manner made him more suited for high society than other National Socialist leaders, in the eyes of conservative circles. In 1931 Karin died of heart disease (to honor her, her widower later named his palatial villa in the Schorfheide KARINHALL). The following year, 1932, the NSDAP became the strongest party in the Reichstag, and Göring was made Reichstag president. There the skilled organizer, good orator, and wily tactician executed critical maneuvers aimed at decisively capturing state power.

When Hitler became Reich chancellor, Göring entered the cabinet as minister without portfolio, and at first was only Reich commissioner for aviation. However, without discernible effort he had already secured for himself the second place in the power hierarchy, less by his performance than by self-promotion, and aided by his lack of scruples. The French ambassador in Berlin, André FRANÇOIS-PONCET, characterized him in retrospect: "He was clever, sly, cold-blooded, brave, and iron-willed. He was free of scruples. He was also cynical. Although he was capable of magnanimous impulses and gallantry, he could also act with pitiless cruelty." Thus, Göring was an unqualified adherent of Hitler's racial doctrine, but could audaciously declare, "I decide who's a Jew!" On that basis he could issue letters of safe conduct that held their force. He enjoyed popularity despite or because of his ostentatiousness, his passion for honorific decoration, his corpulence—and because he was the only one of the principal National Socialists who had a sense of humor, even for whispered jokes hostile to the regime. Nonetheless, he schemed without restraint in the RÖHM AFFAIR and cold-bloodedly supported the murder operation. He took to heart the principle of "live and let live," yet involved himself without hesitation in each of the Third Reich's major operations of inhumane violence. At the end, that rightly made him the first among the principal defendants at Nuremberg.

No other among Hitler's retinue, not even Himmler, took charge, over the course of time—and at times simultaneously—of so many offices. Göring was president of the Reichstag. (At the time of the REICHSTAG FIRE TRIAL in late 1933, his clumsy and threatening manner fed the suspicion, which for a time had subsided, that the National Socialists had been involved in the arson as beneficiaries.) In April 1933 he became Prussian minister president, and for a while he was also interior minister, as such commanding the SECRET STATE POLICE (Gestapo). In May 1933 Göring became Reich minister for aviation, in 1934 Reich chief forester and hunting master, as well as supreme commander

Hermann Göring.

of the Luftwaffe, and in 1936 delegate for the FOUR-YEAR PLAN, which mainly served to prepare for war. In 1936 he put the personnel and matériel of the young Luftwaffe to their first acid test: as the CONDOR LEGION on Franco's side in the Spanish Civil War. In 1938 Hitler named this man who had skipped over the middle and higher ranks of officers as the second field marshal of the Third Reich (after Werner von Blomberg).

After the KRISTALLNACHT pogrom (November 9–10, 1938), Göring forced Germany's Jews out of economic activity altogether and imposed a "restitution" upon the victims: for the undeserved damages they suffered, they had to pay an aggregate special tax of 1 billion RM. In the Polish crisis (August 1939), Göring attempted to avert war and made unsuccessful international contacts (see Birger DAHLERUS). Under the pressure of the British ultimatum of September 3, 1939, Göring allegedly expressed obvious doubt about Germany's ability to pull through: "If we lose this war, then heaven help us." Two days earlier, Hitler had designated him his successor.

The war years displayed Göring in two sharply distinct manifestations. In the Blitzkrieg phase he contributed substantially to the victories, with an innovative cooperation of air and ground combat units. At the apex of his successes he received the highest military rank, created for him: that of *Reichsmarschall* (July 19, 1940). Yet already, in the AIR BATTLE FOR ENGLAND, the decline of the Luftwaffe fighter force had begun. It proved to be technologically inferior—on both out and return flights—and was unable to achieve in combat the air superiority necessary for invading the island or for containing the bomber losses within tolerable limits. Mistaken shifts in armaments for an air war then left the Reich, contrary to Göring's promises, increasingly helpless against bombing raids by the Allied enemies. This evident failure of top leadership in the German Luftwaffe was accompanied by Göring's personal deterioration. He relapsed into his old morphine addiction, which rendered him inactive and blind to reality. Under the euphoric effect of the narcotic he promised to provide the German forces surrounded at Stalingrad with abundant supplies, but this failed totally. The setbacks to Göring's reputation grew through military disasters, augmented by his simultaneous high living, which was financed and embellished by war booty (notably ART PLUNDER). Hitler stood by him, but Göring lost ground against his rivals Martin BORMANN,

Heinrich HIMMLER, and Joseph Goebbels. When he was on the point of entering into negotiations with the western Allies shortly before the war's end, Hitler expelled him from the party in his political testament and ordered his arrest; Göring promptly opted instead for American captivity.

In the NUREMBERG TRIALS Göring self-assuredly assumed the leadership role among the defendants. Despite a skillful defense, under the weight of overwhelming evidence of his complicity in NS mass atrocities and war crimes, especially the FINAL SOLUTION, he was sentenced to death. He received the decision calmly, since he had been able to smuggle poison into the prison (how he did this remains unexplained). Less than three hours before the time set for his execution, he put an end to his life. The corpse was burned along with those of the accused who were hanged, and the ashes were scattered in a tributary of the Isar River.

H. St.

Göring, Karin (née Baroness von Fock; first married name, von Kantzow [divorced]), b. Stockholm, October 21, 1888; d. there, October 17, 1931, first wife of Hermann GÖRING. She met the future second man of the Third Reich at the end of 1920 through relatives, and married him on February 3, 1923, in Munich. Weak in health, she became worn out by the hectic life at the side of her roving husband. Her early death in the midst of a sharp upturn of the NSDAP enmeshed the shattered Göring even more tightly in political work for the party. In her honor, he named his country manor in the Schorfheide KARINHALL and his yacht *Carin* (the name's original spelling).

Göring Works (Reichswerke Hermann Göring), designation for the Hermann Göring Joint Stock Company for Ore Mining and Ironworks, founded by the German Reich on July 15, 1937. Originally intended for mining and smelting unprofitable mineral deposits (in Salzgitter, Baden, and the Upper Palatinate), the Göring Works was the most important expression of the state capitalist economic course in the Third Reich (*see* FOUR-YEAR PLAN). The Anschluss with Austria and the Sudetenland as well as the occupation of Czechoslovakia and Poland led to a gigantic expansion of the concern (which in 1940 had approximately 600,000 employees). The goal of removing bottlenecks in the German supply of iron was not achieved, however, through the creation of the Göring Works.

After its namesake's withdrawal from economic policy in May 1942, a gradual dissolution of the concern took place. In the course of Allied dismantling and decartelization after the war, the Göring Works was liquidated.

R. S.

Götterdämmerung (Twilight of the Gods), melodramatic term for the collapse of the Third Reich, borrowed from the last opera of Richard WAGNER's *Ring of the Nibelung.* It has been applied especially to the circle of leaders around Hitler in the bunker under the Reich Chancellery.

Gottschalk, Joachim ("Joschi"), b. Berlin, April 10, 1904; d. there, November 6, 1941, German actor. Gottschalk was originally a merchant sailor; he launched his acting career in Leipzig and Frankfurt am Main. In 1938 he began acting at the Berlin Theater on the Bülowplatz, where he enjoyed many successes. When he became known also as a film actor, for example as a co-star with Paula WESSELY in Gustav Ucicky's *Ein Leben lang* (A Life Long; 1940), he came to the attention of officialdom—as did his marriage to a Jewish woman. Gottschalk was put under considerable pressure to seek a divorce; his refusal to do so subjected him to economic extortion. Finally the Gestapo resorted to the charge of "racial infamy," of which his wife had purportedly been guilty in an extramarital relationship. With his wife and eight-year-old son, he committed suicide, which sent forth shock waves in the artistic community. Gottschalk's

Joachim Gottschalk.

farewell letter ended with a quotation from the playwright Heinrich von Kleist: "The truth is that nothing on earth could help me."

Government (*Regierung*), in the National Socialist political conception, an obsolete term for the political leadership of a state, as against the apolitical term "administration" (*Verwaltung*). Because the FÜHRER'S WILL was to have become the sole basis for political activity in the Third Reich, any conflict was to have been overcome, and the principle of government had been replaced by that of leadership. Like all administration, government too was only an instrument "in the hand of the Führer of the *Volk* Community."

Graedener, Hermann, b. Vienna, April 29, 1878; d. Altmünster, February 24, 1956, Austrian writer. In novels and dramas, Graedener interpreted the Peasants' War and historical liberation movements in a contemporary sense as struggles for a "new" Reich. In chauvinist essays he spoke for the "Great-German cultural cause" (*Innentum der Deutschheit* [The Inner Being of Germanness]; 1932); he was honored by Hitler with the Goethe Medal in 1938 for his "contributions to the Great-German idea."

Graener, Paul, b. Berlin, January 11, 1872; d. Salzburg, November 13, 1944, German composer. From 1910 to 1913, Graener was director of the Salzburg Mozarteum, from 1920 to 1924 a teacher of composition in Leipzig, and from 1930 to 1935 director of the Sternsches Konservatorium in Berlin. On July 15, 1935, he was

Paul Graener.

made vice president of the REICH MUSIC CHAMBER. Graener's theatrically effective operas enjoyed great popularity during the Third Reich because of what in the official view was their "consciously German attitude." Among his works was *Friedemann Bach*, distinguished by the skillful usage of themes from the works of Johann Sebastian Bach (for example, the chorale "Kein Hälmlein wächst auf Erden" [No Shoot Grows from the Earth]). Graener also wrote successful orchestral music, including *Die Flöte von Sanssouci* (The Flute of Sans Souci), a tribute to Prussia's musician king, Frederick the Great.

Graf, Oskar Maria, b. Berg bei Starnberg, July 22, 1894; d. New York, June 28, 1967, German writer. After apprenticing to be a baker, in 1911 Graf ran away from his parents' home to Munich. He served in the war, but also spent some time in an insane asylum. Graf took part in the revolution of 1918 and collaborated in the Munich Republic of Councils. He made his living as a free-lance "provincial writer," as he himself called it (with *Bolweiser* [translated as *The Station Master*]; 1931), and as a playwright for the Munich Workers' Stage. As a socialist, he was hostile toward National Socialism; he left Germany in February 1933. On May 15, 1933, on the occasion of the BOOK BURNING, Graf demanded, "Burn me!" since the National Socialists had not immediately put his works on the list of undesirable writings. That changed quickly: in 1934 he was deprived of his citizenship, and he had to emigrate through Moscow (1934) and Czechoslovakia (where he lived until 1938) to the United States. In 1947 his small-town novel *Unruhe um einen Friedfertigen* (Commotion over a Peacemaker), which explored fascist roots in the bourgeoisie, was published. In 1958 Graf became an American citizen.

Grafeneck, one of the six "killing facilities" in the EUTHANASIA program. The palatial building (Grafeneck Castle) in the Münsingen district belonged to the Samaritan Foundation in Stuttgart and was originally used as a home for the crippled. In October 1939 the "T4 Organization" refurbished it as a killing facility, which, under the code name "Facility A," began operations in January 1940. Grafeneck was closed in December 1940, and its personnel were transferred to the newly fitted-out facility at HADAMAR, near Limberg. Surviving records indicate that 9,839 people were killed at Grafeneck.

Graff, Sigmund, b. Roth bei Nürnberg, January 7, 1898; d. Erlangen, June 18, 1979, German writer. Graff was the author of much-performed comedies and popular pieces. His major work was his drama based on war experiences, *Die endlose Strasse* (*The Endless Road,* written with Carl E. Hintze, 1926), one of the most frequently performed German theater pieces in the 1930s, for which Graff received the Dietrich Eckart Prize in 1933. In the Third Reich he was a government councillor and a collaborator with the Reich theater adviser in Berlin. While being processed after the war, Graff invoked his contacts with opposition circles and successfully avoided the designation of "Nazi writer."

Grain economy (*Getreidewirtschaft*), particularly sensitive sector of AGRICULTURAL POLICY because of the variations in harvests and plantings, as well as its considerable impact on food supplies. The grain economy was strictly regulated immediately after the Seizure of Power as part of an effort to achieve AUTARKY. The Reich Office for Grain was established by a law of May 30, 1933; as a public corporation, it undertook the direction of the grain economy. A further law of September 15, 1933, merged all mills "for the economic union of rye and wheat mills"; a system of fixed grain prices, introduced on September 26 of that year, was intended to avert speculation. The control of the grain economy was completed on June 27, 1934, by the so-called Grain Constitution (*Getreidegrundgesetz*), which enabled the Reich Ministry for Food and Agriculture, among other departments, to fix quotas, to influence delivery and distribution, and to designate uses for the grain. Complete self-sufficiency, especially in the animal feed sector, was achieved temporarily only after the war began, through exploitation of the occupied territories.

Grand Council of Fascism (Gran Consiglio del Fascismo), central committee, of sorts, of the Italian Fascist party (*see* FASCISM). It was established by Mussolini on December 15, 1922, shortly after his seizure of power. The Grand Council attained constitutional status in 1932 and was expected "to remove any future contradiction between the party and the government." In political practice it played a subordinate role to Mussolini's personal dictatorship. It first achieved significance under increasingly threatening war conditions, when at the initiative of Count Dino GRANDI on the night of July 24–25, 1943, it gave Mussolini a vote of no confidence by a count of 19 to 7, with one abstention. This gave King Victor Emmanuel III the opportunity to depose and arrest the Duce on July 25.

Grandi di Mordano, Count Dino (after 1937), b. Mordano, June 4, 1895; d. Bologna, May 21, 1988, Italian politician. A jurist, Grandi joined the Fascist movement early on, but belonged to the moderate internal party opposition. In 1921 he became a member of the GRAND COUNCIL OF FASCISM. From 1929 to 1932, Grandi was foreign minister, then until 1939 ambassador in London, and thereafter minister of justice until 1943. On July 25, 1943, he introduced the motion in the Grand Council session to remove Mussolini from power. In January 1944, under a death sentence, Grandi fled to Portugal; he moved to Brazil in 1948 and returned to Italy in 1960.

Graziani, Rodolfo, Marquis of Neghelli (as of 1936), b. Filetino, August 11, 1882; d. Rome, January 11, 1955, Italian marshal. Graziani was commander of the colonial troops in Libya, then commander in the war against ABYSSINIA and viceroy there in 1936–1937. He was made supreme commander of Italian troops in North Africa in July 1940, but was recalled in March 1941 because of heavy defeats by the British forces. From September 1943 he was war minister for the Fascist puppet government of SALÒ. In 1950 Graziani was sentenced to 19 years' imprisonment, but he was soon pardoned.

Great Britain (officially, United Kingdom of Great Britain and Northern Ireland), parliamentary monarchy in northwestern Europe; area, 242,632 sq km (approximately 97,200 sq miles); population, 43 million (1930). Between 1914 and 1945, Great Britain experienced the extensive turmoil entailed by its transition from the liberal capitalism of the 19th century to the interventionist welfare state of the 20th century. This development was stimulated by two world wars and the WORLD ECONOMIC CRISIS, which constituted a "watershed" between them. It occurred under the banner of Conservative rule that was interrupted by only two Labour governments and that coincided with the decline of political liberalism.

Significant changes in foreign relations in this period included Britain's transition from empire to commonwealth, its reduction to a medium European power, dissolution of the League of Nations mandate system of 1919 and the beginnings of decolonization, and the challenge to the "workshop of the world" from German, American, and Japanese competition. Meanwhile, there was a concentration on domestic problems and tasks: modernization of the economy; restructuring from old industries (coal, iron and steel, textiles) to new and more dynamic ones (electric appliances, chemicals, precision instruments, mechanical engineering, motors); reduction of social tensions (as were manifested in the 1926 general strike) and of unemployment (which never dropped under 1 million); motorization; urbanization; and so on.

The key ideas of the 1920s—"reconstruction, restoration, recovery"—still pointed to the illusory hope of being able to turn back the clocks to 1914 in domestic and foreign policy (as in the 1925 return to the gold standard). The world economic crisis prompted new emphases in crisis management under the basic concept of "planning": government-subsidized housing construction and expansion of agriculture, a planned economy and welfare-state planning, structural reform for distressed regions, and expansion of unemployment insurance.

In foreign affairs, London in the 1920s considered itself the guarantor of collective security (*see* LEAGUE OF NATIONS; KELLOGG-BRIAND PACT) and of a European balance of power (*see* LOCARNO PACT). It saw itself as a mediator

between French strivings for security and hegemony and German demands for revision of the Versailles treaty and for parity as a political power. Great Britain had supported the Weimar Republic as a reliable bulwark against Bolshevism. After the collapse of the Versailles system of collective security following Hitler's seizure of power, it was forced to seek out bilateral ways for reducing tensions (*see* GERMAN-BRITISH NAVAL AGREEMENT). In light of the failure of international DISARMAMENT and the menace to the worldwide British empire by the three aggressors (Germany, Italy, and Japan), only a dual strategy of APPEASEMENT and a moderate arms buildup enabled Great Britain to safeguard from the outside the previously described transformation and modernization program at home.

A command economy, welfare-state planning, the national coalition in CHURCHILL's wartime cabinet, and the integration of the trade unions in wartime, as well as the Labour party's electoral victory under Clement ATTLEE and Ernest Bevin in July 1945, created the preconditions for the realization of the modern welfare state and—through nationalizations—the "mixed economy," which indeed had been conceived and partially realized between the wars. The

After a bombing raid, customers have salvaged the piano and the Union Jack from the ruins of their pub in London's East End.

consequences of the Second World War for Great Britain were the total exhaustion of national material and financial resources, the final dissolution of the worldwide empire, and the descent into second-class status and international dependency.

B.-J. W.

Great Cross (Grosskreuz), highest category of the IRON CROSS, awarded only once (to Hermann Göring).

Great-German League (Grossdeutscher Bund), alliance of groups from the youth leagues (*bündische Jugend; see* YOUTH MOVEMENT) and the Pathfinders (Boy Scouts) against incursions by the Hitler Youth; it was led by Vice Adm. Adolf von Trotha (1868–1940) and his "Free Brigade of the Young Nation" (Freischar junger Nation). On June 17, 1933, police surrounded a league camp and forced the members to dismantle it. Simultaneously, a decree of the Reich Youth Leadership ordered the dissolution of the Great-German League. Protests were in vain; Trotha himself later made concessions and in 1936 became an honorary member of the Naval Hitler Youth.

Great-German People's Party (Grossdeutsche Volkspartei), Austrian political party founded in 1920 as a collective organization for nationalist groupings; its main platform point was the ANSCHLUSS with Germany. In 1920 the party received 20 mandates in elections to the National Council (Nationalrat); in 1924 it won only 10, and formed a coalition with the Christian Social party. When more and more of its members turned to the NSDAP, the party sought an alliance with the National Socialists, took a confrontational stance toward the DOLLFUSS government, and was banned in 1933.

Great-German Reich (Grossdeutsches Reich; Grossdeutschland), initially a propaganda term; in the Second World War it became the official designation of the National Socialist German Reich (DEUTSCHES REICH). Point 1 of the NSDAP program of February 24, 1920, called for the formation of a great-German state: "We demand the merger of all Germans . . . into a Great-Germany." The party organ, *Völkischer Beobachter* (Völkisch Observer), after 1921 bore the subtitle "Combat Paper of the National Socialist Movement for Great-Germany."

The "great-German" concept had a long history, dating back to the patriotic awakening in the wars of liberation against Napoleonic foreign

rule (1813–1815). The anthem by Ernst Moritz Arndt (1769–1860), "Was ist des Deutschen Vaterland" (What Is the German's Fatherland; 1813), answered: "It must be all Germany [das ganze Deutschland]." Hopes waned in the period of the restoration and foundered anew in 1848–1849 against Prussian-Austrian dualism and the multinational basis of the Danube Monarchy. Bismarck's establishment of a German state in 1871 essentially meant victory for the "small-German" (*kleindeutsch*) solution of a Germany without Austria, but it was attacked for its "narrowness" by disappointed "great-German" supporters. The longing for a Great-German Reich remained alive particularly in German Austria (*see* ALL-GERMAN ASSOCIATION) and, after the downfall of the Habsburg empire in 1918–1919, surfaced as a demand for an ANSCHLUSS with the German state. Because this would have deprived the Allies of the recent war of the power-political fruits of victory, they forbade the union in the peace treaties.

In his "great-German" propaganda, the Austrian Hitler articulated hopes for a "national rebirth." The "merger of people of German nationality [*Deutschtum*] settled in one continuous area" seemed, on the basis of the right of peoples to self-determination propagated by the Allied side, to be the only realistic possibility for loosening the "shackles of the VERSAILLES TREATY." However, after Austria's incorporation into the German Reich on March 13, 1938, the Great-German Reich was mentioned only hesitantly because of Hitler's fundamentally

Great-German Reich (Great-Germany). National Socialist poster.

broader goals. A press advisory issued by the Propaganda Ministry on March 21, 1938, justified the reserve on the basis that "naturally, still other territories" belonged to a genuine Great-German Reich, and "we will lay claim to them at an appropriate time."

Therefore, at first the less binding term "Great-Germany" prevailed, and was not supplanted by the term "Great-German Reich" until after the incorporation of the Sudetenland (October 1938), the MEMELLAND (March 1939), and the *Reichsgaue* DANZIG–WEST PRUSSIA and WARTHELAND (October 1939); the establishment of the "collateral countries" (*Nebenländer*), the PROTECTORATE OF BOHEMIA AND MORAVIA (March 1939) and the GENERAL-GOUVERNEMENT (October 1939); the annexation of EUPEN-MALMÉDY (May 1940); and the appropriation of ALSACE-LORRAINE (July 1940). With this radical expansion of the original notion of a Great-German Reich, the term was distorted by imperialism; after the UNCONDITIONAL SURRENDER (May 8, 1945), it lost all meaning.

Great-German Struggle for Freedom (*Grossdeutscher Freiheitskampf*), propaganda term for the war after 1939. It was meant to suggest that the German attacks were preventive strikes against international ENCIRCLEMENT.

Great-German Volk Community (Grossdeutsche Volksgemeinschaft), a substitute organization of the period when the NSDAP was banned after the Hitler Putsch (*see* NATIONAL SOCIALIST GERMAN WORKERS' PARTY), from November 9, 1923, to the party's reinstitution on February 27, 1925. The Volk Community was the southern branch. Its leaders included Julius STREICHER, Philipp BOUHLER, and Hermann ESSER.

Great-Germany (Grossdeutschland), in the Second World War the name of an infantry division, later a panzer corps (as a political concept, *see* GREAT-GERMAN REICH).

Greece, state in southeastern Europe; area, about 127,000 sq km (approximately 50,800 sq miles); population, 6.2 million (1928). As a result of the First World War, Greece in 1919–1920 won substantial territory, at Bulgaria's expense (southern Thrace) as well as from Turkey (eastern Thrace, Smyrna); however, it lost the Turkish acquisitions after its defeat in the Greek-Turkish War of 1920 to 1922. The existing economic and social problems of the backward country were then increased by new burdens. These included the settlement and integration

of some 1.4 million Greek refugees and a chronic domestic political crisis caused by shifting quarrels between royalists and republicans over the form of the state. On May 1, 1924, a republic was inaugurated, but on November 25, 1935, after a rigged plebiscite, the monarchy was restored under King George II. A politicized and deeply divided army command, ever ready to overthrow the government, was in the background. Some stabilization took place under Prime Minister Eleftherios Venizelos (1928–1932, 1933). But the catastrophic effects of the world economic crisis and the victory of the radical royalists in 1933 brought about renewed internal polarization, which the dictatorship of Gen. Ioannis METAXAS (after a coup on August 4, 1936), following Fascist and National Socialist models, concealed.

In foreign policy, Greece adhered to the traditional policy of compromise and neutrality through bilateral agreements with neighbor-ing states and the Balkan Pact with Yugoslavia, Romania, and Turkey (February 9, 1934). Greece relied heavily on the West, as in an Anglo-French guarantee of Greek independence (April 13, 1939) against Italian imperialism toward the *mare nostrum* (literally, our sea; here, the Mediterranean). It was able to repulse Italy's attack from Albania (October 28, 1940), but not Germany's BALKAN CAMPAIGN in April and May 1941. King George II fled with his government to Egypt under British protection, Greece was occupied by German and Italian troops, and Thrace fell to Bulgaria.

A very repressive occupation regime ensued, with shootings of hostages, mass executions, starvation, and pogroms against Jews (a total of 65,000 victims perished in the FINAL SOLUTION). Fanatically militant resistance groups

Greece. Stamp of a Greek resistance group.

rose up, which, however, were also hostile to one another. The government-in-exile and the British Supreme Command in the Mediterranean, in cooperation with both the republican-nationalist and the revolutionary-Communist groups, made many attempts to impede the civil war and to prepare together for a postwar order. All failed. Only after long struggles and regular campaigns from late 1944 to mid-1949, and with British and American aid, did bourgeois forces prevail and prevent Greece's transformation into a people's republic on the Bolshevik model, as was successfully carried out by the Soviets in the other states of eastern and southeastern Europe.

B.-J. W.

Greek Campaign, conquest of the Greek mainland by the Wehrmacht from April 6 to April 21, 1941, and of Crete between May 20 and July 1 of that year (*see* BALKAN CAMPAIGN).

Green Front (Grüne Front), nationalist conservative alliance of agricultural interest groups (including the REICHSLAND LEAGUE), founded in March 1929. The front's goals included higher agricultural tariffs; it had little political influence, but contributed to the intensified ideological stance of its members along the lines of National Socialist AGRICULTURAL POLICY, and thus to their later move into the REICH FOOD ESTATE.

Greim, Robert Ritter von, b. Bayreuth, June 22, 1892; d. Salzburg, May 24, 1945, German field marshal general (April 28, 1945). A pilot in the First World War, Greim later studied law. From 1924 to 1927 he was in Canton with a commission to build up the Chinese air force. In 1935 Greim became commander of the "Richthofen" Fighter Squadron; in 1938 he was made a major

general in the Reich Aviation Ministry. As General of the Aviators (*General der Flieger*; 1940), he directed the Luftwaffe Eastern Command after April 1942. In April 1945 Greim flew, together with Hanna REITSCH, into besieged Berlin, where he was appointed as Hermann GÖRING's successor to the post of supreme commander of the Luftwaffe. After leaving Berlin on Hitler's order, he fell into captivity and committed suicide.

Greiser, Arthur, b. Schroda (Posen), January 22, 1897; d. Posen (now Poznań), July 14, 1946, German politician and SS-*Obergruppenführer* (1942). During the First World War, Greiser was a pilot, and afterward an unsuccessful businessman. In 1924 he was a co-founder of the STEEL HELMET in Danzig. Greiser joined the NSDAP in 1928, and from 1930 to 1933 he was *Gau* business manager in Danzig. In June 1933 he became vice president of the Danzig senate and head of its Interior desk; on November 24, 1934, he became senate president as the successor to Hermann RAUSCHNING.

When Danzig was reincorporated into the Reich in the wake of the Polish Campaign, Greiser was made head of the civil administration in annexed Posen, on September 21, 1939; on November 2 he became the Reich governor (*Stattshalter*) in the new WARTHELAND *Gau*. Pursuing a brutal policy of RE-GERMANIZATION, he tripled the German segment of the population by 1944, ordered mass deportations of Poles and Jews to slave labor in the Reich or the Generalgouvernement, and transferred sick workers to the extermination camp at KULMHOF.

Robert Ritter von Greim.

Arthur Greiser.

He also made a name for himself, in collaboration with Martin BORMANN, as a persecutor of the churches by making his *Gau* available as a proving ground for planned measures to alienate the population from the church (*see* CHURCH STRUGGLE). Greiser was captured by the Americans in the Alps in 1945 and remanded to Poland. There, after being sentenced to death, he was publicly hanged in front of his former residence.

Grelling, Richard, b. Berlin, June 11, 1853; d. there, January 14, 1929, German pacifist and political journalist. During the First World War, Grelling's book *J'accuse—von einem Deutschen* (I Accuse—by a German) charged Germany's political leadership with having plotted the war; he thus became a mortal enemy in nationalist circles. National Socialist propaganda blamed him for forgeries of "Talmudic cunning," which Grelling was unable to rebut; in 1928 he returned the accusation by publishing an analysis of the falsified semiofficial German historical literature on the war.

Grimm, Friedrich, b. Düsseldorf, June 17, 1888; d. Freiburg im Breisgau, May 16, 1959, German jurist. Grimm practiced law in Essen beginning in 1914, and after 1937 in Berlin; in 1927 he became a professor of international private and trial law in Münster. He acted several times as a defense attorney for Germans living abroad, and also as the plaintiff's attorney on behalf of the widow of Wilhelm GUSTLOFF in the trial of the assailant David FRANKFURTER, whom Grimm tried unsuccessfully to portray as an "agent of world Jewry." A member of the Reichstag from 1933 to 1945, Grimm also made a name for himself as a political commentator: his books include *Der Feind diktiert* (The Enemy Dictates; 1932), on war reparations; *Hitlers deutsche Sendung* (Hitler's German Mission; 1933); and *Wir sind im Recht* (We Are in the Right; 1935), on the reintroduction of universal compulsory military service. Active again as a lawyer after 1949, Grimm wrote *Politische Justiz, eine Krankheit unserer Zeit* (Political Justice, a Disease of Our Times) in 1953.

Grimm, Hans, b. Wiesbaden, March 22, 1875; d. Lippoldsberg an der Weser, September 27, 1959, German writer. Grimm lived for 13 years as a businessman in South Africa and German Southwest Africa, and praised its expanse in many biographically influenced homeland and colonial tales, such as *Der Ölsucher von Duala* (The Oil Prospector from Duala; 1918). On

Hans Grimm.

returning to Germany, he found the "narrowness of the homeland" oppressive, and saw in it the cause of social and political problems that to his mind could find their solution only in *Lebensraum* (LIVING SPACE) in German colonies overseas. Through his presentation of the tragic life of German settlers in British South Africa, he pleaded in his major work for free possibilities of development in Africa. His novel *Volk ohne Raum* (People without Space, 2 vols., 1926) became one of the most frequently read books of the Third Reich, and, as a "classic" of blood-and-soil literature, was required school reading. The title provided National Socialist propaganda and expansionism with an effective slogan. Although never a member of the NSDAP, Grimm represented its chauvinistic and racist thought, and he received numerous prizes and official honors after 1933. In postwar works he justified Hitler ("a reformer," "a good European"), and laid the blame for the Second World War on Great Britain, in *Die Erzbischofsschrift. Antwort eines Deutschen* (1950; translated as *Answer of a German: An Open Letter to the Archbishop of Canterbury*).

H. H.

Gröber, Konrad, b. Messkirch, April 1, 1872; d. Freiburg im Breisgau, February 14, 1948, German Catholic theologian. Gröber was ordained a priest in 1897, made a cathedral canon in Freiburg in 1925, and served as bishop of Meissen in 1931–1932. As archbishop of Freiburg (from 1932), he was closely involved in the establishment of a concordat with the state of

Baden. In 1933 he became a valuable ally of the Roman Curia in winning over the German bishops for a CONCORDAT with the Reich. The sacrifice of political Catholicism that this entailed gained him the nickname "Brown Conrad." Gröber's illusions as to the true character of National Socialism vanished by 1934, after the murder of Erich KLAUSENER during the Röhm Affair. Still, he remained loyal to the state, and in 1937 spoke approvingly of Hitler's fight against Bolshevism; however, he boldly opposed violations of the Concordat and sharply protested against the EUTHANASIA murder program.

Groener, Wilhelm, b. Ludwigsburg, November 22, 1867; d. Bornstedt bei Potsdam, May 3, 1939, German general and politician. During the First World War, Groener was chief of the Railway Department; on October 28, 1918, he became the successor to Erich LUDENDORFF as first quartermaster general. In the following month, Groener pressured for the abdication of Kaiser Wilhelm II and thus invited the hatred of nationalist circles. He played a decisive part in the orderly reduction of the army and in the acceptance of the Versailles treaty. His alliance with Friedrich EBERT cleared the way for parliamentary democracy against attacks from both the Left and the Right. Groener retired from the military on September 13, 1919. He was several times transport minister between 1920 and 1923, armed forces minister from 1928 to 1932, and after October 1931 was simultaneously interior minister. In the BRÜNING cabinet he was, next to the chancellor, the

Wilhelm Groener.

dominant personality. His strong action against the NSDAP and its organizations—ultimately the prohibition of the SA and the SS on April 13, 1932—made him enemies even in the bourgeois camp, which hoped for an arrangement with National Socialism. His resignation as armed forces minister (May 13, 1932) could not avert the fall of the Brüning government, which lost him the Interior Ministry post as well. Thereafter, Groener lived in retirement as a military writer.

Ba.

Gröfaz, ironic and derogatory short form (in the style of the National Socialist passion for such shortenings) of *Grösster Feldherr aller Zeiten* (Greatest Military Commander of All Times), the label for Hitler crafted by Gen. Wilhelm KEITEL after the French Campaign.

Grohé, Josef, b. Gemünden (Hunsrück), November 6, 1902; d. Cologne, January 3, 1988, German politician. A business clerk by occupation, Grohé was a co-founder in 1922 of the Cologne local group of the NSDAP; during the RUHR CONFLICT he took part in acts of sabotage. After the re-establishment of the NSDAP (February 27, 1925), Grohé became business manager for the Rhineland-South *Gau*, editor in chief of the *Westdeutscher Beobachter* (West German Observer), and in 1931 *Gauleiter* of Cologne-Aachen. He advanced to a seat on the Prussian State Council and election to the Reichstag (1933). Later he became Reich Defense Commissioner (1942) and Reich Commissioner for the Occupied Territories of Belgium and Northern France. Following denazification proceedings, he served a prison term until 1950.

Gropius, Walter, b. Berlin, May 18, 1883; d. Boston (Massachusetts), July 5, 1969, German architect. After studies in Berlin and Munich, in 1910 Gropius became an independent professional. In 1919, in Weimar, he was appointed director of the Academy of Fine Arts and the School for Arts and Crafts, which he merged into the BAUHAUS. In 1928 he again set up an independent practice; he emigrated to London in 1934 and, in 1937, to the United States, where he was a professor at Harvard University until 1952. The National Socialists criticized Gropius's architecture as "deliberately alien to the *Volk* in form and material" and lapsing into "the primitive." The best-known Gropius buildings are the "Siemens City" in Berlin (1928–

Walter Gropius.

1933), apartment houses in the Hansa quarter of Berlin (1957), and the Rosenthal porcelain factory in Selb (1963–1967).

Gross, Nikolaus, b. Niederwenigern (Ruhr), September 30, 1898; d. Berlin-Plötzensee (executed), January 23, 1945, German trade unionist. After a trade apprenticeship and work as a miner, Gross helped to found the first youth group in the Christian Miners' Movement. He became a union secretary in Lower Silesia (1922) and in the Ruhr region (1924), and subsequently an editor on the *Westdeutsche Arbeiterzeitung* (West German Workers' Newspaper; WAZ). Gross was then editor of the successor publication to the WAZ, the *Kettler Wacht,* and attacked National Socialism in stirring articles. After his paper was banned he continued his task of enlightenment through lectures; together with others, such as Bernhard

Nikolaus Gross with grandchild.

LETTERHAUS, he concerned himself with upholding the traditions of the Catholic workers' movement. He thus became involved in opposition circles. On August 12, 1944, he fell into Gestapo hands after the failed assassination attempt of July 20. The *Volk* Court sentenced him to death on January 15, 1945. Gross's farewell letter to his wife and seven children radiates the calm and strength of a martyr.

Gross, Walter, b. Kassel, October 21, 1904; d. 1945, German physician. Gross joined the NSDAP in 1925, and became a member of the Reich Directorate of the NATIONAL SOCIALIST GERMAN PHYSICIANS' LEAGUE. In 1933 he established the Information Office for Population Policy and Racial Cultivation, which under his direction became part of the RACIAL POLICY OFFICE of the NSDAP in 1934. A fanatic antisemite, Gross wrote books that included *Rasse und Politik* (Race and Politics; 1934) and *Die rassenpolitischen Voraussetzungen zur Lösung der Judenfrage* (The Racial-Policy Prerequisites for the Solution of the Jewish Question; 1943), in which he argued for the total removal of the European Jews.

Grossdeutsch-. *See* Great-German.

Grossexekution (great [large-scale] execution), National Socialist expression for mass shootings; it was used for purposes of legal camouflage.

Grossnotstand (state of great need), euphemistic Germanization of the word *Katastrophe;* the term was used especially to circumlocute military defeats. Its use is documented beginning in 1943.

Gross-Rosen, National Socialist concentration camp, originally built as a work camp, near Striegau in the Schweidnis district within the former administrative area of Breslau. The camp was at first occupied by only 100 prisoners, who were quartered in wooden barracks. As a result of the shift of the munitions industry toward the east, Gross-Rosen was continually expanded and was set up as an autonomous concentration camp. It ultimately had as many as 70 satellite camps (*Aussenkommandos*), with a total of about 80,000 prisoners. The main camp held about 10,000 prisoners from nearly every European nation; the relatively few German prisoners were predominantly from the prisoner categories of professional criminals, asocials, and homosexuals.

The camp inmates worked mainly for the

German munitions industry, but were also utilized in stone quarries. Food supplies, lodging, and hygienic conditions, as well as all-around treatment, were bad, yet circumstances improved slightly in 1942–1943. Nonetheless, the inhuman and brutal treatment at the hands of SS personnel or specially appointed inmates led to many deaths; prisoners were whipped, shot, hanged, or drowned, or were killed through abuse for the slightest cause. Many died in the punishment squadron or in its special commando, the "intensive punishment squadron," for alleged or actual violations of rules.

In early February 1945, Gross-Rosen was evacuated as the war front pressed closer; the prisoners were dispersed in railway transports (freight cars) and evacuation marches to other concentration camps within the Reich. Many deaths ensued as a result of hunger, exhaustion, and shootings. Between 20 and 30 prisoners, mostly Russian and Polish, hid themselves in the camp in order to elude the evacuation; they were discovered and shot by the SS commando that had remained behind to finish the task of clearing the camp and to burn its written records.

The commandants of Gross-Rosen met diverse fates after the war. Johannes Hassebroek was sentenced to life imprisonment by a British military court, but was released by 1954. His successor, Arthur Rödl, committed suicide in 1945 in Stettin. Preliminary proceedings were conducted by the state prosecutor's office against the last commandant, Wilhelm Gideon, but they were discontinued.

W. D.

Grosz, George, b. Berlin, July 26, 1893; d. there, July 6, 1959, German painter and graphic artist. After studies in art, Grosz served for a while as a soldier (1914–1915 and 1917). A co-founder of the Dadaist circle in Berlin (1917) and a member of the Communist party as of 1918, Grosz developed an unmistakable style, which made him the most trenchant and critical graphic artist and painter of his society, especially in his collections *Ecce Homo* (Behold the Man; 1922), *Der Spiesser-Spiegel* (The Philistine's Mirror; 1925), and *Das neue Gesicht der herrschenden Klasse* (The New Face of the Ruling Class; 1930). In January 1933 he emigrated to the United States, where he worked as an art teacher. In Germany his work was outlawed as "degenerate," and National Socialist critics labeled it as "pictures inciting to class conflict" and as "consciously primitive." Grosz was de-

George Grosz.

prived of his German citizenship in 1938. He returned to Germany only a few weeks before his death.

Grüber, Heinrich, b. Stolberg (Rhineland), June 24, 1891; d. Berlin, November 29, 1975, German Evangelical theologian; an activist in pastoral and social work. In 1937 Grüber established for the Confessing Church the so-called Grüber Bureau for Racially Persecuted Evangelical Christians in his parish at Kaulsdorf, near Berlin. He helped such persons to emigrate and to find employment opportunities abroad, cared for the children of people in jail, and kept up a running battle with Adolf EICHMANN's Jewish bureau in the Reich Security Main Office. For his actions, Grüber was interned in the Sachsenhausen and Dachau concentration camps from 1940 to 1943, yet after his release he immediately resumed his assistance.

In 1945 Grüber was made provost of the Marienkirche (Church of Mary) in East Berlin, and from 1949 to 1958 he was the plenipotentiary of the Evangelical Church to the government of the German Democratic Republic (GDR). Grüber established the Evangelical Aid Office for former racially persecuted people; he also fell out with the GDR authorities over Communist policies. Later, in the Federal Republic of Germany, he opposed militarism and nuclear arms. In 1960 Grüber testified in Jerusalem in the Eichmann trial. To the very end, he remained tireless in warning against the dangers of NEO-NAZISM. He wrote *Erinnerungen aus sieben Jahrzehnten* (Memories of Seven Decades; 1968).

Heinrich Grüber.

Gustaf Gründgens.

"Grün" ("Green"), military code name for an attack on CZECHOSLOVAKIA; it was first ordered on April 21 and May 30, 1938.

Gründgens, Gustaf, b. Düsseldorf, October 22, 1899; d. Manila (Philippines), October 7, 1963 (suicide), German actor, director, and theater head. With experience in provincial theater (Halberstadt and Kiel), in 1923 Gründgens joined the Hamburg Kammerspielen (Intimate Theater), then in 1928 moved to Berlin. From 1925 to 1928 he was married to Erika MANN. Gründgens enjoyed his first triumphs in the 1930s: he was spellbinding as Edelganove in Fritz Lang's film *M* (1931); on the stage he shone especially as Mephisto in Goethe's *Faust* (first performance in this role, 1932). Just as shadowy as the characters he chose and embodied with such verve was the role he played in the Third Reich: a splendid artist in the service of world culture, and simultaneously an irreplaceable culture bearer for the National Socialist state that was precisely the bitter enemy of this world culture.

In spite of his eccentric private life and political thought, Gründgens was made stage manager of the State Theater at the Gendarmenmarkt in 1934, and general manager of the Prussian State Theater in 1936; like all German theaters, these had been "synchronized" under the control of the REICH THEATER CHAMBER. That same year Hermann Göring, his patron, awarded him the title of Prussian state councillor "in grateful appreciation of your services for the cultivation of the performing arts in the National Socialist state." Also in 1936, his former brother-in-law

Klaus MANN, in Amsterdam, portrayed in his novel *Mephisto* the image of the Mephisto Gründgens who, devoured by ambition, becomes an accomplice of National Socialism. It was a caricature arising out of the bitterness of emigrants. What is true is that Gründgens allowed himself to be used by the NS state in order to be able to remain true to his colleagues as a friend and to himself as an artist. To protect his theater company, including its "non-Aryan" members, from the clutches of the regime, he made some reluctant concessions, such as playing the role of the British colonial secretary Joseph Chamberlain in the propaganda film OHM KRÜGER (1941). Yet he preserved "an oasis of the mind in the brown desert" (F. Luft). After a brief internment in a Soviet camp (Russian officers had misunderstood his title of "general" manager [*Generalintendant*]), Gründgens continued his artistic work as director of Düsseldorf's theater, and later of Hamburg's Schauspielhaus. One of the high points of his career, the staging of *Faust* in Hamburg, is preserved in a film version.

M. F.

Grynszpan, Herschel, b. Hannover, March 28, 1921, Jewish assassin. In 1911 Grynszpan's family evaded antisemitic excesses in Poland by going to Germany; there they were overtaken by National Socialism. The young man went in 1936 to stay with relatives in Paris, where he received news of the deportation of former Polish Jews—including his family—from Germany to Poland. In revenge, Grynszpan wanted

Herschel Grynszpan.

to murder the German ambassador in Paris, but on November 7, 1938, he shot Ernst vom RATH, the legation secretary, instead. The National Socialists exploited the assault as a pretext for the KRISTALLNACHT pogrom. In 1940, Grynszpan was delivered to Germany and confined to the concentration camp at Sachsenhausen and later at the Berlin-Moabit Prison. He survived because the National Socialists until the end planned a show trial against him as proof of their thesis of the war guilt of "world Jewry."

Grzesinski, Albert, b. Treptow an der Tollense, July 28, 1879; d. New York, December 31, 1947, German politician and trade unionist (of the metalworkers). Grzesinski was chairman of the Kassel Workers' and Soldiers' Council in 1918–1919. From 1922 to 1924 he was director of the Prussian State Police Office. With an interim appointment (1926–1930) as Prussian interior minister, in 1925–1926 and from 1930 to 1932 he was Berlin's chief of police, a position that made him a main enemy of Berlin Gauleiter Joseph GOEBBELS. Grzesinski strove to democratize the administrative and police apparatus and to keep the National Socialists under control. When the Papen government removed him from office on July 20, 1932 (*see* PRUSSIAN COUP), an important internal political bastion against the spread of the NSDAP fell. Grzesinski emigrated first to Switzerland in 1933, and then to France, where he worked in the exile Social Democratic Party. In 1937 he managed to reach New York via Peru.

Guarantor (*Garant*), word borrowed back from the French language (which had taken it from Old High German) to refer to one who offered security or guarantee (*Bürge; Gewährsmann*). In National Socialist usage it became a favorite term, used especially in cliché formulas referring to (Hitler) youth as a "guarantor of the future." During the war, attempts were made to tone down this hyperbole. A press advisory of February 2, 1940, emphasized that in consideration of the combat troops, such "premature laurels for youth" should be avoided, since the young people had not yet reached the front and thus it was inappropriate to "heroicize" them in advance.

Guardian (*Walter*), term in National Socialist usage for functionaries (*see* SOVEREIGNTY BEARERS) in the NSDAP and its affiliated associations or closely allied organizations. The word *Walter*, which in Middle High German meant something like ruler or master (*Beherrscher*), had long since nearly disappeared from the German language; it was again made fashionable, in keeping with the linguistic enthusiasm for Germanness within National Socialism. It was used to denote functionaries on the level of divisional organizational units (as in *Reichs-Walter, Gau-Walter, Block-Walter*, and the like) or of functional competencies (such as *Kassen-Walter* [guardian of the treasury], *Kultur-Walter* [culture guardian], or *Schulungs-Walter* [schooling guardian]).

Guderian, Heinz, b. Kulm, June 17, 1888; d. Schwangau bei Füssen, May 14, 1954, German general. Beginning in 1919, Guderian served in the Reichswehr. Promoted to colonel in 1933,

Heinz Guderian.

he dedicated himself to building up a modern tank force. "Speedy [*schnelle*] Heinz" developed the concept of tank warfare (in *Achtung, Panzer!* [Attention, Tanks!]; 1937) and, after a series of rapid promotions, became general of the armored troops in 1938. The panzer units that he led were decisively involved in the course of the BLITZKRIEG against Poland and France. Owing to differences with Hitler over the deployment of armored troops during the Russian Campaign, Guderian was relieved of his command on Christmas Day of 1941. In 1943 he was appointed general inspector of the armored troops, and after July 20, 1944, chief of the army's General Staff. As a member of the army's Honor Court, which was established after the TWENTIETH OF JULY, Guderian took part in handing over hundreds of soldiers to the *Volk* Court. After he spoke in favor of a ceasefire with the Western powers in early 1945, he was dismissed on March 28 of that year. In prison until 1948, he engaged afterward in political commentary on the defense situation of the Federal Republic of Germany—for example, in *Kann Westeuropa verteidigt werden?* (Can Western Europe Be Defended?; 1951).

Guernica, northern Spanish town in the Basque region, 20 km (about 12 miles) to the east of Bilbao. During the SPANISH CIVIL WAR, Guernica was destroyed on April 26, 1937, by airplanes of the CONDOR LEGION. The town became known throughout the world as a symbol of barbaric air war, especially through Picasso's painting *Guernica.* The attack, by nine aircraft with a total of 7,950 kg of bombs, was intended to support the advance of Franco's troops toward Bilbao. Instead of military targets outside the town, Guernica itself was hit and 71 percent of it was destroyed. Details of the attack are still being debated: for example, the count of fatalities varies between 100 and 1,600 people. It is also possible that part of the destruction took place only after the bombardment, this time by Republican militiamen and Basque miners (*dinamiteros*), in order to leave behind nothing useful for the advancing enemy, in line with the "scorched earth" principle.

Ba.

Guilt, Confession of. *See* Stuttgart Confession of Guilt.

Gundolf, Friedrich (originally, Gundelfinger), b. Darmstadt, June 20, 1880; d. Heidelberg, July 12, 1931, German literary historian and writer. Gundolf gained his professorial qualification (*Habilitation*) in Heidelberg with a significant work, "Shakespeare and the German Spirit." He was named an assistant (*ausserordentlicher*) professor in 1916, then a full professor in 1920 at Heidelberg. Gundolf was shaped by his friendship with Stefan GEORGE, whom he acknowledged in his *Gefolgschaft und Jüngertum* (Followers and Disciples), and he made a name for himself with unsurpassed biographies of German poets (*Goethe*, 1916; *Kleist*, 1923). As a student, Joseph Goebbels admired Gundolf—into whose seminar he was accepted in 1920—despite the latter's Jewish ancestry, on account of his nationalist utterances during the First World War. Gundolf gave Goebbels the topic for

Guernica. Painting by Picasso.

Friedrich Gundolf.

Hans Friedrich Karl Günther.

his doctoral thesis ("Wilhelm von Schütz—A Contribution to the History of Drama in the Romantic School"). Because he was exempted from the requirement of administering examinations, Gundolf did not serve as Goebbels's doctoral adviser; Professor Max von Waldberg did. Gundolf was in any case little impressed by Goebbels, whose awakening antisemitism was fed by the latent rejection. During the Third Reich, Gundolf's writings were outlawed as "lacking in foundation."

Gunskirchen, annex camp of the MAUTHAUSEN concentration camp; it was the destination of numerous evacuation marches from other camps as Allied troops closed in during 1945. Thousands of inmates perished in these marches, and even after the liberation of the camp by United States troops on May 5, 1945, some 3,000 of the debilitated prisoners died.

Günther, Hans Friedrich Karl, b. Freiburg im Breisgau, February 16, 1891; d. there, September 25, 1968, German anthropologist. With his extremely successful *Rassenkunde des deutschen Volkes* (Race Lore of the German *Volk;* 1922), which by 1943 had been published in 270,000 copies, Günther harked back to the theories of Count Arthur de GOBINEAU and Houston Stewart CHAMBERLAIN. There were, to be sure, no more pure races, but the ideal type of the Nordic Aryan could again be approximated by avoiding further miscegenation, in particular with the "destructive" Jewish elements, and through the single-minded NORDIC UPGRADING of the German *Volk.* Thus Günther provided the ideal theoretical basis for National Socialist racism; he

was appointed to a professorship in Jena by the Thuringian interior minister, Wilhelm Frick, as early as 1930.

After the Seizure of Power, Günther moved to Berlin, becoming director of the Institute for Race Lore, Ethnic Biology, and Regional Sociology there; in 1940 he accepted a teaching post in Freiburg. For developing his theory on the connections between race and character and thereby culture (as in *Führeradel durch Sippenpflege* [Führer Nobility through the Cultivation of Clans]; 1936), Günther—who was known as "Race-Günther"—received numerous honors, including the 1935 Prize of the NSDAP for science and, in 1941, the Goethe Medal. After the war he continued to set down his ideas and republished several of his older titles, such as his 1934 book *Frömmigkeit nordischer Artung* (The Piety of the Nordic Type), in 1963.

Gurs, internment camp in southern France, at the foot of the Pyrenees; it was established at first for the detention of internees during the SPANISH CIVIL WAR. After the French Campaign, the Vichy government pledged to round up the Jews of Alsace-Lorraine (around 8,000), and assembled them in Gurs. Contrary to the agreement that had been made, Gauleiter Josef BÜRCKEL (of Westmark), who was also chief of the civil administration in Lorraine, and his fellow *Gauleiter* Robert WAGNER (Baden), also chief of the civil administration in Alsace, took the opportunity to make their German territories as well "Jew-free." On October 22, 1940, nine transport trains took more than 7,000 Jews deported from the Rhineland into unoccupied

France, where they were brought to the over-crowded Gurs camp over the objections of French officials. By mid-1942, a total of 1,260 of the internees had died. In September of that year several transports went from Gurs through DRANCY to the extermination camps, and in early March 1943, 1,814 more Jewish prisoners from Gurs followed them into the gas chambers of Auschwitz.

Gürtner, Franz, b. Regensburg, January 26, 1881; d. Berlin, January 29, 1941, German jurist and politician. From a petit-bourgeois background, Gürtner was a frontline officer in the First World War, and an (assistant) councillor in the Bavarian Justice Ministry (1909–1914 and 1920–1922). Gürtner belonged to the conservative camp that strove to set aside democracy in favor of an authoritarian regime. In 1922 he became a member of the Bavarian Center party (later the German National People's Party [DNVP]). Personally, he favored a moderate policy of overcoming democracy gradually, but as Bavarian justice minister (from 1922 to 1932) he supported his party in its cooperation with the radical Right. Gürtner favored the growth of the National Socialist movement in that he concealed the unequal handling of the Left and the Right by the justice system, and in his advocacy of tolerance toward armed units, including the SA. In 1932 Papen appointed him Reich justice minister, a post he held until his death.

Initially still believing that the NS regime would return to orderly conditions, Gürtner achieved individual successes in the defense of legal principles: thus, in trials against clergymen (1935–1939), he was able to assure relatively fair treatment, and at times to impose punishments upon party members. On the other hand, he signed NS laws and used his personal mediation to gain cooperation with the regime from conservative jurists. The SS crimes recalled to Gürtner "Oriental sadism," which was alien to "German sensibilities." Nonetheless, his attempts to subordinate the concentration camps to legal control failed. Hitler and the entire party leadership took part in the state ceremony following Gürtner's death.

Sch.

Gusset Decree (*Zwickelerlass*), addition to the police bathing ordinance prescribed by the deputy Reich commissioner for Prussia, Franz BRACHT, on October 24, 1932, and presented to the state legislature on November 1. Never really enforced, the decree produced heated and indeed satirical debates in the media and among the public, since with unconsciously comic precision it prescribed gussets for bathing suits in order to prevent "the delineation of sexual parts."

Gustloff, Wilhelm, b. Schwerin, January 30, 1895; d. Davos (Switzerland), February 4, 1936, German politician. In 1917 Gustloff became an employee of the Swiss Physical and Meteorological Research Institute in Davos, and there became a member in 1921 of the German Völkisch Defensive and Offensive League. In 1929 he joined the NSDAP, and in 1932 he became the Country Group Leader (*Landesgruppenleiter*) of the NSDAP's FOREIGN ORGANIZATION in Switzerland. Gustloff was an unconditional Hitler

Franz Gürtner.

Renaming of a street in honor of Wilhelm Gustloff.

adherent who, along with his fellow believers, became ever more provocative. On February 4, 1936, he was shot in his home by a Jewish student, David FRANKFURTER, who did not know Gustloff but wanted through him to strike a blow at National Socialist persecutors of Jews. German propaganda made a conspiracy of "world Jewry" out of the deed. Because of the imminent RHINELAND OCCUPATION, Hitler behaved discreetly at the state funeral, but he made use of a planned Strength through Joy ship that originally was to have borne his own name by rechristening it the WILHELM GUSTLOFF. To avoid further conflicts with the NSDAP, Switzerland temporarily banned its organization there on February 18, 1936.

Gütt, Arthur, b. Michelau (West Prussia), August 17, 1891; d. Stade, March 2, 1949, German population policymaker. A physician, in 1923 Gütt became a *Kreisleiter* (district leader) of the NSDAP in Labiau, East Prussia. A proponent of RACIAL HYGIENE and the doctrine of hereditary health, in 1933 he became head of the division of public health (*Volksgesundheit*) in the Interior Ministry. He wrote a commentary to the Law for the Prevention of HEREDITARILY ILL OFFSPRING and supported FORCED STERILIZATION. In 1934 he was promoted to ministerial director. The following year he became director of the Office for Population Policy and the Doctrine of Hereditary Health on the staff of the *Reichsführer-SS* (Himmler). Gütt wrote tracts on population policy, including "Culling and Life Selection in Their Significance for the Cultivation of Hereditary Health and Race" (1934) and

Arthur Gütt.

"Service to the Race as the Task of State Policy" (1934). On his own request he retired in 1939, but in 1940 he was promoted to SS-*Gruppenführer.*

Gymnastics (*Gymnastik*), systematic training in the body's movement and stance, without equipment or only with hand-held equipment such as balls or Indian clubs. It was ideologized in National Socialist education as GERMAN GYMNASTICS.

Gypsies (the Sinti and Rom groups; Ger., *Zigeuner*), term for the members of an originally (in some cases, to this day) nomadic ethnic minority that migrated from northwest India into Europe between A.D. 800 and 1000. From the 15th century on, large groups of Gypsies moved into German-speaking areas; because of their alien appearance, speech, and culture they met for the most part with mistrust. For example, as suspected Turkish spies, they were first outlawed by the Reichstag of the Holy Roman Empire in 1496–1497. In the following centuries, various German states issued hundreds of edicts against the Gypsies, who were looked upon as "a plague on the land," cannibals, kidnappers, and poisoners of streams; they were rounded up, "pulverized, branded," and could be executed without a trial. As late as 1899, a "Central Office to Combat the Gypsy Nuisance" (Zentrale zur Bekämpfung des Zigeuner-Unwesens) was founded. By 1926 it had gathered data, photographs, and fingerprints of more than 14,000 Gypsies.

The persecution, broadened by the Law to Combat Gypsies, Vagabonds, and the Work-shy of July 16, 1926, was considerably extended after 1933 by the National Socialists and bolstered by seemingly scientific information on Gypsies (*Tziganologie*). Because of their "alien [*andersartig*] Asiatic progenitors," Gypsies were classified as "racially inferior," and a warning was issued against intermarrying with them (*Archiv für Rassen- und Gesellschaftsbiologie* [Archive for Racial and Social Biology], 1937/1938). Beginning in the mid-1930s, the Research Institute for Racial Hygiene and Population Biology in Berlin-Dahlem, under the leadership of the Tübingen neurologist Robert Ritter, occupied itself with "hereditary research using a breeding population of mixed-breed Gypsies and asocial psychopaths" (financed in part by the German Research Foundation). It reported that the "quarter Gypsies and eighth Gypsies," as "bastards," were bearers of "inferior hereditary matter," and were "highly unbalanced, without character, unpredictable, undependable" (Ritter).

Through methods of racial diagnosis, thousands of such "Gypsy descendants" were tracked down, some of whom for generations had integrated into the "pure German" population, and had even served in the Wehrmacht or were NSDAP members. In contrast to most "Jewish mixed-breeds," they were handed over to concentration camps. The wholesale registration of Gypsies (who were not specifically mentioned in the NUREMBERG LAWS) began on December 8, 1938, with a circular from Himmler; their citizenship, like that of the Jews, was no longer recognized. As early as 1933, large numbers were gathered together in collection camps; from 1936 on, they were brought in increasingly large numbers into concentration camps (chiefly Dachau), and were deported by the thousands into the ghettos of occupied Poland as a result of the Resettlement Decree (*Umsiedlungserlass*) of April 27, 1940. With the goal of "total liquidation," Himmler on December 16, 1942, finally ordered the allocation of all Gypsies and mixed-breed Gypsies to the AUSCHWITZ-Birkenau extermination camp. There they were gassed, became victims of the "extermination through work" programs, suffered epidemics, or died after HUMAN EXPERIMENTS, which Josef Mengele, among others, performed on pairs of twins or in order to test new methods of sterilization. Altogether, National Socialist persecution cost 220,000 Gypsies their lives.

To the present day, Gypsy survivors strive, often fruitlessly, to be recognized as victims of NS tyranny. Their sufferings were long concealed by the millions numbered in the FINAL SOLUTION. The old prejudices have persisted beyond the end of the Third Reich. Even in the 1970s, German authorities, working with data from the NS Institute for Racial Hygiene, the Munich Central Office for Vagabonds, and other police offices, supported their views in part on the basis of documents from the Reich Central Office to Combat the Gypsy Nuisance.

H. H.

H

Habermann, Max, b. Altona (now Hamburg-Altona), March 21, 1885; d. Berlin, November 1944, German trade unionist. Originally a bookseller, Habermann joined the GERMAN NATIONAL SHOP ASSISTANTS' ASSOCIATION in 1907; from 1918 to 1933 he was on its executive committee and that of the German Trade Union Federation. A friend of Heinrich BRÜNING, Habermann hoped for a long while that he might win over at least the National Socialist left wing (*see* Gregor *and* Otto STRASSER) to constructive union work. After the Röhm Affair (June 30, 1934), however, he lost all illusions and sought contact with the opposition to Hitler, through Jakob KAISER. Habermann, who earned his livelihood from a small office-supplies shop, represented, together with Kaiser, the Christian nationalist faction in the social ideology of the conspirators of July 20, 1944. After the failed assassination attempt, he went underground but was captured by the Gestapo; he committed suicide while in prison.

Hácha, Emil, b. Trhové Sviny, July 12, 1872; d. Prague, June 1945, Czechoslovak politician. In 1925 Hácha was named first president of the supreme administrative court in Czechoslovakia. As successor to and opponent of Edvard BENEŠ, he became president of the Czechoslovak Republic on November 30, 1938. Under great pressure from Hitler, he concluded a "treaty of protection" with the German Reich on March 15, 1939, thereafter functioning as puppet president of the PROTECTORATE OF BOHEMIA AND MORAVIA until 1945. After the arrival of the Red Army, Hácha was arrested as a collaborator and killed without trial in prison.

Hadamar (near Limburg an der Lahn), one of the six "killing facilities" in the EUTHANASIA program. Hadamar was established in January 1941 to replace the GRAFENECK institution,

Emil Hácha with Reich Propaganda Minister Goebbels.

closed in December 1940. It opened under the code name "Facility E" (Anstalt E). The personnel came from Grafeneck. Surviving records indicate that 10,072 people were killed at Hadamar.

A. St.

Hadamovsky, Eugen, b. Berlin, December 14, 1904; d. eastern front, 1944, German radio politician. After serving with the free corps, Hadamovsky joined the NSDAP in 1930, becoming co-founder and president (1933) of the REICH ASSOCIATION OF GERMAN RADIO LISTENERS. In 1931 Goebbels put him in charge of radio (with the title *Funkwart* [Radio Warden]) in the Berlin *Gau*, and in 1932 made him head of the radio division in the Reich Propaganda Ministry. Hadamovsky made a name for himself with public attacks against the "mindless perversities" of the "men of the [Weimar] System-radio" (*see* SYSTEM ERA).

Immediately after the Seizure of Power, Hadamovsky organized the direct transmission of Hitler's appearances so perfectly that in 1933 Goebbels made him chief of RADIO GERMANY, and shortly thereafter Reich Program Direc-

Eugen Hadamovsky.

Werner von Haeften.

tor (*Reichssendeleiter*) and director of the Reich Radio Society. In the REICH RADIO CHAMBER Hadamovsky became vice president and chairman of the Television Work Group. As an unscrupulous careerist he "purified" German radio of everything "different, aestheticized, alien to the *Volk*" (*Abseitigen, Ästhetisierenden, Volksfremden*) and made it into a "Brown House of the German spirit," in which "the voice of the Führer" would be "the most important one." Because of personal differences, Hadamovsky fell out of favor with Goebbels in 1942. In late 1943 he volunteered for the Wehrmacht and died in Russia as a tank officer.

H. H.

Haeften, Hans-Bernd von, b. Berlin, December 18, 1905; d. there, August 15, 1944 (executed), German diplomat. Haeften entered the Foreign Service in 1933, and in 1940 became legation councillor for cultural policy in the Foreign Office, establishing ties there to Adam von TROTT ZU SOLZ and Adolf REICHWEIN. Haeften participated in the discussions on a postwar political order in the KREISAU CIRCLE. He was taken into custody after the July 20, 1944, attempt on Hitler's life, for which his brother Werner, an adjutant to Schenk von STAUFFENBERG, was shot. The *Volk* Court, before which Haeften called Hitler a great "executor of evil" (*Vollstrecker des Bösen*), condemned him to death on August 15, 1944.

Haeften, Werner von, b. Berlin, October 9, 1908; d. there, July 20, 1944 (executed), German opposition fighter and jurist. As a soldier,

Haeften was injured in the winter of 1942 and transferred to the Army High Command. He became adjutant to Schenk von STAUFFENBERG, whom he accompanied to the Führer's headquarters at Wolfsschanze on July 20, 1944. After the bomb attack, both men flew back to Berlin. Once its failure became known, Haeften was held at the War Ministry on Bendlerstrasse, on the order of Col. Gen. Friedrich FROMM, and shot shortly thereafter.

Hahn, Otto, b. Frankfurt am Main, March 8, 1879; d. Göttingen, July 28, 1968, German chemist. In 1910 Hahn became a professor in Berlin; from 1928 to 1945 he was director of the Kaiser Wilhelm Institute for Chemistry. Hahn

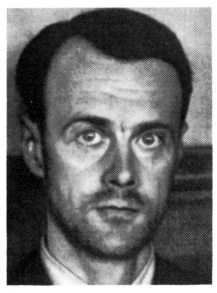

Hans-Bernd von Haeften.

Otto Hahn.

Franz Halder.

conducted research on such topics as the decay products of radioactive elements. In 1938 he and Friedrich Strassmann discovered the splitting of uranium nuclei with neutron bombardment, and thus created the crucial preconditions for building the ATOMIC BOMB. As chief of the institute he kept his distance from the National Socialists, and he helped his Jewish co-worker Lise Meitner to escape abroad. In 1945 Hahn, together with such scientists as Carl Friedrich von Weizsäcker and Werner HEISENBERG, was interned in England. He was allowed to return to Germany in 1946, and became the first president of the Max Planck Society (the successor to the KAISER WILHELM SOCIETY FOR THE ADVANCEMENT OF THE SCIENCES). Hahn received numerous academic honors (notably, a Nobel prize, retroactive to 1944). Under the influence of the war and its effects, as well as the atomic bombardment of Hiroshima and Nagasaki, Hahn began a public campaign against nuclear arms and for the exclusively peaceful use of nuclear energy.

Hakenkreuz. *See* Swastika.

Halder, Franz, b. Würzburg, June 30, 1884; d. Aschau/Chiemgau, April 2, 1972, German colonel general (July 19, 1940). Halder was a General Staff officer in the First World War. In the Reichswehr he served as an instructor in tactics. He was promoted from battery commander to major general (1934), lieutenant general, and quartermaster general (1936). On September 1, 1938, Halder relieved Ludwig BECK as commander of the Army General Staff. (Beck had been forced to step down for opposing Hitler.)

As a nationalist and conservative Prussian officer, Halder did not initially share Hitler's war plans; nonetheless he planned and led Hitler's campaigns in Poland, France, the Balkans, and Russia with "untiring energy."

Halder came into increasing conflict with Hitler over strategic matters once the Führer assumed direct supreme command over the army in 1941. Because Halder opposed the decision to move troops from another front to Stalingrad, he was relieved of duty by Hitler on September 24, 1942. After 1938 Halder maintained loose ties to opposition circles within the military, but as a correct officer who felt bound by the oath of loyalty to Hitler he rejected any active resistance. Nonetheless, after the assassination attempt of July 20, 1944, he was arrested because of his connections to Beck and Erwin von WITZLEBEN, and sent to a concentration camp, where he was later freed by the Americans. After the war Halder wrote several books on military science and biography, including *Hitler als Feldherr* (Hitler as War Lord; 1949).

Half Jew (*Halbjude*), racial category according to the NUREMBERG LAWS (and successive ordinances), in which distinctions were made between the GERMAN-BLOODED, "Jewish MIXED-BREEDS of the second degree" (quarter Jews, with one Jewish grandparent), and "Mischlings of the first degree" (half Jews, with two Jewish grandparents). Anyone with three or more Jewish grandparents counted as a full Jew (*Volljude*). Half Jews were considered only conditionally "worthy of military service" and could at best serve only as reserves ("Ersatzreserve

II'') or with the militia (Landwehr). Half-Jewish children were banned from higher, middle, and upper-level schools after 1941. According to the decisions of the WANNSEE CONFERENCE of February 20, 1942, half Jews were to be "equated with Jews in terms of the FINAL SOLUTION of the Jewish question," although this took place only to a limited extent.

Halifax, Edward Frederick Lindley Wood, Viscount (1934), Earl (1944), b. Powdersham Castle (Devonshire), April 16, 1881; d. Garrowby Hall (Yorkshire), December 23, 1959, English politician. In 1910 Halifax was elected a Conservative Member of Parliament; in 1921–1922 he was parliamentary state secretary for the colonies; from 1925 to 1931, viceroy in India; in 1935 he became war minister. In 1938 Neville CHAMBERLAIN named Halifax to succeed Anthony EDEN as foreign minister; he continued the British APPEASEMENT policy, wishing to avoid military conflict with National Socialist Germany. He did not see through Hitler's plans for conquest: as he wrote later, one tapped about "like a blind man who attempted to find his way through a swamp, while from the shores everyone shouted different information about the nearest danger zones." Because Halifax considered Hitler's revisionist goals to be justified to a certain extent, he hoped to stop German expansionist policies through concessions in the MUNICH AGREEMENT. Only after the "demolition" of so-called rump ("remainder") Czechoslovakia did he recognize that Hitler "could be tamed only with force." In 1940 Halifax resigned as foreign minister and became ambassador to the United States (until 1946).

Halt, Karl Ritter von, b. Munich, June 2, 1891; d. there, August 5, 1964, German sports functionary. Halt's title of nobility (*Ritter,* knight) came from his being awarded the Order of the Knights of Max Joseph in the First World War. He was a member of the eight-man rowing team at the 1912 Olympics, and by 1921 he had several times been German decathlon champion. After studying political science, Halt went into banking, but he also coached German track-and-field athletes at all national competitions from 1924 to 1939. After 1929 he was a member of the International Olympics Committee (IOC), and as president he was in charge of organizing the 1936 Winter Games, as well as being responsible for such organizations as the International Handball Alliance and the German Bobsled and Toboggan Alliance.

Halt was involved in the SYNCHRONIZATION of

Karl Ritter von Halt.

German SPORTS through his work with Hans von TSCHAMMER and as head of the track-and-field division in the National Socialist GERMAN REICH LEAGUE FOR PHYSICAL EXERCISES. His contributions were rewarded when he was named commissioner and Reich Sports Führer (*kommissarischer Reichssportführer*) on September 18, 1944. After the war the Soviets interned Halt at the former Buchenwald camp until 1950. He then resumed his IOC activity. Despite journalistic attacks on his past, he successfully managed Germany's readmission to the Olympics in 1952 and aided in rebuilding the Olympic teams from both Germanys.

Hamm, Eduard, b. Passau, October 16, 1879; d. Berlin, September 23, 1944, German politician. Hamm became Bavarian commerce minister in 1919, state secretary in the Reich Chancellery in 1923, Reich economics minister in 1924, and secretary general of the Congress for Industry and Trade (Industrie- und Handelstag) in 1925; he returned to private life in 1933. Hamm, who at the time of the Hitler Putsch had identified the state based on law as the highest political principle, viewed the National Socialist dictatorship as a national misfortune. He joined the circle around Carl GOERDELER, and was seized on September 2, 1944, in the wave of arrests that followed the failed assassination attempt in July. In order not to compromise others while under torture, he killed himself by jumping out of a window of the Lehrterstrasse jail.

Hammerstein-Equord, Kurt Baron von, b. Hinrichshagen (Mecklenburg), September 26,

Kurt Baron von Hammerstein-Equord.

1878; d. Berlin, April 25, 1943, German colonel general (1934). A General Staff officer in the First World War, after 1918 Hammerstein-Equord served on the staff of Armed Forces Minister Gustav NOSKE, among other posts. He opposed the KAPP PUTSCH in 1920. In 1930 he became chief of the Army Staff through the recommendation of his friend Kurt von SCHLEICHER; both men hoped to "tame" the NSDAP through its participation in government under the "control" of a Reichswehr that was independent of partisan politics. In 1933 Hammerstein-Equord conveyed to President Hindenburg the qualms of the army hierarchy regarding the naming of Hitler to the Reich chancellorship. Thereafter, however, he found little military support; discouraged, he retired in late January 1934. In 1939 Hitler called him back to the army and for a short time gave him supreme command over an army group on the western front. Hammerstein-Equord, who had long been in touch with such representatives of the military opposition as Franz HALDER and Ludwig BECK, planned to take Hitler captive when he visited the troops. Before this was possible, Hammerstein-Equord was permanently relieved of duty; thereafter he lived in self-imposed isolation in Berlin.

Hamsun, Knut, b. Lom (Gudbransdal), August 4, 1859; d. Nørholm, near Grimstad, February 19, 1952, Norwegian writer. After a harsh childhood, work as an occasional laborer, and travels through America, Hamsun achieved a literary breakthrough with the novel *Hunger* (1890; German translation, 1891) and the story "Mysteries" (1892; German translation, 1914). In 1920 he won a Nobel prize for *The Growth of the Soil* (1917; German translation, 1918); his epic masterpiece was a "vagabond" trilogy (1927–1933).

Hamsun's appreciation of the simple life, his closeness to nature, and the anti-American and anticivilization ethos of his "heroes" made him one of the most popular authors in the German YOUTH MOVEMENT and in the *völkisch* camp. The National Socialists, too, praised his "service to the earth," but missed the "will to mastery" expected of the "Northerner," and criticized his attraction "to the mostly inferior . . . woman."

Hamsun saw in National Socialism the hope for opposition to Anglo-Saxon materialism, and thus he took a positive position on Vidkun QUISLING's Norwegian fascist National Unity party. After the German occupation in 1940 Hamsun called for an end to resistance because he believed the National Socialist promises of a privileged position for Norway in the putative future "Great-German World Community." Untiringly he defended his condemned fellow Norwegians with the German authorities, and, at a meeting with Hitler in Vienna in 1943, urged in vain the removal of Reich Commissioner Josef TERBOVEN, whose "Prussianism" he condemned. After the war, Hamsun was defamed for his friendliness toward Germany; in 1947 he was sentenced to a large fine. His report on the trial, *On Overgrown Paths* (1949; German translation, 1950), is a devastating document of wreckage from a political brutality that was never understood.

Knut Hamsun.

Hanfstaengl, Ernst, b. Munich, February 11, 1887; d. there, November 6, 1975, German publicist and politician. Hanfstaengl studied at Harvard and other universities, returning to Germany in 1921. In the same year he joined the NSDAP as a "fervid nationalist." An eccentric and cosmopolite who dabbled in painting and literature and wrote marches for SA bands, he soon became part of Hitler's most intimate circle of friends. Diverting, tending toward clownishness, and sociable, Hanfstaengl (called "Putzi" by his friends) was a favored interlocutor. Hitler also used Hanfstaengl's contacts with the upper bourgeoisie, in part to attract occasional large contributions to the NSDAP.

Because of his good contacts with foreign journalists, Hanfstaengl worked for several years as the party's foreign press chief and propagandist abroad. In 1934 he explained the Seizure of Power to foreign correspondents as a *völkisch* revolution, after which Germans would have to experience a "blood cure" (*Blutkur*) that would transform their "supernational" culture into an "intranational" one with a *völkisch* basis. Hanfstaengl's close relationship with Hitler led finally to jealous intrigues that made him fear for his life. In 1937 he fled to England, later working in the United States as an adviser in psychological warfare against the Third Reich. In 1946 he returned to Germany, where he felt like a "political outsider." His memoirs, *Zwischen Weissem und Braunem Haus* (Between the White and the Brown House; 1970), describe in great detail his relationship with Hitler.

Hanke, Karl, b. Lauban (Silesia), August 24, 1903; d. near Neudorf, June 1945, German politician. In 1928 Hanke became a trade school teacher; he was dismissed in 1931 "for NSDAP activity." After he joined the party in 1928 he quickly worked his way up through the Berlin NSDAP. He became head of the *Gau* organizations, was one of Goebbels's closest associates in the Reich propaganda directorate, and served in the Reichstag after 1932. After the Seizure of Power, Goebbels named Hanke his personal reporter and secretary in the Propaganda Ministry; in 1937 Hanke became ministerial director, then state secretary, and at the same time Reich Senator for Culture and second vice president of the REICH CULTURE CHAMBER.

Hanke's rapid rise to become one of the most influential makers of German culture policy ended because of personal difficulties with Goebbels. In 1941 he was transferred to Lower Silesia as *Gauleiter* and provincial president

Karl Hanke.

(*Oberpräsident*). There he used fanatical slogans to urge the populace to persevere in the struggle for "Fortress Breslau." As a result Hitler, in his 1945 testament, named the zealous National Socialist and SS-*Standartenführer* Himmler's successor as *Reichsführer-SS*. Hanke was able to flee from encircled Breslau, but he was captured by Czech partisans, and was later killed while attempting to flee as an anonymous SS man.

Hans Schemm Prize, most important award for National Socialist books for children and youth. Instituted in 1936 on the first anniversary of the death of Hans SCHEMM, state minister and leader of NS teachers, it was intended as a "means to form the German person, the German *Volk* of the next century." The prize was meant to encourage especially texts that educated youth in the spirit of "the will to defend and the readiness to fight." Prizewinners included some authors remembered after 1945, such as Otto Boris, Fritz Steuben (*see* Erhard WITTEK), and Alfred WEIDEMANN, who won because he glorified labor duty as a "male education community."

Hans Westmar, einer von vielen (Hans Westmar, One of Many), German film (1933), directed by Franz Wenzler, script by H. H. EWERS, with Emil Lohkamp, Carla Bartheel, and Paul WEGENER. The film—its subtitle was "A German Fate from the Year 1929"—was announced in the Berlin *Lokal-Anzeiger* (Local Advertiser) with the words: "At a time when certain segments of the world abroad do not want to see what is beneath a brownshirt, namely, the heart of

Emil Lohkamp as Hans Westmar.

a political fighter, the pulsebeat of a believer, . . . a German film will demonstrate what
it means to conquer Germany." The SA melo-
drama about Hans Westmar, who sacrifices his
life in the struggle for the "Red Berlin of
the SYSTEM ERA," was originally to have been
a Horst WESSEL film. Goebbels, who had
sketched out the idea of a sentimental glorification of "the most famous martyr of the National
Socialist movement," found the film "well
made, but too profane" at its advance showing.
Accordingly, he banned the film on October 9,
1933, and ordered its reworking. On November
2 Goebbels lifted the ban with the explanation
that the new title would avert direct connections with Wessel's life and death. Only the
hero's initials (H. W.), which remained the
same, gave a hint of the original film idea.

M. F.

Hanussen, Jan Erik (pseud. of Herschmann
Steinschneider), b. Bohemia, 1889; d. near Zos-
sen, March 24, 1933, Austrian clairvoyant. Hanussen had begun a criminal career as a pick-
pocket and swindler when, in the late 1920s, he
discovered his talent as a clairvoyant. In Berlin
he founded a "Palace of the Occult" on Lietzen-
burger Strasse. During this time of crisis he
quickly made a career as "adviser" to the rich.
Despite his Jewish background he attempted to
gain a place with the rising National Socialist
movement by calling himself a "Nordic seer"
and cultivating a friendship with SA Gruppenführer Wolf von HELLDORF, whom he several
times helped out of a predicament by extending

credit. When Hanussen began bragging about
this connection, he was taken captive by a mobile SA squad and shot in the woods.

Harbig, Rudolf, b. Dresden, November 8, 1913;
d. eastern front, March 5, 1944 (in combat),
German track-and-field athlete. As a world-
champion middle-distance runner, Harbig was
one of the most popular athletes in the Third
Reich. At the 1936 Olympic Games he won the
bronze in the 4-×-400-m relay; he was seven
times a German champion, and in 1939 he set
world records at 400 m (46.0 seconds) and 800
m (1:46.6 minutes); his 800-m record stood until
1955.

Hardness (*Härte*), catchword from National Socialist propaganda. In general usage, "hardness"
had both positive and negative connotations. To
describe a central character trait of the "combative German," the word was used only in a
positive sense: "The hardest man is just hard
enough for the iron future" (Alfred Rosenberg).
For poetic circumlocutions to describe in particular the toughness required of German youth,
images of military technology served: for example, "hard as Krupp steel," to encompass both
physical hardening and lack of emotional sensi-
tivity. The ultimate purpose of this hardness is
exemplified by Hitler's use of language on August 22, 1939, regarding the Wehrmacht commanders' frame of mind in the Polish Campaign:
"Close your heart to pity. Brutally advance.
Right is with the stronger. The greatest
hardness . . ."

Rudolf Harbig.

Harlan, Veit, b. Berlin, September 22, 1899; d. Capri, April 13, 1964, German actor and director. The son of a banker, Harlan went into the theater as a young man, working as an actor at the Berlin State Theater (1924–1934) and, after 1927, occasionally appearing in films as well. Here he ultimately found the work as a director that suited him best, making his directorial debut in 1934 with *Krach im Hinterhaus* (Noise in the Back Building). Further "little films" (Harlan's term: *Filmchen*) followed, until Propaganda Minister Goebbels discovered him through the Ufa film *Der Herrscher* (The Master; 1937, with Emil JANNINGS), and made him the star director of National Socialism.

Few could use the film medium as unobtrusively as Harlan to convey the opinion of the rulers as the ruling opinion. The director of the antisemitic agitprop film JUD SÜSS (1940), the paean to a hero *Der grosse König* (The Great King; 1940), and the morale-building film KOLBERG (1945) later complained that his art had been misused by the National Socialists; yet his monumental, melodramatic pictures were often in fact aesthetically complicit. Nonetheless, after the war Harlan was classified as "exonerated." With his third wife and favorite actress, Kristina SÖDERBAUM, he continued his work in such films as *Anders als du und ich* (Different than You and I; 1957), a film against homosexuals. His memoirs, *Im Schatten meiner Filme* (In the Shadows of My Films), were published posthumously in 1966.

Harnack, Arvid, b. Darmstadt, May 24, 1901; d. Berlin-Plötzensee, December 22, 1942 (executed), German economist and opposition fighter. Harnack's studies in political economy took him to the United States, where he married an American literature professor, Mildred Fish (b. Milwaukee, September 16, 1902; d. Berlin-Plötzensee, February 16, 1943 [executed]). After his return to Germany, Harnack entered the Economics Ministry. In 1931 he belonged to the "Working Group to Study the Soviet Planned Economy"; he hoped that Germany could play a role as intellectual and economic bridge between East and West.

After the National Socialist Seizure of Power the Harnacks became the center of a small circle of intellectuals, including some Communists, from which an opposition group arose. In 1936 Harnack, who had access to the most secret plans of German heavy industry, including armaments plants, made contact with the Soviet secret service; he thought that the "enormity of National Socialism" could be defeated only with help from outside. In 1939 he made an alliance between his group and that of Harro SCHULZE-BOYSEN; the new group, later persecuted by the Gestapo as the RED ORCHESTRA, combined resistance activities (sabotage, providing safe houses) with espionage for the USSR. After a long period of observation, Harnack, his wife, and numerous friends were arrested in 1942. As a leader of the Red Orchestra, Harnack was tortured, then condemned to death and executed for "high treason."

H. H.

Harnack, Ernst von, b. Marburg, July 15, 1888; d. Berlin, March 3, 1945 (executed), German opposition fighter. After the First World War, Harnack joined the Social Democratic Party (SPD). As a civil servant, he finally became administrative president of Merseburg, then temporarily retired under Franz von Papen, and was dismissed from public service in 1933. As the son of a theology professor, Harnack was compelled by Christian conviction to join the opposition group around Carl GOERDELER: "A system without humility and goodness is condemned to collapse." A longtime friend of Julius LEBER, Harnack mediated contacts among the Goerdeler circle, the SPD underground, and the military opposition. After the assassination attempt of July 20, 1944, Harnack defended the children of the arrested Leber, but was then himself condemned to death "for high treason" by the *Volk* Court on February 1, 1945.

Harnier, Adolf von, b. Munich, April 14, 1903; d. Straubing, May 12, 1945, German jurist.

Veit Harlan.

Adolf von Harnier.

Harnier studied law in Munich, where he was an eyewitness to the HITLER TRIAL in 1924. Converted to the Catholic faith in 1934, he was from the outset an opponent of National Socialism, especially its racial doctrines. As a lawyer he took on the defense of framed Jews and persecuted clerics, and thus came under the suspicion of the Gestapo. Accused by an informer of a conspiracy to promote a constitutional monarchy, Harnier was arrested in August 1939. He was held five years for investigation, and was then sentenced to 10 years in prison in 1944. He survived to be freed by the Americans, but died before his wife could bring him home.

Harris, Sir Arthur Travers, b. Cheltenham, April 13, 1892; d. Goring/Oxfordshire, April 5, 1984, British air marshal (January 1, 1946). In the First World War Harris was chief of a night-flyer squadron. He became commander of the Fourth Bomber Group in 1937, and in 1938–1939 he served as air force commander in Palestine. In 1940 Harris was promoted to deputy supreme commander of the Royal Air Force; in 1942 he was named chief of the British Bombing Command. His declared goal was the "destruction of the morale of the German people" through saturation bombing of Germany's largest cities. To this end he ordered the "thousand-bomber strike" against Cologne and intensified the AIR WAR through the nearly total destruction of such cities as Hamburg; the strategy culminated in the destruction of DRESDEN. Harris, who by the end of the war had become a bugbear ("Bomber Harris") in Germany, was also controversial among the Allies. Accused of the "waste of men and matériel," he was passed over for military decorations when the war ended. In 1953, however, he was made a baron for his accomplishments. In his book *Bomber Offensive* (1947), Harris justified saturation bombing on the ground that it had "shortened [the war] by at least a year."

Hartheim (also Hartheim Castle), located near Linz, Austria, on the Danube River, one of the six "killing facilities" of the EUTHANASIA program. It began functioning in May 1940, under the code name "Facility C" (*Anstalt C*), and operated longer than any other such facility. On December 11, 1944, a transport of "dis-

Ernst von Harnack.

Sir Arthur Travers Harris.

charged" prisoners, some from MAUTHAUSEN, were gassed as part of the so-called INVALID OPERATION. Surviving records indicate that in 1940 and 1941 alone, 18,269 people were killed at Hartheim.

A. St.

Hartmann, Erich, b. Weissach (Württemberg), April 19, 1922, German fighter pilot. Hartmann joined the Luftwaffe in 1940. In 1942 he went to the eastern front with the Fifty-second Fighter Squadron, quickly gaining a reputation there with his enthusiasm and skill. As one of the most decorated pilot officers, he was celebrated as an "ace" by German propaganda. In 1945 he was promoted to group commodore. With 352 officially recognized hits, Hartmann was considered "the most successful fighter pilot in the world." Between 1945 and 1955, he was a Soviet prisoner of war. After his return, he joined the Bundeswehr and became commodore of the "Richthofen" Fighter Squadron. On July 26, 1967, Hartmann was promoted to colonel, and on September 30, 1970, he voluntarily retired.

"Harvest Festival" (Aktion "Erntefest," Operation "Harvest Festival"), SS code name for the extermination of Jews in the Lublin district of the Generalgouvernement in late 1943, ostensibly to suppress terrorist unrest. In the course of 1943 the Jews in the Generalgouvernement manifested increasing resistance to the National Socialist extermination policies. After the WARSAW GHETTO UPRISING the inhabitants of the Białystok ghetto had actively defended themselves against so-called RESETTLEMENT; on August 2, 1943, an uprising took place among the "work Jews" (*Arbeitsjuden*) at the TREBLINKA extermination camp, followed by similar events at the SOBIBÓR camp on October 14. The NS authorities used these uprisings as an occasion to liquidate the Jews remaining in the Lublin district after the REINHARD OPERATION. Exceptions were made for workers needed in the armaments industry. Responsible for planning and directing the "Harvest Festival" operation was SS-Gruppenführer Jakob SPORRENBERG, who had succeeded Odilo GLOBOCNIK as SS and Police Leader in the Lublin district. The murders took place in the MAIDANEK camp, as well as in the Poniatowa and Trawniki camps. In early November 1943 at least 17,000 Jews were shot at Maidanek. A total of some 40,000 people were killed in the operation.

A. St.

Harvest Thanks Day (*Erntedanktag*), one of the most important days among the CELEBRATIONS IN THE NATIONAL SOCIALIST CALENDAR, usually

Harvest Thanks Day.

Erich Hartmann.

in early October. Like MAY DAY, through the expropriation of which workers were to be bound to the "*Volk* Community," the thanksgiving day was elevated to a legal state holiday and placed under NS administration in order officially to honor the peasantry, but also to obligate and integrate them ideologically and politically. Between 1933 and 1937 the central event took place on the BÜCKEBERG. Until the end of the war, the party then promoted local celebrations in cities and in the countryside. It was intended that the harvest celebration would give expression to the BLOOD AND SOIL ideology and would develop into a "SPECIES-RELATED" (*artgemäss*) and "customary" (*see* BRAUCHTUM UND SITTE) festival. Unlike the church-related thanksgiving days, the NS events never really gained a foothold.

K. V.

Harzburg Front (Harzburger Front), alliance between the NSDAP, the GERMAN NATIONAL PEOPLE'S PARTY (DNVP), STEEL HELMET, the ALL-GERMAN ASSOCIATION, and the so-called Fatherland associations. It was agreed to on October 11, 1931, in Bad Harzburg. The meeting included the leaders of the parties named—Hitler, Alfred HUGENBERG, and Franz SELDTE—as well as Hjalmar SCHACHT, Hans von SEECKT and other Reichswehr generals, and leaders of the

REICHSLAND LEAGUE. Initiated by Hugenberg, the meeting was meant to demonstrate the unity of the "National Opposition." Yet the front was united only in opposition to the BRÜNING government and the Weimar Republic itself; and even here the constituents supported no common political program. The bourgeois groups wanted to exploit the popular Hitler and his mass movement as "drummers" for their goals, while Hitler saw the alliance with the right-wing opposition as only a means of advancing his reputation and hiding his real aims from the public. The Harzburg Front could not unite on a common candidate for the election of a Reich president in the spring of 1932, and broke into factions, although it seemed to be revived in the government formed by Hitler on January 30, 1933 (*see* SEIZURE OF POWER).

R. B.

Hase, Paul von, b. Hannover, July 24, 1885; d. Berlin, August 8, 1944 (executed), German general and opposition fighter. On April 1, 1940, Hase was promoted to lieutenant general; the following November 15 he became commandant of Berlin. He was involved in the assassination plot of July 20, 1944; on a sign given by Schenk von STAUFFENBERG, Hase activated the Berlin guard battalion under Otto-Ernst REMER to support the coup and arrest Goebbels. After the

Harzburg Front. Hitler with entourage.

coup's failure, Hase was arrested and condemned to death by the *Volk* Court on August 8, 1944.

Hassell, Ulrich von, b. Anklam, November 12, 1881; d. Berlin-Plötzensee, September 8, 1944 (executed), German diplomat. Hassell entered the diplomatic corps in 1908, serving in various foreign posts, including that of ambassador to Rome from 1932 to 1938. He joined the German National People's Party (DNVP) in 1918, but his Prussian and nationalist convictions soon elicited sympathies for the National Socialists. Hassell joined the party in 1933 despite his disgust with its "vulgarity." A proponent of Germany's continental hegemony, he nonetheless condemned Hitler's risky foreign policy, and was ultimately dismissed as ambassador.

Hassell joined the opposition circles around Ludwig BECK and Carl GOERDELER. Once the war began he tried in vain to win over such generals as Brauchitsch and later Rommel for a negotiated peace. As a member of the executive committee of the Middle-European Economic Congress, Hassell was able to use numerous trips abroad to set forth his ideas for a post-Hitler Germany (such as the restoration of the monarchy); however, neither American representative Alexander Kirk nor British foreign minister Viscount HALIFAX was persuaded. In the case of a successful coup, Hassell was to have been foreign minister in a Goerdeler government. Under suspicion by the Gestapo since 1942, he was arrested shortly after the failed assassination attempt of July 20, 1944, and was condemned to death on September 8. His diaries from the years 1938 to 1944 were published posthumously in 1964 under the title *Vom anderen Deutschland* (From the Other Germany; translated as *The Von Hassell Diaries, 1938–1944*).

Hate (*Hass*), the most extreme degree of dislike or aversion, revalued positively in National Socialist usage as "heroic hate," because it derived from a "consciousness of duty and responsibility" and expressed "inexorable," "honest," and "courageous HARDNESS" (*Meyers Lexikon*, 1938). Contingent on heredity, such hate was imaginable only in the "Nordic race" and stood in "the most extreme opposition" to the "cowardly hate of Jewdom."

Haubach, Theodor, b. Darmstadt, September 15, 1896; d. Berlin, January 23, 1945 (executed), German opposition fighter. Haubach was an officer in the First World War. He then studied philosophy. A Social Democrat, he went from a leadership role in Hamburg's REICH BANNER "BLACK-RED-GOLD" (1923) to an editorial position with the SPD (Social Democratic Party of Germany) paper *Hamburger Echo*. He became press chief in the Berlin Police Presidium in 1930, but lost the post in 1933. Supporting himself as an insurance agent, Haubach was arrested and sentenced several times; his terms included two years in the Esterwegen camp. In 1943 he became involved with the KREISAU CIRCLE, working closely with his old political friends Carlo MIERENDORFF, Julius LEBER, and Wilhelm LEUSCHNER. The Gestapo arrested Haubach on August 8, 1944, after the failed

Ulrich von Hassell.

Theodor Haubach.

assassination attempt of July 20. Regarding the death sentence, he wrote that it could, "to be sure," destroy "the person of the opposition, but not the sentiments [*Gesinnung*] of the opposition."

Hauer, Jakob Wilhelm, b. Ditzingen (Württemberg), April 4, 1881; d. Tübingen, February 18, 1962, German religion scholar. At first a plasterer, Hauer trained to become a missionary, and labored in India from 1907 to 1911. The study of Indian religions relativized his Christianity, which he now understood as only one of the possible expressions of human religiosity. From 1925 to 1927 he was a professor at Marburg, and from 1927 to 1949 in Tübingen. His earlier tolerant and cosmopolitan attitude (in 1927 he founded the "Religious League of Humanity" [Religiöser Menschheitsbund]) became a constricted *völkisch* indolence, which brought him close to the National Socialists. The gathering of many sects into the GERMAN FAITH MOVEMENT (August 1933), which Hauer headed until 1936, stemmed from his initiative. The movement's growing intolerance toward everything Christian led to his withdrawal and to his alienation from National Socialism. Hauer publicly protested the persecution of Jews at the time of Kristallnacht. Nevertheless, through his writings (including *Deutsche Gottschau* [German View of God]; 1934) and early speeches he prepared the way for National Socialist ideology. For that reason he was dismissed as a professor after the war.

Hauptmann, Gerhart, b. Obersalzbrunn (Silesia), November 15, 1862; d. Agnetendorf (Riesengebirge), June 6, 1946, German writer. Hauptmann became one of Wilhelmine Germany's most important dramatists, and gained international acclaim (Nobel prize, 1912) with socially critical, naturalistic dramas such as *Die Weber* (The Weavers; 1892), about the Silesian weavers' uprising of 1844, and *Rose Bernd* (1903). His work, which was multi-layered in both form and content, dealt with mythical, psychological, and biographical themes, contained social criticism, and had a generally humanistic orientation. In 1914 he was drawn for a time into an "intoxication with war," from which, however, he soon distanced himself.

After 1918 Hauptmann acknowledged his support for the Weimar Republic, but as he grew older he removed himself from daily politics in a "stance-above-things." Although he criticized the National Socialist dictatorship, Hauptmann was unable totally to deny those who would use

Gerhart Hauptmann.

his reputation to advance the system. For this he was reproached by critics for his "compromising position." His onetime friend Alfred KERR accused him of "chumminess with the clumsy prison guards of Germany." Yet even in his later work Hauptmann dealt critically with militarism and nationalism, in *Das Abenteuer meiner Jugend* (The Adventure of My Youth, 2 vols., 1937). He dramatized the horror of the Second World War in the "Atriden" tetralogy (1941–1948), in which people are consigned to their fate as "God's impotent instruments."

Hauptschriftleiter (editor in chief), Germanization of *Chefredakteur*. Only persons who fulfilled the criteria of the EDITOR LAW of October 4, 1933, could function under this title.

Hauptschule (upper elementary school), besides the *Volksschule* (elementary school), a further compulsory and "selective school" (*Ausleseschule*); patterned on Austrian and South German traditions, it was established, beginning in 1941, beyond the "Old Reich." Its introduction in some regions of the "Old Reich," which took place until 1943, brought into question the consolidation of the *Mittelschule* (middle school) on the Prussian model, which had only been achieved in December 1939. The municipalities (*Gemeinden*), as the bodies responsible for the *Hauptschule*, would then have had to relinquish fees paid for the *Mittelschulen*. According to a change in the Reich Compulsory Education Law of May 16, 1941, teachers had authority regarding admission to the *Hauptschule*, which was to accept up to a third of the *Volksschule* pupils. The establishment of these central schools (*Mittelpunktschulen*) in the countryside paved the way for bigger changes in the school system.

The *Hauptschule* curriculum represented a compromise: the first two years were intended to make possible the transfer to more advanced secondary schools (*höhere Schulen*) by means of compulsory English instruction, although the total of four years was supposed to give primary attention to practical considerations and prepare for a "National Socialist vocational outlook" guided by a "Germanic-German value system." The regulations developed by the Party Chancellery envisioned "leadership lessons" for pupils in work groups because it was expected that pupils "very often [would take on] political assignments as well as their vocational work." The *Hauptschule* was abolished after the war by the German authorities rather than by the Allied military governments.

H. S.

Haus der Deutschen Kunst. *See* House of German Art.

Haushofer, Albrecht, b. Munich, January 7, 1903; d. Berlin, April 23, 1945 (executed), German geographer, writer, and opposition fighter. From 1928 to 1940, Haushofer was secretary general of the Society for Geographic Knowledge; in 1940 he became a professor of political geography and GEOPOLITICS in Berlin. He was the son of the geopolitical theorist Karl HAUSHOFER. A letter of protection (November 14, 1938) from Rudolf HESS, a family friend, prevented Haushofer from being persecuted be-

cause of his non-Aryan mother. He was himself not without antisemitic sentiments. From 1934 to 1938 he advised the RIBBENTROP OFFICE and at times worked under Ernst von WEIZSÄCKER in the Foreign Office. In 1941 Haushofer was arrested for participating in preparations for Hess's flight to England. While under Gestapo observation, he established contact with opposition circles. After the failed assassination attempt of July 20, 1944, he was captured in December; while imprisoned in besieged Berlin he was murdered by a shot in the nape of the neck by an SS commando. Haushofer, who earlier had written critical dramas in classical guise (*Sulla*, 1936; *Augustus*, 1939), as a prisoner created a touching testimony of resistance, the *Moabiter Sonetten* (Sonnets from Moabit Jail).

Haushofer, Karl, b. Munich, August 27, 1869; d. Pähl (Upper Bavaria), March 13, 1946, German geographer. Haushofer joined the military in 1887; in 1903 he became an instructor in military history. During the First World War he was promoted to major general. After extensive travels in the Far East, Haushofer wrote his dissertation on Japan. In 1921 he became a professor in Munich. His area of expertise was political geography, which as GEOPOLITICS was to become the "geographic knowledge of the state." In 1919 he became acquainted with Rudolf HESS, who was his student and "adoptive son." Despite his many visits with Hess in 1924 in the Landsberg Fortress, where Hitler wrote MEIN KAMPF, Haushofer's influence on Hitler's LIVING SPACE ideology was minimal. On the other hand, his geopolitical theories of "German confinement"

Albrecht Haushofer.

Karl Haushofer.

(*Raumenge*) later served as a "scientific" basis for National Socialist expansionist policies.

Haushofer, who presumably never joined the NSDAP for "camouflage reasons," was celebrated by the National Socialists as an "educator of the *Volk.*" From 1934 to 1937 he was president of the German Academy, and from 1938 to 1941 he presided over the VOLK LEAGUE FOR GERMANDOM ABROAD. After Hess's flight to England he fell into disfavor, and after his son Albrecht participated in the assassination attempt of July 20, 1944, Haushofer was placed in a concentration camp. The Allies indicted him as an instigator of NS imperialism, then withdrew the accusation because of his proven lack of influence. Deeply disturbed by the death of their son, Haushofer and his wife committed suicide.

Hausser, Paul, b. Brandenburg/Havel, October 7, 1880; d. Ludwigsburg, December 21, 1972, German SS general. Hausser went from the STEEL HELMET to the SA in 1933, then transferred to the SS. He was significantly involved in building up the SS STANDBY TROOPS, from which the WAFFEN-SS arose once the war began, and he fought with its units in France and Russia. In 1944 Hausser was promoted to army group chief (*Heeresgruppenchef*) and SS-*Oberstgruppenführer* (colonel general), but toward the end of the war Hitler relieved him of his post. After American captivity, in 1949 Hausser became chairman of the AUXILIARY FELLOWSHIP FOR RECIPROCITY, an organization of Waffen-SS veterans, whom he tried in vain to free of the odium of having been an "ideological army."

Paul Hausser.

Häussler, Willi, b. Hamburg, April 18, 1907; d. there, March 22, 1945, German opposition fighter. A worker, Häussler joined the Social Democratic Party and the Reich Banner in 1925. After the Seizure of Power he was fired for his "subversive attitude." In October 1934 he assumed leadership of an opposition group of former Reich Banner members, which published leaflets against the National Socialist regime and helped victims escape abroad. He himself could not escape when the Gestapo struck on June 13, 1936. Sentenced to seven years in prison, he was then transferred to the Wilhelmsburg camp for foreigners, where he died in the last days of the war, officially "from enemy actions."

Haw-Haw, Lord. *See* Joyce, William.

"Hay Operation" ("Heuaktion"), cover name—made up by Alfred ROSENBERG as minister for the occupied Eastern Territories—for the kidnapping of Russian children aged 10 to 14 into the Reich. Some 40,000 to 50,000 girls and boys who seemed suited to RE-GERMANIZATION fell victim to the operation, which had been planned in 1942. In a letter (July 20, 1944) to Hans Lammers, head of the Reich Chancellery, Rosenberg characterized the goal of the plan as "the creation of apprentices for the German economy."

Health Passport (*Gesundheitspass*), instrument of National Socialist HEALTH POLICY, created in 1937 by the NSDAP Main Office for Volk Health. In keeping with the aims of PERFORMANCE MEDICINE, the document was to be obligatory for all "productive individuals," and was to detail medical diagnoses, therapeutic measures (including participation in "health-promoting Strength through Joy trips"), and also addresses of relevant contacts "from birth to old age." It was always to be carried at work and when visiting a doctor, and was meant to prevent misuse of social institutions. The Health Passport was never completely put into practice because of the coexistence of state and party jurisdictions; especially after the war began, it was no longer consistently used.

Health policy (*Gesundheitspolitik*), characterized in the Third Reich by the social and biological demands of SPECIES UPGRADING (culling out and selection) and the requirements of PERFORMANCE MEDICINE. Health policy was synonymous with the health regimen of the German *Volk.* The duality of state and party institutions, which was also evident in health policy, often stood in the way of success. Besides the Health Offices created by the Law to Unify Health Services, there were *Gau* Offices for Volk Health under the Main Office for Volk Health (Hauptamt für Volksgesundheit) of the NSDAP. Only in 1939 were the two branches unified, at least at the top, with the naming of Leonardo CONTI as Reich Health Führer. Yet this unity was destroyed again in 1942 with the appointment of Karl BRANDT as general commissioner for sanitary and health services, an office that put him directly under Hitler. In September 1943 Brandt was empowered "to centralize the tasks and interests of all sanitary and health services and direct them as instructed."

Aside from RACIAL HYGIENE measures, several other areas were especially important for health policy: the Aid Agency for MOTHER AND CHILD; the institution of "youth doctors" (*Jugendärzte*) to supervise the health of Hitler Youth members (a position that could be realized only in 1940 over the opposition of school doctors); tuberculosis treatment; and the employment of doctors in the workplace to oversee worker morale and health.

R. W.

Health Service Girl (*Gesundheitsdienstmädel*), in the League of German Girls (BDM), term for the medical and technical office assistant of a Hitler Youth physician.

Healthy (*gesund*), fashionable National Socialist word to describe not only a person's nonproblematic medical and biological condition, but beyond that, his or her maximum value for the COMMUNITY. A person was healthy only when he or she fulfilled the racial, eugenic, and political demands placed by National Socialism on the VOLK COMRADE.

Heartfield, John (originally, Helmut Herzfeld), b. Berlin, June 1, 1891; d. there, April 26, 1968, German graphic artist and stage designer. Heartfield studied art and design in Munich and Berlin. Together with his brother Wieland Herzfeld, in 1916–1917 he founded the Neue Jugend (New Youth) and Malik publishing houses. (The latter was the most important German press for socialist and Soviet literature until banned by the National Socialists in 1933.) Heartfield, who joined the Communist party in 1918, under the influence of Dadaism developed the photomontage into an artistic medium for socialist propaganda. By uniting picture and writing, he attempted to make a point about profiteering in the armaments indus-

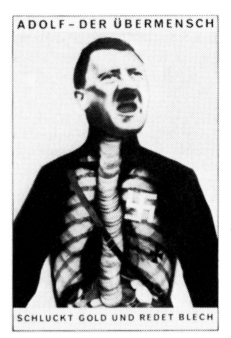

ADOLF - DER ÜBERMENSCH

SCHLUCKT GOLD UND REDET BLECH

Collage by John Heartfield: "Adolf—the Superman. Swallows gold and speaks tin."

try, commented on the events of daily politics, or demonstrated the irrational and ridiculous nature of *völkisch* slogans. With his numerous posters and book and magazine covers, Heartfield was one of the most original political artists of the Weimar Republic. In 1933 he went into exile, first in Prague and then London, where he worked for the German socialist emigré press. In 1950 Heartfield returned to the German Democratic Republic, where he received numerous honors.

Heckel, Erich, b. Döbeln (Saxony), July 31, 1883; d. Radolfzell, January 27, 1970, German painter and graphic artist. Heckel was one of the earliest and most important German Expressionists, and was a founder of the artists' association known as Die Brücke (The Bridge). His landscapes and nudes are characterized by angular forms and strong colors. Considered by the National Socialists as one of the "demolishers of form" and thus an example of DEGENERATE ART, Heckel was able to exhibit only after the war, when he was again recognized (for example, with an appointment as a professor at the Karlsruhe Academy).

Hedemann, Justus Wilhelm, b. Brieg, April 24, 1878; d. Berlin, March 13, 1963, German jurist. From 1906 to 1913, Hedemann was a councillor of the Superior Provincial Court. From 1909 to 1936 he was a professor in Jena, and after 1936, a professor of civil and business law in Berlin. Initially most concerned with the history of civil law, after 1933 Hedemann belonged to those jurists who attempted to provide a formal legal justification for the National Socialist dictatorship, through his university teaching, his many textbooks, and as chairman (after 1933) of a committee on "personal, association, and liability law" of the ACADEMY FOR GERMAN LAW. The National Socialists especially appreciated Hedemann's "effort to adapt the administration of justice to economic interests." He became a professor emeritus in 1946.

Hederich, Karlheinz, b. Wunsiedel, October 29, 1902, German cultural policymaker. Hederich came to the NSDAP as a student who had fought with the free corps. He participated in the Hitler Putsch of November 9, 1923, thereafter becoming a National Socialist university functionary. After the NS takeover, Hederich was given responsibilities for culture and literature. In 1934 he was made business manager of the OFFICIAL PARTY REVIEW COMMISSION FOR SAFE-GUARDING NATIONAL SOCIALIST WRITING, and he later became its deputy chairman. In 1937 he was named to the Reich NSDAP leadership, and in 1938 he became a ministerial councillor in the Reich Propaganda Ministry. Hederich summarized his demands on literature, which aimed at its usefulness to the National Socialists, in his book *Nationalsozialismus und Buch* (National Socialism and the Book; 1938).

Hegehof (cultivated farm), term coined by Reich Peasant Leader Walther DARRÉ for plots created by the HEREDITARY FARM LAW. They were to

Karlheinz Hederich.

foster a new German nobility: the *Hegehof* must become "the reservoir of our best German blood" (*Neuadel aus Blut und Boden* [New Nobility from Blood and Soil]; 1934).

Heidegger, Martin, b. Messkirch, September 26, 1899; d. Freiburg im Breisgau, May 26, 1976, German philosopher. Heidegger studied in Freiburg, where in 1915 he became a lecturer (*Privatdozent*). In 1923 he became a professor in Marburg, and in 1928 succeeded his teacher Edmund Husserl in Freiburg. Along with Karl JASPERS and Jean-Paul Sartre, Heidegger is a founder of Existentialism. With his magnum opus, *Sein und Zeit* (Being and Time; 1927)—which methodologically derives from Husserl's phenomenology, and in terms of the history of ideas, from Kierkegaard, NIETZSCHE, and Wilhelm Dilthey—Heidegger developed a fundamental ontology: the question of the meaning of being. The analysis begins with the "being-in-the-world" (*Dasein*) of the individual, whose existence is portrayed as characterized by anxiety, concern, and the threat of death. The basic theme of all existential philosophy is to encourage one to accept his or her temporal and historical fate and to act accordingly. But because it says nothing about the possible nature of that action, it is vulnerable to ideologies.

Thus Heidegger, in 1933 the first National Socialist rector in Freiburg, became the academic mouthpiece for the new wielders of power. In his inaugural address ("The Self-Affirmation of the German University"; 1933), he acknowledged the "greatness" and "splendor" of the German awakening. He urged youth to "labor [and] military service," as well as to "service to knowledge." He did, however, refuse a call to the University of Berlin in 1934, and thus did not become the star philosopher of National Socialism. In an essay ("Why Do We Remain in the Provinces?") he defended his refusal with arguments from NS BLOOD AND SOIL ideology. Shortly thereafter Heidegger distanced himself from National Socialism: in 1932 he characterized NS philosophies as "nonsensical products." Some of his emigré students, such as Karl Löwith, have never forgiven Heidegger for his mistake at the outset; others have viewed his brief commitment to the National Socialists as insignificant in light of the importance of his total work.

After the war, Heidegger took early retirement. He attained a considerable international reputation, especially in France, Italy, and Japan. In the Federal Republic of Germany during

Martin Heidegger.

the 1950s, more than half of all teaching positions in philosophy were filled with "Heideggerians." Numerous theologians, psychologists, and literary scholars were also influenced by him. Heidegger's connections with National Socialism again became controversial in the 1980s.

I. F.

"Heil Hitler!" (Hail Hitler!), National Socialist greeting, customary after about 1925; combined with a raised right arm, after 1933 it was commonly used as the GERMAN GREETING. The word "Heil" was borrowed from the acclamation of princes according to Old German tradition; it also referred back to the gymnasts' (*Turner*) greeting from 1846, "Gut Heil!" As a form of blessing, through the connection with *heilig* (holy), it had sacred connotations. When used to address Hitler in person, it became "Heil, mein Führer!"

Heilmann, Ernst, b. Berlin, April 13, 1881; d. Buchenwald concentration camp, April 3, 1940, German politician and journalist. Heilmann joined the Social Democratic Party of Germany (SPD) while a student. As a journalist he was editor in chief of the *Chemnitzer Volksstimme* (Chemnitz People's Voice) from 1909 to 1917; after the First World War he was publisher of the *Sozialistische Korrespondenz* and other political newspapers. After 1919 he was a member of the Prussian diet, and after 1925 also chairman of its SPD delegation (from 1928 to 1933 he was simultaneously a Reichstag deputy). Heilmann was a fervent defender of the Weimar Republic. He promoted a politics of compromise

and cooperation with the Center party, which the National Socialists excoriated as "parliamentary horse-trading." In June 1933 Heilmann was arrested; after a dismal trail through various places of incarceration, he was murdered in Buchenwald.

Heim-; Heimat-. *See* Home.

Heines, Edmund, b. July 21, 1897; d. Munich, July 30, 1934, SA *Obergruppenführer* (1933). An officer in the First World War, Heines afterward engaged in free corps activity (with Gerhard ROSSBACH, among others), then joined the NSDAP and SA. The handsome young man soon became part of the homosexual camarilla around Ernst RÖHM. In 1927 Heines was tem-

Reichsleitung

Reichsgeschäftsstelle:
München, Brienerstraße 45
Briefanschrift: München 43, Brieffach 80
Telefon-Nummern: 54901, 58344 u. 56081
Postscheckkonto München 23319

Kampfzeitung d. Partei: „Völkischer Beobachter"
Geschäftsstelle der Zeitung: Thierschstraße 11
Telefon-Nummer 20647
Schriftleitung: Schellingstraße 39
Telefon-Nummer 20501 Postscheckkonto 11346

Der Stellvertreter
des Führers
Stabsleiter

München, den 20.11.1933.

R u n d s c h r e i b e n
an alle Herren Gauleiter.

Dem Stellvertreter des Führers wurde mitgeteilt, über die Frage, ob der Gruss der N.S.D.A.P. "Heil" oder "Heil Hitler" laute, seien an einem grösseren Orte Streitigkeiten entstanden, ja, es sei darüber schon zu handgreiflichen Auseinandersetzungen gekommen und Inschutzhaftnahme von Personen sei beantragt worden, weil diese nur mit "Heil" und nicht mit "Heil Hitler" gegrüsst hätten.
Der Stellvertreter des Führers stellt dazu fest, dass der Gruss "Heil" nie durch eine Anordnung in den Gruss "Heil Hitler" umgewandelt worden ist. Es kann daher ohne weiteres sowohl mit "Heil", wie mit "Heil Hitler" gegrüsst werden.

München, den 20. November 1933.

Zur Kenntnisnahme
an Geheime Staatspolizei, Berlin
" Bayerische Politische Polizei.

Höflichkeitsformeln fallen bei allen parteiamtlichen Schreiben weg.

Circular by Martin Bormann on the use of the greeting "Heil" or "Heil Hitler": "Munich, November 20, 1933. Circular to all *Gau* leaders. The Deputy to the Führer has been informed that disputes have broken out . . . regarding whether the greeting of the N.S.D.A.P. is 'Heil' or 'Heil Hitler,' in fact, that the matter has come to blows and that protective custody has been proposed for persons who use only 'Heil' and not 'Heil Hitler.'

The Deputy to the Führer points out that the greeting 'Heil' has never been changed to the greeting 'Heil Hitler' by any decree. Thus henceforth either 'Heil' or 'Heil Hitler' may be used.
For the attention of:
the Secret State Police, Berlin
the Bavarian Political Police."

Ernst Heilmann as a concentration camp prisoner (1933).

Ernst Heinkel.

porarily expelled from the party; in 1929 he was found guilty of participation in one of the VEHM MURDERS, but he was soon amnestied. After the National Socialist takeover he became police president of Breslau. During the course of Hitler's purge of the SA, Heines was arrested in Bad Wiessee and murdered.

Heinkel, Ernst, b. Grunbach (Württemberg), January 24, 1888; d. Stuttgart, January 1, 1958, German airplane designer and armaments maker. After engineering studies, Heinkel designed aircraft for several firms before founding the Ernst Heinkel Aircraft Factory in Travemünde (later Warnemünde) in 1922. Among numerous specialty aircraft, Heinkel developed, in particular, the first European rapid-transit airplane, the streamlined He 70 (1932), and the two-engine middle-range bomber He 111 (1935), which Göring chose as the standard airplane of German bomber squadrons. Using more power-

ful engines, Heinkel broke international speed records; in 1939 he built the world's first jet airplane, the He 178. Even before the war, armaments contracts allowed him to greatly expand his production facilities, adding new factories in Rostock (1935) and Oranienburg (1936). In 1938 Heinkel was named MILITARY ECONOMY FÜHRER. As a technician and industrialist, he was among the central figures of Germany's preparation for war, and by the end of the war his factories employed over 50 percent ALIEN WORKERS, yet in two hearings before appeals boards he was classified only as a "fellow traveler." Heinkel described his "life for German aeronautics" in his memoirs, *Stürmisches Leben* (A Stormy Life; 1953).

Heisenberg, Werner, b. Würzburg, December 5, 1901; d. Munich, February 2, 1976, German physicist. As director of the Kaiser Wilhelm Institute for Physics in Berlin, Heisenberg was one of the most important German physicists who did not leave the country after the National Socialist takeover. His work in the late 1920s on quantum mechanics, in particular, permanently influenced modern scientific thinking and the development of atomic physics; in 1932 he was awarded a Nobel prize. Heisenberg's NS colleagues, however, defamed him as a "theoretical formalist" and "the OSSIETZKY of physics" because of his unorthodox ideas (*Das Schwarze Korps* [the SS weekly], 1937). Only after a formal proceeding was he allowed to continue lecturing on EINSTEIN's Theory of Relativity. Heisenberg recognized the dangers of a military use of atomic energy, but he continued

Edmund Heines.

Werner Heisenberg.

with his research, which in the long run could have given the Wehrmacht access to atomic weapons. He countered this possibility with evasive maneuvers, and thus was able successfully to slow the tempo of development. After the war, Heisenberg and Otto HAHN were interned in England for a short time. Heisenberg later assumed leadership of the Max Planck Institute for Physics and opposed atomic weapons for the Bundeswehr (the West German military forces).

Heissmeyer, August, b. Gellersen, January 11, 1897; d. Schwäbisch Hall, January 16, 1979, SS-*Obergruppenführer* (1939). A lieutenant in the First World War, Heissmeyer then became a day laborer and a medical student (he never graduated). He joined the NSDAP in 1925, organized the SA in the Hannover-South *Gau* (for a time as deputy *Gauleiter*), and in late 1930 joined the SS. In 1935 Himmler named him a *Gruppenführer* and chief of the SS Main Office, creating after its 1939 reorganization an "Oberführer Heissmeyer Office" (Dienststelle Oberführer Heissmeyer). In this capacity Heissmeyer was in charge of overseeing the NATIONAL-PO-LITICAL EDUCATIONAL INSTITUTES (NPEA); he was also a Higher SS and Police Leader (*Höherer SS- und Polizeiführer*) in Berlin-Brandenburg. Toward the end of the war, when Heissmeyer was organizing the arming of NPEA pupils, he was made a general in the Waffen-SS (November 19, 1944). With his conception of the SS as an "education army" (*Erziehungsarmee*) he failed, because Himmler placed more value on the SS's development as an executive

organ. After the war Heissmeyer and his wife, Reich Women's Führerin Gertrud SCHOLTZ-KLINK, were classified as "major offenders," and punished with internment and loss of assets.

Held, Heinrich, b. Erbach (Hesse), June 6, 1868; d. Regensburg, August 4, 1938, German politician, publicist, and publisher. Active in the Christian workers' movement before the First World War, Held became a Center party deputy in the Bavarian diet. In 1918 he helped found the Bavarian People's Party, and after 1919 he headed its parliamentary delegation. He was elected Bavarian minister president in 1924. A nationalist, but more fundamentally a monarchist, Held supported the extension of the federalist system, proposing a change in the Weimar Constitution to that end in 1928. He even threatened a "revival of the Main [River] line," which had once divided the southern German states from the expanding Prussian empire. As a Christian conservative, Held strongly opposed the National Socialists before 1933, even continuing for a time after the takeover. After the fall of the Bavarian government (March 9, 1933), he retired to Regensburg in resignation.

Helke, Fritz, b. Riesenthal (Mark Brandenburg), May 1, 1905; d. Kriftel, September 13, 1967, German writer and Hitler Youth (HJ) functionary. An HJ leader after 1929, as *Oberbannführer* in the Reich Youth Leadership office Helke was in charge of the Main Bureau for Writing, where he was especially concerned with the "internal reformation of German writ-

Heinrich Held.

ing for youth" (Franz Lennartz), as well as with the Reich youth libraries. In his own books for young people, Helke reworked themes from Brandenburg's history with "Prussian spirit." After the war he concentrated almost exclusively on adventure stories and books for the young, preferably located in the American West, as *Das Blockhaus am Biberfluss* (The Blockhouse on Beaver River; 1953).

Helldorf, Wolf Heinrich Count von, b. Merseburg, October 14, 1896; d. Berlin, August 15, 1944 (executed), German politician. A career officer in the First World War, Helldorf then served in several free corps, participating in the KAPP PUTSCH and in the suppression of Communist uprisings. After a temporary retreat to his estate, in the late 1920s Helldorf began a career with the SA, becoming *Gruppenführer* for Berlin-Brandenburg in 1931. After 1925 he was a deputy for the NSDAP in the Prussian diet (after 1932 deputation chairman); after 1932 he represented the party in the Reichstag. In 1933 Göring made him police president of Potsdam, and in 1935 he became head of the Berlin police. After 1938 Helldorf was in loose contact with opposition circles around Carl Goerdeler. Less from conviction than from opportunistic motives, Helldorf gave support from the Berlin police to the actions of Claus von Stauffenberg and others in the plot of the TWENTIETH OF JULY, 1944, for which he was arrested and, on August 8, 1944, sentenced by the *Volk* Court to death by hanging.

Wolf Heinrich Count von Helldorf.

Hendaye, French bathing resort on the Bay of Biscay at the Spanish border; its population was 5,660 in 1930. On October 23, 1940, Hitler and Foreign Minister Joachim von RIBBENTROP met in Hendaye with the Spanish chief of state, Francisco FRANCO, and his foreign minister, Ramón Serrano Suñer. Germany had been defeated in the AIR BATTLE FOR ENGLAND, and its plan for an invasion (Operation "Sea Lion") had been put on hold; there was thus little likelihood of a direct military defeat of Great Britain. Faced with this dilemma, at a time before the final decision to invade the Soviet Union—the order for Operation "Barbarossa"

Hitler and Franco at the Hendaye railroad station.

was given on December 18, 1940—Hitler decided that autumn, for the time being, on an indirect "peripheral strategy" against the island empire.

The advice of Ribbentrop and of the navy hierarchy were especially important in this plan, which gave a central role to Franco's Spain. After that nation had entered the war through the occupation of Gibraltar, in company with German troops (Operation "Felix," planned for January 1941), the western Mediterranean would be blocked, thus cutting Great Britain off from important overseas connections. Yet because Hitler made no concrete promises regarding Spanish colonial demands for French-held territory in northwest Africa (for the expansion of Spanish Morocco), and above all because the fortunes of war no longer seemed so clearly on Hitler's side, after a few weeks of tergiversation, in December 1940 Franco definitively rejected an entry into the war on Germany's side.

B.-J. W.

Henlein, Konrad, b. Maffersdorf bei Reichenberg, May 6, 1898; d. Pilsen, May 10, 1945, Sudeten German politician. Under the influence of the German gymnastics movement, Henlein developed at an early age into a fervent Great-German nationalist, who wanted to transform the German gymnastics associations of Bohemia and Moravia into "national education and combat organizations." Employed as a gymnastics teacher after 1925, in 1931 he was elected leader of the Sudeten German Gymnastics Alliance in the Czechoslovak Republic. Because Henlein believed that the existing Sudeten German parties could not improve the economic and political situation, and because the Prague government banned the GERMAN NATIONAL SOCIALIST WORKERS' PARTY (DNSAP) in 1933, Henlein founded the Sudeten German Home Front (Sudetendeutsche Heimatfront). This organization, which in 1935 was renamed the SUDETEN GERMAN PARTY (SDP), united German nationalist interests in the Czechoslovak Republic. With the demand for Sudeten German autonomy and the material support of the German Reich, the SDP ultimately represented over two-thirds of the German-speaking population of Czechoslovakia; in the 1935 elections it became the second-strongest party.

In 1935–1936 Henlein supported the SDP's subversion by National Socialist functionaries; he allowed the party to take an openly NS and antisemitic course after 1937, and attempted to

Konrad Henlein.

ignite conflicts with the Czechoslovak government. At a secret meeting with Hitler on March 28, 1938, the strategy of asking Prague for more than it could concede at a given point (*see* SUDETEN CRISIS) was intensified. After the MUNICH AGREEMENT and the entry of German troops into "rump [residual] Czechslovakia," Henlein was named *Gauleiter* and Reich governor (*Reichstatthalter*) in 1939. Although Henlein was promoted to SS-*Obergruppenführer*, Hitler thereafter gave preference to Karl Hermann FRANK. Henlein committed suicide while in an American prison camp after the war.

Hensel, Walther (originally, Julius Janiczek), b. Mährisch-Trübau, September 8, 1887; d. Munich, September 5, 1956, German musical pedagogue. Hensel was a member of the "State Folk-Songs Committee for the German Folk Song in Czechoslovakia," and then a music teacher in the youth music movement. He founded his own music school in Stuttgart in 1932. As an organizer of choral festivals and an editor of numerous folk-song collections, he was one of the most important representatives of a movement for musical renewal, whose nationalist and chauvinist tendencies were exploited and fostered by the National Socialists. Thus Hensel, who after 1938 devoted himself especially to research on folk songs in Sudeten German areas, received the support of National Socialist culture functionaries for works such as *Auf den Spuren des Volksliedes* (On the Trail of the Folk Song; 1944). After the war he worked as a scholarly adviser in the folk-song archive of the Munich Municipal Library.

Herd morality (*Herdenmoral*), pejorative National Socialist cliché for the stance of "followers of the herd" (*Herdenmenschen*), who were not ready to perform exceptional accomplishments for the "*Volk* Community." NIETZSCHE was cited ("Do you want an easy life? Then remain with the herd"), and the term "herd morality" or "slave morality" was applied to anyone who felt more strongly obligated to the Christian ethic (love of one's neighbor) or to "Bolshevist collectivism" than to NS SOCIAL DARWINISM.

Hereditarily Ill Offspring (*Erbkranker Nachwuchs*), according to the National Socialist concept of RACIAL HYGIENE, the children of persons suffering from congenital feeblemindedness, schizophrenia, manic-depressive psychosis, epilepsy, Huntington's chorea, hereditary blindness or deafness, severe hereditary malformations, or severe alcoholism. For persons with these infirmities, FORCED STERILIZATION was ordered in the law of July 14, 1933 (in force on January 1, 1934), "to Prevent Hereditarily Ill Offspring." Some 400,000 people came under this definition in 1934; from their sterilization an immediate increase in the "public health of our race" was expected, as well as a significant decrease in the cost of care in institutions for the handicapped. In a broader sense, the killing operations of the EUTHANASIA program were part of the NS measures against hereditarily ill offspring.

Hereditary Farm Law (*Erbhofgesetz; Reichs-Erbhofgesetz*), legal regulation promulgated on September 29, 1933, which was concerned with "the preservation of the peasantry [*Bauerntum*] as the source of blood for the German *Volk*" and with the protection of peasant holdings from heavy indebtedness and division. The law specified that "only a person of German or related blood" could be a peasant (¶13). This was to be documented by a "large CERTIFICATE OF DESCENT" (tracing back to January 1, 1800). By law, an agricultural property counted as a hereditary farm if it had at least 7.5 hectares (18.5 acres) of arable land—a subsistence plot (*Ackernahrung*)—but no more than 125 hectares (212.5 acres). It had to be cultivated by one farm household and be the sole property of one peasant. According to the Hereditary Farm Law, only the proprietor of a hereditary farm could call himself a *Bauer* (peasant), whereas other farmers were *Landwirte* (agriculturalists).

Hereditary Farm Law. Leather-bound family register.

The Hereditary Farm Law limited the right of inheritance to one sole heir, normally in the male line. The sale of a hereditary farm was forbidden, as was its encumbrance with debt. Exceptions were ruled on by so-called INHERITANCE BOARDS. The forgiveness of debts and protection from foreclosure yielded temporary advantages, but they also limited the peasants' credit opportunities to personal credit, thus impeding agricultural modernization. As did other ideologically tinted economic measures, the Hereditary Farm Law conflicted with National Socialist AGRICULTURAL POLICY and its stated goal of economic self-sufficiency (*see* AUTARKY). It spurred flight from rural areas and could not prevent a decline in living standards among the total of 694,997 (in 1938) hereditary farm proprietors in the "Old Reich" (*see* SOCIAL POLICY).

Hereditary Health Court (*Erbgesundheitsgericht*), judicial body created by the law of July 25, 1933 (*Reich Law Gazette* I, p. 86). The Hereditary Health Court was attached to the lowest court (*Amtsgericht*); it consisted of a lower-court judge as chairman, as well as two doctors, one in a civil service post. It had jurisdiction over FORCED STERILIZATION cases in accordance with the Law to Prevent Hereditarily Ill Offspring of July 14, 1933. Appeals could be made to higher hereditary health courts attached to the higher state courts (*Oberlandesgerichte*).

Heredity cultivation (*Erbpflege*), following Eugen FISCHER in 1934, the term preferred by the National Socialists over "eugenics" for the totality of measures to raise the hereditary health of a people. Because natural SELECTION was largely inoperative with the human species, heredity cultivation and RACIAL HYGIENE were invoked to counteract the danger of an accumulation of unfavorable inherited characteristics. National Socialist POPULATION POLICY intervened here primarily through negative means (*see* CULLING OUT), notably with the Law to Prevent HEREDITARILY ILL OFFSPRING of July 14, 1933, and the MARITAL HEALTH LAW of October 18, 1935. The reproduction of "hereditarily unfit" individuals was thereby to be curbed. On the other hand, such social policy measures as MARRIAGE LOANS and tax advantages were intended to increase the number of "healthy, child-friendly families." According to NS notions, the promotion of "racial purity" also served heredity cultivation, as did the Law to Protect Blood (*see* BLOOD, LAW TO PROTECT) of September 15, 1935, one of the Nuremberg Laws. The most radical consequences of the NS program of heredity cultivation were EUTHANASIA and the FINAL SOLUTION.

Hering, Gottlieb, b. Warmbronn, June 2, 1887; d. Stettin, October 9, 1945, SS-*Hauptsturmführer* (1943) and criminal commissioner. In 1940 Hering was delegated by the Stuttgart criminal police to the "T4" EUTHANASIA organization; he was first deployed in the killing facility at Sonnenstein, and later at Bernburg, as head of the registrar's office. In 1942 he was appointed to "Einsatzstab Reinhard," a task force attached to the office of the SS and Police Leader in Lublin. In early August 1942 Hering was appointed commandant of the BEŁŻEC extermination camp. When he was about to be promoted to *Hauptsturmführer* in acknowledgment of his "services" to the "FINAL SOLUTION of the Jewish question" in the Generalgouvernement in the spring of 1943, it was discovered that he was not a member of the SS, but only a "uniform-wearer." He was ordered to join the SS, and his promotion followed. Before completion of the REINHARD OPERATION, Hering was ordered to Trieste, where he was involved in the persecution of the city's Jews.

A. St.

Hermann, Georg (originally, Georg Hermann Borchardt), b. Berlin, October 7, 1871; d. Auschwitz, November 19, 1943, German author. Hermann became known for his novels of Jewish life in Berlin (such as *Jettchen Gebert;* 1906–1908). He also wrote as an art critic (*Max Liebermann;* 1904). Himself a Jew, in 1933 he fled to the Netherlands. The National Socialists considered him a typical representative of "Jewish defeatism" for his ironic epigram "Better a coward for five minutes than dead for a lifetime." In 1943 he was captured in Holland and deported to the extermination camp at Auschwitz.

Hermann-Göring-Koog, reclaimed land on the western coast of Schleswig-Holstein, created by damming the Wattenmeer as part of the National Socialist WORK CREATION program of 1933 to 1935. As a separate community of 160 inhabitants, it was named Hermann-Göring-Koog on July 1, 1937. After the war, on June 18, 1945, it was renamed the Tümlauer Koog.

Hermann Göring Master School for Painting (Hermann-Göring-Meisterschule für Malerei), art school founded in 1938 in Kronenburg an der Eifel under the leadership of Werner PEINER. The school's mission was to promote "species-true" (*arteigene*) art, which would be the "deepest expression of the *Volk* soul," as against "alien" DEGENERATE ART.

Hermes, Andreas, b. Cologne, July 16, 1878; d. Krälingen/Eifel, January 4, 1964, German politician. A Center party member, Hermes was Reich minister for food and agriculture (1920–1922), then finance minister (1922–1923); he was a Reichstag member from 1928 to 1933. One of the most important agricultural functionaries in the Weimar Republic, after 1928 he was president of the United Association of German Cooperatives–Agricultural Credit Corporation. As a Catholic conservative, Hermes opposed National Socialism and resigned his Reichstag mandate prior to the Enabling Law (March 23, 1933). After several years abroad, he made connections with opposition circles, and was envisaged as agriculture minister in a GOERDELER cabinet. Hermes was arrested immediately after the assassination attempt of July 20, 1944, and condemned to death as an active "conspirator." He barely escaped execution through the entry of Russian troops. In 1945 Hermes was a co-founder of the Christian Democratic Union in the Soviet occupation zone, and its first chairman. He was dismissed by the

Andreas Hermes.

occupation authorities for opposing land reform. He went to West Germany, where he soon became a top functionary in agricultural matters.

Hero cult (*Heldenkult*), mythical exaggeration of soldierly deeds to support military training through the use of models (*see* HEROISM).

Heroes' Memorial Day (*Heldengedenktag*), Sunday commemoration, held yearly as a state holiday after 1934, to honor the soldiers who died in the First World War (after 1940, also the dead of the Second World War), but also those "heroes" who died for the National Socialist movement. In 1939 the date of March 16 was set to commemorate the reintroduction of universal COMPULSORY MILITARY SERVICE in 1935. As an expression of sorrow for the dead of the first war, as of 1923 the fifth Sunday before Easter (*Reminiscere* in the church) had been celebrated as a day of national mourning on the initiative of the National League for the Care of German War Graves. The renaming as Heroes' Memorial Day served to foster psychological assent to a new war and to cultivate an image of those "who were ready to sacrifice themselves to preserve the life of the community" (Hitler, March 10, 1940).

Heroic film (*Heroischer Film*), preferred genre of National Socialist cinematography. Hitler's demand that the German *Volk*'s "truly important men" be artistically interpreted "as supreme heroes in the eyes of the present" was met by heroic film treatments of the lives of German poets and thinkers such as *Friedrich Schiller* (1940) and *Paracelsus* (1943) and those of charismatic leaders of workers and of business such as *Der Herrscher* (The Master; 1937). Heroic films on political leaders included *Bismarck* (1940) and several featuring Frederick the Great and his victories: *Der Choral von Leuthen* (1933), *Der alte und der junge König* (The Old

Heroes' Memorial Day in Berlin (1935).

Heroic film. Emil Jannings as Bismarck.

and the Young King; 1935), and *Der grosse König* (The Great King; 1942). In their protagonists, who alone prevail "against the whole world" and thus legitimize the FÜHRER PRINCIPLE—subordination to the leader whom fate has selected—one finds a constant reference to Hitler, thereby suggesting to the viewer a historical identity among Frederick, Bismarck, and Hitler (*see* FILM).

H. H.

Heroism (*Heroismus; Heldentum*), in the National Socialist worldview, a "racially inborn" aggressive posture exemplifying the "basic type of all Nordic peoples" (Rosenberg). Heroism meant especially the "application of all capacities and energies" from a notion of duty, rather than for a reward. Such self-sacrificial, self-subordinating heroism was necessary both to create an NS dictatorship and to realize a policy of military expansion. In art, literature, film (*see* HEROIC FILM), and SCULPTURE, heroic figures from German history were idealized: "from the noble of the sword Siegfried, . . . to the noble of scientific research Kopperning [NS Germanization and expropriation of the Polish Copernicus], . . . to the noble of religion [Meister] Eckehard, . . . to the political nobles Frederick and Bismarck" (Rosenberg). Through emphasis on the exceptional, every type of expected fulfillment of duty was glorified as "the quiet heroism of daily life."

Herrenklub (Gentlemen's Club; the German *Herr* also has a sense of "master"), informal circle founded in 1924 by Heinrich von Gleichen-Russwurm; formally it was the "German Club," but it was generally known by the masculine designation. Up to 500 members belonged to it and its (for a time) 20 subgroups: leading representatives of heavy industry and of business organizations, high officials and officers, conservative academics and publicists. (Members included Friedrich FLICK, Franz Haniel, Robert Pferdmenges, Fritz THYSSEN, Franz von PAPEN, and Kurt von SCHLEICHER.) The Herrenklub rejected parliamentary democracy and promoted an "authoritarian, hierarchically ordered" nation-state; it supported nationalist-conservative parties (especially the German People's Party and the German National People's Party) and later also the National Socialists. As the most influential combination of big business, big capital, and big agriculture, the Herrenklub at times intervened directly in German politics, as in the formation of the Papen cabinet. In the Third Reich the club quickly lost all influence, and it was dissolved in 1944.

Herriot, Édouard Marie, b. Troyer, July 5, 1872; d. Saint-Genis-Laval, March 26, 1957, French politician and publicist. From 1919 to 1926 and 1931 to 1935 Herriot was leader of the Radical Socialist party. He was foreign minister in 1924–

Édouard Marie Herriot.

1925 and prime minister of a leftist government. It was Herriot who carried out the withdrawal of French forces from the Ruhr (*see* RUHR CONFLICT). Because of his support for the work of the League of Nations and his "pacifist propaganda," Herriot was attacked by German as well as French nationalists, especially when, in 1932, again serving as prime minister, he intensified the relationship with England and sought a French-Soviet alliance. During the occupation of France, Herriot was for a time interned in Germany. After the war he served for many years as president of the French National Assembly.

Hersbruck, satellite camp of the FLOSSENBÜRG concentration camp in Bavaria. Built in May 1944, it was first occupied by 150 prisoners from Flossenbürg. In mid-August there were 1,900 internees, and by the last months of the war some 5,000 to 6,000 of various European nationalities. The prisoners worked in tunnels converted into manufacturing areas, in former mines cut into a mountain, on the production of fighter engines for the Luftwaffe. Inhuman hygienic conditions and poor food and clothing claimed many victims among the sick and exhausted prisoners, as did brutal mistreatment and executions; the death toll from June 1944 to March 1945 was 3,513 prisoners. In mid-April 1945 the prisoners were evacuated on foot in the direction of Dachau; those who were ill were transported in open freight cars of the Reichsbahn.

W. D.

Hertz, Friedrich Otto, b. Vienna, March 26, 1878; d. London, November 20, 1964, Austrian

sociologist, political economist, and historian. From 1930 to 1933 Hertz was a professor of political economy and sociology in Halle. He was vituperously attacked by the National Socialists as a "Jew, Freemason, and pacifist" for his publications on issues of race and nationality. In *Moderne Rassentheorien* (Modern Racial Theories; 1904), Hertz criticized Houston Stewart CHAMBERLAIN's *Foundations of the 19th Century* by showing that the Aryan race had played no "leading role" in the history of humankind, that various races possessed equally valuable qualities, and that members of a particular race could be culturally assimilated by another people.

Hertz, Gustav, b. Hamburg, July 22, 1887; d. Leipzig, October 20, 1975, German physicist. Hertz became a professor in Halle in 1925, and in 1928 went to the Technical University (TU) in Berlin. He devoted his research above all to questions of atomic physics; for his work on the effects of electron bombardment on atoms, he shared a Nobel prize with James Franck (1882–1964) in 1925. Hertz's methods of separating isotopes, which he developed in 1932, had considerable importance for the development of the ATOMIC BOMB. For refusing to sign a loyalty oath to Hitler, he was forced to resign his post as head of the Institute of Physics at the TU in 1934. A "half Jew," Hertz was otherwise protected from pressure, and he continued to investigate the atom as head of a Siemens research laboratory. After 1945 he was taken with other scientists to Sukhumi in the Soviet

Gustav Hertz.

Union, where he applied his experience gained in the Third Reich to research in military technology. In 1945 he returned to Leipzig, where he was a professor and head of the Physics Institute.

Hertz, Paul, b. Worms, June 23, 1888; d. Berlin, October 23, 1961, German politician and publicist. After 1914, Hertz was an editor for the Social Democratic Party (SPD) press. In 1917 he joined the Independent Socialists (USPD). Back in the SPD, he was active in municipal politics, notably as mayor of the Kreuzberg district. From 1920 to June 22, 1933, he was a Reichstag member, after 1922 serving as business manager of that body's SPD delegation. Because he supported a republic of councils (Räterepublik) in Hamburg after the First World War and was one of the first politicians to support acceptance of the Versailles treaty, Hertz was exposed to particularly intensive attacks by the National Socialists. He emigrated to Prague in 1933, and his German citizenship was revoked on March 30, 1934. For several years he belonged to the SPD committee-in-exile. In 1938 he left Prague and emigrated to the United States via Paris. After returning from American exile in 1949, he soon became a leader of the West Berlin SPD, which he represented in the Senate from 1951 to 1953 and from 1955 to 1961.

Hervé, Gustave, b. Brest, January 2, 1871; d. Paris, October 25, 1944, French politician and publicist. Before the First World War, Hervé was considered the most radical pacifist in France; he then became an ardent nationalist. In the 1920s he became a fascist and supported a Rhenish buffer state, although he also promoted German-French rapprochement after 1930.

Herzl, Theodor, b. Budapest, May 2, 1860; d. Edlach (Lower Austria), July 3, 1904, Austrian Jewish publicist and writer. Herzl studied law but switched to journalism, working as Paris correspondent of the Viennese *Neue Freie Presse* (New Free Press). Originally a proponent of Jewish assimilation, during the trial of Capt. Alfred Dreyfus, who was a Jew, Herzl encountered a typical pogrom atmosphere and acknowledged that only their own "homestead" (*Heimstätte*) would be able to protect the Jews from ANTISEMITISM. The vision of such a Jewish exodus was portrayed in Herzl's 1896 book *Der Judenstaat (The Jewish State)*, which became the founding document of ZIONISM.

On Herzl's initiative, the first Zionist Congress met in Basel on August 29, 1897; despite

Theodor Herzl.

strong disagreements it projected the creation of a protected region for oppressed Jews, especially from Poland and Russia. Herzl then negotiated with potential donors of money and land, including the Kaiser, the pope, and the Ottoman sultan, but he died before he could attain any real success. His search for a Jewish homeland, "where we . . . may have curved noses [*krumme Nasen*] without being held in contempt," aimed from the outset at Palestine. This "solution of the Jewish question," the subtitle of his 1896 book, was at first favored by the National Socialist authorities in the Third Reich (*see* PERSECUTION OF JEWS), before they turned to the genocidal program of the FINAL SOLUTION.

Herzogenbusch ('s Hertogenbosch; also Vught), National Socialist concentration camp in the Netherlands, opened on January 5, 1943. The first inmates were German criminals (*BV'er,* from *Berufsverbrecher,* professional criminals), who were employed as KAPOS and as prisoners charged with special functions. In January 1943 the first transport of Dutch prisoners reached Herzogenbusch; they were followed in May by female prisoners, who were housed separately in the women's camp at Vught. Also in January 1943, a transport of Jews from Amsterdam brought "civilian Jews" (*Ziviljuden*), who were housed in the "Jewish Collection Camp" (*Judenauffanglager*), later the "Jewish Transit Camp" (*Judendurchgangslager;* JDL). Several transports went from the JDL to Poland, including one in May 1943 of Jewish children, who almost without exception were killed with their parents (a total of some 3,000 persons) in the SOBIBÓR extermination camp. Further Jewish transports to Auschwitz followed in November 1943 and June 1944 (the last shipment).

In the "Student Camp" at Herzogenbusch oppositional students were interned. A "Political Transit Camp" was created in August 1943 for political detainees from Dutch prisons and arrest facilities who were being held while under investigation. A "Hostage Camp" held mostly women and children who had been arrested in reprisals for acts of sabotage or as family members ("family hostages") of relatives who had fled. Some 29,500 prisoners of various categories were housed at Herzogenbusch.

Some of the prisoners worked at the Philips electrical firm, others at the Escotex textile mill. Living conditions varied greatly from one division of the camp to another, but on the whole were bad. Several hundred people lost their lives to executions or general mistreatment. As Allied troops moved toward southern Holland in September 1944, the prisoners were evacuated by rail. Most of the men were taken to SACHSENHAUSEN, and the women to the women's camp at RAVENSBRÜCK.

W. D.

Hespers, Theo, b. Duisburg, December 12, 1903; d. Berlin-Plötzensee, September 9, 1943 (executed), German opposition fighter. In his youth, Hespers—a retail apprentice—belonged to the WANDERVOGEL and to the Catholic YOUTH MOVEMENT. He opposed National Socialism from the outset. Crossing over the Dutch border in 1933, he agitated from there against the Third Reich. In 1937, supported by Dutch youth organizations, Hespers began publishing the Catholic oppositional paper *Kameradschaft* (Comradeship), which was smuggled into Germany. When the Wehrmacht invaded the Netherlands in 1940, he was on the Gestapo's arrest list. He went underground with Belgian friends for a time, but in February 1942 was arrested, condemned to death in Berlin, and hanged.

Hess, Rudolf, b. Alexandria (Egypt), April 26, 1894; d. Berlin, August 17, 1987, German politician. Hess spent his childhood in Egypt, where his father was in the export-import trade. He attended boarding school in Bad Godesberg in Germany and a business school in Switzerland, then served an apprenticeship in Hamburg. When the war began, Hess dropped the vocational goal, which he disliked, and volunteered for military service. Wounded several times, he became an infantry lieutenant; he switched to the air corps, but by the war's end he had had only one frontline assignment.

In Munich, where he went to study political economy, Hess experienced the turmoil of the republic of councils (Räterepublik) and came under the influence of the radical right-wing THULE SOCIETY, which strengthened his antisemitism. Also influential was the geopolitical theorist Karl HAUSHOFER. Most influential—and from the first moment—was Hitler. Hess joined the NSDAP as early as 1920, promoted the FÜHRER CULT with devotion, and came personally as close to Hitler as the latter's avoidance of personal relationships allowed. Hess participated in the HITLER PUTSCH and was sentenced to 18 months' imprisonment. In the Landsberg prison Hitler dictated MEIN KAMPF to him, accepting many editorial suggestions from Hess, who thenceforth served as Hitler's private secretary. In 1927 Hess married a doctor's daughter, Ilse Pröhl, became a successful avocational pilot, and during the "Time of Struggle" watched as jealously over the activities of his adored Führer as Martin BORMANN did later. Hess also organized the million-mark loan from industry to buy the BROWN HOUSE in Munich.

After the fall of Gregor STRASSER in late 1932, Hess became head of the newly created Political Central Commission of the NSDAP. In 1933 he became Hitler's deputy party leader. As head of the Party Chancellery, he received ministerial rank in the same year. Hess did not, however, have a thirst for power. Thus, although he was Hitler's most loyal promoter to

Rudolf Hess.

power, he was himself easily defeated in a battle of rivals. A contributing factor was the fact that his staff chief, Bormann, zealously controlled the smallest detail in the office and thus indirectly controlled the party itself at an early point. In any case, Hess had no influence on matters of state. He made numerous speeches, which were not very effective, tirelessly propagandized for the Führer cult, and contributed considerably to the climate of antisemitism; thus he was partly responsible for the milieu in which later crimes were committed.

It remains open to question whether the increase in peculiar behaviorial and personality traits manifested by Hess was responsible for Hitler's increasing alienation from his deputy, or whether the distancing was the catalyst for the manifestation of pathological strains in Hess's character. His attempt to regain Hitler's favor may in any case have encouraged Hess's decision to seek peace in London before the planned Russian Campaign. On May 10, 1941, he flew over the North Sea in an Me 110, which he had outfitted himself, and parachuted out over Scotland. There is no indication that Hitler knew anything about this ploy, whose failure threatened considerable loss of prestige. After a period of hesitation, which has been variously interpreted, Hitler had Hess officially characterized as mentally disturbed; the British imprisoned him.

At the Nuremberg Trials Hess was notable for his bizarre behavior, which combined periods of genuine disorientation with acknowledged dissimulation. Legally he was found to be fully responsible for his actions. His imprisonment "for life" exaggerated the real power and influence of the deputy Führer, even though his degree of moral guilt for the evils perpetrated cannot be considered negligible. After co-defendants who had been given the same punishment (Adm. Erich RAEDER, Walther FUNK) were released early, Hess's decades of solitary imprisonment and expiation took on a pronouncedly tragic tone. All attempts from German and Western quarters to amnesty him failed because of a Soviet veto, which was probably a relic of anxiety over German–Anglo-American détente, such as Hess may have imagined when he set off on his flight in 1941. Hess died, an apparent suicide, as the last prisoner in the Spandau Prison.

H. St.

Hesse, Helmut, b. Bremen, May 11, 1916; d. Dachau concentration camp, November 24, 1943, German Evangelical theologian. Hesse grew up in Elberfeld, which became the Rhenish center of the CONFESSING CHURCH, in the parsonage of his father, Hermann. After successful studies, he was ordained only with difficulty because many members of the Hesse family had already come into conflict with church officials and the Gestapo. Hesse participated in efforts to aid Communists and Jews, made contact with the circle around Pastor Heinrich GRÜBER, and did not refrain from using his sermons for extensive attacks on the National Socialist government leadership. While seriously ill, Hesse was arrested in the summer of 1943. His health was completely destroyed by the conditions of imprisonment, and he died in Dachau.

"Heuaktion." *See "Hay Operation."*

Heuschele, Otto, b. Schramberg, May 8, 1900, German writer. Heuschele had lasting success among middle-class readers with his historical prose, poems reflecting "inwardness," and essays in cultural criticism from a traditional perspective, such as *Deutsche Soldatenfrauen* (Wives of German Soldiers; 1940). The National Socialists considered Heuschele a "lyricist with true feeling," and he was able to continue his writing along these lines without difficulty after 1945.

Heusinger, Adolf, b. Holzminden, August 4, 1897; d. Cologne, November 30, 1982, German general. In 1929 Heusinger was posted to the Armed Forces Ministry as a first lieutenant. He became a major in the operations division of the Army High Command in 1937. The division's chief after 1940, he was valued as a strategist by Hitler, who promoted him to lieutenant general in 1943. After the assassination attempt of July 20, 1944, Heusinger was imprisoned for a time under suspicion of being an accessory. Found innocent, he was nonetheless dismissed from his military posts. After postwar internment by the Allies until 1948, the following year Chancellor Konrad Adenauer appointed him as his military adviser. Heusinger played an important role in planning and creating the Bundeswehr, and served as its general inspector from 1957 to 1961.

Heuss, Theodor, b. Brackenheim bei Heilbronn, January 31, 1884; d. Stuttgart, December 12, 1963, German politician and publicist. Heuss joined the Progressive Union (Freisinnige Vereinigung) in 1903. From 1912 to 1918 he was editor in chief of the *Neckar-Zeitung* in Heil-

Theodor Heuss.

Heuss's book *Hitlers Weg* (Hitler's Way).

bronn, and from 1920 to 1933 he lectured at the HOCHSCHULE FÜR POLITIK (College for Politics) in Berlin. A co-founder of the GERMAN DEMOCRATIC PARTY (DDP) in 1918, from 1924 to 1933 he was a Reichstag member. Heuss worked as a journalist and for a time was deputy chairman of the Alliance of German Writers to Defend the Principles of Parliamentary Democracy. As an author (*Hitlers Weg* [Hitler's Way]; 1932) and as a politician he dealt critically with the "wretchedness" (*Kümmerlichkeit*), lack of principles, and irrationalism of National Socialism. Yet despite his principled reservations, he voted for the ENABLING LAW in March 1933 out of party loyalty.

In 1933 Heuss lost his lectureship and his Reichstag seat; his writings were thrown into the flames in the BOOK BURNING, although he was able to write for a considerable time for German newspapers (sometimes under the pseudonym Thomas Brackheim). During the war he occupied himself especially with biographical works. Assisted by the American occupation authorities, Heuss returned to political activity immediately after the war. In 1945 he became culture minister in Württemberg-Baden. As a co-founder and first chairman of the Free Democratic Party (FDP), he successfully worked to unite the liberal parties in the Western zones. On September 12, 1949, Heuss was elected first president of the Federal Republic of Germany (FRG), for which he gained sympathy within the FRG as a folksy father of his country ("Papa Heuss") and international respect as a sophisticated cosmopolitan.

H. H.

Hewel, Walther, b. Cologne, March 25, 1904; d. Berlin (?), May 3, 1945, German politician. While a student, Hewel participated in the HITLER PUTSCH of November 9, 1923. After serving a prison term, he lived abroad as a businessman until 1936. In 1933 he joined the NSDAP Foreign Organization, for which he worked, after his return to Berlin, as a *Gau* main office leader (*Gauhauptstellenleiter*). In 1938 he was made head of the personal staff of the new foreign minister, Joachim von RIBBENTROP. In the Foreign Office Hewel finally rose to be special ambassador and "permanent delegate of the Reich Foreign Minister to the Führer." As foreign-policy liaison at the Führer's headquarters, the ardent National Socialist Hewel met almost daily with Hitler in the last years of the war and belonged to his closest circle. He was counted as missing after early May 1945, presumably a suicide.

Heyde, Werner, b. Forst (Lausitz), April 25, 1902; d. Butzbach, February 13, 1964, German physician. Heyde joined the NSDAP in 1933 after completion of his medical studies, becoming an SS doctor with the rank of SS-*Standartenführer*. He was early on involved in planning the "extermination of unworthy life," after 1939 as a professor of psychiatry and neurology and head of the Reich Association of German Hospitals and Sanatoriums, as well as of the T4 organization (the administrative center of the EUTHA-

Werner Heyde.

NASIA program, located at Tiergartenstrasse 4 in Berlin). In these posts he was thus responsible for the murder of more than 100,000 ill and handicapped persons. Heyde himself headed a group of psychiatrists, with whom he examined inmates in various concentration camps regarding their mental state and "selected" them for killing (*see* INVALID OPERATION).

After the war Heyde was able to escape from American imprisonment. He was condemned to death in absentia by a German court in 1946, but continued to practice for many years in Flensburg as a doctor and state expert under the pseudonym Dr. Fritz Sawade, thereby receiving protection from highly placed officials in Schleswig-Holstein. In 1959 Heyde surrendered himself to the court, his true identity having been revealed, but he committed suicide several days before the trial was to begin.

Heydrich, Reinhard, b. Halle, March 7, 1904; d. Prague, June 4, 1942 (assassinated), German politician. Heydrich's father, Bruno Heydrich, a former Heldentenor, ran a music conservatory. His son Reinhard learned to play the violin well at an early age. He was also active in secondary school (*Gymnasium*) in several sports, notably fencing. In the short navy career (in 1928 he was made first lieutenant) that followed upon his graduation (*Abitur*), he became expert in sailing. The naval career of this Prussian who grew up far from the sea ended abruptly in 1931 before an honor court, in consequence of a broken promise of marriage. In the caste-bound military this charge was considered dishonorable; Heydrich was dismissed for unworthiness.

He applied for entry to the SS and was assigned by Reichsführer Heinrich HIMMLER to form a special SS Security Service (SD). Heydrich created an extensive intelligence service, whose chief he became in July 1932. In 1931 he had married Lina von Osten; four children were born of the marriage. As Himmler's closest collaborator, Heydrich followed one step behind his career path. As the *Reichsführer's* "right hand" at their Munich base in 1933, he helped subjugate the political police (*see* SECRET STATE POLICE [Gestapo]) in all the German states except Prussia. In 1934 Prussia was included, although under Göring's supervision. Heydrich's delegated power was, however, sufficient for successful intrigue in the RÖHM AFFAIR. When Himmler became chief of all German police forces in June 1936, Heydrich combined under his jurisdiction the SD and all political and civil (criminal) secret police (Gestapo and Kripo). His new title was Chief of the Security Police and the SD (*Chef der Sicherheitspolizei und des SD;* CSSD). These offices were combined in 1939, together with several less important functions, in the REICH SECURITY MAIN OFFICE.

The wielders of the greatest power under National Socialism typically championed a fanatic racial consciousness whose criteria they themselves did not satisfy. Externally Heydrich did embody these standards, without representing them internally. According to the criteria for SS selection he was the Nordic ideal—blond, blue-eyed, tall, with sharply chiseled features—but unlike Hitler and Himmler, in

Reinhard Heydrich.

particular, he was not driven in what he did and carried out. Where he exercised power, it was related to the purpose. His decisiveness, high intelligence, and sobriety were employed in a technocratic manner, with no further-reaching goals. To this extent Himmler's perverted idealism was alien to Heydrich. He served the regime with the greatest consistency, without dogmatically committing himself. A "manager of terror," in the words of the Mainz criminologist A. Merge, Heydrich wanted neither to make the world happy nor to transform it. Rather, he wished merely to subordinate it—"a technician of murder for the sake of power." Contemptuous of humanity but not a sadist, cynical but without personal satisfaction in killing, Heydrich became the switchman of mass extermination. It was to him that Göring transmitted the order for the "FINAL SOLUTION of the Jewish question" in July 1941.

Coming from Prague, where since September 1941 he had served as deputy Reich Protector for Bohemia and Moravia in addition to his other duties, Heydrich led the WANNSEE CONFERENCE (January 20, 1942), which translated the program for the Final Solution into a plan for bureaucratic execution. The extermination camps did not, however, come under the Gestapo head, who in September 1941 had been named SS-*Obergruppenführer.*

Heydrich's pragmatic mind resisted the idea of plunder without some compensation, because such measures undercut the desired effect. Thus, after initial single-minded terror (for the purpose of intimidation), he disconcerted the Czechs with extensive social measures. Above all, work for the occupation authorities was paid according to performance. The supply of basic commodities was improved, and industry was given impetus. To a relatively large extent Heydrich satisfied Bohemia and Moravia. This particularly angered the Czech government-in-exile in London: an oppressed people was not supposed to accept its situation. Thus the order went out to eliminate Heydrich. On May 27, 1942, agents who had parachuted in lay in wait for him on the route he traveled daily to his office in the Hradčany Castle. Heydrich was severely wounded and died eight days later of blood poisoning. The SS retribution against the Czech village of LIDICE—whose inhabitants had allegedly aided the perpetrators—was not something on which the government-in-exile had fully reckoned.

H. St.

Heyse, Hans, b. Bremen, March 8, 1891; d. Göttingen, October 19, 1976, German neo-Kantian philosopher. Heyse was a professor in Breslau and Königsberg, and after 1935 in Göttingen. He occupied himself (also after 1945) with questions of the theory of categories. By demarcating classical antiquity and Christianity, he sought to contribute to the philosophical clarification of the Third Reich, which he saw as determined by "basic values of tragic-heroic existence" (*Idee und Existenz* [Idea and Existence]; 1935).

HIAG, acronym of Hilfsgemeinschaft auf Gegenseitigkeit (AUXILIARY FELLOWSHIP FOR RECIPROCITY), an organization of former Waffen-SS members.

"Hib"-Aktion, membership campaign for the NATIONAL SOCIALIST WORKPLACE CELL ORGANIZATION, which used the slogan "Hinein in die Betriebe!" ("Into the Workplaces!").

Hierl, Konstantin, b. Parsberg (Upper Palatinate), February 24, 1875; d. Heidelberg, September 23, 1955, German politician. A General Staff officer in the First World War, Hierl was a free corps leader after the war. In 1919 he returned to the Reichswehr. Discharged from the military as a Ludendorff follower after the HITLER PUTSCH, Hierl joined the NSDAP in 1927 as a "fervent nationalist." In 1929 Hitler appointed him an *Organisationsleiter* II in the Reich administration, in which he developed an "Organization Plan for the REICH LABOR SERVICE" (Reichsarbeitsdienst; RAD). In 1933 Hierl became state secretary in the Reich Labor

Konstantin Hierl.

Ministry and "delegate of the Führer to the RAD," receiving in 1935 the title Reich Labor Führer (*Reicharbeitsführer*) after voluntarism had been replaced by six months of compulsory labor service.

Through the RAD, Hierl wanted to train "German youth in the spirit of National Socialism" for the "experience of the *Volk* Community through work and performance." He also wanted to make "the word 'worker' [*Arbeiter*]" again "a title of honor for every German." Hierl organized the RAD in a strict military fashion according to the Führer Principle. During the war he was put directly under Hitler and in 1945 was made a Reich minister. After 1945 an appeals board classified him as a "major offender" and sentenced him to the loss of half his wealth and five years at hard labor. After his release Hierl worked as a *völkisch* publicist and propagandist, as in his memoirs, *Im Dienst für Deutschland 1918–1945* (In the Service of Germany; 1955).

H. H.

Higher Schools (*Höhere Schulen*), post-elementary (*Volksschule*) educational institutions, such as the *Gymnasium* and the *Ober(real)-*, *Real-*, and *Mittelschulen* (*see* SCHOOL SYSTEM).

Higher SS and Police Leaders (*Höhere SS- und Polizeiführer*; HSSPF), institution whose purpose was the integration of SS and police organizations, as well as their political activation on a regional level. The HSSPF was created through a decree of the Reich interior minister on November 13, 1937. Its original task was to lead all forces (regular police, security police, SS units) under the jurisdiction of the *Reichsführer-SS* and German police chief, Himmler, in case of mobilization. In the course of the war its areas of competence were considerably expanded by Himmler. In particular, it became responsible for pacification and consolidation of the political situation in the occupied territories, which entailed racial purification as well as political control. Its increase in power reached a high point with the assumption of military functions.

A. St.

High finance (*Hochfinanz*), general term, usually with a propagandistic and derogatory intent, for highly capitalized economic sectors, especially for bankers and financiers who used their influence for political ends. "Jewish high finance" played a central role in National Socialist conspiracy theories, and the struggle against it

increasingly replaced the original social-revolutionary demands in the program of the NATIONAL SOCIALIST GERMAN WORKERS' PARTY: as early as April 13, 1928, Hitler declared that Point 17 (expropriation) was directed solely against "Jewish" speculators. After the Seizure of Power, PERSECUTION OF JEWS was substituted for a real attack on the influence of German high finance, which was heavily involved in REARMAMENT and ARYANIZATION, among other programs. The antidemocratic propaganda of National Socialism emphasized the power of "Jewish high finance" in the Western countries in order to label them as plutocracies (*see* PLUTOCRACY).

High treason. *See Volk* treason.

Hildebrand, Friedrich, b. Kiekindemark (Mecklenburg), September 19, 1898; d. Landsberg, 1948 (executed), German politician. Hildebrand was a rural laborer, a war volunteer, and then a free corps member. After the First World War he became a functionary in organizations for agricultural workers. In 1924 Hildebrand entered the Mecklenburg diet as the top candidate on the party list of the German-Völkisch Freedom Movement; he made an alliance with several followers of the NSDAP, himself assuming the office of *Gauleiter* of Mecklenburg-Lübeck (in 1930–1931 he was temporarily suspended). Thanks to his untiring work as a propagandist and campaigner, in 1932 Mecklenburg became one of the first German states in whose *Landtag* (provincial diet) the NSDAP won an absolute majority. On May 12, 1933, Hildebrand became Reich governor in Mecklenburg-

Friedrich Hildebrand.

Lübeck; in 1942 he was promoted to SS-*Ober-gruppenführer* and became Reich defense commissioner. In 1947 an American military court condemned him to death.

Hilferding, Rudolf, b. Vienna, August 10, 1877; d. Paris, February 10, 1941, German-Austrian politician and social scientist. Hilferding was originally a pediatrician in Vienna. Through numerous articles and polemical writings he soon became one of the leading theorists of German Social Democracy, and in 1906 was called to Berlin as a teacher at the party school. He then became editor of the party newspaper *Vorwärts* (Forward). In 1910 Hilferding published his main theoretical work, *Das Finanz-kapital* (translated as *Finance Capital*), in which he revised the Marxist thesis of the unavoidable collapse of the capitalist system. From 1919 to 1922 he was with the Independent Socialists (USPD), but he returned to the Social Democratic Party (SPD) and developed increasingly revisionist positions, which he attempted to realize as Reich finance minister in 1923 and 1928–1929.

Because of his theoretical writings, the National Socialists attacked Hilferding as a "Marxist" and a "dogmatic Israelite," and his agreement to reparations made him a "fulfillment helper" in the "financial bleeding of Germany." In 1933 he had to flee to Switzerland, where he was a primary author of the PRAGUE MANIFESTO, the party program of the exiled SPD. In 1935 he was stripped of his citizenship for "agitation hostile to Germany." He went to France, where

he was arrested by the French police in Vichy on February 9, 1941. Handed over to the Gestapo and mistreated, he died in prison.

Hilfswillige. *See* Volunteer Helpers.

Hilgenfeldt, Erich, b. Heinitz (Kreis Ottweiler), July 2, 1897; d. Regensburg, June 17, 1969, German politician. Hilgenfeldt progressed from salesclerk to manager in a middle-class business operation, then became an employee in the Reich Statistical Office. Politically he was involved in the National Association of German Officers and the STEEL HELMET, until he joined the NSDAP in 1929. Hilgenfeldt made his career as an organizer and propagandist, and in 1933 became *Gau* inspector for Greater Berlin. Through the assumption of various functions and offices he quickly rose to become the most important social policymaker in the Third Reich. As head of the Office for Volk Welfare at Reich NSDAP headquarters and as Reich Leader of the National Socialist Volk Welfare agency (NSV), Hilgenfeldt was entrusted by Goebbels with leadership of the WINTER RELIEF AGENCY, which he built up so successfully in a few weeks that the press was able to celebrate him as "General of the Winter Relief Battle." Hilgenfeldt administered the SYNCHRONIZATION of the independent welfare organizations from his viewpoint of SOCIAL POLICY as primarily a propaganda instrument of the state.

Hilgenreiner, Karl, b. Friedberg (Hesse), February 22, 1867; d. Vienna, May 9, 1948, German theologian and politician. Hilgenreiner was a professor of Catholic moral theology and social

Rudolf Hilferding.

Erich Hilgenfeldt.

doctrine at the German University of Prague. As co-founder, sometime party chairman, and deputy of the German Christian-Social People's Party in the Czechoslovak Republic, he was considered a "zealous promoter of the Sudeten German unity movement" in the late 1930s. In 1938 he effected the merging of the Christian Socials into Konrad Henlein's SUDETEN GERMAN PARTY.

Himmler, Heinrich, b. Munich, October 7, 1900; d. Lüneburg, May 23, 1945, German politician. Himmler grew up in a Catholic middle-class household. His father was a *Gymnasium* teacher. After taking an emergency high school diploma (*Abitur*) during the First World War, Himmler volunteered, but never reached the front. Between 1919 and 1922 he studied agriculture at the Technical University in Munich. After receiving a diploma, he became an agricultural assistant in Schleissheim. Inclined toward conservatism, he sought membership and activity in the nationalist paramilitary group Reich Flag (Reichsflagge) with the ambition of one who came to the war too late. He then joined the Hitler movement and took part in the HITLER PUTSCH as one of the standard-bearers.

Himmler came into close personal contact with Hitler only after the latter's release from the Landsberg prison in 1924. Imbued with a sense of religious conviction, yet not securely rooted in Catholicism, Himmler transferred his search for a spiritual home unreservedly to Hitler and the National Socialist (NS) worldview. Also significant for Himmler was his choice of an agricultural profession at a time when the mythology of BLOOD AND SOIL had taken hold in nationalist circles. Himmler entered into the tightly knit world of the ARTAMANEN, within which he became a *Gauführer* in 1925. In his mid-twenties, he found concrete applications and vivid examples of the general NS notions of *Volk* and race in the elements of freehold farming (*landsässige Kultur*), customs (*see* BRAUCHTUM UND SITTE), selective breeding and upgrading of species, and the neo-Germanic race. The trained agricultural expert became the apostle of a new racial consciousness who used the intellectual categories of his learned profession, and who to a greater degree than his Führer exhibited a sectarian impulse. Whereas Hitler set forth only broad goals and issued general directives, Himmler, with pedantic precision and pedagogic zeal, set about realizing his master's guidelines.

He found the instrument for this in the elite troops of the SS (Schutzstaffeln; Protection Squad). Evolving from the personal staff guard of the party leader (1921) within the paramilitary SA, the SS had its own identity after 1925, but remained an integral part of the SA under its leadership. At this time Himmler achieved his first prominence with general party responsibilities. In 1925 he became general secretary

Heinrich Himmler (fourth from left) at the 1923 Hitler Putsch in Munich.

of the Lower Bavarian *Gau,* and deputy *Gauleiter* and propaganda director (*Obmann*) for Upper Bavaria and Swabia. In 1927 he was named deputy *Reichsführer-SS.* The SS at that point consisted of a few hundred men. Yet Himmler's organizational ability, his hard work, ideological imperturbability, unconditional loyalty to the Führer, and life free of scandal soon brought him attention as a person worthy of promotion. By 1929 he was the (third and last) *Reichsführer-SS.*

Himmler wanted to see his racial ideal incorporated in the SS. His guidelines for selection specified strict "Aryan" criteria: by family origins, "hereditary biology," health, physique, and physiognomy. Like a zealous personnel manager, Himmler himself was fond of poring over passport photos with a magnifying lens— no matter that his own physical type (average height, dark hair, nearsightedness, weak chin) did not bespeak the Nordic ideal. Consciousness of the elite character of the SS allowed Himmler to look down arrogantly on the crude and simple street-brawler types who represented the typical SA man. Nonetheless, photographs from the early 1930s show him, loyally and with an inscrutable expression, in the second row behind SA leader Ernst RÖHM.

The events of the year 1933 at first brought no advance in Himmler's career comparable to that obviously enjoyed by other Hitler grandees. He became police chief in Munich. Yet with circumspection and a view for the long haul, he single-mindedly used this opportunity. For here he had reached a summit of state executive power. From Munich he brought under his control the political police, first of Bavaria, then of all the German states with the exception of Prussia, where Minister President Göring himself controlled the SECRET STATE POLICE (Gestapo). Himmler's right hand became Reinhard HEYDRICH, who built up the SS's internal Security and Intelligence Service after 1931. In 1934 Göring named Himmler as deputy Gestapo chief in Prussia. This key position opened the center of power to Himmler and Heydrich. At the same time, it gave them the opportunity to bring the simmering RÖHM AFFAIR to a boil. With material they themselves had prepared, they convinced Hitler of purported putschist intentions within the SA. After Röhm's removal, the SS was released from the tutelage of the now domesticated SA and elevated as an independent organization (July 25, 1934).

This first decisive step into the power elite of

Heinrich Himmler.

the Third Reich was followed by a second one on June 17, 1936, when the *Reichsführer* was given control of all police forces in the Reich. Himmler's title was now *Reichsführer-SS und Chef der Deutschen Polizei.* Besides the SS, which in the meantime had grown to 50,000 members, Himmler now additionally controlled the entire state security apparatus. A totally pervasive system of control and supervision was at his service, or now developed in consequent elaboration of his tools of power. Himmler created a state within a state, a proliferating growth of interwoven jurisdictions, amid which, with his mastery of bureaucracy and instinct for power, he maintained total and unlimited control. The SS empire reached from the institutes for training future generations (*see* JUNKER SCHOOLS) and the breeding facilities (*see* LEBENSBORN) to the army of millions in the regular police, and on to the vast complex of the CONCENTRATION CAMPS under the jurisdiction of the DEATH'S-HEAD UNITS. Each SS central office, from the personal staff of the *Reichsführer* to the office in charge of "strengthening the German *Volk*" (the latter a wartime creation), was directed by an *Obergruppenführer,* one of Himmler's generals. In the midst of the giant machinery, the motor serviced by Heydrich turned quietly and very efficiently. His office, the REICH SECURITY MAIN OFFICE, had authority over such bodies as the SECURITY SERVICE (SD), as well as the SECURITY POLICE with its Kripo (Criminal Police) and Gestapo subdivisions.

When war broke out Himmler extended his complex apparatus of domination to the occupied territories, grasping the east with particular intensity. Only now did he fully reveal the duplicity of his nature, which here resembled Hitler's: policymaker and executor in one person. On the one hand, "he himself [thought out Hitler's ideas] to the end, but [he] also possessed . . . the power of translating them into reality: this determined his rank and his standing in the hierarchy of the Third Reich" (Joachim Fest). Thoroughly imbued with ideology, he did not exercise power for its own sake, but rather believed that he was serving a mission; in this too he resembled Hitler. The struggle in the east was for both men the struggle of a worldview against Slavic and Jewish "subhumans."

This missionary consciousness explains how Himmler, without inner conflict, could preach moral ideals and yet allow millions of human beings to be exterminated (*see* EINSATZGRUPPEN; FINAL SOLUTION). In many (secret) talks he attempted to harden his SS men against any scruples regarding killing; and without reservation he signed death sentences when his own men enriched themselves with Jewish property. Thus "King Heinrich," as his supporters called him (his mockers said "Reichsheini"), was the overseer of virtue in the SS as well as the greatest organizer of mass murder in the history of the world. The intermixing of the policy of extermination with a legalistic mentality was condensed in his matchless statement (in Posen, October 1943): "If the annihilation were not terrible and so frightful for us, then we would not be Germans."

In his accumulation of offices, Himmler nearly matched Göring. After also becoming Reich Commissioner for the "Fortification of the German Volk-Nation" in 1939, he added the post of interior minister in 1943; after July 20, 1944, he had command over the replacement army (*Ersatzheer*). Thus he once more focused his energies on the inner Reich as the mammoth

territory in the east was lost, concentrating especially on the persecution of the conspirators after the 20th of July, 1944, and on the mobilization of the last fighting reserves, including the VOLK STORM. In 1945 the SS and Police Leader, himself without combat experience, failed as leader of two army groups. Hitler caught word of Himmler's secret armistice negotiations with the West, and in his political testament removed his until then unconditionally loyal lieutenant from all offices and expelled him from the party. Himmler made his way to Flensburg, where the Dönitz government rejected him as a liability. Captured in an attempt to escape through the British lines in disguise, Himmler committed suicide.

H. St.

Himmler Friends' Circle (*Freundeskreis Himmler; Freundeskreis Reichsführer-SS*), circle of leading figures from the business world, government bureaucrats, and high SS leaders, originating from the KEPPLER CIRCLE in 1935. Built up and supervised by a former co-worker of industrialist Wilhelm Keppler, the circle averaged some 44 members (1944). The original purpose of the circle—economic advice and influence over National Socialist policy—was soon subordinated to Himmler's own economic interests, as he used his personal connections with the industrialists to build up SS enterprises. Himmler's circle is an especially striking example of the close cooperation between the state and private economic interests: members of it were involved in the creation and running of state corporations (for example, Braunkohle-Benzin-AG, for production of coal and oil), and figured also in ARYANIZATION. In addition, they supported Himmler through contributions of 8 million RM, which went to SS formations (especially for weapons and other equipment).

R. S.

Hindemith, Paul, b. Hanau, November 16, 1895; d. Frankfurt am Main, December 28, 1963, German composer. Hindemith began his studies (violin and composition) in 1909. In 1915 he became first concertmaster of the Frankfurt Opera Orchestra. He was violist with the Amar Quartet (1922–1929), and taught composition at the Berlin Conservatory (1927–1937). During the 1920s, Hindemith was the guiding spirit of the music festival to "promote contemporary music" in Donaueschingen. Such provocative and satirical works as the opera *Mörder, Hoffnung der Frauen* (Murder, the Hope of Women;

1921) and *Minimax* (1922), a parody on military music, earned him reproach even then in conservative—and especially *völkisch* and nationalist —circles, of "musical Bolshevism." After the Seizure of Power his works were banned, despite the intervention of Wilhelm FURTWÄNGLER. In 1938 Hindemith emigrated to the United States via Switzerland, returning again to Europe only in 1953. He became an American citizen in 1946. His other works include the operas *Mathis der Maler* (Mathis the Painter; 1934) and *Das lange Weihnachtsmahl* (The Long Christmas Dinner; 1960), and numerous symphonies, works for piano, and songs; his writings include *Unterweisungen im Tonsatz* (Instructions in Composition, 3 vols., 1937–1970).

R. H.

Hindenburg, Oskar von, b. Königsberg, January 31, 1883; d. Bad Harzburg, February 12, 1960, German politician. During the First World War, Hindenburg served as adjutant to his father, Field Marshal Paul von HINDENBURG; after the war, he was his father's personal assistant, gaining ever more influence over the man who became Reich president. Cynics spoke of the "constitutionally not-provided-for son of the Reich president." Hindenburg was significantly involved in the intrigues preceding Hitler's appointment as Reich chancellor (January 30, 1933), and rumors persisted that the National Socialists had blackmailed him because of his alleged enrichment through EASTERN AID funds. After the death of his father, Hindenburg used a radio address of August 18, 1934, to urge a vote of "yes" on the referendum to consolidate the offices of chancellor and president in Hitler's hands (*see* FÜHRER UND REICHSKANZLER). His father himself had seen Hitler as his successor, the son asserted.

Hindenburg, Paul von Beneckendorff und von, b. Posen, October 2, 1846; d. Neudeck (West Prussia), August 2, 1934, German field marshal and politician. As a professional officer, Hindenburg participated in the Austro-Prussian (1866) and Franco-German (1870–1871) wars. He made his career in the General Staff, and retired in 1911 as a senior general. In the First World War he was reactivated, and made field marshal general and supreme commander in the east. Through victories over superior Russian forces

At the Hindenburg Neudeck estate. From the right: Oskar von Hindenburg, Otto Meissner (state secretary), Franz von Papen, and Gen. Kurt von Schleicher.

at Tannenberg and the Masurian Lakes in 1914, he became the most popular German military leader. In 1916 Hindenburg, along with First Quartermaster General Erich LUDENDORFF, took over the supreme army command and was able to exercise nearly dictatorial influence over strategic planning and the direction of the war, as well as over industrial production and deployment of the civilian labor force.

In 1918 Hindenburg saw it as his duty to the nation, together with the Social Democrats Friedrich EBERT and Gustav NOSKE, to provide for "peace and order" against revolutionary efforts from the Left. After acceptance of the Versailles treaty, which even the monarchist and nationalist Hindenburg considered "unavoidable," he again retired, while contributing through public declarations to the spread of the STAB-IN-THE-BACK LEGEND.

As the ever-popular symbolic figure of the German Right, Hindenburg allowed himself, after the death of President Ebert in 1925, to be put forward by the combined parties of the Right in the election of a new Reich president. He was elected with 48 percent of the votes, the Centrist Wilhelm MARX receiving 45 percent. Although Hindenburg opposed the Weimar Republic, as president he hewed so closely to the limits set forth in the constitution that the National Socialists reproached him with being only a "protective cover for the worn-out Weimar system." The aging Reich president, slowly losing his own capacity of judgment, fell increasingly under the influence of powerful right-wing agricultural circles (including Franz

Paul von Beneckendorff und von Hindenburg.

von PAPEN) and the Reichswehr leadership (including Kurt von SCHLEICHER). Weary of the continued governmental crisis, Hindenburg together with Heinrich BRÜNING established the first of the PRESIDIAL CABINETS in 1930, thereby undermining the parliamentary system. In 1932 he won re-election against the candidacy of Hitler, but no longer with the support of the parties of the Right alone—rather "mit Sozis und Katholen," as Hitler contemptuously characterized the SPD (Social Democratic Party) and Catholic Centrist support.

For a long time the president fought against giving Hitler governmental responsibility, but he finally chose this path in preference to further elections or manipulations of the constitution. Hindenburg hoped that by naming Hitler as chancellor (January 30, 1933; *see* SEIZURE OF POWER), he could "channel the Nazi flood." Then he once again approved new elections and, with the REICHSTAG FIRE DECREE, gave the new "Government of the National Rising" (*Regierung der nationalen Erhebung*) the instrument with which it could liquidate the Weimar Republic. The National Socialists exploited the imperial nostalgia evoked by the "father figure" Hindenburg to give moral support to their regime, transforming him into the "faithful Eckart of the German *Volk*" (*see* POTSDAM CELEBRATION). In the following months the elderly Hindenburg was increasingly cut off from information and robbed of his opportunities for influence. Weak protests against the onset of the PERSECUTION OF JEWS remained almost without effect; in vain the Evangelical Church turned to Hindenburg in the raging CHURCH STRUGGLE. When Hitler finally secured his power with the murderous operation of the RÖHM AFFAIR, the mortally ill president congratulated the chancellor. After Hindenburg's death Hitler became sole master (FÜHRER UND REICHSKANZLER), using the funeral ceremonies at the Tannenberg Monument as a charade of continuity by celebrating the National Socialists as heirs of the Prussian state.

Hindenburg Fund (*Hindenburgspende*), name of a social fund to support war victims and small pensioners, established in 1927 to honor the Reich president on his 80th birthday; the money was raised by popular subscription. In 1928 the fund became a foundation, with some of the capital placed at Hindenburg's personal disposal. For his 85th and 90th (posthumous) birthdays, new subscriptions were begun, which in 1937 alone brought in nearly 3.2 million RM.

Hindenburg and Hitler in the Garrison Church at the Potsdam Celebration (1933).

"Hinein in die Betriebe!" ("Into the Workplaces!"), motto of the NATIONAL SOCIALIST WORKPLACE CELL ORGANIZATION for a 1931 campaign.

Hinkel, Hans, b. Worms, June 22, 1901, German cultural functionary. Hinkel joined the NSDAP on October 4, 1921. A journalist and editor of several National Socialist newspapers and journals, he was Berlin editor of the VÖLKISCHER

Hans Hinkel.

BEOBACHTER from 1930 to 1932. Until 1933 he was a leading functionary and ideologue in the COMBAT LEAGUE FOR GERMAN CULTURE. After the takeover of power, Goebbels made the ambitious Hinkel a commissioner in charge of surveillance of "non-Aryans active in intellectual and cultural areas," a post in the Propaganda Ministry, where he concerned himself with the "DE-JEWING" of German cultural life, and especially of the universities. In 1935 Hinkel was made chief of the "cultural personnel" division, which was responsible for keeping all "culture creators" under observation. In 1936 he also became secretary-general of the REICH CULTURE CHAMBER. Because Hinkel had proved himself an especially adaptable functionary, Goebbels made him Reich Film Director in 1944, also putting him in charge of the film division in the Propaganda Ministry. There, in the final stages of the war, he was to expedite the politicization of the film industry and to keep up the production of feature films into the last days of the war.

Hinzert, special SS camp near Hermeskeil (Hunsrück), originally built in September 1939 as a so-called work and education camp for German malingerers (*see* WORK-SHY; persons refusing to work who were now laboring in the TODT ORGANIZATION) and others. On July 1,

1940, Hinzert, along with an associated police internment camp, was placed under the Inspectorate of Concentration Camps, and its guard corps was transferred to the SS Death's-Head Units. After a period of temporary jurisdiction under the State Police Office in Luxembourg-Trier (1942), Hinzert finally became an auxiliary camp of the BUCHENWALD concentration camp in January 1945. During the war it received Polish and Russian "work objectors," Polish civilian workers deemed suitable for RE-GERMANIZATION, German foreign legionnaires, Belgians, Dutch citizens, Luxembourgers, Italians, and French victims of the "NIGHT AND FOG" DECREE; an average 600 to 800 prisoners were housed in the various divisions (protective-custody camp, work education camp, and so on).

The camp inmates worked in road construction, in building the WESTWALL, in the forest, on airfields, and in factories. In Hinzert as in other camps, prisoners were killed by brutal mistreatment, shootings, and "injections" of poisonous substances administered to those who were ill or incapable of work. The camp was evacuated on March 3, 1945, with the arrival of Allied troops.

W. D.

Hirsch, Otto, b. Stuttgart, January 9, 1885; d. Mauthausen concentration camp, June 19,

1941, German Jewish politician. Hirsch, who had studied law, was active in Stuttgart's municipal government. In 1933, under Leo BAECK, he became head of the REICH REPRESENTATION OF GERMAN JEWS; during numerous trips abroad he sought help, especially emigration assistance, for German Jews. At the Evian refugee conference in 1938 he appealed, with little success, to potential accepting nations to relax their immigration regulations. Despite repeated arrests and increasing National Socialist terror against Jews, Hirsch rejected tempting offers from abroad and tried to save the greatest possible number of his co-religionists from Germany before the war. In the spring of 1941 he was finally arrested and sent to the Mauthausen concentration camp, where he died from the inhuman conditions.

Hirschfeld, Magnus (pseud., Ramien), b. Kolberg, May 14, 1868; d. Nice (France), May 15, 1935, German sex researcher, neurologist, and publicist. The co-founder of the first journal for the scientific study of sex (*Zeitschrift für Sexualwissenschaft*), Hirschfeld established a neurological practice in Berlin in 1910. Through his campaign against the criminalization of HOMOSEXUALITY, as well as through his support for birth control and easier divorce, Hirschfeld early attracted the hatred of conservative bourgeois circles, although he himself was decided-

Magnus Hirschfeld. In front of his Institute for Sexual Studies, National Socialist students line up before raiding its library.

ly nationalistic in other matters. The Institute for Sexual Studies, founded by Hirschfeld in Berlin in 1918, with which the first German marital counseling agency was affiliated and which devoted itself especially to the counseling of homosexuals, was considered by the National Socialists to be "a singular breeding ground for filth and dirt" (*Der Angriff*, 1933). On May 6, 1933, it was occupied and pillaged by students; its entire library was burned on May 10 (*see* BOOK BURNING). Behind the vilification of the "half Jew" Hirschfeld lay more than the official fight against the "undermining of morality in sexual life." It also revealed the aggression of those who might be caught out, since especially in the SA, homosexual relationships played a significant role (*see* Ernst RÖHM).

Hirschfeld went into exile in France; his German citizenship was revoked in 1934.

H. H.

Hirtsiefer, Heinrich, b. Essen, April 26, 1876; d. Berlin, May 15, 1941, German politician. A locksmith, Hirtsiefer joined the Christian workers' movement. From 1919 to 1933 he served as a Center party deputy in the Prussian diet, and from 1921 to 1933 he was Prussian welfare minister. A deputy to Prussian minister-president Otto BRAUN, he was a strong opponent of the Papen government. After the Seizure of Power, Hirtsiefer was put in "protective custody" and then interned in a concentration camp on false charges of bribery; he was amnestied in 1934.

Adolf Hitler

The founder and destroyer of the Great-German "Third Reich" was born on April 20, 1889, in Braunau am Inn, Austria, and died by his own hand on April 30, 1945, in the bunker below the Reich Chancellery in Berlin. Four stages stand out from one another in his life, which was both a reflection and the motivating force of his epoch: (1) the phase of ideological development in Linz, Vienna, and Munich, which included the First World War; (2) the TIME OF STRUGGLE during the Weimar Republic; (3) the years as chancellor, from 1933 to 1939; and, finally, (4) the military leadership of Germany in the Second World War and the extermination measures against the Jews.

His father, Alois HITLER, born Schicklgruber and later legitimized, was an Austrian customs official. The identity of Alois Hitler's father (Adolf's grandfather) is not completely certain because of incestuous relationships. However, Werner Maser's investigations have thoroughly dispelled persistent speculations regarding Jewish ancestors ("Frankenberger"). Alois Hitler was an ambitious autodidact who wanted his son to continue enjoying the success and security that he himself had gained as a civil servant.

Alois Hitler.

Klara Hitler.

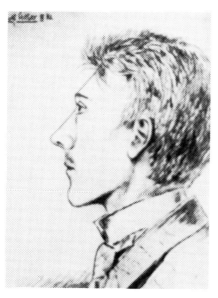

Adolf Hitler. Sketch by a classmate from the year 1905.

When Adolf resisted, severe tensions arose between the authoritarian father and the rebellious son. On the other hand, Adolf had close ties to his mother, Klara HITLER, née Pölzl. Alois died in 1903, ending the authoritarian domestic regime in Hitler's 14th year, after which he was totally indulged.

After repeated moves and changes of school (Passau, Lambach an der Traun, Leonding bei Linz, Linz), Adolf was a student at the *Realschule* at his father's death. He then transferred to the *Oberrealschule* in Steyr an der Enns, remaining there until 1905, when the 16-year-old ended his schooling after the ninth class. The best mark on his graduation certificate was "excellent" (*vorzüglich*), earned in gymnastics and freehand drawing, and confirming his desire to be a professional artist. After two years of doing nothing in his mother's house in Linz, he applied to the Vienna Academy of Art, but failed because his talents pointed him toward architectural drawing more than painting. However, he lacked the *Abitur* certificate necessary for the study of architecture. After his mother's death in 1907 and an unsuccessful second attempt at the academy, Hitler lived in Vienna without a completed education. He supported himself by selling postcards with his own architectural drawings, supplemented by his part of an inheritance from his parents (shared with a sister and two half sisters), as well as an orphan's allowance. His circumstances were adequate.

In addition to art, Hitler developed an increasing "interest in everything connected with poli-

tics." Through his history teacher in Linz, Leopold Poetsch, he had already been influenced by German nationalist, anti-Habsburg views. In order not to serve the Habsburgs, he evaded military duty through repeated and frequent changes of residence until he felt "safe." Hitler admired the fanatic pan-German Georg von SCHÖNERER, who supported the unification of German Austria with the Reich and the exclusion of all non-German parts of the empire. Hitler's Great-German, all-German ideology included two other vital elements: anti-Marxism (as a rejection of supernational, socialist brotherhood) and antisemitism (as a rejection of "un-German" ethnic elements). In May 1913 he moved to Munich in order to elude more serious searches by the Austrian military authorities; he was, however, discovered and ordered to report for military examination in Salzburg. Freed from military service in Austria ("Too weak. Unfit for service"), he nonetheless immediately volunteered for the Bavarian-German army when war broke out in August 1914. He saw meaning only in service in Germany's armed forces.

Promoted to lance corporal, between 1914 and 1918 Hitler was a messenger with the Sixteenth Infantry Regiment (List). He was awarded the IRON CROSS, First Class (August 1918), which was rarely given to noncommissioned ranks. Citations were uniform as to Hitler's bravery, yet "no requisite qualities of leadership" were found to warrant promotion. Moreover, Hitler was said not to want to be promoted. In October 1918 he was gassed in Flanders; temporarily blinded, he recuperated in a military hospital in Pasewalk in Pomerania.

Hitler was in Pasewalk when the war ended. Then and there, he made the decision "to become a politician" in order to avenge the "ignominy" of capitulation (*Mein Kampf*). He firmly believed in the "dagger stab" behind an undefeated front by the Marxist-infected homeland (*see* STAB-IN-THE-BACK LEGEND). In May 1919 Hitler put himself at the service of the Reichswehr, attracting the attention of his superiors as "reliably national." His first successes as a speaker were in the Lechfeld camp before returned prisoners of war who were susceptible to revolution.

On September 12, 1919, Hitler was assigned to report on one of Munich's countless right-wing parties and groups, the GERMAN WORKERS' PARTY (Deutsche Arbeiterpartei; DAP). There he gained attention through his impassioned contribution to the discussions. After a

Hitler (far right) as a lance corporal at his quarters in Frommelles (1916).

period of reflection, he joined the party as its 55th member. His function as chief recruiter (*Werbeobmann*) was to gain new members. He saw this still totally unknown party as an instrument that could be molded to his purposes, unlike an old and established one through whose ranks he would have to climb. This was the beginning of Hitler's career.

He began immediately by making a noise in public. Hitler was organizationally inventive, demagogic, innately gifted with an ability to make contact with a mass audience, an orator with inflammatory and radical black-and-white rhetoric. Condensing all evil into simple formulas and clearly fixing blame (NOVEMBER CRIMINALS, "infamous Versailles treaty," "international Jewry"), he attracted more and more listeners to the DAP, which was renamed the NATIONAL SOCIALIST GERMAN WORKERS' PARTY (Nationalsozialistische Deutsche Arbeiter-Partei; NSDAP) in February 1920. Its 25-point program was written without significant involvement by Hitler, whose tactical thinking shied away from the bonds of paragraphs; the program nonetheless was in keeping with his worldview, especially in regard to Points 1 (Great-German Reich) and 2 (exclusion of Jews, especially from public offices and the press). In July 1921 he appropriated the party leadership for himself. It was then that devoted followers introduced the

FÜHRER CULT. The NSDAP expanded its organization throughout Germany.

The course of nationalistic confrontation between the Bavarian state government (*see* Ritter von KAHR) and the Weimar government, with the former's tendency toward high treason, led Hitler to a false assessment of the balance of power within Germany. He thought the time was ripe for an upheaval, and wanted to use the intentions he attributed to Kahr—in this way

Hitler in 1921.

stealing a march on him—for himself, thereby "overtaking him from the right." Thus the HITLER PUTSCH, precipitate and inadequately prepared, took place on November 8–9, 1923. The resultant trial at times resembled a farce, since the judge was close to Hitler in worldview and allowed him ample opportunity for self-expression. Hitler was sentenced to five years' imprisonment with a prospect of early release.

In Landsberg am Lech, the model prisoner dictated the first volume of MEIN KAMPF. Two key theses in the book prove that Hitler's later policies were already clearly delineated. On the racial question, Hitler argued, the National Socialist movement must "direct universal outrage" against the Jewish race, "the evil enemy of humankind, as the true source of all misery." The future policy of LIVING SPACE was prefigured with the sentence "When today in Europe we speak of new land and soil, we can think in the first place only of Russia and the subject states around it." Thus, undeterred by his political defeat and with no prospect for success, Hitler boldly delineated his program for the future. The ideological receptacle (race and space) would one day be filled with content (Auschwitz and Operation "Barbarossa"; see HITLER'S WORLDVIEW).

Released after nine months, Hitler refounded the collapsed NS movement. In Bamberg, he resolved the ideological struggle between north and south with a clear victory for himself (February 1926) against Gregor STRASSER and Joseph Goebbels. He thereafter won over Goebbels as a follower and sent the capable organizer and demagogue to Berlin as a Gauleiter. Because of Germany's relative economic recovery, these years were the least successful politically for Hitler. This is evidence that the NSDAP was a party of crisis. It thrived less from its convincing ideology than through its radical rejection of the Weimar "system," as an expression of concentrated indignation.

It was the WORLD ECONOMIC CRISIS after the autumn of 1929 that brought the party its second, decisive upturn, with rapid rates of growth in members and voters—all those who doubted that parliamentary democracy could overcome the distress. Hitler, who had learned from the first mistake, wanted to conquer the Republic legally, with its own instruments (see LEGALITY OATH of 1930). Only now did he become a German citizen, through the fictitious post of government councillor (Regierungsrat) in the state of Braunschweig. As a candidate for the office of Reich president in the

spring of 1932, he won a moral victory (over 13 million votes) against the victorious Hindenburg.

In 1932 the Republic became ungovernable. No majority capable of passing legislation could be mobilized against the NSDAP, as the strongest Reichstag delegation, and against the also totally negative Communist party (KPD). In the background were 6 million unemployed. Reich President Hindenburg, after naming two hapless chancellors (Franz von PAPEN and Kurt von SCHLEICHER), under the influence of close advisers (see SEIZURE OF POWER) overcame his reservations toward Hitler, whose person and aims he mistrusted, but whose nationalist language and military orientation were close to his own. On January 30, 1933, he named Hitler Reich chancellor.

Hitler demonstrated tactical considerations in forming his cabinet. With only two NS ministers, the conservatives seemed to dominate, with Papen as vice-chancellor. Yet with one fellow party member as interior minister (Wilhelm FRICK), Hitler controlled the police, and thereby deployable power—a rule of thumb for a dictatorial takeover of a state. Germany was, however, still a multiparty state, and January 30 only a first caesura. But until the elections on March 3 there was unrelenting campaigning. The REICHSTAG FIRE (February 2), an act carried out by the loner Marinus van der LUBBE, was immediately exploited to strengthen the position of the NSDAP (see REICHSTAG FIRE DECREE): the theory of a Communist conspiracy justified a wave of arrests and the de facto destruction of the KPD. The party's new Reichstag mandates were immediately voided, thus giving the NSDAP a slight but absolute majority.

Hitler gained total freedom of action only through the ENABLING LAW (March 23), which completed the Seizure of Power. He gathered together the straitened circumstances he faced, insofar as they seemed to confirm his view of the world, transformed them into compelling oratory, and flung them back, amplified, at the public mind: the ruinous politics of the victors of the First World War; mass misery; a parliament adept at standing pat; weariness with democracy and its failed mechanisms; a damaged sense of self-worth (which he reactivated); fear of Bolshevism, compared to which National Socialism seemed the lesser evil; the longing for a leader as a Kaiser substitute. Hitler duplicated every feeling of discomfort and resentment with an oversimplified, transparent understanding of the state and a well-defined

1

2

3

4

Ein Volk, ein Reich, ein Führer!

5

1
Building in Fournes. Drawing by Hitler from the First World War.
2
"This little book costs twelve marks? A bit expensive, my friend . . . don't you have any matches?" Ridiculing [in thick Bavarian accent] of *Mein Kampf* in *Simplicissimus* (1925).
3
Nazi kitsch: porcelain plate with portrait of Hitler.
4
Hitler slogan as wall decoration: "One *Volk*, one Reich, one Führer!"
5
Hitler with Eva Braun on the Obersalzberg.

notion of the enemy (the Jews and Marxists). As the German politician with the strongest will and the crudest demagogic methods, and with an undeniable charismatic aura, he proved himself a master of psychological mass manipulation. Finally, every historical observer finds it difficult, given the disunity among Hitler's opponents, to imagine alternative scenarios that would have allowed Hitler to be avoided or ignored in 1933.

Through Hitler's dictatorship, the last 12 years of his life and Germany's political history during those years became nearly identical. In his own person he had always been unusually shadowy, even colorless, but from this point on his life was completely absorbed in the state and its purposes. A private sphere, although it existed, manifested—with Eva BRAUN on the Obersalzberg—a monotonous sociability and, later, endless monologues at headquarters in the company of credulous and devoted bit players (see TABLE TALKS). A personal picture of Hitler must also include—along with the Austrian gallantry toward women—a sympathetic, paternalistic concern for and attention toward persons in his immediate circle that could disarm even fanatic prejudices: for example, his promise to protect his former chauffeur Emil Maurice, who had been found out as "non-Aryan," and his personal cook, who had been fired for the same fault.

The academic dispute about the extent to which Hitler was merely an exponent of NS rule—with independently operating power centers—as against his having been the sole center of power, really presents no interpretive problems if properly stated: after the RÖHM AFFAIR (the third victorious internal struggle after the two revolts by Gregor Strasser in 1926 and 1932), Hitler experienced no further confrontations from ideologically antagonistic party members. Until the end, his decisions were not disputed at any level, in the occasional specific instances not even within the Wehrmacht (putsch attempts were directed against his person and the system as a whole). On the other hand, Hitler gave relatively free rein to the power elite. In domestic politics, which did not interest him, he promoted and tolerated rivalries and himself stood untouched above the fray. Hitler was the center of willpower, but he delegated power freely. He scarcely governed, but he did rule and dominate. Primary worldview concerns (the Final Solution, wartime decisions, campaigns) finally remained the decisions of Hitler alone.

Through impressive economic successes, at first even without Germany's rearming, Hitler so strengthened his position with a people surrounded by hoopla that he became a figure of deliverance and salvation for millions. This also proves that his dictatorship, unlike the contemporary one under Stalin, was not felt as oppressive by the majority. Persecuted minorities and various opposition groups remained isolated, bound together in misery, fear, and rejection. The high point of popularity was effected by the successes of 1938, attained without force: the ANSCHLUSS with Austria in March, and the gain of the Sudeten areas through the MUNICH AGREEMENT in September.

In 1939, Hitler focused his plans along two major ideological axes: race and space. After KRISTALLNACHT (November 1938), numerous decrees hastened the revocation of citizenship and civil rights of German Jews and their exile from the intended *Volk* Community of "German blood." Further, as a result of Britain's forbearing APPEASEMENT policy, Hitler believed that his short-range goals, for which he presupposed the use of force—notably the "destruction of Czechoslovakia"—could be approached more quickly than indicated in the HOSSBACH MEMORANDUM (November 1937). All of Hitler's endeavors after 1938 seem by his own admission to have been dictated by his own biological clock (". . . if I remain healthy"); he was convinced that he was ill and did not have much time. After the entry into Prague (March 1939) and the end of British acquiescence, the nonag-

"Reich Chancellor Hitler in his beloved mountains." National Socialist postcard.

gression treaty with the USSR, along with its secret supplementary protocols dividing east-central Europe (August 1939), created a seemingly promising strategic situation. Thus the path was clear for the invasion of Poland, in response to which Hitler speculated that England would do nothing. Stalin, on the other hand, anticipated a Soviet advantage from the expected war in the West, with its mutual capitalist self-laceration. He had no inkling that Hitler's Wehrmacht would prove irresistible and would emerge basically strengthened from the Blitzkriegs of 1939 to 1941.

Hitler the "field marshal" was a two-faceted figure. He could think unconventionally and was open to bold operational plans, as in the attack through the Ardennes in May 1940 (*see* FRENCH CAMPAIGN). With his sense for modern technology, he also encouraged the combined land-and-air mobile warfare. Advantages turned into weaknesses only when the enemies caught up and later became superior in men and matériel. At this point, the autodidact lacked the mental discipline of the General Staff officer. But mistakes now began to accumulate when he rejected experienced advice because of the military's earlier failed predictions against his own better instincts. Deciding everything himself, he degraded his field marshals to underlings. In the distress of defensive battles he returned to the method of the 1914–1918 war of position: hold on at any price. Given the changed rules—regarding military mobility—between 1939 and 1945, and in light of Germany's overextend-

Hitler ten days before his suicide on April 30, 1945.

ed fronts and deficient reserves, this tactic hastened the ultimate disaster.

In the shadow of the ideological war in the east (as of June 1941), Hitler permitted his repeated threats against the "Jewish race in Europe" to become fact. The most terrible program of extermination in world history took place in the years 1941 to 1945—years in which racial insanity and the utopia of *Lebensraum* merged in time and space. The program for the FINAL SOLUTION of the Jewish question, and the war of conquest against Russia after Germany's breach of the nonaggression treaty, were for Hitler historical announcements of the consummation of the program set forth in *Mein Kampf.* Amid the deaths of millions of other people, the originator remained untouched, despite numerous assassination attempts, both planned and carried out. At the end, thirsty for revenge, he dragged an elite of ethically superior personalities into his own ruin. As though to mock all the failed attempts to assassinate him, Hitler died by his own hand in the rubble of what once was to have been his world metropolis, "Germania," after marrying Eva Braun in an apocalyptic bunker scene. His last declaration of political intent (his testament) demanded "ruthless resistance to the worldwide poisoner of all peoples, international Jewry." Hitler remained true to his fixed idea to the end. Unspeakable suffering and the greatest genocide in history remain inseparably bound to his name.

Harald Steffahn

Hitler in 1938.

Hitler, Alois, b. Strones (Waldviertel/Lower Austria), June 7, 1837; d. Leonding, January 3, 1903, Austrian civil servant (customs inspector). Adolf Hitler's father was the illegitimate son of Maria Anna Schicklgruber (1795–1847). In 1842 she married Johann Georg Hiedler, who never adopted or legitimized the stepson. This legal step was first taken in 1876, when Alois was already 39 years old, through the cooperation of Hiedler's brother Johann Nepomuk Hüttler, whom researchers (such as Werner Maser) have meanwhile identified as the natural father of Alois, and thus the grandfather of Adolf Hitler. (The formulation of the name as "Hitler" presumably arose through a hearing error of the pastor filling out the document.)

Ambitious and single-minded, the young Alois Hitler worked his way up in the customs service to become "chief customs official in Rank IX." In 1873 he married Anna Glassl, daughter of a customs official; the marriage was dissolved in 1880. Thereafter he lived with his mistress, Franziska Matzelsberger, whom he married in 1883. They had a son, Alois, born in 1882, and a daughter, Angela, born in 1883. After his wife's death the following year, he received an ecclesiastical dispensation to marry his relative Klara Pölzl.

This third marriage produced, besides Adolf Hitler, Gustav (1885–1887), Ida (1886–1888), Otto (died shortly after his birth), Edmund (1894–1900), and Paula Hitler (1896–1960). In 1895 Alois Hitler chose early retirement.

Hitler, Eva, name of Eva BRAUN on April 29–30, 1945.

Hitler, Klara, née Pölzl, b. Spital (Lower Austria), August 12, 1860; d. Linz, December 21, 1907, Adolf Hitler's mother. Klara Hitler was related to her husband, Alois HITLER: his presumptive father, Johann Nepomuk Hüttler, was also her grandfather. Thus an ecclesiastical dispensation was necessary for the marriage, which took place on January 7, 1885, in Braunau am Inn. Of the six children she had with the man who was 23 years her senior, only two lived, Adolf and Paula. After her husband's death, she moved with them to Linz. Her son, Adolf, said of her: "I respected my father, but loved my mother."

Hitler-Dank (Hitler Appreciation Fund; also Ehrendank der NSDAP, Honorary Fund of the NSDAP), foundation to support needy and worthy party members, founded by Hitler's decree on April 20, 1937; it had a yearly disbursement of 500,000 RM from the party treasury. Funds went only to OLD COMBATANTS who had become needy or suffered in health from their "service to the movement," or to their survivors. Requests for help were evaluated by the NSDAP's national treasurer.

Hitler Diaries (*Tagebücher*), notes from the years 1932 to 1945 attributed to Hitler, publication of which was begun by the West German illustrated magazine *Stern* on April 28, 1983, but which several days later were revealed as clumsy forgeries. As an especially crass example of sensationalism and checkbook journalism (some 9 million DM were paid for 60 notebooks), the Hitler Diaries led to one of the biggest press scandals of the postwar period. The criminal circumstances of their creation, the dilettantish verification, and in particular the unabashedly revisionist marketing of the presumptive diaries ("The history of the Third Reich will to a large extent have to be rewritten") shattered the media world and the credibility of German journalism. The trial that followed was able only to clarify the criminality of the diaries' creation and provenance. Remaining controversial were the psychohistorical reasons for this belated attempt at establishing a "stab-in-the-back legend" for the "Führer" (the excesses of KRISTALLNACHT "went too far for him," he had no "knowledge of the terrorist actions of the SS" when the war began; Hess flew to England with his knowledge, and so on).

Hitler "Free Place" Fund (Hitler-Freiplatz-Spende), aid operation initiated and organized by the NATIONAL SOCIALIST VOLK WELFARE in 1933. Through it, "German families" were to make possible without cost a vacation for "needy" NSDAP members or their families by providing a "free place" for several weeks.

Hitler greeting (*Hitlergruss*), instead of the usual "Good day," a greeting with the words "HEIL HITLER!" while raising the right arm in the post-1933 GERMAN GREETING.

Hitlerjugend. *See* Hitler Youth.

Hitlerjunge Quex, German feature film (1933) directed by Hans STEINHOFF, based on the novel of the same name by Karl A. Schenzinger; with Heinrich George, Berta Drews, and Claus Clausen. The film, rated "artistically outstanding," had its premiere in Munich, on September 16, 1933 (with Hitler present). The propagandistic intent of the film was to capture German youth for the National Socialist movement.

Cover of the novel *Der Hitlerjunge Quex.*

The historical model for Quex was Hitler Youth Herbert NORKUS, who was killed in a Berlin street fight in 1932, thus fulfilling a martyr role for the Hitler Youth similar to that of Horst WESSEL for the SA. The "blood sacrifice" of little Quex, who chooses the NS side against the opposition of family and school, appealed to the "inviolability of the spirit," according to the *Reichsfilmblatt* (Reich Film News); "for good or evil," this spirit "stands by the Führer and fatherland" and has renounced the "unworthy democratic past." The film was accompanied by Baldur von SCHIRACH's Hitler Youth song "Unsre Fahne flattert uns voran" (Our Flag Flutters before Us).

M. F.

Hitler Putsch, attempt of November 8–9, 1923, led by Hitler and retired general Erich LUDENDORFF, in Munich, to overthrow the Bavarian state government and the German national government. The agent of the putsch was the GERMAN COMBAT LEAGUE, whose goal was the establishment of a "national" right-wing dictatorship in Germany.

The events were as follows: on the evening of November 8, at an assembly of "national" leagues in the Munich Bürgerbräukeller, Hitler called for the "national revolution," declared the Bavarian government, the national government, and Reich President Friedrich Ebert deposed, and announced himself as Germany's political "leader" (*Leiter*). He called for a march on Berlin, and had the Bavarian minister president, Eugen von Knilling, the Bavarian ministers present at the meeting, and the Munich police chief arrested. Gustav von KAHR (after September 26, as general state commissioner the effective head of state in Bavaria), who was also present; Gen. Otto von Lossow (Reichswehr defense commissioner in Bavaria); and Col. Hans von Seisser (Bavarian state police chief) agreed to support the putsch under pressure of Ludendorff and Hitler.

However, after they had left the meeting, Kahr and Lossow reneged on their agreement; Kahr banned the NSDAP and the Combat League and transferred the Bavarian government to Regensburg. The Bavarian police and

Hitler Putsch. "Hitler Combat Patrol" in Munich (1923).

Proklamation

an das deutsche Volk!

Die Regierung der Novemberverbrecher in Berlin ist heute
für abgesetzt erklärt worden

Eine provisorische deutsche
National-Regierung
ist gebildet worden.

Diese besteht aus

General Ludendorff, Adolf Hitler
General von Lossow, Oberst von Seisser

Hitler Putsch. Poster by the conspirators: "Proclamation to the German people! The government of the November criminals has today been declared deposed. A provisional national German government has been formed. It consists of General Ludendorff, Adolf Hitler, General von Lossow, Colonel von Seisser."

the Reichswehr then put down the Hitler Putsch. The Reich government under Gustav STRESEMANN, which declared the putsch to be high and state treason and transferred executive power in Germany to Gen. Hans von SEECKT, did not need to intervene.

A column of putschists led by Ludendorff made its way through central Munich to the Feldherrnhalle on November 9, and was broken up by the Bavarian police using armed force; three policemen and 16 putschists were killed, and many (including Hermann Göring) were severely injured. A number of the leaders (notably Ludendorff) allowed themselves to be arrested, while others fled, including Hitler, who was slightly wounded. He was arrested on November 11 at the country home of Ernst ("Putzi") HANFSTAENGL in Uffing am Staffelsee.

The leaders of the Hitler Putsch were charged with high treason and convicted (*see* HITLER TRIAL). Propaganda later made the National Socialist victims of the putsch into "blood witnesses of the movement," and the anniversary was celebrated in the Third Reich.

R. B.

Hitler-Stalin Pact. *See* German-Soviet Nonaggression Pact.

Hitler's Worldview

Hitler spoke repeatedly of his worldview (*Weltanschauung*), but he never defined this term precisely or described its content systematically. His confessional book *Mein Kampf* does, however, allow an already developed ideological structure to be inferred. Although the issue was long disputed, it has been accepted at least since the work of Eberhard Jäckel that Hitler possessed an internally logical and consistent ideology and that he felt committed to its premises and goals to the end.

The beginning point for Hitler was "Nature with its eternally valid laws." In the struggle for existence that governed all beings, the right of the stronger applied to individuals as well as to communities, whereas the weak were destined for destruction. For the "sake of self-preservation" (*Forterhaltungswillens*), a "stronger race will displace the weak ones," and the "ridiculous fetters of so-called humanity" would break asunder, "in order to allow in its place the humanity of Nature, which destroys the weak in

order to make way for the strong." Hitler saw further a "nearly ironclad principle" of "Nature's will to live" (*Lebenswillen der Natur*) in the "internal exclusivity of species among all living beings on earth." Every animal mates only with its own kind: "Titmouse seeks titmouse, finch seeks finch, stork seeks stork, field mouse seeks field mouse, house mouse seeks house mouse, wolf seeks wolf, and so on." If unequal individuals were crossed, the offspring "no doubt will be superior to the racially inferior parental half, but not as advanced as the superior one. As a result it will later lose out in the struggle against a superior type. Such a mating contradicts Nature's will to improve breeds." The result of this "ubiquitous instinct for racial purity in Nature is not only the sharp demarcations dividing individual races, but also their own internally uniform nature."

These "iron laws of Nature" were also responsible for the evolution of human history, in which race and racial purity were allotted decisive significance. Without going into the complex origins and diverse appearances of human races, Hitler reduced them to "three types": the "creators of culture" (*Kulturbegründer*), the "bearers of culture" (*Kulturträger*), and the "destroyers of culture" (*Kulturzerstörer*). Culture creators are "without question only the Aryans; the Japanese are a typical culture-bearing race; the Jews the very embodiment of destroyers of culture." Further: "Everything we see today in the way of human culture, the products of art, science, and technology, is almost exclusively the creative product of the Aryan. . . . If one were to do away with him, then profound darkness would perhaps within a few thousand years again descend upon earth, human culture would cease, and the world become desolate." Moreover, "the Jew is the most powerful antithesis of the Aryan." In Hitler's conceptual world the concrete historical and political situation was conflated with the life-and-death struggle, basic to all human culture, between the superior Aryan and the inferior Jewish race. Endangered by this—lately through the decline in racial purity—was "the Aryan, the genuine creator of culture on earth."

Further: "The mixing of blood and the consequent decline in racial quality is the sole cause of the dying out of all cultures." In order to prevent this, miscegenation must be averted, in order to gain, through struggle, the right to exist for one's own race. For "all worldly occurrences" are in the end only "the expression of the instinct for self-preservation of the races in a good or bad sense."

This racial instinct for self-preservation, the real motivating force of historical development, was accorded by Hitler to the Jews as to every other race. Indeed, he emphasized that the instinct for self-preservation was especially developed among Jews. The strength of this instinct within the Jewish race, coupled with the intention to seek world domination imputed to it by Hitler, constituted the particular danger facing the Germanic-Nordic race and thereby culture itself. (The terms "Aryan," "Nordic," "Germanic," and "Germanic-German" were synonymous for Hitler.) The culture-creating capabilities of the Aryans in fact rested primarily on their "idealistic basic orientation," a race-related tendency "to subordinate one's own ego to the life of the whole, and, if the situation demands, to sacrifice it." This "capacity for self-sacrifice of the individual as against the whole" was itself the necessary precondition for the formation of more highly organized, territor-

ial states, and state formation was itself a precondition for the development of "human culture."

Jews, on the other hand, lacked just this "idealistic mentality" and thus the "most crucial precondition [for being] a people of culture." The will to self-sacrifice within the Jewish people did not go "beyond the naked instinct for individual self-preservation." Therefore, Jews could build neither a territorial state nor their own independent culture. They could live only "as parasites in the body of other peoples." "He [the Jew] is and remains the typical parasite, a sponger [*Schmarotzer*], which spreads more and more like a pernicious bacillus, as soon as a favorable culture medium offers itself. But the result of its presence resembles that of a sponger: where it appears, the productive people die off sooner or later." If the Jew were victorious in the struggle for world mastery he was conducting, then "his crown would be the death dance of humanity," and then "this planet would again, as it did millions of years earlier, make its path through the ether devoid of humans."

As diverse as were the racial characteristics of Jews and Aryans, so diverse were also their methods of realizing their instinct for self-preservation. Nature, according to Hitler, taught not only the inequality (*Ungleichheit*) of races, but also the inequality of individuals within races and peoples. If a people wished to prevail, then "the worth of the individual personality" and "the worth of the people" must relate to one another correctly. The Aryan-Germanic space-bound state must therefore be organized accord-

Behind the "Goddess of the West" lurks the Jew with his weapons for conquering the world. Satirical illustration from *Die Brennessel*.

ing to the "aristocratic principle of Nature," according to the criteria of leadership (*see* FÜHRER PRINCIPLE) and FOLLOWERSHIP, responsibility and trust, authority from above and agreement from below.

The Jew was capable of participating in this eternal struggle of peoples and races only in his own unique way. Since he was incapable of creating a territorial state on account of his racially conditioned "ethnic worth" (*Volkswert*) and his lack of idealism, he necessarily had to grasp other methods in his struggle for existence. Rather than acknowledging the inequality of races and of individual personalities, he preached the unnatural doctrine of equality. The Jew opposed the principle of eternal struggle with the idea of pacifism, the national state based on force (*Machtstaat*) with international solidarity, the authoritarian leadership state with the decadent egalitarian systems of democracy, socialism, and Marxism. For behind all these complex social schemes Hitler saw the "eternal Jew" as the real wire-puller, who in his struggle for world mastery must aim above all at undermining the value of race and individual personality. "With the destruction of personality and race, there falls the most significant barrier against the rule of the inferior—but this is the Jew." To prevent this, the Jewish danger must be recognized and decisively combated. In this Hitler saw his world-historical mission: "By defending myself against the Jew, I am fighting for the work of the Lord" ("Indem ich mich des Juden erwehre, kämpfe ich für das Werk des Herrn").

Besides the elimination of the Jewish racial enemy and the securing of land and soil for his own *Volk*, as well as its establishment as a world power, there were further constituent parts of Hitler's worldview. Still a revisionist in regard to Versailles at the outset of his political career, by the time he wrote *Mein Kampf* Hitler vehemently rejected the return to the boundaries of 1914 as "political nonsense." They neither contained all "persons of German nationality" nor were they "geographically rational in regard to their military efficacy." A rational FOREIGN POLICY should, on the contrary, lead to a boundary adjustment that would secure Hitler's absolute claim to sovereignty. In other words, the boundaries must incorporate a region that could feed the nation and, beyond that, would guarantee the state the necessary geographic basis for military defense. These criteria provided territory and population adequate to establish and maintain a world power.

For Hitler, the only meaningful solution was "consciously [to draw] a line through the foreign-policy direction of our prewar period" and begin anew "where things ended six centuries ago. We will stop the endless stream of Germans toward southern and western Europe and turn our gaze toward the land in the east. We will finally bring a halt to the colonial and trade policies of the prewar period and move on to the land policies of the future. When we in Europe speak today about new land and soil, we can in the first instance think only of Russia and its subject states." Hitler thus rejected all other possibilities in favor of an expansionist policy against Russia. The unbridgeable antagonism between Germany and France ("The implacable mortal enemy of the German *Volk* is and will remain France") meant that the question of potential allies would be answered with Italy and England.

While Italian-French rivalries in the Mediterranean automatically brought Rome to Germany's side, England's traditional balance-of-power policy made London susceptible to an alliance in order to prevent French hegemony in Europe, so long as Germany rejected colonies and naval dominance. The alliance with England would give Hitler the possibility of carrying out "an eastern policy in the sense of gaining the necessary land for our German *Volk*." Through force, the Slavic peoples would make way for the German master race. In the victorious war of plunder and destruction against Russia, Hitler's foreign policy would have its crowning conclusion. Elimination of the Jews and conquest of living space in the east were the ultimate goals of the Hitlerian worldview. Hitler subsumed everything else under the category of means to his end.

Beginning from the fixed idea of the culture-creating Aryan race and the perniciousness of racial mixing, with its concomitant decline in racial quality, the state was to be seen as merely such a means to the end. "Its purpose lies in the preservation and encouragement of a community of physically and intellectually equal living beings. This preservation itself comprises first the racial content and thereby permits the free development of all energies latent in this race." Above all, neither the physically nor the mentally unhealthy might perpetuate their misery through their children. Besides this task of the breeding of a better and purer Nordic-Germanic germ plasm, the state—and all aspects of domestic policy—had the function of creating the preconditions for military expansion. "Domestic policy," according to Hitler's "SECOND BOOK," "must secure for a people the inner strength for its assertion of foreign policy."

If one were to inquire into the origins of this worldview in terms of the history of ideas, Hitler's biologistic assumptions are the most extreme SOCIAL DARWINISM, while his racial conception of history goes back to Count Arthur de GOBINEAU, as popularized in Germany primarily by Houston Stewart CHAMBERLAIN. Agreements are obvious between *Mein Kampf* and Theodor FRITSCH's *Handbuch der Judenfrage* (Handbook of the Jewish Question), which Dietrich ECKART called "our whole intellectual arsenal" in 1920. Since the research of Wilfried Daim, there is much evidence that during his years in Vienna Hitler was influenced by the racial ideas of the former monk Josef LANZ, as published in his *Ostara* journal. At the center of Lanz's ideas was the "blue-blond," the "Aryan race" as the "masterpiece of God," while the "dark races," among which were the Jews, were the "botched job of the Demon." Moreover, "everything hateful and evil [stemmed] from racial mixing." Hitler himself named the antisemites Ritter von SCHÖNERER and Karl LUEGER as his greatest Viennese teachers. In any event, in his "years of apprenticeship and suffering in Vienna," Hitler sought to create "the foundations of a knowledge from which I still draw today." Further, "in this period I formed a world picture and a worldview that have become the granite foundation of my current actions. I have had to learn little more beyond what I already created; I had to change nothing." Certainly, Hitler in Vienna did not yet have ready the worldview evident in *Mein Kampf*. However, during his imprisonment in Landsberg am Lech at the latest, the most significant elements of this worldview had become a certainty that would never be revised.

While the question of Hitler's ideological fixations and the genesis of his worldview is not precisely answerable, the contemporary climate of opinion offered sufficient Social Darwinist and racial-hygienic pronouncements to substantiate his brutal and biologistic ideology of a struggle for existence, not to mention a wealth of writings in racial anthropology with moderate to the most radical antisemitic tendencies. In this confluence of Social Darwinist, racist, antisemitic, and racial-hygienic ideas, Hitler thought he possessed a worldview that was grounded in natural science, although it could not, in fact, stand up to a critique.

When Hitler wrote, "The fox is always a fox, the goose a goose, the tiger a tiger," the implication was obviously: and the human will always remain a human. Yet Hitler did not want to draw precisely this conclusion, and his deficient knowledge of nature necessarily led him to false conclusions. First, Hitler's racial definition is biologically incorrect, for here he confuses or equates the concept of race with the overriding concept of species. Second, his assertion of an eternal law underlying an instinct for racial purity is untenable. To the contrary, the natural evolution of living beings was characterized by a permanent racial splintering through which the formation of new species was itself made possible. The equation of "superior and inferior value" with "stronger and weaker" may have justification in the areas of botany and zoology, but its transference to human society—moreover, one "willed by Nature"—is neither observable nor justified.

To what extent the morphologically or genetically defined races of the human species can be categorized in terms of specific intellectual and emotional qualities is itself a difficult anthropological controversy. Hitler's ideas regarding the nature and importance of races, on the other hand, are basically false. His assertions about the characteristics of the culture-creating Aryan and the constantly culture-destroying Jew, about the decline of all cultures through racial mixing, and about the dying out of productive peoples lack any scientific proof. Finally, the thesis of the Jewish worldwide conspiracy (in this connection, Hitler called the falsified PROTOCOLS OF THE ELDERS OF ZION the "best proof")—that is, a centrally directed, racially determined, consciously planned conquest of the world—is totally absurd. Hitler's racial and antisemitic conceptions are fictions, which he warped until, in conjunction with Social Darwinist ideas and his own paranoid psyche on such matters, they presented a worldview that for him was totally convincing. When it came to a possible (later actual) failure of the policy of winning England as an ally, Hitler refused to blame a realistic British policy that granted a hegemonic position to no European power, including Germany; instead he made fictional Jewish interests responsible. Hitler asked suspiciously "whether the real influence of Jewry is not stronger than all acknowledgments and all goodwill, and thus thwarts and manipulates all plans." Just before the collapse of the Third Reich he complained, "I myself have underestimated one thing: the extent of Jewish influence on the Englishman Churchill."

Roundup in the Warsaw ghetto. Genocide as the ultimate consequence of Hitler's worldview.

That Hitler, once in power, would want his worldview to be solely dominant was clearly expressed in *Mein Kampf:* "For a worldview is impatient and cannot be satisfied with the role of 'one party among others'; rather it jealously demands its own, exclusive, and total recognition." In methods of realization, Hitler was the purest Machiavellian. In the question of political means there was only a "single preconceived thought": "Is it useful to our *Volk* now or in the future, or will it hurt them? Viewpoints from partisan politics, religion, humanity, and so on do not count." The results were the abolition of a state based on laws and democracy, as well as the installation of terror and violence (*see, for example,* CONCENTRATION CAMPS), the extermination of "life unworthy of life" (*see* EUTHANASIA), the preparation and execution of a war of plunder and destruction, and a ruthless racial policy that ended in the genocide of the FINAL SOLUTION. The criminality of the Third Reich finds its deepest roots in Hitler's racial and biologistic worldview, which denied the Christian and humanistic traditions and their appreciation of individual worth even as it denied the universal postulates of freedom, equality, and human worth. In their place, as the logical result of Hitler's worldview, appeared dictatorship, war, and genocide.

Christian Zentner

Hitler Trial (*Hitler-Prozess*), criminal proceeding before the Munich *Volk* Court from February 24 to April 1, 1924, against 10 leading participants of the HITLER PUTSCH: Hitler, Gen. Erich LUDENDORFF, Ernst RÖHM, Wilhelm FRICK, Ernst Pöhner, Hermann Kriebel, Friedrich Weber, Robert WAGNER, Wilhelm BRÜCKNER, and Heinz Pernet; the charge was high treason. After the trial procedure was conducted in a manner favorable to the accused (they had ample opportunity for pointed attacks against the Weimar Republic, and they were conceded to have had honorable motives), Hitler, Pöhner, Kriebel, and Weber were sentenced to the legal minimum of five years' imprisonment (with a prospect of prompt consideration for probation). Röhm, Frick, Wagner, Brückner, and Pernet received 15 months' imprisonment with probation. Ludendorff was acquitted, in consideration of his service as a general in the First World War. The judgment against Hitler, who was then still an Austrian citizen, went against Paragraph 9, Article 2, of the REPUBLIC PROTECTION LAW, which prescribed expulsion from Germany for foreigners convicted of high treason. After approximately one year of imprisonment in the LANDSBERG AM LECH fortress, Hitler was released on December 20, 1924.

R. B.

Hitler Youth (Hitlerjugend; HJ), programmatic term for the totalitarian organization of young people within the National Socialist movement. The HJ's origins were in the Jungsturm [Young Storm] Adolf Hitler, founded in Munich in 1922, an SA organization for recruiting future members. It was first constituted as the HJ in December 1926. After Baldur von SCHIRACH became national party youth leader (*Reichsjugendführer der NSDAP*) on October 30, 1931, a position he held until Arthur AXMANN took

over in 1940, he sought to subordinate to himself all the NSDAP youth leagues, making them independent of the directives of SA and party offices. Besides the HJ, these youth groups included the LEAGUE OF GERMAN GIRLS (BDM), founded in 1929; the National Socialist Schoolchildren's League (Schülerbund); and the German Young Volk (Deutsches Jungvolk). Schirach's goal was attained in September 1932, when NS workplace cells for the young could first be organized.

The HJ experienced its real growth spurt through the surprising success of the Reich Youth Congress (*Reichsjugendtag*) in Potsdam on October 2, 1932. The congress associations were afterward incorporated in the Reich Committee of German Youth Associations (Reichsausschuss der Deutschen Jugendverbände) as the German Youth Agency (Deutsches Jugendwerk). The HJ occupied the committee's headquarters on April 5, 1933, and the Reich government rewarded this coup by naming Schirach as German youth leader (*Jugendführer des Deutschen Reiches*). The REICH YOUTH LEADERSHIP (Reichsjugendführung; RJF), as a "supreme Reich office" (*oberste Reichsbehörde*), thus became both the state organ for youth policy and the Reich

Pernet   Dr. Weber   Frick   Kriebel   Ludendorff   Hitler   Brückner   Röhm   Wagner

The defendants in the Hitler Trial (1924). From the left: Pernet, Weber, Frick, Kriebel, Ludendorff, Hitler, Brückner, Röhm, and Wagner.

1

2

WINTER-KAMPFSPIELE
der Hitler Jugend
GARMISCH-PARTENKIRCHEN 23. FEBR. – 2. MÄRZ 1941

3

4

Reichsparteitag Nürnberg

Reichsberufs-Wettkampf
der deutschen Jugend

1
Jungvolk-Pimpfe [Hitler Youth members aged 10 to 14] on the platform of honor at the Reich Party Congress in Nuremberg.
2–4
Hitler Youth posters.
5
Pimpf on a long march.
6
Appeal for the Reich Vocational Competition of German Youth.
7
Toy model of a Hitler Youth camp.

Hitler Youth. Members of the Drum Corps of the Jungvolk in Nuremberg.

headquarters for the HJ. The HJ at that point encompassed Jungvolk (10- to 14-year-old boys), Jungmädel (10- to 14-year-old girls), the BDM, and the actual HJ (15- to 18-year-old boys). They were organized in 40 regions, themselves subdivided into *Banne* (bans), *Stämme* (tribes), *Gefolgschaften* (followerships), *Scharen* (troops), and *Kameradschaften* (comradeships). The HJ, which was subdivided by age and sex rather than by social group, could present itself as the only state-supported youth organization; through the RJF it exerted influence on various aspects of young people's lives. Its jurisdiction included youth hostels and youth homes, the CHILDREN'S COUNTRY EVACUATION program, supervision of health, youth functionaries in schools and workplaces, and the REICH VOCATIONAL COMPETITION and vocational education; it had the sole right to conduct competitions. Where the HJ encountered limits on its totalitarian claims, it reacted by excluding members who belonged to Catholic youth groups or student corporations. Until enactment of the Law on the HJ in December 1936, the institution of the "State Youth Day," which excused Jungvolk and Jungmädel members from public-school instruction on Saturdays, enabled pupils to enroll in the organizations.

Although emphatically partisan and directed by its educational mandate to oppose parochial schooling, the HJ took upon itself the continuation of the German YOUTH MOVEMENT. Atten-

tion to the principle of "self-direction" (*Selbstführung*) disguised the actual central control over this "youth service." The HJ also promised to realize the "inner unity of the *Volk*" through the younger generation, a dream arising from the state-oriented traditions of German pedagogy, as exemplified by the early 19th-century philosopher Johann Gottlieb Fichte, and from the prewar youth cult. After the legislative prescription of various "duties to serve" (*Dienstpflichten*) for young people (for example, the COUNTRY YEAR, REICH LABOR SERVICE, military service, and DUTY YEAR for girls), the Youth Service Ordinance of March 25, 1939, introduced an HJ obligation. From 1940 on, 10-year-olds were obligated to join the Jungvolk or Jungmädel; to capture older youth, "youth rallies" (*Jugendappelle*) were carried out in the following years.

The areas of activity offered for 14- to 18-year-old Hitler Youths were constantly enlarged and differentiated before the war. Involvement in national policies and physical hardening through service soon developed into the habituation to ritual and the provision of extraordinary experiences through trips and camps: the community of belief (*Gesinnungsgemeinschaft*) was to become a "formation." "Special formations," such as HJ units for pilots, sailors, and auto drivers, developed militarily useful skills; competitions brought those who were not organized together with the HJ; and increasingly the HJ took control of the cultural activities of youth. The difference between schooling and instruction, service and labor, selection of leaders and training, was initially maintained: the political irrationality oriented itself around symbols, on activities and experiences in which political belief could be proved by action. Yet the totalitarian dynamic increasingly negated the difference between school and camp, training (*Ausbildung*) and emotional self-confirmation.

During the war, in the opinion of the RJF, "all work [had] to serve only the conduct of war." But because the HJ had in fact become a compulsory affair, and because the older leaders had been removed, the "self-direction" fell into a crisis. This was met with a "police ordinance," as befit an authoritarian state, and with intensified threats of punishment. The "HJ Patrol" now became an active organ of the Security Police. Especially in its activity in the occupied territories, the HJ increasingly resembled the SS as a pseudo-official totalitarian organization. The RJF apparatus exploited "self-direction" as a compliant instrument for destroying the institutions that were obliged to be concerned about the next generation, in order to mobilize youth for the "final victory" at the earliest possible moment (*see* "HITLER YOUTH"; MILITARY FITNESS CAMPS; FLAK HELPERS; VOLK STORM; WEREWOLF).

H. S.

"Hitler Youth" ("Hitlerjugend"), nickname used first by a tank grenadier division (organized July 1943), later (October 1943) by the Twelfth SS Tank Division under SS-Standartenführer Fritz Witt, and after his death (June 16, 1944) led by SS-Brigadeführer Kurt Meyer ("Panzermeyer"). The creation of an elite unit out of 16- to 18-year-old Hitler Youths went back to an idea of Reich Youth Führer Arthur AXMANN, and was welcomed by Hitler as a test of National Socialist education. About 2,000 volunteers were ultimately recruited, some from MILITARY FITNESS CAMPS of the Hitler Youth (HJ). They were trained by staff personnel from the LEIBSTANDARTE-SS "ADOLF HITLER," and in June 1944 were flung into the front lines against invading armies, where they were mowed down. The fanatic will to fight of these youngsters trained to attack the enemy won them the name "Baby Division" from their opponents. In the Ardennes Offensive, a new SS "Hitlerjugend" Division was largely destroyed.

Hitler Youth Flyers (Flieger-HJ), special Hitler Youth (HJ) unit for "flyer fitness training"

(*fliegerische Ertüchtigung*) of young men. Because motor and air sports were limited to party formations and were no longer possible in clubs, anyone interested in flying had to turn to this HJ group, or, if older, to the NATIONAL SOCIALIST FLYERS' CORPS (NSFK).

Hiwis. *See* Volunteer Helpers.

Hoare, Sir Samuel, b. Cromer (Norfolk), February 24, 1880; d. London, May 7, 1959, British politician. Hoare was head of military intelligence in Russia during the First World War; later he was air minister and state secretary for India. In 1935 he became foreign minister, and in 1936–1937 he was First Lord of the Admiralty. Hoare was one of those British politicians who saw BOLSHEVISM as the real enemy, and he supported—or at least tolerated—National Socialism as a "bulwark against Asia" until the outbreak of the war. As special ambassador in Madrid from 1940 to 1944, Hoare successfully combated German efforts to persuade Spain to enter the war.

Hoche, Alfred (pseud., Alfred Erich), b. Wildenhain, October 1, 1865; d. Baden-Baden, May 16, 1943, German psychiatrist and writer. In 1902 Hoche became a professor of psychiatry in Freiburg. He opposed Freud (an "evil spirit") and psychoanalysis (an "aberration, of interest to cultural history"). His research focused on pathological disturbances of the nervous system and the mind. In public lectures and writings after 1920 he promoted the "legalization of the extermination of life unworthy of life." The National Socialists valued him as an "honorable pioneer" of EUTHANASIA.

Hochlinden, German border station on the boundary between Upper Silesia and Poland; the setting for a fictitious Polish attack on a tollhouse as invented by the Security Service (SD) on August 31, 1939. The Hochlinden incident, like the attack on the GLEIWITZ radio station, served as a propaganda justification for the German attack on Poland the following day.

Hochschule für Politik, Deutsche (German College for Politics), educational institution founded in Berlin in 1920 as a professional academy for political science; it was transformed in 1933 into a National Socialist (NS) teaching and research institute. NSDAP members or members of affiliated organizations followed a three-phase integrated program of study there. The first phase consisted of basics of race lore, German history, and European geography; the second phase dealt with such topics as theories of law and the state, and economic and social policy; in the third phase the student specialized. The curriculum was supplemented by lecture series with "outstanding academicians and politicians of NS Germany," as well as by vacation courses for foreigners. Several NS educational institutions were attached to the Hochschule für Politik: seminars for Hitler Youth and SA leaders, a seminar for the Labor Front, a seminar of the NS teachers' organization in NS pedagogy, and so on. In 1949 the Hochschule was refounded; in 1959 it became part of the Otto Suhr Institute of the Free University of Berlin, and later a separate department of political science.

Hoepner, Erich, b. Frankfurt an der Oder, September 14, 1886; d. Berlin, August 8, 1944 (executed), German colonel general (July 19, 1940). Hoepner joined the army in 1905; he was a General Staff officer in the First World War. Along with Heinz GUDERIAN, Hoepner was considered one of the most experienced tank officers in the Wehrmacht. As a leader of tank units, he played a significant role in the military victories in Poland and France. In late 1941, as supreme commander of the Fourth Tank Army before Moscow, against Hitler's orders he led the retreat of the exhausted troops, for which on January 8, 1942, he was relieved of his post, cashiered from the Wehrmacht for "cowardice and insubordination," and sent to Berlin. There Hoepner, who felt "responsible to a Higher One" for his decisions, made contact through Friedrich OLBRICHT with the circles of the military opposition. Designated "supreme com-

mander of the home military area," he actively participated in the coup attempt of July 20, 1944. On August 8 of that year, he was condemned to death by the *Volk* Court; he was hanged in Plötzensee.

Hoetzsch, Otto, b. Leipzig, February 14, 1876; d. Berlin, August 27, 1946, German historian and politician. A specialist in eastern European history, in 1906 Hoetzsch became a professor in Posen, later going to Berlin. In 1913 he was a co-founder of the German Society for the Study of Eastern Europe. During the First World War, Hoetzsch supported an understanding between Germany and Russia. Politically, he functioned as a "reform conservative" in the German National People's Party (from 1920 to 1930 he was a deputy in the Prussian diet and the German Reichstag). As an opponent of Alfred HUGENBERG's policies of radicalization, he changed to the VOLK-CONSERVATIVE UNION in 1930. Despite his anti-Communist, conservative world outlook, Hoetzsch's portrayals of Russian history were defamed as "pro-Bolshevik" by the National Socialists because of their balanced nature. He was pensioned prematurely in 1935.

Hofacker, Cäsar von, b. Ludwigsburg, March 11, 1896; d. Berlin-Plötzensee, December 20, 1944 (executed), German opposition fighter. Hofacker studied law, then was employed in the steel industry as a head clerk (*Prokurist*). After the occupation of France, he was chief of the "iron and steel" office in the German military government. Through his cousin Schenck von STAUFFENBERG, Hofacker had a contact with the op-

Erich Hoepner.

Cäsar von Hofacker.

position in Germany; in Paris he met with Gen. Otto von STÜLPNAGEL to prepare for the coup of July 20, 1944. After the assassination attempt failed, Hofacker was arrested by the Gestapo. Under torture he divulged the names of several co-conspirators, including Erwin ROMMEL, whom he had won over to the opposition. Found guilty of high treason as "head of the conspiracy in France," he was condemned to death.

Hofer, Franz, b. Hofgastein (Austria), November 27, 1902; d. Munich, February 18, 1975, Austrian politician. A merchant, Hofer became NSDAP *Gauleiter* for the Tyrol and Vorarlberg in 1932. Sentenced to 30 months' imprisonment in 1933, he escaped to Germany. After the Anschluss of Austria he was again appointed *Gauleiter;* in 1940 he became *Reichsstatthalter* (governor). In 1945 Hofer was envisioned as the commander of the never-realized ALPINE FORTRESS.

Hoffmann, Heinrich, b. Fürth, September 12, 1885; d. Munich, December 16, 1957, German photographer. Hoffmann was a military photographer with the Bavarian army during the First World War. In 1919 he first met Hitler, with whom he shared similar artistic and political tendencies. In Munich he soon became one of Hitler's closest confidants, valued for his anecdotes and conversation. It was in Hoffmann's photography studio in the late 1920s that Hitler met Eva BRAUN. As one of the few who possessed Hitler's trust until the end, Hoffmann also concerned himself with the Führer's personal and private life, accompanying him almost constantly on his travels. At the outset of his career Hitler granted Hoffmann nearly exclusive rights to photographs of him; by 1945 Hoffmann had made some 2.5 million photos, which served

Heinrich Hoffmann with Stalin after the signing of the German-Soviet Nonaggression Pact in Moscow (1939).

for both press publicity and picture books. Hoffmann's most successful books included *Hitler, wie ihn keiner kennt* (Hitler, as No One Knows Him; 1933), *Jugend um Hitler* (Youth around Hitler; 1934), and *Hitler befreit das Sudetenland* (Hitler Liberates the Sudetenland; 1938). In 1938 Hitler named his personal photographer a "professor"; in 1940 Hoffmann became a Reichstag deputy. After the war, a Munich appeals board condemned the "beneficiary" (*Nutzniesser*) of the Third Reich to a sentence of hard labor and loss of property.

Hohe Schule der NSDAP (High [Upper] School of the NSDAP), research and teaching institution, planned by Alfred ROSENBERG from 1936, with the intention of establishing totalitarian claims over the formation of the National Socialist worldview. Robert LEY, on the other hand, spoke in 1937 of an "educational path for the selection of National Socialist leaders" that extended from the ADOLF HITLER SCHOOLS and ORDER FORTRESSES to the Hohe Schule. The plans for a building on the Chiemsee (a lake in the Bavarian Alps) suggested a proposal for a party school with educational tasks for the faculty at the schooling site. Rosenberg's vision, on the other hand, foresaw a brain trust, which would provide academic underpinnings for party and government ideological policy; in particular, it would prepare for a "possible church struggle" and give a desired direction to research.

Only in 1940 did the responsible Reich minister approve the creation of branch offices (*Aussenstellen*) of the Hohe Schule, primarily in university cities, to be equipped with books from confiscated libraries. Several universities transferred institute directors or professorships: for the study of religion in Halle, for Indo-Germanic intellectual history in Munich, for the Overseas Institute in Hamburg. Considering the unclear demarcations of responsibility ("German *Volk* lore" in Graz and "National Socialist *Volk* cultivation" in Marburg), the existence of the competing SS ANCESTRAL INHERITANCE institution, and the creation of a central library in Sankt Andrä bei Villach, there could be no thought of a successful coordination by Alfred BAEUMLER. It was all still far removed from an "alternative university" (Bollmus).

H. S.

Hohlbaum, Robert, b. Jägerndorf (Silesia), August 28, 1866; d. Graz (Austria), February 4, 1955, Austrian writer and librarian. Hohlbaum's "borderland tragedies" told of the "struggles of German people" to be included in the Reich. (He dedicated his novel *Grenzland* [Borderland; 1921] to the leader of the Sudeten Germans, Rudolf Lodgmann.) After 1933 Hohlbaum had success with historical stories that glorified *Führertum* (leadership). The National Socialists praised him as a "champion of Great-German ideals." In 1942, Hohlbaum assumed leadership of the Weimar State Library. His postwar work dealt especially with the "problematic life of the genius."

Höhn, Reinhard, b. Graefenthal (Thuringia), July 29, 1904, German jurist. Höhn studied law at various universities, and became a functionary in the YOUNG GERMAN ORDER. After the Seizure of Power, Höhn joined the NSDAP and SS, where he belonged to the group of younger middle-class academics and technocrats who quickly made their careers. In 1934 he became a lecturer in law; in 1935 he was made an adjunct (*ausserplanmässig*) professor and was named head of the main section in the SD Main Office. In 1936 he became a member of the ACADEMY FOR GERMAN LAW, and in 1939, an SS-*Standartenführer* and director of the Institute for Research on the State in Berlin. As an expert in legislation, Höhn defended the "subjugation" of the individual to the National Socialist "*Volk* Community as a species community [*Artgemeinschaft*]," sought to support the FÜHRER PRINCIPLE with a philosophy of law, and, toward the end of the war, supported the increased severity of penal laws for even the "most minor crimes": "We must proceed radically, and death sentences are the best means of squelching every type of opposition." At the war's end, Höhn first went under cover as a lay medical practitioner. In 1956 he took over as head of one of Europe's leading managerial schools.

Holland, name of a province in the NETHERLANDS, often used to stand for the entire country.

Holocaust, English-language term adopted from the Greek *holókauton* (burnt offering; consumption by fire) to designate genocide, especially the extermination of Jews in the FINAL SOLUTION. It has been commonly used in the Federal Republic since the showing of the American television series of that name in January 1979.

Höltermann, Karl, b. Pirmasens, March 20, 1894; d. London, March 3, 1955, German politician and journalist. Höltermann edited vari-

ous Social Democratic newspapers, including *Reichsbanner*. He served as a Reichstag deputy in 1932–1933, and he was a member (after 1931, chairman) of the REICH BANNER "BLACK-RED-GOLD." As a co-founder of the IRON FRONT and one of the most active opponents of National Socialism, Höltermann was forced to flee abroad in 1933. From England he unsuccessfully planned an armed antifascist emigré organization.

Hölz, Max, b. Moritz bei Riesa, October 14, 1889; d. near Gorki (USSR), September 18, 1933, German Communist revolutionary. In 1918 Hölz was in the Falkenstein Workers' and Soldiers' Council; he joined the Independent Socialists (USPD), then the Communists (KPD). As a proponent of anarchic communism, he became one of the most folklike (*volkstümlich*) German Communists in the early 1920s: he extorted tribute from industrialists, divided the money among the poor, and entered into such illegal activities as organizing bank robberies by "expropriation groups." The KPD purged him for "undisciplined behavior." In 1921, during the revolts in the central German industrial regions, Hölz assumed military leadership of the "Red Guards." After their defeat he was charged with high treason and sentenced to life imprisonment, but in 1928 was released. Hölz, who as an anarchist used terrorist methods similar to those of the paramilitary organizations of the Right, was persecuted with particular hate by the National Socialists as a "Communist

Holocaust. Cover of the news magazine *Der Spiegel*: "The murder of the Jews moves the Germans."

Max Hölz.

arsonist." In 1929 he emigrated to the USSR, where he worked for the German section of the Comintern.

Home Economics Year (*Hauswirtschaftliches Jahr*), like the COUNTRY YEAR, a program created in 1934 by the Reich Youth Leadership, Reich Women's Leadership, and Reich Employment Office in order to lessen unemployment among youth, especially girls who had left school. The idea of creating work soon receded into the background, to be replaced by the use of the Home Economics Year to regulate the labor market (*see* LABOR DEPLOYMENT). Under the guidance of the LEAGUE OF GERMAN GIRLS (BDM), political education was also attempted. The "Home Year Girl" (*Hausjahrmädel*) was to be trained in a "domestic area suitable to her nature," and would develop "pleasure and love" (*Lust and Liebe*) for this activity. In return she would receive pocket money and an association with specially selected families. The Home Economics Year was replaced by the DUTY YEAR.

Home-Evening (*Heimabend*), term for the regular membership meetings of the HITLER YOUTH (HJ). Meetings were usually held weekly, apart from other "service"; participation was obligatory. Like all HJ events, they were regarded as an "honorable service to the German *Volk*." The evenings were used first for ideological political SCHOOLING. The Reich Youth Führer promulgated obligatory lesson plans, and HJ leaders received educational folders, especially on themes from German history and race lore; the results of this schooling were examined, and members received certificates of accomplish-

ment. On the other hand, the Home-Evenings were intended to strengthen the feeling of belonging, through songs or craft projects for the Winter Relief Agency. For those who could not attend, the radio brought a weekly program on which the schooling themes were repeated.

Home Flak (*Heimatflak*), air defense units, formed after May 1942, that were entirely or partly staffed with civilian personnel. Workers, apprentices, clerks, and civil servants were drawn into service as "flak-defense men" (*Flakwehrmänner*) in addition to their regular work. The civil defense batteries were classified exclusively as alarm units, which were activated only when needed, and of necessity were in close proximity to their members' posts, for example at antiaircraft stations in factories. Because the civil defense units apparently did not free enough flak soldiers, after February 1943 secondary school students were recruited as FLAK HELPERS with air force and marine units. They were only loosely connected with the home units. Numerous batteries staffed primarily by these helpers were, however, designated as Home Flak units.

Home front (*Heimatfront*), propaganda catchword, cropping up with ever-increasing frequency in the speeches of National Socialist politicians, with which the sense of community between those fighting at the combat front and those at home was to be strengthened: "For the first time in history, a whole *Volk* is involved in the struggle, some at the front, some at home" (Hitler, 1941). In the course of the war, the workplace in the homeland was elevated to the home front, where one was to join in the struggle through special "work details" (*see* LABOR DEPLOYMENT), in order to overcome "insufficiencies" and demonstrate "endurance." The home front concept coincided with NS rejection of the war of combatants and the propagandizing

Home front. Women in the armaments industry.

of a "total war" (*see* INTERNATIONAL LAW), which made no distinction between civilians and combat troops.

Home Guards (*Heimwehren*), armed Austrian defense leagues of the bourgeois political camp after the fall of the Habsburg monarchy in 1918 (*see* AUSTROFASCISM).

Home-Mother Schools (*Heimmütterschulen*), training institutes of the MOTHERS' SERVICE of the German Women's Agency that were to "train physically and spiritually fit mothers" who did not work outside the home; they were especially intended for young women before marriage. The courses usually ran for four to six weeks.

Homestead (*Heimstätte*), one-family house with land that can be farmed by one family without outside help, granted by a state agency. Originating in the United States in 1862 (the Homestead Law), the homestead movement gained ground in Germany only after the First World War, when there were veterans and surviving dependents in need. The Reich Homestead Law of May 10, 1920, was extended in the Third Reich, through a law of November 25, 1937, to "victims of the National Rising and work" as well as to veterans of military service and families with many children. A homestead was obtainable under favorable conditions. It could be bequeathed to heirs, but could not be sold for speculation, because the state retained a right of purchase and offered protection against a distress sale caused by personal indebtedness. A homestead could also be seized, in some cases without compensation, if the homesteader lost Reich citizenship—as Jews and Jewish MIXED-BREEDS did through the Nuremberg Laws—or was responsible for "gross mismanagement."

Because of the great discretionary powers of the Reich Homestead Office (under the Labor Ministry), the homestead was a means for enforcing political discipline. Propaganda constantly stressed that it served to bind "work of hand and head to the home soil"; the homestead was the "entailed estate of the circles of working *Volk* [*werktätige Volkskreise*]." In 1936, some 130,000 homesteaders were organized in the GERMAN SETTLERS' LEAGUE. After the Second World War, homesteads were given to persons driven from their homes, those returning to Germany, and those who had suffered property damage during the war.

Homosexuality, sexual relations between members of the same sex. Not subject to criminal penalties when between women, homosexuality was also not punishable in many German states before 1871 when between men. In the German Empire it was punishable with a prison term as "indecency counter to nature" (*widernatürliches Unzucht;* ¶175, Reich Criminal Code). In criminal law practice, the term applied only to activities "similar to intercourse." On June 28, 1935, the National Socialists strengthened Paragraph 175 so that every "indecency" between men, even thoughts without physical contact (if they were of "some intensity and duration"), could be punished as a "crime" with a prison term of up to 10 years, and in severe cases with "emasculation" (*Entmannung*).

In the National Socialist worldview, homosexuality was considered a "reversal of the sexual instinct"; it undermined the "natural will to live," because it could endanger the "preservation of the *Volk*." Sex researchers who, like Magnus HIRSCHFELD, defended toleration of variant sexual behavior were demonized as "pimps under scientific camouflage." As an "unnatural emotion," homosexuality was considered "curable" by NS physicians; in practice, homosexual men were not treated medically, but were sent to concentration camps (where they were identified by a pink triangle). There, in individual cases (as in Ravensbrück in 1944), the *Reichsführer-SS* or others carried out "renunciation tests" (*Abkehrprüfungen*), which determined who could be "excited by [female] prostitutes" and consequently released from jail as "not really homosexual."

The NS movement as a whole was characterized by a contradictory relationship toward homosexuality: the practice was officially condemned, but internally tolerated. As examined by Klaus Theweleit, MEN'S LEAGUES, which cultivated combative or soldierly "virtues," "lend themselves to the development of homosexual practices." Homosexuality was widespread in the SA and free corps; Ernst RÖHM was named by Hitler to head the SA although he made no attempt to conceal his homosexuality. The loudly proclaimed NS struggle against homosexuality was carried out only halfheartedly even after Röhm's murder. Especially in the sexual deprivation of wartime, homosexual relationships were often quietly tolerated.

H. H.

Honor (*Ehre*), central value in the National Socialist worldview: as the "beginning and end of our entire thought and behavior," honor permitted "no equivalent center of strength . . . other than itself, neither Christian love nor the humanity of Freemasonry" (Alfred Rosenberg). Thus, honor was considered to be racially determined; for the Nordic-Germanic people it meant a special "continuation and preservation of their own type, standing up for and if necessary sacrificing oneself for one's own kind and one's highest values" (*Meyers Lexikon*, 1937). In contrast, blood degeneration and racial decay" were distinctive expressions of an absence of honor.

Honor, protection of (*Ehrenschutz*), general term for laws and official party regulations intended to protect against injuries to honor. Examples of such provisions were:

1. Racial legislation in conformity with the Nuremberg Law to Protect German Blood and German Honor of September 15, 1935 (*see* BLOOD, LAW TO PROTECT)
2. Regulations concerning jurisdiction over matters of honor for the NSDAP, its subdivisions, and its member associations, which was intended to preserve the "mutual honor of the party and . . . of individual party comrades" (*see* PARTY COURTS)
3. Regulations dealing with the HONOR COURTS that presided over honor-related proceedings for occupational or professional associations and the German Labor Front
4. Of lesser importance, criminal law statutes for protecting the honor of individuals.

Honor council (Ehrenrat), committee of three to five officers in every regiment and every independent office of the Wehrmacht that, according to the Order to Preserve Honor of November 1, 1934, was to investigate, clarify, and judge like HONOR COURTS in pertinent matters. Student bodies were also identified as honor councils; they made decisions in affairs of honor, in accordance with a student decree of June 23, 1937.

Honor courts (*Ehrengerichte*), institutions that until 1933 were customary only for professions (such as medicine and the law) traditionally organized as corporative (*ständisch*). Thereafter, other professional groups were so organized, and honor courts were established to monitor and discipline members. Their goal was the "purification of the corporation through the expurgation of incorrigible members." Criminal trial procedure was thus applied to the cases. Above the honor courts stood only the Reich

Honor Court. Punishments levied could include warning, censure, monetary fine, or withdrawal of authorization to practice the profession. Since quicker disciplining was available through labor service, protective custody, and SPECIAL COURTS, the number of trials in the honor courts remained low. Only 251 trials in 1936 and 142 in 1939 ensued from the Law to Structure National Work (*Reich Law Gazette* I, 1934, p. 45), most of them against small-business men. The courts' function can be understood primarily as a demonstration of the regime's sense of social responsibility with respect to the workers.

C. D.

Hoover, Herbert Clark, b. West Branch, Iowa, August 10, 1874; d. New York City, October 20, 1964, American politician. After a career as a mining engineer, Hoover led and organized social welfare programs for Europe during the First World War. As secretary of commerce (1921–1929) and president of the United States (1929–1933), the Republican Hoover worked toward a foreign policy based on a balance of interests. Unlike his successor, Franklin D. ROOSEVELT, Hoover was valued by the National Socialists for his "humanity," especially because in 1932 he was responsive to Chancellor Heinrich BRÜNING's revisionist policies through the moratorium on war debts and reparations, the so-called Hoover Moratorium. During and after the Second World War, Hoover was again active in charitable organizations and was in particular involved with relief of the starvation in postwar Germany.

Herbert Clark Hoover.

Hoppe, Paul-Werner, b. Berlin, February 28, 1910; d. Bochum, July 15, 1974, SS-*Sturmbann-führer* and horticultural technologist. Hoppe joined the NSDAP in November 1932 and the SS in January 1933. In October 1934 he was posted to what was then the SS STANDBY TROOPS (Ver-fügungstruppe); after his promotion to SS-*Hauptsturmführer* on October 1, 1938, he was transferred to ORANIENBURG and the staff of the chief of the SS Death's-Head Unit in charge of concentration camps. As adjutant to the Third SS "Death's-Head" Division, Hoppe took part in the Polish and French campaigns. After several months in Russia he was promoted to SS-*Sturmbannführer* on September 1, 1942, and at the same time was named commandant of the STUTTHOF concentration camp. Through a verdict of the Bochum court on June 4, 1957, Hoppe was sentenced to nine years' imprisonment for complicity in the murder of several hundred people.

Hördt, Philipp, b. Weinheim, December 23, 1891; d. Heidelberg, January 26, 1933, German pedagogue. As a lecturer at the teacher training institute in Heidelberg, Hördt, along with Ernst KRIECK, was one of the *völkisch* pedagogues who during the Weimar Republic developed educational theories based on biology and race; he helped create the postulates for school policy in the Third Reich with his program for a "total education" (*Gesamterziehung*) "based on ethnic identity." In numerous publications, such as *Grundformen volkhafter Bildung* (The Basics of *Volk*-appropriate Education; 1932), Hördt promoted GERMAN LORE as a core subject that would encompass "thinking, feeling, willing, believing," as well as "play, work, classes, and celebration."

Hore-Belisha, Leslie, b. London, September 7, 1893; d. Reims (France), February 16, 1957, English politician and publicist. A National Liberal member of the House of Commons, Hore-Belisha was also war minister from 1937 to 1940. Early on he saw Hitler's Germany as a threat to peace, and sought to respond with an increase in military personnel and stepped-up rearmament; nonetheless, he supported Neville Chamberlain's foreign policy of APPEASEMENT until 1939. Even after Great Britain's entry into the war, Hore-Belisha did not institute significant military measures against the German Reich.

Horney, Brigitte, b. Berlin, March 29, 1911; d. Hamburg, July 27, 1988, German actress. Through sophisticated entertainment films whose popularity was not restricted to the German public, such as *Savoy-Hotel 217* (1936), *Befreite Hände* (Freed Hands; 1939), and MÜNCHHAUSEN (1943), Horney was one of the few German film stars with an international reputation. Treasured by the National Socialists as a "cultivated" actress "with character," along with Zarah LEANDER, Kristina SÖDER-BAUM, and Anny Ondra, Horney was one of the most highly paid actresses in Germany. She portrayed "bar chanteuses of dubious repute" (as in *Liebe, Tod und Teufel* [Love, Death, and the Devil]), as well as "Romanian subhumans" (in *Die Stadt Anatol* [The City of Anatol]). After the war Horney went to the United States, where she occupied herself with the lifework of her mother, the psychoanalyst Karen Horney (1885–1952), who had left Berlin in 1932 because of criticism of her social involvement and her therapeutic methods. Horney accepted a few film and television roles in the Federal Republic (for example, in the anti-Soviet war film *Nacht fiel über Gotenhafen* [Night Fell on Gotenhafen]; 1960).

Hörsing, Otto, b. Gross-Schillingken (East Prussia), July 18, 1874; d. Berlin, August 23, 1937, German politician. Hörsing was employed first as a union functionary, then as a Social Democratic (SPD) functionary before the First World War. After the November Revolution (1918), he was chairman of the workers' and soldiers' coun-

Brigitte Horney.

cil for Upper Silesia. In 1919 he became Reich commissioner for Silesia and Posen, and from 1920 to 1927 he served as governor (*Oberprä-sident*) of the province of Saxony. In 1924 Hör-sing founded the REICH BANNER "BLACK-RED-GOLD" and was elected its first chairman. As a right-wing Social Democrat, he had long been active in the defeat of Communist and socialist actions. Partly because of his drunken state while making Sunday speeches, Hörsing lost his post as governor in 1927, and was forced to leave the SPD as a "right-wing deviant." Karl HÖLTERMANN replaced him as head of the Reich Banner. Hörsing's attempt to found his own Social Republican party remained unsuccessful.

Horst-Wessel-Koog, new land created in the 1930s through dikes along the west coast of Schleswig-Holstein (Kreis Eiderstedt); it was originally called Hever-Sommerkoog. In 1938 it was renamed in honor of the National Socialist "martyr"; today it is Norderhever-Koog.

"Horst-Wessel-Lied" (Horst Wessel Song), name coined by Joseph Goebbels for the poem "Up with the flag . . ." by SA-Sturmführer Horst WESSEL that the National Socialist ANGRIFF published on September 23, 1929. After the death of the author (February 23, 1930), who was then made into a martyr, the text became the official party song of the NSDAP; in the arrangement by the composer Hermann Blume ("Kamerad Horst Wessel") it was often used to open and close celebrations and party congresses. Wessel had used an old sailors' tune as the melody: "For the last time the roll call is blown . . ." After 1933 the Horst Wessel Song became a second national hymn of the German Reich, regularly played after the "Deutsch-landlied" (*see* GERMAN NATIONAL ANTHEM). NS music theory stated that the resounding march music of the Horst Wessel Song was a "song of affirmation born from the heart of the nation."

Horst-Wessel-Studium, National Socialist stipend and program to encourage gifted students, named after the "blood witness" Horst WESSEL. They were supported by the Reich Student Leadership (Reichsstudentenführung; RSF), together with the REICH LABOR SERVICE (RAD) and HITLER YOUTH (HJ), and financed by the Reich Student Agency (Reichsstudentenwerk) and the RSF. The program was intended to facilitate university-level study for "valuable

and gifted members of the *Volk* Community," in particular "peasants' and workers' sons," who for social reasons could not pursue higher education or lacked the economic means to study. Candidates for the stipend were nominated by the NSDAP or its organizations, especially the RAD, the HJ, and the GERMAN LABOR FRONT. During several days in camps, candidates had to prove their "intellectual capabilities"; those selected were prepared for actual study in a one-year course, at the conclusion of which a test was administered to measure "giftedness, behavior, and character" more than knowledge. The most successful graduates could then begin university study, but for another year and a half were under special supervision in groups of 10.

Horthy, Miklós (Nikolaus Horthy von Nagybá-nya), b. Kenderes (Hungary), June 18, 1868; d. Estoril (Portugal), February 9, 1957, Hungarian politician. From 1909 to 1914, Horthy served as an officer (*Flügeladjutant*) attached to Austrian emperor Franz Joseph I. A rear admiral by the end of the First World War, Horthy fought in 1919 as the supreme commander of a counter-revolutionary "National Army" against the Hungarian socialist regime of Béla KUN. In 1920 the Hungarian National Assembly elected Horthy "regent." At first a provisional head of state, he later secured his power with nearly dictatorial authority and sought close cooperation with Fascist Italy and National Socialist Germany. Hungary was repaid with the VIENNA AWARDS, but at the same time was drawn into Axis war

Miklós Horthy.

policies. After the course of war changed in Russia, Horthy attempted to make contact with the Allies. Immediately after beginning armistice negotiations, he was arrested on October 16, 1944, by SS units under Otto SKORZENY and Erich von dem BACH-ZELEWSKI and interned in Hansee Palace (Upper Bavaria). After the liberation he went into exile, first in Switzerland, and then in Portugal.

Höss, Rudolf, b. Baden-Baden, November 25, 1900; d. Auschwitz, April 16, 1947, concentration camp commandant. A First World War volunteer, Höss then joined the ROSSBACH free corps, and in 1922 the NSDAP. For complicity in the murder of the teacher Walter Kadow (the Parchimer Vehm murder; *see* VEHM MURDERS), which also involved Martin BORMANN, Höss was sentenced to 10 years' imprisonment in 1923, but was amnestied on July 14, 1928. He joined the ARTAMANEN, where he came to know Himmler, who persuaded him to join the SS in 1934 and made him *Block- und Rapportführer* (block and mustering chief) in the Dachau concentration camp. Transferred for a time to the Sachsenhausen camp (1938), Höss was promoted to SS-*Hauptsturmführer*, and on May 1, 1940, to commandant of the AUSCHWITZ camp, which he built up to be the largest of the National Socialist extermination camps.

Having received a strict Catholic upbringing, Höss—who lived with his wife and five children in the death factory—never asked about the "why" of his orders to murder. He was only concerned with the greatest possible efficiency; toward this end were devised the ingenious deception maneuvers with which the victims' true fate was hidden from them until the end (such as references to "delousing" and "showering"). It was also Höss who introduced killing with ZYKLON B, which seemed to him "more hygienic" than the bloodbaths of the mass shootings. He was strict regarding the "correct" treatment of prisoners, for whom, as he later wrote, he actually felt "too much pity"; he could not, however, prevent the excesses of such guard personnel as Friedrich Wilhelm BOGER. In late 1943, Höss was relieved of his duties and transferred to the headquarters of Office D (concentration camp administration) in the ECONOMIC-ADMINISTRATIVE MAIN OFFICE, serving there under Richard GLÜCKS. In early May 1944, he returned temporarily to Auschwitz in order to organize the extermination of 400,000 Hungarian Jews.

On March 11, 1946, Höss was finally captured

Rudolf Höss.

by British military police. His testimony at the Nuremberg Trials was among the most shocking of the whole proceeding. He estimated the number of persons gassed in Auschwitz at 2 million. On June 5 of that year Höss was remanded to Poland, where in prison he wrote his memoirs, *Rudolf Höss—Kommandant in Auschwitz* (translated as *Commandant of Auschwitz*), first published in Germany in 1958, in which he attempted to show that he had acted entirely in good faith. On April 2, 1947, Höss was condemned to death by the Supreme People's Court in Warsaw; shortly thereafter he was hanged in front of his former house in Auschwitz.

Hossbach, Friedrich, b. Unna, November 21, 1894; d. Göttingen, September 10, 1980, German infantry general (November 1, 1943). Hossbach entered the Prussian army in 1913; in 1920 he became a Reichswehr officer. He was made division chief in the Army Personnel Office on August 3, 1934, thus becoming Wehrmacht adjutant to Hitler. On November 5, 1937, Hossbach completed the so-called HOSSBACH MEMORANDUM, dealing with conversations between Hitler and political and military leaders during which the offensive character of Hitler's military plans first became clear. Because of his protests against Hitler's actions in the FRITSCH CRISIS, Hossbach was forced to change posts on January 28, 1938. During the Russian Campaign he led various infantry divisions, and after October 1944 he defended East Prussia with the Fourth Army. He was cashiered for insubordinate behavior on January 28, 1945. After the war, Hossbach wrote his memoirs: *Zwischen Wehrmacht und Hitler 1934–1938* (Between Wehrmacht and Hitler; 1949) and *Die Schlacht um Ostpreussen* (The Battle for East Prussia; 1953).

Hossbach Memorandum (*Hossbach-Niederschrift*), protocol of a discussion by Hitler and others in the Reich Chancellery on November 5, 1937, written down on his own initiative by Hitler's Wehrmacht adjutant, Col. Friedrich HOSSBACH. The discussion participants were Hitler, Reich Foreign Minister Konstantin von NEURATH, and Reich War Minister Werner von BLOMBERG, as well as the supreme commanders of the three Wehrmacht forces—Werner von FRITSCH, Erich RAEDER, and Hermann GÖRING—and Hossbach himself. The memorandum was signed on November 10, 1937, and put in the files by Blomberg, the only participant who saw it. A copy from 1943–1944 played a controversial but central role in the NUREMBERG TRIALS of major war criminals in support of the charge of CRIMES AGAINST PEACE.

The discussion concerned the military solution to the "German space question" (*deutsche Raumfrage*), which Hitler had outlined already in *Mein Kampf* and repeated before Reichswehr generals on February 3, 1933. He sketched out three possibilities: (1) a decision on the question no later than 1943–1945, before the German advantage in armaments was lost; (2) moving forward the decision to "use force with attendant risk" against "Tschechei" ("Czechia"; without the Slovaks), in the event that France was sufficiently paralyzed by internal political difficulties; (3) in case of the outbreak of military conflict between Italy and the Western powers (for example, over positions in the Mediterranean), the "lightning-fast" defeat of Austria and Czechoslovakia as early as 1938 in order to do away with the "threat from the flank."

Blomberg and Fritsch raised military objections to such use of force; according to his own testimony the foreign minister was "shaken," and Raeder, the navy chief, pointed to the deficient state of naval armaments. No decisions were made. Nonetheless, Hitler held fast to the program laid down in the Hossbach Memorandum, and during the FRITSCH CRISIS he got rid of his main opponents in the military. In its wake, Neurath also lost his ministerial post.

Hostage Trial (*Geisel-Prozess*; also known as the "Trial of the Southeast Generals"), proceeding of United States Military Court V in Nu-

remberg against former Field Marshal Gen. Wilhelm LIST and others for crimes against humanity and war crimes (Case 7). Charges were brought against 12 generals or officers of equivalent rank in the Wehrmacht. The central charge was that the defendants were perpetrators or accomplices in the murder of thousands of civilians, especially in Greece, Yugoslavia, and Albania.

Before the main proceeding began, Gen. Franz Böhme committed suicide on May 29, 1947. The proceeding against Field Marshal Gen. Maximilian von WEICHS was taken off the agenda because of his inability to stand trial. On October 19, 1948, the court sentenced List and another officer to life imprisonment; six defendants—in part because of acquittal on one charge—were sentenced to 7 to 20 years; two defendants were acquitted. All the limited prison terms were reduced through a pardon on January 31, 1951.

The judgment was sharply criticized in the Eastern European press. The court's determination that an occupation power had the right to shoot hostages under certain circumstances, and that partisans did not have combatant standing, came under particular criticism.

A. St.

House arrest. *See* Residential restriction.

House Flag (*Hausfahne*), swastika flag. As the Reich flag, the House Flag could be displayed on the domicile of every German citizen of the Reich (Reich Flag Law of September 15, 1935). Excluded from this "honor" were Jewish households and houses in which, in addition to "German-blooded" residents, a Jew lived (Flag Decree of December 7, 1936).

House of German Art (Haus der Deutschen Kunst), exhibition hall in Munich, built between 1933 and 1937 according to plans by Paul TROOST. The House of German Art was celebrated in propaganda as "the first beautiful building of the new Reich," whereas the public soon gave it the derogatory nickname "Central Train Station Athens," making fun of the crudely antique, angular, and squat architecture. Intended as a replacement for the Glass Palace, which had burned in 1931, the building served as a representative of the "totality of German artistic creation." Hitler himself laid the cornerstone on October 15, 1933 (on which occasion his silver hammer broke). The building survived the war nearly intact.

House of German Art.

Hübener, Helmuth, b. Hamburg, January 8, 1925; d. Berlin-Plötzensee, October 27, 1942 (executed), German administrative apprentice who became a victim of National Socialism. The Hübener case illustrates National Socialist "administration of justice" in an exemplary fashion: because the defendant was not yet of an age to stand trial, the judgment of the *Volk* Court credited him with intelligence and maturity beyond his years. He was thus sentenced "as an adult," that is, to die, for "listening to a foreign radio transmission . . . and treasonous encouragement of enemies."

Huber, Ernst Rudolf, b. Oberstein, June 8, 1903, German legal theorist. In 1931 Huber became a lecturer in law in Bonn. He became a professor in Kiel in 1933, then went to Leipzig in 1937; he taught in Strasbourg from 1941 to 1945. Huber wrote the leading textbook of National Socialist constitutional law (1937–1939), which propounded the notion that the Führer constituted the true will of the *Volk*, which must be differentiated from the subjective convictions of individual "*Volk* comrades." Furthermore, the economy must be subordinated to the Führer and the totality of political ideas. In 1952 Huber became a professor in Freiburg im Breisgau. He moved to the Institute for Social Science in Wilhelmshaven in 1957, and to Göttingen in 1962. He became known in the Federal Republic as author of the seven-volume *Deutsche Verfassungsgeschichte seit 1789* (German Constitutional History since 1789).

Huber, Kurt, b. Chur (Switzerland), October 24, 1893; d. Munich, July 13, 1943 (executed), German musical theorist and opposition fighter. Huber studied in Munich; in 1926 he became a professor of psychology, specializing in the aesthetics of music and research into folk songs. Huber's conflict with National Socialism, which he opposed from the outset, erupted during a temporary stay in Berlin in 1937–1938, when he observed the misuse of popular customs and art under the National Socialist culture policy. As a Catholic he was also repelled by the new "brown heathenism" and the tyranny of the police state. Huber returned to Munich, and during the war became the center of the WHITE ROSE student resistance group. With his students he organized leafleting actions against National Socialism and the war, first in Munich

Kurt Huber.

and later in Frankfurt, Vienna, Stuttgart, and Augsburg. He was the author of a protest pamphlet that was distributed by Hans and Sophie SCHOLL in early February 1943, and that led to their arrest. On February 27, 1943, the Gestapo also seized Huber. He was sentenced to death in a Munich *Volk* Court proceeding under Roland FREISLER that was held especially for that purpose. Three months later he was guillotined.

Huch, Ricarda, b. Braunschweig, July 18, 1864; d. Schönberg (Taunus), November 17, 1947, German writer. Huch was one of the most productive and respected middle-class authors of the 20th century. Influenced by German Romanticism, her numerous works encompassed lyric poetry, cultural history, and narrative prose. Mussolini honored her for her portrayal of Italy's struggles for unification in the 19th century (*Die Geschichten von Garibaldi* [*Garibaldi and the New Italy;* 1906–1907]); the National Socialists valued her works on such heroic revolutionary figures as Luther and Wallenstein as "innately German" (*urdeutsch*). The novel *Der Fall Deruga* (*The Deruga Trial;* 1917), which dealt with the problem of euthanasia, also found acclaim. Nonetheless, Huch largely rebuffed National Socialist honors. She left the Prussian Academy of Arts in 1933 in protest against totalitarian and anti-Jewish policies, but was allowed to continue publishing during the Third Reich. After the war she was one of the first to demand publicly the honoring as "heroes" of those who resisted National Socialism,

especially the WHITE ROSE (*Der lautlose Aufstand* [The Silent Rebellion]; published posthumously in 1953).

Hugenberg, Alfred, b. Hannover, June 19, 1865; d. Kükenbruch bei Rinteln, March 12, 1951, German politician. From 1909 to 1918, Hugenberg was chairman of the board of the Krupp Works in Essen. During the First World War he became involved with the press. In the early 1920s, aided by the inflation, he bought numerous provincial newspapers, as well as larger newspaper presses such as Scherl, took over news agencies and the Ufa film studios (*see* UNIVERSE FILMS, INC.), and thus built up Germany's largest media and opinion concern. In politics, Hugenberg was one of the founders of the ALL-GERMAN ASSOCIATION in 1890; in 1919 he was elected to the National Assembly for the GERMAN NATIONAL PEOPLE'S PARTY (DNVP), which he represented in the Reichstag after 1920. As a representative of that party's right wing, he gained sufficient influence to become its chairman in 1928.

In the press and as a politician, Hugenberg fought the Weimar Republic, the socialists, and the pacifists. Together with the STEEL HELMET paramilitary organization and the National Socialists, he formed a joint national movement that emerged as the HARZBURG FRONT in 1931. In the illusion that Hitler could be used for his own political interests, Hugenberg deployed the propaganda apparatus of his press and news agencies to aid him. Hitler thereby gained support in industry and among the upper mid-

Ricarda Huch.

Alfred Hugenberg.

dle class, making Hugenberg one of the most important members of the bourgeoisie to prepare the way for the SEIZURE OF POWER. Still needed for a majority after the March 1933 elections, the DNVP lost all influence after the ENABLING LAW. Its chairman, also Minister for Economics and Food in Hitler's first cabinet, became increasingly isolated; he was forced to resign on June 27, 1933, at the same time that his party was dissolved. Hugenberg retained his Reichstag seat as a "guest of the NSDAP" until 1945. Even before the outbreak of war he was forced to sell off important parts of his press concern (Ufa in 1937, Scherl Press in 1944), but he received in return a significant participation in German heavy industry. After the war Hugenberg was interned by the British, but after several trials was classified as "exonerated" in 1951.

Hühnlein, Adolf, b. Neustädtlein bei Kulmbach, September 12, 1881; d. Munich, June 18, 1942, German politician. In the First World War, Hühnlein was an officer with the engineer corps and General Staff; after the war he served in the EPP free corps and then in the Reichswehr. He joined the staff of the SA in 1923. In 1925 Hühnlein became quartermaster of the NSDAP. In 1927 he was put in charge of the SA motor corps, where he founded the SA Motor Troops, the National Socialist Automobile Corps (NSAK), and, in 1931, the NATIONAL SOCIALIST MOTOR CORPS (NSKK).

After 1933 Hühnlein was charged with the "reformation of the entire German motor establishment"; as a *Korpsführer* he was later put

directly under Hitler. "Through the encouragement of automobile use," he wanted "not only to [crank up] the economy, but also . . . to offer . . . masses of our *Volk* the opportunity of acquiring this most modern means of transportation." He was in charge of the "synchronization" of the automobile sector, thereby incorporating many clubs (such as the General German Automobile Club) into the new German Automobile Club (Deutscher Automobil-Club), founded in addition to the NSKK. As president of the "Supreme National Sports Authority for German Automobile Driving" he organized, with industrial support, propaganda-oriented motor sports events, such as the "2,000-km [about 1,200 miles] Drive through Germany." After 1933 a Reichstag deputy and after 1938 a *Reichsleiter*, Hühnlein had numerous responsibilities in transportation policy; during the Second World War he was put in charge of motorized transport in the war economy.

H. H.

Hull, Cordell, b. Overton County, Tennessee, October 2, 1871; d. Washington, D.C., July 23, 1955, American politician. From 1907 to 1921 and from 1923 to 1931, Hull was a Democratic congressman. He served in the Senate from 1931 to 1933, when Roosevelt appointed him secretary of state, a position he held until 1944. During the 1930s, Hull fought for a policy of "moral embargo" against Italy and Germany. When war broke out, he energetically supported aid to Great Britain. His strong opposition was partly responsible for the decision first to soften the MORGENTHAU PLAN in 1944, and finally to

Adolf Hühnlein.

Cordell Hull.

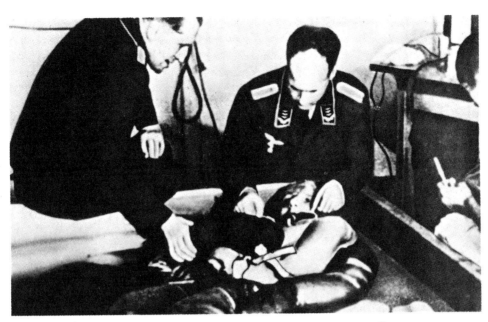

Human experiments. Hypothermia experiment on a Soviet prisoner of war.

abandon it. Hull won the Nobel Peace Prize in 1945 for his part in preparing for and organizing the United Nations.

Human experiments (*Menschenversuche*), medical experiments conducted on human subjects without their prior permission. From 1941 to 1944, experiments were carried out on prisoners in various concentration camps, with three goals: (1) to gain knowledge for the conduct of war; (2) to test medications, toxins, and vaccinations; and (3) to try out racial hygiene measures, especially the FORCED STERILIZATION of entire populations.

1. Low-temperature and low-pressure experiments at Dachau were intended to help save flyers who were shot down; the death of the experimental subjects not only was accepted but was part of the experiment. These experiments were discussed at a scientific congress in Nuremberg in 1942 and reported on in a journal for surgeons (*Zentralblatt für Chirurgie*). Experiments were also conducted at Dachau on the potability of seawater, using prisoners transferred from Buchenwald.

2. Typhus experiments were carried out at the Buchenwald and Struthof concentration camps, and malaria tests were conducted in Dachau; hepatitis experiments were planned for Buchenwald. In order to test the efficacy of sulfa drugs, severe wounds were inflicted on young Polish women in the Ravensbrück concentration camp. These experiments were officially reported as well. Ravensbrück was also the site of experi-

ments in bone regeneration and transplants. Phlegmon (purulent inflammation) experiments were conducted at Dachau, and mustard gas and phosgene were tested at Sachsenhausen and Struthof. In all of these experiments the death of the experimental subjects was willingly risked.

3. Procedures for mass sterilization by means of medications, X rays, and intrauterine inflammation were developed at the Auschwitz and Ravensbrück camps. In this category belongs the Jewish skeleton collection at the Strasbourg Reich University, for which at least 80 Jewish camp prisoners were murdered.

In the Nuremberg DOCTORS' TRIAL of 1946–1947, seven physicians who were involved in human experiments were condemned to death and seven more received life sentences.

R. W.

Humanity (*Humanität*), humane treatment, respect, and encouragement of the uniqueness of an individual; the concept was rejected by the National Socialists as a "destructive" ideal that was "threatening to life and species." They excoriated it as "humanitarian light-headedness" (*Humanitätsduselei*) because of the denial of *völkisch* and racial differences in the idea of humanity. National Socialists blamed the spread of the notion on Freemasons and Jews in particular, but also on the Weimar Republic, with its "feminist and democratic humanity, which feels sorry for every single criminal but forgets the state, the *Volk*—in short, the type [*Typus*]" (Rosenberg).

Human material (*Menschenmaterial*), term used by Karl Marx in 1867 in *Das Kapital* to denote capitalism's reduction of human beings to mere means to an end, and their labor to a ware. The later, totally uncritical use of the word in military jargon ("weapons and human material"), and notably in National Socialist terminology, shows the "internalization" of this inhuman conception of humankind: "We are all steel and iron / We are first-rate material" (Hitler Youth motto). Avoided after 1945, the term resurfaced in West German male adolescent slang in the 1980s, to refer to a girl as "material" (*das Material*) in the sense of an available means of pleasure.

Human rights (*Menschenrechte*), general rights of an individual, preceding and going beyond the rights accorded by a state; in a narrower sense, BASIC RIGHTS.

Humor. *See* Underground humor.

Hungary, state in southeastern Europe; area, 93,073 sq km (about 37,200 sq miles); population, approximately 8.7 million (1930). After republican beginnings (November 16, 1918) and a Communist soviet republic under Béla KUN (March 22–August 1, 1919), Adm. Miklós HORTHY as "state regent" established a kingdom of Hungary with a vacant throne. After the

TRIANON treaty (June 4, 1920), three themes dominated Hungarian policy: (1) revision of the peace treaty, as exemplified by the first of the VIENNA AWARDS (November 2, 1938), the occupation of the Carpathian Ukraine (March 14, 1939), the second Vienna Award (August 30, 1940), and the re-annexation of Yugoslav territories (April 1941); (2) restoration of the Habsburg monarchy, as exemplified by the failed attempt in 1921 to bring back Emperor Karl Franz Josef; and (3) severe social tensions (the domination of feudal estate owners, hunger for land among small peasants, and the rise of a radical right-wing, antisemitic "new middle class").

The liberal-conservative coalition of Count István Bethlen (prime minister from April 4, 1922, to August 19, 1931) stood for an independent foreign policy, moderate revisionism, and domestic consolidation. It was superseded by the exponents of middle-class antisemitism and radical irredentism against the LITTLE ENTENTE. By supporting Prime Minister Gyula Gömbös (September 30, 1932–October 6, 1936), they sought close ties with Fascism and National Socialism. They were influenced by ideological and foreign-policy considerations, as well as by Hungary's increasing dependence on the German market. Berlin itself supported the national socialist ARROW CROSS Party under Ferenc SZÁLASI.

Hungary joins the Three-Power Agreement (November 20, 1940). From the left, seated: German foreign minister Ribbentrop, Italian foreign minister Ciano, and Hungarian foreign minister Bárdossy.

During the Second World War, Horthy aimed at cooperation with Berlin in foreign policy, joining the Anti-Comintern Pact (February 24, 1939) and the Three-Power Agreement (November 20, 1940), and declaring war on Moscow and London (June 27, 1941). He tried to maintain a moderate domestic policy and to keep Hungary's Jewish citizens (6 percent of the population) out of German hands. After the turn in the fortunes of war, German troops occupied Hungary on March 19, 1944, in response to Horthy's failed attempt at an armistice with Moscow. The "state regent" was finally arrested on October 16 of that year and taken to Germany, while the totally isolated Szálasi, as *Staatsführer* (head of state), carried out German policies, including the deportation of Hungary's Jews. Meanwhile, the Soviets established a provisional government under General von Dálnok on territory occupied by the Red Army. On January 1, 1945—behind the facade of a multiparty Independent National Front—they concluded an armistice with Hungary. It was followed by the establishment of a Communist regime, under Mátyás Rákosi, that was dependent on Moscow.

B.-J. W.

Huntziger, Charles, b. Lesneven (Finistère), June 25, 1880; d. near Le Vigan (Gard), November 12, 1941 (in an airplane crash), French army general. Huntziger was supreme commander in Syria from 1934 to 1938. He commanded the French Second Army after September 1939 and the Fifth Army after June 5, 1940, during the FRENCH CAMPAIGN. He signed the French capitulation agreements in the COMPIÈGNE forest on June 22, and in Rome on June 24, 1940. On September 6 of that year he became war minister in the Vichy government, and on August 29, 1941, supreme commander of the troops in North Africa.

Husemann, Friedrich, b. Leopoldsthal (Lippe), September 19, 1873; d. Esterwegen concentration camp, April 15, 1935, German trade unionist. A mason, Husemann was employed in mine work after 1893; active in the mine workers' union, he became the union chairman in 1919. A Social Democrat, he was elected to the Reichstag for the SPD (Social Democratic Party) in 1924. He was a victim of the wave of arrests after the Reichstag fire of February 28, 1933, and was arrested again when the trade unions were abolished (May 2, 1933), and after the SPD was banned (June 22). Husemann flooded the German Labor Front with labor court proceedings for dismissed trade-union employees, until the Gestapo appeared again in March 1935 and took him to the Esterwegen camp, where he was shot "attempting to escape."

Hygiene, care of the body. In National Socialist usage the term was expanded to encompass care of the "body of the *Volk*" (*Volkskörper*), which included RACIAL HYGIENE measures in particular.

Hymmen, Friedrich Wilhelm, b. Soest, June 8, 1913, German writer and journalist. Hymmen took on publicity work in the National Socialist movement out of idealistic impulses. He became a *Bannführer* in the Reich Youth Leadership, and from 1937 to 1939 served as editor in chief of the magazine *Wille und Macht* (Will and Power). As an author (later working free-lance), Hymmen wrote novellas and sentimental dramas, such as *Der Vasall* (The Vassal; 1936), a paean to self-sacrificial faithfulness to the emperor. After the war Hymmen worked for the Information Service of the Evangelical Church in [West] Germany, where he became chief editor and in publications took a critical stance toward the media policy of the Third Reich.

Ich klage an (*I Accuse*), German film (1941) directed by Wolfgang LIEBENEINER and based on the novel *Sendung und Gewissen* (Mission and Conscience) by Helmut Unger; the actors included Heidemarie Hatheyer, Paul Hartmann, and Mathias Wieman. Premiered on August 29, 1941, the film was made in the service of National Socialist propaganda on the theme of EUTHANASIA, which even Goebbels found explosive: "In the treatment of this film," his press release advised, "the greatest tact is appropriate." The plot concerns a woman stricken with multiple sclerosis who pleads for death with two doctors, her husband, and a friend. Her husband finally gives her poison, is charged with murder, and, in a passionate speech in court, acknowledges the mercy killing.

Under the cloak of advocating humane aid in dying, the film (rated as "of particular artistic worth, educational") propagandized for the killing of "life unworthy of life" and served to coalesce opinion in favor of the NS policy of *Ausmerzen* (*see* CULLING OUT). This policy culminated in the FINAL SOLUTION of the Jewish question, in which SS ideologues saw a consistent "racial euthanasia." (The author of the novel on which the film was based himself became a physician "expert" in the NS Euthanasia program.)

Idea (*Gedanke;* also translated as "thought"), general term for a mental process, as well as its result. In terms of ideology it stands for a whole mental construct: in the rhetoric and journalism

Ich klage an. From the left: Charlotte Thiele, Hans Nielsen, and Paul Hartmann.

of the Third Reich, "the National Socialist idea" was favored as a synonym for the cumbersome and dogmatic-sounding "National Socialism."

Identity Card (*Kennkarte*), internal passport introduced in an ordinance of July 22, 1938; it was to be obtained by all German citizens over the age of 14 years. Also required to carry the card were all persons eligible for military service and, after the REICH CITIZENSHIP LAW was put into force, Jews in particular. Issued for a period of five years, the card thus restricted the free movement of particular groups of people.

Ideological acrobats (*Gesinnungsakrobaten*), term popular during the National Socialist "Time of Struggle"; it ridiculed both democratically inclined political opponents, who because they were capable of compromise were said to be without character, and the democratic form of government, which was a "circus" because it was based on a plurality of opinions and the division of power. The term was also applied after the Seizure of Power to so-called *Konjunkturritter* (literally, knights, or riders, of market trends, that is, opportunists), who overnight changed their viewpoint (*see* MÄRZGEFALLENE).

Ideology (*Ideologie*), term for systems of thought, used most often in a derogatory way. National Socialist criticism opposed the Marxist "misuse" of the term as "class consciousness," because all "authentic and spiritual-cultural properties" were thus degraded into mere instruments of domination. Because intellectuals had taken over this linguistic usage and by "ideology" meant the totality of ideas used to obscure sociopolitical reality, the word had been undermined. Against this usage the National Socialists offered the positive term "worldview" (*Weltanschauung*).

Ideology, National Socialist. *See* Fascism; Hitler's Worldview; National Socialism.

I.G. Farben (Interessen-Gemeinschaft Farbenindustrie AG, Frankfurt/Main; Union of Interests of Farben Industries, Inc.), chemical concern founded on December 12, 1925, through the merger of Germany's largest chemical companies (BASF, Bayer, Hoechst, and Agfa, among others). Until late 1932 it was the target of vehement attacks by the NSDAP because of a high degree of Jewish participation (six of its directors were Jewish).

Once a champion of international free trade, I.G. Farben became an advocate of German

AUTARKY. The development of advanced, large-scale techniques for coal liquification, as well as the synthetic production of rubber, initiated with government financial support ("Benzene Agreement," December 14, 1933), assured Farben the leading role in industrial preparations for war foreseen by the FOUR-YEAR PLAN. It also produced a personnel link with the National Socialist state: Farben director Carl Krauch, for example, was also "general plenipotentiary for special issues of chemical production." Aided by the army and the NS bureaucracy, the company plundered the chemical industries of occupied countries during the war. The complicity between Farben (whose DEGESCH subsidiary produced ZYKLON B poison gas) and the National Socialists culminated in the construction of a gigantic plant for the production of synthetic rubber and oil at AUSCHWITZ, where 25,000 forced laborers lost their lives.

On July 29 and 30, 1948, in the I.G. FARBEN TRIAL in Nuremberg, 13 leading employees of the company were condemned to prison sentences of between 18 months and six years for crimes that included "enslavement and murder of the civilian population, prisoners of war, and concentration camp inmates." Through Law No. 35 (August 17, 1950), the Allied High Commission decreed the breaking up of the Farben holdings in the Federal Republic of Germany. The best-known successor enterprises are BASF, Bayer, and Hoechst.

R. V.

I.G. Farben Trial, proceeding before United States Military Court IV in Nuremberg against the chairman of the board of directors, Carl Krauch, and 22 managers, directors, and leading employees of I.G. Farben Industries for crimes against peace, crimes against humanity, and participation in a criminal organization (Case 6). In essence, the defendants were accused of having participated and conspired with Hitler and the military leadership in planning a war of aggression and building up the army to wage it; of having developed plans for the "absorption" of existing industries in countries invaded by Germany; of having carried out these plans after the conquest of those areas; and of having exploited prisoners of war and foreign workers, as well as concentration camp prisoners, for their own uses. Three of the accused were further found guilty of having been members of the SS.

The trial began in August 1947. On July 30, 1948, the court sentenced thirteen defendants to prison for terms ranging from 18 months to six years. Ten defendants were acquitted. When the period of time they had already been detained prior to the investigation was calculated into the sentences, two of those sentenced were immediately released, and five had less than one year to serve. The rest were released early for good behavior.

A. St.

Illustrierter Beobachter (Illustrated Observer; IB), illustrated companion periodical to the VÖLKISCHER BEOBACHTER, published by the Eher Press, and appearing at first monthly and later weekly, from July 1926 on. The IB put photojournalism and photomontage in the service of National Socialist propaganda, and fulfilled the need for "court news" through photographs covering the NS leadership circles. The editor in chief was Dietrich Loder; photographers included Heinrich HOFFMANN. From October 1944 on, because of "restrictions on the press" necessitated by the war, the IB was, along with the BERLINER ILLUSTRIERTE ZEITUNG, the only German illustrated periodical appearing

Illustrierter Beobachter. Cover photo: "The Historical Day. Adolf Hitler, stormily greeted by the people, on the way to his first cabinet meeting on Monday, January 30, 1933, after being appointed Reich chancellor. Inset: calendar in the Reich Chancellery."

until 1945. The circulation as of March 1944 was 1.9 million; the final edition appeared on February 12, 1945.

S. O.

Imbusch, Heinrich, b. Oberhausen, September 1, 1878; d. Essen, January 16, 1945, German trade unionist. After 1897 Imbusch was in the Christian mine workers' movement; from 1920 to 1933, he was a Reichstag deputy for the Center party; from 1929 to 1933, chairman of the GERMAN TRADE UNION FEDERATION. Imbusch worked to establish the welfare state, but he could not stem the countervailing development that set in with the world economic crisis. His struggle against National Socialism too remained fruitless, and consequently Imbusch fled to the Saarland in 1933. Escaping a kidnapping attempt by the SA, he fled on to Luxembourg and France. After the German occupation, Imbusch remained unrecognized; in 1942 he returned secretly to Essen, where he died in hiding.

Immoralism (*Immoralismus*), general philosophical term for a lack of morality or for immorality; it was used by the National Socialists as a catchword—following NIETZSCHE—for a new, more highly evolved moral standard (notably the National Socialist worldview). From the viewpoint of the "previous decadent" morality it would have appeared without moral standards, whereas in reality its standard was "beyond good and evil."

Imperialism (from Lat. *imperium*, state authority, as well as the area of its sway), the striving by states for mastery and expansion, for motives of religion, economics, and/or power politics, necessarily at the expense of other states. The contemporary term "imperialism," most often used negatively in polemics and slogans, is employed by historians to characterize historical tendencies, notably the expansionism of the European Great Powers and the United States in the late 19th and early 20th centuries, the so-called Age of Imperialism, whose rivalries exploded in the First World War, but persisted in a changed form. It expressed itself in the disguised imperialism of Italian FASCISM and German NATIONAL SOCIALISM, which justified its demand for LIVING SPACE as *völkisch* and thus the opposite of the colonial or economic ("dollar imperialism") varieties. "The truly imperialist empires of the future," according to the 1938 *Meyers Lexikon,* "will be those . . . that basically restrict themselves to the space creatively opened up by their own people."

The course of the SECOND WORLD WAR revealed that this thesis cloaked the real, more deeply hidden goal of National Socialism—racist imperialism—which was thus finally discredited. The Marxist interpretation gained impetus after 1945: "Imperialism as the final stage of capitalism" (Lenin, 1916–1917). This purely economic view of imperialism, present in many variations, fails—as does ANTIFASCISM—to recognize the specifically National Socialist aspects in the German imperialism of the Third Reich. The PERSECUTION OF JEWS and the FINAL SOLUTION prove that it was primarily racist, motivated particularly by antisemitism, and thus, in its deluded fixation on a "final struggle between Aryans and Jews," a degenerate form of religious imperialism.

IMT, acronym of INTERNATIONAL MILITARY TRIBUNAL, the court for judging major war criminals in the NUREMBERG TRIALS.

Incorporation. *See* Communal annexation.

Indispensable (*unabkömmlich;* uk), in military law, a category of persons who were exempt from military service because of the crucial nature of their current civilian employment. The opposite category was "kv," fit for active service (*kriegsverwendungsfähig*). During the Second World War, "uk" status could be granted to skilled workers, miners, farmers, engineers, and scientists, among others. Details were stipulated in the Regulations for Uk Determination in Particular Deployments (November 1940) of the Wehrmacht High Command. The essential precondition for "uk" status was that it be "in the interest of the defense of the Reich."

Individualism (*Individualismus*), a worldview placing the greatest importance on the individual personality. It was rejected by the National Socialists as a "degeneration" and the antithesis of the *Volk* Community. In individualism the National Socialist theoreticians saw a "mistaken development" of bourgeois philosophy that would be abolished in the "new state." In this state, "personality and community" would no longer need to be "opposites," since for the individual, "race and *Volk* [constitute] the basis of one's being, yet also at the same time the only possibility of its enhancement" (Alfred Rosenberg).

Induction Order (*Gestellungsbefehl*), notice to report for military service. The term was also applied to the civilian sector, in keeping with the militarization of the National Socialist vocabulary, as in the expression "economic induction order," in connection with LABOR DEPLOYMENT measures.

Industry Letter (*Industriebrief*), document presented to Reich President Paul von Hindenburg on November 19, 1932, in the name of bankers and entrepreneurs (among others, Kurt SCHRÖDER and Fritz THYSSEN). They believed that even the authoritarian PRESIDIAL CABINETS were still too democratic, and anticipated that the naming of Hitler as Reich chancellor would mean the final elimination of the Weimar Republic. Only then, they concluded, could a "recovery of the German economy" be expected. The initiative ultimately failed because of Hitler's extravagant demands and Hindenburg's misgivings. The latter hoped that Hitler could be bypassed with Kurt von Schleicher's idea of a TRADE UNION AXIS.

Inferior race (*Niederrasse*), in National Socialist usage, the opposite in racial ideology to the "Aryan superior race"; it referred especially to the "Jewish race."

Inflation, general term for a steady increase in the price index of a national economy; in particular, for the devaluation of the reichsmark in the first years of the Weimar Republic. This was unleashed by credit financing of war reparations, continuing economic burdens of the First World War, the printing of money (and thus surplus demand), currency speculation, and the flight of capital, among other causes. Creeping inflation between 1918 and 1921 developed into "trotting" inflation in 1922 and then galloping inflation in 1923, as the burden of the RUHR CONFLICT magnified the effect of the factors that fed inflation, but also because the German government, as well as the Reich Bank, welcomed inflation's effect of writing off debt. The dollar, worth 4.2 RM in 1914, had increased by July 1919 to 14.0 RM, and by July 1921 to 76.7 RM. In July 1922 it was worth almost 500 RM; a year later, 353,412 RM, and it reached its peak on November 15, 1923: 4.2 billion RM.

This inflation annihilated both savings and considerable amounts of working capital; it favored indebtedness and capital goods, and led to a far-reaching redistribution of wealth, and the hastening of the process of its concentration in the German economy. For many groups, especially the middle class, this inflation meant a fall

Inflation. Masses of paper money are carried in sacks and laundry baskets.

into a lower class, even proletarianization—a traumatic experience that later, during the WORLD ECONOMIC CRISIS, furthered political radicalization and prepared the ground for National Socialist agitation. This delayed effect took place through the control of inflation by the stabilized mark, the reduction of REPARATIONS in the DAWES PLAN, and the extension of foreign credit; until 1929, there was a short period of modest prosperity. A new but controlled inflation was unleashed by NS WORK CREATION measures through deficit spending and, above all, the financing of REARMAMENT, in part by the printing of money, and especially during the Second World War (*see* ECONOMY UNDER NATIONAL SOCIALISM, THE).

Inheritance, right of (*Erbrecht*), principle of the inheritability of private property (*see* PROPERTY). It was not disputed by the National Socialists, although they did limit it in conformity with the notion of the *Volk* Community (*see, for example,* HEREDITARY FARM LAW).

Inheritance Boards (*Anerbenbehörden*), rural courts set up by the HEREDITARY FARM LAW to adjudicate disputes; they involved peasants and judges. The term derived from Old German (referring to the transmittal of entailed estates)

and reflected National Socialist efforts to revive Germanic legal traditions.

Inherited sin (*Erbsünde*, "original sin"), term from Christian doctrine taken over and radically transformed in meaning by racial ideologists. It no longer meant the unavoidable guilt inherited from the fall from grace of the first humans, but rather the sin against the truths of the laws of heredity, especially that of racial purity: "The sin against blood and race is the inherited sin of this world" (*Mein Kampf*).

Inner Emigration (*Innere Emigration*), term coined by Frank THIESS in 1933 for the oppositional stance taken by writers remaining in Germany after the Seizure of Power. The term was later extended to all those who rejected National Socialism but did not want to leave their homeland. Controversy regarding the virtue of EMIGRATION as against Inner Emigration soon developed, and was not silenced after the war, the more so since even the mere retreat into private life was passed off as Inner Emigration by many. Thus came the accusation that remaining in Germany had made everyone to some degree an accomplice of an unjust regime through such acts as paying taxes, being a consumer, and performing military service. Moreover, what opponents of National Socialism who remained meant by OPPOSITION (*Widerstand*) hardly appeared to be such from the outside, since in a state totally "synchronized" with National Socialist practice, resistance had to camouflage itself in linguistically refined ways, for example, through partial agreement and borrowing the adversary's rhetoric.

Innitzer, Theodor, b. Neugeschrei-Weipert (Bohemia), December 25, 1875; d. Vienna, October 9, 1955, Austrian Catholic theologian. At first a factory worker, Innitzer was ordained in 1902; in 1921 he was made a professor, and in 1928–1929, he was rector at the University of Vienna; in 1929–1930, he was minister for social welfare; on September 19, 1932, he was appointed archbishop of Vienna, and, on March 13, 1933, cardinal. A Sudeten German, Innitzer supported an ANSCHLUSS between Austria and Germany after the First World War. His later support for the authoritarian regimes of Engelbert Dollfuss and Kurt Schuschnigg brought him close to AUSTROFASCISM. After 1932 he warned the Austrian episcopate against National Socialism, and in 1937 he decisively took the side of German Catholics caught up in the CHURCH STRUGGLE.

Nonetheless, Innitzer welcomed the Anschluss in 1938; he visited Hitler on March 15 of that year, and on March 21 called for a "yes" vote in the April 10 referendum as a "self-evident national duty." The illusion that he could win over the new master through such cooperation vanished after Josef BÜRCKEL's hostile measures against the church and Alfred Rosenberg's attacks. When Innitzer defended himself, the archbishop's palace was plundered by Hitler Youth groups. Innitzer retreated from political life, strengthened his pastoral and charitable activities—for persecuted Jews as well as for Christians—and preserved the unity of the Austrian church well into the war, during which National Socialist persecution lessened. Often attacked after 1945—even within the church—because of his early collaboration, Innitzer experienced a kind of rehabilitation with his nomination as papal legate in December 1952.

Inönü (real name, Mustafa Ismet), b. Izmir, September 24, 1884; d. Ankara, December 25, 1973, Turkish general and politician. A General Staff officer in the First World War, Ismet won a victory near Inönü on March 30, 1921, in the Turkish-Greek war; he adopted this name in 1934. As a close associate of President Kemal Atatürk, he served as foreign minister (1922–1924), prime minister (1923–1924 and 1925–1937), and, after Atatürk's death in November 1938, president. Inönü pursued his mentor's course of Turkish modernization. Until early 1945 he was able to keep TURKEY on a course of neutrality, finally entering the war against Germany only to improve his chance of having a say in the creation of the postwar political order. Voted out in 1950, Inönü later served again as prime minister from 1961 to 1965, then led the opposition until 1972.

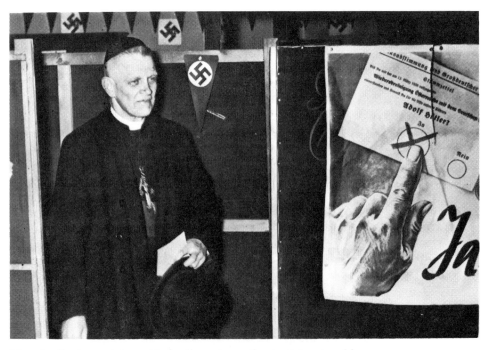

Theodor Innitzer at the polls for the vote on the Austrian Anschluss.

Inquiry and Arbitration Committee (Untersuchungs- und Schlichtungsausschuss; Uschla), internal party arbitration office under Lt. Gen. (ret.) Bruno Heinemann (d. 1938), created after the refounding of the NSDAP (February 27, 1925). The office became truly effective after it was taken over by Walter BUCH on November 11, 1927; on January 1, 1934, it was elevated to the status of Supreme Party Court (*see* PARTY COURTS).

Instinct (*Instinkt*), basic inborn trait, independent of the capacity to reason. National Socialist ideology considered instinct to be determined by "contingencies of race and inheritance," and they classified it as a positive antithesis to "corrosive intellect" and knowledge: "We suffer today from . . . overeducation. . . . The ones too smart for their own good [*Neunmalkluge*] . . . are enemies of the deed. What we need is instinct and will" (Hitler, 1923).

Intellect (*Intellekt*), the faculty of understanding. It was understood by the National Socialists not as a creative ability but, rather, negatively, as "critically divisive" and "destructive." In National Socialist usage, "intellectualism" meant the one-sided development of the powers of understanding, which, to the detriment of CHARACTER, would lead to an "overly critical" stance. Thus, attacks against the state or its representatives (such as the July 20, 1944, assassination attempt against Hitler) were considered "the result . . . of a diabolical intellect" (Goebbels, 1944). In this sense, the terms "intellectual" and "intellectualism" nearly had the connotation of an insult in the Third Reich, and even after 1945 were often used in a derogatory sense.

Intelligence (*Intelligenz*), the faculty of thought. Intelligence as a quality and a goal of education was ranked by the National Socialists as of minor importance—at best, on the same level as will, CHARACTER, and physical traits (E. Krieck, *Völkisch-politische Anthropologie*, 1938). The term was also used as a general derogatory designation for the "bourgeois educated classes," and, in the more intense form "Jewish subversive [*zersetzte*] intelligence," referred especially to critical intellectuals, writers, and scientists.

Intelligence, military. *See* Abwehr.

Intelligentsia Operation (Intelligenz-Aktion), code name for the shooting of Polish intellectuals on Reinhard Heydrich's order after the Polish Campaign. Heydrich was acting on Himm-

ler's, and thus Hitler's, order. The operation began in October 1939 in the annexed territories, especially the *Gaue* of Danzig–West Prussia and Posen, and was carried out by members of EINSATZGRUPPEN, SELF-DEFENSE groups (militia-like units of ethnic Germans), and state police. Heydrich ordered completion of the operation by November 1, 1939, but it ran beyond this deadline. By November 20, some 60,000 physicians, lawyers, government officials, teachers, former officers, and influential businessmen had been shot. The liquidation of clergymen, members of the nobility, and Jews had begun even before the Intelligentsia Operation.

A. St.

Interim Reich (Zwischenreich), National Socialist term for the WEIMAR REPUBLIC, which was thereby denigrated as an episode between the Kaiserreich (Imperial Germany, 1871–1918) and the Third Reich (*see also* SYSTEM ERA).

International, term for the different international socialist federations created for the purpose of overturning capitalism in line with Karl Marx's internationalist motto, "Workers of the world, unite." The First International was formed in London in 1864 (disbanded in 1876). During the Second International, founded in Paris in 1889, May 1 was elevated to a day of struggle for the workers' movement (*see* MAY HOLIDAY). That International ended with the onset of the First World War. One of its successors was the Third or Communist International of 1919 (Comintern), a Communist "world party," in which the Soviet Union in fact claimed the "leading role." In response, Trotsky established a Fourth, Leninist International, which had little influence. The Comintern was sacrificed to the Soviet alliance with the Western powers on May 15, 1943, but was briefly revived from 1947 to 1956 as the Cominform.

For the National Socialists, who rejected any INTERNATIONALISM, all Internationals, particularly the Comintern, were instruments of WORLD JEWRY and of its "plans to take over the world." "International" was thus extended as an insult to the supposedly equally worldwide conspiracies of Catholicism (the Black International), HIGH FINANCE (the Gold International), and the aristocracy (the Blue International).

International Brigades, volunteer units in the SPANISH CIVIL WAR that entered the fight against Franco on the side of the Republic. They were successful in the defense of Madrid in November 1936 and in the battle of Guadalajara in

March 1937. The total strength of the International Brigades came to about 40,000 men. The movement originated among French and Belgian Communists, and the Comintern later took over the greater part of the organizational work. Approximately 3,000 Germans, of whom about half fell in battle, were members of the International Brigades, most of them also Communists and emigrants. In November 1938 the International Brigades were disbanded by a decree of the Spanish government in order to achieve a general prohibition against intervention in the civil war. Their unity had already been shaken by the activity of the Stalinist secret police (through imprisonments and executions on the model of the show trials then taking place in Moscow). Groups of the International Brigades crossed the border into France, where they were interned in camps (among others, GURS).

Ba.

Internationalism (*Internationalismus*), according to the National Socialist view, all international efforts of a political, economic, or cultural kind not linked to the *Volk* or race. Internationalism arose from the basic error, as the National Socialists saw it, that human beings and peoples, or even races, were equal, a fiction that WORLD JEWRY used for the "ruination of *völkisch* communities." To that end it established capitalism (thus undermining national economies through international HIGH FINANCE), just as it did international Marxism (an incitement to class hatred) and also democracy, which was deemed inseparable from internationalism (Hitler, January 27, 1932). Against internationalism's pernicious "ideals of humanitarianism and humanity," National Socialism offered the concepts of the *Volk* nation (*Volkstum*) and race, which share as their point of departure the principle of the difference in nature and worth of all human beings and peoples.

International law (*Völkerrecht*), rules recognized as laws by states in their dealings with one another. National Socialist (NS) international law propagated the idea of the "Reich," which represented a union between a *Grossraum* (domain; literally, "large area")—that is, a geographical sector of the world (such as a *Grossraum Amerika*)—and both a people and a political idea emanating from this domain. This *Grossraum* principle incorporated prohibitions against intervention or interference by outside powers. The intended domain for the German Reich was central and eastern Europe, based on

the presumption of a German right to protect groups of ethnic Germans with foreign citizenship who were living there.

In place of then-existing concepts of warfare (a combatants' war, protection of the civilian population), NS international law offered the notion of "total war," which denied all limitations theretofore drawn by international law to regulate warfare. War could be "total" in the technological, economic, and territorial senses with regard to deployment of men and material, destruction, attitudes toward the enemy, and the protagonist power's own people (that people's "struggle for existence"). NS Germany committed countless infractions of international law: for example, REARMAMENT in defiance of the Versailles treaty, the occupation of Austria and Czechoslovakia, and the initiation of a war of aggression, which violated in particular the KELLOGG-BRIAND PACT of 1928. Most important was the treatment of PRISONERS OF WAR and of civilians in the occupied territories (*see* OCCUPATION POLICY), which ignored all international law and culminated in the systematic murder programs associated with the EINSATZGRUPPEN and the FINAL SOLUTION.

Ha.

International Military Tribunal (IMT; Internationaler Militärgerichtshof), British-American term for the body that in 1945 and 1946 conducted the chief war crimes trial "against Hermann Göring and accomplices" in Nuremberg (*see* NUREMBERG TRIALS). The abbreviation IMT is the usual citation for documents from these trials.

Interzonal Passport (*Interzonenpass*), identity paper prescribed by the Allied Control Council for travel between one occupation zone and another (*see* OCCUPATION ZONES). After creation of the Western Trizone, it was necessary only for travel between that and the Soviet zone.

Interzonal trade (*Interzonenhandel*), originally a term for the exchange of goods among the four OCCUPATION ZONES of Germany. After the unification of the Western zones in a Trizone, it was applied to the economic traffic between this unit and the Soviet zone; finally, after the creation of the Federal Republic of Germany and the German Democratic Republic (GDR), it referred to internal German trade on the basis of exchange units.

Invalid Operation (Invaliden-Aktion; also Aktion 14f13), term for the extension of the EUTHANA-

SIA program to concentration camp inmates. On Himmler's order in the spring of 1941, camp prisoners who were sick and incapable of work began to be separated out for "extermination." The operation went under the code name "Aktion 14f13," taken from the bureaucratic reference number for the Inspectorate of Concentration Camps. Physicians from the T4 Organization conducted the *Selektionen*. There was generally no physical examination; the doctors asked questions about illnesses based on already completed questionnaires, and then made their decision: "mustering out" (*Ausmusterung*) or remaining in the camp. Not only prisoners who were sick or incapable of work were selected; the procedure also took in a diverse group of asocial, criminal, political, and Jewish inmates, with such rationales as "anti-German rabble-rouser," "demanding, lazy, insolent camp behavior," or "repeated camp punishments."

The "experts" (*Gutachter*) sent their questionnaires and decisions to the T4 Organization, where the material was further handled by the subsidiary PUBLIC WELFARE AMBULANCE SERVICE, LTD. (Gekrat). After processing the questionnaires, T4 sent transfer lists of those "mustered out" to the killing facilities at BERNBURG AN DER SAALE, SONNENSTEIN, or HARTHEIM, which themselves contacted the concentration camps and arranged for the transfer of those selected. Probably in April 1943, Himmler ordered that only mentally ill prisoners were thenceforth to be "mustered out." The Bernburg and Sonnenstein killing facilities were closed; Hartheim remained open. In early April 1944, the original "order to exterminate" was again announced, and killings followed in Hartheim. The last transport of selected prisoners was gassed there on December 11, 1944. Prisoners from the MAUTHAUSEN camp were then ordered to dismantle the Hartheim gassing installation.

Only sporadic documentation of the total number of prisoners killed in the Invalid Operation remains. It can, however, be assumed that by April 1943 at least 10,000 persons were murdered in the killing facilities. In Hartheim, in the second phase alone, after April 1944, 3,228 prisoners were killed.

A. St.

Invasion (*Invasion*), general term for military penetration into foreign territory, used in the Second World War more specifically to refer to the landing of British and American troops in German-occupied France, an operation preced-

ed by the invasion of Italy. Three months after the end of the AFRICAN CAMPAIGN, on July 10, 1943, a British and an American army landed on Sicily, which the German and Italian defenders evacuated by mid-August. The real invasion of the Italian mainland began with the passage of the British Eighth Army across the Strait of Messina on September 3 and the landing of the United States Fifth Army in the Bay of Salerno on September 9. German troops had taken over the defense alone after Italy's withdrawal from the war (cease-fire of September 8, 1943); they disarmed their former allies, freed the imprisoned Mussolini on September 12, and established a northern Italian puppet regime in SALÒ for Il Duce. The BADOGLIO government, supported by the Allies, declared war on Germany on October 13. It had authority over the liberated areas in southern Italy as well as over Corsica and Sardinia until the end of 1943.

The Allies made only slow advances against the massive German defense, especially at Monte Cassino. Only at the end of May 1944 did they break through to Rome, which fell on June 4, while the German front fell back across the Arno River into the Apennines. The real invasion began in Normandy on June 6, 1944. With 4,126 landing vehicles and 2,316 transport vehicles, the western Allies established on D Day (D stood for "decision") the second front in Europe (Operation "Overlord") long demanded by Stalin. On the very first day, Allied air support flew 14,674 missions, which were countered by only 319 German responses, and immediately won air supremacy. German counterattacks made no breakthroughs, and by June 18 the Allies (under Supreme Commander Gen. Dwight D. Eisenhower) were able to land 619,000 soldiers and 95,000 vehicles. They had available to them 86 divisions, as against Germany's 56 of very uneven quality.

Cherbourg fell on June 30, 1944. After breaking out of the bridgehead, the Allies began a lightning-fast advance into France on August 2. Paris was occupied on August 25, Brussels on September 3. On August 15, 1944, Allied troops also landed on the French Mediterranean coast, and on September 11 met near Dijon with the American units coming from Normandy. That same day, American troops for the first time reached the Reich's border, northwest of Trier. By that time 360,000 German soldiers had been taken prisoner. Seven Allied armies were ready in the west, four of them American. Their advance once again stalled when a British air-and-land division was wiped out (6,450 prison-

Invasion. American infantrymen land on the beaches at Normandy.

ers) between September 17 and 26, in the course of a large-scale air-and-land operation in southern Holland that was intended to open the way into the Ruhr region. Hitler was encouraged by this successful defense to mount a counteroffensive in the west. The Americans captured the first major German city, Aachen, on October 21; soon afterward the French took Strasbourg (November 23).

A German attack got under way on December 16 between Hohe Venn and northern Luxembourg (*see* ARDENNES OFFENSIVE), carried out by 29 divisions and 1,794 vehicles. Its goal was the supply port of Antwerp. After early successes against a surprised opponent, the German attack collapsed in a few days, as did an offensive in northern Alsace. In these engagements the German army lost 12,652 dead, 30,585 missing, and 38,600 wounded, as well as 222 tanks; the Allies suffered casualties of 8,607 dead, 21,144 missing, and 47,129 wounded, and had to replace 471 Sherman tanks.

G. H.

Iron Cross (Eisernes Kreuz; EK), German, formerly Prussian, war decoration established on March 10, 1813, by King Friedrich Wilhelm III during the wars of liberation against Napoleon. Awarded for combat service without distinction of rank or social standing, it was revived in 1870, 1914, and 1939. In the First World War the EK

was awarded in two classes and as a Great Cross (Grosskreuz). The EK of 1939 had four grades: (1) EK II (red ribbon with black and white borders); (2) EK I (pin); (3) KNIGHT'S CROSS (Ritterkreuz) of the EK; and (4) Great Cross of the EK (sole recipient, Hermann Göring). A law of July 26, 1957, permits the EK to be worn in the Federal Republic of Germany only without the swastika. (*See* CROSS OF HONOR.)

Iron Curtain (*Eiserner Vorhang*), term first coined by Joseph Goebbels on February 25, 1945, in the weekly *Das Reich*, but generally attributed to Winston Churchill (telegram to President Harry S. Truman, May 12, 1945; speech in Fulton, Missouri, March 5, 1946), to refer to the radical Soviet measures to quarantine the Soviet sphere of influence as a sign of estrangement from the western Allies and of the beginning Cold War. The carefully guarded and strongly fortified Iron Curtain divided Germany, especially along the 1,346-km (835-mile) western border of the Soviet occupation zone, from the Bay of Lübeck to the German-Czechoslovak border.

Iron Front (Eiserne Front), organization called into being on December 16, 1931, in Berlin on the initiative of the REICH BANNER "BLACK-RED-GOLD," with the participation of the SPD (Social Democratic Party), trade unions, and workers' organizations. Its emblem consisted of three

Iron Front poster (1931).

arrows, its journal was *Eiserne Front,* and its purpose was to coordinate resistance from supporters of the Weimar Republic to the claims to power of the extreme Right (*see* HARZBURG FRONT). Without the cooperation of significant middle-class support, the Iron Front (led by Karl HÖLTERMANN and Otto WELS) became an inadequately armed combat group of the democratic Left, not equal to the terrorism of the SA and SS, in particular. Before and after the PRUSSIAN COUP (July 20, 1932), the Iron Front broke down, when it renounced a battle for political power outside of legal, parliamentary avenues, in keeping with the fundamentally resigned stance of the SPD. The Iron Front collapsed in May 1933 after the destruction of the trade unions.

M. F.

Iron Guard (Garda de Fier), Romanian party and paramilitary organization that grew out of the "Legion of the Archangel Michael" founded by Corneliu CODREANU. The Iron Guard propagated national renewal on an antisemitic and Christian basis, and fought for this goal with both terrorist attacks and parliamentary means. It chiefly attracted clergymen, officers, and students, but also lured peasants with the promise of radical land reform. In 1932 the Iron Guard won only four seats in the Romanian parliament, but in 1937 it became the third strongest political force, with 16 percent of the vote. After establishment of a royal dictatorship under Carol II (February 1938), it was outlawed and deprived of its leaders through murder and imprisonment. In September 1940, under Horia SIMA, the fascist Iron Guard participated in the overthrow of the king and joined the government of Ion ANTONESCU. An attempt at a coup by Sima in January 1941 was quashed with German help, and the Iron Guard was finally suppressed.

Iron Guard. Illegal demonstration.

Israel, masculine Jewish first name going back to the biblical patriarch Jacob. According to a decree of August 17, 1938, every Jewish man in the German Reich who had a first name forbidden to Jews on the ground that it was not immediately recognizable as Jewish had to add "Israel" to his first name. Women were prescribed the additional name "Sara." This obligation of Jews to thus identify themselves was a result of the NUREMBERG LAWS; it was extended, in the autumn of 1938, by the stamping of a "J" in Jews' passports, and, finally, through the introduction of a JEWISH STAR. All these measures served to deprive Jews of rights as part of the PERSECUTION OF JEWS.

Italy, southern European monarchy [now a republic]; area, approximately 310,000 sq km (about 124,000 sq miles); population, 41.2 million (1931). The triumph of Fascism—marked by the March on Rome (October 28, 1922) and Mussolini's appointment as premier (October 31)—grew out of various conflicts in postwar Italy: disappointment over the "crippled victory" of 1918–1919 and the flaring up of a radical nationalism (*see* Gabriele D'ANNUNZIO); economic and social crises; strike movements; a stalemate in the system of parliamentary democracy, associated with rapidly changing governments and the collapse of the political center; radical Communist and socialist plans for an overthrow; and the fear of revolution among the bourgeoisie and landed property owners. After

Italy. "The Fascist government has given me back my dignity as a worker and as an Italian."

Italy. Propaganda for Mussolini.

1923 the totalitarian Fascist corporatist state was established step by step from within, under the continuing existence of collaborating but autonomous power centers (notably the crown, the church, and industry).

This process at first seemed to accord with a foreign policy that appeared wholly moderate, careful, and based on international cooperation (for example, the LOCARNO PACT of 1925 and the LATERAN TREATIES of 1929), as well as with an estrangement from Berlin, especially after the murder of Austrian chancellor Engelbert DOLLFUSS. It was only the adoption of a policy of imperial conquest on a Roman model (the invasion of ABYSSINIA on December 3, 1935; the occupation of Albania on April 12, 1939) that led to a closer dependency on Germany (*see* AXIS, created on October 25, 1936; SPANISH CIVIL WAR; ANTI-COMINTERN PACT, November 5, 1937; MUNICH AGREEMENT, September 30, 1938; PACT OF STEEL, May 22, 1939).

After a period of "non-*belligeranza*" after 1939–1940, Italy's final entry into the war on June 10, 1940, placed it in a political and military "satellite status" alongside Germany. In the close linkage between Italy's and Germany's fate through Mussolini, Fascist Italy showed itself unequal to the heavy cost of the war and the turn in its fortunes (*see* AFRICAN CAMPAIGN; INVASION). After a vote of no confidence in

On June 10, 1940, Mussolini announces Italy's entry into the war.

Mussolini by the Fascist Grand Council, King VICTOR EMMANUEL III had him imprisoned on July 25, 1943; shortly afterward the king fled with his newly named prime minister, Pietro BADOGLIO, under the protection of the Allies.

Badoglio concluded a cease-fire on September 3, 1943. Together with the Comitato di Liberazione Nationale, newly formed from Italy's anti-Fascist parties, he headed a kind of "dual government" from a provisional seat at Bari. This new Italian government had the status of a "co-*belligeranza*" with the British and Americans.

On September 12, 1943, Mussolini was liberated by German paratroops. As Germany's "puppet," three days later he founded the Fascist Repubblica Sociale Italiana in SALÒ on Lake Garda, in the face of increasing activity in the Po Valley from a partisan movement supported by Yugoslavia. German troops occupied northern "remnant" Italy. They capitulated on April 28, 1945 (officially announced on May 2). On the same day, Mussolini was shot by Communist partisans. On June 18, 1946, Italy became a republic.

B.-J. W.

J

J, abbreviation for "Jew" (*Jude*) in the personal documents and passports of German citizens of Jewish extraction. The distinguishing letter was introduced in late 1938 after KRISTALLNACHT, on the particular recommendation of the Swiss police in charge of foreigners, who wanted to stem the dramatic rise in the tide of refugees fleeing Germany. Swiss border guards received the flat advisement: "Jews are to be turned back." This was because the authorities feared German sanctions, they were opposed to a "flood of foreigners," and, above all, they feared the potential expenses of sheltering and feeding the often penniless refugees. Thus, between 1939 and 1945 only some 28,500 Jews succeeded in escaping through Switzerland, most of whom could offer sufficient financial assurances, such as the persons rescued through the "V7" Operation.

Jablunka Pass, mountain pass on the Polish-Czech border; on August 26, 1939, a German-Slovak special commando group, which had not received word in time of a retraction of the attack command, proceeded over the pass against Poland. The attack through the Jablunka Pass was thus the first battle engagement of the POLISH CAMPAIGN, which actually began on September 1, 1939.

Jackson, Robert H(oughwout), b. Spring Creek, Pa., February 13, 1892; d. Washington, D.C., October 9, 1954, American jurist. Jackson began to practice law in 1913. In 1936 he became an assistant attorney general, in 1938 solicitor general, and in 1940 attorney general under President Franklin D. Roosevelt, who appointed him to the Supreme Court in 1941. Jackson served as chief United States prosecutor at the NUREMBERG TRIALS of the major war criminals in 1945–1946, about which he reported in his book *The Nuremberg Case* (1947).

Jadovno, National Socialist concentration camp in southern Croatia, built shortly after the capitulation of Yugoslavia (April 1941) and put under Croatian control. Some 2,000 Jews who had been interned there following the decreeing of Croatian racial laws perished in 1941 from mistreatment, shootings, and deprivation.

Jäger, Karl, b. Schaffhausen, September 20, 1888; d. June 22, 1959, SS-*Standartenführer*. A businessman, Jäger joined the NSDAP in 1923, and the SS in 1932. By 1935 his primary occupation was that of SS-*Sturmbannführer*, first in Ludwigsburg, then in Ravensburg. In 1938 he was transferred to the Münster SD (Security Service) office, whose leader he became in 1939. After brief service in the Netherlands, he became commander of Einsatzkommando 3 of Einsatzgruppe A at the beginning of the Russian Campaign. Later he was simultaneously commander of the Security Police and the SD for the general district of Lithuania in Kovno (Kowno). Under his command, extensive mass shootings of Jews took place in Lithuania (*see* FINAL SOLU-

Robert H. Jackson (left) with American brigadier general E. C. Betts in Nuremberg.

467

TION). Around the autumn of 1943, Jäger returned to Münster, but he was transferred shortly afterward as police president to Reichenberg (Sudetenland). After the war he worked as a farmhand until his arrest in April 1959, when proceedings were initiated against him for the shooting of Jews in Lithuania. He took his own life while imprisoned and awaiting trial.

A. St.

Jahn, Friedrich Ludwig, b. Lanz bei Ludwigslust, August 11, 1778; d. Freyburg an der Unstrut, October 15, 1852, German pedagogue and politician. Jahn acquired his nickname, "Turnvater [father of gymnastics] Jahn," by founding the German gymnastics movement as a means of making German youth physically fit to fight off Napoleon's foreign rule. In 1811 he founded the first athletic field, on Berlin's Hasenheide. Because of his support for a German national state Jahn was imprisoned from 1819 to 1825. The National Socialists made of him a precursor to Hitler and his unification efforts. Toward the end of the Second World War, a reserve grenadier division was named after Jahn in commemoration of his fight to arm the people. The ideologues of race also harked back to Jahn, who had warned against a "bastardization" of the German people; hence the propaganda motto "Jahngeist—Hitlergeist" ("The Jahn spirit is the Hitler spirit").

Jahnn, Hans Henny, b. Stellingen bei Hamburg, December 17, 1894; d. Hamburg, November 29, 1959, German writer and organ builder. As an ardent pacifist, Jahnn emigrated to Norway in 1915; after returning in 1920, he founded the pacifist community "Ugrino." In 1922 he restored the famous Arp-Schnitger organ in Hamburg. He received the Kleist Prize for his drama *Pastor Ephraim Magnus* in 1920. Jahnn's books were banned in 1933. He himself emigrated to Bornholm, Denmark. In 1950 Jahnn returned to Hamburg. His last years were characterized by his committed struggle against nuclear rearmament.

Jannings, Emil, b. Rorschach (Switzerland), July 23, 1884; d. Strobl am Wolfgangsee (Austria), January 2, 1950, German actor, director, and producer. Jannings's career began in the theater; he was one of the first German silent-movie stars. He had success in such character parts as Professor Rath in *Der blaue Engel (The Blue Angel;* 1930), and in depicting larger-than-life historical characters (Henry VIII and the emperor Nero). The extent to which the general

Emil Jannings as the village magistrate Adam in Heinrich von Kleist's play *Der zerbrochene Krug* (The Broken Jug).

provincialism of the arts in the Third Reich did not affect film was owing to such talented actors as Jannings, along with the cinema's importance as a medium for propaganda. Jannings's depiction of the village magistrate Adam in *Der zerbrochene Krug* (The Broken Jug; 1937) made film history. Although Jannings did not join the NSDAP, he cooperated willingly. He took on parts in propaganda films, and as Hitler's favorite actor, he personified "strong, masterful men" (*Herrenmenschen*) in such a convincing manner —as in *Ohm Krüger* (Uncle Krüger; 1941)— that the National Socialists named him State Actor (*Staatsschauspieler*) and Reich Senator for Culture (*Reichskultursenator*), and put him in charge of the Tobis Film Company. In 1945 Jannings was issued a work prohibition by the Allies.

Japan (officially, Nippon), constitutional empire in eastern Asia; area, 381,814 sq km (about 152,700 sq miles); population, about 64.4 million (1930). Japan's expansionism and nationalism were rooted, first, in its humiliations in the area of foreign policy after 1918: the denial of its claims to China and to equal political and military stature as a victor on the side of the Western powers in the First World War ("Japan's Versailles"). To this were added the social and demographic burdens of forced industrialization and modernization on a Western model and conflicts within the ruling classes. The response to these tensions was the development of a radical *völkisch*-racist sense of mission by the "people of the gods" as the leading eastern Asian power against the "white" colonialists.

With Germany and Italy, Japan shared a nationalistic revisionism and the elevated position of its army, which had been built up on the Prussian model and which served as a voice for déclassé rural and urban lower classes. The army's program proclaimed Japan's "national rebirth" both vis-à-vis the outside world ("living space" on the mainland for the excess population, with a clearly anti-Soviet impetus) and domestically (an authoritarian and anticapitalist course with fascist tendencies, and in 1936 an attempted putsch). The intent was mass mobilization and the solidification of national integration. These forces were opposed by a conservative oligarchy of big business, large landowners, court circles, party politicians, and naval leaders, who defended the domestic social and economic status quo and sought markets for raw materials and products through expansion to the south. Finally, the remote and divine emperor (from 1926, Hirohito) and an underdeveloped parliamentary democracy were unable to coordinate the divergent forces.

As in Germany, constant and severe domestic demographic, political-ideological, and socioeconomic pressures increasingly constrained the government's freedom of movement between the centers of power in Berlin, Moscow, and

On the American battleship *Missouri*, Japanese envoys sign Japan's surrender.

Washington. Under the dictate of the army, expansion on the mainland began in 1931 with the invasion of Manchuria, followed by withdrawal from the League of Nations in 1933 and war with China in 1937. Support was sought from the Berlin-Rome AXIS (the 1936 ANTI-COMINTERN PACT; the 1940 THREE-POWER AGREEMENT) as hostility toward the Soviet Union (in 1938–1939, border conflicts brought heavy losses) and the Western powers increased.

Japan thereby faced a dilemma in 1940–1941. It could yield to the economic sanctions of the United States, the protector of China and the Dutch East Indies, which entailed an embargo of oil, rubber, tin, rice, iron, and steel, as well as the blocking of Japanese funds in the United States. Japan would then have to evacuate its positions in China, French Indochina, and Manchuria. The alternative was to let its economy be "strangled" by diminishing reserves of oil and foodstuffs. Under Gen. Hideki Tojo, the Japanese cabinet chose a "forward escape" with the attack on PEARL HARBOR on December 7, 1941.

Protected by the nonaggression pact with Moscow of April 13, 1941 (the USSR entered the war against Japan only on August 8, 1945), Japan sought a military decision in the Pacific war (*see* SECOND WORLD WAR). After a phase of quick victories and great expansion, often with brutal occupation policies, a turning point came with the air and sea battle near the Midway Islands (June 4–7, 1942) and its heavy losses.

Japan. Victims of the Hiroshima atomic bomb.

The enormous territorial overstraining of Japan's limited resources, the heavy naval losses, bombing raids on Tokyo, shortages of raw materials and food, transport difficulties, and finally the atomic bombs dropped on Hiroshima (August 6, 1945) and Nagasaki (August 9) led to Japan's capitulation on September 2, 1945. The proclamation of a "Greater East Asian Co-Prosperity Sphere" under Japan's leadership, and the slogan "Asia for Asians," had begun the process of decolonization even during the war.

B.-J. W.

Jarres, Karl, b. Remscheid, September 21, 1874; d. Duisburg, October 20, 1951, German politician. Jarres studied law; in 1910 he became mayor of Remscheid, then from 1914 to 1923 and 1925 to 1933 he served as lord mayor of Duisburg. Jarres, who belonged to the right wing of the GERMAN PEOPLE'S PARTY, was sentenced to prison for insubordination in the RUHR CONFLICT. In November 1923 he became Reich interior minister, as well as vice-chancellor under Wilhelm MARX. In 1925 the right-wing parties nominated Jarres for election as Reich president. Although he won a plurality with 10.42 million votes (38 percent), he failed to achieve an absolute majority, and on the second ballot he resigned in favor of HINDENBURG. Jarres then devoted his great energies to municipal politics (including the incorporation of Hamborn). Removed by the National Socialists in 1933, he moved to industry (serving, for example, as chairman of the board of directors of the Klöckner Works). He contributed significantly to the reconstruction of German industry after 1945.

Jasenovac, National Socialist concentration camp in Croatia, established on October 1, 1941. It was intended primarily for Bosnian and Croatian Jews, of whom 20,000 were deported to Jasenovac. In 1942 further deportees came from Dalmatia, which until that time had been occupied by Italy. Most of the inmates survived for only a few months; others—including some 800 on July 15, 1943, alone—were deported to AUSCHWITZ. Only a few hundred lived to see liberation by Soviet troops and Yugoslav partisans on April 30, 1945. Just eight days earlier, 600 inmates had attempted an uprising, but only 80 managed to escape, and the rest were shot.

Jasper, Heinrich, b. Dingelbe (Braunschweig), August 21, 1875; d. Bergen-Belsen concentration camp, February 19, 1945, German politician and lawyer. From 1919 to 1921, 1922 to 1924, and 1927 to 1930, Jasper was the Social Democratic minister president of Braunschweig. After the elections of September 5, 1930, he had to yield to the National Socialist Dietrich KLAGGES, whose vengeance Jasper felt after the Seizure of Power for having actively opposed the NSDAP: he was taken into "protective custody," badly mistreated, released, and immediately arrested again. His path of pain and tribulation led through the concentration camps in Dachau and Oranienburg, until he was released in 1939. Jasper continued to refuse emigration on principle. After the assassination attempt of July 20, 1944, he was again arrested, and did not survive this imprisonment.

Jaspers, Karl, b. Oldenburg, February 23, 1883; d. Basel, February 26, 1969, German philosopher. After studies in medicine, Jaspers worked from 1909 to 1915 at the Psychiatric Clinic in Heidelberg. In 1916 he became professor of psychology, and in 1922 professor of philosophy at the university. Jaspers achieved a reputation both as a psychologist (*Allgemeine Psychopathologie* [General Psychopathology; 1913]) and as a philosopher of existentialism (*Die geistige Situation der Zeit* [The Spiritual Situation of the Age, translated as *Man in the Modern Age*; 1931]). His "rational" perspective on the world could not co-exist with National Socialism, whose proponents reproached him for incomprehension of the "vital-racial basis" of all worldviews and denounced his rejection of general rules of behavior as "the embodiment of helplessness."

Karl Jaspers.

Initially, Jaspers did not recognize the danger of National Socialism both to himself and to academic freedom; he called the Seizure of Power an "operetta," and Hitler's rule "a bad nightmare" (*ein schlechter Spuk*). In 1937, after passage of the CIVIL SERVICE LAW, he was forcibly retired because of his Jewish wife; publication sanctions followed in 1938, and a ban in 1943. Husband and wife were saved from the joint suicide for which they had prepared when United States troops reached Heidelberg on March 30, 1945, before their threatened deportation. In his book *Die Schuldfrage* (*The Question of German Guilt;* 1946), Jaspers opposed the thesis of a COLLECTIVE GUILT, but supported political responsibility. In 1948 he accepted an appointment in Basel.

Jazz, a type of music designated as "undesirable" by National Socialist music criticism and pedagogy. Because of the origins of jazz among Negroes in the American South, it was considered a product of "racially alien" elements. The New Orleans style of jazz was especially criticized; its hard articulation, free improvisations, and stimulating rhythms were irreconcilable with the notions of order of the NS state (*see* MUSIC).

R. H.

Jehovah's Witnesses (Ernste Bibelforscher; International Union of Earnest Bible Students), international faith community founded in 1870 by Charles Taze Russell (1852–1916) and led after 1916 by Joseph F. Rutherford (1869–1942). The Witnesses teach the immediately imminent second coming of Christ and, in strict interpretation of the Bible, reject any action contrary to the sense of biblical proclamation. Despite their usual self-designation after 1931 as "Jehovah's Witnesses," they remained generally known as "Earnest Bible Students." In the context of religious persecution (*see* SECTS, PERSECUTION OF) immediately after the Seizure of Power, they were unremittingly attacked by the National Socialists as "advance agents of world Bolshevism"; they were banned in mid-1933. The situation of the Witnesses was aggravated by their radical pacifism as well as by their rejection of the GERMAN GREETING and the OATH. Furthermore, each member was obligated to bear witness and thus to recruit publicly for the Witnesses, a practice that assured collisions with the Gestapo; the international organization was a particular thorn in the Gestapo's eye for repeatedly raising public protest against the persecution of German Witnesses. When the Congress of Jehovah's Witnesses, held in Lucerne from September 4 to 7, 1936, sent a telegram to "Herr Hitler" with a resolution to this effect, the time was at hand for the extermination blow by the government.

Following upon legislation (*see* MALICIOUS-GOSSIP LAW), 5,911 of the 6,034 (1933) German Witnesses were arrested, sentenced, and detained, after their prison term, in "post-custody" concentration camps. Over 2,000 of the unbending Witnesses did not survive the tortures. Their steadfastness and certain faith provoked mockery ("heavenly clowns"; "sheikhs of Jordan") and harsh mistreatment from their guards; yet paradoxically they also aroused admiration, including that of Himmler: on July 21, 1944 (!), he discussed in a letter to Ernst Kaltenbrunner the possibility of bringing in the peaceful, industrious, honest, antisemitic, and anti-Catholic Witnesses for the "pacification" of the Russian people in the areas under German control.

Jelusich, Mirko, b. Semil (Bohemia), December 12, 1886; d. Vienna, June 22, 1969, Austrian writer. Jelusich gained widespread popularity with his fictional treatments of historical figures (for example, *Cromwell;* 1933), especially in the period after the Anschluss, 1938 to 1945. Often at the expense of historical accuracy, he delineated "ideal Führer portraits" and glorified "heroic warrior types," as in *Hannibal* (1934) and *Der Traum vom Reich* (The Dream of Empire; 1941). In 1938 he directed Vienna's Burgtheater for a time.

Mirko Jelusich.

Jeschonnek, Hans, b. Hohensalza (Posen), April 9, 1899; d. Goldap (East Prussia), August 18, 1943, German colonel general (April 1, 1942). A pilot in the First World War, in the Reichswehr Jeschonnek was involved in the covert creation of an air force. In the spring of 1934, he became squadron leader of one of the Luftwaffe's first bomber squadrons. Promoted to chief of the Luftwaffe General Staff (February 1, 1939), he was significantly involved in all military planning. After the catastrophe at Stalingrad and the heavy bombing of German cities, especially Hamburg (in late July 1943), Jeschonnek took his own life in the East Prussian headquarters of the Luftwaffe, after his demand for a massive buildup of fighter defenses was denied.

Jesuits (Jesuiten; Society of Jesus, S.J.), Catholic religious community founded in 1534 by Ignatius of Loyola, characterized by military-like organization and led by a general elected for life. Heavily involved in the Counter-Reformation, from the beginning the Jesuits have been the object of both admiration and fear. Their departure from monastic clothing and from living in cloisters, together with their duty of absolute obedience to the pope and to their community superiors, made them an elusive group with a sworn purpose. Thus they were often suspected in unexplained situations or reverses as the wire-pullers behind the scenes, and as a result were forced into a scapegoat role. This suited them very well to National Socialist conspiracy theories, exacerbated by the "supranationality" of their organization.

In a secret "background report" by the Security Service (SD) "on the Jesuit Order," issued in August 1937, the Jesuits were termed, with an undertone of undisguised esteem, the "pope's storm troops" with no less a mandate than "to conquer the whole world." With their great mobility, their superior training as specialists in the most varied fields, and the excellent secular cover that was thus available, the Jesuits were the most effective "intelligence service of the Vatican." SD men were warned especially against the Jesuits' unscrupulous exploitation of their opponents' weaknesses (financial problems, women, and so on), and were told that for the "goal of [the Jesuits'] struggle" they were ready to sacrifice any legal or moral reservations. This evaluation and the irreconcilable ideological opposition led to harsh persecution measures in the Third Reich (including the PRIEST TRIALS, confiscation of religious communities' properties, and spying on pastoral activities). All Jesuits, numbering around 23,000 in the Third Reich in 1940, were discharged from the Wehrmacht by a Wehrmacht High Command decree dated May 31, 1941, because of their alleged corrupting influence on the troops; they were transferred to the home reserves (Landwehr II).

Jesus, founder of Christianity. Together with the Old Testament, the Jewish origins—at least on the maternal side—of the religion's founder created ideological difficulties for the National Socialists in their basic affirmation of "positive Christianity" (Point 24 of the Party Program). This led to more intensive attempts at an ARYANIZATION OF JESUS.

Jew-free (*judenfrei*), according to National Socialist terminology, cities or areas from which Jews had been evacuated or, in the course of the FINAL SOLUTION, "resettled" into extermination camps or killed on the spot. Some cities and areas were also identified as "Jew-free" if one or another camp still existed with "worker-Jews" (*Arbeitsjuden*).

Jewish Agency (after 1929, Jewish Agency for Palestine; after 1948, Jewish Agency for Israel), Zionist organization founded in 1922 in the British Mandate area of Palestine to represent the interests of the Jewish population. The Jewish Agency, which in 1929 also accepted non-Zionist "Friends of Rebuilding Palestine," promoted Jewish immigration and pleaded with the British—with little success—for the opening up of Palestine to persecuted German Jews. Through offices in London, New York, and elsewhere, during the war the Jewish Agency trans-

Hans Jeschonnek.

mitted news about the National Socialist FINAL SOLUTION and requests for intercession to Allied governments, but met with little response.

Jewish Councils (Judenräte), bodies established in German-occupied territories during the Second World War on the model of the REICH REPRESENTATION OF GERMAN JEWS. The German authorities demanded the establishment of such councils especially in the ghettos created in the east. Besides internal functions, the councils were responsible for carrying out German ordinances, could express the concerns of the Jewish population, supported the security forces, and also had to cooperate in the preparation and management of deportations. Council members usually were not themselves aware that their co-religionists were being rounded up for EXTERMINATION CAMPS: thus, for example, the Amsterdam council expressed its alarm on September 18, 1942, over one (*sic!*) death in AUSCHWITZ at a time when at least 10,000 of the 15,760 Dutch Jews already deported there had died in the gas chambers.

Jewish Houses (*Judenhäuser*), buildings owned by Jews, into which Jewish tenants could be forcibly moved. Following the restrictions on German Jews after KRISTALLNACHT, the Law on Tenancies for Jews was issued on April 30, 1939. It was intended to separate Jews from non-Jews and eliminated tenant protection for Jews as soon as the landlord could present to the Jewish community a certificate stating that the tenants to be evicted were to be placed somewhere else. The community then was to place the tenants who had been given notice with owners of Jewish Houses, "if necessary, by force." However, no ghetto was to be formed. In mid-1941 the law was applied in many German cities to Jewish property owners as well, and the Jewish population was further crowded together; in Hannover, for example, the Gestapo strictly controlled the 16 Jewish Houses. At the end of 1941 deportations began to move German Jews from the Jewish Houses into the eastern European ghettos and EXTERMINATION CAMPS.

H. O.

Jewish Star, six-pointed star or hexagram made from two equal, equilateral triangles placed one on top of the other; it was made of yellow fabric, with black borders and the inscription "Jew" (*Jude*). By an order of November 23, 1939, the Jewish Star was to be worn on the left side of the chest by all Jews in German-occupied Poland; by a police ordinance of September 2, 1941, it was

Jewish Star. National Socialist inflammatory pamphlet: "When you see this sign . . ."

also to be worn after September 19 by all Jews over the age of six within the German Reich. With this measure (*see* PERSECUTION OF JEWS), the National Socialists harked back to the medieval obligation of Jews to identify themselves. But in order to mock their victims they chose not the previously customary ring symbol or pointed Jewish hat, but rather the national and religious symbol of Judaism, the Star of David, which had also been the emblem of Zionism since 1897. It was distributed to those affected with the instruction to "treat it with care," and sew it on in the prescribed manner. By an order of the Reich Security Main Office (RSHA) of March 13, 1942, the Jewish Star symbol was also to be displayed on Jewish homeowners' and tenants' doors. The star was the last link in a chain of stigmatizations that began with the besmearing of Jewish businesses (*see* BOYCOTT AGAINST JEWS) and continued with the stamping of Jewish passports with a "J" and the compulsory imposition of the Jewish first names ISRAEL and SARA.

Jewization (*Verjudung*), antisemitic catchword. It appeared as early as the late 1870s, in the writings of Paul de LAGARDE, and was then taken up by the National Socialists (for example, in *Mein Kampf*). Jewization was depicted as a vision of cultural horror and a road to *völkisch* destruction.

Jewry. *See* Judaism.

Jews, persecution of. *See* Persecution of Jews.

"Jews Not Wanted!" (*Juden unerwünscht!*), National Socialist campaign slogan. Signs with this or a similar message were placed on the outskirts of Franconian towns and villages after the summer of 1934. The region was under the influence of Julius STREICHER, editor of *Der Stürmer.* After the spring of 1935 the signs also appeared in other places, notably in southern Bavaria. Occasionally the inscriptions were combined with antisemitic graphic illustrations. In places such as Rottach-Egern they were specifically directed against Jewish visitors to the spa. Many German restaurants and hotels also displayed the notice at their entrance. Because of the distasteful impression that the placards made on foreigners and other tourists, they were criticized from various sides, such as the Reich Economics Ministry in July 1934. They were ordered removed before the Olympic Games of 1936, but similar placards reappeared afterward.

Jodl, Alfred, b. Würzburg, May 10, 1890; d. Nuremberg, October 16, 1946 (executed), German colonel general (January 30, 1944). Jodl was an artillery officer in the First World War. He was inducted into the Reichswehr on October 1, 1919, and became head of Department L (home defense) in the Reich War Ministry (July 1, 1935). From March to October 1938 and after August 23, 1939, Jodl was chief of the Wehrmacht Command Office (Führungsamt), renamed the Wehrmacht Command Staff (Führungsstab) on August 8, 1940. He thereby became one of Hitler's closest military advisers, and was also responsible for the western theater of war.

Greifenberg sign: "Jews are not wanted here."

Alfred Jodl.

Jodl participated in all military planning, sometimes contradicting Hitler, but always for practical rather than moral or political reasons. According to his soldierly convictions, such concerns would not have been his business. As a consequence, Jodl had to sign the unconditional surrender in Reims on May 7, 1945, was arrested along with the Dönitz government on May 23, and was put on trial in Nuremberg, found guilty on all counts, and sentenced to death. A German appeals court rehabilitated Jodl posthumously on February 28, 1953, finding him not guilty of breaking international law, as accused, but excluding the disputed charge of CRIMES AGAINST PEACE.

Johst, Hanns, b. Seerhausen (Saxony), July 8, 1890; d. Ruhpolding, November 23, 1978, German writer. Johst was initially a medical student and nurse in Bethel. During the First World War he began writing poetry and plays, which in form and content were first influenced by EXPRESSIONISM. His play *Der junge Mensch. Ein ekstatisches Szenarium* (The Young Person: An Ecstatic Scenario; 1916), directed against bourgeois convention, rose to such outbursts as "It is frantic voluptuousness to be young and to be aware of the ecstasy of death." In his later works Johst accused both profit-oriented capitalist industrial society and proletarian "collectivism." In his essay collection *Wissen und Gewissen* (Knowledge and Conscience; 1924), he declared his faith in the "*völkisch* mission of poetry" and in the National Socialist worldview.

Johst's most famous play, *Schlageter* (1932), one of the most performed pieces in the Third

Hanns Johst.

Reich, depicts the fate of the "martyr" Albert SCHLAGETER, and is dedicated to "Adolf Hitler, with loving respect and unswerving faithfulness." In 1933 Hermann Göring named Johst top dramatic adviser and artistic director of the Berlin Theater. Johst's other titles included those of president of the Academy for German Literature, president of the REICH WRITING CHAMBER, Prussian privy councillor (*Staatsrat*), and SS-*Brigadeführer*. Among his many honors were the Grand Prize of the NSDAP for Art and the Goethe Medal. His writings supported National Socialism until the end of the war; an example was *Ruf des Reiches, Echo des Volkes!* (Call of the Wild, Echo of the *Volk*; 1940), which sang the praises of German farmers resettling "the newly won Eastern Territories." After the war Johst was first classified merely as a "fellow traveler" by a Munich appeals board in 1949; but a further proceeding classified him as a "major offender," sentenced him to a labor camp, and prohibited him from publishing for 10 years.

H. H.

Jokes. *See* Carpet biter; Underground humor.

Joos, Josef, b. Winzenheim, near Colmar (Alsace), November 13, 1878; d. Sankt Gallen (Switzerland), March 11, 1965, German politician and journalist. From 1903 to 1919 Joos was editor and manager of the *Westdeutsche Arbeiterzeitung* (West German Workers' News), the organ of the Catholic workers' organizations. From 1920 to 1933 he was a Reichstag deputy for the Center party, and in 1929 he became chairman of the Catholic Workers' International. Joos advocated international understanding, especially between France and Germany, which the National Socialists denigrated as "pacifist" activity "injurious to the *Volk*." He had to go into exile in 1933, but kept up contact with German Catholic lay groups. Arrested during an illegal visit to Cologne in 1940, he was imprisoned in the Dachau concentration camp from 1941 until 1945. After the war Joos was again active in Catholic men's organizations.

Jordan, Pascual, b. Hannover, October 18, 1902; d. Hamburg, July 31, 1980, German physicist. From 1929 to 1944 Jordan was a professor of physics in Rostock, and in 1944–1945, in Berlin. Together with Max Born and Werner HEISENBERG, he was one of the founders of the quantum theory. Jordan published numerous basic scientific works on theoretical physics, astrophysics, and biophysics. Although he gave adequate credit to the work of Jewish scientists in his most popular book, *Die Physik des 20. Jahrhunderts* (*Physics of the 20th Century*; 1936), he professed active allegiance to the National Socialist state and its leadership, and was therefore able to accept many awards. A professor in Hamburg after 1947, Jordan represented the Christian Democratic Union in the Bundestag from 1957 to 1961.

Jordan, Rudolf, b. Grosslüder bei Fulda, June 21, 1902, German politician and schoolteacher. Jordan joined the NSDAP in 1925; he founded the *völkisch* monthly *Notung*, and in 1929, the *Fuldaer Beobachter* (Fulda Observer). He was dismissed from his teaching post at the end of 1929

Pascual Jordan.

Rudolf Jordan.

William Joyce.

for National Socialist agitation. Appointed *Gauleiter* of Halle-Merseburg in 1931, he entered the Reichstag in 1933. In April 1937 he was appointed Reich governor of Braunschweig and Anhalt, and became an SA-*Obergruppenführer;* the following year, he was made *Gauleiter* of Magdeburg-Anhalt. At the end of the war Jordan was captured by the Soviets, who sentenced him to prison. He returned to Germany in 1955.

Journaille, word used by the National Socialists as a term of ridicule or abuse for journalists (and their products) of a leftist or republican orientation, who consequently opposed the National Socialist movement. The term is derived from the French *canaille* (riffraff, rabble) and was intended to elicit related associations; it was intensified through such prefixes as "stab-in-the-back *Journaille*" (*see* STAB-IN-THE-BACK LEGEND), "fulfillment *Journaille*" (*see* FULFILLMENT POLICY), and "Jewish *Journaille.*"

Joyce, William, b. New York City, April 24, 1906; d. London, January 3, 1946 (executed), Irish-German propagandist. The son of Irish immigrants, Joyce was a United States citizen by birth. In 1909 the family returned to Ireland. Joyce went to England without giving up his American citizenship. A gifted student, he joined the British fascists under Sir Oswald MOSLEY, whose propaganda chief he became. After the fiasco suffered by the fascists in the 1937 elections, Joyce parted from Mosley, obtained a British passport through a swindle, and traveled to Berlin on August 26, 1939. On September 18, he obtained a position at Radio

Germany broadcasting anti-British propaganda programs. He became a German citizen on September 26, 1940.

Joyce's programs were extraordinarily popular in England, where in 1940 up to 50 percent of listeners tuned him in. One of the reasons was his nasal, elitist Oxford intonation, which earned him the nickname "Lord Haw Haw." A fanatical antisemite and admirer of Hitler, Joyce was arrested by a British patrol on May 28, 1945. Taken to London on June 16, he was sentenced to death. The House of Lords rejected an appeal on December 18, 1945. The passport that Joyce had deviously obtained proved disastrous for him, for it made him subject to British jurisdiction.

Juchacz, Maria, b. Landsberg/Warthe, March 15, 1879; d. Düsseldorf, January 28, 1956, German politician, worker, and nurse. Juchacz joined the Social Democratic Party of Germany (SPD) in 1908. During the First World War, she was active in women's war relief. Elected to the Weimar National Assembly in 1919, she became the first woman speaker in a German parliament on February 19 of that year. On January 19, 1920, she founded the Workers' Welfare organization (Arbeiterwohlfahrt), which by 1930 had over 114,000 members. Juchacz also became a member of the new Reichstag. Many social institutions established during the Weimar Republic, such as homes for mothers or for the aged, were her work. Persecuted as a "Marxist," she had to leave Germany. By way of the Saarland and France, in 1945 she fled to the United States, where she organized food parcels for Europe.

On returning to Germany in 1949, Juchacz worked as honorary chairperson for Workers' Welfare.

"Judah, perish!" (*Juda, verrecke!*), NSDAP campaign slogan beginning in the 1920s, often closely connected with the other central party slogan, "Germany, awaken!" (*Deutschland erwache!*). Both slogans, the nationalist and the antisemitic, were meant to fulfill a significant integrative function in National Socialist Germany.

H. O.

Judaism (Jewry; Ger., *Judentum*), originally a Near Eastern people and religion; later, in the Diaspora, a living religious community spread to all parts of the earth with few or no remaining common ethnic characteristics. As the oldest monotheistic religion, the mother of Christianity and Islam, Judaism is characterized by the thesis of a people chosen by God, expressed in the covenant between the patriarch Abraham and Yahweh (God) on Mount Sinai, and in the transmission of the law tablets (Torah) to the people of the God of Israel. Their being the Chosen People was and is perceived by the Jews as a commission toward the entire world; it spurred them on to uncommon accomplishments, but it also led to constant conflicts with other peoples and finally to ANTISEMITISM. The high self-imposed standards and the indomitability of Judaism ultimately unleashed the dispersal of the Jews throughout the world after the Roman empire and the Islamic conquest had destroyed Judaism as an ethnic unity.

A common faith and shared ritual protected the small and scattered Jewish groups from loss of religious identity, but—also because of their defenselessness—brought new hostilities and, in particular, vocational limitations. Jews could participate freely above all in the area of finance, since Christians were forbidden to charge interest. Usurious misuses often produced dependencies that were sensed as threatening and were repeatedly resisted with acts of violence (*see* POGROM). In the Christian environment they could be religiously incited, since Jews could be blamed for the "deicide" of Christ's crucifixion. Judaism's hermetic practices also nourished suspicion of secret organizations and rumors of ritual murders or poisoned wells. Thus the Jews acquired the scapegoat role that jeopardized their existence.

In this situation, many Jews saw their sole salvation in further adaptation (assimilation) to the host peoples. This tendency received strong support during the Enlightenment, when dogmatic barriers were taken down on both sides. In Germany there was widespread emancipation of Jews; the Imperial Constitution of 1871 granted them civil equality. On the other hand, a modern variation of the old antisemitism based on religion and envy developed: racial hatred. After over a millennium of mutual intermixing, in the wake of, and with the irresponsible transfer of, the discoveries of biology, Jewry as a "race" was discovered, one that "from its roots was alien and rotten." Assimilation had no place in this worldview; yet for it to become effective a chain of events was necessary that was not foreseeable toward the end of the 19th century. Thus Theodor HERZL at first found little resonance within Jewry for his Zionist idea. It was the PERSECUTION OF JEWS under National Socialism, to which two-thirds of European Jewry fell victim, that destroyed any assimilationist hopes and that led to the reunion of Jews in their land of origin, Palestine.

Judas Jew (*Judas-Jude*), antisemitic epithet that on phonetic and historical bases was intended to connect the Jewish apostle Judas with the alleged character deficiencies of Jews. The term "Judas Jew," with its juxtaposition of meaning, was propagandistically especially useful for stirring up Christian groups through its appeal to the deicide motif in religious ANTISEMITISM.

Judenräte. *See* Jewish Councils.

Jud Süss (Jew Süss), German movie directed by Veit HARLAN (1940), with Ferdinand Marian, Heinrich GEORGE, Werner KRAUSS, and Kristina SÖDERBAUM. First shown on September 5, 1940, in Venice, it was rated "especially valuable politically and artistically—worthwhile for young people." The film project, which was intensively promoted by Propaganda Minister Joseph Goebbels (with a 2-million-RM budget), was intended as a historical aid in arguing for the antisemitic measures of the regime. The film illustrated the ruinous financial tricks of Joseph Süss-Oppenheimer (1698–1738), the Jewish adviser to Duke Karl Alexander of Württemberg. Süss-Oppenheimer's rapaciousness and moral depravity ("racial infamy") were denounced as "typically Jewish," so that the antisemitic emotions were presented as self-defense.

Because of the great performances of Marian in the title role and of Krauss (both of whom had been made to collaborate on the film under threats by Harlan), the film had a devastating

Ferdinand Marian (right) as Jud Süss, and Werner Krauss as Secretary Levy.

impact in an atmosphere of inflammatory anti-semitism. Attacks against Jews and Jewish establishments were often committed after showings of the film. After the war, Harlan had to defend himself before a law court. Although he personally was acquitted in both March 1949 and May 1950 ("I was only a tool," he testified), the film itself was categorized as "a crime against humanity."

July Agreement (*Juliabkommen*), agreement between Germany and Austria, made on July 11, 1936, but not announced publicly, that was officially termed a "Gentleman's Agreement." Worked out by Franz von PAPEN, the German ambassador in Vienna, and Austrian chancellor Kurt SCHUSCHNIGG, the accord was intended to relax the considerably strained relations between the two countries after the attempted National Socialist putsch on July 25, 1934. It also arose from Italy's desire to form closer ties with Germany following German assistance in the war with ABYSSINIA. The accord's 10 articles stipulated, among other points, mutual admission of printed matter, revitalization of cultural and especially economic relations, coordination of foreign policy, amnesty for the persecuted Austrian National Socialists, and the assumption of political responsibility by the "national opposition." This "nonintervention agreement" became Hitler's lever for massive intervention, since Schuschnigg treated the agreement in a dilatory manner and provoked German warnings. Thus the July Agreement did not fulfill Austria's hope to gain time, but led instead to the BERCHTESGADEN DIKTAT and the ANSCHLUSS.

July Assassination Attempt. *See* Twentieth of July.

July Rising (*Juli-Erhebung*), in National Socialist usage, the common glorified designation for the failed putsch against AUSTRIA's DOLLFUSS government on July 25, 1934.

June Declaration, four declarations issued by the Four Powers—Great Britain, France, the United States, and the USSR—on June 5, 1945, for the purpose of assuming supreme governing power in Germany: (1) the "Declaration in View of the Defeat of Germany," in consequence of which the victorious powers took over all governmental authority, including the Wehrmacht High Command (OKW) and all government offices; (2) establishment of a system of Four-Power control over all of Germany through the ALLIED CONTROL COUNCIL, as well as independent administration of individual OCCUPATION ZONES; (3) final demarcation of these zones; (4) a declaration stating readiness to discuss the German question with all United Nations member states.

Jung, Edgar, b. Ludwigshafen, March 6, 1894; d. Oranienburg, July 1, 1934, German journalist and politician. After studying law, Jung became a pilot in the First World War, and then a free corps member. From 1922 a lawyer in Zweibrücken, he committed himself passionately to fight the separatists in the Palatinate, who were supported by French occupation troops. After murdering separatist leader Franz Josef Heinz-Orbis on January 8, 1924, Jung fled to Munich,

Edgar Jung.

where in 1924 and 1925 he was active in Bavaria's state court and state supreme court. As a nationalist follower of the German People's Party, Jung wrote numerous articles advocating a Christian-conservative revolution to replace the "rule of the inferior"—the title of his 1927 book (*Die Herrschaft der Minderwertigen*). Despite his antidemocratic attitudes, Jung rejected National Socialist activism. His 1933 essay "Sinndeutung der deutschen Revolution" (Exegesis of the German Revolution) criticized racism and the mass character of National Socialism. Meanwhile, he had risen to become speechwriter for Franz von PAPEN, whom he had met in the HERRENKLUB (Gentlemen's Club). Jung wrote Papen's explosive Marburg speech of June 17, 1934, which attacked National Socialism from a conservative viewpoint. Its purpose, to prepare a nationalist-monarchist action against Hitler before Hindenburg's death, was not achieved. Instead, the appeal accelerated the RÖHM AFFAIR and led to Jung's arrest on June 25, 1934, and then his murder.

Jünger, Ernst, b. Heidelberg, March 29, 1895, German writer and essayist. With Gerhart HAUPTMANN and Gottfried BENN, Jünger was among the best-known authors able to remain active and publish in Germany between 1933 and 1945. The early works of this 1914 war volunteer are marked by the idea of "war as a spiritual experience"; his first novel, *Im Stahlgewittern* (*Storm of Steel*, 1920; 28 editions by 1984), was a diary-like, realistically told, unconditional affirmation of war, which describes battle as "a work of art, which gives men joy," and which idealizes valor in the face of the enemy and the "thirst for blood." Jünger was among the most important representatives of the "front generation," which juxtaposed its "heroic realism" to the pacifism of the Weimar Republic. The National Socialists valued him particularly because he saw "war not as an end, but as a prelude" and as the "meaningful force of *völkisch* life."

With his mythic glorification of the "front community," Jünger was among the intellectual precursors of National Socialism, though he himself did not see in it the hoped-for "proud elite." Temporarily espousing the National-Bolshevik ideas of the circle around Ernst NIEKISCH, Jünger refused a seat in the Reichstag in 1933 as well as membership in the Prussian Academy of Writers. His elitist, aristocratic thought brought him increasingly into opposition to the totalitarianism of the National Social-

Ernst Jünger.

ist mass movement, which he felt was "spiritually empty" and which he openly criticized in his *roman à clef, Auf den Marmorklippen* (*On the Marble Cliffs;* 1939). (Hitler appears in the book as head forester.) With his return to a conservative, esoteric position, Jünger remained a productive author even after 1945 and received numerous literary and political honors, including the Federal Republic of Germany's Distinguished Service Cross. To some degree this gave rise to controversy, as when the city of Frankfurt conferred the Goethe Prize on him in 1982, since Jünger did soften some formulations in his early works when they were reissued, but in the end did not distance himself from them. Shortly before his 90th birthday, Jünger described his role as author as that of a "general of the spirit" (*Feldherr des Geistes*).

H. H.

Jünger, Friedrich Georg, b. Hannover, September 1, 1898; d. Überlingen, July 20, 1977, German writer, brother of Ernst Jünger, whose nationalist attitude he shared well into the 1920s. From 1928 to 1935 Jünger maintained contacts with the "national-revolutionary" circle around Ernst NIEKISCH. Because of antifascist poetry such as the elegy "Der Mohn" (The Poppy; 1934), he was arrested for a time and was prohibited from publishing. Jünger's basically esoteric work is influenced by a "feeling for antique life and its forms." His critique of civilization, *Über die Perfektion der Technik* (*The Failure of Technology: Perfection without Purpose;* 1944), after 1945 was overlaid with a magical relationship with nature.

Jungmannen (young men), a striking term, borrowed from German heroic sagas, for the pupils of the NATIONAL-POLITICAL EDUCATIONAL INSTITUTES.

Jungvolk (Young *Volk;* Deutsches Jungvolk), division of the HITLER YOUTH for boys 10 to 14 years old. It was subdivided into the following units: Jungbann (Young Detachment; six Stämme), Stamm (Cadre; four Fähnlein), Fähnlein ("Little Flag"; three Jungzüge), Jungzug (Young Platoon; three Jungenschaften), and Jungenschaft (Boys' Group; 15 boys). The term "Jungvolk" was consciously chosen in keeping with the National Socialist VOLK COMMUNITY, which was meant to overcome age as well as class boundaries.

Junker Schools (*Junkerschulen*), term introduced in 1937 for the SS Leadership Schools established in Bad Tölz and Braunschweig in 1934–1935. (In the ORDER FORTRESSES [*Ordensburgen*], apprentice leaders [*Führeranwärter*] were already called *Ordensjunker.*) About 15,000 participants went through 10 months of training, which was reduced to 4 months during the war; training also took place in Klagenfurt and Prague in 1943–1944. Although comparable to the Wehrmacht "war schools" (*Kriegsschulen*), the Junker Schools did not presuppose a secondary school diploma. Their military training served as a basis for subsequent employment with the police, Security Service (SD), and the like, as well as for the STANDBY TROOPS of the SS (the later Waffen-SS). The model of a trained and intelligent shock-troop leader (*see* Felix STEINER) was only partially valid for the Junker Schools. No great weight was attached to their four hours per week of "ideological education"; the SS, itself organized as an "order," wanted all its members to identify with it. The younger generation that had gone through the Junker Schools rose to higher positions only in small numbers, because the SS in general tried to attract suitable personnel through awarding high ranks. Himmler's plan for a multifaceted seven-year training could not be realized.

H. S.

Junkers, Hugo, b. Rheydt, February 3, 1859; d. Gauting, near Munich, February 3, 1935, German airplane designer and civil engineer (inventor of the gas water heater for bathrooms). From 1897 to 1912 Junkers was a professor in Aachen. In the experimental institute for internal-combustion engines that he founded in Dessau in 1889, he developed the first all-metal airplanes, including the J 1. In 1919, in Dessau, he founded the Junkers Airplane Works, Inc. (Junkers-Flugzeugwerke AG; in 1924 the Junkers Engine Factory, Ltd. [Junkers-Motorenbau GmbH]). This plant produced such planes as the F 13 airliner and the giant G 38 airplane; it also developed the Ju 52 ("Aunt Ju"), which after 1931 long remained the best-known and most widely used passenger and transport plane in the world. After the Seizure of Power, Junkers was forced to transfer the majority of shares in his enterprise to the Reich and to give up the management of factories important to rearmament. After the death of its founder, the Junkers factory produced many military planes, the most famous of which was no doubt the Ju 87 "Stuka" (*Sturzkampfbomber*, dive-bomber).

Jurists' Trial (*Juristen-Prozess*), proceedings by the Third United States Military Court in Nuremberg against (1) Josef Altstötter and 15 other defendants who had been prominent officials of the Reich Justice Ministry; (2) members of the VOLK COURT and of the SPECIAL COURTS; and (3) prominent public prosecutors. They were accused of crimes against peace and humanity, war crimes, and membership in criminal organizations (Case 3). The main indictment was for "judicial murder and other atrocities, which they [had] committed by destroying law and justice in Germany; they [had] then used the empty shells of legal forms to persecute, enslave, and annihilate people on a gigantic scale" (opening speech of the prosecution). In the verdict of December 4, 1947, four of the accused were sentenced to life imprisonment, six

Hugo Junkers.

were sentenced to 5 to 10 years' imprisonment, and four were acquitted. Two of the sentenced served their time; one was released early because of illness. In six cases John J. McCloy, the United States high commissioner, reduced the sentence by a pardon on January 31, 1951.

A. St.

Just, Günther, b. Cottbus, January 3, 1892; d. Heidelberg, August 30, 1950, German anthropologist. A professor in Greifswald from 1928, Just was nominated in 1937 to head the Research Institute for the Science of Heredity (Erbwissenschaftliches Forschungsinstitut) of the Reich Health Office. As one of the most productive researchers on race and heredity in the Third Reich, he contributed to the groundwork of National Socialist racial policies through his numerous experiments and publications, notably as an editor of the *Handbuch der Erbbiologie des Menschen* (Handbook of Human Hereditary Biology, 5 vols., 1939–1940) and as editor of the *Schriften zur Erblehre und Rassenhygiene* (Publications on Genetics and Racial Hygiene).

Justice

Like all state institutions, the German system of justice was so transformed after 1933 that it became a conforming element of the National Socialist (NS) system of authority.

Personnel policy was an effective means of integrating the judicial system into the NS government apparatus. Immediately after January 30, 1933, judges unpopular with the National Socialists (primarily Social Democrats and Jews) were dismissed; many of them were later murdered. A Reichstag decree of April 26, 1942 (*Reich Law Gazette* [*Reichsgesetzblatt;* RGBl] I, p. 247), confirmed the right of political authorities "to impose appropriate punishment" upon any unreliable judge, and in particular to remove him from office. This practice had a restraining effect on those judges who remained in office, since they could expect dismissal if they manifested a critical attitude toward National Socialism, even though the conditions for removal from office had not been clearly defined.

As early as 1933 judges who were not loyal to the regime were deprived of their previous sphere of activity by a change in the distribution of legal functions. After all courts had been subordinated to the Reich Justice Ministry in 1935, their administrative autonomy was abolished in 1937: the ministry now not only named judges, but also assigned their jurisdictions. After 1935 the approval of the relevant *Gau* leadership was required for appointments and promotions.

As of 1935 the Reich Justice Ministry systematically evaluated legal decisions on the basis of reports by presidents of the state supreme courts (Oberlandesgerichte). The results became the basis for a gradually increasing control of justice. In circulars, conferences, individual conversations, and targeted press publications, the ministry's ideas on important matters were conveyed to judges. After 1942 the Reich Justice Ministry sent so-called Judges' Letters (*Richterbriefe*) to all judges through official channels. They contained detailed explanations regarding the interpretation of individual points of law, the measure of punishment for specific crimes, and other judicial issues. These ministerial determinations were binding in practice if not formally. Moreover, after 1942 the politically most important trials were debated, and ultimately binding directives on the continuation of cases were issued in so-called pretrial and posttrial discussions (*Vor- und Nachschaubesprechungen*) chaired by presidents of the respective state courts or state supreme courts.

Through a multitude of changes National Socialism interfered in judicial and legal procedure. For sentencing in political crimes, an order of March 21, 1933 (RGBl I, p. 136), created a Special Court (Sondergericht) in each state supreme court district. It was responsible for offenses against the REICHSTAG FIRE DECREE of February 28, 1933 (RGBl I, p. 83), and the MALICIOUS-GOSSIP LAW of March 21, 1933 (RGBl I, p. 135). The jurisdiction of special courts over political crimes was later broadened considerably. In 1934 the VOLK COURT (Volksgerichtshof) was established. It largely assumed the duties of the Reich Supreme Court (Reichsgericht) in political matters after the REICHSTAG FIRE TRIAL had ended unsatisfactorily from the NS perspective. The Special Courts

Ceremony in the Berlin Criminal Court on October 1, 1936: beginning on this day the National Socialist emblem had to be worn on judges' robes.

and the *Volk* Court were filled with judges of especial political reliability. The accused had no legal recourse against their verdicts.

In matters of administrative and labor law, the legal path to the courts was restricted. For the citizen the legal process was shortened (especially in administrative cases), whereas it was sometimes lengthened for representatives of the "public" interest. In criminal cases two new legal measures were instituted against hitherto valid verdicts that only the chief public prosecutor (*Oberreichsanwalt*) could introduce: an extraordinary objection (*ausserordentlicher Einspruch*) and a nullification complaint (*Nichtigkeitsbeschwerde*). These created additional means for reviewing unwelcome sentences. To allow more effective control over sentences imposed by lower courts, the higher court was permitted to increase the severity of a punishment (*reformatio in peius;* law of June 28, 1935; RGBl I, p. 844). Moreover, numerous changes were made in trial procedures, especially during the war. They were intended to simplify and

expedite proceedings, but at the same time they took away prior protections from those affected.

The practical significance of the judicial system under National Socialism was strongly restricted by the fact that the courts' monopoly over legal decisions had been abolished. Especially in order to secure the sovereign rights of the regime, other institutions were allowed to compete actively in an area of responsibility formerly under exclusive control of the courts. Government authorities and party offices, especially the Gestapo and SS, could obstruct the using of prescribed judicial procedures; they could interfere in pending cases, or could take autonomous measures that disregarded the outcome of a legally valid proceeding. A judicial verdict was often reversed, as when the Gestapo arrested an accused person who had just been acquitted but had not yet left the courtroom, and then dispatched him or her to a concentration camp. To avoid a subsequent reversal by the authorities, courts often used official expectations as the criteria for their decisions.

Prominent National Socialists, especially Hitler, unilaterally ordered punishments, often enough the DEATH PENALTY. National Socialists could transgress laws without prosecution either *de facto* or (because of frequent instances of AMNESTY) *de jure*. Civil law disputes were withdrawn from the courts whenever the immediate interests of the regime were affected. For example, the Reich Interior Ministry could itself decide on civil damage suits raised in connection with the Seizure of Power (law of December 13, 1934; RGBl I, p. 1235). The withdrawal of the courts' monopoly on judicial decisions was sanctioned by legal regulations. Paragraph 7 of the Prussian Law on the Gestapo of February 10, 1936 (1936 Statute Book, pp. 21 and [correction] 28), read as follows: "Orders in matters concerning the Secret State Police are not subject to review by the administrative courts."

As the persecution of Jews intensified, the judicial system directly promoted an important political goal of National Socialism. The laws issued to enforce the regime's antisemitic notions were only partly couched in the precise traditional legal terms that would convey concrete instructions to the judge. On its own, the judicial system manifested considerable initiative and imagination in order to translate the anti-Jewish legislation into reality. Thus administrative and civil courts participated actively in depriving Jews of their rights, and in driving them from economic and social life as a prelude to their later expulsion and murder.

From the outset the criminal justice system cooperated in the suppression of enemies of National Socialism. Sometimes old penal laws were exploited, and other times new crimes were invented, as with the Malicious-Gossip Law or the decree against VOLK VERMIN of September 5, 1939 (RGBl I, p. 1679). The National Socialists found the traditional model of penal law no longer adequate as an instrument of coercion because of its demonstrated biases. Thus they introduced the general clause and the analogy into criminal law. This opened the door to the free construction of criminal acts according to political expediency. The criteria for punishment were in part extended considerably. A regulation of May 5, 1944 (RGBl I, p. 115), allowed military courts to impose any type of punishment for any act, "whenever the regular legal framework provides insufficient expiation [*Sühne*] as judged by the healthy instinct of the *Volk* [*Volksempfinden*]." Thus the criminal facts in the case took on the character of "enabling norms" (*Ermächtigungsnormen*).

Judges in the Special Courts and the *Volk* Court, in particular, allowed themselves to be harnessed to the terrorist system of National Socialism through use of the general clause and analogies, as the regime wished. No exact studies have been made, but estimates are that between 1933 and 1945, regular courts, Special Courts, and the *Volk* Court imposed some 16,000 death sentences, approximately 15,000 of them between 1941 and 1945. More than two-thirds of these sentences were carried out. Moreover, the military justice system imposed some 16,000 death sentences, of which two-thirds again were carried out.

In many areas, primarily in civil, economic, commercial, and tax law, and to an extent even in criminal law, the courts at first continued their earlier practices after 1933, so that the influence of National Socialism was not immediately discernible. The application of previously existing standards was especially necessary in the various legal areas that concerned the economy. The economic system, which in principle continued to be privately organized, depended on the signing of contracts and a legal framework established by the state for traditional safeguards.

Here too, however, the courts had to consider the interests of the community as defined by NS political institutions. The use by the judiciary of traditional legal standards ended where the political interests of National Socialism were affected. As soon as the issue was one of combating the enemies of National Socialism or carrying out its specific goals in such areas as racial policies or rearmament, the possibilities of a legal decision in the previously existing sense were at an end. The judicial system had thus undergone a change of function. It was no longer a guarantor of economic, political, and personal freedom, but only an institution for regulating those conflicts that the regime had left to it.

In isolated cases, judges took part in the opposition activities of other groups. But there were no active opposition groups within the judiciary. Time and again, individual judges helped victims of the system as much as they could. Although the personal courage and moral commitment of these judges was impressive, they could hardly achieve any lasting results because of the Gestapo's practice of "correcting" verdicts.

The party press and prominent representatives of the regime often sharply attacked the judicial system. All in all, however, it fulfilled its tasks in the expected manner. Those judges who were active National Socialists clearly realized the political function of the judicial system. Thus Curt ROTHENBERGER, a longtime president of the Hamburg Supreme Court and later state secretary in the Reich Justice Ministry, wrote: "The law is the Führer's order. The judge who has to apply this law is bound not only to the law, but also to the unified, consistent worldview of the Führer. Thus the judge of the liberal epoch, who was neutral, nonpolitical, and distanced from the state, has evolved into the profoundly political-minded National Socialist, firmly bound to the worldview of the legislator and cooperating in its realization." According to Rothenberger, the judge was "one of the most noble executors of the Führer's will" ("The Position of the Judge in the Führer-State," *Deutsches Recht* [German Law], 1939, p. 831).

To be sure, many judges did not subscribe to such a directly political role for the judicial system. They tried to salvage as much as possible of the traditional concept of justice by confining themselves to a narrow interpretation of the law, and by avoiding any greater inclusion of NS ideals into their verdicts than was absolutely essential. But even with such a position these judges could not extricate themselves from the role set forth for them. For they could apply their norms only insofar as the National Socialists considered them expedient for carrying out their own political goals. No other judicial activity was either legal or in fact possible.

Alexander von Brünneck

K

Kaas, Ludwig, b. Trier, May 23, 1881; d. Rome, April 15, 1952, German Catholic theologian. Kaas studied in Trier and at the Collegium Germanicum in Rome. Ordained a priest in 1906, from 1918 to 1924 he was a professor of canon law in Trier. In 1919 he became Center party deputy in the National Assembly; from 1920 to 1933 he was a Reichstag deputy (party delegation chairman from December 28, 1920, and party chairman after 1929). Kaas, like Konrad ADENAUER, at first favored separatism for the Rhineland; he reluctantly supported Gustav STRESEMANN'S policy of reconciliation with France. For years he was the conservative representative of his party's "Roman" wing as adviser to the papal nuncio, Eugenio Pacelli (*see* PIUS XII). With this background, Kaas was not strongly supportive of the Weimar Republic.

After the fall, in late May 1932, of Chancellor Heinrich Brüning, whose policies he had sup-ported, Kaas recommended the formation of a government of "national concentration" that included the National Socialists. He thought this offered the best chance for achieving one of his main political goals: a CONCORDAT between the Reich and Rome along the lines of the LATERAN TREATIES, which he had favorably evaluated in his tract "Der Konkordatstyp des faschistischen Italien" (The Concordat Model of Fascist Italy) in late 1932. After the Seizure of Power, Kaas opposed Brüning and pushed through his party's assent to the ENABLING LAW, although Hitler had made only vague oral promises. The extent to which a commitment to the Concordat was involved remains debatable. The fact is that it was hastened through at amazing speed, owing to Kaas's decisive participation in Rome. For the sake of the Concordat, he unhesitatingly sacrificed the Center party (dissolved on May 6, 1933, with Brüning as chairman). Kaas remained in exile in Rome. Around 1939–1940, he established loose contacts with the opposition in Germany, yet in general he hewed to the pope's cautious attitude toward National Socialist Germany.

Kaganovich, Lazar, b. Kabany, near Kiev, November 22, 1893; d. after 1957, Soviet politician. A Bolshevik from 1911, Kaganovich was a Central Committee member from 1924 to 1957, a Politburo member from 1930 to 1957, and a minister for several terms. A confidant of Stalin, he was instrumental in forging the latter's personal dictatorship through the bloody "purges." For the National Socialists, Kaganovich's origins proved their thesis that BOLSHEVISM was only a tool of WORLD JEWRY (as outlined in the work by Rudolf Kommoss, *Juden hinter Stalin* [Jews behind Stalin]; 1938). Brought down in the power struggle after Stalin's death, Kaganovich was relieved of all his offices on June 19, 1957, and expelled from the party in 1961.

Ludwig Kaas.

Kahr, Gustav Ritter von, b. Weissenburg (Bavaria), November 29, 1862; d. Dachau, June 30, 1934, German politician and jurist. In 1917 Kahr became chief administrator (*Regierungspräsident*) for Upper Bavaria; after the KAPP PUTSCH in 1920, he became minister president of a middle-class right-wing government in Bavaria. Conservative, nationalist, and monarchist in his attitudes, Kahr wanted to make Bavaria over into a "cell of order" (*Ordnungszelle*) in contrast with Berlin. Toward this end he relied upon the home guard forces (Orgesch) built up by himself and the forestry official Georg Escherich, and sought alliances with all right-wing groups opposed to the Weimar Republic. At first unsuccessful, Kahr resigned on September 11, 1921, but was brought back as general state commissioner on September 26, 1923, as signs appeared of the incipient dissolution of all state order. He bound by oath Gen. Otto von Lossow, recently cashiered by the Reich Defense Ministry, and along with him the Bavarian section of the national armed forces. Kahr was planning to establish a right-wing dictatorship in Germany, starting with Bavaria. These intentions, however, were thwarted by Hitler, who was not content with the role of "drummer" that Kahr had in mind for him. Taken captive at the HITLER PUTSCH on November 8, 1923, and forced to cooperate, on the very next day Kahr disavowed the undertaking and quashed the uprising with Reich soldiers and police. Subsequently, he was president of the Bavarian administrative law courts, from 1924 to 1930.

Gustav Ritter von Kahr.

Hitler's vengeance caught up with Kahr in 1934: he was seized and killed during the murder operation of the RÖHM AFFAIR.

Ba.

Kaiser, Hermann, b. Remscheid, May 31, 1885; d. Berlin-Plötzensee, January 23, 1945 (executed), German opposition fighter. Kaiser had a career as a teacher and reserve officer. He condemned National Socialism's brutalization of political life from the outset, as well as the abuse of soldierly and Prussian virtues. After the outbreak of war in 1939, Kaiser, a captain in the Wehrmacht, came into repeated conflict over his refusal to give the GERMAN GREETING, and over his criticism of the regime in general. At the request of opposition figures in the circle around Ludwig BECK and Carl GOERDELER, he accepted the post of war log officer for Col. Gen. Friedrich FROMM, because it allowed him to work effectively on preparing the reserve army for the overthrow of Hitler. When the attempt of July 20, 1944, miscarried, Kaiser was arrested and then condemned to death on January 17, 1945.

Kaiser, Jakob, b. Hammelburg (Lower Franconia), February 8, 1888; d. Berlin, May 7, 1961, German politician. Kaiser was a bookbinder by training; he joined the Christian trade unions in 1912 and served as their chairman in western Germany from 1918 to 1933; he was a Reichstag deputy (Center party) in 1932–1933. Kaiser protested in vain in May 1933 against the breakup of TRADE UNIONS by the National Socialists. He then maintained contact with Wilhelm LEUSCHNER as a representative of the free (Social Democratic) trade unions and with other figures of the labor movement. He was significantly involved in the sociopolitical program of the OPPOSITION, and was slated to become deputy chairman of a "German Trade Union" free of denominational and ideological ties after July 20, 1944. In 1945 he helped found the East German Christian Democratic Union (CDU), but fell out with the Soviet occupation authorities. In West Germany he was a member of the Parliamentary Council (1948–1949), a deputy in the Bundestag (1949–1961), and minister for all-German affairs (1949–1957). Kaiser resisted the Western orientation of CDU chairman Konrad ADENAUER as jeopardizing German reunification.

Kaiserwald, National Socialist concentration and forced-labor camp near Riga (Latvia), where in 1941–1942, 10,000 Jews, both Latvians and others deported from the Reich, were murdered in gas vans. Forced laborers were made to eliminate traces of the massacre in 1944 as the Red Army approached (*see* EXHUMATION OPERATION). The surviving prisoners were evacuated on September 25, 1944, and transferred to the STUTTHOF camp.

Kaiser Wilhelm Society for the Advancement of the Sciences (Kaiser-Wilhelm-Gesellschaft zur Förderung der Wissenschaften e.V.), association founded in 1911 under the patronage of Kaiser Wilhelm II, at the urging of the German church historian and cultural politician Adolf von Harnack (1851–1931). Its purpose was to establish and administer institutes, especially in the natural sciences, that were dedicated exclusively to research rather than teaching. Apart from contributions by industry, the society was increasingly funded by state money; it promoted both basic research and specific industrial applications, which after 1933 became increasingly military in nature. In 1937, some 38 institutes belonged to the society, including two in legal studies and two in liberal arts. After 1945, Max PLANCK and Otto HAHN attempted to restructure the society. However, the American military government ordered that the name be changed. Thus, in 1948 a successor organization, the Max Planck Society for the Advancement of the Sciences, was founded.

Kalavryta, Greek village in the mountains of the northern Peloponnese; its population was about 1,400 in 1940. The inaccessible area around Kalavryta was an operations base for Greek partisans during the Second World War. In mid-October 1943 they captured a German reconnaissance company (78 troops) and held them in Kalavryta, in order to exchange them for their own people. The German military authorities made a show of negotiations and meanwhile organized a rescue action. As the relief units of the 117th Rifle Division approached, the captives in the mountain were shot. In retaliation, German troops burned the village down on December 13, 1943, herded the women and children together into the school, and shot the men above the age of 13 at the edge of the village. Only 13 escaped the mass shooting, which claimed 511 victims. The fire, along with the ensuing cold and hunger, resulted in the loss of more human life, as did the consequent German "expiation measures" against surrounding villages and cloisters.

According to German accounts a total of 696 civilians died in "Engagement Kalavryta"; the Greek estimate was over 1,200. Material restitution has been meager. Prosecution of the perpetrators bogged down because most of them were later killed in action, but also because inquests were closed, as in a 1974 case held by the state prosecutor's office in Bochum, which classified the actions in Kalavryta as appropriate and necessary according to criteria for reprisals in international law (File 33 Js55/72).

Kalinin, Mikhail, b. Verkhniaia Troitsa (now in Kalinin Oblast [district]), November 19, 1875; d. Moscow, June 3, 1946, Soviet politician. Kalinin was a Bolshevik from 1903; he was editor of *Pravda.* A close associate of Lenin and Stalin, he joined the Communist party's Central Committee in 1919, and the Politburo in 1926. From 1919 to 1946, he was nominal chief of state of the USSR.

Kaltenbrunner, Ernst, b. Ried (Innkreis, Austria), October 4, 1903; d. Nuremberg, October 16, 1946 (executed), SS-*Obergruppenführer* (January 30, 1943). Kaltenbrunner studied law, and practiced in Linz after 1929; he joined the NSDAP and SS in 1932, and was jailed for high treason in 1934–1935. After 1935 he headed the entire Austrian SS. At Göring's direction Kaltenbrunner was brought into the SEYSS-INQUART cabinet as state secretary for public security on March 11, 1938. In the ensuing days he played a decisive part in organizing police activities for the Austrian ANSCHLUSS. Kaltenbrunner built up the Gestapo in what was now called the OSTMARK, inspected the new concentration camp at MAUTHAUSEN, and by the beginning of the war was the Higher SS and Police Leader in the Danube region.

The 6'-6"-tall Kaltenbrunner attracted Himmler's attention with his successes in gathering intelligence; Himmler chose him to be Reinhard Heydrich's successor as director of the Reich Security Main Office and chief of the Security Police and SD, effective January 30, 1943. Kaltenbrunner thus became the superior of Adolf EICHMANN, whom he had known since their school days in Linz. He also became prime mover of the FINAL SOLUTION of the "Jewish question" in the last two years of the war. Kaltenbrunner was responsible for numerous other violations of international law, such as the BULLET DECREE.

With Adm. Wilhelm CANARIS's fall from power in February 1944, Kaltenbrunner forged an intelligence monopoly, through SD absorption of the ABWEHR, that he put to use especially in persecuting the resistance fighters of July 20, 1944 (*see* TWENTIETH OF JULY). The so-called

Ernst Kaltenbrunner.

Kaltenbrunner Reports on these matters showed him to be particularly unscrupulous and malicious. He failed in his attempts in late 1944 to establish contacts with the western Allies, with the aim of establishing a separate cease-fire. In May 1945 Kaltenbrunner, who had transferred his headquarters to Altaussee in Styria near the war's end, was arrested by an American patrol. As one of the major war criminals arraigned before the Nuremberg tribunals, he was judged guilty of crimes against humanity and war crimes, and was sentenced to death by hanging on October 1, 1946.

Kampf (often translated as "struggle"), a central concept of National Socialist ideology. The National Socialists saw as the basic condition of human life the "altercation among opposing powers and forces for dominance or destruction." They appealed on this point to the authority of Heraclitus ("Struggle is the father and master of all things"), Darwin ("struggle for existence"), and Nietzsche (struggle as the manifestation of the "will to power"). In the Social Darwinist sense, struggle was explained as the agent of political and racial selection. Drawing on the traditions of German antiquity and the Middle Ages, ideologists stylized the struggling man as "the Nordic-Germanic ideal of man and his conduct of life" (*Meyers Lexikon*, 1939). [*Kampf* can also be translated as "combat" or "fight"; the word has an aggressive connotation not necessarily present in "struggle."] (*See* MEIN KAMPF.)

Kampfball (also *Raufball*, or battle ball), a team sport whose aim is to move a medicine ball through the opposing goal by any means possible (throwing, rolling, pushing, or carrying). Similarly, any defense is allowed, such as holding or knocking down. *Kampfball* was one of the most popular sports in the Third Reich, especially in the SA and Hitler Youth, since it promoted "decisiveness and a courageous go-ahead style."

Kampfring Deutscher Glaube, name of the GERMAN FAITH MOVEMENT after 1938.

Kampfzeit. *See* Time of Struggle.

Kanzelparagraph. *See* Pulpit Paragraph.

Kapler, Hermann, b. Oels (Silesia), December 2, 1867; d. Berlin, May 2, 1941, German Evangelical Church politician. Kapler studied law and political science; he became a councillor on the High Consistory (1904), and lay vice president of the Evangelical High Church Council (1919). In 1925 Kapler accepted the presidency of the German Evangelical Church Committee, a kind of "government" for the alliance of Germany's 28 Evangelical regional churches (*Landeskirchen*). When in 1933 the negotiations on a concordat with the Catholic church became known, Kapler approached Reich president Paul von Hindenburg, an Evangelical, and requested parallel contractual arrangements for his church. He formed a "three-man committee" with the Lutheran bishop from Hannover, August MARAHRENS, and the Reformed pastor from Elberfeld, Hermann A. Hesse, to conduct negotiations with the Reich government, which for the first time pressed for the establishment of a unified GERMAN EVANGELICAL CHURCH. Conflicts quickly arose over the election of a REICH BISHOP, and during them Kapler's term in office expired. His departure on June 23, 1933, provided the occasion for the appointment of a government church commissioner, and for the hastening of National Socialist efforts toward the SYNCHRONIZATION of the Evangelical Church (*see* CHURCH STRUGGLE).

Kapo (from Ital. *capo*, head), in the National Socialist CONCENTRATION CAMPS, SS and prisoner jargon for an inmate chosen by the SS as a functionary for particular jobs or labor squads. In Germany, the term was used by Italian road crews working in Bavaria in the 1930s. It was first used in the Dachau camp, and later officially adopted for all concentration camps. In large work squads with several Kapos, a head Kapo was occasionally employed.

W. D.

Kappler, Herbert (SS-*Obersturmbannführer*). *See* Ardeatine Caves.

Kapp Putsch, a radical right-wing attempt to overthrow the Weimar Republic in March 1920. It was named for its instigator, the East Prussian general regional director Wolfgang Kapp (1858–1922). The putsch was a response to the reduction of the Reichswehr in compliance with the VERSAILLES TREATY and the consequent decision on March 11, 1920, by Reich armed forces minister Gustav NOSKE to disband the free corps "brigades" headed by Philipp Löwenfeld and Hermann EHRHARDT. Kapp and the head of Reichswehr Group Command I in Berlin, Gen. Walther von Lüttwitz, then had Berlin occupied by the Ehrhardt Brigade, on March 13. The Reich government fled to Dresden and Stuttgart, and, supported by trade unions, the SPD (Social Democratic Party), and the DDP (German Democratic Party), called a general strike. The provisional government formed by self-appointed Reich chancellor Kapp (with Lüttwitz as armed forces minister) had to surrender under this pressure on March 17, since the Reichswehr did not go along with Kapp, and the civil service refused to cooperate. At that point, the right-wing parties and industry also distanced themselves, and Kapp fled to Sweden on March 18. He later appeared before the Reich Supreme Court and died in jail while under investigation. The Kapp Putsch demonstrated the unbroken strength of the political Right and the key role of the Reichswehr in the survival of the Republic.

Wolfgang Kapp.

Kapp Putsch. Members of the Ehrhardt Brigade in Berlin (1920).

Karajan, Herbert von, b. Salzburg, April 5, 1908; d. Anif, July 16, 1989, Austrian conductor. From 1927 to 1934 von Karajan was at the Municipal Theater in Ulm, and from 1935 to 1941, at Aachen; at the age of 27 he was the youngest general music director in Germany. With an eye to his musical work and career, von Karajan adapted himself to the political circumstances of the Third Reich: on May 1, 1933, he became a member of the NSDAP in Austria. After Austria's move into the German Reich, he rapidly secured important positions: as conductor of the Berlin State Opera in 1938, and as State Conductor (*Staatskapellmeister*) on April 20, 1939, the beginning of his rivalry with Wilhelm FURTWÄNGLER. Karajan allowed himself to be put to use for National Socialist cultural propaganda, notably as representative of Germany's official musical culture at many performances abroad.

Karajan's later explanations regarding his motives and his alleged withdrawal from the party in 1942 met with widespread skepticism. During the denazification proceedings, he gained an acquittal at the end of 1945. Soon thereafter he gave his first performance with the Vienna Philharmonic, on January 12, 1946. In 1949 he became director of Vienna's Society of the Friends of Music. After Furtwängler's death in 1954, von Karajan became conductor (for life) of the Berlin Philharmonic, and in 1956 he took over as director of the Vienna State Opera. Much sought after for festival performances, he took part in innumerable concert tours and recordings.

R. H.

Karinhall, Hermann Göring's estate, named after his first wife. It was situated in the Schorfheide, northeast of Berlin, in the Uckermark. In 1934 Göring, as Prussian minister president, acquired a former imperial hunting lodge in the Prussian state forest on the Wackersee. With the help of architects from the construction office of his Interior Ministry, he had it rebuilt according to his own highly detailed plans into a kind of old German manor, where he received state guests, staged hunts, and fulfilled his pronounced need for ostentation. The main building of Karinhall was dominated by an entrance hall 50 m (164 feet) long, which served as a picture gallery; during the war it accommodated the loot (*see* ART PLUNDER) that Göring brought back from occupied countries. For his first wife he had a mausoleum constructed by the entrance; her corpse was transported from Sweden and placed in its vault on April 19, 1934, with Hitler attending. Even the celebration after his wedding to Emmy Sonnemann took place in Karinhall. In January 1945 Göring had the furnishings from Karinhall transported piece by piece to Berchtesgaden for storage. In April of that year the buildings were destroyed on Göring's order by Wehrmacht engineers as the Red Army approached.

Karlsbad Program, list of demands made by the SUDETEN GERMAN PARTY, instigated by Hitler, and presented to the Prague government on April 24, 1938; the first high point of the SUDETEN CRISIS.

Karlshorst, eastern district in Berlin where the Red Army established its headquarters in 1945. In the former school for German army engineers in Karlshorst, Field Marshal Gen. Wilhelm Keitel, Adm. of the Fleet Hans Georg von Friedeburg, and Colonel General Stumpff signed terms for the UNCONDITIONAL SURRENDER of the German armed forces shortly before midnight on May 8, 1945, repeating a ceremony held on May 7 at the Anglo-American headquarters in Reims.

Kästner, Erich, b. Dresden, February 23, 1899; d. Munich, July 29, 1974, German writer. After working as a journalist, Kästner became popular in the 1920s as a poet of political satire, attacking petit-bourgeois fashions and morals, fascism, and militarism in his volumes of poetry ("Do you know the land, where the cannons bloom?"), although with less of a bite than Kurt TUCHOLSKY or Walter MEHRING. With his novels for young people, such as *Emil und die Detektive* (*Emil and the Detectives;* 1928), and his melancholy, moralistic society prose, Kästner was one of the most successful left-liberal authors of the Weimar Republic. In 1933 he was forbidden to publish, and his books were burned. Soon, however, he was able to continue writing, and he penned entertaining nonpolitical novels. With special permission from the Propaganda Ministry, he even wrote the screenplay for the motion picture MÜNCHHAUSEN (1942), produced by Ufa-Jubiläum. Shortly thereafter, he was completely prohibited from writing. After the war, Kästner resumed his prewar success as satirist,

Karinhall. View of the so-called Great or German Hall.

Surrender at Karlshorst. From the left: Generals Stumpff and Keitel, Admiral Friedeburg.

Erich Kästner.

cabaret writer, and juvenile book author. An active pacifist, he took part in campaigns against rearmament. His commitment to moralism is reflected most clearly in *Die Konferenz der Tiere* (*The Animals' Conference;* 1949), a peaceable utopia for children written under the continuing impression of the war.

H. H.

Katyn, village and forest 20 km (12.4 miles) west of Smolensk, in the USSR. In the spring of 1943, German soldiers discovered near Katyn mass graves that, according to German radio reports of April 13, 1943, contained the corpses of Polish officers. A commission established by the Reich government and made up of physicians from Switzerland and occupied countries identified 2,730 out of 4,363 exhumed corpses as Polish officers who were captured by the Soviets during the POLISH CAMPAIGN in 1939 and confined in the Kozelsk camp. Autopsies determined that the Poles had been killed by shots in the napes of their necks prior to the German invasion of Russia, and therefore that they had been killed by the Soviets. When the Polish government-in-exile in London, having tried in vain to learn the whereabouts of 10,000 Polish officers in the Soviet Union, concurred in this opinion, Stalin took the opportunity to break relations with the exiled civilian politicians. The western Allies upheld the claim that the Germans were guilty of the Katyn massacre, out of concern for the wartime coalition with the Soviets. This standpoint was not supported during the Nuremberg Trials in 1946, resulting in the dismissal of Katyn as a count for prosecution, as

Katyn. Mass grave of Polish officers.

demanded by the USSR. In 1952, investigations under American chief prosecutor Robert H. JACKSON confirmed Soviet responsibility for this war crime.

[In April 1990, the Soviet Union officially and publicly acknowledged responsibility for the Katyn massacre.]

Kauen (Pol., Kowno; now Kaunas [Lithuania]), National Socialist concentration camp established on September 15, 1943, in the Jewish ghetto area in the district of Vilijampole. Kauen was filled with several thousand former ghetto inhabitants (men, women, and children), who were put to work in the environs of the city cutting peat and laboring on an airfield and in a cement and lime factory. The SS guards included many ethnic Germans from Hungary, as well as Lithuanian SS members. The housing and provisions were poor.

On October 26, 1943, out of a shipment of 3,500 prisoners being sent to Estonia for labor, those unable to work were sorted out and transported to the camps at Auschwitz and Lublin-Maidanek. On March 27, 1944, Kauen was thoroughly searched; some 1,000 children and 300 elderly persons unable to work were segregated and sent to the extermination camps. A day later, more children and old people were discovered (about 60) and then shot in Fort IX, near the city ("Operation Elderly and Children"). On July 12 of that year, Kauen was evacuated as Soviet troops advanced; the approximately 8,000 prisoners were brought to other concentration camps, with many dying on the way. After the evacuation the area was searched, hiding places and bunkers were blasted, and the camp was burned to the ground. Some 2,000 prisoners still hiding in the camp lost their lives.

W. D.

Kaufmann, Karl, b. Krefeld, October 10, 1900; d. Hamburg, December 4, 1969, German politician. Kaufmann was a free corps volunteer after the First World War. He helped found the NSDAP in the Ruhr area, and was *Gauleiter* for Rhineland-North after 1924. Kaufmann belonged to the avidly anticapitalist STRASSER wing of the party. For that reason, Ruhr industrialist Emil KIRDORF sought his removal as *Gau* leader by Hitler. Kaufmann's replacement was more favorably disposed toward business interests, and Kaufmann was moved to the Hamburg *Gau*, where he remained from 1929 to 1945. In 1933 he also became Reich governor (*Reichsstaathalter*) for Hamburg. In 1942 he was made an SS-*Obergruppenführer* and Reich Commissioner for Overseas Navigation.

Even opponents of the regime regarded Kaufmann as "a relatively decent [*anständig*] person" (a statement made by a Jewish physician). Nonetheless, in 1933–1934 he had a key role in the "defeat of Marxism" in Hamburg, by means of bloody and terroristic arrests and imprisonments unleashed particularly against former Communists and Social Democrats (such as Fritz SOLNITZ). In May 1945, however, Kaufmann refused the order to defend Hamburg, and handed the city over to the British without a struggle. After the war he was repeatedly arrested and accused, each time being released after a short while on grounds of ill health. A denazification proceeding ended in January 1951 with the judgment "lesser offender."

Kaunas. *See* Kauen.

Käutner, Helmut, b. Düusseldorf, March 25, 1908; d. Castellina, Italy, April 20, 1980, German actor, director, and author. After work in theater and cabaret, Käutner in 1939 became a director and screenwriter of ambitious entertainment films, melancholy love stories, and comedies. They earned him recognition both with the German public and abroad, yet some were classified by the Propaganda Ministry as "decadent"; his first film, *Kitty und die Weltkonferenz* (Kitty and the World Conference), was forbidden. With the outlining of official ideology and the retreat into a sphere of private, generally human problems, Käutner's films became some of the most significant examples of "internal emigration" in this medium. The last two films he made during the Third Reich could be shown only after the war: *Grosse Freiheit Nr. 7* (Great Freedom No. 7; 1944, with Hans ALBERS) and *Unter den Brücken* (Under the Bridges; 1945). Their intimacy seemed appropriate for diversion from the miseries of war, but they lacked the requisite "combative stance," and

Karl Kaufmann.

Helmut Käutner.

were thus criticized for "glorification of private life." After 1945 Käutner gained the appreciation of film critics through works that brought the "feelings of living in the immediate postwar period to the screen." Success with the public, however, came his way only in the 1950s, through such unpretentious entertainments as *Der Hauptmann von Köpenick* (The Captain of Köpenick; 1956).

KdF, acronym of the GERMAN LABOR FRONT agency Kraft durch Freude (STRENGTH THROUGH JOY); less frequently, of Kanzlei des Führers (Chancellery of the Führer).

KdF-Wagen, official name for VOLKSWAGEN.

Kehr, Josef, b. Langenau (Upper Silesia), October 17, 1904, SS-*Oberscharführer* (February 1942). A cabinetmaker by trade, Kehr joined both the NSDAP and SS in 1932. After training as a medical orderly he became a guard in the Buchenwald and Dachau concentration camps. In October 1941 he was transferred to Auschwitz, where he served in the infirmary. There he selected prisoners, at times by himself, for killing either by gassing or by phenol injections. Captured by the Americans in 1945, as a Waffen-SS member Kehr received only a standard three-year sentence in a work camp. It was not until September 1960 that he was arrested pending investigation. At the Frankfurt Auschwitz Trial (*see* AUSCHWITZ TRIAL), he was sentenced to life imprisonment on August 20, 1965. The court established that he had committed 475 murders and was an accomplice to murder in at least 2,730 cases.

Keitel, Wilhelm, b. Helmscherode (Harz), September 22, 1882; d. Nuremberg, October 16, 1946 (executed), German field marshal general (July 19, 1940). Keitel entered the army in 1901. An artillery and General Staff officer in the First World War, he was taken into the Reichswehr in 1919. Keitel's theretofore linear career path took a fateful upward turn on October 1, 1935, when he was named head of the Wehrmacht office in the Armed Forces Ministry. After the FRITSCH CRISIS, this office provided the framework for forming the Wehrmacht High Command (OKW); Keitel, as its head, entered Hitler's inner circle.

Promoted to the rank of colonel general on November 10, 1938, Keitel took part in all military planning, yet because he lacked command authority, he could exert only limited influence over operations. His mainly ministerial functions entangled him in National Socialist

Wilhelm Keitel.

(NS) war crimes through his signature on commands contrary to international law, such as the COMMISSAR ORDER, BULLET DECREE, and "NIGHT AND FOG" DECREE. Despite isolated military criticisms of Hitler's decisions, he submitted completely to the latter's "genius," coining the expression "the greatest commander in chief of all time." This earned him the mocking name of "Lakaitel" (from *Lakai*, "lackey") among fellow officers.

As the visible link between the political leadership and the Wehrmacht, which he drew into NS power politics, Keitel accepted the French capitulation at Compiègne on June 22, 1940, as the greatest military triumph. He also signed the UNCONDITIONAL SURRENDER at Karlshorst on May 8, 1945, thereby declaring the bankruptcy of NS imperialism. The Allies arrested him on May 13, 1945. Brought before the tribunal in Nuremberg, he was found guilty on all counts and condemned to death by hanging. His request to be shot as a soldier was turned down.

Kellogg-Briand Pact, an agreement developed from the draft of a Franco-American nonaggression pact, named after United States secretary of state Frank B. Kellogg and French foreign minister Aristide Briand. The pact was signed on August 27, 1928, by 15 countries (including Germany); by 1939 it had been ratified by 63 states (including the Soviet Union). It foresaw the international outlawing of war as "an instrument of national policy" (Article 1) and the resolution of conflicts between states only "by peaceful means" (Article 2). Its lack of enforcement provisions in the event of its violation, its

Last page of the Kellogg-Briand Pact.

reservations for self-defense, and its insufficient coordination with the sanctions mechanisms of the League of Nations Charter (Article 16) rendered the pact politically ineffective. Within international law, it had a controversial influence on the jurisdiction of the NUREMBERG TRIALS. Its material content was integrated into the Charter of the UNITED NATIONS.

B.-J. V.

Kelsen, Hans, b. Prague, October 11, 1881; d. Berkeley, California, April 19, 1973, Austrian jurist. From 1919 to 1930, Kelsen was professor of constitutional law and philosophy of law in Vienna (part of the "Vienna School"). He collaborated on the Austrian federal constitution (1920) and was a professor in Cologne (1930–1933), in Geneva (1933–1940), and also in Prague (1936–1938). Persecuted as a Jew, Kelsen left Germany in 1933 and eventually came to the United States in 1940, obtaining American citizenship in 1945. His *Reine Rechtslehre* (Pure Theory of Law; 1934), which called for the establishment of norms independent of sociological and political conditions, was attacked by the National Socialists as "a typical expression of a destructive Jewish mind" and "ruinous to the community."

Kemna, early National Socialist concentration camp, established in June 1933 in a vacant factory in the village of Kemna (Wuppertal-Barmen) and put under the authority of the administrative president in Düsseldorf. The guard at Kemna consisted of 20 SA men, who were paid as auxiliary police. The camp was occupied by 218 political prisoners (under protective custody), mostly Communists and trade union activists. Living and sanitary conditions in the camp were poor, given the unsuitability of the building. The inmates were brutally mistreated by their SA guards and subjected to general harassment. On January 19, 1934, Kemna was shut down and the prisoners brought to the EMSLAND CAMPS.

W. D.

Kempner, Robert M. W., b. Freiburg im Breisgau, October 17, 1899, German jurist. From 1928 to 1933 Kempner was a lecturer at the Berlin College for Politics and legal adviser to the Prussian Interior Ministry. He fought against Hitler and the NSDAP from the outset, yet his efforts to prosecute them on a charge of conspiracy for high treason proved unsuccessful. After being detained by the Gestapo in 1933, Kempner emigrated through Italy and France to the United States. There he became a government attorney and in 1945 was assigned to the staff of the American chief prosecutor, Robert H. JACKSON, at the NUREMBERG TRIALS. In 1951 he gained admission as a lawyer to the state court (Landgericht) in Frankfurt. In many published works he examined the Third Reich and National Socialist abuses of power, among them *Eichmann und Komplizen* (Eichmann and Accomplices; 1961) and *Das Dritte Reich im Kreuzverhör* (The Third Reich under Cross-examination; 1969).

Keppler, Wilhelm, b. Heidelberg, December 14, 1882; d. Friedrichshafen, June 13, 1960; German politician. An engineer and chemical manufacturer, Keppler joined the NSDAP in 1927, and was appointed the party's economics

Robert Kempner.

Wilhelm Keppler.

adviser by Hitler in December 1931. To strengthen party ties with business and industry, he founded the so-called KEPPLER CIRCLE. In July 1933 Keppler was made commissioner for economic issues (*Kommissar für Wirtschaftsfragen*) in the Reich Chancellery, in charge of all party organizations involved with economic policy. After 1934 he was occupied with the problem of securing and utilizing raw materials (*see* RAW-MATERIALS ECONOMY). An SS member from 1935, Keppler founded the HIMMLER FRIENDS' CIRCLE, which supplied the SS with substantial funds from the private sector. Regarded as weak and slow, Keppler found his functions supplanted in 1936 by the FOUR-YEAR PLAN, and he himself was given the empty title "general expert on German raw and industrial materials." In 1938 he served briefly as Reich commissioner for Austria, and then, until 1945, as state secretary for special duties in the Foreign Ministry. A Nuremberg tribunal sentenced him to 10 years' imprisonment on April 14, 1949; however, he was released on February 1, 1951.

Keppler Circle (Keppler-Kreis), committee of advisers formed in 1932, on Hitler's recommendation, by the chemical manufacturer Wilhelm KEPPLER; it consisted of leading figures in the economy. Their first meeting, attended by Hitler, was held in Berlin on June 20, 1932. The 12 or so members were mainly bankers (such as Hjalmar SCHACHT and Kurt von SCHRÖDER), major industrialists (as Rosberg and Albert VÖGLER), and merchants (such as Helferrich). The circle was officially established to provide eco-

nomic advice to the NSDAP, yet Hitler used it from the beginning to build support among high-level business leaders for his takeover of power. The group's political activities led to a useful alliance between Hitler and Franz von PAPEN at a meeting on January 4, 1933, in the Cologne residence of the banker von Schröder. There the last obstacles to a SEIZURE OF POWER by Hitler were removed. Two years later, the HIMMLER FRIENDS' CIRCLE developed out of Keppler's group.

R. S.

Kerr, Alfred (originally, Kempner), b. Breslau, December 25, 1867; d. Hamburg, October 12, 1948, German writer and critic. From his student days, Kerr worked as a freelance author and theater and literature critic, publishing regularly in the most important German newspapers and magazines. With ambition, aggressiveness, flamboyant phrasing, and self-assuredly subjective opinions, he became one of the most influential and feared critics, a "pope of literature" for the Weimar Republic. Kerr came out against socialist authors such as Bertolt BRECHT, yet he also determinedly combated *völkisch*-nationalistic literature and drama. Until 1933, he pleaded for the unity of the Left against National Socialism through his "Tagesglossen" (Daily Comments) on Radio Berlin. As a Jew and "prime example of a destructive theater critic," he was persecuted by the National Socialists, and his books were burned for their "perversion of language." Forced into exile, after 1935 he worked in London for numerous emigrant periodicals. The years of penurious exile were movingly described by his daughter Judith in her book for young people, *When Hitler Stole Pink Rabbit* (1972).

Kerrl, Hanns, b. Fallersleben, December 11, 1887; d. Paris, December 15, 1941, German politician and judicial official. Kerrl joined the NSDAP in 1923; from 1928 to 1933 he was a deputy in the Prussian legislature, and its president in 1932. Although the WEIMAR COALITION lost its majority in Prussia in April 1932, Kerrl could not form a government either, and therefore he incited Reich Chancellor Franz von PAPEN to engineer the PRUSSIAN COUP against the SPD (Social Democratic Party of Germany) minority government. After the Seizure of Power, Kerrl took over the Prussian Justice Ministry (April 21, 1933, to June 17, 1934), and then became Reich Minister without Portfolio.

On July 16, 1935, Kerrl became Reich Minis-

Hanns Kerrl.

Albert Kesselring.

ter for Church Affairs. Responsible for all religious communities, he considered his principal assignment to be the unification of the Evangelical regional churches into a GERMAN EVANGELICAL CHURCH and the overcoming of resistance within the CONFESSING CHURCH. The Reich Church Committee, of which he was a member, ceased to function on February 12, 1937. Other administrative measures also came to nothing, with the result that Kerrl lost influence with Hitler. Paradoxically, his attempts to "synchronize" the Evangelical Church brought him into some conflict with Martin Bormann and Himmler, who wanted the total elimination of the church and mistrusted any Christian influence. After Kerrl's death no successor was named.

Kesselring, Albert, b. Marktsteft (Lower Franconia), November 30, 1885; d. Bad Nauheim, July 16, 1960, German field marshal general. Kesselring entered the army in 1904 and was an artillery and General Staff officer in the First World War; he was taken into the Reichswehr in 1919. He formally resigned his commission in the fall of 1933, in order to enter the undercover Luftwaffe administration as a "commodore." With the transition to an overt airpower buildup, he became Luftwaffe chief of staff on June 5, 1936. On October 1, 1938, Kesselring took command of Air Fleet 1, and in this capacity participated in the Polish Campaign. In the western and eastern campaigns he commanded Air Fleet 2.

In December 1941, Kesselring became Supreme Commander for the South, with the difficult task of cooperating with the Italian Su-

preme Command and with the self-willed Erwin ROMMEL in Africa. After Italy withdrew from the war (September 1943), Kesselring assumed control in the Mediterranean (November 21, 1943) as Supreme Commander for the Southwest. On March 11, 1945, he became Supreme Commander for the West.

Kesselring was imprisoned by the Americans on May 15, 1945. A British military court sentenced him to death on May 6, 1947; charges included complicity in the ARDEATINE CAVES massacre. However, he was soon pardoned, and in July 1952 was released from the prison at Werl. His rationale for rebuffing opposition attempts to recruit him is expressed in the title of his memoirs: *Soldat bis zum letzten Tag* (A Soldier to the Last Day, 1953; translated as *A Soldier's Record*, 1970).

Kessler, Harry Count, b. Paris, May 23, 1868; d. Lyons, December 4, 1937, German writer and politician. From 1895 to 1900 Kessler was co-editor of the journal *Pan;* until 1906 he was a museum head in Weimar. He founded the Cranach Press in 1913. In 1914 Kessler wrote, with Hugo von Hofmannsthal, the libretto to Richard Strauss's *Josephslegende* (Legend of Joseph). He was ambassador to Poland from 1918 to 1921, president of the German Peace Society, and a member of the German Democratic Party. He emigrated to France in 1933, and lived for a time on Majorca.

Keudell, Walter von, b. Castellamare, near Naples (Italy), July 17, 1884; d. 1973, German politician and jurist. German-nationalist in ideology, Keudell was a district president (*Landrat*) in Königsberg (1916 to 1920), and supervisor of the Oder River dikes (1918 to 1923). In 1924 he entered the Reichstag for the German National People's Party (DNVP). He was Reich interior minister in 1927 and 1928. Keudell left the DNVP in 1929, and for a time belonged to the Countrypeople's Party (*see* COUNTRYFOLK MOVEMENT) and the CHRISTIAN-SOCIAL PEOPLE'S SERVICE. In 1933 he joined the NSDAP. Keudell had a solid reputation as a forestry expert, and served as forester general and state secretary (1933–1937). After the war he was chairman of various refugee organizations.

Keyserling, Hermann Count, b. Könno (Livonia), July 20, 1880; d. Innsbruck, April 26, 1946, German philosopher and natural scientist. Keyserling took a critical view of rationalism and sought "a new synthesis of mind and soul." Although he judged ethnicity and race to be cultural values and compared Jewish character to the "ethos of an intestinal parasite" (in his book *Wiedergeburt* [Rebirth]; 1927), he was at odds with National Socialist criticism, since he accorded mind "preeminence over the powers of blood" and did not distance himself from Jewish colleagues. After 1933, the "School of Wisdom" he founded in Darmstadt was forced to close, and his opportunities for work and publication were restricted.

Kiep, Otto Karl, b. Saltcoats (Scotland), July 7, 1886; d. Berlin-Plötzensee, August 26, 1944 (executed), German diplomat. Kiep served as embassy counsellor in Washington in 1928; in

Harry Count Kessler.

Otto Karl Kiep.

1930 he was consul general in New York. At his own request, he withdrew from active service in 1933 because of the "complete change of political direction." At the outbreak of the war, he allowed himself to be pressed into service in the Wehrmacht High Command, in whose Foreign Division he made contacts with the opposition circle in the ABWEHR. He became a victim of the same informant as Elisabeth von THADDEN, when the Gestapo arrested him for critical statements on the war situation. The result was his death sentence on July 1, 1944.

Killinger, Manfred von, b. Gut Lindigt bei Nossen (Saxony), July 14, 1886; d. Bucharest (Romania), September 3, 1944, German politician. A naval lieutenant captain at the end of the First World War, Killinger fought with the EHRHARDT free corps in Upper Silesia, then was involved in the murder plot against Matthias ERZBERGER. He joined the NSDAP in 1927, and in 1932 became an SA inspector and a Reichstag deputy. On May 6, 1933, he became minister president of Saxony. He entered the diplomatic service in 1935 and was consul general in San Francisco from June 1937 to January 1939. After a post in the Foreign Ministry, Killinger became ambassador to Germany's Romanian ally. He took his life as the Red Army fought its way into Bucharest. Killinger wrote books on the FREE CORPS and the SA, notably *Das waren Kerle* (Those Were Good Fellows; 1937).

Kindermann, Heinz, b. Vienna, October 8, 1894; d. there, October 7, 1985, Austrian literary and theater scholar. Kindermann was a professor in Danzig (1927) and Munster (1936).

He was among the advocates, prized by the National Socialists, of "constructive literary research based on the *Volk*." His works, such as *Dichtung und Volkheit* (Poetry and Ethnicity; 1937), were among the fundamental scholarly studies on literature of the Third Reich. Kindermann made it his particular concern to publish nationalistic poetry by Germans abroad: *Rufe über Grenzen* (Calls over the Borders; 1938) was judged to be the "principal work among the collections of ethnic German poetry" (Langenbucher). Kindermann collected German poems from the "former Poland" in his *Du stehst in grosser Schar* (You Stand with a Great Host; 1939), in which the reader was supposed to "recognize the countenance of the ethnic Germans, who, resolute unto death, endured the bitterest fate for their Germanness, for whose liberation our soldiers streamed forth, for whose salvation many . . . sacrificed their lives." A professor in Vienna from 1953, Kindermann gained international esteem as a historian of the theater, was named to numerous state committees and academies, and received various Austrian awards.

Kirchenkampf. *See* Church Struggle.

Kirchner, Johanna, b. Frankfurt am Main, April 24, 1889; d. Berlin-Plötzensee, June 9, 1944 (executed), German opposition fighter. A Social Democrat, after 1933 Kirchner involved herself with the families of political prisoners, helped endangered people to escape, and finally fled herself in 1934. Through the Saarland she went to France, where she worked in emigré circles, notably with Spanish Civil War volunteers. When the European war broke out she was detained, and after the French surrender the Vichy government handed her over to the German police. The *Volk* Court initially sentenced her to 10 years in prison in May 1943, but when a higher authority ordered a new trial, she was sentenced to death on April 20, 1944.

Kirdorf, Emil, b. Mettmann, April 8, 1847; d. Mülheim/Ruhr, July 13, 1938, German industrialist. Kirdorf apprenticed in his family's textile mill. In 1873 he was co-founder and commercial director of the Gelsenkirchener Bergwerks-AG (Gelsenkirchen Mines, Inc.; GBAG). As general director (after 1892), Kirdorf built the GBAG into one of Germany's largest producers of coal, coke, iron, and steel. Moreover, he created in 1893 the Rhineland-Westphalia Coal Syndicate. In 1926 he helped found the Vereinigte Stahlwerke AG (United Steelworks, Inc.), the largest

Emil Kirdorf.

German steel concern. Since Kirdorf was a professed adversary of the workers' movement and of the Weimar Republic, the National Socialist movement attracted him strongly even in the early phase. After a private meeting with Hitler in 1927, Kirdorf joined the NSDAP and became active as an intermediary with major industry. (He withdrew between 1928 and 1934 to protest the party's socialist Strasser wing.) Kirdorf's highly regarded position in Ruhr industry enabled him to secure Hitler's acceptability in those circles and thus strengthen Hitler's political backing.

R. S.

Kitsch (from Eng. "sketch"), commercial or pseudo-art, characterized by imitation, inappropriate idyllic scenes, superficial sentimental appeal, and "accumulation of effects" (Walther Killy); it is found both in literature and in plastic, graphic, and performing arts, as an adornment for commercial items.

Before and during the First World War, all forms of commercial art reflected an exaggerated patriotism. With the end of the war patriotic kitsch declined in significance, but survived in the form of falsely sentimental, emotional representations of war in literature and in the visual arts. It was not until the "National Awakening" in early 1933 that a sudden boom occurred in political kitsch. Through mass-produced articles with nationalistic and National Socialist symbols, industry sought to express its good conduct with respect to the new rulers. At the same time, it wanted to publicize its nationalist views and

Kitsch. "Adolf the Blacksmith," post-card reproduction from 1933.

advertise in order to improve product sales. By means of ashtrays and breadbaskets in the national colors, thimbles and eggcups with swastikas, table knives and shiny buttons with images of the Führer, citizens sought to display their support of the "new Germany."

Nevertheless, as early as May 19, 1933, Goebbels promulgated the Law to Protect National Symbols, as well as a list of prohibitions for the purpose of keeping the flourishing nationalistic kitsch within bounds. The utilization of nationalist symbols for "advertising purposes," or to decorate "accessories of low value" and thus damage the "dignity of these symbols," was made a punishable offense. Official party symbols and images of the Führer could be used only with the approval of the Reich party leadership. In this way nationalistic kitsch was curbed but not eliminated, the more so since official NS ART also aimed to bypass the intellect in favor of strong sentimental appeal and an effect on the masses.

Kitzelmann, Michael, b. Horben (Allgäu), January 29, 1916; d. Orel (USSR), June 12, 1942 (executed), German officer. Kitzelmann entered the military in 1937, rising to the rank of lieutenant in 1940. He was a company leader in the 199th Infantry Regiment during the Russian

Campaign. A good soldier but not an enthusiastic one, Kitzelmann was taught by the German atrocities in Poland in 1939 to hate the system that made such things possible. He did not always mince words; his criticism reached its peak in the statement "If these criminals win, I no longer want to live!" This utterance led to his court-martial and, on April 3, 1942, to a death sentence for harming the war effort. Kitzelmann's notes from his imprisonment constitute a moving document of struggling with a harsh destiny.

KL, official acronym of Konzentrationslager (*see* CONCENTRATION CAMPS); replaced in common usage by KZ.

Klages, Ludwig, b. Hannover, December 10, 1872; d. Kilchberg bei Zürich, July 29, 1956, German philosopher and psychologist. Klages helped found the German Graphological Society in 1897 and the "Seminar for the Study of Expression [*Ausdruckskunde*]" in 1907. His interests included the biological connection between "handwriting and character" (*Handschrift und Charakter;* 1917). For a long time he belonged to the circle around the poet Stefan GEORGE. Klages's philosophical works expounded the thesis embodied in the title "Mind as the Adversary of Soul" (*Geist als Widersacher der Seele,* 3 vols., 1929–1933): the original unity of soul and body was disturbed by "raw intellect," which as a result degraded into a "life-destroying force." This anti-intellectual, holistic doctrine fit National Socialism's image of humanity, making Klages one of the most widely read and quoted authors of the 1930s.

Ludwig Klages.

Klagges, Dietrich, b. Herringen (Kreis Soest), February 1, 1891; d. Bündheim bei Bad Harzburg, November 12, 1971, German politician. Originally a teacher, Klagges was dismissed without a pension in 1930 for having joined the NSDAP (June 13, 1925). After the National Socialist electoral success in Braunschweig in January 1931, he became a government councillor (*Regierungsrat*), and in September of that year minister of the interior and public instruction. At his request, the Braunschweig government named the Austrian Hitler a councillor on February 25, 1932, thus enabling him to acquire the naturalization necessary for election as Reich president. Klagges became minister president of Braunschweig in 1933; he distinguished himself by his brutal actions against political opponents. He was also a party publicist: his works included *Heldischer Glaube* (Heroic Faith; 1934). In 1950 Klagges was sentenced to life imprisonment for crimes against humanity, but in 1952 the sentence was reduced to 15 years. On October 2, 1957, he was pardoned, at which point he claimed his pension. It was first denied, then approved on July 16, 1970, by a West German administrative court, a decision that unleashed vehement public controversy.

Klamroth, Bernhard, b. Berlin, November 20, 1910; d. August 15, 1944 (executed), German officer. Klamroth was a company commander in the Polish Campaign, then staff officer of the Third and Tenth Panzer Divisions. In 1942 he became a captain and fourth General Staff officer to the Fourth Army High Command outside of Moscow. There he served for a long time with Col. Hellmuth STIEFF, who in early 1943 brought him into the army's organization section in Berlin and convinced him of the need to overthrow Hitler. Klamroth became the liaison with Henning von TRESCKOW and was closely involved with procuring and safeguarding the explosive used in the assassination attempt of July 20, 1944. When the crucial attack failed, Klamroth paid for his collusion with his life.

Klausener, Erich, b. Düsseldorf, January 25, 1885; d. Berlin, June 30, 1934 (murdered), German politician. Klausener studied law and was a First World War volunteer; he became district president (*Landrat*) in Adenau/Eifel (1917) and in Recklinghausen (1919). He was on the central board of the Catholic Academic Union, and in 1924 became ministerial director in the Welfare Ministry. As a Center party member, Klausener became head of the police section in the Prussian Interior Ministry. As a committed Catholic and chairman of CATHOLIC ACTION in the Berlin diocese, he had to vacate this position upon the National Socialist Seizure of Power, and was then shunted over to the merchant marine division of the Reich Transport Ministry. At first vacillating in his judgment of the new regime, the popular orator developed a forceful protest against measures hostile to the church. On June 24, 1934, he assailed NS racial policy before 60,000 people at the Thirty-second Berlin Katholikentag (Catholic Congress). As a consequence, Göring had him put on the death list for the RÖHM AFFAIR. Klausener was shot in his office by two SS men. The official

Dietrich Klagges.

Erich Klausener.

version of "suicide" was refuted by a solemn requiem at Saint Matthias's Church. Nor did the family comply with the ban on death notices. Klausener was one of the first Catholic martyrs of the CHURCH STRUGGLE.

Klausing, Friedrich Karl, b. Munich, May 24, 1920; d. Berlin, August 8, 1944 (executed), German officer. Klausing joined the Wehrmacht in 1938 and was commissioned a second lieutenant after the Polish and French campaigns. He was seriously wounded in Russia, then transferred to the Wehrmacht High Command in 1943. In Berlin he encountered his frontline comrade Friedrich von der SCHULENBURG and became acquainted with Claus Count von STAUFFENBERG. As the latter's adjutant, Klausing was involved in preparing for the assassination attempt of July 20, 1944. He at first fled, but soon surrendered in order to protect his friends. As expected, the *Volk* Court meted out the maximum penalty.

Klee, Paul, b. Münchenbuchsee bei Bern, December 18, 1879; d. Muralto, near Locarno, June 29, 1940, German-Swiss painter and graphic artist. After an early period of drawing that manifested *Jugendstil* (German art nouveau) and other influences, Klee became acquainted with the Expressionist "Der Blaue Reiter" group and dedicated himself to abstract styles of painting. He was particularly successful in incorporating elements of sign and symbol, letters, numbers, eyes, and stars—sometimes with recognizable but ironic and grotesque associations, sometimes completely abstract. As a

teacher at the BAUHAUS (1921–1931) and professor at the Düsseldorf Academy, Klee was one of the most important contemporary art theoreticians. However, his graphic works encountered a complete lack of understanding on the part of the National Socialists, who cited his "childlike drawing style" (*Krikel-Krakel*, "scribble-scrawl"). By the late 1920s, Klee had been declared a "major enemy" by the COMBAT LEAGUE FOR GERMAN CULTURE. In 1933 he had to relinquish state employment and emigrate to Switzerland. His pictures were removed from public museums and were displayed at the Munich DEGENERATE ART exhibit as typical examples. Some were later burned as "worthless sludge."

Kleist, Ewald von, b. Braunfels/Lahn, August 8, 1881; d. Vladimirovka camp (USSR), 1954, German field marshal general. Kleist joined the army in 1899 and was a General Staff officer in the First World War. He was taken into the Reichswehr (1919), and by 1932 was a major general. Kleist was critical of National Socialism; as commander of the Silesian defense district (*Wehrgau*), he fell into vehement conflicts with the SA leadership after 1933. He was cashiered on February 28, 1938, as a consequence of the FRITSCH CRISIS, then was reactivated before the outbreak of the war and commanded the Twenty-second Army Corps in the Polish Campaign. Kleist demonstrated the striking power of concentrated panzer units, commanding his own tank group both in the western and Balkan campaigns, which included the taking of Bel-

Paul Klee.

Ewald von Kleist.

grade. He led tank units in Russia as well, until November 22, 1942, when he became commander in chief of Army Group A, which he led out intact from the Caucasus after the catastrophe at Stalingrad. Held responsible by Hitler for losing the Crimea, Kleist was dismissed from service on March 30, 1944. After the war, the Americans remanded him to Yugoslavia, where he was sentenced to 15 years' hard labor on August 4, 1948. The following year he was passed on to the Soviet Union, where he died in a camp for war criminals.

Kleist-Schmenzin, Ewald von, b. Gross Duberow (Pomerania), March 22, 1890; d. Berlin-Plötzensee, April 9, 1945, German opposition fighter. Kleist-Schmenzin studied law and was a First World War volunteer. A German National People's Party (DNVP) member and a monarchist, he opposed the Weimar Republic and supported the KAPP PUTSCH and the BLACK REICHSWEHR, but rejected National Socialism and its "anticonservative and belligerent goals." His attitude grew into overt hostility after he met Hitler in 1932, expressed in his book *Der National-sozialismus—eine Gefahr* (National Socialism—a Danger; 1932). After the Seizure of Power, Kleist-Schmenzin was repeatedly interrogated and jailed, once for having chased SA troops off his property by force of arms. He made contacts with the OPPOSITION, and in 1938 went to London to campaign unsuccessfully for a hard line in the SUDETEN CRISIS, which he saw as an opportunity for possible action against Hitler. Subsequently, he unflinchingly continued a struggle that he understood as "a God-given command." After the failed assassination attempt of July 20, 1944, Kleist-Schmenzin was arraigned before the *Volk* Court on February 3, 1945. The trial was interrupted by a bomb attack that killed the presiding judge, Roland FREISLER. It resumed on February 23, and delivered a death sentence. Kleist-Schmenzin died on the same day as several of his companions in struggle, including Dietrich BONHOEFFER, Wilhelm CANARIS, and Hans OSTER.

Klemperer, Otto, b. Breslau, May 14, 1885; d. Zurich, July 7, 1973, German conductor. Klemperer began his conducting career in Berlin in 1906, and served as music director in several European opera houses. In 1927 he accepted the directorship of Berlin's Kroll Opera, where he won international acclaim, especially with performances of works by contemporary composers such as Paul HINDEMITH, Arnold Schön-

Otto Klemperer.

berg, and Igor Stravinsky. For his artistic accomplishments, Klemperer received the Goethe Medal (1933), among other awards, but found himself the object of attacks from nationalistic and conservative circles because of his promotion of modern composers. As a Jew, Klemperer saw no possibilities for public work after the Seizure of Power, and consequently in 1933 he went to the United States to continue his career. He returned to Europe in 1946, serving most notably as chief conductor of the London Philharmonic Orchestra until 1970, when he settled in Jerusalem.

Klepper, Jochen, b. Beuthen/Oder, March 22, 1903; d. Berlin-Nikolassee, December 11, 1942, German writer. Klepper studied Evangelical theology and worked in radio broadcasting. He wrote spiritual songs such as "Kyrie" (1938) and novels that, like *Der Kahn der fröhlichen Leute* (The Happy People's Boat; 1933), won positive attention from National Socialist critics for being "popular and humorous stories" (Lennartz). Klepper's tragic historical novel about the soldier-king Friedrich Wilhelm I, *Der Vater* (The Father; 1937), suited the trend toward the encouraged genre of heroic novels with its motto "Kings must be able to suffer more than other people." Nonetheless, Klepper's staunch Christianity and his marriage to a Jewish woman brought him into conflict with the regime: in 1933 he lost his position in radio, and in 1935 he was deprived of further work with his publisher, Ullstein. Expelled from the REICH WRITING CHAMBER in 1937, he could continue working only to a limited extent, with specific

Jochen Klepper.

permission. When Klepper saw no possibility of shielding his Jewish stepdaughter from an announced deportation, he committed suicide along with his family. Diary entries from the last stages of his life, *Unter dem Schatten deiner Flügel* (In the Shadow of Your Wings; 1956) and *Überwindung* (Overcoming; 1958), provide a moving reflection of the desperate lot of the persecuted.

Klepper, Otto, b. Brotterode, August 17, 1888; d. Berlin, May 11, 1957, German politician. Klepper studied law and political science; after 1921 he held several key positions concerned with the financial and structural problems of small and medium landowners and farmers. In the BRAUN government he served as Prussian finance minister after 1931, and supported the cause of Prussian independence. He lost his post as a result of the PRUSSIAN COUP on July 20, 1932. In February 1933 Klepper went into exile, living in China, where he worked as an agricultural consultant; in the United States; in France; and in Mexico, among other places. While in exile Klepper developed his economic and political concepts in various emigré periodicals. In 1947 he returned to Germany as an economic journalist.

Klimsch, Fritz, b. Frankfurt am Main, February 10, 1870; d. Freiburg im Breisgau, March 30, 1960, German sculptor. Klimsch's breakthrough came in 1906 with his victory in the competition for a monument to the German medical researcher and politician Rudolf Virchow. in 1910 Klimsch became a professor in Berlin. He won numerous national and international honors, ranging from the title of senator in 1916 under

the Kaiser's Reich through the Goethe Medal in 1940 under the Third Reich, to the Great Service Cross of the Federal Republic of Germany in 1960. The classical lines that Klimsch employed with ever greater refinement in his numerous female nudes, portrait busts, and monuments matched the desired National Socialist aesthetics. After 1933 Klimsch drew even closer to it through naturalistic concessions, producing statues of combatants and nudes of young women with intensely fervent expressions; in the form of ceramic and porcelain copies, these were sought after as residential decorations. In 1943 Klimsch was bombed out of Berlin and moved to Salzburg; however, in 1946 he was deported from Austria, and passed his final years in the Black Forest.

Klooga, SS labor camp in Estonia, built 44 km (27.3 miles) west of Reval in September 1943, under the supervision of the VAIVARA camp commandant. Klooga held some 2,000 male and female Jewish prisoners, who worked for the TODT ORGANIZATION or for the navy. In September 1944, as Russian troops approached, the prisoners were shot and their bodies burned.

W. D.

Kluft, clothing, especially hiking apparel; a term taken over from slang despite its Jewish origins (Yi., *klaffot*, "rind," "shell"); it was also used in Hitler Youth and League of German Girls (BDM) jargon.

Kluge, Hans Günther von, b. Posen (now Poznań, Poland), October 30, 1882; d. near Metz (Alsace), August 18, 1944, German field marshal general (July 19, 1940). Kluge joined the army in 1901 and served as a General Staff officer in the First World War; he advanced rapidly in the Reichswehr, reaching the rank of major general by 1933. Kluge led the Fourth Army in the Polish and French campaigns, and later in Russia. He became supreme commander of the Middle Army Group on December 18, 1941. On Kluge's 60th birthday, Hitler bestowed on him 250,000 RM for meritorious service. Kluge's first General Staff officer, Henning von TRESCKOW, attempted with little success to win him over to the military opposition.

An automobile accident on October 12, 1943, forced Kluge into long convalescent leave, but on July 7, 1944, he assumed supreme command of the Western Army. After Erwin Rommel's injury he also took command of Army Group B, on July 17. These posts made Kluge a key figure

Hans Günther von Kluge.

in the West for the conspirators of the July 20 assassination attempt. At first he vacillated, but refused cooperation once he learned that Hitler had survived the assault. Nonetheless, he had aroused the suspicions of the Gestapo, and was relieved of his command on August 17. He wrote Hitler a letter of resignation that asserted his unwavering loyalty but also called for an end to the war. On the trip back to Germany Kluge took poison.

Kluge, Kurt, b. Leipzig, April 29, 1886; d. Eben-Emael, near Liège (Belgium), July 26, 1940, German writer and sculptor. Educated in pedagogy and art, Kluge first worked as a sculptor,

Kurt Kluge.

creating metal pieces such as the prisoners' memorial in Güstrow (1932). In 1921 he became a professor in Berlin. He turned to writing in 1930, and produced—besides tales of artisans and nationalistic dramas such as *Ewiges Volk* (Eternal *Volk;* 1933)—some of the most important works to come out of the Third Reich, notably his masterpiece in the tradition of the romantic novel of the outsider, *Der Herr Kortüm* (The Gentleman Kortüm; 1938). Kluge's essentially unpolitical books, for example, *Die Zaubergeige* (The Magic Violin; 1940), were esteemed as "lightly melancholy" and "warmed by humor" (Lennartz); the author was honored with literary prizes. Kluge died of a heart attack during a "German poet's tour of the front."

Knauf, Erich, b. Meerane (Saxony), February 21, 1895; d. Berlin, May 2, 1944 (executed), German journalist. Knauf was a First World War volunteer. From 1922 to 1928 he was editor of the Plauen *Volkszeitung* (People's News); he was a reader for the Gutenberg Book Guild until 1933. His feuilletons and biographies, such as *Daumier* (1932), were highly regarded. However, an unfavorable opera review led to his expulsion from the REICH PRESS CHAMBER and to several weeks' internment in the camps at Oranienburg and Lichtenburg. Afterward, he did motion picture publicity. During this period Knauf became friends with the illustrator E. O. Plauen (pseud. of Erich Ohser), creator of *Vater und Sohn* (Father and Son). Both were indicted for anti-government statements in February 1944. Plauen committed suicide, and Knauf was sentenced to death by the *Volk* Court on April 6, 1944.

Knight's Cross (Ritterkreuz) of the IRON CROSS, war service medal established in 1939, worn around the neck on a black-white-red ribbon. The cross, awarded 7,200 times in all, was larger than the Iron Cross and took the place of the Pour le mérite of the First World War, which was no longer awarded. It received many enhancements in the course of the war: Knight's Cross with Oak-Leaf Cluster (June 3, 1940; 853 recipients), with Swords (July 19, 1940; 150 recipients), with Diamonds (September 28, 1941; 27 recipients), and with Gold Oak-Leaf Cluster, Swords, and Diamonds (December 29, 1944; 1 recipient, Flight Col. Hans-Ulrich RUDEL), allowed to be awarded no more than 12 times. A law of July 26, 1957, permitted the wearing of the Knight's Cross in the Federal Republic of Germany only without a swastika.

Knight's Cross of the Iron Cross, with Oak-Leaf Cluster, Swords, and Diamonds.

Knirsch, Hans, b. Triebendorf (Moravia), September 14, 1877; d. Dux, December 6, 1944, Sudeten German politician. In 1911 Knirsch became a deputy for the German *völkisch* workers' movement in the Vienna Reichsrat; he was a First World War volunteer. He ardently supported an Anschluss of the Sudetenland and Germany after the First World War. Knirsch joined the GERMAN NATIONAL SOCIALIST WORKERS' PARTY (DNSAP), and as a member of the Prague parliament fought for increased autonomy for Czechoslovakia's German population.

Knochen, Helmut, b. Magdeburg, March 14, 1910, SS-*Standartenführer.* Knochen studied English and German philology; he joined the NSDAP in 1932, and the Security Service (SD) in 1936. In late 1939 he was heavily involved in the VENLO INCIDENT, and after the French Campaign was assigned security police tasks such as monitoring Jews and emigrants in the occupied areas. Under Higher SS and Police Leader Carl OBERG, Knochen was chief of the SD and the Security Police in France from 1942. He carried out his duties with so little concern for orders from Berlin that Ernst KALTENBRUNNER removed him from his post on August 18, 1944, and transferred him to the Waffen-SS.

In 1946 a British court sentenced Knochen to life imprisonment for the shooting of downed British aviators; remanded to France, he was given a death sentence on October 9, 1954. The penalty was commuted to life imprisonment on April 10, 1958, then reduced, on December 31, 1959, to 20 years' hard labor. Finally pardoned in December 1962, Knochen returned to Germany.

Koch, Erich, b. Elberfeld (now Wuppertal-Elberfeld), June 19, 1896, German politician. Koch was a railroad official and a First World War volunteer; he was active in the RUHR CONFLICT. In 1922 he joined the NSDAP. Fired in 1926 for anti-Republican activities, he became a *Gau* leader, then in 1933 governor (*Oberpräsident*) of East Prussia. He served in the Reichstag after 1930. Koch was regarded even in party circles as exceedingly uncontrolled and brutal.

As wartime Reich defense commissioner and, after 1942, Reich commissioner for the Ukraine, Koch unleashed a reign of terror that at times provoked opposition even from the SS, and that aroused an avalanche of partisan activity among a population that was at first friendly to the Germans. He applied a policy of massive RE-GERMANIZATION, closed schools on the ground that Russians did not need education, had many thousands deported for slave labor in the Reich, and was responsible for sending uncounted shipments of Jews to extermination camps. In 1944 he returned to Königsberg, where he organized the VOLK STORM against the Red Army, supervised removal of the AMBER ROOM, and then vanished from sight at the war's end. Only in late May 1949 was he arrested by British military police. Remanded to Poland on February 14, 1950, he was sentenced to death in 1959 for complicity in the murders of at least 400,000 Poles (his crimes in the Ukraine were not in-

Erich Koch.

volved). Owing to mental incompetence, however, he was not executed. He is presumed to be still living in a prison in Bartchero (Poland).

Koch, Ilse (née Köhler), b. Dresden, September 22, 1906; d. Aichach prison, September 2, 1967 (suicide), German concentration camp warden. Koch was a secretary by occupation; she joined the NSDAP in 1932. In 1936 she married Karl Otto Koch (b. Darmstadt, August 2, 1897; d. Buchenwald, April 1945), head of the Sachsenhausen concentration camp, who in 1937 was assigned to build the concentration camp at BUCHENWALD. Ilse Koch was feared in the camp because of her brutality (she was known as the "witch [*Hexe*] of Buchenwald"), and her husband was dreaded for a greed that extended even to corpses: he set up a regular warehouse for prisoners' property. In 1942 he was given a punitive transfer, with his family, to the MAIDANEK concentration camp, where he continued with his covert business activities and she with her affairs with SS men.

While uncounted thousands died in the gas chambers, Koch and her husband were arrested in 1943 at the request of SS judge Josias Prince of WALDECK-PYRMONT, she for alleged embezzlement of about 710,000 RM, he for the murders of three prisoners who knew too much. Ilse Koch was acquitted for lack of evidence, but her husband was shot in April 1945. The Americans sentenced Koch to life imprisonment in 1947, but pardoned her in 1949. A German court immediately indicted her for instigation to murder in 135 cases; on January 15, 1951, she was sentenced to life imprisonment for instigation to attempted murder in five cases. (The interrogation of 2,000 witnesses provided no proof of homicide charges.) The defense failed to make its case for an appeal on the ground that the trial was illegal because of prejudicial pretrial publicity in the media.

Koch-Weser, Erich, b. Bremerhaven, February 26, 1875; d. Paraná (Brazil), October 19, 1944, German politician. Koch-Weser studied law; he was mayor of Delmenhorst (1901–1909), Bremerhaven (1909–1913), and Kassel (1913–1919); he was one of the founders of the liberal German Democratic Party (DDP). He served as Reich interior minister (1919–1921), occasionally as vice chancellor, and as Reich justice minister (1928–1929). Along the way he assumed the surname "Weser" (after his electoral district), and became a champion of Reich reform leading to a decentralized unitary state. When in 1930 the DDP, which he headed, merged with the YOUNG GERMAN ORDER to form the GERMAN STATE PARTY, Koch-Weser was seeking a coalition of pro-Republican middle-class voters. However, he had no success in the elections of September 1930, and relinquished his Reichstag mandate as a result. When his license to practice law was revoked in 1933 he emigrated to Brazil, where he attempted to establish himself as a farmer.

Kokoschka, Oskar, b. Pöchlarn an der Donau, March 1, 1886; d. Villeneuve (Switzerland), February 22, 1980, Austrian painter, graphic artist, and writer. Early on, Kokoschka discovered his expressive idiom of color and form. From 1918 to 1924 he was a professor in Dresden. He won international acclaim as one of the most important representatives of Expressionism through his large output of strongly colored paintings with distorted figures and proportions. His works were attacked after 1930 by the COMBAT LEAGUE FOR GERMAN CULTURE as "messes" (*Schmierereien*). Kokoschka's symbolist-Expressionist poems found even less comprehension among the general public. After 1933 the National Socialists labeled him as a typical example of DEGENERATE ART; his pictures were confiscated, and he himself, living again in Vienna from 1931, was deprived of his citizenship after the Anschluss with Austria. He went into exile, and in 1947 accepted British citizenship. Even in his late work Kokoschka remained dedicated to a colorful and spontaneous Expressionist style of painting.

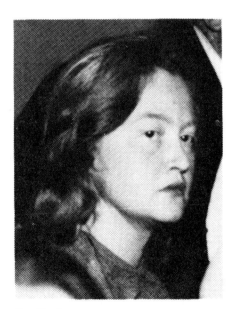

Ilse Koch.

Kolbe, Georg, b. Waldheim (Saxony), April 13, 1877; d. Berlin, November 15, 1947, German sculptor. Influenced by Rodin and by naturalistic concepts, Kolbe became the internationally best known German sculptor after the First World War through his strongly expressive, predominantly female nudes. His classically proportioned and idealized bodies, however, also matched the National Socialist ideal of art (*see* SCULPTURE). After the Seizure of Power, Kolbe received public commissions and awards, and his workshop was frequently visited on art tours of NS educational institutions. During the 1930s Kolbe adapted his work to official expectations; his sculptures lost their rhythmic flow while approaching closer to the expected Nordic-Germanic ideal, although not with the exaggerated monumentality of Arno BREKER or Josef THORAK.

Kolbe, Maximilian, b. Zduńska Wola (Poland), January 8, 1894; d. Auschwitz concentration camp, August 14, 1941, Polish Franciscan and founder of the apostolic association Militia Immaculatae (Militia of Immaculate Mary). In 1941 Kolbe was arrested by the German occupation authorities and sent to AUSCHWITZ. As a reprisal for the escape of a prisoner in July 1941, 10 prisoners were indiscriminately chosen to die of starvation in the cellars of Block II, among them a young Pole, Gajowniczek, the father of a

Maximilian Kolbe.

family. Kolbe volunteered to take his place. He was the only one of the 10 condemned to withstand a month without food in the darkness, and was finally put to death with a phenol injection. He was beatified in 1973, and on October 10, 1982, Pope John Paul II canonized him as a saint. The church dispensed with the normal 50-year waiting period, honoring Kolbe as a symbol of human dignity, self-denial, and solidarity with human beings under inhuman conditions.

Kolbenheyer, Erwin Guido, b. Budapest, December 30, 1878; d. Munich, April 12, 1962, German writer. Kolbenheyer was among the most widely read authors of the Third Reich. His works reflected the exaggerated nationalism of the Sudeten Germans among whom he grew up. In his historical novels such as the *Paracelsus-Trilogie* (1927–1928), which distinguished themselves for their "abundance of historical color" (Loewy), "typical Teutons" do battle with a hostile environment. In his works of philosophy and cultural criticism, he approached the Social Darwinist view of life held by the National Socialists; an example was *Arbeitsnot und Wirtschaftskrise volksbiologisch gesehen* (Unemployment and Economic Crisis from an Ethnic-Biological Standpoint; 1935). Kolbenheyer repudiated the "alien" roots of Christianity and argued for a "belief in God of a purely German kind." In 1931 he withdrew from the Prussian Academy of Letters because of the preponderance of democratic authors in it, but after the initiation of the "New Order" in 1933 he rejoined the academy and became one

Sculpture by Georg Kolbe.

Erwin Guido Kolbenheyer.

Scene from the film *Kolberg*.

of its officials. The National Socialists awarded him various prizes, such as the Eagle's Shield of the German Reich (ADLERSCHILD DES DEUTSCHEN REICHES) and the Goethe Prize. In postwar Germany, after a period of prohibition against publishing, Kolbenheyer was able to rely on a wide readership, leading in 1951 to the founding of the Society of Friends of the Works of E. G. Kolbenheyer: in him they honored a "man who did not grovel before the cross" but who continued openly to avow National Socialism.

Kolberg, German motion picture (1945) directed by Veit HARLAN, with screenplay by Artur Braun, and starring Kristina SÖDERBAUM, Heinrich GEORGE, and Horst Caspar; it premiered on January 30, 1945. The film was rated "especially worthwhile in terms of state policy and artistry—a film for the nation." However, the nation never got to see this color film. Planned as early as mid-1941, filming began in November 1943; however, Propaganda Minister Joseph Goebbels demanded such a monumental work that, despite an immense budget (8.8 million RM) and the assistance of the Wehrmacht (soldiers for mass scenes, transport facilities, 6,000 horses), the premiere could be scheduled no earlier than the 12th anniversary of the SEIZURE OF POWER. The intended connection with the present had in the meantime intensified into a tragic reality: all of Germany now found itself

in the desperate situation of the beleaguered Kolberg Fortress in the movie, which was set during Prussia's war against Napoleon in 1806–1807; the difference was that in 1945 there was no outlook for a happy ending. Moreover, the intended propaganda effect of holding the fort had vanished as well. The only persons who got to see Goebbels's cinematic testament were soldiers in the still-occupied but surrounded Atlantic port of La Rochelle, who received the film reels by parachute, and some party functionaries in the pile of rubble that was Berlin.

Kollwitz, Käthe (née Schmidt), b. Königsberg, July 8, 1867; d. Moritzburg bei Dresden, April 22, 1945, German graphic artist and sculptor. Working-class misery and wartime suffering left their stamp on Kollwitz's work. In graphics dealing with the "weavers' revolt," "war," and "hungry children," she drew impressive images of human need. One of the most important German Expressionist graphic artists, Kollwitz was a professor in Berlin from 1918 to 1933, and a member of the Prussian Academy of the Arts. Appreciated by National Socialist critics as a "strongly expressive" depicter "of big-city misery," she was criticized at the same time for her artistic commitment to national and international humanitarian organizations as one involved in "Communist propaganda work." After the Seizure of Power she withdrew in protest from the

Käthe Kollwitz.

Still from the film *"Kopf hoch, Johannes!"*

academy; she was able to work until 1937, when all her works in public collections were identified as "DEGENERATE ART."

Kommerell, Max, b. Münsingen, February 25, 1902; d. Marburg, July 25, 1944, German literary scholar and writer. While still a student, Kommerell came under the influence of the Stefan GEORGE circle, which had a lasting effect on his early literary scholarship. Kommerell's elitist, *völkisch*-heroic interpretations of writers in *Der Dichter als Führer in der deutschen Klassik* (The Poet as Leader in the German Classical Period; 1928) rank among the fundamental works of *völkisch* German studies. Kommerell welcomed Hitler's dissolution of the "locksmith-and-cobbler governments" of the Weimar period, but as an "aesthete" he distanced himself from the regime's brutalities and moved from irrational and esoteric positions to more mundane conservative ones. After 1941 he was a professor in Marburg. His later works were closely textual, phenomenological, and in part existential; over the years they have influenced West German postwar literary scholarship.

"Kopf hoch, Johannes!" ("Chin up, John!"), German motion picture (1941), with Victor de Kowa and Klaus Detlef Sierck, Otto Gebühr, Albrecht Schoenhals, Dorothea Wieck, and Gunnar Möller; it premiered on February 5, 1941. The narrative deals with the maturing of a spoiled outsider, Johannes, through comradeship and sympathetic teachers in one of

the NATIONAL-POLITICAL EDUCATIONAL INSTITUTES. This recruiting film for National Socialist select schools (its screenplay was partly the work of Konrad Adenauer's later press secretary, Felix von Eckart) avoided the all-too-obvious NS emphases, elaborating instead on the possibilities for self-development in the context of an achieving community (*Leistungsgemeinschaft*). In the early wartime period the turning away from traditional values in life was to be downplayed as much as possible in favor of military preparedness and the demand for a group consciousness. The film's success lagged far behind expectations.

Korczak, Janusz (originally, Henryk Goldszmit), b. Warsaw, July 22, 1878; d. Treblinka, August 5, 1942, Polish physician and educator. After a brief practice as a physician in a pediatric hospital, Korczak became the director of a Jewish orphanage in Warsaw. He described his experiences in books such as *Wie man ein Kind lieben soll* (How to Love a Child; 1926) and *Das Recht des Kindes auf Achtung* (A Child's Right to Respect; 1928). For his children he wrote books of fantasy such as *König Hänschen der Erste* (Little King Hans I; 1923) and *König Hänschen auf der einsamen Insel* (Little King Hans on the Lonely Island; 1923), and appeared as a storyteller on the radio series "Talks for Children about Children." After the German occupation, Korczak's orphanage was first moved into the Warsaw ghetto and then closed down in the summer of 1942. Although offered a chance to escape, Korczak accompanied his 200 children to the Treblinka extermination camp and into the gas chamber. In 1972 he was posthumously awarded the Peace Prize of the German Booksellers' Association.

Körner, Heinrich, b. Essen, April 30, 1892; d. Berlin, April 25, 1945, German trade unionist. A machinist, Körner joined the Christian Metal Workers' Union as a young man; in 1922 he became cartel secretary of the Christian Trade Unions. From 1926 to 1933 he was the unions' regional general secretary for western Germany (with Jakob KAISER); he was also honorary Reich labor arbitrator. Körner was briefly jailed in May 1933 in connection with the destruction of the trade unions. Subsequently he became a traveling salesman, using his trips to make contacts with union opposition groups. This activity led to his arrest after the assassination attempt on Hitler of July 20, 1944. Körner's sentence of four years' imprisonment on April 5, 1945, was ended on April 25 by the Red Army's arrival at the Berlin-Plötzensee prison. Körner was killed on the same day in the fighting in Berlin.

Körner, Paul, b. Pirna, October 2, 1893; d. Tegernsee, November 29, 1957, German politician. Körner was a First World War soldier; he also studied law. He joined the NSDAP in 1928. As an associate of Hermann Göring he was made state secretary in the Prussian State Ministry on April 11, 1933, and from October 1936 was Göring's representative as commissioner for the FOUR-YEAR PLAN. As such, Körner had a significant influence on rearmament and the war economy. In August 1948, the Nuremberg Military Tribunal sentenced him to 15 years in prison; he

Paul Körner.

was soon pardoned, and was released on December 16, 1951.

Korneuburg Oath (*Korneuburger Eid*), program of the Austrian Home Guard of May 18, 1930, conceived largely under the influence of Othmar SPANN (*see* AUSTROFASCISM).

Kortner, Fritz (until 1916, Nathan Kohn), b. Vienna, May 12, 1892; d. Munich, July 22, 1970, German-Austrian actor and director. After performances in Dresden, Vienna, and Hamburg, Kortner was from 1919 to 1933 one of the most important German character actors on the Berlin stage, gaining popularity through roles in expressionistically staged productions. He played Shylock and Othello on the stage, and "demonic background" characters in silent films such as *Orlacs Hände* (Orlac's Hands; 1925), as well as the title roles in *Dreyfus* (1930) and *Dantons Tod* (Danton's Death; 1931). Because of his Jewish ancestry and his support for critical realism, Kortner had to emigrate to the United States in 1933. After returning from exile, he exerted a lasting influence on postwar West German theater as one of the most internationally respected directors.

Kovno. *See* Kowno.

Kowno (Russ., Kovno), Polish name for the Lithuanian Kaunas, where the National Socialist KAUEN concentration camp was built.

KPD. *See* Communist Party of Germany.

Kraft durch Freude. *See* Strength through Joy.

Kraków-Płaszów, National Socialist concentration camp set up in early 1942 on Abraham and Jerosolinska Street in Kraków, first as a forced-labor camp (*Zwangsarbeitslager*) of the SS and Police Leader. After January 1944 it came under the jurisdiction of Administrative Group D of the ECONOMIC-ADMINISTRATIVE MAIN OFFICE (WVHA). The camp was divided into two parts: the smaller was for political prisoners (a maximum of 1,000), and the larger for Jewish prisoners (as many as 25,000). The inmates worked for the German Armament Works and for a textile company, as well as in a quarry and in the munitions industry. Hygiene conditions, food supplies, and housing in the camp were very poor. There were numerous cases of mistreatment of prisoners. Thousands of Jewish prisoners were shot, beaten to death, torn apart by dogs, and otherwise killed. Sick and disabled prisoners were segregated from time to time and shot.   *W. D.*

Kramer, Josef, b. Munich, November 10, 1906; d. Hameln, December 13, 1945 (executed), German concentration camp commandant. After several posts in the camps at Dachau, Esterwegen, and Sachsenhausen, Kramer became adjutant to Auschwitz commandant Rudolf HÖSS in 1940; in 1943 he assumed command of the NATZWEILER concentration camp. There, among other acts, he personally took part in the killing of 80 women, whose skeletons were set aside for the anatomy collection of the Reich University at Strasbourg. In 1944 Kramer was assigned as commandant of the extermination camp AUSCHWITZ II (Birkenau), and on December 1 of that year, commandant of BERGEN-BELSEN. The conditions there when the British liberated the camp on April 15, 1945, epitomized the National Socialist terror system and earned Kramer the nickname "the Beast of Belsen" from the international press. A British military court in Lüneburg sentenced him to death.

Krannhals, Paul, b. Riga (Latvia), November 14, 1883; d. Munich, August 18, 1934, German philosopher. As a culture critic and independent scholar, Krannhals sought from the late 1920s to provide a philosophical foundation for the National Socialist movement, which he supported. In his major work, *Das organische Weltbild* (The Organic Theory of Life, 2 vols., 1928), he attempted to demonstrate, through the example of German culture, that every cultural development was conditioned by "laws rooted in race and ethnicity." As a critic of religion, in *Der Glaubensweg des deutschen Menschen* (The German's Way of Faith; 1934), Krannhals repudiated the "authority based on alien law" and the "one-sided religiosity of redemption" of the Christian churches.

Kraus, Karl, b. Jičin (Bohemia), April 28, 1874; d. Vienna, June 12, 1936, Austrian writer and literary critic. In 1899 Kraus founded the journal *Die Fackel* (The Torch), and was its sole author from 1912 until publication of the last issue in 1936. In many articles of satirical commentary, Kraus fought against the "squandering of the language" in the press and in literature, and argued for the "draining of a great swamp of phrases." The decline of language was for Kraus proof of corruption and "sordidness" in civil society. He took issue with, among other things, the relationship between sensationalistic journalism and the judicial treatment of sex cases, in *Sittlichkeit und Kriminalität* (Morality and Criminality; 1908). In *Literatur und Lüge* (Literature and Lies; 1929) he criticized contemporary

Karl Kraus.

poetry and essays for concealing a lack of moral commitment behind an aesthetic facade.

Kraus's literary masterpiece is his pacifist drama *Die letzten Tage der Menschheit* (1918–1919; translated as *The Last Days of Mankind*). In it, in 200 scenes consisting partly of documentary material and partly of commentary, he polemicized against the journalists responsible for the First World War, and against speculators, military men, and nationalists. Kraus's humanist and radical, highly polished and aphoristically phrased criticism attracted many readers, and made its author a moral authority even beyond the borders of Austria. It also brought down upon him the hatred of broad conservative and nationalistic circles. For the National Socialists, against whose rise to power he had warned for years, he stood out as a typical "Jewish cultural Bolshevik." When Hitler came to power, Kraus wrote a series of antifascist articles on the connections between National Socialism, the "violation of language," and the "atrocity of blood." They were posthumously collected in the book *Die dritte Walpurgisnacht* (The Third Walpurgis Night; 1952).

H. H.

Kraus, Oskar, b. Prague, July 24, 1872; d. Oxford, September 26, 1942, German-Czech philosopher and jurist. From 1909 to 1938, Kraus was a professor of philosophy in Prague. By means of his theses in political philosophy, he questioned the rigid observance of the law ("The state and state authorities, therefore, must be tested as to whether they are to be obeyed"). The National Socialists later branded his thought "crude subjectivism." As a pacifist and author of one of the first standard works on international law, *Jeremy Benthams Grundsätze für ein künftiges Völkerrecht und einen dauernden Frieden* (Jeremy Bentham's Principles for a Future International Law and for Lasting Peace; 1915), as a critic of *völkisch*-racist administration of justice in National Socialist Germany and as a Jew, Kraus was arrested after the occupation of Prague in 1939, but was released into exile in England before the war broke out.

Krauss, Werner, b. Gestungshausern (Upper Franconia), June 23, 1884; d. Vienna, October 20, 1959, German actor. Krauss ranks among the greatest German character actors of the 20th century. He first gained fame in the theater (including work in Berlin with Max REINHARDT), then with more than 100 roles in silent films. He later became one of the most prominent and honored actors of the Third Reich, along with Heinrich GEORGE, Gustaf GRÜNDGENS, and Emil JANNINGS. The National Socialists named Krauss, who was known for his conceit and ambition, Prussian State Actor and a member of the Presidial Council of the REICH THEATER CHAMBER. As a movie idol, Krauss worked in numerous propaganda films, both as a positive hero and as a notably unsympathetic antagonist; examples were *Robert Koch* (1939) and *Bismarck* (1940). His roles included exaggerated caricatures of Jewish characters, as in JUD SÜSS (1940); for this portrayal, he was banned in 1945 from acting for several years. After the war the multifaceted and adaptable Krauss received

Werner Krauss.

honors in Austria and in the Federal Republic of Germany—in the latter, the Service Cross (Bundesverdienstkreuz).

Krebs, Hans, b. Helmstedt, March 4, 1898; d. Berlin, early May 1945, German general. As a major in 1936, Krebs was transferred to the office of the German military attaché in Moscow. There, after service at the front, he became deputy military attaché for a short time in 1941. During the Russian Campaign he held staff positions, then became General Staff chief of Army Group B (Gen. Walter MODEL) on the western front. After his quarrel with Gen. Heinz GUDERIAN, Hitler named Krebs General Staff chief on March 29, 1945. The last to hold this position, Krebs could only keep watch on Germany's collapse from the bunker under the Reich Chancellery. On April 29, he acted as a witness at the signing of Hitler's will. After Hitler's death, Krebs made futile attempts to negotiate with the Red Army. He is believed to have died in the battle for Berlin.

Kreis (district; literally, circle), regional NSDAP division, beneath the *Gau*. Led by a *Kreisleiter* (district leader), it was subdivided into *Ortsgruppen* (local groups).

Kreis, Wilhelm, b. Eltville, March 17, 1873; d. Bad Honnef, August 13, 1955, German architect. Kreis was a professor in Dresden and Düsseldorf; his early tastes inclined toward imposing and monumental buildings. His pre-1914 designs included more than 50 Bismarck towers and plans for national monuments; under the influence of classical and Germanic traditions, he built the Augustus Bridge in Dresden (1904–1908) and a museum of prehistory in Halle (1913–1914). After 1920 Kreis was variously committed to Expressionist, then to functional architecture. As a result, immediately after the Seizure of Power, he did not rank among the preferred architects for state and party buildings (*see* ARCHITECTURE). For the construction of the *Gau* Air Command in Dresden, he reverted to a monumental natural stone building. He supported Albert Speer's planning for the Reich capital, became a Reich Culture Senator in 1938, and in 1941 a member of the board in charge of German military cemeteries. In his few postwar plans, Kreis returned to functional architectural interpretations.

Kreisau Circle (Kreisauer Kreis), OPPOSITION group named after Kreisau, the estate of Helmuth Count MOLTKE in Schweidnitz, Lower

Silesia. The name may have been coined by National Socialist jurist Roland FREISLER, and is first found in one of the so-called Kaltenbrunner Reports to Martin Bormann, dated August 25, 1944. In the Kreisau Circle, representatives of various social groups and political orientations met, beginning in 1940 and then at three large conferences: at Pentecost of 1942, in October 1942, and at Pentecost of 1943. They were predominantly from the younger generation, in their 30s and 40s, and were open to reform: old Prussian nobles such as Peter Count YORCK VON WARTENBURG; Socialists such as Adolf REICHWEIN, Carlo MIERENDORFF, Theodor HAUBACH, and Julius LEBER; clergy of both denominations such as Father Alfred DELP and the Berlin prison chaplain Harald Poelchau; professors; district presidents (*Landräte*) such as Theodor Steltzer, and diplomats such as Hans-Bernd von HAEFTEN and Adam von TROTT ZU SOLZ.

The Kreisau Circle was not primarily interested in the political direction of a *coup d'état;* thus, Moltke rejected "tyrannicide" for reasons of Christian conscience, but also out of fear that such an action would burden any post-Hitler new beginning in Germany with a new STAB-IN-THE-BACK LEGEND. Much more central to the often controversial meetings were Christian socialist–oriented deliberations and reform plans. One of these, set forth in the summer of 1943, consisted of provisional "Principles for the New Order" calling for a social leveling among the classes, a "moral and political renewal," and the reshaping of German and European politics and society after the war. In domestic affairs, discussions developed the concept of autonomous and self-administrating "small communities" (communes, neighborhoods, workplaces) after the American principle of "grassroots democracy" as the basis for a state structure organized from bottom to top, with graduated and indirect elections proceeding upward from the local district (*Kreis*) level. The economic program provided for state control of the raw-material and energy sectors. In foreign affairs, the Kreisau Circle advocated renunciation of national sovereignty, a federally organized European union, and Germany's reconciliation with its western and eastern neighbors.

The Kreisau Circle was virtually broken up by the Gestapo's arrest of Moltke in January 1944. Despite connections among many individuals, it had no part to play on the TWENTIETH OF JULY, 1944.

B.-J. W.

Kreutzberg, Harald, b. Reichenberg (Bohemia), December 11, 1902; d. Gümlingen bei Bern, April 23, 1968, Austrian dancer and choreographer. Originally a fashion illustrator and graphic artist, Kreutzberg studied dancing with Mary WIGMAN. He worked in Hannover as a solo dancer and ballet master. He then moved to Berlin, where he caught the attention of Max REINHARDT, leading to tours through Europe and America. Although totally unpolitical, Kreutzberg let himself be celebrated as a representative figure of National Socialist culture during the Third Reich. In 1941 he became an instructor at the State Academy for Dancing Arts in Vienna. After 1955 he operated his own dance school in Bern.

Krieck, Ernst, b. Vögisheim (Baden), July 6, 1882; d. Moosburg/Isar, March 19, 1947, German educator. As a teacher and professor of pedagogy, Krieck developed as early as the Weimar period the principles of "National Socialist educational theory"; in numerous publications he advocated an EDUCATION aimed at "ordering and subordinating" (*Ein- und Unterordnung*) the individual. After being penalized for making NS propaganda speeches in 1931, he worked off and on as an official propagandist and party functionary. His book *Nationale politische Erziehung* (National Political Education; 1932) served for years as the standard theoretical work of NS pedagogy. According to Krieck, the ground for such education had to be prepared "through appropriate race breeding, race cultivation, race selection, race hygiene." In 1933

Ernst Krieck.

Krieck became the first NS rector of a German university (Frankfurt). He later moved to a professorial chair in Heidelberg, where he wrote his principal work, *Völkische-Politische Anthropologie* (1936–1938). This call for education "in the triad of physical training, spiritual guidance, and intellectual culture" led to controversy with notable race theoreticians of the Third Reich. After the end of the war Krieck was dismissed from university service and died in an internment camp.

Krieg; Kriegs-. *See* War; Wartime.

Kristallnacht (Night of Broken Glass; also Reichs-Kristallnacht), official and intentional euphemism for the pogrom against German Jews staged by the NSDAP on November 9–10, 1938; it was legitimized by an attack by a Jew, Herschel GRYNSZPAN, on Ernst vom RATH, legation secretary at the German embassy in Paris. The signal for Kristallnacht was given by an antisemitic harangue that Goebbels delivered at the traditional "comradeship evening" at Munich's Old City Hall on the evening of November 9, after news of the diplomat's death was brought to him and to Hitler. After the speech, the assembled *Gau* leaders and party officials gave appropriate orders to their local offices, which in turn directed the SA and SS, as well as such groups as the Hitler Youth, to destroy Jewish homes and businesses, and to wreck and set fire to scores of synagogues. The population took a limited part in the pogrom, but the official version of the Kristallnacht events emphasized the "spontaneous" and broad participation of the masses. A total of 7,500 businesses were destroyed, 171 synagogues burned down, and 91 Jews murdered; rapes were also not uncommon. Some 26,000 Jews were confined to concentration camps, although most of them were released after a few weeks.

Grynszpan's assassination of vom Rath provided Hitler with a welcome opportunity for his long-planned intensification of anti-Jewish measures. Since the Seizure of Power in 1933 many laws and regulations had been issued with the objective of social ostracism, yet the Jews' economic position had not changed much. After Kristallnacht, a meeting of various ministers and ministry officials was held on November 12, 1938, at the Reich Air Ministry. At the meeting, conducted by that agency's chief, Hermann Göring, important edicts for the complete expulsion of Jews from the economy were discussed (*see* ARYANIZATION). The insurance indemnifi-

Kristallnacht. Burning synagogue in Berlin.

cation due to Jewish businesses for damages caused by the pogrom was estimated to be more than 100 million RM, a sum that was now ordered to be paid over to the German Reich. Moreover, a "contribution" in the amount of 1 billion RM was imposed "upon Jewry as a punishment" for the assassination. Further decrees strengthened the social discrimination against Jews, such as the decree of November 12 forbidding them to visit theaters, cinemas, concerts, and exhibits, and that of November 15, ordering that all Jewish children be expelled from the schools. By a regulation issued on November 29, the heads of the state governments were authorized to decree a "ban against Jews" and in this way to impose curfews and residential limitations on them. Especially significant was the objective, discussed on November 12, of driving Jews into emigration and therefore organizing a "Jewish emigration central office." Accordingly, in February 1939 the Reich Central Office for Jewish Emigration (Reichszentrale für die jüdische Auswanderung) was opened in Berlin under the direction of Security Police chief Reinhard HEYDRICH; the first managing director was Heinrich MÜLLER, division head of the Gestapo. After October 1939 the post was held by Adolf EICHMANN.

H. O.

Kritikaster (criticaster), epithet for incompetent critics that dates back to the German Enlightenment; it was favored by Hitler for his public speeches. It had a National Socialist connotation of grumbler, spoilsport, or grouser.

Krüger, Gerhard, b. Danzig, December 6, 1908, German cultural politician. Krüger joined the OBERLAND free corps in 1926 and the NSDAP in 1928. A student of history, he headed the German Students' Union from 1931 to 1933. In 1936 he became director of the OFFICIAL PARTY REVIEW COMMISSION FOR SAFEGUARDING NATIONAL SOCIALIST WRITING. A recipient of the Golden Party Badge, Krüger took a post in the Foreign Ministry as legation councillor in the "Germany" section in 1937. In 1941 he was assigned to the German embassy in Paris as a cultural attaché under Otto ABETZ. Discharged for the attempted rape of a secretary, he tried unsuccessfully to secure a teaching position at the "Reich University" in Strasbourg; he then joined the Wehrmacht. His publications, among them *Student und Revolution* (1934) and *Adolf Hitler* (1938), contributed to his postwar classification as an "offender." In the 1950s Krüger

Kritikaster. Poster announcing a National Socialist meeting: "Mass Demonstration against Defeatists and Criticasters."

was active in the neo-Nazi Socialist Reich Party (SRP), which was later banned, and in the radical right-wing German Reich Party.

Krupp Trial (Krupp-Prozess), proceedings of United States Military Court III in 1947–1948 in Nuremberg against Alfried KRUPP VON BOHLEN UND HALBACH and 19 high-level executives of the Krupp firm, on the charges of crimes against peace and crimes against humanity (Case 10). The accused were charged with having planned and carried out a war of aggression, having plundered the occupied countries for property and resources, and having enslaved citizens of those lands.

In contrast with the other NUREMBERG TRIALS, the Krupp Trial was filled with tension: at one point, all the defense attorneys left the courtroom temporarily in protest and were sentenced to jail for contempt of court; one of the attorneys was even excluded from further participation in the trial. Moreover, the accused refused to testify before the court as witnesses in their own case. Having been aquitted of the charge of planning or perpetrating a war of aggression, as well as of other charges, the defendants were sentenced on July 31, 1948, to prison terms ranging from 2 years and 10 months to 12 years (Krupp himself). In addition, the confiscation of Krupp's assets was ordered. One defendant was totally acquitted. Through a pardon granted by United States High Commissioner John J. McCloy on January 31, 1951, all those sentenced who had not yet finished their prison terms were released, and the confiscation of Krupp's assets was rescinded.

A. St.

Krupp von Bohlen und Halbach, Alfried, b. Villa Hügel bei Essen, August 13, 1907; d. Essen, July 30, 1967, German industrialist. The eldest son of Krupp chairman Gustav KRUPP, Alfried Krupp was admitted on October 1, 1938, to the company's board of directors as his father's designated successor. After the conversion of Friedrich Krupp, Inc., into a private concern in December 1943, Krupp was sole owner of the company. At that point, the command economy was so far advanced, especially in the armaments sector, to which Krupp had become heavily committed, that there was scarcely any role for independent entrepreneurial decisions. Krupp was automatically arrested as the Americans invaded Germany. On July 31, 1948, an American military court sentenced him to 12 years' imprisonment and ordered confiscation of

Alfried Krupp von Bohlen und Halbach.

Gustav Krupp von Bohlen und Halbach.

his assets for crimes against humanity (employment of ALIEN WORKERS and prisoners of war) and for plundering economic assets from occupied countries. The Krupp Works, already extensively damaged by the war, was largely restructured through dismantling and divestiture. Amnestied on May 31, 1951, Krupp was able to reassume direction of his firm in 1953, after making a solemn statement that he would never again produce armaments.

Ba.

Krupp von Bohlen und Halbach, Gustav, b. The Hague, August 7, 1870; d. Blühnbach bei Salzburg (Austria), January 16, 1950, German industrialist. Married to Bertha Krupp, sole heiress of Friedrich Krupp, Inc., Gustav joined the management of the family firm in 1906, becoming its chairman in 1909. From 1921 to 1933 he was a member of the Prussian State Council, and after 1931, chairman of the Reich Association of German Industry. Krupp served as a trustee of the ADOLF HITLER DONATION of German businessmen and put his company in the service of National Socialist REARMAMENT as a "weapon smith." In turn, he received the highest honors from Hitler: his company was held up as a "NS model workplace," and he himself was named MILITARY ECONOMY FÜHRER in 1937 and awarded the Golden Party Badge in 1940. In late 1943, Gustav Krupp handed over direction of the company to his son Alfried KRUPP VON BOHLEN UND HALBACH. The elder Krupp was accused of being a principal war criminal before the International Military Tribunal in Nurem-

berg (for preparing a war of aggression), but the charges were dropped because of his inability to stand trial. In the KRUPP TRIAL of 1947–1948, which dealt with the plundering of economic assets from occupied countries, Krupp was again found to be incapable of facing charges. His son Alfried stood accused in his stead.

Ba.

Kube, Wilhelm, b. Glogau, November 13, 1887; d. Minsk (USSR), September 22, 1943, German politician. After studies in history and law, Kube worked in journalism. First active in *völkisch* and antisemitic groups and parties, in 1919 he joined the German National People's Party (DNVP). He founded a DNVP "Bismarck Youth" group, but soon came into conflict with the party for personal reasons and left it in 1923. After several interim stays with other nationalist organizations, in 1924 Kube entered the Reichstag for the National Socialist Freedom Party. In 1928 he switched over to the NSDAP and became its delegation leader in the Prussian legislature. Under his aegis the NSDAP grew from 6 deputies to a total of 162 in April 1932, harried the other parties with meeting-hall brawls, and by means of street terror incited the PRUSSIAN COUP.

In 1932 Kube brought into being the faith movement known as the GERMAN CHRISTIANS as a National Socialist fifth column in the Evangelical Church. In 1933 he became *Gauleiter* of the Ostmark (Frankfurt an der Oder) and governor of Brandenburg. His career came to a temporary end in 1936 when it was discovered that he was

Wilhelm Kube.

the author of an anonymous letter in which "Party Arbitrator" Walter BUCH, Martin Bormann's father-in-law, was accused of being married to a half Jew. Kube lost all his offices, but retained his *Gauleiter* title. He was reactivated on July 17, 1941, as general commissioner for White Ruthenia, with his headquarters in Minsk. A rabid antisemite, Kube experienced there the SS atrocities of the FINAL SOLUTION and began, especially when German Jews were being shot, a vain struggle against the murder operation ("unworthy of a German"). He attempted to rescue Jews by employing them in a horse-cart factory he had established, thus earning the reputation of being "in Jewish bondage." His efforts to conduct moderate occupation policies among the White Russian population ran afoul of Stalin, who feared the effects of a mitigated image of the German enemy. Kube was killed by a Soviet partisan disguised as a housemaid.

Kuckhoff, Adam, b. Aachen, August 30, 1887; d. Berlin-Plötzensee, August 5, 1943 (executed), German writer and actor. After his studies, Kuckhoff was a freelance author and poet, the editor of the religious and nationalist periodical *Die Tat* (The Deed), and a playwright and director at the Berlin Schauspielhaus. In his major work, the society novel *Der Deutsche von Bayencourt* (The German of Bayencourt; 1937), Kuckhoff called for international understanding and the dismantling of nationalism. After 1933 the middle-class intellectual developed into a fervent antifascist. He joined the opposition group associated with Harro SCHULZE-BOYSEN and

Arvid HARNACK (*see* RED ORCHESTRA), for which he wrote appeals, flyers, and material in illegal periodicals. In 1942 he was arrested by the Gestapo and executed for "high treason."

Kugelerlass. *See* Bullet Decree.

Kulmhof (Pol., Chełmno), National Socialist extermination camp in the Reichsgau WARTHELAND. In Kulmhof, a small village near Łódź (Litzmannstadt), an extermination camp was built in October and November 1941 as part of the FINAL SOLUTION. It was planned to absorb Jews removed from the cities and towns of the Warthegau and assembled in the Łódź ghetto. The camp had two parts: a manor house, out of which exterminations took place, and, a few kilometers away, the "forest camp," where corpses were buried in mass graves. Kulmhof was set up and operated by a Special Commando (SK; *see* SPECIAL COMMANDOS) headed by SS-Hauptsturmführer Herbert LANGE, who in 1940 had already directed the murders of mentally ill people in Soldau, East Prussia. The SK had three units: transport, manor house, and forest commandos. The murder of Jews began in December 1941 in two and sometimes three GAS VANS.

The transport commando brought the victims in trucks to the manor house, where they were told they had come to be shipped to the Reich for labor duty: first they were to bathe and have their clothing disinfected. After they had undressed and surrendered their valuables, Polish workers led them into the cellar and from there through a side exit into a waiting gas van. The van's doors were shut and the motor turned on; a hose carried exhaust gases into the van's interior. The victims were dead after about 10 minutes. The truck driver then drove to the forest camp, which police guards secured on all sides. Jewish workers, their feet bound by chains and their own extermination only temporarily delayed, unloaded the corpses and threw them into the waiting graves. The workers cleaned out the van's interior, and the gas van proceeded back to the manor house to pick up more victims. The runs were continued in this way until all the Jews held in Kulmhof that day were killed and deposited in the mass graves in the forest camp.

In the summer of 1942 the EXHUMATION OPERATION began and a switch was made to burning the corpses. At the end of March 1943, Kulmhof was shut down. SK members blew up the manor house and shot the Jewish workers. The SK, which meanwhile had come under the command of SS-Hauptsturmführer Hans BOTH-MANN, was transferred to the "Prinz Eugen" Waffen-SS division in Yugoslavia.

In April 1944 Bothmann and his men were sent back to reactivate the camp. Utilizing the cellar, left undamaged by the demolition, and building some wooden barracks in the court of the manor house and in the forest camp, they began the gassings anew. This time the bodies were burned in an oven in the forest camp by Jewish workers. In August 1944 preparations to shut down the camp began again. As Soviet troops drew nearer, the definitive stoppage order was given. Before the SK withdrew they killed the Jewish workers, despite strong resistance from the latter. In the camp's first period, at least 145,000 Jews were killed; in the second, at least 7,176. According to Polish sources, some 300,000 people were exterminated at Kulmhof.

A. St.

Külz, Wilhelm, b. Borna bei Leipzig, February 18, 1875; d. Berlin, April 10, 1948, German politician. Külz studied law; from 1904 to 1912 he was mayor of Bückeburg. In 1907–1908 he served as Reich commissioner for local administration in German Southwest Africa, and from 1912 he was lord mayor of Zittau. From 1920 to 1933 he was Reichstag deputy for the German Democratic Party. Lord mayor of Dresden from 1931, Külz was removed from office by National Socialist Reich commissioner Manfred von KILLINGER for refusing to raise the NS flag over the city hall.

Kun, Béla, b. Szilágycseh (Hungary), February 20, 1886; d. Moscow, August 29, 1938 (executed), Hungarian politician. Captured by Russian troops in the First World War, Kun became a Bolshevik. On returning home, he organized a Hungarian Communist party. As People's Commissar for foreign affairs, he was strongman of the short-lived soviet republic (March 21–August 1, 1919), whose bloody rule decisively encouraged the fear of BOLSHEVISM in central and western Europe. Kun emigrated via Austria to the Soviet Union, where he fell victim to Stalin's purges.

Kundt, Ernst, b. Böhmisch-Leipa, April 15, 1897; d. Prague-Pankraz, February 15, 1947, German politician. After studying law and national economy, in 1922 Kundt organized and led the Sudeten German youth movement. In 1935 he joined the Sudeten German Home

Front, and in 1935, with Konrad HENLEIN, founded the SUDETEN GERMAN PARTY. In April 1939 Kundt was accepted into the NSDAP; he soon became a Reichstag deputy. After the invasion of Poland, he became city commissioner in Tarnów in September 1939, then the district (*Kreis*) captain in early 1940; in August 1941 he was made governor of the Radom region. Kundt returned to Carlsbad in January 1945, and was arrested in May. A Prague court sentenced him to death three months later; President Edvard Beneš had the sentence carried out the same day.

Kursell, Otto von, b. Saint Petersburg, November 28, 1884; d. Munich, August 30, 1967, German painter and graphic artist. Kursell joined the NSDAP in 1922; after the party's refounding (1925) he renewed his membership in 1932 as honorary member no. 93. In 1933 Kursell, who attacked the Weimar Republic with caricatures and who painted portraits of leading National Socialists, was named a professor at the Berlin Academy of Fine Arts, where he was director in 1944 and 1945.

Otto von Kursell.

Kursk, city in central Russia situated near the site of the largest tank battle in the RUSSIAN CAMPAIGN (July 5–15, 1943). Germany's failure to gain a victory ended its military initiative in the east.

KZ, most common acronym of Konzentrationslager (*see* CONCENTRATION CAMPS); the official acronym was KL.

L

Laban, Rudolf von, b. Pressburg, December 15, 1879; d. Weybridge (England), July 1, 1958, German-Hungarian dance pedagogue and choreographer. Laban studied in Paris. He developed a movement notation (kinetography), the so-called Laban notation, and founded dance schools (including one in Munich in 1910). Laban's ideological view of dance made itself evident as early as 1913, when he established a dance colony with an anticivilization philosophy at Monte Verità, near Ascona (Switzerland). He set forth his "choreosophy," a sort of dance religion, in his apologia, *Die Welt des Tänzers* (The Dancer's World; 1920), written in "thought roundelays." With his "movement choruses" (*Bewegungschören*), Laban gave new life to the amateur dance movement and became the chief ideologue of expressive and group dancing.

As director of the ballet at the Berlin State Opera, Laban demanded the complete withdrawal of the individual in the "we-dance" (*Wir-Tanz*). He agitated against the "racially alien customary motions" in the dances popular at that time, which were said to promote a "rhythm-weary breed." In 1934 he organized the German Dance Festival; he also played a crucial role in the preparation and direction of the gigantic dance productions at the 1936 Olympic Games. Once again he affirmed the "genius of our race, of our blood," before he recognized the shameful misuse of his ideas in National Socialist regimentation and enforcement of uniformity, which smothered any sought-for artistic freedom. In 1938 Laban emigrated to England, where in 1942 he founded the Art of Movement Studio in Manchester.

Labor. *See* Work.

Labor army (*Arbeitsheer*), in military usage, a collective term for the uniformed members of the REICH LABOR SERVICE. When Konstantin HIERL coined the term (in a speech of March 28, 1935), he may not have been aware that it had already been used by Theodor HERZL (in 1895 diary notes on planning for the later Jewish state, published in 1922).

Labor Chamber (*Arbeitskammer*), advisory body from the economy and politics that was supposed to convey "initiatives and requests from the real world of the workplace to the political leadership." Twenty-six Labor Chambers were organized under the umbrella of a Reich Labor Chamber in the Office for Social Self-Sufficiency (Amt Soziale Selbstverantwortung) of the GERMAN LABOR FRONT. The predominance of party representatives in the chambers led to a reversal of the initial direction: the "requests" of the political leadership were increasingly dictated to the workplaces.

Labor Committees (*Arbeitsausschüsse*), advisory bodies organized by trade and region within the GERMAN LABOR FRONT. They were supposed to discuss problems of an economic and sociopolitical nature that went beyond the workplace, and thus aid the TRUSTEES OF LABOR in their decisions. The committees' membership consisted in equal numbers of managers and employees.

Labor Community of the Northwest (*Arbeitsgemeinschaft Nordwest*) of the NSDAP, *Kreis* (district) founded by the north and west German *Gau* leaders on September 10–11, 1925, after the re-establishment of the party. Its statutes were dated October 9, and its general secretary was Joseph Goebbels. It was initiated by the social-revolutionary group around the STRASSER brothers; Hitler ordered its dissolution at the BAMBERG FÜHRER CONFERENCE of the NSDAP on February 14, 1926.

Labor Comrade (*Arbeitskamarad*), Germanization of the word *Kollege* (colleague) with military overtones, as favored in National Socialist usage for terms from the world of work (Labor Front, labor army, labor battle, and so on).

Labor Congress (*Arbeitskongress*), yearly meeting of the GERMAN LABOR FRONT (DAF), which was founded on May 10, 1933, at the first Labor Congress. The site for the meeting, Leipzig, was named the "Nuremberg of the DAF" because of the similarity to the ceremonial displays at the party congresses held there.

Labor deployment (*Arbeitseinsatz*), incursions by the state into the labor market to end UNEMPLOYMENT and for the earmarking and "steering" (*Lenkung*) of workers. Labor deployment measures nullified the liberal foundations of labor law. They can be roughly divided into three phases:

1. Measures related to WORK CREATION to reduce the supply of workers, addressed particularly to the young and to women (*see* MARRIAGE LOANS); in addition, complementary regulations against flight from the countryside, in order to relieve the large cities and industrial centers (Law to Regulate Labor Deployment, May 15, 1934).
2. Limitations on the mobility of workers through labor law regulations of the FOUR-YEAR PLAN, which was in effect after 1935. In this way, despite the growing need for labor power, the armaments industry, in particular, would be assured skilled workers, and the government's wage policy would be supported. Here the EMPLOYMENT BOOK aided in the comprehensive supervision of labor deployment.
3. Further restrictions of mobility for all workers after 1939, and the introduction of possibilities for government conscription (Compulsory Service Decree, February 13, 1939).

Restrictions became more severe during the war through further decrees that required the fulfillment of service and of emergency service, such as the introduction of a general registration obligation (1943). Special conditions obtained for "ethnic alien" workers and prisoners of war. In 1942 the regulation of labor power was transferred to General Plenipotentiary for Labor Deployment Fritz SAUCKEL.

B. W.

Labor Front (*Arbeitsfront*), term devised in keeping with the militarization of language, and used initially for economic functions in general; National Socialist propaganda then applied it to the organization of employees and employers that supplanted the destroyed trade unions—the GERMAN LABOR FRONT.

Labor martyr (*Arbeitsopfer*), term for victims of industrial accidents; it paralleled the term "war martyr" (*Kriegsopfer*), in keeping with the militarization of language and the world of work. Thus work was equated with military service, in fact with compulsory military service.

Labor passport (*Arbeitspass*), certificate of completion of the REICH LABOR SERVICE, a precondition for employment in government service or in the economy.

Labor Regulation Law (*Arbeitsordnungsgesetz*), short designation for the Law to Regulate National Labor of January 20, 1934, the basis of National Socialist labor law. The Labor Regulation Law was intended to achieve an alignment of economic life in keeping with the FÜHRER PRINCIPLE; it defined work as "service to the entirety of the *Volk*." An employer, called a WORKPLACE FÜHRER (*Betriebsführer*), and employees, called the FOLLOWERSHIP (*Gefolgschaft*), were to be connected in a relationship of mutual concern and loyalty (*Fürsorge-Treue-Verhältnis*). To prevent the possibility of democratic cooperation, in operations with over 20 employees a "mutual trust council" (*Vertrauensrat*) was installed, to which belonged the employer and the "mutual trust delegates" (*Vertrauensmänner*) named by him in consultation with functionaries of the GERMAN LABOR FRONT (DAF).

Government TRUSTEES OF LABOR supervised the "workplace regulations" (*Betriebsordnungen*) that were to be issued; they were responsible for "wage regulations" (*Tarifordnungen*); were to be informed regarding terminations, in particular mass layoffs; and in case of conflicts represented the "motion" (*Antrag*; that is, the charge) before the honor courts proposed in the law. This strong position of the trustees made the Labor Regulation Law an effective government instrument for "steering" the economy.

Labor unions. *See* General German Trade Union Federation; Trade unions; Workers' movement.

Lagarde, Paul de (until 1854, Paul de Bötticher), b. Berlin, November 2, 1827; d. Göttingen, December 22, 1891, German orientalist and culture critic. A student of Evangelical theology and philology (his teachers included Jacob Grimm), Lagarde applied critical methods to biblical texts. He first taught in a *Gymnasium* (advanced secondary school), then in 1869 became a professor of oriental languages in Göttingen. In addition to his importance as a scholar,

Paul de Lagarde.

Lagarde became known for essays that expressed a critique of culture, specifically, a polemical analysis of contemporary "symptoms of decline." (They included *Deutsche Schriften* [German Writings]; 1876–1881.)

Lagarde criticized the growing nationalism of his age, demanded a clear division between church and state, opposed the moral decay he thought was caused by industrialization and the unbridled profit seeking of capitalism, rejected moral relativism, and agitated for his nation's renewed role as an "ethical power." His views included a religious and *völkisch* antisemitism, which identified the Jews as foreign bodies obstructing the union of the German people. The National Socialists took up these ideas, as well as Lagarde's massive critique of civilization (*see* Alfred ROSENBERG). They also saw certain of his plans for the mass resettlement of Jews as anticipations of their own ideas for expulsion (*see* MADAGASCAR PLAN). These falsifying interpretations brought Lagarde's ideas close to a boundary between a traditional and a more "modern" racial antisemitism, and made him the "most powerful harbinger of the ideas upon which the German National Socialist Third Reich rests" (Karl August Fischer, Lagarde's editor, 1934).

Lambach, Walther, b. Gummersbach, May 28, 1885; d. Mainz, January 30, 1943, German politician and businessman. In 1914 Lambach became editor of the *Deutsche Handelswacht* (German Business Watch) in Hamburg. In 1919 he became general secretary of the GERMAN NA-

TIONAL SHOP ASSISTANTS' ASSOCIATION (DHV). From 1920 to 1929 he was a Reichstag deputy. As editor of the publication *Politischer Praxis* (Political Practice), Lambach proposed his own "equal-opportunity work for society" (*gleichberechtigte Gesellschaftsarbeit*) and "social working community" as ideal alternatives to both capitalism and socialism. When his attempts to open the German National People's Party (DNVP) to republicanism failed, he founded the Conservative People's Party (Konservative Volkspartei) on July 18, 1930. Allied with the CHRISTIAN-SOCIAL PEOPLE'S SERVICE, it won 18 Reichstag seats in 1930 and 3 in 1932. Lambach was without political influence in the Third Reich, and his DHV was disbanded with the trade unions in 1933.

Lammers, Hans Heinrich, b. Lublinitz (Upper Silesia), May 27, 1879; d. Düsseldorf, January 4, 1962, German politician and jurist. In 1912 Lammers became a rural judge (*Landrichter*) in Beuthen. A volunteer in the First World War, in 1922 he became a ministerial councillor (*Ministerialrat*) in the Interior Ministry. As a national conservative bureaucrat, Lammers joined the German National People's Party (DNVP) and opposed the Weimar Republic both politically and journalistically, while outwardly correctly fulfilling his official duties.

Lammers moved over to the NSDAP in 1932. At Hitler's takeover of power on January 30, 1933, he became head of the Reich Chancellery with the rank of state secretary, a position he held until 1945 (after November 26, 1937, as minister without portfolio). His duties included framing legislative bills, overseeing personnel

Hans Heinrich Lammers.

matters for the ministerial bureaucracy, coordinating the ministries, and briefing Hitler on current government affairs. He thus had considerable influence—above all as "the Reich's notary" (Albert Speer)—on the legal consolidation of the police state and on the decision-making processes within the government, all of which gave him access to Hitler. Once the war began, however, and even more after Martin BORMANN's nomination to the leadership of the Party Chancellery (May 1941), Lammers lost his key role as military considerations assumed paramount importance. Shortly before the end of the war he supported Göring's intention to succeed Hitler, and was arrested in Berchtesgaden on April 23, 1945, on Bormann's radioed order; he escaped being shot only because he was taken prisoner by the Americans. During the WILHELMSTRASSE TRIAL Lammers was condemned on April 11, 1949, to 20 years' imprisonment. A pardon reduced the sentence to 10 years in 1951, and on December 16, 1954, he was declared to have served his sentence and was released from the prison in Landsberg am Lech.

Lampert, Carl, b. Göfis bei Feldkirch, January 9, 1894; d. Halle Penitentiary, November 13, 1944 (executed), Austrian Catholic theologian. In 1930 Lampert took part in the curial tribunal in Rome; in 1938 he returned to Innsbruck with the apostolic administration. Lampert resolutely resisted the National Socialist encroachment upon church life. After many warnings, he spent a year at Dachau because of a memorial address he gave for a fellow priest who had died in a concentration camp. Following his release he was exiled to Stettin, where he ministered in particular to forced laborers and soldiers. A discussion circle he led raised the suspicions of the Gestapo. Material against Lampert procured through an informer led to his imprisonment in February 1943. After months in chains and a farcical trial before a court-martial, he was sentenced to death for "jeopardizing the military" and "aiding and abetting the enemy."

Länder, term in the Weimar Constitution for the constituent states of the German Reich, which had their own constitutions, parliaments, and governments; the REICHSRAT (National Council) represented their interests on the federal level. The *Länder* became the first victims of National Socialist SYNCHRONIZATION, and lost all sovereign rights with the dissolution of the Reichsrat on February 14, 1934.

Landsberg, Otto, b. Rybnik (Upper Silesia), December 4, 1869; d. Baarn, near Utrecht, December 9, 1957, German politician and jurist. From 1903 to 1909, Landsberg was a Social Democratic member of the city council in Magdeburg; from 1912 to 1918 he represented the SPD (Social Democratic Party) in the Reichstag. As a right-wing socialist, he was appointed to the Council of People's Deputies in November 1918. Made Reich justice minister in 1919, he resigned in protest against the Versailles treaty. From 1920 to 1924 he served as ambassador in Brussels, and subsequently was again a Reichstag deputy, until 1933. Landsberg defended his friend Friedrich EBERT in the 1924 Magdeburg trial, in which the former president was accused by the Reich of treason for supporting a strike by munitions workers in 1918. He also appeared as a witness in 1925 in proceedings involving the STAB-IN-THE-BACK LEGEND. After the National Socialist takeover he went into exile in the Netherlands, where he lived in hiding after the German occupation of 1940 to 1945. Landsberg never returned to Germany.

Landsberg am Lech, Upper Bavarian city with some 8,200 inhabitants in 1933. In the former Landsberg castle (fortress), converted into a prison, Hitler and other National Socialists sentenced on April 1, 1924, during the HITLER TRIAL, served their sentences. Hitler's cell, in the so-called generals' wing, which he inhabited until his early release on December 20, 1924, became a shrine during the Third Reich, as well as the destination of the ADOLF HITLER MARCH

Hitler during his imprisonment in Landsberg am Lech.

Landsberg am Lech. Execution of German war criminals in the prison courtyard.

OF GERMAN YOUTH. After the Second World War, the American authorities held Germans accused or found guilty of war crimes at Landsberg; death sentences were also carried out there.

Langbehn, Julius, b. Hadersleben (North Schleswig), March 26, 1851; d. Rosenheim, April 30, 1907, German culture critic and writer. Langbehn studied philology, natural sciences, and the history of art. In 1890, after a trip to Holland, he published anonymously the book *Rembrandt als Erzieher. Von einem Deutschen* (Rembrandt as Teacher: By a German). After his authorship became known, this book won him

Julius Langbehn.

the epithet "the Rembrandt German"; it went through 40 editions in two years. In it Langbehn criticized the "materialist, mechanistic" spirit of the age, called for a return to German simplicity ("What the Germans need is need"), and offered Rembrandt, "the painter of truth and naturalness," as a model.

The demand for a stronger link between modern man and "the sod" had a particular impact on the National Socialist worldview, especially through the YOUTH MOVEMENT. While Langbehn's book was widely read during the Third Reich (85 editions by 1936), and works such as *Dürer als Führer* (Dürer as Leader; published posthumously in 1928) found success, the author's attraction to Catholicism (he became a convert in 1900) was criticized as a backsliding away from the "heroic."

Lange, Herbert, b. Menzlin (Pomerania), September 29, 1909; d. Berlin, April 20, 1945, SS-*Sturmbannführer* (October 1, 1944). Lange studied law (but earned no degree). He joined the NSDAP (May 1, 1932), SA (August 1932), and SS (March 1, 1933). Lange entered the police force, and became a deputy commissioner in May 1935. As an SS-*Untersturmführer* (from November 9, 1939) and criminal commissioner, he was stationed in Poland; after promotion to SS-*Obersturmführer* (April 20, 1940) his posts included that of commandant of the KULMHOF extermination camp (Special Commando Lange). Early in 1942 Lange was transferred to the REICH SECURITY MAIN OFFICE, where his work as criminal investigator (*Kriminalrat*) involved, among other cases, the assassination attempt against

Hitler of July 20, 1944. Promoted in recognition of his work, Lange died in battle-torn Berlin.

Langemarck Ceremonies (*Langemarckfeiern*), commemorative celebrations in the Third Reich organized by students and the Hitler Youth. Even before 1933, the Belgian region of Langemarck had become a "symbol of German love of homeland and a willingness to risk even death for it," because it was here, during the First World War, that a regiment of young Germans, the German national anthem on their lips, had stormed an enemy position with heavy losses on October 22–23, 1914. In 1934, on the 20th anniversary of this event, a "Langemarck Bureau" (Referat Langemarck) was established at the Reich Youth Leadership. It was concerned with "honoring heroes" and "assuming . . . the heritage of the frontline soldiers," since "fulfilling duties on the model" of Langemarck—"service to an idea that is greater than ourselves" (Baldur von SCHIRACH)—was needed from German youth for the impending war.

Langemarck Curriculum (*Langemarckstudium*), "preparatory institutes" named for the place in Flanders where in 1914 a regiment composed largely of student volunteers met their death. First in Königsberg and Heidelberg, the Reich Student Leadership set up such courses to prepare politically deserving, gifted but needy young men between the ages of 17 and 24 who had completed their basic vocational education. By order of the Reich Education Ministry, after 1938 the scope was enlarged to encompass a one-and-a-half-year preparation for the exam for gifted students (*Begabtenprüfung*). This exam, which could be taken outside of the Langemarck program as well, led to university admission for a specific area of study.

During 1939 only 10 students gained admission in this way, but by 1942, 10 university towns offered such courses of instruction, which were intended to effectuate study connected to one's occupation, especially in technical and agricultural fields. Careers in teaching and medicine were also encouraged. Candidates were to be nominated for the "selective camp" (*Ausleselager*) by high functionaries ("sovereignty bearers" [*Hoheitsträger*]) in trade schools, workplaces, and National Socialist organizations, especially in the Reich Labor Service. An edict of April 2, 1942, gave the Langemarck Curriculum the standing of a "selective school" (*Ausleseschule*), thereby establishing a second instructional path.

H. S.

Lanz, Josef (religious name, Georg; nom de plume, Jörg Lanz von Liebenfels), b. Vienna, July 19, 1874; d. there, April 22, 1954, Austrian racial ideologue. In 1893 Lanz entered the Cistercian order. The next year he experienced an "illumination," which in a flash revealed to him that the world was ruled by the opposition between "blue[-eyed]-blond Aryans" and the "inferior race stock" (*Niederrassentum*), which resulted from miscegenation. In 1899 he left the cloister and founded his own "Order of the New Temple," which devoted itself wholly to the struggle for the separation of races and "blue-blond pure breeding."

Illustrations from Josef Lanz's Ostara pamphlets: "Are you blond? Are you a man? Then read the Ostara Library for Blonds and Advocates of Men's Rights!" "Backside shapes: A. the inferior race; B. the superior race."

Josef Lanz.

Lanz bought Castle Werfenstein and designed as the symbol of his growing sect a flag with a red swastika and blue lilies against a golden background. Beginning in 1905 he published OSTARA, a journal series containing variations on his one theme. He had outlined it in 1904, in the tract *Theozoologie oder die Kunde von dem Sodoms-Äfflinge und dem Götter-Elektron* (Theozoology, or the Lore of Sodom's Apes and the Gods' Electron). In this work he sketched out notions of enslaving the "inferior races" that later reappeared in the National Socialist master-race thesis.

Hitler visited Lanz in 1909 because he was missing some Ostara installments, but the role of Lanz's ideas in Hitler's ideology is nonetheless disputed. The ban on Lanz's writings after the Anschluss in 1938 might have been Hitler's attempt to distance himself from the adulatory trappings surrounding the ex-monk. It might also have reflected Hitler's intent to suppress outside elements in his own view of life.

Larenz, Karl, b. Wesel, April 23, 1903, German jurist. Larenz became a university lecturer in Göttingen in 1929, and a professor in Kiel in 1933. After that law faculty had been politically and racially "cleansed," he obtained the post of the philosopher Edmund Husserl. Larenz belonged to the group of militant National Socialists within the legal profession. An adherent of the particularly involved (in the National Socialist sense) "Kiel School," he had considerable influence on the education of jurists and the interpretation of law, and thus indirectly on the courts.

After 1945 Larenz was permitted to retain his chair in the reopened law school in Kiel. In 1960 he accepted a chair for civil law, civil rights, and the philosophy of law at the University of Munich. The lucidity of his post-1945 writings on civil law made them popular as references and textbooks.

C. B.

La Risiera, internment camp southeast of Trieste; it was taken over by German authorities after Italy's capitulation in early September 1943. On October 9, 1943, 3,000 Italian soldiers captured in Dalmatia and Istria were shot in La Risiera; 620 of some 2,000 Jewish residents of Trieste were also murdered.

Lateran Treaties, collective term for three accords concluded in the papal Lateran Palace between Benito Mussolini and secretary of state Cardinal Pietro Gasparri for the Holy See (*see* VATICAN) on February 11, 1929. The first, actual Lateran Treaty (*trattato*) stipulated: recognition of the Holy See's exclusive power over the new, sovereign, and neutral "State of the Vatican City" (Stato della Città del Vaticano), with the pope as head of state and of the Holy See's ownership of churches and palaces in Italian territory (Article 3); and a definitive settlement of the "Roman question," which had been simmering since the new Italian state annexed Rome as its capital in 1870 (Article 26).

The second, financial accord (as Codicil IV, an integral part of the first treaty) stipulated a one-time payment of 1.75 billion lire to the Holy See to compensate it for losses incurred through annexation of church land by the Italian state between 1860 and 1870. The third accord (officially, concordat [*concordato*]) normalized relations between the Italian state and the Roman Catholic church and acknowledged Roman Catholicism as the state religion, with such guarantees as the free exercise of spiritual authority, state protection of church marriage, and the exemption of ordained clerics from military service.

The Lateran accords bolstered the standing and political stability of Mussolini and Fascism within the Catholic world and served as the model for the 1933 CONCORDAT with National Socialist Germany. The treaties were adopted by the Constitutional Assembly into the Constitution of the Italian Republic (Article 7) in 1947.

Latvia (Ger., Lettland), republic on the Baltic Sea, one of the Baltic states; area, 65,800 sq km (about 25,000 sq miles); population, 1.95 million (1935); the capital is Riga. Founded on November 18, 1918, Latvia held out in protracted battles with the Red Army. It expropriated its Baltic-German landed estates, but retained a German minority of some 65,000. In 1934 a coup established an authoritarian regime under Karlis Ulmanis. On May 7, 1939, Latvia concluded a nonaggression pact with Germany for 10 years. It was then effectively nullified by the GERMAN-SOVIET NONAGGRESSION PACT of August 23, 1939, in which Hitler handed the country over to Stalin. The BALTIC GERMANS were resettled in the German Reich.

The Soviet Union annexed Latvia on June 17, 1940. In June 1941, German troops marched in, and the country was joined to the Reich Commissariat OSTLAND as a "General Commissariat." Many Latvians joined the Waffen-SS as volunteers in the Russian Campaign, notably the Fifteenth and Nineteenth SS Waffen Grenadier Divisions. Their hopes that Germany would in return grant national independence were not fulfilled. In the autumn of 1944, Latvia was again occupied by Soviet troops (Riga, on October 13). It then became a Soviet republic within the USSR.

Laue, Max von, b. Pfaffendorf bei Koblenz, October 9, 1879; d. Berlin, April 24, 1960, German physicist. As a professor in Berlin (1919–1943) and as acting director of the Kaiser Wilhelm Institute for Physics (1921–1945), Laue was among the most important German physicists who did not emigrate in 1933. Internationally recognized for his fundamental work in the field of X rays, for which he received a Nobel prize in 1914, he could risk protesting the expulsion of Albert Einstein and other Jewish scientists. He also opposed the National Socialist rejection of the Theory of Relativity as a "worldwide Jewish hoax." As a patriot and scientist, Laue put his work at the disposal of the National Socialists, while resisting their ideological stance. One of the few eminent German scientists who preserved his "human face" (Einstein), Laue served as a frequent witness in postwar denazification trials; he also belonged to the group of scientists who in 1957 openly took a stand against arming the Federal Republic with nuclear weapons.

Laval, Pierre, b. Châteldon, June 26, 1883; d. Paris, October 15, 1945 (executed), French politician and jurist. From 1914 to 1919, Laval was a socialist deputy in the National Assembly. Thereafter he represented no party. Between 1925 and 1931 he held various ministerial posts. In 1931–1932 and 1935–1936, he was prime minister in conservative governments. After France's occupation by German troops in 1940, Laval became deputy prime minister (*vice-président du conseil*) of the VICHY government. Thanks to his eminent "talent for intrigue" (G. de Boitier de Sauvigny), he was able to persuade the National Assembly to entrust the elderly Marshal Henri PÉTAIN with plenary powers and to nominate himself as Pétain's

Max von Laue.

Pierre Laval.

successor. After openly championing his own policy of COLLABORATION with the Germans (critics said of him: "Everything about him was black—his suit, his face, his soul"), Laval was again removed from office in December of 1940.

German pressure made Laval prime minister again in April 1942. He was unable to prevent the conscription of French citizens for forced labor. In August 1944 his government was transferred to Belgium, and in September was removed to Germany. Attempts to escape to Spain and Austria miscarried. American troops arrested Laval and handed him over to France in August 1945. He was convicted and sentenced to death as a collaborator in a controversial proceeding.

Law (*Recht*), the regulation of human relationships by means of laws and binding rules. Under National Socialism, law had the intended function of regulating the VOLK COMMUNITY in line with the views of the leading representatives of the government. Law was no longer the means of securing a minimum of personal, political, and economic freedom, or of mediating the interests of individuals who were perceived as autonomous. Nor was it any longer oriented toward the material notions of justice that were within the European tradition of reason and natural law, which until then had been the rule within the European legal realm. In particular, National Socialism denied the applicability of human and civil rights as they had been recognized in the BASIC RIGHTS of European constitutional documents since the end of the 18th century.

The National Socialists rejected all prior notions of justice in order to replace them with the idea of usefulness to the *Volk* as they defined it at the time. Thus, according to earlier and contemporary standards, they clothed overt injustice in the form of justice and law. This was the case, for example, in the abolition of the rights of Jews through the NUREMBERG LAWS, which contradicted the principle of equality, or in the various terroristic judgments of the SPECIAL COURTS and the VOLK COURT, which ignored the principle of a relationship between crime and punishment.

Even when the law under National Socialism did not in this way contradict traditional conceptions of justice—notably in large areas of civil, economic, commercial, and tax law—its practical significance was changed. It no longer guaranteed a freedom of action and claims vis-à-vis the state or third parties; rather, it merely established what one might expect in a normal legal situation. In this area too, National Socialism did not offer a guarantee of law in the traditional sense of a rule of law or constitutionality, because political agencies claimed for themselves the right to realize the political aims they had set for themselves regardless of any formal and substantial restrictions or limitations.

A. v. B.

Law guardians (*Rechtswahrer*), Germanization of the word *Jurist* that began to crop up as early as the beginning of the 20th century. In National Socialist usage it was applied especially to academically educated WORKERS IN THE LAW. The League of National Socialist Jurists was renamed the NATIONAL SOCIALIST LEAGUE OF LAW GUARDIANS on April 15, 1936.

Laws [and legislation] (*Gesetze [und Gesetzgebung]*), legal axioms promulgated by bodies constitutionally authorized for that purpose. National Socialism purposely destroyed existing guarantees of traditional freedom in order to elevate in their place the promotion of the "community" (by National Socialist definition) as a goal of the state. This changed the very meaning of "law": limitations on freedom and property no longer required a legal basis; Paragraph 1 of the REICHSTAG FIRE DECREE of February 28, 1933 (*Reich Law Gazette* [*Reichs-*

Law guardians. National Socialist poster for the German Law Congress in Leipzig.

gesetzblatt; RGBl] I, p. 83), made them "also permissible outside of until-now-distinct legal boundaries." Ever more vague and inclusive stipulations found their way into laws, thereby endlessly expanding the state's opportunity to infringe upon the individual. In penal law the traditional principle of "NULLA POENA SINE LEGE" (no penalty without a law) was annulled, according to which a punishment could be imposed only if an action's liability for punishment had previously been decided by law. According to Paragraph 2 in the *Criminal Law Gazette,* in the formulation of the law of June 28, 1935 (RGBl I, p. 839), "he who commits an act . . . that according to the fundamental idea of a criminal law or the healthy sentiment of the *Volk* deserves punishment" could also be punished.

No orderly procedure existed for the promulgation of laws that—like the public and contentious discussion in a democratic parliament—might have guaranteed a minimum of justice and legality in their content. Important laws were passed by the Reichstag, which the National Socialists had made their own tool. After the ENABLING LAW of March 24, 1933 (RGBl I, p. 141), the Reich government could also enact laws. Further regulations were promulgated by the FÜHRER'S WILL as well as through decrees issued by diverse government offices; their nature as generally binding rules made them legal prescriptions. The *Reich Law Gazette* usually, although not always, published these regulations.

After the dismantling of orderly legislative procedures, blatant injustice was often disguised by means of legislation, as in the case of the NUREMBERG LAWS or that of the Law on State Self-Defense (*Gesetz über Staatsnotwehr*) of July 3, 1934 (RGBl I, p. 529), which legalized murder in connection with the RÖHM AFFAIR. A large number of NS laws can thus be termed "legal injustice" (Gustav Radbruch).

A. v. B.

Laws to Decrease Unemployment (*Gesetze zur Verminderung der Arbeitslosigkeit*), two programs of the Hitler government, dated June 1, 1933, and September 21, 1933, having the goal of WORK CREATION.

Law to Relieve the Distress of Volk and Reich (*Gesetz zur Behebung der Not von Volk und Reich*), official designation of the ENABLING LAW of March 24, 1933.

Lay theater (*Laienspiel*), term introduced in 1912 by Martin LUSERKE for the types of ama-

teur theater developed in the "league" (*bündisch*) YOUTH MOVEMENT. "Unpolished and folksy," its occasional presentations served to develop a sense of community among participants and at the same time were intended to express the "freshness of natural talent." In the Weimar Republic, lay theater as well as light entertainments such as choral performances, mass spectacles, and the "movement games" (*Bewegungsspiele*) that were part of "gymnastic training" were produced chiefly by church-related and political organizations for youth. Even before 1933 a large number of lay theater authors and theorists came close to a *völkisch* and nationalistic ideology. According to Rudolf Mirbt, for example, "Community needs leadership with a calling."

In 1933 lay theater, along with other manifestations of the "league" youth movement, was annexed and organizationally synchronized by the Hitler Youth, while lay theater publishers were taken over by National Socialist publishing houses. Authors such as Max BARTHEL, who before 1933 had written choral plays and agitprop pieces for the workers' youth movement, now wrote *völkisch* "lay plays" for the National Socialists. Under the shared responsibility of the REICH YOUTH LEADERSHIP, the REICH THEATER CHAMBER, and the STRENGTH THROUGH JOY organization, lay actors were trained and apprenticeship certificates and theatrical props were issued. During the war, lay theater served war propaganda (*see* THEATER).

H. H.

League for a German Church (Bund für Deutsche Kirche), *völkisch* Evangelical group founded in 1921 by the Flensburg pastor Friedrich Andersen. It anticipated the theses and demands of the GERMAN CHRISTIANS: elimination of the Jewish Old Testament from the Bible, and the doctrine of a "variety of Christianity in keeping with the German nature in church and school." Going beyond the program of the German Christians, with whom the League later merged, was the demand for an "introduction to the Savior through the use of German fairy tales."

League for the German East (Bund Deutscher Osten), National Socialist organization founded in 1933 for "*Volk*-Nation [*Volkstum*] and borderland work"; its chairman was Theodor OBERLÄNDER. By propagandizing for a settlement policy (in its organ, *Ostland*), the league sought to combat flight from the countryside and to encourage the opening of new agricultural land. Its *völkisch* ideology—"to educate all Germans in borderland politics"—was anti-Slav and expansionist.

League of Agriculturalists (Bund der Landwirte; BdL), party founded in Czechoslovakia in 1919 to represent the interests of Sudeten German farmers. The BdL attempted at first to cooperate with Czech parties, and achieved some influence in 1925 with its 24 parliamentary seats; however, this influence soon declined (by 1935 the BdL had only 5 seats). The movement was swept up in the Great-German tide, and was dissolved in the spring of 1938 in favor of the SUDETEN GERMAN PARTY.

League of Foreign Germans (Bund der Auslandsdeutschen; BdA), organization representing the interests of FOREIGN GERMANS; it was founded on August 18, 1919, in Berlin. The number of such Germans increased considerably owing to postwar cession of territories (*see* VERSAILLES TREATY). The BdA's goals were preservation of the *Volk*-Nation (*Volkstumspflege*) and economic support for Germans abroad who had lost some or all of their property to confiscation. It was able to obtain indemnities of over 500 million RM by 1928. After the Seizure of Power, BdA activity was limited to providing for the approximately 300,000 Germans who had returned to the Reich. Germans living abroad belonged to the "Foreign *Gau*" (Gau Ausland) of the NSDAP FOREIGN ORGANIZATION, or were organized in the ALLIANCE OF GERMAN ORGANIZATIONS ABROAD. The BdA dissolved itself in 1939. Its publication was *Auslandswart* (The Foreign Watchtower; 1919–1936).

League of German Girls (Bund Deutscher MÄDEL [*Mädel* is a folksy colloquialism for *Mädchen*]; BDM), constituent organization of the HITLER YOUTH (HJ), subdivided into a league for younger girls, from 10 to 13 years (the Jungmädelbund); the BDM itself, for girls aged 14 to 17; and, after 1938, special units for girls 17 to 21 years old (*see* FAITH AND BEAUTY). Precursors of the BDM were separate girls' groups with National Socialist tendencies, which had existed since the 1920s and which were absorbed into the HJ as "sisterhoods" in December 1928. In June 1930 the *Völkischer Beobachter* announced their renaming as the "BDM in the HJ." Although official historiography maintained that the BDM continued an uninterrupted development from this point on,

BDM poster: "All 10-year-olds to us."

there were numerous internal party struggles for leadership and programmatic orientation between 1930 and 1933. The conflicts ended only when Gregor STRASSER ruled that all NS girls' groups be part of the BDM. His independent work with young people began with this declaration of a single official party organization for girls.

Because of problems with organization and orientation, which the BDM could not overcome until 1933, no official pressure to join the BDM was exerted until promulgation of the Law concerning the Hitler Youth (1936). Membership steadily increased, nonetheless, for various reasons: part of the membership was simply taken over from "synchronized" groups; other girls joined because their parents considered it opportune. There were also voluntary registrations; in bourgeois circles, in particular, many girls saw the BDM as a way to escape the rigid conventionality of parental homes.

Organizationally, the BDM remained part of the HJ, by and large adopting parallel subdivisions. The smallest unit was the (*Jung-*)*Mädelschaft*, with approximately 10 girls; 10 of these "girlships" formed a troop (*Schar*), 4 troops formed a group (*Gruppe*), 3 to 5 groups a ring (*Ring*), 4 to 6 rings a sub-*Gau* (*Untergau*), and 20 sub-*Gaue* made up an Upper *Gau* (*Obergau*). On a higher level, women "reporters" (*Referentinnen*) represented the interests of the BDM with the REICH YOUTH LEADERSHIP and its bureaus. The BDM's national official (*Reichsreferentin*) had broad jurisdiction, and she directed the organization with almost independent responsibility.

The aim of the BDM's educational program was to make all German girls, from the youngest on up, into proponents of National Socialist ideas. It was not a matter of winning them through arguments for the NS worldview; unconditionally faithful followers were wanted. Obedience, fulfillment of duty, discipline, self-sacrifice, and physical discipline were the virtues required of every BDM girl. Regardless of her role in later life, the future woman must learn to assume and carry out her duties to the VOLK COMMUNITY with joy and without criticism. In order to achieve this goal, two-thirds of the educational program was devoted to sports and one-third to ideological schooling.

Because of organizational difficulties during the initial phase, the BDM leadership first organized a sports program, although in fact this was thoroughly in tune with an ideology that valued the body over the mind. Sports served both discipline and physical fitness. Only girls accustomed to discipline would be suited to taking orders; only healthy, strong women would be able to fulfill their duties and embody the desired racial ideal. Until 1939 the primary task of a BDM girl was clearly defined: to become the mother of children with hereditary health and to rear them as National Socialists. The emphasis in ideological schooling was thus on the transmission of the *völkisch* cultural heritage, and as of 1936, on fitness as a housewife.

After the reintroduction of universal COMPULSORY MILITARY SERVICE (1935), the tasks of the BDM were broadened. Shortages in the labor force after 1936 brought further new demands: female apprentices had to be channeled increasingly into the armaments industries, although the central concern of the BDM remained the education of girls as housewives and mothers. A reorientation took place only when the war began: the BDM went into the war well prepared, and it quickly succeeded in adapting itself to the new political and military situation. The longer the war continued, the more the BDM became an auxiliary organization in the service of the war effort; its original work with young people receded more and more into the background. As a result, problems of discipline accumulated within the organization; many girls found service obligations boring, and rejected such duties. Although only a few girls consciously resisted, many became increasingly, if privately, alienated from the organization.

D. K.

League of German Officers (Bund Deutscher Offiziere; BDO), anti–National Socialist organization founded by 95 German officers in the Lunevo prisoner-of-war camp near Moscow on September 11–12, 1943. By cooperating with the Soviets, they hoped to preserve the German Reich after the anticipated defeat. Under the leadership of Gen. Walther von SEYDLITZ-KURZBACH, and later supported by Field Marshal

BDM members with the recommended braids and brown mountaineering jackets.

Friedrich PAULUS, the BDO used leaflets and radio broadcasts to call on German soldiers to desert and fight Hitler's dictatorship. Neither these appeals nor attempts to influence Soviet policies with regard to Germany had any effect worth mentioning. After the TEHERAN Conference and Soviet acceptance of the Anglo-American demand for UNCONDITIONAL SURRENDER, the BDO's scope of activity became increasingly narrow. Used by Stalin against the western Allies, the organization lost credibility and was dissolved after uniting with the NATIONAL COMMITTEE FOR A FREE GERMANY on November 2, 1945.

League of Nations (Ger., Völkerbund), worldwide international organization of states, established in 1919–1920, with headquarters in Geneva. The League's Charter was accepted on April 28, 1919, by a plenary session of the Paris Peace Conference. As Part I (Articles 1–26), it was incorporated into all the PARIS SUBURBAN TREATIES and took effect with ratification of the VERSAILLES TREATY on January 10, 1920. United States president Woodrow Wilson initiated the League by calling for such an establishment in the last of his FOURTEEN POINTS of January 8, 1918.

The League's original members were Germany's 32 wartime opponents and the 13 states that had remained neutral in the war. In 1920, Ethiopia, Austria, and Bulgaria were admitted; in 1922, Hungary; on September 8, 1926, Germany (as had been provided for by the LOCARNO PACT); in 1931, Mexico; in 1932, Iraq and Turkey; and in 1934, the USSR. Some of these nations subsequently withdrew from the League: Brazil (1926), Japan (1933), Germany

(October 19, 1933), and Italy (1937). The USSR was expelled because of its WINTER WAR against Finland in 1940. The United States did not ratify the Versailles treaty and never joined the League.

The League bodies were (1) the League of Nations Assembly, which convened once a year and in which every member had one vote; (2) the League of Nations Council, which met many times throughout the year; Great Britain, France, Italy, Japan, and later both Germany and the USSR were standing members, and nine other member states were elected to three-year terms; and (3) the Permanent Secretariat, which was headed by a secretary-general.

The purpose of the League was to promote cooperation among its member states, to assure the preservation of their territorial integrity and political independence, to guarantee their security, and thus to maintain world peace, using such measures as settling international conflicts or making efforts toward international DISARMAMENT. The League was also responsible for administrating the Saarland (until 1935) and the Free City of Danzig, supervising the so-called Mandate Territories (Germany's former colonies in Africa, and Turkey's former territory in Asia), and protecting national minorities. The League succeeded in settling conflicts between smaller states, as well as in cultural, economic, and humanitarian endeavors. In contrast, its efforts at disarmament had no success, nor could it prevent military conflicts involving the major powers (for example, Italy's war against ABYSSINIA in 1935–1936), much less the outbreak of the SECOND WORLD WAR in 1939. On April 18, 1946, the League disbanded. The UNITED NATIONS took its place the same year.

R. B.

"Germany's latest salutation in Geneva." Dutch caricature of Germany's withdrawal from the League of Nations.

Leander, Zarah (née Hedberg), b. Karlstad (Sweden), March 15, 1907; d. Stockholm, June 23, 1981, Swedish actress and singer. After minor stage and film roles, Leander was discovered by Carl August FROELICH as the German cinema's new Marlene DIETRICH. She then began a career as the "loveliest diva" of National Socialist films. Her appearance recalled that of the American vamp (as exemplified by Greta Garbo or Mae West); with erotic radiance she portrayed mainly singers and courtesans, as in *Es war eine rauschende Ballnacht* (It Was an Intoxicating Evening at the Ball; 1939). She won additional popularity in her musical films, with torch songs delivered in a husky voice. Leander incarnated —and not only for male viewers—"the longing

Zarah Leander.

Lebensborn home in Steinhöring (Upper Bavaria).

for an escape from the regimentation of everyday life" (Patalas).

Leander did not openly espouse National Socialism, but along with preponderantly exotic roles, as in *La Habanera* (1937), she appeared in such propaganda films as *Heimat* (Homeland; 1939). In *Die grosse Liebe* (The Great Love; 1945) she was completely transformed from a vamp to a soldier's bride. Her adoption by the National Socialists made it impossible for Leander to regain her earlier renown after the war.

Lebensborn (Fount of Life), registered association established in December 1935 within the SS RACE AND SETTLEMENT MAIN OFFICE (RuSHA). In an extension of the MARRIAGE ORDER of 1932, the Lebensborn statute of September 13, 1936, charged every SS man to produce at least four children, whether in or out of wedlock. The children were to come into the world in well-equipped Lebensborn homes, which protected the mothers from the surrounding world. Lebensborn provided birth documents and the child's basic support, and recruited adoptive parents. Financed by compulsory contributions from the SS Main Office leadership, by 1944 a total of 13 homes were maintained, in which some 11,000 children were born.

Because of the near-total destruction of Lebensborn reports and records, its actual work can be reconstructed only with difficulty. Thus it remains unclear whether Himmler's privately circulated offer "that every unmarried woman who . . . longs for a child can confidently turn

to Lebensborn," which would supply her with a "breeding helper" (*Zeugungshelfer*), was really put into practice. In any case, fartherreaching plans did emerge from Lebensborn, such as Himmler's sketched-out project of May 1942: "In light of the fact that some 400,000 already available women cannot find a husband because of the war and its dead," a central agency should be established "in keeping with the noble idea . . . of the unmarried mother."

Also unclear is the scope of initiative allotted to Lebensborn after the beginning of the Russian Campaign for the RE-GERMANIZATION of children "of Germanic typology." The ideologues of race estimated at 30 million the number of European children "of good blood" who should be taken from their parents, evaluated by Lebensborn, and passed on to adoptive parents. In the RUSHA TRIAL, the Lebensborn authorities shifted responsibility for the kidnappings (estimates of the number of cases vary from several thousand to 200,000) onto other SS organizations and escaped with light sentences.

Ba.

lebensgesetzlich (in accord with the laws of life [or nature]), fashionable term used frequently in National Socialist race lore to denote something biologically or naturally determined: "The relationships among the races as determined by the laws of life" (*Die lebensgesetzliche Verhältnisse unter den Geschlechtern*) should be viewed "from the standpoint of race preservation" (Alfred Rosenberg).

Lebensraum. *See* Living Space.

Lebensunwertes Leben. *See* "Life unworthy of life."

Leber, Julius, b. Biesheim (Alsace), November 16, 1891; d. Berlin-Plötzensee, January 5, 1945 (executed), German politician, political economist, and historian. Leber joined the Social Democratic Party (SPD) in 1913. He volunteered in the First World War. In 1920 he participated in the suppression of the KAPP PUTSCH. Leber was editor of the *Lübecker Volksbote* (Lübeck People's Herald). From 1921 to 1933 he was a member of the Lübeck city council (Bürgerschaft), and from 1925 to 1933 he served in the Reichstag. Leber became the SPD military expert, in which capacity he gradually moved from his beginnings on the Left into the more conservative reform camp. Perhaps 1933 made him receptive to the nationalistic tone of the new regime, which promised the stronger state that he hoped for and that he believed was inevitable. He accused his own party of a "paralysis of action" in light of the National Socialist challenge.

Arrested immediately after the Seizure of Power, Leber sought even in prison to find something positive in the course of events. However, after four years' imprisonment he left the

Julius Leber.

Oranienburg concentration camp an irreconcilable enemy of National Socialism. After his release, Leber lived in Berlin as a coal dealer. He became a leading figure in the opposition, which he tried to establish on a broad democratic basis. Earmarked as interior minister in a future GOERDELER government, he made contact with Communist opposition fighters on July 4, 1944, thereby becoming the victim of a Gestapo spy. Leber's arrest the next day prompted Claus von STAUFFENBERG to speed up his assassination plans. After this attempt failed, Leber was condemned to death by the *Volk* Court in October 1944. "For so good and right a matter, the sacrifice of one's own life is an appropriate price," he wrote shortly before his execution. Leber's speeches, essays, and letters appeared in 1952 under the title *Ein Mann geht seinen Weg* (A Man Goes His Own Way).

Lebrun, Albert, b. Mercy-le-Haut, August 29, 1871; d. Paris, March 6, 1950, French politician. Lebrun served often as a minister (for example, in 1918–1919 for the liberated provinces). After 1920 he served in the Senate (in 1931 as its president). Lebrun became president of the Third Republic on May 10, 1932. Reelected in 1939, he had to hand over his authority to Marshal Henri PÉTAIN after the French defeat on July 10, 1940. In 1944–1945 Lebrun was interned in Germany. After the war he testified in the trial against Pétain and then retired from political life.

Leeb, Wilhelm Ritter von, b. Landsberg am Lech, September 5, 1876; d. Hohenschwangau, April 29, 1956, German field marshal (July 19, 1940). In 1895 Leeb entered the Bavarian army. He was a General Staff officer in the First World War, and afterward a career officer in the Reichswehr (as of February 1, 1929, a major general). In the reshuffling after the FRITSCH CRISIS in March 1938, Leeb was at first retired, but that October he took part (as a colonel general) in the occupation of the Sudetenland with Army Group I.

Leeb assumed supreme command of Army Group C on the Upper Rhine, breaking through the MAGINOT LINE on June 14, 1940. In the Russian Campaign he commanded the Northern Army Group, which attacked Leningrad. Hitler relieved him of duty on January 16, 1942, for an unauthorized change of tactics; he was given no further command. On October 22, 1948, an American military tribunal sentenced him to three years' imprisonment for charges

Wilhelm Ritter von Leeb.

Legality Oath. Hitler as witness for the defense in the Ulm Reichswehr Trial.

that included passing on the COMMISSAR OR-DER. Leeb was considered to have already served that sentence.

Leers, Johann von, b. Vietlübbe (Mecklenburg), January 25, 1902; d. Cairo, March 5, 1965, German antisemitic journalist. Leers initially studied law. As a sworn enemy of the Weimar "Jew Republic," he joined the NSDAP in 1929, becoming chief editor of the National Socialist journal *Wille und Weg* (Will and Way). In numerous books and pamphlets he advocated antisemitic theses, notably in the publication dedicated to Julius STREICHER, *Juden sehen dich an* (Jews Are Watching You; 1933). He also supported the PERSECUTION OF JEWS. At the end of the war Leers fled to Argentina by way of Italy, and in the mid-1950s emigrated to Egypt, where he converted to Islam and continued his anti-Jewish agitation.

Legal Aid (*Gerichtshilfe*), judicial arrangement customary before 1933 for informing the court about the prior record and mental and economic condition of the accused. It was replaced in the Third Reich, as an allegedly absurd (*unsinnig*) protection for "criminals," by DISCOVERY AID.

Legality Oath (*Legalitätseid*), misleading term for Hitler's testimony in the REICHSWEHR TRIAL in late September 1930. During proceedings against three officers for spreading National Socialist propaganda among their units in Ulm, Hitler stated as a defense witness that he sought power exclusively through legal means. On the

other hand, he left no doubt that "heads [would] roll" afterward. The Legality Oath earned him the sobriquet ADOLPHE LÉGALITÉ in social-revolutionary circles of the NSDAP.

Legal reform (*Rechtsreform*), transformation of the German legal system in accordance with the new understanding of LAW and JUSTICE under National Socialism. Legal reform was prepared for in particular by the ACADEMY FOR GERMAN LAW; one of its most active proponents was Curt ROTHENBERGER. Such ideas of reform made the greatest progress in criminal law, although they were never realized. In civil law, plans for a new VOLK LAW CODE came to nothing.

U. B.

Leibstandarte-SS "Adolf Hitler" (SS Bodyguard Unit "Adolf Hitler"; LAH), armed SS troop, formed on March 17, 1933, from 120 men of Hitler's former Munich bodyguard. It was first called the SS-Stabswache Berlin (SS Staff Guard Berlin), then Wachbataillon Berlin (Guard Battalion Berlin), and LAH after September 1933. The unit was garrisoned in the former Main Cadet Academy in Berlin-Lichterfelde. Primarily responsible for Hitler's personal protection, under its commander Joseph ("Sepp") DIETRICH (until July 1943) the LAH took over security measures and served as ceremonial honor guard of the Third Reich (this included garrison duty in the Reich Chancellery).

The LAH took an oath of personal loyalty to Hitler on November 9, 1933, becoming the private army of the Reich Chancellor, in defiance of constitutional law. With the support of the Reichswehr it assumed chief responsibility in the RÖHM AFFAIR for the arrest and liquidation of SA leaders in Bavaria and Berlin. Its "success" in this police-state action led to its merger, along with the POLITICAL SQUADS, into the SS STANDBY TROOPS, within whose compass the LAH was brought to the strength of a motorized infantry regiment. After the Polish Campaign the LAH was attached to the WAFFEN-SS; it became a brigade in 1940 and a division in 1941 (on September 9, 1942, an SS-Panzergrenadierdivision; in February 1944, the First SS-Panzerdivision). It was considered an elite corps in the Waffen-SS and gained renown through often excessively brutal fighting in all theaters of war. Its end came in Austria in April 1945.

Leipart, Theodor, b. Neubrandenburg, May 17, 1867; d. Berlin, March 23, 1947, German trade union leader. A turner (lathe worker), Leipart became head of the turners' union in 1886; in 1890 he became editor of the *Fachzeitung für Drechsler* (Trade News for Turners). He was a Social Democrat, and after the First World War the Social Democratic Party (SPD) named him labor minister in Württemberg (1919–1920).

Theodor Leipart.

Following the death of Carl Legien in 1920, Leipart assumed leadership of the GENERAL GERMAN TRADE UNION FEDERATION (ADGB). He did not succeed in attempts to link the proletariat more closely to the unions during the period of inflation.

In a struggle on multiple fronts against Hitler, employers, and the Communist Party of Germany (KPD), Leipart had difficulties maintaining his pragmatic policy. He was initially favorably disposed toward Chancellor Kurt von Schleicher's plan for a TRADE UNION AXIS, but,

Members of the Leibstandarte-SS "Adolf Hitler."

pressured by the SPD leadership, ultimately refused his support. In May 1933 Leipart was imprisoned during the National Socialist destruction of TRADE UNIONS. He then retreated into private life. In 1946 he joined the Socialist Unity Party (the official Communist party in the German Democratic Republic).

Lejeune-Jung, Paul, b. Cologne, March 16, 1882; d. Berlin-Plötzensee, September 8, 1944 (executed), German politician. Lejeune-Jung studied political economy. Elected to the Reichstag in 1924 for the German National People's Party (DNVP), he left the party in 1929 because of Alfred HUGENBERG's increasingly sharp rightward turn. After the National Socialist takeover, Lejeune-Jung returned to private life. In 1941 opposition circles approached him through Max HABERMANN, a former fellow-DNVP member, to win him over as an economic expert for the political planning of a post-Hitler period. He complied and was earmarked for the post of minister for economics and labor. After the failure of the assassination attempt of July 20, 1944, the Gestapo arrested him in August. A death sentence and his execution followed directly on September 8.

Lenard, Philipp, b. Pressburg, July 6, 1862; d. Messelhausen bei Bad Mergentheim, May 20, 1947, German physicist. Lenard was a professor in Kiel from 1898 to 1907, then in Heidelberg until 1932. He succeeded in elucidating the phenomenon of phosphorescence and explaining the nature of cathode rays. His work on the photon effect provided essential postulates for the theories of Albert EINSTEIN, whose Theory of Relativity Lenard nonetheless rejected as a "Jewish fraud." As an experimental physicist and nationalist, Lenard distrusted theoreticians such as the pacifist Einstein. In the Weimar years, Lenard put his weight as a Nobel laureate (1905) behind antisemitic attacks on Jewish colleagues, and placed himself at the disposal of National Socialist propaganda goals. In *Deutsche Physik* (German Physics; 1936–1937), whose title became an ideological slogan, he tried to establish a *völkisch* and racist basis even for science.

Lend-Lease Act (Ger., *Leih- und Pachtgesetz*), the March 11, 1941, authorization for President Franklin D. Roosevelt to supply, without cash payment, goods vital for the war effort (as weapons, ships, and motor vehicles) to states whose safeguarding he saw as crucial for the defense of the United States. Since entering the war against Germany or even directly supplying arms against it was highly unpopular, Lend-Lease offered the only possibility, given London's desperate financial situation, of supporting a Great Britain made vulnerable by the fall of France. At first a limit of $7 billion was approved, a figure that by 1945 was increased to $50.6 billion. The chief beneficiaries were England and the Commonwealth (about $30 billion); aid to the Soviet Union (a total of $11 billion) was possible only after

Philipp Lenard.

Lend-Lease Act. American war matériel before shipment.

American entry into the war on December 7, 1941. Lend-Lease played a substantial role in turning the course of the war, even though it is difficult to quantify its part in Allied, and particularly Soviet, victories. No substantial repayments were made after the war.

Leningrad, large Soviet city in northern Russia. From September 1941 until January 1943 it was surrounded and cut off from all land connections by German troops during the RUSSIAN CAMPAIGN. Through starvation and bombardment, Leningrad was to be made so weak that it could be taken. But despite some 2 million casualties (most from starvation), it held out until its liberation.

Lenya, Lotte, b. Vienna, October 18, 1900; d. New York, November 27, 1981, Austrian actress and singer. Lenya became known in the 1920s through roles in socially critical plays by authors such as Lion FEUCHTWANGER and Frank Wedekind, which were rejected by the National Socialists as examples of CULTURE BOLSHEVISM. She won particular popularity in her interpretations of Brecht songs, which Kurt WEILL put to music (notably as Jenny Diver in the *Threepenny Opera*). In 1933 Lenya emigrated with Weill (her husband since 1925) to New York. She was naturalized there in 1943, and appeared in plays and musicals until an advanced age.

Lenz, Fritz, b. Pflugrade (Pomerania), March 9, 1887; d. Göttingen, July 6, 1976, German human geneticist. A student of Alfred PLOETZ, from 1913 to 1933 Lenz edited the *Archiv für*

Rassen- und Gesellschaftsbiologie (Archives for Racial and Social Biology). In 1923 he was appointed to the first professorship for RACIAL HYGIENE (in Munich); in 1933 he became a professor of eugenics in Berlin and department head for racial hygiene and heredity research at the Kaiser Wilhelm Institute. Through such writings as *Die Rasse als Wertprinzip* (Race as a Principle of Value; 1933), he had a considerable influence on National Socialist POPULATION POLICY and on the measures to prevent HEREDITARILY ILL OFFSPRING. After the war Lenz was a professor of human heredity in Göttingen (1946–1955).

Leopold III, b. Brussels, November 3, 1901; d. there, September 26, 1983, King of the Belgians as of February 17, 1934. Faced with the nationality problems between the Walloons and the Flemish, as well as Belgium's great economic and political instability, the monarchy gained influence under Leopold in the 1930s. On October 14, 1936, Leopold broke off ties with France and returned to Belgium's traditional neutrality as a signal to Hitler of his peaceful intentions. This did not spare his country occupation by the Germans in the course of the FRENCH CAMPAIGN. Leopold did not join the government-in-exile but rather allowed himself to be interned in Laeken Castle. He tried in vain to obtain the release of Belgian prisoners of war through a visit to Hitler at Berchtesgaden on November 19, 1940. On June 7, 1944, he was brought to Germany, not to be freed until May 8, 1945. When his return to the throne proved impossi-

Lotte Lenya.

Leopold III.

ble, Leopold passed on the crown to his son Baudouin on August 11, 1950, and abdicated on July 11, 1951.

Lersch, Heinrich, b. München-Gladbach (Mönchengladbach), September 12, 1889; d. Remagen, June 18, 1936, German worker-poet. A skilled boilermaker, Lersch became a freelance writer only in 1925. His works were strongly influenced by Expressionism ("Herz! Aufglühe dein Blut" [Heart! Stoke up your blood]; 1916) and were concerned mainly with themes of the working world or recounted war experiences. National Socialist literary history celebrated him as a poet who departed from the depiction of labor in its "class-struggle sense" in order to make "reference to the fate of the entire *Volk.*" His poetry collection *Mensch im Eisen* (Man of Iron; 1925) and his novel *Hammerschläge* (Hammer Blows; 1930) have autobiographical characteristics.

Lersch, Philipp, b. Munich, April 4, 1898; d. there, March 15, 1972, German psychologist. Lersch was a professor in Dresden, Breslau, Leipzig, and, from 1942, Munich. As a journal editor and a scientist, he was among the most important advocates of a psychology of facial expressions and character study. His book *Der Aufbau des Charakters* (The Building of Character; 1938) adopted doctrines of racial biology and sought to demonstrate the interdependence of racial origin and character. Through numerous publications, particularly on themes of so-

cial psychology (as *Vom Wesen der Geschlechter* [*On the Nature of the Sexes*]; 1947), Lersch retained his academic public after 1945.

Les Milles, internment camp and later forced-labor and penal camp near Aix-en-Provence. Immediately after France declared war on September 3, 1939, German citizens were interned in a brickworks at Les Milles. They were chiefly victims of political and racial persecution who had sought refuge in France, and included the painter Max Ernst and the writers Lion FEUCHTWANGER and Walter Hasenclever, who took his own life in Les Milles. After the French defeat the camp became a trap, since according to the terms of the cease-fire the German police had the right to search camps even in unoccupied France. The Vichy government later made Les Milles serve, among other uses, as a camp for Jews, who as early as 1941 were sent from here to forced labor in the French Sahara, and in 1942 were deported to EXTERMINATION CAMPS. In March 1943, after the German occupation of the rest of France, 1,400 Jews from Les Milles were sent to DRANCY. On March 23 they were deported to SOBIBÓR; none survived.

Letterhaus, Bernhard, b. Barmen (now Wuppertal-Barmen), July 10, 1894; d. Berlin, November 14, 1944 (executed), German trade unionist. A volunteer in the First World War, Letterhaus became active in the Catholic workers' movement. In 1928 he became organizational secretary of the West German CATHOLIC WORKERS' ASSOCIATIONS, as well as a deputy in the Prussian legislature. After Hitler's seizure of power

Heinrich Lersch.

Bernhard Letterhaus.

and the destruction of the trade unions, Letterhaus tried to keep together the Catholic opposition. In 1939 he was drafted into the ABWEHR,
where he could make contact with other opposition circles. Imprisoned after the failure of the
assassination attempt of July 20, 1944, he was
sentenced by the *Volk* Court to death by hanging
on November 13, 1944.

Leuninger, Franz, b. Mengerskirschen (Westerwald), December 28, 1898; d. Berlin-Plötzensee, March 1, 1945 (executed), German trade
unionist. A mason, Leuninger became secretary
of the Christian Construction Workers' Association in 1923. In 1933 he was a Center party
Reichstag candidate. Long active in the building
trades in Silesia, Leuninger joined the opposition circles of July 20, 1944, through Friedrich
VOIGT. After the failure of the assassination
attempt, Leuninger was imprisoned on September 26, 1944. On February 28, 1945, the *Volk*
Court sentenced him to death.

Leuschner, Wilhelm, b. Bayreuth, June 15,
1890; d. Berlin, September 29, 1944 (executed),
German politician. A wood-carver, Leuschner
early on became a Social Democrat. From 1924
to 1933 he was an SPD (Social Democratic
Party) member of the Hessian legislature, and
from 1928 to 1932 he served as that state's
interior minister. In 1932 he became Theodor
LEIPART's deputy chairman in the GENERAL
GERMAN TRADE UNION FEDERATION. On May
2, 1933, Leuschner was imprisoned during
National Socialist actions against the TRADE
UNIONS. Forced by Robert LEY to represent Germany and the GERMAN LABOR FRONT at the International Labor Conference in Geneva, he
thwarted this attempt to gain international
credibility for the NS labor organization by his
demonstrative silence, which he then paid for
with two years in the Lichtenburg concentration camp.

As the proprietor of a small business, after his
release Leuschner organized trade union opposition during seemingly innocent business trips.
He linked up with the military opposition
through Ludwig BECK and Carl GOERDELER, in
whose shadow cabinet he was foreseen as vice-
chancellor. After the failure of the assassination
attempt on Hitler of July 20, 1944, Leuschner
could have avoided imprisonment, but he gave
himself up on August 16 because his wife had
been taken hostage. Tortured repeatedly, he was
sentenced to death by the *Volk* Court on September 9, 1944.

Wilhelm Leuschner.

Lewald, Theodor, b. Berlin, August 18, 1860; d.
there, April 15, 1947, German sports official
and jurist. Lewald became active in the Olympics movement as early as 1900. After the First
World War, he and Carl DIEM founded the
German Academy for Physical Exercises in
1922. (For a short time in 1921 he had served
as a state secretary in the Reich Interior Ministry.) From 1919 to 1933 Lewald was president
of the GERMAN REICH COMMITTEE FOR PHYSICAL
EXERCISES, which he helped synchronize with
National Socialist policy in 1933. As president
of the organization committee for the 1936
Olympic Games in Berlin, his duties included
the running of the Olympic torch. After 1924 he
represented Germany in the International
Olympics Committee (IOC). In 1938, under NS
pressure, Lewald had to resign for "reasons of
advanced age."

Lex van der Lubbe, term for the Law on Inflict-
ing and Executing the Death Penalty, promulgated on March 29, 1933. The law increased the
prerogatives of the REICHSTAG FIRE DECREE of
February 28, 1933. It extended back to January
31, 1933 (contrary to the principle of NULLA
POENA SINE LEGE), the threat of the death
penalty for high treason and arson of public
buildings so as to be able to punish the act of
the accused, Marinus van der LUBBE, more
severely during the REICHSTAG FIRE TRIAL.
Franz SCHLEGELBERGER's protests against the
Lex van der Lubbe were unsuccessful, and the
law was supplemented on April 4, 1933, by the
Law to Prevent Political Violence.

Ley, Robert, b. Niederbreidenbach (Bergisches Land), February 15, 1890; d. Nuremberg, October 25, 1945, German politician. In the First World War Ley eventually became a pilot; shot down in 1917, he was a prisoner of war in France. The former chemistry student was employed by I.G. Farben in Leverkusen in 1920. He joined the NSDAP in 1923, and after its reestablishment (February 27, 1925) became *Gauleiter* of the South Rhineland on June 25. Because of his political agitation and his alcoholism (he later earned the nickname "Reich Drunkard" [*Reichstrunkenbold*]), he lost his job.

Together with Josef GROHÉ, Ley founded the *Westdeutscher Beobachter* (West German Observer) as the political and, above all, antisemitic organ of his *Gau*. He became a member of the Reichstag in 1930. As deputy to the Reich party organization director, Gregor STRASSER, Ley to all intents and purposes became Strasser's successor after his removal from power (December 1932)—officially so after Strasser's murder during the RÖHM AFFAIR (June 30, 1934). In between these dates the most decisive event in Ley's life took place: after the takeover of power Hitler named him director of a Working Committee for the Protection of German Labor (Aktionskomitee zum Schutz der deutscher Arbeit). With this organization Ley broke up the TRADE UNIONS on May 2, 1933, replacing them with the GERMAN LABOR FRONT (DAF). It combined employees and employers in the largest mass organization of the Third Reich (some 25 million members in 1942).

Ley thus gained considerable power, which he extended through such spectacular DAF

Robert Ley.

enterprises as the leisure-time organization STRENGTH THROUGH JOY (it named one of its passenger ships after Ley in March 1938). Seeking to strengthen his influence in a more narrow political sphere, he founded the so-called ORDER FORTRESSES and, as preparatory institutions, the ADOLF HITLER SCHOOLS, for the "selection" of the party's future leadership. With the conversion of the German economy to war production, Ley attained, as a member of the General Economic Council (Generalrat der Wirtschaft), the high point of his career, which was shadowed during the war by such rivals as Fritz TODT and Albert SPEER. Fritz SAUCKEL too, in his role as General Plenipotentiary for Labor Deployment, cut into Ley's prerogatives. Ley tried to maintain his position by particularly brutal Jew-baiting. Imprisoned by American troops after the end of the war in May 1945, he hanged himself in his cell before the beginning of his trial.

Liberalism (*Liberalismus*), political movement and theory about government and society that arose in the 18th century and advocated the free development of man, the individual's freedom from religious and governmental guardianship, and an unregulated market economy. As a political movement, liberalism grew ever closer to nationalism beginning in the late 19th century.

According to National Socialist propaganda, liberal principles were the central causes for the political, moral, and cultural "decline" of the Weimar Republic. Politically, the National Socialists equated liberalism with a "uniformity that levels everything," "unrestrained individualism," and "cosmopolitanism." Economically liberalism had led, in the NS view, to the "dependence of the great mass of people," to class struggle, and to catastrophic crises; culturally it had produced "unfettered freedom," "degeneration," and "culture Bolshevism." In contrast to liberalism, the NS worldview was said to derive the worth of the human being not from his rights and freedoms, but "through his duties," his "willing service to the community," and his "readiness to act for the *Volk*," to whom he was bound "by blood ties."

Liberation Law (*Befreiungsgesetz*; officially, Law for the Liberation from National Socialism and Militarism), law of March 5, 1946, promulgated by the three state (*Land*) governments in the American occupation zone in Germany (*see* DENAZIFICATION).

Licensed parties (*Lizenzparteien*), term for the parties newly founded or re-established in Germany after the Second World War; to be politically active, they needed an authorization (license) from the relevant occupying power. At first even licensed parties were restricted in their activities: they had to report all public and internal events; they were prohibited from dealing with matters of occupation policy, foreign policy, or results of the war; and their radio programs were censored. The term "licensed party" was introduced by the political Right in the Federal Republic to discredit the democratic parties, which were said to owe their existence and power not to the German *Volk*, but to the "occupiers." The legitimization earned through many elections was thus intentionally ignored.

Licensed press (*Lizenzpresse*), term for newspapers and periodicals appearing in Germany, Austria, and Italy after the end of the Second World War. Beginning on May 12, 1945, all press releases and all film, theater, music, and recreation establishments in Germany had to be specially authorized (licensed) by the relevant occupying power. Basically, all publishers (holders of licenses) had to demonstrate their political inoffensiveness. In the Western occupation zones the necessity for licensing was abolished by "General License No. 3" of May 2, 1949, and by the Law of the Allied High Commission of May 23, 1959.

Lichtenberg, Bernhard, b. Ohlau, December 3, 1875; d. Dachau concentration camp, November 3, 1943, German Catholic theologian. Lichtenberg was ordained a priest in 1932, and in

Bernhard Lichtenberg.

1938 became a prior at Saint Hedwig's Cathedral in Berlin. From the beginning he actively opposed National Socialist racism, but it was only when he made his strong protests against the EUTHANASIA program (in his letter of August 28, 1941, to Reich Physicians' Führer Leonardo Conti) that the Gestapo came into the picture. The Gestapo reprimanded Lichtenberg for openly praying for Jews and concentration camp prisoners and for including Jews in his appeals to love one's neighbors. On May 22, 1942, Special Court I of the Berlin District Court (*Landgericht*) sentenced Lichtenberg to two years' imprisonment for misuse of the pulpit and breach of the MALICIOUS-GOSSIP LAW. He died in transit to the Dachau concentration camp after serving this sentence.

Lichtenburg, concentration camp near Prettin (Kreis Torgau). The men's camp was established early in 1933, and the women's camp in March 1938 (the women prisoners were transferred from the women's camp in Moringen). Lichtenburg's inmates worked mainly in cleaning and transport details in the plant nursery located within the camp. Some 4,000 inmates are estimated to have inhabited Lichtenburg. The SS guard had separate barracks. Many male and female inmates were beaten to death; two women inmates were torn to pieces by dogs after an escape attempt, by order of the camp commandant. A former SA leader was shot at the camp on June 30, 1934, after the RÖHM AFFAIR. In August 1937 the male inmates were transferred to the Buchenwald concentration camp; the men's camp was disbanded on August 9. The women's camp was disbanded on May 15, 1939, and the inmates were brought to the women's camp at Ravensbrück.

W. D.

Lidice (Ger., Liditz), Czech miners' settlement near Kladno, west of Prague. On an order from Hitler, passed down by telephone through Karl Hermann FRANK to the commanding officer of the security police and the SD (Security Service) in Prague, Lidice was surrounded by German police and SD men on the evening of June 9, 1942. After an army unit had cordoned off the area, the police had the women and children taken away and, according to their own statements, shot "172 adult males with an execution squad composed of one officer, two junior officers, and 20 men." Later that night 11 more workers from the late shift were killed, in addition to 15 relatives of Czech legionnaires

Lidice. Victims of SS reprisals.

serving in England who were already in custody, making the number of those murdered exactly 198. Of the 184 women transported to the Ravensbrück concentration camp and the 11 in prison, 143 women eventually returned. Ninety of the children were taken to a camp in the Wartheland and eight were given to SS families for RE-GERMANIZATION; only 16 could be identified after 1945.

The action, led by SS-Hauptsturmführer Max Rostock (who was executed in 1951), ended with the total destruction of Lidice. It was declared to be a reprisal for the assassination attempt against Reinhard HEYDRICH on May 27, 1942, although no link between the perpetrators and Lidice was proved. The massacre dramatically increased tensions in the PROTECTOR-ATE OF BOHEMIA AND MORAVIA and, together with the killings at ORADOUR-SUR-GLANE in France, became a symbol of National Socialist terrorism. After the war the town was rebuilt nearby as Nové Lidice (New Lidice). The site of the murder is now a memorial.

Liebehenschel, Arthur, b. Posen, November 25, 1901; d. Kraków, January 24, 1948 (executed), SS-*Obersturmbannführer* (January 30, 1941). Liebehenschel attended the Army Technical School for Management and Economics, then worked for the railroads and joined the army (he was discharged in October 1931 as a warrant officer). He joined the NSDAP and SS on February 1, 1932. On August 4, 1934, he joined the

DEATH'S-HEAD UNITS, becoming an adjutant in the commandant's office at the Columbia and Lichtenburg concentration camps. On July 5, 1937, he became a unit leader on the staff of the chief of Death's-Head Units in charge of camps.

Liebehenschel rose further to become chief of staff for concentration camp inspection (May 1, 1940), and then chief official in the SS ECONOMIC-ADMINISTRATIVE MAIN OFFICE. On November 10, 1943, he was appointed commandant of the AUSCHWITZ concentration camp (Auschwitz I, the main camp); on May 19, 1944, he assumed the same post at the MAIDANEK camp. By the war's end he had become a chief of staff in the SS Personnel Main Office. Remanded by American occupation officials to Poland, Liebehenschel was sentenced to death by the Supreme People's Tribunal on December 22, 1947.

Liebeneiner, Wolfgang, b. Liebau (Silesia), October 6, 1905, German actor, scriptwriter, and producer. Liebeneiner joined the Munich Chamber Theater in 1928, then continued his theatrical training at the State Theater in Berlin in 1936. From 1931 on he was active as a film actor, in *Liebelei* (Amours; 1932) and other films. After 1937 he also produced films. From 1938 to 1945 he headed the Film Academy in Babelsberg as a professor, and from 1942 to 1945 he was head of production for Ufa (UNI-VERSE FILMS, INC.).

Liebeneiner demonstrated his independence

by attending the funeral of his colleague Joachim GOTTSCHALK in 1941, despite Goebbels's prohibition, but after the war he was accused of having played into the hands of National Socialist propaganda with his films. In particular, it was claimed that the heroic films *Bismarck* (1940) and *Die Entlassung* (The Dismissal; 1942) had served the FÜHRER CULT, and that ICH KLAGE AN (I Accuse; 1941) had been a justification of the EUTHANASIA program. Aided by his second wife, Hilde Krahl (b. 1917), Liebeneiner carried on his work without a break after the war, making such films as *Liebe 47* (Love 47; 1948), *Die Trapp-Familie* (1958), and *Götz von Berlichingen* (1978). He denied the accusations and saw a contrary significance in his Bismarck movie: Hitler as destroyer of the work of unification. Liebeneiner claimed that in his alleged euthanasia film he had only agitated for the right to choose the manner of one's own death, a right he still upheld.

Liebenfels, Jörg Lanz von (pseud.). *See* Lanz, Josef.

Liebermann, Max, b. Berlin, July 20, 1847; d. there, February 8, 1935, German painter and illustrator. Liebermann studied philosophy. He was strongly influenced by French painters, notably Courbet, and became the spokesman for French Impressionism in Germany. In 1898 he entered the Berlin Academy of Arts, serving as its president from 1920 until he was removed from office in 1933 by the National Socialists, who attacked him for his Jewish origins despite his conservative and patriotic bent. The DEGENERATE ART exhibition contained paintings by

Wolfgang Liebeneiner.

Max Liebermann (self-portrait).

Liebermann. His widow committed suicide in 1943 when threatened with internment in a concentration camp.

Liebermann von Sonnenberg, Max, b. Weisswasser (West Prussia), August 21, 1848; d. Berlin, September 17, 1911, German journalist and politician. First an officer, after 1890 Liebermann von Sonnenberg represented the German-Social Reform Party in the Reichstag, from 1895 to 1900 as its chairman. He was a conservative representative of the antisemitic movement, whose hostility toward Jews he spread after 1884 in his *Deutschsoziale Blätter* (German Social Pages). In 1903 he was a co-founder of the equally antisemitic "Economic Alliance" (Wirtschaftliche Vereinigung).

Lieberose, forced-labor camp north of Cottbus (Brandenburg). Toward the end of 1944, Lieberose was the goal of an evacuation transport from AUSCHWITZ; it was itself evacuated in December 1944. Of 3,500 prisoners, only 900 reached the SACHSENHAUSEN concentration camp; the others were shot during the 140-km (about 84 miles) march for trying to escape or because of exhaustion.

Life celebrations (*Lebensfeiern*), National Socialist substitute ceremonies to supplant church baptisms, weddings, and funerals. (The substitute for confirmation, the "Commitment of Youth," was part of the CELEBRATIONS IN THE NATIONAL SOCIALIST CALENDAR.) During the first years of the Third Reich, NS life celebrations were only partially put into practice, and earliest in the SS. After 1936 (when the designation "GOD-BELIEVING" was introduced), civil marriages of party members were increasingly transformed into NS wedding celebrations. Not until 1942 did Alfred ROSENBERG's office issue comprehensive guidelines for conducting life celebrations, which were intended to assure uniform organization and ideological alignment. Compared to church ceremonies, especially funerals, the proportion of life celebrations remained extremely low: it stayed mostly under 1 percent, and only in a few *Gaue* did it reach 4 percent.

"Life unworthy of life" (*lebensunwertes Leben*), National Socialist cliché for characterizing the incurably ill or mentally handicapped. According to the Law to Prevent Hereditarily Ill Offspring of July 14, 1933, such persons could be subjected to FORCED STERILIZATION; they were later dealt with in the so-called EUTHANASIA operation, which was designated for the "extermination of life unworthy of life."

Light fiction. *See* Trivialliteratur.

"Lili Marleen," poem written during the First World War (1915) by Hans Leip (1893–1983) that, when put to music by Norbert SCHULTZE (1938), became the hit song on all fronts of the Second World War. A recording of the song with Lale Andersen (1919–1972) was by chance played on a program from the German armed forces' station in Belgrade on August 18, 1941. The response was so overwhelming that the station from then on broadcast the song daily at 9:57 p.m. Joseph Goebbels, who called both the text and the music "morbid," and spoke of a "tearjerker that smelled of the dance of death" (*Schnulze mit Totentanzgeruch*), for the moment withdrew his objection. When, after [the defeat at] Stalingrad, broadcasting of the song was suppressed as "undesirable," Allied radio stations long continued to broadcast the English or French version, even though British commanding officers also had expressed reservations about its negative effect on fighting morale.

Lilje, Hanns, b. Hannover, August 20, 1899; d. there, January 5, 1977, German Evangelical theologian. In 1927 Lilje became general secretary of the German Alliance of Christian Students; in 1932, vice president of the International Federation of Christian Students, and in 1935, general secretary of the Lutheran International Assembly. He joined the YOUNG REFORMERS in 1933, became editor of the publi-

Hanns Lilje.

cation *Junge Kirche* (Young Church), and stood firmly on the side of the CONFESSING CHURCH, at whose schism he was named as a "moderate" to the Council of the Evangelical-Lutheran Church on March 18, 1936.

After 1933 Lilje served as a pastor in Berlin. Under suspicion for his international ecumenical connections, he was frequently forbidden to preach. Following the assassination attempt of July 20, 1944, he was arrested and sentenced to time in prison. After the war he took a significant part in rebuilding the Evangelical Church in Germany. He was co-founder of the Lutheran World Federation in 1947 and its president from 1952 to 1957. Lilje was regional bishop of Hannover and, from 1950, abbot of Loccum. His many publications included *Im finsteren Tal* (In the Valley of Darkness; 1947), an account of his imprisonment by the Gestapo.

Limitation [of criminal liability] (*Verjährung*), exclusion from prosecution for criminal acts after the lapse of an established time period. The period of limitation can be based on legal provisions (for example, a statute of limitations) and can be suspended by specific regulations (¶¶78ff., Criminal Code, Federal Republic of Germany).

The role of limitation in the prosecution of National Socialist crimes of violence in the Federal Republic of Germany (FRG) has been considerable. Because the "Führer's will" had the validity of law during the Third Reich, any prosecution had to wait until the end of the war. The onset of the period of liability for prosecution was generally established as May 8, 1945.

As of May 8, 1960, prosecution for all acts except murder (¶211, Criminal Code) became invalid, provided that the period of limitation had not been suspended. For murder the date set was May 8, 1965, for a period of 20 years. However, the Law concerning the Calculating of Penal Statutes of Limitation (March 25, 1965) established that in calculating the time, the period from May 8, 1945, to December 31, 1949, had to be excluded from consideration because of the deficient functioning of the German judicial system during this time.

On November 26, 1968, the General Assembly of the United Nations concluded a convention on the nonapplicability of legal statutes of limitation in cases of WAR CRIMES and CRIMES AGAINST HUMANITY. According to it, even a suspended statute such as the FRG's was retroactively invalid. The FRG and other Western nations did not enter into the convention, on the ground that it was in conflict with the unconstitutionality of retroactive provisions in their own national laws. A similar initiative made by the European Parliament in 1974 was rejected on the same ground by its member nations, except for France.

On August 4, 1969, the West German Bundestag (parliament) passed the 9th amendment to the Criminal Code, in part influenced by the United Nations convention. The statute of limitations in cases of murder, among other crimes, was thereby extended to 30 years. Before this point was reached, a spirited debate arose both in and outside Germany over the limitation of liability for NS crimes. Finally, on July 3, 1979, the Bundestag passed the 16th amendment to the Criminal Code, which abolished any limitation on prosecuting murder and GENOCIDE. A provision on the latter was first adopted in the Criminal Code (¶220a) in 1955.

A. St.

Limpach, Erich, b. Berlin, June 27, 1899; d. Coburg, December 10, 1965, German writer. Limpach's politics were strongly influenced by Gen. Erich LUDENDORFF. After the First World War he composed a series of *völkisch* and nationalistic poems, which were collected as *Deutschland erwache!* (Germany Awaken!; 1924). *Von neuem Werden* (On a New Becoming; 1934) celebrated lyrically the National Socialist state after the Seizure of Power. After 1945 Limpach wrote ostensibly unpolitical stories and aphorisms, but he had difficulty distancing himself from the militaristic and fascist spirit of his earlier works, as proved by his 1959 autobiography, *Volk und Sturm* (*Volk* and Storm).

Linden, Walther, b. Wuppertal, January 26, 1895; d. Paris, July 21, 1943, German literary historian. Linden wrote a series of chauvinistic interpretations of German literary history, especially of the classical period, such as *Goethe und die deutsche Gegenwart* (Goethe and the German Present; 1932). In addition, he tried to engage in theory developing (in the National Socialist sense of the term) through a programmatic work, *Aufgaben einer nationalen Literaturwissenschaft* (Tasks of a National Literary Scholarship; 1933), which was considered to be one of the basic works of *völkisch* literary historiography.

Linke, Johannes, b. Dresden, January 8, 1900; missing since February 1945, German writer. Linke was first an elementary school teacher in Vogtland, then in the Bavarian Forest. As a regional popular poet, he composed peasant chronicles and novels about village communities "sparkling with life," as *Ein Jahr rollt übers Gebirg* (A Year Passes over the Highlands; 1934). He wrote of reverence for war heroes in the "German *Gaue*" in *Das Totenbrünnel* (The Well of the Dead; 1940) and sang of Bavarian trees as "wooden companions" ("Der Baum" [The Tree]; 1934) in prizewinning nature poems.

Linz, Upper Austrian provincial capital on the Danube; in 1934 its population was 115,000. Hitler spent a part of his youth in Linz, attending secondary school (*Realschule*) there without obtaining a diploma. As a dreamy 16-year-old he outlined ambitious urban-planning projects with elegant villas, museums, and a bridge over the Danube, "which 35 years later he built with obstinate pleasure according to his adolescent plans" (Joachim Fest). The young man who had felt repelled and rejected by "cosmopolitan" Vienna sketched out on paper as early as his Munich years the new Austrian metropolis of Linz.

After the Anschluss with Austria, Hitler busied himself intensively with his "favorite project," to make Linz the "cultural center" of Europe, with the largest art and painting gallery in the world. Plans called for an elegant avenue with monumental architecture, at its northeast end a "Hitler Center," next to which would stand the gallery with an immense pilastered facade. Its paintings were to be contributed by other German museums or "acquired" abroad.

Linz. Architectural sketch of the Danube Hotel by Roderich Fick.

During the war this aim was well served by the National Socialist ART PLUNDER from occupied Europe, among other tactics. The director of the Dresden Museum, Hans Posse, became involved with "Special Commission 'Linz,'" on Hitler's explicit command. The expansion of Linz, with which Hitler occupied himself even in the bunker beneath the Reich Chancellery in 1945, never went beyond the planning stage because of the contingencies of war.

H. H.

Linz Program (*Linzer Programm*), 11-point program of the German nationalist movement in Austria, formulated on September 1, 1882. The sociopolitical demands (which included tax reform, trade regulations, and the organization of workers) were decisively influenced by Victor Adler (1852–1918), later a socialist, and the nationalist demands (including a close alliance with the German Empire and naval armaments) were influenced by Georg von SCHÖNERER. Schönerer's influence was also evident in the 12th point, added in 1885: here, for the first time, a kind of ARYAN PARAGRAPH demanded the removal of Jews from the economy and politics.

Lippert, Julius, b. Basel (Switzerland), July 9, 1895; d. Bad Schwalbach, June 30, 1956, German journalist. Lippert was a volunteer in the First World War and then studied law. In 1921 he became a member of the German-Völkisch Freedom Movement; in 1923 he went over to the NSDAP. Joseph Goebbels in 1927 named Lippert chief editor of the newly founded newspaper *Der* ANGRIFF (The Attack), which Lippert made into a feared publication of the yellow press. In March 1933 he was named state commissioner (*Staatskommissar*) for Berlin, and in 1937 he received the title "Lord Mayor and Municipal President of the Reich Capital."

Lippert joined the Wehrmacht in 1940. For a short time he was commandant of the Belgian city of Arlon, and in 1941, during the campaign in the west, he was commander of the southeastern propaganda unit. He later helped establish the soldiers' radio station in Belgrade. Arrested

Julius Lippert.

in 1945, in 1952 he was sentenced in Belgium to seven years of forced labor. That same year he was deported to Germany, where on September 1, 1953, an appeals board classified him as a National Socialist "activist," in part because of his antisemitic book *Im Strom der Zeit* (In the Stream of Time; 1940).

Liquidate (*liquidieren;* from Lat. *liquidus,* liquid), verb borrowed from the commercial vocabulary to denote the dissolution of a business, the conversion of goods into money, or a statement of accounts. In the National Socialist idiom, the term "liquidate" was adopted to denote the execution of opponents, especially by shooting, who were "settled" (*erledigt*) like a business concern. Efforts to eradicate the "brazen" (*nassforsch*) term from war reporting (press advisory of November 15, 1941) proved fruitless.

Lischka, Kurt, b. Breslau, August 16, 1909, SS-*Obersturmbannführer* (April 20, 1942). Lischka was a jurist and lawyer. He joined the SS on June 1, 1933, and the Gestapo on September 2, 1935. In 1938 he was posted to the Gestapo's Section II B 4 (Jewish Affairs), from which he moved to the Reich Central Office for Jewish Emigration, working there in 1938 and 1939. In 1940 he was made head of Gestapo headquarters in Cologne. Lischka was assigned in November of that year to Paris, where he worked as deputy commander of the Security Police and the Security Service (SD) under Helmut KNOCHEN. In charge of internment camps in this capacity, Lischka had a decisive role in the deportation of Jews. Assigned next to the Reich Security Main Office (October 1943), he was responsible for the PROTECTORATE OF BOHEMIA AND MORAVIA.

On December 10, 1945, Lischka was captured by the British, who handed him over to authorities in Prague on May 2, 1947. On August 22, 1950, he was released to the Federal Republic, where he lived undisturbed despite a sentence passed in absentia in France on September 18, 1950. On February 2, 1980, a Cologne state court (*Landgericht*) finally sentenced him to a 10-year term for war crimes, after years of effort by the French-Jewish lawyer Serge Klarsfeld and his German-born wife, Beate Klarsfeld.

List, Wilhelm, b. Oberkirchberg bei Ulm, May 14, 1880; d. Garmisch-Partenkirchen, June 18, 1971, German field marshal general (July 19, 1940). List entered the army in 1898. In the First World War he served as a General Staff officer; afterward he made a career in the

Wilhelm List.

Reichswehr (he was appointed a major general on October 1, 1930). After the Anschluss with Austria, List became commander in chief of Commando Group 5 in Vienna; he led the Fourteenth Army during the Polish Campaign, and the Twelfth Army in the west in 1940 and then in the Balkans. Until October 15, 1941, he was Wehrmacht commander for the southeast.

After a lengthy leave, on July 7, 1942, List took command of Army Group A in Russia, with orders to march toward the Caucasus. From the outset he had warned against overextending forces. Now, on September 10, 1942, he was made to leave his post, despite Gen. Alfred JODL's support, because the offensive had stalled. He received no further assignments. After the war, List was sentenced to life imprisonment by an American military court in Nuremberg on October 19, 1948, in the so-called HOSTAGE TRIAL against generals active on the southeastern front. The charges included reprisal actions after partisan raids. However, on December 24, 1952, List was released from the Landsberg prison for war criminals on grounds of ill health.

Literary prizes, distinctions honoring exceptional literary works or authors (usually carrying monetary awards); in the Third Reich they were used as political instruments to steer literature in the desired direction. The Propaganda Ministry, which was responsible for literary prizes, after 1933 encouraged the Reich government and municipal authorities to endow new prizes and itself staged public award ceremonies. The most important literary prizes of the Third

Reich included the German National Prize for Film and Book, instituted in 1933 by the German Reich for works that represented "the stirring experience . . . of national rebirth," and the German National Prize for Art and Science. Hitler himself arranged for this award in 1937, at the same time prohibiting acceptance of a Nobel prize by any German (a reaction to the conferring of the peace prize on Carl von OSSIETZKY). Recipients of the well-endowed prize (100,000 RM) included Alfred ROSENBERG and Hanns JOHST.

Other important prizes were the Dietrich ECKART Prize, established by the Hamburg Senate for "scholars, poets, and writers" who in their works "symbolize . . . the idea of a National Socialist Germany" (awarded to Adolf BARTELS, Hans BAUMANN, and Edwin E. DWIN-GER, among others); the Goethe Prize of the City of Frankfurt (recipients included Hans CAROSSA and Agnes MIEGEL); the Prize for Foreign German [later Ethnic German] Writing, awarded by the City of Stuttgart; the Literature Prize of the Reich Capital; the Great Poet Prize of the City of Vienna; and the Mozart Prize, for cultural accomplishments "from the *Gaue* of the Ostmark," awarded by the universities of Vienna and Graz. Aside from these literary prizes, the NSDAP and its subdivisions awarded such distinctions as the NSDAP Prize for Science and Art, the Prize of the SA Chief of Staff for Poetry and Writing, and smaller honors such as the HANS SCHEMM PRIZE, for "writing for young people."

H. H.

Literature

What is called "National Socialist literature" encompasses writing that expressed the central content of National Socialist (NS) ideology, and that political and cultural institutions, recognized literary critics, and historians in the Third Reich referred to as "species-true" (*artgemäss*) contemporary literature. [The terms preferred by National Socialists to the "alien" *Literatur* are discussed in DICHTUNG and WRITING.] "National Socialist literature" includes not only works produced during the Third Reich, but also numerous other ideologically correct works appearing before 1933, some of them even before 1918. On the other hand, the designation does not apply to all writers in the Third Reich or all of their works; such borderline and special cases as Hans CAROSSA, Ernst JÜNGER, and Gottfried BENN must be judged individually. The designation chosen follows criteria based on ideology and literary politics. A definition derived from an exclusively aesthetic viewpoint would be difficult, if not impossible. Criteria of valuation in any event lead to the judgment that NS literature in general is of a mediocre, if not miserable, aesthetic quality. Once said, this does not offer a sufficient definition, nor does such a judgment render a confrontation with that literature unnecessary.

The preferred genres can be classified into three major categories, depending on the ideological content at a work's center or which function it performs: (1) the homeland novels (*Heimatromane*), especially peasant novels (*see* PEASANT LITERATURE), as well as most historical novels, revolve around the idea of *Volkstum* (from *Volk*, nationality or ethnic identity); (2) the First World War novels and the NS marching and fighting songs glorify and promote "heroism"; and (3) CHORAL POETRY, a particular variety of "worldview lyric" (*Weltanschauungs-Lyrik*), and THING PLAYS (festival plays) express "belief" in National Socialism and invite "professions of faith." This tripartite division can be supported by the interpretations of NS writers, politicians, and contemporary literary historians, according to whom NS literature represented a "*Volk*-centered poetics" (*volkhafte Dichtung*), a "heroic poetics" (*heldische Dichtung*), and a "poetics of consecration" (*Weihedichtung*). The ideological content and functions expressed in these terms not only undergirded the contemporary literary model but also characterized all NS literature—or should have, according to precepts.

Homeland and peasant novels, in particular, belong to the category of "*Volk*-centered poetics." More generally, this rubric covers all NS literature insofar as it "proclaims the fate of the *Volk* as the most sublime subject matter of art" (Arno Mulot). The demand that art should find inspiration in "the energies of the *Volk*" (Goebbels) meant, in the final analysis, that art and literature should be judged by the criterion of "blood-true substance" (*blutmässige Substanz;*

National Socialist poster: "The Book:
A Source of Strength for the Nation."

Gerhard SCHUMANN). Accordingly, a battle against "mere artistry" (*blosses Artistentum;* Goebbels) ensued; it was motivated on both aesthetic and racial grounds. "*Volk*-centered poetics" thus also had a political function, indeed a double one: on the one hand, it fostered "racial consciousness" in the reader; on the other, the appeal to its alleged value, which was deemed worth defending, served to justify the persecution of "the racially alien literary world" (Alfred Rosenberg).

"Heroic poetics" also designates more than a special category with specific genres. Literary theories made heroism a fundamental quality of NS literature: its expression, style, and general "stance" were supposed to focus on the heroic, while its contents were to portray heroic men. This heroic quality related to a dual political function: the heroic principle led to the suppression of so-called decadent and defeatist literature and authors, and heroic writing fostered a "spirit of valor" in the reader. This prized "heroism" worked hand in hand with the ideology of the "*Volk*-nation"; in the First World War novels that had appeared even before 1933, the frontline community of soldiers was portrayed as the heart of a future *Volk* community, whose organization was ordered on the model of a combat community of leader and followers. Post-1933 literature propagandized the transformation of the *Volk* community into a combat community, as literature became a "weapon."

Finally, the term "poetics of consecration" also has a double meaning. In the narrower sense it refers to the various liturgical texts for NS CELEBRATIONS, including the festival plays; insofar as these texts consecrated the Führer and NS ideology, lent expression to the "belief" in National Socialism, and furnished formulas for suitable "affirmations of faith," one can equally well speak of a "religious poetics." All NS literature had a religious quality (in the sense of "political religiosity"), at least tendentially, since ideology was supposed to govern political and social relationships, as well as to make possible the conferring of spiritual meaning. Erwin KOLBENHEYER ascribed a "transcendental meaning" to NS literature; Herbert BÖHME pronounced the NS poet to be the "herald" of "a new faith." "Heroic poetics" served the function of forging the *Volk* community into a combat community, and the "poetics of consecration" was to transform the *Volk* community into a "community of belief" (*Glaubensgemeinschaft;* Hanns JOHST), that is, into an unconditional FOLLOWERSHIP.

Even before 1918, a series of works appeared that passed for exemplary NS literature in the Third Reich and that had earlier enjoyed considerable public success. These included above all the homeland and historical novels of Ludwig BARTEL, Walter BLOEM, Hermann BURTE, Gustav FRENSSEN, Hermann STEHR, and the previously mentioned Kolbenheyer. Also in this category were certain equally successful works, most of which were tinged with antisemitism and dealt with the history and theory of culture: the *Deutsche Schriften* (German Writings) of Paul de LAGARDE, *Rembrandt als Erzieher* (Rembrandt as Educator) by Julius LANGBEHN, *Die Grundlagen des 19. Jahrhunderts* (Foundations of the 19th Century) by Houston Stewart CHAMBERLAIN, Bartel's *Geschichte der deutschen Literatur* (History of German Literature), and *Die Sünde wider das Blut* (The Sin against Blood) by Artur DINTER. This literature was as a rule seen as a precursor of NS literature and termed *völkisch*-nationalist since National Socialism did not yet exist as a political movement. Yet the ideological content of National Socialism was already present in this literature, which likewise appeared as "*völkisch,*" "heroic," and "religious poetics." It follows that National Socialism did not itself bring forth NS literature; rather, this literature helped to create National Socialism, by making available and propagating the ideology that is identified with that movement.

The ideological positions already developed before 1918 were in any event intensified in the

Quotation from Hitler's *Mein Kampf* as a slogan for the "Week of the German Book": "At that time I read and read, and thoroughly, too. In a few years I thus created the foundations of a knowledge from which I draw even today."

following years under the influence of the lost war and the struggle against the hated Weimar Republic. The tradition of the "*Volk*-centered" homeland novel (Emil STRAUSS, Hans BLUNCK, Will VESPER, and Kolbenheyer) continued, as did that of the colonial novel (Hans GRIMM). The numerous war novels that appeared simultaneously at the end of the 1920s introduced a new genre to the "heroic" category, in works by Werner BEUMELBURG, Josef WEHNER, Edwin Erich DWINGER, Hans ZÖBERLEIN, and Franz Schauwecker. The NS writer and journalist Vesper coined the expression about the "two literatures" of the period; he claimed that leftist and bourgeois-liberal literature had suppressed the other, "genuine German literature." In truth, the quasi-NS homeland and war novels had enjoyed large printings even before 1933.

After 1933 the success of NS literature was achieved through political and administrative means. The production of new works during the Third Reich was relatively modest. The "new guard" NS writers, most of whom appeared only after 1933 (Heinrich ANACKER, Hans BAUMANN, Herbert BÖHME, Kurt EGGERS, Gerhard MENZEL, and Gerhard SCHUMANN, among others), wrote chiefly marching and fighting lyrics, "worldview lyrics," and choral poetry for NS celebrations and festival plays. The functional aspect of literature moved to the fore. It is symptomatic that, almost without exception, these young writers were also functionaries in various government and party policymaking organizations, from the presidial council of the REICH WRITING CHAMBER to Reich Propaganda Headquarters, the Reich Youth Leadership, and the highest SA leadership, all the way to the SS Race and Settlement Main Office.

Klaus Vondung

Literature Bolshevism (*Literaturbolschewismus*), all-inclusive National Socialist polemical term for the development of all non-*völkisch*, non-nationalist literature during the Weimar Republic, from proletarian-revolutionary to republican-humanist. It was used for the most part to discredit Jewish authors (*see* CULTURE BOLSHEVISM).

Lithuania (Ger., Litauen), republic on the Baltic Sea, one of the Baltic states; area, 53,000 sq km (about 21,200 sq miles); population, 2.39 million (1939); the capital is Vilna. Lithuania was founded on December 11, 1917, while under German occupation; after the German collapse it held out against the Poles and the Red Army. It became an authoritarian state after a coup led by Antonas Smetona in 1926. Under German pressure, Lithuania had to cede MEMELLAND— territory it had annexed on January 23, 1939— on March 22 of that year.

The GERMAN-SOVIET NONAGGRESSION PACT

of August 23, 1939, ceded Lithuania to the Soviet sphere of influence; on June 15, 1940, it was annexed. Occupied by the Germans at the outset of the Russian Campaign in June 1941, Lithuania was incorporated into the Reich Commissariat OSTLAND (Eastern Land), and its German population was resettled in the Reich. Harsh years of German occupation, with intense persecution of the Jews, followed the Soviet reprisals. Hopes of regaining independence with German help were not fulfilled. In July 1944, the Red Army once again occupied the country (Vilna was occupied on July 13). Lithuania became a Soviet republic within the USSR.

Litt, Theodor, b. Düsseldorf, December 27, 1880; d. Bonn, July 16, 1969, German philosopher and educator. Litt saw a kinship between his own theoretical views and the thought of Hegel, the phenomenology of Edmund Husserl, and the "philosophy of life" (*Lebensphilosophie*). Litt taught philosophy in Bonn in 1919; from 1920 to 1937 and from 1945 to 1947 he was a professor in Leipzig. In 1947 he returned to Bonn. The National Socialists rejected Litt's philosophy because it lacked the desired "uniform German worldview" with an "active stake in unifying the *Volk.*"

Little Entente, alliance system joining Czechoslovakia, Romania, and Yugoslavia. Directed against efforts to revise the PARIS SUBURBAN TREATIES, especially by Hungary but also by Bulgaria and Italy, it developed from bilateral assistance agreements signed in 1920 and 1921. The initiative for the Little Entente came from Czechoslovak foreign minister Edvard BENEŠ. It was encouraged by France, which allied itself to the entente states in treaties signed between 1924 and 1927, thus building up its system of collective security against the renascent German Reich. (The French system also included a 1921 treaty with Poland and the Franco-Soviet mutual assistance pact of 1935.)

In 1933 the Little Entente was cemented through an organizational pact, which through common institutions (a permanent foreign ministers' council, a secretariat, an economic council) was to create a sort of "fifth great power." But in 1934 Italy, Austria, and Hungary signed the so-called Triple Pact, which, together with the developing Berlin-Rome AXIS, led to erosion of the Little Entente. It finally collapsed owing to minority problems within the member states, the failure of France as a protector in the MUNICH AGREEMENT, and Germany's superior strength after 1938.

Litvinov, Maksim Maksimovich (originally, Max Wallach-Finkelstein), b. Białystok, July 17, 1876; d. Moscow, Dec. 31, 1951, Soviet politician. In 1898 Litvinov joined the Russian Social Democratic party. He emigrated in 1902, then returned in 1917 during the October Revolution. After various diplomatic missions, in July 1930 he became People's Commissar (minister) for foreign affairs. He strove for rapprochement with the Western powers and was the initiator of the Franco-Soviet pact of 1935. Stalin, made uneasy by the MUNICH AGREEMENT, replaced Litvinov with Viacheslav MOLOTOV on May 3, 1939—a sign to Berlin of a willingness to negotiate. After the German attack on Russia (June 22, 1941), Litvinov's advice was again sought. As ambassador to Washington (until 1943), he arranged for extensive American military aid. After the war he again fell into disfavor.

Maksim Maksimovich Litvinov.

Litzmann, Karl, b. Neu-Globnow bei Ruppin, January 22, 1850; d. there, May 28, 1936, German general. On November 24, 1914, Litzmann forced the breakthrough near Brzeziny, which decided the battle of Łódź (thus, he was known as the "Lion of Brzeziny"). Retired from service in August 1918, he joined the NSDAP in 1929, thereafter often representing the party as senior president (*Alterspräsident*) in the Reichstag and the Prussian diet. Like August von MACKENSEN, Litzmann was among the First World War heroes and generals-for-display

Karl Litzmann.

whom the National Socialists liked to use to adorn their parades. In his honor, Łódź, occupied in 1939, was renamed Litzmannstadt on April 12, 1940.

Living Space (*Lebensraum*), popular political slogan at the time of the founding of the German Empire (1870–1871), one that expressed German imperialist claims and originally was to be understood chiefly in a colonial context. The term found acceptance in political geography through the scholar Friedrich Ratzel (1844–1904), who in 1901 published an essay entitled "Der Lebensraum" (The Living Space). Ratzel described human history as a "permanent struggle for living space," but drew no further conclusions for German politics. This was reserved for the GEOPOLITICS of Karl HAUSHOFER and his students. Literary support was found in such works as Hans GRIMM's novel *Volk ohne Raum* (A People without Space), whose title became a National Socialist (NS) slogan. To this colonial orientation was now added a continental European solution, as would define Hitler's FOREIGN POLICY, and which in his view had to do ultimately with *Bodenpolitik* (politics of the soil).

As early as December 10, 1919, Hitler noted "that 18 times more land falls to each Russian than to each German," from which he derived at the very beginning of *Mein Kampf* "the moral right to acquire foreign land and soil." As opposed to the geopoliticians, who viewed military annexation as a last resort, for Hitler force was inherently linked to the plan for acquiring

living space: "The plow is then the sword." He himself indicated that the REVISIONIST POLICY he first adopted was a "cover . . . for an increase in living space," since a war merely to restore Germany's prewar boundaries "would not, God knows, be worth it." Alliances whose "goal did not include war" were "senseless and worthless" (all quotes from *Mein Kampf*). Hitler adduced claims based on colonial policy only as a tactical argument against the colonial powers of the West, while in reality aiming exclusively at "Living Space in the East" (speech before the army generals, February 3, 1933). It only made sense, as he said shortly before the February 7, 1945, collapse, to expand "where geographical contiguity with the motherland is assured" (*Hitlers Politische Testament* [Hitler's Political Testament]). From the beginning, Russia was explicitly meant.

A racist element entered the politics of Living Space through expansion for new sources of food and raw materials; it was implied in the geopoliticians' Social Darwinist schemes but first openly expressed by the National Socialists. According to them, it fell to a "master race" (*Herrenvolk* [*Mein Kampf*]) to promote the subjection and "displacement" (*Verdrängung*) of lesser nationalities and races, even to the extent of extermination. In Hitler's view the Bolshevik Revolution had been nothing more than a Jewish takeover in Russia. But since Jews could never build a state, "the giant empire in the East was ripe for a collapse," which would become the "most powerful confirmation of the correctness of the *völkisch* racial theory" (*Mein Kampf*). The FINAL SOLUTION of the Jewish question was thus an integral part of the war for Living Space, which in February 1945 Hitler was still calling "the holy mission of my life" and the NS "reason for existence."

Lloyd George, David, b. Manchester, January 17, 1863; d. Llanystumdwy, March 26, 1945, British politician. Lloyd George became a Liberal member of Parliament in 1890. From 1905 to 1908 he was president of the Board of Trade. He served as chancellor of the Exchequer from 1908 to 1915, minister of war in 1915–1916, and prime minister from December 1916 to October 19, 1922. In the First World War Lloyd George was the decisive force behind British arms production. He achieved an overwhelming parliamentary victory in the postwar "khaki election" of 1918 (so called after the color of British army uniforms). He strove for a significant softening of the terms of the VERSAILLES

David Lloyd George.

TREATY, but could hardly moderate its basic tenor. Badly defeated in 1922, he remained for a time the Liberal leader, but after 1929 he lost all political influence. In September 1936 Lloyd George visited Germany, where he was deeply impressed by National Socialist "construction work"; after a visit to the Berghof he spoke of Hitler as "the George Washington of Germany." Despite later repudiation of this view, his outburst of enthusiasm remained a black mark in public opinion.

Löbe, Paul, b. Liegnitz, December 14, 1875; d. Bonn, August 3, 1967, German politician. A typesetter, in 1899 Löbe became a journalist with the Social Democratic newspaper *Volkswacht* (People's Watch). His journalistic activity earned him several prison sentences over the years. In 1904 he was elected a councilman for the SPD (Social Democratic Party) in Breslau. He became a member of the National Assembly in 1919, then served from 1920 to 1933 in the Reichstag, where he was elected to the steering committee of the SPD Reichstag delegation; from 1920 to 1932 he served as Reichstag president.

Temporarily imprisoned in 1933, Löbe made contact with the opposition circle around Carl Friedrich GOERDELER, without becoming politically active. After July 20, 1944, he was again imprisoned in a concentration camp. In 1948–1949 he was a member of the SPD's Parliamentary Council, and from 1949 to 1953 he was the senior president (*Alterspräsident*) of the Federal

German Bundestag. After 1954 Löbe led the Curatorium for Indivisible Germany (Kuratorium unteilbares Deutschland).

Loborgrad, National Socialist concentration camp in northern Croatia; it was built immediately after the German occupation of Yugoslavia in April 1941, and put under Croatian control. When the SS deported Jews from Bosnia, especially from Sarajevo, the women in particular were put into Loborgrad. Some 4,000 persons died there through starvation, disease, and general mistreatment.

Local Group (*Ortsgruppe*), organizational unit of the NSDAP and a "sovereign territory" (*Hoheitsgebiet*) in party terminology; it was led by a local leader (*Ortsleiter*) as a "sovereignty bearer" (*Hoheitsträger*). The *Ortsgruppen* did not transcend communal boundaries, insofar as possible; in rural areas, however, they could encompass several communities (*Gemeinden*). Cities could be divided among several *Ortsgruppen*, depending on the density of party membership. An *Ortsgruppe* consisted of at least 150 households, but not more than 1,500; the number of households was the basis of reckoning, not the number of individuals. This related to the tasks of the *Ortsleiter*, which extended to nonmembers: he was to "organize the populace in a National Socialist manner through appropriate events" and was to fill out a questionnaire providing information on the political reliability of nonorganized persons in his district.

The *Ortsleiter*, who was appointed by the *Gauleiter* on recommendation of the *Kreisleiter*

Paul Löbe.

(district leader), worked from the Local Office (*Ortsdienststelle*), as did the local representatives of the German Labor Front, Women's Union, and National Socialist Volk Welfare. Responsible for the "overall political situation" in the *Ortsgruppe*, the leader was to attend to all matters of communal politics, oversee the subordinate cells and BLOCK units, train the POLITICAL LEADERS, and act as an informer. *Ortsgruppe* leaders were often particularly zealous, and were detested by the populace.

Locarno Pact, treaty between Belgium, Germany, France, and Great Britain signed in Locarno, Switzerland, on October 16, 1925, and ratified in London on December 1 of that year. The signatories for Germany were Chancellor Hans LUTHER and Foreign Minister Gustav STRESEMANN (who had prepared the agreement in close cooperation with Great Britain); for Belgium, France, and Great Britain their respective foreign ministers, Emile Vander,velde, Aristide BRIAND, and Austen CHAMBERLAIN; and for Italy, Premier Benito MUSSOLINI.

The terms of the Locarno Pact were:

1. Recognition of the inviolability of Germany's borders with Belgium and France; Germany formally acknowledged her western boundary as established in the Versailles treaty, thus relinquishing claims to ALSACE-LORRAINE
2. Guarantee of these boundaries by Great Britain and Italy
3. Recognition of the demilitarized Rhineland,

as stipulated in Articles 42 and 43 of the Versailles treaty
4. Mutual commitment by Germany and Belgium and by Germany and France "under no circumstances" to begin a war or other warlike action against each other
5. Commitment by the signatories to settle all disputes by peaceful means

At the end of the Locarno Conference (October 5–16), Germany concluded corresponding agreements with both Belgium and France in addition to the Locarno Pact (also known as the "Western," "Rhine," or "Security" Pact). France, moreover, concluded defensive treaties (recognized by Germany) with both Poland and Czechoslovakia. Finally, Germany signed corresponding arbitration treaties with Poland and Czechoslovakia ("Eastern Locarno"), according to which it renounced force in any future revisions of these eastern boundaries.

The Locarno Pact took effect with Germany's entry into the League of Nations on September 8, 1926. On March 7, 1936, Hitler repudiated the pact, ordered the occupation of the Rhineland, and thus destroyed the "Locarno system."

R. B.

Loeper, Wilhelm, b. Schwerin, October 13, 1883; d. Dessau, October 23, 1935, German politician and officer. Loeper was discharged from the Reichswehr for his part in the HITLER PUTSCH (November 9, 1923). He entered the

Locarno Pact. Final session of the conference.

Wilhelm Loeper.

NSDAP in 1925, and in 1928 became *Gauleiter* of Magdeburg-Anhalt. His success there in promoting the party brought him further advancement. In 1930 he became head of the NSDAP Personnel Office, in 1933 Reich governor in Braunschweig and Anhalt, and in 1934, an SS-*Gruppenführer*. In 1935 Loeper was made a member of the Academy for German Law.

Loerzer, Bruno, b. Berlin, January 22, 1891; d. Hamburg, August 22, 1960, German colonel general (February 1943). In 1911 Loerzer became a lieutenant in an infantry regiment. An aviator in the First World War, he won 44 air victories and was awarded the Pour le mérite.

His friendship with Hermann Göring made Loerzer president of the German Air Sports Association in 1933, and on July 26, 1935, Reich Air Sports Führer. In October 1935 Loerzer transferred to the Air Ministry; he became a major general in 1938, and on February 1, 1939, he became commandant of an air force division, which he led in the Polish Campaign. By the war's end he was the commanding general of Air Corps II.

Löhr, Alexander, b. Turnu-Severin, May 20, 1885; d. Belgrade, February 16, 1947 (executed), Austrian colonel general (May 3, 1941). Löhr underwent General Staff training, and in 1918 joined the Austrian air force. As a major general he was made commander in chief of the air force in 1936; after the Anschluss he became head of the Luftwaffe command for the Ostmark. From March 18, 1939, to June 23, 1942, Löhr commanded Air Fleet 4, with which he participated in the campaigns in Poland, the Balkans, and Russia. As commander in chief for the southeast, he next led Army Group E, with which he built a new defensive front in Yugoslavia in January 1945. Cut off from all communications, Löhr and his troops were captured by Yugoslav forces in early May 1945. He was sentenced to death and executed for crimes that included the air attack he led against Belgrade (April 6, 1941).

Lohse, Hinrich, b. Mühlenbarbek bei Itzehoe, September 2, 1896; d. there, February 25, 1964, German politician. Lohse joined the NSDAP in 1925. He became a *Gauleiter* in 1925

Bruno Loerzer.

Alexander Löhr.

Hinrich Lohse.

and governor (*Oberpräsident*) of Schleswig-Holstein in 1933. That same year he was elected to the Reichstag. Lohse became an SA *Obergruppenführer* in 1937, and in 1939 was appointed Reich commissioner for the Ostland, which included chiefly the Baltic states. Despite the objections he made on economic grounds, he did not oppose the SS extermination program; instead, he took part in plundering the Baltic lands through the so-called Ostland Societies. For this he was sentenced to 10 years' imprisonment in 1948, but he was released on grounds of ill health in February 1951. The judicial tug-of-war regarding his pension rights led to heated public controversy. He was finally turned down in 1955.

London Agreement (also known as the London Charter), agreement of August 8, 1945, between Great Britain, the United States, the USSR, and the provisional government of France regarding the prosecution and punishment of the major war criminals of the European Axis. An appended statute established a court to carry out the agreement and regulated its composition, competence, and general procedural principles (*see* NUREMBERG TRIALS).

London Conferences, series of rounds of talks held in London between 1921 and 1924 for the primary purpose of regulating German REPARATIONS. The first London Conference (February 21–March 14, 1921) broke down because the victorious powers found inadequate the German offer of 30 billion gold marks; the occupation of Duisburg, Ruhrort, and Düsseldorf ensued. A

second conference (April 29–May 5, 1921) ended with the London Ultimatum, which was to be accepted by Germany within five days. It stipulated payment of 132 billion gold marks in installments of 2 billion marks each, as well as heavy demands on German exports. This ultimatum led to the resignation of the Fehrenbach cabinet and the beginning of a FULFILLMENT POLICY through Reich Chancellor Joseph WIRTH. A further London Conference (August 7–14, 1922) brought no progress. Finally, the fourth conference (July 16–August 16, 1924) found a lasting solution with acceptance of the DAWES PLAN and the simultaneous conclusion to the RUHR CONFLICT.

London Foreign Ministers' Conferences, two rounds of talks, held in London by the foreign ministers of the four victorious powers after the Second World War, in order to regulate treatment of the defeated countries. The first conference, held from September 10 to October 2, 1945, in which the foreign minister of China also took part, broke down over conflicts concerning Italy's remaining colonies, the Trieste question, Italian reparations, and the establishment of an Allied governing council in Japan. During the second conference, held from November 25 to December 14, 1947, the German question was in the foreground, notably the issues of consolidating the British and American occupation zones, reparations, and the form of a future German state. This second London conference also remained without result.

Lord Haw-Haw. *See* Joyce, William.

Lorenz, Konrad, b. Vienna, November 7, 1903; d. Altenburg, February 27, 1989, Austrian behavioral scientist. In 1937 Lorenz became a university lecturer in Vienna, and in 1940 a professor in Königsberg. He became known through studies of animal behavior, especially that of the gray goose. At the same time he drew problematic parallels to human behavior, thus succumbing to the biological Zeitgeist. In an essay, "Psychologie und Stammesgeschichte" (Psychology and Phylogeny; 1943), he recommended a "sharp demarcation and separation" from "decadent elements of society," and thus played unwittingly into the hands of National Socialist racial policy. He later classified these formulations as "naive."

Lorenz was a Soviet prisoner from 1944 to 1948. In 1949 he founded an institute for comparative behavioral physiology. He held professorships at numerous universities, and from 1961 to 1973 was director of the Max Planck Institute for Behavioral Physiology in Seewiesen. Lorenz was awarded the Nobel prize in physiology and medicine in 1973. He did not accept Simon WIESENTHAL's suggestion that he refuse the prize "as a sign of remorse" for his remarks during the Third Reich. Lorenz's many publications include, most notably, *Das sogenannte Böse* (So-called Evil, 1963; translated as *On Aggression*), *Die acht Todsünden der zivilisierten Menschheit* (*Civilized Man's Eight Deadly Sins;* 1973), and *Der Abbau des Menschlichen* (*The Waning of Humaneness;* 1983).

Lorenz, Werner, b. Gründorf, near Stolp, October 2, 1891; d. Hamburg, March 13, 1974, SS-*Obergruppenführer* (1943). In 1929 Lorenz joined the NSDAP, and in 1931 he joined the SS in Danzig. He was elected to the Reichstag in 1933. From 1934 to 1937, Lorenz served as head of SS Upper Sector North (*Oberabschnitt Nord*) in Altona. Appointed chief of the ETHNIC GERMAN CENTRAL OFFICE in 1937, he organized the relocation of some 900,000 ethnic Germans after 1939. As "Reich Commissioner for the Fortification of the German Volk-Nation" in Himmler's office (as of October 7, 1939), Lorenz was head of the Division for Resettlement and RE-GERMANIZATION, and served as plenipotentiary for international relations in the SS Central Office. Sentenced to 20 years' imprisonment on March 10, 1948, he gained early release in 1955.

Loret, Jean-Marie, b. Saint-Quentin (northern France), March 25, 1918; d. there, February 13, 1985, Hitler's putative son. According to investigations by the German historian Werner Maser, Loret was the product of a liaison between Lance Corporal Hitler and Charlotte Lobjoie, an unmarried Frenchwoman. The evidence offered for this claim does not, however, resolve all questions.

Loyal-Service Medal (Treudienst-Ehrenzeichen), badge issued by Hitler on the occasion of the fifth anniversary of the Seizure of Power in 1938 "in recognition of loyal work in the service of the German *Volk*." It was awarded to officials, employees, and workers in public-service positions; a silver medal represented 25 years of service, and a gold one, 40 years. Persons employed in the private sector received the medal (the silver version, with a gold oak-leaf cluster) after 50 years at the same workplace.

Lubbe, Marinus van der, b. Leiden, January 13, 1909; d. Leipzig, January 10, 1934, Dutch journeyman mason who was unable to work after a construction accident. Van der Lubbe traveled through many European countries, then joined the *Rade* [councils; soviets] Communists, an anarchist splinter group. In early 1933 he decided to assist the German Communists and Socialists in their struggle against the National Socialists. He traveled to Berlin, which he reached on February 18. Van der Lubbe soon realized that the German Left's strength to resist had been paralyzed, and he formed a plan to awaken it with a signal.

Werner Lorenz.

Marinus van der Lubbe.

After his attempts at arson in the Neukölln welfare office, in the town hall, and in the Berlin Palace miscarried on February 25, van der Lubbe broke into the Reichstag building shortly after 9:00 p.m. on February 27. Using coal as an igniter, he was able to set so many fires that despite his prompt arrest at 9:27 p.m., the plenary hall could not be saved. During the REICHSTAG FIRE TRIAL van der Lubbe stood by his story that he had worked alone, which the National Socialists—to no avail—sought to shake on anti-Communist grounds, while the Communists did the same on antifascist grounds. Sentenced to death under the LEX VAN DER LUBBE on December 23, 1933, he was executed by guillotine.

Ludendorff, Erich, b. Kruszewnia bei Posen, April 9, 1856; d. Tutzing, December 20, 1937, German general. A quartermaster general in the Second Army at the outbreak of the First World War, on August 21, 1914, Ludendorff was made chief of the General Staff of the Eighth Army under Paul von HINDENBURG. Victories over the Russians near Tannenberg and at the Masurian Lakes underlay the Ludendorff legend and his own precipitous rise—first to chief of the army's General Staff, and on August 29, 1916, to first quartermaster general and to a kind of military dictatorship. The fall of Reich Chancellor Bethmann Hollweg is traceable back to Ludendorff, who also carried out unrestricted U-boat warfare. He demanded an immediate cease-fire when his last offensives failed in 1918.

Discharged on October 26, 1918, Ludendorff used his popularity to oppose the Weimar Re-

public; he stirred up the STAB-IN-THE-BACK LEGEND and participated in the HITLER PUTSCH on November 9, 1923. Released (unlike Hitler himself), he entered the Reichstag in 1924 and ran unsuccessfully for the office of Reich president in 1925. In 1928 Ludendorff turned his back on the National Socialists. Together with his second wife, Mathilde (1877–1966; née Spiess, widowed Kemnitz), in 1925 he had founded the TANNENBERG LEAGUE, to whose "German acknowledgment of God" he thereafter devoted himself entirely. Although Ludendorff openly opposed Hitler (notably in a telegram to Hindenburg on January 31, 1933), he remained unharassed, and in 1937 was given a pompous state funeral.

Ludwig, Emil (originally, Emil Cohn), b. Breslau, January 25, 1881; d. near Ascona (Switzerland), September 17, 1948, German writer. Ludwig wrote successful biographies of important figures of world history, such as *Goethe* (1920) and *Napoleon* (1925), but he brought down upon himself the accusation of National Socialist critics that he "odiously belittled everything great." Particularly resented was his book *Hindenburg und das Märchen von der deutschen Republik* (Hindenburg and the Fairy Tale of the German Republic; 1935), which was called a "vulgar pamphlet." Ludwig, who had lived in Switzerland since 1932, was stripped of his citizenship; he went to the United States in 1940.

Ludwigsburg Central Office (Ludwigsburger Zentralstelle; ZSt), abbreviated name for the Central Office of State Justice Administrations

Erich Ludendorff.

Emil Ludwig.

for the Investigation of National Socialist Crimes (Zentrale Stelle der Landesjustizverwaltungen zur Aufklärung von national-sozialistischen Verbrechen), an authority founded on November 6, 1958, through administrative agreement of the ministers and senators in charge of justice in the *Länder* (states) of the Federal Republic; it began its activity on December 1, 1958. The mandate of the ZSt is to gather, classify, and evaluate all available material on National Socialist crimes. The main related goal is to establish dossiers of specific criminal acts according to place, time, and circle of perpetrators, and to determine which participants in an event can be prosecuted (*see* STATUTE OF LIMITATIONS). When a group of alleged perpetrators liable for prosecution and the appropriate public prosecutor's office have been determined, the Ludwigsburg office closes its preliminary investigations and turns the proceeding over to this authority. As of January 1, 1985, the ZSt had given 4,899 cases (out of a much larger number of accused individuals) over to the judicial authorities for further investigation. Of the cases passed on, some 13,000 investigations have been pursued by public prosecutors.

A. St.

Lueger, Karl, b. Vienna, October 24, 1844; d. there, March 10, 1910, Austrian politician. In 1874 Lueger became a lawyer. From 1875 he served on Vienna's city council (Gemeinderat), and in 1885 he was elected to the Imperial Parliament (Reichsrat). Lueger's views were initially close to those of the LINZ PROGRAM of

Karl Lueger.

Georg von Schönerer. He then became associated with the Christian-Social movement, which he molded into a mass party in the 1880s. As its spokesman after 1888, Lueger was elected mayor of Vienna in 1895, although he obtained imperial recognition (having been deemed too "vulgar" by Franz Josef) only in 1897. The young Hitler saw the antisemitic and antisocialist demagogue as a model; because of Lueger's extensive community achievements (such as communalizing the provision of energy and water and carrying out administrative reforms), he termed Lueger "the most powerful mayor of all time" (*Mein Kampf*).

Luftalarm (air alarm), official designation for the more usual colloquial term *Fliegeralarm* (literally, flyer alarm; *see* AIR RAID ALARM).

Luftkrieg. *See* Air war.

Luftwaffe. *See* Air Battle for England; Wehrmacht.

Luftwaffe helpers (*Luftwaffenhelfer*), official term referring to school pupils in auxiliary war service who were more generally known as FLAK HELPERS.

Luftwaffe High Command (Oberkommando der Luftwaffe; OKL), name of the highest administrative and command authority of the Luftwaffe under its supreme commanders, Hermann GÖRING (March 1, 1935, to April 23, 1945) and, finally, Robert Ritter von GREIM (April 25 to May 8, 1945). The name was first commonly used as of September 1943.

Luserke, Martin, b. Berlin, May 3, 1880; d. Meldorf, June 1, 1968, German writer. As a teacher in independent schools, Luserke had early become involved in the LAY THEATER; from the 1920s on he was among its most important theorists and authors. He viewed amateur theater as the "original" form of theater, shaped by community work and experience. His romanticizing, sometimes humorous plays were frequently produced before 1933, especially in circles of the young workers' movement, and they later belonged to the permanent National Socialist repertoire. Luserke gained particular popularity in the 1930s and 1940s with numerous novels and stories of seafaring adventure, such as *Hasko wird Geusenkapitän* (Hasko Becomes Captain of the Sea Beggars; 1937), whose "Nordic worldview" (Franz Lennartz) was also prized by NS critics and which after 1945 again found a wide public.

Luther, Hans, b. Berlin, March 10, 1879; d. Düsseldorf, May 11, 1962, German politician. After studying law, from 1913 to 1918 Luther was managing director of the German Städtetag (organization of municipal governments). From 1918 to 1922 he was lord mayor of Essen, in 1922–1923 Reich minister for food and agriculture, and from 1923 to 1925, Reich finance minister. In January 1925 Luther became Reich chancellor, representing no party, but rather a middle-class coalition of the Right. (In 1926 he joined the German People's Party.) With Gustav Stresemann, Luther signed the Locarno accords (*see* LOCARNO PACT). After a new cabinet was formed, Luther had to resign in May 1926 over the Flag Edict, which required German consulates to fly the imperial black-white-red merchant flag as well as the Weimar Republic's black-red-gold colors. From 1930 to 1933 president of the German National Bank, Luther was forced to resign by Hitler, who then made him Germany's ambassador in Washington (1933–1937). After 1945 Luther's activities included work as a consultant on issues of economic reconstruction.

Luther, Martin, b. Berlin, December 16, 1895; d. there, May 13, 1945, German politician. At first a shipping agent, Luther joined the NSDAP and SA on March 1, 1933. In 1936 he was appointed to the RIBBENTROP OFFICE. With his chief he moved to the Foreign Office, where he took over the Deutschlandabteilung (Germany Division) on May 1, 1940. A fanatical National Socialist, Luther worked closely with the SS and was the Foreign Office representative at the

Hans Luther.

WANNSEE CONFERENCE. He was assigned the job of forcing friendly and dependent governments to hand over their Jews. An unsuccessful intrigue against Joachim von Ribbentrop ended Luther's career in April 1943 and led to his imprisonment in the Sachsenhausen concentration camp. He died of a heart attack shortly after the Red Army entered Germany.

Luther Germans (*Luther-Deutsche*), self-designation used after 1938 by the main group of GERMAN CHRISTIANS.

Lütjens, Günther, b. Wiesbaden, May 25, 1887; d. North Atlantic, May 27, 1941, German admiral. Lütjens entered the navy in 1907. A torpedo-boat commander in the First World War, after 1926 he held various command positions, and in 1937 was made rear admiral and chief of torpedo boats. Lütjens led the reconnaissance forces in the NORWEGIAN CAMPAIGN (April 1940). He was promoted to admiral in September 1940, and as head of the fleet led the maneuvers of the battleships *Scharnhorst* and *Gneisenau.*

The high point and, simultaneously, the end of Lütjens's naval career took place when he was supreme commander of Operation "Rhine Exercise" ("Rheinübung"), employing the battleship *Bismarck* and the heavy cruiser *Prinz Eugen* against British supply operations in the North Atlantic. On May 24, 1941, he succeeded in sinking the British battle cruiser *Hood*, but three days later the *Bismarck* was sunk by superior forces. Lütjens and his men fought "to the last grenade," as he had promised Hitler in his final telegram; he went down with his ship and a crew of almost 2,000 men. The Federal Republic's navy named one of its warships, the guided-missile destroyer *Lütjens*, after him.

Lutze, Viktor, b. Bevergern, December 28, 1890; d. near Hannover, May 2, 1943, German politician. Lutze became a career soldier in 1912. He joined the NSDAP in 1922 and the SA in 1923. That same year he was actively engaged in the RUHR CONFLICT. In 1925 he became a *Gauleiter,* and in 1925, SA-*Oberführer* for the Ruhr. Lutze was elected to the Reichstag in 1930. Meanwhile promoted to SA-*Obergruppenführer*, in March 1933 he was named chief of police in Hannover, and, on March 25, governor (*Oberpräsident*) of Hannover province.

After the RÖHM AFFAIR and the bloody purge of the SA, Lutze, who had provided the evidence against Röhm, was named SA chief of staff by Hitler. Although Lutze continually worked in

Viktor Lutze.

bitter opposition to and competition with the SS, he was unable to reconquer the old position of power for his troops. Promoted to *Reichsleiter* of the NSDAP, in April 1941 Lutze on his own initiative resigned his post as provincial governor. His attempt to promote premilitary training within the SA failed. Lutze died in an automobile accident.

Luxembourg, grand duchy bordering on Germany's western border; area, 2,587 sq km (about 1,035 sq miles); population, approximately 300,000 (1930). After the dissolution of an economic union with Germany in 1919 and France's refusal to annex Luxembourg, the grand duchy retained its national independence. (In a referendum of November 28, 1919, nearly 80 percent of its voters supported retaining the dynasty and independence.) Luxembourg also entered into a 50-year tariff and trade union with Belgium on July 25, 1921 (the seed of the postwar Benelux union). Luxembourg's mining industry gave it a significant economic position. After German troops entered on May 10, 1940, in violation of Luxembourg's neutrality, Grand

Duchess Charlotte (1919–1964) and her government went to London via Paris and formed a government-in-exile.

During the war Berlin carried out a single-minded policy of Germanization. On August 30, 1942, Luxembourg was annexed into the German Reich as part of Moselgau Koblenz-Trier under Gauleiter Gustav SIMON. The French language was prohibited, names and place-names were Germanized, German laws were introduced, and the Luxembourg army was annexed into the German forces. In early September 1944 the Allies liberated Luxembourg, but by the end of 1944 it was again briefly a battleground during Germany's Ardennes Offensive. In 1945 the grand duchess returned with the government-in-exile, and national sovereignty was again established.

Bekanntmachung !

DAS

STANDGERICHT

hat wegen Gefährdung des deutschen Aufbauwerkes in Luxemburg durch aufrührerischen Streik und Sabotage im Kriege folgende Personen zum Tode verurteilt und die Einziehung des Vermögens angeordnet.

Dax, Michel,
Eisenbahnarbeiter, Ettelbrück

Schmit, Alfons,
Professor Dr. math., Echternach

Thull, Johann,
Eisenbahnanstreicher, Ettelbrück

Heiderscheid, Emil,
Dachdecker, Diekirch

Ferner wurden elf Angeklagte der Geheimen Staatspolizei überstellt.

Die Todesurteile wurden heute um 6 Uhr durch Erschiessen vollstreckt !

Luxemburg, den 5. September 1942.
Der Vorsitzer des Standgerichts.

Luxembourg. Proclamation by the German occupation authorities of death sentences imposed on four men for strike and sabotage activities. "The death sentences will be carried out today at 6:00 a.m. by shooting!"

THE ENCYCLOPEDIA OF THE THIRD REICH

Volume 2
M - Z

Maass, Hermann, b. Bamberg, October 23, 1897; d. Berlin, October 20, 1944 (executed), German politician. A volunteer in the First World War, Maass then joined the SPD (Social Democratic Party). He also studied philosophy and sociology. In 1924 he was made general secretary of the Reich Committee of German Youth Associations (Reichsausschuss der deutschen Jugendverbände) and editor of the monthly *Das junge Deutschland* (Young Germany). Removed from both positions by the National Socialists in 1933, Maass became associated with Wilhelm LEUSCHNER, in whose small aluminum factory he worked. Above all, he was active in organizing the Social Democratic resistance. After the failure of the assassination attempt of July 20, 1944, Maass was arrested on August 8, and soon afterward was sentenced to death.

Maccabee (Makkabi), Jewish sports organization with a Zionist orientation. Founded in 1921, it grew out of the Jewish Gymnastics Club (Jüdischer Turnverein). The German Maccabee Circle consisted of 25 clubs with 8,000 members in 1933. It purposely kept its autonomy from the German-Jewish SHIELD alliance. When German sports groups adopted the ARYAN PARAGRAPH, Jewish sports enthusiasts had to transfer to Jewish clubs, whose membership rapidly increased. At the same time, their conditions for training deteriorated since public sports facilities were closed to Jews. Until the conclusion of the OLYMPIC GAMES, Maccabee received something of a reprieve. Then police persecution and growing emigration brought an end to Jewish sports activity.

MacDonald, James Ramsay, b. Lossiemouth (Scotland), October 12, 1866; d. during a sea voyage to South America, September 9, 1937, British politician. MacDonald was a co-founder of the Labour party and served as its leader in the House of Commons from 1911 to 1914. He

James Ramsay MacDonald.

broke with the party over its war policies, and held no seat from 1918 to 1922. MacDonald became prime minister and foreign secretary in the first Labour cabinet in January 1924. His conciliatory attitude toward Germany, especially on the issue of reparations, caused him to have foreign-policy problems with Paris. Moreover, his resumption of diplomatic relations with the Soviet Union led to domestic political difficulties and to his fall in October 1924. He again became prime minister in 1929. In 1931, during the world economic crisis, he formed a coalition government with the Conservative and Liberal parties. This cost him his own party's support, and in June 1935 MacDonald resigned.

Machtergreifung. *See* Seizure of Power.

Mackensen, August von, b. Leipnitz Manor, near Wittenberg, December 6, 1849; d. Burghorn bei Celle, November 8, 1945, German field marshal general (June 1915). Mackensen participated in the Franco-German war of 1870–1871. In the First World War he was commanding general of the Seventeenth Army Corps in the battles of Tannenberg and the Masurian

August von Mackensen.

Lakes, and thereafter commander in chief of army groups in Poland and the Balkans. Further victorious campaigns in Serbia and Romania made him a popular army leader. Groups of the nationalist Right, including the NSDAP, later made use of his popularity. As an old man, Mackensen attended the party's celebrations, wearing the snugly fitting uniform of the Death's-Head Hussars. His last major public appearance was at the age of 92, at the funeral of the former emperor Wilhelm II in June 1941.

Madagascar Plan (*Madagaskar-Plan*), proposal first made by Paul de LAGARDE and subsequently by antisemites of the 1920s to resolve the "Jewish question" through the settlement of Jewish citizens in "underpopulated" areas that could be colonized, notably French Madagascar. The Madagascar Plan was discussed officially by the party beginning in the summer of 1938, and received new impetus after the French Campaign. The previously favored idea of forcing the emigration of Jews had become illusory after the conquest of Poland, with its nearly 3 million Jewish inhabitants; a "territorial final solution" was then sought.

In the Jewish Section of the Reich Security Main Office (RSHA), a "provisional plan" (*Nahplan*) was developed to gather all those affected in the Polish GENERALGOUVERNEMENT; this was to be succeeded by the "long-range plan" (*Fernplan*), which would have deported all Jews to the African island-ghetto. The Mada-

gascar Plan, which could hardly have been realized under the most favorable circumstances, failed because of British domination of the seas, the Vichy government's inability to act on the matter, the lack of a German-French peace treaty, and the failure of the German campaign against Russia—all culminating in the genocide of the FINAL SOLUTION. The island of Madagascar as an alternative to Palestine even later played a role in the search for a homeland for the Jewish people.

Mädel, the equivalent of *Mädchen* (girl) in National Socialist usage. The term *Mädel*, which had its origins in dialect, became common around 1900 in the "leagues" within the YOUTH MOVEMENT to describe the somewhat liberated (*burschikose*) type of girl that it idealized. The National Socialists introduced *Mädel* to official jargon through the founding of the Bund Deutscher Mädel (LEAGUE OF GERMAN GIRLS) within the Hitler Youth, and through the subsequent use of compound names for its sub-units: *Mädelschaft* ("Girlship"), *Mädelschar* (Girl Troop), *Mädelgruppe* (Girl Group), and *Mädelring* (Girl Ring).

Maginot Line, belt of fortifications on the French-German border (from Longwy in northeast France to Basel, Switzerland), named after French war minister André Maginot (1877–1932). Construction began in 1929 and was largely completed by 1932, at a cost of nearly 3 billion francs. The Maginot Line consisted of a network of underground passages extending

Brennessel satire of the Madagascar Plan: "They prudently neglected to ask us natives of Madagascar."

Tank fortification on the Maginot Line.

over 150 km (90 miles), with 39 military units, 70 bunkers, 500 artillery and infantry groupings, and 500 casemates, shelters, and observation towers. The belief that the fortifications were impregnable led to a fatally erroneous estimation of France's military position and engendered a defense mentality that could not counter the mobile warfare employed by Germany in the FRENCH CAMPAIGN. In 1940 the Wehrmacht outflanked the Maginot Line by violating the neutrality of the Benelux states. After encircling the main body of the French army, Army Group C broke through the line in a frontal attack on June 16, 1940.

Mahraun, Arthur, b. Cassel, December 30, 1890; d. Gutersloh, March 27, 1950, German politician. Mahraun was a career officer in the First World War. On January 10, 1919, he founded the conservative free corps Kassel Officers' Company (Offizierskompagnie Kassel), which spawned the YOUNG GERMAN ORDER after the KAPP PUTSCH of March 17, 1920. Together with Christian trade unions, Mahraun founded the "People's National Reich Union" (Volksnationale Reichsvereinigung) in 1928; for a short time in 1930 he belonged to the German State Party. In 1930 the order was dissolved; Mahraun was temporarily taken into custody and tortured. Subsequently he worked as a publisher and writer. After the war Mahraun unsuccessfully advocated social reforms, including the creation of "neighborhoods" (Nachbarschaften).

Maid (*Maid*), designation for a girl, derived from Middle High German and used poetically since the 19th century for a maiden or virgin. The National Socialists contrived the compound WORKMAID (*Arbeits-Maid*) for young women in the Reich Labor Service.

Maidanek (Lublin-Maidanek), National Socialist concentration camp on the southwestern outskirts of Lublin, on the Chelm highway. It was built in October 1941 as a prisoner-of-war camp of the Waffen-SS (because of the easier access to financing). According to Himmler's order of July 20, 1941, the camp was intended for 25,000 to 50,000 inmates. Prisoners from Buchenwald, Soviet prisoners of war, and Polish civilian workers were used to build the camp. Its prisoners were mostly Jewish, and came from the concentration camps of Theresienstadt, Auschwitz, Sachsenhausen, and Dachau, as well as from the Warsaw ghetto. German (*Reichsdeutsche*) inmates were given preferential treatment as "prisoners with special assignments" (*Funktionshäftlinge*). In the fall of 1942 a separate women's section was established, which held Polish women and girls who had initially been incarcerated for "political reasons" in various prisons, including Warsaw's notorious Pawiak Prison. Attendance at illegal high schools (only attendance at elementary schools was legal for Poles) was sufficient reason for imprisonment.

The prisoners were assigned to various kinds of work, as in agriculture and forestry (there were ten satellite camps). Clothing, food, housing, and sanitary conditions in the camp were totally inadequate. Many prisoners died from epidemics, starvation, exhaustion, or abuse, were shot "while attempting to escape" (the killer received special leave for this), or were hanged or otherwise killed. Prisoners with contagious diseases or those suspected of having them (especially typhus) were selected out and shot, on the order of the Reich Security Main Office (RSHA).

A gassing facility was put in use in the camp in October 1942. It consisted initially of two gas chambers in a wooden barrack. More gas chambers were later installed in a stone building, and the original chambers used for drying laundry. According to court findings, Maidanek housed "at least three chambers made of concrete, with airtight steel doors." Transports of Jews from Germany, the Netherlands, Italy, and elsewhere underwent a *Selektion* on their arrival, and able-bodied prisoners were assigned to labor commandos. Persons unable to work (women, children, and the elderly) were killed, either with ZYKLON B or carbon monoxide. Prisoners who became ill and unable to work were selected out from time to time and gassed. In May 1943, several hundred Jewish children lost their lives in the gas chambers. Court findings later determined that a minimum of approximately 200,000 persons had been gassed in Maidanek by the fall of 1943.

On November 3, 1943, when the gas chambers were no longer in use, those Jews who were still alive in the camp were shot in an *Aktion* that the SS called "HARVEST FESTIVAL" ("Erntefest"). The evacuation of Maidanek began in April 1944. Just before the capture of Lublin by Soviet troops (July 22, 1944), the last prisoners were marched on foot in the direction of Radom. After taking Maidanek, the Soviets used it for a time as a prisoner-of-war camp. Later, the Polish government built a museum and a memorial for victims of NS tyranny on part of the camp grounds.

The commandants of Maidanek were Karl Otto Koch (*see* BUCHENWALD), Hermann Florstedt (executed on Himmler's orders shortly before the end of the war), Martin Weiss (*see* NEUENGAMME), and Max Koegel (*see* FLOSSENBÜRG).

W. D.

Maidanek Trial, jury proceeding before the state court (*Landgericht*) in Düsseldorf against the former deputy commandant of the MAIDANEK concentration camp, Hermann Hackmann, and other former camp staff. They were charged with murder and with aiding and abetting murder to the detriment of camp prisoners. The Maidanek Trial was the longest in German judicial history. Preliminary inquiries began in October 1960. Charges were brought on November 15, 1974, and July 11, 1975. The trial began on November 26, 1975, and ended with a verdict on June 30, 1981. Originally 17 persons were accused, 11 men and 6 women. Two of the accused were dropped from the case before the main proceedings began because they were found unfit to stand trial. One of the accused died during the trial; the proceedings against another defendant had to be stopped temporarily because of serious illness. Four of the accused, a man and three women, were acquitted in a judgment of April 19, 1979, after their cases were separated from the main proceedings.

In the course of the main trial, more than 340 German and foreign witnesses testified, among them some 215 former inmates and approxi-

mately 85 former SS personnel. Of the former inmates, ill health prevented more than 70 from appearing at the trial. In accordance with international legal procedure, they had to be questioned in the presence of court officials at their current places of residence in Australia, Israel, Canada, Austria, Poland, the USSR, and the United States. The jury trial sentenced one of the nine remaining defendants to life imprisonment, and seven to prison terms of three to seven years. One of the accused was acquitted. An appeal by seven of those convicted was rejected as groundless by the Federal Supreme Court (Bundesgerichtshof) on May 30, 1984.

A. S.

Maikowski, Hans Eberhard, b. Berlin, February 23, 1908; d. there, January 31, 1933, SA-*Sturmführer*. Maikowski was a victim of street fighting after the torchlight parade celebrating the appointment of Hitler as Reich chancellor on January 30, 1933; he was accordingly honored as a "BLOOD WITNESS of the movement."

Malicious-Gossip Law (*Heimtückegesetz; Heimtückeverordnung*), National Socialist criminal measure to combat the expression of opposition views. The Ordinance of the Reich President for the Protection of the German *Volk* (*Reich Law Gazette* I, p. 35) of February 4, 1933, had given the government the possibility of essentially undercutting the freedoms of expression and action of opposition political groups and parties. The REICHSTAG FIRE DECREE (February 28, 1933) had then made any organized political opposition virtually impossible. Now the Ordinance of the Reich President for the Protection against Malicious Attacks of the Government of the National Rising of March 21, 1933 (*Reich Law Gazette* I, p. 135), made it possible to punish remarks critical of the regime made by private persons in private circles. According to Paragraph 3, a person who made "an untrue or a grossly distorted statement" that could harm the prestige of the government or of persons in it could be prosecuted.

After the elimination of former nationalist conservative coalition partners of the NSDAP, the Law against Malicious Attacks on State and Party and for the Protection of Party Uniforms of December 20, 1934 (*Reich Law Gazette* I, p. 1269), replaced the actual Malicious-Gossip Law, that is, the ordinance. This shift exacerbated the legal situation to the extent that, for example, the protection of party insignia was so intensified that wearing a uniform while committing an illegal act could be grounds for a death sentence (¶3). "Private expressions of ill will" were now also punishable "if the perpetrator . . . has cause to expect that the utterance will become publicly known" (¶3, Section 2). The legal door to denunciations was thus opened wide.

To attain the timely and efficient criminal prosecution of political criticism, passage of the Malicious-Gossip Ordinance was accompanied by the creation of SPECIAL COURTS. According to 1933 crime statistics, 3,744 offenses against the law were punished. In later years no statistics on political crimes were kept.

C. S.

Malmédy. *See* Eupen-Malmédy.

Malmédy Trial, proceeding in an American military tribunal in Dachau against 73 former members of the LEIBSTANDARTE-SS "ADOLF HITLER" First SS Tank Division. Charges included the murder of 71 American prisoners of war in Malmédy (in eastern Belgium) on December 17, 1944. This was one of the most controversial war crimes trials. The indictment was based on confessions by the defendants, who claimed during the main trial that they had been subjected to prior psychological pressure and physical coercion. Although other evidence was essentially absent, on July 16, 1946, 43 of the accused were sentenced to death, 22 to life imprisonment, and the rest to long prison terms.

Through the efforts in particular of the chief American defense counsel, Willis M. Everett, Jr., Gen. Lucius Clay, who was in charge of the proceedings, reduced 41 sentences (27 death sentences, 12 life terms, and 2 shorter terms) and quashed 13 sentences (4 death sentences, 8 life terms, and 1 shorter term). On further investigation, conducted in part by a committee of the United States Senate, other sentences were changed. In 1951 Gen. Thomas Handy, the American commander in chief in Europe, commuted the remaining 6 death sentences to life imprisonment. Soon afterward, further reductions of sentences were effected through pardons in 31 cases. One of the main defendants, SS-Standartenführer Joachim PEIPER, was murdered in France by unknown perpetrators in 1976, following a press campaign on the Malmédy case.

A. St.

Malraux, André, b. Paris, November 3, 1901; d. Créteil, November 23, 1976, French writer and politician. During the 1920s Malraux made a

André Malraux.

lengthy stay in China, which he described in *The Conquerors: Red and Yellow Fighting for Canton* (1928). Between 1936 and 1938, he fought on the Republican side in the Spanish Civil War. Malraux resigned from the French Communist party in 1939 because of the German-Soviet Nonaggression Pact. Serving with the French tank corps, he was taken prisoner by the Germans in 1940. He managed to flee, and became active in the RÉSISTANCE (under the pseudonym "Colonel Berger"), for a time as chief of the "Alsace-Lorraine" partisan brigade. As a close party comrade of Gen. Charles de Gaulle, Malraux served as minister several times after the war (notably as minister of culture, 1959–1969). He had an enormous influence on France's intellectual life, both as a writer (as in *The Psychology of Art,* 3 vols., 1947–1950) and a critic.

Mandel, Hermann, b. Holzwickede (Westphalia), December 13, 1882; d. there, April 8, 1946, German theologian and philosopher. As a professor in Kiel (beginning in 1918), Mandel incorporated *völkisch* and nationalist ideas into his philosophy of religion even before 1933. He then departed completely from Christianity and advocated a "Nordic belief in God," alluding to the medieval mystic Meister Eckhart and the young Martin Luther. Mandel distinguished this faith from Christianity and Judaism by means of racial biology, in *Arische Gottschau* (Aryan Vision of God; 1935). In 1934 his appointment in the history of religion was broadened to include the philosophy of religion "with special reference to the intellectual history of race lore."

Mann, Erika, b. Munich, November 9, 1905; d. Zurich, August 27, 1969, German writer. Initially an actress, Mann worked with Max REINHARDT, among others; she was married briefly to Gustaf GRÜNDGENS (1925–1928). Like her father, Thomas MANN, she left Germany in 1933; she went to Switzerland, where she founded the anti–National Socialist cabaret "The Peppermill" (Die Pfeffermühle), with which she traveled throughout Europe. When deprived of German citizenship by the National Socialists, she contracted a marriage of convenience with the English writer W. H. Auden (1907–1973) in order to become a British subject. After 1936 she worked in the United States as a journalist. It was Erika Mann who won over her initially aloof father to the cause of antifascist emigration and agitation. In 1938 she caused a sensation with her book *School for Barbarians*, about NS education. Mann withdrew her application for United States citizenship in 1950 with a pointed attack on official Communist baiters who sought to snoop into private beliefs. Thereafter she lived in Switzerland as a free-lance writer.

Mann, Heinrich, b. Lübeck, March 27, 1871; d. Santa Monica, Calif., March 3, 1950, German writer. From 1893 to 1898 Heinrich Mann lived in Italy together with his brother Thomas MANN. In 1915 he published an antiwar article, "Zola," in the journal *Weisse Blätter* (White Papers); this was an answer to his brother's wildly pro-war essay on Frederick the Great. Mann also aroused attention with his novel *Der Untertan* (The Obedient Subject; translated as *Man of Straw*), the first volume of the trilogy *Das Kaiserreich* (The [German] Empire; 1914). This novel marked him as a defeatist in the eyes of the political Right. The movie version of his novel *Professor Unrat* (1905), filmed as *Der blaue Engel* (The Blue Angel) with Marlene DIETRICH in 1930, made Mann internationally famous. In 1933 he was expelled from the Prussian Academy of Arts by the National Socialists, who also burned his books. Mann fled via France to the United States, where he wrote novels based on France's King Henry IV. In 1950 he was appointed president of the German Academy of Arts in East Berlin, but he died before assuming office.

Mann, Klaus, b. Munich, November 18, 1906; d. Cannes, May 22, 1949, German writer and journalist. The eldest son of Thomas MANN, Klaus Mann was originally a theater critic, notably for *Die* WELTBÜHNE (The World Stage). In the mid-1920s he—together with his sister

Klaus Mann.

Erika MANN, Pamela Wedekind, and Gustaf GRÜNDGENS—founded a theater group. In 1933 he emigrated to Paris, where he published the literary journal *Die Sammlung* (Anthology; 1933–1935). He moved in 1936 to New York, first returning to Germany in 1945 as an American army correspondent. In despair over his personal situation as an intellectual and the hopelessness of the political crisis, he took his life. Mann's best-known works include the novels *Mephisto* (1936), a thinly disguised attack on Gründgens and his career in the Third Reich, and *Der Vulkan* (The Volcano; 1939).

Mann, Thomas, b. Lübeck, June 6, 1875; d. Kilchberg, near Zurich, August 12, 1955, German writer. Mann was the most significant author of the German bourgeoisie in the first half of the 20th century. During the First World War, he championed the "German idea" against Western democratic civilization, notably in his *Betrachtungen eines Unpolitischen* (*Reflections of a Nonpolitical Man;* 1918). Thereafter, however, he became a supporter of the Weimar Republic—one of only a few German artists who accepted the new state without reservations—and represented it convincingly to the outside world. In 1929 he was awarded a Nobel prize for his novels, especially *Buddenbrooks* (1901).

In Switzerland at the time of the Seizure of Power, Mann elected to stay there. In 1936 he was deprived of his German citizenship; in 1938 he emigrated to the United States, the undisputed spiritual head of the EMIGRATION. He fought in numerous lectures and radio speeches against

Thomas Mann.

National Socialism. In his novel *Doktor Faustus* (1947), Mann connected the pact made with the Devil by an artist in the hope of gaining inspiration, to the "pact" between Germany and Hitler. Actual events and persons are artfully interwoven with the plot, and different levels of time are tied together (the action of the novel takes place *before* the Third Reich, while the fictitious narrator is writing during the war). A self-styled representative of a "cosmopolitan German character" (*Weltdeutschtum*), Mann made only short visits to his native country after the war. In 1952 he took up residence in Switzerland.

Ba.

Mannerheim, Carl Gustav Baron von, b. Villnäs (near Turku), June 4, 1867; d. Lausanne, January 27, 1951, Finnish politician. In the First World War Mannerheim fought as an officer in the Russian army until 1917; in 1917–1918, as commander in chief of the Finnish "White" army, he defeated the Finnish "Red" army with German help. He was successful as regent in gaining international recognition of Finnish independence in 1918–1919. As field marshal, Mannerheim took supreme command of his nation's armed forces in the Finnish-Soviet WINTER WAR and in the Second World War. He avoided too close an alignment with National Socialist Germany, and as president (1944–1946) concluded an armistice with the Soviet Union.

Manstein, Erich von (originally, Erich von Lewinski), b. Berlin, November 24, 1887; d. Irschenhausen (Isar Valley), June 10, 1973,

German field marshal (July 1, 1942). Commissioned as an officer in 1906, Manstein served during the First World War on the General Staff. Continuing his career in the Reichswehr (on October 1, 1936, he was appointed a major general), when the war broke out Manstein was chief of staff of Army Group South. After the victory over Poland, he developed the plan of operation for the FRENCH CAMPAIGN: a "sickle-shaped cut" (*Sichelschnitt*) using fast-moving tank units through the Ardennes Forest and Belgium to the Channel. The plan, which the Army High Command (OKH) had viewed with skepticism, was approved by Hitler (*see* MECHELEN INCIDENT) and, after its successful execution, earned Manstein the rank of infantry general (July 19, 1940).

During the RUSSIAN CAMPAIGN Manstein's successes included the conquest of the Crimean peninsula with the Eleventh Army. He became commander in chief of the Don Army Group (later Army Group South) during the Stalingrad crisis. Although he could not break through the Soviet encirclement of the German Sixth Army, he succeeded in saving the Russian southern front (including the retaking of Kharkov on March 16, 1943) with a brilliant "makeshift strategy."

Because of disagreements with Hitler, who now wanted "only dependable supporters" (*nur noch Steher*), Manstein—probably the most able German strategist—was relieved of his duties on March 30, 1944, and given no further assignments. Captured by the British, he was sentenced in Hamburg to 18 years' imprisonment on December 19, 1949. Charges against

Carl Gustav Baron von Mannerheim.

Erich von Manstein.

him included transmitting the COMMISSAR OR-DER and approving the murderous activities of the EINSATZGRUPPEN as a "harsh retribution against Jewry, the spiritual carrier of Bolshevik terror." Manstein was released from prison for reasons of health in May 1953, and wrote his memoirs, *Verlorene Siege* (Lost Victories; 1955). He advised the government of the Federal Republic on issues of rearmament.

Manstein Trial, proceeding by a British military court in Hamburg in 1949 against former field marshal Erich von MANSTEIN, who was charged with war crimes committed in Poland and the USSR. Protests were lodged in both houses of the British Parliament against conducting the trial four years after the war had ended. Lords Bridgemen, De L'Isle, and Dudley assembled a fund for the defense. Winston Churchill, who had repeatedly spoken out against "belated trials of aged German generals," was one of the first contributors. Reginald T. Paget, a member of the House of Commons, offered his free services as defense counsel. The indictment consisted of 17 counts. Acquitted on eight counts, Manstein was sentenced to 18 years' imprisonment on December 19, 1949. The sentence for war crimes was confirmed on nine counts, but the penalty was reduced to 12 years' imprisonment. On May 7, 1953, Manstein was released on probation.

A. St.

Maquis, French term for brushwood or shrub; it became a name for the French underground movement (*see* RÉSISTANCE) because of the lat-ter's undercover tactics against the German occupation forces during the Second World War. The fighters were called *maquisards.*

Marahrens, August, b. Hannover, October 11, 1875; d. Loccum, May 3, 1950, German Evangelical theologian. Marahrens was a military chaplain, then superintendent general for the church in Bremen-Verden (1922–1925) and state bishop of the Evangelical-Lutheran church in Hannover (1925–1947). In the spring of 1933 he belonged to the so-called Dreimännergremium, a three-man committee that negotiated with the Reich government over the formation of a GERMAN EVANGELICAL CHURCH and the choice of a Reich Bishop. After these efforts failed, he joined the CONFESSING CHURCH. When it split in 1936, he became a representative of the "moderates" in the Council of the Evangelical-Lutheran Church of Germany. As president of the Lutheran World Federation (1935–1945), and because of his international connections, he was the object of repeated police persecution, especially during the war.

Marburg Speech (*Marburger Rede*), address given by Franz von PAPEN at the University of Marburg on June 17, 1934. In the speech, written by his collaborator Edgar JUNG, Papen summarized the conservative criticism of National Socialism and condemned the "eternal revolt from below," which he said no *Volk* could afford. Hitler understood the speech, with its monarchist undertone, just as it was meant—namely, as a challenge and an appeal to the ailing and elderly president, Paul von Hindenburg, to bypass, in arranging for his succession, the NSDAP leader. The Marburg Speech thus hastened the RÖHM AFFAIR, which, by taking power from the SA, calmed the president, the Reichswehr, and the business community. Papen, whom Hitler called a "ridiculous dwarf," now found himself in considerable danger. He was put under house arrest and later given a punitive transfer to Vienna, where he was expected to prove himself in the difficult post of ambassador. Jung, the writer of the speech, fell victim to an SS death squad.

March (*Marsch*), like the related verb (*marschieren*), a frequently used word in the National Socialist vocabulary owing to the militarization of the language. The uniform and goal-directed movement of the march, suggesting almost mechanical irresistibility, expressed the idea of SYNCHRONIZATION and the orientation of the individual toward the goals of the "*Volk* Community."

March, Werner, b. Berlin, January 17, 1894; d. there, November 1, 1976, German architect. In 1928 March was commissioned to make proposals for the reconstruction of the German Stadium—built in 1913 by his father, Otto March—for the 1936 Olympic Games. March's plans were approved, and construction at the REICH SPORTS FIELD began in 1932. Hitler reacted ungraciously to the stadium at first, and called March's concrete-and-glass structure a "glass box." Later he accepted the compromise offered by Albert SPEER: to cover up the slender lines with natural stone and thus achieve the desired effect of a powerful and permanent edifice. As the first large National Socialist structure, the Olympic Stadium made a strong impression inside and outside Germany, and earned March numerous commissions, even after the war. He gained further recognition during the postwar reconstruction, and was professor of urban planning at the Technical College in Berlin from 1953 to 1962.

March music, compositions that were among the desired types of MUSIC in the Third Reich, since the regular and even beat could bring large groups into equal step and keep them there. Among the various occasions for march music, military events such as parades were favored. March music was part of the repertoire of all

bands, especially those of the Hitler Youth or the SA. It helped produce an internal alignment, bound the individual to the community, and drowned out doubt and criticism. Nearly all soldiers' songs were written as marches.

March on the Feldherrnhalle (*Marsch auf die Feldhernhalle*), public demonstration of about 1,500 followers of Hitler and Erich Ludendorff on November 9, 1923. It wound its way through Munich, ending near the FELDHERRNHALLE, where it was stopped by the firepower of the Bavarian State Police. In National Socialist propaganda the term "March on the Feldherrnhalle" was also used to designate the entire HITLER PUTSCH. During the Third Reich, an annual memorial march took place on November 9. It ended with a closing manifestation during which the names of the 16 NS victims of the putsch attempt were loudly called out, to the accompaniment of torchlight and the rolling of drums.

Marital fitness (*Ehetauglichkeit*), in the sense of National Socialist HEREDITY CULTIVATION, the racial, physical (in terms of health), and moral qualifications required for marriage. Also to be considered was whether the marriage would be "undesirable for the *Volk* Community." Marital fitness had to be proved by a certificate from the Office of Health when applying for a marriage loan (*see* MARRIAGE LOANS).

Commemoration of the March on the Feldherrnhalle.

Anlage 1
(Zum § 1 vorstehender
Verordnung)

Gesundheitsamt*)

Tgb. Nr. ...., den .... 193 ....
                                        (Anschrift und Fernsprecher)

Ehetauglichkeitszeugnis

Bei dem ....

geb. am .... in ....

wohnhaft in ....

und der ....

geb. am .... in ....

wohnhaft in ....

liegen Ehehindernisse im Sinne des Gesetzes zum Schutze der Erb-
gesundheit des deutschen Volkes (Ehegesundheitsgesetz) vom 18. Ok-
tober 1935 (Reichsgesetzbl. I S. 1246) und des § 6 der Ersten Verordnung vom 14. November 1935 zur Ausführung des Gesetzes zum
Schutze des deutschen Blutes und der deutschen Ehre (Reichsgesetzbl. I
S. 1334) nicht vor.

(Siegel)   ....
                                        (Unterschrift)

Office of Health form for the certificate of marital fitness.

Marital Health Law (*Ehegesundheitsgesetz*), an extension of marital law from the standpoint of HEREDITY CULTIVATION (*Erbpflege*). Issued on October 18, 1935, it was a supplement to the Law for the Prevention of HEREDITARILY ILL OFFSPRING of July 14, 1933. The law prohibited marriages in which there was danger of infection, or where harmful consequences for future generations could be expected. Persons under guardianship or mentally handicapped persons were denied proof of MARITAL FITNESS. Marriages contracted "surreptitiously" to contravene the law were declared void.

Marker, Willi, b. Hofgeismar, August 22, 1894; d. Sachsenhausen concentration camp, April 22, 1940, German municipal politician. After Social Democratic and Independent Socialist Party membership, Marker joined the Communist Party (KPD) in 1922. He was a city councilman in Kassel until 1933. Although Marker managed to escape the hunt for Communists that followed the Reichstag fire, he was arrested on April 11, 1934, and sentenced to 18 months' imprisonment for "preparations to commit high treason." Since his confinement did not result in any "serious inner reform," he was sent to the Esterwegen concentration camp, and then to Sachsenhausen. For aiding Jewish fellow prisoners and for criticizing the abuse of inmates, Marker was put into a disciplinary unit. He was found in the lavatory one night, hanging by the neck: a "suicide," according to the camp administration.

Marr, Wilhelm, b. 1819; d. 1904, German antisemitic journalist. Marr placed on the Jews the responsibility for the economic depression that followed the financial crisis of 1873. He criticized the disproportionate participation of Jews in the government and the press, and demanded a resolute struggle against the impending "Jewish world domination." The persistence of Jewish culture, despite nearly 2,000 years of diaspora, proved to Marr the immutability of the Jewish character, which could not be influenced even by baptism. With this concept, Marr provided the National Socialists with a crucial argument for racial ANTISEMITISM.

Marriage (*Ehe*), legally recognized life partnership of man and woman. According to National Socialist norms, marriage was an "inherent duty," and the refusal to marry meant exclusion from "the bloodstream of the *Volk*" and from the right to participate in the shaping of its fate. To be sure, marriage was desirable only between partners "of healthy heredity and the same race" (*erbgesund und rassegleich*), for marriage was to serve "the reproduction and preservation of the race and species" and therefore had to follow the laws of RACIAL HYGIENE and racial purity. These principles formed the basis for such measures as the Law for the Prevention of HEREDITARILY ILL OFFSPRING of July 14, 1933, and the Law to Protect Blood of September 15, 1935 (*see* BLOOD, LAW TO PROTECT), which prohibited MIXED MARRIAGE. Such marriage was branded a "crime against German blood," just as intentional childlessness was "*völkisch* treason" and allegedly contributed to such morally objectionable life-styles as COMRADELY MARRIAGE. NS legislation and ideology regarding marriage were instruments of a POPULATION POLICY that sought a larger and "improved" stock.

Marriageability Certificate (*Ehefähigkeitszeugnis*), document required after May 31, 1934, for Germans marrying abroad. Issued by the civil registries, the certificate testified that there was no hindrance to a marriage, and in particular, no shortcomings in terms of MARITAL FITNESS.

Marriage Assistance (*Ehestandshilfe*), special tax for financing MARRIAGE LOANS.

Marriage between different faiths (*glaubens-verschiedene Ehe*), term developed to denote a marriage between partners of different denominations or religions after the decree of April 26, 1934, reserved the term MIXED MARRIAGE for marital bonds between partners who were not "racially equal" (*rassegleich*).

Marriage by proxy (*Ferntrauung;* literally, long-distance marriage), possibility for soldiers to marry in absentia, created by the Ordinance on Personal Status of October 17, 1942. It required a declaration of the "wish to marry" before the battalion commander, which led to such a marriage if the prospective bride, within the next six months, gave her agreement before her local civil registry. If her fiancé was killed or declared missing in action in the meantime, the marriage nonetheless took place; the date of marriage was then that of the man's declaration of intent.

It is impossible to determine statistically how many such marriages took place, yet one may assume that there were a considerable number because the constant danger of death at the front and in the "homeland war zone" encouraged quick decisions. Moreover, National Socialist propaganda encouraged marriages by proxy in order to decrease the number of single women, as well as to counteract fraternization with prisoners of war or alien workers.

Marriage loans (*Ehestandsdarlehen*), credits given to promote marriages, based on Paragraph 5 of the first Law for the Reduction of Unemployment. Women who promised to abstain from paid work after marriage, and who were deemed both needy and politically and eugenically reliable, were eligible. The interest-free loan was paid out in the form of coupons (*Bedarfdeck-ungsscheinen*) that entitled the bearer to purchase furniture and housewares. The amount loaned could be as much as 1,000 RM. It was to be repaid at the rate of 1 percent monthly, but the birth of a legitimate child resulted in excusing repayment of a fourth of the amount owed.

Marriage loans were financed through "Marriage Aid" (*Ehestandshilfe*), a special tax levied on all unmarried persons with personal incomes. By 1935 a total of 523,000 loans totaling some 300 million RM had been made. In 1933 more than half of all new couples availed themselves of the loans, but by 1935 the participation rate

Marriage by proxy.

Der Führer
gab euch Ehestandsdarlehen

Von August 1933 bis Ende 1937 wurden 878000 Ehestandsdarlehen im
Gesamtbetrage von weit über einer halben Milliarde RM. ausgezahlt.
Dadurch stieg die Zahl der Eheschließungen von 1932 500000
                                              auf 1937 620000

Der Führer gibt euch Kinderbeihilfen

1938 werden für 2 Millionen Kinder Beihilfen gezahlt.
        Die Zahl der Geburten stieg von 1932 970000
                            auf 1937 1270000

Der Führer
gab euch Freizeit und Erholung

Mit „Kraft durch Freude" reisten seit 1934: 22,5 Millionen Schaffende.

Alle Schaffenden Deutschlands
bekennen sich zu ihm und
stimmen am 10. April mit Ja!

Marriage loans. Poster for the 1938
elections:
   "The Führer gave you marriage
loans. . . . Thereby the number of
marriages increased from 500,000 in
1932 to 620,000 in 1937.
   The Führer gives you child allowances. . . . The number of births
increased from 970,000 in 1932 to
1,270,000 in 1937.
   The Führer gave you freedom and
recreation. With 'Strength through
Joy,' 22.5 million working people have
gone on trips since 1934. All productive Germans declare their faith in him
and vote YES! on April 10."

had fallen to 24 percent. Because of the incipient labor shortage, the prohibition of work for
wives was eliminated as a condition for a loan in
October 1937. In agriculture the prohibition
had been bypassed for some time.

                                                        B. W.

Marriage Order (*Heiratsbefehl*), term for the SS
order of January 1, 1932, that obliged all unmarried SS members to obtain a marriage permit
from the *Reichsführer-SS:* "The desired aim is
a hereditarily healthy and valuable CLAN of
German Nordic type. The permission to marry
is issued only . . . from the viewpoint of race
and hereditary health." This order was supplemented with a regulation termed the "Betrothal Order" (*Verlobungsbefehl*), which obliged
the prospective fiancé to report his "intent" to
the *Reichsführer* (Himmler) three months before the engagement, "since the betrothal is
itself a legal action."

Marriage Schools (*Eheschulen;* also called *Bräuteschulen* [Bridal Schools]), training institutions
for young wives, established in November 1936
by the MOTHERS' SERVICE of the German
Women's Agency. Besides housekeeping and
pedagogical skills, the schools imparted information on ideological matters and the National
Socialist image of woman in their courses,
which lasted four to six weeks. Fiancées of SA
and SS men in particular were urged to attend,
since they had a special need for solid knowledge of the "teachings on race and heredity."

Marschall von Bieberstein, Wilhelm, b. Berlin,
May 9, 1890; d. near Pòdejuch (now in Poland),
January 31, 1935, "Old Combatant" of the
NSDAP. A pilot in the First World War, Marschall von Bieberstein enrolled afterward in a
free corps. He participated in the KAPP PUTSCH,
the RUHR CONFLICT, and the HITLER PUTSCH.
An SA member from 1923, he helped rescue
Hermann Göring when the latter was wounded
in the MARCH ON THE FELDHERRNHALLE during
Hitler's attempted putsch (November 9, 1923).
Marschall von Bieberstein became SA Führer
for Baden, and in 1930 entered the Baden
parliament for the NSDAP. Professionally active
in civil aviation (notably as director of the Königsberg airport), he died in an air crash.

Marseille, Hans-Joachim, b. Berlin, December
13, 1919; d. in North Africa, September 30,
1942, German fighter pilot. Marseille joined the
Luftwaffe in 1941, and became a captain in June
1942. He was the most successful fighter pilot in
the western theater of war, shooting down 17

Hans-Joachim Marseille.

planes on a single day (September 9, 1942) and winning a total of 158 aerial victories. National Socialist propaganda celebrated him as the "Star of Africa," and on September 4, 1942, he was awarded a diamond-studded Knight's Cross with Oak Leaves and Swords. Marseille lost his life when his parachute proved defective while he was attempting to bail out of his burning plane.

Martyr of Labor (Opfer der Arbeit), foundation created by Hitler in May 1933 to support the survivors of workers killed in accidents; it was supplemented, in December 1935, with an additional foundation, "Martyrs of Labor at Sea" (Opfer der Arbeit auf See). The foundations were financed through contributions, and a so-called honorary committee distributed the funds according to political considerations.

Marx, Wilhelm, b. Cologne, January 15, 1863; d. Bonn, August 5, 1946, German politician. Educated in law, Marx became a district court judge (*Landrichter*) in Elberfeld; in 1906 he became councillor of the Superior District Court (Oberlandesgerichtsrat) in Cologne. He was made president (*Landgerichtspräsident*) of the District Court in Limburg in 1921, and in 1922, Senate president at the Supreme Court of Appeals (Kammergericht) in Berlin. A Center party deputy in the Reichstag from 1910, Marx succeeded Gustav Stresemann as Reich chancellor on November 30, 1923. Marx tried to eliminate the consequences of INFLATION and to guarantee the implementation of the DAWES PLAN. Forced to resign as chancellor in January 1925, he became a candidate of the Weimar Coalition

Wilhelm Marx.

in the Reich presidential elections on August 26 of that year. He won 45.3 percent of the vote, only 3 percentage points behind Gen. Paul von Hindenburg. Marx was again chancellor in 1927–1928, but after 1932 he no longer appeared on the political stage.

Marxism, the totality of the theories of Karl Marx (1818–1883) and Friedrich Engels (1820–1895), who, renouncing idealism, outlined a "materialist" model for society and the world. According to these theories human history is a history of class struggle, at the end of which—after a period of dictatorship by the proletariat—the classless society of COMMUNISM will be born.

The complex historical, philosophical, and economic theory of Marxism was evaluated by the ideologues of the NSDAP as an attempt by WORLD JEWRY to divide the *Volk* Communities through class hatred, to undermine them through internationalism, and to make them subservient to the plans for Jewish world domination. As proof of the untenability of Marxism, Marx's Jewish origins were analyzed. Moreover, the National Socialists alleged, despite its thesis of imminent world revolution, Marxism was "as if swept away by the organized fighting force of National Socialist ideas" (*Meyers Lexikon,* 1939), and thus had been brought to the point of absurdity. Marxism as it actually existed—in the form of BOLSHEVISM—had, with its millions of victims during the collectivization of agriculture, revealed the promises of Marxism to be "delusional" utopias. National Socialism juxtaposed to this the organic model of the "*Volk* Community," in which class struggle had been overcome by "*völkisch* rebirth."

Märzgefallene ("the fallen of March"), originally a term of honor for demonstrators shot down by Prussian troops in front of the Berlin Palace on March 18–19, 1848; it was sometimes also used to designate the Viennese victims of the March Revolution of 1848. In *völkisch* circles the term was later applied to persons killed on March 4, 1919, demonstrating for the merger of the Sudetenland with Germany.

As a label of contempt the term was ironically turned around to describe those persons who, out of opportunistic motives, joined the NSDAP after the Reichstag elections of March 5, 1933, and after the final establishment of National Socialist domination with the Enabling Law of March 24. Even the National Socialists called them, in the words of Hans Frank, the "parasites of the revolution" (*Revolutionsschmarotzer*).

Masaryk, Jan, b. Prague, September 14, 1886; d. there, March 10, 1948, Czech politician. The son of Tomáš Garrigue MASARYK, Jan Masaryk entered the diplomatic service in 1918; he was ambassador of the Czechoslovak Republic in London from 1925 to 1939. His advocacy of Czechoslovak sovereignty and his attempts to obtain political and military support from Great Britain were seen by the National Socialists as "animosity toward Germany." After the German occupation of Czechoslovakia, Masaryk became foreign minister of the government-in-exile; he assumed the same post in 1945 in the newly founded Czechoslovak Republic. Following the Communist takeover of power, he lost his life under circumstances that have never been clarified.

Masaryk, Tomáš Garrigue, b. Hodonin, March 7, 1850; d. Lány Castle, near Prague, September 14, 1937, Czech politician, sociologist, and philosopher. As a professor of philosophy at the University of Prague and as a journalist, Masaryk fought equally against German and Hungarian hegemony, as well as against Pan-Slavic tendencies. Because of his support for the Allies, he had to flee abroad after the start of the First World War. He worked toward agreement among Czech and Slovak emigrés, and was substantially involved in the creation of an independent Czechoslovak state in 1918. He became the country's first president, and was repeatedly re-elected (until 1935). Although Masaryk considered himself a humanistic and idealistic democrat, he denied the right to autonomy (on the Swiss model) to the Sudeten Germans and other

national minorities in CZECHOSLOVAKIA, as had originally been promised them. In so doing, he promoted centrifugal forces. Hitler later used the conflicts among national groups to smash the young state.

Mass (*Masse*), term used in psychology and sociology for a crowd of people who at least for a time demonstrate similar or homogeneous behavior, which as group or mass behavior is characterized by a diminished ability to criticize and judge, as well as by a weakened sense of inhibition and responsibility. Especially in situations of crisis and anxiety, the mass lets itself be manipulated by an orientation toward the irrational and by emotional appeals from authoritarian and charismatic political leaders; existing aggressions can be concentrated and then directed against real or imagined enemies.

In the National Socialist worldview the term "mass" was officially applied negatively, to designate an unstructured conglomeration of people. It was sometimes equated with the classless Communist society (*see* COLLECTIVE), and was seen as the opposite of the organic *Volk* Community. In practice, Hitler very early, consciously and unconsciously, adopted the perceptions of mass psychology with regard to the domination and manipulation of crowds. No other politician knew so well how to stage mass rallies and how to mobilize collective instincts and aggressions (*see* FÜHRER CULT). The political and governmental organization of the Third Reich was designed largely to make the individual a member of a uniform mass. In the NS political and cultural self-portrayal, the "mass as ornament" and the arrangement of masses of people had a central function (*see* AESTHETICS; CELEBRATIONS).

Master morality (*Herrenmoral*), National Socialist catchword taken over from Friedrich NIETZSCHE to provide a philosophy for buttressing the theory of racial superiority. He who was selected by heredity and "innate instincts" to exercise "mastery" developed a master morality that was characterized, in contrast to HERD MORALITY, by selfless devotion to the good of the nation. In Nietzsche's words, "He offers his ideals as a sacrifice to that which he loves."

Materialism (*Materialismus*), ideology according to which all reality can be interpreted as matter or material processes. Philosophically, the development of history, humanity, and culture was interpreted by historical and dialectical materialism (that of Marx, Engels, and others) as being

Tomáš Garrigue Masaryk.

the result of material processes. The National Socialists sweepingly equated it with MARXISM; the struggle against "the Jewish-materialist spirit within and outside us" was anchored in the party program (Point 24). Materialism was criticized for its inability to do justice either to the "great ideas" or the "racial-*völkisch* basic forces" that were the true mainsprings of history.

Matern, Hermann, b. Burg bei Magdeburg, June 17, 1893; d. East Berlin, January 24, 1971, German politician. Matern joined the Social Democrats in 1911, but left in 1914 because of the SPD vote for war credits. From 1914 to 1918 he was a soldier. He joined the Independent Socialists (USPD) in 1918 and the Communist Party (KPD) in 1919. A KPD deputy in the Prussian parliament from 1932, Matern was arrested in 1933. He managed to escape, and became head of the Red Relief (Rote Hilfe) in Prague in 1936. After fleeing to the Soviet Union, he disseminated propaganda in prison camps, and helped to found the NATIONAL COMMITTEE FOR A FREE GERMANY. In 1945 Matern returned to Germany, joined the SED (Socialist Unity Party), and was made a member of its Central Committee in 1946; he later joined the Politburo. As chairman of the SED's Central Control Commission, and as a close friend of Walter ULBRICHT, Matern played a considerable role in rendering powerless the enemies of the East German party leader.

Mathematics, as a science, a discipline that remained untouched by National Socialism. Although as a subject of instruction it was ideologically exploited, its limited suitability for such use made its importance slight. Like other subjects, mathematics had to take a back seat to the primacy of physical training in National Socialist education; in the Führer Schools it played hardly any role. This remained so even when individual textbook authors made attempts at ideological ingratiation by incorporating *völkisch*, racial, and military references in their examples. The same was true of geometry, which, as "the natural spatial concept," was alleged to be "a prominent characteristic of the Germanic race." Only the military importance of mathematics, as in ballistics, brought it more attention, especially after the war began.

Matsuoka, Yosuke, b. Yamagutshi, March 4, 1880; d. Tokyo, June 27, 1946, Japanese politician. Matsuoka entered the diplomatic corps in 1901. From 1930 to 1934 he was a deputy for the Conservative party. In 1933, as Japan's delegate to the League of Nations, he declared his country's withdrawal from the organization. Matsuoka became foreign minister in 1940, and as such signed the THREE-POWER AGREEMENT with Italy and Germany in April 1941. He also concluded a nonaggression pact with the Soviet Union. Arrested and accused of war crimes after the war, he died in prison.

Maunz, Theodor, b. Dachau, September 1, 1901, German legal theorist. Maunz worked in the Bavarian state administration from 1927 to 1935. He became a professor of constitutional law (*Staatsrecht*) in Freiburg im Breisgau in 1937. Maunz was the author of the leading book on administrative law during the National Socialist period. In it he justified the unlimited jurisdiction of the central political authorities over the entire departmental and administrative apparatus. In 1943 he wrote *Über Gestalt und Recht der Polizei* (On the Structure and Rights of the Police), in which he maintained that the assignment of tasks by the Führer and by his designees was a sufficient legal basis for police activity.

In 1952 Maunz became a professor of public law in Munich. As a member of the CSU (Christian Social Union), he was Bavarian minister of education and culture from 1957 to 1964. He became one of the most influential teachers of constitutional law in the Federal Republic, notably through his textbook *Deutsches Staatsrecht* (German Constitutional Law) and as co-editor of a standard commentary on West Germany's statutes.

C. B.

Maurras, Charles, b. Martigues (Bouches-du-Rhône), April 20, 1868; d. Saint Symphorien, near Tours, November 16, 1952, French writer and political figure. Maurras was a co-founder of the antisemitic and royalist ACTION FRANÇAISE movement in 1898, and in 1908 of a newspaper with the same name. Through his sharp attacks on Jews, the parliamentary system, the clergy, and the German Empire, he strongly influenced the climate of political opinion in France. Primarily during the 1920s and 1930s, he prepared the way for a French fascism, which was organized, after the defeat of 1940, in the "État Français" of Henri PÉTAIN, whom Maurras supported. Without hiding his hatred of Germany, Maurras furthered by means of his writings the anti-Jewish measures of the occupation power. He also opposed the RÉSISTANCE and Charles de

Gaulle's government-in-exile in London. Because of this COLLABORATION, he was sentenced to life imprisonment in 1945, and was pardoned only in 1952.

Mauthausen, National Socialist concentration camp of category III (for barely "trainable" [*erziehbar*] prisoners); it was built about 20 km (12 miles) east of Linz (Austria) in August 1938. At the outbreak of the war Mauthausen held about 1,500 prisoners; by April 1942 there were 5,500. Toward the end of the war almost 50,000 prisoners were crowded together in the main camp alone. In March 1945, some 24,000 more prisoners were placed in Mauthausen's largest annex camps (*Nebenlager*), Gusen I and II. (Mauthausen had a total of 56 satellite camps and subcamps.) These new inmates represented nearly all European nations, and included German criminals and political prisoners, Danish policemen, Dutch and Hungarian Jews, and Soviet prisoners of war. Especially after July 1943, they were joined by Jewish women with children, and transports of Soviet, Polish, Yugoslav, Italian, and French children and youths, as well as mixed Jewish-Polish Gypsy children (including babies) from the RAVENSBRÜCK camp. According to the last official statistics (March 31, 1945), the camp held more than 1,500 children and young people up to the age of 20, and more than 2,200 women.

In the beginning the prisoners worked primarily on the camp's construction. After 1939 or so, they labored mainly in the granite quarries of the German Earth and Stone Works (Deutsche Erd- und Steinwerke; DEST), which was owned by the SS. From about the autumn of 1943 they worked in the armaments industry (Messerschmitt AG). The food was completely inadequate, and housing and sanitary conditions were as bad as can be imagined. Many people died of hunger and exhaustion. Numerous prisoners were shot, hanged, or fatally abused by SS troops or by KAPOS in the "Wienergraben" quarry.

Prisoners who were ill or incapable of work were separated from the others as part of "Aktion 14f13" (*see* INVALID OPERATION). They were then "euthanized" in special killing facilities, either gassed in the camp's own gas chambers or in a gas van (*see* GAS VANS) that traveled between Mauthausen and the Gusen annex camp, some 5 km (3 miles) away; or they were killed by poison injections in the camp infirmary. In a special place near the crematorium, prisoners were shot in the nape of the neck after being told that they were to have a medical examination. HUMAN EXPERIMENTS (such as surgery performed on healthy prisoners and experiments with tuberculosis serum) claimed more victims. The total number of dead and murdered persons in Mauthausen and its auxiliary camps can no longer be ascertained exactly. The death registers that were kept in the main and secondary camps recorded some 71,000 deaths; the number of unregistered deaths is unknown. After the war a memorial and museum were established on the camp grounds. The commandants of Mauthausen were Albert Sauer (d. in Falkensee in 1945) and Franz Ziereis (shot by American soldiers in 1945 while attempting to escape).

W. D.

May, Karl, b. Hohenstein-Ernstthal, February 25, 1842; d. Radebeul, March 30, 1912, German writer. With his adventure novels, many of which featured American Indians (notably *Winnetou*; 1893), May was one of the most popular "youth and folk authors" in the 1920s. Some National Socialist pedagogues attacked him as an alleged pacifist and "an enemy of the racial idea." But many leaders, including Joseph Goebbels and Rudolf Hess, valued his portrayals of heroic deeds. Immediately after the Seizure of Power, Hitler himself re-read nearly all 70 volumes of May. He saw in Winnetou an example for German youth, and the "model of a company commander." Even in his Table Talks in the 1940s, Hitler referred with gratitude to the fact that his vision of the world, and especially his

Karl May.

vision of America, had been formed, above all, by May.

Nonetheless, once the war began the list of prohibited May volumes grew because of their pacifist and antiracist statements, as in *Und Frieden auf Erden* (And Peace on Earth; 1904). Finally only a part of the complete works were permitted to appear in "new adaptations," shortened, and with antisemitic interpolations (which remained partly intact after 1945). May's Christian and pacifist influence on such youthful protest groups as the EDELWEISS PIRATES is nonetheless not to be entirely discounted.

H. H.

Mayer, Helene, b. Offenbach, December 20, 1910; d. Heidelberg, October 15, 1953, German fencer; world champion with the foil in 1929, 1931, and 1939; winner at the 1928 Olympic Games. Mayer, who went to California to study, was nominated to Germany's national team for the 1936 Olympics, despite her half-Jewish background. The National Socialists hoped in this way to deflect a threatened boycott of the Berlin Olympics by the United States, among others, in retaliation for the persecution of Jews. The plan succeeded. Mayer won a silver medal, emigrated to the United States, and returned to Germany only shortly before her death.

Mayer, Rupert, b. Stuttgart, January 23, 1876; d. Munich, November 1, 1945, German Catholic theologian. Mayer, a Jesuit, opposed the National Socialists as early as 1923 ("A German Catholic can never be a National Socialist"). Several times arrested and banned from preaching, he ignored such measures. On July 22–23, 1937, he was sentenced to six months' imprisonment by a special court in Munich (a sentence still not

Helene Mayer at the honoring of victors in the 1936 Olympic Games.

rescinded). At first incarcerated in Landsberg am Lech, Mayer was interned in the Ettal Cloister from August 1940 until 1945. He was beatified on May 3, 1987.

May Field (Maifeld), parade ground for 210,000 persons behind the Olympic Stadium on the REICH SPORTS FIELD. Completed in 1936, the May Field was intended by Hitler to be used for demonstrations putting National Socialism on display. There were places for 70,000 people in front of the speaker's tribune. The facade was enclosed by the Langemarck Hall and crowned by a Führer Tower 76 m (about 250 feet) high.

May Holiday (*Maifeiertag*), May 1, an international holiday for the labor movement; it was expropriated as early as 1933 by Joseph Goebbels and put under National Socialist management. In order to take the workers by surprise, and also to win them over for the government, the "Day of National Labor" was elevated to the status of a legal holiday comparable to HARVEST THANKS DAY, and became one of the most important holidays of the NS calendar. Its gradual reinterpretation as the "National Holiday of the German *Volk*," as official terminology renamed it, gave the day its new meaning as a celebration of the unified German *Volk* Community. The large demonstrations of the prewar period were discontinued during the war, but MORNING CELEBRATIONS and workplace assemblies were held on May 1 until Albert SPEER, as armaments minister, discontinued them in 1942.

K. V.

Mechelen (Ger., Mecheln; Fr., Malines), Belgian town with 62,000 inhabitants in 1940, located 20 km (12 miles) south of Antwerp. Nearby, during the Second World War, the German occupation authorities operated the Dossin detention camp, through which the SS channeled Belgian Jews scheduled for deportation. The first transports to the EXTERMINATION CAMPS left Mechelen in August 1942 (a total of 5,990 Jews); the last transport (with 563 Belgian Jews) went to the east on July 21, 1944.

Mechelen Incident (*Mechelen-Zwischenfall*), emergency landing of the German Luftwaffe majors Erich Hönmanns and Hellmuth Reinberger near the Belgian town of Mechelen on January 10, 1940. It became an "incident" because the officers were carrying secret data regarding Germany's imminent western offensive. Although the two managed to destroy most of the documents, the Belgian military learned from the remainder that Germany was planning an attack through the Netherlands and Belgium. Only after the Mechelen Incident was Gen. Erich von MANSTEIN's plan for a "sickle-cut" tactic in the FRENCH CAMPAIGN given closer consideration, after Hitler ordered a change in the plan of attack because of the disclosures.

Medicine (*Medizin*), the study of the causes, symptoms, prevention, and treatment of human disease. Under National Socialism medicine was compromised above all by HUMAN EXPERIMENTS in the concentration camps and by the murder of the mentally ill (the so-called EUTHANASIA). It was governed by two basic ideas: (1) SPECIES UPGRADING, notably directed toward the Nordic race, and the simultaneous effort to "cull out" the "alien" and the weak; and (2) the primacy of the *Volk* over the individual; this corresponded to a change in medical ethics that placed responsibility for the collectivity above that for the individual. In both regards, concepts were taken up that had been discussed since the turn of the century, and that had their roots in SOCIAL DARWINISM. The goal of medicine was accordingly to make humans once again subject to those Darwinian laws that cultural influences had repealed for them. RACIAL HYGIENE was to be the primary tool of species upgrading; it was accordingly made mandatory in all medical schools, and was also introduced into the school curriculum. Policy derivations included the HEREDITARY FARM LAW, the LEBENSBORN program, and the NUREMBERG LAWS.

The "culling" process took place in three stages:

1. The Law for the Prevention of HEREDITARILY ILL OFFSPRING (July 1933) created the basis for widespread FORCED STERILIZATION; this program built on earlier efforts made during the Weimar Republic, which, however, had required the consent of the person to be sterilized. The Law for the Protection of Hereditary Health of October 1938 also belongs in this stage.
2. The Euthanasia program began with children in 1939. It was extended as Aktion T4, then as Aktion 14f13, and it later entered its "wild" stage; the victims were, above all, the mentally ill.
3. After the WANNSEE CONFERENCE, Jews, GYPSIES, and other groups were murdered in the EXTERMINATION CAMPS.

The occupational and PERFORMANCE MEDICINE (*Leistungsmedizin*) of the Third Reich

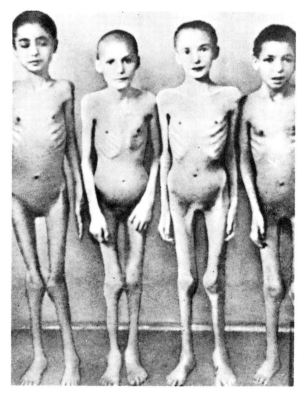

Medicine. Victims of human experimentation in the Auschwitz concentration camp.

should also be understood as an outgrowth of Social Darwinism. In its service were the new public-health organization, the work-force physicians (*Arbeitseinsatzärzte*), and the workplace physicians (*Betriebsärzte*). Their mandate was to strengthen the healthy in their ability and will to produce and perform, and to reduce the incidence of illness in the workplace. From this perspective the human being was no longer the subject, but rather the object, of medicine.

At the beginning of the Third Reich the National Socialists tried to revolutionize medicine, too. Their goal was a NEW GERMAN HEALING LORE (*Neue Deutsche Heilkunde*); promoted by Rudolf HESS and Julius STREICHER in particular, it was to differentiate itself from the allegedly "Jewish" factory medicine (*Fabrik-Medizin*) and from classical medicine. The movement toward lay medicine, which grew during the Weimar period, and the related "healing practitioners" (*Heilpraktiker*) were to be integrated into it. In 1935 the Reich Working Community for a New German Healing Lore (Reichsarbeitsgemeinschaft für eine Neue Deutsche Heilkunde) was created, which, however, soon folded. In the Rudolf Hess Hospital in Dresden an attempt was made to unite classical medicine and a naturopathic approach in the name of a biologistic medicine.

The Healing Practitioner Law of 1939 first recognized this category of healer, which played a special role in the delivery of health care, especially after the exclusion of Jewish and socialist physicians, made final in the fourth ordinance pursuant to the Reich Citizenship Law of July 1939. After September 30, 1938, the licensing of all Jewish physicians was annulled. Of the approximately 9,000 Jewish physicians who on April 1, 1933, had been practicing in Germany, some 709 were now allowed, as "treaters of the ill" (*Krankenbehandler*), to administer to Jewish patients. The exclusion of Jewish doctors was, from the beginning, a basic demand of the NATIONAL SOCIALIST GERMAN PHYSICIANS' LEAGUE, which wanted to place young and unemployed "Aryan" doctors in the vacated positions. It has yet to be clarified to what extent this demand was responsible for the high ranks occupied by doctors in the party and its organizations. Some 45 percent of physicians were party members, about twice the rate among teachers.

The organizational SYNCHRONIZATION of doctors was carried out by destroying the former health insurance plans (*Krankenkassen*) and creating the German Alliance of Fund-Affiliated Physicians (Kassenärztliche Vereinigung Deutschlands), by dissolving the main physicians' organizations, creating a Reich Physicians' Chamber, and promulgating the decree of the Reich Physicians' Ordinance. A Reich Physicians' Führer (*Reichsärzteführer*) now stood at the head of the German medical profession: first Gerhard WAGNER, and after 1939, Leonardo CONTI.

R. W.

Mefo Bills (*Mefo-Wechsel*), sham bills of exchange used for a time to finance REARMAMENT. After taxes and borrowing became insufficient to finance the WORK CREATION programs and arms-related spending, the Armed Forces Ministry and the Reich Bank in May 1933 created the Metallurgical Research, Ltd. (Metallurgische Forschungs-GmbH; Mefo), whose capital of 1 million RM was held by five big armaments firms. Arms suppliers were paid for their contracts in Mefo Bills from the phony firm; the German government guaranteed the bills, which were discounted by the Reich Bank. This secret system of Reich Bank President Hjalmar SCHACHT to disguise arms spending permitted a "noiseless" financing of rearmament. In its initial phase it also strongly spurred the economy (*see* ECONOMY UNDER NATIONAL SOCIALISM,

THE). From 1934 to 1936, Mefo Bills covered about 50 percent of military contracts; in 1938 their issuance was halted after a peak of about 12 billion RM.

V. B.

Mehring, Walter, b. Berlin, April 29, 1896; d. Zurich, October 3, 1981, German writer. Mehring volunteered for the First World War. He then studied art history and took up writing, first as an Expressionist. He became known as the author of satiric and provocative cabaret texts. His drama *Der Kaufmann von Berlin* (The Merchant of Berlin; 1929), about profiteers of the postwar inflation, expressed caustic socialist criticism of the bourgeoisie. This stance earned the author, who was also conspicuous through his antifascist songs, the hatred of the National Socialists.

Mehring, who once called himself "a born and trained emigré," fled to Austria in 1933; his books were banned in Germany. In 1938 he was forced to move to France, where he was detained after the war began. However, he was able to escape to the United States via Marseilles in 1940. After the war Mehring lived in Switzerland, where he wrote *The Lost Library* (English edition, 1951; German edition, *Die verlorene Bibliothek*, 1958), a work of contemporary criticism, which Mehring called "the autobiography of a culture." In 1979 he published fragments from his period of exile under the title *Wir müssen weiter* (We Must Go On).

Meier, in UNDERGROUND HUMOR a nickname for Hermann GÖRING, who on August 9, 1939, said that he could be called "Meier" (chosen for its ordinariness) if an enemy airplane appeared over the Ruhr region. The opportunity to do so presented itself a few days after the war began, at the latest after the beginning of the Allied bombing offensive (*see* AIR WAR), against which German flak and fighter planes were nearly powerless.

Meinecke, Friedrich, b. Salzwedel, October 30, 1862; d. Berlin, February 6, 1954, German historian. Meinecke studied history and philosophy in Bonn and Berlin. From 1887 to 1901, he was employed in the Prussian Archives. He then became a professor in Strasbourg (1901), Freiburg (1906), and Berlin (1914; professor emeritus, 1929). Meinecke's important historical works include *Weltbürgertum und Nationalstaat* (*Cosmopolitanism and the National State;* 1908), in which he interpreted social realities in terms of intellectual history. Despite his conservative tendencies, he supported the Weimar Republic after the First World War and criticized nationalist excesses. The National Socialists accused him of "bloodless intellectualizing," and in 1934 removed him from the editorship of the *Historische Zeitschrift* (Historical Journal), with which he had been associated since 1896. After the war Meinecke was the first rector of the Free University of Berlin, which he helped found. His inquiry into the National Socialist disaster, *Die deutsche Katastrophe* (*The German Catastrophe;* 1946), was given wide attention, and still retains topical interest.

Mein Kampf (My Struggle), book written by Hitler after the failed HITLER PUTSCH (November 9, 1923) while he was confined in the Landsberg fortress. He dictated the first volume, initially to his chauffeur, Emil Maurice, and later to his personal secretary, Rudolf Hess, who typed as Hitler dictated. His first choice of title was "Four and a Half Years of Struggle against Lies, Stupidity, and Cowardice" (*Viereinhalb Jahre Kampf gegen Lüge, Dummheit und Feigheit*). After his early release on December 20, 1924, Hitler dictated the second volume to his secretary and to Max AMANN.

Volume 1, with the subtitle *Eine Abrechnung* (A Settlement of Accounts), appeared on July 18, 1925; volume 2, subtitled *Die national-sozialistische Bewegung* (The National Socialist Movement), came out on December 11, 1926, from the EHER PRESS in Munich. As of 1930 both volumes appeared in a one-volume (782

Jacket of *Mein Kampf.*

pages), Bible-format popular edition. Up to that point, some 23,000 copies of volume 1 and 13,000 copies of volume 2 had been sold. By January 30, 1933, when Hitler assumed power as chancellor, approximately 287,000 copies of *Mein Kampf* had been sold. Subsequent sales were as follows: by the end of 1933, 1.5 million copies; by 1938, 4 million; by 1943, 9.84 million. Sales of the book were deliberately promoted "from above." Thus, the Reich interior minister "recommended" to civil registrars in April 1936 that they give a copy of *Mein Kampf* as a gift to every bride and groom. In October 1938, the president of the Reich Writing Chamber urged book dealers to sell only new editions of the book. A Party Chancellery circular of December 13, 1939, demanded "that someday every German family, even the poorest, should have the Führer's basic work." Despite its publishing records, the book, which was translated into 16 languages, was little read both in Germany and abroad, before and after 1933, as documented by Karl Lange's research.

As noted in his preface, Hitler sought "to clarify the goals of our movement" and "to draw a picture of its development." He also took the opportunity "to give an account of my own development, insofar as is necessary for an understanding of the first and the second volume, and also to destroy the foul legends about my person perpetrated by the Jewish press." Hitler addressed himself in this confession of faith not to "strangers, but to those followers of the movement who belong to it with their hearts, and whose reason now strives for a more penetrating enlightenment."

Hitler regarded his literary achievement (*Mein Kampf* is written in Hitler's typical speaking style) quite critically. "I am no writer," he told Hans Frank in the spring of 1938. "My thoughts run away with me in writing. *Mein Kampf* is a compilation of lead articles for the *Völkischer Beobachter*, and I believe that even there they would be accepted only with reservations because of the language." However: "In terms of content I would not like to change anything." Indeed, despite numerous stylistic corrections in all editions, Hitler's *Mein Kampf* was subject to only one essential change. This was the removal of the last traces of democratic decision making in party and state in favor of an absolute FÜHRER PRINCIPLE. The 1925 and 1928 editions spoke of "Germanic democracy" and "election of the Führer"; after 1930 "the principle of the unconditional authority of the Führer" prevailed.

At their marriage a newly joined couple are given a copy of *Mein Kampf* by the civil registrar.

As a source of information (as in Hitler's autobiographical passages and the descriptions of early NSDAP history), *Mein Kampf* is fragmentary, misleading, obscure, and reticent. It is a markedly stylized self-presentation, which can be used only within limits. In terms of theory and program, however, the utterances on the essence of HITLER'S WORLDVIEW (racist, antisemitic, and based on the conquest of space in the east), as well as on his methods (organization, tactics, and propaganda), could not be clearer. Even the unsystematic structure of the work, and Hitler's long-winded, digressive, repetitive trains of thought, cannot change this. The revolutionary, primitive, and brutal elements of National Socialism are clearly expressed.

After 1945 the copyrights to *Mein Kampf* (the original manuscripts have been missing since the war ended) were transferred to the Free State of Bavaria, which in agreement with the Foreign Ministry has forbidden any new edition out of concern for Germany's reputation abroad. "This decision," according to the historian Eberhard Jäckel in his standard work on Hitler's worldview, "is, however, only enforceable in Germany, and thus the perverse situation arises that in other countries numerous translations are available, some of them with prefaces by totally trustworthy scholars, whereas the original text is available only in the diverse and therefore inadequate versions of the National Socialist editions

found in libraries. However justified the political considerations may appear to many people, in truth the situation is more questionable, in that the state in this way exercises censorship and prevents scholars from making use of an important, available historical source that reveals Hitler's criminal character more persuasively than do many commentaries."

C. Z.

Meiser, Hans, b. Nuremberg, February 16, 1888; d. Munich, June 8, 1956, German Evangelical theologian. Beginning in 1905 Meiser was a curate in various congregations. In 1922 he became director of the Bavarian Seminary in Nuremberg, and in 1928 a member of the High Consistory. From 1933 to 1955 he was bishop (*Landesbischof*) of the Evangelical-Lutheran church in Bavaria. Despite basically nationalist leanings, Meiser opposed National Socialist plans for a SYNCHRONIZATION of the church through creation of an Evangelical Reich Church, and thus he joined the CONFESSING CHURCH. This action cost him his position and put him under house arrest. After considerable public protest from the congregations Meiser was reinstated, and he led his diocese in the struggle against NS persecution of the church throughout the war. In 1949 he became the leading bishop of the United Evangelical-Lutheran Church in Germany.

Hans Meiser.

Meissner, Otto, b. Bischweiler (Alsace), March 13, 1880; d. Munich, May 27, 1953, German politician. In 1911 Meissner became an official (*Regierungsrat*) with the German Railroad Administration in Alsace. First drafted into the infantry in the First World War, after 1918 he served in the military government in the Ukraine. In 1920 Meissner was appointed chief of the Presidial Chancellery, where he became state secretary in 1923 and minister (*Staatsminister*) in 1937. He served under Presidents Friedrich Ebert and Paul von Hindenburg, and after the latter's death, under Hitler as well, until the end of the Third Reich.

Otto Meissner.

Meissner had considerable influence over Hindenburg, whose antiparliamentary prejudices he strengthened. This contributed to the formation of the so-called PRESIDIAL CABINETS, and ultimately to Hitler's nomination as Reich chancellor. Nonetheless, Meissner was acquitted in the postwar WILHELMSTRASSE TRIAL because he had helped many opponents of the regime. Later appellate and judiciary proceedings also ended in acquittal. Meissner's most notable writings were *Staats- und Verwaltungsrecht im Dritten Reich* (Constitutional and Administrative Law in the Third Reich; 1935, with Georg Kaisenberg) and his memoirs, *Staatssekretär unter Ebert, Hindenburg, Hitler* (State Secretary under Ebert, Hindenburg, Hitler; 1950).

Memelland, East Prussian region north of the Memel River, with the Baltic port city of Memel; area, 2,566 sq km (about 1,000 sq miles); population, approximately 140,000 (1919), of whom 71,000 spoke German and 67,000 spoke Lithuanian. The Versailles treaty (Articles 94–99) placed Memelland, without a plebiscite, under the authority of an Allied Commission with a French high commissioner and French occupation troops. LITHUANIA annexed Memelland in 1923 (January 10–16), an act sanctioned by an Allied ambassadors' conference on February 16. On May 8, 1924, the area received a self-government statute under Lithuanian sovereignty, with its own parliament and executive body, and a Lithuanian governor.

Beginning in 1926 a state of emergency existed in Memelland because of constant tensions between the governor and the generally strong German majority in the parliament, a situation exacerbated by numerous infractions of the self-government statute in the course of a deliberate policy of "Lithuanization." This state of affairs also negatively affected German-Lithuanian relations. On March 23, 1939, German troops marched into Memelland in response to a treaty that had been forced upon the Lithuanian government on the previous day, March 22. A Reich law then incorporated Memelland into the German Reich. When the Red Army advanced in 1944, most of the German population left the area. In January 1945 Memelland was joined to the Lithuanian Soviet Socialist Republic, which had been formed in 1944.

B.-J. W.

Mengele, Josef (aliases included José Mengele, Helmut Gregor[i], Dr. Fausto Rindón, S. Josi

Alvers Aspiazu), b. Günzburg, March 16, 1911; d. (it is believed) Embu (Brazil), February 7, 1979, German physician and SS-*Hauptsturm-führer*. Mengele studied philosophy and medicine. He joined the STEEL HELMET in 1931, the NSDAP in 1937, and the SS in 1938. Mengele set up his practice in Frankfurt am Main in 1938. In 1940 he joined the medical corps (Sanitätsinspektion) of the Waffen-SS, and in 1941 became battalion physician for the SS "Viking" Division. After being wounded in the Russian Campaign, on May 30, 1943, Mengele was posted to the office of the "SS Garrison Physician [*Standortarzt*] in AUSCHWITZ." There he took part in numerous *Selektionen*, carried out in order to select for killing those incoming Jews who were incapable of work (these were called "arrival selections" or "ramp selections"). He also carried out *Selektionen* of barracks inmates who were no longer capable of work ("camp selections"). In his HUMAN EXPERIMENTS, which included experiments on twins, Mengele assented to the death of countless prisoners.

After the war Mengele went into hiding. In 1949 he fled to Argentina via Italy, then moved to Paraguay in 1959, and is thought to have ended up in Brazil. Beginning in 1959 he was sought for arrest by criminal prosecutors in the Federal Republic of Germany. In 1964 the Universities of Frankfurt and Munich withdrew his academic degrees. A "Mengele Court" was assembled in Israel in early February 1985 for the purpose of symbolically condemning him. A reward of over 10 million DM was collected from various sources for information leading to

Josef Mengele.

his capture. In the spring of 1985 there seemed reason to believe that Mengele had died years earlier in a swimming accident in Embu, Brazil, and had been buried as Wolfgang Gerhard. His family confirmed this version in a large magazine serial. The body was exhumed on July 5, 1985, and was autopsied by an international panel of forensic pathologists. They concluded that there was a strong probability that these were the mortal remains of Josef Mengele.

A. St.

Men's league (*Männerbund*), organized alliance of men, usually dedicated to a common political ideal and structured hierarchically. Such alliances existed in Germany from the 18th century, partly as political secret societies (*see* FREEMASONRY). After the late 19th century they increasingly manifested a nationalist and militarist bent. The men's league as a paramilitary and ideological association marked by "volitional uniformity, comradeship, discipline, and subordination" is the precursor of, as well as the fundamental form for, fascist organizations in the 20th century. In the National Socialist ideology of manhood, in which women played only a subordinate role, the men's league was highly prized as a "community sworn to loyalty." Sexual segregation was thus one of the NS educational principles (*see* HITLER YOUTH; LEAGUE OF GERMAN GIRLS); uniformed party formations such as the SA and the SS were conceived of as men's leagues. A homoerotic component cannot be overlooked here (*see* HOMOSEXUALITY).

Mentally ill. *See* Euthanasia; Hereditarily Ill Offspring; Psychiatry.

Menzel, Gerhard, b. Waldenburg (Silesia), September 29, 1894; d. Comano (Ticino, Switzerland), May 4, 1966, German writer. Menzel's initial success came with nationalistic plays and novels, such as *Flüchtlinge* (Refugees; 1933), which describes the flight of ethnic Germans living in Russia from the "Bolshevist hell." He then became one of the most popular scriptwriters, dealing in rather unpolitical entertainment movies and would-be heroic material from the German past (as in *Robert Koch*; 1938). After the war Menzel continued without a break as a scriptwriter, notably for the film *Die Sünderin* (The [Woman] Sinner; 1951).

Menzel, Herybert, b. Obornik (Posen), August 10, 1906; killed in action near Tirschtiegel (Posen), February 1945, German writer. Menzel left his law studies to write *völkisch* "homeland" novels (*Heimatromane*) such as *Umstrittene Erde* (Contested Earth; 1933), as well as collections of popular verse from the *Grenzmark* (Posen became a "borderland" when the Versailles treaty transferred parts of it to the Polish Corridor), notably *Der Grenzmark-Rappe* (The Black Horse of the Borderland; 1933). He also wrote numerous poems, cantatas, and hymns in his capacity as National Socialist party bard and lyricist for all occasions; among them were "Im Marschschritt der SA" (In the SA March Step; 1933), "In unseren Fahnen lodert Gott" (In Our Banners God Blazes; 1935), and "Ewig lebt die SA" (Long Live the SA; 1938). Menzel characterized himself politically as a fighter for "Germany's Awakening" and poetically as "messenger of my homeland."

Menzel's "Poem," in the anthology *Künder und Kämpfer* (Heralds and Warriors; 1939), reads: "We are, comrades, / worthy of exaltation / only through pious submission / to the Commandment of God. / And although we are iron-clad, / we each must prove / that pure in all of us / the urge for freedom blazes."

Mercy killing (*Gnadentod;* literally, mercy death), actively aiding a person to die in order to achieve a release from unbearable and incurable suffering. The term was used euphemistically by Hitler in his order of September 1, 1939, to set in motion the EUTHANASIA program.

Messerschmitt, Willy, b. Frankfurt am Main, June 26, 1898; d. Munich, September 15, 1978, German aircraft designer. Messerschmitt studied engineering at the Technical College in Munich, then in 1923 founded the Messerschmitt Flugzeugbau GmbH (Messerschmitt Aircraft Manufacturing, Ltd.). He first concentrated on building recreational aircraft; in 1925 he produced his first engine-powered airplane, and in 1926 he built his first all-metal craft (the M 17). Messerschmitt played a considerable role in building up the German Luftwaffe with his improvements: the Me 109 became the standard fighter plane in the Second World War. In its Me 209 version it attained a record speed for planes with piston engines (755.138 kph [about 450 mph]) that was not exceeded until 1969.

During the war Messerschmitt added the Me 262 ("Swallow"), the first jet-propelled plane adequate for frontline service, as well as numerous other models, including the Me 163 rocket-propelled fighter plane. He was named a MILITARY ECONOMY FÜHRER (*Wehrwirtschaftsführer*) and received the title "Pioneer of La-

Willy Messerschmitt with test pilot Fritz Wendel.

bor" (*Pionier der Arbeit*). In 1938 he was honored with the German National Prize for Art and Science. After the war Messerschmitt—classified as a "fellow traveler" (*Mitläufer*) by a denazification court in 1948—changed over to the manufacture of sewing machines and "bubble cars" (miniature cars with transparent domes). Beginning in 1956 he was involved in the building of jet fighters for NATO and the air force of the Federal Republic. He was a partner in the Messerschmitt-Bölkow-Blohm GmbH concern.

Metal Donation of the German Volk (Metalspende des deutschen Volkes), program for the collection of various metals—nickel, tin, and lead—promoted as of April 20, 1940, to support the German RAW-MATERIALS ECONOMY. The donation was meant to supplement the ordinance of March 15, 1940, dealing with nonferrous metals in buildings and elsewhere; an example was bronze church bells, which were melted "in service to the German armament reserve."

Metallurgische Forschungs-GmbH (Metallurgical Research, Ltd.), corporation for the financing of armaments, founded by the Krupp, Siemens-Schuckert, Deutsche Werke, and Rheinmetall firms in May 1933, on the instigation of Hjalmar SCHACHT (*see* MEFO BILLS).

Metaxas, Ioannis, b. Ithaca (Greece), April 12, 1871; d. Athens, January 29, 1941, Greek politician and general. Metaxas became chief of the Greek General Staff in 1915. After the First World War he held ministerial posts in several governments. As a leader of the monarchists, he engineered the return of King George II. He himself took over the War Ministry, and in 1936 he made himself premier for life by a *coup* *d'état,* introducing a dictatorial, anti-Communist system. As head of state, Metaxas rejected Italy's ultimatum in 1940; his appeal for opposition was so successful that it resulted in Germany's Balkan Campaign. The strong line of fortifications on Greece's northern frontier was named after Metaxas.

Metzger, Max Joseph, b. Schopfheim (Black Forest), February 3, 1887; d. Brandenburg, April 17, 1944 (executed), German Catholic theologian and opposition fighter. Ordained in 1911, Metzger became a field chaplain. In 1917 he helped found the Peace Alliance of German Catholics. As a pacifist he was hostile to the National Socialists, who temporarily imprisoned him in 1936. His ecumenical efforts in founding the "Una Sancta Brotherhood" in 1938 also aroused suspicion. In 1942 Metzger wrote a memorandum for the Swedish bishop Eidem about an eventual postwar Germany, asking his support in future attempts to obtain tolerable peace conditions. The paper fell into Gestapo hands and led to Metzger's arrest on June 29, 1943. The *Volk* Court sentenced him to death for VOLK TREASON on October 14, 1943.

Meyer, Alfred, b. Göttingen, October 5, 1891; d. May 1945 (suicide), German politician. Meyer studied law and political economy. An officer in the First World War, he was a French prisoner of war in 1917. After the war he worked as a mining official in Gelsenkirchen. Meyer joined the NSDAP in 1928, and became a Reichstag deputy and *Gauleiter* for Westphalia-North in 1930. Promoted to the post of *Reichsstatthalter* (governor) for Lippe and Schaumburg-Lippe in 1933, by 1936 he was also a minister of state. In 1938 Meyer became an SS-*Obergruppenführer* as well as *Oberpräsident* (chief administrator) of Westphalia. Beginning in 1941, as state secretary in the Reich Ministry for the Occupied Eastern Territories, he served as Alfred RO-SENBERG's deputy.

Meyer, Arnold Oskar, b. Breslau, October 20, 1877; d. Königsberg (Neumark), June 3, 1944, German historian. The son of the Breslau physicist Oskar Emil Meyer (1834–1909), Arnold Meyer was a member of the Prussian Historical Institute in Rome from 1903 to 1908. He subsequently obtained professorial posts in Rostock (1913), Kiel (1915), Göttingen (1922), Munich (1929), and Berlin (1935). Meyer belonged to the academic elite during the Third Reich: in 1935 he became a member of the advisory council of the "Reich Institute for the History of

the New Germany"; in 1936 he was appointed a senator of the German Academy. Meyer's research concentrated on English history and the Bismarckian period. He lost his life in a riding accident.

Meyerhof, Otto, b. Hannover, April 12, 1884; d. Philadelphia, October 6, 1951, German biochemist. In 1922 Meyerhof received a Nobel prize for research into metabolic processes. At the Kaiser Wilhelm Institute for Biology, where he worked from 1924 to 1938, he was subjected to growing hostility because of his Jewish origins. He finally emigrated to the United States and became a professor in Philadelphia. After the war, as "restitution," he received the professorship at Heidelberg that the National Socialists had denied him.

Otto Meyerhof.

Mickey Mouse (*Mickymaus*), comic figure invented in 1928 by the American film cartoonist Walt Disney (1901–1966). The humanized mouse was presented in early stories as a joker, sometimes down on his luck, who was meant to embody the American Way of Life. This Mickey Mouse belonged more to the "Negro culture" rejected by the National Socialists than to the heroic realism that they advocated. Goebbels called the "filthy mouse" (*schmutzige Maus*) a "most miserable model"; Hitler found Mickey Mouse silly. Nevertheless, his popularity was so great that Mickey Mouse films were shown in Germany until 1940. Other American comic heroes, including Popeye (*Pop, der Seemann*), also found a German audience. Germany's

Fourth Air Squadron had an ax-swinging Mickey Mouse as its emblem during the Second World War.

H. H.

Middle class. *See* Mittelstand.

Miegel, Agnes, b. Königsberg, March 9, 1879; d. Bad Salzuflen, October 26, 1964, German writer. After and together with her journalistic work, Miegel won fame in the 1920s and 1930s as an author closely tied to her East Prussian homeland, about which she wrote ballads, songs, and stories about "Autumn," "Shepherd's Happiness," love, and life. Even before 1933, Miegel sympathized with the National Socialists, who extolled her as a "great master" for her "blood-and-soil romanticism" and her nationalism, as in her glorification of Paul von Hindenburg's First World War East Prussian victory in *Deutsche Balladen* (German Ballads; 1936). In 1940 she was awarded the Goethe Prize for "creating a pure image of the East German." With her celebrations of past East Prussian grandeur, Miegel retained a large circle of readers after the war, especially among Germans expelled from their homes in the east.

Mielert, Fritz Josef Maria, b. Wartha bei Breslau, July 3, 1879; d. Dortmund, August 4, 1947, German writer. As one of the most popular travel writers of the Third Reich, Mielert enjoyed success with numerous illustrated volumes and landscape depictions in which he idealized the "beauties of the homeland"; examples were *Deutsches Ahnengut in Westfalen* (German Ancestral Holdings in Westphalia; 1935) and *Grossdeutschland, erwandert und erlebt* (Great-Germany Traveled Through and Experienced; 1939).

Mierendorff, Carlo, b. Grossenhain (Saxony), March 23, 1897; d. Leipzig, December 4, 1943, German journalist, politician, and opposition fighter. As a disillusioned volunteer in the First World War, Mierendorff became a pacifist, an advocate of reconciliation with France, and a member of the Social Democratic Party (SPD). After working as a trade union secretary and as a journalist with the Social Democratic press, he became press secretary to the Hessian interior minister, Wilhelm LEUSCHNER, and then secretary to the SPD Reichstag delegation. Elected to the Reichstag in 1930, until 1933 Mierendorff was a party spokesman in the fight against National Socialism; in this capacity he initiated the publication of the BOXHEIM DOCUMENTS.

Agnes Miegel.

After a brief period of exile in 1933, Mierendorff was arrested for participating in an illegal opposition group; he remained in various concentration camps until 1938. After his release, he and Theodor HAUBACH built up a Social Democratic opposition organization, maintaining contacts with Julius LEBER and Leuschner, and later with the KREISAU CIRCLE. Mierendorff consistently supported Hitler's removal by force: "Either to power or to the gallows." After the Führer's hoped-for downfall, Mierendorff was to be considered for the post of press secretary under Carl GOERDELER as chancellor. However, he died during a British air raid before the plans for the assassination attempt assumed concrete form.

Carlo Mierendorff.

Miklas, Wilhelm, b. Krems, October 15, 1872; d. Vienna, March 20, 1956, Austrian politician. Beginning in 1918 Miklas was a member of the Austrian National Assembly; in 1923 he became its president. In 1928 he was elected Austria's president as a candidate of the Christian Social party; in 1931 he was confirmed in the post. Although distancing himself from the authoritarian DOLLFUSS and SCHUSCHNIGG governments, Miklas tolerated the suspension of parliament. On March 11, 1938, under Hitler's strong pressure, he named Arthur SEYSS-INQUART to the post of Austrian chancellor; twice before Miklas had refused. But he steadfastly refused to sign the law legitimizing the ANSCHLUSS with the German Reich, and shortly afterward resigned from office, on March 13.

Milch, Erhard, b. Wilhelmshaven, March 30, 1892; d. Wuppertal, January 25, 1972, German field marshal (July 19, 1940). Milch served with the air corps in the First World War, then joined the Junkers aircraft firm. In 1926 he became a member of the board of directors of Lufthansa, and in 1942 its president. On January 30, 1933, Hermann Göring made Milch his deputy, with the title Reich Commissioner for German Aviation (*Reichskommissar für die deutsche Luftfahrt*); a month later Milch became a state secretary. Any objections to Milch's Jewish origins were removed by Göring's sentence: "I determine who is a Jew."

As an air force general (after 1935) and inspector general (after 1938), Milch had a key position in the rebuilding of the Luftwaffe and its preparation for action. After the suicide of

Erhard Milch.

Wilhelm Miklas.

Ernst UDET, Milch assumed the duties of aircraft ordnance general (*Generalluftzeugmeister*). His proposals to shift the Luftwaffe to the defense of the Reich, in view of the steadily increasing stream of Allied bombers, found no response with Hitler and Göring. On the contrary, Milch was blamed for the Luftwaffe's catastrophic failures in 1943–1944, and by January 1945 he had effectively been retired. In the Nuremberg Trials of major war criminals Milch appeared as a witness against Göring. He himself was sentenced on July 17, 1947, in the so-called Milch Trial, to life imprisonment. His sentence was reduced by a pardon to 15 years in 1951, and in 1954 he was released. Thereafter he worked as a consultant to industry.

Military criminal law (*Wehrstrafrecht*), regulations concerning punishable offenses committed by members of the Wehrmacht and, to a degree, by civilians, especially those who were liable for military service but had been granted deferrals. Such law was applied by the MILITARY JURISDICTION. The legal bases for military criminal law were primarily the Military Penal Code (*Militärstrafgesetzbuch* [MilStGB], in the version of the ordinance of October 10, 1940; *Reich Law Gazette* I, p. 1347) and the Penal Code (StGB). The most serious crimes were desertion (*Fahnenflucht*); wartime treason (*Kriegsverrat*), high treason (*Hochverrat*), and state treason (*Landesverrat; see* VOLK TREASON); damage to military matériel; UNDERMINING OF MILITARY STRENGTH; espionage; shirking military or labor service; partisan activity (*Freischärlerei*);

incitement (*Aufwiegelung*); insubordination (*Gehorsamverweigerung*); mutiny; and infractions against the service obligation.

U. B.

Military Economy Führer (*Wehrwirtschaftsführer*), title introduced in 1935 for well-known figures in the armaments industry, such as Friedrich FLICK and Wilhelm ZANGEN. The implementation of REARMAMENT required a close relationship between the Wehrmacht and the economy. Thus the important industrial figures were made responsible as leaders in the military economy through a personal "loyalty relationship" (*Treueverhältnis*). Above all, the influence of the Wehrmacht on the arms industry was in this way to be increased.

V. B.

Military fitness camps (*Wehrertüchtigungslager*), courses of instruction, held over several weeks, in which boys aged 14 to 18 received premilitary training. The camps were organized by the Office for Physical Fitness of the Reich Youth Leadership, as part of the National Socialist military training program as of 1939. They were directed by Hitler Youth leaders and, increasingly, by instructors from the Wehrmacht "with frontline experience." Along with ideological instruction on such subjects as "the Anglo-American striving for world domination," the courses included primarily physical fitness training (long- and short-distance runs, marches with full equipment), military and tactical assignments (such as camouflage and reconnaissance), and the handling of weapons.

Military jurisdiction (*Militärgerichtsbarkeit*), arrangement for sentencing all criminal acts committed by military personnel; it was created by the Military Criminal Court Ordinance of November 4, 1933 (*Reich Law Gazette* I, p. 921). The responsible courts-martial, consisting of a military judge, an officer, and a military justice official, were attached to specific troop units. The commander of such units was in charge of military discipline outside of court proceedings. When the war began the courts were renamed field courts-martial (*Feldkriegsgerichte*). They were staffed with only a wartime judge (*Kriegsrichter*), whose responsibilities included preparing and initiating the arraignment. An independent authority for indictments existed only at the REICH COURT-MARTIAL (*Reichkriegsgericht*), which, together with the Superior Courts-Martial (*Oberkriegsgerichten*), was the channel for legal remedy. With the beginning of the war, a special verification proceeding by the military commander in chief replaced regular legal measures. Some 16,000 death sentences were pronounced under military jurisdiction.

The influence of National Socialism on military jurisdiction was at first small, and is difficult to evaluate for the period after 1939. The general military jurisdiction was supplemented by several measures:

1. In October 1939, a special jurisdiction for SS and police personnel, whose criminal actions were no longer subject to prosecution in regular courts; this jurisdiction also governed civilians in occupied Russian territories who

Military fitness camp of the Hitler Youth.

were charged with committing criminal acts against SS and police;

2. In November 1939, drumhead courts-martial (*see* SUMMARY LAW);

3. In May 1941, the BARBAROSSA JURISDICTIONAL DECREE;

4. In December 1941, the "NIGHT AND FOG" DECREE;

5. As of June 1943, sentencing of political crimes and infractions of the WARTIME SPECIAL CRIMINAL LAW only by the Reich Court-Martial;

6. In July 1944, the TERROR-AND-SABOTAGE DECREE.

C. D.

Military leagues (*Wehrverbände*), general term for the paramilitary organizations that came into being after the First World War; they were overwhelmingly composed of socially alienated former soldiers and officers. The largest military leagues were the STEEL HELMET, the REICH BANNER "BLACK-RED-GOLD," the WEREWOLF, and the Viking, as well as the STURMABTEILUNG (SA). Most of the leagues were imbued with a nationalistic and antiparliamentary spirit. Their reliance on violence, particularly in times of crisis, contributed significantly to the destabilization of the Weimar Republic. In 1922 the right-wing military leagues were joined together in the United Fatherland Leagues of Germany. As a replacement for the Reichswehr (particularly as border patrols) they received official state recognition for a time. In 1933 the leagues were dissolved or were taken over by the paramilitary organizations of the NSDAP.

Military service. *See* Compulsory military service.

Military sports (*Wehrsport*), physical exercises to improve the military fitness of male youth. Since the National Socialists saw EDUCATION primarily in terms of "military fitness" (*Wehrhaftmachung*), all SPORTS in the Third Reich were military sports in the broader sense. This outlook was connected with a bourgeois tradition, as had been expressed in the founding of the REICH CURATORIUM FOR YOUTH FITNESS TRAINING. The premilitary training based on military sports that had begun in the FIELD SPORTS TEAMS of the SA became, after the Seizure of Power, the official program of the Hitler Youth, the SA, SS, National Socialist Motor Corps (NSKK), and National Socialist Flyers' Corps (NSFK).

In the forefront were team sports, which transmitted the community experience and served as education in comradeship, and "hardship sports" (*Strapazensport*) to build endurance, such as marches with full equipment and obstacle races. Technical disciplines such as shooting or throwing hand grenades were also stressed. "Motorized military education" was the responsibility of special units: the Hitler Youth Flyers and Motorized Hitler Youth, the NSFK, and the NSKK. In the SS special elite forms of military sports were cultivated, such as fencing and horseback riding. All these sports were regularly exhibited on such occasions as Military Competition Days of the SA (*Wehrkampftage der SA*) and National Socialist Competitive Games (*NS-Kampfspiele*), which were

Military leagues. In Bad Harzburg, Alfred Hugenberg reviews the Fatherland Leagues.

Military sports. SA men marching with backpacks.

effective recruiting events. Air and motor sports were removed from the authority of the Reich Sports Führer and could be pursued only in National Socialist formations. These gave training to future pilots, and during the war provided some units for special tasks, such as NSKK companies for securing occupied territories.

Military tax (*Wehrsteuer*), a tax introduced by the law of July 20, 1937. It was to be paid by all German citizens subject to taxation who were born after December 31, 1913, and who were not called to a two-year period of active service. The obligation to pay the tax began when the final decision against conscription was made, and it was in force until the age of 45. Exemptions were granted to those disabled in military or labor service. In its first two years, the military tax amounted to 5 percent of the income tax, or at least 4 percent of wages; thereafter it totaled 6 percent of the income tax, or at least 5 percent of wages. On June 1, 1941, assessment of the tax was discontinued for the duration of the war.

Military worthiness (*Wehrwürdigkeit*), official designation for someone considered worthy of serving the *Volk* Community as a soldier; the term was introduced in the Military Law of May 21, 1935. Concomitantly, individuals with prior convictions and non-Aryans were classified as "militarily unworthy."

Militia (*Einwohnerwehren*; also *Bürgerwehren*), self-defense units formed in the revolutionary chaos after the First World War. Created on private initiative, and encouraged by local military authorities or administrations, the militia

units sometimes had access to heavy weapons, joined the FREE CORPS, and were deployed in border patrols. The Armed Forces Ministry had a separate department for militia, which essentially contravened the disarmament provisions of the Versailles treaty. Because the units increasingly developed into an anti-Republican and nationalistic force, especially in Bavaria, the Weimar government bowed to pressure from the victorious powers and decreed their dissolution on April 8, 1920. However, another year passed before the militia in actuality largely disappeared.

Ministerial Council for the Defense of the Reich (Ministerrat für die Reichsverteidigung), body created by Hitler's decree of August 30, 1939, which during the war had legal authority to decree ordinances through an abbreviated legal procedure. Members of the council, under Göring as chairman, included the head of the Party Chancellery, both of the general plenipotentiaries (for the Reich administration and for the economy), the chief of the Reich Chancellery, and the chief of the Wehrmacht High Command (OKW). The REICH DEFENSE COMMISSIONERS were directly responsible to the council as "middle-level authorities."

Minister Presidents' Conference (*Ministerpräsidentenkonferenz*), conference of government heads of the German states (*Länder*), established after the war in 1945. Until 1949 it also included the heads of the German provinces. The importance of the conference was that until 1949 there was no central German government, and the heads of the German states were the most important negotiating partners for, and counterparts to, the military governments of the occupation powers.

Minorities (*Minderheiten*), population groups within a state that distinguish themselves from the majority of citizens through a sense of separate national identity based on language, race, ethnicity, culture, or historical tradition. Minorities presented a considerable problem for European reorganization after the First World War, since the incorporation of alien national groups in the new or enlarged states of eastern and southeastern Europe contravened the right to self-determination demanded by President Woodrow Wilson's FOURTEEN POINTS. The pressures exerted by power politics (as in territorial cessions by defeated Germany) and economic constraints (such as the viability of successor states to the Danubian monarchy) made an alternate path impossible, and they led to multilateral treaties for the protection of minorities. Such treaties were signed between the victorious powers and Poland, Austria, Czechoslovakia, Romania, Greece, Bulgaria, Yugoslavia, Hungary, and Turkey in 1919–1920. Bilateral treaties with the same intent were also signed, such as the agreement on Upper Silesia (May 15, 1922) between Poland and Germany.

The protection of minorities was attempted primarily by guaranteeing and broadening individual BASIC RIGHTS, notably the right to use one's native language; freedom of expression, religion, and cultural associations; and access to public office. Regulations that dealt collectively with national groups were avoided, however, in order not to obstruct the process of integration in the young states. The final appeal for minorities was to the League of Nations, although its covenant did not explicitly protect minorities. Because of the divergent interests of the member states, most complaints on such issues were blocked early on. In effect, individual states could undermine minority rights with impunity. These rights then became an effective lever of National Socialist FOREIGN POLICY, which in its first phase aimed at a revision of the Versailles treaty, and which demanded a judicial solution for German minorities as a first step in destabilizing the small states on Germany's borders.

Behind this tactic was an ideological thrust: according to the NS interpretation, minority protection deriving from the concept of individual rights was a Jewish invention; it led to loss of racial identity (*see* UMVOLKUNG) and thus to a debilitation of the *Volk*. It also encouraged the assimilation that "Jewry" allegedly needed to camouflage its role as a "parasite of peoples" (*Völkerparasit*). NS minority policies during the Second World War were thus characterized by deportations, resettlement and eviction, banishment and annihilation. These measures and the dislocation of peoples following Germany's defeat made the treaties signed to protect national minorities superfluous in post-1945 Europe. The United Nations has thus far been unable to agree on a measure to protect minorities.

Mischling. *See* Mixed-breed.

Mission (*Mission;* also *Sendung, Auftrag, Gesandschaft*), general term for a calling, task, or charge; in the Christian sense, the divine commission to convert the heathen. The term "mission" was secularized in the 18th century in order to emphasize the quasi-divine consecration of an ideological calling or the particular importance of a (life) task. In this sense, "mission" became a National Socialist cliché, which Hitler used constantly, whether speaking of overcoming class struggle as "the great mission of the National Socialist movement" (*Mein Kampf*) or designating eastward expansion as "the holy mission of my life" (*Political Testament*).

Mit brennender Sorge (With Burning Concern), first and only papal encyclical in the German language "concerning the situation of the Catholic church in the German Reich" (March 14, 1937). Based on a draft by Cardinal Michael FAULHABER, the encyclical was secretly rushed to Germany and read from the pulpits of Catholic churches on March 21. It offered strong criticism of the "new heathenism" of National Socialism and its "idolatry" of race, *Volk*, and state. It further regretted that the "tree of peace planted in German earth," represented by the CONCORDAT, had not borne the desired fruits because of the guilt of others (meaning the National Socialists).

Pope PIUS XI warned in the encyclical against "corrosive religious struggles" and admonished the government to fulfill the terms of the Concordat, but he carefully avoided any reference to the concentration camps or to the persecution of Jews in Germany. Moreover, *Mit brennender Sorge* was followed on March 19, 1937, by the encyclical *Divini Redemptoris*, commemorating the common anti-Bolshevik mission of church and National Socialism against atheistic communism. This second missive did not, however, dampen the National Socialist urge for retribution against the earlier one: a wave of

PRIEST TRIALS for morals and currency infractions, restrictions on religious instruction in public schools, and the final liquidation of the CATHOLIC WORKERS' ASSOCIATIONS were among the measures that considerably exacerbated the CHURCH STRUGGLE.

Mitford, Unity Valkyrie, b. London, August 8, 1914; d. Swinbrook, March 28, 1948, English aristocrat. Through her brother-in-law, the British fascist leader Sir Oswald MOSLEY, Mitford came into contact with the German National Socialists and became a fanatical admirer of Hitler, to whose private circle in Munich she belonged as of 1933. Rumors about intimate relations between them were fueled by her "Nordic" outward appearance (buxom, tall, blond), which Hitler valued, and led to Eva BRAUN's jealousy of the "Valkyrie." When Mitford heard of the British declaration of war on September 3, 1939, she attempted to shoot herself. Cared for by Hitler's physicians, she survived, and was sent back to England via Switzerland.

"Mittelbau" ("Central Structure"; also known as "Dora-Mittelbau"), code name for an underground armaments center in the southern Harz mountains, with the focal point in the Nordhausen area. The strictly secret project was put into high gear under the management of a fake, state-owned firm, "Mittelwerk GmbH" (Central Works, Ltd.), after British nighttime air raids were directed against the experimental rocket station in Peenemünde on August 17–18, 1943. The project was intended to mass-produce future "vengeance weapons" (*Vergeltungswaffen;* see WONDER WEAPONS) and provide for their storage in bombproof shafts and tunnels.

By the end of the war, about 30,000 workers were assigned to work on secret weapons in the so-called central space (*Mittelraum*). The overwhelming majority, about 25,000, were forced laborers or prisoners from the Buchenwald concentration camp. The underground manufacturing halls came largely intact into the hands of United States troops. On July 1, 1945, the works were handed over to the Soviets, who transported the remaining German specialists and their families to the USSR. The former camp commandant, Otto Förschner, in December 1945 was sentenced to death by an American military court, as were several former SS guards who had held responsible positions, in a later trial (1947).

Mittelstand, a political and ideological term, rather than an analytical sociological one, for the "middle class" of a society. The old *Mittelstand,* comprising independent artisans, retail merchants, peasants, and the like, was differentiated from a new *Mittelstand* of lower- and middle-level employees (*Angestellte*) and civil servants. Since the world economic crisis, the *Mittelstand,* which was burdened by social anxieties and status problems (notably, the need to distance itself from the proletariat), provided National Socialism with its mass basis. In 1933–1934 the partisan independent employees' associations were "replaced" by the GERMAN LABOR FRONT (DAF). In keeping with its PERFORMANCE-oriented principles, the DAF wanted to dismantle the "differences in standing" (*Standesunterschiede*) between employees and workers, in which, however, it succeeded only to a limited extent.

The old *Mittelstand* was not, to be sure, able to realize its "larger" ideas involving occupational status, but it was able to push through economic and political demands that it thought important,

Hitler with Unity Mitford.

such as compulsory corporations or guilds (*Zwangsinnungen*) and a certificate of qualification (*Grosser Befähigungsnachweis*). Other measures aimed at the *Mittelstand*, such as the HEREDITARY FARM LAW, had ambiguous or even negative effects. The "estate" of artisans and peasants was strongly upgraded socially, and its work was glorified ideologically. The economic situation of the old *Mittelstand* improved somewhat between 1937–1938 and 1941–1942, not least at the expense of the small businesses, which were "combed out" (*ausgekämmt*).

A. v. S.

Mixed-breed (*Mischling*), a person with both Jewish and German ancestry, in the almost chemical National Socialist concept, according to which each person was the product of a chain of blood mixings (*Blutmischungen*). The term was first clearly classified in the NUREMBERG LAWS (September 15, 1935), which defined a Jewish "mixed-breed of the second degree" as someone with only one Jewish grandparent; he was also known as a "quarter Jew" (*Vierteljude*). A "mixed-breed of the first degree" had two Jewish grandparents, and was also known as a "half Jew" (*Halbjude*).

Mixed ethnic marriage (*gemischtvölkische Ehe*), National Socialist term for the marriage bond between partners from different ethnic groups (*Völker*). Such a marriage was in contrast to the MIXED MARRIAGE, between partners who were not "racially equal" (*rassegleich; see also* MARRIAGE BETWEEN DIFFERENT FAITHS).

Mixed marriage (*Mischehe*), term used today and before the Third Reich for the MARRIAGE of partners belonging to different religious faiths. After the decree of April 26, 1935, the term was officially introduced to denote a union between a person of "German or kindred [*artverwandt*] blood and a person of some other racial origin"; it referred especially to German-Jewish marriages. From then on, the usual "mixed marriage" was called a "marriage between different faiths" (*glaubensverschiedene Ehe*). If members of different but "racially equal" (*rassegleich*) peoples married, their marriage was termed a mixed ethnic (*gemischtvölkisch*) marriage.

Mjölnir, the name of the Germanic god Thor's hammer; it was the pseudonym of the National Socialist caricaturist Hans SCHWEITZER.

Model, Walter, b. Genthin bei Magdeburg, January 24, 1891; d. Lintorf bei Düsseldorf, April 21, 1945, German field marshal (March 1,

Walter Model.

1944). Model joined the army in 1909. During the First World War he served in troop and General Staff positions. In 1919 he transferred to the Reichswehr, and on March 1, 1938, he became a major general and chief of staff of the Fourth Army Corps. Model proved himself during the Polish and French campaigns, then led his Forty-first Tank Corps into the vicinity of Moscow during the Russian Campaign, in which he was commander in chief of the Ninth Army during the last German offensive near Kursk (July 1943).

The "master of the defensive position" became chief of Army Group North on January 9, 1944, and on March 31, chief of the North-Ukraine group; on June 28, he took command of Army Group Central. Succeeding Hans von KLUGE, Model was shifted to the west to lead Army Group B (August 17, 1944). Under his command, the Germans repulsed the Allied air landing near Arnheim and the Allied advance in the Ardennes. Finding himself completely encircled in April 1945, Model gave his remaining units (some 300,000 men) the order to disband, and took his own life.

Moeller van den Bruck, Arthur, b. Solingen, April 23, 1876; d. Berlin, May 30, 1925 (suicide), German journalist. Moeller wrote scholarly works on history, art, and literary analysis, notably *Die Deutschen: Unsere Menschengeschichte* (The Germans: Our Human History, 8 vols., 1904–1910). Subsequently, as the leading theoretician of the "young conservative" circle around the journal *Das Gewissen* (Conscience), he turned to political journalism. Influenced by

Arthur Moeller van den Bruck.

NIETZSCHE, Houston Stewart CHAMBERLAIN, nationalist Prussianism, and socialism, he advocated a turn toward the east: "old western Europe" was to be overcome, and a "new order" of "space and peoples" (*Raum und Volk*) was to proceed from the "young peoples of the east," but also from the "technologically advanced North Americans" and the "ideologically and culturally gifted Germans." With his idealistic and programmatic publication *Das Dritte Reich* (The Third Reich, 1923; translated as *Germany's Third Empire*), Moeller gave the National Socialists their handiest catchword. However, they rejected his concept of the "Third Reich," since Moeller relied on a "unified cultural consciousness" as its basis, rather than on ties of "race and blood" (*see* THIRD REICH).

Moldenhauer, Paul, b. Cologne, December 2, 1876; d. there, February 1, 1947, German politician. Moldenhauer studied political science, then became a lecturer (*Dozent*) at Cologne's Commercial College (Handelshochschule) in 1903. Beginning in 1907 he was a professor (*Ordinarius*) in the field of insurance. As a member of the German People's Party (DVP), he was a deputy to the Prussian parliament (1919–1921) and to the Reichstag (1920–1930). In the second MÜLLER cabinet, Moldenhauer became economics minister in November 1929 and, as successor to Rudolf HILFERDING, finance minister on December 23 of that year. He participated in the Second Hague Conference on Reparations in January 1930, and in the Disarmament Conference in 1933. Moldenhauer taught at the Berlin Technical College from 1930 to 1943.

After 1945 he was active in the committee established to break up the I.G. Farben firm.

Mölders, Werner, b. Gelsenkirchen, March 18, 1913; d. Breslau, November 22, 1941, German fighter pilot. Mölders joined the Reichswehr in 1931, and the Luftwaffe in 1935. By downing 14 airplanes in 1938–1939, he became the most successful pilot of the CONDOR LEGION in the Spanish Civil War. In the Second World War he had 115 victories in the air. On July 16, 1941, Mölders became the first officer to be awarded a diamond-studded KNIGHT'S CROSS with Oak Leaves and Swords. He died in a plane crash while en route to Ernst UDET's funeral. Mölders served as a role model for youth in the National Socialist HERO CULT. The Allies exploited his popularity with the so-called MÖLDERS LETTER.

Mölders Letter (*Mölders-Brief*), a letter, forged by British propaganda and dropped over Germany in many thousands of copies in January 1942, allegedly written by Werner MÖLDERS to a clergyman in Stettin. It contained a clear confession of faith in Catholicism by the prominent fighter pilot, and it added new fuel to the rumor that the crash of this idol of young Germans (on November 22, 1941) had been instrumented "from above." The Mölders Letter also played a role in the CHURCH STRUGGLE.

Molotov, Viacheslav Mikhailovich (originally, Viacheslav Mikhailovich Skriabin), b. Kukarka (now Sovetsk, Kirov Oblast [region]), March 9, 1890; d. Moscow, November 8, 1986, Soviet politician. A Bolshevik since 1906, Molotov (his pseudonym; *molot* means "hammer") was editor

Viacheslav Molotov.

Werner Mölders.

of the party newspaper *Pravda* and a close collaborator of Stalin. He was a longtime member of the Central Committee of the Soviet Communist Party (1921–1957) and of the Politburo (1926–1957). From 1930 to 1941 he was chairman of the Council of People's Commissars, and thereafter deputy chairman.

"The Bookkeeper" (as Lenin dubbed Molotov) became foreign minister on May 3, 1939, during prewar negotiations leading up to the GERMAN-SOVIET NONAGGRESSION PACT of August 23, 1939. (Molotov's Jewish predecessor, Maxim LITVINOV, opposed any relaxation of relations with National Socialist Germany.) The German-Soviet agreement and its secret supplementary protocols were primarily Molotov's work. The pact did gain decisive time for the

Red Army, which had been weakened by Stalin's "purges," and gave Hitler the necessary cover to unleash the war. Molotov knew that Hitler would not spare the Soviet Union, and he provided for safeguards in the Far East through a neutrality treaty with Japan. He also saved Moscow in the winter of 1941, after Germany's declaration of war (June 22, 1941). After the war and after Stalin's death (1953), Molotov lost influence—and finally all his positions—in the course of de-Stalinization. He was expelled from the party in 1962, but was reinstated on his 94th birthday in 1984, during a period of détente.

Moltke, Helmuth James Count von, b. Kreisau estate (Lower Silesia), March 11, 1907; d. Berlin-Plötzensee, January 23, 1945 (executed), German jurist and OPPOSITION fighter. After his studies, Moltke worked for a time as an attorney in Berlin, and also engaged in agriculture on his estate. From 1939 to 1944, he worked as an expert in military and international law for the Wehrmacht High Command (OKW).

In the OKW, Moltke became the center of the so-called KREISAU CIRCLE. Its opposition consisted of discussions of a possible post-Hitler Germany, to which Moltke brought his conviction that such a community required a Christian foundation. The involvement of trade unionists such as Wilhelm LEUSCHNER and socialists such as Julius LEBER in these discussions indicates that Moltke was guided by a vision of moral and democratic renewal, rather than by the conservative, restorative intentions of a Carl GOERDELER. Moltke had connections with the military opposition through his work with Adm. Wilhelm Canaris, but he rejected an assassina-

Helmuth James Count von Moltke before the *Volk* Court.

tion attempt out of Christian principles. He was arrested in connection with the breakup of the SOLF CIRCLE on January 19, 1944. Although not involved in the plans for a coup (*see* TWENTI-ETH OF JULY), he was sentenced to death by the *Volk* Court.

Monte, Hilda (originally, Hilda Meisel), b. Berlin, July 31, 1914; d. near Konstanz, April 18, 1945, German opposition fighter. From a Jewish family, Monte joined the International Socialist Combat League; she began writing for its journal *Der Funke* (The Spark) when she was 15 years old. In the early 1930s she moved to England, where she agitated against the Third Reich and helped refugees. At great personal risk, Monte decided during the war to take up the struggle in Germany itself. She was shot to death by an SS patrol during an illegal frontier crossing.

Monte Cassino, Benedictine abbey on the mountain of the same name, 519 m (1,730 feet) above the southern Italian town of Cassino. From January 15 to May 18, 1944, German paratroopers blocked the Allied advance after the INVASION of Italy. The abbey was totally destroyed by bombing and artillery fire.

Montgomery, Bernard Law, Viscount of Alamein and Hindhead, b. Kensington (now London), November 17, 1887; d. Islington Mill (Hamp-

Bernard Law Montgomery.

shire), March 24, 1976, British field marshal (September 1, 1944). In 1939–1940 Montgomery served with the British Expeditionary Forces (Third Division) in France. After Gen. Erwin ROMMEL's amazing successes in North Africa, Montgomery became commander in chief of the British Eighth Army in Egypt on August 13, 1942. He successfully completed the AFRICAN CAMPAIGN after the victory at El Alamein (November 1942). In 1944 he was commander in chief of the British forces at the time of the INVASION. He served as supreme commander of British occupation forces in Germany between the German collapse and June 26, 1946. Montgomery was then commander of the Imperial General Staff, and, for a time, deputy commander of NATO (March 1952–August 1958).

Montoire, small French town in the Loir-et-Cher department. Montoire was the site of a meeting between Hitler, his foreign minister, Joachim von Ribbentrop, and the French vice prime minister, Pierre LAVAL, on October 22, 1940. It was also the site of a meeting between Laval and the Vichy chief, Henri PÉTAIN, on October 24 of that year, after the return of the Germans from a meeting with Francisco Franco in HENDAYE.

Attempts to achieve either a political settlement with Great Britain or its outright military defeat in the summer of 1940 (*see* AIR BATTLE FOR ENGLAND) had failed. This forced Hitler to consider for a time in the autumn of that year the ideas presented by Ribbentrop and the navy command, before he finally decided to attack the Soviet Union. (Directions for Operation "Barbarossa" were given on December 18,

Monte Cassino after it was taken by Allied troops.

1940.) Ribbentrop advised a "continental blockade from Madrid to Yokohama," whereas the navy command had plans for an indirect "war on the periphery" against Great Britain in the Mediterranean. These drafts gave France a role in the Axis military efforts against the island kingdom and its overseas supply lines. France would not enter the war directly, but would use its colonies in North and West Africa as bases. After Winston Churchill ordered the sinking of the French fleet off Oran on July 3, 1940, sentiment for COLLABORATION was strong in France, and Laval in particular favored it. Pétain, however, ultimately prevailed with his shifting course of *attentisme* (waiting).

Thus, despite extremely polite expressions of mutual esteem, the Montoire conferences were complete failures. Hitler refused equal status to Vichy France. Nor did he promise either a binding demarcation of the French, Spanish, and Italian colonial possessions in North Africa or a binding settlement of France's eastern boundary (Alsace-Lorraine and Nice). Finally, Hitler refused to promise the immediate return of French prisoners of war and of civilians deported to Germany.

B.-J. W.

Moorsoldaten. *See* Peat-bog soldiers.

Moravia (Ger., Mähren), "historical region" of CZECHOSLOVAKIA. After its "destruction" in March 1939, it became part of the PROTECTORATE OF BOHEMIA AND MORAVIA.

Moreau, Rudolf von, b. Munich, February 8, 1910; d. Berlin, March 31, 1939, German flyer. In 1931 Moreau flew a round-trip to Africa for the Junkers aircraft firm. He was made a Luftwaffe captain in 1935. Moreau commanded the first unit of the CONDOR LEGION in the Spanish Civil War and directed its further development. He died in a practice flight after returning from Spain.

Morell, Theo, b. Traisa (Hesse), July 18, 1886; d. Tegernsee, May 1948, German physician. As a naval doctor (from 1913), Morell served in military hospitals on the western front in 1915. In 1918 he opened a practice in Berlin for "electrotherapy and urology." Morell, who had a keen business sense, rose to become a fashionable doctor with prominent patients. They included Heinrich HOFFMANN, Hitler's personal photographer, who in 1936 arranged for Morell to be invited to the BERGHOF.

Theo Morell.

Hitler came to trust Morell, who was occasionally able through continuous medication to free his new patient from chronic stomach troubles. Critics such as Karl BRANDT saw this massive chemotherapy as a form of slow poisoning, and bestowed on Morell, who had been given a post as Hitler's personal physician, the nickname *Reichsspritzenmeister* (literally, Reich Master of Injections; *Spitzenmeister* means record holder). Hitler himself, by the end of the war dependent on Morell's treatments for stimulation and relaxation, had faith in his care until the end. Morell left the bunker under the Reich Chancellery on April 21, 1945, and fell into American hands. Held successively in several internment camps and repeatedly questioned, he eventually died in a United States military hospital.

Morgenthau, Henry, Jr., b. New York City, May 11, 1891; d. Poughkeepsie, N.Y., February 6, 1967, American politician. In 1931 Morgenthau became New York state commissioner of conservation under Gov. Franklin D. Roosevelt; under Roosevelt as president, Morgenthau became head of the Farm Credit Administration in 1933, and in 1934 and 1935 served as treasury secretary. He was also an influential adviser to Roosevelt. The MORGENTHAU PLAN, initiated by Morgenthau in 1944, gave unwitting ammunition to National Socialist propaganda for staying the course, even as Morgenthau's Jewish background was exploited as political capital. After the war he headed the American Finance and Development Office for Israel from 1951 to 1954.

Henry Morgenthau, Jr.

Morgenthau Plan, American program for dealing with a defeated Germany, named after Treasury Secretary Henry MORGENTHAU, Jr., on whose initiative it was drafted in August 1944. The 14-point plan, entitled "Program to Prevent Germany from Starting a World War III," stipulated the following:

Germany's total demilitarization;

The DISMANTLING of its industry, distribution of industrial installations among the Allies as reparations, and the closing of its mines (thereby transforming the country into an agricultural state);

Expropriation of large landed estates, collection of Germany's foreign assets, and control of the German economy for at least 20 years;

Cession of East Prussia, Upper Silesia, and the Saarland (to the Moselle and Rhine rivers);

Internationalization of the Ruhr region, Westphalia, the Rhineland, the North Sea coast, and the North Sea–Baltic Sea canal;

Partition of the remaining German territory into two autonomous states and the linking of the southern state with Austria in a customs union;

The sentencing of German war criminals;

Reorganization of the German educational system and RE-EDUCATION of the German population.

The Morgenthau Plan was intended as a corrective to proposals by the United States State Department and the EUROPEAN ADVISORY COMMISSION that Morgenthau considered too moderate. Proposed to President Franklin D. Roosevelt in early September 1944, it was accepted in modified form by him and Winston Churchill at their meeting in Quebec on September 15. However, strong criticism from the secretaries of state (Cordell Hull) and war (Henry Stimson), as well as from the general public, led Roosevelt to withdraw his signature by late September. Publicly as well, the president distanced himself from the plan. Thus neither the Morgenthau Plan itself nor its basic idea of a "hard" (punitive) peace became of any importance in American policy toward Germany. It was, however, constantly conjured up as a bogeyman and as Jewish retribution ("Judah's murderous plan," according to the *Völkischer Beobachter*) by German propaganda, which aimed to promote "staying the course."

R. B.

Morning Celebrations (*Morgenfeiern*), National Socialist ceremonies replacing and competing with morning religious prayers and Sunday church services. During the first years of the Third Reich, Morning Celebrations were performed primarily by the Hitler Youth (HJ) in their camps, as both daily morning flag raisings and larger Sunday morning ceremonies. Other party divisions had similar ceremonies, particularly in their training camps. In 1935 the HJ came forth with a new type of artistically conceived Sunday morning ceremony, which was broadcast over the radio to the wider public at the same time as church services.

In 1940 Joseph Goebbels ordered the implementation of "Celebrations in Honor of Heroes" (*Heldenehrungsfeiern*) as morning ceremonies to commemorate those fallen in battle. Alfred ROSENBERG in 1941 introduced "Hours to Celebrate Worldview" (*Weltanschauliche Feierstunden*), which were a mixture of ideological edification and artistic matinee. Like the religious services, they were intended to take place at the same hour throughout the Reich, down to the level of the local group. Because of their artistic quality, the larger celebrations had temporary success. The heroism celebrations too were accepted among the population for a time, until the war began to demand too many martyrs.

K. V.

Moscow, capital of the Soviet Union. During the RUSSIAN CAMPAIGN, Moscow was the initial military objective of the German attack, although Hitler soon abandoned this plan in favor of a conquest of the Ukraine. In the second attack on Moscow, which started on October 2, 1941, the

German advance halted in early December within a few kilometers of the city. The Soviet government had left Moscow by the end of October.

Moscow, Peace of, treaty signed in Moscow on March 12, 1940, after the end of the WINTER WAR between Finland and the Soviet Union. In the treaty, Finland ceded some islands in the Baltic Sea, Vyborg, the Karelian Isthmus, and areas along the Murman railroad, and leased out the Hangö peninsula as a base for the Red Army. Despite a commitment not to join any coalition directed against the Soviet Union, Finland joined the RUSSIAN CAMPAIGN on the German side on July 26, 1941, thus invalidating the Moscow treaty.

Moscow Foreign Ministers' Conferences, three rounds of talks by the Allied foreign ministers in the Soviet capital. The first conference (October 19–30, 1943) was attended by China's foreign minister, as well as by those of Great Britain (Anthony EDEN), the United States (Cordell HULL), and the USSR (Viacheslav MOLOTOV); its purpose was to prepare for the TEHERAN Conference. It also decided on the restoration of Austria, the purging of Fascism from Italy, the extradition of German war criminals to the countries where they had committed their acts, and the creation of the EUROPEAN ADVISORY COMMISSION; and it strengthened the demand for UNCONDITIONAL SURRENDER.

The second conference (December 16–26, 1945) was attended by Ernest BEVIN (Great Britain), James Byrnes (United States), and Molotov, and was concerned primarily with problems in the Far East. It also planned a peace conference in Paris for all the countries that had been at war with Italy, Bulgaria, Hungary, Romania, and Finland, and it agreed on the creation of an International Atomic Energy Commission.

The third conference (March 10–April 24, 1947) was attended by Bevin, Molotov, George Marshall (United States), and Georges Bidault (France). It contentiously discussed the German question; no agreement emerged, either on the form of the future German state that all wanted, or on Germany's eastern boundary, the reparations, or the issues relating to the German economy.

Mosley, Sir Oswald, b. London, November 16, 1896; d. Paris, December 3, 1980, British politician. Mosley was a member of Parliament from 1918 to 1931, first as a Conservative, then as an independent (1922–1924), and subsequently as a Labourite. He finally left the Labour party as well, in disagreement over the methods to be used in combating unemployment, which he blamed on the ruling cliques ("old gangs").

Sir Oswald Mosley inspects English fascists.

In 1932 Mosley founded a "New Party," on the Italian model, that became the British Union of Fascists (BUF). With it, and in his journal, *Blackshirt*, he fought against the parliamentary system. Although his wife was half Jewish (she died in 1933), Mosley was a radical antisemite. However, he had little success with his antisemitic and anti-Bolshevik slogans. The BUF was prohibited after the war began, and Mosley was detained from 1940 to 1943. In 1948 he founded the Union Movement, a right-radical party that was rumored to have royal support.

Mother and Child Aid Agency (Hilfswerk Mutter und Kind), institution of the NATIONAL SOCIALIST VOLK WELFARE (NSV) organization. The agency was founded in 1934 to care for "needy families that are hereditarily healthy [*erbgesund*] and valuable to the *Volk* Community, especially mothers and children." It provided such services as care by National Socialist nurses, aid in housing and settlement, employment assistance, help in placing children in kindergartens and nursery schools, pediatric care, counseling on child rearing, convalescent homes, and meals for children. The agency was located in the Main Office for Volk Welfare (Hauptamt für Volkswohlfahrt) in the NSDAP Reich headquarters; its work was carried out primarily by volunteers (over 500,000 in 1939). By 1939, some 34,000 offices had been opened, with 1,500 female "care givers" (*Pflegerinnen*).

Mother cult (*Mutterkult*), the revaluation of motherhood demanded and fostered by National Socialist propaganda in order to support the sociopolitical aspects of POPULATION POLICY. Motherhood was extolled as "the greatest mystery on earth" and at the same time was demanded of every married woman as a "natural expectation." Intentional childlessness was said to be "against nature," and ultimately it would lead to "*Volk* death." Accordingly, it was advocated that the Christian concept of sin be abandoned, as well as "Marxist" forms of free love (*see* COMRADELY MARRIAGE). They would be replaced by a return to the values of the Germanic-Nordic peoples, who had always celebrated the mother as the "guardian of the holy hearth fire, of life and honor." As a counterpart, the mother cult praised maternal love, which was frequently depicted in literature and film. MOTHER'S DAY was correspondingly given further development, and the CROSS OF HONOR of the German Mother was awarded as an expression of the new esteem for mothers in the NS state.

Mother's Day (*Muttertag*), holiday to honor mothers; it was inspired by the American journalist Ann Jarvis (1864–1948). Mother's Day was also celebrated in Germany beginning in 1922. After 1933, the National Socialists placed it "in the service of [their] educational policy to deepen family life as the biological and moral foundation of the *völkisch* state" (*Neue Brockhaus* encyclopedia, 1941). Mother's Day was first celebrated on the second Sunday in May, but in 1938 it was moved to the third Sunday. (It

Mother cult. Recipients of the Mother's Cross.

has now returned to the second Sunday.) It was the day for awarding the CROSS OF HONOR of the German Mother. On Mother's Day in 1934, Reich Women's Führerin Gertrud SCHOLTZ-KLINK founded the MOTHERS' SERVICE.

Mothers' Schools (*Mütterschulen*), educational institutions, established in 1936, of the MOTHERS' SERVICE of the German Women's Agency. In 1941 there were about 500 such schools.

Mothers' Service (Mütterdienst), division of the GERMAN WOMEN'S AGENCY as well as of the National Socialist WOMEN'S UNION. It was responsible for the training of mothers in the MARRIAGE SCHOOLS and HOME-MOTHER SCHOOLS, which were established as of November 1936. Their purpose was to teach engaged and married women about the "exalted duties of motherhood" and to train them in housewifely skills. The schools' courses, which ran for several weeks, covered the principles of race and inheritance and *Volk* customs, as well as infant care and sewing. When these schools were located in the workplace, the Women's Office of the GERMAN LABOR FRONT took over the Mothers' Service. The teaching personnel were trained in a Reich School operated by the service.

Motorization, the extraordinarily accelerated supplying of the business sector, the military, and private households with motor vehicles by the National Socialists after the Seizure of Power. Even before 1933, motorized units had largely replaced the cavalry. In preparation for war, trucks had to be produced in especially large numbers, in order to assure rapid and flexible transportation for men and matériel. In the civilian economy, motor vehicles had become the most important means of transportation by the late 1920s, making it necessary to build and enlarge a network of highways in the Third Reich (*see* AUTOBAHN). For private use the public would be offered a standardized and thus inexpensively produced motor vehicle, which could serve for recreation, travel, and other transportation needs (*see* VOLKSWAGEN). Although the war prevented a marked increase in private transportation, the NSDAP and the offices and organizations responsible for motorization (notably the NATIONAL SOCIALIST MOTOR CORPS) could point to considerable success: in 1932 there had been only one vehicle per 44 Germans; by 1938 the ratio was up to one for every 20.

H. H.

Motorization. Hitler inspecting a Mercedes-Benz racing car.

Motorized Hitler Youth (Motor-HJ), special unit of the HITLER YOUTH created for "fitness in motoring skills" (*motorische Ertüchtigung*); it was for boys 16 to 18 years old. In 1934 it had some 100,000 members. Because the motorized youths had only 350 of their own vehicles for training, in that year the NATIONAL SOCIALIST MOTOR CORPS took on this task. Subsequently, up to 10,000 members of the group yearly received their driver's licenses and practiced automotive repairs.

Movement (*Bewegung*), the overall term used by the NSDAP to designate itself with its divisions and affiliated organizations. In National Socialist usage, it derived from a "dynamic striving" that was said to emerge "from the deep fundamental energies of a *Volk*."

Movimento Sociale Italiano. *See* Neofascism.

Muchow, Reinhold, b. December 21, 1905; d. Bacharach, September 12, 1933, German politician. Muchow joined the German National People's Party (DNVP) in 1920, then the free corps OBERLAND League, and in 1925 the NSDAP. In his local party group in the Berlin suburb of Neukölln, Muchow tried out the organizational model of street cells (*Strassenzellen*). His success led Joseph Goebbels to summon him to the Berlin *Gau* headquarters. Muchow was heavily involved in the formation and extension of the NATIONAL SOCIALIST WORKPLACE CELL ORGANIZATION. He founded its journal, *Arbeitertum* (Workerdom), and helped develop the plans to destroy the TRADE UNIONS on May 2, 1933. In the GERMAN LABOR FRONT, which replaced the unions, Muchow became the organizational leader and created the 14 so-called occupational columns (*Berufssäulen*), a division based on branches of work. He died in an automobile accident.

Reinhold Muchow.

Mühsam, Erich, b. Berlin, April 6, 1878; d. Oranienburg concentration camp, July 10, 1934, German writer and political journalist. Beginning in 1901, Mühsam was a freelance writer in Berlin and a contributor to the anarchist journal *Der arme Teufel* (The Poor Devil). He was then editor of the Munich-based journal *Kain: Zeitschrift für Menschlichkeit* (Cain: Journal for Humanitarianism; 1911–1919, but banned during the First World War). In 1918 Mühsam belonged to the "Revolutionary Workers' Council" in Munich, and together with Ernst TOLLER and Gustav LANDAUER was significantly involved in creating the Bavarian Re-

Erich Mühsam.

public of Councils (Räterepublik). Arrested following its fall, Mühsam was sentenced to 15 years' imprisonment. After being amnestied in 1926, he edited the journal *Fanal* (Beacon) until 1931. On February 28, 1933, Mühsam was arrested by the SA; he was detained, tortured, and finally murdered.

Müller, Fritz, b. Berlin, March 11, 1889; d. on the eastern front, September 20, 1942, German Evangelical theologian. A highly decorated volunteer in the First World War, Müller became a clergyman among the working class. In 1933 he was called to Berlin-Dahlem, where (together with Martin NIEMÖLLER) he founded the PASTORS' EMERGENCY LEAGUE. In these circles Müller became an uncompromising fighter for the Confessing Church. After the church's factional split, he took over the chairmanship of the second Provisional Church Directorate in 1936. This group made the clearest Evangelical statement against the National Socialists' destruction of justice, concentration camp terror, and persecution of Jews. Because of a liturgical prayer in which war was called "God's punishment," Müller—whom the Gestapo had already often arrested—lost his position after the Sudeten crisis of 1938. At the outbreak of the war, he volunteered for Wehrmacht service as an officer in charge of burials. He lost his life at the eastern front under circumstances that remain unclarified.

Müller, Heinrich, b. Munich, April 28, 1900; missing since April 29, 1945, German lawyer and SS-*Gruppenführer* (1941). After the First World War, Müller worked in the political section of the Bavarian police. In 1933 he was accepted into the SS Security Service as a detective inspector. He was not admitted into the NSDAP until 1939, because the Munich *Gau* leadership held against him his involvement in pre-1933 judicial proceedings against many National Socialists. Nonetheless, he advanced quickly by demonstrating blind obedience and a lack of scruples. Reinhard Heydrich held him in esteem for his familiarity with Soviet secret police practices; thus Müller was promoted to SS-*Standartenführer* in 1937 and to SS-*Brigadeführer* in 1940.

From 1939 to 1945 Müller was chief of Office IV of the Gestapo (Geheime Staatspolizei; SECRET STATE POLICE) in the Reich Security Main Office (RSHA). His responsibilities included arranging, together with Heydrich, the sham attack on the GLEIWITZ radio station. As "Gestapo-Müller" he became one of the most feared

Heinrich Müller.

Hermann Müller.

figures of the National Socialist dictatorship, both inside and outside Germany. The brutal and arbitrary actions for which he gained this notoriety included the persecution of political enemies and his expert organization of the mass murder of Jews; he personally signed numerous orders for deportation and execution. Müller was last seen by witnesses in the bunker beneath the Reich Chancellery. Rumors that he perished and was buried on May 17, 1945, cannot be confirmed.

Müller, Hermann, b. Mannheim, May 18, 1876; d. Berlin, March 20, 1931, German politician. Originally a commercial apprentice, Müller was editor of the Social Democratic *Görlitzer Volkszeitung* (Görlitz People's News) from 1899 to 1906. In 1906 he became a member of the Social Democratic Party's executive committee; he served in the Reichstag from 1916 to 1918, and from 1920 to 1931 (as head of the parliamentary delegation, from 1920 to 1928). He signed the Versailles treaty as foreign minister in the BAUER cabinet, and as a result was characterized by the right-wing parties as an accomplice of FULFILLMENT POLICY. Supported by the WEIMAR COALITION, which however soon lost its majority support, Müller was Reich chancellor from March to June 1920; he served again from 1928 to 1930. His 21 months in office—a long time for the Weimar situation—were shadowed by the onset of the WORLD ECONOMIC CRISIS and by political radicalization. The Great Coalition led by Müller broke up on March 27, 1930, over the issue of raising contributions for the unemployment insurance fund. From then on,

no government had a parliamentary majority. What did follow were the PRESIDIAL CABINETS that smoothed Hitler's path to dictatorship.

Müller, Josef, b. Steinwiesen (Upper Franconia), March 27, 1898; d. Munich, September 12, 1979, German jurist and politician. Until 1933 Müller was a functionary in the Bavarian People's Party; he then worked as a lawyer for religious institutions. When the war began, he was assigned to the counterintelligence unit (ABWEHR) of the Wehrmacht High Command (OKW). In touch with the military opposition circles around Gen. Ludwig BECK, after 1939 Müller tried to make contact with the British government via the Vatican in order to explore peace terms in case of Hitler's fall. In 1943 Müller was arrested for state treason (*Landesverrat*), and was accused before the Reich Court-Martial of high treason (*Hochverrat*). Although acquitted, he remained in confinement, and was held in the Buchenwald and Dachau concentration camps in 1944–1945. In 1945 Müller helped found the Christian Social Union (CSU), serving as its chairman until 1949. He was also Bavaria's deputy minister president (1947–1949) and justice minister (1947–1952).

Müller, Karl Alexander von, b. Munich, December 20, 1882; d. Rottach-Egern, December 13, 1964, German historian. Müller became a member (*Syndikus*) of the Bavarian Academy of Sciences in 1917 and an honorary member of the Reich Institute for the History of the New Germany in 1935. He was Friedrich MEINECKE's successor as editor of the *Historische Zeitschrift* (Historical Journal) from 1935 to 1945 and president of the Bavarian Academy of Sciences from 1936 to 1945. The renowned scholar and teacher, who joined the NSDAP in 1933, let himself be taken in by the National Socialist regime. He wrote various papers on such current topics as "Problems of the Second Reich in Light of the Third" (1935) and "April 10, 1938, in German History" (on the ANSCHLUSS). After the war he went into forced retirement.

Müller, Ludwig, b. Gütersloh, June 23, 1883; d. Berlin, July 31, 1945, German Evangelical theologian. Müller was ordained in 1908, and in the First World War served as a naval chaplain. From 1918 to 1926 he was a garrison chaplain in Wilhelmshaven, and from 1926 to 1933, a chaplain for the military district (*Wehrkreispfarrer*) in Königsberg. In this last capacity, in 1927 he met Hitler, who in 1933 made this relatively moderate supporter of the GERMAN CHRISTIANS his "representative and plenipotentiary on questions regarding the Evangelical Church." The "pious functionary" (*frommer Routinier*, in Scholder's words) was charged with creating an integrated GERMAN EVANGELICAL CHURCH out of the 28 state regional churches (*Landeskirchen*), and was given full government support for everything from the ouster of Friedrich von BODELSCHWINGH to an ecclesiastical constitution (July 11, 1933) and church elections (July 23, 1933), to his own election as Reich Bishop (*Reichsbischof*; popularly and mockingly shortened to *Reibi*) on September 27, 1933. At this point, however, the opposition to Müller from

Ludwig Müller.

the CONFESSING CHURCH stiffened. Also contested was his centralizing program, which was intended to create a place in the church for such National Socialist policies as the FÜHRER PRINCIPLE and the ARYAN PARAGRAPH. An understanding with the opposition was no longer possible after December 1933, when Müller unilaterally transferred the Evangelical youth organization into the Hitler Youth. Müller was ultimately stripped of any real power after the appointment of Reich Church Minister Hanns KERRL (July 16, 1935), although he did not formally resign. According to information from the Church Chancellery, Müller committed suicide at the end of the war; his family and friends, however, denied it.

Müller, Otto, b. Eckenhagen (Oberberg district), December 9, 1870; d. Tegel Prison (Berlin), October 12, 1944, German Catholic theologian. Müller was known as the "Red Chaplain" because both his doctoral dissertation (in political science) and the greater part of his professional energies were devoted to social problems, notably to the promotion of Christian trade unions. In 1902 he became president (*Präses*) of the Cologne diocese; he also served as secretary general of the Catholic Workers' Associations. In 1929 Müller founded the Ketteler House in Cologne (named after the socially committed Mainz bishop Wilhelm von Ketteler, 1811–1877), which became a center of Catholic opposition to National Socialism. Müller, who termed Hitler "a national disaster," made contact with the military opposition through his friend Bernhard LETTERHAUS, and also with the GOERDELER circle. Imprisoned after the assassination attempt of July 20, 1944, Müller perished from the harsh prison conditions.

Münchhausen, German feature film by Josef von Baky (script by Erich KÄSTNER, under the pseudonym Berthold Bürger); it premiered on March 5, 1943. The film was rated "artistically, especially worthwhile; worthwhile, in terms of *Volk* values." Hans ALBERS played the liar-baron who claimed to have ridden a cannonball and flown to the moon in a balloon. His co-players included Ilse Werner, Brigitte HORNEY, and Käthe Haack. The lavishly produced color film was completed within 16 weeks, after two years of preliminary work, to mark the 25-year jubilee of Ufa (*see* UNIVERSE FILMS, INC.).

Münchhausen, Börries Baron von, b. Hildesheim, March 20, 1874; d. Windischleuba Castle, near Altenburg, March 16, 1945, German

Hans Albers in *Münchhausen*.

writer and jurist. An officer in the First World War, Münchhausen became known primarily for verbally masterful ballads based on heroic legends and fairy tales, German history, and the Bible. He first viewed National Socialism as "a struggle for the spiritual freedom of the world," but became disillusioned and withdrew into his poetic world. He took his own life toward the end of the war.

Munich (München), capital of Bavaria; its population in 1939 was 818,000. Munich had a

multifaceted relationship to the birth, rise, and fall of National Socialism. It was in Munich that Hitler, then an Austrian citizen, reported for military service as a volunteer in 1914. The GERMAN WORKERS' PARTY came into being there in 1919; and after Hitler joined it in 1920, the NSDAP arose there. Munich was the scene of the HITLER PUTSCH and the HITLER TRIAL; the Reich party leadership resided there in the BROWN HOUSE. Hitler lived in various apartments in Munich, and he found patrons in the upper stratum of Munich society. In 1935 he awarded the city the title "Capital of the Movement."

Munich was also the birthplace of Eva BRAUN, whom Hitler met there, and for whom he set up an apartment on Wasserburger Strasse. It was from Munich that Hitler directed the murderous operation concluding the RÖHM AFFAIR on June 30, 1934, during which numerous SA leaders were shot in Munich-Stadelheim. Each year on November 8, Hitler spoke before the "Old Combatants" at the Bürgerbräu, which was destroyed in Johann Georg ELSER's assassination attempt on November 8, 1939. Hitler received Mussolini on a state visit to Munich on September 25, 1937, and a year later celebrated one of his most spectacular foreign-policy successes with the MUNICH AGREEMENT.

Munich was also the location of the ACADEMY FOR GERMAN LAW (founded on June 27, 1933) and of the German Academy for Education. It had more National Socialist architectural showpieces than any other German city, and as the "City of German Art" it boasted the HOUSE OF GERMAN ART (opened on July 16, 1937, there-

The Führer Building on the Königlicher Platz in Munich (as the former and present-day Königsplatz was called at the time).

after commemorated annually as the "Day of German Art"). Munich featured the Temple of Honor (Ehrentempel; opened on November 3, 1935) and numerous party buildings, including the Führer Building (Führerbau; September 24, 1937) on Königlicher Platz; District Aviation Command V (Luftkreiskommando V; May 12, 1937), where the Luftwaffe eagles still stand guard; the SS Main Riding School in Riem (July 25, 1937); and the Riem airport (June 17, 1938). Hitler's regular visits to the BERGHOF on the Obersalzberg took him through Munich. During the Second World War the city was the target of many Allied bombings, which destroyed some 82,000 residences (33 percent of the total). On April 30, 1945, when Hitler committed suicide in Berlin, units of the Seventh United States Army occupied Munich.

Munich Agreement (*Münchener Abkommen*), agreement concluded by the heads of the governments of the German Reich (HITLER), Italy (MUSSOLINI), Great Britain (Neville CHAMBERLAIN), and France (Édouard DALADIER) on September 30, 1938. It forced the Czechs to cede the Sudeten area to Germany between October 1 and 10, to conduct a plebiscite under international supervision in further "German" areas, and to make corresponding arrangements for Polish and Hungarian minorities. It also held out to Czechoslovakia the promise of an international guarantee that was never realized.

Three lines of development culminated in the Munich Agreement:

1. *Domestic Czechoslovak politics.* Although the Czechs had been less than successful with nationalities policies since the multinational republic was founded in 1918, the political and ideological synchronization of the SUDETEN GERMAN PARTY with Berlin's policies since the end of 1933 meant an added burden for internal Czech stability. The SUDETEN CRISIS escalated "according to plan," following Hitler's instruction on March 28, 1938, to the Sudeten German leader, Konrad HENLEIN, to demand more than the Czechs could grant.

2. *Great-German expansionist policies.* Immediately after the annexation of Austria, in his instructions for "Case Green" ("Fall Grün") on April 21 and May 30, 1938, Hitler turned to his plans to "smash" Czechoslovakia (*see* HOSSBACH MEMORANDUM). The skillfully orchestrated and dramatically promoted principle of national self-determination was for him only a lever for reaching further intermediate political and economic goals on his path toward expansion

eastward: destruction of the Soviet Union's advanced Czech bastion, lifting of the threat to Germany's flank, broadening of the German economic base, and creating a staging area to assemble forces for the march eastward.

3. *Anglo-French* APPEASEMENT *policies.* The British government, and the French in its tow, saw no reason to oppose the apparent realization of the principle of self-determination, which they themselves had proclaimed. They evaluated as very slight their ability to give military assistance to Czechoslovakia in case of a conflict, especially since the country was already isolated internationally. In line with "appeasement" they pursued only the peaceful, negotiated, and face-saving settlement of border revisions that had in fact already been conceded long before. During the time between the meetings of Hitler and Chamberlain in Berchtesgaden (September 15) and Godesberg (September 22–24) and the Munich meeting, however, the course of events that had basically been set underwent a dramatic escalation. Hitler's ultimatums for revision seemed to bring Europe to the verge of war (September 26 to 28), until mediation by the Foreign Office and by Mussolini arranged the meeting of the "Big Four" in Munich on September 29.

The Munich Agreement, an early example of modern "summit diplomacy," saved the peace for a year, concluded the "revisionist phase" of Hitler's foreign policy, brought the Czech "remnant state" to the German side as a satellite for a

Last page of the Munich Agreement.

After the signing of the Munich Agreement, Hitler makes a public appearance.

"breathing pause" of barely six months, and created an estrangement between the Western powers and the Soviet Union that was deep and fraught with consequences (*see* GERMAN-SOVIET NONAGGRESSION PACT). No agreement has yet been reached on the question of international law: whether the agreement was invalid from the outset (Prague's view) or was invalidated by its later destruction (Bonn's view).

B.-J. W.

Munich Trial (*Münchener Prozess*), court proceedings against 10 ringleaders of the Hitler Putsch of November 8–9, 1923 (*see* HITLER TRIAL).

Münzenberg, Willi, b. Erfurt, August 14, 1889; d. near Caugnet (France), 1940, German politician. Münzenberg apprenticed in a shoe factory, and joined the Socialist Youth organization in 1906. From 1910 to 1914 he lived in Zurich, working with Lenin; he became secretary of the Socialist Youth International in 1914. Münzenberg then went to Berlin, where he joined the Spartacus League in 1919. In 1921 he founded the International Workers' Aid organization, and was its first chairman. From 1924 to 1933 he served in the Reichstag, and after 1927 he was a member of the Central Committee of the German Communist Party (KPD).

Münzenberg so excelled in producing Com-

munist publications and films that he was named the "Red Press Czar" (*see* ARBEITER-ILLUSTRIER-TE-ZEITUNG). In 1933 he emigrated to France, where he fought against National Socialism as a journalist (notably in his contributions to the BROWN BOOK). He also helped to initiate the POPULAR FRONT. Stalin's purges led to an estrangement between Münzenberg and the KPD, which expelled him in 1937. The German-Soviet Nonaggression Pact led to a complete break. Münzenberg was last seen on June 21,

Willi Münzenberg.

1940, fleeing before the German troops. His corpse was found in November of that year; it is suspected that he was a victim of Soviet agents.

Murr, Wilhelm, b. Esslingen, December 16, 1888; d. May 1945, German politician. A merchant, Murr joined the NSDAP in 1922. In 1928 he became *Gauleiter* of Württemberg, and in 1933 a Reichstag deputy. In March of that year he became Württemberg's minister for the interior and the economy during the "synchronization" of the German states. He became a Reich governor (*Reichsstatthalter*) in May 1933. When the war began, Murr assumed the function of a Reich defense commissioner in Military District V; in 1942 he was named an SS-*Obergruppenführer*. At the war's end, he committed suicide.

Muselmann ("Muslim"), expression used by SS men and inmates in CONCENTRATION CAMPS to describe a prisoner who was near death, totally weakened, apathetic, and indifferent to his fate. Outward symptoms were emaciation, dull skin, large hollow eyes, vacant expression, and uncertain gait. Presumably the term derived from the fact that such prisoners, with their shaking hands and bent posture, gave the impression of Muslims at prayer. In the camps the *Muselmänner* were considered certain candidates for death.

W. D.

Music, tonal art, which National Socialist (NS) cultural policies divided into three categories:

Wilhelm Murr.

desirable, undesirable, and borderline music.

Any music that could serve, stabilize, or embody political authority was considered desirable. It was to be *volkstümlich* (in keeping with the *Volk*), community-building, militant, festive, and heroic, or it was to be relaxing and varied musical entertainment (Goebbels). Types of music considered suitable were the SONG and the MARCH; "festival music" of all kinds, vocal and instrumental, primarily from the Baroque period, or recent compositions; orchestral music and operas by "the great Germans"; and dance and entertainment music. Desirable musical characteristics included the use of traditional keys (major, minor, religious modes), catchy melodies, easily comprehended form, impressive dynamics, "large casts" with massive choirs and ensembles (especially wind instruments), and the "simple" (*ungekünstelte*) setting to music of texts true to the party line.

Such state and party institutions as schools, NS women's groups, the Hitler Youth, the Reich Labor Service, and the armed forces took over the propagation of desirable music. In case of dispute, the REICH MUSIC CHAMBER determined whether a given piece of music was to be considered desirable; as a final resort Goebbels himself, as president of the Reich Culture Chamber, made the decision. The emphases in the music policy, as a manifestation of the new NS authority, first affected marches, cantatas, and festival music, then the works of such "great Germans" as Beethoven, Wagner, and Bruckner, as well as Bach, Haydn, Mozart, Schubert, Schumann, Brahms, Hans PFITZNER,

Music. Taps.

and Richard STRAUSS. As of 1936, greater emphasis was placed on dance and entertainment music, such as that of Werner Bochmann, Michael Jary, Peter Kreuder, Norbert SCHULTZE, and Herms Niel. Once the war began, hit songs promoting homeland sentimentality and "staying the course" acquired greater importance (*see* "REQUEST CONCERT").

The NS rulers declared as "undesirable" Jewish composers (such as Mahler and Mendelssohn) and artists, 12-tone music, and JAZZ, as well as "alien" music, such as Gypsy melodies. The political evaluation of music characterized Jewish music as "saccharine [*süsslich*], weak"; 12-tone music was "chaotic, destructive." It was easy to make such attacks since the general public did not understand this complex world of sound either. Jazz, ecstatic and physically exciting, stood in stark contrast to NS concepts of order, and was therefore denigrated as "nigger music" (*Nigger-Musik*). Among the large number of despised composers besides those already mentioned, Jacques Offenbach, Kurt WEILL, and Hanns Eisler stand out. The numerous ostracized artists include the conductors Fritz Busch, Bruno WALTER, and Otto KLEMPERER, the singers Richard Tauber and Josef Schmidt, and the pianist Rudolf Serkin. Hundreds of soloists, music teachers, and music critics fell into disfavor.

Borderline music (*Musik in Grenzbereichen*) referred to persons, works, and situations that for a variety of reasons could not be easily categorized and were at least temporarily tolerated. Questions of the state's interest and political considerations were decisive here. The international reputation of Strauss, despite his collaboration with Jewish librettists, or of Wilhelm FURTWÄNGLER, despite his support of the unpopular Paul HINDEMITH, forced concessions from the state and party leaders. In the same way, the popularity of such public favorites as Hans ALBERS or Franz Lehár outweighed their marriages to Jewish women. Even the despised jazz was permitted at the time of the 1936 Olympics in order to cultivate an image with the international public. Similar tolerance was exercised on the western front to keep soldiers from listening to "enemy broadcasts" (*see* RADIO).

In general, the daily political situation determined the answer to such questions as the "correct" music for a given event during the war. Still, the considerations described were dominant, even though they sometimes proved helpless against a musical opposition that could never be completely silenced. Considerable leeway was preserved for the initiated with the use of subtle humor, double entendres, and wordplay.

R. H.

Mussert, Anton Adriaan, b. Werkendam, May 11, 1894; d. The Hague, May 7, 1946 (executed), Dutch politician. A hydraulic engineer, Mussert in December 1931 founded the "National Socialist Movement" (Nationaal-Socialistische Beweging; NSB), after the German model, and gained a few parliamentary seats in 1937. After the German occupation of the country in 1940, the NSB was declared to be the only Dutch political party by Arthur SEYSS-INQUART, the Reich governor (*Reichsstatthalter*) in the Netherlands. As the head of the Dutch COLLABORATION, Mussert was named "Leader of the Dutch People" in 1942. He did not have much influence, but he was able to thwart plans for a German annexation of the Netherlands. He did not protest the deportation of Jews. The great majority of his countrymen considered him a traitor. After the war Mussert was arrested and sentenced to death.

Mussolini, Benito, b. Predappio (Forlì), July 29, 1883; d. Giulino di Mezzegra (Como), April 28, 1945, Italian politician. After a harsh youth, Mussolini joined the Italian Socialist Party (PSI) in 1900. He took his teacher's examination in 1901 and spent the years 1902 through 1904 wandering through Switzerland. Back in Italy, he performed his military service with the Bersaglieri (1905–1906). He founded the weekly newspaper *La Lotta di Classe* (Class Struggle) in 1909, and edited it until 1912. Jailed several times for inciting the populace, in 1912 Mussolini became editor in chief of the Socialist organ *Avanti!* (Forward!) and quintupled its circulation within two years. As of 1909 he lived with Rachele Guidi, whom he married in a civil ceremony in 1915 and in a religious one in 1925; they had five children.

More influenced by Vilfredo Pareto's theory of elites, Nietzsche's "master race" (*Herrenmenschtum*), and Georges Sorel's syndicalism than by Marx, Mussolini broke with the Socialists in 1914 and on November 14, 1914, founded his own newspaper, *Popolo d'Italia* (People of Italy). In it, he, like Gabriele D'ANNUNZIO, agitated for Italy's entry into the war on the side of the Entente. Mussolini was a soldier from 1915 until he was wounded in February 1917; thereafter he gathered around himself dissatisfied former combatants and disappointed Socialists, found-

ed on March 23, 1919, the "Fasci di Combattimento" (Combat Leagues), and took up the
struggle against the growing number of Socialist
disturbances, against parliamentarianism, and
against the abuses of capitalism. In November
1921 he consolidated his movement into the
Partito Nazionale Fascista (National Fascist Party; PNF) and had his "Blackshirts" march on
Rome on October 28, 1922. On October 31,
Mussolini became prime minister of a coalition
government.

Mussolini's movement, with its symbol of a
bundle of rods (*fascis*, in Latin; the sign of office
of the lictors in ancient Rome), provided the
name for the tide of events that was pressing
forward even outside Italy. FASCISM defined
itself primarily by identifying its enemies: Socialists, Communists, liberals, and democrats
would have no place in its authoritarian state.
After a brief tactical compromise, Mussolini
built up a corporative (*see* CHARTER OF LABOR)
"totalitarian state," a one-party dictatorship.
In his position in the state he no longer termed
himself prime minister; after 1925 he was
"Capo del Governo" (Head of Government),
and as party chairman, "Il Duce" (The Leader)
since 1922. His absolute political power was
buttressed by his supreme command over the
Fascist militias, his presidency of the GRAND
COUNCIL OF FASCISM, his many ministerial posts
(as many as eight), and his command over the
armed forces as "First Marshal of the Empire"
(as of 1938). But in contrast to Hitler's dictatorship, Mussolini's was limited by alliances with
the traditional elites. He left the monarchy
untouched, as he did heavy industry and the
church, with which he achieved a settlement in
the LATERAN TREATIES of 1929. He thereby
acquired a considerable reserve of trust.

Mussolini was successful in domestic affairs,
particularly in maintaining public order
through the coercive measures of the police
state, and in the economy through the elimination of trade-union elements and through public-works projects (such as the draining of the
Pontine Marshes). As a demagogically skillful
orator he also fascinated the masses with his
promises regarding foreign affairs, notably Italy's new imperial greatness. The conquest of
ABYSSINIA in 1935–1936, Italy's share in Franco's victory in the SPANISH CIVIL WAR, and
the invasion of Albania in 1939 seemed to bring
within reach an Italian hegemony in the Mediterranean, *mare nostro* ("our sea"). The AXIS
with the ascendant National Socialist Germany
promised rich rewards as the Wehrmacht

Benito Mussolini with Hitler in Venice (1934).

seemed to prove its invincibility in the Polish
and French campaigns. Despite the warnings of
many advisers, including Galeazzo CIANO and
Pietro BADOGLIO, Mussolini entered the war on
June 10, 1940, in order to earn the right "with a
few thousand dead" to sit at the victors' table.
This made him a captive of Hitler's ideological
war, which Mussolini never comprehended; Hitler helped him in the BALKAN CAMPAIGN and in
the AFRICAN CAMPAIGN, and tied him irreversi-
bly to himself and to his own downfall.

On July 25, 1943, the Grand Council revoked
confidence in Mussolini and authorized his arrest, but this was not sufficient to extricate Italy
from the war. German paratroopers liberated
the "Duce" on September 12, 1943, and thus
plunged the country into a civil war as well. In
SALÒ, at Hitler's direction, Mussolini established his puppet "Italian Social Republic," had
judgment passed on the "traitors" of July 25
(including his son-in-law Ciano), and brought on
a bloody partisan war. He himself fell victim to

it when, while in flight to Switzerland, he was captured by resistance fighters on April 27, 1945; he was shot the next day, together with his mistress, Clara Petacci. His myth, however, remains alive today in NEOFASCISM.

Müthel, Lothar (originally, Lothar Max Lütcke), b. Berlin, February 18, 1896; d. Frankfurt am Main, September 5, 1964, German actor and producer. Müthel became known for his character and leading roles, and was later in charge of productions that the National Socialists lauded as "exemplary" (*stilbildend*), notably *Die Hermannsschlacht* (The Battle of Arminius) and *Hamlet*, with Gustaf GRÜNDGENS. Müthel became a member of the Presidial Council of the REICH THEATER CHAMBER, was named Reich Culture Senator, and served as director of Vienna's Burgtheater (1939–1945). He gained special popularity for his recitations "in brownshirt" at SA festivities. After the war Müthel was a theater manager in Frankfurt (1951–1956).

Mutschmann, Martin, b. Hirschberg an der Saale, March 9, 1879; d. Dresden, presumably 1948, German politician. A commercial apprentice, Mutschmann was involved in an unsuccessful attempt at lace manufacture. He was a volunteer during the First World War. In 1923 he joined the NSDAP, and by 1925 he had risen to *Gauleiter* of Saxony. In 1933 he became Reich governor (*Reichsstatthalter*) of Saxony, and in March 1935 he replaced Manfred von KILLINGER as head of the Saxon state government. Mutschmann, who was also Reich defense commissioner after 1939, was notorious for his extravagant

Martin Mutschmann.

Lothar Müthel.

life-style, whose expenses he paid with "voluntary" donations from industry, and for particularly brutal measures involving the persecution of Jews. He was captured by Soviet troops while trying to flee westward at the last moment, on May 7, 1945. He allegedly died in Soviet captivity soon after a trial in June 1948.

Mutual Trust Council (*Vertrauensrat*), advisory body required by the LABOR REGULATION LAW of January 20, 1934, in workplaces with more than 20 employees. It consisted of the employer and employees chosen by him in consultation with functionaries from the GERMAN LABOR FRONT and the appropriate TRUSTEES OF LABOR. The Mutual Trust Council replaced the workplace council (*Betriebsrat*), but lacked its participatory rights.

Mythus des 20. Jahrhunderts, Der (*The Myth of the 20th Century*), Alfred ROSENBERG's main work, which appeared in 1930; its subtitle was "A Valuation of the Battles for the Spiritual and Intellectual Shape of Our Times." The work was divided into three "books": "The Struggle of Values," "The Nature of Germanic Art," and "The Coming Reich." Rosenberg, who saw himself as the fulfiller of the racist theories of Houston Stewart CHAMBERLAIN and Paul de LAGARDE, developed the thesis that the cultural development of the West had in its entirety proceeded from the Germanic tribes. The Roman "priestly caste" that had attained influence through Christianity had, in league with Jesuits, Freemasons, and the "conspirators of international Jewry," then caused the decline of this Germanic culture. Now, however, the time was

DEM GEDENKEN DER ZWEI
MILLIONEN DEUTSCHER
HELDEN ⁄ DIE IM WELT-
KRIEG FIELEN FÜR EIN
DEUTSCHES LEBEN UND
EIN DEUTSCHES REICH
DER EHRE UND FREIHEIT

Dedication in Rosenberg's *Mythus des
20 Jahrhunderts:* "In memory of the 2
million German heroes ⁄ who fell in
the world war for a German life and a
German Reich of honor and freedom."

approaching when a racially pure Germanic
empire would be realized with the "myth of
blood": "History and the task of the future no
longer mean the struggle of class against class,
no longer mean the combat between church
dogma and dogma; rather, the contest [will be]
between blood and blood, race and race, people
and people, and this means the struggle between spiritual value and spiritual value."
Rosenberg thought he had discovered the sources of a new religion particularly in the sermons
of the medieval mystic Meister Eckhart: "From
his great soul the new German faith can—and
will—someday be born."

Rosenberg's turgid and hazy presentation was
hardly taken seriously by his own party comrades, even though its content corresponded to
völkisch ideas and to Hitler's thinking. Goebbels
called the *Mythus* an "ideological belch" (*welt-
anschaulicher Rülpser*), and Hitler emphasized
in his Table Talks (April 11, 1942) that he "had at
the time expressly refused to give this book the
status of partisan infallibility [*parteipäpstlicher
Charakter*]." Moreover, he too "had read only
small parts of it, because in [his] opinion as well,
it was written in too incomprehensible a style."

The churches, in contrast, seriously discussed
the book. The Catholic church put it on the
index of forbidden literature on February 7,
1934; church historians and theologians decisively rejected it in *Studien zum Mythus des 20.
Jahrhunderts* (*see* Clemens von GALEN). Evangelical critiques included Walter Künneth's
"reply." Rosenberg took on the Catholics in "An
die Dunkelmänner unserer Zeit" (To the Obscu-
rantists of Our Times), and his "Protestantische
Rompilger" (Protestant Pilgrims to Rome) attacked his Evangelical critics. Hitler attributed
the sale of some 1,080,000 copies of the *Mythus*
by the end of the war to the intensive church
opposition.

C. Z.

Nacht-und-Nebel-Erlass. *See* "Night and Fog" Decree.

Nadler, Josef, b. Neudörfl (northern Bohemia), May 23, 1884; d. Vienna, January 14, 1963, Austrian literary scholar. Nadler was a professor at Fribourg (Switzerland), Königsberg, and elsewhere, and as of 1931, in Vienna. In his major work, *Literaturgeschichte der deutschen Stämme und Landschaften* (Literary History of the German Race and Lands, 4 vols., 1912–1928), he developed the "method of literary observation based on racial stock and landscape," which derived the typical character and the cultural

Josef Nadler. Title page of the first volume of his major work.

value of a literary production from the ethnic and geographical background of its author. This approach thus provided ideological support for the *völkisch* literary interpretations later current among National Socialists.

Nadolny, Rudolf, b. Gross-Stürlack (East Prussia), July 12, 1873; d. Düsseldorf, May 18, 1953, German diplomat. Nadolny entered the foreign service in 1902, became foreign-affairs counselor to the Reich president in 1919, and from 1920 to 1924 was ambassador in Stockholm. From 1924 to 1932, Nadolny represented the German Reich in Turkey; he led the German delegation at the Geneva Disarmament Conference in 1932–1933, was ambassador to the Soviet Union in 1933–1934, and retired in 1937. After the war he attempted to make contact with Moscow in order to set reunification talks in motion.

Naked culture (*Nacktkultur*), derogatory term for what was known as *Freikörperkultur*—literally, the culture of free or liberated bodies (*see* NUDISM). National Socialist morality, with its petit-bourgeois bias, condemned it as an expression of sexual abnormality and the consequence of "Jewish corrosive activity." An ordinance of March 3, 1933, forbade every form of *Nacktkultur* as a "manifestation of the degeneration" of PHYSICAL CULTURE.

Name day (*Namenstag;* also *Namensweihe,* "name dedication"), in the Catholic sense, the feast day of the saint whose name one bears. In the Third Reich, it was one of the so-called LIFE CELEBRATIONS, substituting for baptism. On a child's name day, the parents were to bring him or her to the community and pledge to cultivate the gifts dormant in the child, "so that his name might become deed." In place of baptismal water the father would, within a solemn gathering, ignite a fire next to the child, "so that it might be ignited as part of the whole."

Nation (from Lat. *nasci,* to be born), group constituted by such bonds as common language, history, culture, ancestry, or religion, mostly in one region of settlement. With the weakening of the feudal-dynastic principle through the French Revolution, the nation became the unifying framework for state formation. It led to the unification struggles in Italy and Germany; as a countermovement, it led to the breakup of the multinational state of Austria-Hungary.

In the National Socialist view, nonetheless, the 19th-century concept of the nation was based on the pernicious liberal principle of equality, which in one way led to a "national democracy" and in another to "unbounded deracination" through the recognition of Jews or other "alien" elements as citizens. The nation in the complete sense, however, could be based only on *Volk* and race: the German nation lived by the "instinctive feeling for the togetherness of all people of German blood." A "small-German" solution like Bismarck's, which would accept a Germany that did not encompass all Germans, was just as much to be rejected as the acceptance of people not of "German stock" as citizens in a German state. Proceeding from this, the NSDAP program of February 24, 1920, demanded a "Great-Germany," on the one hand (Point 1), and the banishment of Jews on the other (Point 4). The NS state was to be based on "the unity of the *Volk* in its organic integrity and racial purity." The latter goal was sought through the PERSECUTION OF JEWS, the former through the SECOND WORLD WAR.

National Bolshevism (*Nationalbolschewismus*), designation, used mostly for polemical effect, for efforts made after the First World War to bring about a German communism while renouncing the internationalist element. Left-wing varieties of National Bolshevism, such as the League of Communists, founded in 1919 as a nationalist offshoot of the COMMUNIST PARTY OF GERMANY (KPD), achieved little success and collapsed after a polemic issued by Lenin, "Radicalism, the Childhood Illness of Communism." *Völkisch* expressions of National Bolshevism, like those of Arthur MOELLER VAN DEN BRUCK, which were nourished by the RAPALLO TREATY and the RUHR CONFLICT, lay behind the Reichswehr's contacts with the Red Army. They were also operative in Otto STRASSER's "Black Front." Both elements gained renewed impetus

from criticism (expressed by Ernst NIEKISCH, among others) attacking the rising National Socialism as a betrayal of both nationalism and socialism. Out of this came the persecution of all National Bolshevist groups and movements after the Seizure of Power. Within the NATIONAL COMMITTEE FOR A FREE GERMANY during the war, an initial organizational adaptation of such ideas remained politically insignificant because of the circumstances.

National church (*Nationalkirche*), in the narrow sense, a GERMAN EVANGELICAL CHURCH unified on the Reich level; as a long-range goal of the National Socialists, the German unified church (*Einheitskirche*) transcending all denominational barriers. In order to form such a national church, not only would the German Catholic church have to forsake its ties to Rome, and the Evangelical Church overcome its federalist organization; Christianity itself would have to free itself from its founder. To that extent the propaganda for a national church, on which the policy of overcoming denominationalism was based, aimed at the utter destruction of the large church communities. Under the pretext of seeking to remove from Christianity the "character of a foreign religion" by linking the churches to the "German mission" and by purifying them of "Jewish humbug," a national church would lead to de-Christianization. The plan, which advocates such as the GERMAN CHRISTIANS and their successor organizations (with the motto "One Führer! One *Volk!* One God! One Reich! One church!") never saw through, ran afoul of the resistance of both denominations in the CHURCH STRUGGLE. It also encountered Hitler's lack of interest: his preference was, after a truce during wartime, eventually to resolve the church question by force.

National Committee for a Free Germany (Nationalkomitee "Freies Deutschland"), organization founded on July 12–13, 1943, in Krasnoyarsk, near Moscow (later located in Lunyovo, near Moscow), by prisoners of war (mostly survivors of the German Sixth Army from Stalingrad), members of the Communist exile leadership (among others, Walter ULBRICHT, Wilhelm PIECK, Wilhelm Florin, Anton Ackermann, and H. Matern), and antifascist writers (including Johannes R. BECHER, W. Bredel, Theodor Plievier, and Gustav von Wangenheim). Through its own weekly newspaper, *Freies Deutschland* (Rudolf Herrnstadt, editor in chief), bordered with the German nationalist colors of black, white,

National Committee for a Free Germany. Masthead of the periodical *Free Germany:* "Gen. Field Marshal Paulus, commander of the army at Stalingrad, raises his voice for Germany's deliverance from Hitler."

and red; a radio station of the same name (Anton Ackermann, editor in chief); and pamphlets and loudspeakers, the committee tried to influence German officers and soldiers on the eastern front.

On September 14, 1943, the close collaboration with the LEAGUE OF GERMAN OFFICERS (BDO) was institutionalized by the appointment of its chairman, Gen. Walther von SEYDLITZ-KURZBACH, as a vice president of the National Committee (Erich Weinert was named president). The basic line of the committee's political propaganda was altered as a result of the TEHERAN Conference (November 28–December 1, 1943). Under the banner of the old colors of imperial Germany, and invoking the traditional Prussian-Russian friendship, the earlier catchwords were aimed at the overthrow of Hitler, at cooperation with the German army leadership, and at the Wehrmacht's orderly retreat to the Reich borders with the objective of an honorable separate peace, even respecting the borders of 1937. From the beginning of 1944, after relations improved between the USSR and the Western powers, the appeals were directed toward the German people and its soldiers, and against fascism and its conservative accomplices. They also called for a "popular uprising," for unconditional cessation of the hopeless conflict, and for desertion.

Despite the "Appeal of 50 Generals to the People and the Wehrmacht" for an "act of deliverance against Hitler" (December 8, 1944), frontline agitation remained mostly ineffective. The frontline troops' blind trust in Hitler and their fear of becoming Soviet prisoners of war prevented desertions to the very last. Branded by Hitler as "traitors," the representatives of the National Committee and of the BDO were also criticized by members of the

internal German opposition. After leading Communists of the ULBRICHT GROUP left for Berlin on April 30, 1945, to help establish the postwar order in the Soviet Occupation Zone, the committee and the BDO were dissolved on November 2 of that year.

B.-J. W.

National consciousness (*Nationalbewusstsein*), the sense of belonging to a NATION, including the pride felt in such membership. A German national consciousness developed under the Napoleonic threat, out of the medieval concept of a REICH and out of the cultural and linguistic ties to a common tradition. In the struggle for political unity, and later as a result of the disappointment over the emergence of a "small" Germany (that is, without Austria), national consciousness degenerated into nationalism and then, during and after the First World War, into chauvinism. Within this aggressive climate, Hitler exploited German national consciousness to win over the masses and the nationalistic-conservative elite for his goals, which went far beyond his proclaimed demands for revision of the Versailles treaty. The catastrophic failure enduringly discredited nationalistic plans, which after 1945 were politically obsolete and, economically as well as militarily, illusory in a divided Germany and Europe.

National Day of Mourning (*Volkstrauertag*), commemoration, on the fifth Sunday before Easter (*Reminiscere*), of the dead of the First World War. It was promoted beginning in 1923 by the National League for German War Grave Maintenance (Volksbund deutscher Kriegsgräberfürsorge), and was widely observed beginning in 1926. In 1934 it was recast as the HEROES' MEMORIAL DAY (*Heldengedenktag*), and in 1939 it was standardized as an annual observance on March 17. After the Second World War, the original commemoration was revived in the Federal Republic. Since 1952 it has been observed on the next-to-last Sunday before the first Sunday of Advent. It now commemorates the dead of both world wars as well as the victims of National Socialist tyranny.

National Democratic Party of Germany (Nationaldemokratische Partei Deutschlands; NPD), German right-wing extremist party, founded on November 28, 1964, in Hannover. In both staff and program, it has connections with NEONAZISM.

NPD election poster, 1972: "Renunciation is treason ([Willi] Brandt himself said so in 1963)."

National holidays. *See* Celebrations in the National Socialist Calendar.

National hymn (*Nationalhymne*), after the French Revolution and since the early 19th century, a generally customary national symbol. The German national hymn of the Hohenzollern Empire was the hymn to the Kaiser, "Heil Dir im Siegerkranz" (Hail to Thee in Victory's Crown), with the same melody as the English "God Save the King." The GERMAN NATIONAL ANTHEM ("Deutschlandlied" [Song of Germany]), with lyrics by Hoffmann von Fallersleben (1841) and music by Franz Joseph Haydn (1797), was elevated by President Friedrich Ebert in 1922 to be the national hymn of the new Republican Germany. Despite its democratic associations, it was carried over into the Third Reich because of its great popularity. Nonetheless, on solemn occasions the "Deutschlandlied" was followed by the hymn of the NSDAP, the "HORST-WESSEL-LIED" ("Die Fahne hoch" [Raise the Banner]), which until 1945 had the status of a second German national hymn.

Nationalism (*Nationalismus*), the exploitation of NATIONAL CONSCIOUSNESS for (often aggressive) political ends. Making the nation the object of ideology aids internal integration by diversion from economic and social conflicts. The central role of nationalism in the National Socialist program was demonstrated by the name change of the German Workers' Party (DAP), after Hitler's entry, to the NATIONAL SOCIALIST GERMAN WORKERS' PARTY (NSDAP). That the nationalism had clear precedence over the "socialist" goals was obvious, at the latest, after power was denied to the party's social-revolutionary wing following the BAMBERG FÜHRER CONFERENCE in 1926. Although NS propaganda described German nationalism as "directed inward" and as serving the "formation of a *Volk*" (*Volkwerdung*), it fanned feelings of superiority in preparation for the war and broadened such feelings on a racial basis, by branding enemies as "inferior" or as "subhumans."

Nationalist Action (Nationalistische Aktion; Internationale Arbeitsgemeinschaft der Nationalisten [International Working Community of Nationalists]), alliance of European nationalist groups, founded in Zurich in 1934. Through regular congresses (for example, in 1934 in Berlin), the association intended to prepare the way for a "realm of peoples" (*Reich der Völker*). Given the nationalistic tendencies of the period, notably National Socialism and Fascism, the organization found scant support for its hegemonic goals, and remained politically insignificant.

Nationalities question (*Nationalitätenfrage*), problem that developed in the 19th century for the supranational empires such as the Danube monarchy and the Russian or the Ottoman empire. While a cautious policy of greater autonomy in Austria-Hungary failed to restrain the centrifugal forces released by the nationalities issue, a massive Russification failed similarly in the tsarist realm as an answer to the problem. The First World War then provided the answer by breaking up the multinational states and launching the new revolutionary-ideological structure in the Soviet Union. However, it also created new MINORITIES in the newly formed nations that proved to be sources of new crises. National Socialist FOREIGN POLICY took advantage of this new nationalities question as a revisionist lever against the Versailles system.

Nationalize, to (*nationalisieren*), in National Socialist usage, term for the ideological "alignment" toward the German *Volk*-nation. The nationalization of the ETHNIC GERMANS in particular was promoted, in order to prevent their loss of ethnic identity, or UMVOLKUNG. The term "nationalization" was also used in the sense of RE-GERMANIZATION.

National-Political Educational Institutes (Nationalpolitische Erziehungsanstalten; NPEA [also Napola]), upper-level boarding schools, granted special political status as selective schools by the cultural ministries of the states (*Länder*). The first State Education Institutes were created in Prussia from the cadet academies that had been banned in 1919; they were put directly under the Education Ministry on April 14, 1933. Teachers and pupils were to be "newly constituted" and given "Hitler uniforms." Their curriculum was to be "completely new," but in 1939 it was made to conform to the curricula of upper schools (*Oberschulen*) or *Gymnasien*. Prussia established an "inspectorate" for the association of schools, which as of 1936 was headed by the organizational leader of the SS, August HEISS-MEYER, at first as a branch office. In November 1938, he became supervisor for all schools of the new type, even outside of Prussia. In 1944 there were 13 NPEA schools in Prussia, 9 in the other *Länder*, and 13 outside the OLD REICH, including one for girls. Four schools were *Gymnasien*, 3 were advanced grade schools with six-year college preparation programs (*Aufbauschulen*), and 2 had "special tracks" for flight training.

National-Political Educational Institutes. Pupils at inspection.

The original plan was modeled after that of the English public schools, with extensive initiative given to the institute head. The "national-political" organization of teachers and pupils, with education groups mixed by age and under youth leaders, was soon abandoned in favor of a schematic leadership structure of *Zügen* (columns) and "hundreds" under educator and pupil leaders. In 1936 Heissmeyer arranged for the pupils to join the Hitler Youth (HJ)—but not for the educators to do so, as took place in the rival ADOLF HITLER SCHOOLS. The emphasis on military sports and music education was broadened with three extracurricular assignments (*Einsätze; see* EINSATZ): rural service in the "east," flight training, and factory work; later, mining was added. The tradition of school trips abroad was carried on almost exclusively by the NPEA.

Reich Education Minister Bernhard RUST designated the NPEAs as experimental but model institutions for testing the union of school instruction, National Socialist "formative education" (*Formationserziehung*), and successful achievement in *Einsätze*. This had actually been practiced before 1941 in several types of boarding schools (German Home Schools, TEACHER TRAINING INSTITUTES, and camps of the CHILDREN'S COUNTRY EVACUATION program, for example). The selective schools maintained their prestige in part through strict intrascholastic selection; the graduates (1 percent of those who passed the *Abitur* exam) were free to choose their profession. Participation was made generally free of charge only in 1943. The "Reich schools" (*Reichsschulen*) should also be considered part of the NPEA federation; two were established in the Netherlands and one in Belgium in 1943. Even earlier, "daughter foundations" of individual NPEAs had been established beyond the Reich boundaries. The location of school facilities in politically troubled areas is evidence that as of 1941 their political function as youth garrisons was valued more than the education of an "elite."

H. S.

National Prize for Art and Science (Nationalpreis für Kunst und Wissenschaft; also Deutsche Nationalpreis), substitute award for the Nobel prize; it was established by Hitler on January 30, 1937, when acceptance of that honor was "forbidden to Germans for all time." Specifically, the institution of the prize was a reaction to the "shameful events" connected with the bestowal

National Prize for Art and Science. The 1937 prize recipients are received by Hitler. From the left: the surgeon Ferdinand Sauerbruch, Frau Troost (for her late husband, the architect Paul Ludwig), Alfred Rosenberg, August Bier, and Wilhelm Filchner.

of the Nobel Peace Prize on Carl von OSSIETZKY. Every year at the Reich Party Congress, two "worthy Germans" were to receive such a prize of 100,000 RM each (the prize was divided if there were more than two), as well as a medal.

National Prize for Book and Film (Nationalpreis für Buch und Film), award in the amount of 12,000 RM given to the "creators of the best book and best film" of the prior year. It was established by Joseph Goebbels on May 1, 1933, as a metamorphosis of the former Stefan GEORGE Prize. Among the authors honored by the prize were Richard EURINGER (*Deutsche Passion;* 1935) and Bruno BREHM (*Apis und Este;* 1939). Film directors who won the prize included Leni RIEFENSTAHL (*Triumph des Willens;* 1935) and Carl FROELICH (*Heimat;* 1939).

National Rising (*Nationale Erhebung*), designation, for propaganda purposes, of the SEIZURE OF POWER; it was used, for example, in the "Appeal of the Reich Government to the German *Volk*" of February 1, 1933. By using the term "national rising," the government avoided the label "National Socialist," thereby placating the conservative partners in the coalition. The term set a nationalistic tone, and "rising" signaled the revolutionary aspect of the event and announced the end of parliamentarianism. The catchword "national rising" thus served the same function as the other designation commonly used, the GERMAN REVOLUTION.

National Socialism

The term "National Socialism" refers both to the ideology of the NATIONAL SOCIALIST GERMAN WORKERS' PARTY (NSDAP) and to the party's system of rule in Germany from 1933 to 1945. The term itself came from Bohemia (which at the time belonged to Austria), where in 1904 various political associations that shared both German nationalist and socialist agendas came together in the German Workers' Party (Deutsche Arbeiterpartei). This party renamed itself the German National Socialist Workers' Party (Deutsche Nationalsozialistische Arbeiterpartei) in May 1918. It provided the GERMAN WORKERS' PARTY that was founded in Munich on January 5, 1919, with both the party's symbols (including the SWASTIKA) and its name—which, however, was changed to NSDAP on February 24, 1920. The term "National Socialism" expresses the party's claim that it could achieve a synthesis of the two determinative ideologies and political forces of the 19th century: nationalism and socialism.

National Socialism is a form of FASCISM. Like other European fascist organizations, the NSDAP conceived of itself not as a political party in the traditional sense, but rather as a new social and political "movement." And like them, it found its social support predominantly among those middle-class elements thought of as the petite bourgeoisie: a group whose social status and economic existence had been jeopardized by industrialization and its social and economic consequences, which had become clearly negative after the end of the First World War. Robbed, moreover, of its traditional political ties through the overthrow of the monarchy, this petite bourgeoisie saw in National Socialism a new political home. Like other expressions of the fascist phenomenon, National Socialism was an antimodernist protest movement: against representative democracy and its political institutions (parties, parliaments, and bureaucracies), against modern society and its pluralistic structure, against the capitalist economic system and its large-scale production processes, and against the ideology of political and economic liberalism. With regard to Germany specifically, it stood against the defeat of the German Empire in the world war, against the end of Germany as a major European power and of its imperialist plans, and against the VERSAILLES TREATY, which was felt to be a "national disgrace."

Unlike communism, the other great antidemocratic movement of the 20th century, fascism was unable to develop a concise, internally consistent ideology. The "ideology" of National Socialism consisted rather of a conglomeration of ideological convictions and social and economic concepts and demands, which were largely rooted in the irrationalism of the 19th century. Such a basis was shown by the movement's connections with predemocratic, authoritarian theories of state and society, by the adoption of irrational myths (for example, the worldwide Jewish "conspiracy") and the use of mythical symbols (such as the swastika), and by the development of pseudoreligious rituals (at party congresses, for example) and cults. The National

Socialist (NS) political agenda, which is commonly identified as the NS "ideology," featured the following components, contained partially in the "25-Point Program" of the NSDAP of February 24, 1920 (see PARTY PROGRAM OF THE NSDAP), but above all in numerous NS writings, especially Hitler's MEIN KAMPF (1925):

1. *Antiliberalism and antiparliamentarianism.* On the basis of its opposition to liberal parliamentary democracy, the NSDAP campaigned principally against the results of the November Revolution of 1918 and those who were purportedly responsible for it (see NOVEMBER CRIMINALS), and against the WEIMAR REPUBLIC (the "November Democracy"), its parliamentary "system," and its political institutions, especially the "system parties" (see SYSTEM ERA). The NSDAP's struggle against the "madness of democracy" (Hitler, 1928) did not, to be sure, preclude the use of the political processes of parliamentary democracy after the failed HITLER PUTSCH of 1923 (the so-called tactic of legality). "The NS movement is antiparliamentarian, and even its participation in a parliamentary institution can only have the meaning of an act to destroy it" (*Mein Kampf*).

The antiliberalism of National Socialism was

Photograph from the period when uniforms were prohibited.

also directed against the capitalist economic system. The anticapitalist message of the NSDAP, especially as directed against big business, still occupied considerable space in the 1920 party program; but it played no real practical role after 1926 at the latest, when Hitler prevailed against the party's Left (associated with the brothers Otto and Gregor STRASSER). It did not hinder segments of industry from giving the NSDAP financial support, even before 1933. Nor, after that date, did it stand in the way of close collaboration between the NS dictatorship and big business, especially the capital-goods and armaments industries, or interfere with their privileged position. At no time did National Socialism realize its claim of carrying out a policy that was both nationalist and socialist.

2. *Anticommunism and antisocialism.* From the outset, the NS program, and still more its propaganda, was marked by an aggressive anticommunism and antisocialism, leveled against the German Communist (KPD) and Social Democratic (SPD) parties and the trade unions, as well as against the Soviet Union and the BOLSHEVISM and "world communism" directed from there. Yet the NSDAP subordinated the goal of "destroying Marxism" (Hitler, in an appeal of March 10, 1933) to its primary political goals. To destroy the Republic, it occasionally worked together with the KPD before 1933; to prepare for a war of conquest, the NS dictatorship signed the GERMAN-SOVIET NONAGGRESSION PACT in 1939.

3. *The* FÜHRER PRINCIPLE. National Socialism wanted to replace parliamentary democracy with a dictatorship that was hierarchical, rigidly authoritarian, and based on the principles of leader and followers, command and obedience. It would be led by a Führer who was provided with total power to rule, supported by the state party (NSDAP) acting as a political elite, and legitimized by the (sham) democratic device of plebiscitary approval. This dictatorship would completely encompass society and unite it in a "*Volk* Community" that would be fully directed toward and mobilized for the political goals set by the authoritarian leader.

4. *Nationalism.* Like all the Weimar parties, the NSDAP demanded revision of the Versailles treaty. Beyond that, it demanded the creation of a "Great-German" nation-state extending beyond the borders of the German Empire of 1914 and including "all German tribes."

5. *Racism.* The traditional "Great-German" nationalism was given a *völkisch* emphasis in the

NS program, thus intensifying it to the point of racism. NS racial doctrine seized on racial theories developed during the 19th century by Count Arthur de GOBINEAU and Houston Stewart CHAMBERLAIN, in particular. These ideas were found not only in *Mein Kampf* but in other works, especially Alfred Rosenberg's MYTHUS DES 20. JAHRHUNDERTS (1930). The racial doctrine maintained that there was a progressive "ladder" of human races. It located the "Nordic-Aryan-Germanic" group, the "master race" that alone was capable of creating culture, on the top rung. The "culture-destroying" Jewish race, which had no right to live, occupied the bottom rung. The supreme goals of domestic policy were to be the "preservation of purity" of the "Aryan" race and the implementation and securing of its domination over the other, inferior races. The equivalent goals of foreign policy would then be the primacy of the "Aryan" race and its German primary *Volk* (*Vorvolk*), at least in Europe, and ultimately, Aryan world domination.

6. ANTISEMITISM. An antisemitism based on racism occupied a central role in HITLER'S WORLDVIEW. This hatred of Jews probably provided the crucial motive force of his political desires and actions; it was the central component of NS "ideology" and, after 1933, of the official state doctrine of the Third Reich. NS propaganda effectively united antisemitism with anticommunism (because Marx was a Jew!); the myth of the Jewish "racial enemy" with that of the Bolshevik class enemy; and the traditional hostility toward Jews with the fear of Communists that was rampant in Germany. This last connection was expressed in the thesis of the alleged worldwide "conspiracy" of a "world Jewry" supported by Bolshevik Russia; it was undergirded with such falsifications as the PROTOCOLS OF THE ELDERS OF ZION. The primary goal of NS policy was not only the total abrogation of the rights of German Jews, but beyond that the physical "annihilation of the Jewish race in Europe" (Hitler, on January 30, 1939).

7. *Imperialism.* National Socialism's imperialism was derived from its racism. It demanded the creation of a Great-German imperium that would extend far beyond the boundaries of the German nation and that would offer the German *Volk* the "LIVING SPACE" supposedly necessary for its survival. The goal of German foreign policy was to be an "eastern policy [*Ostpolitik*], in the sense of obtaining the necessary soil for our German *Volk*"; in connection with this, "we are thinking in the first place only of Russia and

the subject states surrounding it" (*Mein Kampf*). This goal could be realized only through a war—of that, Hitler and the other National Socialists had no doubt. The racism of National Socialism was permeated altogether by a primitive Darwinism—the idea that "the most universal, implacable law of life" was the "struggle (of a people) for its existence . . . if necessary, with other peoples who stand in the way of its own development as a people." The war of conquest to acquire "living space" for the German *Volk* was further intended to gain mastery by the "Aryan" German *Volk* and its state over the racially "inferior" Slavic peoples and states of eastern and east-central Europe, and ultimately would lead to German world hegemony.

8. *Militarism.* The preconditions for an imperialistic policy were the militarization of German society, its psychological preparation for a war, and EDUCATION, especially of youth, according to military principles of command and obedience. Force was held in high esteem as the (supposedly) necessary means of settling domestic and international disputes; actual or putative pacifist ideas and positions engendered opposition.

For years, the NSDAP was only a politically insignificant splinter party, scarcely known outside of Bavaria. Only beginning in 1929, during —and in a causal connection with—the WORLD ECONOMIC CRISIS, was it able to acquire the "mass basis" necessary to gain power within the state. The NSDAP owed its electoral successes of 1930 to 1933 less to its program, which differed little in content from those of other right-wing radical parties, than to its support by the "nationalist Right" (*see* HARZBURG FRONT), and above all to the nature and means of its political struggle: its PROPAGANDA and its use of terror.

NS propaganda appealed to the emotions, prejudices, and anxieties of people who saw and understood themselves not as individuals but as a mass. As Hitler had already called for in *Mein Kampf*, it worked with a few easily remembered, emotional formulas, simplified clichés, and popular slogans, repeated again and again; they manipulated, rather than arguing or in-

SA parade in Leipzig (1933). Next to Hitler is the Reich Governor of Saxony, Martin Mutschmann.

forming. The clever use of modern technology and media (colors, music, flags and other political symbols), mass parades and marches, the demagogic skills of Hitler and Goebbels in particular, and even more so, the latter's unscrupulous use of the FÜHRER CULT around Hitler and his person—all this made NS propaganda far superior to the political advertising of any other party.

NS propaganda was particularly effective with the bourgeoisie, especially the lower middle class (*see* MITTELSTAND): independent tradespeople, artisans, clerks, peasants, and the like. Antagonistic to the republican form of government from the outset, still supportive of a state based on principles of authority and obedience, these groups, if not outright monarchist in orientation, saw the economic foundations of their existence endangered by the world economic crisis, and themselves threatened with social decline. Thus they were only too willing to lend credence to the NS slogans, whether about Jewish and Marxist "November criminals" (*see* STAB-IN-THE-BACK LEGEND) or about the incompetent and "corrupt" democratic parties and politicians, and to believe the promises of Germany's resurgence to national greatness, an end to the UNEMPLOYMENT, and the overcoming of the economic crisis.

The tasks of NS propaganda were to win followers for National Socialism, to instill in them the certainty of victory, and to continually mobilize them anew for its goals and against the Weimar "system." The functions of the NS terror—carried out above all by the paramilitary leagues of the NSDAP, and in particular by the Storm Troopers (STURMABTEILUNG; SA)—were to spread alarm among the public, to intimidate government organizations and political opponents, and to cripple their resistance, but at the same time to provide the NSDAP's own members and followers with an image of the unity, energy, and strength of will of the NS movement. Numerous bloody street battles, often approaching civil war (especially those between National Socialists and Communists and their armed leagues), characterized political differences in Germany beginning in 1930.

Supported by its massive electorate, National Socialism won political power with (ostensibly) legal parliamentary means: on January 30, 1933, Hitler, as chairman of the strongest party in parliament, was named Reich chancellor (*see* SEIZURE OF POWER). What distinguished NS fascism from other examples of European fascism (including the Italian variety) was, however,

the positively brutal consistency with which it realized its political platform after 1933—with the exception of anticapitalism:

1. The total destruction of parliamentary democracy, the abolition of a constitutionally governed state, and the establishment of a totalitarian dictatorship—that is, a one-party NSDAP state, created according to the Führer Principle and with the *Führer und Reichskanzler* Hitler at its head—were essentially achieved by the middle of 1934 (*see* SYNCHRONIZATION). Almost all Germans were incorporated in the NSDAP (there were some 2.5 million members in 1935) and/or in its affiliated organizations. They were subjected to a nearly seamless political control by the agencies of state security (especially the SECURITY SERVICE [SD] of the SS), and were totally oriented toward the political goals of the NS regime. The opponents of National Socialism were mostly in foreign exile, incarcerated (the first of the CONCENTRATION CAMPS was set up as early as late February of 1933), or murdered. Meanwhile, Hitler's intraparty competition, especially that from within the SA (*see* RÖHM AFFAIR), was eliminated. Through propaganda in the media (press and radio), which were now state-controlled; through constant mass assemblies of the NSDAP and its organizations, and the rituals that unfolded in particular at the annual REICH PARTY CONGRESSES in Nuremberg; and finally through the manipulated plebiscites in which Hitler and his government found sham democratic legitimation for important political measures—the fiction of a "*Volk* Community" united under Hitler's leadership was constantly generated anew and upheld.

2. The PERSECUTION OF JEWS culminated in the genocide of the "FINAL SOLUTION." A similar fate was suffered by other "racially inferior" population groups, such as the GYPSIES and the mentally handicapped (*see* EUTHANASIA).

3. The preparation for an aggressive war to "conquer new living space in the east, and to achieve its relentless Germanization" (Hitler on February 3, 1933, to the Reichswehr generals), was served by several moves: REARMAMENT, which (at first secretly) had already begun by late 1933; Germany's withdrawal from the LEAGUE OF NATIONS and the international armaments conference (October 1933); and—by breach of the Versailles treaty—the reintroduction of COMPULSORY MILITARY SERVICE (March 1935) and the RHINELAND OCCUPATION (March 1936). On November 5, 1937, Hitler openly announced to the supreme commanders of the Wehrmacht his intention to unleash a war

of aggression (*see* HOSSBACH MEMORANDUM), thus revealing as lies his repeated public assurances of peace. On September 1, 1939, the SECOND WORLD WAR began with the attack on Poland.

4. Even before the war began, NS Germany had already "revised" considerable parts of the Versailles treaty, approaching the goal of a "Great-German" state through the reannexation of the SAAR TERRITORY (January 1935) and through the ANSCHLUSS of Austria (March 1938) and the Sudetenland (October 1938; *see* SUDETEN CRISIS). Germany's *de facto* annexation of the PROTECTORATE OF BOHEMIA AND MORAVIA (formerly "remnant Czechoslovakia") in March 1939 extended this state beyond the boundaries of German nationality. With the conquest of western Poland (October 1939), the building of the Great-German Reich was concluded.

The world war unleashed by National Socialism ended with the total defeat of Germany and the UNCONDITIONAL SURRENDER of its troops on May 7–8, 1945. Germany was occupied by the Allies, and the NSDAP, with all its divisions and member organizations, was banned and dissolved through Law No. 2 of the ALLIED CONTROL COUNCIL (October 10, 1945). Its members (some 8.5 million in 1945) and sympathizers were subjected to a DENAZIFICATION process, and the NS war criminals were indicted and tried (*see* NUREMBERG TRIALS).

Except for the nearly total extermination of European Jewry, Hitler achieved none of his political goals. Rather, the results and consequences of National Socialism, which are still being felt, were the end of a unified German state, the rise of the Soviet Union to a world power, the Sovietization of eastern and east-central Europe, and the division of Europe into a Communist-ruled Eastern Europe and a democratic Western Europe.

National Socialism revived again in the Federal Republic as NEO-NAZISM in the late 1940s and early 1950s, and again after the late 1970s —thus far, to be sure, without significant political importance.

Reinhart Beck

National Socialist Automobile Corps (Nationalsozialistisches Automobilkorps; NSAK), motor squad of the party under the leadership of the Supreme SA-Führer; its establishment was announced by Hitler on April 1, 1930. On April 20, 1931, it was renamed the NATIONAL SOCIALIST MOTOR CORPS (NSKK).

National Socialist Bibliography (*Nationalsozialistische Bibliographie;* NSB), monthly journal of the Review Committee for the Protection of National Socialist Writing, published beginning in January 1936 by Philipp BOUHLER. It carried brief descriptions of all publications that served to "disseminate and deal extensively with National Socialist ideas."

National Socialist Competitive Games (*Nationalsozialistische Kampfspiele*), military sports competitions held in Nuremberg in 1937 and 1938, in conjunction with the Reich Party Congresses. They were directed by the SA, with participation from the SS, Hitler Youth, Reich Labor Service, National Socialist Motor Corps, and National Socialist Flyers' Corps, as well as the NATIONAL SOCIALIST REICH LEAGUE FOR PHYSICAL EXERCISES. The Reich Party Congress Grounds, then under construction, which was referred to as the "greatest stadium in the world" with its 400,000 seats, was intended to be the showplace for the games in the future.

National Socialist Crafts, Trade, and Industrial Organization (Nationalsozialistische Handwerks-, Handels-, und Gewerbeorganisation; NS-Hago), division of the NSDAP created in 1933 for the registration, ideological "alignment," and economic instruction of the MITTELSTAND (middle classes), in line with National Socialism. In 1935 the organization was absorbed into the Reich Workplace Community for Crafts and Trade of the GERMAN LABOR FRONT.

National Socialist Culture Community (Nationalsozialistische Kulturgemeinde), organization of the NSDAP, founded on June 6, 1934, from the Reich Association of the German Stage and the COMBAT LEAGUE FOR GERMAN CULTURE; its purposes included the cultivation of "species-true" art. In 1937 the Culture Community was merged with the German Labor Front agency STRENGTH THROUGH JOY.

National Socialist Flyers' Corps (Nationalsozialistisches Fliegerkorps; NSFK), the "combat organization for air sports" founded by a decree of Hitler on April 17, 1937, with the set purpose of

NSFK badge.

"securing for the German Luftwaffe a numerically strong and technically well-prepared new generation." The founding of the NSFK was coupled with the disbandment of the German Air Sports Association, which had been established in 1933. In the future, air sports activity would be possible only through National Socialist organizations—the NSFK and the Hitler Youth [HJ] Flyers. Both groups worked closely together.

The NSFK provided premilitary training to young people by means of the building and flying of model planes, and by instructing the members of the HJ Flyers in glider and motorized flying; it also provided qualified 18-year-old students with free pilot training in its own flying schools. Among the postmilitary tasks of the NSFK was the "maintenance of flying skills" for flyers returning from military service. The paramilitary character of the NSFK was expressed in its uniforms, in the alignment of its ranks with those of the Wehrmacht, and in the NSFK's subordination to Hermann GÖRING as both aviation minister and supreme commander of the Luftwaffe. Göring ordered that an ideological training program—equal in importance to sports and military training—be incorporated into the NSFK "for maintaining intellectual powers." The corps leader for the NSFK was Gen. Friedrich CHRISTIANSEN.

National Socialist Freedom Movement of Great-Germany (Nationalsozialistische Freiheitsbewegung Grossdeutschlands), one of the two substitute organizations of the NATIONAL SOCIALIST GERMAN WORKERS' PARTY (NSDAP) during the period of the party's banning after the Hitler Putsch of November 9, 1923, until it was refounded on February 27, 1925. The Freedom Movement represented the northern German, as well as the more leftist, branch of the party;

it was led by Gregor STRASSER, Gottfried FEDER, and Wilhelm FRICK, among others. It won 14 mandates in the Reichstag elections of December 1924.

National Socialist German Physicians' League (Nationalsozialistischer Deutscher Ärztebund; NSDÄB), organization of physicians founded at the fourth Reich Party Congress in Nuremberg in 1929. The approximately 50 founding members included Liebl (the first chairman), Gerhard WAGNER, its chairman from 1932 to 1939, and Leonardo CONTI, who succeeded him. At the NSDÄB's first Reich congress in 1930, the organization was opened to dentists, veterinarians, and pharmacists. By late 1932 the membership had grown to 2,786, with 344 applicants. The same year, an instructional course in racial hygiene was instituted, attended by over 300 doctors. In 1934 the Führer Principle was introduced to the organization, when new bylaws automatically made its leader (*Leiter*) the Reich Physicians' Führer (*Reichsärzteführer*). In 1935 the Reich Leadership School for the German Medical Profession (Reichsführerschule der Deutschen Ärzteschaft) in Alt-Rehse (Mecklenburg) was dedicated. The organization's membership meanwhile rose to approximately 30,000 in 1938. The NSDÄB played a significant role in the synchronization of German medicine and in promoting racial hygiene. It was declared illegal and abolished by Control Council Law No. 2 of October 10, 1945.

National Socialist German Students' League (Nationalsozialistischer Deutscher Studentenbund; NSDStB), division of the NSDAP. Even before 1933, the NSDStB gained a reputation as the "shock troop of National Socialists studying in all universities and professional schools," and won majorities in numerous representative student organizations. Among students, dissatisfaction with the Weimar "system"; chauvinistic emotions; antisemitism; and *völkisch* ideals hostile to "civilization" were especially rife, making students particularly vulnerable to National Socialist promises.

National Socialist German University Teachers' League (Nationalsozialistischer Deutscher Dozentenbund; NSD-Dozentenbund), division of the NSDAP, separated from the NATIONAL SOCIALIST TEACHERS' LEAGUE on July 24, 1935; its headquarters was in Munich. The University Teachers' League was intended to spread the National Socialist worldview in universities and colleges by organizing NS teachers in higher education; further functions included ensuring the political good behavior of unorganized colleagues and the ideological saturation of teaching. Members were instructed through participation in meetings, work camps, lecture series, and so on. The chairman from 1935 to 1943 was Reichdozentenführer Walther SCHULTZE. By unifying the positions of leaders of the government university teachers' corporations (*Dozentenschaften*) with those of the league's leaders in the universities and colleges, the party's supervision in matters of teaching and research was assured. [In contrast to the high-status title *Professor*, *Dozent* was more inclusive, as well as inferior in rank in its traditional usage.]

National Socialist German Workers' Party (Nationalsozialistische Deutsche Arbeiterpartei; NSDAP), state party of the National Socialist (NS) dictatorship. On January 5, 1919, Anton DREXLER and Karl Harrer founded the GERMAN WORKERS' PARTY (DAP) in Munich. It was renamed the NSDAP on February 24, 1920. On July 29, 1921, the party elected Hitler, who had joined it in September 1919, as its chairman with almost unlimited authority, including the right to select all party functionaries. After the HITLER PUTSCH (November 8–9, 1923), for which the party was partially responsible, the NSDAP was banned. However, it continued to function in the form of such surrogates as the GREAT-GERMAN VOLK COMMUNITY and NATIONAL SOCIALIST FREEDOM MOVEMENT OF GREAT-GERMANY until it was refounded on February 27, 1925. Beginning in the spring of 1920, the party's emblem was the SWASTIKA; as of December of that year, its publication was the VÖLKISCHER BEOBACHTER (Völkisch Observer).

The NSDAP was a right-wing radical party with a program—spelled out in its "25-Point Program" (*see* PARTY PROGRAM OF THE NSDAP) of February 24, 1920—that included nationalistic and Great-German (irredentist), imperialistic and militaristic, *völkisch* and antisemitic, antiliberal and antiparliamentarian, middle-class (*mittelständisch*) and anticapitalist demands (*see* NATIONAL SOCIALISM). In order to distance itself from the "system parties" of the Weimar Republic (*see* SYSTEM ERA), the NSDAP styled itself as a "new type" of party, a "collective party" (*Sammlungspartei*), and a "movement." Its structure and organization were antidemocratic, centralist, and authoritarian, entirely oriented toward the "Führer," as Hitler was designated after 1922 (*see* FÜHRER PRINCI-

PLE). The highest authority of the party was the Reich Leadership or directorate (Reichsleitung), with the Führer and the chancellery of the Führer (as of 1941, the Party Chancellery) at the apex and, just below, the individual Reich leaders or directors (*Reichsleiter*). These included the deputy to the Führer (*Stellvertreter des Führers:* 1925–1932, Gregor Strasser; 1933–1941, Rudolf Hess) or (after 1941) the secretary to the Führer (Martin Bormann); the Reich Propaganda Leader (*Reichspropagandaleiter*); the Reich treasurer (*Reichsschatzmeister*); the Reich press chief; and so on.

The party's main offices (*Hauptämter*) were the Reich Organizational Directorate (Reichsorganisationsleitung), the Reich Propaganda Directorate (Reichspropagandaleitung; as of 1929 under Joseph Goebbels), the FOREIGN POLICY OFFICE OF THE NSDAP (under Alfred Rosenberg), the Office for Colonial Policy, the Reich Press Office (Reichsleitung für die Presse; under Max Amann), and, as of 1931, the Foreign Division (Auslandsabteilung) of the NSDAP.

Regionally, the NSDAP was organized in *Gaue* (35 in 1935; 41 in 1940), *Kreise* (districts),

NSDAP. Poster announcing the first mass meeting after the re-establishment of the party on February 27, 1925: "Germany's future and our movement."

1
"Who is the most important man in the world?" Hitler with prominent contemporaries (Gerhart Hauptmann, Leon Trotsky, Albert Einstein, Hjalmar Schacht, Paul von Hindenburg, Henry Ford, Benito Mussolini, Max Schmeling, and Aristide Briand). NSDAP election poster (1932).

2
Memorial tablet in Munich's Hofbräuhaus, where Hitler announced the 24-Point Program of the NSDAP on February 24, 1920.

3
Painting of the Hitler Putsch of November 9, 1923, by an unknown artist.

4
Hitler greets a wounded SA man.

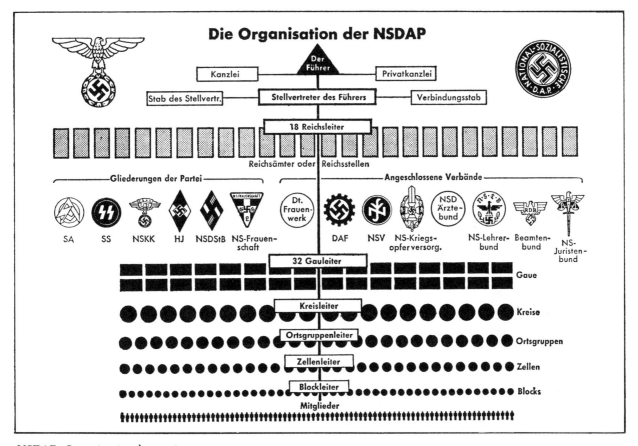

NSDAP. Organizational overview.

Ortsgruppen (local groups), *Zellen* (cells), and *Blocks*. Their leaders (*Gau-, Kreis-, Ortsgruppen-*, and *Zellenleiter*, and *Blockwarte* [block guardians]) together formed the Corps of Political Leaders (Korps der politischen Leiter). Also belonging to (*angeschlossen*) the party were the paramilitary associations of the STURMABTEILUNG (SA), the SS (Schutzstaffel), the NATIONAL SOCIALIST MOTOR CORPS (NSKK), the NATIONAL SOCIALIST FLYERS' CORPS (NSFK), the HITLER YOUTH (HJ), and the National Socialist WOMEN'S UNION (NSF), as well as numerous professional organizations; the GERMAN LABOR FRONT (DAF) was considered a "supporting organization" (*betreute Organisation*). In terms of its membership structure, the NSDAP was a middle-class (*see* MITTELSTAND), petit-bourgeois party in which employees, the self-employed (craftsmen, businessmen), and civil servants were disproportionately represented.

In the 1920s the NSDAP, despite increasing membership (1922: 6,000; 1923: 55,000), was a politically insignificant splinter party. In the 1924 Reichstag elections, the National Socialist Freedom Movement received only 3.0 percent of all votes cast; in 1928 the NSDAP itself

received only 2.6 percent. Only in the final phase of the Weimar Republic did Hitler's tactic of using legal means (attainment of power not through revolution or putsch, but by a legal, parliamentary path) prove itself. Meanwhile, he used such means to prevail against his left-wing intraparty opposition, centered on the brothers Otto and Gregor STRASSER. In the Reichstag elections of September 14, 1930, the NSDAP won 6.4 million votes (18.3 percent) and 107 seats; on July 31, 1932, by garnering 13.8 million votes (37.4 percent) and 230 seats, it became by far the strongest German party. It remained so despite losses in the elections of November 17, 1932 (11.7 million votes [33.1 percent] and 196 seats).

As early as January 1932, Wilhelm FRICK became the first NS member of a state (*Land*) government, in Thuringia. In May of that year the NSDAP first gained an absolute majority in elections to a state legislature, in Oldenburg. Simultaneously, its membership grew from around 400,000 in 1930 to over 800,000 in 1931, then to roughly 1 million in January 1933. The NSDAP owed these successes less to its program—its anticapitalist demands, in partic-

Lagerführerin
des weiblichen Arbeitsdienstes. Arbeitsdienstpflicht für 1 Jahr besteht für die gesamte weibliche Jugend

Sommertracht
des Bundes deutscher Mädel, dem alle Mädchen vom 10. bis 21. Jahre angehören

Trommelbube des Jungvolks
Das Jungvolk ist eine Untergliederung der Hitlerjugend, ihr gehört jeder Junge bis zum 18. Jahre an

Marine-Hitlerjunge,
eine besondere Einheit der HJ. mit einem Schulschiff und einer eigenen kleinen Flottille

Arbeitsmann
des Reichsarbeitsdienstes. Die gesamte männliche Jugend leistet 1 Jahr Arbeitsdienst

Kreisleiter der NSDAP.
Rangunterschiede der Politischen Leiter sind auf den Spiegeln zu erkennen

SS-Oberscharführer
Aufgabe der SS ist der Schutz des Führers und die innere Sicherheit des Reiches

Standartenführer der SA.
Der Dienst in der SA. ist soldatisch und freiwillig. Jeder Deutsche kann ihn zwischen dem 18. und 45. Lebensjahr leisten

Rottenführer
des NS.-Fliegerkorps. Ein freiwilliges Fliegerkorps mit der Aufgabe, die deutsche Jugend im Segel- und Motorflug heranzubilden

Oberscharführer
des NS.-Kraftfahrkorps. Neben der SA. steht als selbständige Gliederung diese motorisierte Einheit

Die Uniformen und Ehrenzeichen der Partei

Das Partei-Abzeichen
Für alle Mitglieder der NSDAP.

Das goldene Ehrenzeichen
Für die ersten 100 000 Mitglieder. Wird außerdem vom Führer verliehen und ist die höchste Zivilorden des Reichs

Der Blutorden
Für Teilnahme am Kampf im November 1923 in München und für besondere Opfer an Blut und Freiheit

Die Dienstauszeichnung in Bronze
Für 10 Jahre aktiven Dienst in der Partei

Die Dienstauszeichnung in Silber
Für 15 Jahre aktiven Dienst in der Partei

ular, fell into oblivion—than to its clever and effective use of PROPAGANDA to exploit mass psychology, the SA's terror tactics in intimidating political opponents, and, not least, the party's alliance with the "national" Right (*see* HARZBURG FRONT). The weaknesses and mistakes of its political opponents must also be taken into consideration.

After Hitler was able to end the financial and political crisis suffered by the party in late 1932 to his own advantage (by Gregor Strasser's relinquishing of his party offices on December 8), he was named Reich chancellor on January 30, 1933 (*see* SEIZURE OF POWER). The NSDAP thus became a ruling party. The law of July 14, 1933 (forbidding the creation of parties), made it the state party, although in the interim, in the Reichstag elections of March 5, 1933, it had failed to gain an absolute majority (43.9 percent of the votes and 288 seats out of 647). As the *Staatspartei*, it was the only legal party; Germany thus became a one-party state, a situation legalized by the Law to Secure the Unity of Party and State of December 1, 1933 (*see* SYNCHRONIZATION). It remained so until

the capitulation of the German Reich on May 8, 1945. Party membership grew to 2.5 million in 1935, and ultimately to 8.5 million in 1945.

In the NS dictatorship, the NSDAP and its divisions had above all the function of totally harnessing the populace and mobilizing it for the aims of NS policy. The annual REICH PARTY CONGRESSES in Nuremberg gained particular significance in this process. After the exclusion of the SA in 1934 (*see* RÖHM AFFAIR), the SS under Himmler became Hitler's most important instrument of authority. The implementation of policy remained largely the preserve of the government bureaucracy. The (partial) conflict and struggles over jurisdiction between bureaucracy and party, as well as the rivalries within the NSDAP and its own bureaucratization, were characteristic of the NS system of domination (the so-called polycracy).

On October 10, 1945, the NSDAP, along with all of its divisions and member associations, was outlawed and dissolved by Law No. 2 of the Allied Control Council (*see* DENAZIFICATION).

R. B.

The Uniforms and Badges of Honor of the Party

(From the illustrated magazine *Signal*)

Camp Führerin of the female Labor Service. All German girls have an obligation to serve for one year.

Summer uniform of the League of German Girls, to which all girls from 10 to 21 belong.

Drummer Boy of the Jungvolk. The Jungvolk is a subdivision of the Hitler Youth. Every boy up to the age of 18 belongs.

Naval Hitler Youth, a special unit of the Hitler Youth, with its own training ship and its own small flotilla.

Workman of the Reich Labor Service. All young men serve one year in the Labor Service.

Kreisleiter of the NSDAP. Distinctions in rank among the political leaders are indicated on the lapels.

SS-Oberscharführer. The task of the SS is the protection of the Führer and the internal security of the Reich.

Standartenführer of the SA. Service in the SA

is military and voluntary. Any German man between the ages of 18 and 45 can serve in it.

Rottenführer of the NS Flyers' Corps. A voluntary flyers' corps with the assignment of training German youth in gliding and motorized flight.

Oberscharführer of the NS Motor Corps. This motorized unit has independent standing as a division at the side of the SA.

The Party Badge. For all members of the NSDAP.

The Golden Badge of Honor. For the first 100,000 members. Furthermore, it is awarded by the Führer and is the highest civil order in the Reich.

The Blood Order. For participants in the combat of November 1923 in Munich and for exceptional sacrifice of blood and freedom.

The Service Award in Bronze. For 10 years of active service in the party.

The Service Award in Silver. For 15 years of active service in the party.

National Socialist League for German Technolo-
gy (Nationalsozialistischer Bund Deutscher
Technik; NSBDT), association of the NSDAP,
organized into Reich- and *Gau*-level specialty
groups (*Fachgruppen*); it was located in the Main
Office for Technology under Fritz TODT. The
NSBDT included all technological and scientific
organizations and associations, and beginning in
1936 had its own Reich School for German
Technology on the Plassenburg (a mountain in
Upper Franconia). It also administered so-called
Gau Houses of Technology in the individual
Gaue. The league's function was to improve
technological performance "in accordance with
the demands of *Volk* and state."

National Socialist League of Law Guardians
(Nationalsozialistischer   Rechtswahrerbund;
NSRB), designation introduced in 1936 for the
League of National Socialist German Jurists
(BNSDJ), the professional organization within
the NSDAP founded by Hans FRANK in 1928.
Until 1933, the BNSDJ functioned as a legal
defense organization for party members; thereafter it was the instrument for the SYNCHRONI-
ZATION of all professional associations involved
with the administration of justice. The associations of judges and of lawyers were at first
joined to it corporately, but by the end of 1934
they were dissolved through the transfer of
their members into the BNSDJ.

This merger of every person active in the
administration of justice was acclaimed as the
achievement of the German Law Front (Deutsche Rechtsfront): the successful unification of
all forces in the struggle for the National Socialist "renewal of law." The BNSDJ dealt with
professional concerns, conducted the honor
court of the German Law Front, and implemented political training. Its name change in
1936 was intended to express the inclusion in
the organization of nonacademic occupations
within the administration of justice. The membership grew from 233 (1930) through 1,374
(1932) to 82,807 (1935). The Führer of all
jurists (*Reichsjuristenführer*), who then became
the Reich Legal Führer (*Reichsrechtsführer*),
was Hans Frank from 1928 to 1942. He was
followed by Otto THIERACK from 1942 to 1945.
The publication of the NSRB was the periodical
Deutsches Recht (German Law).

Sch.

National Socialist Motor Corps (Nationalsozialistisches Kraftfahrkorps; NSKK), special SA unit

under Adolf HÜHNLEIN, established on April 20,
1931, as an outgrowth of the NATIONAL SOCIAL-
IST AUTOMOBILE CORPS. The NSKK was de-
tached from the SA on June 30, 1934, and made
into a distinct division of the party, only to be
merged with the Motorized SA on August 23 of
that year. The creation of the NSKK was initially
promoted by electioneering and propaganda
considerations, which later were superseded by
military goals, since the "defensive power of the
nation" depended upon the level of motorization.

The major aims of the NSKK included teaching "fitness in motoring skills" (*motorische Ertüchtigung*) to young people (*see* MOTORIZED
HITLER YOUTH) and instructing reserve drivers
for the army. By the beginning of the war,
200,000 young men had trained at the 21
NSKK motor-sports schools. Along with educational activities, the NSKK took on traffic-
regulation assignments and provided roadside
assistance for accidents and breakdowns. It was
the only promoter of motor sports, it organized
tours for foreign visitors, and after the AN-
SCHLUSS it switched Austrian traffic from left-
lane to right-lane patterns. Even before the war
it undertook military projects within the TODT
ORGANIZATION in the construction of the
WESTWALL. NSKK units were later assigned to
army and Luftwaffe transport duties; in rare
instances they even undertook security assignments in occupied territories.

At the end of 1931 the NSKK had only 10,000
members, but by the start of the war its membership had grown to 500,000. Admission required
neither a driver's license nor ownership of an
automobile, nor even party membership. What
was required—besides "racial impeccability"
—was "love of motoring and the desire to take
on a higher degree of responsibility as a political soldier." The vehicle pool consisted at first

NSKK badge.

National Socialist Motor Corps. "Motorized troops" in a parade in Nuremberg.

of private cars, but ended with vehicles under corps ownership (several hundred passenger cars and trucks by 1939). The organization's periodicals were *Der NSKK-Mann* (The NSKK Man) and *Deutsche Kraftfahrt* (German Motoring). In the NUREMBERG TRIALS, the NSKK was condemned as a division of the NSDAP.

National Socialist Party Correspondence (Nationalsozialistische Parteikorrespondenz; NSK), information service founded in 1932; its editor was Wilhelm Weiss. The NSK provided the party press, and after the Seizure of Power the nonparty press as well, with reports on the NSDAP. After 1933 all German newspapers had to subscribe.

National Socialist Reich League for Physical Exercises (Nationalsozialistischer Reichsbund für Leibesübungen; NSRL), sports organization of the NSDAP, founded on December 21, 1938; by supplanting the GERMAN REICH LEAGUE FOR PHYSICAL EXERCISES, it completed the synchronization of German sports. The Führer decree founding the NSRL, in the words of the official announcement, expressed the fact that "the marshaling [*Einsatz*] of the millions of German gymnasts and athletes in the NSRL and the work of the organs of this league constitute political activity in the sense of and within the framework of the NSDAP."

National Socialist Reich Soldiers' League (Nationalsozialistischer Reichskriegerbund), organization of former German soldiers; it arose from the Kyffhäuser German Reich Soldiers' Association, and was renamed on March 4, 1938. By October 1 of that year, all other soldiers' associations (including the Reich League of German Officers and the German Officers' League) had been synchronized into the National Socialist organization. Its purposes included the cultivation of COMRADESHIP in the NS sense, and the arousing and strengthening of the "joy of fighting" (*Wehrfreudigkeit*). Its chairman and *Reichskriegerführer* was SS-Gruppenführer Wilhelm Reinhard, who had authority over the regional soldier leaders.

National Socialist Teachers' League (Nationalsozialistischer Lehrerbund; NSLB), member association of the NSDAP, founded in 1929 by Hans SCHEMM as the Organization of National Socialist Educators, with headquarters in Bayreuth (the "House of German Education"). After the Seizure of Power, the NSLB had the special assignment of "aligning" all teachers in terms of the NS worldview. It was organized into 10 divisions, of which the most important was the division for education and instruction, with seven specialty groups (*Fachschaften*) for institutions from universities to special schools. After the death of the founder, Fritz Wächtler assumed the position of *Reichswalter* (Reich administrator) on December 5, 1935. On October 27, 1938, Wächtler dedicated the league's own *Reichsschule* in Bayreuth. Its purpose was the training of functionaries, who were responsible for ideological faithfulness on a regional level, aided by courses, leisure activities, teachers' camps, and similar devices.

National Socialist Volk Welfare (Nationalsozialistische Volkswohlfahrt; NSV), association belonging to the NSDAP (as of March 29, 1935); it arose from the party's social welfare initiatives in the period before the Seizure of Power. It was established by Hitler's decree of May 3, 1933, and had its head office in Berlin. The NSV was responsible "for all matters concerning National Socialist welfare work and social services"; it was directed by the Main Office for Volk Welfare in the party's Reich headquarters. The office chief, Erich HILGENFELDT, personally combined the posts of Reich Administrator (*Reichswalter*) of the NSV and Reich Commissioner for the WINTER RELIEF AGENCY.

The NSV was organized regionally, like the party, into *Gau, Kreis,* and local administrations, and then into cells and blocks. It was divided into six departments (organization, financial administration, welfare work and youth care, public health, propaganda, and training). It attended to "needy *Volk* comrades" (*bedürftige Volksgenossen*), assuming they were politically, racially, and biologically "deserving," in keeping with government welfare arrangements.

Assistance was, moreover, intended as an "education in self-help," and was oriented not toward the needs of the individual, but rather toward helping to secure "the highest possible performance level from the German *Volk.*" Such hopeless cases as drunkards and released convicts were therefore stepchildren of the NSV, which ultimately stood in the service of NS imperialism: "We must have a healthy *Volk* in order to be able to forge our way ahead in the world" (Goebbels, at the Reich Party Congress in September 1938).

In terms of domestic policy, the NSV was an instrument of SOCIAL POLICY. Its numerous aid programs contributed substantially to NS self-promotion as a "socialism of the deed" (*Sozialismus der Tat*). It also facilitated the synchronization in March 1934 of the independent welfare organizations (including Caritas, the Inner Mission, and the German Red Cross) into a Reich association led by the NSV, as well as the synchronization of party and state in the social policy sector. In April 1941 the NSV assumed official jurisdiction over child and youth care; on August 22, 1944, finally, Hitler simply decreed that the NSV was "the organization responsible for assistance to the *Volk.*" In any case, at all levels positions in government welfare work and in the NSV were often held by a single individual.

NSV services were partly financed by the semi-voluntary contributions of its 11 million members (1938), and by Winter Relief Agency receipts. Beyond those sources, they were made

National Socialist Volk Welfare. An NSV nurse distributes vitamin pills.

possible by the unpaid work of nearly 1 million volunteers. Emphasis was given to health care and counseling (*see, for example,* MOTHER AND CHILD AID AGENCY), cures, tuberculosis control, regular dental examinations, and the like, whereas the frequently proclaimed care for the handicapped remained limited. Further, the NSV Railroad Station Service displaced the churches' missions there; an Aid Agency for German Fine Arts was designed to encourage needy artists who met NS standards; and the NUTRITIONAL RELIEF AGENCY supported the campaign for AUTARKY. All the services and programs of the NSV were surrounded by propaganda and tied to ideological indoctrination. Outpatient consultations were supplemented by lectures on racial hygiene, and "mothers' leisure time" was used for political instruction, in keeping with the NSV principle that along with social assistance, the "more valuable political service" must be present.

National Socialist War Martyrs' Welfare (Nationalsozialistische Kriegsopferversorgung; NSKOV), member association of the NSDAP, arising from Main Division IX (War Martyrs), founded in 1930, of the Reich Party Leadership. In 1933 all other related organizations (the Reichsbund, Kyffhäuser, and the like) were synchronized into the NSKOV, so that support payments for soldiers with disabilities from the First World War, and the dependents of that war's casualties, were evaluated in terms of political "worthiness." The NSKOV had some 1.6 million members in 1939; its director (*Reichskriegsopferführer*) was SA-Gruppenführer Hanns Oberlindober.

National Socialist Workplace Cell Organization (Nationalsozialistische Betriebszellenorganisation; NSBO), an alliance, similar to a labor union, of National Socialist–influenced employ-

NSKOV badge.

NSBO badge.

ees, following the Communist model. The NSBO first arose spontaneously from groups that formed in Berlin workplaces (such as the NS Workers' Combat League, 1927–1928), as well as later in some other areas. On July 30, 1928, a Secretariat for Workers' Affairs was established in the Berlin *Gau* that coordinated the work of the individual workplace cells. It was upgraded to the *Gau* Workplace Cell Section on May 1, 1930, in accordance with a plan by Reinhold MUCHOW. For a long time the national leadership of the NSDAP resisted accepting this special organization, but it finally adopted the Berlin model so that the workplace movement would not drift away. The Reich Workplace Cell Section was instituted on January 15, 1931 (on March 8, 1931, it became the NSBO), under Section Leader (as of December 1932, Office Leader) Walter SCHUHMANN as part of the Reich Leadership. Its periodical, which began publication on March 1, 1931, was *Das Arbeitertum* (WORKERDOM).

The NSBO regarded itself, in line with Hitler's intent, as the "SA of the workplace," with the objective of "winning over employees intellectually and politically"; yet it did not consider itself to be a labor union. It took steps to avoid slipping into a futile competition over support benefits with the independent (Social Democratic) and Christian trade unions. On the contrary, the intention was to tap into the unions through dual membership, which led to serious friction and ended by drawing the NSBO into union channels. NSDAP members were singled out for exclusion from the unions at the onset of unemployment, so that the NSBO had to render assistance to them, after it had already helped out in strikes for its members (who totaled about 100,000 in May 1932, and about 730,000 by the end of May 1933).

National Socialist Workplace Cell Organization. Labor squads marching.

This facilitated its equalization with the traditional unions in April 1933 after the Seizure of Power; following the breakup of the unions (May 2, 1933), the NSBO took over some of their functions.

Not all of these functions carried over, however: for example, Hitler viewed strikes as legitimate only as long "as no National Socialist *Volk* state yet exists." In the eyes of the NS leadership, such a state became reality, at the latest, at the point of the ENABLING LAW. This was not, however, the opinion of the party's social-revolutionary wing, in support of which the NSBO stood alongside the SA. Demands were heard from within the NSBO, too, for a SECOND REVOLUTION. They were not quieted until the bloodbath of the RÖHM AFFAIR (June 30, 1934), when Gregor STRASSER and Kurt von SCHLEICHER, the only planners of a TRADE UNION AXIS, were killed. The NSBO consequently lost more and more power, as when it was deprived of the right to levy dues. Finally, in January 1935, it was absorbed as a "main office" into the GERMAN LABOR FRONT.

Natural law (*Naturrecht*), law removed from the disposition of the individual and of the state. As the true, just, and correct law, it can claim unconditional validity (for example, general human and civil rights as they are seen in contemporary thought on natural law). Whether based on divine or human reason, natural law claims precedence over the merely positive statutory law enacted by a state. National Socialist legal theory also claimed to represent a higher and privileged principle of law, as against the earlier "liberalist" constitutional (*rechtsstaatlich*) laws. Here the concern was also to abolish any ethical and normative limits on the state's activities and the political actions of the NSDAP. While natural law, being self-evident, binds everyone— even the supreme government authority—NS legal theory declared the Führer's authority to be beyond such limitations; for example, it acknowledged the political leaders' "right to act" (*Tatrecht*) as the preeminent source of law. By the definition "Law is whatever Aryan men decide is right" (Alfred Rosenberg), the law had annulled itself (*see* LEBENSGESETZLICH).

C. S.

Nature, feeling for (*Naturgefühl*), according to National Socialist ideas, a typical character trait of the GERMAN MAN that was in accordance with his "special racial quality." A German's feeling for nature was said to be "expansive, clear, devotedly austere; religiously and emotionally profound." The emphasis on this feeling for nature derived from the YOUTH MOVEMENT's antipathy to civilization and underlay the cult of BLOOD AND SOIL.

Natzweiler (Struthof), National Socialist concentration camp near the Alsatian village of the same name in the northern Vosges Mountains, about 50 km (approximately 30 miles) southwest of Strasbourg. Officially opened on May 1, 1941, Natzweiler was originally planned for 1,500 prisoners; by the autumn of 1944 it held some 7,000 (including its satellite camps, the total was 20,000 to 25,000). Prisoners of the most varied nationalities worked in the granite quarries of the SS enterprise German Earth and Stone Works (Deutsche Erd- und Steinwerke; DEST), in road building, and in tunnel construction (for underground munitions factories), as well as in shale oil extraction in the Swabian Alps for the German Shale Oil Research Company, Ltd. (Deutsche Ölschiefer-Forschungs-GmbH). Natzweiler had 49 satellite camps and subcamps.

Beginning in the summer of 1943, French and later Norwegian NN PRISONERS (*see* "NIGHT AND FOG" DECREE) were interned and subjected to more intense harassment. Many of the prisoners died of hunger, disease, exhaustion, abuse, shooting "during escape attempts," and hanging. Other prisoners were victims of medical experiments carried out in cooperation with medical researchers at the "Reich University" of Strasbourg. Experiments with mustard gas were conducted by the anatomy professor August Hirt. For Hirt's collection of skulls and skeletons, prisoners from Auschwitz were brought to Natzweiler, then gassed there in a small gas chamber with cyanohydrate salts; the corpses were transported to Strasbourg to be reduced to skeletons. In addition, experiments were conducted on prisoners involving typhus and yellow fever, as well as phosgene gas.

When the Allies pressed closer, the main camp was shut down in September 1944 and the prisoners divided up among the satellite camps. The number of victims who died in Natzweiler has been estimated at between 5,000 and 6,000—by some accounts, 12,000 —including the satellite camps. After the war, a French memorial site, Le Struthof (named after a small locality near the camp), was built on the former camp grounds. The commandants of Natzweiler were Egon Zill (sentenced to life imprisonment in 1955; sentence commuted to 15 years; died in 1974), Fritz Hartjenstein (sentenced to death; died in 1954 in a French prison), Hans Hüttig (sentenced to life imprisonment in France; released in 1956), and Heinrich Schwarz (executed in 1947 in Sandweier).

W. D.

Naujocks, Alfred Helmut, b. September 20, 1911; d. Hamburg, April 4, 1966, German secret agent. After studies in mechanical engineering in Kiel, Naujocks joined the SS in 1931, and was active in the Security Service (SD) beginning in 1934. When the war began he was an SS-*Sturmbannführer* at the SD Main Office in the Foreign Intelligence Service (later RSHA Office VI, "Sabotage"). On August 10, 1939, Reinhard HEYDRICH assigned Naujocks to carry out a faked attack on the radio station at GLEIWITZ on August 31, for the purpose of providing a propaganda cover for the German attack on Poland. Further spectacular operations by Naujocks were the abduction of British agents from the Netherlands in the VENLO INCIDENT on November 9, 1939, and the counterfeit-money "BERNHARD" OPERATION.

Naujocks later fell into disfavor for insubordination; he was assigned to the Waffen-SS, and was wounded on the eastern front. In 1944 he again received an assignment: to counteract resistance organizations (the Danish, among others). On October 19 of that year Naujocks,

whom the American journalist William L. Shirer called an "intellectual gangster," went over to the Americans. Renowned as "the man who unleashed the Second World War," he was nonetheless interned in a camp for war criminals. After his testimony during the NUREMBERG TRIALS he was able to escape; he lived in Hamburg as a businessman and was never called to account in a court.

Naumann, Max, b. Berlin, January 12, 1875; d. there, May 15, 1939, German-Jewish antisemite. Naumann was the leading theorist and one-time chairman of the radical right-wing Association of National German Jews (established in 1921). The highly decorated First World War officer (Iron Cross, First Class) during the Weimar period strongly advocated the "total assimilation of German Jewry into the German nation." He also called for the banishment of Jewish immigrants from eastern Europe, whom he characterized as "harmful bacteria in the body of the German people." In 1933 Naumann, then a member of the German National People's Party (DNVP), celebrated the "national revolution" in glowing terms, yet was in no way able to secure acceptance by the National Socialist leadership of his idea for the assimilation of "purely German Jews" (*rein deutsche Juden*) or otherwise to gain a special status for himself in the Third Reich. In 1935 the Gestapo dissolved Naumann's association on grounds of "attitudes hostile to the state."

Naval war (*Seekrieg*), the combat between the German navy and the naval forces of Germany's opponents, especially the British and American fleets, in the Second World War. Among all branches of the Wehrmacht, the navy was the least prepared for a war in September 1939, especially against the strongest sea power, Great Britain, which at that point had at its disposal 12 battleships, 3 battle cruisers, 3 monitors, 7 aircraft carriers, 15 heavy and 48 light cruisers, 191 destroyers, and 69 submarines. Against this, Germany could summon up only 2 battleships, 3 armored ships, 1 heavy and 6 light cruisers, 21 destroyers, 11 torpedo boats, and 57 U-boats. The major task of these naval forces was to disrupt the enemy supply lines, especially those of Great Britain in the Atlantic.

In the crisis phase before the outbreak of hostilities, the German Naval Command had already dispatched to sea 18 oceangoing U-boats and 2 armored ships. By the end of 1939 the U-boats, suffering 9 losses, sank or captured 147 merchant marine vessels carrying 509,321 gross

Naval war. German U-boat in the Atlantic.

registered tons (GRT), as well as 1 aircraft carrier and 1 battleship. Eleven vessels fell victim to the armored ships, of which 1 was forced to scuttle itself (the *Admiral Graf Spee*, on December 17, 1939). The year 1940 witnessed heavy ship losses for the German navy in the NORWEGIAN CAMPAIGN, and torpedo failures plagued the U-boats, which nevertheless sank 481 freighters with 2,289,547 GRT. Twenty-two U-boats were lost and 50 new ones came into service, along with 1 battleship, 1 heavy cruiser, 3 destroyers, and 8 torpedo boats. The navy's weakness was one reason why Hitler abandoned his plans for the invasion of England.

During 1940, 7 German support cruisers operated successfully overseas, along with an armored ship. In the Atlantic, both of the German battleships carried out an effective economic war. A similar operation by the battleship *Bismarck,* which had sunk the British battle cruiser *Hood,* ended with the loss of the new ship (May 27, 1941). The number of vessels sunk by the German U-boats in 1941 remained slightly under the figure for 1940, even though 199 new submarines had been put into service. A total of 35 were lost; among them, in May 1941, were those of the famous commanders Günther PRIEN, Joachim Schepke, and Otto Kretschmer.

The entrance of the United States into the war, which after PEARL HARBOR became a world war, freed the German U-boat command (under Adm. of the Fleet Karl DÖNITZ) from restrictions in the attacks on shipping. But at the same time, it brought the second largest naval and heavy-industrial power into the naval war against Germany. At first, German U-boat successes increased sharply in 1942 (5,819,065 GRT sunk) against 75 losses; 238 new boats also came into service. However, the interruption of the growing stream of supplies for the USSR through the North Sea never succeeded, and by 1943 it was clear that Germany could never win the tonnage battle. To be sure, in March alone, four Allied Atlantic convoys lost 20 percent of their ships, forcing a re-evaluation of the convoy system, even though the German radio transmission code ("Ultra") was being deciphered. But then the Allied countermeasures took hold, causing the German losses in May 1943 to soar to 41 boats. On May 24, Dönitz (since January 31 of that year the navy's supreme commander) accordingly halted the fighting in the Atlantic. All told, in 1943 the German U-boats sank 2,395,532 GRT, with 239 losses and 283 new boats put into service.

Better defense and Allied radio monitoring during 1944 further prevented the German U-boats from exploiting their earlier successes. They were able to sink only 701,906 GRT; 237 boats remained at sea, and 230 new ones entered service. In this same year the navy lost the *Tirpitz,* its last battleship, along with 7 destroyers, 16 torpedo boats, and 57 patrol boats, mostly in the area of the Allied INVASION. U-boat successes in 1945 were also low (334,681 GRT); the new Type XXI boats, which with their great underwater speed could have imperiled Allied shipping traffic, came too late. In the last phase of the war the navy concentrated all its remaining forces on the rescue of the German population in the east from the Red Army. It brought more than 2.5 million people safely to the west, but with heavy losses (14,000 dead), as with the fate of the WILHELM GUSTLOFF.

G. H.

Navy Helpers (*Marinehelfer*), official designation for the schoolboys more commonly known as FLAK HELPERS, who were deployed with navy flak units during the war.

Navy High Command (Oberkommando der Kriegsmarine; OKM), highest administrative and command authority of the German (combat) navy under its supreme commander: Erich RAEDER (June 1, 1935–January 30, 1943); Karl DÖNITZ (until May 1, 1945); Hans Georg von FRIEDEBURG (until May 8, 1945).

Navy-HJ (Marine-HJ), special unit of the HITLER YOUTH for fitness training through (military) sports and technical instruction; it was intended to train future sailors.

Nazi, short form of *Nationalsozialist;* a form analogous to Sozi (*Sozialist*). It was usually used as a derogatory or polemical term.

Nebe, Arthur, b. Berlin, November 13, 1894; d. there, March 4, 1945 (executed), German police officer. Nebe graduated early from secondary school with a wartime *Notabitur* (examination taken under emergency conditions) and volunteered for the army in 1914. In 1920 he joined Berlin's Criminal Police, becoming an inspector in 1923. He joined the NSDAP and the SA in 1931, and the following year he established a National Socialist civil service association. Under the patronage of Kurt DALUEGE, Nebe became a criminal specialist (*Kriminalrat*) in the Prussian Secret State Police Bureau on April 1, 1933.

Nebe's early enthusiasm for Hitler soon waned, and he developed contacts with the opposition circles around Ludwig BECK, to whom he reported information from police headquarters. Nebe advanced professionally, becoming director of the Prussian State Crime Bureau in 1935, director of the Criminal Police (Kripo) in 1936, and Reich Criminal Director (*Reichskriminaldirektor*) on July 1, 1937. This made him chief of Office V (Kripo) after the

Arthur Nebe.

establishment of the REICH SECURITY MAIN OFFICE (RSHA) in 1939.

Nebe solved the BÜRGERBRÄU ASSASSINATION ATTEMPT case (November 8, 1939), yet his proof that Johann Georg ELSER had acted alone aroused little enthusiasm in Hitler or Himmler. As leader of Einsatzgruppe B (*see* EINSATZGRUPPEN), Nebe took part in the Russian Campaign. Unable to endure the killing operations of his commandos, which claimed—by their own count—45,467 Jewish victims, he arranged to be relieved of his command. Back in his old position in the RSHA, Nebe supported the assassination attempt of July 20, 1944. He remained undiscovered until an impetuous flight on July 27 put him on the wanted list. He was finally captured on January 16, 1945. The *Volk* Court sentenced him to death on March 2 of that year.

Negroization (*Vernegerung*), polemical catchword of National Socialist propaganda denoting the racial intermingling of Europeans with peoples of other—not only black—skin color. Hitler himself used the term primarily with reference to the French, whose colonial possessions favored racial mixing: "This . . . nation, which is becoming a victim of Negroization, is . . . a lurking danger to the existence of the white race" (*Mein Kampf*). The term arose around the turn of the century in *völkisch* circles, together with similar defamatory terms: "France, Italy, Spain, the Balkans, and Hungary are becoming Negroized. . . . Russia, Sweden, Austria, and Germany are becoming Mongolized" (Josef LANZ, 1906).

Neher, Carola, b. Munich, November 2, 1905; d. Orenburg internment camp (USSR), June 28, 1942, German actress. Married to the writer Klabund (1890–1928), by the late 1920s Neher was performing on Berlin stages with success in plays by her husband as well as by Brecht and Shaw. As a sworn opponent of National Socialism, Neher went via Prague to Moscow in 1933. Arrested in 1936 as a suspected counterrevolutionary during the Stalinist purges, she was initially to have been returned to Germany after the GERMAN-SOVIET NONAGGRESSION PACT. However, she remained in Soviet custody and, after refusals to work for the Soviet secret police, was shot.

Neighborly love (*Nächstenliebe*), Christian virtue in accordance with *Matthew* 22:39: "Love thy neighbor as thyself." In the National Socialist view, love of neighbor was a typical relic of "Jewish payment morality" (*Lohnmoral*) in Christianity, since it contemplates a reward. Completely incomprehensible to the National Socialists was the radical Christian extension of the neighborly-love commandment to include love of one's enemies as well, since the "sentiment of the Nordic-German race" knew only love of "comrades in race and *Volk*." For them, a broader love of neighbor contradicted the natural law of love and hate. The humane overcoming of this gap was unthinkable for NS biologism.

Neofascism (*Neofascismus*), all new or resurgent postwar political ideas, ideologies, groups, and organizations in Western Europe, America, and Japan that adhere to the ideology, program, and/or political strategy of Italian FASCISM (neo-Fascism in the narrower sense) or of some other fascist movement (neofascism in the broader sense). In Europe, neofascism is particularly strong in Italy. The Movimento Sociale Italiano (Italian Social Movement; MSI), founded in 1946, draws its members from the petite bourgeoisie, as well as from strongly anti-Communist groups in the upper bourgeoisie. In 1983 the MSI received 6.8 percent of the vote and 42 seats in elections to the Chamber of Deputies, making it the fourth strongest party in Italy.

Other European states, and America as well, have neofascist groups, which are not always easily distinguished from other forms of right-wing extremism. They include the Vlaamse Militanten Orde (Flemish Militant Order; VMO) in Belgium, the Faisceaux Nationalistes Européens (European Nationalist Fascists; FNE) in France, the Europäische Neuordnung (Euro-

pean New Order; ENO) in Switzerland, and the National-Socialistische Deutsche Arbeiterpartei —Auslands- und Aufbauorganisation (National Socialist German Workers' Party—Foreign and Development Organization; NSDAP-AO) in the United States. In the Federal Republic, neofascism is active in the form of NEO-NAZISM. The neofascist organizations also collaborate internationally.

R. B.

Neo-Nazism (*Neonazismus*), all new or resurgent postwar political ideas, ideologies, groups, and organizations that, especially in the Federal Republic of Germany but also in other European states and in the United States, adhere to the ideology, program, and/or political strategy of NATIONAL SOCIALISM and that openly advocate at least some of their ideas.

In the Federal Republic, neo-Nazism was first organized as a political party in 1949 as the Socialist Reich Party (Sozialistische Reichspartei; SRP); that year it received 1.8 percent of the vote for Bundestag seats. It was banned in 1952 by the Federal Constitutional Court (Bundesverfassungsgericht) as a successor organization to the NSDAP and thus as unconstitutional. Until the mid-1970s there was no neo-Nazi organization of significance in West Germany; the National Democratic Party of Germany (National-demokratische Partei Deutschlands; NPD), founded in 1964, has some neo-Nazi features, but can only partially be classified as within that camp. It received 4.3 percent of the vote in the 1969 Bundestag elections, but subsequently was only an insignificant splinter party. Not until 1974–1975 did organized German neo-Nazism again become publicly manifest, through assemblies, parades, demonstrations, graffiti and poster campaigns, distribution of printed materials (including mostly anonymous brochures and pamphlets), and threatening letters. There were also acts of violence, against facilities (for example, dynamite attacks against refugee shelters, foreigners' residences, and United States Army installations) and against individuals.

It is characteristic of current neo-Nazism that its racist hate propaganda and acts of violence no longer apply primarily to "the Jews" but increasingly to foreigners, especially the Turks, and at times also to American soldiers. In 1983 there were 16 neo-Nazi groups in the Federal Republic, including the so-called military/defense sports groups (*Wehrsportgruppen*), with 1,130 active, mostly youthful members. The

Neo-Nazism. ANS leader Kühnen (right) at a meeting in July 1978.

total count of neo-Nazi activists—including the unorganized—amounted in 1983 to about 1,420. The leading organization is the Aktionsfront Nationaler Sozialisten (National Socialist Action Front; ANS), founded in 1977 by M. Kühnen and led by him since then. It was re-established in January 1983 as the Aktionsfront Nationaler Socialisten/Nationaler Aktivisten (National Socialist/National Activists' Action Front; ANS/NA), but then was banned on December 7 of that year. The ANS/NA program contained in the "Frankfurt Appeal" of January 15, 1983 (repeal of the prohibition against the NSDAP, "repatriation" of foreigners, "cultural revolution" against "Americanism," struggle for an "independent socialist Great-Germany"), is typical of the political goals set by neo-Nazism. The German neo-Nazi groups cooperate internationally with other organizations of NEOFASCISM.

R. B.

Nero Command (*Nero-Befehl*; also called Nero Order or Scorched-Earth Command [*Verbrannte-Erde-Befehl*]), designation recalling the megalomaniac Roman emperor Nero; it referred to the "Führer order" of March 19, 1945, which mandated the destruction of all supply facilities in the Reich "that the enemy . . . could use for the continuation of his struggle." This "scorched-earth" tactic (in a Himmler order of September 3, 1943) had been propagandized by Stalin as early as the Russian Campaign and was

applied by the Wehrmacht in its retreat from the east; it was now intended to hinder the Allied invasion of Germany.

The Nero Command contradicted a memorandum that Armaments Minister Albert SPEER had given to Hitler the day before, in which Speer had denied the right of political leaders to destroy the German people's means of existence. Hitler, however, was operating by the slogan "If the war is lost, then the *Volk* will also be lost." In a note of March 29, Speer again pleaded with Hitler to modify the command, and in his implementation instructions on March 30 and April 4, Speer arranged that destruction orders had to be channeled through his ministry. In cooperation with the Wehrmacht and the civil administration, he thus largely succeeded in curbing the Nero Command.

Netherlands, kingdom on Germany's western border; area, 34,222 sq km (about 13,700 sq miles); population, approximately 7.9 million (1930). After a decade of domestic political calm and an untroubled relationship with Germany (including asylum for WILHELM II in Doorn), the world economic crisis and the spread of National Socialism after 1933 provoked changes in the Netherlands. There were increasing fears for the country's neutral independence (a general mobilization was declared on August 28, 1939), economic difficulties, and a radicalization of political life, notably the establishment of the radical right-wing Nationaal Socialistisch Beweging (National Socialist Movement) under Anton MUSSERT. The concern proved to be justified: Germany invaded the Netherlands on May 10, 1940, without a declaration of war and in violation of Dutch neutrality (*see* FRENCH CAMPAIGN). The royal family, headed by Queen Wilhelmina, along with the government, fled to London and established a government-in-exile there. On May 15, 1940, the Netherlands surrendered. A Reich Commissariat for the Netherlands was established on May 25 under Arthur SEYSS-INQUART and with subordinate Dutch state secretaries, as a civilian government alongside the military commander, Gen. Friedrich CHRISTIANSEN.

Germany's harsh occupation policy, especially through the massive Amsterdam pogrom of 1941, progressively involved the Dutch Jews in the FINAL SOLUTION (*see* Anne FRANK). It also sought to Nazify and synchronize the "species-related [*artverwandt*] Germanic country," to undermine its national independence, and to plunder it economically (for example, by the

Netherlands. "Better dead than a slave." Resistance motto pasted over a German occupation proclamation.

abduction of forced laborers to Germany). The occupation left no opportunity for COLLABORATION, aided as it was by Mussert's movement and the Nederlandse Volkunie (Netherlands Volk Union). It constantly provoked responses such as movements of solidarity (with the Jews) and popular strike movements, which had the support of the left-wing parties and the church. Between September 1944 and the German surrender on May 5, 1945, the defense of "Fortress Holland" north of the Rhine delta line inflicted on the Netherlands an eight-month period of suffering. Famine, intensified occupation policies, increasing incidents of sabotage and resistance (for example, a railroad strike of several months' duration), and widespread destruction (especially the flooding of large land areas by opening sluices for defensive purposes) all burdened relations with Germany long after the war's end. In London, the government-in-exile early took significant steps for a supranational alliance among the Benelux countries: a customs union on October 21, 1943, was followed by a tariff treaty on September 5, 1944. Queen Wilhelmina returned to the country on June 28, 1945.

B.-J. W.

Neudeck, manor (*Rittergut*) near Freystadt in West Prussia. It was purchased in 1927 with the aid of a fund-raising campaign by the STEEL HELMET paramilitary organization and presented to Reich President Paul von Hindenburg on his 80th birthday; to avoid inheritance taxes, it was put in the name of his son Oskar. Hindenburg died on the estate, which earlier had been Hindenburg family property, on August 2, 1934.

Neuengamme, National Socialist concentration camp built in December 1938 as a satellite of the Sachsenhausen concentration camp in the village of Neuengamme, just under 30 km (about 18 miles) east of Hamburg. Neuengamme was at first occupied by 500 prisoners who were used to build the camp. Over the course of time, a total of 87,000 male and 13,500 female prisoners from all the European nations passed through the camp. In June 1940 Neuengamme became an autonomous concentration camp. The prisoners worked in a large brickyard, in regulation measures on the Elbe River, and, as time went on, especially in satellite and annex camps—74 in all—for various projects of the munitions industry.

The bad conditions of work, lodging, and sanitation resulted in many deaths, as did abuse and killings by the SS guards. Numerous Soviet prisoners of war and political prisoners were brought to the camp by the Gestapo and shot or hanged there. In April 1945, 20 Jewish children

The Neudeck manor.

up to the age of 12 were hanged in the satellite camp at the Bullenhuserdamm school, so that the tuberculosis experiments that had been performed on them would not become known. That same month, the camp was evacuated. The majority of the prisoners were taken aboard the ships *Deutschland,* CAP ARCONA, and THIELBEK, which were anchored in Neustadt Bay. On May 3 the ships fell victim to British bombardment, and more than 7,000 of the Neuengamme prisoners lost their lives as a result. A total of 56,000 people met their death in the Neuengamme concentration camp.

Today the Neuengamme Penitentiary occupies the camp's stone buildings, constructed by the prisoners. On the grounds, a memorial site and a documentary exhibit stand as reminders of the concentration camp period. The commandants of Neuengamme were Martin Weiss and Max Pauly (both executed in 1946).

W. D.

Neumann, Heinz, b. Berlin, July 6, 1902; d. presumably 1937 in the USSR, German politician. In 1920 Neumann joined the Communist Party of Germany (KPD), which he represented in the Comintern; he took part in a Communist uprising in China in 1928. From 1929 to 1932 he was a member of the KPD Central Committee, and he also served as a Reichstag deputy (1930–1932) and as editor in chief of the party organ, *Die* ROTE FAHNE (The Red Flag). A representative of the party wing loyal to Moscow, Neumann was a follower of Ernst THÄLMANN, who, however, distanced himself after internal party quarrels in April 1932. Neumann then went to Spain as a Comintern functionary, and in 1935 to Moscow. In the course of the Stalinist purges he was arrested there on April 27, 1937, and disappeared.

Neurath, Konstantin Baron von, b. Klein-Glattbach (Württemberg), February 2, 1873; d. Enzweihingen (Württemberg), August 14, 1956, German politician and SS-*Obergruppenführer* (June 19, 1943). Neurath was a legal assistant in the Foreign Office (1901), and then with the German Consulate General in London (1903). He later served as legation counselor (1909) and embassy counselor (1914) in Constantinople, and as ambassador in Copenhagen (1919), Rome (1921–1930), and London (1930–1933). On June 2, 1932, Neurath was appointed Reich Foreign Minister in the cabinet of Franz von Papen. After his term in the Schleicher cabinet, he was retained by Hitler as foreign minister

Konstantin Baron von Neurath.

after the Seizure of Power; his good relations with Great Britain contributed substantially to the increased esteem for National Socialism abroad. He remained in office until February 4, 1938, when he was replaced by Joachim von RIBBENTROP in the shake-up after the FRITSCH CRISIS.

Neurath had not joined the NSDAP until 1937. After his removal from office, he stayed on as Reich Minister without Portfolio until he was named Reich Protector of Bohemia and Moravia on March 18, 1939. He had no particular influence in that post, since the real power lay with his state secretary, Karl Hermann FRANK. On September 27, 1941, Neurath went on leave, ostensibly because of age, but in reality because Hitler found his conduct in office too liberal (despite his role in the persecution of the churches, the racial laws, and so on). He was forced to retire in 1943. In the trial of the main war criminals in Nuremberg, Neurath was sentenced to 15 years' imprisonment. He was granted an early release in 1954 on account of an eye ailment.

New Beginnings (Neu-beginnen), socialist group that arose among young workers in 1931, but first attained political effectiveness in exile in Prague. Its criticism was aimed at the SOCIAL DEMOCRATIC PARTY OF GERMANY (SPD) for its failure to ward off National Socialism. In October 1933, the group's pamphlet "New Beginnings! Fascism or Socialism?" demanded that the SPD executive committee in exile be deposed, and that a single-party state be established as the "democracy of the working people." Nonetheless, New Beginnings did not agitate for cooperative action with the Communists. In 1938 the group had to move to France, and in 1940 to Great Britain and to the United States.

New Financial Plan (Neuer Finanzplan; Law for the Financing of National Political Objectives of March 20, 1939), measure taken by the National Socialist government to provide funding for rearmament. Since the previous method of providing credit (*see* MEFO BILLS) could no longer be utilized in 1939, and since the treasury bonds issued to contractors had substantially increased the national debt, deliveries and services to the Reich were now paid with the aid of tax vouchers that offset 40 percent of the amount billed by each vendor. The vendor could either pass the voucher on to others or could credit it against his own tax liability after six months. This accounting system permitted the "silent" financing of rearmament for the short and medium term without spectacular tax increases or inflationary surges.

V. B.

New German Healing Lore (Neue Deutsche Heilkunde), attempt to establish a *völkisch* medicine that would unite natural methods of healing with academic medicine in a synthesis that aimed to reject "Jewish factory medicine" (*Fabrikmedizin*). Especially encouraged by Rudolf HESS and Julius STREICHER, it led to the founding of the Reich Workshop for a New German Healing Lore in May 1935, on the occasion of the *Volk* Healing Lore from Blood and Soil (Volksheilkunde aus Blut und Boden) exhibition in Nuremberg. The new group was intended to provide an organizational solution to the crisis in medicine. The basis of this new healing lore was to be "the National Socialist worldview of the natural, the biological principles underlying all events" (Reich Physicians' Führer Gerhard WAGNER). The new healing lore attempted, without success, to reclaim as its historical foster father the medieval physician Paracelsus. The desired synthesis was never attained; academic medicine prevailed, and the workshop was dissolved in early 1937. A late result of the efforts for a new therapeutics was the Healing Practitioner Law (*Heilpraktikergesetz*) of 1939. It recognized for the first time the profession of "healing practitioner," but made its exercise dependent on a state license.

R. W.

New Order. *See* European New Order.

New Plan (Neuer Plan), economic program introduced on September 24, 1934, by Hjalmar SCHACHT, Reich Bank president and economics minister, in order to attain complete control of foreign trade through centralized FOREIGN-CURRENCY MANAGEMENT. After only a year of National Socialist rule, a crisis in foreign trade emerged in the summer of 1934. Foreign-currency reserves dwindled rapidly under the pressure of increased domestic demand, which was affected both by accelerated rearmament and declining exports. In order not to jeopardize arms expansion, the government had to take decisive steps to monitor and regulate the totality of FOREIGN TRADE. A comprehensive system of controls aimed at restricting imports to the most important foodstuffs and those raw materials most crucial to the rearmament economy. Because of the shortage of foreign currency, but also for military reasons and ideological concepts regarding "living space," exports were promoted and bilateral compensation arrangements were concluded with nations that could supply raw materials and agricultural products, in exchange for German industrial goods. The shift of foreign trade, to southeastern Europe in particular, did not eliminate the bottlenecks in foreign commerce: a crisis in food supplies arose anew in 1935–1936. Even the subsequent FOUR-YEAR PLAN could not resolve the problem.

V. B.

New Reich Chancellery (Neue Reichskanzlei), as of January 12, 1939, the official headquarters of Reich Chancellor Hitler, located on Vossstrasse at the corner of Wilhelmstrasse, in Berlin. Built by Albert SPEER, the edifice, 220 m (about 730 feet) long, was completed in nine months. The commission was given by Hitler at the end of January 1938; the plans were finished in March, and the topping-off ceremony was held in August. On January 7, 1939, the work was completed, and on January 9, Hitler began his occupancy. For this tempo of construction, 4,000 on-site workers in two shifts were required, aside from the numerous subcontractors.

The chancellery was laid out as a row of various offices and meeting rooms. At its end was a marble gallery 146 m (about 490 feet) long. It provided access to Hitler's office, which was more than 400 sq m (about 1,300 sq feet) in area. The long corridor was intended to intimi-

New Reich Chancellery. Entrance on Vossstrasse.

date visitors and to demonstrate the might of the new Reich. Guards of the LEIBSTANDARTE-SS "ADOLF HITLER," in black uniform, steel helmet, white sword belt, and white gloves, accentuated the imperious appointments of the rooms, with their classicist paintings, Gobelin tapestries, coats of arms, and musclebound statues by Arno BREKER. At the building's opening, Hitler addressed the workers by saying, "This will remain standing here, and through the centuries will give witness to all those who have built it." The New Reich Chancellery was mostly destroyed 76 months later, and was razed down to the ruined FÜHRERBUNKER. Out of the building blocks the Soviets erected the monument to the fallen heroes of the Red Army in Berlin-Treptow.

Newspapers. *See* Press; *articles on individual newspapers.*

Nieden, Wilhelm zur, b. Münster, August 29, 1878; d. Berlin, April 22, 1945 (executed), German engineer. After studies in electrical engineering, Nieden worked first in industry, and then in municipal utilities. He became head of utilities in Barmen (now Wuppertal) in 1910, and in 1927 he went to Leipzig as general director of its municipal utilities. There he came to know Carl GOERDELER. As an opponent of National Socialism, Nieden lost his position in the fall of 1933. He went to Berlin, where he worked as a consultant and for the Audit Office (Rechnungshof). Although not active in the opposition movement, he was arrested on August 20, 1944, because of his connections with

Goerdeler. On January 18, 1945, Nieden was sentenced to death. Released from prison on April 22, he was shot on an expanse of ruins by an SS commando squad, along with numerous other prisoners, including Klaus BONHOEFFER and Albrecht HAUSHOFER.

Niederhagen, National Socialist concentration camp (*see* WEWELSBURG-NIEDERHAGEN).

Niekisch, Ernst, b. Trebnitz (Silesia), May 23, 1889; d. Berlin, May 23, 1967, German politician and writer. An elementary school (*Volksschule*) teacher, Niekisch joined the Social Democratic Party (SPD) in 1917. He was chairman of the Central Workers' and Soldiers' Council of Munich in 1918–1919, then went over to the Independent Socialists (USPD) in 1919. He served as secretary of the German Textile Workers' Union in Berlin from 1922 to 1926. In 1926 Niekisch became a member of the Old Socialist Party, a left-wing splinter group. He also published the periodical *Der Widerstand* (The Opposition), in which he strongly criticized the pro-Western course of Gustav STRESEMANN and advocated displacing the Weimar Republic with NATIONAL BOLSHEVISM. In his perceptive book *Hitler, ein deutsches Verhängnis* (Hitler, a German Fate; 1931), Niekisch early on recognized the danger represented by the National Socialists.

After the Seizure of Power, Niekisch attempted to form resistance groups in various cities. His periodical was banned in 1937, and he himself was jailed. Charged with "literary high treason," he was sentenced to life imprisonment by the *Volk* Court in 1939 and was confined in the Brandenburg Penitentiary.

Niekisch became a member of the German Communist Party (KPD) after the war, and then joined East Germany's Socialist Unity Party (SED). He became a deputy in the People's Chamber (Volkskammer) of the German Democratic Republic (GDR), and also taught at Humboldt University in East Berlin. By sharply criticizing the suppression of the popular uprising of June 17, 1953, in the GDR, he came into conflict with the party, and moved to West Berlin. His analysis of the Hitler era, *Das Reich der niederen Dämonen* (The Empire of the Petty Demons; 1958), has become a standard reference on the subject.

Niemöller, Martin, b. Lippstadt (Westphalia), January 14, 1892; d. Wiesbaden, March 6, 1984, German Evangelical theologian. Niemöller joined the Imperial Navy in 1910 and entered the U-Boat Service in 1915, becoming the commander of UC67 in 1918. Shaken by the "shame of November 9" (1918), and unprepared to serve the Weimar Republic as a soldier, Niemöller gave up his officer's career and began the study of theology in Münster on October 3, 1919. After his ordination on June 29, 1924, he served until 1930 as administrator of the Inner Mission in Westphalia. He then accepted a pastoral post in Berlin-Dahlem.

By his own account, Niemöller always voted for the NSDAP beginning in 1924. Yet he became a source of Evangelical opposition to National Socialist plans for the synchronization of the church, as well as to the ideological undermining of the Christian faith after the Seizure of Power. He therefore joined the YOUNG REFORMERS, and reacted to the GERMAN CHRISTIANS' attempts to introduce the ARYAN PARAGRAPH into the church by founding the PASTORS' EMERGENCY LEAGUE on September 21, 1933. By his request for the removal of Reich Bishop Ludwig MÜLLER, among other demands, Niemöller succeeded in gaining an audience with Hitler on January 25, 1934. During this meeting, which included other church leaders, there was a heated exchange of words between the chancellor and Niemöller. From then on, the Gestapo made frequent visits to the Dahlem parsonage. Niemöller was removed from his post on March 1, 1934, but was restored after protests by his congregation and after the verdict of the Berlin State Court (*Landgericht*) on July 5, 1934.

Extremely popular, in part because of his nationalistic attitudes and military past—in

Martin Niemöller.

1934 his book *Vom U-Boot zur Kanzel* (From the U-boat to the Pulpit) was published—Niemöller subsequently became a point of crystallization for the CONFESSING CHURCH, and belonged to its Fraternal Council from the time of the Barmen Confessional Synod (May 29–31, 1934). In the opinion of his friend Karl BARTH, Niemöller was the personification of the CHURCH STRUGGLE. On July 1, 1937, he was finally arrested on allegations of pulpit abuse, violation of the MALICIOUS-GOSSIP LAW (including defamation of the minister for church affairs, Hanns KERRL), and incitement to disobedience. The Special Court of Berlin-Moabit sentenced him on March 2, 1938, to seven months' detention, which was considered as already served. Nonetheless, immediately after the trial Niemöller was arrested again and sent to the Sachsenhausen concentration camp as "the Führer's personal prisoner."

Despite international protests and numerous petitions, Niemöller remained a prisoner until the war's end. During this period he went through a theological crisis and considered conversion to Catholicism. This led in 1941 to his transfer to Dachau, where he was housed with Catholic priests, since the NS leadership hoped in this way to give the final impetus to his conversion and thus "behead" the Confessing Church. The opposite resulted: Niemöller gained renewed Protestant self-awareness, yet at the same time he became a decisive advocate of the ecumenical movement.

After his liberation, Niemöller became president of the Church Foreign Bureau, was one of the authors of the STUTTGART CONFESSION OF GUILT, and served from 1947 to 1964 as church president of the Hessian regional church. He still remained irksome, struggling against German rearmament, campaigning for an understanding with the East, and in his final years supporting the peace movement with great commitment.

Nietzsche, Friedrich, b. Röcken bei Lützen, October 15, 1844; d. Weimar, August 25, 1900, German philosopher. The son of a Protestant pastor, Nietzsche was educated at the exclusive boarding school of Schulpforta, and then studied theology and classical philology in Bonn and Leipzig. At the age of 24 he became a professor of classical philology in Basel. After falling seriously ill in 1879, he gave up his teaching position and made several sojourns in the Swiss Engadin and in northern Italy. In 1889 he was overtaken by madness, probably as the delayed

Friedrich Nietzsche.

result of a syphilitic infection. Subsequently he lived in Weimar, mentally deranged, until his death.

The young Nietzsche was philosophically influenced by Schopenhauer's pessimism and the artistic theories of Richard WAGNER. As a classical philologist, he was sharply criticized by his colleagues and was increasingly unsuccessful because of his book on the origins of Greek tragedy. He then grew into the role of a philosopher and psychologist critical of the times, predicting with prophetic accuracy developments of the coming century. Nietzsche criticized Christianity and its moral teachings; he also saw in the *décadence* of Europe the collapse of the Western tradition and with it the emergence of NIHILISM in the 20th century. His later works are dominated by the idea of the "will to power" as the mainspring of all life.

Nietzsche's thought had immense influence over several generations of German intellectuals, poets, and artists. Oswald SPENGLER's book *Der Untergang des Abendlandes* (*The Decline of the West*) is unimaginable without Nietzsche, as are the philosophies of Karl JASPERS and Martin HEIDEGGER. Thomas MANN's novels *Der Zauberberg* (*The Magic Mountain*) and *Doktor Faustus* are as much indebted to Nietzsche's spirit and life as are the works of Ernst JÜNGER and Gottfried BENN.

Nietzsche was a harsh critic of the Germans. He attacked the arrogance of Bismarck's partisans and reproached the petite bourgeoisie of the Wilhelmian epoch. He hated all Communist and socialist ideas and was contemptuous of

democracy and parliaments. From the time of his poetic work *Also sprach Zarathustra* (*Thus Spake Zarathustra;* 1883–1885), Nietzsche saw one possibility for overcoming the European crisis: the emergence of a new man, whom he also envisioned as the *Übermensch* (*see* SUPERMAN)—the masterly man, the member of "a race of conquerors and masters, that of the Aryans." However, Nietzsche was not an antisemite in the National Socialist racist sense. Alongside his criticism of Judeo-Christian religion and its "slave morality," his works contain many passages manifesting appreciation of Jewry.

Mussolini declared, with reference to Nietzsche, that the "will to power" was the decisive factor of history. Since Nietzsche did not develop a system, it was as easy for the Italian Fascists as for the National Socialists to extract key ideas for their ideology out of his many fragmentary and often contradictory statements. Whatever in Nietzsche did not match their program was simply suppressed. Nietzsche's immediate influence over Hitler, who certainly was acquainted with some of his works, is nonetheless frequently overestimated (most recently in Ernst Sandvoss's *Hitler und Nietzsche*, 1969). Overall, Nietzsche's thought has left traces for good and for evil in the history of ideas. The Marxist literary scholar Georg Lukács criticized Nietzsche as a precursor of National Socialism because of his irrationalism: "There is no guiltless worldview."

I. F.

Nieviera, Else, b. Pössneck (Thuringia), April 12, 1891; d. Berlin, May 24, 1944, German trade unionist. Nieviera was initially a nurse, and then a factory inspector. A Social Democrat, she was elected to the executive committee of the Textile Workers' Union in 1927. In 1933 she refused an offer from the GERMAN LABOR FRONT to grant her admission in exchange for a loyalty oath. She then became a solderer. Her activity aiding families of the politically persecuted led her to smuggle donations from English Quakers across the border, sometimes from Prague. For this she was sentenced to 30 months' imprisonment in 1939. Subsequently, she cared for Russian forced laborers in a munitions factory. Nieviera died in a bombardment.

"Night and Fog" Decree (*Nacht-und-Nebel-Erlass*), edict issued at Hitler's order on December 7, 1941, by Wilhelm KEITEL, chief of the Wehrmacht High Command (OKW). It directed that in the occupied territories, persons who were charged with "punishable offenses against the German Reich" were to be brought through "night and fog" to Germany, unless they had already received death sentences from military courts. The so-called *NN-Häftlinge* (NN PRISONERS) were then tried by SPECIAL COURTS. Upon acquittal or after serving time for their offenses, they were sent to concentration camps, especially to Natzweiler and Gross-Rosen. On "grounds of deterrence" they were denied any contact with their homeland. Some 7,000 persons were abducted under the terms of the "Night and Fog" Decree, the majority from France.

"Night of the Long Knives" (*Nacht der langen Messer*), general graphic description of an internal settling of accounts or (bloody) purge within a group, organization, or political party. The RÖHM AFFAIR of June 30, 1934, is often cited in historical commentaries as a typical example of a "night of long knives."

Nihilism (from Lat. *nihil*, nothing), term first used in Ivan Turgenev's novel *Fathers and Sons* (1862), and then adopted by socially critical Russian anarchists and by humanists; it seeks to encompass a mental attitude that totally denies any meaning to life. Nihilism passes a "devastating" value judgment on the dominant metaphysical and moral norms, without offering an alternative philosophical or political order; it is discussed in contemporary philosophy (by, for example, Jean-Paul Sartre and Theodor Adorno) as an honorable emancipatory position.

The two-edged nature of the term is made clear by Friedrich NIETZSCHE. On the one hand, he characterizes nihilism polemically as a consequence of the millennia-long reign of a Christianity controlled by "life-denying instincts," and on the other hand he appraises it positively as a "cleansing belief in unbelief" that makes possible a "revaluation of all values" and thus the emergence of a new humanity uncorrupted by power. For all their veneration of Nietzsche, the National Socialists could not go this far. Instead, they preferred a coarsely racist definition of nihilism as "an all-denying decadent mentality in times of racial decay, with its goal the extermination of European culture by Jewry."

M. F.

Nipperdey, Hans Carl, b. Bad Berka, January 21, 1895; d. Cologne, November 21, 1968, German jurist and labor law expert. Nipperdey was a professor in Jena (1924) and Cologne (as of

1925). A recognized scholar of labor law during the Weimar Republic, he valued good relations with trade unions. As late as mid-1933, he advocated that employers and employees should be free to organize and to create their own wage agreements. Toward the end of that year, however, he wrote that the elimination of class struggle in occupation and workplace would leave its mark on the new order (*Neugestaltung*); class struggle had been replaced by the WORKPLACE COMMUNITY. As a member of the Academy of German Law, Nipperdey collaborated on National Socialist legislative proposals. From 1954 to 1963 he was the first president of the Federal Labor Court (Bundesarbeitsgericht).

C. B.

NN Prisoners, abbreviated designation for foreigners incarcerated in German prisons and concentration camps in accordance with the "NIGHT AND FOG" DECREE.

Nobility (*Adel*), term for the leadership stratum; the National Socialist BLOOD AND SOIL ideologists were fond of deriving the German word *Adel* from the Germanic *athala* (inherited land). This was intended to emphasize that true nobility must always have peasant origins; neither granted nor elected, it was the result of "selective racial breeding" (*rassische Hochzucht*). Because of the "generative value of the family tree," Walther DARRÉ wanted to found a "new nobility of blood and soil" (the title of his 1930 book, *Neuadel aus Blut und Boden*).

Nolde, Emil (original surname, Hansen), b. Nolde bei Tondern, August 7, 1867; d. Seebüll, April 15, 1956, German painter, graphic artist, furniture designer, and wood-carver. Nolde was a self-taught artist who lived in Munich and Paris; he was influenced by van Gogh and Munch, in particular. In 1906 he briefly belonged to the avant-garde artists' group "Die Brücke" (The Bridge) in Berlin, and subsequently became one of the most outstanding representatives of German EXPRESSIONISM, although an idiosyncratic one.

Nolde saw himself as the "most Nordic" (*nordischste*) German painter. Imbued with mystical tendencies and antisemitic prejudices, he early found his way to National Socialism, from which he expected a cleansing cultural impact that would overcome materialism. However, among the National Socialist leaders only Goebbels valued his work, which in the 1920s had been bitterly attacked by Alfred Rosenberg's COMBAT LEAGUE FOR GERMAN CULTURE.

Emil Nolde.

In 1933 Nolde's "luridly awful machinations" (*grell-grässliche Machenschaften*) were condemned as "degenerate," and in 1937 his works were removed from all public collections (*see* DEGENERATE ART). For a time Nolde still had supporters within the NS leisure organization STRENGTH THROUGH JOY, which arranged several factory exhibitions of his paintings, until in 1941 an official ban on painting was imposed on him. (Siegfried Lenz used this as a theme in his 1968 novel *Deutschstunde* [*The German Lesson*].) In the seclusion of his North Friesian farm, during the remainder of the war Nolde created some 1,300 watercolors, his so-called unpainted pictures, which are still among his internationally most admired masterpieces.

M. F.

Nordic Faith (*Nordischer Glaube*), in *völkisch* usage, term for the religious views of the Nordic peoples before they were alienated by Christianization. In this interpretation, Nordic Faith, in contrast to the institutional religions, had sprung from the "experience of the universe in its unending breadth, its beauty and discordant order." Without priest or church, Germanic man had developed the Nordic Faith jointly with nature and humans, making him capable of the "natural life-deed [*natürlicher Lebenstat*]." God for him was the "obligatory original source of the everlasting, uncreated world," and his kindred or clan was the "point of contact between being and obligation, between the laws of nature and of culture." Death was a natural occurrence, a "godfather" or a "friend." When

Christianity displaced the Nordic Faith, the latter found refuge for a time in architecture (German Gothic) and mysticism, but it emerged again in the natural sciences, and in National Socialism was experiencing its "great new ascendancy."

Such constructions, passed off as Nordic Faith, found resonance particularly in Alfred ROSENBERG and Heinrich HIMMLER, but their cultivation outside the party, as in the GERMAN FAITH MOVEMENT, was suppressed.

Nordic Movement (*Nordische Bewegung*), the racist branch of the VÖLKISCH MOVEMENT. The adherents of the Nordic Movement, following Count Arthur de GOBINEAU, Paul de LAGARDE, and Houston Stewart CHAMBERLAIN, maintained the thesis that European culture, and therefore any true culture at all, had been achieved by the Nordic race alone. They considered their task to be the freeing of this culture from Christian, liberalist, and materialist "obscurations." The Nordic Movement had followers particularly in the YOUTH MOVEMENT; among the National Socialists it was represented especially by Alfred ROSENBERG and his Combat League for German Culture, whose periodical was *Nordische Blätter* (Nordic Pages). The role of ideologue for the Nordic Movement was filled by the race researcher Hans Friedrich Karl GÜNTHER. Günther headed a "Nordic Ring" (with its periodical, *Rasse* [Race]), which he integrated into the NORDIC SOCIETY.

Nordic race (*Nordische Rasse;* also *Nordrasse,* northern race), designation in race lore (*Rassenkunde*) for the tall, fair-skinned, longheaded (dolichocephalic), blond, and blue-eyed type of human being, as found especially in northern European countries. Racial ideologues and National Socialists considered the Nordic race to be directly descended from the Germanic tribes, who were the true "creators of culture," according to Count Arthur de GOBINEAU and Houston Stewart CHAMBERLAIN, among others. Certain character traits were associated with the Nordic racial attributes, including discretion, courage, hardness, boldness, and decisiveness. Other races, such as the Japanese (mere "culture bearers") and especially the Jews ("culture destroyers" and parasites), manifested these traits only to a limited extent or not at all. In this view, primacy within the Nordic race belonged to the German *Führervolk* (master [leading] people), since "everything that we term German [*deutsch*] is exclusively and solely ac-

Nordic race. "German youth leader from Transylvania."

complished by Germanic people" (Walther DAR-RÉ). The value of a people was accordingly to be measured by its share of Nordic BLOOD, which was the bearer of the Nordic race's characteristics. Among the utopian goals of National Socialist POPULATION POLICY was to increase this percentage of blood through NOR-DIC UPGRADING. This became the basis for banishing Jews from the *Volk* Community, and finally led to the extermination program of the FINAL SOLUTION.

Nordic Society (Nordische Gesellschaft), organi-zation dedicated to cultivating a Nordic world-view (*see* NORDIC MOVEMENT) and relations with peoples of "similar stock"; it was founded in 1921, but became influential only after it was officially sanctioned in 1933. The society served its goals by staging elaborate annual congresses with summer SOLSTICE celebrations in Lübeck, and through films, leisure activities, and the periodicals *Der Norden* (The North) and *Rasse* (Race). Its chairman was Hinrich LOHSE; prominent National Socialists such as Heinrich Himmler, Walther Darré, and Alfred Rosenberg were members of its "Great Council."

Nordic upgrading (*Aufnordung*), according to the racial theorist Hans Friedrich Karl GÜN-THER, the only means of "rescuing true Ger-manness [*Deutschheit*]," by increasing the per-centage of the "Nordic race" in the German *Volk*. RACIAL HYGIENE suggested the ways of carrying this out, such as making a "racially aware choice of mate" and increasing the fruit-fulness of "Nordic families" (*see* SPECIES UP-

GRADING). In colloquial usage, the term was applied ironically to dyeing one's hair blond.

Nordification (*Nordifikation*), term coined by Walther RATHENAU (1908) for a "renewal of the West" (*Erneuerung des Abendlandes*) by hark-ing back to the Germanic ideals of the "coura-geous Nordic race" (*nordische Mutrasse*). The National Socialist racial ideologues were fond of citing Rathenau's concept as Jewish evidence for justifying antisemitism (*see also* NORDIC UP-GRADING).

Norkus, Herbert, b. Berlin, July 26, 1916; d. there, January 24, 1932, Hitler Youth member. Norkus became a victim of street fighting with the Communists that was unleashed by Gaulei-ter Joseph Goebbels in the struggle for the "Red Reich Capital." National Socialist propaganda stylized Norkus as the "blood witness of the movement," and proclaimed his date of death the memorial day for the Hitler Youth. Norkus's fate provided material for the book by Karl A. Schenzinger and for Hans STEINHOFF's film HITLERJUNGE QUEX (1933).

Norway, kingdom in Scandinavia; area, 322,538 sq km (about 129,000 sq miles); population, about 2.8 million (1939). In the interwar period Norway, on the basis of its lumber and hydro-electric power, transformed itself from a coun-try of farmers into an urbanized industrial na-tion with a pronounced welfare-state bias. It also became the fourth largest shipping nation in the world. Externally it adhered, along with Swe-den, to a Nordic policy of neutrality and support for the League of Nations (Fritjof Nansen was the League commissioner for refugees). Yet it manifested its aversion to the National Socialist regime by awarding the Nobel Peace Prize in 1935 to Carl von OSSIETZKY.

The Soviet-Finnish WINTER WAR of 1939–1940, as well as the crucial strategic impor-tance of Narvik as the transfer port for 40 percent of German iron-ore imports from Swe-den, brought Norway to the forefront of atten-tion for both the Germans and the western Allies. On April 8, 1940, Allied ships mined Norway's coastal waters; the next day, the Ger-mans began their NORWEGIAN CAMPAIGN. At the beginning of June, King Haakon, the gov-ernment, and part of the Storting (parliament) left the country and set up a government-in-exile in London. From there they continued the conflict with Norwegian army, navy, and air force contingents, but on June 10 combat oper-ations in Norway came to a halt.

Norway. Ore train at the Rombak fjord.

On April 24, 1940, the *Gauleiter* of Essen, Josef TERBOVEN, was named Reich Commissioner for the Occupied Norwegian Territories. Vidkun QUISLING, the leader of a small fascist splinter party called the Nasjonal Samling (National Assembly) and the self-declared minister of state, was forced to withdraw after only a week (April 9–15) for lack of domestic support. A Norwegian Administrative Council comprised of high civil servants was then installed, to be followed, beginning on September 25, by a 12-member State Council of Commissioners. Simultaneously, the Nasjonal Samling was declared the only "state-competent" party. Beginning on February 1, 1942, Quisling was again premier; on February 7 he declared the Norwegian constitution abrogated. Quisling's increasing isolation within the Norwegian population made it clear that COLLABORATION never had a real opportunity in Norway. Growing resistance to the German occupation, and the activities of an underground movement in continual contact with London, led to mass arrests beginning in 1943 (by the end, some 40,000 Norwegians were prisoners in concentration camps), to the closing of the University of Oslo, to executions, and finally to the deportation of about 900 Jews (of whom 768 were murdered). On May 4, 1945, the German forces, numbering around 40,000, surrendered without a struggle. The government-in-exile returned to Norway on May 31, 1945.

B.-J. W.

Norwegian Campaign, comprehensive designation for the military operations of the German Wehrmacht conducted between April 9 and June 9, 1940, in occupying Denmark and Nor-

way. The aim of the campaign was to secure ore shipments through Norway's northern port at Narvik and through the Baltic Sea waterways. Both avenues were endangered by Allied plans (February 5, 1940) to dispatch help, in the form of an auxiliary corps of three or four divisions, to Finland for its WINTER WAR. The Moscow Peace Treaty of March 12, 1940, averted this plan, but later the Allied Scandinavian operation was rescheduled for April 8.

To forestall this, on March 1 of that year Hitler gave the order for the occupation of Denmark and Norway (Operation "Weser Exercise"). It was implemented on April 9, supported by every navy ship fit to sail: 2 battleships, 7 cruisers, 14 destroyers, 8 torpedo boats, and 31 U-boats. Air cover was provided by the Tenth Flying Corps with 430 aircraft. As Group XXI under Gen. Nikolaus von FALKENHORST, seven German divisions were gradually brought by sea and air to land in Oslo, Kristiansand, Stavanger, Bergen, and Narvik. Denmark was occupied almost without a struggle, but Norway fielded six divisions for defense, and received help from British, French, and Polish troops, which landed between April 14 and 18 at Harstad, Namsos, and Andalsnes.

The German mountain troops and marines under Gen. Eduard DIETL ran into a particularly difficult situation in Narvik. They nonetheless held out against superior Allied forces until

Norwegian Campaign. German paratroopers being briefed.

the latter were compelled to withdraw because of the onset of the FRENCH CAMPAIGN on June 3, 1940. On June 9, King Haakon ordered the cessation of hostilities. The German navy had lost 3 cruisers, 10 destroyers, 1 torpedo boat, and 4 U-boats; the Allies, 1 aircraft carrier, 2 cruisers, 9 destroyers, and 5 submarines. Germany had 3,692 dead, Great Britain 3,349, Norway 1,355, France and Poland 530, and Denmark 26.

G. H.

Noske, Gustav, b. Brandenburg, July 9, 1868; d. Hannover, November 30, 1946, German politician. In 1897 Noske became editor of the Social Democratic Party (SPD) newspaper *Königsberger Volkstribüne* (Königsberg People's Tribune), and beginning in 1902 he managed the *Volksstimme* (People's Voice) in Chemnitz. He served as a war correspondent during the First World War. From 1906 to 1918, Noske represented the SPD in the Reichstag. In November 1918 he became governor of Kiel, where he combated the revolutionary sailors' uprising (and uttered the notorious words "Someone must be the bloodhound"). Beginning on December 29, 1918, he was a member of the Council of People's Deputies in Berlin.

As supreme commander of troops loyal to the government, Noske bloodily suppressed the Spartacus Uprising in Berlin in January 1919, thus bringing upon himself harsh criticism from workers. That February he became Reich armed forces minister, but after the KAPP PUTSCH he

Gustav Noske.

was compelled to resign his office under pressure from the left-wing socialists Carl Legien and Otto WELS. He was governor of Hannover from 1920 until the National Socialists deposed him in 1933. During the Third Reich, Noske was in contact with opposition groups around Wilhelm LEUSCHNER. He was first arrested in 1939, and again after the failed attempt on Hitler of July 20, 1944. Although accused of high treason, he was never brought to trial before the war's end.

November criminals (*Novemberverbrecher*), derogatory term used by the political Right against the Weimar Republic. This invective was aimed primarily at the heralds of the Republic (November 9, 1918), at the members of the Council of People's Deputies, and at the signers of the armistice of November 11, 1918 (hence the name). The intention was to lay the blame for the German collapse on such democrats as Friedrich EBERT, Matthias ERZBERGER, and Philipp SCHEIDEMANN, thus buttressing the STAB-IN-THE-BACK LEGEND. The label was rapidly extended to all representatives of the "November Republic" or the "November system," who were derided as the "November tribe" (*Novembersippschaft*). The November Revolution was downgraded to a "revolt," and the legitimation of the "system" was therefore contested (*see* SYSTEM ERA). The November criminals and their FULFILLMENT POLICY provided Hitler's polemics with a basis for linking the Republic to the "outrage" of November 1918.

NSDAP. *See* National Socialist German Workers' Party.

NSDAP Aid Fund (Hilfskasse der NSDAP), National Socialist social fund, created on the model of the Communist "Red Aid" (Rote Hilfe), to which all members of the party, SA, SS, and NS Motor Corps belonged. It was established on January 1, 1929, through the transformation of the former "SA Insurance" into a party endeavor under Martin BORMANN. The fund was administered by the party's Reich treasurer and was intended to support party members and their dependents in case of accidents or other difficulties encountered while working for the "movement."

NSDAP Program. *See* Party Program of the NSDAP.

NSV piglet (*NSV-Schweinchen*), colloquial term for a placard distributed by the NATIONAL SOCIALIST VOLK WELFARE (NSV) agency. As part

NSV piglet.

of the COMBAT SPOILAGE! campaign, the placard described a pig's diet and promoted the
collection and use of kitchen scraps for this
purpose. Like other such campaigns—for example, that aimed at the COAL THIEF—it was
one of the National Socialist efforts to popula-
rize AUTARKY measures by mobilizing the willingness to save.

Nudism (*Freikörperkultur;* literally, "culture of
free bodies"), movement arising around the turn
of the 20th century to promote the nudity of
both sexes in the outdoors. It was banned on
March 3, 1933, as a "cultural aberration" (*kul-
turelle Verirrung*). (*See also* PHYSICAL CUL-
TURE.)

Nulla poena sine lege (Lat.; "no punishment
without a law"), legal principle according to
which one may be punished for violating a law
only if it was in force at the time of the deed.
During the NUREMBERG TRIALS the defense
unsuccessfully asserted the principle in response to the charges of conspiracy against the
peace and planning for a war of aggression. The
principle had been repeatedly violated by the
National Socialists themselves, as in the death
sentence imposed on the Reichstag arsonist
Marinus van der LUBBE, although life imprisonment was the maximum sentence provided for
this crime at the time it was committed.

Nuremberg (*Nürnberg*), capital of the NSDAP
Gau of Franconia, with 430,851 inhabitants in
1939. Under the "Franconian Führer" Julius
STREICHER, the National Socialists had early on
won votes in Nuremberg; in 1927 it was the
scene of the third, and in 1929 of the fourth,
NSDAP Reich Party Congress. In 1933 Hitler
declared Nuremberg the "city of the REICH PAR-
TY CONGRESSES." They were held there annually until 1938, and led to the enlargement of the
city with the construction of the Luitpold

Arena, the Zeppelin Field, the German Stadium, and the Congress Hall. Further monumental plans were halted by the war. The NATIONAL
SOCIALIST COMPETITIVE GAMES were also held
in Nuremberg.

Nuremberg Laws (*Nürnberger Gesetze*), collec-
tive term for two racial laws of the National
Socialist government that were passed on the
occasion of the NSDAP Reich Party Congress in
Nuremberg on September 15, 1935 (*Reich Law
Gazette* I, p. 1146): the Law to Protect German
Blood and German Honor, and the Reich Citi-
zenship Law.

The so-called Blood Protection Law (*see*
BLOOD, LAW TO PROTECT) stipulated prison
terms for transgressions of the ban on marriage
and extramarital sexual intercourse between
Jews and "German-blooded" individuals. It
was the basis for a number of legal proceedings
against acts of RACIAL INFAMY. The Reich Citizenship Law created for "Aryans" the new
status of Reich citizen (*Reichsbürger*), to which
all political rights were linked, whereas Jews
possessed only state citizenship (*Staatsbürger-
schaft*). A "Jew" was anyone with three Jewish
grandparents, while a person who had two Jewish grandparents and belonged to the Jewish
religious community, or who was married to a
"full Jew," was considered a Jew. This legal
definition in the first ordinance to the citizen-

Adolf Hitler Square in Nuremberg.

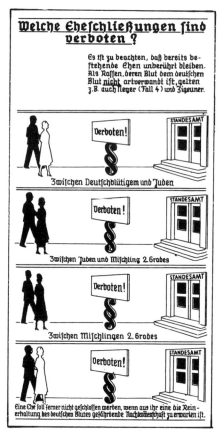

Welche Eheschließungen sind verboten?

Es ist zu beachten, daß bereits bestehende Ehen unberührt bleiben. Als Rassen, deren Blut dem deutschen Blut <u>nicht</u> artverwandt ist, gelten z.B. auch Neger (Fall 4) und Zigeuner.

Verboten! STANDESAMT
Zwischen Deutschblütigem und Juden

Verboten! STANDESAMT
Zwischen Juden und Mischling 2. Grades

Verboten! STANDESAMT
Zwischen Mischlingen 2. Grades

Verboten! STANDESAMT

Eine Ehe soll ferner nicht geschlossen werden, wenn aus ihr eine die Reinerhaltung des deutschen Blutes gefährdende Nachkommenschaft zu erwarten ist.

Nuremberg Laws. Illustration from a National Socialist instructional brochure: "Which marriages are forbidden?"

ship law was the result of a compromise between the NSDAP and the ministerial bureaucracy, which had wanted to define as non-Aryans only persons with four Jewish grandparents, while the NSDAP wanted to equate all "full," "half," and "quarter" Jews.

On the basis of the Nuremberg Laws, further occupations were closed to Jews, and the last Jews were dismissed from public service. Since even the suspicion of "racial infamy" was dangerous, Jews were driven further into a position of isolation and became second-class people. The laws did acknowledge a legal status for Jews—albeit an inferior one—and thus encouraged in them the hope for an end to the anti-Jewish measures. In retrospect, however, the Nuremberg Laws seem to be among the central measures in the constant intensification of the PERSECUTION OF JEWS.

After the first wave of terror in the year 1933, the removal of Jews from public life, and the period of consolidation for the regime that followed, the Nuremberg Laws reflected the renewal of antisemitic demands within the par-

ty only partially, since the position of Jews in the economy remained largely unaffected. Reich Economics Minister Hjalmar Schacht feared negative consequences from too rapid and too radical a policy of exclusion. Moreover, foreign-policy considerations may have held the party and government leaders back from enacting more extensive measures before the Olympic year 1936. At no time did the NSDAP view the Nuremberg Laws as the conclusion of the anti-Jewish measures. The laws became meaningless when, after the completion of rearmament and during the consolidation of Hitler's war plans, the barriers to more radical attacks on the Jews fell away. After KRISTALLNACHT on November 9–10, 1938, and after ARYANIZATION, the Jews became the objects of a total denial of rights.

Nuremberg Trials, legal proceedings held before the International Military Tribunal (IMT) against Hermann GÖRING and others, as well as 12 proceedings held before American military courts against former leaders of the Third Reich from the areas of politics, the SS, the police, the judicial system, the medical profession, the economy, and the Wehrmacht for crimes against peace, war crimes, crimes against humanity, and membership in criminal organizations. The first Nuremberg trial was conducted against the principal war criminals and was based on the LONDON AGREEMENT signed by France, Great Britain, the United States, and the USSR on August 8, 1945. The court's headquarters was in Berlin, yet Nuremberg was chosen as the venue for the trials. The signatory powers assigned judges and prosecutors. The Englishman Lord Geoffrey Lawrence was chosen by the judges themselves as president of the court.

On October 6, 1945, the four chief prosecutors—Robert H. Jackson (United States), François de Menthon (France), Roman A. Rudenko (USSR), and Sir Hartley Shawcross (Great Britain)—handed down indictments against 24 people: Hermann Göring, Rudolf Hess, Joachim von Ribbentrop, Konstantin von Neurath, Erich Raeder, Karl Dönitz, Wilhelm Keitel, Alfred Jodl, Robert Ley, Alfred Rosenberg, Wilhelm Frick, Baldur von Schirach, Ernst Kaltenbrunner, Hans Frank, Walther Funk, Julius Streicher, Fritz Sauckel, Arthur Seyss-Inquart, Albert Speer, Martin Bormann, Franz von Papen, Hjalmar Schacht, Gustav Krupp, and Hans Fritzsche. Six organizations or groups were also indicted:

Nuremberg Trials. The defendants' bench. Lower row, from the left: Göring, Hess, Ribbentrop, Keitel, Kaltenbrunner, Rosenberg, Frank, Frick, Streicher, Funk, Schacht. Upper row: Raeder, Schirach, Sauckel, Jodl, Papen, Seyss-Inquart, Speer, Neurath, Fritzsche.

the SS, SA, General Staff and OKW, Reich Cabinet, Führer Corps of the NSDAP, and Gestapo and Security Service (SD). When the trial began on November 20, 1945, in the Palace of Justice in Nuremberg, three defendants were missing: Ley had committed suicide after the indictment was handed down, BORMANN had not been found, and Krupp was declared unable to stand trial by reason of infirmity. Bormann was nonetheless tried in absentia.

The proceedings lasted 10 months. On October 1, 1946, the IMT imposed the death sentence on 12 defendants (Göring, Ribbentrop, Keitel, Kaltenbrunner, Rosenberg, Frank, Frick, Streicher, Sauckel, Jodl, Seyss-Inquart, and Bormann); 3 were sentenced to life imprisonment (Hess, Funk, and Raeder), and 4 to prison terms ranging from 10 to 20 years (Dönitz, Schirach, Speer, and Neurath). The court acquitted 3 defendants: Schacht, Papen, and Fritzsche. The Allied Control Council ratified all the sentences. The death sentences were carried out on October 16, 1946, with 2 exceptions: Göring

had committed suicide shortly before his scheduled execution, and Bormann remained missing.

The original intention of the Allies to conduct further trials through the IMT was not carried out. Through Control Council Law No. 10 of December 20, 1945, the governors of the four occupation zones instead authorized zone officials to establish "appropriate courts" for passing judgment on war criminals. In the American zone, 12 further trials were conducted in Nuremberg. Indictments were handed down against a total of 185 persons, of whom 177 were actually tried: 4 defendants committed suicide, and 4 were declared incompetent to stand trial. The proceedings began on December 9, 1946, with the DOCTORS' TRIAL; there followed the trial against Erhard MILCH, the JURISTS' TRIAL, the trials of Oswald POHL and Friedrich FLICK, the I.G. FARBEN TRIAL, the trial against the SOUTHEAST GENERALS, the trial against the RACE AND SETTLEMENT MAIN OFFICE, the OH-LENDORF TRIAL of the Einsatzgruppen, the KRUPP TRIAL, the WILHELMSTRASSE TRIAL, and

Nuremberg Trials. 1946 poster: "Guilty!"

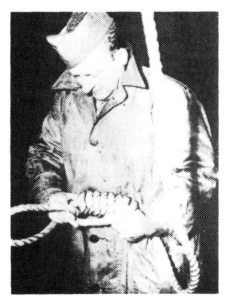

Nuremberg Trials. John C. Wood, the American executioner of the major war criminals.

finally the OKW TRIAL. The last judgment was delivered on April 11, 1949. The death penalty was imposed on 24 defendants; 20 were sentenced to life imprisonment, and 98 to prison terms of between 18 months and 25 years. Acquittal was granted in 35 cases. Of those condemned to death, 12 were executed, 1 was remanded to Belgium (where he died), and 11 received commutations to life imprisonment. With a pardon on January 31, 1951, United States High Commissioner John J. McCloy reduced many sentences.

Parallel to the Nuremberg Trials, many further war crimes trials were conducted before military courts of the occupation powers, pursuant to Control Council Law No. 10. Others were conducted before courts in the countries formerly occupied by the Wehrmacht. All of these proceedings, and especially the Nuremberg Trials, have subsequently been criticized as "victors' [that is, arbitrary] justice," since German jurists were denied participation. In particular, the retroactive introduction of pun-

ishable offenses (such as crimes against peace) and the exclusion of such Allied war crimes as the KATYN massacre have damaged the standing of the Nuremberg Trials. Moreover, they did not serve as the hoped-for model with regard to war crimes committed after the Second World War, especially when superpowers were involved. Nevertheless, the moral value and the historical usefulness of the juridical elaboration achieved through the Nuremberg Trials and later proceedings (*see* LUDWIGSBURG CENTRAL OFFICE) cannot be overestimated.

A. St.

Nutritional Relief Agency (Ernährungshilfswerk; EHW), organization of the NATIONAL SOCIALIST VOLK WELFARE (NSV) agency, created as part of the campaign for AUTARKY. With the motto "Fight Spoilage!" ("Kampf dem Verderb"), it established collection sites for usable leftovers from kitchens and restaurants. These leftovers were to be used for the yearly feeding of up to a million pigs.

Oak Cross (Eichenkreuz), gymnastics association in the German Young Men's Evangelical Associations (Evangelische Jungmännerbünde), consisting of 7,000 groups and 225,000 members in 1933. It sought to attain its educational ideal of "complete Christian manhood" not so much through competitive sports as through communal experiences. When the Evangelical Youth Agency (Evangelisches Jugendwerk) was incorporated into the Hitler Youth (December 20, 1933) by the Reich Bishop, the church abandoned its role in the physical education of youth and dissolved the Oak Cross. The decision was not obeyed everywhere, and only a police prohibition finally closed down the organization, on July 23, 1935.

Oak-Leaf Cluster (*Eichenlaub*), means of increasing the distinction of an award or badge of honor. Beginning in 1870–1871 there was an Oak-Leaf Cluster for the IRON CROSS; in the Second World War, as of June 3, 1940, it was used instead to elevate the KNIGHT'S CROSS by a degree.

Oath (*Eid*), assertion made according to a specific formula before an official authority or a court. On August 20, 1934, a vow of loyalty to the "Führer of the German Reich and of the *Volk*, Adolf Hitler" replaced the Weimar Republic's Constitutional Oath (*Verfassungs-Eid*), by means of the Law concerning the Swearing In of Civil Servants and Soldiers of the Wehrmacht (*Reich Law Gazette* I, p. 785). The vow was intended to reinforce the personal obligation to Hitler. In contrast to the earlier Republican oath, the religious affirmation ("so help me God") could not be omitted. The loyalty oath for public officials was confirmed in Paragraph 4 of the German Civil Service Law of January 26, 1937 (*Reich Law Gazette* I, pp. 41ff.). In accordance with Paragraph 57 of the civil service law, refusal to take the oath was grounds for termination.

Recruit swearing an oath.

For the conspirators of the TWENTIETH OF JULY, 1944, their swearing of the soldier's oath (flag oath) created an obligation to Hitler that constituted a serious moral issue. The only means available of attaining an "oath-free situation" (*eidfreien Zustand*) was to try to kill Hitler. The churches also made an effort at disciplining by the use of an oath, but the 1933 attempt by Reich Bishop Ludwig MÜLLER to introduce a service oath (*Dienst-Eid*) failed, as did a general oath in 1938. Martin Bormann officially distanced himself from the idea, but he made every effort to coerce sect members who declined even to take the accompanying oath when they refused military service for religious reasons. His efforts had little effect. Many JEHOVAH'S WITNESSES, for example, paid for their steadfastness with death in concentration camps or on the gallows.

C. B.

Oberfohren Memorandum (*Oberfohren-Denkschrift*), memorandum concerning the REICHSTAG FIRE of February 27, 1933. It was allegedly written by Ernst Oberfohren (1885–1933), a deputy of the German National People's Party (DNVP). First published in the *Manchester Guardian* on April 27, 1933, the memorandum claimed that the arson plan originated with Joseph Goebbels and had been organized under Hermann Göring's direction by Wolf Heinrich Count von HELLDORF. The "half-crazy" Marinus van der LUBBE was said to have been a tool who was slipped into the parliament building through the underground passage from the palace where Göring's office as Reichstag president was located; he was then made out to be a Communist lackey. The memorandum's theses, presented anew in the BROWN BOOK, could not be verified. They have been regarded as refuted by the research of Fritz Tobias (*Der Reichstagsbrand* [The Reichstag Fire]; 1962) and Hans Mommsen (*Der Reichstagsbrand und die politische Folgen* [The Reichstag Fire and Its Political Consequences]; 1964).

Oberg, Carl Albrecht, b. Hamburg, January 27, 1897; d. June 3, 1965, SS-*Obergruppenführer* (August 1944). After finishing secondary school (he graduated in 1915), Oberg served as a soldier in the First World War; he was discharged as a lieutenant in 1919. He joined a free corps, then held various jobs beginning in 1921.

Carl Albrecht Oberg.

Oberg enrolled in the NSDAP in 1931, and in the SS in 1932. In 1933 he became police chief in Zwickau, and by 1939 he was an SS-*Oberführer*. He was then the SS and Police Leader in Radom (in the Polish Generalgouvernement) from August 4, 1941, to April 5, 1942. Made an SS-*Brigadeführer* in March 1942, he was transferred to France as a Higher SS and Police Leader, remaining there from May 12, 1942, to 1945. After Germany's collapse, Oberg was condemned to death by a French court, but he was eventually pardoned and released in 1962.

A. St.

Obergruppenführer, second-highest rank in the SA and SS (*see* RANKS).

Theodor Oberländer. The federal minister for expellees welcomes refugees in the Friedland reception camp.

Oberland (literally, Upland), a free corps founded in 1919 to combat the Bavarian republic of councils; it was later deployed against revolutionary workers in the Ruhr region and in the defense of Upper Silesia. The OBERLAND LEAGUE grew out of the Oberland free corps in 1921.

Oberländer, Theodor, b. Meiningen, May 1, 1905, German politician. After studies in agronomy and political economy, Oberländer became a professor in Danzig, Königsberg, Greifswald, and then Prague; his main area of specialization was the economy of eastern Europe. He joined the NSDAP in 1933, and from 1939 to 1945 was *Reichsführer* of the LEAGUE FOR THE GERMAN EAST.

After the war, in the Federal Republic, Oberländer was a co-founder and national chairman of the All-German Bloc/League of Persons Expelled from Their Homeland and Deprived of Rights (Gesamtdeutscher Block/Bund der Heimatvertriebenen und Entrechteten). He went over to the Christian Democratic Union (CDU) in 1956. As federal minister for the "expelled" (*see* EXPULSION), he withdrew from office in 1960 in the face of accusations that, as an officer in the German-Ukrainian "Nightingale" unit, he had taken part in shootings of Jews and Poles in the Soviet Union during the autumn of 1941. Preliminary criminal proceedings concerning this were halted by the Public Prosecutor's Office in Bonn. The German Democratic Republic's supreme court, however, sentenced Oberländer in absentia to life imprisonment. The "Oberländer Case" led to vehement public controversies; they flared up anew when he again ran for the Bundestag in 1963.

U. B.

Oberland League (Bund Oberland), (paramilitary) organization with Great-German and *völkisch* goals, founded in 1921. It grew out of a free corps organized in 1919 to combat the Munich republic of councils. The league joined with the NSDAP and the Reich War Flag to form the GERMAN COMBAT LEAGUE on September 2, 1923. It took part in the HITLER PUTSCH, during which four of its members lost their lives. The head of the league, Friedrich Weber, was one of the main defendants in the HITLER TRIAL. Reconstituted in 1925, the Oberland League was incorporated into the NSDAP.

Members of the Oberland League in Munich on November 9, 1923, the day of the Hitler Putsch.

Oberpräsident (governor; literally, high [supreme] president), the administrative head in the Prussian provinces and the representative of Prussia's central government there. A law of December 15, 1933, combined all executive powers in his hands. After the SYNCHRONIZATION of the German states (*Länder*) and the Law concerning the Restructuring of the Reich (second implementation order, November 27, 1934), the *Oberpräsident* became the Reich government's representative in the provinces. To consolidate the unity of party and state, the *Oberpräsident* was in most cases also the NSDAP *Gauleiter* for the same region.

Obersalzberg, mountain ridge northeast of Berchtesgaden, with an altitude of 900 to 1,000 m (about 3,200 feet). Hitler had his BERGHOF built on the Obersalzberg.

Obersturmbannführer, officer rank in the SA and SS (*see* RANKS).

Objectivity (*Objektivität*), the effort to judge a matter or a set of circumstances by screening out subjective and irrelevant influences; the foundation of all scientific research. In the National Socialists' usage, "objectivity" became an outright term of scorn. By citing Friedrich NIETZ-

SCHE, who had mocked objectivity as "the servile groveling before each little fact," they equated it with incompetence. Joseph Goebbels railed against the "fanaticism for objectivity" (*Das Reich*, December 17, 1944); Hitler in *Mein Kampf* remarked on the "craze for objectivity," and taught that "not objectivity, which is weakness, but will and power" would lead to success. This concern over "ruinous" neutrality and factuality applied especially to the administration of justice: Hans FRANK called for the subordination of judicial objectivity to the "interests of the *Volk*" (speech of May 12, 1933).

Obmann (foreman; chairman), National Socialist delegate appointed by the GERMAN LABOR FRONT in places of employment (*see* WORKPLACE FOREMAN).

Occupation policy (*Besatzungspolitik*), the totality of the measures and plans of the German authorities in territories occupied by the Wehrmacht during the Second World War. A consistent occupation policy was created in terms of the economic exploitation of the conquered territories and the persecution of their Jews. Yet even these activities were carried out with regional differences, and they also varied according to the administrator involved (the Wehrmacht, the Reich authorities, the NSDAP, the SS) and with political expediency. Similarly, the subject nations reacted to the German occupation policy in different ways: although resistance movements formed everywhere, only a few achieved the level of activity of the French RÉSISTANCE or of the Soviet and Yugoslav partisans. COLLABORATION also existed in every territory, especially where National Socialist racism and anti-Bolshevism found resonance, as in the Netherlands and Norway; it was least common among the Slavic peoples, which were persecuted as "subhumans."

The sequence according to which the German occupation created victims was as follows:

September 1939. Poland, which was divided between the Soviet Union and Germany, suffered heavy human losses during German rule and sank into misery. The area occupied by Germany was partially annexed (Danzig–West Prussia and the Warthegau) and partially included in the GENERALGOUVERNEMENT. It became the scene for the FINAL SOLUTION in the extermination camps and for radical despoliation through the policy of the *Generalgouverneur,* Hans FRANK.

Obersalzberg. Entrance to Hitler's teahouse.

April–May 1940. Denmark (despite a nonaggression treaty) and *Norway* were treated relatively benignly and did not suffer much from the effects of the war. Because of their comparatively good food supply, they were regarded by the occupation forces as the "butter front."

May–June 1940. Luxembourg was annexed; the *Netherlands* was occupied, as was *Belgium*, which had to cede EUPEN-MALMÉDY. *France* lost ALSACE-LORRAINE, and at first was occupied only as far as the Loire River, with the southern region under the VICHY regime. It was in these western European countries that NS ART PLUNDER was carried out most extensively.

February 1941. Beginning in this month, in *North Africa* only military operations were carried out by the Germans, owing to Italian sovereignty in the area.

April–May 1941. Yugoslavia was occupied and its federation of states was broken up. In *Greece*, numerous war crimes poisoned relations with the occupiers.

June 1941. The *Soviet Union* was the real goal of Hitler's *Lebensraum* policy (*see* LIVING SPACE) and, as the bearer of BOLSHEVISM, was the ruthlessly combated ideological foe of National Socialism. Beginning with the June 22 invasion, the German troops thrust forward to the Leningrad-Moscow-Stalingrad-Caucasus line. The territory behind it was partially annexed (the Białystok district), partially attached to the Generalgouvernement (Galicia), and partially combined into the Reich Commissariats of Ostland (Latvia, Lithuania, Estonia, and western Belorussia) and the Ukraine. The region was subordinate to Alfred ROSENBERG as Reich Minister for the Occupied Territories, and it served Heinrich Himmler and the SS as an experimental proving ground for the occupation goals as established in the GENERAL PLAN FOR THE EAST. The initial enthusiasm for the German "liberators" rapidly yielded to embittered resistance.

November 1942. Vichy France was occupied, in order to forestall an Allied landing.

September 1943. After an Italian–Anglo-American cease-fire was reached, *Italy* was occupied by Germany. Since the Italian troops in southern Europe were disarmed as a result, massacres were perpetrated by the German troops on their former comrades-in-arms; in war-weary Italy this gave rise to a rapidly spreading partisan movement.

In all of the countries affected by the occupation policy, forced laborers were recruited for the German munitions industry (*see* FORCED

Occupation policy. In the east, "ruthless measures" were used against civilians as well. Even the slightest suspicion could mean death.

LABOR). Moreover, prisoners of war were kept in Germany as foreign workers even after an armistice. The VOLUNTEER UNITS were one manifestation of collaboration, especially those of the WAFFEN-SS, which recruited in the western and northern European countries in particular. Without collaboration, the deportation of Jews from the occupied countries could scarcely have been accomplished. It encountered the greatest resistance in Italy and in the countries first occupied by Italy, despite the Fascist anti-Jewish laws. In western and northern Europe it found only scattered support, but it had particular success in the traditionally antisemitic eastern European countries, where numerous Baltic, Ukrainian, and Russian auxiliaries made themselves available.

Occupation Statute (*Besatzungsstatut*) for Germany, statute concluded on May 12, 1949, by the foreign ministers of the western Allies. It was approved and promulgated by the Allied military governors, with the consent of the minister presidents of the West German states. According to the statute, all legislative, executive, and judicial authority was to be transferred to the state organs of the newly emerging Federal

Republic of Germany, with the exception of certain areas for which the occupation powers retained responsibility. The Occupation Statute entered into force on September 21, 1949, thereby dissolving the system of the ALLIED CONTROL COUNCIL, which was replaced by the Allied High Commission.

Occupation zones (*Besatzungszonen*), the four zones occupied, respectively, by French, British, Soviet, and American troops; they were formed after the surrender of the German Reich (May 8, 1945) on the basis of the JUNE DECLARATION of June 5, 1945. In the protocol of the EUROPEAN ADVISORY COMMISSION (EAC) of September 12, 1944, three zones were envisioned; a fourth, the French zone, was first agreed upon at YALTA on February 11, 1945. The zone borders were definitively established in the third Zone Protocol of the EAC (July 26, 1945). It specified that the Soviet zone would comprise the historic German states (*Länder*) of Brandenburg, Mecklenburg, Saxony, Saxony-Anhalt, and Thuringia; the American zone: Bavaria, Hesse, Württemberg-Baden, and (as an exclave) Bremen; the British zone: Schleswig-Holstein, Hamburg, Lower Saxony, and North Rhine–Westphalia; and the French zone: Rhineland-Palatinate, Württemberg-Hohenzollern, and Baden. The occupation zones were formally abrogated by the founding of the Federal Republic of Germany in September 1949 and of the German Democratic Republic in October of that year. In a similar manner, Austria was divided into four occupation zones on July 4, 1945.

Occupied Territories (*Besetzte Gebiete*), parts of Germany located on the left bank of the Rhine River, with bridgeheads on the right bank at Cologne, Koblenz, Mainz, and Kehl. They were occupied by Allied troops on January 10, 1920, in accordance with stipulations of the VERSAILLES TREATY. The areas were to be gradually evacuated by the occupation forces after 5 to 15 years, but if German reparations obligations were not fulfilled they could remain occupied or be reoccupied, as was seen in the RUHR CONFLICT of 1923 to 1925, which extended beyond the actual Occupied Territories. As a rule, the evacuation took place with delays. Complete German sovereignty over the Occupied Territories was achieved only with the RHINELAND OCCUPATION.

Odal, Old German word for the ancestral home of a family; it was also used to refer to one's homeland. Walther DARRÉ wanted to revive

the word, which was used only in scholarly works. Thus, in 1934 he changed the name of his journal *Deutsche Agrarpolitik* (German Agricultural Policy; founded 1932) to *Odal, Monatsschrift für Blut und Boden* (Odal: Monthly for Blood and Soil). The HEREDITARY FARM LAW was to be deliberately based on the Germanic *Odal* law.

Oder-Neisse Line, demarcation line fixed in the POTSDAM AGREEMENT of August 2, 1945 (Chapter IX), between the severed German EASTERN TERRITORIES and the rest of Germany. It was intended to form the western border of Poland until a definitive settlement based on international law could be reached in a peace treaty with Germany. Stalin forced through acceptance of the Oder-Neisse Line with the false claim that the territory east of the Oder River had already been vacated by all the Germans there. The concomitant agreement that the transfer of German segments of the population still remaining in Poland ''should be conducted in an orderly and humane manner'' (Chapter XIII) was repeatedly and grossly violated with the EXPULSION of some 5.6 million Germans in 1945–1946.

The line runs ''from the Baltic Sea immediately west of Swinemünde, and from there along the Oder River up to the mouth of the western (so-called Lusatian) Neisse River, and along the western Neisse up to the Czechoslovak border.'' In the Görlitz Agreement of July 6, 1950, the government of the German Democratic Republic acknowledged the Oder-Neisse Line as the ''inviolable border of peace and friendship,'' without a proviso for a peace treaty.

The governments of the Federal Republic of Germany and of the three Western powers formally maintained their rejection of any border settlement that bypassed a peace treaty, even though leading Western statesmen left scarcely any doubt as to the line's definitive status in international law. Finally, the Federal Republic ratified the inviolability of Poland's existing western border in the German-Soviet Treaty of August 12, 1970 (Article 3), the German-Polish Treaty of December 7, 1970 (Article I), and the 1975 Helsinki Accord, without, however, relinquishing its proviso for a future settlement through a peace treaty negotiated by an all-German government.

B.-J. W.

Oelssner, Fred, b. Leipzig, February 27, 1903; d. East Berlin, November 7, 1977, German politician. Oelssner joined the Communist Party of Germany (KPD) in 1920, and edited various KPD periodicals until 1926. From 1926 to 1932 he studied political economy in Moscow. He emigrated from Germany via Prague to Paris in 1933, and in 1935 went to Moscow. There he directed the Germany Division of the Soviet radio during the war. In 1945 Oelssner returned to Germany and pursued a career in the Socialist Unity Party of Germany (SED); he was a member of the party's executive committee (1947–1958) and of its Politburo (1950–1958). From 1955 to 1958 he was deputy minister president. Although termed the "chief ideologue," Oelssner fell from power because of statements he made criticizing Walter ULBRICHT's policies.

Office "K" (Amt "K"), division in the Reich Ministry for Science, Education, and Public Instruction. Responsible for physical education (*Körperliche Erziehung*), it was headed by Ministerial Director Carl Krümmel. Office "K" developed the guidelines for physical education imposed on schools and universities by the National Socialists. The focus was on "military fitness" (*Wehrhaftmachung*) and the development of the HARDNESS necessary for combat, in which the boundaries between relentlessness and cruelty were deliberately blurred.

Official Party Review Commission for Safeguarding National Socialist Writing (Parteiamtliche Prüfungskommission zum Schutze des NS-Schrifttums; PPK), department established by Rudolf HESS on April 15, 1934, and assigned to his headquarters (and thus to the Reich Leadership of the NSDAP). Its task was to "be on guard . . . lest the National Socialist treasury of ideas be distorted by unauthorized persons and commercially exploited in a way that misleads the general public." The commission's director was Philipp BOUHLER, and his deputy was Karl-heinz HEDERICH. All publications (school and propaganda material, songbooks, guidelines for organizations, and so on) of the NSDAP, its subdivisions, and associated organizations had to be submitted to the commission for examination and release. In addition, publications of other organizations and publishers could be "released as National Socialist in title, in makeup, . . . or in presentation only if they have been submitted to the [PPK] and bear its stamp of unobjectionability." Moreover, the commission had to see to it that the designation "National Socialist" and quotations of NS statesmen were not used misleadingly or "debased." Not least for economic reasons, the commission was

to ensure that all NS publications were issued by the party's central publishing house (*see* EHER PRESS). Finally, it was in charge of compiling all NS printed materials and cataloging them in a bibliography.

H. H.

Ohlendorf, Otto, b. Hoheneggelsen bei Hildesheim, February 4, 1907; d. Landsberg am Lech, June 7, 1951 (executed), SS-*Gruppenführer* (November 1944). Ohlendorf studied law and economics. He joined the NSDAP in 1925 and the SS in 1926. In October 1933 he began work at the Institute for World Economics in Kiel. A consultant to the Security Service (SD) beginning in 1936, he served as the SD director of Section III in the Reich Security Main Office (RSHA) from 1939 to 1945. Although not especially well liked by Heinrich Himmler, Ohlendorf went to Russia in 1941 as chief of Einsatzgruppe D (*see* EINSATZGRUPPEN). By June 1942 he had directed the murders of some 90,000 civilians, mostly Jews.

In the NUREMBERG TRIALS Ohlendorf attached importance to the fact that he had always been strict about ensuring that no "unnecessary agitation" be engendered among the victims, and also had seen to it that the psychological burden on the perpetrators was minimized as much as possible through salvo firing. So that the members of the firing squads, most of them married men, would not have to shoot women and children, such victims were later killed only in GAS VANS. Ohlendorf characterized the extermination of the Jews as historically

Otto Ohlendorf.

necessary, and compared it with America's dropping of the atomic bomb. He was sentenced to death on April 10, 1948, but had to await execution for more than three years.

Ohlendorf Trial (also Einsatzgruppen Trial), proceedings of United States Military Tribunal II in Nuremberg against the former chief of Einsatzgruppe D, Otto OHLENDORF, and 23 other former EINSATZGRUPPEN members on charges of crimes against humanity, war crimes, and membership in criminal organizations (Case 9). The defendants were accused of murdering hundreds of thousands of people on order of the Führer, solely because of their religion, and of murdering an equal number who had been deemed "politically contaminated elements and racially as well as mentally inferior elements." The press characterized the proceedings as the largest murder trial in history. After the indictments were lodged, one defendant committed suicide; during the main trial, the case against the former chief of Einsatzgruppe C, Otto RASCH, was discontinued because of his inability to stand trial. Rasch died on November 1, 1948.

A judgment of April 10, 1948, sentenced Ohlendorf and 13 co-defendants to death by hanging; 2 defendants received sentences of life imprisonment, and 5 received prison terms of 3 to 20 years. One defendant, Matthias Graf, was released, having been sentenced to the time he had already served. The former chief of Einsatzgruppe A, Eduard STRAUCH, already sentenced to death, was remanded to Belgium, where he received another death sentence; he died in prison. Four of the death sentences, including Ohlendorf's, were confirmed. The others were commuted to life imprisonment on January 31, 1951, by United States High Commissioner John J. McCloy, who concurrently reduced all the other penalties.

A. St.

Ohm Krüger, German motion picture (1941) directed by Hans STEINHOFF. Based on the novel *Mann ohne Volk* (Man without a People) by A. Krieger, its stars included Lucie Höflich, Gustaf GRÜNDGENS, Emil JANNINGS, Ferdinand Marian, and Gisela Uhlen. It premiered on April 4, 1941. Rated "politically and artistically especially worthwhile," it was—after KOLBERG—the most expensive movie production during the Third Reich.

Ohm Krüger was an anti-British propaganda film in historical costumes. It narrated the steadfast struggle of the Boer leader "Ohm" (Uncle) Paul Krüger against the brutal British oppressors during the Boer War (1899–1902). Turning "enemy propaganda" around, it denounced English concentration camps (while featuring a commandant who resembled Winston Churchill) and censured the excesses of British troops against civilians. The film owed its success largely to the fine acting of Jannings in the title role, as well as to Gründgens, who went before the camera on the order of Joseph Goebbels. Once the filming was completed, Goebbels used still photos from the movie to intensify the anti-British campaign.

Ohnesorge, Wilhelm, b. Gräfenhainichen bei Bitterfeld, June 8, 1872; d. Munich, February 1, 1962, German politician. After studies in mathematics and physics, Ohnesorge became a postal official, but he also developed inventions relating to the telephone. In 1920 he founded (and led) in Dortmund the first NSDAP local group outside Bavaria. From 1924 to 1929 he held an

Emil Jannings and Lucie Höflich in *Ohm Krüger*.

OKW Trial. Defendants' bench in Nuremberg.

administrative position at Berlin's General Post Office. He became director of the Central Office of the Reich Postal System (Reichspost) in 1929. Ohnesorge subsequently became state secretary in the Postal Ministry (March 1, 1933) and Reichspost minister (February 2, 1937). He unsuccessfully advocated the building of a German ATOMIC BOMB. Arrested at the war's end, he was classified as a major offender in 1948.

Ohrdruf, labor camp established in January 1945 near BUCHENWALD; it held mainly Jews evacuated from the east. Along with Polish and Russian prisoners of war, they were made to work there on an underground headquarters for the Wehrmacht; about 4,000 camp inmates lost their lives during the project. On April 3, 1945, the eve of liberation by American troops, a large number of the prisoners were made to march toward Dachau by way of Plauen. Hundreds of the exhausted prisoners were shot. The Americans, accompanied by their commander in chief, Dwight D. EISENHOWER, were confronted in Ohrdruf for the first time with the entire extent of concentration camp terror. Photographs of the mounds of emaciated corpses went out through the world press, and a British parliamentary group came to inspect Ohrdruf.

OKH. *See* Army High Command.

OKW. *See* Wehrmacht High Command.

OKW Trial, proceedings before United States Military Tribunal V in Nuremberg against Gen. Field Marshal Wilhelm LEEB and 13 other generals or Wehrmacht officers holding the rank of general (Case 12). The defendants were charged with crimes against peace, crimes against humanity, and war crimes. The accusations involved mainly the planning and executing of wars of aggression; the formulation, distribution, and implementation of orders contrary to international law (as the COMMISSAR ORDER); the committing of crimes injurious to prisoners of war and civilians; and the plundering and wanton destruction of cities and villages. Prior to the start of the main trial, the defendant Johannes BLASKOWITZ took his own life, on February 5, 1948.

The court, while acquitting the defendants of the charge of having planned wars of aggression, as well as of some other charges, on October 28, 1948, after eight months of deliberation, sentenced 2 defendants to life imprisonment and 9 to prison terms ranging from 3 to 20 years. Two of the defendants were acquitted. Leeb, who had been found guilty on only one count (transmitting and implementing the BARBAROSSA JURISDICTIONAL DECREE) and who had spent three years in jail, was released in consideration of his pretrial detention. On January 31, 1951, United States High Commissioner John J. McCloy out of clemency reduced the sentences of some of those convicted. By the mid-1950s, all those found guilty had been set free.

Olbricht, Friedrich, b. Leisnig (Saxony), October 4, 1888; d. Berlin, July 20, 1944 (executed), German infantry general (June 1, 1940). In the First World War Olbricht served as a General Staff officer. From 1926 to 1931, he was in the Foreign Armies department of the Armed Forces Ministry. Subsequently he held troop commands

Friedrich Olbricht.

until February 15, 1940, when he became chief of the General Army Office in the Army High Command (OKH). In contact with military opposition circles around Ludwig BECK as early as 1937, Olbricht became the technical organizer of the planned coup. He developed the "VALKYRIE" scheme, under cover of which the NSDAP, SS, and National Socialist government leaders were to be removed from power after Hitler was eliminated. Following several failed attempts, "Valkyrie" was set into motion on the TWENTIETH OF JULY, 1944; however, it was delayed by

mixed signals, and as a result Olbricht could not make up for the lost time. He also tried unsuccessfully to bring the commander of the Reserve Army, Friedrich FROMM, to the side of the opposition fighters, then had him arrested. When the news of Hitler's survival leaked out, Fromm was freed. He in turn had Olbricht and Stauffenberg, among other conspirators, arrested and summarily shot on the evening of the same day as the assassination attempt.

Old Combatants (*Alte Kämpfer*), general term for all members of the NSDAP, the SA, or the SS who had joined the party before January 30, 1933. Thus, it referred to "party comrades" with any membership number under 300,000, as well as to party functionaries (*see* AMTSWALTER) who as of October 1, 1933, had held their post for more than a year. After the SEIZURE OF POWER, many Old Combatants felt that they had been shunted aside and deprived of the fruits of their labors. The call for a SECOND REVOLUTION found many sympathizers among them.

Old Guard (*Alte Garde*), term for the earliest members of the NSDAP (those with membership numbers under 100,000). The Old Guard included all those awarded the BLOOD ORDER and the Golden Badge of Honor of the NSDAP. November 9 was the "Day of the Old Guard."

Old Reich (Altreich), designation for the territory of the German state prior to the ANSCHLUSS with Austria in 1938, as distinguished from the

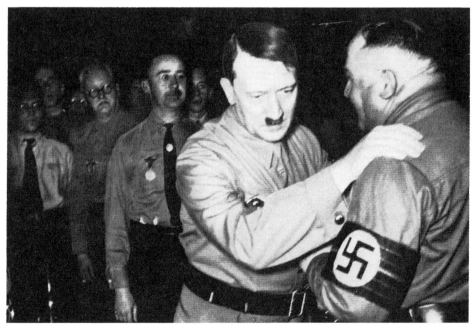

Old Guard. Hitler greets "blood witnesses of the movement" on the Day of the Old Guard.

newly won territories of the GREAT-GERMAN REICH, such as the Sudetenland, Memel, Danzig–West Prussia, and Eupen-Malmédy.

Ollenhauer, Erich, b. Magdeburg, March 27, 1901; d. Bonn, December 14, 1963, German politician. In 1918 Ollenhauer joined the Social Democratic Party (SPD). He became secretary of the Socialist Youth International in 1921, and in April 1933 he was elected to the SPD executive committee. Ollenhauer went to Prague in May 1933 as a member of the SPD's exile leadership. In 1938 he fled to France; after a brief period of detention there in 1940, he went by way of Spain and Portugal to London. Materially supported by the Labour party, he organized emigrants into the Union of German Socialist Organizations in Great Britain, and served as the union's chairman. He refused to cooperate with exiled Communist politicians.

In 1946 Ollenhauer was able to return to Germany, where he served as deputy chairman of the SPD. After Kurt SCHUMACHER's death in 1952, he became chairman and also opposition leader in the Bundestag. He unsuccessfully opposed Konrad ADENAUER's policies of integration with the West and of rearmament. Ollenhauer led the SPD on the road to becoming a people's party (for example, through the Godesberg Program of 1959). In 1961, clearly perceiving his own limited ability to attract voters, he opened the way for Willy Brandt.

Olympic Games (*Olympische Spiele*), the greatest sports event of the Third Reich. In 1936 the Winter Games were held in Garmisch-Partenkir-

Erich Ollenhauer.

Olympic Games. Hitler as a visitor at the Winter Games in Garmisch-Partenkirchen.

chen, with the participation of 756 athletes from 28 countries (February 6–16). The Summer Games took place in Berlin, with 4,069 athletes from 49 countries (August 1–16). The 1916 games had been awarded to Germany, but they were canceled because of the outbreak of war; in 1931 the International Olympic Committee (IOC), meeting in Barcelona, reassigned them to Germany. The games were at first jeopardized by Hitler's Seizure of Power, since to National Socialism the internationalism of the Olympics was suspect, competition with former "enemy powers" was odious, and the participation of Jews and Negroes was undesirable. However, as chancellor, Hitler placed the diplomatic benefits and the possibilities for propagandistic self-display of the Third Reich higher than any ideological reservations. In June 1933 he informed the IOC that Germany would adhere strictly to the Olympic rules and would even allow Jews to compete. At an inspection of the planned Olympic Field on October 5, 1933, he ordered construction of a monumental REICH SPORTS FIELD.

The National Socialist racial policies, however, increasingly invalidated the assertions made for the benefit of the IOC. After passage of the NUREMBERG LAWS (September 15, 1935), a widespread boycott movement developed, especially in the United States, the preeminent sports power. However, through small

1
The dirigible *Hindenburg* over the Reich Sports Field
on the opening day of the 1936 Olympic Games in Berlin.
2
Cover of a special Olympics edition of the *Berliner
Illustrirte Zeitung.*
3–4
The official Olympics posters for Garmisch-Partenkirchen
and Berlin.
5
Austrian poster for the Oympics Fund.

concessions—the acceptance in the German contingent of the half-Jewish fencer Helene MAYER and of the Jewish ice-hockey player Rudi Ball—and with the help of the IOC and of Avery Brundage, the chairman of the United States National Olympic Committee, a boycott was averted. For the duration of the games, anti-Jewish measures were postponed, slogans were removed, and even reportage on the victories of Negro athletes (such as the four gold medals won by the American sprinter Jesse Owens) was positive. This turnabout was easier since the German athletes experienced an unanticipated wave of victories. With 33 gold, 36 silver, and 30 bronze medals, their successes in the Summer Games placed them above the United States, Hungary, and Italy. Hitler, as patron of the games, appeared at the stadium almost daily and showed himself to be an exceedingly popular statesman, to judge from the acclaim of the spectators. The propaganda risk paid off domestically and, within limits, internationally as well, especially since Leni RIEFENSTAHL glowingly preserved the splendor of those days in Berlin with her brilliant and internationally acclaimed film on the Olympic Games.

Olympic Stadium (Olympiastadion), center of the REICH SPORTS FIELD. Completed in 1936, it had 63,500 seats and standing room for 33,500. It was the showplace of the OLYMPIC GAMES.

Olympic Stadium in Berlin.

One-Dish Sunday (*Eintopfsonntag; Eintopf,* literally "one pot," refers to a main dish, such as a stew, that is cooked in a pot), custom introduced in 1933 to promote the idea of a *völkisch* community in the sense of a "socialism of the deed" (*Sozialismus der Tat*). On designated Sundays all Germans were to eat only a stew (*Eintopfgericht*) and to contribute the difference between its cost and that of a regular Sunday dinner to the WINTER RELIEF AGENCY. Leading representatives of the Third Reich tried to capitalize on the folksiness (*Volkstümlichkeit*) of this dish through pub-

One-Dish Sunday. Propaganda photo with Goebbels and Hitler.

licly staged meals and to use it in propaganda as a symbol: in Joseph Goebbels's words (November 7, 1933), "National Socialism is good plain German food, an *Eintopfgericht*" ("National-Sozialismus ist eine gute deutsche Hausmanns-kost, ein Eintopfgericht").

One-price stores (*Einheitspreisgeschäfte*), retail establishments (mostly department stores) that sold commonly used items at uniformly low prices. As early as the period of the Weimar Republic, such stores, many of them owned by Jews, were the object of antisemitic attacks. In 1927 the National Socialists organized a boycott of them on the ground that they were a manifestation of an "insatiable Jewish lust for power." On March 9, 1932, the establishment of one-price stores in large cities was prohibited; this was extended throughout Germany on December 23. The Hitler government on May 12, 1933, declared the ban valid with no time limit, thus fulfilling a promise made to the middle-class retailers (*see* MITTELSTAND), who sought to combat the threat to their specialized stores by the one-price stores. The existing one-price stores and department stores were later "Aryanized" (*see* ARYANIZATION).

Opera Nazionale Dopolavoro. *See* Dopolavoro.

Operation Reinhard. *See* Reinhard Operation.

Opferring (ring of sacrifice), term used from 1924 to 1929 for the group of NSDAP members who paid more than the requested monthly dues.

Opinion, freedom of. *See* Freedom of opinion.

Oppenhoff, Franz, b. Aachen, August 18, 1902; d. there, March 25, 1945, German municipal politician. An attorney, Oppenhoff undertook to defend, among others, clergymen whom the Gestapo had charged with abuse of the pulpit, as well as members of religious orders who were defendants in the PRIEST TRIALS. When American troops occupied Aachen as their first large German city at the end of August 1944, the local bishop recommended Oppenhoff as city administrator. On October 31 of that year Oppenhoff began his service in the severely devastated city, which had long been in the battle zone. He had taken only the first small steps toward reconstruction when he was murdered by a WERE-WOLF commando.

Opposition

Opposition (*Widerstand*; from *widerstehen*, to oppose or resist [literally, "to stand against"]) to National Socialism included a broad spectrum of motives, forms, and goals. It could arise from a conscious decision, but also unintentionally, as when an individual or group withdrew from the prescribed "*Volk* Community." The National Socialist (NS) regime was no more tolerant of opposition to partial aspects of its rule than it was of withdrawal into a sphere of life that excluded party or state. Thus, the consolidation and radicalization of NS rule brought a change in the grounds for conflict that the regime judged as forming opposition. The broad definition of "opposition" enforced by the National Socialists encompassed those persons who did not grasp that their acts constituted opposition. It extended from mere expressions of dissatisfaction, which nevertheless were severely punished, to outspoken rejection and criticism of partial aspects of NS policy, all the way to political struggle aiming to overthrow the regime. The form of resistance (*Resistenz*), from nonconformity to active opposition, that was possible for a person did not depend solely on his or her individual decision.

In envisioning the possibility of resistance and the form it could assume, it was of central importance whether one belonged to some group that could assert itself as an institution. Anyone who by occupation belonged to the ruling apparatus, such as an officer or a civil servant, could develop forms of opposition different from those that were conceivable for someone far from the centers of power. Catholics or Protestants could withdraw into their church organizations and there exercise a form of refusal by participation in processions or by especially active church attendance. Such behavior too was viewed as opposition by the authorities, even if directed not against the regime itself but against its antichurch policy. Communists, socialists, and trade unionists of necessity practiced other forms of opposition: because their organizations were destroyed, they had to function illegally.

On Berlin's Prinz-Albrecht-Strasse, suspects are brought to Gestapo headquarters.

Persons who did not inhabit the protective spaces afforded by such institutions as the military and the established churches, or who could not find a place at least in some informal community of those with similar views, were particularly vulnerable to the regime and its grasp. This was so with the Jews and the JEHOVAH'S WITNESSES. It was also the case with the group of NS enemies known as ASOCIALS, whose definition was extended ever more broadly by the regime, and who were exposed to the terrorist grip of state power: the Sinti and Rom (GYPSIES), homosexuals (*see* HOMOSEXUALITY), and the so-called WORK-SHY. Moreover, these groups stood so far from the opponents of National Socialism that only exceptionally could they count on solidarity. The rule here was not assistance but indifference, so that state terror against such persons evoked no opposition, which was not the case with EUTHANASIA.

The history of the establishment of NS power was not least a history of its underestimation by others. This incorrect assessment initially determined the position of nearly all groups from which opposition developed during the period of NS rule. The abandonment or at least the revision of this original misperception had much to do with the emergence of and changes in opposition and its forms in German society after 1933.

The Communist Party (KPD) leadership initially viewed NS rule totally unrealistically, as a stage on the road to the proletarian revolution. From a position of illegality, the party at first continued its old policy of mass public agitation. As a result, the Communists offered the earliest and most extensive opposition, but they also suffered enormous losses. Of the approximately 300,000 members in 1932, some 150,000 are believed to have been arrested by 1945. A more realistic course was first taken in 1935, when the consolidation of the NS regime was finally acknowledged. New organizational structures for the German opposition groups and for the KPD's exiled leadership were to adapt Communist opposition more successfully to the circumstances of NS rule. This method of distancing from all former models lessened the risks, but it also decreased the possibilities for oppositional agitation.

Hitlerite Germany's attack on the Soviet Union again stimulated Communist opposition. Several large opposition circles arose, working independently of the party in exile. Many of their members paid for their opposition with their lives. Controversy has long surrounded evaluation of the Schulze-Boysen and Harnack groups (*see* RED ORCHESTRA), which combined opposition with espionage for the Soviet Union. Recent studies have recognized, however, that "high treason" against one's country can also be a form of opposition against a totalitarian regime. This was as true of the Communist opposition as it was of the military opposition (*see* Hans OSTER).

The Social Democrats (SPD) and trade unionists also initially misjudged the NS regime. They expected something like the situation under the imperial antisocialist legislation (1878–1890). This and their loyalty to the constitution made it more difficult for them to adjust to opposition from a position of illegality. The path to illegality was, moreover, accompanied by controversies, which constituted one of the reasons why neither in exile nor in Germany did a united opposition of Social Democrats and trade unionists arise. The SPD's exiled leadership concentrated on disseminating information and smuggling reports out of Germany for use abroad. Information flowed back into Germany in the form of brochures, flyers, and magazines (such as *Sozialistische Aktion*). Social Democratic opposition groups have thus far been documented in some 40

Satire in an illegal Communist periodical of 1935: "German ersatz materials. Substitute for freedom. Substitute for the right to organize and to strike. Substitute for public opinion."

German cities. Aside from distributing anti-NS propaganda supported by exiles abroad, their primary goal was to work toward the collapse of the regime.

The trade union leaders, whose ability to act was severely impeded in 1933 by the high unemployment rate, had initially hoped to maintain their organizations in the NS state. This illusion was destroyed when, on May 2, 1933, the National Socialists stormed the trade unions' headquarters and arrested many union leaders. The trade union opposition that then formed expressed itself in many spheres. In the workplaces, the majority of workers refused to give the regime their approval in the elections for workplace delegates of 1933, 1934, and 1935. No further elections were held. Other forms of workplace rejection were difficult to carry out. Under the conditions of the NS dictatorship, strikes were possible only to a limited extent. There were, however, covert forms of labor resistance, from loafing on the job to sabotage or forbidden aid to alien and forced workers. Former union functionaries organized opposition circles on the level of the destroyed individual associations and beyond. An illegal Reich directorate arose that continued earlier attempts to overcome the division of union members into three union networks with different orientations (Social Democratic [or free], Christian, and liberal Hirsch-Duncker) through a united union. In the realistic awareness that they alone could not undermine the regime, trade unionists such as Wilhelm LEUSCHNER and Jakob KAISER, along with Social Democrats, finally made contact with opposition groups from the power elite and took part in preparations for the TWENTIETH OF JULY, 1944. The failure to overthrow the tyrant cost many of them their lives.

Besides the large workers' organizations, small groups offered opposition from the outset. Among them were the Socialist Workers' Party of Germany (SAP), the International Socialist Combat League (ISK), the NEW BEGINNINGS and POPULAR FRONT, and the COMMUNIST PARTY OPPOSITION (KPO). All these groups faced the dilemma that, in the absence of other possibilities for action, they could combat the National Socialists only with propaganda, a tactic that entailed high losses. Or they could retreat into small groups shielded from the outside world, which would limit opposition to self-preservation and preparation for the rebuilding of Germany after the end of the dictatorship.

The Evangelical and Catholic churches in 1933 were also caught in the illusion that they

Kundmachung.

Die am 31. Juli 1942 vom Volksgerichtshof
wegen Vorbereitung zum Hochverrat zum Tode und
zum dauernden Verlust der bürgerlichen Ehrenrechte
verurteilten

Albin Kaiser,

47 Jahre alt, aus Voitsberg,

Johann Jandl,

39 Jahre alt, aus Tregist,

Karl Kilzer,

56 Jahre alt, aus Graz,

sind heute hingerichtet worden.

Berlin, den 30. September 1942.

**Der Oberreichsanwalt
beim Volksgerichtshof.**

Announcement of three death sentences carried out against Austrian opposition fighters.

could maintain or even improve their position in state and society. Parallel to the political synchronization, the SYNCHRONIZATION of the Evangelical Church began in 1933. The partly coerced and partly voluntary Nazification of the Evangelical Church, which included acceptance of the so-called ARYAN PARAGRAPH, gave rise to an internal opposition within the church, which coalesced as the CONFESSING CHURCH. It did not want to conduct political opposition; rather, it claimed a role as guardian, in order to delimit the totalitarian penetration of society. Such a stance nonetheless led to constant conflicts with the state (*see* CHURCH STRUGGLE). Thus, in 1936 this determined wing protested in a memorandum against central tenets of NS ideology (notably, racial doctrine and antisemitism), against the Führer cult and the manipulation of the 1936 Reichstag elections, against acts of injustice committed by the Gestapo, and against the continued existence of the concentration camps. This fundamental ecclesiastical opposition, which extended into the political realm, was, however, shared by only a minority of the Confessing Church's members. Within Protestantism, church opposition meant above all a struggle against the ousting of Christianity from public life, and a religiously based protest against disrespect for human rights. The attempts of Evangelical Church circles to limit NS rule did not, however, sever their loyalty to NS authority, which during the war was strengthened even more. Nonetheless, such ef-

forts were interpreted by the wielders of power as opposition, and were prosecuted accordingly. Evangelical Church groups were not in the forefront of deliberate political opposition, but numerous Evangelical Christians, either as individuals or in opposition groups such as the KREISAU CIRCLE or the FREIBURG CIRCLE, engaged in opposition out of Christian conviction.

The Catholic church seemed to be protected as an institution through the Reich CONCORDAT of July 20, 1933, after the Center party had been abandoned and the Fulda Bishops' Conference had revised its negative position on National Socialism. But the Church Struggle, which began as early as 1933, provoked a church opposition. It was concerned with upholding institutional autonomy and, beyond this, with defending church values. The encyclical MIT BRENNENDER SORGE of 1937 marked an initial high point of this policy of self-preservation, which the Catholic church carried out in a more unified and effective manner than did the Evangelical Church. Yet the Catholic church as well combined its battle for self-preservation with continuing loyalty toward the regime. Within the circle of church leaders, two tendencies opposed one another, unnoticed by the public. Cardinal Adolf BERTRAM was an exponent of the policy of negotiations that prevailed, whereas Cardinal Konrad von PREYSING supported a policy of public protest. Hitler's unleashing of the war did not change the attitude of the Catholic hierarchy, but the radicalization of NS terror that took place during the war did. Episcopal pastoral letters protested publicly, sometimes with success, against the disdain shown for elementary human rights. Thus, Cardinal Clemens von GALEN's famous sermons of 1941 contributed to halting the murder of the mentally ill.

Neither church viewed its struggle for self-preservation and for the defense of Christian values as political opposition, and neither went so far as to renounce, as a matter of principle, obedience to a criminal authority. Yet through their partial opposition they set up a barrier to ideological synchronization that the National Socialists were not able to breach. This may have made it easier for individuals such as Dietrich BONHOEFFER, Alfred DELP, and members of the Catholic workers' movement to join political opposition circles.

The opposition that grew out of the traditional power elites of the military and the upper bureaucracy took for granted a fundamental dissociation from their original expectations. They had, after all, hoped to realize their traditional domestic, foreign-policy, and military-policy goals in league with the National Socialists. The FRITSCH CRISIS in early 1938 had produced a still limited military opposition, and during the Sudeten crisis later that year an antiwar group formed for the first time. In the military it included such figures as the General Staff chief, Ludwig BECK; his successor, Franz HALDER; and the Abwehr chief, Wilhelm CANARIS. Participants from diplomatic circles included State Secretary Ernst Baron von WEIZSÄCKER. But with the MUNICH AGREEMENT, the plans of this group, which extended to a coup, came to nothing. During the war, the nationalist-conservative opposition circles expanded as the growing civilian opposition joined them. But the rapid victories of the German troops weakened the opposition's chances for action. The prestige accruing to the Hitler regime from the lightning victories contributed to this, as did the increase in Germany's great-power status, which even many opposition figures welcomed.

Beginning in early 1942, the resolution of the military opposition to actively resist grew. The group increased and renewed itself politically and also socially, especially when it established contact with the Kreisau Circle, which included Prussian nobles, Catholic and Evangelical clergy, civil servants, Social Democrats, and trade unionists. The Kreisau members drafted plans that sought a renewal of Germany and that became more and more distant from traditional models of the power elites. The ability of the military opposition to act was increased in 1943, when the conspiratorial contacts were extended further in military leadership circles. Moreover, as promoted by Henning von TRESCKOW and Claus Count Schenk von STAUFFENBERG, the conspiracy became infused with the fundamentally ethical conviction that even without a foreign-policy safeguard, the death of the dictator must create the precondition for a revolution.

After several earlier assassination attempts had failed, on July 20, 1944, Stauffenberg's attempt to kill Hitler by means of a bomb fell through. It had been intended to open the way to ending the NS reign of terror with the aid of the Wehrmacht. Thus, within a few years, the nationalist-conservative opposition circles had completed an evolution leading from cooperation with the National Socialists to partial opposition from within the system, to unconditional opposition.

Rebellion of Conscience. Traveling exhibition on the German opposition.

Other forms of opposition arose in other sectors of society. Thus, young people withdrew from the "*Volk* Community" in a variety of ways, ranging from manifesting provocative, nonconformist behavior and sometimes engaging in violent protests, as in the case of the EDELWEISS PIRATES, to organized and informal cooperation among groups hostile to National Socialism (such as church youth and worker and youth circles), to the opposition of the WHITE ROSE. Concentration camp prisoners developed types of opposition, sometimes organized, which helped them to survive the camps. In the final phase of NS rule there were isolated cases of open revolt.

The great extent to which the form of opposition depended on particular circumstances is illustrated by the example of the Jews. There could not be a collective, specifically Jewish opposition, since a homogeneous Jewry existed only in the NS image of the Jew as the enemy. But Jews participated in the entire spectrum between opposition and refusal; they were rep-resented in the various opposition groups according to their political outlook; they carried out opposition in concentration camps, in ghettos, and in the European resistance. Their life in the underground, EMIGRATION, and even suicide—by which 4 percent of the Jews in Berlin avoided government-ordered murder—all were means of self-preservation through refusal.

Thus, there was no united German opposition, but rather a broad and graduated spectrum of conduct, from refusal to active opposition. The continuation of the NS regime was not endangered by it. To this extent, the opposition was in vain. Yet it did help limit the ideological synchronization of the population, and the remembrance of it after 1945 contributed to the establishment of political and moral values that National Socialism had destroyed, aided by many who later, and only through an arduous process, found their way to opposition.

Dieter Langewiesche

Oradour-sur-Glane, French village situated northwest of Limoges, in Limousin. On June 10, 1944, the Third Company of the First Battalion of the "Der Führer" Regiment of the "Das Reich" Second SS Armored Division marched into Oradour-sur-Glane and rounded up all its inhabitants. While the men were being shot in houses and barns, the German soldiers locked 500 women and children in the church and set fire to it, as well as to all the other buildings in the village. Only 36 people survived the massacre; 642 lost their lives either in the fire or in the hail of bullets. Oradour-sur-Glane was officially described as a "retaliatory measure" (*Vergeltungsmassnahme*), since the Second Division, on the march from Toulouse toward the invasion front, had undergone heavy losses through partisan activity. Hitler prevented a judicial inquiry, which in any case would have been impossible owing to the rapid advance of the Allies and the annihilation of the Third Company.

Not until 1953 did 21 former members of the SS unit have to face a military tribunal in Bordeaux. In accordance with the specially formulated Law of Oradour-sur-Glane, which provided that membership in a unit involved in war crimes sufficed for a conviction, the court issued two death sentences, 18 prison terms, and one acquittal; an amnesty immediately mitigated the penalties. In 1983 Heinz Barth, a former pla-

Oradour-sur-Glane after the destruction.

toon leader in the Third Company, was sentenced to life imprisonment in East Berlin. The ruins of Oradour-sur-Glane were left standing as a memorial, and the village was rebuilt nearby.

Oranienburg, concentration camp in the Prussian province of Brandenburg. Established in March 1933, the camp housed political prisoners (Communists, Socialists, trade unionists, and other opponents of the National Socialist regime) who had been sent there as so-called protective-custody prisoners on the basis of the REICHSTAG FIRE DECREE. They were put to work

Oranienburg concentration camp.

on excavation projects in Oranienburg and its environs, as well as on road building and forestry. In June 1934 the Security Service (SA) camp guards were replaced by SS men. Abuse of prisoners (especially under interrogation), sometimes with lethal results, was not uncommon. Oranienburg was closed down in March 1935.

W. D.

Camp money from Oranienburg.

Order Fortresses (Ordensburgen; NS-Ordensburgen), three large facilities financed by the GERMAN LABOR FRONT (DAF) in Sonthofen/Allgäu, at Crössinsee/Pomerania, and at "Vogelsang" (literally, "birdsong"), in the northern Eifel Mountains. They were prestigious institutions, founded by Robert LEY and intended to provide three and a half years of training for *Ordensjunker* ("order nobles"), as a new generation of functionaries for the NSDAP, the DAF, the NATIONAL SOCIALIST VOLK WELFARE, and municipal administrations. Only one two-year course was actually given, from 1937 to 1939. The very heterogeneous "fortress men" (*Burg-*

mannschaft) benefited from a well-rounded physical education and a privileged life-style, along with the usual drill. The political schooling was less concrete, but was meant to strengthen the elite consciousness.

During the war the fortresses served various functions, especially as accommodations for the ADOLF HITLER SCHOOLS. The NSDAP financial administration took over the fortresses only in 1941. In 1943 they added to their original objectives the retraining of the war-disabled. A "training course for the selection of the National Socialist leadership" (in Ley's words), which was to be followed by the NSDAP "college" (HOHE SCHULE DER NSDAP), remained a fiction. Alfred Rosenberg wanted to establish the "college" independently of the fortresses. The Or-

The Order Fortress at Sonthofen.

der Fortresses were intended to attain the prestige of an order for the NSDAP (*see* ORDERS), but in this regard the SS was more successful (*see* JUNKER SCHOOLS).

H. S.

Order-keeping Police (Ordnungspolizei; Orpo), the restructured POLICE under Heinrich Himmler as *Reichsführer-SS* and chief of the German Police (RFSSuChdDtPol), beginning in 1936. The Orpo encompassed all the uniformed police in the cities (Schutzpolizei [protective police]) and in the rural areas (Landespolizei [regional police] and Gendarmerie), as well as various forces of the nonuniformed administrative police (such as building-inspection authorities and health inspectors). In 1940, fire inspectors were incorporated into the overall police.

W. R.

Orders (*Orden*), associations whose members live together under common rules and who have goals or tasks in common, religious communities in particular. Hitler's admiration for the Catholic church with its distinct leadership principle (*see* FÜHRER PRINCIPLE) applied especially to religious orders, whose strict organization and orientation toward community goals corresponded to the National Socialist ideals. Orders whose structure was particularly military, such as the JESUITS or the medieval Teutonic Knights (on whose easterly expansion the LIVING SPACE policy was based), served as models for the organization of the SS "as a soldierly National Socialist order of men of Nordic type" (speech by Heinrich Himmler, November 12, 1935). The SS was to become the germ cell of an NS "state of orders" (*Ordenstaat*), which would revive the Germanic communal mentality and thus enable the *Volk* to develop its highest potential. The concept of dedication and the idea of an order as a sworn community underlay terms such as ORDER FORTRESSES (*Ordensburgen*).

Ordnungspolizei. *See* Order-keeping Police.

Orff, Carl, b. Munich, July 10, 1895; d. there, March 29, 1982, German composer. From 1915 to 1920, Orff was music director in Munich, Mannheim, and Darmstadt. In 1925 he helped found the Günther School for Gymnastics, Music, and Dance in Munich, and from 1932 to 1934 he was director of the Munich Bach Society. Orff worked for the revival of old (folk) musical forms and for the integration of speech and movement in musical events. This brought

him a commission for the 1936 summer OLYMPIC GAMES in Berlin; for the opening ceremonies he wrote "Olympische Reigen" (Olympic Roundelay). Otherwise Orff stayed aloof from National Socialist cultural activity. To be sure, his *Carmina Burana* (1937) won praise, and even more so, his fairy-tale play *Der Mond* (The Moon; 1939), based on the tales of the Grimm brothers, and *Die Kluge* (The Clever Woman; 1943), which was lauded for "overcoming the opera crisis." Nonetheless, the official critics were disturbed by Orff's preference for Latin texts and Italian composers (especially Monteverdi). From 1950 to 1960, Orff was a professor at the Munich Academy of Music; beginning in 1961 he directed the Orff Institute at the Salzburg Mozarteum. His reformist ideas on music pedagogy are set forth in his multivolume *Orff-Schulwerk* (Orff Lessons, 1930–1935; revised edition, 1950–1954).

Organic (*organisch*), National Socialist catchword denoting that which grows in accord with nature, in contrast to that which is constructed in an intellectualistic manner. Thus, a philosophy was identified as "organic" when, in Alfred Rosenberg's words, it rejected the "tyranny of delusions of reason" (*Tyrannei der Verstandesschemen*). Truth was said to be "organic" when it "refer[red] to a specific racial-*völkisch* way of life."

Organisation Todt. *See* Todt Organization.

Organization of the Industrial Economy (Organisation der gewerblichen Wirtschaft), restructuring instituted on February 27, 1934, by the Law to Prepare for the Organizational Reconstruction of the German Economy, which divided the commercial economy into seven Reich groups: industry, crafts, trade, banking, insurance, energy, and tourism. Membership in a Reich group was obligatory for anyone engaged in business, as was membership in regional industry and trade associations or guilds. The Reich Commerce Chamber (Reichswirtschaftskammer) served as an umbrella organization for the regional organizations and the seven Reich groups. Thus, in terms of both region and economic sector, state functionaries concerned themselves with the planned direction of the economy and were able to carry out instructions from the Reich Commerce Ministry.

Ossietzky, Carl von, b. Hamburg, October 3, 1889; d. Berlin, May 4, 1938, German journalist. Originally an employee in Hamburg's municipal administration, Ossietzky in 1911 became a

Carl von Ossietzky as concentration camp prisoner no. 562.

staff member at the weekly newspaper *Das freie Volk* (The Free People). During the First World War he served as an infantryman. After the war he was secretary of the German Peace Society (1919–1920), and as a pacifist participated in the "No More War" movement. Professionally, he was editor of the *Berliner Volks-Zeitung* (Berlin People's News; 1920–1922) and of the periodical *Das Tagebuch* (The Daily Journal; 1924–1926). Beginning in 1927 Ossietzky, in collaboration with Kurt TUCHOLSKY, published the magazine *Die* WELTBÜHNE (The World Stage), and was its editor in chief until 1933.

As early as the Weimar period, in the so-called *Weltbühne* Trial (1931), Ossietzky was sentenced to 18 months' imprisonment for "high treason and betrayal of military secrets" in an article he wrote that exposed the secret rearmament of the Reichswehr. Arrested again by the Gestapo after the REICHSTAG FIRE, he was tortured and incarcerated, first in the Sonnenburg concentration camp and then at the camp in Papenburg-Esterwegen. The National Socialists burned his writings and, on March 13, 1933, banned *Die Weltbühne* (its last issue was that of March 7). In November 1936, Ossietzky was awarded the Nobel Peace Prize for 1935, but the National Socialists forbade him to accept it.

Calling the award "a disgraceful event," they instituted the NATIONAL PRIZE FOR ART AND SCIENCE as a substitute for the Nobel prizes. Ill with tuberculosis, Ossietzky died in a Berlin hospital as a result of his camp internment.

Ostara, series of pamphlets by the racial ideologue Josef LANZ(-Liebenfels), with the subtitle "Briefbücherei der Blonden und Mannesrechtler" (Library for Blonds and Advocates of Male Rights). Published in some 100 issues between 1905 and 1918, it was published again from 1927 to 1930, and was continued in 1933 as the Hertesburger Flugschriften (Hertesburg Pamphlets) and the Luzerner Briefen (Lucerne Letters). The Ostara pamphlets propagated the "planned linebreeding" (*planmässige Reinzucht*) of a "heroic noble race" of "blue-blond" men and women, who were to take up the struggle against the "inferior race" of "Sodom's apes," enslave them, and finally drive them out. Hitler was closely familiar with the series, and even visited the publisher in 1909, since he lacked some issues. The influence of Ostara on HITLER'S WORLDVIEW is, however, difficult to evaluate.

Ostarbeiter. *See* Alien workers; Eastern workers.

Oster, Hans, b. Dresden, August 9, 1888; d. Flossenbürg concentration camp, April 9, 1945, German major general (December 1, 1941) and opposition fighter. Oster was a General Staff officer in the First World War; he subsequently held several command posts in the Reichswehr.

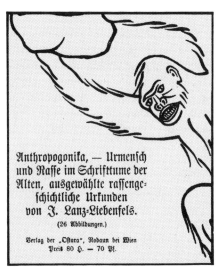

Ostara. 1906 cover: "Anthropogonica—Primitive Man and Race in the Writings of Antiquity: Selected Documents on Racial History," by J. Lanz-Liebenfels.

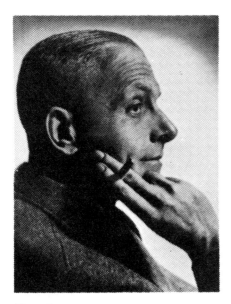

Hans Oster.

He retired in 1932 for personal reasons. Back in service in 1933, he was assigned to the ABWEHR in the Armed Forces Ministry (later the Wehrmacht High Command); in 1939 he became director of its central division. The elegant and nimble-minded Oster had been a fierce opponent of National Socialism at least since the murder of his former superior, Kurt von SCHLEICHER, during the so-called RÖHM AFFAIR (June 30, 1934). He now became friendly with Gen. Ludwig BECK and became the soul of the military opposition.

After the failure of the putsch plans during the SUDETEN CRISIS and once the war began, Oster resorted to direct treason, in line with his motto, "The professional soldier should be the most convinced pacifist, since he knows what war is." He made hints about German attack plans in the west to the Dutch military attaché, Sas, but they did not have the desired effect. Oster then reconsidered the idea of assassinating Hitler, which at first he had rejected, and obtained explosives for several attempts. At the same time, shielded by the Abwehr chief, Wilhelm CANARIS, he sought to help persecuted individuals. He also organized, among other efforts, the "V7" operation. Oster's attempts to defend his arrested collaborator Hans von DOHNÁNYI aroused suspicion and led, on March 31, 1944, to his own dismissal and to Gestapo surveillance. Envisioned by the conspirators of July 20, 1944, as the president of the Reich Court-Martial, Oster was arrested on July 21, after the failed *coup d'état*. Following a summary trial, and shortly before the Americans reached the Flossenbürg camp, he was hanged

along with Canaris, Dietrich BONHOEFFER, and others.

Ostgebiete. *See* Eastern Territories.

Ostindustrie GmbH (Eastern Industries, Ltd.), one of the SS ECONOMIC ENTERPRISES in the Generalgouvernement under the supervision of Odilo GLOBOCNIK.

Ostland (Eastern Land), Reich Commissariat formed on July 17, 1941, during the RUSSIAN CAMPAIGN. It was composed of the former Baltic states of Estonia, Latvia, and Lithuania, together with parts of Belorussia. Hinrich LOHSE became Reich commissioner for the region.

Ostmark (Eastern March), designation for the eastern reaches of the German Reich, as, for example, the Prussian territories ceded to Poland in 1919. In the Third Reich the term was used, in the medieval military sense of an "eastern outpost" of the Reich, to apply to Austria. After the Munich Agreement, it also applied to the Sudeten German territories in southern Bohemia and southern Moravia. By 1940, however, a press advisory demanded that the term "Ostmark" be used sparingly, to be replaced by more frequent use of the individual *Gau* names within it. On January 22, 1942, the press was forbidden to use the name altogether, since Austria (Österreich; literally, "eastern domain") as an entity was to disappear from consciousness. The Bavarian Eastern March (Bayerische Ostmark) was the name of an NSDAP *Gau* with its center in Bayreuth (it was renamed *Gau* Bayreuth on June 15, 1942).

Oświęcim. *See* Auschwitz.

"Otto," military code name for the occupation of Austria at the time of the ANSCHLUSS in March 1938.

Otto, Berthold, b. Bienowitz (Silesia), August 6, 1859; d. Berlin, June 29, 1933, German educator. After studies in language and sociology, Otto worked as a private tutor and a lexicon editor. In 1906 he founded in Berlin-Lichterfelde a "school for tutors" (the Berthold Otto School), in which he propagated his ideas on pedagogic reform. In his belief, the school should contribute to the organic formation of the *Volk* by awakening the "elementary powers of the child" with the help of the "idiom appropriate to his age" (*Altersmundart*). Otto's definition of the *Volk* as a "total organism" (*Gesamtorganismus*) into which the child must grow appealed to the National Socialist educators, who regarded Otto as one of their precursors. His major work, *Volksorganisches Denken* (*Volk*-organic Thought, 4 vols., 1924–1926), was required reading for prospective teachers and educators in the Third Reich.

Otto, Hans, b. Dresden, August 10, 1900; d. Berlin, late November 1933, German actor. In 1924 Otto became an actor at Hamburg's Kammerspiel (chamber theater), and in the late 1920s, at the Berlin State Theater, on the Gendarmenmarkt. In the view of critics one of the period's most talented artists, Otto wanted to act the roles of great heroes of freedom such as Egmont, Don Carlos, and the Prince of Hom-

burg not only on the stage—as a Communist in the theater union, he was politically involved in the struggle against the encroaching National Socialism, continuing his agitation even after the Seizure of Power. He was arrested on November 15, 1933, and abused so severely that he was hospitalized on November 25; there he died from his injuries.

"Our Honor Is Loyalty" ("Unsere Ehre heisst Treue"), SS motto, engraved on belt buckles and "daggers of honor" (*Ehrendolche*). It was the oath by which the unconditional obedience of members of the "Order of the Death's Head" was sworn.

Pacelli, Eugenio. *See* Pius XII.

Pacifism (*Pazifismus;* from Lat. *pax,* peace), a basic attitude of radical peaceableness, as well as the political movements engendered by it. Pacifism as an ideological value was a consequence of the Napoleonic Wars and arose as a term around the middle of the 19th century in international discussions. Peace societies and associations, which emerged in Germany around the turn of the 20th century, made pacifism their program on religious, economic, humanitarian, or general political grounds, and they demanded the outlawing of war and refusal of military service. The First World War was a severe setback for pacifism, especially in Germany, where the agitation of the political Right ascribed the defeat to the influence of pacifism (*see* STAB-IN-THE-BACK LEGEND). Moreover, the pacifist demands for DISARMAMENT in the peace treaties and the League of Nations Charter were applied only to the defeated nations; hence pacifism could be denounced as a "means of strangling the German *Volk.*"

Thus, National Socialist propaganda characterized pacifism as VOLK TREASON and denigrated pacifist authors such as Erich Maria RE-MARQUE and pacifist groups such as the League for Human Rights. After the Seizure of Power they had no further opportunities for activity in Germany. In the NS view, pacifism derived from the fiction of the equality of all human beings; it was therefore internationalistic, indeed directed against the National Socialists' own national characteristics (*Volkstum*), whose will for self-assertion it was undermining. The pacifists were accused of cowardice and of "fomenting despondency and deceitful ideas." They were depicted as failing to see that they were promoting the affairs of Germany's enemies, especially those of WORLD JEWRY.

In fact, pacifism was stronger in the Western democracies than in Germany, and was a sub-stantial force behind APPEASEMENT. In his foreign-policy strategy of threats, Hitler deliberately counted on this "softness" (*Verweichlichung*), which, after many successes, proved in the end to be a mistaken calculation. Yet the retreat before Hitler's policy of violence discredited pacifism far beyond the end of the war; even into the 1980s, it served as an argument against the peace movement. Nonetheless, in the nuclear age, pacifism has no alternative.

Pact of Steel (*Stahlpakt*), term coined by Benito Mussolini to characterize the "strong as steel" solidarity of the German-Italian treaty concluded in Berlin between foreign ministers Joachim von Ribbentrop and Count Galeazzo Ciano on May 22, 1939. With a 10-year term, the Pact of Steel provided for the recognition of common borders (with German renunciation of the South Tyrol), obligatory consultation (Article I), reciprocal political and military support against external threats (Article II), unlimited and unconditional military assistance in the event of "hostile entanglements with another power or powers" (Article III), the establishment of commissions for collaboration with regard to military affairs and a wartime economy (Article IV), and the renunciation of a unilateral separate peace in the event of war (Article V).

The Pact of Steel was based on contradictory motives of the contracting parties. Hitler wanted to utilize it without consultation as a means of political preparation for the long-planned Polish Campaign (on April 11, 1939, the directive for "Case White" was issued) and as a deterrent to the Western powers. Mussolini, however, linked it to the hope of committing the Germans to peace at least until 1942–1943. Germany's evidently aware deception of the Italians, and Italy's completely inadequate military and economic readiness for war, gave Mussolini a justifiable pretext at the outbreak of hostilities on September 1, 1939, for ignoring the Pact of Steel and proclaiming a policy of *non belligeranza.* Later in the war, the pact had still failed to gain any meaning (there was no institutionalization of cooperative conduct of war); it became pointless with the unilateral cease-fire by the Italians on September 3, 1943, in violation of Article V. The Pact of Steel scarcely concealed the extreme fragility of the German-Italian Axis friendship.

B.-J. W.

Padua, Paul Mathias, b. Salzburg, November 15, 1903; d. Tegernsee, August 22, 1981, German painter. Padua was initially self-taught, and then took lessons with Franz von Lenbach. He was already making a name for himself by the 1920s with portraits of prominent individuals and peasant landscapes; in 1930 he won the Albrecht Dürer Prize. In the Third Reich he advanced to become one of the most sought-after artists, as a representative of heroic realism and blood-and-soil painting. Fame ensued as well from his portraits of women and from the painting *Der Führer spricht* (The Führer Speaks; 1937). The latter portrays a peasant family deep in reflection under a radio (*see* VOLK'S RECEIVER), with a portrait of Hitler occupying the traditional place for the crucifix on the wall. After the war Padua was rejected by artists' associations and the media on account of his "court paintings" during the Third Reich. However, he did receive further commissions from prominent people in the worlds of politics, business, and culture, creating portraits

Paul Mathias Padua's *Leda and the Swan.*

of the Bavarian political leader Franz-Josef Strauss, Friedrich FLICK, and Herbert von KARAJAN, among others.

M. F.

Painting (*Malerei*), an art form that was more backward-looking than others in the Third Reich. It had a greater impact on the public (lasting even into the postwar period) as a result of the rejection and destruction of modern art than through its own program and accomplishments. In the campaign of the COMBAT LEAGUE FOR GERMAN CULTURE against DEGENERATE ART, the National Socialists could count on the support of broad circles of the bourgeoisie and working class who, even during the Weimar era, neither understood nor liked modern art. National Socialist aesthetic theories served mainly as demarcation lines: German painters "do not paint absinthe drinkers" or "big-city dens of iniquity. . . . They want to be advocates of a life of positive affirmation" (F. A. Kaufmann, *Neue deutsche Malerei* [New German Painting]; 1941). To express "*völkisch* substance," painters were to depict "men following primeval occupations [*Urberufe*] in closeness to nature," as well as "woman as mother," surrounded by "the sacredness of the natural order" to symbolize the German "will to the future."

The first inclusive and representative Great German Art Exhibition in the summer of 1937 showed that NS aesthetics meant a return to the genre paintings of the 19th century. Idylls of peasants, landscapes, and summer meadows dominated, with titles such as *Homeland, Consoling Nature, Sod,* and *Longing for the Simple Life*; the reality of a modern industrial society was largely left out. Paintings of peasants frozen in lifeless stereotypes by such artists as Adolf Wissel and Hans Thoma were conspicuous in their abundance. They portrayed the "food-growing estate" (*Nährstand,* or peasantry) on "German earth" behind plow horses or with scythe and sword. Still lifes and pictures of artisans, nursing mothers, or women at spinning wheels deliberately portrayed a preindustrial idyll. Only paintings of nudes were allowed to acquire elements of the taboo "degeneracy" during the 1930s. Next to homely "peasant Graces" or Nordic heroines painted with the precision of photographic naturalism (by such artists as Adolf ZIEGLER) were pseudohistorical nudes that to an extent continued the tradition of 19th-century bourgeois salon painting, justifying sultry eroticism with allegorical or mysti-

Painting. *Time of Ripening*, by Johannes Beutner.

cal titles (such as Raffael Schuster-Woldan's *Danae*, 1941).

Paintings that aimed to foster war preparedness and appropriate views of the enemy were encouraged once the war began. At first, historical war motifs were preferred (for example, *Frederick the Great at Kunersdorf* by Werner PEINER, 1940). Later on, representations of actual events, portraits of contemporary soldier-heroes, or battlefield paintings were primarily created (such as B. Franz Eichhorst's *Memory of Stalingrad*, 1943). Monumental painting, which followed in the footsteps of monumental architecture and mainly served to decorate public spaces, in any case preferred martial motifs such as "the *Volk* in combat."

NS painting was presented to the general public through large annual exhibitions and touring shows with such themes as "In Praise of Work," "The Horse in Art," and "Adolf Hitler's Streets." The "Art for the *Volk*" program was in conscious contrast with the individualized, expensive artworks of the Weimar Republic. It provided instead ready-made paintings at relatively low prices, especially paintings on the borderline between artistry and kitsch. They were gladly accepted as a diversion from a daily life ruled by armaments and politics.

H. H.

Palandt, Otto, b. May 1, 1877; d. Hamburg, December 3, 1951, German jurist. Palandt served as a justice on the local (as of 1906), state (1912), and appellate (1916) levels. In 1933 he became president of the Prussian State Judicial

Review Office, and in 1934, of the Reich Judicial Review Office. He was significantly involved after 1933 in new programs "imbued with the purest National Socialist spirit" for the training of jurists. In 1939 he initiated what is today the most frequently published commentary on the German civil code and supplementary legislation, the *Palandt* (44th edition, 1985). In its first six editions (1939–1944), the commentary contained the statements that the "liberalistic" civil law was to be incorporated into the NS interpretation of law and life, and that the "healthy feeling of the *Volk*" and the NSDAP program were to be considered the criteria for judicial decisions. After 1945 the *Palandt* was initially adapted to the changed circumstances without any significant change of editors or contributors; passages containing NS ideology, such as the NUREMBERG LAWS, were simply struck from the laws discussed.

C. S.

Palestine, as of 1920 a territory under British mandate in the Near East, formed from what until then were the Turkish administrative districts of Acre, Nablus, and Jerusalem; area, 26,300 sq km (about 10,400 sq miles); population, 647,500 inhabitants (1919). In accordance with the BALFOUR DECLARATION (1917), Palestine was to provide Jews with a "homeland"; it thus became the goal of a continual wave of Jewish immigration, which increased even more as the National Socialist PERSECUTION OF JEWS intensified. Although in 1919 Jews constituted only 10 percent of the population of Palestine, by 1948 they made up a third. Against this trend, ever since 1920 there had been repeated instances of Arab uprisings and terrorist resistance.

Neither the separation of Transjordan, as a purely Arab territory apart from Palestine, nor limitations placed on Jews' immigrating and buying land brought quiet to the country. In the period leading to the Second World War, however, Great Britain needed this calm; it ordered that the annual number of new Jewish settlers be limited to 10,000, up to a total of 75,000, from which were subtracted the 33,339 Jews who had already immigrated from Germany between 1933 and 1939. The Arab resistance continued, however, and led to the formation of the Jewish defense league (the Haganah) and to counterterror. With no mitigation in the British position against further immigration, few of the persecuted European Jews could escape to Palestine. Many under-

Members of the Haganah militia in Palestine (1932).

went the experience of the passengers on the STRUMA. Only when the full measure of the NS FINAL SOLUTION became public were the borders of Palestine opened to the survivors. Despite the formation of the Jewish state, the region remains a crisis area in world politics.

Papen, Franz von, b. Werl (Westphalia), October 29, 1879; d. Obersasbach (Baden), May 2, 1969, German politician. Papen initially followed an officer's career. During the First World War he served as military attaché in Mexico and the United States. He later joined the German armed forces in Turkey, and finally was chief of staff of the Fourth Turkish Army in Palestine. From 1920 to 1932, he was a Center party deputy in the Prussian parliament. Positioned on the extreme right wing, a monarchist and a member of the exclusive HERRENKLUB with good contacts in industry (through his marriage to an heiress of the Saarland porcelain firm Villeroy & Boch), Papen went counter to his party in the presidential election of 1925 when he supported Paul von HINDENBURG instead of the Center candidate, Wilhelm MARX. In 1932 the break was complete: Reich President Hindenburg dismissed the Centrist Heinrich BRÜNING and named Papen the new Reich chancellor on June 1.

Papen's "Cabinet of National Concentration," mocked as the "Cabinet of Barons" because of its many noble members, followed an authoritarian course, on the basis of the Reich president's emergency decrees. It lifted the ban on the SA and the SS, carried out the PRUSSIAN COUP against the minority Social Democratic government of Otto BRAUN, and in a final blow dissolved the Reichstag after a vote of no confi-

dence on September 12, 1932. Since the new elections in November gave him no majority and Hindenburg refused to grant dictatorial powers, Papen resigned on November 17, and immediately joined in the intrigue that finally brought Hitler to power. On January 4, 1933, Papen reached agreement with the NSDAP Führer during a meeting at the house of the banker Kurt Baron von SCHRÖDER to overthrow Papen's successor, Kurt von SCHLEICHER, and to share in the formation of a cabinet. Papen's expectation of using the post of vice-chancellor (as of January 30, 1933) to "tame" Chancellor Hitler did not work out; on the contrary, the presence of Papen and the other conservative ministers lent respectability to National Socialism. Of special benefit to Hitler was the CONCORDAT with the Catholic church, which Papen mediated.

Franz von Papen.

Papen's polemic in his Marburg speech of June 17, 1934, against the radical forces in the NSDAP accelerated Hitler's settling of scores with the SA leadership (*see* RÖHM AFFAIR) and put the vice-chancellor's own life in danger; several of his collaborators, including Edgar JUNG, were murdered. That July Papen went as ambassador to Vienna, where he helped prepare the JULY AGREEMENT and the ANSCHLUSS. From 1939 to 1944, he was ambassador to Ankara. In 1946 the Nuremberg Military Tribunals acquitted him in the trial of the major war criminals; however, in 1949 a German court sentenced him to eight years in a work camp, which was considered as served by previous confinement. Papen's autobiography, *Der Wahrheit eine Gasse* (A Way to Truth, 1952; translated as *Memoirs*), showed no insight into the fateful role that he had played in the liquidation of the Weimar Republic and the establishment of the NS tyranny.

Ba.

Papenburg, city on the Ems River with a population of 10,680 in 1933. The office of the commandant of the EMSLAND CAMPS was located in Papenburg.

Parades (*Aufmärsche*), propaganda device, often utilized by the NSDAP on a massive scale, that conveyed strong impressions with flags and often torches, as well as with march music. Parades relied on the intimidating effect of closed marching formations and aroused the desire to take part in them. At the same time they assisted in the discipline and inner conviction of those marching.

Pariser Tageblatt (Paris Daily News; *Quotidien en langue allemande,* and as of No. 83/36, *Le quotidien de Paris en langue allemande*), the only large daily newspaper of the German exile press, founded and edited by Georg BERNHARD, the former editor in chief of Berlin's *Vossische Zeitung;* its publisher was Wladimir Poliakoff. It appeared from December 12, 1933, until June 1936 in Paris. After Bernhard wrested its control from Poliakoff on June 12, 1936, it was succeeded by the *Pariser Tageszeitung,* which also carried French articles. Beginning with No. 578/38, the editor in chief was Carl Misch. Its circulation was 14,000, and its last issue was dated February 18, 1940.

S. O.

Paris Suburban Treaties (*Pariser Vorortverträge*), the peace treaties that ended the First World War. Formulated on the basis of the peace conference that opened in Paris on January 18, 1919 (with 27 Allied and associated states participating), they were signed in various suburbs of Paris. They consisted of the treaty with the German Reich, signed on June 28, 1919, in Versailles (*see* VERSAILLES TREATY); the treaty with Austria on September 10, 1919, in Saint-Germain-en-Laye; with Bulgaria on November 27, 1919, in Neuilly-sur-Seine; with Hungary on June 4, 1920, in the Grand Trianon Palace in Versailles; and with Turkey on August 10, 1920, in Sèvres. Austria was required, among other obligations, to cede the South Tyrol, Istria, and Trieste to Italy; to cede Dalmatia and parts of Carinthia and Carniola to Yugoslavia; and to recognize the independence of Hungary, Czechoslovakia, Poland, and Yugoslavia. An ANSCHLUSS with the German Reich was prohibited. Hungary, Bulgaria, and especially Turkey also lost territories. Along with limitations on armaments for these states, the Paris suburban treaties also contained provisions concerning the establishment of the LEAGUE OF NATIONS, the payment of REPARATIONS, and the punishment of alleged war criminals. The United States, which did not ratify the suburban treaties, later concluded separate peace treaties with Germany (1921), Austria (1921), Hungary (1921), and Turkey (1923).

R. B.

Parliamentarianism (*Parliamentarismus*), in the broader sense, a political movement with the goal of securing the participation of the people in the shaping of their destiny through a national representation (a parliament); in the narrower sense, a government system that is the result of this movement. In parliamentarianism, the executive branch is responsible to the parliament, bound to the laws that body makes, and controlled by its majorities. The victory of parliamentarianism in 1918 as the principle of government for the German state remained connected in the minds of broad segments of the populace with the defeat in the First World War and the disorders of the November Revolution. The agitation against parliamentarianism and the Weimar Republic exploited this taint; it also capitalized on the shortcomings of the constitution, which scarcely allowed a stable majority to emerge.

As the vessel of German parliamentarianism, the Reichstag was perceived by many to be a "talk-shop" (*Quasselbude*), which distorted the voters' choices with rapidly changing coalitions.

When coalitions capable of governing could no longer be formed because of a "loss of the middle" and because of the increasing strength of the COMMUNIST PARTY OF GERMANY (KPD) and especially of the National Socialists, parliamentarianism was gradually undermined by the PRESIDIAL CABINETS, finally becoming a victim of the National Socialist SEIZURE OF POWER. In the Third Reich, parliamentarianism was replaced by the FÜHRER PRINCIPLE, since Hitler, despite his legalistic-parliamentarian tactics for winning power, had already rejected parliamentarianism in *Mein Kampf* as a sin "against nature's fundamental idea of aristocracy."

Parti Populaire Français (French Popular Party; PPF), French fascist party founded in 1936 by Jacques Doriot, a onetime Communist functionary. After the French defeat in 1940 it advocated unconditional COLLABORATION with the German occupying power and the transformation of France into a "French people's state" on the National Socialist model. After the liberation in August 1944, the party was banned; many of its members fled to Germany or became victims of the scores settled with collaborators.

Partisans, civilians or combatants not belonging to regular armed forces, who singly or in groups fight an occupying power by means of ambush or attacks on the occupiers' lines of communica-

tion. In international law, partisans are to be considered regular combatants and are to be treated as PRISONERS OF WAR only if they have a responsible leader, wear a recognizable identification mark when seen from a distance, and carry their weapons openly (Article 1 of the Land War Regulation of the Hague [1907]; Article 4 of the Third Geneva Treaty for the Protection of Victims of War [1949]). However, these conditions are normally not met in modern partisan warfare. In the Second World War the German Wehrmacht in the occupied territories had to fend off partisan assaults; the struggle was conducted on both sides with great bitterness and cruelty, and frequently brought barbaric retaliatory operations on the populace.

In January 1943, 57,500 partisans were fighting in Belorussia; by November of that year the number had grown to 122,600. At the beginning of 1944, more than 250,000 Soviet partisans were operating behind German lines. They made considerable trouble for some German units, especially during such major defeats as the collapse of the Central Army Group in the summer of 1944. For 1943, Soviet partisans reported 11,000 railroad track explosions and 9,000 derailments of transport trains, accounting for 6,000 locomotives and 40,000 railroad cars destroyed or damaged; 22,000 German motor vehicles were also destroyed.

Partisans. Discarded munitions are de-activated.

Women members of the Partito Nazionale Fascista.

In the Balkans, Josip TITO had at his disposal in March 1944, according to German estimates, more than 11 corps with 31 divisions, each with 2,000 to 4,000 troops. In German reports, these forces were held responsible for losses amounting to 55,800 dead and 21,500 prisoners between January 1 and August 1, 1944. Tito's partisans were supplied by the Allies, but they also retrieved considerable amounts of arms from the Italian occupation troops and captured others in battles against the Croatian forces. Despite extensive German countermeasures, Tito remained undefeated. On May 25, 1944, German paratroopers just missed seizing his headquarters at Dvar. As the war went on, his troops lost their partisan characteristics and evolved into a regular army.

According to German reports on France and Belgium, between June 6 and August 31, 1944, 11,086 "terrorists" were "cut down" in battle and 4,700 were captured. There were 460 cases of railway sabotage in March 1944, and another 500 in April. The Maquisards (Maquis members) were supplied with arms for the RÉSISTANCE by airlift from Allied airplanes. Partisan warfare developed in Italy as well after its withdrawal from the war in the summer of 1943. German reports had it that 12,582 "bandits" were killed and 8,500 were captured in Italy between May 12 and September 30, 1944. A ruthless guerrilla war raged as well in Greece, where the strongest force was the Communist ELAS, with 22,000 fighters.

G. H.

Partito Fascista Repubblicano (Republican Fascist Party; PFR), Italian Fascist party re-founded by Mussolini after his liberation (September 1943) as the successor organization to the National Fascist Party (PARTITO NAZIONALE FASCISTA; PNF) under Alessandro Pavolini. In the PFR the radical forces in Italian Fascism (which had remained in the shadow of the pragmatists from 1922 to 1943) came to power, supported by the German National Socialist masters, in the Republic of SALÒ. Still, with only 250,000 members (October 1943), the PFR dissipated its energies in combat against the anti-Fascist partisans and in settling scores with the "traitors" of July 25, 1943 (the GRAND COUNCIL OF FASCISM), who were condemned to death in the Verona Trial (January 1944). The attempt to win over the working class through revived programs (such as nationalization) remained totally ineffective.

Partito Nazionale Fascista (National Fascist Party; PNF), Italian party founded in November 1921 and based on the Fascist movement begun by Benito MUSSOLINI in 1919; its membership expanded rapidly, from 21,000 in December 1920 to 322,000 in May 1922. After the March on Rome (October 1922), during the establishment of the Fascist dictatorship the PNF became the state party. Intent only on the concentration of power, Mussolini curbed its radical tendencies by making alliances with the traditional elite, the military, the church, and large industry. Parallel to the establishment of personal rule by "Il Duce," the electoral principle was displaced by that of party appointment; thus the PNF became a kind of state agency, as did its onetime central committee, the GRAND COUNCIL OF FASCISM.

Subsequently, the PNF served mainly to encompass the population, as was reflected in the growth of its membership: in 1927, about 1.1 million; in 1937, 2.2 million; in 1943, 4.8 million. The party worked toward this end through women's and young people's associations, through infiltration of the trade unions, and through the organization of recreation (*see*

DOPOLAVORO). Ultimately, the PNF was little more than a backdrop for the stagings of the Mussolini dictatorship. Only when the worsening military situation exposed the colossus's feet of clay did resistance spring up from within the party, leading to Il Duce's overthrow on July 25, 1943. This event also proved to be the downfall of the party, which Marshal Pietro BADOGLIO's regime outlawed in August 1943. Its revival as the Republican Fascist Party (PARTITO FASCISTA REPUBBLICANO) only aggravated the Italian civil war and was insignificant in terms of politics or programs.

Party Badge (Parteiabzeichen), pin worn on the lapel by NSDAP members. It was a round, white-enameled badge with a black swastika in the center; around the edge was inscribed "Nationalsozialistische D.A.P."

Party Chancellery (Parteikanzlei), designation, as of May 12, 1941, for the office of the deputy to the Führer, who reported personally to Hitler; the change followed Rudolf HESS's flight to England. The director of the Party Chancellery, Martin BORMANN, was equivalent to a Reich minister; he was part of the Reich government, and a member of the MINISTERIAL COUNCIL FOR THE DEFENSE OF THE REICH. He was to be informed of, and consulted on, all decrees of other departments, and all official appointments subject to Hitler's decision had to be submitted with his opinion.

Party Comrade (Parteigenosse), official term for a member of the NSDAP. The term Genosse, which had Middle High German origins, meant "comrade," "companion" (Gefährte), or "participant" (Teilhaber). In the 19th century it became common as a form of address in the workers' movement; it was retained in the workers' parties of the 20th century. The NSDAP

Party Badge of the NSDAP.

continued this tradition, even though it did not consider itself to be a class-based party; rather, it understood the term in a völkisch-nationalist sense (see VOLK).

Party congresses. See Reich Party Congresses.

Party Courts (Parteigerichte), National Socialist HONOR COURTS with the additional jurisdiction to arrest and imprison. The organization and procedure for the Party Courts were regulated not by law but by the guidelines of the Führer's deputy, issued on February 17, 1934. The courts' purpose was to punish party members when their conduct was "contrary to the sense of honor and the views of the NSDAP"; they were also responsible for smoothing out conflicts among party members. The penalties handed down by the courts, particularly expulsion from the party, often had serious consequences for those affected. There were local, district, and Gau courts, and a supreme Party Court under Walter BUCH. Whereas predominantly laypeople worked in the local and district courts, the higher tribunals were staffed mainly by professional jurists who were primarily employed in the regular justice system.

C. D.

Party Program of the NSDAP (Parteiprogramm der NSDAP), 25-point program drawn up by Hitler and Anton DREXLER, under the strong influence of the economic theories of Gottfried FEDER ("breaking interest servitude"). Published on February 24, 1920, it included the following demands: state territory contiguous with the German ethnic boundaries; colonies; a militia (Volksheer); strong central state authority; exclusion of Jews; legislation and cultural policy in line with racial criteria; land reform; elimination of interest; nationalization of trusts; profit sharing by big business; communalization of large retail stores; the death penalty for usurers and for persons committing crimes against the Volk (Volksverbrecher); and confiscation of war profits.

After Hitler's election as party chairman on July 29, 1921, the Party Program was declared to be "unalterable." However, it played hardly any role in the politics of the NSDAP, whose true program beginning in 1920–1921 was much more Hitler's overall political conception, tirelessly expounded in speeches and writings (see HITLER'S WORLDVIEW).

A translation of the Party Program follows.

Party Program

The program of the German Workers' Party is a program for the moment. The leaders refuse, after the goals in the program have been attained, to set new ones merely for the purpose of ensuring the continuation of the party by artificially intensifying the dissatisfaction of the masses.

1. We demand the union of all Germans in a Great-Germany on the basis of the right to self-determination of peoples.
2. We demand equal rights for the German people in relation to those of other nations; nullification of the peace treaties of Versailles and Saint-Germain.
3. We demand land and territory (colonies) to feed our people and provide settlements for our excess population.
4. Only a *Volk* comrade [*Volksgenosse*] can be a citizen; only a person of German blood can be a *Volk* comrade, without regard to religious denomination. Therefore no Jew can be a *Volk* comrade.
5. Anyone who is not a citizen can live in Germany only as a guest, and must be governed by legislation applying to aliens.
6. Only a citizen may have the right to a voice regarding the leadership and laws of the state. Thus we demand that every public office, of whatever type, on the Reich, state, or local level, be filled only by citizens. We oppose the corrupt parliamentary system that fills posts only according to partisan viewpoints, without regard to character and capabilities.
7. We demand that the state pledge to provide above all for the livelihood and living conditions of its citizens.

    If it is not possible to feed the total population of the state, the members of alien nations (non-citizens) must be deported from the Reich.
8. Any further immigration of non-Germans should be prevented. We demand that all non-Germans who have immigrated into Germany beginning on August 2, 1914, be forced immediately to leave the Reich.
9. All citizens must have equal rights and obligations.
10. The first obligation of every citizen must be productivity, mental and physical. The ac-

tivity of the individual may not impinge on the interests of the whole, but rather must be within the whole and for the good of all. *Thus we demand:*
11. Abolition of income without work and effort; breaking interest servitude.
12. With reference to the enormous sacrifice of goods and blood that every war demands of the *Volk*, personal enrichment by means of the war must be classified as a crime against the *Volk*. Thus we demand total expropriation of all war profits.
13. We demand the nationalization of all (heretofore) collectivized enterprises (trusts).
14. We demand profit sharing in large enterprises.
15. We demand a generous expansion of old-age insurance.
16. We demand the creation of a healthy middle class [*Mittelstand*] and its maintenance; the immediate communalization of large retail stores and their rental at low rates to small retailers; the greatest consideration to all small businesses in terms of contracts with the national state, the individual states, and the communes.
17. We demand land reform appropriate to our national needs; the creation of a law for the expropriation without compensation of land for purposes beneficial to the common weal; abolition of the tax on land, and prevention of all speculation in land.
18. We demand a relentless struggle against those whose activity is injurious to the common interests of the whole. Common criminals committing crimes against the *Volk*, usurers, profiteers, and so on, are to be punished with death, without consideration regarding their denomination or race.
19. We demand that a German common law replace Roman law, which serves the materialistic world order.
20. In order to enable every capable and hardworking German to attain higher education and thus to fill positions of leadership, the state must take responsibility for a basic restructuring of public education. The curricula of all educational institutions should be suited to the demands of practical life. The comprehension of the idea of the state must be attained at the beginning of un-

Parteiprogramm.

Das Programm der Deutschen Arbeiterpartei ist ein Zeit-Programm. Die Führer lehnen es ab, nach Erreichung der im Programm aufgestellten Ziele neue aufzustellen, nur zu dem Zweck, um durch künstlich gesteigerte Unzufriedenheit der Massen das Fortbestehen der Partei zu ermöglichen.

1. Wir fordern den Zusammenschluß aller Deutschen auf Grund des Selbstbestimmungsrechts der Völker zu einem Großdeutschland.

2. Wir fordern die Gleichberechtigung des deutschen Volkes gegenüber den anderen Nationen, Aufhebung der Friedensverträge von Versailles und Saint-Germain.

3. Wir fordern Land und Boden (Kolonien) zur Ernährung unseres Volkes und Ansiedlung unseres Bevölkerungsüberschusses.

4. Staatsbürger kann nur sein, wer Volksgenosse ist. Volksgenosse kann nur sein, wer deutschen Blutes ist, ohne Rücksicht auf Konfession. Kein Jude kann daher Volksgenosse sein.

5. Wer nicht Staatsbürger ist, soll nur als Gast in Deutschland leben können und muß unter Fremdengesetzgebung stehen.

6. Das Recht, über Führung und Gesetze des Staates zu bestimmen, darf nur dem Staatsbürger zustehen. Daher fordern wir, daß jedes öffentliche Amt, gleichgültig welcher Art, ob in Reich, Land oder Gemeinde, nur von Staatsbürgern bekleidet werden darf. Wir bekämpfen die korrumpierende Parlamentswirtschaft, eine Stellenbesetzung nur nach Parteigesichtspunkten ohne Rücksicht auf Charakter und Fähigkeiten.

7. Wir fordern, daß sich der Staat verpflichtet, in erster Linie für die Erwerbs- und Lebensmöglichkeit der Staatsbürger zu sorgen.

Wenn es nicht möglich ist, die Gesamtbevölkerung des Staates zu ernähren, so sind die Angehörigen fremder Nationen (Nichtstaatsbürger) aus dem Reiche auszuweisen.

8. Jede weitere Einwanderung Nichtdeutscher ist zu verhindern. Wir fordern, daß alle Nichtdeutschen, die seit dem 2. August 1914 in Deutschland eingewandert sind, sofort zum Verlassen des Reiches gezwungen werden.

9. Alle Staatsbürger müssen gleiche Rechte und Pflichten besitzen.

10. Erste Pflicht jedes Staatsbürgers muß sein, geistig und körperlich zu schaffen. Die Tätigkeit des einzelnen darf nicht gegen die Interessen der Allgemeinheit verstoßen, sondern muß im Rahmen des Gesamten und zum Nutzen aller erfolgen.

Daher fordern wir:

11. Abschaffung des arbeits- und mühelosen Einkommens. Brechung der Zinsknechtschaft.

12. Im Hinblick auf die ungeheuren Opfer an Gut und Blut, die jeder Krieg vom Volke fordert, muß die persönliche Bereicherung durch den Krieg als Verbrechen am Volke bezeichnet werden. Wir fordern daher restlose Einziehung aller Kriegsgewinne.

13. Wir fordern die Verstaatlichung aller (bisher) vergesellschafteten (Trusts) Betriebe.

14. Wir fordern Gewinnbeteiligung an Großbetrieben.

15. Wir fordern einen großzügigen Ausbau der Altersversorgung.

16. Wir fordern die Schaffung eines gesunden Mittelstandes und seine Erhaltung, sofortige Kommunalisierung der Großwarenhäuser und ihre Vermietung zu billigen Preisen an kleine Gewerbetreibende, schärfste Berücksichtigung aller kleinen Gewerbetreibenden bei Lieferungen an den Staat, die Länder oder Gemeinden.

17. Wir fordern eine unserem nationalen Bedürfnis angepaßte Bodenreform, Schaffung eines Gesetzes zur unentgeltlichen Enteignung von Boden für gemeinnützige Zwecke, Abschaffung des Bodenzinses und Verhinderung jeder Bodenspekulation.

18. Wir fordern den rücksichtslosen Kampf gegen diejenigen, die durch ihre Tätigkeit das Gemeinschaftsinteresse schädigen. Gemeine Volksverbrecher, Wucherer, Schieber usw. sind mit dem Tode zu bestrafen, ohne Rücksichtnahme auf Konfession und Rasse.

19. Wir fordern Ersatz für das der materialistischen Weltordnung dienende römische Recht durch ein deutsches Gemeinrecht.

20. Um jedem fähigen und fleißigen Deutschen das Erreichen höherer Bildung und damit das Einrücken in führende Stellungen zu ermöglichen, hat der Staat für einen gründlichen Ausbau unseres gesamten Volksbildungswesens Sorge zu tragen. Die Lehrpläne aller Bildungsanstalten sind den Erfordernissen des praktischen Lebens anzupassen. Das Erfassen des Staatsgedankens muß bereits mit dem Beginn des Verständnisses durch die Schule (Staatsbürgerkunde) erzielt werden. Wir fordern die Ausbildung geistig besonders veranlagter Kinder armer Eltern ohne Rücksicht auf den Stand oder Beruf auf Staatskosten.

21. Der Staat hat für die Hebung der Volksgesundheit zu sorgen durch den Schutz der Mutter und des Kindes, durch Verbot der Jugendarbeit, durch Herbeiführung der körperlichen Ertüchtigung mittels gesetzlicher Festlegung einer Turn- und Sportpflicht, durch größte Unterstützung aller sich mit körperlicher Jugendausbildung beschäftigenden Vereine.

22. Wir fordern die Abschaffung der Söldnertruppe und die Bildung eines Volksheeres.

23. Wir fordern den gesetzlichen Kampf gegen die bewußte politische Lüge und ihre Verbreitung durch die Presse. Um die Schaffung einer deutschen Presse zu ermöglichen, fordern wir, daß

a) sämtliche Schriftleiter und Mitarbeiter von Zeitungen, die in deutscher Sprache erscheinen, Volksgenossen sein müssen;

b) nichtdeutsche Zeitungen zu ihrem Erscheinen der ausdrücklichen Genehmigung des Staates bedürfen. Sie dürfen nicht in deutscher Sprache gedruckt werden;

c) jede finanzielle Beteiligung an deutschen Zeitungen oder deren Beeinflussung durch Nichtdeutsche gesetzlich verboten wird und als Strafe für Übertretungen die Schließung einer solchen Zeitung sowie die sofortige Ausweisung der daran beteiligten Nichtdeutschen aus dem Reich. Zeitungen, die gegen das Gemeinwohl verstoßen, sind zu verbieten.

Wir fordern den gesetzlichen Kampf gegen eine Kunst- und Literaturrichtung, die einen zersetzenden Einfluß auf unser Volksleben ausübt, und die Schließung von Veranstaltungen, die gegen vorstehende Forderungen verstoßen.

24. Wir fordern die Freiheit aller religiösen Bekenntnisse im Staat, soweit sie nicht dessen Bestand gefährden oder gegen das Sittlichkeits- und Moralgefühl der germanischen Rasse verstoßen. Die Partei als solche vertritt den Standpunkt eines positiven Christentums, ohne sich konfessionell an ein bestimmtes Bekenntnis zu binden. Sie bekämpft den jüdisch-materialistischen Geist in und außer uns und ist überzeugt, daß eine dauernde Genesung unseres Volkes nur erfolgen kann von innen heraus auf der Grundlage: Gemeinnutz geht vor Eigennutz.

25. Zur Durchführung alles dessen fordern wir die Schaffung einer starken Zentralgewalt des Reiches. Unbedingte Autorität des politischen Zentralparlaments über das gesamte Reich und seine Organisationen im allgemeinen. Die Bildung von Stände- und Berufskammern zur Durchführung der vom Reich erlassenen Rahmengesetze in den einzelnen Bundesstaaten.

Die Führer der Partei versprechen, wenn nötig unter Einsatz des eigenen Lebens, für die Durchführung der vorstehenden Punkte rücksichtslos einzutreten.

Zu diesem Programm hat Adolf Hitler am 13. 4. 1928 folgende Erklärung verlautbart:

Erklärung.

Gegenüber den verlogenen Auslegungen des Punktes 17 des Programms der NSDAP. von seiten unserer Gegner ist folgende Feststellung notwendig:

Da die NSDAP. auf dem Boden des Privateigentums steht, ergibt sich von selbst, daß der Passus »unentgeltliche Enteignung« nur auf die Schaffung gesetzlicher Möglichkeiten Bezug hat, Boden, der auf unrechtmäßige Weise erworben wurde oder nicht nach den Gesichtspunkten des Volkswohls verwaltet wird, wenn nötig, zu enteignen. Dies richtet sich demgemäß in erster Linie gegen die jüdischen Grundstückspekulationsgesellschaften.

derstanding [*Verständnis*] in the school (through civics). We demand the education of intellectually talented children of poor parents at state expense without regard to their social status or occupation.

21. The state is responsible for improving public health through the protection of mothers and children, through the prohibition of child labor, through the introduction of physical fitness training by means of legislative measures requiring gymnastics and sports, and through the greatest support for all organizations involved in the physical education of youth.

22. We demand the abolition of mercenary troops and the creation of a militia.

23. We demand a legislative struggle against deliberate political lies and their spreading by the press. In order to make the creation of a German press possible, we demand that

   a) all editors of and contributors to newspapers published in the German language must be *Volk* comrades;

   b) non-German newspapers require express state permission to appear. They may not be published in the German language;

   c) any financial participation in German newspapers or influence on them by non-Germans will be legally prohibited; the penalty for infractions will be the closing of such a newspaper, as well as the immediate deportation from the Reich of the non-Germans involved. Newspapers that violate the common good are to be prohibited.

   We demand a legislative struggle against any trend in art or literature that has a corrosive influence on the life of our *Volk*, and the closing of presentations that offend against existing regulations.

24. We demand freedom for all religious denominations in the state insofar as they do not endanger its existence or offend the

sentiments of morality and ethics of the Germanic race. The party itself represents the standpoint of a positive Christianity, without committing itself to the doctrines of a specific denomination. It opposes the Jewish-materialistic spirit within and without us, and is convinced that a lasting recuperation of our *Volk* can succeed only from within, on the foundation of the common good over individual good.

25. To accomplish all this we demand the creation of a strong central power for the Reich. Unconditional authority of the central political parliament over the whole Reich and its bodies in general. The creation of corporatist chambers organized by status and occupation to implement the framework of laws enacted by the Reich in the individual federal states.

   The leaders of the party promise, if necessary with the pledge of their own lives, to relentlessly support the implementation of these points.

On April 13, 1928, Adolf Hitler announced the following clarification regarding this program:

Clarification

The false interpretation of Point 17 of the Program of the NSDAP by our opponents makes the following statement necessary:

Because the NSDAP is based on the foundation of private property, it is implicit that the passage "expropriation without compensation" refers only to the creation of possible legislative measures to expropriate land that had been gained in an unjust manner or was being administered in a way that was not in accord with the viewpoint of the *Volk*'s welfare. Accordingly, this is directed in the first instance against Jewish land-speculation companies.

Pastors' Emergency League (Pfarrernotbund), union of Evangelical clergy founded by the Berlin pastor Martin NIEMÖLLER and his colleagues of the cloth, Gerhard Jacobi and Eitel-Friedrich von Rabenau, on September 21, 1933. It took a stand against the new church order under a Reich Bishop (Ludwig MÜLLER), but above all against the intrusion of National Socialist thought into the church. Upon joining the Emergency League, a minister signed the

following declaration: "(1) I pledge to carry out my office as a servant of the Word, bound only by Holy Scripture and by the confessions of the Reformation as the correct interpretation of Holy Scripture. (2) I pledge that I will protest any violation of this confessional position with unreserved dedication. (3) I am aware that I am responsible, to the extent of my resources, for those who are persecuted for the sake of this confession. (4) Under this obligation I give witness that a violation of this confessional position has taken place with the application of the ARYAN PARAGRAPH within the sphere of the Church of Christ."

This radical reflection on the confession of faith was introduced in the summer of 1933 by Karl BARTH in his essay "Theologische Existenz heute" (Theological Existence Today), which he aimed against the state's attempt to make the church over into an instrument for its own political purposes. The league also wanted to avert the possibility "that a non-Evangelical concept of leader become insinuated into our midst." By January 15, 1934, the league had 7,036 members, comprising nearly half of the Evangelical clergy; from it grew the REICH FRATERNAL COUNCIL, which in turn engendered the BARMEN CONFESSIONAL SYNOD that took the initiative of organizing the CONFESSING CHURCH. Despite uninterrupted persecution during the CHURCH STRUGGLE and despite Niemöller's confinement in concentration camps (1937–1945), the authorities were never able to stamp out the league completely.

Paulus, Friedrich, b. Breitenau (Kreis Melsungen), September 23, 1890; d. Dresden, February 1, 1957, German field marshal general (January 31, 1943). Paulus entered the Prussian army in 1910. He was an officer in the First World War, and afterward served with border security troops in the east. From 1920 to 1939 he held various staff and troop commands in the Reichswehr and the Wehrmacht. As quartermaster general I on the Army General Staff (as of September 1940), Paulus was involved in the preparations for the RUSSIAN CAMPAIGN, during which he took supreme command of the Sixth Army in January 1942. With it he attacked Stalingrad in August of that year. After overcoming nearly the entire city, in November he was surrounded by the Red Army. When Paulus surrendered on February 2, 1943, and was taken captive with the remainder of his army (around 90,000 troops), he was accused of cowardice by Hitler: "The man is supposed to shoot himself!" Paulus took part in the formation of the NATIONAL COMMITTEE FOR A FREE GERMANY and appealed to the German troops on the eastern front to desert. Released from captivity in 1953, he took up residence in the German Democratic Republic. His book *Ich stehe hier auf Befehl* (I Stand Here as Ordered) was published posthumously in 1960.

Ba.

Pavelić, Ante, b. Bradina (Herzegovina), July 14, 1898; d. Madrid, December 28, 1959, Croatian politician. A lawyer, in 1919 Pavelić became a member of the anti-Serbian Croatian Party of Justice, which he represented in the Yugoslav parliament in 1927. In 1929 he went into exile in Italy. Pavelić conspired against the Yugoslav state; his Croatian independence movement, the Ustaša (*see* USTAŠE), for which he found aid in Fascist Italy, engaged in terror and agitation against the Belgrade government (its acts included the 1934 murder of King Alexander I of Yugoslavia in Marseilles). After the collapse of Yugoslavia during the BALKAN CAMPAIGN, Pavelić was able to establish his "Independent State of Croatia," proclaimed on April 10, 1941. As chief of state (*poglavnik*) he followed the pattern of his Fascist and National Socialist protectors, including the establishment of concentration camps for political opponents, the persecution of Serbs and Muslims, and the murder of Jews or their delivery to the SS. Whereas many of his followers fell victim to the wrath of Tito's partisans at the war's end, Pavelić escaped through Austria and Italy to Argentina, where he formed an Ustaša government-in-exile.

Peace Address (*Friedensrede*), designation for Hitler's speech before the Reichstag on May 17, 1933. An aggressive foreign-policy line had been expected from Hitler, but he emphasized, to the applause of all party delegations (those that still remained), the "justified claims to existence of other peoples" and the desire of his government to "work things out" solely "through peaceful and diplomatic means." The Peace Address was a masterpiece of dissimulation. Together with the CONCORDAT (July 20, 1933) and the GERMAN-POLISH NONAGGRESSION PACT (January 26, 1934), it contributed to the fatally erroneous estimation of Hitler and of his FOREIGN POLICY's true goals.

Peace dictates. *See* Friedensdiktate.

Pearl Harbor, naval stronghold of the United States on the Hawaiian island of Oahu. On December 7, 1941, 355 aircraft of the Japanese naval air force attacked Pearl Harbor, sank five battleships, damaged three others, and destroyed as well a great number of ships, airplanes, and military facilities. The American losses were 2,403 dead and 1,178 wounded. Pearl Harbor became the trigger for the American-Japanese war and for the German declaration of war on the United States (December 11,

Ante Pavelić.

1941). President Franklin D. ROOSEVELT was now able to intervene against the AXIS powers in a war that the American public had long supported but had not liked. That the president deliberately sacrificed Pearl Harbor for this purpose remains only speculation.

Peasant Academy (Bauernhochschule), educational institution in Goslar, primarily used for political SCHOOLING and run by the REICH FOOD ESTATE. The academy was intended to educate specially selected young peasant men and women in line with the National Socialist "way of life," and thus to train a cadre of future peasant leaders.

Peasant honor (*Bauernehrung*), bestowal of a document by the Reich Peasant Führer on fami-

December 7, 1941: Japanese surprise attack on Pearl Harbor.

lies that for centuries, in "unbroken generational succession," had worked as farmers "on their own sod for Germany."

Peasant literature (*Bauerndichtung*), general term for the literary presentation of the peasant world. Peasant literature was the literary expression of a countermovement to urbanization and industrialization. In it, the bourgeoisie since the late 19th century had subjected Nature to a cultic glorification, frequently equated the peasantry with naturalness, and idealized peasants as a mythical "source of health," as seen, for example, in the novel *Der Büttnerbauer* (The Cask Maker; 1895) by Wilhelm von Polenz, considered by National Socialist literary scholars to be a classic. NS literary criticism later differentiated between an "opportunistic literature [*Konjunkturschrifttum*], which has not grasped the idea of Blood and Soil," and "valuable" peasant literature directed against the "asphalt mankind of the cosmopolises" (Alfred Rosenberg), such as the novels of Josefa BERENS-TOTENOHL.

Peasant Militia (*Wehrbauer*), official term for the farmers who were to settle the land newly conquered by the German Reich, while also assuming military functions. It was thus that the long-term planning of Heinrich Himmler, as Reich Commissioner for the Fortification of the German Volk-Nation, foresaw sending, "year after year," expeditions of German peasants into the conquered territories in the east. The "borders of the *Volk*-nation" would be shifted forward by settlement of the area "behind the military border" with peasant soldiers. In these lands they would expel the "ethnic aliens," so that ultimately the boundary could be moved further eastward. According to Himmler (August 3, 1944), the Peasant Militia would do for the Führer that which "the Cossacks were able to do for the Russian tsars in gobbling up everything as far as the Yellow Sea and ultimately conquering it." As a reservoir for the Peasant Militia, the members of the Hitler Youth Country Service came into particular consideration. They were repeatedly promised their own land for settlement in return for obedient service, but in practice they functioned as cheap labor for the owners of large estates.

Peasant Physical Education (Bäuerliche Leibeserziehung), National Socialist program for the increased physical fitness of the "for the most part one-sidedly occupied rural population."

For this purpose the REICH FOOD ESTATE set up a Reich School for Physical Exercises near Braunschweig where young peasant men and women were trained in the "practice of species-appropriate [*artgemäss*] physical education."

Peasantry (*Bauerntum*), the estate (*Stand*) designated by the National Socialist BLOOD AND SOIL ideologues as the "blood source" and "most important basic element" of race and nation. Since the end of the 19th century, economic changes—concentration and industrialization—took place more starkly in the country than in the city. Loss of social class led to strong conservative opposition, which in the COUNTRYFOLK MOVEMENT (1928–1930) culminated in local unrest. Land ownership, which was threatened by capitalism, was glorified poetically by the urban bourgeoisie (*see* PEASANT LITERATURE) and mythically by the NSDAP. For political (*see* AUTARKY) as well as ideological reasons the peasantry, which along with "labor and the military" was seen as a state-supporting stratum, was especially encouraged. An Office for Peasant Culture was even established in the Reich Office for Agricultural Policy.

Peasant Schools (*Bauernschulen*), educational institutions of the REICH FOOD ESTATE, in 20 locations by 1936. The schools exclusively served ideological SCHOOLING and PEASANT PHYSICAL EDUCATION. They were intended to convey to the selected students an "understanding of the life and occupation of the National Socialist peasant estate."

Peat-bog soldiers (*Moorsoldaten*), (self-)designation of the prisoners in the EMSLAND CAMPS, who were utilized primarily in the cultivation and cutting of peat in the surrounding moors. The term "peat-bog soldiers" became popular through the song "We Are the Peat-Bog Soldiers," which was written and set to music by prisoners of the Börgermoor camp in the summer of 1933. It was further spread by the actor Wolfgang Langhoff's account of his imprisonment in Börgermoor, *Die Moorsoldaten*, which was published in Switzerland in 1935.

Peenemünde, fishing village on the Usedom peninsula, at the mouth of the Oder River. At Peenemünde the Army Weapons Office in 1936 began construction of a rocket research facility under the direction of Gen. Walter Dornberger and Wernher von BRAUN. It was here that the long-range A-4 rocket (propaganda name, v2)

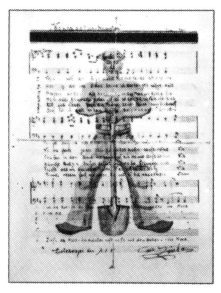

The song of the peat-bog soldiers.

was developed. It belonged to the arsenal of the so-called WONDER WEAPONS in the Second World War, which, however, achieved military and space-technological significance only after the war, through further American development.

Peiner, Werner, b. Düsseldorf, July 20, 1897, German painter. Beginning in 1922 Peiner was an independent artist in Bonn, Düsseldorf, and Kronenburg (Eifel). In Kronenburg he established a "country academy," which quickly fell into difficulties and was rescued only by Hermann Göring's intervention. Renamed the HERMANN GÖRING MASTER SCHOOL FOR PAINTING, it was directed by Peiner after his return from extensive travels in 1938. It was used to train artists in the National Socialist mold, as Peiner had refined it in his "blood-and-soil" paintings. For his patron Göring he produced, among other works of art, *Weibliche Tugenden* (Female Virtues), based on a Gobelin tapestry, which adorned KARINHALL. Peiner expressed his mythological and *völkisch* understanding of art in this way: "Every work of art is a tear that the divine homeland weeps." After the war Peiner settled in Leichlingen, near Cologne. Supported by substantial commissions from rich burghers, he complained about his artistic isolation.

Peiper, Joachim, b. Berlin, January 30, 1915; d. Traves (France), July 13, 1976, SS-*Standartenführer* (colonel) of the Waffen-SS. During the ARDENNES OFFENSIVE, Peiper was the commander of an armored combat group of the LEIB-STANDARTE-SS "ADOLF HITLER" First SS Ar-

Joachim Peiper.

mored Division. He was sentenced to death in the MALMÉDY TRIAL on a charge of prisoner executions; his sentence was later commuted to life imprisonment, and at the end of 1956 he was granted early release. In early 1970 he settled in Traves, in the French Jura mountain range. When it became known who he was, a press campaign against Peiper flared under the leadership of the Communist newspaper *L'Humanité*. Demands arose for his immediate expulsion. After death threats, his house was set afire on the eve of the French national holiday in 1976. Peiper's charred corpse was found in the burned-out structure. An underground organization called Les Vengeurs (The Avengers) took credit for the deed. The perpetrators were never caught.

A. St.

Perels, Friedrich Justus, b. Berlin, November 13, 1910; d. there, April 22, 1945, German jurist and opposition fighter. Involved in church circles even as a law student, after his examinations in 1933 and 1937 Perels worked primarily as an attorney for the PASTORS' EMERGENCY LEAGUE and for the CONFESSING CHURCH. He took as clients the relatives of concentration camp prisoners; he concealed the persecuted and helped Jews to flee. These acts, in addition to his acquaintance with Dietrich BONHOEFFER, Hans von DOHNÁNYI, and other opposition fighters, made Perels an object of suspicion. After the failed assassination attempt of July 20, 1944, he was arrested on October 5; on February 2, 1945, he was sentenced to death for failing to report

the conspiracy. While in transit to another prison in embattled Berlin, he and many other fellow prisoners were shot by an SS commando unit. Perels's motto thus came true: "So many now die fighting for this system. I find it better to die fighting against this system."

Performance (*Leistung;* also translated as "accomplishment" or "efficiency"), a fundamental principle of the National Socialist worldview; it was intended to sum up the "attitude toward the surrounding world" of the "man of the Nordic type" (Ludwig Ferdinand CLAUSS). As a central ideological construct, *Leistung* appeared in numerous combinations. *Leistungsertüchtigung* (training for performance fitness) was an all-encompassing term for "measures that best serve to foster the will to perform [*Leistungswille*] and the capacity to perform [*Leistungsfähigkeit*] of the productive German, and to effect fitness [*Ertüchtigung*] from the inside out" (A. Friedrich, *Grundlegung der Leistungsertüchtigung* [Fundamentals of Training for Performance Fitness]; 1939). *Leistungsethos* (performance ethos) was the readiness to perform or accomplish, said to be manifest as a basic life principle only among the Nordic people. *Leistungsgemeinschaft* (performance community) described common work toward a common goal, which was seen as the basis for a VOLK COMMUNITY. *Leistungsmensch* (person of performance) was a term for the Nordic person as a "racial ideal." *Leistungsprinzip* (performance principle), a social principle fundamental to the Third Reich, determined the individual's place in the *Volk* Community solely by the quality of his or her performance, which in practice, however, took a backseat to political expediency. The *Leistungsrasse* (race of accomplishment) was the Nordic-German race, especially as contrasted to Jewish "drones" and "parasites."

Performance, developmental principle of (*Entfaltungsprinzip der Leistung*), extension of the performance principle to the "developmental foundation of National Socialism." In this view, every "*Volk* comrade" should be rewarded according to his or her performance or accomplishments and should accumulate personal property by the same means. "When all performances of all people active in the *Volk* Community can be developed in accordance with the best respective potential for each," then, in the view of National Socialist economic theory, "the well-being of the *Volk* Community [will be] attained to the fullest possible extent." Because this ideal of community was in opposition to an unchecked development in the liberal sense, the NS developmental principle also included governmental supervision of the economy as well as influence over vocational education and selection.

Performance Book (*Leistungsbuch*), official term for a certificate earned by female trade school pupils and students for several weeks of AID SERVICE in families with many children.

Performance Competition of German Workplaces (*Leistungskampf der deutschen Betriebe*), yearly contest for "model" workplaces and working conditions, instituted in 1936 by the GERMAN LABOR FRONT (DAF). The competition was intended to promote social efforts such as self-improvement, continuing education, work safety, nutrition, company housing, and sports facilities. The programs of the participating workplaces (some 84,000 in 1938) were scrutinized by DAF functionaries and TRUSTEES OF LABOR; the best ones received a regional citation and went on to participate in a Reich-wide selection. Those workplaces that were most successful according to the DAF guidelines then received from Hitler on May 1 the title "National Socialist Model Workshop" (*Nazionalsozialistischer Musterbetrieb*) for the year—in 1938 there were 103 of them—and were permitted to fly the GOLDEN FLAG OF THE GERMAN LABOR FRONT. Workplaces that were exemplary in particular industries received "performance badges" (*Leistungsabzeichen*), of which 266 were awarded in 1938. The Performance Competition was a successful propaganda effort of NS SOCIAL POLICY, but it increasingly lost meaning as the war went on.

Performance medicine (*Leistungsmedizin*), new branch of MEDICINE promoted in 1933, with the goal of "increasing the capacity for performance [*Leistungsfähigkeit*] of every kind to its greatest attainable height." Performance medicine aimed, on the one hand, to maintain the performance capacity of the healthy person and, on the other, to bring about a reduction of illness. Illness was regarded as an insufficient readiness to perform and as a neglect of the "duty to be healthy" (*Pflicht zur Gesundheit*), which was no longer seen as the individual's private concern, but rather as a matter subject to the state's totalitarian claim.

The medical division of the GERMAN LABOR FRONT (DAF) was the standard-bearer of performance medicine. It promoted the introduction of a health card with a "performance diagnosis" (*Leistungsdiagnose*), which would determine the amount of future pensions. The claims of the DAF inevitably produced conflicts with the Reich health leadership (*see* Leonardo CONTI). All measures taken by this new branch of medicine could not prevent the steady rise in the rate of illness during the course of the war.

Performance test (*Leistungsprüfung*), designation borrowed by National Socialist racial researchers from livestock breeding to denote the selection of "breeding stock" (*Zuchtmaterial*): those who, in the words of Walther DARRÉ, "as the new aristocracy will be raised on the cultivation estates [*Hegehöfe*]" and who in future ages would "present the German *Volk* with leaders." "Performance test" was also a term for the athletic tests in which persons belonging to certain age groups or subdivisions of the NSDAP (such as the SA or Hitler Youth) had to demonstrate a particular level of achievement. In this sense it was also used to denote the REICH VOCATIONAL COMPETITION of the German Labor Front.

Periodical Service/German Weekly Service (Zeitschriften-Dienst/Deutscher Wochendienst; ZD), information service for all magazine editors regarding the intentions and aims of the makers of press policy; it was established on May 9, 1939, by Hans FRITZSCHE. The ZD was issued by the Aufwärts-Verlag (Upward Publishing House [as against the Social Democratic *Vorwärts*, or Forward]) in Berlin, and a subscription was required of all periodical publishers. The strictly confidential collections of information and advisories supplanted the oral PRESS ADVISORIES of the Propaganda Ministry's Reich Periodical Conferences and the teletyped advisories of the Reich Propaganda Offices. The ZD's editor in chief was Hans Georg Trurnit, the editor for economic and social policy was Walter Hopf, and those for cultural policy and entertainment were Kurt Lothar Tank and Heinz Vöpel, respectively. The ZD was supplemented for some periodicals with a weekly *Zeitschriften-Information* (Periodical Information), published by the Press Section of the Propaganda Ministry and added without charge by the Reich Propaganda Offices. The final issue of the ZD was that of March 9, 1945.

S. O.

Persecution of Jews

The history of the Jews in the Diaspora is a history of persecution. Religious fanaticism and economic motives led again and again to actions hostile to the Jews, which often ended in massacres. Under the influence of the Enlightenment ideal of tolerance, a process of emancipation began in the late 18th century that finally led to political, economic, and social equality in the course of the 19th century. Emancipation did not, however, eliminate enmity toward Jews; ANTISEMITISM persisted in various guises and levels of activity. Beyond that, a further kind of hostility toward Jews developed: racial antisemitism. It reached its high point in National Socialist Germany with the so-called FINAL SOLUTION of the Jewish question.

Persecution of the Jews constituted one of the basic tenets of the NS worldview. The NSDAP platform of February 24, 1920, stated that only a person of "German blood" could be a VOLK COMRADE. It demanded that Jews be governed by laws for aliens. The first official attack can be found in a legislative initiative by the NSDAP Reichstag delegation on March 13, 1930, that (unsuccessfully) urged punishment for "racial treason" (Rasseverrat). It called for imprisonment—or, in especially severe cases, death —for those "who by mixing with members of the Jewish blood community [Blutsgemeinschaft] (or with colored races) contribute or threaten to contribute to racial deterioration and injury to the German Volk."

After the Seizure of Power the National Socialists soon began to implement their plans for persecution of the Jews. At first their intention was hindered by Article 109 of the Weimar Constitution, according to which all citizens were equal before the law. Exceptive legislation against the Jews would accordingly be unconstitutional. The ground for this was cleared only with the ENABLING LAW (March 24, 1933). A week later followed the so-called first Synchronization Law, according to which the governments of the German states (Länder) could issue laws without prior resolution of the state legislatures (Landtage). The first exceptive law was the CIVIL SERVICE LAW of April 7, 1933, according to which civil servants of non-Aryan extraction, among others, were to be retired or—in the case of honorary unpaid civil servants—

dismissed (see ARYAN PARAGRAPH). On the wish of Reich President Paul von Hindenburg, exceptions were made for those who had held civil service posts since August 1, 1914, who had fought in the First World War on the side of Germany or its allies, or whose fathers or sons had been killed in that war. The first implementation ordinance (April 11, 1933) defined a "non-Aryan" as a person whose parents or grandparents were non-Aryan, especially Jewish; it sufficed to have one non-Aryan parent or grandparent.

Even before the Civil Service Law was issued, individual states and community authorities had issued decrees (without any legal basis) for retiring civil servants. At the state level this involved mainly judges and public prosecutors (Bavaria and Prussia, March 31, 1933); at the community level it affected civil servants of all ranks and professions. Moreover, arbitrary dismissals were often arranged, or civil servants were put under such pressure that they resigned on their own. Parallel with the exceptive law for Jewish civil servants, measures were taken to reduce Jewish activity in many professions: for example, non-Aryan lawyers were not allowed to practice, and under certain circumstances licenses could be withdrawn from lawyers previously admitted to the bar (April 7, 1933); the participation of Jewish physicians, dentists, and dental technicians in the state health insurance plan (Krankenkasse) was terminated, and new licensing was not permitted (April 22, 1933); Jews were no longer issued pharmacy licenses (April 17, 1934). Along with these measures directed against professional groups, the exclusion of Jews from cultural life was begun. The basis for this was the Law to Establish the REICH CULTURE CHAMBER of September 22, 1933. Non-Aryans were not admitted to the chamber.

The restrictive measures of the persecution of the Jews were primarily limited to specific professional groups during the first two years of NS rule. Issuance of the so-called NUREMBERG LAWS of September 15, 1935, namely the Reich Citizenship Law (Reichsbürgergesetz; RBüGes) and the Law to Protect German Blood and German Honor (Gesetz zum Schutze des deutschen Blutes und der deutschen Ehre;

BlSchGes), affected all Jews. Through the former law, Jews were excluded from Reich citizenship (*Reichsbürgerschaft*), although they remained "members of the German state" (*Staatsangehörige*). According to the First Ordinance to Implement the Reich Citizenship Law of November 14, 1935, a Jew was a person with at least three "racially" pure Jewish grandparents or (under certain circumstances) a MIXED-BREED with two fully Jewish grandparents. As noncitizens, Jews had no right to vote in political matters, and they could not hold public office. The remaining Jewish civil servants and other Jews still in public service were to be dismissed. Thus the exemption for frontline veterans and other privileged Jews was abolished. The Law to Protect German Blood and German Honor prohibited marriage between Jews and non-Jews and threatened imprisonment for noncompliance; extramarital liaisons between such persons were also prohibited, under threat of imprisonment.

Not only did the Nuremberg Laws achieve the separation between Jews and non-Jews desired by the National Socialists; they were subsequently also the basis for the systematic exclusion of Jews from the political community.

The wielders of power at first desisted from excluding Jews from economic life. Jewish shop owners and entrepreneurs had variously suffered under restrictive measures (such as the appeal by the NSDAP leadership on March 29, 1933, for an organized BOYCOTT AGAINST JEWS), and in individual cases Jews had been excluded from their area of employment (for example, auctioneering, or the production, repair, and sale of weapons). But for the time being they were left alone in order to ensure an undisturbed recovery from the economic crisis. On June 14, 1938, however, the Reich economics minister declared that the principle of "non-application of the Aryan Paragraph to the economy" was no longer to be upheld; the quickest possible exclusion of Jews from the economy was to be sought. The intervention began with the Law to Change Trade Regulations (*Gesetz zur Änderung der Gewerbeordnung*) of July 6, 1938, which prohibited Jews from practicing a number of trades, and it continued with numerous further measures sanctioned by laws and ordinances. The professional prohibitions that were intended to eliminate Jews from economic life were finally extended to professional groups whose activity was already restricted (such as

Jewish citizens of Vienna are forced to clean the sidewalk with toothbrushes.

physicians on July 25, 1938, and lawyers on September 27 of that year). The confiscation of their property (*see* ARYANIZATION) went hand in hand with the elimination of the Jews from economic life.

All these and other persecution measures were undertaken in order to induce the Jews to leave the German Reich. At first, only Jews who were native to Poland were expelled, among them those who had chosen Germany during the plebiscite on affiliation in the German territories in the east after 1919, but who had been denied citizenship in the German state after 1933. Some 17,000 persons were forcibly deported beyond the Polish border on October 29, 1938. As revenge for this injustice, the young Jew Herschel GRYNSZPAN, whose family members were among the deported, made an attempt on the life of the secretary of the German embassy in Paris, Ernst vom RATH, on November 7, 1938, which unleashed serious consequences for Germany's Jews. At the annual meeting of the so-called Old Combatants in Munich on November 9, Joseph Goebbels made a speech hostile to Jews; it was the signal for a pogrom that began the same night (*see* KRISTALLNACHT), and that lasted until November 11. Now a flood tide of laws and ordinances was issued; they gradually robbed those Jews remaining in Germany of all rights. The measures were accompanied by an unprecedented campaign of harassment by the centrally directed press and the publications of NS organizations.

Despite all this, the authorities came no closer to their goal of solving the Jewish question through emigration. Of the more than 500,000 Jews remaining in Germany in early 1933, only some 180,000 had emigrated by the end of 1938, according to statistics derived from the so-called Reich Escape Tax (*Reichsfluchtsteuer*). Those who remained still hoped for a normalization of conditions; some were unable to leave their homeland because of inadequate means, since many countries were unwilling to accept destitute Jews. To take control over the situation, the Reich Central Office for Jewish Emigration (Reichszentrale für jüdische Auswanderung) was established on January 24, 1939, under the leadership of the chief of the Security Police, Reinhard HEYDRICH; its goal was to prepare, direct, and accelerate Jewish emigration. Toward this end, on July 4, 1939, the Reich Interior Ministry ordered the creation of the Reich Union of Jews in Germany (*see* REICH REPRESENTATION OF GERMAN JEWS), to which all Jews had to belong. With resources that the

Jewish concentration camp prisoners.

Reich Union took exclusively from wealthy Jews, emigration was possible for poor Jews. Nearly 80,000 Jews left Germany in 1939.

After Poland's defeat, Heydrich saw the possibility of solving the Jewish question by evacuations to Poland. However, on March 24, 1940, Göring ordered the deportations stopped for foreign-policy reasons. Heydrich then ordered an increased resumption of emigration. The MADAGASCAR PLAN had not yet been abandoned, but it could not be realized because of the war, and the number of countries admitting Jews had grown smaller. In October 1940 the Jews of Baden, the Palatinate, and the Saar region were abruptly banished into unoccupied France. In view of the imminent Final Solution of the Jewish question, however, the Reich Security Main Office on May 20, 1941, issued an order to stop this "emigration." Finally, on July 31 of that year, Göring gave Heydrich the order to prepare for a "total solution [*Gesamtlösung*] of the Jewish question" within the German sphere of influence in Europe. In mid-October 1941, deportations of Jews began from the Reich territory into the eastern territories, and finally into the EXTERMINATION CAMPS, primarily AUSCHWITZ.

Initially exempt from deportation were (primarily) Jews over the age of 65, those with severe war injuries, those with war decorations, those living in "mixed marriages," and those working in armament plants. The first category was soon transported to the THERESIENSTADT camp, designated as a ghetto for the elderly, in which they had to "buy" a place with so-called home-purchase contracts (*Heimeinkaufsverträge*) by giving up their property. Many ghetto inhabitants died because of poor living conditions or were finally "resettled" into one of the extermination camps. Those Jews who were working under compulsion in the armament plants were eventually removed to Auschwitz beginning in the spring of 1943. Among them were many Jews living in "mixed marriages."

Until the deportation of the last Jews, their living conditions steadily deteriorated. Marked (*see* JEWISH STAR), defamed, harassed, robbed of their property, removed from their professions and homes (*see* JEWISH HOUSES), and employed as forced laborers, they lived without rights in their homeland. Of the 168,972 Jews (by definition of the Nuremberg Laws) still living in the Old Reich in May 1941, only 14,574 were still registered on September 1, 1944. After this date numerous transports went to Auschwitz and, as the Red Army approached, to concentration camps within Reich territory. On March 27, 1945, what is believed to be the last "elderly transport" (*Altertrans-*

port) left Berlin in the direction of Theresienstadt.

Nearly all Jews in the territories occupied by the Wehrmacht or in countries within the German sphere of influence suffered under the NS persecution. Although various governments and populations opposed the NS Jewish policy (as in Denmark and the Netherlands), only rarely was it possible to protect Jews in general from the clutches of the Gestapo (as in Bulgaria outside its occupied areas). Especially tragic was the fate of stateless Jews who found themselves in many of these countries; they included numerous German emigrés whose connection with the German state had been officially severed when they left Germany. No government spoke up for them. They became the first victims of the persecution measures, as in France. The most brutal persecution of Jews was conducted by the National Socialists in Poland and the occupied parts of the USSR. The special political circumstances in these regions gave the NS rulers a free hand in the carrying out of their extermination goals, which had already been begun with the EINSATZGRUPPEN.

Alfred Streim

Persil Certificate (*Persilschein*), ironic term derived from the name of a well-known German laundry detergent and applied to formal exculpations (in the sense of "whitewash"). The term arose during the DENAZIFICATION period, when positive statements on behalf of someone being reviewed, made by a known opponent of National Socialism (ideally, a former concentration camp inmate), had literal exchange value. This created a complex market in favors that further discredited the already problematic denazification procedures.

Personality (*Persönlichkeit*), in National Socialist usage, a substitute for the term "individual" (*Individuum*), which was equated with the "unrestrained and unconnected individualism" of liberalism and which NS propaganda at times used in the sense of "wretch" (*Lump*). The term "personality," on the other hand, implied that the person was bound to the community.

Pétain, Henri, b. Cauchy-la-Tour (Pas-de-Calais), April 24, 1856; d. Port Joinville (Île d'Yeu), July 23, 1951, French marshal (November 1918) and politician. During the First World War, Pétain

initially saw service as commanding general of an army corps. In 1915 he was promoted to commander of the Second Army, and in February 1916 he became supreme commander for the defense of Verdun. On May 15, 1917, he became supreme commander of the French army. From 1922 to 1931 Pétain was inspector general of the army. Elected in 1929 to the Académie Française, he became inspector of air defense in 1931. He served briefly as war minister in 1934.

Pétain's aura as the "victor of Verdun" remained undiminished after the war. In March 1939 he was sent as ambassador to Francisco FRANCO's Spain in order to restore French-Spanish relations, which had been almost totally severed by the SPANISH CIVIL WAR. After the German attack on France (May 10, 1940), Paul REYNAUD appointed Pétain to his cabinet as deputy premier. Having chosen the general as a symbolic national figure, after the fall of Paris on June 16, 1940, Reynaud had to yield to Pétain as head of government. Between June 22 and 24, the general concluded a cease-fire with Germany and Italy. On July 10 he was appointed chief of the "French State" (*État Français*) by the

Henri Pétain.

French National Assembly in VICHY; the vote of 569–80 also gave him dictatorial powers.

Pétain followed a dual policy: limited cooperation with the German occupying powers and simultaneous nonacceptance. In MONTOIRE he was able to keep France out of Hitler's war plans; he did, however, promote the formation of a "French volunteer legion against Bolshevism." For a time he curbed the influence of Pierre LAVAL, the advocate of total COLLABORATION, but on November 8, 1942, Pétain ordered French troops to combat the Allied landing in North Africa. He remained in secret contact with the British government, yet allowed shootings of hostages and the deportation of Jews by the Germans to proceed without protest. Domestically, he worked at consolidating a corporatist state based on the views of the ACTION FRANÇAISE, removed from power all former representatives of the Third Republic, attempted to mitigate the economic consequences of the war, and struggled without success to obtain the release of the French prisoners of war in Germany.

Pétain's double-dealing was not obvious to the French public, and for many of his compatriots he symbolized the legitimization of collaboration (a poster question asked, "Are you more French than he?"). Brought by the Germans on August 20, 1944, to Belfort, and on September 8 to Sigmaringen, Pétain presented himself to the French authorities on April 24, 1945, even though Charles de GAULLE would have preferred that he go into exile in Switzerland. He was tried between July 23 and August 15,

1945; the judges, by a vote of 14 to 13, sentenced him to death. Spared that penalty because of his advanced age, he spent his last years confined to a fortress on the Île d'Yeu.

Pfahler, Gerhard, b. Freudenstadt, August 12, 1897; d. Tübingen, February 20, 1976, German psychologist and educator. Pfahler developed a system of character types according to heredity, in which he categorized different races by hereditary characteristics. He set forth his views in *System der Typenlehren* (Systematic Typology; 1929) and *Vererbung als Schicksal* (Heredity as Destiny; 1932). The National Socialists utilized his books as the basis of a *völkisch* "racial psychology"; they appointed him a professor at Göttingen in 1934 and at Tübingen in 1938. Beginning in 1945, Pfahler occupied himself with issues of heredity from the perspective of depth psychology, publishing *Der Mensch und seine Vergangenheit* (Man and His Past) in 1950.

Pfeffer von Salomon, Franz, b. Düsseldorf, February 19, 1888; d. Munich, April 12, 1968, SA leader. An officer in the First World War, Pfeffer became a free corps leader afterward, taking part in the KAPP PUTSCH and the RUHR CONFLICT. He joined the National Socialists in 1924. Pfeffer von Salomon founded and headed the *Gau* of Westphalia. From 1926 to 1930 he was the SA's supreme head (*Oberster SA-Führer;* Osaf). When Hitler himself assumed this post and placed the SA under its chief of staff, Ernst RÖHM, Pfeffer von Salomon fell by the political wayside. He served as a Reichstag deputy between 1933 and 1942, but was completely without influence during the war, and in 1944 was even imprisoned.

Pfitzner, Hans, b. Moscow, May 5, 1869; d. Salzburg, May 22, 1949, German composer. From 1894 to 1896, Pfitzner was a theatrical music director in Mainz; from 1897 to 1907 he taught composition in Berlin, and from 1908 to 1918 he was municipal music and opera director in Strasbourg. From 1930 to 1934, Pfitzner taught at the Academy of Music in Munich; subsequently he was a conductor, pianist, and opera director. His compositions were especially influenced by Richard WAGNER and German Romanticism, most evidently in his chief work, *Palestrina* (1917). After the First World War, Pfitzner gravitated increasingly toward nationalistic circles, where he found most of his admirers. He regarded himself as a combatant for the protection of German cultural values and considered himself to be Wagner's successor. Pfitz-

Hans Pfitzner.

ner became a convinced supporter of National Socialist ideas. As such, he took part in the cultural propaganda project known as Art for the *Volk* (Die Kunst dem Volke); within that context, in 1937 he conducted a concert of his own compositions in a Reich Railroad improvement project. The National Socialists appreciated his music for its mood, which they called "downright German" and "partly strong in concept, partly childlike and credulous."

Pfitzner, Josef, b. Petersdorf, March 24, 1901; d. Prague, 1945 (executed), German historian and politician. While a professor at the German University of Prague (beginning in 1930), Pfitzner took a special interest in the Sudeten German past and published *Volkstumsschutz und nationale Bewegung* (Ethnic Preservation and National Movement; 1938). Politically he became close to the National Socialists early on. In 1939 he became mayor of Prague, and after the liberation was executed as a war criminal.

Philosemitism (*Philosemitismus*), esteem for Jewry, for Jews, and for the Jewish religion, mainly as a countermovement to ANTISEMITISM. Emerging in antiquity, philosemitism became a stronger movement especially in the Age of Humanism, when its advocates included the young Martin Luther and Johann Reuchlin, and during the Enlightenment, when it was upheld by Gotthold Lessing, among others. Although often arising in reaction to antisemitic excesses, philosemitism had its roots in the Old Testament tradition shared by Judaism and Christianity. This engendered many attempts to proselytize Jews, most of which, however, backfired.

Philosemitism proved to be relatively ineffectual against racial antisemitism. In the Third Reich its only possible foundation was the Christian commandment of neighborly love, which, however, frequently stopped at the church doors. Philosemitic impulses with regard to unbaptized Jews were the exception, since according to the National Socialist racial ideology philosemitism was "considered every bit as dangerous to the *Volk* as Jewry itself," and was persecuted accordingly. Deeply shaken by the Holocaust, many people since the Second World War have subscribed to an uncritical philosemitism, which once again ascribes a special role to the Jews. Many new antisemitic stirrings in Germany can be understood as a reaction to this sort of philosemitism stemming from a bad conscience.

Philosophy (Gr.; love of wisdom), scholarly discipline that was kept on a particularly short rein during the Third Reich. For the totalitarian mind-set of National Socialism (*see* HITLER'S WORLDVIEW), any alternative conceptual structure had to seem dangerous. Thus, philosophical scholarship was assigned special tasks for the purpose of providing underpinnings for National Socialist positions, while original thinkers such as Martin HEIDEGGER and Karl JASPERS were either isolated or persecuted. Epistemological discussions were replaced by the mythological speculations about an "all-life" (*All-Leben*) of Alfred ROSENBERG or Ernst KRIECK; basic ethical questions were answered along the lines of a "political pedagogy," as offered by Alfred BAEUMLER. In philosophical psychology, the "lore of a racial soul" (*Rassenseelenkunde*) as espoused by researchers such as Hans Friedrich Karl GÜNTHER and Ludwig CLAUSS predominated; among the great philosophers of the past, Friedrich NIETZSCHE was especially esteemed by the National Socialists. In order to avoid ideological clashes, academic philosophy occupied itself increasingly with the history of philosophy or with formalized areas of logic.

Photojournalism. *See* Picture reporter; Propaganda Companies.

Physical culture (*Körperkultur*), collective term for such concerns as grooming, personal hygiene, exercise and physical training, awareness of diet and nutrition, and a rational rhythm of life. In National Socialist usage, the term was broadened through a focus on RACIAL HYGIENE, "military fitness," and hereditary health. Thus

Physical culture.

physical culture was at the center of NS training and EDUCATION, which according to the mandate in *Mein Kampf* had as its first priority the "breeding of fit and healthy bodies." Nudism (*Freikörperkultur; Nacktkultur*), on the other hand, was branded as a product of "corrosive Jewish activity" and was banned with an ordinance of March 3, 1933. From the NS perspective, it was one of the modern "degenerate phenomena" of physical culture, as was the "addiction to records" in sports.

Physical exercises (*Leibesübungen*), the totality of sports activities and games aimed at achieving "performance fitness" (*Leistungsfähigkeit*). In National Socialist (and nationalist) usage, the term *Leibesübungen* (literally, body exercises) was preferred to the word *Sport* (*see* SPORTS), with its English origins.

Physics. *See* German physics.

Physical exercises. Swinging with bars.

Picture burning (*Bilderverbrennung*), the destruction of more than 1,000 oil paintings and nearly 4,000 watercolors, drawings, and graphic works on March 20, 1939, "in a symbolic propaganda action on the funeral pyre" in the courtyard of the central fire station in Berlin. The event was similar to the acts of BOOK BURNING, although less spectacular. The "scum of degenerate art" (according to the ministerial councillor Franz Hofmann)—confiscated artworks that could no longer be sold "somehow or other for foreign currency" and that were not needed for defamatory exhibitions—was sacrificed to the flames in a "purifying act."

Picture reporter (*Bildberichter[statter]*), Germanization of *Pressephotograph* (press photographer); the longer form of the term was first mandated, on May 26, 1936. The shorter form became common during the war for the photographers of the PROPAGANDA COMPANIES.

Pieck, Wilhelm, b. Guben, January 3, 1876; d. Berlin, September 7, 1960, German politician. Before the First World War, Pieck was the secretary of the Social Democratic Party (SPD). He went over to the Spartacus League, and in 1919 helped to found the COMMUNIST PARTY OF GERMANY (KPD). Pieck was one of the most important Communist politicians of the Weimar Republic, as a Reichstag deputy from 1928 to 1933, a member of the party's Central Committee, and a director of the "Red Aid."

Pieck was forced into exile in 1933, and after the arrest of Ernst THÄLMANN he assumed the leadership of the exiled KPD. In 1935, along with Walter ULBRICHT, he was able to effect a change in political course after he had confirmed through self-criticism that the party had

Wilhelm Pieck (left) and Otto Grotewohl.

aimed its "main attack against Social Democracy at a time" when it "should have been directed against the fascist movement." In Moscow in 1943, Pieck helped found the NATIONAL COMMITTEE FOR A FREE GERMANY. He returned to Germany in 1946 with the ULBRICHT GROUP; that same year, along with Otto Grotewohl, he assumed the co-chairmanship of the Socialist Unity Party (SED). Pieck was the first president of the German Democratic Republic, serving from 1949 to 1960.

Pierlot, Hubert Count, b. Cugnon (Luxembourg), December 23, 1883; d. Brussels, December 13, 1963, Belgian politician. Pierlot was elected a senator for the Christian Social party in 1926; he served as interior minister (1934–1936) and agricultural minister (1936–1938). He became premier in 1939; together with King LEOPOLD III he attempted unsuccessfully to preserve Belgian neutrality. In contrast to the king, however, after the Belgian defeat (May 28, 1940) Pierlot fled with his cabinet via France to London, where he led the government-in-exile until its return (September 1944). In the meantime he prepared the way for the postwar cooperation of the Benelux countries. He resigned in 1945.

Pillory (*Schandpfahl;* literally, stake of shame/infamy), massive tree trunk, about the height of a man, on which "un-German" books (by authors such as Tucholsky and Marx) and magazines (such as *Die Weltbühne*) were nailed. The pillory played a significant role in the "Operations against the Un-German Spirit" in German colleges and universities in March and April 1933 that culminated in the BOOK BURNING.

Pilsudski, Józef, b. Zulowo (Lithuania), December 5, 1867; d. Warsaw, May 12, 1935, Polish politician. Pilsudski was banished to Siberia form 1887 to 1892 because of subversive activity; on his return he joined the Polish Socialist Party (PPS), becoming its leader in 1894. Against the Russians, Pilsudski built up paramilitary units; he then brought his Polish Legion into the First World War on the side of the central European powers. In 1918 he became the first president of the new Poland. As marshal of Poland he succeeded in forcing back the Red Army in August 1920 (in the "miracle at the Vistula"). He withdrew from politics in 1923. However, on May 12, 1926, supported by the military and aided by his great popularity, Pilsudski overthrew the democratic government and became, without formally being named

Józef Pilsudski.

president, the dictator of Poland, with retention of parliamentary forms. Through his approaches to more powerful neighbors, Pilsudski sought to stabilize the Polish state; thus he concluded nonaggression pacts with the Soviet Union (July 25, 1932) and—through a faulty appraisal of Hitler's true goals—with the German Reich (January 26, 1934).

Pimpf (wolf cub), originally a dialect term for immature young people; in the 1920s it was employed neutrally to designate the youngest in the youth movement. In 1934 *Pimpf* officially became the appellation of the members of the German Jungvolk, the group between the ages of 10 and 14 in the HITLER YOUTH. The recent pejorative use of the term in German (signifying, for example, a half portion or a small sausage)

Pimpf. Admission into the German Jungvolk.

can presumably be traced to a critical attitude among the population toward the paramilitary misuse of children.

Pimpfenprobe, performance test in the German Jungvolk. During the exam, facts from Hitler's biography were used for questions, rote recitation of the "HORST-WESSEL-LIED" was demanded, competitive sporting events were held (for example, a 60-m dash in no more than 12 seconds), and a march with backpack, as well as a "test of courage," was undertaken. After passing the test the youngsters received awards, such as the right to carry a sheath knife.

Pinder, Wilhelm, b. Kassel, June 25, 1878; d. Berlin, May 13, 1947, German art historian. His research on the "nature and evolution of German forms" made Pinder one of the most valued and (with *Festschriften*) honored art scholars. He considered the German sculpture of the Middle Ages to be a "particularly *völkisch* achievement," ranking far above the artworks of neighboring peoples. His works included *Der Naumburger Dom und seine Bildwerke* (The Naumburg Cathedral and Its Art; 1925).

Pitschen, German locality in the Kreuzberg district, on the border between Upper Silesia and Poland. On August 31, 1939, it was the scene of a border incident staged by the Security Service (SD) with SS men dressed as Polish soldiers. The attack on the Pitschen forester's house, like that on the GLEIWITZ radio station, served as propagandistic preparation for the POLISH CAMPAIGN.

Pius XI (originally, Achille Ratti), b. Desio, near Monza, May 31, 1857; d. Rome, February 10, 1939, pope. In 1879 Ratti was ordained a priest; in 1914 he became prefect of the Vatican Library, in 1919 papal nuncio in Poland, and in 1921 cardinal archbishop of Milan. He was elected pope on February 6, 1922. The beginning of Pius's pontificate was concurrent with both the rise of FASCISM in Italy and the shock over Bolshevik persecution of the churches in Russia. All of the church's political measures were thus aimed at agreements that would assure the position of Catholics in the various German states, among them concordats with Bavaria (March 29, 1924), Prussia (June 14, 1929), Baden (October 12, 1932), and Austria (June 5, 1933). In the LATERAN TREATIES (February 11, 1929), Pius also achieved a settlement with Mussolini, whose anti-Communist attitude promised a certain degree of security against socialist revolutionaries.

Pius XI.

Counseled by Eugenio Pacelli (*see* PIUS XII), cardinal secretary of state beginning in 1930, Pius XI at first viewed the National Socialist Seizure of Power from this same perspective. He urged the German bishops to drop their anti-NS opposition, and on July 20, 1933, himself arrived at a CONCORDAT with the German Reich. It required the sacrifice of political Catholicism and yielded considerable international re-evaluation of the Third Reich. Whereas in Italy Pius XI was partially able to offset the loss of a political position through the growth of CATHOLIC ACTION, the German Concordat, intended as a protection, turned out to be the first phase in an intensifying persecution of the churches. Pius endured it for a long time with nothing more than protest notes (34 by 1936), but he finally went public with his grievances in the encyclical letter MIT BRENNENDER SORGE (With Burning Concern). This, however, only aggravated the CHURCH STRUGGLE.

Pius XII (originally, Eugenio Pacelli), b. Rome, March 2, 1876; d. Castel Gandolfo, October 9, 1958, pope. Ordained to the priesthood in 1899, Pacelli served beginning in 1901 in the Papal Secretariat of State and from 1909 to 1914 as a professor at the Vatican's Academy of Diplomats. In 1917 he was made titular archbishop of Sardes and papal nuncio in Munich; from 1920 to 1929 he was the nuncio to the German government. Pacelli was a determined advocate and promoter of the Concordat policy of PIUS XI, and was instrumental in the agreements made with Bavaria (1924), Prussia (1929), Baden (1932), and Austria (1933). Later called the

Pius XII.

"German pope" because of his long years in Germany, as cardinal secretary of state (from 1930) and after the experience with Mussolini in the LATERAN TREATIES, Pacelli took advantage of the authoritarian factor in Germany, and encouraged the Center party chairman, Ludwig KAAS, to make contact with Hitler. The result was the CONCORDAT with the Reich on July 20, 1933, and the renunciation of political activity by the clergy. Although the hopes resting on this arrangement were not fulfilled, and the National Socialist CHURCH STRUGGLE left no doubt about the anti-Christian policy of the Third Reich, Pacelli held fast to his appraisal of National Socialism as a lesser evil than Bolshevism.

Elected pope on March 2, 1939, Pius unsuccessfully appealed to the politicians to avert war. With the means available to the church, in the years that followed he worked to help the persecuted, to alleviate the sufferings of war, to attend to prisoners, and to explore possibilities for mediating a peace (including making contacts between the German military opposition and the British government in 1939–1940 and 1943). Yet he was unable to achieve any great success, especially since he avoided spectacular actions. For example, although he had accurate information, he risked no clear protest against the genocide of the FINAL SOLUTION, "in order to avoid greater evils" (letter of April 30, 1943, to Bishop Konrad PREYSING of Berlin). In 1963 Rolf Hochhuth held this conduct up to ridicule in his drama *Der Stellvertreter—Ein christliches Trauerspiel* (*The Deputy: A Christian Tragedy*). On occasion, Pius himself was in danger; Heinrich Himmler several times urged that he be taken into captivity.

On June 4, 1944, Pius welcomed the entry of the Allies into Rome; this restored him to complete freedom of action. He went on to consolidate the postwar position of the church. He internationalized the College of Cardinals, encouraged the churches of the Third World, and in numerous encyclicals set forth the church's views on ethical, political, social, and dogmatic issues. His name is associated with the intensification of Marian veneration (including the Dogma of the Assumption of Mary, declared in 1950) and the unequivocal turn of Rome toward the Western world.

Planck, Erwin, b. Berlin, March 12, 1893; d. there, January 23, 1945 (executed), German opposition fighter. In 1932 Planck became a state secretary in the German Chancellery, serving under Franz von Papen and Kurt von Schleicher. The son of Max PLANCK, he left public service after the National Socialist Seizure of Power. After travel and further studies, he became active in private commerce. Planck committed himself to the opposition and, under cover of a munitions business, undertook a courier service to the front (to Henning von TRESCKOW, among others). He also took part in the drafting of a constitution for the post-Hitler state. Arrested on July 23, 1944, he was sentenced to death on October 23 of that year.

Planck, Max, b. Kiel, April 23, 1858; d. Göttingen, October 4, 1947, German physicist. From 1885 to 1889 Planck was a professor in Kiel; he then taught in Berlin until he became an emeritus professor in 1928. As the formulator of the quantum theory and of Planck's Law of Radiation, he ranked among the most important physicists at the turn of the century and received a Nobel prize in 1918. In 1930 he became president of the KAISER WILHELM SOCIETY FOR THE ADVANCEMENT OF THE SCIENCES, which after the Second World War would bear his name. No follower of National Socialism, Planck nonetheless remained in Germany after the Seizure of Power for reasons of age and loyalty. He stood up for Jewish colleagues, discussed Einstein's achievements despite such obstacles as hostility in the SS weekly *Das Schwarze Korps*, and sabotaged decisions to dismiss personnel, among other actions. His hope that the National Socialist terror would ebb after a while proved wrong. In the end, Planck lost a son (*see* Erwin PLANCK), his home (which was bombed out),

Max Planck.

and his entire scientific laboratory in the battle against tyranny. Severely infirm with arthritis, he had to flee to the West in 1945.

Plebiscite (*Volksabstimmung*), term current during the Third Reich for "the consultation of the *Volk* by the Führer," in accordance with the Law concerning Plebiscites of July 14, 1933 (*Reich Law Gazette* I, p. 479). The plebiscite was intended to "give visible evidence . . . of

Plebiscite. Poster for the Anschluss with Austria (March 1938).

the existing relationship of trust between the Führer and the *Volk*"; it was the last plebiscitary remnant in the constitutional reality of the National Socialist state. Because the holding of a plebiscite was entirely within the discretion of the government (¶1), it functioned only to acclaim, and was used only three times, with expected results: on November 12, 1933, for withdrawal from the League of Nations (95 percent "yes" votes); on August 19, 1934, for the fusion of the offices of Reich president and head of government as FÜHRER UND REICHS-KANZLER (90 percent); and on April 10, 1938, for the ANSCHLUSS with Austria (99 percent). The large percentages reflected an approval that was surely overwhelming, but they also reflected the political pressure on the electorate: secret voting was frowned upon, opponents were "neutralized" in advance, and there were falsifications (in a few cases proven) of results.

Plebiscite regions (*Abstimmungsgebiete*), selected border areas of the German state where, with regard to the right of popular self-determination, the VERSAILLES TREATY stipulated plebiscites in 1920–1921 over the issue of the regions' remaining in Germany. The areas were North Schleswig, southern East Prussia, West Prussia east of the Weichsel River, Eupen and Malmédy, and Upper Silesia. The German state lost valuable territory—above all the industrial regions of Upper Silesia—which gave further ammunition to the right-wing parties in their fight against Versailles. This was especially so since all charges of arbitrary divisions of the regions and of electoral manipulations (as in Eupen and Malmédy) could be discounted.

Pleyer, Wilhelm, b. Eisenhammer (Bohemia), March 8, 1901; d. Munich, December 14, 1974, German writer. Pleyer engaged in political activity, including service as *Gau* executive secretary (1926–1929) of the German National Party in Czechoslovakia. He later wrote nationalistic poems ("Deutschland ist grösser!" [Germany Is Greater]; 1932) and *völkisch* novels (*Der Puchner. Ein Grenzlandschicksal* [Puchner: A Borderland Destiny]; 1934) on the "struggle of the Sudeten Germans for their nationality." Pleyer's novels and stories published after 1945 concentrate especially on the experiences of expelled Sudeten Germans and make a nationalistic plea for the right to the "old homeland" (*Aus Winkeln und Welten* [From Corners and Worlds]; 1962).

Ploetz, Alfred, b. Swinemünde, August 22, 1860; d. Herrsching am Ammersee, March 20, 1940, German theorist of race lore. Ploetz influenced the concept of RACIAL HYGIENE as a sociopolitical demand, which he sought to derive from genetic research. In 1904 he founded the journal *Archiv für Rassen- und Gesellschaftsbiologie* (Archive for the Biology of Race and Society), and in 1905, the (German) Society for Racial Hygiene. He thus had a long-term influence on National Socialist racial theory (*see* RACE).

Plötzensee, penal institution in northwest Berlin. In a brick warehouse within the sprawling compound was the site where between 1933 and 1945 some 2,400 men, women, and young people were executed for their fight against the dictatorship: persons of German, Dutch, French, Czech, and other nationalities, from all levels of society. The death penalty was at first carried out only with the guillotine, but as of March 29, 1933, hanging was also used. Many of the 200 or so condemned men of the conspiracy of the TWENTIETH OF JULY, 1944, were executed in Plötzensee. On Hitler's express order, those condemned were denied spiritual ministry; their punishment was imposed by hanging on the infamous "meat hooks." Important opponents of the National Socialist regime who met their death in Plötzensee included Carl Friedrich GOERDELER, Ulrich von HASSELL, Julius LEBER, Wilhelm LEUSCHNER, Helmuth James Count von MOLTKE, and Erwin von WITZLEBEN. In 1952, the Berlin Senate erected a public monument to the victims of the Hitler dictatorship on the execution site. The former penitentiary now houses a youth reformatory.

C. B.

Pluralism (*Pluralismus*), the coexistence of differing political and social-interest groups, each striving for a share in government power and legislation. The National Socialists rejected pluralism as a principle of constitutional law because of its inherent requirements for compromise and the granting of basic parliamentary and democratic freedoms. Arguing against it, they claimed that the "fractures within the *Volk*" that produced pluralism had been eliminated by the Seizure of Power; they further maintained that they had formed a *Volk* Community that was eager to subordinate itself to the chosen leadership (Ritterbusch, *Demokratie und Diktatur* [Democracy and Dictatorship]; 1939).

Plutocracy (*Plutokratie;* from Gr. *ploutokratia,* government by the wealthy), catchword that arose in the mid-19th century to describe political systems in which the true power lies in the hands of HIGH FINANCE and business. National Socialist propaganda particularly designated Great Britain and the United States as "plutocracies masked" as democracies, since the only way to political power there was with the capital necessary for electoral campaigns and for bribing the capitalist press in order to manipulate public opinion. The term was a firm element of antisemitic polemics as well, manifest in the stereotypical phrase "Jewish plutocracy." Together with "Jewish BOLSHEVISM," it

Death chamber in Plötzensee.

formed a vise that the National Socialists construed as the conspiracy of WORLD JEWRY, and thus a justification for the aggressive NS policies.

Pogrom (Russ., thunderstorm; devastation), in Russian, initially a term for excesses directed against national and religious minorities; since the persecution of Jews at the end of the 19th century, especially used to denote anti-Jewish attacks. The term has been incorporated into the vocabulary of most languages in this sense. The KRISTALLNACHT pogrom constituted one of the first high points of the National Socialist PERSECUTION OF JEWS in the Third Reich, incited and tolerated by government authorities, as had been the case in previous Russian and Polish pogroms. Despite the later NS policy of annihilation, especially in the USSR, ANTISEMITISM did not die out completely after 1945; isolated instances of pogroms have continued until the present. The term has also been broadened, and is now being used for excesses against other groups, such as the Tamils, Kurds, American Indians, Shiites, and blacks.

Pohl, Oswald, b. Duisburg, June 30, 1892; d. Landsberg am Lech, June 8, 1951 (executed), SS-*Obergruppenführer* (April 21, 1942). A navy official (in 1918 a purser), Pohl joined the NSDAP in 1926 and the SS in 1929. His organizational talents led Heinrich Himmler to assign him as chief of administration at SS headquarters on February 1, 1934. Made an SS-*Standartenführer*, he was responsible for the armed SS units and the concentration camps. As of June 1939, he was also ministerial director in the Reich Interior Ministry. Pohl rapidly built up the SS ECONOMIC ENTERPRISES with the help of experts from industry. On December 31, 1942, these activities were merged into the ECONOMIC-ADMINISTRATIVE MAIN OFFICE (WVHA), enabling him to become one of the most powerful men in the SS state.

Pohl had at his disposal an inexhaustible army of slaves in the concentration camp prisoners: on August 15, 1944, there were 524,286 of them on the rolls, a number that increased to more than 700,000 by the beginning of 1945. Pohl was able to "rent out" prisoners to industry on extremely advantageous terms. With the exploitation of camp inmates, he also fulfilled Himmler's command for "extermination through work": the number of prisoners who died as a result of forced labor is estimated to have been 500,000. Pohl was able to hide until May 1946, when he was identified; at the POHL TRIAL he was sentenced to death on November 3, 1947.

Oswald Pohl as a defendant in Nuremberg.

During his three-year confinement he converted to the Catholic faith; after all his petitions for pardon had been rejected, he was hanged.

Pohl Trial, proceeding before United States Military Tribunal III in Nuremberg against the chief of the ECONOMIC-ADMINISTRATIVE MAIN OFFICE (WVHA) of the SS, Oswald POHL, and 17 of his principal collaborators on charges of crimes against humanity, war crimes, and membership in a criminal organization (Case 4). The defendants were mainly accused of responsibility for murders and other crimes injurious to prisoners in the concentration camps and SS ECONOMIC ENTERPRISES administered by the WVHA.

A judgment handed down on November 3, 1947, sentenced Pohl and 3 other defendants to death by hanging; 11 defendants received prison terms ranging from 10 years to life, and 3 were acquitted. On a motion of the defense, the court revised its judgment on August 11, 1948: one death sentence was commuted to life imprisonment, and three prison terms were reduced. Through a pardon on January 31, 1951, United States High Commissioner John J. McCloy commuted two more death sentences to limited prison terms and reduced all other prison terms. Pohl was executed on June 8, 1951.

A. St.

Poincaré, Raymond, b. Bar-le-Duc (Lorraine), August 20, 1860; d. Paris, October 15, 1934, French politician. Poincaré was elected a nationalist deputy in 1887; he held several ministerial posts and was president of the republic (1913–

Raymond Poincaré.

1920) and premier (1922–1924 and 1926–1929). As chairman of the Reparations Commission after the First World War (February–May 1920), Poincaré uncompromisingly insisted on Germany's fulfillment of its obligations (*see* VERSAILLES TREATY). His policy of "productive seizure" provoked the RUHR CONFLICT and led France into isolation. Only in his second term did Poincaré allow Aristide BRIAND to proceed with his policy of reconciliation; he nonetheless remained one of the most hated French politicians among German nationalist right-wingers.

Poland, neighboring state to the east of Germany; area, 388,390 sq km (approximately 156,000 sq miles); population, about 32 million (1930). Partitioned since the 18th century among Prussia, Russia, and Austria, Poland arose again as a republic on November 11, 1918. After a period of consolidation both internal (the "March Constitution" of March 17, 1921) and external, political destabilization and the ensuing economic problems finally led to a *coup d'état* by Józef PIŁSUDSKI (May 12, 1926). Since Poland was locked in between revisionist powers, its fate remained closely tied to those of Germany and the Soviet Union, and to the development of German-Soviet relations. Closely correlated with this situation was the resolution of domestic political and economic difficulties. Heavily damaged by the war and still economically backward, Poland confronted several issues: (1) agrarian reform, in part used as a weapon against German ownership of landed properties in West Prussia; (2) industrialization and modernization in the shadow of a German-Polish

tariff war between 1925 and 1934; (3) the expansion of Gdynia as a port in competition with the predominantly German Free City of Danzig; and (4) restrictive policies aimed at driving out minorities, especially Germans (some 2.3 percent of the 1921 population).

In foreign affairs, Poland laid claim to a leadership role in the "Third Europe" between the Baltic and Adriatic seas, as expressed in the Polish-Romanian Alliance of February 19, 1921. This eastern European *cordon sanitaire* had been set up by France in 1919 as a barrier against the Soviet Union and Germany; it was solidified through the Polish-French Alliance, also of February 19, 1921. Several developments misled the Polish foreign minister, Józef BECK (since 1932 Piłsudski's "young man"), into conducting an independent policy of balancing between East and West: Piłsudski's unexpected rapprochement with Berlin (on January 26, 1934, the GERMAN-POLISH NONAGGRESSION PACT), after initial plans for a preventive war; the Polish-Soviet Nonaggression Treaty (July 25, 1932); the faith in irreconcilable differences between National Socialism and Bolshevism; and an army that was superior in numbers but inferior in military technology and tactical strategy. When, toward the end of March 1939, Poland resisted German pressure to return Danzig, to concede extraterritorial connections through the Polish CORRIDOR, and to accept a role as a German satellite against the Soviet Union, Hitler abrogated the 1934 pact. After the agreement between Berlin and Moscow (August 23, 1939, the GERMAN-SOVIET NONAGGRESSION PACT), Poland's fate was decided, despite the British-French guarantees and despite a patriotic will to resist that was supported by the Catholic church (*see* POLISH CAMPAIGN).

Nonetheless, the Polish state continued to exist legally and politically with the London government-in-exile and Poland's exile army (*see, for example*, Władysław ANDERS). As a reaction to Germany's ruthless occupation policy in the GENERALGOUVERNEMENT (mass resettlements, forced recruitment of Polish workers, liquidation of the intelligentsia, the FINAL SOLUTION), an underground government and a Polish national Home Army arose (*see* WARSAW UPRISING). Its collapse because of the withholding of Soviet assistance was the result of Moscow's policy of confrontation after the discovery of the mass graves at KATYN. Henceforth Stalin depended only on reliable Polish Communist agencies: from the Lublin Committee, formed with Soviet "assistance" (July 21, 1944), came a

Polish provisional government on January 1, 1945, and on June 28 of that year, the Government of National Unity. At TEHERAN and YALTA, and in the POTSDAM AGREEMENT, the Western powers, under the pressure of the military realities, consented to a "westerly shift" of Poland (between the CURZON LINE and the ODER-NEISSE LINE) and to the EXPULSION of the German population from these newly acquired Polish territories. Stalin, through sham concessions and rigged elections, was able to thwart the demand for a democratic government. Poland became a socialist "people's republic."

B.-J. W.

Police (*Polizei*), government law-enforcement agency that, beginning with the National Socialist New Order, was divided into the ORDER-KEEPING POLICE (Ordnungspolizei; Orpo) and SECURITY POLICE (Sicherheitspolizei; Sipo), with Heinrich Himmler as *Reichsführer-SS und Chef der Deutschen Polizei* (RFSSuChdDtPol). The Sipo comprised the Criminal Police (Kriminalpolizei; Kripo) and the SECRET STATE POLICE (Geheime Staatspolizei; Gestapo). During the NS takeover, arrests and preventive detention of political opponents were carried out with the massive assistance of the SA and SS, appointed as auxiliary police. A few months later, the police leadership restructured the police force in conformity with NS ideology. The ties between SS and police increased until 1943, and uniformed order-keeping police and security police were enrolled in the SS. In November 1937, in consideration of the needs of mobilization, the institution of HIGHER SS AND POLICE LEADERS was created. Beginning in 1940, police commanders were trained at the

SS JUNKER SCHOOLS. These aimed at the "formation of a unified state defense corps [*Staatsschutzkorps*]." The process was completed by Himmler's appointment as Reich interior minister.

In doubtful cases, the police were enjoined to fulfill the Führer's will rather than to uphold the law. The REICHSTAG FIRE DECREE was interpreted (*see* Theodor MAUNZ) as a nationwide general provision that superseded the prevailing legal restrictions in dealing with politically motivated attacks. Laws on political activity were no longer passed to protect the individual, but rather to ensure the security and uniformity of the organizational apparatus. Thus the police, as the most important instrument of authority in the totalitarian state, could base its consolidation of power on extensive insecurity regarding rights.

W. R.

Police state (*Polizeistaat*), political community with an executive that is almost or totally without legal controls or limitations. The Third Reich was a nearly perfect police state owing to the undermining of LAW, a constitutional practice that was determined solely by the Führer's will, the abolition of BASIC RIGHTS, the intrusion of the POLICE in the judicial system, and other such measures.

Polish Campaign, the war on Poland unleashed by Hitler on September 1, 1939, at 4:45 a.m. (not 5:45, as he stated in his Reichstag speech), which was to expand into the SECOND WORLD WAR. Leading up to the Polish Campaign was a phase of hectic attempts at diplomatic mediation aimed at resolving German-Polish differences

Police. SA and SS men are sworn in as "auxiliary police."

(including the CORRIDOR and the DANZIG QUESTION). They ultimately failed because of Hitler's intention to settle the issue of SPACE by force. Yet the order to attack, given for August 26 and then withdrawn—Italy had given notice that it was not yet ready for war—was then issued by Hitler after brief diversionary negotiations, thus setting in motion "Case White" ("Fall Weiss"). The Security Service (SD) furnished the pretext for propaganda purposes with the faked Polish seizure of the German broadcasting station at GLEIWITZ.

The main body of the activated German army (57 divisions) attacked in two assault columns with about 2,500 tanks concentrated in the direction of Warsaw. From Pomerania and East Prussia, Army Group North proceeded under Col. Gen. Fedor von BOCK, and from Silesia and Slovakia, Army Group South attacked under Col. Gen. Gerd von RUNDSTEDT. They were supported by Air Fleets One and Four, with a total of 1,107 aircraft. The Polish Army Command under Marshal Edward RYDZ-ŚMIGŁY had sent the greater part of its forces (26 divisions, 10 brigades) along the border, 1,900 km (about 1,100 miles) in length. Altogether, Poland had mobilized 40 divisions and 16 brigades with 1,132 light armored vehicles. The Polish air force possessed 745 airplanes, but the navy was insignificant and fell victim to German air attacks, with the exception of 5 submarines and 3 destroyers.

By September 7, all Polish armies in the border area had been penetrated, were under attack, or had been forced to retreat. As early as September 9, Rydz-Śmigły was ordering a retreat to beyond the Vistula. For psychological and organizational reasons, and also in the hope of an attack by France in the west, he had overestimated his own strength and had chosen the disastrous border assault. The calamitous outcome could not be altered by the French army's "offensive" on September 6 in the area of Saarbrücken, since it did not compel any transfer of German divisions out of Poland.

Between September 8 and 13, the first battle of encirclement was fought near Radom, during which the German Tenth Army took 65,000 Poles captive. By September 11, the German First Corps had cut Warsaw off from its easterly lines of communication. Between September 17 and 20, Army Group South took 60,000 captives near Lublin. At the same time, the fate of the Polish armies of Posen and eastern Pomerania was sealed: 170,000 Poles were taken prisoner. The Polish air force lost 330 airplanes by September 15, most of them in air combat and not on the ground (only 50), as the German propaganda had reported.

On September 17, the Red Army attacked from the east with two army groups in the areas agreed on in the GERMAN-SOVIET NONAGGRESSION PACT, territory that had been lost to Poland between 1918 and 1920. Against these groups

Polish Campaign. German infantrymen cross the border.

Polish Campaign. Conference of German and Soviet officers about the demarcation lines to be agreed on.

Poland was able to muster only remnants of nine divisions and three brigades. The Polish government fled to Romania on the same day, and the remainder of the air combat forces followed in 116 aircraft. By then, the collapse was only a matter of time: the besieged Polish capital, defended by 120,000 soldiers, surrendered on September 28 after cannonading and heavy air attack. With the surrender of 16,857 Polish soldiers near Kock (east of Deblin) on October 6, the Polish Campaign came to an end. In the fight against Germany the Polish army lost 70,000 dead, 133,000 wounded, and 700,000 prisoners; the Red Army reported another 217,000 captured Poles, along with 737 of its own dead and 1,859 wounded. The Wehrmacht's losses were 10,572 dead, 3,409 missing, and 30,322 wounded, along with 217 tanks, 285 airplanes, and 1 minesweeper boat.

A premonition of the suffering under the forthcoming OCCUPATION POLICY appeared during the Polish Campaign with the terror inflicted by the EINSATZGRUPPEN that followed the attacking German armies and by the Soviet security police, the NKVD. Poland was divided up between Germany and the Soviet Union. The territories occupied by the Germans were in part incorporated into the Reich (around 90,000 sq km [about 36,000 sq miles] with 10 million inhabitants: DANZIG–WEST PRUSSIA and the WARTHELAND); the remainder was organized as the GENERALGOUVERNEMENT on October 10, 1939. The end of the Polish Campaign brought no end to the state of war, since the Western powers rejected both the outcome of

Hitler's policy of violence and his peace proposals.

G. H.

Polish Corridor, Polish territory that as of 1919 separated East Prussia from the rest of Germany (*see* CORRIDOR).

"Polish mess" (*Polnische Wirtschaft*), nationalist-*völkisch* catchphrase, meaning "a total mess" [the German word *Wirtschaft* actually means "economy"]. It emerged in the 19th century to refer to the allegedly chaotic conditions in Poland (as reflected in, for example, Gustav Freytag's novel *Soll und Haben* [Debit and Credit]; 1855). In colloquial German it became an expression for general neglect and confusion. The prejudice underlying the term made it useful in National Socialist propaganda against the neighboring country, especially in 1939; the German attack would free ethnic Germans there from this "mess." The term was a preliminary stage of the NS propaganda theme of the "subhuman."

Polish partition, fourth, a continuation of the first three partitions, which were carried out between 1772 and 1795. The fourth partition was provided for in the secret supplementary protocol to the GERMAN-SOVIET NONAGGRESSION PACT of August 23, 1939.

Political education. *See* Education; Schooling, political.

Political leaders (*Politische Leiter*), term for officeholders in the NSDAP, from the BLOCK WARDENS up to the REICH LEADERS; by 1937 they numbered about 700,000 persons. The Corps of Political Leaders, as they were collectively known, served the purposes of ideological training and political monitoring of the population. According to the party guidelines, a political leader was not a civil servant, although from the district (*Kreis*) level upward, the leaders were employed and paid as full-time officeholders. Nevertheless, the leader was to be "both preacher and soldier." The fact that the lower leaders in particular also had to be informers was not specified, but it was obvious from the files and questionnaires that they had to maintain concerning the residents of their given area of jurisdiction (*Hoheitsgebiet*).

The Corps of Political Leaders was declared in the 1946 Nuremberg Trials to be one of the Third Reich's CRIMINAL ORGANIZATIONS. It was an accessory to the PERSECUTION OF JEWS; down to the local group level it played a significant

Political leaders. Parade in Nuremberg.

role in the exploitation of ALIEN WORKERS; it carried out GERMANIZATION measures; and it was involved in the mistreatment of PRISONERS OF WAR. Since most of these crimes took place during wartime, an exception was made for political leaders whose activity ended before September 1, 1939.

Political poetry (*Politische Dichtung*), in the interpretation of National Socialist theorists or historians of literature, works that were to be perceived as "confessions of political faith" or "appeals to the nation." Examples from the history of literature included Ulrich von Hutten's calls to arms and Hoffmann von Fallersleben's GERMAN NATIONAL ANTHEM. Along these lines Dietrich ECKART, Werner BEUMELBURG, and Edwin Erich DWINGER, in particular, could be seen as representatives of a contemporary political poetry because they were "heralds of Germandom's struggle for existence." In 1939, Heinz KINDERMANN published an anthology of such poetry: *Heimkehr ins Reich—Grossdeutsche Dichtung aus Ostmark und Sudetenland* (Return Home to the Reich: Great-German Poetry from the Ostmark and Sudetenland).

Political police (Politische Polizei), police agencies with authority in political crimes (*see* SECRET STATE POLICE).

Political Squads (Politische Bereitschaften), armed SS units that emerged from the staff guards (Stabswachen) and special commando units formed after the Seizure of Power; they helped local SS leaders consolidate personal power and undertook auxiliary police tasks. Larger special commando units with several companies called themselves Political Squads; they were also intended to win respect from the SA for the SS. The squads spread throughout Germany and were principal actors in the arrest and murder operation against the SA during the RÖHM AFFAIR of June 30, 1934. Later they were combined with the LEIBSTANDARTE-SS "ADOLF HITLER" into SS STANDBY TROOPS, thus becoming forerunners of the WAFFEN-SS.

Politikaster, derogatory term from the 1920s that Hitler favored in referring to what he viewed as incompetent politicians, especially those of the *Systemzeit* (*see* SYSTEM ERA) or those of the Western democracies ("parliamentary *Politikaster*"). Although similar in form to KRITIKASTER, the term did not become part of colloquial speech.

Poll tax (*Bürgersteuer;* literally, tax on citizens), head tax imposed by an emergency decree on July 26, 1930, because of the increasing welfare expenses of localities as a result of the rising UNEMPLOYMENT; the tax was not graduated in line with ability to pay. The National Socialists retained it, but they soon graduated it according to income, and on October 16, 1934, added a family status index. Despite the disappearance of its original rationale by 1937 at the latest, the tax was not abolished until April 24, 1942.

Pölzl, Klara. *See* Hitler, Klara.

Ponten, Josef, b. Raeren bei Eupen, June 3, 1883; d. Munich, April 3, 1940, German writer. After Ponten had described his Rhenish homeland in narrative poetry, he achieved lasting success with "master novellas" on "creative" artist-heroes. His six-volume cycle of novels on the "fateful situation" (*Schicksalhaftigkeit*) of ethnic Germans living abroad, *Volk auf dem Wege* (The *Volk* on the Way; 1933–1942), featured the "*Volk* as protagonist." As a winner of several National Socialist literary prizes, Ponten was honored in the Third Reich along with Hans GRIMM as the "great poet of German *Volk* destinies" (Franz Lennartz).

Popitz, Johannes, b. Leipzig, December 2, 1884; d. Berlin-Plötzensee, February 2, 1945 (executed), German politician. Popitz served as an adviser in the Prussian Interior Ministry from 1914 to 1919 and then in the Reich Finance Ministry until 1929 (beginning in 1925, as a state secretary). Known as a tax expert (*Kommentar zum Umsatzsteuergesetz* [Commentary on the Sales Tax Law]; 1918), he was appointed after the Seizure of Power to the Prussian Finance Ministry (April 21, 1933), even though he did not belong to the NSDAP.

As a nationalist-conservative opponent of the Weimar Republic, Popitz was not unhappy to see it end; yet he swiftly rejected the new regime even more determinedly. In 1938, his attempt to resign over the persecution of the Jews was

Johannes Popitz.

Josef Ponten.

turned down. Through the WEDNESDAY SOCIETY he established contact with Ludwig BECK and Carl Friedrich GOERDELER, and made himself available to their opposition plans. In 1939–1940, under Goerdeler's guidance, he prepared a restorative "provisional basic law" for a post-Hitler Germany. In 1943 he also sounded out Heinrich Himmler on the latter's reaction to an eventual *coup d'état*. Considered by the conspirators of July 20, 1944, for the posts of both minister of ecclesiastical affairs and of finance, Popitz was arrested on July 21, and was sentenced to death on October 3, 1944.

Popular fiction. *See* Trivialliteratur.

Popular front (*Volksfront*), term for a political alliance of left-wing parties with the inclusion of the Communists, who, in contrast to their role in a UNITY FRONT (*Einheitsfront*), renounce any automatic claim to leadership. The Communists' readiness to enter a popular front grew decisively following their experiences with the National Socialist Seizure of Power in Germany, which had exposed the struggle against the alleged "social fascism" of the SPD (Social Democratic Party of Germany) as a tragic error. In France, socialists and Communists formed a tactical alliance "against fascism and war" on July 27, 1934; the following year, after the French-Soviet treaty (May 1935), it was broadened into the Popular Front with the entrance of the middle-class Radical Party. (A common program ensued on January 10, 1936.) On the Communist side, a popular-front policy was sanctioned by the Seventh International Comintern Congress (July 25–August 20, 1935). Nonetheless, the French Left's electoral victory in May 1936 did not lead to a share in the government for the Communist party, which was inclined only to tolerate the government of Léon BLUM.

The Popular Front finally collapsed in 1938 over Blum's refusal to intervene in the SPANISH CIVIL WAR, even though it would have rendered help to another popular-front government. In the summer of 1935, eight Spanish parties had merged in an alliance, which won the election on February 15, 1936; it then formed a government on July 18 of that year, against which Francisco FRANCO aimed his revolt. The concept of a popular front lost most of its credibility after Franco's victory and after the GERMAN-SOVIET NONAGGRESSION PACT of August 23, 1939. In 1945 the Soviets utilized it once more in the ANTIFASCIST-DEMOCRATIC ORDER in their occupation zone, as a preparation for total Communist rule.

Population policy (*Bevölkerungspolitik*), the totality of government measures to direct population movements and to control the population. The National Socialist state intended to expand the merely quantitative population policy of earlier periods—as, for example, Prussian immigration policy—through qualitative population measures, which aimed at a "strengthening of the *Volk* body [*Volkskörper*]"; an "increase in worth" (*Wertsteigerung*) was to complement the "numerical increase." The agency for NS population policy, which accordingly had to aim above all at the "cultivation of the *Volk*" (*Volkspflege*), was—along with the Interior Ministry—the NSDAP's RACIAL POLICY OFFICE.

The goal of quantitative population policy was to reverse the decline in the birthrate during the crisis years 1929 to 1933, through combating birth control (*see* TWO-CHILD SYSTEM) and awakening the "will for a child." This began with the education of girls ("You should want as many children as possible!" was the line in the League of German Girls' "Ten Commandments for Choosing a Husband"). It extended to the new definition of the role of woman as housewife and mother (*see* WOMEN IN THE THIRD REICH). This image was juxtaposed with the cautionary caricature of the liberated old maid who had missed her maternal calling or the young woman living in a morally objectionable COMRADELY MARRIAGE, both "population-policy washouts" (*bevölkerungspolitische Blindgänger*).

In addition to general economic improvement,

childbirth incentives included reform of the tax structure to favor "fertile elements of the *Volk*," MARRIAGE LOANS, which could be paid off with children as well as with money (*see* ABKINDERN), and assistance in purchasing a HOMESTEAD. Side effects of such policies were an easing of pressure on the labor market through the removal of many women and a slowing down of the flight from the countryside.

Qualitative population policy was determined by racial and eugenic considerations: the perspective of animal husbandry was to be applied to human reproduction as well. Because cultural influences stood in the way of a sufficient role for "natural SELECTION," the legislator had to intervene positively. Through increased demands for MARITAL FITNESS and FORCED STERILIZATION, the attempt was made to check the breeding of HEREDITARILY ILL OFFSPRING (law of July 14, 1933); EUTHANASIA—the murder of the handicapped—pursued the same goal. Because the National Socialists considered the "blood poisoning" of miscegenation to be among the damaging influences, and because they viewed the Jews as a race, the measures that served the persecution of Jews—from the Blood Protection Law (*see* BLOOD, LAW TO PROTECT) to the FINAL SOLUTION—were also a part of qualitative population policy, as was the RE-GERMANIZATION of "good blood" in the breeding establishments such as LEBENSBORN.

The motto "*Volk* without Space" stood in seeming contradiction to the NS goals of population increase. However, concerns about an aging population and fears of being overwhelmed by foreigners lay behind the demand for more births (in 1933 there were about 0.9 million births; in 1939, 1.4 million); the argument about tight space came from the arsenal of GEOPOLITICS and served to support territorial demands and the claims for a "more just" division of natural resources and raw materials. The increase in "population pressure" through birth surpluses would take effect only in the long run.

Pornography, texts and pictures aimed at sexual stimulation. Pornography was officially forbidden in Imperial Germany, and in 1911 a German Central Office (as of 1937, the Reich Central Office) was established to "combat obscene pictures, writings, and advertisements." With the removal and easing of censorship after the First World War, the pornography trade increased by leaps and bounds, with several publishers producing material exclusively for this category. Middle-class conservative organizations, especially those composed of women, arose to dedicate themselves to the struggle against pornography and "smut and rubbish" (*see* TRIVIALLITERATUR). In demagogic fashion, to some extent they equated socially critical and socialist literature with pornography. The National Socialists exploited antipornography sentiment for racist purposes by insinuating that the pornography trade lay "overwhelmingly in Jewish hands."

Despite the "preservation of purity in literature and art" proclaimed in 1933, series continued to appear, virtually uncontested, with such titles as Eva-Privatbücher (Eve's Private Books), Mara—Das moderne Magazin, and Potpourri (all from the Eva Press in Leipzig); Ehrlichs Sittenromane (Ehrlich's Novels of Manners and Morals); and the Aphroditenbücherei (Aphrodite's Library). Tighter enforcement of prohibitions in the late 1930s led pornography publishers to give a pseudoscientific embellishment to their series: Beiträge zum Sexualproblem (Contributions to the Sexual Problem; Asa Press, Leipzig) or Allmacht Weib (Omnipotent Woman; Press for Cultural Research, Vienna). The pornography traffic shifted somewhat to "under the counter," yet new titles continued to appear, as the prohibition lists of 1940 and 1942 attest.

In the 1970s, the pornography taboo intersected with the taboo on the Third Reich itself: purveyors used forbidden National Socialist accessories such as SS daggers, swastikas, uniforms, and insignia as props for a particularly brutal sadomasochistic or homophile pornography, not even shrinking from so-called *KZ-Pornographie* (concentration camp pornography).

H. H.

Porsche, Ferdinand, b. Maffersdorf (Bohemia), September 8, 1875; d. Stuttgart, January 30, 1951, German automobile maker. Trained as a plumber, Porsche advanced his training through self-study to become an engineer. He found employment at the Löhner Automobile Factory in Vienna, for which he built an electric car with a rotary motor in 1900. In 1906 he switched to the Austro-Daimler firm, becoming its general director in 1916, and built automobiles with internal combustion engines that attracted international attention. Employed as of 1923 at the Daimler plant in Stuttgart, he built a sports car for Auto Union in 1933 that for years won all the international races and secured Porsche's reputation at the highest levels of the sport.

In the spring of 1937, Hitler commissioned

Ferdinand Porsche.

Porsche to construct a small vehicle for the masses that anyone could afford. The project was underwritten with 50 million RM from the German Labor Front. By Hitler's birthday in 1938 Porsche was able to present the VOLKSWAGEN (at first, called the "KdF-Wagen"; *see* STRENGTH THROUGH JOY). Shortly afterward he assumed the management of the newly founded Volkswagen Company, Ltd. Hitler decorated Porsche in 1938 with the NATIONAL PRIZE FOR ART AND SCIENCE. During the war he was less successful as a tank manufacturer (one failed project was a 100-ton combat vehicle). In 1945 he shifted over to sports-car manufacture.

Porten, Henny, b. Magdeburg, January 7, 1890; d. Berlin, October 15, 1960, German actress. Trained as a singer and dancer, Porten performed in silent films. In 1921 she and Carl August FROELICH founded the Porten-Froelich Production Company. Porten's greatest period came with sound films. She played in many light feature films, which especially during the war were received enthusiastically as welcome diversions: *Krach im Hinterhaus* (Noise in the Rear House; 1937), *Der Optimist* (1938), and *Komödianten* (Comedians; 1941), among others. After her great success with *Familie Buchholz* (The Buchholz Family; 1943), Hermann Göring invited Porten to Karinhall and demanded that she divorce her Jewish husband, Wilhelm von Kaufman. Despite her refusal, she and her husband were left untouched. Only after being bombed out of her home on February 14, 1944, did Porten experience problems, since giving shelter to homeless Jews was forbidden. After

Henny Porten in her double role as Kohlhiesel's daughters in the film of the same name (*Kohlhiesels Töchter*).

the war Porten was still to be seen in such films as *Das Fräulein von Scuderi* (Miss von Scuderi; 1955).

Portugal, republic on the Iberian peninsula; area, 88,500 sq km (about 35,400 sq miles; with the Azores and Madeira, 91,631 sq km [about 36,600 sq miles]); population, 6.2 million (1930). After several revolutions and military coups, a military dictatorship came to power on July 9, 1926, under Gen. Oscar Antonio Carmona (president, 1928–1941). On April 27, 1928, Antonio de Oliveira SALAZAR was appointed finance minister; beginning in 1932 he ruled as premier with dictatorial powers. Through the constitution of 1933 he established a permanent authoritarian "new state"

Portugal. Recruitment poster for the Portuguese Legion.

on the fascist corporatist model, without democratic parties or parliamentarianism, but with a secret police and a ban on strikes and lockouts.

A close ideological relationship and the fear of domestic destabilization as a result of the SPANISH CIVIL WAR led Salazar to side with Gen. Francisco Franco. Portugal broke off diplomatic relations with the Spanish Republic in October 1936, sent a Portuguese legion to take part in the conflict, and signed a pact of friendship and neutrality with Spain on March 17, 1939. Salazar performed a skillful balancing act between the Axis powers and the western Allies (he delivered strategic tungsten to the Third Reich, but leased support facilities in the Azores to the British), an approach that was dictated by the great strategic vulnerability of both the mother country and its far-flung colonial empire. He thus led his country through the Second World War under a neutrality that was respected by all sides. Lisbon became the favorite playground of international secret services, but also a "window" of rescue for many emigrants.

B.-J. W.

Positive Christianity (*Positives Christentum*), religious position of the NSDAP in Point 24 of the Party Program formulated on February 24, 1920. An elaboration of what was meant by Positive Christianity was never issued, since the plan was to avoid denominational commitments and to keep open antichurch options. By pointing to its Positive Christianity, National Socialism could brush aside church objections and dispel the reservations of devout party members. The CHURCH STRUGGLE exposed the program point's camouflage function.

Postage stamps. [The illustration on the facing page shows examples of postage stamps issued during the Third Reich. Note the falsified stamp in the lower right-hand corner.]

Potempa (as of 1936, Wüstenrode; now Potępa), village in Upper Silesia. On the night of August 9–10, 1932, in Potempa, five SA men assaulted a Communist worker and kicked him to death before his mother's eyes. On the basis of the Emergency Decree against Political Terror dated August 9, 1932 (repealed on December 19 of that year), the killers were sentenced to death on August 22 by the Special Court at Beuthen. Hitler expressed solidarity with the perpetrators in a telegram assailing "this atrocious death sentence," and termed their liberation a "matter of our honor." The Papen government recom-

English counterfeit stamp with
the legend "Vanished Reich"
(Futsches Reich).

mended on September 2 that the sentence be commuted to life imprisonment. In mid-March of 1933, the Hitler government released the killers.

Potsdam Agreement, closing communiqué of the conference that took place in Potsdam from July 17 to August 2, 1945. It was signed by the heads of government of Great Britain (Clement ATT-LEE), the Soviet Union (Joseph STALIN), and the United States (Harry S. TRUMAN); their respective foreign ministers also took part. Preceding the conference were the surrender of the German Reich on May 7–8, 1945, and the assumption of government authority in Germany by the ALLIED CONTROL COUNCIL on the basis of the JUNE DECLARATION of June 5.

The most important part of the Potsdam Agreement, Article 3, dealt with the territorial, political, and economic principles for dealing with conquered Germany; it provided measures "that are necessary so that Germany can never again threaten its neighbors or the preservation of peace in the whole world." At the same time, such measures were to prepare Germany "to reconstruct its life on a democratic and peaceful foundation," so that it "might eventually be able to take its place among the free and peace-loving peoples of the world."

The political provisions of Article 3 were: (1) total disarmament and demilitarization of Germany, that is, the destruction of all its weapons and military facilities and the disbandment of all its fighting forces; (2) DENAZIFICATION, that is, dissolution of the NSDAP and its organizations, repeal of National Socialist laws, internment of leading National Socialists and of influential supporters of the NSDAP, removal of active NSDAP members from public offices, and the arrest and trial of war criminals; (3) democratization, partly through allowing the formation of democratic parties and labor unions and the election of local, district, provincial, and state parliaments; (4) decentralization, or the setting up of a decentralized German administration—only in the sectors of the economy and of traffic and transport systems were central German administrative offices to be maintained or newly established.

The economic provisions were: (1) prohibition against armaments production; (2) breakup of cartels and (partial) DISMANTLING of the German economy; (3) promotion of peacetime industry and of the consumer and agricultural economies; (4) Allied control of the overall German economy; (5) as an urgent task, restoration or new construction of roadways, dwellings, and public facilities; (6) management of Germany as a single economic unit; (7) levy of reparations: each of the four occupying powers could withdraw reparations (in goods) only from its own occupation zone. In addition, the USSR was to receive industrial facilities that had been left intact and that were not needed for peaceful production in the American, British, and French zones: 15 percent in exchange

Potsdam Agreement. From the left: Stalin, Truman, and Churchill (who was later replaced by Attlee).

The "historic handshake" between Hitler and Hindenburg at the Potsdam Celebration.

for other goods, and another 10 percent without any exchange. The amount of reparations was not fixed; yet it was "to leave the German people enough means to exist without help from outside."

The territorial provisions were: (1) the ceding of Königsberg (later Kaliningrad) and the surrounding area of northern East Prussia to the Soviet Union, "contingent on the definitive settlement of the territorial questions at the peace conference"; (2) subordination of the German territories east of the ODER-NEISSE LINE, including the former Free City of Danzig (now Gdansk), "under the administration of the Polish state," but with a "definitive fixing of Poland's western border" to be deferred until the peace conference; (3) removal of the German population from Poland, Czechoslovakia, and Hungary and their resettlement in Germany "in an orderly and humane fashion" (see EXPULSION).

The provisional government essentially approved the Potsdam Agreement on August 4. The agreement established the legal basis for the common responsibility of the Four Powers (Great Britain, France, the USSR, and the United States) for Germany as a whole and for the restoration of its unity as a state. [The USSR has viewed the territorial arrangements of the Potsdam Agreement as definitive, as did the German Democratic Republic until the events

of 1989. While it did not dispute its eastern boundaries, the GDR's readiness to enter into negotiations for German unification put it into a position of conflict with the USSR over the related implications of the Potsdam Agreement.] The Western powers (as well as the Federal Republic of Germany) have maintained that these matters are to be given final legal validity only through a final peace treaty.

R. B.

Potsdam Celebration (*Tag von Potsdam*), ceremony elevating the solemn opening of the Reichstag that had been elected on March 5, 1933; Hitler and Goebbels chose as the showplace the Prussian capital outside the gates of Berlin. March 21 was selected as the date because, 62 years earlier on that day, Otto von Bismarck had convened the first Reichstag of the "Second Reich." Broadcast in its entirety on radio, the staging—from which only the Communist and Social Democratic parties were missing—aimed at enthroning the Third Reich as the legitimate heir of the Kaiser's Reich and at weakening objections to the revolutionary aspects of the SEIZURE OF POWER. The "day of Potsdam" was introduced with religious services: for the Evangelical deputies (including Göring), in the Church of Saint Nicholas (with the sermon by Otto DIBELIUS); and for the Catholics, in the parish church. Hitler and Goebbels stayed away from the mass, thereby branding the German bishops as saboteurs of the "NATIONAL RISING," since they upheld the ban against the National Socialists.

A state ceremony in the garrison church followed, with addresses by the Reich president and by Hitler, who in contrast with his uniformed party comrades came dressed in a cutaway. A solemn handshake between the president and the chancellor sealed the "marriage of old grandeur and new power." Hindenburg laid a wreath on the tomb of Frederick the Great as a 21-gun salute was fired. Then, together with Hitler, he reviewed the parade of Reichswehr, police, SA, SS, and Steel Helmet units. The day ended with the return of the deputies to the Kroll Opera House, where the Reichstag was convened. Two days later, with its acceptance of the ENABLING LAW, it relinquished its own power. The basis for this victory by Hitler had been set in Potsdam; 12 years later, Potsdam was the site where his defeat was sealed by means of the POTSDAM AGREEMENT.

Pound Donation (Pfundspende), monthly collection campaign of the WINTER RELIEF AGENCY, introduced in 1934–1935. All households were asked to contribute prepackaged small items suitable for transmitting to needy persons; monetary donations could be substituted.

"Pour le sémite," cynical term for the JEWISH STAR; it was a pun on the highest German military award from the First World War, the Pour le mérite.

Prague Manifesto (*Prager Manifest*), appeal by the exiled executive committee of the SOCIAL DEMOCRATIC PARTY OF GERMANY (SPD) for resistance against National Socialism, and at the same time a programmatic statement regarding the "struggle and goal of revolutionary socialism." The Prague Manifesto, formulated by Friedrich STAMPFER and Rudolf HILFERDING, was issued on the first anniversary of the Seizure of Power, on January 28, 1934, in the periodical *Neues Vorwärts* (*see* VORWÄRTS); it leveled self-criticism on the mistaken tactics of the party during the Weimar Republic. The SPD now proposed the "common front of all antifascist ranks," including the Communists, that earlier had been spurned, as well as a true "socialist organization of the economy." The Prague Manifesto had little resonance even within the SPD because of disunity over the strategy for struggle (*see* NEW BEGINNINGS).

Presidial cabinets (*Präsidialkabinette*), term for the BRÜNING, PAPEN, and SCHLEICHER governments. Having no Reichstag majorities, they depended for support upon the Reich president's right to issue emergency decrees in accordance with ARTICLE 48 of the Weimar Constitution. The presidial cabinets undermined the authority of the parliament and thus the foundation of the Weimar Republic.

Press, during the Third Reich, a means of rule and an instrument of indoctrination at the disposal of the National Socialist (NS) leaders for attaining their political goals and interests; it was thus no longer the free conveyer of public opinion. Freedom of the press was denigrated as a liberal aberration; the work of journalists and editors was defined as an assignment in the service of the *Volk* and the state; the exercise of the publishing trade was made dependent upon reliability and suitability from the NS viewpoint. The goal of NS press policy was to make all journalistic products politically and, as far as possible, economically dependent upon the state, and in this way to dominate the public forum.

In the last phase of the Weimar Republic, the basic legal status of the press had already been restricted through emergency decrees. The Third Reich brought the final suspension of the freedom of the press, notably through the REICHSTAG FIRE DECREE and the suppression of the left-wing press. Steering and control of the press was organized and coordinated by the Press Section of the Propaganda Ministry, which was headed by Kurt Jahncke (May 29, 1933–March 1936), Alfred-Ingemar Berndt (until November 1938), Hans FRITZSCHE (until 1942), and Erich Fischer. They served under State Secretary Walther FUNK and, as of 1938, his successor Otto DIETRICH, each of whom in turn was concurrently press chief for the Reich government; Dietrich was also Reich Press Chief of the NSDAP.

News material had to be acquired from the GERMAN NEWS BUREAU (DNB) and from the NATIONAL SOCIALIST PARTY CORRESPONDENCE (NSK). Oral briefings were provided for the major German daily newspapers through the so-called BERLIN PRESS CONFERENCE. Press instructions for the provincial papers were issued through the Reich propaganda offices. Other conferences dealt with magazines, cultural and economic news, and special occasions. Even prior to the war there was an unmistakable development toward greater and more detailed

Press. Goebbels speaks to the Foreign Press Association in 1933.

regulation. For the supervision of magazines a PERIODICAL SERVICE was organized in 1939. Military censorship was instituted on August 26, 1939.

The EDITOR LAW obligated managing editors to follow the state press policy. The compulsory professional organization for journalists and publishers was the REICH PRESS CHAMBER, within the REICH CULTURE CHAMBER. In terms of economics, the gradual concentration of all newspaper and magazine publishers in NS hands was nearly accomplished. Press enterprises of the Social Democratic and Communist parties and of the trade unions were confiscated without indemnification, to the advantage of the NS party press. The middle-class press, however, was at first tolerated within limits, since the demand of radical party groups for its immediate absorption by the party press could not be achieved; domestic as well as foreign-policy considerations of the German national interest were involved. The party press was subsequently reorganized, and in 1935 the Reich Press School was established in Berlin to provide training for a new generation of journalists.

The systematic liquidation of the competing private publishers of the Catholic press and of the provincial press, along with the companies of the general-circulation newspapers, such as Huck, Girardet, and Leonhardt, was carried out through the orders issued by Max AMANN on April 24, 1935. They made possible forced closings and financed buyouts through ostensibly neutral holding and finance companies, set up by Amann's staff directors Rolf RIENHARDT and Max WINKLER. Only parts of the HUGENBERG concern remained intact by 1944. Three newspaper shutdown operations, partly political and partly war-related (May 1941, February–April 1943, and July–August 1944), finally reduced the circulation share of private newspapers throughout the Reich to 17.5 percent in October 1944. The few weekly newspapers and illustrated magazines still publishing in 1944 were totally in party hands. Magazines were reduced to a small vestige (in October 1944, 10 percent of the 1939 level).

The weaknesses of press control arose from the characteristic structural principle of the NS system of rule: to divide up functions to the vanishing point and to unify party and state posts in individual hands at all levels. The results were overlapping jurisdictions and rivalries, as among Goebbels, Amann, and Dietrich, or between the Propaganda Ministry and the Foreign Office. Nevertheless, apart from the resistance of small groups, the goal of a synchronized public forum was achieved in the press sector.

The result was a uniformity of the press in expression and in format that Goebbels himself complained about early on; it led to losses in readership of the regulated press publications by 1939. It was only the heightened demand for information during the war that produced increases in circulation. In order to win over certain population groups as well as other nations, a sort of "pluralism of opinions" was officially tolerated within strict limits for the purpose of manipulation. Varying modes of expression in the press on current issues and political situations should be seen in this light: a play with delegated roles was staged to include such surviving middle-class press publications as the *Frankfurter Zeitung* and new NS creations such as *Das* REICH, along with *Der* STÜRMER and *Das* SCHWARZE KORPS.

S. O.

Press, freedom of the. *See* Freedom of the Press.

Press Advisories (*Presseanweisungen*), obligatory and strictly confidential government directives and rules regarding expression for the German daily press; they were transmitted at the BERLIN PRESS CONFERENCE, held daily beginning in July 1933 by the Press Section of the Propaganda Ministry for the reception, organization, and placement of news and commentaries. The advisories presented a compilation of factual and political information from the government offices involved, as set forth in preliminary conferences. Advisories to the provincial press and to periodicals followed by teletype through the state offices (Landesstellen; as of 1937, Reichspropagandaämter [Reich Propaganda Offices]). Magazines were informed at Reich Periodical Conferences, and as of May 9, 1939, through the PERIODICAL SERVICE. Themes to be adopted immediately were marked with a double border, and texts to be adopted bore the code word "alignment" (*Ausrichtung*). Beginning in November 1940, instead of the individual advisories a "Daily Word from the Reich Press Chief" was dictated for the daily press and supplemented with oral information and further rules regarding the choice of wording.

S. O.

Preysing, Konrad Count von, b. Schloss Kronwinkl (Lower Bavaria), August 30, 1880; d. Berlin, February 21, 1950, German Catholic theologian. After studies in law Preysing served as Bavarian embassy secretary in Rome. He began theological studies in 1910 and was ordained a priest in 1912. From 1917 to 1932, he was a preacher and cathedral canon in Munich; in 1932 he was appointed bishop of Eichstätt, and in 1935, bishop of Berlin. Preysing assumed leadership of the diocese of the Reich capital just as the National Socialist attack on church institutions was being fully unleashed. He defended himself through pastoral letters, evaded teaching prohibitions against priests by the use of Catholic laity for instruction, and publicly

Konrad von Preysing.

denounced NS violations of the CONCORDAT. This led to harassment (for example, a temporary ban on the diocesan newspaper) and to closer monitoring of his preaching. Nevertheless, because of wartime considerations Preysing was left largely undisturbed, even when he sharply protested against the EUTHANASIA measures in a sermon in March 1941.

Preysing tried without success to halt the deportation of Jews; his call for help to Pope PIUS XII, with whom he had been friends for years, produced only expressions of consolation in late April 1943. Similarly, Preysing's hopes for the success of the opposition, with which he was connected through the KREISAU CIRCLE, were not fulfilled. After the end of the war Preysing criticized the excesses of the occupying powers as vigorously as he had those of the National Socialists; he also appealed for aid for the starving population. At Christmas 1945 Preysing was named a cardinal.

Price control (*Preisstopp*), regulatory measure to check price increases, such as the Price Control Ordinance of November 26, 1936 (*see* WAGE-PRICE POLICY).

Prien, Günther, b. Osterfeld (Thuringia), January 16, 1908; d. North Atlantic Ocean, March 7, 1941, German corvette captain (March 1, 1941). After service in the merchant marine, Prien became a naval ensign in 1935. A lieutenant commander at the outbreak of the war, he was in command of a U 47 submarine when, on October 14, 1939, it penetrated the heavily defended port of the British Home Fleet at

Günther Prien.

Scapa Flow and sank the battleship *Royal Oak.*
This made Prien one of the first naval war heroes
to be singled out for propaganda use. He received several decorations (including the
Knight's Cross with Oak Leaves) and became a
best-selling author with *Mein Weg nach Scapa
Flow* (My Path to Scapa Flow; 1940), which was
a postwar success in England under the title *I
Sank the Royal Oak.* During 1940–1941 he sank
more ships, with a total tonnage of 160,935
gross registered tons. Prien ultimately fell a
victim to depth charges from the British destroyer *Wolverine.*

Priest trials (*Priesterprozesse*), in general, the
proceedings held against clergy because of violations of such laws as the PULPIT PARAGRAPH or
the MALICIOUS-GOSSIP LAW; in the narrower
sense, prosecution of Catholic priests and members of religious orders in the years 1935 to
1937 for currency violations and offenses
against morals. A first wave of such prosecutions
dealt with "currency smuggling," especially by
religious communities, and began with the sentencing of a Daughter of Charity of Saint Vincent de Paul on May 17, 1935, to a prison term
of five years and a fine of 140,000 RM. Since the
German religious orders had both revenues and
liabilities in currency abroad, they were particularly affected by the measures for FOREIGN-CUR-
RENCY MANAGEMENT that began to take effect
as early as 1931. They evaded the measures by
transfers through the Hosius Bank, which had
offices in Berlin and Amsterdam. When the
situation became risky, the bank attempted to
ward off penalties by reporting itself, but in

doing so it delivered complete documentation
to the Gestapo that was then used to prosecute
60 priests. The bishops were unable to defend
the accused, and could only protest against the
media's exploitation of the priests' trials and
against the spread of so-called currency-smug-
gling songs (*Devisenschieberlieder*), such as:
"Yes, life in the cloister, / Yes, life there is swell,
/ Yes, more than praying there / They smuggle
currency well! / Tra la la. . . ." In the wake of
these trials the religious orders were also defenseless against confiscations, which had been
prepared for some time (advisory of the NSDAP
treasurer, October 20, 1934).

The trials of priests on morals charges had also
been planned for some time; some had even
begun, when the encyclical letter MIT BRENNEN-
DER SORGE (March 14, 1937) provided a favorable opportunity for a counterstroke. In the
ensuing period the press gave extensive coverage, with many titillating details about the
moral lapses of monks, nuns, and priests. Goebbels spoke of "thousands of cases," and the
Reich Minister for Church Affairs, Hanns
KERRL, mentioned 7,000; the newspapers
heightened this impression. Yet only a total of 49
diocesan priests and 9 priests in orders were
involved, some of whom had already been punished with ecclesiastical sanctions. The propaganda objective of driving a wedge between the
clergy and their parishes was not successful.
Indeed, the malicious portrayals and the wholesale defamation of monasteries and convents as

Priest trials. National Socialist brochure: "The Truth about the Morals
Trials."

(in Wilhelm Frick's words) "breeding grounds of vice" often had the opposite effect. Subsequently the priest trials quickly disappeared from the headlines.

Primo de Rivera, José Antonio, b. Madrid, April 24, 1903; d. Alicante, November 20, 1936, Spanish politician. Son of the military dictator Miguel Primo de Rivera (1870–1930), José Antonio was a jurist by profession. He ran unsuccessfully for the Cortes, the Spanish parliament, in 1931. On October 29, 1933, he founded the fascist FALANGE, which he was able to combine with the nationalist wing of the syndicalists. In February 1936, the Republican government banned the movement; it had Primo de Rivera arrested in March. At first sentenced to a prison term, he was blamed after the start of the SPANISH CIVIL WAR for having plotted the revolt, and was sentenced to death and shot. Gen. Francisco Franco had his body laid to rest in 1940 during a solemn state ceremony in Madrid.

Princes, expropriation of. *See* Expropriation of princes.

Prisoners of war (*Kriegsgefangene*), enemy combatants placed in custody to prevent their further participation in battle. The treatment of such prisoners during the Second World War was governed by the GENEVA CONVENTIONS of July 27, 1929, insofar as the belligerents had entered into them. In addition, the Hague Land-War Regulation (1907) was to be applied. The Soviet Union had not ratified the Geneva agreements, and did not consider itself bound by the Hague regulation, since it had renounced all treaties concluded by the tsarist empire. Nonetheless, at the outbreak of the German-Soviet war, the USSR announced to the government of the German Reich, in a note dated July 17, 1941, and handed to the Swedish representative in Moscow, that it would observe the Hague regulation on condition that the enemy do likewise. This note was not answered by the German government.

The treatment of western Allied prisoners of war under German custody basically conformed to the international agreements, with certain exceptions. In line with the COMMANDO ORDER, for example, commando troops were to be shot, and "terror pilots" who were forced down were to be handed over to the lynch justice of the local population. Moreover, in some instances Hitler ordered reprisals such as the shooting of recaptured escapees, which as a rule were forbidden against prisoners of war.

José Antonio Primo de Rivera.

Violations of international agreements were more common in the treatment accorded to war prisoners from the eastern countries. However, the treatment of Soviet prisoners of war violated all the principles of international law. One reason for this was that Hitler did not see himself bound by the Geneva Conventions, which Russia had not signed. Another reason was the escalation of the struggle in the east as a "war of two worldviews."

The ordeal of the Soviet soldiers began immediately after their capture. After the battles of encirclement they lay by the tens of thousands, exhausted, sick, or wounded, in the roundup centers and transit camps for army prisoners. The needed provisions were not available owing to supply difficulties or other reasons. Mass death was the result. A great number of other prisoners died in transit to the main camps in the rear areas or in the Reich. Conditions did not improve upon their arrival, since at times the food supply was restricted by special order. Indeed, officers and contractors active at the prisoner-of-war camps, under whom the prisoners were placed in labor assignments, sought to profit from the prisoners' lot. Only when the shortage of labor began to make itself felt and the prisoners of war became urgently needed for the war economy did a change in treatment slowly set in.

At the same time, and up to the collapse of the Third Reich, orders were given for the physical extermination of certain groups of Soviet prisoners of war. Thus, in compliance with the so-called COMMISSAR ORDER of June 6, 1941, captured commissars were to be "taken care of" (*zu erledigen*) while still on the battlefield.

When the troops carried out the order only hesitantly and many commissars were sent off to camps, SD Chief Reinhard Heydrich sent EINSATZKOMMANDOS to the prisoner-of-war camps to search out commissars as well as any other politically "intolerable" prisoners of war. These prisoners were turned over to SPECIAL HANDLING. Immediate liquidation sometimes gave way to making selected prisoners of war available for "scientific experiments" likely to be fatal. Disabled, sick, and wounded prisoners of war in the occupied regions of the USSR were at times handed over to the HIGHER SS AND POLICE LEADERS, who had the "useless eaters" shot. Escaped and recaptured prisoners of war were shot in compliance with the BULLET DECREE. Prisoners of war who violated the restrictions imposed on them—such as the prohibition against intimacy with German women and girls—were hanged. The same fate awaited Polish and Serbian prisoners of war. Western prisoners of war, on the other hand, could expect only a punishment for disobedience. It can be estimated that at least 2,530,000 of the minimum of 5,400,000 Red Army soldiers who fell into German captivity died or were killed.

The treatment of German prisoners of war by the Allies varied. The Western powers adhered basically to international law, with the exception of excesses committed by smaller units or individuals. To be sure, infringements and harsh conduct increased against German prisoners of war in the final phase of the war and after the surrender, especially with regard to members of the WAFFEN-SS. Transgressions multiplied as well in reaction to revelations of National Socialist crimes. But the frequent charge of inadequate food supplies and lodging cannot, taking into account the overall situation, be sustained. Investigations have shown that these conditions existed only around the time, shortly before and after the surrender, when the Americans and British seized some 4 million German prisoners of war and encountered serious difficulties in providing them with food and shelter. Efforts to overcome the shortages were successful, averting the fear of mass deaths. Shortly after the surrender the western Allies began to release prisoners, the Americans as early as May 1945. By the end of 1948 all the German prisoners of war in the custody of the Western powers had been freed, in accordance with the agreements of the Moscow Foreign Ministers' Conference of 1947 (*see* MOSCOW FOREIGN MINISTERS' CONFERENCES), with the exception of those who had been sentenced for war crimes.

Prisoners of war. Homecoming (1945).

The fate of the German prisoners of war in Soviet hands, like that of their counterparts in German hands, was catastrophic. The "conventionless war," the ideological warfare, and especially the terrible living conditions under which the Soviet civilian population also had to suffer claimed many victims among German captives. From the first months after the invasion of the USSR and into 1942, German soldiers were at first frequently, then later sporadically shot immediately after capture on the order of commissars and fanatic officers. This apparently stemmed at first from the Commissar Order issued on the German side, and later from the inflammatory Soviet propaganda campaign led by Ilya Ehrenburg. Many thousands died of exhaustion in transit to permanent

German prisoners of war in Russia.

camps. Housing, food supplies, and medical care were extremely bad, a situation exacerbated by hard labor under often unaccustomed weather conditions, until around 1948; the mortality was correspondingly high. Of the German soldiers who fell into captivity in 1941–1942, 90 to 95 percent died; in 1943, 60 to 70 percent; in 1944, 30 to 40 percent; and in 1945, 20 to 25 percent. Only in 1949 did the death rate drop to a normal level as a consequence of the generally improved living conditions in the USSR.

The USSR took its time releasing the prisoners of war, who provided cheap labor for reconstruction. Still, even in the early postwar years, German prisoners of war were released, the overwhelming majority of them disabled. The Soviet Union did not subscribe to the agreement concluded at the Moscow Foreign Ministers' Conference. As late as May 1950, transports of homecoming prisoners of war were arriving in the Federal Republic. The prisoners left behind were those sentenced for war crimes; some of these returned in 1953–1954. Only after negotiations concluded in Moscow with Chancellor Konrad ADENAUER in September 1955 did the USSR declare itself ready to return the remaining "criminal elements" as well. By West German reckoning there re-

mained a total of 130,000 prisoners of war in Soviet custody, whereas the Soviets counted only 9,628 remaining, in penal camps. These prisoners of war returned home in 1956. Of a total of 3,060,000 German soldiers who had been taken prisoner by the Soviets, 1,094,250 died or lost their lives in other ways.

A. St.

Profit sharing (*Gewinnbeteiligung*), the demand in Point 14 of the NSDAP Program of February 24, 1920; it was applied to "big businesses" (*Grossbetriebe*) without a more precise definition. After the defeat of the social-revolutionary wing of the party at the BAMBERG FÜHRER CONFERENCE (February 14, 1926), and in the conflict over the so-called TRADE UNION AXIS at the end of 1932, the demand for profit sharing remained unfulfilled owing to Hitler's arrangement with industry after the Seizure of Power. Point 14 was from then on reinterpreted: true profit sharing would be the "determination of fair wages by performance [*Leistungslöhne*]," and also the development of workplace social services, as guaranteed by National Socialist SOCIAL POLICY.

Progress (*Fortschritt*), a higher development of humanity that, in the National Socialist view, was attainable only through the "generative energies and laws of race and *Volk.*" The National Socialists rejected the optimistic belief in progress according to which this development toward higher levels would emerge "by itself." They based their view on what they saw as the global menace to humanity of "raceless [*rasselos*] international powers" such as Jewry, Marxism, and Jesuitism. These would destroy any progress if not stopped by "racially aware" powers such as National Socialism.

Propaganda

Propaganda played a central role in securing and asserting National Socialist (NS) rule. In domestic policy it served as the most important means for imposing the NSDAP's demands for power as well as its ideological and political viewpoints upon the entire populace. It also worked to indoctrinate the people, to totally envelop them, and to manipulate them in line with the regime's purposes. In this way it partially succeeded in averting potential opposition, since it was able to depend on already existing authoritarian attitudes and on the aversion of wide sectors of the population toward minorities, for example on a latent ANTISEMITISM. Nonetheless, the "element of coercion," extending even to terror, was also an indispensable component of NS propaganda (J. Hagemann). Indeed, it was able to legitimate autocracy through pseudodemocratic and pseudoplebiscitary devices, and to dampen or eliminate the public and private articulation and advocacy of all divergent opinions and attitudes. All "VOLK COMRADES," both men and women, were to subordinate themselves without reservation to the so-called opinion leadership (*Meinungsführung*). Propaganda was, however, not only the instrument of domestic rule for the regime; at the same time it was—especially in wartime—the government's means of exercising power in foreign policy. Therefore, as Joseph Goebbels noted in his daily journal on May 10, 1942, news policy during wartime had the purpose of waging the war, not of conveying information.

The procedural motto after the Seizure of Power derived from Hitler's statement in *Mein Kampf:* "The victory of an idea becomes all the more possible the more completely propaganda works upon people taken as a whole, and the more exclusive, strict, and solid is the organization that finally carries through the struggle." Goebbels's Reich Ministry for Volk Enlightenment and Propaganda was established on March 13, 1933, by decree of the Reich president. Augmented by its state-level offices in the *Gaue* (as of 1937, Reich Propaganda Offices), the ministry assured the "ubiquity of influence through organization," as Reich Broadcasting Leader Eugen HADAMOVSKY later expressed it. For this reason, state and party jurisdictions were combined as a matter of principle under leading officials in all instances, in order to ensure a maximum of control. Propaganda Minister Goebbels himself combined government and party functions as both president of the REICH CULTURE CHAMBER and Reich Propaganda Leader of the NSDAP.

According to Goebbels's ideas, propaganda had to "encompass domestic, cultural, economic, social, and foreign policies"—in other words, areas of responsibility that until that point had belonged to other ministries. Hitler's order of June 30, 1933, provided greater precision. Goebbels succeeded only partially in asserting control over all the areas he claimed in the perpetual competitive struggle. Still, he remained the central figure in the NS propaganda machinery, which controlled the nation's entire cultural life through the Culture Chamber.

At the same time, other party and government agencies claimed and maintained important jurisdictions. Although control over teachers and faculties in the art academies was taken away from Bernhard RUST's Ministry of Science, Education, and Public Instruction (May 15, 1935), Goebbels did not manage to gain supervision over the universities. Protracted power struggles went on with Alfred Rosenberg, the Führer's Plenipotentiary for the Supervision of All Intellectual and Ideological Schooling and Education in the NSDAP, and his Office for the Cultivation of Writing (*see* WRITING, CULTIVATION OF). Functions also overlapped with Philipp BOUHLER's OFFICIAL PARTY REVIEW COMMISSION FOR SAFEGUARDING NATIONAL SOCIALIST WRITING. Further ongoing conflicts took place with the Foreign Office, the Reich War Ministry, and the Wehrmacht. The order of June 30, 1933, concerning the responsibilities of the

Propaganda Ministry stated expressly that "the news and information services abroad, the art, art exhibits, film, and sports abroad" were to be moved from the Foreign Office to the Propaganda Ministry. However, the Foreign Office successfully maintained authority in the press sector with its "Diplomatic Correspondence," news material that Goebbels had to disseminate through his GERMAN NEWS BUREAU, and with its press conferences for foreign journalists. Goebbels, however, prevailed as the authority with sole supervision over foreign radio broadcasts.

It was a severe setback for the Propaganda Ministry, therefore, when the Führer decree of September 8, 1939, transferred responsibility for the conduct of foreign propaganda to the Foreign Office under Ribbentrop after the outbreak of war. The Propaganda Ministry was only to make the existing apparatus available, and the propaganda facilities of the Foreign Office were not to be expanded. Still, the rivalries continued, and each ministry tried to expel the other from the area of foreign broadcasting. The propaganda for the occupied Eastern Territories finally fell to Rosenberg's ministry.

Disagreement arose among the Propaganda Ministry, the War Ministry, and the Wehrmacht over control of the PROPAGANDA COMPANIES, which had been in existence since 1936, and over "the conducting of propaganda in wartime." An agreement was reached in 1938 that "the propaganda war" was to be regarded as a "means of war equivalent to war with weapons"; at home the Propaganda Ministry had sole authority, but in the frontline areas it was to act in accord with the Wehrmacht High Command (OKW). The Wehrmacht gained the monopoly over war reporting until shortly before the war's end, with the Propaganda Ministry providing some of the experts. On April 1, 1939, the first Propaganda Companies were unified under the command of the newly formed Division of Wehrmacht Propaganda and attached to the Wehrmacht Command Office (as of August 8, 1940, the Wehrmacht Command Staff). This was the source of the daily WEHRMACHT REPORT, from whose compilation Goebbels was excluded. Nevertheless, he was able to issue guidelines for its treatment in the media. As late as September 1943 he was still trying in vain to have Hitler transfer the Wehrmacht propaganda to his own ministry. Quarrels over jurisdiction, power struggles, and excessive organization made any unified propaganda approach difficult

Propaganda slogan: "One *Volk*, one Reich, one Führer!"

Social policy in the service of propaganda: street collection for the Winter Relief Agency.

in practice, leaving room for exploitation by opponents.

However, Goebbels did essentially succeed in making propaganda "one of the supporting pillars of National Socialist rule and power expansion" (Boelke). Alongside the extensive control and guiding apparatus, the content and methods of propaganda, developed in line with data on mass psychology, played an important role. NS propaganda utilized the most primitive clichés, suggestive catchwords, and slogans ("Ein Volk, ein Reich, ein Führer," or "The Jews are our misfortune") and applied the principle of continual repetition of the simplest trains of thought and content, which were to be imprinted in the allegedly limited minds of the masses. Appeal was made more to mass and class instincts than to intellect. Propaganda relied upon preexisting popular prejudices to conjure enemy images, which it then hammered into the consciousness. An example was the "bogeyman of the Jewish-plutocratic-Bolshevik conspiracy" (J. Hagemann), which could be identified with any internal or external political opponents as need required. Propaganda was significantly applied in constructing the Führer myth, and in the figure of Horst WESSEL it fashioned a symbol of the movement that "became an essential component of National Socialism's visions of the

future" (Ernst Bramsted). Historical parallels were sought and used in indoctrination, while domestic and foreign political events that militated against the propaganda version were passed over in silence or disguised.

All propaganda devices were, insofar as possible, deployed everywhere and at the same time, in order to achieve an effect on the public. Speeches, the daily press, books, films, and radio—the importance of each was measured by the extent of its influence. The spoken word counted for more than the written one, and direct contact with the masses was the aim. Consequently, the modern mass media of radio and cinema were declared to be "means of journalistic leadership in the service of leading the *Volk.*" The GERMAN WEEKLY NEWSREEL, which was placed under the personal control of Goebbels and at times even of Hitler, became "the acknowledged place for propagandistic influence with the purpose of bringing the Führer's world closer to all *Volk* comrades and making palpable his essence as the embodiment of all-German being" (Ludwig Heyde). Along with the taken-for-granted daily ubiquity of NS propaganda, along with the obligatory parades and the annual CELEBRATIONS of the Führer's birthday, the solstice, and November 9, the Harvest Thanks Days and the launchings of the

WINTER RELIEF AGENCY drives, propaganda operations and campaigns were staged for current political goals and aims, only a few of which have been closely analyzed. Thus, in the context of the Catholic CHURCH STRUGGLE, the approximately 250 morals trials conducted against Catholic priests and lay brothers in 1936 and 1937 became a prominent occasion for, and object of, "a propaganda campaign that was as vast and spectacular as it was risky" (Hockerts), with the aim of upsetting the cohesion between churchgoers and the institutional church.

In 1938, in domestic and foreign policy, propaganda prepared for, supported, and accompanied the so-called Sudeten crisis. The concerted operations of the Propaganda Ministry that lasted for several months after KRISTALLNACHT had only superficially the task of countering foreign criticism and justifying the ensuing antisemitic measures; they also served to camouflage the actual events. ARYANIZATION did not become known to the general public, emigration statistics were not announced, and the deportations to the CONCENTRATION CAMPS were concealed. It was understood that nothing about the staging of such actions or about the techniques and practices used in propaganda should, insofar as possible, be allowed to reach the public, both to ensure the propaganda's effectiveness and to avoid disillusionment.

Successful propaganda work, however, presupposed knowledge about the opinions and attitudes of the population or population groups, so that they could be specifically addressed and influenced. In this connection Goebbels and others made use of secret situation reports concerning the various sectors of public life that were prepared by government and party offices, and after 1935 especially by the Security Service (SD). The propaganda was accompanied by overt or hidden violence, yet it was increasingly conducted without any competition. Where, when, and how this situation began to provoke detachment, skepticism, and opposition may be seen in incipient form in such tendencies as the Church Struggle, or in the influence that propaganda had on foreign political and military reactions. As for the wholesale assertion that "the long years of Nazi propaganda had brought most people to the point of accepting the official line" (Bramsted), more discriminating studies would be required.

Sibylle Obenaus

Propaganda Companies (Propagandakompanien; PK), special units set up in 1938 in the army general commands (after the start of the war, also in the navy and the Luftwaffe) and consisting of military and technical personnel, to ensure "cooperation between warfare with propaganda and warfare with weapons in the area of operations." The companies were first put to use when German soldiers marched into the Sudetenland. The Propaganda Companies were divided into teams: one each for supply, labor, and loudspeaker equipment, and three for war reporting; the last had squads for text, film, photographs, and radio. The material produced by the Propaganda Companies, after passing military censorship, was forwarded to the Propaganda Ministry. Films, for example, were prepared there for showing in the programs of the GERMAN WEEKLY NEWSREEL. At first subordinate to Signal Corps units, in 1943 the Propaganda Companies were made into a separate section, with a staff of around 15,000 until the war's end.

Propaganda Ministry (Propagandaministerium), the usual shortened designation of the Reich Ministry for Volk Enlightenment and Propaganda (Reichsministerium für Volksaufklärung und Propaganda; Promi), established on March 13, 1933, under Joseph GOEBBELS. The ministry derived its authority from several spheres, and was intended to put into action Hitler's ideas for effective PROPAGANDA, as he had described it in *Mein Kampf.* Initial operations toward this end were the SYNCHRONIZATION of all makers of opinion (the press, radio, and cinema), as well as the monopolization of all cultural activity (literature, the theater, art, and music). The lever for this was the law of September 22, 1933, for the unification of all "culture-creating" people (*Kulturschaffenden*) into corporate bodies under public law beneath the umbrella of a REICH CULTURE CHAMBER, of which Goebbels became president. By controlling the exercise of the professions and by means of censorship, the chamber conducted defensive propaganda through filtering out unwanted elements.

The positive presentation of the regime, as in the mass media, was furthered by the various forms of PRESS ADVISORIES, which penetrated into every corner of the Reich by means of the Propaganda Ministry's state offices (as of 1937, the Reich Propaganda Offices). The ministry

Propaganda Ministry. Goebbels's office in Berlin.

was also responsible for the grandiose stagings at the REICH PARTY CONGRESSES and at the National Socialist CELEBRATIONS, as well as for developing the FÜHRER CULT. Goebbels never succeeded entirely in shunting aside competing agencies such as the Foreign Office and the Wehrmacht. Nevertheless, his high rank in the NS hierarchy assured the participation of his ministry in all matters concerning influence over opinion. The monolithic image of the Third Reich, which endures even today, is his handiwork.

Property (*Eigentum*). Despite the original declaration of intentions in the NSDAP Program of 1920 and the official emphasis on the social bond of property (*see* VOLK COMMUNITY), property ownership remained a basic right that the National Socialists infringed upon only in limited areas. The socialist nationalization plans of the early period were sacrificed to political expediency, and encroachments on private property in land or in terms of the means of production were undertaken only for military reasons during the war or as a weapon in the persecution of Jews (*see* ARYANIZATION).

Prostitution, commercial, paid "surrender" of the (female) body for sexual intercourse. In German law it was termed "commercial indecency" (*Gewerbeunzucht*), and was not punishable as of February 18, 1927, but it was subject to health control. The medical supervision of "persons with frequent change of sexual partners" and regulations governing the "public display" of prostitution were intensified under the Third Reich. Criminal penalties were possible for "anyone who invites indecency or offers [her/

him]self for such, publicly in a conspicuous manner or in a manner that offends an individual or the general public" (law of May 26, 1933). The National Socialists made the claim that they had eliminated prostitution through work creation and social policy and through measures designed to protect "blood" and youth. The decrease in prostitution during the 1930s, however, took place simultaneously with an increased promiscuity in and around the National Socialist organizations, camp life, and large-scale events. The outbreak of war, increasing poverty, and the difficult postwar years under the occupation broke down the barriers between commercial prostitution and "selling oneself" out of economic distress.

H. H.

Protective custody (*Schutzhaft*), institution established before the First World War for taking persons into police custody. In Prussia its imposition was based initially on the General Law Code (Allgemeines Landrecht; Article 10 II 17). A further Prussian regulation was the Police Administration Law of July 1, 1931. Thereafter, the police could place a person in protective custody only for his or her own protection, to remove a previously occurring disturbance of public safety or order, or, if it were necessary, to ward off an immediate security threat, if there was no alternative solution. In any event, the prisoner was to be released no later than the following day (with the exception of mentally ill persons who endangered the public).

The National Socialist Seizure of Power significantly increased the possibility of taking persons into protective custody: the Decree to Pro-

Protective custody. Headlines of the *Berlin Stock Market Courier* of May 2, 1933: "All Leaders of Independent Trade Unions in Protective Custody."

tect the German *Volk* of February 4, 1933 (*Reich Law Gazette* I, p. 35), gave the police authority for a longer detention period without a warrant of arrest from a judge. The arrested person could still—besides complaining to supervisory personnel—appeal to the judge of the district where the arrest was carried out. Moreover, the detention presupposed the commission of a punishable act (for example, the unauthorized carrying of weapons) and was limited to a maximum of three months. This early regulation lost its significance with the REICHSTAG FIRE DECREE of February 28, 1933, which permitted confinement for an unlimited period and gave the prisoner no legal recourse. It was initially used against Communist activities in the broadest sense, but finally it came to apply to anything that offended the regime. On this basis, some of those locked up were troublesome Evangelical and Catholic clergy, Center party members, socialists, trade unionists, newspaper publishers, journalists, alcoholics, asocial persons, malingerers, alimony delinquents, "unsocial" manufacturers, and relatives of fugitive opponents of the regime (*see* CLAN LIABILITY). The confinement of an individual for his own protection—supposedly against the "indignation" of the people—played a subordinate role in practice.

Prisoners in protective custody were at first housed in police jails and penitentiaries. Since these filled up quickly, prisoners were then confined in old factories or in other penal camps, the early CONCENTRATION CAMPS, almost all of which were shut down between 1933 and 1935. A final great wave of arrests passed through Germany after the so-called RÖHM AFFAIR (June 30, 1934). Thereafter the SS took control of the camps, which until then had been guarded mostly by SA auxiliary policemen. In 1933 the following statistics on protective-custody prisoners were published in the press: by April, in Bavaria, about 5,400 people, and in the whole Reich, some 16,000; by October, in Prussia, about 15,000 persons. It must also be taken into account that for propaganda reasons the numbers announced had probably been reduced. Moreover, the Interior Ministry—as was established by postwar verdicts—was not able to obtain accurate reports on the number of prisoners, in view of the many arrests made by all possible party and police offices. Immediately after the Seizure of Power and after the Reichstag Fire Decree there were many cases of completely arbitrary and unauthorized arrests (as by SA and SS members wanting to take revenge on political opponents), by means of which those arrested were brought to hastily improvised "wild" concentration camps (old barns, sheds, empty halls, back rooms, and so on), and were often severely abused or even killed there.

Early concentration camps that served for protective custody were:

Ahrensbök (Schleswig-Holstein)
Ankenbuck (Baden)
Augustusburg (Saxony)
Bad Sulza (Thuringia)
Benninghausen (Lippstadt district)
Bornim bei Potsdam
Brandenburg an der Havel
Brauweiler, near Cologne
Breitenau (Hesse-Nassau)
Bremen-Ochtumsand (on a ship)
Bremerhaven ("Langlütjen")
Breslau-Dürrgoy
Chemnitz and Colditz (satellite camps of Sachsenburg)
Columbia-Haus in Berlin (not closed until November 5, 1936)
Dresden (jail)
Dresden-Drachenberge (part of Sachsenburg)
Fuhlsbüttel (Hamburg)
Gollnow (Pomerania)
Gotteszell bei Schwäbisch Gmünd
Hainewalde (Saxony)
Hainichen (Saxony)
Hammerstein (Posen–West Prussia)
Heuberg bei Stetten am Kalten Markt (Württemberg)
Hohenstein (Saxony)
KEMNA
Kislau (Baden)
Königstein (Saxony)
Leipzig (women's concentration camp in St. George's Hospital)
Leschwitz bei Görlitz
LICHTENBURG
Moringen (Northeim district)
ORANIENBURG
Osthofen bei Worms

Quedenau (East Prussia)
Reichenbach (Vogtland)
Rosslau (Anhalt)
Sachsenburg (not closed until the summer of 1937)
Sonnenburg (Neumark)
Stettin-Bredow
Taufkirchen (Bavaria)
ULM-KUHBERG and the Garrison Guardhouse
Werden (Rhine Province)
Wittmoor (Hamburg)
Zschochau (Saxony)
Zwickau (Saxony)

W. D.

Protective custody camp (*Schutzhaftlager*), actual prisoner area in the CONCENTRATION CAMPS.

Protectorate of Bohemia and Moravia (Protektorat Böhmen und Mähren), "protected territory" (*Schutzgebiet*) incorporated into the German Reich by Hitler's decree of March 16, 1939, consisting of the "historic lands" of CZECHOSLOVAKIA, which the day before had been "smashed" by the entry march of the German military; area, 48,927 sq km (about 19,600 sq miles); population, 7.5 million (1940), including 225,000 Germans. Virtually unlimited power in the Protectorate was held by the Reich Protector (until September 27, 1941, Konstantin Baron von NEURATH; from August 25, 1943, Wilhelm FRICK) and his deputy (until June 4, 1942, Reinhard HEYDRICH; thereafter Kurt DALUEGE). Emil HÁCHA, who continued in office as "president," had practically no influence.

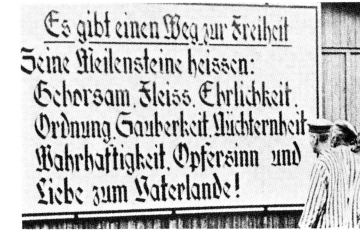

Protective custody. Prisoners in the Dachau concentration camp. The sign reads: "There is one road to freedom. Its milestones are: obedience, hard work, honesty, order, cleanliness, sobriety, truthfulness, self-sacrifice, and love of the fatherland!"

Protectorate of Bohemia and Moravia. Entry of German troops into Prague.

The German rule in the Protectorate was marked by a ruthless synchronization of its administration; imposition of the FÜHRER PRINCIPLE; reduction of the Czechs, in comparison with the Reich Germans, to persons with fewer rights; and open terror against the Czech intelligentsia and middle class. The Protectorate was an especially valuable area for the German war economy because of its productive and labor resources and because of its relative safety from air attacks. For this reason the labor pool was treated relatively well and materially rewarded. Yet the situation, already tense because of the National Socialist persecution of Jews (see THERESIENSTADT), became aggravated after the assassination attempt on Heydrich (May 27, 1942) by the SS reprisal operations (including that at LIDICE). Some 65,000 Jews and 40,000 Czechs had died as a result of the NS tyranny by 1945. The excesses against the German population during the EXPULSION can be traced to this. The territory of the Protectorate was re-incorporated into Czechoslovakia after the Soviet occupation in May 1945.

B.-J. W.

Protein gap (*Eiweisslücke*), shortage in the consumer economy of foodstuffs containing protein. Efforts were made to fill the gap as part of the campaign for agricultural AUTARKY by promoting a "battle for production" (*Erzeugungs-*

schlacht), by increasing the cultivation of protein-rich plants for human and animal consumption, and by the "Fight Spoilage!" (*Kampf dem Verderb*) campaign of the NUTRITIONAL RELIEF AGENCY. Like the battle against the FAT GAP, these efforts met with success only at the outset, and during the war only temporarily by exploitation of the food reserves of the occupied territories.

Protocols of the Elders of Zion (*Protokolle der Weisen von Zion*), falsified transcripts of speeches in which a member of the "Elders of Zion," an alleged Jewish secret government, explains the plan for gaining world dominion. The *Protocols* were among the texts on which antisemites based their claims that there was a "Jewish world conspiracy" (see ANTISEMITISM). The usual version of the text consists of 24 protocols (speeches or chapters), and is about 100 printed pages in length. The main themes include the role of liberalism, the methods for establishing Jewish world rule, and finally a description of the coming world state. Especially important was the work's critique of liberalism, since that was regarded as the way to chaos and anarchy, out of which only despotism could result; at the same time, it offered an opportunity for Jewish world rule. To attain this, Jews would support all liberal movements, all revolutions and political turmoil.

The *Protocols* were probably produced in the Paris foreign office of the tsarist secret police, the Okhrana. The first publication was in 1903, in an antisemitic newspaper in Saint Petersburg. The falsifiers used as a model the tract written by Maurice Joly in 1864 against Emperor Napoleon III. In August 1921 the plagiarism was first exposed, by the British newspaper the *Times*, but this information did nothing to interrupt the spread of the *Protocols*. Russian immigrants brought them in 1918 to Germany, where they were first published in January 1920 by the antisemitic journalist Ludwig Müller. The *Protocols* attracted much attention, and their reference to the Jewish world conspiracy provided an explanation for Germany's defeat in the First World War. Until Hitler's Seizure of Power, Müller's text appeared in 33 editions; a popular edition from the Hammer Press in Leipzig produced 100,000 copies by 1933.

The *Protocols* were very significant in the development of the antisemitic programs in the Weimar Republic. Hitler mentioned them in *Mein Kampf* and characterized them as genuine. Perceived as instructions for action on the part of Jewry, they required counteraction. Thus, from the circle of the murderers of Walther RATHE-NAU came the declaration that the murdered man had been considered one of the "Elders of Zion." The "Jewish world conspiracy" and the *Protocols* were repeatedly invoked as legitimation by the instigators and organizers of the NS PERSECUTION OF JEWS.

H. O.

Prussian Coup (*Preussenschlag*), designation for the removal from office of the Prussian government under the Social Democratic (SPD) minister president Otto BRAUN by Reich Chancellor Franz von PAPEN on July 20, 1932. In the Prussian legislative elections of April 24, 1932, the WEIMAR COALITION (consisting of the SPD and the Center and State parties) had lost its majority. However, the Braun government, in office since April 6, 1925, and composed of ministers from these parties, remained in charge. On the ground that public security and order in Prussia were endangered by street fights between National Socialists and Communists that approached civil war—the most serious incident was ALTONA BLOODY SUNDAY on July 17, 1932—Papen invoked an emergency decree of the Reich president on July 20. He deposed all Prussian ministers (Braun himself had been out of office since June 6 for reasons of health) as well as the Berlin police president,

Albert GRZESINSKI, and the commander of Berlin's municipal police, Magnus Heimannsberg. Papen made himself Reich commissioner in Prussia, appointed the lord mayor of Essen, Franz BRACHT, as both his deputy and interior minister, and entrusted him with government authority in Prussia.

The Prussian Coup was Papen's advance concession to Hitler; with it he hoped to win the latter and his party over to toleration of Papen's minority cabinet. He eliminated, along with the democratic government in Germany's largest state, one of the most important and final bulwarks of the Weimar Republic. In doing so, he cleared the way for the NSDAP's SEIZURE OF POWER.

Instead of resisting the coup with force, the Prussian government merely appealed to the state court (Staatsgerichtshof). On October 25, 1932, the court did indeed establish that the Braun government remained in office and could represent Prussia in the REICHSRAT, yet otherwise declared the coup to be legitimate. Braun's definitive removal from office took place on February 6, 1933, by order of the Reich president.

R. B.

Psychiatry, the science of mental illnesses and their cure. Like all MEDICINE under the Third Reich, psychiatry was linked with a biologistic–Social Darwinist program, within which the concept of psychopathology and the doctrine of the "born criminal" had arisen before

Prussian Coup. "Papen and Schleicher, always fresh and merry." French cartoon.

the end of the 19th century, with the Italian Cesare Lombroso. As early as 1911 a prize competition posed the question: "What do inferior elements cost the state and society?" In 1920 the psychiatrist Alfred Hoche urged legalization of the extermination of "life unworthy of life."

According to National Socialist thought, this extermination should affect not only the mentally ill, but also all psychopaths and, indeed, all "individuals incapable of community life" (*Gemeinschaftsunfähigen*). Psychiatric therapy was to be used only for patients who had some value within the *Volk* Community; those who were worthless were to be "culled out." This led to a transformation in the program of therapy that was greeted as a "revolutionary change," and that was summed up in the motto "Away with life unworthy of life—onward to treatable and curable *Volk* comrades. Away with the biologically inferior—onward to biological superiority." The CULLING OUT (*Ausmerze*) of the inferior was begun with FORCED STERILIZATION, continued with the EUTHANASIA program, and reached its culmination in the FINAL SOLUTION of the Jewish question. Some 50 psychiatrists participated actively; few distanced themselves unequivocally.

R. W.

Psychoanalysis, therapeutic treatment for neurotic illnesses by bringing into the conscious mind those elements of experience that have been repressed; it was created by Sigmund FREUD. Psychoanalysis was rejected under the Third Reich as a "Jewish-Marxist concoction" (as seen in the burning of Freud's writings on May 10, 1933, during the BOOK BURNING). Instead of psychoanalysis, a German psychotherapy was to be created, the protagonist of which was Carl Jung. In place of the internationally oriented General Medical Society for Psychotherapy, a nationalist German General Medical Society was founded, which was to create a "German Psychology" (*Deutsche Seelenkunde*). In the space of the famous Berlin Psychoanalytic Institute, a German Institute for Psychological Research and Psychotherapy was founded in 1936; its head, Matthias Heinrich Göring, was a cousin of the National Socialist minister. Within this framework psychoanalysis was at first tolerated. The term "psychoanalysis" could, however, no longer be used; the German Psychoanalytical Society took on the name Working Group for Analysis, and later that of Lecture Evening for Case Histories [*Kasuistik*]

and Therapy. The term "analysis" had to be circumlocuted with the term "genuine depth-psychological treatment of long duration." Even though German psychotherapy subordinated itself to the biologistic interpretation of MEDICINE and made performance (*Leistung*) and fitness the goals of its treatment, it remained afflicted with the blemish of a "Jewish seditious" science, according to NS categorization.

R. W.

Psychology, the science of human experience and behavior in the surrounding world. In Germany it arose as a subdiscipline of philosophy, and established itself as an academic subject at the end of the Weimar period. National Socialist civil service legislation resulted in the dismissal of more than 30 percent of the college and university teachers of psychology; the vacated positions were filled above all according to political considerations. By 1937 a new appreciation of psychology was oriented toward practical applications, with the goal of securing new psychologists for the Wehrmacht. For the first time, psychology was made into a preprofessional subject; this eventually led to the introduction of a diploma examination with accompanying regulations in 1941. For Wehrmacht psychology, by 1937 a candidate's examination (*Assessorexamen*), as a kind of second state examination, had been added after graduation (*Promotion*). The Luftwaffe and army psychology staffs were discontinued in 1942, but new areas of employment opened up in educational counseling and personnel training in the NS welfare organization (NSV) and in the psychology-of-work division of the German Labor Front. This made possible (according to U. Geuter) the professionalization of German psychology in the Third Reich.

R. W.

Public benefit, for the (*Gemeinnützigkeit*), with regard to tax liability, economic activity that is privileged because of its officially recognized usefulness to the common welfare. As a National Socialist cliché, it was an invocation of the "genuinely human[e] community that we Germans . . . again recognize in the *Volk* through Adolf Hitler." The idea of public service or public-spiritedness could thus be found in the demand of the NSDAP Party Program of February 24, 1920, for "activity of the individual . . . for the good of all" (Point 10), as well as in its calls for land reform (Point 17), for the combating of "common criminals . . .

usurers, [and] profiteers" (Point 18), and for replacement of the allegedly materialistic Roman law with a "German common law" (Point 19). Further, the demand for freedom of religious expression (Point 24) was made under the dictate of a public-spiritedness in the sense of the "*Volk* Community": "the common good over individual good." The NS interpretation of the idea thus transcended the demand for a social dimension to economic and political action, and provided a legal justification for the subordination of individual rights to a common welfare that in the Third Reich was defined exclusively by the political leadership.

Public Welfare Ambulance Service, Ltd. (Gemeinnützige Krankentransport GmbH; Gekrat), subdivision of the T4 EUTHANASIA organization. As part of the so-called INVALID OPERATION, Gekrat was responsible for assembling the transports for the various killing facilities, and for such tasks as transfer of the victims; administration; contact with family members; and budget estimates.

Public Welfare Homestead, Savings, and Building Corporation (Gemeinnützige Heimstätten-Spar- und Bau-AG; Gehag), the "Homestead Office" of the GERMAN LABOR FRONT (*see* HOMESTEAD).

Pulpit Paragraph (*Kanzelparagraph*), designation for the imperial statute (¶130a of the Criminal Law Code) passed on December 10, 1871, at the beginning of Otto von Bismarck's so-called struggle for culture (*Kulturkampf*). Clergy who expressed themselves in their capacity as such, orally or in writing, on state affairs "in a way that endangers the public peace" could, in line with the paragraph, be punished with imprisonment of up to two years. Such a punishable act was known as "misuse of the pulpit" (*Kanzelmissbrauch*). The vagueness of the elements constituting the offense made the paragraph an effective instrument of the National Socialist CHURCH STRUGGLE (*Kirchenkampf*) against insubordinate pastors. Martin NIEMÖLLER, for instance, was indicted in July 1937 on the basis of this paragraph, among other charges. It was not revoked in the Federal Republic of Germany until 1953.

Purchase permit (*Bezugsschein*), proof of the right to obtain certain products. Introduced on August 28, 1939, after the introduction of planning measures associated with the WAR ECONOMY, it was intended to regulate consumption. The permit was applied to an increasing number of products as the war continued.

Purveyance duty (*Andienungspflicht*), obligation imposed on members of the REICH FOOD ESTATE to offer their products first to the appropriate association and in accordance with its directives. It was intended to check intermediate trade and avoid distribution bottlenecks.

Quadragesimo anno (Lat.; In the Fortieth Year), title of a social encyclical by Pope PIUS XI dated May 15, 1931, "in the fortieth year" after Pope Leo XIII's encyclical *Rerum novarum* (Of New Things), which also had taken positions on social problems. In *Quadragesimo,* the Catholic church eased its attitude on issues of nationalization and on the participation of employees in the management, means of production, and profit of businesses. Nonetheless, a reconciliation between socialism and the church's positions was ruled out for the future. *Quadragesimo* influenced the constitution of the Austrian COR-PORATIST STATE, but it was rejected by the National Socialists as "alienated from life," since it disdained the "tasks of the national and *Volk*-conscious state." Moreover, *Quadragesimo* was seen as a typical manifestation of political Catholicism and therefore an impermissible meddling in state affairs.

Quakers, originally a derisive name ("those who quake [or shake]," later a self-designation, for a Christian sect (the Society of Friends) that arose in England in the 17th century. The charitably oriented Quakers became widely spread, especially in the United States. They adhered strictly to moral postulates such as the refusal to swear oaths and to perform military service. This rigorous posture led to severe conflicts for the German Quakers in the Third Reich, and for that reason it was officially relaxed by the sect so that it did not result in a high number of martyrs, as was the case with the JEHOVAH'S WITNESSES. Nonetheless, because of their international ties the Quakers were watched with suspicion, especially since they repeatedly organized assistance drives for persecuted people, working with the Evangelical pastor Heinrich GRÜBER, among others. As they had done after the First World War with the Quaker Food Relief, after 1945 the Quakers set about helping the needy European population and were instrumental in the CARE aid program.

Quebec conferences, two rounds of talks held by Allied politicians during the Second World War, in the Canadian provincial capital of Quebec. The first conference (code name, "Quadrant") was held from August 17 to 24, 1943, and was attended by Winston Churchill, Franklin D. Roosevelt, their foreign ministers, the Canadian prime minister, and the Chinese foreign minister. It agreed on the "Germany first" strategy—the priority of defeating Germany. An INVASION via France was planned for May 1944, supported by a landing in the Mediterranean. At the second conference (September 11 to 16, 1944), Roosevelt and Churchill discussed issues relating to the defeat of Japan and the occupation of Germany (including the MORGENTHAU PLAN).

Quedenau, locality in East Prussia. In 1933 and 1934 a concentration camp for protective-custody prisoners was situated there.

Questionnaire (*Fragebogen*), method of investigation for obtaining personal data during the DENAZIFICATION program. It was developed for the American occupation zone and was systematically used only there. An extremely detailed questionnaire had to be filled out by every public officeholder and by every person wanting to hold such a position. He or she was then ranked in one of six categories: "to be arrested automatically," "must be discharged," "recommended for discharge," "not recommended for discharge," "no evidence of National Socialist activity," "evidence of anti–National Socialist activity." In March 1946 the questionnaire system was replaced by court proceedings (*see* APPEALS BOARDS). By then some 120,000 people had been interned, and about 300,000 discharged from public service. Ernst von SALOMON attacked the snooping via questionnaires in his sarcastic novel *Der Frage-bogen* (translated as *Fragebogen: The Question-naire;* 1951).

Quisling, Vidkun, b. Fyresdal (Telemark), July 18, 1887; d. Oslo, October 24, 1945 (executed), Norwegian politician. An army officer, from

Vidkun Quisling.

1922 to 1926 Quisling aided Fridtjof Nansen (the League of Nations high commissioner for refugees) in providing aid to the starving Soviet population; he then was the legation secretary at the Norwegian embassy in Moscow in 1927–1928. At first enthusiastic about the Russian Revolution, after his return home in 1930 Quisling became a radical anti-Bolshevik. In 1933 he founded the fascist Norwegian Popular Awakening movement, which he later called the Nasjonal Samling (National Unity) party. However, as party chairman Quisling was unable to win a seat in the parliament even once. In the war he staked everything on collaboration with the Germans: he was received by Hitler on December 14, 1939, and he warned against a British invasion of Norway. After the German landing (April 9, 1940), he called for the end of resistance and placed himself at the service of Reich Commissioner Josef TERBOVEN. Quisling's party was declared to be the only one allowed. In 1942 he was made premier of a "national government," but his influence on German occupation policy was insignificant. He was arrested on May 9, 1945, and sentenced to death on September 10 of that year. The international press made his name a general term for a collaborator and traitor.

R

Raabe, Peter, b. Frankfurt an der Oder, November 27, 1872; d. Weimar, January 12, 1945, German conductor and musicologist. In 1894 Raabe became a conductor (*Kapellmeister*); in 1907 he was appointed court conductor in Weimar and curator of the Liszt Museum there. From 1920 to 1934 he was general music director in Aachen; beginning in 1924 he was also a professor at the Technical College. After Richard STRAUSS's resignation, Raabe became president of the REICH MUSIC CHAMBER in 1935. He deliberately maintained a low political profile, however, even though he too made concessions to the *Zeitgeist* in his writings (as in *Musik im Dritten Reich* [Music in the Third Reich]; 1935). Otherwise, he largely avoided attention by withdrawing into historical studies, chiefly his Liszt research. Raabe made numerous appearances as a guest conductor both in Germany and abroad.

Peter Raabe.

Race (*Rasse*), in biology, a subspecies. The term "race" was taken over by anthropology to designate particular morphologies within the species *Homo sapiens.* The racism that arose in the 18th and 19th centuries and the National Socialist racial doctrine that came from this tradition falsified the term by equating it with that of SPECIES: from the fact that the human races by and large preserved typical characteristics, it was inferred that reproductive boundaries divided races as they did biological species. The fact that totally different factors underlay this observed stability (for example, very low population densities for thousands of years, natural barriers to migration, low mobility, and cultural barriers) was ignored, despite increasing counterevidence. Rather, such indications were interpreted as alarm signals for a threatened bastardization of mankind.

This danger was supported by the observation that cultural development correlated with race. In 1775, for example, the noted philosopher Immanuel Kant had written: "Mankind reaches its highest level of perfection in the white race." In the wake of the Enlightenment, this argument supplanted outdated religious justifications for the suppression of other peoples and for colonialism and slavery. The pseudoscientific logic made such arguments especially successful, since the loss of myths owing to rationalism and technological progress led in the 19th century to a faith in science that was still unafflicted by recognition of the tentative nature of even scientific data. In particular, the research of Charles Darwin (1809–1882) in *On the Origin of Species* [*by Means of Natural Selection*] (1859) seemed to substantiate the view that the "successful" white race was especially valuable, especially its "Nordic" component. Count Arthur de GOBINEAU introduced the term "Aryan," initially with linguistic connota-

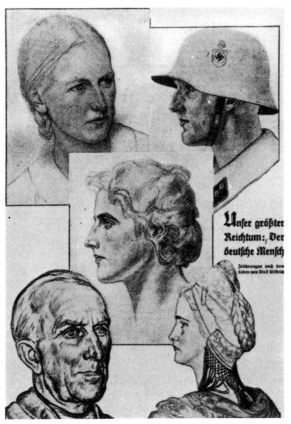

Race. Germanic heads in a National Socialist instructional pamphlet: "Our greatest wealth: the German."

From this set of metaphors arose the notion that BLOOD was the carrier of racial characteristics and attributes. A mixing of blood, on the other hand, meant the "decline of the racial level." All the measures available to RACIAL HYGIENE accordingly had to be mobilized against it. This kind of radical racial antisemitism was the ideology of a minority, but it could depend on the antisemitic prejudices of a majority. Even in the shaping of National Socialism by HITLER'S WORLDVIEW, the biologistic argument remained foreign to most antisemites. Yet as the official doctrine of the Third Reich it had the power to determine history, since Hitler in *Mein Kampf* identified its aim as the "preservation of the racial existence of mankind" (*Erhaltung des rassischen Daseins der Menschen*). In this view race, along with its biological meaning, assumed an almost mythical connotation as the destiny and mission of the "Nordic people." Accordingly, ETHICS was oriented entirely toward the well-being of the race.

Behind the hierarchy of the value of the various races, according to Hitler's view, operated the "aristocratic master plan of nature," from which was derived an unequal valuation of individual humans. The members of inferior races were also inferior as individuals. Since Hitler viewed the "Aryan" as the sole "founder

tions, to characterize this "culturally creative" group. Houston Stewart CHAMBERLAIN then identified the Aryans more precisely as *Germane* (belonging to the Germanic tribes). In this interpretation of history, the Germans (*die Deutschen*) assumed the role of a chosen people because they had preserved in its most nearly pure form the "Germanic essence."

A plan of action inevitably followed this interpretation: victory in the "struggle of races" could be secured only by preserving the purity of the race. At this point ANTISEMITISM intruded, and augmented its traditional religious and economic arguments with racial components. The historical process that had led to the special role of the Jews was again ignored. Instead, Jews were characterized as a race, and their special role explained as a result of their pernicious racial characteristics. The fact that they could not immediately be identified visually as a separate race made them especially dangerous, and in a kind of vicious circle this was introduced as proof of their perfidy. Racial policy thus meant above all the "expurgation" (*Ausscheidung*) of Jews from the "body of the Volk."

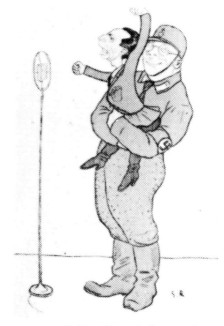

Race. "Tall; blond hair; light eyes; long skull; oval face; and high, narrow nose are characteristic for the Aryan." Satire on National Socialist racial ideology from the *Nebelspalter,* using Goebbels as an exemplar.

of a higher humanity" and as the "prototype of that which we today understand by the word 'man' [*Mensch*]," he denied Jews the status of humans, labeling them "subhumans." The racial barrier between "German-blooded" humans and Jews was thus more formidable than the inhibition against killing. From judicial convictions for the crime of RACIAL INFAMY it was only a step to the extermination policy of the FINAL SOLUTION.

Race and Settlement Main Office (Rasse- und Siedlungshauptamt; RuSHA), office of the SS Reich Leadership; it was established in 1931 and elevated to the status of a Main Office on January 30, 1935. The functions of the RuSHA concerned basic issues of SS ideology: the "alignment [*Ausrichtung*] of the SS in terms of race," issues dealing with peasants and settlements, "CLAN cultivation" (*Sippenpflege*), and instruction. To translate these tasks into reality the RuSHA used advisers on racial and peasant matters in every SS-Oberabschnitt (Higher Section) and instructional leaders in the individual units; it established "clan cultivation offices" (Sippenpflegestellen) in the SS Standarten (regiments) and published "SS guidebooks."

Tensions between Heinrich Himmler and Walther DARRÉ, the independently minded chief of the RuSHA, led to the latter's dismissal in the summer of 1938. His successor was Günther Pancke, who was followed by Otto Hofmann in 1940 and Richard HILDEBRANDT in 1943. Even before Darré's departure, the work of the RuSHA, which was often imbued with unreal "blood-and-soil" romanticism, was faced by increasing pressure from competing offices. Thus, the Main Office lost much of its initial influence in the ensuing years. For example, instructional matters were gradually shifted to the SS Main Office beginning in 1939, since that office had assumed control over the so-called Germanic labor in the occupied countries of western and northern Europe because of its responsibility for recruiting foreign Waffen-SS volunteers. The Settlement Office by the beginning of the war had created an elaborate administrative apparatus through establishing a series of SS-controlled settlement societies, among other measures. In early 1940 it was removed from the RuSHA and given over to the newly created command staff of the Reich Commissioner for the Fortification of the German Volk-Nation. Further responsibilities were transferred to the ETHNIC GERMAN CENTRAL OFFICE and the LEBENSBORN organization. Thus, during the war the responsibili-

ties of the RuSHA were increasingly concentrated on such areas as the processing of marriage applications and certificates of descent, the carrying out of investigations into the racial-biological background of Waffen-SS volunteers and resettlers in particular, and the recruitment and technical instruction of would-be settlers. In 1942 it was put in charge of social welfare, and temporarily even of social services, for the SS. It also had specific war-related functions. For example, it served as the main office for the burial and cemetery functionaries of the Waffen-SS and as an information office dealing with SS war casualties.

We.

Racial hygiene (*Rassenhygiene*), term coined by Alfred PLOETZ to denote the "doctrine of the conditions underlying the optimum preservation and perfection of the human race." Its aims were to promote families of "fit" individuals with many children; to establish a counterforce to the protection of the weak by preventing reproduction among the "inferior"; to combat "germ toxins" (*Keimgifte*)—syphilis, tuberculosis, and alcohol; to care for and encourage the peasantry; and to maintain military fitness. In order to promote these aims, in 1904 the journal *Archiv für Rassen- und Gesellschaftsbiologie* (Archive for Racial and Societal Biology) was founded, and in 1905, the GERMAN SOCIETY FOR RACIAL HYGIENE. The ideas of racial hygiene were continued especially by Fritz LENZ, a student of Ploetz, who from 1913 to 1933 was editor of the *Archiv*. In 1921, together with Erwin Baur and Eugen FISCHER, he wrote *Grundriss der menschlichen Erblichkeitslehre* (Foundation of the Theory of Human Inheritance), which was considered a classic even during the Third Reich.

In 1923 Lenz was appointed Germany's first professor of racial hygiene, and in 1933 he became director of the Division for Racial Hygiene at the Kaiser Wilhelm Institute for Anthropology, Human Inheritance Theory, and Eugenics in Berlin. In the words of the Reich Physicians' Führer, Gerhard WAGNER, racial hygiene became the "underlying foundation for today's reason of state [that is, motive for government action]" under National Socialism. To implement the ideas of racial hygiene, the Expert Committee for Population and Racial Policy was created. It was responsible for the Law to Prevent HEREDITARILY ILL OFFSPRING (1933), the Law against Dangerous Habitual Criminals (1933), the HEREDITARY FARM LAW (1933), the

Law to Encourage Marriages (1933), the Income Tax Law (1934), the Law to Protect the Hereditary Health of the German Volk (1935), and the NUREMBERG LAWS (1935).

R. W.

Racial infamy (*Rassenschande*), a criminal act according to the Law to Protect Blood (*see* BLOOD, LAW TO PROTECT) of September 15, 1935 (*Reich Law Gazette* I, p. 1146); it was concerned with marriage as well as with "extramarital intercourse between Jews and citizens of the state who are of German or species-related blood." Since marriages of this kind were prohibited, extramarital intercourse constituted the crime, for which by law only the man could be punished. In the numerous proceedings against racial infamy, most of them instigated through denunciations inspired by revenge or jealousy, women were in fact often prosecuted. Most of the proceedings ended with drastic punishments, especially prison terms; during the war they were made more severe. According to the Ordinance against VOLK VERMIN of September 5, 1939, even a death sentence was not unusual

Racial infamy. A "delinquent" being displayed by SS men. The sign reads: "I am the biggest swine in town for getting involved with Jews."

if the defendant could be accused of exploiting the circumstances of wartime, such as blackouts or economic deprivation. Racial infamy charges often led to concentration camp internment without a trial (as in the case of ALIEN WORKERS). The term was initially created to apply to Jews, but it was also used for relationships with other "alien" categories.

Racial Laws (*Rassengesetze*), the totality of legislation during the Third Reich bearing on the PERSECUTION OF JEWS, especially the NUREMBERG LAWS.

Racial[ly] (*Rasse-; Rassen-*), adjectival and adverbial prefix frequent in racist and National Socialist usage because of the central ideological importance of RACE. Some examples were:

racially true (*rassenecht*): unadulterated; in a figurative sense, having character

racially healthy (*rassengesund*): morally pure; eugenically impeccable

racial nucleus (*Rassenkern*): the foundation of the racial essence

racial consciousness; racial feeling (*Rassenbewusstsein; Rassengefühl*): pride in racial membership

racial mush; racial chaos (*Rassenbrei; Rassenchaos*): the pernicious mixing of races in a territory, as well as miscegenation altogether

racial character (*Rassencharakter*): racially determined characteristics

racial protection (*Rassenschutz*): a guarantee against the mixing of blood, as provided, for example, by the Law to Protect Blood (*see* BLOOD, LAW TO PROTECT)

racial barrier (*Rassenschranke*): the taboo against interracial intercourse

racial soul (*Rassenseele*): "the flame of brotherly feeling" (Alfred Rosenberg), as engendered by membership in a common race; also, the collective will of a people as expressed in culture

racially negligent (*rassevergessen*): negligence of, or even indifference to, racial duties.

Racial policy. See Race; Persecution of Jews; Final Solution.

Racial Policy Office (Rassenpolitisches Amt) of the NSDAP, party office created by Rudolf Hess on May 1, 1934; it was located in Berlin. The Racial Policy Office was preceded by the Information Office for Population Policy and Racial Cultivation (Aufklärungsamt für Bevölkerungspolitik und Rassenpflege), founded by Walter

GROSS. The tasks of the successor office were above all propagandistic and instructional: it sponsored courses, film evenings, and recreation for party functionaries, and provided guidance for the "work with women and girls" of the NATIONAL SOCIALIST VOLK WELFARE agency, and for racial policy legislation. With leaflets, slide shows, its own publication series, and the "Neues *Volk*" calendar, the office was to be the "central point of all worldview-related and practical efforts to cultivate and augment the racial strength of the nation," thus transforming the "racial idea" within the *Volk*.

Racial psychology (*Rassenpsychologie*), in the Third Reich, a discipline consisting of the specialties that dealt with the racial soul, racial abilities, and racial performance or accomplishments. Its aim was to investigate human character traits, talents, and cultural accomplishments in terms of their racial determinants. Because the outcome was already set forth in this assignment, the "research" conducted in racial psychology simply confirmed prejudices. Collections of material underpinned the already dogmatically established worldview that RACE was the engine of historical and cultural change, as well as the individual's personal fate and mission. In this purely genetic argument there was no place for issues of environmental influence; individuals and collective groups were changed not by learning but by SELECTION and CULLING OUT. Therapy for faulty developments could consist only of disciplinary correction.

Racial treason (*Rasseverrat*), equivalent in the National Socialist vocabulary to RACIAL INFAMY.

Racism (*Rassismus*), the ideological and political instrumentalization of race lore (*Rassenkunde*; *see* RACE).

Rademacher, Franz, b. Neustrelitz (Mecklenburg), February 20, 1906; d. Bonn, March 17, 1973, German diplomat and jurist. In March 1933 Rademacher joined the NSDAP. He became legation secretary in the Foreign Office in November 1937, and in 1938 he was posted to the German embassy in Uruguay. Rademacher returned to Germany in May 1940 to take over the Jewish desk in the Germany Division of the Foreign Ministry. He was the author of the so-called MADAGASCAR PLAN for the deportation of the Jews, which he developed together with Adolf EICHMANN after the German victory over France. Initially something of a "salon antisemite," Rademacher later took part without hesitation in the FINAL SOLUTION. In Octo-

ber 1941 he personally managed the deportation of Serbian Jews from Belgrade, in the course of which 449 were killed on the spot.

Rademacher fell into disfavor in 1943. He became a naval officer, then went underground after the end of the war. Arrested and sentenced in 1952, he escaped to Syria, from which he returned in ill health in 1966. Despite a renewed sentence, he remained free because the sentence (five and a half years) was considered to have been served. The verdict was set aside in 1971 and a new trial was ordered, but he died before it opened.

Radio (*Rundfunk*), like all media in the Third Reich, a tool for domination used by government leaders to realize political goals and interests; according to Joseph Goebbels, it was the "most modern and most important instrument for influencing the masses" in terms of propagandistic mobilization. As early as November 18, 1932, the Radio Ordinance created, in Lerg's words, a "government information organization system" (*staatspublizistisches Organisationsgebilde*). Immediately after the Reichstag election of March 5, 1933, numerous employees in programming, technical services, and administration were let go, and all key posts were filled with National Socialists. In November 1934, the Radio Trial was staged in Berlin; though hardly successful, it was an attempt to prove that leading contributors to Weimar radio, among them Hans Bredow, the founder of German radio, constituted a "swamp of corruption."

The Radio Division of the Propaganda Ministry (Division III) served as the "command center" of German radio. In March 1933 it took over the radio responsibilities of the Interior and Postal ministries. Resistance in the individual states (*Länder*) was undercut by the final establishment of the Propaganda Ministry's jurisdiction (June 30, 1933). The legal liquidation of the various state radio systems followed, until May 1934; the Reich Radio Company (Reich-Radio-Gesellschaft; RRG), the administrative authority for German radio, took over the property of the regional radio facilities. Beginning on April 1, 1934, they were administered as "Reich Broadcasting Companies" (Reichssender), and thus as dependent subsidiaries of the RRG, by their respective directors.

The central radio news service was the Wireless Service (Der Drahtlose Dienst; DDD), whose editor in chief until 1938 was Hans FRITZSCHE, and then Walter Wilhelm Dittmar. Horst Dressler-Andress headed the Radio Divi-

Radio. Reich Station Manager Heinrich Glasmeier (left) and Reich Program Director
Eugen Hadamovsky during a news broadcast on May 1, 1937, in Berlin.

sion until May 1937, followed by Hans Kriegler (until August 1939), Alfred-Ingemar Berndt (1939 to 1941; with an interruption), Eugen HADAMOVSKY (February to August 1940), Wolfgang Diewerge (September 1941 to 1942), and finally Fritzsche, from November 3, 1942, until the end of the war in 1945.

The RRG itself was reorganized: it was given a five-person administrative council made up of three representatives from the Propaganda Ministry and one each from the Postal and Finance ministries. It was chaired by a state secretary from the Propaganda Ministry— Walther FUNK until 1937, and then Karl HANKE until the council's dissolution in April 1940. The board of directors of the RRG consisted of the Reich Program Director (*Reichssendeleiter*), Hadamovsky, who was in overall charge of programming; the technical director, Claus Hubmann; and the business director, Hermann Voss. Not until April 1, 1937, was the RRG given a general director: Reichsintendant (Reich Station Manager) Heinrich Glasmeier.

Once the war began, power was gradually consolidated in the Propaganda Ministry itself, and the RRG with its general director was increasingly relegated to the background. In October 1941 Hans HINKEL assumed responsibility for entertainment and artistic programming, and the head of the Radio Division himself took over political and propaganda broadcasting; initially this was Wolfgang Diewerge, and then Fritzsche. Hadamovsky left the RRG in June 1942, and went to the Reich Propaganda Leadership as chief of staff. Even the remaining foreign-radio responsibilities

were taken from the RRG general director in 1941, and handed over to Toni Winkelnkemper, who was directly responsible to the Propaganda Ministry.

To make mass radio reception actually possible, the REICH RADIO CHAMBER (the compulsory professional organization for all radio workers) aided in sponsoring the development of "political radio equipment" (*politische Radiogeräte*): the VOLK'S RECEIVER (1933), the Labor Front Receiver for communal listening at the workplace (1935), and the German Mini-Receiver (1938), also called "Goebbels's Snout" (*Goebbels' Schnauze*). With this inexpensive equipment, which required only the simplest technical apparatus, anyone could receive broadcasts from the nearest Reich station and also from Radio Germany, which broadcast on long waves.

On September 1, 1939, the Ordinance on Extraordinary RADIO MEASURES prohibited Germans from tuning in to foreign radio stations. For domestic radio, the consolidation of programming had the most immediate priority. Beginning in May 1940 all the German radio stations were "synchronized together in an unvarying Reich broadcast" (Diller); the resulting uniform program of "Great-German Radio" was increasingly reduced to news reports, the WEHRMACHT REPORTS, political commentary, reportage, and music. With regard to foreign radio (shortwave broadcasting), which until 1939 was under the sole authority of the Propaganda Ministry, there were constant struggles over jurisdiction among the Propaganda Ministry, the Wehrmacht, and the Foreign Office, which under Gerd Rühle created its own radio department in May 1939 (*see* PROPAGANDA).

During the war, foreign radio broadcasting had several important spheres of responsibility aside from carrying on with the official government foreign program. Among them were the implementation of the "New Order" for radio in occupied Europe. Stations in these areas were incorporated into the Reich Radio network (as in the cases of Austrian radio and Prague's Station II in the Protectorate of Bohemia and Moravia), were placed under the authority of the military administration (as in Belgium), or were under the local German Reich commissioner (as in Denmark, the Netherlands, France, and Norway). Foreign broadcasting also exerted an influence on the radio programming of Germany's European allies and of neutral countries, through exchanges, joint broadcasting, and subsidies, among other means. Interference devices and secret transmitters were organized under the code name "Concordia" and directed by Erich Hetzler; an example of "Concordia" activity was the New British Broadcasting Station (NBBS), whose contributors included the notorious "Lord Haw-Haw" (*see* William JOYCE). Finally, interception services were established, of which the best known was Sonderdienst Seehaus (Lake House Special Service), on Berlin's Grosser Wannsee. From October 1941 to April 1945 it functioned under the joint responsibility of the Propaganda Ministry and the Foreign Office.

S. O.

Radio Germany (Deutschlandsender), supraregional German radio station, set up near Königs Wusterhausen on December 20, 1927, as Europe's most powerful long-wave transmitter. After the nationalization of German radio under Chancellor Franz von Papen, beginning on January 31, 1933, Radio Germany was given the assignment of being the "representative of the Reich and of German culture," in contrast to the mission of the individual German stations, which was to adapt their programs to "the character of their *Gau* landscape." Thus, during the Third Reich, Radio Germany had particular significance for propaganda within Germany and beyond its borders. In 1939 the transmitter was moved to Harzburg an der Elster; after 1945 it was initially merged with Radio Berlin (Berliner Rundfunk) in the Soviet occupation zone. In 1971 it was renamed Voice of the GDR.

Radio Measures (*Rundfunkmassnahmen*), circumlocution for the prohibition against listening to foreign (and neutral) broadcasting stations that was announced in an ordinance of September 1, 1939. The "Extraordinary Radio Measures" were justified on the ground that each word of such programs was "obviously a lie." All radio receivers were to bear a sticker with the Radio Measures on it as a brief warning; "enemy listeners" (*Feindhörer*) were threatened with severe punishments.

Radio play (*Hörspiel*; originally also called radio drama [*Funkdrama*] or broadcast play [*Sendungsspiel*]), genre of dramatic literature presented exclusively by acoustic means, through word, sound, and music; it was introduced to German radio in 1924. In the beginning, a good many experimental and critical plays were broadcast; authors such as Bertolt BRECHT, Erich KÄSTNER, and Franz MEHRING wrote for radio. However, even before 1933 an anti–Weimar Republic and *völkisch* tendency dominated the German radio play, which was systematically promoted by National Socialist radio functionaries after the takeover of power.

From 1933 on, radio plays dealt especially with such subjects as the peasant world; thematically and by making nature mysterious, they corresponded to the "blood-and-soil literature." In numerous historical plays, Germanic or German history was religiously elevated. Increasingly, the radio play was given an ideological function. Plays dealing with such topical events as the Spanish Civil War served as psychological preparation for war; adventure plays (for example, Günter Eich's *Aufstand in der Goldstadt* [Revolt in the City of Gold]; 1940) were meant to intensify anti-English enemy stereotypes. The literary radio play disappeared almost completely once the war began, to be replaced by "didactic plays" (*Lehrstücken*) about the theory of inheritance, for example, or warning against enemy spies, as well as by mixed forms: choral spoken plays and consecration plays, which by emotionally linking music and text transfigured German history into myth; from 1933 on, they were broadcast especially during NS CELEBRATIONS. Joseph Goebbels was far more interested in film as a medium of mass persuasion. He "fundamentally reject[ed] the radio play" (memorandum, 1940), presumably because as an art form it was apprehended individually rather than collectively.

H. H.

Radio Steward (*Funkwalter*), person in an enterprise responsible for the radio. After the takeover of power, the National Socialists set up a network of Radio Stewards through the GERMAN LABOR FRONT. "In the service of radio leadership," they were to direct the "will of the *Volk* toward the radio" (speech by Horst Dressler-Andress) by organizing group audiences in such places as workshops and factories for speeches by Hitler.

Raeder, Erich, b. Wandsbek (now Hamburg-Wandsbek), April 24, 1876; d. Kiel, November 6, 1960, German First Lord of the Admiralty (April 1, 1939). Raeder entered the navy in 1894; in the First World War he was Admiralty staff officer and eventually commander of the light cruiser *Cöln*. In postwar Germany he served in the Naval Office; as an admiral (from October 1, 1926), he was made chief of naval operations, and on January 1, 1935, commander in chief of naval forces. Even during the Weimar period, Raeder had built up the German navy with battleships beyond the quota allowed by the Versailles treaty. He welcomed Hitler's rearmament policy, but steadfastly warned against a conflict with British sea power. By the outbreak of the war he reluctantly confirmed that because of its wholly inadequate level of arms, the navy could only "go down with honor."

Hitler at first followed Raeder's advice in the NORWEGIAN CAMPAIGN, but the alienation between them grew; rather than being able to concentrate on the British enemy, the navy was constantly burdened with new assignments that dissipated its strength. An open quarrel erupted when Hitler ordered the scrapping of large surface conveys in favor of U-boat tactics. Because Raeder opposed the shift, he was replaced as commander in chief by Adm. Karl DÖNITZ on

January 31, 1943. Nonetheless, Raeder's role in the war preparations brought him to the defendants' bench in Nuremberg in 1945. Sentenced to life imprisonment on October 1, 1946, he was released early from the Spandau Prison on grounds of poor health on September 26, 1955.

Railroad, German. *See* Deutsche Reichsbahn.

Ranking order (*Rangordnung*), term introduced by Friedrich NIETZSCHE, with political and moral connotations; it referred to a "superior, equal, and inferior ordering of values, moral duties, and people." The National Socialists invoked the concept as the philosophical foundation for their nationalist and racist perception of the world when they placed the Germans at the top in a "ranking order of peoples."

Ranks. Hierarchies played a central role in the National Socialist Führer state. The thicket of service ranks in the Wehrmacht, police, and some NS organizations is shown in Table 1.

Rapallo Treaty, agreement concluded on April 16, 1922, in Rapallo (northern Italy) between Germany and the Russian Soviet Federated Socialist Republic during the World Economic Conference in Genoa (April 10–May 19); it was signed by foreign ministers Walther RATHENAU and Georgi Vasilievich Chicherin. The Rapallo Treaty served to regulate German-Soviet relations. Both states reciprocally renounced any compensation for their war costs and for military and civilian war losses, and Germany furthermore renounced compensation for the German

Erich Raeder.

Rapallo Treaty. Chancellor Joseph Wirth (center) in conversation with the Russian envoys L. B. Krasin (right) and G. V. Chicherin.

TABLE 1. *National Socialist Service Ranks*

Navy	Army/Luftwaffe	Police	SS/Waffen-SS	SA (Sturmabteilung)	National Socialist Motor Corps (NSKK)/ National Socialist Flyers' Corps (NSFK)
	Reichsmarschall (Reich marshal)				
Grossadmiral (First lord of the admiralty)	*Generalfeldmarschall* (Field marshal general)	*Reichsführer-SS*		*Stabschef* (Chief of staff)	*Korpsführer* (Corps Führer)
Generaladmiral (Admiral of the fleet)	*Generaloberst* (Colonel general)		*Oberstgruppenführer* (Supreme group Führer)		
Admiral	*General*			*Obergruppenführer* (High group Führer)	
Vizeadmiral (Vice admiral)	*Generalleutnant* (Lieutenant general)			*Gruppenführer* (Group Führer)	
Konteradmiral (Rear admiral)	*Generalmajor* (Major general)			*Brigadeführer*	
				Oberführer (High Führer)	
Kapitän zur See (Sea captain)	*Oberst* (Colonel)			*Standartenführer* (Standard Führer)	
Fregattenkapitän (Frigate commander)	*Oberstleutnant* (Lieutenant colonel)		*Obersturmbannführer* (High storm unit Führer)		*Oberstaffelführer* (High flight Führer)
Korvettenkapitän (Corvette commander)	*Major*		*Sturmbannführer* (Storm unit Führer)		*Staffelführer* (Flight Führer)
Kapitänleutnant (Lieutenant captain)	*Hauptmann* (Captain)			*Hauptsturmführer* (Chief storm Führer)	
Oberleutnant zur See (First lieutenant)	*Oberleutnant* (First lieutenant)			*Obersturmführer* (High storm Führer)	
Leutnant zur See (Lieutenant)	*Leutnant* (Lieutenant)		*Untersturmführer* (Lieutenant storm Führer)	*Sturmführer*	
	Stabsoberfeldwebel (Staff sergeant major)		*Sturmscharführer* (Storm squad Führer)	*Haupttruppführer* (Chief troop Führer)	
Oberfähnrich zur See (Senior grade midshipman)	*Oberfähnrich* (Senior cadet)				
	Oberfeldwebel (Sergeant major)		*Hauptscharführer* (Chief squad Führer)	*Obertruppführer* (High troop Führer)	
	Feldwebel (Sergeant)	*Meister* (Master)	*Oberscharführer* (High squad Führer)	*Truppführer* (Troop Führer)	
Fähnrich zur See (Midshipman)	*Fähnrich* (Ensign)				
Obermaat (Chief petty officer)	*Unterfeldwebel* (Sergeant)	*Hauptwachtmeister* (Chief of patrols)	*Scharführer* (Squad Führer)	*Oberscharführer* (High squad Führer)	
Maat (Seaman)	*Unteroffizier* (Noncommissioned officer)	*Revier Oberwachtmeister* (Precinct commander)	*Unterscharführer* (Lieutenant squad Führer)	*Scharführer* (Squad Führer)	
Hauptgefreiter (Chief lance corporal)	*Stabsgefreiter* (Staff lance corporal)				
Obergefreiter (Corporal)		*Oberwachtmeister* (Chief patrolman)			
Gefreiter (Lance corporal)		*Wachtmeister* (Patrolman)	*Rottenführer* (Battalion Führer)		
Obersoldat (Private first class)		*Rottwachtmeister* (Battalion patrolman)	*Sturmmann* (Storm [attack] man)	*Obersturmmann* (Storm [attack] man first class)	
Matrose (Sailor)	*Soldat* (Private)	*Unterwachtmeister* (Lieutenant patrolman)	*SS-Mann*	*Sturmmann*	
			SS-Anwärter (SS aspirant)	*SA-Anwärter* (SA aspirant)	

property nationalized in the Soviet Union. Both agreed to regulate their economic relations according to the principle of preferential treatment and to initiate diplomatic and consular relations. Through an agreement concluded in Berlin on November 5, 1922, the Rapallo Treaty was extended to include the other Soviet republics; it was ratified in Berlin on January 31, 1923. With the Wehrmacht's attack on the Soviet Union on June 22, 1941, the treaty was nullified.

R. B.

Rasch, Otto, b. Friedrichsruhe, December 7, 1891; d. Wehrstedt, November 1, 1948, SS-*Brigadeführer* and major general in the police (1940). Rasch took part in the First World War as a naval lieutenant. He then studied philosophy, law, and political science. Active in the private sector, in 1931 he became a lawyer in Dresden. In 1933 he became mayor in Radeberg, and in 1935, lord mayor of Wittenberg. Rausch had joined the NSDAP in 1931 and the SA in 1933. Beginning in 1936 he was employed full-time by the SD. On October 1, 1937, as commissioner, he took over the leadership of the State Police (Stapo) in Frankfurt am Main; in March 1938 (again as commissioner), he became the director of security, based in Linz, for Upper Austria. Beginning in June of that year he was assigned various responsibilities within the Reich Security Main Office (RSHA), as well as in the office of the commander of the Security Police (Sipo) and SD in Prague.

In 1940, as inspector of the Sipo and the SD, Rasch was transferred to Königsberg. Shortly before the beginning of the Russian Campaign, he took over Einsatzgruppe C (*see* EINSATZGRUPPEN), with which he carried out extermination operations against the Jews. Discharged in October 1941, at the beginning of 1942 he became the director of Continental Oil, Inc., in Berlin. At the end of September 1947 the Americans brought charges against him and others in Nuremberg for crimes against humanity, war crimes, and membership in a criminal organization (*see* OHLENDORF TRIAL). Rasch's case was severed from the others on February 5, 1948, because it could not be tried [owing to the defendant's illness].

A. St.

Rasse; Rasse-; Rassen-. *See* Race; Racial.

Rassemblement National Populaire (National Popular Assembly; RNP), party founded in Paris on December 1, 1941, by the former socialist Marcel Déat. It strove for unrestricted COLLABORATION with the German occupying power. The Rassemblement, with its approximately 20,000 members, first sought to return Pierre LAVAL to the Vichy regime, which it saw as reactionary and inconsistent, and tried to form an alliance with all the pro-German forces in France. It fell apart, however, because of internal struggles for power between the left fascists, who were eventually victorious, and the nationalistic units of frontline fighters.

Rath, Ernst vom, b. Frankfurt am Main, June 3, 1909; d. Paris, November 9, 1938, German diplomat. Rath, who had been legation secretary in the German embassy in Paris since October 1936, was shot on November 7, 1938, by Herschel GRYNSZPAN, who had confused him with the German ambassador. The National Socialists used the attack, from which Rath died two days later, as an excuse for the KRISTALLNACHT pogrom. Hitler furthermore named Rath legation councillor. The National Socialist cult surrounding the "martyr" concealed the fact that the young diplomat had been considered "politically unreliable" by the Gestapo.

Rathenau, Walther, b. Berlin, September 29, 1867; d. there, June 24, 1922, German industrialist and politician. The son of the industrial magnate Emil Rathenau, Walther Rathenau became a director of Allgemeine Elektricitäts-Gesellschaft (General Electric of Germany; AEG) in 1899. From 1902 to 1907 he was bank director of the Berliner Handelsgesellschaft (Berlin Mercantile Company), and in 1915 he became the president of AEG. During the First World War, as head of the Raw Materials Division in Prussia's War Ministry, he was in charge of building up Germany's war economy. In 1918 he defended the idea of a general conscription of the population (*levée en masse*).

After the war Rathenau joined the German Democratic Party (DDP). He served as an expert for the preliminary discussions of the peace treaty and took part in the Spa Conference in 1920. In the Wirth cabinet he was minister for reconstruction, but he withdrew in protest against the Allied decision to divide Upper Silesia. In January 1922 he was Germany's representative at the Cannes Conference; as foreign minister in the Wirth government he took part in the World Economic Conference, held in Genoa in April 1922, at which he signed the RAPALLO TREATY. Nationalistic German circles

Walther Rathenau.

Ration cards. Coupons being counted at the end of the business day.

opposed Rathenau because of his FULFILLMENT POLICY and his Jewish background. He was murdered in Berlin by two radical right-wing officers who were members of the secret CONSUL ORGANIZATION.

Ration cards (*Lebensmittelkarten*), authorizations to buy foodstuffs. In the course of long-term preparations for war, ration cards were printed as early as 1937 and handed out for the first time a few days before the beginning of the war, on August 27, 1939. At first one card was valid for different foods and consumer goods, but during the war more and more goods were rationed and sold in exchange for coupons from different cards. Thus, there were Reich cards for bread, fat, and so on. The ration cards were often valid for different lengths of time; their colors were keyed according to different kinds of goods and the age of the person entitled to purchase them.

Jews, ALIEN WORKERS living in the Reich, and the civilian populations of the occupied territories received special cards with smaller ration allotments. "Special supplemental" cards were given to small children, young people, persons working at heavy labor and those working at night, and pregnant women and nursing mothers. There were also separate ration cards for soldiers on home leave ("Reich cards for those on leave") and for travelers. Some foodstuffs (potatoes and vegetables) did not have to be rationed, and others were distributed evenly according to the supply at a given time. This meant in ever-decreasing amounts toward the end of the war: in 1945 an adult received

weekly 125 g (4.38 oz) of fat, 250 g (8.75 oz) of meat, and 1,700 g (3.72 lbs) of bread. Owing to inadequate supplies, even after 1945 the majority of necessities and luxuries were rationed. Only on January 10, 1950, were ration cards finally done away with in the Federal Republic.

Ratti, Achille. *See* Pius XI.

Raubal, Angela ("Geli"), b. Linz, January 4, 1908; d. Munich, September 18, 1931, Hitler's niece (daughter of his half sister, Angela Raubal). The pretty, dark-haired Raubal began musical studies in Munich. There she again encountered her uncle, who had been particularly fond of her when she was a child. She became his lover (*Geliebte*). Her mother took over the running of Hitler's household (until 1935). The politician, under great pressure during the period of the rise of the NSDAP, was seldom present, but he jealously watched (or had watched) every movement his niece made. His regimentation and the blossoming affair with Eva BRAUN in 1929 led to many confrontations and finally to Raubal's suicide in Hitler's apartment on Prinzregentenplatz. Hitler never fully overcame the shock; no one but himself was allowed to enter Geli's room from that time on. Josef THORAK received a commission for a bust of Raubal, which was placed in

Angela (Geli) Raubal.

the New Reich Chancellery. Her portrait, by Adolf ZIEGLER, always decorated with flowers, hung in the large chamber of the Berghof.

Rauff, Walther, b. Köthen (Anhalt), June 19, 1906; d. Las Condes (Chile), May 14, 1984, SS-*Standartenführer* (June 21, 1944). Rauff was a naval officer (a lieutenant commander as of April 1, 1935). He entered the NSDAP on May 1, 1937. On December 31 of that year, Rauff retired from the navy on his own initiative and found a position with the Security Service (SD); he also joined the SS as a *Hauptsturmführer*, on April 20, 1938. Completing his military service on April 1, 1941, with the rank of commander in the reserves, he was released to join the Waffen-SS and was posted to the Security Police.

As an SS-*Obersturmbannführer* in the Reich Security Main Office (RSHA), Rauff headed Group II D (Technical Matters), to which Section II D 3a (Motor Vehicles) was subordinated. It developed the so-called gas van (*see* GAS VANS), which was to facilitate the "work" of the EINSATZGRUPPEN in the murder of Jews in the east. Beginning in the summer of 1942, Rauff led an Einsatzkommando in Tunis and later in northern Italy. Taken into American custody after the war, he was able, presumably with the help of Catholic clergymen, to escape to South America; from 1958 on he lived in Chile. A German extradition attempt was rejected on April 26, 1963, by the highest Chilean court, because the crimes Rauff was charged with were past the statute of limitations according to Chilean law. Rauff once again attracted inter-

national attention when neo-Nazi demonstrations took place at his burial in Santiago.

A. St.

Raum. *See* Space.

Rauschning, Hermann, b. Thorn (West Prussia), August 7, 1887; d. Portland (Oregon), February 8, 1982, German politician. Rauschning studied musicology. After volunteer service during the First World War, in 1918 he joined the German Ethnic Group in Posen, as reflected in his publication *Die Entdeutschung Westpreussens und Posens* (The De-Germanization of West Prussia and Posen; 1929). Rauschning acquired a farm in Danzig in 1926. He became attracted to the NSDAP; however, he joined the party not in 1926, as has commonly been asserted, but in 1931, when its eventual victory became obvious. As a prominent conservative figurehead, he became its top candidate in the elections to the Danzig Volkstag in May 1933.

As president of Danzig's senate beginning on June 20, 1933, Rauschning carried out a rigorously National Socialist (that is, antisemitic) policy ("purging the *Volk* of alien/foreign, destructive personalities") and fostered an extravagant FÜHRER CULT. He fell out with Gauleiter Albert FORSTER over economic issues and ultimately had to resign under pressure from Hitler.

Rauschning fled via Poland to Switzerland and published a settling of accounts with National Socialism, *Die Revolution des Nihilismus* (The Revolution of Nihilism; 1938). By his own

Hermann Rauschning.

admission, "only with great difficulty" had he been able to "separate [himself] internally." The book was extremely successful, although it completely misunderstood National Socialism in its accusation that Hitler embraced an opportunism without program or principle.

Rauschning's next publication, *Gespräche mit Hitler* (Conversations with Hitler; translated as *Hitler Speaks* and as *The Voice of Destruction*), was written down toward the end of 1939, on the suggestion of the Hungarian press magnate Emery Reves. It too became a best-seller, and has influenced historiography on Hitler to the present day. The book's literal worth as a source has been questioned, but its "inner truthfulness" is highly valued. The research of the Swiss educator Wolfgang Hänel has made it clear that the "conversations" were mostly free inventions; according to Rauschning's testimony (in a private letter), he relied on "scanty notes." Remarkably, the Hitler profile as revealed by the conversations, and the later Hitler of the TABLE TALKS, are practically interchangeable (as on the theme of the churches). Rauschning settled in the United States in 1948; his publications included works on German political issues.

Ravensbrück, National Socialist women's concentration camp north of Fürstenberg an der Havel. It was established on May 15, 1939, and housed inmates from the LICHTENBURG concentration camp. By the end of 1939, Ravensbrück held approximately 2,000 women; at the end of 1942 there were 10,800, and in 1944 some 70,000 prisoners were admitted. According to the evidence of the International Search Service of the Red Cross, from the time Ravensbrück was opened, 107,753 women were admitted to the main camp and its 42 satellite camps. The inmates belonged to various European nationalities and had been brought to Ravensbrück as political prisoners, Jews, Gypsies, Jehovah's Witnesses, prostitutes, and criminals. They worked in the SS-operated German Research Institute for Nutrition and Provisioning, on private farms, and in local industries and workshops. A small men's camp was joined to the women's camp in March and April 1941. The guards in the women's camp were mainly female SS auxiliaries; the camp was supervised by a commandant.

Insufficient lodging and food, as well as poor hygienic and sanitary conditions, were the chief reasons for the high mortality rate among the Ravensbrück inmates. Punishments, abuse, and heavy physical labor did the rest. Many victims were claimed by HUMAN EXPERIMENTS (including those involving gas gangrene and deliberately infected wounds, as well as experiments in sterilizing Gypsies). Other victims were inmates judged "incapable of work" and "mentally defective"; beginning in 1942 they were selected out—allegedly for admittance into sanatoriums—by a commission of doctors involved in Operation 14f13 (*see* INVALID OPERATION). In actuality, the prisoners were transferred to the extermination establishments of the EUTHANASIA operation (T4) and gassed there. Early in 1945, Heinrich Himmler ordered that the sick inmates and those incapable of work be killed in the camp itself. Thus, a gas chamber was built near the crematorium. According to statements by the former head of the protective-custody camp, Schwarzhuber, be-

Women in the Ravensbrück concentration camp.

tween 2,300 and 2,400 people were gassed in the gas chamber.

Thanks to the intervention of the Swedish Red Cross, in March 1945 French and Swedish women inmates were freed. In April the inmates were evacuated on foot, but during the evacuation march they were run down by Soviet troops. Sick inmates and those unable to walk had been left behind in the camp and were freed on April 29–30 by troops of the Red Army. The commandants of Ravensbrück were Max Koegel (committed suicide in 1946) and Fritz Suhren (executed in 1950).

W. D.

Raw-materials economy (*Rohstoffwirtschaft*), the intensified concentration of the National Socialist economy on procuring and finding substitutes for raw materials, particularly those necessary for armaments (*see* ECONOMY UNDER NATIONAL SOCIALISM, THE). Because of Germany's insufficient supply of industrial raw materials, the NS government was forced to take advantage of all possibilities for providing them. In the context of the AUTARKY concept, the German economy was to be made independent of foreign countries, and the raw materials necessary for REARMAMENT were to be produced in Germany itself.

The growing demand for foreign raw materials, intensified by the increase in armaments production, had to accommodate itself to government control over FOREIGN TRADE. Such control included strict currency regulations, since the dependence of heavy industry on imports, for example, still amounted to 60 percent in 1928. Measures for government control of raw materials became the most important instrument for the regulation of industrial production. The fixing of quotas on raw materials was introduced in 1934 (*see* NEW PLAN), yet from 1935 on, the shortage of raw materials became more acute, proving that control over raw materials up to that time had been insufficient. Beginning in 1936, the FOUR-YEAR PLAN was intended to provide new regulation of the foreign as well as the domestic raw-materials economy.

Thus, the development of artificial and substitute materials, such as synthetic fuels, textiles, and rubber (*see* BUNA), was promoted. As early as 1933 a "gasoline agreement" was concluded between the government and I.G. Farben. Domestic raw materials such as iron ore were smelted totally unprofitably at the Hermann GÖRING WORKS. Among the population, exten-

Raw-materials economy. National Socialist poster: "Scrap from fences helps protect Great-Germany!"

sive scrap-metal drives were regularly conducted through propaganda. Despite these measures, at the outbreak of the war 45 percent of the iron ore required still had to be imported. Ultimately, the raw-materials problem was to be solved only through the conquest of foreign lands.

V. B.

Rearmament (*Aufrüstung*), general strengthening of a state's military potential, with a view to increasing its readiness for defense and/or its offensive strength. The DISARMAMENT propagated after the First World War affected only the vanquished states, particularly Germany. Thus, even during the Weimar Republic, efforts toward rearmament were set into motion, as through cooperation between the Reichswehr and the Red Army, and through covert development of an air force. Hitler's expressed goal was rearmament as a way to regain Germany's "military sovereignty" and military parity, demands that met with understanding even abroad, particularly in Great Britain. Behind them, however, lurked the aggressive, expansionist National Socialist concept of *Lebensraum* (LIVING SPACE).

As early as February 3, 1933, Hitler revealed to the Reichswehr leadership his program for rearmament, although he still hesitated regarding a considerable increase in armaments expenditures. Only in 1934 did these outlays rise dramatically, indeed fivefold. They doubled again by 1936, although by 1937 they constituted no more than 5 percent of the total

1
First raising of the Reich War flag, commissioned
by Hitler, on November 7, 1935.
2
After Hindenburg's death in 1934, Hitler as Supreme Commander reviews a Reichswehr parade.
3
The U-boat parent ship *Saar* with boats of the
Weddingen U-boat flotilla. Painting by Alex Kircher, 1938.

German gross national product. In figures, German prewar arms expenditures were: 1933, 0.746 billion RM; 1934, 4.197 billion; 1935, 5.87 billion; 1936, 10.273 billion; 1937, 10.961 billion; 1938, 17.247 billion; 1939, 11.906 billion (April 1 through August 31).

Additional indirect rearmament spending went for such purposes as the building of the AUTOBAHN and paramilitary training in the Hitler Youth, the SA, and the Reich Labor Service. Hitler's claim of September 1, 1939, that he had "already spent over 90 billion for the rebuilding of our Wehrmacht" was propagandistic hyperbole, intended to inspire fear. Until the war, German armaments did not reach an impressive level, and even then they gained momentum only slowly: for example, from September 1 to December 31, 1939, the 247 tanks produced were only 30 more than were lost in the Polish Campaign.

The first clearly evident indication of Germany's rearmament was the reintroduction of a COMPULSORY MILITARY SERVICE on March 16, 1935. The army's strength at 36 divisions, as stipulated in Paragraph 2 of the law, was

Rearmament. Newly assembled light field howitzers in the assembly hall of a German weapons factory.

reached only in 1936. In 1939 the German peacetime army had 52 divisions, including five tank divisions, and by the time of the mobilization in August 1939, a further 52 divisions were formed. Naval rearmament increased noticeably only after the GERMAN-BRITISH NAVAL AGREEMENT of June 18, 1935, but it was limited because the German shipyards were working to full capacity on currency-producing foreign orders. Thus, by the beginning of the war only 57 U-boats were ready for use, and the planned 35:100 ratio of strength of the German vis-à-vis the British fleet was not achieved. Only in the air did Germany gain an advantage, mainly in weapons technology. Abroad, greatly exaggerated ideas of the Luftwaffe's strength and attack capability arose through clever propaganda; in reality, the Luftwaffe suffered from confusion in terms of models, and from high accident rates in training maneuvers.

All in all, by 1939 German rearmament had not attained a level sufficient for the far-reaching goals of NS imperialism. Hitler nonetheless decided to use the narrow "strategic window" opened by means of rearmament and his FOREIGN POLICY. His decision was based on politically incorrect calculations about the supposed unreadiness to act on the part of the "flabby democracies" and on an overestimation of the state of German rearmament and especially of German resources.

G. H.

Re-articulation (*Rückgliederung*), propaganda term to denote annexations such as the ANSCHLUSS of Austria, which was to be brought "back home to the Reich." It was used correctly during the re-integration of the Saarland, and in later occupations such as those of the Sudetenland, the Memel region, and the Polish Corridor, it was meant to underscore the historical claim of the German Reich to the area in question.

Reche, Otto Carl, b. Glatz (Silesia), May 24, 1879; d. Grosshansdorf bei Hamburg, March 23, 1966, German anthropologist and proponent of racial hygiene. After conducting ethnographic research, Reche turned to conceptions of *völkisch* racial theories in *Die Bedeutung der Rassenpflege für die Zukunft unseres Volkes* (The Importance of Racial Cultivation for the Future of Our *Volk*; 1925). He was editor of the journals *Volk und Rasse* (*Volk* and Race; from 1927), *Zeitschrift für Rassenphysiologie* (Journal for Racial Physiology; from 1928), and *Studien zur Rassenkunde* (Studies on Race Lore; from 1934). In his editorial work as well as in his own research, Reche made crucial contributions toward supporting National Socialist racial delusions. After 1945 he initially published only studies on blood-type research, but his later work involved the biology of heredity as well. Reche's anthropological testimony gained international attention in 1959 in the Anastasia Trial, over the alleged survival of a daughter of the last tsar.

Reck-Malleczewen, Friedrich, b. Estate [Gut] Malleczewen (East Prussia), August 11, 1884; d. Dachau concentration camp, February 17, 1945, German journalist. Reck-Malleczewen studied medicine; he was also a world traveler. He moved from East Prussia to Bavaria, and shortly before the First World War took up a career as a writer, producing essays on cultural history and plays. He experienced the downfall of the monarchy as a catastrophe for his conservative worldview. Reck-Malleczewen's alienation from his political surroundings grew dramatically with the National Socialist Seizure of Power. He described it in a disguised form in the book *Bockelson—Geschichte eines Massenwahns* (Bockelson: History of a Mass Delusion; 1937) through a portrayal of the 16th-century Anabaptists' reign of terror. The book was banned.

Reck-Malleczewen made himself even more unpopular with the authorities by refusing to write the scenario for the film JUD SÜSS (Jew Süss), and he was imprisoned after a denunciation in 1944. He had been able to deliver his *Tagebuch eines Verzweifelten* (*Diary of a Man in Despair*; 1936–1944) into safety prior to his imprisonment. Published in 1947, it stirred up attention as much for its clear-sighted analysis of National Socialism as for its attacks on those participating in the attempt on Hitler's life of July 20, 1944. Reck-Malleczewen accused them of having first followed Hitler, and of then having betrayed "the company as it fell into bankruptcy."

Red Cross (International Red Cross), umbrella organization of all national and international Red Cross associations. In line with the GENEVA CONVENTIONS, they have taken as their mission the provision of protection and humanitarian aid in international and civil conflicts. The Red Cross is both the symbol of these organizations and the overall symbol of protection for medical efforts in wartime. The national Red Cross organization in Germany was the GERMAN RED CROSS (DRK).

Reder, Walter, b. Freiwaldau (northern Moravia), February 4, 1915, SS-*Sturmbannführer*. In September 1944, Reder commanded the reconnaissance patrol division of the Sixteenth SS Armored Infantry Division in northern Italy, in the battle against the "Stella Rossa" partisan brigade. At the end of the month, in reprisal for partisan attacks, he ordered the destruction of the town of Marzabotto, near Bologna, and of several neighboring villages. In this five-day operation, which Reder led from a command post 40 km (about 25 miles) away, his men killed, according to official Italian statements, 1,830 civilians, most of them women, children, and the elderly. The Germans burned down houses, machine-gunned those fleeing, and threw hand grenades into buildings.

Captured in 1945 by British soldiers, Reder was sentenced to life imprisonment in Bologna in 1951 and was brought to the Gaeta fortress. Appeals for a pardon, even from Austrian government offices, remained unsuccessful. In 1980, Reder's sentence was given a time limit ending July 15, 1985; at the end of January of that year he was released early, although survivors among the victims had spoken out against his release shortly beforehand. His welcome in Austria by the defense minister led to a government crisis in Vienna.

Red Frontline Fighters' League (Roter Frontkämpferbund; RFB), Communist paramilitary organization created by a resolution of the KPD (Communist Party of Germany) in May 1924. Its membership grew from 15,000 in 1925 to more than 100,000 in 1928, of whom approximately half were KPD members. Conceived of as a response to the STEEL HELMET and the REICH BANNER "BLACK-RED-GOLD," the RFB became an instrument of the Moscow faction within the KPD, whose chairman, Ernst THÄLMANN, led the RFB beginning in February 1925. Thälmann founded auxiliary organizations such as the Red Youth Storm, the Red Navy, and the Red League of Women and Girls. He deployed his combat groups, along with musical groups, in propaganda parades on such occasions as the annual Reich conferences, or in street fights with political opponents. The bloody confrontation on May Day of 1929 in Berlin led to the banning of the RFB. After the National Socialist takeover it was persecuted with especial zeal and was soon destroyed.

Red Frontline Fighters' League. Parade in Berlin.

Red Orchestra (Rote Kapelle), term coined by the Gestapo for the largest spy and opposition organization during the Second World War. In 1938 the Polish Communist Leopold TREPPER received a commission from the Soviet secret service to build up an information network for keeping Moscow up to date on the war preparations of National Socialist Germany. As a cover, Trepper founded in Brussels a company for importing and exporting trench coats, and he recruited agents in Belgium, the Netherlands, and France. Since Stalin wanted to avoid any provocation of Hitler because of the nonaggression pact with Germany, for the time being no Soviet agents were to work directly on German soil. For that reason, Trepper concentrated the work of the Red Orchestra in Paris after the occupation of France.

In the meantime, a group of politically very diverse leftist intellectuals, writers, artists, and journalists had come together around Harro SCHULZE-BOYSEN and Arvid HARNACK, and had made contact with Trepper's Red Orchestra. Some of them occupied influential government positions and edited illegal pamphlets such as "Agis Writings," "Letters to the Eastern Front," and "The Inner Front." They put up anti–National Socialist posters, helped opponents of the system to escape, and organized acts of sabotage in the war industry. In addition to an inner circle, which restricted itself to active opposition within the Reich, there also existed from 1940 on an outer circle, whose members maintained radio contact with the outside. The radio personnel of the Red Orchestra, called

"pianists," between 1940 and 1943 sent approximately 1,500 radio messages to the Moscow central office. They betrayed German deployment plans and agents, revealed plans for new weapons such as the "Tiger" armored combat vehicle, and warned about the German attack on the USSR. Beginning in 1941, the German ABWEHR collected these radio messages, and in July 1942 it organized the Red Orchestra Special Commando, which soon identified the leaders. That August, more than 100 persons were arrested and tortured; most of them were sentenced to death as "traitors and Bolsheviks." Hitler himself in many instances pressed for more severe sentences, and prescribed the means by which the sentence should be carried out (by hanging or by beheading).

The blanket NS defamation of the Red Orchestra as a Communist spy organization shaped the evaluation of this group for many years after the war. In fact, opposition and espionage were combined in the work of the Red Orchestra. In the group's self-perception, sharing information with the USSR was not treason; rather, it served to free Germany from Hitler's dictatorship.

H. H.

Re-education (*Umerziehung*), term denoting the programs and plans of the Allies for extirpating National Socialist ideas in Germany; for leading the Germans back to democracy, the rule of law, and a mentality based on human rights; and for preparing peaceable German involvement in international political and cultural life after 1945. To be sure, what "procedure" would best achieve such a re-education was not only a matter of controversy among the Allies but was subject to changes according to political circumstances (*see* DENAZIFICATION). The initially chosen path of shock treatment through the accusation of COLLECTIVE GUILT for NS crimes of violence led chiefly to defensive behavior and made re-education a negative concept, especially in right-wing circles. Following the postwar alienation between East and West, re-education propaganda was soon modified, and ultimately was dropped.

Refugees (*Flüchtlinge*), persons forced to flee their home or their home country for political, racial, or religious reasons. The refugee problem is one of the most acute issues of the 20th century and was exacerbated in particular during and after the Second World War. It affected Germany especially, through the EXPULSION from the Eastern Territories and eastern Europe of over 12 million Germans, of whom 7.7 million came to the Federal Republic of Germany (constituting 16.1 percent of the population). In addition, by 1951 about a million refugees had fled to West Germany from the Soviet zone or, subsequently, the German Democratic Republic.

Re-Germanization (*Eindeutschung;* also *Rückdeutschung*), National Socialist plans and measures to "increase the growth of the racially desirable population" in territories occupied by the Wehrmacht during the Second World War. Re-Germanization was placed under the jurisdiction of Heinrich Himmler, who on October 7, 1939, was named Reich Commissioner for the Fortification of the German Volk-Nation (*Reichskommissar für die Festigung des deutschen Volkstums*). It affected persons—especially ETHNIC GERMANS (*Volksdeutsche*)—who could prove their German origin with a CERTIFICATE OF DESCENT.

The provisions of the German *Volk* List of March 4, 1941, divided these persons into four groups:

1. Individuals suitable for **NSDAP** membership
2. Persons who could "prove that they [had] retained their Germanness [*Deutschtum*]" and thus automatically became German citizens
3. German-minded persons (*deutsch gesinnte Personen*) with "ethnically alien" (*fremdvölkisch*) connections, who could receive rev-

ocable German citizenship after passing a racial-hygiene investigation
4. "Individuals who [had] become alienated from their German origins [*überfremdete Deutschstämmige*]," who could attain re-Germanization only by fulfilling achievements for Germany, following re-education (*see* EDUCATION).

Persons who were questionable in terms of heredity and race were excluded from re-Germanization, which, however, could be extended to "racially valuable" children belonging to foreign peoples (*see* GERMANIZATION). In 1944 the German *Volk* List enumerated some 2.75 million persons eligible for re-Germanization.

Reich, in National Socialist usage, a term for the "sovereign living space [*Herrschafts- und Lebensraum*] won with the blood of the German *Volk* and the mission willed by destiny to the Germans" (*Meyers Lexikon,* 1942). The term *das Reich* was intended to supplant the designation THIRD REICH, as well as the term GREAT-GERMAN REICH. [*Reich* in German can have the meaning of either "state" or "empire," and frequently connotes both.]

Reich, Das, representative political and cultural newspaper founded by Rolf Rienhardt and patterned on a foreign model. It was intended for foreign readers and for the German intelligentsia; the subtitle was "Deutsche Wochenzeitung" (German Weekly). *Das Reich* was published in Berlin beginning on May 26, 1940, by the Deutscher Verlag (German Publishing Company; until 1934, the Ullstein publishing house), which belonged to the National Socialist press trust. The author of the lead articles was Joseph Goebbels. Eugen Mündler was the editor in chief until January 31, 1943; he was followed, beginning on February 14 of that year, by Rudolf Sparing, the magazine's co-founder. Both these men, as well as the majority of the highly gifted contributors, were renowned journalists from former liberal and conservative papers. E. O. Plauen (pseudonym of Erich Ohser) and Hans Erich Köhler were the caricaturists.

Das Reich was given extensive freedom from the Propaganda Ministry's press restrictions, a freedom that was taken advantage of by the editorial staff; they were granted special material and sensitive information denied other publications. The intellectually pretentious newspaper, articulating NS content in traditional bourgeois forms, was completely successful. Its

DAS REICH

DIE ÄUSSERSTE ANSTRENGUNG

Führen wir einen totalen Krieg?

Front page of the weekly newspaper *Das Reich*: "The utmost effort: Are we waging a total war?"

circulation in October 1940 was 500,000, and in March 1944, 1.4 million. The last regular issue appeared on April 15, 1945, and the final issue, printed but not distributed, came out on April 22.

Reich Academy for Physical Exercises (Reichsakademie für Leibesübungen), training academy for teachers of gymnastics and sports, established in 1936 in the "House of German Sports" at the REICH SPORTS FIELD. It was also the "instructional steward" (*Lehrwarte*) of the GERMAN REICH LEAGUE FOR PHYSICAL EXERCISES. The academy's head was the ministerial director Carl Krümmel. Its functions included the cultivation of the "best traditions of Hellenic-Nordic education," in Krümmel's words. It also provided political and ideological instruction for sports teachers and was intended to create the prototype of the National Socialist physical education instructor, in whom a "combative mind and body [*kämpferische Leibseele*] prevail[ed]." Only the first steps toward this goal were taken, since the academy ceased operations at the end of the 1939 summer semester because of the war.

Reich Air Defense League (Reichsluftschutz-

bund; RLB), organization of the Reich Aviation Ministry that was created on April 29, 1933 (*see* AIR DEFENSE).

Reich Association of German Industry (Reichsverband der deutschen Industrie; RdI), umbrella organization and representative of special interests in German industry. Founded on February 4, 1919, the RdI was organized into 27 industrial divisions and was led by a presidium (Gustav KRUPP VON BOHLEN UND HALBACH was made chairman on September 25, 1931). In regular meetings of its members, the RdI, which was dominated by heavy industry, laid down its political agenda. Initially, the Weimar Republic was rejected. The state was affirmed after its consolidation, but in the wake of the world economic crisis, the RdI made an appeal for an authoritarian state. Especially at the time of the Schleicher government, the struggle against the trade unions brought the RdI in close proximity to the NSDAP. It gave the party substantial financial support and unconditional political support, however, only after the Seizure of Power. The RdI was finally merged with the Union of Employers' Associations; it was supplanted in 1934 by the Reich Group for Industry during the ORGANIZATION OF THE INDUSTRIAL ECONOMY.

Reich Association of German Radio Listeners (Reichsverband Deutscher Rundfunkteilnehmer; RDR), alliance of radio listeners founded on August 12, 1930, by middle-class conservatives and National Socialists. Its goal was to effect a nationalistic impact on RADIO programming. Through various intrigues, the RDR came under the complete control of the NSDAP in 1931; until 1933 it fought, with little success, for a "National Socialist radio revolution." In 1935 the RDR was disbanded, since NS radio functionaries believed that a representation of radio listeners was superfluous. Instead, they wanted organizational support for the RADIO STEWARD, so as to introduce the largest possible number of listeners to the radio as an instrument of propaganda.

Reich Authorities

(as of 1941)

The Reich authorities (*Reichsbehörden*) were those authorities that carried out the affairs of the German Reich. Thus, in the narrower sense,

they consisted of the Reich Chancellery and the Reich ministries. The conflation of party and state was expressed above all through frequent personal unions of functions, and through the elevation of party offices to the rank of Reich authority. They were:

1. The Führer und Reichskanzler: Hitler as chief of state and government head, with the Reich Chancellery (under Hans Lammers), the Wehrmacht High Command (OKW; Gen. Wilhelm Keitel), and the Presidial Chancellery (Otto Meissner). Immediately subordinate were the following offices: the General Inspector for Highways; Reich Office for Regional Planning (Reichsstelle für Raumordnung); Reich Youth Leadership; General Inspector for the Reich Capital; General Construction Councillor for the Capital of the Movement [that is, Munich]; and Reich Construction Councillor for the City of Linz on the Danube.

2. The Deputy for the Four-Year Plan: Hermann Göring.

3. The Privy Cabinet Council, which was to advise Hitler in foreign-policy matters and thus in fact had no function: Konstantin von Neurath.

4. The Reich Protector for Bohemia and Moravia (Neurath), as well as the Generalgouverneur for occupied Poland (Hans Frank).

5. The Reich government, consisting of the Reich ministers and the head of the OKW (Keitel), the chief of the Reich Chancellery (Lammers), the chief of the Party Chancellery (Martin Bormann), the Reich Master Forester (Göring), the president of the Reich Treasury (Müller), the president of the German Reich Bank (Walther Funk), and the Reich Ministers without Portfolio (Neurath, Frank, Hjalmar Schacht, Arthur Seyss-Inquart). There were 15 cabinet bureaus (Fachressorts):

a) The Reich Foreign Minister (Reichsminister des Auswärtigen): Joachim von Ribbentrop, subordinate to whom were such posts as the head of the NSDAP Foreign Organization (Ernst Bohle), the diplomatic corps, and the Reich Office for Foreign Trade.

b) The Reich Interior Minister (Reichsminister des Innern): Wilhelm Frick, under whom were the Prussian Interior Minister and the head of the Reich Labor Service (Konstantin Hierl). Formally part of the Interior Ministry were also the bureaus of the Reichsführer-SS and Chief of the German Police (Heinrich Himmler), over whom the ministry in fact had no real authority. The numerous agencies within the Interior Ministry included the Office for Clan Research, the Reich Publishing Office, the Reich Health Office, the

Reich Archive, and the Reich Sports Office. A series of institutes were also supervised by the Interior Ministry, such as the Reich Physicians' Chamber and the German Red Cross.

c) The Reich Minister for Volk Enlightenment and Propaganda (Reichsminister für Volksaufklärung und Propaganda): Joseph Goebbels (see PROPAGANDA MINISTRY).

d) The Reich Minister for Aviation (Reichsminister für Luftfahrt): Hermann Göring, who was simultaneously Supreme Commander of the Luftwaffe, and as Reich Marshal the highest officer in the Wehrmacht (even superior to the OKW chief).

e) The Reich Minister of Finance (Reichsminister der Finanzen): Lutz Schwerin von Krosigk, who aside from the usual duties had responsibility over such matters as marriage loans, child subsidies, and the promotion of agriculture.

f) The Reich Minister of Justice (Reichsminister der Justiz): Franz Schlegelberger as acting head (until Otto Thierack, in August 1942), under whose supervision were the Academy for German Law and the Reich Patent Office, among other agencies.

g) The Reich Economics Minister (Reichswirtschaftsminister): Funk (simultaneously Prussian Minister for the Economy and Labor), who was responsible for the customary functions, as well as for managing foreign currency and raw materials; he also had responsibilities for issues concerning the war economy.

h) The Reich Minister for Nutrition and Agriculture (Reichsminister für Ernährung und Landwirtschaft): Walther Darré (simultaneously Prussian Agricultural Minister), who as Reich Peasant Führer led the Reich Food Estate and supervised the Reich Hereditary Farm Court, among other agencies.

i) The Reich Labor Minister (Reichsarbeitsminister), who was also the Prussian Labor Minister: Franz Seldte. Along with the traditional functions he had responsibilities for administering the Organization for Labor Deployment, settlers' affairs, the jurisdiction of social honor courts, and the like.

j) The Reich Minister [also Prussian Minister] for Science, Education, and Public Instruction (Reichsminister für Wissenschaft, Erziehung, und Volksbildung): Bernhard Rust. His responsibilities included the organization of the Country Year of service; he was the principal official of the Reich Institute for the History of the New Germany and the supervisor of the Kaiser Wilhelm Society for the

Encouragement of Science and its member institutes.

k) The Reich Minister for Ecclesiastical Affairs (*Reichsminister für kirchlichen Angelegenheiten*): Hanns Kerrl (after his death in December 1941 he was replaced only by a state secretary).

l) The Reich Transportation Minister (*Reichsverkehrsminister*), also Prussian Transportation Minister: Julius Dorpmüller, who was also General Director of the German Railroad (Deutsche Reichsbahn).

m) The Reich Postal Minister (*Reichspostminister*): Wilhelm Ohnesorge, whose research bureau developed such military improvements as intelligence-related technology and

radar equipment, and which for a time considered the building of an atomic bomb.

n) The Reich Minister for Weapons and Munitions (*Reichsminister für Bewaffnung und Munition*; established March 17, 1940): Fritz Todt (as of 1942, Albert Speer).

o) The Reich Minister for the Occupied Eastern Territories (*Reichsminister für die besetzten Ostgebiete*; established November 17, 1941): Alfred Rosenberg, responsible for the Reich Commissioners, who, however, largely evaded Rosenberg's supervision.

[Most of the persons, organizations, and bureaus referred to above are the subjects of individual entries.]

Reich authority (*Reichsgewalt*), the unification, sought by National Socialism, of all government power in a unified and hierarchically organized authority. Its exercise was derived from the FÜHRER'S WILL. National Socialism abolished the separation of powers among legislation (*see* LAWS), ADMINISTRATION, and JUSTICE that reciprocal controls were meant to achieve. SYNCHRONIZATION additionally abolished the division of government power among the central state, the individual states, and the organizations of communal self-government, as had been characteristic of the German constitutional tradition.

A. v. B.

Reich Banner "Black-Red-Gold" (Reichsbanner "Schwarz-Rot-Gold"), republican defense organization founded on February 24, 1924, by Otto HÖRSING (its chairman until 1932), among others, with headquarters in Magdeburg. It was supported chiefly by the Social Democratic

Party (SPD), but also by the other parties of the WEIMAR COALITION. The Reich Banner, which at one point had more than 3 million members, formed a militarily organized fighting arm, the so-called Schufo (Schutzformation, or Defense Formation), with as many as 400,000 troops. Its hour came with the growth of the radical parties, especially the NSDAP, during the course of the world economic crisis beginning in 1930.

The Reich Banner in the final analysis remained unsuccessful, like the IRON FRONT, to which it gave substantial support. This was because of the inhibiting supra-party organization; the SPD's indecisive leadership; and the unscrupulousness of the National Socialist adversary, which until then had not been recognized. In June and July 1932, eight Reich Banner members lost their lives in street brawls, and many others (over 3,000) were summarily convicted by biased courts. At the time of Franz von Papen's PRUSSIAN COUP (July 20, 1932), the fighting groups of the Reich

Reich Banner "Black-Red-Gold." Parade in Berlin.

Banner remained inactive because there were no orders to intervene. Afterward, neither a rapprochement with the army nor (on a regional level) one with the STEEL HELMET could save the situation. Almost without resistance, the Reich Banner disbanded in March 1933. Many of its members emigrated, and others were imprisoned.

Reich Basic Laws (*Reichsgrundgesetze*), in the absence of a CONSTITUTION, the term used by National Socialism for especially important laws of the Third Reich based on the REICHSTAG FIRE DECREE and the ENABLING LAW. They included the Law to Secure the Unity of Party and State of December 12, 1933, the Law against the Formation of New Parties of July 14, 1933, the HEREDITARY FARM LAW of September 29, 1933, the Law on the Rebuilding of the Reich of January 30, 1934 (*see* SYNCHRONIZATION), the Law on the Head of State of the German Reich of August 1, 1934 (*see* FÜHRER UND REICHSKANZLER), the LABOR REGULATION LAW of January 20, 1934, the GERMAN COMMUNAL ORDINANCE of January 30, 1935, the Law for the Creation of the Wehrmacht of March 16, 1935, and the NUREMBERG LAWS of September 15, 1935.

Reich Bishop (*Reichsbischof*), the head of a united GERMAN EVANGELICAL CHURCH, sought by the GERMAN CHRISTIANS in particular. Even before the passage of the Reich Ecclesiastical Constitution, which would have been a necessary preliminary step, the representatives of the 28 Evangelical local churches (*Landeskirchen*) agreed on May 27, 1933, to appoint Friedrich von BODELSCHWINGH to the post of Reich Bishop. When Bodelschwingh resigned under political pressure, and after the ecclesiastic elections of July 23, 1933, had produced a clear German Christian majority, the National Synod, meeting in Wittenberg on September 27 of that year, chose Ludwig MÜLLER as Reich Bishop. The CONFESSING CHURCH closed ranks against Müller, and as a result he was unable to consolidate his control. On November 24, 1935, his authority was withdrawn, although he nominally remained in the post.

Reich Bridal Schools (*Reichsbräuteschulen*), representative educational institutions; they were a component of the MARRIAGE SCHOOLS of the MOTHERS' SERVICE within the German Women's Agency, with locations in Berlin-Wannsee and Edewecht (Oldenburg).

Reich Chamber of Fine Arts (Reichskammer der bildenden Künste), one of the seven chambers of the REICH CULTURE CHAMBER. It was founded on November 1, 1933, through the First Decree for the Implementation of the Reich Culture Law, which came from the Reich Cartel of Fine Arts. In 1937 the Reich Chamber of Fine Arts was itself organized into seven divisions, which in their totality encompassed all the professional groups, institutions, and associations that were concerned with the "creation of culture" and the "advancement of culture." The president from 1933 to 1936 was Eugen Hönig, and from 1937 to 1945, Adolf ZIEGLER. Walter Hofmann was the managing director. The chamber created the post of "Reich Delegate for Artistic Realization" (*Reichsbeauftragter für künstlerische Formgebung*) and filled it in 1935 with Hans SCHWEITZER, a caricaturist from the Time of Struggle. He was to set the political guidelines of the chamber and supervise their implementation.

Membership in the Reich Chamber of Fine Arts was an obligation for all those involved in the fine arts, and it was impossible to practice one's profession without belonging. A supposedly extensive occupational self-government in the chamber was, however, a sham. In reality, like the other Reich chambers, the Reich Chamber of Fine Arts was an important instrument of the Propaganda Ministry for cultural control and manipulation of access to information.

S. O.

Reich Chancellery (Reichskanzlei), Hitler's office (*see* REICH AUTHORITIES) as government chief, headed by Hans LAMMERS, as well as Hitler's official headquarters. Until January 1939 Hitler resided in the Old Reich Chancellery on the Wilhelmstrasse in Berlin, but he felt increasingly uncomfortable in that Wilhelmine-era building. It was perhaps "appropriate for a soap company," but not for a Reich on the move. Consequently, in 1938–1939 he had Albert Speer build the NEW REICH CHANCELLERY on Vossstrasse.

Reich Chancellor (*Reichskanzler*), chief of the Reich government. According to the Weimar Constitution he was responsible to the parliament, was appointed by the Reich president, and could be dismissed by him. The PRESIDIAL CABINETS had already undermined the connection between the Reichstag and the chancellor's office by the time Hitler was named to the post on January 30, 1933. The ENABLING LAW of March 24 of that year completely did away with any responsibility on the part of the parliament, and in August 1934 it transformed the office into the personal dictatorship of the FÜHRER UND REICHSKANZLER.

Reich Citizenship Law (*Reichsburgergesetz*), along with the Law to Protect Blood, the primary component of the NUREMBERG LAWS of September 15, 1935.

Reich Clothing Card (*Reichskleiderkarte*), permit for the purchase of textiles. After the beginning of the Second World War it was distributed to all Germans not serving in uniform, in order better to plan and ensure a more or less equitable and sufficient supply for the civilian population. The cards, valid for one year, contained 100 coupons or points, which had to be handed in when buying textile goods. A dress, for example, required 20 points, and a summer coat, 35 points. During the course of the war, supplemental cards were handed out for the young, as were special authorizations for winter clothing and professional uniforms. From 1940 on, Jews received no clothing cards.

Reich commissioner (*Reichskommissar*), position provided for in the Weimar Constitution and retained in the Third Reich: a delegate (*Beauftragter*) of the Reich government or the Reich president, with extensive authority to supervise or assume control of regional offices or authorities, to look after the rights of the Reich in certain areas, or to take on special assignments. The commissioner was a crucial instrument of

Reich Clothing Card.

SYNCHRONIZATION. Already utilized successfully by the Papen government in the PRUSSIAN COUP, after the Seizure of Power the Reich commissioners were used in the Reich's takeover (*Verreichlichung*) of the judicial system by Hans Frank; as a preliminary step to a ministerial post for Hermann Göring (the Reich Commissioner for Aviation); to discipline the Evangelical Church; in sports; and so on.

In abolishing the sovereignty of the individual states (*Länder*), the Office of the Reich Commissioner was created as an interim arrangement. Appointed Reich commissioner, Josef BÜRCKEL managed the return of the Saarland to the Reich (January 1, 1935) and the merger of Austria (April 23, 1938). Commissioner Konrad HENLEIN brought in the Sudetenland (October 1, 1938). During the war, commissioners were installed as heads of the civil administration with the occupation authorities in the conquered territories: Josef TERBOVEN in Norway (April 24, 1940), Arthur SEYSS-INQUART in the Netherlands (May 18, 1940), and Gustav SIMON in Luxembourg (August 8, 1940); and in addition, Robert WAGNER in Alsace and Bürckel in Lorraine. In Russia two commissioners were installed on November 14, 1941: Hinrich LOHSE for the Ostland and Erich KOCH for the Ukraine. Heinrich Himmler undertook special assignments as Commissioner for the Fortification of the German Volk-Nation (October 7, 1939), as did Robert LEY as Commissioner for the Construction of Social Housing (November 19, 1940). Reich defense commissioners also functioned as Reich commissioners.

Reich Commissioner for the Fortification of the German Volk-Nation (*Reichskommissar für die Festigung des deutschen Volkstums*), post assigned to Heinrich HIMMLER on October 7, 1939, for which he established an SS Main Office. The commissioner was responsible for the repatriation settlement, resettlement, and new settlement of German citizens or ETHNIC GERMANS, especially in the occupied territories in the east. He also directed RE-GERMANIZATION and promoted the program for GERMANIZATION.

Reich Consistory. *See* Reich Fraternal Council.

Reich Country League (Reichslandbund), national conservative interest group for German agriculture; it was founded in 1921. With approximately 5 million members in 1928, the Reich Country League, whose chief concerns were promoting a protective tariff and ensuring prices and markets, was the largest agricultural organization. It affiliated itself with the GREEN FRONT in 1929, participated in the HARZBURG FRONT, and backed Hitler's election as Reich president in 1932. The league's good relations with the NSDAP led to its cooperation with the party's AGRICULTURAL POLICY apparatus and, ultimately, to its smooth integration into the REICH FOOD ESTATE on December 8, 1933.

Reich Court (*Reichsgericht*), from 1875 to 1945 the appellate court for civil and criminal matters; it was located in Leipzig. Until the establishment of the VOLK COURT, it was the sole court of appeal for cases involving high, state, and wartime treason. With the introduction of SPECIAL COURTS, it lost its appellate jurisdiction with regard to political crimes, except for prosecutions under the NUREMBERG LAWS. In proceedings using the plea of nullity, introduced in 1940, the Reich Court could reverse nearly any decision of a lower court. As early as 1939 the Special Panel (*Besonderes Senat*) was created to adjudicate extraordinary objections, which were permissible against any legal criminal verdict, and to rule on matters that because of their "particular significance" could be prosecuted there. In civil law, which remained largely unaltered, the judicial system subordinated itself to political and ideological requirements only upon demand, through an extensive interpretation. In criminal law, however, especially in prosecutions of RACIAL INFAMY, it often abandoned the principles of the rule of law, making use of retroactive punishment, prohibition against the use of analogies, and expansion of the definition of a crime.

C. D.

Reich Court in Leipzig.

Reich Court-martial (*Reichskriegsgericht*), the highest military court, established in Berlin in 1936. Before the war it was the appellate court for matters under MILITARY JURISDICTION, and it had immediate jurisdiction in matters of high treason, treason against the states (*Landesverrat*), and treason committed in wartime by military personnel, as well as in cases of refusal to perform military service for religious reasons. After the war began, the Reich Court-martial was the sole court of appeal in the military sphere for espionage, industrial sabotage, and offenses involving the UNDERMINING OF MILITARY STRENGTH. By permitting the public almost unrestricted access to its proceedings concerning this last charge beginning in 1939, the Reich Court-martial demonstrated that it was clearly influenced by National Socialist ideology. In 1943 the Special Standing Court for the Wehrmacht was established in the Reich Court-martial.

C. D.

Reich Culture Chamber (Reichskulturkammer), public corporation established by a law of September 22, 1933, and by its implementation decrees of November 1 and 9 of that year. The Reich Culture Chamber encompassed everyone involved in the cultural professions; it established working conditions in the branches of trade and industry placed under it, and made decisions regarding the opening and closing of enterprises. It was organized into seven separate chambers: the REICH FILM CHAMBER, REICH MUSIC CHAMBER, REICH THEATER CHAMBER, REICH PRESS CHAMBER, REICH WRITING CHAMBER, REICH CHAMBER FOR FINE ARTS, and the REICH RADIO CHAMBER, which was dissolved in 1939.

The president of the Reich Culture Chamber was Joseph GOEBBELS, and its vice presidents (who also bore the title of state secretary in the Propaganda Ministry) were Walther FUNK (1933–1937), Karl HANKE (1937–1940), Leopold Gutterer (1940–1944), and Werner Naumann (May 1944–1945). Until 1938 there were three managing directors (*Reichskulturverwalter*), and then general secretaries functioned as chairmen of the main directorate: Hans Schmidt-Leonhard (until April 1938), Franz Moraller (October 1934–1938), Hans HINKEL (May 1935–April 1938), Erich Schmidt (1938–1939), again Hans Hinkel (1940–1941), and Hans Erich Schrade (from July 1944 on).

The formulated purpose of the Reich Culture Chamber was "to promote German culture in a position of responsibility to *Volk* and Reich [*in*

Verantwortung für Volk und Reich], to regulate the economic and social affairs of the cultural profession, and to ensure agreement among all the efforts of its constituent groups." As of February 12, 1934, the chamber was a corporative member of the GERMAN LABOR FRONT. Its actual responsibility was to organize and supervise the entire cultural life of the nation. Membership in one of the individual chambers was the prerequisite for any cultural activity in the Third Reich. From June 20, 1934, the official organ of the Reich Culture Chamber was the *Völkischer Beobachter*.

S. O.

Reich Curatorium for Youth Fitness Training (Reichskuratorium für Jugendertüchtigung), foundation that aimed to create uniformity in programs for the premilitary training of young men. Founded by a decree of Reich President Paul von Hindenburg on September 14, 1932, its president was Gen. Otto von STÜLPNAGEL. The highest educational aim of the Reich Curatorium was "military fitness" (*Wehrhaftigkeit*) resulting from "physical and spiritual manliness" (*körperliche und geistige Mannhaftigkeit*). It became superfluous by 1933 since its functions were taken over by the Hitler Youth, SA, and SS.

Reich Defense Commissioners (*Reichsverteidigungskommissare*), organizers of the civil defense administration; their function was established by an ordinance of September 1, 1939. At first, those *Gau* leaders who were also Reich governors (*Reichsstatthalter*) served as defense commissioners; as of November 16, 1942, all the other *Gau* leaders assumed this additional duty. In their defense function they served under the authority of the MINISTERIAL COUNCIL FOR THE DEFENSE OF THE REICH and worked together with commanders of the military districts. When consultation was required, they convened defense committees.

Reich Dramaturge (*Reichsdramaturg*), post created within the PROPAGANDA MINISTRY in 1933 for the supervision and guidance of the repertoire of the German stage.

Reich Drunkard (*Reichstrunkenbold*), nickname for the head of the German Labor Front, Robert LEY, who was considered to be extremely susceptible to the pleasures of alcohol.

Reich Economic Council (Reichswirtschaftsrat), central institution for the regulation of economic matters. A law of April 5, 1933, disbanded the old Provisional Reich Economic Council, and founded a new one. The 60 new members were all appointed by the Reich president on the recommendation of the Reich government. The council was disbanded, however, by a law of March 23, 1934. A law of March 21, 1935, then regulated the representation of private industry and its cooperation with the German Labor Front (DAF). It established the Reich Labor and Reich Economic Council in accordance with National Socialist principles. Like its precursor, this council had no executive apparatus of its own; accordingly, it gained no particular importance. Any practical work was carried out primarily in the seven central organizations—specialized by branch—of the industrial economy (joined together in the Reich Economic Chamber) and in the branch offices (*Fachämter*), or in the central office of the DAF.

A. v. S.

Reichenau, Walter von, b. Karlsruhe, October 8, 1884; d. Poltava, January 17, 1942, German field marshal (July 19, 1940). A career officer, Reichenau entered the army in 1903. He was a battery commander and General Staff officer in the First World War. A friend of Armed Forces Minister Werner von BLOMBERG, Reichenau was made chief of staff of the Ministerial Office (as of March 1935, the Wehrmacht Office) on February 1, 1933. He shared his superior's concerns over the plans of the SA leader, Ernst RÖHM, for a popular militia. At Röhm's liquidation on June 30, 1934, Reichenau tacitly supported the benevolent nonintervention of the military leadership. Once again the military

Walter von Reichenau.

could regard itself as the "sole bearer of arms of the nation." Immediately after Paul von Hindenburg's death on August 2, 1934, it showed its gratitude to Hitler by swearing the troops' allegiance to the Führer.

Reichenau also proved his loyalty to the National Socialist government during the FRITSCH CRISIS. After it he took command of the Tenth Army for the occupation of the Sudetenland, the "crushing of the remnant of the Czech state," and the Polish Campaign. In France and Russia he led the Eighth Army, which later was destroyed at Stalingrad. Reichenau adopted Hitler's thesis of an "ideological war" (*Weltanschauungskrieg*) in the east: on October 10, 1941, he announced in an order of the day that the soldier too was "the bearer of a relentless *völkisch* idea" and must have a complete understanding of "the necessity of the harsh but justified expiation of Jewish subhumanity." In December 1941 Reichenau took over the supreme command of Army Group South, but he suffered a stroke shortly afterward.

Reich Film Chamber (Reichsfilmkammer), one of the seven chambers of the REICH CULTURE CHAMBER, but instituted even before the latter, by a law of July 14, 1933. The Reich Film Chamber was subdivided in 1937 into 10 sections (specialty groups), which encompassed all

Reich Film Chamber. From the left: Weidemann, Hans Hinkel, Lehnich, and Scheuermann.

persons involved in the production and distribution of films. The presidents of the chamber were Fritz Scheuermann (1933–1935), Oswald Lehnich (1935–1939), and Carl August FROELICH (1939–1945). The vice presidents were Arnold Raether (1933–1935), Hans Weidemann (1935–1939), and Karl Melzer (1939–1945). Melzer also served as executive director until 1939, followed by Heinz Tachmann (until 1945). Membership in the chamber was a requirement for all persons active in the film sector; professional activity without membership was not possible. A supposedly extensive professional autonomy was, however, only a pretense. In reality the Reich Film Chamber, like the other individual chambers, was an important instrument of the Propaganda Ministry for the cultural control and manipulation of the public.

S. O.

Reich Flag Law (*Reichsflaggengesetz*), regulation promulgated on September 15, 1935, simultaneously with the NUREMBERG LAWS. It made Germany's colors the old imperial black, white, and red, and the Reich or national flag the swastika flag, which also served as the commercial flag. Implementation decrees proclaimed that the Reich flag was to be raised on privately owned buildings on the following holidays: the Day of the [Imperial] Reich's Founding (January 18 [1871]), the Day of the National Rising (the Seizure of Power, January 30), the HEROES' MEMORIAL DAY, the Führer's Birthday (April 20), the MAY HOLIDAY, the HARVEST THANKS DAY, and the Memorial Day for the Fallen of the Movement (the Day of the Hitler Putsch, November 9). The flying of the flag could also be ordered on special occasions; compliance was zealously supervised by local groups and block leaders. Even accidental failure to raise the flag could lead to a detailed interrogation; a dirty or torn flag could result in a charge of breach of the MALICIOUS-GOSSIP LAW. Jews were forbidden to show the Reich flag.

Reich Food Estate (Reichsnährstand), monopoly organization established by law on March 19, 1933; it included all persons and businesses involved in agricultural production, cultivation, and processing, as well as the marketing of farm products. Membership was obligatory. The Food Estate incorporated the agricultural-interest organizations that were disbanded in the course of SYNCHRONIZATION and the agricultural institutions under public law, such as the agricultural

Reich Food Estate. Göring announces the program for the 1937–1938 "Battle for Production."

chambers (*Landwirtschaftskammern*). It was the organization that undergirded all National Socialist AGRICULTURAL POLICY.

At the head of the Food Estate was Reich Peasant Führer and Agriculture Minister Walther DARRÉ, with his own subordinate administrative apparatus. Beneath it, in a strictly hierarchical structure, were the state (*Land*), district (*Kreis*), and local peasant unions (*Bauernschaften*). Horizontally, the Food Estate was divided on the levels of Reich, state, and district into three bureaus.

1. The "Der Mensch" [The Human Being] Main Division inherited the functions previously fulfilled by independent agricultural organizations, clubs, and associations. In addition, it had the tasks of checking the flight from the countryside and implementing the blood-and-soil ideology through such programs as the HEREDI-

TARY FARM LAW and the remolding of the German peasantry.

2. The "Der Hof" [The Farmstead] Main Division dealt with the professional and managerial concerns of agriculture, particularly the direction and implementation of the "Battle for Production," which previously had been the task of the agricultural chambers.

3. The "Der Markt" [The Market] Main Division had responsibility for organizing and supervising all agricultural markets. This included the regulation of imports and the collection of data on domestic production and its total distribution. The division also managed production and sales in conformity with the sought-after AUTARKY by controlling the relationship between market and prices (establishing processing quotas, delivery terms, and market margins).

R. S.

Reich Fraternal Council (Reichsbruderrat), institution of the CONFESSING CHURCH. It arose in March 1934, even before the church's own establishment, from Fraternal Councils (Brüderräte) that members of the PASTORS' EMERGENCY LEAGUE had formed in the Evangelical regional churches. The council first appeared in public on April 22, 1934, at the jubilee celebration of the Ulm cathedral, when it called for opposition to the synchronization measures of the Reich Church government under Ludwig MÜLLER, and convoked the BARMEN CONFESSIONAL SYNOD, to be held at the end of that May. Given legitimacy there by 19 regional churches, the Fraternal Council coordinated the struggle against the GERMAN CHRISTIANS, and after the second confessional synod, held in Berlin-Dahlem that October, it gave the Confessing Church a Provisional Church Government (VKL). The Fraternal Council was divided over the election of the Hannoverian regional bishop, August MARAHRENS, as chairman of the VKL (*see* Martin NIEMÖLLER). It consulted with the VKL and saw to it that the synodal decisions were implemented. After the split in the Confessing Church it remained the church's most important unifying body, and following the collapse of Germany in 1945 it provided leadership for the rebuilding of the Evangelical Church in Germany.

Reich Gau (*Reichsgau*), administrative district, immediately beneath the national Reich level, into which territory annexed to the Reich beginning in 1938 was divided. The 10 *Reichsgaue* were Vienna, Carinthia, Lower Danube, Upper

Danube, Salzburg, Styria, Tyrol, Sudetenland, Danzig–West Prussia, and Wartheland. They were identical with the respective NSDAP *Gaue*, unlike the situation within Germany's original 1933 borders. On the government level they were led by a Reich governor, and politically by a party *Gauleiter*, who governed together in a personal union. This Reich *Gau* principle was to have become the organizational basis in the projected Reich reform.

Reich Germans (*Reichsdeutsche*), in the Weimar period and during the Third Reich, the designation for German citizens who lived within the borders of the German Reich, unlike the FOREIGN GERMANS (*Auslandsdeutsche*). The term was occasionally used after the war began in the narrower sense of German citizens in the so-called OLD REICH. Germans with foreign citizenship were called ETHNIC GERMANS (*Volksdeutsche*).

Reich government (Reichsregierung), according to the Weimar Constitution, the cabinet of Reich ministers under the chairmanship of the REICH CHANCELLOR. The Reich government acted according to the principles of majority rule and loyalty toward colleagues; department heads conferred legality on the decrees of the Reich president by their COUNTERSIGNATURE. Until 1930 the governments were supported by Reichstag majorities and were correspondingly unstable. After the ability to create parliamentary majorities was lost, the so-called PRESIDIAL CABINETS formed the Reich governments, whose rights to participate in government diminished to purely advisory functions within a few months after the Seizure of Power. After the attainment of Hitler's dictatorship (August

2, 1934), there were almost no joint sessions of the Reich government (the last took place at the beginning of 1938). To the ministers were added other functionaries of the National Socialist state (*see* REICH AUTHORITIES).

Reich governors (*Reichsstatthalter*), supervising authorities of the Reich government, with control over the state (*Land*) governments, whose members could be dismissed by a governor. The Reich governors' authority was created by the Second Law for the SYNCHRONIZATION of the States with the Reich of April 7, 1933. After the states lost their sovereign rights through the Law on the New Organization of the Reich of January 30, 1934, the governors became representatives of the Reich's authority, under the supervision of the Reich Interior Ministry. Almost without exception, they were also *Gau* leaders of the NSDAP and thus directly under Hitler, a fact that led to much friction with the Interior Ministry. Minister President Hermann Göring became the Reich governor of Prussia, as the most important of the states. In the REICH GAUS, established beginning in 1938, the Reich governors were at the apex of the administrative hierarchy, and as *Gau* leaders at the same time, were also at the top of the party hierarchy.

Reich Homestead Office (Reichsheimstättenamt), division of the NSDAP and German Labor Front for administering HOMESTEADS and providing for homestead settlers; it was subordinated to the Reich Labor Minister.

Reich Institute for the History of the New Germany (Reichsinstitut für Geschichte des neuen Deutschlands), research institute, located in Berlin, that was founded on July 1, 1935, on

Reich governors. Swearing-in by Reich Interior Minister Frick (right). From the left: von Epp, Mutschmann, Wagner, Sprenger, and Hildebrandt. Next to Frick: Hitler and Lammers.

the initiative of the National Socialist historian Walter FRANK after the dissolution of the Reich Commission for History (founded in 1928). It was responsible to the Reich Minister for Science, Education, and Public Instruction. The institute's self-imposed mission was to provide new impetus to academic history and to "unite [it] with the living energies of the National Socialist Reich." In other words, it was to interpret modern (post-1789) German history in a way that would make the Third Reich appear to be its culmination. The results of such research were published in the Schriften des Reichsinstituts; naturally, they often dealt with problems of the "Jewish question."

Reich Labor Chamber (Reichsarbeitskammer), economic and sociopolitical advisory body in the Office for Social Self-Responsibility (Amt Soziale Selbstverantwortung) of the GERMAN LABOR FRONT (*see* LABOR CHAMBER).

Reich Labor Service (Reichsarbeitsdienst; RAD), general obligation for all healthy males between the ages of 18 and 25 to serve in self-contained units so as to achieve socially useful tasks; it was established by a law of June 26, 1935. Aside from isolated efforts before the First World War, the ideas of a labor service and an obligation to serve went back chiefly to the model of the Auxiliary Service to the Fatherland (Vaterländischer Hilfsdienst) of 1916–1917. In the Weimar Republic, discussions about a labor service were always closely linked with times of economic crisis, such as the early postwar

period. The subject gained renewed impetus through the world economic crisis. Unemployment, especially among young people, was to be combated in this way. A labor service duty was promoted by such groups as the STEEL HELMET, ARTAMANEN, and the YOUNG GERMAN ORDER.

In 1930 the Reich Working Group for a German Labor Service Obligation (RADA) was formed, as was the National League for Labor Service. An emergency decree of June 5, 1931, created the legal basis for a voluntary labor service, and the Institute for Employment Services and Unemployment Insurance took over the advancement of these efforts. Participation in the labor service camps was limited to 20 weeks. The NSDAP was one of the supporters of this voluntary service. At first only the unemployed were to participate, but eventually all young men between the ages of 18 and 25 were included. Their activity was to include agricultural service in particular.

After the takeover of power, Hitler appointed Col. Konstantin HIERL, who had retired, to head the labor service on March 31, 1933. Later made a Reich commissioner, Hierl initially had the rank of a state secretary, at first in the Reich Labor Ministry and later in the Interior Ministry. Only in 1943 did the labor service become a Supreme Reich Authority (*Oberste Reichsbehörde*), directly responsible to Hitler. The Führer saw in the RAD an ideal vehicle for the "alignment" (AUSRICHTUNG) of young men, in the National Socialist sense of the word. Its paramilitary training was to serve the Wehr-

Reich Labor Service. Roll call of Labor Service members in Nuremberg (1934).

macht well later on. But the RAD suffered from a constant lack of suitable leaders, and consequently the hoped-for political schooling was scarcely achieved. Nonetheless, the RAD was used as a public display of "German socialism." At the Reich Party Congress in 1934, when 52,000 identically uniformed Labor Service men paraded by, Hitler proclaimed: "Through your school, the entire nation will pass." The length of this "service of honor to the German *Volk*" was set at a half year.

Hierl eliminated the denominational and other organizers of labor service programs, and created an NS monopoly. He divided the RAD into 30 *Gau* units (*Arbeitsgaue*), 182 RAD groups, and 1,260 RAD divisions. As early as 1934 a service duty of half a year was established for persons who had an *Abitur* diploma. On April 1, 1936, a women's labor service, based on voluntary enlistment, was joined to the RAD. Not until 1939 was labor service made obligatory for women. Including permanent staff, the strength of the RAD by October 1, 1935, came to approximately 200,000; between then and October 1, 1939, the RAD grew by 350,000 participants yearly. With a budget of approximately 1.70 RM daily per person, it was especially active in farm labor. It was also utilized for building the AUTOBAHN and the WESTWALL. The "work maidens" mainly helped the "overburdened German mother in the settlement areas" and assisted in agriculture.

After the outbreak of the war, the RAD came largely under the control of the Wehrmacht; even the labor service draft was the responsibility of the military district commands. Labor service men occupied themselves with spades and weapons from the North Pole to the Cyclades in the Aegean. They manned anti-aircraft guns, built V1 firing ramps, and in 1944–1945 were assigned to the VOLK STORM.

The labor service, originally conceived as a means for combating unemployment, developed under the National Socialists into an instrument that trained young people in the spirit of the *Volk* Community and above all prepared them for war.

B. W.

Reich Leaders (*Reichsleiter; Leiter* is commonly translated as "director"), as of 1933, the term for the highest POLITICAL LEADERS of the NSDAP, with specific spheres of responsibility. Such persons would formerly have been called *Referenten* (councillors) or *Amtsleiter* (office directors). Nominated by Hitler, they formed the Reich Leadership (*Reichsleitung*), a purely collective term without the character of a standing committee or even a council. The Reich Leadership had its headquarters in the BROWN HOUSE in Munich, although some Reich Leaders had their offices in Berlin because of their additional government duties. It was the task of the Reich Leaders, whose authority was not based on a "sovereign territory" (locality, district, or *Gau*), to establish the "political direction of the German *Volk*" according to Hitler's directives, to fulfill special party assignments, and to ensure "that in all areas of life a leadership is available that unerringly stands by the National Socialist worldview." Thus, they were to remain "in the closest possible touch with the life of the *Volk*," an obligation that required a straightforward folksiness (*Volkstümlichkeit*), as well as the development of an airtight supervisory apparatus.

In 1940 the title of *Reichsleiter* was held by such men as the head of the Führer's Chancellery (Philipp BOUHLER), the Führer's deputy (Rudolf HESS) and chief of staff (Martin BORMANN), the head of the Reich party organization (Robert LEY), the Reich party treasurer (Franz Xaver SCHWARZ), the Reich propaganda chief (Joseph GOEBBELS), the supreme party judge (Walter BUCH), the Reich press chief (Otto DIETRICH), the *Reichsleiter* for the press (Max AMANN), and the heads of the Reich Office for Agricultural Policy (Walther DARRÉ), the Reich Legal Office (Hans FRANK), the Foreign Policy Office (Alfred ROSENBERG), the Office for Colonial Policy (Franz Xaver EPP), and the Reichstag delegation (Wilhelm FRICK).

Reich Leadership Schools (*Reichsführerschulen*), term for the instructional institutes of the POLITICAL LEADERS of the NSDAP; it also referred to training institutions for future party leaders such as the ORDER FORTRESSES.

Reich League for German Naval Prestige (Reichsbund Deutscher Seegeltung), association founded in Berlin in 1934, to which Hitler gave the task of creating propaganda for the navy. Its chairman was Adm. Adolf von TROTHA, and after his death in 1941, Rear Admiral Busse. The Reich League was in the tradition of the Wilhelmine navy ("Germany's future is on the seas") and the Great-German ideology. However, it gained little response with its Institute for Naval Prestige in Magdeburg, since in National Socialist rearmament the emphasis was definitely placed on the army and air force.

Reich League of German Civil Servants (Reichsbund der Deutschen Beamten; RDB), affiliated association of the NSDAP. Founded in 1933 as a unified organization of civil service employees, it was under the auspices of the Main Office for Civil Servants in the Party Leadership. The Reich League's functions were to educate its members (who were not required to belong to the party) to become "exemplary National Socialists," to "infuse" the civil service with ideology, and to share responsibility for government civil service policy. The league was subdivided into 14 occupational categories (*Fachschaften*) and was organized in accordance with the FÜHRER PRINCIPLE.

Reich League of Jewish Frontline Soldiers (Reichsbund Jüdischer Frontsoldaten; RJF), organization of German Jews founded on February 8, 1919, for such goals as fostering comradeship, caring for Jewish war casualties, and promoting settlement projects and athletic competitions. The Reich League, which in 1936 had approximately 30,000 members, published the weekly magazine *Der Schild* (The Shield; 1921–1938), and sought to gain sympathy for the Jewish cause with the documentary work *Die jüdischen Gefallenen des deutschen Heeres* (The Jews in the German Army Who Fell in Action; 1932). At the beginning of the Third Reich, especially with the support of Reich President Paul von Hindenburg, the league was able to obtain for its members exemptions from anti-Jewish measures such as the ARYAN PARAGRAPH. But at the latest by the time of the NUREMBERG LAWS it too was included in National Socialist antisemitism, and in 1938 it was dissolved.

Reich League of the Child-Rich (Reichsbund der Kinderreichen; RDK), organization, founded in 1920, of German families with many children (*see* CHILD-RICH). Its publication was the *Völkischer Wille* (*Völkisch* Will).

Reich Literature Chamber. *See* Reich Writing Chamber.

Reich Marshal (*Reichsmarschall*), highest rank in the German Wehrmacht, conferred by Hitler on Hermann Göring (July 19, 1940), as the sole bearer of the title. It was awarded "for his services to the *Volk* and the Reich, and above all as creator of the German Luftwaffe." The title was meant to evoke the rank of *Reichsfeldmarschall* (Imperial Field Marshal), which in 1707 was conferred on Prince Eugen of Savoy in the days of the Holy Roman Empire.

Reich Master Forester (*Reichsforstmeister*), Hermann Göring's official title as head of the Reich Forestry Office, with the rank of a Reich minister. In matters concerning hunting, he had the title of Reich Master of the Hunt (*Reichsjägermeister*). The Reich Master Forester was responsible for all forest-related matters, from the lumber business to nature conservation.

Reich League of Jewish Frontline Soldiers. Poster, 1924: "To German mothers! Seventy-two thousand Jewish soldiers fell on the field of honor for Germany. Christian and Jewish heroes fought together and rest together in foreign earth. One hundred and twenty thousand Jews fell in battle! Partisan hatred, blind with rage, does not halt before the graves of the dead. German women, do not allow Jewish mothers to be mocked in their grief."

Reich Marshal Hermann Göring.

Reich Master Forester Hermann Göring.

Reich Master of the Hunt (*Reichsjägermeister*), title of REICH MASTER FORESTER Hermann Göring in matters relating to hunting.

Reich ministers. *See* Reich Authorities.

Reich Ministry for Volk Enlightenment and Propaganda, official designation of the Propaganda Ministry.

Reich Mothers' School (*Reichsmütterschule*), "institution for continuing education" in Berlin-Wedding. Its task was to train the teachers employed by the MOTHERS' SERVICE in the German Women's Agency.

Reich Music Chamber (Reichsmusikkammer), professional union founded as a corporation under public law by the First Ordinance to Implement the Reich Culture Chamber Law, promulgated on November 1, 1933. The largest in membership of the seven chambers in the REICH CULTURE CHAMBER, the Reich Music Chamber emerged from the Reich Cartel of German Musicians, founded in May 1933. Its president until 1935 was Richard STRAUSS, followed by Peter RAABE. The Music Chamber was in reality a subordinate bureau of the Propaganda Ministry. Organized according to state (*Land*) and *Gau*, it was divided into the leadership (Presidial Council and Administration), five central offices for coordination, and seven divisions: (1) the Professional Guild of German Composers; (2) the Reich Musicians' Union; (3) the Office for Concerts; (4) the Office for Choral and Folk Music; (5) the German Organization of Music Publishers; (6) the Reich Association of Music Managers; and (7) the Working Communi-

ties. Thus, the Reich Music Chamber was an all-encompassing, obligatory professional union outside of which it was impossible to practice one's profession in music. As an instrument of the cultural SYNCHRONIZATION, it was "to embrace music and musical life in their totality," in the words of Gustav Havemann, a chamber member (1934).

R. H.

Reich Office for Agricultural Policy (Reichsamt für Agrarpolitik), office in the Reich Leadership of the NSDAP that emerged from the AGRICULTURAL POLICY APPARATUS OF THE NSDAP in 1933. It was located in Munich, and its head was Walther DARRÉ. The office's functions were to advise Hitler on agricultural issues, to support government measures in this sector by means of propaganda, and to work jointly with the REICH FOOD ESTATE and the Reich Ministry for Nutrition and Agriculture, both of which were under Darré's personal supervision. The office's publication was the *NS-Landpost* (NS Rural Post).

Reich Office for Military and Economic Planning (Reichsamt für wehrwirtschaftliche Planung), administrative authority formed in 1938 within the Reich Economics Ministry. It concerned itself with statistics and plans related to the preparations for a WAR ECONOMY.

Reich Office for the Promotion of German Writing (Reichsstelle zur Förderung des deutschen Schrifttums), agency created on July 1, 1933, for the overall encouragement of the production and dissemination of *völkisch* writing; it was a joint creation of the Propaganda Ministry and the Combat League for German Culture. The office was later transferred (under the leadership of Hans Hagemeyer) as a division for "special assignments" to Alfred Rosenberg's Office for the Cultivation of Writing (*see* WRITING, CULTIVATION OF).

Reich Offices (*Reichsstellen*), administrative departments for managing the economy; they were established during the transition to a WAR ECONOMY. They included Reich offices for grain and feed, eggs, milk, oil, fats, horticultural products, beverages, wool, metal, leather, lampblack, tobacco, coal, furs, paper, coffee, salt, and wood. Besides these, there were Reich offices for resettlement, foreign trade, and area planning; in the sphere of cultural affairs there were Reich offices for the cultivation of literature, schoolbooks, films and art, library affairs, nature conservation, genealogical research, emigration, and so on.

Reich Party Congresses (*Reichsparteitage*), NSDAP assemblies that, in contrast to congresses of democratic parties, did not serve to develop political objectives, but rather were held for purposes of self-presentation, proclamation of slogans, and demonstrations of the party's own power. Beginning in 1927, the Reich Party Congresses were held in Nuremberg; from 1933 to 1938 they took place annually at the beginning of September, and lasted for a week. The city chosen was an early National Socialist stronghold, and was also favored because the imperial assemblies of "the first Reich of the Germans" had met there. The Reich Party Congresses were to be installed in this tradition.

The Congress Grounds were built southeast of Nuremberg on a grandiose scale by Albert SPEER. In 1935 the Luitpold Arena was ready, and a Congress Hall for 60,000 spectators was under construction. The party formations marched in 1936 on the Zeppelin Field, which held several hundred thousand persons. It was bordered by ramparts with stone turrets topped by banners, and also contained a main platform with an imposing portico. A parade ground (*champ de Mars*) and stadium completed the setting, to which a large ceremonial boulevard

led. Although no party congresses were held during the war, the construction continued.

The rituals of the party congresses were unchanging: endless columns of the SA, SS, National Socialist Motor Corps, and Hitler Youth, who had staged an **ADOLF HITLER MARCH OF HITLER YOUTH** to Nuremberg, passed by Hitler. They were later joined by Wehrmacht units, to which a separate day was devoted during the congresses. The marchers formed vast blocks of humanity on the Congress Grounds. There, as the climax, Hitler gave his programmatic speeches, to which the diplomatic corps and foreign dignitaries were invited. Banners were consecrated, sports demonstrations given, vows of fidelity made, and ceremonies to honor the dead celebrated. A blood-red sea of banners waved among the masses, and a ring of anti-aircraft spotlights arched over the evening parade with a "vault of light." This stage setting, totally calculated for propagandistic effect, was intended to display Hitler as the undisputed Führer of the *Volk* and to reinforce the sense of community.

The first Reich Party Congress took place from January 27 to 29, 1923, in Munich, and the second after the re-establishment of the party in

Reich Party Congresses. Hitler speaks to 151,000 *Amtswalter* (office stewards) on the Zeppelin Field.

After the surrender in 1945: Americans on the Reich Party Congress grounds.

Weimar on July 3–4, 1926. Two other party congresses followed in Nuremberg (August 19 to 21, 1927, and August 1 to 4, 1929) before the congresses attained a quasi-official character as important CELEBRATIONS after 1933. Subsequently, they were given individual mottoes: August 31 to September 3, 1933, "Victory of Faith," to celebrate the Seizure of Power; September 4 to 10, 1934, "Triumph of the Will," after the attainment of Hitler's dictatorship; September 10 to 16, 1935, "Reich Party Congress of Freedom," to promulgate the NUREMBERG LAWS on discrimination against the Jews; September 8 to 14, 1936, "Reich Party Congress of Honor," after the successful OLYMPIC GAMES and the RHINELAND OCCUPATION; September 6 to 13, 1937, "Reich Party Congress of Labor," to announce the FOUR-YEAR PLAN; and September 5 to 12, 1938, "Reich Party Congress of Great-Germany," after the ANSCHLUSS with Austria. The congress planned for 1939 (the eleventh), the "Reich Party Congress of Peace," did not take place owing to the outbreak of the war.

Reich Party of the German Middle Class (Reichspartei des deutschen Mittelstands), party oriented toward the middle class (*see* MITTELS-TAND). Appealing to such groups as homeowners and medium and small businessmen and tradesmen, it was founded in 1920 as the Wirtschaftspartei (Economic Party; that is, party concerned with economic policy), and was renamed in 1925. Its program remained hazy. The party attained its best election results in 1930, when it won 23 Reichstag seats. It then fell victim to the radicalization of politics, and in November 1932 gained only one seat. Drift-

ing toward the right, it succumbed to the embrace of the NSDAP. It dissolved itself on April 13, 1933.

Reich Peasant Führer (*Reichsbauernführer*), leadership position created on September 13, 1933, within the REICH FOOD ESTATE; after January 1934 it was occupied by Walther DAR-RÉ. The Peasant Führer was personally responsible to Hitler, or to the Reich Minister for Nutrition and Agriculture as Hitler's representative. Since it was Darré who held this office, the Peasant Führer effectively combined in himself official party functions and governmental and corporative ones.

Reich President (*Reichspräsident*), Germany's head of state from 1919 to 1934, in accordance with the WEIMAR CONSTITUTION. The president was elected directly by the people for a seven-year term. Besides ceremonial duties, he had considerable political power as the highest state authority. The powers of the office included the right to appoint and recall the REICH CHANCELLOR, to dissolve the Reichstag, and to declare a temporary dictatorship in accordance with AR-TICLE 48 of the Constitution. To this was added supreme command over the armed forces. Under these circumstances, the possibilities of removing the Reich president from office (by plebiscite or by indictment before the Supreme Court) were negligible.

The first Reich president was Friedrich EBERT, who was voted in by the National Assembly, rather than by the people. He put his authority to use very cautiously to stabilize the Weimar Republic. Ebert's early death, on February 28, 1925, deprived the Social Democratic Party (SPD) of its most promising candidate. In the elections on March 29 of that year, Otto BRAUN received only 29 percent of the vote for the SPD. When the parties of the Right made Gen. Paul von HINDENBURG their candidate on the second ballot, on April 26, 1925, the WEIMAR COALITION was defeated. Although strictly faithful to the Constitution, Hindenburg was rooted in the mentality of the Wilhelmine Empire. Consequently, the masses made of him an "imitation emperor" (*Ersatzkaiser*), and thus he contributed unwittingly to a further erosion of the democratic principles of the Republic.

What was wanted, however, was the removal of power from a Reichstag that was increasingly incapable of achieving a majority. This was accomplished beginning in 1930 by the PRESIDIAL CABINETS. Hitler saw the office of Reich president as the shortest legal path to power, and he contested the election in 1932. Although he came in second to Hindenburg, who received 53 percent of the votes, by gaining 36.8 percent of the votes in the second ballot on April 10, Hitler achieved a remarkable result. Reassured, he could follow the "detour" by way of the chancellorship to his dictatorship. After Hindenburg's death on August 2, 1934, Hitler combined the offices of Reich president and head of government to create a new position with unlimited powers: FÜHRER UND REICHSKANZLER.

Reich Press Chamber (Reichspressekammer), one of the seven chambers of the REICH CULTURE CHAMBER. Established as a corporation under

"Amman rages in the German newspapers [*Blätterwald*]." Anti–National Socialist satire of the Reich Press Chamber.

public law by the First Ordinance to Implement the Reich Culture Chamber Law of November 1, 1933, the Reich Press Chamber emerged from the Reich Working Group of the German Press. In 1937 it was organized into 14 occupational groups (*Fachschaften*) or professional associations (*Fachverbände*), which together encompassed all groups involved in the production and distribution of periodical publications. These included the Reich Association of German Newspaper Publishers, the Reich Association of German Periodical Publishers, and the Reich Association of the German Press, the federation of all journalists. The president of the Reich Press Chamber was Max AMANN, who as the Reich Leader for the NSDAP press was responsible for all party-owned press enterprises. Its vice president was Otto DIETRICH, and its executive directors were Ildephons Richter (1936–1939) and Anton Willi (1939–1945).

Membership in the Press Chamber was obligatory for all persons active in the press sector, and it was impossible to practice one's profession without this membership. In the Press Chamber, as a part of the cultural Labor Front, all antagonistic group interests of employers and employees were to seem resolved, and a supposedly extensive professional autonomy was pretended. In fact, the Press Chamber, like all the other individual chambers, was an important instrument of the Propaganda Ministry for the control and cultural manipulation of the public.

Reich President Hindenburg on his deathbed.

S. O.

Reich Press Chief (*Reichspressechef*), title of the NSDAP press chief (beginning in 1931, Otto DIETRICH). He was simultaneously the press chief of the Reich government, a Reich Leader in the party, and state secretary in the Propaganda Ministry (*see* PRESS).

Reich Protectorate of Bohemia and Moravia (Reichsprotektorat Böhmen and Mähren), official name for the territory of the RESIDUAL CZECH STATE ("remnant Czechia") after its takeover by the German Reich in March 1939. In ordinary usage the name was usually shortened to PROTECTORATE OF BOHEMIA AND MORAVIA.

Reich Radio Chamber (Reichsrundfunkkammer), one of the seven chambers of the REICH CULTURE CHAMBER. It was established as a corporation under public law on November 1, 1933, by the First Ordinance to Implement the Reich Culture Chamber Law. The Radio Chamber emerged from the National Socialist Radio Chamber (a registered association), which was founded on July 3, 1933, by the Reich Broadcasting Leader, Eugen HADAMOVSKY. Joseph Goebbels's goal of creating a "radio monopoly" (*Rundfunkeinheit*) in the Radio Chamber soon proved to be illusory; the Economics Ministry laid claim to the industry and commerce in the radio sector, so that this area was removed from the chamber on March 19, 1934. In addition, the listeners' associations disbanded.

In 1937 the Radio Chamber was organized into five divisions: administration, propaganda, economy and technology, law, and culture. The Radio Guild (Fachschaft Rundfunk), established on September 3, 1935, included all workers in the field, from directors and production managers to sound technicians and announcers. It was impossible to practice one's profession without membership. From 1933 to 1937 the president was Horst Dressler-Andress, followed from May 1937 to 1939 by Hans Kriegler; both men concurrently headed Division III (Radio) in the Propaganda Ministry and the NSDAP radio. The chamber's vice president was Hadamovsky, and the executive directors were Bernhard Knust (1933–1935) and Herbert Packebusch (1935–1939). The Radio Chamber was significantly involved in the development, promotion, and sales of the VOLK'S RECEIVER. Goebbels dissolved the chamber on October 28, 1939; its individual members were dispersed among the music, theater, and literature chambers.

S. O.

Reich Radio Chamber. Goebbels opens the 1936 Berlin Radio Exhibition. The sign reads: "The radio forms the German man in the spirit of Adolf Hitler."

Reich Reform (*Reichsreform*), a territorial reorganization of the German state, and a redefinition of the relationship between the national state (the Reich) and the constituent states (the *Länder*), as provided for in Article 18 of the Weimar Constitution. Although the Thuringian territories were merged in 1920, the union of Coburg with Bavaria took place the same year, and Prussia annexed Pyrmont in 1922 and Waldeck in 1929, such reforms remained a matter of declarations of intent. Despite the initiatives made by the League to Renew the Reich (founded by Hans LUTHER in 1928), the breakup of disproportionately large Prussia, in particular, did not occur, owing to the opposition of the Social Democratic Party (SDP), which dominated there.

After the Seizure of Power, the SYNCHRONIZATION of the states was chiefly represented as the fulfillment of a constitutional obligation, although National Socialism's centralism was the exact opposite of the federalist views of the 1919 National Assembly. Hitler understood Reich Reform to mean the hierarchical organization of the Reich on the model of the REICH GAU.

Reich Representation of German Jews (Reichsvertretung der deutschen Juden), umbrella association of Jewish organizations founded in 1933 (its president was Leo BAECK). Its aim was to ward off National Socialist racial antisemitism, while downplaying Zionist or assimilationist positions. At the time of the NUREMBERG LAWS, the Reichsvertretung was forced to change its name to the Reich Representation of Jews in Germany (Reichsvertretung der Juden in Deutschland); as a result of the Tenth Ordinance to the Reich Citizenship Law of July 4, 1939, it became the Reich Alliance of Jews in Germany (Reichsvereinigung der Juden in Deutschland). These changes of nomenclature in themselves ᐟreflect the gradual loss of legal rights: the assertion of nationality gave way to a localization, and a representative body (with rights and claims) became a nonbinding alliance. These changes were accompanied by a narrowing of the organization's possibilities for effectiveness and a change in its functions.

Initially the priority was for a separate school and educational system, because the restrictions imposed were first felt in the area of education. Soon, however, economic difficulties became even more pressing, because of the prohibitions against holding certain occupations (*see* ARYAN PARAGRAPH). Thus, the primary tasks of the Reichsvertretung were in the area of social assistance, which was financed through inherited wealth and foreign contributions. After KRISTALLNACHT, the organization concentrated on encouraging Jews to emigrate from Germany, a goal that required cooperation with SS offices. Until emigration was prohibited on October 23, 1941, some 300,000 Jews left Germany (out of a total of half a million). After the prohibition, deportations to ghettos and EXTERMINATION CAMPS replaced emigration. The Reichsvertretung, which was unaware of the actual aims, was forced to assist in the deportations, by maintaining order and in other ways. In June 1943 its dissolution put an end to its activities.

Reich Research Council (Reichsforschungsrat), institution established in 1937 by the Reich Ministry for Science, Education, and Public Instruction, to coordinate research in the natural sciences as part of the FOUR-YEAR PLAN. Its chairman was Professor Karl Becker (1879–1940), and then Bernhard RUST.

Reich Seal (*Reichssiegel;* also called *Staatssiegel,* state seal), official seal for executing and authenticating official documents. After a decree of March 16, 1937, the Great Reich Seal (*Grosse*

Reichssiegel) was to be used for investitures, laws, and ceremonial pronouncements. It depicted a Reich eagle with a garlanded swastika in its talons and encircled with oak-leaf clusters. For other administrative documents a simpler Small Reich Seal (*Kleine Reichssiegel*) was used as an embossing or ink seal.

Reich Security Main Office (Reichssicherheitshauptamt; RSHA), administrative body created on September 27, 1939, as "an amalgamation of the central bureaus of the SECURITY POLICE and the SECURITY SERVICE [SD] of the *Reichsführer-SS.*" With the establishment of the RSHA, the process of integrating government offices with offices of the National Socialist movement, sought chiefly by Heinrich Himmler, was completed. The RSHA was placed under Himmler. It was first headed by Reinhard HEYDRICH (until his death on June 4, 1942), then temporarily by Himmler himself, and from January 30, 1943, by Ernst KALTENBRUNNER.

The RSHA was at first organized into six offices, and as of 1940, into seven:

Office I, under Bruno Streckenbach, was responsible for personnel matters, and above all for the selection and political reliability of the RSHA members.

Office II, under Werner BEST (later under Hans Nockmann), was the legal division, responsible for organization, law, and administration.

Office III, under Otto OHLENDORF, originally

Reich Security Main Office. Himmler and Heydrich.

the SD, was the Domestic Intelligence Service (Inlandsnachrichtendienst).

Office IV was the SECRET STATE POLICE (Gestapo), under Hermann MÜLLER.

Office V was the Reich Criminal Police Office, under Arthur NEBE.

Office VI was the Foreign Intelligence Service, under Heinz Jost (later under Walter SCHELLENBERG).

Office VII, under Franz Six (later under Paul Dittel), was responsible for "research and evaluation from the perspective of worldview." It was an archive for material and literature on and by political and ideological opponents.

The RSHA was the central office for the extra-judicial NS measures of terror and repression from the beginning of the war until 1945. Offices III and IV in particular were notorious for terror at home and in the occupied territories. The RSHA methods in the latter included mobile EINSATZGRUPPEN for "combating the adversary." In mid-1941 the "technical implementation" of the FINAL SOLUTION was handed over to the RSHA. As of September 1942, the RSHA could "correct" judicial sentences "through special handling"—that is, by liquidating those involved. The RSHA intervened in the jurisdiction of the judicial system, as in pending proceedings. As of November 1942, it constituted the entire criminal justice system for Poles and Jews in the occupied territories, and beginning in the summer of 1943, in the Reich as well.

                                                                              U. B.

Reich Set Designer (*Reichsbühnenbildner*), delegate of the REICH THEATER CHAMBER for creating and supervising stage sets in German theaters. The office of the Reich Set Designer was established in 1936 under Benno von ARENT.

Reichsführer-SS and Chief of the German Police (*Reichsführer-SS und Chef der Deutschen Polizei*; RFSSuChdDtPol), Himmler's official title as of June 17, 1936; with it he achieved the long-sought "merger of SS and POLICE." Officially the title included "in the Reich Interior Ministry," which had no real significance. Because Himmler as RFSS was directly responsible to Hitler, as head of the German police he was not obliged to approach Hitler by way of the interior minister; Hitler, moreover, also used the direct route. The creation of this post was the logical consequence of Himmler's career path: from the SS chief who was subordinate to the SA (1929) he progressed through the leadership of the Bavarian police (April 1933) to the destruction of SA power (June 30, 1934) and the separation of the SS from its SA association (July 20, 1934), finally taking over the political police (*see* SECRET STATE POLICE) in all the German states in 1933 and 1934.

Reichsland League. *See* Reich Country League.

Reich Sports Field (Reichssportfeld), sports facility built for the 1936 OLYMPIC GAMES on the site of the earlier German Stadium and the Grunewald Racetrack west of Berlin. It covered an area totaling 132 hectares (about 50 sq miles), with the Olympic Stadium (having a seating capacity of 97,000) as its centerpiece.

Reichsführer-SS and Chief of the German Police. Himmler and Hitler inspect an SS unit.

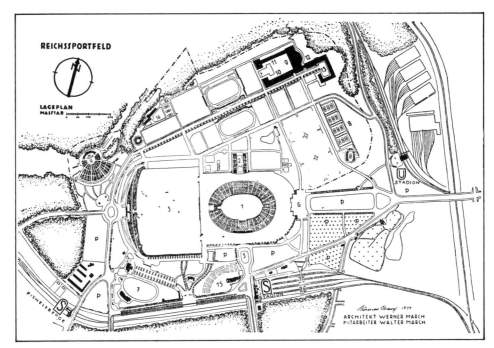

Reich Sports Field. (1) German (Olympic) Stadium; (2) Swimming Stadium; (3) May Field; (4) Dietrich Eckart Open-Air Theater; (5) South Gate; (6) East Gate; (7) Equestrian Ring; (8) Tennis Courts; (9) House of German Sports; (10) Gymnastics Building; (11) Swimming Pool Building; (12) German Gymnastics School; (13) "Friedenhaus" Student Residence; (14) Women Students' Residence; (15) Main Restaurant; (P) Parking area; (S) Rapid Transit [*Schnellbahn*] station; (U) Subway [*U-Bahn*] station.

Other facilities of the Reich Sports Field were the swimming stadium (17,000 seats), the riding track (2,000), the hockey stadium (16,500), the tennis stadium (3,300), the May Field (70,000; it was a parade ground for over 200,000 people), the Dietrich Eckart Open-Air Theater (20,000), and the Stadium Terrace restaurant for 5,000 patrons. In addition, there was the House of German Sports with the Sports Forum (the central office of the GERMAN REICH LEAGUE FOR PHYSICAL EXERCISES and the REICH ACADEMY FOR PHYSICAL EXERCISES).

Paradoxically, the Sports Field was the first architectural monument undertaken by the profoundly anti-Olympic National Socialism. After visiting the site on October 5, 1933, Hitler decreed: "We will build it." He had Werner MARCH's design reworked by Albert SPEER, who gave the concrete-and-glass structures a sheath of natural stone. Speer also topped the May Field's rostrum with the "Führer Tower," 76 m (about 250 feet) in height, and underscored the National Socialist will to build with immense statues, among them *The Boxer*, by Josef THORAK. NS propaganda called the Sports Field "the largest, most practical, and most beautiful sports complex in the world."

Reich Sports Führer (*Reichssportführer*), the head of the GERMAN REICH LEAGUE FOR PHYSICAL EXERCISES, the NATIONAL SOCIALIST REICH LEAGUE FOR PHYSICAL EXERCISES, and the Reich Sports Office. As such, the Reich Sports Führer was a state secretary in the Reich Interior Ministry. The first Sports Führer was Hans von TSCHAMMER UND OSTEN, originally called the Reich Sports Commissioner, from April 28

Reich Sports Führer. Hitler and von Tschammer und Osten.

to July 19, 1933. After his death on March 25, 1943, he was succeeded by Arno Breitmeyer. As of September 18, 1944, Karl Ritter von HALT was the Reich Sports Führer.

Reich Sports Office (Reichssportamt), office directed by the REICH SPORTS FÜHRER; it was established within the Reich Interior Ministry on April 23, 1936.

Reichsrat (Reich Council), according to the WEIMAR CONSTITUTION, the body that represented the constituent states (*Länder*) in the legislation and administration of the national state. The Reichsrat had the right to propose laws to the REICHSTAG and could raise objections to draft laws introduced by the Reichstag or by the government. It also had the right to ratify changes in the budget. Administrative ordinances, especially concerning the postal service or the railroads, required the approval of the Reichsrat. It was composed of 66 representatives of the 17 states, allotted according to population: 17 from Prussia, 11 from Bavaria, 7 from Saxony, and so on. The Reichsrat lost importance as early as 1933 during the course of SYNCHRONIZATION, and totally forfeited it as a result of the Law to Restructure the Reich of January 30, 1934, which transferred all the states' sovereign rights to the Reich. The Reichsrat was dissolved on February 14, 1934.

Reichssicherheitshauptamt (RSHA). *See* Reich Security Main Office.

Reichstag (Reich Assembly), Germany's parliament since 1871. The Reichstag gained considerably broader authority through the WEIMAR CONSTITUTION. As the legislative branch, it was elected every four years by all enfranchised men and women, through universal, equal, secret, and direct balloting, according to a system of proportional representation; it was the supreme bearer of state authority. The Reich government required the confidence of the Reichstag, which could formally impeach the president (through a plebiscite or an indictment before the Supreme Court). In actuality, this was an ineffective instrument, since the president had the right to dissolve the Reichstag, as granted in Article 25.

The election law had no clause barring parties with less than a minimum of support from Reichstag representation; this resulted in a considerable splintering of factions and, ultimately, in the inability to form legislative majorities. Disdained by the Right in particular as a "blather-shop" (*Quasselbude*), the Reichstag was increasingly bypassed beginning in 1930 by EMERGENCY DECREES issued by the Reich president. Meanwhile, it tolerated the so-called PRESIDIAL CABINETS because of the National Socialist threat. After the final Reichstag election of March 5, 1933, it was again convened for the POTSDAM CELEBRATION on March 21 of that year. Two days later it relinquished its authority by accepting the ENABLING LAW. It formally survived as a one-party legislature in the Third Reich (its last session was held in 1942), but it had no legislative powers and served as a stage for Hitler's programmatic pronouncements. After the REICHSTAG FIRE it met at Berlin's Kroll Opera House.

Reichstag. National Socialists on the way to the Kroll Opera House.

Reichstag fire (*Reichstagsbrand*), the destruction by fire of large parts (especially the plenary assembly hall) of the Reichstag building in Berlin, on the evening of February 27, 1933. The Dutch anarchist Marinus van der LUBBE had broken into the parliament building shortly after 9:00 p.m. and with coal igniters had set numerous fires, which he spread with rag torches. When he was found at 9:27 the plenary hall could no longer be saved, despite the extensive response of the fire brigades, since the dome had caved in, precipitating a so-called chimney-flue effect (*Schlot-Effekt*).

Hitler and the National Socialist leaders, who appeared on the scene immediately afterward, right away called the Reichstag fire a "Communist signal" for an uprising against the new government of the "national rising." They made use of the opportunity to launch sudden mass arrests of approximately 4,000 persons—mainly Communist functionaries, but also some from the Social Democratic Party (SPD), using lists that had been made up beforehand. On the following day, the REICHSTAG FIRE DECREE abrogated fundamental laws. The Communists' campaign for the Reichstag election of March 5, 1933, was halted, and the SPD's campaign was severely impeded by prohibitions against newspapers and public gatherings, among other measures.

The Reichstag fire.

In accordance with the classical question "cui bono"—whom the Reichstag fire had benefited—immediately after this well-planned government reaction, the suspicion arose that the fire had been set by the National Socialists. Contributing to this conclusion was the fact that an underground passage led from the palace occupied by the Reichstag president, Hermann Göring, into the Reichstag building. It could have been an ideal escape route for arsonists who had merely exploited Lubbe to their own advantage. Moreover, it seemed difficult to imagine that a single person could have engulfed the huge building in flames.

Nonetheless, neither side could prove its version: neither the Communists with their BROWN BOOK, nor the National Socialists. The latter in the REICHSTAG FIRE TRIAL charged, besides Lubbe, Ernst Torgler, the head of the Communist Party (KPD) Reichstag delegation, who had been the last to leave the building that evening, and three Comintern officials then in Berlin: Georgi DIMITROV, Blagoi Semyonovich Popov, and Vasil Konstantinov Tanev. Moreover, a postwar historical commission directed by a Swiss professor, Walther Hofer, could not undermine Lubbe's stubborn assertion at the time that he had acted alone.

Reichstag Fire Decree (*Reichstagsbrandverordnung*), emergency decree promulgated on February 28, 1933, and titled Decree of the Reich President for Protecting the *Volk* and the State. It was issued following the REICHSTAG FIRE of February 27, which the National Socialists had blamed on the Communists. "To ward off Communist acts of violence endangering the state" (so stated the preamble), the decree abrogated basic rights, notably those of personal freedom; inviolability of the home; privacy of letter, post, telegraph, and telephone; freedom of opinion; freedom of assembly and association; and the guarantee of private property, as assured in Articles 114, 115, 117, 118, 123, 124, and 153 of the WEIMAR CONSTITUTION. In order to "restore public security and order" in the states (*Länder*), the decree gave the national Reich government the right "temporarily to assume" the powers of the *Land* governments. It also increased the sentences for certain crimes, such as introducing the death penalty for high treason and arson.

The Reichstag Fire Decree gave the government led by Hitler an ostensibly legal basis for the SYNCHRONIZATION of the states, as well as for the persecution of real or supposed opponents of National Socialism. In 1933 alone, the decree was used for 3,584 criminal proceedings, which resulted in 3,133 sentences. Above all, it abolished basic elements of the rule of law and thus, together with the ENABLING LAW of March 24, 1933, formed the legal basis for the National Socialist dictatorship.

R. B.

Reichstag Fire Trial (*Reichstagsbrandprozess*), proceeding against "Van der Lubbe and Accomplices" for an act of arson against the Reichstag building on February 27, 1933. It was held from September 21 to December 23, 1933, before the Fourth Criminal Panel of the Leipzig Supreme Court under the presiding judge, Wilhelm Bünger. The accused were Marinus van der LUBBE, the Communist Reichstag deputy Ernst Torgler, and the Bulgarian Comintern functionaries Georgi DIMITROV, Blagoi Semyonovich Popov, and Vasil Konstantinov Tanev. The National Socialist leadership, especially Hermann Göring, who was called as a witness, tried to make the proceeding into a show trial against communism, but instead it drew international suspicions of complicity onto itself (*see* BROWN BOOK).

Van der Lubbe's claim that he had acted alone was in the end impossible to disprove. Despite considerable restrictions placed on the defense, the accused Communist officials had to be acquitted owing to lack of evidence. This result led to the establishment of the VOLK COURT, to which (in place of the Supreme Court) responsibility for cases of high treason and state treason was transferred. The death

sentence against the convicted arsonist was based on the LEX VAN DER LUBBE, which made possible the illegally retroactive death penalty for his act. In 1967 the sentence was posthumously decreased to eight years in prison, and a restoration of civil rights was ordered; in 1980 the Berlin State Court (*Landgericht*) declared the sentence invalid, a decision that was overturned by an appeals court in 1981.

C. S.

Reichsvereinigung der Juden in Deutschland (Reich Union of Jews in Germany), designation imposed as of July 4, 1939, for the Reichsvertretung der Juden in Deutschland, which was originally the Reichsvertretung der deutschen Juden (REICH REPRESENTATION OF GERMAN JEWS).

Reichswehr (Reich Armed Forces), the name of Germany's military forces from 1919 to 1935. In accordance with the terms of the VERSAILLES TREATY, the Reichswehr was limited to an army of 100,000 men and a navy of 15,000; an air force was forbidden. Despite its numerical weakness, the Reichswehr represented a significant military instrument owing to the high level of training of its career soldiers as the nucleus of a later large army. Because of the prohibition against such offensive weapons as tanks, poison gas, and U-boats, the Reichswehr was built up through secret rearmament measures in cooperation with the Red Army (from 1924 on, tank training; from 1930, air force training). The Reichswehr was under the supreme command of the Reich president, whose orders had to be

Reichstag Fire Trial. Goebbels at the witness stand.

countersigned by the armed forces minister. In this post were Gustav NOSKE (1919–1920), Otto GESSLER (1920–1928), Wilhelm GROENER (1928–1932), Kurt von SCHLEICHER until the Seizure of Power, and afterward Werner von BLOMBERG. The military leaders were at the head of the army command: Walther Reinhardt (1919–1920), Hans von SEECKT (1920–1926), Wilhelm Heye (1926–1930), and Kurt Baron von HAMMERSTEIN-EQUORD; and at the head of the navy command: Adolf von TROTHA (1919–1920), Paul Behncke (1920–1924), Zenker (1924–1928), and Erich RAEDER.

Composed of former members of the imperial army and navy and of the FREE CORPS and other volunteer units, the Reichswehr was infused with an anti-Republican spirit. During the first crisis years it held to the terms of its constitutional mandate. However, after Paul von Hindenburg's assumption of the Reich presidency (1925), hopes developed in the Reichswehr for a new authoritarian state; these gained new impetus in the period of the PRESIDIAL CABINETS.

To be sure, Hitler was not unconditionally the Reichswehr's man, although he courted it assiduously. Yet his takeover of power was welcomed, especially since he immediately announced steps toward REARMAMENT (in his speech to the Reichswehr generals on February 3, 1933). After the removal of power from the SA and the liquidation of its plans for a popular militia in the RÖHM AFFAIR (June 30, 1934), the Reichswehr finally made its peace with the National Socialist government and itself introduced the soldiers' oath of loyalty to Hitler personally. From the moment when compulsory military service was reintroduced (March 16, 1935), the Reichswehr was officially called the WEHRMACHT.

Reichswehr Trial (*Reichswehrprozess*), criminal proceeding held before the Leipzig Supreme Court (September 23 to October 4, 1930) against three young officers of the Fifth Ulm Artillery Regiment for conspiring to commit high treason. They were accused of distributing National Socialist propaganda in the Reichswehr, and thus of having worked toward the overthrow of the government. The defense attorney, Hans FRANK, called Hitler as a defense witness; the latter took the famous LEGALITY OATH before the court, stating that he sought power exclusively through legal means. The accused were subsequently sentenced to 18 months' imprisonment in a fortress. One of them, embittered, went over to the Communist party, and justified this in a telegram to Joseph Goebbels: "Hitler betrayed the revolution."

Reichswerke Hermann Göring. *See* Göring Works.

Reich Theater Chamber (Reichstheaterkammer), one of the seven chambers of the REICH CULTURE CHAMBER; it was established on November 1, 1933, by the First Ordinance to Implement the Reich Culture Chamber Law. The Reich Theater Chamber was organized in 1937 into seven divisions or occupational categories that encompassed all professional groups

Reichswehr. President Friedrich Ebert and Armed Forces Minister Gessler inspecting an honor company of the Reichswehr (1922).

engaged in the theater, vaudeville, cabaret, and dance. From 1933 until his death in October 1935, the president was Otto Laubinger; he was followed by Rainer Schlösser, until April 1938. Both were concurrently the head of the Theater Section (Section VI) in the Propaganda Ministry. Ludwig Körner was the next president, followed from April 1942 to 1945 by Paul Hartmann. The vice presidents were Werner KRAUSS (1933 to 1935), Rainer Schlösser (June to November 1935), and finally Eugen Klöpfer. The executive directors were Gustav Assmann, from June 1935 Alfred Eduard FRAUENFELD, and from April 1942 to 1945, Hans Erich Schrade. The Reich Theater Law of May 15, 1934, created the Office of the Reich Drama Critic (Amt des Reichsdramaturgen), and the post was filled by Schlösser. The censorship of stage productions was assigned to him, rather than to the Reich Theater Chamber.

Membership in the Theater Chamber was obligatory for all persons active in the theater, and it was impossible to practice one's profession without belonging. A supposedly considerable autonomy in the chamber was a pretense. In actuality it, like the other individual chambers, was an important instrument of the Propaganda Ministry for the cultural control and manipulation of the public.

S. O.

Reich Vocational Competition (Reichsberufs-wettkampf), program proposed in 1933 by Arthur AXMANN, the head of the Social Services Office in the REICH YOUTH LEADERSHIP, and carried out in concert with the GERMAN LABOR FRONT (DAF). Its purpose was to encourage young people in their vocations and to exercise control over vocational training. The competitions were held in the spring from 1934 to 1939; in 1938 and 1939, as well as in the "Wartime Vocational Competition" in 1944, young adults also took part. The criteria for judging performance included a heavily weighted practical section (valued at 70 points), job-related theory (professional knowledge, technical mathematics, and an essay: 30 points), and a "worldview" (political) exercise (20 points). For girls there was an additional home economics section (30 points). Certain minimum standards had to be met in the sports section.

More than half a million assistants were required to conduct the competition in 1938, which involved some 2.2 million competitors in 1,600 vocational categories, and took place at

Apprentice in the Reich Vocational Competition.

the local, *Gau*, and Reich levels. This outlay did not replace vocational training programs, but it served to motivate a desire for accomplishment and performance. It aided in creating a basis for trust in the system on the part of the "nonorganized," and in arousing hopes for individual advancement in the "victors." Moreover, conspicuous propaganda effects could be achieved through a "showcase competition." Thus the inadequate services provided by the Hitler Youth were revalued, and the sociopolitical situation of apprentices and young workers could be as controlled as were the effects of political propaganda.

H. S.

Reich War Damage Office (Reichskriegsschädenamt), department attached to the Reich Administrative Court on April 15, 1941. Its purpose was to verify and classify damage resulting from combat or from evacuation for military reasons.

Reichwein, Adolf, b. Bad Ems, October 3, 1898; d. Berlin-Plötzensee, October 20, 1944 (executed), German educator and opposition fighter. After involvement as a youth in the WANDERVOGEL, Reichwein joined the workers' movement; he became a member of the Social Democratic Party (SPD) in 1930. He viewed the "overcoming of differences in class, education, and consciousness . . . in the German people" as both a pedagogical and a sociopolitical task, one that he sought to address first in adult education, and then (until his dismissal in 1933) in the "red" teacher training college in Halle.

Adolf Reichwein.

After his demotion to the post of a village schoolteacher, Reichwein for a short time retreated into the inner emigration, but in 1938 he established contact with the opposition through Helmuth Count von MOLTKE. As one of his opposition activities, Reichwein developed ideas for a democratic reorganization of German schooling after the demise of Hitler for the KREISAU CIRCLE; he himself was discussed as a possible Reich minister of culture for that future time. Together with Julius LEBER, Reichwein sought an alliance with the Communist underground (the Saefkow-Jacob-Bästlein group) in 1944. He was arrested while on the way to a meeting on July 4 of that year. After being tortured, he was condemned to death on October 20.

Reich Women's Führerin (*Reichsfrauenführerin*), as of November 1934 the official title of Gertrud SCHOLTZ-KLINK as leader of all the women's organizations in the Third Reich. They were united in the GERMAN WOMEN'S AGENCY, from the National Socialist WOMEN'S UNION to the Women's Office of the German Labor Front and Office III of the German Red Cross. The respective leaders of these organizations constituted the "staff" of the *Führerin*. Scholtz-Klink was responsible to the Reich Leadership of the NSDAP.

Reich Writing Chamber (Reichsschrifttumskammer), one of the seven chambers of the REICH CULTURE CHAMBER; it was established on November 1, 1933, by the First Ordinance to Implement the Reich Culture Chamber Law. The Writing Chamber was organized in 1937

into seven divisions that together encompassed all professional groups and institutions involved in the production, distribution, and sales of nonperiodical literature (with the exception of academic literature). It included the Writers' Group, which emerged from the Reich Association of German Writers, disbanded in October 1935; the Book Trade Group, which grew out of the Reich League of German Book Dealers, Inc.; and the Library Section, which originated from the Association of German Public Librarians.

The first president of the Reich Writing Chamber was Hans Friedrich BLUNCK (as of October 3, 1935, honorary president), and from 1935 to 1945, Hanns JOHST. The vice presidents, who concurrently headed Section VIII (Writing) of the Propaganda Ministry, were P. Wismann (1933–1936), Karlheinz HEDERICH (1936–1939), Alfred-Ingemar Berndt (1939–1941), and until 1945, Wilhelm Haegert. The executive directors were Gunther Haupt (until 1935), and then Richard Suchenwirth, Eduard Koelwel, and Wilhelm Ihde.

Beginning on April 25, 1934, the Writing Chamber produced a "list of harmful and undesirable writing," and thus engaged in book censorship in close cooperation with the Reich Writing Office of the Propaganda Ministry. Membership in the Writing Chamber was obligatory for anyone active in the field of literature, and it was impossible to practice one's profession without membership. In the Writing Chamber, as a part of the cultural Labor Front, all antagonistic group interests of employers and employees were to appear absent, and a supposedly extensive autonomy was a pretense. In actuality the Writing Chamber, like all the other individual chambers, was an important instrument of the Propaganda Ministry for the control and cultural manipulation of the public.

S. O.

Reich Youth Leadership (Reichsjugendführung), department established under Baldur von SCHIRACH on October 30, 1931, within the Reich Leadership of the NSDAP (*see* REICH LEADERS). The Youth Leadership sponsored the National Socialist Secondary School Students' League, the National Socialist Students' League, and the HITLER YOUTH (HJ). On June 17, 1933, it achieved government status through Schirach's nomination as "Youth Führer of the German Reich," which made him the leader of all the German youth organizations. On December 1, 1936, the Youth Leadership became a Supreme Reich Authority (*see* REICH AUTHORITIES)

Reich Youth Leadership. Baldur von Schirach at a Hitler Youth meeting.

through the Law on the Hitler Youth (*Reich Law Gazette* I, p. 993). When Schirach was replaced as Youth Führer by Arthur AXMANN in 1940, all German young people were synchronized into the HJ. Service in it was made "a service of honor to the German *Volk*" (Implementation Ordinance to the Hitler Youth Law of March 25, 1939).

Reinecker, Herbert, b. Hagen/Westphalia, December 24, 1914, German writer. Reinecker first worked as a journalist; he edited the Hitler Youth journal *Jungvolk* (Young *Volk*) in Berlin for the Reich Youth Leadership. His first dramatic work, *Das Dorf bei Odessa* (The Village near Odessa; 1942), became one of the most frequently produced plays of the Third Reich. During the Second World War Reinecker was a war correspondent; in addition, he wrote scripts for feature films. With Alfred WEIDEMANN, he wrote the script for the propaganda film *Junge Adler* (Young Eagles; 1944). After 1945 Reinecker wrote many novels and movie scripts. In particular, his crime series "Der Kommissar" (The Commissioner) and "Derrick" made him by far the most active author in the Federal Republic to write for television.

Reinerth, Hans, b. Bistriţa (Transylvania), May 13, 1900, German historian. Reinerth's research on German prehistory and early Germanic histo-

ry gained him recognition in nationalist and National Socialist circles as a specialist on "Nordic Indo-Germanic peoples" who did not hesitate to make *völkisch* and racist reflections. He was also editor of the periodicals *Germanen-Erbe* (Germanic Heritage) and *Mannus*. In 1933 he was named the leader of the Reich League for German Prehistory, and in 1934 he became a professor in Berlin. After 1945 Reinerth served for many years as head of the Open-Air Museum of German Prehistory on the Bodensee.

"Reinhard," code name for the extermination of Jews in the Generalgouvernement; *see* Reinhard Operation.

Reinhard Operation (*Aktion Reinhard*), camouflage name for the FINAL SOLUTION of the Jewish question in the Generalgouvernement (of Poland), named after Reinhard HEYDRICH, chief of the Reich Security Main Office (RSHA), who had fallen victim to an assassination in late May 1942. To carry out the operation, Heinrich Himmler appointed the SS- *und Polizeiführer* (SS and Police Leader; SSPF) of the Lublin district, Odilo GLOBOCNIK. His assignment consisted primarily of the overall planning for deportations, the construction of extermination camps, the coordination of transports of Jews from the various administrative districts into the camps, the killing of the Jews, and the securing of the property that resulted from the operation and its transfer to the appropriate Reich authorities. To administer all these functions Globocnik added to his office a major division (Einsatz Reinhard), whose administration he gave to Sturmbannführer Hans Höfle (committed suicide in 1962 while in investigative custody in Vienna).

Globocnik's personnel included former workers in the T4 EUTHANASIA operation, whom he installed in key positions. One of the first of them was Christian WIRTH, later a police major (*Kriminalrat*) and SS-*Sturmbannführer,* who first set up the BEŁŻEC extermination camp, then supervised the construction of the camps at SOBIBÓR and TREBLINKA, and in August 1942 became inspector of the camps. In March 1942 Bełżec began "operations" with the extermination of some 35,000 Jews from the ghetto of the city of Lublin. In early May 1942, Sobibór was completed and in July, Treblinka. The task of the remaining SSPFs was to seize the Jews in their respective districts and send them to the extermination camps under the jurisdiction of the SSPF for Lublin. These Jews were deported in special trains with sealed freight cars under the camouflage term *Aussiedlung* ("resettlement"). Because of transportation difficulties caused by the war, the decision was later made not to transport the Jews from the smaller ghettos to the extermination camps; they were shot on the spot. Exempted from the "resettlement" were Jews working in factories important to the war effort. They were put into work camps under the jurisdiction of the SSPFs.

On July 19, 1942, Himmler set December 31 of that year as the date by which the "resettlement" was to be concluded. Except for the inmates in the work camps, at this point there were to be no more Jews left in the Generalgouvernement. At the end of December, Bełzec was the first camp to halt its operations. In Sobibór and Treblinka the deadline was delayed. Not until November 4, 1943, could Globocnik report to Himmler that he had concluded the Reinhard Operation on October 19 of that year and had closed down the camps. A total of at least 1.75 million Jews had fallen victim.

In conclusion, Globocnik put together a report on the "administrative liquidation of the Reinhard Operation," which estimated the "total value of the acquired objects . . . at roughly 180,000,000 RM." It was stressed that this was a conservative estimate and that the market value would be significantly higher. The report made no mention of the immovable property of those who had been murdered. In accordance with Himmler's decree of December 15, 1942, it was put at the disposal of the "fortification of the German *Volk*-nation," especially for resettlers and other preferred applicants.

A. St.

Reinhardt, Fritz, b. Ilmenau, April 3, 1895; d. 1969 (?), German politician and SA-*Obergruppenführer* (November 9, 1937). Reinhardt was trained in business; from 1919 to 1924 he was director of the Thuringian Business School and a tax agent. In 1924 he founded the German Foreign Trade School in Herrsching am Ammersee, where he was also the mayor from 1929 to 1932. He was the NSDAP *Gauleiter* of Upper Bavaria from 1928 to 1930, and a Reichstag deputy from 1930 to 1933. On April 1, 1933, he became a state secretary in the Reich Finance Ministry. Reinhardt was significantly involved in the programs for WORK CREATION and in the financing of REARMAMENT. Sentenced to a prison term in 1945, he was released in 1949. In 1950 an appeals board classified him as a "major offender."

Fritz Reinhardt.

Reinhardt, Max (original surname, Goldmann), b. Baden, near Vienna, September 9, 1873; d. New York, October 30, 1943, Austrian actor, director, and theater manager. After successes as a character actor, from the turn of the century on Reinhardt won a reputation through extravagant productions of the classics, as well as of such socially critical plays as Maxim Gorky's *Night Asylum* (1903). As a theater director in Vienna and Berlin, Reinhardt gave the German-language stage of the 20th century decisive impetus. His penchant for modern works and topically critical plays by such authors as Oscar Wilde, Frank Wedekind, and August Strindberg,

Max Reinhardt.

his unconventional, fantasy-like productions, and his Jewish background led the National Socialists to see him as an "eclectic director" and a "prime example of the Jewization [*Verjudung*] of the German stage." After 1933 he was able to work in Vienna under restricted circumstances for a few more years before finally emigrating to the United States.

Reitsch, Hanna, b. Hirschberg (Silesia), March 29, 1912; d. Frankfurt am Main, August 24, 1979, German aviatrix. Reitsch set numerous glider records in the 1930s, and in 1937 was appointed the first female flight captain. In 1938, as a test pilot with Berlin's Deutschlandhalle (Germany Hangar), she flew the first really practical helicopter in the world, the Fw 61. Later, after entering the Luftwaffe, she tested a very wide range of military equipment: the Me 163 rocket fighter plane, the Me 323 "Giant" large-capacity aircraft, and the Fi 103 "Cherry Pit" bomber, better known as the V1.

Reitsch was an avid admirer of Hitler, who awarded her the Iron Cross, First Class, in 1942. As Field Marshal Robert von GREIM's pilot, she visited the Führer in the bunker under the Reich Chancellery from April 26 to 29, 1945. Afterward she was miraculously able to take off and fly out of embattled Berlin. After 15 months of American internment, Reitsch was freed in 1946, and devoted herself once again to motorless flight. At the age of 58 she set a German record. She viewed the Third Reich more critically in her memoirs (1975).

Hanna Reitsch.

Relativity Theory (*Relativitätstheorie*), theory of physics developed by Albert EINSTEIN in 1905 and 1915; it explains the structure of space and time, and has become the basis of the modern scientific view of the world. Because of the Jewish origins of its discoverer, the Relativity Theory was seen by the National Socialists as a typical example of the "undermining of the lucid, unifying Germanic-German view of the world and nature, which honors the great laws of nature, by abstract, fragmentizing Jewish thought, which disregards these laws." Research on the consequences of the Relativity Theory was thus as unwelcome in the Third Reich as publications or instruction on it. Werner HEISENBERG, for example, won the right to speak about the Relativity Theory in his lectures only through a court trial.

Religious instruction (*Religionsunterricht*), a controversial topic in the CHURCH STRUGGLE for both of the large denominations, Catholic and Protestant, during the Third Reich. From the outset, National Socialist school authorities attempted to check the influence of the churches over religious instruction [which in Germany was conducted in the public schools], even though it was guaranteed in the CONCORDAT and at first was actually encouraged, although the aim was to remove it from the clergy insofar as possible. Moreover, through deliberate pressure, the intention later was to put an end to religious instruction by organizing service in the Hitler Youth in such a way that conflicts would be created. At the age of 14 [the beginning of compulsory Hitler Youth membership], it was traditional for a schoolboy to announce his readiness to join the church; in Austria, where the German Concordat did not apply, one had to register to join (according to a decree of August 29, 1939).

During the war, religious instruction was often enough simply not given, owing to the lack of teachers. Offers by the church to assist with volunteers were simply not answered or were criticized as an inappropriate intervention in school matters. Especially in rural areas, however, the authorities had only partial success in their efforts to stifle religious instruction, because the population complained and the clergy countervened the persecutions with activities such as private Bible study.

Remagen, city north of Koblenz on the left bank of the Rhine, with a population of 5,505 in 1939. The Ludendorff Bridge, 330 m (about 1,100 feet) long, which crossed the Rhine at

American troops on the railroad bridge at Remagen.

Erich Maria Remarque.

Remagen, had been built between 1916 and 1918. It became the springboard for the American entry into central Germany on March 7, 1945. The German engineers failed to blow up the bridge in time, so that the Ninth United States Armored Division was able to convey 8,000 men to the eastern bank of the Rhine within 24 hours. They succeeded in securing the bridgehead against German air attack by means of antiaircraft fire and fighter planes. Even a German bombardment with 11 V2 rockets from Arnheim accomplished nothing. By the time the Remagen bridge collapsed under the weight of transport vehicles and as a result of bomb strikes on March 17, 1945 (leaving 46 dead), 18 American battalions had crossed the Rhine. Germany's collapse was thus accelerated by many weeks. Hitler had five officers assigned to the bridge area sentenced to death; four of the sentences were carried out.

Remarque, Erich Maria (originally, E. P. Remark), b. Osnabrück, June 22, 1898; d. Locarno (Switzerland), September 29, 1970, German writer. Remarque's novel *Im Westen nichts Neues* (*All Quiet on the Western Front;* 1929) made him famous—or, from the National Socialist perspective, infamous—overnight. The book portrayed the war without cosmetics, and depicted the "hero's death," so often and readily glorified, as a miserable biting of the dust. For that reason, NS criticism accused Remarque of creating "tendential caricatures of frontline soldiers" and "corroding the *Volk* spirit."

At the first showing of the film version of the antiwar novel, in Berlin early in December 1930, the SA created a demonstration by setting off stink bombs and releasing white mice in the movie house. At the request of two state (*Land*) governments, the film was finally banned. In 1931 Remarque went to Switzerland; in 1938 the National Socialists revoked his citizenship. He emigrated to the United States in 1939, although he later returned to Switzerland. Remarque's other novels include *Der Weg zurück* (*The Road Back;* 1931), *Drei Kameraden* (*Three Comrades;* 1938), *Arc de Triomphe* (*Arch of Triumph;* 1946), and *Die Nacht von Lissabon* (*The Night in Lisbon;* 1962).

Remer, Otto-Ernst, b. Neubrandenburg, August 18, 1912, German major general (January 31, 1945). As the commander of the Berlin Guard Battalion, Remer became a key figure in the failure of the coup of the TWENTIETH OF JULY, 1944. Ordered by the city commandant, Paul HASE, to arrest Joseph Goebbels, the young major let himself be persuaded by the propaganda minister to telephone the Führer's headquarters. Remer spoke directly with Hitler, who promoted him to colonel on the spot. Remer then carried out the opposite order, arresting the conspirators. This was relatively easy, since the news of Hitler's survival made the putsch crumble quickly. After the war, Remer helped found the later prohibited radical right-wing Socialist Reich Party (SRP); up until the 1980s he attracted attention as an agitator on the extreme Right. In 1985 he was sentenced to pay a fine for defaming the memory of the dead (the martyrs of July 20).

Otto-Ernst Remer.

"Remnant Czechia." *See* Residual Czech state.

Renn, Ludwig (originally, Arnold Vieth von Gols-senau), b. Dresden, April 22, 1889; d. Berlin, July 21, 1979, German writer. Renn was a battalion commander in the First World War, and until 1920 a captain in the Dresden security police. After studies in the theory and history of culture, he gained an impressive success in 1928 with his first book, *Krieg* (War), a sober and realistic antiwar novel, although because of it he was exposed to incessant attacks from nationalist circles. That same year, Renn joined the Communist Party (KPD) and the Red Frontline Fighters' League. He became secretary of the

Ludwig Renn.

league's proletarian-revolutionary writers, and editor of the Communist literary periodicals *Linkskurve* (Curve to the Left) and *Aufbruch* (New Start).

Through his other, socialist-oriented works, like *Nachkrieg* (Postwar; 1930) and *Russland-fahrten* (Russia Voyages; 1932), Renn became one of the most important Communist writers of the Weimar Republic. His travels in the USSR were interpreted in 1932 as "literary high treason," and after the Reichstag fire he was sentenced to two and a half years in prison. Subsequently, he fought as chief of staff of the Eleventh International Brigade in the Spanish Civil War, and then lived in Mexico until 1947. There, among other posts, he served as president of the antifascist emigré-organization movement Freies Deutschland (For a Free Germany). After returning to Germany, Renn assumed numerous high functions in the cultural life of the German Democratic Republic.

H. H.

Renner, Karl, b. Untertannowitz (Moravia), December 14, 1870; d. Vienna, December 31, 1950, Austrian politician and jurist. In 1907 Renner was a Social Democratic deputy in the Reichsrat. After the collapse of the monarchy he was state chancellor from 1918 to 1920, and in 1919–1920 he was foreign minister. As head of the Austrian peace delegation in Saint-Germain, Renner fought passionately but in vain for an ANSCHLUSS with the German state. From 1920 to 1934 he was a deputy in the National Council (Nationalrat), and from 1931 to 1934, its president. He withdrew from politics after the victory of AUSTROFASCISM and numerous arrests. Renner welcomed 1938, despite his criticism of the military form that the Anschluss ultimately took. Even before the end of the war, he formed a provisional Austrian government, on April 27, 1945. He was one of the founders of the Social Democratic Party of Austria. From the end of 1945 until his death Renner was the first president of the new Republic of Austria.

Renteln, Theodor Adrian von, b. Khodzi (Russia), September 15, 1897; d. in the Soviet Union, 1946 (executed), German politician. Renteln studied law and economics, then became a journalist. He joined the NSDAP in 1928, and from 1929 to 1932 was Reich Leader of the National Socialist Secondary School Students' League. In 1931–1932 he was Führer of the Hitler Youth, in 1932 a Reichstag deputy, and from June 1933 to 1935 president of the German Council of

Theodor Adrian von Renteln.

Industry and Trade. He was then staff leader in the German Labor Front (DAF), and in 1940, head (*Hauptamtsleiter*) of the Trade and Artisanship Section of the NSDAP Reich Leadership. Renteln's numerous other offices included the chairmanship of the Supreme Honor Court of the DAF. In 1941 he was appointed general commissioner in Lithuania (Reich Commissariat Ostland). There he was involved in the plundering that formed part of German occupation policies, as well as in the persecution of Jews. After the war, the Soviets hanged him as a war criminal.

Reparations, term introduced in 1918–1919 to denote compensatory payments imposed on the loser after a war. Judging Germany as bearing the entire responsibility for the First World War, as charged in ARTICLE 231 of the Versailles treaty, the victorious powers gave Germany the sole responsibility for paying reparations for Allied war costs and losses. These payments were at the same time thought of as a punishment, and were meant to weaken Germany to the extent that it could never again take up arms. Even among the victors there was no agreement over the amount of reparations. At first a preliminary payment of 20 billion gold marks for the years 1919–1921 was decided on; then a series of meetings resulted in a total demand of 226 billion gold marks (January 1921), to which the Germans counteroffered 30 billion. The conflict escalated in the RUHR CONFLICT and could not be settled even through an Allied ultimatum of 132 billion gold marks at

the conclusion of the second London Conference on May 5, 1921 (*see* LONDON CONFERENCES).

The economic consequences of Germany's overburdening (in particular, INFLATION) became a threat to the victorious powers as well, and in 1924 the DAWES PLAN created an accommodation of reparations that was more in keeping with Germany's ability to pay. In 1929 the YOUNG PLAN set forth a final regulation of reparations: 34.5 billion RM, in 59 yearly installments. This schedule was soon undermined by the world economic crisis. On July 1, 1931, the one-year so-called Hoover Moratorium for all inter-Allied war debts and reparations took effect. The obligations were then totally canceled by the Lausanne Agreement of July 9, 1932 (after a final German payment of bonds worth 3 billion RM). According to German figures, the Weimar Republic up to that point had made reparations payments totaling 53 billion gold marks, a bloodletting whose political price was a growing radicalization. The reparations, as the most visible and painful consequence of the Versailles treaty, contributed significantly to the rejection of the Republican system in Germany and fostered National Socialist agitation, in particular.

Reprisal (*Repressalie*), in international law, a retaliation measure that is not bound by international law when proclaimed and carried out in reaction to a breach of international law suffered by the perpetrator. Examples of reprisals are the occupation of foreign territory, the taking and executing of hostages (in set quotas), the seizure

Reparations. A French sentry guards a coal shipment destined for France.

of property from the government that provoked the reprisal, and a blockade. It is counter to international law to continue a reprisal after the cessation of its cause, or to carry out a reprisal on the order of, or with the intent to harm, a third state. In the Second World War, reprisals were chiefly an instrument for combating partisan resistance, but they often escalated to pure terrorism.

Repubblica Sociale Italiana (RSI), official designation for the Republic of SALÒ.

Republican Judges' League (Republikanischer Richterbund), organization of judges and members of other law-related professions, founded in 1922 as an antipode to the reactionary German Judges' League (Deutscher Richterbund). The Republican Judges' League called for an express profession of belief in the Weimar Republic and its constitution, supported legal reform in its spirit, and viewed criticism of the judicial system as one of its primary tasks. Thus, it characterized the 1924 HITLER TRIAL as a farce and called the judgment against Friedrich EBERT in the treason trial of December 1924 a "shameless judicial decision." The mouthpiece of such criticism was the journal *Die Justiz* (Justice), founded in 1925.

With some 800 members in 1931, the Republican Judges' League represented approximately 5 percent of the judiciary. For a considerable period it believed in the possibility of a judicial restraint of National Socialism; only as of 1930 did it recognize the full extent of the political danger. One of the league's members, Robert KEMPNER, in 1932 wrote the lucid analysis *Justizdämmerung—Auftakt zum 3. Reich* (Twilight of Justice: Prelude to the Third Reich). By dissolving itself in March 1933, the league avoided being closed down by the state. Unlike the German Judges' League, it was not reconstituted after the war in 1945.

Republic Protection Law (*Republikschutzgesetz*), designation for the constitution-amending Law for the Protection of the Republic (*Gesetz zum Schutze der Republik*) of July 21, 1922. The law was promulgated with a validity of five years, after numerous attacks from the Right and the Left against the Weimar Republic in 1921–1922, and after the assassination of Foreign Minister Walther RATHENAU on June 24, 1922. It was revised on March 31 and July 8, 1926, and extended by the Reichstag for a further two years on June 2, 1927. It was then replaced by a considerably weaker set of provisions in the

Second Law for the Protection of the Republic. This law became invalid on December 20, 1932. In the meantime, the German government had come to depend more heavily on the use of emergency decrees as provided in Article 48 of the Weimar Constitution.

The Republic Protection Law protected the life and honor of members of the national and state (*Land*) governments. It imposed sanctions for condoning acts of violence and for disparaging and libeling the Republican form of government, the Constitution, or the Republic's colors. The law gave the central governments of the constituent states full authority to prohibit political parties, meetings, and publications that were inimical to the Constitution (an example was the prohibition of the *Völkischer Beobachter* in 1923). On November 15, 1923, Prussia prohibited the NSDAP on the ground that it violated the terms of the law; corresponding bans were promulgated by the states of Saxony, Thuringia, Baden, Hesse, Braunschweig, and Hamburg. The State Court for the Protection of the Republic (Staatsgerichtshof zum Schutz der Republik) was established in the Supreme Court to execute the law and to function as an appeals court; on June 2, 1927, its jurisdiction was transferred to the regular courts. According to the remarks of Reich Justice Minister Gustav Radbruch, the law was initially promulgated against the threat from the Right, but it was increasingly used against dangers from the extreme Left. It proved useless as a weapon against National Socialism, since it could not compensate for the failing democratic and Republican convictions of the majority of the population.

B.-J. W.

"Request Concert" ("Wunschkonzert für die Wehrmacht"), by far the most popular entertainment program on German radio during the Second World War; it was a continuation of the "Request Concert for the WINTER RELIEF AGENCY." The moderator was Heinz Goedecke. The program was first broadcast on October 1, 1939, and every Sunday thereafter from 4:00 to 8:00 p.m. from the Great Broadcasting Studio in Berlin. Its motto was: "The front now reaches out its hands to the homeland; the homeland, however, gives the front a hand." Within the framework of a musical program, requests, greetings, and news were exchanged between soldiers in the field and listeners at home, often the first contact in a long time.

The "Request Concert" naturally presented chiefly happy and good news, such as its "Regis-

Heinz Goedecke in the film *Wunschkonzert.*

try of Births": introduced by a baby's cry, it announced to many infantrymen that they had become fathers. The program, in which renowned artists took part, also broadcast donation drives for soldiers, emergencies, and the Winter Relief Agency. It transmitted a popular musical blend of classics, tearjerkers, and regional and marching songs. The biggest hits included "Erika" and "That Can't Shock a Sailor." The goal of the strictly censored live broadcast (in case of a hitch, a censor could cause a technical malfunction) was to reinforce the sense of community. Its success in this endeavor was substantiated by a Security Service (SD) report of April 1940, according to which the program awakened "in thousands the experience of the *Volk* Community." *Wunschkonzert* was also the name of a much-celebrated film romance of 1940, starring Ilse Werner and Carl Raddatz.

R. H.

Resettlement (*Umsiedlung*), the assignment of new places of residence to certain groups of people or nationalities. Resettlement as it was carried out after the First World War or according to agreements between states (as in the cases of the SOUTH TYROL and ESTONIA) served to mitigate the problems of certain MINORITIES. Compulsory resettlement, as ordered in the course of the German conquests or with the advance of the Red Army during and after the Second World War, constitutes EXPULSION, which is prohibited by international law. In National Socialist usage, the term "resettlement" also served as a synonym for deportation, and often for the extermination that took place at the destination (*see* FINAL SOLUTION).

Residential restriction [house arrest] (*Aufenthaltsbeschränkung*), limitation of freedom of

movement in order to discipline objectionable critics; it was often combined with police surveillance. Residential restriction was frequently imposed on oppositional clergy to prevent their contact with their congregations. The legal basis was the REICHSTAG FIRE DECREE of February 28, 1933.

Residual Czech state (Resttschechei, or "remnant Czechia"), dismissive National Socialist propaganda term for the territory of the Czechoslovak state in the wake of the MUNICH AGREEMENT. It intentionally omitted the Slovak component since Slovakia was the next area to be split off. Thus, the "destruction of the residual Czech state" (March 1939) could be passed off as an act carried out to maintain order (*see* CZECHOSLOVAKIA).

Résistance, the French resistance organization in the Second World War. The Résistance arose as a response to Charles de Gaulle's June 18, 1940, call to resist, issued from London. From isolated, uncoordinated beginnings in 1941–1942 it developed into a regionally organized underground movement that transcended parties, although it was not without inner tensions. It resisted the encroachments of the German occupation army in the occupied northern zone (the forcible recruiting of work forces, economic plundering, and the shooting of hostages) and also the COLLABORATION in Vichy France and Algeria.

The Résistance gained important reinforcements after the German attack on the Soviet Union of June 22, 1941, through the disciplined underground cadres of the Communist party with their own fighting forces, the Franc-Tireurs Partisans Français (French Partisan Snipers; FTPF). The range of operations of the Résistance encompassed passive opposition; strikes; the organizing of escapes, assassinations, and sabotage; the transmittal of information to Allied secret services; and contacts with the London government-in-exile. It also involved the delivery of weapons from London for the Maquis operations, which often cut off German supplies and contained strong German forces. German retaliatory measures reached their culmination on June 10, 1944, in ORADOUR-SUR-GLANE.

Although the Résistance originated chiefly with politicians, military men, and intellectuals, later on all levels of the population, across party lines, found themselves united in it. On May 27, 1943, de Gaulle, through his emissary Jean Moulin, achieved a merger of most of the resistance groups in the Conseil National de la Résistance (CNR), and the latter's subordination to France Libre (Free France). The FTPF and numerous other resistance groups on February 1, 1944, were merged in the Forces Françaises de l'Intérieur (French Home Army; FFI). Dwight D. Eisenhower estimated that they represented a combat equivalent of about 15 divisions; they were later merged with the regular army.

After the Allied landing on June 6, 1944, France demonstrated its claim to an international role as a Great Power by the participation of the fighting forces of France Libre, the FFI, and the Maquis in the liberation of France. De Gaulle brought many members of the Résistance into his first cabinet on September 9 of that year. After the failure of the Third Republic, there developed from the Résistance members, and particularly from their leftist intellectual representatives, a strong, progressive impulse as a kind of "spiritual conscience of the nation." It called for the spiritual and moral self-assertion and political renewal of France in the Fourth Republic, as well as for a modernized economy and social reforms.

Estimates of the Résistance dead vary considerably. They are believed to number between 20,000 and 30,000 executed and some 75,000 more who were deported and did not survive

Résistance. Members of the FFI.

imprisonment in the German concentration camps. Besides the German occupation forces, French collaborators and the gendarmerie took part in the executions. After the liberation this led to a bloody legal and illegal "settling of accounts" between resistance fighters and collaborators that is said to have resulted in a further 8,000 to 10,000 victims. This topic, as well as the difficult question of a clear-cut demarcation between Résistance and collaboration, has in recent years been the subject of controversy in France.

B.-J. W.

Restitution (*Wiedergutmachung*), financial payments made by the Federal Republic of Germany to victims of National Socialist violence, or to their survivors. They received or receive individual payments in the form of restitution of expropriated assets and/or compensation for property or personal losses. The restitution was initially regulated in the Western occupation zones by laws of the Allied military government, and in Berlin by an order from the Allied commandant's office. It was then provided for by the Federal Restitution Law (*Bundesrückerstattungsgesetz*; BRÜG) of July 19, 1957. The right to compensation was at first included in various state and federal laws and is now guaranteed in the Federal Compensation Law (*Bundesentschädigungsgesetz*; BEG) of June 29, 1956. According to it, anyone who was persecuted on political, racial, religious, or ideological grounds by National Socialist tyranny and who as a result suffered harm to his or her life, health, freedom, or property, or in his or her professional or economic advancement, has a right to compensation as long as his claim was submitted by April 1, 1958. Former members of the NSDAP or its divisions (except for merely nominal members), and persons who supported the NS tyranny, cannot receive restitution. By 1981 approximately 3.9 billion DM had been paid in restitution on the basis of the BRÜG, and another 50.1 billion DM on the basis of the BEG.

A distinction must be made between individual restitution and global restitution. The latter is based on bilateral treaties according to which the Federal Republic makes payments to numerous states affected by NS terror and to international organizations. They include, above all, 3 billion DM to Israel and 450 million DM to the Jewish worldwide organization, in accordance with the German-Israeli Restitution Agreement of September 10, 1952. This treaty was especially controversial in Israel because of what some saw as an underlying German ransom mentality, in light of the unatonable wrong of the FINAL SOLUTION. Other recipients of restitution include the United Nations High Commission for Refugees, Yugoslavia, Poland, Czechoslovakia, Hungary, Austria, Great Britain, France, the Netherlands, Belgium, Greece, Italy, Switzerland, Luxembourg, Norway, and Sweden. By the end of 1980, total restitution payments amounted to approximately 63.4 billion DM; the total amount of restitution made is estimated at more than 85 billion DM.

[In early 1990, both Austria and the German Democratic Republic acknowledged for the first time that those of their citizens who had suffered from NS persecution were due restitution from the successor governments.]

R. B.

Revaluation of all values (*Umwertung aller Werte*), National Socialist slogan taken over from the late works of Friedrich NIETZSCHE. In revaluing all values, Nietzsche wanted to juxtapose new values "beyond good and evil" to the "senselessness" of the world, by demanding an elite of the "physically and intellectually strong." For him the mass, the "slaves and herd animals," counted for nothing. Only the SUPERMAN, the "hero" and tyrannical ruler, was important: "The Revolution made Napoleon possible: that is its justification. For a similar prize one would wish for an anarchistic collapse of our whole civilization." This concept of an elite was converted into the NS ideology of the elect, with its demand for a "new justice": "Domination for the strong, slavery for the weak" (Alfred Baeumler, in *Nietzsche. Der Philosoph und Politiker;* 1931).

H. H.

Reventlow, Ernst Count von, b. Husum, August 18, 1869; d. Munich, November 21, 1943, German politician. Reventlow retired from naval service as a lieutenant commander, and then became a freelance writer. He sharply criticized the policies and governing style of Wilhelm II, but after the First World War just as uncompromisingly criticized the Weimar Republic. Reventlow joined the VÖLKISCH MOVEMENT and in 1924 was elected to the Reichstag as a deputy for it. In 1928 he was elected for the NSDAP, which he had joined the previous year. His publications included *Deutscher Sozialismus* (German Socialism; 1930). In the journal *Der Reichswart* (The Reich Guardian), which he founded in 1920, Reventlow evolved from a social revolutionary to a nationalist, and from a

proponent of the GERMAN FAITH MOVEMENT, in which he played a leading role from 1934 to 1936, to a practicing Christian.

Revisionist policy (*Revisionspolitik*), comprehensive term for efforts made from 1919 on to correct those terms of the Versailles treaty that were felt to be especially discriminatory toward Germany. Revisionist policy was directed chiefly against territorial losses, against the WAR GUILT LIE and the COLONIAL LIE, and against the military-political restrictions (*see* DISARMAMENT) and the heavy REPARATIONS. The Weimar government pursued its revisionist policy through peaceful means and through negotiations in order to facilitate Germany's return to the concert of the Great Powers. It was able to achieve considerable success in this area by the end of 1932, such as the initially temporary regulation of reparations (*see* DAWES PLAN; YOUNG PLAN) and later their final regulation in the Lausanne Agreement of July 9, 1932; the early withdrawal of Allied troops from the Rhineland by 1930; and the fundamental recognition of German equality at the Geneva Disarmament Conference on December 11, 1932.

For National Socialist FOREIGN POLICY, on the other hand, revisionist policy served a threefold and far more aggressive function: (1) as an important preliminary step for German hegemony on the Continent and the conquest of "living space in the east"; (2) as a domestic-policy means of winning over the conservative elite and the population as a whole, and a propagandistic preparation for the attack on Poland in 1939; (3) seen from without, as a way of disguising expansionist aims toward the Western governments (*see* APPEASEMENT).

The individual stages of revisionist policy from 1933 on should be evaluated in terms of this triple function. They were: the reintroduction of COMPULSORY MILITARY SERVICE (March 16, 1935), the RHINELAND OCCUPATION (March 7, 1936), the ANSCHLUSS with Austria (March 14, 1938), the annexation of the Sudetenland according to the terms of the MUNICH AGREEMENT (early October 1938), and the reannexation of MEMELLAND (March 22, 1939). The German entry into Prague on March 15, 1939, clearly overstepped revisionist policy. The GERMAN-POLISH NONAGGRESSION PACT of January 26, 1934, the renunciation of rights to the SOUTH TYROL, and the inconsistent treatment of colonial demands vis-à-vis England prove beyond a doubt the functional character that revisionist policy had for Hitler: revisionist demands could fade in or fade out according to foreign-policy expediency.

B.-J. W.

Revue film (*Revuefilm*), popular genre of film entertainment in which the story serves merely as an excuse for music and dance scenes. It was particularly successful during the Third Reich. At the end of the 1920s, the early talking films created the prerequisites for the revue film, which in Germany carried on the traditions of the operetta and the vaudeville, but which after 1933 modeled itself after the Hollywood classics. (American musicals were shown in movie houses in major German cities until 1939.)

The German revue film suffered from the fact that international stars avoided Germany after 1933, or, if they were "non-Aryan," could not even appear in films there. As a result, the German film industry promoted popular favorites who were considered more "homemade," such as Marika RÖKK or Johannes Heesters. The German revue film composers had to lag behind the vivacity of their American models, since even the smallest borrowings from JAZZ could lead to objections. In décor, costumes, and scenery, however, no expense was spared. *Der weisse Traum* (The White Dream) in 1943 was one of the most expensive productions, at over 2 million RM. Especially during the war, the revue film served as a diversion from everyday routine. It conformed to National Socialist collectivism in its rhythmic crowd scenes, and

portrayed women with the desired combination of erotic stimulus and servile femininity, as in the most successful film during the Third Reich, *Die grosse Liebe* (The Great Love; 1942), with Zarah LEANDER, which was seen by 27 million spectators. Most of the directors, composers, and actors associated with the German revue film were able to continue their work without a break in the 1950s. (*See also* FILM.)

Rexists, followers of the Walloon authoritarian, antidemocratic Christ-the-King Movement, founded in Belgium in 1930 by Léon DE-GRELLE. The Rexists were named after the Christus Rex publishing house, which issued the group's periodical, *Rex.* They emerged from the militant youth wing of Catholic Action and distanced themselves from their church roots by means of nationalistic demands and denominational open-mindedness. They advocated a corporatist order based on the principle of "natural communities" (family, work, and *Volk*), and in so doing found a resonance in the Flemish sector of the population. (In the elections of May 24, 1936, the Rexists elected 21 deputies and 12 senators.) Drifting ever closer to the fascist camp, the Rexists lost considerable sections of the vote as early as 1938. After the German occupation of Belgium in May 1940, they formed the backbone of the COLLABORATION; many voluntarily joined the Waffen-SS and

Revue film. Zarah Leander and Viktor Staal in *Die grosse Liebe.*

Arrest of two Rexists in Belgium.

fought in the "Wallonie" armored infantry division. After the war numerous Rexist leaders were brought to trial, and most were given death sentences.

Reynaud, Paul, b. Barcelonette, October 15, 1878; d. Paris, September 21, 1966, French politician and jurist. Reynaud was a Democratic Alliance deputy from 1919 to 1940. He held various ministerial posts from 1930 to 1932, and for a time was chairman of the League to Combat Antisemitism. From 1938 to 1940 Reynaud served successfully as minister of finance. An opponent of the APPEASEMENT course followed by Prime Minister Édouard DALADIER, Reynaud himself assumed this post in March 1940.

Reynaud was also minister of defense when the German offensive began on May 10, 1940. He could not deflect the catastrophe, since his support for Gen. Charles de Gaulle's concept of a massing of tanks came too late. Reynaud fled with the government to Bordeaux, but he was unable to carry out his plan to continue the war from the colonies and had to cede to Marshal Henri PÉTAIN. Arrested by the Vichy government and handed over to Germany in 1942, Reynaud was imprisoned in concentration camps (Buchenwald and Sachsenhausen, among others). After the war he again served (from 1946 to 1962) as a deputy (Independent Republican). He was an advocate of European unification, one of the architects of the Fifth Republic, and a critic of de Gaulle.

Paul Reynaud.

Rhineland occupation (*Rheinlandbesetzung*), the entry of German troops (joyously greeted by the population), amounting to about one division, into the demilitarized Rhineland zone on March 7, 1936. In terms of international law, the Rhineland occupation represented a unilateral violation of the VERSAILLES TREATY (Articles 42ff.) and of the freely contracted LOCARNO PACT of October 16, 1925 (Articles 1, 2, and 4). Thus, for the contracting parties it constituted a kind of "aggressive action" that undermined the alliance. The Western powers, however, reacted only with a special session of the Council of the League of Nations and a condemnation of the German action (on grounds of both international law and morality). Italy remained wholly on the sidelines because of its own involvement in the war in ABYSSINIA.

Hitler carried out the surprise move, which he later called "the most tense period of my life," like a gambler, entirely on his own initiative and against the explicit verdict of his military and political advisers. Aware of the army's totally inadequate level of rearmament, he gave the order to immediately withdraw the troops at the first sign of "contact with the enemy." Having astutely calculated the pacifist mood in the Western states, he linked the breach of the treaty on March 7 to a new offer of a treaty: a 25-year nonaggression pact with France, Belgium, and the Netherlands, to be guaranteed by England and Italy. It would provide for a demilitarized zone on both sides of the western border; an air pact; equality of colonial rights; and Germany's return to a reorganized League of Nations.

The ratification of the Franco-Soviet Treaty of Alliance on February 27, 1936, and the accusation that with it Paris had harmed European security interests, were merely pretexts for the Rhineland occupation. The occupation was, moreover, only superficially an instance of REVISIONIST POLICY against the Versailles treaty. Behind it, with an eye to war, loomed Germany's aims of freedom of action in the east and southeast through securing the western border (*see* WESTWALL), and the intention of assuring the regime both the loyalty of the masses at home and legitimacy through foreign successes. (In the Reichstag elections of March 29, 1936, the action was approved by the usual 98.3 percent of the votes.) The APPEASEMENT policy of the Western powers was based on a general overestimation of German military strength, on domestic difficulties (particularly in France), on a strong belief in defensive warfare (the Magi-

Rhineland occupation. German troops cross the Rhine near Cologne.

not Complex), and on a certain recognition of the legitimacy of the German demands for revision "in its own backyard."

Beyond the relatively meaningless act of the occupation itself, the Rhineland occupation had very far-reaching consequences. Hitler's triumph and the considerable growth of his prestige both domestically and internationally are believed to have enormously fostered his overestimation of himself and his claim to infallibility. He became increasingly deaf to the advice and warnings of military and political experts. At the same time, the occupation overturned a pillar of the 20th-century European system of alliances and security. There prevailed a general shock over the inaction of the Western powers, especially France, and the view that the fortification of Germany's western border would make an active French intervention on behalf of the threatened powers almost impossible in the future. These factors induced the small and medium-sized countries between the Baltic Sea and the Balkans increasingly and henceforth very quickly to turn away from the West and toward Berlin. We know today that an energetic military reaction by the Western powers to the breach of the treaty would have led, within a few days, to the military collapse of the German Reich.

B.-J. W.

Ribbentrop, Joachim von, b. Wesel, April 30, 1893; d. Nuremberg, October 16, 1946 (executed), German politician. Ribbentrop had little success in school, as a bank trainee, and as a casual laborer in Canada and the United States. In the First World War he ended up as a first lieutenant. The handsome Ribbentrop in 1920 married Annelies Henkell, the daughter of an extremely wealthy champagne maker. Ribbentrop took over as the company's agent in Berlin (and thus acquired his nickname, "the traveling wine salesman"). In 1925, after being adopted by an aristocratic aunt, he was able to add "von" to his name; he headed a large household in Dahlem, outside Berlin. There, after Ribbentrop joined the NSDAP (May 1, 1932), Franz von

Joachim von Ribbentrop.

Papen and Hitler often met to prepare for the Seizure of Power, after which Ribbentrop advanced quickly (*see* RIBBENTROP OFFICE).

As Hitler's foreign-policy adviser, Ribbentrop had an astounding diplomatic success on June 18, 1935, with the GERMAN-BRITISH NAVAL AGREEMENT, which led to his appointment as German ambassador to London (August 1936–January 1938). Because of his arrogant and tactless behavior, he continually met with rejection, which he interpreted as proof of irreconcilable German-British differences.

This conviction later influenced Ribbentrop as foreign minister (as of February 4, 1938), although in his pliability toward Hitler he was hardly more than a special envoy. Ribbentrop saw the GERMAN-SOVIET NONAGGRESSION PACT of August 23, 1939, which covered Hitler's rear for the Polish Campaign, as a personal victory for himself. During the war he suffered as a result of the declining importance of his office. Such treaties as the THREE-POWER AGREEMENT and the VIENNA AWARDS did not alter the situation at all, especially since Ribbentrop, as a representative of a Wilhelmine imperialism, scarcely understood the true goals of Hitler's FOREIGN POLICY. In order not to lose his connection, he placed himself and his office wholly at the service of the FINAL SOLUTION, exerting pressure on dependent and allied countries to hand Jewish citizens over to the SS. Arrested on June 14, 1945, Ribbentrop was found guilty of all charges in the Nuremberg trial of the major war criminals, and was sentenced to death. His memoirs, *Zwischen London und Moskau* (Between London and Moscow; translated as *The Ribbentrop Memoirs*), appeared posthumously in 1953.

Ribbentrop-Molotov Pact. *See* German-Soviet Nonaggression Pact.

Ribbentrop Office (Dienststelle Ribbentrop), Joachim von RIBBENTROP's foreign-policy institution; it competed with Alfred Rosenberg's FOREIGN POLICY OFFICE OF THE NSDAP and the Foreign Ministry under Konstantin von NEURATH. The Ribbentrop Office was located on the Wilhelmstrasse in Berlin, in the former Prussian Foreign Ministry. Developing in 1934 from the office that Ribbentrop headed as delegate for disarmament issues, it was particularly involved with German-British relations. It prepared the GERMAN-BRITISH NAVAL AGREEMENT and was Ribbentrop's stepping-stone for the posts of ambassador to London (1936–1938) and foreign minister (as of February 4, 1938). The

Ribbentrop Office, financed by special donations (among them the ADOLF HITLER DONATION), at times had as many as 300 employees, among them businessmen with good contacts abroad. After Ribbentrop took over the Foreign Office, the Ribbentrop Office closed.

Richthofen, Wolfram Baron von, b. Barzdorf (Silesia), October 10, 1895; d. Lüneburg, July 12, 1945, German field marshal (February 16, 1943). Initially a hussar in the First World War, in 1917 Richthofen became a fighter pilot in the Richthofen Squadron of his cousin Manfred von Richthofen (d. April 21, 1918). After the war he studied mechanical engineering and later joined the Weapons Office of the Armed Forces Ministry; in 1933 he became head of the Testing Division in the Reich Air Ministry. In January 1937 Richthofen became chief of staff of the CONDOR LEGION in the Spanish Civil War, leading it in the last months of the war until its return in May 1939. After the Polish Campaign he took over the Eighth Air Corps, which he commanded in France, the Balkans, and Russia. In June 1942 Richthofen became commander in chief of Air Fleet 4 in the east, and a year later he commanded Air Fleet 2 in Italy. A serious illness (a brain tumor) ended his military career in October 1944, and shortly after the end of the war it led to his death.

Riefenstahl, Leni, b. Berlin, August 22, 1902, German actress, dancer, and film director. Riefenstahl was discovered for the cinema in the 1920s. She had roles in *Der heilige Berg* (The Holy Mountain; 1926) and *Die weisse Hölle vom Piz Palü* (The White Hell of Mount Palü; 1929),

Wolfram von Richthofen.

Leni Riefenstahl.

among other films. The first feature film she directed, *Das blaue Licht* (The Blue Light; 1932), brought her to Hitler's attention. He entrusted her with National Socialist propaganda films, which eventually included *Sieg des Glaubens* (Victory of Faith; 1933) and *Triumph des Willens* (TRIUMPH OF THE WILL; 1934), about the first two Reich Party Congresses of the NSDAP after the Seizure of Power; *Tag der Freiheit—unsere Wehrmacht* (The Day of Freedom: Our Wehrmacht; 1935), about the reintroduction of compulsory military service; and *Fest der Völker* (Festival of the Nations) and *Fest der Schönheit* (Festival of Beauty) in 1936, on that year's Olympic Games. The last two films in particular won international acclaim and honors (in 1948 from the International Olympics Committee) since Riefenstahl had captured the glorious Berlin days with inimitable forcefulness.

After 1945 Riefenstahl was repeatedly reproached for her complicity with National Socialist tyranny. Unperturbed, she always referred to her artistic duty. She could not, however, refute the accusation that she had recruited Gypsies from a concentration camp for her film *Tiefland* (Lowlands; 1940–1944). In the postwar period she gained prominence as a successful still photographer, particularly with the book *Die Nuba von Kau* (The People of Kau; 1973).

Rienhardt, Rolf, b. Bucha, July 2, 1903, German jurist. In 1932 Rienhardt was the legal counsel for the EHER PRESS, and became friendly with Gregor Strasser. In 1932 he was a Reichstag

deputy for the NSDAP. Rienhardt became chief manager in the Press Office of the Reich Leadership of the NSDAP under Max AMANN. He was the true builder of the National Socialist press monopoly, wrote the speeches for his chief, and formulated his directives. Amann viewed Rienhardt as a rival, however, and in 1943 removed him from office on a pretext. Rienhardt was an officer in the Waffen-SS until the end of the war.

Rintelen, Anton, b. Graz, November 15, 1876; d. there, January 28, 1946, Austrian politician and jurist. In 1903 Rintelen became a professor in Prague, and in 1911 in Graz. He was elected a deputy in the provincial parliament for the Christian-Social Party in Styria in 1918; from 1919 to 1926 and from 1928 to 1933 he was governor of the provincial administration. He was also Austrian minister of education in 1926 and in 1932–1933. Rintelen was sympathetic to AUSTROFASCISM and he favored the Austrian National Socialists, who had designated him as chancellor in the event that they succeeded in their putsch against Engelbert DOLLFUSS on July 25, 1934. After they failed, Rintelen was sentenced to life imprisonment for high treason in March 1935. Following the 1938 ANSCHLUSS he was released, but he played no further political role.

Ritter, Gerhard, b. Bad Sooden(-Allendorf), April 6, 1888; d. Freiburg im Breisgau, July 1, 1967, German historian. In 1921 Ritter became a lecturer (*Privatdozent*) in Heidelberg; in 1924 he was a professor in Hamburg, and from 1925 to 1957, in Freiburg. A national-conservative scholar whose historical writings (such as *Luther*; 1925) were in the Prussian tradition, Ritter soon revealed the patriotic tones of National Socialist propaganda to be a ploy. His famous memorial address on Paul von Hindenburg (1934) criticized the lack of an ethical foundation in Hitler's power politics, especially in light of the murders in the Röhm Affair. After the war, Ritter's thoughts on the subject appeared under the title *On the Ethical Problem of Power* (1948), a meditation on his experiences with the opposition. As the main figure in the so-called Freiburg Circle of conservative opponents of National Socialism, Ritter spent several months in prison because of his connection with Carl Friedrich GOERDELER in 1944–1945. He published further research on the subject in his 1958 book, *Goerdeler und die deutsche Widerstandsbewegung* (translated as *The German Resistance*).

Ritter, Karl, b. Würzburg, November 7, 1888; d. Buenos Aires, April 7, 1977, German film director and producer. Ritter was a career officer and one of the first German military pilots. After the First World War he was initially a draftsman and graphic artist, and then a public-relations manager with Südfilm. Following the takeover of power, the committed National Socialist was named by Joseph Goebbels as chief of production and director of Ufa (UNIVERSE FILMS, INC.). As a producer (notably of HITLERJUNGE QUEX; 1933) and a director, Ritter made a series of NS propaganda films; militaristic paeans to the Luftwaffe (*Pour le Mérite*, 1938; *Stukas*, 1941); anti-Communist melodramas such as *GPU* [the precursor to the KGB] (1942); and appeals to German willingness for self-sacrifice, as *Unternehmen Michael* (Assignment: Michael; 1937).

Although Hitler was not entirely satisfied with Ritter's films, Goebbels valued Ritter's ability to produce atmospheric films and movies in the Hollywood style, as well as feature films such as *Hochzeitsreise* (Wedding Trip; 1939) and *Bal paré* (Full-Dress Ball; 1940). He appointed Ritter to the Presidial Council of the Reich Film Chamber and made him a Reich Culture Senator and a professor. After the war, Ritter emigrated to South America. In the 1950s he made films in the Federal Republic of Germany with his own production company, among them *Staatsanwältin Corda* (The Lady Public Prosecutor Corda; 1953). Subsequently he went definitively into exile.

Ritterkreuz. *See* Knight's Cross.

Röchling, Hermann, b. Völklingen, November 12, 1872; d. Mannheim, August 24, 1955, German industrialist. In 1898 Röchling took over his father's foundry. Röchling was able to keep his firm the only large production facility in the SAAR TERRITORY free of French involvement after 1918, but he lost his participation in French firms. Subsequently he carried out continuous efforts toward German re-annexation of the Saar territory. Röchling sought out Hitler in April 1933, and upon the latter's request he promoted the formation of the GERMAN FRONT. After the annexation of the Saarland on March 1, 1935, Röchling became the leading figure in the German coal and steel industry, and during the war he had the status of a MILITARY ECONOMY FÜHRER. On his 70th birthday he was honored by Hitler with the Eagle Shield of the German Reich (*see* ADLERSCHILD DES DEUTSCHEN REICHES). In 1947 a French court sentenced Röchling to 10 years' imprisonment and loss of property. His release on August 18, 1951, came about on the intervention of his former coworkers. Röchling did not live to see the restoration of his companies following the reincorporation of the Saarland into the Federal Republic of Germany on January 1, 1957.

R. S.

Röhm, Ernst, b. Munich, November 28, 1887; d. there, July 1, 1934, Sturmabteilung (SA) chief of staff. Röhm belonged to the "lost generation" of combatants. Unprepared to find a role for themselves in civilian life again after the end of hostilities in 1918, and filled with contempt for the Weimar Republic, they joined the NSDAP

Karl Ritter.

Hermann Röchling.

Ernst Röhm.

by way of national military associations. From a family of Bavarian civil servants, Röhm had reached the rank of captain during the First World War. Afterward he joined the EPP Free Corps in deposing the Munich republic of councils (May 2, 1919), and took part in forming and arming home guard units. In 1919 he met Hitler and joined the GERMAN WORKERS' PARTY. He retired from the army on September 26, 1923. Röhm's participation in the HITLER PUTSCH resulted in a sentence of 15 months' imprisonment, on probation. After Hitler's release at the end of 1924, differences developed between the two: Röhm had nothing but contempt for the legalistic tactics that the party leader was then following. Despite a close friendship, the alienation grew to such a degree that Röhm withdrew from political life in April 1925. After uneventful intervening years, in his own words, "leading the life of a sick animal," he went to Bolivia as a military adviser.

In the autumn of 1930 Hitler summoned Röhm back and made him chief of staff of the SA after the resignation of Ernst PFEFFER VON SALOMON. Hitler believed he would be able to outmaneuver his highest SA man's unchanged plan for revolution. He gave Röhm a largely free hand, and also tolerated his homosexual tendencies, which were widely known and ridiculed. Röhm's brutally unscrupulous mercenary manner rapidly caught on in the SA, and it made Hitler's private army the terror of the late Weimar period.

After the SEIZURE OF POWER, Röhm demanded a SECOND REVOLUTION and recognition of his SA as a national army. Hitler put him off,

even appointing him Reich Minister without Portfolio in December 1933, but he then decided on a forceful solution to the problem: Röhm was arrested on June 30, 1934, as part of a large-scale assassination operation (*see* RÖHM AFFAIR), and on the next day he was shot in his cell. In light of this ending, the title of his 1929 autobiography, *Geschichte eines Hochverräters* (History of a Traitor), seems almost tragicomic.

Röhm Affair (*Röhm Affäre*), the conflict between Hitler and the SA under Ernst RÖHM; it entered its critical phase in 1934 and culminated in the assassination operation of June 30 and July 1, 1934. At the end of 1930, Hitler won Röhm over as chief of staff of the STURMABTEILUNG (SA) and, in actuality, as its leader. Hitler believed that the SA's structure was so sound, and that it was so absorbed by its tasks of political agitation, that it would withstand Röhm's inclination (known to Hitler) to transform it into a militia. A series of high-ranking SA leaders had resisted Röhm's appointment from the outset. The opposition to Röhm was directed against his person and his ideas, but also against his leadership: envisioning a people's army, he exhorted not only confirmed National Socialists and opportunists, but also persons with other political views and those who (from a bourgeois perspective) had been led astray, to join together in the SA combat community.

Initially these reservations seemed groundless. In the course of the terror and synchronization following the Seizure of Power, some 25,000 SA men were deployed as Prussian auxiliary police, and others as concentration camp personnel. The remaining men, numbering approximately 500,000, carried on more intensively the political agitation and lawlessness of the earlier years, but now as legitimate wielders of power. In the autumn of 1933 these activities were called off; the auxiliary police were dismissed, and the SA concentration camps were dissolved or handed over to the SS, which continued the terror in a more organized manner.

The SA's aggressiveness (which, however, had been the organization's *raison d'être*) was suppressed and repressed at the height of its fury. It sought substitute objects, which it found in the demand for a new wave of revenge, the so-called SECOND REVOLUTION, against more subtle political antagonists. This revolutionary rhetoric also articulated the disappointment of the numerous unemployed men within the National Socialist movement—who were disproportionately represented in the SA—whom the Seizure of Power had not yet provided for. Consequently, it gained a sociopolitical dimension that alarmed Hitler's conservative supporters and began to alienate them. The old insubordination that had appeared in 1929–1930 in the conflict over the "legality course" and that had been quelled with the dismissal of the Supreme SA Führer, Franz PFEFFER VON SALOMON (*see* STENNES RE-VOLTS), was now revived against Hitler himself. Because of this attack on National Socialism's alliance with the establishment and the conservatives, the crisis concerning the SA's function grew into a governmental crisis.

Most dangerous was the SA's collision course with the Reichswehr. In the spring of 1933 Röhm had reached an understanding with Gen. Walter von REICHENAU of the Armed Forces Ministry that the Reichswehr would provide military training for the SA, but that the SA would be armed and outfitted only for deployment in domestic assignments. In return, it would be allowed to absorb the paramilitary organizations and soldiers' clubs—with the exception of the STEEL HELMET, which the Reichswehr viewed as a valuable auxiliary and ally. After clashes with the Steel Helmet, the SA absorbed this military movement, too, cleverly exploiting its voluntary surrender to National Socialism. Now, approximately 4.5 million men served under Röhm, most of them experienced soldiers who had fought in the First World War. With them he turned again to his old plans for a militia.

The two-component army, as modeled according to the ideas of Hans von SEECKT, creator of the Reichswehr, played a large role in the thinking of the time: a relatively small elite army conducted offensive warfare, and a militia manned the defensive fronts. On this basis a compromise between the SA and the Reichswehr might have been possible. However, Hitler and Gen. Werner von BLOMBERG, the armed forces minister, were stubbornly fixed on the classic army of cadres. Röhm went to the opposite extreme: on February 1, 1934, he demanded that the Reichswehr be merged into the SA, while the standing army would be reduced to a military training organization for his Home Defense–SA force. As a result, tensions grew between the SA officer corps—which consisted mostly of imperial officers who had never been incorporated into the "Republican" Reichswehr—and the military establishment. Röhm's demand was very clearly an expression of what the historian Martin Broszat has termed the "dynamic for its own sake, without regard to

content" that had characterized the SA since the fall of 1933. For the building of a militia army, whose own unwieldiness would not permit the adventure of a war, ultimately had to lead to its joining the ranks of the "peaceable International of the frontline soldiers" (Salewski) toward which the survivors of the First World War trenches were inclined, often with a romanticizing and anti-civilian attitude. Thus Hitler saw his program endangered, while the Reichswehr feared for its very existence.

Important SA leaders such as the *Obergruppenführer* for the North, Viktor LUTZE, and the head of the SA training division (attached to the Reichswehr), Friedrich Wilhelm Krüger, warned Hitler about Röhm's intentions. Hitler now realized definitively that it was no longer possible to rein in the SA, as he had sought to do by tying Röhm down as a minister in the Reich government (through the Law to Secure the Unity of Party and State of December 1, 1933) and by making SA plenipotentiaries jointly responsible for administration. Pressured by Göring, Wilhelm Frick, Goebbels, Reichenau, Himmler, and Reinhard Heydrich, beginning in March 1934 Hitler steered toward a violent confrontation, having it prepared for in advance with media propaganda. Competing "blacklists" generated by party, SS, and Gestapo circles identified the SA candidates for death. To them were added the names of conservatives who were too openly disgruntled, such as Vice Chancellor Franz von Papen and those around him. The Political Police were placed under

"And the Führer spoke: 'Only death can separate us!'" Satire on the Röhm Affair in the Swiss *Nebelspalter*.

Himmler, who as a result could deploy the SS as he wished.

Papen's MARBURG SPEECH of June 17 openly expressed conservative disenchantment and was received with applause. It forced Hitler to act, although the situation had eased off since the SA—which for its part had no actual intention of fighting—was on furlough. The SS received arms from the Reichswehr, which on the appointed day mobilized in support in some places. Hitler summoned the unsuspecting SA leaders to a meeting at Bad Wiessee, where he then had Röhm and his followers dragged out of bed on the morning of June 30, 1934. They were brought to Munich and shot there, Röhm himself only after some hesitation. Those leaders who were still in transit were seized in the Munich train station, and most of them were imprisoned. These arrests unleashed throughout the Reich the planned operation, which quickly extended beyond its intended limits and claimed hundreds of additional victims. The official death lists contained 83 names, including all the members of the SA leadership who had not set themselves clearly against Röhm, as had the new chief of staff, Lutze. Those on the lists who were not SA members included the former chancellor Gen. Kurt von SCHLEICHER; the conservative journalist Edgar JUNG; the Catholic activist Erich KLAUSENER; Gustav von KAHR, the betrayer of the Hitler Putsch; and the "left-wing" National Socialist Gregor STRASSER. Papen escaped. Unrecorded were the countless victims of arbitrary decisions by SS death squads, especially in Silesia.

The Reich government's Enabling Law of July 3, 1934, retroactively legalized the massacre as having constituted a response to a state emergency, an alleged "Röhm Putsch," which in fact Heydrich had fabricated on the basis of the vaguest indications. The most significant source of unrest and willfulness in the first phase of the Third Reich had been eliminated, and the beneficiary was the cold-blooded police state of the SS, with which the Reichswehr soon had to share its monopoly of arms. Hitler's last antagonist had been removed.

W. P.

Rökk, Marika (originally, Ilona Rökk), b. Cairo, November 3, 1913, German dancer, actress, and singer of Hungarian background. Rökk was discovered for the movies in Budapest in 1933. She acted mainly under the direction of her husband, G. Jacoby, in the large-scale dance spectacles of Universe Films, Inc. (*see* REVUE FILMS).

Marika Rökk in *Es war eine rauschende Ballnacht.*

They included *Es war eine rauschende Ballnacht* (It Was an Intoxicating Night at the Ball; 1939), *Wunschkonzert* ("Request Concert"; 1940), and *Die Frau meiner Träume* (The Woman of My Dreams; 1944). Rökk's ebullience and talent were retained even in the postwar period.

Roma, self-designation of the GYPSIES (*rom* means "man" or "husband").

Romania, state in southeastern Europe; area, 294,967 sq km (about 120,000 sq miles); population, approximately 18 million (1930). Beginning in the late 1930s Romania underwent several changes in its form of government: from 1918 to 1938 it was a constitutional monarchy; from February 1938 to September 1940 it had a monarchical dictatorship under Carol II; and from September 1940 to August 23, 1944, an authoritarian regime under Ion ANTONESCU. Domestically unstable, Romania was shaken by crises beginning in 1918. These included the issue of agrarian reform; antisemitism; the rise of fascist groups such as the IRON GUARD alongside the two large blocs of the National Peasants' Party and the Liberal Party; rapidly shifting coalitions; corruption; and the problems of integrating national minorities. In foreign policy Romania was able to maintain a balance until 1940. Its need to defend its large territorial gains resulting from the peace treaties of 1919–1920 (Transylvania, the western Banat, Buko-

Romania. Latticed cross on the "Green House" of the Romanian fascists in Bucharest.

vina, Bessarabia, and southern Dobruja) against the revisionist demands of Hungary, the Soviet Union, and Bulgaria directed its policy toward the LITTLE ENTENTE and toward alliances with Poland (March 3, 1921) and France (June 10, 1926).

Romania's drastically worsening economic crisis was marked by a fall in the price of petroleum and agricultural products, market stagnation, the inability to make debt payments, and high unemployment. Agrarian reform was one cause of the dislocations, which were then exacerbated by the worldwide depression of 1929–1932. These difficulties propelled Bucharest both economically and politically ever closer to National Socialist Germany, with its nearly unlimited and crisis-proof market (based on petroleum and wheat) and its possibilities for currency-free deferred payments through clearings. On March 23, 1939, Romania signed an economic treaty with Germany, and on May 27, 1940, the two nations concluded an Oil Pact.

Romania became definitively aligned with the Axis camp as a consequence of France's capitulation, Great Britain's retreat from the Continent, and the annexation of Bessarabia and northern Bukovina by the Soviet Union on June 28, 1940, in accordance with the terms of

the GERMAN-SOVIET NONAGGRESSION PACT (August 23, 1939). On August 30, 1940, Romania participated in the second of the VIENNA AWARDS; on November 23 it acceded to the THREE-POWER AGREEMENT; and on November 25, to the ANTI-COMINTERN PACT. Antonescu proclaimed a "holy war" against the Soviet Union on June 24, 1941. The war's turning point at Stalingrad in the winter of 1942–1943, the heavy losses among Romanian troops, and the breakthrough of Soviet units toward Romania led to Antonescu's arrest on August 23, 1944, and to a declaration of war against Germany on August 28. On September 12, Romania and the USSR signed a cease-fire agreement. In the following period, under constant Soviet pressure, Romania was transformed into a Communist people's republic.

B.-J. W.

Roman Protocols (*Römische Protokolle*), term for the treaty-like final declarations of two rounds of conferences held in Rome. In the first Roman Protocol of March 17, 1934, the heads of the governments of Hungary (Gyula Gömbös), Austria (Engelbert Dollfuss), and Italy (Benito Mussolini) announced first the signing of a consultative pact to coordinate political activities, and second, mutual trade concessions. Italy wanted the protocol to secure its influence in the Danube region and to support Austria in its efforts to defend itself against German plans for an Anschluss. The Second Roman Protocol of January 7, 1935 (also called the Roman Pact), also served this end, in that France and Italy initiated a convention to assure the status quo in central Europe, especially with regard to Austria. This went no further than an exchange of opinions, since the Italian war against ABYSSINIA destroyed any further cooperation.

Römer, Josef ("Beppo"), b. Altenkirchen bei Freising, November 17, 1892; d. Brandenburg, September 25, 1944 (executed), German opposition fighter. Römer was an officer in the First World War. Subsequently, as a member of the Oberland Free Corps, he took part in suppressing the Munich republic of councils and in battles in Upper Silesia. Römer studied law and political science, and in the 1920s he evolved from a nationalist to a socialist. He then began to write for the Communist periodical *Aufbruch* (New Start). In 1932 he joined the Communist Party (KPD) and took over the supervision of *Aufbruch*.

As early as 1934, Römer planned an assassina-

Josef Römer.

tion attempt on Hitler, but he was arrested and imprisoned in Dachau until 1939. He then immediately re-established contact with the workers' opposition; in 1940 founded the *Informationsdienst* (Information Service), distributed monthly; again prepared an assassination attempt; and created a network of opposition workplace cells. The Gestapo was nonetheless able to infiltrate an informant, and it crushed the organization. Römer was arrested in the spring of 1942 and after a two-year imprisonment was sentenced to death on June 16, 1944.

Rommel, Erwin, b. Heidenheim/Brenz, November 15, 1891; d. near Herrlingen bei Ulm, October 14, 1944, German general field marshal (June 22, 1942). Rommel joined the Württemberg army in 1910. During the First World War, in 1917, he was awarded the Pour le mérite for the storming of Monte Matajur, the "miracle of Good Friday." Pursuing a Reichswehr career, he taught military tactics in the Infantry School at Dresden from 1929 to 1933. Rommel welcomed the National Socialist Seizure of Power and was soon "discovered" by Hitler, who in 1935 appointed him liaison officer for the Reich Youth Leadership in the Armed Forces Ministry. In 1938–1939 Hitler made Rommel commander of the Führer Headquarters during the Sudeten crisis, for the march into the residual Czech state (Resttschechei), and in the Polish Campaign. In France Rommel received his first frontline command. As a major general (from August 1, 1939), in May 1940 he took command of the Seventh Panzer Division, which gained the nick-

name "Ghost Division" (Gespensterdivision) because of its rapid surprise advances.

Its "lightning" tactics in North Africa, where Rommel's next assignment took him in February 1941, made him the legendary "Desert Fox" (Wüstenfuchs), who was able once again to save the already hopeless Italian situation during the AFRICAN CAMPAIGN. With his German Africa Corps (DAK), Rommel brought the British Eighth Army near the brink of defeat after the capitulation of Tobruk (June 21, 1942). He had to admit defeat only in the spring of 1943, following the Anglo-American landing in Morocco (November 8, 1942).

As supreme commander of Army Group B, Rommel organized the defense of Italy beginning on August 18, 1943, and as of December 1 of that year, he prepared the defense against the INVASION. His efforts did not prevail, however, because of tensions with the supreme commander in the west, Field Marshal Gerd von RUNDSTEDT, and above all because of the Allies' overwhelming air superiority. Rommel, who had for a long time criticized Hitler's irresponsible military leadership, gradually joined the opposition, but at that point he strictly opposed an assassination attempt. In a letter of July 15, 1944, he urged Hitler to draw for himself the political consequences of battles that had grown futile. Two days later he was severely wounded in a dive-bombing attack near Lisieux. His connection to the conspirators of July 20, 1944, who had designated him as supreme commander of the army if the *coup d'état* were successful, led on October 14 of that year to a visit paid to

Erwin Rommel.

the recuperating Rommel in his hometown of Herrlingen by Generals Burgdorf and Meisel. They conveyed Hitler's order: either suicide or a trial before the *Volk* Court and corresponding consequences for his family. Rommel decided on the proffered poison. Hitler ordered a state burial.

Roosevelt, Franklin Delano, b. Hyde Park (New York), January 30, 1882; d. Warm Springs (Georgia), April 12, 1945, American politician. Roosevelt was a lawyer. Elected as a Democrat to the New York Senate in 1910, from 1913 to 1920 he was under secretary of the navy. In 1919 he directed America's postwar demobilization in Europe. Roosevelt's career met with two setbacks in 1920 and 1921: he ran unsuccessfully for the vice presidency, and he was then confined to a wheelchair by polio. Until 1928 he practiced law. The following year he was elected governor of New York, and at the end of 1932 he became the 32nd president of the United States, defeating the incumbent, Herbert HOOVER. Roosevelt was the only American president to be re-elected three times (1936, 1940, and 1944). Thus, his years in office coincided almost to the day with those of the Third Reich and with Hitler's tenure of office.

Like Hitler, upon his entry into government Roosevelt was faced with the problem of overcoming the WORLD ECONOMIC CRISIS, and like Hitler he ultimately succeeded in doing this only through a policy of rearmament. This took effect in the United States considerably later because of isolationist public opinion that large-ly tied Roosevelt's hands. Nonetheless, he was successful in using his "New Deal" programs to effect a gradual change of course from total economic liberalism to a welfare state (unemployment insurance and Social Security, in particular), which mitigated social antagonisms and assured Roosevelt's popularity. This permitted him increasingly to face head-on the expansionist policy of Germany, Italy, and Japan, and to support England generously once the war broke out (*see* LEND-LEASE ACT). After the German attack on the Soviet Union (June 22, 1941), this policy crystallized in the ATLANTIC CHARTER and culminated in America's entry into the war after the Japanese attack on PEARL HARBOR. The mobilization of the entire American economy finally decided the Second World War in favor of the Allies.

The "Germany first" strategy agreed upon at conferences in Casablanca, Teheran, and Yalta is traceable to Roosevelt, as is the demand for an UNCONDITIONAL SURRENDER of the Axis powers. It was Roosevelt, too, who against Winston CHURCHILL's warnings left eastern Europe to the Red Army because he wanted to win Joseph STALIN over for an engagement against Japan. Roosevelt did not suspect that he would not need Stalin at all for that task, since he did not survive to see the gigantic advance in weaponry signified for the United States by the development of the ATOMIC BOMB that he himself had commissioned. His premature death, which aroused hopes in beleaguered Berlin for a collapse of the Allied war coalition, tipped the Western political scales to Stalin's side, as the POTSDAM AGREEMENT would demonstrate.

Rosenberg, Alfred, b. Reval (now Tallinn, Estonia), January 12, 1893; d. Nuremberg, October 16, 1946 (executed), German politician. Rosenberg studied architecture in Riga and in Moscow. He fled to Germany in 1918 and became a member of the *völkisch* THULE SOCIETY in 1919. He joined the GERMAN WORKERS' PARTY (DAP) shortly after Hitler, as member no. 625. Rosenberg had already made a name for himself as an antisemitic journalist with works such as *Die Spur des Judentums im Wandel der Zeiten* (The Tracks of Jewry through the Ages; 1919). He was introduced to National Socialist circles by Dietrich ECKART. In 1921 he assumed the chief editorship of the VÖLKISCHER BEOBACHTER, acting as its publisher from 1938 on. After taking part in the failed Hitler Putsch (November 9, 1923), he helped found the GREAT-GERMAN VOLK COMMUNITY, a surrogate organiza-

Franklin Delano Roosevelt.

Alfred Rosenberg.

tion for the banned NSDAP; he attempted to portray himself as the chief ideologue of the party. Hitler, impressed by Rosenberg's cultivation, promoted him and protected him from the attacks of prominent party members, who did not get along with the "foreigner," a humorless doctrinaire.

Becoming prominent early on as a self-appointed censor with the COMBAT LEAGUE FOR GERMAN CULTURE that he had founded, Rosenberg attempted in 1930 to codify the pure NS doctrine in his main work, *The Myth of the 20th Century* (MYTHUS DES 20. JAHRHUNDERTS, DER). His racist and anti-Christian constructions, however, met with reservations even from Hitler, who nevertheless chose to indulge Rosenberg and did not officially distance himself from the book. Since a confrontation with the churches was not desired at first, even after the Seizure of Power, Rosenberg seemed to Hitler to be made to order as an image of the enemy to distract the theologians. In 1934 Hitler named him "Delegate of the Führer for the Supervision of All Spiritual and Worldview-related Schooling and Education of the NSDAP" (*Beauftragter des Führers für die Überwachung der gesamten geistigen und weltanschaulichen Schulung und Erziehung der NSDAP*). This position placed Rosenberg in rivalry with the guardians of *Weltanschauung* in the SS, with Bernhard RUST as Reich Minister for Science, Education, and Public Instruction, and with Martin Bormann and Joseph Goebbels. Rosenberg also had ambitions in the area of foreign policy. In 1933 he was put in charge of the party's FOREIGN POLICY OFFICE, where he came into competition with

Joachim von RIBBENTROP. In all these roles Rosenberg became a typical figure in the jurisdictional jungle of the Third Reich's "polycracy," which was carefully maintained by Hitler.

Rosenberg also continued in this role after the war began, when he was named Reich Minister for the Occupied Eastern Territories on November 17, 1941. In this post he became involved in a war of multiple fronts, against the Foreign Office, the SS, the Wehrmacht, and even against his formal subordinates, the Reich Commissioners for the Ukraine, Erich KOCH, and for the Ostland, Hinrich LOHSE. Although personally not fastidious in his choice of means, Rosenberg believed that the reign of terror exercised by the German occupation in Russia was politically wrongheaded. But he could obtain no hearing with Hitler for his reservations. He did not understand that the GERMANIZATION being propagated meant above all the extermination of the indigenous population, rather than their conversion to the German cause. Rosenberg came into conflict even with the powerful Hermann Göring when his ROSENBERG OPERATION STAFF did not sufficiently respect the Reich Marshal's wishes in the NS ART PLUNDER. All these conflicts could not tip the scales of justice in Rosenberg's favor at the Nuremberg Trials, in light of the overwhelming evidence of his guilt. He was sentenced to death on October 1, 1946. Rosenberg's *Letzte Aufzeichnungen* (Last Notes) and *Politisches Tagebuch* (Political Diary; translated as *Memoirs of Alfred Rosenberg*) appeared posthumously in 1955.

Rosenberg Operation Staff (Einsatzstab Reichsleiter Rosenberg), "mobile" (*fliegende*) panel of experts on fine arts and decorative arts created during the French Campaign in 1940. Under the pretext of "securing" "abandoned Jewish property" for the Reich, the Einsatzstab conducted plunder operations first in France (despite strong protests by the Vichy government), and then in other occupied territories. The booty came initially from Jewish art collections (including that of the Rothschilds), and later from those of real or putative enemies of the German occupation power. With his Einsatzstab, Alfred ROSENBERG played a significant role in National Socialism's wartime ART PLUNDER, which was also carried out by other agencies (including the Foreign Office). During the Nuremberg Trials he defended the operation as an attempt to protect irreplaceable art treasures from war-related damage and destruction.

Rossbach, Gerhard, b. Kehrberg (Pomerania), February 28, 1893; d. Hamburg, August 30, 1967, German politician. Rossbach was a career officer. In 1918 he founded a free corps and fought in West Prussia and in the Baltic area. He took part in the KAPP PUTSCH with the Rossbach Detachment. Despite many orders to disband, Rossbach kept his men together in "teams," and in 1921 deployed them during the unrest in Upper Silesia as the Silesia Volunteer Division. With their remnants, he took part in the Hitler Putsch (November 9, 1923). Rossbach escaped to Austria and was amnestied. From 1926 to 1933 he was active in the youth movement. In 1933 he became a training inspector in the newly founded Reich Air Defense League. During the Röhm Affair (June 30, 1934), he was temporarily jailed. Later he retreated into private life as an insurance salesman. After the war Rossbach was successful in promoting the reinstitution of the Bayreuth Festival. He published his memoirs, *Mein Weg durch die Zeit* (My Path through Time), in 1950.

"Rot" ("Red"), military code name for the second phase of the German FRENCH CAMPAIGN.

Rote Fahne, Die (The Red Flag; as of 1920 subtitled "Official Publication of the Communist Party of Germany/Section of the Communist International"), Berlin daily newspaper, founded in 1918 by Rosa Luxemburg and Karl Liebknecht. It was published beginning in February 1919 by the publishing house of the same name. *Die Rote Fahne*, like the entire rigidly centralized Communist Party (KPD) press of the Weimar Republic, considered itself the "mouthpiece of the masses" and a weapon in the class struggle. Its circulation on October 1, 1920, was 30,000; by 1933 it was 130,000.

Die Rote Fahne, official publication of the German Communist party: "Tomorrow show fascism our strength! Red Berlin, come out for the storm week of the antifascist operation!"

Like all the Communist newspapers, *Die Rote Fahne* was at first banned for four weeks by the REICHSTAG FIRE DECREE, and then definitively suppressed. Its last Berlin issue was dated February 26/27, 1933. It continued to appear as the newspaper of the exiled KPD beginning in mid-July 1933, from one to three times a month—

Gerhard Rossbach (center) with his followers during the Hitler Putsch on November 9, 1923, in Munich.

first in the Saarland, then in 1935 and 1936 in Czechoslovakia, and in Alsace-Lorraine, Belgium, and Holland. The print matrixes were set simultaneously in different countries, mainly on thin paper; the publication information was often fictitious and the articles unsigned. Alexander Abusch was the editor in chief beginning in March 1935. Between 1933 and 1939 the circulation of *Die Rote Fahne* varied from 40,000 to 50,000. Its last issue appeared in June 1939 with no date.

S. O.

Rote Kapelle. *See* Red Orchestra.

Rothenberger, Curt Ferdinand, b. Cuxhaven, June 30, 1896; d. Hamburg, September 1, 1959, German jurist. Rothenberger studied law in Berlin, Kiel, and Hamburg. He became a judge in Hamburg's state court (*Landgericht*) in 1925, and in 1931, its presiding judge. In 1933 he was appointed Hamburg's judicial senator, and in 1935, president of the Hanseatic Superior Court. At the beginning of the Otto THIERACK era at the Reich Justice Ministry, Rothenberger was made Thierack's state secretary on August 20, 1942. He left in 1943 because of disagreements, and settled in Hamburg as a notary. After the war he was active as a lawyer and a tutor for law examinations.

A National Socialist of an intellectual bent, Rothenberger had a reputation as an excellent jurist. He had comprehensive plans for reforming the German judicial system, and for this reason Hitler named him state secretary. On the one hand, Rothenberger wanted to strengthen the position of the judge, but he also wanted the judge to be dependent on "the Führer's will." Judicial independence thus existed only vis-à-vis a third party, such as the police; Hitler would remain the "supreme judge." Rothenberger viewed the magistrate as the "executor of the Führer's will"; even as judicial senator he had pleaded for broader jurisdiction for the SPECIAL COURTS. In the Nuremberg JURISTS' TRIAL he was sentenced to seven years' imprisonment, of which he served five years. His works included *Der deutsche Richter* (The German Judge; 1943).

U. B.

Rotterdam, largest port city in the Netherlands; its population in 1940 was approximately 600,000. Despite the surrender negotiations that were in progress, on May 14, 1940, Rotter-

dam became the victim of a German air attack (carried out by Combat Squadron 54), which could not be halted in time. More than 900 people were killed, and the historical Old City was totally destroyed. In the AIR WAR the attack on Rotterdam, like that on COVENTRY, was a prelude to warfare conducted against the civilian population as well.

Rottleberode, National Socialist concentration camp located 15 km (about 9 miles) east of Nordhausen/Harz. Rottleberode was established in March 1944 as a satellite of BUCHENWALD; beginning in late October and early November of that year, it was a satellite of MITTELBAU. Together with the Stempeda subsidiary camp, about 2–3 km away, Rottleberode was occupied by some 1,400 prisoners, among them Jews, Gypsies, Germans, Poles, Russians, Czechs, and Frenchmen, who were employed in machine-building factories and in the airplane industry. Many of the inmates died of abuse and of exhaustion caused by overwork.

At the beginning of April 1945, Rottleberode was evacuated along with several other nearby Mittelbau camps, first in trucks and later on foot. Prisoners who could not keep up the pace of the march or who tried to escape were shot by the guards. During the evacuation, prisoners from other concentration camps joined the group. On April 13, all the prisoners were brought—supposedly to spend the night—into a large barn on the Isenschnibbe estate, near the outskirts of Gardelegen, and locked inside. The guards then set the building on fire and machine-gunned those prisoners who tried to escape. Altogether, more than 1,000 people lost their lives.

A memorial today commemorates the terrible incident.

W. D.

Röver, Carl, b. Lemwerder (Oldenburg), February 12, 1889; d. 1942, German politician and businessman. In the First World War, Röver served in the Propaganda Section of the Army High Command from 1916 to 1918. He joined the NSDAP in 1923. In 1928 he became *Gauleiter* of Weser-Ems (the "Führer of East Frisia"), and in 1930 he was elected to the Reichstag. On June 16, 1932, Röver became the first National Socialist minister president of a German state (Oldenburg). Immediately after he took office he began a quarrel with the Evangelical Church over a sermon given by a black pastor (terming it "culture infamy"), a demonstration of what was

Carl Röver.

to be expected of NS cultural policy. Röver became a Reich governor in Oldenburg and Bremen in 1933.

RSHA. *See* Reich Security Main Office.

Rubble women (*Trümmerfrauen*), colloquial term for the women in a postwar Germany with a shortage of men who were primarily responsible for clearing away the rubble in bombed-out German cities. Of a total of 19 million residences in 1939, by the end of the war (excluding the Eastern Territories) some 3.5 million were destroyed or heavily damaged.

Rudel, Hans-Ulrich, b. Konradswaldau (Silesia), July 2, 1916; d. Rosenheim, December 18, 1982, German Luftwaffe colonel (January 1, 1945). In 1937 and 1938 Rudel underwent flight training with Stukas and reconnaissance planes. With his specially armed Stuka, he specialized in pursuing tanks in the east; by the end of the war he had made 519 hits in 2,530 missions. Added to this were 800 destroyed vehicles, a sunken cruiser, and a heavily damaged battleship. The most highly decorated soldier in the Wehrmacht (he was awarded the Knight's Cross with Gold Oak-Leaf Cluster, Swords, and Diamonds), Rudel fell into Soviet imprisonment in March 1944. In February 1945 he lost his right leg, and on May 8 of that year he was taken captive by the Americans. After the war Rudel lived for a long time in National Socialist emigré colonies in Argentina, meanwhile supporting extremist right-wing organizations in the Federal Republic of Germany. In 1976 two Luftwaffe generals were forced to resign because they had not prevented Bundeswehr officers from participating in a Rudel testimonial. There was another scandal at Rudel's burial, when West German air force planes flew over his grave.

Rüdin, Ernst, b. Saint Gall (Switzerland), April 19, 1874; d. Munich, October 2, 1952, German

Rubble woman.

Hans-Ulrich Rudel.

specialist in human genetics. Rüdin became a professor in Munich in 1915; he taught in Basel from 1925 to 1928. In 1935 he became director of the German Research Institute for Psychiatry, and in 1938, of the Institute for Racial Hygiene in Munich. Rüdin, together with Alfred PLOETZ, founded the German Society for RACIAL HYGIENE. In 1933 Rüdin became its chairman, and he was appointed by Reich Interior Minister Wilhelm Frick to the Advisory Council for Population and Racial Policy.

Rüdin developed an "empirical heredity prognosis," according to which the inheritability of illnesses and deformities could allegedly be predicted; it became the foundation of the Law to Prevent HEREDITARILY ILL OFFSPRING of July 14, 1933. He collaborated in writing the standard commentary to this law, which he praised as a liberation from the "terrible situation" of the handicapped. In 1939 Hitler honored Rüdin with the Goethe Medal for Art and Science, and in 1944 bestowed on him the Eagle Shield of the German Reich.

Ruf, Ludwig, b. Seckenheim (now Mannheim-Seckenheim), February 12, 1898; d. Mannheim, May 20, 1936, German opposition fighter. Ruf was a railway worker. In 1918 he joined the Social Democratic Party (SPD). He belonged to a workplace council, and was active in his trade union. Following the destruction of the trade unions (May 2, 1933), Ruf became involved in creating a Social Democratic opposition cell; he distributed informational pamphlets. After attending a conference with emigrés in Antwerp in December 1934, he fell into the clutches of the Gestapo on February 14, 1936. He died in prison, presumably as a result of abuse, although the official cause of his death was suicide.

Rühmann, Heinz, b. Essen, March 7, 1902, German actor. Rühmann had his first acting engagement in Breslau in 1921; he subsequently appeared on the stage in Hannover, Bremen, Munich, and ultimately Berlin. He worked with the director Falckenberg, who developed his talents as a comedian, and with Max REINHARDT, who expanded his acting repertoire. Rühmann became known nationwide through the film *Die Drei von der Tankstelle* (The Three from the Gas Station; 1930). Other film roles followed, but after the National Socialist Seizure of Power, the fact that he had a Jewish wife, Maria (née Bernheim), was frowned on.

Rühmann ultimately bowed to the pressure, especially from Hermann Göring, and divorced

Heinz Rühmann.

his wife, after which his career advanced brilliantly. His other films included *Wenn wir alle Engel wären* (If We Were All Angels; 1936), *Der Mustergatte* (The Model Husband; 1937), *13 Stühle* (13 Chairs; 1938), and *Lauter Lügen* (Nothing But Lies; 1938), in which he directed for the first time and during which he met Hertha Feiler, who became his second wife on July 1, 1939. Although as a "quarter Jew" she too was frowned on, for the sake of wartime morale no one wanted to forego Rühmann's genius for entertaining. He later appeared in *Wunschkonzert* (1940; *see* "REQUEST CONCERT"), *Quax der Bruchpilot* (Quax the Crash Pilot; 1941), and *Die Feuerzangenbowle* (Burnt Punch; 1944). After a few postwar flops, Rühmann once again became perhaps the most popular German actor, starring in character roles in such films as *Charley's Tante* (Charley's Aunt; 1955), *Der Hauptmann von Köpenick* (The Captain from Köpenick; 1955), and *Der Kapitän* (The Captain; 1971).

Ruhr conflict (*Ruhrkampf*), German opposition to the occupation of the Ruhr territory on January 9, 1923, by French and Belgian troops on the pretext that Berlin was in arrears with its reparations deliveries of wood, telegraph poles, and coal (representing the policy of "productive seizure"). The Ruhr conflict for most of the population was a matter of "passive resistance,"

Ruhr conflict. French soldiers at the German Corner (the confluence of the Rhine and Moselle rivers) at Koblenz.

involving the suspension of reparations and service payments to the occupying powers and the shutting down of mines, factories, and railways. To a smaller extent, it meant active measures of sabotage as well: sinking inland ships, blocking canals, and blowing up railway lines. For a time it even brought about a working alliance between National Socialists (*see* Albert SCHLA-GETER) and Communists, who were following the national-Communist "Schlageter course" under Karl Radek.

The use of counterterror, reprisals, and expulsions by the occupying powers led to hatred and bitterness among the population; the Weimar government's financial support of the conflict made the value of the reichsmark fall through the floor (*see* INFLATION). The French encouraged separatist movements in the Rhineland and in the Palatinate. Reich Chancellor Gustav Stresemann was induced by the political and economic dangers to put an unconditional end to the resistance on September 26, 1923. The HITLER PUTSCH on November 9 of that year was one reaction to this decision. Ultimately, the resumption of the FULFILLMENT POLICY led to Germany's breaking out from international moral isolation, and to efforts by England and the United States to mediate the reparations issue (*see* DAWES PLAN). France and Belgium evacuated the Ruhr area by July 1925.

B.-J. W.

Runciman, Sir Walter, b. South Shields (Durham), November 19, 1870; d. Doxford (Northumberland), November 14, 1949, British politician. With few interruptions (for example, his activity as a shipowner), Runciman was a Liberal member of the House of Commons, and several times a minister, between 1899 and 1937. From 1931 to 1937 he was the trade and economics minister. His government sent him to Prague during the SUDETEN CRISIS in 1938 to test the situation and, wherever possible, to pour oil on the troubled waters as an "independent mediator." This did not succeed, particularly since Berlin suspected that Runciman's mission was a trick on London's part to gain time. Runciman later retreated from political life.

Rundstedt, Gerd von, b. Aschersleben, December 12, 1875; d. Hannover, February 24, 1953, German field marshal (July 19, 1940). Rundstedt entered the army in 1892. He was a General Staff officer during the First World War, and afterward quickly advanced in the Reichswehr. As an infantry general (October 1, 1932), he was made commander in chief of Group Command 1 in Berlin. Despite reservations toward National Socialism, Rundstedt continued to advance in the Third Reich. Only when he criticized the German action against Czechoslovakia in late 1938 was he retired as a colonel general.

Rundstedt was ordered back into service at

Gerd von Rundstedt.

the time of the Polish Campaign as commander in chief of Army Group South, and was then assigned to France and Russia as commander of Army Group A. Following disagreements with Hitler, he was relieved of his command at his own request after the withdrawal of his troops from Rostov on December 12, 1941. Nonetheless, from March 1, 1942, to March 10, 1945, he was commander in chief in the west, with an interruption after the successful Allied INVASION, when he pressed for an end to the war. During this period he headed the Wehrmacht "Honor Court" that expelled from the forces those officers who were suspected of having been connected with the conspirators of the July 20, 1944, attempt on Hitler's life. A prisoner of the British after the war, Rundstedt served a sentence for transmitting the COMMANDO ORDER of October 18, 1942. He was ultimately released on May 5, 1949, because of serious illness.

Runes (*Runen*; from Goth. *rûna*, "secret"), term for the oldest written characters, used by all the

Runes. SS collar insignia.

Germanic tribes. Runes were rediscovered and used as a symbol at the end of the 19th century as a consequence of the Germanic cult in nationalist and *völkisch* circles. National Socialist organizations used runes in emblems, pamphlets, and pennants; the best known was the SS rune as a "symbol of the struggle," on banners, ceremonial daggers, and the collar insignia of SS men. NS researchers devoted themselves to the investigation of the different Nordic rune alphabets, since these "constitute[d] one of the most important components of Aryan culture." Thus, "primeval values [would] be reintroduced" with their use "that too long [had] been buried and forgotten" (K. Renk-Reichert, *Runenfibel* [The Rune Primer]; 1935).

RuSHA. *See* Race and Settlement Main Office.

RuSHA Trial, proceeding before United States Military Tribunal I in Nuremberg against the head of the Main Staff Office of the Reich Commissariat for the Fortification of the German Volk-Nation, Ulrich Greifelt, and 13 others, on charges of crimes against humanity, war crimes, and membership in a criminal organization (Case 8). The accused were 14 high-ranking members of different SS organizations —such as the RACE AND SETTLEMENT MAIN OFFICE (RuSHA) and the ETHNIC GERMAN CENTRAL OFFICE—whose purpose, according to the indictment, was to promote and safeguard the alleged superiority of the Nordic race, as well as to suppress and extirpate all those forces that resisted it.

The verdict, on March 10, 1948, sentenced Greifelt to life imprisonment; 12 of his co-defendants, partly acquitted of charges, received prison terms ranging from 2 years and 8 months to 25 years. The sole female defendant, Inge Viermetz, from the LEBENSBORN program, was acquitted. Five of those sentenced were immediately released because their period of imprisonment during the trial "represented a sufficient punishment." A former RuSHA head, Richard Hildebrandt (sentenced to 25 years' imprisonment), was handed over to Poland, and there was sentenced to death and executed, on March 10, 1951. Greifelt died while serving his term. The sentences of the others were terminated by a pardon from the United States High Commissioner, John J. McCloy, on January 31, 1951.

A. St.

Russia. *See* Soviet Union.

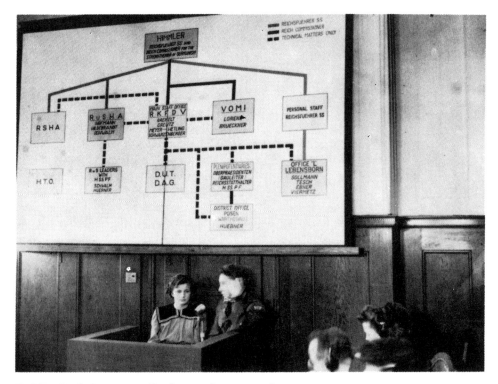

RuSHA Trial. Survivors of Lidice in the witness box.

Russian Campaign, term for the conflict between the German Wehrmacht and its allies against the Red Army from 1941 to 1945. After it became clear to Germany that England could not be conquered, the Russian Campaign was to decide the outcome of the war and also to actualize the program for LIVING SPACE, which Hitler called "the holiest mission of my life." Thus, he declared the Russian Campaign to be a "war of two worldviews," in which chivalry and traditional military concepts of honor would play no role (*see* COMMISSAR ORDER; EINSATZGRUPPEN). The aim of the conquest was to be "ruthless Germanization," which Hitler had spoken of before military leaders as early as February 3, 1933; its details were contained in the GENERAL PLAN FOR THE EAST. Hitler disregarded the GERMAN-SOVIET NONAGGRESSION PACT without qualms since he believed that he had to forestall a Soviet attack.

German preparations for a Russian campaign had begun as early as the summer of 1940 (the "Buildup in the East," August 5, 1940; *see* "AUFBAU OST"). They became concrete with Directive 21 of December 18, 1940 (Case "Barbarossa"): "in a rapid advance," troops were to reach the Arkhangelsk-Astrakhan line before the USSR could mobilize its immense reserves of 12 million soldiers. Delayed by the BALKAN CAMPAIGN, the attack began on June 22, 1941

—without a preliminary declaration of war. It was carried out by approximately 75 percent of the German field army (3 million men with 3,580 tanks and assault weapons) in three army groups, with a total of 152 divisions. Army Group North, under Gen. Field Marshal Wilhelm Ritter von LEEB, thrust toward the Baltic states and Leningrad; the Central Army Group, under Gen. Field Marshal Fedor von BOCK, moved in the direction of Minsk-Smolensk-Moscow; and Army Group South, under Gen. Field Marshal Gerd von RUNDSTEDT, pushed toward Kiev and the bend in the Dnieper River. On July 2 the "Antonescu" Romanian army group joined the Germans with 15 divisions. The German attack encountered five Soviet army groups, consisting of 15 armies with 149 divisions. The German Luftwaffe, in Air Fleets 1, 2, 4, and 5, mobilized a total of 1,945 bombers, Stukas, destroyers, and fighters; the Soviet Union, over 8,000 aircraft.

The 1941 summer campaign brought the German armies great territorial gains: the Baltic states, Belorussia, and the Ukraine. In the encirclement of Białystok and Minsk (July 9), 324,000 Soviet soldiers were taken prisoner; near Smolensk (August 5), a further 310,000; and in the twin battles of Viazma and Briansk (concluded October 15), as many as 673,000 more. These early successes misled Hitler into assuming that the Russian Campaign had been won. An edict of July 14 ordered that the emphasis in arms production be shifted to the construction of U-boats and planes, to the detriment of the army.

On October 2, the Central Army Group began the attack on Moscow, advancing so easily that the Soviet government withdrew from the city on October 16 and went to Kuibyshev. After the onset of winter, for which the German army was unprepared, the German momentum died out 27 km (about 16 miles) from the Kremlin, on December 1. By that point the eastern army had already lost 158,773 dead, 31,191 missing, and 563,082 wounded, and the Luftwaffe had lost 2,093 planes. A Soviet winter offensive began on December 5–6, 1941, with fresh Siberian troops, who were available in the Far East thanks to the Soviet-Japanese Neutrality Pact (April 13, 1941). The offensive inflicted heavy losses on the Germans (21,808 dead, 5,247 missing, and 75,169 wounded) and forced them to relinquish large areas.

The campaign of 1942 began with the encirclement battle south of Kharkov (May 17–26) and the defeat of Soviet troops in the Crimea. Then the German army began a summer offensive in the south on June 28: Army Group B reached the Don near Voronezh on July 3, and in the Crimea, Sevastopol was taken on July 1. The Soviet front reeled, but the considerably lower numbers of prisoners taken indicated that the

opponent was not defeated. During a second phase of operations, Rostov was occupied on July 23. In contrast to the planned tactics used up to that point, Hitler decided on operations against Stalingrad and simultaneously against the Caucasus that deviated from the norm (Directive 45, July 23). After reaching the North Caucasus (Mount Elbrus, August 22), Army Group A came to a standstill at the Terek River. Army Group B reached Stalingrad in mid-September and became entangled in a costly house-to-house battle lasting for weeks. In the fall of 1942 the Red Army front seemed to invite a large-scale pincer operation. The northern and southern flanks each had an Italian, a Hungarian, and two Romanian armies, altogether constituting 37 divisions. On November 19 they encountered the full force of a Soviet offensive: the German Sixth Army, with 250,000 men, was cut to pieces. Hitler, misled (not for the last time) by Hermann Göring's promises of air support, forbade the breakout that would still have been possible. The German resistance in Stalingrad collapsed on February 2, 1943: 91,000 defenders fell into Soviet hands, of whom only 6,000 later returned home. The Red Army pressed forward everywhere toward the west in the winter of 1942–1943. In the German-occupied areas, moreover, the barbaric treatment of the population by the National Socialist administration (particularly in the central areas) led to partisan activity that grew like an avalanche.

Russian Campaign. Soldiers advancing in the Ukraine (1941).

Russian Campaign. German motorized unit.

Local successes (on February 8, Kursk was retaken; on February 9, Belgorod; and on March 16, Kharkov) created in 1943 the prerequisites for Hitler's last attempt at an offensive. However, he himself jeopardized the operations by interfering in the smallest details and constantly replacing army leaders who did not suit him. After many delays the German attack, long expected by the enemy, began on July 5 near Kursk, against a large Soviet front with 33 divisions, 2,000 tanks, and 1,800 aircraft. After initial successes it came to a standstill. In the fall the Kuban bridgehead had to be evacuated by sea (September 7–October 9).

On January 4, 1944, the Red Army crossed the former Polish-Soviet border near Sarny (in Volhynia). At the same time it finally broke through the German hunger blockade around Leningrad, which had been surrounded since August 1941; a spring offensive in the Ukraine began on March 4. It forced the German front back over the Prut River, in the direction of Romania and the Carpathians and toward Eastern Galicia, where the Germans were able to consolidate their forces for a short while. By May 12, the Soviet troops had destroyed in the

Crimea the decimated Seventeenth Army, whose timely evacuation Hitler had prohibited. The Red Army no longer ceded the initiative. On June 1 it possessed 476 divisions, 37 tank and mechanized corps, 93 artillery divisions, and a total of 14,787 combat planes. A large-scale offensive against the German Central Army Group on June 22 led by July 8 to the destruction of 28 divisions with 350,000 men, a catastrophe that outdid Stalingrad.

In the north as well, the Red Army pushed far westward, took Estonia and the greater part of Latvia and Lithuania, and reached the Bay of Riga on July 29, 1944. The WARSAW UPRISING, begun on August 1 in expectation of aid from Soviet troops (which had reached the Vistula near Sandomierz), remained without their support and collapsed on October 2. So did the Slovak uprising of August 28 to October 29. In the south the next blow fell against the German Army Group South Ukraine on August 20. In a few days the Sixth Army, with 18 divisions, was destroyed, and on August 25 Romania, a former ally, declared war on Germany. The oil fields of Ploeşti were lost (August 30), and on August 31 Bucharest was occupied.

These developments forced Hitler to give up southeastern Europe step by step: on September 16, 1944, Soviet troops marched into Sofia; the Romanian army was now joined by the Bulgarian army in taking up the battle against the Wehrmacht. To the north, Finland had to give up the fight after the loss of Karelia on September 4. Hungary then remained as the last ally; it had been occupied by the Germans since March 19, 1944. In October the Red Army bore down on Hungarian territory (taking Debrecen on October 20) and conquered part of Yugoslavia (occupying Belgrade on October 20). By the end of 1944, Germany's situation on all fronts was hopeless.

Between January 12 and 14, 1945, four Soviet army groups with 25 armies began a major offensive between Memelland and the Carpathian Mountains. The German front collapsed; on January 17 the Red Army entered Warsaw, and on January 19, Kraków and Łódź. It reached the Oder north and south of Breslau on January 22. The Upper Silesian industrial region was lost, and on January 26 the land connection with East Prussia was cut through. In East Prussia and Silesia countless streams of refugees were drawn into this inferno, their timely evacuation obstructed by the political leadership, the *Gau* leaders Erich KOCH and Karl HANKE.

G. H.

Rust, Bernhard, b. Hannover, September 30, 1883; d. Berne (Oldenburg), May 8, 1945, German politician. Rust studied German and classical philology and philosophy. He became an assistant schoolmaster, and after the First World War was active in the *völkisch* military movement. Rust joined the NSDAP immediately after its re-establishment (February 27, 1925). From 1925 to 1940 he was *Gauleiter* of Hannover (as of 1928, South Hannover-Braunschweig). Dismissed from teaching in 1930 "on grounds of health" (rumors spoke of his sexual misdemeanors), that same year he became a Reichstag deputy. On February 4, 1933, he was named a Reich Commissioner in the Prussian Culture Ministry. His unconditional loyalty to Hitler was repaid on April 30, 1933, with the post of Reich Minister for Science, Education, and Public Instruction.

Totally unsuited for this post and an alcoholic in addition, Rust ran into considerable difficulties with competing education functionaries, notably Baldur von SCHIRACH (Hitler Youth), Robert LEY (Order Fortresses), Alfred ROSENBERG (ideological matters), and Heinrich Himmler (JUNKER SCHOOLS). He tried with frantic measures and reorientation efforts to bring the German school system into line with the National Socialist course. Rust provincialized research and science by dismissing political and racial undesirables. He was caricatured in underground humor as a unit of measure: "One Rust equals the smallest unit of time between a decree and the reversal of an order." Rust shot himself upon hearing the news of the German capitulation.

Rydz-Śmigły, Edward, b. Brzeżany (eastern Poland; today in the Ukrainian SSR), March 11, 1886; d. Warsaw, December 12, 1941, Polish marshal (1936) and politician. Rydz-Śmigły was at first an artist. He was close to Marshal Jözef PIŁSUDSKI, and from 1919 to 1921 fought against the Red Army. In 1921 he became an army inspector; as inspector general and supreme commander from 1936 to 1939, he also played a crucial political role in the events leading to the war. When defeat in the Polish Campaign became clear in September 1939, Rydz-Śmigły escaped to Romania. In 1940 he returned to Poland under cover in order to organize the resistance against the German occupation. While doing so, he lost his life under mysterious circumstances.

Bernhard Rust.

Edward Rydz-Śmigły.

S

SA. *See* Sturmabteilung.

Saar Territory (Saargebiet), region with an area of almost 2,000 sq km (about 800 sq m; present-day Saarland, 2,567 sq km) and a population of 800,000, formed from five Prussian and two Bavarian districts (*Landkreisen*) by the VER-SAILLES TREATY. Although France's plan for annexation ran afoul of British and American resistance, the region was removed from German sovereignty and assigned to France for economic exploitation to compensate for war damage. A League of Nations governing commission under the Frenchman Victor Rault assumed supreme state authority. After 15 years, a plebiscite was to decide the Saar's further political destiny. The Saar belonged to the French customs system and the franc was the only legal tender; these and other measures of *de facto* French rule, as well as the pressure of Frenchification, did not make the Saar Statute popular, especially since the German parties had no right to participate in the government through the essentially advisory State Council (Landesrat), established in 1922. German efforts to achieve an early return of the Saar Territory, including those by Gustav STRE-SEMANN, failed in 1929–1930.

The political landscape in the Catholic Saar region differed considerably from that in Germany proper until the Seizure of Power. The unchallenged leader of opinion was the Center party, which in the State Council elections of March 1932 received 43.2 percent of the votes, as against 23.1 percent for the Communist Party (KPD); the Social Democratic Party (SPD) received only 9.6 percent, and the NSDAP, soon to be the strongest party in the Reichstag, garnered only 6.7 percent. The rapid turnabout in Germany changed the picture rapidly, since the leading politicians, including the major industrialist Hermann RÖCHLING, sought support from Hit-

ler and indeed received pledges on condition that, following the German pattern, all "nationalist forces" would unite in preparation for the plebiscite scheduled for January 13, 1935. After serious intraparty conflicts, particularly in the Center, a GERMAN FRONT, with massive financial and propaganda support, had been formed by the autumn of 1933. The political battle ran its course after the precedent set in the final phase of the Weimar Republic: the National Socialists occupied key positions in the party and the economy, an SA-like order-keeping force intimidated opponents, firms put pressure on their employees to join the German Front so as to ward off disadvantages after the Saar was united with Germany, and so on.

The promoters of an "Anschluss" encountered no meaningful opposition: with an unemployment rate of 24.4 percent in December 1934, the opponents had little with which to counter the tidal effect of the upswing in the German economy. They had tardily forged their own unified SPD-KPD front that summer, but were left with only the unpopular alternative of advocating maintenance of the status quo. In contrast, the Catholic church was spreading the nationalist motto "When his loyalty to the Fatherland one breaks, the same deed to the Lord God he makes" ("Wer seinem Vaterland die Treue bricht, hält sie auch unserem Herrgott nicht"). Appeals by such prominent German emigrants as Heinrich MANN, Bertolt BRECHT, Lion FEUCHTWANGER, Anna Seghers, and Alfred KERR, among many others, proved ineffective, as did hints about National Socialist tyranny and concentration camps. On January 13, 1935, the German Front received over 90 percent of the plebiscite votes; 8.8 percent were for the status quo, and only 0.4 percent for union with France. On March 1 of that year, with Hitler present to celebrate his first foreign-policy tri-

Saar Territory. Hitler's entry into Saarbrücken on March 1, 1935.

umph, the Saar Territory was brought "home to the Reich." From then on it and the Palatinate formed the Saar-Palatinate (Saarpfalz) *Gau*, which after December 7, 1940, was called "Westmark" (Western March).

Sabotage, criminal act prosecuted in the Third Reich according to the Ordinance against VOLK VERMIN of September 5, 1939, or as VOLK TREASON.

Sachsenhausen, National Socialist concentration camp about 25 km (approximately 15 miles) northeast of Berlin, built in August and September 1936 by inmates from the Emsland camp in Esterwegen. It was secured by a wall 2.5 m (about 8 feet) high, reinforced with an electric fence and eight watchtowers. Built originally to hold around 8,000 to 10,000 prisoners, by the end of the war 35,000 people were imprisoned there. By mid-February 1945, a total of more than 135,000 prisoners had passed through the camp.

In the early period, mainly political prisoners (especially Communists, Socialists, and Center party members) were interned in Sachsenhausen, but later prisoners included Jews, Gypsies, "asocials," criminals, Jehovah's Witnesses, homosexuals, soldiers discharged from the Wehrmacht, SS members undergoing punishment, Soviet prisoners of war, and captives from the occupied territories (Czech, Polish, Dutch, Belgian, French, and Norwegian prisoners). Camp inmates worked mostly in factories of the German Armament Works and in a clothing factory that was also known as the shoe factory. Especially feared was the so-called shoe-walkers' squad (Schuhläufer-Kommando), in which prisoners had to test the durability of Wehrmacht boots by means of long marches. The most important of Sachsenhausen's 61 satellite and annex camps were the large units at the Heinkel Works in Germendorf, the Klinker Works in Oranienburg, and the DEMAG Works (Deutsche Maschinenfabrik AG) in Falkensee.

Sachsenhausen contained a special camp for notable prisoners and their families; its internees included former Austrian chancellor Kurt SCHUSCHNIGG and the industrialist Fritz THYSSEN. The overall conditions of lodging, food supply, work, and hygiene were catastrophic. Many prisoners died from hunger, cold, exhaustion, inadequate medical care, shooting, hanging, or mistreatment at the hands of SS members or prisoner functionaries. Sick and disabled prisoners (*see* MUSELMANN) were periodically separated out and killed in the course of "Operation 14f13" (*see* INVALID OPERATION) or in the camp itself, by poison injection or in the gas chamber, built in 1943. In the fall of 1941, in compliance with the COMMISSAR ORDER of June 6, 1941, over 11,000 Soviet prisoners of war were shot in the nape of the neck in the camp's execution building, disguised as a medical outpatient facility, under the guise of medical research. During the ensuing period the execution building was used in the same way for the killing of persons who had been transferred to Sachsenhausen for SPECIAL HANDLING on order of the Reich Security Main Office (RSHA).

As in all the large concentration camps, medical experiments were conducted at Sachsenhausen. For example, prisoners were deliberately wounded so that artificial contamination could generate a gangrenous infection on which to test a newly developed antiseptic; some deaths ensued. In the summer of 1944, four out of eight prisoners died from experiments of an unknown kind. That September, prisoners were inflicted with gunshot wounds, not lethal in themselves but using poisoned ammunition, in order to test the rapidity of the poison's effect. Soviet prisoners of war died in the trial of a newly constructed gas van (see GAS VANS) in the autumn of 1941. When the Soviet army approached in early 1945, the SS killed a large number of seriously ill prisoners in the infirmary who were incapable of marching. Less seriously ill inmates were evacuated in freight cars to other camps within Reich territory (Bergen-Belsen, Dachau, and Mauthausen). Some 3,000 prisoners, most of them ill, remained behind and were liberated by Soviet troops on April 22–23. Most of the prisoners were evacuated on foot that month. Those who could not keep up with the march were, on Himmler's specific order, shot on the side of the road by an SS squad. The evacuation march ended in Schwerin, where the exhausted surviving prisoners were freed by American soldiers.

Camp commandants of Sachsenhausen were Hermann Baranowski (d. 1939), Hans Loritz (committed suicide in 1946 in the Neumünster internment camp), Walter Eisfeld (d. 1940), and Anton Kaindl (sentenced to life imprisonment by a Soviet military court; d. in the USSR).

W. D.

Sacrifice (*Opfer*), the cultic presentation to a deity of a feat, of something valuable, or of a person (human sacrifice). Sacrifice in this sense was, in the National Socialist view, typical of the "payment morality" (*Lohnmoral*) of the Jewish religion in particular, and of the Christianity it had spawned, whereas this kind of "bribery of God" was said to be alien to the priestless NORDIC FAITH. Sacrifice was for the Germanic people a "gift out of friendship for the friend-gods [*Freundgötter*]"; for the GERMAN MAN in the present age it received "its value and dignity only from the sense of community." Readiness to sacrifice thus was among the central virtues of National Socialism, as exemplified by the NS movement's dead (see BLOOD SACRIFICE; BLOOD WITNESS; WAR MARTYR). During the war sacrifice for *Volk* and fatherland was unstintingly demanded and praised. Goebbels decreed: "There must be certain words that are reserved exclusively for the Front. Among these is the word 'sacrifice'" (*Das Reich*, December 28, 1942). Sacrifice nonetheless also became a synonym for donation (*Spende*).

Sahm, Heinrich, b. Anklam, September 12, 1877; d. Oslo, October 3, 1939, German politician. In 1912 Sahm became mayor of Bochum; from 1920 to 1930 he was the (unaffiliated) senate president of the Free City of Danzig. He followed a policy of compromise between Poles and Germans, and understood how to protect their rights. After the National Socialist electo-

Roll call in the Sachsenhausen concentration camp.

ral victory in 1930, he was compelled to resign. Within the year he was elected lord mayor of Berlin, but here too he finally (in 1935) had to yield to NS pressure, personified by State Commissioner Julius LIPPERT. Sahm was then appointed German ambassador to Oslo.

Saint-Germain-en-Laye, suburb of Paris where the final peace conditions for Austria were set forth by the Allies on September 2, 1919, and were signed by Austria under protest on September 10. The treaty stipulated the dissolution of Austria-Hungary and restriction of the Austrian state to the territory settled by Germans, except for the South Tyrol and the German-speaking areas of Bohemia and Moravia, which were awarded to Italy and the newly created Czechoslovakia, respectively. In strict adherence to the VERSAILLES TREATY, reparations were imposed on Austria, its army was kept to a maximum of 30,000 troops, and any union with Germany (*see* ANSCHLUSS) had to be approved by the League of Nations, which was tantamount to forbidding it. The Treaty of Saint-Germain-en-Laye, which took effect on July 16, 1920, was both an economic and a psychological catastrophe for Austria. It thereby created an international crisis point that would significantly contribute to the failure of the security systems of the PARIS SUBURBAN TREATIES.

Salazar, Antonio de Oliveira, b. Vimeiro (Beira Province), April 28, 1889; d. Lisbon, July 27, 1970, Portuguese politician. A political economist, in 1928 Salazar became finance minister, and in 1932 premier, remaining in office until 1968. In his domestic policies Salazar, who held dictatorial powers after 1933, stood close to the corporatist state autocracies of Franco's Spain and Italian Fascism; in foreign affairs he pursued a strict neutralist policy during the Second World War in order to protect Portugal's colonial empire from international turmoil. His maneuvering space depended on simultaneous good relations with the Western democracies (especially traditionally friendly England) and with Spain and the Axis powers.

Salò, Republic of (officially, Repubblica Sociale Italiana), term for the Fascist republican countergovernment established on September 15, 1943, by Benito Mussolini (after his liberation on September 12), whom the Germans would not permit to return to Rome; it was named after its capital on Lake Garda. Mussolini's attempts to win over the working class of northern Italy by reviving the socialist and republican origins

Antonio de Oliveira Salazar.

of FASCISM found no response and were greeted with mistrust by German authorities concerned with maintaining production capacity.

The sovereignty of the Salò government was substantially compromised by its total dependence on German supervision: industry fell under the German military command (Reich Plenipotentiary, Ambassador Rudolf Rahn; Supreme SS and Police Leader Karl WOLFF), and the South Tyrol, Trentino, and Venezia Giulia (eastern Venetia, including the Julian Alps and Istria, now mostly in Yugoslavia) were placed under German *Gau* leaders as a first step toward annexation. Moreover, partisan activity was intensifying in northern Italy, and a reign of terror was unleashed by the radical Fascist Partito Fascista Repubblicano (PFR), established on the German model under Alessandro Pavolini. Acts of terror included death sentences against the "traitors" of July 24, 1943, who had deposed MUSSOLINI, and the attempt to draw rump ("residue") Italy into the FINAL SOLUTION. The effort to build a republican army utterly failed, undermined by mass desertions. Finally, the German front was pushed back. The uprising of the resistance (April 24, 1945), Mussolini's execution by partisans (April 28), and Germany's separate armistice in northern Italy (April 28) sealed the fate of the Salò republic.

B.-J. W.

Salomon, Ernst von, b. Kiel, September 25, 1902; d. Winsen an der Luhe, August 9, 1972, German writer. Salomon took part in FREE CORPS conflicts in the Baltic region and in Upper Silesia

Ernst von Salomon.

in 1919, then in the KAPP PUTSCH in 1920. He made no secret of his rejection of the Weimar Republic or of his antisemitic prejudices. In 1922 he was involved in the murder of Walther RATHENAU, for which he was sentenced to five years' imprisonment. Despite his nationalist and conservative posture, Salomon stayed aloof from the National Socialists, whose practices contradicted his notion of a national "awakening" dedicated to Prussian ideals. Nevertheless, the regime celebrated his books, especially *Die*

Geächteten (The Outlaws; 1930), a novel about the free corps, as national documents promoting Germany's renewal. During the Third Reich, Salomon worked mostly outside politics as a screenwriter. After the war he was interned by the Americans until 1946. In 1951 he published his sarcastic novel on denazification, *Die Fragebogen* (translated as *Fragebogen: The Questionnaire*), which became one of the most successful postwar books in Germany (*see* QUESTIONNAIRE).

SA-Mann Brand, German feature film (1933) directed by Franz Seitz and starring Heinz Klingenberg, Otto Wernicke, and Elise Aulinger. Rated "artistically very worthwhile; of instructional value to the *Volk*," it premiered on June 15, 1933. In order to make the National Socialist Seizure of Power appear as an act of salvation, the film glorified the Time of Struggle with operetta-like clichés. The hero of the title plays the role of a noble knight; the girl of his choice is a young Communist, who along with her heart gradually loses her "red" beliefs to Brand as well. His protégé is a Hitler Youth from poor circumstances whose mother secretly sews at night in order to come by the money for a brown shirt. The Communists, in the role of villains, have the upper hand in the section of town and attempt to cut down the ranks of the SA men with murder and mayhem. During the first NS

Still from the film *SA-Mann Brand*.

procession the Hitler Youth, proud in his new brown shirt, is struck by a fatal bullet. With the words "I'm now going to meet the Führer" ("Ich geh' jetzt zum Führer"), he breathes his last breath. His personal tragedy pales in the final scene before the "awakening Germany" in the background, on the day of Hitler's takeover of power.

M. F.

SA Military Badge (SA-Wehrabzeichen), the former Sports Badge, renamed and broadened by a decree of Hitler on January 19, 1939. The military badge was awarded in three ranks (bronze, silver, and gold) after completion of premilitary training for 18-year-olds and postmilitary schooling for men who had completed their compulsory military service. Acquiring it was promoted as a "moral duty of all young German men," and eligibility was limited to Germans free of any "racially alien admixture." They also had to pass tests in three areas: track and field events, military exercises, and field training. A certificate, which also attested to the badge holder's "bearing as to character and worldview," documented successful participation in the "Führer's" program for bringing up a "hardy and tough generation through combat training for the body and the training of a spirit fit for battle."

San Francisco, city in California, chosen at the YALTA Conference as the site for the conference that was to found the UNITED NATIONS.

Sara, biblical woman's name. According to an ordinance of August 17, 1938, "Sara" was to be added in official papers to the first name of all Jewish women who were citizens of the German state (*Staatsbürger*). (*See also* ISRAEL.)

Sauckel, Fritz, b. Hassfurt (Lower Franconia), October 27, 1894; d. Nuremberg, October 16, 1945 (executed), German politician. A merchant seaman, during the First World War Sauckel was in French civilian internment; after the war he became an apprentice locksmith. He became involved in the VÖLKISCH MOVEMENT, joined the SA in 1922, and the NSDAP in 1923. In 1925 he became *Gau* party administrator in Thuringia, and two years later replaced Artur DINTER, who had run into conflict with Hitler, as *Gauleiter*. After 1929 Sauckel was NSDAP leader in the Thuringian legislature. In 1932 he became minister-president for that state and, in the course of the synchronization of the *Länder*

Fritz Sauckel.

(states), Reich governor (*Reichsstatthalter*) in May 1933 (for Anhalt as well, from 1935 to 1937).

Following his appointment as Reich defense commissioner for Military District IX (Kassel) in 1939, Sauckel was designated general plenipotentiary for LABOR DEPLOYMENT on March 21 of that year. For Germany's war economy he organized an army of millions of ALIEN WORKERS, not even a fraction of whom came willingly to Germany. Amid ruthless exploitation under miserable working conditions, amid terror and mistreatment, they suffered devastating losses. The record-breaking recruitment statistics that Sauckel time and again proudly reported ultimately led to his death sentence on October 1, 1946, during the Nuremberg Trials, on counts of war crimes and crimes against humanity.

Sauerbruch, Ferdinand, b. Barmen (now Wuppertal-Barmen), July 3, 1875; d. Berlin, July 2, 1951, German surgeon. In 1908 Sauerbruch became a professor in Marburg; he then taught in Zurich, Munich, and (after 1927) Berlin, where he was affiliated with the Charité hospital. Sauerbruch attained renown with his discovery of the differential pressure procedure in thorax operations. He also developed an improved hand-and-lower-arm prosthesis (the Sauerbruch hand), which enabled many war amputees to return to employment. In 1933, Sauerbruch welcomed the Seizure of Power. As one of the most prominent physicians in the Third Reich, he treated Joseph Goebbels and Paul von Hindenburg, among others, and in 1937 was awarded the National Prize for Art

Ferdinand Sauerbruch.

and Science. Soon disappointed by National Socialism, Sauerbruch did not refrain from incisive critical remarks and was connected with Gen. Ludwig BECK and other opposition fighters in the WEDNESDAY SOCIETY; still, he remained largely untouched. A postwar denazification proceeding acquitted him. In 1951 Sauerbruch published his memoirs, *Das war mein Leben* (That Was My Life; translated as *Master Surgeon*). It was made into a film in 1954.

Sawade, Fritz (alias, 1945–1959). *See* Heyde, Werner.

SB, acronym of *Sonderbehandlung; see* Special Handling.

Schachleiter, Albanus (originally, Jakob Schachleiter), b. Mainz, January 20, 1861; d. Feilnbach (Upper Bavaria), June 20, 1937, German Catholic theologian. Ordained a priest in 1886, Schachleiter in 1908 became abbot of the Benedictine Abbey of Saint Emaus in Prague. A militant German nationalist, he left Czechoslovakia in 1920 and went to Munich to direct the Schola Gregoriana for Catholic church music. He was a popular preacher, and officially declared his support for the NSDAP beginning in 1926, as a result encountering all kinds of difficulties with the official church. His celebratory article on Hitler's seizure of power, published in the *Völkischer Beobachter* on February 2, 1933, led to his suspension and gained Schachleiter a monthly pension of 200 RM from the NSDAP. Hitler demonstratively visited him on May 13, 1933, and obtained his reinstatement that Au-

gust. As a National Socialist showcase-Catholic, Schachleiter was always insistent on demonstrating the party's posture of POSITIVE CHRISTIANITY. At his death, Hitler ordered a state funeral.

Schacht, Hjalmar, b. Tinglev (North Schleswig), January 22, 1877; d. Munich, June 3, 1970, German politician and financial expert. Schacht obtained a doctorate in economics. After his studies he was employed by the Dresdner Bank, and was a deputy director by 1908. From 1916 to 1923 he was director of the (private) National Bank for Germany. In November 1923 he was appointed national currency commissioner, and in December, president of the Reichsbank. In these posts he made a significant contribution to the stabilization of the currency. After 1924 he played a leading role in negotiations on German reparations, but he resigned in 1930 over differences with the Weimar government regarding the YOUNG PLAN. A founder of the German Democratic Party (DDP) in 1918, Schacht withdrew from it in 1926. Politically he leaned increasingly to the right: he was involved in the HARZBURG FRONT, and he helped to introduce Hitler to industrial and financial leaders, notably through the KEPPLER CIRCLE. Moreover, in a petition to Paul von Hindenburg as early as November 1932, Schacht pressed for Hitler's designation as Reich chancellor.

As Reichsbank president (1933–1939), Reich economics minister (1935–1937), and general plenipotentiary for the war economy (1935–1937), Schacht became the central figure in National Socialist rearmament, which he financed through the system of MEFO BILLS that

Hjalmar Schacht.

he created. Under his supervision, German foreign trade (*see* NEW PLAN) was subjected to comprehensive regulation (*see* FOREIGN-CURRENCY MANAGEMENT), bilateralization, and shifting in direction, particularly toward southeastern Europe. Jurisdictional quarrels with Hermann Göring and criticism of the FOUR-YEAR PLAN finally led to Schacht's gradual withdrawal; until then he had stood out for his exaggerated advocacy of colonial and expansionist ideas. After his dismissal as Reichsbank president (January 2, 1939), Schacht remained Reich minister without portfolio until 1943. His loose contacts with the opposition movement of July 20, 1944, led to his imprisonment (July 29), which lasted until the war's end. After acquittal by the International Military Tribunal in Nuremberg on September 30, 1946, a denazification court in Stuttgart sentenced him to eight years in a work camp; he was released in 1948. Absolved of all accusations related to his activities during the Third Reich, in 1950 Schacht began a successful second career as an economic and financial consultant for developing countries.

R. S.

Schäfer, Wilhelm, b. Ottrau (Upper Hesse), January 20, 1868; d. Überlingen, January 19, 1952, German writer. Schäfer taught elementary school (*Volkschule*), and then became editor of the periodical *Die Rheinlande* (The Rhine Lands). After naturalistic beginnings, his art developed along increasingly *völkisch* and nationalistic lines, especially pronounced in the *Dreizehn Bücher der deutschen Seele* (Thirteen

Books of the German Soul; 1922), of which 170,000 copies were in print by 1940. In protest against its democratic leadership, Schäfer, along with Erwin Guido KOLBENHEYER, left the Prussian Academy of Letters in 1931. In 1933 he published an omnibus volume of symbolic *Deutsche Reden* (German Talks). During the Third Reich he was honored with the Rhenish Literature Prize (1937) and Frankfurt's Goethe Prize (1941). Even after the war his books continued to be successful.

Schar (troop), smallest unit (8 to 10 men) in the SA, SS, National Socialist Motor Corps (NSKK), and National Socialist Flyers' Corps (NSFK).

Scheel, Gustav Adolf, b. Rosenberg (Bavaria), November 22, 1907; d. Hamburg, March 23, 1979, German politician. Scheel joined the NSDAP in 1930, and in 1931 was elected chairman of the Heidelberg Student Association by its National Socialist majority. As a student leader, he took a leading role in "cleansing" the University of Heidelberg of "Jewish, pacifist, and Marxist elements." In appreciation of his activism, he was appointed *Reichsstudentenführer* on November 6, 1936. After completing his medical studies, he became inspector of the Security Police and the Security Service (SD) in Stuttgart.

As inspector, Scheel was an instigator in the 1938 KRISTALLNACHT ("I have no patience for restraint!"). On November 27, 1941, he became *Gauleiter* and Reich governor (*Reichsstatthalter*) in Salzburg; at the end of June 1944, he also became Führer of Germany's university teachers (*Reichsdozentenführer*). He was slated

Wilhelm Schäfer.

Gustav Adolf Scheel.

on April 29, 1945, to succeed Bernhard RUST as Reich minister for science, education, and public instruction. Active as a physician after the war, Scheel was classified as an "offender" in a denazification proceeding and was sentenced to five years in a work camp and partial confiscation of his assets. Later, he was accused of collaboration with illegal right-wing extremist organizations, but was acquitted.

Scheidemann, Philipp, b. Kassel, July 26, 1865; d. Copenhagen, November 29, 1939, German politician. Scheidemann joined the Social Democratic Party (SPD) in 1883. He served in the Reichstag from 1903 to 1933, and in 1911 was made a member of the party's executive committee. As his party's spokesman in the Reichstag, Scheidemann spoke out during the First World War against pan-German propaganda advocating war, and called for a negotiated peace. After the SPD split in 1917, he advanced—by the side of Friedrich EBERT—to become the party's recognized leader.

On November 9, 1918, Scheidemann proclaimed the German Republic (without Ebert's agreement) in order to avert incipient revolution. After election of a National Assembly, on February 13, 1919, he formed Germany's first democratic government, comprised of the SPD, the Center party, and the German Democratic Party (DDP). On May 11, 1919, with the words "What hand would not wither, which lay with us in these chains," he undertook rejection of the Versailles treaty. He resigned in June and dedicated himself to municipal politics, serving as lord mayor of Kassel from 1920 to 1925.

Scheidemann remained a political figure influential throughout Germany, as evidenced, for example, by his harsh criticism of cooperation between the Reichswehr and the Red Army (1926). In 1933 he went into exile. After sojourns in France and the United States, he settled in Denmark. He published *Memoiren eines Socialdemokraten* (translated as *The Making of a New Germany: Memoirs of a Social Democrat*) in 1928.

M. F.

Schellenberg, Walter, b. Saarbrücken, January 16, 1910; d. Turin (Italy), March 31, 1952, German secret agent. Schellenberg studied medicine, then law. He joined both the NSDAP and the SS in May 1933. He began work at the Security Service (SD) headquarters in the summer of 1934, becoming an administrative councillor in 1937. Schellenberg played a major role in the merger of all Security Police offices with the SD to create the REICH SECURITY MAIN OFFICE (RSHA), within which he took charge of Office Group (Amtsgruppe) IV E (Domestic Counterespionage) in 1939. He was then an *SS-Obersturmbannführer*. For his achievement in abducting British agents from the Netherlands in the VENLO INCIDENT (November 9, 1939), he was promoted to *SS-Standartenführer* and assigned to prepare security police measures for an eventual German invasion of Great Britain.

At the end of 1941, Schellenberg became director of Office VI (Foreign Intelligence) in the RSHA, as well as an *SS-Brigadeführer*. He crushed the RED ORCHESTRA, a Communist re-

Philipp Scheidemann.

Walter Schellenberg.

sistance and espionage organization; played a substantial part in subordinating the ABWEHR (military intelligence); and personally arrested Adm. Wilhelm CANARIS. With defeat looming, Schellenberg expedited Himmler's plans for separate surrender efforts with the Western powers; in this connection, he procured the release of many captives. This worked in his favor in his trial before Military Court IV in Nuremberg; on April 11, 1949, he was sentenced to a six-year term, despite charges that included aiding and abetting the murder of Soviet prisoners of war. He was pardoned in December 1950.

Schemann, Ludwig, b. Cologne, October 16, 1852; d. Freiburg im Breisgau, February 13, 1938, German race-lore specialist and librarian. In 1894 Schemann founded the Gobineau Union, and served as its chairman until 1920. He also translated the principal work of Count Arthur de GOBINEAU (*Essay on the Inequality of Human Races*) and published Gobineau's papers, thus contributing to the dissemination of his racist ideas. Schemann himself published a three-volume work, *Die Rasse in der Geisteswissenschaft* (Race in Scholarship; 1928–1931).

Schemm, Hans, b. Bayreuth, October 6, 1891; d. there, March 5, 1935, German cultural and educational policymaker. An elementary school (*Volksschule*) teacher, Schemm joined the NSDAP in 1923. He became the local group leader for Bayreuth in 1925, and in 1928 *Gauleiter* of Upper Franconia (which was combined with the Upper Palatinate–Lower Bavaria *Gau* to form a Bavarian "Ostmark" in 1932). Schemm became Bavarian minister for instruction and worship on April 13, 1933.

Known to the public as "Handsome Hanni" ("Schöne Hanni"), Schemm made Bayreuth a National Socialist stronghold as early as the 1920s with his organizational and demagogic talent. In 1929 he founded the NATIONAL SOCIALIST TEACHERS' LEAGUE; he was its "Reich steward," or administrator (*Reichswalter*), until his death. His popularity, which he owed to a blend of pastoral officiousness and antisemitic agitation (as manifested in his book *Gott, Rasse und Kultur* [God, Race, and Culture]; 1933), long remained undiminished. In 1936 a prize for authors of juvenile books was named the HANS SCHEMM PRIZE. After the war, and indeed until 1966, the Bayreuth quarters of the United States Army was called the Hans Schemm Barracks.

Hans Schemm.

Schicklgruber, original last name of Alois HITLER; it was used to make fun of Hitler (as by changing the Hitler greeting into "*Heil Schicklgruber!*") and his fanaticism about heredity.

Schiftan, Hans, b. Berlin, December 8, 1899; d. Mauthausen concentration camp, November 3, 1941, German opposition fighter. Schiftan was a Berlin businessman. A Social Democrat, after 1933 he was the liaison with the exiled SPD (Social Democratic Party) in Prague. Following Germany's march into the Czechoslovak Republic, he fell into the Gestapo's hands on April 13, 1939. He spent a two-year term in the penitentiary and then was taken into "protective custody" in the Mauthausen concentration camp, since "he gave reason to fear that he would . . . resume activities for Marxist aims." Schiftan did not survive the harsh internment conditions; the official cause of his death was given as "general sepsis."

Schirach, Baldur von, b. Berlin, May 9, 1907; d. Kröv/Mosel, August 8, 1974, German politician. Schirach was the son of the Weimar theater director Friedrich Karl von Schirach (1842–1907) and his American wife, Emma. The young Schirach met Hitler in 1925, joined the NSDAP (as member no. 17,251), and after beginning his studies in German philology and art history in Munich, dedicated himself in 1927 to building up the National Socialist German Students' League. His organizational successes as leader of this group beginning in 1928 led to his appointment as Reich Youth Führer (*Reichsjugendführer*) in the NSDAP. He soon secured for himself the leadership of the Hitler Youth (HJ), the National Socialist Schoolboys' League, the League of German Girls (BDM), and the Jungvolk, and shook off any subordination to the SA. After the Seizure of Power, Hitler named Schirach Youth Führer of the German Reich (*Jugendführer des Deutschen Reiches*) on June 18, 1933. Schirach thus became responsible for all extracurricular training of young people, particularly after the Law on the State's Youth of December 1, 1936.

With his unconditional, even unrestrained veneration of Hitler, as well as with the heartfelt pathos of his speeches, Schirach knew how to captivate young people. He considered himself a "priest of the National Socialist faith" and an "officer in National Socialist service." Just as little as he himself corresponded to the ideal of manhood that he promoted—he was rather fat and was often mocked as "effeminate"—did he all the more intensively advocate education for hardness and military fitness. In numerous writings, including *Die Hitler-Jugend* (1934) and *Revolution der Erziehung* (Revolution in Education; 1939), and in songs such as "Unsere Fahne flattert uns voran" (Our Flag Flutters Ahead of Us), he invoked the heroic ideals of the warrior caste, issued antisemitic slogans, and dedicated himself and his organizations completely to the "Führer." Together with his father-in-law, Heinrich HOFFMANN, Hitler's photographer, Schirach published flattering picture books with such titles as *Hitler, wie ihn keiner kennt* (Hitler as No One Knows Him) and *Jugend um Hitler* (Youth around Hitler).

In the long run, Schirach was no match for the crude power plays of his rivals in the NS hierarchy. In 1940 Arthur AXMANN replaced him as Reich Youth Führer. After brief frontline service, Schirach went to Vienna as *Gauleiter* and Reich governor (*Reichsstatthalter*), remaining there until the end of the war, even though his willful conduct in office provoked new intrigues against him. He lost any remaining influence when he and his wife, during a visit to Hitler's Berghof residence, criticized Germany's occupation policy and the harsh methods of deporting Jews. At the same time, Schirach himself shared responsibility for the eastward removal of 185,000 Austrian Jews. In the Nuremberg Trials of major war criminals he denied having had any knowledge of the extermination camps in the east. However, as he first admitted in his own confession of guilt to the court, he had trained German youth "for millionfold murder." Schirach spent the 20-year sentence imposed on October 1, 1946, in the Spandau Prison. His memoirs, *Ich glaubte an Hitler* (I Believed in Hitler), published after his release in 1966, failed to shed much light.

Schlabrendorff, Fabian von, b. Halle an der Saale, July 1, 1907; d. Wiesbaden, September 3, 1980, German jurist. Even before the Seizure of Power, Schlabrendorff was among the conservative opponents of Hitler and of National Socialism. After that point he continued to express his viewpoint in publications, thereby incurring official governmental prohibition. In London he later tried unsuccessfully to gain support for the German opposition. During the war he was the ordnance officer for Henning von TRESCKOW,

Baldur von Schirach.

Fabian von Schlabrendorff.

and as such was involved in the failed assassination attempt of March 1943. After the further thwarted attempt of July 20, 1944, he was arrested. He escaped a death sentence only because his trial was interrupted on February 3, 1945, by the bombardment that killed Roland FREISLER. Schlabrendorff was freed from concentration camp confinement by American troops. Later, he was among the most distinguished jurists of the Federal Republic of Germany, from 1967 to 1975 serving as a judge in the Federal Constitutional Court. He published the studies *Offiziere gegen Hitler* (Officers against Hitler; 1946) and *Gerstenmaier im 3. Reich* (Gerstenmaier in the Third Reich; 1966).

schlagartig (at one fell swoop; suddenly), National Socialist term used in the sense of "well prepared," "surprising"; it was favored for its dynamic sound and its tone of resonant inexorability.

Schlageter, Albert Leo, b. Schönau (Black Forest), August 12, 1894; d. Golzheimer Heide (now part of Düsseldorf), May 26, 1923 (shot), German officer. A volunteer in the First World War, Schlageter advanced to lieutenant, and was awarded the Iron Cross, First Class. From 1919 to 1921 he was active with the free corps, fighting in the Baltic region and Upper Silesia, and suppressing a Communist uprising in the Ruhr. After the outbreak of the RUHR CONFLICT over the French occupation, he campaigned for a transition from passive to active resistance and became involved in acts of sabotage. A member of the Great-German Workers' Party, an offshoot of the NSDAP, Schlageter was the victim of spies in his own ranks, who betrayed him to the French authorities after a successful attack on the Düsseldorf-Duisburg railroad line near Kalkum. He was tried and sentenced to death on May 8, 1923. Despite massive German protests, French president Raymond POINCARÉ confirmed the sentence as a sign of implacability. The parties of the Right, especially the National Socialists, held up Schlageter as a "martyr." In 1931 they placed a cross of honor 30 m (about 100 feet) high at the site of his execution. Hanns JOHST in 1933 wrote and dedicated to Hitler a drama about Schlageter.

Albert Leo Schlageter.

Schlegelberger, Franz, b. Königsberg (Prussia), October 23, 1876; d. Flensburg, December 14, 1970, German jurist. Schlegelberger studied in Königsberg and Berlin, and then became a counselor (*Kammergerichtsrat*) at the Prussian appeals court. In 1918 he transferred to the Reich Justice Ministry as an adviser (*Vortragender Rat*). He became ministerial director in 1927, and from 1931 to 1942 was a state secretary. Beginning in 1922 he was also a professor at the University of Berlin. After Justice Minister Franz GÜRTNER's death, Schlegelberger was in charge of the ministry, from January 29, 1941, until August 20, 1942, with the appointment of Otto THIERACK. He then retired with a grant of 100,000 RM.

Schlegelberger joined the NSDAP on January 30, 1938. Other judges regarded him as a good jurist and a defender of judicial independence when he assumed the ministerial post. However, as the ministry's highest official he did not live up to this reputation. Since Hitler treated him with mistrust and suspicion, Schlegelberger conducted himself with great submissiveness. He significantly increased the severity of the penal code and instigated the systematic dismantling of procedural guarantees. He sought to control sentencing directly through so-called previews and postviews of court judgments, and pressed for the harshest implementation of wartime penal law. In the Nuremberg JURISTS' TRIAL, Schlegelberger was sentenced to life imprisonment, but he was released in 1951 owing to ill health. His writings included *Das Recht der Gegenwart* (Law Today), a loose-leaf work that went through its 16th edition in 1985.

U. B.

Schleicher, Kurt von, b. Brandenburg an der Havel, April 7, 1882; d. Neubabelsberg (now Potsdam-Neubabelsberg), June 30, 1934, German general (1929) and politician. During his training, which began in 1900, Schleicher became acquainted with Kurt Baron von HAM-MER-STEIN-EQUORD and Oskar von HINDENBURG, son of the general. During the First World War Schleicher was assigned to the Supreme Army Command, and for a time was on the staff of Wilhelm GROENER. Like Groener, he was an advocate of a postwar alliance between the Social Democratic Party (SPD) and the military. In 1920 Schleicher became director of the Office for Domestic Affairs in the Armed Forces (Reichswehr) Ministry, and in 1929, chief of the newly formed Military Forces (Wehrmacht) Division, which reported directly to the minister. In these posts he developed his political and economic ideas for a reinvigoration of Germany. Schleicher's office was upgraded in 1929 to a ministry; he thereby became a state secretary and adviser to the minister, who was then Groener. Thus the highest levels of leadership were opened to him.

Together with his chief and with Heinrich BRÜNING, the new Reich chancellor (as of March 28, 1930), Schleicher followed an authoritarian policy and, in view of the crippling of the Reichstag, consolidated the authoritarian model of the PRESIDIAL CABINETS. Brüning's emphasis on foreign affairs nonetheless led to a rapid estrangement between them, and then to a break over the issue of fending off the NSDAP. After Brüning's fall on May 30, 1932, and Groener's removal from power, Schleicher was the key figure in naming Franz von PAPEN as chancellor; Schleicher pushed him forward in order to pull the strings from behind the scenes. In this way he assured himself of the post of armed forces minister. When Papen took an unexpected reactionary course and the National Socialist danger seemed to dwindle after the party's losses in the elections of November 1932, Schleicher himself assumed the leadership of government affairs on December 3. He sought to form a majority with a TRADE UNION AXIS, extending from the NSDAP left wing to the GENERAL GERMAN TRADE UNION FEDERATION, in order to fight unemployment and boost the economy. Yet both the splitting of the NSDAP, attempted with the help of Gregor STRASSER,

Kurt von Schleicher.

and the enticement of the unions failed, when the SPD leadership pressured the unions to break off their flirtation with the general.

Hitler and Papen exploited these weaknesses in a new intrigue with the Reich president against Schleicher; Hindenburg now denied Schleicher his request for a temporary suspension of the constitution, and dismissed him on January 28, 1933. Schleicher rejected the idea of a putsch, suggested to him by Hammerstein (since December 1929 chief of the Army Command), by pointing to his own oath of office. He thus cleared the way for Hitler's SEIZURE OF POWER, and retired to private life. Hitler's revenge for the general's assault on the unity of the NSDAP caught up with Schleicher during the so-called RÖHM AFFAIR. On June 30, 1934, SS men broke into his house and shot both him and his wife, as she ran for help.

Schmaus, Anton, b. Munich, April 19, 1910; d. Berlin, January 1934, German victim of National Socialism. A carpenter, Schmaus was the son of Berlin trade union secretary Johannes Schmaus and, like him, a member of the REICH BANNER "BLACK-RED-GOLD." During the course of SA raids on real or alleged political opponents after the Seizure of Power, Schmaus was attacked in his apartment in Köpenick; his mother was beaten, and his father was hanged. In an exchange of gunfire that killed four SA men, Schmaus was able to escape, and then went to the police. Despite strong pressure they did not hand him over to the SA, which therefore staged an attack as Schmaus was being transferred to the main police headquarters. Seriously wounded, he died in the police infirmary; the exact date is unknown.

Schmaus, Michael, b. Oberbaar bei Augsburg, July 17, 1897, German Catholic theologian. Schmaus became a professor of dogmatics in Prague in 1929, and in Münster in 1933. His primary field was medieval studies, in which he was notable for, among other writings, *Die psychologische Trinitätslehre des heiligen Augustinus* (Saint Augustine's Psychological Teaching on the Trinity; 1927) and his four-volume major work, *Kathologische Dogmatik* (Catholic Dogma; 1937–1941). In 1933 he took a position on Hitler's seizure of power with *Begegnungen zwischen katholisches Christentum und nationalsozialistische Weltanschauungen* (Encounters between Catholic Christianity and National Socialist Worldviews). Schmaus openly welcomed National Socialism as the "most incisive and most vigorous protest against the spiritual climate of the 19th and 20th centuries," and saw in its "decisive 'No' to liberalism" complete agreement with Catholicism.

In *völkisch* thought, too, Schmaus agreed with the National Socialists in his statement that the love of the believer for his *Volk* was "rooted in rushing blood [*rauschenden Blut*] and sustaining soil, both of which are God's work." From this it was only a step to placing values on races, which Schmaus took with his thesis that one must "accord to the German nation a different rank . . . than the Negro Republic of Liberia." The theologian Schmaus was particularly attracted

by the FÜHRER PRINCIPLE, in which he perceived a parallel with the authority of the pope. In 1946 Schmaus became a professor in Munich. He was appointed rector there in 1951, and in 1952 was named a papal domestic prelate by Pope PIUS XII.

Schmeling, Max, b. Klein-Luckow (Uckermark), September 28, 1905, German boxer. Schmeling became light heavyweight champion of Germany in 1926 and of Europe in 1927; in 1928 he became German heavyweight champion. On June 12, 1930, he became world champion in all classes with his victory over the American boxer Jack Sharkey; overnight Schmeling became far and away Germany's most popular athlete. This did not change, even after his unlucky defeat in their rematch on June 21, 1932. With his knockout defeat, on June 19, 1936, of the "Brown Bomber," Joe Louis, who had been regarded as unbeatable, Schmeling—whose manager, Joe Jacobs, was Jewish—involuntarily became a symbol of the National Socialist thesis of the superiority of the "Nordic race." But Schmeling lost their rematch by a knockout in only two minutes and four seconds on June 22, 1938, in New York. NS propagandists circulated rumors of "Jewish trickery." In the Second World War the prominent sportsman had to pose as a hero (including posing as a paratrooper in the Crete operation for the cover of *Signal* magazine), but he was not very cooperative. After the war Schmeling continued his boxing career out of necessity, with varying success, and he retired

Max Schmeling and his wife, Anny Ondra, with Hitler.

in 1948. Married since 1932 to the actress Anny Ondra, he has remained undiminished in popularity.

Schmidt, Guido, b. Bludenz, January 15, 1901; d. Vienna, December 5, 1957, Austrian politician. In 1927, Schmidt took a post in the Austrian president's chancellery, carrying out liaison tasks with the chancellor's office. Valued as a diplomat by Kurt SCHUSCHNIGG, Schmidt directed his efforts toward a settlement with the Third Reich, which was realized in the JULY AGREEMENT of 1936. Subsequently he was state secretary in the Foreign Ministry, and served as foreign minister after Hitler's BERCHTESGADEN DIKTAT until the Anschluss of March 12, 1938. Active in industry during the war (in the Hermann Göring Works, among other places), Schmidt was indicted in 1947 because of his pro–National Socialist politics, but he was acquitted after a short proceeding.

Schmidt, Paul Otto, b. Berlin, June 23, 1899; d. Munich, April 21, 1970, German diplomat. After language studies, Schmidt became an interpreter in the Foreign Language Office of the German government in 1924, and later, chief interpreter for the Foreign Office. With Gustav STRESEMANN, Schmidt took part in all the important international conferences and retained his position under Hitler as well, whom he assisted as interpreter at the MUNICH AGREEMENT. Schmidt also functioned at the center of power during the critical phase at the outset of the war. In 1943 he joined the NSDAP. His fascinating memoirs, *Statist auf diplomatische*

Bühne (An Extra on the Diplomatic Stage; 1949), were often criticized as superficial, yet they provide a good reflection of the period's atmosphere and of the main protagonists on the political stage.

Schmidt-Rottluff, Karl, b. Rottluff bei Chemnitz, December 1, 1884; d. there, August 10, 1976, German painter; co-founder of the Expressionist artists' group "Die Brücke" (The Bridge). Art criticism in the Third Reich found fault with Schmidt-Rottluff because his paintings and large-scale woodcuts diverged from "every German tradition" and did violence to "the portrayal of nature to the most extreme degree." In 1941, as a "degenerate," he was forbidden to paint. Schmidt-Rottluff became a professor at the Berlin Academy of Fine Arts in 1947. His pictures are among the most coveted works in the international art market.

Schmitt, Carl, b. Plettenberg (Westphalia), July 11, 1888; d. there, April 7, 1985, German jurist specializing in constitutional and international law. Between 1921 and 1945 Schmitt was a professor in Greifswald, Bonn, Cologne, and Berlin. He developed his theories in confrontation with the workers' movement. During the Weimar Republic the cardinal points of his thought were the relation between a state of emergency and the norm, the nature of parliamentarianism and pluralism, and the concept of the political, which he determined through the differentiation between friend and enemy.

Schmitt was an adviser to Chancellor Kurt von SCHLEICHER, yet in early 1933 he joined the

Paul Otto Schmidt.

Carl Schmitt.

NSDAP. He became a Prussian state councillor and, until publication of an anonymous attack on him in the SS organ *Das Schwarze Korps* (The Black Corps) in December 1936, was the definitive legal theoretician of the National Socialist regime. He defended the state-perpetrated murders occasioned by the RÖHM AFFAIR in an article entitled "Der Führer schützt das Recht" (The Führer Protects the Law; 1934), and in 1936 advocated cleansing German law "of Jewish influence." In 1940, Schmitt argued against "positive normativism" (*positiver Normativismus*). After 1945 he was without a post, but not without influence. He modified his positions and ideas partially, and now spoke of containing enmity and war; in 1950 he wrote about a new *Nomos der Erde* (Law of the Earth).

J. S.

Schmitt, Kurt, b. Heidelberg, October 7, 1886; d. there, November 22, 1950, German politician, economics expert, and attorney. Schmitt was seriously wounded in the First World War. In 1915 he was appointed to the board of directors of the Alliance Insurance Company (Allianz-Versicherung); he became its general director in 1921. On June 29, 1933, Hitler appointed him Reich economics minister, succeeding Alfred HUGENBERG. This was meant as a signal to the private economy, intended to relieve industry's fears regarding any National Socialist plans for social revolution. When these fears were rendered groundless by the suppression of the SA in the RÖHM AFFAIR (June 30, 1934), Hitler replaced the not very active Schmitt with Hjalmar SCHACHT, at first provisionally on July 30, 1934, then permanently on January 1, 1935. Schmitt returned to private business.

Schmundt, Rudolf, b. Metz, August 13, 1896; d. Rastenburg (East Prussia), October 1, 1944, German officer. In January 1938 Schmundt succeeded Friedrich HOSSBACH as "chief adjutant of the Wehrmacht appointed to the Führer." He was then quickly promoted, becoming a lieutenant general on April 1, 1943. Schmundt was severely injured in the assassination attempt on Hitler of July 20, 1944, and subsequently died in the Rastenburg military hospital.

Schneider, Paul, b. Pferdsfeld bei Bad Kreuznach, August 28, 1897; d. Buchenwald concentration camp, July 18, 1939, German Evangelical theologian. Schneider was a volunteer in the First World War. After his studies, he became a

Paul Schneider and his wife.

pastor in Hochelheim bei Wetzlar in 1926. On October 8, 1933, he was reprimanded by his bishop for criticizing an appeal made by SA chief Ernst RÖHM; nonetheless, Schneider did not stop his attacks on the National Socialist worldview or on the GERMAN CHRISTIANS influenced by it. This resulted in his transfer to the isolated village of Dickenschied, in the Hunsrück Mountains. By June 1934, Schneider had come into conflict with the local NSDAP district leader, who put him in "protective custody." The strong protest of the community, which included many SA members, regained him his freedom until 1937, when his resistance to an order expelling him from the Rhineland brought him to the Buchenwald concentration camp. There he provided his fellow prisoners with Christian consolation from his cell window and put up with harassment and abuse. He ultimately died of an overdose in a strophanthin injection after a severe beating.

Scholarly Evaluation (*Wissenschaftliche Auswertung*), camouflage term for the confiscation of items of cultural value in the German-occupied territories during the Second World War (*see* ROSENBERG OPERATION STAFF; ART PLUNDER).

Scholl, Hans, b. Ingersheim (now part of Crailsheim), September 22, 1918; d. Munich-Stadelheim, February 22, 1943 (executed), German opposition fighter. A leader in the Hitler Youth, Scholl was temporarily incarcerated in 1938 for "leaguist" youth work (*see* YOUTH MOVEMENT). While a medical student, he changed from an enthusiastic supporter of National Socialism to a dedicated enemy. A primary reason for the change was his Catholic upbringing, which clashed with his experiences of the war. After service as a medical corpsman in France and a period of studies at the University of Munich, he was transferred to the eastern front. There he came to realize that National Socialism was conducting an outright extermination campaign against Jews and Slavs, and his decision to fight against Hitler's dictatorship matured.

In the autumn of 1942, Scholl returned to Munich for another study period. There, together with his sister Sophie SCHOLL and others, he founded the WHITE ROSE opposition group. He organized the distribution of leaflets, some previously written and others new, that denounced National Socialist crimes, whose true scale the writers did not even suspect, and that called for overthrow of the regime. During a new leaflet campaign after the Stalingrad catastrophe, on February 18, 1943, Scholl and his sister were observed by the school janitor in the main court of the University of Munich, and turned in. Their death sentence was carried out immediately by beheading on February 22.

Scholl, Sophie, b. Forchtenberg (Württemberg), May 9, 1921; d. Munich-Stadelheim, February 22, 1943 (executed), German opposition fighter. Like her brother Hans, Sophie Scholl freed herself from her fascination with National Socialism only under the impact of the war. During her labor service and her WAR AID SERVICE, she recognized that Hitler's aggressive policies could lead only to ruin. She entered the University of Munich in 1942 as a student of biology and philosophy, and established contact between her opposition group, the WHITE ROSE, and her mentor, Professor Kurt HUBER.

With a youthful rigor that made her almost more daring than her male comrades, she undertook to transport secretly printed leaflets calling for the overthrow of the National Socialist regime, and helped in their distribution as well. Like her whole circle, Scholl hoped that the spark for an uprising against the criminal political leadership would spread from the academic community. Neither she nor the others adequately recognized the system's deep hold on the structures of German society. Yet even such an awareness could hardly have dissuaded her from her struggle, which ended on February 18, 1943, when she and her brother were apprehended in the midst of a leaflet campaign at the University of Munich. Their death sentence, pronounced by the *Volk* Court four days later, was carried out within a few hours.

Scholtz-Klink, Gertrud, b. Adelsheim (Baden), February 9, 1902, German politician. Scholtz-Klink joined the NSDAP in 1928, and became leader of the National Socialist WOMEN'S UNION

Hans Scholl.

Sophie Scholl.

Gertrud Scholtz-Klink.

Georg von Schönerer.

(NSF) in Baden in 1930. In 1931 she took over NSF leadership in the Hessen *Gau* as well, and on January 1, 1934, she became leader of the women's labor service. After lengthy internal jurisdictional disputes, on February 24, 1934, Scholtz-Klink became *Reichsführerin* (female Führer) of the NSF and of the GERMAN WOMEN'S AGENCY (DFW). That November she received the title "Reich Women's Führerin" (*Reichsfrauenführerin*).

Although over the years Scholtz-Klink came to control all matters relating to women, she and the organizations she led remained totally without political importance. She made no attempt to broaden the narrow sphere that the party allowed her. Her scanty ability to prevail within the NSDAP no doubt predestined her for her post in the eyes of her supporters (Rudolf HESS and Erich HILGENFELDT), as did her external "Aryan" appearance and the fact that, as the mother of numerous children, she could be presented to women as a model. In 1950 Scholtz-Klink was characterized as a "major offender" because of her NS activity, and as a result lost her civil rights. As is clear from her 1978 book, *Die Frau im Dritten Reich* (Women in the Third Reich), she continues even today to evaluate the central ideas of the NS worldview as positive.

Schönerer, Georg Ritter von, b. Vienna, July 17, 1842; d. Rosenau (Lower Austria), December 14, 1921, Austrian politician. Schönerer spent his school and university years in Germany. From 1873 to 1888, he represented the Waldviertel (Forest District) in the Reich Council

(Reichsrat) in Vienna. He initially took liberal positions, but rapidly shifted to a nationalist stance (he published the journal *Unverfälschte deutsche Worte* [Unadulterated German Words] until 1912) and to antisemitism, while resorting increasingly to racist arguments. In 1882 he helped formulate the LINZ PROGRAM and developed a Germanic cult to venerate Richard WAGNER.

When the *Neue Wiener Tageblatt*, a Viennese daily newspaper, in 1888 prematurely reported the death of the popular German emperor, Wilhelm I, Schönerer was angered to the point of assaulting the editors. This earned him a four-month prison term and caused him to lose his seat in the Reich Council and his title of nobility (*Ritter* means "knight"). Nonetheless, from 1897 to 1907 he again sat in the Reich Council, this time representing Eger (now in Hungary), and portrayed himself as a "fighter for an all-German state." Because of the Catholic clergy's alleged Slavophile attitude, Schönerer converted to Protestantism and founded an "Away-from-Rome" movement. After the introduction of universal male suffrage in 1907, the personally abrasive zealot was not re-elected, although he continued to have significant influence on *völkisch* and antisemitic ideology. In *Mein Kampf* Hitler referred explicitly to Schönerer, whom he criticized only for not having correctly evaluated the labor question.

Schooling, political (*politische Schulung*), ideological education in the spirit of National Socialism. Schooling, in conjunction with "organization and propaganda" (Hitler's words), influenced attitudes and behavior so as to prepare individuals for releasing radical tendencies or carrying through a plan of action. The success of "schooling evenings" was ensured by reorientation derived from military EDUCATION (such as the wearing of uniforms), by creation of a relationship of obedience toward leaders, and by rituals of acceptance into a particular group that influenced personal conduct (the "community of comrades"). The learning of a repertoire of "confessional" songs was also part of the program. Schooling built on this base was to proclaim slogans and to intensify the pressure of group opinion toward a radical espousal of "principles." This viewpoint was the main criterion for the selection of leaders (*Führerauslese*), which took place in a hierarchical series of schooling camps. They stressed distance from everyday behavior and provided a model for behavior in "service." Schooling in a narrow sense was attuned to this type of political practice as an instructive demonstration of ideological orientation. Appropriate forms for such were hortatory speeches; lectures that did not inform or instruct but instead were intended to stimulate a desire for prescribed "combat goals"; and "working communities" (*Arbeitsgemeinschaften*) with concrete aims.

To secure the dictatorship of the Führer, the party program had been declared "immutable" as early as 1926. Schooling could therefore aim only to strengthen attitudes and values, not to

develop a political program. "A worldview cannot be learned and taught; rather, where there is faith, it can be academically fortified or can be exercised by appropriate methods" (Robert LEY, 1936). In the NSDAP's SCHOOLING FORTRESSES under Ley's jurisdiction, and in the Reich or *Gau* schools of such affiliated associations as the Labor Front (DAF) or the National Socialist Volk Welfare (NSV) agency, such "education" took place. Hitler's perspective as developed in *Mein Kampf* was interpreted with regard to individual subjects (but rarely to basic problems).

On the other hand, divisions such as the SA and Hitler Youth were not bound by the directives of the Main Schooling Office (Hauptschulungsamt). The Rosenberg Office was responsible for supervising them, but it limited itself to providing professional experts, and did not regard itself as competent to set up curricula for ideological schooling. More weight was allotted to the manipulation of speech, which issued from the Propaganda Ministry. It was typical of the restraint on political education after 1936, which went hand in hand with the consolidation of the dictatorship, that the introduction of citizenship training in all schools, demanded in the party program, never took place, whereas total instruction on "ideological foundations" was to be carried out. Thus the arbitrary exercise of power could elude rational political control, and there remained room for subjective identification with the "Führer's will."

H. S.

Schooling. *The Schooling Bulletin*, official monthly publication of the NSDAP: "Thousand-year struggle for the western border."

Schooling Fortresses (*Schulungsburgen*), political educational institutions of the NSDAP, hierarchically organized on Reich, *Gau*, and *Kreis* levels. In the "fortresses" the next political generation was given orientation in a worldview by means of camp rituals, comradeship evenings, working communities, and premilitary exercises. The party's divisions, such as the SA and Hitler Youth, had their own Schooling Fortresses.

School system (*Schulsystem*), the organization and determination of the functions of schools in the Third Reich. In 1933 the NSDAP postponed the solution of controversial questions regarding the school system that had arisen during the Weimar Republic, notably structural reform and ecclesiastical influence. This was done despite the fact that in 1930 the party had promised to establish an eight-year "basic school" (*Grundschule*), to eliminate more elite schools (*höhere*

Schulen), and to reject the Concordat. In fact, the first measures carried out by the government proved to be determined by the pragmatism of power: closing down the "secular" schools (those without religious instruction), conclusion of a CONCORDAT with the Vatican, dismissal of teachers having no denominational ties, and intensification of restrictive selection after the fourth school year, albeit according to the new criteria of physical, character-based, and *völkisch* suitability (ordinance of March 27, 1935). Instead of the ninth elementary school year, Prussia in 1934 instituted the COUNTRY YEAR.

These first decisions regarding school policy served to consolidate the system; most of them were later revised. In 1936 campaigns were started to introduce a "community school" (*Gemeinschaftsschule*), which would no longer be tied to a denomination and which became the norm for all elementary schools until 1941. Religious instruction was reduced, and church-related boarding schools were confiscated or were subjected to inspection by the SS. Teacher training was first transferred to "colleges" (*Hochschulen*) throughout the whole Reich, then after 1941 to TEACHER TRAINING INSTITUTES. Similarly, the consolidation of the middle school (*Mittelschule*) during the war was followed by the introduction of the "Main School" (HAUPTSCHULE), and thereby the abandonment of educational privilege structured according to profession and class. Whether the Main School would assume the tasks of the secondary school in the ninth and tenth school years remained unclear throughout the war. Simultaneously, the many restrictions on access to higher education were eased as new paths for obtaining an academic diploma (*Reifeprüfung*) were opened up for those who had completed vocational training and for the war-disabled, through correspondence and evening courses and the LANGEMARCK CURRICULUM. During the last year of the war, more women students matriculated than ever before.

The strengthening of sex segregation, at least in urban schools (both elementary and more advanced), brought with it a consolidation of the system of girls' schools. The earlier "Women's Schools" (*Frauenschulen*), with their requirement of one foreign language, were recognized as leading to a first-class diploma (*Abitur*). The exclusion of girls from taking Latin at boys' schools was reversed in 1940. In the "Upper School for Boys" (*Oberschule für Jungen*), in contrast to the "German Upper School" of the Weimar period, Latin was obligatory for every-

one. The number of classical, "humanistic" high schools (*Gymnasien*) was sharply reduced, but their prestige thereby increased. Beginning in 1937, the elimination of the 13th school year made the higher schools more uniform. Except for the classical high schools, the boys' schools had two tracks: foreign language, and mathematics and natural science. The girls' schools had tracks for foreign language and for domestic science. Continuation schools (*Aufbauschulen*), which sent some graduates on to higher education, were also retained; they were now separated by sex, and were reserved primarily for pupils from the country schools, whose organization remained less complex. The distribution of courses was intended to keep a balance between the various groups of subjects. But it considerably reduced the proportion of natural science subjects, and a revision was made in 1941. The introduction to citizenship that had been promoted in the NSDAP program was not realized. "Worldview" was not intended to be "a subject or area of applied instruction"; rather, it was meant to be a prerequisite. ("Instruction in worldview" was introduced only in Württemberg-Hohenzollern.) The comprehensive regulations for "Education and Instruction in the Higher School," in comparison with the brief guidelines for other types of schools, clearly contradicted the "revaluation" (*Umwertung*) of all traditional valuations (*Wertsetzungen*) (*see* EDUCATION).

The Reich Law for Compulsory Education of July 6, 1938, not only established eight years of elementary school attendance, but also required the expansion of vocational schools, especially for agricultural occupations. The dual system of instruction was preserved, but the choice of vocational, technical, and engineering schools was expanded. The League of German Girls (BDM) set up its own home economics schools. Instead of continuation schools, teacher training institutes (two-thirds of them for young women) were preferentially promoted. Twelve ADOLF HITLER SCHOOLS were considered to be "party continuation schools" (*Aufbauschulen der Partei*), and the Country Year camp offered the possibility of transferring to one of the NATIONAL-POLITICAL EDUCATIONAL INSTITUTES. German "home schools" (*Heimschulen*), especially for ethnic Germans, were in part organized as comprehensive schools (*gesamtschulartig*). By establishing the Main School as a "selective and compulsory school" (*Auslese-Pflichtschule*), access to further education was to be under stricter political

School system. "Great-Germany. What we must now *learn anew* in fatherland lore." From a National Socialist propaganda pamphlet.

control after 1941. The plans of Baldur von SCHIRACH to limit such education to persons under 16 years of age during the war became reality in 1943 when pupils were called up to become FLAK HELPERS.

Despite inconsistencies, the result of school policies should be interpreted as a consistent application of Hitler's maxims: instruction shortened but expanded with ideology; more physical education; separation of the sexes; elimination of Jews; curbing of church influence; safeguarding of political control over school selection processes; differentiation of vocational training; fostering of enthusiasm for war among boys and preparing girls to be mothers. German occupation policies were far more restrictive with regard to the school system in Poland, where education in schools was reduced to a minimum. In the course of realizing these tendencies, however, impulses were released that only to a limited extent functioned in support of the political system, and that consequently encountered some repression during the war. Notable among them were the opening up of the school to political activities; an increase in the self-confidence and mobility of young people, especially girls; the tendency among teachers to develop an attitude of partnership with pupils and to make

instruction more varied; a shift from demanding rote learning on the part of pupils to requiring performance that involved them more as individuals. Although pressures on young people increased, challenging demands were accepted insofar as they could be related to hopes for advancement. Personal expectations were thus closely tied to the goal of a "final victory."

H. S.

Schörner, Ferdinand, b. Munich, June 12, 1892; d. there, July 2, 1973, German field marshal (April 5, 1945). A highly decorated officer in the First World War (he received the Pour le mérite), Schörner became a career officer in the Reichswehr. He was promoted to major general on August 1, 1940, but his true career took off only after the war's turning point in 1942–1943, when his tough leadership style struck Hitler as most suited to executing the motto of "Hold the line at all costs." Schörner was supreme commander of various army groups: Army Group South, as of March 31, 1944; Army Group North, July 20, 1944; Army Group Central, January 18, 1945. A fanatic National Socialist, Schörner was chief of the National Socialist Command Staff in the Army High Command (OKH) for a brief period in February 1944. At first "successful" with his brutal disciplinary measures (shootings, death-or-glory squads, and so on), he later often strained his collapsing units pointlessly. Named in Hitler's will as supreme commander of the army, Schörner abandoned his troops in Bohemia on May 11, 1945, and set out for Austria in civilian

Ferdinand Schörner.

clothes. Late that month, the Americans handed him over to the Soviet Union, where he remained confined in prisons and camps for war criminals until 1955. After his return to Germany, he was sentenced in October 1957 to four and a half years' imprisonment for manslaughter, but was released for reasons of health in 1960.

Schörzingen, satellite camp of the NATZWEILER concentration camp in Württemberg (Swabian Alps), established in February 1944 as part of the planning for the "Geilenberg Wilderness Work Staff" (Project "Wilderness" [*Wüste*]), on the road from Schörzingen to Wilfingen. Occupied at first by 70 prisoners, the camp held 180 in June 1944, and 200 from almost all of the European countries at the time of the last camp situation report, in August of that year. The prisoners worked at extracting oil shale for the Deutsche Ölschiefer-Forschungsgesellschaft mbH (German Oil Shale Research, Ltd.), the Kohle-Öl-Union (Coal-Oil Union), and the TODT ORGANIZATION. The poor sanitary conditions and inadequate food supplies led to high mortality rates through hunger and exhaustion; mistreatment and killings also took their toll. In mid-April 1945, the camp was evacuated by a foot march in the direction of Lake Constance; on April 23, the prisoners were liberated by the Americans near the village of Ostrach. Other camps of the "Wilderness Group" were Bisinen (Hohenzollern), Dautmergen and Dormettingen (Swabian Alps), Erzingen, Frommern, and Schömberg (Balingen District).

W. D.

Schröder, Kurt Baron von, b. Hamburg, November 24, 1889; d. there, November 4, 1966, German banker. After incomplete law studies in Bonn, Schröder served as a General Staff officer in the First World War. From a banking family, he became co-owner of the J. H. Stein Banking House in Cologne in 1921. With time he joined numerous boards of directors, and was one of the initiators of the KEPPLER CIRCLE. In an attempt to find a solution to the long-standing government crisis that was favorable to industry, he worked after 1932 to place Hitler in the chancellorship.

Schröder arranged the January 4, 1933, meeting at his home in Cologne between Franz von PAPEN and Hitler that was crucial in setting into motion the fall of Chancellor Kurt von SCHLEICHER and the establishment of a government of the "national rising" under Hitler's

leadership, with agreement of the parties present. After the successful SEIZURE OF POWER, Schröder joined the NSDAP on February 1, 1933. He received several honorary posts in the Third Reich. On September 13, 1936, he joined the SS, rising to the rank of *Brigadeführer;* he was also a member of the HIMMLER FRIENDS' CIRCLE. This led to his sentencing in a postwar court proceeding. In his last years Schröder lived in seclusion near Eckernförde.

Schuhmann, Walter, b. Berlin, April 3, 1898, German politician. Schuhmann was a volunteer in the First World War and then worked as a mechanic. He joined the NSDAP in 1925 and was a party section leader in Berlin-Neukölln from 1926 to 1929. Himself a worker, Schuhmann was involved from the outset in setting up the NATIONAL SOCIALIST WORKPLACE CELL ORGANIZATION (NSBO); he assumed control of it within the party leadership in 1931, and in 1933 took over its direction within the Reich government. From this position he was the crucial figure among those organizing the coup against the TRADE UNIONS on May 2, 1933. In the subsequent GERMAN LABOR FRONT (DAF), Schuhmann took control of the general organization of German workers, but he lost influence during the course of the integration of the NSBO. On March 1, 1936, he became a Trustee of Labor in Silesia (*see* TRUSTEES OF LABOR).

Schulenburg, Friedrich Bernhard Count von der, b. Bobitz (Mecklenburg), November 21, 1865; d. Sankt Blasien, May 19, 1939, German officer. Schulenburg entered the army in 1888;

Walter Schuhmann.

from 1902 to 1906 he was military attaché in London. During the First World War he was a General Staff officer, ultimately serving as artillery general and chief of staff in the army group of the German crown prince. Schulenburg resigned his commission in 1919. He was a Reichstag deputy for the German National People's Party (DNVP) from 1925 to 1928, and joined the NSDAP in 1931. Although a high SA leader on Ernst Röhm's staff, he escaped the massacre during the RÖHM AFFAIR (June 30, 1934). He later moved to the SS, within which he rose to *Obergruppenführer*.

Schulenburg, Friedrich Werner Count von der, b. Kemberg (Saxony), November 20, 1875; d. Berlin-Plötzensee, November 10, 1944 (executed), German diplomat. Schulenburg studied law and political science, then entered the diplomatic service in 1901. An officer in the First World War, he became ambassador in Teheran in 1923, and was ambassador in Bucharest from 1931 to 1934. That year he was appointed ambassador to Moscow just as the anti-Bolshevik propaganda of the National Socialists, now in power, was reaching new peaks. Nonetheless, he was able to maintain the lines of communication and thereby contribute to the success of the GERMAN-SOVIET NONAGGRESSION PACT of August 23, 1939. He considered Germany's attack on the USSR on June 22, 1941, to be a disaster, and in 1942 he appealed for a positive answer to Stalin's efforts toward a separate peace settlement. Brusquely rebuffed by Hitler and Ribbentrop, Schulenburg offered his services to

the opposition circle around Carl Friedrich GOERDELER, and went so far as to suggest that he be slipped through the front lines by Henning von TRESCKOW. The conspirators of July 20, 1944, planned to make Schulenburg foreign minister. After the *coup d'état* failed, he was sentenced to death by the *Volk* Court.

Schulenburg, Fritz-Dietlof Count von der, b. London, September 5, 1902; d. Berlin-Plötzensee, August 10, 1944 (executed), German jurist and opposition fighter. Because of his sympathies with the workers' movement, Schulenburg was nicknamed the "Red Count"; he joined the NSDAP in 1932 and was a partisan of Gregor STRASSER. In 1933, as a civil servant in the office of the governor of East Prussia, Schulenburg observed the brutal methods of Gauleiter Erich KOCH with growing disgust. This led to his total alienation from the NSDAP after Strasser's murder during the so-called RÖHM AFFAIR (June 30, 1934). In 1937 Schulenburg, then deputy police president of Berlin under Wolf Heinrich Count von HELLDORF, established contact with the military resistance around Gen. Ludwig BECK. In 1939 he became deputy governor (*Oberpräsident*) of Silesia. He withdrew from the party in 1940 and became an officer on

Friedrich Werner von der Schulenburg.

Fritz-Dietlof von der Schulenburg before the *Volk* Court.

the "mopping-up" staff of Gen. Walter von Un-
ruh ("The Hero Thief") in Paris. In the preparations for the coup of the TWENTIETH OF JULY,
1944, Schulenburg belonged to the inner leadership circle (for example, he helped draft a
conservative constitution). After the coup's failure he was sentenced to death on the gallows.

Schulte, Karl Joseph, b. near Meschede, September 14, 1871; d. Cologne, March 10, 1941,
German Catholic theologian. A professor at the
Philosophical-Theological Academy in Paderborn from 1903, Schulte was made bishop of
that city in 1909. In 1920 Pope Benedict XV
appointed him archbishop of Cologne; the following year he was made a cardinal. In the Third
Reich, Schulte belonged to the moderate wing of
the German episcopacy, as did its chairman,
Cardinal Adolf BERTRAM. Nonetheless, Schulte
fearlessly rejected any assault on the substance
of the Christian message. For example, in a
personal conversation with Hitler on February
7, 1934, he secured the withdrawal of the
recommendation that all school pupils should
read Alfred Rosenberg's *Myth of the 20th Century* (MYTHUS DES 20. JAHRHUNDERTS). Shortly
before his death, Schulte protested against the
National Socialist EUTHANASIA program.

Schultze, Norbert, b. Braunschweig, January 26,
1911, German composer, cabaret performer,
and conductor in Darmstadt and Munich.
Schultze's first success was with the opera
Schwarzer Peter (Black Peter; 1936). His breakthrough came with his music for the Hans Leib
lyric "LILI MARLEEN" (1938), which became an
international hit of the Second World War and
won him exemption from military service as a
"creative artist." Thereafter he wrote propaganda songs such as "Bomben auf Eng(e)land"
(Bombs over England [*Engel* means "angel"])
and "Panzer rollen in Afrika" (Tanks Roll in
Africa). After the war he was successful with
musicals such as *Käpt'n Bay-Bay* and film
scores, among them *Das Mädchen Rosemarie*
(The Girl Rosemarie; 1957).

Schultze, Walther, b. Hersbruck (Middle Franconia), January 1, 1894; d. Krailling, near Munich,
August 16, 1979, German physician. An aviator
in the First World War, Schultze was then a
member of the EPP free corps. He belonged to
the NSDAP from its very beginning, and played
a part in the HITLER PUTSCH. From 1926 to
1931 he was a deputy in the Bavarian parliament
(*Landtag*). In 1933 he became director of public
health for Bavaria, and in 1935 he was made

Walther Schultze.

Reich University Teachers' Führer (*Reichsdozentenführer*), a post he held until 1943. Schultze sought to orient teachers in higher education
along rigid National Socialist lines. Because of
his involvement in the EUTHANASIA program he
was sentenced to four years' imprisonment in
1960. At least 380 cases of aiding and abetting
the killing of handicapped persons were traced
to him.

Schultze-Naumburg, Paul, b. Altenburg bei
Naumburg an der Saale, June 10, 1869; d. Jena,
May 19, 1949, German architect. From 1901 to
1903 Schultze-Naumburg was a professor at the
Weimar Art Academy; he was also director of
the Saaleck Workshops that he established. He
built many country homes and manors in a
deliberate departure from putatively "*Volk-
alien*" architecture: both the turn-of-the-
century "bourgeois un-culture" and the "art-
Bolshevik" tendencies he found embodied in
the BAUHAUS, in particular. Schultze-Naumburg
joined the NSDAP and fought against the "Judaized and depraved art of the SYSTEM ERA"; in
1930 he was appointed director of the State
Academy of Architecture and Handicrafts in
Weimar by the Thuringian interior minister,
Wilhelm FRICK. In 1932 Schultze-Naumburg
was elected to the Reichstag.

The great respect enjoyed by Schultze-Naum-
burg under the official cultural policies of the
Third Reich can be seen in the titles of his
books: *Kunst und Rasse* (Art and Race; 1928),
Kunst aus Blut und Boden (Art from Blood and
Soil; 1934), *Rassegebundene Kunst* (Race-linked

Paul Schultze-Naumburg.

Art; 1934), *Nordische Schönheit* (Nordic Beauty; 1937), and so on. In 1945 one of his buildings received an honor surely unwanted by the architect: the government heads of the victorious powers held their meetings in his Cecilienhof, built between 1913 and 1917. (*See also* ARCHITECTURE.)

Schulze-Boysen, Harro, b. Kiel, September 2, 1909; d. Berlin-Plötzensee, December 22, 1942, German officer and opposition fighter. As a journalist, Schulze-Boysen managed the left-liberal periodical *Der Gegner* (The Opponent;

1932–1933). Through family connections of his wife, Libertas (b. Paris, November 20, 1913; d. Berlin-Plötzensee, December 22, 1942), with Hermann Göring, he secured a post in the Reich Air Ministry as a lieutenant colonel in the Intelligence Division. From 1935 on, Schulze-Boysen, who had no party affiliation, gathered around himself opponents of National Socialism, whether journalists, artists, or even Communist workers, for such activities as distributing illegal publications.

In 1939 Schulze-Boysen joined forces with the resistance group of Arvid HARNACK. In that group, labeled the RED ORCHESTRA by the Gestapo, Schulze-Boysen used his key position in the Air Ministry to acquire sensitive war information; he transmitted it to the Soviet Union, with which he was in continuous contact beginning in 1941. His reports revealed, among other things, the impending German attack, which Stalin nonetheless did not take seriously enough. In 1942 Schulze-Boysen was apprehended along with many active members of the Red Orchestra. He was tortured by the Gestapo and sentenced to death by hanging for high treason.

Schumacher, Kurt, b. Kulm, October 13, 1895; d. Bonn, August 20, 1952, German Social Democratic politician. Schumacher joined the Berlin Workers' and Soldiers' Council in 1918. In 1924 he helped found the REICH BANNER "BLACK-RED-GOLD"; from 1924 to 1931 he was a state legislative deputy in Württemberg. Schumacher was elected in 1931 to the Reichstag, where

Harro Schulze-Boysen with his wife, Libertas.

Kurt Schumacher.

he distinguished himself as an aggressive and shrewd orator, particularly in fierce exchanges with the National Socialist faction. His unforgettable comment on NS agitation as a "persistent appeal to the inner dirty dog [*innerer Schweinehund*] in people" (February 1932) gained him a 10-year concentration camp term. After his arrest on July 6, 1933, Schumacher was interned in Dachau and Flossenbürg, among other camps; there he was subjected to torture and confinement in darkness, and he was seriously ill by the time of his release in March 1943.

After the war's end Schumacher organized from Hannover the reconstruction of the SOCIAL DEMOCRATIC PARTY OF GERMANY (SPD); he decisively opposed unification with the COMMUNIST PARTY OF GERMANY (KPD). As SPD party chairman, member of the Parliamentary Council, and opposition leader in the Bundestag, he labored energetically for the democratization and reunification of Germany, which he considered to be irreconcilable with Adenauer's policy of integration with the West.

M. F.

Schumann, Gerhard, b. Esslingen, February 14, 1911, German writer. Schumann studied German literature (*Germanistik*) in Tübingen. During the Third Reich he was principal dramatic adviser for the Württemberg State Theater. He made a name for himself as a National Socialist with his lyric poems and SA songs. He celebrated Great-Germany in *Lieder vom Reich* (Songs of the Reich; 1935), and its "freedom struggle" in *Leider vom Krieg* (Songs of the War; 1941); he

also wrote cantatas, such as *Sonnwendfeier* (Solstice Celebration; 1936), and CHORAL POETRY, as *Volk ohne Grenzen* (A People without Borders; 1938). Schumann's attempts at drama, including *Entscheidung* (Decision; 1939), were less successful. After the war he was manager of the European Book Club in Stuttgart, and later founded the Hohenstaufen Publishing House. His literary production consisted mainly of light verse with a tone at times humorously critical: examples were *Stachel-Beeren-Auslese* (Gooseberry Picking; 1960) and *Der Segen bleibt* (The Blessing Remains; 1968).

Schuschnigg, Kurt (Edler von [Nobleman of]), b. Riva/Lake Garda (now in Italy), December 14, 1897; d. Mutters (Austria), November 18, 1977, Austrian politician. Schuschnigg studied jurisprudence. In 1927 he was elected to the Austrian National Council (Nationalrat) for the Christian Social party. He was minister of justice from 1932 to 1934, and after 1933 also minister of education. As the successor to Engelbert DOLLFUSS, he became chancellor of Austria on July 30, 1934; for a time he was also foreign minister and defense minister.

Although Schuschnigg sympathized with the idea of a Great-German Reich, he was firmly opposed to the *völkisch* and National Socialist worldviews. His domestic policy measures against the ever more influential National Socialists proved as ineffectual as his foreign policy: at first he relied on Italy for protection, but when the Berlin-Rome AXIS took shape, he was

Gerhard Schumann.

Kurt Schuschnigg. Election poster.

forced to make an arrangement with Germany in order to preserve Austrian independence (*see* JULY AGREEMENT). Pressured by Hitler and without backing from Mussolini, Schuschnigg agreed in the BERCHTESGADEN DIKTAT (February 12, 1938) to accept Hitler's Austrian protégé Arthur SEYSS-INQUART into the cabinet. His attempt to renege on the agreement through a plebiscite on Austrian independence was exploited by Hitler as the occasion to invade Austria (March 12, 1938). Schuschnigg was arrested and interned in a concentration camp between 1941 and 1945. After the war he taught history in Saint Louis, Missouri, and wrote his memoirs, *Ein Requiem in rot-weiss-rot* (A Requiem in Red-White-Red [translated as *Austrian Requiem*]; 1946) and *Im Kampf gegen Hitler* (Struggling against Hitler; 1969).

M. F.

Schutzhaft. *See* Protective custody.

Schutzstaffeln. *See* SS.

Schwab, Alexander, b. Stuttgart, July 5, 1887; d. Zwickau Penitentiary, November 12, 1943, German journalist. Schwab was a teacher. In 1918 he moved from the Independent Socialists (USPD) and the Spartacus League to the Communist Workers' Party (KAP), which rejected the parliamentary tactics of the Communist Party (KPD). Sharply critical of the Bolshevik dictatorship, Schwab became an economics journalist, broke away from the KAP, and took charge of the press office of the Reich Employment Exchange (Reichsanstalt für Arbeitsvermittlung), which he was forced to leave after the CIVIL SERVICE LAW of 1933. He organized contacts with emigré groups, published an illegal periodical, and approached Social Democratic Party (SPD) opposition groups. He was arrested in 1936 and, after a year of pretrial detention, was sentenced to eight years' imprisonment. Schwab's health collapsed from harsh mining labor in the Börgermoor concentration camp.

Schwamb, Ludwig, b. Untenheim (Rhine-Hesse), July 30, 1890; d. Berlin, January 23, 1945 (executed), German jurist. In 1921 Schwamb became a lawyer in Mainz. A Social Democrat, in 1928 he was appointed by Wilhelm LEUSCH-NER to the Hessian Interior Ministry along with Carlo MIERENDORFF. He was discharged after the Seizure of Power, and worked in private business. Schwamb maintained contact with the Social Democratic opposition; his home in Wil-

mersdorf was the scene of many secret meetings of the group around Julius LEBER, and its hideout. After the failed attempt on Hitler's life in July 1944, the Gestapo arrived and took Schwamb away on July 23, delivering him up to National Socialist justice of vengeance. His death sentence on January 23, 1945, was carried out the same day.

Schwarz, Franz Xaver, b. Günzburg (Danube), November 27, 1875; d. Regensburg internment camp, December 2, 1947, German politician. From 1900 to 1924, Schwarz was an administrative official in Munich's city government. He joined the NSDAP in 1922, and was discharged from his job after the HITLER PUTSCH (November 9, 1923). During the period when the party was illegal, he belonged to the directorate of the substitute organization, the Great-German Volk Community. When the NSDAP was refounded, he became its first treasurer.

Addressed within the party as Reich treasurer (*Reichsschatzmeister*), Schwarz was a pedantic administrator; as of September 16, 1931, he represented the party in all financial matters as "General Plenipotentiary of the Führer" (*Generalbevollmächtiger des Führers*). He eventually also took control of the NSDAP AID FUND and the Reich Ordnance (*Reichszeugmeisterei*), which until then had been run by the SA leadership. The entire party organization, including the armed SS units, was financed from the budget administered by Schwarz until the beginning of the Third Reich, when it was partially absorbed into the Reich budget. In 1935

Franz Xaver Schwarz.

Schwarz, who from 1933 was a Reichstag member and a "Reich leader" (*Reichsleiter*), was also given responsibility for the finances of associations allied with the NSDAP. Well above the average age for National Socialist leaders, he avoided intraparty political wrangles. Nonetheless, he was posthumously classified as a "major offender" by a Munich court in September 1948, resulting in confiscation of his estate.

Schwarze Korps, Das (The Black Corps), the SS weekly newspaper, subtitled "Newspaper of the Schutzstaffeln of the NSDAP, Organ of the SS Reich Leadership." *Das Schwarze Korps* began publishing in early 1935 through the initiative of Max AMANN; its first issue appeared on March 6 of that year. It was published on Thursdays by the EHER PRESS. The editor in chief was Gunter d'ALQUEN; the assistant editor was Rudolf aus den Ruthen. The paper's circulation in November 1935 was 200,000, and in 1944, 750,000; the final issue was that of April 12, 1945. *Das Schwarze Korps* benefited from the intelligence apparatus of the Security Service (SD) and won a reputation among the public as the "only oppositional newspaper" because it did not hesitate to criticize intraparty problems. This posture arose from its claim to be the guardian of authentic National Socialist doctrine, which was frequently reflected in its biting and often vulgar attacks on such targets as the Catholic church and the Jews.

S. O.

Das Schwarze Korps. Masthead.

Schweitzer, Hans, b. Berlin, July 25, 1901, German graphic artist. As early as the 1920s, Schweitzer took sides with the NSDAP and published crude but memorable caricatures of its opponents. As a pseudonym (and program), he chose "Mjölnir," the name of the Germanic god Thor's hammer. Schweitzer became a star caricaturist in the Third Reich; he was named a professor in 1937, and became a "Reich Delegate for Artistic Expression" and chairman of the Reich Committee of Press Illustrators. After the war he worked as an illustrator.

Schwerin von Krosigk, Johann Ludwig (Lutz) Count von (title received in 1925 through adoption), b. Rathmannsdorf (Anhalt), August 22, 1887; d. Essen, March 4, 1977, German politician. After studies in law and political science, Schwerin von Krosigk served as an officer in the First World War. In 1920 he became an administrative counselor in the Peace Treaty Division of the Reich Finance Ministry; in 1929 he was promoted to ministerial director of the Budget Office. Renowned as a financial expert and with no party affiliation, he was given the finance post in Franz von Papen's "Cabinet of Barons." He

"With unbroken strength!" From *Das Schwarze Korps* (1945).

Hans Schweitzer.

Lutz Schwerin von Krosigk.

Ulrich-Wilhelm Schwerin von Schwanenfeld.

retained the post under both Kurt von Schleicher and Hitler up until the collapse of 1945,
even though he never joined the NSDAP.

Schwerin von Krosigk kept a low political
profile. On the one hand, he maintained contacts with opposition circles, but on the other,
he never protested against the National Socialist
persecution of Jews. Without his skillful management the financing of REARMAMENT would
have been much more difficult. When the war
was ending, in order to avoid being designated
chancellor in the DÖNITZ government he became director of the "Acting Reich Government for Conduct of the Affairs of the Reich
Foreign Ministry and the Reich Finance Ministry." Interned after his arrest on May 23, 1945,
he was sentenced on April 11, 1949, during the
WILHELMSTRASSE TRIAL, to 10 years' imprisonment, but he won early release in January 1951.
His volumes of memoirs of the Third Reich era,
particularly *Es geschah in Deutschland* (It Happened in Germany; 1951), are distinguished for
their succinct portraits of leading personalities.

**Schwerin von Schwanenfeld, Ulrich-Wilhelm
Count,** b. Copenhagen, December 21, 1902; d.
Berlin-Plötzensee, September 8, 1944 (execut-
ed), German opposition fighter. After agricul-
tural studies in Munich (where he observed the
Hitler Putsch of November 9, 1923) and in
Breslau, Schwerin von Schwanenfeld managed
his estates in West Prussia and Mecklenburg. In
contact since his student years with Peter Count
YORCK VON WARTENBURG and Adam von TROTT
ZU SOLZ, he rejected National Socialism from
the start; as early as 1935 he maintained that

only by assassinating Hitler could Germany be
spared from ruin. After the failure of the first
putsch plans during the SUDETEN CRISIS,
Schwerin von Schwanenfeld joined the Wehrmacht as an officer. Until 1942 he was an
ordnance officer with Field Marshal Erwin von
WITZLEBEN, and then a captain in the Army
High Command. He was important as a liaison
between military and civilian opposition groups.
Although as a conservative he called for a "revolution from above" to follow a successful *coup
d'état*, he also advocated agrarian reform. Arrested on the day of the failed assassination
attempt of July 20, 1944, Schwerin von Schwanenfeld was sentenced to death on September 8.

Science fiction. *See* Futuristic novels.

Scorched earth (*Verbrannte Erde*), military tactic
during retreats to make the abandoned area
useless for the enemy's supply and transport
needs. In the Russian Campaign, the Red Army
was to have used this method, on Stalin's order,
to hinder the German advance. It failed, owing
largely to the high speed of the German offensive. The Wehrmacht, for its part, counted on
the scorched-earth method to check the Soviet
offensive (according to Himmler's order of September 3, 1943) after the German defeat at the
battle of Kursk (July 1943). The tactic achieved
its goal only in some localities, since commanding officers disregarded the orders for destruction or because partisan units were able to
secure bridges, railroads, and industrial installations in time. Finally, according to Hitler's in-

tention, as expressed in the NERO COMMAND of March 19, 1945, the scorched-earth policy was intended to hold back the Allies in the final struggle in Germany.

Scrip (*Bedarfsdeckungsscheine*), noncash form of payment, subsidization, or loan forgiveness having a particular purpose. Scrip could be used to buy clothing, furniture, and household appliances; according to the Law to Reduce Unemployment of June 1, 1933, it was distributed to unemployed persons conscripted for agricultural service, to relief agencies, and to the recipients of MARRIAGE LOANS.

Sculpture (*Bildhauerkunst*), art form whose public nature and ability to influence the masses made it equally important with ARCHITECTURE as a means of (self-)presentation for the cultural policy of the Third Reich. As monumental plastic art (sometimes actually combined with architecture) of similarly awe-inspiring effect, sculpture was to create "images of a community united in a common ideal." Building facades and open squares were embellished with large sculptures; offices and meeting rooms, with reliefs and busts. In sculpture, more than in other branches of the arts, the National Socialists were able to connect with prior stylistic developments. Sculpture was an art form traditionally favored by those in authority; it was usually too large and too expensive for private ownership. Moreover, as a form of public art, statues were usually figurative and thus comprehensible to the masses. After 1933, internationally recognized sculptors such as Georg KOLBE and Fritz KLIMSCH created with state support realistic human figures conforming to an image of the classical antiquity toward which National Socialist aesthetics was primarily oriented; in sculpture, "classical Greek" was to be not an "unattainable ideal" but a "living reality." Sculptors who departed from strict attention to form were banned—as "destroyers of form" and "art-Bolsheviks"—from working.

Thus, figures of a stereotypical GERMAN MAN (or woman) came to dominate sculpture as a central motif. Whether soldier, peasant, or hero, he was a model and a "racial ideal"; sculptures of nudes, often bearing torches, flags, and swords, personified "the Wehrmacht," or "Young Germany." Particularly popular were the muscle-bound nude athletes of Arno BREKER and Josef THORAK: masterful male figures meant to embody the pride and strength of the "new Germany." Female figures, on the other hand, were characterized by "grace and devotion,"

Sculpture. *The Avenger*, relief by Arno Breker.

and based on a concept of their traditional role as childbearer. Idealized nudes that avoided any individual features sought to emphasize the timelessness of the NS state and its institutions. Not least for this reason, one finds hardly any full-length sculptures of contemporary personalities; but on the other hand, political figures of the Third Reich were abundantly portrayed in busts. Busts of the Führer were made in multiple copies as solemn decorations for public rooms. They frequently suggested "imperial greatness" through their exaggerated dimensions.

H. H.

SD, acronym of Sicherheitsdienst des Reichsführers-SS; *see* Security Service.

Seasonal state (*Saisonstaat*), in the vocabulary of National Socialist propaganda, a term of derision used after about 1939 for countries created in 1918 that because of German expansion had again disappeared, such as Czechoslovakia or Poland.

Sea war. *See* Naval war.

"Second Book" (*Zweites Buch*), typescript of Hitler's from the holdings of the United States National Archives (catalog number EAP 105/

40). First published in 1961 by the American historian Gerhard L. Weinberg, with a preface by German historian Hans Rothfels, it evidently dates from the summer of 1928. Hitler himself mentioned the 324-page work on February 17, 1942, in the TABLE TALKS; in connection with MEIN KAMPF, he spoke "of another, not published manuscript." Weinberg claims that the work was not published because of the slow sales of *Mein Kampf* at the time, and because the unstable political situation would have rendered unavoidable major revisions of the text, for which Hitler had neither the time nor, probably, the interest.

As for its content, the "Second Book," which deals primarily with foreign-policy issues, confirms the components of HITLER'S WORLDVIEW as already set forth in *Mein Kampf*. The basic theme of his FOREIGN POLICY, in particular the solution on Russian soil to the "need for space," is developed with an incisiveness and range of variations that exceed even the well-known selections from *Mein Kampf*. The "Second Book" demonstrates, in Rothfels's words, the "consistency of Hitler's foreign-policy principles, as against the view of him as a mere opportunist or the view of the nihilistic revolution for its own sake; and particularly as against the underestimation of the content of his program." Hitler's basic principles "might permit opportunistic deviations in their realization, but in the final analysis they remain bound up in a rigid neo-Darwinism of fanatical proportions, with all its consequences."

C. Z.

Second Revolution (*Zweite Revolution*), slogan widely propagated after the Seizure of Power by the social-revolutionary wing of the NSDAP. This faction saw the political victory of National Socialism as only the first step toward a radical restructuring of society and a massive redistribution of wealth. The spokesmen for a Second Revolution were to be found chiefly in the NATIONAL SOCIALIST WORKPLACE CELL ORGANIZATION (NSBO) and the STURMABTEILUNG (SA). The unemployed masses in the party organizations also understood by this term their totally concrete claims for the material support that they had earned in the struggle for the streets. Hitler met the demands, which endangered his alliance with industry, business, and above all the Reichswehr, with measures of WORK CREATION and with unconcealed threats. On July 6, 1933, he announced in a speech before the Reich governors (*Reichsstatthaltern*) the end of the "national revolution" and explained that if there were a Second Revolution, "we leave no doubt that we would drown such an attempt in blood, if necessary." The RÖHM AFFAIR showed that he meant this literally. It put an end to demands for a Second Revolution and eliminated the social-revolutionary wing of the party.

Second World War

The historian Ludwig Dehio has made the controversial claim that the two world wars are connected "in the interlinked chain of European wars of hegemony like two acts of the same drama." So seen, the Second World War is thus a result and continuation, as it were, of the First World War—although in a radicalized form. Thus the central question of continuity or break in German history between 1914 and 1945 is thrown open. It must be answered on three levels: on that of the war's goals, on that of its leaders, and on that of its political and military implementation.

In territorial terms, National Socialist ambitions transcended the dimensions of a relatively restricted traditional policy of revisionism and national political hegemony, even if one cites for comparison imperial Germany's already very extensive war-goal planning for Russia, France, and central Africa: after the military subjugation of the Soviet Union, a German-ruled continental European "living space," from the Bay of Biscay to the Urals, was to furnish the provisions for the final struggle for world ascendancy against the United States that was seen as the ultimate goal. Once again, as in 1914, the key to the success of this global strategy lay with Great Britain. Would it place itself and the resources of its empire on the side of Germany as a "junior partner," or would it, together with the United States, again block a new German thrust for world predominance? If the latter were the case, then the destruction of the British empire, which in and of itself Hitler constantly rejected, stood next on the program, directly after that of the Soviet Union and before that of the United States.

These war aims, totally overambitious even in territorial terms, meant a permanent overextension and squandering of Germany's limited forces. As in the First World War, the radical dynamism and immutability of German war aims, which ultimately ruled out alternatives by excluding any timely political compromise solution until the bitter end, rested on the demands of Germany's power elites for political power and economic hegemony (*see* AUTARKY). But above all, and for the first time, they derived from a dogmatic racial ideology as official government doctrine, which from the "eternal struggle for existence" (*see* SOCIAL DARWINISM) inferred a natural right to "living space in the east" and to the enslavement of the indigenous population based on the alleged "superiority" of the Nordic-Germanic race. The ineluctable consequence of this racial utopia was an unprecedented ideological intensification, fanaticization, and brutalization of warfare in the east as an anti-Bolshevik "struggle for extermination" and "struggle of two worldviews" (Hitler on March 30, 1941), and of occupation policies in Poland and the Soviet Union (*see* GENERAL PLAN FOR THE EAST, June 12, 1942). The goal no longer consisted merely of the military subjugation of the enemy, territorial gains, and economic exploitation. Rather, the intent was reduction of the population to a helot-like existence and, in part, even its physical annihilation, to this end ignoring all traditional norms of international law (*see* Decree on Wartime MILITARY JURISDICTION, May 13, 1941; COMMISSAR ORDER, June 6, 1941). The invasion of the Soviet Union on June 22, 1941, and the first dramatic intensification of the war situation that autumn made it clear that the unexpectedly unfavorable course of the war was postponing far into the future the "ghetto solution" in Siberia that for a time had been considered, or the MADAGASCAR PLAN solution. It was not by chance that concurrently the decisive steps were taken toward the physical FINAL SOLUTION of the Jewish question.

At least an initial realization of all these war aims, including the "final solution," was made possible only with close cooperation between the new National Socialist power elite and the old ruling strata in the army, the bureaucracy, and the private economy. Except for a few individuals involved in active opposition, even in the occupied territories the latter groups fully identified themselves with the planning and actions of the regime, and, indeed, lent their assistance.

The new character of the Second World War also revealed itself in the abolition—incipient already in 1917–1918—of the traditional separation between the military and the civilian realm in the modern, technological people's war. Preeminent examples of this "qualitative leap" were Germany's OCCUPATION POLICY and, in response to it, new forms of political and military warfare behind the fronts without a clearcut definition of combatant status, such as the fighting by PARTISANS and the French RÉSISTANCE (*see also* WARSAW UPRISING, August 1–October 10, 1944). Other manifestations of this transformation were the "total war" proclaimed by Joseph Goebbels after the defeat at Stalingrad, in his Sports Palace speech of February 18, 1943; the NERO ORDER of March 19, 1945; and the mobilizations of boys born in 1928 and of the "last reserves" near the end of the war (*see* VOLK STORM), as well as the weapons and tactics of the strategic AIR WAR against civilian populations. (This form of aerial warfare did not achieve its goals, either in the AIR BATTLE FOR ENGLAND or in the Allied bombing war from 1942 to 1945.) In addition, the measures of forced resettlement and expulsion, affecting millions (which had their trial run in 1939–1940 by joint agreement of the Germans and the Soviets, and which the victors then exercised against the defeated in 1945), should be seen in the context of a war that inflicted severe suffering on civilian populations. The "qualitative leap" already mentioned had as its prerequisite the revolutionary technological development of modern techniques for warfare and mass extermination. The modern tank (*see* Heinz GUDERIAN) permitted a wide-ranging operational strategy of encirclement (*see* BLITZKRIEG); long-range bombers and fighter planes with a large radius of action were the foundations of strategic bombing; German remote-controlled rockets (*see* WONDER WEAPONS) and American atomic bombs introduced the modern "scenario" of missiles and nuclear war. Finally, the Holocaust too was the product of a machinery of death technically perfected by industry.

The fundamental resolution of the NS leadership to realize expansive goals, if necessary with military force, should not divert attention from a careful analysis of the Second World War, its final outcome, and its important turning points from the perspectives of politics, military strategy, and social history. Thus, the war situation impelled the aggressor more and more into a kind of objective compulsion to open new fronts and to include ever more extensive territories in his war plans and actions. He thus saw himself increasingly restricted in his autonomous freedom of decision.

In contrast to the "war guilt debate" of 1914, the "unleashing of the Second World War" by Germany on September 1, 1939, inspired no comparable controversies. The date of the German attack on Poland with a "reversed front formation" toward the west and east, rather than toward the east alone as originally planned, and the motives behind it, do need some explanation. Reasons for the attack (even before the onset of the autumn mud season) must be sought in Hitler's expectations from the GERMAN-SOVIET NONAGGRESSION PACT of August 23, 1939 (specifically, Poland's isolation, intimidation of the Western powers, and the neutralization of the Soviet Union), as well as in his calculations as to timing: that he could take advantage of an optimal "strategic window." For a short time, Germany's "broad-based armaments" would be at their peak; the world powers and particularly the United States, in contrast, had not yet developed their eventually superior powers.

In view of Germany's limited resources and a war economy that, in comparison with the practically unlimited goals, had relatively limited productive and expansion capabilities, the German leadership drew the strategic consequence: to utilize a high level of military mobilization, a partial technological superiority, and the element of surprise to overcome the enemies one after another in small "Blitzkriegs" (*see* POLISH CAMPAIGN; NORWEGIAN CAMPAIGN; FRENCH CAMPAIGN) and thereby successively to expand the supply of provisions for Germany's war economy. When this "Blitzkrieg plan" stalled in the autumn of 1941 in the mud and ice outside Moscow (*see* RUSSIAN CAMPAIGN), and when a year later the war finally changed into a dogged and hard war of attrition and defense, a large-scale and consistent concept of an alternative military or political strategy for the defense of "Fortress Europe" was lacking. The slogans that emerged from Berlin, such as "Persevere" (*Durchhalten*), "Unite" (*Einigeln*), or "Hold fast to each square centimeter of soil," expressed from 1943 on a desperate protest, not flexible strategic thinking. Moreover, the "European New Order" envisaged by Hitler was based on a German *Diktat* and racial biology; it permitted large-scale organized human roundups of forced laborers (*see* Fritz SAUCKEL) and Jews, and it was imbued with obvious contempt for what Hitler termed the "trash" (*Gerümpel*) of Europe's small states, and also for Germany's satellites and the countries it had conquered.

On September 1, 1939, Hitler announces to the Reichstag the beginning of the war with Poland.

7

8

9

1
Hitler reviews the victory parade in
Warsaw on October 5, 1939.
2
African Campaign. German cannon in
the desert sand.
3–6
German war propaganda posters:
(3) "Germany's victory: Europe's freedom."
(4) "Watch out for spies. Be careful in
conversations!" (5) "Victory at any price."
(6) "Help. Give. Textiles, linens, and clothing
collection."
7
One of millions.
8
Russian Campaign. German tanks in
the Ukraine.
9
Naval war. Encounter at sea.
10
German infantry.
11
Air war. Briefing of a combat unit.

10

11

Despite a few instances of COLLABORATION, this "new order" offered no real likelihood of united European cooperation based on equal rights, perhaps under the banner of a common "crusade against Bolshevism." National Socialism had no constructive or attractive program for Europe.

The question as to the decisive turning points of the Second World War and the openness of the situation at each brings forth for consideration three phases: the summer of 1940, the autumn and winter of 1941–1942, and the winter of 1942–1943. It became clear that Great Britain under its new prime minister, Winston Churchill, was not willing to conclude peace even after France's capitulation on June 22, 1940, and that the United States was moving more menacingly to the fore as an eventual enemy through its ever closer military cooperation with London. This evoked for one last time a broad palette of varying conceptions for the victorious ending of the war: unification of "central Europe" under German hegemony, supplemented by peripheral "large economic domains" in southeast Europe and a colonial empire in central Africa; a direct landing in England (Operation "Sea Lion" ["Seelöwe"]) after achieving air supremacy, starving out the island empire, and halting the supply of provi-

From the beginning to the end of the Second World War, propaganda manifested total confidence in victory: "Germany is victorious on all fronts."

sions from the United States through an accelerated buildup of the U-boat weapon (*see* NAVAL WAR); destruction of the British empire and the approaches to it through a "peripheral strategy" with bases in West Africa, the Mediterranean (*see* AFRICAN CAMPAIGN), and the Near East by building up a superior battleship fleet; the development, favored by Foreign Minister Joachim von Ribbentrop, of a Eurasian continental bloc, extending from Madrid to Yokohama, against Great Britain and the United States, based on the THREE-POWER AGREEMENT of September 27, 1940, with the inclusion of Spain (*see* HENDAYE; October 23, 1940), Vichy France (*see* MONTOIRE; October 24, 1940), and the Soviet Union (Molotov's visit to Berlin on November 12–13, 1940); and, finally, indirect warfare against the two Anglo-Saxon powers through an attack on the Soviet Union.

The attack on the Soviet Union (the instructions for Operation "Barbarossa" were dated December 18, 1940) was truly "Hitler's real ideological war," and as such was planned long in advance. It resulted, however, both from an assuredly real exigency—having "securely won" in the west without any prospect of a decisive victory in the war, and with the nightmare of being exposed in the rear to potential political and economic pressures from Stalin—and from the energetic proclamation by Foreign Minister Viacheslav Molotov in Berlin of a Soviet offensive security zone stretching from Finland by way of the Baltic Sea outlets to Romania and the Balkans, and as far as the Turkish straits. The BALKAN CAMPAIGN (April 6–June 1, 1941) from this perspective had a more defensive character—to safeguard the southern flank for "Barbarossa" and to protect the Romanian oil fields at Ploieşti from English bomber attacks originating in Crete.

The "turning point outside Moscow" at the end of 1941, and the simultaneous entry of the United States into the European war (December 11, 1941; the declaration of war by Germany and Italy), aroused among contemporaries and allegedly even in Hitler the first real doubts as to the "final victory" and, above all, great perplexity as to how the United States could be defeated. Rivalries between the Axis partners involving power politics, as well as mutual distrust and also the great geographical distance between Germany/Italy and Japan, stood in the way of planning a common global strategy and a coordinated war strategy in Europe/North Africa and the Far East, despite the political agreement of February 18, 1942, on the mutual delineation of

German infantry advancing in Russia.

the theater of operations. The German armies and their allies ran into stiff Soviet resistance along the entire eastern front in the autumn of 1942, and despite a rigid and unimaginative "holding strategy," had to swallow their first reverses. Meanwhile, Tokyo affirmed its friendship toward Moscow (April 14, 1941; the Japanese-Soviet Nonaggression Pact) and unilaterally realized its "Greater Asian Co-Prosperity Sphere," from the Aleutian Islands to New Guinea and from Burma to the Marshall Islands in the Pacific, as a mighty reservoir of raw materials and at the same time as a market for its industrial products and surplus population. It was only the loss of the naval battle near the Midway Islands (June 3–7, 1942) and then the costly defeat at Guadalcanal (August 7, 1942–February 8, 1943) that led to a turning point in the Far East that was contemporaneous with developments in the Euro-African theater of war. The autumn and winter of 1942–1943 brought the most decisive turnaround on all fronts: Stalingrad (surrounded November 19–23, 1942; German capitulation, January 31–February 2, 1943); El Alamein (Rommel's retreat, November 3, 1942; capitulation in Tunisia, May 13, 1943); northwest Africa (Anglo-American troop landings and thus the opening of a "second front," November 7–8, 1942); the conference at CASABLANCA (demand for UNCON-DITIONAL SURRENDER, January 14–24, 1943); and the Battle of the Atlantic (for the first time the Allies produced more ships than the Germans sank).

Following a final, unsuccessful German offensive at Kursk (Operation "Citadel"; July 5–15, 1943), "Fortress Europe" was breached in the east in a step-by-step process that began at the Dnieper (by the end of 1943), then moved to the Budapest–Weichsel–East Prussian border (end of 1944). The Russians launched their final pincer attack on Berlin from their Oder bridgehead on April 16, 1945, culminating in the German capital's surrender on May 2. From the southeast, Soviet thrusts and partisan activity in the Balkans, augmented by the Anglo-American INVASIONs from Italy and France, brought the German fronts to the point of collapse.

After the turn in the fortunes of war in 1942–1943, Hitler persisted ever more inflexibly in his radical political and strategic stance, which excluded any political compromise and which he was able to force by suggestion on his entourage as a maxim of behavior; this was the effect of the "Führer myth." Feelers for a separate peace put out by Stalin from the end of 1942, probably out of anger over the nonappearance of the second front in France, were ignored. Acts of opposition (notably the assassination attempt of July 20, 1944) and protest were met

1
Volk Storm, 1945.
2
"Total war is the short-
est war!" War poster,
1944.
3
After the air raid on
Dresden, the bodies of
the victims are burned
on gratings made of rail-
road tracks.
4
March 20, 1945. In the
courtyard of the Reich
Chancellery, Hitler
greets young wearers of
the Iron Cross, Second
Class.
5
Collapse. Germany,
1945.

German soldiers on the way to captivity.

with terror and executions. Overall movements to overthrow satellite regimes (Romania, August 23, 1944; Bulgaria, September 8; Finland, September 19) were, insofar as possible, answered with military occupation and the forced installation of puppet governments. Uprisings behind the front (the Warsaw Uprising, August 1–October 2, 1944; the uprising in SLOVAKIA, September 1944) were put down with bloodshed. A clearly grotesque expression of the total loss of contact with reality and the willful blindness prevailing in the Berlin Führer bunker's world of illusion was Goebbels's attempt in the final hour to falsify for propaganda purposes the news from TEHERAN (November 28–December 1, 1943) and YALTA (February 4–11, 1945) about increasing conflicts among the "Big Three" concerning the new postwar order in Europe, particularly with regard to Germany, Poland, and the Balkans, so that he might portray it as the hour of rebirth for Germany as a great power between East and West.

The capitulations of Germany (May 8, 1945) and Japan (September 2, 1945) ended a world war whose highest blood tolls were paid by the Soviet Union (between 10 million and 13 million soldiers and 7 million civilians dead) and, at a certain remove, Poland (5 million to 6 million dead, of whom approximately 3 million were Jews; altogether, 20 percent of the population), and by Germany (3.8 million soldiers and 1.65 million civilians). The defeat in 1918, after the retreat of the United States into isolation as a political power and the self-isolation of the revolutionary Soviet Union, had bequeathed to the defeated Germany in the center of Europe sovereign unity and every possibility of rising again to great-power status within a relatively short period. After 1945, the rapid alienation among the victorious powers (the POTSDAM AGREEMENT, July 17–August 2, 1945) led to the division of the world into two power blocs and, with the creation of a border between these blocs in central Europe, to the *de facto* obliteration of the German nation-state only 75 years after its establishment by Otto von Bismarck in 1870–1871.

Bernd-Jürgen Wendt

Secret Service, British agency, subordinate to the Joint Intelligence Bureau, that coordinates military counterintelligence and state security operations; it was pilloried by National Socialist propaganda as the instigator of "nefarious crimes." Among the most spectacular Secret Service operations in the Second World War were the assassination of Reinhard HEYDRICH in 1942, and the disinformation that misled Germany's ABWEHR regarding the Allied invasion of Normandy in 1944. On the other hand, despite orders from the highest level, the REICH SECURITY MAIN OFFICE (RSHA) was unsuccessful in trying to prove that the Secret Service participated in the BÜRGERBRÄU ASSASSINATION ATTEMPT made by the cabinetmaker Johann Georg ELSER on November 8, 1939.

Secret State Police (Geheime Staatspolizei; Gestapo), agency of the SECURITY POLICE (Sicherheitspolizei; Sipo) that emerged from the Secret State Police Office (Geheimes Staatspolizeiamt; Gestapa), which was founded in Prussia in 1933. Rudolf DIELS was the first Gestapa director. The Gestapa office grew out of the Prussian Political Police, which after the PRUSSIAN COUP had shifted its attention from the right wing of the political spectrum to the left because of infiltration of its leadership by reactionaries and National Socialists. In this way a foundation was laid for the successful National Socialist revolution, especially when augmented by SA and SS personnel who were deputized as auxiliary police. During the revolution the Gestapa used the REICHSTAG FIRE DECREE to place numerous political opponents in police and SA jails, under the rubric "PROTECTIVE CUSTODY." Later in 1933 the political police forces of the German

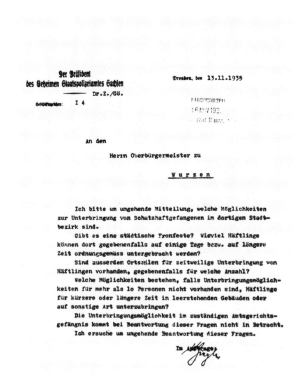

Secret State Police. Gestapo query to the mayor of Wurzen (Saxony) about the setting up of a concentration camp in his town "for the lodging of protective-custody prisoners. . . . Is there a public jail? How many prisoners can . . . be housed there for several days or a longer period? Are there also cells . . . , and how many? If there are not facilities for more than 10 persons, could prisoners be housed . . . in empty buildings?"

states were synchronized under Heinrich Himmler, and in 1934 Reinhard HEYDRICH replaced Diels as Gestapa head.

By the Prussian Secret State Police Law of February 10, 1936 (*Statute Book* [*Gesetzsammlung*], p. 21), the Gestapo's assignments were to investigate and combat all activities hostile to the state, to conduct and evaluate the results of investigations, to report to the government, and also to provide other administrative authorities with relevant information and to give them advice. To implement its goals the Gestapo relied in large measure on so-called Protective Custody Orders (*Schutzhaftbefehle*), which formally derived from the Reichstag Fire Decree and resulted in immediate internment in a concentration camp or other confinement facility. Instructions involving the Gestapo were exempt from judicial control. Here, however, the law simply followed prior practice and the highest judicial interpretations.

In its area of competence the Gestapo had authority over the ORDER-KEEPING POLICE. The inspector of the state concentration camps was directly under the Gestapo. From the beginning of the war it formed the fourth department of the REICH SECURITY MAIN OFFICE (RSHA). If Gestapo agents fulfilled requirements for the SS, they were also accepted into the SECURITY SERVICE (SD) of the *Reichsführer-SS*.

The Gestapo implemented its own punishments of criminal acts and politically objectionable behavior, bypassing the state prosecutors and courts. Punishments ranged from physical abuse, to concentration camp incarceration, to summary execution. If a judicial sentence was too mild by NS standards, the Gestapo "correctively" intervened—in the case of an acquittal, for example, by arrest and internment in a concentration camp. Thus to protect its own prestige, the judicial system often anticipated Gestapo measures. Aside from combating political opponents, the primary assignments of the Gestapo included sending such categories as Jews, Gypsies, homosexuals, and Freemasons to the concentration camps. The domestic terror unleashed by the Gestapo increased in direct proportion to the decline in Germany's fortunes at war. (*See also* GESTAPO.)

W. R.

Sects, persecution of (*Sektenverfolgung*), the totality of measures taken against the small religious communities in the Third Reich; unlike the two large churches, they were not public corporate bodies. The persecution of sects at times took more dramatic forms than did the CHURCH STRUGGLE. Although in accordance with Article 137 of the Weimar Constitution the sects came under the protection of religious freedom and could appeal to the FREEDOM OF BELIEF called for in the NSDAP program, they still had no connection with the state beyond the provisions of civil law. They had to raise their own contributions and could bring in supplementary income only from the donations of foreign members or from the sale of printed materials. Restrictions came into play at this point, since the international connections of many groups aroused the particular suspicions of National Socialist authorities. Currency controls and legal limitations on associations undermined their economic bases and seriously hindered their missionary activity.

A further step toward persecution was taken by the state if a religious community omitted the required loyalty declaration. According to the Ordinance of the Reich President for the Preservation of Internal Peace of December 19, 1932 (*Reich Law Gazette* I, p. 548), as well as the REICHSTAG FIRE DECREE, such sects were declared to be forbidden organizations, their assets were confiscated, and their presses shut down. Members who continued to work for their communities were confined in PROTECTIVE CUSTODY. A typical example of their tribulations was the fate of the JEHOVAH'S WITNESSES. Yet other sects too felt the full weight of persecution. Nonetheless, some groups endured until the war's end, since they were obstructed by administrative harassment and thus evaded a prohibition (as was the case with the QUAKERS), or because the "preservation of harmless sects" seemed to promote a desired "fragmentation in the area of church and religion." Even *völkisch* groups such as the GERMAN FAITH MOVEMENT were liable to persecution.

Secular (*säkular*), in the sense of "long-term duration," a favorite foreign word in the National Socialist vocabulary. It was used to signify in a lofty manner the transcendent importance of an event or decision.

Secure, to (*sicherstellen*), National Socialist euphemism for the verb "to confiscate" (*beschlagnahmen*), especially with regard to the taking of Jewish property in the course of ARYANIZATION or ART PLUNDER.

Security Police (Sicherheitspolizei; Sipo), after the ORDER-KEEPING POLICE (Orpo) the second

pillar of the police forces, following the reorganization of the German POLICE. It included the SECRET STATE POLICE (Gestapo), the Criminal Police (Kripo), and the Border Police (Grenzpolizei). Reinhard HEYDRICH was chief of the Sipo as well as of the SECURITY SERVICE (SD) of the SS. He merged the two organizations in establishing the REICH SECURITY MAIN OFFICE (RSHA) on September 27, 1939. They were the sources of the EINSATZGRUPPEN that followed the Wehrmacht on German military campaigns and that fulfilled both security police tasks and operations involving the persecution and liquidation of Jews.

Security Service (Sicherheitsdienst; SD) of the *Reichsführer-SS*, intelligence and surveillance organization established in 1931, first as the "Ic-Dienst," under Reinhard HEYDRICH. Within two years it covered the entire Reich territory. SD sectors (*Abschnitte*) and upper sectors (*Oberabschnitte*; later called leading sectors [*Leitabschnitte*]) were also established, parallel to those of the General SS (Allgemeine SS). After taking over competing authorities (including the FOREIGN POLICY OFFICE OF THE NSDAP), by 1934 the SD was the only counterespionage and intelligence service in the National Socialist movement. Although in the ensuing years it also assumed government control functions, it remained *de jure* an agency of the party, and as such received its budget from the NSDAP treasurer.

The agency's goal was to subject the entire German population to total surveillance, yet even the SD was unable to accomplish this, given the regime's structure of authority. For example, any meddling with internal party procedures was forbidden. In the areas of politics and police, the SD ran into conflict with the interests of state executive agencies such as the Gestapo, the Criminal Police, and the Security Police. In 1937 their various jurisdictions were accordingly more strictly delineated. The SD, within the realm of executive police measures, was given particular responsibility for keeping watch on the enemies of National Socialism, reporting on the state of opinion among the German populace (in the "Reports from the Reich"), evaluating the political reliability of individual "*Volk* Comrades," and gathering relevant foreign news. With regard to this last task, even before the war the SD influenced German foreign and domestic policy through contacts with foreign sympathizers and ethnic Germans, and also through its planning of sabotage acts (as at the GLEIWITZ radio station). In addition, in February 1944 the ABWEHR was placed under its control.

The close technical interdependence and the personnel connections between the SD and the SECURITY POLICE (Sipo) led to their merger on September 27, 1939, in the REICH SECURITY MAIN OFFICE (RSHA). The SD thus penetrated more deeply than before into the operational area of the Sipo, which itself became increasingly an instrument of Hitler's direct power as Führer, beyond party and state. This proved to be especially important in the role played in the occupied territories by those installed as "commanders of the Sipo and the SD," as well as in the murder operations of the EINSATZGRUPPEN, whose leaders were frequently higher SD functionaries.

We.

Seeckt, Hans von, b. Schleswig, April 22, 1866; d. Berlin, December 27, 1936, German general. Seeckt was a General Staff officer in the First World War (a major general by 1915). In 1919 he headed the military contingent in the German peace delegation at Versailles. He then became chief of the newly established Troop Office in the Armed Forces Ministry of the Weimar Republic, and in 1920, chief of the army command. With the standing army limited by the victors to 100,000 men, the monarchist Seeckt, as "creator of the Reichswehr," set up a cadre force in lieu of the forbidden conscript army. Insulated from the democratic system as a "state within the state," it played a political role that was only formally neutral.

In 1923 Seeckt, in effect a military dictator with full authority conferred by Reich president Friedrich EBERT, had leftist uprisings put down in Saxony and Thuringia, but he refused to intervene in revolts from the Right (notably the KAPP PUTSCH and HITLER PUTSCH), invoking the motto "Troops do not fire upon troops." After a conflict with armed forces minister Otto GESSLER, he was discharged from service in 1926. He remained active as a politician (he was a Reichstag deputy for the German People's Party, 1930–1932), as a military adviser to Chiang Kai-shek in China (1934–1935), and as a military author (*Gedanken eines Soldaten* [*Thoughts of a Soldier*]).

"Seelöwe" ("Sea Lion"), military code name for the planned landing of German troops in England in 1940–1941. The operation had to be abandoned because of the loss of the AIR BATTLE FOR ENGLAND.

Seidel, Ina, b. Halle an der Saale, September 15, 1885; d. Schäftlarn/Isar, October 2, 1974, German writer. Seidel first wrote religious lyrics and later, patriotic poems during the First World War. She achieved success with such novels as *Das Labyrinth* (*The Labyrinth;* 1921) and especially *Das Wunschkind* (*The Wish Child;* 1930). The mystical tenor of her prose grew stronger in her novel *Lennaker* (1938), and was commended by National Socialist reviewers as an effort to "portray bloodline as a law of life." This esteem was made manifest by her election to the Academy of Letters and her award of the Poetry Prize of the City of Vienna

Hans von Seeckt.

Ina Seidel.

in 1941; Seidel reciprocated it by penning hymns to Hitler. She later regretted this "mistake," but even after 1945 did not alter her poetic tone of believing and commanding (*Wähnen und Walten*), as in *Das unverwesliche Erbe* (The Incorruptible Inheritance; 1954) and *Michaela* (1959).

Seizure of Power (*Machtergreifung*), in the narrower sense, the takeover of governing power in Germany by the NSDAP on January 30, 1933, when the party's Führer, Hitler, was named Reich chancellor; in the broader, actual sense, the process of establishing the National Socialist dictatorship and destroying democracy in Germany during 1933 and 1934. Preliminary to the Seizure of Power was the dissolution of the WEIMAR REPUBLIC between 1929 and 1933: first the transition from a parliamentary system to PRESIDIAL CABINETS under Heinrich BRÜNING (chancellor, March 30, 1930–May 30, 1932); then the openly antidemocratic policy of Franz von PAPEN (chancellor, June 1–November 17, 1932), who sought the establishment of an authoritarian regime, and his policy of concessions to Hitler and the NSDAP (June 14, lifting

of the ban on the SA and SS; July 20, the PRUSSIAN COUP); the concomitant rise of the NSDAP from the status of an unimportant splinter party (1928: 12 Reichstag seats) to that of the strongest political power (July 1932: 230 out of 608 Reichstag seats); and finally, on December 3, 1932, the appointment of Gen. Kurt von SCHLEICHER as Reich chancellor.

In contrast with Papen, Schleicher had a plan to obstruct a seizure of power by Hitler— namely, the splitting of the NSDAP and the formation of a "trade union axis" made up of the General German Trade Union Federation and the left wing of the NSDAP as represented by Gregor STRASSER. In the election of November 6, the NSDAP had sustained a loss of votes (falling to 196 seats out of 584) and had slipped into a crisis because of large debts. Yet Hitler succeeded in isolating Strasser within the party leadership: on December 7, Strasser announced his resignation from all party posts. Schleicher's plan thus foundered on Strasser's weakness, but also on the resistance of the Social Democratic Party (SPD) and the trade unions. At a meeting between Hitler and German industrialists arranged by Papen and held on January 4, 1933, in

Seizure of Power. Group portrait of January 30, 1933. From the left: Wilhelm Kube, Hanns Kerrl, Goebbels, Hitler, Röhm, Göring, Darré, Himmler, Hess. Seated in front: Frick.

the home of the banker Kurt Baron von SCHRÖ-
DER in Cologne, they apparently assured him of
further financial support. Agreements were also
reached there concerning the formation of a
Hitler-Papen government. As the final possibility for blocking such a government, Schleicher
suggested to Reich President Hindenburg on
January 23 that the Reichstag once again be
dissolved, that any new election be indefinitely
postponed, that a state of emergency be declared, and that both the NSDAP and the
Communist party be banned. Hindenburg rejected this "plan for dictatorship," as he had
already done in the case of a similar plan of
Papen's; Schleicher therefore resigned on January 28. On January 30, Hindenburg, reluctant
to the last but pressured by Papen and his
associates, named Hitler as Reich chancellor,
supported by a coalition of the NSDAP and the
GERMAN NATIONAL PEOPLE'S PARTY (DNVP).
Papen became vice chancellor and Alfred HU-
GENBERG, the DNVP chairman, became economics minister. Indeed, in this "cabinet of
national concentration" in which the HARZBURG
FRONT seemed to come into new life, the bourgeois minority held the majority. Aside from
Hitler, the NSDAP was represented only by
Wilhelm Frick (interior minister) and Hermann
Göring (minister without portfolio). Yet Frick
and Göring (who was also made Prussian interi-
or minister) possessed the key domestic political
positions. The conviction of the middle-class
"nationalist" Right that it had "tamed" the
National Socialists in the new government and
had "engaged" them for its own political goals
(Papen) quickly proved to be a fiction.

January 30, 1933, celebrated by the NSDAP
as the "NATIONAL RISING" and the onset of the
"National Socialist revolution," was in reality
only the beginning of the Seizure of Power. In
the succeeding months democracy was conclusively extinguished in Germany while a totalitarian dictatorship was put together in stages:

1. Under Göring's direction and with the
assistance of the SA and the SS ("auxiliary
police" in Prussia since February 11), the replacement of democratic by NS bureaucrats
began immediately in February, ratified by the
CIVIL SERVICE LAW of April 7.

2. The REICHSTAG FIRE on February 27
provided the pretext for banning the Communist press and part of the Social Democratic
press, as well as for the REICHSTAG FIRE DECREE
of February 28, which invalidated important
constitutional laws. Real and suspected opponents of National Socialism were taken into

After the Seizure of Power, Hitler appears before a
jubilant crowd.

"PROTECTIVE CUSTODY." This action, the simultaneous establishment of the first concentration camp, and also the boycott of Jewish
businesses on April 1, marked the start of the
NS system of terror.

3. The Reichstag was dissolved immediately
on February 1, in accordance with an agreement
made in forming the Hitler government. Although the election that followed violated the
fundamental laws of a free election—the Communist Party (KPD) was banned and SPD electioneering was curtailed—the NSDAP won
"only" 288 seats out of 647, with 43.9 percent
of the vote, so that it needed the 52 votes of the
DNVP for an absolute majority. On March 21,
the new Reichstag was opened in the Potsdam
Garrison Church in the presence of the Reich
president, solemnly and with great pomp, which
was meant to symbolize the bond between the
old (Prussian monarchist) and the new (NS)
Germany (see POTSDAM CELEBRATION).

4. With the installation of NS Reich commissioners (Reichskommissaren) as executive heads
of the individual states (Länder) between March
5 and 10, their SYNCHRONIZATION began. Germany for the first time became a centralized
state.

5. The ENABLING LAW of March 24 definitively eliminated the state governed by law (*Rechtsstaat*).

6. On May 2, trade unions were banned, and on May 10 employers and employees were forcibly united in the GERMAN LABOR FRONT.

7. In June and July 1933, the surviving parties were forbidden or they dissolved themselves under NS pressure; the law of July 14 forbade the formation of new parties. Germany had become a one-party state, as legalized by the Law to Secure the Unity of Party and State of December 1, 1933.

8. The Reich Culture Chamber Law of September 22 and the EDITOR LAW of October 4 initiated cultural synchronization.

9. The Reich government was in fact already synchronized: ministers who were not NSDAP members were removed and were replaced by National Socialists; the Propaganda Ministry emerged as a new entity.

10. Under the pretext of an alleged SA conspiracy, between June 30 and July 2, 1934, Hitler had Ernst RÖHM, other SA leaders, and others out of favor with the regime murdered. He thus removed the SA as an independent power factor (*see* RÖHM AFFAIR). In its stead, the SS became the most important support for the regime.

11. After Hindenburg's death on August 2, 1934, indeed on that very day, the offices of Reich president and Reich chancellor were by law combined in the person of Hitler as FÜHRER UND REICHSKANZLER. The establishment of the NS dictatorship was complete.

R. B.

Seldte, Franz, b. Magdeburg, June 29, 1882; d. Fürth, April 1, 1947, German politician. Seldte's studies were in chemistry. He served as an officer in the First World War, in which he was seriously wounded. He then took over his father's chemical factory. On December 25, 1918, Seldte founded the STEEL HELMET (Stahlhelm), an anti-Republican military organization of former frontline soldiers that he used in his fight against the "November democracy" (that is, the WEIMAR REPUBLIC). Leading the Steel Helmet after 1924 together with Theodor DUESTERBERG, Seldte fought against the YOUNG PLAN in the 1929 referendum and made common cause with Hitler in the HARZBURG FRONT in 1931.

On January 30, 1933, Hitler made Seldte Reich labor minister in his new cabinet. Seldte

Franz Seldte.

joined the NSDAP on April 27, and brought the Steel Helmet into the SA. From March 1933 to July 1934 he was Reich commissioner for the Labor Service; he later took charge of the Prussian Economics Ministry as well. Nonetheless, his influence ebbed continuously as the Labor Front, Göring's Office for the FOUR-YEAR PLAN, and finally Fritz SAUCKEL, as general commissioner for labor deployment, all absorbed more and more of his jurisdiction. Hitler rejected Seldte's attempt to resign in 1935. Imprisoned at the war's end, Seldte was to have been indicted as a war criminal, but he died in an American military hospital.

Selection (*Auslese*), central concept of the National Socialist biologistic worldview. In the application of Darwin's Theory of DESCENT to human history and society (*see* SOCIAL DARWINISM), the political and racial status quo was interpreted as the result of a constant struggle for existence. In this way a beneficial natural selection was increasingly superseded by a counterselection process that was destructive of culture, but that could be checked through HEREDITY CULTIVATION and RACIAL HYGIENE. Venereal diseases, especially among active individuals, costly "preservation of the hereditarily unfit," wars, emigration of vigorous citizens, late marriage among the especially capable—all these factors were responsible for the increasing reproduction of unsuitable, hereditarily ill persons, who were gradually destroying the racial germ of the *Volk*. NS population policymakers thus saw their task in reversing this trend through such breeding-related measures as the Law to Prevent HEREDITARILY ILL OFFSPRING,

FORCED STERILIZATION, and the EUTHANASIA program.

The concept was also used in pedagogy, in the "selective schools" (*Auslese-Schulen*), and in party schooling to develop leaders (*Führer-Auslese*). (*See also* EDUCATION; SCHOOLING, POLITICAL.)

Selection, Theory of (*Selektionstheorie*), the foundation of Charles Darwin's Theory of DESCENT, according to which the biological status quo of races and species is the result of natural SELECTION. The theory was applied to human evolution and history by SOCIAL DARWINISM; it considerably influenced National Socialist POPULATION POLICY.

Selektion (Latin-derived term for *Auslese; see* SELECTION), in National Socialist usage, aside from its biological meaning, a term customarily used in the EXTERMINATION CAMPS to designate the separation of prisoners capable of work from those slated to be killed. In AUSCHWITZ, for example, at the "ramps," the *Selektion* often took place when deportation trains arrived, as SS men glanced over the newcomers and made their decisions. Not infrequently, entire transports were sent to the gas chambers without any *Selektion*. In the barracks housing prisoners who had initially been classified as capable of work, doctors and SS medical personnel regularly made further *Selektionen* in order to separate out for killing exhausted and ill persons ("useless eaters"). The term *Selektion* had previously been used in this sense in the EUTHANASIA program.

Self-Defense (*Selbstschutz*), militia-like units of ethnic Germans in Poland. After German troops marched into Poland in September 1939, groups of ethnic Germans banded together in order to maintain peace and order in their communities and to prevent assaults by the Polish population upon the German minority. Heinrich Himmler took up the idea and in mid-September 1939 ordered Gottlob BERGER, at the time an SS-*Brigadeführer*, to set up a Self-Defense presence in the occupied Eastern Territories with the use of SS staff. To be sure, this Self-Defense force did not limit itself to its primary tasks: in numerous instances it engaged in "vengeance operations" against Poles hostile to Germans, liquidated many Jews, and took part in the so-called INTELLIGENTSIA OPERATION. The Self-Defense operation, numbering around 45,000 men, finally became a burden to the military. Even SS notables termed it "a band of murderers" (Hans

FRANK). By a decree of November 8, 1939, Himmler ordered its dissolution, to be effective as of November 30. Self-Defense members were to be transferred to the SA, the National Socialist Motor Corps, and the National Socialist Flyers' Corps. Nonetheless, in reality Self-Defense units remained in some areas of Poland until the spring of 1940.

Self-determination of peoples, right to (*Selbstbestimmungsrecht der Völker*), principle of international law according to which, on the one hand, each state is free to determine its internal form of organization and, on the other, each people has the right to be embodied in a state. The unification movements of the 19th century derived from the demand for self-determination, and the FOURTEEN POINTS of the American president, Woodrow Wilson, made it the guiding principle for the new order in Europe after the First World War.

The prospects were favorable, since the principle of sovereignty that stood in opposition to self-determination carried little weight, at least in the case of the defeated states. The multinational states of Russia, the Ottoman Empire, and Austria-Hungary were either dissolved or severely truncated. However, for reasons of security and economic policy the principle of self-determination could not be applied without compromise in the ethnic mixture of southeastern Europe above all, a situation that created new MINORITIES. In some cases, the interests of the victorious powers stood in the way of a full realization of self-determination: for example, Germany had to relinquish considerable territory without any inquiry being made among the populace, and territories subject to a PLEBISCITE were not always fairly demarcated. Austria lost South Tyrol to Italy, a victorious but still unsatisfied power; the Sudeten territory was attached to the new state of Czechoslovakia for its security; and an ANSCHLUSS of Austria with Germany was prohibited.

The attempt was made to defuse these conflicts by establishing the rights of minorities to autonomy; however, the forcible treatment of self-determination issues brought lasting discredit on the peace treaties. In this way self-determination became one of the most effective arguments of REVISIONIST POLICY, especially as Hitler successfully manipulated it. After the conclusion of this first phase of his FOREIGN POLICY, when the self-determination of peoples impeded further German expansion, it was degraded to a mere right to a homeland (*Recht auf*

Heimat), without the option of a state or else with only limited sovereignty. Finally, it disappeared completely from German political argumentation.

During the conferences at Teheran, Yalta, and Potsdam, the Allied response to new territorial and ethnic problems was influenced only to a limited extent by concern for self-determination, an issue that would have complicated reparations settlements and security considerations. To be sure, the German Federal Republic's Basic Law appeals to self-determination in its mandate for German reunification, even as the associations of expelled persons (*see* EXPULSION) see the right to a homeland rooted in it. But with the totally different constellation of powers in Europe after the Second World War, these demands no longer have the same political explosiveness that they did in 1918. However, in the postwar period the right to self-determination did become the incentive to decolonization and found its way into the United Nations Charter.

Self-synchronizer (*Selbstgleichschalter*), ironic term for the people who in 1933 quickly began serving the new wielders of power and who submitted to SYNCHRONIZATION, for example the MÄRZGEFALLENE.

Seraphim, Peter Heinz, b. Riga (Latvia), September 15, 1902, German political economist. In 1937 Seraphim became a university lecturer in Königsberg. From a *völkisch* and chauvinistic perspective he developed analyses and theories of political economy in *Polen und seine Wirtschaft* (Poland and Its Economy; 1937). He then devoted himself mainly to antisemitic historical interpretation, in *Das Judentum im osteuropäischen Raum* (Jewry in the Eastern European Area; 1938) and *Die Wanderungsbewegung des jüdischen Volkes* (The Migration Movement of the Jewish People; 1940). Beginning in 1945 Seraphim was a university-level teacher in Munich and Bamberg; he published critical interpretations of the Eastern European, especially the East German, economy.

Serbia. *See* Yugoslavia.

Severing, Carl, b. Herford, June 1, 1875; d. Bielefeld, July 23, 1952, German politician. A locksmith by trade, Severing joined the Social Democratic Party (SPD) in 1893. In 1901 he became a trade union functionary, and in 1912, editor of the Bielefeld *Volkswache* (People's Watch). From 1907 to 1912 he was a delegate in the Reichstag, where he was considered part of

Carl Severing.

the SPD's revisionist wing. In 1919 he was elected to the National Assembly.

As Reich commissioner in the Ruhr region in 1919–1920, Severing was able to ward off a miners' strike, but in 1920 he put down a Communist uprising with force. From 1920 to 1933, he was again in the Reichstag. He was also Prussian interior minister (1920–1926 and 1930–1932). As Reich interior minister in the Great Coalition cabinet (1928–1930), he improved the training and strength of the municipal police; he was able to increase the loyalty of both the police and the civil service to the Weimar Republic. The Prussian cabinet finally came to be called simply the Braun-Severing government, since, next to Minister President Otto BRAUN, the interior minister had the highest profile. Nonetheless, they both—taking a legalistic stance—acquiesced in Franz von Papen's PRUSSIAN COUP in 1932 with virtually no resistance. Severing withdrew from political life, and during the Third Reich did not allow himself to be drawn into active opposition. In 1950 his memoirs were published under the title *Mein Lebensweg* (My Path through Life).

Sèvres, suburb of Paris where the peace treaty between the Allies and Turkey was signed on August 10, 1920. Turkey had fought on the side of the Central Powers during the First World War, and the humiliating provisions of the Sèvres treaty (such as extensive territorial losses, including some to Greece even in the Near East) ignited a Turkish-Greek war in 1921–1922. The treaty was considered typical of the ill-conceived PARIS SUBURBAN TREATIES.

Seydlitz-Kurzbach, Walther von, b. Hamburg, August 22, 1888; d. Bremen, April 28, 1976, German artillery general (June 1942). Seydlitz-Kurzbach joined the army in 1908, serving as an officer in the First World War. From 1920 to 1929 he was a battery commander in the Reichswehr, and from 1930 to 1933 he served in the Armed Forces Ministry. He then was a troop commander until 1939, and by the start of war had been promoted to major general. Seydlitz-Kurzbach led the Twelfth Infantry Division in France, later commanding it in the east as well. In February 1942 he distinguished himself with the Seydlitz-Kurzbach Group by liberating the forces surrounded at Demiansk.

At Stalingrad, Seydlitz-Kurzbach led the Fifty-first Army Corps; as early as November 22, 1942, he advised Gen. Friedrich PAULUS to attempt a breakout from the surrounded city against Hitler's orders. When this was rejected, he halted the pointless fighting on January 25, 1943, one of the first to do so. He was taken into captivity on January 31. Seidlitz-Kurzbach made himself available for anti-Hitler propaganda as chairman of the LEAGUE OF GERMAN OFFICERS and vice president of the NATIONAL COMMITTEE FOR A FREE GERMANY; he declined, however, to declare himself a Communist, and later also rejected an offer to cooperate in establishing the Soviet occupation zone in Germany. Sentenced to death in absentia by a Reich military court in April 1944, in 1950 he was sentenced to death by the Soviets. This was later commuted to 25 years, and in 1955 he was released to the Federal Republic.

Seyss-Inquart, Arthur, b. Stannern bei Iglau (Moravia), July 22, 1892; d. Nuremberg, October 16, 1946 (executed), Austrian politician. Seyss-Inquart was a lawyer in Vienna beginning in 1921. As a champion of an Austrian AN-SCHLUSS with Germany, he became involved in nationalist associations, including the Austrian-German National League and the Styrian Homeland Defense. In 1931 he formed close ties with the NSDAP. Nonetheless, since he was not yet a party member, Chancellor Kurt SCHUSCHNIGG chose him as his liaison with the nationalist opposition. As a consequence of the 1936 JULY AGREEMENT, in June 1937 the chancellor named Seyss-Inquart a state councillor (*Staatsrat*) in order to reduce tensions with Berlin and to fend off more extensive concessions.

After the BERCHTESGADEN DIKTAT of February 12, 1938, Schuschnigg was compelled to appoint Seyss-Inquart as minister for internal administration and security. In this post he had command of the police. On March 11 of that year Seyss-Inquart became chancellor as a result of German pressure; he then summoned into his country German troops that were already on the march, bringing Austria officially into the German Reich. On March 16, he was appointed Reich governor (*Reichsstatthalter*) for Austria, a position he held until April 30, 1939. He was also commissioned an SS-*Obergruppenführer*. In May 1939 he was made a Reich minister without portfolio. After the Polish Campaign he became deputy to Generalgouverneur Hans FRANK, before being appointed Reich commissioner for the occupied NETHER-

Walther von Seydlitz-Kurzbach.

Arthur Seyss-Inquart.

LANDS in May 1940. Seyss-Inquart governed there until the war's end, sharing responsibility for the deportation of Jews to extermination camps, the shooting of hostages, the exploitation of the Dutch economy, the abduction of ALIEN WORKERS, and the suppression of all political groups except for Anton Adriaan MUSSERT's National Socialist Movement. Arrested by Canadian troops in 1945, Seyss-Inquart was indicted at Nuremberg as a major war criminal and sentenced to death on October 1, 1946.

Shield (Schild), Jewish sports organization with some 7,000 members in 1933; it was founded in 1919 by the REICH LEAGUE OF JEWISH FRONT-LINE SOLDIERS. The Shield was German-Jewish in orientation and, in contrast to the MACCABEE Association, strove for integration into German sports activities. In the course of adoption of the ARYAN PARAGRAPH by the GERMAN REICH LEAGUE FOR PHYSICAL EXERCISES, Jewish athletes from German sports clubs joined the Shield in large numbers, causing its membership to increase sharply (to about 40,000 in 1935, together with the Maccabees). Despite more difficult training conditions, Shield athletes achieved remarkable performances (including the German high-jump record for 1936, achieved by Gretl Bergmann of Stuttgart's Shield club). After the OLYMPIC GAMES, however, police harassment and emigration losses brought an end to the Shield's activities.

Sicherheitsdienst. *See* Security Service.

Sicherheitspolizei. *See* Security Police.

Sieburg, Friedrich, b. Altena (Sauerland), May 18, 1893; d. Gärtringen (Böblingen district), July 19, 1964, German writer. Sieburg studied political economy, history, and literature in Heidelberg. From 1924 to 1939 he was a foreign correspondent for the *Frankfurter Zeitung* in Copenhagen, Paris, and London, among other places. A student of Friedrich GUNDOLF almost concurrently with Joseph Goebbels, Sieburg developed an expressly elitist sensibility, which he learned from Stefan GEORGE and which was based especially on French culture. After some insignificant poetry, in 1929 Sieburg wrote *Gott in Frankreich?* (God in France? [translated as *Is God a Frenchman?*]), and in 1933, *Es werde Deutschland* (Germany Becomes [translated as *Germany: My Country*]). These works manifested what Sieburg called a "confession of faith in Germany" and what amounted to an aesthetic glorification of National Socialism.

After the French Campaign, Sieburg came to Germany's Vichy embassy under Otto ABETZ and promoted German-French cooperation. In 1945 the French military government imposed a ban on his professional work (until 1948). During the 1950s Sieburg directed the literary supplement of the *Frankfurter Allgemeine Zeitung* and was one of the most influential critics. His biographies, including *Napoleon* (1956) and *Chateaubriand* (1959), are regarded as paragons of the genre.

Siegfried Line, English name for the WESTWALL, alluding to Germany's "Siegfried" position behind the Somme front in the First World War. To

Siegfried Line. Tank barriers on Germany's western frontier.

the tune of "Glory, glory, hallelujah," British soldiers sang "We're gonna hang out the washing on the Siegfried Line" in an effort to make light of the SITTING WAR of 1939–1940.

Signal, illustrated showcase magazine for foreigners put out as German war propaganda; it was founded in April 1940. *Signal* was designed to advertise National Socialist Germany, support the countries allied with it, gain "the trust and willingness to work of the population in occupied territories," and influence neutral states toward a "pro-German and anti-inimical opinion." *Signal* was intended to be the "magazine of the New Europe." Like *Das* REICH, *Signal* received special reports; with a view to its foreign readership, it avoided the antisemitic propaganda campaigns of the domestic press. European youth were the magazine's special target.

Signal appeared as the fortnightly supplement of the BERLINER ILLUSTRIERTE ZEITUNG (BI), and both were products of the "German Press" (Deutscher Verlag; before 1934, Ullstein) in Berlin. The periodical came out at one time or another in 20 languages, under the authority of the Wehrmacht Propaganda Department (director, Hasso von Wedel) of the Wehrmacht Command Staff. Its total circulation in 1943 was around 2.5 million copies, with about a fifth in German and 800,000 in French. Its editor in chief until September 1941 was Harald Lechenberg; Heinz von Medefind acted in his place until the spring of 1942; Wilhelm Reetz then held the position until the February 1945 issue; finally it went to Giselher WIRSING, who had been the *de facto* editor in chief since May 1943. Responsible for the excellent technical quality of *Signal* was Franz Hugo Mösslang. The magazine's contributors included Heinrich Hunke, Walter Kiaulehn, Walter Grävell, Kurt Zentner, and Alfred Ernst Johann. Its artists included P. Ellgaard and Hans Liska. The last issue was that of April 13, 1945.

S. O.

Sikorski, Władysław, b. Tuszów Narodowy, May 20, 1881; d. Gibraltar, July 4, 1943, Polish general and politician. A civil engineer, during the First World War Sikorski was director of the Military Division in the Supreme National Committee and a comrade-in-arms of Józef PIŁSUD-SKI. Sikorski was chief of the General Staff in 1921–1922, prime minister in 1922–1923, war minister in 1924–1925, and commander of the Lvov Military District in 1925–1926. He resigned in 1929 after a falling-out with Piłsudski. Sikorski emigrated in 1939 to France, where he

Signal. Front page of the first issue, April 1940.

formed a Polish government-in-exile even as the Polish Campaign was in progress. He then went to London as the government-in-exile's prime minister and head. In 1941 he acquiesced to the British agreement with Moscow, but disavowed it following the discovery of the mass graves at KATYN. His death in an airplane crash soon afterward aroused rumors of murder that have still not been laid to rest.

Władysław Sikorski.

Sillein Agreement (*Silleiner Abkommen*), agreement reached on October 6, 1938, under the pressure of the MUNICH AGREEMENT, in the central Slovak city of Sillein (now Žilina), between the Slovak People's Party (SVP) and other Slovak political organizations. Its purpose was to accept a draft passed by the SVP "for the proclamation of a legal constitution for the autonomy of Slovakia." The Sillein Agreement thus became the basis for the demand for the federalization of CZECHOSLOVAKIA and the autonomy of SLOVAKIA that was presented to the weak central government in Prague as an ultimatum by united Slovak autonomists. (Through the merger of the Slovak parties on October 6, 1938, the "Slovak Front" had become the only state party.) It was realized on October 7. A Slovak state government was formed under Jozef TISO, and on October 22 the Autonomy Law was passed. The Sillein Agreement was therefore an important step toward the declaration of full independence for Slovakia that was promulgated under German pressure on March 14, 1939.

B.-J. W.

Sima, Horia, b. Bucharest, July 3, 1906, Romanian politician. A teacher, Sima joined the fascist IRON GUARD in 1927 and became its leader in 1938. Forced into exile from 1938 to 1940, when the guard was outlawed, he then reached an agreement with King Carol II by which the group was renamed the Romanian Legionnaire

Horia Sima with Romanian legionnaires.

Movement. In 1940–1941 Sima was deputy prime minister under Ion ANTONESCU. Sima's attempt to take power himself via a putsch failed, and his flight to Germany that followed ended in the Buchenwald concentration camp. He managed to escape to Italy, but was sent back to Germany, where he was again interned in a camp. After the loss of Romania he was allowed to form an exile government in Vienna in late 1944; he remained in Austria after the war. In 1946 he was condemned to death in absentia in Bucharest.

Simon, Gustav, b. Saarbrücken, August 2, 1900; d. Koblenz, April 1945, German politician. A teacher of commercial subjects, Simon joined the NSDAP in 1925. He became the full-time *Bezirksleiter* (district leader) of the party in Trier-Birkenfeld in 1928, then of Koblenz-Trier in 1929. He was elected to the Reichstag in 1930 and was named *Gauleiter* in Koblenz-Trier-Birkenfeld in 1931 (renamed *Gau* Moselland in 1942). In 1940 he took over the civil administration of Luxembourg and was a Reich defense commissioner as of 1942. At the end of the war he took his own life.

Simon, Sir John, b. Manchester, February 28, 1873; d. London, January 11, 1954, British politician and jurist. A Liberal member of the House of Commons from 1906 to 1918 and from 1922 to 1940, Simon was foreign secretary from 1931 to 1935 and home secretary from 1935 to 1937. As a committed advocate of APPEASEMENT, in March 1935 Simon initiated the GERMAN-BRITISH NAVAL AGREEMENT during a visit

Gustav Simon.

to Hitler. From 1937 to 1940 Simon was chancellor of the Exchequer. He served as lord chancellor during the war (1940 to 1945).

Simplicissimus, satirical illustrated weekly magazine founded by Albert Langen in Munich in 1896; it rapidly became an institution in Imperial Germany. From a National Liberal standpoint, *Simplicissimus* criticized state and society in Wilhelmian Germany. To assure the independence of the editorial staff from their advertising agent, Mosse, the firm was converted into a limited corporation in 1906. The stockholders were Langen and the permanent staff members. Up to 1914 the circulation varied between 80,000 and 100,000 copies.

After a nationalist phase during the First World War, the magazine reverted to the old anticonservative line. In fundamental support of the Weimar Republic, *Simplicissimus* spoke out against extremes of both the Right and the Left. This stance gradually caused a loss of importance that was exacerbated by growing competition from other illustrated magazines. *Simplicissimus*'s contributors included the renowned artists Karl Arnold, Olaf Gulbransson, Thomas Theodor Heine, Bruno Paul, Erich Schilling, and Eduard Thöny. The editors until 1924 were Heine and Arnold; from 1924 to 1929, H. Sinzheimer; from 1929 to 1933, Franz Schoenberner.

In 1933 *Simplicissimus* was immediately "synchronized." After it was banned and had its editorial staff changed, on April 16, 1933, it published a public declaration of loyalty to the authorities. Heine, who as a Jew was especially imperiled, emigrated. The corporation was dissolved, and beginning with issue no. 28/1936, *Simplicissimus* was taken over as of December 1935 by the Munich publisher Knorr und Hirth, part of the EHER PRESS. It became a National Socialist showcase for foreign consumption; *Die* BRENNESSEL, the party's own satirical imitation of *Simplicissimus*, ceased publication. The drawings of Hans SCHWEITZER now appeared in *Simplicissimus*. After the outbreak of war its illustrations had German and Italian captions, and like all illustrated magazines and newspapers, it was subject to prior censorship by the Propaganda Ministry. The editors between 1933 and 1944 were Ernst Blaich, Anton Rath, Hermann Seyboth, and, finally, Walter Foitzick. Its 1937 circulation was 11,822; the last issue was published on September 13, 1944.

S. O.

Simplicissimus. Front page for December 3, 1923: "The man from Munich [in Bavarian dialect]: 'I want my quiet and a revolution, / And there must be order and a Jewish pogrom, / We need a dictator, too, and beatings: / I'll show you how to build Germany!'"

Sinti, self-designation of the ethnic group of GYPSIES who in the 14th century migrated into the German-speaking areas.

Sitting war (*Sitzkrieg*), term for the nearly combatless phase of the war on the western front, from the British-French declaration of war on September 3, 1939, until Germany's western offensive on May 5, 1940. The sitting war corresponded to the French term *drôle de guerre* ("comic war" [or, in the rhyming German translation, *Witzkrieg*]). Aside from local forays and reconnaissance flights, isolated artillery exchanges and leaflet operations, during and after the POLISH CAMPAIGN all was quiet on the WESTWALL, giving the Wehrmacht the breathing pause it needed. The sitting war was the result of France's fateful fortress mentality, which was based on the protection afforded by the presumably impregnable Maginot Line.

Situation reports (*Ereignismeldungen*), reports of the EINSATZGRUPPEN and Security Service (SD) posts in the occupied territories that were collected in Bureau IV A 1 of Office IV (Gestapo) of the REICH SECURITY MAIN OFFICE (RSHA). They were sent on to specific National Socialist

Sitting war. French soldiers playing cards at the Maginot Line.

leaders as well as to certain offices and bureaus in the RSHA. They contained mainly descriptions of the activity of the Einsatzgruppen and their commandos, and reports on morale and conditions, opponents, cultural topics, economic matters, the local populace, and the like. They also related incidents from within the Reich and the occupied western and southeastern territories. Recipients were primarily Heinrich Himmler, Reinhard HEYDRICH, office chiefs of the RSHA, group leaders (*Gruppenleiter*) of Office IV, and certain bureau heads. The last situation report appeared on April 24, 1942. They were replaced by the "Reports from the Occupied Eastern Territories" (*Meldungen aus den besetzten Ostgebieten*).

A. St.

Skilled worker (*Facharbeiter*), a technically trained and—usually after a three-year apprenticeship—tested worker. As a consequence of National Socialist rearmament, a shortage of skilled workers became evident very early, especially in metalworking and the construction trades. It was met with a systematic, legally regulated LABOR DEPLOYMENT program. A generational bottleneck also existed, owing to the reduced birthrate during the First World War; this was counteracted by procedures for training more apprentices. To assure fulfillment of the FOUR-YEAR PLAN, enterprises critical for rearmament were preferentially provided with skilled workers. In addition, non-wage incen-

tives were utilized that were otherwise scarcely possible (*see* SOCIAL POLICY).

Skorzeny, Otto, b. Vienna, June 12, 1908; d. Madrid, July 6, 1975, SS-*Standartenführer* (February 1945). A professional engineer, Skorzeny joined the NSDAP in 1930, and the LEIBSTANDARTE-SS "ADOLF HITLER" bodyguard in 1939; in 1940 he joined the Waffen-SS Division "Das Reich." He became known as the "rescuer of Mussolini," although he merely accompanied the paratroopers who accomplished the actual liberation of Il Duce, imprisoned since July 25,

Otto Skorzeny.

on September 12, 1943. Skorzeny played a major role in the October 1944 arrest of the Hungarian head of state, Miklós HORTHY, in the Budapest Castle (Operation "Mailed Fist"). At the beginning of the ARDENNES OFFENSIVE in December 1944, Skorzeny led the SS Panzer Brigade 150, a force of English-speaking men disguised as GIs who were to mislead the enemy. Operation "Griffin" ("Greif") had little success, but it stirred up the fear of secret agents among the Americans. Captured in Styria on May 15, 1945, Skorzeny was acquitted by an American military court on August 9, 1947. He fled from the internment camp at Darmstadt and settled in Spain.

Slovakia, until 1939 a part of CZECHOSLOVAKIA; thereafter, until 1945, a neighboring state south of the German Reich; area, 38,000 sq km (about 15,200 sq miles), population, approximately 2.6 million (1940). Slovakia gained its autonomy after the MUNICH AGREEMENT, on October 6, 1938. On March 14, 1939, in accord with Berlin, it declared its independence under (Prime Minister) President Jozef TISO. Through a "treaty of protection" dated March 18, 1939, it became a formally sovereign "protected state" (*Schutzstaat*) occupied by German troops in a western "protected zone" (*Schutzzone*), closely dependent on Germany in foreign, military, and economic affairs. Germany wanted to display Slovakia as a "model" for the planned National Socialist New Order in Europe. The constitution of July 31, 1939, was a combination of authoritarian-Catholic and corporatist-state principles with those of a presidential democracy.

Recognized by Italy, Switzerland, Sweden, Spain, Poland, the Soviet Union (until 1941), and *de facto* even by the Western powers, Slovakia at first conducted a scanty political life of its own, but it slipped by force of circumstances into an ever stronger dependence on the German Reich. On November 24, 1940, it entered into the Tripartite Pact, then into the Anti-Comintern Pact after declaring war on the USSR (June 24, 1941); it provided troops for the Russian Campaign. Finally, Slovakia lost all room for maneuvering, even in internal policies. At first still a refuge for politically and (despite a statute on Jews dated November 10, 1941) racially persecuted people, in 1942 it was swept into the FINAL SOLUTION. An uprising against the Germans as the Red Army approached in September and October 1944 was stifled by the Wehrmacht and the SS. In May 1945 a Slovak

National Council again proclaimed unity with the Czech people and state.

B.-J. W.

Smolensk Committee (Smolensker Komitee), body of Russian military men and politicians, founded in Smolensk in September 1941 on the initiative of a German officer, Henning von TRESCKOW. The group sent a memorandum to Hitler and proposed cooperation with the Wehrmacht. It was rejected by Hitler, whose OCCUPATION POLICY had very different goals and who believed that the Red Army had already been defeated. Nonetheless, high German officers encouraged the formation of Russian volunteer units. The Soviet general Andrei VLASOV, who was captured in July 1942, embraced the suggestions of the Smolensk Committee; in the spring of 1943 he had copies of a "Smolensk Manifesto" dropped behind Soviet lines. In the precarious situation after Stalingrad, it had been signed by Rosenberg's Ministry for the Occupied Eastern Territories. The manifesto called for a struggle against Stalin and promised an honorable peace with Germany. However, it had not been approved by Hitler, who rejected it definitively on June 8, 1943.

Sobibór, the smallest extermination camp of the REINHARD OPERATION, functioning as part of the "FINAL SOLUTION of the Jewish question." For the construction of Sobibór a forest tract was chosen in a thinly settled area on the eastern border of the Lublin district. Management of the project was first assigned in March 1942 to SS-Obersturmführer Richard Thomalla (later presumed dead). In early April he was replaced by SS-Obersturmführer Franz STANGL, who at the same time was named camp commandant. Stangl first set about studying camps and camp management in BEŁŻEC, which had already started extermination activity; he then accelerated the completion of Sobibór. After the main construction work was finished, a "test gassing" took place in the gassing facility, which consisted of three chambers, each with a capacity of around 150 to 200 people, in the presence of the Bełżec commandant, Christian WIRTH. The subjects were about 30 or 40 Jewish women. They were killed by exhaust gases from tank and automobile engines that had been brought into the gas chambers.

The mass exterminations began in May 1942. After the unloading at the Sobibór railroad station, the Jews were led into the camp, calmed by a talk, and asked to undress for bathing and to deposit their valuables. They were then driven in groups into the gas chambers, which were located in a secluded part of the camp. After the gassing, the corpses were piled into mass graves by a Jewish work squad that had been temporarily spared from extermination. When transport difficulties arose in July 1942, the opportunity was taken to expand the capacity of the gassing facility. From August 1942 on, SS-Hauptsturmführer Franz Reichleitner (killed on January 3, 1944, during a raid against partisans) took command of the camp; Stangl was transferred to Treblinka.

In the autumn of 1942, the SS began to remove the traces of the mass murder. The victims' corpses were exhumed and burned on grates in pits. New corpses were brought by the corpse squads directly from the gas chambers to the incinerators. In July 1943 Himmler ordered that Sobibór be converted into a concentration camp for the storage and processing of captured munitions. During the construction of the munitions camp the exterminations continued on a lesser scale. On October 14, 1943, the Jewish prisoners revolted against the SS. An undetermined number of Jews managed to flee, and the remaining prisoners were shot. The camp was then shut down.

In addition to the inhabitants of the General-gouvernement's ghettos, Jews from the Reich (Austria), from the Protectorate of Bohemia and Moravia, and from Slovakia, Holland, and France were killed at Sobibór. The exact number of victims can no longer be established, but documentary material indicates that at least 150,000 Jewish persons were killed there. According to Polish allegations based on the statements of Polish railway officials concerning the number of transports to the camp, the victim count in Sobibór amounted to around 250,000. This figure does not include the people who were brought on foot, in horse-drawn conveyances, or in trucks to the camp for extermination.

A. St.

Social Darwinism (*Sozialdarwinismus*), application of the Darwinian laws to humankind and society. The principles of selection and the struggle for existence were considered to be particularly applicable to humans and society, which was itself perceived as a kind of organism. SELECTION (*Auslese*), CULLING OUT (*Ausmerze*), and the Right of the Stronger were viewed as scientific givens, not only in nature but also in relation to human individuals and collec-

tivities (races, peoples). They were to be employed by the state against the counterselective influences of culture and civilization. In combination with racial anthropology (which attested to the Nordic race's natural claim to leadership) and with RACIAL HYGIENE (which strove for a general qualitative improvement of the human gene pool), demands were raised for SPECIES UPGRADING and for "culling out" bad hereditary material.

In Germany, Social Darwinism was promoted as early as 1863 by Ernst Haeckel. It was popularized in particular by the physician Wilhelm Schallmeyer, the first-prize winner of a 1900 essay contest on the theme "What we can learn from the principles of the Theory of Descent with regard to domestic-policy development and state law," and by Alfred PLOETZ, the founder of racial hygiene. Social Darwinism found followers in all segments of the bourgeoisie, but also among the working classes and among youth of all social groups. It provided the ideological and practical preconditions for such National Socialist programs as FORCED STERILIZATION of the hereditarily ill, the murder of the mentally ill under the rubric EUTHANASIA, and the murder, during the course of the FINAL SOLUTION, of Jews and other groups perceived as racially inferior.

R. W.

Social Democratic Party of Germany (Sozialdemokratische Partei Deutschlands; SPD) political party established in 1875 through the unification of the General German Workers' Association (founded in 1863) and the Social Democratic Workers' Party (founded in 1869), resulting in the Socialist Workers' Party; in 1890 it became the SPD. The SPD was a founding party of the Weimar Republic. It provided Friedrich EBERT as the first Reich president (1919–1925) and, four times, the Reich chancellor: Philipp SCHEIDEMANN (1919), Gustav BAUER (1919–1920), and Hermann MÜLLER (1920 and 1928–1930), mostly in a so-called WEIMAR COALITION. In the elections for the constituent National Assembly in 1919 the SPD received 37.9 percent of the votes. It did not match this figure again in the Reichstag elections of 1920 (21.7 percent), May 1924 (20.4 percent), December 1924 (26 percent), and 1928 (29.8 percent), yet until 1932 it remained the strongest German party both in voters and in members (over 1 million in 1931). The March 27, 1930, collapse of the Great Coalition government led by Hermann Müller, the last parlia-

SPD. The cabinet of Hermann Müller. Standing, from the left: Hermann Dietrich (DDP), Rudolf Hilferding (SPD), Julius Curtius (DVP), Carl Severing (SPD), Theodor von Guérard (Center party), Georg Schätzel (BVP). Seated, from the left: Erich Koch-Weser (DDP), Hermann Müller (SPD), Wilhelm Groener (independent), Rudolf Wissel (SPD).

mentary government of Weimar Germany, marked the beginning of the Republic's crisis.

Between 1930 and 1932, the SPD suffered heavy losses of votes in the Reichstag elections (1930: 24.5 percent; July 1932: 21.6 percent; November 1932: 20.4 percent), especially to the KPD (COMMUNIST PARTY OF GERMANY). The SPD proved unable to avert the NSDAP's SEIZURE OF POWER, whether by its tolerance of the government of Heinrich BRÜNING (1930–1932), through the formation of the IRON FRONT (1931), or through its determined opposition to the governments of Chancellors Franz von Papen and Kurt von Schleicher (1932–1933). As shown by its acquiescence in the deposition of the Prussian government of Otto Braun by Papen in July 1932 (*see* PRUSSIAN COUP), the SPD bore these developments rather passively; even after Hitler took office, it adhered to its policy of a strictly legal (and thus ineffective) opposition. Nonetheless, despite National Socialist election terror (including the banning of the SPD party organ, VORWÄRTS, on February 28), the party received 18.3 percent of the vote and 120 of the seats in the Reichstag election of March 5. On March 23, it was the only party to vote as a solid bloc against the ENABLING LAW, a stance that Otto WELS (one of the party executive members since 1919) justified in a courageous speech.

The SPD was banned on June 22, 1933. Earlier, on May 4, the newly elected party executive committee had established a "foreign

representation" in the Saarland, which moved its seat to Prague at the end of May, constituting itself anew there as the Executive Committee of the Exile SPD ("Sopade"). Its membership included Wels, Erich OLLENHAUER, and Friedrich STAMPFER. From 1938 to 1940 it conducted its affairs from Paris, and between 1940 and 1945, from London. There a faction of the Social Democrats merged with the Socialist Workers' Party (which split off in 1931 from the SPD), the NEW BEGINNINGS group, and other non-Communist socialist organizations to form,

SPD. Election poster. 1932: "The worker in the land of the swastika!"

Verbot schafft klare Bahn!

Während dieses Blatt gedruckt wird, kommt die Nachricht vom Verbot der Sozialdemokratischen Partei. Seit Tagen wußte man, daß die wirtschaftlichen Schwierigkeiten Deutschlands und die Spannungen innerhalb der nationalsozialistischen Bewegung so groß geworden sind, daß die

gewaltsame Unterdrückung aller politischen Parteien

als Ablenkungsmanöver in Aussicht genommen war. Schon in einer Unterredung, die vor etwa drei Wochen zwischen Hitler und Brüning stattgefunden hat, hat Hitler diese Absicht angekündigt.

Mit der gewaltsamen Entfernung der am 5. und 12. März rechtmäßig gewählten sozialdemokratischen Volksvertreter aus den öffentlichen Körperschaften ist der

letzte Schein demokratischer Legalität vernichtet

SPD declaration in the *Neuer Vorwärts* on the occasion of the banning of the party on June 22, 1933: "The ban clears the path! While this paper was being printed we received word of the banning of the Social Democratic Party. For days we have known that Germany's economic difficulties and the tensions within the National Socialist movement had become so great that the suppression of all political parties by force was being considered. . . . With the forcible removal of the . . . legally elected Social Democratic representatives . . . the last pretense of democratic legality has been destroyed."

in March 1941, the Union of German Socialist Organizations in Great Britain. Attempts by the KPD to form a united front had already been rejected by the SPD executive committee in 1935–1936. In Germany itself the Social Democratic opposition movement, which had sprung up in particular from working-class youth groups, was largely extinguished under Gestapo terror around 1936. It was reinvigorat-

ed only during the Second World War. Social Democrats such as Wilhelm LEUSCHNER, Hermann MAASS, Adolf REICHWEIN, Carlo MIERENDORFF, Theodor HAUBACH, and Julius LEBER belonged to the opposition circle of the TWENTIETH OF JULY, 1944.

Once the NS dictatorship had ended, the SPD emerged anew on local and regional levels by the summer and fall of 1945. In the Soviet zone it was forcibly united with the KPD on April 21, 1946, as the Socialist Unity Party of Germany (Sozialistische Einheitspartei Deutschlands). In the Western occupation zones the SPD, in its first party assembly on May 9, 1946, in Hannover, elected Kurt SCHUMACHER as its party chairman.

R. B.

Socialist Reich Party (Sozialistische Reichspartei; SRP), party founded on October 2, 1949, in the Federal Republic of Germany; it split off from the right wing of the German Justice Party (Deutsche Rechtspartei). The SRP program advocated neo-Nazi positions (*see* NEO-NAZISM). It was particularly successful among refugees, former professional soldiers, people who had suffered in the DENAZIFICATION process, and other discontented individuals. In the state legislative elections in Bremen and Lower Saxony in 1951, the SRP received 7.7 percent and 11 percent of the vote, respectively. As a successor organization to the NSDAP, the SRP was banned by a federal constitutional court on October 23, 1952.

Social Policy

The social policy of the Weimar Republic had gone beyond the framework established in the 19th century for the solution of the "social question" and had expanded in the direction of a policy for "shaping society." Partly through the influence of the trade unions, objectives were set for substantial improvements, particularly in the policy areas of labor law, housing construction, and communal welfare. Still, the expansion of the social network was opposed, especially by business associations, as an "overextension." Against the background of increasing costs, they demanded a subordination of social policy to economic policy. This was ac-

complished in the last phase of the Weimar Republic under the PRESIDIAL CABINETS, and a reduction in social ownership ensued.

The attitude of the National Socialists to this issue was most ambivalent. From one angle they recognized a great potential for political and societal identification with sociopolitical demands, and they exploited the crisis in social policy for agitation. From another angle they railed against the state's "welfare establishment" and called for eliminations and reductions. At no point did National Socialism develop a unified and comprehensive program of economic and social policy. Even after the Seizure of Power, the Hitler regime at first avoided any firm position on basic issues of economics, society, and social welfare.

A principle of National Socialist policy was the idea of the VOLK COMMUNITY. The interests of the individual, of groups, and of classes were to be subordinate to the "common good" (*Gesamtwohl*) of the community. Any emerging disagreements were subject to the state's authoritarian decision since it was the state that was to decide this "common good." As a social policy guideline for the *Volk* Community, it was held that social progress was achieved not by the demands of the individual, but only by his or her subordination to the community. Social policy with all its institutions yielded precedence to state policy and was at the disposal of the state's goals. Through such steps as the REICHSTAG FIRE DECREE, the ENABLING LAW, the dissolution of the Reichstag, and the SYNCHRONIZATION of the states, the Hitler government secured dictatorial powers for itself, extending to the field of social policy. As time went on, the effects of this policy were to become manifest for certain social groups to whom National Socialism had particularly appealed: workers, the middle strata, and peasants.

The forcible breakup of the trade unions eliminated representation for the interests of the workers and deprived them of their rights and means of struggle. The subsequent founding of the GERMAN LABOR FRONT (DAF), into which employers' associations were later also merged, was extolled by the government as the fulfillment of the demand for a unified trade union. The DAF declared every business to be a community of "workplace leaders" (*Betriebsführer*) and "followership" (*Gefolgschaft*), and thus a fundamental building block of the *Volk* Community. In this system the employer was again accorded the traditional "master-of-the-house position." A firm's wages were decided by the employer alone. Regulations exceeding the employers' authority on minimum wages and pay structures were handled by the TRUSTEES OF LABOR, a state agency. It became rapidly evident, however, that the conflicts over wages and distribution in a highly industrialized society could not be eliminated simply by the destruction of workers' organizations, the self-abolition of employers' associations, and the introduction of government regulation. After the Seizure of Power the open supression of labor, and government-ordered wage cap, and a high rate of unemployment were utilized to secure quiet on the "wage front."

The NS regime was aware of the positive psychological effect of eliminating UNEMPLOY-

Mobile theater of the German Labor Front.

MENT, and it cleverly connected measures for WORK CREATION with the planned rearmament from the outset. The Hitler government followed up on the later Weimar Republic's presidial cabinets' programs and plans for work creation policy. However, it removed the employment issue from the narrow economic field and promulgated a "battle for work" (*Arbeitsschlacht*), the successes and "frontline reports" of which were announced to Germans daily in the press. Benefiting from the recovery in business conditions that had become evident as early as 1932, Hitler was able by 1936 to have himself celebrated as the victor in that battle, thus gaining great credence among the workers. The conditions for workers in the employment program were extremely poor: their compensation hovered close to the subsistence minimum, and labor law guarantees had been curtailed. Still, the regulated work was tied to hopes and expectations for a better future. In contrast, the situation of the unemployed worsened as the unemployment rate sank, the ranks of those entitled to state support were systematically reduced, and the promised reform of unemployment insurance went unfulfilled.

For pensioners as well the situation became ever worse, since the already low level of pensions from the time of the world economic crisis was undercut by new settlements. The conditions for granting pensions became tighter. With the accelerating of rearmament, the assets of social insurance were utilized to finance the arms buildup, and the insurance carriers were converted into credit institutions of the state. The pension policy stood at the service of the arms policy insofar as people were pressured to work longer. Moreover, the high premiums and low benefits meant that purchasing power in the incipient prosperity of 1936 came to be siphoned off. Not until 1942 did a perceptible rise in pensions take place. The fear of political conflicts and the trauma of refusals to work in the First World War compelled this social policy concession. The two-sided concern for discipline and control, but also for the satisfaction of sociopolitical demands, was characteristic of NS social policy as a whole.

The reduced state social welfare payments were replaced by the voluntary donations of the NATIONAL SOCIALIST VOLK WELFARE (NSV) agency, which was financed by contributions. Propaganda that extolled "supplementary" payments was intended to give the population the illusion of social improvement. Yet the support provided by the NSV emphasized not the need of the individual but the usefulness to the state.

As the labor market recovered, renewed conflicts over distribution and wages arose in the state-regulated compulsory community. With the onset of full employment and the resulting labor shortages, employees no longer accepted the low wage level, which in part had fallen beneath the 1932 level and thus was 20 percent below 1929 wage rates. Business leaders sought to stay under the state-ordered wage cap and to hold on to their labor resources with performance bonuses, family supplements, in-house old-age pension plans, and the like. Such supplements, however, were only voluntary, not a matter of legal entitlement, so that real wages were contingent upon an employee's good behavior and an employer's goodwill. From 1938 on, the growth in wages threatened rearmament, and the labor trustees received wider authority to intervene in wage structures. In 1939 these rights were expanded and all non-wage supplements were forbidden. The trustees nevertheless had a certain amount of room for maneuvering in practice, and they applied the measures to the individual branches in very different ways, since wage incentives were still to be utilized to assure productivity in especially important areas of the armaments industry. The policy of segmenting wages was an important basis for upholding a system that depended on disinformation and obfuscation in wage issues. Real net weekly wages increased by 1941 to approximately the same level as in 1929, whereas the nominal hourly pay stagnated. The increases in earnings resulted for the most part from the extension of work time, which by the end of the war came to 60 hours a week. The ratio of wages to national income clearly sank between 1932 and 1938.

Through its wage-policy measures the government managed to limit private consumption to the advantage of arms investments. At the same time, collections for the NSV, for the WINTER RELIEF AGENCY (WHW), and for the wartime "Conserve Iron" drive were designed to soak up cash that, despite the restrictive wage policy, was still disposable. This same goal was pursued by the tax reform of 1934, which laid a heavier burden especially on single people and childless couples. The government wage policy was supported by LABOR DEPLOYMENT measures. Changes of workplace were submitted to state control initially in certain areas of the economy, then during the war in all areas.

A farther-reaching measure of state wage policy was the regulation of prices. A 1936 prohibition against price increases intended both to give the impression that the state was securing wages by means of prices, and to counteract the widespread fear of inflation. The War Economy Ordinance of 1939 provided for a lowering of prices, but it was no more consistently applied than was the wage cap. The official cost-of-living index rose from 118 (1933) to 141.1 (1944), while the price index went from 104.9 to 129. Nonetheless, during the war the prices for some important foodstuffs rose sharply higher. The indexes merely reflected the prices allowed by the state.

In order for the rearmament policy to succeed, the Hitler government needed heavy industry, whose monopolization proceeded apace, resulting in damages to medium and small businesses. Preferences in the world of *Realpolitik* contradicted the economic and sociopolitical demands of the middle stratum (*see* MITTELSTAND), which before 1933 had constituted a main feature of the NS program. Some concessions, such as the Law for the Protection of Retail Trade in 1933, compulsory guild membership (*Pflichtinnung*) in the artisan trades (*Handwerk*) in 1934, regulations that restricted activities of large department stores, and the introduction of major certificates of qualification for certain trades in 1935 could not conceal this fact. They remained gestures that proved to have no impact in comparison with the dominance of heavy industry. For all that, until 1936 a certain amount of "social elbowroom" was conceded to the middle classes. After that, requirements for fulfillment of the FOUR-YEAR PLAN prevailed even here. Raw-materials management and the shifting of labor resources into heavy industry drained the trades and small businesses. As a result of the "shakedown" in the trades after 1939, many businesses not involved in militarily important production shut down. Yet even during this phase, important sociopolitical decisions were made in favor of the middle stratum of society. Voluntary enrollment of the self-employed into social insurance in 1936 and the introduction of mandatory old-age pension plans in 1938 fulfilled long-standing middle-class demands.

Like the middle stratum, the peasantry too had invested great expectations in the Seizure of Power. Even after 1933, the NS government clung to its romantic notions of the peasantry, although the agrarian-biased ideal of state and society also stood in stark contradiction to the accelerated industrialization. As in the case of middle-class policies, here too the contradiction between practical politics and ideology quickly became manifest. In order to secure farm income, the government controlled markets and prices and decreed protective trade measures against other countries. This policy of limiting the risks of business for farmers was carried out at the expense of consumers. Attempts to achieve AUTARKY led to constant bottlenecks in the supply of foodstuffs (*see* FAT GAP). Prices of agricultural products rose by 25 percent from the beginning of 1933 to the end of 1939. Another attempt to restore farming was the HEREDITARY FARM LAW (1933), which was intended to shelter family farms from parceling and mortgaging. However, it achieved only short-term relief for peasant farms. The flight from the land, which reached record levels between 1933 and 1938, went against the attempted ruralization of society. During the Third Reich even fewer new farmsteads were started than during the Weimar Republic. The utilization of land for industrial and military purposes took clear precedence. The ratio of farm income to the national product steadily declined in comparison with wages and prices after 1935. Following a brief improvement, the mortgaging of smaller and medium-sized farms continued to increase. The living standard among peasants remained far under the general level.

Still, this was only one aspect of social policy. In the popular consciousness these everyday experiences were entwined with the propaganda claims of "National Socialism." It promised the classless equality of all "VOLK COMRADES" who, with no differences in status, were to enjoy the social benefits of the *Volk* Community. Status in this community would no longer depend on education or class membership, but on belief and membership in the "German race." Thus the social status of workers and peasants was elevated by the establishment of holidays and by mass marches for the Harvest Thanks Festival and on the "Day of National Labor," when the National Socialists cleverly maintained continuity with the traditions of the workers' movement. Welfare and relief programs such as the NSV and the WHW, the model workplaces of the DAF, the STRENGTH THROUGH JOY organization, coupled with exemplary vacation arrangements, and the seemingly classless community in the NS organizations—all these did not fail to have their effect on employees, even though participation was often compulsory and

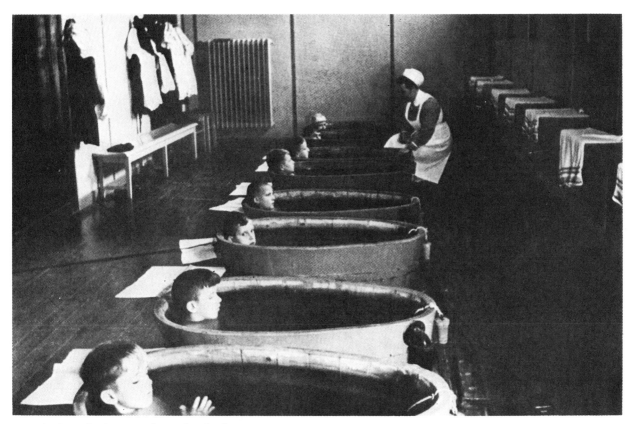

NSV bathing facilities at the Bad Salzuflen spa.

served the ends of control and war mobilization.

A special place in this system was occupied by the NS policy on women and the family. It emphasized the family as the smallest cell of the *Volk* Community and endorsed the traditional stereotypes that placed woman as wife and mother at the service of the long-range goals of racial and population policy (*see* WOMEN IN THE THIRD REICH). Connected with this was the drive to remove women from the workplace, which had only incipient success: the only groups that were consistently dislodged from their occupations were women academicians and civil servants. Women were allowed to enter the civil service only after the age of 35, and they received lower pay than their male colleagues. The National Socialists also instituted overt occupational restrictions: for example, women could no longer serve as judges or lawyers, and higher education had admissions quotas for women. Measures were inaugurated in health policy to improve prenatal care and job safety, a campaign against birth control was instituted, and a monthly child subsidy was introduced. Even as the ideal of motherhood collided with the growing labor shortage toward the end of the 1930s and as work by women once again became an economic necessity, the goals of population policy still took precedence. During the war fewer women were employed in Germany than in the other warring countries.

In a closing reflection on the main points of NS social policy, the conclusion can be drawn that the individual experienced improvements only to a limited extent. In each phase political considerations, namely the goals of rearmament and expansionism, took precedence. The individual was bound to the system by force, by partial concessions, by social welfare measures, and by opportunities for identification with the system. The psychological factor of the political utilization of mass propaganda, which yielded an uninterrupted stream of success reports, must also not be underestimated. Largely isolated from other sources of information, the populace found itself in a system that promised it social order and community, and that above all guaranteed it security.

Birgit Wulff

Sod (*Scholle*), in mythical National Socialist usage a term counter to ASPHALT, which was the metaphor for civilization and degeneracy. Sod was earth that was cultivated as a source of strength for the *Volk* and the foundation of nourishment. To restore or to strengthen the connection with the sod was the goal of BLOOD AND SOIL ideology (*see* HOMESTEAD).

Söderbaum, Kristina, b. Stockholm, September 5, 1912, German-Swedish actress. Söderbaum went to Berlin in 1930 for studies in art history and immediately won her first film role, in *Onkel Bräsig* (Uncle Bräsig). Her career stalled until the director Veit HARLAN discovered and hired her, and shortly thereafter married her. Their first film together, *Jugend* (Youth; 1938), was followed by further tendentious National Socialist films, including *Das unsterbliche Herz* (The Immortal Heart; 1939), JUD SÜSS (Jew Süss; 1940), *Der grosse König* (The Great King; 1942), and KOLBERG (1945). Söderbaum's main character portrayal was the naive and lovable blonde; she was given the nickname "Reich Water Lily." Together with her husband she continued to make movies after the war, although with less success. After his death in 1964 she became a photographer. She reappeared in 1974 in the Hans Jürgen Syberberg film *Karl May.*

Sohnrey, Heinrich, b. Jühnde bei Göttingen, June 19, 1859; d. Neuhaus im Solling, January 26, 1948, German writer. By the end of the 19th century Sohnrey had become one of the most popular German *Volk* writers, with novels and stories that glorified country life in the Weser mountain region, notably *Friedesinchens Lebenslauf* (Little Friedesin's Life Story; 1887). After 1896 he published the *Deutsche Dorfzeitung* (German Village News), which in 1934 was renamed *Neues Bauerntum* (New Peasantry). National Socialist critics admired the "simple, pleasing form" of his poetry. For his commitment to the *Volk,* Sohnrey received several honorary doctorates, and in 1938 the Eagle Shield of the German Reich.

Soldiers' songs (*Soldatenlieder*), repertoire of songs written especially for soldiers, encouraging them through the rhythm of words and music to march in step. During the Third Reich old and new soldiers' songs appeared in numerous collections, such as *Morgen marschieren wir* (Tomorrow We March; 1939), published by Hans BAUMANN. They propagandized ideological bonds to the homeland, as in "Westerwaldlied" (Westerwald Song), readiness for sacrifice ("Heilig Vaterland" [Holy Fatherland]), or hatred of the enemy ("Englandlied"). The individual branches of the armed forces, as well as the SA, SS, and Hitler Youth, all had their own soldiers' songs. Along with the official songs, some popular hits also became favorite soldiers' songs, notably "LILI MARLEEN."

Solf Circle (*Solf-Kreis*), opposition group that formed around the diplomat W. H. Solf (1862–1936) and his wife, Johanna (1887–1954). After her husband's death, Frau Solf carried on in a more informal way with the group that was known in Berlin as "Frau Solf's Tea Society" and contemptuously termed the "Fronde Salon" by the Gestapo. It was frequented by, among others, Countess Hannah von Bredow, a granddaughter of Bismarck; the diplomat Otto Karl KIEP, a close friend of Helmut James Count von MOLTKE; the Jesuit priest Friedrich Erxleben; and Elisabeth von THADDEN, headmistress of a well-known girls' school near Heidelberg. Frau Solf and her daughter, a Countess Ballestrem, made use of their wide-ranging contacts abroad (where Herr Solf was remembered with high esteem everywhere), especially in Switzerland, to aid victims of persecution and assist them in their flight. The Gestapo's infiltration of an agent provocateur at the end of 1943 resulted, in January 1944, in the arrest of most members of the group, including Count Moltke, and in their execution. Through the intervention of the

Kristina Söderbaum and Rudolf Prack in *Die goldene Stadt* (The Golden City).

Solf Circle. Hanna Solf.

Japanese ambassador and owing to the war's end, the mother and daughter themselves eluded death.

B.-J. W.

Solidarism (*Solidarismus*), polemical and derogatory National Socialist term referring to political and philosophical demands for a rapprochement between capitalism and socialism based on Christian love of neighbor and a community of solidarity among trades, professions, and classes. Solidarism, which derived mainly from Roman Catholic social doctrine, with its goal of the "solidarity of peoples and of humanity," contradicted the aim propagated by National Socialists of a "socialism of *Volk* comrades on the basis of blood and soil."

Solidarity (*Solidarität*), term to describe a sense of unity and a community of interests. It was a catchword from the 19th-century workers' movement, especially in the combinations "proletarian solidarity" (workers standing together in a strike) and "international solidarity" (a unity among workers that transcended all national borders). In order to present itself as the party of the workers' interests, the NSDAP from its beginnings employed "solidarity" as a catchword in its propaganda, but invested it with a purely nationalistic meaning. Hitler saw in the "supposedly international solidarity only the enemy of a genuine nationalist attitude . . . a phantom that leads people astray from the only rational solidarity, the solidarity that is ever

rooted in blood"; he defined this as "the idea of sacrifice" (speech for the WINTER RELIEF AGENCY, 1933–1934).

Solmitz, Fritz, b. Berlin, October 22, 1893; d. Fuhlsbüttel concentration camp, September 19, 1933, German victim of National Socialism. Solmitz studied political economy. Beginning in 1924 he was, together with Julius LEBER, political editor of the *Lübecker Volksbote* (Lübeck People's Herald). As a pacifist and Social Democrat, Solmitz viewed the rise of the NSDAP with deep concern, and in February 1933 he exhorted the workers of Lübeck to actively resist Hitler's incipient dictatorship. As a Jew, Solmitz was in any case endangered by the wave of arrests that followed the Reichstag Fire Decree. On March 11, 1933, he was arrested and sent to the Fuhlsbüttel concentration camp. After many appeals by his wife, his release seemed imminent, but he died of severe abuse on the night of September 19, 1933.

Solstice (*Sonnwend*), holiday particularly cultivated among the CELEBRATIONS IN THE NATIONAL SOCIALIST CALENDAR. Between 1933 and 1944 the Summer Solstice was celebrated on June 23 with great fires (Saint John's Fire, Midsummer Fire) on mountains, hills and riverbanks, and with THING PLAYS and musical performances. It was the mandatory event for the Hitler Youth (HJ). The Winter Solstice on December 21 was intended, as a yule feast, to replace secular and Christian observances of Christmas, with anonymous exchange of gifts within the celebrating group (HJ units, school classes, businesses, and so on). The attempt, however, did not even begin to succeed.

Sonderbehandlung. *See* Special Handling.

Song (*Lied*), art form with a high pedagogical status, used explicitly by National Socialist EDUCATION for purposes of indoctrination and community cohesiveness. The desired song had various origins: the repertoire of patriotic songs of the 19th century (such as "Flamme empor" [Flames rise up]), the YOUTH MOVEMENT and the youth leagues ("Aus grauer Städte Mauern" [From the Walls of Gray Cities]), the NS "Time of Struggle" (the "HORST-WESSEL-LIED"), and the period of the Seizure of Power, when many NS texts were put to music (as Baldur von Schirach's Hitler Youth song, "Vorwärts, Vorwärts! schmettern die hellen Fanfaren" [Forward! Forward! the bright fanfares blare]). Notable composers from the "new times" included Werner Altendorf, Hans BAUMANN, Georg Blumensaat, Hans-Otto Borgmann, Paul Dorscht, Reinhold Heyden, Fritz Sotke, and Heinrich SPITTA. Popular songs were appropriated and reworked as another song form. Even some songs of Communist origin were supplied with new texts, such as "Brüder, zur Sonne, zur Freiheit" (Brothers, to the sun, to freedom), which became "Brüder, in Zechen und Gruben" (Brothers, in mines and pits).

Singing was given the musical-political aims of reinforcing the *völkisch* sense of community, portraying a society that was free of conflict, creating emotional fervor, and firmly establishing an image of the enemy. The song as credo also served to exclude outsiders and to isolate those who rejected National Socialism ("Die Fahne ist mehr als der Tod" [The Banner is more than Death]). According to the motto "To each his own song," the repertoire of songs was organized for particular groups: children, the Hitler Youth, the Reich Labor Service, women, and the Wehrmacht, among others. A flood of songbooks appeared for numerous occasions, such as celebrations, community evenings, hiking, and marches. The traditional church hymn was also to be replaced, as with "Hohe Nacht der klaren Sterne" (Sublime Night of Clear Stars), the Christmas song of 1936. Hit songs and songs from film scores attained particular importance, especially during the war. Conspicuous in many of the battle and party songs were symbols, which also appeared as book illustrations: the circle, signifying inclusiveness, comradeship, and faithfulness; the flag, symbolizing the NS movement and its guidance; and the fire, standing for vigilance but also for natural change, struggle, and revolution.

R. H.

"Sonnenblume" ("Sunflower"), military code name for the attack of the German Africa Corps in Libya in February 1941 (*see* AFRICAN CAMPAIGN).

Sonnenstein (near Pirna), one of the six "killing facilities" in the EUTHANASIA program and the so-called INVALID OPERATION. In April 1940 the Sonnenstein Hospital and Nursing Facility was converted to a euthanasia facility under the camouflage name "Facility D." After the curtailment of the Invalid Operation in the spring of 1943, Sonnenstein was closed. According to surviving records, in 1940–1941 alone 13,720 people were killed in Sonnenstein.

Sorge, Richard, b. near Baku (USSR), October 4, 1895; d. Tokyo, July 9, 1944 (executed), German journalist and spy. The son of an engineer in Russian service who returned to Germany in 1898, Sorge volunteered in the First World War, then studied political economy. He joined the Independent Socialists (USPD) in 1917, and the Communist party in 1919. Sorge was editor in 1920–1921 of the *Bergische Arbeiterstimme* (Mine Workers' Voice). He played a leading role in the Communist uprisings of 1920 in the Ruhr region and of 1923 in Hamburg. Entering the service of the Comintern in 1925, he became a Soviet citizen. As a correspondent of the *Frankfurter Zeitung* and other publications, Sorge went in 1929 to China and in 1933 to Japan, where he built up a network of Soviet agents.

A man of the world, Sorge gained access to the highest Japanese circles and made excellent connections with the German embassy; in May 1941 he was able to report to Moscow the forthcoming German attack on the Soviet Union almost to the day. Stalin ignored the warning, but he did profit from Sorge's report that the Japanese Kwantung Army would not be deployed against the USSR; this enabled him to hurl Siberian troops against the Wehrmacht and thus ward off collapse. Sorge then reported the imminent Japanese strike against PEARL HARBOR before he was arrested on October 16, 1941. His death sentence was not carried out until nearly three years later.

Richard Sorge.

Soul (*Seele*), in Greek thought, the life principle inherent in the human organism, defined by the Stoics as an emanation from the material world soul, and termed by Aristotle a part of the immortal intellect that is realized in matter (the body). In Christian thought, the soul represents man's spiritual essence, created by God, which determines one's independent and unmistakable individuality. In National Socialist ideology, the soul appears as the reflection of racial qualities and is extensively equated with the "life force." In this way, the unresolved contradiction in Christianity between body and soul is resolved in favor of that which is material, and the concept of race simultaneously receives pseudo-religious exaltation: "Soul means race as seen from within, and race is reciprocally the externalization of soul" (Alfred Rosenberg). National Socialism's tendency to bestow a mystical and sentimental aesthetic on its racist worldview is evident in such neologisms as *Seelenstil* ("soul-style," or racial culture) and *Seelentum* ("soul-hood," or racial character).

M. F.

Southeast Generals (*Südostgeneräle*), collective term for the Wehrmacht commanders in southeastern Europe during the Second World War who were prosecuted in the so-called HOSTAGE TRIAL after the war.

South Tyrol (Südtirol; Ital., Alto Adige), part of Tyrol lying south of the Brenner Pass. Despite its overwhelmingly German-speaking population, the South Tyrol was promised to Italy by the London Treaty of 1915 as compensation for its entering the war on the side of the Entente; it was transferred in 1919 by the Treaty of SAINT-GERMAIN-EN-LAYE. The South Tyrol problem became aggravated because of a strict policy of Italianization under Benito Mussolini: a ban on the German language in public offices and schools, changes in place-names, extensive Italian settlement, and so on. Hitler's seizure of power and his policy of ANSCHLUSS with Austria accelerated the program, since Rome feared a demand from Great-Germany for the return of the South Tyrol and wanted to have on hand a fait accompli.

Hitler, however, deliberately left the South Tyrol question out of his REVISIONIST POLICY, in order to win Italy over as an alliance partner. After the formation of the AXIS, he consequently concluded a treaty with Mussolini on October 21, 1939, that offered resettlement to the South

South Tyrol. A settler family leaves their farm.

Tyrolians. By 1943, 70,000 had taken advantage of the offer, going mainly to Austria and Bavaria; 25,000 later returned. After Italy's withdrawal from the war (September 1943), the South Tyrol was placed under German civil administration. Despite the Italian alliance with Hitler, after 1945 the region remained part of Italy. Following long and sometimes terroristic struggles, a solution to the conflict was reached in 1969 by broadening the South Tyrol's rights of autonomy.

Sovereignty Badge (Hoheitsabzeichen), service uniform badge (Reich eagle with swastika) for the army, navy, and air force. In the German Wehrmacht the badge, silver gray in color, was worn on the left side of the steel helmet, on the cap over the cockade, and on field jacket, jacket, and shirt at the right side of the chest. For officers the badge was embroidered in silver, except for generals and naval officers, whose badges were embroidered in gold. For army and Luftwaffe troops, silver gray thread was used, and for navy men, yellow thread.

Sovereignty bearers (*Hoheitsträger*), in the NSDAP, term for regional or jurisdictional leaders (*Gebietsleiter*) of the party. On the Reich level they bore the title "Führer"; on the GAU level they were *Gauleiter* (*Gau* leaders), with the district (*Kreis*), local group (*Ortsgruppe*), base (*Stützpunkt*), cell (*Zell*), and block (*Block*) leaders under them. Every sovereignty bearer was responsible to the one immediately above him, in accordance with the FÜHRER PRINCIPLE, and was responsible for supervising all party agencies in his jurisdiction. In the one-party state this amounted to total political responsibility, especially since the party sovereignty bearers usually also held state offices.

Soviet Military Administration (Sowjetische Militäradministration; SMAD), the supreme military and political power in the SOVIET OCCUPATION ZONE, formed on June 9, 1945. Its headquarters was in Berlin-Karlshorst; its commander was Gen. Vasily Ivanovich Chuikov. The SMAD was dissolved on October 10, 1949, after the founding of the German Democratic Republic.

Soviet Occupation Zone (Sowjetische Besatzungszone; SBZ, also called the Sowjetzone), one of the four OCCUPATION ZONES in Germany after the Second World War; area, 107,862 sq km (about 43,100 sq miles); population, 18.3 million (1946). The Soviet Zone encompassed the territory of the German Reich between the ODER-NEISSE LINE in the east and the line through Lübeck-Helmstedt-Hof in the west

SMAD. Col. Sergei Tulpanov, the head of SMAD, conveys the good wishes of the Soviet Military Administration on the first anniversary of the Socialist Unity Party (SED). In the background: "Through plebiscite, the unity of Germany."

(with the exception of West Berlin). The parts of Mecklenburg, Saxony, and Thuringia that were at first occupied by American and British troops were evacuated by them on July 1, 1945, and these areas were immediately occupied by the Soviets. Supreme military and political authority in the SBZ was assumed on June 9, 1945, by the SOVIET MILITARY ADMINISTRATION (SMAD). Under its rule the economy of the SBZ was systematically exploited and a Communist societal and economic order was established. Among other measures, schools and the justice system were restructured; landed properties were confiscated, as was the property of "war criminals and Nazi activists," and distributed among peasants, farm workers, and expelled persons; and heavy and key industries were nationalized. The Social Democratic Party and the Communist Party were merged into the Socialist Unity Party (Sozialistische Einheitspartei Deutschlands; SED). From the SBZ arose the German Democratic Republic in 1949.

Soviet Union (since 1922, officially the Union of Soviet Socialist Republics; USSR), European-Asian state; area, almost 22 million sq km (about 8.8 million sq miles); population, 164 million (1932); its capital is Moscow. After the end of wartime communism (1917–1921), of the Civil War, and of outside intervention (March 18, 1921, the Peace of Riga, conceding Galicia and a strip of White Russia to Poland), and after the introduction of an internal consolidation in 1921 through Lenin's New Economic Policy (NEP), the Soviet Union began to break down its foreign political isolation. With the RAPALLO TREATY of 1922 (confirmed in 1926 by the BERLIN TREATY), it began a close political, economic, and military cooperation with the Weimar Republic. In 1924 it gained recognition from France, Great Britain (interrupted in 1927–1929), and most of the European states.

The fundamental ambiguity of Soviet foreign policy—political and ideological aggression and a need for national security—always matched an ambivalence in its relations with the capitalist states: correct relations with other governments along with strict ideological demarcation. Stalin's policy, introduced in the first Five-Year Plan (1928–1933), of forced industrialization, arms buildup (in cooperation with the Reichswehr), and forced collectivization—along with his temporary abandonment of world revolution through the avowal of "building socialism in one country"—had far-reaching foreign-policy consequences. The So-

Soviet Union. Cartoon by the Englishman David Low on the Hitler-Stalin pact of 1939. The dictators greet each other over the corpse of Poland. [The original English wording was: "The Scum of the Earth, I believe?" "The Bloody Assassin of the Workers, I presume?"]

viet Union became an attractive site for Western, especially German, industrial investments, in return for Soviet deliveries of raw materials and foodstuffs; it thus was forced into a defensive security policy toward the outside world.

The strong position of the National Socialist regime, contrary to expectations, and the rapid chill in German-Soviet relations after 1933 as Hitler turned to Poland (*see* GERMAN-POLISH NONAGGRESSION PACT, 1934), led to a policy shift under Foreign Minister Maksim Maksimovich LITVINOV. To defend against the fascist danger, an ideological shift produced the strategy of a "popular front" among Communist, Socialist, and left-wing middle-class parties. A change of course toward collective security led to entry into the League of Nations (September 18, 1934) and an opening up to the West (1933, recognition by the United States; 1935, French-Soviet and Soviet-Czechoslovak aid pacts).

A new change in direction for Soviet foreign policy then developed, which was to lead into the Second World War. It was prepared for by the bloody "purges" between 1935 and 1937 in the government, party, and military apparatuses; by Stalin's rise to sole power; and by the political and diplomatic isolation of the Soviet

Union on the part of the Western powers in 1938 (*see* APPEASEMENT; MUNICH AGREEMENT). It was reflected in Soviet officialdom by the replacement of Litvinov with Viacheslav Mikhailovich MOLOTOV (May 3, 1939). After alternative negotiations with London/Paris and with Berlin, these shifts were followed in the summer of 1939 by the GERMAN-SOVIET NONAGGRESSION PACT, on August 23.

Up into 1941 the Soviet Union was able to occupy—with the exception of Finland (*see* WINTER WAR)—the buffer zone provided to it by treaties: September 17, 1939, its march into Poland; June 27, 1940, its annexation of BESSARABIA and Northern Bukovina; July–August 1940, its annexation of the Baltic states. The nearly four-year-long defensive struggle against the German invasion (June 22, 1941) was proclaimed to be the "Great Patriotic War" (*see* RUSSIAN CAMPAIGN). Through the mobilization of national patriotism, the great number of war victims, the partisan struggle, Germany's brutal war conduct and occupation policy (*see* GENERAL PLAN FOR THE EAST), and then finally victory, the Stalin regime gained a high domestic level of mass loyalty and legitimacy. In foreign relations as well—on the basis of the often unilaterally interpreted accords of TEHERAN (1943) and YALTA (1945), and of the POTSDAM AGREEMENT—it gained an expansion of the Soviet sphere of influence deep into central and southeastern Europe.

B.-J. W.

Space (*Raum*), in the sense of LIVING SPACE (*Lebensraum*), a frequently used word in the National Socialist vocabulary. Taken over from GEOPOLITICS, the term—like other NS key words (RACE, BLOOD, SOD, and the like)—gained a nearly mythical life of its own in descriptions of the "primeval essence" (*Urgrund*) of the *Volk*. "Space" in this context referred not only to material resources, but also to the fundamental soul and the basis of the *Volk*'s strength. The answer to the question of space (that is, expansion) became in this sense, along with the racial question, the second pillar of NS politics. It was invoked in ever new combinations: regional planning (*Raumordnung*); idea of space (*Raumgedanke*); space revolution (*Raumrevolution*); tightness of space (*Raumenge*); spatial tie or confinement (*Raumgebundenheit*); alienation from a space (*Raumfremdheit*); responsibility for a space (*Raumverantwortung*); large space, in the sense of a territorial unit (*Gross-Raum*), and so on.

Spain, state in southwestern Europe; area, approximately 505,000 sq km (about 200,000 sq miles); population, 24 million (1930). From the turn of the 20th century, internal fronts and political-social contradictions in Spain blocked the functioning of a parliamentary democratic system, civil reforms, and economic and societal modernization. They finally exploded in the SPANISH CIVIL WAR. The upper middle class, the predominantly middle-class and agrarian-capitalist large landowners, and the Catholic church were the dominant economic powers; arrayed against them were the landless rural proletariat and a working class that was divided ideologically and regionally between socialism and anarcho-syndicalism. A weakly developed industrial middle class lacked the political framework of a national middle-class democratic party. The traditionalist and antiprogressive army leadership stood in the background.

Neither the military dictatorship under José Antonio PRIMO DE RIVERA (1923–1930) nor the Second Republic (1931–1939) was able to defuse the long-standing crises in state and society embodied by such problems as the land question, economic backwardness, church-state relations, the social question, separatism, and corruption. Nor could they break down the extreme political and societal polarization between Socialists, Communists, and anarchists, on the one hand, and the nationalist and conservative Catholic Right and the anti-Republican military, on the other. After the election of a popular front of left-wing Republicans, Socialists, and Communists on February 16, 1936, these contradictions forced a settlement through armed conflict. The Spanish Civil War began as a conservative-nationalist military revolt (July 17–18, 1936) and was originally a purely internal Spanish conflict. It escalated through the outward expansion of its internal fronts, as the stage was being set for the Second World War, into the first rehearsal for the struggle between the fascist and democratic powers in Europe.

After the war ended, the victorious Francisco FRANCO avoided too close a dependence on his National Socialist and Fascist alliance partners. In domestic policy he renounced a uniform recognized ideology for his authoritarian-restorative government by dictatorship. In foreign policy he aligned himself with the idea of an anti-Bolshevik "crusade" (April 7, 1939, entry into the ANTI-COMINTERN PACT; sending of the BLUE DIVISION against Russia). Nonetheless, he steadfastly refused to enter the war on the side of the Axis (*see* HENDAYE, October 23, 1940), and in so doing was able to consolidate his rule.

B.-J. W.

Spandau, since 1920 a district of Berlin, with 170,000 inhabitants (1940). The seven major war criminals who were sentenced to prison terms on October 1, 1946, in the Nuremberg Trials were remanded on July 18, 1947, to the Spandau Prison, which had originally been constructed to hold 600 inmates, to serve their terms. In the hermetically sealed facility, with its electric fences and walls with watchtowers, units of the victorious powers in monthly rotation guarded the prisoners:

1. Baldur von SCHIRACH (sentenced to 20 years; released in 1966)
2. Karl DÖNITZ (10 years; released in 1956)
3. Konstantin von NEURATH (15 years; released in 1954)
4. Erich RAEDER (life term; released in 1955)
5. Albert SPEER (20 years; released in 1966)
6. Walther FUNK (life term; released in 1957)
7. Rudolf HESS (life term; as the sole inmate

from 1966 until his death on August 17, 1987, termed "the world's most expensive prisoner").

The conditions of imprisonment were relatively strict: twice-daily walks in the yard, one letter a week to relatives, severely limited visiting opportunities, limited and censored reading, prohibition against conversations between guards and prisoners, arising at 6:00 a.m., and turning lights off at 10:00 p.m. In his *Spandauer Tagebücher* (Spandau Diaries, 1975; translated as *Spandau*), Speer gave a descriptive portrayal of the daily routine.

Spanish Civil War, conflict that took place in Spain between 1936 and 1939, between nationalist, traditionalist, Falangist-fascist, and conservative forces on the one side, and Republican, Socialist, Communist, and anarchist forces on the other. The war began with an uprising, especially of the troops stationed in North Africa (*see* Francisco FRANCO), against the Republican government after the murder of monarchist leader José Calvo Sotelo on July 13, 1936. A march on Madrid came to a standstill in November 1936; during the war the Nationalist troops were unable to take the capital. Instead, the Republican bastions in the northern provinces, Aragon and Catalonia, gradually fell. In March 1939 the resistance collapsed; Franco declared the civil war over on April 1 of that year, and established a dictatorial regime that was to last for 40 years. The war, waged with the greatest cruelty, cost the lives of more than a half million people.

Among the European and American public the Spanish Civil War aroused intense sympathy, mostly for the besieged Republic. Thousands of volunteers enrolled in the INTERNATIONAL BRIGADES, which first saw action in November 1936 in the defense of Madrid. Mexico and the USSR delivered war matériel. On Franco's side Germany and Italy intervened with extensive military aid. Italy dispatched some 20,000 regular soldiers and a "voluntary militia" of 27,000 men, and Germany sent the CONDOR LEGION, with a complement of around 6,000 men, who were rotated in rapid succession. Several motives lay behind the German commitment to Spain: along with the ideological motive (to combat the "spread of communism") there were foreign-policy considerations (improvement of relations with Mussolini, detachment of Italy from British influence), economic reasons (expansion of the raw-materials supply by means of Spanish mines), and military interests (testing of new weapons systems). The non-involvement of the Western powers in the Spanish Civil War and the obvious toleration of German and Italian intervention strengthened Hitler in his risk-taking FOREIGN POLICY.

Ba.

Spann, Othmar, b. Vienna, October 1, 1878; d. Neustift (Burgenland), July 8, 1950, Austrian sociologist and philosopher. In 1908 Spann became a professor in Brünn (now Brno [Czechoslovakia]); from 1919 to 1938 he taught in Vienna. In his major work, *Der wahre Staat— Vorlesungen über Abbruch und Neubau der Ge-*

Spanish Civil War. Nationalists lead away Republican prisoners.

sellschaft (The True State: Lectures on the Breakdown and Reconstruction of Society; 1921), Spann developed the plan of a conservative revolution with a return to the Catholic universalism of the Middle Ages. His antidemocratic, antiliberal, and anti-Marxist positions made him an ideological forerunner of AUSTROFASCISM and the Austrian CORPORATIST STATE. According to Spann, society is the "first essential" and is more than the sum of its parts (individuals). The National Socialists at first made use of Spann's thought, but they rejected as a "misapprehension of *völkisch* interests" its Catholic elements and its strict adherence to a corporatist and federalist structure for society. Spann's call for a separate Jewish territory on German soil in the form of a "great ghetto" was too moderate for National Socialist racist antisemites. After the ANSCHLUSS in 1938, Spann was temporarily detained in the Dachau concentration camp and then was prohibited from teaching.

SPD. *See* Social Democratic Party of Germany.

Special Commandos (Sonderkommandos; SK), along with the Einsatzkommandos, units of the EINSATZGRUPPEN. As a rule all smaller units with specific assignments were designated as SKs, for example SK 1005, which carried out the EXHUMATION OPERATION.

A. St.

Special Courts (*Sondergerichte*), criminal courts established in 1933 for the special purpose of removing political opponents. During the war they were on the way to becoming the typical criminal court of the National Socialist state.

Special Court. Pronouncement of a death sentence in Holland.

The number of such courts started out as 26 and rose to 74 by the end of 1942. Their competence was at first limited to individual political crimes, but after 1938 the prosecutor's office made the decision whether a case was to be tried in them, regardless of the jurisdiction of local or state courts. After 1940 they had exclusive jurisdiction over WARTIME SPECIAL CRIMINAL LAW and criminal law within the scope of the MALICIOUS-GOSSIP LAW. The proceedings were rapid, in the style of a summary court; there were no pretrial procedures, and waiting time was short. The defense was increasingly weakened and the prosecution inversely strengthened. After 1940 immediate sentencing was possible (often to death sentences). Judgments gained legal force upon their promulgation and at times were carried out immediately. The customary legal remedies were not permitted. Special Court sentences could be reversed only by the REICH COURT, after submission of an extraordinary appeal or declaration of nullification.

C. D.

Special Handling (*Sonderbehandlung;* also Special Treatment), camouflage term used by the National Socialist authorities to denote the physical extermination of human beings. The term was probably introduced in a teletype dated September 20, 1939, from Reinhard HEYDRICH to all State Police commands and stations, concerning the "principles of internal security during the war." The message stated that in order "to rule out misunderstandings," it was necessary to distinguish between those cases "that can be settled in what have been the usual ways, and those that must be given special handling." These were cases that "in consideration of their reprehensibility, their risk, or their suitability for propaganda are appropriate, without regard for the person, for culling out [*ausgemerzt*] through ruthless action (namely, through execution)" (*see* CULLING OUT).

The camouflage designation was used during the ensuing years especially in many decrees of the chief of the Security Police and the Security Service (SD), in instructions, orders, and notices addressed to subordinate stations and units. Over the course of time the meaning of the term apparently became so well known that other code words came into use. From about the autumn of 1941, for example, in preparing and carrying out the mass murder of Jews and others, the words "resettlement" (*Umsiedlung*) and "transfer" (*Aussiedlung*) were applied. Finally, Heinrich Himmler forbade that any mention be made of the "special handling" (of Jews), and ordered that the term be replaced by others (note from the Personal Staff of the *Reichsführer-SS* to its inspector of statistics, April 10, 1943). In fact, however, it remained a fixture in specifically National Socialist language.

A. St.

Special Purchase Permit for the Aircraft-damaged [that is, air raid victims] (*Sonderbezugsschein für Fliegergeschädigte*), PURCHASE PERMIT for victims of the AIR WAR. Because more and more Germans lost their clothing and household possessions owing to the increase in air raids, as of March 1, 1943, they could apply for such a permit at distribution offices (*Wirtschaftsämter*). The certificate also authorized the purchase of textiles and household items as a supplement to the REICH CLOTHING CARD.

Special Report (*Sondermeldung*), official designation for news on the course of the war, and especially the wartime bulletins that were read over all Reich broadcasting stations by interrupting the radio program in progress. A fanfare preceded the Special Report, and march or funeral music would follow the reading. In the early war years only victories of the German troops were broadcast as Special Reports; later, defeats were also announced, although often with a delay or embellished by propaganda.

Species (*Art*), in biology, the totality of individuals that resemble one another in all significant characteristics and that reproduce or could reproduce under natural conditions. In the biologistic worldview of National Socialism, the concept of species—contrary to the scientific definition—was equated with RACE. Racial mixing was accordingly degeneration (*Entartung*), because it ignored the limits on reproduction. Preservation of a species could therefore be assured only through its purity. The concept of species narrowed in this way provided the foundation of the NUREMBERG LAWS; it also provided the pseudoscientific rationale for the PERSECUTION OF JEWS. In the National Socialist vocabulary "species" turned up in numerous combinations: species-conscious (*artbewusst*), "proud of the racial qualities of one's own people"; species-German (*artdeutsch*), "nationally conscious in a racial sense"; species joy (*Artfreude*), "the serene typical characteristic of the 'heroic person' and the 'Northern race' [*Nordrasse*]"; spe-

ciesless (*artlos*), "unnatural," "negligent of race"; species will (*Artwille*), "a driving force that renews a people or a race 'from buried depths'" (a Germanization of the philosophical term *élan vital*).

Species-alien (*artfremd*), neologism based on the National Socialist definition of SPECIES, referring to everything opposed (hostile) to one's own race. It was used particularly in conjunction with the term BLOOD, which would be "corroded" (*zersetzt*) by the admixture of species-alien fluid. This "poisoning" could take place through sexual intercourse between persons of different races, during which, along with the "species-alien protein" in the semen, "the alien soul too" penetrates (Julius STREICHER). Such relations were branded as RACIAL INFAMY.

Species-related (*artverwandt*), term devised in line with the National Socialist definition of SPECIES; it applied to everything resembling and "compatible" with one's own racial characteristics. BLOOD was thus considered to be "species-related" if, when mixed with that of a particular race, it caused no "problems and tensions" (*Hemmungen und Spannungen*). The Nordic, East Baltic, Dalo-Nordic (*fälisch*), Western, Eastern, and Dinaric races were considered to be "species-related." The term was crucial in the CERTIFICATE OF DESCENT and the Law to Protect Blood (*see* BLOOD, LAW TO PROTECT).

Species-true Christianity (*arteigenes Christentum*; also *artgemässes* [species-appropriate] *Christentum*), a demand of the GERMAN CHRISTIANS, who understood the term to mean separation from the "Old Testament and its Jewish money morality [*Lohnmoral*]" and the prophecy of "a heroic Jesus figure." The CONFESSING CHURCH turned against this kind of doctrine, which defined "service to our *Volk* comrades as the only true service to God."

Species-true faith (*arttreuer Glaube*), in *völkisch* usage the religiosity "rooted in the racial essence of man," in opposition to grafted-on Christianity, with all its Jewish and oriental influences: "German space and the German *Volk* as divine revelations; service to the earth, *Volk*, and Reich as divine service; race as mission." Species-true faith remained confined to *völkisch* sects, for in spite of linguistic borrowings, the National Socialists sought to keep their conflict with the churches within bounds until after the war.

Species upgrading (*Aufartung*), in the biologistic terminology of National Socialism, the improvement of a species through deliberate breeding (*züchterische*) practices that aim to eliminate harmful traits and encourage valuable ones. Among humans, species upgrading, by means of HEREDITY CULTIVATION and RACIAL HYGIENE, was to attain the goal of "keeping the blood pure." A parallel term, relating to the perfecting of the Nordic race, was NORDIC UPGRADING.

Speer, Albert, b. Mannheim, March 19, 1905; d. London, September 1, 1981, German politician. Speer studied architecture in Karlsruhe, Munich, and Berlin, and became a licensed engineer in 1927. Born into a liberal family, he was not inclined toward National Socialism initially, but when he heard Hitler speak to a group of students he was seized by his "special magic" and joined the NSDAP in 1931. Architectural commissions from the party caused his abilities and his preference for large-scale designs and huge dimensions to become recognized. In part this derived from influences during his studies, which taught and practiced the monumental style (not restricted to Germany) of the 1930s. Speer went far beyond this, and aroused Hitler's parallel interests. Thus was Speer directed toward his career as an architect in the service of the Third Reich, especially after the early death of Hitler's admired master builder, Paul Ludwig TROOST.

Speer's engaging outward appearance, his energy, his appreciation of contemporary art, his veneration of Hitler, and Hitler's own sympa-

Albert Speer. Zeppelin Field rostrum in Nuremberg.

thetic response, together with Speer's special organizational abilities (particularly the punctuality with which he completed large building projects), assured him a sharply rising career. Hitler, who wanted to leave behind himself structures that would last for centuries, recognized in Speer a virtually ideal instrument for executing his own architectonic plans for domination. Not counting the gigantic stage for party congresses and the technical lighting effects that went with these triumphal self-presentations of the regime, Speer's greatest project—aided by unlimited resources—was the NEW REICH CHANCELLERY, completed in 1939. His greatest uncompleted project was the re-creation of Berlin as the world capital, "Germania." Only its beginnings were realized; the war interrupted and terminated the gigantesque plan. The preliminary drawings display its excesses, which beggar comparison with anything before it in the history of municipal construction.

At the age of 37, Speer became the successor to Fritz TODT as Reich Minister for Armaments and Munitions in February 1942. For the second time he assumed the post of a predecessor highly regarded by Hitler, and each time he exceeded expectations, independently of their worth or worthlessness. Speer increased arms production more and more under ever worsening conditions, so that it actually reached its peak in 1944, in the midst of uninterrupted bombardments. With astounding organization-

Albert Speer.

al skill he marshaled the very last production reserves, thus surely prolonging a war that had long since been lost. Only when he himself recognized this did his personal attitude toward Hitler change, and in March 1945 he sabotaged Hitler's NERO COMMAND, thus helping to mitigate the ruin in the last stage of the war. His conscience won over his loyalty.

As a result of his inner transformation, Speer confessed his share of guilt at the Nuremberg Trials, the only defendant other than Baldur von SCHIRACH to do so. His repentance may have been the reason why, despite his unscrupulous utilization of forced laborers, he came away with a 20-year prison sentence. He served his term in SPANDAU until October 1966. Three years after his release, his memoirs appeared. *Inside the Third Reich* is by far the most important book among the autobiographies of National Socialist leaders. The author hewed without reservation to the line of his self-criticism at Nuremberg. In 1975, Speer's *Spandauer Tagebücher* (Spandau Diaries; translated as *Spandau*) was published. He compiled it from many thousands of notes that he had smuggled out and that his family had collected. The *Diaries* continue his earlier tone: "Never will I get over having served in a leading position in a regime whose real energies were dedicated to the extermination of human beings." His summary of Hitler, among whose few friends Speer numbered, amounts to sheer perplexity: "All reflection makes him more incomprehensible."

H. St.

Speer Legion (Legion Speer), uniformed transport unit formed in September 1942 under National Socialist Motor Corps (NSKK) Gruppenführer Jost. It used almost exclusively foreign personnel, since the NSKK as a party division could employ only Germans. Named after Albert SPEER, the legion recruited volunteers from all over Europe, as well as Soviet prisoners of war and VOLUNTEER HELPERS. Only the command positions were held by Germans.

Speidel, Hans, b. Metzingen, October 28, 1897; d. Bad Honnef, November 28, 1984, German lieutenant general (January 1, 1944). Speidel entered the army in 1914, later becoming an officer in the Reichswehr. He studied political economy and history, and in 1936 was attached to the Army High Command (OKH), in charge of foreign armies in the west. A good friend of Ludwig BECK, during the war Speidel was Gen-

Hans Speidel.

eral Staff chief with the military commander for France, the Lanz Army Division, and Army Group South in Russia. As of April 14, 1944, he was back in France, with Army Group B under Gen. Erwin ROMMEL. For some time, Speidel had been on the side of the military opposition, but during the Gestapo interrogations after the failure of the assassination attempt of July 20, 1944, and his arrest on September 7, he was able to play down his role and was thus merely confined in prison without sentencing until the end of the war. In the Federal Republic, Speidel became an adviser to Chancellor Konrad Adenauer regarding the creation of the Bundeswehr. From 1957 to 1973 he was the first German supreme commander of the NATO land forces in Central Europe.

Spengler, Oswald, b. Blankenburg/Harz, May 29, 1880; d. Munich, May 8, 1936, German philosopher of history. Spengler was originally a high school (*Gymnasium*) teacher in Hamburg (1908–1911), then a freelance journalist. Drawing on Friedrich NIETZSCHE's cultural pessimism, Spengler, in *Der Untergang des Abendlandes* (*The Decline of the West*), his major work, propounded a vision of the decay of European (termed "Faustian") culture as a consequence of the continent's self-laceration, of the increasing role of technology in life, and of the concomitant depersonalization of human beings in the "culturally uprooted" mass democracies. He predicted a new age of Caesarism, characterized by progressively more primitive forms of political behavior. The book made an enormous impres-

Oswald Spengler.

sion, especially because it was published immediately after Germany's defeat in the world war (vol. 1, 1918; vol. 2, 1922).

As a suitable model for the future of Germany, Spengler advocated in *Preussentum und Sozialismus* (Prussiandom and Socialism; 1920) an alliance between the intellectual elite and the non-Marxist workers' movement on the basis of classic Prussian ideals. A harsh critic of liberal parliamentary democracy, he provided the radical Right with effective arguments for agitation against the Weimar Republic. Like Knut HAMSUN and, to an extent, Martin HEIDEGGER, Spengler was at first attracted by the "primitive might" of National Socialism because of his hostility toward civilization. His 1933 work *Jahre der Entscheidung* (Years of Decision; translated as *Hours of Decision*) celebrated the National Socialist upheaval, in contrast to his substantive evaluation of the movement. The NS idealization of "mass and race" seemed to Spengler to be "childish nonsense": "One who talks too much about race is without any." Thus in the Third Reich, which he had prophesied, Spengler remained isolated as "the eternal man of yesterday" (*Ewig-Gestriger*).

M. F.

Sperr, Franz, b. Karlstadt (Lower Franconia), February 12, 1878; d. Berlin, January 23, 1945 (executed), German diplomat. Speer was a General Staff officer in the First World War. He then served in the Bavarian embassy and the Reichsrat (Reich Council) in Berlin from 1918 to 1934.

In the name of the Munich government he bitterly opposed the National Socialist synchronization of the German states in 1933. After the Röhm Affair (June 30, 1934) he utilized his contact with Reich President Paul von Hindenburg to protest Hitler's arbitrary rule, albeit unsuccessfully. Sperr resigned his post and prepared himself and others of like mind for the time to come after Hitler. Although Sperr saw no possibilities for a violent overthrow, he was not spared a death sentence from the *Volk* Court (January 11, 1945). The court alleged that shortly before the assassination attempt of July 20, 1944, he had met with Claus von Stauffenberg, and that he had maintained ties with the KREISAU CIRCLE through Alfred DELP.

Sperrle, Hugo, b. Ludwigsburg, February 7, 1885; d. near Landsberg am Lech, April 2, 1953, German field marshal general (July 19, 1940). Sperrle entered the army in 1903, served as a flight officer during the First World War, and then held various troop command positions in the Reichswehr. He had much to do with the covert buildup of an air force, and became commander of Air *Gau* V (Munich) in 1935. In 1936–1937 he led the CONDOR LEGION in the Spanish Civil War, but he was promoted to another post because of his warnings against military adventures. On July 1, 1938, he took command of Air Fleet 3, which he also led during the French Campaign. In 1944 Sperrle directed the Luftwaffe operations for warding off the Allied invasion of France; when his measures failed, he was relieved of his post and

Hugo Sperrle.

discharged on August 22, 1944. In the OKW TRIAL, Sperrle was acquitted of all charges on October 22, 1948.

Spitta, Heinrich, b. Strasbourg, March 19, 1902; d. Lüneburg, June 23, 1972, German composer. In 1933 Spitta was appointed a teacher at the State Academy for Music in Berlin, and at the same time to the Cultural Office of the Reich Youth Leadership. Spitta first wrote music for youth, especially choral works, including "Heilig Vaterland" (Sacred Fatherland; 1934) and "Jahr überm Pflug" (Year at the Plow; 1936). The critics praised them as "austere and powerful," and as constituting a "declaration of the new German will." Beginning in 1950 Spitta taught at the Pedagogical Institute in Lüneburg, where he became a professor in 1957.

Sporrenberg, Jacob, b. Düsseldorf, September 16, 1902; d. Warsaw, 1950 (executed), SS-*Gruppenführer* and lieutenant general of the police (1941). A mechanic by trade, Sporrenberg served after the First World War on the border patrol. He was then accepted into the Reichswehr, and in 1921 he joined the postal service. As a member of the illegal "SCHLAGETER Memorial League" in the Rhineland, he was sentenced to two years' imprisonment by the French occupation authorities on May 14, 1924. Released early, after the French withdrawal in August 1935 he helped build up the NSDAP in Düsseldorf. On October 1, 1930, the SS accepted him as a *Sturmführer,* and he was rapidly promoted.

In 1933 Sporrenberg became leader of SS Section [*Abschnitt*] XX (Schleswig-Holstein). After several assignments, including at the Security Service (SD) headquarters in Berlin, in early 1937 he went to Königsberg as SD chief. At the start of the war he was appointed *Höherer SS- und Polizeiführer* (HSSPF; *see* HIGHER SS AND POLICE LEADERS) in Defense District II (Wiesbaden), and in June 1941, in Königsberg. From August 1941 to about August 1943, with brief intervals, Sporrenberg was active in combating partisans in the USSR. He was then appointed SS and Police Leader in Lublin, where his assignments included Operation "HARVEST FESTIVAL." On November 5, 1944, he was sent to Oslo with the same leadership role for southern Norway. Captured there, he was remanded to Poland by the Allies. In 1950 he was executed after being sentenced by a Polish court.

A. St.

Sports (*Sport*), the main subject in National Socialist education, in which, according to Hitler in *Mein Kampf,* the "raising [*Heranzüchten*] of totally sound bodies [is] the first concern." Because of the English origin of the word and its original meaning ("disport" means "pleasure"), the term "physical exercises" (*Leibesübungen*) was preferred.

The NS sports organizers and ideologues built upon long-standing traditions, which they often could utilize with only light retouches. Like *völkisch* and bourgeois sports educators during the Weimar period, they invoked the "father of gymnastics," Friedrich Ludwig JAHN, and his idea of defense preparedness, which had experienced a renaissance after the 1918 defeat. The restrictions on defense policy imposed by the Versailles treaty also contributed to the interest, as did the soon-glorified FRONT EXPERIENCE. The military terminology used to describe sports even during the Weimar Republic anticipated the official NS vocabulary: the national sports festival established in 1922 was called the GERMAN COMPETITIVE GAMES, and in 1932 the Republic's president created the REICH CURATORIUM FOR YOUTH FITNESS TRAINING.

Only the workers' sports movement (with some 1.3 million members in 1933) stood aloof from ties with military policy. It became the first victim of the "synchronization" of German sports by Reich Sports Commissioner Hans von TSCHAMMER UND OSTEN in the spring of 1933. The workers' sports clubs and organizations were banned, their facilities closed or taken over, and their property confiscated. Middle-class sports groups were also expected to acknowledge the political and ideological ideas of the new holders of power. In line with their traditions, they met the new sports commissioner far more than halfway. Even before von Tschammer instituted the new order of the GERMAN REICH COMMITTEE FOR PHYSICAL EXERCISES (DRA), procedures for self-dissolution had begun. The leading representatives of the DRA supported the centralization of the network of German sports clubs and organizations.

Whereas middle-class sports lacked the will to resist, the denominational sports organizations lacked the power to do so. The Evangelical OAK CROSS was handed over to the Hitler Youth by the church leadership itself. The Catholic GERMAN YOUTH FORCE made little use of the Concordat for protection against harassment. Both Catholic and Evangelical sports ended when the ban on any independent sports activity was issued on July 23, 1935. Paradoxically, the Jewish sports clubs (MACCABEE and SHIELD) had initially experienced a "flowering," since Jewish athletes were excluded from German clubs by the ARYAN PARAGRAPH. Out of concern for foreign opinion, the National Socialists postponed the elimination of Jewish sports until after the 1936 OLYMPIC GAMES.

The new organization of German sports in the NS state went through two phases. In the first, a Reich Führer Ring, made up of 16 representatives of the sports specialty associations (*Fachverbände*), was established under the chairmanship of von Tschammer (May 24, 1933). All associations had to transfer their administrative offices to Berlin. At the same time, the associations were divided up, following the new political divisions of the Reich, into 16 *Gaue*, which in turn were subdivided into regions (*Bezirke*) and districts (*Kreise*). On January 30, 1934, the GERMAN REICH LEAGUE FOR PHYSICAL EXERCISES (DRL) was founded under the chairmanship of von Tschammer (by then named Reich Sports Führer). This umbrella organization was comprised of 25 specialty offices (*Fachämter*), corresponding essentially to the old specialty associations. The Reich Sports Office in Berlin became the new central authority and organization.

In the second phase of the new order, after the Olympics—when political reasons seemed to favor a delay—von Tschammer strove to integrate sports more closely with the party. The first step toward this end was a new coordinating office, with von Tschammer as bureau head, in the Reich Interior Ministry. This was followed in late 1938 by the founding of the NATIONAL SOCIALIST REICH LEAGUE FOR PHYSICAL EXERCISES (NSRL), a party organization. The process culminated in 1939 with the appointment of the Sports Führer as "Plenipotentiary for Physical Exercises in the NSDAP" on the staff of the deputy to the Führer. Thus independent sports, which had until then been self-governing, were synchronized.

Sports were now totally at the disposal of the ideological orientation toward the principles of race, authoritarian leadership, and defense preparedness. "*Volk* guardians" (DIETWARTE) oversaw political schooling in the sports clubs and attended to the conveying of the "political soldier" model cultivated in the sports programs of the Hitler Youth, SA, SS, NS Motor Corps, and NS Flyers' Corps. Key passages from Hitler's *Mein Kampf* provided the ideological basis for a system of physical education that was to serve the regime's political goals and to prepare for the "emergency" (*Ernstfall*): "The greatest physical readiness is achieved precisely for deployment in an emergency" (von Tschammer). Sports also served the internal orientation toward this emergency: in schools, clubs, and party groups they increasingly became MILI-

Sports. Mass gymnastics.

TARY SPORTS. The success of German athletes was exploited as a nationalistic stimulant, and sports were glorified in wartime as "the workshop of victory." The war ended with the destruction of more than 40 percent of all sports facilities and with the "total destruction of the moral substance of sports" (Willi Daume).

Sports Palace Speech (*Sportpalastrede*), mass rally convoked by Joseph Goebbels in the Berlin Sports Palace on February 18, 1943, at which he called for TOTAL WAR in reaction to the catastrophe at Stalingrad. In rhetorically masterful fashion, the Sports Palace Speech pledged readiness for combat and sacrifice, and exploited the Allied demand for UNCONDITIONAL SURRENDER to energize the will to resistance. The fanaticized crowd (mostly party functionaries or at least party members) allowed itself to be swept along into a thunderous "Yes!" by 10 questions that Goebbels hurled into the hall ("Do you want total war . . . ?"). With the charge "*Volk*, stand up! And storm, break forth!" Goebbels released his listeners and rang in a struggle literally unto ruin.

Sports Palace Speech. Fanatic applause from the public.

SS

The SS (Schutzstaffeln, or Defense/Protection Squads) of the NSDAP was, like no other institution of the Third Reich, the embodiment of National Socialist master-race ideology. The early history of the SS reaches back to Munich in 1923, when Hitler set up a "Staff Guard" (*Stabswache*) under the leadership of Josef Berchtold. Banned after the Hitler Putsch of November 9, 1923, it was re-established in early 1925 under Julius Schreck. *Staffeln* (squads) were soon formed in other localities, each with a complement of one Führer and 10 men. The primary tasks of these guard units, called *Schutzstaffeln* from the summer of 1925 on, were to protect eminent party personages, to protect gatherings, and to conduct recruitment operations for the party. They did not fall within the tradition of armed or military units (*Wehrverbände*) but were party cadres. Their significance for Hitler lay in their unconditional loyalty to his person, something that was not assured from the SA (STURMABTEILUNG).

The real history of the SS begins with the appointment of Heinrich HIMMLER as—the

third after Berchtold and Erhard Heiden—*Reichsführer-SS* (RFSS) on January 6, 1929. Parallel with the general ascendancy of the NSDAP and the SA, Himmler succeeded in expanding SS membership from a few hundred to about 52,000 by the end of 1932. New areas of responsibility also began to be delineated: with the suppression of the intraparty STENNES REVOLTS and with the buildup (begun in 1931 by Reinhard HEYDRICH) of the "Ic-Dienst," a cadre that was the germ of the later SECURITY SERVICE (SD), the SS established itself as the "party police" of the NSDAP. At the same time, the establishment of the "Race and Settlement Office" (1931) documented the determination of the new RFSS to forge by means of the SS a leadership order on the basis of "biological selection."

Despite the repeated quadrupling of the membership to about 209,000 by the end of 1933, the rise of the SS in power politics after the Seizure of Power initially proceeded in relative quiet. Himmler's appointment to the obscure post of police commissioner of Munich

1

1
SS march at the party
congress in Nuremberg
(1933).
2
"My Honor Is Loyalty."
SS dagger.
3
SS insignia.
4
"You too." Recruiting
poster for the Waffen-SS.
5
Propaganda poster for
the Flemish "Lange-
marck" volunteer divi-
sion.

(March 9, 1933) proved to be the starting point of a development that enabled the SS chief within 15 months to rise to the level of master of the political police in all the German states. In this way Himmler not only obtained the use of an instrument of power with great striking force; more importantly, with the transfer of increasingly broader party and state functions into the hands of the SS, a "Führer executive" took shape that typified the organizational structure of that regime. It was distinguished by the fact that its actions were no longer legitimized and defined by general norms of justice and law, but only by the will of the "Führer" (see FÜHRER'S WILL).

In this connection, the SS passed its test of trustworthiness with the liquidation of the SA leadership on June 30, 1934, in the RÖHM AFFAIR, which resulted in the upgrading of the SS—which was subject up to that point to the highest SA command—into an autonomous organization within the NSDAP (July 20, 1934). Freed from SA supervision, Himmler could now build the all-encompassing system of control and rule that would later be called the "SS state." Three lines of development mark this process, which aimed at the creation of a unified "state defense corps" (Staatsschutzkorps). First, the meshing of the SS and the police was extended. Himmler's designation as "Reich Führer of the

Oath of the SS man: "I swear to you, Adolf Hitler, as Führer and Chancellor of the Reich, loyalty and bravery. I vow to you and to the authorities appointed by you obedience unto death, so help me God."

SS and Chief of the German Police" (Reichsführer-SS und Chef der Deutschen Polizei; RFSSuChdDtPol) on June 17, 1936, as well as the establishment of the Main Office of the Order-keeping Police (Hauptamt Ordnungspolizei) and of the Reich Security Main Office (Reichssicherheitshauptamt; RSHA), constituted the institutional basis for the increasing fusion of personnel as well. At the same time the SD, which since 1934 had held a monopoly on intelligence-gathering within the NSDAP, was expanded. After the autumn of 1938 it was also officially empowered to act with a state mandate, and in February 1944 the ABWEHR (counterintelligence), which until then had reported to the Wehrmacht High Command (OKW), was also subordinated to it. Third, the CONCENTRATION CAMPS, some of which had been taken over by the SA in the summer of 1934 and placed under Theodor EICKE as inspector, underwent a thorough reorganization based on the "model" camp at Dachau. The result was tighter control over the camps and their guards (see DEATH'S-HEAD UNITS), more effective exploitation of prisoner labor, and also the deliberate isolation of this sector from the jurisdiction of the Justice and Interior ministries.

Whereas the SS quickly established its monopoly in the area of the regime's internal security, its military ambitions encountered stiffer resistance. With the LEIBSTANDARTE-SS "ADOLF HITLER" bodyguard, organized at Hitler's behest in March 1933, and with the "political squads," which quickly arose in many places and were combined in the autumn of 1934 into STANDBY TROOPS, the SS early on had at its command militarily organized volunteer units. They were largely removed from army control, as were the SS leadership schools (see JUNKER SCHOOLS), founded in 1934–1935. The military function of these institutions was expressly acknowledged in a decree of Hitler on August 17, 1938, after a years-long tug-of-war between the SS and the army command. Their importance lay not so much in their strength (some 14,000 men as of January 1, 1939) as in the fact that their existence represented an irreversible breach of the Wehrmacht's monopoly on arms.

The influence of the SS did not confine itself, however, to authority over some central instruments of power. Himmler's "Black Order" considered itself to be much more: in deliberate imitation of the nobility and knighthood of past times, it thought of itself as a leadership elite for the entire society. As such, it claimed to be the model for and teacher of the entire Volk,

Hitler reviews SS formations as they march past.

with the aim of restoring to the *Volk* its "extra-Christian and species-true ideological principles for the conduct of life," which had been buried under a thousand-year course of error throughout Western Christian history. By such an entanglement of goals, the SS exerted considerable influence over propaganda and culture, religion and learning. The SS Main Office and the RACE AND SETTLEMENT MAIN OFFICE (RuSHA) produced for these purposes a multitude of books, pamphlets, and motion pictures; the NATIONAL-POLITICAL EDUCATIONAL INSTITUTES (NPEA), controlled by the SS, as well as the LEBENSBORN (Fount of Life) and ANCESTRAL INHERITANCE organizations, served to promulgate the SS worldview.

This outlook on life and the claim to rule that

derived from it constituted, along with the person of the RFSS himself, the only unifying framework for the SS, which was otherwise as heterogeneous in its functions as in its social composition. To cultivate it, Himmler resorted to means both scurrilous and pedantic. He gave the SS a kind of order-like rule, created a spiritual center for it at the Wewelsburg in Westphalia, and, in imitation of various historical precedents, introduced pseudoreligious rituals and dedication ceremonies, symbols and cultic objects (including the honorary dagger, the death's-head ring, and the yule candle-holder). All this was intended not only to satisfy the mystical needs of the religiously alienated SS tribe (*see* CLAN), but also to provide a framework of traditions that would ensure individual conduct proper to the SS within an SS empire that was becoming more and more diverse.

As the war continued, these efforts underwent setbacks. The aspect of the SS changed, but its set goals as determined by power politics did not alter. In particular, the nonprofessional General SS (Allgemeine SS), the ideological core of the order before the war, now lost its earlier significance, since with few exceptions its members had been summoned to war service. On the other hand, the WAFFEN-SS (Armed SS), formed in the autumn of 1939 by a merger of the Standby Troops, the Death's-Head Units, and the Junker Schools, rapidly increased in importance and scope. As a consequence, the military wing of the SS was transformed from an elite Praetorian Guard into a multinational army consisting partly of "Germanic" and eastern European volunteers, and partly of German and ethnic German "forced volunteers" (*Zwangsfreiwilligen*), whose soldiers by and large did not meet the requirements of the SS order. In military politics, the SS first gained crucial importance when, following the putsch attempt of July 20, 1944, the position of "Commander of the Reserve Army [Ersatzheer] and Chief of Army Munitions," along with other important functions in the area of army command, was given to Himmler.

The SS's historically most fateful role was in the area of OCCUPATION POLICY, precisely

Decorative page from the SS Songbook: "Our honor is loyalty."

where interests involving population policy, foreign policy, security police, the military, and economics all overlapped. Determined to make itself the motive force of the NS "New Order" in Europe, the SS strove, in often sharp competition with military and civilian authorities, to monopolize the control and exploitation of the occupied territories. Particular advocates of these ambitions were the HIGHER SS AND POLICE LEADERS (HSSPF); wherever possible, they were installed as the extended arm of the RFSSuChdDtPol and were provided with comprehensive authority that was never clearly defined. The main feature of this authority was the political administration and the "pacification" by police of the occupied territories, as well as their GERMANIZATION through programs of population transfer, displacement, and colonization, as ordered by Himmler in his capacity as Reich Commissioner for the Fortification of the German Volk-Nation.

The consequences of all these measures attained, from 1941 at the latest, a dimension that exceeded any comparison with the repressive policies of the prewar years. The aim was no longer primarily to protect the regime, but rather to collectively segregate and "cull out" entire groups of the population (Jews, Gypsies, Slavs, and so on), along with exploitation of their labor ("extermination through work"). This dual approach was reflected in the development of the concentration camps, where the prisoner count, despite a high mortality rate, went from around 25,000 at the start of the war to over 700,000 in early 1945. In view of the labor shortage in the free economy, caused by the war, this source of labor offered an increasingly irresistible potential that Himmler planned to exploit for building up an SS-owned armaments industry, over the opposition of Albert SPEER's Armaments Ministry.

Nevertheless, for camps such as MAIDANEK the typical economics-related outcome of extermination was a secondary phenomenon. This was not the case with the FINAL SOLUTION of the Jewish question, which the SS did not devise but nonetheless carried out without any objection. The operations of the EINSATZGRUPPEN of the Security Police and the SD, which began at the outbreak of war in Poland and in the Soviet Union, and which by November 1942 had claimed over 800,000 victims, served no economic, military, or otherwise war-related purpose, but only extermination itself. This was particularly so with regard to the genocide perpetrated in the extermination camps, primarily in Chełmno, Bełżec, Sobibór, Treblinka, and Auschwitz, as a consequence of the **WANNSEE CONFERENCE** (January 20, 1942). Through it all, the SS once more proved itself to be the unconditionally loyal "executive organ of the Führer," and could entertain the justifiable hope of administering the now "cleansed eastern space" under its own rule after the end of the war.

Only a minority of SS members took direct part in the execution of the Final Solution. It was perhaps not even the most typical of the many functions that the SS performed, but it was certainly the most significant in terms of the impact on history. Indeed, all of the SS functions, as varied as they were, arose from and served the same racist ideological will to domination; its point of reference for the SS was always Hitler himself. His death therefore also meant the end for the SS, which the Nuremberg Trials of major war criminals classified as a "criminal organization."

Bernd Wegner

"Without sentiment [Sans Sentiment]—without feeling." French cartoon on the SS.

SS Economic Enterprises (*SS-Wirtschaftsunternehmen*), conglomerate of more than 40 different individual enterprises, mostly in the form of corporations (*Handelsgesellschaften*) and limited companies (GmbH and AG), with a total of 150 factories and plants. The capital for the establishment of these enterprises came at first from the compulsory savings of SS members, and later mainly from private bank credits extended by the Dresdner Bank (about 30 million RM). The starting points for the economic activities of the SS were (1) the workshops that had existed from the beginning at the concentration camps, established since the spring of 1933; and (2) Himmler's personal preferences and his cultural and ideological goals (such as the establishment of the Allach porcelain factory, the Nordland Press, and the Society for the Support and Care of German Cultural Monuments). Both types of enterprise were subordinated in 1938 to the SS Administrative Office (as of 1942, the SS Economic-Administrative Main Office [WVHA]) and were integrated in terms of organization, personnel, and budget.

With the establishment of more concentration camps in 1938–1939, economic aspects became more significant, although a reasoned-out economic-political concept never lay at the basis of the expansion of enterprises. The concentration camps were transformed from an instrument of police and political goals to one of forced labor. Those SS prisoner industries that became the largest were (1) the German Earth and Stone Works (Deutsche Erd- und Steinwerke; DEST), with quarries and plants for granite, bricks, gravel, and construction materials near the concentration camps at Flossenbürg, Gross-Rosen, and Neuengamme, among others; (2) the German Armament Works (Deutsche Ausrüstungswerke; DAW), which took over the already existing SS workshops in the concentration camps; (3) the German Research Institute for Nutrition and Diet (Versuchsanstalt für Ernährung und Verpflegung), whose goal was autarky in the area of spices and medicinal herbs; and (4) the Textile and Leather Processing Company (Gesellschaft für Textil- und Lederverarbeitung), which produced clothing for prisoners and soldiers. On July 26, 1938, all of the SS industries were merged into the German Economic Industries (Deutsche Wirtschaftsbetriebe; DWB) umbrella organization. The DWB directorate was identical with the top echelon of the SS administration in the later WVHA (the WVHA chief, Oswald **POHL**, was also the administrative head of the DWB). In the same way, the individual SS industries were directed by leading SS officers of the WVHA.

In the territories annexed by Germany beginning in 1938–1939 (especially the Sudeten-

SS Economic Enterprises. Quarrying in the Mauthausen concentration camp.

land) and, once the war began, in the occupied
Polish territories, the SS acquired immense
wealth, thanks to its influential political position, when Jewish firms there were "Aryanized"
and Polish or "enemy" concerns were confiscated. These included especially furniture and
ceramics companies and mineral-water springs,
in which the SS industries ended up holding a
near monopoly, with a 75 percent market share
in the German Reich. In the Generalgouvernement the economic activity of the SS (Ostindustrie [Eastern Industries]) was closely connected with the ruthless use of deported Jewish
concentration camp inmates for forced labor,
until the mass extermination measures beginning in 1942–1943. In general, the use of
prisoners was a central economic factor for the
SS enterprises, since the amount of compensation credited to the Reich Treasury was substantially beneath the wage level in private industry,
which successfully protested against the unfair
competition. The growing deterioration of the
war situation beginning in 1943 led many SS
industries to convert to the production of armaments, whereas the overall wartime shortages
favored the economic expansion of the SS industries.

R. S.

SS-Totenkopfverbände. *See* Death's-Head Units.

Stab-in-the-Back Legend (*Dolchstosslegende;* literally, dagger-stab legend), thesis disseminated
by nationalist circles after the First World War
that the failure on the home front was responsible for the military collapse of Germany in the
autumn of 1918. In the words of Gen. Paul von
HINDENBURG before the parliamentary investigation committee of the National Assembly on
November 18, 1919, the "army that was undefeated in the field" was "stabbed from behind"
by means of the November Revolution. During
the following years, the legend became a standard component of the Right's agitation, especially that of the German Nationalists (DNVP)
and the National Socialists, whose intent was to
defame the democratic politicians of the Weimar Republic as "November criminals."

In actuality, for reasons of military strategy
and the war economy, the German army faced
immediate defeat in the autumn of 1918, as
Gen. Erich LUDENDORFF, later one of the
foster-fathers of the legend, himself had demonstrated by his precipitate resignation at the end
of September 1918, as well as by his demand for
an "immediate armistice." The fact that politicians could be found who would relieve the
military of the signing of the unavoidable armistice gave the legend added support. The legend
could not be eradicated despite the clear proof
of its untenability (as in the "Stab-in-the-Back
Trial," held from October 19 to November 20,
1925, in Munich), and it continued to poison the
atmosphere. The total collapse of the German
Wehrmacht in 1945 prevented the emergence of

Stab-in-the-Back Legend. Cover of the
nationalistic *South German Monthly.*

a new stab-in-the-back legend after the Second World War.

Stabswachen, early SS formations; *see* Leib-standarte-SS "Adolf Hitler"; SS.

Städteordnung (city ordinance), municipal constitution for communes having the rights of a city (*Stadtrecht*) (*see* GERMAN COMMUNAL ORDINANCE).

Staffelmann, National Socialist jargon for *Schutzstaffelmann* (SS man).

Stage director (*Spielleiter*), Germanization of the word *Regisseur* (director) in National Socialist reference works and pronouncements.

Stahlhelm. *See* Steel Helmet.

Stahlpakt. *See* Pact of Steel.

Stalin, Joseph (originally, Iosif Dzhugashvili), b. Gori (Georgia), December 21, 1879; d. Kuntsevo (now part of Moscow), March 5, 1953, Soviet politician. The son of a shoemaker, Stalin was educated in the Orthodox Christian seminary in Tiflis (1894–1898) but was dismissed because of his Marxist agitation. He became a member of the Social Democratic Workers' Party of Russia in 1898 (as of 1904, the majority [Bolshevik] faction), and was several times arrested and banished to Siberia. He was made a member of the Central Committee in 1912, and assumed the surname Stalin ("man of steel [*stal'*]"). He also helped found the party newspaper, *Pravda.* Banished again from 1913 to 1917, Stalin did not return to Saint Petersburg (from 1914, Petrograd) until March 1917, after the February revolution. He first followed a moderate course, but then accepted Lenin's demand for a violent seizure of power, accomplished in the October Revolution. In 1922 Stalin, then People's Commissar for Nationality Issues (1917–1923), rose to the post of general secretary of the Central Committee, a position of power he kept despite warnings made by the dying Lenin. By 1929 Stalin had outmaneuvered all rivals, particularly Trotsky, and in the 1930s he built up his personal dictatorship on the basis of police-state terror.

Through forced collectivization of agriculture and an expansive industrialization program, Stalin sought to secure independence in foreign affairs with economic recovery and an arms buildup. The SPANISH CIVIL WAR and the MUNICH AGREEMENT, however, made the danger to the young Soviet Union evident. On one level, the armaments gap with the fascist states was

Joseph Stalin.

still substantial, and on another, a coalition of the Western powers with Hitler stood out as a threat. Accordingly, in 1939 Stalin replaced his pro-Western foreign minister, Maksim Maksimovich LITVINOV, with Viacheslav Mikhailovich MOLOTOV. Despite the ideological contradictions, the GERMAN-SOVIET NONAGGRESSION PACT of August 23, 1939, gained Stalin considerably more time, and Hitler's consent allowed Stalin to expand his territorial base through annexations (including eastern Poland, Bessarabia, and the Baltic states) and the WINTER WAR with Finland. Nonetheless, the Soviet Union came to the brink of collapse in the RUSSIAN CAMPAIGN after a German attack (June 22, 1941) that Stalin had not yet expected. But the Soviet nonaggression pact with Japan (April 1941) held up, an alliance with England (and thus with the United States) helped, and the appeal to Russian patriotism finally brought about the turning point.

Although at first Stalin (after 1941 also premier, and after 1943, marshal) still considered a possible separate peace with Germany, like his Allies he soon decided on UNCONDITIONAL SURRENDER. He even refused Germany's offer to exchange his captured son Yakov, who died in German custody in 1943. At the conferences of TEHERAN, YALTA, and Potsdam (*see* POTSDAM AGREEMENT), Stalin proved to be the most skillful negotiator, securing the positions he had won through a policy of "fait accompli" (including the EXPULSION of Germans from areas occupied by the Red Army). In this role he benefited from changes of leadership in the

United States and in Great Britain in 1945, as well as from a Red Army whose potential had grown mightily during the war. This enabled him to follow a course of conflict that led to the desired Cold War with his former allies and to a partitioning off by means of the IRON CURTAIN. Stalin could then pursue undisturbed his program for the Bolshevization of eastern and southeastern Europe.

Stalingrad (until 1925, Tsaritsyn; now Volgograd), Soviet city on the lower Volga River, with 450,000 inhabitants in 1940. Stalingrad was the objective of a German offensive in the autumn of 1942, during the RUSSIAN CAMPAIGN. The resulting Battle of Stalingrad is generally regarded as the turning point of the Second World War, a crucial turn that in any event had already begun to take shape in the winter crisis outside of Moscow in 1941–1942. On November 19, 1942, the Red Army began a pincer movement that cut off the German Sixth Army, which had already advanced to Stalingrad. After German relief efforts failed, and under Hitler's order forbidding a breakout, the Sixth Army was forced to surrender between January 31 and February 2, 1943. Some 146,000 German soldiers had died, and 90,000 were taken into Soviet captivity; only 6,000 returned home after the war. In his SPORTS PALACE SPEECH on February 18, 1943, Goebbels exploited the catastrophe of Stalingrad with a fanatic appeal to fight to the end.

Stalingrad. National Socialist propaganda poster: "Stalingrad—deathless example of German warriordom."

Stampfer, Friedrich, b. Brünn (now Brno, Czechoslovakia), September 8, 1874; d. Kronberg (Taunus), December 1, 1957, German journalist and politician. A member of the Social Democratic Party (SPD) since his school days, Stampfer studied political economy. From 1900 to 1902 he was an editor with the *Leipziger Volkszeitung*, and then a free-lance journalist. Between 1916 and 1933 he was editor in chief of

Stalingrad. Dead Soviet and German soldiers.

the main SPD newspaper, VORWÄRTS. From 1920 to 1933 he was also a Reichstag deputy, and from 1926 to 1933, a member of the SPD Executive Committee.

A member of the reformist wing of the party, Stampfer wanted to remain in Germany after the National Socialist Seizure of Power, but he submitted to the party executive's decision to continue political activity from exile. He went in May 1933 to Prague, where he edited the *Neues Vorwärts* until 1938, when he escaped with it to France. In 1940 he had to flee further to the United States, where he collaborated on the *Neue Volkszeitung* (New People's News) and appealed for a reasonable peace treaty with a Germany liberated from National Socialism. From 1948 to 1955 Stampfer lectured at the Academy of Labor in Frankfurt am Main.

Stamps. *See* Postage stamps.

Standarte, SA and SS unit having the approximate strength of a regiment. It was led by a *Standartenführer* (colonel).

Standby Troops (*Verfügungstruppe;* VT [officially, SS Standby Troops]), armed SS units, quartered in barracks. They were developed from the LEIBSTANDARTS-SS "ADOLF HITLER" and the POLITICAL SQUADS in accordance with guidelines of the Armed Forces Ministry of September 24, 1934, and the directive of December 12, 1934. They were themselves the basis for the WAFFEN-SS. Although Hitler had assured the Reichswehr that it would remain "the sole arms-bearer of the nation," the experience of the RÖHM AFFAIR made the desire for a state police troop prevail. In any event, until the war the VT were not allowed to form divisions or use heavy arms, although their leaders, under former Reichswehr general Paul HAUSSER, saw to their military training. Moreover, the JUNKER SCHOOLS provided elite schooling for future VT leaders.

Thus the Standby Troops became guards of the National Socialist regime. The military athlete type was dominant, but the troops were also imbued by ideological fanaticism. An outspokenly anti-Christian attitude, for example, prevailed in the VT, leading to collective withdrawals from the churches; by the end of 1938 every second VT soldier had no formal denomination. The troops were particularly well suited for Hitler's assignment of August 17, 1938, both with regard to "domestic-policy tasks" and to "mobile deployment within the fighting forces." The latter usage came during the Pol-

ish Campaign, in which the SS regiments that had meanwhile been formed were divided among the attack armies. Later they were merged with the DEATH'S-HEAD UNITS in the Waffen-SS.

Stangl, Franz, b. Altmünster (Austria), March 26, 1908; d. Düsseldorf, June 28, 1971, SS-*Hauptsturmführer* (February 12, 1943). A weaver by trade, Stangl joined the Austrian police in 1931, and was accepted by the Criminal Police in 1935. After Austria's Anschluss he was assigned to the Stapo (State Police) in Linz, where for a time he was posted to the Jewish Bureau (Judenreferat). He joined the NSDAP on May 1, 1938. In early 1940 he was given instructions to report for work at the Public Service Foundation for Institutional Care (Gemeinnützige Stiftung für Anstaltspflege), a front organization in the EUTHANASIA program (T4). In the uniform of a first lieutenant in the regular police (Schupo), Stangl went first to the "killing facility" at HARTHEIM, then, in the late summer of 1941, to BERNBURG.

In the spring of 1942, as part of the REINHARD OPERATION, Stangl became commandant of the extermination camps at SOBIBÓR and TREBLINKA. Along with his superior Odilo GLOBOCNIK, he was transferred in August 1943 to Trieste. Because of illness he returned to Vienna in early 1945 and served in the "ALPINE FORTRESS." After the end of the war he was interned, and in 1947 was placed in detention pending investigation in Linz. He managed to escape on May 30, 1948, and made his way via Italy to Syria. In 1951 he emigrated to Brazil, but in 1967 he was

Franz Stangl.

extradited to the Federal Republic. On December 22, 1970, he was sentenced to life imprisonment after a jury trial in the state court (*Landgericht*) in Düsseldorf, for taking part in the murder of at least 400,000 people. He died in prison.

A. St.

Starhemberg, Ernst Rüdiger Prince, b. Eferding (Upper Austria), May 10, 1899; d. Schruns (Vorarlberg), March 15, 1956, Austrian politician. A frontline soldier for a short time in the First World War, Starhemberg then studied law in Innsbruck and Munich. Connected with radical right-wing circles, he was a member of the "Tyrolean Storm Platoon" (Sturmzug Tirol), associated with the OBERLAND free corps. Starhemberg took part in Hitler's putsch attempt in November 1923, and returned to Austria after its failure. In 1928 he joined the Homeland Defense (Heimatschutz), and from 1930 to 1936 served as its president. A representative of the Home Guards (*see* AUSTROFASCISM), he became interior minister in 1930, supported Engelbert DOLLFUSS in the establishment of an Austrian CORPORATIST STATE, and as leader of the FATHERLAND FRONT was vice chancellor from 1934 to 1936. As a convinced opponent of National Socialism and a champion of Austrian independence, Starhemberg sought support from Fascist Italy, but he lost influence as a result of the German-Italian rapprochement; he went into exile in 1937. In 1940 he fought with the French against the Wehrmacht, then escaped to England and South America. He returned home in 1956.

Stark, Johannes, b. Thansüss (Upper Palatinate), April 15, 1874; d. Traunstein, June 21, 1957, German physicist. Stark was a professor in Hannover (1906–1909), Aachen, Greifswald (1917–1920), and Würzburg (until 1922). In 1905 he discovered the optical Doppler effect (the shift in wavelength in moving sources of light rays) on channelized light, and in 1913, the effect (named after him) of splitting spectral lines in an electric field. He received a Nobel prize in 1919. At first an advocate of the quantum theory and the special Theory of Relativity, in 1922 Stark turned against theoretical physics in a pamphlet, an act that cost him his professorial chair. He became increasingly extreme in his stance, and intensified his polemic with antisemitic invective. This commended him to the NSDAP, which he joined on April 1, 1930, and earned him the presidency of the Physical-

Johannes Stark.

Technical Reich Institute (1933–1939) and the chairmanship of the German Research Society (1934–1936). With his works *Nationalsozialismus und Wissenschaft* (National Socialism and Science; 1934) and *Jüdische und Deutsche Physik* (Jewish and German Physics; 1941), Stark became, next to Philipp LENARD, the most determined proponent of a racist interpretation of even the natural sciences. On July 20, 1947, an appeals board classified him as a major offender and sentenced him to a labor camp.

Stark, Jonathan, b. Ulm, July 8, 1926; d. Sachsenhausen concentration camp, late October 1944, Jehovah's Witness and German victim of National Socialism. Like thousands of his fellow believers, Stark was arrested for refusing to swear the oath of loyalty to Hitler. He withstood the worst harassments in the Sachsenhausen punishment company. The camp chief (*Lagerführer*) finally had him hanged for refusing to obey orders.

State; state concept (*Staat[sbegriff]*), the totality of institutions whose collaboration is meant to ensure the lasting and orderly coexistence of a state's populace (*Staatsvolk*) within that state's territory. National Socialism wanted to eliminate traditional individual freedom and the (in principle) autonomous society characterized by opposing interests, in order to replace them with the fiction of a unified VOLK COMMUNITY. As a result, the theory and practice of statecraft also changed. The activity of the state no longer resulted from open political discussions that were resolved in democratic decision-making processes. Instead, the FÜHRER'S WILL defined statecraft in an authoritarian manner that required no agreement with the actual opinions of the people. Behind this construct was an image of humanity that denied to the individual the majority (*Mündigkeit*) that would allow for responsible political participation.

In order to implement the political goals of National Socialism, constitutional restraints that had previously limited state activity were abolished. By appealing to the interests of the *Volk* Community as it had defined them, National Socialism justified its intervention in every individual and societal sector without restriction by formal or material barriers. On the pretext of the benefit to the *Volk* Community, National Socialism legitimized the arms buildup and the waging of war in particular, as well as the total deprivation of the rights of the regime's opponents, leading eventually to their mass murder.

The NS state acknowledged no democratic or constitutional controls, but rather regarded itself as empowered by the interests of the *Volk* Community (as it saw them) to intrude in all personal and social areas without restriction. Ernst FORSTHOFF thus termed the regime a "total state" (1933). The initial period might have been regarded, according to Ernst Fraenkel, as still being a DUAL STATE, within which a certain obligation to norms held true, at least in the economic sector. But the system developed increasingly into the state based on injustice, designated by Franz Neumann as the BEHEMOTH.

A. v. B.

States. *See* Länder.

Statute of limitations. *See* Limitation [of criminal liability].

Stauffenberg, Claus Count Schenk von, b. Jettingen bei Günzburg, November 15, 1907; d. Berlin, July 20, 1944 (executed), German officer and opposition fighter. As a boy Stauffenberg was influenced by the elitist-conservative circle around the poet Stefan GEORGE. In 1926 he joined the Bamberg Seventeenth Cavalry Regiment. He became a teacher at the War Academy in Berlin in 1936, and in 1938 was appointed to the staff of Erich HOEPNER's Armored Division, with which he took part in the Polish Campaign in 1939 and the French Campaign in 1940. Stauffenberg was initially fascinated by National Socialism; on the day of the Seizure of Power (January 30, 1933), he organized a demonstration of public rejoicing in Bamberg. Yet by

Claus Schenk von Stauffenberg.

KRISTALLNACHT (November 9–10, 1938) at the latest, he had come to regard Hitler's course with deep mistrust and growing abhorrence. That the persecution of Jews in Germany was only a minor prelude to something far more atrocious was a fact that Stauffenberg realized in the Russian Campaign, when he collaborated with the SMOLENSK COMMITTEE in setting up units of Russian volunteers and became aware of Hitler's estimate of "Jewish and Slavic subhumans."

In February 1943 Stauffenberg, as a lieutenant colonel, was transferred to the staff of the Tenth Panzer Division in Africa. He was severely wounded on April 7, losing one eye, one hand, and two fingers of the other. During his long convalescence his decision to eliminate Hitler matured; unless it were done, he regarded any overthrow attempt as useless. On October 1, 1943, he became chief of staff at the General Army Office under Friedrich OLBRICHT. Within a relatively short period of time Stauffenberg succeeded with his contagious energy in binding together the divergent groups of the opposition. His conservative attitude made him acceptable to the circle around Carl Friedrich GOERDELER, his social openness commended him to the Social Democrat Wilhelm LEUSCHNER, and his personal bravery predestined him for the carrying out of the assassination attempt. The opportunity for it arose after July 1, 1944, when Stauffenberg became a colonel and chief of staff to the Reserve Army commander, Friedrich FROMM, and thus gained access to the situation conferences in the Führer's headquar-

ters. After two failed attempts, on the TWENTI-
ETH OF JULY, 1944, Stauffenberg brought a time
bomb in a briefcase into the command barracks
of the "Wolfsschanze," near Rastenburg (East
Prussia). He left the room before the detonation,
and flew to Berlin convinced that Hitler was
dead. Contrary to plan, however, the code word,
"VALKYRIE," was released with a substantial
delay, so that the news of Hitler's survival led
to the collapse of the *coup d'état.* Stauffenberg
was arrested by Fromm, and together with Olbricht and other conspirators was summarily
shot.

Steel Helmet (Stahlhelm; also Bund der Frontsoldaten [League of Frontline Soldiers]), soldiers'
league founded on December 25, 1918, by
Franz SELDTE. It was conceived as a military
force against Socialist and Communist uprisings
and was intended to bring the "spirit of frontline
comradeship" over into politics. From this programmatic standpoint there soon evolved an
anti–Weimar Republic bias, which manifested
itself in the Steel Helmet's struggle against "the
System" and the forces supporting it. The
league adopted other positions of the nationalist
and authoritarian parties, and it declared its
opposition to "cosmopolitan" Catholicism and
to Jews, who were excluded from membership
by an early version of the ARYAN PARAGRAPH.
With some 400,000 members (1925), the Steel
Helmet attacked the DAWES PLAN in 1924,
banded together with the right-wing parties

Steel Helmet. Recruiting poster, 1929.

against the YOUNG PLAN in 1929, and finally
entered into a pact with them in the HARZBURG
FRONT. It thus became one of the lackeys of
National Socialism, quickly succumbing to its
embrace after the Seizure of Power. Seldte became labor minister in Hitler's government, and
the league's younger cohorts were integrated
directly into the SA by April 1933. The remaining groups, after being renamed the "National Socialist German Frontline Combatants'
League" (March 1934), were dissolved in No-

Steel Helmet. Consecration of flags.

vember 1935. The re-establishment of the Steel Helmet in the Federal Republic of Germany in 1951 met with little success.

Steering (*Lenkung*), term taken from the language of technology, and in National Socialist usage applied to social, economic, and political processes. It became a fashionable term for emphasizing the technocratic, goal-oriented character of leadership and hierarchical leadership structures.

Stegerwald, Adam, b. Greussenheim (Lower Franconia), December 14, 1874; d. Würzburg, December 3, 1945, German politician. In 1903 Stegerwald became general secretary of the Alliance of Christian Trade Unions; from 1919 to 1929 he served as its chairman. He was elected to represent the Center party in the Weimar National Assembly in 1919, and he then represented the party in the Reichstag from 1920 to 1933. He became transportation minister in 1929, and in 1930, labor minister under Wilhelm Brüning. Stegerwald resigned in 1932. Through conversations with Hitler, he sought to secure the continued functioning of the trade unions in the Third Reich. Forced to recognize the futility of such initiatives, he withdrew to private life. His loose contacts with the opposition landed him in jail for a time in 1944. In 1945 Stegerwald helped found the Christian Social Union (CSU), the Bavarian sister party of the Christian Democratic Union (CDU).

Steguweit, Heinz, b. Cologne, March 19, 1897; d. Halver (Westphalia), May 25, 1964, German writer. Steguweit had his first literary successes with Rhenish folk stories and anecdotes, published as *Das Laternchen der Unschuld* (The Lamp of Innocence; 1925). With sentimental and nationalistic glorifications of war experiences he became the "poet of the frontline generation," in *Der Jüngling im Feuerofen* (The Young Man in the Furnace; 1932). Along with humorous prose and "lay plays," during the Third Reich Steguweit composed *völkisch* poems, for which he received several literary prizes and was appointed a state (*Land*) director of the Reich Writing Chamber. After 1945 Steguweit continued to find a public with genre poetry and with books for children and adolescents, such as *Eulenspiegel darf nicht sterben* (Eulenspiegel Must Not Die; 1955).

Stehr, Hermann, b. Habelschwerdt, February 16, 1864; d. Oberschreiberhau (Silesia), September 11, 1940, German writer. Stehr wrote his major works, influenced by traditional Sile-

Hermann Stehr.

sian mysticism, in the years before 1933. His tendency toward subjectivity made him a "favorite author of the German philistine" (Ernst Loewy). The National Socialists valued his antidemocratic mystification of man and soil as "*völkisch* earthboundness" (*Erdverbundenheit*) and awarded to "the greatest living German poet" (Hanns Johst) the Goethe Prize, the Eagle Shield, honorary doctorates, and the like. In the late 1930s Stehr in public speeches stated his view that "Germandom . . . and . . . *Volk* [could be] fulfilled and maintained only . . . as the Followership of the Führer." His books found a wide readership even after 1945 in the Federal Republic; to preserve his memory, his readers founded the Hermann Stehr Society.

Steil, Ludwig, b. Lüttringhausen, October 29, 1900; d. Dachau concentration camp, January 17, 1945, German Evangelical theologian. A pastor in a Westphalian industrial district, Steil was a member of the PASTORS' EMERGENCY LEAGUE from its beginnings. He was also a delegate to the first Westphalian Confessional Synod in March 1934, and a member of the Fraternal Council there. He struggled against the National Socialist–influenced German Christians and promoted the Confessing Church, positions that brought him into repeated conflict with the SA and the party. Despite a ban, he persisted in announcing from the pulpit the names of imprisoned brothers of the cloth so that prayers of intercession might be said for them. As a result, he was finally arrested in the summer of 1944. Confined in the Dachau concentration camp, he died in a typhus epidemic.

Stein, Edith, b. Breslau (now Wrocław, Poland), October 12, 1891; d. Auschwitz concentration camp, August 9, 1942, German philosopher. From an Orthodox Jewish family, Stein studied in Breslau, Göttingen, and Freiburg, where, upon completing her doctorate, she became assistant to the philosopher Edmund Husserl (1859–1938). Stein converted to Catholicism in 1922, and made a scholarly contribution in 1929 with her edition of the letters of Cardinal John Henry Newman. In her philosophical writings, including *Endliches und ewiges Sein* (Final and Eternal Being; published posthumously in 1950), she attempted to build a bridge between Scholasticism and modern philosophy.

Appointed a lecturer at the Pedagogical Academy in Münster in 1932, Stein lost her post in 1933 because of the ARYAN PARAGRAPH. She became a Carmelite nun in Cologne, taking the religious name Teresia Benedicta of the Cross. When her presence became a hazard for the convent after KRISTALLNACHT, on November 9–10, 1938, Stein went to Echt, in the Netherlands. In January 1942 the SS apprehended her there. As a response to a critical pastoral letter issued by the Dutch bishops, they deported her along with many other Jews to Auschwitz, where immediately after her arrival she died in the gas chamber. [A Carmelite convent at Auschwitz, dedicated in part to Edith Stein, became a center of controversy in the late 1980s when Jews protested the reneging of an agreement to move it.]

Stein, Fritz (originally, Friedrich Wilhelm), b. Gerlachsheim (Main-Tauber district), December

Edith Stein.

Fritz Stein.

17, 1897; d. Berlin, November 14, 1961, German musicologist and conductor. As a professor of music and, after 1925, as general music director in Kiel, Stein often addressed issues of "*völkisch* musical education." Through theoretical as well as practical work on this theme, he became after 1933 one of the most important music functionaries of the Third Reich. He was director of the State Academy for Music in Berlin (1933–1945), director of the Office for Choirs and Volk Music in the REICH MUSIC CHAMBER (as of 1934), and also president of the Reich Association for Evangelical Church Music. After 1945 Stein limited himself to works of systematization and to formal studies of individual musicians and works, especially of Max Reger.

Steiner, Felix, b. Stallupönen (East Prussia), May 23, 1896; d. Munich, May 17, 1966, SS-*Obergruppenführer* and general of the Waffen-SS (July 1, 1943). Steiner, a regiment commander at the beginning of the war, in contrast to Paul HAUSSER wanted to implement an elitist program in the WAFFEN-SS. In November 1940 Steiner became a major general and commander of the Fifth SS Armored Division "Viking," which consisted of European (Flemish, Walloon, Dutch, Danish, Norwegian, and Finnish) volunteers. In November 1942 he assumed command of the Third Armored Corps, in May 1943 he became commanding general of the Third SS Armored Corps, and in the spring of 1945, supreme commander of several armies and army groups. On May 3, 1945, he was taken into

British captivity, from which he was released on April 27, 1948.

Steinhoff, Hans, b. Pfaffenhofen, near Munich, March 10, 1882; d. near Luckenwalde, May 1945 (in an airplane crash), German motion-picture director. After working in the theater, Steinhoff came late to films, where he found a wide public with routine entertainment films such as *Gräfin Mariza* (Countess Maritza; 1925). In 1933, in HITLERJUNGE QUEX, Steinhoff made one of the first and cleverest National Socialist propaganda films. He fulfilled a particular demand of the NS leaders with historical (*Der alte und der junge König* [The Old and the Young King]; 1935) and biographical (*Robert Koch*, 1939; OHM KRÜGER, 1941) movies. Regarded as "the most politically reliable star director of the Third Reich" (Tichy), Steinhoff knew better than anyone else how to use expressive images that invoked the proletariat and Hollywood, and also how to use formal brilliance to conceal anti-Communist or antisemitic biases and defamations of political opponents and enemies of war.

Stellbrink, Karl Friedrich, b. Münster, October 28, 1894; d. Hamburg, November 10, 1943 (executed), German Evangelical theologian. Stellbrink was a volunteer in the First World War. After serving as a vicar, he was ordained in 1921 for the overseas service of the Evangelical Church. He worked as a pastor among German settlers in Brazil until 1929, then returned to Germany. On June 1, 1934, Stellbrink became pastor of the Luther Church in Lübeck, where

Hans Steinhoff.

he acquired a reputation as a fearless and critical preacher. Long under Gestapo surveillance, on March 29, 1942, he interpreted Lübeck's recent heavy bombardment as God's warning of a need for moral regeneration. The investigators were certain that this message was aimed at National Socialist policies, since the pastor had distributed the anti-EUTHANASIA sermons of Bishop Clemens August Count von GALEN to his congregation. Stellbrink was arrested on April 7, 1942, along with three Catholic colleagues who were similarly charged. On June 24, 1943, he was sentenced to death in Lübeck by a specially convened *Volk* Court, and later executed in Hamburg.

Stennes Revolts (*Stennes-Revolten*), protest actions by the Berlin SA (STURMABTEILUNG) against the NSDAP in 1930–1931. Since the onset of the world economic crisis, a host of unemployed men had streamed into the SA, which presented itself as a social collecting basin (*Auffangbecken*) and as a militant organization opposed to the social system, which it blamed for their calamities. The NSDAP evolved in a contrary direction: Hitler managed to impose upon the party his strategy of a "legal seizure of power" through his ability to form coalitions with the bourgeois Right, while eliminating Otto STRASSER's nationalist and revolutionary wing in the summer of 1930. This tactic, along with the denial to the SA of funds and Reichstag seats even as it became ideologically more radical and politically stronger, led to Hitler's conflict with the Supreme SA Leader (*Oberster SA-Führer*; Osaf), Franz PFEFFER VON SALOMON, which took concrete shape in Berlin.

In the capital a particularly radical SA group under the eastern Osaf deputy, Walter Stennes (b. 1895; d. May 9, 1973), demanded independence from Berlin *Gauleiter* Joseph Goebbels as well as payment for its own services. As the promising September elections approached, the Berlin SA went on a campaign strike. On August 30, 1930, it even assailed the SS and broke into the *Gau* headquarters. Goebbels called in the police to drive out the SA, but Hitler temporarily gave in so as not to endanger the NSDAP's expected political breakthrough, and consented to Stennes's demands. At the same time he dismissed Pfeffer von Salomon, who was caught in the middle, and himself assumed the position of Osaf, bringing in Ernst RÖHM as SA chief of staff. The latent conflict flared up again on April 1, 1931, when Hitler removed Stennes for resisting Röhm's authority. The events of August repeated themselves when Stennes gained approval and support from all of eastern Germany. Despite recourse to the police, it took weeks for the SA leadership to impose itself everywhere. The expelled "Stennesians" came together—without much success—as the "Independent National Socialist Militant Movement [*Kampfbewegung*] of Germany." Even under Röhm the SA remained the left wing of the NS movement and absorbed the corresponding revolutionary potential (*see* RÖHM AFFAIR).

W. P.

Sterilization. *See* Forced sterilization.

Stettinius, Edward Reilly, b. Chicago, October 22, 1900; d. Greenwich, Conn., October 31, 1949, American businessman and politician. Stettinius joined General Motors in 1924, becoming a vice president in 1931. In 1938 he became chairman of the board of U.S. Steel. After 1939 he held various government positions concerned with military production. In 1941 President Franklin D. Roosevelt appointed Stettinius director of priorities in the Office of Production Management, in which capacity he was in charge of the Lend-Lease program (*see* LEND-LEASE ACT). In 1943–1944 he served as under secretary of state and in 1944–1945 as secretary of state, in this position advising the president at YALTA. Stettinius was closely involved with the establishment of the UNITED NATIONS and was the first chief delegate of the United States to the organization, in 1945–1946. In 1946 he became the United States delegate to the Security Council.

Steuben, Fritz. *See* Wittek, Erhard.

Stieff, Hellmuth, b. Deutsch-Eylau, June 6, 1901; d. Berlin-Plötzensee, August 8, 1944 (executed), German officer. As a major in Poland in 1939, Stieff witnessed with incomprehension German atrocities ("I am ashamed to be a German"), but he advanced rapidly as an excellent General Staff officer. By the time he was a colonel with the Fourth Army outside Moscow in 1941–1942, he recognized that catastrophe could be averted only by eliminating Hitler. Appointed chief of the Organizational Section of the Army General Staff in October 1942, Stieff procured the explosive for Henning von TRESCKOW's assassination attempt of September 1943. Then, as the army's youngest major general (January 30, 1944), he worked tirelessly as well in preparation for Claus von Stauffenberg's attempt of July 20, 1944. After its failure the *Volk* Court sentenced Stieff to death.

Hellmuth Stieff.

Stimson, Henry Lewis, b. New York City, September 21, 1867; d. Huntington, N.Y., October 20, 1950, American jurist and politician. Stimson practiced law beginning in 1891. He then served as secretary of war (1911–1913) and as governor-general of the Philippines (1928–1929). As Herbert HOOVER's secretary of state he succeeded in reaching a solution on the issue of German REPARATIONS, but he was not able to advance the disarmament negotiations. The Stimson Doctrine (1932)—named for him—aimed to avert war and contain expansionism, especially by the Japanese, but it proved to be an ineffective instrument when challenged, as by the Italian attack on ABYSSINIA. From 1940 to 1945 Stimson was again secretary of war. He worked unsuccessfully against an excessively close alliance with Moscow, thwarted the MORGENTHAU PLAN, and supported dropping the atom bomb on Japan.

St. Louis, passenger ship of the Hapag Line, with a gross registered tonnage of 16,732. Under Capt. Gustav Schröder the *St. Louis* sailed on May 13, 1939, from the harbor of Hamburg. On board were 937 Jews, mostly well to do, who had been promised emigration to Cuba. However, while lying at anchor in Havana, the ship was detained and the passengers were forbidden to disembark in Cuba; their dearly acquired visas proved to have been falsified by Cuban police. Schröder turned next to the United States, which also refused to accept the Jews. After a five-week odyssey, the *St. Louis*—called by the international press "the ship of the damned"—was able to set its passengers ashore at the port

St. Louis.

of Antwerp. Belgium, Holland, France, and England each accepted groups of the refugees. [The difficulties of the *St. Louis* were allegorized in Katherine Anne Porter's *Ship of Fools* (1962).]

Ba.

Stoecker, Adolf, b. Halberstadt, November 11, 1835; d. Bolzano (Italy), February 7, 1909, German Evangelical theologian and politician. Stoecker became a pastor in 1863, and from 1874 to 1890 he was a cathedral and court preacher in Berlin. As a preacher and publicist, he strove to win back the masses to the church, and toward this end promoted the idea of an Inner Mission with a social and political objective. But since the arch-conservative Stoecker was also involved in the struggle against Social

Democracy, he railed against the Jews as the real culprits responsible for the distress of the proletariat. He argued this mainly from an economic and social perspective, yet as a talented demagogue he became a forerunner of the antisemitic campaign of nationalist and National Socialist orators. Stoecker served in the Reichstag from 1881 to 1893 and from 1898 to 1908, representing the German Conservative Party. Although he failed in his objective of binding the masses to the monarchic nation-state, he did win over a broad spectrum of the middle class to his antiliberal ideas, which had a long-range effect and continued to burden the political and social climate of the Weimar period.

Stosstrupp Adolf Hitler (Adolf Hitler Patrol), guard troop established by Hitler in 1922, under his exclusive command, in reaction to the development of the SA. It was the nucleus for the ss of the NSDAP.

Strassburger Sender (Radio Strasbourg), French state radio station, located in Strasbourg; it was established in 1930. The German-language programs of this station were, for many German listeners before 1940, an important source of information suppressed in the Third Reich. Consequently, the National Socialist government opposed the station and demanded, without success, that it close down.

S. O.

Strasser, Gregor, b. Geisenfeld (Upper Bavaria), May 31, 1892; d. Berlin, June 30, 1934, German politician. Strasser initially worked as a pharmacist in Landshut. An officer in the First World War, he subsequently became ringleader of the Lower Bavarian Storm Battalion. He joined the NSDAP in 1921, became *Gauleiter* for Low-

Adolf Stoecker.

Gregor Strasser.

er Bavaria, and took part in the Hitler Putsch of November 9, 1923. He was spared an 18-month prison term by his election to the Bavarian legislature in April 1924. During the period when the NSDAP was banned, he built up one of its replacement organizations, the NATIONAL SOCIALIST FREEDOM MOVEMENT OF GREAT- GERMANY. As of December 1924 Strasser was a Reichstag deputy, retaining the seat after the re-establishment of the NSDAP (February 27, 1925), until December 1932. This gave him considerable influence in the party leadership, which made him responsible for organizing in northern Germany.

Strasser's responsibility gave him a private empire, which he imbued with his own social-revolutionary ideas, thus bringing him into conflict with the more nationalistic Hitler wing. Strasser called for the nationalization of banks and heavy industry. In the organs of the Kampf-Verlag (Militant Press), founded by him on March 1, 1926, in Berlin, he criticized the "System." He also promoted the building of an "organic" *Volk* Community to overcome the fetishes of productivity and profits, as well as both capitalism and Bolshevism. Despite his ideological differences with Hitler, which continued to fester even after the BAMBERG FÜHRER CONFERENCE (February 14, 1926), Strasser was named Reich Propaganda Leader (*Reichspropagandaleiter*) in September 1926, a post he held until he was replaced by Joseph Goebbels in 1930. In December 1927 Strasser was given the influential post of a Reich Organization Leader (*Reichsorganisationsleiter*). The Hitler-Strasser conflict was quelled once again when his more

dogmatic brother, Otto STRASSER, withdrew from the party in July 1930. It flared up again in December 1932, when Chancellor Kurt von SCHLEICHER sought to win Strasser over for his own so-called TRADE UNION AXIS by offering him the posts of vice chancellor and Prussian minister president. Hitler's superior tactics and Strasser's indecisiveness thwarted this attempt to split off the party's left wing. On December 8, Strasser withdrew from all party posts and resigned. Because Hitler continued to regard him as dangerous, he was murdered, like Schleicher, during the RÖHM AFFAIR.

Strasser, Otto, b. Windsheim (Middle Franconia), September 10, 1897; d. Munich, August 27, 1974, German politician. A First World War volunteer, Strasser then studied political economy. He joined the Social Democratic Party (SPD) for a time in 1920, and from 1921 to 1923 worked as an assistant researcher (*Hilfsreferent*) in the Reich Food Ministry. Strasser began to promote the NSDAP as early as 1924 with articles in the *Völkischer Beobachter* (Völkisch Observer) even before he joined the party in 1925. Beginning on March 1, 1926, he managed the Kampf-Verlag (Militant Press) in Berlin for his brother Gregor, and sought to foster a "socialist" orientation for the NSDAP. Like Gregor, he advocated the socialization of heavy industry and warned against the Italian Fascist model, whose social peace was but the stillness of a graveyard at the expense of the workers.

Strasser's pro-Soviet and anti-Western foreign-policy line further exacerbated the conflict with Hitler; a conversation between the two on May

Otto Strasser.

21–22, 1930, failed to lessen the tension. On July 4 of that year Strasser left the party to found the "Militant Community [Kampfgemeinschaft] of Revolutionary National Socialists," which combined with other groups (National Bolsheviks, disillusioned Communists, and so on) in the "Black Front." After the Seizure of Power Strasser emigrated and continued the war of words against Hitler from Austria, Switzerland (1938), and Portugal (1940). In 1943 he gained admission to Canada, and in 1955 returned to Germany. His publications, including *Hitler and I* (1940; German edition, 1948) and *Exil* (1958), and his political initiatives (among them the founding of the insignificant German Social Union in 1956), were witness that Strasser clung to his early National Socialist and antisemitic ideas.

Strauch, Eduard, b. Essen, August 17, 1906; d. Belgium, 1955, SS-*Obersturmbannführer*. After studies in law, Strauch joined the SA and the NSDAP on August 1, 1931, and the SS on December 1. After a post with the Security Service (SD), in 1939 he was made a government councillor and a *Sturmbannführer*. He took part in the Polish Campaign as a member of the Wehrmacht. In March 1941 he was transferred to State Police headquarters in Königsberg.

Early in November 1941 Strauch took command of Einsatzkommando 2 (Latvia), serving under the commander of the Security Police (Sipo) and the SD for Ostland (Einsatzgruppe A); his responsibilities included supervising shooting operations against Jewish civilians. In February 1942 he became commander of the Sipo and the SD in White Ruthenia (Minsk). Strauch was posted in July 1943 as an intelligence officer (*Ic-Offizier*) to be "Plenipotentiary of the Reichsführer-SS for Combating Banditry." Effective April 5, 1944, the Reich Security Main Office (RSHA) relieved him of this post and at the same time appointed him the delegate of the chief of the Sipo and the SD for Belgium and northern France.

After the war Strauch was sentenced to death at the OHLENDORF TRIAL (the Einsatzgruppen Trial) in Nuremberg on April 10, 1948, for crimes against humanity, war crimes, and membership in a criminal organization. At Belgium's request he was remanded there to be prosecuted for activities in that country. A Belgian military court passed a second death sentence. [The execution was stayed owing to the defendant's insanity.]

Strauss, Emil, b. Pforzheim, January 31, 1866; d. Freiburg im Breisgau, August 10, 1960, German writer. In extremely varied, literarily pretentious works, often oriented toward *völkisch* "homeland" literature, Strauss contrasted an idealized rural life with urban "ASPHALT." In the novel *Das Riesenspielzeug* (The Giant Plaything; 1934) an intellectual finds his way to an unalienated, vegetarian way of life: the "German man" finds renewal in the peasantry. Together with Erwin KOLBENHEYER and Wilhelm SCHÄFER, Strauss withdrew from the Prussian Academy of Letters in 1931 because of its supposedly leftist leadership, returning after its "cleansing" in 1933. As a "fighter for the renewal of the *völkisch* German life community," he was honored with numerous literary prizes and appointment to the Reich Cultural Senate. Racist ideas and cooperation with the National Socialists did not, however, diminish Strauss's reputation after 1945. Until his death he was considered one of the most distinguished German writers (as reflected in an honorary degree in 1956).

Strauss, Richard, b. Munich, June 11, 1864; d. Garmisch-Partenkirchen, September 8, 1949, German composer. Strauss was especially renowned as a composer of operas, notably *Salome* (1905), *Der Rosenkavalier* (1911), *Ariadne auf Naxos* (1912), *Die Frau ohne Schatten* (The Woman with No Shadow; 1919), and *Arabella* (1933). He also composed orchestral music, including *Till Eulenspiegels lustige Streiche* (*Till Eulenspiegel's Merry Pranks*), *Also sprach Zarathustra* (*Thus Spake Zarathustra*), and *Der Bür-*

Emil Strauss.

Richard Strauss.

ger als Edelman (*The Bourgeois Gentleman*). In 1884 he made his debut as a conductor in Munich, and in 1889, as a musical assistant in Bayreuth. Strauss considered himself committed to German music, and he distanced himself from 12-tone music (such as that of Arnold Schönberg) and from "operetta trash" (as that of Franz Lehár). Politically, he underestimated the consequences of National Socialist music policy and thus, as an allegedly unpolitical musician, helped the Third Reich to gain considerable prestige. On November 15, 1933, Strauss took over the leadership of the REICH MUSIC CHAMBER as president, and set as his goal the reduction by one-third of "the foreign repertoire" in German opera houses.

As early as 1935, however, Strauss came into conflict with the regime by standing up for his Jewish librettist, Stefan ZWEIG, at the debut of Strauss's opera *Die schweigsame Frau* (*The Silent Woman;* July 24, 1935). At first he was able to prevail, but after four performances he had to accept the work's removal. On July 14, 1935, his withdrawal from the presidency of the Music Chamber "on grounds of health" was announced. This reflected the ambiguous relationship between Strauss and National Socialism. Strauss was self-willed and purposeful in musical matters, but naive and ready to make political concessions. The party distanced itself from Strauss's person, but it took advantage of the world renown of his works. A secret order from Heinrich Himmler of January 24, 1944, prohibited personal dealings with Strauss, but approved the presentation of his works. Strauss

owed to his prestige the fact that his Jewish daughter-in-law was spared from NS persecution. At an appeals board proceeding in May 1948, Strauss was classified as "exonerated."

R. H.

Strauss und Torney, Lulu von, b. Bückeburg, September 20, 1873; d. Jena, June 19, 1956, German writer. Strauss und Torney was connected with the circle of writers around Börries von MÜNCHHAUSEN and was friendly with Agnes MIEGEL. In novels, in novellas, and particularly in ballads, Strauss und Torney idealized the world of the peasant as "a dream of root and sod," as seen in "Reif steht die Saat" (The Corn Is Ripe; 1919). Honored in the Third Reich as a venerable and great "homeland" poet, Strauss und Torney reciprocated with poems celebrating the National Socialist "Germany of tomorrow" as "the dream of your fathers."

Streicher, Julius, b. Fleinhausen bei Augsburg, February 12, 1885; d. Nuremberg, October 16, 1946 (executed), German politician and publisher. Originally an elementary school (*Volksschule*) teacher, Streicher volunteered for the First World War. In 1919 he helped found the antisemitic and nationalist German Social Party, with which he joined the NSDAP in 1921. In 1923 he established the antisemitic newspaper *Der* STÜRMER (The Stormer/Militant). Streicher was suspended from schoolteaching for his participation in the Hitler Putsch of November 9, 1923. During the period when the NSDAP was prohibited following the putsch, he was active as a leader of the substitute organization, the

Lulu von Strauss und Torney.

Julius Streicher.

GREAT-GERMAN VOLK COMMUNITY. He was elected to the Bavarian legislature in 1924, remaining a member until 1932.

After Hitler's release from prison, Streicher became *Gauleiter* in Franconia ("the Führer of Franconia") and a Reichstag deputy on January 12, 1933 (until 1945). Although he was not highly regarded within the party, he remained a protégé of Hitler, who viewed Streicher's primitive Jew-baiting as useful for winning over the populace for harsher measures (*see* PERSECUTION OF JEWS). In 1933 Streicher became director of the "Central Committee for Deflecting Jewish Atrocity- and Boycott-Mongering" (Zentralkomitee zur Abwehr der jüdischen Greuel- und Boykotthetze), which organized the BOYCOTT AGAINST JEWS of April 1, 1933. Streicher was also heavily involved in bringing about the NUREMBERG LAWS, which he thought did not go nearly far enough.

Having become rich through the journalistic success of *Der Stürmer* and through his other publishing acquisitions (including the *Fränkische Zeitung*), Streicher used his position to amass greater wealth, in part through ARYANIZATION. He lived like a prince and gained notoriety for his erotic excesses. Hitler long overlooked Streicher's personal defects until Streicher himself took aim at the highest party leaders, such as Göring. On February 13, 1940, the Supreme Party Court under Walter BUCH found Streicher to be "unsuited for leadership," removed him from his party posts, and banished him to a country estate. Hitler ordained, however, that he be permitted to continue publishing

Der Stürmer and to retain the title of *Gauleiter.* At the war's end, Streicher disguised himself as an artist (*Kunstmaler*), but he was recognized by an American army major in Berchtesgaden on May 23, 1945, and was put on trial in Nuremberg. On October 1, 1946, Streicher, clinging to the end to his near-religious antisemitic mania, was sentenced to death for crimes against humanity.

Strength through Joy (Kraft durch Freude; KdF), recreational organization within the GERMAN LABOR FRONT (DAF), established on November 27, 1933. The name was said to originate with a suggestion by Hitler. Following the model of the Italian Fascist organization DOPOLAVORO (After Work), KdF was designed to win over the working class, still aloof from National Socialism, through an ample offering of leisure activities. By doing so, it was applying a proven socialist practice (such as the workers' educational associations), as well as putting to use the confiscated facilities and property of the abolished trade unions.

KdF consisted of the following offices:

1. The "After Work" (*Feierabend*) office presented such attractions as theater performances and concerts, which by 1938 had been attended by 38 million people; in addition, it organized the political courses of the GERMAN PUBLIC INSTRUCTION AGENCY;

Strength through Joy. Employees' sports.

1
Hitler and Himmler with chauffeur in a KdF car.
2
"Strength through Joy *Volk* Festival." Poster of the German Labor Front.
3
"Toward the sun. German workers travel to Madeira." Travel report on the first trip of the KdF fleet to Madeira.

2. The Sports office directed workplace sports for "military fitness training" and "racial improvement";
3. The "BEAUTY OF WORK" office concerned itself with improving working conditions and the aesthetic appearance of the workplace;
4. The "Wehrmacht Homes" (*Wehrmachtsheime*) office linked the Wehrmacht and the Reich Labor Service;
5. The "Travel, Hiking, and Vacation" office arranged (by 1938) vacation trips for approximately 10 million people, especially in areas barely open to tourists such as the Bavarian Forest or the Masurian Lakes in East Prussia, as well as to other countries (notably Italy) and overseas. Its cruises especially contributed to the popularity of the KdF; the white "Peace Fleet" of KdF ships (including the **WILHELM GUSTLOFF**) was purposely sent on foreign tours as an ambassador of National Socialism.

The ultimate goals of the highly subsidized leisure programs in the context of war preparations were openly conceded by leading officials after the war began: "We did not send our workers on vacations aboard their own ships and build them huge seaside resorts just for the fun of it. . . . We did it only so that we might bring [them] back to [their] workplaces with new strength and purpose" (DAF press secretary Gerhard Starcke, 1940). The KdF facilities

proved their usefulness for wartime ends. The passenger steamships were put into service as troop transports, the vacation lodgings at the shore were remodeled into military hospitals, and the KdF Auto (*see* **VOLKSWAGEN**), toward which 300,000 customers were saving, left the KdF Works in Stadt des KdF-Wagens (City of the KdF Car; later Wolfsburg) as the Wehrmacht's jeep.

Ba.

Stresa, Italian health resort on Lake Maggiore with about 4,000 inhabitants in 1935. In Stresa the heads of government from England (James Ramsay MacDonald), France (Pierre-Étienne Flandin), and Italy (Mussolini) met from April 11 through April 14, 1935, in order to confer on common measures against German revisionism (most immediately, reintroduction of **COMPULSORY MILITARY SERVICE**) and Hitler's anticipated expansionist foreign policy (including his threatening stance toward Austria and the murder, on July 25, 1934, of Engelbert **DOLLFUSS**). In a joint statement, the conferees declared their regret over Germany's unilateral moves toward rearming at the time when discussions were being held on arms limitations. They also made known their intention "to oppose with all appropriate means any unilateral abrogation of treaties that could endanger the peace of Europe."

The three participating powers further con-

Strength through Joy. German vacationers in Madeira.

Stresa. Conference participants. From the left: James Ramsay MacDonald (Great Britain), Baron Pompeo Aloisi (Italy), Pierre Flandin and Pierre Laval (France).

firmed their determination to stand up for the independence and territorial integrity of Austria, and to fulfill their obligations under the LOCARNO PACT in the event of Germany's unilateral remilitarization of the Rhineland. Finally, they underscored the efforts to achieve collective security in eastern Europe, an air pact in western Europe, and international disarmament. The announced steps appeared quite vague and nonbinding, and the "antirevisionist front" of Stresa soon dissolved by itself through London's unilateral conclusion of the GERMAN-BRITISH NAVAL AGREEMENT of June 18, 1935, and the consequent sanctioning of German rearmament, as well as through the Italian attack on ABYSSINIA in early October 1935 and the tensions between Britain and France.

B.-J. W.

Stresemann, Gustav, b. Berlin, May 10, 1878; d. there, October 3, 1929, German politician. Stresemann became a member of the National Liberal Party in 1903, and represented it in the Reichstag from 1907 to 1912 and from 1914 to 1918. A friend of Erich LUDENDORFF, he hoped for a "victorious peace" up until the final phase of the First World War; after Germany's defeat he changed from an authoritarian monarchist into an advocate of the Weimar Republic. In

1918 Stresemann helped found the GERMAN PEOPLE'S PARTY, which he represented in the Weimar National Assembly, and beginning in 1920 he was the party's leader in the Reichstag. On August 13, 1923, he became Reich chancellor of a cabinet of the Great Coalition. Although he was in office for only 100 days, he achieved a decisive turning point both in politics (through suppressing the HITLER PUTSCH and Communist uprisings in Saxony, and ending the RUHR CONFLICT) and in economics (through overcoming

Gustav Stresemann.

INFLATION). When the Social Democrats left the coalition, Stresemann had to resign, on November 23, 1923.

Stresemann remained as foreign minister in all the succeeding governments until his death, pursuing a modified FULFILLMENT POLICY in order to bring Germany back into harmony with the Great Powers. He accomplished the beginnings of this in such achievements as the LOCARNO PACT of 1925, Germany's admission into the League of Nations in 1926, and the BERLIN TREATY of 1926. Stresemann's policies were oriented toward the long term and required patience, something that the nationalist Right in particular was not prepared to muster. The understanding that Stresemann reached with Aristide BRIAND (gaining them the Nobel Peace Prize of 1926) collapsed with the untimely death of its initiator and the political radicalization in the ensuing world economic crisis.

Stroop, Jürgen, b. Detmold, September 26, 1895; d. Warsaw, March 6, 1952 (executed), SS-*Gruppenführer* (1943). At the beginning of the war Stroop was an SS-*Oberführer*. He distinguished himself in the "struggle against banditry," which included security-police measures in the occupied territories, fighting partisans, and resettling or liquidating Jews. On April 19, 1943, Stroop received orders to put down the WARSAW GHETTO UPRISING, and until May 16 he carried out this assignment, with unparalleled brutality. He reported on it in great detail in his journal, the so-called *Stroop Report* ("The Jew-

Jürgen Stroop (left) during the police operation in the Warsaw ghetto.

ish quarter of Warsaw is no more"), published in 1976 in a facsimile edition. Later he was transferred to Greece as a Higher SS and Police Leader. An American military court sentenced him to death on March 21, 1947, for the shooting of captured Allied pilots, but then remanded him to Poland, where he was again sentenced to death and was hanged.

Struggle for existence (*Kampf ums Dasein*), those activities and protective measures of plant and animal organisms that serve the purposes of further evolution and of self-preservation. According to evolutionary theory (*see* DESCENT, THEORY OF), this struggle constituted the motive force of SELECTION through the success of those individuals that were best adapted. SOCIAL DARWINISM applied this struggle and the "right of the stronger" that allegedly supported it to human and ethnic communities. From this, the National Socialists derived the justification for their policies of expansion and conquest as the "struggle for existence of the German *Volk.*"

Struma, Romanian ship that in 1941 was boarded by Jewish refugees who wanted to reach safety in Palestine, away from the growing persecution of Jews. On December 12, 1941, the *Struma* sailed under Panamanian registry from the Romanian port of Constanţa with 750 Jews on board, arriving at Istanbul on December 15. However, the Turkish authorities allowed only one passenger, a pregnant woman, to land. Finally, under pressure from London, which feared Arab protests and further fleets of refugee ships, the Turks in mid-February 1942 sent the *Struma* back into the Black Sea, where it presumably was sunk by a Soviet submarine on February 24, 1942. Only one refugee survived the catastrophe. Although British officials pledged that there would be no more *Strumas*, they continued to block the escape routes to Palestine for European Jews menaced by the German FINAL SOLUTION.

Strünck, Theodor, b. Kiel, April 7, 1895; d. Flossenbürg concentration camp, April 9, 1945 (executed), German opposition fighter. A lawyer specializing in the insurance industry, Strünck came to know Hans OSTER, who brought him into the ABWEHR as a reserve officer in 1937. As early as 1938, Strünck took part in the plans for overthrowing Hitler in connection with the SUDETEN CRISIS. Appointed to the Wehrmacht High Command (OKW) in 1939, he passed on valuable information to the conspirators planning the assassination attempt of July 20, 1944. He also made his inconspicuous apartment on Nürnberger Strasse, in Berlin W 30, available for secret meetings. After the attempt failed, Strünck turned himself in and was sentenced to death on October 10, 1944.

Struthof, National Socialist concentration camp in the Vosges Mountains; *see* Natzweiler.

Stuckart, Wilhelm, b. Wiesbaden, November 16, 1902; d. near Hannover, November 15, 1953 (automobile accident), German jurist. After studies in Frankfurt am Main and Munich, Stuckart joined the NSDAP in 1922. He became a legal adviser to the party in 1926, a judge in 1930, an attorney and legal counsel to the SA in Pomerania in 1931. In June 1933 Stuckart became a state secretary in the Prussian Ministry of Public Worship, in September 1933 a member of the Prussian State Council, and in 1934, state secretary in the Reich Education Ministry.

In March 1935, as a state secretary in the Reich Interior Ministry, Stuckart became director of the Division for the Constitution and Legislation, and he had a decisive part in drafting the NUREMBERG LAWS. He joined the SS in 1936. In January 1942, Stuckart took part in the WANNSEE CONFERENCE, where he approved the plans for the FINAL SOLUTION of the Jewish question; he also proposed the forced sterilization of all non-Aryans, and the dissolution of all MIXED MARRIAGES. Together with Hans GLOBKE he wrote the *Kommentare zur deutschen Rassengesetzgebung* (Commentary on German Racial Legislation; 1936); he himself wrote several

works on National Socialist legal theory. Stuckart was arrested in 1945. Owing to lack of evidence, he was sentenced to only four years' imprisonment in 1949, which he had already served.

U. B.

Stülpnagel, Karl Heinrich von, b. Darmstadt, January 2, 1886; d. Berlin-Plötzensee, August 30, 1944 (executed), German infantry general (April 1, 1939) and opposition fighter. Stülpnagel entered the army in 1904, and was a major general by 1935. On October 21, 1938, he became quartermaster general I on the Army General Staff, and on May 30, 1940, he assumed command of the Second Army Corps. After the French Campaign he headed the German-French Cease-fire Commission in Wiesbaden. On February 15, 1941, he took command of the Seventeenth Army, which he led in the Russian Campaign until November 25 of that year. On February 13, 1942, he was made military commander in France as successor to his cousin, Otto von STÜLPNAGEL. Despite his rejection of Hitler and of National Socialism, he maintained a harsh occupation regime while still actively participating in the opposition. On the TWENTIETH OF JULY, 1944, Stülpnagel succeeded in arresting the most important SS, Security Service (SD), and Gestapo members in Paris (about 1,200) before the news of the failed *coup d'état* came through. Summoned back to Berlin, he attempted to take his life but only blinded himself with the shooting. He was then sentenced to death by the *Volk* Court.

Wilhelm Stuckart.

Karl Heinrich von Stülpnagel.

Stülpnagel, Otto von, b. Berlin, June 16, 1878; d.
Paris, February 6, 1948, German infantry general (1932). Stülpnagel joined the army in 1898.
He rose to the rank of major during the First
World War, then held various command posts in
the Reichswehr. He retired on April 1, 1931, as
a lieutenant general. (The following year he
received his final promotion.) An opponent of
the Weimar Republic from the outset, Stülpnagel was summoned back to the Wehrmacht in
1935 and made commander of the Air War
Academy. Again retired on March 31, 1939, he
returned to duty once more when the war broke
out. As military commander of France (as of
October 25, 1940), he made himself hated
through his draconian punitive measures, deportations, and shootings of hostages. The reign
of terror stopped on January 31, 1942, but it led
to his arrest and extradition to France after the
war. He took his own life before his trial began.

Otto von Stülpnagel.

Sturmabteilung

Terror in the form of battles in assembly halls
and in the streets characterized the public emergence of National Socialism from the outset. The
well-prepared and compact deployment of soldiers assigned for this purpose by Reichswehr
Capt. Ernst RÖHM in Munich proved itself to be
especially able. On August 3, 1921, Hitler
brought together tested brawlers who, after the
Bürgerbräu Cellar fight (November 4, 1921),
called themselves the Sturmabteilung (Storm
Division; SA, known as the Storm Troopers).
Officers from the covert right-wing league of
free corps under Hermann EHRHARDT (see CON-
SUL ORGANIZATION) undertook the formation of
the SA, which Röhm strongly urged and promoted. Under their first leader, Hans-Ulrich
Klintzsch, who was still on Ehrhardt's payroll,
the SA easily entered the mainstream of nationalist military leagues. It was given military training by the local Reichswehr and was used for
regular national defense duty during the RUHR
CONFLICT.

Hermann Göring, as the second SA leader
(1923), did not alter this arrangement, which
had proved itself useful in recruiting for the
NSDAP. The SA, in its forays as an unarmed
party troop in 1921–1922, had demonstrated
the required striking power and had created the
desired sensation. Hitler, however, took offense
at its twofold character, which allowed him only

partial political control. He thus formed his own
guard with the "Adolf Hitler Shock Troop," the
nucleus of the ss.

After the HITLER PUTSCH of November 8–9,
1923, during which the SA's surprise attack on

SA man. Sketch by Adolf Hitler, 1920.

the Munich Reichswehr Barracks was repulsed and the SA itself was routed in front of the Feldherrnhalle, it was banned and dissolved. Röhm kept a nucleus together and built it up throughout the Reich as the "Frontline Unit" (Frontbann). After his release from prison in 1925, Hitler gave Röhm the mandate to rebuild the SA, but he rejected Röhm's revival of the paramilitary concept. The SA units, which spontaneously arose—in part, together with the Frontbann units—alongside the new local revivals of the NSDAP, oriented themselves toward their political task: to conduct marches and brawls. The only military traces were elements of presentation and appearance, such as the uniforms, which came in 1924 from German East Africa colonial defense troop surpluses. However, the coexistence of the Frontbann units and the SA did not end immediately, even after Röhm departed in April 1925. Hitler's views won out only when the previously unconnected SA units were centralized under Supreme SA Führer [Osaf] Franz PFEFFER VON SALOMON (1926–1930).

The coordination of the buildup proceeded in accordance with "fundamental directives" (*Grundsätzliche Anordnungen;* GRUSA) and "SA Orders" (*SA-Befehlen;* SABE) from the Osaf, for which Hitler's wishes served only as guidelines. Altogether, the political organization at all levels, even the highest, could only designate the tasks; their execution lay within the sole competence of the SA. Conflicts with government authorities were thus carefully avoided, although Pfeffer von Salomon went so far as to issue a draft statute that was in fact invalid (GRUSA II). He kept the subdivisions very flexible, so that, according to local circumstances, units from the brigade level down to the platoons varied greatly in size. He combined the hierarchy of the command levels with the egalitarian homogeneity of the leadership corps, in which honors and badges were conferred for service rather than for rank. The SA men themselves had to bear equipment and service expenses, as well as obligatory party dues. After 1929, however, Pfeffer von Salomon was able to provide subsidies and to come up with some social benefits.

Under these conditions the SA could exploit the unemployment, caused by the world economic crisis, as the source of a mass influx. Its growth paralleled the first great electoral victories of the NSDAP, which the SA attributed to its own activities: disciplined demonstrations as well as unbridled street terror. Nonethe-

"A little SA man." Propaganda postcard.

less, Hitler rebuffed the sometimes rabid claims that the SA men made as they demanded what they saw as their due for conducting such activities (*see* STENNES REVOLTS), and himself assumed the post of Osaf. The SA chief of staff, in 1929–1930 Otto Wagener (1888–1971), gained in importance through this move. Yet since Wagener was overstrained by the dynamism of this self-radicalizing party army, Hitler again handed the actual direction of the SA to Röhm, who agreed on condition of extensive autonomy.

With Röhm as chief of staff in the hectic period from 1931 to 1934, the SA experienced explosive growth. Its membership increased from 260,000 at the end of 1931 to 600,000– 700,000 in January 1933. It also experienced extreme fluctuations, especially if compared with the Communist Party (KPD) and the RED FRONTLINE FIGHTERS' LEAGUE. In its goals the SA became even more unpredictable; it remained clearly faithful only to its purpose as an instrument of propaganda and terror. Röhm even lifted the requirement of party membership for SA men, an act that brought a huge influx into the SA after the NSDAP suspended new admissions (May 1, 1933). The temporary ban on the SA (April–June 1932) did not hinder its activities but rather incited a wave of terror that did not ebb until the Seizure of Power. From March until the autumn of 1933, the SA,

1
The first four standards on the Champ de Mars in Munich (1923).
2
"The terror from the Left can be met only with greater terror." From the cigarette-card album "Germany Awakens."
3
Poster for the SA Sports Badge: "German, show your military readiness."

SA men at a mass meeting.

made up mainly of the unemployed and sometimes even infiltrated by criminals, took uninhibited revenge on its political opponents and
ideological enemies: it held some 50,000 prisoners in its own partially "wild" concentration
camps (*see* PROTECTIVE CUSTODY). Its concrete
demands for power and material provisions ran
into opposition from the government, which
wanted SYNCHRONIZATION, not upheaval. When
the SA called for a SECOND REVOLUTION in
order to still have some task, it was excluded
from power to the advantage of the SS, through
the *Aktion* (operation) of June 30, 1934 (*see*
RÖHM AFFAIR).

The murder of some 50 SA leaders by the SS
was followed by a rapid shrinkage of the organization. The SA now found itself freed from its
most compromising personalities—above all
Röhm—and could finally expel those who opposed justice and morality. The sharp decline in
numbers resulted in part from the excision of
already inactive units such as the former
Kyffhäuser League, with 1.5 million members,
and from the mass dismissal of hangers-on and
meal-seekers. The SS and the Hitler Youth (HJ),
nominally subordinated to the SA chief of staff,
now became formally autonomous. On the other
hand, granting the National Socialist Motor
Corps (NSKK) its independence and incorporating the SA Sharpshooters Corps into the regular
police meant a real loss for the SA. The latter
change subordinated the SA to police control,
and through conclusively denying to the SA its
own internal jurisdiction, subordinated it to the
public judicial system or to the SS. New admissions were now screened: applicants had to have

previously belonged to the Wehrmacht or the
HJ. This put an end to the uncontrolled mass
influx with its radicalizing consequences. From
4.5 million in June 1934, the membership decreased by September 1934 to 2.6 million, by
October 1935 to 1.6 million, and by 1938 to 1.2
million.

With its complete disarmament and the surrender of its arsenals to the Reichswehr (whose
rearmament was perceptibly advanced), the SA
lost its potential as a threat. The limitation to
self-defense weapons for leaders and a few staff
guards destroyed not only its character as a
paramilitary organization, which had been restored under Röhm, but also curbed its sports
training with military equipment.

The exclusion of rowdyism by discipline and
by the merger with the former STEEL HELMET
altered the SA only slowly. Incidents of violence,
and especially its decisive participation in the
pogrom of November 9, 1938 (*see* KRISTALL-
NACHT), showed that the terrorist energy of the
NS movement remained more or less latently
stored and available in the SA, until the war
gave it another kind of outlet. The SA thus
retained, in contrast to its loss of power under
Röhm's successor, Viktor LUTZE (chief of staff,
1934–1943), an important political function
that for the regime thoroughly justified its
continued existence. Along with such activities
as marches and fund collections, premilitary
training was seen by National Socialism as one
of the SA's major responsibilities. This strengthened the influence of militarily experienced
former Steel Helmet members, since Lutze
phased out the historic "Old SA" and Steel
Helmet units to make way for units with mixed
origins and standardized complements. On
February 15, 1935, Hitler reinstituted the SA
Sports Medal (as of January 19, 1939, the SA
Military Medal), but he ruled that it could be
won by nonmembers of the SA. The fact that SA
membership gave evidence of approved NS
"sentiments" without any need for further activities in the "movement" made the organization quite attractive. Although it was openly
regarded as "politically the most innocuous
program of the party" (Army Adjutant Engel,
1939), by the beginning of the war 1.5 million
young men laid claim to it as proof of their
conformity to the system.

With the outbreak of war, the SA took over
the training of military conscripts whose training had been deferred. It was conducted within
"SA Military Teams" (*SA-Wehrmannschaften*);
by April 1940 the program included 1.5 million

volunteers. Moreover, 60 percent of the team members and 80 percent of the leaders enrolled in the Wehrmacht, since SA service did not exempt one from military service. Separate SA field units similar to the Waffen-SS were not formed; only in the Sudetenland and in Danzig were SA free corps temporarily mustered. Those SA members who were not conscripted provided auxiliary services to the Wehrmacht, the police, the customs and border patrol, air defense, the SS, and so on. Some 80,000 armed members were at the command of *Gau* leaders in "special-assignment companies" (*Stürmen z. b. V.*) as police reinforcements against uprisings. When the VOLK STORM was formed in 1944–1945, the SA served merely as a source of personnel. Its last chief of staff, Wilhelm Schepmann (1943–1945), was bypassed by the organization and did not even achieve the status of Reich leader (*Reichsleiter*) in the party. In the Nuremberg Trials, the SA was classified as not guilty in the sense of the indictment charges.

Wolfgang Petter

Sturmbannführer (Stubaf), SA and SS rank (major).

Stürmer, Der (The Stormer), antisemitic and pornographic newspaper of the National Socialist militant press. Founded in 1923 by Julius STREICHER in Nuremberg, it aimed at the political mobilization of the masses. Its subtitle read: "German [until 1933, "Nuremberg"] Weekly for the Struggle for Truth." *Der Stürmer* was banned after the HITLER PUTSCH, but it reappeared beginning March 24, 1925. Published until 1934 by the nationalist Wilhelm Härdel Press in Nuremberg, as of 1935 it came out of Streicher's own publishing house. In the early years its circulation was around 2,000 to 3,000, and by 1933, around 20,000. Its main editors were Streicher, Karl Holz, Ernst Hiemer, and Erwin Kellinek. The collaborators followed Streicher's guidelines as to choice of topics and formulations. Special note should be taken of the cartoonist "Fips" (Philipp Rupprecht), on the staff from November 1925, who created the infamous caricature of the "*Stürmer* Jew," and of the Jewish journalist from Fürth, "Fritz Brand" (Jonas Wolk), who collaborated from 1934 to 1938.

Der Stürmer was not a party newspaper even after January 30, 1933, but remained Streicher's private property. It enjoyed a circulation increase that was substantial but not precisely determinable: estimates show an average yearly circulation of about 600,000 until 1940, the year when Streicher was removed as *Gauleiter* of Franconia; after 1940 it declined, reaching 398,500 in 1944. Conceived in its external format as a paper for the masses (black and red type, and illustrations), *Der Stürmer* dealt with only one theme: Jew-baiting. As of 1927 it bore a quotation from Heinrich von Treitschke at the foot of the front page: "The Jews are our misfortune" ("Die Juden sind unser Unglück"). The same motto was on the *Stürmer-Kästen* (*Stürmer* display cases), in which, as of 1933, the newspaper was posted in all German cities and villages. One of *Der Stürmer*'s many sources of notoriety was its stories about alleged Jewish ritual murders. The newspaper's last issue was published on February 1, 1945.

S. O.

Der Stürmer. Front page, May 1938. At the bottom: "The Jews are our misfortune."

Sturmmann ("storm man"; "stormer"), general term, dating back to the "father of gymnastics," Friedrich Ludwig JAHN, referring to a combatant or soldier. In the SA, *Sturmmann* became a service rank that could be attained by an ordinary recruit as a first promotion after a half-year's service.

Stuttgart Confession of Guilt (*Stuttgarter Schuldbekenntnis;* also *Stuttgarter Schulderklärung*, or Stuttgart Declaration of Guilt), avowal dated October 19, 1945, that was formulated by the newly constituted Council of the Evangelical Church of Germany (EKD). It admitted the church's failure under the moral challenge of National Socialist tyranny: "For long years we may have fought in the name of Jesus Christ against the spirit that found its terrible expression in the National Socialist rule of violence; yet we accuse ourselves for not speaking out more courageously, praying more faithfully, believing more gladly, and loving more ardently." The proponents of this confession were clergymen such as Martin NIEMÖLLER, who in the CHURCH STRUGGLE had spared no personal sacrifice. Since it was precisely they who accepted responsibility for the NS calamity, the declaration put a decisive stamp on the church's new beginning and established new bridges for ecumenical relations. The confession, despite the interpretation read into it by critics, did not assign a wholesale German COLLECTIVE GUILT in the sense of personal complicity or even of failure to give aid.

Stutthof, National Socialist concentration camp located 36 km (about 22 miles) east of Danzig on the edge of the village of Stutthof. The camp was set up in September 1939, first as a civilian internment camp, and from November 1941 as a special SS camp. On January 13, 1942, it was taken over as a government-run concentration camp. The facility, originally surrounded by a barbed-wire fence (the "old camp"), was supplemented in early 1943 by the "new camp" built alongside it, surrounded by an electric fence and designed for 25,000 prisoners, although it was never entirely completed. The SS provided the guards and camp staff.

In early 1942 Stutthof was occupied by about 3,000 prisoners. At the end of May 1944 the camp's roll included about 8,000 people. This number increased sharply beginning in the summer of 1944 with the arriving transports of Jewish prisoners (above all, Hungarian Jewish women). Eventually, in December 1944–January 1945, Stutthof, including its more than 100 satellite camps (*Aussenkommandos*), held over 52,000 prisoners (among them more than 33,000 women). In all, over 100,000 prisoners passed through Stutthof, belonging to the most diverse European nationalities (Germans, Poles, Russians, French, Dutch, Belgians, Czechs, Latvians, Lithuanians, Danes, Norwegians, and

Gypsies). Some worked in SS-owned businesses such as the German Armament Works (DAW), built near the camp. Others labored in local brickyards, in private industrial enterprises, in agriculture, or in the camp's own workshops.

Mortality was high. It resulted partly from the bad conditions of work, lodging, and food supply, but especially from the totally inadequate hygiene. A great many of the sick died during a typhus epidemic in the winter of 1942–1943 and during a typhoid epidemic in the second half of 1944, particularly since the SS medical personnel were prohibited from caring for Jewish prisoners. Many deaths also resulted from shootings (in the camp's execution facility, among other places), from gassings, and from abuse. The gassings (with ZYKLON B) began in Stutthof no later than June 1944, in a gas chamber built that spring; it was also utilized for delousing clothing. Other gassings were carried out in sealed railroad cars equipped for this purpose, situated on a narrow-gauge track leading into the camp. Sick prisoners were killed in the infirmary with injections of poison or gasoline.

In January 1945 the first columns of evacuation marches out of Stutthof were set in motion. Many of the exhausted prisoners were shot by the guards for being unfit for the march. The prisoners remaining in the camp were evacuated by ship in April 1945, some to Flensburg, most into Lübeck Bay, off Neustadt. The ships CAP ARCONA and THIELBEK, among other vessels, were anchored there, but they were already loaded with prisoners from other concentration camps, and their captains refused to take on more people. Many prisoners succeeded in reaching the shore, but some 400 were shot there by the SS. The main camp at Stutthof was occupied on May 1, 1945, by Soviet troops. They liberated some 120 prisoners who had managed to hide.

The commandants of Stutthof were Max Pauly (sentenced to death in 1946 in the first NEUENGAMME Trial and executed) and Paul Werner HOPPE.

W. D.

Subhuman (*Untermensch*), term arising as early as the end of the 18th century, to denote a being (*Wesen*) to whom full human status cannot be conceded. The term reappeared in the 1920s in *völkisch*-racist propaganda as a complementary designation to the SUPERMAN in Friedrich Nietzsche's sense. National Socialist propaganda appropriated the label for the allegedly

Subhuman. Cover of an SS pamphlet.

racially and morally inferior Jews. It used the term particularly during the TIME OF STRUGGLE, but continued to make use of the emotions it generated in connection with the PERSECUTION OF JEWS (notably in Himmler's speech of November 12, 1935) and in order to devalue the Poles and Russians as "Slavic subhumans."

Thus, a press advisory of October 24, 1939, stated: "It has to be made clear to the last dairymaid [*Kuhmagd*] in Germany that being a Pole is equivalent to being subhuman." In 1942 the SS Main Office under Gottlob BERGER published a brochure entitled "The Subhuman." Jürgen STROOP's report on the suppression of the WARSAW GHETTO UPRISING noted among its observations the destruction of numerous "Jews, bandits, and subhumans." The reduction of the enemy to a nonhuman was intended to destroy among soldiers and SS men inhibi-

tions against murder. The ATROCITY STORIES of the First World War had been similar, and the Soviet propagandist Ilya Ehrenburg had similarly defamed the Germans as "fascist animals." Most campaigns aimed at destruction (such as Vietnam or the war in the Persian Gulf) are justified in like manner even today.

Sudeten Crisis (*Sudetenkrise*), conflict over the German-settled areas of Czechoslovakia, the so-called Sudetenland, with some 26,000 sq km (about 10,400 sq miles) and 3.3 million German inhabitants. The conflict smoldered beginning in 1919, then erupted acutely in 1937–1938. After demands by the SUDETEN GERMAN PARTY for autonomy grew stronger and its leader, Konrad HENLEIN, turned to National Socialism in November 1937, the first voices were raised for an Anschluss with the German Reich. Hitler encouraged Henlein to make unacceptable demands of the Prague government, much as those formulated in the Karlsbad Program of April 24, 1938: the most extensive autonomy, with the "freedom of declaring . . . for the German worldview," that is, for the National Socialist Great-German program. German propaganda responded to the government's rejection with half-true reports of excesses against the German minority. Meanwhile, Berlin supported the revisionist demands of Czechoslovakia's Polish and Hungarian minorities.

Western mediation efforts, such as those of Lord RUNCIMAN, were unsuccessful. Hitler, already determined to "destroy" Czechoslovakia (his instructions for "Case Green" ["Fall Grün"] of April 21 and May 30, 1938), inflamed the mood into a rebellious frenzy through offers of military support to the Sudeten Germans (in his speech of September 12). In two personal visits to Hitler, in Berchtesgaden (September 15) and Bad Godesberg (September 22–24), the British

Sudeten Crisis. Members of the Sudeten German Self-Defense.

prime minister, Neville Chamberlain, obtained only a delay of the Sudetenland annexation that was insistently demanded by Hitler. The Western powers averted a European war at the last moment by their total acceptance of the German demands in the MUNICH AGREEMENT.

Sudeten German Party (Sudetendeutsche Partei; SdP), unification movement in Czechoslovakia established on October 1, 1933, by Konrad HENLEIN in Eger (Hungary) as the Sudeten German Home Front (Sudetendeutsche Heimatfront; renamed the SdP on April 19, 1935). It regarded itself as a "community of German culture and destiny" (*deutsche Kultur- und Schicksalsgemeinschaft*). Fighting for reparations for the "injustice done since 1918–1919" to the Sudeten Germans, as well as for autonomy, it moved increasingly into the National Socialist mainstream. In 1935 the SdP, now financed by Berlin, won two-thirds of the German vote (gaining 44 of 300 seats in the Czechoslovak parliament). Its membership rose from 70,000 in October 1934 to 1.3 million in July 1938. It thus became a useful instrument for Hitler in igniting the SUDETEN CRISIS. The SdP was absorbed into the NSDAP on December 11, 1938; a subsidiary group, the Carpathian German Party, continued to operate in SLOVAKIA.

Suicide (*Selbstmord;* also *Freitod*), the intentional destruction of one's own life. Although characterized as "un-German" by its nature, suicide

Sudeten German Party election poster: "German! Your vote only to the Sudeten German Party of Konrad Henlein."

was not rejected in principle by National Socialism as it is by Christianity but was assessed differently according to the motive. Thus "responsible" suicide was held to be morally unobjectionable, as in the case of an incurable illness (sanctioned as a kind of "self-euthanasia"). Sacrificial actions in war ("suicide commandos") and "self-executions" out of a sense of honor (as when threatened by capture) were praised as "heroic suicides" (*Heldenfreitode*). Suicide "out of despair," committed because of lover's grief "by persons like [Goethe's] Werther," or because of social need, were to be regarded as "fundamentally overcome" in National Socialist Germany through the "provision of a healthy mode of life as developed in the *Volk* Community and through education in firmness of character and self-discipline."

M. F.

Summary law (*Standrecht*), the authority to make judicial judgments through an abbreviated court procedure by means of a summary court during an exceptional, wartime, or siege situation. By an ordinance of November 1, 1939 (*Reich Law Gazette* I, p. 2131), a Paragraph 13a ("Summary Courts") was inserted into the Ordinance Regulating Military Criminal Proceedings during Wartime and in the Case of Special Deployment (*bei besonderem Einsatz*). Henceforth, independently of general MILITARY JURISDICTION, the most immediately available regimental commander, or a troop commander who had been granted equivalent disciplinary authority, could act as a judge.

Summary court jurisdiction could be utilized when compelling military reasons forbade postponement and a judge was not available, so long as witnesses and other evidentiary materials were immediately available. The necessity of notifying the otherwise responsible judge, and his right to take over the proceedings, were not annulled. On June 21, 1943, the central Special Summary Court [*Sonderstandgericht*] for the Wehrmacht was created within the central court-martial, the REICH COURT-MARTIAL; its assignment was to use summary proceedings to judge political crimes. On March 9, 1945, a "flying staff court" (*fliegendes Stabsgericht*)— named the Special Summary Court of the Führer—was created outside the structure of Wehrmacht justice. There are no reliable statistics on summary court actions. The Geneva Accord of August 12, 1949, disallowed summary court proceedings.

C. B.

Summary law. Firing squad in action.

Summer Day (*Sommertag*), holiday celebrating the beginning of spring. During the Third Reich, it was normally held on the fourth Sunday after Shrove Tuesday. On Summer Day, regional folk customs were revived: children went with decorated staffs from house to house; in Lausitz, summer songs were sung; and in Franconia, an image of Death was carried. In many localities a straw effigy of Winter was burned. (Derived from this was the "Judas burning" among *völkisch* church groups.)

Summer Time (*Sommerzeit*), the moving forward of the clock by one hour in order to make better use of the daylight. Introduced in Germany in the First World War, Summer Time was also put to use during the Second World War by an order of January 23, 1940, to foster efficiency in the WAR ECONOMY. It generally extended from around mid-March to early October. Germany's Summer Time led to confusion in the dating of the surrender in 1945. According to Summer Time the surrender took effect on the first minute of May 9, while according to the document it came into force at 23:01 hours (11:01 p.m.) on May 8.

Superman (*Übermensch*; literally, "over-man"), term coined by Friedrich NIETZSCHE in his main philosophical work, *Also sprach Zarathustra* (*Thus Spake Zarathustra*; 1883–1885) to denote a superior human being (*Elitemensch*) who breaks through the limits of normal human existence, who serves no ideal, who pays homage to no god, for whom the meaning of life lies in the exercise of power, and who possesses the virtues of "the warrior and the soldier." "Man is something that has to be overcome. . . . The superman is the meaning of this earth." With his vision of the superman, Nietzsche unleashed an enduring literary fashion; in turn, the literary representations of the superman influenced the *völkisch*-racist theories that arose around the turn of the 20th century. For the National Socialists the superman was no longer the image of "disciplined power," as he had been with Nietzsche; instead, he became a racist slogan that was intended to justify claims for power and domination.

Suprastate Powers (*Überstaatliche Mächte*), term coined by the *völkisch* movement and propagated especially by Gen. Erich Ludendorff and his TANNENBERG LEAGUE. It was used to designate political, religious, and ideological groupings that laid claim to authority beyond governmental and "popular spheres of life and exigencies." "Suprastate Powers" included the Roman Catholic church, Freemasons, Jews, Bolshevism, and high finance. Regarded as pulling the wires behind the political scene, they were made responsible for the "German disgrace," as well as for present-day "moral and cultural decay." By offering a personal image of the enemy rather than intangible opinions, ANTISEMITISM played a particular role in these conspiracy theories. Their racist foundations eliminated the last loophole, since the stigma of Jewish descent could be combated neither by recantation nor by baptism. World Jewry thus became the prototype of a Suprastate Power, and the struggle

Suprastate Powers. Cartoon in the *Brennessel* on the international Jewish conspiracy: "The suprastate wall."

against it prepared the way for the PERSECUTION OF JEWS in the Third Reich, although the National Socialists themselves avoided the use of the concept because of its sectarian onus.

Supreme Commander of the Wehrmacht (*Oberster Befehlshaber der Wehrmacht*), Hitler's title and function as of August 2, 1934. After the dissolution of the Reich War Ministry and the

Supreme Commander of the Wehrmacht. "These military idiots can be trusted not to observe any boundaries!" Cartoon in the Swiss *Nebelspalter* (1944).

creation of the WEHRMACHT HIGH COMMAND (OKW), Hitler assumed direct control over Germany's armed forces.

Supreme Judge (*Oberster Gerichtsherr;* literally, Most High Lord of the Court), function officially granted to Hitler by the Reichstag at its last session (April 26, 1942), but which he had held *de facto* at least since achieving his dictatorship through the combined offices of FÜHRER UND REICHSKANZLER. As the ultimate judge, Hitler was placed above law and JUSTICE, as he had demanded during and after the RÖHM AFFAIR. At that time, on July 3, 1934, speaking as the "Supreme Judge of the German *Volk*," he retroactively declared the murder operation "justified" because it was "necessary for the state's defense."

Supreme SA Führer (*Oberster SA-Führer;* Osaf), term for the chief of the SA's Supreme Command, formed on November 1, 1926. Franz PFEFFER VON SALOMON was Osaf until August 29, 1930, when Hitler himself assumed the position. Hitler then used only chiefs of staff to lead the SA (Ernst RÖHM until June 30, 1934; Viktor LUTZE until May 2, 1943, and subsequently Wilhelm Schepmann). (*See also* STURMABTEILUNG.)

Surén, Hans, b. Berlin, June 10, 1885; d. there, May 25, 1972, German pedagogue. An officer in the First World War, Surén advanced to major. As an educator, he concerned himself with issues of physical fitness through gymnastics. He developed a program of army gymnastics, and in 1921 outlined a "schooling for body and character" in his book *Deutsche Gymnastik* (German Gymnastics). It fit National Socialist pedagogical concepts, as did his next work, *Der Mensch und die Sonne* (Man and the Sun), which in a completely revised 1936 edition bore the subtitle "Aryan-Olympic Spirit." Although Surén was the longtime director of the Army Sports School in Wünsdorf, as well as inspector for physical exercises with the Reich Labor Service (with the title *Oberarbeitsführer*), he nonetheless ran into conflict with the regime. Because of alleged ties to the opposition, he was confined to the Brandenburg/Havel penitentiary after the assassination attempt of July 20, 1944. He lived in seclusion after the war, writing further works on sports pedagogy.

Sütterlin Script (*Sütterlinschrift*), script developed by the German graphic artist and designer

Sütterlin Script. "That is Streicher!" Page from a National Socialist children's book.

Ludwig Sütterlin (1865–1917). The script was tried out in several of the German states in the early 1930s; in 1935, as the "German script," it was made the obligatory normal script in German schools. Although many picture books and children's books were published in this script, willingness to adopt the complicated style was lacking, and in 1941 it was replaced by a Latinate "German Normal Script."

Swastika (*Hakenkreuz*), the official symbol of the NSDAP and of National Socialist Germany. There is evidence of the swastika in Europe since the fourth millennium B.C. As the *svastika* (a Sanskrit word meaning "salutary sign") and in slightly altered forms of it, the symmetrical cross, with its four arms extending at right or acute angles in the same rotary direction, appears often in Asiatic cultures and less often in African or Central American ones. The swastika is interpreted mainly as a solar disk, and even today in India and Japan is regarded as a solar symbol "promising good luck and warding off disaster." In the Germanic tradition, the swastika (*fyrfos*; "fourfoot") can be seen as Thor's hammer or as a doubled wolf trap; in Germanic folk art the swastika was retained as a decorative element even after Christianization.

In the course of renewed nostalgia for Germanic origins, nationalist circles around the "father of gymnastics," Friedrich Ludwig JAHN, rediscovered the swastika in the 19th century and used it as a symbol of their "confession of German nationality." By the end of the 19th century it had become the official emblem of the German Gymnasts' League. Later it was adopted by the Wandervogel (*see* YOUTH MOVEMENT)

and by free corps units, and it acquired a clearly nationalistic and antisemitic character. Hitler became familiar with the symbol used in this sense, especially through the periodical OSTARA and the insignia used by the THULE SOCIETY. In search of a symbol that would have "great impact on posters," Hitler decided in favor of the swastika and designed the swastika flag himself: "In red we see the social idea of the movement, in white the nationalist, in the swastika the mission of struggle for the victory of the Aryan and . . . the victory of the idea of productive work, which itself was always antisemitic and will always be antisemitic."

At the Salzburg Congress of August 7, 1920, the swastika flag became the official banner of the NSDAP. In 1933 it became the Reich flag alongside the black, white, and red flag, and on September 15, 1935, it was declared to be the only national flag (Reich Flag Law). The National Socialists had stylized the swastika symbol and made it uniform; all the subdivisions embodied it in their insignia. The swastika flag became an important propaganda tool: in marches during the "Time of Struggle" it was an expression of elitist consciousness and cohesion; in later mass marches, seas of flags contributed to eliminating thought by "overwhelming the senses." After 1933 the swastika became overall the object of a "quasi-religious symbol cult." The level of cultic worship of the flag was most clearly expressed in Baldur von Schirach's Hitler Youth anthem, "Unsre Fahne flattert uns voran" (Our Flag Flutters before Us): "the flag is greater than death."

After 1945 the use of the swastika and other NS signs and symbols was forbidden by the Allies. Fascist organizations throughout the world had adopted the swastika as a symbol

Swastika. Führer banner.

during the 1930s and 1940s. Even today anti-semites use it as an international distinctive sign.

H. H.

Sweden, kingdom in Scandinavia; area, 448,439 sq km (about 180,000 sq miles); population, about 6.1 million (1930). In the interwar period, under predominantly or partially Social Democratic governments, Sweden made the transition to a social welfare state. It also became the leading industrialized nation in Scandinavia, while simultaneously achieving a high level of agricultural self-sufficiency after bitter experiences in the First World War. Sweden was located at the intersection point of competing Great Power interests, with established foreign trade and capital involvements with both Great Britain and Germany.

After the outbreak of war in 1939, Sweden used skillful delaying tactics to maintain its constantly imperiled neutrality against both National Socialist claims to power and Allied threats of economic warfare and blockades. In a "Supplementary Grand-scale Economic Domain of Northern Europe" (Ergänzungs- und Grosswirtschaftsraum Nordeuropas), which was dominated by Germany and protected by blockades, and whose aim was continental AUTARKY, the Swedish economy was accorded a key position in Germany's war economy as the supplier of high-grade iron ore (30 percent of German military stores), ball bearings, machinery, wood, foodstuffs, and ships. It was also the financier for German delivery of war equipment, coal, coke, textiles, tools, and electrical appliances. Until 1939 Sweden was able to offset the peril of dependence on one side through economic treaties with Great Britain (1933) and the United States (1935), and even during the war it conducted a scrupulously limited foreign trade via Göteborg under British and German control.

After the occupation of Denmark and Norway and after Finland's entry into the war as a German ally, the surrounding of Sweden by the Third Reich and Sweden's severance from the West between 1940 and 1943 set the stage for the maintenance of a precarious neutral independence. It was made possible only at the price of uninterrupted deliveries to the German war economy, extensive credit for goods, and guaranteed transit of German military and freight transports through northern Sweden. Only after the war's turning point in 1943 did Sweden succeed in gradually extricating itself from the German political and commercial web and in turning toward the Western powers, until the

traffic toward Germany virtually collapsed by New Year's Day of 1945. From 1943 onward, when the FINAL SOLUTION was being carried out in Denmark as well, Sweden became a haven for many Danish Jews.

B.-J. W.

Switzerland (officially, Swiss Confederation), federal state in central Europe; area, 41,288 sq km (about 16,400 sq miles); population, approximately 4 million (1930). Switzerland joined the League of Nations in 1920 and declared its "differentiated" neutrality (its commitment to economic sanctions), but in 1938 it reverted to "integral" (unconditional) neutrality. Under Federal Councillor [*Bundesrat*] Giuseppe Motta as director of the Political Department (1920–1940), even after the deterioration of its military and strategic situation through Austria's AN-SCHLUSS, Switzerland continued to maintain its policy of independence in foreign affairs vis-à-vis Fascist Italy (in 1936 it recognized the Impero [Empire of Italy]) and National Socialist Germany, with the goal of preserving its national existence and its liberal-democratic way of life. Fascist and National Socialist–oriented renewal movements ("frontism") did not find much resonance, particularly after the economic upswing beginning in 1936. But a "fifth column" (*see* Wilhelm GUSTLOFF) under tight control from Berlin was perceived as a serious threat to Swiss national independence and statehood.

After the outbreak of the Second World War,

Switzerland. "I sing the song of him whose bread I eat!" *Nebelspalter* satire on the Swiss National Socialists.

and especially after the capitulation of France, neutral Switzerland, now completely isolated, evaded the pincer-like political and military grip of the Axis by a dual strategy of adaptation and resistance. On the one hand, it maintained press censorship, strictly emphasized its neutrality (despite many violations of it on all sides), and made the Gotthard Railway available for German and Italian transport of materials, in exchange for keeping foreign-trade connections in essential commodities open. On the other hand, there was general mobilization, a wartime economy, an alliance spanning Left to Right for a "spiritual defense of the country," and a military strategy of the *Réduit national* (National Redoubt; that is, expansion of the Alpine [central] defense perimeter)—all measures that would have made any attack a costly and troublesome undertaking. During the war as well, Switzerland played an important role as a country that accepted political refugees despite many restrictions, as a European haven for free speech in German (the Zurich Theater), and as the preferred place for secret contacts between the hostile powers (it was the site of the liaisons between the German opposition and the West, and of the preparations for the German surrender in Italy at the end of April 1945). The common external threat reinforced a collective Swiss solidarity and sense of identity, and it obstructed thenceforth any tendencies toward irredentism or union with Germany.

B.-J. W.

Symbols (*Sinnbilder*), signs and emblems from the early Indo-Germanic period that were put to new use by the National Socialists. The ancient symbols were found variously in the stitching and weaving patterns of garments, in family and village coats of arms, and in ornamentation on buildings, household furnishings, and jewelry. Most of them developed during the Neolithic age and the period of mass tribal migrations. They can be subdivided into stylized, abstract symbols and naturalistic symbols. Examples of the former were the SWASTIKA as a solar symbol, the rhombus as a sign of the womb and fertility, the pentagram for warding off evil influence, and RUNES such as the SS emblem, a protective symbol. Symbols from nature were the oak leaf or wreath, the four-leaf clover, fountains, flowers, and trees. National Socialist organizations utilized symbols in their coats of arms, and symbols adorned public buildings as well as reception and assembly halls, in the form of friezes and decor. Particularly in the late

Symbols. Visigothic gravestone from the seventh century.

1930s, symbols became common in commercial and applied art: in fabrics and rugs, on vases and cigarette boxes, and as typographical ornaments in books and magazines. ANCESTRAL INHERITANCE, the research and education society in Berlin, in 1938 established in Horn (in the state of Lippe) a special department for the systematic classification and study of symbols.

H. H.

Synchronization (*Gleichschaltung*), word used in electrotechnology, referring to currents (*Schalter* means "switch"), that was appropriated by National Socialist (NS) propaganda to refer to the alignment of associations, organizations, political parties, and, ultimately, every individual citizen toward the goals of NS policy. The term was coined by Reich Justice Minister Franz GÜRTNER for the formulation of the Law of March 31, 1933, for the Synchronization of [the German] States [*Länder*] with the Reich.

Thus the first victim of synchronization was federalism: as early as the week after the Reichstag election of March 5, 1933, all the state parliaments were forced by NSDAP pressure to constitute themselves in line with the Reich-

Synchronization. Reich Propaganda Minister Goebbels gives instructions to representatives of the German press.

level results. On April 4, a second Synchronization Law ordered the installation of REICH GOVERNORS (*Reichsstatthalter*). They were named by the Reich president on recommendation of the chancellor (Hitler). These governors then had a right to appoint the state governments and their officials; except for Franz Xavier Ritter von EPP they were all party *Gau* leaders as well. Thereby the REICHSRAT lost all significance as a constitutional body; it was made totally superfluous on January 30, 1934, through the Law on the Restructuring of the Reich, which transferred all sovereign rights of the states to the Reich. The synchronization of the states was concluded with the dissolution of the Reichsrat on February 14, 1934, and the Reich's takeover of the state justice departments (*see* VERREICHLICHUNG) on April 1, 1935.

The plural party system disappeared even more quickly. The synchronization of parties too began in March 1933, when the REICHSTAG relinquished its own power in the ENABLING LAW. The Communist Party (KPD) had in fact been eliminated since the REICHSTAG FIRE DECREE, and it was definitively banned on March 28. The Socialist Party (SPD), which alone had offered opposition to the Enabling Law, was prohibited on June 22, after many of its leaders had already been lost through flight and arrest. The members of the middle-class parties flocked in droves to the NSDAP. One by one, these parties dissolved themselves: on June 27 the German National People's Party (DNVP), the next day the State Party, on July 3 the Center, and the day after that the Bavarian People's Party. After promulgation of the Law against the New Formation of Parties of July 14, only the

NSDAP existed. A law of December 1, 1933, then elevated it to the status of a public corporation (*Körperschaft öffentliches Rechts*). The Law on the Head of State [*Staatsoberhaupt*] of the German Reich of August 1, 1934, concluded the synchronization of the party state by merging the offices of Reich president and head of government. Thus Hitler became "FÜHRER UND REICHSKANZLER" (Leader and Reich Chancellor).

The instruments for synchronizing associations were the CIVIL SERVICE LAW and the ARYAN PARAGRAPH. The pattern was always the same: under pressure by NSDAP members, the executive committee of a professional organization was restructured and National Socialists were admitted. They "purged" (*säuberte*) the committee and led the association under the umbrella of the party. Where this was not possible, the NS leadership resorted to force: for example, on May 2, 1933, the buildings and offices of the trade unions were occupied by SA and police personnel, their records impounded, and their assets confiscated; the organizations themselves were merged into the GERMAN LABOR FRONT. The fate of the farmers' organizations was similar; on September 15, 1933, they all found themselves forcibly united in the REICH FOOD ESTATE. The industrial economy held out somewhat longer, but in August 1934 it too was bound closer to the state, when it was divided into Reich groups that were considerably influenced by the Economics Ministry. The FOUR-YEAR PLAN then obligated them, on October 15, 1936, to pursue the (war-related) goals of the NS leadership.

For the purpose of synchronizing opinion and

culture, on March 13, 1933, Hitler made Joseph GOEBBELS head of a separate Ministry for Volk Enlightenment and Propaganda. Anyone who wanted to professionally write, play music, make films, paint, or act had to become a member of the appropriate subdivision of the REICH CULTURE CHAMBER by September 22, 1933, at the latest. The conditions for acceptance, notably the Aryan Paragraph, made certain that those out of favor would no longer have an audience in Germany.

It was only the synchronization of the churches that was not entirely successful, although in the CHURCH STRUGGLE everything was tried to abolish this last corner of possible opposition. Neither the appointment of Hanns KERRL as Minister for Churches on July 16, 1935, nor the PULPIT PARAGRAPH was able to break the refractoriness of the CONFESSING CHURCH, nor did the PRIEST TRIALS force the Catholic church to its knees.

Nonetheless, after the summer of 1934 there was scarcely a German who was not connected to the party in some way, whether through profession or job, position, or organization. After the reintroduction of universal COMPULSORY MILITARY SERVICE (March 16, 1935), the REICH LABOR SERVICE duty (July 1, 1935), and the Law on State Youth (December 1, 1936; *see* HITLER YOUTH), the bond between the younger generation and the new state was complete. Hitler outlined his vision of the total capture of the *Volk* in a speech to district leaders on December 4, 1938: he would get children at age 10 into the Jungvolk, at 12 into the Hitler Youth, then there would be the party, the SA or SS, then the Labor Service, the Wehrmacht, and again the party divisions. Hitler concluded with the words, "and they will not be free again as long as they live."

System Era (*Systemzeit*), in the official National Socialist vocabulary of 1933, the increasingly common term for the period of the Weimar Republic, by then said to be past and "overcome." The term "system" as signifying something arranged by prior planning was here given a negative connotation of something artificially constructed and propped up. Conservative and *völkisch* groups had coined the term in the 1920s to deride the Republican state as the "November system" or the "system of infamy" (*Schandsystem*). The National Socialists contrasted this "intellectualist rubbish heap" (*intellektualistischer Schutthaufen;* Alfred Rosenberg's term) to the "organic" *Volk* Community, which was being built on "feeling and belief" rather than on "abstract knowledge." They cited the NS motto: "He who thinks, already doubts" ("Wer denkt, zweifelt schon"). The term "system" was accordingly used in various compounds referring to the Republic and its institutions: "system" Germany, "system" political parties, politicians, press, governments, and so forth.

Szálasi, Ferenc, b. Košice, January 6, 1897; d. Budapest, March 12, 1946 (executed), Hungarian politician. In 1935 Szálasi called into existence the nationalist and antisemitic movement of the Hungarists (later the ARROW CROSS), but he held little influence in Miklós HORTHY's authoritarian government and was periodically imprisoned. Only after the overthrow of the chief of state (October 16, 1944) did the German military authorities bring Szálasi back and hand the government over to him, even though the country was already largely occupied by the Soviets. Despite the hopeless situation, he called for the continuation of the war and became an accomplice in the persecution of the Jews. Apprehended by the Americans in Austria at the end of the war, Szálasi was remanded to Hungary and sentenced to death.

Szenes, Hanna, b. Budapest, 1921; d. there, November 7, 1944, Jewish partisan. Szenes emigrated in 1939 to Palestine, but she decided in 1943 to return to Hungary in order to help her co-religionists, particularly her mother, to emigrate or flee. She joined the British army, which assigned her to a paratroop commando. In early March 1944 the unit landed in Yugoslavia, established contact with Tito's partisans, and took on the task of freeing Allied aviators who had been shot down. When German troops occupied Hungary on March 19, 1944, Szenes quickly separated from the partisans and crossed the Hungarian border on June 7. She was captured, but despite torture and threats kept silent about her mother's whereabouts and the assignment of her commando unit. The Szálasi government finally had her executed.

T

T4, code name for the killing activities of the EUTHANASIA program. It was taken from the address of the program's office at Berlin's Tiergartenstrasse 4.

Table Talks (*Tischgespräche*), Hitler's remarks at the Führer's headquarters during lunch and dinner, as well as at the evening teatime. Immediately after the beginning of the Russian Campaign, Martin Bormann suggested taking down the conversations in writing, and instructed his aide, the ministerial councillor Heinrich Heim, to do so. Heim's note-taking began on July 5, 1941, was interrupted on March 12, 1942, and continued again from August 1 to September 7 of that year. During Heim's absence his representative, government councillor Henry Picker, took notes from March 21 to July 31. They ended when, in early September 1942, a severe crisis developed at the Führer's headquarters over the conduct of war in the east and Hitler ceased taking his meals in the company of others.

Picker's notes, which have been published several times, were at his personal disposal, but Heim's notes are available only in a collection of "Führer Conversations" that Bormann began compiling and then sent to his wife for safekeeping. Following Frau Bormann's death (on March 23, 1946), these notes came into the hands of an Italian government official in a prisoner camp in Merano, who sold them to the Swiss publisher François Genoud. After they had appeared in French and English translations, the notes were first published in German by Werner Jochmann in 1980.

Neither Heim nor Picker used shorthand or verbatim transcription, but rather wrote down only summaries giving the sense of Hitler's utterances; moreover, these were written after the meals, using notes. The Table Talks should actually be termed "Monologues," since Hitler essentially spoke alone. "The conversation at the table resembled a subdued whispering, which ceased as soon as Hitler said anything. The whole atmosphere was one of deference toward Hitler, which caused even gray-haired generals and politicians to occasionally knock over their glasses out of nervousness when he greeted them" (Picker).

In terms of content, the Table Talks confirm everything that made up HITLER'S WORLDVIEW. Antisemitic remarks run through them like a red thread: "When we eradicate this pest [the Jews] we will have achieved a feat for humanity" (October 21, 1941). The conquest of space in the east was of decisive strategic importance: "The struggle for hegemony in the world will be resolved for Europe by possession of the Russian domain" (September 17–18, 1941). In his intimate circle Hitler was more critical of the church than elsewhere: "The war will come to an end, and the final task of my life will be to settle the church problem." Indeed, the church would have to "rot off like a gangrenous limb. It must come to the point where only outright dolts [*lauter Deppen*] will stand at the pulpit, and only old maids [*alte Weiblein*] will sit before them. The healthy young people are with us" (December 13, 1941).

Otherwise, Hitler chatted, sometimes changing his themes abruptly, sometimes going more deeply into one thought, covering nearly all areas of life and knowledge. He played the role of the sociable, joking, obliging host, as well as of the uncompromising fanatic whose favorite word was "ice-cold." The Table Talks handed down by Heim and Picker (Jochmann lists another 10 Table Talks produced by Bormann) are, despite the fact that they were written down after the event, important "primary testimony" (Percy Schramm) for Hitler research. They convey a sense of Hitler's nature, his emotional and mental makeup, and the content and character of his autodidactic education.

C. Z.

Tag der nationalen Arbeit (Day of National Labor), May 1, elevated by the National Socialists to the status of a state holiday as early as 1933 (*see* MAY HOLIDAY).

"Tannenberg" ("Tannenberg" Operation), code name for the deployment of EINSATZGRUPPEN (task forces) and Einsatzkommandos (operational squads) under the chief of the Security Police during the Polish Campaign. In mid-August 1939, five task forces were set up, consisting primarily of personnel from the State Police (Stapo), the Criminal Police (Kripo), and the Security Service (SD). They were initially designated by the names of the cities where they were organized, but were later assigned Roman numerals (Vienna: I; Oppeln: II; Breslau: III; Dramburg: IV; and Allenstein: V). After hostilities began, these groups were joined by the Einsatzgruppe z.b.V. (*zur besonderen Verfügung*, or "on special assignment") and by Einsatzgruppe VI. One or more Einsatzkommandos were under the control of each task force. An independent Einsatzkommando 16 operated in the jurisdiction of the military commander for West Prussia. The total task force strength was about 2,700 men.

The purpose of the "Tannenberg" Operation was "to combat all elements hostile to the Reich and to Germans in the rear of the fighting troops." This included the "political consolidation of land" (*politische Flurbereinigung*) desired by Hitler, which led to the mass shooting of thousands of Poles and Jews (notably in the INTELLIGENTSIA OPERATION). Later, according to Himmler's decree of November 20, 1939, the task forces and squads were to be dissolved. Most of their members were transferred to the newly established offices of the chief of the Security Police and the SD in the incorporated Eastern Territories (Eastern Upper Silesia, the Danzig–West Prussia Reich *Gau*, and the Posen Reich *Gau* [later the Wartheland]) and in the so-called Generalgouvernement of Poland. Wehrmacht and army commanders sharply protested (sometimes even during the campaign) against the liquidations carried out by the Einsatzgruppen and other affiliated units subordinate to Himmler.

A. St.

Tannenberg League (Tannenbergbund), umbrella organization of *völkisch* military and youth leagues, initially with some 30,000 members. It was founded by Erich LUDENDORFF in 1925, and was named after the site of a victory over the Russians in 1914. In terms of ideology, the league saw itself as a militant community of persons "freed from Christian influence," who confronted the "SUPRASTATE POWERS" (notably the Roman Catholic church, Marxists, Jews, and Freemasons) while supporting a "German perception of God." As such, the Tannenberg League was a harbinger of National Socialism, although the NSDAP kept a careful distance out of deference to the churches. After seizing power, the party saw to the league's decline through administrative persecution and re-

Victims of the "Tannenberg" Operation.

cruitment from its ranks. In September 1933, the league was finally prohibited. Ludendorff and his wife, Mathilde, the ideological "brain" of the Tannenberg League, remained unmolested because of the general's popularity.

Tarnung (camouflage), translation of the French *camouflage;* the word was created by reviving the Old German word *tarnen* (to hide). It appeared as a technical military term in the First World War, and became widely used in a figurative sense in the National Socialist vocabulary: it conformed with the NS conspiracy and persecution fantasies, which saw Jews everywhere.

Tat Circle (*Tatkreis*), term for the editors of and the broader group of contributors to the *völkisch* magazine *Die Tat* (The Deed), founded in 1909. Oriented especially toward the middle-class nationalist intelligentsia, it supported the "molding of a new reality" and the "struggle against Versailles and Weimar." Under Hans ZEHRER as editor in chief (1929–1933) and with contributors such as Giselher WIRSING, the *Tat* Circle called for an antidemocratic elitism, for economic autarky, and for the establishment of a permanent nation-state with anticapitalist features.

Although the magazine consciously distanced itself from National Socialism, at least until 1933, as the "center of the conservative revolution" it nonetheless was an important intellectual precursor of National Socialist rule. Under Wirsing as editor after 1933, *Die Tat* conformed to ideological demands until it ceased publication in 1937. In addition to *Die Tat*, which was influential until 1933, the *Tat* Circle also published a *Korrespondenz* for "leading personalities" in Germany between 1929 and 1932, and a number of individual titles, such as Ferdinand FRIED's *Das Ende des Kapitalismus* (The End of Capitalism; 1931).

H. H.

Teachers. *See* Education; National Socialist Teacher's League.

Teachers' Camp (*Lehrerlager*), occasional vacations organized by the NATIONAL SOCIALIST TEACHERS' LEAGUE (NSLB); they were held in instructional camps or *Gau* schools to facilitate the "alignment of the teaching faculty" in terms of worldview and to reinforce the teachers' sense of togetherness.

Teacher Training Institutes (Lehrerbildungsanstalten; LBA), educational institutions introduced in 1941 as substitutes for the 28 Teachers Colleges (Hochschulen für Lehrerbildung; HfL) that had trained elementary school (*Volksschule*) teachers throughout the Reich since 1937. The prerequisite for the two-year course had been an academic diploma (*Abitur*). Additionally, in 1939 Continuation Instructional Courses (Aufbaulehrgänge) were instituted to prepare elementary and middle school (*Mittelschule*) students for study at the Teachers Colleges. By 1943, 257 of the new LBA had been created, 130 of them for girls only. They offered courses of instruction varying in length: five years for those who had completed elementary school, four years for those who had completed the COUNTRY YEAR, and three years for middle- and upper-level secondary students; for students with an *Abitur*, the course was shortened to one year. Twenty of the pedagogical institutes also trained "school aides" (*Schulhelfer*) ranging in age from 19 to 30, who were instructed in three-month preparatory courses. After in-school apprenticeships of one to two years, these aides then had a final nine-month training course. Some of the LBA also had classes for *technische Lehrerinnen* (women teachers in technical subjects) and for kindergarten teachers.

As far as possible, housing for the LBA students was provided in dormitories. The institutes were organized on the model of the Continuation Instructional Courses, which had adopted the idea of "formation education" (*Formationserziehung*; that is, molding) from the NATIONAL-POLITICAL EDUCATIONAL INSTITUTES. Recruitment was carried out mainly by the Hitler Youth (HJ), which was also in charge of the "selection" (*Auslese*) in "recruitment camps" (*Musterungslager*). Because of the varied periods of training, the influence of the HJ, and the relatively large enrollment of girls (in 1943 they amounted to 63.1 percent of the 44,157 trainees), the LBA differed appreciably from earlier German normal schools (*Lehrerseminare*). It was the Party Chancellery, under Martin BORMANN, and not the Reich Education Ministry, that issued the LBA guidelines. The chancellery was concerned less with the quality of training than with the early and comprehensive political socialization and mobilization of young people from upwardly mobile social groups. They could also be tapped for "deployment" (EINSATZ) beyond the Reich frontiers, where 43 of the LBA were located, and (beginning in 1943) for auxiliary war service.

H. S.

Teheran, capital of Iran. From November 28 to December 1, 1943, the heads of state of Great Britain (Winston CHURCHILL), the USSR (Joseph STALIN), and the United States (Franklin D. ROOSEVELT) met in Teheran. The meeting had been prepared by the first of the MOSCOW FOREIGN MINISTERS' CONFERENCES, held by the three states in October 1943. The conference covered three main areas. First, Roosevelt and Churchill agreed to establish a second European front in May 1944 with a landing by the western Allies in France (*see* INVASION), and thus to relieve the Soviet military forces. Stalin, who had demanded a second front since July 1941, promised a simultaneous Soviet offensive on the German eastern front, as well as support for the United States in its war with Japan, once the war in Europe had ended. Second, the participants agreed in principle to a westward shift of Poland's borders: the CURZON LINE was to be Poland's approximate eastern boundary, and the ODER-NEISSE LINE (which Stalin proposed) its western frontier. Stalin in addition laid claim to the German Baltic Sea ports of Königsberg and Memel, as well as the surrounding area of East Prussia.

The Teheran Conference also agreed in principle to the division of Germany, although not to the form it would take. Churchill's idea of a division along the Main River line to form a northern part ("Prussia") and a southern part,

which would belong to a Danubian Confederation, was rejected by Stalin and Roosevelt. They recommended instead the formation of five individual German states and the internationalization of the Ruhr and Saar regions, as well as of the North Sea–Baltic Sea canal area, including Hamburg. The participants also established a EUROPEAN ADVISORY COMMISSION to deal further with the German problem. Besides the Polish and German questions, the conference's topics included Roosevelt's idea of a world peace organization that would include the USSR (*see* UNITED NATIONS).

R. B.

Temperament (*Gemüt*), term for human qualities such as character, depth of feeling, and fortitude, which together constitute the essence (*Kern*) of a person in relation to the surrounding world. Traditionally, the word was associated with a romantic, conciliatory, and peaceful human disposition. In National Socialist usage, *Gemüt* was ideologically appropriated to designate a depth of soul characteristic only of the German, and determined by his "racial feelings and values."

Terboven, Josef, b. Essen, May 23, 1898; d. Oslo, May 11, 1945, German politician and SA-*Obergruppenführer* (1936). A lieutenant by the end of the First World War, Terboven began but did

Teheran. From the left: Stalin, Roosevelt, and Churchill. Behind them: Molotov, Sir Archibald Clark Kerr, and Anthony Eden.

Josef Terboven.

not complete studies in political economy. He then went into commercial banking. In Munich he entered NSDAP circles, and participated in the Hitler Putsch. He built up the SA in Essen, became a *Gauleiter* in 1928, and was elected to the Reichstag in 1930. At Terboven's wedding, which Hitler attended as a sign of his personal esteem, the final decision for the murder operation of the RÖHM AFFAIR was taken on June 29, 1934.

Terboven became governor (*Oberpräsident*) of the Rhine province on February 5, 1935, and on April 24, 1940, Reich commissioner for Norway. As commissioner he put the Norwegian economy entirely at the service of the German Four-Year Plan, promoted collaborators in Vidkun QUIS-LING's entourage, and with the aid of the SS suppressed any hint of opposition with harsh measures. The Norwegian writer Knut HAMSUN unsuccessfully intervened with Hitler against this reign of terror. Terboven took his own life at the end of the war.

Terezín. *See* Theresienstadt.

Terror-and-Sabotage Decree (*Terror- und Sabotageerlass*), directive issued in July 1944 that in cases of terrorist attacks and acts of sabotage restricted MILITARY JURISDICTION over German civilians. According to the directive, all other persons caught in the act were to be "subdued" (*niederzukämpfen*) on the spot; those caught later were to be handed over to the Security Police or SD.

Terwiel, Maria, b. Boppard, June 7, 1910; d. Berlin, August 5, 1943 (executed), German opposition fighter. Terwiel studied law, but as a half Jew she was not permitted to take the examination, and she thus became a secretary. A practicing Catholic, she came in contact with the opposition group around Harro SCHULZE-BOYSEN during the war, circulated anti-Nazi pamphlets, and provided identity cards for Jews in danger. The Reich Court-martial punished her and her fiancé, Helmut Himpel, with death for these actions.

Tetzner, Lisa, b. Zittau, November 10, 1894; d. Corona (Switzerland), July 2, 1963, German writer. After becoming socially committed, beginning in 1918 Tetzner traveled on foot throughout Germany as a narrator of stories and fairy tales. She also contributed with her own texts to the creation of a socialist and realist German children's literature in the 1920s. From 1927 to 1933 she was in charge of the children's hour on Radio Berlin, but she then had to emigrate to Switzerland together with her husband, Kurt Kläber (pseud., Kurt Held), a working-class writer. It was there that she wrote her main work between 1933 and 1949, the nine-volume *Odyssee einer Jugend—Erlebnisse und Abenteuer der Kinder aus Nr. 67* (Odyssey of a Childhood: Impressions and Adventures of the Children at No. 67). By portraying the individual lives of a group of children from a Berlin tenement house (*Hinterhaus*), Tetzner sketches a realistic and harsh picture of the period from the beginnings of National Socialism to the first

Lisa Tetzner.

postwar years, depicting terror and opportunism, flight and exile, in a manner comprehensible to children. Her cycle is among the earliest and still most important German children's books about the Third Reich.

Thadden, Elisabeth von, b. Mohrungen (East Prussia), July 29, 1890; d. Berlin, August 8, 1944 (executed), German victim of National Socialism. An educator of youth, Thadden founded an Evangelical rural boarding school (*Landerziehungsheim*) at Wieblingen Castle near Heidelberg in 1927. A member of the Confessing Church, she left the school in 1941 because of pressure from the government. She then worked with the Red Cross in convalescent homes for soldiers in France. A spy who had infiltrated the circle of her friends by posing as an enemy of National Socialism turned her over to the Gestapo after she had given him access to the Christian conservative opposition in Berlin. Arrested in January 1944, Thadden was imprisoned in the Ravensbrück concentration camp, then sentenced to death by the *Volk* Court on July 1, 1944, for allegedly undermining military strength and attempting high treason.

Thälmann, Ernst, b. Hamburg, April 16, 1886; d. Buchenwald concentration camp, August 18, 1944, German politician. Thälmann was a longshoreman and transport worker. He joined the Social Democratic Party (SPD) in 1903, the Independent Socialists (USPD) in 1917, and the Communist Party (KPD) in 1920, in 1921 becoming its party chairman in Hamburg. He supported the (unsuccessful) October uprising

Ernst Thälmann.

in that city in 1923, against the line taken by the party leadership. In 1924 Thälmann advanced to the executive committee of the Comintern, assumed the leadership of the RED FRONTLINE FIGHTERS' LEAGUE on October 31 of that year, and became chairman of the KPD in September 1925. He had meanwhile become known beyond party circles as a candidate for the office of Reich president in April 1925, when he won 1.9 million votes. He was able regularly to increase the number of KPD votes until 1932, when he received 4.9 million ballots in the presidential contest.

Thälmann's absolute party loyalty vis-à-vis Stalin proved fatal. Both men assessed National Socialism and the political situation incorrectly when they perceived the SPD as the left arm and the NSDAP as the right arm of the same bourgeoisie. Consequently, there could be no joint action with the "social fascists" against Hitler. The "overtaxed but steadfast worker" (in the words of Willy Brandt) was arrested after the Reichstag fire, on March 3, 1933. After 11 years of imprisonment, he was murdered by SS guards who took advantage of an air raid on the Buchenwald concentration camp. Thälmann had refused release after the conclusion of the German-Soviet Nonaggression Pact in 1939, since he was unwilling to sign a promise to abstain from political activity.

Theater, the art of acting and the place for its presentation, as well as the totality of intellectual and organizational prerequisites required by them. The German theater had gained interna-

Elisabeth von Thadden.

tional prestige during the Weimar Republic through Expressionist and socially critical plays, as well as through works that were avant-garde in form and content; it boasted authors such as Bertolt BRECHT and Lion FEUCHTWANGER, and producers such as Max REINHARDT. As a whole, however, the theater had remained a medium of the educated middle class, and classical authors and shallow entertainment dominated the repertoires.

There was no dearth of plays with *völkisch* tendencies soon after the takeover of power. In the words of Heinrich MANN: "The political system obtains its literary offspring from the ranks of the old and half-forgotten. . . . They tremble with excitement when their turn comes." Many bourgeois-conservative authors readily demonstrated their jubilant patriotism and their "close relationship with the sod." The synchronization of the German theatrical profession proceeded smoothly as well. The REICH THEATER CHAMBER prescribed which National Socialist holidays should be marked by special productions. The Theater Law of May 15, 1934, placed all German theaters under the authority of the Propaganda Ministry. Audience organizations such as the People's Stage (Volksbühne), which had originated with the workers' movement, were synchronized into the NS cultural community. Public educational institutions with a new emphasis on the *Volk* (*Volksbildungseinrichtungen*), and "culture overseers" (*Kulturwalter*) in factories, arranged theater visits. The impact of theater on the masses

was to be increased by new sites and forms. For example, 200 open-air amphitheaters came into being by 1936, for staging the choral THING PLAYS that were favored for mass audiences. Numerous traveling companies were founded to bring didactic and entertaining NS plays to the provinces, or—in the case of the "Reich Autobahn Theater"—to bring "the German worker into contact with theater for the first time." The "Borderland Theaters" (*Grenzland-Theater*) enjoyed particular support; their repertoire was oriented toward "nationalizing" the German minorities in neighboring countries. After the war began, many traveling companies went on tour, providing entertainment for the troops, in order to bring ideology and recreation to the front.

Artists were tied to the system by means of prize competitions (for example, the Dietrich ECKART Competition of the Philipp Reclam, Jr., Publishing House), well-endowed honors (*see* LITERARY PRIZES), improved social protection (minimum salaries, long-term contracts, old-age provisions), and material and political privileges. Stars such as Werner KRAUSS willingly played roles that were interpreted in line with antisemitism, and Gustaf GRÜNDGENS within four weeks produced a play on Mussolini according to ministerial instructions.

The repertoire of German theater in the Third Reich continued its bourgeois-conservative orientation. In first place were traditional productions of the classics (notably Goethe and Schiller), along with light comedies. There fol-

Theater. Performance of the play *Der Weg ins Reich* (The Path to the Reich) in the *Thing* site on Heidelberg's Heiligenberg.

Theater. Gustaf Gründgens as Mephisto. Berlin State Theater, 1941–1942 season.

lowed coarse popular plays such as *Die Frösche von Büschebüll* (The Frogs of Büschebüll; 1934), by the "poet of weddings and wedding-eve parties," Bruno Wellenkamp. Only then came actual NS drama, as celebrated annually at the Reich Theater Weeks. In the tradition of theater in the Weimar period, it often consisted of "action dramas" with heroic and militant figures of soldiers or leaders, the prime example being Hanns JOHST's *Schlageter* (1933). A series of "Sturmabteilung plays" after the takeover of power featured storm troopers who "went to a hero's death with a smile." The central themes of the NS worldview were given dramatic form in plays such as *Opferstunde* (Hour of Sacrifice; 1934) by Helmut Unger, later an expert in the EUTHANASIA program, who propagandized against "hereditarily ill offspring" and praised the "blessings of the sterilization law" (*see* FORCED STERILIZATION). [The screenplay for the pro-euthanasia film ICH KLAGE AN was also based on Unger's writings.]

In theoretical discussions the creation of a new "National Theater" was proposed, which would simultaneously demonstrate the superiority of German culture and the ideology of the *Volk* Community. After the war broke out, an intertwining of the tragic and the heroic already predominating in NS drama was intensified. It provided an aesthetic undergirding for the will-

ingness to sacrifice that was demanded in political propaganda: he who "stood before fate" and let himself be "imbued" by it would "gratefully accept the terrible as a favor" (Curt Langenbeck, *Wiedergeburt des Dramas aus dem Geist der Zeit* [Rebirth of the Drama from the Spirit of the Age]; 1940). In the final analysis, NS theoreticians of drama demanded "optimistic tragedies."

H. H.

Theresienstadt (Czech, Terezín), National Socialist ghetto, originally intended for elderly Jews as an *Altersgetto*. It was established on November 24, 1941, in the former garrison town of Theresienstadt, which was evacuated of its approximately 7,000 inhabitants toward this end. Located about 60 km (some 36 miles) north of Prague, it was in an area subject to flooding by the Eger River. In reality, Theresienstadt served primarily as a transit camp within the general plan for the FINAL SOLUTION of the Jewish question: deportation transports left the ghetto for the death camps in the east, among them Auschwitz. The word "ghetto" served to obscure the real function of the camp. For propaganda purposes, terms such as "preferential camp" (*Vorzugslager*) or "Reich Home for the Elderly" (*Reichsaltersheim*) were also sometimes used.

Theresienstadt. *A Transport to the East.* Pencil drawing by a girl inmate, 1942–1943.

Initially Theresienstadt held Jewish people
from the Protectorate of Bohemia and Moravia;
German Jews (*Reichsdeutsche Juden*) over the
age of 65 and handicapped Jewish persons over
the age of 55, with their Jewish spouses and
their children under the age of 14; Jewish
veterans of the First World War with military
decorations or badges awarded as a result of war
injuries; and groups of Jewish people from western Europe. Later on, in 1943–1944, Jews in
these categories were joined by Jews from the
liquidated ghettos in the east and from assembly
camps in Hungary. Shortly before the end of the
war, evacuation transports from concentration
camps in the east (including non-Jews) arrived at
Theresienstadt.

A total of 152,000 persons were sent to the
camp. The largest number of inmates there at
one time was 58,000 men, women, and children,
in September 1942. More than 30,000 people
remained in Theresienstadt at the time of its
liberation. Although the inmates were unsuited
for labor because of their age and state of health,
they were made to work at mining, forestry, and
gardening, among other occupations, both in the
camp and in some nine satellite camps, up to the
time when they were sent away.

Theresienstadt was under the authority of the
Central Office for Jewish Emigration (Zentralstelle für jüdische Auswanderung) in Prague,
which around 1943 was renamed the Central
Office for the Settlement of the Jewish Question
in Bohemia and Moravia (Zentralamt für die
Regelung der Judenfrage in Böhmen und Mähren). This office in turn was under the jurisdiction of Adolf Eichmann's Section IV B 4 in the
Reich Security Main Office (RSHA) in Berlin.
Through misrepresentations, many of the camp's
inmates had been prevailed on to put all their
financial resources into "Home Purchase Agreements" (*Heimeinkaufsverträge*), which supposedly assured them of an old-age pension and the
right to lifelong care in the "Reich Home for
the Elderly" at Theresienstadt, which was de-

Theresienstadt. Distribution of rations.

scribed to them as a kind of health resort. In
reality, conditions in the camp were catastrophic. The town's houses and apartments, which
were for 7,000 inhabitants, were overcrowded
with tens of thousands of elderly and frail people, many of whom were lodged in cellars and
drafty attics. Insufficient food (at times, 225 g
[about 7.9 oz] of bread, 60 g [2.1 oz] of potatoes,
and a watery soup daily), a shortage of water,
and primitive sanitary conditions contributed to
raising the death rate in the camp. Altogether,
34,000 people died in Theresienstadt.

Ghetto inmates were also taken at times for
SPECIAL HANDLING to the nearby police prison
or the "Little Theresienstadt Fortress" camp,
which was under the authority of the State
Police Directorate (Stapo-Leitstelle) in Prague,
and was not administratively connected with
the ghetto. They included some 30 to 40 children from a children's transport (*Kindertrans-
port*) from the Białystok ghetto. They had arrived at Theresienstadt in August 1943 and had
become ill in the camp. In all, 85,934 persons
were deported from Theresienstadt to extermination camps, of whom nearly 84,000 were
killed there. In 1944 a National Socialist propaganda film with the title *Der Führer schenkt den
Juden eine Stadt* (The Führer Makes a Gift of a
City to the Jews) was produced in the camp. For
this purpose, and in order to deceive a Danish
Red Cross commission about conditions in the
ghetto, appropriate measures were carried out
to refurbish the buildings, inmates were temporarily well clad, sports and music events were
held, and so on. On May 8, 1945, Soviet troops
liberated Theresienstadt.

Theresienstadt. Camp currency.

The ghetto's first commandant was Siegfried Seidl (November 1941 to July 5, 1943), who was sentenced to death by the *Volk* Court in Vienna in October 1946 and executed on February 4, 1947. Anton Burger (July 1943 to the end of January 1944) was captured after the war and was to be extradited to Czechoslovakia, but he managed to escape. Searches for him have been unsuccessful. He was sentenced to death in absentia by the Special *Volk* Court in Leitmeritz. Finally, Karl Rahm, the commandant from February 1944 to May 1945, was sentenced to death by the same Czechoslovak court in Leitmeritz, and was executed.

W. D.

Thielbek, freighter of the German merchant fleet, with 2,800 gross registered tons; it was used to transport German refugees from the east to the west during the last weeks of the war on orders from the German navy. Like the CAP ARCONA, the *Thielbek* was requisitioned by Karl KAUFMANN, the Reich Commissioner for Navigation, at the end of April 1945. It was ordered to take on board 2,800 prisoners from the NEUENGAMME concentration camp, which had been evacuated; the prisoners were crammed into the ship's hold with indescribable brutality. Clearing Neustadt Bay on May 2, 1945, on the following day the *Thielbek* became the target of a British air raid directed against "concentrations of enemy ships." Hit by rockets, bombs, and aircraft weapons, she sank within a quarter of an hour. There was no chance of escape from the ship's hold, and nearly all the prisoners lost their lives. The SS guards had fled earlier.

Thierack, Otto, b. Wurzen (Saxony), April 19, 1889; d. Eselheide camp (Senne camp), near Paderborn, November 22, 1946, German lawyer. Thierack studied law and political science in Marburg and Leipzig. After volunteering in the First World War, he became a public prosecutor in Leipzig in 1921. In 1926 he began serving in Saxony's Superior State Court in Dresden, and in 1933 he became that state's provisional justice minister. He had joined the NSDAP in 1932. In 1935 Thierack became vice president of the Supreme Reich Court (Reichsgericht) in Leipzig, and in 1936, president of the VOLK COURT in Berlin.

Hitler made Thierack Reich justice minister in August 1943, an office he held until 1945. Concurrently, he headed the Reich Legal Office (Reichsrechtamt) of the Reich Leadership

Otto Thierack.

of the NSDAP and was president of the ACADEMY FOR GERMAN LAW. Thierack had the reputation of being Hitler's faithful follower. As head of the *Volk* Court he was not as brutal as his successor, Roland FREISLER, but even during his own term, punishment was biased toward the maximum penalty, and procedural guarantees were systematically eliminated. Thierack attempted "to forge martial law anew in order to make it a weapon sufficient to all requirements." As justice minister he uncompromisingly continued the efforts of the National Socialist regime to directly control the system of JUSTICE and to transform it into an instrument of power and terror. Thus, he increased the use of the so-called preview (*Vorschau*) and review (*Nachschau*) of sentences by supervisors of the judge involved, a procedure already being followed under Franz SCHLEGELBERGER; he also introduced the so-called judges' letters (*Richterbriefe*). Above all, Thierack carried out a personnel policy designed to favor younger "proven National Socialists," and changed the competency of law courts, especially through transfers to SPECIAL COURTS and reliably National Socialist administrative offices, in particular the Gestapo and SS. Thierack declared the German judge to be the "indirect assistant in government leadership." He committed suicide before he could be put on trial.

U. B.

Thiess, Frank, b. Eluisenstein bei Uexküll (Livonia), March 13, 1890; d. Darmstadt, December 22, 1977, German writer. After working as a

Frank Thiess.

journalist, playwright, and theater critic, Thiess wrote stories and novels, primarily about "borderline situations of human emotional life," and also on topics involving cultural history. Although he was not convinced of the *völkisch*-national vision of the world in 1933, Thiess attempted to "pay his respects to the new regime by supplying his socially critical novel from the period of the great inflation (*Der Leibhaftige* [The Devil Incarnate]; 1924) with an introduction that was meant to recommend him to the rulers" (Ernst Loewy).

Thiess refrained from political activity and utterances during the Third Reich, residing primarily in Vienna and Rome. However, because of its veiled criticism of the totalitarian state, his novel *Das Reich der Dämonen* (The Realm of Demons; 1941), which immediately sold out, was prohibited. After the war Thiess was one of the spokesmen for the INNER EMIGRATION. In public discussions with figures such as Thomas Mann, he reproached emigré authors for having "fled." For his work, which was esteemed as "refined" by conservative critics in particular, Thiess was awarded the Konrad Adenauer Prize of the Germany Foundation (Deutschland Stiftung) in 1968.

H. H.

Thing plays (*Thingspiel*), special form of National Socialist outdoor theater, conceived as an alternative to the proscenium stage. [The *Thing* was an old German public assembly.] The architecture of the "*Thing* places" (*Thingstätten*) and the novel productions that were to take place in them were meant to erase the barrier between actors and audience and thus represent the "*Volk* Community." The model, as propagandized by Hanns JOHST in particular, was the "cultic" theater of the Greeks; precursors were the representatives of a "*völkisch* world stage" and the LAY THEATER movement with its community orientation.

The outdoor theaters built by the REICH LABOR SERVICE (RAD) beginning in 1933 were termed "*Thing* places" because their layout was compared to Germanic cult sites. On June 5, 1934, the first of these theaters was dedicated in

Thing plays. Dietrich Eckart Stage in Berlin.

Brandbergen bei Halle; that same year another one was completed on the "Holy Mountain" (Heiliger Berg), near Heidelberg. In 1935, 10 *Thing* places were opened. The ideal form for the *Thing* play was thought to be CHORAL PO-ETRY, for with the use of the choir the "*Volk* Community" could be celebrated particularly well. The presentations were less a matter of drama than of ritual, and the spoken word was not so much dialogue as a confession-like procla-mation. To this extent the *Thing* plays represent-ed another variety of the NS CELEBRATIONS; the terms "cult play" and "cult place" were often used for their *Thing* equivalents.

Yet it was precisely the "cultic" character of such performances that soon cooled the interest of the public. The choral presentations offered little action, and there was a dearth of good and gripping plays. Joseph Goebbels, who had en-couraged the *Thing* movement by means of a "Reich league," in 1935 forbade the use of the terms "cult" and "*Thing.*" The "*Thing* places" were henceforth to be known as "open-air stag-es" (*Freilichtbühnen*). At the time of the Olym-pic Games in 1936, the Dietrich Eckart Stage (today the Waldbühne) in Berlin was inaugurat-ed with Eberhard Wolfgang Möller's *Franken-burger Würfenspiel* (Frankenburg Dice Game), but in 1937 Goebbels halted his promotion of the *Thing* movement.

K. V.

Third Reich (*Drittes Reich*), at first the self-designation of the National Socialist state, it has now become the standard term for the epoch in German history extending from 1933 to 1945. The National Socialists borrowed the phrase in the 1920s from the title of a 1923 book by Arthur MOELLER VAN DEN BRUCK. Initially, they meant to imply a continuity from the First Reich, the Holy Roman Empire of the German nation (962 to 1806), to the Second Reich, the Hohenzollern empire (1871 to 1918), to the Third Reich, the coming rule of Hitler. The Weimar period was considered an INTERIM REICH. (*See also* DEUTSCHES REICH.)

But at the same time, the National Socialists linked the concept to medieval Christian ex-pectations of salvation, which longed for a third kingdom of the Holy Spirit as the fulfillment of human and world history, after the first king-dom of the Father and the second of the Son. It would be the epoch when ideas and reality would be reconciled. This prophetic concept has often been borrowed and transformed, as in the work of the Norwegian dramatist Henrik Ibsen, who fused antiquity and Christianity. The hope for eternity (*see* THOUSAND-YEAR REICH) was combined with the notion, as was the call for a messiah, which was the way NS propaganda portrayed Hitler.

Yet as useful as the slogan of a Third Reich was during the period of the acquisition of power, it wore out quickly when confronted with the reality of National Socialism in prac-tice; indeed, it invited scorn. The Propaganda Ministry thus prohibited the term's use by the German press on July 10, 1939. On March 21, 1942, it was announced that in future, just as the British used the term "Empire," "the term 'Das Reich' [would] be used" to show "the world at large the new Germany with all its possessions as a united national unit [*geschlos-sene staatliche Einheit*]." A numbered Reich no longer suited National Socialism's imperial con-cept of itself as the culmination of German history.

Thorak, Josef, b. Salzburg, February 2, 1889; d. Hartmannsberg (Upper Bavaria), February 26, 1952, German sculptor. Thorak was initially influenced by Auguste Rodin. He was successful in the 1920s with neoclassical sculptures and busts, for which he was awarded the State Prize of the Prussian Academy of Arts in 1928. His monumental, grandiose sculptures—primarily nudes in bronze and marble, the men bulging with muscles, the women submissive and "heavy-hipped"—made Thorak, next to Arno BREKER, the sculptor most esteemed and pro-

Josef Thorak (right) and Albert Speer.

moted by National Socialist leaders. Hitler himself selected statues by Thorak for an award as examples of "healthy Nordic eroticism," and had a huge studio set up for him, where Thorak could create his oversized (up to 16 meters [over 50 feet] in height) heroic figures to grace such large-scale projects as the Reich Sports Field and the Autobahn. Thorak, who had served the NS state with conviction, was classified as "exonerated" by a Munich appeals board, and was able to work again after the war, even on official projects.

H. H.

Thought. *See* Idea.

Thousand-Year Reich (*Tausendjähriges Reich*), in the philosophy of history of the Christian Middle Ages, the reign of Christ after the first "resurrection of the righteous," anticipated as the THIRD REICH of the Holy Spirit. National Socialist propaganda fashioned the term into a catchword for the alleged completion of German history through National Socialism. Hitler himself rejected the expression, but at the Reich Party Congress in 1934 he proclaimed that "in the next thousand years [there would be] no more revolutions in Germany." Moreover, at the beginning of the Western Campaign (May 10, 1940), he said that the campaign would determine Germany's fate "for the next thousand years." Despite habituation to the inflated use of grandiose words, the term "Thousand-Year Reich" was often derided among the general public as ridiculous.

Three-Power Agreement (*Dreimächtepakt*), treaty agreement of 10 years' validity between Italy, Japan, and the German Reich; it came into being on Hitler's initiative on September 29, 1940. It promised to Germany hegemony over continental Europe (excluding the USSR); to Italy, over the Mediterranean area; and to Japan, over the "greater East Asian" area. The three powers committed themselves to use "all political, economic, and military means" in mutual support against aggressors who up until then had not been involved in the European and Asian (Sino-Japanese) wars. Directed particularly against the United States, the agreement supplemented the ANTI-COMINTERN PACT. The initial three signatories were joined by Hungary (November 20, 1940), Romania (November 23, 1940), Slovakia (November 24, 1941), and Bulgaria (March 1, 1941). Yugoslavia signed the agreement on March 25, 1941, but withdrew on March 27 after a coup in Belgrade, thus contributing to the unleashing of the BALKAN CAMPAIGN. The autonomous Croatian state that resulted from Germany's invasion signed the agreement on June 15, 1941.

The hoped-for culmination of the Three-Power Agreement was to be its signing by the Soviet Union, whose relations with the three powers were expressly excluded from the agreement. This possibility foundered during Viacheslav Molotov's visit to Berlin on November 12–13, 1940. Although war between the United States and Japan broke out after the attack on Pearl Harbor (December 7, 1941), Germany and Italy themselves declared war on the United States on

After the signing of the Three-Power Agreement, von Ribbentrop reads a clarification by the Reich government. Next to Ribbentrop: Hitler, Count Ciano, and the Japanese ambassador, Kurusu.

December 11, while Japan made use of the provisions of the agreement and stayed out of the Russo-German war. On January 18, 1942, the pact was supplemented with a military agreement, and on June 2 of that year, with economic provisions. But it collapsed in September 1943 with Italy's unilateral armistice, and on May 9, 1945, with Germany's capitulation, which Tokyo characterized as a "breach of treaty." It formally ended with the Japanese capitulation of September 2, 1945.

Thule Society (Thule-Gesellschaft), cover and successor organization, similar to the Freemasons, to the Germanic Order (Germanenorden); it was founded by Rudolf von Sebottendorff in 1918. The Thule Society strove to rally all nationalist and *völkisch* groups and subgroups in Bavaria. It was involved in the founding of FREE CORPS after the First World War to fight the Bavarian republic of councils (*Räterepublik*), and it published antisemitic propaganda in its newspaper, the *Münchner Beobachter* (Munich Observer), established in 1918 and the precursor of the NSDAP's VÖLKISCHER BEOBACHTER.

The membership of the Thule Society amounted at times to 1,500, and included Dietrich ECKART, Alfred ROSENBERG, Rudolf HESS, Anton DREXLER, and Gottfried FEDER. The society tried to gain influence in working-class circles through the GERMAN WORKERS' PARTY, but it also gave financial support to other *völkisch* groups. Altogether, the Thule Society was one of the most important organizational precursors of the NSDAP, although the National Socialists resolutely suppressed and eliminated its influence.

Thyssen, Fritz, b. Styrum bei Mühlheim/Ruhr, November 9, 1873; d. Buenos Aires, February 8, 1951, German industrialist. After the death of his father, August, the founder of the family firm, Fritz Thyssen took over its management. That same year the Thyssen concern merged into the United Steel Works, Inc. (Vereinigte Stahlwerke AG). Thyssen headed the board of directors until 1935. Already a zealous nationalist, in 1923 he had 100,000 gold marks given to Erich LUDENDORFF, then Hitler's comrade-in-arms. Until 1933 Thyssen remained one of the largest financiers of the NSDAP and its promoters (above all, Hermann Göring), although he himself joined the party only on March 1, 1933.

Along with Emil KIRDORF, Thyssen helped Hitler open the doors to heavy industry along the Rhine and Ruhr rivers, and assisted in smoothing his path to the chancellorship. Al-

Fritz Thyssen.

though Thyssen's services to National Socialism were recognized (in 1933 Göring made him a Prussian state councillor, and on November 12, 1933, he became a Reichstag deputy), after 1935 there were clear differences of opinion between him and the regime.

As a champion of corporatist ideas in the economy (*see* ECONOMY UNDER NATIONAL SOCIALISM, THE; CORPORATIST STATE), Thyssen turned against the extensive rearmament policy of the National Socialists and their persecution of Jews. The GERMAN-SOVIET NONAGGRESSION PACT then led to the final break. Thyssen emigrated to Switzerland on September 2, 1939 (whereupon his assets in Germany were confiscated), and then to France in 1940, where his memoirs, titled *I Paid Hitler*—a controversial historical source—were published. He and his wife were arrested in Vichy France in 1941. They were handed over to Germany and placed in a concentration camp. After denazification proceedings in 1948, in which he was classified as a "minor offender," Thyssen emigrated to Argentina.

R. S.

Time of Struggle (*Kampfzeit*), in National Socialist usage, a retrospective term for the years before the Seizure of Power; it was also used to refer to the activities of Austrian National Socialism up to the ANSCHLUSS. The Time of Struggle was stylized as the continuation of the FRONT EXPERIENCE and was intended to evoke an NS "combat community" (*Kampfgemeinschaft*). After the victory within Germany it

Group photo from the Time of Struggle. First row, from the left: Himmler, Frick, Hitler, von Epp, Göring. Second row, from the left: Mutschmann, Goebbels, Schaub. In back: K. Fritsch.

would become the vehicle for new German greatness abroad, thus recapturing the lost victory of the First World War and wiping out the "ignominy of Versailles." The cult of the OLD COMBATANTS served the same goal; the fact that they had survived the harsh "selection" proc-

ess of the Time of Struggle justified their "political leadership." The history of the Time of Struggle was one of the main topics of political schooling. Its central event, the failed HITLER PUTSCH of November 8–9, 1923, was celebrated yearly with the memorial march to the FELDHERRNHALLE. This glorification gave the Time of Struggle a nostalgic aura of the "good old days" that party circles were fond of cultivating, especially during the war years.

Tischgespräche. *See* Table Talks.

Tiso, Jozef, b. Velka Bytča, October 13, 1887; d. Pressburg, April 18, 1947 (executed), Slovak politician. A priest, in 1918 Tiso helped found the Slovak People's Party. In 1925 he was its representative in the Prague parliament, and in 1927–1928 he served as Czechoslovakia's minister of health. After the MUNICH AGREEMENT, Tiso became president of an autonomous SLOVAKIA on October 6, 1938. When the Prague government declared him deposed on March 10, 1939, he placed Slovakia under German protection and proclaimed its independence on March 14.

Subsequently, Tiso became Slovakia's president on October 26, 1939, and a willing and compliant assistant of Berlin. He joined the Three-Power Pact and the Anti-Comintern Pact, supplied troops for the German campaign against Russia, and did not resist including his country in the FINAL SOLUTION of the Jewish question. During the Slovak uprising of August 1944, he supported its suppression by the SS.

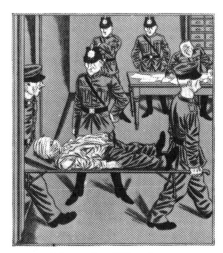

Time of Struggle, "Was the man run over by a car?" "No, by the National Socialists." Cartoon from *Simplicissimus*, 1932.

Jozef Tiso in his study.

Tiso fled to the West on April 5, 1945; he fell into Allied captivity, and was extradited to Czechoslovakia. Indicted in December 1946, he was sentenced to death for high treason and executed.

Tito, Josip (b. Josip Broz), b. Kumrovec (Croatia), May 25, 1892; d. Ljubljana, May 4, 1980, Yugoslav marshal (1943) and politician. Originally a mechanic, Tito fought in the Austrian army in the First World War. He was a Russian prisoner of war from 1915 to 1917, and after the Russian Revolution he joined the Red Army. Returning to the new state of YUGOSLAVIA in 1920, he helped to found the Yugoslav Communist Party (KPY). In 1927 Tito became a trade union secretary, but in 1928 he was arrested; he spent the years until 1934 in prison. Upon his release, he emigrated. In Moscow he became a member of the exiled Politburo of the KPY in 1934 and its secretary general in 1937. Between 1936 and 1938 Tito recruited volunteers for the International Brigades in the SPANISH CIVIL WAR, and himself fought against Franco. Returning to Yugoslavia before the outbreak of the Second World War, after the German BALKAN CAMPAIGN he organized the struggle of the PARTISANS against the occupying forces.

Together with bourgeois politicians, Tito formed a provisional Yugoslav government in 1943. He became prime minister and head of state of the Federative People's Republic of Yugoslavia after a bloody settling of accounts with collaborators and after ousting bourgeois elements from the government. Designated as president in 1953 (in 1963 he was made presi-

Josip Tito.

dent for life), Tito kept his unstable multiethnic state together by virtue of his personal authority and his prestige as the liberator from foreign fascist tyranny. His disengagement from Soviet patronage in 1948 contributed further to his popularity, as did his neutral political line between East and West and his avoidance of collectivization and a radical planned economy.

Tobruk, port city in Libya, fortified by the Italians as a fortress; the British took it on January 22, 1941. It was won back by Gen. Erwin Rommel during the AFRICAN CAMPAIGN on June 21, 1942, and on November 13 of that year was retaken by the British Eighth Army.

Todt, Fritz, b. Pforzheim, September 4, 1891; d. near Rastenburg (East Prussia), February 8, 1942, German engineer and politician. After studies in underground mining, Todt served as an officer in the First World War. He joined the NSDAP on January 5, 1922, and in 1931 was admitted to the SS supreme command as a *Standartenführer.* On July 5, 1933, he was given the post of General Inspector for German Highways, which had been created a few days before. (On November 30, 1933, it was made a Supreme Reich Authority [*Oberste Reichsbehörde*].) In his capacity as general inspector, he was put in charge of building a network of highways (*see* AUTOBAHN). After being named Plenipotentiary for Regulating the Construction Industry (December 1938), Todt was effectively in charge of coordinating the entire German construction industry as part of the FOUR-YEAR PLAN. For this purpose he made use of the TODT ORGANIZATION, which he had founded to accomplish the building of the WESTWALL. Todt's authority was broadened on March 17, 1940, to include management of the entire WAR ECONOMY when he became head of the Reich Ministry for Armaments and Munitions. In 1941 he was also made General Inspector for Water and Energy Resources.

Todt and his organization were active throughout the occupied territories. He began by building the so-called Atlantic Wall from the North Cape to southern France; he further adapted the Russian railroad system to the German broad-gauge track, and undertook to repair streets and bridges that had been destroyed. As an SS-*Obergruppenführer* he held a high rank in the party hierarchy as well as in the military (in which he was a Luftwaffe major general). The reticent technocrat avoided involvement in the daily political routine. At the

Fritz Todt.

end of 1941 he viewed the war situation as being extremely critical. After a visit to the Führer's "Wolfsschanze" headquarters, Todt lost his life in an airplane accident. He was given a state funeral in Berlin with Hitler present. Todt's successor in nearly all his offices and as minister was Albert SPEER.

Todt Organization (Organisation Todt; O.T.), state construction organization, named after its director, Fritz TODT. Established in 1938 for the construction of military facilities, the O.T. was especially active in the occupied areas, both shortly before and during the war. One of the principal reasons for its creation was the need to make use of the numerous service obligations of workers and employees and the commissioning of private construction firms, according to the Ordinance for "Securing the Required Forces for Tasks of Special National Political Responsibility." These were first employed in the construction of the WESTWALL in 1938–1939.

Beginning with the onset of the war, the O.T. was used primarily for reconstructing streets, bridges, and railroad lines destroyed in the conflict. After Todt's appointment as Reich Minister for Armaments and Munitions in 1940, the O.T. was increasingly utilized as a construction unit for military-related projects. Ultimately, it was placed under the authority of the Wehrmacht's engineer units. The O.T. workers wore uniforms and were under quasi-military discipline. At construction sites in the occupied areas and in the Reich, the organization also employed hundreds of thousands of foreign civilian workers and prisoners of war (*see* ALIEN WORKERS); in places close to concentration camps, it used the slave labor of Jews and other inmates.

Todt's extensive administrative authority derived from a number of positions, including those of General Inspector of German Highways, General Plenipotentiary for the Regulation of the Construction Industry, and Reich Minister. This placed his organization in an extraordinarily strong position that was largely free of bureaucratic encumbrances. Such an advantage made the O.T.—above all because

Todt Organization workers building a bridge in Russia.

of its great efficiency in carrying out its construction assignments—one of the most important specialized organizations in the Third Reich.

R. S.

Toller, Ernst, b. Samotchin bei Bromberg, December 1, 1893; d. New York City, May 22, 1939, German writer. The experiences of the First World War made Toller a firm pacifist. As a member of the Independent Socialists (USPD) and a representative of an idealistic socialism, he was a leader of the 1918 revolution in Munich (the "revolution of love"). After Kurt Eisner's assassination, he became head of state of the Bavarian republic of councils (*Räterepublik*). Toller contributed to the failure of that republic with his romantic unworldliness. During the next five years, which he spent confined in a fortress, he wrote a series of pacifist and socially critical works, notably the drama *Der deutsche Hinkemann* (translated as *Hinkemann*; 1923). His play *Der entfesselte Wotan* (Wotan Unfettered; 1923), a satirical story of a swindling hairdresser, anticipated the rise of Hitler. Toller also contributed to such leftist journals as *Die* WELTBÜHNE. Deprived of his citizenship in 1933, he emigrated to the United States. The consolidation of the National Socialist dictator-

Ernst Toller. "Wanted" notice in the *Bavarian Police Gazette*, May 15, 1919: "10,000-mark reward. For high treason."

ship in Germany made him question the sense of his own peaceful policy and ultimately drove him to suicide.

Torchlight parade (*Fackelzug*), custom of honoring "worthy" personages that was encouraged by the National Socialists. With allusions to the cults of antiquity, in which the torch was an "emblem of deities," masses of people holding lighted wax or pitch torches were intended to present an image that was especially imposing, solemn, and impressive to the onlookers. The best-known example was the "Honoring of the Führer" with a torchlight parade on the evening of January 30, 1933.

Torgau, *Kreis* (district) administrative center on the Elbe River, between Dessau and Dresden, with 17,700 inhabitants in 1942. In Torgau, on April 25, 1945, at about 4:00 p.m., troops of the Soviet First Ukrainian Front and those of the Sixty-ninth United States Infantry Division made contact, thereby cutting the remainder of the German theater of military operations in two parts. Torgau is officially considered the first point of contact by the Allies, although several hours earlier (at 11:30 a.m.) another American patrol had met Red Army troops near Strehla, 30 km (about 18 miles) south of Torgau. However, it had not been able to report this because of defective wireless equipment. Subsequently, for symbolic reasons, the middle of the Elbe was chosen as the place for the meeting, rather than the actual spot (the eastern shore).

Totalitarianism (*Totalitarismus*), scholarly term and political catchword to denote political systems that are characterized by the (forcible) synchronization of all social, cultural, and individual manifestations in accordance with a prescribed ideology. The term arose in the 1920s with the criticism of Italian FASCISM and of its claim to total authority. Using it in a positive sense, Mussolini appropriated it for his dictatorship, wanting thereby to emphasize its "inexorable, totalitarian determination." After the practical experience of Bolshevist Stalinism and of German NATIONAL SOCIALISM (to which Carl SCHMITT and Ernst FORSTHOFF, among others, applied the term), the Italian version seems to have been a preliminary form, since it did not attempt to eliminate pluralist elements related to the crown and the church. Even National Socialist totalitarianism manifested intentionally cultivated gaps in its internal party "polycracy." These then required decisions by

Torgau. Meeting of American and Soviet soldiers.

Hitler to bridge, thus introducing an element of occasionalism [a doctrine that intervention from on high is required for mind and matter to affect each other] into the seemingly monolithic Führer State.

The term "totalitarianism" must therefore be applied only with a sense of nuance, even to its prototypes. The polemical misuse of the term (especially in the East-West confrontations after 1945) and the divergence in theories of totalitarianism have led to a loss of the term's meaningfulness. The placing of systems as divergent in substance as Bolshevism and National Socialism under this common rubric has facilitated impermissible equations (red equaling brown) and has undermined the objective basis for the discussion of totalitarianism. The lowest common denominator of its definition would today include the following features: an all-embracing worldview and its implementation by the terroristic means of a police state; a planned economy; one-party rule; censorship; a monopoly on weapons; and revolution from above.

Total War (*Totaler Krieg*), term coined by Erich LUDENDORFF to denote the intensification of warfare, which demanded "literally the total strength of a people" (*Der Totaler Krieg* [translated as *The Nation at War*]; 1935). The concept of total war was disseminated by means of the SPORTS PALACE SPEECH of Propaganda Minister

Joseph Goebbels on February 18, 1943. The speech had been preceded by Hitler's January 13 order for a "total mobilization" and by a regulation issued on January 27 by the plenipotentiary for labor deployment, Fritz SAUCKEL, "regarding the reporting of men and women for assignments in defense of the Reich." As a result, a "service duty" was imposed on men between the ages of 16 and 65 and women from 17 to 45, with some exemptions (such as pregnancy). The Reich Economics Ministry, moreover, on February 4, 1943, ordered the closing of all militarily nonessential industries and of all restaurants. Working shifts in the armaments industry gradually increased to 12 and more hours daily, and the forced recruitment of ALIEN WORKERS reached new heights.

Cultural life largely came to a halt, insofar as it was not essential to the maintenance of working and fighting morale. In order to carry out the measures for total war, the WARTIME SPECIAL CRIMINAL LAW was made harsher, and more and more statutory offenses were sentenced as instances of UNDERMINING OF MILITARY STRENGTH or were punished according to the September 5, 1939, regulations against VOLK VERMIN.

With the proclaiming of total war, the German military command, which had already overstepped all the rules of war—in particular in the east—totally severed ties to INTERNATIONAL

Total War. Goebbels's Sports Palace Speech, February 18, 1943. The banner reads: "Total War—Shortest War!"

LAW and the GENEVA CONVENTIONS. The peak of total war was reached in 1944, when Goebbels was made General Plenipotentiary for the Total War Effort (*Generalbevollmächtigter für den totalen Kriegseinsatz*). He sought to mobilize the last reserves with every possible propaganda tool (including the promise of WONDER WEAPONS) and with disciplinary measures (including CLAN LIABILITY, which provided for the imprisonment of relatives). This effort led to senseless losses among soldiers (*see* VOLK STORM) and civilians. The latter were exposed to the Allied AIR WAR, which at least in part was a response to Germany's declaration of total war.

Totenkopfverbände. *See* Death's-Head Units.

Trade Union Axis (*Gewerkschaftsachse*), designation for a plan of Gen. Kurt von SCHLEICHER in late 1932 that was intended to thwart both a National Socialist seizure of power and any putschist intentions of the Reich chancellor at the time, Franz von PAPEN. The idea of such an axis arose from the recognition that (1) in the long run no policy would be feasible that was opposed by the workers, and (2) given the inability of the parties to form a coalition, an agreement might be reached among their associations and workers' branches. Schleicher envisioned an axis extending from the Social Democratic GENERAL GERMAN TRADE UNION FEDERATION (ADGB) to the Christian trade unions, and all the way to the left wing of the NSDAP.

Schleicher proposed the plan to Reich President Paul von Hindenburg on December 1, 1932, but first promoted it actively when Papen could find little cabinet support for his manipulations of the constitution. On December 3,

Schleicher himself became chancellor, but his attempts to sell Hitler on the idea fell on deaf ears. Schleicher then attempted to split the NSDAP and ally himself with Gregor STRASSER, who did support the plan. Strasser, however, was unable to prevail against Hitler, and consequently relinquished all his party offices on December 8. On the political Left, the ADGB finally rejected the axis under pressure from the Social Democratic Party (SPD), which categorically refused to enter in an alliance with the authoritarian general. Thus in January 1933 Schleicher faced the same dilemma that Papen had earlier, and now proposed in his turn a solution by force, which the Reich president then turned down. The path to Hitler's SEIZURE OF POWER was open.

Trade Union Federation of Employees (Gewerkschaftsbund der Angestellten; G. d. A.), organization close to the GERMAN DEMOCRATIC PARTY (DDP) that represented the interests of sales, technical, and office employees. The federation lost significance along with the DDP. Like all the trade unions, it was crushed on May 2, 1933, and on May 10 it was absorbed into the GERMAN LABOR FRONT.

Trade unions (*Gewerkschaften*), organizations of employees that arose in the 19th century in order to fight for the economic and social interests of wage earners. The German unions, after a wartime "truce" in 1914, first obtained state recognition in 1916 and experienced rapid growth after the end of the First World War. By far the largest group consisted of the Social Democratic–oriented Free Trade Unions (Freie Gewerkschaften), which were united in the GEN-

ERAL GERMAN TRADE UNION FEDERATION (ADGB). In 1923 the ADGB expanded to include the AFABUND. In addition, there were the Christian trade unions, the liberal Hirsch-Duncker trade unions, and other smaller groups.

In the first years of the Weimar Republic, the influence and membership (over 10 million) of the unions grew, marked by the recognition of the right to bargain for wage agreements, the final establishment of the eight-hour day, and the unified rebuff of the KAPP PUTSCH through a general strike in 1920. This trend reversed itself when, with the incipient world economic crisis (1930–1932), employment declined and many social gains were cut back (by 1932 there were fewer than 7 million organized workers and employees). The partisan trade unions, bound by political and ideological ties, were unable to work their way through to a common position, even in the face of threats posed by the emerging Communist and fascist rivals, including the NATIONAL SOCIALIST WORKPLACE CELL ORGANIZATION (NSBO).

The ADGB still had 4.6 million members in 1931 and it was a participant in the militant organization of the IRON FRONT, but it lost its room for maneuvering both in terms of wages and in politics, and it rejected the TRADE UNION AXIS planned by Chancellor Kurt von SCHLEICHER. Since a common front with the Communists was completely ruled out, nearly all the trade unions sought to reach some arrangement with the National Socialists after the Seizure of Power, despite all the warning signs.

Although the so-called people's houses (Volkshäuser) of the Free Trade Unions were occupied by the SA as early as March 8–9, 1933, the ADGB leadership undertook talks with the NSBO. The workplace council (Betriebsrat) elections of April 1933, which resulted in 73.4 percent for the Free Trade Unions and only 11.7 percent for the NSBO, lulled the union functionaries into a sense of security, while leading to an acceleration of the National Socialist plans for the "crushing" of the unions. As a clever gambit, it was announced that May 1 would be elevated to the status of a "Day of National Labor" (Tag der nationalen Arbeit; see MAY HOLIDAY), something expressly welcomed by the ADGB and for which the labor movement had struggled for generations.

Yet on April 21, 1933, even before the parades began, an order was issued to the SA and the SS "for occupying the trade union headquarters and taking into protective custody the persons under suspicion," with the planned

date of "Tuesday, May 2, 1933, at 10:00 a.m." The SYNCHRONIZATION of the unions was punctually carried out, and encountered only negligible resistance. An Action Committee for the Protection of German Labor, previously formed under Robert LEY, took over the offices. On May 10 the GERMAN LABOR FRONT (DAF) was founded; on May 12 the assets of the unions were confiscated on grounds of alleged irregularities. Finally, all the workers' organizations were incorporated into the DAF on June 28, as were all employee organizations on July 1.

Treblinka, one of the extermination camps of the REINHARD OPERATION, in the scope of the "Final Solution of the Jewish question." The construction of Treblinka, located north of Warsaw, was begun in late May and early June 1942 under the supervision of the SS Central Construction Division of the SS and Police Leader of Warsaw. The work force consisted of Poles and Jews, some of whom were inmates of nearby work camps. When completed, the camp consisted of three parts: (1) the living area (Wohnlager, or residential camp), which included SS quarters, service buildings, barracks for Polish and Ukrainian workers and for Jewish prisoners, stables, and a zoo; (2) the reception area (Auffanglager) for the arriving Jews, which included the railroad ramp, the reception square, a barrack for the articles taken from the Jews, barracks for undressing, a "selection" area (see SELEKTION), and an "infirmary" (Lazarett); and, finally, (3) the so-called upper or "death camp" (Totenlager), which included gas chambers, pits, lodging for the Jewish Sonderkommando (special commando), and, later, cremation facilities.

The camp staff consisted of about 40 Germans and approximately 120 Ukrainian VOLUNTEER HELPERS. The latter served primarily as guards, but they were also utilized in the extermination of the Jews. The camp's first commandant was Irmfried EBERL, who was removed from his post for "unfitness" after a few weeks. He was succeeded by Franz STANGL, who was later promoted to SS-Hauptsturmführer. Finally, in August 1943, Kurt Hubert FRANZ assumed the leadership post at Treblinka.

The camp was "ready for operation" (betriebsbereit) in July 1942. Beginning on July 23, transports of Jews arrived continuously, especially from Warsaw and the surrounding district, the "catchment area" (Einzugsgebiet) for Treblinka. The extermination process was similar to that of Bełżec and Sobibór. After their arrival

Treblinka. Model of the reception area.

the Jews were separated into groups on the square of the reception camp: men, and women and children. They were informed that they would be transported further to work camps, but that they first had to bathe, hand over their clothes and luggage for disinfection, and leave any gold, money, foreign currency, and jewelry at the cashier's office for security reasons.

The women and children were then taken to a barrack, where they were told to undress for a "shower." The men waited in front of the barrack until the women and children had been driven with clubs, whips, and rifle butts by German and Ukrainian members of the camp staff through the "tube" (*Schlauch*; also called the "road to Heaven" ["Himmelfahrtstrasse"] or the "path with no return" ["Weg ohne Rückkehr"])—a narrow fenced-in passage leading from the reception camp to the "death camp"— and into the gas chambers. After the women and children had been gassed and the gas chambers had been cleared, the men, who meanwhile had undressed themselves, were in their turn flogged into the "death camp." There they were either gassed or were shot at the pits situated there for corpses. Sick and frail Jews were taken to the "infirmary," which was marked with a red cross and surrounded by a high barbed-wire fence into which brushwood had been interwoven to conceal the area within. Inside was a large pit, in which a fire burned almost continuously. The sick people were shot and thrown into the pit.

From time to time the SS separated out men—

more rarely women—who were capable of work, to form labor units for work inside the camp. They included "court Jews" (*Hofjuden*), who worked as craftsmen in the SS workshops; "gold Jews" (*Goldjuden*), who sorted and packed valuables and foreign currency; sorting squads, who sorted and stacked the clothing that had been left behind; and "dentists," who removed gold teeth from the corpses. All had to carry out their tasks under constant abuse. Especially feared was the last commandant, Franz, whose dog, "Barry," attacked prisoners on command and injured them severely. To be conspicuous in any way meant punishment, "normally" death. Otherwise, there were constant *Selektionen* among the workers; those weeded out were for the most part shot in the "infirmary."

The gassing, by means of exhaust fumes from truck motors, initially took place in three small gas chambers; in September 1942 the capacity was considerably enlarged by the construction of larger chambers. At least three huge pits had been dug for the corpses of the Jews who were killed. When Treblinka was to be disbanded, the EXHUMATION OPERATION began: two installations for burning were constructed from railroad tracks, and the dug-up corpses as well as the new ones were burned on them. A rebellion by the inmates on August 2, 1943, accelerated the dissolution of the camp. The buildings were torn down, the entire camp area was leveled, and lupine was sown. A peasant farmstead was built with the bricks from the gas chambers; it was to be managed by members of the Ukrainian guard staff. The last (30, at the most) Jews in the labor squads were shot on November 17, 1943, and their bodies were burned on makeshift grates. At the end of that month the camp was disbanded and its staff was transferred to Trieste.

At least 700,000 Jews were killed in Treblinka.

A. St.

Trenker, Luis, b. Sankt Ulrich (South Tyrol), October 4, 1892; d. Bolzano (Italy), April 13, 1990, Austrian film director, actor, and screenwriter. After playing leading roles in films involving mountains, such as *Der Kampf ums Matterhorn* (The Struggle for the Matterhorn; 1928), Trenker directed a series of movies that glorified nature, the homeland (*Heimat*), and Germanness (*Deutschtum*). *Der Rebell* (The Rebel; 1932) extolled the National Socialist movement and outlined the vision of a Great-German Reich through the example of the Tyrolean peasant rebellion against Napoleon's troops. Hitler saw the movie several times, and "each time found new pleasure" (*Film-Kurier*, August 23, 1933). In the 1930s Trenker was among the most patronized directors; his mountain, war, and history films, like those of Leni RIEFEN-STAHL, are characterized by "breathtakingly beautiful pictures." Trenker did not let himself be taken in by the goals of NS policies without contradiction; in 1940 he came into such sharp conflict with the regime that he was scarcely

Luis Trenker in the film *Berge in Flammen* (Mountains in Flame).

able to work until the end of the war. After 1945 he resumed his career of directing homeland films.

H. H.

Trepper, Leopold, b. Novy Tary (Neumarkt), February 23, 1904; d. Jerusalem, January 19, 1983, Polish journalist and secret agent. Trepper belonged to the Polish workers' movement from his youth, and was arrested for participating in workers' riots. He emigrated in 1925 to Palestine, where he helped found the Communist Party of Palestine and became a member of its directorate. The British expelled him for anti-English activities. Trepper was active in several places as a Communist party functionary, including France and the USSR. As a colonel in the Soviet secret service, he built up the successful RED ORCHESTRA espionage network in Brussels in 1938. Among other accomplishments, he was able to warn Moscow of the impending German attack in 1941, although his warning was not taken seriously.

The Gestapo arrested Trepper on November 27, 1942. He pretended to switch sides, and was able to escape in 1943. On returning to Moscow, however, he was imprisoned. He was rehabilitated only in 1954, after many years of imprisonment. In 1957 Trepper moved to Poland, where he worked as a journalist. By 1967–1968, he felt under such pressure from antisemitism that he finally emigrated to Jerusalem in 1975. He described his espionage work against the Third Reich in an autobiography that appeared in German in 1975, *Die Wahrheit—Ich war Chef der Roten Kapelle* (The Truth: I Was Chief of the Red Orchestra), and in memoirs published in English as *The Great Game: Memoirs of the Spy Hitler Couldn't Silence.*

Tresckow, Henning von, b. Magdeburg, January 10, 1901; d. near Białystok (Belorussia), July 21, 1944, German major general (January 30, 1944) and opposition fighter. Tresckow was an officer in the First World War. He then undertook studies in banking, but joined the Reichswehr in 1924. He initially welcomed the National Socialist takeover of power, but distanced himself from the movement as early as the aftermath of the RÖHM AFFAIR (June 30, 1934). He broke with the National Socialists completely after the KRISTALLNACHT pogrom (November 9–10, 1938), which led him to consider a removal of Hitler from power by political means. In the course of the war this thought solidified into

Henning von Tresckow.

the conviction that only the killing of the tyrant could prevent Germany's moral and military downfall.

At the beginning of the war, Tresckow was an officer with the General Staff. With the help of Fabian von SCHLABRENDORFF, he organized an attack on Hitler's airplane on March 13, 1943. However, the time fuse did not work. After further assassination attempts failed, Tresckow (since November 20, 1943, chief of staff of the Second Army) agreed to Claus von STAUFFEN-BERG's plan for a *coup d'état*. When this too failed on July 20, 1944, and the outlook for a deliverance from National Socialism by their own power seemed hopeless, Tresckow chose suicide.

Treviranus, Gottfried, b. Schieder (Lippe), March 20, 1891; d. near Florence, June 7, 1971, German politician. A naval officer in the First World War, Treviranus then studied agricultural science. In 1924 he joined the German National People's Party (DNVP), but he resigned from the party in 1929 in disagreement over its opposition to the YOUNG PLAN, and founded the People's Conservative Union (Volkskonservative Vereinigung). Although this party had only the status of a splinter group during the 1930 Reichstag elections, Chancellor Heinrich BRÜNING brought Treviranus into his cabinet as minister for the occupied territories and Reich commissioner for implementation of the EAST-ERN AID program. Treviranus was among the closest associates of the chancellor and was his personal friend. He became transportation minister in Brüning's second cabinet. Both men left the political arena together in 1932, and both were put on the National Socialist "hit list." Treviranus barely escaped Hermann Gö-ring's hatchet men during the so-called RÖHM AFFAIR (June 30, 1934). He fled to Great Britain, and from there to the United States, returning to Germany in 1949. His memoirs, *Das Ende von Weimar* (The End of Weimar), were published in 1968.

Trianon, pleasure palaces in the park at Versailles. In the Grand Trianon, built in 1687–1688, a peace treaty was signed on June 4, 1920, between the Allied powers of the First World War and Hungary as a legal successor to the Danubian monarchy, and as such, a defeated state. The Peace of Trianon was modeled on the VERSAILLES TREATY, with a war-guilt clause, restrictions on armaments, and obligations regarding reparations and territorial cessions. Violating the right to SELF-DETERMINATION OF PEO-PLES, the treaty assigned 60 percent of the Hungarian population to foreign states. As a result, Hungarian policies were shaped by demands for revision well into the Second World War, and they brought the country close to Fascist Italy and National Socialist Germany.

Triumph of the Will (*Triumph des Willens*), slogan of the 1934 Reich Party Congress (*Reichsparteitag*) and the title of a film by Leni RIEFEN-STAHL, who received the National Film Prize for it for 1934–1935. Joseph Goebbels called the propaganda work, which Hitler had personally commissioned, a "great film vision of the Füh-rer, who appears here for the first time graphically, with a forcefulness that has never before been seen." The film also received numerous foreign prizes, including that of the Venice Film Festival. Its production involved the work of 30 cameramen and a multitude of extras.

Like the party congress, *Triumph des Willens* was completely cut to Hitler's measure. His "liberating deed" in the recent RÖHM AFFAIR was particularly emphasized in order to demonstrate the movement's cohesiveness. Hitler's arrival by airplane in Nuremberg appeared as an epiphany of a higher being. That which appeared distant and small from the perspective of the participants at the congress grew in the film into an overwhelming center of attention demanding veneration: the "Führer" holding a military review before never-ending marching columns, surrounded by fluttering banners, illuminated with the light from torches and floodlights. *Triumph des Willens* became an impressive document of the FÜHRER CULT.

Trivialliteratur (light fiction), a type of writing, published in mass editions, that was stereotyped in content and form. In the Weimar Republic it enjoyed wide circulation, particularly in cheap paperbacks; bourgeois critics and educators attacked it as "filth and trash." Initially rejected in the Third Reich, *Trivialliteratur* was soon discovered by propagandists to be useful. It was then justified, as in the case of adventure stories, which represented "a first step toward the heroic, . . . insofar as a life of danger . . . is being lived in the service of an idea, a task, a community" (Eduard Rothemund). After the war began, Joseph Goebbels devoted "Weeks of the German Book" to the promotion of light reading on the ground that the German *Volk* was "so run down by the serious business of war" that "relaxation had to be found in art" (*see* FILM).

Both National Socialist critics and the public praised books describing idyllic and unscathed worlds (as against everyday reality) as "good" light reading; examples were the humorous novels of Heinrich Spoerl, such as *Feuerzangenbowle* (Fire-Tong Punch; 1933), and Kurt KLUGE's *Der Herr Kortüm* (1938). Major publishers of cheap fiction such as Martin Kelter in Hamburg and Arthur Moewig in Dresden published millions of sentimental paperbacks every week on such themes as love and the homeland, up into the 1940s. The obligatory happy ending was now often presented as a reward for soldierly heroism or exemplary "German" conduct. Willingness to sacrifice and renunciation in favor of the community became the popular themes: "We must sacrifice much on the altar of the homeland" (Rudolf Utsch in *Heimkehr* [Return Home]; 1940). Besides the fiction paperbacks, serial novels in the popular illustrated magazines were also successfully used to propagate the NS worldview.

The borderline between light fiction and "high literature" (*Hochliteratur*) remained fluid because the *völkisch* works of the Third Reich often manifested hackneyed characteristics (*see* LITERATURE). Moreover, the National Socialists utilized the mediums and aesthetic standards of light fiction to create a new *völkisch* variety: series of softcover books with titles such as Aus Deutschlands Werden (From Germany's Becoming), Kleine Kriegshefte (Little War Booklets), and Junges *Volk* (Young *Volk*), which were to supplant less political homeland (*Heimat*) and adventure series. As a tool of literary propaganda, specific categories of "official light fiction" were initiated: softcover books with realistic or fantasy figures (such as the COAL THIEF), which were intended to demonstrate, for example, that happiness in love depends on properly observed air raid precautions. A similar official light fiction was created within and for NS organizations, such as the brochure sponsored by the German Labor Front: "Hau Ruck! Der Westwall steht! Unser Schachtmeister schreibt.

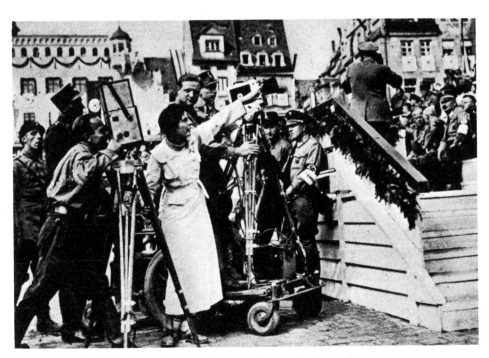

Triumph of the Will. Leni Riefenstahl during filming in Nuremberg.

Ein launiges Buch von den Männern mit Schippe und Hacke" ("Ho-heave-ho! The Westwall stands! Our crew foreman writes. A humorous Book about the Men with Shovels and Pickaxes").

H. H.

Trizone, unified economic region created by the addition of France to the BIZONE on April 8, 1949. This union of the American, British, and French occupation zones in Germany was the preliminary stage for the Federal Republic of Germany.

Troop recreation (*Truppenbetreuung*), entertainment and cultural program during the Second World War for frontline soldiers and those at the rear; it was directed by Hans HINKEL. Groups of singers, dancers, musicians, and actors were assembled and then brought by bus or train to individual frontline sectors or to the centers for German occupation troops throughout Europe. Even the most highly paid stars had to render this service, although less often because they were needed for films back home, and under less taxing conditions. Performances of particularly high quality were transmitted over the military broadcasting stations, and even the most remote combat areas were included by radio linkup. Soldiers exhausted by the daily grind of war took

in most programs with enthusiasm, and the leadership therefore promoted them in order to raise the fighting morale. Participants in the recreation program welcomed their assignment, since it freed them from military service and gave them the opportunity to buy (or obtain by barter) in the occupied territories goods that were in short supply at home. The preferred assignments were thus naturally in the West. The sentimental film *Fronttheater*, with René Deltgen and Heli Finkenzeller, was made on the subject of troop recreation. It premiered in movie theaters in October 1942, but did not attain the success of the feature film *Wunschkonzert* (REQUEST CONCERT), on a related theme.

Troost, Paul Ludwig, b. Elberfeld, August 17, 1878; d. Munich, January 21, 1934, German architect. Prior to 1914 Troost tended toward classical and traditional forms, in a desire to juxtapose a functional, non-ornamental architecture to the *Jugendstil* (German art nouveau). Hitler admired his work. In 1930 Troost drafted plans for an enlargement of the BROWN HOUSE for Hitler, as well as plans for the proposed HOUSE OF GERMAN ART in Munich. In part together with other National Socialist architects, he planned and built many administrative buildings and dwellings, as well as Autobahn

Troop recreation. Theater at the front.

Paul Ludwig Troost and Hitler at the laying of the foundation stone for the House of German Art.

bridges. Until Troost's death, Hitler often visited his office personally, to study and discuss the latest plans.

Trophy Commission (Trophäenkommission), colloquial term for the staff set up by the Soviet occupying power in the Soviet zone of defeated Germany for the purpose of confiscating private and public money and property for shipment to the USSR.

Trotha, Adolf von, b. Koblenz, March 1, 1868; d. Berlin, October 11, 1940, German vice admiral. Trotha joined the imperial navy in 1886. In 1900 he served during the Boxer Rebellion in China, and in the First World War he distinguished himself in the 1916 Battle of Skagerrak. Having risen to chief of staff of Germany's High Seas Fleet in the war, he retired from naval service in 1920. Trotha became leader of the Great-German Youth League and waged a struggle for a national restoration, as seen in his 1924 work, *Grossdeutsches Wollen* (Great-German Aspiration). Hoping that the National Socialists would restore Germany's position as a great power, in 1934 he let himself be enlisted in their rearmament campaign as chairman of the REICH LEAGUE FOR GERMAN NAVAL PRESTIGE.

Trott zu Solz, Adam von, b. Potsdam, August 9, 1909; d. Berlin-Plötzensee, September 26, 1944 (executed), German diplomat and opposition fighter. Trott zu Solz studied law, then spent a long sojourn in England as a Rhodes scholar. He returned to Germany in 1934 and became a judge's assistant (*Assessor*) in 1936. After further studies in East Asia and the United States, he entered the diplomatic service in the Foreign Ministry's information office in 1940.

Trott zu Solz rejected National Socialism because of his profoundly Christian outlook. He joined the KREISAU CIRCLE and used his broad international connections to solicit support and understanding for the German opposition. In July 1939 he met with British prime minister Neville Chamberlain, and in October of that year he tested the atmosphere in Washington. He met with British and American diplomats in Switzerland in 1943–1944, and made a final attempt to come to some agreement in June 1944 in Sweden. A patriot, Trott zu Solz wanted to obtain an honorable peace for a Germany liberated from National Socialism, and in seeking it he did not shy away from using even the "Soviet card." This, however, aroused suspicion. He was sentenced to death on August 15

Adam von Trott zu Solz.

after the failure of the coup attempt of July 20, 1944, having let go all the opportunities available to him of saving himself.

Truman, Harry S., b. Lamar (Missouri), May 8, 1884; d. Kansas City (Missouri), December 26, 1972, 33rd president of the United States (1945–1953). Truman served as an officer in France during the First World War, and subsequently became a haberdasher in Kansas City. After undergoing bankruptcy in 1921, he became a judge. In 1935 he was elected a Democratic senator from his home state; he was re-elected in 1940. Beginning in 1941 he headed the Truman Committee to control American military expenditures. On November 7, 1944, Truman was elected vice president, and as such he became Franklin D. ROOSEVELT's successor at the president's death on April 12, 1945. (He was re-elected in 1948.)

The change in presidents weakened the position of the United States at the time of the POTSDAM AGREEMENT, despite the successful first uses of the ATOMIC BOMB that Truman had ordered to be dropped on Hiroshima and Nagasaki in August 1945. In the ensuing Cold War, Truman followed the course of containing Soviet expansion; he strengthened the Western European states through economic assistance (the Marshall Plan) and through the founding of NATO (1949). Finally, in the Korean War, he resorted to military action to ward off communism.

Trustees of Labor (*Treuhänder* [or *Reichs-Treuhänder*] *der Arbeit*), members of a Reich Department for "Maintaining Labor Peace" under the authority of the Reich Labor Ministry; the position was established by the Law on Trustees of Labor of May 19, 1933. The LABOR REGULATION LAW of January 20, 1934, assigned them their functions as authorities for social control: the establishment of wage rates; the supervision of plant regulations; participation in the formation of MUTUAL TRUST COUNCILS; the supervision of dismissals, especially mass layoffs; and representation of the plaintiff in proceedings before the social HONOR COURTS. One trustee was assigned to each of the 14 economic regions (*Wirtschaftsgebiete*) of the Reich (by 1941 there were 22 such regions). The installation of trustees ended the autonomous setting of wage rates. National Socialist propaganda extolled their institution as a decisive step toward "overcoming class struggle" by "eliminating all one-sided interests."

Tschammer und Osten, Hans von, b. Dresden, October 25, 1887; d. Berlin, March 25, 1943, German politician. An intelligence officer in the First World War, Tschammer und Osten later engaged in agriculture at the ancestral estate of his parents. From 1923 to 1926, he served as leader of the Saxon YOUNG GERMAN ORDER, and in 1929 he joined the NSDAP. He became a Reichstag deputy on March 5, 1933. Hitler appointed Tschammer und Osten Reich Sports Commissioner with the assignment of synchronizing German SPORTS, a task he carried out without encountering major resistance. On July 14, 1933, he took over leadership of the German Gymnasts' League. He became *Reichssport-*

Hans von Tschammer und Osten.

führer on July 19, 1933, becoming head of the GERMAN REICH LEAGUE FOR PHYSICAL EXERCISES, which he made into the NATIONAL SOCIALIST REICH LEAGUE FOR PHYSICAL EXERCISES in 1938.

As "deputy for the total physical education of German youth," Tschammer und Osten supervised intraparty sports in the Hitler Youth and in the SA (as head of the Main Office for Competitive Games). As president of the Reich Academy for Physical Exercises, he implemented the National Socialist program of military sports in teacher training. He was president of the German Olympics Committee, and as such had considerable influence on the organizing of the Berlin OLYMPIC GAMES in 1936. After the Olympics, Tschammer und Osten devoted himself to the definitive elimination of Jewish athletes and to the allover physical-fitness training of the entire German *Volk* as head of the sports section of the STRENGTH THROUGH JOY German Labor Front agency.

Tucholsky, Kurt, b. Berlin, January 9, 1890; d. Hindas, near Göteborg (Sweden), December 21, 1935, German writer. After studying law, Tucholsky began his literary career in 1911 with commentaries, poems, and reviews for the Social Democratic Party (SPD) newspaper VORWÄRTS (Forward). His breakthrough came in 1912 with the amusing and playful summer sketch *Rheinsberg—Ein Bilderbuch für Verliebte* (Rheinsberg: A Picture Book for Lovers). He found his real stature as a satirist and political writer after a meeting with Siegfried Jacobsohn (1881–1926), who hired him for his journal *Schaubühne* (Theater; as of 1918 called *Die* WELTBÜHNE). (He briefly served as its editor in 1926.) Tucholsky became one of the journal's most productive contributors, hiding behind four pseudonyms to avoid authorial monotony (Peter Panter, Ignaz Wrobel, Kaspar Hauser, and Theobold Tiger).

After the war, Tucholsky gained prominence as a radical pacifist. He joined the Independent Socialists (USPD) in 1920, and then the SPD. He polemicized against the weaknesses of the Weimar Republic: its toleration and support for its own gravediggers in the guises of militarism, partisan justice, a radical right-wing press, philistinism, and nationalism. Tucholsky elaborated on this theme in collaboration with John HEARTFIELD in *Deutschland, Deutschland über alles!* (Germany, Germany above All!; 1929). With effervescent Berlin wit and biting mockery, he also turned against the rise of National Social-

Kurt Tucholsky.

ism, as in "Hitler und Goethe—Ein Schulauf-satz" (Hitler and Goethe: A School Essay; 1932), but with little result.

Tucholsky spent more and more time abroad, in order "to rest from my fatherland," and lived in Sweden beginning in 1929. His love story *Schloss Gripsholm* (*Gripsholm Castle*; 1931) was written there. On May 10, 1933, his writings were victims of the National Socialist BOOK BURNING, the more so because of his Jewish origins. He was deprived of his German citizenship on August 25 of that year, and thenceforth bitterly called himself a "discontinued German" (*aufgehörter Deutscher*). He sank into an increasingly deeper depression, and finally poisoned himself.

Turkey, republic in the Near East; area, 772,340 sq km (approximately 309,000 sq miles); population, about 13.6 million (1927). Turkish politics after the First World War was dominated by territorial issues. The dictated Peace of SÈVRES was revised through the Turkish-Greek war (1919–1922) and the Peace of Lausanne (July 24, 1923), which resulted in the expulsion of Greeks from Asia Minor and the regaining of eastern Thrace. On November 1, 1922, the Sultanate was abolished, and on October 29, 1923, the republic was proclaimed. Under its founding president, Kemal Atatürk (1923–1938), and his successor, INÖNÜ (1938–1950), Turkey underwent an unparalleled process of Europeanization, modernization, secularization, and the beginnings of industrialization. At the same time it experienced a swift rise to the

position of the strongest power in the Near East, and also became a respected and courted member in the concert of European nations.

The maintenance of Turkish neutrality and independence in the interwar period, and then between the belligerent camps during the Second World War, was achieved through the relatively quick reduction of traditional tensions with Greece (exemplified by a treaty of friendship and neutrality on October 30, 1930); through dependence on the Western powers, especially Great Britain; and through an artfully woven net of treaties in all directions: with the Soviet Union (friendship treaty, March 16, 1921); acceptance into the League of Nations (July 18, 1932); the Balkan Pact with Yugoslavia, Greece, and Romania (February 9, 1934); the international convention of Montreux, with the gaining of the right to refortify the straits (July 20, 1936); the Eastern Pact with Iran, Iraq, and Afghanistan (July 8, 1937); a treaty of alliance with Great Britain and France (October 19, 1939); and a treaty of friendship with Germany "subject to the existing commitments" (June 16, 1941).

Turkey turned away from Germany (whose ambassador was Franz von PAPEN) only after strong pressure from London (at a meeting between Churchill and Inönü on January 30–31, 1943), and as a result of the changing fortunes of war. On May 1, 1944, Turkey ceased delivery of the chrome shipments vital to Germany's military production. Diplomatic relations were broken off on August 2 of that year, and on March 1, 1945, Turkey finally declared war on Germany in order to be able to participate in the San Francisco conference as a founding member of the UNITED NATIONS.

B.-J. W.

Twentieth of July (1944; *Zwanzigster Juli*), the day of the failed assassination attempt on Hitler's life at the Führer's headquarters near Rastenburg, in East Prussia. After several fruitless attempts in the fall of 1938, during the winter of 1939–1940, and in 1943, preparations for a coup by senior military men, former politicians, trade unionists, and diplomats were consolidated beginning in the fall of 1943. Active coordination and planning with the General Staff was carried out by Claus Count Schenk von STAUFFENBERG. Stauffenberg was a lieutenant colonel in the General Staff until July 1, 1944, and then colonel and chief of staff under the commander of the Reserve Army, Col. Gen. Friedrich FROMM, in Berlin. The decision for active OPPOSITION had its origin in the political and moral rejection of Germany's war conduct and its occupation policies, especially in the east and in connection with the treatment of the Jews. Other factors were the doubts as to Hitler's qualifications for leadership, and the awareness that the war had reached a turning point.

The military, above all, faced a dilemma. If the coup were successful, they would have to prove convincingly to the German people that defeat was impending and the regime bankrupt, and at the same time they had to defend enough room for maneuvering against the enemy forces to ensure an honorable armistice despite the Allied demands for UNCONDITIONAL SURRENDER. They even consciously risked a new STAB-IN-THE-BACK LEGEND. The conspirators' immediate aims were to eliminate Hitler; to take over power in the Reich by means of the Wehrmacht after issuing the "VALKYRIE" order; to arrest the leadership of the state, the party, the SS, the Security Service, and the Gestapo; to restore justice and freedom; to assume authority over the concentration camps; to institute a provisional government authority (as Reich Regent, Ludwig BECK; as Reich Chancellor, Carl Friedrich GOERDELER; as Vice Chancellor, Wilhelm

Fahndung nach Dr. Goerdeler
Mittäterschaft am Attentat — 1 Mill. RM. Belohnung

Berlin, 2. 8.

Wegen Mittäterschaft am Attentat auf den Führer am 20. Juli 1944 ist seit diesem Tage flüchtig geworden:

Twentieth of July. "Search for Dr. Goerdeler. Complicity in the assassination attempt—1 million RM reward."

LEUSCHNER; as Interior Minister, Julius LEBER; as Foreign Minister, Ulrich von HASSELL; and as Wehrmacht Supreme Commander, Field Marshal Erwin von WITZLEBEN); and to immediately begin negotiations toward a separate peace treaty in the West.

Early on, the Gestapo broke up centers of opposition, through the arrest in January 1944 of Count Helmuth von MOLTKE, leader of the KREISAU CIRCLE, and through the removal of Adm. Wilhelm CANARIS as chief of the ABWEHR in February. On July 18, Goerdeler was uncovered with an arrest warrant, and Leber and Adolf REICHWEIN were arrested as well. As a result of the Allied landings at Normandy (June 6) and the Soviet breakthrough at the middle section of the eastern front, Germany's military and political scope for maneuvering was narrowed with dramatic rapidity. All these factors forced the conspirators finally—after two delays on July 11 and 15—to go into action.

Stauffenberg undertook the extremely difficult dual role of carrying out the actual assassination attempt and directing the coup d'état in Berlin. Adverse circumstances at the Führer's headquarters (the war conference was held in a wooden barrack rather than in a bunker, as was usual, and the briefcase containing the time bomb was placed unfavorably) led to Hitler's surviving with only slight wounds. Moreover, the news blackout that had been ordered by Gen. Fritz FELLGIEBEL was lifted too soon.

These circumstances had fateful consequences for the coup's Berlin leaders, assembled in the building of the Army High Command (OKH) on Bendlerstrasse (now Stauffenbergstrasse). The initiative here lay with Witzleben, Col. Gen. Erich HOEPNER, Gen. Friedrich OLBRICHT (chief of the Army Office), and, above all, Stauffenberg, who had left Rastenburg by air at 1:15 p.m. and arrived in Berlin at 3:45 p.m. Stauffenberg was convinced that he had killed Hitler, although he had left the barrack a few minutes before the detonation. The password, "Valkyrie," was issued around 4:00 p.m., but when the news of Hitler's survival emerged, opposing forces loyal to the regime formed around the Berlin Guard Battalion under Maj. Otto-Ernst REMER and on the initiative of Gen. Wilhelm KEITEL.

By 11:00 p.m. the putsch in Berlin had been thwarted. Stauffenberg, Olbricht, First Lt. Werner von HAEFTEN, and Col. Albrecht Mertz von Quirnheim were shot "by court-martial" that same night; after an unsuccessful attempt at

Twentieth of July. Headline of the *Völkischer Beobachter:* "The traitors are sentenced. The proceeding before the *Volk* Court reveals the cowardly criminality of the conspirators."

suicide, Beck too was killed. The coup attempt was at least temporarily successful only in Paris (under the military commander for France, Karl Heinrich von STÜLPNAGEL, who was ready to act), Vienna, Prague, Kassel, and Frankfurt. Some 200 conspirators fell victim to the blood justice of the *Volk* Court over the following months, and approximately 7,000 were arrested.

The reasons for the failure of the Twentieth of July are manifold. Above all, Hitler had survived, and no prominent frontline commanders with troops put themselves at the plot's disposal. Other significant factors include a certain hesitancy among many of the conspirators in Berlin; the excessive demands placed on Stauffenberg by his dual function; the fact that the radio stations were not occupied; the failure of the attempt to seize Goebbels; and the early lifting of the ban on reports about Rastenburg. Despite its failure, the Twentieth of July, through the great courage and moral integrity of its martyrs,

continues to the present day to bear witness to the "other Germany." In the words of Henning von TRESCKOW, "What counts now is not the practical goal, but the fact that the German opposition, before the world and before history, has ventured to make the decisive move."

B.-J. W.

Two-child system (*Zweikindersystem*), trend to limit the number of children in a marriage to two. National Socialist POPULATION POLICY fought this "deplorable custom" (*Unsitte*), allegedly caused by the "urbanization and streamlining of life," on the ground that it stood in the way of "a healthy increase in population." The RACIAL POLICY OFFICE of the NSDAP in January 1937 even urged the REICH CHAMBER OF FINE ARTS to see to it that family portrayals henceforth showed "at least four German children."

U

Überfremdung (over-alienation), National Socialist propaganda catchword that addressed the fear of the alien and incomprehensible. It was intended to be channeled in the form of hatred toward minorities: "The *Überfremdung* of Germany's intellectual life by international Jewry" (Goebbels).

Übermensch. *See* Superman.

Udet, Ernst, b. Frankfurt am Main, April 26, 1896; d. Berlin, November 18, 1941, German colonel general (July 19, 1940). In the First World War Udet was leader of a fighter squadron. As Germany's most successful surviving ace pilot (62 hits), he was awarded the Pour le mérite, and he left the service as a first lieutenant. During the 1920s he won a reputation as a brave stunt pilot and a skilled test pilot. In 1935 Hermann Göring brought Udet into the Reich

Ernst Udet.

Aviation Ministry as a colonel. The following year he was appointed Inspector of Military Fighters and Dive-bombers, and in 1939 Göring made him an aircraft ordnance general (*Generalluftzeugmeister*).

Udet's ideas on air strategy, which emphasized fighters, Stukas, and light bombers, proved themselves in the first phase of the war, but they were not equal to the strategic challenge of even the AIR BATTLE FOR ENGLAND, much less the totally unanticipated demands created by the Russian Campaign. Udet capitulated when confronted with severe blame on the part of Hitler and Göring, and took his own life. National Socialist propaganda camouflaged his death, stating that it resulted from an airplane accident. Udet was Carl ZUCKMAYER's model for the hero in his drama *Des Teufels General* (The Devil's General).

Ufa. *See* Universe Films, Inc.

Ukraine, area in the southern part of the Soviet Union, on both sides of the Dnieper and Dniester rivers and extending to the Black Sea and the Sea of Azov; area, about 900,000 sq km (some 360,000 sq miles); population, 45 million (1940); the capital is Kiev. After great initial success in the RUSSIAN CAMPAIGN, Hitler ordered the tank units that were pressing toward Moscow to turn around, in order to secure Ukrainian industry and agriculture for supplying the German military. After the region was conquered, it was unified as a Reich Commissariat (Reichskommissariat Ukraine) under Erich KOCH. Alfred Rosenberg's proposal to create an independent Ukrainian satellite state was rejected by Hitler for both racial reasons (the Ukrainians were "subhumans") and economic ones (exploitation could then proceed unhindered). German settlement of the Ukraine by the South-

Ukraine. Civilians capable of work being put on a train at Kiev's main station for forced labor in Germany.

Ukraine. "Germany's might is growing every day . . . that is why Germany will win!" German propaganda poster for the Ukraine.

ern Tyrolese, among others, had been envisaged in the GENERAL PLAN FOR THE EAST, but it did not proceed beyond insignificant beginnings. In the autumn of 1943 the Red Army retook the Ukraine.

Ulbricht, Walter, b. Leipzig, June 30, 1893; d. Berlin, August 1, 1973, German politician. A cabinetmaker by trade, Ulbricht joined the Social Democratic Party (SPD) in 1912 and the Communist Party (KPD) in 1919. In 1920 he became a full-time party functionary. He represented the KPD in the Reichstag from 1928 to 1933. Ulbricht's communism was flexible enough to adapt to the fluctuating dominant trends within the party. As head of the KPD's Berlin-Brandenburg district from 1929 to 1933 he was the antagonist of Joseph Goebbels, the NSDAP's *Gauleiter* for Berlin, yet despite numerous street battles between their respective parties, the two leaders made common cause in the BERLIN TRANSIT WORKERS' STRIKE (November 1932). This cooperation did not, of course, protect Ulbricht from persecution in 1933.

Walter Ulbricht.

Ulbricht was forced to emigrate, first to France and, in 1937, to the Soviet Union. During the war he agitated against Hitler in prisoner-of-war camps, helped establish the NATIONAL COMMITTEE FOR A FREE GERMANY, and on April 30, 1945, returned to Berlin as head of the ULBRICHT GROUP in order to organize the administration and political alignment of the Soviet occupation zone.

Ulbricht initiated the fusion of the SPD and KPD in the Soviet zone into the SED (Socialist Unity Party), which he led from 1950 to 1971. For two decades he was the most powerful and least popular figure in the newly founded German Democratic Republic (GDR). He survived the popular uprising of June 17, 1953, and also de-Stalinization; by building the Berlin Wall on August 13, 1961, he put an end to the mass exodus to the West. He thus uncoupled the GDR, destabilized in this way, from German history, making the "capitalist" Federal Republic the sole heir of National Socialist guilt. At the same time, he contested West Germany's claim to be the sole political representation of Germany.

Ulbricht Group (Gruppe Ulbricht), the first group of Communist emigrés to return from Moscow to Berlin, on April 30, 1945; it was named for their leader, Walter ULBRICHT. The group's 10 members included Otto Winzer, Karl Maron, Gustav Gundelach, and Wolfgang Leonhard, author of the best-selling autobiography *Die Revolution entlässt ihre Kinder* (The Revolution Dismisses Its Children, 1955; translated as

Child of the Revolution). Under instructions from the SOVIET MILITARY ADMINISTRATION (SMAD), the group's mission (as first delineated) was to introduce a bourgeois-democratic and antifascist restructuring into Greater Berlin (the municipal council) and the city's 20 municipal districts.

Ulbricht followed the principle of demonstrating to the outside world the broad democratic and antifascist foundation of these new organs by including Social Democrats and representatives of the bourgeoisie, and by filling only the key positions (personnel, public instruction, police) with reliable Communists. Initial plans for establishing an antifascist unity organization—a "Bloc of Militant Democracy" (Block der kämpferischen Demokratie)—were dropped, and the Ulbricht Group dissolved itself when the KPD was refounded on June 11, 1945, by a single-minded group from the Moscow emigration headed by Wilhelm PIECK. KPD representatives moved into central positions in the municipal council (Winzer and Maron), in radio (Hans Mahle), in the press (Leonhard), and then in the government and party apparatus of the SOVIET OCCUPATION ZONE and of the GDR. The activity of the Ulbricht Group has long remained in obscurity, so as to camouflage its close connection with the Moscow emigration and the fact that it often brutally suppressed, with Soviet backing, spontaneous reconstruction initiatives of popular committees and of committees of the antifascist opposition within Germany.

B.-J. W.

Ulm Agreement (*Ulmer Einigung*), declaration of the Evangelical regional churches of Bavaria and Württemberg against the synchronization measures of Reich Bishop Ludwig MÜLLER. It was published on the occasion of the jubilee celebration of the Ulm cathedral, on April 22, 1934 (*see* REICH FRATERNAL COUNCIL).

Ulm-Kuhberg, early National Socialist concentration camp (a "protective-custody" camp), established in November 1933 in the fortified enclosures of the former Upper Kuhberg fort. The camp was first occupied by about 30 "political" prisoners (mostly Communists) from the Heuberg concentration camp. Prisoners from the concentration camp at the Ulm Military Garrison who had helped to build the Kuhberg camp were added to the first group. Further enemies of the NS regime, including clergymen, journalists, and trade unionists, were transferred to Ulm-Kuhberg over the course of time. The most prominent prisoner there was the Social Democrat Kurt SCHUMACHER.

The prisoners worked in a Wehrmacht repair shop at the nearby motor transport depot. They were also utilized in quarries and in a plant nursery. Some of the camp guards were regular police officers, and the others were SA men employed as auxiliary police. After the RÖHM AFFAIR (June 30, 1934), the camp was put under the SS. The living conditions at Ulm-Kuhberg were poor. The prisoners were housed in the damp and unhealthy rooms of the fort, and were often subjected to persecution and abuse by the guards. There were, however, no deaths. In July 1935 the camp was dissolved and its remaining prisoners (about 30) were taken to the Dachau concentration camp. Today the former camp grounds are the site of a memorial and a documentation center.

Umrath, Oskar, b. Chemnitz, June 9, 1913; d. Berlin, March 6, 1943, German opposition fighter and lawyer. A Social Democrat, Umrath studied political economy in London, Vienna, and Bern. Convinced of the "absolute lack of importance of one's own existence," he returned to National Socialist Germany after his studies despite his half-Jewish background. He took a job in a bank and dedicated himself totally to the work of the NEW BEGINNINGS opposition group. He became friendly with Fritz Erler. In the militant publication "5 Jahre National-sozialismus" (Five Years of National Socialism), Umrath wrote a politico-economic analysis that accused the regime of "robbery," "cold-blooded inflation," and a boundlessly corrupt economy (*Pfründerwirtschaft*). Arrested on November 4, 1938, he was sentenced for his attacks to prison, where he perished from the harsh conditions.

Umsiedlung. *See* Resettlement.

Umvolkung (re-ethnicization), term in National Socialist POPULATION POLICY used to describe the loss of a people's racial identity through ÜBERFREMDUNG (over-alienation). According to this idea, *Umvolkung* threatened above all the FOREIGN GERMANS and ETHNIC GERMANS who became acculturated to the customs of their host countries, or who even mixed with "ethnically alien elements." Such mixing could lead ultimately to *Entvolkung* (de-ethnicization), a complete merging into the host people.

Unconditional Surrender (*Bedingungslose Kapitulation*), Allied demand first raised at the CASA-

BLANCA conference on January 24, 1943. It stipulated that hostilities against the Axis powers would cease only after the latter placed their military and political fate completely in the hands of the victors. This demand for global authority, explicitly adopted by the Soviet Union on May 1, 1943, was problematic from the point of view of international law. It encountered criticism even in Western military circles, supplied ammunition for the National Socialist TOTAL WAR propaganda, and made the position of the German OPPOSITION more difficult. The main advocate of Unconditional Surrender was United States president Franklin D. Roosevelt, who opposed all proposals for modification and adhered to the concept of a "total victory." The capitulation documents of May 7–8, 1945, and the POTSDAM AGREEMENT are strongly influenced by this idea.

Underground humor (*Flüsterwitz*; literally, "whispered humor"), the only possible kind of political joke at a time when humor that did not support the National Socialist system was considered "subversive" and was subject to criminal punishment. In the Third Reich, underground humor flourished under the pressure of censorship and persecution. It served as a mark of identification for the like-minded, was an outlet for repressed criticism, strengthened the powers of resistance, and constituted an act of liberation. It could, however, also feed the illusion that things were not really so bad. To this extent, underground humor was acceptable, and rumor had it that Hermann Göring always wanted to hear the latest jokes over breakfast. With time, however, such joviality faded when it was recognized that laughter could develop considerable subversive strength; and it was replaced by merciless revenge.

During the war, death sentences were pronounced for jokes about the NS leaders, and the cabarets and theater clubs that at first were only censored and spied on were finally banned. This did not halt the jokes, which were a means of survival for people now burdened by the daily routines of war. Humor ranged from making fun of the "Gröfaz" (*Grösster Feldherr aller Zeiten*, "greatest commander of all times") and "Reich Marshal Meier" (because of Göring's boast that he could be called "MEIER" if enemy aircraft appeared over Germany) to equivocal parodies of official fervor ("Hold your brownshirt high and don't forget the Movement"). Jokes that at the time seemed most daring often appeared quite crude—even insipid—after the war, because they depended for their effect on the mood of fear.

Undermining of military strength (*Wehrkraftzersetzung*), a new criminal offense according to Paragraph 5, Section 1, No. 1, of the Special Wartime Criminal Law Ordinance (*Kriegssonderstrafrechtsverordnung*) of August 17, 1938 (first published on August 26, 1939; *Reich Law Gazette* I, p. 1455). It stipulated the death penalty for anyone who publicly encouraged or incited another to refuse his obligation to serve in the German or an allied military force, or for anyone who otherwise publicly attempted to paralyze or undermine (*zersetzen; see* CORROSION) the will of the German *Volk* or their allies for military self-affirmation. In less serious cases, punishment could be a term in a house of correction or a prison. An ordinance of November 25, 1939 (*Reich Law Gazette* I, p. 2319), further broadened the criminal regulations "to protect the military strength of the German people."

The criminalization of the undermining of military strength is an example of the National Socialist method of lawmaking, whereby offenses were defined as broadly as possible in order to make them open to unrestricted interpretation. The courts themselves broadened the criteria for the offense still further, as with regard to the concept of "publicly": thus, comments made within a private circle could be considered "public" if they might go beyond that group, a possibility that could never be discounted. Nearly all critical comments were interpreted as undermining military strength. Along with desertion, it was the criminal offense that led to the greatest number of death sentences. Responsible for trying such cases were, in the first instance, the REICH COURT-MARTIAL, then the SPECIAL COURTS, and finally, by an ordinance of January 29, 1943 (*Reich Law Gazette* I, p. 76), the VOLK COURT.

U. B.

Unemployment (*Arbeitslosigkeit*), state of being without work among persons who would otherwise be employed. At the time of the Seizure of Power there were 6,013,612 unemployed persons in the German Reich, corresponding to about 19 percent of the work force. At this level, unemployment had surpassed the 1932 extent: in that year, the average was 5.5 million. The economic depression and the mass unemployment that accompanied it were caused by the WORLD ECONOMIC CRISIS, which, along with the

United States, had hit Germany particularly hard. Employees in commerce, unskilled workers, laborers in the iron and other metal industries, and also skilled construction workers suffered in particular from the crisis. The statistics reflected only those unemployed persons seeking employment who were registered with the employment and welfare offices, so that the real numbers were far higher. Because the chance of finding work was slight, fewer and fewer of the unemployed registered during the course of the crisis. The "invisible" unemployed were primarily women, young people, and older workers. If they were counted, then unemployment in the spring of 1933 would have been around 7.8 million.

Beginning with the establishment of the Reich Agency for Employment and Unemployment Insurance (Reichsanstalt für Arbeitsvermittlung und Arbeitslosenversicherung) in 1927, the principle of insurance prevailed in providing for

Unemployment. Millions of citizens of all classes and occupations found themselves subjected to this fate. "Hire me! I am looking for work of any kind, and am accustomed to good, hard work. Fluent command of: French, Dutch, Russian, Polish, German, and English. Experienced in the hotel and restaurant business. Good credentials and references available."

the unemployed. Unemployment benefits were initially limited to 26 weeks, although in times of especially high unemployment a "crisis support" was granted. The longest coverage for unemployment and crisis payments for workers under 40 years of age was 58 weeks; for older workers it was 71 weeks. In the course of the crisis, a verification of need was introduced after 6 weeks of coverage. At the end of the eligibility term, a person still out of work received welfare support from the local community (*Gemeinde*). These localities were soon unable to handle the burden caused by a steady increase in the number of unemployed on welfare.

In November 1932, the time limits for crisis-assistance eligibility were lifted. The National Socialists retained this provision. But the rate of assistance for the unemployed had already been reduced several times during the crisis. It was calculated according to the previous wage, the locality, and the number of eligible dependents. An unmarried unemployed person in a large city received a basic weekly support of 5.10 RM; the highest rate in this category was 11.70 RM. Welfare support levels too were constantly decreased. The rates, which barely exceeded the minimum for existence, were taken over by the National Socialists, who then raised them slightly in 1937 and 1939 by increasing the family allowances.

After the assumption of power, unemployment fell rapidly in Germany. This was due first to the overall improvement in economic conditions, to WORK CREATION measures, and above all to the onset of armaments production. In 1933 unemployment stood at a yearly average of 4.8 million; by 1934 it was down to 2.7 million. This decline was intensified in 1935 by the introduction of the REICH LABOR SERVICE and of COMPULSORY MILITARY SERVICE. But the reduction in unemployment figures was also due to changes in the basis for statistical calculation. Young people temporarily working as farm help, youths in the Labor Service, and the unemployed who were being utilized in state job creation projects were, in part, no longer counted as unemployed, although their activity was only supplementary or temporary and their compensation did not exceed the level of welfare support.

By these criteria, unemployment sank by 1937 to a yearly average of 0.9 million. The remaining unemployed were "combed through" (*durchkämmt*) after 1936 because of the scarcity of workers, and were increasingly used under the rubric LABOR DEPLOYMENT. A redefinition of the term "unemployed" achieved a further reduction in figures. Only those persons who were in the labor market and who were "politically reliable" were deemed "unemployed." Those who did not fit labor deployment requirements lost eligibility for unemployment compensation.

The impoverishment of broad groups as a result of the world economic crisis during the final years of the WEIMAR REPUBLIC had greatly contributed to the radicalization of the political spectrum; it was crucial in bringing new followers to the NSDAP. The elimination of unemployment accordingly contributed to the stabilization of the National Socialist system of domination.

B. W.

Union of Soviet Socialist Republics. *See* Soviet Union.

Union of the Victims of Nazi Persecution (Vereinigung der Verfolgten des Naziregimes [literally, Union of Those Persecuted by the Nazi Regime]; VVN), organization of persons persecuted and arrested in the Third Reich, as well as of opposition fighters. It was founded on February 22, 1947, in East Berlin, and between March 15 and 17 of that year in Frankfurt am Main. In the German Democratic Republic it was superseded in 1953 by the Committee of Antifascist Opposition Fighters (Komitee der Antifaschistischen Widerstandskämpfer). Beginning as an organization that represented the political and economic interests of those persecuted by the National Socialist regime, it became a general pacifist and radical democratic union, the VVN —Bund der Antifaschisten (League of Antifascists). In numerous publications the VVN has documented active political opposition in the Third Reich; it also seeks in particular to counter "the undermining of the Basic Law" of the Federal Republic and "a potential neofascist development." Conservative circles, as well as the West German agency in charge of protecting the constitution, consider the VVN to be "Communist-infiltrated."

United Nations (UN; also United Nations Organization, UNO [Ger., Vereinte Nationen]), organization of nearly all the nations of the world, with its headquarters in New York City. The UN was founded on June 26, 1945, with the signing of the Charter of the United Nations by 50 states (all opponents of the German Reich in the Second World War), at the end of a conference in San Francisco (April 25–June 26). Its charter took effect on October 24 of that year. The

United Nations. Conference session in the San Francisco Opera (1945).

initiative for the UN's founding came from United States president Franklin D. ROOSEVELT, who is also credited with originating the concept of the UN. The term "United Nations" was first used to designate the opponents of the Axis Powers in the Declaration of the United Nations of January 1, 1942, which appeared at the end of the ATLANTIC CHARTER.

The UN Charter identified as the goals of the United Nations the securing of peace and international security; the establishment of friendly relations among peoples; their cooperation in resolving international political, economic, social, and cultural problems; and the promotion of respect for human rights. The basic principles of the UN are: the equal rights of all member states; their obligation to settle disagreements peacefully and to refrain from the use or threat of force among one another, as well as to support the procedures of the UN; the nonintervention of the UN in the internal affairs of a state; and the right of all states recognizing the UN Charter to membership in the organization. The originally anti-German intention of the UN, expressed in the so-called ENEMY-STATE CLAUSES, was overcome at the latest when the Federal Republic and the German Democratic Republic were accepted into the organization in 1972.

R. B.

United States of America (USA), federal democracy, headed by a president, in North America; area, approximately 7.8 million sq km (about 3 million sq miles); population, 123 million (1930). The United States Senate's rejection, on March 19, 1920, of the VERSAILLES TREATY and President Wilson's foreign policy (1913 to 1921) was not followed by the country's retreat into isolationism. The chief creditor nation of the First World War participated in international disarmament conferences, the KELLOGG-BRIAND PACT (1928), and activist Latin American policies. Above all, it was involved in the economic and political stabilization of Europe after 1919, notably through the DAWES PLAN (1924) and the YOUNG PLAN (1929). This involvement led Washington and Berlin (until the period of the Brüning government, in 1930–1932) to a close community of interests. Presidents Herbert Hoover (1929–1933) and Franklin D. ROOSEVELT (1933–1945) made efforts to combat the WORLD ECONOMIC CRISIS that followed "Black Friday" at the New York Stock Exchange (October 24, 1929) with high protective tariffs and a government program (the New Deal) to revive and reform the American economy. But these attempts met with only limited success (there remained over 10 million unemployed in 1938), and led to severe domestic conflicts.

Roosevelt and his secretary of state, Cordell HULL, believed that in order to overcome the crisis, preserve the economic and political primacy of the United States, and maintain international peace, it was necessary to rebuild and stabilize a worldwide, multilateral, liberal-capitalist trade economy based on the principle of the "Open Door" (formulated and made binding in 1899–1900). Domestic welfare and order, as well as Roosevelt's political career, depended on this goal of American foreign-economic and security policy.

Yet Americans saw this goal as threatened in many respects by the National Socialist regime,

United States of America. Donald Duck in an anti-Hitler cartoon.

although until 1941, despite provocations, Germany treated the "American factor" with great circumspection. The perceived threat was multifaceted. In terms of foreign trade, it reflected Germany's policy of a self-contained, large-scale economic realm, of economic expansion toward South America, among other places, and of bilateralism (as in the NEW PLAN of September 24, 1934). Geostrategically, there was concern over Germany's offensive posture toward the Western Hemisphere, especially Latin America, and its close cooperation with Japan (as witnessed by the ANTI-COMINTERN PACT of November 25, 1936). In terms of security policy, Americans were disturbed by Germany's rapid rearmament and preparation for war, especially after 1936; and ideologically, by Germany's totalitarianism, its aggressive militarism, and its antisemitism, which stood in contrast to the American system of values. On November 10, 1938, the American ambassador in Berlin was recalled in protest against KRISTALLNACHT.

The president had already been harmed domestically by the partial failure of the New Deal. The neutralist legislation of 1935 and 1937, an ingrained pacifism and isolationism among the American population, and Congress's declared aim of closely restricting the president's foreign policy all made it impossible for him to steer American foreign policy on a clear course alongside the Western powers against the Third Reich. Roosevelt could not go beyond making warnings to the aggressors (as in his

so-called quarantine speech of October 5, 1937), among whom Hitler, from the beginning, had seemed to him to be a "pure unadulterated devil." The president had to confine himself to building up an "arsenal of democracy" through resolute rearmament from 1936 on, to economic cooperation (he concluded a trade agreement with Great Britain on November 2, 1938), and to secret but ultimately nonbinding treaty arrangements with London for the eventuality of war. Only after the defeat of France did Roosevelt—in consistency with his prewar stance—lead his nation in an "undeclared war" (Langer and Gleason) step by step to the brink of war (see LEND-LEASE ACT, March 11, 1941; ATLANTIC CHARTER, August 14, 1941). Finally, Japan

United States. Roosevelt (right) with Vice President Truman.

(with the attack on Pearl Harbor, December 7, 1941) and Germany and Italy (with their declarations of war on December 11 of that year) on their own took the final, decisive step into the Second World War.

B.-J. W.

Unity Front (*Einheitsfront*), political slogan from the 1920s, used especially in Communist propaganda to describe the union of all antifascist forces (*see* ANTIFASCISM). It was adopted by the National Socialists because of its military sound (*Einheit* also denotes a [military] unit). The sense of the term was transformed to refer to uniform mentality and conduct within a VOLK COMMUNITY, as in Hitler's *Mein Kampf*: "The great Unity Front of Germans who are truly loyal in their heart."

Universe Films, Inc. (Universum-Film-Aktiengesellschaft; Ufa), German film company. It was founded on December 18, 1917, on the initiative of the Supreme Army Leadership, and especially of Gen. Erich Ludendorff, who wanted to exploit film as a propaganda tool during the First World War. Partly with government money, film production firms and theaters were bought up and combined into Ufa. The enterprise came completely into the hands of the Deutsche Bank after the war. It became the most important German film company, producing spectacular historical films (notably *Madame Dubarry*, 1919), but also such artistically significant works as *Das Kabinett des Dr. Caligari* (*The Cabinet of Dr. Caligari;* 1919–1920).

Ufa expanded rapidly, but it could not compete with the American film industry, despite increasingly extravagant productions such as *Metropolis* (1927). After it had lost millions, Alfred

Ufa film poster: *A Woman for Three Days.*

HUGENBERG bought Ufa in 1927 and incorporated it into his press combine. Ufa's program became more and more nationalistic in orientation; besides folksy comedies and filmed operettas, it included a number of war films that were close in spirit to the National Socialist ideology, among them *Die letzte Kompanie* (The Last Company; 1930).

Because of the "cleansing [*Säuberung*] of film art and the film industry of elements alien in race and nature," Ufa was automatically incorporated into the NS propaganda apparatus after 1933. Yet because Joseph Goebbels wanted the total centralization of the German film industry, in 1936–1937 he had Ufa's stock shares purchased (at first anonymously). In 1937 he nationalized the major German film companies, and he definitively merged the individually owned firms into the parent company, Ufa Films, Ltd. (Ufa-Film GmbH; Ufi), in 1938. During the remainder of the Third Reich, Ufi controlled all film production as well as most film theaters.

After the Second World War, the victorious powers insisted that the German film monopoly be divested. In the German Democratic Republic, German Films, Inc. (Deutsche Film-AG; DEFA), established in 1946, took over Ufi's holdings. In the Federal Republic, Ufa Theaters, Inc. (Ufa-Theater AG), and the production company Universe Films, Inc. (Universum-Film AG), were newly established in 1955 and 1956, respectively. They were not, however, able to capitalize on the prewar successes of the

Universe Films, Inc. Sound truck for outdoor filming.

German cinema, and in 1964 were acquired by the Bertelsmann Publishing Group (*see* FILM).

H. H.

Universities, scholarly advanced schools whose purpose is to provide comprehensive education and research facilities. Into the 1920s, the German universities had a worldwide reputation as exemplary educational institutions, in particular because of their system of administrative autonomy and the high scholarly level of many academics. At the same time, however, the universities had been a stronghold of nationalism for many decades, and therefore were vulnerable to the National Socialist vision of a new national beginning directed toward a Great-Germany. This had been the demand of a large group of university professors in 1915, in a petition to the Kaiser supporting ambitious German war aims. Meanwhile, the student body was attracted by the seemingly social-revolutionary program of the NSDAP and by the party's ideology of a *Volk* Community. The prevalence of *völkisch* ideas and the YOUTH MOVEMENT had prepared the ground for this.

After the NATIONAL SOCIALIST GERMAN STUDENTS' LEAGUE had attained a majority in student associations at numerous universities, even before the Seizure of Power (January 30, 1933), the political synchronization of the universities met little opposition. This synchronization consisted first in the "cleansing" of the universities by means of the ARYAN PARAGRAPH, to which some 1,200 university teachers fell victim during the first year, among them first-rate scholars, and through the elimination of politically unde-

sirable lecturers. This action led to a distinct decline in the level of scholarship, especially since the young professors promoted to replace those forced out had few demonstrable qualifications other than political reliability. The Law against the Overcrowding of German Schools and Universities of April 1933 was a means of sorting out students. Its applications included a reduction in the number of women students (*see* WOMEN IN THE THIRD REICH), and it was followed in December of that year by a maximum quota (*numerus clausus*) for women of 10 percent. This was lifted in 1936 after a drastic reduction in the number of women students took place.

Like the BOOK BURNING, which was staged primarily by universities, these events indicated the imminent alignment of the content of research and instruction with the spirit of National Socialism (*see* HITLER'S WORLDVIEW). In 1935 the FÜHRER PRINCIPLE was introduced into the universities; according to it, the rector (chosen on the basis of political considerations) appointed the deans, who designated the heads of departments, and so on. It also permitted direct state interference in teaching. Excessive deviations from the desired line of thought led to suspension of the instructor, especially in the humanities, although the natural sciences were also affected (*see* GERMAN PHYSICS). The NATIONAL SOCIALIST GERMAN UNIVERSITY TEACHERS' LEAGUE infiltrated university committees with its functionaries. It also saw to indoctrination through numerous "voluntary" training courses, and used threats to achieve internalization of the desired ideological censorship.

Universities. Matriculation at the University of Berlin (1937).

The norms of NS EDUCATION were thus meant to prevail on the university level as well as below.

Untermensch. *See* Subhuman.

Upper School of the NSDAP. *See* Hohe Schule der NSDAP.

Urbanization (*Verstädterung*), term used in a negative sense by the National Socialist sociologists Hans Friedrich Karl GÜNTHER and Ernst KRIECK to describe the growth of large cities, conformity to urban life-styles in rural localities, and the increasing alienation of man from nature. The National Socialists ascribed to urban ASPHALT practically all the characteristics of capitalism and the Weimar Republic that they censured as urbanization. Urbanization was to be overcome by a mythical "repatriation" (*Zurückführung*) of man back to nature and to the "soil" (*see* BLOOD AND SOIL).

Ustaše (from Croat. *ustaša*, "insurgent," "rebel"), Croatian autonomist movement of a fascist nature. Founded on January 7, 1929, by the lawyer Ante PAVELIĆ, it was patterned on the model of Balkan conspiratorial groups. It was directed against the "royal dictatorship" of Alexander I of Yugoslavia and Belgrade's policy of centralism. With financial aid from Fascist Italy, the Ustaše strove for the complete independence of Croatia from Yugoslavia through terrorist bombings (notably the October 1934 assassination of Alexander I in Marseilles) and attempts at violent revolution.

After Yugoslavia was militarily smashed, the "Independent State of Croatia" (1941–1944) was founded by the grace of Mussolini and Hitler. Pavelić became head of state (*poglavnik*), and after the fall of the war minister, Slavko Kvaternik, he also (following Hitler's example) became supreme commander of the Croatian armed forces, as of October 6, 1942. The bloody suppression policy of the fascist and antisemitic Ustaše regime was directed against Orthodox Serbs, Jews, Muslims, and Yugoslav partisans, by means of the Ustaše's own battalions and concentration camps and by mass executions. At the time when Pavelić emigrated in 1945 via Austria and Italy to Argentina and founded an Ustaše government-in-exile there in 1949, a large number of his supporters whom the English had handed over to TITO's partisans in 1945 were killed.

Ustaše. Arrest of a Serbian resistance fighter by a member of the Ustaše militia.

Üxküll-Gyllenband, Nikolaus Count von, b. Güns (Hungary), February 14, 1877; d. Berlin-Plötzensee, September 14, 1944 (executed), German opposition fighter. Üxküll was an officer in the Austrian army, and then a businessman. As early as 1938 he tried to persuade his nephew Claus Count von STAUFFENBERG to act against Hitler. He later encouraged the young officer in his plans for assassinating and overthrowing Hitler during the war: "We Germans can no longer look a foreigner in the eye if we do not make an attempt on our own!" Üxküll assisted Stauffenberg, who had been severely disabled in the war, until the very end. After the failure of the attempt of July 20, 1944, Üxküll refused to have his sentence lessened on grounds of advanced age, virtually provoking his death sentence by acknowledging that he would act in the same manner at any time.

V1, propaganda term for the Fieseler Fi 103 *Kirschkern* ("Cherry Pit") flying bomb; the V stood for *Vergeltung* (vengeance). (*See also* WONDER WEAPONS.)

V2, propaganda term for the A4 (*Aggregat* 4) long-range rocket; the V stood for *Vergeltung* (VENGEANCE). The V2 was one of the heralded WONDER WEAPONS that in 1944–1945 was intended to bring a turn in the course of the war and result in the "final victory."

"V7," code name for a rescue operation carried out by the ABWEHR for German Jews in the fall of 1942. As early as 1941, several hundred Dutch Jews had been able to escape to South America as "agents" (*Vertrauensleute*). In similar fashion, seven adults (hence the name) and seven children from among the Jewish acquaintances of Adm. Wilhelm CANARIS and Hans von DOHNÁNYI were brought to Switzerland. Since that country did not recognize people persecuted on racial grounds as political refugees, the Abwehr had to provide financial guarantees. The Gestapo found out about the foreign-exchange transactions that were required, and this put them on the trace of the opposition elements in the Abwehr. Dohnányi's arrest placed extensive incriminating material into the hands of the Gestapo.

Vacation camp (*Ferienlager*), means of EDUCATION intensively utilized by the National Socialists, especially for the HITLER YOUTH (HJ). In the vacation camps, children were removed from parental influence; they experienced the comradeship and romantic spirit of camp life, and were prepared for military life by means of the regulated daily routine, roll calls, marches, and quartering in barracks. They were given strictly circumscribed tasks and learned to carry out responsibilities according to the HJ motto: "Youth will be led by youth."

Vaivara, National Socialist concentration camp in Estonia, established on September 15, 1943. It was initially occupied by Jews from the ghettos of Vilna and Kovno, and later also by Jews from the then Reich territory and from THERESIENSTADT, Poland, and Hungary. The number of inmates fluctuated between 1,200 and 2,000 (including women and children). Vaivara and its satellite camps were controlled and administered by the Kommandantur Konzentrationslager V (Headquarters for Concentration Camp V) of the SS Office. The guards were Estonian policemen under the authority of the Security Police (Sipo) and the Security Service (SD) in Reval (now Tallinn).

The prisoners were utilized in woodcutting, cement making, transport, work on railroad tracks, and fortification work, as well as in the extraction of oil shale (for the Baltic Oil Company, Ltd.). Conditions in Vaivara were poor, as was usual in concentration camps. Many prisoners died of starvation, epidemics, and the after-effects of abuse. Prisoners who were ill and unable to work were routinely selected out (as were children) and shot as "useless eaters." Conditions in the satellite camps, such as Narva, Kiviöli I and II, and KLOOGA, were similar. In 1944, when the war front came closer, Vaivara and its annex camps were abandoned. Most of the prisoners were taken via the Stutthof concentration camp to an auxiliary camp of the Natzweiler concentration camp in the Württemberg oil-shale area of the Swabian Alps.

W. D.

"Valkyrie" ("Walküre"), code name for the instructions regarding countermeasures to be taken in case of internal disturbances or uprisings in Germany (such as those that might be caused by ALIEN WORKERS); they were issued on July 31, 1943. After the instructions were issued, fighting cadres were to be formed from the Field Army and were to be put in a state of alert in two stages. The military district (*Wehrkreis*) units were to take extensive measures to secure all vital installations. During the attempted coup on the TWENTIETH OF JULY, 1944, the conspirators attempted to gain control over Berlin and the Reich by issuing the "Valkyrie" code.

Vansittart, Robert Gilbert, b. Farnham, June 25, 1881; d. Denham (Buckinghamshire), February 14, 1957, British diplomat. In 1902 Vansittart became an attaché, and filled posts in Cairo, Stockholm, and Paris; from 1930 to 1938 he was permanent under secretary of state in the Foreign Office. A Francophile, he regarded the rise of the Third Reich with deep distrust. In May 1935 he received Foreign Minister Joachim von RIBBENTROP, who had come to London to negotiate the GERMAN-BRITISH NAVAL AGREEMENT; Vansittart later described him as a politically "clumsy lightweight" (*schwerfälliges Leichtgewicht*). Vansittart's visit to the Berlin Olympic Games in 1936 increased his anti-Nazi ill feelings, which grew into a criticism ("Vansittartism") of the APPEASEMENT policy. He was therefore demoted to the non-influential post of a foreign-policy adviser to the British government prior to the MUNICH AGREEMENT.

Vapniarka, concentration camp under Romanian administration in Transnistria (USSR), between the Dniester and Bug rivers, on the Shmerinka-Odessa railroad line. On September 16, 1942, some 1,200 men and women (including young people up to the age of 15), mainly Romanian Jews, were transported to Vapniarka. The prisoners were guarded by Romanian gendarmes and were made to work at loading and unloading freight cars, along with other tasks. Besides a little barley bread, their food ration consisted primarily of cooked field peas (*Latyrus sativus*), a poisonous legume that causes lathyrism, a disease known in central Europe since the 17th century, whose symptoms include paralysis. After consuming these peas for about six weeks, the prisoners experienced intestinal disturbances and painful muscular contractions in their arms, legs, stomach, and back, in addition to bladder dysfunction, including urine blockage; high blood pressure; circulatory disturbances in the feet; and finally severe paralysis. Several of the inmates died from this toxin. On January 16 and 30, 1943, and on February 22 of that year, the prisoners' condition was checked by medical commissions. Their diet may have been planned from the beginning, as a nutritional or medical experiment.

Before the arrival of the above-mentioned transport of September 16, 1942, about 900 Romanian Jews from earlier deportations were apparently executed. In March 1944, the camp (according to the statements of witnesses) was dissolved. Many of the survivors emigrated after the war to Israel, where most of them suffered permanent disabilities (paralysis of the extremities, crippling, and heart and lung diseases) as lasting consequences of lathyrism. These so-called Vapniarka patients were aided by private and church relief agencies in the Federal Republic of Germany after their fate became known.

W. D.

Vatican, shortened term for the highest authority in the Roman Catholic church; named after the pope's residence (also called the Apostolic See or Holy See) in Rome. After the dissolution of the ecclesiastical state, the Vatican state was created (officially, Stato della Città del Vaticano; Vatican City), with an area of 0.44 sq km (about 0.18 sq miles) and a population of around 1,025 (1932). The LATERAN TREATIES of February 2, 1929, made it a sovereign and neutral state and an absolute monarchy (statute of June 7, 1929), with the pope as head of state and a government body (the Curia), appointed by and dependent on him. The Holy See is a sovereign state in terms of international law. From 1920 to April 1943, the German ambassador to the Vatican was Carl-Ludwig Diego von Bergen, followed by Ernst Baron von WEIZSÄCKER from July 1943 until May 1945.

Under the pontificates of PIUS XI (1922–

Vatican. The apostolic nuncio in Berlin, Cesare Orsenigo, in 1937 at a reception given by Hitler.

1939) and PIUS XII (1939–1958), the Vatican policy toward National Socialist Germany is particularly controversial, beginning with the CONCORDAT of 1933. The paramount goal of the Vatican was and remains the contractual guarantee of freedom of confession and the public exercise of religion by means of concordats. This need to protect the faith was especially acute under the totalitarian challenge of National Socialism and the threats posed by the CHURCH STRUGGLE in Germany. Hitler's repeated affirmations to both Christian denominations that they were the "most important factors in upholding our *Volk*-nation" (March 23, 1933), his clearcut rejections of "Marxist heresy" and of materialism, atheism, and liberalism, as well as his anti-Bolshevik "crusade ideology"—despite the constant intensification of the church struggle—made the Vatican continue to hope for a possible compromise with the National Socialist regime even after the war had begun. The Vatican's readiness to compromise, and its renouncing of any public and international denunciation of the PERSECUTION OF JEWS and the Holocaust (especially under Pius XII), subjected it after 1945 to sharp accusations of having failed to extend aid to the victims of National Socialist tyranny (as seen, for example, in Rolf Hochhuth's play *Der Stellvertreter. Ein christliches Trauerspiel* [*The Deputy: A Christian Tragedy*]; 1963).

On the other hand, from the side of the church, the Vatican's sharp criticism of the NS church policies and of the increasingly frequent violations of the Concordat led to the German-language encyclical MIT BRENNENDER SORGE of March 14, 1937, attributed to Cardinal Michael FAULHABER's influence, and culminated in its being publicly read from all the Catholic pulpits in Germany. Moreover, it has been pointed out that during the Second World War, the Vatican provided a point of liaison for feelers from the German opposition to the West. Moreover, after the fall of Italy and the occupation of Rome by German troops, who respected the extraterritoriality of the neutral Vatican state, the Vatican offered sanctuary to many victims of political and racial persecution until the Allies liberated Rome on June 4, 1944.

B.-J. W.

Veesenmayer, Edmund, b. Bad Kissingen, November 12, 1904, SS-*Brigadeführer* (March 15, 1944) and diplomat. Veesenmayer studied economics, and then became a university instructor (*Dozent*) in Munich. He joined the NSDAP in

Edmund Veesenmayer.

1925. Through good connections with influential business circles, Veesenmayer succeeded in entering the diplomatic service. He worked at the Foreign Ministry after 1932, and was posted to the German Embassy in Zagreb in May 1941. Already occupied with "Jewish affairs" at that time, Veesenmayer became German ambassador to Hungary in March 1944. He was nominally under the authority of the Foreign Ministry, but continued to work primarily on the managing of the FINAL SOLUTION of the Jewish question, which was directed by Adolf EICHMANN. For his activities, Veesenmayer was sentenced to 20 years' imprisonment in Nuremberg on April 2, 1949. He was released as early as December 1951, through the general amnesty issued by the United States high commissioner, John J. McCloy.

Vehm murders (*Fememorde*), term originating under the influence of the medieval German secret tribunals, the *Femegerichte*. It referred to the vigilante political justice exercised by secret leagues and underground organizations. Vehm murders were committed above all by members of the FREE CORPS and the BLACK REICHSWEHR between 1919 and 1923, as punishment of alleged "military traitors" who, for example, had given information about weapons caches to the authorities. Only a few of the approximately 300 Vehm murders were punished with the usual severity of the national-conservative system of justice. Even one of the main culprits, First Lt. Paul Schultz, was merely imprisoned after being sentenced to death in 1927, and was then amnestied according to the Reich law of October

24, 1932. During the Second World War there were isolated instances of Vehm murders in Allied prisoner-of-war camps, committed by fanatical National Socialists against comrades who doubted the "final victory" and who collaborated with their captors.

Vengeance (*Vergeltung*), in the sense of international law, a REPRISAL to compensate for injustice suffered as a result of enemy acts of violence. Through the term's inflationary use in propaganda to cover up acts of aggression, it became devalued. National Socialist propaganda, in particular, contributed to the process of its undermining. For example, as early as Hitler's Reichstag speech of September 1, 1939, Germany's attack on Poland was portrayed as an act of vengeance for the raid on the GLEIWITZ radio transmitter. The flying bombs and long-range rockets deployed toward the end of the war were called vengeance weapons (*Vergeltungswaffen; see* WONDER WEAPONS) in response to the Allied air offensive.

Venlo Incident (*Venlo-Zwischenfall*), secret service incident that took place after the Polish Campaign of October–November 1939. It began as an attempt to investigate the British SECRET SERVICE in Holland through contacts that were to be established by SS-Obersturmführer Walter SCHELLENBERG, who pretended to be a member of the military opposition. But after the BÜRGERBRÄU ASSASSINATION ATTEMPT on November 9, neither Hitler nor Himmler was inclined to believe that the explosion was the solitary act of Johann Georg ELSER. Suspecting backing by the British Secret Service, they instructed Schellenberg to lure his English contacts to the German border.

There, behind the border barricade, SS-Sturmbannführer Alfred NAUJOCKS and an assault commando were waiting. After a short exchange of fire, two British agents, Capt. S. Paine Best and Maj. Richard Stevens, as well as a Dutch colleague, were abducted across the border. Their statements provided no evidence for the theory of British instigation, but at the time of the German attack in the west (May 10, 1940), Hitler used the alleged proof of the Dutch-British "conspiracy against the Reich" as a pretext to accuse Holland of "the most flagrant violation of the most basic neutrality obligations," and thus justify the German assault. Schellenberg was promoted to the rank of SS-*Standartenführer*, and the English agents remained imprisoned in concentration camps until the end of the war.

Veradelung (approximate meaning, "ennoblement"), unsuccessful attempt, made by the publicist Walter Best in 1939, at a Germanization of the word *Kultur;* it never gained currency.

Vercors, valley in the French western Alps, southwest of Grenoble. In the Second World War, beginning in 1942 it was one of the first centers of the RÉSISTANCE. The plateau, surrounded by peaks 2,000 m (about 6,700 feet) high, was

Vengeance. Shooting of hostages in Greece.

planned as a base for sorties by Allied paratroops against the German communication lines in the Rhône valley. After the Allied invasion it was occupied by the MAQUIS in June 1944 and declared the republic of France. The revolt was put down by SS paratroops and Russian volunteer units; during the struggle, 201 civilians and 639 underground fighters were killed.

Vermisste, persons whose whereabouts are unknown for an extended time period; *see* DISAPPEARANCE.

Vernichtungslager. *See* Extermination camps.

Vernordung, term coined by Hans Friedrich Karl GÜNTHER in 1925; it was the equivalent of NORDIC UPGRADING (*Aufnordung*).

Verona, city in northern Italy. The trial against 19 members of the former GRAND COUNCIL OF FASCISM took place in Verona from January 8 to 10, 1944. The council had signed a resolution by Count Dino Grandi against Mussolini in a session of July 24–25, 1943. Of the 19 defendants tried, 18 were sentenced to death, 13 of them in absentia. On the morning of January 11, 1944, the following men were executed: Count Galeazzo CIANO, the foreign minister; Marshal Emilio de BONO; Giuseppe Pareschi, the minister of agriculture; Giovanni Marinelli, the administrative head of the Fascist party; and Luciano Gottardi, the head of the Association of Italian Industry.

Verpflichtung der Jugend (Commitment of Youth), National Socialist replacement ceremony for confirmation (*see* CELEBRATIONS IN THE NATIONAL SOCIALIST CALENDAR).

Verreichlichung, term for measures that standardized individual regional features in administration and justice on the Reich level; it also referred to the assumption of state (*Land*) responsibilities by the Reich. It was an important aspect of SYNCHRONIZATION.

Versailles, suburb of Paris in which the VERSAILLES TREATY was concluded. The name "Versailles" often serves as an abbreviated designation for the treaty.

Versailles treaty (officially, Treaty of Versailles), peace treaty signed on June 28, 1919, by Germany and its opponents in the First World War. Like the other PARIS SUBURBAN TREATIES, the Versailles treaty was negotiated at the Paris

Peace Conference, which opened on January 18, 1919. The 27 participants were the Allies and their associated states. The decision-making body was the Supreme Council, made up of the heads of government of the United States (Woodrow Wilson), France (Georges Clemenceau), Great Britain (David Lloyd George), and Italy (Vittorio Orlando).

Germany was not allowed to participate in the negotiations. The German delegation, headed by Foreign Minister Ulrich Count von Brockdorff-Rantzau, was given the final draft of the treaty on May 7. On June 16 the victorious powers agreed to a few insignificant points in the German counterproposals of May 29. In view of the Allied ultimatum threatening the resumption of hostilities, the German National Assembly empowered the Reich government (237 votes for, 138 against) to sign the treaty. This was done at the Palace of Versailles on June 28, by Foreign Minister Hermann MÜLLER and Transportation Minister Johannes Bell. The Versailles treaty took effect on January 10, 1920.

In 15 sections with a total of 440 articles, the Versailles treaty contained:

1. The statutes of the LEAGUE OF NATIONS.
2. *Territorial settlements:* Without plebiscites, Germany had to cede (1) Alsace-Lorraine to France; (2) Posen and West Prussia to Poland; (3) the small territory of Hultschin to Czechoslovakia; (4) the Memel territory to the Allies (it was transferred to Lithuania in 1923); (5) Danzig,

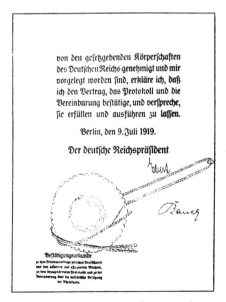

Versailles treaty. Ratification document, signed by Ebert and Bauer.

1

2

3
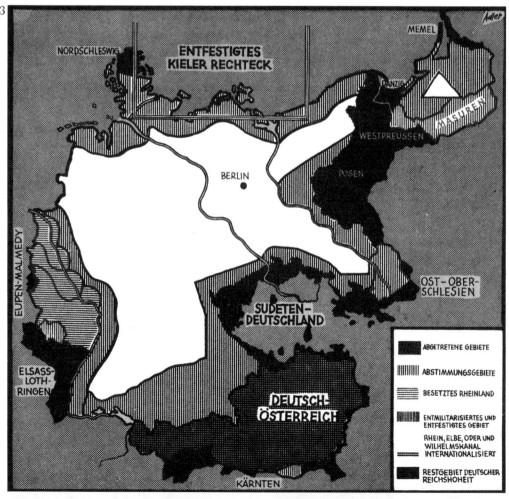

1
Clemenceau, flanked by Wilson (left) and Lloyd George, receives the German signature to the treaty in the Hall of Mirrors at Versailles.
2
Propaganda postcard assailing the Versailles treaty.
3
"The Versailles Solution of 1919." Map from the Third Reich period.

which was declared a Free City; and (6) all its overseas colonies, which as mandate territories came under the supervision and authority of the League of Nations. On the basis of plebiscites, Germany had to cede (7) eastern Upper Silesia to Poland; (8) Eupen-Malmédy to Belgium; and (9) northern Schleswig to Denmark (*see* PLEBISCITE REGIONS). Further, (10) the SAAR TERRITORY (Saarland) was placed under the administration of the League of Nations until a plebiscite, 15 years in the future; (11) the Elbe, Oder, Memel, Danube, Rhine, and Mosel rivers were internationalized; and (12) Austria was forbidden to carry out a union (ANSCHLUSS) with the German Reich. The total German losses were 73,845 sq km (about 29,600 sq miles) and some 7.3 million inhabitants.

3. *Military stipulations:* (1) Allied troops were to occupy the left bank of the Rhine, with bridgeheads on the right bank at Kehl, Cologne, Koblenz, and Mainz; the occupation troops would be removed in stages, at intervals of 5, 10, and 15 years; (2) a demilitarized zone on the left bank of the Rhine would be created, along with a strip 50 km (30 miles) wide on the right bank; (3) universal military service was abolished; the German army was limited to a maximum of 100,000, and the navy to 15,000, career men; (4) the air force and naval air force were disbanded; (5) the production and use of "heavy" weapons

"The Origin." Cartoon on the Versailles treaty in the *St. Louis Post-Dispatch*, October 18, 1930.

(such as airplanes and tanks) were prohibited; (6) German war matériel and the control of German arms and arms production were to be surrendered to the Allies; (7) the German General Staff and German military schools were to be dissolved.

4. *Economic stipulations:* (1) Germany was obliged to pay REPARATIONS and to supply goods (including coal, machinery, factory installations, and underwater cable) and livestock (for example, 140,000 dairy cows) to the Allies; (2) Germany had to surrender nearly its entire merchant fleet; (3) German assets abroad (including private assets) were to be confiscated. The imposition of reparations was justified by the assignment to Germany and its allies of sole responsibility for the war, as stated in Article 231, and Germany was forced to acknowledge it (*see* WAR GUILT QUESTION).

5. The (former) German emperor, Wilhelm II, and other persons alleged to have violated international law, were to be indicted before a court of law (to be formed) and handed over to it.

The Versailles treaty was almost unanimously rejected in Germany as a "dictated peace" (*Diktatfrieden*) and the "infamous diktat of Versailles" (*Schanddiktat von Versailles*). It constituted a heavy and lasting liability for the WEIMAR REPUBLIC. The treaty provided a foothold for antidemocratic forces, especially for the NSDAP, in their struggle against the Republic (*see* STAB-IN-THE-BACK LEGEND; WAR GUILT LIE). Among the Allies as well, the treaty did

"This is what disarmament looks like." Cartoon on the Versailles treaty.

not meet with universal approval. The United States, for example, did not ratify it, and in 1921 concluded a separate peace treaty with Germany.

R. B.

Vesper, Will, b. Barmen, October 11, 1882; d. Gut [estate] Triangel, near Gifhorn, March 14, 1962, German writer. After the First World War, Vesper was head of the feuilleton (feature supplement) section of the *Deutsche Allgemeine Zeitung* (German General News). He was then particularly successful as the author of chauvinistic novels about the Germanic past. In his poetry, stories, and adaptations, he manifested increasingly antisemitic and National Socialist tendencies. As a result, after the takeover of power he was appointed to the Prussian Academy of Letters and to the post of *Gau* chairman (*Obmann*) of the National Socialist Reich Association of German Writers.

In 1933 Vesper was among the official speakers at the BOOK BURNING celebrations. In the leading literary magazine of the Third Reich, *Die Neue Literatur* (New Literature), of which he was also the publisher, he attacked those of his colleagues who had emigrated. As one of the most zealous court poets to the National Socialist leadership, Vesper celebrated Germany in odes and hymns as "a Reich armed, wished for by One Man [*von Einem*], and created by One Man" ("Das Neue Reich" [The New Reich]; 1939). He sang the praises of the "Duke of the Reich [*Herzog des Reiches*]," who as the "fittest son" (*tüchtigster Sohn*) "arises . . . from the midst of the *Volk*" ("Dem Führer" [To the Führer]; 1943). Beginning in 1938 Vesper lived primarily as a farmer on his estate, where after the war he assembled an informal circle of like-minded men. In his postwar works he did not disown his basic National Socialist attitude.

H. H.

Vialon, Friedrich Karl, b. Frankfurt am Main, July 10, 1905, German lawyer. Vialon joined the NSDAP in 1933 and began working at the Reich Finance Ministry in 1937. Temporarily drafted into the Wehrmacht at the beginning of the war, on May 1, 1942, he was ordered to join the office of the Reich Commissioner for the Eastern Territory (*Reichskommissar für das Ostland*) in Riga. As a senior government councillor (*Oberregierungsrat*), he directed the Finance Department in the Ostland, and was appointed a government director (*Regierungsdirektor*).

After the collapse of the Third Reich, Vialon was active in business and industry. He joined the Federal Republic's Finance Ministry in 1950, and the Federal Chancellor's Office in 1958. From 1962 to 1966 he was a state secretary in the Federal Ministry for Economic Cooperation and an honorary professor of public financial law. The Eastern bloc states, in particular, accused Vialon of having at least had knowledge of the extermination actions against the Jews. However, no evidence of his culpability could be found that would make him liable for legal proceedings.

A. St.

Vichy, shortened term for the government of Henri PÉTAIN and the authoritarian-bureaucratic "État Français" it represented as the successor to the Third Republic (*see* FRANCE). After the military defeat of France, the government was relocated to the spa town of Vichy, in the Allier department, northeast of Clermont-Ferrand. On July 10, 1940, at the last session of the French National Assembly, held in Vichy, Pétain by a vote of 569 to 80 received unlimited powers as head of state, independent of parliament, to make use of the executive authority and develop a new constitution (which never became operative).

The Vichy government, which was formally sovereign but in fact heavily dependent on Germany, had authority over about 40 percent of the territory of the French state, an army of 100,000 men, and the French colonies; the navy had been neutralized in its home ports. The United States, the USSR, and the Vatican, among other states, gave diplomatic recognition to Vichy France.

Initially greeted by most French citizens as a salvation-bringing incarnation of "eternal France," the Vichy regime, supported by conservative politicians and notables, the bourgeoisie, the peasantry, and the Catholic church, proclaimed a "National Revolution." It was to achieve a sweeping moral renewal and rebirth of France on a conservative foundation, under the motto "Work, Family, Fatherland" ("Travail, Famille, Patrie"). In so doing, the Vichy government decisively opposed the revolutionary-republican and parliamentary tradition of 1789, with its slogan of "Liberty, Equality, Fraternity," as well as the parliamentarianism, socialism, and POPULAR FRONT of the Third Republic. Vichy strove to overcome the Republic's alleged *décadence* through an active policy of promoting

The Pétain government in Vichy. Front row, from the left: Pierre Caziot, Paul Baudouin, Laval, Pétain, Weygand, Henri Lémery, Colson. Back row, from the left: Darlan, François Piétri, Rafaël Alibert, Adrien Marquet, Yves Bouthillier, Émil Mireaux, Jean Yharnégaray, Pujo.

large families and the physical-fitness training of its young people.

The Vichy regime's policies were characterized by strong press censorship, suppression of the opposition, a leadership cult surrounding Pétain, a corporatist anticapitalism (as exemplified by a "Charter of Labor"), legislation against the Jews, and partial cooperation with the Gestapo and Security Service (SD) in their persecution. Nevertheless, the regime should be termed conservative-authoritarian rather than fascist. To the outside world, Pierre LAVAL (vice-premier until December 13, 1940; premier as of April 18, 1942) and Adm. François DARLAN (vice-premier from 1941 to April 1942 and Pétain's designated successor) represented a clear anti-British and pro-German policy of political, economic, and military COLLABORATION, intended to secure for France the second place in a National Socialist Europe. Pétain, on the other hand, pursued a more neutralist policy of stalling (*attentisme*), in order to spare his country the fate of Poland (*see* MONTOIRE).

With the passage of time, more and more French citizens came to reject Vichy as synonymous with a hated collaboration. The occupation of the hitherto unoccupied southern zone by German troops on November 11, 1942, in response to the Allied landing in North Africa decisively narrowed the Vichy government's scope for maneuvering. After the installation of a provisional French government under Gen. Charles de Gaulle on August 25, 1944, France's liberation by the Allies, and the Germans' forcible removal of Pétain and his associates via

Belfort (August 26) to Sigmaringen in Württemberg-Hohenzollern (September 7), the Vichy government ceased its activity, which had lasted for over four years and which remains controversial even today.

B.-J. W.

Victor Emmanuel III, b. Naples, November 11, 1869; d. Alexandria (Egypt), December 28, 1947, king of Italy (1900–1946). Victor Emmanuel was an advocate of Italy's entrance into the war on the side of the Entente in 1915. Despite his considerable distrust of FASCISM, he named Benito Mussolini as prime minister on October 31, 1922, fearing a civil war if he did not do so. He continued to support Il Duce out of fear of the republican forces in the anti-Fascist camp. He became emperor of Ethiopia in 1936, and king of Albania in 1939. Throughout his long years in the shadow of the Fascist dictatorship, Victor Emmanuel nevertheless retained enough authority to succeed in arresting Mussolini and depriving him of power, with the aid of the GRAND COUNCIL OF FASCISM, on July 25, 1943. After conclusion of a separate armistice on September 8 with the Allies through the BADOGLIO government that Victor Emmanuel had installed, the king fled to Brindisi the following day to avoid German revenge. Many Italians felt that this was a "desertion," and it ultimately led to the fall of the monarchy, which in any case had been damaged by its complicity with Mussolini. Victor Emmanuel's abdication in favor of his son Umberto on May 9, 1946, changed nothing in this regard.

Victor Emmanuel III with his wife. At the left: Hitler and Mussolini.

Vienna Awards (*Wiener Schiedssprüche*), two German-Italian agreements for settling Hungary's claims, dating from the Peace of Trianon (1920), against Czechoslovakia and Romania for territorial revision. A supplementary declaration to the MUNICH AGREEMENT (September 29, 1938), issued under Hungarian pressure, was intended to solve the problem of Czechoslovakia's Hungarian minority through bilateral negotiations. When this failed to materialize, foreign ministers Joachim von Ribbentrop and Count Galeazzo Ciano, on the request of the Prague and Budapest governments, struck an arbitration settlement on November 2, 1938. The first Vienna Award gave to Hungary an agriculturally and industrially important strip of southern Slovakia and the Carpatho-Ukraine, with an area of 12,009 sq km (some 4,800 sq miles) and 1.04 million inhabitants (including 590,000 Magyars).

The second Vienna Award addressed conflicting claims against Romania by Hungary, the USSR (for Bukovina and Bessarabia), and Bulgaria (for Dobruja). In the summer of 1940 these claims threatened to lead to conflict in the Danube region that could disrupt Germany's supply of oil. When bilateral negotiations could not settle the disputes, the German and Italian foreign ministers on August 30, 1940, decreed the second Vienna Award in order to maintain calm in southeastern Europe. In exchange for a German-Italian guarantee of its new border, Romania had to cede to Hungary northern Transylvania and the Székely Land, with 43,000 sq km (about 17,200 sq miles) and 2.53 million inhabitants. The two awards were revoked in Article 13 of the January 20, 1945, Hungarian cease-fire with the Soviet Union,

Great Britain, and the United States. The Paris Peace Treaty of February 10, 1947 (Article 1), confirmed the revocation.

B.-J. W.

Vierjahresplan. *See* Four-Year Plan.

Vieth von Golssenau, Arnold, real name of the author Ludwig Renn.

Vilna, National Socialist ghetto for Jews, established in September 1941 in a quarter of the Lithuanian city (now Vilnius; in 1938, it had around 208,000 inhabitants). The area was surrounded with a wall and barbed wire and was divided by a street into a large and a small ghetto. In the large one, about 45,000 Jews "lived," and in the small one, about 15,000, in an area where previously some 4,000 people had resided. The Vilna ghetto was controlled by the German city commissariat; guards were supplied by the SS and the Lithuanian auxiliary police. There was a Jewish ghetto administration, and a Jewish camp police that dealt with local security. The inhabitants worked in fur factories, at the railway station, at the airport, in the army motor depot, in German offices, and in various workshops inside and outside the ghetto. They were checked at the gate as they returned from outside work. Anyone trying to bring in food—an act tolerated at the beginning—was abused or shot.

The population in Vilna was sharply reduced by repeated mass shootings, which were directed above all against persons unable to work (up to a thousand a week). Special shooting operations on a larger scale were not infrequent. For example, on October 1, 1941, on the Jewish holy day of Yom Kippur, several thousand Jews were herded to the suburb of Ponary and killed there. In mid-October, the small ghetto was dissolved through the shooting of all its 15,000 inhabitants. At the end of that month, skilled workers received yellow work permits (*Scheine*) that were also valid for their immediate families. On October 24, some 5,000 to 8,000 Jews who did not have such a permit were segregated and then shot in Ponary. A similar massacre claimed another 3,000 Jewish victims on November 5. These killings were known as the "yellow-*Schein* operations" ("Aktionen der gelben Scheine"). In December the yellow permits were replaced by pink ones, and all ghetto dwellers who did not have them were then shot, in the "Aktion der rosa Scheine."

Until August 1943, individual Jews were continually being abused or killed for petty offenses. In other respects, however, a mild normalization set in: handicrafts workshops were established, Jewish schools were opened, and there were even concert and theater performances. That August the German occupation authority decided to resettle Vilna's Jewish inhabitants in Latvia and Estonia. Since no one volunteered, a thousand Jews were seized on their way to work and deported to Estonia. In September security forces combed through the ghetto for four days, dragged 6,000 people—some of whom put up resistance—out of their hiding places, and deported them to Estonia. Buildings from which shots came were blown up, killing many inside. From September 23 to 27, the last inhabitants of the Vilna ghetto were seized; some were transported to the other two Baltic states, and others were sent to the Treblinka extermination camp.

In the middle of September 1943, some 1,500 Jews were allocated to the army motor depot and another 1,500 to the fur factory in Kailis. There, on March 27, 1944, the elderly and sick men and women, as well as all the children, were separated out and then shot in Ponary. The same fate befell the ghetto's last inhabitants in early July of 1944. On July 12–13 the Red Army reached Vilna.

W. D.

Vlasov, Andrei, b. Lomkino, near Nizhni Novgorod, September 1, 1900; d. Moscow, August 2, 1946 (executed), Soviet lieutenant general. Vlasov joined the Red Army in 1919. At the time of the Russian Campaign, he was the commanding general of the Fourth Tank Corps; he defended Kiev in September 1941 as supreme commander of the Thirty-seventh Army. After successes in the battle for Moscow (December 1941), Vlasov

Andrei Vlasov.

was flown on March 21, 1942, to the Volkhov front, which was encircled by the Germans. There he fell into the hands of the surrounding German troops on July 11 of that year. He then put himself at the disposal of the SMOLENSK COMMITTEE. On September 10 he wrote his first pamphlet urging Soviet soldiers to desert, and he sought to create a volunteer army of Soviet prisoners of war to free Russia from Bolshevism. The National Socialist leadership used him solely for propagandistic ends, put him off, and permitted the creation of two divisions (the Vlasov army) only when the situation became hopeless. Captured by American troops in 1945, Vlasov was handed over to the Soviet Union.

Vocational competition (*Berufswettkampf*), competition of "all productive Germans as an expression of National Socialist readiness to perform in a vocation." It was organized beginning in 1934 by the German Labor Front (*see* REICH VOCATIONAL COMPETITION).

Vocational training, continuing (*Berufsschulung, zusätzliche*), continuation courses for industrial workers and artisans offered by the GERMAN LABOR FRONT (DAF) to promote and select new generations of skilled craftsmen. The training was conducted partly in cooperation with the Hitler Youth, on the principle that the "struggle for the best vocational performance" was part of the political struggle for the VOLK COMMUNITY. Thus, vocational training camps, especially for apprentices, were organized by the Reich Youth Leadership.

Vögler, Albert, b. Borbeck, February 8, 1877; d. near Herdecke, April 14, 1945, German industrialist and politician. Even before the First World War, Vögler, a metallurgical engineer, was a prominent representative of the steel industry. From 1906 to 1912 he was director of the Union Corporation for the Iron and Steel Industry (Union AG für Eisen- und Stahlindustrie), and from 1915 to 1926 he was general director of the United Steel Works, Inc. (Vereinigte Stahlwerke AG), Germany's largest steel concern. He was also active in politics. In 1919 he became a member of the National Assembly, and from 1920 to 1924 he represented the German People's Party (DVP) in the Reichstag.

Between 1930 and 1933, Vögler was one of the first representatives of German business circles to give money to the NSDAP. He joined the KEPPLER CIRCLE in 1932. In January 1933 Vögler, along with other representatives of the steel industry, supported Hitler's nomination as Reich chancellor. In the Third Reich he was chairman of numerous boards of directors (including those of the Ruhr Gas Company, Inc., and Gelsenkirchen Mines, Inc.) and a member of economic coordinating councils (among others, the General Council for the Economy). He was a Reichstag delegate from 1933 to 1945, although not a member of the NSDAP. Toward the end of the war, Vögler was interned as an American prisoner of war. He committed suicide in captivity.

R. S.

Albert Vögler (left) with Hitler and Borbet.

Voigt, Friedrich, b. Treba bei Nordhausen, November 18, 1882; d. Berlin, March 1, 1945 (executed), German opposition fighter. A construction worker, in 1909 Voigt became a trade union secretary in Kiel. In 1913 he moved to Breslau. From 1914 to 1918 he served at the front, and in 1918 he became chairman of the Soldiers' Council for Silesia. A Social Democrat, he was police president of Breslau in 1919–1920, then had a leading role in the development of communal nonprofit construction organizations. Voigt lost all his offices in 1933, and was temporarily interned in concentration camps; he became friends with the opposition figure Oswald WIERSICH. Voigt's contacts with Friedrich Werner Count von der SCHULENBURG and the conspirators of July 20, 1944, led to his arrest. The *Volk* Court on February 28, 1945, condemned him to death.

Volk (folk, people), one of the most frequently used catchwords in the Third Reich. The word, which acquired multiple meanings, came from the Old High German, and referred originally to a troop of warriors or a human crowd (*Menschenhaufen*). In the 18th century it was used in a largely negative connotation for the lowly, common folk, as distinct from the upper orders. The word *Volk* then acquired new significance from the philosophers and writers of German Romanticism, a tradition that appealed to the National Socialists.

The *Volk* thus became: (1) the "nucleus of all social groupings" (*Kern aller Stände*) in the sense of the basic and original social order, a positive contrast to the "decadent" cultures of the bourgeoisie, the aristocracy, the "educated," and the intellectuals; (2) a political, cultural, and linguistic unit, in the sense of a NATION or nation-state (*Staats-Volk*); (3) an ideal or metaphysically transfigured entity, a "sublime community of a long succession of past, now-living, and yet-to-be-born generations, which are all connected in a great and intimate union of life and death" (Adam Müller); this concept was expanded by the National Socialists to a "fateful idea" (*schicksalshafte Idee*), which found its most notable expression in the "Führer" predestined by "Providence"; (4) a "community of blood" or race; the National Socialists used the term in this sense with particular frequency, often in derivations and compound terms.

[In a sense closer to the original meaning, but with positive and class-conscious connotations, the word *Volk* was historically part of the basic vocabulary of the German Left, as in *Berliner Volksblatt*, the subtitle of the Social Democratic Party's newspaper, VORWÄRTS. This is the "news of the people," in the sense of the common or "real" people; *see also* PARTY COMRADE; VOLK COMRADE.]

Volk Community (*Volksgemeinschaft*), official National Socialist designation for the model of society being promoted: "Transcending classes and social orders, occupations, religious denominations, and all the usual confusion of life, the social unity of all Germans arises, without regard to social status or origins, grounded in blood, united by a thousand-year history, bound together by fate in success and in ruin" (Hitler, 1940). A similarly transfigured *Volk* Community based on the so-called "front community" (*see* FRONT EXPERIENCE) of the First World War trenches was offered as the solution to the conflicts of political and economic interests in the Weimar Republic and as a means to overcome class conflict. With their program of the *Volk* Community as the "community of all *Volk* comrades," the National Socialists wanted to foster in the masses the readiness to sacrifice for higher ideals—the goals of the NS policies— and to conform to the demands of the state as a community. The basic structures of bourgeois society and the conflicts of economic interest remained untouched: "We are no egalitarians [*Gleichmacher*] and idolizers of humanity," remarked Joseph Goebbels in 1928. "We want a stratification of the *Volk*, high and low, above and below."

H. H.

Volk Comrade (*Volksgenosse, Volksgenossin* [f.]), regularly used form of address during the Third Reich, in National Socialist propaganda, in speeches, in appeals, and in laws. It was intended to underline a sense of community and the abolition of social and status differences. In terms of its etymology, "*Volk* Comrade" was initially used only to refer to citizens of the same country or region, in the sense of *Landsmann*. During the First World War the term was intended to emphasize the common effort for the fatherland: "In this war . . . millions of *Volk* Comrades are on the battlefield" (Wilhelm II, 1917).

In *völkisch*-nationalist circles the term began to be used early in the 20th century as a racist, positive term, as contrasted to "people of alien and other ethnic groups." This *völkisch* conno-

tation, together with a revolutionary-socialist one (because of the practice, in the workers' movement and workers' parties, of addressing one another as "comrade" [*Genosse*]), was of greatest importance for the National Socialists: "Only a *Volk* Comrade can be a citizen. Only a person with German blood, without regard to religious denomination, can be a *Volk* Comrade. Therefore no Jew can be a *Volk* Comrade" (Point 4 of the PARTY PROGRAM OF THE NSDAP of February 24, 1920). Because of the exceptionally frequent use of the term, however, it eventually lost its political and ideological meaning, so that "*Volk* Comrade" became one of the typically empty formulas of the Third Reich.

Volk-Conservative Union (Volkskonservative Vereinigung), splinter group from the German National People's Party (DNVP) under Gottfried TREVIRANUS; it was established on January 28, 1930. The union's intention was to be a conservative reservoir containing forces from the political center to the Right; it sought a constitutional monarchy. On July 30, 1930, it accepted a further group of DNVP dissidents. As the Conservative People's Party (Konservative Volkspartei) it took part in the elections of September 14, 1930, with little success (only four mandates). The group did not participate in the elections of 1932–1933. Under the National Socialist ban on parties it was dissolved on July 14, 1933. Of its some 10,000 members (1933), many found their way into the opposition (*see, for example,* Paul LEJEUNE-JUNG; Max HABERMANN).

Volk Court (Volksgerichtshof), court created in 1934, with its headquarters in Berlin; its function was to pass sentence on certain political crimes. It was first founded as one of the SPECIAL COURTS to judge cases of high and state treason by a law of April 24, 1934 (*Reich Law Gazette* I, p. 341). By a law of April 18, 1936 (*Reich Law Gazette* I, p. 369), the *Volk* Court became a regular court. Its jurisdiction was gradually broadened, particularly in the areas of UNDERMINING OF MILITARY STRENGTH, espionage, and damage to Wehrmacht property.

The occasion prompting the creation of the *Volk* Court was the REICHSTAG FIRE TRIAL, which the National Socialists found unsatisfactory; it was held before the REICH COURT, which up until then had had jurisdiction over such matters. The actual purpose of the *Volk* Court's establishment was to give the political leadership direct influence over its composition:

Volk Court. Roland Freisler before the opposition fighters of July 20.

in a departure from the Law on Judicial Organization, the members of the *Volk* Court were appointed by Hitler. The court had six panels (senates), each with five judges, only two of whom had to be professional judges. These lay judges served as honorary members and came from the Wehrmacht, the police, or party organizations. The prosecution authority was the Supreme Reich Prosecutor (*Oberreichsanwalt*). The court's first president in 1936 was the later Reich justice minister Otto THIERACK, under whose leadership the court's sentences became increasingly harsh. After Roland FREISLER became president in 1942, the *Volk* Court became a pure instrument of terror for annihilating political opponents; between 1942 and 1944 it imposed a total of 4,951 death sentences. The proceedings—above all those of the First Senate under Freisler as chief judge—were characterized by the total abandonment of constitutional procedural guarantees and the rules of criminal procedure. The *Volk* Court presided over the prosecutions of the opposition fighters of the TWENTIETH OF JULY and of the members of the WHITE ROSE group.

Despite the dominant role played by the *Volk* Court during the war years, it did not shape the JUSTICE system under the Third Reich, though today this is often assumed to have been the case. Rather, this was done by the traditional courts, whose judicial decisions were merely overshadowed by the brutality of the *Volk* Court.

West Germany's supreme Federal Court (Bundesgerichtshof; BGH)—like other courts—has concerned itself repeatedly with *Volk* Court decisions, and has particularly criticized the latter's misuse of penal code paragraphs and its extraordinarily heavy punishments (BGHSt 3, 110; 4, 66; 9, 302): the BGH has stated that the *Volk* Court's misuse of paragraphs in the penal code was an "exploitation of legal forms for illegal killing" and had nothing to do with the administration of justice. The only criminal judgment against a *Volk* Court member was, however, reversed by the BGH in 1968 (the Rehse decision; *see Neue Juristische Wochenschrift*, 1968, p. 1339). In 1979 the state prosecutor's office in Berlin again took up the investigation of the 74 former members of the *Volk* Court who were still living. On January 25, 1985, the Bundestag passed a resolution (BT-Drs. 10/2368, Plenary Protocol 10/118, p. 8761) stating that "the institution known as the *Volk* Court was not a court in the constitutional sense, but rather an instrument of terror for implementing National Socialist tyranny." *Volk* Court decisions thus had no legal validity.

U. B.

[**Volk-Germans**, the literal sense of the National Socialist term *Volksdeutsche*. It referred to noncitizens of the German state who, however, ethnically belonged to the German nation. The term, which is still in use today, is more familiarly translated as ETHNIC GERMANS.]

Volkhafte Dichtung (writing infused with qualities of the *Volk*), term introduced by nationalistic literary history (as Hellmuth Langenbucher's *Volkhafte Dichtung der Zeit* (*Volkhaft* Literature of the Era). It was initially applied to the homeland literature (*Heimatliteratur*) that became popular around 1890, and was later extended to all contemporary, nationalist, and National Socialist literature.

völkisch, National Socialist catchword with a positive connotation frequently used in the Third Reich in ideological contexts, although its meaning was not sufficiently defined. Even Hitler (in *Mein Kampf*) criticized the "conceptual boundlessness" of the word *völkisch*. Originally it meant only *volkstümlich* (folksy, popular, simple), but beginning in the late 19th century it also acquired a nationalist sense. After 1918 it became generally accepted above all as a comprehensive term for the nationalistic and racist groups and movements in the German-speaking areas. In NS usage it acquired first and foremost the meanings of antisemitic, chauvinist-nationalistic, and true to blood and species (*blut- und artgemäss*).

Völkischer Beobachter (Völkisch Observer; VB), the central organ of the NSDAP. It was acquired at the end of 1920, and beginning in 1923 it was published daily by the EHER PRESS. As of 1921 it bore the subhead "Militant Paper of the Great-German National Socialist Movement" (*Kampfblatt der national-sozialistischen Bewegung Grossdeutschlands*). In its external makeup as well, it was conceived as a political paper for the masses, with oversize format, black and red type, and illustrations. During the TIME OF STRUGGLE the VB was, next to the party's gatherings, the most important propaganda medium for spreading National Socialist ideology. Within the party it was regarded as the "connecting link between the Führer and his followership."

The Eher Press director as of 1922 was Max AMANN, and the VB's editor in chief beginning in July–August 1921 was Dietrich ECKART, until his replacement in March 1923 by Alfred ROSENBERG. Its regular contributors were journalists from the VÖLKISCH MOVEMENT, as well as nonprofessionals from Hitler's immediate circle. The VB was banned after the HITLER PUTSCH, to be re-established in February 1925. Hitler himself took responsibility as publisher of the paper until April 30, 1933. Its circulation in 1925 was 4,000 copies, a figure that increased to 126,000 in 1932. Beginning in February 1927 a Reich edition was printed along with the Bavarian one, and as of March 1930 there was a separate Berlin edition, which lasted a year. In 1933 the VB established its

Völkischer Beobachter. "Gauleiter Bürckel speaks today on the Heldenplatz. German Vienna answers the black agitators. Gauleiter Globocnik warns the politicized clergy."

own editorial office and press in Berlin, where the North German edition came out.

As of January 30, 1933, the VB became a quasi-government organ, and its articles had an official character. To stress its universal appeal it published many supplements, especially between 1933 and 1938, such as "The German Woman," "The Film Observer," and the like. Wilhelm WEISS became editor in chief in 1938. After the annexation of Austria, a branch office was established in Vienna in 1938. A VB FIELD POST edition began publication in Munich in 1941.

In 1938, some 600,000 copies of the VB were printed (a much higher number than were sold). Of these, the Berlin–North German edition consisted of 410,000 copies, the Munich edition of 150,000, and the Vienna edition of 40,000. In 1944 the press run was 1.7 million copies. The last copy of the North German edition was dated April 27, 1945, and of the South German edition, April 30.

S. O.

Völkischer Wille (Völkisch Will), journal of the Reich League of the Child-Rich.

Völkisch Movement (*Völkische Bewegung*), collective term for *völkisch*-antisemitic and all-German-nationalistic parties and organizations that entered into frequently shifting alliances, while generally manifesting an exclusive, doctrinaire, and sectarian character. The intellectual roots of the Völkisch Movement and of its Austrian variant reach back to the 19th century (and to the "father of gymnastics," Friedrich Ludwig JAHN, among other sources). Its organizational origins can be traced to the fusion of the German Social Party with the German Reform Party, which produced the German Völkisch Party—the proponent of aggressive annexationism and racist antisemitism at the time of the First World War. During the Weimar Republic its heirs included such groups as ARTAMANEN, the THULE SOCIETY, the German Völkisch League for Defense and Offense, and the German Völkisch Freedom Party.

The German Völkisch Freedom Party (DVFP; *see* GERMAN-VÖLKISCH MOVEMENT) originated as a splinter group from the German National People's Party (DNVP), under the special aegis of Gen. Erich LUDENDORFF. Its base was in the northern and eastern German regions dominated by large estates. Like the NSDAP, the DVFP was banned for a time in 1923–1924 in Prussia and several other states. In the chaos after the

Völkisch Movement. Election poster of the Völkisch Bloc, 1924: "The wire-puller. Workers of head and hand vote Völkisch Bloc."

HITLER PUTSCH and the ringleader's incarceration, loose alliances formed between the DVFP and some National Socialists in northern Germany. In the south, the National Socialists were variously known as the Völkisch Bloc or the GREAT-GERMAN VOLK COMMUNITY. The *völkisch* forces coalesced tenuously, first in the National Socialist Freedom Party, which later, in 1924, became the NATIONAL SOCIALIST FREEDOM MOVEMENT OF GREAT-GERMANY, in an effort to assume leadership in the Völkisch Movement. Although the National Socialists stayed mostly aloof from these organizations, the *völkisch* forces in general reached an electoral high point in the Reichstag elections of May 4, 1924, when they won 32 seats (10 to the National Socialists) and 6.5 percent of the votes cast. In the next elections, on December 7, 1924, the *völkisch* mandates dropped to 14 (including 4 to the National Socialists). After the election, any idea of a real alliance with the NSDAP collapsed, an inevitable outcome after Hitler's release from prison. The German Völkisch Freedom Movement that arose in early 1925 remained largely confined to northern Germany.

From 1918 to 1924 the Völkisch Movement was the political and ideological pioneer, the source of members, and, often enough, the financial and social midwife (the role of the Thule Society) for the NSDAP and its predecessor, the German Workers' Party (DAP). The movement also served the NSDAP during the period of its prohibition (1923 to 1925) by providing camouflage and substitute organizations. Despite its internal heterogeneity and its lack of organizational stability, the movement was held together programmatically by its sense of German-*völkisch* mission and superiority. Other unifying factors were its rejection of a "foreignization" from the West (*westliche Überfremdung*), its belief in "*völkisch* species purity" as the basis of national greatness, its fanatic hatred of Jews and Bolshevism, and its common opposition to democracy, the "November criminals," and the "Versailles diktat."

Hitler dismissively characterized the Völkisch Movement as consisting of "*völkisch* sleepwalkers," "itinerant preachers," and theoretical hypocrites, and as an organization of "highly honorable but eccentric and naive academics, professors, district officials, assistant headmasters, and judicial councillors." He utilized the movement only as a springboard to power and as a tool enabling him to seem "respectable" in bourgeois salons, especially in Munich, so that he might solicit sources of money for his own "movement." On the other hand, the Völkisch Movement for a time harbored the illusion that Hitler could be used as a *Massentrommler*—a drummer whom the masses would follow into its own camp. After the re-establishment of the NSDAP on February 27, 1925, Hitler quickly succeeded in usurping the legacy of the Völkisch Movement. Its representatives were integrated into the NSDAP or marginalized until the remainder of the movement was synchronized or prohibited in 1933.

B.-J. W.

Volk Law Code (*Volksgesetzbuch;* VGB), the rewriting of civil (private) law, planned but never carried through, as part of the National Socialists' effort at LEGAL REFORM. The National Socialists were inspired by their antipathy toward the Civil Code (Bürgerliches Gesetzbuch; BGB) and the liberalism that underlay it, which in their view one-sidedly emphasized the sovereignty of the individual will. Instead, they wanted to create a legal work that—in language comprehensible to the *Volk*—would facilitate the development of *völkisch* law and give precedence to the idea of community. The birthplace of this endeavor was the ACADEMY FOR GERMAN LAW under Hans Frank. The new code was first discussed in 1933, and the actual work on it began in 1939.

Difficulties in realizing the project developed, however, once the war began. Aside from disagreements among the academy, the Reich Justice Ministry, and Hitler, the quantity of material to be dealt with, above all, presented a problem. The intention of creating a law code close to the people with fewer paragraphs than the BGB, which comprehensively regulated the legal affairs of the *völkisch* community, proved scarcely feasible. When Otto THIERACK became Reich justice minister in 1942, work on the code took second place to judicial reform. The only part that was published, in late 1942, was the first: Basic Law and Book I, written by Justus HEDEMANN, Wolfgang Siebert, and Heinrich Lehmann, three leading German theorists of civil law. Thierack soon realized that the new code would not become law before the end of the war.

U. B.

Volk League for Germandom Abroad (Volksbund für das Deutschtum im Ausland; VDA), organization for fostering the cultural and social life of FOREIGN GERMANS and ETHNIC GERMANS; it was founded in 1881 as the German School Organization (Deutscher Schulverein). In 1933 the VDA supported 9,200 German schools in other countries; it also promoted ethnic German literature and established libraries. Synchronized after the Seizure of Power, it played a considerable role in the National Socialist propaganda promoting the idea of a *Volk*-nation.

Volk officer (*Volksoffizier*), derogatory term in Wehrmacht jargon for a National Socialist upstart in the officer corps. They were also ridiculed with the acronym Vomag (Volksoffizier mit Arbeitergesicht [*Volk* officer with a worker's face]).

"Volk ohne Raum" (*Volk* without Space), frequently used propaganda slogan, borrowed by the National Socialist makers of population policy from the title of the 1926 novel by Hans GRIMM. Applied to the Germans, it was intended to justify the demand for more LIVING SPACE (*Lebensraum*).

Volksaufklärung und Propaganda (*Volk* [Public] Enlightenment and Propaganda), ministry newly created in Hitler's government on March 13, 1933 (*see* PROPAGANDA MINISTRY).

Volk sentiment (*Volksempfinden*), catchword used to defame modern, socially critical, and socialist art, which supposedly was in conflict with *Volk* sentiment; it was used almost exclusively in the combination "healthy *Volk* sentiment" (*gesundes Volksempfinden*). After 1933 the term even found its way into the judicial system: following the amendment of the penal code on June 28, 1935, punishment could be levied not only for a breach of law "according to the fundamental idea of a penal law," but for any act that "deserves punishment according to healthy *Volk* sentiment." Since "healthy *Volk* sentiment" was not to be confused with "*Volk* sentiment as such," courts were to make the "authoritative proclamations of the Führer's will" the ultimate standard: "Whether the sentiment is healthy," stated Roland FREISLER, "must be tested against the standards and guidelines that the Führer himself has repeatedly given to the *Volk* in important questions affecting the life of the *Volk*."

Volksgemeinschaft. *See Volk* Community.

Volksgerichtshof. *See Volk* Court.

Volkskanzler (*Volk* [people's] chancellor), term favored by Joseph Goebbels for Hitler, especially in the early phase of the Third Reich; it was meant to emphasize the popularity of the "Führer."

Volk soldier (*Volkssoldat*), term coined by former Reich bishop Ludwig MÜLLER (in *Der deutsche Volkssoldat* [The German *Volk* Soldier]; 1940). It was taken over by National Socialist propaganda to emphasize the "intimate involvement" between the military and the *Volk* in the Third Reich. The term was also intended to reflect the extension of military concerns to all areas of life. Accordingly, every German who "[did] his duty for the building of the *Volk* Community" (*Das Reich*, August 4, 1940) was a *Volk* soldier.

Volk soul (*Volksseele*), among the German writers and philosophers of the 19th century who were oriented toward the nation-state, a term used to denote the spiritual and cultural factors shared by those who made up the nation. The National Socialists added a more mythical layer ("with primeval racial origins"). They also used the term in the sense of VOLK SENTIMENT, mainly in the combination "seething *Volk* soul" (*kochende Volksseele*).

Volk's receiver (*Volksempfänger*), official designation for a technically simple and outwardly plain and unornamented radio set; it was designed and built in 1933 on the request of the Propaganda Ministry. By means of standardization and mass production, the usual price for a radio, which was between 200 and 400 RM at

Volk's receiver. National Socialist poster: "All of Germany hears the Führer with the *Volk's* receiver."

that time, could be lowered to 76 RM (including an antenna). The radio received only medium wavelengths, so that foreign broadcasting stations could scarcely be heard. However, its low price made it accessible for most Germans: the number of households with radios rose from 25 percent in 1933 to 65 percent in 1941. Behind the promotion of the *Volk's* receiver lay Joseph Goebbels's view that RADIO was "the most important instrument for influencing the masses."

Volk Storm (*Volkssturm*), troops assembled from previously nonconscripted men between the ages of 16 and 60, for the purpose of defending the "home soil"; it was created by a Führer decree of September 25, 1944. After invoking the German victories of the years 1939 to 1941, the decree stated that for the "second large-scale operation [*Grosseinsatz*] of our *Volk*," the *Gau* leaders, as Reich Defense Commissioners (*Reichsverteidigungskommissare*), would be responsible for organizing and leading the *Volk* Storm; that the party and its divisions were to give unstinting help; and that Reichsführer-SS Heinrich Himmler would assume the military leadership, and Reichsleiter Martin Bormann, the political and organizational leadership. Those affected were some 6 million men, who were called up in three levies: (1) all men born between 1884 and 1924 who had been exempted from military service for reasons of age or health (the average age was 52); (2) men previously classified as in indispensable occupations; and (3) young men born between 1925 and 1928, who were to be trained in MILITARY FITNESS CAMPS of the Hitler Youth or by the REICH LABOR SERVICE.

It was the required instruction in particular that created difficulties: because of the bloodletting caused by the war, the work week for most of the men designated for the *Volk* Storm had increased to over 70 hours; in addition, there was a lack of weapons and even more so, of ammunition. This deficiency could not be overcome, so that the military value of the *Volk* Storm units, for all their personal courage, remained minimal. They fought with captured weapons and a specially developed "*Volk* rifle" (*Volksgewehr*) that economized on materials, with antitank rocket launchers, and above all with picks and shovels. They built tank barricades, dug trenches at the front, and put up emergency shelters.

Because the *Volk* Storm men had combatant status, they shared the fate of regular soldiers— or worse—if captured. Their field gray party uniforms and their armbands with the legend "German *Volk* Storm Wehrmacht" often caused them to be mistaken for partisans. Especially in the east, they suffered enormous casualties. Primarily deployed in areas close to home, many *Volk* Storm units defended themselves against the Red Army with the courage of despair. In the west, on the other hand, the panic fear of the enemy was absent. Altogether, the deployment of the *Volk* Storm proved to be meaningless and irresponsible. The last reserves of the defeated National Socialist Reich bled to death: tens of thousands fell, and after the war 175,000 were listed in the files as missing.

Volkswagen (VW; literally, the *Volk*'s car), automobile designed by Ferdinand PORSCHE. It was offered at affordable prices and was intended to introduce mass MOTORIZATION to Germany. In the VW's creation, an industrial investment program was united with a sociopolitical goal: the automobile lost its character as a status symbol for wealthy people. The idea and even the first conception of the (beetlelike) shape of the VW allegedly originated with Hitler ("It should look like a beetle [*Maikäfer*]; one needs only to observe nature to realize how it produces a streamlined form"). Porsche's design of an automobile accommodating four persons, with rear-wheel drive, air-cooled engine, top speed of 100 km/hr (about 60 mph), and 8-liter (2.11-gallon) gas tank, at a price of 1,000 RM, was presented as early as January 1934. Prototypes of the sedan, coupe, and convertible models were ready by 1936.

The automobile industry, which was to finance the VW and produce it in its own factories, delayed the project. Hitler then transferred production to a private factory, founded by the GERMAN LABOR FRONT in the "City of the KdF-car" (*Stadt der KdF-Autos*), now Wolfsburg. The STRENGTH THROUGH JOY (KdF) leisure-time organization issued savings certificates ("5 Mark die Woche musst du sparen, willst du im eigenen Wagen fahren!" ["Save 5 marks a week if you want to drive your own car!"]). Yet none of the 336,000 people who placed an order for the VW ever saw one; the car was ultimately produced only as a jeep (*Kübelwagen*) for the Wehrmacht after the war had begun.

In 1944, after heavy air attacks, production of the VW was halted. It was quickly started again

Volk Storm. Young and old with antitank rocket launchers in the trenches.

Volkswagen. Presentation of the three models at the laying of the foundation stone of the Volkswagen factory (1938).

after the war, now with real VWs, which as "beetles" began their triumphal march around the world: the total production by 1981, in Wolfsburg and in foreign branch factories, was 20 million cars. Those who had joined the KdF savings plan were compensated in 1961 with a price reduction of 600 DM toward the price of a new car.

Ba.

Volk treason (*Volksverrat*), in National Socialist legal thought, "crime against the state" as such; *Volksverrat* was a generic term for the "phenomena" (*Erscheinungsformen*) of high treason, state treason, and territorial treason (*Hoch-, Landes-, Gebietsverrat*), among other such crimes. Any attack on the authority of the state or on the "idea of the *Volk* Community" that underlay National Socialism constituted treason against the *Volk*. According to this argument, the traitor to the *Volk* (*Volksverräter*) breaks asunder "the awareness of his sacred bond" with the "state as a sworn community of loyalty." High treason and state treason were by nature the same crime; any differences were insignificant, since an attack on the state's inner stability would always undermine its outer stability, and vice versa.

National Socialist CRIMINAL LAW from the outset accorded the highest priority to the prosecution of *Volk* treason. As early as 1933, the death penalty was introduced for high treason (law of February 28, 1933; *Reich Law Gazette* I, p. 85). In 1934 the provisions on high treason and state treason were made considerably more severe (¶¶80–93 of the Criminal Code; law of April 24, 1934; *Reich Law Gazette*

I, p. 34). The supreme REICH COURT was deprived of jurisdiction over such legal proceedings. They were transferred to the VOLK COURT, which had been newly created expressly for such cases as the court of first and last instance. The facts in these treason cases were increasingly interpreted by the courts in a totally unrestrained manner, and thus could be applied as was convenient. According to the *Volk* Court judge Roland FREISLER, the legal decisions were to be inspired "by the firm desire to root out treason." The National Socialist Guidelines for a New German Criminal Law, issued by the Reich Legal Office of the NSDAP, defined *Volk* treason as "the crime committed directly against the German *Volk* by a *Volk* Comrade [*Volksgenosse*] who is seeking to upset [*erschüttern*] the political unity, freedom, and strength of the German *Volk*." This definition made any unfavorable utterance or attitude punishable as *Volk* treason.

U. B.

Volk vermin (*Volksschädlinge*), application of the agricultural-pest concept to human beings, a usage that arose around the turn of the 20th century. It soon became a favored term in the antisemitic and nationalist repertoire of catchwords. The National Socialist ideology of the *Volk* Community in particular favored the vermin rhetoric for segregating those whom it hated. The Ordinance against Volk Vermin of September 5, 1939 (*Reich Law Gazette* I, p. 1679)—a particularly significant usage—drastically expanded the possibilities of criminal prosecution and culpability. According to this law, almost all criminal acts committed by someone exploiting the special circumstances of war were punishable by death. The law's Paragraph 2 stipulated the most severe punishment for any crime against person or property; its Paragraph 4 made the same stipulation for other crimes "when [demanded] by healthy VOLK SENTIMENT because of the particular heinousness of the criminal act."

After the war began, the state prosecutor had the authority to prosecute a crime with normal procedures and sentencing, or to prosecute it by means of the Ordinance against Volk Vermin before the Special Court to which that ordinance (¶1, Section 2) assigned jurisdiction (*see* SPECIAL COURTS). Protections for the defendant were abolished in Paragraph 5 if he or she were caught committing the act, or if "guilt [is] otherwise evident." The defendant then had to be sentenced immediately. The Ordinance against Volk Vermin was probably the most frequently used "legal" basis for the approximately 15,000 death sentences imposed in civil courts between 1941 and 1945.

                                             C. S.

Volkwerdung (*Volk* becoming), National Socialist catchword for the desired overcoming of class antagonism and class distinctions in a German VOLK COMMUNITY.

Vollsieg (total victory), attempt to Germanize the foreign word "triumph."

Voluntariness (*Freiwilligkeit*), a hollow term in the collectivist National Socialist system, since refusal of the desired behavior, especially the making of contributions, was threatened with what could be severe sanctions. For example, Hitler addressed his appeal for the Winter Relief Agency in 1937 as follows: "You must step forward and make a voluntary sacrifice!" ("Du musst herantreten und freiwilling Opfer bringen!").

Volunteer Helpers (Hilfswillige; Hiwis), term for foreign (*fremdvölkisch*) auxiliaries of the Wehrmacht, police, and SS during the Second World War. Persons of Russian, Ukrainian, Polish, and Latvian nationality (some of them prisoners of war) were especially likely to be won over as volunteers. They were generally deployed for civilian police activities, rather than with combat troops. The volunteers served in concentration camps, in EINSATZGRUPPEN *Aktionen*, in "resettlement" operations, and so on. Occasionally actual "Hiwi" units were formed, as for

Volunteer Helpers. Ukrainians from Lemberg apply for the Waffen-SS.

transport and supply functions, in the manner of the VOLUNTEER UNITS. During the Wehrmacht's retreat from the east it was joined by the volunteers, who could expect immediate execution if they were captured by the Red Army.

Volunteer Units (Freiwilligen-Verbände), term for the field divisions composed of nationals of countries occupied by or allied with Germany that fought with the Wehrmacht in the Second World War. They served as VOLUNTEER HELPERS with the supply columns, at the front with the army, and especially with the WAFFEN-SS. They also worked with the TODT ORGANIZATION or assumed police functions, as in combating partisans.

By 1945 some 1 million men were serving in volunteer units. Among the first such divisions was the Spanish BLUE DIVISION, which had by then withdrawn; the last such large unit was the VLASOV army. The genuine volunteers among the members of these units (of whom many had been subjected to considerable pressure) had streamed to German recruiting stations after the start of the Russian Campaign in order to participate in the "crusade against Bolshevism." Their disillusioned reports about the anti-Christian atmosphere in the SS units soon made the job of recruiters in the SS Main Office (under Gottlob BERGER) increasingly difficult. Nonetheless, the Waffen-SS formed a total of 21 volunteer units from men of nearly 30 nationalities.

Volunteer Units. Russian Hiwis in German uniform.

Vorwärts (Forward; subhead: Berlin People's Paper; Central Organ of the Social Democratic Party [SPD] of Germany), newspaper founded in 1891 in Berlin. Published until 1910 by Wilhelm Liebknecht, it was then put out by a collective committee. Beginning in 1902 it was printed by a publishing house with the same name. The 1914 circulation was 154,000. After the 1916 split in the SPD, Friedrich STAMPFER served as editor in chief (except for a brief interruption) between 1919 and 1933. As of October 1, 1922, Vorwärts for a time had as a subhead: "Central Organ of the United Social Democratic Party of Germany." Beginning on June 29, 1932, its headline bore the emblem of the IRON FRONT: three black arrows on a white background. By the end of 1918, circulation was 400,000; by 1933, it had fallen to 100,000. The REICHSTAG FIRE DECREE prohibited Vorwärts from publishing for four weeks, after which it was completely suppressed. The last issue—printed but not distributed—in Prussia was that of March 28, 1933.

An exile newspaper of the SPD was published in Prague as the Neuer Vorwärts (New Vorwärts) beginning on June 18, 1933. Its editor in

Vorwärts. First issue of the Neuer Vorwärts. "Break the chains! The vanquished of today will be the victors of tomorrow."

chief was again Stampfer; from 1935 to 1940 he was joined by Curt Geyer and Rudolf HILFER-DING as the leading regular contributors. The 1935 printing was 10,000 copies. The newspaper *Sozialistische Aktion* was distributed illegally in Germany from October 29, 1933, to March 1938; its editor in chief was Paul HERTZ. In 1934–1935, 10,000 to 25,000 copies were being printed. Beginning in 1938 the *Neuer Vorwärts* appeared biweekly in Paris in an edition of some 5,000 copies. After the German occupation it had to cease publication, in 1940. The last issue was dated May 12 of that year.

S. O.

Vught, alternate name for the Herzogenbusch concentration camp, especially its women's camp.

V weapons, abbreviated term for the Wonder Weapons intended as "vengeance" (*Vergeltung*) weapons.

Wachenfeld, house on the Obersalzberg, near Berchtesgaden, acquired by Hitler in 1927 and refurbished at considerable expense as the BERGHOF.

Waffen-SS (Armed SS), from November 1939 the usual collective designation for the armed units of the SS and the police. [*Waffen* means "weapons."] The Waffen-SS was thus comprised of the former STANDBY TROOPS, the DEATH'S-HEAD UNITS, and the JUNKER SCHOOLS; it also included a newly instituted police division made up of forces from the Order-keeping Police, as well as members of the responsible central offices (especially the recruitment, weapons, and personnel offices of the Waffen-SS). Soon afterward, partly out of budgetary considerations and partly in order to shelter certain groups of people from conscription into the Wehrmacht, further SS departments—notably various training centers, as well as all concentration camps—were declared to be parts of the Waffen-SS. Although it did not forfeit its autonomy, the Inspectorate for Concentration Camps too, in August 1940, was temporarily (until its incorporation in March 1942 into the ECONOMIC-ADMINISTRATIVE MAIN OFFICE) integrated into the newly established SS Command Main Office, which was conceived as the military command center for the Waffen-SS. Even with regard to the combat units of the Waffen-SS, the competence of this main office was severely limited, since the combat units were incorporated mainly into the field army and were tactically subordinate to the relevant army command authorities. Beyond that, these units, as parts of the overall SS, were also subject to the directives of other SS offices in personnel, training, disciplinary, and penal matters.

The buildup of an SS-controlled army foundered before the war, owing to resistance from the army command in particular. But the latter's loss of influence, in connection with the war pressures, made possible a fundamentally new development. The armed SS, which before the war had never even reached the level of a divisional unit, had at its disposal toward the end of the war a total effective strength of more than 600,000 men (January 1, 1939, 22,700) in (nominally) 38 divisions, 16 general commands, and one army high command (the Sixth SS Panzer Army).

The price for this tumultuous development was, especially from the beginning of the war against the Soviet Union, an increasing deviation from the (never formally abandoned) principle of volunteerism. Simultaneously, the suitability requirements were lowered and a growing number of ethnic German and foreign volunteers from nearly all the European countries were drawn into service. The conversion of the Waffen-SS from a small praetorian guard into a multinational mass army with, at the end, only a minority of totally German soldiers led—particularly given the wartime circumstances—both to a gradual erosion of the organization's ideological uniformity and to extensive loss of its military elitist character. The consequence of this development was a separation of the Waffen-SS into three parts, undertaken by the SS command in 1944. Thereafter the core consisted of "SS divisions" made up only of SS men "suitable for order membership" (*ordenfähig*). Alongside these were the "volunteer divisions" comprised of Germans not suitable for the SS, and "Germanics" (*Germanen*, that is, western and northern Europeans), as well as the "armed divisions" of the SS manned by non-"Germanic," mostly eastern European, volunteers.

The military quality of all these units was extremely variable, depending on the composition of their personnel, their equipment, their training level, and the quality of their collectively very heterogeneous leadership corps. The reputation of the Waffen-SS (which was used on

Himmler inspects members of the Waffen-SS.

all the fronts except for North Africa) as a military elite is based on the outstanding performances of those relatively few units that were best equipped with personnel and matériel. Most of these—such as the "Leibstandarte" (Bodyguard), "Das Reich," "Death's-Head," and "Viking" divisions—came from the cadres of the prewar SS.

The obverse side of the readiness for self-sacrifice characteristic of these units was war conduct that was often ruthless against the enemy and against civilian populations, as was demonstrated in a long list of war crimes, among them those of Le Paradis, Klisura, ORADOUR-SUR-GLANE, and Malmédy (*see* MALMÉDY TRIAL). For this reason, and because of the organizational and personnel ties with other parts of the SS, including the extermination apparatus (*see especially* EINSATZGRUPPEN; CONCENTRATION CAMPS), in the Nuremberg Trials against major war criminals the Waffen-SS was declared one of the CRIMINAL ORGANIZATIONS. In actuality the Waffen-SS, although in official and budgetary matters legally a state agency, and formally subordinate to the jurisdiction of the Reich Interior Ministry, was always a part of the allover SS, and as such the military exponent of an executive authority fixated on the person of Hitler. Regardless of its service at the front with the combat army and the often close cooperation between army and SS units, the Waffen-SS was not, either legally or by its historical evolution, a "fourth branch of the Wehrmacht."

We.

Wage-price policy (*Lohn-Preis-Politik*), measures taken by the National Socialist government to avert rises in wages and prices. Expanded production capacity connected with REARMAMENT, and related shortages of raw materials and manpower, involved the danger of wage and price increases. The government supervision of prices (under Reich Commissioner Carl Friedrich GOERDELER), which had been introduced as early as 1931, was therefore replaced by an active price structuring. An ordinance of October 29, 1936, established the post of Reich Commissioner for Price-setting, a position with extensive authority and a mandate to establish "economically fair prices" (*volkswirtschaftlich gerechte Preise*). One measure in this direction was an ordinance of November 26, 1936, which froze all prices and to a large extent stabilized the level of prices. The price index for the cost of living rose by barely 5 percent between 1934 and 1939.

A freeze was also ordered for wages and salaries. Because the state needed a growing share of the national income for rearmament, a redistribution ensued that was to the detriment of employees. In some sectors the ceiling on wages was evaded because of the increased labor shortage; extra pay and bonuses were used in an effective competition for workers. The state hesitated to take steps against such practices, in order to avoid tensions in the period prior to the war (*see* SOCIAL POLICY). Instead, it preferred managerial tactics involving the raw-materials economy and FOREIGN TRADE in order to ensure the production of armaments.

V. B.

Wager, Bebo, b. Augsburg, December 19, 1905; d. Munich, August 12, 1943 (executed), German opposition fighter. A mechanical engineer, at age 17 Wager joined the Young Socialist Workers and the Social Democratic Party (SPD). After the SPD was proscribed in June 1933, he founded the Revolutionary Socialists (Revolutionäre Sozialisten) opposition group. Maintaining steady contact with the foreign central office in Prague, he kept the left-wing opposition alive in Bavaria. Although his hope to avert the war was futile, Wager prepared his associates with information and arms for a "shortening of the final catastrophe." After he had conducted underground activities for nine years, in the spring of 1942 the Gestapo discovered repositories with plans for an overthrow of the regime. The *Volk* Court in Innsbruck sentenced Wager to death.

Wagner, Adolf, b. Algringen (Lorraine), October 1, 1890; d. Munich, April 12, 1944, German politician. Wagner was an officer in the First World War, then became director of a small mine in the Upper Palatinate. In 1922 he joined the NSDAP, and the following year he participated in the Hitler Putsch. Wagner in 1929

Adolf Wagner.

became *Gauleiter* of Munich–Upper Bavaria (after 1930 called the *Gau* of Tradition). On April 12, 1933, he became interior minister and deputy minister-president of Bavaria, and in 1936, minister of culture and religious affairs.

A dynamic man whom Hitler called his "best, most beloved, and most idealistic collaborator in Bavaria," Wagner became the real strongman in that state and probably the most powerful *Gauleiter* of the Third Reich. (Officially, he ranked after Bavarian minister-president Ludwig Siebert [d. 1942] and Reich governor [*Statthalter*] Ritter von EPP.) Despite the SYNCHRONIZATION of the German states (*Länder*), which he vigorously advocated, Wagner knew how to override advisories from the ministries in Berlin. In cases of conflict he turned directly to Hitler. He had constant access to the Führer's circle of intimate friends at the Obersalzberg; indeed, Hitler often put the Führer Airplane at Wagner's disposal for trips to Berlin.

Wagner had over 100 dealers in provisions sent to the Dachau concentration camp for having raised the price of butter excessively. He personally supervised the removal of crucifixes from schools, although he stopped the practice during the Russian Campaign. He was a fanatic instigator of the PERSECUTION OF JEWS and of ARYANIZATION, and he kept up a permanent feud with Cardinal Michael FAULHABER. Not without unintentionally comic effects, Wagner passed himself off as a patron of the arts. The career of this "despot of Munich" ended when he had a stroke in June 1942. After an illness of 20 months, he died and was given a state funeral

Bebo Wager.

at the FELDHERRNHALLE, with Hitler in attendance.

Wagner, Gerhard, b. Neu-Heiduk (Upper Silesia), August 18, 1888; d. Munich, March 25, 1939, German physician. After studies in Munich, Wagner was a highly decorated medical officer in the First World War (Iron Cross, First Class). After the war he joined the EPP and OBERLAND free corps; he established a general medical practice in Munich in 1919. He joined the NSDAP in 1924, and again in 1929, after its banning was rescinded. Along with Leonardo CONTI and other medical men, Wagner founded the NATIONAL SOCIALIST GERMAN PHYSICIANS' LEAGUE in 1929, assuming its leadership in 1932. In 1933 he was named Reich Physicians' Führer (*Reichsärzteführer*). He supported the Nuremberg Laws and recommended possible methods for FORCED STERILIZATION of Jews and the handicapped. In Wagner's program for *Volk* health—his sphere of responsibility within the Reich NSDAP leadership—there was no room for the mentally ill either. Thus, supported by Rudolf HESS, his patron and patient, he early on supported a EUTHANASIA program.

Wagner, Gustav, b. Vienna, July 18, 1911; d. Itatiaia (São Paulo, Brazil), October 15, 1980 (suicide), SS-*Sturmscharführer* (September 1943). In 1931 Wagner joined the Austrian NSDAP. After being arrested for proscribed National Socialist agitation he fled to Germany, where he joined the SA and later the SS. In May 1940 Wagner began working at the HARTHEIM

Gerhard Wagner.

killing facility near Linz, within the EUTHANASIA program.

Because of his experience at Hartheim, Wagner was assigned to establish the extermination camp at SOBIBÓR in March 1942. After completion of the killing installations there he became deputy commandant of the camp, and as such was responsible for selecting which incoming prisoners were to be used as workers, and which were to be put to death immediately. Survivors of the camp described him as a cold-blooded sadist.

After a prisoner uprising on October 14, 1943, Wagner received an order to close the camp. He was transferred to Italy, where he participated in the deportation of Jews. When the war ended he succeeded in fleeing from an American prison camp. Together with Franz STANGL he escaped to Italy, and then to Brazil (by way of Syria) with the help of ecclesiastics. Wagner lived undisturbed in Brazil until his arrest on May 30, 1978. Demands by Israel, Austria, and the Federal Republic of Germany that he be extradited were refused, and Wagner was again set free.

Wagner, Josef, b. Algringen (Lorraine), January 12, 1899; d. presumably in Berlin, late April 1945 (executed?), German politician. An army volunteer in the First World War, Wagner was severely wounded in 1918 and taken as a French prisoner of war. He underwent teacher training, and in 1922 founded a local NSDAP group in Bochum. In 1928 he became one of the first National Socialist members of the Reichstag, and in October of that year was made *Gauleiter* in Westphalia (as of 1930, in Westphalia-South). Despite his well-known loyalty to the church and to Roman Catholicism, Wagner gained further promotions. In December 1934 he became, in addition to his Westphalian post, governor (*Oberpräsident*) and *Gauleiter* of Silesia. He was also named Reich Commissioner for Pricesetting on October 29, 1936.

Only after the war had begun did the party leadership take exception to Wagner's position on Christianity. They deprived him of his Silesian posts in January 1941, and, at the end of the year, of the *Gau* leadership in Westphalia as well. Against the verdict of the Supreme Party Court, Hitler on October 12, 1942, decreed Wagner's expulsion from the NSDAP, and in the autumn of 1943 ordered that he be kept under Gestapo surveillance. Since his personal assistant during his tenure as price commissioner had been Peter Count YORCK VON WARTENBURG,

Josef Wagner.

Richard Wagner.

Wagner was arrested after the assassination attempt of July 20, 1944. He probably fell victim to his SS captors during the last days of the war.

Wagner, Richard, b. Leipzig, May 22, 1813; d. Venice, February 13, 1883, German composer. No artist was as revered by Hitler and the National Socialists as was Wagner. Both the form and the message of his works contributed to this admiration, as did the cult that surrounded him even during his lifetime.

After years of privation, Wagner achieved an artistic breakthrough with his opera *Rienzi* in 1842. With financial support from Bavaria's King Ludwig II, he achieved monetary success by 1864. This connection to the "fairy-tale king," to whom Wagner owed the building of both his own festival theater in Bayreuth (1872–1876) and his villa there, "Wahnfried" (1873–1874), by itself contributed substantially to the Wagner legend.

His ideological appropriation by the National Socialists was facilitated by his antisemitic writings—for example, *Das Judentum in der Musik* (Jewry in Music; 1850)—and by the near-religious glorification of the German *Volk* in his operas. Wagner, who also wrote all of his own texts, wanted to create with his operas "total works of art" (*Gesamtkunstwerke*) that would reunite poetry, music, and mime, and in which artists and *Volk* would again find one another. Thus came about such monumental works as *Der Ring des Nibelungen* (The Ring of the Nibelungs; 1854–1874), which corresponded to the National Socialist predilection for the super-dimensional.

The celebration of Wagner's operas in the Third Reich as expressions of the "heroic-German worldview" was also a result of Wagner's preference for reworking materials from the German Middle Ages (*Parsifal*; 1882), and of his reliance on Old German alliterative verse. To this he added a turning toward the *Volk* in his most successful opera, *Die Meistersinger von Nürnberg* (The Master Singers of Nuremberg; 1867), which NS interpreters evaluated as "a strong profession of Germanness" and as "art nourished from the primeval spring of *Volk* energy." The figure of Hans Sachs was deemed to be the ideal embodiment of energy, order, and guild honor. According to Joseph Goebbels (1933), no work was so close to "our age in its spiritual and intellectual tensions."

In his later years, by adopting the racial theories of Count Arthur de GOBINEAU, Wagner also laid the foundation for the antisemitic exploitation of his fame. His son-in-law and fervent admirer, Houston Stewart CHAMBERLAIN, who was a personal acquaintance of Hitler's after 1923, steered the perception of Wagner in this direction. The BAYREUTH FESTIVALS, which the leading National Socialists used for self-display, served their ideological ancestor as well.

Wagner, Robert, b. Lindach (North Baden), October 13, 1895; d. Strasbourg, August 14, 1945 (executed), German politician. Without having completed his teacher's training, Wagner volunteered in the First World War, becoming an officer in the Reichswehr. He was a lieutenant in the Munich Infantry School when Hitler attempted his insurrection of November 8–9,

Robert Wagner.

1923, which Wagner joined with enthusiasm. At the HITLER TRIAL he was therefore sentenced to a short period of confinement in a fortress, and was discharged from the army with the rank of captain. When the NSDAP was re-established in February 1925, Wagner was involved with it from the beginning. He became *Gauleiter* in Baden, and, after May 5, 1933, Reich governor (*Statthalter*) as well.

After the French Campaign, Wagner also assumed leadership of the German civilian administration in Alsace, on August 2, 1940, with the goal of complete RE-GERMANIZATION of the area as a preparatory step before annexation. One of his measures in this regard was the deportation of Jews into unoccupied France; they were followed on October 22, 1940, by Jews from his Baden *Gau*, who were interned in GURS. Wagner's harshness escalated to a brutal die-hard policy (*Durchhaltepolitik*) of no concessions when the Allied forces were approaching in 1944. This made him a wanted man after the end of the war. After several months in hiding, he was finally apprehended by the United States military police. Extradited to France, he was sentenced to death and was shot in a summary proceeding.

Wagner, Winifred (née Williams), b. Hastings, June 23, 1897; d. Überlingen, March 5, 1980, English daughter-in-law of Richard WAGNER; a friend of Hitler. At the age of 10 Winifred Williams was adopted by a relative in Germany who was one of the early friends and supporters of Richard Wagner. She married the composer's son Siegfried in 1915. She was on friendly terms with Hitler, an admirer of Wagner's music, starting in 1923. Indeed, while Hitler was incarcerated in Landsberg she sent him food packages and manuscript paper (for *Mein Kampf*); in later years their friendship was so close that rumors of a marriage circulated from time to time. Even after 1933, the Wagner house in Bayreuth, "Wahnfried," remained for Hitler a valued retreat and shelter.

In 1930, Wagner took over the management of the BAYREUTH FESTIVALS, for which she received Hitler's generous support (both subsidies and tax exemptions). The Festival Opera House was elevated to a place of worship in the Third Reich. After 1945 Wagner had to relinquish the management of the festivals, and she retired almost completely from public life. In an interview that she gave in 1975, she continued to declare her friendship and affection for Hitler.

H. H.

Waldeck-Pyrmont, Josias, Hereditary Prince of, b. Arolsen, May 13, 1896; d. there, November 30, 1967, SS-*Obergruppenführer* (1936). After agricultural studies, Waldeck-Pyrmont joined the NSDAP on November 1, 1929, and the SS on March 2, 1930. He became an aide-de-camp to Joseph DIETRICH, and, in 1933, a member of the Reichstag. In 1939 Waldeck-Pyrmont became a Higher SS and Police Leader in Military District (*Wehrkreis*) IX (Weimar), where the Buchenwald concentration camp was located. Although he himself was hardly less devoid of scruples, Waldeck-Pyrmont turned against the methods of private enrichment practiced by the Buchenwald commandant, Karl Koch, and his wife, Ilse KOCH. Waldeck-Pyrmont succeeded in having them transferred for disciplinary reasons to Maidanek, and finally in having them sentenced by an SS court. He also opposed the brutal methods of soliciting recruits practiced by the Waffen-SS, and as a result incurred the wrath of Gottlob BERGER. Waldeck-Pyrmont's own account of offenses was so large that an American court in Dachau sentenced him on August 14, 1947, to life imprisonment. He was, however, released for reasons of ill health as early as September 1950.

Waldorf Schools (*Waldorf-Schulen*), educational institutions of the Anthroposophical Society (*see* ANTHROPOSOPHY); both the schools and the society were prohibited on November 1, 1935.

"Walküre." *See* "Valkyrie."

Wallot Building (*Wallot-Bau*), designation of the Reichstag building, after its builder, Paul Wallot (1841–1912). It was burned down in the REICHSTAG FIRE on February 27, 1933.

Walter, Bruno (originally, Bruno Walter Schlesinger), b. Berlin, September 15, 1876; d. Beverly Hills (California), February 17, 1962, German-American orchestra conductor. As chief music director (*Generalmusikdirektor*) in Munich and Berlin, and as conductor (*Kapellmeister*) of the Gewandhaus Orchestra in Leipzig from 1929 to 1933, Walter was one of the most distinguished German conductors, with an international reputation. He was known especially for promoting works by modern composers (Bruckner, Mahler, and Pfitzner). Because of his love for musical experimentation and his Jewish origin, the "lousy bum" (*Lauselump*, in Richard STRAUSS's words) Walter had to cancel his concerts after the takeover of power. He was at the Vienna State Opera until 1938, and then emigrated to the United States.

Wandering Jew (*Ewiger Jude*; literally, eternal Jew), legendary figure of the Jew condemned to eternal wandering. The legend was known since the 6th century from various traditions, and was circulated throughout Europe in the 17th century as the *Chapbook of the Wandering Jew*. It tells of the shoemaker Ahasuerus, who is condemned forever to ceaseless roaming for turning away Christ from his door as the latter went to his crucifixion. Romantic literature interpreted the motif as a vision of human suffering; in later

Bruno Walter.

works it symbolized in particular the tragic fate of the Jewish people.

Antisemitic propaganda and literature appropriated the Wandering Jew as a symbol of the racially bound vileness of Jewry. At its most extreme, this was shown in the prizewinning National Socialist film of the same name, which was intended to justify to a general public a policy aimed at the physical annihilation of the Jews. This and similar films, such as JUD SÜSS, by portraying the Jews as "subhumans" generated in a broad audience the desired emotional reactions: fear, disgust, envy, and hatred.

Wandervogel (literally, bird of passage), organization formed around 1895 as a schoolboys' group in Berlin-Steglitz; in 1901 its name was changed to the Wandervogel Committee for Schoolboy Excursions. It became the starting point for the German YOUTH MOVEMENT after the turn of the century. The Wandervogel rejected bourgeois culture and big-city civilization, seeking out instead an encounter with, and shared adventure in, nature. The group strove for an alternative culture specifically for young people, with hiking, camping in tents, folk songs, and folk dancing. During the First World War, some army volunteers joined in a "Field-Wandervogel."

After 1918 the Wandervogel broke up into various groups, and *völkisch*-nationalist organizations split off from the overall group. In 1929 the Wandervogel Leagues had a total membership of 30,000. After the takeover of power, the Wandervogel groups joined—some of them voluntarily—the Hitler Youth (HJ), which also

Poster for the exhibition The Wandering Jew in Munich (1937).

Wandervogel members in Imperial Germany.

offered hiking and camp life. Officially, the Wandervogel Leagues were dissolved in June 1933, and their members were transferred to the HJ. Individual groups, however, remained in contact with their members, and eventually became nuclei for youthful opposition in the Third Reich.

H. H.

Wannsee Conference (*Wannsee-Konferenz*), meeting of Reinhard HEYDRICH, chief of the Security Police and the Security Service (SD), and representatives of ministries, party offices, and SS offices on the implementation of the FINAL SOLUTION of the "European Jewish question." The conference took place on January 20, 1942, in Berlin, in a building of the Criminal Police (Am Grossen Wannsee 56/58). On July 31, 1941, Hermann Göring had appointed Heydrich as the delegate for preparing the "complete solution of the European Jewish question." Thus, Heydrich invited to the conference representatives of the Reich Ministry for the Occupied Eastern Territories, the Reich Interior Ministry, the delegate for the Four-Year Plan, the *Generalgouverneur*, the Foreign Ministry, the Party Chancellery, the Reich Chancellery, the Race and Settlement Main Office (RuSHA), the Reich Security Main Office (RSHA), and the commanders of the Security Police (Sipo) and the SD for the Reich Commissariat of the Ostland and the Generalgouvernement. The purpose of the conference was to coordinate the planned measures with these central institutions, which were directly involved in the Final Solution.

Heydrich first presented an overview of the measures that had been taken against the Jews up to that point, and stated in conclusion that despite numerous difficulties, some 537,000 Jews had been made to emigrate (this figure probably included deportees) by October 31, 1941. Of them, about 360,000 came from the "Old Reich" (Altreich; pre-Hitler Germany), about 147,000 from the Ostmark (Austria), and about 30,000 from the Protectorate of Bohemia and Moravia. Instead of emigrating, he reported, Jews were now being evacuated to the east, although this represented only an interim solution until the coming final one, for which practical experience was being collected. About 11 million Jews would be involved in the Final Solution, which would resemble the following scenario: "Under suitable supervision, the Jews shall . . . be taken to the east and deployed in appropriate work. Able-bodied Jews, separated by sex, will be taken to these areas in large work details to build roads, and a large part will doubtlessly be lost through natural attrition. The surviving remnants, since they will no doubt be the most resistant, will have to be treated appropriately, since—representing a natural selection [*natürliche Auslese*]—if released they must be considered the germ cell [*Keimzelle*] of a new Jewish rebuilding [*Aufbau*]."

Heydrich stated that the precise determination of the group of persons to be considered for evacuation was the most important prerequisite for the procedure. The NUREMBERG LAWS were to be the basis. In order to achieve "a complete clearing up of the problem," the settlement of the issue involving mixed marriages and mixed-breeds was, he noted, of fundamental importance. Heydrich then opened the topic for discussion. State Secretary Wilhelm STUCKART of the Reich Interior Ministry and SS-Gruppenführer Otto Hofmann of RuSHA proposed FORCED STERLIZATION for biological reasons. A decision on the issue was not, however, made. After a discussion about implementing the Final Solution in the individual European countries, State Secretary Josef Bühler of the *Generalgouverneur*'s office declared that the removal of 2.5 million Jews from the Generalgouvernement as soon as possible would be welcomed: apart from the fact that as "carriers of contagion" they presented an imminent danger, the majority of them were unsuitable for work. In conclusion, the possibilities of "carrying out certain preparatory work in line with the Final Solution in the affected areas" was discussed, "during which the alarming of the population must be avoided."

A. St.

War (*Krieg*), solution by force of conflicts between cultures, states, peoples, or systems of alliance. War was a central concept in the Social Darwinism of HITLER'S WORLDVIEW, which transferred the "eternal struggle for existence" in nature to human society, in which the stronger would prevail in the final analysis. Readiness for war was allegedly based on the elementary realization that "only by risking one's life can one ensure that it will endure" (*Brockhaus* [Encyclopedia] *on Current Events*, 1942). Referring to the authority of Clausewitz, who categorized war as "a continuation of political intercourse with the addition of other means," the National Socialist perception saw war as a legitimate instrument of politics. Hitler himself viewed assurances of peace during the first years of his rule as a simple matter of tactics, which had forced him to "talk nearly constantly about peace for a decade," whereas the true "goal of this system" was "to make the people ready to stand straight even when thunder and lightning strike" (secret speech before the German press on November 11, 1938).

War Aid Service (Kriegshilfsdienst), an additional labor obligation, at first for young women, justified by the burdens of war. The program was introduced by an edict of July 29, 1941, but it had been temporarily practiced at the beginning of the war; it became a six-month extension of the REICH LABOR SERVICE. Officially, social work, and perhaps office work with the Wehrmacht, was envisioned. However, of the approximately 50,000 young women who were inducted into the War Aid Service in 1942–1943, more than 50 percent were working in the armaments industry, at a daily wage of 1.70 RM. Duty as a Flak Helper (*see* FLAK HELPERS) was later also designated as War Aid Service.

War crimes (*Kriegsverbrechen*), violation of laws and customs of war; one of the four main points of indictment at the NUREMBERG TRIALS, according to Control Council Law No. 10. The rules of conduct for warring parties arise from international agreements, customary law, and general principles of law. Actions that violate these rules are war crimes. According to the statute for the International Military Tribunal (IMT)—a supplement to the LONDON AGREEMENT of August 8, 1945—this category includes, "without being limited to them: murder, mistreatment, or deportation for slave labor or for any other purpose of members of the civilian population of or in occupied territories; murder or mistreatment of prisoners of war or of persons on the high seas; killing of hostages; plundering of public or private property; deliberate destruction of cities, market towns, or villages; or any devastation not justified by military necessity." Control Council Law No. 10 repeated these definitions, but clarified at the outset which legal possessions have to be injured by deeds of violence: body, life, or property.

War crimes. Murdered civilians.

The USSR was a signatory power to the London Agreement, and as an occupying power had enacted Control Council Law No. 10 along with the others. Yet the concept of war crimes was broadened in Soviet proceedings because of a special evaluation of international law that no longer corresponded to international concepts. Any German soldier who had participated in the Russian Campaign was subject to punishment. After the Second World War, only the war crimes of the defeated were punished; the violations of international law by the victors remained unexpiated.

A. St.

War economy (*Kriegswirtschaft*), the complete alignment of the National Socialist economy with military needs. Despite the fact that NS policy was designed for REARMAMENT and war from the beginning, the economy in 1939 was not sufficiently prepared for a war of lengthy duration. Because of Hitler's concept of a BLITZ-KRIEG, it had been adjusted for a major spurt in armaments production at the beginning of the war. Although it thus had at its disposal a high level of armaments, it lacked the necessary potential for an extended war, which would use a large amount of matériel.

The onset of war did not bring about any essential reorientation toward a comprehensive war economy; state-run planning and "steering" had not been intensified, and fundamental modernization of the production facilities had not been carried out. Despite the establishment of the Ministry for Armaments and Munitions under Fritz TODT on March 17, 1940, armaments production was not increased. For over two years, Germany kept to a strategy of diversified armaments (material superiority); the production of weapons and ammunition at the beginning of 1942 was still at the same level as at the beginning of the war. For domestic-policy reasons, production of civilian goods was hardly reduced at all; despite a permanent labor shortage the potential was not fully exploited. The employment of women in particular scarcely increased during the war, and working hours were not drastically extended.

After the failure of the Blitzkrieg in the winter of 1941 (through the defeat outside of Moscow and the entry of the United States into the war), the economy had to be adapted to a war footing. The accession of a new armaments minister, Albert SPEER, Todt's successor, initiated a new period in the German war economy in February 1942. Building on Todt's preliminary

steps, armaments production under Speer rose threefold by mid-1944. Speer centralized the production of goods vital to the manufacture of armaments, and installed cheap and simple facilities for mass production that could be operated by unskilled laborers, ALIEN WORKERS, and forced laborers, as well as by concentration camp inmates. The uncoordinated assignment of slave laborers by Gauleiter Fritz SAUCKEL, the general plenipotentiary for labor deployment, went counter to Speer's idea, according to which foreign skilled workers were to produce for Germany in their own homelands. Economic difficulties increased with the loss of occupied territories, as well as with intensified Allied bombing. Constant shortages of raw materials and manpower could no longer be compensated for after military defeats.

V. B.

War films (*Kriegsfilme*), motion-picture genre preferentially promoted and utilized for propaganda by the National Socialists. As early as the 1920s, numerous German war films represented war as a "purifying bath of steel [*Stahlbad*]," and even before the Seizure of Power propagandized *völkisch*-militaristic heroism: "I could die 10 deaths for Germany, even a hundred," declared the sinking U-boat commander in *Morgenrot* (Dawn; 1933). In the prewar period, war films served as a central means for psychological war preparation, and glorified the sense of duty and readiness to sacrifice (*Urlaub auf Ehrenwort* [Furlough on Parole]; 1937). At times they exaggerated their chauvinism to a point beyond belief: the film *Unternehmen Michael* (Operation Michael; 1937), about the 1918 spring offensive, gave the viewer the impression that "Germany won the First World War" (Erwin Leiser). War films issued after the onset of the Second World War celebrated German military superiority (*Feuertaufe* [Baptism of Fire]; 1940) or extolled a hero's death (*Stukas* [Dive Bombers]; 1941). According to Goebbels, the "hardness and greatness" of war were to be shown, but not films that "would elicit terror of war."

H. H.

War guilt lie (*Kriegsschuldlüge*), slogan in the political fight against the terms of the VERSAILLES TREATY. It referred to ARTICLE 231, which assigned to Germany the sole guilt for unleashing the First World War. This article was not only perceived as a lie in nationalist circles, but it embittered the large majority of the German population, and was even disputed among the victorious powers. An objective answer to the WAR GUILT QUESTION in the long term was thereby hindered.

War guilt question (*Kriegsschuldfrage*), one of the most burning political topics in the Weimar Republic. By signing the Versailles treaty, Germany had—even though under protest and strong pressure (the Allied diplomatic "cover note" of June 16, 1919)—acknowledged its sole guilt for the outbreak of the First World War. From this acceptance, the victorious powers deduced (according to ARTICLE 231 of the peace treaty) their right to German reparations and to military limitations. The majority of the German population treated the one-sided apportionment of guilt as a WAR GUILT LIE, not only because of its economic consequences, but also for its implied moral denigration.

The Weimar governments repeatedly attempted to achieve a revision of the judgment against Germany. A War Guilt desk in the Foreign Ministry was established in 1919; it financed the Central Office for Research on the Causes of the War (Zentralstelle zur Erforschung der Kriegsursachen), which published the journal *Die Kriegsschuldfrage* (as of 1927, *Berliner Monatshefte* [Berlin Monthly Bulletin]). These efforts were unsuccessful, since the entire Versailles system depended on the question of war guilt. The issue provided the parties of the Right, especially the National Socialists, with effective ammunition against "the fetters of the infamous diktat" and thereby against the Republic as well. At the opening session of the Reichstag on March 21, 1933 (*see* POTSDAM CELEBRATION), Hitler rejected the Versailles guilt clause outright, making opposition to it the basis of his REVISIONIST POLICY. He formally withdrew Germany's signature on the Versailles treaty on January 30, 1937.

Today the question of guilt for the 1914 war is being answered in a more complex way: although historians in general dispute Germany's sole guilt, they clearly assume a higher level of German guilt than did the apologists of the 1920s and 1930s. A war guilt question for the Second World War does not present itself in the same way, since the causal factors are unavoidably found in the National Socialists' aggressive foreign policy and in their demands for "living space."

War Library for German Youth (Kriegsbücherei der deutschen Jugend), title of a series of softcover books popular with young people; they were published weekly beginning in 1939 by the REICH YOUTH LEADERSHIP. Since children of workers, in particular, were difficult to reach with hardcover books, adventurous war stories on the model of popular, trite series of cheap novels were intended to awaken enthusiasm for war. Typical titles were *Deutsche Tanks fahren zur Hölle* (German Tanks Drive to Hell) and *Flammenwerfer vor!* (Flamethrowers Ahead!). The authors were often distinguished writers of books for youth using pseudonyms, such as Alfred WEIDEMANN, who published *Ich stürmte Fort III* (I Stormed Fort III; 1940) as M. Derfla.

War novel (*Kriegsroman*), heavily promoted genre of National Socialist LITERATURE. In reaction to a growing number of pacifist novels in the late 1920s, notably Erich Maria REMARQUE's *Im Westen nichts Neues* (In the West There Is Nothing New, 1929; translated as *All Quiet on the Western Front*), numerous NS novels dealt with the First World War even before 1933. Authors such as Werner BEUMELBURG, Edwin Erich DWINGER, and Hans ZÖBERLEIN aesthetically glorified struggle and force, and offered the "cleansing and renewing" effect of war as a solution to current social problems. During the lengthy psychological preparation for war, the war novel received particular support through propaganda measures and literary prizes. In youth, popular, and entertainment series, the war novel by far outpaced such other genres as Wild West or crime novels during the 1930s.

At a "Meeting of War Writers" in 1936, 50 authors formed a "War Writers' Squad" (Mannschaft Kriegsdichter). After the outbreak of the war, "authors' tours" (*Dichterfahrten*) to the war front were organized for selected writers. The results of these tours were recorded in literary "experience reports" (*Erlebnisberichte*), which were committed to specific contemporary political goals and which played down the war (as in a passage by Otto Paust: "Let's go! Tackled that bit of a war. Spit in my hands"), or else put forth slogans for holding out. After 1945 such softcover series as Der Landser (The GI) and SOS continued the tradition of the trite war novel.

H. H.

War reporters (*Kriegsberichter[statter]*), term employed first in its longer form, then shortened to denote the reporters using the media of words, pictures, film, and radio who comprised PROPAGANDA COMPANIES (in the Luftwaffe called War Reporter Companies). The war reporters belonged to the frontline troops, carried weapons, and used motorized transportation. Their texts and pictures were subject to military and political censorship.

War sacrifice (*Kriegsopfer*; also translated as "war victim" or "war martyr"), official term as of 1933 for persons permanently injured in the First World War, as well as for widows and orphans of the war dead who had a claim to assistance. The term was meant to ennoble everything related to war and replaced the previously used *Kriegsbeschädigte* (war-damaged). Its extension to persons with war injuries, in addition to those fallen in combat, occurred first in popular speech, and then made its way into official terminology with the establishment of the National Socialist War Martyrs' Welfare organization (Nationalsozialistische Kriegsopferversorgung; NSKOV). It remains the current term.

Warsaw Ghetto Uprising (*Warschauer Getto-Aufstand*), armed uprising of the inhabitants of the Warsaw ghetto against their "resettlement" to the extermination camps of the REINHARD OPERATION. After more than 310,000 Jews had been "resettled" in the TREBLINKA extermination camp between the end of July and the beginning of October 1942, the Jewish organizations represented in the ghetto decided to resist with force any further deportations. Un-

der the leadership of a Coordinating Committee, the Jewish Fighting Organization (Żydowska Organizacja Bojowa; ŻOB) was put together. Its total of 22 units, comprising about 1,500 men and women, were commanded by the 24-year-old Mordecai Anielewicz. Nationalist Jews of the Revisionist party did not join the ŻOB. Their military organization, Irgun Tseva'i Le'ummi, had its own three fighting groups. Under the pretext that they were air raid shelters, several hundred bunkers were built that were partly connected with the sewer system. Primarily the Polish Home Army (Armia Krajowa) put arms and explosives at the disposal of the ghetto inhabitants.

Of the approximately 75,000 Jews still living in the ghetto, 6,500 were unexpectedly deported in January 1943. During the operation, resistance was offered; a police captain was seriously injured, and 1,171 Jews were shot as a countermeasure. After this incident Himmler ordered the dissolution and destruction of the ghetto. On April 19, 1943, at 3:00 a.m., the SS and Police Leader of Warsaw, Ferdinand von Sammern-Frankenegg (d. in combat, September 20, 1944, in Croatia), ordered that the ghetto be cleared within three days. When the units under his command advanced into the ghetto at 6:00, they were met by the concerted fire of the ŻOB combat units, and had to retreat with casualties. Around 8:00, Sammern-Frankenegg was re-

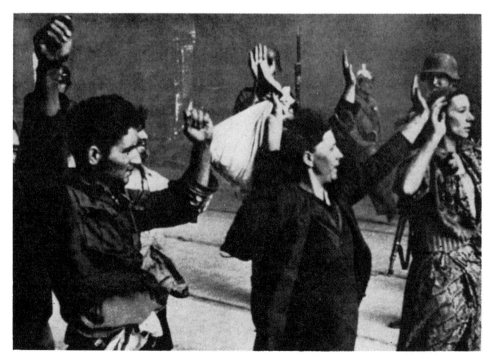

Warsaw Ghetto Uprising. Jewish resistance fighters surrender.

Warsaw Ghetto Uprising. Last page of the *Stroop Report:* "The Jewish quarter of Warsaw no longer exists."

placed by SS-Brigadeführer Jürgen STROOP, who ordered new attacks. His units were repeatedly forced to retreat. On April 23 he ordered that the buildings be set on fire. The ghetto became a sea of flames. Many Jews fled into the sewer system, but because parts of it were flooded and blasted, they suffered heavy losses. Finally Stroop had the remaining bunkers systematically smoked out by attack troops. The ranks of the fighting Jews rapidly thinned. On May 8, Anielewicz was killed.

By mid-May, the resistance of the ŻOB was broken. As a sign of the defeat of the Jews, Stroop had the large Tłomacki Synagogue, which was located in the "Aryan" part of Warsaw, blown up on May 16, 1943. In the so-called *Stroop Report*, he reported to his superior, the Higher SS and Police Leader in the Generalgouvernement, Friedrich-Wilhelm Krüger (presumably committed suicide, May 10, 1945): "The Jewish quarter of Warsaw no longer exists." Of the 70,000 Jews who had been in the ghetto when the operation began, about 56,000 were taken prisoner; 7,000 of these were shot, 7,000 more were "resettled" in Treblinka, and 15,000 went to the extermination camp of Lublin-Maidanek. The rest were put into labor camps. Losses among the German troops and their VOLUNTEER HELPERS (one battalion of Ukrainians and Polish police) were 16 dead and 90 wounded.

A. St.

Warsaw Uprising (*Warschauer Aufstand*), uprising of the underground Polish national Home Army (Armia Krajowa) under the command of Count Tadeusz Komorowski (code name, "Bor" ["forest"]) against the German occupation forces from August 1 to October 2, 1944. Although the uprising (under the code name "Burza" ["thunderstorm"]) had been agreed upon in general terms with the London-based government-in-exile, it was begun independently by the underground leadership. The action was initiated by some 14,000 inadequately armed men and women, whose numbers rose to 36,000 toward the end. Their aim was to liberate Warsaw from the retreating German troops before the arrival of the Red Army, which had broken through the middle section of the eastern front on June 22, 1944. In addition, they hoped to establish a government administration by the government-in-exile before Stalin's Polish satellites, the so-called Lublin Committee and the Berling Army, could establish themselves in the capital. Both aims failed because of the attack by the Ninth German Army under Gen. Erich von dem BACH-ZELEWSKI of the Waffen-SS, augmented by SS and police units and the Luftwaffe.

After initial successes, the Poles were unable to occupy the Warsaw airport and the bridges over the Vistula River. By August 4, the Polish units were scattered throughout the city. The Red Army occupied the Praga suburb on the right bank of the Vistula on September 14, and ferried a battalion of the Berling Army across the river to the south of the city, but otherwise it remained halted at the river. Thus the underground army had to capitulate.

Through the intervention of the Wehrmacht, the Foreign Ministry, and Generalgouverneur Hans FRANK, who tardily wanted to introduce a "new occupation policy" in opposition to the SS, the prisoners were given the status of combatants. German losses in the Warsaw Uprising were 2,000 dead and 9,000 wounded; on the Polish side, 16,000 were killed and 6,000 wounded. Some 16,000 Polish civilians were allegedly killed, and 60,000 to 80,000 deported to German concentration camps and armaments factories. On Hitler's orders, the Germans evacuated Warsaw and razed it to the ground (incidentally destroying irreplaceable art treasures), insofar as was possible during the brief time until the Soviet army entered the city.

Profound differences of opinion persist between Western and Eastern historians regarding the reasons for Stalin's passive behavior. The Soviet side explains its tactics by referring to the allegedly inadequate state of arrangements with the Polish underground army, as well as to the unfavorable disposition of the Soviet troops and

Warsaw Uprising. Polish national machine gunners.

their plans of operation. The Soviets can also assert that the Germans brought the Red Army advance to a temporary halt with a counterdrive southeast of Warsaw on August 3. On the other hand, Stalin broke off relations with the Polish government-in-exile in London after the disclosing of the KATYN massacre on April 13, 1943, and beginning in the summer of 1944 he backed only the Lublin Committee, with a view to Poland's political future. He strictly refused to grant landing rights at Soviet airstrips to the western Allies so that they could supply and aid the Warsaw Uprising. These facts strengthen Western conjectures that the bleeding to death of Poland's national anti-Communist forces to the advantage of a Sovietization of east-central Europe was not unwelcome.

B.-J. W.

Wartheland (Reich *Gau* Wartheland; Warthegau), region to the south of the Vistula and Netze rivers, with the administrative districts of Posen, Hohensalza, and Łódź (the last was renamed Litzmannstadt as of April 12, 1940); area, approximately 44,000 sq km (about 17,600 sq miles); population, 4.7 million (of whom 327,000 were German). After the Polish Campaign, the region was annexed by the German Reich, on October 8, 1939. In the Wartheland (known as Reich *Gau* Posen until January 1940), Arthur GREISER was given the dual function of *Gauleiter* and Reich governor (*Reichsstatthalter*) on October 26, 1939, and with it the assignment to "re-Germanize" (*regermanisieren*) the area.

To this end, all imaginable coercive measures were applied: the expulsion of the approximately 380,000 Jews, or their concentration (primarily in the Łódź ghetto) and murder in the EXTERMINATION CAMPS; the nearly total smashing of the Catholic church organization as a bulwark of Polish nationalism; and the murder (*see* INTELLIGENTSIA OPERATION) or expulsion of the Polish clergy.

In order to strengthen the German position, Baltic Germans and other ethnic German groups were settled in the region; in addition, by 1944 some 630,000 Poles had been forced into the GENERALGOUVERNEMENT. The Wartheland was a sort of model National Socialist *Gau*, in which the fusion of party and state functions, the separation of state and church (reduced to the status of mere associations), and total police-state control were intended to create an NS community "free of all traditional bureaucratic obstructions" (Greiser). The experiment ended in January 1945 with the entry of the Red Army and the flight, expulsion, or death of the German population.

Wartime law (*Recht im Kriege*), special legal regulations for wartime situations, especially WARTIME SPECIAL CRIMINAL LAW.

Wartime Material-Damage Claim Ordinance (*Kriegssachschädenverordnung*), provision that was passed on November 30, 1940, to compensate for material damages caused by the war, especially through air attacks (*see* BOMBED OUT). It provided for compensation at replacement value, though "in accord with economic contingencies and possibilities," which as the war wore on effectively nullified the ordinance. Jews were not permitted to apply for the "wartime compensation proceeding" that was necessary for compensation.

Wartime Model Workplace (*Kriegsmusterbetrieb*), title awarded by the GERMAN LABOR FRONT from May 1, 1942, as part of the PERFORMANCE COMPETITION OF GERMAN WORKPLACES. Its purpose was to acknowledge socially and economically successful enterprises.

Wartime Special Criminal Law (*Kriegssonderstrafrecht*), criminal law regulations issued shortly before or during the Second World War and stipulating draconian punishments. In particular, they threatened the death penalty with an altogether unheard-of frequency. The Wartime Special Criminal Law Ordinance of August 17, 1938 (first published on August 26, 1939, *Reich Law Gazette* [*Reichsgesetzblatt; RGBl*] I, p. 1445), contained regulations on espionage and partisan activity, among other matters. In particular, it introduced a new category of criminal activity, UNDERMINING OF MILITARY STRENGTH (*Wehrkraftzersetzung*). The chief of the Wehrmacht High Command (OKW) was authorized to change or supplement the ordinance insofar as the demands of the conduct of war required. In the legal history of modern times, this granted to the military a unique authority: to enact penal regulations that affected civilians as well as military personnel.

An Ordinance regarding Extraordinary Radio Measures of September 1, 1939 (RGBl I, p. 1683), threatened severe penalties for listening to foreign broadcasts. The Ordinance against VOLK VERMIN of September 5, 1939 (RGBl I, p. 1679), contained penal regulations on plundering and crimes committed under cover of blackouts, as well as "crimes endangering the general public." The Ordinance to Supplement the Penal Regulations to Protect the Military Strength of the German *Volk* of November 25, 1939 (RGBl I, p. 2319), stipulated high penalties for damaging military equipment, hindering the operation of an important production facility, participating in an antimilitary organization, and the like. The Ordinance against Violent Criminals of December 5, 1939 (RGBl I, p. 2378), established the death penalty for crimes committed with a weapon, even if committed prior to the law's date of effectiveness. Finally, various regulations were enacted to ensure the supply of essential goods for the population,

such as the War Economy Ordinance of September 4, 1939 (RGBl I, p. 1609), and the Criminal Ordinance for Regulating Consumption of November 26, 1941 (RGBl I, p. 734).

The keystone of these special laws was the Ordinance to Supplement the Wartime Special Criminal Law Ordinance of May 5, 1944 (RGBl I, p. 115), which allowed imposition of the death penalty for any criminal act "whenever, according to a positive *völkisch* viewpoint, the regular punishment is inadequate for expiation." Special legislation was finally created to be deployed against so-called ETHNIC ALIENS (*Fremdvölkische*), as in the Polish Criminal Law Ordinance (*Polenstrafrechtsverordnung*) of December 4, 1941 (RGBl I, p. 759), against Jews and Poles. In criminal procedural law, constitutional guarantees were further abolished. The wartime ordinance of August 17, 1938 (first published on August 26, 1939; RGBl I, p. 1457), introduced a simplified so-called wartime procedure (*Kriegsverfahren*), which curtailed the rights of the defense counsel and re-ordered the judicial competencies.

U. B.

Wartime Winter Relief Agency (Kriegswinterhilfswerk), intensification of the WINTER RELIEF AGENCY in the special emergency situation of the war.

Wealth (*Reichtum*), the accumulation of property in the hands of the few. As a general principle it was not touched by the National Socialists, although their programmatic statements repeatedly demanded "the most multilayered possible structure of wealth in the national economy" and the "greatest possible number of economically independent persons." National Socialist theories held the bourgeois democratic parliamentary system largely responsible for the rise of a wealthy class, allowing the wealthy to influence parliamentary legislation in the interest of their profits. In order to conceal the persistence of wealth and of conflicting economic interests in the Third Reich, the National Socialists designated as wealth not money, "but rather work": "Productivity [*Leistungsfähigkeit*], as well as the will to perform [*Wille zur Leistung*], is the true wealth of every people" (*Meyers Lexikon*, 1942; *see* PERFORMANCE).

Wednesday Society (Mittwochsgesellschaft), "Free Society for Scholarly Discussion" founded in 1863, to which at any given time 16 leading Berliners belonged: scientists, artists, officers, politicians, and the like. The society met every second Wednesday, to listen to talks by members and to discuss all topics "with the exception of the politics of the day." This restriction remained intact after 1933, but only superficially, since men involved in the OPPOSITION increasingly became members of the elitist circle: along with rather nonpolitical scientists such as Werner HEISENBERG or Ferdinand SAUERBRUCH, active conspirators such as Ludwig BECK, Johannes POPITZ, and Ulrich von HASSELL. Scholarly meetings were especially suited to camouflage. The Wednesday Society was disbanded after the failure of the assassination attempt of July 20, 1944. The last meeting, its 1,056th, took place on July 26 of that year.

Wegener, Paul, b. Bischdorf Estate [*Rittergut*] (East Prussia), December 11, 1874; d. Berlin, September 13, 1948, German actor and film producer. Wegener first worked as an actor in the theater (from 1906 to 1920, with Max REINHARDT in Berlin); he then had success abroad as an actor and producer, mostly of fantasy films, notably *Der Student von Prag* (The Student from Prague; 1913) and *Der Golem* (1914). He was considered one of the first great German film actors. After 1933, Wegener let himself be harnessed to the National Socialist propaganda apparatus. As a producer he made rather trite movies, such as *August der Starke* (August the Strong; 1936), about the Saxon elector and king of Poland, and diverse patriotic films, including *Ein Mann will nach Deutschland* (A Man Wants to Come to Germany; 1934). However, it was as an expressive actor that Wegener had a decisive role in the propagandistic vitality of such popular NS films as HANS WESTMAR (1933), *Der Grosse König* (The Great King; 1937), and KOLBERG (1945).

Josef Magnus Wehner.

Wehner, Josef Magnus, b. Bermbach/Rhön, November 14, 1891; d. Munich, December 14, 1973, German writer. After literary beginnings "imbued with Catholic mysticism" (Franz Lennartz), Wehner gained prominence as a *völkisch* author with works such as *Die Sieben vor Verdun* (The Seven before Verdun; 1930) and "patriotic fantasies," among them *Die Wallfahrt nach Paris* (The Pilgrimage to Paris; 1932). The National Socialists honored him with appointment to the German Academy of Letters in 1933. In a series of "Addresses to the German People" over Radio Cologne in the early 1940s, he tried to arouse confidence in the war "in [these] hard times." A dedicated opponent of "anal art" (*Afterkunst*), Wehner found himself outside the literary mainstream after the war. He tried to find a public with smaller, Catholic, idyllic, legendlike works.

Wehrmacht (literally, military or defense power), term for Germany's military forces, previously the REICHSWEHR (Reich military or defense force). It was first used in the Law for the Creation of the Wehrmacht (*Gesetz für den Aufbau der Wehrmacht*) of March 16, 1935. The Wehrmacht was comprised of the army (Heer), the navy (Kriegsmarine), and the air force (Luftwaffe). The national defense regulations of May 21, 1935, stipulated: "Paragraph 3: The supreme commander of the Wehrmacht is the Führer and Reich chancellor. Paragraph 4: Below him, the Reich war minister, as commander in chief of the Wehrmacht, exercises authority over the Wehrmacht."

Paul Wegener (left) as a Bolshevik leader, with Emil Lohkamp as Hans Westmar.

The former armed forces (Reichswehr) minister, Field Marshal Gen. Werner von BLOMBERG, remained Reich war minister. Col. Gen. Werner Freiherr von FRITSCH became supreme commander of the army, and Adm. of the Fleet Erich RAEDER continued to lead the navy. Col. Gen. Hermann GÖRING became supreme commander of the new air force. By means of the dual intrigue of the FRITSCH CRISIS, Hitler undermined the Wehrmacht leadership through the dismissals of Fritsch and Blomberg, and on February 4, 1938, he decreed: "Command over the entire Wehrmacht will from now on be exercised personally by me." The former Wehrmacht Office in the Reich War Ministry thus came directly under Hitler's command, and became Hitler's military staff as the Wehrmacht High Command (OKW). Gen. Wilhelm KEITEL became chief of the OKW, and Col. Gen. Walther von BRAUCHITSCH became the new supreme commander of the army.

[The two-page illustration on pages 1028–1029, "Flags and Uniforms of the Wehrmacht," shows the flags and insignia of the army, the navy, and the air force.]

G. H.

Wehrmacht, Women in the (*Wehrmachthelferinnen*, or Wehrmacht women's auxiliary), collective term for the female "helpers" in the army, navy, and air force. Female auxiliary personnel served in intelligence, staff posts, naval and air force posts, nursing, antiaircraft posts, and antiaircraft batteries. They were civilian employees of the Wehrmacht and, despite their uniforms, had no military status, serving as a "female Wehrmacht retinue" (*weibliche Wehrmachtsgefolge*). After the French Campaign in the summer of 1940, the first women auxiliary intelligence personnel (*Nachrichtenhelferinnen*) were attached to the army from the personnel reserves of the GERMAN RED CROSS. They were trained at the Intelligence School in Giessen. Toward the end of 1941, the use of women auxiliary staff personnel (*Stabshelferinnen*) made it possible to "disengage" soldiers from the administrative offices of the Wehrmacht. *Flakhelferinnen* (women flak helpers) served at searchlight posts and reported the approach of aircraft. On October 16, 1943, Hermann Göring ordered the deployment of a Flakwaffenhelferinnenkorps to serve at antiaircraft batteries. In accordance with Hitler's edict on total war of July 25, 1944, the formation of a Wehrmachthelferinnenkorps was ordered on November 29 of that year.

Wehrmacht women auxiliaries in the Luftwaffe.

At the outbreak of the war, some 140,000 women were already employed by the army. In 1943–1944 approximately 300,000 women held jobs related to the reserve army, half of them in compulsory labor service. Some 8,000 women served in intelligence, and 12,500 in staff posts with the field army and in the occupied territories. With the navy there were some 20,000 women, including the *Marinehelferinnen*, and the Luftwaffe employed about 130,000 women during the war. The fate of these women at the war's end was often no less hard than that of the soldiers, and included internment and deportation for forced labor. There are no exact figures on the considerable number of casualties in the Wehrmacht women's auxiliary.

G. H.

Wehrmacht High Command (Oberkommando der Wehrmacht; OKW), the highest administrative and command level of the German armed forces, formed as a result of the FRITSCH CRISIS on February 4, 1938. It was headed by Gen. Wilhelm KEITEL, who in turn reported directly to Hitler as supreme commander of the Wehrmacht. Keitel received the rank of a Reich minister and was made responsible for overseeing the affairs of the Reich War Ministry. The OKW organization consisted of four departments. The Wehrmacht Command Office (Wehrmachtführungsamt; as of 1940, the Wehrmacht Command Staff [Wehrmachtführungs-

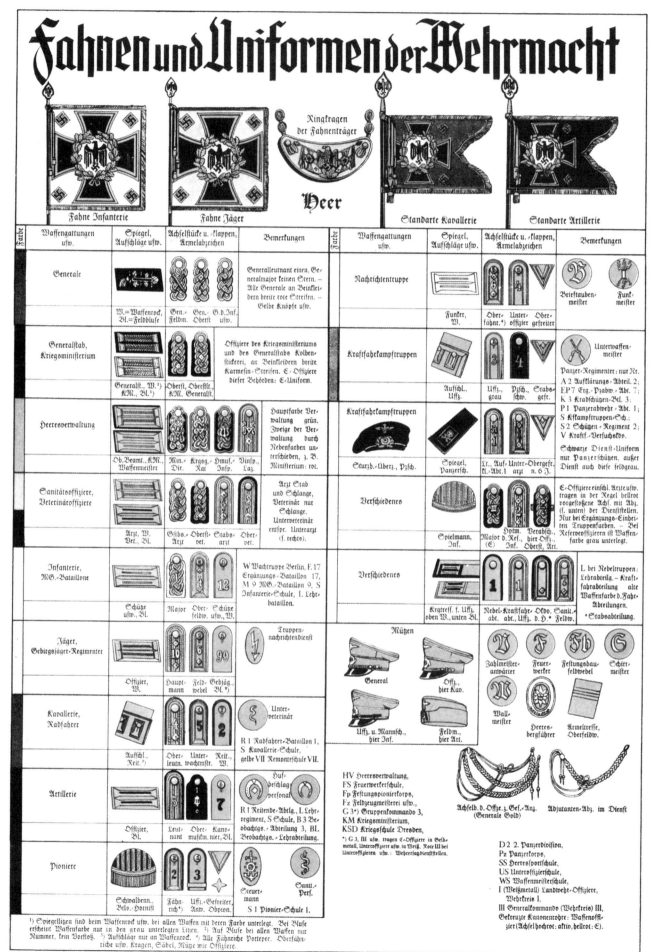

Fahnen und Uniformen der Wehrmacht

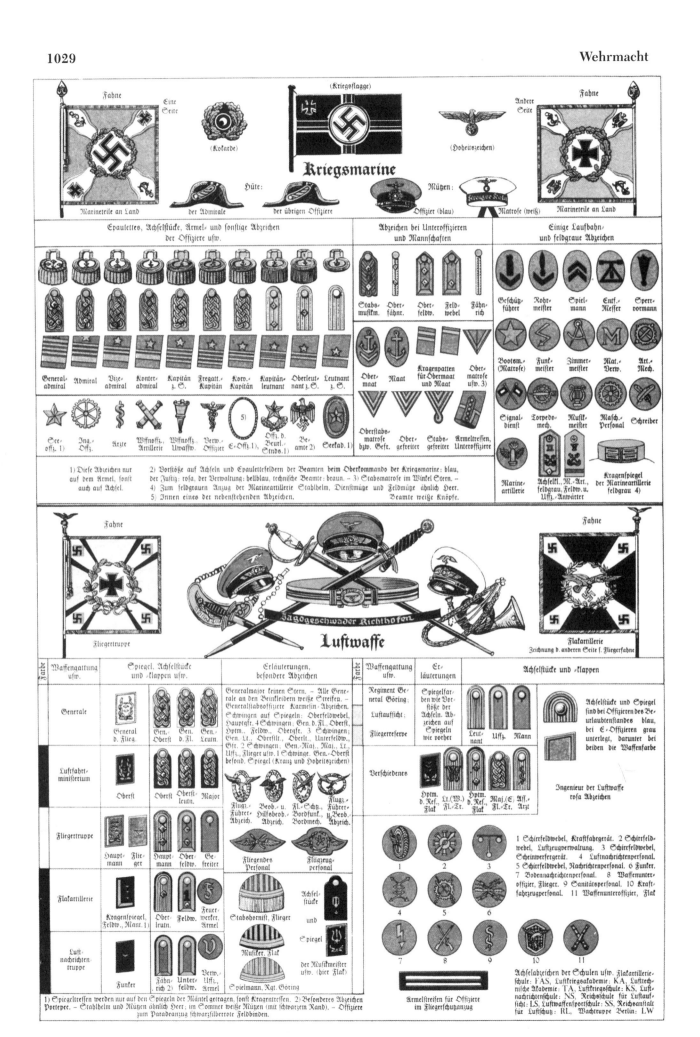

stab]), under Alfred JODL, was Hitler's military staff. The Foreign/ABWEHR Office was headed by Adm. Wilhelm CANARIS until February 1944. In addition, there were two administrative divisions: a General Wehrmacht Office and the Office for War Industry and Armaments.

The OKW formulated Hitler's "Instructions for the Conduct of War" and transmitted his orders to the branches of the armed forces, though without having direct authority over them. It controlled only the military planning for the Wehrmacht's branches, in accord with Hitler's general instructions. During the Nuremberg Trials in 1945, the OKW was accused of such acts as having relayed the COMMISSAR ORDER and the BULLET DECREE, but it was ultimately not classified among the CRIMINAL ORGANIZATIONS. As in the case of the GENERAL STAFF, the tribunal ruled that the OKW was not an "organization," and recommended the prosecution of individual participants to punish its crimes.

Wehrmacht Investigation Office (Wehrmachtuntersuchungsstelle; WUSt), office created on September 4, 1939, in the legal department of the Wehrmacht High Command. Its task was "to determine the offenses against international law committed by enemy military and civilian personnel in relation to members of the German Wehrmacht, and to clarify accusations in this respect made against the German Wehrmacht by the outside world." The head of the office was the Berlin lawyer Johannes Goldsche, who had been deputy director of the Military Investigation Office for Violations of Military Law in the

Wehrmacht Investigation Office. Murdered German soldiers.

Prussian War Ministry during the First World War. The Wehrmacht Investigation Office was transferred from Berlin to Torgau, on the Elbe River, in August 1943, and transferred further to Langensalza, in Thuringia, at the end of February 1945. Some of the office's documents were burned during the approach of the American forces, and the rest were captured on April 9, 1945. Of the original inquiries (about 8,000), 4,000 have been preserved, in 226 files. They were returned by the United States to the Federal Republic of Germany in 1968, and are now kept in the Federal Archives/Military Archives in Freiburg im Breisgau.

G. H.

Wehrmacht Report (*Wehrmacht Bericht*), military report made by the WEHRMACHT HIGH COMMAND (OKW), intended for the public. Such reports were read over the radio daily as part of the midday news from September 1, 1939, to May 9, 1945 ("The Wehrmacht High Command announces . . ."). The 2,080 publicized Wehrmacht Reports originated in the Wehrmacht Propaganda Office of the OKW; the responsible officer was Maj. Gen. Hasso von Wedel. From September 1939 to May 1940, the largely accurate reports showed careful restraint, then, until November 1941, exuberance born of success. Thereafter, until the autumn of 1944, they served (more or less successfully) to camouflage reverses, and finally became sober liquidation reports. The portrayal of developments at the fronts was generally reliable, though the numbers of sunken enemy ships and downed enemy aircraft were very often magnified, since information on actual results usually required more time to arrive at than was available before the next broadcast. The OKW was successful in warding off the attempts of the Propaganda Ministry to involve itself in the wording of the Wehrmacht Reports.

G. H.

Weichs, Maximilian Baron von, b. Dessau, November 12, 1881; d. Rösberg Estate [Gut Rösberg], near Bonn, September 27, 1954, German field marshal general (February 1, 1943). Weichs joined the army in 1902; in the First World War, he was an ordnance officer. He then made his career in the Reichswehr, in 1933 becoming a major general. On October 1, 1937, Weichs became commanding general of the Thirteenth Army Corps, which he led in the Polish Campaign. On October 20, 1939, he was given supreme command of the Second Army,

Maximilian von Weichs.

which as a unit of Army Group A participated in the French Campaign. With the Second Army, Weichs contributed to the quick success of the Balkan Campaign in April 1941. He also led the army at the beginning of the Russian Campaign, until he was given supreme command of Army Group B on July 15, 1941. After the reverses in the east, Weichs became supreme commander of the Southeast Army, and also of Army Group F, on August 26, 1943. He led these units until they disbanded on March 25, 1945. Weichs was arrested at the end of the war, but his poor state of health led to his release on November 3, 1948, even before the beginning of the HOSTAGE TRIAL against the generals of the Southeast Army.

Weidemann, Alfred, b. Stuttgart, May 10, 1918, German writer and film producer. After journalistic beginnings, Weidemann made his career in the Third Reich as the author of several Hitler Youth stories and other books for young people. He glorified the National Socialist worldview without reservation, and with the motto "To serve is to be silent" ("Dienen ist Schweigen") propagandized unconditional obedience in works such as *Trupp Plessen* (1937) and *50 Jungen im Dienst* (50 Boys in Service), which won the 1937–1938 HANS SCHEMM PRIZE. Under the pseudonym M. Derfla, Weidemann contributed a series of softcover stories to the WAR LIBRARY FOR GERMAN YOUTH; among other themes, they justified the German attack on Poland.

The best known of his screen works was the propaganda film *Junge Adler* (Young Eagles; 1944), whose screenplay he wrote together with Herbert REINECKER; Joseph Goebbels thought highly of it. Although successful after the war as an author of books for young people (for example, *Gepäckschein 666* [Baggage Ticket 666]; 1953), Weidemann turned increasingly to films, producing *Canaris* (1954) and *Der Stern von Afrika* (The Star of Africa; 1956), among other works. During the 1960s and 1970s he became especially popular with his contributions to the television series *Der Kommissar* (The Commissioner).

Weill, Kurt, b. Dessau, March 2, 1900; d. New York City, April 3, 1950, German composer. Starting in the 1920s, Weill sought to combine popular and serious music, becoming famous primarily with compositions for the music theater that were critical of contemporary mores. Together with Bertolt BRECHT he wrote, most notably, *Die Dreigroschenoper* (The Three-penny Opera; 1928) and *Aufstieg und Fall der Stadt Mahagonny* (Rise and Fall of the City of Mahagonny; 1930). Early on, the National Socialists subjected the "notorious Jew Kurt Weill" and his "repulsive bungled works" (*widerwärtige Machwerke*) to the sharpest attacks: "vulgar jazz and Negro rhythms, abominable, completely senseless dissonances . . . trivial banalities, the most common street-ballad melodies . . . without any artistic finish, pasted together in deadening primitiveness . . . complete and absolute impotence" (*Deutsche Bühnenkorrespondenz* [German Stage Letter], 1932). In 1933 Weill had to emigrate, along

Kurt Weill.

with his wife, Lotte LENYA, the apt interpreter of his songs. In the United States he wrote musicals for Broadway that were commercially successful, yet had socially critical content.

Weimar Coalition, coalition of the SOCIAL DEMOCRATIC PARTY OF GERMANY (SPD), the CENTER party, and the GERMAN DEMOCRATIC PARTY (DDP; after 1930, the German State Party) in the Weimar Republic—that is, the parties that alone were strongly in favor of a republican form of state and government from the outset. The (later) Weimar Coalition had first been delineated in the July 1917 Peace Resolution of the majority parties in the Reichstag: the SPD, the Center, and the Progressive People's Party (Fortschrittliche Volkspartei, the predecessor of the DDP). Of the 19 governments during the Weimar Republic, the first one (February 1919) and 4 others (until 1922) were formed by the Weimar Coalition. The SPD, the Center, and the DDP participated in 3 later governments of the so-called Great Coalition (in 1923 and from 1928 to 1930), which also included the GERMAN PEOPLE'S PARTY.

During the elections to the National Assembly, which was to draft the constitution (January 1919), the parties of the Weimar Coalition received a total of 76.2 percent of the vote. However, they lost this majority in the subsequent Reichstag elections. Their share of votes sank from 43.6 percent in 1920 to 33.3 percent in November 1932. The loss of votes by the DDP (in 1919, 18.6 percent; in 1932, 1.0 percent) and also by the SPD (in 1919, 37.9 percent; in November 1932, 20.4 percent) benefited the radical parties, especially the Communist Party (KPD), and even more the NSDAP.

R. B.

Weimar Constitution (*Weimarer Verfassung*), the constitution of the WEIMAR REPUBLIC, which was adopted with a vote of 262 to 75 by the German National Assembly, meeting in Weimar, on July 31, 1919. Voting for it were the Social Democratic Party (SPD), the Center party, and the German Democratic Party (DDP); opposed were the Independent Socialists (USPD), the German People's Party (DVP), and the German National People's Party (DNVP). The constitution was proclaimed on August 11, and took effect on August 14. Its draft was written primarily by the constitutional law specialist Hugo Preuss. The constitution was divided into a preamble, two main sections, and final provisions. The first main section (Articles 1 to 108)

Weimar Constitution. "From the parliamentary amusement park." Cartoon from the *Kladderadatsch.*

described the "structure and purposes of the state" (*Aufbau und Aufgaben des Reiches*); the second section (Articles 109 to 165) contained the "Basic Rights and Basic Duties of Germans" (*Grundrechte und Grundpflichten der Deutschen*).

The Weimar Constitution (Article 1) made the German state (*see* REICH) into a republic for the first time in its history, consisting of 18 member German states (*Länder;* Article 2) and having the republican national colors black, red, and gold (Article 3). The new state was federal in structure and its system of government was that of a parliamentary democracy, although interspersed with elements of presidial and direct democracy (for example, a strong Reich president who was popularly elected, as well as the possibility of initiative and referendum).

The deficiencies of the Weimar Constitution were several: election by proportional representation, which led to a multiparty system (Article 22); the purely destructive vote of no confidence against the Reich chancellor and every Reich minister (Article 54); the absence of any possibility of prohibiting a party; and the Reich president's right to issue emergency decrees (ARTICLE 48). In combination, these deficiencies contributed to the dissolution of the Weimar Republic and to the National Socialist SEIZURE OF POWER. The Weimar Constitution was *de facto* abolished by the Decree of the Reich President to Protect the People and the State of

February 28, 1933, by the ENABLING LAW of March 24, 1933, and by the NS SYNCHRONIZA-TION. It was never formally invalidated during the Third Reich.

R. B.

Weimar Republic, the first all-German republic, which existed from 1919 to 1933; it was named after the place of its founding, Weimar. The birth of the Weimar Republic was a consequence of the First World War (1914–1918) and of the defeat of the German Empire. After the outbreak of the November Revolution (on October 28, 1918), Reich Chancellor Max von Baden on November 9 announced the abdication of Kaiser Wilhelm II, and transferred the duties of the Reich chancellor to the chairman of the Social Democratic Party (SPD), Friedrich EBERT. The Council of People's Deputies (Rat der Volksbeauftragten), which was led by Ebert, took over the tasks of the government. On the same day, Philipp Scheidemann (SPD) proclaimed the "German Republic."

On February 11, 1919, the National Assembly (which had been elected on January 19) met in Weimar, chosen in part because of the revolutionary unrest in Berlin. It elected Ebert president of the new state (*Reich*). On February 13, Scheidemann formed a government, made up of the SPD, the German Democratic Party (DDP), and the Center party (the WEIMAR COALITION). The National Assembly on July 31, 1919, adopted the WEIMAR CONSTITUTION, which was signed by the president on August 11, and took effect on August 14.

The Weimar Republic was a parliamentary republic in the form of a federal state made up of 18 member states (*Länder*). Its government apparatus consisted of the Reichstag as parliament; the Reich Council (Reichsrat), which offered parliamentary representation to the *Länder*; the Reich president as head of state; and the Reich government, made up of the Reich chancellor and the Reich ministers. The Reich president had considerable political powers: nomination and dismissal of the Reich chancellor and ministers; supreme command of the armed forces, or REICHSWEHR; dissolution of the Reichstag; and executive and legislative authority in emergency situations, according to Article 48 of the constitution. As a result, the parliamentary system of government had elements of a presidial government, and also of a direct democracy, through various participatory rights of the people (election of the Reich president and the possibility of a demand for plebiscite and referendum, in accordance with Article 73).

The crucial political forces in the Weimar

Weimar Republic. After the swearing-in of Reich President Ebert in 1919 in Weimar.

Republic were the political parties, which were not mentioned in the Weimar Constitution. They were numerous because the system of proportional representation and the lack of a minimum vote barrier for parliamentary representation (a *Sperrklausel*) led to crippling fragmentation. Since there was also no possibility of banning parties, the democratic parties (especially the SPD, the Center, and the DDP) were irreconcilably confronted with antidemocratic parties: on the left, the Communist Party (KPD) and the Independent Socialists (USPD), and on the right, the German National People's Party (DNVP) and the NSDAP. The SPD, Center, and DDP garnered a total of 76.2 percent in the 1919 elections to the National Assembly, but they lost their majority as early as the first Reichstag elections in 1920 (44.6 percent). In the November 1932 Reichstag elections they received only 33.3 percent of the vote, whereas the NSDAP, KPD, and DNVP gained a total of 58.9 percent. The deficiencies in the Weimar Constitution also encouraged the frequent dissolutions of and new elections to the Reichstag (between 1920 and 1932 there were seven elections), as well as the frequent changes of government (from 1919 to January 1933, there were 20 cabinets with 12 different chancellors).

The history of the Weimar Republic can be divided into three periods:

1. *Years of crisis, 1919–1923.* They began with revolutionary unrest and uprisings on the Left, as Berlin's Spartacist Uprising in 1919 and Munich's temporary "soviet" (council) republic (*Räterepublik*) that same year. The Ruhr region experienced unrest in 1919 and 1920, central Germany and Hamburg in 1921 and 1923, and Saxony and Thuringia in 1923. On the Right, there were two significant putsch attempts (the KAPP PUTSCH in 1920 and the HITLER PUTSCH in 1923), as well as right-radical agitation against the Republic (*see* STAB-IN-THE-BACK LEGEND; NOVEMBER CRIMINALS). Polish attempts at uprisings took place in Upper Silesia in 1919, 1920, and 1921. Disputes divided the government and the Reichswehr leadership, as well as the national government and the individual states, especially Bavaria in 1923. The same year saw the so-called RUHR CONFLICT. Numerous political murders were carried out: in 1919 against the Communist leaders Rosa Luxemburg and Karl Liebknecht, in 1921 against Matthias ERZBERGER, and in 1922 against Walther RATHENAU. Finally, the political, economic, and financial consequences of the war heavily burdened

Facing page:
3
"Enough of this system." Election poster for the KPD, 1932.
4
"Our last hope: Hitler." Election poster for the NSDAP, 1932.

Weimar Republic. The parliamentary governments, 1919–1933.

1
"They are carrying the letters of the firm—
but who is carrying the spirit?" Cartoon by
Th. Th. Heine.
2
"Cheers to the New Year! Papen (right): 'And
so we wish for you in the New Year that you
won't experience what I did—in the past
year.' Brüning (left): 'And I hope that out of
old habit you won't be tempted to topple
yourself.'" Satire of the new Reich chancellor,
Kurt von Schleicher (seated), 1933.
3–4
(See facing page.)

the young Republic and endangered its existence, especially the payment of REPARATIONS to the Allies, which after mid-1922 contributed significantly to the galloping INFLATION.

2. *Consolidation, 1924–1929.* The end of the Ruhr conflict in August 1923, the dampening of inflation through introduction of a new currency (the Rentenmark) in November 1923, and settlement of the conflict between Bavaria and the national government in February 1924 introduced a phase of economic and political consolidation and stability in the Weimar Republic. The DAWES PLAN of 1924 and, still more, the YOUNG PLAN of 1929, which superseded it, eased Germany's reparations burden. The foreign policy conducted by Gustav STRESEMANN from 1923 to 1929 normalized Germany's relations with its former wartime enemies. High points of this policy were the treaties of Locarno (1925; *see* LOCARNO PACT); the BERLIN TREATY with the USSR (1926), which had been preceded by the RAPALLO TREATY (1922); the Allied evacuation of the Rhineland (1925–1930); and Germany's admission to the LEAGUE OF NATIONS. The most important event in domestic politics during this period was probably the election of Field Marshal Paul von HINDENBURG as Reich president on April 26, 1925.

3. *Dissolution, 1929–1933.* This last phase of the Weimar Republic was marked by the WORLD ECONOMIC CRISIS, the transition from a parliamentary system of government to a presidial system, and the growth of political extremism from the Left and still more from the Right. On October 25, 1929, BLACK FRIDAY at the New York Stock Exchange ushered in the world economic crisis, which hit Germany especially hard and led, among other effects, to massive UNEMPLOYMENT (over 2 million out of work at the end of 1929, and over 6 million at the beginning of 1932). The breakup of the coalition government led by Hermann MÜLLER over issues of unemployment compensation on March 27, 1930, marked the end of the parliamentary system of government. The minority government formed under Heinrich BRÜNING (Center party) on March 30 was the first of several PRESIDIAL CABINETS. After the Reichstag was dissolved on July 18, 1930, the new elections on September 14 brought about an abrupt rise of the NSDAP from an insignificant splinter party to the second strongest German party, with 18.3 percent of the vote and 107 (of 577) seats. The electoral success of the NSDAP had been preceded by the referendum against the Young Plan, which with 4.1 million signa-

tures had been barely successful, and which had first brought the NSDAP and its leader, Hitler, to the attention of the broad public.

On October 11, 1931, the NSDAP, the DNVP, and the STEEL HELMET joined forces against the Republic in the HARZBURG FRONT. The SPD, the trade unions, and the REICH BANNER "BLACK-RED-GOLD" responded on December 16 with the IRON FRONT. Brüning, who remained chancellor, tried to master the crisis by resorting to a deflationary economic policy, which ultimately did not succeed. The SPD initially tolerated his minority cabinet. On April 10, 1932, Hindenburg was re-elected president (with 19.4 million votes), this time as candidate of the Republican parties; he defeated Hitler (who received 13.4 million votes). Shortly thereafter, Hindenburg, under the influence of intrigues within his entourage, withdrew his confidence from Brüning. The chancellor resigned on May 30, 1932, and was succeeded on June 1 by Franz von PAPEN, a member of the Center party until June 3, and thereafter without party affiliation. Only the DNVP supported Papen's conservative "cabinet of barons" and his openly anti-Republican policies, which aimed at restoration of the monarchy or the establishment of an authoritarian system. Consequently, he dissolved the Reichstag on June 4. In order to win the NSDAP's toleration of his policies, on June 14 Papen lifted the prohibition of the SA and the SS, which had been proclaimed by the Brüning government on April 13. On July 20 he removed from office the Prussian caretaker government under Otto Braun (SPD). By removing the democratic government in Germany's largest state, the so-called PRUSSIAN COUP eliminated one of the last and most important bulwarks of the Republic.

In the Reichstag elections of July 31, the NSDAP was able to double its share of votes: gaining 37.4 percent of the ballots and winning 230 (of 608) seats, it was now by far the largest party in Germany. After a new conflict, Papen again had the Reichstag dissolved, on September 12. The NSDAP lost some votes in the following Reichstag elections on November 6 (receiving "only" 31.1 percent and 196 mandates). But because the DNVP registered simultaneous gains (8.9 percent) and the KPD rose to 16.9 percent, this changed nothing with regard to the clearly anti-Republican majority in the Reichstag. Nor did it give the Papen government a majority: the DNVP (52 seats) remained its only parliamentary support. Papen resigned on November 17, and was succeeded by Gen. Kurt von SCHLEICHER on December 3.

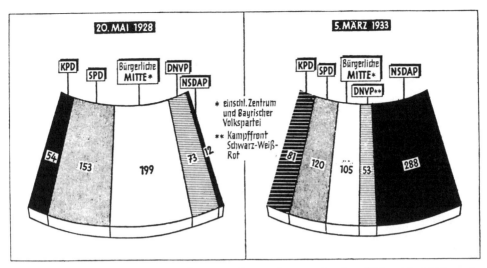

Weimar Republic. Comparison of the Reichstag election results of May 20, 1928, and March 5, 1933. [Single asterisk: "including the Center and the Bavarian People's Party"; double asterisk: "Black-White-Red Combat Front."]

Schleicher had the idea of splitting the NSDAP and forming a "trade union axis" to support his government by using the GENERAL GERMAN TRADE UNION FEDERATION (ADGB) and the left wing of the NSDAP, as represented by Gregor STRASSER. This plan failed, both because of Strasser's weakness and because of the opposition of the ADGB and the SPD. Schleicher resigned on January 28, 1933, after Hindenburg rejected his plan to declare a state of emergency as a final possibility of thwarting a Hitler government. On January 30, Hindenburg named Hitler Reich chancellor. This National Socialist SEIZURE OF POWER brought about the end of the Weimar Republic.

The reasons for the failure of the Weimar Republic were many: the lack of a democratic tradition in Germany (it could hardly develop in the empire); the stigma of the Republic's origin as the consequence of German defeat in the First World War; the burden imposed by the war's political and economic consequences, especially through the VERSAILLES TREATY; the shortcomings of the WEIMAR CONSTITUTION; the lack of able and popular democratic leaders (which became blatantly evident by 1925 at the latest, when Hindenburg was chosen Reich president); the insufficient willingness and/or ability of the Republican parties and party leaders to compromise (as became evident in the numerous changes in and failures of government, especially in the resignation of the Müller government in 1930); and the failure, the mistakes, and the erroneous estimations by those at the helm of the Republic between 1930 and 1933, especially Hindenburg, Papen, and Schleicher.

The decisive fact was that the Weimar Republic was a "republic without republicans." The bureaucracy and judiciary, and the officer corps as well, remained for the most part monarchist and authoritarian in their sentiments. The majority of the population, especially the bourgeoisie, regarded the Republic with aversion from the very beginning, and after 1930 openly went over to the anti-Republican parties under the effect of the world economic crisis. The bourgeoisie went over primarily to the NSDAP, since the democratic parties could not or would not find anything with which to counteract its demagogic propaganda. The workers, who were in any case disappointed by the absence of a real social and economic revolution after 1918, went over in part to the KPD.

R. B.

Weinheber, Josef, b. Vienna, September 9, 1892; d. Kirchstetten, April 8, 1945, Austrian writer. A post-office worker, Weinheber had his first literary success with the autobiographical prose work *Das Waisenhaus* (The Orphanage; 1924). He then embarked "on the hard path of one who [wants] to serve the essence [*Wesen*] of his people with the spirit of language" (Franz Lennartz). Weinheber wrote numerous elegies and hymns, such as "Den Gefallenen" (To the Fallen) and "Dem kommenden Menschen" (To the Coming Man; 1936), for which he received several National Socialist literary prizes. Other works included a consecration play about Reich insignia, *Die hohen Zeichen* (The Lofty Badges; 1939), written for radio. Weinheber distanced

Josef Weinheber.

himself from the National Socialists beginning in 1943. He committed suicide during the advance of the Red Army.

Weismantel, Leo, b. Obersinn im Spessart, June 10, 1888; d. Rodalben (Palatinate), September 16, 1962, German writer. As a reform-minded educator and founder of a research and teaching institute, Weismantel wrote numerous plays for amateur and school theater, as well as ambitious prose with humanistic Catholic tendencies. The National Socialists liked his fiction about the Reformation and the Peasant War, with the Rhön mountain range as a background—notably his trilogy *Vom Sterben und Untergang eines*

Volkes (On the Death and Fall of a People; 1928–1933), which they ideologically misconstrued as "blood and soil" literature. His social and educational commitment brought Weismantel repeatedly into conflict with the system; in 1939 and again in 1944 he was in Gestapo custody. After the war Weismantel became a school administrator (*Schulrat*) in West Germany, and then a professor of art history. He opposed "an uncreative Christian policy of restoration" and espoused the cause of international understanding.

"Weiss" ("White"), military code name for the German attack on Poland (*see* POLISH CAMPAIGN).

Weiss, Wilhelm, b. Stadtsteinach (Upper Franconia), March 31, 1892; d. Wasserburg am Inn, February 24, 1950, German journalist. Weiss was an enthusiastic soldier in the First World War. When it ended, he joined a free corps and paramilitary right-wing organizations. In 1921 he became managing editor of *Heimatland* (Homeland), the magazine of the Bavarian Home Guards. He joined the NSDAP in 1922, participated in the MARCH ON THE FELDHERRN-HALLE, and was chief editor of the *Völkischer Kurier* from 1924 to 1926. The *Kurier* temporarily replaced the banned VÖLKISCHER BEOBACHTER, and when the latter resumed publication, Weiss (a close colleague of Alfred ROSENBERG) joined its editorial staff, on January 1, 1927. In 1933 he became its deputy editor, and in 1938 its editor in chief. In addition, he was editorial chief of the EHER PRESS and chairman of the Reich Association of the German Press.

Leo Weismantel.

Wilhelm Weiss.

As one of the most important press functionaries of the Third Reich, Weiss saw to it that journalism was no longer a "middle-class business" practiced by "gentle souls." He received numerous tributes and medals for his services during the Synchronization of the German PRESS. He became a member of the Reichstag and was appointed to the Reich Culture Senate. After the war, a Munich appeals court sentenced him to 3 years in a labor camp, partial confiscation of property, and 10 years' prohibition from practicing his profession.

Weissler, Friedrich, b. April 28, 1891; d. Sachsenhausen concentration camp, February 19, 1937, German Evangelical jurist. Weissler was a district court administrator (*Landgerichtsdirektor*) in Halle and Magdeburg. Because of his Jewish background he was dismissed from government service in 1933, and became a legal assistant (*juristischer Mitarbeiter*) of the Provisional Directorate of the CONFESSING CHURCH. He was significantly involved in writing a memorandum, addressed to Hitler in the summer of 1936, that sharply criticized National Socialist de-Christianization and antisemitic racism. When the document passed into the hands of the foreign press, the Gestapo arrested Weissler on October 8, 1936, although he was demonstrably innocent of its distribution. On February 13, 1937, Weissler was sent to the concentration camp in Sachsenhausen, where he was murdered after several nights of torture. A Jew had become the first martyr of the Evangelical Church.

Friedrich Weissler.

Chaim Weizmann.

Weizmann, Chaim, b. near Pinsk (Belorussia), November 27, 1874; d. Rehovot (Israel), November 9, 1952, Israeli politician. Weizmann studied chemistry in Berlin and Freiburg. In 1903 he left for England, where he later became a lecturer in biochemistry in Manchester. From 1916 to 1919 he served with the British admiralty. Weizmann was a follower of ZIONISM and one of the initiators of the BALFOUR DECLARATION. In 1918 he founded the Hebrew University in Jerusalem. He was president of the World Zionist Organization from 1920 to 1931, and again from 1935 to 1946. Weizmann demanded the establishment of a Jewish state in Palestine, and became its first president in 1948.

Weizsäcker, Ernst Baron von, b. Stuttgart, May 12, 1882; d. Lindau, August 4, 1951, German diplomat. From 1933 to 1936 Weizsäcker was chargé d'affaires in Switzerland. In 1936 he became head of the political section of the Foreign Ministry, and in 1938, state secretary under Foreign Minister Joachim von Ribbentrop. As a conservative nationalist, Weizsäcker kept his distance from National Socialist policy; on the other hand, as a conscientious official he was careful to carry out such policy. He maintained contacts with the opposition, and in the hope of preventing something worse let a warning be passed to the British foreign secretary, Lord Halifax, about the imminent attack on Czechoslovakia and the planned outbreak of war.

Nevertheless, Weizsäcker later initialed "illegitimate orders" (*Unrechtsbefehle*) and accepted the honorary rank of SS-*Führer*, probably not merely (as he claimed) for "decorative reasons." In 1947 Weizsäcker, who had served as ambas-

Ernst von Weizsäcker.

Otto Wels.

sador to the Vatican during the last two years of the war, was arrested by the Allies. As a main defendant in the WILHELMSTRASSE TRIAL, he was sentenced to seven years' imprisonment. In 1950 he received an early pardon. He tried in his *Erinnerungen* (*Memoirs;* 1950) to justify his conduct in the Third Reich.

Welles, Sumner, b. New York City, October 14, 1892; d. Bernardsville (New Jersey), September 24, 1961, American politician. In 1915 Welles joined the diplomatic service; from 1933 to 1937 he was deputy under secretary and from 1937 to 1943 under secretary in the State Department. As Roosevelt's confidant, Welles explored the European situation for the president in 1940, and accompanied him at the meeting with Churchill on August 14, 1941, during which the ATLANTIC CHARTER was proclaimed.

Wels, Otto, b. Berlin, September 15, 1873; d. Paris, September 16, 1939, German politician. Even before the First World War, Wels had worked his way up to become one of the leading functionaries of the Social Democratic Party (SPD). A fervent enemy of the party's left wing, as city commandant of Berlin he impeded the radicalization of the November Revolution in 1918. As the speaker of the SPD Reichstag delegation, he effectively influenced the Weimar Republic's foreign policy, notably by safeguarding the LOCARNO PACT. Essentially pragmatic and oriented toward the party apparatus, Wels sought an SPD policy that was more aligned with the middle class. He tolerated Hein-

rich Brüning's cabinet (1930–1932) and campaigned for Paul von Hindenburg's re-election as Reich president in 1932. On March 23, 1933, Wels gave a courageous speech before the Reichstag explaining his party's opposition to the ENABLING LAW. By a decision of the SPD leadership, on May 1 of that year he went to Prague, where, together with Erich OLLEN-HAUER and Friedrich STAMPFER, he built up the foreign directorate of the SPD. In 1938 he fled to Paris, where he headed the SPD in exile until his death.

Weltbühne, Die (The World Stage), weekly magazine for politics, art, and economics that grew out of the theatrical journal *Die Schaubühne* (The Stage). It was first published on April 4, 1918; its office was in Berlin, and its 1925 circulation was approximately 12,600 copies. After the death of Siegfried Jacobsohn on December 3, 1926, the journal was "under the editorship of Carl von OSSIETZKY, with Kurt TUCHOLSKY as contributor" (masthead as of October 11, 1927). The main targets of this critical intellectual review of the Left, whose authors included the best journalists of the Weimar Republic, were the administration of justice based on class bias, the VEHM MURDERS, and covert REARMAMENT.

Ossietzky was sentenced to 18 months in prison by the Supreme Court (Reichsgericht) in Leipzig for "betrayal of military secrets" after a *Weltbühne* article referred to the collaboration of the Reichswehr with the Red Army. He began

Die Weltbühne. Cover of the November 24, 1925, issue.

serving the term on May 10, 1932, and was amnestied on December 22. Helmut von GER- LACH took over as editor during his incarceration. Ossietzky was again arrested after the Reichstag fire, and sent to a concentration camp. The magazine was banned on March 13, 1933, its last issue having appeared on March 7.

Die neue Weltbühne (The New World Stage) appeared in Prague on April 6, 1933, as an antifascist newspaper in exile. It arose from the merger of the banned Berlin journal and its affiliate, the *Wiener Weltbühne,* which had been published in Vienna since September 1932. The editor of *Die neue Weltbühne* was initially William S. Schlamm, and as of March 1934 Hermann Budzislawski, who from 1936 owned the copyright jointly with Helen Reichenbach. Its circulation was approximately 5,000 to 9,000. The *Neue Weltbühne* was ideologically close to the German Communist Party (KPD) and promoted the policies of the POPULAR FRONT. Beginning in June 1938 it was published in Paris, until suppressed by the Daladier government on August 31, 1939.

S. O.

Werewolf (Werwolf), German partisan organization active in the last phase of the Second World War. The first Werewolf was a military organization that was formed in the summer of 1944 under the General Inspector for Special Defense [*Spezialabwehr*] in the Office of the *Reichsführer-SS,* Obergruppenführer Hans-Adolf Prütz-

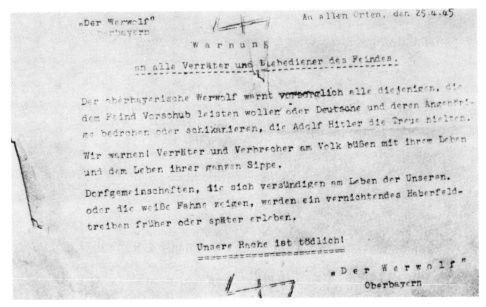

Werewolf. Flyer of April 25, 1945. "To all localities, April 25, 1945. Warning to all traitors and toadies of the enemy. The Upper Bavarian Werewolf warns in advance all those who would do the enemy's bidding, or who would threaten or harass Germans and their relatives who remain loyal to Adolf Hitler. We warn! Traitors and criminals against the *Volk* will pay with their lives and the lives of their entire clan. Village communities that sin against the life of one of us, or that wave the white flag, will sooner or later experience a devastating retribution. *Our vengeance is deadly!* 'The Werewolf,' Upper Bavaria."

mann (d. May 1945); the training center was at Hülchrath Castle. The second Werewolf was a revolutionary political movement staged as a "*Volk* uprising." It was proclaimed by Joseph Goebbels on the evening of April 1, 1945 (Easter Sunday), over the Werewolf radio station, using the frequency of the old RADIO GERMANY (Deutschlandsender).

Neither organization got off the ground, owing to lack of personnel and equipment. The Werewolf commandos distinguished themselves less through combating occupation troops then through liquidating "internal enemies" of National Socialism. Their most spectacular operation was the assassination of the American-appointed mayor of Aachen, Franz Oppenhoff, on March 25, 1945, by SS-Unterscharführer Josef Leitgeb (d. March 27, 1945) and a group consisting of five men and one woman. They had left Hildesheim on March 20 in a captured B-17. After landing by parachute, they shot the Belgian border guard Jost Saive. Another murderous act was the "execution" of eight citizens of the Bavarian city of Penzberg by a Werewolf commando led by SA-Brigadeführer Hans ZÖBERLEIN on April 28–29, 1945. As late as April 1985, former Lt. Kurt Rahäuser was sentenced in Waldshut for having ordered his Werewolf group to shoot eight Lithuanian and Russian "alien workers" in Wiesental, in the southern Black Forest, late in April 1945.

"Werewolf" was also the name of the FÜHRER'S HEADQUARTERS near Vinnitsa in the Ukraine.

G. H.

Werfel, Franz, b. Prague, September 10, 1890; d. Beverly Hills (California), August 26, 1945, Austrian writer. His early poetry made Werfel one of the first proponents of Expressionism ("Der Weltfreund" [Friend of the World]; 1911). During the First World War he caused a sensation with "radical pacifist" works, such as his translation of Euripides' *Die Troerinnen* (*The Trojan Women;* 1915–1916). In November 1918, he participated in revolutionary activities. During the 1920s Werfel won international acclaim as one of the most important German-language authors, with a varied body of works imbued with a strong religious feeling.

The National Socialists censured the expressive and symbolist form of Werfel's prose, as well as its humanistic content. His most important novel, *Die 40 Tage des Musa Dagh* (*The Forty Days of Musa Dagh;* 1933), used the example of the Turkish oppression of the Arme-

Franz Werfel.

nians to attack "barbaric nationalism." Not least because of his Jewish heritage, Werfel was excluded from the Prussian Academy of Letters in 1933; most of his works were then banned. After the annexation of Austria, Werfel had to go into exile, where he wrote poems against war and inhumanity, anti-Hitler pamphlets, and, ultimately, works that bespoke a resigned and mystical Catholicism. Most notable of these was *Das Lied von Bernadette* (1941), which as *The Song of Bernadette* became a best-seller in the United States.

"Weserübung" ("Weser Exercise"), code name for the operations of the German Wehrmacht in the occupation of Denmark and Norway (*see* NORWEGIAN CAMPAIGN).

Wessel, Horst, b. Bielefeld, October 9, 1907; d. February 23, 1930, SA man. The son of an Evangelical pastor, Wessel went to Berlin to study, but entered the NSDAP there in 1926 and took over SA Storm Unit 5 in the Communist stronghold of Friedrichshain. His political activities flagged, however, when he became enamored of a prostitute, with whom he moved into an apartment. They were ferreted out there by a pimp, Ali Höhler, accompanied by several Red Front militants; Wessel was shot in the mouth. Joseph GOEBBELS, *Gauleiter* of Berlin, turned the drama of jealousy into a political sacrifice and reported daily in *Der* ANGRIFF on Wessel's condition. Wessel's death transformed him into a "blood witness for the movement," and Goebbels exploited his burial to create a political

Horst Wessel.

demonstration. A poem that Wessel had published in the *Angriff* of September 23, 1929, was set to the catchy march melody of a sailors' song; as the "HORST-WESSEL-LIED," "Die Fahne hoch" (Up with the flag) became the second GERMAN NATIONAL ANTHEM after 1933. Many streets, ships, and events were named after Wessel.

Wessely, Paula, b. Vienna, January 10, 1907, Austrian actress. After successes on the Viennese stage, Wessely was discovered for the German cinema. Through her work in more demanding entertainment films (*So endete eine*

Paula Wessely.

Liebe [Thus Ended a Love]; 1934), Wessely ranked among the most popular and best-paid actresses of the Third Reich; her expressive and acting talents earned her international recognition. Wessely also accepted leading roles in political propaganda films such as *Heimkehr* (Return Home; 1941), which justified the occupation of Poland. After the war's end, and since 1953 at Vienna's Burgtheater, Wessely has been one of Austria's most important character actresses (in such works as *Jedermann* [Everyman]; 1961).

West, the (*Abendland*; literally, "land of the evening"), common term since the 16th century for Europe as the western half of the Old World, in contrast—indeed in opposition—to the Orient (*Morgenland*; "land of the morning"). After the First World War, the National Socialists used the slogan "decline of the West" (after the title of the book by Oswald SPENGLER) to make propaganda against the VERSAILLES TREATY, which was said to be a continuation of the "self-laceration of the cultured peoples of the West." They could be saved only by a new order arising "from the midst of Europe." Germany's demand for hegemony, paraphrased in this way, became the basis of the racist EUROPE IDEOLOGY, which was promoted after the beginning of the war in 1939 and intensified after the attack on the Soviet Union.

Westerbork, police detention camp and transit camp for Jews in the Drenthe Moors (Netherlands). It was originally built in the spring of 1939 for Jewish refugees who since the end of 1938 had fled Reich territory. From May 18, 1940, to June 30, 1942, Westerbork was subordinate to the Dutch Justice Ministry under the command of the German occupation authority. Effective July 1, 1942, the camp was taken over by the commander of the Security Police in The Hague. At the beginning of 1942 there were about 1,600 Jewish men, women, and children in Westerbork; by the end of that June, more barracks were constructed, with a capacity of at least 10,000 people. They were used to quarter Jews of various nationalities, as well as Gypsies.

The prisoners worked in the camp's autonomous administration; as artisans and laborers in various camp workshops (metal sorting, for example); and in fields, gardens, and road construction. Conditions in the camp were relatively good. The prisoners were properly lodged, hygienic and sanitary facilities were provided, food supply and clothing were adequate, and the prisoners were treated essentially according to regulations. The camp personnel consisted of around 10 SS members, some with serious war disabilities. They were at first assisted in the administrative work by Dutch personnel, but later the tasks of the latter were assumed by the Jewish self-government in the camp. The camp's external security was assigned to Dutch police officers.

On July 15, 1942, deportations from Westerbork began, headed for the EXTERMINATION CAMPS of the east, especially Sobibór and Auschwitz. A total of about 69,000 Jewish men, women, and children were taken away, of whom 68,000 are believed to have perished. A small number of those interned in Westerbork were deported to THERESIENSTADT, BERGEN-BELSEN, and Vittel (France). The camp was liberated by the Allies in April 1945.

Western Campaign (*Westfeldzug*), term for the military operations after the German attack in the west on May 10, 1940. They continued until the collapse of the Netherlands (May 14), Belgium (May 28), and France (June 22; *see* FRENCH CAMPAIGN).

Westmark (Western March), as of December 7, 1940, the name of the NSDAP Saarpfalz (Saar-Palatinate) *Gau*, consisting of the SAAR TERRITORY and the Palatinate.

Westphal, Max, b. Hamburg, September 30, 1895; d. Berlin, December 28, 1942, German opposition fighter. A worker, Westphal became chairman of the Hamburg Socialist Worker Youth in 1920. He joined the executive committee of the Social Democratic Party (SPD) in 1927, and in 1932 became a deputy in the Prussian parliament. In 1933 Westphal lost his job, but not his courage to combat the National Socialist dictatorship, even after spending June to September of that year in jail. He sought the cooperation of his former comrades, gathered donations—even abroad—for the persecuted, and maintained contacts with emigré circles. On December 19, 1938, he was arrested and charged with having worked for the banned SPD. Although acquitted, he was kept in protective custody at the Sachsenhausen concentration camp. Ruined in health, he was released only in May 1940.

West Prussia (Westpreussen), former Prussian province between Pomerania (Pommern) and East Prussia (Ostpreussen). After 1918 it was ceded to Poland; following Poland's defeat in 1939 it became the Danzig-Westpreussen *Reichsgau* (*see* DANZIG–WEST PRUSSIA).

Westwall, the fortified line along Germany's western border, from the Swiss border through the Upper Rhine, the Palatine Forest, and the Saar Territory, up to the area north of Aachen. Along this distance of some 630 km (about 400 miles), between May 1938 and September 1939 around 14,000 bunkers, battle positions, and dugouts, as well as the characteristic antitank "dragon's teeth," were put into place. The expenditure came to around 3.5 billion RM. Materials consumed included 8 million metric tons of cement (20 percent of Germany's yearly production), 1.2 million metric tons of iron (5 percent of the yearly production), 20.5 million metric tons of filler materials, and .95 million cu m of wood (8 percent of the yearly wood consumption). Every day some 8,000 railway freight cars reached the construction sites with materials (for a total of 1.01 million cars). By ship and truck, 4.5 million metric tons of material were delivered.

Along with the REICH LABOR SERVICE and transport organizations, some 100,000 workers from the fortification engineering corps of the army and 350,000 from the TODT ORGANIZATION were utilized. Characterized as impregnable in a mammoth propaganda campaign, the Westwall had an intimidating effect on the Western powers in 1939–1940. When it was put to the test in 1944–1945 against the Allied invasion, some of the installations turned out to be useless. Many bunkers were too small for modern weapons and others had been stripped of weapons and equipment in the course of the war, so that the troops often preferred to hold their ground in field trenches alongside the fortifications. (The English name for the Westwall was the SIEGFRIED LINE.)

G. H.

Wewelsburg-Niederhagen, National Socialist concentration camp near Paderborn (Westphalia), between the village and fortress of Wewelsburg and the Niederen-Hagen [Lower Hagen] Forest. It was built in January 1940 as a satellite of the Sachsenhausen concentration camp and was initially occupied by 300 prisoners, almost exclusively JEHOVAH'S WITNESSES. Beginning on September 1, 1941, Wewelsburg was an autonomous concentration camp with a population of about 1,200 prisoners, both German and foreign, of the most diverse categories (political, criminal, asocial, and homosexual), who had been brought in from other camps. In May 1943 Wewelsburg was downgraded from its autonomous status and became a small annex satellite of the Buchenwald camp, with about 50 Witnesses. Allied troops reached the camp on April 2, 1945.

The prisoners worked at constructing and expanding the camp barracks, and were involved in work on the SS Reich Leadership School that had been built at the Wewelsburg Fortress in 1933–1934. They were also put to use in various labor squads on tracts in the village, where eventually an SS settlement was to have been developed. The provisions for the prisoners—especially in view of the hard working conditions—were totally inadequate. Many of the forced laborers starved to death, or died from exhaustion or abuse by SS guards or kapos. In despair, many attempted to escape through the sentry post barriers, and were routinely shot without warning.

Weygand, Maxime, b. Brussels, January 21, 1867; d. Paris, January 28, 1965, French army general. In the First World War Weygand was chief of the General Staff for Marshal Ferdinand Foch. He served in 1920–1921 as an adviser to Marshal Józef PIŁSUDSKI in the Polish-Soviet war. In 1923–1924 he was high commissioner for Lebanon and Syria, as well as commander of the French Army of the Levant. Thereafter a member of the Supreme War Council, in 1930 he was chief of the General Staff, and in 1931 inspector general of the army. He retired in 1935, but was summoned back at the outbreak of war.

Weygand became Maurice-Gustave GAMELIN's successor as supreme commander of the Allied troops on May 19, 1940, during the FRENCH CAMPAIGN. Yet even the hasty formation of an initial position along the Somme River (the Weygand Line) could not halt the German advance any longer; thus, on June 12, Weygand recommended cease-fire negotiations. From June to September 1940 he was defense minister in the PÉTAIN government, then commissioner in French North Africa. He was ordered back on November 20, 1941, under German pressure, because of his contacts with the Anglo-Americans, and arrested on November 12, 1942. The Americans freed Weygand from German captivity in May 1945, but his countrymen brought him to trial for COLLABORATION. Spared imprisonment, on May 6, 1948, Wey-

gand was rehabilitated by France's highest court.

"White Jews" (*Weisse Juden*), term used in the SS weekly, *Das Schwarze Korps* (as on July 15, 1937), to designate German physicists who occupied themselves with the "detailed expositions" of the "relativity Jew" (*Relativitäts-Jude*) Albert EINSTEIN. (The latter epithet originated with the Nobel laureate Philipp LENARD.)

White Rose (Weisse Rose), student opposition group in Munich, formed around Hans SCHOLL and his sister Sophie SCHOLL, Christoph Probst, Willi Graf, Alexander Schmorell, and the philosophy professor Kurt HUBER. Its contacts extended to student groups in Hamburg, Freiburg, Berlin, and Vienna. Indignant over the moral and political capitulation of Germany's educated middle class, the White Rose in 1942–1943 turned to the public, and especially to students, with leaflets and inscriptions on walls such as "The spirit lives" ("Der Geist lebt") and "Down with Hitler." They wanted to inform others of the terror committed by the National Socialist tyranny, of its crimes against Jews and Poles, the spiritual corruption of youth, and the deteriorating military situation. The White Rose wanted to break the vicious circle in which "each waits for the other to begin," and thus makes everyone guilty.

The White Rose did not attempt a coup, although its members knew that "National Socialist power must be broken militarily." They wanted instead to instigate sabotage and passive resistance in order to "bring down National Socialism" and "achieve a renewal from inside out of the badly wounded German spirit." The last White Rose leaflet, which the Scholls scattered in large numbers at the entrance hall of the University of Munich on February 18, 1943, aroused a particular stir. It led to their immediate arrest through a denunciation by the janitor. The leaflet exhorted: "The day of reckoning has come, the reckoning of German youth with the most abominable tyranny that our people have ever suffered." It demanded "the fight for our free self-determination, without which spiritual values cannot be created," and the "destruction of National Socialist terror by the power of the spirit." The Scholls and Probst were executed on February 22, 1943, after a trial by the *Volk* Court under Roland FREISLER. In the following months their friends followed them in death.

B.-J. W.

White Rose. Hans and Sophie Scholl with Christoph Probst (right).

Wiechert, Ernst, b. Kleinort Forestry (Forsthaus), near Sensburg (East Prussia), May 18, 1887; d. Uerikon (Switzerland), August 24, 1950, German writer. Wiechert devoted himself, in his early work especially, to the poetic expression of his "East Prussian homeland of forests, lakes, and moors." His heroes withdrew from hectic city life back into "nature and genuine life." For this reason National Socialist criticism classified him with the "blood and soil" writers. Although Wiechert was initially able to continue working unhampered after the

Ernst Wiechert.

Seizure of Power, criticism increased over his Christian outlook and his scarcely heroic, even somewhat pacifist, representation of frontline experience in *Die Majorin* (The Major's Wife; 1934).

In 1937 Wiechert warned in a public lecture that the nation was standing on the "edge of an abyss" and would be "condemned by the eternal Judge" if it did not learn "to distinguish between justice and injustice." He was imprisoned in the Buchenwald concentration camp for several months as a "seducer and perverter of youth," and afterward was kept under Gestapo surveillance. After the war, Wiechert was regarded as one of the most important representatives of INNER EMIGRATION in the Third Reich. He described his Buchenwald experiences in the narratives *Der Totenwald* (*The Forest of the Dead;* 1946) and *Häftling Nr. 7188* (Prisoner No. 7188; published posthumously in 1966).

Wiedemann, Fritz, b. Augsburg, August 16, 1891; d. Fuchsgrub (Bavaria), January 17, 1970, German officer. Wiedemann became a lieutenant in 1912, and in the First World War was a battalion adjutant in the List Regiment, in which Hitler also served. Wiedemann later reported that there had been an intention to promote the lance corporal to noncommissioned officer, but "no appropriate leadership qualities" could be found in him. Wiedemann joined the NSDAP in 1934, served as Hitler's adjutant from 1935 to 1939, and was assigned to various missions,

Fritz Wiedemann.

including one involved with preparations for the ANSCHLUSS of Austria. In 1939 he became general consul in San Francisco, and in 1941 in Tientsin (China), where he was captured by American troops at the war's end. He was later a farmer in Bavaria.

Wiener, Alfred, b. Potsdam, March 16, 1885; d. February 4, 1964, German historian. In 1919, Wiener became the representative and the executive director of the CENTRAL ASSOCIATION OF GERMAN CITIZENS OF THE JEWISH FAITH. As a leading Jewish functionary, he had to flee abroad in 1933. In Holland he established the Jewish Central Information Office and gathered material on every sort of National Socialist lawbreaking and crime, especially on the PERSECUTION OF JEWS. In 1939 he moved to London. There, with his collection of materials (then called the Wiener Library), he supplied the British government with information for the struggle and the propaganda campaign against the Third Reich. After 1945, Wiener provided incriminatory material for war crimes trials, and developed his institute into one of the most important research centers for the history of Jews in the 20th century, as well as for National Socialism and the Third Reich.

Wiersich, Oswald, b. Breslau, September 1, 1882; d. Berlin-Plötzensee, March 1, 1945 (executed), German trade unionist. A machinist, even before 1914 Wiersich was often reprimanded for union activities. In 1923 he became district secretary (*Bezirkssekretär*) of the General German Trade Union Federation (ADGB) in Silesia and a member of its executive committee;

he was also a member of the Prussian State Council. Wiersich was arrested immediately in 1933 because of his known anti-Nazi attitude, and after his release he was kept under police surveillance. He then worked as a union representative and was able to maintain contacts with his former union colleagues. They put him in touch in 1935 with Wilhelm LEUSCHNER, who drew Wiersich into the opposition circles, notably the group around Col. Gen. Ludwig BECK. After the July 1944 assassination attempt, Wiersich was arrested, on August 22; following detention in the Gross-Rosen concentration camp, he was sentenced to death.

Wiesenthal, Simon, b. Buczacz (Galicia; now in Russia), December 31, 1908, Austrian archivist. An architect, Wiesenthal was apprehended by German security forces in 1941 and confined in various jails and concentration camps. Shortly before the war's end, American troops liberated the Mauthausen concentration camp, where Wiesenthal was being held. In 1947 he established in Linz a documentation center on National Socialist persecution of Jews. Discouraged by the limited official support, he emigrated to Israel in 1954. There he contributed greatly to the tracking down of Adolf EICHMANN. In 1962, Wiesenthal returned to Austria and established in Vienna the Documentation Center of the Union of Jews Persecuted by the Nazi Regime. It was financed primarily by donations, and provided material for over a thousand cases against NS criminals. Wiesenthal was successful in capturing, among others, Franz STANGL, the former commandant of the Treblinka concentration camp, as well as former SS leaders who were being traced. In later years he sought in particular Josef MENGELE, who had been the concentration camp physician in AUSCHWITZ.

Wigman, Mary (originally, Marie Wiegmann), b. Hannover, November 13, 1886; d. Berlin, September 19, 1973, German dancer and choreographer. A student of Rudolf von LABAN, in 1920–1921 Wigman established her own dance school in Dresden (the Wigman-Schule). After the First World War she had continual success. The founder of a "German dance art" (*deutsche Tanzkunst*)—mainly scenes accompanied by percussion or danced without music—she created individual and group dances, such as "Schicksalslied" (Song of Fate; 1935) and "Totenklage" (Lament for the Dead; 1936), that were darkly visionary and laden with mythology. Wigman found an enthusiastic public in the Third Reich, for whom she staged operas and oratorios in the 1940s. She reopened her dance school after the war, at first in Leipzig and then in West Berlin in 1949. In later years she expanded it into the Center for Modern Dance.

Wild concentration camps (*wilde KZ*), designation for the improvised camps set up immediately after the Seizure of Power and without any legal basis by SS and SA troops. Political or private enemies were mistreated there and kept incarcerated in disregard of the provisions of PROTECTIVE CUSTODY.

Wilhelm, b. Potsdam, May 6, 1882; d. Hechingen, July 20, 1951, German crown prince, son of Kaiser WILHELM II. In the First World War, Wilhelm was at first supreme commander of the Fifth Army without adequate qualifications, and later of his own "German Crown Prince" Army Group. In 1918 he pursued unsuccessful plans to succeed his abdicated father, then accompanied him to Holland in exile. After returning to Germany in 1923 with the help of Gustav STRE-SEMANN, Wilhelm joined the STEEL HELMET and worked toward a restoration of the monarchy. One ploy he considered was becoming a candidate for the office of Reich president in 1932, but his father forbade it. Thereupon Wilhelm promoted Hitler's candidacy, hoping through the latter's seizure of power for the restoration of the German Empire. However, in contrast to his brother AUGUST WILHELM, Wilhelm remained aloof from the party and joined only the NATIONAL SOCIALIST MOTOR CORPS (NSKK) before turning away in disappointment. Later he even established loose contacts with the opposition movement. He never enjoyed great popularity.

Wilhelm II, b. Potsdam, January 27, 1859; d. Doorn (Netherlands), June 4, 1941, German emperor (Kaiser) and king of Prussia (1888–1918). Imbued with a strong sense of destiny as a monarch, after ascending the throne Wilhelm rapidly came into conflict with Chancellor Otto von Bismarck, the Reich's founder. In domestic affairs Bismarck opposed the Kaiser's drive for popularity (a pretense at social and political progressivism); in foreign affairs, Wilhelm believed that the chancellor lacked assertiveness. The post-Bismarck era was then characterized by social and political regression and pointless martial displays. Whereas the domestic political conflicts could be kept under control through relative prosperity, the aggressive foreign policy (fleet buildup, shifting rapprochements, "Nibe-

Wilhelm II in the uniform of a fleet admiral.

lung loyalty" to Vienna, and naive tactlessness) resulted in Germany's diplomatic isolation and the First World War.

After the overthrow of the monarchy, Wilhelm left for exile in Holland on November 10, 1918. He abdicated soon afterward, on November 28, but sought a prompt restoration in Germany. From National Socialist successes he hoped in particular to be recalled (Hermann Göring visited Doorn in January 1931 and May 1932), but he had to put that illusion to rest after Paul von Hindenburg's death (August 2, 1934). Thereafter, Wilhelm spoke of the Third Reich only as the "mustard republic" ("brown and sharp"). When German troops marched into Holland in 1940, higher-ranking officers were forbidden contact with Wilhelm, although he was accorded military honors at his burial. A reader of Wilhelm's speeches and pronouncements today might find their similarity with Hitler's simplifications astounding. Unlike those of the dictator, however, Wilhelm's were merely a pose.

Wilhelm Gustloff, passenger ship of the German Labor Front commissioned on January 22, 1936, and launched on July 5, 1937. Built for the

Burial of Wilhelm II (1941). From the left: the former empress Hermine, Crown Prince
Wilhelm, Arthur Seyss-Inquart, August von Mackensen.

"Peace Fleet" (Flotte des Friedens) of the
STRENGTH THROUGH JOY (KdF) organization,
the ship had a gross registered tonnage of
25,484, a length of 208.5 m (about 700 feet), a
width of 23.5 m (about 80 feet), 10 decks, and
space for 417 crew members and 1,465 cruise
guests. Originally intended to bear Hitler's
name, the *Wilhelm Gustloff* was named after
the Swiss National Group Leader of the NSDAP
Foreign Organization, Wilhelm GUSTLOFF, who
was assassinated on February 4, 1936. The

Members of the Condor Legion on the
Wilhelm Gustloff.

maiden voyage began on March 23, 1938, after
the Anschluss of Austria, with 1,000 *Ostmärker*
(Austrians) heading into the North Sea. On April
10, 1938, the ship lay at anchor off London as a
floating polling place where Germans in England could vote on the Anschluss. Thereafter it
made KdF trips to Madeira and to the Norwegian fjords, and in May 1939 brought the CON-
DOR LEGION back from Spain.

At the outbreak of the war the *Wilhelm
Gustloff* was declared an auxiliary ship of the
navy, and put to use first as a hospital ship and
then in 1940 as a barracks ship anchored in
Gotenhafen (Gdingen; now Gdynia). There it
was damaged by a bomb in 1944 and given
makeshift repairs. On January 30, 1945, the
ship put out to sea for Kiel-Flensburg with
4,974 refugees and 1,626 women naval auxiliaries (*Marinehelferinnen*), wounded persons, soldiers, and crew members. The temperature
stood at −18°C (about 0°F). At 9:08 p.m. the
ship was hit by three torpedoes from a Soviet
S 13 submarine and sank off Stolpmünde within
62 minutes. A total of 5,348 people lost their
lives, and 1,252 were rescued. Today the *Wilhelm Gustloff* is marked on Polish sea charts as
"Navigation Obstacle No. 73."

Wilhelmstrasse, street crossing the Allee Unter
den Linden and the Stresemannstrasse, east of
the Brandenburg Gate in Berlin (in the GDR,
Otto-Grotewohl-Strasse). After the German unification in 1871, Wilhelmstrasse was the address

of several ministries, including the Foreign Office. The administration of German foreign policy until 1945 was therefore often simply called "the Wilhelmstrasse."

Wilhelmstrasse Trial (*Wilhelmstrassen-Prozess*), proceeding held before United States Military Court V against the state secretary in the Foreign Office, Ernst Baron von WEIZSÄCKER, and 20 others, so called because of the location of the Foreign Office and other ministries. It was the largest and the last of the NUREMBERG TRIALS (Case 11). Of the 21 defendants, 18 were ministers and high officials in the civil administration of the Third Reich. They were charged with crimes against peace, war crimes (including complicity in the lynching of downed aviators and the murder and mistreatment of war prisoners), crimes against humanity (particularly against the civilian population in the occupied territories), and with having been members of a criminal organization.

In a decision handed down on April 11, 1949, 19 defendants, partially acquitted of some charges, were sentenced to prison terms of between 46 months (3 years, 10 months) and 25 years, and 2 defendants were found not guilty. Through a supplementary decision of December 12, 1949, the penalties of 3 of those convicted, including Weizsäcker, were reduced from 7 to 5 years. In a pardon issued on January 31, 1951, United States High Commissioner John J. Mc-Cloy reduced the parts of the sentences that had not yet been served.

A. St.

Wilhelm Tell, play by Friedrich Schiller (1804) that celebrates the Swiss fight for freedom from foreign rule (in the 14th century) and from tyranny. Hitler, who called Switzerland an "anachronism" and its national hero a "sniper" (February 4, 1942), gave an order on June 3, 1941, that prohibited performances of the play, as well as teaching it in classrooms. The case of the would-be assassin Maurice BAVAUD had a direct bearing on this measure.

Winckler, Josef, b. Rheine, July 6, 1881; d. Bergisch Gladbach, January 29, 1966, German writer. A dentist by profession, in 1912 Winckler helped found the so-called Nyland League, which devoted itself to the poetic rendering of the modern (industrial) world (as in *Eiserne Sonette* [Iron Sonnets]; 1904). In 1924 Winckler became well known for his picaresque Westphalian novel *Der tolle Bomber* (The Wild Bomber), which even during the Third Reich went

through several editions and was made into a film. His energetic language, which "draws from the richness of the *Volk*," was especially esteemed. Further works included the novel *Dr. Eisenbart* (1929) and the stories in *Die goldene Kiepe* (The Golden Basket; 1941).

Winkler, Max, b. Karresch/West Prussia, September 7, 1875; d. Düsseldorf, October 12, 1961, German cultural and financial policymaker. A deputy of the German Party in the Prussian parliament, in 1919 Winkler became Reich trustee for the German territories ceded in the Versailles treaty, and director of the Cura-Revisions und Treuhand GmbH (Cura Audit and Trust Company, Ltd.), which supported German newspapers in these and other territories with German minorities. At Joseph Goebbels's special request, Winkler handled the details of the Synchronization and concentration of the German PRESS, and then focused his work on FILM. In 1937, as a new party member, he was given the recently created post of Reich Commissioner for the German Film Industry. He implemented the cinema's nationalization, generously paid off private owners, and discreetly brought the film industry under control. In 1939 Winkler was also made the Leader of the Main Trustee Office for the East (HTO), responsible for the administration of confiscated industrial and landed properties in the conquered Eastern Territories. In 1945 he was interned for a time, then successfully denazified. He began work again in the film sector, this time for the German federal government, dismantling the unified film organization that he had built up.

H. H.

Winnig, August, b. Blankenburg/Harz, March 31, 1878; d. Bad Nauheim, November 3, 1956, German politician and political journalist. A mason by trade, and a member of the Social Democratic Party (SPD), in 1912 Winnig became chairman of the German Construction Workers' Association and publisher of its periodical, *Der Grundstein* (The Cornerstone). In 1918 he became plenipotentiary of the Reich in the Baltic territory (Baltikum), then envoy in Latvia and Estonia, and in 1919 governor (*Oberpräsident*) of East Prussia. Because of his support for the KAPP PUTSCH, he lost all his offices in 1920 and was expelled from the SPD.

In his writings, Winnig drew increasingly closer to conservative positions, as in *Das Reich als Republik* (The Reich as Republic; 1928), and to NATIONAL BOLSHEVISM, notably in *Vom Prole-*

August Winnig: *The Distant Path* (1932).

tariat zum Arbeitertum (From Proletariat to Workerdom; 1930). This brought him for a time in contact even with the NSDAP; however, Winnig declined their offer to give him leadership of the GERMAN LABOR FRONT. His Christian principles led him into the INNER EMIGRATION in the Third Reich, even though at times he expressed himself in a nationalist sense on political questions, as in his *Europa—Gedanken eines Deutschen* (Europe—A German's Thoughts; 1937).

Winter Relief Agency (Winterhilfswerk; WHW), organization that came into being during the crisis winter of 1931–1932 to provide unemployed and needy people with money, groceries, meals, clothing, and fuel. A reaction to the world economic crisis, the WHW was jointly maintained by private welfare associations, including the GERMAN RED CROSS, the Nondenominational Welfare Association (Paritätischer Wohlfahrtsverband), the German-Israelite Community, Workers' Welfare, Inner Mission (Evangelical), and Caritas (Catholic), as well as governmental social service agencies.

Even before 1933, the NSDAP had organized its own, competing winter relief measures. A proclamation by Hitler and Goebbels on September 13, 1933, introduced the first National Socialist WHW for the winter of 1933–1934. Although officially proclaimed as a broad-based

organization of all welfare resources, in reality the WHW was subordinate to the NATIONAL SOCIALIST VOLK WELFARE agency (NSV) as the leading organization for voluntary welfare services, a status favored by a monopoly on collections of funds. Those organizations that had not yet been "synchronized," such as the Inner Mission, Caritas, and the Red Cross, played only a subordinate role. While the WHW was granted its own legal rights in 1936, the ties between it and the NSV were also evident in their parallel hierarchical structures (*Gau, Kreis,* and *Bezirksstelle*) and in the dual positions held by officials on parallel levels.

The activities of the WHW were multifarious: street and house-to-house collections for money and clothing, the monthly ONE-DISH SUNDAY, obligatory wage and salary deductions, collection cans in stores for a "winter pfennig," and a Reich Winter Relief Lottery. The donation revenues from 1933–1934 to 1938–1939 amounted to 2.5 billion RM. The allocation of the support was carried out in cooperation with government social service agencies through the regional offices (*Bezirksstellen*). The originally very wide

Winter Relief Agency. Street collection.

Winter Relief Agency wooden figures.

range of recipients was soon narrowed to politically, racially, and biologically "worthy persons" (*würdige Personen*). As the core component of NS SOCIAL POLICY, the WHW was in various ways designed to further the internal stabilization of the regime as well as its totalitarian infiltration. It served to eliminate material need, as the preeminent prestige objective of the authorities; to mobilize the population and facilitate total, close-knit control even within the private sphere of the home; to stimulate a sense of national awakening; to synchronize and encourage voluntary conformity of the independent social service organizations; to portray the Propaganda Ministry as responsible for the WHW by means of film, newspaper, poster, and radio publicity; to appeal to such concepts as "*Volk* Community," "national solidarity," and "readiness for sacrifice"; and to document a "socialism of deeds" that transcended groups and classes (K. Kaufmann). On the other hand, the sorting out (*Selektion*) of "asocial" and "racially and biologically inferior" people, as well as the campaign against the "nuisance of begging" (*Bettelunwesen*), turned the WHW into a means of political and ideological oppression.

The continual badgering for donations, privately and on the job, and the financial burden involved, especially for people at lower income levels, led increasingly to exasperation and to a decline in "voluntary" willingness to donate. Countless instances of quarrels between the NSV/WHW and government agencies over authority and jurisdiction, as well as over dual responsibility, point to a basic and ultimately unresolved structural defect of the Third Reich: the dualism between party and state (*see* DUAL STATE).

B.-J. W.

Winter War (*Winterkrieg*), designation for the hostilities between Finland and the Soviet Union from November 30, 1939, to March 12, 1940. In October 1939 Moscow issued an ultimatum to Finland, which the GERMAN-SOVIET NONAGGRESSION PACT had given over to the Soviet sphere of interest. Finland's rejection of the Soviet demands—strongholds for the Red Army and border adjustments—provoked an attack. The rapid Finnish collapse that had been anticipated did not occur, even though the Soviets moved 450,000 men with massive air and tank support against Finland's poorly armed reserve army of 215,000 men. The Arctic cold, down to $-50°C$ ($-58°F$), and an officer corps weakened by the Stalinist purges, impeded Soviet successes.

Only the mobilization of another 500,000 Red Army troops under Marshal Semyon Timoshenko brought a decision in the Winter War, although not to the extent desired by Stalin. He found himself forced into a quick peace because of British-French plans for a relief corps that at the same time could have cut Germany off from its Swedish ore deliveries. With the loss of (according to Soviet accounts) 207,000 soldiers, as opposed to 25,000 Finnish dead, the Soviet Union obtained a territorial gain of 35,000 sq km (about 14,000 sq miles), some strongholds, and a nonaggression treaty, which Finland revoked on June 26, 1941, after the German attack on Russia. It was an attack that Hitler risked in part because of the Red Army's failure in the Winter War. The Wehrmacht High Command had stated on December 31, 1939, that the Soviet armed forces were "no opponent."

Wireless Service (Der Drahtloser Dienst; DDD), the central radio news service of the National Socialist government. The DDD developed out of the Wireless Service, Inc. (Drahtloser Dienst AG; Dradag) of the Weimar Republic, which at first was legally autonomous although supervised by the Reich, the states, the parties, and the press associations. As the DDD, it was incorporated in 1932 into the Reich Radio Company (Reichs-Rundfunk-Gesellschaft; RRG), the administrative head of German RADIO. From May 1, 1933, to September 15, 1939, the DDD belonged to the press section of the Propaganda Ministry, but it was then once again placed under the RRG. Its editor in chief until 1938 was Hans FRITZSCHE, and then Walter Wilhelm Dittmar.

S. O.

Wirmer, Josef, b. Paderborn, March 19, 1901; d. Berlin-Plötzensee, September 8, 1944 (executed), German jurist. A Berlin lawyer, Wirmer was a member of the Center party. He was a representative of the Catholic Student Associations from the early 1930s until their synchronization. Wirmer rejected National Socialism out of Christian conviction. Beginning in 1934 he was in contact with Jakob KAISER and the Catholic workers' opposition. Because of Wirmer's defense of Jewish clients, he was excluded from the NATIONAL SOCIALIST LEAGUE OF LAW GUARDIANS. Conscripted for work in the chemical industry during the war, he joined the opposition group around Carl GOERDELER, in whose post-overthrow government he was slated to be justice minister. When the assassination plot of July 20, 1944, failed, Wirmer was arrested on August 4 and condemned to death. In the proceeding before the *Volk* Court, Roland FREISLER characterized Wirmer as the "personification of obstinate hatred of our Führer." Wirmer had proposed a flag for a Germany liberated from National Socialism: it combined the republican black-red-gold with the Christian cross.

Wirsing, Giselher, b. Schweinfurt, April 15, 1907; d. Stuttgart, September 23, 1975, German political journalist. As a foreign-affairs editor, Wirsing was one of the leading figures of the TAT CIRCLE, which was associated with Hans ZEHRER. Parallel with National Socialism, Wirsing even before 1933 developed an expansionist program of conquest with anticapitalist leanings, as seen in *Zwischeneuropa und die deutsche Zukunft* (Interim Europe and the German Future; 1932). After the Seizure of Power, Wirsing placed himself unreservedly on the side of National Socialism. He joined the SS in 1933, and as an SS-*Sturmbannführer* worked intermittently in the National Socialist Institute for Research on the Jewish Question.

Wirsing was one of the Third Reich's representatives of an outstanding and intellectually more demanding NS political journalism, not least as editor of the illustrated magazine for readers abroad, SIGNAL (1943–1945). A recurrent hostility toward England and America evident in travel reports, article series, and foreign-affairs publications was continued by Wirsing after the war in several works on Third World developments and in his position as editor in chief of the conservative weekly newspaper *Christ und Welt* (The Christian and the World; 1954–1970).

H. H.

Wirth, Christian, b. Oberbalzheim, November 24, 1885; d. Trieste, May 26, 1944, SS-*Sturmbannführer* (May 1943). A skilled sawyer, Wirth entered police service in 1910. After serving in the First World War, he transferred to the Criminal Police (Kripo). He became a member of the NSDAP on January 1, 1931, and of the SA on June 30, 1933; he was accepted by the SS in 1939. In 1940, having risen to the rank of criminal commissioner, Wirth became part of the T4 EUTHANASIA organization. Shortly afterward, in the context of the REINHARD OPERATION, he was put in charge of setting up the BEŁŻEC extermination camp, and from August 1942 served as inspector of the extermination camps. Wirth fulfilled with brutal consistency his mandate for killing. According to statements of his subordinates, he was a shouting and cursing "fiend" (*Unhold*); wherever he appeared, he spread fear and horror. His nickname was "Christian the Terrible" (*Christian der Grausame*) or "wild Christian."

Promoted to criminal inspector on January 30, 1943, Wirth was transferred along with other staff members under his superior, Odilo GLOBOCNIK, to Trieste toward the end of the Reinhard Operation. There, following the overthrow of the Italian Fascist government, he was to implement the now possible "population transfer" of Jews. He was shot by partisans on an official trip to Fiume.

A. St.

Wirth, Joseph, b. Freiburg im Breisgau, September 6, 1879; d. there, January 3, 1956, German politician. A teacher, Wirth was from 1914 to 1933 a member of the Reichstag for the Center party; he was Reich finance minister in 1920–1921. He became Reich chancellor on May 10, 1921, without a majority in the Reichstag, but with the help of the WEIMAR COALITION. He then accepted the ultimatum of the London Conference of May 5, 1921 (*see* LONDON CONFERENCES), on the reparations issue and thus introduced the FULFILLMENT POLICY. Together with his foreign minister, Walther RATHENAU, he balanced this policy with an opening to the east in the RAPALLO TREATY.

In domestic policies Wirth strove for stabilization of the democratic system; after Rathenau's murder, he brought to passage the REPUBLIC PROTECTION LAW (slogan: "The enemy is on the right!"). Having failed to broaden his parliamentary base toward a Great Coalition, Wirth resigned on November 14, 1922. From 1929 to 1931 he was a minister under Hermann MÜLLER

Joseph Wirth.

and Heinrich BRÜNING. After the Seizure of Power, he went into exile in Switzerland, where he founded the Democratic Germany group. After the war he opposed the integration of the Federal Republic into the West, but found little response to his political initiatives (including his founding of the Union of the Middle in 1948).

Wirtschaftspartei (Economic Party), middle-class party founded in September 1920; in 1925 it was renamed the REICH PARTY OF THE GERMAN MIDDLE CLASS.

Wirtschafts-Verwaltungshauptamt. *See* Economic-Administrative Main Office.

Wisliceny, Dieter, b. Regulowken (East Prussia), January 13, 1911; d. Pressburg, February 27, 1948 (executed), SS-*Hauptsturmführer* (1944). Wisliceny studied theology without taking a degree, then joined the NSDAP in 1931 and the SS in 1934. In June of that year he joined the Security Service (SD), for a time serving as Adolf EICHMANN's superior. In September 1940 Wisliceny was assigned to the Slovak government in Pressburg as a "Jewish expert" (*Judenberater*); he organized the deportations of Greek Jews in 1943–1944, and participated in Eichmann's program for exterminating the Hungarian Jews beginning in March 1944. His corruptibility, which the Jews in Slovakia had capitalized on, fed Hungarian hopes as well, especially those of Joel BRAND, but these hopes remained unrealized. After giving his testimony in the NUREMBERG TRIALS, Wisliceny was remanded to Czechoslovakia and there sentenced to death.

Wittek, Erhard, b. Wongrowitz (Posen), December 3, 1898; d. Pinneberg, June 4, 1981, German writer. Wittek was the author of widely read children's books about the Indian chief Tecumseh, which he wrote under the pseudonym Fritz Steuben. Also popular during the Third Reich were his "heroic" anecdotes, *Männer* (Men; 1936); the First World War novel *Durchbruch anno achtzehn* (Breakthrough in the year '18; 1933); and sentimental stories such as *Bewährung der Herzen* (Hearts' Confirmation; 1937) and *Dem Vaterland zugute . . .* (For the Sake of the Fatherland . . . ; 1943).

Witzleben, Erwin von, b. Breslau, December 4, 1881; d. Berlin-Plötzensee, August 8, 1944 (executed), German field marshal general (July 19, 1940) and opposition fighter. Witzleben was a major general and commander in Military District III. Since the Sudeten crisis in 1938, he had been among those supporting an overthrow of Hitler. He went to war in September 1939 as commander of the First Army in the Polish Campaign. After being active in the French Campaign in May and June 1940, he became supreme commander of Army Group D in France on October 26 of that year; on May 1, 1941, he was promoted to supreme commander in the west. Relieved of his duties on March 21, 1942, because of suspicions against him, Witzleben worked for the military opposition. He finally made up his mind to agree to an assassination attempt on Hitler, despite reservations on religious grounds. In case of its success he was slated to be the supreme commander of the Wehrmacht. The *coup d'état* of July 20, 1944,

Erwin von Witzleben.

miscarried, however; Witzleben was arrested the next day and sentenced to death on August 8.

Wolff, Karl, b. Darmstadt, May 13, 1900; d. Rosenheim, July 15, 1984, German SS-*Führer*. Wolff was an officer (a lieutenant of the guard) in the First World War. From 1918 to 1920 he was a member of the Hessian Free Corps. He then worked as a businessman, and joined the NSDAP and the SS in 1931. As early as July 1933 Wolff became Heinrich Himmler's personal adjutant. He advanced quickly in the SS: on January 30, 1937, he was promoted to *Gruppenführer*, and on January 30, 1942, to *Obergruppenführer* and general in the Waffen-SS. Himmler appointed Wolff chief of his staff in 1937 and in 1939 made him his liaison to the Führer Headquarters. Wolff was thus more or less the third man in the SS, after Reinhard HEYDRICH.

On September 23, 1943, Wolff went to Italy as the Highest SS and Police Leader. From July 26, 1944, as plenipotentiary general of the German Wehrmacht, he directed Mussolini's puppet regime in SALÒ. In view of Germany's certain defeat, on his own initiative Wolff put himself in contact with the United States secret service in Switzerland and arranged an early German capitulation in Italy on May 2, 1945. In exchange, the Allies spared him the dock at Nuremberg and allowed him to appear as a witness in full SS uniform. Less forbearing was the German appeals chamber in Hamburg in 1949, which sentenced Wolff to four years' imprisonment. Only a trial before the Munich court of assizes (*Schwurgericht*) made it clear that he was not the "SS general with the white vest." Because of his involvement in at least 300,000 cases of murder (deportations of Jews to TREBLINKA), Wolff was sentenced on September 30, 1964, to 15 years in prison. In 1971 he was released from imprisonment.

"Wolfsschanze" ("Wolf's Lair"), one of the FÜHRER'S HEADQUARTERS, located near Rastenburg in East Prussia. It was the scene of the assassination attempt on Hitler on the TWENTIETH OF JULY, 1944.

Wöllersdorf, Austrian commune (*Gemeinde*) in Lower Austria, with 1,900 inhabitants in 1933. The DOLLFUSS government built its largest detention camp (*see* DETENTION CAMPS) in Wöllersdorf; until its dismantling in February 1938, it held mainly Austrian National Socialists.

Women, employment of (*Frauenberufstätigkeit*), in the context of WORK CREATION measures, initially the decreased employment of women. Owing to the scarcity of labor, however, women's contributions to the work of the *Volk* Community were soon encouraged again, especially in jobs that encouraged "their maternal capacity to help, heal, and teach." (*See also* WOMEN IN THE THIRD REICH; SOCIAL POLICY.)

Women in the Third Reich

The NSDAP, which saw itself as a "militant party" (*Kampfpartei*), initially had little interest in winning over women for its movement. Women with National Socialist (NS) leanings were tolerated as volunteers, but a confrontation with issues of particular concern to women began only in the early 1930s, when there were indications that a parliamentary victory for the party might really be possible. On the path to a legal takeover of power, women as voters would have to be addressed more clearly than before. Because of these pragmatic considerations, the NSDAP was obliged to develop a message regarding women's roles in the *völkisch* state. While continuing to see itself as a men's party, and presenting itself as such, it was able to claim success in competing for women's votes in the early 1930s, although the thesis that "women brought Hitler to power" must be rejected as greatly exaggerated.

The ideology with which the National Socialists hoped to win over women was in no way original: similar ideas could be found among other conservative groups. Political emancipation was rejected as a mistake, and woman's appropriate arena of activity was located within the family circle. As a mother she was valuable for the nation, and in fulfilling her maternal duties she fulfilled herself. For those women who, because of the lack of marriageable men, were unable to attain the ideal state, ideology offered a way out: in occupations "appropriate to their nature" (*arteigene*), women would have the opportunity to transfer their innate maternal feelings and instincts (in spiritual motherhood). The woman who did not accept such ideas for

1

Schütze Mutter und Kind, das kostbarste Gut deines Volkes!

2

Die schöne Aufgabe:

R.A.D. Führerin
Ein Ruf der Zeit!

3

Hilf siegen
als Luftnachrichtenhelferin

Auskunft erteilt jede Luftwaffendienststelle

4

Deutsche Heringe gut u. frisch

Mutter bringt Hering auf den Tisch

5

MÄDEL, DEIN BERUF, WERDE SCHWESTER!

DER SCHÖNSTE DIENST AN DER GESUNDHEIT DEINES VOLKES

1–5

Posters for the image of women propagandized in the Third Reich: (1) "Protect mother and child, the most valuable possession of your *Volk!*" (2) "The fine mission: Reich Labor Service Führerin—a calling of the times!" (3) "Hasten victory as an air intelligence (See facing page.)

6

herself was not, in NS eyes, a true woman. This restriction of the female population to an existence as housewives and mothers was justified by "typical" feminine characteristics. Standing intellectually between man and child, a woman offered ideal qualities for the education of children; at the same time, her capacities were sufficient to enable her to stand beside her man as an understanding comrade.

One should not condemn this ideal as solely the expression of a conservative mentality within the party, since it seized upon subconscious fantasies of many women, and thus became effective as propaganda. In reality, the rights given to women by the WEIMAR CONSTITUTION were often enough burdens, rather than opportunities, for those affected. The economic crises of the Weimar Republic often led to a heavy double burden for women, who all too frequently were the sole support of themselves and their families. The NSDAP promised relief to these overextended women by dangling an ideal picture before them and conveying the impression that the party would see to it that this utopia was realized.

After 1933 the NSDAP intensified its message that "woman belongs at home," while strengthening its emphasis on the notion of duty. Marriage and motherhood would no longer serve to create individual happiness; rather, they now related to the fulfillment of obligations to the VOLK COMMUNITY. Marriage had value for the NS state primarily in terms of the birth and rearing of genetically healthy Aryan children. To ensure the quantity and quality of offspring, the state intervened extensively in private life. Women were repeatedly enjoined to keep themselves "pure" out of responsibility to the community, and to think of themselves as guardians of the nation. Married couples were warned against misusing married life for the satisfaction of their sexual needs, since the primary purpose of one's sex life was to preserve the nation. Basically, reproduction and the rearing of children were to take place within marriage; the ground was not yet prepared for the later demand for motherhood out of wedlock, as was encouraged in part within the LEBENSBORN program.

Facing page:
1–5 (cont.)
women's auxiliary." (4) "German herring—good and fresh. Mother brings herring to the table." (5) "Young woman, your vocation—become a nurse! The finest service for the health of your Volk!"
6
Hitler in a circle of young admirers.

The NS state used numerous measures to increase the birthrate. The closing of birth-control centers made it difficult to obtain information about contraception. The authorities zealously pursued transgressions against Paragraph 218 (see ABORTION). "Refusal to reproduce" (Fortpflanzungsverweigerung) became a ground for divorce, along with infertility. On the other hand, married couples with children received tax deductions, and large families could count on aid. But because the goal was not simply to raise the overall birthrate, but rather to encourage the birth of Aryan and genetically healthy children, legislation even in the first years of the regime began to select for "CULLING OUT" certain offspring. Persons with hereditary illnesses could be subjected to FORCED STERILIZATION. Marriages between Jews and persons of "German blood" were forbidden after 1935, and the Marital Health Law (1935) was intended to prevent any marriage that was undesirable from the standpoint of health.

In the education of these genetically healthy children, the mother was given considerable—propagandistic—significance, because she had responsibility for the biological and spiritual existence of the Volk, as well as the duty to rear these children for the Volk Community. To be sure, a mother's rights remained sharply circumscribed. Within the marriage, she did share in the right to custody, but the father alone had parental authority. Despite the attempt to tie women as educators of children closer to the system by ideologically upgrading their role, leading representatives of the regime viewed education within the family with undisguised mistrust because such endeavors were so far removed from public controls. In order to mold true Germans, the movement would have to take into its own hands the education of the first generation of National Socialists.

In keeping with the ideology, from their earliest years young girls were to be reared to fulfill correctly and dutifully their later roles as housewives and mothers. This goal permeated the public and informal education of girls. School organization, curriculum, and course content were to be arranged accordingly; coeducation was banned from the outset. In general, girls were allowed an adequate elementary school (Volksschule) education, which would enable them to satisfy the demands of motherhood or specialized women's occupations. But the higher education and academic training that had been won with so much effort since the 19th century were rejected as unsuited to women's nature. Only a few graduates of secondary schools, having passed the *Abitur* examination, were allowed university study before the war; and they were excluded from some occupations. Outside of the school, the NS girls' organization (*see* LEAGUE OF GERMAN GIRLS) provided a training for girls in keeping with the ideology. At an age when children are still easily influenced, the party attempted to remove them from the parental household and mold them. In the process, the authorities did not hesitate to exploit generational conflict in their own favor. Parents had few possibilities of keeping their children out of the Hitler Youth, since in the view of the National Socialists, only the *Volk* Community had the right to educate children. In order not to harm her children, even a woman with little interest in politics had to come to some kind of understanding with National Socialism and acknowledge its influence.

In 1933, it appeared at first that the NS ideology concerning women would exercise a permanent influence on economic policies. The party's wish to return woman to her proper place confronted two circumstances: women's work outside the home had become largely a reality during the First World War, but the debate over such activity had by no means ended. Influential voices were still loud against women's economic and political emancipation, and even some of those affected saw employment as only a burden. Moreover, the economic crisis meant that the government could count on widespread public support when it attempted to replace women workers with men. It soon became clear, however, that for economic reasons cheap female labor would not be eliminated, and attempts to do so did not extend beyond the point, around 1936, when the reserve labor pool was rapidly being exhausted. The conquest of

Reich Organization Leader Robert Ley visits women working in war production.

"living space" now proved to be more valuable to the NS leadership than their ideology of woman's place.

In the interest of the *Volk* Community, women therefore were to shoulder a temporary expansion of their field of activity. But despite the propaganda efforts to acknowledge the unique value of the employed woman, even in this phase the mother was at the apex on the scale of social prestige. The efforts to mobilize a reserve army of women workers aroused a meager response: low wages and poor chances for advancement would not entice a financially secure woman into the workplace. Because volunteers were lacking, in 1939 the government found itself forced to promulgate a compulsory service ordinance for women with an EMPLOYMENT BOOK. Thus, the total burden of the war-related intensification of labor affected solely those women who, for financial reasons, had been obliged to seek work even before the war. A further handicap was the increasing amount of time required for housekeeping caused by shortages of consumer goods and foodstuffs. Inadequate nourishment, lines in front of and inside shops, poor transportation connections to the workplace, and long hours once there—all were the lot of the employed woman. Meanwhile, labor reserves still remained within the female population. In 1943 there was an attempt to mobilize the last reserves by requiring women aged 17 to 45 to report for work. It did not, however, achieve success, since the government, despite the tight labor market, abstained from rigorously applying the provisions.

Although NS ideology and practice aimed at excluding women from economic and political life, this should not be understood as an encouragement to them to retreat entirely into a private sphere. Instead, women too were exhorted to make the interests of the entire community the measure of their actions, and to subordinate themselves to these interests. Under the leadership of the party's organization for women, the NS WOMEN'S UNION, the GERMAN WOMEN'S AGENCY (DFW) attempted to win over to this ideal the as yet unorganized housewives and mothers. As a point of departure, they used

themes and issues specific to women. The practical courses offered by the DFW, as well as its cultural and sports events, excited avid interest, but any lasting organizational involvement of the intended audience proved to be difficult. The indifference toward political issues, but even more the remaining church ties of many women, presented the female propagandists with a huge task.

Even though one must agree with the usual assertion that "women were without rights or influence in the Third Reich," it does not follow that women were unimportant: objectively observed, they too contributed to the upholding of a system of injustice. For the National Socialists, one characteristic in particular gave women an enormous importance: their insignificance in the public consciousness. The National Socialists found an arena here that made it possible for them to implement their harshly regressive social and political notions without having to fear public opinion; indeed, they could count on the agreement of broad sectors of the population. "Women's policies" (*Frauenpolitik*) thus became a proving ground for strategies of persuasion; attempts were made to determine how far the state could intervene in private life and the right to a private self without repercussions.

The results of such policies are ambiguous: on the one hand, women as a group proved difficult to encompass. A segment of the female population was able to avoid being used by the regime and thus retained a certain free space; the idea of the *Volk* Community evidently had not fallen on fertile ground. On the other hand, it appeared that the patriarchal ideal of womanhood gained ground again during the Third Reich. In contrast to their mothers and grandmothers, women clearly did not gain any new self-confidence through their efforts during the Second World War and the postwar period. It was their daughters who succeeded in again calling forth a women's movement in order to struggle for a different image of women.

Dorothee Klinksiek

Women's camps (*Frauenlager*), term for concentration camps with exclusively female prisoners, such as LICHTENBURG or RAVENSBRÜCK.

Women's Labor Service (Frauenarbeitsdienst), a "Labor Service for Female Youth" first intro-

duced on April 1, 1936, initially on a voluntary basis, as part of the REICH LABOR SERVICE. By 1939 it encompassed some 30,000 "workmaidens" (*Arbeitsmaiden; see* WORKMAID). Organized in camps of some 40 women, the workers were employed especially in agriculture.

Women's Union, National Socialist (National-sozialistische Frauenschaft; NSF), organization founded by the NSDAP on October 1, 1931; after March 29, 1935, it was a division of the party. The NSF was at first a union of all female party members, but beginning in 1933 entry into it was no longer linked to party membership. Also in 1933, the NSF became an organization of women Führers, claiming to lead and direct all other women's groups ("responsible for the ideological, cultural, and economic leadership"). In practice, its work was limited largely to training housewives and countrywomen, since employed women were organized in the GERMAN LABOR FRONT. Working closely with the GERMAN WOMEN'S AGENCY, the NSF implemented a program that limited itself completely to preserving the "species" (*Art*), home economics, and welfare. Under the leadership of Gertrud SCHOLTZ-KLINK (1934–1945), the NSF was totally without political importance.

D. K.

Wonder Weapons (*Wunderwaffen*; popularly and mockingly shortened to Wuwa), general propaganda term for newly developed German weapons or battlefield techniques that were intended to turn the fortunes of war in Germany's favor between 1943 and 1945. Joseph Goebbels disseminated the slogan as a response to the widespread fear of Allied material superiority: what the enemy could offer in terms of quantity, German ingenuity could offset with quality. Those Wonder Weapons that played a role in this propaganda strategy of consolation (or empty promises) chiefly included the V1 flying bomb, first deployed in June 1944, and the V2 long-range rocket (V stood for "vengeance"

[*Vergeltung*]), which was launched against England for the first time in early September 1944, and against whose supersonic speed there was no defense.

Also extolled as Wonder Weapons were the Messerschmitt Me 262 jet fighter; the Heinkel He 162 (the "*Volk*'s fighter"), which also had a jet engine; naval weaponry such as one-man torpedoes (*Sprengboote*) and midget submarines; long-range artillery such as the "Fleissiges Lieschen" ("Eager Lizzie"), with a range of 150 km (about 60 miles); airborne rockets such as the R4M (R stood for "rocket" [*Rakete*], 4 referred to 4 kg [8.8 lbs], and M stood for "mine-head" [*Minenkopf*]); and collision bombers such as those of the "Special Commando Elbe," modeled after the kamikaze. Even the bazooka was praised as a "*Volk*'s weapon." All these Wonder Weapons could not significantly delay the Allied victory, and still less affect the fortunes of war.

Work (*Arbeit* [in some contexts better translated as "labor" or "employment"]), central concept of the National Socialist worldview, which posited a Right to Work as a "manifestation of inborn vital energies," but also posited a "socialist duty" (*sozialistische Pflicht*) to work; work became meaningful only as a "service to the entirety of the *Volk*." All the attempts to transfigure work into a quasi cult could not conceal the fact that in NS practice it was almost exclusively a matter of duty. The high cultural level of work tended to be emphasized when increased performance was desired without equivalent increase in compensation. Here, what would have been blamed on "the Jews" as exploitation was called "fulfillment of duty to maintain the *Volk*

Wonder Weapons. The V1 in action.

Work creation. State-subsidized private housing development.

Community"; a restrictive wage policy became "liberation from the devaluation of labor to a product," as propagandized in Marxist ideology. The propagandists of National Socialism made great efforts, moreover, to overcome the opposition between physical and mental work as different but equally valuable kinds of service to the whole.

Work, Duty to (*Arbeitspflicht*), obligation to engage in mentally and physically productive activity; it was Point 10 in the Program of the NSDAP. The Duty to Work was called "the first duty of every citizen," and by means of National Socialist education it was to become a "self-evident duty of honor." It was the logical consequence of the Right to Work (Point 7 in the party program).

Work Bill (*Arbeitswechsel*), Reich treasury bill issued from 1933 to 1936 to finance WORK CREATION measures during the so-called Battle for Work.

Work creation (*Arbeitsbeschaffung*), measures for decreasing UNEMPLOYMENT. Work creation was one of the primary tasks of the National Socialists after the Seizure of Power, since they had made the promise that they would provide work and bread for everyone. The Hitler government was able to appropriate the program of its predecessors in this area. Two approaches had previously been tried: (1) indirect measures, such as tax concessions or the granting of loans to encourage private investment; and (2) direct

measures, notably government-sponsored projects, particularly those that primarily employed persons out of work. The PAPEN government had carried out such a government program to the amount of 302 million RM, but it had relied primarily on indirect means such as tax credits. The SCHLEICHER cabinet had proposed an emergency program (*see* Günther GEREKE), which made available 500 million RM for public works.

Thus the path to work creation was already laid out for the National Socialists. The Hitler government initially limited its efforts to continuing the emergency program, which it increased by 100 million RM and put in the service of rearmament. A separate National Socialist work creation program was not announced until June 1, 1933, with the first Law to Decrease Unemployment. According to its first section, which covered direct measures, 1 billion RM was to be made available for repairing and restoring private and public buildings, and for building small settlements, mining projects, and the like. Also proposed were in-kind payments to the needy, MARRIAGE LOANS, a fund to promote national work, and tax concessions. On September 21, 1933, a second Law to Decrease Unemployment was passed. It provided for 500 million RM and, through subsidies and tax subventions, promoted repair and restoration projects for buildings. It also provided tax cuts for agriculture and for new construction.

The National Socialists also relied on established means for financing their programs: they made use of prior financing based on bills of exchange by dealing with the credit institutions (especially the GERMAN SOCIETY FOR PUBLIC WORKS) that took part in the programs. The bills could be discounted by the Reich Bank and could be renewed. The Reich guaranteed the bills' redemption at the end of fixed terms. They were covered by so-called labor treasury bills (*Arbeitsschatzanweisungen*).

Both types of NS work creation programs were expanded with further measures. The national railroad (*see* DEUTSCHE REICHSBAHN) and postal service (Reichspost) supported government policy with their own projects, and the Law to Establish the Reich Autobahn Undertaking of June 27, 1933, served the same end. Tax measures to stimulate the market were another device. In a parallel effort, the "steering" maneuvers of LABOR DEPLOYMENT were intended to decrease the labor supply. Emergency projects of the states and municipalities created further jobs, some with the encouragement of the Reich Employment Agency. The total budget for work creation efforts may have amounted to some 5.5 billion to 6 billion RM.

The effect of these programs on the labor market is difficult to estimate with precision because other factors contributed significantly to the decline in unemployment—for example, the increase in armaments production and the economic trend toward a world market. The contribution of work creation measures was certainly important in integrating a segment of the working class into the system, aided by the clever propagandistic exploitation of the program's successes.

B. W.

Worker (*Arbeiter*), in National Socialist usage, a leveling term for all "creative" or "productive" people, whether their work was mental ("worker of the forehead") or physical ("worker of the fist"), as contrasted to the parasitic existence of "grasping" people. The differences in labor law between the wage worker and the salaried employee were in actuality reduced only through the general curtailment of employees' rights in the LABOR REGULATION LAW.

Workerdom (*Arbeitertum*), Germanization of the word *Proletariat* that at the same time de-ideologized it as a term related to the class struggle. The word was coined by Eugen DÜHRING in 1881 and entered the National Socialist vocabulary through the title of a book by August WINNIG, *Vom Proletariat zum Arbeitertum*

National Socialist slogan of the week: "Honor labor and respect the worker."

(From the Proletariat to Workerdom; 1930). Beginning in 1931, the journal of the NATIONAL SOCIALIST WORKPLACE CELL ORGANIZATION was called *Das Arbeitertum.*

Worker opposition (*Arbeiterwiderstand*), general term for the opponents of National Socialism who came from the Communist and Social Democratic parties and the trade unions; it also referred to unorganized anti-Nazi workers such as Johann Georg ELSER. Owing to overemphasis on the TWENTIETH OF JULY, 1944, and the OPPOSITION activity that led up to it, the opposition by workers was insufficiently recognized in the Federal Republic in the period after the war. This began to change in the late 1960s.

Workers in the law (*Arbeiter am Recht*), National Socialist generic term for all persons employed in jurisprudence, including the academically educated LAW GUARDIANS (that is, jurists). The term reflected the endeavor to place intellectual and physical activity on the same level.

Workers' movement (*Arbeiterbewegung*), the alliance of dependent wage workers that had been in existence since the 19th century; its goal was to change the existing economic, social, and political conditions. National Socialism asserted that the path chosen—that of class struggle—was the "historical tragedy" of the workers' movement, which had allowed "rootless Jewish intellectuals" such as Marx and Ferdinand Las-salle to alienate them from the *Volk* and lead them into the homelessness of internationalism. The "national socialism" of the VOLK COMMUNITY in the Third Reich had then finally succeeded in overcoming exploitation and thus the class struggle.

Workers of forehead and fist (*Arbeiter der Stirn und der Faust*), expression made popular through Hitler's speeches (it was first used on August 12, 1922). Behind it was the attempt to value intellectual and physical activity equally and to overcome the traditional opposition between them. The slogan was often mocked with the observation that it was difficult to work with one's fist.

Work extension (*Arbeitsstreckung*), WORK CREATION measure achieved through reducing the hours of work (without adjusting wages). Another work extension measure was the granting of leave to employees from time to time.

Work Fund (*Arbeitsspende*), misleading designation for a levy, introduced in a law of June 1, 1933, to finance public works. The "voluntary" nature of the contribution implied in the name existed only on paper, since significant pressure was exerted in the workplace to participate, as was clear from the first year's income of 140 million RM.

Workmaid (*Arbeitsmaid*), official designation for members of the female REICH LABOR SERVICE. National Socialism was indebted to German social theorist Ida von Kortzfleisch (1850–1915) for both the term "maid" and the idea of a female labor service. Kortzfleisch founded the first "countrywomen's school" (*Landfrauenschule*) in 1897. Her choice of word suited the National Socialists' preference for Old German, even as her rendering of *Maid* as an acronym of "Mut, Aufopferung, Idealismus und Demut" ("courage, self-sacrifice, idealism, and modesty") suited their ideal concept of woman (*see* WOMEN IN THE THIRD REICH).

Workman (*Arbeitsmann*), official designation for a member of the male REICH LABOR SERVICE. According to Konstantin HIERL (speech of March 28, 1935), the workman was, moreover, to represent a new National Socialist type of man, like the English gentleman but with militant ideals, as a "fusion of soldier, farmer, and worker." The word's plural was *Arbeitsmänner* (workmen), not *Arbeitsleute* (working folk) or *Arbeitsmenschen* (working people).

Workplace block (*Betriebsblock*), subdivision of the work force of an enterprise into groups of 20 to 25 persons, under the leadership of a WORKPLACE FOREMAN of the German Labor Front. A workplace cell was made up of two to six such blocks.

Workplace cell (*Betriebszelle*), designation, borrowed from Communist usage, for a unit of the National Socialist political organization in industrial enterprises; it was supervised by a workplace foreman (*see* NATIONAL SOCIALIST WORKPLACE CELL ORGANIZATION).

Workplace community (*Betriebsgemeinschaft*), the "cell of working life" (*Zelle des Arbeitslebens*), in the National Socialist charter for labor brought into being by the LABOR REGULATION LAW of January 20, 1934. It was based in a feudal manner on the duty of the WORKPLACE FÜHRER to "provide for the welfare of the FOLLOWERSHIP," and the reciprocal "obligation of the followership to loyalty." The workplace community was organized in accordance with the FÜHRER PRINCIPLE, in that the work force's rights to participate were limited to advisory functions in the MUTUAL TRUST COUNCIL, whereas government TRUSTEES OF LABOR had superior authority. In agreement with a trustee, the manager of a company provided basic workplace regulations for the community, which in larger firms was subdivided into so-

Workmaids on the way to their day's work.

called workplace blocks and workplace cells, each under the leadership of a functionary from the GERMAN LABOR FRONT. Thus, the workplace community reflected on a small scale the ideal of the VOLK COMMUNITY that the National Socialists hoped to achieve as a result of "overcoming class struggle."

Workplace council (*Betriebsrat*), according to the Workplace Council Law of February 4, 1920, the elected representatives of employees, even those not organized in trade unions, in industrial enterprises, as well as the body composed of these employee representatives. The LABOR REGULATION LAW of January 20, 1934, abolished the workplace council as an elected organ representing the employees and replaced it with an appointed MUTUAL TRUST COUNCIL.

Workplace exchange (*Arbeitsplatzaustausch*), one of the WORK CREATION measures in the Law to Decrease Unemployment.

Workplace foreman (*Betriebsobmann*), "GUARDIAN" appointed in a company with four or more employees; he was selected by the German Labor Front from the ranks of the work force. His duties included the ideological "alignment" (in the National Socialist sense) of the other employees, as well as political and social control. The foreman had to be consulted in appointments to the MUTUAL TRUST COUNCIL, to which he himself belonged.

Workplace Führer (*Betriebsführer*), term for the responsible manager of a firm, especially the employer himself; it was introduced by the LABOR REGULATION LAW of January 20, 1934. In keeping with the FÜHRER PRINCIPLE, he alone was responsible for making decisions and competent to make them. He also was at the head of the MUTUAL TRUST COUNCIL, the employees' representative body, and was himself only under the government supervision of the TRUSTEES OF LABOR. According to the ordinance of November 12, 1938, Jews could no longer hold the position of Workplace Führer as of January 1, 1939, even when they were the owner (*see* ARYANIZATION).

Workplace roll call (*Betriebsappell*), lineup of all employees before beginning work, a measure initiated by the GERMAN LABOR FRONT in order to strengthen the WORKPLACE COMMUNITY. At the roll call, the WORKPLACE FÜHRER was to "align" (*see* AUSRICHTUNG) the work force toward the goal of common work.

Work-shy (*Arbeitsscheue*), according to a decree of January 26, 1938, all unemployed men who were capable of work but who had twice rejected offers of employment or had twice left jobs shortly after beginning them. It was not a matter of concern if the work offered was unsuitable or did not match the person's qualifications. The Gestapo was instructed to send the work-shy to the Buchenwald concentration camp. The Labor Offices and the EMPLOYMENT BOOK were of assistance in detecting such individuals. There was no legal recourse against arrest. The campaign against the work-shy served to utilize the labor market reserves for the fulfillment of the FOUR-YEAR PLAN.

Work squads (*Werkscharen*), uniformed groups of the GERMAN LABOR FRONT in the workplace. They were intended to be "ideological shock troops" (*weltanschauliche Stosstrupps*) of the NSDAP in industry. The work squads were to bring National Socialist ideas to the "members of the followership" in an enterprise, and to contribute to the desired organization of the WORKPLACE ROLL CALL and of joint leisure time. Membership in the work squads was voluntary, but it was encouraged by benefits to one's career.

World economic crisis (*Weltwirtschaftskrise*), the greatest crisis up until then of the international capitalist system (1929–1933). Structural and cyclical defects with cumulative effects in the various sectors of the economy (production, the credit system, and international trade) coincided in the emergence and spread of the crisis. Both agrarian and industrial countries were affected by it, although its extent varied from country to country. Outside of the United States, Germany in particular suffered greatly during the crisis (6 million were unemployed in 1932). Given Germany's political instability and the general lowering of its standard of living because of the lost war and inflation—important differences compared with the United States!—the economic crisis soon expanded into a general crisis. On the political level, this led to the PRESIDIAL CABINETS and finally to Hitler's Seizure of Power.

The world economic crisis was set off by an American financial and speculative crisis (*see* BLACK FRIDAY). The following months witnessed massive withdrawals of credit from Germany, partly in response to the large number of votes gained by the National Socialists in the 1930 Reichstag elections. By July 1931, German banks had begun to fail. International

World economic crisis. Demonstration by impoverished winegrowers in front of the town hall in Cochem an der Mosel.

trade suffered a simultaneous major crisis (the index of world market values at the current rate of exchange was 100 in 1926 and 39.2 in 1932). Agricultural overproduction led to a collapse of prices for farm products in world markets. Many agrarian countries ran into economic difficulties and reduced purchases of products from industrial countries. The German economy, however, was dependent on exports to a particularly high degree (the export rate in 1928 was 21 percent).

The rationalization investments undertaken by German industry between 1926 and 1928 had been predicated on increased exports and economic growth. Yet production capacities grew faster than the income-dependent flow of demand. Despite the attempts of the Brüning government to lower production costs (the wage component, above all) through EMERGENCY DECREES, German exports rapidly declined: in 1932 they were at half the 1928 value. German industrial production sank—as expressed in index values—from 100 (1928) to 61.2 (1932). Moreover, the Brüning government failed in its attempt to shelter the distressed German agricultural economy from the consequences of worldwide agricultural overproduction by means of a high protective tariff system and subsidies (see EASTERN AID). Thus, force was lent to those elements in economics and politics that sought a relative decoupling of the German economy from the world economy (see AUTAR-

KY) or else a shift of German foreign trade, mainly to southeastern Europe.

After the failure of Heinrich Brüning's deflationary policy (his government fell in May 1932), the governments of Franz von Papen and Kurt von Schleicher adopted the then highly controversial path of an active trade cycle policy (deficit spending), although with diverse concentrations of focus. But it was only through the massive rearmament policy for which Hitler gave the green light when he entered the government (aside from the initial strengthening of the ongoing WORK CREATION program) that the crisis and its consequences were "overcome," using different means at different times.

A. v. S.

World ice theory (*Welteislehre*), cosmological theory advanced by the Austrian engineer Hanns Hörbiger; it was favored by Himmler and later also by Hitler. The theory explained the geological configuration of the earth as the consequence of collisions with ice-covered planets, among which Hörbiger included the moon; he understood hail as a form of cosmic ice. At the basis of the theory was the hypothesis that cosmic ice counteracted the heat of the giant suns; the driving force of all cosmic events was the conflict between ice and heat. Although, or precisely because, the world ice theory was rejected by established science, Himmler made it a branch of research in the ANCESTRAL INHERI-

TANCE society, where "conflict theory" was prominent. The world ice theory was propagated there as a "Nordic view of the world" in which a "Nordic-heroic basic attitude" was realized. As a bonus, it was hoped that the theory would yield practical advantages in weather forecasting.

Ba.

World Jewish Congress (WJC), umbrella organization of Jewish groups, founded in August 1936 in Geneva. It arose from the American Jewish Congress, founded in 1918, and the Comité des Délégations Juives (Paris), formed in 1919. It was intended to represent Jewish interests vis-à-vis international public opinion. The WJC, which had offices in many Western capitals, spread news about the PERSECUTION OF JEWS in the German Reich, and was one of the first voices to warn the world by providing details about National Socialist genocide (*see* FINAL SOLUTION). However, it attained little more than support for individual aid and rescue actions. After the war the WJC dedicated itself to the prosecution of war criminals and to RESTITUTION.

World Jewry (*Weltjudentum*), antisemitic term for the alleged alliance of all Jews, to which was attributed a joint policy and, finally, the collective plan of attaining world rule. As evidence for the existence of such an alliance, alleged discoveries were cited, such as the PROTOCOLS OF THE ELDERS OF ZION, which dealt with plans for a Jewish "world conspiracy." The notion of uniform conduct by international Jewry reappeared in other forms, such as the alleged existence of "interest-rate servitude," into which "pan-Jewish HIGH FINANCE" had cast the peoples of the world (*see* Gottfried FEDER on the NSDAP program). The term "World Jewry" represents an exaggerated and purposefully incited fear of a Jewish menace that was typical especially of the ANTISEMITISM of the NSDAP. Harsher measures against the Jews, leading up to their extermination, were thus legitimized.

H. O.

World-political triangle (*Weltpolitisches Dreieck*), term used after 1940 in German propaganda and journalism for the relations between Germany, Japan, and Italy as a result of the ANTI-COMINTERN PACT (*see* THREE-POWER AGREEMENT; AXIS).

World Relief Committee for the Victims of German Fascism (Welthilfskomitee für die Op-

fer des deutschen Fascismus), organization founded in 1933 by the Communist publisher Willi MÜNZENBERG. Its members also included numerous middle-class German emigrés and Western politicians, in particular many Britons. With the aid of a so-called BROWN BOOK as well as a "counter trial" against the REICHSTAG FIRE TRIAL, they sought in vain to prove the National Socialists guilty of setting the REICHSTAG FIRE.

Worldview, Hitler's. *See* Hitler's Worldview.

World War (*Weltkrieg*), until 1945 the conventional term for the First World War (1914–1918), and since then also for the war of 1939 to 1945, the SECOND WORLD WAR. The numbering has an inner logic, since the Second World War in many ways was a continuation of the First World War, which failed to resolve the conflicts that had caused it to break out. Above all, the vengeful peace of the VERSAILLES TREATY of 1919 and the one-sided assessment of war guilt (*see* WAR GUILT LIE) created new potential for aggression. The WEIMAR REPUBLIC fell victim to it, and in Hitler's hands it became a welcome instrument for his war policy.

Writing (*Schrifttum*), Germanization of the foreign-derived word *Literatur*. In National Socialist usage, "writing" consisted of all written productions in the form of books, booklets, and periodicals, from technical works to imaginative literature. The task of a National Socialist cultural policy was to redirect writing, which was to reflect the national character, "into the indispensable, profound interrelationship of blood (race) and fate." Responsible for this assignment was the Propaganda Ministry with its REICH WRITING CHAMBER.

Writing, cultivation of (*Schrifttumspflege*), official term during the Third Reich for surveillance over the entire body of literature and the encouragement of the desired kinds. As early as 1932 there was an office with this mission, the Stelle zur Schrifttumspflege, within the COMBAT LEAGUE FOR GERMAN CULTURE; from it arose the related bureau (Amt Schrifttumspflege) in Alfred ROSENBERG's party office. It was headed by Hans Hagemeyer (who also directed the Reich Office for the Promotion of German Writing), a deputy to the literary scholar Hellmuth Langenbucher.

Hagemeyer's Office for the Cultivation of Writing housed a central review board. In 1940 it consisted of some 1,400 readers, who examined and evaluated every item in the German book and periodical market "according to the perspectives of politics, worldview, public instruction, technical accuracy, and aesthetics." It published its own review journal, *Bücherkunde* (Book Lore), and organized book exhibitions to promote "worthwhile German writing" on specific themes, such as "The Struggle for Europe's Fate in the East" in 1942.

Wurm, Theophil, b. Basel, December 7, 1868; d. Stuttgart, January 28, 1953, German Evangelical theologian. Wurm became a pastor in 1899. In 1920 he was made a deacon in Reutlingen, in 1929 a church president, and in 1933 the state bishop (*Landesbischof*) of Württemberg. Through his vacillating stance on the issues of nominating a REICH BISHOP and church elections, Wurm initially encouraged the rise of the GERMAN CHRISTIANS. As early as the autumn of 1933 he became one of the spokesmen of the church opposition against the National Socialist plans for synchronizing the church.

Wurm joined with the CONFESSING CHURCH, and was put under house arrest in 1934 because of his resistance to the church government of Ludwig MÜLLER, but he was released after tumultuous protests. Although one of the more moderate church leaders, he protested more loudly than most against the EUTHANASIA program, and he was one of the very few to sharply attack the NS PERSECUTION OF JEWS. Wurm was only partially successful during the war in his

Theophil Wurm.

efforts to overcome the division of the Confessing Church, but he laid the ground for a reconstruction after 1945. In August 1945 he became the representative of the Council of the Evangelical Church in Germany and was crucially involved in drawing up the STUTTGART CONFESSION OF GUILT.

WVHA. *See* Economic-Administrative Main Office.

Yalta, Soviet city on the southern shore of the Crimean peninsula. From February 4 to 11, 1945, the heads of state of Great Britain (Winston CHURCHILL), the USSR (Joseph STALIN), and the United States (Franklin D. ROOSEVELT) met in Yalta, assisted by their foreign ministers, Anthony EDEN, Viacheslav MOLOTOV, and Edward R. STETTINIUS. After some discordant discussions, especially between Churchill and Stalin, the Yalta Conference decided on the following points:

1. Improved coordination of military planning among the Allies in the final struggle against Germany;

2. Germany's partition after the war into American, British, Soviet, and French occupation zones, as well as coordination of occupation policy by an ALLIED CONTROL COUNCIL; the French zone, considered at Yalta for the first time, was to be formed from parts of the British and American zones;

3. Complete DEMILITARIZATION and DENAZIFICATION of Germany by the abolition of all German military forces, elimination of all other military installations, destruction of the armaments industry, dissolution of the NSDAP and its organizations and institutions, and the trial of all German war criminals (*see* WAR CRIMES);

4. Imposition of reparations upon a defeated Germany; the exact details were left to a reparations conference to be held in Moscow;

5. Fixing of Poland's eastern frontier approximately along the CURZON LINE; the western frontier was to be determined only at a peace conference, since Stalin's demand for the ODER-NEISSE LINE met with resistance, primarily from Churchill; in any case, Poland would be com-

Yalta Conference. From the left: Stalin, Roosevelt, and Churchill.

pensated with "considerable" territory in the north and west at Germany's expense;

6. Recognition of the (Communist) Lublin Committee, which was to be enlarged by members of the Polish government-in-exile in London, as the provisional Polish government;

7. The calling of a conference in San Francisco to establish the UNITED NATIONS;

8. Entry of the USSR into the war against Japan after Germany's capitulation.

The conference's results were recorded in a final communiqué, the Yalta Declaration. The decrees concerning Germany became legally binding through the JUNE DECLARATION (June 6, 1945) and the POTSDAM AGREEMENT (August 2, 1945). Stalin was the real victor at Yalta. In exchange for the Soviet promise to enter the war against Japan, which was Roosevelt's main concern, the United States and Great Britain made concessions in matters concerning the United Nations, and accepted the spread of Soviet spheres of power and influence in eastern Asia and eastern Europe, especially in Poland.

R. E.

Yiddish, the language, written in Hebraic letters, of unassimilated Jews, especially from eastern Europe, who were driven from Germany by pogroms during the period of the Crusades and by the plague, taking with them a Middle High German interspersed with Hebrew. Yiddish was later heavily enriched by Slavic elements, without the displacement of its German base. Strong pressures to assimilate in the 19th and 20th centuries in many instances made Yiddish decline to the status of a secondary language, while a conscious revival led to a rich Yiddish literature.

National Socialist antisemites saw Yiddish as a "violation" (*Vergewaltigung*) of the German language, and established "revealing" connections between Yiddish and "German thieves' cant, or '*Rotwelsch*.'" The 1939 conquest of Poland, the occupation by German troops of western Russia from 1941 to 1944, and the resultant persecution and destruction of eastern European Jewry destroyed the base for Yiddish. Those who managed to survive or escape were from then on uprooted, and were further decimated by the Stalinist campaign against intellectuals in 1948. Yiddish is still spoken by Jews throughout the world, but its vitality seems to have been destroyed with the loss of its cultural background.

Yorck von Wartenburg, Peter Count, b. Klein-Oels (Silesia), November 13, 1904; d. Berlin-

Peter Yorck von Wartenburg before the *Volk* Court.

Plötzensee, August 8, 1944 (executed), German opposition fighter. Yorck von Wartenburg studied law and government, then became a civil servant in the office of the chief administrator (*Oberpräsident*) in Breslau. After 1938 he served in the office of the Reich commissioner for price controls, Josef WAGNER. On grounds of Christian conscience, Yorck von Wartenburg rejected the National Socialist claim to absolute sovereignty and repudiated its racism and expansionism. He was a co-founder of the KREISAU CIRCLE. During the war, in which he participated first as a frontline officer and then in the Military Economy Office of the Wehrmacht High Command, he overcame his religious scruples against tyrannicide. Beginning in 1943–1944, he was often in contact with his cousin Schenk von STAUFFENBERG, with whom he helped prepare the attempted coup of July 20, 1944. After its failure, he was imprisoned and sentenced to death.

Young German Order (Jungdeutscher Orden; Jungdo), national militant league, founded in 1920 by Arthur MAHRAUN under the influence of the romantic social ideas associated with the YOUTH MOVEMENT and the FRONT EXPERIENCE. Its membership, which at times amounted to 200,000, came predominantly from the middle classes. The Young German Order was organized on the model of the medieval Teutonic Order; its chairman was the "grand master," its regional units were Balleien ("commanderies"), and its local groups were "brotherhoods." In domestic policy, Jungdo stood equally for antiparliamentary and anticapitalist goals, advocating the reform of the Weimar Republic along the lines of a national *Volk* community. In foreign policy, it pleaded for reconciliation and a pact with France, notably in its daily, *Der Jungdeutsche* (The Young German). While initially supporting the "Führer State," when the order began to lose influence it tried to come to terms with the parliamentary system. Together with the GERMAN DEMOCRATIC PARTY (DDP), it joined the GERMAN STATE PARTY in 1930 and participated in the Reichstag elections, although without success. Because of its clear-cut distancing from National Socialism, it was prohibited in 1933. After 1945 there was a temporary revival of the Young German Order in West Germany under the name "Young German League" (Jungdeutscher Bund).

Young people, literature for. *See* Children's and young people's literature.

Young Plan, program signed on June 7, 1929, to adjust the REPARATIONS that the German state owed its former enemies according to the stipulations of the VERSAILLES TREATY. The Young Plan, which replaced the DAWES PLAN of 1924, was worked out initially by a conference of experts that convened in Paris on February 9, 1929, under the chairmanship of the American banker Owen D. Young (1874–1962). Germany participated, with Hjalmar SCHACHT as head of its delegation. Two concluding conferences took place at The Hague (August 6–31, 1929, and January 3–20, 1930). The plan, which went into effect retroactively on September 1, 1929, set the total reparations bill for the German Republic at 34.5 billion RM, to be paid in 59 yearly installments (until 1988). The BANK FOR INTERNATIONAL SETTLEMENT was created to handle the payments.

The Young Plan was tied to the lifting of Allied controls over the German economy and the early suspension of the Rhineland occupation (until 1930). After Germany was forced to suspend reparations payments on July 1, 1931, owing to the WORLD ECONOMIC CRISIS, the Young Plan was formally canceled by the Lausanne Agreement of June 9, 1932. More important than its economic significance was the role played by the Young Plan in domestic politics: the referendum initiated by the "national opposition" (NSDAP, German National People's Party, and Steel Helmet) against the plan (gaining narrow success with 4.1 million signatures) made Hitler and the

NSDAP known to a wide public in Germany, even though the subsequent referendum on December 22, 1930, failed (with 5.8 million votes).

R. B.

Young Reformers (*Jungreformatoren*), self-designation of a group of Evangelical theologians and pastors who on May 9, 1933, intervened in the discussion concerning an Evangelical Reich Church and the election of a REICH BISHOP with an "Appeal for Rebuilding the Church." Led by a group of Berlin clergy such as Künneth, from the Center for Apologetics; Riethmüller, from the Burckhardt House; and the general secretary of the German Christian Student Union, Hanns LILJE, the Young Reformers, like the GERMAN CHRISTIANS, called for a "glad 'yes' to the new state." Yet in a clear counterposition, they emphasized that ecclesiastical decisions could proceed "only from the structure of the church," that is, from the denomination itself (Article 1). They wanted a Reich bishop to be chosen immediately, without "preliminary elections" (Article 2); the introduction of the ARYAN PARAGRAPH into the church sphere was unthinkable (Article 7). The Young Reformers thus energetically promoted the election of Friedrich von BODELSCHWINGH as Reich bishop. In the church elections of July 23, 1933, they stood on the "Gospel and Church" candidate list as the only important competition against the German Christians. Martin NIEMÖLLER had in the meantime been pushed into a leadership position. After the Reformers' election defeat, he gathered opponents of the German Christian advocates of Synchronization into the PASTORS' EMERGENCY LEAGUE.

Youth, recommended for (*jugendwert*), rating introduced in the Third Reich for films that were considered educational in terms of National Socialist ideals, and particularly exemplary in their effect on children and young people. Tax advantages went with the rating.

Youth movement (*Jugendbewegung*), movement, burgeoning after 1900, of an elite group of young people from the "new middle class" and also from the working class to organize independently their leisure activities. Only middle-class groups were able successfully to emancipate themselves from the state-supported adult-led organizations for youth ("Jugendpflege") and, especially through hiking and group trips, to create a neo-romantic "youth culture." However, the farewell to political, economic, and denominational dogmas announced at the "Con-

Youth movement. Wandervogel outing (1913).

gress of Free German Youth" in 1913 proved to be illusory in the First World War. The political debate between the old-timers from the "Field WANDERVOGEL" was answered by a younger group with the demand for "leagues" organized by age cohort (see YOUNG GERMAN ORDER). The idea of the "leaguers" (*Bündische*) of creating a basis for uniting the nation through life-styles "suitable for youth" was increasingly taken up by adult organizations charged with helping youth, as observed in *Weimar der arbeitenden Jugend* (The Weimar of Working-Class Youth; 1920).

Toward the late 1920s these life-styles became more modern. Alongside the camp romanticism there arose a willingness to practice "socialism" in work camps. The group lost in significance as against the collective self-presentation of uniformed marching columns, which was connected with the turn to technology and sports. This development was portrayed in the first phase of the National Socialist Seizure of Power as the need of the entire younger generation; it was responded to with overtures from the new state. The "branches" of the NSDAP were portrayed to sympathizers as "leagues" for men and youth. However, "leaguist intrigues" (*bündische Umtriebe*) that resisted Synchronization were condemned. Thus, some adherents of the youth movement rose to high positions in the SS, while others became victims of the system of terror.

H. S.

Youth protest, increasing antagonism in circles of working-class young people and among secondary school students (*Oberschülern*) as National Socialist rule continued, especially during the war (*see, for example,* EDELWEISS PIRATES). The protests were directed against the tiresome drills in the Hitler Youth, the cultural desolation, and the constant control by the party. Organized OPPOSITION finally arose, which was answered by the Gestapo with brutal intervention, including the creation of special concentration camps such as that in Neuwied for young men under the age of 20, as well as numerous executions.

Youth Steward (*Jugendwalter*), organizer and custodian of young workers in an enterprise; through the GERMAN LABOR FRONT, workplace youth stewards (*Betriebs-Jugendwalter*) were introduced especially in larger firms and factories. Their tasks included organizing workplace meetings with management for their charges, as well as inspirational ceremonies on National Socialist holidays and memorial days, and general responsibility in questions of the ideological schooling of the "young FOLLOWERSHIP" (*junge Gefolgschaft*).

Yugoslavia, state in southeastern Europe; area, approximately 250,000 sq km (about 100,000 sq miles); population, 13.9 million (1931). Yugoslavia came into being on December 1, 1918, through proclamation of "the Kingdom of the Serbs, Croats, and Slovenes," a constitutional monarchy with strong centralist leanings (Constitution of June 28, 1921). It was formed from the kingdoms of Serbia and Montenegro, as well as from parts of Austria-Hungary, and assumed the name Yugoslavia on October 3, 1929. Great internal political instability (there were a total of 44 cabinet crises between 1918 and

1929) was due to tensions between proponents of a Greater Serbian centralist state (advocated by Serbians) and supporters of a South Slavic federalist state (advocated by Croatians). It was further exacerbated by minority problems, diverse historical and cultural experiences, the economic difficulties of an agrarian society, and border disputes, all of which had direct influence on internal policies.

Aiming to achieve internal consolidation on a centralized, bureaucratic, and antihistorical foundation, King Alexander I established an authoritarian "Royal Dictatorship" with a *coup d'état* on January 6, 1929. After his murder in Marseilles on October 9, 1934, a regency council with Prince-Regent Paul (acting for the minor King Peter II) followed. In foreign-policy matters Yugoslavia protected itself against revisionist claims of neighbor states by joining the LITTLE ENTENTE and signing a treaty with France (November 11, 1927), the Balkan Pact with Romania, Greece, and Turkey (February 9, 1934), and individual treaties. Mussolini's steps to realize the *mare nostro* concept (the occupation of Albania on April 7, 1939, and the attack on Greece on October 28, 1940), and Yugoslavia's increased economic dependence (the German-Yugoslav trade agreement of May 1, 1934), led to ever-closer political dependence on Berlin in the years 1939 to 1941, despite formal neutrality: on March 25, 1941, Yugoslavia joined the THREE-POWER AGREEMENT. This provoked a military putsch with an anti-German bias on March 27, which in turn contributed to the unleashing of the BALKAN CAMPAIGN and thus to the fall of the Yugoslav state. On April 10, 1941, Ante PAVELIĆ proclaimed an "Independent State of Croatia"; Montenegro became an independent state. The remaining Yugoslav territory was divided among Germany, Italy, Hungary, and Bulgaria.

According to international law, Yugoslavia

Yugoslavia. Ribbentrop greets the Yugoslav prime minister, Dragiša Cvetković, in Germany on February 16, 1941.

continued to exist in the form of a government-in-exile in London, under Peter II. However, it was dropped by Moscow and the Allies at TEHE-RAN in 1943. Its place was taken by TITO's Communist partisan movement. Tito gradually prepared a postwar regime for Yugoslavia: on November 29, 1943, he formed a provisional government, and on March 8, 1945, a coalition government—headed by himself—with representatives of the London exiles and earlier parties. By November 29, 1945, the transformation into the Communist unity state, the Federative People's Republic of Yugoslavia, was completed. For a long time the country suffered from the heavy losses experienced under foreign rule and the bitter civil war between Communist and non-Communist partisans. The collaboration chapter was closed with a bloody settlement of accounts.

B.-J. W.

Z

Zangen, Wilhelm, b. Duisburg, September 30, 1891; d. Düsseldorf, November 25, 1971, German industrialist. Zangen was trained in business, and made his career in various enterprises. From 1925 to 1929 he was a director of the Schiess-Defries Corporation, and from 1929 to 1934, of DEMAG (Deutsche Maschinenfabrik AG; German Machine Factory, Inc.); after 1934 he was chairman of the board and general director of the Mannesmann Tubing Corporation (Mannesmann-Röhrenwerke AG). An early member of the NSDAP and SS (1927), in the Third Reich Zangen held the title of MILITARY ECONOMY FÜHRER. Besides numerous other functions (such as those of deputy head of the Reich Economics Chamber in Berlin and chair of the Export Company for War Equipment), in 1938 he assumed the chair of the influential Reich Group for Industry. In close cooperation with National Socialist policy, Zangen proved to be an especially successful advocate, among the Ruhr industrialists, of economic expansion in such occupied areas as the Sudetenland. He continued to run the Mannesmann concern after the war, until 1957, when he became chair of the board of trustees (*Aufsichtsrat*), a post he retained until 1966. In 1956 Zangen received the Grand Cross with Star for Service to the Federal Republic.

Zehrer, Hans, b. Berlin, June 22, 1899; d. there, August 23, 1966, German journalist. In 1929 Zehrer succeeded the leftist romantic poet Adam KUCKHOFF as editor of *Die Tat* (The Deed). By 1933 he had made it a "center for the right-wing intelligentsia" (*see* TAT CIRCLE). In 1932 Zehrer became editor in chief of the *Tägliche Rundschau* (Daily Review) of Gen. Kurt von Schleicher, whom he supported in efforts to "blow up" the NSDAP. However, Zehrer ended up merely making National Socialism generally acceptable to polite society for the first time. He did this, according to Carl von OSSIETZKY, by

Hans Zehrer.

"out-Hitlering Hitler" and "translating him into modern, educated language."

In 1933 Zehrer welcomed the "New State," but unlike other members of the Tat Circle, he did not join the SS, for which he was classified as an "insubordinate conservative" (*Das Schwarze Korps*) in party circles. He retreated from journalism and became director of the Stalling Publishing Company. In 1943–1944 the young publisher Axel Springer contacted Zehrer and entrusted him with organizing, after the war, the first publication of the daily *Die Welt* (The World). As its chief editor from 1953 to 1966, Zehrer definitively molded the paper's conservative line. In a popularized form, he circulated his message of restoration in Springer's tabloid *Bild-Zeitung* (Picture News) as commentary under the title "Hans im Bild" (1952–1961).

H. H.

Zeitenwende ("change of era"; *Zw.*), term occasionally used in National Socialist historiography to avoid using the term "B.C." for the beginning of the modern reckoning of time. Dates prior to this point were designated *v. Zw.* (*vor*, "before"), and those afterward, *n. Zw.* (*nach*, "after").

Zeitzler, Kurt, b. Cossmar (Brandenburg), June 9, 1895; d. Hohenaschau (Upper Bavaria), September 25, 1963, German colonel general (January 30, 1944). In the First World War, Zeitzler was an officer. He was accepted into the Reichswehr, but made his real career during the Third Reich, in 1937 becoming a lieutenant colonel in the Army High Command (OKH). Zeitzler had significant successes as chief of staff of the Twenty-second Army Corps in the Polish Campaign (September 1939), of the Kleist Panzer Group in the French Campaign (May–June 1940), and of the First Panzer Army, after October 1941 fighting in the Russian Campaign. He became general chief of staff of Army Group D in occupied France (April 1, 1942), and on September 24, 1942, he was named general chief of staff of the army as Gen. Franz HALDER's successor. Hitler hoped for more agreement with his risky warfare tactics from the energetic Zeitzler (nicknamed "lightning ball"), but ran into serious conflicts with him during the Stalingrad crisis. After Zeitzler had rejected four such requests, Hitler finally cashiered him on July 10, 1944 (made final on January 31, 1945). In February 1947 Zeitzler was released from British imprisonment.

Zemun, National Socialist concentration camp in Yugoslavia, to which Serbian Jews (principally from nearby Belgrade) were deported after the Balkan Campaign. Systematic killings were carried out in Zemun by means of GAS VANS disguised as Red Cross vehicles; at least 15,000 people fell victim between December 1941 and June 1942. Later thousands of GYPSIES lost their lives in Zemun, where they were assembled under inhuman conditions.

Zentrale Stelle der Landesjustizverwaltungen zur Aufklärung von NS-Verbrechen. *See* Ludwigsburg Central Office.

Zentrum. *See* Center.

Zerkaulen, Heinrich, b. Bonn, March 2, 1892; d. Hofgeismar, February 13, 1954, German writer. Zerkaulen, who had been wounded as a volunteer in the First World War, was first a journalist. In the 1920s he won a broad public chiefly with descriptions of his Rhenish homeland. His popular historical novels made him one of the most widely read authors of the Third Reich. During

Heinrich Zerkaulen: *Anna and Sigrid: Novel of a Marriage.*

the war years he tried to stir up aggression and self-sacrifice through flat propaganda tales: "We want to reconquer Germany, to which we returned after the war without finding it" (*Der Kaiser Jäger* [The Kaiser Hunter]; 1942). After 1945 Zerkaulen was classified as "exonerated" in an appeals court proceeding, but he had literary success again only with the republication of his Beethoven novel, *Der feuerige Gott* (The Fiery God; 1943).

Zetkin, Clara (née Eissner), b. Wiederau (Saxony), July 5, 1857; d. Arkhangelskoe, near Moscow, June 20, 1933, German politician. Zetkin joined the Social Democratic Party of Germany (SPD) in 1878. After 1891 she edited the party's journal for women, *Die Gleichheit* (Equality). In 1900 Zetkin organized the first SPD women's conference. A member of the party's left wing, in 1918 she moved to the Communist Party of Germany (KPD), which she represented in the Reichstag from 1920 to 1933.

[Zetkin is generally classified as a feminist, although she herself abjured the label "Frauenrechtlerin" (advocate of women's rights) for reasons of class consciousness.] She was an engaged pacifist. For these reasons, and because of her frequent visits to the Soviet Union, she was sharply (at times personally) attacked by the National Socialists. As senior president (oldest

Clara Zetkin.

member) of the Reichstag, she opened the session of August 30, 1932, in which, with its 230 seats, the NSDAP constituted the largest delegation by far. Despite tumultuous disturbances from the Right, she called for the formation of an antifascist unity front. Seriously ill, she left Germany shortly afterward.

Zhukov, Georgi Konstantinovich, b. Strelkova (Kaluga), December 11, 1896; d. Moscow, June 18, 1974, Soviet marshal (1943). Trained as a furrier, in 1915 Zhukov entered the army. In 1928 he took part in a Reichswehr training course for officers of the Red Army. From 1932 to 1936 he was a division commander, in 1940

he became commander in chief of the Kiev military sector, and on February 1, 1941, he was made chief of the General Staff. During the winter of 1941–1942, Zhukov commanded the Red Army's counterattack before Moscow, which achieved broad breakthroughs in the center section of Germany's eastern front. In 1942–1943 he coordinated the Soviet offensives at Stalingrad, Leningrad, and Kursk. He entered the capital of the Reich in 1945 as the "victor of Berlin," accepted the German capitulation in Karlshorst, and until April 1946 was commander in chief of the Soviet troops in Germany. Zhukov was minister of defense after 1955 and a member of the Politburo, but he fell into disfavor in 1957, and was removed from all his posts.

Ziegler, Adolf, b. Bremen, October 16, 1892; d. Varnahlt bei Baden-Baden, September 18, 1959, German painter and art functionary. In 1925 Ziegler met Hitler, who was impressed by his classically influenced works and later appointed him art expert of the NSDAP and, in 1933, a professor in the Munich Academy of Art. Ziegler specialized in allegorical, "penetratingly naturalistic" female nudes (his nickname was "master of the curly pubic hair") and portraits (among others, of Geli RAUBAL). He had more impact as the leading art functionary of the Third Reich than through his art. As president of the REICH CHAMBER OF FINE ARTS from 1936 to 1943, he polemicized against modern art that was critical of both its time and society, calling it the "pacemaker of international Jewry." With Hitler's mandate Ziegler "cleansed"

Georgi Konstantinovich Zhukov.

Adolf Ziegler.

German museums and galleries of DEGENERATE ART in 1937, and brought together examples of it in a propagandistic exhibition in Munich.

Ziesel, Kurt, b. Innsbruck, February 25, 1911, Austrian-German writer. As a journalist, Ziesel early on joined the Austrian National Socialists. A novelist (*Verwandlungen der Herzen* [Transformations of Hearts]; 1938), publicist, and editor (*Krieg und Dichtung* [War and Poetics]; 1940), he devoted himself especially to *völkisch* and nationalist themes. After 1941 he was in a war correspondent unit of the Wehrmacht. In the *Völkischer Beobachter* of September 3, 1944, Ziesel characterized the men of the TWENTIETH OF JULY as "egoists" who had acted out of "depravity or mental derangement."

After 1945 Ziesel published numerous anti-Communist writings, maintained contacts with right-radical and conservative circles, and through such books as *Der rote Rufmord* (The Red Slander; 1962) attempted to rehabilitate Theodor OBERLÄNDER, the minister for expellees' affairs. As business manager of the "Germany Foundation" (Deutschland-Stiftung e.V.) and editor of *Deutschland-Magazin*, Ziesel campaigned particularly against recognition of the German Democratic Republic (GDR) and the ODER-NEISSE LINE. Because of his radical right-wing and antisemitic connections, his official participation in Chancellor Helmut Kohl's trip to Israel in 1984 aroused international protests. According to a judgment of a state court in Munich (Landgericht München I: AZ 46Bs 344/67; XIV Qs 70/68), Ziesel may be called a "notorious National Socialist."

Zillich, Heinrich, b. Kronstadt (Transylvania), May 23, 1898, German-Austrian writer. In novels and stories that appeared beginning in the early 1920s, Zillich described the people and landscapes of his Transylvanian homeland (*Wälder und Laternenschein* [Woods and Lantern Glow], 1923; *Der Toddergerch*, 1930). The National Socialists treasured and honored these works as *völkisch* writing. (Zillich's honors included the Ethnic German Writing Prize of the City of Stuttgart.) Living in Bavaria after 1936, he remained true to his homeland theme even after the war (*Siebenbürgen, ein abendländisches Schicksal* [Transylvania: A Western Fate]; 1957).

Zinn, Karl, b. Frankfurt am Main, July 22, 1906; d. Berlin, August 24, 1943, German opposition fighter, bank employee, and Social Democrat. After Hitler's seizure of power, Zinn was

shocked by the defeatism of the Left, whose leadership he saw as "rotten and useless." In April 1933, he joined the resistance group "Red Shock Troop," which organized workplace cells, supported the persecuted, and through pamphleteering urged "no" votes in the plebiscite of November 1933. This was Zinn's last effort. Arrested directly afterward, he was sentenced to a five-year term in the penitentiary; subsequently, he was under Gestapo surveillance. He died while clearing rubble after a bomb attack.

Zionism, political and social movement that aimed for the establishment of a Jewish state in PALESTINE as a "national homeland" for all Jews scattered around the world. Zionism was a reaction to new forms of ANTISEMITISM in late 19th-century Europe. Developing at the same time as nationalist movements, it was a kind of Jewish nationalism, in which religious ideas (about the Promised Land of Israel) and political goals were linked. As the real founder of Zionism, Theodor HERZL, beginning in 1897, convoked the first Zionist congresses, as a result of which an emigration of Jews into predominantly Arab-occupied Palestine slowly began.

In Germany the National Socialist takeover of power and the connected failure of Jewish assimilation led to a strengthening of Zionist organizations. They countered antisemitic defamation with a conscious emphasis on the elect nature of their Jewishness and rejected all hopes for an "accommodation" with Hitler: "There are no more hiding places for us. Instead of

Heinrich Zillich: *Transylvanian Yarns.*

Zöberlein, Hans

Zionism. Proclamation of the state of Israel by David Ben-Gurion on May 14, 1948.

assimilation we want something new: the recognition of a Jewish nation and Jewish race" (Rabbi Joachim Prinz). The SS, too, promoted the expulsion of Jewish citizens as a "solution to the Jewish question" and supported Zionist emigration propaganda. In annexed Austria, Adolf EICHMANN set up a Central Office for Jewish Emigration in 1938, and later in Berlin a corresponding Reich Central Office, which (with the help of the REICH REPRESENTATION OF GERMAN JEWS) drained hundreds of thousands of Jews out of the Reich, Austria, Bohemia, and Moravia until emigration was prohibited on October 23, 1941 (*see* PERSECUTION OF JEWS).

Emigration into Palestine, increasing by leaps and bounds, led to growing Arab resistance and to considerable restrictions on the part of the British Mandate authority; but after 1945, under the impact of National Socialist genocide, Zionist groups found support, particularly in the United States. Finally, on May 14, 1948, the "founding of a Jewish state" sought by Zionism was achieved through the proclamation of the state of Israel.

H. H.

Zöberlein, Hans, b. Nuremberg, September 1, 1895; d. Munich, February 13, 1964, German writer. In the First World War Zöberlein received the highest war decorations. He was a

member of the EPP Free Corps, and in 1921 joined the NSDAP and the SA (where he rose to *Brigadeführer*). As an author, Zöberlein won recognition in *völkisch* circles through chauvinistic war novels, one of which, *Der Glaube an Deutschland* (Belief in Germany; 1931), was even favored with a foreword by Hitler. Zöberlein was honored by National Socialist literary prizes and NSDAP decorations for his racist-propaganda novels, among them *Der Befehl des*

Hans Zöberlein.

Gewissens (Conscience's Order; 1937). When citizens in Bavarian Penzberg capitulated prematurely shortly before the end of the war in order to spare the city further battles, Zöberlein, as leader of one of the commandos sent by the Reich defense commissioner, had those who were "politically untrustworthy" shot. For this, Zöberlein—who before a court acknowledged himself as a convinced National Socialist and antisemite—was sentenced to death in 1948. This was commuted to life imprisonment, but he was released in 1958 "on grounds of health."

Zonal border (*Zonengrenze*), original postwar term for the boundary lines between the four OCCUPATION ZONES in Germany; after the merger of the three Western zones into the Trizone and ultimately the Federal Republic of Germany, the border became the demarcation line for the German Democratic Republic (GDR). After November 16, 1957, the GDR termed the border its "western state border" (*Staatsgrenze West*), whereas the Federal Republic designated it the "internal German border" (*Innerdeutsche Grenze*) after the Foundation Treaty (*Grundlagenvertrag*) went into effect on June 21, 1973.

Zuckmayer, Carl, b. Nackenheim (Rhine-Hesse), December 27, 1896; d. Visp (Switzerland), January 18, 1977, German writer. Under the impact of the horror of the First World War, Zuckmayer (a volunteer in that war) wrote expressionistic texts against "the barbarism of warfare." As a theater and film dramatist, he wrote the screenplay for *Der blaue Engel* (The Blue Angel; 1930), among other works. He had particular success with realistic and humorous plays about simple folk, such as *Der fröhliche Weinberg* (The Happy Vineyard; 1925), *Schinderhannes* (Knacker Hans; 1927), and, most important, *Der Hauptmann von Köpenick* (The Captain of Köpenick; 1931). The true story of a shoemaker and convict, to whom all authorities show respect once he dons the uniform of a captain, it was a satirical attack on the German spirit of subordination to authority and militarism.

After 1932, Zuckmayer, a social critic who was also a half Jew, was the target of increasing National Socialist attacks. The staging of his plays was prohibited in 1933, and he himself had to flee after Germany's entry into Austria in 1938. One of the most discussed plays of the postwar period, *Des Teufels General* (The Devil's General; published in 1946, filmed in 1955), was written by Zuckmayer in American exile in 1942. It treats the conflict between opposition

Carl Zuckmayer.

and obedience in NS Germany through the tragic example of a daredevil air force general (patterned on Ernst UDET).

Zwangsglaubensatz (forced article of faith), polemical Germanization of the foreign word *dogma*, used in Alfred Rosenberg's MYTHUS DES 20. JAHRHUNDERTS, for example.

Zweig, Arnold, b. Glogau, November 10, 1887; d. East Berlin, November 26, 1968, German writer. In 1918 Zweig was a member of the Soldiers' Council of Vilna. In 1923 he became editor of the *Jüdische Rundschau* (Jewish Review) in Berlin, and in 1929, chairman of the German Writers' Trade Protection Society. Zweig's various literary labors reflect his development from a pacifist and Zionist to a "Marxist socialist." From 1925 on, he was exposed to National Socialist attacks (some physical), especially after the appearance of his famous novel *Der Streit um den Sargeanten Grischa* (The Case of Sergeant Grischa; 1927), in which he described the judicial murder of a Russian prisoner of war. Zweig's later realistic works, such as *Erziehung vor Verdun* (Education before Verdun; 1935), also attempted to counteract the glorification of war.

Zweig had to emigrate in 1933, and he lived in Palestine until 1948; he was involved with many exile periodicals. His novel *Das Beil von Wandsbek* (The Axe of Wandsbek; published in Hebrew in 1943, in German in 1947) was the first psychologically complex literary depiction of fellow travelers in the Third Reich. After his return from exile, Zweig was one of the most important authors of the German Democratic Republic (GDR), where he was president of the Academy of Arts and of the PEN Center; he was also a deputy in the People's Chamber (Volkskammer) from 1949 to 1967.

Zweig, Stefan, b. Vienna, November 28, 1881; d. Petropolis, near Rio de Janeiro, February 23, 1942, Austrian writer. During the First World War, Zweig, whose friends included Romain Rolland, had to emigrate to Switzerland because of his advocacy of a "just people's peace." After a rather impressionistic early work, he won international recognition through his antiwar drama *Jeremias* (Jeremiah: A Drama in Nine Scenes, 1917; first produced in 1919). His prose had psychological and biographical dimensions and humanist ambitions, as demonstrated most notably in the "historical miniatures" of the volume *Sternstunden der Menschheit* (Celestial Hours of Mankind, 1927; translated as *The Tide of Fortune*).

Zweig became one of the internationally most widely read German-language authors of the 1920s. As translator and editor of the most important French and Russian writers, he sought above all to promote understanding among peoples. After the February revolts of 1934 in Austria, Zweig, who was persecuted by the country's National Socialists, took up a second residence in England; he finally went into exile in 1938. One of his last works was *Schachnovelle* (Chess Novella; 1941), which describes the Gestapo methods of destroying a personality. Zweig finally took his life in exile out of "despair over the breakdown of his humanitarian ideals."

Zyklon B, trade name of an agent for gassing based on hydrocyanic (prussic) acid and used for such purposes as disinfecting ships against rat-borne plague. Produced by the DEGESCH firm (Frankfurt am Main), which was a subsidiary of Degussa/I.G. Farben, and by Tesch and Stabenow (Hamburg), Zyklon B was first tried out on human beings in the killing facilities of the EU-THANASIA operation; it was later produced in industrial quantities for the EXTERMINATION CAMPS. It was delivered in cans in crystalline form (absorbed in siliceous earth) and thrown through openings into the GAS CHAMBERS. In air, the crystals formed hydrogen cyanide (prussic acid) clouds that killed anyone in the chambers within a few minutes (a form of death by suffocation).

Stefan Zweig.

Zyklon B poison gas.

Bibliography

This bibliography includes most of the entries in the German-language *Lexikon*. Existing English translations of these works have been listed, and editions that first appeared in English have been substituted for any German translation. Some books have been omitted because they duplicate material in others, or because they are difficult to obtain. Additional works, marked with an asterisk*, have been added, the majority of them important books in the English language, but also a few significant German-language books published since the *Lexikon* appeared. German journal articles have been omitted, but a small number of English-language articles are included where they provided coverage not available elsewhere.

As in the *Lexikon* bibliography, works are divided by topic. The categories have been broadened somewhat to avoid duplicate or multiple listings of a work. Since a number of these categories overlap, the reader is sometimes referred to other headings for related references.

General Works on National Socialism and Third Reich Historiography

*Aycoberry, Pierre. *The Nazi Question: An Essay on the Interpretations of National Socialism (1922–1975)*. New York, 1981.

Beck, Johannes, et al. *Terror und Hoffnung in Deutschland 1933–1945: Leben im Faschismus*. Reinbek bei Hamburg, 1980.

*Berghahn, V. R. *Modern Germany: Society, Economy and Politics in the Twentieth Century*. Cambridge, 1982.

Bracher, Karl Dietrich. *The German Dictatorship: The Origins, Structure, and Effects of National Socialism*. New York, 1970.

Broszat, Martin, and H. Möller, eds. *Das Dritte Reich*. Munich, 1983.

Broszat, Martin, and N. Frei, eds. *Das Dritte Reich*. Freiburg im Breisgau, 1983.

Broszat, Martin, Elke Fröhlich, and Anton Grossmann, eds. *Bayern in der NS-Zeit*. 6 vols. Munich, 1977–1984.

*Craig, Gordon A. *The Germans*. New York, 1982.

*Craig, Gordon A. *Germany, 1866–1945*. Oxford, 1978.

*Dahrendorf, Ralf. *Society and Democracy in Germany*. Garden City, N.Y., 1967.

*Eley, Geoff. *From Unification to Nazism: Reinterpreting the German Past*. London, 1986.

*Evans, Richard J. *In Hitler's Shadow: West German Historians and the Attempt to Escape from the Nazi Past*. London, 1989.

*Freeman, Michael. *An Atlas of Nazi Germany*. New York, 1987.

Friedländer, Saul. *Reflections of Nazism: An Essay on Kitsch and Death*. New York, 1986.

Glaser, Hermann. *Das Dritte Reich*. Freiburg im Breisgau, 1979.

*Grunberger, Richard. *The 12-Year Reich: A Social History of Nazi Germany, 1933–1945*. New York, 1971.

*Hartman, Geoffrey H., ed. *Bitburg in Moral and Political Perspective*. Bloomington, 1986.

*Hiden, John, and John Farquharson. *Explaining Hitler's Germany: Historians and the Third Reich*. Boston, 1984.

Hirschfeld, Gerhard, and Lothar Kettenacker, eds. *Der "Führerstaat." Mythos und Realität: Studien zur Struktur und Politik des Dritten Reiches*. Stuttgart, 1981. (Some of the articles are in English.)

*Holborn, Hajo, ed. *From Republic to Reich: The Making of the Nazi Revolution*. New York, 1972.

Huber, H., and A. Müller. *Das Dritte Reich*. 2 vols. Munich, 1964.

*Iggers, Georg. *The Social History of Politics: Critical Perspectives on West German Historical Writing since 1945*. New York, 1986.

*Kershaw, Ian. *The Nazi Dictatorship: Problems and Perspectives of Interpretation*. London, 1985.

*Koch, Hansjoachim W., ed. *Aspects of the Third Reich*. New York, 1986.

Krausnick, Helmut, et al. *Anatomy of the SS State*. New York, 1968.

*Maier, Charles S. *The Unmasterable Past: History, Holocaust and German National Identity.* Cambridge, Mass., 1988.

*Noakes, Jeremy, and Geoffrey Pridham, eds. *Nazism: 1919–1945: History in Documents and Eyewitness Accounts.* 2 vols. New York, 1990 [1984].

*Shirer, William. *The Rise and Fall of the Third Reich.* New York, 1960.

Speer, Albert. *Inside the Third Reich.* New York, 1971.

*Stark, Gary D., and Bede Karl Lackner, eds. *Essays on Culture and Society in Modern Germany.* College Station, Tex., 1982.

*Stern, Fritz. *Dreams and Delusions: The Drama of German History.* New York, 1987.

*Turner, Henry A., ed. *Nazism and the Third Reich.* New York, 1972.

*Weizsäcker, Richard von. *A Voice from Germany.* New York, 1986.

Zentner, Christian. *Illustrierte Geschichte des Dritten Reiches.* Munich, 1983.

Agricultural Policy

Barmeyer, Heide. *Andreas Hermes und die Organisation des deutschen Landwirtschaft: Christliche Bauernvereine, Reichstagsbrand, Grüne Front, Reichsnährstand 1928–1933.* Stuttgart, 1971.

*Bramwell, Anna. *Blood and Soil: Walther Darré and Hitler's Green Party.* Bourne End, England, 1985.

*Evans, Richard J., and W. R. Lee, eds. *The German Peasantry: Conflict and Community in Rural Society from the Eighteenth to the Twentieth Centuries.* New York, 1986.

*Farquharson, John E. *The Plough and the Swastika: The NSDAP and Agriculture in Germany, 1928–45.* Beverly Hills, 1976.

Grundmann, Friedrich. *Agrarpolitik im "Dritten Reich": Anspruch und Wirklichkeit des Reichserbhofgesetzes.* Hamburg, 1979.

Klais, E. *Geschichte der deutschen Landwirtschaft im Industriezeitalter.* Wiesbaden, 1973.

*Moeller, Robert G., ed. *Peasants and Lords in Modern Germany: Recent Studies in Agricultural History.* Boston, 1986.

Tornow, W., ed. *Chronik der Agrarpolitik und Agrarwirtschaft des Deutschen Reiches von 1933–1945.* Hamburg, 1972.

*Wunderlich, Frieda. *Farm Labor in Germany, 1810–1945.* Princeton, 1961.

Allied Occupation, Denazification, and Re-education

*Bower, Tom. *Blind Eye to Murder: Britain, America, and the Purging of Nazi Germany—A Pledge Betrayed.* London, 1981.

*Hearnden, Arthur, ed. *The British in Germany: Educational Reconstruction after 1945.* London, 1978.

Pakschies, Günther. *Umerziehung in der Britischen Zone 1945–1949.* 2nd ed. Cologne, 1984 [1979].

*Peterson, Edward N. *The American Occupation of Germany: Retreat to Victory.* Detroit, 1977.

Ruge-Schatz, A. *Umerziehung und Schulpolitik in der französischen Besatzungszone 1945–1949.* Frankfurt, 1977.

*Salomon, Ernst von. *Fragebogen: The Questionnaire.* Garden City, N.Y., 1955.

*Sharp, Tony. *The Wartime Allies and the Zonal Division of Germany.* Oxford, 1975.

*Tent, James F. *Mission on the Rhine.* Chicago, 1982.

Antisemitism

*Arendt, Hannah. *The Origins of Totalitarianism.* 2nd ed. New York, 1958.

Boehlich, Walter, ed. *Der Berliner Antisemitismusstreit.* Frankfurt, 1965.

Bunzl, John, and Bernd Martin. *Antisemitismus in Österreich.* Innsbruck, 1983.

*Cohn, Norman R. C. *Warrant for Genocide: The Myth of the Jewish World Conspiracy and the Protocols of the Elders of Zion.* New York, 1967.

*Gordon, Sarah Ann. *Hitler, Germans, and the "Jewish Question."* Princeton, 1984.

Greive, Hermann. *Geschichte der modernen Antisemitismus in Deutschland.* Darmstadt, 1983.

*Low, Alfred D. *Jews in the Eyes of the Germans: From the Enlightenment to Imperial Germany.* Philadelphia, 1979.

Nipperdey, Thomas, and Reinhard Rürup. "Antisemitismus." In *Geschichtliche Grundbegriffe*, vol. I. Stuttgart, 1972.

Pulzer, Peter G. J. *The Rise of Political Anti-Semitism in Germany and Austria.* New York, 1964.

Reichmann, Eva. *Hostages of Civilization: The Social Sources of National Socialist Anti-Semitism.* Westport, Conn., 1970 [1949].

Ruether, Rosemary R. *Faith and Fratricide: The Theological Roots of Anti-Semitism.* New York, 1974.

Rürup, Reinhard. *Emanzipation und Antisemitismus.* Göttingen, 1975.

Spira, L. *Feindbild "Jud'": 100 Jahre politischer Antisemitismus in Österreich.* Vienna, 1981.

Austria

Anschluss 1938: Protokoll des Symposiums in Wien am 14. und 15. März 1978. Munich, 1978.

*Bukey, Evan B. *Hitler's Hometown: Linz, Austria, 1908–1945.* Bloomington, 1986.

*Carsten, Francis L. *Fascist Movements in Austria: From Schönerer to Hitler.* Beverly Hills, 1977.

*Gehl, Jurgen. *Austria, Germany, and the Anschluss, 1931–1938.* New York, 1963.

*Herzstein, Robert E. *Waldheim.* New York, 1988.

Kadrnoska, Franz, ed. *Aufbruch und Untergang: Österreichische Kultur zwischen 1918 und 1938.* Vienna, 1979.

Konrad, Helmut, ed. *Sozialdemokratie und "Anschluss."* Vienna, 1979.

*Luža, Radomir. *Austro-German Relations in the Anschluss Era.* Princeton, 1975.

*Luža, Radomir. *The Resistance in Austria, 1938–1945.* Minneapolis, 1984.

*Pauley, Bruce F. *Hitler and the Forgotten Nazis: A History of Austrian National Socialism.* Chapel Hill, 1981.

Schausberger, Norbert. *Der Griff nach Österreich.* Vienna, 1978.

*Wagner, Dieter, and Gerhard Tomkowitz. *Anschluss: The Week That Hitler Seized Vienna.* New York, 1971.

See also under Antisemitism; Fascism; Foreign Policy.

Biography
General
Fest, Joachim C. *The Face of the Third Reich: Portraits of the Nazi Leadership.* New York, 1970.

Peuschel, H. *Die Männer um Hitler: Braune Biographien.* Düsseldorf, 1982.

Wistrich, Robert S. *Who's Who in Nazi Germany.* New York, 1982.

Martin Bormann
Besymenski, L. *Die letzten Notizen von Martin Bormann.* Stuttgart, 1974.

Decaux, A. *Rätsel in verstaubten Akten.* Bayreuth, 1970.

Lang, Jochen von. *The Secretary: Martin Bormann, the Man Who Manipulated Hitler.* New York, 1979.

Wulf, J. *Martin Bormann. Hitlers Schatten.* Gütersloh, 1962.

Adolf Eichmann
*Arendt, Hannah. *Eichmann in Jerusalem: A Report on the Banality of Evil.* Rev. ed. New York, 1964.

Kempner, Robert M. W. *Eichmann und Komplizen.* Zurich, 1961.

Lang, Jochen von, and Claus Sibyll, eds. *Eichmann Interrogated: Transcripts from the Archives of the Israeli Police.* New York, 1983.

Oppenheimer, M., ed. *Eichmann und die Eichmänner.* Ludwigsburg, 1961.

Joseph Goebbels
Boelcke, W., ed. *"Wollt Ihr den totalen Krieg?" Die Geheimen Goebbels-Konferenzen 1939–1943.* Munich, 1969.

Goebbels, Joseph. *Final Entries, 1945: The Diaries of Joseph Goebbels.* Edited by Hugh Trevor-Roper. New York, 1978.

Goebbels, Joseph. *The Goebbels Diaries, 1939–1941.* New York, 1982.

Goebbels, Joseph. *The Goebbels Diaries, 1942–1943.* Garden City, N.Y., 1948.

Heiber, Helmut. *Goebbels.* New York, 1972.

Reimann, Viktor. *Goebbels.* Garden City, N.Y., 1976.

See also under Culture; Propaganda.

Hermann Göring
Frischauer, Willi. *The Rise and Fall of Hermann Göring.* Boston, 1951.

Göring, Emmy. *An der Seite meines Mannes.* Göttingen, 1967.

*Irving, David. *Göring: A Biography.* New York, 1989.

Lee, Asher. *Goering: Air Leader.* New York, 1972.

*Leffland, Ella. *The Knight, Death, and the Devil.* New York, 1990. (A fictionalized biography.)

Manvell, Roger, and Heinrich Fraenkel. *Göring.* New York, 1962.

*Mosley, Leonard. *The Reich Marshal: A Biography of Hermann Göring.* Garden City, N.Y., 1974.

*Overy, R. J. *Goering: The "Iron Man."* Boston, 1984.

Rudolf Hess
Bird, Eugene. *Prisoner #7: Rudolf Hess—The Thirty Years in Jail of Hitler's Deputy Führer.* New York, 1974.

Douglass-Hamilton, James Lord. *Motive for a Mission: The Story behind Hess's Flight to Britain.* New York, 1971.

Hess, Wolf R. *My Father, Rudolf Hess.* London, 1986.

*Hutton, Joseph B. *Hess: The Man and His Mission.* New York, 1971.

Manvell, Roger, and Heinrich Fraenkel. *Hess: A Biography.* New York, 1973.

Schwarzwäller, Wulf. *Rudolf Hess: The Last Nazi.* Bethesda, Md., 1988.

Reinhard Heydrich
Calic, Edouard. *Reinhard Heydrich: The Chilling Story of the Man Who Masterminded the Nazi Death Camps.* New York, 1985.

Deschner, Günther. *Reinhard Heydrich: A Biography.* New York, 1981.

Heydrich, Lina. *Leben mit einem Kriegsverbrecher.* Pfaffenhofen, 1976.

*MacDonald, Callum. *The Killing of SS Obergruppenführer Reinhard Heydrich.* New York, 1989.

Heinrich Himmler
Frankel, Heinrich, and Roger Manvell. *Himmler.* Frankfurt, 1965.

Heiber, Helmut, ed. *Reichsführer! . . . Briefe an und von Himmler.* Stuttgart, 1968.

Smith, Bradley F. *Heinrich Himmler: A Nazi in the Making, 1900–1926.* Stanford, 1971.

Smith, Bradley F., and Agnes F. Peterson, eds. *Heinrich Himmler: Geheimreden 1933–1945.* Frankfurt, 1974.

Wykes, Alan. *Reichsführer SS Himmler.* Rastatt, 1981.

See also under SS.

Adolf Hitler
*Binion, Rudolph. *Hitler among the Germans.* New York, 1976.

*Breiting, Richard. *Secret Conversations with Hitler: The Two Newly Discovered 1931 Interviews.* New York, 1971.

Bullock, Alan. *Hitler: A Study in Tyranny.* Rev. ed. New York, 1962.

*Davidson, Eugene. *The Making of Adolf Hitler.* New York, 1977.

Fest, Joachim C. *Hitler.* New York, 1974.

*Flood, Charles B. *Hitler: The Path to Power.* Boston, 1989.

Haffner, Sebastian. *The Meaning of Hitler.* New York, 1979.

*Heiden, Konrad. *Der Fuehrer: Hitler's Rise to Power.* Boston, 1969 [1944].

Hillgruber, Andreas. *Hitlers Strategie: Politik und Kriegsführung 1940–41.* Frankfurt, 1965.

Hitlers politischen Testament: Die Bormann Diktate von Februar und April 1945. Hamburg, 1981.

*Jäckel, Eberhard. *Hitler in History.* Hanover, N.H., 1984.

Jäckel, Eberhard, and A. Kuhn, eds. *Hitler: Sämtliche Aufzeichnungen 1905–1924.* Stuttgart, 1980.

Jenks, William A. *Vienna and the Young Hitler.* Chicago, 1976 [1960].

Jones, J. Sydney. *Hitler in Vienna, 1907–1913.* New York, 1983.

Kardel, Hennecke. *Hitlers Verrat am Nationalsozialismus.* Geneva, 1981.

Knopp, G., ed. *Hitler heute: Gespräche über ein deutsches Trauma.* Aschaffenburg, 1979.

*Langer, Walter C. *The Mind of Adolf Hitler: The Secret Wartime Report.* New York, 1972.

*Lewin, Ronald. *Hitler's Mistakes.* London, 1984.

Maser, Werner, ed. *Hitler's Letters and Notes.* New York, 1974.

*McRandle, James H. *The Track of the Wolf: Essays on National Socialism and Its Leader, Adolf Hitler.* Evanston, Ill., 1965.

Olden, Rudolf. *Hitler.* Hildesheim, 1981.

Schwind-Waldeck, P. *Wie deutsch war Hitler?* Frankfurt, 1979.

Stern, J. P. *Hitler: The Führer and the People.* Berkeley, 1975.

Stierlein, Helm. *Adolf Hitler: A Family Perspective.* New York, 1976.

*Wagener, Otto. *Hitler—Memoirs of a Confidant.* New Haven, 1985.

See also under Ideology; Jews; NSDAP; Second World War.

Other Significant Figures

*Black, Peter R. *Ernst Kaltenbrunner: Ideological Soldier of the Third Reich.* Princeton, 1984.

Friedländer, Saul. *Kurt Gerstein: The Ambiguity of Good.* New York, 1969.

Padfield, Peter. *Dönitz: The Last Führer.* New York, 1984.

Schirach, Baldur von. *Ich glaubte an Hitler.* Hamburg, 1968.

Schmidt, Matthias. *Albert Speer: The End of a Myth.* New York, 1984.

*Stachura, Peter D. *Gregor Strasser and the Rise of Nazism.* Boston, 1983.

*Wortmann, Michael. *Baldur von Schirach: Hitlers Jugendführer.* Cologne, 1982.

The Churches and National Socialism

Protestant and Catholic Churches; Confessing Church

*Bethge, Eberhard. *Dietrich Bonhoeffer: Man of Vision, Man of Courage.* New York, 1970.

Conway, John S. *The Nazi Persecution of the Churches, 1933–1945.* New York, 1968.

Denzler, G., and V. Fabricius. *Die Kirchen im Dritten Reich.* 2 vols. Frankfurt, 1985.

*Dietrich, Donald. *Catholic Citizens in the Third Reich: Psycho-Social Principles and Moral Reasoning.* New Brunswick, N.J., 1988.

Gotto, K., and Konrad Repgen, eds. *Kirche, Katholiken und Nationalsozialismus.* Mainz, 1980.

*Helmreich, Ernst Christian. *The German Churches under Hitler: Background, Struggle, and Epilogue.* Detroit, 1979.

Hockerts, Hans G. *Die Sittlichkeitsprozesse gegen katholische Ordensangehörige und Priester 1936/1937.* Mainz, 1971.

Kirche und Nationalsozialismus in Deutschland und Österreich. Aschaffenburg, 1980.

Klempner, B. M. *Nonnen unter dem Hakenkreuz.* Würzburg, 1979.

Lenz, Hans F. *"Sagen Sie, Herr Pfarrer, wie kommen Sie zur SS?"* Giessen, 1982.

*Lewy, Günther. *The Catholic Church and Nazi Germany.* London, 1966.

*Matheson, Peter, ed. *The Third Reich and the Christian Churches.* Grand Rapids, Mich., 1981.

Meier, Kurt. *Der evangelische Kirchenkampf.* 3 vols. Göttingen, 1976–.

Müller, Hans Michael, ed. *Katholische Kirche und Nationalsozialismus: Dokumente 1930–1935.* Munich, 1963.

Niemöller, Martin. *"God is my Fuehrer," being the last twenty-eight Sermons by Martin Niemöller.* Preface by Thomas Mann. New York, 1941.

Niesel, Wilhelm. *Kirche unter dem Wort. Der Kampf der Bekennenden Kirche der altpreussischen Union 1933–1945.* Göttingen, 1978.

Oehme, W. *Märtyrer der evangelischen Christenheit 1933–45.* Berlin, 1980.

Prolingheuer, Hans. *Der ungekämpfte Kirchenkampf, 1939–1945: Das politische Versagen der Bekennenden Kirche.* Cologne, 1983.

See, Wolfgang, and Rudolf Weckerling. *Frauen im Kirchenkampf: Beispiele aus der Bekennende Kirche Berlin-Brandenburg 1933 bis 1945.* Berlin, 1984.

Zahn, Gordon C. *German Catholics and Hitler's War: A Study in Social Control.* New York, 1962.

Zimmermann-Buhr, B. *Die Katholische Kirche und der Nationalsozialismus in den Jahren 1930–1933.* Frankfurt, 1982.

Zipfel, Friedrich. *Kirchenkampf in Deutschland 1933–1945.* 2 vols. Berlin, 1965.

The Churches and the Jews

Busch, Eberhard. *Juden und Christen im Schatten des Dritten Reiches.* Munich, 1979.

*Gutteridge, Richard. *The German Evangelical Church and the Jews, 1879–1950.* New York, 1976.

*Littell, Franklin H., and Hubert G. Locke, eds. *The German Church Struggle and the Holocaust.* Detroit, 1974.

German Christians

Döring, D. *Christentum und Faschismus.* Mainz, 1982.

Meier, Kurt. *Die Deutschen Christen.* Göttingen, 1964.

Norden, Günther von, ed. *Der deutsche Protestantismus im Jahr der nationalsozialistischen Machtergreifung.* Gütersloh, 1979.

Sonne, H.-J. *Die politische Theologie der Deutschen Christen.* Göttingen, 1982.

See also under Antisemitism; Medicine and Biology; Opposition.

Concentration Camps and Extermination Camps

Antoni, E. *KZ: Von Dachau bis Auschwitz.* Frankfurt, 1979.

Auschwitz: Geschichte und Wirklichkeit des Vernichtungslagers. Hamburg, 1980.

Demant, E., ed. *Auschwitz: "Direkt von der Rampe weg . . ."* Reinbek bei Hamburg, 1979.

Drobisch, K. *Widerstand in Buchenwald.* Frankfurt, 1978.

Fénelon, Fania. *Playing for Time.* New York, 1977.

*Ferencz, Benjamin B. *Less Than Slaves: Jewish Forced Labor and the Quest for Compensation.* Cambridge, Mass., 1979.

Gilbert, Martin. *Auschwitz and the Allies.* New York, 1981.

Grünewald, P. *KZ Osthofen: Material zur Geschichte eines fast vergessenen Konzentrationslagers.* Frankfurt, 1979.

Hilberg, Raul. *Sonderzüge nach Auschwitz.* Mainz, 1981.

*Hirschfeld, Gerhard. *The Politics of Genocide: Jews and Soviet Prisoners of War in Nazi Germany.* Boston, 1986.

Hoess, Rudolf. *Commandant of Auschwitz.* Cleveland, 1959.

Horbach, Michael. *So überlebten sie den Holocaust.* Munich, 1979.

Jentzsch, Bernd, ed. *Der Tod ist ein Meister aus Deutschland: Deportation und Vernichtung in poetischen Zeugnissen.* Munich, 1979.

Kaminski, Andrzej. *Konzentrationslager 1896 bis heute.* Stuttgart, 1982.

*Kieler, Wieslaw. *Anus Mundi: 1,500 Days in Auschwitz/Birkenau.* New York, 1970.

Kogon, Eugen. *The Theory and Practice of Hell: The German Concentration Camps and the System behind Them.* New York, 1973 [1950].

Kogon, Eugen, Hermann Langbein, Adalbert Rückerl et al. *Nationalsozialistische Massentötungen durch Giftgas.* Frankfurt, 1983.

Kolb, Eberhard. *Bergen-Belsen: Vom "Aufenthaltslager" zum Konzentrationslager 1943–45.* 3rd ed. Hannover, 1988.

*Kraus, Ota B., and Erich Kulka. *The Death Factory: Document on Auschwitz.* New York, 1966.

Kühnrich, Heinz. *Der KZ-Staat: Die faschistischen Konzentrationslager 1933 bis 1945.* 5th ed. East Berlin, 1988.

Langbein, Hermann. *Der Auschwitz-Prozess.* Vienna, 1965.

*Lanzmann, Claude. *Shoah: An Oral History of the Holocaust.* New York, 1985.

Lenner, H. D. *Gerettet vor dem Holocaust: Menschen, die halfen.* Munich, 1979.

Lichtenstein, Heiner. *Mit der Reichsbahn in den Tod: Massentransporte in den Holocaust 1941 bis 1945.* Cologne, 1985.

Lichtenstein, Heiner. *Warum Auschwitz nicht bombardiert wurde: Eine Dokumentation.* Cologne, 1980.

Marszalek, Josef. *Majdanek: Geschichte und Wirklichkeit des Vernichtungslagers.* Reinbek bei Hamburg, 1982.

*Müller, Filip. *Eyewitness Auschwitz: Three Years in the Gas Chambers at Auschwitz.* New York, 1979.

*Naumann, Bernd. *Auschwitz: A Report on the Proceedings against Robert Karl Ludwig Mulka and Others before the Court at Frankfurt.* New York, 1966.

Pingel, Falk. *Häftling unter SS-Herrschaft.* Hamburg, 1978.

*Rubenstein, Richard L., and John Roth. *Approaches to Auschwitz: The Holocaust and Its Legacy.* Atlanta, 1987.

Rückerl, Adalbert, ed. *NS-Vernichtungslager.* Munich, 1977.

Scheuer, L. *Vom Tode, der nicht stattfand—Theresienstadt, Auschwitz, Freiberg, Mauthausen: Eine Frau überlebt.* Reinbek bei Hamburg, 1983.

*Segev, Tom. *Soldiers of Evil: The Commandants of the Nazi Concentration Camps.* New York, 1987.

*Smith, Marcus J. *The Harrowing of Hell: Dachau.* Albuquerque, N.M., 1972.

*Smolen, Kazimierz, ed. *From the History of KL-Auschwitz.* New York, 1982 [1967].

*Steiner, Jean-François. *Treblinka.* New York, 1967.

Zentner, Christian, ed. *Anmerkungen zu "Holocaust."* Munich, 1979.

   See also under Biography: Eichmann *and* Himmler; Economy; Gypsies; Jews; Medicine and Biology; Repression; SS.

Culture and Cultural Policy

General

Brenner, Hildegard. *Die Kunstpolitik des Nationalsozialismus.* Hamburg, 1963.

Düwell, Kurt, and Werner Link, eds. *Deutsche auswärtige Kulturpolitik seit 1871.* Cologne, 1981.

Kinser, Bill, and Neil Kleinmann. *The Dream That Was No More a Dream: A Search for Aesthetic Reality in Germany, 1890–1945.* New York, 1969.

Mosse, George, ed. *Nazi Culture: Intellectual, Cultural and Social Life in the Third Reich.* New York, 1966.

Poliakov, Leon, and Josef Wulf. *Das Dritte Reich und seine Denker: Dokumente.* Berlin, 1959.

Richard, Lionel. *Deutscher Faschismus und Kultur.* East Berlin, 1982.

Schäfer, Hans Dieter. *Das gespaltene Bewusstsein: Über deutsche Kultur und Lebenswirklichkeit 1933–1945.* Munich, 1981.

Schnell, R., ed. *Kunst und Kultur im deutschen Faschismus.* Stuttgart, 1978.

*Sontag, Susan. "Nazi Kitsch." In *Under the Sign of Saturn.* New York, 1972.

   See also under Emigration; Ideology; Weimar Republic.

Architecture

Arnst, Karl, et al. *Albert Speer: Arbeiten 1933–1942.* Frankfurt, 1978.

*Lane, Barbara Miller. *Architecture and Politics in Germany, 1918–1945.* Rev. ed. Cambridge, Mass., 1985 [1968].

Rasp, Hans-Peter. *Eine Stadt für tausend Jahre—München: Bauten und Projekte für die Hauptstadt der Bewegung.* Munich, 1982.

Schönberger, Angele. *Die neue Reichskanzlei von Albert Speer: Zum Zusammenhang von nationalsozialistischer Ideologie und Architektur.* Berlin, 1981.

*Taylor, Robert B. *The World in Stone: The Role of Architecture in National Socialist Ideology.* Berkeley, 1974.

Teut, Anna, ed. *Architektur im Dritten Reich 1933–1945.* Frankfurt, 1967.

Art

Damus, Martin. *Sozialistischer Realismus und Kunst im Nationalsozialismus.* Frankfurt, 1981.

Die dreissiger Jahre—Schauplatz Deutschland. Munich, 1977. (Exhibition catalog of Haus der Kunst.)

Entartete Kunst: Bildersturm vor 25 Jahren. Munich, 1962. (Exhibition catalog of Haus der Kunst.)

Frankfurter Kunstverein. *Kunst im 3. Reich: Dokumente der Unterwerfung.* 2nd ed. Frankfurt, 1980.

*Grosshans, Henry. *Hitler and the Artists.* New York, 1983.

Hinz, Berthold. *Art in the Third Reich.* New York, 1979.

Hinz, Berthold, et al., eds. *Die Dekoration der Gewalt: Kunst und Medien im Faschismus.* Giessen, 1979.

Liska, Pavel. *Nationalsozialistische Kunstpolitik.* Berlin, 1974.

Merker, Reinhard. *Die bildende Künste im Nationalsozialismus.* Cologne, 1983.

Steinberg, R., ed. *Nazi-Kitsch.* Darmstadt, 1975.

Thomas, O. *Die Propaganda-Maschinerie: Bildende Kunst und Öffentlichkeit im Dritten Reich.* Berlin, 1978.

Wulf, Josef. *Die Bildenden Künste im Dritten Reich—Eine Dokumentation.* Gütersloh, 1963.

Film

Albrecht, Gerd. *Nationalsozialistische Filmpolitik: Eine soziologische Untersuchung über die Spielfilm des Dritten Reiches.* Stuttgart, 1969.

Albrecht, Gerd, ed. *Film im Dritten Reich: Eine Dokumentation.* Karlsruhe, 1979.

Courtade, Francis, and P. Cadars. *Geschichte des Films im Dritten Reich.* Munich, 1975.

*Hull, David S. *Film in the Third Reich: Art and Propaganda in Nazi Germany.* New York, 1973.

*Infield, Glenn. *Leni Riefenstahl: The Fallen Film Goddess.* New York, 1976.

*Kracauer, Siegfried. *From Caligari to Hitler: A Psychological History of the German Film.* Princeton, 1947.

Leiser, Erwin. *Nazi Cinema.* New York, 1974.

Spiker, J. *Film und Kapital: Der Weg der deutschen Filmwirtschaft zum nationalsozialistischen Einheitskonzern.* Berlin, 1975.

*Taylor, Richard. *Film Propaganda: Soviet Russia and Nazi Germany.* New York, 1979.

*Welch, David. *Propaganda and the German Cinema.* Oxford, 1983.

Wetzel, Kraft, and Peter A. Hagemann. *Zensur: Verbotene deutsche Filme 1933–1945.* Berlin, 1978.

Literature

Aley, Peter. *Jugendliteratur im Dritten Reich: Dokumente und Kommentare.* Hamburg, 1965.

Denkler, Horst, and Kurt Prümm, eds. *Die deutsche Literatur im Dritten Reich.* Stuttgart, 1976.

Geissler, Rolf. *Dekadenz und Heroismus: Zeitroman und völkisch-nationalsozialistische Literaturkritik.* Stuttgart, 1964.

*Gray, Ronald. *The German Tradition of Literature, 1871–1945.* Cambridge, Mass., 1965.

*Kamenetsky, Christa. *Children's Literature in Hitler's Germany: The Cultural Policy of National Socialist Germany.* Athens, Ohio, 1984.

Ketelsen, Uwe K. *Völkisch-nationale und nationalsozialistische Literatur in Deutschland 1890–1945.* Stuttgart, 1976.

Loewy, Emil. *Literatur unterm Hakenkreuz: Das Dritte Reich und seine Dichtung.* Frankfurt, 1966.

Sander, G., ed. *Die Bücherverbrennung.* Munich, 1983.

Schnell, Ralf. *Literarische Innere Emigration 1933–1945.* Stuttgart, 1976.

Schöffling, K., ed. *Dort wo man Bücher verbrennt.* Frankfurt, 1983.

Serke, J. *Die verbrannte Dichter.* Weinheim, 1977.

Strothmann, Dietrich. *Nationalsozialistische Literaturpolitik: Ein Beitrag zur Publizistik im Dritten Reich.* Bonn, 1960.

Vondung, Klaus. *Völkisch-nationale und nationalsozialistische Literaturtheorie.* Munich, 1973.

Walberer, U., ed. *10 Mai 1933: Bücherverbrennung in Deutschland und die Folgen.* Frankfurt, 1983.

Wulf, Josef. *Literatur und Dichtung im Dritten Reich.* Gütersloh, 1963.

Zimmerman, P. *Der Bauernroman: Antifeudalismus—Konservatismus—Faschismus.* Stuttgart, 1975.

Music

*Heister, Werner, and Hans-Gunter Klein, eds. *Musik und Musikpolitik im faschistischen Deutschland.* Frankfurt, 1984.

*Lidtke, Vernon L. "Songs and Nazis: Political Music and Social Change in Twentieth-Century Germany." In *Essays on Culture and Society in Modern Germany*, edited by Gary D. Stark and Bede Karl Lackner. College Station, Tex., 1982.

*Meyer, Michael. "The Nazi Musicologist as Myth Maker in the Third Reich." *Journal of Contemporary History* 10 (1975): 649–665.

*Prieberg, Fred K. *Musik im NS-Staat.* Frankfurt, 1982.

Wulf, Josef. *Musik im Dritten Reich: Eine Dokumentation.* Gütersloh, 1963.

Theater

Fischli, Bruno. *Die Deutschen-Dämmerung: Zur Genealogie des völkisch-faschistischen Dramas und Theaters 1897–1933.* Bonn, 1976.

*Innes, C. D. *Erwin Piscator's Political Theatre: The Development of Modern German Drama.* Cambridge, 1972.

Ketelsen, Uwe K. *Heroisches Theater: Untersuchungen zur Dramentheorie des Dritten Reichs.* Bonn, 1968.

Wardetzky, J. *Theaterpolitik im faschistischen Deutschland.* East Berlin, 1983.

*Willett, John. *The Theatre of the Weimar Republic.* New York, 1988.

See also under Ideology; Opposition; Propaganda.

Czechoslovakia

*Brügel, Johann W. *Czechoslovakia before Munich: The German Minority Problem and British Appeasement Policy.* Cambridge, 1973.

Franke, Reiner. *London und Prag: Materalien zum Problem eines multinationalen Nationalstaats 1919–1938.* Munich, 1982.

*Luža, Radomir. *The Transfer of the Sudeten Germans: A Study of Czech-German Relations, 1933–1962.* New York, 1964.

Mamatey, Victor S., and Radomir Luža, eds. *A History of the Czechoslovak Republic, 1918–1948.* Princeton, 1973.

Smelser, Ronald M. *The Sudeten Problem, 1933–1938: Volkstumspolitik and the Formulation of Nazi Foreign Policy.* Middletown, Conn., 1975.

Welisch, S. A. *Die Sudetendeutsche Frage 1918–1928.* Munich, 1980.

*Wiskemann, Elizabeth. *Czechs and Germans: A Study of the Struggle in the Historic Provinces of Bohemia and Moravia.* 2nd ed. New York, 1967.

See also under Foreign Policy; Occupation Policy.

Daily Life in National Socialist Germany

*Bessel, Richard, ed. *Life in the Third Reich.* Oxford, 1987.

Engelmann, Bernt. *In Hitler's Germany: Daily Life in the Third Reich.* New York, 1985.

Huck, Gerhard, ed. *Sozialgeschichte der Freizeit: Untersu-chungen zum Wandel der Alltagskultur in Deutschland.* 2nd ed. Wuppertal, 1982.

*Kardorff, Ursula von. *Diary of a Nightmare: Berlin 1942–1945.* New York, 1966.

*Krüger, Horst. *A Crack in the Wall: Growing Up under Hitler.* New York, 1986.

Peukert, Detlev J. K. *Inside Nazi Germany: Conformity, Opposition, and Racism in Everyday Life.* New Haven, 1986.

Peukert, Detlev J. K., and Jürgen Reulecke, eds. *Die Reihen fast geschlossen: Beiträge zur Geschichte des Alltags unterm Nationalsozialismus.* Wuppertal, 1981.

*Shirer, William. *Berlin Diary: The Journal of a Foreign Correspondent, 1934–1941.* New York, 1988 [1941].

Steinbach, Lothar, ed. *Ein Volk, ein Reich, ein Glaube? Ehemalige Nationalsozialisten und Zeitzeugen berichten über ihr Leben im Deutschen Reich.* Bonn, 1983.

*Vassiltchikov, Marie. *Berlin Diaries, 1940–1945.* London, 1985.

The Economy

Weimar Germany and Economic Crisis

*Abraham, David. *The Collapse of the Weimar Republic: Political Economy in Crisis.* Rev. ed. New York, 1986.

Becker, J., and R. Wenzel, eds. *Internationale Beziehungen in der Weltwirtschaftskrise 1929–1933.* Munich, 1980.

Evans, Richard, and Dick Geary, eds. *The German Unem-ployed.* New York, 1987.

Holl, Karl, ed. *Wirtschaftskrise und liberale Demokratie.* Göttingen, 1978.

*Kindleberger, Charles Poor. *The World in Depression, 1929–1939.* Berkeley, 1973.

*Ringer, Fritz, ed. *The German Inflation of 1923.* New York, 1969.

*Stachura, Peter D., ed. *Unemployment and the Great Depression in Weimar Germany.* New York, 1986.

Treue, Wolfgang, ed. *Deutschland in der Weltwirtschafts-krise in Augenzeugenberichten.* Düsseldorf, 1967.

*Turner, Henry A. *German Business and the Rise of Hitler.* New York, 1985.

See also under Seizure of Power; Weimar Republic.

The National Socialist Economy: Rearmament and Autarky

Bagel-Bohlau, Anja E. *Hitlers industrielle Kriegsvorberei-tungen 1936–1939.* Koblenz, 1975.

Barkai, Avraham. *Das Wirtschaftssystem des Nationalsozia-lismus.* Cologne, 1977.

Borkin, Joseph. *The Crime and Punishment of I.G. Farben.* New York, 1978.

*Carroll, Berenice A. *Design for Total War: Arms and Economics in the Third Reich.* The Hague, 1968.

Dubiel, Helmut, and A. Söllner, eds. *Wirtschaft, Recht und Staat im Nationalsozialismus: Analysen des Instituts für Sozialforschung 1939–1942.* Frankfurt, 1981.

Eichholtz, Dietrich. *Geschichte der deutschen Kriegswirt-schaft 1939–1945.* Berlin, 1969.

Forstmeier, Friedrich, and Hans-Erich Volkmann, eds. *Kriegswirtschaft und Rüstung 1939 bis 1945.* Düsseldorf, 1977.

Forstmeier, Friedrich, and Hans-Erich Volkmann, eds. *Wirtschaft und Rüstung am Vorabend des Zweiten Welt-krieges.* Düsseldorf, 1975.

Geyer, Michael. *Aufrüstung oder Sicherheit: Die Reichswehr in der Krise der Machtpolitik 1924–1936.* Wiesbaden, 1980.

Geyer, Michael. *Deutsche Rüstungspolitik 1890–1980.* Frankfurt, 1981.

Hentschel, Volker. *Deutsche Wirtschafts- und Sozialpolitik 1815 bis 1945.* Königstein, 1980.

Herbst, Ludolf. *Der totale Krieg und die Ordnung der Wirtschaft.* Stuttgart, 1982.

*Overy, Richard J. *The Nazi Economic Recovery, 1932–1938.* London, 1982.

Petzina, Dieter. *Autarkiepolitik im Dritten Reich: Der natio-nalsozialistische Vierjahresplan.* Stuttgart, 1968.

Sator, Klaus. *Grosskapital im Faschismus: Dargestellt am Beispiel der IG-Farben.* Frankfurt, 1978.

*Schweitzer, Arthur. *Big Business in the Third Reich.* Bloomington, 1964.

Speer, Albert. *Infiltration.* New York, 1981.

Thomas, G. *Geschichte der deutschen Wehr- und Rüstungs-wirtschaft 1918–1943/45.* Boppard am Rhein, 1966.

Volkmann, Hans-Erich. *1933–1939.* Vol. 1 of *Wirtschaft im Dritten Reich: Eine Bibliographie.* Munich, 1980.

*Zilbert, E. R. *Albert Speer and the Nazi Ministry of Arms: Economic Institutions and Industrial Production in the German War Economy.* Rutherford, N.J., 1981.

Zumpe, Lotte. *Wirtschaft und Staat in Deutschland 1933–1945.* Vaduz, Lichtenstein, 1980.

See also under Concentration Camps; Labor Policy; Pris-oners of War; Second World War; Technology and Science; Weimar Republic.

Education and Schools

Arbeitsgruppe Pädagogisches Museum. *Heil Hitler, Herr Lehrer: Volksschule 1933–45.* Reinbek, 1983.

*Blackburn, Gilmer W. *Education in the Third Reich: A Study of Race and History in Nazi Textbooks.* Albany, N.Y., 1985.

Dithmar, R., and J. Willer, eds. *Schule zwischen Kaiserreich und Faschismus.* Darmstadt, 1981.

Eilers, Rolf. *Die nationalsozialistische Schulpolitik.* Cologne, 1963.

Feiten, Willi. *Der Nationalsozialistische Lehrerbund.* Wein-heim, 1981.

Flessau, Kurt-Ingo. *Schule der Diktatur: Lehrpläne und Schulbücher des Nationalsozialismus.* Munich, 1977.

Genschel, Helmut. *Politische Erziehung durch Geschichts-unterricht.* Frankfurt, 1980.

Heinemann, Manfred, ed. *Erziehung und Schulung im Drit-ten Reich.* 2 vols. Stuttgart, 1980.

Lingelbach, Karl. *Erziehung und Erziehungstheorien im nationalsozialistischen Deutschland.* Kronberg, 1970.

*Mann, Erika. *School for Barbarians.* Introduction by Thomas Mann. New York, 1938.

Nyssen, Elke. *Schule im Nationalsozialismus.* Heidelberg, 1979.

Ottweiler, O. *Die Volksschule im Nationalsozialismus.* Wein-heim, 1979.

Platner, Geert, ed. *Schule im Dritten Reich—Erziehung zum Tod?* Munich, 1983.

*Samuel, R. H., and R. Hinton Thomas. *Education and Society in Modern Germany.* Westport, Conn., 1971.

Scholtz, Harald. *NS-Ausleseschulen.* Göttingen, 1973.

Steinhaus, H. *Hitlers pädagogische Maximen: "Mein Kampf" und die Destruktion der Erziehung im Nationalsozialismus.* Frankfurt, 1981.

See also under Culture; Hitler Youth; Ideology; Universities; Women and Girls.

Emigration and Exile

*Berghahn, Marion. *German-Jewish Refugees in England: The Ambiguities of Assimilation.* London, 1984.

*Boyers, Robert, ed. *The Legacy of the German Refugee Intellectuals.* New York, 1972.

Fabian, Ruth, and Corinna Coulmas. *Die deutsche Emigration in Frankreich nach 1933.* Munich, 1978.

Frühwald, W., and Wolfgang Schieder, eds. *Leben im Exil: Probleme der Integration deutscher Flüchtlinge im Ausland 1933–1945.* Hamburg, 1981.

Hardt, H., E. Hilscher, and Winfried B. Lerg, eds. *Presse im Exil.* Munich, 1979.

Hilchenbach, Maria. *Kino im Exil.* Munich, 1982.

*Hirschfeld, Gerhard, ed. *Exile in Great Britain: Refugees from Hitler's Germany.* Atlantic Highlands, N.J., 1984.

Kantorowicz, Alfred. *Politik und Literatur im Exil.* Hamburg, 1978.

Kettenacker, Lothar, ed. *Das "Andere Deutschland" im Zweiten Weltkrieg: Emigration und Widerstand in internationaler Perspektive.* Stuttgart, 1977.

*Koepke, Wulf, and Michael Winkler. *Exilliteratur 1933–1945.* Darmstadt, 1989.

*Krispyn, Egbert. *Anti-Nazi Writers in Exile.* Athens, Ga., 1978.

Kunst und Literatur im antifaschistischen Exil 1933–1945. 7 vols. Frankfurt, 1979–1981.

Lacina, Evelyn. *Emigration 1933–1945.* Stuttgart, 1982.

*Lixl-Purcell, Andreas, ed. *Women of Exile: German-Jewish Autobiographies since 1933.* Westport, Conn., 1988.

Stephan, Alexander. *Die deutsche Exilliteratur 1933–1945.* Munich, 1979.

Winkler, Michael, ed. *Deutsche Literatur im Exil.* Stuttgart, 1977.

See also under Opposition.

Expulsion and Population Transfers

Ahrens, Wilfred, ed. *Verbrechen an Deutschen: Dokumente der Vertreibung.* 2nd ed. Arget, 1989.

Arndt, W. *Ostpreussen, Westpreussen, Pommern, Schlesien, Sudetenland 1944/45: Die Bild-Dokumentation der Flucht und Vertreibung aus den deutschen Ostgebieten.* Friedberg, 1981.

Böddeker, Gunter. *Die Flüchtlinge der Deutschen—Die Vertreibung im Osten.* Frankfurt, 1985.

*De Zayas, Alfred M. *Nemesis at Potsdam: The Anglo-Americans and the Expulsion of the Germans.* 3rd rev. ed. Lincoln, Nebr., 1989.

De Zayas, Alfred M. *Zeugnisse der Vertreibung.* Krefeld, 1983.

Hupka, Herbert, ed. *Letzte Tage in Schlesien.* Munich, 1982.

*Marrus, Michael. *The Unwanted: European Refugees in the Twentieth Century.* New York, 1985.

Mühlfenzl, Rudolf, ed. *Geflohen und vertrieben: Augenzeugen berichten.* Königstein, 1981.

See also under Czechoslovakia; Occupation Policy; Poland; Second World War.

Fascism

Abendroth, Wolfgang, ed. *Faschismus und Kapitalismus.* Frankfurt, 1967.

Bataille, Georges. *Die psychologische Struktur des Faschismus.* Munich, 1978.

Brüdigam, Heinz, ed. *Faschismus an der Macht.* Frankfurt, 1982.

*Carsten, Francis L. *The Rise of Fascism.* 2nd ed. Berkeley, 1980.

Felice, Renzo de. *Interpretations of Fascism.* Cambridge, Mass., 1977.

*Gregor, A. James. *The Ideology of Fascism: The Rationale of Totalitarianism.* New York, 1969.

*Laqueur, Walter. *Fascism: A Reader's Guide.* Berkeley, 1976.

Mann, Reinhard, ed. *Die Nationalsozialisten: Analysen faschistischen Bewegungen.* Stuttgart, 1980.

Neulen, Hans W. *Eurofaschismus und der Zweite Weltkrieg.* Munich, 1980.

Nolte, Ernst. *Marxismus, Faschismus, Kalter Krieg.* Stuttgart, 1977.

Nolte, Ernst. *Three Faces of Fascism: Action Française, Italian Fascism, National Socialism.* New York, 1965.

*Payne, Stanley G. *Fascism: Comparison and Definition.* Madison, Wis., 1980.

*Poulantzus, Nicos. *Fascism and Dictatorship: The Third International and the Problem of Fascism.* Atlantic Highlands, N.J., 1974.

*Reich, Wilhelm. *The Mass Psychology of Fascism.* New York, 1970.

Saggan, W. *Faschismustheorien und antifaschistische Strategien in der SPD.* Cologne, 1981.

Schieder, Wolfgang, ed. *Faschismus als soziale Bewegung: Deutschland und Italien im Vergleich.* Hamburg, 1976.

*Weber, Eugen. *Varieties of Fascism: Doctrines of Revolution in the Twentieth Century.* Princeton, 1964.

Wippermann, Wolfgang. *Europäischer Faschismus im Vergleich 1922–1982.* Frankfurt, 1983.

*Wippermann, Wolfgang. *Faschismustheorien: Zum Stand der gegenwärtigen Situation.* 5th rev. ed. Darmstadt, 1989.

Wippermann, Wolfgang. *Zur Analyse des Faschismus: Die sozialistischen und kommunistischen Faschismustheorien 1921–1945.* Frankfurt, 1981.

Foreign Policy

General

Bollmus, Reinhard. *Das Amt Rosenberg und seine Gegner.* Stuttgart, 1970.

Browning, Christopher. *The Final Solution and the German Foreign Office: A Study of Referat DIII of Abteilung Deutschland, 1940–43.* New York, 1978.

*Carr, William. *Arms, Autarky and Aggression: A Study in German Foreign Policy.* New York, 1972.

*Craig, Gordon A., and Felix Gilbert, eds. *The 1930s.* Vol. 2 of *The Diplomats.* New York, 1953.

Documents on German Foreign Policy, 1918–1945: From the Archives of the German Foreign Ministry. Series C: *1933–1937.* Series D: *1937–1941.* Washington, D.C., 1949–.

Forndran, Erhard, G. Golczewski, and D. Riesenberger, eds. *Innen- und Aussenpolitik unter nationalsozialer Bedrohung.* Opladen, 1977.

Funke, Manfred, ed. *Hitler, Deutschland und die Mächte: Materialien zur Aussenpolitik des Dritten Reiches.* Düsseldorf, 1976.

Hildebrand, Klaus. *The Foreign Policy of the Third Reich.* Berkeley, 1973.

Hillgruber, Andreas, ed. *Staatsmänner und Diplomaten bei Hitler.* Frankfurt, 1967.

Jacobsen, Hans-Adolf. *Die nationalsozialistische Aussenpolitik 1933–1938.* Frankfurt, 1968.

*Kimmich, Christoph. *Germany and the League of Nations.* Chicago, 1976.

Michalka, Wolfgang, ed. *Nationalsozialistische Aussenpolitik.* Darmstadt, 1978.

*Weinberg, Gerhard L. *The Foreign Policy of Hitler's Germany: Diplomatic Revolution in Europe, 1933–36.* Chicago, 1970.

See also under Austria; Second World War.

Appeasement: The West and Hitler

*Cowling, Maurice. *The Impact of Hitler.* Cambridge, 1976.

*Eubank, Keith. *Munich.* Norman, Okla., 1963.

Gilbert, Martin, and Richard Gott. *The Appeasers.* London, 1963.

Hauser, Oswald. *England und das Dritte Reich.* 2 vols. Göttingen, 1982.

Hildebrand, Klaus, and K. F. Werner, eds. *Deutschland und Frankreich. 1936–1939.* Munich, 1981.

MacDonald, C. A. *The United States, Britain and Appeasement, 1936–1939.* London, 1981.

*Middleman, Robert K. *The Strategy of Appeasement: The British Government and Germany, 1937–39.* Chicago, 1972.

*Mommsen, Wolfgang J., and Lothar Kettenacker, eds. *The Fascist Challenge and the Politics of Appeasement.* Boston, 1983.

*Murray, Williamson. *The Change in the European Balance of Power, 1938–1939: The Path to Ruin.* Princeton, 1984.

Rock, W. R. *British Appeasement in the 1930s.* London, 1977.

Rohe, K., ed. *Die Westmächte und das Dritte Reich 1933–1939.* Paderborn, 1982.

Schmidt, Gustav. *England in der Krise: Grundzüge und Grundlagen der britischen Appeasement-Politik 1930–1937.* Opladen, 1981.

Wehner, Gerd. *Grossbritanien und Polen 1938–1939.* Frankfurt, 1983.

See also under Czechoslovakia; France; Poland; Second World War.

Balkan Peninsula and Southeastern Europe

Hoppe, H. J. *Bulgarien—Hitlers eigenwilliger Verbündeter.* Stuttgart, 1979.

*Littlefield, Frank C. *Germany and Yugoslavia, 1933–1941: The German Conquest of Yugoslavia.* Boulder, 1988.

*Miller, Marshall L. *Bulgaria during the Second World War.* Stanford, 1975.

Hungary

*Fenyo, Mario D. *Hitler, Horthy, and Hungary: German-Hungarian Relations, 1941–1944.* New Haven, 1972.

See also under Fascism; Second World War.

Italy

*Deakin, Frederick W. *The Brutal Friendship: Mussolini, Hitler and the Fall of Italian Fascism.* New York, 1962.

Petersen, J. *Hitler-Mussolini: Die Entstehung der Achse Berlin-Rom 1933–1936.* Tübingen, 1973.

Plehwe, Friedrich-Karl von. *The End of an Alliance: Rome's Defection from the Axis in 1943.* New York, 1971.

Steurer, Leopold. *Südtirol zwischen Rom und Berlin 1919–1939.* Munich, 1980.

*Toscano, Mario. *The Origins of the Pact of Steel.* Baltimore, 1967.

*Wiskemann, Elizabeth. *The Rome-Berlin Axis.* London, 1966.

See also under Fascism; Italy; Second World War.

Poland

Broszat, Martin. *Nationalsozialistische Polenpolitik.* Frankfurt, 1965.

*Kimmich, Christoph M. *The Free City: Danzig and German Foreign Policy, 1925–1939.* New Haven, 1968.

See also under Foreign Policy: Appeasement; Poland.

Rhineland Occupation

Emmerson, J. T. *The Rhineland Crisis, 7 March 1936.* London, 1977.

Reimer, Klaus. *Rheinlandfrage und Rheinlandbewegung 1918–1933.* Frankfurt, 1979.

Saar Territory

Jacoby, Fritz. *Die nationalsozialistische Herrschaftsübernahme an der Saar.* Saarbrücken, 1973.

Schock, Ralph, ed. *Haltet die Saar, Genossen! Antifaschistische Schriftsteller im Abstimmungskampf 1935.* East Berlin, 1984.

Zenner, Maria. *Parteien und Politik im Saargebiet unter dem Völkerbundsregime 1920–1935.* Saarbrücken, 1966.

Zur Mühlen, Patrik von. *"Schlagt Hitler an der Saar": Abstimmungskampf, Emigration und Widerstand im Saargebiet 1933–1935.* Bonn, 1979.

See also under Foreign Policy: Appeasement; France.

Soviet Union

Allard, S. *Stalin und Hitler: Die sowjetrussische Aussenpolitik.* Munich, 1974.

Fabry, Philipp W. *Der Hitler-Stalin-Pakt 1939–1941: Ein Beitrag zur Methode sowjetischer Aussenpolitik.* Darmstadt, 1962.

Fleischhauer, J. *Das Dritte Reich und die Deutschen in der Sowjetunion.* Stuttgart, 1983.

Hillgruber, Andreas. *Sowjetische Aussenpolitik im Zweiten Weltkrieg.* Königstein, 1979.

Hillgruber, Andreas, and Karl Hildebrand. *Kalkül zwischen Macht und Ideologie—Der Hitler-Stalin-Pakt: Parallelen bis heute?* Osnabrück, 1980.

Kennan, George. *Soviet Foreign Policy, 1917–1941.* New York, 1960.

*Laqueur, Walter. *Russia and Germany: A Century of Conflict.* London, 1965.

*Leonhard, Wolfgang. *Betrayal: The Hitler-Stalin Pact of 1939.* New York, 1989.

*Read, Anthony, and David Fisher. *The Deadly Embrace: Hitler, Stalin, and the Nazi-Soviet Pact, 1939–1941.* New York, 1988.

*Roberts, Geoffrey. *The Unholy Alliance: Stalin's Pact with Hitler.* Bloomington, 1990.

Spain

*Borkenau, Franz. *The Spanish Cockpit: An Eye-Witness Account of the Political and Social Conflicts of the Spanish Civil War.* Ann Arbor, 1963.

Dahms, Hellmuth. *Der spanische Bürgerkrieg 1936–1939.* Tübingen, 1962.

Degen, H.-J., and H. Ahrens, eds. *"Wir sind es leid, die Ketten zu tragen . . .": Antifaschisten im Spanischen Bürgerkrieg.* Berlin, 1979.

*Harper, Glenn T. *German Economic Policy in Spain during the Spanish Civil War, 1936–1939.* The Hague, 1967.

*Proctor, Raymond L. *Hitler's Luftwaffe in the Spanish Civil War.* Westport, Conn., 1983.

*Puzzo, Dante A. *Spain and the Great Powers, 1936–1941.* New York, 1962.

Ruhl, K.-J. *Der politische Konflikt.* Vol. 1 of *Der Spanische Bürgerkrieg.* Munich, 1982.

*Southworth, Hubert R. *Guernica! Guernica! A Study of Journalism, Diplomacy, Propaganda, and History.* Berkeley, 1977.

*Thomas, Hugh. *The Spanish Civil War.* Rev. ed. New York, 1977.

See also under Fascism.

United States

*Compton, James. *The Swastika and the Eagle: Hitler, the United States, and the Origins of the Second World War.* London, 1968.

Economides, S. *Der Nationalsozialismus und die deutschsprachige Presse in New York, 1933–1941.* Frankfurt, 1982.

Friedländer, Saul. *Prelude to Downfall: Hitler and the United States, 1939–41.* New York, 1967.

*Gatzke, Hans. *Germany and the United States.* Cambridge, Mass., 1980.

*Herzstein, Robert E. *Roosevelt & Hitler: Prelude to War.* New York, 1990.

*Jonas, M. *The United States and Germany: A Diplomatic History.* Ithaca, N.Y., 1980.

Knapp, M., et al. *Die USA und Deutschland 1918–1975.* Munich, 1978.

France

Benoist-Méchin, Jacques. *Sixty Days That Shook the West: The Fall of France, 1940.* New York, 1963.

*Bower, Tom. *Klaus Barbie: The "Butcher of Lyons."* New York, 1984.

*Cobb, Richard. *French and Germans: A Personal Interpretation of France under Two Occupations, 1914–1918/ 1940–1944.* Hanover, N.H., 1983.

*Dank, Milton. *The French against the French: Collaboration and Resistance.* Philadelphia, 1974.

*Gordon, Bertram. *Collaborationism in France during the Second World War.* Ithaca, N.Y., 1980.

*Heller, Gerhard. *NS-Kulturpolitik in Frankreich.* Cologne, 1982.

Heller, Gerhard, and J. Grand. *In einem besetzten Land: Zensur in Frankreich 1940–1944.* Cologne, 1979.

*Kedward, Harry. *Resistance in Vichy France: A Study of Ideas and Motivation in the Southern Zone.* Oxford, 1978.

Klarsfeld, Serge, ed. *Die Endlösung der Judenfrage in Frankreich.* Paris, 1977.

*Marrus, Michael R., and Robert O. Paxton. *Vichy France and the Jews.* New York, 1981.

*Milward, Alan S. *The New Order and the French Economy.* Oxford, 1970.

*Paxton, Robert O. *Vichy France: Old Guard and New Order, 1940–1944.* New York, 1972.

Sartre, Jean-Paul. *Paris unter der Besatzung: Artikel, Reportagen, Aufsätze, 1944–1945.* Reinbek bei Hamburg, 1980.

*Schoenbrun, David. *Soldiers of the Night: The Story of the French Resistance.* New York, 1980.

See also under Concentration Camps; Fascism; Foreign Policy; Occupation Policy; Prisoners of War.

Government and Bureaucracy

Broszat, Martin. *The Hitler State: The Foundation and Development of the Internal Structure of the Third Reich.* New York, 1981.

*Caplan, Jane. *Government without Administration: State and Civil Service in Weimar and Nazi Germany.* Oxford, 1988.

*Fraenkel, Ernst. *The Dual State: A Contribution to the Theory of Dictatorship.* New York, 1969 [1941].

*Franz-Willing, Georg. *Die Reichskanzlei, 1933–1945: Rolle und Bedeutung unter der Regierung Hitler.* Tübingen, 1984.

*Mommsen, Hans. *Beamtentum im Dritten Reich.* Stuttgart, 1966.

Neumann, Franz. *Behemoth: The Structure and Practice of National Socialism, 1933–1944.* 2nd ed. New York, 1966 [1944].

*Peterson, Edward N. *The Limits of Hitler's Power.* Princeton, 1969.

*Stachura, Peter, ed. *The Shaping of the Nazi State.* London, 1978.

See also under Biography: Bormann *and* Hitler; Foreign Policy; Jews; Justice; NSDAP; Police; SS.

Gypsies (Sinta and Roma)

Hohmann, Joachim S. *Geschichte der Zigeunerverfolgung in Deutschland.* Frankfurt, 1981.

Hohmann, Joachim S. *Zigeuner und Zigeunerwissenschaft: Ein Beitrag zur Grundlagenforschung und Dokumenta-*

tion des Völkermords im "Dritten Reich." Marburg, 1980.

*Kendrick, Donald, and Gratton Puxon. *The Destiny of Europe's Gypsies.* New York, 1972.

Kendrick, D., G. Puxon, and T. Zülch. *Die Zigeuner: Verkannt, verachtet, verfolgt.* Hannover, 1980.

Soest, G. von. *Zigeuner zwischen Verfolgung und Integration.* Weinheim, 1979.

Völklein, U. *Zigeuner: Das verachtete Volk.* Oldenburg, 1981.

Vossen, R. *Zigeuner—Roma, Sinti, Gitanos, Gypsies: Zwischen Verfolgung und Romantisierung.* Frankfurt, 1983.

See also under Concentration Camps; Medicine and Biology; Repression.

Hitler Youth

Blohm, Erich. *Hitler-Jugend: Soziale Tatgemeinschaft.* 2nd ed. Vlotho, 1979.

Boberach, Heinz. *Jugend unter Hitler.* Düsseldorf, 1982.

Brandenburg, Hans-Christian. *Die Geschichte der HJ: Wege und Irrwege einer Generation.* Cologne, 1968.

Burger, Horst. *Warum warst du in der Hitler-Jugend? Vier Fragen an meinen Vater.* Reinbek bei Hamburg, 1978.

Giesecke, Hermann. *Vom Wandervogel bis zur Hitlerjugend.* Munich, 1981.

Huber, Karl H. *Jugend unterm Hakenkreuz.* Frankfurt, 1982.

*Laqueur, Walter Z. *Young Germany: A History of the German Youth Movement.* New York, 1962.

Klönne, Arno. *Jugend im Dritten Reich.* Cologne, 1982.

Klose, Werner. *Generation im Gleichschritt: Ein Dokumentarbericht.* Oldenburg, 1964.

*Koch, Hansjoachim. *The Hitler Youth: Origins and Development, 1922–45.* New York, 1965.

*Rempel, Gerhard. *Hitler's Children: The Hitler Youth and the SS.* Chapel Hill, 1989.

*Stachura, Peter. *Nazi Youth in the Weimar Republic.* Santa Barbara, Calif., 1975.

Ideology

Precursors

Bergmann, K. *Agrarromantik und Grossstadtfeindschaft.* Meisenheim, 1970.

*Eley, Geoff. *Reshaping the German Right: Radical Nationalism and Political Change after Bismarck.* New Haven, 1980.

*Field, Geoffrey. *Evangelist of Race: The Germanic Vision of Houston Stewart Chamberlain.* New York, 1981.

*Gasman, Daniel. *The Scientific Origins of National Socialism: Social Darwinism in Ernst Haeckel and the German Monist League.* New York, 1971.

Glaser, Hermann. *The Cultural Roots of National Socialism.* Austin, 1978.

Haack, Friedrich W. *Wotans Wiederkehr: Blut-, Boden- und Rasse-Religion.* Munich, 1981.

*Klemperer, Klemens von. *Germany's New Conservatism: Its History and Dilemma in the Twentieth Century.* Princeton, 1956.

*Meyer, Henry Cord. *Mitteleuropa in German Thought and Action, 1815–1945.* The Hague, 1955.

*Mosse, George L. *The Crisis of German Ideology: Intellectual Origins of the Third Reich.* New York, 1964.

*Mosse, George L. *Fallen Soldiers: Reshaping the Memory of the World Wars.* New York, 1990.

*Mosse, George L. *Masses and Man: Nationalist and Fascist Perceptions of Reality.* New York, 1980.

*Mosse, George L. *The Nationalization of the Masses: Political Symbolism and Mass Movements in Germany from the Napoleonic Wars through the Third Reich.* New York, 1975.

*Mosse, George L. *Toward the Final Solution: A History of European Racism.* New York, 1978.

See, Klaus von. *Deutsche Germanen-Ideologie vom Humanismus bis zur Gegenwart.* Frankfurt, 1970.

Stern, Fritz. *The Politics of Cultural Despair: A Study in the Rise of the Germanic Ideology.* Berkeley, 1961.

*Theweleit, Klaus. *Male Phantasies.* 2 vols. Minneapolis, 1987–.

*Vondung, Klaus. *Die Apokalypse in Deutschland.* Munich, 1988.

National Socialist Ideology

*Baird, Jay W. *To Die for Germany: Heroes in the Nazi Pantheon.* Bloomington, 1990.

Breitling, R. *Die nationalsozialistische Rassenlehre.* Meisenheim, 1971.

*Cecil, Robert. *The Myth of the Master Race: Alfred Rosenberg and Nazi Ideology.* New York, 1972.

Daucet, F. W. *Im Banne des Mythos: Die Psychologie des Dritten Reiches.* Esslingen, 1979.

Gamm, Hans Jochen. *Der braune Kult: Das Dritte Reich und seine Ersatzreligion.* Hamburg, 1962.

Heer, Friedrich. *Der Glaube des Adolf Hitler: Anatomie einer politische Religiosität.* Munich, 1968.

Hitler, Adolf. *Mein Kampf.* Translated by Ralph Manheim. Boston, 1943.

Jäckel, Eberhard. *Hitler's Weltanschauung: A Blueprint for Power.* Middletown, Conn., 1972.

Maser, Werner. *Hitlers "Mein Kampf."* Munich, 1966.

Poliakov, Léon. *The Aryan Myth: A History of Racist and Nationalist Ideas in Europe.* New York, 1974.

*Sklar, Dusty. *Gods and Beasts: The Nazis and the Occult.* New York, 1977.

*Smith, Woodruff. *The Ideological Origins of Nazi Imperialism.* New York, 1986.

*Staudinger, Hans. *The Inner Nazi: A Critical Analysis of Mein Kampf.* Baton Rouge, La., 1981.

Tautz, J. *Der Eingriff des Widersachers: Fragen zum Okkultenaspekt des Nationalsozialismus.* Freiburg, 1980.

Thöne, A. W. *Das Licht der Arier. Licht-, Feuer- und Dunkelsymbolik des Nationalsozialismus.* Munich, 1979.

Vondung, Klaus. *Magie und Manipulation: Ideologischer Kult und politische Religion des Nationalsozialismus.* Göttingen, 1971.

Zentner, Christian, ed. *Adolf Hitlers "Mein Kampf": Eine kommentierte Auswahl.* Munich, 1974.

See also under Biography: Hitler; Culture; Language; Medicine and Biology.

Italy

*De Grazia, Victoria. *The Culture of Consent: Mass Organization of Leisure in Fascist Italy.* New York, 1981.

Domarus, Max. *Mussolini und Hitler.* Würzburg, 1977.

*Finer, Herman. *Mussolini's Italy.* Hamden, Conn., 1964.

*Gallo, Max. *Mussolini's Italy: Twenty Years of the Fascist Era.* New York, 1973.

Der italienische Faschismus: Probleme und Forschungstendenzen. Munich, 1983.

*Koon, Tracy H. *Believe, Obey, Fight: Political Socialization of Youth in Fascist Italy, 1922–1943.* Chapel Hill, 1985.

Kuby, Erich. *Verrat auf deutsch: Wie das Dritte Reich Italien ruinierte.* Hamburg, 1982.

*Leeds, Christopher. *Italy under Mussolini.* New York, 1972.

*Lyttle, Richard B. *Il Duce: The Rise and Fall of Benito Mussolini.* New York, 1987.

Mack Smith, Denis. *Mussolini.* New York, 1981.

Miccoli, Giovanni. *Kirche und Faschismus in Italien.* Wiesbaden, 1977.

Mussolini, Rachele. *Mussolini: An Intimate Biography.* New York, 1974.

*Webster, Richard. *The Cross and the Fasces: Christian Democracy and Fascism in Italy.* Stanford, 1960.

*Wiskemann, Elizabeth. *Fascism in Italy: Its Development and Influence.* New York, 1970.

*Zuccotti, Susan. *The Italians and the Holocaust: Persecution, Rescue, and Survival.* New York, 1987.

See also under Fascism; Foreign Policy; Second World War.

Japan

*Barnhart, Michael J. *Japan Prepares for Total War: The Search for Economic Security, 1919–1941.* New York, 1987.

*Crowley, James B. *Japan's Quest for Autonomy: National Security and Foreign Policy, 1930–1938.* Princeton, 1966.

*Dower, John W. *War without Mercy: Race and Power in the Pacific War.* New York, 1986.

Ienaga, Saburō. *The Pacific War: World War II and the Japanese, 1931–1945.* New York, 1978.

Nish, Ian. *Japanese Foreign Policy, 1869–1942.* London, 1977.

Shillony, Ben-Ami. *Politics and Culture in Wartime Japan.* Oxford, 1981.

See also under Foreign Policy; Second World War.

Jews in Germany and Europe

Adam, Uwe D. *Judenpolitik im Dritten Reich.* Düsseldorf, 1972.

Adler, H. G. *Der Kampf gegen die "Endlösung der Judenfrage."* Bonn, 1958.

*Barkai, Avraham. *From Boycott to Annihilation: The Economic Struggle of German Jews, 1933–43.* Hanover, N.H., and London, 1989.

Billig, Joseph. *Die Endlösung der Judenfrage.* Frankfurt, 1979.

*Browning, Christopher. *Fateful Months: Essays on the Emergence of the Final Solution.* New York, 1985.

Dawidowicz, Lucy S. *The War against the Jews.* Rev. ed. New York, 1986.

Deutschkron, Inge. *Outcast: A Jewish Girl in Wartime Berlin.* New York, 1989.

Eschwege, Helmut, ed. *Kennzeichen J.: Bilder, Dokumente, Berichte zur Geschichte der Verbrechen des Hitlerfaschis-*

mus an den deutschen Juden 1933–1945. Frankfurt, 1979.

*Fleming, Gerald. *Hitler and the Final Solution.* Berkeley, 1984.

Fruchtmann, Karl. *Zeugen: Aussagen zum Mord an einem Volk.* Cologne, 1982.

Genschel, H. *Die Verdrängung der Juden aus der Wirtschaft im Dritten Reich.* Göttingen, 1966.

*Gilbert, Martin. *Atlas of the Holocaust.* London, 1982.

*Gilbert, Martin. *The Holocaust.* New York, 1985.

*Graml, Hermann. *Reichskristallnacht: Antisemitismus und Judenverfolgung im Dritten Reich.* Munich, 1988.

*Henry, Frances. *Victims and Neighbors: A Small Town in Nazi Germany Revisited.* South Hadley, Mass., 1984.

Hilberg, Raul. *The Destruction of the European Jews.* Rev. ed. 3 vols. New York, 1985.

*Kiret, Konrad, and Helmut Eschwege. *Selbstbehauptung und Widerstand: Deutsche Juden im Kampf um Existenz und Menschenwürde 1933–45.* Hamburg, 1984.

Lauber, H. *Judenpogrom: "Reichskristallnacht," November 1938 in Grossdeutschland.* Gerlingen, 1981.

Leo Baeck Institute Year Book. London, 1956–.

Lipscher, Ladislav. *Die Juden im Slowakischen Staat 1939–1945.* Munich, 1980.

*Marrus, Michael R. *The Holocaust in History.* Hanover, N.H., 1987.

*Mayer, Arno J. *Why Did the Heavens Not Darken? The "Final Solution" in History.* New York, 1988.

Metzger, Hartmut, ed. *Kristallnacht: Dokumente von Gestern.* Stuttgart, 1978.

*Mosse, George L. *Germans and Jews: The Right, the Left, and the Search for a "Third Force" in pre-Nazi Germany.* New York, 1970.

*Niewyk, Donald. *The Jews in Weimar Germany.* Baton Rouge, La., 1980.

*Paucker, Arnold, ed. *The Jews in Nazi Germany, 1933–43.* Tübingen, 1986.

*Pehle, Walter H., ed. *Der Judenpogrom 1938.* Frankfurt, 1988.

*Read, Anthony, and David Fisher. *Kristallnacht: The Nazi Night of Terror.* New York, 1989.

Reitlinger, Gerald. *The Final Solution: The Attempt to Exterminate the Jews of Europe, 1939–1945.* 2nd rev. ed. South Brunswick, N.J., 1981.

*Richarz, Monika, ed. *Jüdisches Leben in Deutschland: Selbstzeugnisse und Sozialgeschichte 1918–1945.* Stuttgart, 1982.

Rosenkranz, Herbert. *Verfolgung und Selbstbehauptung: Die Juden in Österreich 1938–1945.* Munich, 1978.

Rosenthal, L. *"Endlösung der Judenfrage"—Massenmord oder "Gaskammerlüge"?* Darmstadt, 1980.

Rosenthal, L. *Wie war es möglich? Zur Geschichte der Judenverfolgungen.* Darmstadt, 1981.

*Schleunes, Karl A. *The Twisted Road to Auschwitz: Nazi Policy toward German Jews, 1933–1939.* Urbana, Ill., 1970.

Schoenberner, Gerhard. *Der gelbe Stern: Die Judenverfolgungen in Europa 1933–1945.* Munich, 1978.

*Thalmann, Rita, and Emmanuel Feuermann. *Crystal Night.* New York, 1974.

*Walk, Joseph. *Jüdische Schule und Erziehung im Dritten Reich.* Frankfurt, 1989.

Walk, Joseph. *Das Sonderrecht für die Juden im NS-Staat.* Heidelberg, 1981.

See also under Antisemitism; Concentration Camps; Government and Bureaucracy; Ideology; Occupation Policy; Repression; SS; Women and Girls.

Justice

Anderbrügge, Klaus. *Völkisches Rechtsdenken: Zur Rechtslehre in der Zeit des Nationalsozialismus.* Berlin, 1978.

Bendersky, Joseph W. *Carl Schmitt: Theorist for the Reich.* Princeton, 1983.

Boberach, Heinz. *Richterbriefe.* Boppard am Rhein, 1975.

Buchheit, Gert. *Richter in roter Robe.* Munich, 1968.

Echterhölter, R. *Das öffentliche Recht im nationalsozialistischen Staat.* Stuttgart, 1970.

*Engelmann, Bernt. *Die unsichtbare Tradition.* 2 vols. Cologne, 1988–1989.

Fieberg, Gerhard. *Justiz im nationalsozialistischen Deutschland.* Cologne, 1984.

Friedrich, J. *Freispruch für die Nazi-Justiz.* Reinbek bei Hamburg, 1983.

*Gruchmann, Lothar. *Justiz im Dritten Reich, 1933–1940: Anpassung und Unterwerfung in der Ära Gürtner.* Munich, 1988.

Güstrow, D. *Tödlicher Alltag: Strafverteidiger im Dritten Reich.* Berlin, 1981.

Hillermeier, H., ed. *"Im Namen des deutschen Volkes": Todesurteile des Volksgerichtshofs.* Darmstadt, 1980.

Hirsch, M., et al., eds. *Recht, Verwaltung und Justiz im Nationalsozialismus.* Cologne, 1984.

Institut für Zeitgeschichte. *NS-Recht in historischer Perspektive.* Munich, 1981.

Johe, Werner. *Die gleichgeschaltete Justiz.* Hamburg, 1983.

Kaul, F. K. *1937–1945.* Vol. 4 of *Geschichte des Reichsgerichts.* Glashütten im Taunus, 1971.

*Koch, Hansjoachim W. *In the Name of the Volk: Political Justice in Hitler's Germany.* London, 1989.

Münch, J. V., and U. Brodersen, eds. *Gesetze des NS-Staates.* Paderborn, 1982.

Redaktion Kritische Justiz. *Der Unrechts-Staat.* 2 vols. Baden-Baden, 1983.

Reifner, U., ed. *Das Recht des Unrechtsstaates.* New York, 1981.

Reiter, E. *Franz Gürtner: Politische Biographie eines deutschen Juristen 1881–1941.* Berlin, 1976.

Robinsohn, H. *Justiz als politische Verfolgung.* Stuttgart, 1977.

Rottleuthner, H., ed. *Recht, Rechtsphilosophie und Nationalsozialismus.* Wiesbaden, 1983.

Schweling, Otto Peter, and Erich Schwinge. *Die deutsche Militärjustiz in der Zeit des Nationalsozialismus.* Marburg, 1978.

Staff, Inge. *Justiz im Dritten Reich: Eine Dokumentation.* Frankfurt, 1978.

*Stolleis, Michael, and Dieter Simon, eds. *Rechtsgeschichte im Nationalsozialismus.* Tübingen, 1989.

Wagner, W. *Der Volksgerichtshof im nationalsozialistischen Staat.* Stuttgart, 1974.

See also under Government and Bureaucracy; Jews; Police; Repression.

Labor Policy

Buchholz, W. *Die Nationalsozialistische Gemeinschaft "Kraft durch Freude."* Munich, 1976.

*Honze, Edward L. *Foreign Labor in Nazi Germany.* Princeton, 1967.

*Kele, Max H. *Nazis and Workers: National Socialist Appeals to German Labor, 1919–1933.* Chapel Hill, 1972.

Kocka, Jürgen. *Die Angestellten in der deutschen Geschichte 1850–1980.* Göttingen, 1981.

Köhler, H. *Arbeitsdienst in Deutschland.* Berlin, 1967.

Lärmer, Karl. *Vom Arbeitszwang zur Zwangsarbeit.* Berlin, 1961.

*Smelser, Ronald M. *Robert Ley: Hitler's Labor Front Leader.* Leamington Spa, England, 1988.

Stelling, W., and W. Mallebrein. *Männer und Maiden: Leben und Wirken im Reichsarbeitsdienst in Wort und Bild.* Preussisch Oldendorf, 1979.

Stupperich, Amrei. *Volksgemeinschaft oder Arbeitersolidarität: Studien zur Arbeitnehmerpolitik in dem Deutschnationalen Volkspartei 1918–1933.* Göttingen, 1982.

See also under Concentration Camps; Economy.

Language of National Socialism

Ach, Manfred, and Clemens Pentrop. *Hitlers "Religion": Pseudoreligiöse Elemente im nationalsozialistischen Sprachgebrauch.* Munich, 1972.

Berning, Cornelia. *Die Sprache des Nationalsozialismus.* Berlin, 1961.

Berning, Cornelia. *Vom "Abstammungsnachweis" zum "Zuchtwart": Vokabular des Nationalsozialismus.* Berlin, 1964.

*Betz, Werner. "The National Socialist Vocabulary." In *The Third Reich,* edited by Maurice Beaumont, John H. E. Fried, and Edmond Vermeil. New York, 1955.

*Childers, Thomas. "The Social Language of Politics in Germany." *American Historical Review* 95 (April 1990): 331–358.

Ehlich, Konrad, ed. *Sprache im Faschismus.* Frankfurt, 1989.

Faye, Jean-Pierre. *Totalitäre Sprachen.* Frankfurt, 1977.

Seidel, E., and J. Seidel-Slotty. *Sprachwandel im Dritten Reich.* Halle, 1961.

Winckler, Lütz. *Studie zur gesellschaftlichen Funktion faschistischer Sprache.* Frankfurt, 1970.

See also under Culture; Ideology.

Medicine and Biology

Baader, Gerhard, and U. Schultz, eds. *Medizin im Nationalsozialismus.* Berlin, 1980.

*Bock, Gisela. *Zwangssterilisation im Nationalsozialismus: Untersuchungen zur Rassenpolitik und Frauenpolitik.* Berlin, 1985.

*Cocks, Geoffrey. *Psychotheraphy in the Third Reich: The Göring Institute.* New York, 1985.

Dörner, Klaus, et al. *Der Krieg gegen die psychisch Kranken.* Rehburg-Loccum, 1980.

*Gallagher, Hugh Gregory. *By Trust Betrayed: Patients, Physicians, and the License to Kill in the Third Reich.* New York, 1990.

*Kater, Michael H. *Doctors under Hitler.* Chapel Hill, 1989.

Kaul, Friedrich K. *Die Psychiatrie im Strudel der "Eutha-nasie."* Frankfurt, 1979.

Klee, Ernst. *"Euthanasie" im NS-Staat: Die "Vernichtung lebensunwerten Lebens."* Frankfurt, 1985.

Klee, Ernst, ed. *Dokumente zur "Euthanasie" im NS-Staat.* Frankfurt, 1985.

Lifton, Robert J. *The Nazi Doctors: Medical Killing and the Psychology of Genocide.* New York, 1986.

Müller-Hill, Benno. *Murderous Science: Elimination by Sci-entific Selection of Jews, Gypsies, and Others—Germany, 1935–1945.* New York, 1988.

Nowak, Kurt. *"Euthanasie" und Sterilisation im "Dritten Reich": Die Konfrontation der evangelischen und katho-lischen Kirche mit . . . der "Euthanasie" Aktion.* 3rd ed. Göttingen, 1984.

Pommerin, Reiner. *"Sterilisierung der Rheinlandbastarde": Das Schicksal einer farbigen deutschen Minderheit 1918–1937.* Düsseldorf, 1979.

*Proctor, Robert. *Racial Hygiene: Medicine under the Nazis.* Cambridge, Mass., 1988.

Schwarberg, Günther. *The Murders at Bullenhuser Damm.* Bloomington, 1984.

*Seidler, Horst, and Andreas Rett. *Rassenhygiene: Ein Weg in den Nationalsozialismus.* Vienna, 1988.

Seidler, Horst, and Andreas Rett. *Das Reichssippenamt entscheidet: Rassenbiologie im Nationalsozialismus.* Vien-na, 1982.

Wuttke-Groneber, Walter, ed. *Medizin im Nationalsozialis-mus.* 2nd ed. Tübingen, 1982.

See also under Concentration Camps; Ideology; Universi-ties.

National Socialist German Workers' Party (NSDAP)

*Abel, Theodore. *Why Hitler Came into Power.* Cambridge, Mass., 1986 [1938].

*Childers, Thomas. *The Nazi Voter: The Social Foundations of Fascism in Germany, 1919–1933.* Chapel Hill, 1983.

*Childers, Thomas, ed. *The Formation of the Nazi Constitu-ency, 1919–1933.* London, 1986.

Franz-Willing, Georg. *Putsch und Verbotszeit der Hitlerbe-wegung.* Preussisch Oldendorf, 1977.

Gordon, Harold J., Jr. *Hitler and the Beer Hall Putsch.* Princeton, 1972.

*Grill, Johnpeter H. *The Nazi Movement in Baden, 1920–1945.* Chapel Hill, 1983.

*Hamilton, Richard F. *Who Voted for Hitler?* Princeton, 1982.

Horn, Wolfgang. *Führerideologie und Parteiorganisation in der NSDAP (1919–1933).* Düsseldorf, 1972.

*Kater, Michael H. *The Nazi Party: A Social Profile of Members and Leaders, 1919–1945.* Cambridge, Mass., 1983.

*Koshar, Rudy. *Social Life, Local Politics, and Nazism: Bourgeois Marburg, 1880–1935.* Chapel Hill, 1986.

Neebe, Reinhard. *Grossindustrie, Staat und NSDAP, 1930–1933.* Göttingen, 1981.

*Noakes, Jeremy. *The Nazi Party in Lower Saxony, 1921–1933.* London, 1971.

*Nyomarkay, Joseph. *Charisma and Factionalism in the Nazi Party.* Minneapolis, 1967.

*Orlow, Dietrich. *The History of the Nazi Party.* 2 vols. Pittsburgh, 1969–1973.

Pätzold, Kurt, and M. Weissbecker. *Geschichte der NSDAP 1920–1945.* Cologne, 1981.

*Paul, Gerhard. *Die NSDAP des Saargebietes, 1920–1935: Die verspätete Aufstieg der NSDAP in der katholischen-proletarischen Provinz.* Saarbrücken, 1987.

*Pridham, Geoffrey. *Hitler's Rise to Power: The Nazi Move-ment in Bavaria, 1923–1933.* New York, 1974.

Das Schriftgut der NSDAP, ihrer Gliederungen und ange-schlossenen Verbände. Düsseldorf, 1981.

See also under Biography: Hitler; Fascism; Repression; SA; Seizure of Power; Weimar Republic.

Neo-Nazism

*Ashkenazi, Abraham. *Modern German Nationalism.* New York, 1976.

Broder, Henryk M., et al. *Deutschland erwacht: Die neuen Nazis—Aktionen und Provokationen.* Bornheim-Merten, 1978.

Filmer, Werner, and Heribert Schwan. *Was von Hitler blieb: 50 Jahre nach der Machtergreifung.* Frankfurt, 1983.

Ginzel, Günther. *Hitlers (Ur)enkel—Neonazis: Ihre Ideolo-gien und Aktionen.* Düsseldorf, 1981.

Lersch, P., ed. *Die verkannte Gefahr: Rechtsradikalismus in der Bundesrepublik.* Reinbek bei Hamburg, 1981.

Plack, Arno. *Wie oft wird Hitler noch besiegt? Neonazismus und Vergangenheitsbewältigung.* Frankfurt, 1985.

Pomorin, Jürgen, and Reinhard Junge. *Die Neonazis und wie man sie bekämpfen kann.* Dortmund, 1978.

*Tetens, Tete H. *The New Germany and the Old Nazis.* New York, 1961.

Vinke, H. *Mit zweierlei Mass: Die deutsche Reaktion auf den Terror von rechts.* Reinbek bei Hamburg, 1981.

See also under Allied Occupation; Fascism.

Occupation and Population Policy

Dallin, Alexander. *German Rule in Russia, 1941–45: A Study of Occupation Policies.* London, 1957.

*De Jaeger, Charles. *The Linz Files: Hitler's Plunder of European Art.* Exeter, England, 1981.

Dress, H. *Slowakei und faschistische Neuordnung Europas 1939–1941.* Berlin, 1972.

Geiss, Immanuel, and Wolfgang Jacobmeyer, eds. *Deutsche Politik in Polen 1939–1945: Aus dem Diensttagebuch von Hans Frank, Generalgouverneur in Polen.* Opladen, 1980.

Grassmann, G. O. *Die deutsche Besatzungsgesetzgebung während des 2. Weltkrieges.* Tübingen, 1958.

*Hirschfeld, Gerhard. *Nazi Rule and Dutch Collaboration: The Netherlands under German Occupation, 1940–1945.* New York, 1988.

*Kamenetsky, Ihor. *Secret Nazi Plans for Eastern Europe: A Study in Lebensraum Policies.* New York, 1961.

Koehl, Robert L. *RKFDV—German Resettlement and Popu-lation Policy, 1939–1945: A History of the Reich Commis-sion for the Strengthening of Germandom.* Cambridge, Mass., 1957.

*Komjathy, Anthony, and Rebecca Stockwell. *German Mi-norities and the Third Reich: Ethnic Germans of East Central Europe between the Wars.* New York, 1980.

*Madajczyk, Czeslaw. *Die Okkupationspolitik Nazideutschlands in Polen 1939-1945.* Cologne, 1988.

Majer, Diemut. *"Fremdvölkische" im Dritten Reich.* Boppard am Rhein, 1981.

*Mastny, Vojtech. *The Czechs under Nazi Rule: The Failure of National Resistance, 1939-1943.* New York, 1971.

*Milward, Alan. *The Fascist Economy of Norway.* Oxford, 1978.

Müller, N., ed. *Okkupation, Raub, Vernichtung: Dokumente zur Besatzungspolitik der faschistischen Wehrmacht auf sowjetischem Territorium 1941 bis 1944.* East Berlin, 1980.

*Petrow, Richard. *The Bitter Years: The Invasion and Occupation of Denmark and Norway.* New York, 1974.

*Schulte, Theo S. *The German Army and Nazi Policies in Occupied Russia.* New York, 1989.

Thomsen, E. *Deutsche Besatzungspolitik in Dänemark 1940-1945.* Düsseldorf, 1971.

Umbreit, Hans. *Deutsche Militärverwaltungen 1938/39: Die militärische Besetzung der Tschechoslowakei und Polens.* Stuttgart, 1977.

*Warmbrunn, W. *The Dutch under German Occupation.* Stanford, 1963.

Zorn, N. *Nach Ostland geht unser Ritt.* Bonn, 1980.

See also under Concentration Camps; Czechoslovakia; Economy; Expulsion; Foreign Policy; France; Ideology; Poland; Police; Second World War; SS; Wehrmacht.

Opposition in Germany

*Balfour, Michael. *Withstanding Hitler in Germany, 1933-1945.* New York, 1988.

Beier, Gerhard. *Die illegale Reichsleitung der Gewerkschaften 1933-1945.* Cologne, 1981.

Berthold, Will. *Die 42 Attentate auf Adolf Hitler.* Munich, 1981.

Blank, A. S., and J. Mader. *Rote Kapelle gegen Hitler.* Berlin, 1979.

*Deutsch, Harold C. *The Conspiracy against Hitler in the Twilight War.* Minneapolis, 1968.

Duhnke, Horst. *Die KPD von 1933 bis 1945.* Cologne, 1972.

Elling, Hannah. *Frauen im deutschen Widerstand 1933-1945.* Frankfurt, 1981.

*Finker, Kurt. *Geschichte des Roten Frontkämpferbundes.* Frankfurt, 1981.

Finker, Kurt. *Stauffenberg und der 20. Juli 1944.* Cologne, 1985.

Fraenkel, Heinrich, and Roger Manvell. *Der 20. Juli.* Berlin, 1964.

*Graml, Hermann, et al. *The German Resistance to Hitler.* Berkeley, 1970.

*Grant Duff, Sheila. *A Noble Combat: The Letters of Sheila Grant Duff and Adam von Trott zu Solz, 1932-1939.* New York, 1988.

Hoffmann, Peter. *German Resistance to Hitler.* Cambridge, Mass., 1988.

Hoffmann, Peter. *The History of the German Resistance to Hitler, 1933-1945.* Cambridge, Mass., 1977.

*Höhne, Heinz. *Codeword—Direktor: The Story of the Red Orchestra.* New York, 1971.

Holmsten, Georg. *Deutschland Juli 1944.* Düsseldorf, 1982.

Jahnke, Karl-Heinz. *Entscheidungen: Jugend im Widerstand 1933-1945.* Frankfurt, 1976.

Kerschbaumer, Marie Th. *Der weibliche Name des Widerstandes.* Freiburg im Breisgau, 1980.

*Kershaw, Ian. *Popular Opinion and Political Dissent in the Third Reich: Bavaria, 1933-1945.* New York, 1983.

Kettenacker, Lothard, ed. *Das "Andere Deutschland" im Zweiten Weltkrieg: Emigration und Widerstand in internationaler Perspektive.* Stuttgart, 1977.

Klessmann, Christoph, and Falk Pingel, eds. *Gegner des Nationalsozialismus: Wissenschaftler und Widerstandskämpfer auf der Suche nach der historischen Wirklichkeit.* Frankfurt, 1980.

Leber, Annemarie. *Conscience in Revolt.* London, 1954.

Lill, Rudolf, ed. *20. Juli: Portrait des Widerstands.* Düsseldorf, 1984.

Löwenthal, Richard, and Patrik von zur Mühlen, eds. *Widerstand und Verweigerung in Deutschland 1933 bis 1945.* Berlin, 1982.

Markmann, Hans J. *Der deutsche Widerstand gegen den Nationalsozialismus 1933-1945: Modelle für den Unterricht.* Mainz, 1984.

Meienberg, Niklaus. *Es ist kalt in Brandenburg: Ein Hitler-Attentat.* Zurich, 1980.

Naumann, U. *Zwischen Tränen und Gelächter: Satirische Faschismuskritik 1933 bis 1945.* Cologne, 1983.

*Perrault, Gilles. *The Red Orchestra.* New York, 1969.

Peukert, Detlev. *Die Edelweisspiraten—Protestbewegungen jugendlicher Arbeiter im Dritten Reich: Eine Dokumentation.* 2nd ed. Cologne, 1983.

Ritter, Gerhard. *The German Resistance: Carl Goerdeler's Struggle against Tyranny.* Freeport, N.Y., 1970.

Roon, Ger van. *Widerstand im Dritten Reich: Ein Überblick.* 4th rev. ed. Munich, 1987.

*Rothfels, Hans. *German Opposition to Hitler.* Chicago, 1962.

Schafheitlin, S. *Gewerkschaften in Exil und Widerstand 1939-1945.* Hamburg, 1979.

*Scholl, Hans, and Sophie Scholl. *At the Heart of the White Rose: Letters and Diaries of Hans and Sophie Scholl.* New York, 1987.

Scholl, Inge. *The White Rose: Munich, 1942-1943.* Middletown, Conn., 1983.

Stroech, J. *Die illegale Presse: Eine Waffe im Kampf gegen den deutschen Faschismus.* Frankfurt, 1979.

Uhlmann, W. *Metallarbeiter in antifaschistischen Widerstand.* Berlin, 1982.

Urner, K. *Der Schweizer Hitler-Attentäter.* Frauenfeld, 1980.

Zeller, Eberhard. *The Flame of Freedom: The German Struggle against Hitler.* Coral Gables, Fla., 1969.

Zentner, Christian. *Illustrierte Geschichte des Widerstands in Deutschland und Europa.* Munich, 1966.

See also under Churches; Emigration; Wehrmacht.

Poland

Bartoszewski, Wladyslaw. *Das Warschauer Ghetto—wie es wirklich war.* Frankfurt, 1983.

*Bethell, Nicholas. *The War Hitler Won: The Fall of Poland, September 1939.* New York, 1972.

*Ciechanowski, Jan M. *The Warsaw Rising of 1944.* Cambridge, 1974.

*Davies, Norman. *Poland: God's Playground.* 2 vols. New York, 1982.

*Gross, Jan Tomasz. *Polish Society under German Occupation.* Princeton, 1979.

*Hanson, Joanna. *The Civilian Population and the Warsaw Uprising of 1944.* New York, 1982.

Hrabar, Roman, Zofia Tokarz, and Jacek E. Wilczur. *The Fate of Polish Children during the Last War.* Warsaw, 1981.

Krannhals, H. von. *Der Warschauer Aufstand 1944.* Frankfurt, 1964.

Wolff, K., ed. *Hiob 1943: Ein Requiem für das Warschauer Ghetto.* Neukirchen-Vluyn, 1983.

*Zawodny, Janusz. *Nothing but Honor: The Story of the Warsaw Uprising, 1944.* Stanford, 1978.

See also under Concentration Camps; Jews; Occupation Policy; Repression.

Police

Buchheim, Hans. *SS und Polizei im NS-Staat.* Bonn, 1964.

Delarue, Jacques. *The Gestapo: A History of Horror.* New York, 1964.

Krausnick, Helmut, and Hans-Heinrich Wilhelm. *Die Truppe des Weltanschauungskrieges: Die Einsatzgruppen der Sicherheitspolizei und des SD 1938–1942.* Stuttgart, 1980.

*Liang, Hsi-huey. *The Berlin Police Force in the Weimar Republic.* Berkeley, 1970.

Manvell, Richard. *Die Herrschaft der Gestapo.* Rastatt, 1982.

*Mosse, George, ed. *Police Forces in History.* 2 vols. London, 1975.

*Tuchel, Johannes. *Zentrale des Terrors: Prinz-Albrecht-Strasse 8.* Berlin, 1987.

*Weyrauch, Walter O. *Gestapo V-Leute.* Frankfurt, 1989.

See also under Biography: Himmler; Concentration Camps; Government and Bureaucracy; Justice; Occupation Policy; Repression; SS.

Prisoners of War

Berthold, E., ed. *Kriegsgefangene im Osten.* Königstein, 1981.

*Durand, Arthur H. *Stalag Luft III: The Secret Story.* Baton Rouge, La., 1988.

*Foy, David A. *For You the War Is Over: American Prisoners of War in Nazi Germany.* New York, 1984.

Frieser, Karl H. *Krieg hinter Stacheldraht: Die deutschen Kriegsgefangenen in der Sowjetunion und das Nationalkomitee "Freies Deutschland."* Mainz, 1981.

*Gansberg, Judith. *Stalag U.S.A.: The Remarkable Story of German POWs in America.* New York, 1977.

*Koop, Allen V. *Stark Decency: German Prisoners of War in a New England Village.* Hanover, N.H., 1988.

*Krammer, Arnold. *Nazi Prisoners of War in America.* New York, 1979.

Lang, Martin. *Stalins Strafjustiz gegen deutsche Soldaten.* Herford, 1981.

*Letulle, Claude J. *Nightmare Memoir: Four Years as a Prisoner of the Nazis.* Baton Rouge, La., 1987.

Maschke, Erich, ed. *Die deutschen Kriegsgefangenen des Zweiten Weltkrieges.* 15 vols. Bielefeld, 1962–1974.

Maurach, Reinhart. *Die Kriegsverbrecherprozesse gegen deutsche Gefangene in der Sowjetunion.* Hamburg, 1950.

Schramm, Hanna. *Menschen in Gurs: Erinnerungen an ein französisches Internierungslager 1940–1941.* Worms, 1977.

*Semprun, Jorge. *What a Beautiful Sunday!* New York, 1982.

Streim, Alfred. *Die Behandlung sowjetischer Kriegsgefangener im "Fall Barbarossa."* Heidelberg, 1981.

*Sullivan, Matthew B. *Thresholds of Peace: Four Hundred Thousand German Prisoners and the People of Britain, 1944–1948.* London, 1979.

Ziock, H. *Jeder geht seinen Weg allein: Tagebuch eines deutschen Kriegsgefangenen.* Sankt Michael, 1981.

See also under Concentration Camps; Second World War.

Propaganda and Public Opinion

General

*Baird, Jay W. *The Mythical World of Nazi War Propaganda, 1939–1945.* Minneapolis, 1974.

Boberach, Heinz, ed. *Meldungen aus dem Reich: Auswahl aus den geheimen Lageberichten des Sicherheitsdienstes der SS 1939–1944.* Neuwied, 1965.

Boelcke, Willi A., ed. *Kriegspropaganda 1939–1941: Geheime Ministerkonferenzen im Reichspropagandaministerium.* Stuttgart, 1966.

Bramsted, Ernest Kohn. *Goebbels and National Socialist Propaganda, 1925–1945.* East Lansing, Mich., 1965.

Buchbinder, O., and H. Schuh, eds. *Heil Beil! Flugblattpropaganda im Zweiten Weltkrieg: Dokumentation und Analyse.* Stuttgart, 1974.

*Hadamovsky, Eugen. *Propaganda and National Power: The Organization of Public Opinion for National Politics.* New York, 1954 [1933].

*Kershaw, Ian. *Der Hitler-Mythos: Volksmeinung und Propaganda im Dritten Reich.* Stuttgart, 1980.

*Kirchner, Klaus. *Flugblätter: Psychologische Kriegsführung im Zweiten Weltkrieg in Europa.* Hanser, 1974.

*Lasswell, Harold D. *Propaganda Technique in the World War.* Cambridge, Mass., 1971.

*Steinert, Marlis G. *Hitlers Krieg und die Deutschen: Stimmung und Haltung der deutschen Bevölkerung im Zweiten Weltkrieg.* Düsseldorf, 1970.

Thomas, O. *Die Propaganda-Maschinerie: Bildende Kunst und Öffentlichkeit im Dritten Reich.* Berlin, 1978.

*Zeman, Z. A. B. *Nazi Propaganda.* 2nd ed. New York, 1973.

Poster Art

Arnold, Friedrich. *Anschläge: 220 politische Plakate als Dokumente der deutschen Geschichte 1900–1980.* Berlin, 1985.

Schockel, Erwin. *Das politische Plakat: Eine psychologische Betrachtung.* Munich, 1939.

Press

Abel, Karl D. *Presse-Lenkung im NS-Staat: Eine Studie zur Geschichte der Publizistik in dem nationalsozialistischen Staat.* 2nd ed. Berlin, 1987.

Berglund, G. *Der Kampf um das Leser im Dritten Reich.* Worms, 1980.

*Eksteins, Modris. *The Limits of Reason: The German Democratic Press and the Collapse of Weimar Democracy.* London, 1975.

Frei, Norbert. *Nationalsozialistische Eroberung der Provinzpresse: Gleichschaltung, Selbstanpassung und Resistenz in Bayern.* Stuttgart, 1980.

Hagemann, Jürgen. *Die Presselenkung im Dritten Reich.* Bonn, 1970.

Hale, Oren J. *The Captive Press in the Third Reich.* Princeton, 1964.

Koszyk, Kurt. *Deutsche Presse 1914–1945.* Berlin, 1972.

Radio and Television

Boelcke, Willi A. *Die Macht des Radios.* Frankfurt, 1977.

Dahl, P. *Arbeitersender und Volksempfänger: Proletarische Radio-Bewegung und bürgerlicher Rundfunk bis 1945.* Frankfurt, 1978.

Dahl, P. *Radio: Sozialgeschichte des Rundfunks für Sender und Empfänger.* Reinbek bei Hamburg, 1983.

Diller, Ansgar. *Rundfunkpolitik im Dritten Reich.* Munich, 1980.

*Gombrich, E. H. *Myth and Reality in German War-Time Broadcasting.* London, 1970.

*Kris, Ernst, and Hans Speier. *German Radio Propaganda: Report on Home Broadcasts during the War.* London, 1944.

Lerg, Winfried B., and Rolf Steininger, eds. *Rundfunk und Politik 1923–1973.* Berlin, 1975.

Pohle, H. *Der Rundfunk als Führungsmittel der Politik: Zur Geschichte des deutschen Rundfunks von 1923–38.* Hamburg, 1955.

Reiss, E. *"Wir senden Frohsinn." Fernsehen unterm Faschismus.* Berlin, 1979.

See also under Biography: Goebbels; Culture; Ideology; Second World War.

Repression and Terror

Bayer, J., ed. *Ehe alles Legende wird.* Baden-Baden, 1979.

*Bessel, Richard. *Political Violence and the Rise of Nazism: The Storm Troopers in Eastern Germany, 1925–1934.* New Haven, 1984.

Focke, Harald, and Uwe Reimer. *Alltag der Entrechteten: Wie die Nazis mit ihren Gegnern umgingen.* Reinbek bei Hamburg, 1980.

Mausbach, H., and B. Mausbach-Bromberger. *Feinde des Lebens: NS-Verbrechen an Kindern.* Frankfurt, 1979.

*Merkl, Peter H. *Political Violence under the Swastika: 481 Early Nazis.* Princeton, 1975.

*Mommsen, Wolfgang J., and Gerhard Hirschfeld, eds. *Social Protest, Violence and Terror in Nineteenth and Twentieth Century Europe.* London, 1982.

*Plant, Richard. *The Pink Triangle: The Nazi War against Homosexuals.* New York, 1986.

*Rector, Frank. *The Nazi Extermination of Homosexuals.* New York, 1981.

*Rosenhaft, Eve. *Beating the Fascists? The German Communists and Political Violence, 1929–1933.* New York, 1983.

See also under Concentration Camps; Daily Life; Gypsies; Jews; Justice; Police; SA; SS.

Second World War

Origins and Causes

*Bell, P. M. H. *The Origins of the Second World War in Europe.* New York, 1986.

Eichholtz, Dietrich, and Kurt Patzold, eds. *Der Weg in den Krieg.* Cologne, 1989.

Hofer, Walther. *Die Entfesselung des Zweiten Weltkrieges: Eine Studie über die internationalen Beziehungen im Sommer 1939.* Frankfurt, 1964.

*Kaiser, David E. *Economic Diplomacy and the Origins of the Second World War: Germany, Britain, France, and Eastern Europe, 1930–1939.* Princeton, 1980.

*Overy, Richard, and Andrew Wheatcroft. *The Road to War: The Origins of World War II.* London, 1989.

*Taylor, A. J. P. *The Origins of the Second World War.* London, 1961.

*Watt, Donald Cameron. *How War Came: The Immediate Origins of the Second World War, 1938–1939.* New York, 1989.

*Weinberg, Gerhard. *World in the Balance.* Hanover, N.H., 1981.

*Wendt, Bernd Jürgen. *Grossdeutschland: Aussenpolitik und Kriegsvorbereitung des Hitler-Regimes.* Munich, 1987.

Whiting, C., and F. Gehendges. *Jener September: Europa beim Kriegsausbruch 1939.* Düsseldorf, 1979.

See also under Foreign Policy.

Course of the War

Bartov, Omer. *The Eastern Front, 1941–1945: German Troops and the Barbarization of Warfare.* New York, 1986.

Berghahn, Volker, and Martin Kitchens, eds. *Germany in the Age of Total War.* London, 1981.

Böll, Heinrich, and Lev Kopelev. *Warum haben wir aufeinander geschossen?* Bornheim-Merten, 1981.

Bolz, Rüdiger. *Synchronopse des Zweiten Weltkrieges.* Düsseldorf, 1983.

Cartier, Raymond. *La Second Guerre mondiale.* 2 vols. Paris, 1965–1966.

Churchill, Winston. *The Second World War.* 6 vols. Boston, 1948–1953.

Dahms, Hellmuth G. *Die Geschichte des Zweiten Weltkrieges.* Munich, 1983.

Dahms, Hellmuth G. *Der Zweite Weltkrieg in Text und Bild.* Rev. ed. Berlin, 1989.

Filmer, Werner, and Heribert Schwan. *Mensch, der Krieg ist aus! Zeitzeugen erinnern sich.* Düsseldorf, 1985.

Görlitz, Walther. *Der Zweite Weltkrieg 1939–1945.* 2 vols. Stuttgart, 1951–1952.

Gruchmann, Lothar. *Der Zweite Weltkrieg: Kriegsführung und Politik.* Munich, 1967.

Hillgruber, Andreas. *Der Zweite Weltkrieg: Kriegsziele und Strategien der grossen Mächte.* Stuttgart, 1982.

Hillgruber, Andreas, ed. *Probleme des Zweiten Weltkrieges.* Cologne, 1967.

Hillgruber, Andreas, and Gerhard Hümmelchen. *Chronik des Zweiten Weltkrieges.* Düsseldorf, 1978.

Irving, David. *Hitler's War.* New York, 1977.

Jäckel, Eberhard, and Jürgen Rohwer, eds. *Kriegswende Dezember 1941.* Koblenz, 1984.

Jacobsen, Hans-Adolf. *Der Weg zur Teilung der Welt: Politik und Strategie 1939–1945.* Koblenz, 1977.

Jacobsen, Hans-Adolf, and Gerhard Hümmelchen. *Chronology of the War at Sea, 1939–1945.* Rev. ed. 2 vols. New York, 1972–1974.

Jacobsen, Hans-Adolf, and Hans Dollinger. *Der Zweite Weltkrieg in Bildern und Dokumenten.* 3 vols. Munich, 1962.

Jacobsen, Hans-Adolf, and Jürgen Rohwer, eds. *Decisive Battles of World War II: The German View.* New York, 1965.

*Jukes, Geoffrey. *Hitler's Stalingrad Decisions.* Berkeley, 1985.

*Kahn, David. *Hitler's Spies: German Military Intelligence in World War II.* New York, 1978.

*Keegan, John. *The Second World War.* New York, 1989.

Kissel, H. *Der deutsche Volkssturm 1944/45.* Frankfurt, 1962.

Liddell Hart, Basil. *History of the Second World War.* 2nd ed. Hicksville, N.Y., 1972.

*Milward, Alan S. *The German Economy at War.* London, 1965.

Neulen, Hans Werner. *An deutscher Seite: Internationale Freiwillige von Wehrmacht und Waffen-SS.* Munich, 1985.

Nicholaisen, Hans-Dietrich. *Der Einsatz der Luftwaffenhelfer im 2. Weltkrieg: Darstellung und Dokumentation.* Büsum, 1981.

Nicholaisen, Hans-Dietrich. *Die Flakhelfer: Luftwaffenhelfer und Marinehelfer im Zweiten Weltkrieg.* Berlin, 1981.

Paul, Wolfgang. *Der Heimatkrieg 1939 bis 1945.* Esslingen, 1980.

Piekalkiewicz, Janusz. *The Air War, 1939–1945.* Harrisburg, Pa., 1985.

Piekalkiewicz, Janusz. *Sea War, 1939–1945.* Harrisburg, Pa., 1987.

Piekalkiewicz, Janusz. *Tank War, 1939–1945.* Harrisburg, Pa., 1986.

Piekalkiewicz, Janusz. *Der Zweite Weltkrieg.* Düsseldorf, 1985.

*Rich, Norman. *Hitler's War Aims.* 2 vols. New York, 1973–1974.

*Sorge, Martin K. *The Other Price of Hitler's War: German Military and Civilian Losses Resulting from World War II.* Westport, Conn., 1986.

*Wehrmacht, OKW. *Hitler Directs His War: The Secret Records of His Daily Military Conferences.* Edited by Felix Gilbert. New York, 1982 [1950].

*Weingartner, James J. *Crossroads of Death: The Story of the Malmédy Massacre and Trial.* Berkeley, 1979.

Whiting, Charles. *Hitler's Werewolves: The Story of the Nazi Resistance Movement, 1944–1945.* New York, 1972.

*Whiting, Charles. *Siegfried: The Nazis' Last Stand.* New York, 1982.

Wright, Gordon. *The Ordeal of Total War, 1939–1945.* New York, 1968.

*Zhukov, Georgii K. *Marshal Zhukov's Greatest Battles.* Edited by Harrison E. Salisbury. New York, 1969.

See also under Biography: Hitler; Occupation Policy; Police; SS; Wehrmacht; Women and Girls.

End of the War and Collapse

Dollinger, Hans. *The Decline and Fall of Nazi Germany and Imperial Japan: A Pictorial History of the Final Days of World War II.* New York, 1968.

*Feis, Herbert. *Between War and Peace: The Potsdam Conference.* Princeton, 1960.

Glaser, Hermann. *The Rubble Years: The Cultural Roots of Postwar Germany.* New York, 1986.

Gosztony, Peter, ed. *Der Kampf um Berlin 1945 in Augenzeugenberichten.* Düsseldorf, 1970.

Klein, Friedrich, and B. Meissner, eds. *Der Potsdamer Abkommen und die Deutschlandfrage.* Stuttgart, 1977.

*Kuby, Erich. *The Russians and Berlin, 1945.* New York, 1968.

Luedde-Neurath, Walter. *Regierung Dönitz: Die letzten Tage des Dritten Reiches.* 4th ed. Göttingen, 1980.

*Mee, Charles L., Jr. *Meeting at Potsdam.* New York, 1975.

*Ryan, Cornelius. *The Last Battle.* New York, 1966.

Sanakojew, S. P., and B. L. Zybulewski, eds. *Teheran, Jalta, Potsdam.* East Berlin, 1978.

*Trevor-Roper, Hugh R. *The Last Days of Hitler.* New York, 1947.

See also under Allied Occupation; Expulsion; War Crimes Trials.

Seizure of Power and Synchronization

*Allen, William S. *The Nazi Seizure of Power: The Experience of a Single German Town, 1930–1935.* Rev. ed. New York, 1984.

Becker, J., and R. Becker, eds. *Hitlers Machtergreifung 1933.* Munich, 1983.

Brüdigam, Heinz. *Das Jahr 1933: Terrorismus an der Macht.* Frankfurt, 1978.

Eschenhagen, W., ed. *Die "Machtergreifung."* Darmstadt, 1982.

Focke, Harald, and M. Strocka. *Alltag der Gleichgeschalteten.* Reinbek bei Hamburg, 1985.

Heuss, Theodor. *Die Machtergreifung und das Ermächtigungsgesetz.* Tübingen, 1967.

Höhne, Heinz. *Die Machtergreifung.* Reinbek bei Hamburg, 1983.

Internationales Komitee zur wissenschaftlichen Erforschung der Ursachen und Folgen des Zweiten Weltkrieges Luxemburg. *Reichstagsbrand: Die Provokation des 20. Jahrhunderts.* Munich, 1978.

Karasek, H. *Der Brandstifter.* Berlin, 1980.

Machtverfall und Machtergreifung: Aufstieg und Herrschaft im Nationalsozialismus. Munich, 1983.

Matthias, Eric, and Rudolf Morsey, eds. *Das Ende der Parteien 1933.* Düsseldorf, 1960.

Megerle, Klaus. *Die nationalsozialistische Machtergreifung.* Berlin, 1982.

Morsey, Rudolf, ed. *Das "Ermächtigungsgesetz" vom 24. März 1933.* Göttingen, 1976.

Niess, W. *Machtergreifung 33: Beginn einer Katastrophe.* Stuttgart, 1982.

The Path to Dictatorship, 1918–1933: Ten Essays by German Scholars. Introduction by Fritz Stern. Garden City, N.Y., 1966.

Pentzlin, H. *Wie Hitler an die Macht kam.* Bergisch Gladbach, 1983.

Rittberger, Volker, ed. *1933: Wie die Republik der Diktatur erlag.* Stuttgart, 1983.

Tobias, F. *Der Reichstagsbrand: Legende und Wirklichkeit.* Rastatt, 1962.

See also under Government and Bureaucracy; Justice; NSDAP; Weimar Republic.

Social Policy

Beuys, Barbara. *Familienleben in Deutschland.* Reinbek bei Hamburg, 1980.

Bluel, Hans-Peter. *Sex and Society in Nazi Germany.* New York, 1974.

Hennig, Eike. *Bürgerliche Gesellschaft und Faschismus in Deutschland.* Frankfurt, 1981.

Hennig, Eike. *Thesen zur deutschen Sozial- und Wirtschaftsgeschichte 1933 bis 1938.* Frankfurt, 1973.

Majer, Diemut. *"Fremdvölkische" im Dritten Reich.* Boppard, 1981.

Mason, Tim W. *Sozialpolitik im Dritten Reich: Arbeiterklasse und Volksgemeinschaft.* Opladen, 1977.

Otto, Hans-Uwe, and Heinz Sünker, eds. *Soziale Arbeit und Faschismus.* Frankfurt, 1989.

Saldern, Adelheid von. *Mittelstand im "Dritten Reich."* Frankfurt, 1979.

Schneider, Christian. *Stadtgründung im Dritten Reich: Wolfsburg und Salzgitter.* Munich, 1979.

Schoenbaum, David. *Hitler's Social Revolution: Class and Status in Nazi Germany, 1933–1939.* Garden City, N.Y., 1967.

Stolleis, Michael. *Gemeinwohlformen im nationalsozialistischen Recht.* Berlin, 1974.

Walz, Manfred. *Wohnungsbau- und Industrieansiedlungspolitik in Deutschland 1933–1939.* Frankfurt, 1979.

Weber-Kellermann, J. *Die deutsche Familie.* Frankfurt, 1976.

See also under Economy; Labor Policy; Women and Girls.

Sports

Bernett, Hajo. *Der jüdische Sport im nationalsozialistischen Deutschland 1933–1938.* Schorndorf bei Stuttgart, 1978.

Bernett, Hajo. *Nationalsozialistische Leibeserziehung.* Schorndorf bei Stuttgart, 1966.

Bernett, Hajo. *Sportpolitik im Dritten Reich.* Schorndorf bei Stuttgart, 1971.

Bohlen, F. *Die XI. Olympischen Spiele.* Cologne, 1979 [1936].

Friese, G. *Anspruch und Wirklichkeit des Sports im Nationalsozialismus.* Ahrensburg bei Hamburg, 1974.

*Hart-Davis, Duff. *Hitler's Games: The 1936 Olympics.* New York, 1986.

*Hoberman, John M. *Sport and Political Ideology.* Austin, Tex., 1984.

Krüger, A. *Theodor Lewald: Sportführer ins Dritte Reich.* Berlin, 1975.

Mandell, Richard D. *The Nazi Olympics.* New York, 1971.

Mengden, G. von. *Umgang mit der Geschichte und mit Menschen: Ein Beitrag zur Geschichte der Machtübernahme im deutschen Sport durch die NSDAP.* Berlin, 1980.

See also under Ideology; Medicine and Biology; SA; SS.

SS

Artzt, Heinz. *Mörder in Uniform: Nazi Verbrecher-Organisationen.* Munich, 1979.

Birn, Ruth Bettina. *Die Höheren SS- und Polizeiführer: Himmlers Vertreter im Reich und in den besetzten Gebieten.* Düsseldorf, 1987.

*Dicks, Henry V. *Licensed Mass Murder: A Socio-Psychological Study of Some SS Killers.* New York, 1972.

Georg, Enno. *Die wirtschaftliche Unternehmungen der SS.* Stuttgart, 1963.

Haupt, Werner. *Gliederung und Organisation der SS.* Stuttgart, 1981.

Höhne, Heinz. *The Order of the Death's Head: The Story of Hitler's SS.* New York, 1971.

Hüser, K. *Wewelsburg 1933 bis 1945: Kult- und Terrorstätte der SS.* Paderborn, 1982.

*Kater, Michael. *Das "Ahnenerbe" der SS 1935–1945: Ein Beitrag zur Kulturpolitik des Dritten Reiches.* Stuttgart, 1974.

Kempner, Robert M. W. *SS im Kreuzverhör.* Munich, 1964.

Koehl, Robert L. *The Black Corps: The Structure and Power Struggles of the Nazi SS.* Madison, Wis., 1983.

*Reitlinger, Gerald. *The SS: Alibi of a Nation, 1922–1945.* New York, 1957.

Schulze-Kossens, Richard. *Führernachwuchs der Waffen-SS: Die Junkerschulen.* Osnabrück, 1982.

*Snydor, Charles W., Jr. *Soldiers of Destruction: The SS Death's Head Division, 1933–1945.* Princeton, 1977.

*Stein, George H. *The Waffen-SS: Hitler's Elite Guard at War, 1939–1945.* Ithaca, N.Y., 1966.

Wegner, Bernd. *The Waffen-SS: Ideology, Organization and Function.* Cambridge, Mass., 1990.

*Weingartner, James J. *Hitler's Guard: The Story of the Leibstandarte SS Adolf Hitler, 1933–1945.* Carbondale, Ill., 1974.

See also under Biography: Himmler; Concentration Camps; Jews; Medicine and Biology; NSDAP; Occupation Policy; Propaganda; Repression; SA; Second World War.

Sturmabteilung (SA)

Bennecke, H. *Hitler und die SA.* Munich, 1962.

Bennecke, H. *Die Reichswehr und der "Röhm-Putsch."* Munich, 1964.

Bloch, C. *Die SA und die Krise des NS-Regimes 1934.* Frankfurt, 1970.

*Fischer, Conan. *Stormtroopers: A Social, Economic and Ideological Analysis, 1929–1935.* London, 1983.

Gallo, M. *Der Schwarze Freitag der SA: Die Vernichtung des revolutionären Flügels der NSDAP durch Hitlers SS in Juni 1934.* Munich, 1972.

*Merkl, Peter H. *The Making of a Stormtrooper.* Princeton, 1980.

Werner, A. *SA und NSDAP.* Erlangen, 1964.

See also under NSDAP; Repression; SS.

Technology and Science

Bellon, Bernard P. *Mercedes in Peace and War: German Automobile Workers, 1903–1945.* New York, 1990.

Beyerchen, Alan D. *Scientists under Hitler: Politics and the Physics Community in the Third Reich.* New Haven, 1977.

Bornemann, M. *Geheimprojekt Mittelbau: Die Geschichte der deutschen V-Waffen-Werke.* Munich, 1971.

Bower, Tom. *The Paperclip Conspiracy: The Hunt for the Nazi Scientists.* Boston, 1987.

Dornberger, Walter. *V-2.* New York, 1954.

Etzold, Hans-Rüdiger. *The Beetle: The Chronicle of the People's Car.* Newbury Park, Calif., 1988.

Heisenberg, Elisabeth. *Inner Exile: Recollections of a Life with Werner Heisenberg.* Boston, 1984.

Hopfinger, K. B. *The Volkswagen Story.* 3rd ed. Cambridge, Mass., 1971.

Johnson, Brian. *The Secret War.* New York, 1978.

Klee, Ernst, and Otto Mark. *The Birth of the Missile: The Secrets of Peenemunde.* New York, 1965.

Lärmer, Karl. *Autobahnbau in Deutschland 1933 bis 1945.* Berlin, 1975.

Lundgreen, P., ed. *Wissenschaft im Dritten Reich.* Frankfurt, 1985.

Mehrtens, H., and S. Reichter, eds. *Naturwissenschaft, Technik und NS-Ideologie.* Frankfurt, 1980.

See also under Economy; Second World War; Universities.

Universities

Bergmann, W., et al. *Soziologie im Faschismus 1933–1945.* Cologne, 1981.

Bleuel, Hans Peter. *Deutschlands Bekenner: Professoren zwischen Kaiserreich und Diktatur.* Bern, 1968.

Corino, K., ed. *Intellektuelle im Bann des Nationalsozialismus.* Hamburg, 1980.

*Giles, Geoffrey. *Students and National Socialism in Germany.* Princeton, 1985.

*Hartshorne, Edward Y., Jr. *The German Universities and National Socialism.* Cambridge, Mass., 1937.

Lundgreen, P., ed. *Wissenschaft im Dritten Reich.* Frankfurt, 1985.

*Ringer, Fritz K. *The Decline of the German Mandarins: The German Academic Community, 1890–1933.* Cambridge, Mass., 1969.

*Steinberg, Michael S. *Sabers and Brown Shirts: The German Students' Path to National Socialism, 1918–1935.* Chicago, 1977.

*Weber, R. G. S. *The German Student Corps in the Third Reich.* New York, 1986.

See also under Education; Ideology; Opposition; Technology and Science; Women and Girls.

Versailles Treaty

*Craig, Gordon A., and Felix Gilbert, eds. *The Twenties.* Vol. 1 of *The Diplomats, 1919–1939.* Princeton, 1953.

Gunzenhäuser, M. *Die Pariser Friedenskonferenz und die Friedensverträge 1919/20.* Frankfurt, 1970.

Haffner, Sebastian, et al. *Der Vertrag von Versailles.* Munich, 1978.

*Holborn, Hajo. *The Political Collapse of Europe.* New York, 1951.

*Keynes, John Maynard. *The Economic Consequences of the Peace.* Introduction by Robert Lekachman. New York, 1988 [1920].

Lloyd George, David. *The Truth about the Peace Treaties.* London, 1938.

*Mayer, Arno J. *Politics and Diplomacy of Peacemaking: Containment and Counterrevolution at Versailles, 1918–1919.* New York, 1968.

Schreiber, G. *Revisionismus und Weltmachtstreben.* Stuttgart, 1978.

War Crimes Trials

*Benton, Wilbourn E., and Georg Grimm, eds. *Nuremberg: German Views of the War Trials.* Dallas, Tex., 1955.

*Davidson, Eugene. *Trial of the Germans: An Account of Twenty-two Defendants before the International Military Tribunal at Nuremberg.* New York, 1966.

Maser, Werner, *Nuremberg: A Nation on Trial.* New York, 1970.

Przybylski, P. *Zwischen Galgen und Amnestie: Kriegsverbrecherprozesse im Spiegel von Nürnberg.* East Berlin, 1979.

Ratz, M., et al. *Die Justiz und die Nazis: Zur Strafverfolgung von Nazismus und Neonazismus seit 1945.* Frankfurt, 1979.

*Rückerl, Adalbert. *The Investigation of Nazi Crimes, 1945–1978: A Documentation.* New York, 1980.

*Taylor, Telford. *Nuremberg Trials: War Crimes and International Law.* New York, 1949.

United States Government Printing Office. *Trials of War Criminals under Control Council Law No. 10: Nürnberg, October 1946–April 1949.* 15 vols. Washington, D.C., 1949–1953.

Westphal, Siegfried. *Der Deutsche Generalstab auf der Anklagebank: Nürnberg, 1945–1948.* Mainz, 1978.

See also under Concentration Camps; Second World War; Wehrmacht.

Wehrmacht

Absolon, Rudolf. *Die Wehrmacht im Dritten Reich.* Boppard, 1979.

Buchbender, Ortwin, and Reinhold Sterz, eds. *Das andere Gesicht des Krieges: Deutsche Feldpostbriefe 1939–1945.* 2nd ed. Munich, 1983.

*Craig, Gordon. *The Politics of the Prussian Army, 1640–1945.* New York, 1955.

*Deist, Wilhelm, ed. *The German Military in the Age of Total War.* Leamington Spa, England, 1985.

De Zayas, Alfred M. *The Wehrmacht War Crimes Bureau, 1939–1945.* Lincoln, Nebr., 1989.

*Görlitz, Walter. *History of the German General Staff.* New York, 1953.

Kern, Wolfgang. *Die innere Funktion der Wehrmacht 1933–1939.* East Berlin, 1979.

Müller, K.-J. *Armee, Politik und Gesellschaft in Deutschland 1933–1945.* Paderborn, 1979.

*O'Neill, Robert J. *The German Army and the Nazi Party, 1933–1939.* London, 1966.

Stumpf, R. *Die Wehrmachtselite.* Boppard, 1982.

*Taylor, Telford. *Sword and Swastika: Generals and Nazis in the Third Reich.* New York, 1952.

Vogelsang, Thilo. *Reichswehr, Staat und NSDAP.* Stuttgart, 1962.

Warlimont, Walter. *Inside Hitler's Headquarters, 1939–1945.* New York, 1964.

*Wheeler-Bennett, John W. *The Nemesis of Power: The German Army in Politics, 1918–1945.* New York, 1964.

See also under Opposition; Second World War; SS.

Weimar Republic

*Bessel, Richard, and E. J. Feuchtwanger, eds. *Social Change and Political Development in Weimar Germany.* London, 1981.

Bracher, Karl Dietrich. *Die Auflösung der Weimarer Republik: Eine Studie zum Problem des Machtverfalls in der Demokratie.* 2nd ed. Stuttgart, 1957.

Carlebach, Emil. *Hitler war kein Betriebsunfall: Hinter den Kulissen der Weimarer Republik.* Frankfurt, 1978.

*Deak, Istvan. *Weimar Germany's Left-Wing Intellectuals: A Political History of the Weltbühne and Its Circle.* Berkeley, 1968.

*Dorpalen, Andreas. *Hindenburg and the Weimar Republic.* Princeton, 1964.

Eyck, Erich. *A History of the Weimar Republic.* 2 vols. Cambridge, Mass., 1962.

*Fritzsche, Peter. *Rehearsal for Fascism: Populism and Political Motivation in Weimar Germany.* New York, 1990.

*Gay, Peter. *Weimar Culture: The Outsider as Insider.* New York, 1968.

Haffner, Sebastian. *1918/19: Eine deutsche Revolution.* Reinbek bei Hamburg, 1981.

Heiber, Helmut. *Die Republik von Weimar.* Munich, 1982.

Hermand, Jost, and Frank Trommler. *Die Kultur in der Weimarer Republik.* Munich, 1978.

*Hunt, Richard N. *German Social Democracy, 1918–1933.* New Haven, 1964.

Italiaander, R., ed. *Wir erlebten das Ende der Weimarer Republik: Zeitgenossen berichten.* Düsseldorf, 1982.

*Jacobson, John. *Locarno Diplomacy: Germany and the West, 1925–1929.* Princeton, 1972.

Koebner, T., ed. *Weimars Ende: Prognosen und Diagnosen in der deutschen Literatur und politischen Publizistik 1930–1935.* Frankfurt, 1982.

*Kolb, Eberhard. *The Weimar Republic.* London, 1988.

*Laqueur, Walter. *Weimar: A Cultural History.* New York, 1975.

Larsen, Egon. *Weimar Eyewitness.* London, 1976.

*Maier, Charles J. *Recasting Bourgeois Europe: Stabilization in France, Germany, and Italy in the Decade after World War I.* Princeton, 1975.

*Mitchell, Allen. *Revolution in Bavaria, 1918–1919: The Eisner Regime and the Soviet Republic.* Princeton, 1965.

*Morgan, David W. *The Socialist Left and the German Revolution: A History of the German Independent Social Democratic Party, 1917–1922.* Ithaca, N.Y., 1975.

Overesch, Manfred, and F. W. Saal. *Die Weimarer Republik.* Düsseldorf, 1982.

*Phelan, Anthony, ed. *The Weimar Dilemma: Intellectuals in the Weimar Republic.* Manchester, England, 1985.

Rosenberg, Arthur. *Entstehung und Geschichte der Weimarer Republik.* Frankfurt, 1982 [1928–1934].

*Turner, Henry A. *Stresemann and the Politics of the Weimar Republic.* Princeton, 1963.

*Waite, Robert G. L. *Vanguard of Nazism: The Free Corps Movement in Germany, 1918–1923.* Cambridge, Mass., 1952.

*Winkler, Heinrich A. *Mittelstand, Demokratie und Nationalsozialismus: Die politische Entwicklung von Handwerk und Kleinhandel in der Weimarer Republik.* Cologne, 1972.

See also under Economy; Foreign Policy; NSDAP; Seizure of Power.

Women and Girls

*Bridenthal, Renate, Atina Grossmann, and Marion Kaplan, eds. *When Biology Became Destiny: Women in Weimar and Nazi Germany.* New York, 1984.

Frauengruppe Faschismusforschung. *Mutterkreuz und Arbeitsbuch.* Frankfurt, 1981.

*Higonnet, Margaret, et al. *Behind the Lines: Gender and the Two World Wars.* New Haven, 1987.

*Kaplan, Marion. "Jewish Women in Nazi Germany: Daily Life, Daily Struggles, 1933–1939." *Feminist Studies* (Fall 1990): in press.

*Kirkpatrick, Clifford. *Nazi Germany: Its Women and Family Life.* Indianapolis, 1938.

Klaus, Martin. *Mädchen im Dritten Reich: Der Bund Deutscher Mädel (BDM).* Cologne, 1983.

Klaus, Martin. *Mädchen in der Hitlerjugend: Die Erziehung zur "deutschen Frau."* Cologne, 1980.

Klinksiek, Dorothee. *Die Frau im NS-Staat.* Stuttgart, 1982.

*Koonz, Claudia. *Mothers in the Fatherland: Women, the Family and Nazi Politics.* New York, 1987.

Kuhn, Annette, and Valentine Roth. *Frauen im deutschen Faschismus.* 2 vols. Düsseldorf, 1982.

Laska, Vera, ed. *Women in the Resistance and in the Holocaust.* Westport, Conn., 1983.

Lück, Margret. *Die Frau im Männerstaat: Die gesellschaftliche Stellung der Frau im Nationalsozialismus.* Frankfurt, 1979.

Macciocchi, Maria-A. *Jungfrauen, Mütter und ein Führer.* Berlin, 1976.

Mason, Tim W. "Women in Germany, 1925–1940: Family, Welfare, and Work." *History Workshop* 1 (Spring 1976): 74–113; 2 (Autumn 1976): 5–32.

*Rupp, Leila. *Mobilizing Women for War: German and American Propaganda, 1939–1945.* Princeton, 1978.

*Sachse, Carola. *Industrial Housewives: Women's Social Work in the Factories of Nazi Germany.* New York, 1987.

Scholtz-Klink, Gertrud. *Die Frau im Dritten Reich.* Tübingen, 1978.

Schüddekopf, Charles, ed. *Der alltägliche Faschismus: Frauen im Dritten Reich.* Bonn, 1982.

*Stephenson, Jill. *The Nazi Organization of Women.* New York, 1981.

*Stephenson, Jill. *Women in Nazi Society.* New York, 1985.

Winkler, Dörte. *Frauenarbeit im "Dritten Reich."* Hamburg, 1977.

Wittrock, Christine. *Weiblichkeitsmythen.* Frankfurt, 1983.

See also under Churches; Daily Life; Education; Jews; Opposition; Second World War; Social Policy.

Index

The index does not attempt to list systematically all the encyclopedia's articles. Those articles not in the index will be found alphabetically throughout the encyclopedia.

Page numbers in **boldface** refer to (1) main articles on major National Socialist figures; or (2) longer, in-depth articles or articles with a special focus.

Berlin Sports Palace, 47, 901
  see also Reich Sports Field
Berlin State Opera, 310, 489, 521
Berlin Theater, 475
Berlin Transit Authority, 82
Berlin Transit Workers' Strike (1932),
  976
Berlin Treaty (1926), 82, 926, 1036
Berlin Wall, 977
Bernadotte, Folke, 82, 260
Bernburg an der Saale, 82, 106, 213,
  314, 461, 910
Berndt, Alfred-Ingemar, 724, 750,
  790
Bernhard, Georg, 82–83, 687
"Bernhard" Operation, 83, 639
Bernstein-Zimmer. *See* Amber Room
Bertelsmann Publishing Group, 984
Bertram, Adolf, 83, 675, 848
Bertram, Ernst, 83
Berufsbeamtengesetz. *See* Civil
  Service Law
Besatzungspolitik. *See* Occupation
  policy, German
Besatzungsstatut. *See* Occupation
  Statute (1949)
Bessarabia, 83–84, 119, 221, 341,
  810, 891, 996
Besson, General, 297
Best, S. Paine, 990
Best, Walter, 990
Best, Werner, 84, 104, 191, 782
Bethel Institute for the Handicapped,
  95
Bethge, Friedrich, 84
Bethlen, Count István, 450
Beumelburg, Werner, 85, 552, 716,
  1021
Bevin, Ernest, 85, 359, 603
Bevölkerungspolitik. *See* Population
  policy
BGAG. *See* Gelsenkirchener
  Bergwerks-AG
BGB. *See* Civil Code
BGH. *See* Federal Court (West
  Germany)
BI. *See* Berliner Illustrierte Zeitung
Białystok, 384, 663, 820, 951
Bianchi, Michele, 85
Bibelforscher. *See* Jehovah's Witnesses
Bidault, Georges, 603
Bie, Oskar, 85–86
Bierut, Bolesław, 86
Big Three alliance, 86, 140
Bild-Zeitung (publication), 1075
Billotte, Gaston, 297
Binding, Rudolf Georg, 68, 86
Birkenau, 50–52, 53, 86, 267, 512
Bisinen, 846
Bismarck (battleship), 562, 640
Bismarck (film), 178, 263, 399, 513,
  545
Bismarck, Otto von, 400, 723, 741,
  863, 1048
Bis zum bitteren Ende (Gisevius), 346
BIZ. *See* Bank for International
  Settlement

Bizone, 968
Black Corps, The. *See Schwarze
  Korps, Das*
Black Front, 87–88, 231, 618
Black International, 459
"Black List," 88
Black Order, 903–904
"Black-Red-Gold." *See* Reich Banner
  "Black-Red-Gold"
Black Reichswehr, 989
Black Sea, 171
Blackshirt (publication), 604
Black-White-Red Combat Front, 89
Blaich, Ernst, 876
Blanc, Giuseppe, 345
Blaskowitz, Johannes, 89–90, 667
Blass, Ernst, 90
Blaue Boll, Der (Barlach), 67
Blaue Engel, Der (film), 197, 570,
  1080
Bleeding Germany (film), 94
Blei, Franz, 90
Blitzkrieg, 90, 287, 856, 857
Blitzmarsch nach Warschau
  (Hadamovsky), 90
"Blitz." *See* Air Battle for England
Blobel, Paul, 61, 90, 228, 246, 266
Bloch, Ernst, 99, 256
Bloem, Walter, 91, 551
Blomberg, Werner von, 91, 301–302,
  355, 445, 770, 788, 808, 1027
Blomberg-Fritsch Crisis. *See* Fritsch
  Crisis
Blondi (Hitler's dog), 91
Blood. *See* Race
Blood, Law to Protect (1935), 92,
  347, 398, 441, 574, 655–656,
  700, 718, 748, 895
Blood Order, 62, 93
Bloody Sunday, 93, 115
  see also Altona Bloody Sunday;
  Bromberg Bloody Sunday
Blue Angel, The (film), 197, 570,
  1080
Blue Division. *See* División Azul
Blue International, 459
Blüher, Hans, 93
Blum, Léon, 93–94, 718
Blume, Hermann, 443
Blumenkriege. *See* Flower Wars
Blumensaat, Georg, 888
Blunck, Hans Friedrich, 94, 332, 552,
  790
Blutendes Deutschland (film), 94
Blutschutzgesetz. *See* Blood, Law to
  Protect
BNSDJ. *See* League of National
  Socialist German Jurists
Board of German Broadcasters, 309
Bock, Fedor von, 94, 297, 714, 820
Böckel, Otto, 95
*Bockelson—Geschichte eines
  Massenwahns* (Reck-
  Malleczewen), 761
Bodelschwingh, Friedrich von, 95,
  142, 163, 327, 767, 1071
Boeselager, Baron von, 48

Boger, Friedrich Wilhelm, 53, 95,
  444
Bohemia, 175, 622, 828
Bohemia and Moravia, Protectorate of,
  96, 128, 176, 290–291, 299,
  361, 375, 407, 544, 549, 601,
  627, 737–738, 781
Bohle, Ernst Wilhelm, 96, 276, 282,
  283
Böhme, Franz, 445
Böhme, Herbert, 96, 139, 551, 552
Bolivia, 66–67
Bologna, 151
Bolshevik Revolution, 554
Bolshevism, 96–97, 154, 244, 435,
  436, 487, 519, 552, 577, 624,
  663, 710, 960–961
  see also Comintern; Communism;
  Communist Party of Germany;
  National Bolshevism
Bolz, Eugen, 97
Bomber Offensive (Harris), 383
Bonhoeffer, Dietrich, 98, 99, 144,
  165, 205, 275, 503, 675, 681
Bonhoeffer, Klaus, 98–99, 647
Bono, Emilio de, 99, 991
Bonomi, Ivanoe, 62
Book Burning, 88, 99–100, 110, 114,
  233, 247, 284, 299, 357, 405,
  417, 495, 570, 706, 740, 971,
  994
Book Trade Group, 790
Booty operations (Soviet Union), 100
Borchardt, Georg Hermann, 100, 398
Borchardt, Rudolf, 100–101
Border Police, 865
Börgermoor, 101
Borgmann, Hans-Otto, 888
Boris III (king of Bulgaria), 101,
  119
Boris, Otto, 380
Bormann, Martin, 5, 80, **101–103**,
  118, 121, 144, 165, 167, 192,
  308, 355, 363, 403–404, 444,
  514, 518, 629, 654, 656–657,
  659, 690, 813, 943
Born, Max, 475
Borowski, Tadeusz, 103
Bosch, Carl, 3, 291
Bosnia, 555
Bothmann, Hans, 103, 267, 519
Botschafterkonferenz. *See*
  Ambassadors' Conference
Bottai, Giuseppe, 103
Bouhler, Philipp, 103–104, 105–106,
  245, 361, 665, 731
Boxer, The (Thorak sculpture), 784
Boxheim Documents, 84, 104, 590
Boycott against Jews (1933), 31,
  104–105
Bracher, Karl Dietrich, 256–257
Bracht, Franz, 105, 371, 739
Brack, Viktor, 105–106
Brackheim, Thomas. *See* Heuss,
  Theodor
Bradfisch, Otto, 106
Brandbergen bei Halle, 954

Death's-Head Units, 73, 159, 177, 184, 226, 442, 544, 903, 905, 910, 1011

Decker, Will, 184

Declaration of the Rights of Man of the United Nations (1948), 276

Decline of the West, The (Spengler), 92, 649, 897–898, 1043

Decree of the Reich President for Protecting the *Volk* and the State. *See* Reichstag Fire Decree (1933)

Decree on Wartime Military Jurisdiction (1941), 856

Deeg, Peter, 184–185

DEFA. *See* German Films, Inc.

De Gaulle, Charles. *See* Gaulle, Charles de

Degenerate Art exhibition (1937), 74, 185–186

DEGESCH. *See* German Society for Vermin Control

Degrelle, Léon, 76, 150, 187, 801–802

Degussa/I.G. Farben, 1081

Dehio, Ludwig, 855

Delbrück, Schickler and Co., 1

De L'Isle, Lord, 572

Delitzsch, Friedrich, 188

Delmer, D. Sefton, 125

Delp, Alfred, 188–189, 514, 675, 898

DEMAG (Deutsche Maschinenfabrik AG), 826, 1075

Demilitarization of Germany, 189, 1069

Demilitarized Zone, 189

Democracy, 189

Democratic Germany group, 1054

Denazification, 34, 189–190, 627, 702, 743, 829, 1069

Denmark, 28, 82, 84, 150, 191, 653, 663, 939

Deportation, 191–192
    see also Extermination camps; Final Solution; *specific camps*

Deputy, The: A Christian Tragedy (Hochhuth), 708, 989

Derna, 10, 11

Deruga Trial, The (Huch), 447

Descent, Theory of, 192, 246, 870
    see also Social Darwinism

Desperate Struggle of the Aryan Peoples with Judaism (Ahlwardt), 13

DEST. *See* German Earth and Stone Works

De Staline à Hitler (Coulondre), 168

Detention camps (Austria), 192, 1055

Detten, Georg von, 192–193

Deutsch, Ernst, 193

Deutsch-Britisches Flottenabkommen. *See* German-British Naval Agreement (1935)

Deutsche Agrarpolitik. *See Odal, Monatsschrift für Blut und Boden* (publication)

Deutsche Ahnenstammkartei. *See* German Ancestral Catalog

Deutsche Allgemeine Zeitung (publication), 193, 194

Deutsche Angestelltengewerkschaft. *See* German Employees' Union

Deutsche Ansiedlungsgesellschaft. *See* German Colonization Society

Deutsche Arbeiterpartei. *See* German Workers' Party

Deutsche Arbeiterpartei Österreichs. *See* German Workers' Party of Austria

Deutsche Arbeitsfront. *See* German Labor Front

Deutsche Ausrüstungswerke. *See* German Armament Works

Deutsche Bank, 1, 2, 831–832, 983

Deutsche Bauernpartei. *See* German Peasants' Party

Deutsche Bodenpolitik. *See* German Soil Policy

Deutsche Christen. *See* German Christians

Deutsche Demokratische Partei. *See* German Democratic Party

Deutsche Dorfzeitung (publication), 886

Deutsche Erd- und Steinwerke. *See* German Earth and Stone Works

Deutsche Evangelische Kirche. *See* German Evangelical Church

Deutsche Film-AG. *See* German Films, Inc.

Deutsche Front. *See* German Front

Deutsche Gemeindeordnung. *See* German Communal Ordinance (1935)

Deutsche Gesellschaft für öffentliche Arbeiten AG. *See* German Society for Public Works

Deutsche Gesellschaft für Rassenhygiene. *See* German Society for Racial Hygiene

Deutsche Gesellschaft für Schädlingsbekämpfung (DEGESCH). *See* German Society for Vermin Control

Deutsche Gesellschaft für Wehrpolitik und Wehrwissenschaften. *See* German Society for Military Policy and Military Studies

Deutsche Glaubensbewegung. *See* German Faith Movement

Deutsche Gottschau (Hauer), 387

Deutsche Hinkemann, Der (Toller), 960

Deutsche Hochschule für Politik. *See* Hochschule für Politik, Deutsche

Deutsche Jugendkraft. *See* German Youth Force

Deutsche Kampfspiele. *See* German Competitive Games

Deutsche Katastrophe, Die (Meinecke), 584

Deutsche Kraftfahrt (publication), 635

Deutsche Lied, Das (Bie), 85

Deutsche Maschinenfabrik AG. *See* DEMAG

Deutsche Nationalsozialistische Arbeiterpartei. *See* German National Socialist Workers' Party

Deutsche Ölschiefer-Forschungs-GmbH. *See* German Shale Oil Research Company, Ltd.

Deutsche Passion (Euringer), 243–244, 305, 622

Deutsche Physik (Lenard), 538

Deutsche-Polnischer Nichtangriffspakt. *See* German-Polish Nonaggression Pact

Deutscher Akademischer Austauschdienst. *See* German Academic Exchange Service

Deutscher Aufbruch (Bertram), 83

Deutscher Automobil-Club. *See* German Automobile Club

Deutscher Christenbund. *See* German Christians' League

Deutsche Rechtsfront. *See* German Law Front

Deutsche Reden (Schäfer), 832

Deutsche Reichsbahn, 114, 193, 207, 231, 267, 1062

Deutscher Gewerkschaftsbund. *See* German Trade Union Federation

Deutscher Heimstättensiedler, Der (publication), 340

Deutscher Juristentag. *See* German Congress of Jurists

Deutscher Kampfbund. *See* German Combat League

Deutscher Ostbund. *See* German Eastern League

Deutscher Reichsausschuss für Leibesübungen. *See* German Reich Committee for Physical Exercises

Deutscher Reichsbund für Leibesübungen. *See* German Reich League for Physical Exercises

Deutscher Richterbund. *See* German Judges' League

Deutscher Siedlerbund. *See* German Settlers' League

Deutscher Verlag, 194, 225, 874

Deutscher Werkbund. *See* German Arts and Crafts League

Deutsches Afrika-Korps. *See* German Africa Corps

Deutsches Berufserziehungswerk. *See* German Vocational Education Agency

Deutsche Schriften (Lagarde), 551

Deutsches Frauenwerk. *See* German Women's Agency

Deutsches Institut für national-sozialistische technische Arbeitsschulung. *See* German Institute for National Socialist Technical Vocational Training

Deutsches Jugendwerk. *See* German Youth Agency

League for a German Church, 328, 530

League for the German East, 330, 530–531, 661

League of Agriculturalists, 30, 531

League of Communists, 618

League of Foreign Germans, 276, 531

League of Frontline Soldiers. *See* Steel Helmet

League of German Girls (BDM), 66, 120, 125, 133, 223, 251, 257, 332, 390, 431, 439, 531–532, 566, 718, 835, 844

League of German Officers (BDO), 532–533, 619, 872

League of National Socialist German Jurists (BNSDJ), 329, 634

see also National Socialist League of Law Guardians

League of Nations, 3, 25, 112, 121, 181, 200–201, 286, 533, 556, 595, 626, 652, 687, 709, 802, 891, 991, 993, 1036

League of Proletarian Revolutionary Writers, 72

League to Combat Antisemitism, 802

League to Renew the Reich, 781

Leander, Zarah, 197, 442, 533–534, 801

Lebensborn (program), 333, 534, 582, 747, 819, 904

Lebensraum. *See* Living Space

"Lebensraum, Der" (Ratzel), 554

Leber, Julius, 239–240, 352, 382, 386, 514, 535, 590, 599, 710, 790, 851, 881, 887, 972

Lebrun, Albert, 535

Lechenberg, Harald, 874

Lecture Evening for Case Histories [*Kasuistik*] and Therapy, 740

Leeb, Wilhelm Ritter von, 297, 535–536, 667, 820

Leers, Johann von, 536

Leffler, Siegfried, 327

Legal Aid (Gerichtshilfe) office, 201

Legality Oath (1930), 8, 420

Legien, Carl, 319, 654

Legion Condor. *See* Condor Legion

Legion of the Archangel Michael, 149, 463

Legion Speer. *See* Speer Legion

Legislation. *See* Laws and legislation; *specific laws and ordinances*

Lehár, Franz, 613

Lehmann, Heinrich, 1003

Lehnich, Oswald, 771

Lehrerbildungsanstalten. *See* Teacher Training Institutes

Leib, Hans, 848

Leibhaftige, Der (Thiess), 953

Leibstandarte-SS "Adolf Hitler," 197, 536–537, 569, 647, 696, 716, 903

Leip, Hans, 546

Leipart, Theodor, 319, 537–538

Leipzig, 151, 351

Leistungskampf der deutschen Betriebe. *See* Performance

Competition of German Workplaces

Leiter des SS-Hauptamtes. *See* SS Headquarters

Leitgeb, Josef, 1042

Lejeune-Jung, Paul, 538

Lenard, Philipp, 229, 337, 538, 1045

Lend-Lease Act (1941), 140, 538–539, 917

Lenin, V. I., 88, 96, 127, 908

Leningrad, 539, 822, 1077

Leninist International, 459

Lennaker (Seidel), 866

Lenya, Lotte, 539, 1032

Lenz, Fritz, 539, 747

Lenz, Siegfried, 651

Leo XIII (pope), 743

Leo Baeck Institute, 63

Leonhard, Wolfgang, 977

Leopold III (king of Belgium), 76, 297, 539–540, 706

Lersch, Heinrich, 540

Lersch, Philipp, 540

Les Milles (camp), 540

Lessing, Gotthold, 704

Letter from Home. *See Heimatbrief*

Letterhaus, Bernhard, 540–541, 608

Letters and Papers from Prison (Bonhoeffer), 98

Letzte Aufzeichnungen (Rosenberg), 813

Letzte Kompanie, Die (film), 983

Letzten Tage der Menschheit, Die (Kraus), 512

Letzte Versuch, Der (Dahlerus), 179

Leuninger, Franz, 541

Leuschner, Wilhelm, 386, 486, 541, 565, 590, 599, 654, 674, 710, 881, 912, 972, 1047

Leutheuser, Julius, 327

Lewald, Theodor, 337, 541

Lex van der Lubbe (1930), 40, 541, 787

Ley, Robert, 5, 101, 437, 541, 542, 656–657, 678, 768, 770, 823, 843, 963

L'Humanité (publication), 697

Libau, 270

Liberalism, 542

Liberation Law (1946), 34, 190, 542–543

Libya, 11, 62, 64

Lichtenberg, Bernhard, 543

Lichtenburg, 543, 757, 1059

Liddell Hart, Sir Basil, 90

Lidice, 180, 290–291, 407, 543–544, 738

Liebehenschel, Arthur, 52, 53, 544

Liebeneiner, Wolfgang, 178, 263, 453, 544–545

Liebenfels, Jörg Lanz von (pseud.). *See* Lanz, Josef

Liebermann, Max, 545

Liebermann von Sonnenberg, Max, 545

Lieberose (camp), 545

Liebknecht, Karl, 125, 293, 814, 1034

Lied von Bernadette, Das (Werfel), 1042

Life Celebrations, 617–618

"Lili Marleen" (song), 546, 848, 886

Lilje, Hanns, 546, 1071

Limpach, Erich, 547

Lindemann, Fritz, 348

Linden, Walther, 547

Lingen, Theo, 263

Linke, Johannes, 547

Linz, 547–548

Linz Program (1882), 548, 561, 842

Lippert, Julius, 548–549

Lipski, Józef, 337

Lischka, Kurt, 549

Liska, Hans, 874

List, Wilhelm, 445, 549

Literature, **550–552**

see also specific authors, titles, and organizations

Literature Prize of the Reich Capital, 550

Literaturgeschichte der deutschen Stämme und Landschaften (Nadler), 617

Lithuania, 113, 341, 467–468, 491, 552–553, 586, 663, 681, 796, 822, 996–997

Litt, Theodor, 553

Little Entente, 77, 175, 450, 553, 810, 1073

Little Man, What Now? (Fallada), 253

"Little Theresienstadt Fortress" (camp), 951

Litvinov, Maksim Maksimovich, 553, 599, 891, 908

Litzmann, Karl, 553–554

Litzmannstadt. *See* Łódź

Living Space, 56, 86, 97, 153, 183, 277, 282, 285, 321, 322, 332–333, 339, 363, 420, 423, 428, 445, 455, 554, 624–625, 626, 663, 679, 714, 718, 758, 820, 855–856, 892, 1003

Lloyd George, David, 554–555, 991

Löbe, Paul, 555

Lobjoie, Charlotte, 559

Loborgrad (camp), 555

Locarno Pact (1925), 21, 76, 82, 114, 135, 177, 200, 533, 556, 562, 802, 925, 926, 1036, 1040

Loder, Dietrich, 113, 455

Łódź, 106, 267, 269, 270, 518, 553, 554, 822, 1024

Loeper, Wilhelm, 556–557

Loerzer, Bruno, 557

Loewe Weapons Factory, 13

Lohkamp, Emil, 380

Löhr, Alexander, 557

Lohse, Hinrich, 557–558, 652, 681, 768, 813

Lombroso, Cesare, 740

London, 14

London, Jack, 99

London Agreement (1945), 171, 558, 656, 1019–1020

London Conferences (1921–1924), 558, 796

Other titles of interest

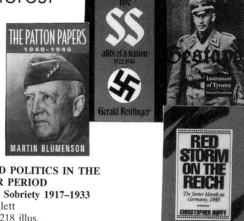

FRANKLIN D. ROOSEVELT:
HIS LIFE AND TIMES
An Encyclopedic View
Edited by Otis L. Graham, Jr.
and Meghan Robinson Wander
512 pp., 250 illus.
80410-7 $22.50

GESTAPO
Instrument of Tyranny
Edward Crankshaw
281 pp., 12 photos
80567-7 $13.95

THE GI's WAR
American Soldiers in Europe
During World War II
Edwin P. Hoyt
638 pp., 29 illus.
80448-4 $16.95

GOEBBELS
A Biography
Helmut Heiber
398 pp., 19 photos
80187-6 $9.95

THE GUINNESS BOOK
OF ESPIONAGE
Mark Lloyd
256 pp., 100 photos
80584-7 $16.95

HITLER'S WAR
Edwin P. Hoyt
432 pp., 65 photos
80381-X $14.95

ROMMEL
Battles and Campaigns
Kenneth Macksey
226 pp., 162 photos, 22 maps
80786-6 $15.95

STRONG MEN ARMED
The United States Marines
vs. Japan
Robert Leckie
600 pp., 56 illus., 16 maps
80785-8 $17.95

THE WAR, 1939–1945
A Documentary History
Edited by Desmond Flowers
and James Reeves
New introduction by
John S. D. Eisenhower
1,142 pp., 20 maps
80763-7 $24.95

IN SEARCH OF LIGHT
The Broadcasts of
Edward R. Murrow,
1938–1961
Edward Bliss, Jr.
402 pp.
80762-9 $14.95

MEMOIRS
Ten Years and Twenty Days
Grand Admiral Karl Doenitz
Introduction and Afterword
by Jürgen Rohwer
New foreword by John Toland
554 pp., 18 photos, 5 maps
80764-5 $16.95

LIBERATION WAS
FOR OTHERS
Memoirs of a Gay Survivor
of the Nazi Holocaust
Pierre Seel
translated from the French by
Joachim Neugroschel
200 pp.
80756-4 $13.95

THE NIGHT OF
LONG KNIVES
June 29–30, 1934
Max Gallo
346 pp., 32 photos
80760-2 $14.95

ART AND POLITICS IN THE
WEIMAR PERIOD
The New Sobriety 1917–1933
John Willett
272 pp., 218 illus.
80724-6 $17.95

THE BITTER WOODS
The Battle of the Bulge
John S. D. Eisenhower
New introduction by
Stephen E. Ambrose
550 pp., 46 photos & 27 maps
80652-5 $17.95

THE BRAVEST BATTLE
The 28 Days of the Warsaw
Ghetto Uprising
Dan Kurzman
400 pp., 51 photos
80533-2 $14.95

THE COLLAPSE OF
THE THIRD REPUBLIC
An Inquiry into the Fall
of France in 1940
William L. Shirer
1,082 pp., 12 maps
80562-6 $22.95

DEATH DEALER
The Memoirs of the SS
Kommandant at Auschwitz
Rudolph Höss
Edited by Steven Paskuly
Translated by Andrew Pollinger
New foreword by Primo Levi
416 pp., 42 photos & diagrams
80698-3 $15.95

THE DEFEAT OF IMPERIAL
GERMANY, 1917–1918
Rod Paschall
Introduction by
John S. D. Eisenhower
288 pp., 61 photos, 14 maps
80585-5 $13.95

EISENHOWER AS
MILITARY COMMANDER
E. K. G. Sixsmith
264 pp., 35 photos, 11 maps
80369-0 $12.95

THE FALL OF BERLIN
Anthony Read and David Fisher
535 pp., 17 photos, 5 maps
80619-3 $16.95

JAPAN'S WAR
The Great Pacific Conflict
Edwin P. Hoyt
560 pp., 57 photos, 6 pp. of maps
80348-8 $16.95

THE LUFTWAFFE
WAR DIARIES
The German Air Force in
World War II
Cajus Bekker
447 pp., 119 photos, 20 maps
80604-5 $15.95

THE MEMOIRS OF
FIELD MARSHAL
MONTGOMERY
508 pp., 61 photos
80173-6 $10.95

MEMOIRS OF
HARRY S. TRUMAN
Volume II. 1946–1952:
Years of Trial and Hope
608 pp.
80297-X $14.95

THE MIGHTY ENDEAVOR
The American War in Europe
Charles B. MacDonald
621 pp., 78 photos, 10 maps
80486-7 $16.95

A MILITARY HISTORY OF THE
WESTERN WORLD
J. F. C. Fuller
Vol. I: From the Earliest Times to
the Battle of Lepanto
602 pp. 80304-6 $15.95
Vol. II: From the Defeat of the
Spanish Armada to the
Battle of Waterloo
562 pp. 80305-4 $15.95
Vol. III: From the American
Civil War to the
End of World War II
666 pp.
80306-2 $15.95

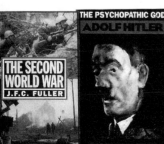

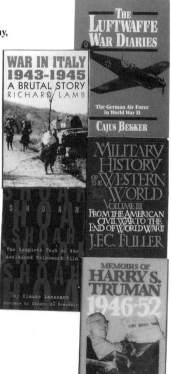